A

TOPOGRAPHICAL DICTIONARY

OF

IRELAND,

COMPRISING THE

SEVERAL COUNTIES, CITIES, BOROUGHS, CORPORATE, MARKET, AND POST TOWNS, PARISHES, AND VILLAGES,

WITH

HISTORICAL AND STATISTICAL DESCRIPTIONS;

EMBELLISHED WITH

ENGRAVINGS OF THE ARMS OF THE CITIES, BISHOPRICKS, CORPORATE TOWNS, AND BOROUGHS; AND OF THE SEALS OF THE SEVERAL MUNICIPAL CORPORATIONS:

WITH AN

APPENDIX,

DESCRIBING THE ELECTORAL BOUNDARIES OF THE SEVERAL BOROUGHS, AS DEFINED BY THE ACT OF THE 2d & 3d OF WILLIAM IV.

BY SAMUEL LEWIS.

IN TWO VOLUMES.

VOL. I.

Originally published: London, 1837
Reprinted: Genealogical Publishing Co., Inc.
Baltimore, Maryland, 1984, 1995
Library of Congress Catalogue Card Number 83-82827
International Standard Book Number, Volume I: 0-8063-1061-8
Set Number: 0-8063-1063-4
Made in the United States of America

YUBA COUNTY LIBRARY
MARYSVILLE, CA

PREFACE.

The publication of similar works on England and Wales, forming portions of a great national undertaking, intended to embrace Topographical Dictionaries of England, Wales, Ireland, and Scotland, had in some measure prepared the proprietors for the difficulties which they have encountered in their recent survey of Ireland. The numerous county histories, and local descriptions of cities, towns, and districts of England and Wales, rendered the publication of their former works, in comparison with the present, an easy task. The extreme paucity of such works, in relation to Ireland, imposed the necessity of greater assiduity in the personal survey, and proportionately increased the expense. But if the labour was thus augmented, the generous encouragement which the proprietors received animated them to a continuance of those exertions which have at length brought this portion of their undertaking to a close. To distinguish all to whom they are indebted for assistance in affording local information and facilitating their researches, would present a record of the names of nearly all the most intelligent resident gentlemen in Ireland: this fact, therefore, must be admitted as an apology for expressing, in a general acknowledgment, their gratitude for such disinterested services. They can with confidence assure their numerous subscribers, that, in the discharge of their arduous duties, they have unremittingly endeavoured to present every fact of importance tending to illustrate the local history, or convey useful information respecting the past or present state, of Ireland: fabulous tales and improbable traditions have generally been intentionally omitted; the chief aim being to give, in a condensed form, a faithful and impartial description of each place.

To render the account of every town and place of importance as correct as possible, prior to its being finally put to press, proof sheets were forwarded to those resident gentlemen who had previously furnished local information, in order that, in their revisal of them, they might introduce any changes which had subsequently taken place, or improvements that might be at that time in progress: these were, with very few exceptions, promptly examined and returned, but in some instances inevitable delay was occasioned by the absence of the parties to whom they were addressed. Though this essential precaution may have retarded the publication, it has conduced materially to the accuracy of the work. For a similar reason, the time employed in the survey has been longer than was at first anticipated; it having been thought advisable that the persons engaged in that arduous and important service should protract the period originally prescribed for their researches, rather than compromise the interests of the work by omitting to avail themselves of every possible source of intelligence.

The unsettled orthography of names rendered it somewhat difficult to select a standard of arrangement calculated to afford facility of reference. That mode of spelling was therefore adopted which, after careful examination and inquiry, appeared to be sanctioned by general usage; and where a name was found to be spelt in two or more ways, a reference has been given from one to the other. On this head, two points may require explanation, as a guide to reference:—The final *l* in the prefix *Kill* has been dropped when followed by a consonant, and retained when followed by a vowel. The ultimate of the prefix *Bally* (a corruption of *Baile*) is written variously, the letter *i* being sometimes substituted for *y*, but the latter is by far the more general; in respect to names compounded of this and other simple terms, the non-discovery of a place under the head *Bally* will lead to the inference that it is given as *Balli*.

It is necessary to state that all distances are given in Irish miles; glebes, and every other extent of lands, except when otherwise expressed, in Irish plantation acres; grants and sums of money, unless the standard be specified, may be generally regulated, as regards their amount, by the period to which they refer, in its relation to the year 1826, when the assimilation of the currency took place. Numerous Reports to Parliament, of recent date, have been made available for supplying much useful statistical information. The Ordnance survey, so far as it has extended, has been adopted as the best authority for stating the number of acres which each parish comprises. As regards other parishes, the number of acres given is that applotted under the tithe composition act, which in some cases embraces the entire superficies of the parish, in others excludes an unproductive tract of mountain waste, of which the estimated value is too small to admit of its being brought under composition. The amount of parochial tithes was derived from parliamentary returns of the sums for which they have been compounded. In case of a union of parishes forming one benefice, and of which the incumbent only receives a portion of the tithes, the parishes constituting the benefice are enumerated under the head of that which gives name to it; the tithes of the latter of which, and their application, are first stated; then, the gross tithes of the benefice payable to the incumbent, the appropriation of the remaining portions of the tithes of the other parishes being detailed under their respective heads.

The Presbyterian congregations are divided into classes corresponding with the sum which each receives from the annual parliamentary grant called the Regium Donum. Those in connection with the Synod of Ulster, Presbytery of Antrim, and Remonstrant Synod, consist each of three classes; each congregation of the first class has an annual grant of £92. 6. 2. (British currency); of the second, £69. 4. 8.; and of the third, £46. 3. 1. The Presbyterian Synod of Ireland, generally styled the Seceding Synod, is also divided into congregations of the first, second, and third classes, respectively receiving £64. 12, 4., £46. 3. 1., and £36. 18. 6. each per annum. Each congregation is designated in the work as being of one of these three classes, thus indicating the amount which it receives. Those in connection with the Synod of Munster, few in number, not being classed, the sum which each receives is stated.

The census of 1831 has been adopted with reference to the population and number of houses; and the Reports of the Commissioners on Ecclesiastical Revenue and Patronage, of Ecclesiastical Inquiry, and of Public Instruction, have furnished much valuable matter relative to the Church. The number of children educated in the several schools in connection with the Board of National Education is given from the Report of the Commissioners. With respect to other schools, the numbers are generally those reported by the Commissioners of Public Instruction, which, being the numbers entered upon the books of the different schools, must be regarded as exceeding those in actual attendance. In cases where the information obtained on the spot materially differed from that contained in the Reports, the former has been adopted; but the introduction of the National system has caused such numerous alterations, as to render it extremely difficult to state with any degree of precision the exact number of children at present receiving instruction in each parish.

The Arms and Seals of the several cities, boroughs, corporate towns, bishoprics, &c., are engraved from drawings made from impressions in wax, furnished by the respective corporate bodies; and, notwithstanding they have generally been either enlarged or reduced to one scale, for the sake of uniformity, great care has been taken to preserve, in every instance, an exact *fac-simile* of the original.

The Proprietors cannot indulge the hope that, in a work of such magnitude, containing notices so numerous and diversified, some errors may not be found: indeed, the information collected upon the spot, even from the most intelligent persons, has frequently been so contradictory, as to require much labour and perseverance to reconcile and verify it. They have, however, regardless of expense, used the most indefatigable exertions to attain correctness, and to render the work as complete as possible; and they, therefore, trust that occasional inaccuracies will receive the indulgence of the Subscribers.

SUBSCRIBERS.

HER MOST GRACIOUS MAJESTY THE QUEEN,

HIS LATE MOST GRACIOUS MAJESTY WILLIAM THE FOURTH,

HER MAJESTY DOWAGER QUEEN ADELAIDE,

*HIS MAJESTY THE KING OF HANOVER
*HER MAJESTY THE QUEEN OF HANOVER
*HIS MAJESTY THE EMPEROR OF AUSTRIA
*HIS MAJESTY THE EMPEROR OF ALL THE RUSSIAS
*HIS MAJESTY THE KING OF BELGIUM
*HIS MAJESTY THE KING OF SWEDEN AND NORWAY
*HIS ROYAL HIGHNESS THE DUKE OF SUSSEX
*HIS ROYAL HIGHNESS THE DUKE OF CAMBRIDGE
*HER ROYAL HIGHNESS THE PRINCESS AUGUSTA
*HER ROYAL HIGHNESS THE DUCHESS OF KENT

Abbott, J., Esq., Gov. of the Lunatic Asylum, Maryboro', Queen's co.
Abbott, J. Tydd, Esq., Barnagrotty, Moneygall, King's county
Abbott, Samuel, Esq., Horse-head-cottage, Passage West, Co. Cork
*Abbott, Messrs. S. & Co., Cork
*ABERCORN, The Most Noble the Marquis of
Abraham, The Rt. Rev. W., D.D., R.C. Bishop of Waterford and [Lismore
*Ackland, Lieut. Edward, R.N., Moville, co. Donegal
*Ackland, Graves, Esq., Drogheda, co. Louth
*Acres, Thomas, Esq., Tullamore, King's county
Acton, Lieut.-Col. William, D.L. and J.P., West Aston, Rathdrum, [co. Wicklow
Adair, George, Esq., J.P., Bellegrove, Ballybrittas, Queen's county
Adair, Henry, Esq., Templepatrick, Antrim
*Adair, Thomas, Esq., Greenvale, Cookstown, co. Tyrone
*Adair, Thomas Benjamin, Esq., J.P., Loughinmore, co. Antrim
Adams, Anthony, Esq., Horsehill-house, Kinsale, co. Cork
*Adams, Rev. Charles, Newtown-stewart, co. Tyrone
*Adams, Charles James, Esq., J.P., Retreat, Cootehill, co. Cavan
Adams, Rev. Charles Robert, Aghada-glebe, near Cloyne, co. Cork
Adams, George Hill, Esq., M.D., Portglenone, co. Antrim
Adams, George M., Esq., Aclare-lodge, Ardee, co. Louth
*Adams, George Esq., Pembroke-street, Cork
Adams, James, Esq., Ballyannan, Midleton, co. Cork
*Adams, James B., Esq., Clarence-street, Cork
Adams, Mr. James, Exchequer-street, Dublin
Adams, John James, Esq., Watercourse, Cork
Adams, Richard, Esq., Glandore-lodge, Rosscarbery, co. Cork
Adams, Robert, Esq., Newcastle-lodge, Galway
*Adams, R. W. G., Esq., J.P., Jamesbrook-hall, Cloyne, co. Cork
*Adams, The Very Rev. Samuel, A.M., & J.P., Dean of Cashel, [Northlands, near Kingscourt, co. Cavan
Adams, Samuel Wallis, Esq., J.P., Kilbree, Cloyne, co. Cork
*Adams, T. T., Esq., Annagurra, Kilfinane, co. Limerick
Adamson, Rev. Arthur, Glebe-house, Phibsborough, near Dublin
*Adamson, Christopher, Esq., Ballinalack, Moate, co. Westmeath
*Adamson, Rev. William, Loughill, near Glin, co. Limerick
Adamson, Rev. W. A., B.A., Green-park, Ennis, co. Clare
*Adamson, William Gustavus, Esq., Cairn-park, co. Westmeath
Addenbrooke, H. Esq., Field-house, Hagley, Worcestershire
*ADMIRALTY, The Rt. Hon. the Lords Commissioners of the
*Agnew, Edward Jones, Esq., Killwaughter-castle, co. Antrim
Agnew, James, Esq., Mossvale, Lisburn, co. Down
Ahearne, John, Esq., South-mall, Cork
Aherin, Maurice, Esq., Hernsbrook, Newcastle, co. Limerick
*A'Hern, William, Esq., Bishopstown, near Cork
*A'Hmuty, Arthur, Esq., M.D., J.P., Kilmore-house, Kilmore, co. [Roscommon
*A'Hmuty, William S., Esq., Loy-house, Cookstown, co. Tyrone
Aickin, P., Esq., J.P., Harryville, Ballymena, co. Antrim
*Aickin, William, Esq., M.D., Broughshane, co. Antrim
Aiken, Miss, Pettigo-house, Kesh, co. Fermanagh
*Aiken, Irvine, Esq., Lifford, co. Donegal
Alcock, Rev. Alexander, J.P., Fethard-castle, co. Wexford
Alcock, Harry, Esq., Wilton, near Enniscorthy, co. Wexford
*Alcock, J. H., Esq., Richmond, Cappoquin, co. Waterford
Alcock, Maskelyne, Esq., J.P., Roughgrove, near Bandon, co. Cork
Alder, Rev. Samuel, M.A., Glebe-house, Saul, near Downpatrick
*Aldworth, Robert R., Esq., Newmarket-house, co. Cork
Aldworth, Lieut. St. Leger, R.N., J.P., Newmarket, co. Cork
Alexander, Arthur, Esq., South-park, Gort, co. Galway
*Alexander, Rev. James, Killucan, co. Westmeath
*Alexander, Mr. John, Castletown, near Londonderry
*Alexander, Mr. John, Knockbrack, near Londonderry
*Alexander, Mr. John, Londonderry
Alexander, Lesley, Esq., Foyle-park, near Londonderry, & 6 York-terrace, Regent's-park, London
Alexander, Rev. Nat., Crumlin, Co. Antrim
Alexander, Rev. Robert, J.P., Black-heath, Coleraine, co. Derry
Alexander, Rev. Robert, J.P., Portglenone, co. Antrim
*Alexander, Robert, Esq., Landville, Strabane, co. Tyrone
Alexander, Thomas, Esq., Buncrana, co. Donegal
*Alexander, William John, Esq., Caledon, co. Tyrone
*Algeo, Lewis, Esq., Glenboy, Manorhamilton, co. Leitrim
*Algeo, William Whitelaw, Esq., J.P., Pavilion, Armagh

Those marked with an Asterisk (*) are Subscribers for large paper Copies.

Allan, John, Esq., Blackwell, Darlington, Durham
Allan, W., Esq., Blackwell Grange, Darlington, Durham
Allen, A. W., Esq., Garryduffe, Douglas, co. Cork
Allen, Major Edward, West-view-house, Glandore, Rosscarberry,
*Allen, F., Esq., Glandore, Rosscarbery, co. Cork, and South- [terrace, Cork
Allen, Rev. F., M.A., Castletown, Pallaskenry, co. Limerick
Allen, Mr. George, Parliament-street, Dublin
*Allen, J., Esq., Lisconnan, near Dervock, co. Antrim
*Allen, Mr. John, Ballymagrorty, Templemore, near Derry
Allen, John, Esq., Breckanhill, Ballyclare, co. Antrim
Allen, Mr. John, Londonderry
*Allen, John, Esq., Retreat, near Armagh
Allen, Major John, Stone-hall, Glandore, Rosscarbery, co. Cork
*Allen, John Reed, Esq., Mount Panther, Clough, co. Down
Allen, John Richmond, Esq., Ballystraw, Fethard, co. Wexford
*Allen, Kyrle, Esq., Clashenure, near Ovens, co. Cork
Allen, Mr. Samuel, jun., Midleton, co. Cork
*Allen, Timothy, Esq., Camden-street, Dublin
Allen, William, Esq., Carnisle, Trim, co. Meath
*Allen, William, Esq., Recorder, Sligo
Allen, William, Esq., J.P., Liscongill, Kanturk, co. Cork
*Allen, the Misses, Lakeview-house, Blackrock, Cork
Alley, Rev. George, Moymett, Trim, co. Meath
*Alley, Rev. Henry, George's-hill, Dublin
*Alley, Thomas, Esq., Artaine-house, co. Dublin
*Alley, Thomas, Esq., Primrose-cottage, Rathgar-road, near Dublin
Alleyne, Samuel, Esq., Tipperary
Alleyne, William, Esq., Tipperary
*Allgood, R. L., Esq., Nunwick-park, Hexham, Northumberland
Allin, James, Esq., Shannonvale, near Cloghnakilty, co. Cork
Allin, John, Esq., Fermoy, co. Cork
*Allingham, Edward, Esq., Willybrook, Ballyshannon, co. Donegal
Allingham, E. H., Esq., Dromahaire, co. Leitrim
Allman, James C., Esq., Bandon, co. Cork
Allman, John, Esq., J.P., Woodview, near Eyrecourt, co. Galway
Alloway, A. W., Esq., Kilbracken, Ballybrittas, Queen's county
*Alloway, Robert M., Esq., J.P., The Derries, Ballybrittas, Queen's co.
Alma, Mr. E. L., Blackrock, co. Dublin
Alsop, John, Esq., Darley-dale, Derbyshire
*Althorpe, J. C., Esq., Dinnington, Worksop, Nottinghamshire
Ambrose, Thomas, Esq., Abbeyfeale, co. Limerick
*Ames, George, Esq., Clifton, Bristol
*AMIENS, The Right Honorable Lord
Anders, John, Esq., Wyndham-street, Bryanston-square, London
Anderson, A., Esq., Delgany, co. Wicklow
Anderson, Barton, Esq., Dungarvan, co. Waterford
Anderson, Charles Frederick, Esq., Tipperary
*Anderson, The Rev. Sir C. J., Bart., Lea-house, Gainsborough
*Anderson, Francis, Esq., Eastham, Drogheda, co. Louth
*Anderson, Sir James C., Bart., Buttevant-castle, co. Cork
Anderson, John, Esq., C.C.P., Midleton, co. Cork
Anderson, John, Esq., Bantry, co. Cork
Anderson, John William, Esq., Ashfield, Fermoy, co. Cork
Anderson, M., Esq., Hoayfield, Bray, co. Wicklow
*Anderson, Richard, Esq., Sligo
*Anderson, Rev. Robert, Rathmullen, co. Donegal
Andrews, John, Esq., J.P., Comber, co. Down
Andrews, John, Esq., Ratheny-cottage, Moneygall, King's co.
*Andrews, Maunsell, Esq., J.P., Ratheny-house, do. do.
*Andrews, Michael, Esq., Ardoyne, Belfast
*Andrews, Rev. Nicholas, R.C.C., Meath-street, Dublin
*Andrews, William, Esq., Upper Ormond Quay, and Haymount, [Castleknock, co. Dublin
*Anketell, Matthew, Esq., Anketell-grove, co. Monaghan
*Anketell, R., Esq., Mount Anketell, Emyvale, co. Monaghan
*Anketell, R. C., Esq., J.P., Anketell-lodge, Stewartstown, co. Tyrone
*Anketell, Thomas, Esq., J.P., Dungillick, Emyvale, co. Monaghan
*Anketell, W., Esq., J.P., & D.L., Anketell-grove, do.
*ANNESLEY, The Right Honorable the Earl
*Annesley, Lieut.-Gen. The Hon. A. G., J.P., Annesgrove, co. Cork
Annesley, Arthur, Esq., Bletchington-park, near Woodstock, Ox- [ford, & Eaton-square, London
Annesley, Lawson, Esq., Derramore, Belfast
*Annesley, Richard A., Esq., Castlewellan, co. Down
Annesley, Rev. William, A.M., Ardilea, Clough, co. Down
Anthony, Thomas, Esq., Cork
Anthony, Thomas, Esq., Ring-mount, Dungarvan, co. Waterford
Antisell, Thomas, Esq., Sraduff (Parsonstown), co. Tipperary
Applegath, Augustus, Esq., Crayford, Kent
*Appleton, R. W., Esq., Everton, near Liverpool

*Arabin, Henry, Esq., Clondalkin, co. Dublin
*Archbold, Rev. Charles, A.M., J.P., Rathmullen, Downpatrick
Archbold, J., Esq., Waterford
*Archbold, Richard, Esq., Capel-street, Dublin
*Archbold, Robert, Esq., J.P., Davidstown, co. Kildare
*Archdall, Charles, Esq., J.P., Riverstown, Irvinestown, co. Ferma- [nagh
*Archdall, Edward, Esq., D.L. & J.P., Riversdale, Enniskillen, do.
*Archdall, E. M., Esq., Lincoln's-inn-fields, London
*Archdall, General Mervyn, M.P., Castle Archdall, co. Fermanagh
Archdall, Rev. William, Fethard, co. Wexford
*Archdall, Rev. Francis J., P.P., Blessington, co. Wicklow
*Archdeacon, James, Esq., Cooper-hill, Limerick
*Archer, Henry, Esq., Ballyseskin, Wexford
*Archer, Rev. William, A.M., Newcastle, co. Wicklow
Ardagh, William Marchant, Esq., Waterford
*ARDEN, The Right Honorable Lord
*Ardill, Rev. Richard, Harrington-street, Dublin
*Arkwright, Peter, Esq., Rock-house, Cromford, Derbyshire
*Arkwright, Richard, Esq., Willersley Castle, Derbyshire
Arkwright, Robert, Esq., Stoke, Bakewell, Derbyshire
*ARMAGH, His Grace the Lord Archbishop of
*Armit, John, Esq., J.P., Newtown-park-house, near Stillorgan, co. [Dublin
*Armit, John Lees, Esq., Kildare-street, Dublin
Armor, Rev. Samuel, Drumquin, near Omagh, co. Tyrone
*Armstrong, Major Gen. A., Elm-mount, near Artaine, co. Dublin
*Armstrong, Mr. A., Anglesea Arms Hotel, Kingstown, co. Dublin
*Armstrong, A., Esq., C.C.P., Cottage-grove, Ballyshannon, co. [Donegal
Armstrong, Alexander, Esq., Cavan
*Armstrong, Andrew, Esq., Gallen, Ferbane, King's county
Armstrong, Andrew, Esq., Kilsharvan, Drogheda, co. Louth
*Armstrong, Benjamin, Esq., Summer-hill, Dublin
Armstrong, Charles, Esq., Rock-island, Skibbereen, co. Cork
*Armstrong, Charles, Esq., Aughamore, Mohill, co. Longford
*Armstrong, Rev. Charles, A.M., Glanealy, co. Wicklow
Armstrong, Chas. W., Esq., J.P., Cherry-valley, Crumlin, co. Antrim
*Armstrong, Edmund J., Esq., J.P., Willow-bank, Ennis, co. Clare
Armstrong, H. Esq., Bishopwearmouth, Durham
*Armstrong, Henry R., Esq., Mount Venus-house near Rathfarnham, [co. Dublin, and Merchant's Quay, Dublin
Armstrong, James W., Esq., Culmore, Kilrea, co. Derry
*Armstrong, John, Esq., Mountjoy-square South, Dublin
*Armstrong, John, Esq., J.P., Chaffpool, Ballymote, co. Sligo
Armstrong, John, Esq., J.P., Kilclare, Durrow, King's county
*Armstrong, Rev. J., J.P., Kiltoom-glebe, Athlone, co. Roscommon
*Armstrong, John, Esq., Knockballymore, Clones, co. Fermanagh
Armstrong, Lieut.-Col., Portarlington, Queen's county
*Armstrong, Montgomery, Esq., Bumper-lodge, Florence-court, co. [Fermanagh
Armstrong, Philip A., Esq., Castletown, co. Cork
*Armstrong, Richard, jun., Esq., Clonbolt, Longford
Armstrong, Robert, Esq., Ardnaree, Ballina, co. Mayo
*Armstrong, S., Esq., J.P., Hollymount, Manorhamilton, co. Leitrim
Armstrong, Rev. Thomas B., P.C. of Churchtown, co. Wexford
*Armstrong, T. K., Esq., J. P., Fellows-hall, Armagh
*Armstrong, William Andrew, Esq., J.P., Rathmacknee, co. Wexford
*Armstrong, W. B., Esq., Castle Iver, Banagher, King's county
Armstrong, Rev. W. C., Moydow-glebe, Longford
*Arnold, William F., Esq., Little Missenden-abbey, Bucks.
*Arthur, James, Esq., Bush, near Antrim
Arthur, Patrick, Esq., C.C.P., Ballinasloe, co. Galway
Arthur, Robert, Esq., Lower Dominick-street, Dublin
Arthur, William, Esq., White-rocks, Belfast
*Arthur, Walter, Esq., Molesworth-street, Dublin
*Arthure, B., Esq., Dominick-street, Dublin
*Arthure, J., Esq., J.P., Seafield, near Swords, co. Dublin
Ash, Rev. George H., Glebe-house, Bellaghy, co. Derry
*Ash, W. H., Esq., J.P., Ash Brook, Glendermott, near Derry
*Ashe, Rev. Henry, Curate of Croagh, Rathkeale, co. Limerick
Ashe, Norman, Esq., Galway
Ashe, Richard, Esq., J.P., Glebe-house, Macroom, co. Cork
*Ashe, Richard, Esq., J.P., Coolehane, Macroom, co. Cork
Ashe, Robert Henry, Esq., Downshire-place, Newry, co. Down
*Ashe, Rev. Trevor Lloyd, Castle Mary, Ashe-grove, co. Tipperary
*Ashlin, J. M., Esq., J.P., Carrigrenane, near Cork
*Ashton, Herbert, Esq., Sandaway-lodge, near Northwich, Cheshire
*Ashton, Messrs. William and Co., Derry
*Ashworth, James, Esq., Celbridge-abbey, co. Kildare
Askham, W., Esq., Eckington, Chesterfield, Derbyshire
Atbridge, Arthur, Esq., River-view, Skibbereen, co. Cork
*Atchison, Robert, Esq., Glenglush, Strabane, co. Tyrone
*Athawes, Rev. John, M.A., Loughton, near Stoney-Stratford, Bucks
*ATHENRY, The Right Honorable Lord

*Atkin, John Drew, Esq., South-mall, Cork
Atkin, Thomas, Esq., Portadown, co. Armagh
*Atkin, Walter, Esq., Careystown, Cloyne, co. Cork
*Atkin, W. F., Esq., Fern-hill, Cloghnakilty, co. Cork
*Atkin, Mrs. Atkin-ville, Douglas, near Cork
Atkins, Mr. Henry, Hotel, Dunmanway, co. Cork
*Atkins, Lieut. John, R.N., Wicklow
Atkins, Stephen H., Esq., J.P., Bird-hill, Killaloe, co. Clare
Atkins, Major Thomas, E.I.C.S., Killynhanvagh, co. Armagh
Atkins, Mr. W., Sandymount, co. Dublin
Atkinson, Capt. Sir Henry Escli, R.N., Cowes, Isle of Wight
*Atkinson, Charles, Esq., Green-hall, Moy, co. Tyrone
Atkinson, Chas., Esq., J.P., South-park, Burrisokane, co. Tipperary
Atkinson, Charles, Esq., Woodland, Firbane, King's county
*Atkinson, Rev. C., LL.D., and J. P., Rector of Creggan, Dundalk
*Atkinson, Rev. Edward, Strabane, co. Tyrone
Atkinson, Messrs. Edward & Charles, Ballina, co. Mayo
*Atkinson, Francis, Esq., Tullyvea, Cookstown, co. Tyrone
Atkinson, George Grindall, Esq., Cordery, Lurgan-green, co. Louth
*Atkinson, Guy, Esq., J.P., Cangort, Shinrone, King's county
*Atkinson, Henry, jun., Esq., Brookfield, Moy, co. Tyrone
Atkinson, Rev. James, Curate of Dunleckney, co. Carlow
Atkinson, John, Esq., New Bliss, co. Monaghan
Atkinson, John, Esq., St. Mary's Gate Academy, Chesterfield
*Atkinson, J., Esq., J. P., Crow-hill-house, Loughall, co. Armagh
*Atkinson, Joseph, Esq., Barberstown, Celbridge, co. Kildare
*Atkinson, Thomas J., Esq., J.P., Cavangarden, Ballyshannon, co. Do-
*Atkinson, William, Esq., J. P., Rehins, Ballina, co. Mayo [negal
*Atlas Fire & Life Assurance Company, London
Atthill, Robert, Esq., Trillick, co. Tyrone
Atthill, Rev. W., A.B., Brandiston-hall, Aylsham, Norfolk
Attwood, C. Esq., Whickham, Gateshead, Durham
*Aubrey, Sir Thomas, Bart., Oring-house, Aylesbury, Bucks.
*Auchinleck, Daniel, Esq., Omagh, co. Tyrone
Auchinleck, James Richard, Esq., Mulvin, Strabane, co. Tyrone
Auchinleck, Rev. John, Rector of Killesk, co. Wexford
*Auchmuty, Thomas, Esq., J.P., Brianstown, Longford
*AUDLEY, The Right Honorable Lord [nedy, co. Wicklow
*Audouin, James Lamb, Esq., J.P., East-hill, Newtown-Mount-Ken-
*Auglen, Rev. Robert, J.D., C.C., Exchange-st., Dublin
*Augustinian Library, Cork
*Aull, Miss Mary, Newtown-Limavady, co. Derry
*Aungier, Peter, Esq., Lays, Swords, co. Dublin
Austen, Samuel Adams, Esq., Ballyphilip, co. Cork
Austin, George, Esq., Deer-park, Newtown-Stewart, co. Tyrone
*Austin, James H., Esq., Newtown-Stewart, co. Tyrone
*Avary Jordan, Esq., Race-course-lodge, near Cashel, co. Tipperary
*AVONMORE, The Right Hon. Viscount
Aylmer, Rev. C., Hardwick-street, Dublin
*Aylmer, Edmond F., Esq., Mullafin, Ashbourne, co. Meath
*Aylmer, Sir Gerald George, Bart., D.L. and J.P., Donadea-castle, [Kilcock, co. Kildare
Aylmer, Gerald, Esq., Painstown, Kilcock, co. Kildare
*Aylmer, John, Esq., J.P., Courtown, Kilcock, co. Kildare
Aylmer, J., Esq., Blessington-street, Dublin
Aylmer, Rev. William Josiah, Rector of Donadea & Balraheen, [Woodside, Kilcock, co. Kildare

Babington, Rev. H., A. B., Moviddy Glebe, Crookstown, co. Cork
*Babington, Humphrey, Esq., Greenfort, Ramelton, co. Donegal
*Babington, Michael, Esq., Fort View, Cavan
Babington, Murray, Esq., Bonny Glen, co. Donegal
Babington, Richard, Esq., Summer Hill, Dublin, and Londonderry
Backhouse, Thomas, Esq., Havenfield Lodge, Gt. Missenden, Bucks.
*Badham, W. L., Esq., Stormanstown, Santry, co. Dublin
*Baggallay, Richard, Esq., King-st., Cheapside, London
*Bagge, Simon, Esq., Ardmore, Youghal, co. Waterford
Baggs, George, Esq., Short Castle, Mallow, co. Cork
*Bagnell, Rev. J. Armstrong, Attaugh Glebe, Durrow, King's county
Bagot, C. H., Esq., J.P., Ennis, co. Clare
*Bagot, James John, Esq., Castle Bagot, Rathcoole, co. Dublin
*Bagwell, Captain, R.N., Castle View, Kilkenny
*Bagwell, John, Esq., Glenconner, Clonmel, co. Tipperary
*Bagwell, John, Esq., J.P., Marlfield, Clonmel, co. Tipperary
*Bagwell, The Right Honorable W.
*Bailey, Mr. Robert, Doey, Coleraine, co. Derry [nagh
Bailey, Thomas, Esq., J.P., Mulladuff, Newtown-Butler, co. Ferma-
Bailie, Rev. John, Clonaleenan, Dundalk, co. Louth
Bailie, Major James, J. P., Carrig Hill, Belturbet, co. Cavan
Bailie, James, Esq., J.P., Ringdufferin, Killyleagh, co. Down

Bailie, Robert, Esq., Shortstone, Dundalk, co. Louth
*Bailie, William, Esq., Toye House, near Killyleagh, co. Armagh
*Baird, Andrew, Esq., R.N., Donoghenry, near Stewartstown, co.
Baird, Mr. James, Cloghfin, near Derry [Tyrone
*Baird, T. M., Esq., Merchants'-quay, Dublin
*Bairston, John, Esq., Preston, Lancashire
*Baker, Abraham Whyte, Esq., Ballytobin, Callan, co. Kilkenny
*Baker, Andrew, Esq., Redhill, Boyle, co. Roscommon
*Baker, Arthur, Esq., Balheary House, near Swords, co. Dublin
*Baker, Rev. Francis, Vicar of Balrothery, co. Dublin
*Baker, George, Esq., Ballydavid, Tipperary
*Baker, Rev. George C., Portmarnock-glebe, near Cloghran, co. Dublin
*Baker, Hugh, Esq., Lismacue, near Tipperary
*Baker, John, Esq., Kilcoran, Callan, co. Kilkenny
Baker, Richard, Esq., Baker Place, Limerick
Baker, Richard, Esq., Thomas-steet, Limerick
*Baker, Robert, Esq., Belmont, near Clogheen, King's county
*Baldwin, Mr. Henry, Mt. Pleasant, Bandon, co. Cork
Baldwin, Henry, Esq., Skibbereen, co. Cork
*Baldwin, Rev. John, Incumbent of Clonaslee, Queen's county
*Baldwin, Richard, Esq., Lower Gardiner-street, Dublin
*Balfe, Christopher, Esq., Curramore, Athleague, co. Roscommon
*Balfe, James, Esq., J.P., Runnemead, co. Roscommon
*Balfe, John, Esq., J.P., Lisdurn, Elphin, co. Roscommon
*Balfe, Michael, Esq., Southpark, Castlerea, co. Roscommon
Balfour, B., Esq., D.L. and J.P., Townley Hall, Drogheda, co. Louth
Ball, James C., Esq., Shannon, Strabane, co. Donegal
Ball, Rev. John Gage, Churchtown, near Cookstown, co. Derry
Ball, John William, Esq., Fitzwilliam Square West, Dublin
*Ball, Lawrence, Esq., Wintergrass, Duleek, co. Meath
*Ball, Robert Stawel, Esq., Youghal, co. Cork
Ball, Robert, Esq., Fownes-street, Dublin [near Drogheda
*Ball, Shirley W., Esq., Harcourt-st., Dublin, and Cowslip Lodge,
Ball, T., Esq., Wood-street, London
*Ball, Thomas P., Esq., Little Stanhope-street, May-Fair, London
*Bamber, Richard, Esq., Eustace-street, Dublin
Banan, Rev. Patrick, P.P., Louth [naghan
*Banan, Robert, Esq., Longfield Cottage, Carrickmacross, co. Mo-
*BANDON, The Right Honorable the Earl of
BANGOR, The Right Honorable Viscount
*Banks, Charles, Esq., Royal Hospital, Kilmainham, co. Dublin
Banks, Rev. Langrishe, Curate of Rosbercon Grammar School, New [Ross, co. Wexford
Banks, Perceval, Esq., M.D., Rose Bank, Ennis, co. Clare
Bannan, Rev. T., P.P., Bourna, and Corbally, Roscrea, co. Tipperary
Banon, Rev. Michael, R.C.C. Moyne, Thurles, co. Tipperary
*Banon, Thomas, Esq., Rathcaslin, Mullingar, co. Westmeath
*Banting, Mr. Thomas, Pall Mall, London
*BANTRY, The Right Honorable the Earl of
Barber, J. M., Esq., New Inn, London
*Barber, Joseph, Esq., Clapham Rise, Surrey
*Barber, Thomas, Esq., Greasley, near Nottingham
*Barber, Mr. Thomas, Mobury, Faughanvale, co. Derry
*Barber, Rev. William, Prebendary of Crosspatrick, and Rector of [Kilcommon, co. Wicklow
*Barbor, Robert C., Esq., Rathmore, Nougheval, co. Longford
Barbour, William, Esq., Hildon, near Lisburn, co. Antrim
Barclay, Rev. Joseph, Curate of Raphoe, co. Donegal
*Barclay, Richard, Esq., J.P., Ballyartney, Kildysart, co. Clare
Barclay, Thomas, Esq., Castlebar, co. Mayo
Bardin, Rev. Charles, D.D., Rector of Derryloran, co. Tyrone
*Barker, Richard, Esq., Great Britain-street, Dublin
*Barker, W. Esq., J P., Kilcooly Abbey, Johnstown, co. Tipperary
Barklie, Alexander, Esq., Mullamore, Coleraine, co. Derry
Barklie, Archibald, Esq., Inver House, co. Antrim
Barklie, Archibald, Esq., Larne, co. Antrim
*Barlow, A., Esq., Gt. George-street, North, Dublin
*Barlow, Arthur C., Esq., Saunderscourt, near Wexford
*Barlow, J., Esq., J.P., Bushy Park, Tessara, co. Roscommon
*Barlow, John, Esq., Sybil Hill, Howth Road, co. Dublin
*Barlow, John Wilson, Esq., Upper Pembroke-st., Dublin, and Riversdale, co. Dublin [rary
Barnan, Rev. T., P.P., Bourney and Corbally, Roscrea, co. Tippe-
Barnes, Mr. Edward, Wicklow Copper Mine Co., near Rathdrum,
Barnes, G., Esq., Christ Church College, Oxford [co. Wicklow
*Barnes, John, Esq., J. P., Armagh
Barnes, John, Esq., Baggot-street, Dublin
*Barnes, John Coote, Esq., Newtown Kells, co. Meath
*Barnes, Capt. J., J.P., Gort, co. Galway
Barnes, John, Esq., Mount Emla, Douglas, near Cork
*Barnes, Thomas, Esq., J.P., Westland, Moynalty, co. Meath

Barnes, Thomas R., Esq., View-mount, Cloghjordan, co. Tipperary
Barnes, Messrs. Thomas A. and Co., Cork
Barnett, James, Esq., Carrickfergus, co. Antrim
*Barnett, Rev. John, Moneymore, co. Derry
*Barnett, John, Esq., Redcliff Parade, Bristol
Barnett, John, Esq., Belfast
*Barnewall, The Hon. Thomas, Turvey-house, near Swords, co. Dublin
*Baron, J. C., Esq., Merrion-avenue, near Dublin
*Barras, John, Esq., Farnacres, Gateshead, Durham
Barrett, Jacob, Esq., Armagh
Barrett, Rev. John, P.P., Crossmolina, co. Mayo
Barrett, Richard, Esq., Mallow, co. Cork
*Barrett, S., Esq., Greenhills, Kilconnell, co. Galway
Barrett, William, Esq., York-street, Dublin
*Barrie, Capt. Sir R., R.N., Swerthdale, near Lancaster
*Barrington, The Honorable Russell
*Barrington, Daniel, Esq., J.P., George's-street, Limerick
Barrington, Sir Joseph, Bart., Limerick
*Barrington, Manleff, Esq., Glendruid, near Cabinteely, co. Dublin
Barrington, Nicholas, Esq., Ballycogley Castle, co. Wexford
Barrington, Mr. Richard, Ballymacane, co. Wexford
Barron, Rev. Edward, St. John's College, Waterford
Barron, Henry Winston, Esq., M.P. and D.L., Belmont House, co. Kilkenny
*Barron, J., Esq., J.P., Georgestown, Kilmacthomas, co. Waterford
*Barron, John N., Esq., J.P., Ballydavid House, near Waterford
*Barron, Pierse George, Esq., D.L. and J.P., Eastland, Tramore, co. Waterford
*Barron, Pierse R., Esq., Fahagh, Kilmacthomas, co. Waterford
*Barron, Pierse Marcus, Esq., J.P., Glenview, Kilmacthomas, co. Waterford, and Stephen's Green, Dublin
*Barron, Philip, Esq., Seafield, co. Waterford, and Chronicle Office, Waterford
*Barron, William H., Esq., Fitzwilliam-square, Dublin
Barron, William Henry, Esq., Hermitage, Dungarvan, co. Waterford
Barron, Captain, Belmont House, co. Waterford
Barronneau, Mrs., New Lodge, Barnet, Herts.
Barrow, G. H., Esq., Ringwood-hill, Chesterfield, Derbyshire
Barry, Augustus W., Esq., Rosehill House, Midleton, co. Cork
Barry, C., Esq., Ely Place, London
Barry, D., Esq., Swinton Place, London
Barry, D., Esq., M. D., Rathealy, Fermoy, co. Cork
*Barry, David, Esq., Barry's Lodge, Carrigtohill, co. Cork
*Barry, David J., Esq., C.C.P., Swinford, co. Mayo
*Barry, Rev. Edward, P.P., Fermoy, co. Cork
*Barry, Edward, Esq., M.D., Rathcormack, co. Cork
Barry, Gerard P., Esq., M.D., Kanturk, co. Cork
*Barry, Major-General, H. G., J.P., Ballyclough House, Fermoy, co. Cork
Barry, James, Esq., Macroom, co. Cork
Barry, James, Esq., Rock Lodge, Castlelyons, co. Cork
Barry, James, Esq., Kilbarry, Macroom, co. Cork
*Barry, James, Esq., Cahir, co. Tipperary
Barry, James Redmond, Esq., Glandore, Rosscarbery, co. Cork
*Barry, James Smith, Esq., Lota Lodge, near Cork
Barry, Rev., John, P.P., Droumtarriffe, Kanturk, co. Cork
Barry, Rev. John, P.P., Lislee, Timoleague, co. Cork
Barry, Rev. John, Skull, Ballidahol, co. Cork
*Barry, J., Esq., Sandville, Bruff, co. Limerick
*Barry, John H., Esq., Ballyvouere-house, near Doneraile, co. Cork
*Barry, John Smith, Esq., J.P., Foaty, Cove, co. Cork, 2 copies
*Barry, Joseph, Esq., M.D., Midleton, co. Cork
*Barry, Rev. Patrick, P.P., Clara, King's county
*Barry, Paul, Esq., Barry's-row, Rathmines, co. Dublin
*Barry, Richard, Esq., Grand Parade, Cork
Barry, Richard, Esq., Greenville, Midleton, co. Cork
*Barry, Thomas, Esq., Ann Grove, near Carrigtohill, co. Cork
*Barry, Mr. Thomas, sen., Grange, Burt, co. Donegal
*Barry, Rev. Thomas, V.F. & P.P., Bantry, co. Cork
*Barry, Valentine, Esq., George's Quay, Cork
Barry, Captain, Kilbolane House, co. Cork
*Barry, Mrs., Sea View, near Delgany, co. Wicklow
Barry, Messrs. James and Son, Mitchellstown, co. Cork
Barry, Ring and Burke, Messrs., Cove, near Cork
Barter, B., Esq., Bally William, Kinsale, co. Cork
Barter, Joseph M., Esq., Dromcarra House, Macroom, co. Cork
Barter, J. W., Esq., Grandcloyne, Midleton, co. Cork
Barter, Thomas, Esq., North Main-street, Bandon, co. Cork
Barter, Richard, Esq., Inniscarra, co. Cork
Barter, Thomas B. P., Esq., Clifton, near Bristol
*Bartlett, Edward, Esq., Buckingham
*Bartlett, Rev. R. J., Buckingham
*Barton, Folliott Warren, Esq., D.L. & J.P., Clonelly, Kish, co. Fermanagh
*Barton, Hugh, Esq., Straffon-house, Clane, co. Kildare
*Barton, Hugh H., Esq., Armagh
*Barton, John, Esq., Stone-house, near Donnybrook, co. Dublin
Barton, John Bayer, Esq., Cove, near Cork
*Barton, Samuel, Esq.
*Barton, William, Esq., Grove, Fethard, co. Tipperary
*Bartree, Simon, Esq. Cohanan, Moy, co. Tyrone
*Bashford, J., Esq., Donaghmoyne, Carrickmacross, co. Monaghan
*Baskirville, T. B. M., Esq., Rockley House, Wilts
*Bassett, J. D., Esq., Leighton Buzzard, Bedfordshire
*Bastable, Daniel Charles, Esq., William-street, Dublin, and Egent Place, Kanturk, co. Cork
*Bastable, Henry, Esq., Heathfield, Kinsale, Cork
Bastable, Mr. H., Trinity-place, Dublin
Batchelor, Edward S., Esq., Moneymore, co. Derry
*Batchelor, Henry John, Esq., Abbeville near St. Doulough, co. Dublin
*Bateman, John, Esq., Oak Park, Tralee, co. Kerry
Bateman, T., Esq., Middleton-hall, Bakewell, Derbyshire
*Bateman, Thomas G., Esq., Alta villa, near Rathkeale, co. Limerick
Bateman, W. W., Esq., M. R. C. S., Green House, Clara, King's co.
Bates, Rev. C. C., Vicar of Castleton, Derbyshire
Bates, John, Esq., Belfast
Bateson, Sir Robert, Bart., M.P. and J.P., Belvoir Park, near Belfast
*Bateson's Arms Hotel, Moira, Co. Down
*Bath, Joseph Henry, Esq., Mecklenburgh-st., Dublin, and Eyre-street, Galway
*Batt, Mr. Benjamin E., Banagher, King's county
*Batt, Narcissus, Esq., Purdysburn, Belfast
*Batt, Thomas, Esq., Donegal Place, Belfast
Batt, Thomas, Esq., Abergavenny
*Batten, Mr. David, Library, Clapham Common, Surrey
*Batten, Mr. H. N., Clapham, Surrey
*Battersby, Lieut.-Col. C. B., Listoke, Drogheda, co. Louth
Battersby, Lieut.-Col. Bobsville, Crossakeel, co. Meath
*Battersby, Edwin, Esq., Lower Merrion-street, Dublin
*Battersby, Henry, Esq., Blessington-street, Dublin
*Battersby, John, Esq., Lakefield, Crossakeel, co. Meath
Battersby, Rev. J. F., Clough Cottage, Clones, co. Monaghan
*Battersby, Thomas, Esq., J.P., Newcastle House, Oldcastle, co. Meath
Battersby, Rev. W., Drumrany Glebe, co. Westmeath
*Battersby, William, Esq., Freffans, Trim, co. Meath
Batteson, David, Esq., Saltergate, Chesterfield, Derbyshire
Batteson, W., Esq., Chesterfield, Derbyshire
*Batty, Arthur Henry, Esq., Brohatna Lodge, Dundalk, co. Louth
*Batwell, Andrew, Esq., Fortlands, near Charleville, co. Cork
*Baylee, H. W., Esq., Larne, co. Antrim
*Baylee, John Tyrrel, Esq., Academy, Baker Place, Limerick
*Bayley, John W., Esq., New-grove, Birr, King's county
*Baylie, Mrs. Sexton, West-grove, Douglas, near Cork
Baylor, Peter, Esq., Wood Side, Fermoy, co. Cork
Baylor, Messrs. Peter & Arthur, Fermoy, co. Cork
*Bayly, Clayton, Esq., Kilcreen, co. Kilkenny
Bayly, Rev. Edward, Rector of Horetown, Taghmon, co. Wexford
*Bayly, Edward Symes, Esq., Ballyarthur, co. Wicklow
*Bayly, John, Esq., Debsborough, Nenagh, co. Tipperary
Bayly, Lieut. Peter, R.N., Hazle Point, Nenagh, co. Tipperary
*Bayly, Richard N., Esq., Ballynaclough, co. Tipperary
*Bayly, Thomas, Esq., Wallstown Castle, Doneraile and Riverdale House, Bandon, co. Cork
*Bayly, Thomas, Esq., Kells, Kilkenny
*Bayly, W., Esq., D.L. & J.P., Norelands, Thomastown, co. Kilkenny
*Bayly, William, Esq., Rose Bank, near Clondalkin, co. Dublin
*Beach, Sir M. H. Hicks, Bt., Williamstrife Park, Gloucestershire
Beahan, Owen and Son, Drogheda, co. Louth
Beale, Abraham, Esq., Patrick's Quay, Cork
Beale, Mr. William, Anne Grove, Mountmelick, Queen's county
Beamish, Mr. A. C., Sun-view, near Inchkinny, Cork
*Beamish, Adderley, Esq., Kilcoleman, Bandon, co. Cork
Beamish, B. Swayne, Esq., South-mall, Cork
Beamish, Charles, Esq., Parade, Cork
Beamish, George, Esq., Lake Mount, Skibbereen, co. Cork
Beamish, J. Newman, Esq., Parade, Cork
Beamish, Mrs. Henry, Muckcross, Clonakilty, co. Cork
Beamish, James Caulfield, Esq., Ringacoultig, Cove, Cork
Beamish, Major, North Ludlow, Belview, Cove, Cork
Beamish, Richard, Esq., Sans Souci, Cork
*Beamish, Samuel Bernard, Esq., Mamore, near Bandon, co. Cork
Beamish, Samuel George, Esq., Rockvale House, Mallow, co. Cork
Beamish, Sampson, Esq., Kilmolodey House, Timoleague, co. Cork
Beamish, Rev. Thomas, Glenview, near Cork
*Beamish, William, Esq., Beaumont, near Cork
*Beamish, William, Esq., Springmount, Clonakilty, co. Cork
Beamish and Crawford, Messrs., Cork
Beare, Richard, Esq., Bruin Lodge, Cork

*Beatty, D., Esq., Upper Gardiner-street, Dublin, and Sligo
Beatty, David, Esq., J.P., Borodale, Enniscorthy, co. Wexford
Beatty, Rev. James, M.A., Dundalk, co. Louth
Beatty, Rev. J., Perpetual Curate of Convoy, co. Donegal
Beatty, Rev. J., Rector of Donaghcloney, co. Down
*Beatty, James, Esq., Governor of Sligo Prison, Sligo
Beatty, Mr. Nathaniel, Grange, Gernan-lane, Dublin
*Beatty, Rev. Thomas, J.P., Moira, co. Down
Beaufort, Rev. William Lewis, Prebendary of Cork, Glanmire, Cork
*Beauman, W., Esq., Furness, Naas, co. Kildare
*Beauman, John, jun., Esq., Hyde Park, Gorey, co. Wexford
*Becher, Edward, Esq., Rock Castle, near Innishannon, co. Cork
*Becher, Henry, Esq., Aughadown, near Skibbereen, Cork
*Becher, Michael Alleyn, Esq., Ballidevane House, Clonakilty, co. Cork
*Becher, Richard, H. H., Esq., J.P., Hollybrook, Skibbereen, co. Cork
*Becher, Sir W. W., Bart., J.P., Ballygiblin, near Kanturk, co. Cork
*Beck, James, Esq., Islandreagh, co. Antrim
*BECTIVE, The Right Honorable the Earl of
*Beddan, Matthew, Esq., Shannon View, Scariff, co. Clare
*Beddy, Joseph, Esq., Cronakiry, near Wicklow
*BEDFORD, His Grace the Duke of
Bedingfeld, Lieut.-Col. F., Thornton-lodge, Thornton-le-Bears, [Northallerton, Yorkshire
*Beechinor, Rev. Jeremiah, P.P., of Newmarket, co. Cork
Beere, Rev. Gerald, Kilbixy-glebe, near Mullingar, co. Westmeath
*Beere, Usher, Esq., Holles-st., Dublin, & Liskeveen Castle, co. Tip- [perary
*BEERHAVEN, the Right Honorable Viscount
*Beers, John, Esq., J.P., Leslie Hill, Manor Cunningham, co. Do- [negal
*Beers, Rev. J. A., Hilltown-glebe, co. Down
*Begg, Oliver William Costello, Esq., Mount Dalton, Rathconrath, [co. Westmeath
Begley, Mr. Charles, Ballymullimber, co. Derry
Begley, Rev. Patrick, Ballinadee, Bandon, co. Cork
Behan, James, Esq., Derryallen, Tandragee, co. Armagh
*Behan, T. S., Esq., Blessington-street, Dublin
Belcher, Robert T., Esq., Bandon, co. Cork
*BELFAST, The Right Honorable the Earl of
*Belfast Historic Society
*Belfast Society for Promoting Knowledge
Bell, Rev. A., Cuba House, Banagher, King's county
*Bell, Andrew, Esq., J. P., Kilmainham House, Cavan
*Bell, Andrew Thomas, Esq., Belmont, co. Tyrone
Bell, Rev. Daniel, Aghnadaragh, Glenavy, co. Antrim
*Bell, David, Esq., Newry, co. Down, & Gardiner's Place, Dublin
*Bell, Edward D. Gonne, Esq., J.P., Farmhill, Claremorris, co. Mayo
Bell, Mr. Henry, Crumlin, co. Antrim
*Bell, Captain James, J.P., Ardcarn, Ballinasloe, co. Roscommon
Bell, James Chapman, Esq., Brown's Mills, Kinsale, co. Cork
Bell, James, Esq., J.P., Bank of Ireland, Ballinasloe, co. Galway
*Bell, John, Esq., Omeath, Co. Louth
Bell, John, Esq., Ballyclare, co. Antrim
*Bell, John, Esq., Halliwell Dean, Hexham, Northumberland
Bell, John, Esq., H.C., Belmount, Gort, co. Galway
*Bell, John, Esq., Thirsk, Yorkshire
Bell, Mr. Joseph, Limabella, Moira, co. Down
*Bell, Matthew, Esq., M.P., Woolsington, Newcastle-on-Tyne
*Bell, R., Esq., Drumheel-house, co. Cavan
*Bell, Robert, Esq., M.D., Hume-st., Dublin
Bell, Rev. Robert, D.D., Clonmel, co. Tipperary
Bell, Robert, Esq., Bellbrook, Glenavy, co. Antrim
*Bell, Mr. Robert, Crumlin, Glenavy co. Antrim
Bell, S., Esq., Finstown-lodge, near Lucan, co. Dublin
Bell, S. A., Esq., Ahascragh, co. Galway
Bell, Thomas, Esq., J.P., Casino, Castlemartyr, co. Cork
*Bell, William, Esq., Cavan
*Bell, William, Esq., Drumhill, Cavan
Bell, William, Esq., M.D., Clonmel, co. Tipperary
Bell, William, Esq., Bellview, Abbeyleix, Queen's county
*Bellew, John, Esq., Blackrock, near Dublin
*Bellew, Sir Patrick, Bart., M.P., Barmeath, Dunleer, co. Louth
*Bellew, Michael D., Esq., J.P., Mount Bellew, Castle Blakeney, [co. Galway
*Bellew, R. M., Esq., M. P., Eccles-street, Dublin
*Bellingham, Lady, Castle Bellingham, co. Louth
*Bellingham, A. O'Bryen, Esq., J.P., Castle-Blayney, co. Monaghan
BELMORE, The Right Honorable the Earl of
Belton, Captain, Ballykilmurry, Tullamore, King's county
Belton, Mr. Henry, Belleck, Tullamore, King's county
*Belton, Samuel, Esq., Blackhall-street, Dublin
*Benison, James, Esq., Ballyshannon, co. Donegal
*Benison, Richard, Esq., Ravensdale, Flurry Bridge, co. Louth
Benn, B. W., Esq., Mansfield, Nottinghamshire
*Benn, John, Esq., Ballygrennan, near Limerick, co. Clare

Bennett, Rev. Edward Leigh, Vicar of Lechlade, Gloucestershire
Bennett, Mr. G. J., Ballincollig, co. Cork
Bennett, John, Esq., Riverston, Nenagh, co. Tipperary
*Bennett, J. B., Esq., Church-street, Dublin
Bennett, J. H., Esq., Ballymore, Cove, co. Cork
Bennett, John William, Esq., Sligo
Bennett, John, Esq., Church-street, Dublin
Bennett, Richard, Esq., Ardverness, Coleraine, co. Derry
*Bennett, J. and J., Messrs., Turnlee, Glossop, Derbyshire
Bennett, Richard, Esq., Aungier-street, Dublin
Bennett, Samuel, Esq., M.D., Bruff, co. Limerick
Bennett, Valentine, Esq., D.L. and J.P., Thomastown-House, [Frankford, King's county
*Bennett, Thomas, Esq., J.P., Ballydevitt, Coleraine, co. Derry
Bennitt, W., Esq., Dudley, Worcestershire
Benson, Mr. George, Essex-quay, Dublin
*Benson, Rev. Hill, Kilchar-glebe, Killybegs, co. Donegal
Benson, John, Esq., Henry-street, Limerick
*Benson, Rev. M., Leighton Buzzard, Bedfordshire
*Benson, Mr. William, Saly Park, near Dolphins Bain, Dublin
*Bentley, G., Esq., Fleet-st., Dublin, & Ballinastoe House, co. Wick- [low
Bently, Rev. John, Rector of Donaghclony-Waringstown, co. Down
*Bently, John, Esq., Hurlston, Broadford, co. Clare
*BERESFORD, The Right Honorable Lord John
*BERESFORD, The Right Honorable Lord George
*BERESFORD, The Right Honorable Lord William
Beresford, Barre, Esq., Learmont, co. Derry
*Beresford, Rev. Charles Cobbe, J.P., Rector of Termon McGuirk, [Termon-glebe, Omagh, co. Tyrone
Beresford, Rev. Charles C., A.M., Kinawly, Ballyconnell, co. Cavan
*Beresford, Hon. & Rev. G. De-la-poer, Fenagh-glebe, co. Leitrim
Beresford, Rev. J., Donoughmore Glebe, Rathdown, Queen's county
Beresford, J. C., Esq., Coleraine, co. Derry
*Beresford, Rev. Marcus G., M.A., Kilmore Palace, Cavan
*Beresford, Major William, Templecarig, near Bray, co. Wicklow
*Beresford, Rev. William, Ballincollig, co. Cork
Berkeley, Rev. G., LL.D., Chaplain of the Foundling, Cork
Bermingham, M., Esq., J.P., Dolgin, near Tuam, co. Galway
Bermingham, Thomas, Esq., Caramana, Kilconnell, co. Galway
*Bermingham, Rev. Thomas, R.C., Curate of Castle-Town-Delvin, [co. Westmeath
Bernard, Hon. and Very Rev. Richard Boyle, D.D., Dean of [Leighlin, Leighlin-bridge, co. Carlow
*Bernard, Arthur B., Esq., J.P., Palace Anne, near Bandon, co. Cork
*Bernard, Hon. Charles L., Lotamore, Cork
Bernard, Edward, Esq., Limerick
*Bernard, Rev. Joshua L., Curate of St. Mary's, Donnybrook, Dublin
*Bernard, Thomas, Esq., Castle-Bernard, Kinnety, King's county
*Bernard, Hon. William S., J.P., The Farm, Bandon, co. Cork
Berry, James, Esq., Drumcree, co. Westmeath
Berry, Mr. Joseph, Moira, co. Down
*Berry, Lieut. Patrick, Revenue Police, Swinford, co. Mayo
Berry, Rev. Philip, Vicar of Castle-Lyons, Rathcormack, co. Cork
*Berry, T. S., Esq., Hume-street, Dublin
Besnard, Julius Cæsar, Esq., Town Clerk of Cork
*Best, Benjamin, Esq., Congreves, Rowley-Regis, Staffordshire
Bestall, W. L., Esq., Templelyon, near Redcross, co. Wicklow
Bethell, R. R., Esq., Ballincollig, co. Cork
Betty, John, Esq., Ashford, Enniskillen, co. Fermanagh
Betty, William, Esq., Irvinstown, co. Fermanagh
*Bevan, Godfrey, Esq., Thomas-street, Limerick
Bevan, Rev. Henry, Vicar of the union of Dromtariffe, co. Cork
Bevan, Joseph, Esq., Glen-bevan, Croom, co. Limerick
Bevan, M., Esq., Carrass, Bruff, co. Limerick
*Bevan, Rev. R., Rector of Carne, near Broadway, co. Wexford
Bevan, Robert, Esq., Limerick
*Bewley, Joseph, Esq., William-street, Dublin
Bewley, Thomas, Esq., Whitechurch, co. Dublin
Bickford, Robert John, Esq., The Mount, Kinsale, co. Cork
*Bickerstaff, John C., Esq., J.P., Lislea, near Ballymahon, co. Long- [ford
Bickersteth, R., Esq., Rodney-street, Liverpool
Biddulph, Nicholas, Esq., Kingsborough, King's county
*Biddulph, R. M., Esq., M.P., Chirk Castle, Denbighshire
*Bigger, William, Esq., Ellerslie, near Little Bray, co. Dublin
*Biggs, G. W., Esq., Bellevue, Borrisokane, co. Tipperary
Biggs, Richard, Esq., Devizes, Wiltshire
*Biggs, William, Esq., Burris Castle, Queen's county
Biggs, Messrs. William, Jacob, and John, Bandon Mills, Bandon, [co. Cork
*Bingham, Sir G. R., J.P.
*Bingham, C., Esq., Kilrush, co. Clare
*Bingham, Major Dennis, J.P., Bingham Castle, Belmullet, co. Mayo

*Bingham, Rev. J. B., Great Gaddesden, Hertfordshire
Bingham, W. B., Esq., M.D., Downpatrick, co. Down
Bingham, William, Esq., Bay-view, Binghamstown, co. Mayo
Birch, Mr. D., Londonderry
*Birch, George, Esq., Monaincha, Roscrea, co. Tipperary
Birch, Henry, Esq., Ashfield, Ballybrittas, Queen's county
Birch, James, Esq., Ballybeen, Belfast, co. Antrim
Birch, Rev. P., C.C. Inistiogue, co. Kilkenny
*Birch, Robert, Esq., Church-street, and Richmond-house, near [Drumcondra, co. Dublin
*Birch, W. H., Esq., Birch-grove, near Roscrea, co. Tipperary
Bird, John S., Esq., Bantry, co. Cork
Birmingham, Rev. George, A.M., Prebendary and Vicar of the union [of Lackan, Lackan-glebe, Rathlackan, co. Mayo
Birmingham, Rev. James, C.C., Roscrea, co. Tipperary
Birney, James, Esq., J.P., Oakley, co. Down
*Birney, Rev. Thomas, M.A., Aghavea-glebe, Brook-borough, co. Fer- [managh
*Birnie, Sir R. Knt., Bow-street, London
Bishopp, Edward, Esq., M.D., Kinsale, co. Cork
*Bisshopp, Very Rev. Sir G., Bart., Dean of Lismore, Bagot street, [Dublin
Black, Adam, Esq., Newry, co. Down
Black, George, Esq., Stranmillis, Belfast
*Black, Henderson, Esq., J.P., Larkfield, Belfast
Black, James, Esq., Kinsale, co. Cork
Black, John, Esq., Aughnaskeagh, Dundalk, co. Louth
Black, Joseph, Esq., Sligo
*Black, Thomas, Esq., Eccles-street, Dublin
Black, Thomas, Esq., Lodge, Coleraine, co. Derry
*Black, William, Esq., Ballymena, co. Antrim
*Blackburne, The Right Honorable Francis, Roebuck, co. Dublin
Blackburne, George F., Esq., Mornington-house, Drogheda, co. Louth
*Blacker, Lieut.-col. William, D.L. and J.P., Carrick, co. Armagh
*Blacker, Rev. James S., A.M., J.P., Rector of Keady, co. Armagh
Blackham, John, Esq., Antrim
Blackmore, Henry, Esq., Kilshane-cottage, Tipperary
Blackstock, Thomas, Esq., Ballinasloe, co. Galway
*Blackstone, W. S., Esq., Castle-priory, Wallingford, Berkshire
*Blackwall, S. W., Esq., Colamber, Edgeworthstown, co. Longford
Blackwell, J. C., Esq., Elmfield, Armagh
Blackwood, Rev. William S., Rector of Armoy, co. Antrim
Blair, James, Esq., Wheatfield, Belfast
Blair, Richard L., Esq., Blair's-cove, Bantry, co. Cork
Blair, William, Esq., Iron-works, Lucan, co. Dublin
*Blake, A. R., Esq., J.P., Stillorgan, co. Dublin
Blake, Charles, Esq., Tuam, co. Galway
Blake, Charles, jun., Esq., D.L. and J.P., Merlin-park, Galway
Blake, Edmund, Esq., National Bank, Galway
Blake, H., Esq., J.P., Hartfield, Loughrea, co. Galway
Blake, Henry Joseph, Esq., Springvale, Ballinrobe, co. Mayo
Blake, Isidore, Esq., C.C.P., Benlevy, Cong, co. Mayo
*Blake, James, Esq., Vermont, Castle-Blakeney, co. Galway
Blake, The Very Rev. Michael, Vicar-General, St. Michael's and [St. John's, Dublin
Blake, John F., Esq., Newtown Smyth, Galway
*Blake, M., Esq., Killeen-castle, near Galway
*Blake, Maurice, Esq., Ballinafad, Ballyglass, co. Mayo
*Blake, M. J., Esq., M.P., Brooklodge, Dangan, co. Galway
*Blake, Nicholas, Esq., Frenchfort, Oranmore, co. Galway
*Blake, Patrick, Esq., J.P., Gortnamona, Balliuasloe, co. Galway
*Blake, Richard, Esq., J.P., Garracloone, Cong, co. Mayo
*Blake, Rev. Thomas, P.P., Borrisokane, co. Tipperary
Blake, Thomas Joseph, Esq., Holly-park, near Loughrea, co. Galway
Blake, Sir Valentine, Bart., J.P., Menlough-castle, near Galway
Blake, Walter J., Esq., Rosslodge, near Headford, co. Galway
*Blake, Walter, Esq., Queensfort, Tuam, co. Galway
*Blakeney, Charles William, Esq., Holywell, near Roscommon
Blakeney, J. H., Esq., J.P., Abbert, Castle-Blakeney, co. Galway
*Blakeney, Robert, Esq., Fitzwilliam-square West, Dublin
*Blakeney, Robert, Esq., Dundermott, Ballymoe, co. Galway
Blanchfield, Patrick, Esq., Clifden, Kilkenny
*Bland, Francis C., Esq., D.L. & J.P., Derriquin, Kenmare, co. Kerry
*Bland, John Thomas, Esq., Blandsfort, Abbeyleix, Queen's county
*Bland, Loftus Henry, Esq., Upper Pembroke-street, Dublin
Bland, Rev. R. W., Perpetual Curate of St. George, Belfast
*Bland, Rev. Thomas, Killarney, co. Kerry
Blaquiere, E., Esq., Rendifin, Gort, co. Galway
Blathwaite, G. W., Esq., J. P., Farnhill, Magherafelt, co. Derry
BLAYNEY, The Right Honorable Lord
*Blayney, Robert, Esq., Umrigar, near Carnew, co. Wicklow
Bleazby, John, Esq., Ballinacurra, Kinsale, co. Cork
*Bleckley, Rev. John, M.A., Monaghan
*Blennerhassett, Arthur, Esq., D.L., J.P., Ballyseedy-house, Tralee, [co. Kerry
Blennerhassett, Gerald, Esq., D.L. and J.P., Riddlestown, co. Li- [merick
Blennerhassett, Henry, Esq., M.D., Dingle, co. Kerry
*Blennerhassett, John, Esq., J.P., Rockview, Limerick
*Blick, T. C., Esq., Newport Pagnell, Bucks
*Bligh, Thomas, Esq., Brittas, co. Cavan
Blood, Bindon, Esq., J.P., Cranaher, Ennis, co. Clare
*Blood, FitzGerald, Esq., Ballykilty, Newmarket-on-Fergus, co. Clare
*Blood, Michael, Esq., Galway
Blood, Neptune, Esq., Ormond Quay, Dublin
Blood, Neptune, Esq., Curraugh, Kanturk, co. Cork
Blood, Thomas, Esq., J.P., Roxton, Corofin, co. Clare
*BLOOMFIELD, The Right Honorable Lord
*Bloomfield, Major John Colpoys, J.P., Castle-Caldwell, Ballyshan- [non, co. Fermanagh
Blow, James, Esq., Dunadry, co. Antrim
*Bluett, Matthew, Esq., Newcastle, co. Limerick
*Blundell, Rev. William, D.D., Castlerea, co. Roscommon
*Boardman, Robert, Esq., Woodville-house, Loughbrickland, co. Down
Boate, Beresford, Esq., Tournore, Dungarvan, co. Waterford
*Boate, George, Esq., Abbey-side, Dungarvan, co. Waterford
Bodel, Michael, Esq., Dromore, co. Down
*Bodkin, John, Esq., Annagh, co. Galway
Bodkin, John D., Esq., Bengurra, Athenry, co. Galway
Bodkin, J. E., Esq., Fleet Street, London
*Bodkin, John J., Esq., M.P. and J.P., Quarrymount, near Tuam, [co. Galway
*Bodkin, Thomas, Esq., Rahoon, Galway
Boggs, Gard, Esq., Wall, Londonderry
*Boggs, George Hill, Esq., Ballybrack-house, Moville, co. Donegal
*Bogue, Rev. Thomas, P.P., of Clones East, Lake-view, co. Ferma- [nagh
*Boileau, George Wilson, Esq., Stillorgan, co. Dublin
*Boileau, Simon, Esq., Lakelands, near Stillorgan, co. Dublin
*Boland, Thomas, Esq., Sligo
Boland, Rev. John, P.P., Killconly, Tuam, co. Galway
*Boland, Rev. M., A.B., & J.P., Killynumery-glebe, Dromahair, co. [Sligo
Boland, T. Parsons, Esq., Pembrook-passage, co. Cork
Boles, Rev. William, Springfield, near Castlemartyr, co. Cork
Bolger, Paul, Esq., Enniscorthy, co. Wexford
*Bolger, Richard, Esq., Ballard, Kilbeggan, co. Westmeath
*Bolingbroke, John, Esq., J.P., Oldcastle, Swinford, co. Mayo
Bolster, Mr. Humphrey, Great-George-street, Cork
*Bolton, Captain Edward, Knock Robbin, Kinsale, co. Cork
*Bolton, Chichester, Esq., Upper Temple-street, Dublin
*Bolton, Henry, Esq., Ballywillan, Sligo
*Bolton, Rev. L. H., Carrickmines, co. Dublin
Bolton, Rev. Peter, A.M., Camira, Nenagh, co. Tipperary
*Bolton, Richard, Esq., Gorey, co. Wexford
*Bolton, Richard, Esq., Bective, Navan, co. Meath
Bolton, Richard, Esq., Castlering, Dundalk, co. Louth
Bolton, Thomas, Esq., Ballykisteen, Tipperary
Bolton, William, Esq., J.P., Island, near Oulart, co. Wexford
*Bompas, George G., Esq., M. D., Fish-ponds-house, near Bristol
Bond, Andrew, Esq., Pennyburn, Londonderry
*Bond, Major A. P., J.P., Ardglass, Rathowen, co. Westmeath
*Bond, Henry M., Esq., Newtown-bond, Edgeworthstown, co. Longford
*Bond, Henry Coote, Esq., Bondville, Tynan, co. Armagh
*Bond, J. W., Esq., Cartron Card, Edgeworthstown, co. Longford
*Bond, Joseph Moffatt, Esq., Mortimer, Berks.
*Bond, Thomas W., Esq., Aungier-st., Dublin, & Newtown Bond, [Edgeworthstown, co. Longford
*Bond, Walter McGeough, Esq., Argory, co. Armagh
Bond, Rev. William, A. M., Glebe-house, Ballee, co. Down
*Bond, Willoughby, Esq., Farra, Longford
Bonham, Rev. J., Willow-brook, Ballitore, co. Kildare
Booker, Rev. John, A.M., Vicar of Killurin, co. Wexford
Booker, William, Esq., Bensford, Kells, co. Meath
*Bookey, Richard, Esq., Donistall, near Carnew, co. Wicklow
*Bookey, W. T., Esq., Derrybane, near Glendalough, co. Wicklow
*Boomer, James, Esq., Sea-view, Belfast
*Booth, Sir Robert Gore, Bart., J.P., Lissadell, Sligo
Booth, George, Esq., Brunswick-st., Liverpool
*Booth, George Thomas B., Esq., J.P., Drumcorbin, Crossdoney, co. [Cavan
*Booth, Joseph, Esq., Darven-castle, Lurgan-green, co. Louth
Booth, William, Esq., South-view cottage, near Ballincollig, co. Cork
*Boothby, B., Esq., Christ-church, Oxford, & Ashbourn-hall, Derby
*Borough, Randal, Esq., J. P., Cappa-lodge, Kilrush, co. Clare
*Borrowes, Rev. Sir Erasmus Dixon, Bart., Lauragh, Emo, Queen's co.
Borthwick, J., Esq., Kilroot Bleachgreen, Carrickfergus, co. Antrim
*Boston, John, Esq., M.D. and A.B., Midleton, co. Cork
*Boswell, John, Esq., Athlone, co. Westmeath
*Boswell, T. A., Esq., The Grange, North Crawley, Buckinghamshire
Bottomley, John, Esq., Belfast, co. Antrim
Bouchier, Rev. James Henry, Rathkeale, co. Limerick

Bourke, George, Esq., Queen-street, Cheapside, London
Bourke, Hon. and Rev. George T., Kilmacon, Waterford
*Bourke, Isidore, Esq., Ballina, Co. Mayo, and Mountjoy-st., Dublin
*Bourke, Rev. Miles, P.P., Clonmeen, & Kilcorney, Kanturk, co. [Cork
*Bourke, Oliver, Esq., Heathfield, Killala, co. Mayo
*Bourke, Rev. Robert, R.C., Vicar of St. Patrick's, & Kilmuny, Li- [merick
*Bourke, Ulick., Esq., Grove-hill, near Bray, co. Wicklow
Bourke, W., Esq., Mountjoy-st., Dublin, & Carrowkeel, co. Limerick
*Bourke, Rev. W., P.P. of Buiounagh and Templetoher, Dunmore [Mayo
*Bourke, Walter J., Esq., The Castle, Killalla, co. Clare
Bourke, Rev. J. W., Vicar of Offerlane, Mountrath, Queen's county
*Bourne, F., Esq., Terenure, near Roundstown, co. Dublin
*Bourne, P., Esq., Fieldstown, Swords, & York-street, Dublin
*Bourne, Richard, Esq., Lynnbury, Mullingar, co. Westmeath
Bourne, Timothy, Esq., Liverpool
Bourne, Rev. William, A. M., Rathcormac, co. Cork
*Bourne, W., jun., Esq., Harcourt-st., Dublin
*Bourne, Thomas, Esq., Killincoole, Dundalk, co Louth
Bournes, David, Esq., Ardglass, near Carrick on Shannon, co. Ros- [common
*Bourns, Charles, Esq., Toomavara, co. Tipperary
Bourns, Mr. F., Deputy-Governor of Newgate, Dublin
Bourns, Henry, Esq., Crossmolina, co. Mayo
Bourns, Matthew, Esq., Belmullet, co. Mayo
*Bouverie, T. K., Esq., Castle-Dawson, co. Derry
*Bouwens, Rev., Theodore, Rector of Stoke-Hamond, Buckinghamshire
*Bowden, J. B., Esq., Southgate-house, Chesterfield, Derbyshire
*Bowden, J. W., Esq., Aldermanbury, London
Bowden, Thomas, Esq., Coleshill, Amersham, Buckinghamshire
*Bowden, Robert F., Esq., Blackrock, Cork
Bowen, Anthony E., Esq., J. P., Annefield, Hollymount, co. Mayo
*Bowen, Charles Jones, Esq., St. Stephen's Green, Dublin
Bowen, Rev. Christopher, A.M., Kilcommon-glebe, Hollymount, [co. Mayo
*Bowen, Rev. Edward, Bogay-house, Londonderry
Bowen, Henry Cole, Esq., J.P., Bowens-court, near Doneraile, co. [Cork
*Bowen, John, Esq., Oakgrove, Killinardrish, co. Cork
Bowen, Robert, Esq., Greham, Hollymount, co. Mayo
Bowens, Samuel, Esq., Rossport, Erris, co. Mayo
Bower, J. S., Esq., Broxholme, Doncaster, Yorkshire
*Bowes, John, Esq., Streatham-castle, Durham
Bowles, Spotswood, Esq., Ahern-house, Fermoy, co. Cork
Bowles, Rev. W., Springfield, Cloyne, co. Cork
Boxwell, John, Butlerstown-castle, near Wexford
Boxwell, Samuel, Esq., Campfield-house, near Dundrum, co. Dublin
*Boxwell, William, Esq., M.D., Abbeyleix, Queen's county
*Boyce, Samuel, Esq., Brook-hall, Coleraine, co. Derry
Boyd, C., Esq., Lisburne, co. Antrim
*Boyd, A., Esq., Williamstown Castle, near Dublin, and Ballycastle, [co. Antrim
*Boyd, Ezl. D., Esq., J. P., Ballycastle, co. Antrim
*Boyd, G. A., Esq., Belvidere-house, Great Denmark-street, Dublin
Boyd, Hugh, Esq., Ashgrove, near Newry, co. Down
Boyd, Rev. H. E., J.P., Prebendary of Dromaragh, co. Down
Boyd, J., Esq., Stephen's-green, Dublin
Boyd, J., Esq., J.P., Rosslare-house, near Wexford
Boyd, Captain James, Loughbrickland, co. Down
*Boyd, James B., Esq., Ballier, Armagh
*Boyd, Mr. James B., Limerick
*Boyd, Rev. John, C. C., Castlerea, co. Roscommon
*Boyd, John, Esq., J.P., Coleraine, co. Derry
Boyd, John, Esq., Hill-street, Newry, co. Down
Boyd, John, Esq., Clementstown, Cootehill, co. Cavan
Boyd, John William, Esq., Roscrea, co. Tipperary
*Boyd, Joseph Hall, Esq., Lurgan, co. Armagh
*Boyd, Matthew, Esq., Lurgan, co. Armagh
Boyd, Rev. Ralph, Prebendary of Taghmon, co. Wexford
*Boyd, Robert, Esq., Marlocoo, Tandragee, co. Armagh
*Boyd, Mr. Robert, Newtown-Limavady, co. Derry
*Boyd, William, Esq., J.P., Fort Breda, Belfast
*Boyd, Lieut. W., R. I. Fuzileers
*Boyd, Rev. W., J. P., Kiltoe-lodge, Letterkenny, co. Donegal
Boyd, W., Esq., Ballinaslce, co. Galway
Boyes, Rev. William, Curate of Dunean, Toome, co. Antrim
*Boylan, Rev. Daniel, P.P., Maheracloon, Carrickmacross, co. Mo- [naghan
*Boylan, Felix, Esq., Stephen's-green West, Dublin
*Boylan, Nicholas, Esq., Hilltown-house, Drogheda, co. Louth
Boylan, John, Esq., Blakestown, Ardee, co. Louth
*Boylan, Patrick, Esq., North Quay, Drogheda, co. Louth
Boylan, R. Dillon, Esq., Lower Baggott-st. Dublin
*BOYLE, The Right Honorable Lord
*Boyle, Alexander, Esq., College-green, Dublin
*Boyle, C., Esq., The Rock, Cookstown, co. Tyrone
Boyle, James, Esq., Boyle Grove, Macroom, co. Cork
Boyle, Mr. James, Sligo
*Boyle, Hon. John, Hamilton Place, London
*Boyle, Maxwell James, Esq., J.P., Tullyvin House, Cootehill, co. [Cavan
*Boyse, John, jun., Esq., Limerick
*Boyse, S., Esq., The Grange, Bannow, Taghmon, co. Wexford
Boyton, Rev. Charles, Glendoven, Letterkenny, co. Donegal
*Brabazon, Sir William, Bart., M.P., Brabazon Park, Swinford, co. [Mayo
*Brabazon, Charles, Esq., Charleville, Dalkey, co. Dublin
*Brabazon, Henry J., Esq., D.L. and J. P., Dromisken House, Castle [Bellingham, co. Louth
*Brabazon, Harry L., Esq., Seafield, Dunleer, co. Louth
Brabazon, Mrs. Margaret, Rath House, Termon Fechin, Drogheda
*Bracken, William Henry, Esq., J.P., Recorder of Kilkenny
*Brackenbury, Mrs. William, Lincoln
Brackin, Patrick, Esq., Athlone Bridge, co. Westmeath
Brackwell, J. C., Esq., Elmfield, near Armagh
Braddell, Messrs. George & Thomas, Prospect, Clonegal, co. Wexford
Braddell, W., Esq., Lower Bullingate, near Carnew, co. Wicklow
Braddell, Mrs. H., Rahangrany, near Carnew, co. Wicklow
*BRADFORD, The Right Honorable the Earl of
Bradford, John, Esq., Cavananore, Dundalk, co. Louth
*Bradley, George, Esq., Omagh, co. Tyrone
*Bradley, Henry, Esq., Rockingham Hall, Hagley, Worcestershire
*Bradshaw, A. H., Esq., Charles-st., St. James's square, London
Bradshaw, Benjamin Bennett, Esq., J.P., Clonmel, co. Tipperary
*Bradshaw, Rev. Benjamin W., Curate of Abington, near Limerick
*Bradshaw, Messrs. H. A. & Co., Donegal
Bradshaw, H., Esq., Culcavy Cottage, Hillsborough, co. Down
Bradshaw, Hugh B., Esq., Philipstown, Tipperary
*Bradshaw, George, Esq., Pegsboro, near Tipperary
*Bradshaw, W. H., Esq., J.P., Summerville, Clonmel, co. Tipperary
*Brady, Denis C., Esq., M.P. and J.P., Newry, co. Down
*Brady, Rev. Hugh, Ballinamore, co. Leitrim
*Brady, John D., Esq., Keon Brook, Carrick-on-Shannon, co. Leitrim
*Brady, Rev. Joseph, P.P. of New Bridge, near Arklow, co. Wicklow
*Brady, Rev. Philip, P.P. of Donabate & Portrane, co. Dublin
Brady, Rev. P. J., R. C. C., Athboy, co. Meath
*Brady, Raheens Hugh, Esq., Tomgrany, Scariff, co. Clare
*Brady, Rev. Thomas B., M. A., Raheens, Killaloe, co. Clare
Brady, William, Esq., Nuns Island, Galway
Brady, William, Esq., Mill View, Mallow, co. Cork
Brady, W., Esq., Sandymount Avenue, co. Dublin
Bransfield, Mr. John, Castle Lake, near Cashel, co. Tipperary
Bramston, Rt. Rev. James Yorke, D. D., R.C. Bishop of London [Golden-square, London
*Brandling, John, Esq., Kenton-lodge, Newcastle-on-Tyne
Brangan, Lawrence, Esq., Collinstown, near Cloghran, co. Dublin, [& N. King-street, Dublin
*Branston, Mrs. Elizabeth, Micklefield Green, Hertfordshire
*Branton, Mrs. E., Micklefield-green, Hertfordshire
*Brass, Mrs. Mary Anne, Revelscourt, near Redcross, co. Wicklow
*Brassington, Charles, Esq., Dominick-street, Dublin
Bray, Reginald, Esq., Great Russel-st., Bloomsbury, London
*Brayne, Robert, Esq., Banbury, Oxfordshire
Brayne, Thomas, Esq., Banbury, Oxfordshire
Breakey, Mr. W., Breakeys Rocks, near Rockcarry, co. Monaghan
*Bredin, Rev. James A. M., Nurney, near Leighlin Bridge, co. Carlow
Breen, Patrick, Esq., Castle-bridge, Wexford
Brenan, Rev. G. J. M., Cove-street, Cork
Brenan, George, Esq., Ableny Cottage, Skibbereen, co. Cork
*Brenan, James, Esq., Ballina, co. Mayo
*Brenan, John, Esq., Kingstown Lodge, co. Dublin
Brenan, Rev. Michael, P.P., Goresbridge, co. Kilkenny
Brenan, R. Esq., Great Eastcheap, London
*Brenan, Rev. Thomas, P. P., Johnstown, co. Kilkenny
Brenan, Thomas, Esq., Wexford
Brenan, Rev. William, P.P., New Ross, co. Wexford
*Brennan, Denis, Esq., Coolbane, Brennan's Glen, Killarney, co. [Kerry
*Brennan, F., Esq., Kilglass-house, Ahascragh, co. Galway
Brennan, James, Esq., Pitt-street, Dublin
*Brennan, John, Esq., Springlawn, Castle-Blakeney, co. Galway
*Brennan, Rev. Patrick, R.A. of Killian and Kilronan, co. Galway
Brennan, Rev. Patrick, P.P., Kildare
*Brennan, Rev. Malachi, P.P., Kilpatrick, Carney, co. Sligo
*Brennan, Rev. Peter, P.P. of Killaraght, Boyle, co. Sligo
*Brennan, Peter. Esq., Harristown, near Finglass, co. Dublin
*Brennan, Rev. P., P.P., Aughnamullan West, Ballybay, co. Monaghan
*Brennan, Robert, Esq., Hermitage, near Lucan, co. Dublin
Brereton, Captain Henry, J.P., Mount Rath, Queen's county
Brereton, Mr. John, Mountmellick, Queen's county
*Brereton, R. P., Esq., Shannon Park, & Castletown co. Sligo

*Brereton, Thomas, Esq., Rathurlys, Nenagh, co. Tipperary
Brett, John, Esq., Tubbercury, co. Sligo
Brett, Mr. John, Hotel, Killaloe, co. Clare
*Brett, William Gore, Esq., Roslea, co. Monaghan
*Brettle and Co., Messrs. G., Wood-street, London
Brew, Rev. Richard, A. B., Tulla-glebe, co. Clare
Brew, Tomkins, Esq., J.P., Ennis, co. Clare
*Brewster, Edward, Esq., French-street, Dublin
Brice, W., Esq., Excise-office, Gort, co. Galway
*Bricknell, J. J., Esq., J.P., Loughrea, co. Galway
*Bride, Rev. Edward, Urney, Strabane, co. Tyrone
Bridge, Rev. Ralph, Lisburn, co. Antrim
Bridge, Vizer, Esq., Ashbury, Roscrea, co. Tipperary
*Bridgeman, H. O., Esq., Fairy-mount, Castle Connell, co. Limerick
*Bridgeman, Hewitt, Esq., M.P., Tierna, near Ennis, co. Clare
*Brien, John, Esq., J. P., Castletown, Enniskillen, co. Fermanagh
Brien, Lowther, Esq., Lower Rutland-st. Dublin, & Ardverney [West, co. Fermanagh
Brierly, Mr. John, King's court Baths, Clontarf, co. Dublin
Brindley, J. N., Esq., Temple, London
Brinkley, Rev. John, Rector of Glanworth, co. Cork
*Briscoe, Edward, Esq., J.P., Grangemore, near Mullingar, co. West- [meath
*Briscoe, George, Esq., Willmount, Pilltown, co. Tipperary
*Briscoe, Henry Harrison, Esq., Cloncunny, Clonmore, co. Kilkenny
*Briscoe, Henry W., Esq., Tinvane House, Carrick-on-Suir, do.
Briscoe, James, Esq., Rosse, Tullamoore, King's county
*Briscoe, Robert, Esq., Fermoy, co. Cork
*Briscoe, William Nugent, Esq., J.P., Mount Briscoe, near Philips- [town, King's co.
*Briscoe, William T., Esq., Riverdale, nr. Mullingar, co. Westmeath
Briton, John, Esq., Londonderry
*Broadley, H., Esq., Milton-hill, Hull, Yorkshire
*Broderick, Major Edward, J.P., Maryborough-house, & Castletown [Cottage, co. Cork
Brodigan, Thomas, Esq., Pilltown, Drogheda
Bromehead, Rev. A. C., Rectory-house, Eckington, Chesterfield
Bromhead, Major S., Cairnsfoot, Sligo
*Brooke, Sir Arthur B., Bart., J.P., Colebrooke, Brookboro, co. Fer- [managh
*Brooke, Sir Arthur de Capell, Bart., Ahadoe, co. Cork
*Brooke, Rev. Butler, A.B., Trory-glebe, Enniskillen, co. Fermanagh
*Brooke, Rev. Hugh, Burt, co. Donegal
Brooke, Richard, Esq., Liverpool
*Brooke, Thomas, Esq., J.P., Lough Eske, Donegal
*Broomfield, A. S., Esq., Hollywood, Glanealy, Ashford, Co. Wicklow
*Brough, Rev. Grainger, LL.D., Dundalk, Co. Louth
Brough, J., Esq., Kiltegan, near Baltinglass, co. Wicklow
*Broughton, Rev. Thomas Delves, Rector of Bletchley, near Fenny [Stratford, Buckinghamshire
Broughton, Capt. W. E. Delors, Stranorlar, co. Donegal
Brown, Alan, Esq., Glengormley-house, Belfast
*Brown, David, Esq., Ballyarnet, Templemore, co. Derry
Brown, Francis, Esq., Mount-Southwell, Rathkeale, co. Limerick
Brown, Rev. G. B., Tideswell, Derbyshire
Brown, Hugh, Esq., Glenconway, Glenavy, co. Antrim
Brown, J., Esq., J.P., Roscommon
*Brown, Rev. James, A. M., Garva, co. Derry
Brown, James, Esq., Grange Moy, co. Cork
Brown, Mr. James Corballis, Castledermot, co. Kildare
*Brown, James S., Esq., J. P., Mount Brown, and Castlematrix, [Rathkeale, co. Limerick
Brown, James Grier, Esq., Summer Hill, Antrim
*Brown, John, Esq., J. P., Clonboy, Castleconnell, co. Limerick
*Brown, Mr. John, Randalstown, co. Antrim
*Brown, Mathew, Esq., Bolton-street, Dublin, & Augher, co. Tyrone
Brown, Pearce, Esq., Brown Ville, Rathkeale, co. Limerick
*Brown, R., Esq., Rosey-park, near Blackrock, co. Dublin
*Brown, Thomas D., Esq., Church-street, Fenchurch-street, London
*Brown, William, Esq., Regent-street, London
Brown, William, jun., Esq., Passage West, co. Cork
*Brown, William K., Esq., Wilton, Rathkeale, co. Limerick
Browne, Lieut-General, Sir Thomas, K. C. H., Knockduffe-house, [on the Oyster Haven, near Kinsale, co. Cork
*Browne, Hon. & Rev. Henry M., Mullingar, co. Westmeath
Browne, Right Rev. George J.B., R. C. Bishop of Galway
*Browne, Major Edmund, J. P., Breafy Lodge, Castlebar, co. Mayo
Browne, Capt., Janeville, Killough, co. Down
*Browne, Alexander, Esq., Heathfield, Tyrrelspass, co. Westmeath
*Browne, Arthur, Esq., J.P., Roxborough, near Roscommon
*Browne, B. G., Esq., Baggott-street, Dublin
*Browne, Rev. Chaworth, J.P., Wilson's Hospital, near Mullingar, [co. Westmeath
*Browne, G., Esq., J.P., Annefield, Pilltown, co. Kilkenny
Browne, Henry, Esq., Youghal, co. Cork
*Browne, Right Rev. James, D. D., R. C. Bishop of Kilmore, Coote- [hill, co. Cavan
Browne, B., Esq., Mount-Bernard, Castle-Blakeney, co. Galway
Browne, Rev. John, Kildare
Browne, Rev. James, P.P., Kilmain, Hollymount, co. Mayo
Browne, James, Esq., Ardskea, Dangan, co. Galway
*Browne, Rev. James Thomas, Vicar of Kinsale, co. Cork
*Browne, Jemmett, Esq., J.P., Riverstown, near Cork
*Browne, John, Esq., J.P., Mount Browne, Westport, co. Mayo
*Browne, John, Esq., Eccles-street, Dublin
Browne, Rev. John, LL.D., Bandon, co. Cork
*Browne, John Francis, Esq., Tuam, co. Galway
*Browne, John H., Esq., Comber House, near Derry
Browne, Joseph, Esq., Rosemount, near New Ross, co. Wexford
Browne, Joseph, Esq., Elm Grove, Trim, co. Meath
*Browne, Michael Joseph, Esq., J.P., Moyne, Dangan, co. Galway
Browne, Michael P., Esq., Curcullen, near Galway
*Browne, Robert, Esq., Riverstown, Monastereven, co. Kildare
*Browne, R. Clayton, Esq., J.P., Viewmount, Carlow
Browne, The Hon. Thomas, J.P., Prospect Hall, Killarney, co. Kerry
*Browne, William, Esq., Granby Row, Dublin
Browne, Rev. William, Keady, co. Armagh
*Browning, William, Esq., Ardinade, Kilcullen, co. Kildare
*Brownlow, Charles, Esq., D.L. and J.P., Lurgan House, co. Armagh
Brownlow, Rev. Francis, Alla Rectory, Derry
Brownlow, Rev. J., Ballynascreen Glebe, Tobermore, co. Derry
Brownrigg, Rev. Abraham, C.C., Tomacork, co. Wicklow
Brownrigg, Anneiby B., Esq., Bishop Hall, co. Kilkenny
Brownrigg, Henry, Esq., Wingfield, near Tinahely, co. Wicklow
*BRUCE, The Right Honorable Lord Ernest
*Bruce, Sir James Robert, Bart., V.L. and J.P., Downhill, near [Derry
*Bruce, Edward, Esq., Scout Bush, Carrickfergus, co. Antrim
Bruce, George, Esq., Milltown Castle, near Charleville, co. Cork
Bruce, Rev. Jonathan, A.M. and J.P., Springfort, co. Cork
*Bruce, Samuel, jun., Esq., Belfast, co. Antrim
Bruce, Stewart C., Esq., Millburn, Coleraine, co. Derry
*Bruce, W. F., Esq., Auburn, near Athlone, co. Westmeath
*Bruen, Col. H., M.P. and J.P., Oak Park, near Carlow
Brunett, W. K., Esq., Springfield, Cloyne, co. Cork
*Brunker, Edward George, Esq., M.D., Dundalk, co. Louth
*Brunker, Thomas, Esq., Milmore, Ballibay, co. Monaghan
Brunskill, Rev. John, A.M., Kilquain, Loughrea, co. Galway
Brunton, W. H., Esq., Herbertstown, Newbridge, co. Kildare
*Brush, Crane, Esq., Rathfryland, co. Down
Brush, Crane Richard, Esq., Dromore, co. Down
*Bryan, John, Esq., Millnell, Monaghan
*Bryan, William, Esq., Magherafelt, co. Derry
Bryce and Brown, Messrs. Limerick
*Brydges, Col. Sir John William Head, Knt., Wootton Court, Kent
Bryson, Edward, Esq., Antrim
Bryson, Harper C., Esq., Randalstown, co. Antrim
*Buchanan, Charles W., Esq., M.D., Omagh, co. Tyrone
*Buchanan, J. W., Esq., Nuneaton, Warwickshire
Buchanan, Rev. Thomas, Cullen-glebe, Tipperary
*Buchanan, Mr. William, Springtown, Templemore, co. Derry
*Buchanan, W. B,, Esq., J.P., Shannon-grove, Banagher, King's [county
*Buckley, Rev. Charles, P. P., Buttevant, co. Cork
*Buckley, Henry, Esq., Hillsboro', Roscrea, co. Tipperary
Buckmaster, William, Esq., Youghal, co. Cork
*Bucknall, Samuel Lindsey, Esq., Lower Gardiner-street, Dublin, [and Turin Castle, co. Mayo
*Budd, Rev. James, Rathmullen, co. Donegal
Budd, Rev. Richard, A.B., Stradbally, Queen's county
*Bulfin, Thomas, Esq., J.P., Castlebar, co. Mayo
*Bulkley, Rev. D., R.C.R., Darra, and Kilflynn, Kilfinane, co. [Limerick
Bull, J., Esq., Cittadella, Blackrock-road, Cork
*Bullen, William, Esq., M.D., Cork
*Bulmer, William, Esq., Watling-street, London
*Bunbury, Benjamin, Esq., Johnstown, co. Kilkenny
Bunbury, Henry, Esq., Bunbury-lodge, Carlow
Bunbury, Sir James Mervyn Richardson, Bart., D.L. and J.P., [Augher Castle, co. Tyrone
Bunbury, Thomas, Esq., Moyle, Carlow
Bunbury, Thomas, Esq., Lisbryan, Burrisokane, co. Tipperary
Burbigh, W., Esq., St. Catherine's, Carrickfergus, co. Antrim
Burdekin, G., Esq., Manchester
*Burges, John Ynyr, Esq., J.P., Parkanour, Dungannon, co. Tyrone
*Burges, R., Esq., J.P., Mullaghmore, Omagh, co. Tyrone
Burgess, Henry, Esq., Lombard-street, London
Burgess, Richard, Esq., Clonmel, co. Tipperary
Burgh, Walter Hussey, Esq., J.P., Donore, Naas, co. Kildare
Burgoyne, Sir John James, Knt., J.P., Strabane, co. Tyrone
*Burgoyne, Rev. T. N., Donagheady, Altrest, Strabane, co. Tyrone

*Burk, Patrick, Esq., Belfast
*Burke, Right Rev. Patrick, D.D., R.C. Bishop of Elphin
*Burke, Charles Granby, Esq., Marble Hill, co. Galway
*Burke, Edmund, Esq., Tyaquin, near Monivoe, co. Galway
Burke, Rev. Edward, R.C.C., Cork
Burke, James P., Esq., Tuam, co. Galway
*Burke, James, Esq., Sweetmount, near Dundrum, co. Dublin
Burke, James, Esq., Clonmel, co. Tipperary
Burke, James Ulick, Esq., Carrowkeel, Loughrea, co. Galway
*Burke, John, Esq., J.P., Moyglass, Woodford, Loughrea, do.
*Burke, John, Esq., J.P., Ower, Headford, co. Galway
Burke, Rev. John, Usk, Monmouthshire
*Burke, J., Esq., Upper Rutland-st., Dublin, and Rosduff, co. Mayo
Burke Rev. John A.M., Kilcolgan Vicarage, Oranmore, co. Galway
*Burke, Joseph, Esq., Lower Gardiner-st., Dublin, and Elm Hall,
[Parsonstown, co. Tipperary
Burke, J. F., Esq., Becan, Claremorris, co. Mayo [Galway
Burke, J. Hardiman, Esq., J.P., St. Clerans near Loughrea, co.
*Burke, Patrick, Esq., Galway
*Burke, P. M., Esq., D.L. & J.P., Danesfield, Moycullen, co. Galway
*Burke, Rev. Redmond, Fethard, co. Tipperary
Burke, Redmond, Esq., Galway
*Burke, Theobald, Esq., Burke-ville, Aughrim, co. Galway
Burke, Theobald, Esq., J.P., Woodville, Castlebar, co. Mayo
*Burke, Lieut.-Col. Thomas, Prospect Villa, Carrigaline, co. Cork
*Burke, Thomas, Esq., Kilmain, co. Mayo
Burke, Thomas, Esq., Fort-hall, Gort, co. Galway, and Gloucester-
[place, Dublin
Burke, Thomas, Esq., Ballydoogan, Loughrea, co. Galway, and
[Belvedere-place, Dublin
*Burke, Ulic, Esq., M.D., Swinford, co. Mayo
Burke, W. B., Esq., Queensborough-lodge, Eyrecourt, co. Galway
Burke, William, Esq., J.P., Tuam, co. Galway
Burke, William, Esq., M.D., Dundrum, co. Dublin
Burke, Rev. William J., R.C.C., Liscannor, co. Clare
Burleigh, William, Esq., J.P., St. Catherine's, Carrickfergus, co.
*Burnard, Major William, Kinsale, co. Cork [Antrim
*Burne, Edward, Esq., J.P., Athlone, co. Westmeath
*Burnett, Rev. James, Rathfarnham, co. Dublin
*Burniston, Lieut. H. S., R.N., Raven-lodge, Kingstown, co. Dublin
Burns, Lieut., Manor Hamilton, co. Leitrim
Burns, Robert, Esq., High-street, Belfast
Burnside, Mr. James, Capel-street, Dublin
*Burr, Richard, Esq., Nenagh, co. Tipperary
*Burriss, Charles, Esq., Frankford, King's county [co. Kilkenny
*Burroughs, Rev. W. K., Curate of Grange Silvea, Goresbridge,
*Burrowes, Alexander, Esq., Fernsboro', Granard, co. Longford
*Burrowes, Rev. Sir E. D., Lauragh, Emo, Queen's county
*Burrowes, Mrs. John, General Post Office, Dublin
*Burrowes, Peter, jun., Esq., Grange Ville, Rochetown Avenue,
[near Killiney, co. Dublin
Burrowes, Robert, Esq., Lara House, near Annamoe, co. Wicklow
Burrowes, Rev. Robert, D.D., Rector of Drumragh, Omagh, co.
Burrowes, The Very Rev. R., D.D., Dean of Cork [Tyrone
*Burrowes, Robert, Esq., Stradone House, co. Cavan
*Burrowes, S., Esq., M.D., Bideford, Devonshire
*Burrowes, Major Thomas, D.L. & J.P., Stradone House, co. Cavan
*Burrowes, T., Esq., Grange-ville, Rochestown-avenue, co. Dublin
Burrowes, William, Esq., J. P., Cavan
Burtchaell, David, Esq., J.P., Brandon-dale, Graig, co. Kilkenny
*Burton, The Right Honorable Judge, Dublin
*Burton, Henry Stuart, Esq., West Mall, Clifton, near Bristol
Burton, Rev. J. E., Clonakilty, co. Cork
Burton, Rev. Nathaniel, Royal Hospital, Kilmainham, Dublin
*Burton, Rev. Philip, R.C.C., Cloyne, co. Cork
*Burton, Rev. Robert William, Rathmelton, co. Donegal [dare
*Burton, William F., Esq., J.P., Burton Hall, Castledermot, co. Kil-
*Burtt, Mr. James, Clifton, near Bristol
*Bury, Capt. George, J.P., Mount Avon, near Rathdrum, co. Wicklow
*Bury, John, Esq., Woodville, Clane, co. Kildare
Bury, Michael, Esq., J.P., Downings House, Clane, co. Kildare
*Bury, Phineas, Esq., Little Island, Cork
*Bury, Robert, Esq., Killora Lodge, Cahirlog, co. Cork
*Bury, T. S., Esq., Hume-street, Dublin
*Bury, William, Esq., New Bridge-street, Blackfriars, London
*Bushe, Arthur, Esq., Lower Gloucester-street, Dublin
*Bushe, Arthur, Esq., Upper Fitzwilliam-street, Dublin
*BUSHE, Lord Chief Justice
*Bushe, Thomas, Esq., Fitzwilliam-square, North, Dublin
*Bussell, H., Esq., Abbey-ville, Cross-avenue, Booterstown, Dublin
Busher, Rev. Thomas, R.C.C., Lady's Island, co. Wexford
3

*Butler, Sir Thomas, Bart., J.P., Ballin Temple, near Tullow, co.
[Carlow
*Butler, Augustin, Esq., J.P., Ballyl'ne Knock, co. Clare
*Butler, Capt. Edward, Ballyadams Castle, Ballylinan, Queen's co.
*Butler, Edward, Esq., Mt. Anville, co. Dublin
*Butler, Capt. F., J.P., Cregg, Gort, co. Galway
*Butler, Rev. Hans, Lismore, co. Waterford
*Butler, James, Esq., Kilmagar, Kilkenny [co. Galway
Butler, J. F., Esq., M.D., Mount-Bellew-bridge, Castle-Blakeney,
*Butler, James, Esq., J.P., Broomville, Tullow, co. Carlow
*Butler, James, Esq., D.L. & J.P., Waterville, Cahirciveen, co. Kerry
*Butler, J. Archer, Esq., Garnavella, Cahir, co. Tipperary
*Butler, James Blake, Esq., Glen William, Ennis, co. Clare
Butler, R., Esq., Maryboro', Queen's county [Dublin
*Butler, The Honourable T. Fitzwalter, Rathmines-terrace, near
*Butler, Rev. Richard, Vicar of Trim, co. Meath
Butler, Richard, Esq., Ballyslatteen, near Cashel, co. Tipperary
Butler, Rev. Richard, Burnchurch-glebe, Kilkenny
*Butler, Robert, Esq., Blessington-street, Dublin
*Butler, Theobald, Esq., Kemsey, near Worcester
*Butler, Rev. Theobald, J.P., Blanchville, Gowran, Kilkenny
Butler, Rev. Theobald, Besborough, Knock, co. Clare
*Butler, Thomas, Esq., Ballycarron, Golden, co. Tipperary
Butler, Thomas, Esq., Ballyconra, Ballyragget, Kilkenny
Butler, Rev. William, Spring Cottage, Fermoy, co. Cork
Butler, William, Esq., Rosemount, Phillipsburgh Avenue, Dublin
*Butler, William, Esq., White Hall, near Baltinglass, co. Wicklow
*Butler, Mr. W. H., Mt. Merrion, co. Dublin
Butler, W., Esq., J.P., Bunnahow, Gort, co. Galway
*Butson, The Ven. J. S., LL.D., Archdeacon of Clonfert, co. Galway
Butt, Benjamin E., Esq., Banagher, King's county
*Byde, Rev. John, Hertford
Byrne, Anthony, Esq., Claragh Castle, Kilkenny
Byrne, Edward, Esq., Ballyrogan, near Arklow, co. Wicklow [mon
*Byrne, Francis Tyrrell, Esq., Currisdoona, Ballymoe, co. Roscom-
Byrne, Gerald, Esq., Sleaty, Carlow
Byrne, James, Esq., Ennis, co. Clare
*Byrne, Rev. John, C.C., Bray, co. Wicklow
*Byrne, John, Esq., J.P., Kilpatrick, near Arklow, co. Wicklow
*Byrne, James R., Esq., Gt. Brunswick-street, Dublin
*Byrne, Lawrence, Esq., Cronybyrne, near Rathdrum, co. Wicklow
*Byrne, Rev. Patrick, P.P. of Castletown, co. Westmeath
*Byrne, Thomas, Esq., Ballyboghill, co. Dublin
*Byrne, Timothy, Esq., Ellen and Alicia Cottages, Dalkey, and
[Grafton-street, Dublin
Byrne, Thomas T., Esq., Tenny Park, co. Roscommon
Byrne, Rev. William, P.P., Ballina, Killaloe, co. Tipperary
*Byrne, Messrs. Patrick and Son, Mabbot-street, Dublin
*Byrne, Daniel, Esq., Brook Ville, near Moate, King's county
Byron, L., Esq., M.D., Navan, co. Meath

*Caddell, Michael O'Farrell, Esq., Harbourstown, near Balbriggan, co.
Cadge, Rev. R., A.M., Ahascragh, co. Galway [Meath
*Cæsar, H. A. Esq., M.D., South-mall, Cork
Caffray, James, Esq., Bridgefoot-street, Dublin
Caffry, Rev. Atkinson, A.M., J.P., Mullagh, co. Cavan
*Cahill, Rev. D. W., Seafort Seminary, Williamstown, near Dublin
*Cahill, Rev. David L., R.C.C., Bantry, co. Cork
Cahill, James, Esq., Crinlin-lodge, near Little Bray, co. Dublin
*Cahill, John, Esq., Thurles, co. Tipperary
*Cahill, Rev. John, P.P., Inniscarra, Cork
*Cahill, Michael, Esq., Dublin
Cahill, T. W., Esq., M.D., Blarney, co. Cork
Cainen, Rev. John, R.C.C. of Lucan, co. Dublin
Caincy, Patrick, Esq., Marlborough-street, Dublin
*Cairnes, William, Esq., Drogheda, co. Louth
Cairns, William, Esq., Belfast
Caldbeck, John F., Esq., Rathmines-road, Dublin
*Caldbeck, W. Esq., Moyle Park, Clondalkin, co. Dublin
*Caldwell, James, Esq., Sligo
Caldwell, Robert, Esq., Mary-street, Dublin
Caldwell, W., Esq., C.C.P., Ballina
Caldwell, Mr. W., Faughanvale, co. Derry
*CALEDON, The Right Honorable the Earl of
Caley, Digby, Esq., Ripon, Yorkshire
*Callaghan, G., Esq., Sidney-house, Cork
*Callaghan, H. H. O., Esq., Grafton-street, Dublin
Callaghan, John, Esq., Ballinhassig, co. Cork
*Callaghan, Mathew, Esq., Midleton, co. Cork
*Callaghan, Mathew, Esq., Artaine, co. Dublin

*Callanan, Rev. James P.P., Clontarf, co. Dublin
*Callanan, Peter, Esq., Skecur, Eyrecourt, co. Galway
Callannan, Michael, Esq., Blackpool, Cork
*Callery, W. T., Esq., Clonona, King's county
*Callwell, Rev. J., Hermitage, Newtown-Mount Kennedy, co. Wicklow
Callwell, R., Esq., Lismoine, near Belfast
*Calvert, Frederick, Esq., Lincoln's-Inn, London
Camack, W., Esq., River-view, Buncrana, co. Donegal
Cambie, Charles, Esq., J.P., Castletown, Burrosokane, co. Tipperary
Cambie, S.L., Esq., Killoran, near Thurles, co. Tipperary
Camble, Mr. Daniel, Coagh, co. Tyrone
CAMDEN, The Most Noble the Marquess of
Campbell, Mr. Alexander, Omagh, co. Tyrone
*Campbell, Rev. Charles, LL.D. & J.P., Vicar of Newry, co. Down
*Campbell, D., Esq., Provincial Bank of Ireland, Cavan
Campbell, E. H., jun., Esq., Newcastle-on-Tyne, Northumberland
*Campbell, Rev. James, P.P. of St. James', Dublin
*Campbell, Rev. James, LL.D. & J.P., Rector of Forkhill, co. Armagh
*Campbell, James, Esq., Wine-street, Sligo
Campbell, James, Esq., Cottage, Ballykelly, Newtownlimavady, co. Derry
Campbell, James, Esq., Belfast
*Campbell, John, Esq., Danesfield, near Clontarf, & Sackville-st., Dublin
Campbell, Mr. Mathew, Burt, co. Donegal
*Campbell, Robert W., Esq., Distillery, Enniskillen, co. Fermanagh
Campbell, Rev., W., White-abbey, Belfast
Campbell, W., Esq., M.D., Fermoy, co. Cork
*Campbell, William, Esq., Antrim
Campbell, W., Esq., Drogheda
*Campin, Henry, Esq., St. Paul's-church-yard, London
Campin, Luke Graham, Esq., Gurteen-house, Fermoy, co. Cork
*Campion, C. W., Esq., French-street, Dublin
Campion, Robert, Esq., Cromore, Doneraile, co. Cork
Campion, Rev. Robert Deane, A.B., Knockmourne Parsonage, Tallow, co. Cork
Campion, R. G. Esq., Bushy-park, Rathcormac, co. Cork
*Canavan, Rev. George, P. P. of Damastown, Naul, co. Dublin
Canavan, Rev. John, P.P. of Menna, co. Galway
Canavan, Rev. Patrick, P.P. of Bellclare, Tuam, co. Galway
*Cane, Richard, Esq., St. Wolstans, Celbridge, co. Kildare
Cane, Major Stopford, Sunville-house, Cloyne, co. Cork
*Cann, John M., Esq., Farmley, near Cahir, co. Tipperary
Cannan, D., Esq., Lothbury, London
Canning, Rev. James Alfred, A.M., Downpatrick
Canning, Rev. John, Rockville, Carndonagh, co. Donegal
*Cannon, Charles, Esq., Moyglare, Maynooth, co. Meath
Cannon Rev. Peter, Castlebar, co. Mayo
Cannon, Philip, Esq., Shamble-street, Ballymena
Cannon, Philip, sen., Esq., Ballymena-castle, co. Antrim
Cannon, Philip, jun., Esq., M.D., Ballymena-castle, co. Antrim
Canny, Dennis, Esq., J. P., Clonmony, Bunratty, co. Clare
Canny, John, Esq., Ballyglass, Killeagh, co. Cork
Canny, John, Esq., Ballyglass-house, Killeagh, co. Cork
Canny, Mr. W., High-st., Ennis, co. Clare
Cantillon, John, jun., Esq., Rockfarm, Little-island, Cork
Cantrell, Henry, Esq., Youghal, co. Cork
Cantwell, James, Esq., Carrick-on-Suir, co. Tipperary
Cantwell, The Right Rev. John, D.D., R.C. Bishop of Meath
*Cantwell, Rev. Nicholas, P.P., Tramore, co. Waterford
Caraffa, Mr. Paolo, Exchequer-street, Dublin
*Caraher, James, Esq., Cardistown, Ardee, co. Louth
*CARBERY, The Right Honorable Lord
*Carbery, Rev. Peter, R.C.C., Kilbeggan, co. Westmeath
*Carbery, W. Esq., Youghal, co. Cork
*Carden, Sir H. R., Bart, D.L. & J.P., Priory, Templemore, co. Tipperary
*Carden, R. M., Esq., Fithmoyne, co. Tipperary
Cardiff, Robert, Esq., M.D., Wexford
*Cardwell, William, Esq., Tully-Elmer, Armagh
CAREW, The Right Honorable Lord
*Carew, Alexander, Esq., Kilcarron, Burrosokane, co. Tipperary
Carew, Lynn, Esq., Upper Rutland-street, Dublin
Carew, Robert, Esq., J.P., Woodinstown, near Cashel, co. Tipperary
*Carew, Thomas, Esq., J.P., Ballinamona, near Waterford
Carew, T. M., Esq., Drummond-lodge, Rockfort-bridge, co. Westmeath
*Carew, Walter John, Esq., Loscairne, Dungarvan, co. Waterford
Carey, Edward K., Esq., Carey's-ville-castle, Fermoy, co. Cork
*Carey, Capt. John W., Cork
Carey, Joseph, Esq., Curraghmore, Fermoy, co. Cork
Carigan, Rev. P., P. P., Kilamery, Callan, Kilkenny
Carleill, W., Esq., Longstone-hall, Bakewell, Derbyshire
Carleton, Rev. E. M., Woodside, near Cork
Carleton, Rev. R., Killead, Crumlin, co. Antrim
*Carlile, Rev. James, Upper-Merrion-st., Dublin
*Carmichael, James, Esq., Stephen's-green, Dublin
Carmichael, John, Esq., Cork
*Carmichael, Richard, Esq., Rutland-square, Dublin
*Carmichael, Samuel, Esq., Ballylawn, Moville, co. Donegal
*Carmichael, Rev. Thomas, Ennis, co. Clare
Carmody, Michael, Esq., Ennis, co. Clare
*Carmolt, Thomas, Esq., Brook-hill, near Londonderry
*Carncross, Col. Sir J. H., K.C.B., Rose Lawn, near Celbridge, co. Kildare, and Booterstown, co. Dublin
*Carnegie, J. Esq., North-Esk, near Cork
Carney, Redmond, Esq., Castlebar, co. Mayo
*Carolin, Charles, Esq., Abbey-street, Dublin
Carolin, Frederick, Esq., Talbot-street, Dublin
*Carpendale, Rev. Maxwell, A.M., Mullyvilly-glebe, co. Armagh
Carpendale, Rev. Thomas, Donaghmore, Dungannon, co. Tyrone
Carpenter, Richard, Esq., Usher's-quay, Dublin
*Carpenter, Rev. Robert, Coollattin, Tinahely, co. Wicklow
Carpenter, Mr. W., City Marshalsea, Dublin
Carr, Captain Dawson, Ballynook, Youghal, co. Cork
Carr, Frederick, Esq., C.C.P. Castlerea, co. Roscommon
Carre, Rev. Henry, Fanet, Ramelton, co. Donegal
*CARRICK, The Right Honorable the Earl of
*Carrick, P., Esq., Ennis, co. Clare
Carrigg, Charles, Esq., Ennis, co. Clare
*Carroll, Henry, Esq., Ballynure, near Baltinglass, co. Wicklow
*Carroll, George, Esq., Boston, Wetherby, Yorkshire
Carroll, James, Esq., Dundalk, co. Louth
*Carroll, John, Esq., Great-Charles-st., Dublin
*Carroll, Redmond, Esq., Upper-Rutland-street, Dublin
*Carroll, Rev. T., R.C.C., Townsend-street, Dublin
Carroll, Thomas F., Esq., Waterford
*Carroll, Mrs. Mary, Carollina, Cork
*Carruthers, James, Esq., Galwally, near Belfast
Carruthers, William, Esq., Knockbeg, Carlow
Cart, Robert, Esq., Woodlawn-cottage, Newcastle, co. Limerick
Carte, Thomas E. Esq., Upper Cecil-street, Limerick
*Carter, Charles, Esq., St. Katharine-dock-house, London
Carter, R. H., Esq., Gloucester
Carter, S. R., Esq., M.D., Castledermot, co. Kildare
*Carter, T., Esq., Edgcott, Northamptonshire
*Carter, The Very Rev. Thomas, Dean of Tuam, & Prebend & Rector of Ballymore Glebe-house, Tandragee, co. Armagh
Carter, W. H., Esq., New-park, near Stillorgan, co. Dublin
Carter, W. H., Esq., J.P., Castlemartin, near Kilcullen, co. Kildare
Carthy, Ross, Esq., Carlingford, co. Louth
*Cartwright, Rev. S. R., Aynhoe Rectory, Northamptonshire
*Cartwright, W. R., Esq., Aynhoe, near Brackley, Northamptonshire
Cary, D., Esq., C.C.P., Maryborough, Queen's county
Carty, Mr. Denis, Rathyark, near Bridgetown, co. Wexford
*Carty, Rev. H., P. P., Castletown, Kilpatrick, Nobber, co. Meath
Carty, Robert J., Esq., Wexford
*Carty, Thomas, Esq., Drogheda, co. Louth
Cary, Rev. Anthony G., Glendermot-glebe, Londonderry
Cary, John, Esq., Silver-brook, Dunnamanna, co. Tyrone
*Cary, Lucius, Esq., J. P., Carmaguigly, Moville, co. Donegal
Cary, Rev. Oliver, York-crescent, Clifton, near Bristol
*Cary, Robert, Esq., Tunalague, Carndonagh, co. Donegal
*Casebourne, Thomas, Esq., Caledon, co. Tyrone
*Casement, Francis, Esq., Ballee-cottage, Ballymena, co. Antrim
*Casement, John M., Esq., J.P., Invermore, Larne, co. Antrim
Casement, Thomas, Esq., Ballymena, co. Antrim
*Casey, E. H., Esq., Newbrook, Coolock, co. Dublin
*Cash, Lieut.-Col. H., Belville, Rochestown Avenue, Killiney, co. Dublin
*Cash, John, Esq., Esker-house, near Lucan, co. Dublin
*Cashel, Rowan, P., Esq., Lissen-hall, Nenagh, co. Tipperary
*Casserley, Mr. Myles, Roscommon
*Cassidy, Andrew, Esq., Bruckless, Donegal
Cassidy, John James, Esq., Carrickmacross, co. Monaghan
*Cassidy, Robert, Esq., Monastereven, co. Kildare
*Cassidy, S. J., Esq., Mount-Aeriel, Magherafelt, Londonderry
Cassidy, Rev. Thomas, Harolds-cross, near Dublin
*Caswell, Samuel, Esq., Blackwater-mill, and Bank-place, Limerick
*CASTLEMAINE, The Right Honorable Viscount
*CASTLESTUART, The Right Honorable Lord
*Catharine Hall Library, Cambridge
Cathcart, Mr. Alexander, Curragh, Coleraine, co. Derry
Cather, W., Esq., Newtown-li-mavady, co. Derry
*Cathrew, James, Esq., Ballyowen-lodge, near Lucan, co. Dublin
*Caulfield, The Honorable Henry, Hockley, co. Armagh
Caulfield, Rev. John, R. C. C., of Monaghan

*Caulfield, Peter, Esq., Castle of Kilkea, Castledermot, co. Kildare
*Caulfield, Rev. T. G., Benowen-glebe, near Athlone, co. Westmeath
Caulfield, W., Esq., Livitstown, Athy, co. Kildare
*Cavanagh, Edward, Esq., Drimna Castle, co. Dublin
Cave, Mr. Thomas, Darley-dale, Derbyshire
*CAVENDISH, The Right Honorable Lord William
*Cavendish, The Honorable George, J.P., Leixlip Castle, co. Kildare
*Cavendish, The Honorable & Rev. Thomas, J.P., Cahir, co. Tipperary
Ceely, Robert, Esq., Aylesbury, Bucks
*Chadwick, A. C., Esq., Dameville, Tipperary [mines, co. Dublin
*Chadwick, John, Esq., Grafton-street, and Greenville, near Rath-
*Chaine, Rev. John, Oakfield, Carrickfergus, co. Antrim
*Chaine, W., Esq., Ballycraigy, co. Antrim
*Chaine, W., jun., Esq., Moilena, Antrim
*Chaloner, Richard, Esq., Kingsfort, Moynalty, co. Meath [ford
*Chaloner, Robert, Esq., J.P., Coollattin Park, near Carnew, co. Wex-
*Chambers, Daniel, Esq., J. P., Gartan, Letterkenny, co. Donegal
*Chambers, David, Esq., Magherafelt, co. Derry
Chambers, Mr. Francis, Londonderry
Chambers, J., Esq., Dundalk, co. Louth
*Chambers, James, Esq., Kilrush, co. Clare [co. Donegal
*Chambers, John, Esq., Rutland-square North, Dublin, & Red Castle,
*Chambers, John, Esq., Fox Hall, Letterkenny, co. Donegal
*Chambers, Rev. John, J.P., do. do.
Chambers, Rev. John, Ballinderry, co. Antrim
*Chambers, W., Esq., Llanelly House, Carmarthenshire
*Chambers, W. C., Esq., Clover Hill, Sligo [Armagh
*Chambré, H. W., Esq., J. P., Hawthorn Hill, Flurry Bridge, co.
*Chamley, Rev. Francis, Gaybrook, near Malahide, co. Dublin
*Chamney, John, Esq., Lower Gardiner-street, Dublin
Chamney, John, Esq., Coolboy, Tinahely, co. Wicklow
*Chamney, Thomas, Esq., Ballyrahine, near Tinahely, co. Wicklow
Chandlee, Mr. Thomas, Baltinglass, co. Wicklow
*Chandler, G., Esq., Treeton, Rotheram, Yorkshire
Channer, W. Esq., C. C. P., Kilrush, co. Clare
Chapman, George, Esq., Water-View-Lodge, Fermoy, co. Cork
*Chapman, John, Esq., J.P., Portland, Burrosokane, co. Tipperary
Chapman, Rev. Joseph, Bagnalstown, co. Carlow
*Chapman, Robert, Esq., J.P., Castle Mitchell, Athy, Queen's co.
*Chapman, Sir Thomas, Bart., Killua Castle, Clonmellon, co. West-
*CHARLEMONT, The Right Honorable the Earl of [meath
CHARLEVILLE, The Right Honorable the Earl of
*Charley, Hill, Esq., Belfast, co. Antrim
Charley, Mathew, Esq., Woodbourne, near Belfast, co. Antrim
Charley, W., Esq., Seymour Hill, Lisburne, co. Antrim
*Charlton, Edward, Esq., Sandhoe, Hexham, Northumberland
Charters, James, Esq., Glendona, Glenavy, co. Antrim
*Charters, Robert, Esq., Athlone, co. Westmeath
Chartres, Capt. W., J.P., Curragh, Lisnaskea, co. Fermanagh
*CHATTERTON, The Dowager Lady
*Chaytor, J. M., Esq., Heath-ville, Monkstown, co. Dublin
Chaytor, W., Esq., Clonmel, co. Tipperary
*Chaytor, W. C., Esq., Durham
*Chearnley, Anthony, Esq., Salterbridge, Cappoquin, co. Waterford
Cheevers, Rev. Conolly, Glebe House, All Saints, co. Donegal
*Cheevers, John, Esq., J.P., Killyon, Ballinamore, co. Galway
Cherry, Mr. John, Lomona, near Newtownlimavady, co. Derry
Cherry, Thomas R., Esq., Waterford
*Cherry, Mr. Thomas R., New Ross, co. Wexford
Chester, Henry, Esq., J.P. & D.L., Cartown, Drogheda, co. Louth
*Chester, Rev. John, J.P., Vicar of Ballyclough, near Mallow, co. Cork
*Chester, Lieut.-Col. John, Chicheley Hall, Bucks
*Chester, Michael, Esq., J.P., Stone House, Dunleer, co. Louth
*Chetwood, Major J., J.P., Woodbrook, Portarlington, Queen's county
*CHETWYND, The Right Honorable Viscount
CHICHESTER, The Right Honorable Lord Arthur
*CHICHESTER, The Right Honorable and Rev. Lord E.
Chittick, James, Esq., Manor Cunningham, Letterkenny, co. Donegal
*Chittock, J., Esq., Upper Dominick-street, Dublin
Cholmeley, Francis, Esq., Brandsby, near York
*Cholmley, Lewin, Esq., Gunby Park, near Spilsby, Lincolnshire
*Christie, Rev. James, P.C. of Faughanvale, co. Derry
Christie, Mr. James, Gracehill, Ballymena, co. Antrim
Christie, Mr. Robert., Barrack-street, Belfast, co. Antrim
*Christmas, William, Esq., D.L. and J.P., Tramore, co. Waterford
Christy, Mr. James, Kircassock, Moira, co. Down
*Christy, John, Esq., Stramone, near Gilford, co. Down
Christy, John, Esq., Fort Union, Adare, co. Limerick
*Church, Rev. James, A.B., Loughill, Dunbo, co. Derry
*Church, John, Esq., Oatlands, near Newtownlimavady, co. Derry
Church, Robert H., Esq., Drumvan, Magilligan, co. Derry

*Church, Thomas, Esq., Magilligan, near Newtownlimavady, co. Derry
Church, Thomas, Esq., Thistlefield, near Newtownlimavady, co. Derry
*Church, Miss Mary, Newtownlimavady, co. Derry
Churley, John, Esq., Finaghey, near Belfast, co. Antrim
*Chute, Capt. Francis, Spring Hill, Tralee, co. Kerry
*Chute, Rev. J.P., A.M. & J.P., Ballyheigue, near Tralee, co. Kerry
Chute, Rev. John L., Castlerea, co. Roscommon
*CLANCARTY, The Right Honorable the Earl of
Clanchy, Daniel, Esq., J.P., National Bank, Charleville, co. Cork
Clancy, Francis, Esq., M.D., Ballinhassig, co. Cork
Clanny, W. Reid, Esq., M.D., F.R.S., Sunderland
*CLARE, The Right Honorable the Earl of
Clare, Benjamin, Esq., Claremount, Drogheda, co. Louth
*Clare, H. J., Esq., Laurel-grove, near Delgany, co. Wicklow
*CLARINA, The Right Honorable Lord [perary
*Clark, Charles, Esq., J.P., Graignoe-park, near Thurles, co. Tip-
Clark, G. J., Esq., J.P., Steeple, near Antrim
Clark, Mr. Jackson, Kilmore, Lurgan, co. Armagh
*Clark, John, Esq., Sessions-house, Old Bailey, London
*Clark, Joseph, Esq., Ballymoney, co. Antrim
Clark, Lieut. W., R.N., Langhaugh, Galashiels, Selkirk, N.B.
*Clarke, Alexander, Esq., Maghera, co. Derry
*Clarke, General Andrew, Belmont, Lifford, co. Donegal
*Clarke, Mr. Andrew, Porthall, Lifford, co. Donegal
*Clarke, G. K., Esq., Ringsend, Dublin
Clarke, Charles, Esq., Rathdrum, co. Wicklow
*Clarke, Denis, Esq., Flood-street, Galway, and Larch Hill, Loughrea
*Clarke, Edward, Esq., Ballinagh, co. Cavan
Clarke, Rev. Eugene, R.C.C. of Clondalkin, co. Dublin
Clarke, Rev. E. A., Prior of Straid Abbey, Foxford, co. Mayo
Clarke, Rev. E. M., Curate of Clonleigh, Lifford, co. Donegal
Clarke, George, Esq., Emo, Queen's county
*Clarke, Mr. H, Carraroe-lodge, Marble-hill, Woodford, co. Galway
Clarke, J. G., Esq., Benwell-lodge, Newcastle-on-Tyne, Northum-
Clarke, J., Esq., Esker-house, near Lucan, co. Dublin [berland
*Clarke, J. D., Esq., J.P., Recorder of Portarlington, Queen's county
*Clarke, Mr. James, Rathmelton, co. Donegal
Clarke, James, Esq., Abbey-street, Dublin, & Weldrum, Westmeath
*Clarke, James, Esq., County Surveyor, Omagh, co. Tyrone
*Clarke, Joseph, Esq., Mount-prospect, Killaloe, co. Clare
Clarke, Rev. Mark, Shronell-glebe, near Tipperary
*Clarke, Robert, Esq., Bansha-house, Killardry, Tipperary
Clarke, Samuel, Esq., Newtown Butler, co. Fermanagh
Clarke, W., Esq., Mount-pleasant, Ballinasloe, co. Galway
*Clarke, Walter, Esq., Eagralough, Loughall, co. Armagh
Clarke, W., Esq., Rathleague, Maryborough, Queen's county
Clarke, W., Esq., Youghal, co. Cork
Clarke, William, Esq., College Hill, Galway
*Classon, John, Esq., Northumberland-buildings, Eden-quay, Dublin
*Clay, W. W. P., Esq., Southwell, Notts. [hall, Lancashire
Clayton, Lieut.-Gen. B., Carrickburn, co. Wexford, & Adlington-
Clealand, James Rose, Esq., J.P., Rath-Gael-house, Bangor, co.
*Cleaver, Rev. W., Delgany, co. Wicklow [Down
*Cleburne, Christopher, Esq., Belgouly-mills, near Kinsale, co. Cork
Cleburne, Joseph, Esq., M.D., Grange, Ballincollig, co. Cork
Cleland, Rev. Andrew, Ballintemple-glebe, near Newry, co. Down
Clements, Rev. A., Beech-cottage, Moville, co. Donegal
Clements, Henry, Esq., Milltown, near Wicklow
*Clements, Col. H. John, J.P., Ashfield-lodge, Cootehill, co. Cavan
Clements, Hill, Esq., C.E., Thomas-street, Limerick
Clements, James, Esq., C.C.P., Limerick
*Clements, Col. J. M., Wilton-crescent, London
*Clements, T., Esq., Rakenny, Stradone, co. Cavan
*Clendining, Alexander, Esq., I. P., Westport, co. Mayo
Clerke, David Horan, Esq., Weston-lodge, Skibbereen, co. Cork
Clerke, John, Esq., Mills, Skibbereen, co. Cork
Clerke, John W., Esq., Agricultural Bank, Skibbereen, co. Cork
Clerke, W., Esq., Clountis-house, Rosscarbery, co. Cork
*Clewlow, Miss Anne, Claremont, Belfast, co. Antrim
Clibborn, Barclay, Esq., Anner-mills, near Clonmel, co. Tipperary
Clibborn, E. C., Esq., Banbridge, co. Down
Cliffe, Anthony, Esq., D.L and J.P., Belleview, Wexford
Cliffe, Richard, Esq., Lismore, co. Waterford
Clifford, The Honorable C.F., Irnham-hall, Colsterworth, Lincoln-
Clifford, Lieut. H. I., R.N., Thornhill, Sligo [shire
*Clifford, Captain Robert, Carn-cottage, Ballyconnell, co. Cavan
Clifford, W., Esq., Millview, Thomastown, co. Kilkenny
Clifton, John, Esq., Leyburn, Bedale, Yorkshire
Clinch, Thomas, Esq., Mer-view, Booterstown, co. Dublin
*Clindining, Henry, Esq., Wheatfield, Richill, co. Armagh
*CLOGHER, The Right Honorable and Rev. Lord Bishop of

*CLONBROCK, The Right Honorable Lord
CLONCURRY, The Right Honorable Lord
*Close, H. V., Esq., Merrion-square East, Dublin
*Close, Rev. John F., A.M., Morne Rectory, Kilkeel, co. Down
*Close, Lieut.-Col. Maxwell, J.P., Drumbanagher-castle, co. Armagh
*CLOYNE, The Right Rev. Lord Bishop of
*Clutterbuck, Lorenzo, Esq., Killemley, near Cahir, co. Tipperary
*Coast, W., Esq., Cairn-lodge, Fermoy, co. Cork
*Coates, Arthur, Esq., Newtown-prospect, Kilcock, co. Kildare
Coates, Charles, Esq., Tankersley, near Tinahely, co. Wicklow
Coates, John, Esq., Carrickfergus, co. Antrim
*Coates, Samuel, Esq., Cloncurry, Enfield, co. Kildare
*Coates, Samuel, Esq., New-park, Kilcock, co. Kildare
*Coates, Thomas, Esq., Lincoln's-inn-fields, London
*Coates, William, Esq., J.P., Knockanally, Kilcock, co. Kildare
*Coates, William, Esq., Rockspring, Longford
*Cobbe, Charles, Esq., Newbridge, near Swords, co. Dublin
*Cochran, Mr. Edward, sen., Glendermot, Londonderry
*Cochran, Mr. Edward, jun., Glendermot, Londonderry [Down
*Cochran, Rev. Henry S., Rector of Killygarvan, Rathmullen, co.
Cochran, Mr. James, Carrokeel, Glendermot, Londonderry
Cochran, James, Esq., Gortlee, Letterkenny, co. Donegal
*Cochran, John, Esq., J.P., Edenmore, Stranorlar, co. Donegal
*Cochran, Mr. John, Coleraine, co. Derry
*Cochran, Mr. Samuel, Crislaghmore, Fahan, co. Donegal
Cochran, W., Esq., Leek, Glasslough, co. Monaghan
Cochrane, John L., Esq., Westport, co. Mayo
*Cochrane, Robert, Esq., City-quay, Dublin
*Cochrane, Thomas, Esq., Ballinasloe, co. Galway
*Cochrane, Thomas, Esq., Ballyconnell, co. Cavan
Cockburn, General Sir G., J.P., Shanganagh, Bray, co. Dublin
*Cockburn, Gilbert, Esq., Rathmines and Dublin
Codd, Mr. Francis, Ballytory, near Broadway, co. Wexford [meath
*Codd, F., Esq., Old Dominick-st., Dublin, & Kilbeggan, co. West-
Codd, Rev. Nicholas, P.P., Monageer, Clone, co. Wexford
*Codd, William, Esq., Kilbeggan, co. Westmeath
*Coddington, H. B., Esq., Old Bridge, Drogheda, co. Louth
*Coddington, Rev. Latham, Timolin-glebe, co. Kildare
Cody, Mr. Michael, Chapel-street, Cork
*Coen, Rev. Thomas, R.C.A., Portumna, co. Galway
Coffee, Rev. James, Ennistymon, co. Clare
Coffee, Rev. John, Newmarket-on-Fergus, co. Clare
Coffey, Rev. N. J., P.M., Merchants' Quay, Dublin
Coffey, W., Esq., C.C.P., Gort, co. Galway
*Coffy, Edward, Esq., Clonkeen, Noughoval, co. Westmeath
*Cogan, Bernard Owen, Esq., Lisconney-house, Collooney, co. Sligo
*Cogan, Edward H., Esq., Rockbrook, Collooney, co. Sligo
Cogan, Mr. James Carr, St. Stephen's-hospital, Cork [Dublin
*Coghill, Sir J. C., Bart., J.P., Belvidere-house, Drumcondra, co.
*Coghlan, Rev. Charles, D.D., Timoleague, near Bandon, co. Cork
*Coghlan, Rev. C. T., A.M., Glebe-castle, Rathkeale, co. Limerick
*Coghlan, John, Esq., Bride-park, near Ballinrobe, co. Mayo
*Coghlan, John, Esq., Kilcop-house, near Waterford
Coghlan, Rev. John, Oldtown, Ballinacargy, co. Westmeath
*Coghlan, John P., Esq., M.D., Kilmacthomas, co. Waterford
*Coghlan, Joseph, Esq., Ballygarvan, Ballymartle, co. Cork
*Coghlan, Michael, Esq., Loughrea, co. Galway
Coghlan, Owen, Esq., Huntstown, near Finglas, co. Dublin
Coghlan, Richard, Esq., Ballinvilla, Claremorris, co. Mayo
Coghlan, Rev. Thomas Lloyd, A.M., Spy-hill, Cove, co. Cork
Cohen, The Right Rev. Dr., R.C. Bishop of Clonfert, Loughrea, co.
Coin, Mr. Myles, Galway [Galway
*Coke, Edward, Esq., Longford-hall, near Ashbourne, Derbyshire
*Coke, John, Esq., Debdale, Mansfield, Nottinghamshire
*Colahan, W., Esq., M.D., Ballinasloe, co. Galway
Colburn, John, Esq., South-mall, Cork
Colburn, Rev. W., Blackrock, near Cork
*COLCHESTER, The Right Honorable Lord
Colclough, Beauchamp, Esq., Mount Sion, Carlow
*Cole, E. H. Esq., J.P., Moore-abbey, Monasterevin, co. Kildare
*Cole, Owen Blayney, Esq., Brandiim, co. Monaghan
Cole, T. C., Esq., Clifton-lodge, Blackrock-road, Cork
*Coleman, Mr. John, Hotel, Portstewart, Coleraine, co. Derry
Coleman, Rev. John, P.P., Swinford, co. Mayo
Coleman, John, Esq., Rathory, Ardee, co. Louth
*Coleman, Neale Thomas, Esq., Church-park, co. Louth
*Coleman, The Very Rev. P., V.G. & P.P. of St. Michan's, Dublin
Coleman, Rev. P., P.P., Lough-harbour-cottage, Keady, co. Armagh
*Coleman, The Very Rev. T. A., Aungier-street, Dublin
*Coleman, Thomas D., Esq., Bolton-street, Dublin
*Colgan, Rev. A., Firr-house-convent, co. Dublin
Colgan, Rev. James, P.P., Edenderry, King's county
Colgan, John, Esq., Kilcock, co. Kildare
Colguitt, Thomas, Esq., Liverpool
*Colhoun, Charles King, Esq., J.P., Letterkenny, co. Donegal
*Colhoun, A. W., Esq., J.P., Cross-house, N. T. Stewart, co. Tyrone
*Coll, The Very Rev. Thomas, Vicar-general, Newcastle, co. Limerick
Colles, John, Esq., Grangemore, Kilcullen, co. Kildare
Collett, Ebenezer, John, Esq.
Collett, Edward, Esq., Seneschal of Kilworth, co. Cork
*Collett, E. M., Esq., Great-George-street, Westminster, London
*Collins, Charles J., Esq., Drogheda, co. Louth
Collins, Rev. James, A. M., Cavan
*Collins, John, Esq., Baltimore-house, near Skibbereen, co. Cork
Collins, Mr. John, Spa-house, Lucan, co. Dublin
Collins, John, Esq., Cookstown, co. Tyrone
Collins, Rev. John, D.D., New Glanmire-lodge, near Cork
Collins, Rev. John, Curate of Donaghmore, Castlefin, co. Donegal
Collins, Rev. Mortimer, P.P., Shanagolden, co. Limerick
*Collins, Thomas, Esq., Baltimore-house, near Skibbereen, co. Cork
Collins, Rev. Timothy, P.P., Kilgobbin, Tralee, co. Kerry [Dublin
Collins, W., Esq., College-green, Dublin, and Crumlin-house, co.
*Collins, W., Esq., Spring-lodge, Kilfinane, co. Limerick
Collins, Rev. William, A.B., Carrigtwohill-glebe, Midleton, co. Cork
Collis, Rev. George Gun., A.M., Mountford-lodge, Fermoy, co. Cork
Collis, Maurice Atkin, Esq., Trinity-college, Dublin
*Collis, Rev. R., A.B., the Glebe, Kilconnell, co. Galway
*Collis, Stephen E., Esq., Gurtenard, Listowel, co. Kerry
Collis, Captain W., Dingle, co. Kerry
*Collis, Captain W. Cooke, J.P., Castle Cooke, Kilworth, co. Cork
*Collum, John, Esq., Capel-street, Dublin, and Enniskillen
Colthurst, C., Esq., J.P., Clonmoyle, Coachford, co. Cork
Colthurst, Rev. John, J.P., Boveva-glebe, Dungiven, co. Derry
*Colthurst, Sir N. C., Bart., Ardrum, Ballincollig, co. Cork
*Colthurst, W., Esq., J.P., Baltinglass, co. Wicklow
Coltsmann, John, Esq., Flesk-castle, co. Kerry
Colvan, John, Esq., M.D., Armagh
*Colvill, W. C., Esq., Elm-view, near Clontarf, co. Dublin, & [Batchelor's-walk, Dublin
Comerford, Mr. James, Roscrea, co. Tipperary
Commander in Chief's Office, Her Majesty's
Commins, Mr. Edward, Hotel-quay, Waterford
*Comyn, Francis, Esq., Woodstock, co. Galway
Comyn, James P., Esq., Ballinderry, Kilconnell, co. Galway
Comyn, Rev. Michael, P.P., Ballard-house, Kilkee, co. Clare
*Conan, Rev. John, Rector of Upper Badoney, Omagh, co. Tyrone
Condon, Rev. Eugene, P.P., Tallow, co. Waterford
Condon, R. L., Esq., Kilsconnell, Rathkeale, co. Limerick
Coneys, John, Esq., Cluankin, Tuam, co. Galway
Congreve, J. F., Esq., Stony Stratford, Bucks.
*Conlan, W., Esq., Barton-lodge, near Rathfarnham, co. Dublin
*Conlan, Messrs. W. E. and J., New-row, Dublin
Connell, Charles, Esq., Clover-hill, Blackrock, Cork
Connell, W., Esq., Rathcormac, co. Cork
*Connell, W., Esq., South-mall, and Woodbine-lodge, Cork
*Connell & Fitzgerald, Messrs., Limerick
Connelly, Rev. Martin, P.P. of Achill, Newport-Pratt, co. Mayo
*Conner, Daniel, Esq., J.P., Manch-house, Dunmanway, co. Cork
*Conner, Daniel, Esq., J.P., Ballybricken, near Monkstown, co. Cork
Conner, John, Esq., Pallas, Ahascragh, co. Galway
*Conner, Rev. R. L., Downdaniel, Innishannon, co. Cork
*Conner, W. Esq., Inch, Athy, co. Kildare
Conner, W., Esq., J.P., Mishells, near Bandon, co. Cork
*Connery, Rev. Edmund, P.P., Kildimo, Pallaskenry, co. Limerick
Connick, Rev. W., P.P., Old Ross, co. Wexford
*Conniff, Rev. P., P.P. of Tessaragh, Mount Talbot, co. Roscommon
*Connison, Mr. Waller, Donnemanna, co. Tyrone
*Connolly, Mrs. Anne, Clondalkin, co. Dublin
*Connor, E., Esq., William-street, Dublin
*Connor, Roderick, Esq., Seafield, near Donnybrook, Dublin
Connor, Thomas, Esq., Redbow, near Clondalkin, co. Dublin
*Conolly, Col. Edward, M.P. D.L. & J.P., Cliff, Ballyshannon, co.
*Conolly, Rev. Felix, Riverstown, Collooney, co. Sligo [Donegal
Conolly, Mr. John, Galway
*Conolly, Terence, Esq., Mount Prospect, Ballyshannon, co. Leitrim
*Conolly, Mr. Thomas, Dalkey, co. Dublin
Conran, M., Esq., Knockrigg, Baltinglass, co. Wicklow
Conron, W., Esq., Grange, near Douglas, co. Cork
*Conroy, Mr. John, Killeigh, Tullamore, King's connty
*Conroy, Rev. John, Curate of Urney, Strabane, co. Tyrone
*Conroy, Messrs. Edward & John, Mount-Mellick, Queen's county
*Conry, Thomas, Esq., Strokestown, co. Roscommon

Constable, William, Esq., Prior-park, Clonmel, co. Tipperary
Constant, Rev. John, Fermoy, co. Cork
Conway, J., Esq., Rose-view, Blackrock-road, Cork
*Conway, Rev. Michael, P.P., Killala, co. Mayo
*Conway, Robert, Esq., Chatham-street, Dublin
*Conway, Rev. Thomas, Convent, Multifarnham, co. Westmeath
Conyers, C., jun., Esq., Castletown-Conyers, Charleville, co. Cork
CONYNGHAM, The Most Noble The Marquis of
*Conyngham, W. L., Esq., J.P., Spring-hill, Moneymore, co. Derry
*Cook, Robert, Esq., Kiltinan-castle, Fethard, co. Tipperary
*Cook, Capt. S. E., Carlton-hall, Richmond, Yorkshire
Cook, Thomas, Esq., M.D., Fever-hospital, Youghal, co. Cork
Cooke, B. C., Esq., M.D., Castletownroche, co. Cork
*Cooke, Edward, Esq., Bachelor's-walk, Dublin
*Cooke, Edward, Esq., Kilkenny
Cooke, George, Esq., Windsor, Douglas, co. Cork
Cooke, Rev. J. P., St. John's-college, Waterford
Cooke, Michael, Esq., Griffinstown, near Dunlaven, co. Wicklow
*Cooke, Rev. Peter, P.P. of Bohola, Swinford, co. Mayo
*Cooke, Phanuel, Esq., Poyntstown, New Birmingham, co. Kilkenny
*Cooke, Rev. Richard, Rector of Thomastown, co. Kilkenny
Cooke, Richard, Esq., Waterford
*Cooke, Thomas L., Esq., Parsonstown, King's county
*Cooke, W., Esq., J.P., The Cottage, near Athlone, co. Westmeath
Cooke, W., Esq., Griffinstown, near Dunlavin, co. Wicklow
*Cookman, Edward R., Esq., Monart-house, Enniscorthy, co. Wexford
Coombe, John, Esq., Waterford
*Cooper, Rev. Austin, Landscape, Pallas-green, co. Limerick
*Cooper, Austin, Esq., Kilmore, Cashel, co. Tipperary
Cooper, A. B., Esq., J.P., Cooper's-hill, Collooney, co. Sligo
*Cooper, A. P., Esq., White-hill, Great-Berkhampstead, Herts.
Cooper, C., Esq., Earlstown, Portumna, co. Galway, and Harcourt-[street, Dublin
*Cooper, E. W., Esq., Abbey-street, Dublin
Cooper, Rev. Francis, A.B., Drishane-glebe, Mill-street, co. Cork
Cooper, H. Herring, Esq., Shruel-castle, Carlow
*Cooper, John, Esq., J.P., Beamore, Drogheda, co. Louth
*Cooper, John, Esq., Cooper-hill, Drogheda, co. Louth
*Cooper, John T., Esq., Wentworth-place, Dublin
Cooper, Robert, Esq., Dundrum, co. Dublin
*Cooper, R. W., Esq., Dunboden, Mullingar, co. Westmeath
*Cooper, Samuel, Esq., Wexford
*Cooper, W., Esq., J.P., Killenure-castle, Cashel, co. Tipperary
*Cooper, W. Cope, Esq., D.L. and J.P., Cooper-hill, Carlow
Cooper, Rev. W. H., Kings-Inns-street, Dublin
Cooper, W. Warsop, Esq., Cooper-ville, Macroom, co. Cork
*Coote, Sir C. H., Bart., M.P., D.L., and J.P., Ballyfin-house, near [Mountrath, Queen's co.
*Coote, C. H., Esq., Trinity-college, Cambridge
Coote, Rev. C. P., Doone Glebe, Pallas Green, co. Limerick
*Coote, Eyre, Esq., J.P., Bellamont-forest, co. Cavan
*Coote, Rev. Ralph, Lynally, Tullamore, King's county
*Coote, Robert Eyre Purdon, Esq., Royal York-crescent, Clifton, [near Bristol
*Coote, Thomas, Esq., J.P., Lislea, Cootehill, co. Cavan
*Coote, W., Esq., Baggot-street, Dublin, & Letterkenny, co. Donegal
*Cope, Mrs. Arabella, Drumilly, near Loughal, co. Armagh
*Copeland, W. T., Esq., M.P., Lincoln's-inn-fields, London
*Copinger, R. John, Esq., South-mall, Cork
*Copley, Edward, Esq., Croft, Darlington, Durham
Copley, John, Esq., Ballyclough, Askeaton, co. Limerick
*Coppinger, Francis H., Esq., J.P., Myross-wood, Rosscarbery, co. [Cork
Coppinger, Rev. J., P.P., Aughadown, Skibbereen, co. Cork
Coppinger, Rev. S., Midleton, co. Cork
*Coppinger, Thomas S., Esq., J.P., Sandy-hill, Macroom, co. Cork
Coppinger, W., Esq., Barry's Court, near Midleton, co. Cork
Coppinger, W. Joseph, Esq., Glenmore-cottage, Cove, co. Cork
*Corballis. J. R., Esq., Upper Mount-street, Dublin
Corballis, James J., Esq., Manor-house, Ratoath, co. Meath
*Corbally, Elias, Esq., Corbalton-hall, Dunshaughlin, co. Meath
*Corbally, E. T., Esq., Rathkeale, near Swords, co. Dublin
*Corbally, Henry, Esq., Roden-place, Dundalk, co. Louth
*Corbally, M. E., Esq., Corbalton-hall, near Dunshaughlin, co. Meath
Corban, Lawrence, Esq., J.P., Maryville Mills, Kilworth, co. Cork
*Corbet, W., Esq., Churchtown, near Dundrum, co. Dublin
Corbet, Capt. W., Grange, Gorman-lane, Dublin
Corbet, Mrs. M. A., Edge-hill, near Clonaslee, Queen's county
*Corbett, Edwin, Esq., Darnall-hall, Winsford, Cheshire
*Corbett, H., Esq., Londonderry, & Ravenscliff, Moville, co. Derry
Corbett, John, Esq., Newry, co. Down
Corbett, Nicholas, Esq., Askeaton, co. Limerick
Corbett, Rev. Patrick, P.P. of Quinn, co. Clare
Corbett, Richard, Esq., M.D., Innishannon, co. Cork

*Corcoran, Rev. Anthony, P.P. of Killala, co. Mayo
*Corcoran, John, Esq., Grafton-street. Dublin, & Enniscorthy, co. [Wexford
Corcoran, John, Esq., Enniscorthy, co. Wexford
Cordner, Rev. E. J., M.A., Lisburn, co. Antrim
Corish, Rev. Peter, P.P., of Bannow, co. Cork
Cork, The Corporation of the City of
CORK, The Right Honorable the Earl of
CORK AND ROSS, The Right Rev. Lord Bishop of
*Cork, Augustinian Library
*Cork, Presentation Schools, Douglas-street, Cork
Corkerry, John B., Esq., Bantry, co. Cork
Corkran, Rev. Cornelius, Tracton-vicarage, near Kinsale, co. Cork
*Corley, Rev. John, R.C.C. of Kilshalvy, Ballymote, co. Sligo
*Cormick, Major Michael, I. P., Castlehill, Crossmolina, co. Mayo
*Cornock, Rev. Zachariah, J.P., Cromwelsfort, Wexford
*Cornwall, George, Esq., Woodlands, Bandon, co. Cork
*Cornwall, John, Esq., Rutland-square West, Dublin
Corr, Henry, Esq., Durham, Killbride, near Roscommon
*Corrigan, J. S., Esq., J.P., Rockview, Parsonstown, co. Tipperary
*Corry, Smithson, Esq., J.P., Old-hall, Rosstrevor, co. Down
*Corry, Trevor, Esq., J.P., Abbey-yard, Newry, co. Down
*Corry, T. C. Stewart, Esq., D.L. and J.P., Rock Corry Castle, [Cootehill, co. Monaghan
*Corry, W. J., Esq., Ivy-lodge, Drumcashlone, Newry, co. Down
Corscaden, James, Esq., Londonderry
Corvan, Rev. John, Vicar of Ballyvalden, co. Wexford
*Cosby, Sidney, Esq., J.P., Stradbally-hall, Stradbally, Queen's county
*Cosby, Rev. W., Killermogh-glebe, near Durrow, Queen's county
*Cosgrove, Thomas, Esq., Tuam, co. Galway
*Cosgrove, Rev. W., Aghada, co. Cork
*Costello, Very Rev. B. Vicar Capitular of Killala, co. Mayo
Costello, Edward, Esq., D.C.P., Bank-place, Limerick
*Costello, John, Esq., M.D., Spanish Point, Miltown Malbay, co. [Clare
Costello, Mr. John, Dominick-street, Galway
*Costello, John, Esq., Gort, co. Galway
Costello, Philip, Esq., Lower Dominick-street, Dublin
*Costello, Very Rev. T. O'Brien, V.F., Castle Comfort, Barrington's-[bridge, co. Limerick
Costello, William, Esq., Ballina, and Bellmullet, co. Mayo
*Costigan, Rev. A., C.C., Halston-street, Dublin
Costigan, John, Esq., Harcourt-terrace, Dublin
Cotter, Rev. G. E., Templenacarriga, Midleton, co. Cork
*Cotter, Captain G. S., Heathfield, near Youghal, co. Cork
*Cotter, Sir James L., Bart., Rockforest, Mallow, co. Cork
Cotter, Rev. James L., LL.D., Vicar of Buttevant, co. Cork
Cotter, John, Esq., Clonmore Mill, near Cork
Cotter, Rev. John R., J.P., Rector of Templetrine, Kinsale, co. Cork
*Cotter, Richard, Esq., Coolawinney, near Wicklow
Cotter, R. B., Esq., Cork
Cotter, Mr. Thomas, Tipperary
Cotter, Rev. W., P.P. of Kilworth, co. Cork
*Cottingham, John, Esq., Hardwick-hall, Chesterfield, Derbyshire
Cottingham, Captain E., Belfield, near Drumcondra, co. Dublin
Cottingham, Thomas, Esq., Cottage, Little Neston, Cheshire
Cottnam, Captain, Minow, Cootehill, co. Cavan
*Cotton, F. R., Esq., Allenton, near Tallaght, co. Dublin
*Cottrell, M. C., Esq., Ballydulia, Cove, near Cork
*Coulson, Col. F., Belfast
*Coulter, R., Esq., Carnmeen, near Newry, co. Down
*Coulter, Robert, Esq., Dundalk, co. Louth
Coulter, Samuel, Esq., M.D., Carney Dispensary, Sligo
Coulter, Thomas, Esq., Newtown, Dundalk, co. Louth
Coulter, W., Esq., Ballygawley, co. Tyrone
*Coulton, Thomas, Esq., Lennox-place, Golden-bridge, Dublin
Courtenay, Rev. A. Lefroy, Sandymount, Dublin
Courtenay, David, Esq., Mount Bagly, near Dundalk, co. Louth
Courtenay, Rev. D. C., Ballyclare, co. Antrim
*Courtenay, G. W., Esq., J.P., Dromadda, near Castlemartyr, co. Cork
Courtenay, James, Esq., J.P., Glenburn, co. Derry
Courtenay, Robert, Esq., Bishop-street, Dublin
*Courtenay, Robert, Esq., J.P., Bally Edmond, near Midleton, co. [Cork
Courtenay, Thomas, Esq., Upper Pembroke-street, Dublin, and [Rockmount, near Dundrum, co. Dublin
Courtney, Sampson, Esq., Randalstown, co. Antrim
Courtney and Stephens, Messrs., Blackhall-place, Dublin
*COURTOWN, The Right Honorable the Earl of
Couts, W., Esq., Snugbrooke, Belfast
Cowan, James, Esq., Barn-cottage, Carrickfergus, co. Antrim
*Cowan, Mr. John, Greenan, Faughanvale, co. Derry
Cowan, Rev. John, Coagh, co. Tyrone
Cowan, Joseph H., Esq., Eyrecourt, co. Galway

*Cowdroy, Alfred, Esq., Millifont Mills, near Drogheda, co. Louth
*Cower, John, Esq., Capel-street, Dublin, & Waterford
Cowran, M., Esq., Knockrigg, near Baltinglass, co. Wicklow
Cox, Benjamin Lentaigne, Esq., Dublin
*Cox, Douglas, Esq., Carrickfergus, co. Antrim
*Cox, Edward, Esq., J.P., Clara-house, Clara, King's county
*Cox, Michael, Esq., Castletown, Carrick-on-Suir, co. Kilkenny
Cox, Sir W., Knt., D.L. & J.P., Coolcliffe, Taghmon, co. Wexford
*Cox, W., Esq., Ballynoe, Ballingarry, co. Limerick
Coxon, John Stuart, Esq., Flesk Priory, Killarney, co. Kerry
Coyle, Thomas, Esq., Rose Ville, near Cork
*Coyle, Walter, Esq., Lougher, Slane, co. Meath
*Coyne, Mr. Richard, Capel-street, Dublin
Craig, Mr. David, Foyle-street, Londonderry
Craig, Rev. George, Macosquin-glebe, Coleraine, co. Derry
Craig, Mr. J. H., Hotel, Ballinasloe, co. Galway
Craig, Mr. John, Craigstown, Randalstown, co. Antrim
Craig, Stewart, Esq., Banbridge, co. Down
*Craig, W., Esq., Swan Nest, near Coolock, co. Dublin
Cramer, John Thomas, Esq., J. P., Rathmore-house, Kinsale, co. [Cork
Crampton, George, Esq., J. P., Nymphsfield, Cong, co. Mayo
Crampton, Rev. Josiah, A.M., Castle Connell, co. Limerick
*Crampton, P. C., Esq., M.P., Merrion-square West, Dublin
Crampton, Philip, Esq., Merrion-square North, Dublin
Cramsie, Messrs. John & W., Jamaica, & Belfast
Crane, J. R., Esq., Wexford
Cranston, John, Esq., Cranebrook, Coal Island, Dungannon, co. [Tyrone
*Cranston, W., Esq., Belfast
*Cranston, W. F., Esq., Ardmoulin, Belfast
Crawford, A., Esq., Dawson-street, Dublin
*Crawford, B. H., Esq., Camden-street, Dublin
Crawford, E., Esq., Wellington Quay, Dublin
*Crawford, Rev. George, LL.D. and J.P., St. Anne's-hill, Newtown-[Forbes, co. Longford
*Crawford, J., Esq., J.P., Tullamore, King's county
*Crawford, Rev. James, Glebe-house, Athleague, co. Roscommon
*Crawford, John L., Esq., Grange, Moy, co. Tyrone
*Crawford, Jones, Esq., J.P., Newtownstewart, co. Tyrone
Crawford, Mr. Robert, Ballyrobin, Antrim
Crawford, Samuel L., Esq., Londonderry
Crawford, T. W., Esq., Rockville, Ballyshannon, co. Donegal
Crawford, Thomas, Esq., Lambton, Chester-le-street, Durham
*Crawford, W., Esq., Lakelands, near Cork
Crawford, Rev. W., Rector of Skerry & Rathcaven, co. Antrim
*Crawford, W. C., Esq., Rapla, Nenagh, co. Tipperary
Crawford, William Sharman, Esq., M.P. & J.P., Crawfordsburn, [Bangor, co. Down
*Crawford, Messrs. G. & T., Ballievy, near Banbridge, co. Down
*Creagh, A. G., Esq., Doneraile, co. Cork
*Creagh, Benjamin B., Esq., Doneraile, co. Cork
*Creagh, G. W. B., Esq., J.P., Creagh-castle, Doneraile, co. Cork
Creagh, John, Esq., Mallow, co. Cork
Creagh, Rev. John B., Rector of Kincurran, near Kinsale, co. Cork
*Creagh, Michael, Esq., J.P., Laurentinum, Doneraile, co. Cork
Creagh, P. W., Esq., Landscape, Limerick
*Creagh, Pierce, Esq., J.P., Rathbane, Ennistymon, co. Clare
Creagh, Pierce, Esq., Summer-hill, Mallow, co. Cork
Creaghe, Pierse, Esq., Rathbayne, Ennistymon, co. Clare
*Creaghe, Richard, Esq., J.P., Castle-park, Golden, co. Tipperary
*Crean, Francis, Esq., J. P., Prospect, Claremorris, co. Mayo
Crean, Mr. M., Lower Abbey-street, Dublin
*Creanè, Stephen, Esq., Cartoon, Aughrim, co. Galway
*Creed, John, Esq., College-green, Dublin, & George-st., Limerick
*Creed, Rev. John C., A.M., Newcastle, co. Limerick
Creery, Charles A., Esq., Tanderagee, co. Armagh
Creery, John, Esq., Orange-hill, Tanderagee, co. Armagh
Creery, The Venerable Archdeacon, Billy, near Bushmills, co. Antrim
Creevy, Mr. George, Killaloe, co. Clare
*Cregan, Rev. Claud, J.P., Cappagh Mount Pleasant, Omagh, co. [Tyrone
*Creight, W. M., Esq., Gilford, co. Down
Creighton, Mr. Robert J., Londonderry
Creighton, G. W., Esq., Upper Pembroke-street, Dublin
*Cremen, Mr. Jeremiah, Woodview, Templemichael, co. Cork
*Cremen, John F., Esq., Killelan-cottage, Newcastle, co. Limerick
*CREMORNE, The Right Honorable Lord
*Crewe, Sir George, Bart., Calke-abbey, near Ashby-de-la-Zouche, [Leicestershire
*Crips, Alderman John, Cahirnarry-house, Limerick
*Croffts, Rev. John, Rathpeacon, near Cork
*CROFTON, The Right Honorable Lord
*Crofton, A. B., Esq., Roebuck-castle, co. Dublin
*Crofton, Duke, Esq., J.P., Lakefield, Mohill, co. Leitrim
Crofton, Freke L., Esq., Liscormick, near Ballymahon, co. Longford
*Crofton, Rev. H. W., Inchinappa, Ashford, co. Wicklow
*Crofton, Sir James, Bart., J.P., Longford-house, Sligo
Crofton, Captain Thomas, Dorset-lodge, Killiney, co. Dublin
Crofton, Captain W. E., Rowens Gift, Castledawson, co. Derry
*Crofts, C. T., Esq., Prospect-lodge, Blackrock, Cork
*Crofts, Rev. F. W., Churchtown-house, Buttevant, co. Cork
Crofts, George, Esq., Stream-hill, Doneraile, co. Cork
Crofts, James, Esq., Grenagh, near Cork
*Crofts, W., Esq., Ballinure, Blackrock, Cork
*Crofts, Rev. W., Curate of Whitechurch, co. Cork
Croke, Rev., John, P. P., Donohill, near Tipperary
*Croke, Rev. Thomas, P. P., Charleville, co. Cork
Croke, Rev. W., R.C.C., Kingstown, co. Dublin
Croker, Captain Charles, R.N., Lissa, Doneraile, co. Cork
Croker, Eyre Coote, Esq., Laura-ville, Mallow, co. Cork
*Croker, G. J., Esq., Scart, Rathkeale, co. Limerick
*Croker, Rev. John, Fort-Elizabeth, near Croom, co. Limerick
*Croker, John, Esq., J.P., Ballyneguard, near Limerick
*Croker, The Right Honorable J. Wilson
Croker, Rev. R., A.M., Athlacca Glebe, Bruff, co. Limerick
Croker, Richard, Esq., Athlacca, Bruff, co. Limerick
*Croker, Robert, Esq., Ballyboy, Clogheen, co. Tipperary
Croker, Samuel, Esq., Kilmacthomas, co. Waterford
Croker, Thomas Swan, Esq., Tankerville, Balbriggan, co. Dublin
*Croker, Captain Walter, Lisnabrin-house, Tallow, co. Waterford
*Croker, W. R., Esq., Mary-street, Dublin
*Crolly, Henry, Esq., Drogheda, co. Louth
Croly, H., Esq., M.D., Mountmellick, Queen's county
Crombie, Miss Maria, Golden Bridge, co. Dublin
*Cromie, Charles H., Esq., J.P., Rathgraher, Hollymount, co. Mayo
Cromie, John, Esq., Draper-hill, Ballynahinch, co. Down
*Cromie, John, Esq., Cromore, Portstewart, co. Derry
*Crompton, A., Esq., Lincoln's-Inn, London
Crompton, Lieut. John, Dromore West, co. Sligo
Crondace, W., Esq., Pelton, Chester-le-street, Durham
Crondace, Mr. W., Bunker-hill, Durham
*Cronin, Rev. John, Clondrohid, Macroom, co. Cork
Cronin, John Joseph, Esq., M.D., Cove, near Cork
Cronin, Rev. Michael, Clonmult, near Midleton, co. Cork
Cronin, W. James, Esq., Cove, near Cork
Cronin, W. James, Esq., M.R.C.S.L., Cove, near Cork
*Crooke, Rev. G. D., Merrion-avenue, Dublin
Crooke, R. B., Esq., Kilenardrish, near Macroom, co. Cork
Crooke, Thomas E., Esq., Ahavrin, Coachford, co. Cork
Crooke, W., Esq., J.P., Derreen, Coachford, co. Cork
Crosbie, Pierce, Esq., Lislaghtin-abbey, Ballylongford, co. Kerry
*Crosbie, William Talbot, Esq., Ardfert-abbey, co. Kerry
*Crosier, John, Esq., Gartra, Clones, co. Monaghan
*Croskell, Rev. W., Durham
Cross, Alexander, Esq., Portnelligan, co. Armagh
*Cross, Mr. Henry, Coachford, co. Cork
*Cross, Maxwell, Esq., J.P., Dartan, Tynan, co. Armagh
Crossle, Rev. Charles, Curate of Cappagh, near Omagh, co. Tyrone
*Crossle, Henry, Esq., J.P., Anahoe-house, Ballygawley, co. Tyrone
*Crossley, A., Esq., C.M.P., J.P., Elphin, co. Roscommon
Crossley, J., Esq., C.C.P., Portadown, co. Armagh
Crossley, Mr. John, Lisburn, co. Antrim
*Crossley, W., Esq., J.P., Garvagh-cottage, co. Derry
Crothers, John, Esq., Blackwatertown, co. Armagh
Crotty, Rev. Barth., President R. C. College, Maynooth (2 copies)
Crotty, John, Esq., Roscrea, co. Tipperary
Crotty, Rev. M., Parsonstown, King's county
Crowe, George, Esq., Mount-Evans, Kilconnell, co. Galway
Crowe, Thomas, jun., Esq., Abbey-ville, Ennis, co. Clare
*Crowly, Mr. Daniel, Inchy Mills, Timoleague, co. Cork
Crowly, Rev. David, P.P. of Courcey, near Kinsale, co. Cork
*Crozier, W., Esq., Fortfield-lodge, near Rathfarnham, co. Dublin
Crozier, Rev. W., Kilmore, near Ballinahinch, co. Down
Cruikshank, Mr., Lower Gardiner-street, Dublin
Cruise, Mr. Edward, Hotel, Limerick
*Cruise, Peter, Esq., Greenville, Castle-Blakeney, co. Galway
*Cruise, W., Esq., Cruise-lawn, Castle-Blakeney, co. Galway
*Cruise, Richard, Esq., Rathhood, Nobber, co. Meath
*Cuddy, Rev. James, St. Mary's, Kilkenny
*Cuff, James, Esq., J. P., Creagh, Ballinrobe, co. Mayo
Cuff, St. George, Esq., Deel-castle, co. Mayo
*Cuffe, William, Esq., Killbeggan, co. Westmeath
Culbert, Mr. James, Newtown Cunningham, All Saints, co. Donegal
Culbertson, David, Esq., Sligo
Culkin, Michael, Esq., Excise-office, Kilmallock, co. Limerick

*Cullen, Cam Cross, Esq., J.P., Glenade, Manor Hamilton, co. Leitrim
Cullen, Captain Edward, Westgate, Wexford
*Cullen, F. N., Esq., J.P., Cony-lodge, Manor Hamilton, co. Leitrim
Cullen, Captain H. F., Rockwood, Manor Hamilton, co. Leitrim
Cullen, John, Esq., Bridgefoot-street, Dublin
*Cullen, Mr. John, Newport, co. Tipperary [co. Leitrim
*Cullen, Lieut.-Col. J. J., J. P., Skreeny-house, Manor Hamilton,
Cullen, Rev. Philip, C.C., Rathangan, co. Wexford
Cullen, Thomas, Esq., Piercetown, Kilcock, co. Kildare
*Cullen, W., Esq., North Cumberland-st., Dublin, & Arbutus-lodge,
Cullinan, Rev. Daniel S., P.P. of Athenry, co. Galway [co. Dublin
Cullinan, James, Esq., M. D., Freshford, co. Kilkenny
Cullinan, Rev. Luke, Killross, Collooney, co. Sligo
Cullinan, Rev. P. J., R.C.C., Bridge-street, Dublin
Cullinan, Ralph, Esq., Magowna, Ennis, co. Clare
Cullinan, Thomas, Esq., Bushy-park, Ennis, co. Clare
Cuming, James, Esq., Belfast
Cuming, John, Esq., Greys-Wood, near Haslemere, Surry
*Cummin, George, Esq., J.P., Ballynrowan, near Baltinglass, co.
Cummins, Mr. Denis, Rathcormac, co. Cork [Wicklow
Cummins, Henry, Esq., Leinster-street, Dublin
Cummins, Rev. L., Myshall, co. Carlow
*Cummins, Richard, Esq., Whitehall, near Tallaght, co. Dublin
*Cummins, Robert King, Esq., Belmont, Cork
*Cummins, Samuel, Esq., Mutryn, Strabane, co. Tyrone
*Cuningham, Mr. Andrew, Burt, co. Donegal
Cuningham, Hugh, Esq., M. D., Castlecooly, Burt, co. Donegal
Cuningham, John, Esq., Dunevin, Ballymena, co. Antrim
*Cuningham, Joseph, Esq., Carnaveagh, Ballibay, co. Monaghan
Cuningham, Michael, Esq., Ballynoe-house, Cove, co. Cork
*Cuningham, Robert G., Esq., D.L. and J.P., Mount Kennedy, co. [Wicklow
Cuningham, Samuel, Esq., Fenaghy, near Ballymena, co. Antrim
Cunliffe, Mr. W., Glynn, Larne, co. Antrim
Cunningham, John, jun., Esq., Belfast
Cuppage, General A., Clare Grove, Coolock, co. Dublin
Cuppage, Henry, Esq., Lurgan, co. Armagh
Cuppage, John, Esq., Lurgan, co. Armagh
Cuppaidge, George, Esq., Wood-quay, Galway
Cupples, Rev. Edward, LL.B., Vicar of Glenavy, co. Antrim
Cupples, Rev. Thomas, Ballyrashane Rectory, co. Derry
Curell, Daniel, Esq., Ballygarry, near Ballymena, co. Antrim
Curell, John, Esq., Belfast
Curoe, Rev. Richard, P. P. of Kilkeel, co. Down
*Curran, Rev. John, P.P. of Killucan, co. Westmeath
*Curran, Mrs. Mary J., Sienna Convent, Drogheda, co. Louth
*Currey, W. S., Esq., Lismore-castle, co. Waterford
*Curry, John, Esq., Drummarton-house, near Dundrum, co. Dublin
Curry, Rev. John M., Buncrana, co. Donegal
Curry, W., Esq., Siskenore-cottage, Fintona, co. Tyrone
*Curry, Messrs. W., jun., and Co., Sackville-street, Dublin
Curteis, Edward, Esq., Glenburn, near Belfast
Curtin, C. J., Esq., Carrigoon-house, Mallow, co. Cork
Curtin, Daniel, Esq., Mount Eaton, Cove, co. Cork
Curtin, P., Esq., Ennis, co. Clare
Curtis, Francis, Esq., William-street, Dublin, & Schenagh, Cork
Curtis, Rev. John, Tullabeg College, Tullamore. King's county
Curtis, Patrick, Esq., Moorefield, near Roebuck, co. Dublin
Curtis, T. A., Esq., Southgate, Middlesex [co. Limerick
Curtis, Rev. W., B. A., Rector & Vicar of Rathronan, Newcastle,
Curwen, M., Esq., Stella-lodge, near Artaine, co. Dublin
*Curzon, The Honorable Nathaniel [Dublin
*Cusack, John, Esq., Artaine cottage, co. Dublin, & Linen-hall,
*Cusack, P., Esq., Spring-park, Athlone, co. Westmeath
Cussen, Robert, Esq., B.A., Newcastle, co. Limerick
Cuthbert, John, Esq., J.P., Green-hill, Kinsale, co. Cork

Dacre, E. M., Esq., Bandon, co. Cork
Dakeyne, E., Esq., Darley Dale, Derbyshire
Dallan, Mr. John, Knightsbrook, Trim, co. Meath
*Dalrymple, Captain Charles, Gills-cottage, Coleraine, co. Derry
*Daltera, W. R., Esq., Abbey-street, Dublin, & South Mall, Cork
*Daltera, W. R., Esq., Darling-hill, Monkstown, co. Westmeath
*D'Alton, Count, J.P., Greenanstown House, Nenagh, co. Tipperary
Dalton, Mr. Andrew, Tuam, co. Galway
Dalton, George, Esq., Carracastle, Ballaghaderren, co. Mayo
*Dalton, M. A., Esq., Auburne-cottage, near Malahide, co. Dublin
*Dalway, Marriott, Esq., Bella-hill, near Carrickfergus, co. Antrim
Daly, Arthur Gore, Esq., Ballydavid, Loughrea, co Galway
Daly, Charles, Esq., Skibbereen, co. Cork
*Daly, Edward, Esq., Lake-view, near Mullingar, co. Westmeath
Daly, Edward, Esq., Kinsale, co. Cork
Daly, Rev. Eugene, Enfield, Clonakilty, co. Cork
Daly, Rev. Eugene, R.C.C., Carrigtohill, near Midleton, co. Cork
*Daly, Rev. H., P.P., Barrindarrig, near Wicklow
Daly, Lieut. Hugh, Ballinamore, co. Leitrim
*Daly, Hyacinth, Esq., J. P., Raford, near Loughrea, co. Galway
*Daly, Rev. James, P.P. of Ovens & Aglish, co. Cork
Daly, Rev. James, R.C.C. of Doneraile, co. Cork
Daly, James, Esq., Ballina, co. Mayo
*Daly, James, Esq., J.P., Dunsandall, near Loughrea, co. Galway
*Daly, J. M., Esq., J.P., Castle Daly, near Moate, co. Westmeath
Daly, Mr. John, Hotel, Tuam, co. Galway
Daly, Rev. Joseph M., Moystown, Cloghan, King's county
Daly, Peter, Esq., Cloncha, Loughrea, co. Galway
*Daly, Mr. Robert, Drogheda
*Daly, S. A., Esq., Dalymount, near Dublin
*Dalys Club, Cork
Dames, Francis L., Esq., J.P., Green-hill, Edenderry, King's Co.
*Dames, Joseph A., Esq., C.C.C., Dunlavin, co. Wicklow
*Danaher, John, Esq., Capel-street, Dublin
Dance, G. M., Esq., Hill-castle, near Tagoat, co. Wexford
*Dancer, Sir Amyrald, Bart., Modereney, Cloghjordan, co. Tipperary
*Dane, Paul, jun., Esq., Killyhevlin, Enniskillen, co. Fermanagh
*Dane, R., Esq., J.P., Killyhevlin, Enniskillen, co. Fermanagh
*Daniel, F. J., Esq., Mary-street, Dublin
*Daniell, Captain Edward, Rock-lodge, Cookstown, co. Tyrone
*Daniell, Rev. H., Portneshangan-glebe, Mullingar, co. Westmeath
*Daniell, John, Esq., Bellvue, Crossakeel, co. Meath
*Daniell, Robert, Esq., J.P., New-forest, near Kilbeggan, co. West-
*Daniell, Thomas, Esq., Little Berkhamstead, Hertford [meath
Daniell, Sir William, Knt., Cove, near Cork
Daniels, Henry, Esq., Ballyclough-castle, Mallow, co. Cork
*Danks, Josiah, Esq., Stourport, Worcestershire
*Darby, Rev. C., Vicar of Kells, co. Kilkenny
*Darby, H., Esq., Leap-castle, Roscrea, co. Tipperary
*Darcus, S., Esq., Larne, co. Antrim
*D'Arcey, Capt. Edward, Royal Hospital, Kilmainham, Dublin
*D'Arcy, Burton, Esq., Ennis, co. Clare
*D'Arcy, James, Esq., J.P., Newforest, Castle-Blakeney, co. Galway
*D'Arcy, John, Esq., Hyde-park, near Kinnegad, co. Westmeath
D'Arcy, John, Esq., Ennis, co. Clare
D'Arcy, John, Esq., J.P., Clifden-castle, near Ougtherard, co. Galway
*D'Arcy, John S., Esq., Lodge-park, Trim, co. Meath
*D'Arcy, Messrs. John and Co., Usher-street, Dublin
*D'Arcy, Nicholas, Esq., Ballinlass, Ballinamore, co. Leitrim
*D'Arcy, Rev. Patrick, Limerick
*Darcy, Patrick, Esq., Carlingford, co. Louth
*Darley, Alderman F., Swanbrook, Dublin
*Darley, Capt. Arthur, R.N. & J.P., Buncrana, co. Donegal
*Darley, Frederick, jun., Esq., Lower Fitzwilliam-street, Dublin
*Darley, Henry, Esq., Stillorgan Brewery, & Bray, co. Wicklow
*Darley, Henry, Esq., Beaufield, near Stillorgan, co. Dublin
*Darley, Henry Fanan, Esq., York-street, Dublin
*Darley, Rev. John R., Dungannon, co. Tyrone
Darley, Rev. John, Artrea, Stewartstown, co. Tyrone
*Darling, George, Esq., Prospect, near Killiney, co. Dublin
*DARNLEY, The Right Honorable The Earl of
*Dartnell, E. Taylor, Esq., Catherine-place, Limerick
Dartnell, Edward, Esq., Newcastle, co. Limerick
*Dashwood, Sir G., Bart., Kirtlington-park, Oxfordshire
Dashwood, Rev. Henry, Rector of Halton, Buckinghamshire
*Daunt, Lieut. A. de Courcy, Carragaline, co. Cork
*Daunt, George, Esq., Broomley, near Kinsale, co. Cork
Daunt, George A., Esq., Newborough, near Kinsale, co. Cork
Daunt, George Digby, Esq., Kinsale, co. Cork
Daunt, W. J. O'Neill, Esq., Kilcascan, Dunmanway, co. Cork
Daven, John, Esq., Tuam, co. Galway
*Davenport, B., Esq., Church-row, Hampstead, Middlesex [Limerick
Davenport, T. E., Esq., J. P., Ballynacourty, Pallas-Kenry, co.
Davidson, C. C., Esq., Moy, co. Tyrone
*Davidson, William, Esq., Cookstown, co. Tyrone
Davies, Captain Alfred, Kilgariffe-house, Clonakilty, co. Cork
*Davies, Capt. Francis, Hampstead, Castle-Blakeney, co. Galway
*Davies, Geoffry, Esq., Kentstown, Castle-Blakeney, co. Galway
*Davies, Rev. J. J., Tottenham, Middlesex
*Davies, James, Esq., Threadneedle-street, London
*Davies, Rev. Richard, J.P., Macroom-castle, Cork
*Davies, Rev. Stephen, Rector of Bow Brickhill, Bucks.
Davies, William, Esq., M.D., Kilcondy, Cookstown, co. Cork
Davis, Rev. Charles, R.C.C., Cove, near Cork

Davis, Charles, Esq., Cloragh, near Rathfarnham, co. Dublin
Davis, Rev. James, A.M., Banbridge, co. Down
*Davis, James, Esq., Great Brunswick-street, Dublin
Davis, James, Esq., Belmullet, co. Mayo
*Davis, Rev John, M.A. & J.P., Chancellor of Dromore, co. Down
*Davis, Rev. John, jun., Warrenspoint, co. Down
*Davis, John, Esq., The Park, Rathfarnham, co. Dublin
Davis, John, Esq., Cloonshanville, near Frenchpark, co. Roscommon
Davis, John Snow, Esq., Summer-hill, Thomastown, co. Kilkenny
*Davis, Matthew, Esq., J.P., Ballyshannon, co. Donegal
Davis, Neal, Esq., Castlebar, co. Mayo
*Davis, Patrick, Esq., Carrick, Foxford, co. Mayo
*Davis, Robert, Esq., Newry, co. Down [Youghal, co. Cork
Davis, Roger Green, Esq., Drumdihey-house, Killeigh, near
*Davis, Sydenham, Esq., Dangan, Thomastown, co. Kilkenny
*Davis, Gray, & Hughes, Messrs., Coal-island, Dungannon, co. Tyrone
Davis, Strangman, & Co., Messrs., Waterford
*Davison, Alexander, jun., Esq., Knockboy, Broughshane, co. Antrim
Davison, John, Esq., Tullymore-cottage, Broughshane, co. Antrim
Davison, Thomas, Esq., J.P., Glenarm, co. Antrim
*Davison, Thomas, Esq., Durham
Davock, Mr. Thomas, Coleraine, co. Derry
Davoren, Basil, Esq., Henry-street, Dublin, and Glenwood, co. Clare
Dawe, E. M., Esq., Bandon, co. Cork
Dawes, James, Esq., Dublin Castle
*Dawson, Abraham, Esq., Newcastle-on-Tyne, Northumberland
Dawson, G. R., Esq., Upper Grosvenor-street, London
Dawson, Rt. Hon. George R., Castledawson, co. Derry
*Dawson, Arthur, Esq., Magherafelt, co. Derry
*Dawson, Charles P., Esq., Rutland-square, Dublin
*Dawson, Charles, Esq., J.P., Tanagh, Cootehill, co. Monaghan
*Dawson, Edward V., Esq., Athlone, co. Westmeath
*Dawson, Rev. John, A.M., Easkey Vicarage Dromore West, co. Sligo
Dawson, John H., Esq., Richardson-castle, Dunleer, co. Louth
*Dawson, Richard Thomas James, Esq., Forkhill-lodge, co. Armagh
*Dawson, Thomas, Esq., Lisnamorrow, Magherafelt, co. Derry
*Dawson, Walter James, Esq., Forkhill-lodge, co. Armagh
Dawson, William, Esq., Forest View, Cootehill, co. Cavan
Dawson, William, Esq., Noghaville, near Ballymahon, co. Westmeath
Dawson, W. G., Esq., Donegal, & Londonderry [co. Mayo
Dawson, Rev. William Paul, A.B., Tarmoncarra-glebe, Bellmullet,
*Day, Rev. Andrew, Aungier-street, Dublin
*Day, Mr. Charles, Worcester
Day, Rev. Edward, J.P., Roscommon
Day, Rev. Edward, Kilgobbin-glebe, co. Kerry
*Day, James Richard, Esq., Grange-house, Douglas, co. Cork
Dea, Martin, Esq., Castlebar, co. Mayo
*Deacon, Col. Charles, Manor-house, Berkhamstead, Hertfordshire
Deacon, Col., per Mr. Nichols, Farnham, Surrey
*Dean, Thomas, Esq., Sligo
Deane, Edmund, Esq., Carragann, Foxford, co. Mayo
Deane, George, Esq., Berkely, New Ross, co. Wexford
Deane, Hugh, Esq., Crofton-park, Ballina, co. Mayo
Deane, Joseph, Esq., Stokestown, near New Ross, co. Wexford
Deane, K. Allen, Esq., Pembroke-street, Cork
Deane, Sir Thomas, Knt., Dundanion-castle, Cork
*Dease, Gerald, Esq., J.P., Turbotstown, Castle-Pollard, co. West-
Dease, Thomas, Esq., Clonakilty, co. Cork [meath
Deaves, Messrs., Cork
*Debasterot, The Baron James, Durras-house, Kinvarra, co. Galway
*Debine, Lieut. Thomas D. J., R.N., Bray, co. Wicklow
*Decie, Henry, Esq., Douglas, Kilworth, co. Cork
*Decluzeau, John James, Esq., Virginia, co. Cavan
De Courcy, Maurice, Esq., Molahiffe-castle, Killarney, co. Kerry
D'Courcy, Matthew H., Esq., Limerick
*Deehan, Thomas, Esq., Lower Gardiner-st., Dublin, & Banagher, King's co. [house, co. Fermanagh
Deering, John, Esq., J.P., Mount-Joy-square North, & Derrybrusk-
*Deirue, F.. Esq., Ballymun, near Santry, co. Dublin
De La Charois Daniel, Esq., Donaghadee, co. Down
De La Cour, Newnham Robert, Esq., Ballincollig, co. Cork
De La Cour, Robert, Esq., Beareforest, Mallow, co. Cork
De Lacy, Rev. Hugh, P.P., Glenade, Manor-Hamilton, co. Leitrim
Delahunty, Pierce, Esq., Waterford [nedy, co. Wicklow
*Delamere, Rev. Lewis Roland, Holywell, nr. Newtown-Mount-Ken-
*Delaney, John, Esq., Air-park, near Rathfarnham, co. Dublin
Delannoy, William, Esq., Friday-street, London
*Delany, Rev. D. B., R.C. Chaplain, House of Industry, Dublin
Delany, H. P., Esq., Millbrook, Maryboro', Queen's county
Delany, Thomas, Esq., Court House, Galway
*Delap, Rev. John, M.A., Drumrusk, Kish, co. Fermanagh

*Delap, William Drummond, Esq., Monasterboice, Collon, co. Louth
Delay, Mr. Michael, Cork
Delmege, Christopher, Esq., Castle-park, Limerick
Delmege, Julius, Esq., Rathkeale, co. Limerick [Kilkenny
*De Montmorency, Harvey, Esq., Castle Morris, Knocktopher, co.
*De Montmorency, W., Esq., Upperwood, Freshford, co. Kilkenny
Dempsey, Rev. E. H., Ballyfin, Mountrath, Queen's county
*Dempsey, Rev. Luke D., Denmark-street, Dublin
Dempster, Mr. R., Brighton, Sussex
Denham, J., Esq., J.P., Fairwood-park, Enniskillen, co. Fermanagh
*Dennehy, Thomas, Esq., Bellevue, Fermoy, co. Cork
Dennehy, Walter, Esq., Fermoy, co. Cork
Denney, Rev. Henry, Churchill Rectory, Tralee, co. Kerry
*Dennis, Rev. G. M., Lynn-house, near Mullingar, co. Westmeath
Dennis, John Irwin, Esq., Tuam, co. Galway
Dennis, Rev. M. P., Donard, near Baltinglass, co. Wicklow
Dennis, Thomas Stratford, Esq., J.P., Fort Granite, near Baltinglass,
Denny, Rev. Barry, Frogmore-lodge, Tralee, co. Kerry [co. Wicklow
Denny, Rev. Edward May, Vicar of Listowel Union, co. Kerry
Denny, Henry, Esq., Queen-street, Waterford
*Denny, William, Esq., J.P., Tralee, co. Kerry
*Derinzi, Benjamin S., Esq., Baltinglass, co. Wicklow [co. Wexford
Derinzy, Thomas, Esq., D.L. and J.P., Clobemon-hall, near Ferns,
Derinzy, William S., Esq., Secretary to Grand Jury, Wexford
*DERRY, The Honorable and Right Rev. Lord Bishop of
Derry, Rev. Dean, P.P. of Ballymacward and Clonkeen, Woodview, [Kilconnell, co. Galway
*D'Esterre, R. Ker, Esq., Rossmanahir, co. Clare, and George's-
*DE SALIS, The Countess [street, Limerick
*DESART, The Right Honorable The Earl of
*Despard, George, Esq., Trim, co. Meath
*Despard, John, Esq., Killaghy-castle, near Callan, co. Tipperary
*Despard, W. W., Esq., J.P., Donore, Mountrath, Queen's county
*De Verdon, Richard, Esq., J. P., Manksland-house, Carlingford,
De Vere, Sir Aubrey, Bart., Currah, co. Limerick [co. Louth
Devereux, Rev. Aidan, St. Peter's College, Wexford
*Devereux, Major John, Ballyrankin-house, near Ferns, co. Wexford
*Devereux, Rev. John, LL.D., Stradbally, near Kilmacthomas, co.
*Devereux, Rev. John, O. S. F. C., Church-st., Dublin [Waterford
Devereux, Michael, Esq., M.D., Wexford
*Devereux, Rev. Nicholas, Cremorne-cottage, Cootehill, co. Monaghan
Devereux, William, Esq., Wexford
*Devereux, Harvey, & Co., Messrs., Wexford
Devereux, Richard, Esq., Tallow, co. Cork
*DE VESCI, The Right Honorable Viscount
Devine, Charles, Esq., Killininny, near Firr-house, co. Dublin
*Devine, Francis, Esq., Ballymeen, near Santry, co. Dublin
Devine, Rev. M. G., P.P., Boyle, co. Roscommon
Devine, Rev. Michael, P.P., Castletown-Berehaven, co. Cork
Devitt, Mr. James, Bridgend, Burt, co. Donegal
*Devitt, Thomas, Esq., George's-street, Limerick
Devonshir, A., Esq., Glenville, Cork
Devoy, Mr. Joshua, Exchequer-street, Dublin
*Dick, John, Esq., J.P., Bellefield, co. Wicklow
Dickey, Adam, Esq., Hollybrook-cottage, Randalstown, co. Antrim
Dickey, John, Esq., Leghinmore, Ballymena, co. Antrim
*Dickey, Rev. W., Carnone, Castlefin, co. Donegal
Dickey, Mrs. Jane, Myrtlefield Malone, Belfast, co. Antrim
*Dickie, Robert, jun., Esq., Killen, Dundalk, co. Louth
Dickinson, Rev. D., Vicar of Seapatrick, co. Down
Dickman, J., Esq., Newgate-street, London
*Dickson, Lieut.-Col., Corcreevy-house, Five-Mile Town, co. Tyrone
Dickson, Alexander, Esq., Riversdale, Belturbet, co. Cavan
*Dickson, Joseph, Esq., J.P., Ballyfree, Glanealy, co. Wicklow
*Dickson, Rev. J. L., Dungarberry-lodge, Ballyshannon, co. Leitrim
*Dickson, Rev. R., J.P., Rector and Vicar of Kilkeedy, near Limerick
Dickson, Rev. Stephen, Vicar of Dungarvan, co. Waterford
Dickson, T., Esq., Cookstown, co. Tyrone
*Dickson, Rev. W., Ratharkin, co. Antrim
Dickson, W., Esq., Cavan-house, Fintona, co. Tyrone
Dickson, Mrs., Glenconway, Antrim
*Digby, Rev. John, Landerstown, near Naas, co. Kildare
*Digby, Rev. William, Templeton-glebe, Killashee, Longford
*Digges, De La Warr, Esq., Chilham-cottage, Eyrecourt, co. Galway
Dignam, Thomas, Esq., Little Distaff Lane, London
Dignan, Christopher, Esq., Parsonstown, co. Tipperary
*Dilke, William, Esq., Maxstoke-castle, near Coleshill, Warwickshire
Dill, Moses, Esq., Springfield, Rathmellon, co. Donegal
*Dill, Rev. Richard, Muff, co. Donegal
Dill, Rev. S., Berwick-hall, Donaughmore, Castlefin, co. Donegal
*DILLON, The Right Honorable Viscount

*Dillon, Charles Henry, Esq., Athlone, co. Westmeath
Dillon, James, Esq., Cahir-house, Ballinasloe. co. Galway
*Dillon, Mr. John H., Donegal
Dillon, Very Rev. L., R.C. Archdeacon of Clonfert and P.P. of [Ballinasloe, co. Galway
Dillon, Michael, Esq., M. D., Elphin, co. Roscommon
Dillon, Rev. Michael, D.D. & P. P., Kilcluney, co. Armagh
*Dillon, O'Brien, Esq., Nenagh, co. Tipperary
Dillon, Rev. R. M., Dundonald, co. Down
Dillon, Rev. Thomas, P.P., Ballintubber, Ballymoe, co. Galway
Dillon, Thomas, Esq., M..D, Castlebar, co. Mayo
Dillon, Thomas, Esq., Clonferte, Leighlin-bridge, co. Carlow
Dillon, Thomas, Esq., Insulavita-cottage, Parsonstown, Kings' co.
*Dillon, Capt. W., Sandymount-park, Dublin
Dillon, William, jun., Esq., Lisburn, co. Antrim
*DIMSDALE, The Honorable Baron
Dinleany, Rev. James, P. P. of Sligo
DINORBEN, The Right Honorable Lord [Dublin
*Disney, Rev. Brabazon W., Archdeacon of Raphoe, Rutland-square,
*Disney, R. A., Esq., Westland-row, Dublin
*Disney, Thomas, jun., Esq., Westland-row, Dublin
Disney, W., Esq., Somerset, near Blackrock, Dublin
Divir, Anthony, Esq., Donegal
*Dixon, Henry, Esq., Great George-street, Cork
Dixon, Rev. T., Waterford
*Dobb, Rev. John, Vicar of Glynn, near Carrickfergus, co. Antrim
*Dobbin, Clotworthy, Esq., Belfast
Dobbin, Mr. Hugh, Ballymagaraghan, Moira, co. Down [Dublin
*Dobbin, Leonard, jun., Esq., J.P., Armagh, and Gardiner's-place,
*Dobbin, Thomas, Esq., Armagh
*Dobbs, Conway R., Esq., J.P., Acton-house, Loughbrickland, co.
Dobbs, Rev. Francis, Curate of Derrykeighan, co. Antrim [Down
*Dobbs, Richard, Esq., J.P., Castle Dobbs, Carrickfergus, co. Antrim
*Dobbyn, Michael, Esq., Woodlands, Kil, St. Nicholas, Waterford
Dockrall, Mr. William A., Kanturk, co. Cork
*Dodd, John, Esq., Sackville-street, Dublin
*Dodd, Patrick J., Esq., Tommontown, near Ballyboghill, co. Dublin
*Dodwell, George, Esq., Kivinsfort, Sligo [mon
*Dodwell, J. C., Esq., J.P., Knockranny, near Keadue, co. Roscom-
Doheny, Rev. James, P. P., Fanlobus, co. Cork
Doherty, Counsellor, Nelson-street, Dublin
*Doherty, James, Esq., North Frederick-street, Dublin
*Doherty, Michael, Esq., Glen-house, Carndonagh, co. Donegal
*Doherty, Rev. Michael, P. P. of Mohill, co. Leitrim
*Doherty, Mr. Michael, Coleraine, co. Derry
Doherty, Mr. Owen, Firmane, Clonmany, Carndonagh, co. Donegal
Doherty, Mr. William, Buncrana, co. Donegal
Dolan, Terence, Esq., Mount-pleasant, Ranelagh, co. Dublin
*D'Olier, Isaac M., Esq,, Collegnes, Booterstown, co. Dublin
*Domville, Sir Compton, Bart., Santry-house, co. Dublin
*Donagh, Francis, Esq., J.P., Newtown, Drogheda, co. Louth
Donahoo, Lieut. James, R.P., Galway
*Donald, Rev. A., St., Albans, Hertfordshire
Donaldson, Rev. D., A.M., Tartaraghan, Loughall, co. Armagh
*DONEGAL, The Most Noble the Marquis of
Donelan, Anthony, Esq., Galway
Donelan, Dermot, Esq., Silane, Tuam, co. Galway
Donelan, E. H., Esq., Hillswood, Kilconnel, co. Galway
Donkin, W., Esq., Sandhoe, Hexham, Northumberland
Donlevy, Rev. La Touche D., Kilcar-glebe, Killybegs, co. Donegal
Donnellan, Rev. John, C. C. St. Mary's, Drogheda, co. Louth
Donnellan, J. H. Esq., Kildare-street, Dublin
Donohoe, Thomas, Esq., Dowdstone, Maynooth, co. Kildare
Donohoe and Co., Messrs. Thos., South Earl-street, Dublin
*Donolan, S., Esq.
*DONOUGHMORE, The Right Honorable the Earl of
*Donovan, Rev. C., P.P., Rathcormac, co. Cork
Donovan, Daniel, Esq., M.D., Woodview, near Skibbereen, co. Cork
Donovan, Mr. Daniel, jun., Killumney, co. Cork
Donovan, Rev. I.I., Convent, Athlone, co. Westmeath
Donovan, Rev. Patrick, R.C.C., Newmarket, Kanturk, co. Cork
*Donovan, R., Esq., Ballymore, near Ferns, co. Wexford
Donovan, Richard, Esq., Lisheens-house, Ballincollig, co. Cork
Donovan, Rev. Solomon, Killanne, near Enniscorthy, co. Wexford
*Donovan, Messrs. Simon & James, Ovens, co. Cork
*Doolan, Thomas, Esq., Fairy-hill, Portumna, co. Galway
*Dooley, Thomas, Esq., Queen-street, Dublin, & Clonturk-house, co.
*Dooner, John, Esq., Gloucester-place, Dublin [Dublin
*Dopping, John, Esq., J.P., Erne-head, Granard, co. Longford
*Dopping, William, Esq., Lotown-house, near Kinnegad, co. West-
*Doran, Edmund E., Esq., Ninch, near Drogheda, co. Louth [meath
*Doran, Rev. James, P.P.C. Ballylinen, King's county
*Doran, Rev. T. C. C., Halston-street, Dublin
*Dore, Rev. David, P.P., Caharagh, Skibbereen, co. Cork
Dorman, John, Esq., Kinsale, co. Cork
Dorman, William B., Esq., Kinsale, co. Cork
Douglas, Charles, Esq., Dervock, co. Antrim
Douglas, Sir James, Bart., Limerick
*Douglas, James, Esq., Rosebrook, near Dungiven, co. Derry
Douglas Rope Walk Company, Cork
Douglas, Rev. A., A.M., Cootehill, co. Cavan
Douglass, Charles, Esq., J. P., Grace-hall, Lurgan, co. Armagh
*Douglass, Mr. John, Lissaghmore, Glendermott, co. Derry
*Dowall, Bernard, Esq., Castlecoote, near Roscommon
Dowdall, Henry, Esq., Upper Dominick-street, Dublin
Dowdall, Rev. Launcelot, Magherafelt, co. Derry
Dowdican, Rev. Peter, P. P. of Dromard, co. Sligo
Dowley, Rev. P., St. Vincent's, Castleknock, co. Dublin
Dowling, Rev. Cornelius H., P. P., Stradbally, Queen's county
*Dowling, Rev. James, P. P. of the Union of Multifarnham, Mul- [lingar, co. Westmeath
*Dowling, John, Esq., Newcastle, co. Limerick
Dowling, John, Esq., Castle Lyon, co. Cork
Dowling, John, Esq., Longford Castle, Eyrecourt, co. Galway
*Dowling, Rev. P., P.P., Durrow, co. Kilkenny
*Dowling, Rev. Patrick O.S.A., John-street, Dublin
*Dowling, Peter, Esq., Lower Ormond-quay, Dublin
Dowling, William D., Esq., Eyrecourt, co. Galway
*Dowman, Mrs. Jane, Wilsfort, Douglas, near Cork
*DOWN & CONNOR, The Right Rev. Lord Bishop of
*DOWNES, The Right Honorable Lord [co. Tipperary
Downes, Rev. Joseph, P.P. of Knigh, &c., Ballyhogan, Nenagh,
*Downes, Rev. William, P.P. of Kilkeedy, &c., near Limerick
Downing, Francis Henry, Esq., Kenmare, co. Kerry
*Downing, Henry, Esq., French Walls Iron and Steel Works, [near Birmingham
Downing, Rev. Samuel, Fennagh-glebe, Leighlin-bridge, co. Carlow
Downing, Thomas, Fitzgerald, Esq., M.D., Fermoy, co. Cork
*DOWNSHIRE, The Most Noble the Marquis of
*Dowse, Richard B., Esq., Lower-Dorset-street, Dublin
Dowse, Robert, Esq., Baradawn, near Tinahely, co. Wicklow
Dowse, William, Esq., Springfield, near Tinahely, co. Wicklow
Doyle, Rev. C. M., A.M., The Rectory, Castle-Blakeney, co. Galway
*Doyle, Rev. Charles, P.C., Ballyfinn, near Mountrath, Queen's Co.
*Doyle, Edward, Esq., Nelson-st., Dublin, & Eyrecourt, co. Galway
*Doyle, Rt. Rev. Francis, D.D., R.C. Bishop of Kildare and
*Doyle, Rev. Gerald, C.R., Naas, co. Kildare [Leighlin
*Doyle, James, Esq., Lower Bridge-street, Dublin
Doyle, James, Esq., Cloyne, co. Cork
*Doyle, Gen. Sir John, Bart., Somerset-street, Portman-square, London
*Doyle, Rev. John, C.C., of St. James's, Dublin
Doyle, Capt. M. T., Ballincollig, co. Cork
*Doyle, Rev. Patrick, C. C., Kilpipe, near Tinahely, co. Wicklow
*Doyle, Rev. Patrick, C. C. of Rathmines, near Dublin
*Doyle, Rev. Peter, C. C., Killavaney, near Tinahely, co. Wicklow
*Doyle, R., Esq., Caroline-lodge, Williamstown, co. Dublin
Doyle and Co., Messrs. J. P., Upper Church-street, Dublin
*Doyle, Richard, Esq., Willfield, near Ballymore-Eustace, co. Dublin
Doyle, Messrs. R.& W., Grantstown Convent, Taghmon, co. Wexford
*Doyle, Rev. W., P.P. of Rathdrum, co. Wicklow
Doyne, Rev. Charles William, Prebendary of Fethard, co. Wexford
*Doyne, Charles, Esq., Newtown-park, near Dublin
*Doyne, Robert, Esq., J.P., Borris, co. Carlow
Drake, Christopher, Esq., Roristown-house, Trim, co. Meath
Draper, James, Esq., Crampton-court, Dublin
Draper, Samuel, Esq., Royal-canal-house, Dublin
*Drax, I. S. W. S. E., Esq., Charborough Park, Dorsetshire
Drew, Barry, jun., Esq., Flower-hill, near Lismore, co. Waterford
*Drew, Francis, Esq., D.L. and J.P., Mocollop, Fermoy, co. Cork
*Drew, Francis, Esq., Drewsborough, Scariff, co Clare
*Drew, Francis, Esq., Flower-hill, Lismore, co. Waterford
Drew, Rev. Pierce William, A.B., Youghal
Drew, Patrick, Esq., Monknewtown, Drogheda, co. Louth
*Drewe, Capt. E. W., Valetta, Kingstown, co. Dublin
*DROMORE, The Right Rev. Lord Bishop of
*Drought, Rev. Adolphus, Castle-Pollard, co. Westmeath
*Drought, Capt. G. M. J., J.P., Glencainy, Wicklow
Drought, Mr. James, Kilbredy, Rathdowney, Queen's county
*Drue, Richard, Esq., Portyana, Portstewart, Coleraine, co. Derry
Drummond, James L., Esq., M.D., Belfast
*Drummond, John, Esq., Trinity-street, Dublin
*Drury, Capt. H., R.N., Bundoran, Ballyshannon, co. Donegal

* DUBLIN, His Grace the Lord Archbishop of
* Dublin Royal Society
Dublin Steam Packet Company, Liverpool
Dubourdieu, Capt. Francis, Sligo
Dubourdieu, Rev. John, Rector of Drumgooland, Rathfriland, co. Down
Dubourdieu, Saumarez, Esq., Derryloran, Cookstown, co. Tyrone
Duckett, Jonas, Esq., Bellview, Castle Dermott, co. Kildare
Duckett, J. D., Esq., J.P., Duckett's Grove, Castle Dermott, co. Kildare
* Duckett, W., Esq., Stapelstown-park, Carlow
* Duckworth, Capt. John, Mount Erris, near Boyle, co. Roscommon
Duddell, Rev. John, M.A., Prebendary of St. Munchin's, Limerick
* Dudding, John, Esq., Lincoln
Dudgeon, Alexander, Esq., Capel-street, Dublin, and Sterling-lodge, Clones, co. Monaghan
* Dudgeon, Rev. Michael Fox, Carrowbarrow, Monaghan
* Dudgeon, Capt. Ralph, J.P., Rosefield, Monaghan
* Dudgeon, Samuel, Esq., Middle Gardiner-street, Dublin
* DUDLEY, The Right Honorable the Earl of
* Duff, C. N., Esq., Corrig Castle, Kingstown, co. Dublin
Duff, Mr. John, Coagh, co. Tyrone
* Duff, V., Esq., North Earl-street, Dublin
Duffy, Rev. E., P.P. of Fohenagh, Ahascragh, co. Galway
* Duffy, Rev., Thomas, P.P., Clones West, co. Monaghan
* DUFFERIN, The Right Honorable Lord
Duffin, Rev. William, Maghera-glebe, Castlewellan, co. Down
Duffy, The Very Rev. M., P.P. & V.G., Kilmacduagh, near Gort, co. Galway
* Dugdale, Mr. Thomas, Clara, King's county
* Duggan, Mr. John, New Ross, co. Wexford
* Duggan, Rev. Malachy, C.R. of Moyarta and Kilballyowen, Kilrush, co. Clare
Duggan, Rev. Patrick, Ballinamona, Mallow, co. Cork
Duggin, John, Esq., Elmvale, Mallow, co. Cork
Duke, John, Esq., Ciogher, near Boyle, co. Roscommon
* Dumas, Henry, Esq., C.C.P., Cootehill, co. Cavan
* DUNALLEY, The Right Honorable Lord
Dunbar, Hugh, Esq., Huntley Glen, Banbridge, co. Down
Dunbar, Mr. Patrick, Ballincollig, cc. Cork
* Dunbavin, William, Esq., Willmount, near Blesington, co. Wicklow
Duncan, James. Esq., Kilkenny
Duncan, John, Esq., Magherafelt, co. Derry
* DUNCANNON, The Right Honorable Lord
* Duncombe, Philip Duncombe Pauncefort, Esq., Great Brickhill Manor, Bucks
* Dundas, Capt. Francis, Sea View, near Clontarf, co. Dublin
* Dundas, R. A., Esq., Eaton-square, Pimlico, London
Dungan, J. M., Esq., M.D., Castle Connell, co. Limerick
* Dungan, Rev. Michael, R.C.C., Meath-street, Dublin
* Dunkin, Rev. David, Agherton Glebe-house, Coleraine, co. Derry
* DUNLO, The Right Honorable Viscount
Dunlop, Charles, Esq., Edenderry-house, Belfast
Dunlop, David, Esq., Coleraine, co. Derry
Dunlop, Mr. Robert, Taumnie, Moira, co. Antrim
Dunn, Rev. Charles, Roscommon
Dunn, Edward, Esq., Luke-street, Dublin
* Dunn, Mr. George, Kilmainham, near Dublin
* Dunn, Rev. John, D.D., Palmerstown, near Chapelisod, co. Dublin
* Dunn, Rev. John P., St. Catherine's, Meath-street, Dublin
* Dunn, Josias, Esq., Kildare-street, Dublin
Dunn, Mr. Michael, Cork
Dunn, Rev. Patrick, Chaplain to the Monastery of St. Joseph, Clondalkin, co. Dublin
Dunn, Robert L., Esq., Kinsale, co. Cork
Dunn, Stuart, Esq., Farmhill, Carrickfergus, co. Antrim
Dunne, Andrew, Esq., Dollardstown, near Athy, co. Kildare
Dunne, Rev. D., P.P., Allen, co. Kildare
* Dunne, Gen. Edward, Brittas, Clonaslee, Queen's county
* Dunne, Rev. F. C., P.P., Dunsany, & Kilmesson, co. Meath
* Dunne, Capt. F. P., Brittas, near Clonaslee, Queen's county
Dunne, Rev. J., P.P., Clonmore, Clonbulloge, Queen's county
Dunne, James, Esq., Rathleix, Portarlington, Queen's county
* Dunne, Rev. John, P. P., Saggard, co. Dublin
* Dunne, J. H., Esq., Rocklands, near Stillorgan, co. Dublin
Dunne, Lawrence, Esq., Benfield, near Portarlington, King's co.
Dunne, Rev. Lawrence, P.P., Castle-Dermott, co. Kildare
* Dunne, Rev. Michael, Newbridge, co. Kildare
* Dunne, Michael, Esq., Ballymanus, Stradbally, Queen's county
Dunne, Mr. Patrick, Kilkea-house, Castle-Dermott, co. Kildare
* Dunne, W., Esq., Molesworth-street, Dublin
Dunne, William, Esq., Tully, Kildare
Dunphy, Michael, Esq., Westfield, near Booterstown, and North Cumberland-street, Dublin
* DUNRAVEN, The Right Honorable the Earl of
* Dunscombe, C. W., Esq., Cork
* Dunscombe, N., Esq., Mount Desert, near Cork
* Du Pre, James, Esq., Wilton Park, Beaconsfield, Bucks
* Durcan, Rev. P., P.P., Ballisodare, Collooney, co. Sligo
DURHAM, The Right Honorable the Earl of [Two copies.]
Durham, Andrew, Esq., Belvidere, near Belfast
Durkan, John, Esq., Swinford, co. Mayo
Durreux, Richard, Esq., Tallow, co. Waterford
* Dwyer, Francis, Esq., Elm Green, Castleknock, co. Dublin
* Dwyer, Rev. Geo., A.M. & J.P., The Rectory, Ardrahan, co. Galway
* Dwyer, James, Esq., Lower Gardiner-street, Dublin
Dwyer, James, Esq., South Main-street, Cork
* Dwyer, Robert D., Esq., Kilternan Cottage, co. Dublin
* Dwyer, Thomas, Esq., Lower Mount-st., Dublin, & Ellen-ville, Johnstown, co. Kilkenny
Dwyer, Messrs. Thomas & Joseph, Midleton, co. Cork
Dyas, Capt. Joseph, Ennis, co. Clare
* Dysart, Mr. James, Ballynagallaugh, Templemore, co. Derry
* Dysart, John, Esq., J.P., Londonderry
Dysart, J. Mitchell, Esq., Foyle-street, Londonderry
Dysart, Rev. William, Curate of Desertmartin, co. Derry

Eade, George, Esq., Upper Thames-street, London
Eagar, Henry, Esq., Palmyra, Ballina, co. Mayo
* Eagar, Rev. J., R.C.C., Midleton, co. Cork
* Eagle, George, Esq., Dublin
* Eagle, W., Esq., Gravesend, Kent
Eames, Rev. Benjamin, M.A., Killala, co. Mayo
Eames, Mr. Edward, Sullivan's-quay, Cork
* Earl, Rev. Edward, P.P., Castle-carberry, Edenderry, co. Kildare
* Eason, W. M., Esq., Baggot-street, Dublin
East India Company, The Honorable. [Three copies.]
* Eastwood, Francis, Esq., Falmore, Dundalk, co. Louth
* Eastwood, James, Esq., J.P., Castletown-castle, Dundalk, co. Louth
* Eccles, Charles, Esq., Ecclesville, Fintona, co. Tyrone
Eccles, Isaac Ambrose, Esq., J.P., Cronroe, near Wicklow
Eccles, Mr. James, Fairview, Ballygruby, Randalstown, co. Antrim
Echlin, John, Esq., Echlinville, Kirkcubbin, co. Down
Eckland, Lieut. Edward, R.N., Moville, co. Donegal
Edgar, John P., Esq., M.D., Ballyhooly, co. Cork
Edgar, Rev. John Ware, M.A., High-park, Fermoy, co. Cork
Edge, John, Esq., Knockrath, near Rathdrum, co. Wicklow
* Edgeworth, Lovell, Esq., J.P., Edgeworthstown, co. Longford
Edie, A. C. D. L., Esq., Thorn-hill, Strabane, co. Tyrone
Edington, Charles, Esq., Knockadown, Youghal, co. Cork
Edmonds, Charles, Esq., Change-alley, London
Edmundson, W., Esq., Capel-street, Dublin
* Education, The Commissioners of, Upper Merrion-street, Dublin
Edwards, Rev. Edward, Castlederg, co. Tyrone
* Edwards, F. W., Esq., Woodford, near Santry, co. Dublin
* Edwards, Major J. K., Old-court, near Bray, co. Wicklow
* Edwards, John, Esq., J.P., Camolin-park, co. Wexford
* Egan, The Rt. Rev. Cornelius, D.D., R.C. Bishop of Kerry
* Egan, Howard N., Esq., Borrisokane, co. Tipperary
* Egan, Rev. John, Curate of St. Finbarr's, Cork
Egan, Mr. Joseph, Hotel, Eyrecourt, co. Galway
Egan, Rev. Kinan, R.C.C., Cloghan, King's county
Egan, Rev. L., P.P., Leitrim, Loughrea, co. Galway
Egan, Stephen, Esq., Cottage, Sans Souci, Roscrea, co. Tipperary
* Egan, Terence, Esq., Borrisokane, co. Tipperary
Egan, Timothy, Esq., North Ann-street, Dublin
Egan, W., Esq., Mount-Eagle, Kilkenny
Ekin, Mr. Thomas, Ballyscullion, Bellaghey, Londonderry
Elgee, Rev. R. W., Rector of Killinick, Wexford
* Ellard, Rev. James, A.B., Vicar of Kilfinan & Darra, co. Limerick
Ellard, J. D., Esq., J.P., Swinford, co. Mayo, & Kenmore, Galway
Elliott, Alexander, Esq., Tanavalla, Listowel, co. Kerry
Elliott, Francis, Esq., Fennor, Slane, co. Meath
* Elliott, James, Esq., Sackville street, Dublin
Elliott, James, Esq., Cavan
* Elliott, John, Esq., M.D., Kilrush, co. Clare
Elliott, Mr. John, Moira, co. Down
* Elliott, Samuel, Esq., J.P., Kilmany, Carlow
Elliott, Thomas, Esq., Johnstown, co. Carlow
Elliott, Mr. W., Letterkenny, co. Donegal
Elliott, W., Esq., Strabane, co. Tyrone
Elliott, W., Esq., Clare-street, Dublin, & Racroge, co. Carlow
* Ellis, Alexander, Esq., Rathdrum, co. Wicklow
Ellis, Charles, Esq., Soho-square, London
Ellis, Henry, Esq., Glanmire, co. Cork
Ellis, James S., Esq., Ward-house, Bundoran, Ballyshannon, co. Donegal
Ellis, John, Esq., Westport, co. Mayo

Ellis, Mr. Robert, Leans-mount, Lurgan, co. Armagh
*Ellis, Thomas H., Esq., Hermitage, Clongesh, co. Longford
*Ellis, Thomas J., Esq., Sligo
*Ellis, Rev. V., Rector of Walton, Stoney-Stratford, Bucks.
*Ellison, Rev. John, J.P., Killymard-glebe, Donegal
*Ellison, Thomas, Esq., The Hall, Glossop, Derbyshire
*ELPHIN, The Rt. Rev. Lord Bishop of
*Elphinstone, John G., Esq., Passage West, co. Cork
*Elrington, Rev. C. R., D.D., Regius Professor of Divinity, Trinity [College, Dublin
Elrington, Rev. H. P., A.M., Precentor of Ferns, co. Wexford
Elstob, George, Esq., Bridge-end, Hexham, Northumberland
*Elwood, Rev. James, Ballymore, Boyle, co. Roscommon
*Elwood, Thomas, Esq., J.P., Strand-hill, Cong, co. Mayo
*ELY, The Right Reverend Lord Bishop of
ELY, The Dean & Chapter of
*ELY, The Most Noble the Marquess of
*Emerson, Arbuthnot, Esq., Beech-park, Belfast
Emerson, John Jervis, Esq., Rochfort, Wexford
*Emly, Henry, Esq., Middle Temple-lane, London
*Emmerson, John, Esq., Royal Exchange-square, Glasgow
*Enery, John, Esq., Ballyconnell-house, co. Cavan
Ennis, James, Esq., Claristown, Drogheda, co. Louth
*Ennis, John, Esq., Roebuck, co. Dublin
Ennis Rev. John, Townsend-street, Dublin
Ennis, Richard, Esq., Essex-quay, Dublin
Ennis, Richard, Esq., Cellar, Nobber, co. Meath
*Ennis, Mr. W., Kingstan, near Dundrum, co. Dublin
*ENNISKILLEN, The Right Honorable the Earl of
ENNISMORE, The Right Honorable Viscount
Enraght, Rev. T., P.P., Mohoonogh, Newcastle, co. Limerick
Enright, Thomas, Esq., M.D., Glin, co. Limerick
Ensor, George, Esq., Ardress-house, Loughgall, co. Armagh
ERROLL, The Right Honorable the Earl of
*Erskine, James, Esq., Carrickfergus, co. Antrim
*Erskine, W., Esq., Treasurer of the county, Cavan
*Erson, Paul, Esq., Askeaton, co. Limerick
*Esmonde, Rev. B., D.D., Dublin
*Esmonde, James, Esq., J.P., Pembrokestown, near Waterford
*Esmonde, Sir Thomas, Bart., J.P. Ballynastragh, Gorey, co. Wexford
Espinasse, Richard, Esq., Kill-abbey, near Monkstown, co. Dublin
Espinasse, Richard, Esq., Newcastle, co. Wicklow
ESSEX, The Right Honorable the Earl of
Eustace, John, Esq., Youghal, co. Cork
*Eustace, Robert, Esq., J.P., Newtown, Tullow, co. Carlow
*Evans, Arthur, Esq., Lower Mallow-street, Limerick
*Evans, Charles, Esq., Brown-street, Manchester
Evans, Rev. Edward, P.C., of Newmarket, Flintshire
Evans, Edward, Esq., J.P., Dungannon, co. Tyrone
Evans, Eyre, Esq., J.P., Ash-hill, Kilmallock, co. Limerick
*Evans, Eyre, jun., Esq., The Towers, Kilmallock, co. Limerick
*Evans, Francis, Esq., Mountjoy-square East, Dublin
*Evans, George, Esq., Farm-hill, Athy, co. Kildare
*Evans, George, Esq., M.P., Portrane, co. Dublin
*Evans, G. W., Esq., Drogheda, co. Louth
Evans, H., Esq., Copse, near Rathdrum, co. Wicklow
*Evans, Rear-Adm. H., Old Town, near Doneraile, co. Cork
*Evans, John, Esq., Broad-street, Worcester
Evans, John, Esq., Mallow, co. Cork
*Evans, John Freke, Esq., The Towers, Kilmallock, co. Limerick
*Evans, Nicholas, Esq., J.P., Lough-park, Castle Pollard, co. West- [meath
Evans, N. G., Esq., Carker, Doneraile, co. Cork
*Evans, Ralph, Esq., Carker, Doneraile, co. Cork
*Evans, Mrs. Sophia, Portrane, co. Dublin
*Evans, T. D'Arcy, Esq., Knockaderry-house, Newcastle, co. [Limerick
Evans, Thomas P., Esq., J.P., Ashrow, Newport, co. Tipperary
Evans, T. Williams, Esq., M.P., Ash Hill Towers, Kilmallock, co. [Limerick
*Evans, W., Esq., Allestree, Derbyshire
*Evans, W., Esq., Carrana, Kilconnell, co. Galway
Evans & Son, Messrs., Galway
Evanson, Rev. Alleyn, A. B., J.P., Four-mile-water-court, Ban- [try, co. Cork
*Evanson, Lieut. Alleyn, R.N., The Castle, Beerhaven, co. Cork
Evanson, Richard J., Esq , Ardoguina, Bantry, co. Cork
Evatt, Rev. Charles, Rector of Monaghan
*Evatt, S. R. B., Esq., J.P., Mount Louise, near Monaghan
*Ewart, John, Esq., Mosley-hill, near Liverpool
*Ewing, Mr. Alexander, Burt, co. Donegal
Ewing, Rev. G. T., Londonderry
*Ewing, Rev. W., All Saints-glebe, Newtowncunningham, near Lon- [donderry
Exchange Assurance Company, London
EXCISE, The Hon. the Commissioners of Her Majesty's

Eyles, James, Esq., Coleshill, near Amersham, Bucks.
Eyre, Edmund, Esq., Middle Gardiner-st., Dublin, & Gort, co. [Galway
Eyre, Rev. Giles, Athenry, Co. Galway
*Eyre, John, Esq., Hassop-park, Eyrecourt, co. Galway
Eyre, Richard, Esq., Boras-house, Borrisokane, co. Tipperary
Eyre, Rev. R. B., Vicar of Eyrecourt, co. Galway
*Eyre, R. H., Esq., Macroom-castle, co. Cork
Eyre, Thomas Stratford, Esq., J.P., Eyreville, Ballinasloe, co. Gal- [way

Fagan, James, Esq., Prospect, near Roundtown, and Bridgefoot- [street, Dublin
*Fagan, Rev. Matthew, C.C., Arklow, co. Wicklow
Fagan, Patrick, Esq., Balsaw, Navan, co. Meath
Fagan, Stephen, Esq., M.D., Sidney-place, Cork
*Fagan, William, Esq., Filtrim, Cork
Fahey, Rev. James, R.C.C. of Bolea and Killoran, co. Sligo
Fahey, James, Esq., A. B., College, Fermoy, co. Cork
*Fahy, Very Rev. Charles, V.G. & P.P., Tulla, co. Clare
*Fahy, Rev. Mordachy, P.P., Gambo, near Elphin, co. Roscommon
Fahy, Rev. P., R.C.C., Galway
Fair, Campbell, Esq., Lavally, Hollymount, co. Mayo
Fair, James, Esq., Fairhill, near Cong, co. Mayo
*Fair, Robert, Esq., Carraville, Hollymount, co. Mayo
*Fair, Thomas, Esq., Fortville, Hollymount, co. Mayo
*Fairchild, George, Esq., Ballina, co. Mayo
Fairfield, C. G., Esq., Mount Eagle, Castle Island, co. Kerry
Fairtlough, Rev. Edward, M.A., Ballidihob, Skibbereen, co. Cork
Fairtlough, Latham, Esq., Drogheda, co. Louth
Fairtlough, Rev. S. Gerrard, Ahinagh-glebe, Killinardrish, co. Cork
Faithfull, Edward C., Esq., King's-road, Bedford-row, London
Falkiner, Daniel, Esq., Beechwood, Nenagh, co. Tipperary
*Falkiner, John, Esq., Willsborough, Burris-o'-kane, co. Tipperary
*Falkiner, Joseph, Esq., Rodeen, Burris-o'-kane, co. Tipperary
*Falkner, Francis, Esq., Lower Gardiner-street, Dublin
*Fallon, Edward, Esq., Upper-Gloster-street, Dublin, & Roscommon
Fallon, Rev. Patrick, P.P., Kiltarton, co. Galway
Fallon, Rev. Thomas, P.P., Ballinakill, & Donena, Queen's county
Fallow, John, Esq., Banagher, King's county
Falls James O'Neill, Esq., Belfast
*Falls, John, Esq., Dungannon, co. Tyrone
FALMOUTH, The Right Honorable the Earl of
Falvey, Rev. John F., P.P., Glanmire, co. Cork
*Fanelly, Rev. Thomas, R.C. Dean of Ardagh, Longford
*Fanning, Messrs. J. & C., Cork
*Fant, Rev. P., P.P., Templemore, co. Tipperary
Farange, Henry, Esq., Clonliffe-house, near Dublin
*Faris, Alexander, Esq., Hardwicke-st., Dublin, & Summerhill, near [Carrick-on-Shannon, Co. Leitrim
Farmar, William R., Esq., Bloomfield, Enniscorthy, co. Wexford
*FARNHAM, The Right Honorable Lord
Farquharson, R., Esq., Christ Church College, Oxford
*Farran, Charles, Esq., M.D., Feltrim, near St. Doulough's, co. Dublin
*Farran, J., Esq., Rathgar, near Dublin
Farran, Mark, Esq., Drumnigh, near St. Doulough's, co. Dublin
*Farrell, Charles, Esq., M.D., Minard, Longford
Farrell, Mr. John, Doagh, co. Antrim
Farrell, James, Esq., R.N., Kingstown, co. Dublin
*Farrell, John, Esq., Moynalty, co. Meath
Farrell, Matthew Wood, Esq., Waterford
*Farrelly, Rev. Dean, P.P., Ardagh, Edgeworthstown, co. Long- [ford
*Fate, Mr. Christy, Kilfennon, Glendermott, co. Derry
*Faunt, Col., Myrtle Grove, Youghal, co. Cork
*Fausset, Charles, Esq., Upper Gloucester-street, Dublin
Fausset, Charles, Esq., J.P., Lisbofin, Enniskillen, co. Fermanagh
Fausset, John, Esq., J.P., Mount-Glynne, Killala, co. Mayo
*Fausset, W., Esq., J.P., Willsboro', Sligo
Faussett, Richard, Esq., M.D., Ardnaree, Ballina, co. Mayo
Fauvel, Rev. T., Glossop, Derbyshire
Fawcett, John, Esq., Durham
Fearon, R. J., Esq., Lower Gardiner-street, Dublin
Feehan, Mrs. T., Carrickbegg, Carrick on Suir, co. Tipperary
Feely, Rev. William, Franciscan Convent, Galway
Feeney, Rev. Owen, C.C., Sligo
Feeney, Rev. William, R.C.C., Westport, co. Mayo
Fenamore, George, Esq., The Cottage, Clonaslee, Queen's county
*Fendall, Rev. John, Miserden, Gloucestershire
*Fennell, John, Esq., Sub-Inspector of Revenue police, Loughrea, [co. Galway
Fennell, William J., Esq., J.P., Carrigataha, Cahir, co. Waterford
*Fenton, Rev. Galbraith, Balbriggan, co. Dublin
*Fenton, George, Esq., Dromore West, co. Sligo, & Summer-hill, [Dublin
Fenton, John, Esq., J.P., Dromore-house, Dromore West, co. Sligo

*Fenton, Richard, Esq., Ballinclea, near Baltinglass, co. Wicklow
*Fenton, Thomas, Esq., Castleton, Dromore West, co. Sligo
Fenton, Mr. W., Lifford, co. Donegal
Fenwick, Rev. M.G., Nenagh-glebe, Ballintra, co. Donegal
*Fenwick, William, Esq., J.P., Greenhills, Raphoe, co. Donegal
*Ferguson, Andrew, Esq., J.P., Burt-house, Burt, co. Donegal
Ferguson, Henry, Esq., Belfast
Ferguson, James, Esq., Shannon-st., Limerick
Ferguson, James, Esq., Newforge-green, Belfast
*Ferguson, John, Esq., Rathkeale, co. Limerick
Ferguson, John, Esq., Candleriggs-st., Glasgow
Ferguson, Joseph, Esq., Oatlands, Abbeyleix, Queen's county
Ferguson, J. S., Esq., Belfast
Ferguson, Sir R. A., Bart., M.P. and J.P., The Farm, Londonderry
Ferguson, T. P., Esq., Strade, Manor Hamilton, co. Leitrim
Ferguson, William, Esq., Parkgate, co. Antrim
Ferguson & Sons, Messrs., Newforge-green, Belfast
*Fergusson, Lieut.-Gen. A., Dunfallandy, Dunkeld, Perthshire
Ferrall, James J. C., Esq., Gibraltar-house, Sligo
Ferrall, Rev. Richard, P.P., of Killashee, Longford
Ferrar, Michael, Esq., Belfast
*Ferrier, James, Esq., Willow-park, Booterstown, co. Dublin
Ferrier, John, Esq., Kilrea, co. Derry
*Fetherston, Sir G. R., Bart., Ardagh, Longford
Fetherston, Robt., Esq., J.P., Bruree-house, Charleville, co. Cork
*Fetherston H., C., Esq., J.P., Dardistown, near Castletown Delvin,
[co. Westmeath
*Fetherston H., Rev. Cuthbert, Hacketstown, co. Carlow
Fetherston H., Francis, Esq., Cassino, nr. Rathdrum, co. Wicklow
Fetherston H., G., Esq , North Great, George-street, Dublin
Fetherston H., John, Esq., Griffinstown-house, near Kinnegad, co. Westmeath
[Westmeath
Fetherston H., Theobald, Esq., J.P., Mosstown, near Moate, co.
Fetherston H., T. J., Esq., J.P., Bracklyn Castle, Kinnegad, co. Westmeath
[Westmeath
*Fetherston H., William, Esq., Ballintobber, near Moate, co.
Fetherston H., W., Esq., J.P., Carrick, Mullingar, co. Westmeath
*Fetherston H., Mrs. R, Rockview, Castletown Delvin, co. Westmeath
Feuge, Thomas, Esq., Rockville, Youghal, co. Cork
*Fewtrell, Samuel, Esq., Aungier-street, Dublin
Ffolliott, William, Esq., M.D., Clonakilty, co. Cork
*FFRENCH, The Right Honorable Lord
Ffrench, Right Rev. Edmund, D.D., R.C. Bishop of Kilmacduagh
Ffrench, Rev. Edward, P.P., Moycullen, co. Galway
*Ffrench, The Honorable Gonville, J.P.
*Ffrench, The Honorable Martin, J.P.,
Ffrench, The Honorable and Rev. N.
*Ffrench, N. Joseph, Esq., J.P., Fortwilliam, Athleague, co. Ros-
Ffrench, The Honorable Thomas [common
Fiddes, Edward, Esq., Clenamully, Monaghan
Field, Mr. C. J., William-street, Dublin
*Field, H. C., Esq., M.D., Field-villa, Blackrock, and Lower Bag-
Field, James, Esq., Lothbury, London [got-street, Dublin
Field, James, Esq., Adelaide Place, London Bridge
Field, Rev. Michael, P.P., Innishannon, co. Cork
*FIFE, The Right Honorable the Earl of
Filgate, Charles, Esq., J.P., Ahascragh, co. Galway
*Filgate, William, Esq., J.P., Lisreigny, Ardee, co. Louth
*Finch, George, Esq., Burley-on-the-Hill, Oakham, Rutland
*Finch, Hugh F., Esq., Mary Ville, Limerick
*Finch, William, Esq., J.P., Tullaghmore, Nenagh, co. Tipperary
Finch, W., Esq., M.D., Salisbury
*Finegan, Mr. Bernard J., Drogheda, co. Louth
*Finegan, Mr. Lawrence, Drogheda, co. Louth
Finegan, Mr. Philip, Navan, co. Meath
*Finey, Captain A. G., Beechwood, near Bray, co. Wicklow
*Finigan, Rev. James Berd, Merchants Quay, Dublin
*Finlay, John, Esq., Argyll-street, Glasgow
Finlay, John, Esq., LL.D., North-Cumberland-street, Dublin
*Finlay, Rev. John William, A.M., Derryheen, Cavan
Finlay, Mr. Robert, Jervis-street, Dublin
*Finlay, Thomas, Esq., J.P., Sugar-loaf, Belturbet, co. Cavan
Finlay, Colonel Thomas, Dublin
*Finley, Col., Port-Stewart, Coleraine, co. Derry
Finley, John, Esq., Trinity College, Cambridge [street, Dublin
*Finn, John J., Esq., Mary Ville, near Clonturk, and Henrietta-
*Finn, Lawrence, Esq., Eden-park, near Dundrum, co. Dublin
Finn, Rev. Thomas, LL.D., Williamstown-avenue, near Dublin
Finnegan, Rev. Dennis, P.P., Killany, Carrickmacross, co. Monaghan
Finnemore, J., Esq., J.P., Ballyward, Blessington, co. Wicklow
Finney, James, Esq., Curnocreen, Tuam, co. Galway

Finnimore, Mr. W., Ashton Academy, near Bristol
Finucane, John, Esq., Ennistymon, co. Clare
*Finucane, Michael, Esq., Stamer-park, Ennis, co. Clare
*Fishbourne, James, Esq., Moorefield, Carlow
Fishbourne, Rev. Robert, Coolkenno-glebe, Tullow, co. Carlow
Fishbourne, William, Esq., J.P., Hollymount, Carlow
*Fisher, Rev. James, Duckinfield, Cheshire
Fisher, Joseph, Esq., Austin Friars, London
Fisher, Robert, Esq., Provincial Bank, Galway
Fisher, Robert, Esq., Fenchurch Street, London
Fisher, Thomas, Esq., Caroline-street, Cork
*Fitt, Mr. Matthew, Newgate, Limerick
*FITZ-GERALD & VESEY, The Right Honorable Lord
Fitz-Gerald, Rev. Andrew, D.D., Carlow
*Fitz-Gerald, Augustine, Esq., Belmont, Miltown-Malbay, co. Clare
*Fitz-Gerald, Rev. Edward, Loughlinstown-house, co. Dublin
*Fitz-Gerald, Edward, Esq., Spring Mount, Ballingarry, co. Limerick
Fitz-Gerald, G., Esq., J.P., Cashel, co. Tipperary
*Fitz-Gerald, G. Blakeney, Esq., White Gate-house, Cloyne, co. Cork
*Fitz-Gerald, Gerald B., Esq., Ballinvera, Adare, co. Limerick
Fitz-Gerald, Lieut. Henry, R.N., Maryland, Cloyne, co. Cork
*Fitz-Gerald, Rev. H., Castletown-Delvin, co. Westmeath
*Fitz-Gerald, The Honorable and Very Rev. Henry Vesey, LL.D.,
[Dean of Kilmore, Danesfort, Cavan
*Fitz-Gerald, Rev. J., P.P., Castletown-Delvin, co. Westmeath
*Fitz-Gerald, Rev. James, Keadue, co. Roscommon
*Fitz-Gerald, Rev. John, P.P. of the Union of Killenvoy, near Ath-
[lone, co. Roscommon
Fitz-Gerald, John, Esq., M.D., M.R.C.S., Carrick-on-Suir, co.
[Tipperary
Fitz-Gerald, Sir J. J., Bart., J.P., Lisheen, Cashel, co. Tipperary
Fitz-Gerald, Rev. John R., Nohoval, near Castle Island, co. Kerry
*Fitz-Gerald, Joseph C., Esq., Cloghroe, near Cork
*Fitz-Gerald, The Right Honorable M.
Fitz-Gerald, Maurice, Esq., Bandon, co. Cork [co. Cork
*Fitz-Gerald, Captain Michael, R.N., Ballykinnelly, near Cloyne,
*Fitz-Gerald, Rev. Richard, Tarbert, co. Kerry
Fitz-Gerald, Richard, Esq., Listowel, co. Kerry
Fitz-Gerald, Richard, Esq., Castle-Richard, near Youghal, co. Cork
*Fitz-Gerald, Robert, Esq., North-Earl-street, Dublin
*Fitz-Gerald, Robert, Esq., J.P., Navanstown, Kildare
Fitz-Gerald, Robert, Esq., Cavan
*Fitz-Gerald, R. U. Penrose, Esq., Corkbegg, near Cloyne, co. Cork
*Fitz-Gerald, Col. Thomas, Geraldine, Athy, co. Kildare
Fitz-Gerald, Thomas, Esq., Echo-lodge, Ballingarry, co. Limerick
Fitz-Gerald, Rev. Thomas, P.P. of O'Dorney, co. Kerry
*Fitz-Gerald, Thomas Joseph, Esq., Ballinaparka, near Cappoquin,
Fitz-Gerald, William, Esq., Castle Lyons, co. Cork [co. Waterford
*Fitz-Gerald, W. B., Esq., Rutland-square West, Dublin
*Fitz-Gerald, W. Crofton, Esq., Jonesborough, Kells, co. Meath
*Fitz-Gerald, Rev. W. M., Limerick
Fitzgerald, F. J., Esq., J.P., Adelphi, Corofin, co. Clare
Fitzgerald, Capt. Garrett Hugh, Richmond-place, Limerick
Fitzgerald, Gerald, Esq., Newpark, Rathkeale, co. Limerick
Fitzgerald, John, Esq., M.D., Bruff, co. Limerick
*Fitzgerald, M., Esq., Floraville, Donnybrook, co. Dublin
Fitzgerald, Rev. P., Vicar of Cahirconey, Bruff, co. Limerick
Fitzgerald, R., Esq., M.D., Dispensary, Croom, co. Limerick
Fitzgerald, Tobias, Esq., Newpark, Rathkeale, co. Limerick
*Fitzgerald, W., Esq., Georges-street Limerick
*Fitzgerald, W. M., Esq., Clerk of the Peace, Limerick
Fitz-Gibbon, Mr. Edward, Aharenagh, near Coachford, co. Cork
Fitz-Gibbon, Rev. Maurice, P.P., Adare, co. Limerick
Fitz-Gibbon, Michael, Esq., Mitchelstown, co. Cork
Fitz-Gibbon, The Honorable R. H., M.P.
Fitz-Gibbon, Thomas, Esq., Rosscarbery, co. Cork
*Fitz-Gibbon, Thomas G., Esq., Ballyseeda, near Limerick
Fitzgibbon W., Esq., Woodville, and Great George-street, Cork
Fitzmaurice, Harman, Esq., Carlow
Fitzmaurice, James, Esq., Shrule Turrett, Carlow
Fitzmaurice, William, Esq., Mallow, co. Cork
Fitzpatrick, Mr. A. D., Laurel-hill, near Wexford
Fitzpatrick Rev. Bartholomew, P.P., Mount-Bellew, co. Galway
*Fitzpatrick, Rev. Frederick, A.M. & J.P., Shercock-glebe, co.
*Fitzpatrick, Henry, Esq., Jervis-street, Dublin [Cavan
Fitzpatrick, Rev. J., Skibbereen, co. Cork [co. Tipperary
Fitzpatrick, James, Esq., Suir-mount, Kilronan, near Clonmel,
Fitzpatrick, Rev. James, C.R. of Castletown-Roche & Ballyhooly,
[co. Cork
Fitzpatrick, James, Esq., Capel-street, Dublin, and Ennis, co. Clare
*Fitzpatrick, J. W., Esq., Westfield Farm, Mountrath, Queen's county

*Fitzpatrick, Patrick, Esq., Dominick-street, Dublin, and Newford, [Athenry, co. Galway
Fitzpatrick, Rev. Patrick, Millstreet, co. Cork
Fitzpatrick, Samuel, Esq., French-street, Dublin
*Fitzpatrick, Rev. William, C.C., Rathfarnham, co. Dublin
Fitzpatrick, Mr. William, Roscrea, co. Tipperary
*Fitzsimon, C., Esq., J.P., Glancullen, Golden-ball, co. Dublin
*Fitzsimon, Rev. Hugh, P.P., Annagh, co. Cavan
Fitzsimon, John, Esq., Governor of the county Gaol, Galway
Fitzsimon, Rev. M., P.P., Shannon-bridge, Ballinasloe, co. Galway
*Fitzsimon, N., Esq., M.P., Castlewood, Frankford, King's county
*Fitzsimons, John, Esq., Cook-street, Cork
Fitzsimons, Mr. John, Kilkenny
*Fitzsimons, Rev. Patrick, C.C., Drung, co. Cavan
Fivey, William, Esq., Union-lodge, Loughbrickland, co. Down
Flanagan, Mr. Edward, Londonderry
Flanagan, Rev. John, Fuerty-glebe, near Roscommon
Flanagan, Mr. Matthew, Ballinasloe, co. Galway
*Flanagan, Nicholas, Esq., Cabra, co. Dublin
Flanagan, Rev. Richard, R.C. Curate of Dunleer, co. Louth
Flanagan, Rev. William, P.P., Mullinahone, Callan, co. Tipperary
Flanaghan, Rev. Matthew, Francis-street, Dublin
Flannelly, Rev. Patrick, P.P. of Easky, co. Sligo
*Flannery, Rev. Thomas, D.D., Clonmel, co. Tipperary
Flattery, Daniel, Esq., Ballinasloe, co. Galway
Flaxman, Mr. T. C., Fermoy, co. Cork
*Fleetwood, James, Esq., Willow-lodge, Cloghjordan, co. Tipperary
*Fleming, George, Esq., Athlone, co. Westmeath
Fleming, Lionel, J., Esq., J.P., Ballydevlin, Skibbereen, co. Cork
Fleming, Mr. W., Richmond, near Longford
*Fleming, W., Esq., Ashfield, Moynalty, co. Meath
Fleming, William, Esq., Blessington-street, Dublin, and Ashfield, [co. Meath
Flemyng, Richard B., Esq., Lower-Gloucester-street, Dublin
Flemyng, W. H., Esq., Nullamore, Classon's-bridge, near Dublin
*Fletcher, Rev. John Joseph, D.D., Dunran, near Wicklow
*Fletcher, P., Esq., Mount Pleasant, Carrickfergus, co. Antrim
*Fletcher, Robert B., Esq., C.C.P., Ennis, co. Clare
*Fletcher, W., Esq., Merrion-square South, Dublin
Fletcher, Rev. W., F.R.A.S., Stone, Buckinghamshire
Fletcher, W. P., Esq., Foster-place, Dublin
Flinn, Rev. Edmund, P.P., Newinn, Cashel, co. Tipperary
Flood, Christopher, Esq., Lower Sackville-street, Dublin
*Flood, Edward, Esq., Kells, co. Meath
Flood, John, Esq., D.L. and J.P., Flood-hall, near Knocktopher, co. [Kilkenny
Flood, P. F., Esq., Summer-hill, near Enniskerry, co Wicklow, and [Lower Mount-street, Dublin
*Flood, Richard, Esq., Trim, co. Meath
*Floyd, Mr. John, Londonderry
Flyme, Rev. Thomas, Kildare-place, Dublin
*Flyn, Edward, Esq., Marlborough-street, Cork
Flynn, Charles A., Esq., Liscarroll, co. Cork
Flynn, Rev. Edward, P.P., Riesk, near Waterford
*Flynn, Mr. James, Youghal, co. Cork
Flynn, Rev. J. O., Moate-convent, co. Westmeath
Flynn, Rev. Martin, Waterford
*Flynn, Mr. Michael, Royal Hotel, Roscommon
Fogarty, James, Esq., Kilrush, Thurles, co. Tipperary
Fogarty, M., Esq., Ballinlonty, Burrisoleigh, co. Tipperary
*Fogarty, Rev. Mark, P.P., Lusk, near Swords, co. Dublin
Fogarty, Rev. P. R., C.C., Dungarvan, co. Waterford
*Fogarty, Philip, Esq., Upper-Mount-street, Dublin
*FOLEY, The Right Honorable Lord
Foley, Rev. Daniel, R.C.C., Ballyhooly, Fermoy, co. Cork
Foley, Daniel B., Esq., Evergreen-house, near Cork
*Foley, Rev. John, R.C.C., Youghal, co. Cork
Foley, R. Allen, Esq., Dromineen, near Nenagh, co. Tipperary
Foley, Romney, Esq., New Ross, co. Wexford
*Foley, Thomas, Esq., Great-Brunswick-street, Dublin, and Tour- [tane, Lismore, co. Waterford
*Foley, Rev. Timothy, P.P., Stonehall, Pallas-Kenry, co. Limerick
Folingsby, Thomas G., Esq., Belfast
*Foot, Simon, Esq., Somerton-lodge, Rocherstown, co. Dublin
Foot, Mrs. E., Ballykane, near Redcross, co. Wicklow
Foot, Messrs. Lundy and Co., Essex-street, Dublin
Foott, Henry B., Esq., J.P., Carrigacunna Castle, Castletown Roche, [co. Cork
Foott, James, Esq., Springfort, Mallow, co. Cork
*Foran, Very Rev. Dr., P.P., Dungarvan, co. Waterford
Forbes, Arthur, Esq., J.P., Crag-a-vad, Holywood, co. Down
*Forbes, John Tilly, Esq., Chantinee, Carrickmacross, co. Monaghan
Forbes, W., Esq., Sleaford, Lincolnshire
Forbes, Mrs., Antrim
Ford, Alfred, Esq., Manchester
Ford, James, Esq., South Terrace, Cork
Ford, Rev. John, R.C.R., Kilbeaconty, Gort, co. Galway
Ford, Rev. John, jun., R.C.C., Kilbeaconty, Gort, co. Galway
*Ford, Rev. Thomas, P.P. of Drumlease, Dromahair, co. Leitrim
Forde, Edward, Esq., Sea-view, Ballyshannon, co. Donegal
Forde, James, Esq., J.P., Rauglin, near Lurgan, co. Armagh
*Forde, Matthew, Esq., J.P., Seaforde, Clough, co. Down
Forde, Rev. Patrick, R.C.C., Beagh, Gort, co. Galway
*Forde, Thomas A., Esq., Mountjoy-square South, Dublin
Forde, Rev. William B., Anahilt, near Lisburn, co. Antrim
Foristall, Mr. Thomas, George-street, Waterford
Forrest, Edward Young, Esq., Gullanagh, Monaghan
Forrest, James, P., Esq., Barlboro, Chesterfield, Derbyshire
Forrest, John, Esq., Chetwynd, Old Kinsale-road, near Cork
Forrest, Rev. Thomas, A.B., Mitchelstown, co. Cork
Forrester, Robert, Esq., Clover-hill, Maghera, co. Derry
*Forster, A. M., Esq., Nelson-street, Dublin
*Forster, George M., Esq., Gardiner's-place, Dublin
Forster, Perceval, Esq., Durham
*Forster, Robert, Esq., Springfield, Dungannon, co. Tyrone
Forster, Rev. T., Kilmainham Wood, King's Court, co. Cavan
*Forster, William, Esq., J.P., Ballynure, Clones, co. Monaghan
*Forsyth, George, Esq., M.D., Rosebrook, Carrickfergus, co. Antrim
*Fortescue, Faithful, Esq., J.P., Corderry, Lurgan-green, co. Louth
Fortescue, J. M., Esq., C.C.P., Westport, co. Mayo
*Fortescue, Matthew, Esq., Stephenstown, Dundalk, co. Louth
*Fortescue, Thomas, Esq., Ravensdale-park, and Clermont, Dun- [dalk, co. Louth
Fortune, William, Esq., Mount Mary, Ballinhassig, Cork
Fosbery, W., Esq., Ash-grove, Pallas-Kenry, co. Limerick
*Foslowe, Rev. F., Stavely-hall, Chesterfield, Derbyshire
*FOSTER, The Honorable Baron
Foster, Rev. Charles S., Termoneeny-glebe, Portglenone, co. Derry
*Foster, Rev. F. W., Ockbrook, Derbyshire
Foster, George, Esq., Londonderry
*Foster, The Venerable and Rev. James W., LL.D., Archdeacon of [Aghadoe, and Vicar General of the diocese of Limerick
*Foster, James, Esq., Stourton Castle, Kinfare, Stourbridge, Wor- [cestershire
*Foster, Robert Blake, Esq., Abbey, Knockmoy, Dangan, co. Galway
Foster, Thomas, Esq., Liverpool
*Foster, William, Esq., Athlone, co. Westmeath
Foster, W. K., Esq., Bandon, co. Cork
Fottrell, Capt. C., Harold's Grange, Rathfarnham, co. Dublin
*Foulke, Cosens, Esq., Young-grove, Midleton, co. Cork
Fowke, John, Esq., Antrim
Fowle, M., Esq., Seaford, Clough, co. Down
*Fowler, Richard T., Esq., M.D., Lower Glanmire Road, Cork
*Fowler, Villiars Bussy, Esq., Mecklenburgh-street, Dublin
*Fox, Rev. A. J., C.C., Phibsborough, Dublin
*Fox, Capt. Burry, Annaghmore, Tullamoore, King's county
*Fox, Charles Joseph, Esq., M.B., Brislington-house, near Bristol
*Fox, George Lane, Esq., Bramham-house, Wetherby, Yorkshire
*Fox, James, Esq., Galtrim-house, Summerhill, co. Meath
*Fox, James D'Arcy, Esq., Foxbrook, Trim, co. Meath
*Fox, Rev. J. James, M.A., Kinawly-glebe, Ballyconnell, co. Cavan
Fox, Joseph, Esq., Doolistown-house, Trim, co. Meath
Fox, Matthew, Esq., Moyally-house, Moate, King's county
Fox, Robert, Esq., Wendover-lodge, Wendover, Bucks.
*Fox, Rev. S. W., Richview, Rathmines, near Dublin
*Foxall, Powell, Esq., Killevey Castle, Newry, co. Armagh
Franklin, Rev. A., Denzile-street, Dublin
*Franklin, Denham, Esq., South Mall, Cork
Franklin, Rev. G., Kildrine-glebe, Pallas-Kenry, co. Limerick
*Franklin, W., Esq., Strabane, co. Tyrone
*Franklyn, Richard, jun., Esq., Royal Mint London
Franks, George, Esq., Londonderry
Franks, Robert, Esq., Leeson-street, Dublin
Fraser, Mr. A. G., D'Olier-street, Dublin
*Fraser, James, Esq., Lower-Dorset-street, Dublin
Fraser, James, Esq., M.D., Newmarket-on-Fergus, co. Clare
Fraser, Rev. Robert, Tullynure-lodge, Dungannon, co. Tyrone
Frayne, Rev. Nicholas, Newbridge, co. Kildare
*Frayne, Robert, Esq., Upper-Ormond-quay, Dublin
Frazer, Samuel Livingston, Banbridge, co. Down
*Freeman, Rev. Daniel, R.C.C., Killeagh, near Castlemartyr, co. [Cork
*Freeman, Edward Deane, Esq., Sandfield, Mallow, co. Cork
Freeman, John Deane, Esq., Castle-Cor, Mallow, co. Cork
*Freeman, Major J. D., Retreat, Cove, near Cork
Freeman, J. J. B., Esq., Youghal, co. Cork
Freeman, Rev. Richard Deane, A.M., Charleston, Midleton, co. [Cork

*French, Arthur, Esq., Carney-castle, Nenagh, co. Tipperary, and [Blessington-street, Dublin
*French, Charles, Esq., Farmley, co. Dublin
French, Dawson, Esq., Ballintoher, Monastereven, Queen's county
French, Digby, Esq., M.D., Monivea, co. Galway
*French, E., Esq., J.P., Bella, near Frenchpark, co. Roscommon
*French, Rev. Edward, Dungiven, co. Derry
French, E. Hyde, Esq., Hyde-park, Monivea, co. Galway
French, Fitz, Esq., M.P. and J.P., Frenchpark, co. Roscommon
French, George, Esq., Mountjoy-square, Dublin
*French, George Jones, Esq., North-Frederick-street, Dublin
French, Mr. Henry, French-park, Randalstown, co. Antrim [mon
*French, The Very Rev. John, Deanery-house, Elphin, co. Roscom-
French, Rev. John, A.B., the Glebe, Kilkerrin, Dangan, co. Galway
*French, Rev. John, J.P., Frenchpark-house, co. Roscommon
French, Rev. John, P.P. of Kilrush, co. Wexford
French, Savage, Esq., Cuskinny, Cove, near Cork
French, Thomas George, Esq., Marino, Passage West, co. Cork
French, Rev. William, Glebe-house, Frenchpark, co. Roscommon
*Frend, Benjamin, Esq., Rocklow, Fethard, co. Tipperary
Frew, Rev. J. J., Belvidere-house, Great-Denmark-street, Dublin
Fripp, Thomas Esq., Brookfield, Belfast
Frizell, Mr. George, Old Ross, co. Wexford
Frizell, John, Esq., New Ross, co. Wexford
*Frodsham, R., Esq., Liverpool
Frood, James N., Esq., J.P. Bailiff of Dundalk co. Louth
Frost, Matthew, Esq., Calvee, Bakewell, Derbyshire
*Fry, Henry, Esq., Frybrook, Boyle, co. Roscommon
*Fry, Mrs. B., Rockbrook, near Rathfarnham, co. Dublin
Fulham, Matthew, Esq., Tribly, Trim, co. Meath
*Fullam, Rev. John R.,C.C. of Lusk, co. Dublin
Fuller, Thomas, Esq., Prospect, near Dolphin's Bain, Dublin
Fullerton, John, Esq., Thyburgh Castle, Doncaster, Yorkshire
*Fullerton, Rev. Thomas, Rector and Vicar of Stranorlar, co. Donegal
*Fulton, Mr. James, Gortinleave, Londonderry
Funston, Mr. Thomas, Castlederg, co. Tyrone
*Furlong, Alfred, Esq., J.P., Courtenay-castle, Newcastle, co. Limerick
Furlong, Charles, Esq., Convamore, Fermoy, co. Cork
Furlong, Mr. John, Dananstown-mills, Castletown-Roche, co. Cork
Furlong, John, Esq., M.D., Verona, near Enniscorthy, co. Wexford
Furlong, Rev. Jonathan, R.C.C., Ennis, co. Clare
Furlong, J. J., Esq., Tulliline-house, Newcastle, co. Limerick
*Furlong, N., Esq., Talavera, near Baldoyle, co. Dublin
Furlong, Mr. Nicholas, Knockahone, Arcandrisk, co. Wexford
Furlong, Rev. Thomas, P.P. of Killegny, Enniscorthy, co. Wexford
Furlong, W., Esq., M.D., Coolalta, Killinardrish, Cork
*Furnace, N., Esq., Talavera, near Baldoyle, co. Dublin
*Furnell, George, Esq., Thomas-street, Limerick
Furnell, Michael, Esq., J.P., Cahir-Elly, Limerick
Fyffe, John, Esq., Liggertown, Strabane, co. Tyrone
Fynn, John, Esq., J.P., Ballymagibbon, Cong, co. Mayo

Gabbett, The Very Rev. John, LL.D., Vicar General of Killaloe, and Rector and Vicar of the union of Castletown, Nenagh, co. Tipperary
Gabbett, Rev. Joseph, Cahirnarry-glebe, Limerick
Gabbett, Rev. Joseph, A. B., Kilmallock, co. Limerick
*Gabbett, Poole, Esq., J.P., Corbally-house, Limerick [Tipperary
Gabbett, Rev. Robert, LL.D., Glebe-house, Castletown, Killalce, co.
*Gabbett, W. H., Esq., Caherline, nr. Castle Connell, co. Limerick
Gadsden, Charles E., Esq., Greenbank-cottage, near Waterford
GAGE, The Right Honorable Viscount
*Gage, Marcus, Esq., Streeve-hill, Newtownlimavady, co. Derry
Gaggin, Henry, Esq., Ballybane, Cloyne, co. Cork
Gaggin, Thomas, Esq., Ballybane, Cloyne, co. Cork [Dublin
Gahan, James, Esq., Anne-mount, near Tallaght, and Francis-street,
*Gahan, Rev. John, Rathvilly, Baltinglass, co. Wicklow
*Gainford, George, Esq., Ballycrummeg, near Armagh
*Galbraith, Lady, Urney-park, Strabane, co. Tyrone
Galbraith, Mr. James, Drumaneeny, Faughanvale, co. Derry
*Galbraith, James, Esq., Upper-Rutland-st., Dublin, & Gortmore, [Omagh, co. Tyrone
*Galbraith, Morgan, Esq., J.P., Mackenwood, Killysandra, co. Cavan
*Galbraith, Samuel, Esq., J.P., New-grove, Omagh, co. Tyrone
Galbraith, Mr. Samuel, Faughanvale, co. Derry
*Galbraith, Captain W., Castlerea, co. Roscommon [ford
*Galbraith, W. L., Esq., Curraghgrane, Edgeworthstown, co. Long-
*Gale, Peter, Esq., J.P., Ashfield, Carlow
*Gale, Samuel, Esq., Dominick-street, Dublin
Gale, Mr. S., Fleet Street, London

Gallagher, Andrew, Esq., Ballina, co. Mayo
*Gallagher, Francis, Esq., Lenyghack, Letterkenny, co. Donegal
*Gallagher, Rev. J., P.P. of Mullinabreenagh, Tobbercorry, co. Sligo
*Gallagher, Matthew, Esq., J.P., Laragon, near Foxford, co. Mayo
*Gallagher, W., Esq., Ballyarnet, Templemore, co. Derry
*Gallagher, Mr. W., Burt, co. Donegal
Gallaher, Andrew, Esq., Richmond, Castlebar, co. Mayo
Gallaher, Mr. Anthony, Ruskey, All Saints, co. Donegal
Gallaher, Mr. John, Ruskey, All Saints, co. Donegal
Gallery Mr. E., Ennis, co. Clare
*Galloway, Rev. James, Aldbury, near Tring, Hertfordshire
Gallwey, Bryan, Esq., Marlboro'-street, Cork
*Gallwey, Christopher, Esq., Killarney, co. Kerry
*Gallwey, Major J., Ballincollig, co. Cork
Gallwey, John, Esq., Greenpark, Skibbereen, co. Cork
*Gallwey, Michael, Esq., Kilkeran-house, Ross, co. Cork
Gallwey, Michael, Esq., J.P., Ballina-house, Clonakilty, co. Cork
Galt, W., Esq., Ballysally, Coleraine, co. Derry
*Galvin, Bartholomew, Esq., French-street, Dublin
*Galvin, Rev. Patrick, P.P. of Kiltormer, Laurencetown, co. Galway
Galvin, Rev. P., P.P., Portumna, co. Galway
*GALWAY, The Right Honorable Lord
*Galway, The Commercial Society of
Galway Amicable Society
Galwey, Rev. Charles, Gortgowan, Moville, co. Donegal
*Galwey, Edward, Esq., Lower Mallow-street, Limerick
Galwey, James, Esq., M.D., Lisnashandrum, Cork
Galwey, John, Esq., Rock-lodge, Passage West, co. Cork
Galwey, St. John, Esq., M.D., Mallow, co. Cork
*Gamble, Andrew W., Esq., Killooly-hall, Frankford, King's county
*Gamble, James, Esq., Dromore, co. Derry
Gamble, Robert, Esq., Belfast
*Gamble, W. Esq., R.N., Strabane, co. Tyrone
Gamble, Rev. W., Green-hill, Letterkenny, co. Donegal
*Gannon, Rev. A., P.P., Rathowen, co. Westmeath
*Gannon, James, Esq., J.P., Laragh, near Kilcock, co. Kildare
Gannon, The Very Rev. Miles, Prior of the Abbey, Loughrea, co. [Galway
Gannon, W., Esq., Clonfert, co. Galway
Gard, Thomas, Esq., A.B. & M.D., Knockane, co. Cork
Garde, C. B., Esq., Balindinnass, Castlemartyr, co. Cork
Garde, Henry, Esq., M.D., Lochcarrig, Midleton, co. Cork
*Garde, W., Esq., Stephens-green, Dublin
Garde, Rev. John, A.B., Killeagh, co. Cork
*Gardiner, Charles, Esq., Cloonee, Ballina, co. Mayo
*Gardiner, Major John, J.P., D.L., Farmhill, Killala, co. Mayo
Gardner, John, Esq., Royal-Gunpowder-Mills, Ballincollig, co. Cork
Gardner, William, Esq., Youghal, co. Cork
Gargan, Patrick, Esq., Cromwell's-Bush, Duleek, co. Meath
*Garland, Captain J. G., Poole, Dorsetshire
*Garmany, Hugh, Esq., Mountain-lodge, Keady, co. Armagh
Garner, Captain J. H., Garnerville, Belfast
*Garnett, Cope, Esq., Green-park, Dunshaughlin, co. Meath
*Garnett, Rev. George, Williamston, co. Meath
*Garnett, Hamlet, Esq., Teltown, Kells, co. Meath
*Garnett, John Paine, Esq., Arch-hall, Navan, co. Meath
*Garnett, Samuel, Esq., Summerseat, Clonee, co. Meath
*Garnett, W., Esq., Donover-house, Moynalty, co. Meath
*Garrard, Lieut.-Col. Thomas, Boyne-hill, Navan, co. Meath
*Garratt, Richard, Esq., Granite-hall, near Kingstown, co. Dublin
*Garrett, Henry, Esq., Ballymote, co. Sligo
Garrett, J., Esq., Queen's College, Oxford
*Garrett, Rev. J., Vicar of Emlafad, Ballymote, co. Sligo
*Garrett, Rev. J. P., Jane-ville, co. Carlow
Garrett, R., Esq., New Broad-street court, London
*Garrett, Thomas, Esq., Cromac, near Belfast
Garrett, W., Esq., Janeville, Leighlin-bridge, co. Carlow
*Gartlan, T. E., Esq., Monalty, Carrickmacross, co. Monaghan
*GARVAGH, The Right Honorable Lord
Garvey, George, Esq., J.P., Thorn-vale, Moneygall, King's county
*Gascoigne, R. O., Esq., Partington-hall, Yorkshire
Gash, Rev. Benjamin, A.M., Ballytrasna, Macroom, co. Cork
*Gason, John, Esq., M.D., Enniskerry, co. Wicklow
*Gason, R. W., Esq., D.L. & J.P., Richmond, Nenagh, co. Tipperary
Gatchell, George, Esq., Waterford
*Gatchell, Isaac, Esq., Coolegegan, Clonbulloge, King's county
*Gates, Benedict Arthur, Esq., Moone-abbey, Ballitore, co. Kildare
Gath, Samuel, Esq., Erskine-street, Liverpool
*Gaussen, David, Esq., Lakeview, Ballyronan, co. Derry
*Gaussen, James, Esq., Lake-lodge, Magherafelt, co. Derry
*Gaussen, W., Esq., Magherafelt, co. Derry
Gavan, Rev. John, A.M., Rector of Wallstown, Doneraile, co. Cork

*Gavin, Rev. John, Chaplain to the Cab:a Nunnery, co. Dublin
Gawly, Eccles, Esq., Swinford, co. Mayo
Gayer, Rev. Charles R., M.A., Dingle, co. Kerry
*Gaynor, Captain, Killiney-house, Killiney, co. Dublin
Gaynor, John, Esq., Athlone, co. Westmeath
Gaynor, Rev. Thomas, C.C., Castlepollard, co. Westmeath
*Geale, Piers, Esq., Mountjoy-square West, Dublin
Gearty, Rev. G., P.P. of Annaluff, Drumsna, co. Leitrim
Geary, James, Esq., Kildysart, co. Clare
Geary, John, Esq., M.D., William-street, Limerick
*Geary, Sir W. P., Bart., Morristown, co. Wicklow
*Geary, Sir W. R. P., Bart., Oxon-heath, Kent
Gee, John, Esq., Mayfield, near Youghal, co. Cork
Geekir, John, Esq., Cushendall, co. Antrim
Gegan, Mr. Joseph, Ennis, co. Clare
Gell, Rev. R., Wirksworth, Derbyshire
Geoghgan, Capt., Galway
Geoghegan, C., Esq., Blackhall-street, Dublin
*Geoghegan, Rev. P. M. B., O.M., Merchants-quay, Dublin
Geoghegan, Rev. T., P.P., Craughwell, Eyrecourt, co. Galway
*Geoghegan, W. M., Esq., Rathmines, near Dublin
George, M., Esq., Seafield-cottage, Monkstown, co. Dublin
*Geraghty, Mr. John, Inchicore, near Dublin
*Geraghty, Michael, Esq., Clover-hill, near Clondalkin, co. Dublin
Geraghty, Philip, Esq., Dungannon, co. Tyrone
*Geran, Daniel, Esq., Rushmount-house, Kilworth, co. Cork
Germaine, John, Esq., Grangecon, near Baltinglass, co. Wicklow
*Gernon, James, Esq., Athcarne-castle, Duleek, co. Meath
*Gernon, John, Esq., Wilville, Carlingford, co. Louth
*Gernon, T., Esq., Grange, Carlingford, co. Louth
*Gerrard, John N., Esq., Gibbstown, Navan, co. Meath
*Gerrard, T. F., Esq., Tallyho, near Mullingar, co. Westmeath
*Gervais, Rev. Francis., J.P., Cecil, Aughnacloy, co. Tyrone
Getty, Edmund, Esq., Belfast
*Gibbings, R., Esq., Gibbings-grove, Charleville, co. Cork
Gibbings, Rev. Thomas, A.M., Charleville, co. Cork
*Gibbon, Thomas, Esq., Kinlough, Ballyshannon, co. Donegal
Gibbons, James, Esq., Castlerea, co. Roscommon
Gibbons, James B., Esq., Ballinspittle-house, Kinsale, co. Cork
Gibbons, John, Esq., Enver, Belmullet, co. Mayo
Gibbons, Rev. John, R.C.C., Moylough, co. Galway
*Gibbons, Captain John, Castlerea, co. Roscommon
Gibbons, Joseph, Esq., Toxteth-park, Liverpool
Gibbons, Matthew, Esq., Castlebar, co. Mayo
*Gibbons, Mr. Patrick, Montgomery-street, Dublin
Gibbons, Rev. Richard, P.P., Castlebar, co. Mayo
Gibbs, John Bennett, Esq., J.P., Derry, Coachford, co. Cork
*Gibbs, Thomas, Esq., Deddington, Oxfordshire
*Gibson, Edward, Esq., Hull, Yorkshire
*Gibson, Rev. James, A.M., Lisloone, Tynan, co. Armagh
Gibson, Mr. James, Crislaughkeel, Upper Fahan, co. Donegal
Gibson, Mr. John, Crislaughkeel, Upper Fahan, co. Donegal
*Gibson, Mr. J., Tamlaghtfinlagan, Newtown-Limavady, co. Derry
Gibson, Mr. Joseph, Coagh, co. Tyrone
Gibson, Lewis, Esq., Kilboy, Cloyne, co. Cork
Gibson, Peter, Esq., Ennis, co. Clare
*Gibson, Rev. W., Crieve, Ballibay, co. Monaghan
Gibson, W. R., Esq., Rathcullen, co. Cork
Gifford, Rev. W., Ballysop, near New Ross, co. Wexford
Gihon, W., Esq., J.P., Hill-head, Ballymena, co. Antrim
Gilberson, Mr. Michael, Kilmallock, co. Limerick
*Gilbert, John, Esq., North-lodge, near Kilgobbin, co. Dublin
Gilborne, Edward, Esq., Philipsburgh Avenue, Dublin
Gildea, Rev., G.R., M.A., Kilmaine-glebe, co. Mayo
*Gildea, J. Knox, Esq., Closecormack-house, Hollymount, co. Mayo
*Gildea, Rev. P., P.P. of Kilcommin, Erris, Belmullet, co. Mayo
Giles, Richard, Esq., Chantry, Youghal, co. Cork
*Giles, Walter, Esq., J.P., Coolnagower, Dungarvan, co. Waterford
*Gilfellan, Alexander, Esq., M.D., Glendermott, Londonderry
*Gilfilland, George, Esq., M.D., Killylane, Faughanvale, co. Derry
Gilfoyle, W., Esq., Loughrea, co. Galway
Gill, Mr. Joshua, Hotel, Ballinasloe, co. Galway
Gill, Rev. Thomas, E., P. P., Zephyr Lodge, Oranmore, Co. Galway
Gill, Thomas, Esq., Drogheda, co. Louth
Gillan, James, Esq., Ballina, co. Mayo
*Gillespie, Joshua, Esq., J.P., Londonderry
Gillespie, Mr. Richard, Patrick-street, Cork
Gillett, William, Esq., Northampton
*Gilliatt, W. H., Esq., Liverpool
*Gillichan, Joseph, Esq., M.D., Dundalk, co. Louth
Gilligan, Mr. Michael, Coolmine, near Kilgobbin, co. Dublin
Gillis, Mr. J., Tanderagee, co. Armagh
Gillis, Joseph, Esq., North-street, Belfast
*Gillkrest, George, Esq., Kanturk, co. Cork
Gillman, Edward, Esq., Dunmanway, co. Cork
Gillman, Edward, Esq., Leoffney-house, Kinsale, co. Cork
Gillman, Herbert, Esq., J.P., Bennett's-grove, Clonakilty, co. Cork
Gillman, Herbert, jun., Esq., Wood Brook, Dunmanway, co. Cork
Gillman, James, Esq., Oak Mount, Dunmanway, co. Cork
Gillman, John, Esq., Rock-house, Bandon, co. Cork
*Gillman, John, Esq., Belle-vue, Cross-avenue, Booterstown, co. Dublin
*Gilmour, P., Esq., Londonderry
Gilpin, Rev. J., Tedbury-park, Richmond, Yorkshire
*Gilson, Thomas, Esq., Bucklersbury, London
*Giltrap, Mr. John, Humphrystown, Blessington, co. Wicklow
Girvin, William, Esq., Roan, co. Armagh
Gisborne, T., Esq., M.P., Horwick-house, near Chapel-en-le-Frith
*Gist, Samuel Gist, Esq., Dixton, Gloucestershire
*Givens, Matthew, Esq., Woodville, near Tipperary
Givin, Benjamin, Esq., Liscommon, Ballymoney, co. Antrim
Gladwin, Mr. Samuel, Wexford
Glaister, H. R., Esq., Bedale, Yorkshire
Glaister, Rev. W., Vicar of Kirkby Fleetham, Catterick, Yorkshire
*Glancy, Francis, Esq., Wellsgrove, Castlerea, co. Roscommon
Glascott, George, Esq., Fruit-hill, New Ross, co. Wexford
*Glascott, John, Esq., Leeson-street, Dublin
*Glascott, W. M., Esq., J.P., Pill Town, New Ross, co. Wexford
Gledstanes, A. Upton, Esq., Dollandstown, Kilcock, co. Kildare
Gledstanes, George, Esq., Fortland-cottage, Manorhamilton, co. Leitrim
Gleeson, Rev. D., P.P., Clonrush, Woodford, co. Galway
Gleeson, John, Esq., William-street, Limerick
*Gleeson, Robert, Esq., National Bank, Castlerea, co. Roscommon
*GLENGALL, The Right Honorable the Earl of
Glenn, Mr. James, Londonderry
*Glenny, Isaac, Esq., J.P., Glenville, co. Down
Glenny, Isaac W., Esq., J.P., Newry, co. Down
*Glin, The Knight of, Glin, co. Limerick
*Globe Insurance Company, London
*Gloster, George, Esq., York-street, Dublin, and Limerick
Gloster, George, Esq., Derryknockane, Limerick
Glynn, Patrick, Esq., Gort, co. Galway
Godbey, Robert, Esq., Dundalk, co. Louth
Godfrey, Sir John, Bart., J.P., Kilcoleman-abbey, co. Kerry
Godfrey, Edward, Esq., Cove, near Cork
*Godfrey, T., Esq., M.D., Beechmount, near Coachford, co. Cork
*Godley, John, Esq., Oatlands, near Castlenock, co. Dublin
*Godley, John, Esq., J.P., Killigar, Killeshandra, co. Leitrim
*Goff, Rev. Patrick, Curraha, Ashbourne, co. Meath
Goff, Robert, Esq., Carrow-park, Roscommon
Goff, Stevens, Esq., Enniscorthy, co. Wexford
*Goff, Rev. Thomas, Carriglea, Blackrock, near Dublin, and Eccles-street, Dublin
Gog rty, P., Esq., Templeoge-house, Dublin
Goggan, James, Esq., Belmont, Navan, co. Meath
Goggin, G. Morgan, Esq., Shannon-view, Limerick
*Going, Ambrose, Esq., J.P., Ballyphilip, Killenaule, co. Tipperary
Going, Rev. James, A.B., Kilkeedy, Limerick
*Going, John, Esq., J.P., Cragg Castle, Newport, co. Tipperary
Going, Robert, Esq., Cragg, Newport, co. Tipperary
*Golding, G. R., Esq., J.P., Lime-park-lodge, Caledon, co. Tyrone
Gollock, Rev. James, Cloughroe, Inniscarra, Cork
*Gollock, Thomas, Esq., Leemount, near Coachford, co. Cork
*Gondy, Rev. Alexander, P., Strabane, co. Tyrone
*Gondy, John, Esq., Coolmain-house, Monaghan
Good, E. H., Esq., Phale-house, Inniskeen, co. Cork
Good, John, Esq., Rockgrove, Coachford, co. Cork
Good, William, Esq., Ardnaneen, Macroom, co. Cork
*Goodhall, H. H., Esq., Crutched-friars, London
*Goodlatte, D. R., Esq., Callan-hill-villa, Moy, co. Tyrone
*Goodricke, Sir F. L. Holyoake, Bart., Studley Castle, Warwickshire
Goodwin, Charles, Esq., Ballyvay-house, Castlebar, co. Mayo
Goodwin, Rev. John, P.P. of Currin, co. Monaghan
Goold, George, Esq., Old Court, near Cork
Goold, Mr. George, Antrim
Goold, Henry, Esq., Goold's-hill, Mallow, co. Cork
Goold, Rev. P., Glebe-house, Finnoe, Burris-o'-kane, co. Tipperary
Goold, Pierce Purcell, Esq., Curriglass, Charleville, co. Cork
Goold, Thomas, Esq., Carysfoot-lodge, Stillorgan-park, co. Dublin
GORDON, His Grace the Duke of
Gordon, David, Esq., J.P., Florida, near Killinchy, co. Down
Gordon, George, Esq., J.P., Downpatrick
*Gordon, Lieut.-Col. John, Cremona, near Swords, co. Dublin
*Gordon, John, Esq., Wendover Dean, Wendover, Bucks.

*Gordon, Rev. J. C., Rector of Loughinisland, co. Down
*Gordon, J. E., Esq., St. James'-place, London
*Gordon, Rev. R. B., Rector of Duncormack, co. Wexford
Gordon, Robert, Esq., J.P., Summerfield, co. Down
Gordon, R. F., Esq., Castle-place, Belfast
Gore, Rev. Annesley, Vicar of Mungret, near Limerick
*Gore, Lieut.-Col. F. A. Knox, Belleek, near Ballina, co. Mayo
Gore, The Honorable and Very Rev. George
Gore, Henry, Esq., J.P., Kilkenny
Gore, Rev. Thomas, Rector of Mulrancan Union, Wexford
Gorman, Edward, Esq., Benekerry-lodge, Carlow
Gorman, Mr. Ferdinand, Levetstown, Athy, co. Kildare
Gorman, William, Esq., Broommount, Moira, co. Down
Gorsuch, Roger, Esq., Castlemartyr, co. Cork
GORT, The Right Honorable Viscount
GOSFORD, The Right Honorable the Earl of
Gosnell, Mr. W., North-Main-street, Cork
Gosselin, Thomas, Esq., Grangemore, Kilcullen, co. Kildare
Gosselin, William, Esq., Fortland, Ballyjamesduff, co. Cavan
*Gossett, Sir W., Knt., Dublin Castle
*Gough, George, Esq., Annsgift, Fethard, co. Tipperary
*Gough, Lieut.-Col. George, J.P., Ardsalla, Fethard, co. Tipperary
*Gough, Major-Gen. Sir Hugh, K.C.B., D.L. and J.P., Rathronan-
[house, Clonmel, co. Tipperary
*Gough, Rev. John, P.P. of Rush, co. Dublin
Gould, Ignatius, Esq., West-Grove-cottage, Cork
Gouldsbury, John, Esq., Church-hill, Letterkenny, co. Donegal
*Gower, Henry, Esq., Glosthule, and Lower-Ormond-quay, co.
*Gower, John, Esq., Roundwood Park, co. Wicklow [Dublin
*Grabham, W., Esq., Woodville-cottage, Howth-road, co. Dublin
Grace, John, Esq., jun., Pelaw-house, Chester-le-street, Derbyshire
Grace, John E., Esq., Nenagh, co. Tipperary
*Grace, O. D. J., Esq., J.P., Mantua, Shankill, co. Roscommon
*Grace, Rev. W., P.P., Ballycallan, Kilkenny
*Grace, William, Esq., J.P., Kilkenny
Gracey, Thomas, Esq., Ballyhosset, near Downpatrick
*Grady, J. H., Esq., Mount-Eagle, near Stillorgan, co. Dublin
Grady, John, Esq., Pratt-street, Lambeth, Surrey
*GRAFTON, His Grace the Duke of
*Graham, A., Esq., Newtownstewart, co. Tyrone [shire
*Graham, Sir Bellingham R., Bart., Norton Conyers, Ripon, York-
*Graham, Abraham, Esq., Hampstead, Middlesex
Graham, Mr. David, Newpark, Antrim
Graham, Mr. Edward, Lower Sackville-street, Dublin
*Graham, Rev. E., P.P. of Knocklong and Glonbrolane, Limerick
Graham, Garret, Esq., M.D., Gurteen-lodge, Drumcolloher, co.
*Graham, George, Esq., Clonmel, co. Tipperary [Limerick
*Graham, Henry Torrens, Esq., Margaret's-place, Dublin
Graham, Mr. John, Londonderry
Graham, Mr. John, Cove, near Cork [co. Derry
Graham, Rev. John, Magilligan-glebe, near Newtownlimavady,
*Graham, Robert, Esq., Drumgoon, Maguires-bridge, co. Fermanagh
*Graham, Mr. Thomas, Mountjoy Forest, Omagh, co. Tyrone
*Graham, Major T. C., Gartgranagh, co. Monaghan
*Graham, Mr. W., Lisburn, co. Antrim
*Graham, Capt. W., J.P., Oakley-park, Moynalty, co. Meath
Graham, Messrs. W. and W., Westport, co. Mayo
Grant, Rev. D., Naas, co. Kildare
Grant, James, Esq., Great-Brunswick-street, Dublin
Grant, Jasper, Esq., Lismore, co. Waterford
*Grant, Joseph, Esq., Hilton-lodge, Rathmines-road, Dublin
*Grant, Rev. John, P.P. of Wicklow [Down
Grant, Rev. J. B., Curate of Drumgooland, near Rathfriland, co.
Grant, Thomas St. John, Esq., Kilmurry, near Fermoy, co. Cork
*Grantham, R. B., Esq., Lower Mallow-street, Limerick [Wicklow
*Grattan, H., Esq., M.P., Glenwood-cottage, near Rathdrum, co.
Grattan, J., Esq., Thornfield, Chesterfield, Derbyshire
Grattan, Richard, Esq., M.D., J.P., Drummin-house, Edenderry,
[co. Kildare
*Grattan, Thomas, Esq., Coolville, Edenderry, co. Kildare
*Graves, A., Esq., Derrynaseera, Mountrath, Queen's county
*Graves, Capt. J. B., J.P., Dunsinane, near Enniscorthy, co. Wexford
Graves, Rev. James W., A.M., Ightermurrough, co. Cork
Graves, John, Esq., Mill-view, Killeigh, Tullamore, King's county
Graves, R. D., Esq., Woodstock, Ballingarry, co. Limerick [Cork
Graves, Rev. R. H., D.D., Rector of Brigown, Mitchelstown, co.
Graves, W., Esq., J.P., Castle-Dawson, co. Derry
Gray, Alexander G., Esq., Newcastle-on-Tyne, Northumberland
*Gray, George, Esq., High-park, near Drumcondra, co. Dublin
*Gray, John, Esq., Upper Leabeg, near Newcastle, co. Wicklow
*Gray, John, Esq., J.P., Dealfield, Castlerea, co. Roscommon

Gray, Roderick, Esq., Enniskillen, co. Fermanagh
Gray, R. R., Esq., M.D., Dominick-street, Galway
Gray, W., Esq., Greencastle, Belfast
Gray, Rev. W., Vicar of Brafferton, Thirsk, Yorkshire
Gray, Mr. W., Ballibay, co. Monaghan [low
*Graydon, L., Esq., Toomon, Newtown-Mount-Kennedy, co. Wick-
*Graydon, Richard, Esq., Ballymorris, near Bray, co. Wicklow
*Graydon, T. Hughes, Esq., Ballinasloe, co. Galway
Green, Mr. Francis, Marahinch, Moira, co. Down
*Green, John, Esq., Greenmount, Patrickswell, co. Limerick
*Green, John, Esq., Nelson-hill, near Youghal, co. Cork
*Green, Murdock, Esq., Greenville-street, Dublin
Green, Rev. Pierce, P.P., Carrigadrohid, Macroom, co. Cork
*Green, Thomas M., Esq., Killeagh, co. Cork
Greene, A., Esq., Tooting, Surrey
Greene, George, Esq., Powerstown, Clonmel, co. Tipperary
Greene, H., Esq., Court-hill, Dunboyne, co. Meath
*Greene, Rev. Henry, Ballyclog-glebe, Stewartstown, co. Tyrone
Greene, John, Esq., Wexford
*Greene, John, Esq., Millbrook, Castledermot, co. Kildare
*Greene, John, Esq., Kilrisk, near St. Margaret's, Dublin
Greene, John, Esq., A.M., Fortlands, Loughrea, co. Galway
*Greene, Lieut., 82nd Regiment
*Greene, Lieut.-Col. N., D.L. and J.P., Kilmanahan-castle, Clonmel,
Greene, R. George, Esq., Ennis, co. Clare [co. Tipperary
*Greene, R. W., Esq., St. Stephen's-green, Dublin
Greene, Rev. Walter, Curate of St. Iberius, co. Wexford
Greene, W., Esq., Comptroller of Customs, Pembroke-road, Mount-
*Greene, William, Esq., French-street, Dublin [Vernon, Liverpool
*Greene, William, Esq., Kilrisk, near St. Margarets, co. Dublin
Greene, Rev. William, Vicar of Antrim
Greene, W. Francis, Esq., Ballymoney, co. Antrim
*Greene, W. Hastings, Esq., Lota-house, near Cork
*Greene, W. P., Esq., J.P., Collon, co. Louth [Kildare
Greenham, Mr. Leonard, Inchaquire-cotton-mills, Ballitore, co.
Greenham, Robert, Esq., Mountrath, Queen's county
*Greenwood, Cox and Co. Messrs., Craigs-court, London
*Greer, Alfred, Esq., Dripsey-paper-mills, Cork
*Greer, David, Esq., Omagh, co. Tyrone
*Greer, Mr. James, Stranorlar, co. Donegal
*Greer, James, Esq., Omagh, co. Tyrone
*Greer, Joseph, Esq., J.P., Desertcreight, Cookstown, co. Tyrone
*Greer, Thomas, Esq., Rhone-hill, Dungannon, co. Tyrone
*Greer, Thomas, Esq., Clonmel, co. Tipperary
Greer, Thomas, Esq., Tullylogan, Dungannon, co. Tyrone
Greer, Thomas, Esq., J.P., Randalstown, co. Antrim
Greer, William, Esq., Milton, Dungannon, co. Tyrone
Greer, W. J., Esq., Moy, co. Tyrone
*Greer, W. J., Esq., M.D., Lifford, co. Donegal
*Gregg, W., Esq., Londonderry
*Gregg, W. H., Esq., Peter-street, Dublin
Gregg, W. and Son, Messrs., South Mall, Cork
Gregory, Major David, Youghal, co. Cork
Gregory, Rev. James, Upper Fitzwilliam-street, Dublin
*Gregory, Richard, Esq., F.R.S., F.S.A., Coole, near Gort, co.
Galway, and Berners-street, London
Gregory, Rev. W., Fiddown-glebe, Pilltown, co. Kilkenny
Gregory, W., Esq., Belle-Vue, near Finglass, co. Dublin
Greham, Rev. M., P.P., Clonaslee, Queen's county
*Grenfell, P. S. L., Esq., Lombard-street, London
Grennan, Rev. W., P.P., Dunboyne and Kilbride, co. Meath
*GRENVILLE, The Right Honorable Lord
*Gresham, T., Esq., Sackville-street, Dublin
*Gresham, T. M., Esq., Rahiny-park, near Dublin
Gresley, R. A. Douglas, Esq., Bishop-Auckland, Durham
Gresson, Rev. G. L., J.P., Ardnorcher-glebe, Kilbeggan, King's co.
Grey, A., Esq., New Broad Street, London
*Grey, Rev. J., R.C.C., Collinstown, Castlepollard, co. Westmeath
Grey, John, Esq., Dilston-house, Hexham, Northumberland
Grey, Patrick, Esq., National Bank, Dingle, co. Kerry
Gribban, James, Esq., Coleraine, co. Derry
*Grier, John, Esq., Bolton-street, Dublin
*Grier, Rev. J. W., East Acton, near Redcross, co. Wicklow
*Grier, Thomas, Esq., Upper-Dominick-street, Dublin
Grierson, John, Esq., Drumawier-house, Moville, co. Donegal
*Grieves, W. and Co. Messrs., Galway, and Covent Garden, London
Griffin, D., Esq., M.D., Pallas Kenry, co. Limerick
Griffin, James, Esq., Corgrigg-house, Shanagolden, co. Limerick
Griffin, John, Esq., City Road, London
Griffin, John, Esq., M.D., Kilrush, co. Clare
Griffin, Mr. John, Ballytrasna, Tuam, co. Galway

Griffin, Rev. John, P.P. of Abbeygormican and Killoran, Loughrea, co. Galway
Griffin, M., Esq., New Bond Street, London
Griffin, Michael, Esq., Ballybane, Killarney, co. Kerry
Griffin, P., Esq., Fairy-lawn, Glin, co. Limerick
Griffin, W., Esq., M.D., Limerick
*Griffith, A. A., Esq., North-Frederick-street, Dublin
Griffith, Rev. George, Danby, Ballyshannon, co. Donegal
*Griffith, Richard, Esq., Fitswilliam-place, Dublin
*Griffith, W. D., Esq., South-Frederick-street, Dublin
*Griffiths, Henry, Esq., Ballytevreare-house, Sligo
Grimshaw, Robert, Esq., J.P., Belfast
Grogan, Rev. Charles J., Bagnalstown, co. Carlow
Grogan, Edward, Esq., Harcourt-street, Dublin
*Grome, Edward, Esq., Cloncondra-house, Eyrecourt, co. Galway
*Grome, Rev. T. M., A.M., Kiltonner Glebe, Ballinasloe, co. Galway
Grove, W., Esq., Dromore West, co. Sligo
Grove, Rev. W., M.A. and J.P., Charlesfort, Dromore West, co. Sligo
Grubb, Joseph, Esq., Clonmel, co. Tipperary
*Grubb, Richard, Esq., Cahir Abbey, co. Tipperary
*Grubb, Samuel, Esq., Claishleigh, Clogheen, co. Tipperary
*Grueber, Thomas, Esq., Torrington, Devonshire
*Grueber, W. F., Esq., M.D., Springfield, Rathmullen, co. Donegal
*Gubbins, Joseph, Esq., D.L., Kilfrush, Bruff, co. Limerick
GUILDFORD, The Right Honorable the Earl of
*GUILLAMORE, The Right Honorable Viscount
*Guinness, Arthur, Esq., Beaumont, co. Dublin
Guinness, R. S., Esq., Kildare-street, Dublin, and Ballinroan-lodge, co. Wexford
Guinness, Edward, Esq., Upper Fitzwilliam-street, Dublin
Guinness, J. G., Esq., Montpelier-parade, Dublin
*Guinness, W. S., Esq., Mountjoy-square, Dublin
*Guinness, Rev. W. S., Rector of Rathdrum, co. Wicklow
*Guinness, Arthur and Co. Messrs., James' Gate, Dublin
Guinty, Rev. Patrick, R.C.C., Moyne, Castlepollard, co. Westmeath
Guise, Sir B. W., Bart., M.P., Rencomb-park, Gloucestershire
Gumbleton, Rev. George, A.B., Belgrove, Cove, near Cork
*Gumbleton, R. H., Esq., Curriglass-house, Tallow, co. Cork
*Gumbleton, W., Esq., Curriglass-house, Tallow, co. Cork
*Gumley, J., Esq., Lower-Gardiner-street, Dublin
*Gumley, John, Esq., J.P., Belturbet, co. Cavan
*Gun, George, Esq., Plover-hill, Tralee, co. Kerry
Gun, John, Esq., Churchtown, Newcastle, co. Limerick
*Gun, W. Townsend, Esq., J.P., Ratloo-lodge, Tralee, co. Kerry
Gunning, Mr. John, Stranorlar, co. Donegal
*Gunson, R. and J., Messrs., Limerick
Guthrie, James, Esq., Coleraine, co. Derry
Gwydir, D., Esq., Grove-lodge, Littleton, co. Tipperary
*Gwyn, Mr. Alexander, Waterside, Glendermott, co. Derry
Gwyn, Mr. John, Drumskillin, Muff, co. Donegal
Gwynn, Rev. John, Prebendary of Kilroot, Carrickfergus, co. Antrim
Gwynn, Rev. S., Agherton Rectory, Coleraine, co. Derry
Gwynne, Rev. George J., A.B., Curriglass, Tallow, co. Cork
*Gwynne, W., Esq., Strabane, co. Tyrone
*Gwynne, Rev. W., D.D., Castlenock-house, co. Dublin

*Hacket, Messrs. E. and Co., Merchant's Quay, Cork
*Hackett, Edward, Esq., Cork
*Hackett, J., Esq., Clonmel, co. Tipperary
*Hackett, James & Co., Midleton, co. Cork
*Hackett, John, Esq., Mount-prospect, Rathpatrick, near Waterford
*Hackett, Capt. John, R.N., Musick-hall, Maynooth, co. Kildare
*Hackett, Michael, Esq., Brooklawn, Palmerstown, co. Dublin
*Hackett, Simpson, Esq., J.P., Riverstown, Parsonstown, King's co.
Hackett, William, Esq., Midleton, co. Cork
Hadden, Thomas Leys, Esq., Aberdeen
*HADDINGTON, the Right Honorable the Earl of
Hadley, Joseph, Esq., Smethwick, near Birmingham
*Hadnett, Richard, Esq., Barringtons-bridge, co. Limerick
Hagan, Sir Robert, R.N., Cove, near Cork
Haig, Robert, Esq., Dundalk, co. Louth
*Haigh, James, Esq., Dublin
*Haire, Rev. H., A.M., Aghabog-glebe, Newbliss, co. Monaghan
*Halanan, Rev. John, P.P. of Ballinhassig, near Cork
Hale, Rev. F., M.A., Lisburn, co. Antrim
*Halford, Sir H., Bart., M.D., F.R.S.,, G.C.H., Wistow-hall, Leicestershire
Haliday, Robert, Esq., Belfast
Hall, Rev. Bond, Taghmon-glebe, near Mullingar, co. Westmeath
Hall, G. C., Esq., Alfreton, Derbyshire
*Hall, John, Esq., Banagher, King's county
Hall, Richard, Esq., Cottage, Killeagh, co. Cork
Hall, Robert, Esq., Little Rath, Naas, co. Kildare
*Hall, R., Esq., D.L. and J.P., Narrow-water-house, WarrenPoint, co. Down
*Hall, Samuel, Esq., M.D., Roseborough, Naas, co. Kildare
*Hall, W., Esq., Mountjoy-square North, Dublin
Hall, William, Esq., Upper Gloucester-street, Dublin
*Hall, William Henry, Esq., Francis-street, Limerick
Hall, William, Esq., Burgess-house, Killeagh, co. Cork
*Hallaran, Rev. William, Macroom, co. Cork
Halliday, John, Esq., Ballicassidy-mills, Enniskillen, co. Fermanagh
*Halliday, Rev. Walter S., M.A., Glenthorn, Lynton, Devonshire
*Halligan, Rev. William J., R.C.C., Trim, co. Meath
*Halliwell, John, Esq., Red-mills, near Chapelizod, co. Dublin
Hally, Rev. Jeremiah, R.C.C., Dungarvan, co. Waterford
*Halpin, Mr. James, Wicklow
*Halpin, Rev. John, P.P., Nobber, co. Meath
*Halpin, Rev. Nicholas J., A.B., Vicarage, Oldcastle, co. Meath
*Haly, Rev. F., P.P., Kilcock, co. Kildare
*Haly, F. B., Esq., Kingstown, co. Dublin
Haly, Henry, Esq., Kilmurry, Crookstown, co. Cork
Ham, Thomas, Esq., Ballina, co. Mayo
Hamill, David, Esq., Ruskey, Clones, co. Monaghan
Hamill, Robert Henry, Esq., Mountjoy-street, Dublin
Hamilton, A., Esq., M.D., Londonderry
*Hamilton, Alexander, Esq., J.P., Cox Town, Donegal
*Hamilton, Rev. A. R., Vicar of Castledermot, co. Kildare
*Hamilton, A. W. Cole, Esq., D.L. and J.P., Beltrum, Gortin, co Tyrone
*Hamilton, Charles, Esq., Dominick-street, Dublin
Hamilton, Rev. Charles, Curate of Upper Badoney, co. Tyrone
Hamilton, Dacre, Esq., J.P., Newpark, Cootehill, co. Cavan
Hamilton, Rev. Edward, Philipstown, King's county
*Hamilton, Francis, Esq., Dominick-street, Dublin
*Hamilton, Frederick, Esq., Londonderry
*Hamilton G. A., Esq., Hampton-hall, Balybriggan, co. Dublin
*Hamilton, Gustavus, Esq., South Frederick-street, Dublin
*Hamilton, H. H., Esq., Upper Merrion-street, Dublin
Hamilton, Capt. Henry, Wexford
Hamilton, Henry, Esq., J.P., Tullylish-house, Gilford, co. Down
Hamilton, Hill, Esq., Mount-Vernon, Belfast
Hamilton, Rev. Hugh, A.M. and J.P., Benmore, Churchill, co. Fermanagh
*Hamilton, James, Esq., Newtown Stewart, co. Tyrone
*Hamilton, James, Esq., Fintra-house, Killybegs, co. Donegal
*Hamilton, James, Esq., Lake Mount, Dromore, co. Down
*Hamilton, James, Esq., Strabane, co. Tyrone
Hamilton, Rev. James, M.A., Castlebar, co. Mayo
Hamilton, James, Esq., M.D., Cottage, Gorey, co. Wexford
Hamilton, Rev. James, R.C.C., Bridge-street, Dublin
*Hamilton, James, Esq., Larkfield, near Clondalkin, co. Dublin
*Hamilton, James Hans, Esq., Sheep-hill, Castlenock, co. Dublin
*Hamilton, Rev. John, Marlborough-street, Dublin
*Hamilton, Very Rev. John, R.C. Archdeacon of Dublin
*Hamilton, John, Esq., Glentaugher-house, Carndonagh, co. Donegal
*Hamilton, John, Esq., Omagh, co. Tyrone
*Hamilton, John, Esq., J.P., St. Ernan's, Donegal
Hamilton, John, Esq., J.P., Villa, Glin, co. Limerick
Hamilton, John P., Esq., J.P., Oakfield, Clones, co. Fermanagh
Hamilton, Micah Cary, Esq., Ballyfatton, Strabane, co. Tyrone
Hamilton, Patrick, Esq., M.D., Ballinrobe, co. Mayo
*Hamilton, R., Esq., North Great George-street, Dublin
*Hamilton, Rev. R. Rector of Culdaff and Cloncha, Redford, Moville, co. Donegal
Hamilton, S., Esq., Broad Street, London
Hamilton, S., Esq., M.D., Loughrea, co. Galway
Hamilton, Rev. Sackville Robert, Rector of Mallow, co. Cork
*Hamilton, Samuel, Esq., M.D., Kilrush, co. Clare
*Hamilton, Thomas C., Esq., Hampton-hall, Balbriggan, co. Dublin
Hamilton, Capt. W. A. B., R. N., Dublin Castle
*Hamilton, Rev. William, Donabate, co. Dublin
*Hamilton, William, Esq., Sligo
*Hamilton, William, Esq., J.P., Cooltrim-lodge, Castle-blayney, co. Monaghan
*Hamilton, William, Esq., Peafield, Borris in Ossory, Queen's county
Hamilton, William, Esq., M.D., Ballintra, co. Donegal
Hamilton, W. H., Esq., Sunbury, Blarney, co. Cork
Hamilton, William R., Esq., Observatory, near Dublin
Hamilton, Mrs., Moneymore, co. Derry
*Hammersley, Richard, Esq., Corolanty, Shinrone, King's county
*Hammond, Thomas, Esq., Drogheda, co. Louth
Hampston, Rev. James, Castlegregory, near Tralee, co. Kerry
Hanan, Denis, Esq., M.D., Tallow, co. Cork
Hancock, C., Esq., Hall Leys, Whitwell, Chesterfield, Derbyshire
*Hancock, William John, Esq., J.P., Lurgan, co. Armagh
*Handcock, E. B., Esq., Rathmoyle-house, Abbeyleix, Queen's co.
Handcock, G., Esq., J.P., Millmount-ho., Randalstown, co. Antrim
*Handcock, Henry H., Esq., Grange-park, Dungannon, co. Tyrone

*Handcock, Mr. Hugh H., Upper Cumber, Londonderry
*Handcock, Rev. J. G., Rector and Vicar of Annaduff, co. Leitrim
*Handcock, John S., Esq., East-prospect, Nenagh, co. Tipperary
Handcock, Mr. Thomas, Upper Cumber, Londonderry
*Handcock, William Elias, Esq., Sally-park, Firhouse, near Dublin
Handfield, Commander Edward, R.N., Seaforth, near Liverpool
*Handy, John, Esq., Barraghcore, Goresbridge, Kilkenny
*Handy, Rev. R. F., Mayne-glebe, Castle Pollard, co. Westmeath
*Handy, S., Esq., J.P., Bracca-castle, Kilbeggan, co. Westmeath
*Hanks, J., Esq., Colomore, co. Dublin, and Gardiner's-pl., Dublin
*Hanly, James, Esq., Kilroe, Headford, co. Galway
Hanley, Mr. William, Murphystown, near Kilgobbin, co. Dublin
*Hanlon, Rev. Matthew, P.P. of Duleek, co. Meath
*Hanlon, Mr. Samuel, Mill Bairne, near Drumcondra, co. Dublin
Hanly, James, Esq., Glanmire-factory, near Cork
Hanly, Rev. James, P.P. of Latten, near Tipperary
*Hanly, Rev. John P., Church-street, Dublin
*Hanna, James, Esq., Blackwatertown, co. Armagh
Hanna, Mr. John, Whitehouse, Killea, co. Donegal
Hanna, Rev. Samuel, D.D., S.S., Theological Professor, Belfast
Hannagan, Rev. Michael, P.P. of Castlemartyr, co. Cork
Hannagan, Rev. Michael, R.C.C., Mitchelstown, co. Cork
Hannan, Rev. Daniel Joseph, O.S.D., Limerick
*Hannay, Capt. J., Castleroe, Coleraine, co. Derry
*Hannigan, Rev. J., A.M., Somerset-glebe, Ballinasloe, co. Galway
Hanning, James, Esq., Kilcrone, Cloyne, co. Cork
Hanrahan, C. J., Esq., Limerick
*HARBERTON, The Right Honorable Viscount
Harden, John H., Esq., Summer-hill, Burrisoleigh, co. Tipperary
*Harden, Robert, Esq., D.L. & J.P., Harrybrook, Tandragee, co. Armagh
*Hardey, James J., Esq., Nassau-street, Dublin
Hardiman, James, Esq., Middle Gardiner-street, Dublin
*Harding, Rev. Henry S., Black Rock, Dublin
Harding, Philip, Esq., J.P., Firville, Macroom, co. Cork
*Harding, Robert, Esq., Bruree, near Bruff, co. Limerick
Harding, Robert, Esq., Ballycastle, co. Antrim
*Harding, Samuel, Esq., Rock-lodge, Loughill, near Glin, co. Limerick
*Harding, Thomas, Esq., M.D., Limerick
Hardinge, Rev. N., C.C., Maryborough, Queens county
Hardman, Patrick, Esq., Togher, Dunleer, co. Louth
Hardum, Mess. J. & R. Fair Brook-paper-mill, Kilmeadon, Waterford
*Hardy, Charles, Esq., Coalisland, Dungannon, co. Tyrone
*Hardy, James, Esq., Drumart, Tandragee, co. Armagh
*Hardy, John, Esq., J.P. Loughall, co. Armagh
*Hardy, Robert Cope, Esq., Armagh
Hare, Rev. David, A.B., Kilworth, co. Cork
Hare, Rev. George, Portarlington, Queen's county
*Hare, Rev. John, Rector of Tully Corbet, Ballibay, co. Monaghan
*Hare, Sir Thomas, Stow-hall, Norfolk
*Harford, Mr. Thomas, Verbina-lodge, near Artane, co. Dublin
Hargreave, Abraham, Esq., Ballynoe, Cove, near Cork
*Harke, Rev. C. F., Gracehill, Ballymena, co. Antrim
*Harkin, Michael, Esq., M. D., Omagh, co. Tyrone
*Harle, John, Esq., Newcastle-on-Tyne, Northumberland
Harley, John, Esq., Clonroad, Ennis, co. Clare
*Harman, William Smith, Esq., Upper Crossdrum, co. Meath
*Harman and Co., Messrs., Adam's-court, Old Broad-street, London
*Harmon, Rev. John, R.C.C., St. James, Dublin
Harmon, Rev. R., R.C.C., Ballinahinch, near Ashford, co. Wicklow
Harnett, E., Esq., Newcastle, co. Limerick
*Harnett, John D., Esq., Academy-street, Cork
*Harnett, John, Esq., Newcastle, co. Limerick
*Harnett, Rev. L., P.P. of Croom, &c., co. Limerick
*Harnett, Maurice, Esq., Milltown, near Dublin
Harnett, Robert Fuller, Esq., Deelis, Macroom, co. Cork
Harnett, Rev. T., P.P. of Dunagh, near Listowel, co. Kerry
Harnett, William, Esq., Moynsha, Abbeyfeale, co. Limerick
*Harold, Rev. Dr., Denmark-street, Dublin
Harper, Francis, Esq., Wexford
Harper, Rev. James, R.C.C., Bannow, near Taghmon, co. Wexford
Harpur, Rev. Walter, R.C.C. of Barentown, near Wexford
Harris, Rev. George, A.B., Rector of Derrycrust, co. Fermanagh
*Harris, Rev. George, M.A., Templecarne, Kish, co. Fermanagh
*Harris, Hugh, Esq., Ashfort, Tynan, co. Armagh
Harris, Rev. John, A.M., Ashfield-glebe, Cootehill, co. Cavan
Harris, John, Esq., Winchester-place, Southwark, Surrey
*Harris, M., Esq., Eden, near Rathfarnham, co. Dublin, and Upper Merrion-street, Dublin
Harris, W. P., Esq., Lake-view, near Blackrock, co. Cork
Harris, Thomas, Esq., J.P., Bathview, Mallow, co. Cork
Harris, Rev. W., P.P. of Killevan and Aughabeg, co. Monaghan
Harris, Rev. W. W., LL.D., Elton, near Arklow, co. Wicklow
Harris, Walter W., Esq., M.D., Cork
Harrison, Rev. C. B., A.M., Monivea, co. Galway
Harrison, Edward, Esq., Emla, near Roscommon
*Harrison, Hugh, Esq., Hugomont, Ballymena, co. Antrim
Harrison, Rev. John, Vicar of Bodinstown, and P.C. of Sherlockstown, Naas, co. Kildare
Harrison, Capt. J. Rhincrew-cottage, Youghal, co. Cork
*Harrison, Michael, Esq., Glenmona, Cushindall, co. Antrim
*Harrison, Richard, Esq., Wolverton, near Stoney Stratford, Bucks.
Harrison, Robert, Esq., Rair View, Broughshane, co. Antrim
Harrison, S., Esq., Garna-villa, near Douglas, co. Cork
Harrison, Capt. Seymour, Killane-lodge, Kilconnell, co. Galway
Harrison, T., Esq., M.D. Killane-lodge, Kilconnell, co. Galway
Harrison, Thomas, Esq., Saithaelwyd, Holywell, Flint
*Harrison, William, Esq., Grace-park, Richmond, near Dublin
*Harrower, Mr. Thomas, Drogheda, co. Louth
*Harry, Rev. Richard, Richmond Convent, Dublin
Hart, General G. V., Kilderry, near Derry
*Hart, Capt. E., Glen-villa, Glandore, Roscarbery, co. Cork
Hart, Rev. George Vaughan Ledwick, Glenallo, co. Donegal
Hart, J. Esq., M.D., Portarlington, Queen's county
*Hart, John, Esq., Sligo
*Hart, Rev. M., P.P. of Dunfeeny and Kilbride, Ballycastle, co. Mayo
Hart, Philip, Esq., Richmond-avenue, near Dublin
Hart, Mr. P. H., Faughanvale, near N. T. Limavady, co. Derry
Hart, Mr. R., Gower Street, London
Harte, Rev. Charles, A.M., Lisquinlan, near Cloyne, co. Cork
*Harte, Henry, Esq., Gortree-cottage, Ballingarry, co. Limerick
Harte, Rev. Henry H., Rector of Cappagh, Ergennagh Glebe-house, Omagh, co. Tyrone
*Harte, R., Jun., Esq., Limerick
*Harte, Richard, Esq., J.P., Coolruss, near Croom, co. Limerick
Harte, Thomas, Esq., Phipsbourg-avenue, co. Dublin
Hartford, George, Esq., Rathmines, near Dublin
*Hartigan, W., Esq., Mount Sion, Pallas Green, co. Limerick
*Hartley, Major George, Middleton-lodge, Richmond, Yorkshire
Hartnett, Rev. Patrick, Bally Quane, near Fermoy, co. Cork
*Harton, John Luke, Esq., Banagher, King's county
*Hartstonge, M. Weld, Esq., M.R.I.A., Molesworth-street, Dublin
Harty, W., Esq., M.D., Middle Gardiner-street, Dublin
Harty, Lady, Prospect-house, Roebuck, co. Dublin
*Harty, Mr. Michael, Medical Hall, Nenagh, co. Tipperary
Harvey, C. G., Esq., Kyle, near Wexford
Harvey, George, Esq., Sligo
Harvey, Henry, Esq., Cove, near Cork
*Harvey, James, Esq., Limerick
*Harvey, Capt. James William, Park-house, near Wexford
*Harvey, John, Esq., Wexford
*Harvey, John, Esq., Ickwell Bury, near Biggleswade, Bedfordshire
Harvey, John, Esq., J.P., Malin-hall, Carndonagh, co. Donegal
Harvey, John, Esq., Goorey, Carndonagh, co. Donegal
Harvey, Mr. John, Bateson's-quay, Moira, co. Down
Harvey, J. R. Esq., M.D., Upper Glanmire-road, Cork
Harvey, Nicholson, Esq., Londonderry
Harvey, Rev. Robert, Raymochy, Manor Cunningham, co. Donegal
Harvey, Thomas, Esq., Youghal, co. Cork
*Harvey, W. G., Esq., Lombard-street, London
*Harvey, Rev. William Henry, Linsfirt, co. Donegal
*Harvey, W. G., Esq., Edwardes-square, Kensington, Middlesex
Haslett, Rev. Henry, Knock, Belfast
*Haslett, James, Esq., Dublin
Haslett, Rev. James, Curate of Donaghedy, Donamana, co. Tyrone
*Hassard, A., Esq., J.P., Garden-hill, Enniskillen, co. Fermanagh
Hassard, Rev. Edward, Curate of the Union, Collon, co. Louth
*Hassard, Jason, Esq., Cara-house, Clones, co. Monaghan
Hassard, Jason, Esq., Levagby, Enniskillen, co. Fermanagh
*Hassard, William, Esq., Garden-hill, Enniskillen, co. Fermanagh
Hastings, Charles, Esq., M.D., Worcester
Hastings, Rev. Henry James, Arely Kings, Worcestershire
Hatch, John, Esq., M.D., Dunlavin, co. Wicklow
*Hatch, William, Esq., Castle Ardee, co. Louth
*Hatchell, George, Esq., Ludford-park, near Dundrum, co. Dublin
*Hatchell, Henry Melville, Esq., Lough Guir Castle, Bruff, co. Limerick
*Hatchell, John, Esq., Monaghan
*Hatrick, Mr. Ezekiel, Glebes, Glendermott, co. Derry
*Hatton, Robert, Esq., Lee-bank, Cork
*Haughton, Benjamin, Esq., Banford-house, Gilford, co. Down
*Haughton, J., Esq., Jonestown, Edenderry, King's county
*Haughton, Rev. R., Phipsborough, co. Dublin
*Haughton, Thomas, Esq., J.P., Carlow
*Haughton, Messrs. James and William, City-quay, Dublin

Havanagh, Rev. James, C.C., Ballymore, co. Wexford
* HAWARDEN, The Right Honorable Viscount
* Hawkes, George, Esq., Sirmount, Ballincollig, co. Cork
* Hawkes, John, Esq., J.P., Grange, near Cork
* Hawkes, John, Esq., Kilcrea, near Ovens, co. Cork
* Hawkes, Rev. Lewis, Faragher-lodge, near Roscommon
* Hawkes, Samuel, Esq., Kilcrea, near Ovens, co. Cork
* Hawkes, William, Esq., Rose Mount, near Ovens, co. Cork
* Hawkesworth, John, Esq., Forest, Mountrath, Queen's county
* Hawkesworth, William, Esq., Woodbrook, Mountrath, Queen's co.
* Hawkins, The Very Rev. Dean, Dunkerrin-glebe, Moneygall, King's co.
Hawkshew, Charles, Esq., Dromore, Monaghan
* Hawthorne, Charles Stewart, Esq., Belcamp-house, co. Dublin
Hayden, Rev. John, A.B., Killaloe-glebe, Upper Cumber, co. Derry
Hayden, Rev. Timothy, P.P. Hospital, near Bruff, co. Limerick
Haydin, Rev. J., C.C. Clonaslee, Queen's county
Haydn, Joseph, Esq., Francis-street, Limerick
Hayes, E., Esq., Gardiner's-place, Dublin
* Hayes, Mr. E., Royal Hotel, Kingstown, co. Dublin
* Hayes, Sir Edmund S., Bart., M.P., Drumboe, Stranorlar, co. Donegal
Hayes, Frederick W., Esq., Seapatrick, Banbridge, co. Down
* Hayes, Sir H. B. Knt., Vernon Mount, near Cork
Hayes, James, Esq., Castle View, Clonakilty, co. Cork
Hayes, Mr. James John, Parade, Cork
Hayes, O., Esq., Vernon-mount, Cork
* Hayes, P., Esq., Abbeyfeale, co. Limerick
Hayes, Patrick, Esq., Usher's-quay, Dublin
* Hayes, Patrick, Esq., Westmoreland-street, Dublin
Hayes, Richard, Esq., Millmount, Banbridge, co. Down
* Hayes, T. P., Esq., Wood-park, Rathmines, co. Dublin
* Hayman, Matthew, Esq., Youghal, co. Cork
* Hayman, Samuel, Esq., M.D., Prospect-hill, Youghal, co. Cork
Haynes, J. W. H., Esq., Mont-de-Piete, Limerick
Haynes, Joseph, Esq., Maryland-house, Cloyne, co. Cork
Haynes, Michael, Esq., Inchigaggin, Carrigrchane, co. Cork
Haynes, M. P., Esq., Galway
* Haynes, Rev. Thomas, R.C.C., Cahirlog, co. Cork
* Hayward, Charles, Esq., Lincoln
Hazlett, John, Esq., Lurgan, co. Armagh
* Hazlett, J. H., Esq., J.P., Carnisk, Ramelton, co. Donegal
Hazlewood, Rev. George, Sackville-street, Dublin
* Hazlewood, Mr. Henry, Navan, co. Meath
Hazlewood, Rev. William, Donamore, Gorey, co. Wexford
* Head, The Very Rev. John, Dean of Killaloe, Ballinaclough-glebe, [Nenagh, co. Tipperary
* HEADFORT, The Most Noble the Marquis of
* HEADLEY, The Right Honorable Lord
* Healy, Rev. A., P.P., Mount Mellick, Queen's county
* Healy, Francis, Esq., Mogullane, Newmarket-on-Fergus, co. Clare
Healy, Michael, Esq., M.D., Manus-house, Ennis, co. Clare
* Healy, Rev. P., P.P. Monastereven, co. Kildare
* Healy, Rev. Thomas, P.P. of Killshaloy, Ballymote, co. Sligo
Healy, Messrs. W. and S., Lock-quay, Limerick
Heaney, Rev. Edward, R.C.C., Drogheda, co. Louth
Heard, Edward, Esq., Kinsale, co. Cork
Heard, John, Esq., J.P., Fermoy, co. Cork
Heard, John, Esq., Ballybrack, near Douglas, co. Cork
Heard, John Isaac, Esq., J.P., Kinsale, co. Cork
* Hearn, J. O'Grady, Esq., Shanakill, Carrick on Suir, co. Waterford
Hearn, John, Esq., Dungarvan, co. Waterford
* Hearn, Owen W., Esq., Richmond-avenue, Dublin
* Heath, Joseph, Esq., Chesham, Bucks
Heath, Richard, Esq., Stourport, Worcestershire
Heathcote, Rev. E., Chesterfield, Derbyshire
* Heatly, Rev. Samuel S., Randalstown, co. Antrim
Heatty, J. H., Esq., South-Cumberland-street, Dublin
Heeney, Francis, Esq., Portglenone, co. Antrim
Hegarty, Mr. William, Letterkenny, co. Donegal
Hehir, Mr. Mort, Miltown Malbay, co. Clare
Heinekey, Mr. Robert, Bilton Hotel, Sackville-street, Dublin
* Heise, William, Esq., M. D., Ballinasloe, co. Galway
* Helden, Cornelius, Esq., Bessvill, Granard, co. Longford
Helsham, George, Esq., Mallardstown, and John-street, Kilkenny
* Hely, Charles, Esq., Melross, Johnstown, co. Kilkenny
* Hely, Gorges, Esq., Violet-hill, Johnstown, co. Kilkenny
Hely, Pierce, Esq., D.L. and J.P., Rockfield, near Cappoquin, co. [Waterford
Heming, Rev. John, Cloughjordan, co. Tipperary
Hemphill, James, Esq., Aughadory-house, Coleraine, co. Derry
* Hemsworth, T. G., Esq., Abbeville, Borrisokane, co. Tipperary
* Henderson, J., Esq., Upper-Dorset-s., Dublin, and Tuam, co. Galway
* Henderson, James, Esq., Brownstown, Navan, co. Meath
* Henderson, J., Esq., Hollybrook, Ballicumber, Clara, King's co.
* Henderson, Mr. John, Londonderry
Henderson, Rev. L. J., R.C.C. of St. Finbarr's, Cork
* Henderson, Richard, Esq., Waterford
Henderson, Samuel, Esq., Rathmullen, co. Donegal
Hendley, Matthias, Esq., J.P., Mount Rivers, Fermoy, co. Cork
* Hendrick, Rev. W. F., R.C.C., Booterstown, co. Dublin
* Heneage, G. F., Esq., Hainton-hall, Wragby, Lincolnshire
Henery, Messrs. J. and D., Sligo
Heney, Mr. James, Cashel, co. Tipperary
Henn, Richard, Esq., Upper-Merrion-street, Dublin
* Henn, William, Esq., Merrion-square South, Dublin
Hennesy, Rev. L., C.C., Portarlington, Queen's county
Hennesy Rev. T., C.C., Clonmore, Clonbullage, King's county
Hennessy, James, Esq., Ballymacmoy-house, Mallow, co. Cork
* Hennessy, Maurice, Esq., Youghal, co. Cork
Hennessy and Sheehan, Messrs., South Mall, Cork, 2 copies
* HENNIKER, The Right Honorable Lord
Henri, Lieut. Alphonso B., R.N. and J.P., Sans Souci-cottage, [Doonkeeghan, Killala, co. Mayo
Henry, Arthur, Esq., J.P., Lodge-park, Celbridge, co. Kildare
* Henry, D., Esq., Stephen's-green, South, Dublin
* Henry, J., Esq., Harrington-street, Dublin
* Henry, Rev. James, P.P. of Foxford, co. Mayo
* Henry, John, Esq., Rathmestin, near Louth
* Henry, John, Esq., Sand-hill, Castle-Blayney, co. Monaghan
Henry, L. L., Esq., Clonmaskill, Castletown Delvin, co. Westmeath
Henry, Michael William, Esq., Swinford, co. Mayo
* Henry, Rev. Richard, Richmond-convent, Dublin
Henry, Rev. Robert, M.A., Rector of Jonesborough, co. Armagh
Henry, Thomas E., Esq., York-street, Dublin
* Henry, Thomas G., Esq., J.P., Mile-street, Newry, co. Down
Henry, W., Esq., Broomfield, Castle-Blayney, co. Monaghan
* Henry, William, Esq., Armagh
* Henry, William, Esq., Island-bridge, near Dublin
Henry, William Wentworth, Esq., Killiney, co. Dublin
* Henry, William, Esq., Millbrook-house, Oldcastle, co. Meath
Henson, Rev. F., Rector of South Kilvington, Thirsk, Yorkshire
* Henson, I., Esq., Bouverie-street, Fleet-street, London
* Henwood, Charles, Esq., Gas and Water-works, Limerick
* Henzell, Rev. Bigor, Rector and Vicar of Kilmahon, Cloyne, co. Cork
* Herbert, Rev. Arthur, J.P., Cahirnane, Killarney, co. Kerry
* Herbert, Henry Arthur, Esq., Muckross, co. Kerry
* Herbert, Rev. Nicholas, J.P., Rector of Knockgraffon and Dogs- [town, near Cahir, co. Tipperary
Herbert, Rev. E., A.M., Kilpeacon-glebe, Limerick
Heron, John, Esq., M.D., Portumna, co. Galway
Heron, John, Esq., Belfast
Heron, Robert, Esq., J.P., Ardigon, Killyleagh, co. Down
* Heron, Thomas, Esq., Belfast
Heron, William C., Esq., J.P., Altafort, Dromore, co. Down
Herrick, E. H., Esq., Ballyduvane, Cloghnakilty, co. Cork
Herrick, Henry, Esq., Farnalough, Bandon, co. Cork
* Herrick, T., Esq., J.P., Coolkirky, Ballymartle, near Kinsale, co. [Cork
Herrick, Thomas, Esq., Bellmount, Crookstown, Cork
* Herrick, William Henry, Esq., J.P., Shippool, Innishanon, co. Cork
Herring, Mr. Jamieson, Cork
Herron, Hugh, Esq., Banbridge, co. Down
* Hesketh, Mrs., Tulketh-park, near Preston, Lancashire
Hewgill, Rev. James, Rector of Great-Smeeton, Yorkshire
Hewitt, The Honourable and Rev. John P., Rector of Desertlyn, [Moneymore, co. Derry
Hewitt, Charles, Esq., M.D., Maryland-cottage, Cloyne, co. Cork
Hewitt, Thomas, Esq., St. Patrick's-hill, Cork
Hewitt, T. H., Esq., Watercourse Distillery, Cork
Hewitt, T. S., Esq., Token-house-yard, London
Hewitt, The Misses, Marine-cottages, Monkstown, co. Cork
Hewson, Edward, Esq., Ballystool, Pallas-Kenry, co. Limerick
* Hewson, James, Esq., Rathkeale Abbey, co. Limerick
* Hewson, James, Esq., Hollywood, near Adair, co. Limerick
Hewson, John, Esq., Enniscoush, Rathkeale, co. Limerick
Hewson, John, Esq., Island-castle, near Dungarvan, co. Waterford
Hewson, John F., Esq., J.P., Ennismore, Listowel, co. Kerry
* Hewson, Rev. Robert, Kilcoleman-glebe, Milltown, co. Kerry
Heyland, Lieut. James, R.N., Clogher-lodge, Belmullet, co. Mayo
Hezlet, Robert, Esq., Coleraine, co. Derry
* Hickey, Rev. Patrick, P.P. Doon, co. Limerick
* Hickey, Rev. William, Rector of Wexford
* Hickie, W., Jun., Esq., Jane-mount, Glanmire, near Cork
* Hickman, H. B., Esq., Thonock-hall, Gainsborough, Lincolnshire

*Hickman, P., Esq., D.L. and J.P., Kilmore, Knock, co. Clare
*Hicks, W. W., Esq., Kilmacanogue-house, near Bray, co. Wicklow
*Hickson, George, Esq., J.P., Stradbally-lodge, Tralee, co. Kerry
*Hickson, George Blake, Esq., North Great-George-street, Dublin
Hickson, John, Esq., J.P., Grove, Dingle, co. Kerry
Hickson, John James, Esq., Tralee, co. Kerry
*Hickson, S. Murray, Esq., Balintagart, Dingle, co. Kerry
Hickson, Mr. Stephen R., Glanmire-road, Cork [low
*Higginbotham, J. W., Esq., Castle Ruddery, Baltinglass, co. Wick-
Higgins, George, Esq., Hillsboro', Kilcullen, co. Kildare
*Higgins, James, Esq., Ballina, co. Mayo
Higgins, James, Esq., Maragall-house, Lisburn, co. Antrim
Higgins, John, Esq., Ross, Killala, co. Mayo
Higgins, Rev. Michael, Kilworth, co. Cork
Higgins, Mr. Paullet, Araglen-woollen-mills, Kilworth, co. Cork
*Higgins, Mr. Thomas, Ballinderry, co. Antrim
*Higgins, Thomas Charles, Esq., The Cottage, Turvey, Bedfordshire
Higgon, Lieut. H. M., R.N., Pullorheny, Dromore West, co. Sligo
*Higinbotham, Henry, Esq., Church-view, Cross-avenue, Dublin
Hildebrand, George, Esq., Westport, co. Mayo
Hildebrand, Henry, Esq., Boffin Island, Westport, co. Mayo
*HILL, The Right Honourable Lord Arthur
Hill, Lieut.-Col. Arundel, J.P., Cloheen, Buttevant, co. Cork
*Hill, Arundel, Esq., Bolane-cottage, Pallas-Kenry, co. Limerick
Hill, Beauchamp, Esq., Armagh
Hill, Boyle, Esq., Hampstead, near Douglas, co. Cork
*Hill, E. T. M., Esq., Ross-bank, Belfast
*Hill, The Rt. Hon. Sir F. G., Bart., Brooke-hall, near Londonderry
*Hill, George, Esq., Clonsilla-cottage, co. Dublin
*Hill, George, Esq., J.P., St. Columbs, Londonderry
*Hill, G. S., Esq., Newtown Hamilton, co. Armagh
*Hill, J., Esq., J.P., Bellaghy-castle, co. Derry
Hill, J., Esq., Graig, near Doneraile, co. Cork
*Hill, James, Jun., Esq., Lower-Pembroke-street, Dublin
Hill, Rev. James, Knocklofty-glebe, Clonmel, co. Tipperary
Hill, James, Esq., Abbey-hall-school, Omagh, co. Tyrone
*Hill, John, Esq., Limerick
*Hill, Mr. John, Wicklow
Hill, John, Esq., Moneyglass, near Randalstown, co. Antrim
Hill, Rev. John, M.A., Vicarage, Donaghadee, co. Down
*Hill, Nathaniel, Esq., Drogheda, co. Louth
Hill, Richard, Esq., Doneraile, co. Cork
Hill, Rev. Robert, A.M., Aghalee-glebe, Moira, co. Antrim
Hill, Rev. T., B.D., Vicar of Chesterfield, Derbyshire
Hill, Rev. T., Vicar of Badgeworth, Shurdington, Gloucestershire
Hill, Thomas, Esq., Mount-pleasant, Pallas-Kenry, co. Limerick
*Hill, The Right Honourable William, 43rd Regt., Cork
*Hill, William, Esq., Crescent, Salford, near Manchester
Hill, William, Esq., Donnybrook, Doneraile, co. Cork
Hill, Mr. William, Yewtree-hill, Moira, co. Antrim
*Hillas, William Hutchinson, Esq., J.P., Seaview-house, co. Sligo
*Hinch, Thomas, Esq., Rathsallagh, near Dunlavin, co. Wicklow
Hincks, Rev. Edward, D.D., Killyleagh, co. Down
Hincks, Ralph, Esq., Rosegarland-cottage, Taghmon, co. Wexford
Hincks, Rev. Thomas, Belfast
Hind, Rev. John, M.A., F.R.A.S., Cambridge
*Hindes, Rev. George, A.M., Ballycan, Mount-Nugent, co. Cavan
*Hinds, George, Esq., Green-park, Mullingar, co. Westmeath
Hingston, The Very Rev. James, LL.D. and J.P., Vicar General of [Cloyne, co. Cork
Hingston, Rev. James, Rector of Youghal, co. Cork
Hinson, Rev. W., Rector of Rossdroit, near Enniscorthy, co. Wexford
*Hitchcock, John, Esq., Anglesea-street, Dublin
Hoare, Rev. E. N., A.M., Limerick
*Hoare, Capt. E. W., R.N., J.P., Carrigrenane, LittleIsland, Cork
Hoare, Henry Hugh, Esq., Wavendon-house, Bucks
Hoare, Rev. Thomas, Glenamore, Castletown-Roche, co. Cork
Hoare, Rev. W. W., A.B., Kilmallock, co. Limerick
Hobbs, Capt, Greenhills, Ballyboy, King's county
Hobbs, Henry William, Esq., Prospect, Parsonstown, King's co.
Hobbs, W., Esq., Marlborough-street, Cork
Hobbs, Robert, Esq., Borrisokane, co. Tipperary
Hobbs, Thomas, Esq., Greenhills, Frankford, King's county
Hobson, Rev. H. T., Jenkinstown-glebe, Flurrybridge, co. Louth
Hodder, Francis, Esq., Ballea-castle, Carrigaline, co. Cork
*Hodder, Rev. H. T. M., Cork
*Hodder, Col. W. H. M., Hoddersfield, near Carrigaline, co. Cork
*Hodgens, Robert, Esq., Beaufort, near Rathfarnham, co. Dublin
*Hodgens, W., Esq., Blackrock, near Dublin [Two copies.]
Hodges, George Crowe, Esq., Donogrogue-castle, Knock, co. Clare
Hodges, Alderman W., Sackville-street, Dublin
*Hodges, W., Esq., Willow-mount, near Roundtown, co. Dublin
*Hodgkinson, Francis, Esq., LL.D., and V.P.T.C., Dublin
Hodgson, Mr. John, Belfast
Hodnett, Charles, Esq., Mary's-street, Cork
Hodnett, Mr. James, Sallybrook-paper-mills, near Cork
Hodson, Edward, Esq., J.P., Twyford, Athlone, co. Westmeath
*Hodson, Rev. Edward, A.M., Twyford, Athlone, co. Westmeath
Hodson, Sir G.F., Bart., D.L. and J.P., Hollybrooke-house, co. Wicklow
*Hodson, Leonard, Esq., Hodson's-bay, near Athlone, co. Roscommon
Hogan, C., Esq., Newport, co. Tipperary
Hogan, Edmund, Esq., Carahan-house, Ennis, co. Clare
*Hogan, John, Esq., J.P., Auburn, near Athlone, co. Westmeath
*Hogan, Rev. M., P.P. Croagh, &c., near Rathkeale, co. Limerick
*Hogan, Matthew G., Esq., Bank-place, Limerick
*Hogan, The Very Rev. Patrick, D. D., Vicar General, and P. P. of
*Hogan, Patrick James, Esq., Limerick [St. Michael's, Limerick
*Hogan, The Very Rev. Thomas, Vicar General, and P. P. Rath-
*Hogan, W. C., Esq., York-street, Dublin [keale, co. Limerick
*Hogan, William C., Esq., Fairyland, co. Dublin
*Hogan, Rev. W., R.C.C., Conna, co. Cork
*Hogg, James, Esq., Gilstown, near Strokestown, co. Roscommon
Hogg, Mr. James, Ballydawly, Moneymore, co. Derry
*Holahan, Rev. James, R.C.C., Bruff, co. Limerick
Holahan, Capt. John, Limerick
Holburd, Rev. Robert, Curate of Dunderrow, near Kinsale, co. Cork
*Hole, Henry, Esq., Ebberley-house, Devonshire
*Holford, R. S., Esq., Westonbrit, near Tetbury, Gloucestershire
Holland, Rev. Edward, P.P. of Carlingford, co. Louth
Holland, Rev. Jeremiah, C. R., Inchigeela, Macroom, co. Cork
*Holland, John, Esq., Carryreagh, Ballymoney, co. Antrim
*Holland, Rev. John, R.C.C. of North Parish, Cork
*Holland, P. H., Esq., Thomas-street, Limerick
Holland, W. H., Esq., New-grove, Ballincollig, co. Cork
Hollingsworth, Rev. H. G. H., Vicar of Monkstown, Passsage, co.
*Holloway, Mrs., Bloxham, near Banbury, Oxfordshire [Cork
*Holmes, Alexander, Esq., Scribblestown, co. Dublin
Holmes, Rev. Arthur, Templeharry-glebe, King's county
*Holmes, Benjamin Hayes, Esq., Dunmanway, co. Cork
Holmes, The Very Rev. Gilbert, Dean of Ardfert, J.P., Kilmore, [Nenagh, co. Tipperary
Holmes, Henry Joy, Esq., Holywell, Antrim
*Holmes, John, Esq., Southwark, Surrey
*Holmes, Richard, Esq., Clogher, co. Sligo
Holmes, Robert, Esq., Springfield, Cove, near Cork
Holmes, Robert Low, Esq., Maiden-hall, Charleville, co. Cork
Holt, Mr. Samuel, Sallins-lodge, near Naas, co. Kildare
*Holton, William, Esq., Athlone, co. Westmeath
Homan, C. E. Esq., M.D., William-street, Limerick
*Homan, Edward, Esq., Rutland-street, Limerick
Homan, Travers, Esq., Colga, Sligo [Cork
*Homan, Sir W. Jackson, Bart., J.P., Clifton-house, Youghal, co.
Hone, Joseph, Esq., Rockfield, near Stillorgan, co. Dublin
*Hooman, George, Esq., Kidderminster, Worcestershire
Hope, Ralph James, Esq. J.P., Urelands, near Carnew, co. Wicklow
*Hopes, William, Esq., Mulnahinch, near Monaghan
*Hopkins, Rev. Andrew, P.P. of Castleconnor, Ballina, co. Sligo
*Hopkins, Andrew, Esq., Blackhall-street, Dublin
*Hopkins, D.D., Esq., Davies-street, Berkeley-square, London
*Hopkins, John, Esq., Rockfield, Nobber, co. Meath
Hopkins, Rev. John, R.C.C., Kilbegnet, Roscommon
Hopkins, Mr. John, Shop-street, Tuam, co. Galway
Hopkins, Joseph F., Esq., Possextown, Nobber, co. Meath
*Hopper, H., Esq., Roscommon
*Hopper, W., Esq., Shangannagh-house, near Killiney, co. Dublin
Horan, Austin, Esq., Newport Pratt, co. Mayo
Horan, James, Esq., Ballinakill, Queen's county
Horan, Thomas, Esq., Loughrea, co. Galway
Horan, Thomas J., Esq., Cootehill, co. Cavan
Hore, Captain J. S., R.N., Emerald-cottage, Bray, co. Wicklow
*Hore, Captain Samuel, R. N., J.P., Lambarton, near Arklow, co.
Hore, Rev. Thomas, R.C.C., Camolin, co. Wexford [Wicklow
*Hore, Walter, Esq., J.P., Seafield, Gorey, co. Wexford
*Hore, Walter, Esq., J.P., Harperstown, near Taghmon, co. Wexford
*Horgan, Rev. Daniel, P.P. of Mogealy, Connogh, &c., co. Cork
Horgan, Rev. David, Crookstown, co. Cork
Horgan, John, Esq., Knucknagoun, Macroom, co. Cork
*Horgan, Rev. Mathew, P.P., Blarney, near Cork
*Horgan, Rev. M., P.P of Whitechurch and Garrycloyne, co. Cork
*Horgan, Paul, Esq., Carrigayulla, Macroom, co. Cork
Horn, William, Esq., Sligo
Horn, William, Esq., Cheapside, London

Horne, C., Esq., Newtown-mills, near Rathfarnham, co. Dublin
Horner, Mr. Francis, Ballybay, co. Monaghan
*Horner, Rev. James, D.D., Dorset-street, Dublin
*Horner, John, Esq., Bucklersbury, London
Horner, John, Esq., Grove-hill, Camberwell, Surrey
*Horner, Joshua, Esq., Twyvale, Dungannon, co. Tyrone
Horner, Rev. R. N., Glebe-hill, Dungannon, co. Tyrone [Wicklow
*Hornidge, Richard, Esq., J.P., Tulfarris, near Blessington, co.
*Hort, F., Esq., Leopardstown, near Stillorgan, co. Dublin
*Houghton, Henry, Esq., Dundrum, co. Dublin
*Hourigon, Rev. Nicholas, P.P. Shinrone, King's county
Houston, Rev. Clarke, Mount-pleasant, Ballymena, co. Antrim
Houston, Messrs. John and Samuel, Larne, co. Antrim
*Houston, John, Esq., Prospect-villa, Rathgar-road, Dublin
Hovenden, Pierce, Esq., North Infirmary, Cork
How, Thomas, Esq., Belfast
How, Mr. Thomas F., Glenavy, co. Antrim
*Howard, The Honorable Col. H., Bushy-park, Enniskerry, co. Wicklow
*Howard, The Hon. and Rev. F., Swords Vicarage, co. Dublin
Howard, Colonel Robert, M.P., Rathdrum, co. Wicklow
Howard, John P., Esq., Eyne-house, Mountmelick, Queen's county
Howard, W. H., Esq., Newry, co. Down
*Howe, Edmond, Esq., Aungier-street, Dublin
Howe, Mr. M., New Bond Street, London
Howell, George, Esq., Molesworth-street, Dublin
*Howlett, Messrs. and Co., New Ross, co. Wexford
*Howly, Arthur V., Esq., Ballina, co. Mayo
*Howly, Edward, Esq., J.P., Belleek-castle, Ballina, co. Mayo
*Howly, John, Esq., Upper Fitzwilliam-street, Dublin
*Howly, P. Culkin, Esq., J.P., Broadlands-park, Ballina, co. Mayo
*Howly, Patrick Irwin, Esq., Seaville, Ballina, co. Mayo
*Howly, William, Esq., Rich-hill, near Castle-Connell, co. Limerick
*HOWTH, The Right Honorable the Earl of
*Hoy, Mr. Thomas H., Westmorland-street, Dublin
*Hudson, H., Esq., Grafton-street, Dublin
Hubbard, Lieut. James, R.N., Ballybeg, near Ballina, co. Mayo
*Hubert, Rev. Michael, P.P. of Aughalurcher, The Hill, Maguire's- [bridge, co. Fermanagh
*Hudson, Alexander, Esq., J.P., Enniskillen, co. Fermanagh
Hudson, Rev. E.G., J.P., Glenville, co. Cork
*Hudson, George, Esq., Mount-Joy-square South, Dublin
*Hudson, James, Esq., Stranorcum-house, Ballymoney, co. Antrim
Hudson, John, Esq., Dungarvan, co. Waterford
Hudson, Michael, Esq., Killiniskyduff, near Arklow, co. Wicklow
*Hudson, R., Esq., J.P., Springfarm, N. T. Mt. Kennedy, do.
*Hudson, Robert, Esq., Seabank, near Arklow, co. Wicklow
*Huggins, J., Esq., M.D., Richmont, near Colehill, co. Longford
*Hughes, Henry, Esq., Killenley-hall, near Cahir, co. Tipperary
*Hughes, Rev. Henry, Merchants'-quay, Dublin
*Hughes, Rev. James, P.P. of Newport-Pratt, co. Mayo
Hughes, James, Esq., Oberstown, Ardee, co. Louth
Hughes, James, Esq., Capel-street, Dublin [co. Galway
Hughes, Rev. Mark, P.P., Killane-grange, and Bullane, Kilconnell,
*Hughes, John, Esq., The Grove, near Stillorgan, co. Dublin
*Hughes, Robert, Esq., J.P., Ely-house, Wexford
*Hughes, Samuel, Esq., Greenfield, Strabane, co. Tyrone
Hughes, Rev. William, Aghanloo, Newtownlimavady, co. Derry
Hughes, Rev. William, Newtownstewart, co. Tyrone
Hull, John, Esq., Crosshaven, Cove, near Cork
Hull, R. E., Esq., Lemcon-house, Skull, near Skibbereen, co. Cork
Hulls, John, Esq., Gloucester
*Hulme, J. H., Esq., Crescent, Salford, near Manchester
*Hume, Gustavus, Esq., Dawson-street, Dublin
*Hume, John S., Esq., Janeville, Kingstown, co., Dublin
*Hume, Rev. Robert, Rector of Urney, Strabane, co. Tyrone
Humfrey, A. J., Esq., Summer-hill, Dublin
Humfrey, B Geale, Esq., J.P., Cavanacor, Strabane, co. Donegal
Humphreys, Daniel, Esq., Broomfield-house, Midleton, co. Cork
*Humphreys, Major John, Ballykeane-house, co. Wicklow
*Humphreys, J., Esq., Claremont Institution, nr. Glasnevin, co. Dublin
*Humphreys, W., Esq., J.P., Ballyhaise-house, co. Cavan
*Humphrys, John, Esq., J.P., Strabane, co. Tyrone
*Hungerford, Thomas, Esq., J.P., The Island, Clonakilty, co. Cork
Hungerford, Thomas, Esq., Cahirmore, Rosscarbery, co. Cork
Hungerford, Thomas J., Esq., Lakelands, Skibbereen, co. Cork
*Hunloke, James, Esq., Budholme, Chesterfield, Derbyshire
*Hunt, Charles, Esq., Blessington-street, Dublin
*Hunt, E. Lombard, Esq., Ballymantane, Gort, co. Galway
Hunt, Edward, Esq., Jerpoint, Thomastown, co. Kilkenny
Hunt, Edward, Esq., J.P., Kinsale, co. Cork
*Hunt, Rev. John, Rathmichael-glebe-house, Bray, co. Dublin
Hunt, John, Esq., Hammersmith, Middlesex
*Hunt, John, Esq., Aungier-street, Dublin, and Thurles, co. Tipperary
Hunt, Martin Joseph, Esq., Riverview, Headford, co. Galway
Hunt, Robert, Esq., J.P., Inchirourk, Askeaton, co. Limerick
Hunt, Robert, Esq., Oaklands, Knock, co. Clare
Hunt, W. Henry, Esq., J.P., Jerpoint-house, Thomastown, co. Kil-
*Hunt, W. S., Esq., Upper Merrion-street, Dublin [kenny
*Hunt, W., Esq., Friarstown-abbey, Limerick
*Hunter, G., Esq., Pencher Colliery, Chester-le-Street, Derbyshire
*Hunter, John, Esq., Greenhill, Coleraine, co. Derry
Hunter, Mr. John, Hill-hall, Lisburn, co. Down
Hunter, Mr. Joseph, Kilrea, co. Derry
Hunter, Rev. Stevenson, Rector of Loughgill, co. Antrim
Hunter, William, Esq., Dunmurry, near Lisburn, co. Antrim
*HUNTINGDON, The Right Honorable the Earl of
*Hurford, Lieut. J., Royal Barracks, Dublin
Hurley, Francis, Esq., Derra-cottage, Ballymoe, co. Galway
Hurley, Mr. John, Bandon, co. Cork
Hurly, Rev. R. Conway, A.M., Tralee, co. Kerry
Hurst, Hugh, Esq., Ballincarrig, Pallas-Kenry, co. Limerick
Hurst, John, Esq., Cloverhill, near Roscommon
*Hurt, C., Esq., Wirksworth, Derbyshire
*Huskisson, Captain Thomas, R.N., Greenwich Hospital
Huson, Charles, Esq., Broomley, near Wexford
*Hussey, Anthony S., Esq., Westown, near Naul, co. Dublin
Hussey, Mr. Patrick, Kilmallock, co. Limerick
*Hussey, P. B., Esq., D.L. and J.P., Farinikilla, Dingle, co. Kerry
*Hussey, Thomas, Esq., Castlecore, Ballymahon, co. Longford
*Hutton, Robert Todd, Esq., M.D., Tynan, co. Armagh
*Hutchinson, The Hon. Capt. C.H., Rathgar-house, near Dublin
*Hutchinson, Dawson, Esq., Mount-Heaton, Roscrea, co. Tipperary
Hutchinson, Hicks, Esq., Muff-cottage, Cookstown, co. Tyrone
*Hutchinson, James, Esq., Stranocum-house, Ballymoney, co. Antrim
*Hutchinson, John D., Esq., Timoney, Roscrea, co. Tipperary
Hutchinson, John, Esq., Durham
Hutchinson, R., Esq., Durham
*Hutchinson, Rev. Sir S. Synge, Bart., D.D., Dublin
*Hutchinson, W., Esq., Seaview-house, Dromore, co. Sligo
Hutchinson, W., Esq., Bullock Castle, near Dublin
Hutchinson, W. H., Esq., Liverpool
*Hutchinson, William Henry, Esq., Rockforest, Roscrea, co. Tipperary
*Hutton, Timothy, Esq., Clifton Castle, Masham, Yorkshire
*Hutton, Thomas, Esq., Elm-park, near Drumcondra, co. Dublin
Hutton, W., Esq., Gate Burton, Lincolnshire
Hyde, Rev. A., Vicar of Killarney, co. Kerry
*Hyde, Rev. Arthur, Drumkillan-glebe, Mohill, co. Leitrim
*Hyde, George, Esq., Tintwistle-hall, near Mottram, Cheshire
Hyde, John, Esq., Castle-hyde, Fermoy, co. Cork
Hyde, William L. Esq., Templenoe, Fermoy, co. Cork
Hyland, Rev. John, R.C.C., Carrick-on-suir, co. Tipperary
Hyland, Rev. John, P.P. of Dunlavin, co. Wicklow
*Hyland, Lawrence, Esq., Castle-blunder, Kilkenny
*Hyland, W., Esq., Lower Gardiner-street, Dublin
*Hyndman, John E., Esq., Roebuck-lodge, co. Dublin
*Hynes, John, Esq., Rockview-lodge, Dalkey, co. Dublin
Hynes, Patrick, Esq., Gort, co. Galway
Hynes, Mr. Thomas, Kinvara, co. Galway

Inch, Rev. Nathaniel, Kililagh, Maghera, co. Derry
Ingham, Captain G. R.N., Loughrea, co. Galway
*Ingilby, Sir W. Amcotts, Bart., Ripley Castle, Yorkshire
Ingram, Rev. James, D.D., Trinity-college, Oxford
Ireland, Captain, J.P,, Bayview-house, Belmullet, co. Mayo
Ireland, John, Esq., J.P., Eyre-square, Galway
Ireland, W., Esq., Robertstown-house, Rathangan, co. Kildare
*Ireland, William, Esq., Gloucester-street, Dublin, and Doro-ville, Robertstown, co. Kildare [Wicklow
*Ireland, William W., Esq., Ballyorsey, near NT. Mt. Kennedy, co.
*Irish Office, London
*Irish Society, Honorable the, London
*Irvine, Major, Green-hill, Lisnaskea, co. Fermanagh [Fermanagh
Irvine, Rev. A. H., A.M., and J.P., Corkhill, Enniskillen, co.
*Irvine, Edward C., Esq., Spring-park, Tynan, co. Armagh
*Irvine, Major G., St. George, Owenevarra, Newtownbarry, co. Wexford
*Irvine, Henry, Esq., Hardwicke-place, Dublin
*Irvine, John, Esq., Moville, co. Donegal
*Irvine, John, Esq., J.P., Rockfield, Enniskillen, co. Fermanagh
*Irvine, John C., Esq., Grove-hill, Passage West, co. Cork
*Irvine, Rev. William John, Cookstown, co. Tyrone
Irving, Mr .Charles, Carnone, Castlefin, co. Donegal

*Irving, Rev. Charles, Rector of Donaghmore, Castlefin, co. Donegal
*Irving, J., Esq., Richmond-ter., London, & Magramorne, co. Antrim
*Irwin, Rev. A., Howth, co. Dublin
Irwin, Rev. Charles King, A.M., P.C. of Portadown, co. Armagh
*Irwin, Rev. Francis, A.M., Castlerea, co. Roscommon
*Irwin, George, Esq., Digges-street, Dublin
Irwin, Rev. Henry, Sandford, Dublin
*Irwin, Henry, Esq., M.D., Sligo
Irwin, Henry, Esq., Sligo
*Irwin, Rev. J., Master of the Royal School, and Surrogate of the [diocese of Raphoe, co. Donegal
*Irwin, Colonel John, J.P., Kilkenny
*Irwin, Rev. John, Bara, Enniskillen, co. Fermanagh
*Irwin, John, Esq., Camlin, near Boyle, co. Roscommon
Irwin, John, Esq., Malin, co. Donegal
*Irwin, Rev. John L., Christ's Church College, Oxford, and Kilkenny
Irwin, Jones, Esq., Mackata, Tubbercorry, co. Sligo
*Irwin, Lieut. Joseph, R.N., Soldiers-point, Dundalk, co. Louth
*Irwin, Richard, Esq., Rathmile-house, Frenchpark, co. Roscommon
Irwin, Rev. Thomas, Raphoe, co. Donegal
Irwin, Mr. Thomas, Bottear-house, Moira, co. Down
*Irwin, Major William, Cloncorrick-castle, Carrigallen, co. Leitrim
*Irwin, W. G., Esq., Anagola, Tynan, co. Armagh
*Irwin, William W., Esq., Castle-blayney, co. Monaghan
Isdell, Charles C., Esq., Conlanstown, Ballinacargy, co. Westmeath
Ivatts, Mr. James, Clifton Hotwells, near Bristol
Ivers, Rev. William, R.C.C., Kildorrery, near Fermoy, co. Cork
*Izod, William, Esq., Chapel-Izod-house, Knocktopher, co. Kilkenny

*Jackson, Colonel, J.P., Curramore, Ballina, co. Mayo
Jackson, Clark, Esq., Kilmore, Lurgan, co. Armagh
*Jackson, Rev. David, M.A., Stratton-audley, Oxfordshire
Jackson, David, Esq., Tuam, co. Galway
*Jackson, George Vaughan, Esq., J.P., Christ's College, Cambridge, [and Enniscoe, Crossmolina, co. Mayo
Jackson, Mr. James, Tuam, co. Galway
Jackson, James Eyre, Esq., J.P., Tullydoey, Blackwatertown, co. [Armagh
Jackson, James Kennedy, Esq., Belfast
*Jackson, John, Esq., Cremorne Green, Ballibay, co. Monaghan
*Jackson, John, Esq., Lunatic Asylum, Limerick
Jackson, Rev. John, Rector of Tullow, co. Carlow
Jackson, Rev. John, A.M., Rector of Tallow, co. Waterford
*Jackson, Lloyd, Esq., Tamnamore, Moy, co. Tyrone
*Jackson, Peter, Esq., Lower Gardiner-street, Dublin
*Jackson, P. W., Esq., Fairy-hill, near Bray, co. Wicklow
*Jackson, Richard, Esq., Liscabeck, Clones, co. Monaghan
*Jackson, S. B., Esq., New Inn, London
*Jackson, Thomas, Esq., District Asylum, Armagh
Jackson, Rev. W., A.B., Headford, co. Galway
*Jackson, William, Esq., Red-mills, Ballibay, co. Monaghan
*Jackson, William, Esq., Lower-ormond-quay, Dublin
Jackson, William, Esq., Hermitage, Nenagh, co. Tipperary
Jackson, Mr. William, Ballynona-cottage, Midleton, co. Cork
Jacob, A., Esq., M.D., Willow-lodge, Booterstown, and Ely-place, [Dublin
Jacob, Charles, Esq., Bushville, near Wexford
Jacob, John, Esq., M.D., Maryboro', Queen's county
*Jacob, Matthew, Esq., J.P., Mobarnan, Fethard, co. Tipperary
*Jacob, Rev. Thomas J., Littlewood-glebe, near Carnew, co. Wick- [low
Jagoe, Nicholas B., Esq., Kilronan, Dunmanway, co. Cork
Jago, Robert P., Esq., Kinsale-mills, co. Cork
Jagoe, J. H., Esq., M.D., Ballineen, near Dunmanway, co. Cork
James, James, Esq., Aylesbury, Buckinghamshire
James, Rev. John, Rawmarsh Rectory, Rotheram, Yorkshire
James, Sir J. K., Bart., Treasurer to the Corporation of Dublin
James, William, Esq., Bannow Grammar-school, Scaween-house, [Taghmon, co. Wexford
Jameson, Andrew, Esq., Daphne, near Enniscorthy, co. Wexford
*Jameson, James, Esq., Mount-rose, near Donnybrook, co. Dublin
*Jameson, William, Esq., York-street, Dublin
Jamieson, Mr. William, Warren-place, Cork
*Jandles, James, Esq., at Messrs. Burnetts, Vauxhall, Surrey
*Jebb, The Honorable Judge, Dublin
Jebb, Rev. Ross, Rector of Glenaven, co. Antrim
Jeffares, Mr. Danby, Cornwall, near Killurin, co. Wexford
Jeffares, Rev. Samuel, Vicar of Kilpatrick, Wexford
Jefferyes, St. John, Esq., Cork
*Jeffrey and Barton, Messrs. Bishopsgate-street, London
*Jeffreys, M., Esq., Christ Church College, Oxford, and Barnes, Surrey
Jelly, Rev. Robert B., Portarlington, Queen's county
*Jenings, Benjamin, Esq., Mount-jenings, Hollymount, co. Mayo
*Jenings, Messrs. R. and G., Blessington-street, Dublin
Jenings, Theobald, Esq., Fountain-hill, Kilmain, co. Mayo
*Jenkins, Edward, Esq., J.P., Dundalk, co. Louth
Jenkins, George, Esq., Blarney, Cork
*Jenkins, John, Esq., Slaines, Blarney, near Cork
Jennings, Rev. John, P.P. of Clontuskert, Ballinasloe, co. Galway
Jennings, Ulick, Esq., Ironpool, near Tuam, co. Galway
*Jephson, C. D. O., Esq., M.P., The Castle, Mallow, co. Cork
*Jervis, Sir H. M. J. W., Bart, Belcamp, near Artane, co. Dublin, [and Bally-ellis, co. Wexford
Jervis, Alderman Thomas, Limerick
Jervois, Rev. Joseph, A.M., J.P., Rector of Ardagh, Youghal, co. [Cork
*Jessop, A. P., Esq., Shanderry, Mountrath, Queen's county
*Jessop, Francis, Esq., Mount-Jessop, near Longford
*Jessop, Rev. Robert F., Killglass-glebe, Colehill, co. Longford
Jesus College, Oxford, per the Librarian, Rev. — Reynolds
Jevers, Rev. Colin, A.B., Tartaraghan, Loughall, co. Armagh
Jevers, Cornelius, Esq., Askeaton, co. Limerick
Jevers, Eyre, Esq., Bradagh-cottage, Drumculloher, co. Limerick
Jevers, James, Esq., Glenfield, Kilmallock, co. Limerick
*Jevers, Richard, Esq., Green-park, near Bruff, co. Limerick
*Jevers, Robert W., Castle-jevers, near Bruff, co. Limerick
Jeyner, Joseph Sumpner, Esq., Ballina, co. Mayo
Jogo, Edward, Esq., M.D., Kinsale, co. Cork
John, Thomas, jun., Esq., Youghal, co. Cork
Johnson, Rev. Benjamin Burton, Roseville, Mallow, co. Cork
Johnson, Benjamin, Esq., M.D., Passage West, co. Cork
*Johnson, Charles F., Esq., Capel-street, Dublin, and Tullylost, [Rathangar, co. Kildare
*Johnson, Edward, Esq., J.P., Ballymacash, co. Antrim
Johnson, Edward, Esq., Clash-cottage, near Rathdrum, co. Wicklow
Johnson, Edward, Esq., Enniscorthy, co. Wexford
Johnson, Mr. Francis George, Duntaheen, Fermoy, co. Cork
*Johnson, George, Esq., Richmond-avenue, near Dublin
*Johnson, George, Esq., Wellington, Newcastle, Northumberland
Johnson, Rev. H., Parsonage, Bangor, co. Down
*Johnson, Rev. J., P.P., Glendalough, co. Wicklow
Johnson, James B., Esq., Killeagh, co. Cork
*Johnson, John, Esq., J.P., Thorn-hill, Monaghan
*Johnson, John, Esq., C.C.P., Ballymoney, co. Antrim
Johnson, Mr. John, Pine-hill, Drumbo, co. Down
Johnson, John, Esq., Dree-hill, Moy, co. Tyrone
*Johnson, The Honorable Judge, Dublin
Johnson, Noble, Esq., Rockenham-passage, near Cork
Johnson, Mr. R., Cronebane-mine, near Arklow, co. Wicklow
*Johnson, Robert, Esq., Patna, East Indies
*Johnson, Robert, Esq., Mount-pellier-terrace, Cork
Johnson, S. E., Esq., Fort-anne, Rathkeale, co. Limerick
Johnson, Rev. Walter, P.P. of Knockcommon, Slane, co. Meath
Johnson, William, Esq., Fortfield, Belfast
*Johnson, William Bradford, Esq., Patna, East Indies
Johnston, Rev. A., North Bank, Newbliss, co. Monaghan
Johnston, Archibald, Esq., Middletown, co. Armagh
*Johnston, Arthur, Esq., Carrickbrede-house, near Newry, co. [Armagh
Johnston, Christmas, Esq., Coolafancy, near Tinahely, co. Wicklow
Johnston, Capt. Francis, Brookvale, near Monaghan
*Johnston, Rev. G. H. M'Dowel, Ballywillwill, Castlewellan, co. [Down
*Johnston, Graham, Esq., Dundalk, co. Louth
*Johnston, Rev. H., Mullaboden, near Ballymore-Eustace, co. Dublin
Johnston, Henry, Esq., M.D., Adare, co. Limerick
Johnston, James, Esq., J.P., Woodlands, Stranorlar, co. Donegal
*Johnston, John, jun., Esq., Lurgan, co. Armagh
Johnston, John, Esq., Naveny, Stranorlar, co. Donegal
Johnston, J. B., Esq., Ballykilbeg-house, Downpatrick, co. Down
*Johnston, John F., Esq., Laputa, Ballyshannon, co. Donegal
*Johnston, Joseph, Esq., J.P., Glenaule, Blackwatertown, co. Armagh
*Johnston, Matthew, Esq., Middletown, co. Armagh
Johnston, Peter, Esq., Newtownards, co. Down
Johnston, Peyton, Esq., Drumbawn, near Longford
*Johnston, R., Esq., Mountjoy-square East, Dublin, and Kinlough- [house, Ballyshannon, co. Donegal
*Johnston, Randall W., Esq., J.P., Glynn, near Larne, co. Antrim
*Johnston, Capt. Robert, Brook-hill, Ballyshannon, co. Leitrim
*Johnston, Robert, Esq., Kinlough-house, Bundoran, co. Leitrim
*Johnston, Robert, Esq., Great-charles-street, Dublin
Johnston, Robert, Esq., Cashill, Dunfanaghey, co. Donegal
Johnston, Robert, Esq., Cranagill, Loughall, co. Armagh
Johnston, Mr. Samuel, Belfast
*Johnston, Thomas, Esq., J.P., Fort-Johnston, Glasslough, co. [Monaghan
*Johnston, Thomas, Esq., Rossnaree, Slane, co. Meath
*Johnston, Thomas, Esq., Oak-park, Letterkenny, co. Donegal
*Johnston, William, Esq., Kish, co. Fermanagh

*Johnston, William, Esq., Greenfield, Antrim
Johnston, William, Esq., Downpatrick, co. Down
*Johnston, William, Esq., Lurgan, co. Armagh
*Johnston, William, Esq., Greenfield, near Ballymena, co. Antrim
*Johnston, Rev. W. Henry, Skerries, co. Dublin
*Johnston, W., Esq., Marlborough-street, Dublin
*Johnston, William J., Esq., Mountjoy-square South, Dublin, and Magheremena, co. Fermanagh [co. Tyrone
*Johnston, Morrison, and Co., Messrs., Coalisland, near Dungannon,
*Johnstone, Capt. C., Moatfield-cottage, Little Bray, co. Dublin
*Johnstone, James, Esq., Dromore-lodge, Cootehill, co. Cavan
*Johnstone, John, Esq., Francis-street, Dublin
*Johnstone, John D., Esq., Snow-hill, Lisnaskea, co. Fermanagh
*Johnstone, J. W., Esq., Portarlington, Queen's county
Joly, Rev. Henry Edward, Clonbulloge, King's county
*Jones, Arthur, Esq., Lower Dominick-street, Dublin
*Jones, Arthur, Esq., J.P., Killincarrick-house, near Delgany, co.
*Jones, Booth, Esq., Streeda, near Sligo [Wicklow
*Jones, Capt. Charles, J.P., Russian, Enniskillen, co. Fermanagh
*Jones, D., Esq., Janeville, near Wexford
*Jones, Edward, Esq., Upper Gloucester-street, Dublin
Jones, Rev. Francis, A.M., Midleton-glebe, co. Cork
*Jones, George Charles, Esq., Malahide, co. Dublin
Jones, Rev. Harry, A.B., Lisgoold-glebe, Midleton, co. Cork
Jones, Henry H., Esq., Ballybrennan, co. Wexford
*Jones, Humphreys, Esq., Cameron-lodge, near Coolock, co. Dublin
Jones, J., Esq., Ystrad, near Carmarthen
*Jones, James, Esq., Tibradon, near Whitechurch, co. Dublin
*Jones, James, Esq., Lower-Newcastle, co. Wicklow
Jones, James, Esq., Mount-Ruby, Mallow, co. Cork
Jones, Lieut. James, R.N., Bennetstown, near Broadway, co. Wexford
*Jones, Jeremy, Esq., J.P., Sea-mount, Sligo
*Jones, John, Esq., Rockley-lodge, Sligo
*Jones, Mr. John, Campsey, Faughanvale, co. Derry
Jones, John Gore, Esq., J.P., Castle, Dublin
*Jones, John Hawtrey, Esq., J.P., Mullinabro, near Waterford
*Jones, John, Esq., Peter-street, Dublin
Jones, Rev. Jonas Travers, Dromley, Rosscarbery, co. Cork
Jones, John Joseph, Esq., Clino-cottage, Limerick
*Jones, Rev. Joseph, M.A., Ashfort-house, Limerick
Jones, Lewis, Esq., Donnybrook, Douglas, near Cork
*Jones, Capt. Michael, Lisgoole-abbey, Enniskillen, co. Fermanagh
*Jones, P., Esq., Nutgrove-school, near Rathfarnham, co. Dublin
*Jones, Robert, Esq., Ardnaree-cottage, Ballina, co. Mayo
*Jones, Robert, Esq., Dorrington-house, near Athlone, co. Westmeath
*Jones, Robert, Esq., J.P., Fortland, Dromore West, co. Sligo
Jones, Rev. S., A.M., Prebendary and Rector of Ardcanny, Pallaskenry, co. Limerick
*Jones, Rev. Thomas, Rector of Hempstead, near Gloucester
*Jones, Rev. Thomas, Drumliffin-glebe, Carrick-on-Shannon, co.
*Jones, Thomas, jun., Esq., Stapleton, near Bristol [Leitrim
*Jones, Thomas, Esq., Ardnaree, Ballina, co. Mayo
Jones, Rev. Travers, A.M., the Rectory, Ballinasloe, co. Galway
*Jones, Vaughan, Esq., Donahantra, Dromore West, co. Sligo
Jones, Walter, Esq., Harcourt-street, Dublin
Jones, William, Esq., Kilkenny
Jones, William, Esq., Sweet-farm, near Enniscorthy, co. Wexford
*Jordan, Christopher, Esq., Drogheda
*Jordan, R., Esq., Rich-view, Monkstown, co. Dublin
*Jourdain, W. C., Esq., Artillery-place, Finsbury-square, London
*Journeaux, F., Esq., Mount-shannon-mills, Golden-bridge, co. [Dublin
*Joy, The Right Honorable Henry, Lord Chief Baron, Exchequer [of Ireland
*Joy, G., Esq., J.P., Galgorm-castle, Ballymena, co. Antrim
Joy, Henry, Esq., Belfast
Joyce, Capt. D., Limerick [co. Galway
Joyce, James, Esq., C.C.P., Mount-Bellew-bridge, Castle-Blakeney,
Joyce, John, Esq., J.P., Enniskillen, co. Fermanagh
*Joyce, Patrick, Esq., Galway
*Joyce, Patrick James, Esq., Caltra-lodge, Castle-Blakeney, co. Galway
*Joyce, Walter, Esq., Corgorry-house, Castle-Blakeney, co. Galway
*Joyce, William, Esq., Athlone, co. Westmeath
Joyes, Stephen J., Esq., Castlebar, co. Mayo
*Judge, Arthur, Esq., Wicklow
Julian, Christopher, Esq., J.P., Tullamore-house, Listowel, co.
Justice, Thomas H., Esq., M.D., Mallow, co. Cork [Kerry

Kainan, Rev. Matthias, P.P., Laracor, Summerhill co. Meath
*Kane, Daniel R., Esq., Upper Fitzwilliam-street, Dublin
*Kane, John, Esq., Baggot-street, Dublin
Kane, John, Esq., Turf-lodge, Belfast
*Kane, Richard, Esq., Glentworth-street, Limerick
*Kane, R. D., Esq., Molesworth-street, Dublin, and White-hall, co.
Kavanagh, George, Esq., M.D., New Ross, co. Wexford [Limerick
Kavanagh, Rev. J., R.C.C., Ballymore, nr. Broadway, co. Wexford
*Kavanagh, T., Esq., J.P., Borris-house, co. Carlow
Kean, William, Esq., Hermitage, Ennis, co. Clare
Keane, James, Esq., Combermere-cottage, and Grand Parade, Cork
*Keane, John B., Esq., Mabbot-street, Dublin
*Keane, Robert, Esq., J.P., Beechpark, Ennis, co. Clare
*Keane, Thomas I., Esq., Shanagary-house, Cloyne, co. Cork
Keane, Rev. William, P.P., Bansha, near Tipperary
Kearney, Rev. Henry, P.P., Faughard, Mountpleasant-cottage, [Dundalk, co. Louth
*Kearney, Rev. Dr. H., Kilterman-glebe, co. Dublin
*Kearney, H., Esq., Belleview, Williamstown, co. Dublin
Kearney, James, Esq., Dungarvan, co. Waterford
*Kearney, Hickman, Esq., Williamstown, co. Dublin
*Kearney, Major Gen. Sir James, K.C.H., Merrion-square, Dublin, [and Blanch-ville, co. Kilkenny
*Kearney, Rev. J., P.P. of Kilkenny-west, Athlone, co. Westmeath
*Kearney, Rev. John, Chancellor of the Diocese of Ossory, Bamfort, [co. Kilkenny
Kearney, John, Esq., Miltown-house, Crossakeel, co. Meath
Kearney, Mr., Tramore, co. Waterford
*Kearney, Rev. P., R.C.C., Newbridge, near Arklow, co. Wicklow
Kearney, Patrick, Esq., Lake-view, Blackrock, Cork
Kearney, Patrick, Esq., Birmingham-cottage, Tuam, co. Galway
*Kearney Thomas, Esq., J.P., Ballinakill, co. Kildare
*Kearney Rev. P., P.P. of Cooly, Monkland, Carlingford, co. Louth
Kearny, Thomas Cuthbert, Esq., J.P., Garrettstown, nr. Kinsale, co.
Keating, Bryan, Esq., Lismore, co. Waterford [Cork
Keating, Rev. Geo., Glebe-house, Edgeworths-town, co. Longford
*Keating, Capt. Henry, Crover, Mount-Nugent, co. Cavan
*Keating, The Right Rev. James, D.D., R. C. Bishop of Ferns
Keating, Leonard, Esq., Garranler, Cashel, co. Tipperary
Keatinge, John, Esq., Springmount, near Clonmel, co. Tipperary
Keays, Messrs. Samuel and Sons, Cork
*Keck, Samuel, Esq., Maghera, co. Derry
*Keenan, The Very Rev. John S., D.D., President of Dromore [Seminary, Newry, co. Down
*Keene, James, Esq., Academy-street, Cork, and Green-hill, near [Passage, co. Cork
*Keher, Rev. Bartholomew H., P.P. of Athleague, co. Roscommon
Kehoe, Rev. Jeremiah, R.C.C., Bagnalstown, co. Carlow
Kehoe, P., Esq., M.D., Cork
Keightley, William S., Esq., Springfield, Stradbally, Queen's-county
*Keily, Arthur, Esq., Ballysaggartmore, near Lismore, co. Waterford
*Keily, John, Esq., Baymount-house, Clontarf, co. Dublin
*Keily, John, Esq., J.P., Strancally-castle, Tallow, co, Waterford
Keily, John, Esq., Limerick
Keily, Rev. M., P.P. of Castletown, Kilmeady, and Drumcolloher, [Feenah Cottage, Newcastle, co. Limerick
Keily, Thomas Edward, Esq., Springmount, near Dungarvan, co.
*Keily, Wm. Henry, Esq., Clifton, Cork [Waterford
Keiran, Rev. Michael, R.C.C., Drogheda, co. Louth
Kelehero, Rev. John, R.C.C., Kilmurry, Crookstown, co. Cork
Kelleher, Rev. John O'Connell, R.C.C., Glauntane, near Mallow,
Keller, Daniel, Esq., Tuligmore, Ballinhassig, co. Cork [co. Cork
Kellett, Lieut. Arthur, R.N., Wexford
*Kellett, Edward, Esq., Westland-cottage, Moynalty, co. Meath
*Kellett, Rev. John, Rector of Agher, Summerhill, co. Meath
*Kellett, Richard, Esq., Blessington-street, Dublin
*Kellett, Robert, Esq., Waterstown, Moynalty, co. Meath
Kellett, Wm. Henry, Esq., Great-clonard, near Wexford
Kelly, A., Esq., Camphill, Collooney, co. Sligo
Kelly, Arthur Irwin, Esq., J.P., Armagh
*Kelly, Mr.
Kelly, Mr. B., Wood-quay, Dublin
*Kelly, Burrowes, Esq., Stradbally, Queen's-county
*Kelly, D. B., Esq., Johnstown-house, near Athlone, co. Roscommon
*Kelly, Dr. Dillon, Moate, co. Westmeath
*Kelly, Edmund W., Esq., J.P., Ballymurry, near Roscommon
Kelly, Rev. Edward, R.C.C., Buncrana, co. Donegal
Kelly, Edward, Esq., Sligo
Kelly, Edward, Esq., Killeen, Portumna, co. Galway
*Kelly, Rev. George, curate of St. Mary's, Dublin
Kelly, Rev. H., P. P. Kilkeran and Clonbern, Mylough, co. Galway
*Kelly, Hugh, Esq., Woodmount, (near Ballinasloe) co. Roscommon
*Kelly, James, Esq., Newtown, Dangan, co. Galway

Kelly, James, Esq., Tuam, co. Galway
*Kelly, James D., Esq., Athlone, co. Westmeath
*Kelly, J. H., Esq., Glencarry, Ballinacargy, co. Westmeath
*Kelly, Capt. John S., Ballaghadinea, co. Mayo
Kelly, James, Esq., Ballinanty, Bruff, co. Limerick
*Kelly, John W., Esq., Tully-house, near Drumsna, co. Roscommon
Kelly, Mr. John, Portarlington, Queen's county
Kelly, John, Esq., Roscommon
*Kelly, John, Esq., J.P., Caltra-house, Castle-Blakeney, co. Galway
*Kelly, John, Esq., Ballybane, Ahascragh, co. Galway
*Kelly, Joseph, Esq., Henrietta-street, Dublin
*Kelly, Joseph, Esq., Westport, co. Mayo
*Kelly, Rev. Joseph, R.C.C. of St. Paul's, Queen-street, Dublin
*Kelly, Laurence, Esq., Seneschalston, Slane, co. Meath
Kelly, Mark, Esq., Templemacateer, Kilbeggan, co. Westmeath
Kelly, Rev. Michael, P.P. of Kilcommon, Belmullet, co. Mayo
Kelly, Matthew, Esq., Kilrush, co. Clare
*Kelly Michael N., Esq., River-view, near Rathfarnham, co. Dublin
*Kelly, Rev. M. B., R.C.C., Rathfarnham, co. Dublin
*Kelly, Nicholas, Esq., J.P., Carrickmacross, co. Monaghan
Kelly, Patrick, Esq., Midfield-house, near Swinford, co. Mayo
*Kelly, Rev. Patrick, P.P. of Lusk, co. Dublin
Kelly, Rev. Patrick, P.P. of Eyrecourt, co. Galway
Kelly, Patrick, Esq., Tuam, co. Galway
Kelly, Rev. Patrick, R.C.C., Kilskyre, Crossakeel, co. Meath
Kelly, Lieut.-col. R., York-crescent, Clifton, near Bristol
Kelly, Richard, Esq., Dundermott, near Ballymoe, co. Roscommon
*Kelly, R. H., Esq., Eccles-street, Dublin
Kelly, Major S. D., Longford-lodge, near Eyrecourt, co. Galway
Kelly, Mr. Thomas, Eyrecourt, co. Galway
Kelly, Thomas, Esq., Drogheda, co. Louth
Kelly, Thomas B., Esq., Kellyville, Stradbally, Queen's county
Kelly, Thomas, Esq., Capel-street, Dublin
*Kelly, Tobias Joseph, Esq., Clondoyle, Dunmore, co. Galway
*Kelly, Capt. W., Cloncannon, Ahascragh, co. Galway
*Kelly, W. J., Esq., Kelly's grove, Ballinasloe, co. Galway
Kelly, Walter, Esq., Eskar, Faughmaconnell, co. Roscommon
Kelly, William, Esq., Maddenstown-house, Kildare
*Kelly, W. Bennett, Esq., Georges-street, Limerick
*Kelly, Messrs. James and Son, Lower Dominick-street, Dublin
Kelsey, John, Esq., Drumbridge, Lisburn, co. Antrim
Kelso, John J., Esq., M.D., Lisburn, co. Antrim
Kemmis, Rev. G., Vicar of Rosinallis, Mountmellick, Queen's co.
Kemmis, Henry, Esq., Merrion-square East, Dublin
Kemmis, Joshua, Esq., J.P., Knightstown, Emo, Queen's county
Kemmis, Thomas, Esq., Shane Castle, near Emo, Queen's county
*Kemmis, W., jun., Esq., Ballinacor, near Rathdrum co. Wicklow
Kemp, James, C. Esq., Mount-pleasant, Dysart, co. Derry
*Kempston, John, Esq., Clonmel, co. Tipperary
*Kempston, N., Esq., Connerce Mines, nr. Rathdrum, co. Wicklow
Kempston, Mr. Robert, Lower Sackville-street, Dublin
Kempthorn, Lieut. C. H., R.N., Mill-cove, Rosscarbery, co. Cork
Kenah, Thomas Webb, Esq., Youghal, co. Cork
*KENMARE, The Right Honorable the Earl of
*Kennan, George, Esq., Newtown-cottage, Enniskerry, co. Wicklow
*Kennedy, C. E., Esq., Peamount, near Rathcoole, co. Dublin
*Kennedy, Edward, Esq., Cabinteely, co. Dublin
Kennedy, Edward, Esq., Cloghjordan, co. Tipperary
Kennedy, Evory, Esq., M.D., Lying-in-hospital, Dublin
*Kennedy, Francis, Esq., Coppa-lodge, Kilrush, co. Clare
Kennedy, Francis, Esq., Ballinamultina, Clashmore, co. Waterford
*Kennedy, Rev. J., D.D., Ardtrea-house, Stewartstown, co. Tyrone
*Kennedy, Rev. Joseph, P.P., Ardbraccan, Navan, co. Meath
*Kennedy, Rev. P., P.P., Birr, King's-county
Kennedy, William, Esq., Glanahelty-castle, Nenagh, co. Tipperary
*Kennett, Capt. Charles L., Portglenone, co. Antrim
Kenney, Rev. Edward Herbert, J.P., Kilmeen-glebe, co. Cork
*Kenney, N. W., Esq., Rocksavage, Carrickmacross, co. Monaghan
Kenny, Courtney, Esq., J.P., Riverbank, Ballinrobe, co. Mayo.
*Kenny, Edward, Esq., Roe-house, Ennis, co. Clare
Kenny, James, Esq., Merrion-square, Dublin
*Kenny, Rev. John, V.G. and P.P. of Kilrush, co. Clare
Kenny, Joseph, Esq., Clonmel, co. Tipperary
Kenny, Martin, Esq., Elm-villa, Serpentine-avenue, co. Dublin
*Kenny, Richard, Esq., Limerick
*Kenny, Rev. Terence, R.C.C., Ballyrush, Boyle, co. Sligo
*Kenny, Thomas Lee, Esq., Belin, Monasterevan, co. Kildare
Kent, Bamlet, Esq., Curragh, Ballymartle, co. Cork
Kent, Benjamin Archer, Esq., M.D., Walsall, Staffordshire
*Kent, Rev. Edward, A.M., Glebe-house, Lurgan, co. Armagh
Kenyon, W. Smith, Esq., Ballina, co. Mayo

*Keogh, Rev. E., P.P. of Kilmore, near Drumsna, co. Roscommon
*Keoghoe, Capt. Thomas, Ballinclare, near Rathdrum, co. Wicklow
Keoughy, John, Esq., Galway
Keowen, Mrs. J., Tollymore, near Newcastle, co. Down
Keown, John, Esq., Corrogs, Castlewellan, co. Down
Kepple, Rev. John, R.C.C., Grenogh, near Cork
*Ker, Andrew, Esq., M.D. & J.P., Newbliss-house, co. Monaghan
*Ker, Lieut.-Col. J., J.P., Mountain-lodge, Cootehill, co. Cavan
Ker, W., Esq., Liverpool
Ker, William, Esq., Covent-garden, London
Kerans, L. C., Esq., M.D., Ahascragh, co. Galway
Kerin, Rev. John, M.A., Hillsborough, Tralee, co. Kerry
*Kerman, R., Esq., Blessington-street, Dublin
*Kernan, Right Rev. Edward, D.D., R.C. Bishop of Clogher
*Kernan, J. B., Esq., J.P., Cabragh-lodge, Carrickmacross, co. [Monaghan
*Kernan, Randall, Esq., Enniskillen, co. Fermanagh
KERR, The Right Honorable Lord Mark
*Kerr, Rev. John, Rector of Termonfechin, nr. Drogheda, co. Louth
*Kerr, Mark, Esq., Tokay-lodge, near Dublin
*Kerry County Club, Tralee, co. Kerry
*Kershaw, John, sen., Esq., Hurst, Glossop, Derbyshire
Kettlewell, Evans, Esq., Thomastown, Duleek, co. Meath
*Kettlewell, Capt. Thomas, Rich-view, near Bray, co. Wicklow
*Kidd, James Alexander, Esq., Greenmount, Keady, co. Armagh
Kidd, John, Esq., Grafton-street, Dublin
*Kidd, Joseph, Esq., Armagh
Kidd, Josiah, Esq., Keady, co. Armagh
*Kidd, Samuel, Esq., Dundrum, Keady, co. Armagh
*Kidd, Messrs. Thomas and Osborne, Armagh
*Kieran, A., Esq., Legga, Nobber, co. Meath
*Kieran, Lawrence, Esq., Collon, co. Louth
*Kieran, Owen, Esq., Rabrist, near Louth
*Kiernan, Francis, Esq., St. Andrew's-street, Dublin
*Kiernan, Rev. Patrick, Skryne, Dunshaughlin, co. Meath
*Kilbee, Henry T., Esq., J.P., Bingfield, Crossdoney, co. Cavan
Kilbee, James, Esq., Mine-view, near Arklow, co. Wicklow
Kilbee, William, Esq., Canny-court, Kilcullen, co. Kildare
Kilfenora, The Very Rev. the Dean of, Deanery, Ennistymon, co. [Clare
*Killaloe, Clonfert, &c., The Right Rev. Lord Bishop of
KILLEEN, The Right Hon. Viscount
Killeen, Rev. Austin, Augustinian Convent, Galway
Killeen, Edward, Esq., Galway
*Killeen, Martin, Esq., Banagher, King's county
Killikelly, Hubert, Esq., Derrywillan, Loughrea, co. Galway
Killikelly, Capt. Michael, Youghal, co. Cork
*KILMORE, The Right Rev. Lord Bishop of
*Kilpatrick, William, Esq., Dundalk, co. Louth
Kilroe, Rev. K., P.P., St. Mary's, Athlone, co. Westmeath
Kimberley, G., Esq., Emscote-lodge, near Warwick
*Kinahan, George, Esq., Roebuck-park, co. Dublin
Kinahan, Rev. John, Knock-Breda Rectory, Belfast
*Kincaid, Messrs. D. and R., Ballyholly, Letterkenny, co. Donegal
Kincaid, Rev. John, P.C. of Rossnowlagh, co. Donegal
*Kinchant, R. H., Esq., St. Leonard's near Wendover, Bucks.
*King, Arthur, Esq., Donaghmede, near Coolock, co. Dublin
King, Mr. Bryan, Bigfurze, Termonfeckan, co. Louth
*King, Sir Gilbert, Bart., Charlestown, Drumsna, co. Roscommon
*King, Rev. Gilbert, J.P., Rector of Lower Longfield, co. Tyrone
King, Rev. H., Ballylin, Ferbane, King's-county
King, Henry, Esq., J.P., Castle Caulfield, Dungannon, co. Tyrone
*King, the Hon. James, Mitchelstown-castle, co. Cork
King, James, Esq., Donaghmore, Dungannon, co. Tyrone
King, John, Esq., Donegal
King, Mr. Michael, Tuam, co. Galway
*King, Rev. R., Woodville, Barony of Forth, co. Wexford
*King, Rev. Richard, Woodville, co. Wexford
*King, Hon. Robert, J.P., Craig, Sligo
*King, Samuel, Esq., Mount-Pleasant, near Waterford
*King, Rev. Samuel, Rector of Latimers, near Chesham, Bucks
King, Rev. Thomas, P.P. of Aughrim, near Elphin, co. Roscommon
King, Thomas Mills, Esq., J.P., Kingston, near Rathdrum, co. Wicklow
*King, W., Esq., Trimra, Letterkenny, co. Donegal
King, Lieut. W. H., R.N., Baltinglass, co. Wicklow
Kinkead, Rev. Francis, A.M., Athenry, co. Galway
*King's College Library, Cambridge, per Rev. George Thackeray, [D.D., F.L.S.
*KINGSALE, The Right Hon. Lord
*KINGSBOROUGH, The Right Honorable Viscount
*KINGSLAND, The Right Honorable Viscount
Kingsmill, Sir John, Knt., Merrion-square, Dublin
Kingsmore, Rev. R., Tullaghniskin-glebe, Duncannon, co. Tyrone
*KINGSTON, The Right Honorable the Earl of

*Kingston, Arthur Johnston, Esq., Mosstown, Longford
Kingston, John Young, Esq., Bantry, co. Cork
Kingston, Mr. Paul, Bantry, co. Cork
Kingston, W. H., Esq., Bandon, co. Cork
*Kington, Thomas, Esq., Bristol
*Kinsela, The Very Rev. William, Aungier-street, Dublin
*Kinsella, Rev. James, P.P., Killeigh, Tullamoore, King's-county
*Kinsella, The Right Rev. William, D.D., R.C., Bishop of Ossory
Kinsella, Rev. William, P.P., Rathrush, Tullow, co. Carlow
*Kinsella, Rev. W. J., Clarendon-street, Dublin
Kinsey, H., Esq., Green-lanes, Clontarf, co. Dublin
*Kinsey, Richard, Esq., Green-lanes, Clontarf, co. Dublin
Kirby, John, Esq., LL.D., M.D., Harcourt-street, Dublin
Kirby, John, Esq., Limerick
Kirby, Rev. John, P.P., St. Catherine's, Ennistymon, co. Clare
Kirby, Rev. John, P.P. of Ballintubber and Boncarra, Ballyglass, [co. Mayo
*Kirby, Nicholas, Esq., Carhue, near Cork
*Kirby, Richard, Esq. Carhue, Inniscarra, Cork
Kirby, Wm., Esq., J.P., Park, Fermoy, co. Cork
Kirchhoffer, Rev. R., J.P., Clondrohid-glebe, Macroom, co. Cork
Kirchoffer, Rev. Richard W., A.M., Ballincollig, co. Cork
Kirk, D., Esq., Moorefield, co. Antrim
Kirk, Daniel, Esq., Tannybrake-house, near Ballymena, co. Antrim
*Kirk, J. J., Esq., Wood-park, Rochestown-avenue, near Killiney, [co. Dublin
Kirk, Mr. Patrick, Drogheda, co. Louth
*Kirk, Thomas, Esq., M.D., Kingstown, co. Dublin
Kirk, William, Esq., Arunvale, Keady, co. Armagh
*Kirkaldy, Alexander, Esq., Monk-Wearmouth, Durham
Kirkaldy, G. D. H., Esq., J.P., Hearnsbrook, Portumna, co. Galway
*Kirkpatrick, A., Esq., Coolmine-house, near Castleknock, co. Dublin
Kirkpatrick, Rev. Geo., Ahoghill-glebe, Ballymena, co. Antrim
Kirkpatrick, Mr. James, Kildrum, Killea, co. Donegal
*Kirkpatrick, James, Esq., Enniskillen, co. Fermanagh
Kirkpatrick, Mr. John, Waterside, Londonderry
Kirkpatrick, Thomas, Esq., M.D., Larne, co. Antrim
*Kirkpatrick, Rev. William B., Mary's Abbey, Dublin
Kirkwood, Joseph, Esq., Killala, co. Mayo
*Kirkwood, S., Esq., Cottlestown, Ballina, co. Mayo
*Kirkwood, T., Esq., J.P., Lakeview, co. Roscommon
Kirkwood, Thomas, Esq., M.D., Rathfarnham, co. Dublin
Kirkwood, Thomas, Esq., The Lodge, Killala, co. Mayo
*Kirkwood and M'Cune, Messrs., Glass-works, Newry, co. Down
Kirsopp, John, Esq., Hexham, Northumberland
Kirwan, Rev. A. L., A.B., Pallaskenry, co. Limerick
Kirwan, Andrew, Esq., Waterford
*Kirwan, Capt. E. S., Hume-street, Dublin
*Kirwan, Major John, J.P., Castle Hackett, Tuam, co Galway
Kirwan, John A., Esq., J.P., Hillsbrook, Dangan, co. Galway
*Kirwan, Rev. Joseph, D.D., P.P., Oughterard, co. Galway
Kirwan, Martin, Esq., Bantry, co. Cork
Kirwan, Martin Staunton, Esq., J.P., Blindwell, co. Galway
Kirwan, Patrick, Esq., Thurles, co. Tipperary
*Kirwan, Rev. Peter, P.P., Mount-Talbot, co. Roscommon
*Kirwan, Rev. W., P.P., Bohirlahan, Cashel, co. Tipperary
*Kirwan, William, Esq., Well-park, Drumcondra, co. Dublin
Kittyle, Mr. Maxwell, Letterkenny, co. Donegal
*Knight, James J., Esq., Green-cottage, Clones, co. Monaghan
*Knipe, Geo. M., Esq., J.P., Erne-hill, Belturbet, co. Cavan
*Knipe, John, Esq., Spring-hill, Burros-in-Ossory, Queen's-county
*Knolles, Capt. Thomas, Oatlands, near Kinsale, co. Cork
*Knott, Edward, Esq., M.D., Sligo
Knott, Edward, Esq., Atville, Boyle, co. Roscommon
*Knott, James, Esq., Battlefield, do.
Knowles, James, Esq., Dundalk, co. Louth
Knowles, William, Esq., Clifton, near Bristol
Knowlton, Thomas B., Esq., Darley Dale, Derbyshire
*Knox, Annesley, Esq., J.P., Rappa Castle, near Ballina, co. Mayo
*Knox, Annesley, Esq., J.P., Bushfield, Hollymount, co. Mayo
Knox, Annesley, Esq., Ballina, co. Mayo
*Knox, Charles James, Esq., Cranaghmore, Coleraine, co. Derry
*Knox, Charles Nesbitt, Esq., J.P., Castle Lacken, co. Mayo
*Knox, Rev. Edmond, Archdeacon of Killaloe, Lorrha-glebe, Bor- [risokane, co. Tipperary
Knox, Rev. E. D. H., Kilfyn Rectory, Kilfinane, Kilmallock, co. [Limerick
*Knox, George, Esq., Lifford, co. Donegal
Knox, Rev. George, Donamon Castle, near Roscommon
Knox, George, Esq., Belle-vue, Enniskillen, co. Fermanagh
*Knox, Rev. G. N., Rector of Termonamongan, co. Donegal
*Knox, H., Esq., Trinity Coll., Cambridge, and Netly-park, co. Mayo
*Knox, Henry W. Esq., J.P., Netley-park, Ballina, co, Mayo
*Knox, Capt. John, Greenwood-park, Crossmolina, co. Mayo
Knox, John, Esq., J.P., Castle Rea, Killala, co. Mayo
Knox, John, Esq., Rushbrook, co. Derry
*Knox, Lieut. John Chichester (Queen's Bays), Gort, co. Galway
*Knox, John F., Esq., J.P., Mount-Falcon, Ballina, co. Mayo
*Knox, Rev. J. S., J.P., Maghera, co. Derry
*Knox, Nathaniel Alexander, Esq., Agivey, Coleraine, co. Derry
*Knox, Samuel Wright, Esq., Coleraine, co. Derry
*Knox, The Honorable Thomas
*Knox, Rev. Thomas, Toomavara, Nenagh, co. Tipperary
*Knox, Thomas, Esq., Stone-hall, Crossmolina, co. Mayo
Knox, Rev. W., J.P., Rector of Clonleigh, Lifford, co. Donegal
*Knox, Walter T., Esq., Caledon, co. Tyrone
*Knudson, St. George, Esq., Glendarragh, co. Wicklow
Kough, Edward, Esq., New Ross, co. Wexford
*Kyd, Mr. William, Dungiven, co. Derry
*Kyle, Mr. Arthur, Dungiven, co. Derry
*Kyle, C., Esq., Londonderry
*Kyle, Henry, Esq., Laurel-hill, Coleraine, co. Derry
Kyle, The Very Rev. S. M., LL.D., Archdeacon of Cork
*Kyle, W. Cotter, Esq., Gardiner's-place, Dublin

*Labarte, Edward, Esq., Clonmel, co. Tipperary
*Lacey, Patrick, Esq., Inchicore, near Dublin
Laffan, Rev. Michael, P.P. of Fethard, co. Tipperary
*Laffan, Thomas J., Esq., Holles-street, Dublin
*Laffan, Timothy, Esq., Whitehall, near Rathfarnham, co. Dublin
La Grange, C., Esq., Riversdale, near Little Bray, co. Dublin
Lahey, Thomas, Esq., Middle Gardiner-street, Dublin
Lahiff, Capt. Thomas, Russan, Gort, co. Galway
*Laing, Joseph, Esq., North Shields, Northumberland
Laird, John G., Esq., Ballybofey, co. Donegal
*LAKE, The Right Honorable Lord
*Lalor, Rev. Daniel, P.P. of Baltinglass, co. Wicklow
*Lalor, John, Esq., Gurteen, Parsonstown, King's county
Lalor, Richard, Esq., Cascade, Freshford, Kilkenny
*Lamb, G. A., Esq., J.P., East-hill, Newtown-Mount-Kennedy, co. [Wicklow
*Lambert, A. C., Esq., J.P., Ballinrobe, co. Mayo
*Lambert, H., Esq., Carnagh, New Ross, co. Wexford
*Lambert, John, Esq., Upper Buckingham-street, Dublin
*Lambert, John, Esq., Edmonstown, near Rathfarnham, co. Dublin
*Lambert, Joseph, Esq., J.P., Brookhill, Claremorris, co. Mayo
*Lambert, J. S., Esq., J.P., Cregclare, near Ardrahan, co. Galway
Lambert, Peter, Esq., J.P., Castle Ellen, Athenry, co. Galway
*Lambert, Richard, Esq., York-street, Dublin, and Woodville, near [Granard, co. Longford
*Lambert, Walter, Esq., Castle Lambert, Athenry, co. Galway
Lambert, William, Esq., Fish-street, Cork
Lamprey, Rev. G. W., Ballintemple-glebe, Arklow, co. Wicklow
*Lanauze, Daniel, Esq., Larne, co. Antrim
Lander, Robert, Esq., Kinsale, co. Cork
Landles, James, Esq., Messrs., Burnett's, Vauxhall, London
Lane, Abraham, Esq., Devonshire-square, Bandon, co. Cork
Lane, Ambrose, Esq., Clonmel, co. Tipperary
Lane, E. D., Esq., Ballynock-cottage, Youghal, co. Cork
Lane, Henry, Esq., Air-mount, Tramore, co. Waterford
Lane, Hugh, Esq., Newtown-Limavady, co. Derry
*Lane, James, Esq., Riverstown-lodge, co. Cork
Lane, Rev. J. L., Rector of Withington, Gloucestershire
*Lane, James S., Esq., Shipton, Callan, Kilkenny
Lane, John, Esq., Rock-hill, Kinsale, co. Cork
Lane, Rev. M., P.P., Ballyvourney, Macroom, co. Cork
*Lane, Mr. Maurice, Cnockanmore, near Cork
*Lane, Rev. Michael, R.C.C., Aghabologue, Magourney, co. Cork
Lane, Samuel, Esq., Frankfield, co. Cork
Lane, Mr. Thomas, Coolebanagh, Clonaslee, Queen's county
*Lane, W., Esq., Rose-hill, Douglas, near Cork
*Lane, W., Esq., Newtown-Limavady, co. Derry
*Langan, Rev. John, P.P., Ardcath, Duleek, co. Meath
*Langan, Patrick, Esq., Butteramstown, Duleek, co. Meath
Langan, Richard, Esq., Cruiserath, near Mullihuddart, co. Dublin
*Langdon, A., Esq., F.A.S., York-terrace, Regent's-park, London
Langford, E., Esq., J.P., Stone-hall, Pallaskenry, co. Limerick
Langford, Rev. F., M.A., Castletown, Pallaskenry, co. Limerick
*Langford, Rev. Fras., Morristown Biller, Newbridge, co. Kildare
Langford, George, Esq., Kenmare, co. Kerry
Langford, G. W., Esq., M.D., Askeaton, co. Limerick
Langford, J. E. Esq., J.P., Cartown, Pallaskenry, co. Limerick
Langford, James, Esq., Ballyellis, Mallow, co. Cork
*Langley, Henry, Esq., Coal Brook, New Birmingham, co. Tiperary
*Langley, John, Esq., Coal Brook, New Birmingham, co. Tipperary

Langley, Rev. P., Vicar of Ballymore Eustace, South Cumberland-[street, Dublin
*Langrishe, Rev. Hercules, A.B., Rector and Vicar of Ballybay, co. [Monaghan
*Langtry, George, Esq., Fort William, Belfast
Langtry, George, Esq., Bellview, Richill, co. Armagh
Lanigan, John, Esq., Richmond, Templemore, co. Tipperary
Lanphier, J. P., Esq., Parkstown, Littleton, co. Tipperary
*Lanphier, Capt. S., Ballyfermot-castle, co. Dublin
Lanphier, Vernon, Esq., Laurel-lodge, Littleton, co. Tipperary
Lapham, J. D., Esq., Waterford
*Laphen, Rev. J. T., C.C., Marlboro'-street, Dublin
Laracy, Rev. Richard, P.P., Freshford, Kilkenny
Large, John, Esq., Westport, co. Mayo
*Larkin, Mr. Denis, Loughrea, co. Galway
*Larkin, Mr. Henry, Kilmore-lands, near Artaine, co. Dublin
Larkin, Rev. James, P.P., Pastorville, Newcastle, co. Tipperary
Larkin, P., Esq., Old Orchard, Rathfarnham, & Thomas-st., Dublin
*Larkin, Rev. Patrick, C.C., Thurles, co. Tipperary
Larminie, Charles, Esq., Westport, co. Mayo
Larminie, John Charles, Esq., Rocklands, Castlebar, co. Mayo
Laron, Samuel, Esq., Frankfield, Cork
Lascelles, The Hon. Arthur, Ribston-hall, Wetherby, Yorkshire
Lascelles, Rev. F. E., J.P., Vicar of St. Andrews, Kircubbin, co. [Down
*Lascelles, Francis, Esq., Newry, co. Down
Latham, W., Esq., M.D., Antrim
*La Touche, David, Esq., Luggelaw, co. Wicklow
La Touche, P., Esq., Corpus Christi College, Oxford
*La Touche, Mrs. Peter, Bellview, near Delgany, co. Wicklow
*Latouche, Messrs. and Co., Dublin
*Latouche, John David, Esq.
*Latouche, Robert, Esq.
*Latouche and Co., Messrs. John David
*Lauder, Robert, Esq., J.P., Moyclare, Farbane, King's-county
Laurie, A, Esq., C.C.P., Tully-cottage, Ballinasloe, co. Galway
Lavelle, Rev. E., P.P. of Kilglass, Dromore West, co. Sligo.
*Lavens, James, Esq., Milford, Ramelton, co. Donegal
Law, John, Esq., Woodlawn, Castlewellan, co. Down
*Law, Michael, Esq., Cottage, near Coolock, co. Dublin
*Lawder, W., Esq., Mough, Ballinamore, co. Leitrim
*Lawe, Robert, Esq., Lawciston, near Glanmire, co. Cork
Lawes, W., Esq., Prudhue Castle, Northumberland
*Lawford, Edward, Esq., Draper's-hall, London
Lawler, Rev. John, Glebe-house, Clonard, co. Meath
Lawler, Mr. Thomas, Mabbott-street, Dublin
Lawless, Barry E. Esq., Harcourt-street, Dublin
Lawless, Rev. J. P., A.B. Rector of Inch, Woodview, Cloyne, co. [Cork
Lawless, Peter A., Esq., Cherryfield, nr. Rathfarnham, co. Dublin
Lawless, Rev. Thomas, P.P. of Killaghton, Aughrim, co. Galway
*Lawlor, Rev. Denis, P.P., Hacketstown, co. Carlow
Lawlor, Denis Shyne, Esq., Castle Lough, Lakes of Killarney, co. [Kerry
Lawlor, Mr. John H., Timolin, co. Kildare
Lawlor, P., Esq., Ardo, near Youghal, co. Waterford
*Lawlor, Rev. Thomas, P.P., Athy, co. Kildare
*Lawlor, W. D., Esq., M.D., Stradbally, Queen's-county
Lawrence, Mr. Charles, Island Effrick, Coleraine, co. Derry
Lawrence, John, Esq., Magherafelt, co. Derry
*Lawrence, Capt. S. H., Belmont-cottage, Douglas, near Cork
Lawrence, Samuel, Esq., Coleraine, co. Derry
*Lawrence, Walter, Esq., J.P., Bellevue, Laurencetown, co. Galway
Lawrence, W., Esq., Silver-mines-cottage, Nenagh, co. Tipperary
*Lawrenson, Robert, Esq., J.P., Castlewood, Durrow, Queen's-county
*Lawson, W., Esq., Brough-hall, Catterick, Yorkshire
Lawton, Hugh, Esq., Castle Jane, Glanmire, co. Cork
Lawton, Hugh, Esq., J.P., Lake marsh, Skibbereen, co. Cork
Lawton, John Lindsay, Esq., Springhill-cottage, Glanmire, co. Cork
Lawton, Robert Esq., Eastferry, Cove, co. Cork
*Layton, Capt. H., R.N., Killybegs, co. Donegal
*Leadbitter, Robert, Esq., Newcastle-on-Tyne, Northumberland
Leader, H., Esq., Dromore West, co. Sligo
*Leader, Henry, Esq., J.P., Mount-leader, Millstreet, co. Cork
Leader, John, jun., Esq., J.P., Keale-house, nr. Millstreet, co. Cork
*Leader, Nicholas P., Esq., M.D., Kanturk, co. Cork
*Leaf, William, Esq., Old-change, London
Leahy, Daniel, Esq., Shanakill, co. Cork
Leahy, Daniel, Esq., J.P., Rossacon, Kanturk, co. Cork
Leahy, Edmund, Esq., Court-house, Cork
Leahy, Henry, Esq., Berkeley-square, London
*Leahy, John, Esq., Eglantine, Douglas, near Cork
*Leahy, Mr. Patrick, Cork
Leake, G. D., Esq., Garyduff-cottage, Newcastle, co. Limerick
Leathem, Rev. Moses, Desertegney-glebe, co. Donegal
Leathem, Mr. Thomas, Crumlin, co. Antrim
Leathem and Armstrong, Messrs., Enniskillen, co. Fermanagh
*Leathley, Rev. Joseph F., Glebe-house, Rathowen, co. Westmeath
*Leathley, Mrs. Echo-cottage, Kingstown, co. Dublin
Leavy, Rev. John, P.P. of Moyne, Castle-Pollard, co. Westmeath
Leche, T. Hurleston, Esq., Carden Park, Chester
*Leckie, W., Esq., Crab-lake, Clontarf, co. Dublin
*Lecky, Hugh, Esq., J.P., Black-rock, co. Antrim
*Lecky, John James, Esq., J.P., Ballykealy, Tullow, co. Carlow
*Lecky. W., Esq., Coalisland, co. Tyrone
*Lecky, W. R., Esq., Ballinacarrig, Carlow
*Ledger, G. W., Esq., Dovor, Kent
*Ledwick, James, Esq., York-street, Dublin
*Ledwith, W., Esq., Ledwithstown, Ballymahon, co. Longford
*Lee, Rev. Charles, Stagshaw-house, Hexham, Northumberland
*Lee, Edward, Esq., Jervis-street, Dublin
*Lee, Edward, Esq., Nenagh, co. Tipperary
Lee, Edward, Esq., Corrin-lodge, Killybegs, co. Donegal
*Lee, Francis, Esq., Ballylekin, Edenderry, co. Kildare
Lee, Henry, Esq., J.P., Barna, Newport, co. Tipperary
*Lee, Mr. Peter, Summerstown, near Cork
*Lee, Rev. P. D., R.C.C., Ballyloughloe, co. Westmeath
*Lee, Robert, Esq., Hull, Yorkshire
Lee, Mr. Thomas, Marlboro'-street, Dublin
*Lee, Rev. Thomas, Berrings, Inniscarra, co. Cork
Lee, The Very Reverend Usher, Dean of Waterford
*Lee, Rev. W., A.M., Churchtown, Ardee, co. Louth
Leech, Capt. John, Bally-edikin, Midleton, co. Cork
Leech, Mr. J. H., Main-street, Carrick-on-Suir, co. Tipperary
*Leech, Mr. Joshua, Gracehill, Ballymena, co. Antrim
Leech, J. R., Esq., Milltown-mills, Midleton, co. Cork
*LEEDS, His Grace the Duke of
Leek, W. Cochran, Esq., Glaslough, co. Monaghan
Lees, Edward, Esq., Ashton-under-Lyne, Staffordshire
*Lees, Rev. Sir Ha court, Bart., Blackrock-house, near Dublin
*Lees, John, Esq., Padfield-brook, Glossop, Derbyshire
Lees, T. O., Esq., Bloomfield, Merrion, near Dublin
*Lees, W., Esq., Tower, London
*Lees, W. H., Esq., Gorton, near Manchester
*Leeson, John, Esq., Burris-o'-kane, co. Tipperary
Le Fanu, The Very Rev. Thomas Philip, LL.D., Dean of Emly and Rector of Abington, co. Limerick
*Lefroy, A. T., Esq., C.C., Rathdrum, co. Wicklow
*Lefroy, Rev. Jeffry, A.B., Mullavilly, Tanderagee, co. Armagh
*Lefroy, The Rt. Hon. Thomas, M.P., LL.D , Leeson-street, Dublin
Legg, David, Esq., Lisburn and Carrickfergus, co. Antrim
*Legg, John, Esq., Carrickfergus, co. Antrim
Legge, The Honorable and Rev. H.
*Legge, W. Wallace, Esq., Malone-house, near Belfast
Legoe, Thomas, Esq., Conorraugh-house, Rosscarbery, co. Cork
*Le Hunte, Capt. Francis, R.N., Artramont, co. Wexford
Le Hunte, George, Esq., Artramont, co. Wexford
*Leigh, Chandos, Esq., Stoneleigh-abbey, nr. Coventry, Warwicksh.
*Leigh, Francis, Esq., Merrion-square South, Dublin
*Leigh, Francis, jun., Esq., J.P., Rosegarland, Taghmon, co. Wex-[ford
*Leigh, John, Esq., Moor-hall, Ormskirk, Lancashire
*LEIGHLIN and FERNS, The Right Rev. Lord Bishop of
Leighton, Hugh, Esq , Sligo
*LEITRIM, The Right Honorable the Earl of
Leland, Francis W., Esq., Drogheda, co. Louth
Lemon, James, Esq., Belfast
Lemon, Mr. James, Donaghadee, co. Down
Lendrum, George, Esq., J.P., Jamestown, Enniskillen, co. Fer-[managh
*Lenigan, James, Esq., Castle-fogerty, Thurles, co. Tipperary
Lennan, Rev. Michael, P.P., of Upper Cregan, co. Armagh
Lennard, Mr. John, Listowell, co. Kerry
Lennon, T. N., Esq., J.P., Colehill-house, Ballymahon, co. Long-[ford
Lentaigne, John, Esq., Tallaght-house, co. Dublin
Leonard, Dennis, Esq., Listowel, co. Kerry
*Leonard, Rev. George, P.P., of Oldcastle, co. Meath
*Leonard, Maurice, Esq., Listowel, co. Kerry
Leonard, Rev. S. B., A.M., Tuagh-house, Adare, co. Limerick
Leonard, S. I., Esq., Queensfort, Tuam, co. Galway
*Lepper, Robert, Esq., Foyle-view, Moville, co. Donegal
*Leslie, The Honorable Lady Mary
*Leslie, Blayney T., Esq., Rahinstown-house, Summerhill, co. Meath
Leslie, David, Esq., Leslie-hill, Keady, co. Armagh
*Leslie, Rev. Edward, Rector of Dromore, co. Down
Leslie, The Very Rev. H., Dean of Connor
*Leslie, Rev. H., Kilclief-glebe, near Downpatrick
Leslie, James, Esq., Leslie-hill, Ballymoney, co. Antrim

Leslie, John, Esq., Courtmasherry, Clonakilty, co. Cork
Leslie, Rev. John, Vicar of Kilcredan, Castlemartyr, co. Cork
Leslie, Rev. John, B.A., Carews-wood, Castlemartyr, co. Cork
*Leslie, Matthew, Esq., Wilton, near Cork
*Leslie, Pierce, Esq., Tarbert, co. Kerry
*Leslie, P. A., Esq., Woodley, near Stillorgan, co. Dublin
*Leslie, P. A., Esq., Bride-street, Dublin
Leslie, Capt. S., R.N., Donaghadee, co. Down
*Leslie, Samuel. Esq., Drumcanver, Derrynoose, co. Armagh
*Leslie, Mrs., Upper Harley-street, London
*L'Estrange, Very Rev. F. J., V.P.O.C.D., Clarendon-street, Dublin
*L'Estrange, Geo. Esq., J.P., Lisnamandra, Crossdoney, co. Cavan
L'Estrange, H. P., Esq., Moytown, Cloghan, King's-county
L'Estrange, R. A., Esq., William-street, Dublin
Lett, Mr. Joshua, Enniscorthy, co. Wexford
*Lett, Richard, Esq., Balloghten, near Taghmon, co. Wexford
Lett, William, Seafield, Wexford
*Levens, James, Esq., Milford, Ramelton, co. Donegal
*Levinge, M. A., Esq., Enniscoffey-house, near Rochfort-bridge, co. [Westmeath
Levis, Samuel, Esq., Glenview, Skibbereen co. Cork
*Lewen, Thomas, Esq., Cloghan's-house, Kilmain, co. Mayo
Lewin, Capt. James, Kilsharney-lodge, Kilmain, co. Mayo
Lewis, A. G., Esq., J.P., The Terrace, Monaghan
Lewis, Stephen, Esq., Rockfort, Innishannon, co. Cork
Lewis, W., Esq., Sub-Inspector of Police, Loughrea, co. Galway
*Lewis, Rev. W., Rector and Vicar of Killeely, Limerick
*Lewis, Mr. W., Primrose-grange, Sligo
Lewis, Mr. W., Clohamon Cotton-mills, near Newtownbarry, co. [Wexford
*Leycester, Joseph, Esq., East-view, Cork
Leycester and Cotter, Messrs., Cork
Leyne, Capt. R., Tralee, co. Kerry
Lightburne, Joseph, Esq., Harcourt-lodge, Trim, co. Meath
*LIMERICK, The Right Rev. Lord Bishop of
*LIMERICK, The Right Honorable the Earl of
Limerick, Mr. Samuel, Ballykerly, co. Derry
*Lindesay, John, Esq., D.L. and J.P., Loughry, Dungannon, co. [Tyrone
*Lindesay, Rev. Thomas, Tamlaght-glebe, Moneymore, co. Derry
Lindley, Thomas, Esq., Lower Sackville-street, Dublin
*Lindsay, Mr. Alexander, Elaghmore, Templemore, co. Derry
*Lindsay, David, Esq., Ashfield, Dromore, co. Down
*Lindsay, Henry Lill, Esq., Armagh
Lindsay, John, Esq., J.P., Tullyhenan, near Banbridge, co. Down
Lindsay, Rev. Robert H., Galway
*Lindsay, Walter, Esq., Great Charles-street, Dublin, and Rath- [drummin, Dunleer, co. Louth
Lindsay, William, Esq., Wilfort, Tuam, co. Galway
Lindsey, Henry John, Esq., Myshell, Coachford, co. Cork
*Lindsey, T. S., Esq., J.P., Hollymount-house, co. Mayo
*Linihan, Cornelius, Esq., Killura, near Mallow, co. Cork
Lipsett, Mr. James, Portrush, co. Antrim
Lipsett, Lewis E., Esq., Roebuck, co. Dublin
*Lipsett, Michael, Esq., Ballyshannon, co. Donegal
*LISMORE, The Right Honorable Viscount
*Lister, John, Esq., Blackburn, Lancashire
Liston, Rev. R., R.C.C., Ashford, Newcastle, co. Limerick
*Litchfield, W., Esq., Factory-hill, Glanmire, near Cork
Lithgow, Mr. Henry, Carn, Glendermott, co. Derry
Lithgow, John, Esq., Lisnagelvin, Glendermott, co. Derry
*Little, Archibald, Esq., Newry, co. Down
*Little, George, Esq., Cullentra, near Wexford
*Little, James, Esq., J.P., Loughbrickland, co. Down
Little, John, Esq., Stewartstown, co. Tyrone
*Little, Thomas, Esq., M.D., J.P., Sligo
Litton, James, Esq., Kilcorkin, near Chapelmidway, co. Dublin
Liverpool, the Corporation of
Livesay, Edward, Esq., Mountjoy-square, Dublin
*Livingston, Mr. Jacob, Carrickhue, Faughanvale, co. Derry
*Livingston, William, Esq., Westport, co. Mayo
*Lloyd, Rev. B., Trinity College, Dublin
*Lloyd, Edward, Esq., Upper Mount-street, Dublin
Lloyd, Edward, Esq., Heathfield, Ballingarry, co. Limerick
*Lloyd, Erasmus, Esq., Fortview, near Drumsna, co. Roscommon
*Lloyd, George, Esq., Limerick
*Lloyd, Guy, Esq., J.P., Croghan-house, near Boyle, co. Roscommon
Lloyd, Hardress, Esq., D.L. & J.P., Gloster, Shinrone, King's-county
*Lloyd, Jackson, Esq., Tamnamore, Moy, co. Tyrone
*Lloyd, John, Esq., J.P., Lisheen-castle, Templemore, co. Tipperary
*Lloyd, John, Esq., Lloydsboro, Templemore, co. Tipperary
Lloyd, Rev. John, Smithhill, Elphin, co. Roscommon
*Lloyd, John Thomas, Esq., Herbert's-place, Dublin
*Lloyd, Owen, Esq., J.P., Knockadoo, Boyle, co. Roscommon

Lloyd, Robert, Esq., M.D., Roscommon
*Lloyd, Rev. Richard, A.B., J.P., Passage-west, co. Cork
*Lloyd, Rev. T., J.P., Killyglass-glebe, near Strokestown, co. Ros- [common
Lloyd, Thomas, Esq., Clifford, Castletown-Roche, co. Cork
*Lloyd, Thomas W., Esq., J.P., Hermitage, near Boyle, co. Roscom- [mon
*Lloyd, W., Esq., J.P., Rockville, near Drumsna, co. Roscommon
Lloyd, W., Esq., Belle-isle, co. Clare, and Clare-street, Limerick
*Lloyd, W., Esq., Arm-lodge, Castlerea, co. Roscommon
*Lloyd, Rev. W. E., Rector of Tennor, Johnstown, Kilkenny
Lloyd, Lieut. W. H., R.N., Millfield-house, Rosscarbery, co. Cork
*Lloyds, The Committee for managing the affairs of
Loane, George, Esq., M.D., Bandon, co. Cork
Locke, Rev. Thomas, Newcastle, co. Limerick
Locke, W., Esq., Balbriggan, co. Dublin
Lockwood, Rev. W., Easingwold, Yorkshire
*Lodge, Rev. F., A.M., Rathsaran-glebe, Rathdowney, Queen's-co.
Lodge, Mr. R. F., Prospect, Durrow, Queens-county
*Lodge, Rev. W., J.P., Killea-glebe, Killea, co. Donegal
Loftie, John H., Esq., Tanderagee, co. Armagh
*LOFTUS, The Right Honorable Lord
*Logan, James, Esq., Smithstown, Dunshaughlin, co. Meath
*Logan, James, Esq., Nowhead, Broughshane, co. Antrim
Logan, W. C., Esq., Ballincurrig-cottage, Douglas-road, Cork
Logue, Mr. Joseph, Drumahoe, Glendermott, co. Derry
Lombard, Rev. John, M.A., J.P., Harrietville, Mallow, co. Cork
*LONDONDERRY, The Most Noble the Marquess of
Long, Mr. Edward, White-house, Belfast
Long, John, Esq., Mary-street, Dublin
*Long, Rev. J. D., Buckingham-street, Dublin
*Long, Rev. P., Meath-street, Dublin
*Long, Rev. Paul, P.P. of St. Catharines, Dublin
*Long, Richard, Esq., J.P., Longfield, near Cashel, co. Tipperary
*Long, Samuel, Esq., Thomastown-house, Rathangan, co. Kildare
Longan, Robert, Esq., J.P., Ballinacourty, Dungarvan, co. Water- [ford
Longfield, Rev. M., J.P., Church-hill, Bandon, co. Cork
Longfield, Col. John, Longueville, Mallow, co. Cork
*Longfield, Rev. R. Castle-Mary, near Cloyne, co. Cork
Longford, George, Esq., Kenmare, co. Kerry
*Lopdell, John, Esq., J.P., Derryowen, Gort, co. Galway
*Lopdell, John, Esq., Prospect-house, Athenry, co. Galway
Lord, Rev. John, A.B., J.P., Mitchelstown, co. Cork
Lordan, John, Esq., Kinsale, co. Cork
Lorimer, Mr. John, Glenavy, co. Antrim
*LORTON, the Right Honorable Viscount
Lough, James, Esq., Clones, co. Monaghan
Loughnan, Peter, Esq., Crohill-lodge, Freshford, Kilkenny
Loughran, Rev. Bernard J., P.P. of Tynan, co. Armagh
*Loughry, Michael, Esq., Binion, Clonmany, co. Donegal
*LOUTH, the Right Honorable Lord
Love, Mr. James, Ballyboe, All Saints, co. Donegal
Lovell, Edwin, Esq., Coventry-street, London
*Lovely, Robert, Esq., Locke-street, Dublin
Lovett, Jonathan, Esq., Youghal, co. Cork
Low, Francis, Esq., Merrion Castle, near Dublin
*Low, George Bond, Esq., Clogher, near Doneraile, co. Cork
*Low, John, Esq., J.P., Spring-house, Killshane, near Tipperary
*Low, Richard H., Esq., Kilmahon, Cloyne, co. Cork
Low, R. B. H., Esq., J.P., Kenilworth, Clonmel, and Bay-view, [Dungarvan, co. Waterford
*Lowndes, Rev. Robert, Rectory, North Crawley, Bucks
*Lowndes, W., Esq., The Bury, Chesham, Bucks
*Lowndes, W. S., Esq., Whaddon-hall, Stony Stratford, Bucks
*Lowney, William, Esq., Limerick
*Lowry, James, Esq., J.P., Rockdale-house, Cookstown, co. Tyrone
Lowry, John, Esq., Ballytrim-house, Killyleagh, co. Down
Lowry, John, Esq., Capel-street, Dublin
*Lowry, R. W., Esq., D.L. and J.P., Pomeroy-house, co. Tyrone
*Loyd, Edward, Esq., King-street, Manchester
*Luby, Rev. M.A., Ennis, co. Clare
*Lucas, B., Esq., D.L. and J.P., Mount-Lucas, Philipstown, King's [county
Lucas, Charles R., Esq., J.P., Cavan-lodge, Fintona, co. Tyrone
*Lucas, Davis, Esq., Dromenargoole, Poyntz-pass, co. Armagh
*Lucas, E., Esq., M.P., D.L., and J.P., Castle-Shane, co. Monaghan
*Lucas, John, Esq., Rathealy, Fermoy, co. Cork
Lucas, Rev. John, B.A., Kilrush, co. Clare
*Lucas, Lieut.-Col. Robert, Raconnel, Monaghan
*Lucas, Rev. Samuel, Castlelost-glebe, Tyrrelspass, co. Westmeath
*Lucas, Thos., Esq., M.D., Richfordstown, Clonakilty, co. Cork
*Lucette, Edward, Esq., Bellevue, near Douglas, co. Cork
Lucey, Rev. Samuel, P.P. of Glauntane, and Little Island, nr. Cork
Lucie, Rev. Samuel, P.P. of Lower Glanmire, Cork

*Lumley, J. O., Esq., New Inn, London
Lumm, W. Purefoy, Esq., Leitrim-house, Edenderry, King's-county
Luther, John, Esq., Main-street, Clonmel, co. Tipperary
*Lyddy, Rev. Daniel, P.P., Abbeyfeale, co. Limerick
*Lyde, Lionel, Esq., Regent-street, London
*Lyle, Hugh, Esq., J.P., Knockintern, Coleraine, co. Derry
*Lyle, H., Esq., J.P., Oaks-lodge, co. Derry, and Lusnagariff, co. Donegal
Lymbery, Rev. G., Vicar of Kilrossinty, Kilmacthomas, co. Waterford
*Lynar, Sir W. Wainwright, Knt., Kingstown, co. Dublin
Lynch, Alexander, Esq., Garrorine, Castle-Blakeney, co. Galway
*Lynch, A. C., Esq., J.P., Hollybrook, Hollymount, co. Mayo
Lynch, Capt. Anthony Francis, Loughrea, co. Galway
*Lynch, A. H., Esq., M.P., Galway
Lynch, Charles, Esq., Petersburgh, Cong, co. Mayo
*Lynch, David, Esq., Churchtown-house, near Dundrum, co. Dublin
Lynch, Mr. Edward, Athlone, co. Westmeath
*Lynch, Eyre, Esq., Rathglass, Aughrim, co. Galway
Lynch, George, Esq., Castlebar, co. Mayo
*Lynch, Mr. George Alexander, Everton, Carlow
Lynch, James, Esq., Dominick-street, Galway
Lynch, James, Esq., Loughrea, co. Galway
*Lynch, James M., Esq., White Leys, near Ballymore-Eustace, co. Dublin
*Lynch, John, Esq., Rosslea, co. Fermanagh
*Lynch, John, Esq., Bridge-place, Tralee, co. Kerry
Lynch, John, Esq., M.D., A.B., Charleville, co. Cork
*Lynch, Mark, Esq., J.P., Dominick-street, Galway
*Lynch, Capt. Martin, Roseberry, Ballymoe, co. Galway
*Lynch, Nicholas, Esq., Barna, near Galway
Lynch, Owen, Esq., Wood-park, Ballinasloe, co. Galway
*Lynch, P., Esq., Ballycurrin Castle, co. Mayo
*Lynch, Capt. P., Ballycurrin Castle, co. Mayo
Lynch, Philip, Esq., Stephen's-green, Dublin
Lynch, Richard, Esq., R.N, William-street, Limerick
*Lynch, Richard M., Esq., Galway
*Lynch, Major Thomas, Oatfield, Aughrim, co. Galway
Lynch, Thomas, Esq., Portglenone, co. Antrim
Lynch, W., Esq., Blackhall-street, Dublin
*Lyndsey, Michael, Esq., Balaheragh, Hollymount, co. Mayo
Lynn, Adam Loftus, Esq., Innyard, Fethard, co. Wexford
Lynn, John, Esq., Downpatrick, co. Down
*Lyon, George, Esq., Londonderry
*Lyon, John, Esq., Portarlington, King's-county
Lyons, Henry, Esq., Old Park, Belfast
Lyons, James, Esq., Trafalgar, Cork, and Glanmire Woollen Factory, near Cork
Lyons, James D., Esq., D.L. and J.P., Tworine, Croom, co. Limerick
Lyons, Philip, Esq., M.D., Cecil-street, Limerick
Lyons, Thomas, Esq., Trafalgar, Cork, and North Main-st. Cork
*Lyons, Rev. T. A., A.M., Cavan
Lyons, Messrs., John and Co., Camden Quay, Cork
Lysaght, C. A., Esq., Rockforest, Corofin, co. Clare
Lysaght, Daniel, Esq., Knockaloo, Gort, co. Galway
Lysaght, George, Esq., Kilcorney, Burren, co. Clare, and Glentworth-street, Limerick
Lysaght, James, Esq., Erina-house, Castle-Connell, co. Limerick
Lysaght, John, Esq., Stafford-street, Dublin
*Lysaght, Thomas, Esq., M.D., Roscommon
Lysaght, William, Esq., Hazlewood, Mallow, co. Cork
*Lyster, James, Esq., Lysterfield, near Athleague, co. Roscommon
Lyster, Lyttleton, Esq., J.P., Union-hall, Rosscarberry, co. Cork
*Lyster, Rev. Mark, Stratford-glebe, co. Wicklow
*Lyster, William, Esq., Clomanty Mills, Freshford, co. Kilkenny
*Lyte, Rev. H. F., M.A., Burton-house, Brixham, Devonshire

*Macan, Major T., Greenmount-lodge, Castle-Bellingham, co. Louth
*Macarthy, John Eugene, Esq., Newtown, Roscarberry, co. Cork
Macartney, Rev. A. C., Vicar of Belfast
Macartney, F., Esq., M.D., Enniscorthy, co. Wexford
Macartney, George, Esq., J.P., Lisanour-castle, co. Antrim
Macartney, Rev. H. B., B.A., Creagh-glebe, Skibbereen, co. Cork
*Macartney, J., Esq., Abbey-lodge, Maguires-bridge, co. Fermanagh
Macartney, Joseph, Esq., Hollywood, co. Down
*Macartney, Rev. W. G., Vicar of Killead, Crumlin, co. Antrim
*Macartny, Joseph, Esq., Upper Gloucester-street, Dublin
Macaulay, Frederick W., Esq., Antrim
Macaulay, Messrs. Robert and Son, Crumlin, co. Antrim
*Macbeth, John, Esq., Ennis, co. Clare
*Mac Carthy, M. F., Esq., Air-hill-house, Kingstown, co. Dublin
*Mac Donagh, Peter, Esq., Jervis-street, Dublin
Mac Dermott, James, Esq., Rathmore, co. Galway
*Mac Donnell, Sir Francis, Knt., J.P., Donforth-house, Enfield, co. Kildare
Mac Donnell, Francis, Esq., Ballina, co. Mayo
Mac Donnell, Rev. G., A.B., Crossdoney, co. Cavan
Macdonnell, Joseph A., Esq., Abbeyville, Newport, co. Mayo
Mac Donnell, Rev. L. G., Favorita, near Glanealy, co. Wicklow
Macdonnell, R. F., Esq., Collon, co. Louth
*Mac Donogh, Charles S. Esq., North Great George-street, Dublin
*Mac Dougall, W., Esq., Hollybrook-house, Howth-road, co. Dublin
Macentegart, Mr. John Thomas, Ardee, co. Louth
Mac Grath, Joseph, Esq., Dublin
Mac Hale, Rev. James, P.P., Hollymount, co. Mayo
*Mac Hale, The Right Rev. John, D.D., R. C. Bishop of Killala
Mac Inorny, Rev. James, Clare
Macintosh, Rev. A., Tralee, co. Kerry
Mackay, Mr. A., Belfast
Mackay, Michael, Esq., Ballyroberts Castle, Fermoy, co. Cork
*Mackenzie, Alex., Esq., J.P., Donaghmore, Dungannon, co. Tyrone
Mackenzie, Mr. W., O'Brien's Bridge, Castle-Connell, co. Limerick
Mackeon, Rev. A., P.P., Ballynahown, nr. Athlone, co. Westmeath
Mackesy, Rev. William, J.P., Clashmore-glebe, co. Waterford
*Mackey, Mr. Alexander, Cairnalbany, Coleraine, co. Derry
Mackey, Capt. A. J., Lena Dergh, Banbridge, co. Down
*Mackey, James, Esq., Ballyards, Armagh
*Mackey, Mr. James, Gallagh, Templemore, co. Derry
Mackey, Mr. James, Coshquin, Templemore, co. Derry
Mackey, Rev. John, P.P., Clerihan, Clonmel, co. Tipperary
*Mackey, Mrs. Elogh, Stewastown, co. Tyrone
*Macklin, Gerard, Esq., Lake Park, near Roundwood, co. Wicklow
Macklin, Rev. John, Loughrea, co. Galway
*Macklin, Rev. R., Glebe-house, Lusk, co. Dublin
*Mackmurdo, Edward, Esq., Broad-street, London
*Mac Lean, Rev. Henry, Rathfarnham, co. Dublin
Macleod, Rev. Dennis F., O.S.F., Cork
Mac Leod, John, Esq., J.P., Cavan
*Mac Mahon, The Right Rev. P., D.D., R. C. Bishop of Killaloe
*Mac Mahon, John, Esq., Firgrove-house, Bunratty, co. Clare
*Mac Mahon, Patrick, Esq., Ennis, co. Clare
Macmullen, Rev. D. W., Ardmore-glebe, near Lurgan, co. Armagh
*Macnaghten, E. C. Esq., Beardiville, Coleraine, co. Derry
*Macnaghten, Sir F. Workman, Bart., D.L. and J.P., Bushmills-house, near Coleraine, co. Antrim
Mac Nally, John, Esq., Upper Dominick-street, Dublin
*Macnamara, Dillon, Esq., York-street, Dublin
Macnamara, Francis, Esq., J.P., Arran-view, Ennistymon, co. Clare
Macnamara, J., Esq., Moher, near Ennistymon, co. Clare
*Macnamara, The Very Rev. P., R.C. Dean, and V.G. of Limerick, and P.P. of Bruff, co. Limerick
Mac Namara, Patrick, Esq., Limerick
*Macnamara, R., Esq., Loughscur, Carrick-on-Shannon, co. Leitrim
Macnamara, Thomas, Esq., Rutland, near Dolphin's Barn, co. Dublin
*Macnamara, Major W. N., M.P. and J.P., Doolin, co. Clare
*Macnaughton, Mr. John, Leixlip, co. Kildare
*Mac Neale, J. W. Esq., Ballymascanlon-house, Dundalk, co. Louth
*Macneill, John, Esq., St. Martin's-place, London
*Maconchy, John, Esq., Edenmore, near Raheny, co. Dublin
Maconchy, Rev. Wm., Glebe, Coolock, co. Dublin
Macoun, Mr. John, Shankil, Lurgan, co. Antrim
*Mac Owen, James, Esq., Castle-moat, Cloghran, co. Dublin
*Mac Owen, Nicholas, Esq., Midleton, near Cloghran, co. Dublin
McAdam, Philip, Esq., Spring-hill, Limerick
*McAlteser, J., Esq., Cambrickvale, Dundalk, co. Louth
*McAlroy, Rev. A., R.C.C., Navan, co. Meath
McArdle, Rev. Arthur, D.D., Loughbrickland, co. Down
McArdle, Edward, Esq., Ardee, co. Louth
*McAuley, Mr. Charles, Cotton-mills, Randalstown, co. Antrim
McAuley, Rev. Matthew, Corvoam, Ballibay, co. Monaghan
McAuliff, Rev. J., P.P. of Kilmine, near Clonakilty, co. Cork
McBirney, Mr. Samuel, White-abbey, Belfast
McBride, Robert, Esq., Alistragh, near Armagh
McBurney, John, Esq., Saintfield, co. Down
McCabe, Rev. Felix, P.P. of Killersherdiny, near Cootehill, co. Cavan
*McCabe, Rev. Patrick, P.P. of Killesandra, co. Cavan
*McCabe, Rev. P. A., Adam and Eve Chapel, Merchant's-quay, Dublin
*McCafferty, Rev. Eugene, P.P. of Donegal
McCall, Samuel, Esq., Belle Vue, Rosstrevor, co. Down
*McCally, Robert Richard, Esq., Furry-park, Granard, co. Longford
McCalmont, Hugh, Esq., Abbey-lands, Belfast
McCalmont, Rev. Thomas, White-abbey, near Belfast
McCambridge, Messrs. John and Alexander, Larne, co. Antrim
McCammon, Thomas, Esq., Belfast
McCance, John, Esq., Suffolk, Belfast

*McCann, Rev. C. J., R.C.C., Halston-street, Dublin
*McCann, James, Esq., Drogheda, co. Louth
McCann, Joseph, Esq., Beaumont, Drogheda, co. Louth
McCann, Mr. Thomas, Armagh
McCann, Rev. Thomas, D.D., Dundalk, co. Louth
McCarthy, A. C., Esq., Queen-street, South-mall, Cork
McCarthy, Alexander, Esq., South-mall, Cork
*McCarthy, A. C., Esq., Altonville, Douglas road, Cork
*McCarthy, Callaghan, Esq., Dublin-street, Cork
McCarthy, Charles, Esq., Leadenhall Street, London
*McCarthy, Rev. Charles, R.C.C. of Buttevant, co. Cork
McCarthy, Capt. Charles C., Kinsale, co. Cork
*McCarthy, Rev. C. J., P.P., Ballingarry, Rathkeale, co. Limerick
McCarthy, D., Esq., Loughrin-cottage, Skibbereen, co. Cork
McCarthy, D., Esq., M.D., Newcastle, co. Limerick
*McCarthy, D., Esq., Lower Gardiner-street, Dublin
*McCarthy, Rev. Daniel, P.P., Ballylongford and Tarbert, co. Kerry
McCarthy, Denis, Esq., Rathroe, Millstreet, co. Cork
*McCarthy, Rev. E., Bridestown, Ardnageehy, co. Cork
McCarthy, Rev. Edward, Convent, Newbridge, co. Kildare
McCarthy, Rev. Eugene, P.P., Ballyheigue, co. Kerry
*McCarthy, F., Esq., Skibbereen, co. Cork
McCarthy, James, Esq., Goleen-house, Skibbereen, co. Cork
*McCarthy, Jeremiah, Esq., Dawson-street, Dublin
McCarthy, John, Esq., Kinsale, co. Cork
McCarthy, John, Esq., Carrignavar, near Cork
McCarthy, Rev. Justin, R.C.C., Rathcormac, co. Cork
*McCarthy, Mr. S., Carrigeen Paper Mills, and Malor-street, Cork
*McCarthy, Samuel, Esq., Spring-mount, near Ovens, co. Cork
McCarthy, S., Esq., Lucan, co. Dublin
McCarthy, Thos., Esq., M.D., Dispensary, Rathkeale, co. Limerick
McCarthy, Timothy, Esq., Harbour-view, Youghal, co. Cork
*McCarthy, William, Esq., Newcastle, co. Limerick
McCarthy and Murphy, Messrs., South-mall, Cork
McCartie, Daniel, Esq., Church-hill, Millstreet, co. Cork
McCartie, Denis, Esq., Derrigh, Millstreet, co. Cork
McCartie, Jeremiah, Esq., Woodview, Kanturk, co. Cork
*McCarty, Rev. Charles, R.C.C. of Buttevant, co. Cork
*McCarty, Justin, Esq., Carrignavar, co. Cork
*McCasky, John, Esq., Fern-hill, near Dundrum, co. Dublin
*McCaull, Michael, Esq., Willington-lodge, Kingstown, co. Dublin
*McCausland, Alexander, Esq., J.P., Omagh, co. Tyrone [Derry
McCausland, M., Esq., J.P., Fruit-hill, Newtown-Limavady, co.
McCausland, Rev. O., Finlagan, near Newtown-Limavady, co. Derry
*McCausland, W. J., Esq., Merville, near Stillorgan, co. Dublin
*McCaw, Wm., Esq., Belfast
McCawley, Rev. William, P.P. of Lacken, Rathlacken, co. Mayo
*McCay, Mr. Archibald, Fersaghmore, Letterkenny, co. Donegal
*McCay, Henry, Esq., Jervis-street, Dublin, and Londonderry
McCay, Mr. Scott, Newtown-Cunningham, co. Donegal
*McClatchy, J., Esq., Digges-street, Dublin
*McClea, Mr. Andrew, Crislaghkeel, Fahan, co. Donegal
*McClea, Mr. James, Crislaghkeel, Fahan, co. Donegal
McClean, William, Esq., M.D., Ballibay, co. Monaghan
*McCleery, John, Esq., Moneycarrie, Coleraine, co. Derry
*McCleland, Rev. William, Athlone, co. Westmeath
McClellan, Carey, Esq., Larch-mount, Londonderry [Tyrone
*McClellan, Rev. Thomas, Curate of Leckpatrick, Strabane, co.
*McClelland, William, Esq., Clanmurray, Dromore, co. Down
McClintock, Rev. A., Rector of Newtown-Barry, co. Wexford
*McClintock, John, Esq., Newtown-house, Drogheda, co. Louth
*McClintock, John, Esq., J.P., Drumcar-house, Dunleer, co. Louth
*McClintock, Robert, Esq., J.P., Dunmore, Londonderry
*McClintock, Samuel, Esq., Termonfeckan, Drogheda, co. Louth
McClintock, Samuel, Esq., Granshogh, Londonderry
*McClintock, William Kerr, Esq., J.P., Greenhaw-house, London-
McClury, Mr. David, Crampton-court, Dublin [derry
McComas, Mr. Francis, Westmoreland-street, Dublin
McConiloque, Rev. B., R.C.C., Cumberclady, co. Derry
McCorkell, Mr. John, Skeag, Burt, co. Donegal
McCorkell, William, Esq., Londonderry
McCormick, Rev. John, A.M., Coleraine, co. Derry
McCormick, Rev. Joseph, Dungiven-glebe, Fintona, co. Tyrone
*McCormick, Rev. Patrick, R.C.C., Ballymore, co. Westmeath
*McCormick, Mr. Thomas, Marlboro'-street, Dublin
McCormick, W. James, Esq., M.D., Kilpatrick, Mallow, co. Cork
McCoy, John, Esq., Waterfoot, Crumlin, co. Antrim
McCracken, Francis, Esq., Belfast
*McCracken, John W., Esq., Belfast
McCraith, John, Esq., J.P., Kilkenny
McCraith, Thomas, Esq., Newenham-street, Limerick
*McCrea, Rev. J. B., Gortnasheelagh, Rathmines, near Dublin
*McCrea, Mr. James, Glencush, Strabane, co. Tyrone
*McCreery, James, Esq., Kilkenny
McCreight, Rev. A., M.A., Brookhill, Ballyhaise, co. Cavan
McCreight, Rev. James, Glebe-house, Caledon, co. Tyrone
*McCreight, William, Esq., Gilford, co. Down
*McCrum, William, Esq., Milford, co. Armagh
McCullagh, E. J., Esq., Toolstown, Maynooth, co. Kildare
*McCullagh, James, Esq., Ballibay, co. Monaghan
McCullagh, James, Esq., Corfadd, Ballibay, co. Monaghan
McCullagh, Rev. John, R.C.C., Termonamongan, co. Tyrone
*McCullagh, Thomas, Esq., Derryvally, Ballibay, co. Monaghan
*McCullagh, Thomas, Esq., Dunrimond-house, Ballibay, co. Mo-
McCulloch, John, Esq., Ballina, co. Mayo [naghan
McCulloch, John, Esq., Larne, co. Antrim
McCulloch, John Shaw, Esq., Drogheda, co. Louth
*McCulloch, Rev. Thomas, M.A., Newmarket-on-Fergus, co. Clare
McCune, William, Esq., Downpatrick, co. Down
McCurdy, John, Esq., Magilligan, near N. T. Limavady, co. Derry
McCusker, Rev. John, P.P., Ballibay, and Tullycorbet, co. Mo-
McDaniel, Lieut. J., R.N., Kinsale, co. Cork [naghan
*McDavitt, Rev. James, P.P., Culdaff, co. Donegal
*McDennott, W., Esq., Mountjoy-square South, Dublin
*McDermott, Rev. B., P.P. of Kilglass, co. Roscommon
*McDermott, Rev. Charles, P.P. of Errigal-Trough, co. Monaghan
*McDermott, G., Esq., Caldra-lodge, Carrick-on-Shannon, co. Leitrim
McDermott, James, Esq., Rathmore, Eyrecourt, co. Galway
*McDermott, Rev. M., P.P., Strokestown, co. Roscommon
McDermott, Rev. M., P.P. of Ballycroy, Newport-Pratt, co. Mayo
*McDermott, M., Esq., Tubberpatrick, Strokestown, co. Roscommon
*McDermott, W., Esq., Springfield, Ballymoe, co. Galway
*McDermott, William, Esq., M.D., Rose-cottage, Knock, co. Clare
*McDermott, William, Esq., Springfield, co. Galway
*McDermott-Roe, Thomas, Esq., Alderford, Keadue, co. Roscommon
*McDonagh, Peter, Esq., Jervis-street, Dublin, and Londonderry
*McDonagh, William, Esq., Wilmont, Portumna, co. Galway
McDonald, Rev. John, R.C.C., Doneraile, co. Cork
*McDonald, M., Esq., Buckroney-house, near Arklow, co. Wicklow
McDonald, Thomas U., Esq., M.D., Crumlin, co. Antrim
McDonald, William, Esq., Lisburn, co. Antrim
McDonnell, Alexander, Esq., Belfast
McDonnell, A., Esq., Darlington-lodge, Ballymore, co. Westmeath
McDonnell, J., Esq., North Cliffe, Blackrock, Cork
*McDonnell, Mr. James, Limerick
McDonnell, James, Esq., M.D., Belfast
*McDonnell, Michael, Esq., Oldbawn, near Tallaght, co. Dublin
*McDonnell, Michael, Esq., William-street, Dublin [co. Limerick
McDonnell, Rev. Michael, R.C.C., Drumcolloher, near Newcastle,
McDonnell, Owen R., Esq., Sligo
*McDonnell, P., Esq., Cannaghannally, Dromore West, co. Sligo
*McDonnell, R. W. D., Esq., Mullaghmore-villa, co. Monaghan
*McDonnell, Messrs. Christopher and Sons, Merchants-quay, Dublin
McDonogh, James, Esq., Galway [common
*McDonogh, Rev. M. D., P.P., Frenchpark, Golderfort, co. Ros-
*McDonough, Edward, Esq., Lower Sackville-street, Dublin
*McDonough, Rev. John, Townsend-street, Dublin
*McDonough, Mr. Mathew, Drogheda, co. Louth
*McDougall, James, Esq., Artigarvan, Strabane, co. Tyrone
*McDowell, C., Esq., Imperial Clarence Hotel, Cork, and Colum-
[bine, Cove, near Cork
McDowell, Mr. John, Fairview, Lisburn, co. Down
McDowell, Robert, Esq., Belfast
McElrath, Mr. William, Millfarm, Dungonnell, Antrim [Monaghan
*McEnally, J., Esq., M.D. and J.P., Prospect Villa, Cootehill, co.
McEnnrv, Very Rev. J. G., Vicar General, Tralee, co. Kerry
McEntire, Robert J., Esq., Belfast
McEvilly, Rev. W., P.P. of Moore, Ballinasloe, co. Galway
McEvoy Rev. John, R.C.C., Geashill, King's county
McEwen, Rev. W., A.M., Beauhill-house, Killeevan, co. Monaghan
*McFadzen, John, Esq., M.D., Buttevant, co. Cork
*McFarland, Armar, Esq., Straree, Gortin, co. Tyrone
*McFarland, James, Esq., Camus, near Coleraine, co. Derry
*McFarland, Mr. Robert, Cloon, Killea, co. Donegal
McFeeters, Mr. Robert, Newtown-Stewart, co. Tyrone
*McGann, James, Esq., Phœnix-park, Dublin
McGarry, Rev. Daniel, P.P. of Aughagallon, Lurgan, co. Antrim
*McGauley, Rev. James W., R.C.C. Marlborough-street, Dublin
*McGaver, Rev. E., P.P. of Carrickedmond, Colehill, co. Longford
*McGeough, Miss Eliza, Drumsill-house, Armagh
*McGhee, John, Esq., Hollymount, Rathmullen, co. Donegal
*McGhee, Rev. R. J., Enniskerry, co. Wicklow

McGhee, W., Esq., Hammersmith, Middlesex
*McGildowney, C., Esq., J.P., Clare-park, Ballycastle, co. Antrim
*McGillycuddy of the Reeks, co. Kerry
McGonegal, David, Esq., Attly, Coleraine, co. Derry
McGowan, William, Esq., Manorhamilton, co. Leitrim
*McGrane, C., Esq., Edmonstown, near Rathfarnham, co. Dublin
McGrath, Rev. Jeremiah, P.P., Macroom, co. Cork
McGrath, Rev. P., P.P. of Ardmore (near Youghal), co. Waterford
*McGrath, W. H., Esq., North Great George-street, and Summer-hill, Dublin
McGreal, Patrick, Esq., Westport, co. Mayo
*McGuire, Rev. A., P.P., Ballyhand, near Mullingar, co. Westmeath
*McGusty, George, Esq., J. P., Derefalone, Dundalk, co. Louth
*McGusty, Robert, Esq., Dundalk, co. Louth
*McGwiness, Rev. Edmund, P.P., Tullylish, co. Down
*McGwire, Rev. F., Shruel-glebe, Ballymahon, co. Longford
*McGwire, Joseph, Esq., J.P., Cavan
McGwire, Walter, Esq., Clonea Castle, Dungarvan, co. Waterford
*McGwire, William J., Esq., Crayfield, Rosstrevor, co. Down
McHale, Rev. Patrick, P.P. of Skreen, co. Sligo
McHenry, Rev. J. L., Curate of Culdaff, co. Donegal
*McHugh, Rev. John, P.P. of Ahamplish, Cliffoney, co. Sligo
*McHugh, T., Esq., M.D., Ballina, co. Mayo
*McIlwain, Rev. John, Morne, Kilkeel, co. Down
*McInerny, Rev. Thomas, P.P. of Feakle, Tulla, co. Clare
*McIntosh, Richard, Esq., Anglesea-street, Dublin
McKay, Mr. George, Little Bray, co. Dublin
McKay, Rev. M., M.A., Master of the Endowed School, Kinsale, co. Cork
McKay, Rev. W. K., Portglenone, co. Antrim
*McKean, Henry, Esq., Darkley, Keady, co. Armagh
*McKean, Lieut. J., R.N., New Holland-mills, Keady, co. Armagh
*McKee, Henry H., Esq., Armagh
McKee, Mr. John, Coleraine, co. Derry
*McKee, Joseph, Esq., Millview, Keady, co. Armagh
McKee, Rev. Joseph, Glebe-lodge, Killead, co. Antrim
McKeirnan, Rev. James, P.P. of Cloone, Mohill, co. Leitrim
*McKenna, Rev. James, R.C.C., Cabinteely, co. Dublin
*McKenna, Robert, Esq., North-wall, Dublin
*McKennally, J., Esq., French-st., Dublin, and Crusheen, Ennis, co. Clare
McKenny, Sir Thomas, Bart., Fitzwilliam-street, Dublin
*McKeon, Rev. P., P.P. of Drumlish, Newtown-Forbes, co. Longford
*McKibbin, Mr. James, Bushmills, co. Antrim
McKiernan, John B., Esq., Manager of the Connaught Lunatic Asylum, Ballinasloe, co. Galway
*McKillop, John, Esq., Ballygarvey, Ballymena, co. Antrim
*McKinstry, John, Esq., Armagh
*McKinstry, John, jun., Esq., Armagh
McKone, Owen, Esq., Belrobin, Dundalk, co. Louth
*McKowan, John, Esq., Shamrock-hill, near Donnybrook, co. Dublin
McLaine, Alexander, Esq., Belfast
McLamon, Miss Susan, Ballykelly, N. T. Limavady, co. Derry
McLaughlin, Right Rev. P., D.D., R.C., Bishop of Derry
*McLaughlin, Mr. Richard, Glenleary, Coleraine, co. Derry
McLaughlin, Rev. R. G., R.C.C. of Kiltoon, co. Roscommon
*McLaughlin, W. J., Esq., Castlecoote-mills, near Roscommon
McLeod, N. B., Esq., Mitchelstown, co. Cork
*McLeroth, Thomas, Esq., Killynether-house, Comber, co. Down
McLester, Edward, Esq., Sligo
*McMahon, Alexander St. Leger, Esq., Cloydale-glebe, co. Carlow
McMahon, Mr. Anthony, Anderson's-court, Dublin
McMahon, Bernard, Esq., Ballibay, co. Monaghan
McMahon, James, Esq., Diocesan Registrar of Limerick
McMahon, John, Esq., Youghal, co. Cork
McMahon, John, Esq., Camden-street, Dublin
*McMahon, Rev. M., P.P., Doonass, co. Clare
McMahon, Patrick, Esq., Lakeview, Rathkeale, co. Limerick
McMahon, Rev. Peter, P.P., Tyhollan, co. Monaghan
McMahon, Peter, Esq., Rossgrove, near Enniscorthy, co. Wexford
McMahon, Thomas, Esq., Kilfinane, co. Limerick
McMahon, The Right Honorable Sir W., Bart., Dublin
McMahon, Mr. William, Spring Hill, Louth
McManus, Alexander, Esq., D.L. & J.P., Mount Davies, co. Antrim
*McMaster, Alexander, Esq., Antrim
*McMaster, Hugh, Esq., Armagh
*McMath, H., Esq., Thornford, Castle-Blayney, co. Monaghan
McMechan, John, Esq., M.D., Whitehouse, Belfast
McMullan, Alexander, Esq., Cabra-house, Castlewellan, co. Down
McMullan, Owen, Esq., Castlewellan, co. Down
*McMullen, Mr. James, Exchequer-street, Dublin
McMullen, Joseph, Esq., Clonakilty, co. Cork
McNaier, James, Esq., M.D., Crossmolina, co. Mayo
*McNamara, Rev. John, P.P., Ballygarvan, co. Cork
McNamara, Rev. Justin F., P.P. of Kinsale, co. Cork
*McNamara, Rev. J. S., Chaplain of Warren Mount Convent, Dublin
*McNaughten, Rev. R., R.C.C. of Kilmeen, Kanturk, co. Cork
*McNeale, J., Esq., J.P., Ballycastle, co. Antrim
*McNeale, Neale, Esq., J.P., Faughart, Dundalk, co. Louth
*McNeale, S. Wilson, Esq., Ballymoney, co. Antrim
*McNeile, James N., Esq., Rutland-square West, Dublin
*McNeill, John, Esq., Parkmount, Belfast
McNeill, W. W., Esq., Larne, co. Antrim
McNemara, Mr. John, Fitton-street, Cork
*McNevin, Daniel, Esq., Middle Gardiner-street, Dublin, and Rose-park, Gort, co. Galway
*McNicholas, Rev. T., P.P. of Carncastle, Ballaghadireen, co. Mayo
McNolty, Rev. Neal, P.P. of Ballysakeery, Ballina, co. Mayo
McNulty, Bernard, Esq., George's-street, Limerick
*McNulty, Rev. John, P.P. of Killasser, Swinford, co. Mayo
*McO'Boy, Michael F., Esq., South-mall, Cork
*McParlan, Patrick, Esq., Newry, co. Down
*McQuestion, W., Esq., Rathmines, Dublin
McQuillan, Mr. John, Londonderry
*McQuiston, Mr. W., Lark Hill, Portstewart, Coleraine, co. Derry
*McSheffrey, James, Esq., Drumaville, Carndonagh, co. Donegal
*McSherry, Rev. A., P.P. of East Aughnamullen, Ballibay, co. Monaghan
McSweeny, Rev. D., R.C.C., Ballyclough, Mallow, co. Cork
McSwiney, Rev. D., P.P. of Bandon, co. Cork
McSwiney, John, Esq., Macroom, co. Cork
McSwiney, Morgan John, Esq., Killarney, co. Kerry
McSwiney, Paul, Esq., King-street, Iron-works, Cork
McSwiney, Rev. Peter, Rest-ville, Kinsale, co. Cork
McTier, James, Esq., Vernant-lodge, Belfast
*McTiernan, Hugh, Esq., Mount Allen, co. Roscommon
Macrory, A. J., Esq., Duncairn, Belfast
Madden, Daniel, Esq., Ballycastle, Rathlacken, co. Mayo
Madden, Francis, Esq., Ballydonagh, Laurencetown, co. Galway
Madden, John, Esq., Donnybrook, co. Dublin
*Madden, Rev. John, P.P., Roscommon
*Madden, J. F., Esq., Denzill-street, Dublin
Madden, Owen, Esq., Mallow, co. Cork
Madden, Peter, Esq., Simmons-court, near Donnybrook, co. Dublin
*Madden, Martin, and Co., Messrs., Sligo
Madder, Rev. Geo., Precentor of Emly, co. Limerick
*Maddock, Robert, Esq., Shankill, near Little Bray, co. Dublin
*Magan, F., Esq., J.P., Emoe, near Moate, co. Westmeath
*Magauran, Rev. Andrew, P.P., Abbeylara, co. Longford
*Magauran, Rev. J., P.P., Killasnet, Manorhamilton, co. Leitrim
*Magauran, Rev. Patrick, P.P., Carrigallen, co. Leitrim
Magauran, Rev. Patrick, P.P. of Caltra, Castle-Blakeney, co. Galway
*Magauran, Rev. Peter, P.P. of Killery, Collooney, co. Sligo
*Magauran, Rev. Philip, R.C. Rector of Templeport, Springhill, co. Cavan
Magee, Rev. Thos., P.P., Dunleer, co. Louth
*Magee, Rev. T. P., LL.D., Archdeacon of Kilmacduagh, Wicklow
*Magee, Rev. William, Rector of Dunganstown, co. Wicklow
*Magill, James, Esq., Fairview-house, Carndonagh, co. Donegal
Magill, James, Esq., Belfast
*Magill, Samuel R., Esq., J.P., Cookstown, co. Tyrone
*Maginis, Richard, Esq., Grosvenor-place, London
*Maginis, Roger, Esq., Ballyaby, Dromore, co. Down
Maginn, Rev. E., P.P. of the Fahans, Desertegney and Buncrana, [Cottage, Buncrana, co. Donegal
Maginn, Rev. John, M.A., Rector of Castletown-Roche, co. Cork
Magle, James, Esq., Midleton, co. Cork
Magrane, Christopher, Esq., Balbriggan, co. Dublin
Magrath, Daniel, Esq., Olive-vale, Woodtree, Liverpool
*Magrath, Rev. Matthew, P.P., Kilmurry, near Macroom, co. Cork
*Maguire, B., Esq., Belmont, Kilbeggan, co. Westmeath
*Maguire, Bernard, Esq., Upper Dorset-street, Dublin
*Maguire, Edward, Esq., College-green, Dublin
*Maguire, Constantine, Esq., J.P., Newry, co. Down
*Maguire, Constantine, Esq., Kilmoylermore, Cahir, co. Tipperary
Maguire, Edward, Esq., Dame-street, Dublin
*Maguire, Rev. F., R.C.R. of Rathcline, Lanesborough, co. Longford
Maguire, Rev. John, P.P., Cashcarrigan, co. Leitrim
*Maguire, Richard, Esq., Newgrange, Drogheda, co. Louth
*Maguire, Rev. T., P.P. of Innismagrath, Keadue, co. Leitrim
Mahan, John, Esq., Upper Gardiner-street, Dublin
*Maher, Rev. Daniel, P.C., Jamestown, Ballybrittas, Queen's-county
*Maher, John, Esq., Kilkenny
Maher, John, Esq., Ballinkeele, Wexford
*Maher, John, Esq., Ballinasloe, co. Galway
*Maher, John, Esq., J.P., Tullamaine, Fethard, co. Tipperary
*Maher, Nicholas, Esq., Thurles, co. Tipperary

*Maher, Richard, Esq., J.P., Killermin, Aughrim, co. Galway
*Mahon, Bartholomew, Esq., J.P., Strokestown, co. Roscommon
Mahon, Charles, Esq., J.P., Cahircalla, Ennis, co. Clare
Mahon, Edward, Esq., Newmarket-on-Fergus, co. Clare
Mahon, Henry, Esq., Limerick
*Mahon, Rev. Henry, Killigally-glebe, Farbane, King's-county
Mahon, James, Esq., Mount-William, near Tipperary
*Mahon, James, Esq., Northampton, Gort, co. Galway
*Mahon, James C., Esq., Beech-hill, Loughrea, co. Galway
Mahon, John, Esq., Upper Gardiner-street, Dublin
*Mahon, O'Gorman, Esq., Fitzwilliam-square, Dublin
*Mahon, Sir Ross, Bart., Castlegar, co. Galway
*Mahon, Ross, Esq., Tarmon, near Gort, co. Galway
Mahon, William R., Esq., J.P., New-park, Ennis, co. Clare
Mahoney, Daniel, Esq., J.P., Dunloh Castle, Killarney, co. Kerry
Mahony, Rev. A., Vicar of St. Finbarr's, Cork
Mahony, Rev. Darby, P.P., Listowel, co. Kerry
*Mahony, Rev. Denis, J.P., Dromore Castle, Kenmare, co. Kerry
Mahony, Rev. Denis, Aghabollogue, Coachford, co. Cork
*Mahony, D. F. G., Esq., Limerick
*Mahony, J. R., Esq., Raheen Wood, near Rathkeale, co. Limerick
*Mahony, Pierce, Esq., Merrion-square North, Dublin
*Mahony, Rev. Thomas, P.P., Pallasgreine, co. Limerick
Mailleure, Capt. J. M., John's-grove, Doneraile, co. Cork
Maister, General J. M., Littlethorp, Ripon, Yorkshire
*Major, James, Esq., North Great George-street, Dublin
*Major, Thomas, Esq., Tullybrisland, Faughanvale, co. Derry
*Major, W. E., Esq., Blessington-street, Dublin
*Maker, J., Esq., Batchelor-walk, Dublin
Malassez, Capt. N., Green-lanes, Clontarf, co. Dublin
Malcolm, Mr. William, Hillhall, Lisburn, co. Down
*Malcomson, David, Esq., Clonmel, co. Tipperary
Malcomson, Joseph, Esq., Mayfield, near Waterford
*Maley, Richard, Esq., Bicester, Oxfordshire
Mallan, Mathew, Esq., Haggerstown, Dundalk, co. Louth
Malley, William, Esq., Ballina, co. Mayo
*Mallow Club, co. Cork, per Capt. R. P. Davies, R.N.
*Mally, Charles, Esq., Castlebar, co. Mayo
Mally, William, Esq., Holly-hill, Turlow, Castlebar, co. Mayo
Malone, Edmond, Esq., Antrim
*Malone, Edmond, Esq., Moate, co. Westmeath
Malone, Rev. James, P.P. of Doora, co. Clare
Malone, J. P., Esq., Killaloe, co. Clare
*Malone, Rev. M., P.P., Cratloe, near Limerick
*Malone, Rev. Michael F., Limerick
*Malone, Rev. Nicholas, Church-street, Dublin
*Malone, Mrs. O'Connor, Baronstown, nr. Mullingar, co. Westmeath
Maltby, Rev. W., Terrace, Chesterfield, Derbyshire
*Manders, Isaac, Esq., Castlesize, Naas, co. Kildare
*Manders, Richard, Esq., Brackenstown, near Swords, co. Dublin
*Manders, Robert, Esq., Merville, near Roebuck, co. Dublin
*MANDEVILLE The Right Honorable Countess
*Mandeville, Rev. N. H., A.M., Ville-house, Carrick-on-Suir, co. [Tipperary
Mangan, Rev. Cosby, Stopford, Armagh
Mangan, John, Esq., Gort, co. Galway, and Ennis, co. Clare
Mangan, Michael, Esq., Ballina, co. Mayo
Manleverer, Rev. W., M.A., J.P., Rector of Tynan, co. Armagh
*Manly, J. H., Esq., Ferney, Blackrock, Cork
Manly, Mr. Michael, Sligo
Mann, Mr. Edward, Hotel, Banagher, King's county
Mann, John, Esq., Londonderry
*Manning, A., Esq., Corballis-castle, nr. Rathdrum, co. Wicklow
Manning, Patrick, Esq., Foxford, co. Mayo
Manning, Thomas S., Esq., Ruan-lodge, near Tipperary
Mannix, Henry, Esq., Richmond, near Cork
Mansel, J. C., Esq., Cosgrove-mansion, Stony Stratford, Bucks.
*Mansel, Lieut.-Col. R. C., Limerick
*Mansergh, R. S., Esq., J.P., Greenane, near Tipperary
Mansfield, Alexander, Esq., Morristown-house, co. Kildare
Mansfield, B., Esq., Castlewray, Letterkenny, co. Donegal
Mansfield, F., Esq., J.P., Castlewray, Letterkenny, co. Donegal
*Mansfield, H. C., Esq., Magheramore, co. Donegal
Mansfield, Johnston, Esq., J.P., Killygordon, Castlefin, co. Donegal
Mansfield, Robert, Esq., Castle-Blayney, co. Monaghan
Mant, The Venerable and Rev. Walter B., Archdeacon of Connor, [Bally-parsonage, Bushmills, co. Antrim
*Mapother, J. E., Esq., Kiltiven-house, near Roscommon
Marchant, William, Esq., Kiltra, Taghmon, co. Wexford
Margrane, C., Esq., Balbriggan, co. Dublin
Markey, James, Esq., Glaspistol, Drogheda, co. Louth
Marks, John, Esq., Cook-street, Cork

Markey, Owen, Esq., Reynoldstown, Dunleer, co. Louth
Markham, John, Esq., Youghal, co. Cork
*Marrett, W. C., Esq., J.P., Square, Kilrush, co. Clare
*Marron, James, Esq., Ballibay, co. Monaghan
Marsden, Col. F., Brook-lodge, Youghal, co. Cork
*Marsh, H., Esq., M.D., Molesworth-street, Dublin
*Marsh, Mr. W., Salt-hill, Monkstown, co. Dublin
Marshall, Rev. Cornelius, Cottage, Ballygawley, co. Tyrone
*Marshall, Rev. Geo., Donagh-glebe, Carndonagh, co. Donegal
Marshall, Rev. H., A.M., Incumbent of Calary, co. Wicklow
Marshall, James E., Esq., Cork, and Lower Gardiner-street, Dublin
*Marshall, James Jackson, Esq., Molesworth-street, Dublin
*Marshall, John, jun., Esq., Headingly, Leeds, Yorkshire
Marshall, Jos., Esq., George's-street, Limerick
Marshall, W., Esq., Bond Street, London
Marshall, William, Esq., Castle-Forward, near Londonderry
Marshall, Messrs. John, J., and Hugh, Dunsilly, Antrim
*Marston, Mr. J. E., Penitentiary, Smithfield, Dublin
Martelli, Francis G., Esq., Spring-cottage, Tralee, co. Kerry
*Martin, Adam, Esq., M.D., Chatham, Kent
Martin, Mr. H., Carramuddle, Newtown-Limavady, co. Derry
*Martin, Rev. H., A.M., Aughrim-glebe, co. Galway
Martin, Hughes, Esq., Tulligreen, near Midleton, co. Cork
Martin, James, Esq., Ballynahinch, co. Down
Martin, Rev. James, A.B., J.P., Kilmurry-glebe, Knock, co. Clare
*Martin, John, Esq., M.P. and J.P., Sligo
*Martin, John, jun. Esq., Shrigley, Killyleagh, co. Down
*Martin, John, Esq., Culmore, near Newtown-Limavady, co. Derry
*Martin, John, Esq., Argomal, Tynan, co. Armagh
Martin, John, Esq., Upper Riverstown, Cork
Martin, Mr. John, Dundalk, co, Louth
Martin, John, Esq., Lake-lodge, Glanmire, co. Cork
*Martin, John Charles, Esq., Ellen-villa, Sligo
Martin, Mr. Joseph, Ballibay, co. Monaghan, and Drumlane, near [Lisbellaw, co, Fermanagh
Martin, J. J., Esq., Ham-court, Upton-on-Severn, Worcestershire
Martin, Nathaniel C., Esq., Butlerstown-house, Glanmire, co. Cork
Martin, Richard, Esq., Flaxforth, Little Island, Cork
Martin, Robert, Esq., Brooklodge, Glanmire, co. Cork
Martin, Robert, Esq., Castle Jane Cottage, Glanmire, co. Cork
Martin, Robert, Esq., Bushy Park, Galway
Martin, S. D., Esq., C.C.P., Rathcoole, co. Dublin
*Martin, Thomas, Esq., Ballinahinch-castle, Oughterard, co. Galway
*Martin, Thomas, Esq., Omagh, co. Tyrone
Martin, Rev. Thomas B., Ballitrain, co. Monaghan
*Martin, Rev. Thomas F., Rathrowel-lodge, Lurgan-green, co. Louth
*Martin William, Esq., Belfast
Martin, W. K., Esq., M.D., Hillmount-house, near Larne, co. Antrim
Martin, W. H., Esq., Castlewellan, co. Down
Martin, Messrs. N. and T., Springmount-cottage, Glanmire, co. [Cork
*Martin, Messrs. John and Son, North Wall, and Santry, Dublin
*Martley, John, Esq., Rutland-square, Dublin
Martyn, Geoffrey, Esq., Galway
Martyn, John, Esq., Tillyra, Gort, co. Galway
Marum, Rev. Pierce, P.P., Conetry, Ballyragget, co. Kilkenny
Mason, E. G., Esq., Dellbrook, Ballally, Dundrum, co. Dublin
*Mason, Joseph, Esq., Cooline, near Bruff, co. Limerick
Mason, Joshua, jun., Esq., Waterford
Mason, Richard, Esq., J.P., Capanihane, Charleville, co. Cork
Mason, Rev. Robert, Wellclose-square, London
*Mason, Samuel, Esq., Cosey-lodge, near Rathfarnham, co. Dublin
Mason, Rev. S. H., Dundrum, co. Dublin
Mason, W. Jackson, Esq., Castle Jackson, Charleville, co. Cork
Massey, Francis, Esq., Gaulty View, Cashel, co. Tipperary
*Massey, Godfrey, Esq., Prospect, Castle-Connell, co. Limerick
*MASSY, The Right Honorable Lord
Massy, The Hon. John, J.P., Georges-street, Limerick
*Massy, The Hon. G. W., J.P., Belmont, near Castle-Connell, co. [Limerick
*Massy, Sir Hugh Dillon, Bart., D.L. and J.P., Doonass-house, [near Limerick
Massy, Eyre, Esq., Glanduff-castle, Newcastle, co. Limerick
Massy, George, Esq., Woodfort, Fermoy, co. Cork
Massy, Rev. Godfrey, A.B., Vicarage, Bruff, co. Limerick
Massy, Rev. G. M., A.B., Bruree-glebe, Charleville, co. Cork
Massy, Hugh, Esq., Riversdale, near Tipperary
Massy, Hugh, jun., Esq., Stoneville, Rathkeale, co. Limerick
Massy, Hugh Dillon, Esq, Summerhill, Castle-Connell, co. Limerick
*Massy James F., Esq., J.P., Cloughnarold, Rathkeale, co. Limerick
*Massy, John, Esq., Killcullane, Bruff, co. Limerick
Massy, John, Esq., Tipperary
*Massy, John B., Esq., Ballywire, near Tipperary

*Massy, Richard, Esq., M.D., Upper Cecil-street, Limerick
*Massy, T., Esq., M.D., Brookville-cottage, Kilfinane, co. Limerick
Massy, William, Esq., J.P., Stagdale, near Tipperary [Limerick
Massy, William H., Esq., J.P., Glenwilliam-castle, Ballingarry, co.
Masters, H. P., Esq., Clonakilty, co. Cork
*Masters, Stephen, Esq., J.P., Cregane, Ballinasloe, co. Galway
*Masterson, Rev. B., P.P. of Fore and Kilcumney, Castle-Pollard, co. Westmeath [co. Meath
*Masterson, Rev. John, R.C.C., Ballinlough, Painstown, Slane,
*Mathew, Lady, Thomastown-house, near Cashel, co. Tipperary
*Mathew, C., Esq., Lehonagh, near Douglas, co. Cork [perary
Mathew, Francis, J., Esq., Golden-mills, near Cashel, co. Tip
[Cork, 2 copies
*Mathew, Very Rev. Theobald, Provincial of the Capuchins Order,
*Mathew, Thomas, Esq., Castlelake, near Cashel, co. Tipperary
*Mathews, James, Esq., Mount-Hanover, Drogheda, co. Louth
*Mathews, Rev. John, P.P., Castleterra, co. Cavan
Mathews, John, Esq., Tuam, co. Galway
Mathews, Patrick, Esq., Annagor, Drogheda, co. Louth [Derry
Mathews, Mr. Robert, Millfield-paper-mill, Upper Cumber, co.
Mathews, Rev. Robert, A.M., Ballymena, co. Antrim; Master of
[the Diocesan-school of Armagh and Connor
*Mathews, Thomas, Esq., Castlevilla, Castleknock, co. Dublin
Mathews, W., Esq., Sally-park, Philipsburgh Avenue, Dublin
*Mathews, William T., Esq., Dublin Castle
Mathewson, Lavens, Esq., Newtown-Stewart, co. Tyrone
*Matterson, Joseph, Esq., Limerick
*Matthews, John, Esq., Kilmartin, near Newcastle, co. Wicklow
*Matthews, John Echlin, Esq., White-abbey, Belfast [co. Donegal
*Maturin, Rev. H., Rector of Clondevadock, Fanet-glebe, Ramelton,
*Maturin, Rev. H., jun., Rector and Vicar of Gartan, Letterkenny, co.
*Maughan, Rev. John Dixon, Bellevue, Londonderry [Donegal
*Maughan, N., Esq., Newburgh-lodge, Hexham, Northumberland
*Maunsell, C., Esq., Foster-place, Dublin, and Derriheen, Cappo-
*Maunsell, Rev. D. H., Balbriggan, co. Dublin [quin, co. Waterford
Maunsell, Rev. E. Eyre, A.M., Fort Eyre, Galway
*Maunsell, Henry, Esq., Limerick
Maunsell, Rev. Horatio, Drumbo Rectory, Belfast
*Maunsell, Nicholas, Esq., Newry, co. Down
*Maunsell, R. G., Esq., Richmond-place, Limerick
*Maunsell, Robert, Esq., Merrion-square, Dublin
*Maunsell, Rev. R., Vicar of Drehidtarsna, near Adare, co. Limerick
Maunsell, Rev. Richard, A.B., Sackville, Tralee, co. Kerry
*Maunsell, Robert, Esq., Merrion-square South, Dublin
*Maunsell, Samuel, Esq., Ballybrood-house, co. Limerick
Mawe, Thomas, Esq., M.D., Tralee, co. Kerry
Max, John, Esq., Ballytarsna, near Cashel, co. Tipperary
*Maxwell, Albert F., Esq., Glen Albert, Roscrea, co. Tipperary
Maxwell, Frederick, Esq., Moneymore, co. Derry
*Maxwell, Henry, Esq., M.P. and J.P., Farnham, Cavan
Maxwell, James, Esq., Belfast
Maxwell, J. W., Esq., J.P., Finnebrogue, Downpatrick, co. Down
*Maxwell, Robert, Esq., Middle Gardiner-street, Dublin
Maxwell, Mr. Robert, Templemoyle, Faughanvale, co. Derry
Maxwell, Robert, Esq., J.P., Charleville, co. Cork
*Maxwell, R. W., Esq., J.P., Killyfaddy, Clogher, co. Tyrone
*Maxwell, Thomas, Esq., Magheramorne, Carrickfergus, co. Antrim
Maxwell, Zachariah, Esq., Moneymore, co. Derry
*Mayers, Rev. M J., Ballymoney, near Arklow, co. Wicklow
Maynagh, Rev. Patrick, P.P. of Donagh, co. Monaghan
Maynard, J. C., Esq., Harsely-hall, Cleveland Inn, Yorkshire
Maynard, T. Christopher, Esq., Durham
*Mayne, Rev. E., M.A., Lakeview, Carrickmacross, co. Monaghan
*Mayne, John, Esq., J.P., French-street, Dublin
Mayne, John R., Esq., Cootehill, co. Cavan
Mayne, Richard, Esq., J.P., Freame-mount, Cootehill, co. Cavan
Mayne, William H., Esq., Laurel-hill, Aughnacloy, co. Tyrone
Maynooth College Library, per Rev. B. Crotty
Maziere, William, Esq., North Great George-street, Dublin
Meade, Rev. John, J.P., Ballintober, co. Cork
Meade, Patrick, Esq., M.D., Dromin, Newcastle, co. Limerick
Meade, Mr. Walter, Raduff, near Golden, co. Tipperary [Cork
Meade, Rev. William, A.B., Vicar of Fanlobbus, Dunmanway, co.
Meade, Rev. William, B. A. Derry-cottage, Donoughmore, Cork
Meade, Rev. W. R., A.M., Rector of Templemichael-de-Duagh,
[Innishannon, co. Cork
Meadows, A., Esq., Hermitage, Wexford
*Meagher, Rev. John, Clarendon-street, Dublin
Meagher, Rev. John, P.P., Toomavara, co. Tipperary
*Meagher, Rev. P., P.P. of Tipperary, and Vicar General of the Diocese of Cashel and Emley

*Meany, Rev. P., P.P., Kilrossanty, Dungarvan, co. Waterford
*Meara, George, Esq., J.P., May-park, co. Waterford
Meara, Rev. John, A.M., Headford Rectory, co. Galway [meath
*Meares, J. D.. Esq., J.P., Mearescourt, near Mullingar, co. West-
Mease, Rev. James, Curate of Killygarvan, co. Donegal
*MEATH, The Right Honorable and Right Rev. Lord Bishop of
Mecklin, Counsellor, St. George's-place, Dublin [co. Down
*Mecredy, W. H., Esq., Summer Hill, Dublin, and Rathfriland,
Medlecott, Graydon, Esq., Dunmurry, Kildare
Mee, J., Esq., Balbriggan, co. Dublin
Mee, Rev. M. J., Donaghmore-glebe, Newry, co. Down
Meehan, Rev. P., Exchange-street, Dublin
Meehan, Terence, Esq., Ennis, co. Clare
*Meehan, Rev. Thomas, Possextown, Enfield, co. Meath
*Meekins, Robert, Esq., Glasthule-house, co. Dublin
Megarry, Mr. Bennett, Broomhedge, Lisburn, co. Antrim
Mehan, Mr. James, Londonderry [Tipperary
*Meighan, Rev. M., P.P., Gurthnahoe, &c., New Birmingham, co.
Meilleure, Capt. John, Johnsgrove, near Doneraile, co. Cork
Meing, Mr. John S, Limerick
*MELBOURNE, The Right Honorable Viscount
*Meldon, James D., Esq., Capel-street, Dublin
Melling, John, Esq., Newry, co. Down
*MELVILLE, The Right Honorable Viscount
Menzies, James, Esq., Ennis, co. Clare
*Mercer, Mrs. Elizabeth, East Farleigh, Kent
Meredith, E. J., Esq., Presteign, Radnorshire
*Meredith, George D., Esq., Primrose Grange, Sligo
Meredith, J., Esq., Reary-More, Mountmellick, Queen's county
*Meredith, Joseph, Esq., Cloonamahin, Collooney, co. Sligo
Meredith, Matthew, Esq., Belmullet, co. Mayo
Meredith, R., Esq., Reary-vale, Mountmellick, Queen's county
*Meredith, Richard, Esq., J.P., Dicks-grove, Castle Island, co. Kerry
Meredith, Thomas, Esq., Lower Ormond-quay, Dublin
*Meredyth, Sir H., Bart., LL.D., Judge of the High Court of Admi-
[ralty, Dublin
*Meredyth, Henry, Esq., Randillstown, Navan, co. Meath
*Merrick, Mrs. E., Clonmana, Carndonagh, co. Donegal
Merry, Mr. John, Youghal, co. Cork
*Metcalf, C., Esq., Peace-ville-lodge, Castleruddery, co. Wicklow
Metcalfe, Thomas L., Esq., Dresden, co. Donegal
*Metge, Peter Ponsonby, Esq., Athlumney, Navan, co. Meath
*Meux, Sir Henry, Bart., Theobalds, Hertfordshire
*Meyler, George, Esq., Laurel-lodge, near Dundrum, co. Dublin
*Meyler, Very Rev. W., D.D., Vicar General, P.P. of St. Andrews,
*Michell, H., Esq., M.D., Booterstown-avenue, Dublin [Dublin
Middleton, James, Esq., Dangan-lodge, Roscrea, co. Tipperary
Middleton, Thomas B., Esq., Upper Camden-street, Dublin
Middleton, William, Esq., Kilkenny
*Miles, William, Esq., Manilla-hall, Clifton, near Bristol
Mill, Rev. William, Ballywillan-rectory, co. Derry
*Millar, Jesse, Esq., Dundrum, near Ballymena, co. Antrim
Millar, Mr. John, Lisburn, co. Antrim
*Millar, William, Esq., J.P., Ross-lodge, Ballymena, co. Antrim
Millar, William, Esq., Templemoil, co. Antrim
Millar, William, Esq., Ahoghill, Ballymena, co. Antrim
Millar, W., Esq., Belfast
*Miller, Mr. Alexander, Lissaughmore, Glendermott, co. Derry
*Miller, Alexander, Esq., Ballycastle, co. Antrim
Miller, Alexander, Esq., J.P., Downpatrick, co. Down
Miller, Rev. Alexander, A.B., Keady, co. Armagh
Miller, Mr. George, Glendermott, Londonderry
Miller, Rev. J., D.D., Pittington, Durham
Miller, Rev. J., Rector of Whitechurch and Kilmokea, co. Wexford
*Miller, John, Esq., Rossyvoelan, Donegal
Miller, John, Esq., Comber, co. Down
*Miller, J. E., Esq., M.D., Londonderry
Miller, Rev. John H., Leck-glebe, Letterkenny, co. Donegal
Miller, Robert, jun., Esq., Cookstown, co. Tyrone
Miller, Major William, J.P., Cork
Miller, Captain, J.P., Ennis, co. Clare
*Millet, James, Esq., St. Johnstown-castle, co. Tipperary
*Millet, John, Esq., Lismontagh, Fethard, co. Tipperary
*Millifont, The Hon. Mrs., Eccles-street, Dublin
Milliken, William, Esq., Mallow, co. Cork
*Millikin and Son, Messrs., Grafton-street, Dublin
*Mills, J., Esq., Middle Gardiner-street, Dublin, and Fassaroe-
[cottage, co. Wicklow
Mills, J. F., Esq., Lexden-park, near Colchester, Essex
Mills, John Scott, Esq., Denzille-street, Dublin
*Mills, Rev. M. R., R.C.C., Halston-street, Dublin

Mills, Mr. Robert, Ballyongary, co. Derry
*Mills, Wilson, Esq., Glasnevin-road, Phibsboro, co. Dublin
*MILTOWN, The Right Honorable the Earl of
Minchin, Boyle, Esq., Mallow, co. Cork
Minchin, Charles H., Esq., J.P., Rutland, Shinrone, King's county
*Minchin, Humphrey, Esq., Woodville, Nenagh, co. Tipperary, and [Stephen's-green, Dublin
*Minchin, John, Esq., Annah, Nenagh, co. Tipperary
*Minchin, W., Esq., Eversham, near Stillorgan, co. Dublin
*Minchin, Rev. William, Green-hills, Moneygall, King's county
*Minnitt, J. R., Esq., Annabeg, Nenagh, co. Tipperary
Minnitt, R. A., Esq., Derrygoonly, Carrickmacross, co. Monaghan
*Mint Office, Her Majesty's
Mitchel, Rev. John, Newry, co. Down
Mitchel, Samuel, Esq., Millfield, Buncrana, co. Donegal
*Mitchel, Messrs. W. and J., Dungiven, co. Derry
*Mitchell, Alexander, Esq., J.P., Shirley-house, Carrickmacross, co. [Monaghan
Mitchell, Alexander, Esq., Coleraine, co. Derry
*Mitchell, Rev. Allen, B.A., Drumsnat-glebe, Monaghan
Mitchell, D., Esq., Strabane, co. Tyrone
*Mitchell, Edward, Esq., Sorris-grove, co. Kilkenny
*Mitchell, Edward, Esq., Castlestrange, Athleague, co. Roscommon
*Mitchell, Henry, Esq., J.P., Drumreaske, Monaghan
*Mitchell, H. B., Esq., J.P., Mitchellsfort, Rathcormac, co. Cork
Mitchell, Rev. John, M.A., Newry, co. Down
Mitchell, John, Esq., Gosford, Markethill, co. Armagh
*Mitchell, Mr. Robert, Frankford, King's county
Mitchell, Thomas, Esq., Lower Rutland-street, Dublin
Mitchell, Mr. Walter, Galway
Mockler, Rev. James, Rockville, co. Cork
Moclair, Thomas D., Esq., Castlebar, co. Mayo
Moffat, Rev. Charles J., Chaplain to the Garrison, and Curate [of Newry, co. Down
Moffatt, Rev. G. B., B.A., Drumlane, Belturbet, co. Cavan
*Moffatt, Graham Little, Esq., Banagher, King's county
*Moffatt, Lieut.-Col. J., Parsonstown, King's county
*Moffatt, Rev. J. R., J.P., Rectory, Athlone, co. Westmeath
*Moffett, Rev. James, Ballymahon, co. Longford
*Moffitt, John, Esq., Coltstown, Castledermot, co. Kildare
*Molling, Frederick, Esq., Eltham, Kent
*Molloy, B., Esq., J.P., Millicent, co. Kildare, and Belvidere-place, [Dublin
Molloy, Rev. Francis L., Carndonagh, co. Donegal
*Molloy, Rev. John, P.P., Skerries, co. Dublin
Molloy, John, Esq., Strawberry-hill, King's county
*Molloy, John, Esq., Banagher, King's county
Molloy, Paul, Esq., Rockvalley, Nenagh, co. Tipperary
Molloy, Richard, Esq., Tipperary
*Molony, Croasdaile, Esq., Gloucester-street, Dublin
Molony, James, Esq., J.P., Kiltanon, near Tulla, co. Clare
*Molony, Rev. Jeremiah, P.P., Rosscarbery, co. Cork
*Molony, John, Esq., J.P., Ballinaboy, co. Cork
Molony, John J., Esq., Clonakilty, co. Cork
Molony, Walter, Esq., J.P., Castlecomer, Kilkenny
*Molyineaux, Mr. John, Beechfield, Antrim
Molyneux, Andrew A., Esq., Antrim
*Molyneux, Mr. Samuel, Ballyharvey, Antrim
*Molyneux, Lieut.-Gen. Sir T., Bart., Castle-Dillon-park, Armagh
Monaghan, Rev. H., R.C.C. of Cloncha, Malin, co. Donegal
*Monahan, Rev. M., Tahergar Convent, Ballinamore, co. Leitrim
Monahan, Michael, Esq., Heathlawn, Portumna, co. Galway
*Monck, Hon. Charles J. K., Belleville, Templemore, co. Tipperary
Monck, Rev. G. S., Coolfin, Portlaw, co. Waterford
*Monck, Rev. Marcus, Rathdowney, Queen's county
Monckton, Miles, Esq., Thomas-street, Limerick
*Mongan, Thomas, Esq., Abington, near Killiney, co. Dublin
*Monks, Rev. James, P.P. of St. Andrew's, Dublin
Monks, John, Esq., Cook-street, Cork
*Monks, Thomas, Esq., Summer-hill, Dublin
Monsell, The Rev. T. B., Archdeacon of Derry, Dunloe, co. Derry
*Monsell, William, Esq., Tervoe, near Limerick
*MONTAGU, The Right Honorable Lord W.
*Montague, Rev. M., Maynooth-college, co. Kildare
*Montague, Rev. Patrick, P.P. of Finglass, co. Dublin
*Montfort, Henry, Esq., Middletown, Longford
*Montgomery, The Hon. Mrs., Tyrella, co. Down
*Montgomery, Alexander, Esq., Antrim
*Montgomery, Alexander, Esq., Mill-view, Killead, co. Antrim
*Montgomery, Alexander, Esq., Rutland-square, Dublin
Montgomery, Alexander, Esq., Belmont, Belfast
*Montgomery, Rev. Alexander J., Beaulieu, Drogheda, co. Louth
*Montgomery, A. M., Esq., Glynn, Larne, co. Antrim

*Montgomery, Major A.N., J.P., Bessmont-park, Monaghan
Montgomery, Andrew T., Esq., The Knocks, Naas, co. Kildare
*Montgomery, Rev. C. L., J.P., Vicar of Innismagrath, co. Leitrim
*Montgomery, Hugh, Esq., Ballydrain, Belfast
Montgomery, James, Esq., Belfast
Montgomery, James, Esq., Garvey, Aughnacloy, co. Tyrone
*Montgomery, John, Esq., J.P., Benvarden, co. Antrim
Montgomery, John, Esq., Locust-lodge, Belfast
Montgomery, John, Esq., Eyrecourt, co. Galway
*Montgomery, Robert, Esq., D.L. and J.P., Convoy-house, Raphoe, [co. Donegal
Montgomery, R. G., Esq., M.D., Eyrecourt, co. Galway
*Montgomery, Rev. Samuel, Moville, co. Donegal
Montgomery, Thomas, Esq., J.P., Mitchelstown, co. Cork
*Montgomery, Rev. T. H., Rutland-square North, Dublin
Montgomery, Rev. William J., J.P., Kiilee-castle, Mitchelstown, co. [Cork
*Moody, T., Esq., Dominick-street, Dublin
Moody, William, Esq., Roe-house, Newtown-Limavady, co. Derry
Moone, Rev., J., R.C.C. of Killascobe, Castle-Blakeney, co. Galway
*Mooney, John, Esq., Newmarket Brewery, Dublin
Mooney, Rev. John, R.C.C., Clane, co. Kildare
*Mooney, Rev. P., R.C.C., Meath-street, Dublin
*Mooney, Rev. Peter, Crosspatrick, near Tinahely, co. Wicklow
*Mooney, T., Esq., Killmacud-house, near Stillorgan, co. Dublin
Mooney, Rev. Thomas, A.M., Monaghan
*Moony, Francis E., Esq., Retreat, near Athlone, co. Westmeath
*Moony, R. J. E., Esq., The Doon, Moate, co. Westmeath
*Moore, Sir Emanuel, Bart., Trevara, Bandon, co. Cork
Moore, Alexander, Esq., M.D., Ballymoney, co. Antrim
*Moore, Rev. Charles, J.P., Monasterevan, co. Kildare
Moore, Christopher, Esq., Kilmacthomas, co. Waterford
*Moore, Edward, Esq., J.P., Bawn, Aughnacloy, co. Tyrone
*Moore, Edward, Esq., Lower Gardiner-street, Dublin
*Moore, Edward, Esq., J.P., Aughnacloy, co. Tyrone
*Moore, Garrett, Esq., Richmond Barracks, Dublin
*Moore, George, Esq., Durham
*Moore, George, Esq., Moore-lodge, Kilrea, co. Antrim
*Moore, George, Esq., Moore-hall, Ballyglass, co. Mayo
*Moore, Rev. G. B., J.P., Bawnmore, Longford
*Moore, Rev. H., Carnew-castle, co. Wicklow
Moore, H., Esq., J.P., Eglantine, Hillsborough, co. Down
Moore, Mr. Henry, Ramelton, co. Donegal
Moore, Rev. J., A.M., Rossory-glebe, Enniskillen, co. Fermanagh
*Moore, J., Esq., Newcastle, near Rathcoole, co. Dublin
Moore, Rev. James, P.P., Mungrett and Creehora, Limerick
*Moore, James, Esq., Strandfield, Dundalk, co. Louth
Moore, Mr. James, Crookedstone, Antrim
Moore, James, Esq., Moore Fort, co. Antrim
*Moore, John, Esq., Manor-street, Dublin
Moore, John, Esq., Glendaragh-cottage, Crumlin, co. Antrim
*Moore, John S., Esq., Shannon-grove, Kilkeel, co. Down
Moore, John, Esq., Blessington-street, Dublin
Moore, John, Esq., Governor of City Gaol, Limerick
*Moore, Joseph, Esq., Ballintree, near Clonee, co. Meath
*Moore, J.S., Esq., J.P., Ballydivity, co. Antrim
*Moore, Rev. J. T., Eirke Rectory, Rathdowney, Queen's county
*Moore, J. W., Esq., Rutland-square, Dublin
Moore, Lewis, Esq., D.L. and J.P., Cremorgan, Queen's county
Moore, Rev. M., A.M., Parsonage, Cahirconlish, co. Limerick
Moore, Rev. Michael, R.C.C., Mitchelstown, co. Cork
Moore, O., Esq., Carrickmeane, near Killiney, co. Dublin
*Moore, Rev. Ogle W., Vicar of Blessington, co. Wicklow
Moore, Patrick, Esq., Bridgefoot-street, Dublin
*Moore, Ponsonby, Esq., D.L. & J.P., Moorefield-house, co. Kildare
Moore, Lieut.-Col. Richard, Lawnsdown, Portarlington, Queen's co
Moore, Richard, Esq., Glen-cottage, Watercourse, Cork
Moore, Rev. Richard, A.M., St. Patrick's, Limerick
Moore, Robert, Esq., Athlone, co. Westmeath
*Moore, R. Montgomery, Esq., Storm-hill, Aughnacloy, co. Tyrone
*Moore, S., Esq., Ballynacree, co. Antrim
*Moore, Samuel, Esq., J.P., Cullies-house, Cavan
*Moore, Rev. Samuel, Rockcorry, co. Monaghan
Moore, Mr. Samuel, Ballyharvey, Antrim
*Moore, Stephen, Esq., D.L. and J.P., Barn, Clonmel, co. Tipperary
*Moore, Stephen C., Esq., Coolgrena, Cove, near Cork
*Moore, Rev. Thomas Duke, A.M., Aghadown-glebe, Skibbereen, [co. Cork
Moore, Rev. T. O., Ferns, near Gorey, co. Wexford
Moore, Messrs. T. and J., Belfast, co. Antrim
Moore, W., Esq., Cavan
*Moore, William, Esq., J.P., Castle-view, Carlingford, co. Louth
Moore, Mr. William, Crookedstone, Antrim
Moore, William, Esq., M.D., Dungiven, co. Derry

*Moore, Rev. William Prior, A.B., The College, Cavan
Moorhead, Charles, Esq., Aughless, Dromore, co. Tyrone
*Moorhead, William, Esq., Drumoconner, Monaghan
*Moorsom, Sir R., K.C.B., Cosgrove Priory, Stoney Stratford, Bucks
Moran, Rev. J. F., Curate of Woodford, co. Galway
Moran, John S., Mucknish, Burrin, co. Clare
Moran, J.T., Esq., Summerville, Rathfarnham, co. Dublin
Moran, Rev. Martin, R.C.C., Galbally, Wexford
Mordaunt, Sir J., Bart., Walton, Stratford-on-Avon, Warwickshire
Moreland, James C., Esq., Carnbane, co. Antrim
*Morell, Rev. John H., Fairview, Ballibay, co. Monaghan
Moreton, Mr. Thomas, Rathdrum, co. Wicklow
Morewood, Rev. James, Dunluce Rectory, co. Antrim
Morgan, Francis, Esq., Arran-quay, Dublin
*Morgan, G. G., Esq., Ardcandrisk, Wexford
*Morgan, George, Esq., Bidellesden-park, Bucks
*Morgan, H. K. G., Esq., Johnstown-castle, Wexford
Morgan, James, Esq., Limerick
Morgan, Rev. James, Incumbent of Ross Union, co. Wexford
*Morgan, William, Esq., Ravensdale, co. Dublin
Morgan, William, Esq., Navan, co. Meath
Morgan, William, Esq., Old Abbey, Shanagolden, co. Limerick
*Morgan, Captain, Monksfield, Loughrea, co. Galway
Moriarty, Rev. T., R.C.C., Bridge-street, Dublin
Moriarty, Rev. Martin, R.C.C. of Aghabologue, Coachford, co. Cork
Moriaty, Sir Thomas, Knt., M.D., Abbeytown-house, Roscommon
Morissey, Rev. P., P.P., Kilmurry, and Grange Macler, near Carrick-on-Suir, co. Tipperary
*Morony, F. G., Esq., J.P., Seaview, Miltown-Malbay, co. Clare
*Morony, John, Esq., Westpark, Miltown-Malbay, co. Clare
Morony, T. H., Esq., J.P., Limerick, and Miltown-house, co. Clare
Morow, John, Esq., Deputy Clerk of the Peace, Roscommon
Morressy, Patrick, Esq., Tipperary
*Morris, A., Esq., J.P., Dunkettle, Cork
*Morris, Andrew, Esq., Ballyman, near Little Bray, co. Dublin
*Morris, Rev. B., J.P., Newtown, Callan, co. Kilkenny
Morris, Rev. J., P.P. Roscommon
Morris, James, Esq., Waterford
Morris, Rev. John, P.P., Ballinrobe, co. Mayo
Morris, John, jun., Esq., Prospect-house, Glandore, Rosscarbery, co. Cork
*Morris, Lewis, Esq., Rathdown, near Bray, co. Wicklow
*Morris, Maynard D., Esq., Tralee, co. Kerry
Morris, Rev. Patrick, R.C.C., Ballynoe, co. Cork
*Morris, Richard, Esq., Ballycanvan, near Waterford
*Morris, Samuel, Esq., Fort-view, Clontarf, co. Dublin
Morris, T. F., Esq., Post-master, Gort, co. Galway
Morris, W., Esq., Rathdown, near Bray, co. Wicklow
*Morrison, Mr. Gabriel, Ballymagroarty, Templemore, co. Derry
Morrison, Mr. John, Crookedstone, Antrim
Morrogh, Henry, Esq., Park-farm, Cork
*Morrogh, John, Esq., Sydney-place, Cork
*Mortimer, Thomas Hill, Esq., Albany, Piccadilly, London
*Morton, Francis H., Esq., Fort Town, near Tinahely, co. Wicklow
Morton, Henry, Esq., Town-view, Tinahely, co. Wicklow
*Morton, Rev. James, Navan, co. Meath
*Morton, Rev. James, Vicar of Timmahoe, Clonmel, co. Tipperary
*Morton, James, Esq., Clonmel, co. Tipperary
*Morton, John, Esq., Castlenode, co. Roscommon
*Morton, Captain Moses, Lifford, co. Donegal
Morton, Samuel, Esq., Strabane, co. Tyrone
*Morton, Capt. Thomas, Little Island, Clonmel, co. Tipperary
*Morton, W., Esq., Fairview, co. Roscommon
Morton, William J., Esq., Upton, co. Wexford
*Moss, Mr. Samuel, Kilternan Cotton-mills, co. Dublin
Mosse, A. M., Esq., Annefield, Maryborough, Queen's county
*Mosse, John, Esq., Ballyconra-mills, Ballyraggett, co. Kilkenny
Mostyn, F. T., Esq., Lower Dominick-street, Dublin
*Mostyn, Thomas, Esq., Sligo, and Lower Gardiner-street, Dublin
Mothersill, R., Esq., Washington, Kildare
*Mould, Lieut. Thomas R., Chatham
*MOUNTCASHEL, The Right Honorable the Earl of
*MOUNTCHARLES, The Right Honorable the Earl of
MOUNTMORRES, The Right Honorable Viscount
Mountmorris, Rev. V., Flower-grove, Rochestown-avenue, co. Dublin
*Moutray, J. C., Esq., D.L. and J.P., Favour Royal, Aughnacloy, co. Tyrone
*Mowld, W. T., Esq., Milltown, near Dublin
Mowlds, G. F., Esq., North Cumberland-street, Dublin
Mox, John, Esq., Ballytaisna, Cashel, co. Tipperary
Moyle, Rev. James, P.P. of Ardagh, Ballina, co. Mayo
Mulhall, Thomas, Esq., Stephen's-green, Dublin
Mulcahy, Edmund, Esq., Ballymakee, Clonmel, co. Tipperary
*Mulcahy, Rev. J., P.P., Castlehaven, and Myross, Castletownsend, co. Cork
*MULGRAVE, The Right Honorable the Earl
Mulhallen, Edward, Esq., Ballintubher, near Midleton, co. Cork
Mulhallen, J. G. H., Esq., Royal Oak, Bagnalstown, co. Carlow
Mulholland, Andrew, Esq., Belfast
Mulholland, Mr. Henry, Lisburn, co. Antrim
*Mulholland, Mr. John, Byron-lodge, near Howth, co. Dublin
*Mulholland, Mr. Richard, Lisburn, co. Antrim
Mulholland, S. K., Esq., Belfast
Mullally, Rev. James, R.C.C., Golden, co. Tipperary
Mullanny, Rev. T., P.P., Kilgarrin, Ballina, co. Mayo
Mullany, Rev. Thomas, P.P., Drom, Templemore, co. Tipperary
Mullarky, Rev. D., P.P. of Kilmactigue, Banada, co. Sligo
Mullen, Rev. Michael, P.P., Ballynacargy, co. Westmeath
Mulligan, George, Esq., Newcastle, near Castlewellan, co. Down
*Mulligan, Rev. P. J., Capuchin Convent, Kilkenny
*Mullin, Alexander, Esq., Ballibay, co. Monaghan
*Mullins, Bernard, Esq., Fitzwilliam-square South, Dublin
*Mullins, Mr. James, Athlone-bridge, co. Westmeath
*Mullins, James, Esq., Lombard Street, London
Mullins, Rev. John, P.P., Callan, co. Kilkenny
Mullins, Rev. Patrick, P.P. of Kildinest, Loughrea, co. Galway
*Mullins, Mr. T., Laraghaleas, Faughanvale, co. Derry
Mullock, Rev. J. T., Adam and Eve Chapel, Merchants-quay, Dublin
*Mulloy, C., Esq., J.P., Hughestown, co. Roscommon
*Mulloy, W., Esq., J.P., Oakport, near Boyle, co. Roscommon
Mulock, T. H., Esq., Bellair, Ballycumber, King's county
*Mulock, W. H., Esq., Ballinagore, Kilbeggan, co. Westmeath
*Mulreany, Hugh, Esq., Mount Charles, Donegal
*Mulreany, Michael, Esq., Donegal
Mulreany, Michael, Esq., Beakstown-mills, Thurles, co. Tipperary
Mulvany, Mr. Bernard, Lower Abbey-street, Dublin
Mulville, W., Esq., M.D., M.A., Gort, co. Galway
*Munn, John, Esq., Londonderry
Murdock, W., Esq., Salt-hill, Donegal
Murland, Henry, Esq., Castlewellan, co. Down
*Murland, James, Esq., Annsbro', Castlewellan, co. Down
Murphy, Right Rev. John, R.C., Bishop of Cork
Murphy, Mr. Andrew, Cork
Murphy, Charles, Esq., M.D., Fermoy, co. Cork
*Murphy, Rev. Daniel, P.P., Youghal, co. Cork
Murphy, Daniel, Esq., Belleville, Cork
*Murphy, Rev. Denis, Enniskeen, co. Cork
*Murphy, Rev. Dennis, R.C.C., Kinneigh, Bandon, co. Cork
Murphy, Rev. Dominick, Cooldrahy, Macroom, co. Cork
Murphy, Mr. Edward, Killaloe, co. Clare
Murphy, Rev. E. J., R.C., Vicar of Fermoy, co. Cork
Murphy, F. C., Esq., Ballinderry-house, Enfield, co. Meath
*Murphy, F. D., Esq., Governor of Convict Depot, Cork
Murphy, Rev. James, R.C.C., Riverchapel, co. Wexford
*Murphy, James, Esq., Midleton, co. Cork
*Murphy, James, jun., Esq., Midleton, co. Cork
Murphy, James, Esq., Liverpool
Murphy, Rev. Jeremiah, Ballinamona, Mallow, co. Cork
*Murphy, Jeremiah Stack, Esq., South Main-street, Cork
*Murphy, Rev. John, Adam and Eve Chapel, Merchants-quay, Dublin
Murphy, John, Esq., Cove, co. Cork
Murphy, John, Esq., Woodford, Cashel, co. Tipperary
Murphy, John, Esq., Governor of County Gaol, Cork
Murphy, John Fish, Esq., Sir John Rogerson's-quay, Dublin
Murphy, John, Joseph, Esq., Capel-street, Dublin
Murphy, Rev. Lawrence, P.P., Castleconner, Kilkenny
*Murphy, M., Esq., J.P., Annilea, Cootehill, co. Cavan
*Murphy, M., Esq., Temple-ville, Blackrock-road, Cork
Murphy, Michael, Esq., South Main-street, Cork
Murphy, Rev. Michael, P.P. of Carnew, and Crosspatrick, co. Wicklow
*Murphy, Nicholas D., Esq., South-mall, Cork
Murphy, Rev. P., D.D., Bridge-street, Dublin
Murphy, Rev. P., P.P. of Glynn, co. Wexford
Murphy, Rev. P., P.P. of Monasterevan, &c., co. Kildare
Murphy, Rev. P., P.P., Clonallan, co. Down
Murphy, Mr. Patrick, The Farm, Ballincollig, co. Cork
Murphy, Patrick, Esq., Tuam, co. Galway
Murphy, P. E., Esq., J.P., Ballincloon, near Mullingar, co. Westmeath
*Murphy, P. M., Esq., Bagot-street, Dublin
*Murphy, R., Esq., Caius-college, Cambridge
*Murphy, Robert F., Esq., Elm-cottage, Roundtown, near Dublin
*Murphy, Samuel, Esq., Rathfriland, co. Down
*Murphy, Rev. Stephen, P.P., Kildorrery, co. Cork
*Murphy, Thomas, Esq., Clonmel, co. Tipperary
*Murphy, Thomas, Esq., Carrickmacross, co. Monaghan

Murphy, W., Esq., Woodford, co. Galway
Murphy, Walter William, Esq., M.D., Killarney, co. Kerry
Murphy, William, Esq., Ballinamona, near Cashel, co. Tipperary
Murphy, Rev. William, P.P. of Murragh, co. Cork
Murphy, and O'Connor, Messrs., Marlbro'-street, Cork, 2 copies
Murphy and Co., Messrs., Sligo
* Murray, His Grace the Most Rev. Daniel, D.D., R.C. Primate of [Ireland
* Murray, Lieut.-Gen. Sir George
* Murray, Alexander, Esq., Cally Gate-house, Scotland
* Murray, Rev. D., D.D., Mountjoy-square South, Dublin
* Murray, Edward, Esq., Letterkenny, co. Donegal
Murray, Rev. Edward, Vicar of Kilmore Erris, co. Mayo
Murray, Edward, Esq., Ballinasloe, co. Galway
* Murray, Sir James, Knt., M.D., Merrion-square, Dublin
* Murray, Rev. James, P.P. of Clonmellon, co. Westmeath
* Murray, Rev. James, R.C.C., Ratoath, Ashbourne, co. Meath
* Murray, James, Esq., Londonderry
Murray, James, Esq., J.P., Tullay, Crumlin, co. Antrim
* Murray, John, Esq., Marlfield, Clonmel, co. Tipperary
* Murray, John, Esq., Blessington, co. Wicklow
* Murray, John, Esq., Londonderry
* Murray, John S., Esq., J.P., Forren-hill, Dungannon, co. Tyrone
* Murray, Rev. Joseph, P.C., Monasterevan, co. Kildare
Murray, Major-Gen., J.P., Killinore-house, Athlone, co. Westmeath
Murray, J. W. S., Esq., J.P., Dungannon, co. Tyrone
* Murray, Rev. Michael J., P.P. of Skerries, co. Dublin
* Murray, Patrick, Esq. North Brunswick-street, Dublin
* Murray, The Very Rev. R., Dean of Ardagh, co. Longford
Murray, Rev. Richard, R.C.C., St. Nicholas without, Dublin
* Murray, Robert, Esq., A.M., M.D., Beech-hill, Monaghan
Murray, Thomas, Esq., Sheepwalk, near Arklow, co. Wicklow
Murray, Rev. Thomas, P.P., Garristown, co. Dublin
Murray, Rev. Thomas, Macroom, co. Cork
* Murray, William, Esq., Bank of Ireland, Dublin
Murray, William, Esq., Eccles-street, Dublin
* Murray, William T., Esq., Cloncallow, Ballymahon, co. Longford
Murry, John, Esq., Sunderland
Murtagh, Rev. J., P.P. of Kilcullen, co. Kildare
* Musgrave, Sir R., Bart., M.P. & J.P., Tourin, Cappoquin, co. Wa- [terford
* MUSKERRY, The Right Honorable the Earl of
* Mussenden, William, Esq., D.L. & J.P., Larchfield, co. Down
Musters, Henry P., Esq., Clonakilty, co. Cork
Myers, Mrs., Grantham, Lincolnshire

* Naghten, E. H., Esq., Thomastown-park, Athlone, co. Roscommon
Nagle, G., Esq., Ballynamona-castle, near Mallow, co. Cork
Nagle, James, Esq., Midleton, co. Cork
* Nagle, Pierce, Esq., Anakissy, Mallow. co. Cork
* Naish, Carrol, Esq., Ballycullen, near Askeaton, co. Limerick
Nangle, B., Esq., Midleton, co. Cork
* Nangle, Charles, Esq., New Haggard, Trim, co. Meath
* Napier, W. Z., Esq., Littleton-lodge, near Ballymahon, co. West- [meath
* Nash, Cornelius, Esq., Limerick
* Nash, Rev. D. H., Rector of Templeomalus, co. Cork
* Nash, Capt. Edmund, Charleville, co. Cork
Nash, Rev. H. M., J.P., Fairview, Bundoran, Ballyshannon, co. [Leitrim
Nash, Richard, Esq., Borrisokane, co. Tipperary
Nash, Rev. R. H., D.D., Rector of Ardstraw, Moyle, co. Tyrone
* Nash, Rev. R. S., Hamerton Rectory, near Huntingdon
* Nash, Richard West, Esq., Upper Mount-street, Dublin
Nash, S., Esq., Knockreagh, near Douglas, co. Cork
Nash, Rev. Thomas E., A.M., Cove, co. Cork
Nash, Rev. W. R., Barnstead, Blackrock, co. Cork
Nash, William, Esq., Doneraile, co. Cork
* Nason, Henry, Esq., Newtown-lodge, Tallow, co. Cork
Nason, Lieut. H. T. King, R.N., Kinsale, co. Cork
* Nason, John, Esq., Newtown, Tallow, co. Cork
Naters, Ralph, Esq., Newcastle-on-Tyne, Northumberland
National Bank, Dublin
* NAVY, The Rt. Hon. the Lords Commissioners of Her Majesty's
* Navy Pay Office, Her Majesty's
Neale, George, Esq., Coolraine Mills, Mountrath, Queen's county
* Neale, George Penrose, Esq., Kilmoney, Rathangan, co. Kildare
Neale, Samuel, Esq., Newington, Rathangan, co. Kildare
Need, John, Esq., Mansfield-Woodhouse, Nottinghamshire
Neeson, H., Esq., M.D, Randalstown, co. Antrim
Neilan, Andrew, Esq., Spring-mount, Gort, co. Galway
Neill, Miss H., Ballymoney, co. Antrim
* Neilson, Andrew, Esq., Craigmonaghan, Castlederg, co. Tyrone
Neilson, Charles, Esq., M.D., Killala, co. Mayo
Neilson, William, Esq., Abbey-street, Dublin
Neligan, Lieut. Thomas, George-street, Cork
Neligan, Rev. W. C., Curate of St. Peters, Cork
Nelley, Rev. Michael, P.P., Ennistymon, co. Clare
* Nelson, Rev. J., D.D., Downpatrick, co. Down
Nelson, Joseph, Esq., Lower Gardiner-street, Dublin, and May- [street, Belfast
* Nesbitt, J. D., Esq., J.P., Tubberdaly, Edenderry, King's county
* Nesbitt, R. W., Esq., Bruckless, Dunkanely, co. Donegal
* Nesham, J. D., Esq., Blackwell and Houghton-le-Spring, Durham
* Nesham, R., Esq., Darlington, Durham
* Ness, J. B., Esq., Shanagolden, co. Limerick
Nettles, R. N., Esq., J.P., Nettleview-house, Killenardrish, co. Cork
* Nevill, W., Esq., Maiden-lane, London
Neville, Rev. Richard, A.M., Ahadoe-house, Killeagh, co. Cork
Neville, Robert, Esq., J.P., Marymount, Johnstown, co. Kilkenny
Nevin, Rev. John L., Portglenone, co. Antrim
* Nevin, P., Esq., Crumlin-road, Dublin
* Newbald, Charles, Esq., Pottersfields, Tooley-street, London
* NEWBURGH, The Right Honorable the Earl of
* Newburgh, Captain, J.P., Marino, Bantry, co. Cork
Newcomb, George, Esq., Hollywood, Clonbulloge, co. Tipperary
* Newdick, Shirley, Esq., Sidmouth, Devonshire
Newell and Grant, Messrs., Distillery, Tralee, co. Kerry
Newenham, Charles, Esq., Snugmore, near Kinsale, co. Cork
* Newenham, Capt. E. W., Talbot-lodge, Stillorgan-park, co. Dublin
Newenham, E. Eyre, Esq., Maryborough, near Douglas, co. Cork
Newenham, George, Esq., Summerhill, Cork
Newenham, Rev. Thomas, Rector of Kilworth, co. Cork
Newland, Rev. Henry, D.D., Ferns, co. Wexford
* Newman, George, Esq., Kinsale, co. Cork
Newman, George, Esq., New Road, London
Newman, Rev. Horatio T., Rector of Kilbrogan, Bandon, co. Cork
Newman, J., Esq., Cardiffe-bridge, near Dublin
* Newman, John, Esq., Town-hall, Southwark, Surrey
Newman, John Spiller, Esq., Kinsale, co. Cork
Newman, W., Esq., Castlemartyr, co. Cork
Newman, W., Esq., J.P., Kinsale, co. Cork
* Newman, W. L., Esq., Guildhall, London
* Newport, The Right Honourable Sir J., Bart., J.P.
* Newport, Simon, Esq., Brook-lodge, near Waterford
* NEWRY, The Right Honorable Viscount
* Newson, Robert, Esq., Mount Wilson, Edenderry, King's county
Newson, Thomas, Esq., Great George-street, Cork
Newton, B. B., Esq., Rathwade, Bagnalstown, co. Carlow
* Newton, George, Esq., Darragh-villa, near Kilcoole, co. Wicklow
Newton, Rev. Thomas, Incumbent of Coxwold, Thirsk, Yorkshire
Newton, Walter, Esq., J.P., Dunleckney, Bagnalstown, co. Carlow
* Neynoe, Col. W. B., J.P., Castle Neynoe, Collooney, co. Sligo
Niblock, Rev. W., Donegal
Nicholas, John, Esq., Mount-pleasant, Liverpool
Nicholl, J. R., Esq., Exeter-college, Oxford
Nicholson, Rev. A. A., P.C. of Moylary, Dunleer, co. Louth
* Nicholson, Capt. B. W., Quatrebras, near Dalkey, co. Dublin
* Nicholson, C. A., Esq., Belrash, near Kells, co. Meath
Nicholson, Harvey, Esq., Londonderry
* Nicholson, John, Esq., Tall-bridge, Loughall, co. Armagh
* Nicholson, J., Esq., Boldbrook-mills, Tallaght, and Cook-st., Dublin
Nicholson, Richard, Esq., Town Clerk, Ripon, Yorkshire
Nicholson, Robert, Esq., Belfast, co. Antrim
Nicholson, Robert, Esq., Clanwilliam-place, Dublin
* Nicholson, R. Jaffray, Esq., Stramore-house, Gilford, co. Down
Nicholson, W. Steele, Esq., J.P., Ballow, Bangor, co. Down
Nightingale, Miss, Bryan-house, Blackheath, Kent
* Nimmo, George, Esq., Marlborough-street, Dublin
* Nisbett, Francis, Esq., Derrycarne, Dromod, co. Leitrim
Nisbett, Rev. R. W., A.M., O'Gonnelloe-glebe, Killaloe, co. Clare
Niven, Richard, Esq., Chrome-hill, Lisburn, co. Antrim
* Nixon, A., Esq., D.L., and J.P. Ballanaleck, Enniskillen, co. Fer- [managh
* Nixon, Adam, Esq., Gran, Enniskillen, co. Fermanagh
* Nixon, Allan, Esq., Blackpark, Manorhamilton, co. Leitrim
Nixon, Edward, Esq., Abbey-street, Dublin
Nixon, George Alcock, Esq., M.D., Enniskillen, co. Fermanagh
Nixon, James, Esq., Prospect, Enniskillen, co. Fermanagh
* Nixon, James, Esq., Mountjoy-square South, Dublin
Nixon, Rev. R. H., Marino, Booterstown, near Dublin
* Nixon, Mr. Robert, Aylesbury, Bucks
* Nixon, Thomas, Esq., J.P., Dunbar-house, Enniskillen, co. Ferma- [nagh
* Noble, Major Samuel, Cavan
* Noble, William, Esq., Greenmount, near Dundrum, co. Dublin
* Noblett, Henry, Esq., South-mall, Cork
* Noel, C. Henry, Esq., Wellingore-house, Sleaford, Lincolnshire

*Nogueras, Rev. C., Clarendon-street, Dublin
*Nolan, Rev. A., P.P. Dunkerrin, Roscrea, co. Tipperary
*Nolan, Rev. E., St. James'-college, Kilkenny [Leighlin
Nolan, The Right Rev. E., D.D., R.C., Bishop of Kildare and
*Nolan, E. J., Esq., Woodview, Donnybrook, co. Dublin, and Logboy,
Nolan, Rev. James, R.C.C., Bagnalstown, co. Carlow [co. Mayo
*Nolan, John, Esq., J.P., Ballinderry, Tuam, co. Galway
Nolan, J. D., Esq., Grenville-street, Dublin
*Nolan, Luke, Esq., Tinneclash, Carlow
Nolan, Rev. P., P.P. of Balla, and V.G. of Tuam, co. Mayo
Nolan, Rev. Thomas, P.P. of Kill and Lyons, near Naas, co. Kildare
Nolan, Rev. Thomas, R.C.C., Tullow, co. Carlow
Nolan, Rev. Thomas, Curate of Conwall, Letterkenny, co. Donegal
*Nolan, William, Esq., Wicklow
Noonan, Rev. John, R.CC. of Kildorrery, co. Cork
*Noone, Rev. Dominick, R.C.C. of Ahamplish, Cliffoney, co. Sligo
Noone, Rev. J. J., R.C.C. of Killescobe, Castle-Blakeney, co. Gal-
*NORBURY, The Right Honorable the Earl of [way
*Norcott, Lieut. E., R.N.
Norcott, John, Esq., M.D., Cottage, Doneraile, co. Cork
Norcott, R. B., Esq., Clonakilty, co. Cork
Norcott, W., Esq., Villa, Kilworth, co. Cork
Norman, Charles, Esq., J.P., Fahan, Londonderry
Norman, Robert, Esq., Stafford-street, Dublin
*Norman, Rev. Robert, Ratoath, Ashbourne, co. Meath
*Norman, T. Lee, Esq., J.P., Corballis, Ardee, co. Louth
*Norris, James J., Esq., Keiran, Ardee, co. Louth
*Norris, John, Esq., Hughenden-house, near High Wycombe, Bucks
North, Isaac, Esq., Ferrans, Kilcock, co. Meath
*NORTHAMPTON, The Most Noble the Marquis of
*Norton, John, Esq., Williamstown, near Dublin
*Norton, Capt. T., Wainsfort, near Rathfarnham, co. Dublin
Norton, Josh. E. and Co., Messrs., Clifton, near Bristol
*Norwich Union Fire and Life Insurance Company
Notter, John, Esq., Rock Island House, near Skibbereen, co. Cork
*Notter, Richard, Esq., Carrigduve, Cork
*Nowell, R., Esq., Essex-street, London
Nowlan, Rev. E., P.P. Gowran, Kilkenny
*Nowlan, Rev. Patrick, P.P. Stamullen, Balbriggan, co. Meath.
Nowlan, Captain Thomas, Golden-bridge, co. Dublin
Nowlan, Rev. Thomas, P.P. of Kill, near Naas, co. Kildare
Nowlan, Rev. Thomas, P.P. of Newbridge, co. Kildare
*Nugent, Colonel Andrew, J.P., Portaferry-house, co. Down
*Nugent, The Honorable Anthony, Tynagh
*Nugent, C. E. J., Esq., J.P. Bobsgrove, Mount Nugent, co. Cavan
*Nugent, Sir Edmond, Knt.
Nugent, George Lucas, Esq., Castle Rickard, near Trim, co. Meath
*Nugent, Capt. J., Mill-view, near Malahide, co. Dublin
*Nugent, James, Esq., Kingstown, co. Dublin
*NUGENT, The Count
*Nugent, James, Esq., Streamstown, near Killbeggan, co. Westmeath
*Nugent, Sir Percy, Bart., D.L. and J.P.
Nugent, Walter, Esq., Mallow, co. Cork
Nugent, Walter, Esq., Leamington Spa, and Westmeath
Nunn, John, Esq., Silverspring, near Wexford
Nunn, Capt. John N., J.P., Enniscorthy Castle, co. Wexford
Nunn, Rev. Loftus, Curate of Whitechurch, New Ross, co. Wexford

Oakes, Charles Henry, Esq., Mitcham-hall, Surrey
*Oakes, W., Esq., Shirland-house, Alfreton, Derbyshire
*Oakley, George, Esq., Crumlin-lodge, co. Dublin
*Oates, Very Rev. James, O.D.C., Clarendon-street, Dublin
O'Beirne, Rev. A., LL.D., Portavo-house, Enniskillen, co. Fer-
*O'Beirne, Edmund, Esq., Lower Gardiner-street, Dublin [managh
O'Beirne, Francis, Esq., J.P., Jamestown-lodge, Drumsna, co. Lei-
*O'Beirne, John, Esq., Athlone, co. Westmeath [trim
*O'Beirne, Rev. Michael, P.P. of Newtown Forbes, co. Longford
O'Beirne, T., Esq., Belleville, Sligo [Wicklow
*Obins, Lieut.-Col. H., Ballyronane, N. T., Mount-kennedy, co.
*Obrie, Edward, Esq., Clantileu, Loughgall, co. Armagh
*O'Brien, Acheson, Esq., J.P., Drumsilla, Carrigallen, co. Leitrim
*O'Brien, Cornelius, Esq., J.P., Birchfield, co. Clare
O'Brien, Rev. Cornelius, C.C. Roscrea, co. Tipperary
O'Brien, Cornelius, Esq., M.P., Kilcor, Rathcormac, co. Cork
O'Brien, Rev. D., St. John's College, Waterford
O'Brien, Denis, Esq., Ballinvillin-house, Mitchelstown, co. Cork
O'Brien, Dennis, Esq., Jervis-street, Dublin
*O'Brien, D. C., Esq., Waterloo-cottage, Caher, co. Tipperary
*O'Brien, Sir E., Bart., J.P., Dromoland, Newmarket-on-Fergus, co.
O'Brien, Edward, Esq., Mitchelstown, co. Cork [Clare

*O'Brien, George, Esq., Cheshunt, Hertfordshire
O'Brien, George W., Esq., M.D., Ennis, co. Clare
O'Brien, Henry, Esq., Lisurland, Newcastle, co. Limerick
*O'Brien, James West, Esq., Drumregan, Mohill, co. Leitrim
O'Brien, Rev. J., P.P. of Knockany and Patrickswell, Bruff, co.
*O'Brien, James John, Esq., Academy-street, Cork [Limerick
*O'Brien, Jeremiah, Esq., Ryninch, Killaloe, co. Clare
*O'Brien, Rev. John, R.C.C., Croghan, near Boyle, co. Roscommon
*O'Brien, John, Esq., J.P., Drumrahan, Drumsna, co. Leitrim
*O'Brien, John, Esq., Mountjoy-square East, Dublin
O'Brien, John, Esq., Fox-hall, Newport, co. Tipperary
O'Brien, John, Esq., Larogh, Tullow, co. Carlow
*O'Brien, John, Esq., Fairfield, Ahascragh, co. Galway
O'Brien, John, Esq.. Elmvale, co. Clare
*O'Brien, John B., Esq., J.P., Turtulla, Thurles, co. Tipperary
*O'Brien, Rev. Kenedy, R.C.C. of Macroom, co. Cork
*O'Brien, Lucius, Esq., Dromoland, co. Clare
O'Brien Rev. M., P.P., Kilkeedy, Corofin, co. Clare
*O'Brien, Mathew, Esq., Newcastle, near Limerick
O'Brien, Rev. Michael, P.P. of Timoleague, near Bandon, co. Cork
O'Brien, Michael, Esq., Ballinvullen-cottage, Mitchelstown, co. Cork
*O'Brien, P., Esq., Sexton-street, Limerick
*O'Brien, P., Esq., M.D., Johnstown-bridge, Enfield, co. Kildare
*O'Brien, Richard, Esq., Ballinasloe, co. Galway
O'Brien, Richard, Esq., Kilshanna-house, Mitchelstown, co. Cork
O'Brien, Richard, Esq., Lansdowne, near Nenagh, co. Tipperary
*O'Brien, Stafford, Esq., J.P., Cratloe-woods, co. Clare, and Blather-
[wycke-park, Northamptonshire
O'Brien, Thomas, Esq., Rockvale, Castlemartyr, co. Cork
O'Brien, W., Esq., Rossmanagher-cottage, Six-mile-bridge, co.
*O'Brien, Rev. W., P.P. of Lurgan, co. Armagh [Clare
O'Brien, Rev. W., Tobber-house, near Moate, co. Westmeath
O'Brien, W., Esq., M.R.C.S., Mitchelstown, co. Cork
*O'Brien, W. L., Esq., Mount Francis, Boyle, co. Roscommon
*O'Brien, Rev. Mr., R.C.C., Kells, co. Meath
O'Bryen, Hewitt, Esq., Foyle-street, Londonderry
*O'Callaghan, C., Esq., Riverstown, Cork
*O'Callaghan, Mr. Cornelius, Brookville, co. Cork
*O'Callaghan, Denis, Esq., J.P., Cadogan, Rathcormac, co. Cork
O'Callaghan, Rev. Denis, P.P. of Carron, near Corofin, co. Clare
O'Callaghan, Mr. Eugene, Ballyclough, Mallow, co. Cork
O'Callaghan, George, Esq., Mary-fort, Tulla, co. Clare
*O'Callaghan, H. H., Esq., Georges-st., and Castle-Connell, Limerick
*O'Callaghan, James, Esq., Lower Fitzwilliam-street, Dublin
*O'Callaghan, J. O., Esq., Lower Mount-street, Dublin
*O'Callaghan, Rev. Michael, P.P. of Drumcliff, co. Sligo [Dublin
*O'Callaghan and McShean, Messrs. W., Lower Gardiner-street,
*O'Connell, Rev. Andrew, Exchange-street, Dublin
O'Connell, Charles, Esq., J.P., Bahoss, Cahirciveen, co. Kerry
*O'Connell, Rev. Daniel, R.C.C., Bantry, co. Cork
*O'Connell, Daniel Esq., M.P. & J.P., Derrynane-abbey, Cahirciveen,
*O'Connell, David, Esq., Marlboro'-street, Cork [co. Kerry
O'Connell, Denis, Esq., M.D., Flintfield, Millstreet, co. Cork
O'Connell, Rev. Jeremiah, P.P. Lixnaw, co. Kerry
*O'Connell, Rev. John, P.P. Mitchelstown, co. Cork
O'Connell, Mr. John, Marlboro-street, Dublin
*O'Connell, Rev. John, O.S.F., Cork
*O'Connell, John, Esq., Bantry, co. Cork
*O'Connell, John, Esq., John-street, Cork (2 copies)
O'Connell, John, Esq., Watercourse, Cork
O'Connell, John, Esq., M.P. & J.P., Grena, near Killarney, co. Kerry
*O'Connell, Morgan John, Esq., M.P., Grena, near Killarney, co. Kerry
*O'Connell, Philip, Esq., Sullivans' Quay, Cork
O'Connell, Rev. T., P.P., Portarlington, Queen's county
*O'Connell, Timothy, Esq., Kilfinane, near Kilmallock, co. Limerick
O'Connell, W., Esq., Rathcormac, co. Cork
O'Connor, Very Rev. A., P.P. Maryboro', Queen's county
O'Connor, Mr. Bernard, Mecklenburgh-street, Dublin
O'Connor, Charles, Esq., Churchill-house, Sligo
O'Connor, Rev. C. J., Tralee, co. Kerry
*O'Connor, Mr. Daniel, Bruff, co. Limerick
O'Connor, Mr. Edward, Mecklenburgh-street, Dublin
*O'Connor, Rev. George, Castlenock, co. Dublin
*O'Connor, Rev. George, R.C.C. of Glendalough, co. Wicklow
*O'Connor, Henry, Esq., Baronston, near Mullingar, co. Westmeath
O'Connor, Henry, Esq., Sligo
O'Connor, Rev. James, A.M., Tubbercorry, co. Sligo
*O'Connor, John, Esq., Gravelmount, Nobber, co. Meath
O'Connor, Maurice, Esq., J.P., Tralee, co. Kerry
O'Connor, Rev. Michael, D.D., Cove, co. Cork
*O'Connor, Rev. Patrick, P.P. Peterswell, Gort, co. Galway

O'Connor, Rev. Patrick, P.P. Kilcloon, Maynooth, co. Kilkenny
O'Connor, Rev. Peter, P.P. Croghan, near Boyle, co. Roscommon
O'Connor, Peter, Esq., Sligo
O'Connor, R., Esq., Gloster-place, Dublin [hill, Dublin
O'Connor, R., Esq., Milton, Tulske, co. Roscommon, and Summer-
* O'Connor, Rev. Thomas, Thurles, co. Tipperary
O'Connor, Rev. W., Vicar of St. Finbarr's, Cork
O'Connor, William, Esq., Cork
O'Conor, E, Esq., J.P., Belanagare, French-Park, co. Roscommon
* O'Conor, Rev. James, P.P. Ahascragh, co. Galway
* O'Conor, Matthew, Esq., Mountjoy-sq., South, Dublin, and Mount [Druid, co. Roscommon
* O'Conor Don. The, M.P., Blenagare, French-Park, co. Roscommon
* O'Corcoran, Rev. G. D., Dominican-convent, Drogheda, co. Louth
* O'Croly, Rev. David, P.P. Ovens and Aglish, co. Cork
* Odell, Edward, Esq., J.P., Carriglea, near Dungarvan, co. Waterford
* Odell, John, Esq., J.P., Carriglea, near Dungarvan, co. Waterford
Odell, John, Esq., Shannon-vale, Nenagh, co. Tipperary
* Odell, John, Esq., Odellville, Ballingarry, co. Limerick
Odell, Robert, Esq., M.D., Ballingarry, co. Limerick
Odell, Thomas A., Esq., Odellville, Ballingarry, co. Limerick
* O'Dell, Major, The Grove, Ballingarry, co. Limerick
* Odlim, Digby, Esq., Ballymorin, Edenderry, King's county
Odlum, E. J., Esq., Old Connall-house, Newbridge, co. Kildare
* O'Doherty, Charles, Esq., The Cottage, Londonderry
O'Doherty, Rev. James, Clonmany, Carndonagh, co. Donegal
O'Doherty, Mr. Neil, Gaddyduff, Clonmany, co. Donegal
* O'Doherty, Rev. Patrick, C.C. Wicklow
O'Donell, Dominick, Esq., Cross cottage, Belmullet, co. Mayo
O'Donnell, Rev. David, P.P. Kilkeedy, co. Kerry
* O'Donnell, Ignatius P., Esq., Fahyness, Swinford, co. Mayo
O'Donnell, James, Esq., Sligo
O'Donnell, John, Esq., Kilbreedy, Kilmallock, co. Limerick
O'Donnell, Rev L., R.C. Vicar-General of the Diocese of Galway
O'Donnell, Maurice, Esq., Carrick-on-Suir, co. Tipperary
O'Donnell, Rev. P., R.C.C. of Clonmany, Carndonagh, co. Donegal
O'Donnell, Rev. Patrick, P.P. Tubrid, near Caher, co. Tipperary
* O'Donnell, Robert, Esq., Greyfield, near Keadue, co. Roscommon
O'Donnell, Terence, Esq., Sligo
* O'Donnell, Rev. W., P.P. of Clonmany, Carndonagh, co. Donegal
O'Donoghue, Lieut.-Col. D., J.P., Portarlington, Queen's county
* O'Donoghue, Rev. P., P.P. Dungimmar, Mount Nugent, co. Meath
* O'Donoghue, Robert J., Esq., Mount Vernon, near Cork
O'Donoghue, Robert J., Esq., Killinardrish, co. Cork
* O'Donohoe, Rev. James, P.P. of Longford
* O'Donovan, Rev. C., P.P. Rathcormac, co. Cork
* O'Donovan, Daniel, Esq., M.D., Bantry, co. Cork
O'Donovan, Jeremiah, Esq., Midleton, co. Cork
* O'Donovan, Rev. Morgan, Montpelier, Douglas, near Cork
O'Donovan, T., Esq., J.P. O'Donovan's Cove, Bantry, co. Cork
O'Donovan, Rev. Timothy, R.C.C. of Dunmanway, co. Cork
* O'Dowd, James, Esq., Lakemount, Ballyglass, co. Mayo
* O'Dowda, Thaddeus, Esq., O'Dowdas Town, Ballina, co. Mayo
O'Driscoll, Alexander, Esq., J.P., the Hill, Passage-road, near Cork
O'Driscoll, Alexander, Esq., Gurnasreena, Skibbereen, co. Cork
O'Driscoll, Rev. James, P.P. Kilmichael, Macroom, co. Cork
O'Driscoll, Timothy, Esq., Old Court, Skibbereen, co. Cork
O'Dwyer, Rev. James, P.P. Clare Island, Westport, co. Mayo
O'Dwyer, Rev. Thomas, R.C.C. Skerries, co. Dublin
* O'Farrell, Michael James, Esq., Marlboro-street, Dublin
* O'Fay, The Count, D.D., K.G.S., Galway
* O'Ferrall, Hugh, Esq., North Frederick-street, Dublin [Longford
* O'Ferrall, John L., Esq., Baggot-street, Dublin, and Lissard, co.
* O'Ferrall, Rev. Mark, R.C.C. Moate, co. Westmeath [ford
* O'Ferrall, Rev. M., R.C.C. of Killyglass, Edgeworthstown, co. Long-
* O'Ferrall, R. More, Esq., M.P., D.L., & J.P., Balyna-house, co.
O'Fflahertie, Thomas, Esq., J.P., Lemonfield, co. Galway [Kildare
O'Flaherty, Anthony, Esq., J.P., Knockbane, Moycullen, co. Galway
O'Flaherty, Rev. Edward, Littlegraigna, near Fethard, co. Wexford, [P.P. of the Union of Fethard, St. James, and Templetown
* O'Flaherty, Thomas, Esq., Limerick
O'Flanagan, Captain J. F., Fermoy, co. Cork
* O'Flanagan, Matthew, Esq., Crescent, Limerick
* O'Flinn, Rev. Daniel, P.P. of Aghada, near Cloyne, co. Cork
* O'Flynn, Rev. Patrick, Bantry, co. Cork
* O'Gara, Rev. R. Dominick, P.P. of Clontead, co. Cork
* O'Gara, Rev. P., R.C.C. of Ardcarne, near Boyle, co. Roscommon
* Ogden, Robert, Esq., Ardwick, Manchester
* Ogden, Robert, Esq., Portland-place, Manchester
* Ogilby, Robert, Esq., Pellipar-house, Dungiven, co. Derry, 2 copies
Ogle, Arthur Knox, Esq., Newry, co. Down
* Ogle, Francis, Esq., Newry, co. Down
* Ogle, N., Esq., J.P., Dysart, Castletown-Delvin, co. Westmeath
* O'Grady, The, D.L. and J.P., Kilballyowen, co. Limerick, and Carrigmahon, co. Cork [Cork
O'Grady, Carew, Esq., J.P., Aghamarta-castle, near Carrigaline, co.
* O'Grady, Daniel, Esq., J.P., Shore-park, Kildysart, co. Clare
O'Grady, Darby, Esq., D.L., Linfield, Pallas Green, co. Limerick
O'Grady, Henry, Esq., Grange, Limerick
O'Grady, J., Esq., Ballinasloe, co. Galway
* O'Grady, John Waller, Esq., Fort Etna, Patrickswell, near Limerick
O'Grady, Rev. John Decourcy, Vicar of Any, Bruff, co. Limerick
* O'Grady, Michael Martin, Esq., M.D., Swords, co. Dublin
* O'Grady, Richard, Esq., Carabeg, Ballaghaderran, co. Mayo
* O'Grady, The Hon. Col. S., D.L. and J.P., Rockbarton, co. Lime-
O'Grady, Rev. Thomas, Rock Island, Skibbereen, co. Cork [rick
* O'Grady, Waller, Esq., Stephen's-green, Dublin, and Castlegarde, [Pallas-greine, co. Limerick
O'Halloran, Rev. E., P.P., Killeedy, co. Limerick
* O'Halloran, John, Esq., Killarem, Listowel, co. Kerry
O'Halloran, Peter, Esq., North Great George-street, Dublin
* O'Hanlon, James, Esq., Mount Bagnal, Dundalk, co. Louth
* O'Hanlon, Philip, Esq., Rathkeale, co. Limerick
* O'Hanlon, Rev. R. J., Clarendon-street, Dublin
* O'Hara, A., Esq., J.P. Gloonan-lodge, Ballymena, co. Antrim
* O'Hara, Charles, Esq., O'Hara-brook, Ballymoney, co. Antrim
* O'Hara, Charles, Esq., Blackall-street, Dublin
* O'Hara, C. K., Esq., J.P., Annachmore, Colooney, co. Sligo
O'Hara, Constantine, Esq., Essex-quay, Dublin, and Galway
* O'Hara, H., Esq., Patrick-street, Cork
* O'Hara, H., Esq., Prospect, Portstewart, Coleraine, co. Derry
* O'Hara, James, Esq., Leneboy, Galway
* O'Hara, Rev. James, P.P. of Drumratt, Ballymote, co. Sligo
* O'Hara, John, Esq., Limerick
O'Hara, John, Esq., Galway
O'Hea, Rev. Eugene, R.C.C. Castle Lyons, co. Cork
O'Hea, Matthew, Esq., R.N., Cottage, Cloyne, co. Cork
O'Hea, Rev. Michael, R.C.C. Castlelyons, co. Cork
O'Hea, Michael, Esq., George's-quay, Cork
O'Kaine, Rev. Dennis, P.P. of Attymas, Ballina, co. Mayo
O'Kane, Rev. John, R.C.C. Lixnaw, Listowel, co. Kerry
O'Keane, Rev. P. J., P.P. Clare, Galway
O'Keeffe, Charles, Esq., Thurles, co. Tipperary [co. Cork
* O'Keeffe, Rev. D., R.C.C., P.P. of the Islands of Sherkin and Clear,
* O'Keeffe, Rev. Joseph, P.P. of Kilshannick, Kanturk, co. Cork
O'Keeffe, Rev. M., C.C. Lisquinlan, Castlemartyr, co. Cork
O'Keeffe, Menus, Esq., J.P. Mount Keeffe, Newmarket, co. Cork
* O'Keeffe, P., Esq., Abbeyview, near Waterford
* O'Keeffe, Very Rev. T., R.C. Dean of Cork, and P.P. of St. Finbars,
* O'Keene, Rev. Bernard, P.P., Ballymote, co. Sligo [co. Cork
* O'Kelly, Cornelius T., Esq., Tycooly, Castle-Blakeney, co. Galway
O'Kelly, David, Jun., Esq., Charleville, co. Cork
* O'Kelly, George, Esq., Ballysax-house, Kilcullen, co. Kildare
* O'Kelly, P. F., Esq., Kevinsport, Dublin
Okill, Charles, Esq., Town-hall, Liverpool
* Oldham, James, Esq., Cork
* Oldham, James, Esq., Roseville, near Cork
* Oldman, Henry, Esq., Faversham, Kent
O'Leary, Rev. D., Currymount, Buttevant, co. Cork
O'Leary, Rev. Jeremiah, P.P., Castle Island, co. Kerry
* O'Leary, M'Carthy, Esq., J.P., Coomlagane, Millstreet, co. Cork
Oliver, A. Morris, Esq., Towermore, Fermoy, co. Cork
* Oliver, Joseph, Esq., Tullymore, co. Armagh
* Oliver, Vice-Admiral Robert Dudley, Fitzwilliam-square, Dublin
Oliver, William, Esq., Laragh, Carrickmacross, co. Monaghan
Oliver, William, Esq., Spa-hill, Kilfinane, co. Limerick
O'Loghlen, Donat, Esq., M.D., Castle Connell, co. Limerick
O'Loghlen, Hugh, Esq., J.P., Port, co. Clare
O'Loghlen, Ryan, Esq., Rockview, Ennis, co. Clare [Armagh
* Olpherts, W., Esq., J.P., Dartrey-lodge, Blackwatertown, co.
* O'Malley, Andrew C., Esq., J.P., Newcastle, Swinford, co. Mayo
O'Malley, Charles A., Esq., Prospect-house, Eyrecourt, co. Galway
* O'Malley, Rev. Edward, R.C.C. of Belmullet, co. Mayo
O'Malley, James, Esq., Cloonane, Castlebar, co. Mayo
* O'Malley, Major Owen, D.L. and J.P., Spencer-park, Castlebar, co.
* O'Malley, St. Clair, Esq., Castlebar, co. Mayo [Mayo
O'Meagher, Lieut. James, Gort, co. Galway
* O'Meagher, Stephen, Esq., J.P., Kilmoyler, near Caher, co. Tipperary
O'Meara, Mrs. Eliza, Shally, Nenagh, co. Tipperary
* O'Moore, Garrett, Esq., Cloghan-castle, Banagher, King's county

O'Neil, John, Esq., Garrivoe-lodge, Castlemartyr, co. Cork
*O'NEILL, The Right Honorable Earl [Antrim
*O'Neill, The Hon. J., B.R., Tallymore-lodge, Broughshane, co.
O'Neill, Mr. Edward, Clonmel, co. Tipperary
O'Neill, Eugene, Esq., M.D. and J.P., Mitchelstown, co.Cork
O'Neill, Francis, Esq., Mount-pleasant, Strabane, co. Tyrone
O'Neill, Francis J., Esq., Limerick
*O'Neill, Rev. Henry Hugh, Monastereven, co. Kildare
O'Neill, James, Esq., Jervis-street, Dublin
*O'Neill, John, Esq., Larch-hill, near Whitchurch, co. Dublin
O'Neill, N. J., Esq., Gloster-street, and Hartfield, co. Dublin
O'Neill, Rev. T. G., P.P. Kiltomb, near Athlone, co. Roscommon
O'Neille, Rev. W., P.P. of Ferns, co. Wexford [Kidderminster
Onslow, The Venerable Archdeacon, Newent, Gloucestershire, and
O'Regan, Rev. Anthony, St. Jarlath's-college, Tuam, co. Galway
O'Regan, Rev. James, R.C.C. Dunmanway, co. Cork
*O'Regan, Rev. James, P.P. of Dromin, near Bruff, co. Limerick
*O'Regan, Rev. P. D., R.C.C. Fermoy, co. Cork
O'Regan, Thomas, Esq., Mount-earl, Adare, co. Limerick
*O'Reilly, Anthony, Esq., Beltrasna, Oldcastle, co. Meath
*O'Reilly, D., Esq., D.L. and J.P., Kildangan-castle, co. Kildare
O'Reilly, Rev. Eugene, P.P., Denn, Ballyjamesduff, co. Cavan
*O'Reilly, Hugh, Esq., Thornhill, Clontarf, co. Dublin, and Mount-[joy-square North, Dublin
*O'Reilly, Hugh, Esq., Newgrove, Kells, co. Meath
O'Reilly, Rev. Hugh, P.P. of Kinlough, Ballyshannon, co. Leitrim
*O'Reilly, James, Esq., Beltrasna, Oldcastle, co. Meath
*O'Reilly, Rev. John, P.P. of Killoe, Killiter, Longford
*O'Reilly, Rev. John, P.P. Virginia, co. Cavan
*O'Reilly, Lawrence, Esq., M.D., Ratoath, Ashbourne, co. Meath
*O'Reilly, Martin, Esq., Lispopple, near Swords, co. Dublin
O'Reilly, Mr. Nugent, Waterford [Kilkenny
*O'Reilly, P., Esq., Williamstown-avenue, Dublin, and Johnswell,
*O'Reilly, Rev. Patrick, R.C.C. of St. James', Dublin
*O'Reilly, Rev. Patrick, P.P. of Cavan, Dromelis-house, Cavan
O'Reilly, Rev. Patrick, P.P. of Killargy, Dromahair, co. Leitrim
*O'Reilly, Rev. Peter, P.P. of Drung, co. Cavan
*O'Reilly, R., Esq., Sackville-street, Dublin
O'Reilly, Rev. Robert, R.C.C. Trim, co. Meath
*O'Reilly, Rev. T., P.P. Ballymartle, near Carrigaline, co. Cork
*O'Reilly, Terence, Esq., Ballybeg, Kells, co. Meath
O'Reilly, Rev. Terence, P.P. of Lary, co. Cavan
*O'Reily, Hunter, Esq., Kilquade-house, near Delgany, co. Wicklow
O'Reily, The Very Rev. Phill., P.P. Balieboro', co. Cavan
O'Riordan, Rev. R., R.C.R. of Kilbolane, &c., co. Limerick
*Orme, Edward, Esq., J.P., Ballycorroon, Crossmolina, co. Mayo
*Orme, W., Esq., Glenmore, Crossmolina, co. Mayo
*Orme, W., Esq., J.P., Belleville, Crossmolina, co. Mayo
Ormsby, Arthur, Esq., Brookdale, Castlemartyr, co. Cork
Ormsby, George, Esq., Castle Lucas, Ballyglass, co. Mayo
*Ormsby, John, Esq., Ballywaltrim, near Bray, co. Wicklow
Ormsby, John, Esq., J.P., Castledargan, Collooney, co. Sligo
Ormsby, Robert, Esq., Brookboro', Lisnaskea, co. Fermanagh
Ormsby, Robert, Esq., M.D., Durrow, Queen's county
*Ormsby, Thomas, Esq., Cummin, Sligo
Ormsby, Thomas, Esq., Marino-cottage, Dromore West co. Sligo
Ormsby, W., Esq., J.P., Knockbrandane, Ballina, co. Sligo
Ormsby, W., Esq., J.P., Crossmolina, co. Mayo
Ormsby, W., Esq., Fare M^cfare, Dromore West, co. Sligo
O'Rorke, Rev. E, P.P. of Rathconnell, Mullingar, co. Westmeath
*O'Rorke, Rev. James, R.C.C., Fedamore, Bruff, co. Limerick
*O'Rorke, Rev. John, A.M., Moylogh-house, co. Galway
*O'Rorke, Rev. T., A.B., Lougheren-glebe, Oldcastle, co. Meath
O'Rourke, Rev. Patrick, R.C.C., Celbridge, co. Kildare
Orpen, Thomas Hungerford, Esq., M.D., Mallow, co. Cork
Orpin, Basil, Esq., Lower Mount-street, Dublin
Orr, Andrew, Esq., J.P., Keely, Coleraine, co. Derry
Orr, James, Esq., Donegal-place, Belfast
Orr, James, Esq., Course-lodge, Richill, co. Armagh
Orr, James, Esq., M.D., Ballylesson, Belfast
*Orr, Robert, Esq., Lisdogan, Ballymote, co. Sligo
*Orr, Samuel, Esq., Flowerfield, Coleraine, co. Derry
*Orr, William, Esq., Ballymena, co. Antrim
Orr, William, Esq., Glenalena, Belfast
Orr, Mr. William, Ballymoney, co. Antrim
*Orr, W. T., Esq., Stratford-upon-Slaney, co. Wicklow
*Orr, Mrs. Mary, Strabane, co. Tyrone
*O'Ryan, E., Esq., Bansha-castle, Tipperary
O'Ryan, Francis, Esq., Cashel, co. Tipperary
*Osborn, Colonel D. T., J.P., Ballyduff, Inistioge, Kilkenny
*Osborne, Lady
*Osborne, Rev. Charles, Kilskyre-glebe, Crossakeel, co. Meath
Osborne, John, Esq., Ardfallen, and Warren's-place, Cork
*Osborne, Rev. Joseph, Altmore, near Dungiven, co. Derry
*Osborne, Rev. W., Ballyhargan, near Dungiven, co. Derry
*Osburne, Thomas C., Esq., M.D., Lindville, Blackrock-road, Cork
Osburne, T., Esq., Regent Street, London
*O'Shaughnessey, Rev. Michael, R.C.R., Beagh, or St. Ann, Gort, [co. Galway
*O'Shaughnessy, J. R., Esq., Bruree, co. Limerick
*O'Shaughnessy, James R., Esq., Charleville, co. Cork
*O'Shaughnessy, John, Esq., Lower Gardiner-street, Dublin
*O'Shaughnessy, The Very Rev. Terence, R.C. Dean of Killaloe, and [P.P. of Ennis, co. Clare
O'Shaughnessy, Mark T., Esq., Henry-street, Limerick
O'Shea, H. Esq., Limerick
O'Shea, Henry, Esq., Lower Mallow-street, Limerick
O'Shea, Rev. Michael B., P.P. of St. Peter and St. Paul, Cork
O'Shea, Rev. Timothy, R.C.C., North Presbytery, Cork
*O'Shee, J. P., Esq., Gardenmorris, Kilmacthomas, co. Waterford
*O'Shee, Rev. Robert, R.C.C., St. Mary's, Kilkenny
*OSSORY, The Right Honorable Lord
*O'Sullivan, Daniel, Esq., Marlboro'-street, Cork
O'Sullivan, Mr. Daniel, Skibbereen, co. Cork
O'Sullivan, Denis, Esq., Liscahane-house, Millstreet, co. Cork
*O'Sullivan, Rev. D. A., Vicar of Bandon, co. Cork
O'Sullivan, Eugene, Esq., Castletown-Berehaven, co. Cork
*O'Sullivan, Rev. Francis R.C.C., Youghal, co. Cork
O'Sullivan, Rev. George, R.C.C. of Prior, Cahirciveen, co. Kerry
O'Sullivan, Henry, Esq., Limerick
*O'Sullivan, Rev. J. A., P.P., Enniskeen, Bandon, co. Cork
*O'Sullivan, James, Esq., Limerick
*O'Sullivan, James, Esq., Roaringwater-house, Skibbereen, co. Cork
*O'Sullivan, James, Esq., Clare-street, Limerick
O'Sullivan, Rev. James, R.C.C., St. Peter's and St. Paul, Cork
*O'Sullivan, Rev. Jeremiah, P.P., Ardfert, co. Kerry
O'Sullivan, Jeremiah D., Esq., Brennybeg, Bantry, co. Cork
O'Sullivan, John, Esq., Moherea-house, Castlelyons, co. Cork
O'Sullivan, John, Esq., Cametringane, Castletown-Berehaven, co.
O'Sullivan, Rev. Laurence, P.P. of Kilmoe, Skull, co. Cork [Cork
O'Sullivan, Rev. Michael, Bantry, co. Cork
O'Sullivan, Rev. Michael, P.P., Ballymac-Elligott, Tralee, co. Kerry
*O'Sullivan, P., Esq., Mill-cove, Castletown-Berehaven, co. Cork
*O'Sullivan, Rev. P. J., Vicar of the Union of Passage West and [Shanbally, Cork
*O'Sullivan, Roger, Esq., Reendonegan-house, Bantry, co. Cork
O'Sullivan, Rev. W., R.C.C., Killurey, co. Kerry
*O'Sullivan, Rev. W., R.C. Chaplain of City Gaol, Cork
*O'Sullivan, Rev. W., R.C.C. of the North Parish, Cork
*Otley, Richard, Esq., Darlington, Durham
*Ottley, Brook T., Esq., Delaford, near Fir-house, co. Dublin
Ould, Rev. Fielding, P. Curate of Lucan, co. Dublin
*Ovenden, Charles, Esq., M.D. and J.P., Enniskillen, co. Fermanagh
Ovens, Rev. James, Curate of Inver, Mountcharles, co. Donegal
Owen, Mr. James, Kilmore, Lurgan, co. Antrim
*Owen, W. H., Esq., Thomas-street, Limerick
*Owens, Henry, Esq., Stephenstown, Nobber, co. Meath
Owens, Henry, Esq., Mallow-street, Limerick
*Owens, J., Esq., J.P., Holestone, co. Antrim
*Owens, Simon, Esq., Julianstown, Nobber, co. Meath
*Oxley, Thomas, Esq., Martello-farm, Killiney, co. Dublin
*OXMANTOWN, The Right Honorable Lord

*Pack, Rev. Anthony, D.D., Vicar-General of Ossory, Glebe-house
*Pack, Thomas, Esq., M.D., Kilkenny [Inistioge, co. Kilkenny
Pack, W., Esq., Hampstead, Middlesex
Packenham, Rev. Robert, Rector of Celbridge, co. Kildare
Page, Mr. Edward, Beau Parc, Slane, co. Meath
*Page, T., Esq., Ringsend, near Dublin
Paget, James, Esq., J.P., Kinnaird, Ballina, co. Mayo
*Paget, Thomas, Esq., J.P., Knockglass, Crossmolina, co. Mayo
*Paige, Rev. Lewis, A.B., Kildare
Pain, James, Esq., Limerick
Paine, George, Esq., Ballinacarrig, co. Kildare
Paine, G. R., Esq., Cork
*Paisly, Rev. L., R.C.C. St. Pauls, Arran-quay, Dublin
Pakenham, The Honorable Col. Hercules, D.L. & J.P., Langford-[lodge, near Antrim
*Pakenham, Rev. Robert, Vicar of Kildrought, co. Kildare

Paley, Rev. Edward, Vicar of Easingwold, Yorkshire
* Palles, A. J. Esq., Lower Gardiner-street, Dublin
* Palliser, Hugh, Esq., Castle Coarden, Rathcoole, co. Kildare
* Palliser, Rev. J. B., Rector of Kill, St. Nicholas, and Faithleg, near [Waterford
Palliser, Mathew W., Esq., Grange, near Wexford
* Palmer, Sir William H., Bart., Kenure-park, Rush, co. Dublin
* Palmer, H., Esq., Dromahaire, co. Leitrim
* Palmer, Major James, Milltown, co. Dublin
Palmer, Joseph, Esq., Cuffsboro', Rathdowney, Queen's county
Palmer, Samuel, Esq., Palmerston, Portumna, co. Galway
Palmer, Sandford, Esq., Laurel-hill, Roscrea, co. Tipperary
* Palmer, Thomas, Esq., J.P., Summerhill, Killala, co. Mayo
Palmer, Thomas, Esq., Coolraine-house, Mountrath, Queen's county
Park, Rev. Robert, A.M., Ballymoney, co. Antrim
* Park, Mr. William, Ballybigley, near Londonderry
* Park, Messrs. William and Robert, Ballybigley, near Londonderry
Parke, Henry, Esq., Park-view, Camolin, co. Wexford
* Parke, Thomas, Esq., Cornhill, London
* Parker, A., Esq., Castlelough, Killaloe, co. Tipperary
Parker, Anthony, Esq., Fort William, Nenagh, co. Tipperary
* Parker, Captain H., R.N., Green-park, Youghal, co. Cork
Parker, James, Esq., Mount Kearney, near Newry, co. Down
* Parker, John, Esq., Upper Fitzwilliam-street, Dublin
* Parker, John, Esq., Mountmellick, Queen's county
* Parker, Nicholas, Esq., Suffolk-street, Dublin
* Parker, R. Nevill, Esq., South-mall, Cork
* Parker, R. Twiss, Esq., Castleconnell, co. Limerick
* Parker, Thomas, Esq., Old Connaught, near Little Bray, co. Dublin
Parker, Thomas, Esq., Carrigrohane, co. Cork
Parker, W., Esq., Marlbro-street, and Sundays-well, Cork
Parkes, Harry, Esq., Copperfield Iron Works, Bilston, Staffordshire
Parks, John, Esq., Balley-castle, Carlingford, co. Louth
* Parnell, John, Esq., Avondale, co. Wicklow
* Parr, John J., Esq., Meath Hospital, Dublin
* Parr, Mr. William, Throgmorton-street, London
Parris, George, Esq., Thomas-street, Limerick
Parry, E. L. H., Esq., Cumberland-street, Cork
Parry, Rev. Thomas, B.A., Cirencester, Gloucestershire
Parsons, Samuel, Esq., Temple-Gowran and Newry, co. Down
* Parsons, Rev. William, Parsonstown, King's county
* Parsonstown Reading Room, King's county
* Partridge, J. A., Esq., Breakspears, near Uxbridge, Middlesex
* Partridge, W. H., Esq., Birmingham
* Pasley, Rev. Henry, A.M. and J.P., Castlebar, co. Mayo
* Pasley, William, Esq., Balbriggan, co. Dublin
* Pasley, Rev. William, A.M., Rathaspick, Athy, co. Kildare
Paterson, Irvin W., Esq., Cottage, Kilrush, co. Clare
* Paterson, W., Esq., Mason-lodge, Newtown-Cunningham, co. Do- [negal
Paterson, W. F., Esq., Newmarket-on-Fergus, co. Clare
Paterson and Son, Messrs. James, Westmoreland-street, Dublin
Paton, William, Esq., Provincial Bank of Ireland, Armagh
* Patrick, John, Esq., Ballymena, co. Antrim
* Patrick, T. C., Esq., Wakefield, Yorkshire
* Patten, William, Esq., Tamlaghtfinlagan, co. Derry
Patten, William Moore, Esq., Westport, co. Mayo
Patten, Mrs. Sarah, Streamville, co. Antrim
Patterson, Rev. Alexander, Rosebank, co. Antrim
Patterson, Rev. Alexander, Ballymena, co. Antrim
Patterson, Charles, Esq., M.D., Rathkeale, co. Limerick
Patterson, Edward, Esq., Shannon, Sligo
Patterson, George, Esq., Belfast, co. Antrim
Patton, George Washington, Esq., M.D., Tanderagee, co. Armagh
Patton, Mr. James, Glendermott, co. Derry
* Patton, Robert H., Esq., Crohan-house, Ramelton, co. Donegal
Paxton, Mr. Jos., Chatsworth, Bakewell, Derbyshire
* Paul, Sir Joshua, Bart., Ballyglan, near Waterford
Paul, Rev. J. T., Kilcronaghan-glebe, Tobermore, co. Derry
Paye, Thomas, Esq., M.D., Kilworth, co. Cork
Paye, William, Esq., Mitchelstown, co. Cork
* Paymaster General's Office, Her Majesty's
Payne, J. R., Esq., Camden-place, Cork
* Payne, Rev. Somers, J.P., Upton, Bandon, co. Cork
* Peacock Lane Schools, Cork
* Peard, Henry Hawke, Esq., J.P., Coole-abbey, Fermoy, co. Cork
* Peard, R. F., Esq., Bellvidere, Tallow, co. Waterford
Pearson, John, Esq., Mount Cross, Macroom, co. Cork
Pease, J. R., Esq., Hessle-wood, Hull, Yorkshire
* Peebles, Hans, Esq., Mill-bank, Omagh, co. Tyrone
* Peel, Henry, Esq., Aylesmore, near Coleford, Gloucestershire
Peele, George, Esq., Dublin
Peet, Francis, Esq., Arabella, Tralee, co. Kerry

* Peirce, John, Esq., M.D., Newcastle, co. Limerick
* Pelham, The Hon. C. A. W., Manby-hall, Brigg, Lincolnshire
Pelican Life Insurance Office, London
Pemberton, Thomas, Esq., Barnes, Sunderland
* PEMBERTON, The Right Honorable the Earl of
* Pendred, Vaughan, jun., Esq., Barraderry, Baltinglass, co. Wicklow
Pendregast, Rev. Martin, R.C.C., Kilcoran, Oranmore, co. Galway
* Pennefather, Rev. John, LL.D., J.P., Glebe-house, Newport, co. [Tipperary
* Pennefather, Lysaght, Esq., Newport, co. Tipperary
* Pennefather, Mathew, Esq., D.L. and J.P., New-park, Cashel, co. [Tipperary
Pennefather, R., Esq., Ballynira, Thurles, co. Tipperary
* Penefather, The Right Honorable Richard, Third Baron, Exchequer [of Ireland
* Pennefather, W., Esq., J.P., Lakefield, Fethard, co. Tipperary
Penrose, George, Esq., Rehely-cottage, Fermoy, co. Cork
* Penrose, James, Esq., Hadwell, Cloyne, co. Cork
* Penrose, Joseph, Esq., Philipstown, co. Kildare [Cork
Penrose, Rev. J. D., A.B., Castlemagner-glebe, Cecilstown, co.
Penrose, S., Esq., J.P., Shandangan, Crookstown, co. Cork
* Penrose, S., Jun., Esq., Farren-lodge, Ballincollig, co. Cork
* Penrose, Samuel N., Esq., Youghal, co. Cork
Penrose, William, Esq., Ballymountain, Bandon, co. Cork
Pentland, Robert, Esq., Drogheda, co. Louth
Pentony, Rev. John, P.P., Clogher, co. Louth
Peppard, John, Esq., M.D., Limerick
* Pepper, George, Esq., Mosney-house, Balbriggan, co. Meath
Pepper, Captain Theobald, Rathcormac, co. Cork
* Perceval, The Hon. and Rev. Charles G., Calverton-rectory, Bucks
Perceval, Major James, Barntown-house, near Wexford
* Perceval, John, Esq., Northampton
Percival, William, Esq., J.P., Woodville, Queen's county
* Percival, Capt., Woodville, Maryboro, Queen's county
* Percy, William C., Esq., J.P., Gorradise, co. Leitrim
Perkins, John, jun., Esq., J.P., Ballybroony, Killala, co. Mayo
Perkins, Percival, Esq., Birtley-hall, Durham
Perrin, James, Esq., Leinster-lodge, Athy, co. Kildare
Perrott, Richard, Esq., Cork
Perrott, Thomas, Esq., J.P., Upland, Fermoy, co. Cork
Perry, Rev. Henry P., Clonmel, co. Tipperary
* Perry, Richard, Esq., Newtown-park, near Stillorgan, co. Dublin
* Perry, Rev. Richard N., Ballinadea-glebe, co. Cork
Perry, Mr. Robert, Rathdowney, Queen's county
Perry, S., Esq., Liverpool
* Perry, W., Esq., J.P., Woodrooff, near Clonmel, co. Tipperary
* Perry, Mr. William, Rathdowney, Queen's county
Persse, Burton, Esq., J.P., Moyode-castle, Craughwell, co. Galway
* Persse, R. H., Esq., J.P., Castle Boy, Loughrea, co. Galway
Persse, W. B., Esq., Athenry, co. Galway
Peter, Richard, Esq., Lower North Cumberland-street, Dublin, and [Merville, near Clontarf, co. Dublin
* Peters, George, Esq., Bishport-lodge, Bedminster, Somerset
Petit, Rev. Clement, P.P., Oilgate, co. Wexford
Pettit, Matthew, Esq., Wexford
Peyton, Rev. Alexander James, R.C.C., Blarney, co. Cork
* Peyton, C. R., Esq., Castlecarrow, Carrick-on-Shannon, co. Lei- [trim
* Peyton, J. H., Esq., Port, Carrick-on-Shannon, co. Leitrim
* Peyton, J. R., Esq., J.P., Laheen, Cashcarrigan, co. Leitrim
* Peyton, Wynne, Esq., Springfield, near Carrick-on-Shannon, co. [Leitrim
Phair, William, Esq., Millview, Cork
Phayre, Thomas R., Esq., M.D., Newcastle, co. Limerick
Phelan, Rev. Andrew, R.C.C., Thomastown, co. Kilkenny
Phelan, Rev. Andrew, R.C.C., Bagnalstown, co. Carlow
* Phelan, Bernard, Esq., Rock-abbey, Cashel, co. Tipperary
Phelan, Mr. David, Tramore, co. Waterford
Phelan, Mr. J., Carrick-on-Suir, co. Tipperary
Phelan, Rev. James, Glebe-house, Finglas, co. Dublin
* Phepoe, Richard, Esq., Taptoe, Maynooth, co. Kildare
* Phibbs, William, Esq., Seafield, Sligo
* Phibbs, Lieut. W. H., 25th Regiment
Philips, John, Esq., Bushfield (Killaloe), co. Tipperary
* Philips, Samuel W., Esq., Oakhampton, Newport, co. Tipperary
* Phillips, Henry, Esq., Kilcarbery, near Clondalkin, co. Dublin
Phillips, Rev. J. G., Ardmayle-glebe, Cashel, co. Tipperary
Phillips, John, Esq., Lower Mount-street, Dublin
Phillips, Lodge, Esq., Lodgefield, Rathdowney, Queen's county
* Phillips, Michael, Esq., Newcastle, co. Wicklow
* Phillips, Richard, Esq., Mount Rivers, Newport, co. Tipperary
* Phillips, Captain Robert, Johnstown, Fermoy, co. Cork
Phillips, Capt. R. J., Dundalk, co. Louth
* Phillips, Samuel, Esq., J.P., Gaile, near Tipperary
* Phillips, Thomas, Esq., Drumbrain, Newbliss, co. Monaghan

Phillips, W., Esq., St. Andrew-street, Dublin, and Rathronan, [Newcastle, co. Limerick
*Pickering, Charles, Esq., Capel-street, and Rathgar-road, Dublin
*Picknoll, W. B., Esq., Clover Eden-house, Loughall, co. Armagh
Piddell, Samuel, Esq., M.D., Kildorrery, co. Cork
Pidgeon, John, Esq., Sydney-avenue, Booterstown, near Dublin
Pierce, Edward, Esq., M.D., Rathmacknee, near Wexford
*Pierce, James, Esq., Crampton-court, Dublin
*Piercy, John, Esq., J.P., Limerick
*Piercy, William, Esq., Limerick
*Piers, Edward, Esq., Lower Gloucester-street, Dublin
*Pigott, Capt. Henry, Eagle-hill, near Woodford, co. Galway
*Pigott, John, Esq., D.L. & J.P., Capard, Rosinallis, Queen's county
*Pigott, John, Esq., Capard, Mountmellick, Queen's county
Pigott, Lieut.-Col. William P., Slevoy-castle, co. Wexford
*Pike, E., Esq., Besborough, Blackrock, Cork
*Pilkington, A. J., Esq., Kilbride-castle, co. Westmeath
*Pilkington, Henry, Esq., Tore, co. Westmeath
*Pilkington, Rev. J., Rector of Upper Langfield, Omagh, co. Tyrone
Pilkington, R., Esq., Woodmount, co. Galway
*Pilkington, W., Esq., Thorne, Doncaster, Yorkshire
*Pilson, Aynsworth, Esq., Downpatrick, co. Down
*Pim, George, Esq., Brenanstown-house, co. Dublin
*Pim, J., Esq., Bloomsbury, Monkstown, and William street, Dublin
*Pim, John, Esq., J.P., New-park, Kildare
*Pim, John, Esq., Laca, Queen's county
Pim, Messrs. James and Sons, Mountmelick, Queen's county
*Pim, W. Harvey, Esq., William-street, Dublin
*Pinchin, George, Esq., J.P., Pallas Kenry, co. Limerick
Pineau, Daniel, Esq., Stephen's-green, Dublin
*Plant, W., Esq., M.D., Plantation, near Kingstown, co. Dublin
Platt, Mr. W., Hadfield-lodge, Glossop, Derbyshire
Plummer, B., Esq., Mount Plummer, Newcastle, co. Limerick
Plummer, Rev. R., J.P., Killeiny-glebe, Tralee, co. Kerry
*PLUNKETT, The Right Honorable Lord
*Plunkett, The Honorable H. L., Louth-hall, co. Louth
*Plunkett, The Honorable Mrs., Plunket-lodge, Kingstown, co. Dub- [lin, and Killough Castle, Thurles, co. Tipperary
*Plunkett, The Hon. Randal E., Dunsany-castle, co. Meath
*Plunkett, The Hon. John, Upper Fitzwilliam-street, Dublin
*Plunkett, The Hon. and Rev. W. C., Old Connaught, co. Dublin
*Plunkett, Christopher, Esq., Castlebellingham, co. Louth
*Plunkett, G., Esq., Mount Plunkett (near Athlone), co. Roscommon
*Plunkett, Henry, Esq., Plunket-lodge, Kingstown, co. Dublin
*Plunkett, John, Esq., Cabra-house, co. Dublin
Plunkett, Robert, Esq., Millbrook, near Londonderry
Plunkett, Thomas, Esq., Corbally, Tulsk, co. Roscommon
*Poe, J. P., Esq., J.P., Hailey-park, co. Tipperary
*Poer, Samuel, Esq., Belleville-park, near Cappoquin, co. Waterford
*Pollard, W. D., Esq., D.L. and J.P., Kinturk, co. Westmeath
*Pollock, A. H. C., Esq., Mountainstown, Navan, co. Meath
*Pollock, David, Esq., F.R.S., M.R.A.S., R.S.L., V.P.S.A., Dart- [mouth-street, Westminster
Pollock, Figgis and Co., Messrs., Capel-street, Dublin
*Pollock, H., Esq., J.P., Castle-Wilder, near Ballymahon, co. Long- [ford
*Pollock, John, Esq., Youghal, co. Cork
*Pollock, M., Esq., Oatlands, near Stillorgan, co. Dublin
Pollon, Mr. Frederick, Limerick
*Pomeroy, The Hon. and Rev. A. W., Rector of Desertmartin, [co. Derry
*Ponsonby, C. B., Esq., Little Dargle, co. Dublin
*Ponsonby, Thomas C., Esq., J.P., Crotto-house, Tralee, co. Kerry
*Poole, Thomas, Esq., Cahirmore, near Midleton, co. Cork
*Poole, William, Esq., Ballyroan, near Rathfarnham, co. Dublin
Pope, Alexander Richard, Esq., Waterford
Pope, Capt. E. H., Popefield, Athy, co. Kildare
Pope, George, Esq., Muff, co. Donegal
Popham, Capt. Charles, Cove, near Cork
Porter, Rev. Clapon, Larne, co. Antrim
*Porter, Edward Robert, Esq., New Court, Temple, London
*Porter, Mr. James, Elaghmore, Templemore, co. Derry
Porter, Rev. James, Drumlee, Castlewellan, co. Down
*Porter, Mr. John, Burt, near Londonderry
Porter, Rev. John, Belfast
*Porter, Mr. Joseph, Ballymoney, Burt, co. Donegal
*Porter, Rev. Philip, R.C.C. of Ardstraw East, co. Tyrone
*Porter, Mr. William, Burt, near Londonderry
*Porter, William, Esq., Stratford-on-Avon, Warwickshire
*Potter, Rev. F. A., Rathconrath-glebe, Mullingar, co. Westmeath
*Potter, Robert, Esq., George's-street, Limerick
Potter, Robert, Esq., Ardview, Killinchy, co. Down
Potter, Robert, Esq., Limerick

Potter, Samuel L., Esq., M.D., Gortalowry-house, Cookstown [co. Tyrone
Potter, Thomas H., Esq., Farm-lodge, Adare, co. Limerick
*Potterton, H., Esq., Moyrath-castle, Athboy, co. Meath
Potterton, Rev. John, M.A., Slacksgrove, Monaghan
*Potterton, Thomas, Esq., Balatalion, Trim, co. Meath
*Potterton, Thomas, Esq., Clarkstown, Kilcock, co. Meath
*Pottinger, Thomas, Esq., Rathbride-house, Kildare
*Potts, John, Esq., New-mills, Derbyshire
*Potts, W. W., Esq., New-mills, Derbyshire
*Potts, William, Esq., Thornfield, near Donnybrook, co. Dublin
Poulette, The Hon. Thomas Orde, Bolton-hall, Leyburn, Yorkshire
*Pounder, Rev. Patrick, Ballinasloe, co. Galway
Pounder, Thomas, Esq., Enniscorthy, co. Wexford
Powell, Caleb, Esq., Kildare-street, Dublin
Powell, Edmund, Esq., Fountain, Ennis, co. Clare
*Powell, Major Edward, Bunlahan, Rosscarbery, co. Cork
*Powell, Rev. John, Lea Glebe-house, Ballybrittas, Queen's county
*Powell, J. L., Esq., Mecklenburgh-street, Dublin
*Powell, John, Esq., Peel-street, Manchester
*Powell, M., Esq., Richview, near Roebuck, co. Dublin
Powell, P., Esq., Poplar, Corofin, co. Clare
*Powell, Rev. P. B., Dundrum, co. Dublin
Powell, Mr. Thomas, Bride-street, Dublin
Powell, Thomas, Esq., Newmarket-on-Fergus, co. Clare
Powell, T. E., Esq., P.J., Great Connell-lodge, Kilcullen, co. Kildare
Power, The Venerable A., Archdeacon of Lismore
Power, D. D., Esq., Glenwilliam Castle, Ballingarry, co. Limerick
*Power, E., Esq., Carrick-on-Suir, and Abbey-street, Dublin
*Power, Major Ed., Townend, Longford
*Power, E. O'Neil, Esq., Newtown, Tramore, co. Waterford
*Power, Hugh, Esq., Carrig Castle, Kilmacthomas, co. Waterford
*Power, Rev. John, P.P., Ballyhea, &c., co. Cork
*Power, John, jun., Esq., J.P., Kilfane, Thomastown, co. Kilkenny
Power, John, Esq., Churchtown, Carrick on-Suir, co. Tipperary
Power, John, Esq., Mount-Richard, Carrick-on-Suir, co. Tipperary
Power, John, Esq., Waterford
Power, Lorenzo, Esq., J.P., Mahon-lodge, Kilmacthomas, co. Wa- [terford
*Power, Rev. Maurice, P.P. of Skibbereen, co. Cork
Power, Maurice, Esq., M.D., Castle-house, Glandore, co. Cork
Power, Rev. Michael, Carrickbegg, co. Waterford
Power, Michael, Esq., Cashel, co. Tipperary
Power, Rev. N., Navan, co. Meath
*Power, Nicholas, Esq., D.L. and J.P., Faithlegg, near Waterford
*Power, P., Esq., Bellevue, near Waterford
*Power, Pierce, Esq., J.P., Rosskeen, co. Cork
*Power, Pierce, Esq., Monroe, Nenagh, co. Tipperary
*Power, Pierce, Esq., Park-street, Dublin
Power, Richard, Esq., Carrigmore, Tallow, co, Waterford
Power, Richard, Esq., Monroe, Nenagh, co. Tipperary
*Power, Robert, Esq., Clashmore-house, co. Waterford
Power, Thomas, Esq., Beech-hill, Freshford, co. Kilkenny
Power, William, Esq., Dunhill-lodge, Tramore, co. Waterford
*POWERSCOURT, The Right Honorable Viscount
*Praed, J. B., Esq., Tyringham, Bucks
*Prangnall, Lieut. F., R.N., Woodview, near Fermoy, co. Cork, and [Alresford, Hants.
*Pratt, Lieut.-Col. C., Stoneville, Rochestown-avenue, Killiney, co. [Dublin
Pratt, James, Esq., Kinsale, co. Cork
*Pratt, James, Esq., Farm-hill, near Roebuck, co. Dublin
*Pratt, John, Esq., J.P., Corinsica, King's-court, co. Cavan
*Pratt, Mervyn, Esq., J.P., Enniscoe, Crossmolina, co. Mayo
Pratt, Rev. R., Prebendary of Desertmore, Ballincollig, co. Cork
*Pratt, Rev. W. H., A.M., Vicar of Donagh, co. Monaghan
*Pratt, Col., J.P., Cabra Castle, Kingscourt, co. Cavan, and the [Hall, Donegal
*Prendergast, Rev. E., P.P., Ballingarry, co. Tipperary
Prendergast, Rev. Francis, P.P., Davidstown, co. Wexford
*Prendergast, J. S., Esq., Johnstown-park, Nenagh, co. Tipperary
*Prendergast, John, Esq., Bettyville, Ballinasloe, co. Galway
*Prendergast, William Kelly, Esq., Bettyville, Aughrim, co. Galway
*Presentation Schools, Douglas-street, Cork
*Presly, Rev. L., St. Paul's, Arran-quay, Dublin
*Prest, John, Esq., Masham, Yorkshire
*Preston, The Very Rev. A. J., Dean of Limerick
Preston, Rev. A. J., Rector of Kilmeague, Rathernan-glebe, Rath- [angan, co. Kildare
*Preston, Rev. Joseph, Ballinter, Navan, co. Meath
Preston, Rev. P., Prebendary of Edermine, co. Wexford
*Price, J. R., Esq., Westfield-farm, Mountrath, Queen's-county
*Price, James, Esq., Cromwell-lodge, Monkstown, co. Dublin

*Price, Nicholas, Esq., J.P., Saintfield-house, co. Down
Prickett, Edward, Esq., Aylesbury, Bucks
*Pring, Elijah, Esq,, Westmoreland-street, Dublin, and Seafort-lodge, [Williamstown, co. Dublin
Pringle, Michael, Esq., The Grange, Armagh
Prior, Rev. G., Curate of Tullyaughnish, Ramelton, co. Donegal
*Prior, Rev. Hugh Edward, Wicklow
*Prior, Rev. John, Mount Dillon, near Roebuck, co. Dublin
Prior, Rev. Michael, P.P. of Ballincollig, co. Cork
*Prior, Rev. Thomas, Mount Dillon, near Roebuck, co. Dublin
Pritchett, William, Esq., Worcester
Prittie, Henry, Esq., J.P., Corville, Roscrea, co. Tipperary
Privy Council Office, Her Majesty's [co. Wicklow
Proby, The Hon. Capt. G. J., D.L. and J.P., Glenart, near Arklow,
Proctor, George, Esq., Newtown Limavady, co. Derry
*Provis, Henry Thomas, Esq., Sandymount, Dublin
*Pugh, Arthur, Esq., J.P., Lissadrone, Rathlacken, co. Mayo
Purcell, George, Esq., Lohort Castle, Cecilstown, co. Cork
*Purcell, Ignatius, Esq., Prospect Point, near Swords, co. Dublin
*Purcell, Rev. James G., Foxboro', Monegal, King's-county
Purcell, John, Esq., Doon-cottage, Kinsale, co. Cork
Purcell, John F., Esq., A.B., M.D., Carrick-on-Suir, co. Tipperary
Purcell, Rev. M., P.P. of Ringagona, Dungarvan, co. Waterford
Purcell, Peter, Esq., Halverstown, co. Kildare
*Purcell, Richard, Esq., M.D, Highfort, Buttevant, co. Cork
*Purcell, R. H., Esq., Annabella, Mallow, co. Cork
*Purcell, Rev. Thomas, Cloyne, co. Cork
Purcell, Thomas, Esq., Upper Fleet-street, Dublin [co. Louth
Purcell, T. J., Esq., Lower Gardiner-street, Dublin, and Dundalk,
Purcell, William, Esq., J.P., Altimira, near Buttevant, co. Cork
*Purdon, Edward, Esq., Lisnabin, near Killucan, co. Westmeath
Purdon, Mr. Henry, Ardrums, Kilcock, co. Meath
Purdon, Henry, Esq., M.D., Belfast
*Purdon, R., Esq., M.D., Tralee, co. Kerry
*Purdon, Simon, Esq., Tamar-terrace, Stoke, near Plymouth
*Purdon, S. G., Esq., J.P., Tinciana, Killaloe, co. Clare
*Purdon, Thomas, Esq., Richmond Penitentiary, Dublin
Putland, Charles, Esq., Fitzwilliam-square West, Dublin
*Putland, George, Esq., Bray Head, co. Wicklow
*Putland, George, Esq., Lower Mount-street, Dublin
*Puxley, Edward, Esq., Oak-lodge, Castletown-Berehaven, co. Cork
*Pyne, Jasper, Esq., Ballyvolane, Rathcormac, co. Cork
Pyne, John, Esq., Cottage, Coachford, co. Cork
Pyne, John George, Esq., Ballinacariga, Kilworth, co. Cork

*Quarter Master General's Office, Dublin
Quartley, Rev. Henry, Rector of Wicken, Northamptonshire
Quill, David, Esq., M.D., Tralee, co. Kerry
Quillinan, Rev. I., P.P., Knockaderry and Clouncagh, Newcastle, [co. Limerick
Quin, Rev. Andrew, P.P., Kilfenora, co. Clare
*Quin, Mr. Edward, Meadow-brook, near Dundrum, co. Dublin
*Quin, J., jun., Esq., Bray, co. Wicklow
Quin, Rev. J., P.P., Loughgall, co. Armagh
*Quin, John, Esq., Douglass, Newtown Stewart, co. Tyrone
*Quin, John, Esq., Campsey-house, co. Derry
Quin, Rev. John, P.P., Kilgobinet, Dungarvan, co. Waterford
Quin, John, Esq., Corvally, co. Monaghan
*Quin, Joseph, Esq., Mullinahinch (Clones), co. Fermanagh
Quin, Mr. Michael, Limerick
Quin, Rev. Patrick B., P.P., Ardrahan, co. Galway
*Quin, Rev. Peter, P.P., Union of Backs, co. Mayo
Quin, R., Esq., J.P., Fir-grove, Innishannon, co. Cork
*Quin, Rev. Richard, P.P., Durras, co. Cork
*Quin, Terence, Esq., Ballymore-Eustace, co. Dublin
Quin, Rev. Thomas, Wingfield, co. Wicklow
Quinan, Rev. C., Holles-street, Dublin
Quinlan, Mr. James Thomas, Limerick
Quinlan, Mathew, Esq., M.D., Ballyrafter, Lismore, co. Waterford
Quinlan, Rev. Michael, P.P., Golden, co. Tipperary
Quinlan, Mr. William, Great George-street, Cork
Quinlivan, Rev. P., P.P., Kilmore, Nenagh, co. Tipperary
*Quinn, Rev. Andrew, R.C.C., Townsend-street, Dublin
Quinn, Rev. John, R.C.C., Faughmaconnell, co. Roscommon
Quinn, Rev. John Campbell, Newry, co. Down
*Quinn, William Henry, Esq., J.P., Newry, co. Down
Quirke, Rev. Patrick, P.P., Clashmore, co. Waterford

*Radcliff, John, Esq., J.P., Willmount, Kells, co. Meath
Radcliff, Rev. Richard, Rector of Enniscorthy, co. Wexford
*Radcliff, Rev. Thomas, Prebendary of Clonmethan, co. Dublin
*Radcliffe, The Right Honorable John, LL.D., Hume-street, Dublin
Rafferty, John, Esq., Willow-terrace, Williamstown, near Dublin
*Rafter, Rev. M., P.P., Killeshin, Old Derig, Carlow
*Raikes, Robert, Esq., Welton-house, Yorkshire
Rainey, John Ash, Esq., Magherafelt, co. Derry
*Rait, George, Esq., Rathmoyle, Edenderry, King's-county
*Rait, S., Esq., Clonin, Rockfort-bridge, Edenderry, King's-county
Raleigh, Rev. James, Castle Mahon, and Limerick
Raleigh, John F., Esq., National Medical Hall, Limerick
*Ralph, J., Esq., Baldoyle, co. Dublin
*Ralph, John, Esq., Thornfield, Killbarrick, near Dublin
*Ram, Rev. Abel John, Lichfield, Staffordshire,
*Ramsay, Sir James, Bart., Bamff-house, Perthshire
*Ramsay, Rev. T., P. C. of Kilteevock, Stranorlar, co. Donegal
*Rance, Henry, Esq., Cambridge
*RANFURLY, The Right Honorable the Earl of
*Rankin, Messrs. W. and Co., Donegal
*Rathborne, Henry, Esq., Dunsinea, nr. Blanchardstown, co. Dublin
Rathborne, R., Esq., J.P., Ballimore, near Craughwell, co. Galway
*Rathborne, W., Esq., Scripplestown, nr. Cardiffe Bridge, co. Dublin
*RATHDOWNE, The Right Honorable the Earl of
*Ravenscroft, John, Esq., Ballinderry, co. Antrim
*Rawlins, Rev. Charles, Ramelton, co. Donegal
Rawlins, George H., Esq., Peafield-house, Bandon, co. Cork
Rawson, Richard, Esq., Aungier-street, Dublin
Rawson, Robert, Esq., Glassealy, Ballitore, co. Kildare
Raymond, Capt. James, J.P., Dromin, Listowel, co. Kerry
Raymond, Samuel S., Esq., Bedford-house, Listowel, co. Kerry
Raymond, Capt. W., Listowel, and Spray-mount, Ballybunnian, co. [Kerry
*Rea, Charles, Esq., J.P., Fort Royal, Rathmullen, co. Donegal
*Rea, John, Esq., Grayfort, Ballymote, co. Sligo
*Rea, Mr. John, Islandreigh, Antrim
Read, A. H., Esq., Gosean, Killyleagh, co. Down
Read, Capt. John, Ballycarroll, Monastereven, Queen's-county
*Read, Nicholas, Esq., Elenborough, near Tallaght, co. Dublin
*Read, Thomas, Esq., M.D., Coleraine, co. Derry
Read, Thomas, Esq., Chamber-street, Dublin
*Read, Thomas and Co., Parliament-street, Dublin
Read, Mrs. Mary, Read's-vale, Dundrum, co. Dublin
Reade, Rev. Charles T., Curate of Maynooth, co. Kildare
*Reade, Edward, Esq., Kilrateera, Scariff, co. Clare
Reade, Rev. G. H., Stonewold-cottage, Ballyshannon, co. Donegal
Reade, Rev. John, LL.D., Vicar and Rector of the Union of Clon-[dalkin and Prebendary of Kilmactalway, co. Dublin
*Reade, Rev. Loftus, A.B., and J.P., Levelly-glebe, Enniskillen, co. [Fermanagh
*Reade, Philip, Esq., J.P., Wood-park, Scariff, co. Clare
*Reade, Richard H., Esq., White Abbey, Belfast,
*Reade, W. Morris, Esq., J.P., Rossenarre, Carrick-on-Suir, co. Kil-[kenny
Ready, Mr. Jeremiah, Mitchelstown, co. Cork
*Reardan, Robert, Esq., M.D., Doneraile, co. Cork
*Reay, Joseph, Esq., Customs, Youghal, co. Cork
*Reay, Robert, Esq., Hylton-hall, Sunderland
*Reddan, Matthew, Esq., Shannon-view, Scariff co. Clare
*Redington, John Joseph, Esq., Tuam, co. Galway
*Redington, T. M., Esq., J.P., Kilcornan, Oranmore, co. Galway
*Redmond, Rev. E., P.P., Arklow, co. Wicklow
Redmond, Rev. E., P.P., Suttons Parish, New Ross, co. Wexford
*Redmond, H. T., Esq., J.P., Killoughton-house, near Wicklow
*Redmond, J. E., Esq., J.P., Wexford
Redmond, Philip, Esq., Wexford
Redmond, Mrs., Summer-hill, near Wexford
*Reed, Capt. Abraham, Sligo
Reed, Rev. J., Enniscoffey-glebe, Rochfort Bridge, co Westmeath
Reed, Capt. J. R., Allihies Mines, Castletown-Berehaven, co. Cork
*Reedy, M. O'K., Esq., M.D., Carysfoot-avenue, Blackrock, Dublin
*Reeves, Edward Hoare, Esq., Ballyglissane, Rathcormac, co. Cork
*Reeves, Rev. P., P.P., Drumcoloher, and Broadford, co. Limerick
*Reeves, Peter, Esq., Cottage, near Cork
Reeves, T. S., Esq., Tramore, Douglas, Cork
*Reeves, W. Maunsell, Esq., Vostersberg, Cork
Reford, Lewis, Esq., Beechmount, near Belfast
*Reid, Andrew, Esq., Weston-park, co. Kildare
*Reid, Capt. Henry, Phibblestown, near Clonsilla, co. Dublin
Reid, J. H., Esq., Weston-park, near Lucan, co. Dublin
*Reid, Rev. James, Castlenock, co. Dublin
Reid, James, Esq., Millbank, Fermoy, co. Cork
*Reid, James M., Esq., J.P., Castle Blayney, co. Monaghan

* Reid, Samuel, Esq., Newry, co. Down
Reilly, Rev. Charles, P.P., Ematriss, near Cootehill, co. Monaghan
* Reilly, Cornelius, Esq., Caledon, co. Tyrone
Reilly, Edward, Esq., Summer-hill, Ballyglass, co. Mayo
Reilly, J. Lushington, Esq., Collector of Customs, Galway
* Reilly, James, Esq., Brook-lodge, near Blanchardstown, co. Dublin
Reilly, J. L., Esq., Scarvagh-house, nr. Loughbrickland, co. Down
Reilly, J. M., Esq., Scarvagh-house, co. Down
* Reilly, Rev. John, PP., Virginia, co. Cavan
* Reilly, Miles, Esq., Pill-lane, Dublin
Reilly, Thomas, Esq., Hollymount, co. Mayo
* Reilly, W., Esq., Belmont, Mullingar, co. Westmeath
* Reilly, William E., Esq., J.P., Hillsborough, co. Down
Reily, Samuel, Esq., Summer-hill, Cork
* Renny, G., Esq., M.D., Dublin
Rentoul, Rev. James, Presbyterian Minister, Ramochy, Letterken-
* Revell, John, Esq., Seapark, near Wicklow [ny, co. Donegal
* Revell, Rev, Henry, Ballydonarea, Delgany, co. Wicklow
Revell, Rev. S., Wingerworth, Chesterfield, Derbyshire
* Reynell, Cooke, Esq., Woodfort, Mullingar, co. Westmeath
* Reynell, Richard Winter, Esq., J.P., Killymon, near Mullingar, [co. Westmeath
Reynolds, C., Esq., Berryburn, Glendermott, co. Derry
* Reynolds, Rev. Francis, P.P., of Fenagh, Cashcarrigan, co. Leitrim
* Reynolds, E., Esq., Fitzwilliam-square East, Dublin
Reynolds, James, Esq., Dispensary, Middletown, co. Armagh
* Reynolds, John, Esq., J.P., Coolbeg, Ballyshannon, co. Donegal
* Reynolds, Rev. M., R.C.C. of Newtownforbes, co. Longford
* Reynolds, Robert, Esq., Mullins, Ballyshannon, co. Donegal
* Reynolds, R. Young, Esq., Fort-lodge, Cavan
* Reynolds, W., Esq., Feduff, Tynan, co. Armagh
* Rhoades, Rev. J. P., Rectory, Clonmel, co. Tipperary
Riall, Arthur, Esq., Westgrove, Clonmel, co. Tipperary
* Riall, Charles, Esq., Heywood, Clonmel, co. Tipperary
* Rice, The Right Honorable Thomas Spring, M.P., J.P.
* Rice, Henry, Esq., Scart, Clogheen, co. Tipperary
* Rice, Stephen B., Esq., Carrickfergus, co. Antrim
* Rich, Sir George, Knt., Cavendish-row, Dublin
Richards, Rev. Edward, Loughbrickland, co. Down
Richards, Rev. G., Prebendary of Coolstuffe, Taghmon, co. Wexford
* Richards, John, Esq., Sun Fire Office, London
* Richards, J. B., Esq., Mateelah Cottage, Gorey, co. Wexford
* Richards, John Goddard, Esq., J.P., Ardemine, co. Wexford
Richards, Solomon, Esq., J.P., Owenavara, co. Wexford
* Richards, Thomas, Esq., Fitzgibbon-street, Dublin
* Richardson, Charles, Esq., J.P., Annagh, Aughnacloy, co. Tyrone
* Richardson, Major Edward, J.P., Poplar-vale, Monaghan [ford
* Richardson, J. A., Esq., J.P., Richfort, Edgeworthstown, co. Long-
* Richardson, John, Esq., Hammersmith, Middlesex
* Richardson, Major John, Rosfad, Enniskillen, co. Fermanagh
Richardson, John, Esq., J.P., Coal-Island, Dungannon, co. Tyrone
* Richardson, Rev. Thomas, J.P., Somerset, Coleraine, co. Derry
* Richardson, Capt. W. S., Oaklands, Cookstown, co. Tyrone
Richardson, W. T., Esq., Rehobeth-place, South Circular-road,
Richardson, Mrs. C., Lakefield, Belfast [Dublin
Richardson, Messrs. James N. Son and Co., Lisburn, co. Antrim
Richardson, Messrs. Jonathan and James, Lisburn, co. Antrim
Rickard, Rev. James, P.P., Athboy, co. Meath
Rickard, Rev. James, R.C.C., Francis-street, Dublin
Rickard, Rev. John, R.C.C. of Gobbinstown Chapel, New Ross, [co. Wexford
Riddell, Rev. William, Newcastle-on-Tyne, Northumberland
Riddle, James, Esq., Mount Pleasant, Rich Hill, co. Armagh
* Ridley, Biggs and Co., Messrs., Newcastle-on-Tyne, Northumber-
* Ridgway, Henry, Esq., Blenheim, near Waterford [land
Riedy, John, Esq., Tally-ho-lodge, Rathkeale, co. Limerick
Rigden, W., Esq., Faversham, Kent
Riggs, W. N., Esq., Bruff, co. Limerick
* Rigney, Rev. Patrick, P.P., Philipstown, King's-county
Rimer, Mr. W., Muff, near Derry, co. Donegal
* Ring, Richard, Esq., Farra, near Mullingar, co. Westmeath
Ring, Mr. Thomas, Mecklenburgh-street, Dublin
Riordan, Rev. D. Twiss, The Abbey, Tipperary
* Riordan, Rev. James L. O., Cork
Riordan, Mr. John, Killarney, co. Kerry
Riordan, Rev. John, P.P., Castlemagner, near Mallow, co. Cork
* Riordan, Rev. Robert, P.P., Kilbolane, Drumcolloher, co Limerick
* Riordan, Thomas Travers, Esq., M.D., Limerick
* Rippon, Cuthbert, Esq., Stanhope Castle, Durham
* Risley, Rev. W. C., Souldern Rectory, Deddington, Oxfordshire
Ritchie, Mr. W., Belfast

* RIVERSDALE, The Right Honorable Lord
* Robbins, Rev. G., R.C.C., of Castlelost, West-lodge, Rochfort [Bridge, co. Westmeath
* Robeck, The Baron de, Merrion Square, East, Dublin [Cork
* Roberts, Sir Thomas, Bart., J.P., Britfieldstown, nr. Carrigaline, co.
* Roberts, Captain H. W., Fairfield-house, Fermoy, co. Cork
* Roberts, Miss Jane, Old Connagh-hill, near Bray, co. Dublin
* Roberts, John, Esq., Belmont, near Waterford
Roberts, John, Esq., J.P., Ardmore, near Passage, Cork [dare
Roberts, Rev. J. Cramer, J.P., Sallymount, Kilcullenbridge, co. Kil-
Roberts, Lieut. Horatio, Ballinasloe, co. Galway
* Roberts, Michael, Esq., J.P., Mount Rivers, Carrigaline, co. Cork
* Roberts, Michael, Esq., J.P., Kilmoney, Carrigaline, co. Cork
* Roberts, Rev. R. Vicar of Haverhill, Suffolk
* Roberts, Robert, Esq., Drogheda, co. Louth
Roberts, Rev. Samuel, B.A., Cavan [Carlow
Roberts, Rev. S. T., LL.D., J.P., Ravindon, Leighlin Bridge, co.
Roberts, Thomas, Esq., Coleville, Clonmel, co. Tipperary
Roberts, Mr. Thomas, Nore Mills, Mountrath, Queen's-county
Roberts, Thomas Pepper, Esq., Mota, Burris-o'-kane, co. Tipperary
Roberts, Walter, Esq., Collin, near Belfast
* Roberts, Rev. Walter Cramer, Glasnevin, co. Dublin
* Roberts, Watkins, Esq., Shanbally-house, Doneraile, co. Cork
Roberts, Messrs. T. and D., Hibernian Foundry, Mountmellick,
* Robertson, John, Esq., Green Bank, Londonderry [Queen's co.
Robertson, John, Esq., J.P., Abbey, Boyle, co. Roscommon
Robertson, Thomas J. Esq., Merino-crescent, Dublin
* Robinson, Rev. C., A.M., Tynagh-glebe, Loughrea, co. Galway
* Robinson, Rev. Christopher, J.P., Granard-glebe, co. Longford
Robinson, James, Esq., Hull, Yorkshire
Robinson, James, Esq., Priest-house, near Donnybrook, co. Dublin
* Robinson, De la Pere A. J., Esq., Park-house, Cloghjordan, co.
Robinson, George, Esq., Blessington, co. Wicklow [Tipperary
Robinson, H., Esq., Upper Temple-street, Dublin
* Robinson, James, Esq., Main-cottage, Ballymena, co. Antrim
Robinson, John, Esq., Shamrock-lodge, Athlone, co. Westmeath
* Robinson, J. P., Esq., Coolderry, Parsonstown, King's-co.
* Robinson, J. R., Esq., Lisglassick, Ballymahon, co. Longford
Robinson, P. F., Esq., Lower Brook-street, London
Robinson, Rev. R., Whittington, Chesterfield, Derbyshire
* Robinson, Richard, Esq., Oakley-park, Parsonstown, King's-co.
Robinson, Richard, Esq., Royal Phœnix Iron Works, Dublin
* Robinson, Robert, Esq., Tinnakilly, Birr, King's-co.
* Robinson, Samuel, Esq., J.P., Cloonbarry, Tubbercurry, co. Sligo
Robinson, Mr. Samuel, Clara Mills, Clara, King's-county
* Robinson, Thomas, Esq., Sally Mount, co. Monaghan
* Robinson, W., Esq., J.P., Annaville, Mullingar, co. Westmeath
* Robinson, Rev. W., Vicar of Tallaght, co. Dublin
* Robson, Michael, Esq., West Chirton, Newcastle, Northumberland
* Roch, George, Esq., Woodbine-hill (near Youghal), co. Waterford
Roche, Rev. B. J., P.P., St. Nicholas, Galway
* Roche, Charles W., Esq., Rockville, near Kilternan, co. Dublin
* Roche, David, Esq., M.P., Carass, Croom, co. Limerick
* Roche, E., Esq., Trabolgan, Cloyne, co. Cork
Roche, Rev. E., P.P., Aglis, Cappoquin, co. Waterford
Roche, Rev. George T., Temple Michael, Youghal, co. Cork
* Roche, Rev. James, R.C.C., Francis-street Chapel, Dublin
Roche, Rev. James, Enniscorthy, co. Wexford
Roche, Rev. James, P.P. of Carrigtoohill, Midleton, co. Cork
Roche, James H., Esq., Clonakilty, co. Cork
* Roche, Rev. John F., Ballinteer, near Dundrum, co. Dublin
* Roche, J. J.. Esq., J.P., Aghada-house, Cloyne, co. Cork
* Roche, J. W., Esq., Rochemount, Cloyne, co. Cork
* Roche, Rev. L., P.P., Rathfarnham, co. Dublin
* Roche, Rev. N., R.C.C. of Rathmines, co. Dublin
Roche, N. W., Esq. M.D., R.N., Fermoy, co. Cork
* Roche, W., Esq., M.P., Limerick [Mountjoy-street, Dublin
Rochfort, C., Esq., Altymon-cottage, Athenry, co. Galway, and
* Rochfort, John, Esq., Altymon-cottage, Athenry, co. Galway, and [Mountjoy-street, Dublin
Rock, John, Esq., National Bank, Ballinasloe, co. Galway
* Rodanghan, Rev. Bernard, P.P. of Kilronan, near Keadue, co.
Rodgers, Mr. William, Belfast [Roscommon
* Roe, George, Esq., Thomas-street, Dublin
* Roe, George, Esq., Lorn-park, Roscrea, co. Tipperary
* Roe, George, Esq., Nutley, near Donnybrook, co. Dublin
Roe, George, Esq., M.D., Cavan
* Roe, Henry, Esq., Fitzwilliam-square East, Dublin
* Roe, James, Esq., J.P., Roe'sborough, near Tipperary
* Roe, John, Esq., J.P., Belmont, Rathdowney, Queen's-county
* Roe, Michael, Esq., Ballytrain, Ballibay, co. Monaghan

* Roe, Robert, Esq., Sans Souci, Booterstown, co. Dublin
* Roe, W., Upper Ormond-quay, Dublin
* Roe, W., Esq., J.P., Rockwell, near Cashel, co. Tipperary
Rogan, Rev. J., Manor Hamilton, co. Leitrim
Rogan, John, Esq., Killough co. Down
* Rogan, W., Esq., Killough, co. Down
Rogers, Rev. John, P.P, of Dromisken, co. Louth
Rogers, Major J. Hingston, Cloyne, co. Cork
Rogers, John Martin, Esq., Castlebar, co. Mayo
Rogers, Rev. R., Rocksmount, Carndonagh, co. Donegal
* Rogers, Rev. R. H., LL.D., Parsonage, Killeagh, co. Cork
* Rogers, Rev. S. G., Tullycleagh-glebe, Enniskillen, co. Fermanagh
Rogers, Rev. W., A.M., Surrogate of the Dioce e of Cloyne, [co. Cork
* Rogers, W. C., Esq., Henrietta-street, Dublin
Rogers, W. F., Esq., Peter-street, Dublin
* Rogers, W. R., Esq., Dundalk, co. Louth
Rohan, Rev. Michael, P.P., Knock, co. Clare
* Rolleston, J. F., Esq., Franckfort Castle, Moneygall, King's-county
Rolleston, Rev. Thomas, Greenfield, Coleraine, co. Derry
Ronaldson, Mr. John, Barbarasfort, Tuam, co. Galway
* Ronayne, D., Esq., Upper Rutland-street, Dublin
Ronayne, James, Esq., Youghal, co. Cork
* Ronayne, James, Esq., Berry Hill, Cove, co. Cork
* Ronayne, Patrick, Esq., Ann Brook, Cove, co. Cork
Ronayne, Patrick, Esq., Castleview, Macroom, co. Cork
* Ronayne, Richard, Esq., Nicholas-street, Cork
* Ronayne, R. Power, Esq., D.L. and J.P., D'Laughtane-house, [Youghal, co. Cork
Ronayne, W. Crooke, Esq., South-mall, Cork
* Roney, E. H. W., Esq., Sothern, Ashbourne, co. Meath
Rooney, Rev. C., R.C.C., Townsend-street, Dublin
Roose, Sir D. C., Knt.,Upper Fitzwilliam-street, Dublin
Rooth, Samuel, Esq., Walton, Chesterfield, Derbyshire
Roper, Mr. Richard, Forestown, Kilcock, co. Meath
Roper, Rev. W., A.M., Aughnamullin, Ballibay, co. Monaghan
* Rorke, Andrew, Esq., Tyrrelstown, Mullahuddart, co. Dublin
* Rorke, Edmund, Esq., Clonsilla, near Castlenock, co. Dublin
* Rorke, John, Esq., Jamestown, near Kilternan, co. Dublin
* Rorke, John, Esq., Finstown-house, Lucan, co. Dublin
* Rorke, L., Esq., Neilstown-house, near Clondalkin, co. Dublin
* Rorke, P. C., Esq., Nanger near Clondalkin, co. Dublin
Rose, Alderman H. Ballyclough, Limerick
Rose, Rev. H. H., A.M., Gable-ville, Limerick
* Rose, Richard, Esq., Lower Gloster-street, Dublin and Limerick
Rose, Simon, Esq., Thomas-street, Limerick
Rose, Thomas, Esq., Aghoberg, near Limerick
* Rose, W. Anderson, Esq., Fox-hall, Newport, co. Tipperary
Ross, Rev. A., Banagher-glebe, Dungiven, co. Derry
Ross, Mr. Francis A., Lisneal, Glendermott, co. Derry
Ross, Rev. G. F., Hathersage, Derbyshire
* Ross, Major James, Liscarney, Monaghan
* Ross, John, Esq., Ardsalla, Navan, co. Meath
Ross, John Higgins, Esq., Killala, co. Mayo
Ross, Rev. Michael, Kildorrery, co. Cork
Ross, Rev. Richard, A.M., Drumbrain-cottage, Newbliss, co. [Monaghan
* Ross, Mrs., Bladensburg, Rosstrevor, co. Down
* ROSSE, The Right Honorable the Earl of
Rossiter, Tobias, Esq., Newbawn, New Ross, co. Wexford
Rossiter, Mr. W., Wexford
Rothe, Rev. R. J., Macloneigh-glebe, Macroom, co. Cork
* Rotheram, Edward, Esq., J.P., Crossdrum, Oldcastle, co. Meath
* Rotheram, G. S., Esq., J.P., Sallymount, co. Westmeath
* Rotheram, Thomas, Esq., J.P., Triermore, Athboy, co. Meath
Rothwell, Hugh, Esq., Brownstown, Navan, co. Meath
* Rothwell, Peter, Esq., Sunning Hill, Bolton, Lancashire
* Rothwell, Richard, Esq., Rockfield, Kells, co. Meath
Rowan, Rev. A. B., Belmont, co. Kerry
* Rowan, A. H., Esq., Rathcoffy-house, Maynooth, co. Kildare
Rowan, Hill W., Esq., J.P., Carrick-on-Suir, co. Waterford
Rowan, John, Esq., Merville, Belfast
Rowe, John, Esq., Blessington-street, Dublin
Rowe John, Esq., Ballycross, Wexford
Rowe, Rev. Walter, P.P., Tagoat, co. Wexford
Rowland, Francis, Esq., J.P., Kilbay-house, Cloyne, co. Cork
Rowland, Michael, Esq., Mucknagh, Castlebar, co. Mayo
Rowland, Richard, Esq., Creslow, Aylesbury, Bucks
* Rowley, Rev. John, LL.D. and J.P., Lurgan-glebe, Virginia, co. [Cavan
* Rowsell, Thomas S., Esq., Wandsworth, Surrey
Roy, Messrs. A. and Co., John's-gate Brewery, Limerick
* Royal Exchange Assurance Company, London
Royse, Thos. Esq., J.P., Ballinvirick, Rathkeale, co. Limerick
Royse, Thomas, Esq., Fenchurch Street, London
Royse, T. H., Esq., J.P.,Nantenan-house, Rathkeale, co. Limerick
* Rule, Mr. James, Castle-Blayney, co. Monaghan
Rumley, Thomas H., Esq., Ballinacurra-lodge, Midleton, co. Cork
* Rumley, Thomas, Esq., Stephen's-green, Dublin
Rush, Francis French, Esq., Cloonkeelly, Tuam, co. Galway
* RUSSELL, The Right Hon. Lord C. J. F.
* Russell, Francis Philip, Esq., Limerick
Russell, George, Esq., Charleville, co. Cork
* Russell, James, Esq., J.P., Mount-Russell, Charleville, co. Cork
* Russell, Rev. John, Belcamp, near St. Douloughs, co. Dublin
* Russell, John, Esq., Limerick
Russell, Rev. John, P.P. of Cloyne, co. Cork
* Russell, John N., Esq., Askeaton and Limerick
Russell, Peter, Esq., St. Cloud, Slane, co. Meath
Russell, Vincent, Esq., Youghal, co. Cork
* Rutherfoord, A. H., Esq., Ravensdale, Flurrybridge, co. Louth
* Rutherfoord, J., Esq., St. Doulough's-lodge, & Rutland-sq., Dublin
* Rutherford, John, Esq. Rathmines, co. Dublin
* Rutherford, John, Esq., Lower Sackville-street, Dublin
* Rutherford, Thomas, Esq., Annisborough-house, Lurgan, co. Antrim
* Ruthven, E. S., Esq., J.P., Ballyfair, Kilcullen, and Downpatrick
* Rutson, W., Esq., Newby-Wiske, Northallerton, Yorkshire
Ruttle, D., Esq., Glocester-st., Dublin, and Rathkeale, co. Limerick
* Ruttledge, Rev. F., J.P., Bloomfield, Hollymount, co. Mayo
* Ruttledge, George, Esq., Castle Connor, Ballina, co. Mayo
Ryall, J., Esq., Brook-lodge, Kilrossenty, co. Waterford
Ryan, Charles, Esq., Crodenstown, Newbridge, co. Kildare
* Ryan, Daniel, Esq., Rye Vale, Leixlip, co. Kildare
* Ryan, George, Esq., J.P., Inch-house, Thurles, co. Tipperary
Ryan, Rev. James, P.P. of Bruree, co. Limerick
Ryan, James, Esq., Clone-lodge, Templemore, co. Tipperary
* Ryan, Rev. James, P.P., Kanturk, co. Cork
* Ryan, Rev. James F., R.C.C., Thomastown, Kilkenny
Ryan, Mr. John, Ballyroan, Abbeyleix, Queen's-county
* Ryan, Rev. John, P.P., Cappamore, co. Limerick
* Ryan, The Right Rev. John, D.D., R.C. Bishop of Limerick
Ryan, Rev. John, P.P., Kilmoyler, Cahir, co. Tipperary
* Ryan, Rev. J. J., R.C.C., St. Pauls, Arran-Quay, Dublin
Ryan, Rev. J. J., P.P., Carrigaline, co. Cork
* Ryan, Jos., Esq., O'Briery-bridge, co. Clare
* Ryan, Malachi, Esq., Tyone Mills, Nenagh, co. Tipperary
Ryan, Michael, Esq., Lower Dominick-street, Dublin
Ryan, Rev. P., R.C.C. of Adamstown, New Ross, co. Wexford
* Ryan, Rev. Philip, A.M., Lime Hill, near St. Douloughs, co. Dublin
* Ryan, Thaddeus R., Esq., J.P., Castle Jane, Pallas-Griene, co. [Limerick
Ryan, Rev. T., P.P., of Fahil and Kilquane, Eyrecourt, co. Galway
Ryan, W. H., Esq., Larchfield, Abbeyleix, Queen's-county
* Ryder, John, Esq., Ballinahinch, near N. M. Kennedy, co. Wicklow
Ryder, Rev. Joshua Brown, J.P., Castlelyons-house, co. Cork
Ryder, The Venerable Rev. W., Archdeacon of Cloyne, J.P., Bal- [linterry, Rathcormac, co. Cork
* Rye, John Tonson, Esq., Rye-court, near Ovens, co. Cork
Rynd, Christopher, Esq., Mount-Armstrong, Clane, co. Kildare
* Rynd, Robert, Esq., Ryndville, Enfield, co. Meath
* Ryves, Massy, Esq., Limerick and New Garden, Castle-Connel. [co. Limerick
* Ryves, W., Esq., Ryves Castle, Limerick, & Regent's-park, London

Sadleir, Rev. F., D.D., S.F.T.C.D., College, Dublin
* Sadleir, James, Esq., Brookville, Tipperary
* Sadleir, Thomas, Esq., Salisbury, Clonmel, co. Tipperary
* Sadleir, Thomas, jun., Esq., Ballinderry, Burris-o'-kane, co. Tippe- [rary
* Sadleir, William, Esq., J.P., Sadleir's Wells, Tipperary
* Sadler, Benjamin, Esq., Belfast
* Salvin, B. J., Esq., Burn-hall, near Durham
* Salvin, W. T., Esq., Croxdale-hall, Durham
St. Clair, Major W., Ballinteer-lodge, near Dundrum, co. Dublin
St. Edmund Hall Library, Oxford, per Rev. J. Hill
* St. George, Acheson, Esq., J.P., Woodpark, Tynan, co. Armagh
St. George, Nelson, Esq., Altamount, Tullow, co. Carlow
St. George, Robert, Esq., J.P., Balief-castle, Freshford, Kilkenny
St. George, R. J. Mansergh, Esq., D.L. and J.P., Headford-castle, [co. Galway
St. George, Rev. Thomas, A.B., Killaloe, co. Clare
* St. George, Thomas B., Esq., Esker, co. Kilkenny, and Dawson- [street, Dublin
* St. Georgio, John N., Esq., Frederick-street, Dublin
* St. Lawrance, Rev. R. K., Murragh-glebe, near Bandon, co. Cork
* St. Leger, A. B., Esq., Chicheley, Bucks
St. Leger, B., Esq., Ballyheragh St. Leger, Hollymount, co. Mayo
* Salmon, John, Esq., Derryville, Killaloe, co. Tipperary

Salmon, John, Esq., Jamaica, per E. J. Green, Esq., Leadenhall-street, London
*Sampson, Denis, Esq., St. Catherines, Scariff, co. Clare, and St. [Stephen's-green, Dublin
Sampson, Rev. M., J.P., Rector of Annacloan, co. Down
*Samson, G., Esq., Ballycastle, co. Antrim
*Samuell, W. L. W., Esq., Upton-hall, near Northampton
*Sanders, James, Esq., Wellington Farm, near Artaine, co. Dublin
*Sandersan, A., Esq., Ballyshannon, co. Donegal
*Sanderson, J., Esq., D.L. and J.P., Cloverhill, Belturbet, co. Cavan
*Sanderson, Mr. John, Old Jewry, London
*Sandes, C. L., Esq., J.P., Indiaville, Portarlington, Queen's-county
Sandes, George, Esq., Dunowen, Clonakilty, co. Cork
*Sandes, Pigott, Esq., Geashill, King's-county
*Sandes, Thomas William, Esq., Sallow Glen, co. Kerry
*Sandes, William, Esq., Pyrmont, co. Kerry
*Sandes, William, Esq., Sallow Glen, Tarbert, co. Kerry
Sandes, William, Esq., Mount Pleasant, Askeaton, co. Limerick
Sandiford, Rev. Samuel, B.A., Bantry, co. Cork
Sands, John, Esq., Limerick
Sands, William G., Esq., Greenville, Listowel, co. Kerry
*Sandys, Rev. F. R., Prebendary of Mayne, Kilkenny
*Sandys, Robert, Esq., Dargle-cottage, near Enniskerry, co. Wicklow
*Sandys, W., Esq., Drimnacor, Ballymahon, co. Longford
*Sankey, M. V., Esq., J.P., Coolmore, Fethard, co. Tipperary
*Sargent, Rev. Robert, M.A. and J.P., Eites, Virginia, co. Cavan
*Sarsfield, D., Esq., Doughcloyne, Old Kinsale-road, Cork
*Saunders, Arthur, Esq., Annamore, Castleisland, co. Kerry
Saunders, Joseph, Esq., J.P., Ardglass, co. Down
*Saunders, J., Esq., Park-gate Iron Works, Rotheram, Yorkshire
Saunders, Lieut.-Gen. J. S., D.L. and J.P., Golden Fort, Baltinglass, [co. Wicklow
Saunders, Rev. J. T. C., Borris, co. Carlow
*Saunderson, Alexander, Esq., D.L. and J.P., Castle-Saunderson, [co. Cavan
*Saunderson, Rev. F., A.M., J.P., Bocade, Killeshandra, co. Cavan
Saunderson, Rev. J. H., Fairy-mount, Shinrone, co. Tipperary
Saunderson, James Johnston, Esq., C.C., Portarlington, Queen's co.
Saurin, The Venerable, Archdeacon of Dromore, Seagoe, co. Armagh
*Sausse, Matthew Richard, Esq., Hume-street, Dublin
Savage, Benjamin, Esq., Kanturk, co. Cork
*Savage, Francis, Esq., Fitzgibbon-street, Dublin
Savage, Francis, Esq., Dundrum, co. Down
Savage, Francis, Esq., J.P., Glastry, Kircubbin, co. Down
*Savage, James, Esq., Finglas Wood, co. Dublin
Savage, Richard, Esq., Tuam, co. Galway
*Savage, Rev. W. W., Rector of Union of Shinrone, King's-county
Sayers, Capt. Arthur, Limerick
*Sayers, W., Esq., Crebilly House, Ballymena, co. Antrim
Sayers, Capt. W., Curriglass, Tallow, co. Cork
Scallan, Rev. John, P.P., Taghmon, co. Wexford
Scallan, Mr. Nicholas, Spa-well-brewery, near Wexford
Scanlan, Anthony, Esq., Ballycahan Castle, Croom, co. Limerick
Scanlan, Rev. Michael, P.P., Castle-Connel, co. Limerick
Scannill, Rev. Michael, Mallow, co. Cork
*SCARSDALE, The Right Honorable Lord
Schoales, Adam, Esq., Londonderry
*Schoales, John, Esq., S. Fitzwilliam-square, Dublin
Scmullen, Thomas, Esq., Villa, near Lucan, co. Dublin
Scollard, Nicholas, Esq., Camden-place, Cork
*Scott, Major-Gen. Sir H. J., K.C.B., Woodville, co. Dublin
Scott, Alexander, Esq., Belfast
Scott, Barnaby, jun., Esq., S. Frederick-street, Dublin, and Kilkenny
*Scott, Charles, Esq., Straghroy, Omagh, co. Tyrone
Scott, David H., Esq., M.D., Cove, co. Cork
Scott, Rev. George, A.M., Balteagh, co. Derry
Scott, George Henry, Esq., Devonshire-place, London
*Scott, Henry, Esq., Bank of Ireland, Clonmel, co Tipperary
Scott, Henry, Esq., Oulston, Easingwold, Yorkshire
*Scott, Rev. J., R.C.C. of St. Paul's, Arran-Quay, Dublin
*Scott, James, Esq., J.P., Bloomhill, Dungannon, co. Tyrone
*Scott, James E., Esq., J.P., Ann-grove-abbey, Queen's-county
Scott, Rev. J. R. W., Drumbeg Rectory, Lisburn, co. Down
Scott, James S., Esq., Delgany, co. Wicklow, and Merrion-square [South, Dublin
*Scott, Mr. John, Ballymecran, co. Derry
*Scott, John, Esq., J.P., Cahiracon, Kildysart, co. Clare
Scott, Rev. John, Curate of Carndonagh, co. Donegal
Scott, John, Esq., Admiralty, Somerset House, London
Scott, John James, Esq., Devonshire-place, London
*Scott, Rev. Joseph, Statford-upon-Slaney, co. Wicklow
Scott, Major Matthew, Gortaglanna, Bandon, co. Cork
*Scott, Patrick, Esq., Palace-street, Dublin
Scott, Mr. P., Whitechapel, London
Scott, Rev. Robert, Vicar of Clondulane, Fermoy, co. Cork
*Scott, Thomas, Esq., D.L. and J.P., Willsborough, Londonderry
*Scott, Rev. Thomas, A.M., Curate of St. Audoens, Dublin
Scott, Lieut. Thomas, R.P., Ballycastle, co. Mayo
Scott, Thomas, Esq., Rathfriland, co. Down
*Scott, Capt., W H., J.P., Banagher, King's county
*Scott, Rev. William, Rectory, Pallasgreine, co. Limerick
*Scott, W., Esq., J.P., Scottsborough, Clones, co. Fermanagh
Scroder, Jacob, Esq., Waterford
*Scroope, Henry, Esq., Roscrea, co. Tipperary
*Scully, Rev. C., P.P. of Ballyclough and Kilbrin, co. Cork
*Scully, James, Esq., J.P., Tipperary
Scully, Jeremiah, Esq., Silverfort, Cashel, co. Tipperary
Scully, John, Esq., Dually, Cashel, co. Tipperary
Scully, Rody, Esq., Hymenstown, Cashel, co. Tipperary
Scully, Roger, Esq., J.P., Tipperary
Sealy, Jonas M., Esq., Gortnahorna, co. Cork
Sealy, William, Esq., Maug House,-Tralee, co. Kerry
*Searancke, Samuel S., Esq., Trim, co. Meath
*Seaver, Jonathan, Esq., J.P., Heath Hall, Newry, co. Down
Seaver, Lieut. Joseph, R.P., Newport, co. Mayo
Seely, Francis, Esq., Woodview, Innishannon, co. Cork
*Segrave, H. J., Esq., J.P., Glencarrig, near Glanealy, co. Wicklow
*Segrave, John, Esq., New Barn, co. Dublin
*Segrave, W. P., Esq., Borranstown, near Ashbourne, co. Dublin
Semple, Charles, Esq., J.P., Furlough House, Castlebar, co. Mayo
*Semple, Rev. Edward, Rector of Kilcormuck, co. Wexford
*Semple, Major John, Castletown, Strabane, co. Tyrone
Senior, Lieut. James, R.N., Coast Guard, Bantry, co. Cork
*Senior, Richard, Esq., J.P., Moorfield, Mountrath, Queen's-county
Senior, Thomas, Esq., Ballycastle, co. Antrim
Senior, W., Esq., Knockacollar, Mountrath, Queen's-county
Service, Mr. John, Drunmurry, co. Antrim
*Seton, Anketell, Esq., Merino-crescent, Dublin
*Severne, Samuel A., Esq., Thenford, near Banbury, Oxfordshire
*Seward, Thomas, Esq., Seafield, co. Cork
*Seymour, Rev. David, A.M., Abbeyland, Eyrecourt, co. Galway
*Seymour, Francis, Esq., Theatre-Royal, Limerick
*Seymour, Rev. G. T., Marksbury, near Bath
*Seymour, Henry, Esq., York-street, Dublin
*Seymour, Rev. Joseph J., A.M., Carane, Kilconnell, co. Galway
*Seymour, Joseph, Esq., Blessington, co. Wicklow
*Seymour, Rev. J. H., Northchurch, Great Berkhampstead, Herts
Seymour, Rev. M. H., A.M., Ballinrobe, co. Mayo
Seymour, Nicholas, Esq., Custom House, Cove, co. Cork
Seymour N. G., Esq., Moeneroe, Carrigaline, co. Cork
Seymour, Rev. R., R.C.C., Carrigdowning Cottage, Kildorrery, co. [Cork
*Seymour, Simeon, Esq., Somerset-house, Laurencetown, co. Galway
*Seymour, T., Esq., J.P., Ballymore Castle, Laurencetown, co. Galway
Shackleton, Ebenezer, Esq., Moone-mills, Ballytore, co. Kildare
Shafts, D. R. E., Esq., Whitworth-park, Bishop-Auckland, Durham
Shalloway, Mr. Christopher, North-Wall-Baths, Dublin
Shanahan, Rev. John, P.P., Abbeyside, Dungarvan, co. Waterford
*Shanks, W. G., Esq., West Auckland, Durham
*Shanley, J., Esq., J.P., Norman's grove, Clonee, co. Meath
Shanly, W., Esq., Kilrush, Ballinamore, co. Leitrim
*SHANNON, The Right Honorable the Earl of
*Shannon, Pierce, Esq., Limerick
Shannon, Oliver, Esq., Mount-Brown, near Kilmainham, co. Dublin
Sharkey, Rev. Daniel, R.C. Rector of Ballinahinch, co. Down
Sharkey, Edmund, Esq., M.D., Allihies-mines, Castletown-Bere-[haven, co. Cork
Sharky, Michael, Esq., St. Helena-lodge, Roscommon
*Sharpe, Ingham, Esq., Limerick
*Sharpe, Robert, Esq., Coleraine, co. Derry
*Shaw, Sir Robert, Bart, Bushy-park, Dublin
Shaw, Archibald C., Esq., Glanmire, Cork
*Shaw, B., Esq., Stamp-office, Cork
Shaw, Charles, Esq., Austin Friars, London
*Shaw, George, Esq., Mosley-hall, Manchester
Shaw, George, Esq., Kilsellagh, Sligo
Shaw, George, Esq., Fermoy-lodge, Fermoy, co. Cork
*Shaw, J., Esq., Lower-ormond-quay, and Merrion Avenue, Dublin
Shaw, John, Esq., Newport, co. Tipperary
Shaw, Mr. Lorenzo F., Bachelor's-walk, Dublin
*Shaw, Ponsonby, Esq., Friarstown, near Tallaght, co. Dublin
Shaw, Robert B., Esq., Monkstown-Castle, co. Cork
*Shaw, Robert, Esq., Meath Hospital, Dublin
*Shaw, W., Esq., Gracefield-lodge, Balbriggan, co. Dublin
*Shaw, W., Esq., Greenwood, near St. Doulough's, co. Dublin
*Shaw, Mrs. Grace, St. Doulough's, co. Dublin

Shaw, Messrs. Robert and Co., Cloghroe-mills, co. Cork
*Sheahan, Rev. J., P.P., Kilmacabea, co. Cork
Sheahan, Rev. Jeremiah, P.P., Glengariff, co. Cork
*Sheahan, Rev. Michael, P.P., Mahonagh, co. Limerick
Sheane, Henry, Esq., Banagher, King's county
*Sheane, Mr. Samuel, Mountmelick, Queen's-county
Shearman, Alexander H., Esq., Waterford
*Shee, John, Esq., J.P., Sheestown, Kilkenny
*Shee, Rev. John, President, St. James's College, Kilkenny
Sheehan, A., Esq., Ennis, co. Clare
Sheehan, Rev. G., R.C.C. of St. Peter's and St. Paul's, Cork
Sheehan, Rev. John, P.P., Killeilagh, co. Clare
Sheehan, Rev. M., P.P. of Killeagh, co. Cork
Sheehan, The Very Rev. Patrick, Vicar General of Cloyne, and [P.P. of Rathcormac, co. Cork
*Sheehy, Rev. Edmund, P.P., Parteen, near Limerick
Sheehy, Rev. John, P.P., Kilfinane, and Ardpatrick, co. Limerick
Sheehy, John K. Esq., Newcastle, co. Limerick
Sheehy, John, Esq., Thomas-street, Limerick
Sheehy, Rev. Patrick, P.P. of Andfield, Clonakilty, co. Cork
*Sheehy, R. K., Esq., J.P., Liskennett, Croom, co. Limerick
Sheehy, W. J., Esq., Bloomfield, Douglas, Cork
Shefley, Mr. James, Roscrea, co. Tipperary
*Shegog, Richard, Esq., Drogheda, co. Louth
Sheil, Mr. George, Lower Abbey-street, Dublin
*Sheil, Mr. James, Constitution-hill, Dublin
*Sheil, John, Esq., J.P., Castle-Dawson, co. Derry
Sheil, John B., Esq., M.D., Ballyshannon, co. Donegal
Sheil, The Very Rev. Patrick, Vicar General of Clonfert, and P.P. [of Portumna, co. Galway
*Sheil, Simon, Esq., Port Nasson, Ballyshannon, co. Donegal
*Shekleton, A., Esq., Dundalk, co. Louth
Shekleton, James, Esq., Bleach-green, Collon, co. Louth
*Shelden, E., Esq., Brailes, Warwickshire
Shelton, Capt. J. W., J.P., Rossmore-house, co. Limerick
*Shepard, James, Esq., Sheep-hill, near Wicklow
*Shepard, William, Esq., Oatlands, near Wicklow
*Shepheard, Robert, Esq., Bettystown, Drogheda, co. Louth
Shepheard, Capt. W., R.N., Insp. Com. Coast Guard, Listowel, co. [Kerry
*Shepherd, James, Esq., Lime-street-square, London
*Shepherd, Mr. J. G., Faversham, Kent
*Shepley, Robert, Esq., Glossop, Derbyshire
*Sheppard, Thomas, Esq., John's-hill House, Waterford
*Sheppard, William, Esq., York-crescent, Clifton, near Bristol
Sheridan, James, Esq., Eden-ville, Kingstown, co. Dublin
*Sheridan, Rev. B., R.C.R., Lodge-park, Kingstown, co. Dublin
Sheridan, Rev. Farrell, P.P., Granard, co. Longford
Sheridan, Rev. John, P.P., Dulane and Loughan, Kells, co. Meath
Sheridan, Rev. Myles, R.C. Administrator, Kilmeena, and Kilma- [classan, Westport, co. Mayo
Sheridan, Messrs. Martin and Michael, Castlebar, co. Mayo
*Sherlock, Alexander, Esq., Killaspy, near Waterford
Sherlock, Edward, Esq., Coolgrove, Stradbally, Queen's-county
Sherlock, J. W., Esq., Fermoy, co. Cork
*Sherlock, R., Esq., Springvale, and Edmonstown-mills, near Rath- [farnham, co. Dublin
*Sherlock, Thomas, Esq., Mount-Anville, co. Dublin
Sherlock, Thomas, Esq., Bandon, co. Cork
*Sherlock, W. R. Esq., Sherlockstown, Naas, co. Kildare
*Sherlock, W. T., Esq., Mount-Irwin, Ballymoate, co. Sligo
Sherrard, Mr. Conolly, Lomond, co. Derry
*Sherrard, D. H., Esq., Thorndale, co. Dublin
*Sherrard, Thomas, Esq., Coolock-lodge, co. Dublin
*Sherrard, William, Esq., Marlay, Dunleer, co. Louth
*Sherwood, A. B., Esq., M.D., Redcross, co. Wicklow
Sherwood, Rev. Jos., Aiskew, Bedale, Yorkshire
Sherwood, Richard N. Esq., Barracks, near Carnew, co. Wicklow
Shew, Barnett, Esq., Newtown, near Finglas, co. Dublin
*Shew, Mrs. Jane, Jamestown, near Finglas, co. Dublin
*Shickle, Charles, Esq., Norwich
*Shiel, J. H., Esq., Cottage, near Rochfort-Bridge, co. Westmeath
*Shield, Jos., Esq., Field-house, Gateshead, Durham
*Shieldham, William L., Esq., Dunmanway, co. Cork
Shields, Rev. James, Newry, co. Down
Shine, James, Esq., Ballymacreese-house, Limerick
Shine, Jeremiah, Esq., Coolyhenan-house, Limerick
Shine, Michael, Esq., Edwardstown, Limerick
Shipperdson, Edward. Esq., Durham
Short, Lawrence, Esq., Chesterfield, Derbyshire
Short, Mr. T., Aldermanbury, London
Shortridge, Richard, Esq., South Shields, Durham
*Shortt, James, Esq., Newtown, Mountrath, Queen's-county
*Shortt, P. H., Esq., Centry-lodge, Burros-in-Ossory, Queen's-county
Shortt, W. T., Esq., Summerhill, Moneygall, co. Tipperary
*SHREWSBURY, The Right Honorable the Earl of
*Shulze, Rev. J. G. F., Ranelagh, co. Dublin
*Sibthorpe, Rev. H. W., M.A., Washingborough, Lincolnshire
*Sidley, George, Esq., Glendermott, co. Derry
*Siex, Michael, Esq., Drynam-house, co. Dublin
Silk, Eyre, Esq., Loughrea, co. Galway
Sim, Alexander, Esq., Ballisadare-villa, Collooney, co. Sligo
*Simcoe, Rev. H. A., Penheale-house, Launceston, Cornwall
*Simeon, Captain, R.N., J.P., Thornhill, Templemore, co. Derry
*Simmonds, D., Esq., Collinstown, (Leixlip) co. Dublin
*Simmonds, Joseph C., Esq., Sligo
Simms, Messrs. William and Son, Belfast
*Simpson, Hugh, Esq., Aughnacloy, co. Tyrone
Simpson, James C., Esq., Millbrook, Sligo
Simpson, James, Esq., Dough Cloyne, Old Kinsale-road, near Cork
*Simpson, Rev. John, LL.D., Worcester
*Simpson, John, Esq., Ballyards, Armagh
Simpson, John, Esq., Millview, Aughnacloy, co. Tyrone
Simpson, Joseph, Esq., Drumskil, Cootehill, co. Cavan
*Simpson, Robert, Esq., Sea-view, Carrickfergus, co. Antrim
*Simpson, Robert, Esq., Bellgrove, Clontarf, co. Dublin
Simpson, Rev. S., A.M., Queen-street, Dublin
Simpson, Rev. Samuel, Keady, co. Armagh
*Simpson, Thomas, Esq., Beech-hill, Armagh
Simpson, Thomas, Esq., College-green, Dublin
Simson, John, Esq., Bowmore, Island of Islay, Scotland
*Sinclair, James, Esq., D.L. and J.P., Holy-hill, Strabane, co. Tyrone
*Sinclair, Rev. R. H., Cashel-glebe, Lanesborough, co. Longford
*Sinclaire, John, Esq., Belfast
*Singleton, John, Esq., J.P., Quinville-abbey, Quin, co. Clare
*Singleton, T., Esq., J.P., Fort Singleton, Emyvale, co. Monaghan
Sinnott, Rev. James, R.C.C. of Cushinstown, co. Wexford
Sinnott, Rev. James, C.C. of Old Ross, &c., New Ross, co. Wexford
Sinnott, Rev. John, President of St. Peter's College, Wexford
*Sinnott, Mr. Patrick, Wexford
Sinnott, Mr. Peter, Carrickfergus, co. Antrim
Sirr, Rev. Joseph D'Arcy, Kilcoleman Parsonage, co. Mayo
*Skaife, John, Esq., Blackburn, Lancashire
*Skelly, F. J., Esq., Ballymena, co. Antrim
*Skelten, Samuel, Esq., Antrim
Skelton, H., Esq., Jonesborough-house, Flurry-bridge, co. Louth
Skerrett, Patrick, Esq., Loughrea, co. Galway
*Skerrett, William, Esq., Carnacrow, Headford, co. Galway
Skiddy, Mr. Morgan, Church-street, Cork
Skidmore, Emmott, Esq., Rickmansworth, Hertfordshire
Skinner, Edward, Esq., Antrim
Skinner, Mr. M., Cronebane and Tigrony-mines, co. Wicklow
Skipsey, Rev. R., Incumbent of South Cowton and Enyholme, [Northallerton, Yorkshire
*Skipton, Conolly, Esq., Brook-hill, Glendermott, co. Derry
*Skipton, Captain V., J.P., Springfield, Longford
Skipwith, Sir G., Bart., Newbold-hall, Kirby Monks, near Coventry
Skottowe, Sir Edmund, Knt., Waterford
*Slacke, Thomas, Esq., Eccles-street, Dublin
*Slacke, W. R., Esq., Annadale, Carrick-on-Shannon, co. Leitrim
*Slade, Hercules Henry, Esq., J.P., Mount-Shannon, Sligo
Slark, Mr. William, Piccadilly, London
*Slator, Bevan C., Esq., J.P., Clinan, Colehill, co. Longford
*Slator, Henry B., Esq., White-hill, Edgeworthstown, co. Longford
Sleater, Rev. Charles, Killiney, Kingstown, co. Dublin
Sleater, Rev. Welbore H., Lacka, Kildare
*Slee, Noah, Esq., Bermondsey-street, London
*Slevin, The Rev. F., D.D., Vicar General, Lismore-House, Carrick- [on-Shannon
*SLIGO, The Most Noble the Marquess of
*Sloan, George, Esq., Coalisland, Dungannon, co. Tyrone
*Sloane, Rev. S. Hans, LL.D., Nullamore, Sunday's Well, Cork
Small, Rev. H. A., Haversham-rectory, Stoney Stratford, Bucks.
Smiley, S., Esq., Cork-harbour, Cove, co. Cork
*Smith, Rev. Ambrose, Incumbent of Templeudigan, co. Wexford
Smith, Anthony, Esq., Ardee, co. Louth
Smith, B., Esq.,*Adelphi Iron Works, Chesterfield, Derbyshire
Smith, C., Esq., Rosemount, Booterstown, co. Dublin
*Smith, Rev. Charles, Vicar of Kilnemanagh, Elphin, co. Roscommon
*Smith, Rev. Charles, Rector of Arklow, co. Wicklow
Smith, C. L., Esq., Christ-college, Cambridge, and Shurdington, [near Cheltenham
*Smith, David, Esq., J.P., Lakeview, Clones, co. Monaghan
*Smith, E. J., Esq., North Frederick-street, Dublin
*Smith, Francis, Esq., Flora-ville, near Clondalkin, co. Dublin

Smith, F. P., Esq., J.P., Larkfield, near Mullingar, co. Westmeath
Smith, George, Esq., Castletown-Roche, co. Cork
Smith, George, Esq., Gurteen, (Parsonstown) co. Tipperary
Smith, Rev. George, Rector of Castlemartyr, co. Cork
Smith, Rev. Godfrey C., Lisnabrinny, Clonakilty, co. Cork
Smith, Lieut.-Colonel H., Baltiboys, co. Wicklow
*Smith, Henry, Esq., Annsbrook, Duleek, co. Meath
*Smith, Henry, Esq., Clareen, Shinrone, King's county
Smith, Henry, Esq., Drogheda
Smith, J. Esq., Brookfield, Milltown, co. Dublin
*Smith, James, Esq., Lincolns Inn, London
*Smith, James, Esq., Fort-lodge, Ballinacargy, co. Cavan
*Smith, James, Esq., Salford, near Manchester
Smith, Rev. James, Rector of Camus-juxta-Mourne, Strabane, co. Tyrone
Smith, James, Esq., J.P., New-park, Mountrath, Queen's county
*Smith, John, Esq., Blossomfort, co. Cork
*Smith, John, Esq., Ballymount-castle, near Clondalkin, co. Dublin
*Smith, John, Esq., Henrietta-street, Dublin
*Smith, John, Esq., Leamore, near Newcastle, co. Wicklow
*Smith, John, Esq., Shinrone, King's county
*Smith, Captain John, Ardverness, Coleraine, co. Derry
*Smith, John, Esq., Annaville, King's county
Smith, John, Esq., Kells, co. Meath
Smith, John, Esq., Gravesend, Kent
Smith, John, Esq., Newcastle, Nobber, co. Meath
Smith, Rev. John, A.B., Ahavrin-cottage, Coachford, co. Cork
*Smith, John H., Esq., Elphin, co. Roscommon
*Smith, Marmaduke, Esq., Jamestown, near Finglas, co. Dublin
Smith, Matthias, Esq., Rock-cottage, Blackrock, Cork
*Smith, Rev. P., R.C.C., Francis-street Chapel, Dublin
Smith, Rev. P., A.B., Nantenan-glebe, Rathkeale, co. Limerick
*Smith, Patten, Esq., Saggard-house, co. Dublin
*Smith, Philip, Esq., Cherry-mount, Moynalty, co. Meath
Smith, Rev. Philip, A.M., Moynalty, co. Meath
Smith, R., Esq., Milford, co. Tipperary, and Buckingham-street, Dublin
*Smith, Richard, Esq., Newmarket, co. Cork
*Smith, Robert, Esq., Crumlin, co. Dublin
*Smith, Robert, Esq., Upper Fitzwilliam-street, Dublin
*Smith, S., Esq., Stone-view, co. Dublin
Smith, Samuel, Esq., Headford, co. Galway
*Smith, St. George, Esq., Green-hills, Drogheda, co. Louth
*Smith, Rev. S., A.M., Drumlion-cottage, Ballintemple, co. Cavan
*Smith, T., Esq., Heaton-hall, Newcastle-on-Tyne, Northumberland
*Smith, Thomas, Esq., Bolton-street, Dublin
*Smith, Thomas, Esq., J.P,, Rathmullen, co. Donegal
Smith, Thomas, Esq., M.D., Bellmont, Kilgobbin, co. Donegal
Smith, Thomas, Esq., Macroom, co. Cork
*Smith, Mr. Thomas D., Waterford
*Smith, Thomas W., Esq., Craigmore-cottage, Ramelton, co. Donegal
Smith, U. T., Esq., Rathmelton, co. Donegal
Smith, W., Esq., J.P., Rathkeale, co. Limerick
*Smith, W., Esq., Upper Ormond-quay, Dublin
*Smith, The Right Hon. Sir William Cusack, Bart., late Second Baron, Exchequer of Ireland
*Smith, William, Esq., Lisaniskea, co. Dublin
*Smith, Rev. William, Rector of Glebehill, Garvagh, co. Derry
Smith, William, Esq., J.P., Northland, Cloghjordan, co. Tipperary
Smith, William, Esq., Lisduff, Moneygall, co. Tipperary
Smith, William, Esq., Agricultural-bank, Mallow, co. Cork
*Smithson, T. B., Esq., Woodbine-lodge, Rathfarnham, co. Dublin
*Smithwick, Edward, Esq., Kilkenny
*Smithwick, Rev. G., Rector of Leckpatrick, Strabane, co. Tyrone
Smithwick, George, Esq., Cottage, Tipperary
*Smithwick, Henry, Esq., Mount Catherine, co. Limerick
*Smithwick, Rev. P., R.C.C., Irishtown, Dublin
*Smithwick, W., Esq., Youghal, Nenagh, co. Tipperary
Smyly, Rev. Cecil, Lisburn, co. Antrim
Smyly, John George, Esq., North Great George-street, Dublin
*Smyth, Brice, Esq., Brookfield, Banbridge, co. Down
Smyth, Charles, Esq., Kingstown, co. Dublin
Smyth, Charles, Esq., Rathkeale, co. Limerick
Smyth, Charles. Esq., Killala, co. Mayo
*Smyth, C. G., Esq., Lower Dorset-street, Dublin, and Ballinasloe, co. Galway
Smyth, David, Esq., Strabane, co. Tyrone
Smyth, Eyre, Esq., South-hill, near Limerick
*Smyth, Henry, Esq., J.P., Mount Henry, Queen's county
*Smyth, Henry, Esq., Strabane, co. Tyrone
Smyth, Henry, Esq., Richmond, co. Cork
Smyth, Henry M., Esq., Castle-widenham, co. Cork
*Smyth, Rev. James, P.P. of Street, Rathowen, co. Westmeath
*Smyth, Mr. James, Gracehill, Ballymena, co. Antrim
Smyth, James, Esq., Dysartlin-cottage, Moneymore, co. Derry
Smyth, James, Esq., Midleton, co. Cork
Smyth, James G., Esq., Ashfield, Clones, co. Monaghan
Smyth, James, Esq., Masonbrook, Loughrea, co. Galway
*Smyth, Rev. John, P.P. of Balrothery, co. Dublin
*Smyth, Rev. John, R.C.C., St. Michael's and St. John's, Dublin
Smyth, John, Esq., Rathcoursey, Midleton, co. Cork
Smyth, John, Esq., Millbrook, Newtownstewart, co. Tyrone
Smyth, John, Esq., Milltown, Banbridge, co. Down
Smyth, John, Esq., Loughrea, co. Galway
Smyth, John, Esq., Castle-widenham, Castletown-Roche, co. Cork
Smyth, John Freke, Esq., Easton-house, Rosscarbery, co. Cork
*Smyth, Jonathan, Esq., Urken-house, Crossmaglen, co. Armagh
*Smyth, L. C., Esq., Snugboro', Ashbourne, co. Meath
*Smyth, Rev. Mitchell, Rector of Arrigal, Garvagh, co. Derry
*Smyth, Rev. P., P.P. of Sandiford, near Dundrum, co. Dublin
Smyth, R. Croker, Esq., Ballylin, Rathkeale, co. Limerick
*Smyth, Ralph, Esq., J.P., Ralphsdale, near Drumcree, co. Westmeath
*Smyth, R., Esq., D.L. & J.P., Ballynatray, Youghal, co. Cork
Smyth, Richard, Esq., J.P., Castle Dooneen, Rosscarbery, co. Cork
*Smyth, Robert, Esq., Portlick Castle, near Athlone, co. Westmeath
*Smyth, Robert, Esq., J.P., Gaybrook, Mullingar, co. Westmeath
*Smyth, Robert, Esq., Fitzwilliam-square North, Dublin
Smyth, Robert, Esq., Cross, Lower Cumber, co. Derry
Smyth, Robert, Esq., Portadown, co. Armagh
Smyth, Samuel, Esq., Westport-lodge, Westport, co. Mayo
*Smyth, Rev. T., J.P., Benison-lodge, Castlepollard, co. Westmeath
*Smyth, Rev. W., Lathbury, Bucks
Smyth, Rev. W. St. John, A.M., Rectory, Portaferry, co. Down
Smyth, Miss M. J., Longfield, Faughanvale, co. Derry
Smyth, Mrs. Rebecca, Carrowreagh, Burt, co. Donegal
*Smythe, Rev. John, M.A., Dromisken Rectory, co. Louth
*Smythe, Captain Ralph, Glasnevin, co. Dublin
Smythe, Rev. S., Carnmoney, near Belfast
*Smythe, W. B., Esq., Ch. Ch. College, Oxford, and Westmeath
*Smythe, Mrs., Newpark, near Athlone, co. Roscommon
*Sneyd, H. R., Esq., Ravenhill, Belfast
Sneyd, Nathaniel, Esq., Sackville-street, Dublin
Snoddon, Mr. Samuel, sen., Glenvale, Drumbo, co. Down
*Snoulten, O., Esq., Oaten-hill, Canterbury, Kent
Soden, James, Esq., Moneygold, Sligo
*SOMERVILLE, The Right Honorable Lord
*Somerville, Sir Marcus, Bart., Somerville, Navan, co. Meath
*Somerville, James, Esq., J.P., Ross, co. Meath
Somerville, P., Esq., Union-hall, Rosscarbery, co. Cork
Somerville, Robert, Esq., C.C.P., Ballincollig, co. Cork
*Somerville, Thomas, Esq., Drishane, Skibbereen, co. Cork
*SOUTHAMPTON, The Right Honorable Lord
*Sowerby, W., Esq., Putteridge-bury, Herts
*Sowerby, William, Esq., Clifford-street, London
Spain, Rev. John, P.P. of Lorrha, Burris-o'-kane, co. Tipperary
Speck, Lieut. W., R.N., Gally-head, Clonakilty, co. Cork
*Speer, John, Esq., M.D., Sussex-parade, Kingstown, co. Dublin
*Speer, R. D., Esq., Granitefield, Rochestown-avenue, Kiliney, co. Dublin
Spence, W. McClintock, Esq., Lifford, co. Donegal
*SPENCER, The Right Honorable Earl
Spillan, Daniel, Esq., A.M. and M.D., Kildare-street, Dublin
Splaine, James, Esq., J.P., Garrane, near Bandon, co. Cork
*Spooner, John, Esq., Frith-hill, Great Missenden, Bucks
*Spotswood, A., Esq., Magherafelt, co. Derry
*Spotswood, C., Esq., Mary-street, Dublin
*Spottiswoode, Andrew, Esq., Bedford-square, London
*Spowart, Mr. David, Limerick
Spratt, Harmer Devereux, Esq., Monte Video, Mallow, co. Cork
*Spratt, The Very Rev. John, S.T.M., Aungier-street, Dublin
*Spray, Rev. John, Kinneagh-glebe, Castledermot, co. Kildare
*Spring, Rev. Edward, Charleville, co. Cork
*Spring, J., Esq., Esker-cottage, Lucan, and Francis-street, Dublin
Sproul, Edward, Esq., Spamount, Castlederg, co. Tyrone
*Sproule, James, Esq., Grove, near Athlone, co. Roscommon
Sproule, Mr. Robert, Cloverhill, Drumquin, co. Tyrone
Sproule, Samuel, Esq., Rathmelton, co. Donegal
*Sproule, Thomas, Esq., Drumgallan, Castlederg, co. Tyrone
Sproule, William, Esq., Athlone, co. Westmeath
*Sproull, Moses, Esq., Inchiney, Strabane, co. Tyrone,
*Spunner, Thomas, Esq., Clyduffe, Roscrea, co. Tipperary
*Stable, G. W., Esq., Newcastle-on-Tyne, Northumberland
*Stack, C. M., Esq., Upper Merrion-street, Dublin
Stack, Edward, Esq., M.D., Listowel, co. Kerry
Stack, Eyre W., Esq., Ballyconry, Listowel, co. Kerry
Stack, James, Esq., Drumcolloher, co. Limerick

*Stack, Rev. John, M.A., J.P., Dromard-glebe, Collooney, co. Sligo
*Stack, Rev. Thomas, J.P., Omagh, co. Tyrone
Stack, Rev. W. Horatio, Londonderry
Stacpoole, Andrew, Esq., J.P., Ballyally, Ennis, co. Clare
*Stacpoole, Richard, Esq., Ennis, co. Clare
*Stacpoole, R. J., Esq., D.L., J.P., Eden-vale, Ennis, co. Clare
Stafford, Berkeley B., Esq., Maine, Dundalk, co. Louth
Stafford, Rev. P., P.P., Ballymore Eustace, co. Dublin
Stafford, Major Randal, Tully-house, Crossdoney, co. Cavan
*Stafford, Rev. W., P.P. of Rathmines, co. Dublin
*Stamer, John, Esq., Clare-castle, co. Clare
*Stamer, Captain L., Beauchamp, near Little Bray, co. Dublin
*STAMFORD, The Right Honorable Lord
Stamper, Mr. T. J., Monaline, Newtown-Mount-Kennedy, co. Wicklow
Standish, John, Esq., Glin-lodge, Glin, co. Limerick
Standish, John, Esq., Rathbeggan-house, Dunshaughlin, co. Meath
Standish, Richard, Esq., Frankfort, Ballingarry, co. Limerick
*Stanford, Robert, Esq., The Castle, Aughrim, co. Galway
Stanistreet, Mr. Thomas, Midleton, co. Cork
*Stanton, Thomas, Esq., Clonmel, co. Tipperary
*Staples, Sir Thomas, Bart., Lissan, near Moneymore, co. Derry
Staples, Rev. Alexander, D.D., J.P., Gowran-glebe, co. Kilkenny
*Staples, Edmund, Esq., J.P., Donmore, Durrow, Queen's county
*Staples, Rev. J. Molesworth, J.P., Moville, co. Donegal
*Staples, Samuel, jun., Esq., Staples-inn, London
*Stapleton, George, Esq., Casino, near Dublin
Stapleton, Gilbert, Esq., The Grove, Richmond, Yorkshire
Starkie, Robert, Esq., Cregane, Rosscarbery, co. Cork
*Starkie, Captain Walter, The Hill, Rosscarbery, co. Cork
Starkie, W., Esq., Ross-abbey, Rosscarbery, co. Cork
Staunton, Edward H., Esq., Galway
*Staunton, Michael J., Esq., Ballysimon, Limerick
*Staunton, Myles, Esq., Tinny-park, Newtown-Mount-Kennedy, co. Wicklow
Stavely, Mr. James, Ballymoney, co. Antrim
*Steedman, John, Esq., Lifford, co. Donegal
*Steele, Sir Richard, Bart., Fitzwilliam-square South, Dublin
Steele, Lieut. F. E., Loughrea, co. Galway
*Steele, Isaac, Esq., Poole, Dorset
Steele, James, Esq., Greenvale, Castlewellan, co. Down
Steele, Richard, Esq., Skirke, Burros-in-Ossory, Queen's county
Steele, Robert, Esq., Rosselougan, Donegal
Steele, Mr. Samuel, Wellington-quay, Dublin
Steele, Thomas, Esq., Lough O'Connell, Ennis, co. Clare
Steell, Mr. John, Cork
*Steen, Alexander, Esq., Clady, Antrim
*Steen, Rev. G., Newtownlimavady, co. Derry
Steen, James, Esq., Belfast
Steen, Mr. John, Mandistown, Ardee, co. Louth
Stein, Brown and Co., Messrs., Limerick
*Stennett, Rev. C. B., R.C. Rector of Kilquane and Kilmurray, co. Wicklow
*Stephens, Gilbert, Esq., Doughty-street, London
*Stephens, John, Esq., Thames-street, London
Stephens, John, Esq., Patrick-street, Cork
Stephens, Richard, Esq., Hermitage, Crossdoney, co. Cavan
*Stephens, Lieut. W. L., R.N., Dunfanaghy, co. Donegal
Stephenson, George, Esq., Lisburn, co. Antrim
Stephenson, James A., Esq., Kilcally, near Crumlin, co. Antrim
Stephenson, John, Esq., Curraheen, Rathkeale, co. Limerick
*Stephenson, Mr. Standish, Limerick
*Stephenson, S. M., Esq., M.D., Belfast
Stephenson, Rev. W., Clonmel, co. Tipperary
*Sterne, Captain, Gola, Brookborough, co. Fermanagh
*Sterne, Lieut. W., R.N., Thornhill, Ballycastle, co. Mayo
*Steuart, The Hon. A. G., D.L. and J.P., Lisdhue, Dungannon, co. Tyrone
Steuart, Mr. Charles, Kilrea, co. Derry
*Steuart, Robert, Esq., Alderston, near Haddington, N.B.
Steuart, W. R., Esq., Steuart's-lodge, Leighlin-bridge, co. Carlow
*Stevelly, R. J., Esq., J.P. Glanduff-castle, Drumcolloher, co. Limerick
*Stevens, J. D., Esq., Sarratt, Hertfordshire
*Stevens, Mr. Montague, Frogmoor-mill, Two Waters, Herts.
Stevenson, Rev. Henry F., Castle Dawson, co. Derry
*Stevenson, Mr. Jacob, Tullyalley, Glendermott, co. Derry
Stevenson, James, Esq., Ashpark, Dungiven, co. Derry
*Stevenson, John, Esq., J.P., Fort William, Tobermore, co. Derry
Stevenson, Joseph, Esq., Springfield, near Belfast
*Stevenson, Sir J. A., Knight, Lower Mount-street, Dublin
*Stevenson, Mr. W., Tullyalley, Glendermott, co. Derry
Stevenson, W., Esq., Strabane, co. Tyrone
Stewart, Alexander, Esq., Trinity-college, Dublin
*Stewart, Alexander, Esq., Ligoneil, Belfast
Stewart, D., Esq., Great Russell-street, London
*Stewart, Rev. Henry, J.P., Vicar of Rathbarry, Rosscarbery, co. Cork
*Stewart, Rev. Henry, Rector of Leixlip, co. Kildare
Stewart, Henry, Esq., J.P., Tyrcallen, Stranorlar, co. Donegal
Stewart, Henry Hutchinson, Esq., M.D., Killucan, co. Westmeath
Stewart, Rev. James, Vicar of Leslie, Clonakilty, co. Cork
Stewart, Rev. J., Presbyterian Minister, Portstewart, co. Derry
*Stewart, J. V., Esq., J.P., Rock-hill, Letterkenny, co. Donegal
*Stewart, Mr. Robert, Altrest, Strabane, co. Tyrone
*Stewart, Colonel Thomas, Enniskillen, co. Fermanagh
Stewart, Thomas L., Esq., Belfast-castle
Stewart, W., Esq.
Stewart, Rev. W., Henry-street, Cork
Stewart, Major W., Harrymount, Kingstown, co. Dublin
*Stewart, W., Esq., Killymoon, Cookstown, co. Tyrone
*Stewart, Colonel W., J.P., Creg, near Fermoy, co. Cork
*Stewart, W., Esq., J.P., Killymoon, co. Tyrone
Stewart, W., Esq., M.D., Lisburn, co. Antrim
Stewart, W., Esq., J.P., Horn-head, Dunfanaghy, co. Donegal
Stewart, W., Esq., J.P., Sea-park, Carrickfergus, co. Antrim
Stewart, W., Esq., Drumnagessan, Bushmills, co. Antrim
*St. George, A. F., Esq., D.L. and J.P., Tyrone-house, Oranmore, co. Galway
*St. George's Steam Packet Company's Office, Cork
Stitt, John, Esq., Tynan, co. Armagh
Stitt, Mr., Lower Abbey-street, Dublin
Stock, Rev. Samuel, A.M., Vicar of Kilcommon, Belmullet, co. Mayo
Stocks, Benjamin, Esq., Hull, Yorkshire
*Stokes, John Whitby, Esq., Stephen's-green, Dublin
Stokes, Rev. J. W., Ardcolme-parsonage, Wexford
Stokes, W., Esq., O'Brien's-bridge, Castle Connel, co. Limerick
Stokes, Rev. W. R., Grammar School, Lismore, co. Waterford
*Stone, Mr. Samuel, Mountmellick, Queen's county
*Stoney, Isaac, Esq., Mount-pleasant, Gilford, co. Down
*Stoney, J. J., Esq., M.D., Burris-o'-kane, co. Tipperary
*Stoney, Johnston, Esq., Emell-castle, Cloghjordan, co. Tipperary
*Stoney, Rev. Ralph, A.M., Terryglass, Burris-o'-kane, co. Tipperary
*Stoney, R. Johnston, Esq., J.P., Killavalla, Burris-o'-kane, co. Tipperary
Stoney, Thomas, Esq., Portland, co. Tipperary
*Stoney, Thomas G., Esq., Arran-hill, Burris-o'-kane, co. Tipperary
Stoney, Rev. W. B., Rector of Burrishoole, Newport-Pratt, co. Mayo
*STOPFORD, The Right Honorable Viscount
Stopford, Rev. Edward A., Caledon, co. Tyrone
*Story, Abraham, Esq., Durham
Story, Rev. J., A.M. and J.P., Cranaghan, Ballyconnell, co. Cavan
*Story, Thomas, Esq., C.E., St. Helen's, Auckland, Durham
Stotesbury, R. and Co., Messrs., Kyrels-quay, Cork
*Stothard, John, Esq., Dromore, co. Down, and North Cumberland-street, Dublin
Stoughton, Thomas A., Esq., J.P., Ballyhorgan, Listowel, co. Kerry
Stout, Nicholas P., Esq., Newtown, Youghal, co. Cork
Stowards, Robert, Esq., Ballymacowen, Clonakilty, co. Cork
Stoyle, Rev. John, Rector of Ballymartle, near Kinsale, co. Cork
Stranbanzee, H. V., Esq., Spennithorne, Bedale, Yorkshire
*Strangman, Joshua W., Esq., Waterford
*Strangman, Mrs. Mary Christy, Melbrook, Clonmel, co. Tipperary
*Strangways, T., Esq., Rowan-tree-hill, Ballyshannon, co. Donegal
Straton, John, Esq., Dundalk, co. Louth
*Strean, Rev. Annesley, D.D., J.P., St. Peter's, Athlone, co. Westmeath
*Stretton, C., Esq., Llangoed-castle, near Hay, Brecknockshire
Strickland, E., Esq., York
*Stringer, Francis, Esq., J.P., Tassagh, Keady, co. Armagh
Stringer, John, Esq., Nelson-street, Dublin
*Stringer, Miles, Esq., Russell-square, London
*Stritch, Captain W. L., Saintbury, Killiney, co. Dublin
*Strogin, Samuel, Esq., Dove-hall, Foxford, co. Mayo
Strong, John H., Esq., Fassaroe, near Little Bray, co. Dublin
*Strong, Joseph, Esq., Glanamuck, near Kilternan, co. Dublin
*Stronge, Sir James, Bart., D.L. & J.P., Tynan-abbey, co. Armagh
*Stronge, J. Calvert, Esq., J.P., Northland-house, Dungannon, co. Tyrone
Stuart, Rev. Alexander, Monkstown-glebe Cork
Stuart, Rev. A. G., Desertcreight, Cookstown, co. Tyrone
*Stuart, The Very Rev. Charles, John-street, Dublin
Stuart, Rev. H., Incumbent of Lower Fahan, Buncrana, co. Donegal
Stuart, James T. S., Esq., J.P., Tymore, Newport Pratt, co. Mayo
*Stuart, James, Esq., LL.D., Belfast, co. Antrim
*Stuart, John S., Esq., Bruff, co. Limerick
Stuart, W., Esq., Carrickfergus, co. Antrim
*Stuart, William Villiers, Esq., D.L. & J.P., Dromana House, near Lismore, co. Waterford
*Stubber, R. H., Esq., D.L. & J.P., Moyne, Durrow, co. Kilkenny
Stubber, Sewell, M., Esq., Monaclare, Ballynakill, Queen's county
*Stubbs, J. W., Esq., Rawlestown, near Swords, co. Dublin

Stubbs, Captain Thomas, J.P., East Hill-house, Cove, co. Cork
Stubbs, Captain Thomas, Rosseanna, near Athlone, co. Westmeath
*Stubbs, Thomas Trowbridge, Esq., Ballyshannon, co. Donegal
*Studdert, Rev. George, Ballywilliam, Rathkeale, co. Limerick
Studdert, George, Esq., J.P., Clonderlaw, Knock, co. Clare
Studdert, Ion, Esq., J.P., Elm-hill, Rathkeale, co. Limerick
Studdert, Jonas, Esq., Riverston, Corofin, co. Clare
Studdert, Jonas, Esq., J.P., Atlantic-lodge, Kilkee, co. Clare
Studdert, Joseph G., Esq., Woodlawn, Knock, co. Clare
Studdert, Rev. Richard, A.B., Quin-glebe, co. Clare
Studdert, Richard, Esq., Kilrush, co. Clare
Studdert, W., Esq., Thornbury, Knock, co. Clare
Studdy, John, Esq., Youghal, co. Cork
*Sturgeon, T. S., Esq., Esker Abbey, near Lucan, co. Dublin
Style, Sir T. C., Bart., D.L. and J.P., Cloghan-lodge, Stranorlar, co. [Donegal
*Style, Charles, Esq., Glenmore, Stranorlar, co. Donegal
Suffern, George, Esq., College-square North, Belfast
*Sullivan, Cornelius, Esq., Upper Mount-street, Dublin
Sullivan, Francis, Esq., J.P., Banmore, Drumcolloher, co. Limerick
*Sullivan, George, Esq., Limerick
*Sullivan, James, Esq., J.P., Chesterfield, Newcastle, co. Limerick
*Sullivan, J. J., Esq., Tullilease-house, Drumcolloher, co. Limerick
Sullivan, J. J., Esq., Camas, Newcastle, co. Limerick
*Sullivan, Jos., Esq., Cecil-street, Limerick
Sullivan, P., Esq., Hely's-bridge, Cork
Sullivan, Rev. Patrick, P.P. of Cove, co. Cork
Sullivan, P. K., Esq., Camas, Newcastle, co. Limerick
Sullivan, Mr. Thomas H., Cork
*Supple, Daniel, jun., Esq., Tralee, co. Kerry
*Sutton, Cæsar, Esq., J.P., Longgrage, near Taghmon, co. Wexford
Sutton, Mr. Cæsar, Ballylannon, Fethard, co. Wexford
*Sutton, Rev. John, Rossway, Great Berkhampstead, Herts
Sutton, Mr. Richard, Clonmines, Fethard, co. Wexford
Sutton, Mr. Richard, Oak-hall, near Enniscorthy, co. Wexford
*Swaby, James, Esq., Thorne, near Chesham, Bucks
*Swan, E. L., Esq., Allworth, Abbeyleix, Queen's county
*Swan, Hugh, Esq., Clady, near Antrim
Swan, Thomas, Esq., Tombreen, Carnew, co. Wexford
*Swan, W., Esq., Islandreagh, Antrim
Swan, Mr. W. B., Capponellan, Durrow, co. Kilkenny
Swanston, John, Esq., Laragh, near Bandon, co. Cork
Swanton, James H., Esq., Ballydehob, Shibbereen, co. Cork
Swanton, Robert, Esq., Ratruane, Ballydehob, co. Cork
*Swanzy, Andrew, Esq., J.P., Millmount, co. Monaghan
Swanzy, Henry, Esq., Rockfield, Castle-Blayney, co. Monaghan
*Swanzy, Samuel, Esq., Cavan
Swayne, George, Esq., Redmond-cottage, Midleton, co. Cork
Swayne, James, Esq., Youghal, co. Cork
Sweeney, Rev. —, R.C.C., Ahada, co. Cork
*Sweeny, James, Esq., Castle-Bellingham, co. Louth
Sweeny, James, Esq., Clonakilty, co. Cork
Sweeny, John, Esq., Old Orchard, near Rathfarnham, co. Dublin
*Sweeny, John, jun., Esq., Windy-harbour, near Dundrum, co. Dublin
*Sweetman, J. A., Esq., Fox-house, near Raheny, co. Dublin
*Sweetman, Michael, Esq., J.P., Longtown, Clane, co. Kildare
Sweetman, Michael, Esq., Poole, Dorsetshire
*Sweetman, Pierce, Esq., Blenheim-lodge, near Waterford
*Sweetman, W., Esq., Raheny-house, co. Dublin
*Sweetman, Walter, Esq., Mountjoy-square, Dublin
*Sweetman, Messrs. P. and J., Francis-court Brewery, Dublin
Sweetnam, John, Esq., Clover-hill, Skibbereen, co. Cork
Sweny, Rev. J., A.M. and J.P., Cleenish-glebe, Enniskillen, co. Fer- [managh
*Swete, Benjamin, Esq., Greenville, Macroom, co. Cork
*Swete, Rev. Benjamin, Prebendary of Kilbrittain, Bandon, co. Cork
Swete, John, Esq., J.P., Bandon, co. Cork
Sweetman, Mr. Edmund, Sweetmount, New Ross, co. Wexford
*Swift, Richard, Esq., Lynn Lamancha, Mullingar, co. Westmeath
*Swift, Richard, Esq., J.P., Lynn-lodge, Mullingar, co. Westmeath
Swinburne, James, Esq., Limerick
Swindell, Rev. R. F., A.B. and J.P., Tullam, Tralee, co. Kerry
Swire, Rev. J., Mansfield Vicarage, Darlington, Durham
Swords, Thomas, Esq., Crowhill, Maynooth, co. Kildare
*Sykes, John, Esq., Sheffield, Yorkshire
*Sykes, Richard, Esq., West Ella, near Hull, Yorkshire
Symes, Glascott, Esq., Kingstown, co. Dublin
*Symes, J., Esq., Hillbrook, near Carnew, co. Wicklow
*Symes, John, Esq., Bally Britton, Edenderry, King's county
Symes, S., Esq., Hill-view, near Tinahely, co. Wicklow, and Domi- [nick-street, Dublin
*Symmers, A., Esq., Aungier-street, Dublin, and Tierillan, co. Galway
*Synan, Henry, Esq., Limerick

Synge, F. H., Esq., East Cranmore, Somerset
*Synge, John, Esq., J.P., Glanmore, near Wicklow
*Synnot, Marcus, Esq., J.P., Ballymoyer-lodge, co. Armagh
Synnott, Rev. P., P.P., Kilcavan, Taghmon, co. Wexford
Synnott, Rev. Patrick, P.P. of Little Limerick, Gorey, co. Wexford

Taaffe, George, Esq., D.L. & J.P., Smarmore-castle, Ardee, co. Louth
*Taaffe, Patrick, Esq., Foxborough, Elphin, co. Roscommon
Taaffe, Captain W., J.P., Cappa-lodge, Strokestown, co. Roscommon
Tabuteau, A. S., Esq., M.D., Portarlington, Queen's county
Tagert, Robert M., Esq., Wood Brook, Newtownstewart, co. Tyrone
Taggart, John, Esq., Coleraine, co. Derry
*TALBOT, The Right Honorable Lord
TALBOT, DE MALAHIDE, The Right Hon. Lord
*Talbot, James, Esq., Mary-ville, New Ross, co. Wexford
*Talbot, John Hyacinth, Esq., D.L. and J.P., Talbot-hall, New Ross, [co. Wexford
*Talbot, W., Esq., D.L. and J.P., Mount Talbot, co. Roscommon
Talbot, W., Esq., J.P., Rockland-hall, co. Wexford
*Tall, John, Esq., Hull, Yorkshire
Tallent, Rev. Edward, R.C.C., Knock, co. Clare
Tallon, Dominick, Esq., Lacken-lodge, Dungarvan, co. Waterford
*Tandy, Burton, Esq., Mornington, Drogheda, co. Louth
*Tandy, Charles, Esq., Prospect-cottage, Bray, co. Wicklow
Tandy, C. S., Esq., Sion-lodge, Waterford
*Tandy, Edward, Esq., Mountjoy-square South, Dublin
Tarleton, John, Esq., Limerick
*Tarleton, Rev. J. R., Clogher, co. Tyrone, and Congor, Burris-o'- [kane, co. Tipperary
*Tarleton, J. W., Esq., J.P., Killeigh, Tullamore, King's county
Tarrant, Thomas Hoskin, Esq., Cove, co. Cork
*Tate, Abraham Augustus, Esq., Rathdrum, co. Wicklow
*Tatlow, John Charles, Esq., J.P., The Rocks, Crossdoney, co. Cavan
*Tawney, Henry, Esq., Banbury, Oxfordshire
Tayler, W., Esq., M.D., Ballymoney, co. Antrim
*Taylor, The Hon. and Rev. Edward, Ardgillan-castle, near Bal- [briggan, co. Dublin
*Taylor, A. E., Esq., J.P., Woodcliff, Shanagolden, co. Limerick
*Taylor, Rev. Edward M., A.B., Kilmore, co. Armagh
*Taylor, Mr. E., Bridge Street, Blackfriars, London
Taylor, Edwin, Esq., J.P., Clogheen, co. Tipperary
*Taylor, George, jun., Esq., Rathmines-road, Dublin
*Taylor, Godfrey, Esq., J.P., Cashel, co. Tipperary
*Taylor, Hugh, Esq., Earsdon, near Newcastle, Northumberland
Taylor, Mr. J., Tanlaght-cottage, Coagh, co. Derry
*Taylor, James, Esq., J.P., Raphoe, co. Donegal
Taylor, James, Esq., Moor-green, near Birmingham
*Taylor, Rev. John, A.M., Clones, co. Monaghan
*Taylor, John, Esq., Strencham-court, Pershore, Worcestershire
*Taylor, Major-Gen. Sir John, J.P., Castle-taylor, Galway
*Taylor, John, Esq., Cork
Taylor, John Fogg, Esq., Wigan, Lancashire
*Taylor, John, Esq., Strencham-court, Pershore, Worcestershire
Taylor, Ralph, Esq., Kilcavan, near Carnew, co. Wicklow
*Taylor, Robert, Esq., Carrickmines, near Cabinteely, co. Dublin
Taylor, Rev. Robert, P.P. of Kilbrittain, Bandon, co. Cork
Taylor, Robert, Esq., Fort-hill, Ballymena, co. Antrim
Taylor, Rev. Thomas, Knockrigg, near Baltinglass, co. Wicklow
Taylor, Thomas Robert, Esq., Maryville, Youghal, co. Cork
Taylor, Mrs. Sarah, Wexford
Tedlie, Mr. John, Ballyowen, Glendermott, co. Derry
Tedlie, Miss Mary, Trench, Faughanvale, co. Derry
Tefalliott, W., Esq., M.D Clonakilty, co. Cork
Telford, Mr. John, Kilnabin, Tullamore, King's county
Tempany, Myles, Esq., Sligo
Temple, Sir Edmond, K.C.S., Peruvian-lodge, Athlone, co. West- [meath
*Temple, G. H., Esq., Loughree-lodge, near Athlone, co. Westmeath
*Temple, R. H., Esq., J.P., Waterstown, near Athlone, co. Westmeath
*Templeman, John, Esq., Pulteney-street, Bath
*TEMPLEMORE, The Right Honorable Lord
Templeton, Mrs. Katharine, Cranmore, Belfast
Tench, Higatt, Esq., Ballyhealy, near Wexford
*Tenisson, William Barton, Esq., J.P., Lough Bawn, Carrickmacross, [co. Monaghan
*Tennent, J., Esq., Stanmore, Middlesex, and Russell-place, London
Tennent, J. E., Esq., M.P., D.L., and J.P., The Lodge, Belfast
*Tennent, James T., Esq., Belfast
*Tennent, Robert, Esq., M.D., Belfast
*Tennent, Robert J., Esq., Belfast
*Tennent, William, Esq., Belfast
*Tenor, John K., Esq., Moree, Dungannon, co. Tyrone

*Ternan, Patrick, Esq., J.P., Green-hills, Drogheda, co. Louth
*Ternan, Mr. Thomas, Ardee, co. Louth
*Terry, Carden, Esq., Morrison's Island, Cork
Terry, J. Beevers Esq., Ripon, Yorkshire
Tetley, W., Esq., Asenby-lodge, Thirsk, Yorkshire
Teulon, Major Peter, Ennismore-cottage, Cove, co. Cork
*Teulon, W., jun., Esq., Patrick-street, Cork
*Tewhy, Rev. Michael, P.P., Cahirnarry, near Limerick
Thacker, Mr. Alexander, Killowen, near Wexford
*Thacker, B., Esq., J.P., Ballymellish, Burros-in-Ossory, Queen's co.
*Thackeray, Rev. Elias, A.M., Rector of Louth, and Vicar of Dundalk, co. Louth
*Thackwray, Jos., Esq., Harrogate, Yorkshire
Therry, James, Esq., Bettyville, Kanturk, co. Cork
Thomas, Rev. A., A.M., Rector and Vicar of the Union of Ballinakill, co. Galway
*Thomas, Benjamin, Esq., Lower Mount-street, Dublin
Thomas, Rev. Charles P., Carlow
*Thomas, Rev. E., M.A., and J.P., Ballynacourty-glebe, Tralee, co. Kerry
*Thomas, F. E., jun., Esq., Upper Gardiner-street, Dublin
Thomas, F. E., Esq., Lower Dominick-street, Dublin
*Thomas, Rev. F. H., Swords, co. Dublin
Thomas, Lieut.-Col. H., Kinsale, co. Cork
*THOMOND, The Most Noble the Marquess of
Thompson, Adam, Esq., M.D., Ballymoney, co. Antrim
*Thompson, B., Esq., Oatlands-house, Navan, co. Meath
Thompson, Rev. David, Curate of Wexford
*Thompson, David Peter, Esq., J.P., Burnham-house, Dingle, co. Kerry
*Thompson, Capt. E. C., Edmundsbury, Durrow, co. Kilkenny
*Thompson, Capt. Francis, J.P., Cavan
Thompson, Rev. George, Presbyterian Seceding Minister, Moneymore, co. Derry
Thompson, George, Esq., Clonskeagh-castle. co. Dublin
*Thompson, G. J., Esq., Grangecon, near Baltinglass, co. Wicklow
*Thompson, Henry, Esq., Fitzwilliam-place, Dublin
*Thompson, Henry, Esq., New-grove, near Coolock, co. Dublin
Thompson, Rev. James, A.M., Fort Henry, Cootehill, co. Cavan
*Thompson, James Allen, Esq., Letterkenny, co. Donegal
*Thompson, John, Esq., Rathnally, Trim, co. Meath
*Thompson, John, Esq., J.P., Clonfin, Granard, co. Longford
*Thompson, John, Esq., J.P., Glinch-lodge, Clones, co. Monaghan
*Thompson, Joseph, Esq., Com. R.N., Makeestown, Antrim
*Thompson, Joseph, Esq., Ballyarnet, Templemore, co. Derry
*Thompson, Joseph, Esq., Upper Ormond-quay, Dublin
Thompson, Mr. Joseph, Cork
Thompson, Rev. M. N., Cranagh, Templemore, co. Tipperary
*Thompson, Peter, Esq., J.P., Tralee, co. Kerry
*Thompson, Robert, Esq., J.P., Annagassan, Castle-Bellingham, co. Louth
Thompson, Richard, Esq., Durham
*Thompson, Rev. R., J.P., Rector of Navan, Athlumney, co. Meath
*Thompson, Rev. Samuel, Tullybrook, Donegal
*Thompson, Rev. S., Broomfield, near Castleknock, co. Dublin
Thompson, W., Esq., M.D., Lisburn, co. Antrim
*Thompson, Major W., Hollywood, Rath, co. Dublin
Thompson, W., Esq., Ballintra, co. Donegal
Thompson, W. P., Esq., Rush-hall, Ballynakill, Queen's county
Thompson, Mr. W. P., Ralish, Abbeyleix, Queen's county
*Thomson, Col. A., C.B., Woodlands, near Santry, co. Dublin
Thomson, Benjamin, Esq., Ravensdale, Flurrybridge, co. Louth
*Thomson, E.P., Esq., Manchester
Thomson, James, Esq., Ballymoney, co. Antrim
Thomson, John, Esq., Low-wood, Belfast
Thomson, John J., Esq., Bandon, co. Cork
Thomson, Rev. P., Silvermines, Nenagh, co. Tipperary
*Thomson, Robert, Esq., J.P., Jennymount, Belfast
Thomson, S. J., Esq., M.D., Belfast
Thomson, Rev. W., Ballinderry, Lisburn, co. Antrim
*Thorman, J., Esq., Lawrence-place, London
*Thornhill, E. Badham, Esq., Castle Kevin, Mallow, co. Cork
*Thornhill, H. B., Esq., Castle Kevin, Mallow, co. Cork
*Thornhill, Rev. Jonathan, Durrow, co. Kilkenny
*Thornley, Thomas, Esq., Talbot-street, Dublin
*Thornley, Lieut. Thomas, Sligo
*Thornton, M. B., Esq., Ballyhue, Ballyconnell, co. Cavan
Thornton, Perrott, Esq., J.P., Greenville, Ballyconnell, co. Cavan
*Thorpe, Charles, Esq., Phibsborough-lodge, co. Dublin
Thunder, Michael, Esq., New Church-street, Dublin
Thwaites, Major, Portarlington, Queen's county
Tierney, Rev. James, R.C.C., Drogheda, co. Louth
*Tierney, Rev. Thomas, P.P., Clontibret, Castleblayney, co. Monaghan
Tighe, Rev. Denis, P.P. of Ballaghadireen, co. Mayo
*Tighe, Rev. Hugh Usher, Clonmore Rectory, Dunleer, co. Louth
*Tighe, James, Esq., Durrow, Queen's county
*Tighe, Rev. John, P.P., Strokestown, co. Roscommon
*Tighe, W. Fownes, Esq., D.L. & J.P., Woodstock, Inistioge, co. Kilkenny
*Tilly, Robert, Esq., Upper Merrion-street, Dublin
*Tilly, Thomas, Esq., Henrietta-street, Dublin
Tindal, Thomas, Esq., Aylesbury, Bucks
*Tinley, Rev. G., A.B., J.P., Rector of Faughart, near Dundalk, co. Louth
*Tinley, John, Esq., North Shields, Northumberland
*Tiplady, John, Esq., Durham
*Tipping, Edward, Esq., Bellurgan-park, Dundalk, co. Louth
*Tipping, James, Esq., Lisnawilly, Dundalk, co. Louth
*Tisdall, Edward, Esq., Rathcoole-house, Dunleer, co. Louth
*Tisdall, Rev. James, Ballinderry-glebe, Moneymore, co. Derry
*Tisdall, Lieut.-Col. Thomas, J.P., Charleville, Dunleer, co. Louth
Tittle, John Moore, Esq., Farmhill, Coleraine, co. Derry
Tivy, Philip Ryder, Esq., Newmarket, Kanturk, co. Cork
Tobin, James, Esq., Limerick
Tobin, Rev. Michael, P.P. Cahir, co. Tipperary
*Tobin, Thomas, Esq., Ballincollig, co. Cork
*Todd, Joseph, Esq., Coleraine, co. Derry
Tollett, George, Esq., Morahan, Belmullett, co. Mayo
*Tomb, George, Esq., Temple-street, Dublin
*Tomlinson, John, jun., Esq., Luke-street, Dublin
Tonson, The Hon. and Rev. Ludlow, Ahern, co. Cork
Toohey, Jeremiah, Esq., Milgrove, Moneygall, co. Tipperary
*Toole, Charles, Esq., Wilfort, Bray, co. Dublin
Toole, Edward, Esq., Bandon, co. Cork
Topp, J. W., Esq., Mardyke-parade, Cork
*Topp, R. W., Esq., Rochelle, near Cork
Torbuck, Graham, Esq., Youghal, co. Cork
Toris, Rev. James, P.P., Ballymakenny, Drogheda, co. Louth
Torrance, John, Esq., Mondella, Adare, co. Limerick
*Torrens, The Right Honorable Judge, Dublin
Torrens, Rev. Thomas H., Rector of Carnalvay, near Naas, co. Kildare
*Tottenham, Charles, Esq., Mac Murrough, New Ross, co. Wexford
Tottenham, Charles, Esq., Ballycurry, co. Wicklow, and New Ross, co. Wexford
*Tottenham, Charles Henry, Esq., J.P., Glenfarne-hall, Florence-court, co. Fermanagh
Tottenham, C. J., Esq., J.P., Woodstock, co. Wicklow
Tottenham, George, Esq., Tottenham-green, Rathangan, co. Kildare
Tottenham, Capt. J. L., Mac Murrough, New Ross, co. Wexford
*Tottenham, R., Esq., Trinity-college, Cambridge
*Tottenham, Rev. R., L., M.A., Rector of Rossory, Enniskillen, co. Fermanagh
Toutcher, Capt. R., R.N., Rumley-avenue, Kingstown, co. Dublin
Townley, Rev. C. G., LL.D., Limerick
Townley, John, Esq., Dundalk, co. Louth
*Townsend, Henry, Esq., Ennis, co. Clare
Townsend, Rev. Horace, M.A., J.P., Derry, Rosscarberry, co. Cork
Townsend, Rev. Horatio, Belgrove, Great Island, co. Cork
Townsend, J. Fitzhenry, Esq., Glandore-cottage, Rosscarberry, co. Cork
Townsend, Richard, Esq., M.D., Merville, Cove, co. Cork
Townsend, Richard, Esq., Laurel-mount, Dunmanway, co. Cork
*Townsend, R. B., Esq., J.P., Point-house, Castle Townsend, do.
Townsend, Samuel, Esq., D.L., and J.P., White-hall, Skibbereen, do.
Townsend, Thomas, Esq., Smithville, Skibbereen, co. Cork
*Townshend, Rev. Thomas, Curate of Nathlash, Rock-mills, co. Cork
Tracy, W. S., Esq., J.P., Sligo
*Tracy, W. W., Esq., Summer-hill, Dublin
*Trail, Rev. Robert, J.P., Rector of Ballintoy, Mount Druid, co. Antrim
Trail, Rev. Robert, M.A., Skull-glebe, Skibbereen, co. Cork
*Trail, W., Esq., Ballylough, Bushmills, co. Antrim
*Trant, John, Esq., D.L. and J.P., Dovea, Thurles, co. Tipperary, and Mountjoy-square, Dublin
Travers, Abraham Henry, Esq., Cloyne, co. Cork
*Travers, Capt. Boyle, Beechmount, Cove, co. Cork
Travers, George, Esq., Lissicrineen, Timoleague, co. Cork
Travers, J. Moore, Esq., Clifton, near Cork
Travers, Lieut. James Walter, R.N., Bandon, co. Cork
*Travers, John, Esq., J.P., Garrycloyne-castle, Cork
*Travers, Jonas, Esq., J.P., Butlerstown, Timoleague, co. Cork
*Travers, R. Hennessy, Esq., Moses Town-house, Cloyne, co. Cork
*Travers, Lieut.-Col. Robert, Timoleague-house, near Bandon, co. Cork
*Travers, Capt. Thomas Otho, Leemount, Cork
Trayer, Thomas, Esq., Castle Treasure, Cork
*Tredennick, Rev. G. N., Rector of Kildoney, co. Donegal
*Tredennick, John, Esq., J.P., Camlin, co. Donegal
*Tredennick, W., Esq., Fort William, co. Donegal
*Trench, Charles, Esq., Farmley, near Castlenock, co. Dublin
Trench, F. M., Esq., Sopwell-hall, Roscrea, co. Tipperary
Trench, John Eyre, Esq., Clonfert-house, Eyrecourt, co. Galway
*Trench, Rev. F. S., Kilmoroney, Athy, co. Kildare

*Trench, H., Esq., Ballybrittas, Queen's county [common
*Trench, Rev. J. Le Poer, Ballinlough-house, Castlerea, co. Ros-
*Trench, Thomas, Esq., J.P., Rath, Ballybrittas, Queen's county
*Trench, The Hon. W. Le Poer, Dalystown, Loughrea, co. Galway
Trench, Rev. W. Le Poer, A.M., Garbally, Ballinasloe, co. Galway
Trenor, Rev. V., James-street, Dublin
*Trevor, Andrew Marcus, Esq., J.P., Loughbrickland, co. Down
Trevor, The Hon. Arthur, M.A., F.A.S., Wicken-park, Stoney-
Stratford, Bucks [Down
Trevor, Edward Hill, Esq., Lisnagade, near Loughbrickland, co.
Trew, Rev. J. M., Chantilly-glebe, Tynan, co. Armagh
*Trinity House, Newcastle-on-Tyne
*Trinity House, The Honorable the Corporation of the
Tripp, Thomas, Esq., Brookfield, Belfast
*Tristan, Richard, Esq., M.R.C.S., Athleague, co. Roscommon
*Trotter, W., Esq., Bishop-Auckland, Durham
Trousdell, Richard, Esq., Forte, Kilrush, co. Clare
Trousdell, Rev. Henry, A.B., Kilkeady-glebe, Corofin, co. Clare
Trownsell, W., Esq., Millstreet, co. Cork
*Trowsdell, John, Esq., Ennis, co. Clare, and Abbey-street, Dublin
*Troy, J. J., Esq., Collector of Customs, Cork
Troy, Rev. Robert, R.C.C., Lower Aghada, Cloyne, co. Cork
Trulock, Rev. George, A.M. and J.P., Skreen Rectory, co. Sligo
*Trumbull, N. J., Esq., Beechwood, near Malahide, co. Dublin
*Trye, H. N., Esq., Leekhampton Court, Gloucestershire
*Tuam, The Very Rev. the Dean of, Prebend and Rector of Bally-
[more, Glebe-house, Tanderagee, co. Armagh
Tucker, Thomas, Esq., Petersville, Moynalty, co. Meath
*Tucker, W., Esq., Dominick-street, Dublin, and Petersville, Moy-
[nalty, co. Meath
*Tudor, John, Esq., Beachfield, near Clontarf, co. Dublin
Tuite, C., Esq., Lower Mount-street, Dublin, and Tralee, co. Kerry
*Tuite, Hugh M., Esq., J.P., Sonna, near Mullingar, co. Westmeath
Tuite, Jeremiah, Esq., M.D., Tralee, co. Kerry
*Tully, Lieut. John, R.N., Killaloe, co. Clare [Cavan
*Tully, Mathew, Esq., Bolton-street, Dublin, and Ballyhaise, co.
Tully, Thomas T., Esq., Rathfaran, Loughrea, co. Galway
Turle, Mr. Robert, Keady, co. Armagh
Turner, Abraham, Esq., Kidderminster, Worcestershire
*Turner, Rev. C., Balrothery-glebe, near Balbriggan, co. Dublin
*Turner, Rev. Power, M.A., Hogston, near Winslow, Bucks
*Turner, R., Esq., Hammersmith Iron Works, Balls-bridge, Dublin
Turner, Robert, Esq., Bansha-mill, near Tipperary
*Turner, Samuel, Esq., Haymarket, London
*Turner, Thomas, Esq., London Wall, London
Turnly, John, Esq., Rockport, Belfast
*Turpin, Rev. Charles B., Rahan-glebe, Tullamore, King's county
Turpin, John, Esq., M.A., College, Midleton, co. Cork
*Turpin, Thomas D., Esq., Killurin-house, Tullamore, King's county
Turpin, Rev. W. P., Ballycommon-glebe, King's-county [managh
Tuthill, Rev. J. B., M.A., J.P., Belleck-glebe, Enniskillen, co. Fer-
Tuthill, J., Esq.,Woodlands, near Castle-Connel, co. Limerick
Tuthill, John, Esq., Kilmore-house, Croom, co. Limerick
*Twigg, Paul, Esq., Hartfield, near Drumcondra, co. Dublin
Twigg, Rev. Thomas, Thornhill, Dungannon, co. Tyrone
*Twiss, Francis, Esq., Tralee, co. Kerry
*Twiss, Robert, Esq., Parteen, Castle-Connel, co. Limerick
Twiss, W. M., Esq., Ballyheigue Castle, co. Kerry
Twohig, Mr. Daniel, Crookstown, co. Cork
Twomey, Rev. Timothy, P.P., Monanimy, Mallow, co. Cork
Twycross, Edward, Esq., Upper Ormond-Quay, Dublin
Tydd, Thomas, Esq., Clonmel, co. Tipperary
*Tyler, Robert George, Esq., Sligo
*Tymons, James, Esq., Baskin Hill, near Cloghran, co. Dublin
*Tyndall, Lieut. Peter, Stranorlar, co. Donegal
Tyner, Rev. R. L., Rector of Cloghane, Dingle, co. Kerry
TYRCONNEL, The Right Honorable the Earl of
Tyrrell, Edward, Esq., Kinvarra, co. Galway
Tyrrell, Mr. Gerrard, Lower Sackville-street, Dublin
Tyrrell, James, Esq., Dunloe-street, Ballinasloe, co. Galway
*Tyrrell, Rev. M. E., R.C.C., Newbridge, co. Kildare
Tyrrell, Rev. Thomas, P.P., Tinryland, Carlow
Tyrrell, Rev. W., Curate of St. Paul's, Dublin
*Tyrrells, The Misses, Ballinderry, Edenderry, King's-county

*Underwood, J. T., Esq., Farmley, near Dundrum, co. Dublin, and
[Lower Mount-street, Dublin
Uniacke, Crofton, Esq., Ballyrea, near Youghal, co. Cork
Uniacke, James, Esq., Glengarra, near Youghal, co. Cork
*Uniacke, Norman, Esq., Mount Uniacke, Killeagh, co. Cork
*Uniacke, Norman, Esq., Castletown, Castlemartyr, co. Cork
Uniacke, R., Esq., J.P., Woodhouse, near Dungarvan, co. Waterford
*Unthank, Robert S., Esq., Marine-villa, Kilrush, co. Clare
Unwin, E., Esq., Sutton-hall, Alfreton, Derbyshire
Unwin, G., Esq., Whitwell, Chesterfield, Derbyshire
Uprichard, James, Esq., Banvale, Gilford, co. Down
*Upton, Arthur, Esq., Woodlodge, Stradone, co. Cavan
Upton, Arthur, Esq., Kilsaran, Castle Bellingham, co. Louth
Upton, John Furlong, Esq., Ballybrahir, Cloyne, co. Cork
*Upton, William, Esq., Herald Office, Limerick
Upton, William, Esq., Ballygranymore, and Midleton, co. Cork
*Upton, W. Bayly, Esq., Cashel, co. Tipperary
*Ure, John, Esq., Distillery, Dundalk, co. Louth
Ursuline Convent, The, Blackrock, near Cork
*Urwick, Rev. W., D.D., Minister of York-street Chapel, Dublin
Usher, Rev. George, R.C.C. of Rahoon, co. Galway
*Usher, Thomas, Esq., Lower Rutland-street, Dublin
*Ussher, Rev. C. H., D.D., Rector and Vicar of Tullyaughnish,
[Ramelton, co. Donegal
Ussher, Rev. Henry, Ballaghneillmore, Magherafelt, co. Derry
Ussher, The Venerable and Rev. John, Archdeacon of Raphoe,
Ussher, John, Esq., Eastwell, co. Galway [Sharon, co. Donegal
*Ussher, Richard, Esq., Cappagh, near Dungarvan, co. Waterford

*Vallancey, Richard, Esq., Killaloe, co. Clare
Vance, James, Esq., Cuffe-street, Dublin
Vance, John, Esq., Sussex-parade, Kingstown, co. Dublin
*Vandeleur, The Honorable Judge, Dublin
*Vandeleur, Crofton M. Esq., J.P., Kilrush-house, co. Clare
Vandeleur, Capt. T. P., Cragbeg, Patrickswell, co. Limerick
*Vandeleur, Rev. W., Julianstown-glebe, Balbriggan, co. Meath
*Vanderkiste, F. W., Esq., Limerick
*Vardon, W., Esq., Gracechurch-street, London
*Vaughan, Arthur, Esq., Essex Bridge, Dublin
Vaughan, Charles, Esq., M.D., Cashel, co. Tipperary
Vaughan, John, Esq., Villa, Dromore, co. Down
Vaughan, Thomas, Esq., Londonderry
*Vaughan, William Paisly, Esq., D.L. and J.P., Golden Grove,
[Roscrea, co. Tipperary
Vereker, Amos, Esq., M.D., Cecil-street, Limerick
*Vereker, Major J., Limerick
*Vereker, John, Esq., Comptroller of Customs, Limerick
Vereker, The Hon. J. P., J.P., Roxborough, near Limerick
Verling, B., Esq., Hill-house, Cove, co. Cork
Verling, Bartholomew, Esq., Heathfield, co. Cork
*Verling, Rev. Patrick, R.C.C., Charleville, co. Cork [Armagh
*Verner, Col. William, M.P., D.L., & J.P., Churchill, Moy, co.
*Vernon, Henry, Esq., Marine Cottage, Sligo
Vernon, John, Esq., Clontarf Castle, co. Dublin
*Verschoyle, John, Esq., Stillorgan-house, co. Dublin
Verschoyle, Rev. Joseph, A.M., Ardnaree-glebe, Ballina, co. Mayo
*VERULAM, The Right Honorable the Earl of
*Vesey, Rev. Dr., Merrion-square South, Dublin
*Vesey, George, Esq., Lucan, co. Dublin
Vesey, Rev. George, Curate of Maghera, co. Derry
*Vesey, Samuel, Esq., J.P., Derrabard-house, Fintona, co. Tyrone
*Vesey, Rev. Thomas A., Rector of Magherafelt, co. Derry
Vicars, Robert, Esq., Grantstown, Rathdowney, Queen's-county
Vicary, James M., Esq., Rosslare, near Wexford
*Vickers, John, Esq., Surrey-square, Kent-road, London
Vignoles, J., Esq., Mount Pleasant, Tullamore, King's-county
*Villar, Rev. J. G., Bishop's Cleeve, Worcestershire
*Vincent, Rev. George, J.P., Vicar of Shanagolden, co. Limerick
Vincent, John, Esq., Kildare-street, Dublin
*Vincent, Messrs. N. and R., South-mall, Cork
*Vintners Company, The, Dublin
*Vizer, Robert W., Esq., Doughty-street, London
Voelke, Charles, Esq., St. Domingo-house, Everton, near Liverpool
Vogan, Josiah, Esq., Armagh
Vokes, T. P., Esq., J.P., Limerick

*Wackerbath, George, Esq., Parson's-street, London
Waddell, Cosslett, Esq., Newforge, Moira, co. Down
*Wade, George, Esq., Glyde Farm, Louth
Wade, George, Esq., Omagh, co. Tyrone
*Wade, James, Esq., Ash Tree Cottage, Saggard, co. Dublin
*Wade, John, Windfield Mills, Castle-Blakeney, co. Galway
Wade, John, Esq., Bachelor's-lodge, Navan, co. Meath
*Wade, Thomas, Esq., Fairfield, Aughrim, co. Galway

* Wade, W. B., Esq., Clonebrany, Crossakeel, co. Meath
* Waggett, W., Esq., Kitsborough, near Cork
Waggett, Rev. Thomas, Rector of Rathclaren, co. Cork
Wakefield, T. C., Esq., Moyallon, Gilford, co. Down
Wakefield, T. C., jun., Esq., Moyallon-house, co. Down
Wakeham, W. J., Esq., Springhill, Midleton, co. Cork
* Wakely, J., Esq., J.P., Ballyburly, Edenderry, King's county
* Wakely, Rev. W. G., Rector of Ballyburly, Monasteroris-house, [Edenderry, co. Kildare
* Wakeman, W. F., Esq., D'Olier-street, Dublin
* Waldron, Francis, Esq., Drumsna, co. Leitrim
* Waldron, H. K., Esq., J.P., Ashfort-house, Drumsna, co. Roscom- [mon
* Waldron, Thomas, Esq., Lissmoyle, Drumsna, co. Leitrim
Waldron, Thomas, Esq., Athleague, co. Roscommon
* Waldron, Thomas, jun., Esq., Athleague, co. Roscommon
* Walkden, G., Esq., Mansfield, Nottinghamshire
* Walker, Abraham, Esq., Loughall, co. Armagh
* Walker, Alexander, Esq., Clare Island, Granard, co. Westmeath
* Walker, C., Esq., Woodfield, Broadford, co. Clare, and Limerick
* Walker, David, Esq., Baggot-street, Dublin
* Walker, Rev. David J., Hollymount, Dunnamanna, co. Tyrone
* Walker, George, Esq., Eastwood, Nottinghamshire
* Walker, The Hon. Henry, D.L. & J.P., Castle Durrow, Durrow, co. [Kilkenny
Walker, Henry, Esq., Anna Hill, Richhill, co. Armagh
* Walker, John, Esq., Limerick
* Walker, John, Esq., Magherafelt, co. Derry
* Walker, John Cotton, Esq., Baggot-street, Dublin
* Walker, Joseph T., Esq., Pitchfordstown, Kilcock, co. Kildare
* Walker, R. Chambers, Esq., Granby-row, Dublin
* Walker, Samuel E., Esq., Forkhill, near Dundalk, co. Louth
* Walker, Thomas, Esq., Ravenfield-park, Doncaster, Yorkshire
Walker, Rev. Thomas, J.P., Rector of Kilmolooda, co. Cork
* Walker, Rev. T. F., Belgriffin-park, co. Dublin
Walker, W. F., Esq., Austin-friars, London
Walkington, T., Esq., Oatland-cottage, Ballinderry, co. Antrim
Walkinshaw, Clotworthy, Esq., Forthill, co. Antrim
* Wall, C. W., Esq., J.P., Coolnamuck-court, Carrick-on-Suir, co. [Waterford
Wall, Rev. Edward, P.P., Lismore, co. Waterford
* Wall, H. H., Esq., Bessina, near Baltinglass, co. Wicklow
* Wall, James, Esq., Knockrigg, co. Wicklow
Wall, James, Esq., Cloyne, co. Cork
* Wall, James A., Esq., Stephen's-green, Dublin
Wall, James B., Esq., M.D., Doneraile, co. Cork
* Wall, Rev. R. H., Hume-street, Dublin
* Wallace, Charles, Esq., J.P., Lime-park, Ardrahan, co. Galway
* Wallace, D. C., Esq., Richmond-villa, co. Limerick
Wallace, Horatio, Esq., Lime-park, Ardrahan, co. Galway
Wallace, Hugh, Esq., Downpatrick, co. Down
Wallace, John, Esq., Clover-hill, Cootehill, co. Cavan
Wallace, John, Esq., Belfast
Wallace, Mr. Samuel, Fair View, co. Donegal
* Wallace, Thomas, Esq., Stephen's-green, Dublin
Wallace, Mr. Thomas, Coshquin, Templemore, co. Derry
Wallen, John, Esq., Drumboe Abbey, Stranorlar, co. Donegal
Waller, Bolton, Esq., J.P., Shannongrove, co. Limerick
* Waller, Sir Edmund, Bart., J.P., Newport, co. Tipperary
Waller, John, Esq., J.P., Castletown, co. Limerick
* Waller, S., Esq., Ormond-cottage, Burris-o'-kane, co. Tipperary
* Waller, T., Esq., J.P., Finnoe-house, Burris-o'-kane, co. Tipperary
* Waller, Rev. W., Copsewood-cottage, Pallas Kenry, co. Limerick
Waller, William, Esq., Prior-park, Nenagh, co. Tipperary
* Waller, W. H., Esq., Allanstown, Navan, co. Meath
* Wallis, Henry, Esq., J.P., Drishane Castle, Mill-street, co. Cork
Wallplate, Joseph, Esq., J.P., Grange, Castle-Connel, co. Limerick
* Walmsley, George, Esq., Boleswoith Castle, Cheshire
* Walpole, J., Esq., Hampstead-house, near Glasnevin, co. Dublin
Walpole, Mr. R., Monderhilt, Burros-in-Ossory, Queen's-county
Walsh, Charles, Esq., Castlewellan, co. Down
* Walsh, Rev. D., P.P., Clonakilty, co. Cork
* Walsh, Sir Edward, Bart., Ballykilcavin, Stradbally, Queen's county
Walsh, Rev. E., P.P., Kilteely, New Palace, co. Limerick
* Walsh, Henry T., Esq., Stedalt Mills, Balbriggan, co. Meath
Walsh, J., Esq., J.P., Fanningstown, Pilltown, co. Kilkenny
Walsh, Rev. James, P.P., Midleton, co. Cork
Walsh, Rev. James, P.P., Kilmore, co. Wexford
Walsh, Rev. James, P.P., Newtownbarry, co. Wexford
Walsh, Rev. James, P.P., Macroom, co. Cork
Walsh, Rev. James, P.P., St. Athnassey and Kilbreedy Major, Kil- [mallock, co. Limerick
Walsh, J. H., Esq., Kilduff, Tyrrels Pass, and Gardiner-st, Dublin
* Walsh, Rev. John, P.P., Lisgoold, co. Cork
* Walsh, Rev. John, P.P., Borris, co. Carlow
* Walsh, Rev. J., P.P., of Rollestown, and Oldtown, Swords, co. Dub- [lin
Walsh, Rev. John, St. John's, Kilkenny
Walsh, Rev. John, R.C.C., Borris, co. Carlow
Walsh, John, Esq., Cahergall, Tuam, co. Galway
* Walsh, Mrs. Mary, Kingswood, near Rathcoole, co. Dublin
* Walsh, Matthew, Esq., Glen-house, Sligo
* Walsh, M., Esq., Mount-Michael, Rathfarnham, co. Dublin.
Walsh, Rev. Michael, R.C.C., Ardfinan, near Cahir, co. Tipperary
Walsh, Rev. Nicholas, P.P., Clondrohid, co. Cork
* Walsh, Rev. P., North Ann-street, Dublin
* Walsh, Patrick, Riverstown-house, Ardree, co. Louth
* Walsh, Rev. Patrick, P.P., Urlingford and Tobrid, co. Kilkenny
Walsh, Rev. Patrick, R.C.C., Lady's Island, Broadway, co. Wexford
* Walsh, Philip, Esq., Leeson-street, Dublin
Walsh, Philip N., Esq., Midleton, co. Cork
* Walsh, Rev. Richard, R.C.C. of Ovens, near Ballincollig, co. Cork
* Walsh, Rev. Richard, Convent, Wexford
Walsh, Rev. Richard, P.P., Headford, co. Galway
* Walsh, Rev. Robert, LL.D., Glasnevin, co. Dublin
Walsh, Rev. Stephen, P.P. of Rath and Kilnaboy, Corofin, co. Clare
Walsh, Robert W., Esq., Tullowherin, Thomastown, co. Kilkenny
* Walsh, Rev. Thomas, R.C.C., Backs, Ballina, co. Mayo
Walsh, Rev. Thomas, R.C.C., Glenville, Cork
Walsh, Thomas, Esq., Philpotstown, Kilcock, co. Meath
* Walsh, Rev. William, R.C.C. of Clontarf, &c., co. Dublin
* Walsh, William, Esq., Holywell, near Dundrum, co. Dublin
Walsh, William, Esq., Youghal, co. Cork
* Walsh, W. H., Esq., J.P., Gortalowry-house, Cookstown, co. [Tyrone
Walsh, Mr. W. Horatio, Muff, co. Derry
Walsh, Messrs. John and Co., Patrick-street, Cork
* Walshe, Lieut.-Col., Silver-Stream-house, Belfast
* Walshe, John, Esq., Hume-street, Dublin
* Walters, Henry, Esq., J.P., Staplestown-lodge, Carlow
* Walters, Patrick, Esq., Kilkenny
* Walters, Ralph, Esq., Newcastle-on-Tyne, Northumberland
Walton, Josiah Dunn, Esq., Kinsale, co. Cork
Wanchob, Samuel, Esq., Essex-bridge, Dublin
WAR OFFICE, Her Majesty's
* Warburton, Capt. B., J.P., Ballinasloe, co. Galway
Warburton, The Venerable and Rev. C., Archdeacon of Tuam, [Glebe, Rathkeale, co. Limerick
Ward, Rev. D., Leney-glebe, near Mullingar, co. Westmeath
* Ward, Mr. Francis, Limerick
Ward, Mr. Francis D., Bushmills, co. Antrim
Ward, Rev. Henry, Killinchy, co. Down
* Ward, Mr. James, Dame-street, Dublin
Ward, Col. John R., J.P., Castle, Bangor, co. Down
Ward, Rev. Ralph, Curate of Cairncastle, co. Antrim
* Ward, W. R., Esq., Baggot-street, Dublin
* Ward, Pring and Co., Messrs., Westmoreland-street, Dublin
Ware, N. Webb, Esq., J.P., Woodfort, Mallow, co. Cork
* Ware, W., Esq., South-mall, Cork
* Waring, Rev. Holt, J.P., Waringstown, Banbridge, co. Down
* Waring, James, Esq., J.P., Downshire-road, Newry, co. Down
* Waring, Thomas, Esq., Waringfield, co. Down
* Waring, Thomas, Esq., J.P., Newry, co. Down
* Warmsley, John, Esq., Belvidere-road, London
* Warne, J., jun., Esq., Leadenhall-street, London
Warner, H. B., Esq., Dances-court, Athboy, co. Meath
* Warner, Peter, Esq., Castle-view, Midleton, co. Cork
* Warner, Simeon, Esq., Colonnade-house, Blackheath, Kent
* Warren, Sir A., Bart, J.P., Warren's-court, Crookstown, co. Cork
* Warren, Brisbane, Esq., Castle Townsend, co. Cork
* Warren, Edward, jun., Esq., Parsonstown, King's county
Warren, Mr. George, Rylandville, Newtownbarry, co. Wexford
Warren, James, Esq., Royal Arcade, Dublin
Warren, Mr. John, Powers-grove, Athy, co. Kildare
* Warren, John, Esq,, Codrum, co. Cork
* Warren, John, Esq., Kilgariff-cottage, Clonakilty, co. Cork
Warren, J. B., Esq., J.P., Warren's-grove, Crookstown, co. Cork, [and Sillerdane-cottage, Kenmare, co. Kerry
* Warren, Robert, Esq., Cavendish-row, Dublin
* Warren, Robert, jun., Esq., Castle Warren, co. Cork
Warren, Robert, Esq., M.D., Kinsale, co. Cork
Warren, Mrs. Midleton, co. Cork
Warton, Matthew, jun., Esq., Stepney Causeway, Middlesex
* Wasse, J., Esq., M.D., Moat-hall, Borobridge, Yorkshire
* WATERFORD, The Most Noble the Marquess of
* Waterford Chamber of Commerce
Waterford County and City Club

Waterson, Henry, Esq., Belfast
* Watkins, Joseph, Esq., Elm-park, Merrion, near Dublin
* Watkins, Richard, Esq., Ardee-street, Dublin
Watkins, Westropp Peard, Esq., Bandon, co. Cork
Watson, A. J., Esq., Limerick
* Watson, George, Esq., Ashgrove, Rathmines, co. Dublin
* Watson, Henry, Esq., J.P., Limerick
Watson, James, Esq., J.P., Brookhill, co. Antrim
* Watson, James, Esq., Millbrook, Killaloe, co. Clare
Watson, Mr. Moses, Maragale, co. Antrim
Watson, S. E., Esq., Larch-hill, Kilcock, co. Meath
Watson, Thomas, Esq., Aldermanbury, London
Watson, T. H., Esq., J.P., Lumclone, Leighlin-bridge, co. Carlow
Watson, William, Esq., Glensiskin-house, Kilworth, co. Cork
* Watt, Andrew A., Esq., Londonderry
Watt, James, Esq., Springvale, co. Antrim
Watt, James, Esq., Clara, Ramelton, co. Donegal
Watts, Thomas, Esq., Hartstown, near Castlenock, co. Dublin
Wawn, John T., Esq., West Bolden, Newcastle, Northumberland
Wayland, F. V., Esq., Ballywaler, Cashel, co. Tipperary
Wayland, P., Esq., Knockavilla, near Cashel, co. Tipperary
Webb, Arthur, Esq., Cork
* Webb, D. J., Esq., J.P., Woodville-lodge, Templemore, co. Derry
* Webb, John, Esq., Daisyhill, Clogher, co. Tyrone
* Webb, Rev. John, LL.D., J.P., West-hill, Ballincollig, co. Cork
Webb, Rev. John, Vicar of Killeighley, King's county
Webb, Rev. J. B., Curate of Ringroan, co. Cork
* Webb, Rev. R. H., A.B., Parsons-green, Belturbet, co. Cavan
Webb, Robert, Esq., Castletown-Roche, co. Cork
Webb, Rev. R. F., Caherah, Skibbereen, co. Cork
* Webb, T. M., Esq., Wardinstown, co. Westmeath
Webb, Mr. T., Lower Sackville-street, Dublin
Webb, William, Esq., Castle-Nugent, Granard, co. Longford
* Webb, William, Esq., J.P., Hilltown, Castlepollard, co. Westmeath
* Webb, William, Esq., J.P., Castlecorr, Oldcastle, co. Meath
Webbe, Rev. H. G., Rector of Gilbertstown, co. Wexford
Webster, Erasmus, Esq., Chapel-en-le Frith, Derbyshire
* Webster, Rowland, Esq., Bishopwearmouth, Durham
Weekes, W. S., Esq., Castle Kevin, co. Wicklow
Weir, John, Esq., Gardiner's-place, Dublin
Weir, Mr. R., Coleraine, co. Derry
* Weir, Thomas, Esq., Lenaderg, Banbridge, co. Down
Welbank, W., Esq., Northallerton, Yorkshire
Welburn, Thomas, Esq., Excise Office, Loughrea, co. Galway
* Welch, Joseph T., Esq., Whitechapel, Lon on
Welch, Thomas, Esq., Fleet Street, London
Weld, Isaac, sen., Esq., Hon. Sec. to the Royal Dublin Society, [M.R.I.A., F.G.S.D. Ravenswell, Bray, co. Dublin
* Weldon, Lieut.-Col., Rahin, Ballylinan, Queen's county
Weldon, Mr. Francis, Lisburn, co. Antrim
Weldon, Thomas, Esq., Riversfield, Kilmallock, co. Limerick
* Welfit, Rev. W., Pelham, near Gainsborough, Lincolnshire
* Welford, Edward, Esq., Hexham, Northumberland
* Welland, Joseph, Esq., Upper Rutland-street, Dublin
Welland, Rev. William, A.M., Residentiary-house, Cloyne, co. Cork
Welland, William, Esq., Killeagh-farm, Midleton, co. Cork
* Weller, John, Esq., Amersham, Bucks.
* Weller, W., Esq., Amersham, Bucks.
* WELLESLEY, The Most Noble the Marquess of
* Wellington, Jonathan, Esq., Richmond-house, Templemore, co. [Tipperary
Wells, Major, Sutton, Surrey
* Welply, Rev. M., R.C.C., St. Catherine's, Meath-street, Dublin
Welsh, C. H., Esq., Mogeely, near Tallow, co. Cork
* Welsh, Rev. J., J.P., Rector and Vicar of Killaghtee, Duncanely, [co. Donegal
Welsh, Mr. John, King's Arms, Tuam, co. Galway
* Welsh, Thomas, Esq., Woodstock, Cappoquin, co. Waterford
Welstead, William, Esq., Lismore, co. Waterford
Welsted, R., Esq., Ballywalter, Castletown-Roche, co. Cork
* Wemys, Henry, Esq., J.P., Danesfort, Kilkenny
West, Rev. Charles, Grange, Sligo
* West, Jacob, Esq., Springfield, co. Wicklow
* West, James, Esq., Coolafinny, near Londonderry
West, James, Esq., J.P., Rath, co. Westmeath
* West, J. R., Esq., Alscot, Stratford-on-Avon, Warwickshire
* West, M., Esq., Foxhall, Edgeworthstown, co. Longford
West, Richard, Esq., Weston-cottage, Newtownbarry, co. Wexford
West, William B., Esq., Wexford
* West, Miss, Donaghadee, co. Down
* Westby, E. H., Esq., High-park, co. Wicklow
Westby, Percival, Esq., D.L. and J.P., Knightsbrook, Trim, co. [Meath
* Westby, William, Esq., Merrion-square, Dublin
* Westenra, Lieut.-Col., Sharavogue-house, Roscrea, co. Tipperary
* Westenra, H., Esq., J.P., Camla, Monaghan
* Westenra, The Honorable H. R., M.P., D.L., and J.P.
Westenra, Capt. R., Kinsale, co. Cork
Weston, W., Esq., Northfield, Worcestershire
* Westrop, John, Esq., Attyflin, Limerick
Westropp, Edmund, Esq., J.P., Ballystein, co. Limerick
Westropp, Capt. H., Newlawn, Tulla, co. Clare
* Westropp, John, Esq., Limerick
Westropp, M., Esq., Mellon-house, Pallas Kenry, co. Limerick
Westropp, Rev. Thomas, jun., A.M., Mungrets-glebe, Limerick
Wetherall, Thomas, Esq., Cork
Wethered, Thomas, Esq., Lisburn, co. Antrim
Wetherell, Rev. R., Rectory, Newtown Longville, Bucks.
Wexford Union Club
* Whaley, John, Esq., Stephen's-green, Dublin
* Whaley, Richard William, Esq., Whaley-abbey, Rathdrum, co. [Wicklow
* Wharton, J. L., Esq., York-street, and Meadow-bank, co. Dublin
Wharton, Rev. W., Vicarage, Gilling, Richmond, Yorkshire
* Whatley, Thomas Clifford, Esq., Cheltenham, Gloucestershire
* Wheeler, James, Esq., Cork
Wheeler, James, Esq., Brickfields, Cork
Wheeler, W., Esq., Catherine-street, Limerick
Whelan, The Very Rev. W. J., O.D.C., Clarendon-street, Dublin
White, Lieut.-Col., Rockbridge-cottage, Killinardrish, co. Cork
* White, Andrew, Esq., Frederick-lodge, Hexham, Northumberland
White, Barnwall, Esq., M.D., Londonderry
White, David, Esq., Omagh, co. Tyrone
White, George, Esq., Douglas, near Cork
White, H., Esq., Somerset, Ballinasloe, co. Galway
* White, Henry, Esq., Peppards-castle, co. Wexford
White, J. E., Esq., M.D., Wexford
White, Mr. James, Ballitore, co. Kildare
White, Rev. James, P.P., Kilmacshalgan, Dromore West, co. Sligo
White, James G., Esq., Kilburn, Doneraile, co. Cork
White, John, Esq., Shannon-lodge, Castle Connell, co. Limerick
* White, John, Esq., J.P., Divernagh, near Newry, co. Armagh
* White, Rev. John, R.C.C., St. Michael and St. Johns, Exchange- [street, Dublin
* White, John, Esq., White-hall, co. Antrim
White, Mr. John, Ballymoney, co. Antrim
* White, John William, Esq., Limerick
White, Matthew Edmond, Esq., A.M., M.D., Wexford
* White, Newport, Esq., Kilmoylan, co. Limerick
* White, R., Esq., Coolrain-house, Mountrath, Queen's county
* White, Richard, Esq., J.P., Inchiclough, Bantry, co. Cork
* White, Richard, Esq., Abbeyville, Croom, co. Limerick
* White, R. H. E., Esq., Monkstown, co. Cork
* White, Robert, Esq., Scotchrath, Abbeyleix, Queen's county
* White, Robert, Esq., J.P., Old-park, Rathdowney, Queen's county
* White, Robert, Esq., Virginia, co. Cavan
* White, R. H. E., Esq., Glengarriff-castle, Bantry, co. Cork
* White, Samuel, Esq., Fitzwilliam-street, Dublin
White, Samuel, Esq., Killikee, Rathfarnham, co. Dublin
White, Mr. S. J., Whitefield, co. Wexford
* White, Simon, Esq., J.P., Glengarriff-castle, Bantry, co. Cork
* White, Rev. Thomas, Ferns Diocesan School, Wexford
White, Thomas, Esq., J.P., Ballybrophy, Burros-in-Ossory, Queen's [county
* White, Thomas, Esq., Woodlands, near Dublin
White, Rev. T. J., Curate of Arboe, co. Tyrone
* White, T. W., Esq., Bonnybrook, near Artane, co. Dublin
* White, W., Esq., Richmond Avenue, Dublin
White, W., Esq., Springmount, Cashel, co. Tipperary
* White, Mr. William Duckett, Cork
White and Borrett, Messrs., Frederick's-place, London
* Whitehead, Richard, Esq., Mecklenburgh-street, Dublin
Whiter, Rev. C. W., Rector of Clown, Chesterfield, Derbyshire
* Whitla, George, Esq., Inver lodge, co. Antrim
Whitla, James, Esq., Gobrana, Crumlin, co. Antrim
* Whitla, Mr. Thomas, Aughacomon, co. Antrim
Whitla, Valentine, Esq., Belfast
* Whitmore, Edward, Esq., Lombard-street, London
Whitmore, Frederick, Esq., Lombard-street, London
Whitmore, Wells and Whitmore, Messrs., Lombard-street, London
Whitney, Mr. John, Moneytucker, co. Wexford
Whitney, Thomas, A. Esq., J.P., Merton, co. Wexford
Whittle, Francis, Esq., J.P., Muckamore-lodge, Antrim
* Whittle, James, Esq., Thistleborough, Crumlin, co. Antrim
Whitton, Charles, Esq., Lower Gardiner-street, Dublin
* Whittsit, Joseph, Esq., Salloo, Monaghan
Whitty, Rev. G., P.P., Castlebridge, Wexford
* Whitty, Mr. Philip, Wexford

Whitty, Thomas R., Esq., Balli'ore-house, co. Kildare
Whitty, W., Esq., Wexford
* Whyte, Capt. Edward, R.N., Johnstown, near Cabinteely, co. Dublin
Whyte, N. C., Esq., Loughbrickland-house, co. Down
* Wickham, Mr. Michael, Wexford
Wickings, William, Esq., Barnsbury-place, Islington, Middlesex
WICKLOW, The Right Honorable the Earl of
Wigelsworth, Joseph, Esq., Churchpark, near Roscommon
Wigmore, Henry, Esq., Ballyvodock, Midleton, co. Cork
Wigmore, Henry, Esq., Kilbarry, co. Cork
Wigmore, Henry, Esq., Ballynona, Castlemartyr, co. Cork
Wigmore, Robert, Esq., Ballynona-cottage, Castlemartyr, co. Cork
Wildman, Mr. W., Mabbott-street, Dublin
* Wilkin, Thomas H., Esq., Leinster-street, Dublin
* Wilkinson, G. Hutton, Esq., Harpeale-park, Bishop Auckland, Durham, and Eldon-square, Newcastle-on-Tyne
* Wilkinson, James, Esq., M.D., Blackrock, near Dublin
* Wilkinson, Rev. John Mevagh, Kilmacrenan, co. Donegal
* Wilkinson, Rev. P. S., Mount-Oswald, Durham
* Wilkinson, T., Esq., Drumglass-colliery, Dungannon, co. Tyrone
* Wilkinson, Thomas W., Esq., Anglesea-street, Dublin
* Wilkinson, W., Esq., Old Broad-street, London
* Willan, Thomas, Esq., Hansfield, near Clonsilla, co. Dublin
* Willans, Thomas, Esq., Hibernian-mills, Kilmainham, Dublin
* Willcocks, John, Esq., J.P., Tipperary
Willcocks, Rev. William, Palmerston, near Chapelizod, co. Dublin
* Willes, W., Esq., Astrop-house, Northamptonshire
* Williams, A., Esq., Talbot-street, Dublin
* Williams, Benjamin, jun., Esq., Broughton-bridge, near Manchester
* Williams, John, Esq., Yew-hill, co. Cork
* Williams, John, Esq., Harrogate, Yorkshire
* Williams, Rev. R., Rector of Aber, near Bangor, Carnarvonshire
* Williams, Mr. Thomas, Londonderry
Williams, Thomas, Esq., Great George-street, Cork
* Williams, W. B., Esq., Radical-cottage, Mallow, co. Cork
Williamson, A., Esq., Albany-house, Monkstown, co. Dublin
Williamson, A., Esq., Lambeg, Lisburn, co. Antrim
* Williamson, Rev. B., Rector and Vicar of Mourne Abbey, co. Cork
* Williamson, J., Esq., Lakelands, Sandymount, near Dublin
Williamson, John, Esq., Melbeach, Monkstown, co. Dublin
Williamson, Rev. W. C., P.C. of Temple Bready, co. Cork
Williamson, William G., Esq., Antrim
* Williamson, Mr. W., Derrycrenard-cottage, Rockcorry, co. Monaghan
* Willington, J., Esq., Killoskehane, Burrisoleigh, co. Tipperary
* Willington, J., Esq., J.P., Castle Willington, Nenagh, co. Tipperary
* Willington, J., Esq., Richmond-house, Templemore, co. Tipperary
Willis, Mr. Hamilton, Johnstown-castle, Wexford
Willis, Richard, Esq., Rockfield-house, near Monmouth
Wills, James, Esq., J.P., Carrickfergus, co. Antrim
* Wills, W. R., Esq., Castlerea-house, co. Roscommon
Willson, James, Esq., Holly-ville, Rathmines, co. Dublin
* Wilmot, Henry, S., Esq., Chaddesdin-hall, Derbyshire
* Wilson, A., Esq., Governor of County Gaol, Maryboro, Queen's county
* Wilson, Benjamin, Esq., Sledagh, co. Wexford
* Wilson, Campbell, Esq., Weybourne, Larne, co. Antrim
Wilson, Charles, Esq., Newborough, Adare, co. Limerick
Wilson, Charles, Esq., Fethard, co. Tipperary
Wilson, Rev. Charles, A.M., Rector of Achill, Newport-Pratt, co Mayo
Wilson, Mr. David, Dungonnal, near Antrim
Wilson, Rev. Edward, Killbeggan-glebe, co. Westmeath
Wilson, Captain Edward, J.P., Shenan-house, Shercock, co. Cavan
Wilson, Hugh Gilmer, Esq., Rashee, co. Antrim
* Wilson, James, Esq., Clonleek, Glasslough, co. Monaghan
* Wilson, James, Esq., Omagh, co. Tyrone
* Wilson, James, Esq., Meath-park, near Coleraine, co. Derry
* Wilson, Mr. James, Strabane, co. Tyrone
* Wilson, Rev. James, Tandragee, co. Armagh
* Wilson, James G., Esq., Charlemont Mall, Dublin
* Wilson, Rev. John, M.A., Brookeborough, co. Fermanagh
* Wilson, John, Esq., Wilmington-square, London
Wilson, Mr. John, Seacash, near Antrim
Wilson, John, jun., Esq., Barronstown, co. Wicklow
* Wilson, Mr. Joseph, Ballygallon, co. Derry
* Wilson, Rev. Joseph, Cottage, near Kildare
* Wilson, Joseph, Esq., Ballycrana, Midleton, co. Cork
Wilson, Joseph, Esq., Lurgan, co. Armagh
* Wilson, Mr. Myrry, Adderbury, Oxfordshire
Wilson, S., Esq., The Hall, Bomboa-hall, Baltinglass, co. Wicklow
* Wilson, Thomas M., Esq., Cahirconlish-house, near Limerick
* Wilson, W., Esq., M.D., Littleton, near Stillorgan, co. Dublin
* Wilson, William, Esq., Farloe, co. Derry
Wilson, Mr. William, Shenington, Oxfordshire
Wilsone, Mr. W., Bolton Street, Dublin
* Wingfield, Rev. J. D., J.P., Geashill-glebe, King's county
Winslow, B., Esq., Mount-prospect, Lisnaskea, co. Fermanagh
Winslow, D. T., Esq., Dresternan, Ballyconnel, co. Fermanagh
* Winter, John Pratt, Esq., J.P., Agher, Summerhill, co. Meath
* Winter, Mr. Robert, Dundalk, co. Louth
* Winter, Samuel, Esq., J.P., Tullaghard, Trim, co. Meath
Winwood, Henry Q., Esq., Henbury-hill, near Bristol
Wire, Thomas, Esq., Ballysone, Ardee, co. Louth
Wisdom, John, Esq., Clonliffe, near Dublin
Wise, Francis, Esq., Anngrove, co. Cork
* Wise, Rev. Henry, Offchurch, near Warwick
* Wise, Henry C., Esq., Woodcote, near Warwick
* Wise, Rev. John, Lillington, near Warwick
* Wise, Messrs. and Co., Cork
Wiseman, Jonathan F., Esq., Paul-street, Cork
Witham, Henry, Esq., Lismore, co. Waterford
Witherby, Charles, Esq., Panton-street, London
Witherby, Charles, Esq., Guildford, Surrey
Wogan, John, Esq., Carrick on Suir, co. Tipperary
* Wolfe, John, Esq., North Frederick-street, Dublin
* Wolfe, John, Esq., Arran-quay, Dublin
Wolfe, Rev. Richard, Forenaughts, Naas, co. Kildare
* Wolfe, Robert, Esq., Tentower, Queen's county
Wolfe, William, Esq., Cashil-house, Rosscarberry, co. Cork
* Wollaston, G. H., Esq., Clapham-common, Surrey
Wolseley, Captain R. B., Youghal, co. Cork
Wolseley, Rev. John, Portarlington, Queen's county
Wolseley, Rev. William, Rector of Dunaghy, co. Antrim
Wood, Rev. J., D.D., Master of St. John's-college, Cambridge
* Wood, James, Esq., Woodville, Sligo
* Wood, John, Esq., Howardtown, Glossop, Derbyshire
Wood, Mr. Joseph, Kilkenny
* Wood, Rev. Joshua, Rosscarbery, co. Cork
Wood, S., Esq., A.M., M.B., Woodville, Ballinspittle, Bandon, co. Cork
* Wood, N. Esq., Killingworth, Newcastle-on-Tyne, Northumberland
Wood, Thomas, Esq., Woodville, near Skibbereen, co. Cork
Wood, Thomas, Esq., Chesterfield, Derbyshire
* Wood, W., Esq., Georges-place, Dublin
* Wood, William C., Esq., Finisklin, Sligo
Woodburn, Henry, Esq., Governor of the County Gaol, Limerick
Woodcock, Mr. Francis, Nore-ville, Queen's county
Woodcock, Mr. Thomas, Noneville, Abbeyleix, Queen's county
Woodhouse, Archibald, Esq., Castletown, co. Cork
* Woodhouse, J. O., Esq., St. Andrew-street, Dublin, and Portadown, co. Armagh
Woodley, William, Esq., Anne Brook, Cove, co. Cork
Woodley, William, Esq., Northesk, Cork
Woodroffe, Rev. J. N., A.M., Woodland-cottage, Glanmire, co. Cork
* Woodroffe, J., Esq., Capel-street, Dublin, and Killiney, co. Dublin
Woodroffe, J., Esq., M.D., South-mall, Cork
* Woods, George, Esq., Milverton, co. Dublin
Woods, James, jun., Esq., Tamnalannan, Stewartstown, co. Tyrone
Woods, John, Esq., Grace-ville, Merrion, near Dublin
* Woods, Rev. Patrick, St. Mary's Parish, Dublin
Woods, W., Esq., Keave-house, Castle-Blakeney, co., Galway
* Woodthorpe, Henry, Esq., Guildhall, London
* Woodward, Henry, Esq., Drumbarrow, Kells, co. Meath
* Woodwright, Henry, Esq., J.P., Gola, co. Monaghan
* Wooler, W. C., Esq., Durham
* Woolmore, John, Esq., Trinity House, London
* Woolsey, John, Esq., Milestown-park, Castle-Bellingham, co. Louth
* Woolsey, Jameson and Co., Messrs., Drogheda, co. Louth
WORCESTER, The Right Rev. Lord Bishop of
Worcester, The Venerable Archdeacon of
Workman, Robert. Esq., Belfast
Worrall, W. P., Esq., Clonmel, co. Tipperary
* Worrall, W., Esq., Upper Cecil-street, Limerick
Worthington, Jonathan, Esq., Stourport, Worcestershire
Wray, G. A., Esq., Cromore, Coleraine, co. Derry
* Wray, H. B., Esq., J P., Maryborough, Queen's county
* Wray, James T., Esq., Leyburn, Bedale, Yorkshire
Wray, W., Esq., J.P., Oak-park, Letterkenny, co. Donegal
Wren, G., Esq., Litton, Ballylongford, co. Kerry
Wright, Charles, Esq., Richmond, Yorkshire
Wright, David, Esq., Emma-vale, near Arklow, co. Wicklow
* Wright, J., Esq., Antrim
* Wright, J., Esq., Butterfield-house, Rathfarnham, co. Dublin
* Wright, John, Esq., Cartron, co. Longford
* Wright, John, Esq., Springfield, near Dunganstown, co. Wicklow
* Wright, Captain John, Enniskillen, co. Fermanagh

Wright, Rev. John, A.M., J.P., Killcevan, co. Monaghan
*Wright, Joseph, Esq., Carachor, Monaghan
*Wright, Joseph John, Esq., Bishopwearmouth, Durham
Wright, Rev. Joseph, M.A., J.P., Killincool, Lurgan-green, co. Louth
*Wright, J. Smith, Esq., Rempstone-hall, Nottinghamshire
Wright, Joseph W., Esq., Corlatt, Monaghan
*Wright, Nathaniel, Esq., Barrington's-bridge, co. Limerick
Wright, Richard, Esq., Fethard, co. Tipperary
*Wright, Captain Robert, The Garrison, Carlow
*Wright, Robert, Esq., Mespil, Dublin
*Wright, Thomas, Esq., Foulksrath-castle, Freshford, co. Kilkenny
Wright, Thomas E., Esq., Hardwicke-place, Dublin
*Wright, Travers, Esq., Dundalk, co. Louth
*Wright, William, Esq., York-street, Dublin
Wrigley, Mr. S., Dublin
Wyatt, Rev. C. F., Broughton Rectory, Oxfordshire
Wybrants, George S., Esq., Peter-street, Dublin
Wynne, Rev. Arthur, Enniskerry, co. Wicklow
*Wynne, Mr. Edward, Shankill, co. Kilkenny
*Wynne, Mr. Edward, Kellymont, Goresbridge, co. Carlow
*Wynne, Rev. Henry, Killanne, Enniscorthy, co. Wexford
Wynne, Major John, Ardmanah-house, Skibbereen, co. Cork
*Wynne, O., Esq., J.P., Hazlewood, Sligo
*Wynne, Owen, Esq., Customs, Sligo
Wynne, Richard Beavor, Esq., Sligo
Wynne, Rev. W. H., A.M., Vicar of Tullylish, Gilford, co. Down
*Wynne, Mrs., Lislea, Armagh
Wyse, Thomas, Esq., Manor of St. John, Waterford

*YARBOROUGH, The Right Honorable Lord
*Yates, Benedict, A., Esq., Moone Abbey, co. Kildare
*Yeats, John, Esq., Dundalk, co. Louth
Yerbury, John, Esq., Shirehampton, Gloucestershire
*Yore, Rev. Mr., Queen-street, Dublin
Young, Rev. Arthur, J.P., Clogherney, Omagh, co. Tyrone
Young, David E., Esq., Ballygibbon, Nenagh, co. Tipperary
Young, Rev. E. N., Quainton-rectory, near Aylesbury, Bucks
*Young, George, Esq., J.P., Culdaff-house, Moville, co. Donegal
Young, Rev. G. H., Killough, co. Down
Young, Rev. James, R.C.C. of Baldoyle, and Howth, co. Dublin
*Young, Mr. James, Capel-street, Dublin
*Young, James W., Esq., Culdaff-house, Moville, co. Donegal
*Young, Rev. John, Rector of Killishil, Ballygawley, co. Tyrone
*Young, Rev. J., A.M., Multifarnham-glebe, Mullingar, co. West- [meath
*Young, John, Esq., North Earl-street, Dublin
Young, John, Esq., Shamrock-lodge, Ballymacarett, Belfast
Young, Rev. J. R., A.B., Rector of Tidavnet, Monaghan
*Young, John T., Esq., Philpotstown, Navan, co. Meath
*Young, Owen, Esq., Harristown, Castlerea, co. Roscommon
*Young, Richard, Esq., J.P., Lakeville, Crossdoney, co. Cavan
*Young, Richard, Esq., J.P., Coolkeragh-house, Londonderry
*Young, Rev. Robert A., Lackland, Rathdowney, Queen's county
*Young, Rev. Robert, Steele-grove, Carrickfergus, co. Antrim
*Young, Robert, Esq., Glenview, near Glanmire, co. Cork
Young, Samuel, Esq., Bantry, co. Cork
Young, Rev. Walter, M.A., Lisbellan, Enniskillen, co. Fermanagh
Young, W., Esq., Capnagh, co. Carlow
Young, W., Esq., Mount-hall, Killygordon, co. Donegal
*Young, W. B., Esq., New-mills, Glasslough, co. Monaghan
Young, Messrs. J. and R., Ballymoney, Ballymena, co. Antrim
Young and Murdock, Messrs., Upper Gardiner-street, Dublin
Yourell, Michael, Esq., Newelswood, Clonee, co. Meath
Yourell, Mr. Patrick, Quarryland, Clonee, co. Meath

A

TOPOGRAPHICAL DICTIONARY

OF

IRELAND.

ABBEY, a parish and village, in the barony of BURREN, county of CLARE, and province of MUNSTER; containing, with the post-town of Burren, 2493 inhabitants, of which number, 128 are in the village. This place, which is situated on the shores of the harbour of Burren in the bay of Galway, and on the road from Galway to Ennistymon, derives its name from an ancient Cistertian abbey founded here, either by Donald O'Brien, King of Limerick, in 1194, or by his son Donough Carbrac O'Brien, in the year 1200. This establishment, designated the abbey of Corcomroe, Corcomruadh, or *De Petra fertili*, and called also Gounamonagh, or "the Glen of the Monks," is said to have been a sumptuous edifice, dedicated to the Blessed Virgin, and dependent on or connected with the abbey of Suire, or Innislaunaght, in the county of Tipperary: it was afterwards made subject to the celebrated abbey of Furness, in Lancashire, and had a cell annexed to it in Kilshanny, in the adjoining barony of Corcomroe. The remains are extensive, forming an interesting object as seen from the road, and presenting evident traces of its former splendour: a fine pointed arch is still tolerably perfect, and is particularly admired for the beauty of its proportions; and there are some remains of the stately tomb of the King of Thomond, who was killed in a battle fought near this place, in 1267. The parish extends along the southern shore of the bay, on the confines of the county of Galway, and comprises 5545 statute acres, as applotted under the tithe act. The greater portion is under tillage; the land along the coast produces good crops of wheat, but that in the interior is hilly and unproductive, adapted only for grazing; the system of agriculture has been greatly improved through the exertions of Burton Bindon, Esq., and Messrs. Hynes and Moran. There are some limestone quarries of excellent quality, and sea manure is found in abundance on the shore. The principal seats are Finvarra House, the residence of — Skerret, Esq.; and Curranroe, of Burton Bindon, Esq. The small port of New Quay is situated about a quarter of a mile to the north of the village of Burren; a constant intercourse is kept up with Galway, on the opposite side of the bay, and a considerable trade in corn and fish is carried on; the boats employed in the Galway bay fishery rendezvous here, and more than 100 of them have at one time taken shelter in stormy weather. The port affords great facilities for commerce, as vessels of considerable burden can approach at any time of the tide: the coast is well adapted for sea bathing. The great oyster bed, called the Red Bank, to the east of Burren, and said to be one of the most extensive on the Irish coast, was established some years since by Mr. Bindon, and is now in great celebrity: it is stocked with young oysters, chiefly from Connemara, aud more than 150 persons, chiefly women and children, are regularly employed. A considerable trade is also carried on in sea-weed with the farmers of the interior, which has been greatly increased since the construction of a new line of road from this place leading through the parishes of Kinvarra and Killeny, in the county of Galway, and of Kilkeady and Inchicronan, in the county of Clare. The harbour of New Quay, or Burren, called also Curranroe, is one of the several inlets of the bay of Galway: it lies to the south of Aughnish Point, and extends four miles up to Curranroe Bridge. The late Fishery Board built a small quay in the narrow part of the channel, at the village of New Quay (so called from the construction of this quay, about eight years since), a little to the east of an older one, of which there are still some remains: vessels of 100 tons' burden can come close up to it and deliver their cargoes. A court is held at Burren by the seneschal of the manor, about once in six weeks, for the recovery of small debts. The parish is in the diocese of Kilfenora, and is a rectory, partly without provision for the cure of souls: the tithes, with the exception of those of the townlands of Aughnish, Finvarra, Behagh, and Kilmacrane, which are annexed to the parish of Kilcorney, are impropriate in Pierse Creagh, Esq., and amount to £120. In the R.C. divisions it is the head of a union or district, comprising also the parish of Oughtmanna; the chapel is situated in the village of Behagh, and it is intended to establish a school connected with it. There is a pay school, in which are about 30 boys and 15 girls. On the summit of Rosraly mountain is a well springing from the solid rock; it is dedicated to St. Patrick, and produces water of the purest quality, which is conveyed by pipes to the road side at the foot of the mountain.—See Burren.

ABBEYDORNEY, a village, in the parish of O'Dorney, barony of Clanmaurice, county of Kerry, and province of Munster, 7½ miles (N. N. E.) from Tralee; containing 338 inhabitants. This place, which is situated at the intersection of the old and new roads from Tralee to Listowel, takes its name from the ancient abbey of Kirie Eleyson, or O'Dorney, founded here in 1154 by some person unknown, for Cistertian monks, who were brought from the abbey of Magio, in the county of Limerick; the abbot was a lord in parliament. The remains are situated a little to the north of the village, but retain few vestiges of its original character. The village, which consists mostly of thatched houses, is a constabulary police station; a penny post from Tralee has been established, and a manorial court is held occasionally. The R. C. parochial chapel, built here in 1826, at an expense of £600, is a spacious and handsome edifice fronted with stone, in the later English style, and embellished with a fine altar-piece and painting. Near the village is a flour-mill.—See O'Dorney.

ABBEYFEALE, a parish, in the Glenquin Division of the barony of Upper Connello, county of Limerick, and province of Munster, 10 miles (W. by S.) from Newcastle, on the mail coach road from Limerick to Tralee; containing 4242 inhabitants, of which number, 607 are in the village. This place obviously derives its name from a Cistertian abbey founded here, in 1188, by Brien O'Brien, and from its situation on the river Feale: the abbey, in 1209, became a cell to that of Monasternanagh, or Nenay, in the barony of Pubblebrien. The village, situated in a wild mountainous district, was almost inaccessible, but since the construction of the new lines of road, great alterations have taken place; great improvement in the condition of the people has resulted from the facilities thus afforded of taking their little produce to market; and the inhabitants are now industriously and profitably employed. Here is a large and commodious hotel, and some respectable houses, but the greater number are thatched cabins. The village has a penny post dependent on Newcastle, and is a constabulary police station. Fairs are held on the 29th of June and Sept. 24th, chiefly for cattle, sheep, and pigs. The parish comprises 17,659 statute acres, as applotted under the tithe act, of which 1620 acres are arable, 12,800 pasture, and about 3500 waste land and bog: a considerable portion of the waste land is gradually being brought into cultivation, and the system of agriculture is steadily improving. From long previous neglect, the lands in many parts have become marshy and cold, and in some places are covered to the depth of several feet with a loose turbary, which, in the total absence of timber, affords excellent fuel, of which great quantities are sent to Newcastle, whence limestone is brought in return and is burnt with coal of indifferent quality procured here for that purpose only. The farms have generally large dairies, and a considerable quantity of butter is sent to Cork and Limerick. On the great line of road from Limerick to Tralee is Wellesley bridge, a handsome structure, about a mile and a half to the west of the village; and at the same distance to the east is Goulburn bridge. The new line of road leading through the heart of the mountains from Abbeyfeale to Glin, a distance of 12 miles, was opened after the spring assizes of 1836, previously to which there was scarcely any possibility of access to this secluded district, which for that reason was, in the year 1822, selected as their head-quarters by the Rockites, who dated their proclamations "From our camp at Abbeyfeale." The living is a vicarage, in the diocese of Limerick, and in the patronage of Lord Southwell, during whose legal incapacity the Crown presents; the rectory is impropriate in Richard Ellis and Thomas G. Bateman, Esqrs. The tithes amount to £320, payable to the impropriators; the clerical duties of the parish are performed by the curate of an adjoining parish, who is paid by Lord Southwell. The church, a small edifice in the early English style, with a lofty square tower, was erected near the village in 1812, for which the late Board of First Fruits gave £800. There is neither glebe-house nor glebe. The R. C. parish is co-extensive with that of the Established Church; the chapel, situated in the village, was erected on the site of the ancient monastery, a small portion of which is incorporated with it. There are four pay schools, in which are about 100 boys and 50 girls. On the bank of the river, one mile from the village, are the ruins of Purt Castle, built by a branch of the Geraldine family, to command the pass of the Feale; it is strongly built, and occupies a bold situation.

ABBEYGORMAGAN, a parish, partly in the barony of Leitrim, but chiefly in that of Longford, county of Galway, and province of Connaught, 8¼ miles (W. by N.) from Eyrecourt, on the road from Banagher to Tralee; containing 2858 inhabitants. This place, called also "Monaster O'Gormagan," or "de Via Nova," derives its name from a monastery founded here for canons regular of the order of St. Augustine, and dedicated to the Blessed Virgin, by O'Gormagan, head of that sept, which at the dissolution was granted by Hen. VIII. to Ulick, first Earl of Clanricarde. The parish comprises 8865 statute acres, as applotted under the tithe act: about one-third is arable. Brooklawn is the seat of T. Blake, Esq. It is in the diocese of Clonfert; the rectory is partly appropriate to the see, the deanery, and the archdeaconry, and to the prebends of Fenore, Kilquaine and Kilteskill, in the cathedral church of St. Brandon, Clonfert, and partly united with the vicarage, which forms a portion of the union of Kiltormer. The tithes amount to £218. 15. 4½., of which £23. 1. 6½. is payable to the bishop, £4. 12. 3¾. to the dean, £13. 16. 11. to the archdeacon, £50. 15. 4½. to the prebendary of Fenore, £8. 6. 1¾. to the prebendary of Kilquaine, £10. 3. 1. to the prebendary of Kilteskill, and £108 to the incumbent. In the R. C. divisions it is the head of a union or district, comprising also the parish of Killoran, in each of which there is a chapel: that for this parish is situated at Mullagh. There are two private pay schools, in which are about 100 boys and 46 girls.

ABBEY-JERPOINT, a parish (anciently a corporate town), in the barony of Knocktopher, county of Kilkenny, and province of Leinster, 1½ mile (W. S. W.) from Thomastown; containing 367 inhabitants. This place is situated on the river Nore, and derives its name from an abbey founded here, in 1180, by Donogh O'Donoghoe, King of Ossory, for monks of the Cistertian order, whom he removed from a distant part of Ossory. It was dedicated to the Blessed Virgin, and was amply endowed by the royal founder, who was interred here in 1185; and its possessions were subsequently confirmed by John, Lord of Ireland. In 1202, Felix O'Dullany, Bishop of Ossory, was interred here, at whose tomb many miracles are said to have been wrought; and the abbey became a favourite place of sepulture with all the great families in the surrounding country. The abbot was a lord in parliament, but in 1395 obtained exemption from his attendance, on the plea that his house was subject to the abbey of Baltinglass, the abbot of which performed the parliamentary duties. The abbey continued to flourish till its dissolution in the 31st of Hen. VIII., when it was surrendered into the king's hands by Oliver Grace, the last abbot; and its possessions were subsequently granted by Philip and Mary to James, Earl of Ormonde, and his heirs male, to be held *in capite* at an annual rent of £49. 3. 9. The present ruins are very extensive, and display some fine specimens of the later Norman passing into the early English style of architecture, but are rapidly falling to decay through neglect and wanton injury: the most perfect portion is a well-proportioned, square, embattled tower. The parish is in the diocese of Ossory, and is a vicarage and one of the eighteen denominations, or reputed parishes, that constitute the union of Burnchurch: the tithes amount to £70. In the R. C. divisions it is part of the union or district of Thomastown.

ABBEYKNOCKMOY, a parish, in the barony of TYAQUIN, county of GALWAY, and province of CONNAUGHT, 7 miles (S. E.) from Tuam, on the road from Newtownbellew to Galway; containing 2866 inhabitants. This place derives its name from the abbey of Knockmoy, called by some writers Cnoc Mugha, signifying in the Irish language "the Hill of Slaughter," and by others *Monasterium de Colle Victoriæ*. It was founded here, in 1189, by Cathol O'Connor, surnamed Croove-Dearg, or "the Red Hand," King of Connaught, in fulfilment of a vow made by him previously to a battle with the English forces under Almeric de St. Lawrence, in which he obtained the victory; and was occupied by Cistertian monks from the abbey of Boyle. In 1620, its site and extensive possessions were granted by Jas. I. to Valentine Blake, Esq., and are now the property of Francis Blake Forster, Esq., of Ashfield. Near the summit of Knockroe hill is a subterraneous river, or stream, which was discovered some years since by the late Mr. Browne, of Moyne; and an opening having been made, it now supplies the neighbourhood with water: near the top of this hill are several limestone caverns. There are about 500 acres of bog in the parish. The gentlemen's seats are Moyne, the residence of M. J. Browne, Esq., a handsome mansion pleasantly situated in a fine demesne; Newtown, of Jas. Kelly, Esq.; and the Abbey, belonging to F. B. Forster, Esq. The intended railway from Dublin to the western coast is proposed to terminate here, with branches to Galway, Tuam, and the county of Mayo. Fairs are held on June 24th, Aug. 21st, and Nov. 1st. There is a constabulary police station at Moyne; and petty sessions are also held there. The parish is in the diocese of Tuam, and is a rectory and vicarage, forming part of the union of Killereran: the tithes amount to £220. In the R. C. divisions it is the head of a union or district, comprising also the parish of Monivae, and containing a chapel in each, situated at Abbey and Rye Hill; the former is a neat edifice with a steeple, recently erected on an eminence. At Briarsfield is a school, in which 70 boys and 43 girls are instructed. There are some very interesting remains of the ancient abbey, which show it to have been extensive in its dimensions and elegant in its design: several capitals of pillars beautifully sculptured lie scattered about the churchyard; the chancel is vaulted with stone, and on the north wall is the tomb of the founder, ornamented with some rude paintings in fresco, which, from some inscriptions on the walls, still legible, appear to be the work of the 13th century; they are partly defaced, and are rapidly going to decay.

ABBEYLARAGH, a parish, in the barony of GRANARD, county of LONGFORD, and province of LEINSTER, 6½ miles (N. W. by W.) from Castlepollard, on the road from Granard to Dublin; containing 3112 inhabitants, of which number, 316 are in the village. The monastery of Lerha, at this place, is said to have been founded by St. Patrick, who appointed St. Guasacht its first abbot: it was refounded for monks of the Cistertian order, and dedicated to the Blessed Virgin, in 1205, by Lord Richard Tuit, who settled here soon after the first invasion of Ireland by the English, and being killed by the fall of a tower at Athlone, was interred here in 1211. The parish is divided into two nearly equal parts by that of Granard, which intersects it from north to south; the eastern division is situated on Lough Keinaile, and the western on Lough Gownagh; both together comprise 5715 statute acres, as applotted under the tithe act. The lands are chiefly under tillage; the principal crops are wheat and oats; and there are large tracts of bog and abundance of limestone. The gentlemen's seats are Newgrove, the residence of R. J. Hinds, Esq.; Fernsboro', of A. Burrowes, Esq., situated in a finely planted demesne; and Kilrea, of H. Dopping, Esq., pleasantly seated on Lough Gownagh. The village, in 1831, contained 66 houses: a market and fairs are about to be established here by Capt. Ball, to whom the fee simple partly belongs, and who is making great improvements. Here is a station of the constabulary police. The living is a vicarage, in the diocese of Ardagh, and in the patronage of the Bishop; the rectory is impropriate in the Marquess of Westmeath and Messrs. Armstrong. The tithes amount to £260, of which £110 is payable to the Marquess of Westmeath, £45 to Messrs. Armstrong, and £105 to the vicar. The church, a neat plain edifice, was erected about thirty years since; and divine service is performed twice in the week in two school-houses, respectively situated at the extremities of the parish. There is a glebe-house, with four acres of glebe. In the R. C. divisions the western portion of the parish is included in the union or district of Columbkill; and to the eastern is united the northern part of the parish of Granard; the chapel in the village is a large and well-built edifice. There are two schools, in which 37 boys and 40 girls receive gratuitous education; and three pay schools, in which are 98 boys and 65 girls. Of the ancient monastery, a fine arch supporting one side of the conventual church, several smaller arches (all of which, except one, are blocked up), and a winding staircase still entire, are the only remaining portions.

ABBEYLEIX, a market and post-town, and a parish, partly in the barony of FASSADINING, county of KILKENNY, and partly in the barony of MARYBOROUGH-WEST, but chiefly in that of CULLINAGH, QUEEN's county, and province of LEINSTER, 7 miles (S. S. E.) from Maryborough, and 47½ miles (S. W.) from Dublin; containing 5990 inhabitants, of which number 1009 are in the town. This place, called also *Clonkyne Leix*, or *De Lege Dei*, was the site of a monastery founded about the year 600, but of which there is no further account till the year 1183, when it was refounded and dedicated to the Blessed Virgin by Conogher or Corcheger O'More, who placed in it monks of the Cistertian order from Baltinglass, in the county of Wicklow, and was himself interred within its precincts. It maintained a high degree of reputation; and the town adjoining it, which took its name from the abbey, gradually rose to be the principal place in the territory of Leix, now Queen's county. In the 5th of Elizabeth, the abbey and some of its possessions, which were large, were granted to Thomas, Earl of Ormonde, and now form part of the estate of Viscount De Vesci. The town is situated on the mail road from Dublin, through Athy, to Cashel, and contains about 140 houses, of which the greater number are neatly built: the late Lord De Vesci caused the old town to be entirely rased, and laid out the present on a more eligible site. There are two woollen manufactories; a large worsted-mill and factory has been recently established near the town, which affords employment to about 200 persons in combing, weaving, and spinning yarn; and on the river Nore, which passes near the town, is a boulting-mill. The market is on Saturday; and fairs are held on Jan. 26th, March 17th, May 5th, July 20th, Sept. 20th, and Nov. 4th. The market-house is a good building. The quarter sessions for the county are held in the town in June and December; petty sessions are held every Saturday; a court is also held by the seneschal of the manor; and here is a chief constabulary police station. The sessions-house is a commodious building, and a new bridewell has been erected.

The parish comprises 11,974 statute acres, as applotted under the tithe act: there are about 400 acres of bog and 300 of woodland; the soil is in general light and sandy, and the system of agriculture is improving. Limestone of very good quality abounds, and is quarried for building and for burning into lime; there is also a curious freestone quarry, and excellent potters' clay is found here. The gentlemen's seats are Abbey Leix, the residence of Viscount de Vesci, a spacious and handsome mansion, pleasantly situated in a demesne of about 1135 statute acres, embellished with thriving plantations and with timber of stately growth; Bellview, of W. Bell, Esq.; Thornberry, of Capt. Croker; Farmley, of — Roe, Esq.; Rathmoyle House, of E. B. Handcock, Esq.; and Oatlands, of J. Ferguson, Esq. The living is a vicarage, in the diocese of Leighlin, and in the patronage of Viscount De Vesci, who is impropriator of the rectory. The tithes amount to £507. 13. 10¼., of which £338. 9. 2¾. is payable to the impropriator, and the remainder to the vicar. The parish church, recently erected, is a very handsome building, in the later English style, with a vaulted roof of stone and an elegant spire: the old church, which has an endowment by Lord De Vesci, is not generally used. The glebe-house was built in 1810, for which the late Board of First Fruits gave £400; the glebe comprises 5 acres. In the R. C. divisions this parish is partly in the diocese of Ossory, but chiefly in that of Leighlin; the former in the union or district of Ballyragget, and the latter the head of a district, comprising also the parish of Ballyroan, and containing a chapel in each. There is a place of worship for Wesleyan Methodists. There are a parochial and an infants' school, a work school for girls, and another aided by subscription, together affording instruction to nearly 300 children: a school-house was erected for the parochial school by Lord de Vesci, at an expense of £250: there are also two pay schools. An almshouse for poor widows is maintained by Lady De Vesci; and a dispensary and an infirmary are supported in the usual way. The tomb of Malachi O'More, with an inscription, is in the gardens of Lord De Vesci, near the site of the old abbey. There is a fine chalybeate spring in the parish.

ABBEYMAHON, a parish, in the barony of IBANE and BARRYROE, county of CORK, and province of MUNSTER, 1½ mile (E. S. E.) from Timoleague; containing 3563 inhabitants. This parish is situated on the north-west side of Courtmacsherry bay, on the south coast: it formerly constituted part of the parish of Lislee, from which it was separated on the erection of an abbey by some Cistertian monks, which stood close to the shore, and was endowed by Lord Barry with 18 ploughlands, but was not entirely completed at the general suppression of monasteries, when its possessions were seized by the Crown and granted to the Boyle family, and are still the property of the Earl of Shannon. The parish comprises 3475 statute acres: the land is in general good, and under an improving system of tillage: there is a considerable extent of bog, which supplies plenty of fuel. The ordinary manures are sand and sea wrack afforded by the shore of the bay, in collecting which, during the season, numerous persons find employment. The living is an impropriate cure, in the diocese of Ross, and in the patronage of the Earl of Shannon, in whom the rectory is wholly impropriate, and who allows the curate a voluntary stipend; the tithes having merged into the rent, the parish is now considered tithe-free. There is no church; but divine service is regularly performed in a private house licensed by the bishop. In the R. C. divisions this parish is the head of a union or district, comprising also Lislee, Kilsillagh, and Donoghmore, and containing two chapels, situated respectively at Abbeymahon and Lislee. The parochial schools are principally supported by the Cork Diocesan Association; the school-house was given by C. Leslie, Esq. There are also a Sunday school and a hedge school. The ruins of the abbey consist of the walls of the church, which are tolerably entire, and a square tower mantled with ivy.

ABBEYSHRULE, or ABBEYSHRUEL, a parish, in the barony of ABBEYSHRULE, county of LONGFORD, and province of LEINSTER, 1½ mile (S. W.) from Colehill, on the road from Longford to Moyvore; containing 1233 inhabitants. It is situated on the river Inney, which divides it into two parts, connected by a stone bridge of ten arches; and derives its name from the monastery of Shrowl, or Shruel, founded here prior to the tenth century, and refounded for monks of the Cistertian order and dedicated to the Blessed Virgin, by O'Ferrall, according to Sir James Ware's conjecture, about the year 1150 or 1152. The monastery subsisted till the dissolution, when it was granted to James, Earl of Roscommon; and, in 1569, it was granted by Queen Elizabeth to Sir Robert Dillon, Chief Justice of the Common Pleas. In the village is a large flour-mill, also a station of the constabulary police, and a fair is held on the first Wednesday after Trinity. The Royal Canal passes through it, and at a short distance is carried over the river Inney by a handsome aqueduct. The parish comprises 1390 statute acres, a small portion of which is bog, but scarcely sufficient to supply the inhabitants with fuel: on the confines of the county there is a quarry of black stone. It is in the diocese of Ardagh, and is a rectory and vicarage, forming part of the union of Tashinny: the tithes amount to £87. 13. 10½. In the R. C. divisions it is part of the union or district of Carrickedmond, or Teighshinod; the chapel is situated in the village. There are two schools aided by grants from the Countess of Rosse, the rector, and the Ardagh Association, which afford instruction to 45 boys and 45 girls; and a pay school of 20 boys and 20 girls. Some remains of the ancient abbey yet exist; and there is a large square tower, to which is attached an extensive cemetery.

ABBEYSIDE, a village and suburb of the borough of DUNGARVAN, in the barony of DECIES-without-DRUM, county of WATERFORD, and province of MUNSTER, containing 1859 inhabitants. This place derives its name from the remains of an ancient abbey, which is described in the article on Dungarvan; it is situated on an inlet of the bay, and is included within the electoral boundary of the borough of Dungarvan. The R. C. chapel for the district of East Dungarvan is situated here.

ABBEYSLUNAGH.—See INNISLONNAGH.

ABBEYSTROWRY, a parish, in the Eastern Division of the barony of WEST CARBERY, county of CORK, and province of MUNSTER; containing, with part of the market and post-town of Skibbereen, 5570 inhabitants. This parish is situated near the southern coast, on the road from Cork to Baltimore, and is intersected by the river Ilen. It contains 9362 statute acres, as applotted under the tithe act; and is said to derive its name from a religious house, the ruins of which are situated close to the northern bank of the Ilen, one mile west from Skibbereen, but of the origin of which no particulars are on record. About one-third is waste land or bog, the former consisting of rocky elevations which in some parts afford tolerable pasturage; the bog is only of small extent, and peat is becoming somewhat scarce. Generally the system of agriculture is not much improved: the heavy old wooden plough is still used. The substratum is entirely of the schistus formation: there are quarries of excellent slate at Derrygoole, but not much worked; and throughout the parish is found clay-slate for building and repairing the roads. There are numerous large and handsome residences: the principal are Hollybrook, the seat of R. Becher, Esq.; Lakelands, of T. J. Hungerford, Esq.; Coronea, of Mrs. Marmion; Gortnamucalla, of H. Newman, Esq.; Carriganare, of Mrs. Evans; Laghartydawley, of A. McCarthy, Esq.; Mill House, of J. Clark, Esq.; Clover Hill, of J. Sweetnam, Esq.; Weston, of D. H. Clarke, Esq.; the glebe-house, the residence of the Rev. R. B. Townsend; Abbeyville, the seat of G. Brenham, Esq.; and Rossfort, of J. Ross, Esq.; The living is a vicarage, in the diocese of Ross, and in the patronage of J. S. Townsend, Esq., the impropriator of the rectory: the tithes amount to £647, of which £200 is payable to the impropriator, £20 to the vicar (under an appropriation grant of the late Earl of Shannon), and the remainder to the lessees of Col. Townsend. The church, situated in the town of Skibbereen, is a large edifice, in the early English style of architecture, with a lofty square tower at the east end: it was built on a new site in 1827, at an expense of £1200, of which £900 was given by the late Board of First Fruits; and the Ecclesiastical Commissioners have recently granted £180 for its repair. The glebe-house, near the town, was built in 1824, by aid of a gift of £450 and a loan of £50 from the same Board, on a glebe of fifteen acres purchased by the Board and subject to a rent of £13. 7. per annum. In the R. C. divisions this parish is united to those of Creagh and Tullagh, under the denomination of the union of Skibbereen: the chapel in that town is a spacious and handsome structure, in the Grecian style, with an elegant altar; there is also a chapel in the parish of Tullagh. The male and female parochial schools are situated near the church, and were built in 1825, at the expense of the vicar. An infants' school was built in 1835, and is supported by subscription; and there is a Sunday school for both sexes, under the superintendence of the vicar.—See SKIBBEREEN.

ABINGTON, a parish, partly in the barony of OWNEY-ARRA, county of TIPPERARY, partly in the county of the city of LIMERICK, and partly in the barony of CLANWILLIAM, but chiefly in that of OWNEY-BEG, county of LIMERICK, and province of MUNSTER, 7 miles (E. by S.) from Limerick; containing 7564 inhabitants. This place, anciently called Wotheney or Woney, attained considerable importance at a very early period, and was celebrated for a Cistertian abbey founded, according to some, in 1189, and to others, in 1205, and provided with monks from the abbey of Savignac, in France, by Theobald Fitz-Walter, Lord of Carrick, and ancestor of the Butlers, Earls of Ormonde, who was interred here in 1206. To this abbey King John made extensive grants of land in the kingdom of Limerick, with the advowsons of several parishes; and the abbot sat as a spiritual peer in the Irish House of Lords. The abbey, with all its possessions, was granted by Elizabeth, in the 5th year of her reign, to Capt. Walshe, who erected a handsome modern house near the ancient buildings; but in the war of 1641 these estates were forfeited to the Crown. There are only some small fragments remaining, situated near the present church, and also a portion of the mansion of the Walshe family; but neither are adequate to afford any idea of their original character. The parish comprises about 32,200 statute acres, of which 12,920 are in the county of Tipperary, 708 are in the liberties of the city of Limerick, and the remainder are in the county of Limerick: of its entire extent, 10,317 statute acres are applotted under the tithe act. Towards its north-eastern boundary it includes a large portion of the Sliebh Phelim mountains, which rise to a considerable height, in many parts affording good pasturage for numerous herds of young cattle and flocks of sheep. The fields are generally well fenced, and the lands are in a good state of cultivation. There are some excellent meadows, mostly attached to the dairy farms; and the farm-houses are comfortable and of neat appearance. The seats are the Glebe-House, the residence of the Very Rev. Thos. P. Le Fanu, Dean of Emly; Borroe Ville, of Dr. Wilkins; Maddebuoy House, of Capt. Wickham; Balovarane, of T. Holland, Esq.; Ash Row, of T. Evans, Esq.; Farnane, of Mrs. Costello; Lillypot, of Mrs. Bradshaw; Castle Comfort, of the Rev. T. O'Brien Costello; and the Deer-Park, the property of Lord Carbery. Fairs are held on May 29th and Aug. 31st; besides which there are fairs at Murroe on April 29th and Oct. 27th. Petty sessions are held every alternate Tuesday; and here is a station of the constabulary police. The living is a rectory, in the diocese of Emly, with the rectory and vicarage of Tuough united, by act of council in 1776, together forming the union of Abington, in the patronage of the Archbishop of Cashel: the tithes amount to £650, and of the entire benefice, to £900. The church is a neat small edifice, without tower or spire. The glebe-house is situated on a glebe of 20 acres. In the R. C. divisions this parish is the head of a district, comprising also Clonkeen and a small portion of Doone. The chapel at Murroe is a large and handsome edifice, built in 1811, and enlarged in 1836: there is another old chapel at Borroe. The parochial schools are chiefly supported by the rector; there is another school of about 60 boys and 60 girls, also three pay schools. Two handsome school-houses have been erected at Kisikerk.

ACHILL, a parish, in the barony of Burrishoole, county of Mayo, and province of Connaught, 14 miles (W.) from Newport-Pratt; containing 5277 inhabitants. This district comprehends the islands of Achill and Achillbeg, and the peninsula of Coraan Achill. The island of Achill, which is the largest off the Irish coast, is situated in the Atlantic Ocean, and is separated from the mainland by a narrow sound, of which the southern part, at a place called Pollyranney, is fordable at low water. It is bounded on the north by Blacksod and on the south by Clew bays, and is 16 miles in length and about 7 miles in breadth, forming a line of coast about 80 miles in circuit, and comprising 46,401 statute acres, chiefly the property of Sir Richard A. O'Donnell, Bart., and partly belonging to the Marquess of Sligo. The western side is mostly a precipitous range of cliffs, but the eastern is in every part well sheltered. Achill Head, a bold promontory, is situated on the south-western extremity of the island, in lat. 53° 58′ 30″ (N.), and lon. 10° 12′ 20″ (W.); and at the northern extremity is Saddle Head, at the entrance of Blacksod bay. Between this and the smaller island of Achillbeg, which is described under its own head, is a channel called Achill Hole, where vessels drawing ten or twelve feet of water may ride in safety in all states of the weather. The peninsula of Coraan Achill, also called the Hook of Achill, lies to the east of the island, and is connected with the mainland by the narrow isthmus of Pollyranney; a powerful tide runs in the sound at the narrows called the Bull's Mouth. The surface is very elevated, rising into lofty eminences, of which the highest is the hill of Coraan, 2254 feet above the level of the sea. There is but little arable land, which is chiefly in the valleys and near the shore. In addition to the mountains of Coraan and Slievemore is Menal Hill, on which is a precipice rising abruptly from the sea to the height of 700 feet. Till within the last fifteen years there were no roads in this retired district; the Sound is about a mile across, and a house has been built and a ferry boat established for the accommodation of travellers. There are several good and safe harbours; and the Fishery Board built a landing pier at this place. Keel is a coast-guard station, and is one of the six that constitute the district of Newport; and at Dugarth there is another, which is one of the six included in the district of Belmullet. The living is a rectory, in the diocese of Tuam, and in the patronage of the Archbishop: the tithes amount to £100. There is neither church, glebe-house, nor glebe: divine service is performed at the house of the Achill mission, at Dugarth, twice every Sunday, in the English and Irish languages. In the R. C. divisions this forms a separate and distinct parish: there are two places of worship, one at Kildavenet and the other at Dookenella, but no regular chapel has been built. There are schools at Dugarth, Slievemore, Keel, and Cashel, in which about 380 children receive instruction; also two pay schools, in which are 80 boys and 6 girls. There are remains of old churches, with burial-grounds attached, at Kildurnet and Slievemore; and at the former place are also the remains of an ancient castle, which originally belonged to Grace O'Malley.

ACHILLBEG, an island, in the parish of Achill, barony of Burrishoole, county of Mayo, and province of Connaught, 22 miles (W.) from Newport-Pratt: the population is returned with the parish. This island is situated on the western coast, and on the north side of the entrance of Clew bay; it is separated from the larger island of Achill by a narrow sound, which in some parts is fordable and almost dry at low water. The western shore is very wild, and, in consequence of the swells running to a great height, is unapproachable even in the calmest weather. It comprises about 200 statute acres, the property of Sir Richard A. O'Donnell, Bart.; a small portion of the land is arable, and the remainder is rocky pasture. A coast-guard station has been established here, and is one of the six stations constituting the district of Westport.

ACHONRY, a parish and the head of a diocese, in the barony of Leney, county of Sligo, and province of Connaught, 6 miles (W. S. W.) from Ballymote; containing 15,481 inhabitants. This place, anciently called *Achad*, *Achad-Conair*, and *Achad-Chaoin*, was granted about 530, by the chief of the territory of Luigny, to St. Finian, Bishop of Clonard, who founded an abbey here and placed over it his disciple St. Nathy, who was afterwards made Bishop of Achonry. In 1798, the French invaders marched from Castlebar through Tubbercurry, where a slight skirmish took place. The parish is situated on the river Moy, and on the roads from Boyle to Ballina and from Sligo to Swinford; and comprises 40,500 statute acres, of which, 19,827 are applotted under the tithe act: about 24,300 acres are arable and pasture land, and 16,200 are mountain and bog, much of which the peasantry are reclaiming. The land is generally good, and the system of husbandry is improving: there are quarries of excellent limestone and granite. The principal seats are Chaffpool, the property of J. Armstrong, Esq.; Muckalta, of Jones Irwin, Esq.; Achonry, of T. Rice, Esq.; Roadstown, of D. O'Connor, Esq.; Corsalla, of D. O'Connor, Esq.; Doornon, of H. Gray, Esq.; and Carrounaleck, of J. Gray, Esq. Petty sessions are held at Tubbercurry very Thursday. There are also weekly markets at that place and Bellaghy; and several fairs are held here and at Bellaghy and Curry, *which see*.

The DIOCESE is one of the six constituting the ecclesiastical province of Tuam: it comprehends a large portion of the county of Sligo and part of that of Mayo, and xtends about 35 miles in length and 27 in breadth, omprising by estimation a superficial area of 207,650 plantation acres, of which 113,950 are in Sligo, and 93,700 in Mayo. From about the commencement of the 7th century it was held with the see of Killala, as one bishoprick, till 1833, when they were both annexed, under the provisions of the Church Temporalities' Act 3rd of Wm. IV.), to the archiepiscopal see of Tuam. The chapter consists of a dean, precentor, archdeacon, and the three prebendaries of Ballysodere, Killaraght, and Kilmovee: there are neither minor canons nor vicars choral. The cathedral, dedicated to St. Nathy, and called the cathedral church of St. Crumnathy, Achonry, is parochial: it is kept in good repair by an assessment on the parishioners, but in future the expenses will be defrayed by the Ecclesiastical Commissioners; there is no economy fund. The diocese comprehends 25 parishes, of which three are consolidated rectories and vicarages, two appropriate rectories, and the remainder are vicarages of which the rectories are impropriate: the number of benefices is thirteen, all of which, with the dignities and prebends, are in the patronage of the Archbishop of Tuam, except the deanery, which is in the gift of the Crown; there is one perpetual cure dependent on the deanery and in the patronage of the Dean; the number of churches is eleven, and of glebe-houses, six. The see lands comprise 11,784 acres, of which 8391 are profitable land; and the glebe lands of the benefices consist of $187\frac{1}{4}$ Irish acres. The gross annual revenue of the diocese payable to the bishop is, on an average, £1481. 6. $9\frac{1}{2}$.; and the entire tithes amount to £7354. 0. 5. per annum, of which £4549. 9. $11\frac{1}{2}$. is payable to the clergy, and the remainder to lay impropriators. In the R. C. divisions this diocese includes also the parishes of Kilgarvan and Attymass (which in the Protestant church form part of the adjoining diocese of Killala), and, as originally founded, continues a distinct bishoprick, suffragan to that of Tuam, and comprising 19 parochial unions or parishes, containing 35 chapels, which are served by 19 parish priests and 18 curates or coadjutors.

The living is a rectory and vicarage, in the diocese of Achonry, with the rectory and vicarage of Cloonoghill and the rectories of Killoran and Kilvarnet united, together constituting the corps of the deanery of Achonry, which is in the patronage of the Crown. The tithes amount to £646. 3. 1.; and the gross revenue of the deanery, or union, is £920 per annum, out of which the dean allows an annual stipend of £75 to the perpetual curate of Tubbercurry. The church is a plain edifice with a tower and spire, for rebuilding which the late Board of First Fruits, in 1822, granted a loan of £1066. The glebe house was built by a gift of £100 and a loan of £1500 from the same Board: the glebe comprises 20 acres. In the R. C. divisions this parish forms the benefice of the dean, and is divided into three portions, called the Upper, Middle, and Lower Divisions; the first is Curry, in which there are two chapels, one at that place and the other at Moylough; the second is Cloonacool, in which also are two chapels, one there and the other at Tubbercurry; and the third is Mullinabriny, which has one chapel. There are schools for both sexes at Chaffpool, Tubbercurry, Achonry, and Carrowmore: the first is partly supported by J. Armstrong, Esq., who also gave the school-house. The ruins of the old church are situated near the present edifice: there are also ruins of the abbey of Court, founded by O'Hara for Franciscan friars of the third order; of an old church and burial-place at Kilcummer; and of an ancient fortified residence at Castlelough. There is a mineral spring at Ballincurry.

ACTON, a parish, in the barony of LOWER ORIOR, county of ARMAGH, and province of ULSTER, 3 miles (S. S. E.) from Tanderagee, on the old road from Newry to that place; containing 3843 inhabitants, of which number, 257 are in the village. The village was originally founded by Sir Toby Pointz, who, for his military services, obtained a grant of 500 acres of land, part of the forfeited estates of the O'Hanlons, and erected a bawn 100 feet square, a house of brick and lime for his own residence, and 24 cottages for so many English settlers, and called the place Acton, after his own native village in England. It consists of one main street, and at present contains about 50 houses indifferently built. Under the authority of an order of council, in 1789, nineteen townlands were severed from the parish of Ballymore, and erected into the parish of Acton, which comprises 4395 statute acres, and is intersected by the Newry canal. The improved system of agriculture has been extensively introduced, the lands are well drained and fenced, and the bogs have been all drained and brought into cultivation by the proprietor, Col. Close. The weaving of linen cloth, diapers, checks, and calicoes is extensively carried on by the small farmers and cottiers in the parish. The principal gentlemen's seats are Acton House, the residence of R. Conway Dobbs, Esq.; and Drominargoole, of D. Lucas, Esq. The living is a perpetual curacy, in the diocese of Armagh, and in the patronage of the Prebendary of Ballymore in the cathedral church of St. Patrick, Armagh: the income arises from a fixed stipend of £50 per annum, payable by the rector or prebendary of Ballymore, and an augmentation of £25 per annum from Primate Boulter's fund. The church, erected at Pointz Pass in 1789, is a neat edifice, in the early English style. The glebe-house, situated about half a mile from the church, is a handsome residence; and the glebe comprises 21 acres of good land. In the R. C. divisions this parish is in the union or district of Ballymore: the chapel is a small building, situated at Pointz Pass. There are two places of worship for Presbyterians in connection with the Seceding Synod, situated respectively at Tanniokee and Carrickbrack, or Tyrone's Ditches, the latter of the first class. There are four schools, of which two are aided by annual donations from Col. Close and the Rev. Mr. Darby, and in which are about 220 boys and 160 girls; also a private pay school of about 30 boys and 30 girls. The remains of a church built by Sir Toby Pointz, in 1684, under the chancel of which he lies interred, are situated in the midst of a wood, and have a very interesting appearance; a tablet is still preserved, with an inscription to his memory.

ADAM'S ISLE, an islet in the parish of CASTLEHAVEN, Eastern Division of the barony of WEST CAR-

BERY, county of CORK, and province of MUNSTER. It is situated in the harbour of Castlehaven, off Shillenragga Head.

ADAMSTOWN, or MURNEVAN, a parish, in the barony of BANTRY, county of WEXFORD, and province of LEINSTER, 6 miles (E. N. E.) from New Ross, on the road from that place, by way of Old Ross, to Enniscorthy; containing 1857 inhabitants. It comprises 7941 statute acres: the surface is diversified with gentle elevations, contrasting strikingly with the rocky hill of Carrigburn in the vicinity; the land is chiefly under an improving system of tillage; limestone for manure is brought from New Ross. Merton, the seat of T. Annesley Whitney, Esq., is in this parish. The living is a rectory, in the diocese of Ferns, to which part of Inch, called Newbawn, has been united time immemorially, together constituting the corps of the archdeaconry of Ferns, in the patronage of the Bishop: the tithes of the parish amount to £410. 13. 1., and of the benefice, to £770. 17. 9. The church, towards the erection of which the late Board of First Fruits gave £500, in 1805, is a neat edifice, in the later English style, with a square embattled tower; the Ecclesiastical Commissioners have lately granted £259 for its repair. There are two glebes, containing 13 acres, of which 10 acres are held under the Earl of Rathdown, at a rental of £6, which is paid to the master of the parochial school; and on this portion are situated the church, glebe-house, and school premises. The glebe-house was built by Archdeacon Barton, in 1803, by aid of a gift of £100 from the same Board. The parish is within the R. C. union or district of Newbawn: the chapel is a spacious and handsome edifice, with a tower 56 feet high, built by local subscription, and is one of the largest in the diocese. A parochial school-house, in which about 60 boys and 20 girls are taught, with apartments for the master, was lately built at the expense of the Earl of Rathdown and Archdeacon Barton. There are also two private pay schools, in which are about 70 children; and a Sunday school, under the superintendence of the Protestant clergyman. Here are the remains of a castle, built in 1556 by Nicholas Devereux and his wife Katherine, as appears by a Latin inscription on a shield over the gateway, which is also charged with the armorial bearings of that family: they consist of a square tower in the centre of a quadrangle surrounded by a high wall flanked with turrets at the angles. In the ancient burial-ground is a Roman cross, supposed to be of considerable antiquity.

ADARE, a post-town and parish (anciently a corporate town), partly in the barony of KENRY, and partly in the Eastern Division of UPPER CONNELLO, but chiefly in the barony of COSHMA, county of LIMERICK, and province of MUNSTER, 8 miles (S. W.) from Limerick, and 102 miles (S. W. by W.) from Dublin; containing 4913 inhabitants, of which number, 776 are in the town. The early history of this place, of which the name signifies "the ford of the oaks," is involved in great obscurity. On the arrival of the English, in the reign of Hen. II., it appears to have been distinguished as having a castle and a church. In the following century it became the property of the Fitzgeralds, of whom John, first Earl of Kildare, founded a monastery here in 1279, which he dedicated to the Holy Trinity and amply endowed, for the redemption of Christian captives. This establishment, which is now called the Black Abbey, and is situated in the town, continued to flourish till the dissolution, when, with the other religious houses subsequently founded here, it was granted by Elizabeth, in the 37th of her reign, to Sir Henry Wallop, Knt., to be held for ever in fealty, in free and common socage, at a yearly rent of £26. 17. 8., on condition of his maintaining two able horsemen on the premises. The remains consist of the tower, nave, and part of the choir of the church, which were fitted up in 1811 for a R. C. chapel by the present Earl of Dunraven; the tower, which is embattled, is in a very perfect state, and is one of the most massive in the South of Ireland; the prevailing style of architecture is the early English, which has been tolerably well preserved in its restoration. There are several extensive ruins on the north side, probably the remains of the domestic buildings. Another abbey was founded here, the remains of which, situated within the demesne of Adare Castle, on the bank of the river, are very extensive and highly interesting: they consist of the nave, choir, and south transept of the church, which, with the exception of the roof, are tolerably entire. From the intersection rises a beautiful slender square tower; in the choir are several stalls, niches, fonts and stoups of elegant design; and on the east side of the transept, in which also are niches and fonts, are two chantry chapels, or oratories, and also one on the west side. The cloisters are nearly in a perfect state, and round them are arranged the principal offices, the refectory, and various other domestic buildings; in the centre of the enclosure is a stately and venerable yew tree, but inferior in growth to that at Muckross. The prevailing style of architecture is the later English, of which these remains display some very elegant details. A Franciscan abbey was also founded on the south side of the river, by Thomas, seventh Earl of Kildare, who married Joan, daughter of the Earl of Desmond. The remains, situated close to the bridge, consist of the lofty and slender square tower, the nave, and part of the choir of the conventual church, fitted up by the Earl of Dunraven as the parochial church; the cloisters on the north side, which are perfect, having been restored by the earl (who has erected adjoining them a splendid mausoleum for his family), and in which, and over the doorway, are several shields with the arms of Kildare and Desmond alternately; the refectory, and part of the domestic buildings, which have been recently restored and appropriated as a school-house by the Countess of Dunraven: the prevailing style is the later English, which has been carefully preserved throughout.

Some time prior to the year 1310 the town appears, from ancient records, to have been incorporated, as in that year a grant of murage and customs was made by Edw. II. to "the bailiffs and good men of the town of Adare;" and in 1376 Edw. III. issued a writ to the sheriff of the county and all officers connected with the subsidies, &c., prohibiting them under heavy penalties from demanding from the provost or commonalty of Adare any services or customs, until the town, which had been then recently burned and destroyed by the "Irish enemy," should be fully rebuilt and inhabited. The castle was originally erected by the O'Donovans, rebuilt by the second Earl of Kildare in 1326, and enlarged and fortified by several of his successors. When Turlough O'Brien was ravaging this part of the country, he burned the castle, which was soon afterwards repaired by Thomas, Earl of Kildare. Gerald, a subsequent earl, having countenanced the second attempt of Perkin Warbeck, was accused of treasonable practices, and the castle and all his possessions were forfeited to the Crown; but he was restored to his estate by favour of Henry, Prince of Wales, who made him his deputy-governor of Ireland. In 1519, the earl set out from this castle on his route to London, to meet the accusations of Cardinal Wolsey; and having vindicated his innocence was, on his return to Ireland, appointed lord-deputy, and ordered to secure the person of his nephew, the Earl of Desmond, who had departed from his allegiance and joined Francis I. of France, and was taking refuge in the castle of Askeaton. The lord-deputy, on his arrival at the castle of this place, finding that the earl had retired to his strong holds, returned to Dublin; and for this neglect, in connection with other charges, he was sent to the Tower of London, where he died in confinement; and on the rebellion of his son, better known by the appellation of Silken Thomas, this castle and the family estates again escheated to the crown. During the wars in the reign of Elizabeth the castle was frequently attacked by the English forces without success; but in the summer of 1578 it was taken, after a siege of eleven days, and in the following year was garrisoned by a powerful body of English troops, under the command of Captain Carew. Sir John Desmond soon after assaulted it, but was repulsed with great loss by the garrison, and compelled to seek protection from his friend and kinsman, the Knight of Glin. In 1581 the castle was again besieged by the Earls of Desmond and Kerry, with a numerous and powerful army, who succeeded in reducing the garrison, and put every man to the sword. Upon this occasion the English forces, under Col. Zouch, marched from Cork to the relief of the garrison, but arriving too late, they attacked the confederate earls, whom they defeated with great slaughter, and retook the castle. It was again besieged in 1600, when the garrison suffered greatly, being without food for many days, and obtaining a supply of water only by excavating a subterraneous passage to the bed of the river. In 1641 the castle was seized by the insurgents and held for some time, till they were at last driven out by the Earl of Castlehaven; in 1657 it was dismantled by Cromwell's orders. The remains are of considerable extent, and the walls of great strength, but notwithstanding the efforts of its noble proprietor to preserve this interesting relic of antiquity, it is rapidly falling into decay. This was the scene of much confusion and many atrocities during the prevalence of Whiteboyism in 1786, and of Defenderism in 1793; and also under the system of the Rockites many persons were destroyed near the place, on the chapel of which were posted notices, signed, "John Rock, R. C. B., Commander-in-chief of the army in Ireland."

The ancient town of Adare was situated on the eastern bank of the river Mague, near the castle and the ancient parish church, which are now within the demesne of the Earl of Dunraven, and about half a mile distant from the present town, which is situated on the western bank of the river, over which is a fine bridge of fourteen arches. The bridge is quite level, and, though narrow, is generally admired; it was built by the fifth Earl of Kildare, and is still in a good state of preservation. The river is here broad, and from several artificial weirs appears like a succession of lakes, but beyond the bridge it becomes very shallow. The present town has the appearance of an old village whose growth has been gradual: it contains 114 houses, many of which are old and badly built; several houses have been taken down already, and others will be also removed as the leases fall in, under the improvements intended by the proprietor, Lord Dunraven, which have been already commenced by the erection of an hotel, post-office, and several other substantial houses. The mail coach from Limerick to Tralee passes daily through it. A constabulary police force has been established here; petty sessions are held fortnightly; and fairs are held on Jan. 20th, Feb. 21st, March 27th, April 27th, May 27th, Sept. 15th, Oct. 14th, and Dec. 15th, for the sale of farming stock and implements, which are well attended.

The parish comprises 10,202 statute acres, as applotted under the tithe act. The land is every where fertile, and is under an improved system of cultivation: about two-fifths are in tillage, and the remainder is rich meadow and pasture land; there is neither bog nor waste land. Black, grey, and porphyritic limestone of good quality abounds; the black is most esteemed for building, and the grey for agricultural purposes. The Maigue is navigable up to the town by means of a short canal, and there are two quays, one at the termination of the canal in the town, the other about a mile down the river, both constructed at the expense of Lord Dunraven. The surrounding scenery is finely diversified and embellished with handsome seats and highly ornamented demesnes. The principal seat is Adare Castle, the property and residence of the Earl of Dunraven: of this noble edifice, the centre and north wing only are completed; the style of architecture is that of the more enriched period of the later English, and when finished it will be one of the most splendid mansions in the country. It is built of hewn limestone found upon the estate, and is situated on the western bank of the river, in a very extensive and finely wooded demesne, commanding a beautiful view of the interesting remains of the ancient castle and of the several abbeys; and near the house still stands the venerable ash tree under which the family papers, with other things of value, were hastily hidden by Lord Dunraven's ancestor, on the approach of a party of marauders during the Revolution of 1688. Not far distant is Currah, the elegant residence of Sir Aubrey de Vere, Bart., in the centre of a wide, fertile, and undulating demesne, enriched with luxuriant woods and plantations, and embellished with a picturesque lake: the mansion is of hewn limestone, with a front of beautiful design commanding the lake; there are three entrances to the park, of which the lodge at that from Adare is the most handsome. Sir Aubrey is author of "Julian the Apostate" and other minor poems. Near Currah is Currah Bridge, the neat residence of G. Fosbery, Esq.; and within the parish is Tuagh House, the residence of the Rev. S. B. Leonard. The farm-houses, generally small, have gardens and orchards attached, and are mostly occupied by Palatines, originally German Protestants, who settled here about the year 1740, since which time they have greatly increased in numbers, but continue a distinct body. The living is a vicarage, in the diocese of Limerick, and in the patronage of John Croker, Esq.; the rectory is impropriate in the Earl of Dunraven. The tithes amount to £808. 5. 5., of which £506. 8. 6. is payable to the impropriator, and the remainder to the vicar. The church, part of the Franciscan abbey, has been already noticed: there is neither glebe nor glebe-house. In the R. C. divisions the parish is the head of a union or district, comprising also Drehidtarsna and Clounshire, and parts of two other parishes; the chapel is part of the ancient abbey of the Holy Trinity, previously noticed. The refectory of the Franciscan abbey, adjoining the church, was restored and fitted up for a school by the Countess of Dunraven, in 1815; it is a spacious apartment lighted by fifteen windows, each of which is of a design different from the rest; and, in 1825, the countess built a good residence for the master and mistress, in the same style as the refectory, with a garden attached. There are 300 children in the school, which is wholly supported by the countess. The parochial school, in which are about 80 boys and 50 girls, is supported by Lord Dunraven; and there is a private pay school of about 30 boys and 6 girls. A fever hospital and dispensary, with a house adjoining for a resident physician, has been recently erected by his lordship, and is supported in the customary manner. Adare gives the titles of Baron and Viscount to the ancient Irish family of Quin, Earls of Dunraven and Mountearl; the present Earl constantly resides here.

ADDERGOOLE, a parish, in the barony of TYRAWLEY, county of MAYO, and province of CONNAUGHT, 5 miles (S. by E.) from Crossmolina; containing 6725 inhabitants. This parish is situated on Lough Conn, by which it is bounded on the north, and on the road from Crossmolina to Castlebar: it contains within its limits the greater portion of the stupendous mountain of Nephin, which rises to a height of 2640 feet above the level of the sea. The land generally is under an improved system of tillage; there are large tracts of bog and mountain, which have been reclaimed to a great extent; and limestone abounds in the parish. Castle Hill is the seat of Major Cormick; Woodpark, beautifully situated on Lough Conn, of J. Anderson, Esq.; and Carrowkeel, of W. Bourke, Esq. A fair is held at Laherdane on the 29th of June, and at Ballagheen on the 24th of June. The parish is in the diocese of Killala; the rectory is partly appropriate to the precentorship, and partly to the vicars choral, of the cathedral of Christchurch, Dublin; the vicarage forms part of the union of Crossmolina. The tithes amount to £250, of which £13. 10. is payable to the precentor, £111. 10. to the vicars choral, and £125 to the vicar. The R. C. parish is co-extensive with that of the Established Church; the chapel is at Laherdane. There are two public schools, in which are about 130 boys and 30 girls; and six hedge schools, in which are about 160 boys and 70 girls. There are some remains of an old abbey at Addergoole, and also at Bofinan; and near Castle Hill are vestiges of an ancient castle.

ADNITH, or ATHNETT, a parish, in the barony of ELIOGARTY, county of TIPPERARY, and province of MUNSTER, 4¼ miles (S. by E.) from Templemore, on the river Suir, and on the road from Thurles to Templemore and Rathdowney; containing 253 inhabitants. It comprises 826 statute acres, and in the Down survey and county books is not noticed as a parish, but as forming a part of the parish of Rahelty, which was part of the possessions of the abbey of Woney. It is a vicarage, in the diocese of Cashel, and forms part of the union of Thurles; the rectory is impropriate in Edward Taylor, Esq. The tithes amount to £72, of which £39 is payable to the impropriator, and the remainder to the vicar. In the R. C. divisions also it is part of the union or district of Thurles.

ADREGOOLE, or ADDERGOOLE, a parish, in the barony of DUNMORE, county of GALWAY, and province of CONNAUGHT, 4 miles (W.) from Dunmore, on the river Clare, and on the road from Dunmore to Castlebar; containing 2842 inhabitants. A constabulary police force has been stationed here; and petty sessions are held every alternate week. It is a vicarage, in the diocese of Tuam, and forms part of the union of Tuam; the rectory is appropriate partly to the deanery and partly to the archdeaconry of Tuam. The tithes amount to £137. 8. 2½., of which £103. 1. 1½. is payable to the dean and archdeacon, and £34. 7. 1. to the incumbent. At Kilconly there is a chapel of ease. In the R. C. divisions the parish is the head of a union or district, comprising also that of Liskeevy; the chapel, a large slated building recently erected, is situated at Milltown. There are three pay schools, in which are about 170 boys and 60 girls.

AFFANE, a parish, in the barony of DECIES-without-DRUM, county of WATERFORD, and province of MUNSTER, 4 miles (E. by S.) from Lismore, on the mail road from Waterford, through Youghal, to Cork; containing 1879 inhabitants. This place, called anciently *Arthmean*, or *Aghmean*, was, in 1564, the scene of a battle between the Earls of Desmond and Ormonde, in which the Earl of Ormonde was defeated with the loss of 280 of his men. It is chiefly distinguished as containing Dromana, which was for a long time the chief seat of the Fitzgeralds of the Decies, who were descendants of James, the seventh Earl of Desmond, and one of whom, in 1569, was created "Baron of Dromany and Viscount Desses," which titles became extinct at his decease. His nephew and second successor in the estate entertained at this place the celebrated Sir Walter Raleigh, who introduced here a fine species of cherry, which has continued to flourish in the neighbourhood to the present day, and is still in high estimation. The old castle having been burnt down in a period of hostility, the present mansion was erected on its site, and is now the property of H. Villiers Stuart, Esq., a descendant of the original possessors. The parish is bounded on the south-west by the river Blackwater, which is here navigable; it comprises 7530 statute acres, as applotted under the tithe act; the land is in general fertile. The mansion of Mr. Stuart overhangs the Blackwater, which winds round the base of a precipitous ascent clothed with thriving plantations, and with its hanging gardens presents a picturesque and interesting feature. The other seats are Belleville Park, the residence of S. Poer, Esq., pleasantly situated amidst thriving plantations; Richmond, of Major Alcock; Mountrivers, of the Rev. G. Gumbleton, the vicar; Affane, of S. Power, Esq.; and Derriheen, of C. Maunsell, Esq. Fairs are held on May 14th, Aug. 12th, and Nov. 22nd. The living is a vicarage, in the diocese of Lismore, to which the vicarage of Aglish was episcopally united in 1817, forming the union of Affane, in the patronage of the Duke of Devonshire, in whom the rectory is impropriate. The tithes amount to £369. 4. 7., payable in moieties to the impropriator and the vicar; and the gross amount of tithe for the whole benefice is £344. 12. 3½. The church is a neat building, for the erection of which the late Board of First Fruits granted a loan of £500, in 1819. There is no glebe-house; the glebe contains only 2 roods and 20 perches. In the R. C. divisions this parish is one of the two which form the union of Modeligo; the chapel is at Boharavaughera. A school of 250 boys and 80 girls, at Carrageen, is aided by a legacy of £20 per annum from the late Mr. Magner.

AGHA, or AUGHA, a parish, in the barony of Idrone East, county of Carlow, and province of Leinster, comprising part of the market and post-town of Leighlin-bridge, and containing 1739 inhabitants. This parish is situated on the east side of the river Barrow, which is navigable to Waterford, and on the road from Carlow to Kilkenny. An abbey, called Achad-finglass, was founded here at a very early period by St. Fintan, and in 864, in which year it was plundered by the Danes, had risen into some note; its site is now unknown. The parish contains 4028 statute acres, as applotted under the tithe act, and is wholly under cultivation; the system of agriculture is improving. Limestone for burning is procured within its limits. The principal seats are Rathwade, the residence of B.B. Newton, Esq., and Steuart Lodge, of W. R. Steuart, Esq. Fairs for the sale of live stock are held on Easter-Monday, May 14th, Sept. 23rd, and Dec. 27th; and there are two at Orchard on Whit-Tuesday and Oct. 2nd. It is a vicarage, in the diocese of Leighlin, and forms part of the union of Dunleckney; the rectory is impropriate in A. Weldon, Esq. The tithes amount to £415. 7. 8¼., of which £276. 18. 5½. is payable to the impropriator, and £138. 9. 2¾. to the vicar. The church is in ruins. In the R. C. divisions it is partly in the union or district of Dunleckney, and partly in that of Old Leighlin: the chapel, situated at Newtown, is a handsome edifice lately erected. There are two schools for boys and girls; one situated at Leighlin-bridge, and the other, a large and handsome edifice lately built, near the R. C. chapel; they afford instruction to 120 boys and 230 girls. There is also a private pay school, in which are about 20 children; and a dispensary.—See Leighlin-bridge.

AGHABOE, or AUGHAVOE, a parish, in the barony of Upper Ossory, Queen's county, and province of Leinster, on the road from Dublin to Roscrea; containing, with the post-town of Burros-in-Ossory, 6196 inhabitants. This place, originally called *Achadh-Bho*, and signifying in the Irish language "the field of an ox," derived that name from the fertility of its soil and the luxuriance of its pastures. It was celebrated at a very early period as the residence of St. Canice, who, in the 6th century, founded a monastery here for the cultivation of literature and religious discipline; and so great was his reputation for learning and sanctity, that a town was soon formed around it for the reception of his numerous disciples. The town soon afterwards became the seat of a diocese, comprehending the district of Ossory, and the church of the monastery was made the cathedral of the see of Aghaboe. This see continued, under a succession of bishops, to retain its episcopal distinction till near the close of the 12th century, when Felix O'Dullany, the last bishop, was compelled, by the submission of Donchad, Prince of Ossory, to Hen. II., to remove the seat of his diocese to Kilkenny. The parish comprises 17,311 statute acres, as applotted under the tithe act. The rich and extensive vale in which it is seated lies between the mountains of Cullahill, on the south-east, and the Slieve Bloom range on the north-west, which separates the Queen's from the King's county. The soil is generally fertile, and in a tract of about 40 acres behind the church, said to have been the site of the ancient town, and afterwards of the abbey gardens, it is remarkably rich: the system of agriculture is improving, and there is a considerable tract of bog, but not sufficient to provide fuel for the use of the inhabitants. The substratum is limestone, of which there are several quarries; at Knockaruadh is found a brown slate; and at Carrig and Carrigeen are some rocks of granite. The gentlemen's seats are Ballybrophy, the residence of T. White, Esq.; Old Park, of — Roe, Esq.; Middlemount, of Capt. Moss; Carrick, of — Pilkington, Esq.; and Cuffsborough, of J. Palmer, Esq. Fairs are held at Burros eight times in the year; and petty sessions are held every alternate week there and at Cuffsborough. The living is a vicarage, in the diocese of Ossory, and in the patronage of the Rev. Thomas Carr; the rectory constitutes part of the corps of the deanery of St. Canice, Kilkenny, in the patronage of the Crown. The tithes amount to £789. 4. 7½., of which £526. 3. 1. is payable to the dean, and the remainder to the vicar. The parish church appears to be the chancel of the old cathedral, the west end having an arch of red grit-stone, now filled up with masonry; and there are foundations of walls, clearly indicating a continuance of the building towards the west; it was enlarged, or partly rebuilt, about 1818, for which purpose the late Board of First Fruits granted a loan of £500. Divine service is also performed in the court-house of Burros. The glebe-house was built by aid of a gift of £100 and a loan of £1350 from the same Board, in 1820; there are two glebes in the parish, comprising together 185 acres, which belong to the vicarage. In the R. C. divisions the parish is the head of a union or district, which comprises also the parishes of Killermagh and Boardwell, and parts of those of Kildellig and Coolkerry, and contains four chapels, three of which are at Knockrea, Ballincolla, and Burros-in-Ossory, in this parish. There are two schools, in which are about 80 boys and 50 girls, and of which one at Cuffsborough is principally supported by Jas. Grattan, Esq.; and there also eight private schools, in which are about 230 boys and 160 girls; and a Sunday school. At the distance of a few yards from the parish church are the remains of the Dominican abbey church; and at Lismore are the remains of an ancient oratory of stone, supposed to have been attached to a residence of the Fitzpatricks; adjoining it is an old burying-ground. To the north of the church is a large artificial mount, surrounded by a fosse and encircled with a wall near the summit; and at some distance from it is an ancient fortification, called the "rath of Lara," or the "moat of Monacoghlan." At Gurtneleahie is an ancient square castle; and at Ballygihin are the remains of an ancient fortress, of which there were formerly many others in the parish.—See Burros-in-Ossory.

AGHABOG, a parish, in the barony of DARTRY, county of MONAGHAN, and province of ULSTER, 1 mile (W.) from Newbliss, on the road from Clones to Ballybay; containing 7442 inhabitants. It comprises, according to the Ordnance survey, 11,543½ statute acres, of which 222½ are covered with water, and 10,484 are arable and pasture land, applotted under the tithe act; there are also from 16 to 20 acres of woodland, and about 243 of bog. The soil is a rich but shallow loam on a deep, stiff, and retentive clay, which renders it wet unless drained and manured with lime and marl, but it produces naturally an abundant herbage: the inhabitants are nearly all engaged in the linen manufacture. Within the limits of the parish are five lakes, of which that near Leysborough demesne is the largest. Drumbrain is the neat residence of T. Phillips, Esq. The living is a rectory and vicarage, in the diocese of Clogher, and in the patronage of the Bishop: the tithes amount to £331. 3. 3. The church is a plain edifice, built in 1775, for which purpose the late Board of First Fruits gave £390. There is a glebe-house, with a glebe of 40 acres. In the R. C. divisions this parish forms part of the union of Killeevan: the chapel is a neat modern building, situated on the townland of Lathnamard. At Drumkeen there is a Presbyterian meeting-house, in connection with the Seceding Synod, and of the second class. There are seven public and two private schools in the parish. James Woodwright, Esq., of Gola, bequeathed £10 per ann. for the poor.

AGHABOLOGUE, a parish, in the barony of EAST MUSKERRY, county of CORK, and province of MUNSTER, 5 miles (E. N. E.) from Macroom; containing 5054 inhabitants. It comprises 18,130 statute acres, as applotted under the tithe act, and valued at £6712 per annum. Its surface is very uneven and soil various: in the western and northern parts are several lofty hills, of which Knockgaun and Knockroer are the highest. On part of its eastern boundary, near the Dripsey, the soil is very productive; and the lands around Ahavrin are in a high state of cultivation. The state of agriculture has been much improved by the exertions of Capt. Crooke, Mr. Colthurst, and other proprietors, who have introduced a practical system of irrigation and draining, and the culture of green crops. The glen of Mullinassig abounds with beautiful and romantic scenery; both its sides are richly adorned with wood, and at its head, deeply seated amid towering rocks, is a little mill, below which the river forms a fine cascade, and a little lower falls into a beautiful lake. Numerous large and elegant houses are scattered over the parish: the principal are Clonmoyle, the seat of C. Colthurst, Esq.; Ahavrin House, of Capt. T. E. Crooke; Leeds, of F. Woodley, Esq.; Cooper's Ville, of W. Warsop Cooper, Esq.; Deelis, of R. Fuller Harnett, Esq.; Mountrivers, of N. Whiting, Esq.; Kilberehert, of R. B. Crooke, Esq.; the Cottage, of J. Pyne, Esq.; Rock Ville, of T. Radley, Esq.; Ahavrin Cottage, of the Rev. I. Smith; and Carrigadrohid, of the Rev. Pierce Green, P.P. The small demesne of Ahavrin is well planted; and on an isolated rock at its southern extremity stands a picturesque castellated tower, surmounted by a light and graceful turret. The living is a rectory and vicarage, in the diocese of Cloyne, and in the patronage of the Bishop: the tithes amount to £750. 0. 5½. The church is a small dilapidated structure, and is about to be rebuilt by the Ecclesiastical Commissioners. There is no glebe-house; but adjoining the churchyard is a glebe of five acres, and another glebe of thirty acres was purchased at Ahavrin by the late Board of First Fruits, subject to an annual rental, which being too high, the rector never took possession of it. In the R. C. divisions this parish is the head of a union or district, which comprises also the parish of Magourney and a moiety of Aghinagh, and contains two chapels, situated at Aghabologue and Magourney: the former is a large and handsome edifice, in the pointed style of architecture, with a broad, flat, castellated bell turret. The parochial school for boys and girls is built on the glebe adjoining the church, and is endowed by the rector with the entire plot of glebe: there are also two hedge schools in the parish. Near the church is a celebrated well, dedicated to St. Olan. In the churchyard is St. Olan's Cap, a square stone, six feet high, inscribed with a number of Ogham characters, perfect and legible, with several others on the base covered by the soil; and close to the doorway leading into the church is a large ancient square font of grey marble, curiously moulded at the corners.

AGHACREW, or AUGHACREW, a parish, in the barony of KILNEMANAGH, county of TIPPERARY, and province of MUNSTER, 7 miles (N. N. E.) from Tipperary, on the new line of road from that place to Nenagh; containing 390 inhabitants. It comprises only 364 statute acres, as applotted under the tithe act; and contains High Park, the residence of the Rev. John Hunt. It is in the diocese of Cashel, and the rectory is wholly appropriate to the Archbishop's mensal: the tithes amount to £40. 10. 4. There is no church: the Protestant inhabitants attend divine service at Toam, about three miles distant.

AGHACROSS.—See AHACROSS.

AGHADA, or AHADA, a parish, partly in the barony of BARRYMORE, but chiefly in that of IMOKILLY, county of CORK, and province of MUNSTER, 4 miles (S. W. by W.) from Cloyne; containing 2512 inhabitants. This parish, which includes the small fishing village of Whitegate, is situated on the south side of Cork harbour, and on the road from Cloyne to Carlisle Fort. The village of Aghada occupies an elevated site, and contains the parish church and R. C. chapel. The village of Whitegate is a small fishing port, where several boats are employed in raising sand from the harbour, which is used for manure. On the north side of the parish a neat small pier has been constructed by subscription, where a steam-boat from Cork or Cove calls every Tuesday during the summer, and where coal and sand are occasionally landed. About 50 females are employed in platting Tuscan straw for exportation, and a few in platting the crested dog's tail, or "traneen," grass found here. The parish comprises 2331 statute acres, as applotted under the tithe act: the greater part is under tillage, and nearly the whole of the remainder is pasture; there is very little waste land or bog. At Whitegate are two quarries of stone used for building. There are several handsome houses within its limits: the principal are Aghada House, the residence of J. Roche, Esq.; Whitegate House, of Mrs. Blakeney Fitzgerald; Careystown, of Mrs. Atkin; Hadwell Lodge, of J. Penrose, Esq.; Hadwell, of the Rev. Dr. Austen; Maryland House, of J. Haynes, Esq.; Rathcourcy, of J. Smith, Esq.; and the glebe-house, of the Rev. J.

Gore. There is a coast-guard station at East Ferry. The living is a rectory and vicarage, in the diocese of Cloyne; it was united in the reign of Chas. II. to the rectories and vicarages of Corkbeg, Rostellan, Inch, and Kilteskin or Titeskin, which, from the time of Bishop Crow, in the reign of Anne, were held in commendam by the Bishop of Cloyne, till the death of Dr. Brinkley in 1835, when they were disunited by the Ecclesiastical Commissioners, and made separate benefices, in the patronage of the Crown: the tithes amount to £292. 15. 6. The church, a neat structure, situated on an eminence above the harbour of Cove, was erected in 1812. The glebe-house adjoins it, and for its erection the late Board of First Fruits, in 1814, granted a loan of £1000 and a gift of £100: the glebe comprises 20 acres of profitable land. In the R. C. divisions the parish forms the head of a union or district, also called Saleen, which comprises the parishes of Aghada, Rostellan, Corkbeg, Inch, and Garranekenefeck, and contains three chapels, situated respectively in Aghada, Rostellan, and Inch; the first is a small plain edifice, built by the late John Roche, Esq., who, in 1818, founded a school. The parochial school at Farcet was founded by the late Bishop Brinkley, who endowed it with two acres of land from the glebe, and is further supported by the Marchioness of Thomond. A school at Whitegate Hill was founded in 1827, for 50 boys, by the late R. U. Fitzgerald, Esq., who endowed it with £500; and female and infants' schools have been built and are supported by his widow, Mrs. Blakeney Fitzgerald. In these schools about 100 boys and 50 girls receive instruction: there are also two private schools, in which are about 50 boys and 40 girls. In the village of Aghada are the picturesque ruins of the old church.

AGHADE, a parish, in the barony of Forth, county of Carlow, and province of Leinster, 2¾ miles (S.) from Tullow, on the river Slaney, and on the road from Tullow to Newtownbarry; containing 368 inhabitants. It comprises 1614 statute acres, as applotted under the tithe act: the land is partly arable and partly pasture; a great portion of the latter is marshy, but might be improved by draining; the state of agriculture is very good. There are quarries of limestone and of a fine species of granite for building. Ballykealy is the residence of J. J. Lecky, Esq. The living is an impropriate curacy, endowed with two-thirds of the entire tithes, to which the vicarage of Ballon was recently united, and in the diocese of Leighlin and patronage of the Bishop; the remainder of the tithes are impropriate in Lord Downes. It was episcopally united, in 1710, to the rectory of Gilbertstown and the vicarages of Ardristin and Ballon, which union was dissolved in 1830, and divided into three distinct benefices. The tithes amount to £135, of which £45 is payable to the impropriator and £90 to the incumbent; and the entire tithes of the benefice amount to £170. The church, which is pleasantly situated on rising ground above a small stream, is a plain old building in indifferent repair, and is about to be newly roofed, for which the Ecclesiastical Commissioners have lately granted £591. There is neither glebe-house nor glebe. In the R. C. divisions the parish forms part of the union of Ballon and Ratoe, or district of Gilbertstown. There is a school, in which 57 boys are taught.

AGHADERG, or AGHADERRICK, a parish, partly in the barony of Lower but chiefly in that of Upper Iveagh, county of Down, and province of Ulster, on the road from Newry to Belfast; containing, with the towns of Loughbrickland and Scarvagh, 8981 inhabitants. This place formed part of the grant made by Queen Elizabeth, in 1585, to Sir Marmaduke Whitchurch, who built a castle on the shore of Loughbrickland, which was dismantled by Cromwell's army, and remained in ruins till 1812, when it was taken down and a dwelling-house erected on its site. In 1690 William III. encamped here with his army from the 14th to the 25th of June, on his march to the Boyne: vestiges of the camp may still be traced, and Dutch coins are frequently found in the neighbourhood. The parish, according to the Ordnance survey, comprises 13,919 statute acres, of which 119¼ are covered with water, and 11,772 are applotted under the tithe act; of waste and bog there is one acre to every twenty of arable land, and the pasture land is in the proportion of one to every five acres in tillage. The land is extremely fertile, and under a highly improved system of tillage: the bog is very valuable, being estimated at 32 guineas per acre. Great quantities of clay-slate are raised here for mending the roads and for building purposes; and slate quarries have been formerly worked, but are now discontinued. The Newry Canal, in its progress to Lough Neagh, forms the western boundary of the parish and the county. There are two lakes; Loughbrickland, which forms the summit level of the canal, is skirted on its western shore by the road from Dublin to Belfast; Loughadian, near the western boundary of the parish, is rendered highly picturesque by the beautiful grounds and rich plantations of Union Lodge, the seat of W. Fivey, Esq. Among the other gentlemen's seats are Scarvagh House, the handsome residence of J. Lushington Reilly, Esq.; Loughbrickland-House, of N. C. Whyte, Esq.; Lisnagrade, of E. H. Trevor, Esq.; and Woodville House, of R. Boardman, Esq. The manufacture of linen is carried on to a considerable extent, many persons being employed at their own houses in weaving damask, diapers, drills, shirtings, and sheetings, for the Banbridge manufacturers. The living is a vicarage, in the diocese of Dromore, and in the patronage of the bishop; the rectory is united, by charter of the 7th of Jas. I., to the rectories of Seapatrick, Drumballyroney, and Tullylish, and part of those of Drumgooland and Magherally, together constituting the corps of the deanery of Dromore, in the patronage of the Crown. The tithes amount to £746. 14. 3., of which £497. 16. 2. is payable to the dean, and £248. 18. 1. to the vicar. The gross annual value of the deanery, as returned by the Commissioners on Ecclesiastical Revenues, is £1483. 19. The church is a large handsome edifice, in the early English style, erected in 1688, and a lofty square tower surmounted by an octagonal spire of hewn stone was added to it, for which the late Board of First Fruits, in 1821, granted a loan of £500. The glebe-house is a handsome residence; the Board, in 1801, gave £100 towards its erection, and also purchased a glebe of 24 acres for the vicar. The R. C. parish is co-extensive with that of the Established Church, and is the benefice of the Vicar-general; there are two chapels, one in Loughbrickland, a large and handsome edifice, and a smaller at Lisnagead. There are three places of worship for Presbyterians, one near the lake in connection with the Synod of Ulster, another at Glascar with the Seceding Synod, and a third at Scarvagh, all of the first class; one for Covenanters near Scarvagh, and one for Primitive Methodists at Loughbrickland. There are two public schools, in which are about 100 boys and 70 girls; and eleven private pay schools, in which are about 400 boys and 290 girls. Some remains of an ancient church exist in the townland of Drumsallagh; and about half a mile to the south-west of Lough-brickland are three upright stones, called "the three sisters of Greenan," apparently the remains of an ancient cromlech: they are situated on a gentle eminence, and near them is a fourth lying in a ditch. In 1826, a canoe formed out of a solid piece of oak was found in Meenan bog; and in a small earthwork near it were found several gold ornaments, earthen pots, and other relics of antiquity. At Drummillar is a vast cairn of loose stones, 60 feet high and 226 feet in circumference.—See LOUGHBRICKLAND and SCARVAGH.

AGHADOE, a parish, in the barony of MAGONIHY, county of KERRY, and province of MUNSTER; containing, with part of the town of Killarney, 4796 inhabitants. This place was formerly the head of a bishop's see, merged from time immemorial into that of Ardfert, which, with Limerick, forms the bishoprick of Limerick, Ardfert and Aghadoe. The annals of Innisfallen state that a son of O'Donoghue was buried in an abbey founded here by him, which was standing in 1231. The only traces of its ancient dignity are the ruins of its cathedral, and the archdeaconry of Aghadoe, of which it still forms the corps. The parish is situated chiefly on the road from Killarney to Milltown and Tralee, and partly on that from Killarney to Cork: it comprehends within its limits the Island of Innisfallen, and part of the lakes of Killarney, and comprises 17,720 statute acres, as applotted under the tithe act. The lands consist of a ridge of shaly rock bounding and overlooking the lake; and of a flat spreading towards the north into a wide expanse of wet bog, with shoals of gravel. On the expiration of the lease of this manor, held under its proprietor, Lord Headley, in 1826, his lordship took the estate under his own management; the farms, previously consisting of small portions of land held under middlemen by cottier tenants, were surveyed and improved upon an arrangement adapted to the mutual benefit of landlord and tenant, and let on leases of 21 years in portions varying from 100 to 200 acres, with stipulated allowances for building comfortable farm-houses, making fences and drains, and drawing the requisite quantities of lime for the improvement of the soil. Several miles of new road have been constructed, and extensive plantations made solely at his lordship's expense. The hovels formerly occupied by the cottier tenants have been superseded by good farm-houses built of stone and roofed with slate; attached to each are orchards and gardens, and the whole face of the district presents an appearance of improvement. Lord Headley has a pattern farm of considerable extent adjoining his demesne, and has erected a splendid villa in the Italian style of architecture, commanding an interesting and extensive view over the great Lower Lake of Killarney; the approach is by a small but elegant bridge across a ravine, leading from the entrance gate and lodge, which are both in a corresponding style of architecture. The plantations of Aghadoe House comprise about 100 acres, extending along the hill overlooking the lake. [For Lord Headley's other improvements see the articles on Castleisland and Glanbegh.] Grena, the seat of John O'Connell, Esq., is pleasantly situated on the river Laune, near its outlet from the lake: this river is considered capable of being made navigable from Castlemaine bay to the lake. The other seats are Lakeville, the residence of James O'Connell, Esq., so called from its proximity to the Lower Lake; Fossa Cottage, of W. B. Harding, Lord Headley's agent; Lakelands, at present unoccupied; Gurtroe, of S. Riordan, Esq.; Prospect Hall, of the Hon. T. Browne, brother of the Earl of Kenmare, commanding a fine view of the lake and its numerous islands; and, on the opposite side of the lake, Tomies, the seat of D. J. O'Sullivan, Esq. Near the town of Killarney, but within the limits of this parish, are the extensive flour-mills of Messrs. Galway and Leahy, worked by the small river Dinagh.

The living is a rectory, in the diocese of Ardfert and Aghadoe, forming the corps of the archdeaconry of Aghadoe, in the patronage of the Bishop, and partly impropriate in the Earl of Donoughmore and H. Herbert, Esq., of Muckross. The tithes, including those of "the five plough-lands of Killarney," amount to £552. 4. 7½., of which £447. 4. 7½. is payable to the archdeacon, and of the remainder, £55 is payable to the lessee of Lord Donoughmore, and £50 to H. Herbert, Esq., as abbot of Innisfallen. A glebe of 10¾ acres, and one-third of the tithes of the "Church Quarter" in the parish of Kilgarvan, with tithes in Tuosist amounting to £15. 6. 11½. late currency, belong also to the archdeacon. There is at present neither church nor glebe-house: the ancient and much used burial-ground adjoining the ruins of the cathedral of Aghadoe has been enlarged by the addition of a slip of ground given by Lord Headley. It is in contemplation to erect a church on a site to the west of the ancient cathedral, presented by Lord Headley, who has also contributed £100 towards a subscription now in progress for this purpose, and at present amounting to about £700, to which the archdeacon, who has appointed a curate, subscribed £100, and the Countess of Rosse, £50. In the R. C. divisions this parish forms part of the unions or districts of Killarney, Killorglin, and Glenflesk; the chapel for the portion of the parish in the district of Killarney is at Fossa, to the north of the lake, adjoining the plantations of Lord Headley; and at Barraduff is also a chapel for that part of the parish which is in the district of Glenflesk. In that part of the town of Killarney which is within this parish is a convent for nuns of the order of the Presentation, in which is a school of nearly 400 girls, who are gratuitously instructed by the ladies of the convent, and to the support of which the Earl of Kenmare contributes £100 per annum. There is also a school supported partly by an annual donation of £5 from his lordship, and by subscription. The venerable remains of the ancient cathedral are situated on the summit of a range of low hills, sloping gradually towards the northern shore of the great Lower Lake. Near them are the ruins of an ancient round tower, of which about 20 feet are yet standing; and at a short distance are those of an ancient castle, usually called "the Pulpit."

AGHADOWN.—See AUGHADOWN.

AGHADOWY, or AGHADOEY, a parish, in the half-barony of COLERAINE, county of LONDONDERRY, and province of ULSTER, 6 miles (S. by W.) from Coleraine, on the road from that place to Dungannon; containing 7634 inhabitants. This parish, which is bounded on the north-east by the river Bann, is $10\frac{3}{4}$ miles in length from north-west to south-east; and $4\frac{1}{2}$ miles in breadth from north-east to south-west; and, with the extra-parochial grange or liberty of Agivey, which is locally within its limits, and has since the Reformation been attached to it, comprises, according to the Ordnance survey, $18,115\frac{3}{4}$ statute acres, of which $1727\frac{3}{4}$ are in Agivey, $119\frac{1}{2}$ are covered with water, and 16,290 are applotted under the tithe act. Its western extremity is mountainous and barren, but eastward towards the river the soil is fertile; the lands are generally in a high state of cultivation, particularly in the neighbourhood of Keeley, Ballybrittan, Rushbrook, Flowerfield, and Mullamore; in the valley where the Agivey and Aghadowy waters meet, the soil is very rich. Previously to the year 1828, no wheat was grown in this parish; but since that period the system of agriculture has been greatly improved, and, in 1832, Mr. James Hemphill introduced the cultivation of mangel-wurzel and turnips, which has been attended with complete success. There are considerable tracts of bog, but they will soon be exhausted by the large quantities annually consumed in the bleach-greens; and in the western or mountainous parts are large tracts of land which, from the depth of the soil, might easily be brought into cultivation. Ironstone is found in several parts, but is more particularly plentiful in the townland of Bovagh. The greater portion of the parish formed part of the lands granted, in 1609, by Jas. I. to the Irish Society, and is now held under the Ironmongers' Company, of London, by whom, on the expiration of the present leases, the lands will be let, as far as may be practicable, on the English principle: the Mercers' Company, the Bishop of Derry, and the Rev. T. Richardson are also proprietors. There are numerous gentlemen's seats, of which the principal are Rushbrook, the residence of J. Knox, Esq.; Landmore, of Geo. Dunbar, Esq.; Flowerfield, of J. Hunter, Esq.; Flowerfield, of Mrs. Hemphill; Keeley, of Andrew Orr, Esq.; Ballydivitt, of T. Bennett, Esq.; Mullamore, of A. Barklie, Esq.; Moneycarrie, of J. M'Cleery, Esq.; Meath Park, of J. Wilson, Esq.; Bovagh, of R. Hezlett, Esq.; and Killeague, of Mrs. Wilson. Previously to 1730 the parish was for the greater part unenclosed and uncultivated; but three streams of water which intersect it attracted the attention of some spirited individuals engaged in the linen trade, which at that time was coming into notice, and had obtained the sanction of some legislative enactments for its encouragement and support. Of these, the first that settled here with a view to the introduction of that trade were Mr. J. Orr, of Ballybrittan, and Mr. J. Blair of Ballydivitt, who, in 1744, established some bleach-greens; since that time the number has greatly increased, and there are at present not less than eleven in the parish, of which ten are in full operation. The quantity of linen bleached and finished here, in 1833, amounted to 126,000 pieces, almost exclusively for the English market; they are chiefly purchased in the brown state in the markets of Coleraine, Ballymoney, Strabane, and Londonderry, and are generally known in England as "Coleraines," by which name all linens of a similar kind, wherever made, are now called, from the early celebrity which that town acquired for linens of a certain width and quality. In addition to the bleaching and finishing, Messrs. A. and G. Barklie have recently introduced the manufacture of linens, and have already 800 looms employed. Coarse kinds of earthenware, bricks, and water pipes, are manufactured in considerable quantities; and when the navigation of the river Bann is opened, there is every probability that this place will increase in importance.

The living is a rectory, in the diocese of Derry, constituting the corps of the prebend of Aghadowy in the cathedral church of that see, and in the patronage of the Bishop: the tithes amount to £500. The church, situated in a fertile vale near the centre of the parish, and rebuilt in 1797, is a small neat edifice with a handsome tower, formerly surmounted by a lofty octagonal spire, erected at the expense of the late Earl of Bristol (when bishop of Derry), but which was destroyed by lightning in 1826; the tower, being but slightly injured, was afterwards embattled and crowned with pinnacles: the Ecclesiastical Commissioners have lately granted £183 for the repair of the church. The late Board of First Fruits granted £100 towards the erection of a glebe-house, in 1789; and in 1794 the present house, called Blackheath, was built by the late Sir Harvey Bruce, Bart., as a glebe-house for the parish. It is a handsome residence; over the mantel-piece in the drawing-room is an elegant sculpture, representing Socrates discovering his pupil Alcibiades in the haunts of dissipation, which was brought from Italy by Lord Bristol, and presented to Sir H. Bruce. The glebe lands comprise 403 statute acres, exclusively of a glebe of 121 acres in Agivey; and the gross value of the prebend, as returned by His Majesty's Commissioners on Ecclesiastical Revenues, is £880 per annum. In the R. C. divisions this parish forms part of the union or district of Killowen, or Coleraine, and contains a small chapel at Mullaghinch. There are places of worship for Presbyterians of the Synod of Ulster (of the first class), Seceders in connection with the Associate Synod (of the second class), and Covenanters, situated respectively at Aghadowy, Ringsend, Ballylintagh, and Killeague. There are five schools, situated respectively at Mullaghinch, Droghead, Collins, Drumstaple, and Killeague, supported by the Ironmongers' Company; two free schools at Gorran and Callyrammer, and two schools situated at Blackheath and Ballynakelly, of which the former, for females only, is supported by the rector's lady, and the latter is aided by an annual donation from Mr. Knox. About 530 boys and 350 girls are taught in these schools; and there is a private school of about 16 boys and 20 girls. A religious establishment was founded here, in the 7th century, by St. Goarcus, as a cell to the priory or abbey founded by him at Agivey, the latter of which became a grange to the abbey of St. Mary-de-la-Fouta, or Mecasquin, in 1172. A very splendid lachrymatory or double patera of pure gold, of exquisite workmanship and in good preservation, was found at Mullaghinch in 1832, and is now in the possession of Alexander Barklie, Esq. In the townland of Crevilla is a large druidical altar, called by the country people the "Grey Stane;" and on the mountains above Rushbrook is a copious chalybeate spring, powerfully impregnated with iron and sulphur held in solution by carbonic acid gas.

AGHAGALLEN, or AUGHAGALLON, a parish, in the Upper half-barony of MASSAREENE, county of ANTRIM, and province of ULSTER, 2 miles (N. W. by N.) from Moira, on the road from that place to Antrim; containing 3574 inhabitants. It is bounded on the west by Lough Neagh, and comprises, according to the Ordnance survey, 7885 statute acres, of which 2415 acres are in the lough: the land is chiefly under an improved system of tillage; there are about 300 acres of bog, but no waste. Many of the inhabitants are engaged in weaving linen and cotton, and some in spinning. The parish is intersected by the Lagan canal from Lough Neagh to Belfast. It is a vicarage, in the diocese of Connor, and is part of the union of Magheramesk; the rectory is impropriate in the Marquess of Hertford. The tithes amount to £66. 10., of which £26. 10. is payable to the impropriator, and the remainder to the vicar. The church has long been in ruins. In the R. C. divisions it is the head of a union or district, called also the union of Ballinderry, which comprises the parishes of Aghagallen, Aghalee, Ballinderry, and Magheramesk, and contains two chapels, one of which is in this parish. The parochial school is principally supported by the vicar; and there are three private schools and a Sunday school.

AGHAGOWER.—See AUGHAGOWER.

AGHALEE, or AGHANALEE, a parish, in the Upper half-barony of MASSAREENE, county of ANTRIM, and province of ULSTER, 1 mile (N. by W.) from Moira, on the road from that place to Antrim; containing 1411 inhabitants. This place obtained the name of Soldiers'-town from its having had, during the war in 1641, a barrack in the village, in which were quartered two troops of horse and foot belonging to the royal army. The parish is bounded on the west by Lough Neagh, and comprises, according to the Ordnance survey, 2499½ statute acres: the land is fertile and in a very high state of cultivation; there is neither bog nor waste land. Limestone abounds, and great quantities are shipped off by the Lagan canal from Lough Neagh to Belfast. Broommount House is the property and residence of Stafford Gorman, Esq. Many of the working class are employed at their own houses in weaving linen and cotton for the manufacturers of Belfast. The parish is in the diocese of Dromore; the rectory is impropriate in the Marquess of Hertford; the vicarage forms part of the union of Magheramesk. The tithes amount to £100. 16., of which £21. 16. is payable to the impropriator, and the remainder to the vicar. The church of the union, situated here, is a small plain edifice in substantial repair. The glebe-house, about half a mile from the church, was built in 1826; and the glebe contains 13*a.*, 3*r.*, 9*p.*, valued at £12. 8. 6. per annum. In the R. C. divisions it forms part of the union or district of Aghagallen, or Ballinderry. The parochial school, near the church, is principally supported by the vicar; and there are two other public and two private schools. A finely wrought and flexible piece of gold, shaped like a gorget, was found near this place a few years since.

AGHALOO.—See AUGHALOO.

AGHALURCHER, a parish, partly in the barony of CLOGHER, county of TYRONE, but chiefly in that of MAGHERASTEPHENA, county of FERMANAGH, and province of ULSTER, on the mail coach road from Cavan to Enniskillen; containing, with the towns of Maguire's-bridge and Lisnaskea, 15,218 inhabitants. This parish is situated on Lough Erne, and is 17 miles in length (extending from the island of Cordillar, near Crumcastle, to Ballaghlough, within two miles of Clogher), and 5 miles in breadth. It comprises, according to the Ordnance survey, 47,015¾ statute acres (including 3157¼ covered with water), of which 4708¼ are in Tyrone, and 42,307½ in Fermanagh, and of which also, about one-fourth are pasturable mountain and bog. The system of agriculture is greatly improved, and the crops and stock are generally productive and of good quality; the peasantry, in addition to their agricultural pursuits, are employed in spinning and weaving, and are generally industrious and in comfortable circumstances. Limestone and limestone gravel abound, and there are some good quarries of freestone and of mill-stone. Slushill quarry is considered one of the best in the North of Ireland, and produces freestone of excellent quality. The only river of note is Maguire's river, which runs nearly the whole length of the parish; it is navigable, and abounds with pike, perch, trout, and eels. There are two bridges over this river, one at Maguire's-bridge (which is a flourishing market-town), and one at Ballindanaford, between that place and Lough Erne, a substantial structure of seven large arches, on the great line of road. Lough Erne, in which are seven islands included within this parish, abounds with salmon, pike, eels, perch, and bream; it is navigable from Belleek, and affords a facility of supplying the barracks of Belturbet with turf from this place. The principal seats are Cole-Brooke, the residence of Sir A. B. Brooke, Bart.; Drumgoon, of R. Graham, Esq.; Curragh, of Capt. Chartres; Nutfield, of Lady Brooke; Shebrag, of H. Gresson, Esq.; and Holybrook, of H. Leslie, Esq. The living is a rectory and vicarage, in the diocese of Clogher, and in the patronage of the Provost and Fellows of Trinity College, Dublin: the tithes amount to £831. The church, a plain building at Coletrain, for the erection of which the late Board of First Fruits, in 1762, gave £200, was, by an act of the 7th of Geo. III. (1767), constituted the parish church: the Ecclesiastical Commissioners have lately granted £142 for its repair. There is also a chapel of ease at Lisnaskea. The glebe-house, with a glebe comprising 518 statute acres, of which two-thirds are arable land, and one-third moor and bog, is situated within a mile and a half from the church; there is also another glebe, which is from 5 to 6 miles distant from either the church or chapel. The R. C. parish is co-extensive with that of the Established Church; there are two chapels, one at Maguire's-bridge, and the other called the Moate Chapel, near Lisnaskea. There are also places of worship for Presbyterians and Primitive Wesleyan Methodists at Maguire's-bridge; the former is in connection with the Synod of Ulster, and of the third class. There are seven public schools, affording also instruction to about 440 boys and 200 girls; also six Sunday schools, and ten private schools, in which latter are about 300 boys and 160 girls. Within two miles of Lisnaskea are the venerable ruins of the ancient church of Aghalurcher, said to have been built towards the close of the 9th century, and dedicated to St. Ronan. There are some remains of an old castle on the townland of Aheter, within a mile of Five-mile-town, on the Cole-Brooke estate, in which the insurgents are said to have sustained a siege in the last rebellion of the Maguires. There are two old castles in Largy deer-park; and one in the town of Brookboro', in the parish of Aghaveagh, all of which belonged to the Maguire family; and on Naan, an island in Lough Erne, are the remains of a very extensive castle, which in remote times was a formidable strong hold, surrounded on all sides by water of the lake more than a mile in breadth. There are numerous sulphureous and chalybeate springs in the parish.—See MAGUIRE'S-BRIDGE and LISNASKEA.

AGHAMACART.—See AUGHAMACART.

AGHAMORE.—See AGHAVOWER.

AGHANAGH.—See AUGHANAGH.

AGHANCON, a parish, partly in the barony of CLONLISK, but chiefly in that of BALLYBRITT, KING'S county, and province of LEINSTER, $3\frac{1}{2}$ miles (N.) from Roscrea, on the road from Parsonstown to Mountrath; containing 1378 inhabitants. It comprises 3000 statute acres, as applotted under the tithe act: the land is mostly poor, and the state of agriculture is not much improved; there is some bog, and gritstone used for building is found. The principal seats are Leap Castle, the residence of H. Darby, Esq.; and Summer Hill, of F. Freeman, Esq. The living is a rectory and vicarage, in the diocese of Killaloe, and in the patronage of the Bishop: the tithes amount to £150. The church is a neat edifice in good repair: it was built in 1786, at the joint expense of Dr. Pery, then Bishop of Limerick, and Jonathan Darby, Esq., with the aid of a gift of £390 from the late Board of First Fruits. The glebe-house was built by the late incumbent, and has been much improved and enlarged at the expense of the Rev. R. M. Kennedy, the present incumbent; the glebe comprises 15 acres. The parochial school, in which 22 boys and 17 girls are at present taught, is supported by Mr. Darby; the school-house is a good slated building near the church. There are also two private pay schools, in which are about 50 boys and 30 girls. The ruins of Ballybrit castle yet exist; and on the townland of Garryhill is a mineral spring.

AGHANLOO, or AGHANLOE, a parish, in the barony of KENAUGHT, county of LONDONDERRY, and province of ULSTER, 2 miles (N.) from Newtown-Limavady; containing 2159 inhabitants. It comprises, according to the Ordnance survey, $8251\frac{1}{4}$ statute acres, of which $50\frac{3}{4}$ acres are under water. On the plantation of Ulster in the reign of Jas. I., the lands of this parish and several others were allotted to the Haberdashers' Company, of London, who selected this as the head of their territory, and built a bawn and castle for its defence, in 1619, which was called Bally Castle, or "the Castle of the Town," and placed under the custody of Sir Robt. M'Lellan, who had a garrison of 80 able men and arms for its protection. In the war of 1641 the castle was besieged by the insurgents, headed by Capt. O. Hagan, but was bravely defended by Capt. Philips, its governor, till May in the following year, when it was relieved by the united Derry and Strabane troops, under the command of Col. Mervyn, and the assailants put to flight; but in the contentions which afterwards ensued it was destroyed, and has ever since been in ruins. The lands are of variable quality; in the district bordering on the Roe the soil is fertile, being principally composed of gravel, with a mixture of clay, and produces abundant crops of wheat, oats, &c.; towards the mountains it is a stiff marl, with a substratum of white limestone, and produces excellent crops of flax and oats. The mountain of Benyevenagh, consisting entirely of basalt, and rising to the height of 1260 feet above the level of Lough Foyle, which washes its base, affords excellent pasturage, and is cultivated on the western side nearly to its summit. Limestone abounds, and is found ranging immediately under the basalt throughout the whole length of the parish. The living is a rectory, in the diocese of Derry, and in the patronage of the Bishop: the tithes amount to £315. The church, a small neat edifice in the early English style, was erected in 1826, by aid of a grant from the late Board of First Fruits; it has a lofty square tower crowned with pinnacles, and is situated about a quarter of a mile to the south of the ruins of the old church. Divine service is also performed in two school-houses, in distant parts of the parish, alternately once every Sunday, in summer, and twice in winter. The glebe-house, nearly adjoining the church, is a handsome residence; the glebe comprises 32*a.* 1*r.* 19*p.* of excellent land. In the R. C. divisions the parish is included partly in the union or district of Magilligan, and partly in that of Newtown-Limavady. There are schools at Lisnagrib, Stradragh, and Ballycarton, in which are about 140 boys and 90 girls; and there is also a private school of about 11 boys and 7 girls. The parochial school, supported by the rector, is at present discontinued, in consequence of the erection of a new school-house now in progress at the expense of the Marquess of Waterford. A portion of the south wall of the old church is still remaining; it was destroyed by the insurgents in 1641, and was rebuilt from the produce of forfeited impropriations, by order of Wm. III. The Rev. G. V. Sampson, author of a "Map and Memoir of the County of Derry," was rector of this parish, and his statistical survey is dated from the glebe of Aghanloo.

AGHARNEY.—See AHARNEY.

AGHAVALLIN, or AGHAVALAH, a parish, in the barony of IRAGHTICONNOR, county of KERRY, and province of MUNSTER, $4\frac{1}{2}$ miles (W. S. W.) from Tarbert; containing, with the town of Ballylongford and the island of Carrigue, 5688 inhabitants. This place anciently belonged to the O'Connors of Kerry, whose principal seat, Castle Carrig-a-foile, signifying in the Irish language "the rock of the chasm," was situated on the south-west side of the inlet between the main land and the small island of Carrigue, which is encircled by the river Shannon. This castle was defended on the land side by a double wall flanked with circular and square bastions, which are still remaining, and was fortified against Queen Elizabeth by O'Connor, who placed in it a garrison under the command of Julio, an Italian officer. The castle, with the entire barony, excepting only one estate, was forfeited by the O'Connors of Kerry, in 1666, and conferred by the act of settlement upon the Provost and Fellows of Trinity College, Dublin. The parish is situated on the river Shannon, and within a mile and a half of the high road from Tralee to Limerick, and comprises 15,152 statute acres, as applotted under the tithe act. About one-third of it is good arable land, rather more than one-third of a coarser quality, and the remainder is mountain pasture and bog. Limestone for manure is brought from Askeaton by turf boats returning from Limerick; and sea manure is also extensively used. A species of brown stone of good quality is quarried for building. The principal seats are Kiletton, the residence of W. Hickey, Esq.; Litter, of G. Wren, Esq.; Rusheen, of F. Crosbie, Esq.; Rushy Park, the property of Godfrey Leonard, Esq., at present occupied by Terence O'Connor, Esq.; Ahanogran, the seat of J. O'Connor, Esq.; and Asdee, of Barry Collins, Esq. A steam-boat passes daily from Kilrush to Tarbert and Limerick, and vessels of 30 tons enter the creek for potatoes and turf, in which a considerable traffic is carried on. Dredging for oysters off the island of Carrigue, and fishing, employ several persons in the season. The living is a vicarage, in the diocese of Ardfert and Aghadoe, to which those of Liseltin, Killehenny, Galey, Murhir, Kilnaughten, Disert, Finuge, Listowel, and Knockanure are united, constituting the union of Aghavallin, in the patronage of Anthony Stoughton, Esq., in whom the rectory is impropriate. The tithes amount to £304. 12. 2., of which £152. 6. 1. is payable to the impropriator, and the remainder to the vicar: the gross amount of tithes of the union payable to the incumbent is £774. 17. 11. The church, having been condemned, is about to be rebuilt by the Ecclesiastical Commissioners. There are churches at Liseltin, Kilnaughten, and Listowel. There are several glebes in the union, but all in the possession of the impropriator. In the R. C. divisions this parish is the head of the union or district of Ballylongford, also called Tarbert, which comprises the parishes of Aghavallin and Kilnaughten: a chapel has been recently erected at Asdee, as a chapel of ease to that at Ballylongford; and there is also a chapel at Tarbert, in the parish of Kilnaughten. A large and commodious school-house has been erected at Ballylongford: but the Protestant children of the parish attend a school at Sallow Glin, the demesne of Mr. Sandes, on the border of the adjoining parish; there are six pay schools.—See Ballylongford and Carrigue.

AGHAVOWER, or AGHAMORE, a parish, in the barony of Costello, county of Mayo, and province of Connaught, 4½ miles (N.) from Ballyhaunis, on the road from that place to Swinford; containing 7062 inhabitants. St. Patrick is said to have erected a monastery here, for his disciple St. Loarn. The surface of the parish is varied with several small lakes; the lands are chiefly under tillage; there is a considerable quantity of bog, also a quarry of black marble. The gentlemen's seats are Cooge, the residence of James Dillon, Esq.; Annach, of Thomas Tyrrell, Esq.; and Oahil, of James McDonnell, Esq. Fairs are held at Ballinacostello on June 3rd, Aug. 8th, Oct. 19th, and Dec. 18th. The parish is in the diocese of Tuam, and is a rectory and vicarage, forming part of the union of Kiltullagh: the tithes amount to £158. 4. 10. The ancient church is in ruins, but the cemetery is still used. In the R. C. divisions it is part of the district of Knock; the chapel is an old thatched building. There are seven pay schools, in which are about 550 children. At Cloonfallagh there is a mineral spring.

AGHER, a parish, in the barony of Upper Deece, county of Meath, and province of Leinster, 2½ miles (S. S. W.) from Summerhill; containing 360 inhabitants. It is situated on the road from Summerhill to Edenderry, and from the latter town to Dunboyne, and contains 1900 statute acres, as applotted under the tithe act. Its surface gently undulates, and the soil consists of loam of different qualities: about one-third of the land is under tillage, and the remainder, with the exception of about 100 acres of bog, half of which is cut away and partly planted, is good grazing land. There are quarries of limestone; the Royal Canal passes near the southern extremity of the parish. Agher House, the residence of J. P. Winter, Esq., occupies a beautiful situation in a demesne of about 650 statute acres, containing some fine timber: the gardens are extensive and well laid out; and the neat appearance of the cottages on the estate manifests the proprietor's regard for the comforts of the peasantry. The living is a rectory, in the diocese of Meath, and in the patronage of the Crown: the tithes amount to £80. The church is a neat edifice, erected by voluntary contributions and a parochial rate, in 1804: it contains a window painted by Gervaise, representing Paul preaching at Athens, from the cartoons of Raphael, which was formerly in the private chapel at Dangan, in the adjoining parish, when that place was the seat of the Wellesley family. There is a glebe-house, with a glebe of 12½ acres. In the R. C. divisions this parish forms part of the union or district of Laracor, or Summerhill: the chapel is situated on the townland of Agher, on ground given by the family of Winter. The parochial school for both sexes is aided by annual donations from Mr. Winter and the rector, and there is a private pay school; also a dispensary.

AGHERN, or AHERN, a parish, in the barony of Kinnataloon, county of Cork, and province of Munster, 5 miles (E.) from Rathcormac; containing 1367 inhabitants. This parish is situated on the river Bride, over which is a bridge of three arches of stone, and on the mail car road from Rathcormac to Castle Martyr, and the direct road from Cork to Tullow. A castle was erected here, in 1389, by one of the Fitzgeralds, to command the pass of the river, on which was an ancient ford at that time of great importance: it was of great strength, and was powerfully garrisoned by the Earl of Desmond against the forces of Elizabeth. At no great distance were the castles of Duneen and Conna, both founded by the Fitzgeralds for the defence of other passes of the Bride, of which there are some picturesque remains. The parish comprises 3480 statute acres, as applotted under the tithe act, and valued at £2296 per ann.: 2855 acres are arable and pasture land; 425 are coarse land and bog, but capable of being improved; and 200 consist of waste and mountain. The soil is in general fertile, particularly in the Vale of the Bride, where the substratum is limestone; the land is principally under tillage, and the system of agriculture is rapidly improving under the exertions of Spotswood Bowles, Esq., and the Hon. and Rev. L. Tonson. Ahern House, the residence of Mr. Bowles, is pleasantly situated near the picturesque ruins of the ancient castle, and the grounds comprise some interesting and beautiful scenery. There is a constabulary police station; and petty sessions are held on the first Thursday in each month. The living is a rectory and vicarage, in the diocese of Cloyne; the rectory united from time immemorial to that of Ballynoe, and in the patronage of the Crown; and the vicarage episcopally united for many years to the entire rectory of Britway, and in the patronage of the Bishop. The tithes amount to £370. 18. 5½., which is equally divided between the rector and the vicar; and the gross tithes of the union, payable to the incumbent, amount to £456. 17. 4½. The church, situated near the bridge, at the extremity of the parish, is a neat edifice, built in 1817, for which the late Board of First Fruits granted a loan of £500. The Board also granted a gift and loan, each of £300, for the erection of the glebe-house, in 1822: the glebe comprises seven acres of profitable land. In the R. C. divisions the parish forms part of the union or district of Knockmourne, also called Ballynoe. The parochial school, in which are about 20 boys and 20 girls, is endowed with an acre of land by the Duke of Devonshire; there are also a Sunday school and two hedge schools, in which latter are about 80 boys and 40 girls.

AGHERTON, or BALLYAGHRAN, a parish, in the liberties of COLERAINE, county of LONDONDERRY, and province of ULSTER, 3 miles (N. N. W.) from Coleraine; containing, with the town of Portstewart, 2746 inhabitants. This parish occupies the whole of the promontory between the Bann and the Atlantic, comprising, according to the Ordnance survey, 3896¾ statute acres, of which 3709 are applotted under the tithe act, and valued at £2831 per annum. With the exception of about 320 acres, the whole is arable; there is a small portion of unenclosed land, part of which is light and sandy, and chiefly a rabbit warren, and part affords excellent pasture. The cultivation of wheat was introduced by Mr. Orr, in 1829, and great quantities are now annually raised. Similar success attended the cultivation of barley, potatoes, mangel-wurzel, and turnips; and the agriculture of the parish is at present in a very flourishing state. Iron-ore is found in great quantities, and might be worked to great advantage, but no works have yet been established. There are several gentlemen's seats, the principal of which are Cromore, an elegant mansion, the residence of J. Cromie, Esq., the principal proprietor in the parish, who has recently planted several acres with forest and other trees; Flowerfield, of S. Orr, Esq.; O'Hara Castle, of H. O'Hara, Esq.; Low Rock, of Miss M'Manus; and Black Rock, of T. Bennett, Esq. There are also several villas and handsome bathing lodges at Portstewart, a pleasant and well-attended watering-place. A small manufacture of linen and linen yarn is carried on, and many of the inhabitants are employed in the fisheries, particularly in the salmon fishery on the river Bann. Of late, great quantities of salmon have been taken along the whole coast, by means of a newly invented net; and the sea fishery is continued for a long time after that on the river is by law compelled to cease. The Bann, which is the only outlet from Lough Neagh, discharges itself into the Atlantic at the western point of the parish; it appears to have changed its course, and now passes close under the point of Down Hill, the celebrated mansion erected by the Earl of Bristol, when Bishop of Derry. The living is a rectory, in the diocese of Connor, united by charter of Jas. I., in 1609, to the rectory of Ardclinis, together constituting the union of Agherton, and the corps of the treasurership in the cathedral church of St. Saviour, Connor, in the patronage of the Bishop. The tithes amount to £240; and the tithes of the union, including glebe, amount to £470, constituting the gross income of the treasurership, to which no duty is annexed. The church, a small edifice, was erected in 1826, at an expense of £960, of which £100 was raised by subscription, £800 was a loan from the late Board of First Fruits, and £60 was given by John Cromie, Esq., who also paid the interest on £700 of the loan until the debt was cancelled in 1833. Divine service is also performed by the curate every Sunday in the school-house at Portstewart. The glebe-house, a handsome residence close adjoining the church, was built in 1806, for which the Board granted a gift of £250 and a loan of £500; the glebe comprises 20 acres of profitable land, valued at £80 per annum. In the R. C. divisions the parish forms part of the union or district of Coleraine. There are places of worship for Presbyterians and Wesleyan Methodists, the former in connection with the Synod of Ulster and of the third class. There is a male free school, and a female and two infants' schools are supported by Mrs. Cromie, who has built a large school-room for one of the latter: 275 children are taught in these schools; and there are four private schools, in which are about 130 children, and four Sunday schools. Mark Kerr O'Neill, Esq., in 1814, bequeathed £40 per ann. to the poor. There are some remains of the ancient castle of Mac Quillan on the glebe land adjoining the church. Near them are the gabled walls of the old church, still tolerably entire; and in the adjoining field is an extensive cave formed of uncemented walls covered with large flat stones, one of the largest and most perfect yet known in this part of the country: there are also several other caves in the parish. In the townland of Carnanee is a very fine triangular fort, called *Craig-an-Ariff*; it is defended by fosses and breastworks, and is the only fort so constructed in this part of Ireland; within the enclosure are two cairns or tumuli. Dr. Adam Clarke, whose father kept a school for several years in the old parish church, received the rudiments of his education here; and in the latter part of his life spent much of his time in the summer at Portstewart, where during his stay in 1830, he built a handsome house, and erected in the gardens of Mr. Cromie a curious astronomical and geographical dial, which is still preserved there.—See PORTSTEWART.

AGHIART, a parish, in the barony of KILLIAN, county of GALWAY, and province of CONNAUGHT, 12 miles (E. S. E.) from Tuam, on the road from that place to Ballinasloe; the population is returned with the parish of Ballinakilly. It comprises 3203 statute acres, as applotted under the tithe act: the soil is fertile, the land generally in a good state of cultivation, and the bogs are all reclaimable. Mount Bellew is the seat of M. D. Bellew, Esq., and Bellew's Grove, of Mrs. Bellew. The parish is in the diocese of Tuam, and is a rectory and vicarage, forming part of the union of Moylough: the tithes, which also include those of Ballinakilly, amount to £148. 10. 8¼. In the R. C. divisions it is the head of a union or district, also called the union of Mount Bellew, which comprises the parishes of Aghiart, Killascobe, and Moylough, and contains three chapels, situated respectively at Mount Bellew, Menlo, and Moylough; the first is a handsome slated edifice, erected at the sole expense of C. D. Bellew, Esq.

AGHNAMADLE, a parish, in the barony of UPPER ORMOND, county of TIPPERARY, and province of MUNSTER, 3½ miles (S.) from Moneygall, on the mail coach road from Limerick to Dublin; containing, with the town of Toomavara, 3577 inhabitants. This place was formerly the residence of the O'Egan family, and there are still considerable portions of the old Court of Aghnamadle remaining. The parish, which is bounded on the east by King's county, comprises 6076 statute acres, as applotted under the tithe act. The living is a rectory and vicarage, in the diocese of Killaloe, and in the patronage of the Bishop: the tithes amount to £369. 4. 7½. The church is a small edifice, situated at Toomavara. There is neither glebe nor glebe-house. In the R. C. divisions it is the head of a union or district, which comprises also the parish of Ballymackey, and is called the union of Toomavara, in which are two chapels, one at Toomavara, a large building, and one at Ballymackey. About 120 boys and 120 girls are taught in two public schools; and there are also three private schools, in which are about 170 children. A poor fund has been established here on Dr. Chalmers' plan. There are remains of Blane castle, and of the old church, near which is an oratory apparently of great antiquity; and at Ballinlough is a chalybeate spring.—See TOOMAVARA.

AGHNAMOLT.—See ANNAMULT.

AGHNAMULLEN.—See AUGHNAMULLEN.

AGHOLD, or AGH-UAILL, a parish, in the half-barony of SHILLELAGH, county of WICKLOW, and province of LEINSTER, 5 miles (E. by S.) from Tullow; containing 2977 inhabitants. This parish, which is situated on the south-western boundary of the county, comprises 7978 statute acres, as applotted under the tithe act. The state of agriculture is improving; there is a considerable quantity of mountain land and bog. The gentlemen's seats are Munny, the residence of Capt. A. A. Nickson; the Hall, of A. Haskins, Esq.; and Killenure, of A. Muntford, Esq. A constabulary police station has been established here; and petty sessions are held at Coolkenno every alternate Monday. The living is a rectory, in the diocese of Leighlin, constituting the corps of the prebend of Aghold in the cathedral church of St. Lazerian, Leighlin, and episcopally united, in 1714, to the impropriate curacies of Mullinacuff, Crecrim, and Liscoleman, which four parishes form the union of Aghold, in the patronage of the Bishop. The tithes amount to £464. 3. 3¾.; and the gross tithes of the union, payable to the incumbent, amount to £674. 9. 9¼. The church was erected in 1716, and enlarged by aid of a loan of £350 from the late Board of First Fruits, in 1814. The glebe-house was built by a gift of £100 and a loan of £1350 from the same Board; the glebe comprises 10 acres. In the R. C. divisions this parish is included in the union or district of Clonmore; the chapel is at Kilquigan. There are five schools, of which the parochial school is under the Trustees of Erasmus Smith's Charity, and another is aided by the Governors of the Foundling Hospital, and in which about 160 boys and 120 girls are taught.

AGHOUR.—See FRESHFORD.

AGHRIM.—See RATHDRUM.

AGHULTIE.—See BALLYHOOLEY.

AGIVEY, a grange, or extra-parochial district, locally in the parish of AGHADOWY, half-barony of COLERAINE, county of LONDONDERRY, and province of ULSTER, 6 miles (S. S. E.) from Coleraine; containing 938 inhabitants. This place appears to have been the site of a religious establishment, by some called a priory and by others an abbey, the foundation of which, about the beginning of the seventh century, is attributed to St. Goarcus, who afterwards founded a cell at Agha-Dubthaigh, now Aghadowy. This establishment subsequently became dependent on the abbey of St. Mary-de-la-Fonta, or Mecasquin, which was founded in the year 1172, and to which this district became a grange. There are still some slight remains of the ancient religious house, with an extensive cemetery, in which are some tombs of the ancient family of the Cannings, ancestors of the present Lord Garvagh. The liberty is situated on the western bank of the river Bann, and on the road from Newtown-Limavady to Ballymoney, which is continued over the river by a light and handsome bridge of wood, of 6 arches 203 feet in span, erected in 1834 at the joint expense of the counties of Londonderry and Antrim. It comprises, according to the Ordnance survey, 1727¾ statute acres, the whole of which is free from tithe or parochial assessment, and forms part of the estates of the Ironmongers' Company, of London. The land is fertile, but being divided into small holdings in the occupation of tenants without capital to expend on its improvement, has been greatly neglected, and no regular system of agriculture has been adopted; there is a small tract of bog, which is now nearly worked out for fuel. Potters' clay of good quality is found here in great abundance; and a considerable manufacture of coarse earthenware, bricks, and water pipes is carried on for the supply of the neighbourhood. Iron-stone is found near the Aghadowy water, and there are also some indications of coal. A fair is held on Nov. 12th, under a charter granted to the monks of Coleraine at a very early period, and is chiefly for the sale of cattle and pigs. There is neither church nor any place of worship in the district; the inhabitants attend divine service at the several places of worship in Aghadowy.

AGLISH, a parish, partly in the barony of BARRETTS, but chiefly in that of EAST MUSKERRY, county of CORK, and province of MUNSTER, 10 miles (W. by S.) from Cork; containing 2782 inhabitants. It is situated on the south bank of the river Lee, between it and the Bride, which winds pleasantly on its southern border; and contains 6701 statute acres, as applotted under the tithe act, and valued at £6527 per annum: 5000 acres are arable, 1481 are pasture, 150 are woodland, and 70 are waste land and bog. The land is generally fertile, and the state of agriculture is improving; irrigation is practised very advantageously on the grass lands. On the south side of the parish lies an extensive marsh, reclaimable at a small expense. The gentlemen's seats are Curihaly, that of H. Penrose, Esq.; Farren Lodge, of S. Penrose, jun., Esq.; Elm Park, of Valentine Barry, Esq.; and Rose-Mount, of W. Hawkes, Esq. Here is a station of the constabulary police. The living is a vicarage, in the diocese of Cork, and in the patronage of the Bishop: the rectory is partly impropriate in P. Cross, of Shandy Hall, Esq., and partly appropriate to the prebend of Kilbrogan in the cathedral church of St. Finbarr, Cork. The tithes amount to £573. 3. 11¾., of which £152. 6. 1¾. is payable to the impropriator, £379. 1. 1. to the prebendary, and £41. 16. 9. to the vicar. The church is in ruins, and until it can be rebuilt divine service will continue to be performed in a house licensed by the bishop. There is no glebe-house.

In the R. C. divisions this parish forms part of the union or district of Ovens: the chapel is a large old plain building. Besides the parochial school for boys and girls, a school in which are about 60 boys is partly supported by an annual donation of £8. 8. from Mr. Rye: there are also two other pay schools.

AGLISH, a parish, in the barony of MAGONIHY, county of KERRY, and province of MUNSTER, 4 miles (S. E.) from Milltown, on the north-east side of the river Laune, and on the road from Killarney to Milltown; containing 1901 inhabitants. It comprises 4924 statute acres, as applotted under the tithe act: the greater part of the land is of the best quality and chiefly under tillage, and the system of agriculture has been greatly improved within the last few years; there are about 100 acres of bog. At Barleymount is a quarry of excellent building stone, from which the stone was taken for Lord Headley's mansion at Aghadoe. The living is a vicarage, in the diocese of Ardfert and Aghadoe, and in the patronage of the Earl of Cork, in whom the rectory is impropriate: the tithes amount to £156. 18. 4½., one-half of which is payable to the impropriator, and the other to the vicar. The church is a neat structure, with an octagon tower on a square base, and for its erection the late Board of First Fruits gave £600, in 1822. The glebe-house was built about the same time, the Board having granted a gift of £337 and a loan of £142: the glebe comprises 14*a.* 3*r.* 1*p.* In the R. C. divisions the parish is included in the union or district of Fieries; the old chapel is disused, and a chapel was built within the last fourteen years at Ballyhar, on the border of this parish, but within the limits of the parish of Kilcredane. A school, in which are 50 boys and 6 girls, is supported by Lord Kenmare; and there is a pay school, in which are about 30 boys and 20 girls. Immediately adjoining the church are the remains of the ancient structure, completely mantled with ivy, and forming an interesting appendage.

AGLISH, or AGLISHMARTIN, a parish, in the barony of IVERK, county of KILKENNY, and province of LEINSTER, 3 miles (W.) from Waterford, on the river Suir, and on the road from Waterford to Carrick-on-Suir; containing 401 inhabitants, of which number, 142 are in the village. It comprises 2414 statute acres, and is a rectory, in the diocese of Ossory, and in the patronage of the Crown: the tithes amount to £96. 18. 5½. There is neither church nor glebe-house; the glebe consists of 2½ acres. In the R. C. divisions it is part of the union or district of Moncoin.

AGLISH, county of MAYO.—See CASTLEBAR.

AGLISH, a parish, in the barony of DECIES-within-DRUM, county of WATERFORD, and province of MUNSTER, 8 miles (W.) from Dungarvan; containing 3689 inhabitants, of which number, 302 are in the village. This parish is situated on the river Blackwater, by which it is bounded on the west, and comprises about 7800 statute acres of arable, pasture, and meadow land, 810 of woodland, 1393 of waste, and 1296 of bog and marsh, the greater portion of which affords good pasturage for cattle: of its entire extent, 6706 acres are applotted under the tithe act. Part of it is mountainous, but towards the river the soil is generally fertile. It is in the diocese of Lismore, and is a vicarage, forming part of the union of Affane; the rectory is impropriate in the Duke of Devonshire. The tithes amount to £480, of which £320 is payable to the impropriator, and the remainder to the vicar. There is a chapel at Villierstown independent of the vicarage, founded and endowed by John, Earl of Grandison; the living is a donative, in the patronage of H. V. Stuart, Esq. In the R. C. divisions the parish is the head of a union or district, which comprises also the parish of Whitechurch and part of the parish of Ardmore, and contains three chapels, situated respectively at Aglish, Ballynamileach, and Slievegrine also a friary chapel. There are two schools, supported by H. V. Stuart, Esq., in which 183 children are instructed; and five pay schools, in which are about 220 boys and 85 girls.

AGLISHCLOGHANE, or EGLISH, a parish, in the barony of LOWER ORMOND, county of TIPPERARY, and province of MUNSTER, 3 miles (N. E.) from Burris-o-kane, on the road from Roscrea to Portumna; containing 1961 inhabitants. It comprises 4474 statute acres, as applotted under the tithe act. The system of agriculture is improving, and a considerable portion of moor land, formerly waste, has been reclaimed and brought into cultivation: there is an abundance of bog. Limestone of superior quality abounds, and is quarried for building. Milford, pleasantly situated in a well-planted demesne, is the occasional residence of Ralph Smith, Esq. The living consists of a rectory, vicarage, and perpetual curacy, in the diocese of Killaloe; the vicarage, with cure of souls, forms the corps of the archdeaconry of Killaloe, with which are held, without cure, the rectories of Aglishcloghane, Lorrha, and Dorrha, episcopally united in 1785, and by act of council in 1802, and in the patronage of the Bishop; the perpetual curacy is in the patronage of the Archdeacon. The tithes amount to £161. 10. 9¼., and of the entire union, to £1013. 7. 8¾. The church of the union is at Lorrha, where is also the glebe-house of the archdeaconry; and there are two glebes, comprising together about 43 acres, situated respectively near the sites of the old churches. The church of the perpetual curacy, a neat modern building, for the erection of which the late Board of First Fruits gave £800, in 1813, is situated near the ruins of the old church, in the churchyard of which is a very old ash tree of large dimensions. The glebe-house was built by aid of a gift of £450 and a loan of £50 from the same Board, in 1816; the glebe comprises 13½ acres; and the stipend of the perpetual curate is £100 per ann., paid by the archdeacon. This is one of the three parishes which constitute the R. C. union or district of Burris o-kane: the chapel is situated in the village of Eglish. The parochial school is supported under the patronage of the perpetual curate; and there is also a school in the R. C. chapel.

AGLISHCORMICK, or LISCORMUCK, a parish, partly in the barony of COONAGH, but principally in that of CLANWILLIAM, county of LIMERICK, and province of MUNSTER, 2½ miles (W. S. W.) from Pallas-Greine, on the road to Bruff; containing 316 inhabitants. It comprises 1020¼ statute acres, as applotted under the tithe act: the land is in general of good quality. The living is a rectory and vicarage, in the diocese of Emly, and forms part of the corps of the precentorship in the cathedral church of St. Alibeus, Emly, in the patronage of the Archbishop of Cashel. The tithes amount to £138. 9. 2¾.: there is neither church, glebe-house, nor glebe. In the R. C. divisions the parish is included in the union or district of Kilteely, or Listeely. A school-house is now being erected; and there is a pay school of about 30 boys and 12 girls. There are some remains of the old parish church.

AGLISHDRINAGH, or AGLISHDRIDEEN, a parish, in the barony of ORRERY and KILMORE, county of CORK, and province of MUNSTER, 3½ miles (S. W. by W.) from Charleville, on the road from that place to Buttevant; containing 973 inhabitants. It comprises 4770 statute acres, as applotted under the tithe act, and valued at £4228 per ann.: the land under tillage is in general of good quality, but a very large portion of the parish consists chiefly of hilly pasture. The living is a rectory, in the diocese of Cloyne, and in the patronage of the Bishop: the tithes amount to £240. There is neither church, glebe-house, nor glebe. In the R. C. divisions this is one of the six parishes that constitute the union of Ballyhea, or Newtown. There are some vestiges of the ancient parish church.

AGLISHMARTIN. — See AGLISH.

AGLISHVENAN. — See BALLYMACART.

AHACROSS, or AGHACROSS, a parish, in the barony of CONDONS and CLONGIBBONS, county of CORK, and province of MUNSTER, 4 miles (W. by N.) from Mitchelstown: the population is returned with the parish of Templemolloga. This parish, which is situated on the confines of the county of Limerick, and near the road from Kildorrery to Mitchelstown, comprises only 356½ statute acres, as applotted under the tithe act, and valued at £445 per annum: it consists chiefly of mountainous pasture, and for all civil purposes has merged into the parish of Templemollogga, of which it is now regarded only as a townland. Fairs are held on Jan. 20th and Oct. 3rd, chiefly for cattle. It is a rectory, in the diocese of Cloyne, and forms part of the union of Clenore, from which it is detached by the intervention of several other parishes: the tithes amount to £30. 5. 7. The nearest church is at Marshalstown. In the R. C. divisions it is included in the union or district of Kildorrery.

AHAMPLISH, a parish, in the barony of LOWER CARBERY, county of SLIGO, and province of CONNAUGHT, 9 miles (N. N. W.) from Sligo; containing, with the villages of Ballintample and Grange, and the islands of Innismurray and Dernish (which are separately described), 7483 inhabitants. It is situated on the northwest coast, near the entrance to the bay of Sligo, and on the road from Sligo to Ballyshannon; and comprises 9286 statute acres, of which 6509 are applotted under the tithe act, and of which, also, 7311 are arable and pasture, and 1975 bog and waste. The surface is naked and unadorned, having only one small wood on the lands of Grellagh, near the river Bunduff, the estate of Viscount Palmerston, who is proprietor of the greater part of the parish. The mountain of Benbulbin extends in a direction from east to west, and separates this parish from Drumcliffe. The principal village is Grange, consisting of one street, in which are only four decent houses, and the rest are thatched cabins. Some improvement in the mode of tillage has taken place of late years, but the system of husbandry is comparatively still very deficient, and the farming implements are of a very inferior kind: limestone and turf are plentiful. A great extent of bog has been reclaimed by Lord Palmerston, who has also planted large scopes of sandy banks with bent. Considerable improvements at Mullaghmore have been made exclusively by the direction and at the expense of that nobleman, which are noticed under the head of that place. There is a salmon fishery in the river Bunduff; and at Mullaghmore several boats were formerly employed in taking turbot, cod, and other kinds of fish, which abound on this part of the coast. There are some corn-mills in the parish. The principal seats are Moneygold, the residence of J. Soden, Esq.; Streeda, of Booth Jones, Esq.; Grange, of the Rev. C. West, the incumbent; and Creenymore, of the Rev. J. McHugh, P.P. Seven fairs for live stock are held at Grange; and a fair on Feb. 1st is held at Cliffony, which has also a penny post from Sligo. Grange is both a coastguard and a constabulary police station. The living is a vicarage, in the diocese of Elphin, and in the patronage of the Bishop; the rectory is impropriate in Lord Palmerston. The tithes amount to £221. 10. 9., divided in moieties between the impropriator and the incumbent. The church is a plain edifice, built in 1813, for which the late Board of First Fruits granted a loan of £700, and Lord Palmerston contributed £100: it contains a marble monument to the Soden family, with an inscription recording the death of James Soden, in 1705, at the age of 109 years: the Ecclesiastical Commissioners have lately granted £119 for its repair. There is neither glebe nor glebe-house. The R. C. parish is co-extensive with that of the Established Church: there are two chapels, situated at Grange and Cliffony, and built at the sole expense of Lord Palmerston. Three schools are supported principally by his lordship, each of which has a house and garden, and in which are 170 boys and more than 100 girls; and in other private schools are taught more than 100 boys and 60 girls.

AHARA, otherwise AUGHARA, a parish, in the barony of ABBEYSHRUEL, county of LONGFORD, and province of LEINSTER, 4½ miles (N.E.) from Ballymahon, on the mail coach road from that place to Mullingar: the population is returned with Kilglass. It comprises 2277 statute acres, as applotted under the tithe act: the land is principally under tillage, but there is a large tract of bog. Castle-Wilder is the residence of H. Pollock, Esq. Petty sessions are held at Castle-Wilder every alternate week. It is in the diocese of Ardagh, and is part of the union of Kilglass, to which the vicarage is attached; the rectory is impropriate in Col. Fox. The tithes amount to £108. 15. 4¼., of which £37. 7. 8¼. is payable to the impropriator, and the remainder to the vicar: the glebe comprises 37 acres, valued at £59. 19. 2. per annum. In the R. C. divisions it is also united to Kilglass. There are five hedge schools, in which are 96 boys and 56 girls. The remains of the church are still visible at Ahara, and there are also ruins of the ancient castle of Ardandra.

AHARNEY, or AGHARNEY, also called LISDOWNEY, a parish, partly in the barony of UPPER OSSORY, QUEEN'S county, but chiefly in that of GALMOY, county of KILKENNY, and in the province of LEINSTER, 3 miles (S. by E.) from Durrow, on the road to Kilkenny; containing 2156 inhabitants. It comprises 6809 statute acres, as applotted under the tithe act, and valued at £4616 per ann., and is nearly equally divided between tillage and pasturage; there is plenty of limestone, used both for building and burning. At Ballyconra is an extensive flour-mill, capable of manufacturing 16,000 barrels of flour annually; and there is another at the bridge of Ballyragget, both carried on by John Mosse, Esq. Ballyconra, situated in a fine demesne on the banks of the Nore, is the ancient seat of the family of Butler, Earls of Kilkenny, and is the occasional residence of the Hon. Col. Pierce Butler. A manor court is held at Clontubrid once a month, the jurisdiction of which extends over part of this parish. The living consists of a rectory and a vicarage, in the diocese of Ossory, the former united to the rectory of Attanagh, and the latter forming part of the vicarial union of Attanagh: the tithes amount to £340, of which £226. 13. 4. is payable to the rector, and the remainder to the vicar. In the R. C. divisions this parish is the head of a district, called the union of Lisdowney, comprising the parishes of Aharney, Sheffin, Balleen, Coolcashin, and parts of Rathbeagh and Grange, and containing three chapels; that of Lisdowney, with a school-house attached, was built by subscription. About 100 boys and 100 girls are taught in the school, and about 80 boys and 40 girls in two pay schools; there is also a Sunday school. The parochial church is in ruins; on the demesne of Ballyconra, where is the burial-place of the family of Butler, are other remains; and on the opposite side of the river there is a Danish fort.

AHASCRAGH, a post-town and parish, partly in the baronies of KILCONNELL and KILLIAN, but chiefly in that of CLONMACNOON, county of GALWAY, and province of CONNAUGHT, 30 miles (E. N. E.) from Galway, and 78 miles (W.) from Dublin, on the road from Ballinasloe to Castlebar; containing 5205 inhabitants, of which number, 851 are in the town, which contains about 120 houses. It is situated in a fine corn country and there are some large oatmeal-mills. Fairs are held on Easter-Monday, Wednesday after Trinity, Aug. 25th, and Nov. 24th. Petty sessions are held fortnightly and here is a station of the constabulary police. The parish comprises 10,692 statute acres: there are quarries of excellent limestone, also a large tract of bog, which might be reclaimed. A branch of the Grand Canal approaches within six miles, and a drawback on the carriage of goods is allowed by the company. The principal seats are Castle Ffrench, the residence of Lord Ffrench; Weston, of the Very Rev. Jas. Mahon, Dean of Dromore; Crigane, of S. Masters, Esq.; and Castlegar, of Sir Ross Mahon, Bart. Part of the demesne of Clonbrock, the seat of Lord Clonbrock, is also within the parish. The living is a rectory, in the diocese of Elphin, and in the alternate patronage of the Crown and the Bishop: the tithes amount to £323. 1. 6½. The church is a neat building, erected at an expense of £1500, of which £1000 was granted on loan by the late Board of First Fruits, in 1814. The glebe-house was built in 1804, and the same Board gave £100 towards defraying the expense: the glebe comprises 24 acres. The R. C. parish is co-extensive with that of the Established Church: the chapel is a large building, with a burial-ground annexed. In addition to the parochial school, there is one for boys and girls, supported by Lord Clonbrock, by whom a few of the children are clothed; and a male and female school are also supported by Sir Ross Mahon. About 170 boys and 90 girls are instructed in these schools; and there are also five hedge schools, in which are about 200 boys and 70 girls.

AHINAGH, or AGHINAGH, a parish, in the barony of EAST MUSKERRY, county of CORK, and province of MUNSTER, 4 miles (S. E.) from Macroom; containing 2442 inhabitants. This parish, anciently called *Omai*, contains the village of Carrigadrohid, which has a penny post, and through which the mail coach from Cork to Tralee passes. It comprises 9080 statute acres, as applotted under the tithe act, and valued at £5321 per annum: the land is generally good and is well sheltered, particularly towards its southern boundary; about four-fifths are under a good system of cultivation; the remainder is rough pasture and bog. There are stone quarries, which are worked only for building. The river Lee is crossed at the village of Carrigadrohid by an old bridge, built by order of Cromwell, which connects the parish with the pretty modern village of Killinardrish. The banks of the river are here adorned with several elegant houses. Oakgrove, the residence of John Bowen, Esq., is a handsome modern mansion, situated in a richly ornamented demesne containing some of the finest oaks in the county. Coolalta, the residence of W. Furlong, Esq., M. D., is a pretty villa in the midst of some picturesque ground stastefully planted; and contiguous to the church is the glebe-house, a handsome edifice, the residence of the Rev. S. Gerrard Fairtlough. Besides the oak woods of Oakgrove, there are flourishing plantations of young timber at Carrigadrohid and Umery, the former of which is very extensive. The living is a rectory and vicarage, in the diocese of Cloyne, and in the patronage of the Bishop: the tithes amount to £738. 3. 11. The church is a small plain edifice with a square tower, erected in 1791, for which the late Board of First Fruits gave £500. The glebe-house was built in 1814, by a gift of £100 and a loan of £1500 from the same Board: the glebe comprises 24 acres. In the R. C. divisions one-half of this parish is comprised within the union or district of Aghabologue, which has a chapel at Rusheen, and the other is united to Macroom, for which there is a chapel at Caum: it is also in contemplation to erect a third chapel, by subscription, on ground given by Mr. Bowen. The parochial school for boys and girls is supported by contributions from resident gentlemen, and a neat building has been erected as a school-house: there are also an infants' school, a Sunday school, and a private pay school. The principal remains of antiquity are the ruined castles of Carrigadrohid and Mashanaglass; the former, according to some writers, built by a branch of the Macarthy family, and by others ascribed to the family of O'Leary: it is a massive structure, situated on a rock in the river Lee, with some modern additions, including an entrance opened from the bridge. The owner of the lands of Carrigadrohid has a patent for a fair, which is now held in a field in the parish of Cannaway. The castle of Mashanaglass is a lofty square tower of gloomy aspect, built by the Mac Swineys. Smith, in his history of Cork, mentions a letter addressed by Jas. I. to the Lord-deputy Sydney, directing him to accept the surrender of the lands of Owen Mac Swiney, otherwise "Hoggy of Mashanaglass." A little to the north of this ruin is *Glen Laum*, "the crooked glen," now called Umery, through which the mail coach road is carried: it is enclosed by precipitous rocky heights covered with valuable plantations, the property of Sir Thomas Deane, Knt., of Dundanion Castle, near Cork. On the glebe are the remains of a cromlech;

and several single stones, called "Gcllanes," are standing in the parish. Raths or Danish forts are numerous, and there are several artificial caves.

AHOGHILL, a parish, partly in the barony of LOWER ANTRIM, partly in that of KILCONWAY, partly in that of UPPER TOOME, but chiefly in the barony of LOWER TOOME, county of ANTRIM, and province of ULSTER, 4 miles (E. S. E.) from Portglenone; containing 14,920 inhabitants, of which number, 421 are in the village. The district around this place appears, from the numerous remains of forts and the great number of *tumuli* and human bones found, to have been the scene of much early warfare. During the war of 1688, the ford of the river Bann at Portglenone was regarded as a very important pass between the counties of Antrim and Derry; and Sir I. Magill and Capt. Edmonston were, in 1689, despatched to defend it against the Irish army on their march towards the Bann, in order to enter the county of Derry. In 1760, when the French under Thurot made a descent on Carrickfergus, the inhabitants of this place rose in a body for the defence of the country: a well-appointed force marched to Belfast, numerous parties proceeded to Carrickfergus, while others patroled the country nightly, and these irregular levies had a powerful effect in repelling the invaders. About the year 1771, an organised system of outrage pervaded the whole of this parish, in common with other parts of the county: the persons who thus combined, called themselves "Steel Men," or "Hearts of Steel," and executed their revenge by houghing cattle and perpetrating other outrages; they attacked the house of Paul M'Larnon, Esq., who, in defending himself, was shot. In 1778, a corps was raised by John Dickey, Esq., of Cullybackey, and called the Cullybackey Volunteers; a similar corps was embodied the following year by T. Hill, Esq., of Drumra, called the Portglenone Volunteers, to which was afterwards added a second corps by — Simpson, Esq.; and a corps, called the Ahoghill Volunteers, was raised by Alexander M'Manus, of Mount Davies.

The parish, anciently called *Maghrahoghill*, of which the derivation is unknown, is bounded by the river Bann, which flows out of Lough Neagh in a direction from south to north, and is intersected by the river Maine, which flows into that lough in a direction from north to south. It was formerly more extensive than at present, having included Portglenone, which, in 1825, was, together with 21 townlands, severed from it and formed into a distinct parish. According to the Ordnance survey, including Portglenone, it comprises 35,419 statute acres, of which 14,954 are applotted under the tithe act, and 145¾ are covered with water. The system of agriculture is in a very indifferent state; there is a considerable quantity of waste land, with some extensive bogs, which might be drained. The surface is hilly, and many of the eminences being planted, render the valley through which the Maine flows beautiful and interesting. The village is neatly built, and the neighbourhood, is enlivened with several gentlemen's seats. The castle of Galgorm, a seat of the Earl of Mountcashel, is a handsome square embattled edifice, erected in the 17th century by the celebrated Dr. Colville; the rooms are wainscoted with Irish oak from the woods of Largy and Grange. The other principal seats in the parish and neighbourhood are Mount Davies, the residence of Alex. M'Manus, Esq.; Low Park, of J. Dickey, Esq.; Ballybollan, the property of Ambrose O'Rourke, Esq.; Lisnafillen, of W. Gihon, Esq., of Ballymena; Fenaghy, the residence of S. Cuningham, Esq.; Leighnmore, the property of J. Dickey, Esq.; and Drumona, built by Alex. Brown, Esq. The linen trade appears to have been introduced here by the ancestor of John Dickey, Esq., of Low Park, and now in its several branches affords employment to the greater number of the inhabitants. There are several bleach-greens on the river Maine: and a good monthly market is held in the village, for the sale of linens, on the Friday before Ballymony market. Fairs for cattle and pigs are held on June 4th, Aug. 26th, Oct. 12th, and Dec. 5th. The manorial court of Fortescue, anciently Straboy, has jurisdiction extending to debts not exceeding £5 late currency; and the manorial court of Cashel is held monthly at Portglenone, for the recovery of debts to the same amount. Two courts leet are held annually; and petty sessions are held every alternate Friday.

The living is a rectory, in the diocese of Connor, and in the patronage of the Crown: the tithes amount to £1015. 7. 8. The church is an ancient edifice; the walls have within the last few years been raised and covered with a new roof. The glebe-house was built by a gift of £100 and a loan of £1500 from the late Board of First Fruits, in 1815; the glebe comprises 138½ acres. In the R. C. divisions this is the head of a union or district, comprising also Portglenone, and containing three chapels, one about half a mile from the village, another at Aughnahoy, and a third at Portglenone. There are places of worship for Presbyterians in connection with the Synod of Ulster at Ahoghill and Cullybackey, both of the third class: in the former are also two places of worship for Seceders of the Ahoghill Presbytery, each of the second class, and in the latter is one for Covenanters; there is also a place of worship for Independents, and a Moravian meeting-house at Gracehill. There are 15 schools in different parts of the parish, in which are about 400 boys and 330 girls; and there are also 12 private schools, in which are about 300 boys and 150 girls; and 16 Sunday schools. John Guy, in 1813, bequeathed £12 per ann. to the Moravian establishment, which sum is now, by the death of his adopted heir, augmented to £45 per annum. There are some remains of Rory Oge Mac Quillan's castle of Straboy, and some tumuli at Moyessit.

·ALISH.—See RATHKYRAN.

ALLEN, Isle of.—See RATHERNON.

ALL SAINTS, a parish, in the barony of RAPHOE, county of DONEGAL, and province of ULSTER, 6 miles (W.) from Londonderry, on Lough Swilly, and on the road from Londonderry to Letterkenny; containing 4066 inhabitants. It consists of several townlands formerly in the parish of Taughboyne, from which they were separated and formed into a distinct parish, containing, according to the Ordnance survey, 9673¾ statute acres, of which 102 are covered with water. The land is generally good and in a profitable state of cultivation; the system of agriculture is improving; the bog affords a valuable supply of fuel, and there are some good quarries of stone for building. Castle Forward, the property of the Earl of Wicklow, is at present in the occupation of W. Marshall, Esq. A distillery and a brewery are carried on to some extent; and petty sessions are held on the first Friday in every month. The living is a perpetual curacy, in the diocese of Raphoe, and in the patronage of the Incumbent of Taughboyne. The church, a neat small edifice, was formerly a chapel of ease to the church of Taughboyne. In the R. C. divisions this parish is the head of a union or district, called the union of Lagan, and comprising also the parishes of Taughboyne, Killea, and Raymochy; there are three chapels, situated respectively at Newtown-Conyngham (in All Saints), Raymochy, and Taughboyne. There are two places of worship for Presbyterians, one in connection with the Synod of Ulster, of the third class; and the other with the Seceding Synod. The parochial school is aided from Robinson's fund; a school of 28 girls is supported by Lady Wicklow, and a school is supported by subscription; there are also three pay schools, in which are about 90 boys and 20 girls, and a Sunday school. The interest of £200, bequeathed by a respectable farmer, is annually divided among the poor.

ALL SAINTS, an island, in the parish of Cashel, barony of Rathcline, county of Longford, and province of Leinster; the population is returned with the parish. This island, which is situated in Lough Ree, comprises only 291 statute acres, divided into several small farms, and contains eight houses.—See Cashel.

ALMORITIA, or MORANSTOWN, a parish, in the barony of Rathconrath, county of Westmeath, and province of Leinster, 4½ miles (N. E.) from Ballymore, on the road from Mullingar to Athlone; containing 675 inhabitants. This parish, which is also called Ballymoran, comprises 2330 statute acres, as applotted under the tithe act, and is principally under an improving system of tillage: there is but an inconsiderable portion of bog; limestone of very good quality abounds, and is quarried chiefly for building. The Royal Canal passes within four miles of the parish, affording great advantages to this district, which is wholly agricultural. The principal seats are Glencarry, the residence of J. H. Kelly, Esq., surrounded with flourishing plantations; Darlington Lodge, of A. McDonnell, Esq.; and Halston, of H. Boyd Gamble, Esq. On a stream which runs from Ballinacurra lake, through the parish, into the river Inney, is a large flour-mill. The living is a rectory, in the diocese of Meath, to which that of Piercetown was united episcopally in 1791, and in the patronage of the Bishop: the tithes of the parish amount to £70, and of the entire benefice to £165. The church was rebuilt in 1816, for which the late Board of First Fruits granted a loan of £600, obtained by the bishop, through the representation of Mr. Kelly, of Glencarry. The glebe-house was built in 1820, the Board having granted a loan of £600 and a gift of £200. The glebe comprises 28 acres, valued at £56 per annum; and there is also a glebe of 12½ acres at Piercetown, valued at £24. 10. per annum. In the R. C. divisions the parish forms part of the union or district of Rathconrath, also called Miltown. There is a pay school, in which are about twelve children.

AMBROSETOWN, a parish, in the barony of Bargy, county of Wexford, and province of Leinster, 6 miles (S. by W.) from Taghmon; containing, with the extra-parochial townlands of Ballingeal and Rochestown, 1045 inhabitants. This parish comprises 2274 statute acres, as applotted under the tithe act: it is partly under tillage and partly in pasture, and contains an entirely exhausted bog, part of which has been reclaimed and is now under cultivation, and the remainder is grazed. It is a rectory, in the diocese of Ferns, and fomrs part of the union of Duncormuck: the tithes amount to £138. 9. 2¾. In the R. C. divisions it is partly within the union or district of Rathangan, or Duncormuck, but chiefly in that of Carrig. A school, in which are about 50 boys and 30 girls, is aided by Mr. Morgan, of Johnstown; and there is a private school of about 20 children.

ANACLOAN, or ANNAGHLONE, a parish, in the barony of Upper Iveagh, county of Down, and province of Ulster, 3 miles (S. E. by E.) from Banbridge, on the river Bann, and on the road from Banbridge to Castlewellan, containing 3426 inhabitants. It comprises, according to the Ordnance survey, 6544½ statute acres: the lands are fertile and in a high state of cultivation; there is no waste land, and only about 200 acres of bog, which is daily becoming more scarce and valuable. The living is a rectory, in the diocese of Dromore, and in the patronage of the Bishop: the tithes amount to £188. 3. 8. The church is a neat small edifice in good repair. The glebe-house was built by aid of a gift of £200 and a loan of £600 from the late Board of First Fruits, in 1818: the glebe comprises 204 acres. In the R. C. divisions the parish is the head of a union or district, comprising also that of Drumballyroney, and containing a chapel in each parish. There are places of worship for Presbyterians in connection with the Synod of Ulster and the Seceding Synod; the former of the third, and the latter of the second class. There are three schools, affording instruction to about 190 boys and 100 girls; also four private schools, in which are about 90 boys and 60 girls. Near the church is Tanvally fort, one of the largest and most perfect in this part of the country, and within sight of it are many others of smaller dimensions.

ANADORN, a village, in the parish of Lougham Island, barony of Kinelearty, county of Down, and province of Ulster, 3 miles (N.) from Clough; containing 93 inhabitants. This place, with an extensive surrounding district, formerly belonged to the ancient and powerful family of the McCartans, who had a castle here, situated on an eminence, or mound, now called Castle-hill; but McCartan having joined in the rebellion of the Earl of Tyrone, his estates became forfeited to the crown. The village is situated on the road from Ballynahinch and Hillsborough to Downpatrick: it appears to have been much neglected, but it has been recently purchased by Col. Forde, who has already commenced a series of improvements. Fairs are held on May 14th and Nov. 8th.—See Lougham Island.

ANAHILT, a parish, partly in the barony of Kinelearty, but chiefly in that of Lower Iveagh, county of Down, and province of Ulster, 3 miles (E. S. E.) from Hillsborough; containing 3755 inhabitants. This parish is intersected by numerous roads, of which the principal are those leading respectively from Hillsborough and Dromore, and from Lisburn to Downpatrick, and from Belfast and Lisburn to Rathfriland. It comprises, according to the Ordnance survey, 6777¼ statute acres, of which 6069 are in Lower Iveagh, and 708½ in Kinelearty, and is principally arable and pasture land, but mostly under tillage: 6202 acres are applotted under the tithe act. The lands are in a state of excellent cultivation: under-draining is well understood and extensively practised. In the townland of Cluntogh there is a fine slate quarry. The inhabitants combine with agricultural pursuits the weaving of linen and cotton for the manufacturers of the neighbouring towns, and the women and girls are employed in spinning. A penny post has been lately established from Hillsborough. The principal seats are Larchfield, the handsome mansion and extensive demesne of W. Mussenden, Esq., and Lough Aghery, the residence of James Magill, Esq. The living is a rectory and vicarage, in the diocese of Dromore, and in the patronage of the Bishop: the tithes amount to £367. 5. 4. The church was built in 1741, at the sole expense of the Rev. T. Smith, then rector of the parish; and the tower was added to it by the Marquess of Downshire, in 1768. The glebe-house was built, in 1793, by the Rev. J. Doubourdieu, then rector, at an expense of £845. 16. 2.: the glebe comprises 60 acres, contiguous to the church. In the R. C. divisions the parish forms part of the union or district of Magheradroll, also called Dunmore. There is a place of worship near Hillsborough for Presbyterians in connection with the Synod of Ulster, also one for those in connection with the Seceding Synod, at Lough Aghery, both of the first class. A free school of about 150 boys and 100 girls was founded in 1796, by Thos. Jamieson, Esq., who bequeathed £1000 for its support; it is further endowed with four acres of land given by the Marquess of Downshire, who also contributed towards defraying the expense of building the school-houses. Near Larchfield are two schools, supported by W. Mussenden, Esq., and Mrs. Forde, in which about 80 boys and 70 girls are educated and partly clothed; and there are also three private schools, in which are about 120 boys and 70 girls. Robert Sharland, Esq., a native of Barnstaple, Devon, who died on the 6th of May, 1833, bequeathed from £2000 to £3000 in trust to the clergy of the parish and the proprietor of one or two townlands, for the erection of ten almshouses for ten aged men and ten aged women, and a house for the housekeeper, to each of whom he assigned £5 per ann.: the buildings were about to be commenced in the spring of 1835. The burial-ground about the church occupies the site of an ancient fort, which is the innermost of four enclosures, the whole occupying about 9 acres, and sloping to the east in a regular glacis. There are also numerous forts on the hill, all within view of each other, and several relics of antiquity have been discovered here.

ANBALLY, a village, in the parish of Kilmoylan, barony of Clare, county of Galway, and province of Connaught, 7 miles (S.) from Tuam, on the road to Galway, containing 224 inhabitants. It consists of 54 cottages, and is only remarkable for the ruins of an ancient castle in excellent preservation, which, during winter, are completely surrounded by water from the turlough in the immediate vicinity.

ANDREW'S. (ST.), a parish, in the barony of Ardes, county of Down, and province of Ulster, comprising the post-town of Kirkcubbin, and containing, with the parishes of Ballywalter or Whitechurch, Ballyhalbert, and Innishargy, 7618 inhabitants. This parish, together with those which are now united with it, formed part of the possessions of a Benedictine monastery founded as a cell to the abbey of St. Mary, at Lonley, in Normandy, by John de Courcey, who died in 1210; and though designated, in the charter of foundation, the abbey of St. Andrew de Stokes, is more generally known by the appellation of the Black Abbey. It was seized into the king's hands as an alien priory in 1395, and was granted to the Archbishop of Armagh, who annexed it to his see; and after the dissolution it fell into the hands of the O'Neils. On the rebellion of O'Neil it escheated to the crown, and was granted to Sir James Hamilton, who assigned it to Sir Hugh Montgomery, Lord of the Ardes; but in 1639 it was finally awarded to the Archbishop of Armagh. The parishes of Ballywalter or Whitechurch, Ballyhalbert, and Innishargy are all included under the general name of St. Andrew's, and comprise, according to the Ordnance survey, 12,907 statute acres, of which 4012 are in St. Andrew's (including Ballyhalbert) and its islands. The land is fertile and in a high state of cultivation; but the fences are in bad condition, and in many places the system of draining is very inefficient. A large quantity of bog has been lately reclaimed by the Rev. Hugh Montgomery, which is now under cultivation and produces good crops. There are several gentlemen's seats, of which the principal are Spring Vale, the residence of G. Matthews, Esq.; Echlinville, of J. Echlin, Esq.; Glastry, of F. Savage, Esq.; and the Roddens, of J. Blackiston, Esq., all handsome and spacious mansions ornamented with thriving plantations. The post-town of Kirkcubbin is situated on the shore of Strangford Lough, on the west, and is separately described; and off the coast, on the east, are two islets, called respectively Green Island and Bur or Burrial, the former connected with the shore by a strand which is dry at low water; and the latter is remarkable as being the most eastern point of land in Ireland. There are some yawls and fishing smacks belonging to these islands; and about a mile to the north of Green Island is John's port, a small harbour for fishing boats, sheltered by a rock, called the Plough. On this coast is also a creek called Cloughy bay, having a bottom of clean sand; it has several fishing boats and wherries, and a coast-guard station has been established there, which is one of the twelve forming the district of Donaghadee. At the commencement of the last century, the churches of these parishes were in ruins; and, in the 2nd of Anne, an act was obtained for uniting the parishes and erecting a church in the centre of the union. The living is denominated the vicarage of St. Andrew's, or the union of Ballywalter, in the diocese of Down, and in the patronage of the Lord-Primate: the tithes amount to £1200, of which, £800 is payable to the Primate, as rector, and £400 to the vicar. The church, a spacious structure, was erected in the year 1704. The glebe-house, a handsome residence close to the town of Kirkcubbin, and about 2¼ miles from the church, was built about 50 years since, and has been greatly improved by the Rev. F. Lascelles, the present incumbent, at an expense of nearly £400: the glebe comprises about 30 acres, valued at £77. 18. per annum. In the R. C. divisions this union forms part of the district of Upper Ardes, also called Portaferry. There are three places of worship for Presbyterians in connection with the Synod of Ulster, situated respectively at Ballywalter, Kirkcubbin, and Glastry, all of the second class; one at Ballyhamlin in connection with the Remonstrant Synod, and one for Independents. There are six schools, two of which are supported by Lord Dufferin and J. Echlin, Esq., respectively, and two are infants' schools, supported by Miss Keown. In these schools are about 550 children of both sexes; and there are also four private schools, in which are about 100 boys and 80 girls. The sum of £50 per ann., payable out of the estate of Ballyatwood, was bequeathed by the Countess of Clanbrassil for clothing the poor on that estate. At Cloughy are the extensive ruins of a commandery of the Knights of St. John of Jerusalem, founded in 1189, by Hugh de Lacie, and called Castlebuoy; not far from which are the ruins of Slane church. Kirkstown castle, a heavy pile of building, erected in the reign of Jas. I., is in tolerable repair, and the tower in excellent preservation.—See KIRKCUBBIN.

ANEY, or KNOCKANEY, a parish, in the barony of SMALL COUNTY, county of LIMERICK, and province of MUNSTER, 3 miles (E.) from Bruff; containing 4542 inhabitants, of which number, 514 are in the village. This place, which is situated on the river Commogue, and bounded on the north by Lough Gur, appears to have been distinguished at a very early period of Irish history. Its parish church and a monastery, or college, are said, by ecclesiastical writers, to have been founded about the time of St. Patrick; but the earliest authentic notice of the place occurs in 941, when a convent for nuns of the order of St. Augustine was founded, but by whom is not recorded. This establishment, which was called *Monaster-ni-Cailliagh Juxta Aney*, and was situated on Lough Gur, was destroyed in the Danish irruption, but was refounded, in 1283, by a branch of the Fitzgibbon family, and appears to have subsisted till the dissolution: of the building, only some small fragments are remaining. In 1226, a preceptory was founded here, which subsequently became the property of the Knights of St. John of Jerusalem; and, in 1349, a friary for Eremites of the order of St. Augustine was founded by John Fitzgerald, or, as he was sometimes called, Fitz-Robert, which, after the dissolution, was granted by Queen Elizabeth to Edward, John and Mary Absley. This place was equally celebrated for its numerous stately castles; the most important was a spacious and very strong fortress, erected in 1248 by John Fitzgerald, sometimes called John of Callan, on the western bank of the river Commogue, in which the founder died in 1296; some very inconsiderable fragments only are remaining. In the fourteenth century the same powerful family erected two very strong castles on the shores of Lough Gur, called respectively Doon and the Black castle, to defend the two entrances to Knockadoon, a lofty eminence nearly surrounded by the lake, and by most writers considered as an island. The present castle of Doon, supposed to have been erected on the site of the original by Sir George Boucher, in the reign of Jas. I., is in a very perfect state; but the Black castle is a heap of ruins. A smaller castle was built in the village, soon after the erection of those on Lough Gur, probably by the family of O'Grady, who also built a very extensive castle at Kilballyowen: the former is, with the exception of the roof, in a very perfect state; and the latter has been incorporated with the modern dwelling-house, and contains four rooms in perfect order. Though the surrounding neighbourhood is fertile, and the inhabitants in general opulent, yet the village, which is the property of the Provost and Fellows of Trinity College, and of the Earls of Aldborough and Kenmare, is in a state of neglect and ruin. The parish comprises 8312 statute acres, as applotted under the tithe act: the land is remarkably productive, particularly round Kilballyowen; about one-fifth is under tillage, more than three-fifths are meadow and pasture land, and there is a small tract of very valuable bog. The great fertility of the soil seems to have obviated the necessity of paying much attention to the improvement of agriculture, which throughout the district is generally disregarded. The surface is adorned with rich plantations: the principal seats are Kilballyowen, the residence of De Courcy O'Grady, Esq. (who retains the ancient title of O'Grady of Kilballyowen), a handsome modern building in a richly planted demesne; Elton, of Mrs. Grady; Lough Gur Castle, of Miss Bailie; Baggotstown, of J. Bouchier, Esq.; Milltown Lodge, of T. D. O'Grady, Esq.; and Rathaney, of T. Bennett, Esq.

The living is a vicarage, in the diocese of Emly, with the vicarages of Ballynard, Ballynamona, Long or Knocklong, Kilfrush, Ballinlough, and Hospital, which seven parishes constitute the union of Aney, in the patronage of the Crown during the legal incapacity of the Earl of Kenmare; the rectory is impropriate in E. Deane Freeman, Esq. The tithes amount to £860, of which £573. 6. 8. is payable to the impropriator, and the remainder to the vicar; and the entire tithes of the benefice amount to £748. 0. 4½. The church is a neat edifice, with a handsome octagonal spire of hewn stone, and the Ecclesiastical Commissioners have lately granted £183 for its repair. The glebe-house, nearly adjoining the church, but not habitable for a family, is built on a glebe of *7a. 1r. 38p.* The R. C. parish is co-extensive with that of the Established Church, the chapel is in the village of Aney, and has been rebuilt and was consecrated on the 9th of October, 1836; there is also another at St. Patrick's Well. There is a school aided by a donation from the parish, which is held in the R. C. chapel; and a school is also supported by the Count de Salis. In these schools are about 220 boys and 130 girls; and there is also a pay school of 20 boys and 8 girls. Lough Gur, the only lake of importance in the county, is about four miles in circumference, and bounds the parish for nearly three miles; it has two beautiful small islands, and is of very picturesque and romantic character. On one of the islands are the remains of ancient fortifications; and midway between Knockadoon and Knockfennel is the other, about three-quarters of an acre in extent, which was strongly fortified, and the walls are now nearly in a perfect state. Not far from the Black castle are the interesting ruins of the New Church, so called from its being founded by the Countess of Bath, when resident at Doon Castle, by whom it was also endowed with £20 per annum for the support of a chaplain; but the property having descended to the Count de Salis, and the church not being registered in the diocesan records, that nobleman discontinued the appointment of a chaplain, and the church has fallen into ruins. The plate presented to this church by the Countess of Bath is now used in the parish church of Aney. At St. Patrick's well are some remains of a church, with an extensive burial-ground; and near Elton are also some fragments of another, in a churchyard. Not far distant are the picturesque ruins of Baggotstown castle, built by one of the Baggot family in the reign of Chas. I., and forming, with its lofty gables and chimneys, a singular object when viewed from a distance. On the hill of Knockadoon, just over the lake, are some rude traces of an ancient fortress.

ANHID, or ATHNETT, a parish, in the barony of COSHMA, county of LIMERICK, and province of MUNSTER, 1¼ mile (S.) from Croom; containing 475 inhabitants. This parish, which is situated on the western bank of the river Maigue, and on the new road from Charleville to Limerick, by way of Croom, comprises 928 statute acres, as applotted under the tithe act. The land is very fertile: about one-half of it is under tillage, and the remainder is good meadow and pasture. A new line of road is now in progress from Croom to Charleville, which will be intersected by the direct mail coach road from Cork to Limerick. Athnett is a prebend in the cathedral church of St. Mary, Limerick, which has, from time immemorial, been annexed to the bishoprick, and gives to the bishop a seat in the chapter: the tithes amount to £42. There is neither church nor glebe-house. In the R. C. divisions it forms part of the union or district of Croom.

ANNADUFF, or ANNAGHDUFF, a parish, partly in the barony of MOHILL, but chiefly in that of LEITRIM, county of LEITRIM, and province of CONNAUGHT; containing, with the post-town of Drumsna, 5858 inhabitants. This place is situated on the mail coach road from Dublin to Sligo, and on the river Shannon, which here forms the beautiful and picturesque loughs of Bodarig and Boffin. An abbey was founded here in 766; but there are no further accounts of it, and the only vestiges are a few curious stones worked into the window in the south gable of the ancient parish church, the ruins of which are in the present churchyard. In the reign of Jas. II. a skirmish took place here between the partisans of that monarch and the troops of Wm. III., at a ford over the river Shannon, near Derrycarne, and the spot is still called James's Heap. The parish comprises 8428 statute acres, as applotted under the tithe act, and valued at £6871. 4. 10. per annum: it is principally under an improving system of tillage. There is a tract of bog, affording a good supply of fuel: limestone of inferior quality is quarried, and freestone is found in the vicinity of Drumod. Iron ore exists in various parts, particularly near Drumod. The principal seats are Mount Campbell, the handsome residence of Admiral Sir Josias Rowley, Bart.; Derrycarne, of F. Nisbett, Esq., surrounded by a well-planted demesne and picturesquely situated between the two loughs, Bodarig and Boffin; Lismoyle, of T. Waldron, Esq.; and the residence of Messrs. Walsh, near Drumsna, commanding extensive views of the Shannon and surrounding country. The living is a rectory and vicarage, in the diocese of Ardagh, and in the patronage of the Bishop: the tithes amount to £262. 13. 1. The church is a neat edifice, in the later English style, with a square tower crowned with minarets, for the erection of which the late Board of First Fruits, in 1815, granted a loan of £1600. There is also a chapel of ease at Drumod. The glebe-house is a good residence, and the glebe comprises 300 acres. The R. C. parish is co-extensive with that of the Established Church: the chapel, at Aughamore, is in a very bad state of repair, and it is in contemplation to erect a new one as soon as a convenient site can be obtained. Divine service is also performed in a school-house. There are four schools, affording instruction to about 120 boys and 180 girls; also six pay schools, in which are about 270 boys and 100 girls, and two Sunday schools.—See DRUMOD and DRUMSNA.

ANNAGASSON, a village, in the parish of DRUMCAR, barony of ARDEE, county of LOUTH, and province of LEINSTER, 8 miles (S.) from Dundalk; containing 235 inhabitants. This place is situated on a pleasant beach, forming part of Dundalk bay; it comprises 38 houses, which are neatly built, and the handsome residence of Robert Thompson, Esq., who has some extensive mills, and is proprietor of the shipping, which afford employment to the inhabitants. The river Drumcar abounds with salmon and trout, and is here crossed by a substantial bridge. There is a beautiful drive along the sea-side to Dundalk, and to Clogher Head, where regattas are annually held; and the view of the bay and the sea, with steam-boats and other craft daily passing and repassing, give an air of cheerfulness to the place. The principal import is coal for the supply of the neighbourhood. Fairs are held on March 17th, May 7th, July 22d, and Nov. 8th.—See DRUMCAR.

ANNAGELIFFE, a parish, in the barony of UPPER LOUGHTEE, county of CAVAN, and province of ULSTER, 1 mile (N. E. by E.) from Cavan, on the road from that place to Virginia; containing 4341 inhabitants. It comprises, according to the Ordnance survey, 8260¼ statute acres, of which 5096 are applotted under the tithe act. The living is a vicarage, in the diocese of Kilmore, forming, with that of Urney, the union of Urney and Annageliffe, in the patronage of the Bishop; the rectory is impropriate in the Representatives of Richard, Earl of Westmeath. The tithes amount to £217. 16. 11½., of which £62. 2. 2½. is payable to the impropriator, and £155. 14. 9. to the vicar. In the R. C. divisions this parish forms part of the union or district of Urney, or, as it is more commonly called, Cavan: the chapel is a large building, situated at Stragolla. There are a parochial school, and a school on the townland of Curlurgan; also four hedge schools.

ANNAGH, or BELTURBET, a parish, partly in the barony of LOWER LOUGHTEE, but chiefly in that of TULLAGHGARVEY, county of CAVAN, and province of ULSTER, on the road from Ballyconnell to Cavan; containing, with the greater part of the market and post-town of Belturbet, 12,269 inhabitants. It comprises, according to the Ordnance survey, 19,145¼ statute acres, of which 12,340 are in Tullaghgarvey; about 16,000 are arable and pasture, 2000 are bog and waste, 300 are woodland, and 200 are common: of its entire area, 14,936 acres are applotted under the tithe act. The principal seats are Castle Saunderson, the residence of A. Saunderson, Esq.; Erne Hill, of G. M. Knipe, Esq.; Clover Hill, of J. Saunderson, Esq.; and Red Hill, of — White, Esq. The living is a rectory and vicarage, in the diocese of Kilmore, and in the patronage of Lord Farnham: the tithes amount to £384. 4. 7½. The church is a handsome edifice, for the repairs and enlargement of which the late Board of First Fruits granted £2600, in 1812 and 1814; and the Ecclesiastical Commissioners have recently granted £112 for its further repair. The glebe-house was purchased by aid of a loan of £844, in 1810, from the same Board; the glebe comprises 400 acres. In 1813, forty-seven townlands of he parish were disunited, to form the perpetual cure of Killoughter. This parish is divided into the two R. C. districts of Annagh West and Annagh East, or Killoughter, the former containing a chapel at Drumalee, and the latter at Red Hill. There are two places of worship for Wesleyan Methodists, one of which belongs to the Primitive class. A school is supported by the Trustees of Erasmus Smith's charity; and there are schools at Drumlaney, Killoughter, and Drumloor; also an infants' and two other schools, besides six private pay schools. The ruins of the old church yet exist.—See BELTURBET.

ANNAGH, or ST. ANNA, a parish, in the barony of TRUGHENACKMY, county of KERRY, and province of MUNSTER, 6¼ miles (W. S. W.) from Tralee; containing, with the town of Blennerville, 3253 inhabitants. This parish, which is situated on the bay of Tralee, and on the high road from Tralee to Dingle, extends for some miles between a chain of mountains and the sea, and comprises 17,967 statute acres, as applotted under the tithe act, about 11,400 of which consist of rough mountain pasture, and the remainder of arable land. It is a rectory, in the diocese of Ardfert and Aghadoe, and forms part of the union of Ballynahaglish: the tithes amount to £332. 6. 1. The church, situated in the town of Blennerville, is a neat modern structure with a square tower; and about half a mile distant are the ruins of the old church, with the burial-ground, in which is a stone bearing a rude effigy of an armed horseman. There is neither glebe nor glebe-house. In the R. C. divisions it is included in the unions of Tralee and Ballymacelligot; the chapel is at Curragheen, 1½ mile to the west of Blennerville. A school is supported by the R. C. clergyman; and at Curragrague is one under the Trustees of Erasmus Smith's charity; in which, together, are about 170 boys and 110 girls.—See BLENNERVILLE.

ANNAGH, a parish, in the barony of COSTELLO, county of MAYO, and province of CONNAUGHT, on the road from Castlebar to Frenchpark; containing, with the post-town of Ballyhaunis, 6885 inhabitants. This place was chiefly distinguished for a cell of Franciscan friars, though by some writers said to have been founded by Walter de Burgh for brethren of the order of St. Augustine, as a cell to the abbey of Cong, and to have been the burial-place of Walter, Lord Mac William Oughter, who was interred here in 1440. The parish comprises 16,325 statute acres, as applotted under the tithe act: it is principally under tillage; and there is a sufficient quantity of bog. Logboy is the residence of E. Nolan, Esq., and Hollywell, of J. Bourke, Esq. A weekly market and annual fairs are held at Ballyhaunis, which see. It is a rectory and vicarage, in the diocese of Tuam, and forms part of the union of Kiltullagh: the tithes amount to £194. 19. 11. The R. C. parish is co-extensive with that of the Established Church; there are chapels at Ballyhaunis and Tulrahan. The old monastery at the former place is still occupied by friars of the order of St. Augustine. There are eight pay schools in the parish, in which are about 390 boys and 230 girls.

ANNAGH, an island, in the parish of KILCOMMON, barony of ERRIS, county of MAYO, and province of CONNAUGHT, 23 miles (S. by E.) from Belmullet; containing 6 inhabitants. This island is situated in the bay of Tulloghane, on the western coast, and near the entrance of the sound of Achill; it is separated from the mainland of Ballycroy by a narrow sound to which it gives name, and is the property of Sir Richard O'Donnell, Bart., from whom it is rented by the inhabitants of the village of Claggan-Caferky. The greater portion of the land is mountainous, but affords very good pasture; and there is a salmon and herring fishery, which, if properly managed, might be rendered very lucrative.

ANNAGHCLONE.—See ANACLOAN.

ANNAGHDOWN, or ENAGHDUNE, a parish, in the barony of CLARE, county of GALWAY, and province of CONNAUGHT, 7½ miles (N.) from Galway, on the road from Galway to Headford; containing 6093 inhabitants. This parish is bounded on the west by Lough Corrib, and comprises 16,508 statute acres, as applotted under the tithe act. It is a place of considerable antiquity, and was formerly the seat of an independent bishoprick, of which some notice will be found in the account of the archiepiscopal see of Tuam, with which it has for centuries been incorporated. St. Brendan of Clonfert built a nunnery here under the invocation of the Blessed Virgin, for his sister Briga, which, in 1195, was confirmed by Pope Celestine III., together with the town of Kelgel, to nuns of the Arroasian order: at the suppression it was granted to the Earl of Clanricarde. An abbey, dedicated to St. Mary, and called the abbey of St. Mary *de portu patrum*, was founded at an early period for White Premonstratensian canons; and here was a Franciscan friary, the head of a custody, to which the monasteries of Connaught and Ulster were subordinate. There was also another religious house, called the College of St. Brendan, in which four priests or vicars were supported, and which was not subjected to royal inquisition until the 28th of Elizabeth; and at Kilcoonagh, in the vicinity, was an abbey, which Tipraid, Prince of Hy Fiacrja, granted to St. Columb, who placed over it St. Cuannan, from whom it derived its name. The seats are Cregg Castle, that of Fras. Blake, Esq., and Waterdale, of Jas. Blake, Esq. The living is a vicarage, in the diocese of Tuam, to which those of Killascobe and Laccagh are episcopally united, and in the patronage of the Archbishop; the rectory is impropriate in John Kirwan, Esq. The tithes amount to £553. 16. 11¼., of which £138. 9. 3. is payable to the impropriator, and the remainder to the incumbent; and of the entire union, to £675. 9. 4¾. The church is a small neat building, for the erection of which the late Board of First Fruits gave £500, in 1798. The glebe-house was also built by aid of a gift of £350 and a loan of £450, in 1818, from the same Board: the glebe comprises 20 acres. The R. C. parish is co-extensive with that of the Established Church: the chapel is at Corondola, and divine service is also regularly performed in a school-house at Woodpark. Schools at Annaghdown and Woodpark were each endowed with £100 late currency by the Rev. Redmond Hardagan, for the gratuitous instruction of 30 children in each; about 160 children are at present taught in these schools. There are also six hedge schools, in which are about 300 children; and a Sunday school is supported by the vicar.

ANNAMOE, a village, in the parish of DERRALOSSORY, barony of BALLINACOR, county of WICKLOW, and province of LEINSTER, 6¼ miles (S. W.) from Newtown-Mount-Kennedy; containing 67 inhabitants. This small village is situated in a sequestered spot, where a small valley opens on the east into the beautiful and romantic vale through which the river Annamoe flows in its descent from Lough Dan. The scenery is richly diversified, and in the vicinity are several gentlemen's seats, among which is Castle Kevin, the residence of Dr. Frizell, occupying a lofty eminence richly planted with firs and other forest trees, and commanding an extensive and delightful view. About half a mile to the northwest of the village is Dromeen, the seat of Captain Hugo, situated in a demesne tastefully laid out; near it is the glebe-house of Derralossory, and in the neighbourhood is Lara House, the residence of Robert Burrowes, Esq., from which is a most extensive mountain view. A daily penny post from Newtown-Mount-Kennedy has been established; and here is a small neat R. C. chapel belonging to the union or district of Glendalough. At a short distance up the valley, at the head of which the village is situated, is the site of Castle Kevin, supposed to have been originally built by the O'Tooles, a spacious quadrangular area encompassed by a deep ditch and rampart, which, with some of the foundations, is all that remains of that ancient fortress. Lawrence Sterne, when a child, was on a visit with his father at the parsonage-house for about six months, during which period occurred the circumstance which he relates of his falling through a mill-race, while the mill was at work, and being taken up unhurt.—See DERRALOSSORY.

ANNAMULT, otherwise AGHNAMOLT, a parish, in the barony of SHILLELOGHER, county of KILKENNY, and province of LEINSTER, 6 miles (S.) from Kilkenny; containing 458 inhabitants. It is situated on the river Nore, which here receives the King's river, on the high road from Stoneyford to Kilkenny by Bennett's-Bridge, and contains 1664 statute acres. An extensive Merino factory for superfine cloth, with a farm attached, was established here about 20 years since, at an expense, including the machinery, of nearly £30,000, and a further sum of £10,000 was subsequently expended on additional buildings and machinery. This excellent establishment, in which about 800 persons were employed and every process of the manufacture was carried on, was conducted on a plan which afforded to the children of the neighbouring peasantry the means of acquiring not only a knowledge of the trade, but also an useful elementary education; but from unavoidable losses and want of sufficient encouragement the undertaking was abandoned by its projectors, in 1822, and the works were subsequently taken by a firm in Dublin and Leeds, which, in 1826, being unable to obtain a satisfactory lease, discontinued them, and they are now unoccupied. Except about 25 acres of woodland attached to Annamult, the handsome residence of T. Neville, Esq., and to the residence of the Rev. Dr. Butler, the lands are all arable and pasture; about one-half are held immediately from Major Wemyss, and the other half under the lessees of Sir J. Blunden, Bart. The parish is tithe-free: it is a rectory, in the diocese of Ossory, and forms part of the union of Kells. In the R. C. divisions it is united to Danesfort.

ANNASCALL, or AUNASCALL, a hamlet, in the parish of BALLINACOURTY, barony of CORKAGUINEY, county of KERRY, and province of MUNSTER, 9 miles (E. by N.) from Dingle; containing 11 houses and 92 inhabitants. This place is situated in a pleasant valley on the new mail coach road from Tralee to Dingle, to each of which it has a penny post recently established. It is a constabulary police station; and petty sessions are held generally on alternate Mondays. The parish church, a small plain edifice with a square tower, is situated here; and a R. C. chapel has been recently erected. In the vicinity is a beautiful lake, about a mile in circumference; and in a glen among the mountains in its neighbourhood, bordering on Ballyduff, it is said the last wolf in Ireland was killed; the particular spot is called the "Wolf Step."—See BALLINACOURTY.

ANNESBOROUGH.—See DROMARAGH.

ANNESTOWN, a village, in the parish of DUNHILL, barony of MIDDLETHIRD, county of WATERFORD, and province of MUNSTER, 6 miles (S. W.) from Tramore; containing 232 inhabitants. This place is situated on the south coast, and on the western side of a pleasant valley, which extends for a considerable distance inland. The village contains 31 houses, and possesses some natural advantages as a place of resort during summer; and a few lodging-houses have been established for the accommodation of visiters. Its situation and appearance are highly picturesque; the vicinity presents an extensive line of coast, consisting of stupendous rocks rising abruptly from the sea. On the east the view is bounded by the isles of Icane, and on the opposite side the headland of Dungarvan is seen stretching far to the southwest. The parish church, a neat edifice, erected by aid of a gift of £900 from the late Board of First Fruits, in 1822, is situated in the village.—See DUNHILL.

ANTRIM (County of), a maritime county in the province of ULSTER, bounded on the north by the Northern Ocean, or Deucaledonian Sea; on the north-east and east, by the North Channel; on the south-east, by the lough or bay of Belfast and the river Lagan, separating it from the county of Down, which likewise borders it on the south; on the south-west, by Lough Neagh; on the west, by Lough Beg and the river Bann, which separate it from the county of Londonderry; and on the north-west, by the liberties of Coleraine. It extends from 54° 26′ to 55° 12′ 16″ (N. Lat.), and from 5° 47′ to 6° 52′ (W. Lon.); and, exclusively of the extensive parish of Carrickfergus (which is a county of a town in itself), comprises, according to the Ordnance survey, 761,877¾ statute acres, of which 466,564 are cultivated land, 53,487½ are under water, and the remainder unimproved mountain and bog. The population, in 1821, was 262,860; and in 1831, 316,909.

In the ancient division of the island the southern and south-western parts of this county were included in the territory called *Dalaradiæ*, or *Ulidia*, the western and north-western were designated *Dalrieda*, and the name of the whole was *Endruim* or *Andruim*, signifying the "habitation upon the waters," and strikingly descriptive of its situation. It was afterwards divided into the three districts of *North* or *Lower Clan-Hugh-Boy*, *Claneboy*, or *Clandeboy*; the *Glynnes*; and the *Reuta*, *Route*, or *Rowte*. North or Lower Clandeboy, so called to distinguish it from South or Upper Clandeboy, now included in the adjacent county of Down, extended from Carrickfergus bay and the river Lagan to Lough Neagh, and consisted of the tract now forming the baronies of Belfast, Massareene, and Antrim: the Glynnes, so called from the intersection of its surface by many rocky dells, extended from Larne, northward along the coast, to Ballycastle, being backed by the mountains on the west, and containing the present baronies of Glenarm, and part of that of Carey: the Route included nearly all the rest of the county to the west and north, forming the more ancient *Dalrieda*, and, in the reign of Elizabeth, occasionally called "Mac Sorley Boy's Country." Within the limits of Clandeboy was a minor division, called "Bryen Carrogh's Country," won from the rest by the Scots. At what precise period Antrim was erected into a county is uncertain: it was divided into baronies in 1584, by the lord-deputy, Sir John Perrot, but this arrangement was not until some time afterwards strictly observed.

The earliest inhabitants of this part of Ireland on record were a race of its ancient Celtic possessors, designated by Ptolemy *Darnii* or *Darini*; and it deserves notice that Nennius mentions the "regions of Dalrieda" as the ultimate settlement of the Scythian colony in Ireland. According to the Irish annalists, Murdoch Mac Erch, chief of the Hibernian Dalaradians, early in the fourth century, by a series of conquests extended his dominions in the north of Antrim and the adjacent districts, while his brother Fergus succeeded in establishing a colony in North Britain. The first intruders upon these earliest settlers were probably the Danish marauders, to whose desolating descents this coast was for several ages peculiarly exposed. Subsequently the northern Scots harassed the inhabitants by numerous plundering inroads, and ultimately accomplished permanent settlements here, maintaining for a long time a constant intercourse with their roving countrymen of the isles. A right of supremacy over the lords of this territory was claimed by the powerful family of the northern O'Nials (now written O'Neill), who were at length deprived of the southern part of this county by the family of Savage and other English adventurers. Early in the 14th century, Edward Bruce, the Scottish chieftain, gained possession of this district by the reduction of Carrickfergus, which had long resisted the most vigorous assaults of his troops. The English, however, shortly afterwards recovered their dominion; but in 1333, William de Burgho, Earl of Ulster, being assassinated at Carrickfergus by his own servants, and his countess, with her infant daughter, seeking safety by escaping into England, the sept of O'Nial rose suddenly in arms, and, falling furiously upon the English settlers, succeeded, notwithstanding a brave and obstinate defence, in either totally extirpating them, or reducing them within very narrow bounds. The conquerors then allotted amongst themselves the extensive possessions thus recaptured from the English, and the entire district received the name of the Upper and Lower Clan-Hugh-Boy, from their leader, Hugh-Boy O'Nial. During the successful operations of Sir John Perrot, lord-deputy in the reign of Elizabeth, to reduce the province of Ulster into allegiance to the English government, he was compelled to lay siege to Dunluce castle, on the northern coast of Antrim, which surrendered on honourable terms: this fortress having been subsequently lost through treachery, in 1585, was again given up to the English by Sorley Boy O'Donnell or Mac Donnell, the proprietor of a great extent of the surrounding country, to whom it was returned in charge.

This county is in the diocese of Connor, except part of the parish of Ballyscullion in the diocese of Derry, Lambeg in that of Down, and Aghalee in that of Dromore. For purposes of civil jurisdiction it is divided into the baronies of Upper Belfast, Lower Belfast, Upper Massareene, Lower Massareene, Upper Antrim, Lower Antrim, Upper Toome, Lower Toome, Upper Glenarm, Lower Glenarm, Upper Dunluce, Lower Dunluce, Kilconway, and Carey. It contains the borough, market, and sea-port town of Belfast; the borough and market-town of Lisburn; the ancient disfranchised borough and market-towns of Antrim and Randalstown; the sea-port and market-towns of Ballycastle, Larne, and Portrush; the market and post-towns of Ballymena, Ballymoney, Broughshane, and Glenarm; and the post-towns of Ballinderry, Ballyclare, Bushmills, Crumlin, Cushendall, Dervock, Glenavy, Portglenone, and Toome. Connor, the ancient seat of the diocese, is now merely a village: the largest villages are Ballykennedy, Templepatrick, Whitehouse, Dunmurry, Kells (each of which has a penny post), Doagh, Dunethery, Eden, Massareene, and Parkgate. Prior to the Union, this county sent ten members to the Irish parliament,—two knights of the shire, and two representatives for each of the boroughs of Antrim, Belfast, Lisburn, and Randalstown: from that period until 1832 it returned four members to the Imperial parliament,—two for the county, and one each for the boroughs of Belfast and Lisburn; but, by the act to amend the representation, passed in that year (2 Wm. IV., c. 88), an additional member has been given to Belfast. The county constituency (as registered in October, 1836,) consists of 598 £50, 562 £20, and 2246 £10 freeholders; 6 £50 and 19 £20 rent-chargers; and 59 £20 and 337 £10 leaseholders; making a total of 3827 registered voters. The election for the county takes place at Carrickfergus. It is included in the north-east circuit: the assizes are held at Carrickfergus, and the general quarter sessions at Belfast, Antrim, Carrickfergus, Ballymena, and Ballymoney, at which the assistant barrister presides. The county court-house and gaol is situated at Carrickfergus, the house of correction at Belfast, and there are bridewells at Antrim, Ballymena, and Ballymoney. The number of persons charged with criminal offences and committed to these prisons, in the year 1835, was 202; and the commitments under civil bill decrees amounted to 106. The local government is vested in a lieutenant and thirteen deputy-lieutenants, who are all justices of the pacee: the entire number of magistrates is 84, including the mayor of the town and county of the town of Carrickfergus, and the "sovereign" of Belfast, who are *ex-officio* magistrates of the county; besides whom there are the usual county officers, including two coroners. There are 29 constabulary police stations, having a force of a stipendiary magistrate, sub-inspector, pay-master, 6 chief and 33 subordinate constables, and 165 men, with 8 horses, the expense of whose maintenance is defrayed equally by grand jury presentments and by Government. Along the coast are 16 coast-guard stations,—8 in the district of Ballycastle, having a force of 8 officers and 54 men,—and 8 in the district of Carrickfergus, with a force of 8 officers and 51 men; each district is under the control of a resident inspecting commander. The district lunatic asylum and the county fever hospital are at Belfast, the county infirmary is at Lisburn, and there are two dispensaries at Belfast, and others at Crumlin,

Ballymoney, Ballymena, Larne, Doagh, Randalstown, Whitehouse, Antrim, Connor, Ahoghill, Loughguile, Bushmills, Ballycastle, Broughshane, and Cushendall, supported by equal grand jury presentments and private subscriptions. The amount of grand jury presentsentments, for 1835, was £41,002. 16. 1., of which £5230. 7. 10. was for the public roads of the county at large; £14,072. 4. 4. for the public roads, being the baronial charge; £7666. 8. 2. in repayment of loans advanced by Government, £3802. 11. 8. for police, and £10,231. 4. 1. for public establishments, officers' salaries, buildings, &c. In military arrangements this county is included in the north-eastern district: there are barracks for artillery and infantry at Belfast; and Carrickfergus Castle, in which the ordnance stores are deposited, is appropriated as a barrack for detachments from Belfast.

The most striking features of the surface of this county are its mountains, which stretch in a regular outline from the southern to the northern extremity, terminating on the shore in abrupt and almost perpendicular declivities: they attain their greatest elevation near the coast, and have a gradual descent inland; so that many of the principal streams have their source near the sea, and run directly thence towards Lough Neagh: exclusively of the valleys embosomed amid them, these mountains are computed to occupy about one-third of the superficial area of the county. Between this range and the shore, in some places, are tracts of very fertile land, especially from Belfast to Carrickfergus, and thence to Larne, near which the mountains project in rugged grandeur so as nearly to overhang the sea. From Glenarm round to Bengore Head this succession of rocky headlands presents numerous striking and picturesque views broken by narrow valleys watered by mountain torrents, which give a diversified character to the romantic scenery by which this part of the coast is distinguished. The most remarkable ranges of cliffs are those of perpendicular basaltic columns, which extend for many miles, and form a coast of surpassing magnificence: their arrangement is most strikingly displayed in Fair Head and the Giant's Causeway, which project several hundred feet into the sea, at the northern extremity of the county. On the western side of the mountain range the valleys expand to a considerable width, and are of great fertility: that of the Six-mile-water, stretching towards the town of Antrim, is particularly distinguished for its beauty and high state of cultivation. The valley of the Lagan merits especial notice for its beautiful undulating surface, its richness, the enlivening aspect of its bleach-greens, and the numerous excellent habitations, with their gardens and plantations, which impart an air of cheerfulness and industry to this interesting vale. The general inclination of the surface of the mountainous region becomes less rapid as it approaches the river Bann: the flattest parts of this elevated tract are composed of turf bogs, which occupy a great space, but are mostly susceptible of improvement. In the southern part of the barony of Toome, along the shore of Lough Neagh to the east of Shane's Castle, the surface consists of numerous detached swells, and presents a remarkably pleasing aspect. Thence southward, along the shore of Lough Neagh to the confines of the county, lies the most extensive level tract within its limits, which for fertility and cultivation is nowhere surpassed. Detached basaltic eminences, in some instances attaining a mountainous elevation, are conspicuous in several parts of the county, of which Slemish, to the south-east of Broughshane, and 1437 feet high, is the most remarkable: and in divers places, but generally in the lower tracts, are scattered gravelly knolls, which from Antrim to Kells are particularly striking. Off the northern extremity of the county, nearly seven miles distant from the town of Ballycastle, lies the island of Rathlin, about 6½ miles in length by 1½ in breadth, the shores of which are principally composed of precipitous basaltic and limestone rocks, rearing their heads in sublime grandeur above the waves of a wild and turbulent ocean. Off this part of the coast are some small islets, and a few others lie off the eastern shore, and in Lough Neagh.

Lough Neagh, which is the largest lake in the British islands, is chiefly in this county, but extends into several others:—it is traditionally stated to have been formed in the year 62, by an irruption of the sea, but is obviously formed by the confluence of the Blackwater, Upper Bann, and five other rivers. This lake is about 20 British miles in length from north-east to south-west, about 12 miles in extreme breadth from east to west, 80 miles in circumference, and comprises about 154 square miles: its greatest depth in the middle is 45 feet. According to the Ordnance survey, it is 48 feet above the level of the sea at low water, and contains 98,255½ statute acres, of which 50,025 are in this county, 27,355½ in Tyrone, 15,556¾ in Armagh, 5160 in Londonderry, and 138 in Down. The only outlet is the Lower Bann, which being obstructed by weirs and rocks prevents the free egress of the waters, and causes the surrounding country to be injuriously inundated in winter. In some places the waters possess medicinal properties, which they are supposed to derive from the adjacent shore. They have also petrifying powers, but these are supposed to exist in the soil, as petrifactions are only found in the lake near the shore of this county, while they are found at considerable heights and depths and at some distance from the coast inland. Valuable hones are made of the petrified wood, and in the white sand on the shore very hard and beautiful stones, known by the name of Lough Neagh pebbles, are found: they are chiefly chalcedony, generally yellow or veined with red, susceptible of a fine polish, and highly valued for seals and necklaces. Besides the fish usually caught in fresh water lakes, Lough Neagh has the char, a species of trout called the dollaghern, and the pullan or fresh water herring. Swans, teal, widgeon, herons, bitterns, and several other kinds of birds frequent its shores. Canals connect it with Belfast, Newry, and Coal island, and a steam-boat is employed in towing trading vessels across its surface, which, although sometimes violently agitated, is scarcely ever visited by tempests, from the absence of mountains from its borders. This vast expanse of water was frozen in 1739 and 1784, and in 1814 the ice was sufficiently thick for Col. Heyland to ride from Crumlin water foot to Ram's Island, which is the only one of any importance in the lake, and contains the remains of a round tower. Sir Arthur Chichester, in 1604, received from James I. a grant of the fisheries and of the office of Admiral of Lough Neagh, which have been held by his successors and are now vested in the Marquess of Donegal. Lough Neagh gives the title of Baron to Viscount Masareene. North of this lake, and connected with it by a narrow channel about a mile long, over which is the handsome bridge of Toome, is Lough Beg, or "the small lake," containing 3144¾ acres, of which 1624 are in this county, and 1520¾ in Derry. This lake, which is generally 15 inches lower than Lough Neagh, contains four small islands, and its banks are more diversified and pleasing than those of the larger lake.

The soils are of considerable variety: that of the plains and valleys is a strong loam upon clay, capable of being rendered very fertile, and in many parts interspersed with whinstones lying on or near the surface, the removal of which is necessary preparatory to tillage. On the rising grounds this kind of soil assumes a different quality, the vegetable mould diminishing in quantity, and being lighter in texture and colour; and the substratum deteriorates into a brown or yellow *till.* Still nearer the mountains this change becomes more apparent from the coarse and scanty produce, rocks and stones in many parts occupying nearly the entire surface, and the soil gradually acquiring a mixture of peat, and thus forming extensive moors. To the north of the Lagan, at a short distance from Belfast, commences a sandy loam which extends, with occasional interruptions, to the Maze-course, and under good management is very productive: on the shores of Lough Neagh are likewise some tracts of a similar soil: and small stripes of sand are found on different parts of the sea shore. Gravelly soils prevail on the irregularly disposed swells above mentioned, which are composed of water-worn stones of various dimensions, with a loamy covering. There are several detached tracts of soils of various texture, of a superior quality, resting on a substratum of limestone; one of the most extensive lies in the parishes of Maheragall and Soldierstown. Besides the turf, a prevailing soil upon the mountains is a peculiar loam without either cohesion or strength, which appears to be only a rust or oxyde of the softer parts of the ironstone, and under tillage yields exceedingly scanty crops of grain, but an abundance of straw, and tolerably good crops of potatoes: its herbage forms excellent pasturage.

The main feature in the tillage system of a great part of Antrim is the potatoe fallow, to which it owes nearly as much as Norfolk does to the turnip fallow. The principal wheat district extends along the shore of Lough Neagh and the course of the Lagan river, stretching as far north as Cairdcastle, in approaching which its extent is greatly reduced by the projection of the mountainous districts. Much barley of the four-rowed or Bere species is grown on the dry and gravelly swells; but the cultivation of oats is most extensive, the straw being used as fodder for cattle, and the meal, together with potatoes, the chief food of the great body of the people. The other crops of common cultivation are potatoes and flax: turnips have been grown by some agriculturists since 1774, and the quantity is yearly increasing. In some districts the grass lands are extensive and productive, although a considerable portion formerly employed as grazing pastures is now under tillage: the mountains and high lands also are constantly stocked with either the cattle of the proprietors, or those taken in from distant owners. Much butter is made throughout the county, and is packed in firkins containing from 60 to 80lb., and sold at Belfast, whence a considerable quantity is exported. Carrickfergus and Antrim have long been celebrated for cheese, some of which rivals in quality that of Cheshire.

The principal manure, besides that of the farm-yard, is lime, the produce of the county; but the quarries being situated at its extremities, it requires much labour and expense to convey it into the interior. Near the coast, shells and sea-sand are applied; and sea-sand is also used even where it contains few shells. Great improvement has of late years been made in the agricultural implements, by introducing the best Scotch and English modes of construction. The soil being particularly favourable to the growth of the white thorn, the numerous hedges planted with it greatly enrich the appearance of the lower districts: the mountain fences consist either of loose stones collected from the surface of the ground, or of drains (called shoughs) with banks of earth. The breed of cattle has been very much improved within the last few years, particularly in the more fertile districts; the most esteemed English and Scottish breeds have been introduced, and by judicious crosses stock of the most valuable kind are becoming general. In several parts is a Bengal breed, imported by Sir Fras. McNaghten, Bart., from which several crosses have been tried, but they appear too tender to endure the cold of winter. Generally, little attention is paid to the improvement of the breed of sheep, though on the rich lands of Muckamore and Massareene it has been very much improved: the old native sheep are principally found in and near the barony of Carey. A very hardy and strong, though small, race of horses, partly bred in the county and partly imported from Scotland, is employed on the northern and north-eastern coast, and among the mountains; and in Rathlin island is a breed similar to these, but still smaller. In other parts of the county the horses are of a good size and valuable kinds, but are chiefly introduced by dealers from other counties. The long-legged flat-sided hogs formerly reared have been superseded by the best English breeds: the bacon and pork of more than 100,000 are annually exported from Belfast.

There is but little natural wood in the county, the greater portion being that which surrounds Shane's Castle, and the scattered trees on the steep banks of a few rivers. Numerous, and in some instances extensive, plantations have, however, been made in various parts; and, though there are still many wide naked tracts, there are others well clothed with wood, especially adjoining Lough Neagh, the vicinities of Moneyglass and Drumraymond, the valleys of the Six-mile-water, Kells-water, and the Braid, the whole extent from Lisburn to Carrickfergus, the neighbourhood of Bella hill and Castle Dobbs, of Larne, Glenarm, Benvarden, O'Hara-brook, Ballynacre, Leslie hill, and Lisanoure. The greatest tracts of waste land are the highest portions of the mountain range: even the irreclaimable bogs of these elevated tracts produce a coarse herbage, and many of the bogs which overspread to a considerable extent the plains between the mountains and the Bann are likewise covered with verdure. Towards the southern part of the county most of the bogs have been exhausted. Coal is furnished to the northern and eastern coasts from the mines of Ballycastle, but the chief supply is from England, Wales, and Scotland.

The geology of Antrim presents a great variety of the most interesting features, and its mineral productions are of considerable importance. With the exception of a diversified district on the eastern coast and the entire vale of the Lagan, nearly the whole is occupied by basaltic beds, presenting abrupt declivities on the eastern and northern coasts, which are truly magnificent. These secondary beds consist of enormous unstratified masses, the average depth of which is about 300 feet, though in the north, at Knock-laid, it is 980 feet; the base of that mountain is composed of mica slate. The island of Rathlin is principally occupied by these basaltic beds, which are classified by Dr. Berger under the following heads: — tabular basalt, columnar basalt, green-stone, grey-stone, porphyry, bole or red ochre, wacke, amygdaloidal wacke, and wood coal: and imbedded in them are granular olivine augite, calcareous spar, steatite, zeolite, iron pyrites, glassy feldspar, and chalcedony. The beds of columnar basalt occur almost exclusively towards the northern extremity of the county, and form an amazing display of natural grandeur along the shore. Besides the well-known columnar strata composing the Giant's Causeway and the adjacent cliffs, similar strata are seen in divers parts of the county, particularly near Antrim and Kilroot: the pillars composing the Giant's Causeway (which is minutely described in the article on Billy), are irregular prisms standing in the closest contact, and of various forms, from three to nine sides, the hexagonal equalling in number all the rest. Slievemish, or Slemish, mountain is an enormous mass of greenstone, which likewise occurs in other situations. Porphyry occupies a considerable district to the south of Connor and Kells, and is met with in several other places, particularly near Cushendall. The remarkable substance called wood coal occurs in thin strata at Portnoffer, Kiltymorris, Ballintoy, and elsewhere. All the other rocks of Antrim are beneath the basaltic beds in geological position. The first is hard chalk, sometimes called white limestone, which does not average more than 200 feet in thickness, and occurs on the eastern and southern sides of the county, and on the southern coast of Rathlin island. Mulattoe, or green sandstone next occurs in the neighbourhood of Belfast, to the north of Carrickfergus, near Larne, at Garron Point, &c.; and under this are found lias beds on the coast between Garron Point and Larne, and in other places. These, together with the chalk and basalt, are based upon beds of reddish and reddish-brown sandstone of various textures, which are found under the entire south-eastern border of the county, in several detached spots along the eastern coast, and in considerable tracts from Red bay to Ballycastle: the upper strata form a marl, in which are veins of gypsum. The coal district of Ballycastle comprises an extent of about two miles along the coast; the beds crop out above the level of the sea, dipping to the south-east about one foot in nine, and alternate with others of sandstone and slate clay, being themselves of a slaty quality. The only rocks lying under the strata of the great coal district, besides the primitive rocks of mica-slate, &c., already mentioned, are those of "old red sandstone," between the bays of Cushendall and Cushendun. All the above-mentioned strata are occasionally intersected and dislocated by remarkable dykes of basalt or whinstone, varying from three inches to sixteen feet in width. Sometimes very minute dykes or veins of greenstone penetrate these enormous beds of basalt, and are particularly observable near Portrush, where they are seen in the face of the cliff not more than an inch broad. Chert is also found in abundance and variety at Portrush. Fullers' earth exists in the basaltic district, in which also a rough tripoli is found at Agnew's Hill, and a vein of steatite or French chalk in the path to the Gobbins. In Belfast Lough, lying under the level of the ordinary tides, but generally left bare at the ebb, is a stratum of submarine peat and timber, in which nuts are singularly petrified on the east and west sides of the Lough. Numerous organic remains are also found in the beds of chalk, &c.; large and beautiful crystals in the basaltic region, particularly near the Giant's Causeway, where agates, opal, and chalcedony are met with in different situations. Of all this variety of subterranean productions, the coal has been procured to the greatest extent. The collieries of Ballycastle, once flourishing, are now but little worked; they were formerly twelve in number, and exported from 10,000 to 15,000 tons annually. Gypsum or alabaster is dug in different places, and the various species of stone are quarried in spots convenient for building and other purposes.

As this county is situated in the centre of the district in which the linen and cotton manufactures are most vigorously carried on, a brief historical view of the progress of these branches of industry, the most valuable in the island, may here be introduced. The linen manufacture, of which Belfast is the grand mart, is most extensively carried on at Lisburn and the surrounding country: it is of remote antiquity in Ireland, but appears to have been first particularly encouraged in the north about 1637, by Lord Strafford, who induced the Scottish and English settlers, then recently established in Ulster, to cultivate flax, offering them every facility in exporting the yarn. But this rising trade was for some time entirely destroyed by the civil war which speedily followed, and its revival effectually prevented by the competition of the French and Dutch in the English market. In 1678, an act prohibiting the importation of linen from France was passed, which was soon afterwards disannulled by Jas. II., who afforded great encouragement to the French manufacturers. The first parliament of Wm. III. declared the importation of French linens highly injurious to the interests of the three kingdoms; and the progress of the woollen trade in Ireland having alarmed the English manufacturers, the king was prevailed upon to suppress it, and re-establish in lieu the manufacture of linen, which was accordingly so much encouraged as to induce many of the Hugonots to emigrate hither from France, several of whom had carried on the trade extensively in their native country. Amongst these emigrants was Mr. Crommelin, who received from Government a grant of £800 per annum, as an equivalent for the interest of capital to be expended by him in establishing the linen manufacture at Lisburn, with a patent for its improvement, and an additional salary of £200, on condition that, with the assistance of three other persons, also remunerated from the public purse, he should instruct the Irish farmers in the cultivation of flax, which had been altogether neglected for upwards of half a century. These and similar efforts, aided by protecting legislative enactments, produced the most important results: a board of trustees of the linen and hempen manufactures was established under an act passed in 1711, at which period the value of the exports did not exceed £6000 per annum. But in the early part of the reign of Geo. I., a linen-hall having been erected in Dublin, and a Board of Management appointed, authorised by parliament annually to employ a large specific sum in the importation and gratuitous distribution of flax seed, and in awarding premiums for the extension and improvement of the trade, the annual imports, before the year 1730, had increased in value to upwards of £400,000; in twenty years more they exceeded one million sterling; and of such importance was the success of this staple manufacture deemed, that £12,000 was annually granted by parliament for its better protection. During this rapid growth, numerous abuses crept in, and the most obnoxious frauds were practised by the weavers in the length and quality of their webs; for the suppression of which several acts were passed in vain, until the provisions of the act of the 33rd of Geo. II. were enforced, on the southern border of this county, by Lord Hillsborough and Mr. Williamson, whose persevering activity rendering it impossible for the weavers any longer to evade the law, while the bleachers and merchants were convinced of the advantages to be derived from its observance, the sealing of brown linen by deputed responsible officers, to attest its quantity and quality, became general throughout the whole province, and continues to be practised with equal strictness at present. In 1784, the value of brown linens sold in the markets of Ulster was £1,214,560; and for several years prior and subsequent to the Union, the total exports amounted in value to upwards of £2,600,000, of which nearly one-half was the produce of the county of Antrim. Some conception of the present extent of the manufacture may be derived from the fact that at one only of the numerous bleach-greens about 80,000 pieces of linen are finished annually, and at many others nearly the same number. Prior to the accession of Geo. II., every branch of the manufacture was performed by the same parties. Machinery was first invented and applied in the operation of washing, rubbing and beetling at Ballydrain, in the parish of Belfast, in 1725, and, as the manufacture extended, the process of bleaching became a separate business; the bleacher became merchant, bought the brown linens in the open market, and has made this business one of the most important branches of the trade. Owing to the improvements in machinery, and the aid afforded by the application of chymical preparations, the present number of bleach-greens is not so great as formerly, notwithstanding the vast increase in the produce of the manufacture. So late as 1761, the only acid used in bleaching was buttermilk: in 1764, Dr. James Ferguson, of Belfast, received from the Linen Board a premium of £300 for the successful application of lime, and in 1770 he introduced the use of sulphuric acid; ten years subsequently, potash was first used, and, in 1795, chloride of lime was introduced: the articles now generally used are barilla, American ashes, chloride of lime, and vitriol. The fine material which first induced competition and the offer of a bounty was cambrics: the attention of the Board was next directed to the production of damasks and diapers, and many looms were given to the weavers in the counties of Down and Antrim; and so great a degree of perfection has the weaving of damasks attained, that the Lisburn and Ardoyne manufactures adorn the tables of most of the sovereigns of Europe. Every species of fabric, from the coarsest canvas to the finest cambric, is now manufactured here, from flax which is cultivated and prepared in all its stages in the province of Ulster.

The cotton trade, which has become of so great importance in the North of Ireland, was introduced in 1777, merely as a source of employment for the children in the poor-house at Belfast, by Mr. Robt. Joy and Thos. McCabe, who, unable to secure individual co-operation, offered the machinery, which was then of the most improved description, to the managers of the charitable institution at prime cost. But the latter refusing to embark in a speculation altogether novel in Ireland, Messrs. Joy, McCabe, and McCracken formed themselves into a company, erected buildings, introduced new machinery, and generously opened their works to the public, at a time when it was endeavoured in England to keep the nature of the improved machinery a secret. In 1779 they commenced the manufacture of calico, dimities, and Marseilles quilting; and introduced the use of the fly shuttle. This branch of the trade soon acquiring considerable celebrity, many persons were induced to embark in it: the first mill for spinning twist by water was erected at Whitehouse, near Belfast, in 1784, from which period may be dated the fixed establishment of the cotton manufacture; and so rapid was thenceforward its progress that, in 1800, in Belfast and the surrounding country within a circuit of ten miles, it furnished employment to upwards of 13,000 individuals, or, including those indirectly connected with it, to 27,000. In 1811, the number of bags of cotton wool imported into Belfast was 14,320, and the number exported, 3007; leaving for home consumption 11,313, worth £226,260, and, when manufactured, worth about one million sterling. The number of spinners in the mills, at the same period, was estimated at 22,000; of weavers, including attendants on looms, 25,000; and engaged in bleaching, embroidery, making looms, reels, &c., about 5000 more. The manufacture has been since still further extended, and every description of cotton fabric is now produced. In addition to the two above-named important branches of manufacture, there are, in this county, at Belfast, canvas and rope manufactories, and extensive paper-mills in various places. Woollen stockings are woven in several of the towns; soap and candles are made for exportation and home consumption; the manufacture of chloride of lime and vitriol, for which there is a great demand in the bleach-greens, has long been carried on at Lisburn and Belfast; and the manufacture of leather, though not so extensive as formerly, is still considerable throughout the county. At Belfast are several large iron-foundries and glass-manufactories; and at Lisburn are works for turning and fluting iron. Hence the commerce of this county is very extensive: the exports are linens, linen yarn, cotton goods, all kinds of grain, pork, bacon, hams, beef, butter, eggs, lard, potatoes, soap, and candles; and the imports consist of the raw materials for the cotton manufacture, also coal and the various foreign articles of consumption required by the numerous population. There is an extensive salmon fishery along the coast at Carrickarede, between Ballintoy and Kenbane Head, and this fish is also caught at different places along the entire coast north of Glenarm, and also in the rivers Bann and Bush: all the other rivers, except the Lagan, are likewise frequented by salmon; and all abound with eels, which are taken at weirs in the Bann. There is a great variety of other valuable fish off the coast; of testaceous fish this shore affords the lobster and the crab, and oysters of superior size and flavour are found in Carrickfergus bay; the seal is common.

The two largest rivers are the Lagan and the Bann, both of which rise in the county of Down: at Belfast the Lagan spreads into the wide æstuary called the bay of Belfast, or Belfast Lough, and above it, with the aid of several cuts, has been made navigable to Lisburn, forming part of the navigation between Belfast and Lough Neagh: the Bann flows through Lough Neagh and Lough Beg, and continues its course to Coleraine, below which it falls into the sea. Most of the rivers strictly belonging to the county rise in the mountains on the coast, and owing to the rapidity and shortness of their currents are unnavigable. The Bush runs westward from the mountains of Lisanoure to Benvarden, and then northward to the sea at Port Ballintrae: the Main flows southward into Lough Neagh, and has three copious tributaries, the Ravel, the Braid, and the Glenwherry: the Six-mile-water also falls into Lough Neagh, at Antrim, and the Camlin, or Crumlin, and Glenavy rivers at Sandy-bay. The rapidity of these and the smaller rivers renders their banks peculiarly advantageous sites for bleach-greens, cotton-mills, and flour and corn-mills, of which the last are especially numerous. The only artificial line of navigation is the Belfast Canal, or Lagan Navigation. The Lagan Navigation Company were incorporated by an act of the 27th of Geo. III., empowering them to levy a duty of one penny per gallon on beer, and fourpence per gallon on spirits, in the excise district of Lisburn; but these duties having recently been repealed, an equivalent sum was annually paid to the Company by Government, until the year 1835, when their right ceased: it is navigable for vessels of fifty tons' burden, and the entire length from Lough Neagh to the quays of Belfast is twenty-two miles: its construction was powerfully aided by the noble family of Chichester, and the expense amounted to £62,000, raised by debentures. The roads of late years have been gradually improved, the materials existing within the county for making and repairing them being of the best quality. An important and very difficult work, called the Antrim Coast Road, from Larne to Ballycastle, has been lately executed under the immediate control of the Board of Public Works, opening an improved communication with a fine tract of country comprehended between the coast and the range of mountains from Carrickfergus to Ballycastle, and hitherto cut off from any reasonable means of intercourse by the badness of the roads over those mountains, some of which were conducted for miles at slopes varying from one yard in six to one in twelve. Many projects had been formed, at different times, for an improved line, but were abandoned on account of the great expense involved in the execution of them; but at length a plan with a moderate estimate was sanctioned by the Commissioners, and they and the grand jury granted about £18,000 for carrying it into effect. The new road proceeds from Larne close along the shore to Black Cave, where it winds round the promontory of Ballygalley Head, passing by Glenarm, Cairnlough, Garron Head, and Waterfoot, to Cushendall, where it strikes off inland to its northern terminus at Ballycastle, taking in the few portions of the old line that were available. The greatest difficulties encountered in its formation arose from the necessity of conducting the road, in part of its line, under a considerable extent of rock, some hundreds of feet in height, having its base washed by the open sea; and from its passing along portions of very steep hills of moving clay bank. The former obstacle presented itself at the bold headland of Glenarm deer-park, where about 30,000 cubic yards of rock were, by blasting with great care and judgment, hurled in immense masses down upon the shore; and the road, 21 feet in clear width and 10 feet above the highest tides, has been floored partly on the loose and partly on the solid rock. The latter occurred more particularly at the base of the hill of Cloony, and was by far the more serious obstacle, from the slippery nature of the clay banks and their tendency to move over the road. To counteract this inconvenience the engineer proposed, after having thrown down very large masses of detached rock, which were found strewed over the face of the bank (so as to form a sufficient flooring), to construct a revetment wall, from the summit of which any gradual accumulation of the slippery bank might from time to time be removed. Very solid piers of heavy rough blocks were deeply bedded into the bank, 30 feet apart, to be connected by substantial walls having a vertical curvilinear batter combined with an arched horizontal curve, to which the piers form the abutments. The entire distance being also concave, affords a powerful combination of resistance against the pressure. The old road passes over the hill at an elevation of nearly 200 feet above the sea, with slopes of one in six and upwards; while the new line along the coast is nearly level. A new line of road has been opened from Belfast to Lisburn; another from Belfast to Antrim, which is to be immediately continued to Ballymoney, Ballymena, and Coleraine; and a third recently from Belfast to Crumlin. A new line has been made from Ballymoney to Dervock, crossing a large and valuable tract of bog; and others are in progress leading respectively from Whitewell-brae to Ballyclare and Ballymena, from Belfast to Carrickfergus and Larne, from Glenavy to Moira, from Doagh to Ballymena, and from Ballymena to Cushendall. But the most important and expensive is the mail coach road from Belfast to Derry, now in progress. The lines from Belfast to Carrickfergus and Larne, and from Antrim to Coleraine (the latter being the Derry road), have been undertaken with the sanction of the Commissioners of Public Works. A double line of railway is in progress from Belfast to Cave Hill, which was the first undertaken in Ireland, but for want of funds was abandoned for some years; the operations have, however, been resumed. Railways are also contemplated from Belfast to Carrickfergus, from Belfast to Armagh (being the Dublin line), and from Armagh to Portrush; the last will only pass about two miles through this county.

The remains of antiquity of earliest date consist of cairns or barrows, cromlechs, raths or intrenchments, and mounts differing in magnitude and form. The most remarkable of the cairns is that on Colin mountain, about three miles north of Lisburn; there is also one on Slieve True, to the west of Carrickfergus, and two on Colinward. Near Cairngrainey, to the north-east of the old road from Belfast to Templepatrick, is the cromlech most worthy of especial notice: it has several table stones resting on numerous upright ones; and near it is a large mount, also several fortified posts different from all others in the county. There is likewise a large cromlech at Mount Druid, near Ballintoy; another at the northern extremity of Island Magee; and Hole Stone, to the east of the road from Antrim to Glenavy, appears to be a relic of the druids. Of mounts, forts, and intrenchments, there is every variety which exists in Ireland; and so numerous are they, that the parishes of Killead and Muckamore alone contain two hundred and thirty, defended by one or more ramparts; and ten mounts, two of them containing caves, of which that called Donald's Mount is a fine specimen of this kind of earthwork. Among the most remarkable of the rest are, one at Donegore, one at Kilconway, one at the Clough-water, one at Dunethery, the last of which is planted with trees; one with a square outwork at Dunmacaltar, in the parish of Culfeightrin; Dunmaul fort, near Nappan; one at Cushendall, having a castle within its defences, and probably a Danish relic; one at Drumfane on the Braid, one at Camlent-Oldchurch, and another in a bog near Ballykennedy: one near Connor has outworks exactly resembling that at Dromore, and in another near Carrickfergus have been found several curious Danish trumpets. Stone hatchets or celts of various sizes have been discovered in several places, but in the greatest numbers near Ballintoy; arrow heads of flint, spear heads of brass, and numerous miscellaneous relics have been found. There have also been discovered a Roman torques, a coin of Valentinian, fibulæ, and other Roman antiquities, supposed to be relics of the spoil obtained by the Irish Scots in their plunder of South Britain, in alliance with the Picts. Of the singular round towers, the original purpose of which has been a fertile source of almost innumerable conjectures, there are at present four in this county; *viz.*, one at Antrim, one on Ram's Island in Lough Neagh, a fragment of one near the old church at Trummery (between Lisburn and Moira), and one in the churchyard of Armoy.

Archdall enumerates forty-eight religious establishments, as having existed in this county, but adds, that twenty of them are now unknown, and scarcely can the existence of half the entire number be now established by positive evidence. There are still interesting remains of those of Bonamargy, Kells, Glenarm, Glynn near Larne, Muckamore, and White Abbey, to the west of the road from Belfast to Carrickfergus; and extensive ruins of other religious edifices, in the several townlands of Dundesert, Ballykennedy, and Carmavy, in the parish of Killead. Of ancient fortresses, that of Carrickfergus, which has always been the strongest and most important, is the only one in complete preservation: there are interesting ruins of Green Castle, to the west of the road between Belfast and Carrickfergus; Olderfleet Castle, situated at the extremity of the peninsula which forms one side of the harbour of Larne; Castle Chichester, near the entrance to the peninsula of Island Magee; Red Bay Castle; and the Castle of Court Martin, near Cushendall. Near the northern coast are likewise several old castles, some of which are very difficult of access, and must have been fortresses of great strength prior to the use of artillery: of these the principal are Dunluce, remarkable for its amazing extent and romantic situation, also Dunseverick, Kenbane, Doonaninny, and Castle Carey; in Rathlin Island are the remains of Bruce's Castle. Inland there are also many remains of fortified residences, of which Shane's Castle, the venerable seat of the O'Nials, was destroyed by fire in 1816: Castle Upton is the only mansion of this kind at present habitable. Lisanoure, the beautiful seat of George Macartney, Esq., on the banks of Lough Guile, is so called from an old fort in the vicinity. Near the summit of White Mountain, two miles north of Lisburn, are the extensive remains of Castle Robin; and at Portmore, near the Little Lough in Ballinderry, are similar remains. Among the mansions of the nobility and gentry, few are splendid, though many are of considerable elegance; they are noticed under the heads of the parishes in which they are respectively situated. There are numerous mineral springs: one near Ballycastle is chalybeate, another aluminous and vitriolic, and a third, on Knocklaid mountain, chalybeate; at Kilroot there is a nitrous water of a purgative quality; and near Carrickfergus are two salt springs, one at Bella hill, and the other in Island Magee. There are also various natural caverns, of which the most remarkable are those of the picturesque mountain called Cave Hill; a curious and extensive cavity at Black-cave-head, to the north of Larne; a cave of larger dimensions under Red Bay Castle; one under Dunluce Castle; the cave at Port Coon, near the Giant's Causeway; and those of Cushendun and the white rocks, near Dunluce; besides which there are numerous artificial caves.

ANTRIM, a market and post-town, and a parish (formerly a parliamentary borough), partly in the barony of Upper Antrim, and partly in that of Upper Toome, county of Antrim, and province of Ulster, 13 miles (N. W. by W.) from Belfast, and 94 miles (N.) from Dublin; containing 5415 inhabitants, of which number, 2655 are in the town. This place was anciently called *Entruim, Entrumnia,* or *Entrum Neagh,* signifying, according to some writers, "the habitation upon the waters," probably from its contiguity to Lough Neagh. The earliest notice of it occurs in the year 495, when Aodh, a disciple of St. Patrick, founded a monastery here, which was destroyed during the Danish incursions, and of which no further mention appears till the foundation of Woodburn Abbey, to which it became an appendage. A sanguinary battle between the native Irish and the English took place near the town, when Sir Robert Savage, one of the earliest English settlers, is said with a small party of his forces to have killed more than 3000 of the Irish army. In the 13th of Jas. I., the town and sixteen townlands of the parish, together with the advowson of the living and the rectorial tithes, were granted to Sir Arthur Chichester. A naval engagement took place on Lough Neagh, in 1643, when Col. Conolly and Capt. Longford gave battle to a party of Irish marauders, who at that time had possession of the fort of Charlemont, near the shore of Clanbrassil, on which occasion the Irish were defeated, and their fleet brought by the victors in triumph up to the town. In 1649 the town was burnt by Gen. Monroe; and in 1688 a party of Lord Blayney's troops, being separated from the main body of the army, crossed the river Bann at Toome, and were made prisoners in a skirmish near this place. During the disturbances of 1798 it was the principal scene of the hostilities which took place in the county: the insurgents had planned an attack on the 7th of June, by marching their forces in four columns respectively by the Belfast, Carrickfergus, Ballymena and Shane's Castle roads; but their design becoming known to the military commanders of the district, troops were hastily assembled in the town, and the inhabitants were also mustered for its defence. The conflict was obstinately maintained on both sides, but at length the insurgents fled in all directions, leaving behind them about 3000 pikes and muskets: more than 900 of them were slain in the town and many killed in the pursuit.

The town is situated on the banks of the Six-mile-water river, on the great road from Belfast to Londonderry, and in one of the most fertile and beautiful valleys in the county: it consists of two principal streets, with others branching from them; many of the houses are modern, and well built of stone and roofed with slate, and several are ancient, of timber frame-work and plaister, with gable fronts, of which the upper projects over the lower story: the inhabitants are amply supplied with water from conduits in the streets. The manufacture of paper is carried on to a very great extent; mills for that purpose were first erected about the year 1776, but were burnt down a few years after; they were, however, rebuilt on a very extensive scale, and the first machinery used in the North of Ireland for the making of paper was introduced and is now employed in manufacturing paper of every description. Attached to these and belonging to the same proprietors, Messrs. Ferguson and Fowke, are a large brewery, flour and meal mills, malt-kilns, stores for grain, and other appendages, the whole affording employment to a great number of the industrious poor. At Boghead, one mile distant, and on the same stream, is another paper-mill on a smaller scale: there are also several bleach-greens in the parish; and the weaving of linen, calico, and hosiery is carried on in the dwellings of many of the poor both in the town and neighbourhood. The situation of the town within a quarter of a mile of the north-eastern portion of Lough Neagh, where a small rude pier or quay has been constructed, is favourable to the increase of its trade, from the facility of water conveyance afforded by the lake, the Belfast canal, and the Upper Bann. Several patents granting fairs and markets are extant, of which the earliest, granting to Sir James Hamilton a market on Thursday, is dated Feb. 14th, 1605. The market is still held on Thursday, and there is a market for grain every Tuesday, but, although the town is situated in a fine grain country, the market is very small. Fairs are held on Jan. 1st, May 12th, Aug. 1st, and Nov. 12th; those in May and August are well supplied with black cattle and pigs. Tolls were formerly levied, but were discontinued about fourteen years since, by direction of Viscount Ferrard. This is a chief or baronial station of the constabulary police. Chas. II., in the 17th year of his reign (1666), granted the inhabitants letters patent empowering them to send two members to the Irish parliament, which they continued to do till deprived of the privilege at the time of the Union, when the compensation grant of £15,000 for the abolition of the franchise was assigned in equal shares to Clotworthy, Earl of Massareene, and three members of the Skeffington family. The seneschal of the manor of Moylinny, within which the town is situated, is appointed by the Marquess of Donegal, and holds a court once in three weeks, under charter of the 21st of Chas. II., granted to Arthur, Earl of Donegal, for determining pleas "not exceeding £20 current money in England," with power of attachment of goods: he also holds a court-leet annually. Petty sessions are held every alternate Tuesday; and the quarter sessions for the county are held here in April and October. The court-house is a large and handsome building nearly in the centre of the town; and part of the market-house is appropriated as a county district bridewell.

The parish comprises, according to the Ordnance survey, 8884¼ statute acres, of which about three-fourths are arable and one-fourth pasture land, and 200 acres are under plantations; there is little waste and no bog. The scenery is diversified and embellished with several gentlemen's seats, and derives much interest from Lough Neagh, which is partly within the limits of the parish. Closely adjoining the town is Antrim Castle, the ancient residence of the Earls of Massareene, and now, by marriage, the property and residence of Viscount Ferrard: it appears to have been originally built in the reign of Chas. II. by Sir John Clotworthy, and has been enlarged and partly rebuilt. It occupies an elevated situation above the precipitous banks of the Six-mile-water, commanding a fine view of the lake and of the surrounding country. Not far from the town are Steeple, the residence of G. J. Clark, Esq.; Ballycraigy, of W. Chaine, Esq.; Spring Farm, of Lewis Reford, Esq.; Birch Hill, of A. Montgomery, Esq.; Greenmount, of W. Thompson, Esq.; Muckamore, of S. Thompson, Esq.; the Cottage, of F. Whittle, Esq.; Moilena, of W. Chaine, jun., Esq.; and Holywell, of H. Joy Holmes, Esq. The living is a vicarage, in the diocese of Connor, and in the patronage of the Marquess of Donegal; the rectory is impropriate in Lord Ferrard. The tithes amount to £598. 2. 10., of which sum, £318. 18. 8. is payable to the impropriator, and the remainder to the vicar. The church, originally built in 1596, was destroyed by fire in 1649, and remained in ruins till 1720, when it was rebuilt; a lofty square embattled tower, surmounted by an elegant octagonal spire of freestone, was added in 1812, for which the late Board of First Fruits granted a loan of £1500. There is a glebe-house, but no glebe. In the R. C. divisions the parish forms part of the union or district of Drumaul, also called Randalstown: the chapel is a spacious and handsome edifice. There are two meeting-houses for Presbyterians; one, in Main-street, in connection with the Synod of Ulster and of the second class, was built in 1613; and the other, in Mill-row, in connection with the presbytery of Antrim and of the third class, was built in 1726. There are also two places of worship for Primitive Wesleyan Methodists, and one for the Society of Friends. A free school on the foundation of Erasmus Smith was established in 1812, and is supported by annual grants of £30 from the trustees and £2 from the rector: the school-house was built at an expense of £800, of which £200 was given by Lord Ferrard. On the same foundation is also a school for girls, to which the trustees contribute £27. 10. per annum; and there are an infants' school, supported by subscriptions amounting to about £15 per ann., and two Sunday schools. The total number of children on the books of these schools, exclusively of the Sunday schools, is about 300; and in the private pay schools are 230 boys and 100 girls. A mendicity society has been established for some years; a temperance society was formed in 1829; and a branch savings' bank, in connection with the Belfast savings' bank, was established here in Dec. 1832, in which the deposits during the first half year amounted to £1369. 9. 3. About half a mile to the north-east of the church, and in the middle of the plantations of G. J. Clark, Esq., in a part of the valley leading to Lough Neagh, is one of the most perfect round towers in the island: it is built of unhewn stone and mortar, perfectly cylindrical in form, and is 95 feet in height and 49 feet in circumference at the base; the summit terminates with a cone 12 feet high; the door is on the north side, and at a height of 7 feet 9 inches from the ground; the walls are 2 feet 9 inches in thickness, and the tower contains four stories, the ascent to which appears to have been by a spiral staircase; each of the three lower stories is lighted by a square window, and the upper story by four square perforations, corresponding with the cardinal points; immediately above the doorway is a Grecian cross rudely sculptured in alto relievo on a block of freestone, which appears to be part of the original building. Around the base of the tower great quantities of human bones and some vestiges of the foundations of buildings have been discovered; the latter are supposed to indicate the site of the ancient monastery founded by Aodh. In a garden adjoining the tower is a large detached mass of basalt, having nearly a level surface, in which are two cavities or basins, evidently the work of art, of which the larger is 19 inches in length, 16 inches wide, and 9 inches deep, and during the driest seasons is constantly filled with fine clear water. There is a very powerful chalybeate spring in the garden of Frederick Macauley, Esq. John Abernethy, Esq., the eminent surgeon, was a native of this place. Antrim gives the title of Earl to the family of Macdonnel, of which the present representative is the Countess of Antrim and Viscountess Dunluce, in the peerage of Ireland, who succeeded her father, Randal William, Marquess and sixth Earl of Antrim, in 1791, in the earldom and viscounty only, by virtue of a new patent which the earl, having no son, obtained in 1785, with remainder to his daughters and their heirs male.

ARBOE, or ARDBOE, a parish, partly in the barony of LOUGHINSHOLIN, county of LONDONDERRY, but chiefly in the barony of DUNGANNON, county of TYRONE, and province of ULSTER, 5 miles (E. N. E.) from Stewartstown; containing 8148 inhabitants. A monastery was founded here by St. Colman, son of Aidhe, and surnamed Mucaidhe, whose reliques were long preserved in it: it was destroyed in 1166, by Rory Makang Makillmory Omorna, but there are still some remains. The parish is situated on the shore of Lough Neagh, by which it is bounded on the east, and comprises, according to the Ordnance survey, 33,504 statute acres, of which 21,000 form part of Lough Neagh, and 56 are in small islands. The greater portion is under tillage, and there are some tracts of good meadow, about 50 acres of woodland, and 1000 acres of bog. The system of agriculture is improved; the soil is fertile, and the lands generally in a high state of cultivation. There are several large and handsome houses, the principal of which is Elogh, the residence of Mrs. Mackay. The living is a rectory, in the diocese of Armagh, and in the patronage of the Provost and Fellows of Trinity College, Dublin: the tithes amount to £507. 13. 10½. The church, a neat small edifice, was erected in the reign of William and Mary, on a site two miles westward from the ruins of the ancient abbey. The glebe-house is a handsome building; and the glebe comprises 212 acres. The R. C. parish is co-extensive with that of the Established Church; the chapel, a spacious and handsome edifice, is situated at New Arboe; and there are two altars in the open air, where divine service is performed alternately once every Sunday. There is a place of worship for Presbyterians in connection with the Seceding synod. There are four public schools, in which about 320 boys and 240 girls are taught; and there are also five private schools, in which are about 140 boys and 50 girls, and five Sunday schools. On the western shore of Lough Neagh are the ruins of the ancient abbey, which form an interesting and picturesque feature; and the remains of an old church, of which the walls are standing. Near them is an ancient ornamented stone cross in good preservation.

ARDAGH, a parish, in the barony of IMOKILLY, county of CORK, and province of MUNSTER, 3 miles (N. W.) from Youghal, on the new mail-coach road from that place to Tallow; containing 2658 inhabitants. This parish is situated on the confines of the county of Waterford, and comprises 7629 statute acres, as applotted under the tithe act, and valued at £3402 per annum. The general aspect is mountainous, and a large portion of its surface is unreclaimed, affording a plentiful supply of turf. The soil is for the most part poor and stony; and excepting the waste, the land is wholly in tillage and only indifferently cultivated. The living is a rectory, in the diocese of Cloyne, and in the patronage of the Crown: the tithes amount to £600. The church is an old plain building of small dimensions. There is no glebe-house; the glebe comprises five acres. In the R. C. divisions this parish forms part of the union or district of Killeigh: the chapel is a small thatched building, situated at Inch. There is a school for boys and girls at Killeigh, aided by a donation of £5 per ann. from Lord Ponsonby, who also gave the school-house rent-free, and contributes to another school for both sexes; there is only one pay school in the parish. On the banks of the Turra, which runs through the centre of the parish, is the ruined castle of Kilnaturra, a massive square tower in excellent preservation.

ARDAGH, a parish, in the Shanid Division of the barony of LOWER CONNELLO, county of LIMERICK, and province of MUNSTER, 3 miles (N. W.) from Newcastle, on the road from that place to Shanagolden; containing 2197 inhabitants, of which number, 415 are in the village. This place is situated in the heart of an interesting and fertile district; the village consists of one long irregular street, containing 65 houses, which are in a very ruinous condition. Near it are the interesting remains of the old parish church, which was destroyed in the insurrection of 1641, and has not been rebuilt. Fairs are held on the 11th of May, Aug. 14th, and Nov. 21st, chiefly for the sale of cattle, pigs, and pedlery.

The parish comprises 6572 statute acres, as applotted under the tithe act, exclusively of a considerable tract of bog; the land is some of the best in the county and finely planted; the system of agriculture is little improved, the fertility of the soil and the abundance of the crops rendering the farmer unwilling to change his plans. On the west it is bounded by heathy and boggy mountains, which contain several strata of coal, but the two upper strata, which are very thin, are alone worked: the only pits now open are at Carrigkerry. Iron-stone and fire clay of very superior quality are also abundant, but no attempt has yet been made to work them. The seats are Ardagh Lodge, the residence of T. Fitzgibbon, Esq.; and Ballynaborney, of W. Upton, Esq. The parish is in the diocese of Limerick, and the rectory forms part of the union of St. Michael and corps of the archdeaconry, in the patronage of the Bishop: the tithes amount to £184. 12. 3¾. In the R. C. divisions it is the head of a union or district, comprising also the parish of Rathronan and part of the parish of Kilscannell; the chapel, a large but old and neglected building, is situated in the village, where a school-house is now in course of erection. There are two schools, in which are about 100 boys and 80 girls.

ARDAGH, a parish, partly in the barony of MOYDOW, but chiefly in that of ARDAGH, county of LONGFORD, and province of LEINSTER, 4 miles (W. S. W.) from Edgeworthstown; containing 4980 inhabitants, of which number, 142 are in the village, which comprises 25 houses and is wholly in the latter barony. This ancient place derives its name from its elevated situation, and its origin may at the latest be ascribed to the middle of the fifth century, when its church was founded. Subsequently here was a friary of the third order of St. Francis, founded at Ballynesaggard by the family of O'Ferrall, and reformed in 1521 by the friars of the Strict Observance. The parish is situated on the nearest road from Mullingar to Longford over Ballicorkey bridge, but the coach road is through Edgeworthstown, from which there is a penny post. It comprises 10,063 statute acres, as applotted under the tithe act, and valued at £8073 per annum; there is a moderate extent of bog, but no waste land. The land is good, and is principally under tillage, and the system of agriculture, though still very backward, has considerably improved. Ardagh House is the seat of Sir G. R. Fetherston, Bart.; Richfort, of J. A. Richardson, Esq.; Oldtown, of Thornton Gregg, Esq.; and Drumbawn, of Peyton Johnston, Esq. Fairs are held on April 5th and Aug. 26th. Petty sessions are held every Thursday; and here is a constabulary police station.

The DIOCESE of ARDAGH appears to have been founded either by St. Patrick or by his disciple and nephew, St. Mell, a Briton, who became bishop and abbot of Ardagh before the year 454. Of his successors until the arrival of the English, in the reign of Hen. II., little with certainty is known, and nothing remarkable is recorded of any. Near the close of the fifteenth century the bishoprick was held by William O'Ferrall, who was also dynast of the surrounding territory; and Richard O'Ferrall combined these two dignities from 1541 to 1553. It was held jointly with the diocese of Kilmore by royal patent from 1603 till 1633, when it was voluntarily resigned by William Bedell, Bishop of Kilmore; and John Richardson, D.D., Archdeacon of Derry, and a native of Chester, was advanced to the see of Ardagh. This prelate, apprehensive of the insurrection which broke out towards the close of 1641, withdrew with all his substance into England in the summer of that year; and having a short time before his departure recovered some lands in his diocese from one Teigue O'Roddy, the latter applied for relief to the British House of Commons, and a summons was sent to the bishop requiring his appearance on a certain day; but on application to the Irish House of Lords, the lord-chancellor was ordered to write to the Speaker of the English House, asserting their privileges, and refusing to permit the bishop's compliance; and on a motion of the Bishop of Clonfert an order was resolved on to prevent such grievances in future. After his death, in 1653 or 1654, the see continued vacant and its revenues sequestrated until the Restoration of Chas. II., when the dioceses were again united and so continued until the deprivation of Bishop Sheridan, in 1692. Ulysses Burgh, D.D., was then promoted to Ardagh; and dying in the same year the union was restored, but was ultimately dissolved in 1742, on the translation of Bishop Hart to the archiepiscopal see of Tuam, with which Ardagh has been since held *in commendam*, the archbishop being suffragan to the Lord-Primate for this see. Under the provisions of the Church Temporalities Act (3rd of Wm. IV.) this diocese, on the death of the present Archbishop of Tuam, will be again permanently united to that of Kilmore. It is one of the ten which constitute the ecclesiastical province of Armagh, and comprehends part of the counties of Sligo, Roscommon, and Leitrim, in the civil province of Connaught; part of Cavan, in Ulster; and part of Westmeath and nearly the whole of Longford, in Leinster. It comprises, by estimation, 233,650 acres, of which 4400 are in Sligo, 8700 in Roscommon, 71,200 in Leitrim, 10,600 in Cavan, 8900 in Westmeath, and 129,850 in Longford. A dean and an archdeacon are the only dignitaries, but have no official duties to perform, and the latter has no emoluments: there is no chapter, but in cases of necessity a majority of the beneficed clergymen of the diocese represent that body; the parochial church of Ardagh serves as the cathedral. It was divided into four rural deaneries prior to the year 1819, when the diocesan dispensed with the services of the rural deans and has since discharged their duties himself. The diocese comprises 38 parishes, of which 20 are rectories or united rectories and vicarages, 17 vicarages, and 1 impropriate cure: the total number of benefices is 26, of which 8 are unions consisting of 20 parishes, and the remainder consist of single parishes, and of which 1 is in the gift of the crown, 22 in that of the diocesan, and 3 are in lay patronage; the number of churches is 33, and of glebe-houses 22. The see lands comprise 22,216 statute acres, of which 13,194 are profitable land, and 9022 are unprofitable; and the gross annual revenue payable to the archbishop is, on an average, £3186. 2. 6¾. In the R. C. divisions this diocese and a few parishes in Meath constitute the see, which is suffragan to Armagh; it contains 65 chapels, served by 42 parish priests and 42 coadjutors and curates.

The living is a rectory and vicarage, in the diocese of Ardagh, and constituting the corps of the deanery, which is in the patronage of the Crown. The tithes amount to £482. 11. 5½.: and the mensal and other lands of the deanery, exclusively of several houses, tolls of fairs, a plot of nearly two acres on which the deanery-house is built, a farm of 13*a.* 1*r.* 10*p.*, and a large bog, comprise 714*a.* 2*r.* 35*p.*, (statute measure) producing, with the annual renewal fines, a rental of £292. 11. 2. per annum. The church is a plain commodious building with a square tower, for the erection of which the late Board of First Fruits granted a loan of £900, in 1812, and the Ecclesiastical Commissioners have lately granted £301 for its repair. The deanery-house was built in 1823, by a gift of £100 and a loan of £1200 from the same Board. In the R. C. divisions this parish is the head of a union or district, which includes also the adjoining parish of Moydow, in each of which is a chapel; that of Ardagh is situated near the village. The parochial school for boys is principally supported by a grant of £40 per ann. from Dr. Murray, the present dean, who also contributes annually £15. towards the support of the girls' school, which is further aided by an annual grant of £5 from the Ardagh Diocesan Society: the school-house is a good slated building of two stories, with apartments for the master and mistress, erected by Dr. Murray at an expense of £400, and attached to it is an acre of land. There are 40 boys and 30 girls in this school, and in the private pay schools are about 290 boys and 170 girls: there is also a Sunday school for boys and girls. Some remains of the old cathedral church, a small edifice rudely built of fragments of rock of a large size, are still visible; it was superseded by another church, now also in ruins, and the present edifice was erected near its site. St. Mell was interred here, and his festival is annually celebrated on Feb. 6th. The comedy of the "Mistakes of a Night," written by Dr. Goldsmith, derives its plot from an incident that occurred at this village to the author, who, on passing through it, having inquired for the "head inn," was directed by a humorous individual to the residence of the proprietor of the place, Mr. Fetherston, who perceiving the delusion, nevertheless indulged it, and hospitably entertained his guest; and it was not until next morning that, on finishing his breakfast and calling for the bill, the poet discovered his mistake.

ARDAGH, a parish, in the barony of TYRAWLEY, county of MAYO, and province of CONNAUGHT, 2¾ miles (W. S. W.) from Ballina; containing 1813 inhabitants. This parish is situated on the shores of Lough Conn and the river Deel, and on the road from Ballina to Crossmolina: it comprises 3215 statute acres, as applotted under the tithe act, and valued at £1794 per annum; the land is chiefly under tillage. There are large tracts of bog, furnishing abundance of fuel. Deel Castle, the seat of St. George Cuff, Esq., is delightfully situated on the river Deel, and in a fine demesne. Fairs are held at Newtown on the 4th of Aug. and the 1st of Nov. The living is a vicarage, in the diocese of Killala, with the vicarages of Ballynahaglish, Kilbelfad, Kilmoremoy, Attymass, and Kilgarvan episcopally united, constituting the union of Ardagh, in the patronage of the Bishop: the rectory is partly appropriate to the precentorship of the cathedral of Killala, and partly to the vicars choral of the cathedral of Christchurch, Dublin. The tithes amount to £110. 15. 4½., of which £38. 10. 10. is payable to the precentor of Killala, £13. 16. 11. to the vicars choral, and £55. 7. 8½. to the vicar. The glebes, which are detached, comprise together 31 acres; and the gross tithes payable to the incumbent amount to £948. 19. 2¼. The church of this parish is in ruins, and the church of the union is situated at Kilmoremoy. An episcopal chapel has been partly built at Deel Castle, but is not yet roofed. The R. C. parish is co-extensive with that of the Established Church: the chapel, a neat slated building, is situated at Newtown. Here is a school of 60 boys and 30 girls.

ARDAGH, a parish, partly in the barony of MORGALLION, but chiefly in that of LOWER SLANE, county of MEATH, and province of LEINSTER, 2 miles (E. S. E.) from Kingscourt; containing 2408 inhabitants. This parish, which is situated on the road from Drumconra to Kingscourt, and on the confines of the counties of Louth, Monaghan, and Cavan; comprises 3290 statute acres, as applotted under the tithe act, of which 2835 are arable, 324 are pasture, 112 are bog, and 19 woodland. Here are extensive quarries of limestone, of which a large quantity is sent into the county of Cavan to be burnt for manure. The living is a perpetual cure, in the diocese of Meath, and in the patronage of the Bishop, to whom the rectory is appropriate; the tithes amount to £207. 6. 5½., which is payable to the Bishop. The church is a plain edifice, built in 1805, for the repair of which the Ecclesiastical Commissioners have lately granted £125. There is a glebe-house, with a glebe of ten acres. In the R. C. divisions this parish is united to Drumconra: the chapel, a plain building, is situated at Ballinavoren. There are three hedge schools in the parish. On the townland of Cloughrea are the remains of an old castle; and at the northern extremity of the parish, but principally in the county of Monaghan, there is a considerable lake, called Rahans.

ARDAMINE, a parish, in the barony of BALLAGHKEEN, county of WEXFORD, and province of LEINSTER, 3¾ miles (S. S. E.) from Gorey; containing 1535 inhabitants. This parish is situated near the coast of the Irish sea, and comprises 4078 statute acres, as applotted under the tithe act; the soil is generally a strong marl favourable to the growth of wheat, and the system of agriculture is improving. A fishery in the bay of Ardamine promises to become very valuable when the harbour of Courtown, which is now in progress, shall be completed. Ardamine, the seat of J. Goddard Richards, Esq., is beautifully situated at a short distance from the sea; and the grounds have been recently embellished with thriving plantations and other improvements. Owenavarra Cottage, the residence of Mrs. Richards, sen., is also in the parish. The living is an impropriate curacy, in the diocese of Ferns, with that of Killenagh episcopally united, and in the patronage of the Bishop; the rectory is impropriate in H. K. G. Morgan, Esq. The tithes amount to £190, payable to the impropriator, who allows £23. 1. 6½. per ann. for the performance of the clerical duties of both parishes to which has been lately added an annual grant of £25 from Primate Boulter's fund. The church is situated on the confines of both parishes; there is neither glebe nor glebe-house. In the R. C. divisions the parish is the head of a union or district, also called River chapel, comprising the parishes of Ardamine and Donaghmore, in each of which is a chapel: that in this parish, with a comfortable residence for the clergyman adjoining it, was erected by subscription, together with a school-house for boys superintended by him, and another for girls under the patronage of Mrs. Richards. There is also a Sunday school, besides two private pay schools in which are about 30 children. Near the demesne of Ardemine is a large high tumulus, called the "Moat of Ardemine," considered to be one of the most perfect of its kind in Ireland: it is traditionally said to mark the burial-place of a Danish chief.

ARDARA, a post-town and district parish, in the barony of BANNAGH, county of DONEGAL, and province of ULSTER, $7\frac{1}{2}$ miles (N.) from Killybegs, and $134\frac{1}{2}$ miles (N. W.) from Dublin; containing 456 inhabitants. This place is situated on the river Awinea, at the bottom of Lockrusmore bay on the northern coast, and on the road from Narin to Killybegs. The village consists of 85 houses: it is a constabulary police station, and has a fair on the 1st of November; petty sessions are held at irregular intervals. The parochial district was formed by act of council in 1829, by disuniting 38 townlands from the parish of Killybegs, and 49 from that of Inniskeel. The living is a perpetual curacy, in the diocese of Raphoe, and in the alternate patronage of the Rectors of Killybegs and Inniskeel. The income of the curate is £90 per annum, of which £35 is paid by each of the rectors of the above-named parishes, and £20 is given from Primate Boulter's augmentation fund. The church is situated in the village. The R. C. parochial district is co-extensive with that of the Established Church, and contains a chapel. The Wesleyan Methodists assemble in a school-house once every alternate Sunday. A parochial school is aided by an annual grant from Col. Robertson's fund; and there is a school under the Wesleyan Missionary Society. In these schools are about 160 boys and 80 girls; and there are also two pay schools, in which are about 70 boys and 20 girls, and a Sunday school. On an island in the lake of Kiltorus, off Boylagh, near Mr. Hamilton's, of Eden, are the ruins of an old fortified building, near which were formerly some rusty cannon.

ARDBOE, county of TYRONE.—See ARBOE.

ARDBRACCAN, a parish, in the barony of LOWER NAVAN, county of MEATH, and province of LEINSTER, $2\frac{1}{2}$ miles (W.) from Navan; containing 3798 inhabitants. This place derived its name, signifying, in the Irish language, "the Hill of Braccan," from St. Braccan, who presided over a monastery here, and died in the year 650. The establishment subsequently became the seat of a small bishoprick, which flourished under a series of prelates, many of whom are noticed as eminent ecclesiastics, till the twelfth century, when, with several other small bishopricks, it was included in the diocese of Meath. The monastery was frequently plundered and laid waste by the Danes, and repeatedly destroyed by fire, from the 9th to the 12th century; and, in 1166, Moriertach, King of Ireland, granted to it in perpetuity a parcel of land at an annual rent of three ounces of gold. The village, which was anciently a place of some importance, especially during the existence of the see, appears to have declined since the period of the English invasion, and is no longer of any note. About one-half of the parish is under tillage, two-fifths in pasture, and the remainder meadow land. The only remarkable elevation is Faughan Hill, the conical summit of which being well planted, is conspicuous over the surrounding flat districts; and on the western border of the parish is a chain of bogs. Limestone is quarried for building; and at a place called White Quarry is found a particular kind of limestone, of which the bishop's palace is built. Limestone, gravel, and marl are also raised for manure. The bishop's palace, one of the most elegant ecclesiastical residences in Ireland, was erected by the late Bishop Maxwell: it is beautifully situated, and the grounds and gardens are tastefully laid out; the demesne is embellished with forest trees of stately growth, among which are some remarkably fine horse-chestnut trees; and there are also two very beautiful cedars of Lebanon, planted by the late Bishop Pococke. Oatland House, the residence and demesne of Blennerhasset Thompson, Esq., is also within the parish; and Dormerstown Castle is an old fortified residence. The weaving of linen cloth is carried on to a small extent, and some cotton looms are also employed by the inhabitants.

The living is a rectory, in the diocese of Meath, united by act of council, in 1771, to the rectories of Liscarton and Rataine, the chapelry of Churchtown, and the vicarage of Martry, and by the same authority, in 1780, to the rectory of Clonmacduff, which six parishes constitute the union of Ardbraccan, in the patronage of the Crown. The tithes amount to £433. 16. $10\frac{3}{4}$.: the gross amount of tithes payable to the incumbent is £820. 15. $5\frac{1}{4}$. The church is a handsome edifice, erected in 1777, under the auspices of the late Bishop Maxwell. The glebe-house is situated about half a mile from the church: the glebe comprises 33 acres of profitable land. The R. C. union or district of Ardbraccan, called also Bohermein, includes the parishes of Ardbraccan, Martry, Rathboyne, and parts of the parishes of Moyagher and Liscarton: there are two chapels in Ardbraccan and one in Rathboyne. The male and female parochial school is principally supported by the rector, and is aided by an annual donation from the Bishop of Meath; and there are two free schools at Byerstown and Bohermein, supported by bequests from the late Rev. Mr. Brannigan, P. P., and by annual subscriptions from Earl Ludlow and the parishioners. In these schools are about 300 boys and 160 girls; and there are also two private schools, in which are about 60 children. Dr. Chetwood, formerly rector of this parish, left £500, and Dr. Sterne, Bishop of Clogher, left £30 per annum, for apprenticing the children of Protestant inhabitants of the diocese to Protestant masters and mistresses; about 30 children are annually apprenticed from these funds. In the churchyard is a square tower with a spire and vane, forming a pleasing object. There is also a monument to Bishop Montgomery, who died in London, on the 15th of January, 1620, and was buried here; and on the south side of it is a small tablet to the memory of that celebrated traveller, Bishop Pococke, who presided over the see of Meath, and died in 1765.

ARDCANDRIDGE, or ARDCANDRISK, a parish, in the barony of SHELMALIER, county of WEXFORD, and province of LEINSTER, $3\frac{1}{2}$ miles (W. by N.) from Wexford, containing 242 inhabitants. This parish is situated on the river Slaney, by which it is bounded on the north, and on the road from Wexford along the south bank of the river, by way of Clonmore, to Enniscorthy: it comprises 1144 statute acres, as applotted under the tithe act, and is chiefly under tillage, which has gradually improved since the introduction of the drill system of husbandry. Ardcandrisk House, the seat of G. Grogan

Morgan, Esq., the proprietor of the soil, was built in 1833, and is beautifully situated on a wooded eminence rising above the Slaney, and commanding a very fine and extensive prospect. The Slaney is navigable for lighters up to Enniscorthy, affording facility for the conveyance of corn and other agricultural produce to Wexford, and for bringing coal and other commodities from that port. The parish is in the diocese of Ferns, and the rectory is one of the sixteen denominations constituting the union of St. Patrick's, Wexford: the tithes amount to £48. 18. 6½. In the R. C. divisions it is included in the union or district of Glyn, a village in the parish of Killurin.

ARDCANNY, a parish, in the barony of KENRY, county of LIMERICK, and province of MUNSTER, 10 miles (W. by S.) from Limerick; containing 1318 inhabitants. This parish is bounded on the north by the river Shannon, and on the east by the river Maigue, the banks of which are embellished with flourishing plantations and elegant seats. It comprises 3256 statute acres, as applotted under the tithe act: the land is remarkably good, being based on a substratum of limestone; about one-fourth is under an excellent system of tillage, and the remainder is meadow, pasture, and demesne, except about 48 acres of woodland, 10 acres of bog, and a very small portion of waste. Among the principal seats are Cartown, the residence of J. E. Langford, Esq.; Mellon, of M. Westropp, Esq.; Ballincarriga House, of — Dawson, Esq.; Rockfield, of E. Fitzgerald, Esq.; Shannon Grove, the old family mansion of the Earls of Charleville, and now the residence of Bolton Waller, Esq.; Mount Pleasant, the residence of Mrs. Hill; Ballystool, of E. Hewson, Esq.; and Ballincarreg, of H. Hurst, Esq.; besides which there are many substantial houses. The living is a rectory and vicarage, in the diocese of Limerick, forming the corps of the prebend of Ardcanny in the cathedral of Limerick, and in the patronage of the Bishop: the tithes amount to £300. The church is a spacious edifice, built in 1738, but in a very dilapidated condition. The glebe-house was built in 1791, by aid of a gift of £100 from the late Board of First Fruits, and has been greatly improved by the late and present incumbents: the glebe contains 52 statute acres. In the R. C. divisions this parish forms part of the union or district of Kildeemo, or Kildimo. A male and female parochial school, for which a house was built by the rector, has been discontinued, and the building is now used as a court-house. There is a private school, in which are about 90 children. In the demesne of Rockfield is a very capacious and ancient fortress, constructed of large blocks of stone very ingeniously put together without mortar, and forming walls of great thickness: there are also numerous earthworks in the parish.

ARDCARNE, a parish, in the barony of BOYLE, county of ROSCOMMON, and province of CONNAUGHT, 3½ miles (E. S. E.) from Boyle, on the road to Carrick-on-Shannon; containing 7673 inhabitants. An abbey of Regular canons was founded here, probably in the early part of the 6th century, of which, according to the Annals of the Four Masters, Beaidh died bishop in 523: its possessions were granted, in the 39th of Elizabeth, to the Provost and Fellows of Trinity College, Dublin. Here was also a Benedictine nunnery, a cell to the abbey of Kilcreunata, in the county of Galway; and at Knockvicar was a monastery of the third order of Franciscans, which at the suppression was granted with other possessions on lease to Richard Kendlemarch. The parish is situated on the shores of Lough Key: it is partly bounded by the Shannon on the east, and comprises 11,460 statute acres, as applotted under the tithe act. The land is principally under an improving system of tillage; there is a considerable extent of reclaimable bog, and part of the plains of Boyle is included within the parish. Limestone and freestone of the best description for architectural purposes abound; indications of coal have been discovered on the lands of Ballyfermoyle, the property of W. Mulloy, Esq., where shafts have been sunk, but the operations are discontinued. The Boyle river runs through the parish, and a project is in contemplation to render it navigable from its junction with the Shannon, near Carrick, to Lough Gara: this river is crossed by a bridge at Knockvicar, where its banks are adorned with some pleasing scenery. Rockingham House, the elegant mansion of Viscount Lorton, is beautifully situated on the south-east side of Lough Key, in a gently undulating and well-wooded demesne of about 2000 statute acres, tastefully laid out in lawns and groves descending to the water's edge: it is of Grecian Ionic architecture, built externally of marble, with a portico of six Ionic columns forming the principal entrance, on each side of which are corresponding pillars ornamenting the façade, and on the north side is a colonnade supported by six Ionic columns: adjoining the house is an extensive orangery, and numerous improvements have been made in the grounds by the present noble proprietor. Oakport, the seat of W. Mulloy, Esq., is a large edifice in the ancient or Gothic style of architecture, occupying a beautiful situation on the margin of a large expanse of water formed by the Boyle river: the demesne comprises about 1200 statute acres, beautifully wooded, and from the inequality of its surface presents many picturesque and commanding views. The other seats are Knockvicar, the residence of C. J. Peyton, Esq., and Mount Francis, of W. Lloyd O'Brien, Esq. Petty sessions are held every Tuesday at Cootehall. That place was formerly called *Urtaheera*, or O'Mulloy's Hall, and was, early in the 17th century, together with the manor attached to it, the property of William, styled "the Great O'Mulloy;" but in the war of 1641 it came into the possession of the Hon. Chidley Coote, nephew of the first Earl of Mountrath, and from that family took its present name. The parish is in the diocese of Elphin, and the rectory forms part of the union of Killuken: the tithes amount to £280. The church is an ancient structure, which was enlarged by a grant of £600 from the late Board of First Fruits, and the Ecclesiastical Commissioners have lately granted £234 for its further repair. The glebe-house was built by aid of a gift of £100 and a loan of £300 from the same Board, in 1807: the glebe comprises 20 acres, subject to a rent of £8. In the R. C. divisions the parish is also called Crosna, and comprises the parish of Ardcarne and part of that of Tumna, containing two chapels, situated at Cootehall and Crosna. The parochial free school is supported by Lord Lorton, who built the school-house at an expense of £120; and a school for girls is supported by Lady Lorton, and is remarkably well conducted. At Derrygra is a school aided by the Elphin Diocesan Society, to which the bishop gave a house and an acre of ground; and three Sunday schools are held in the parish, two under the patronage of Lady Lorton, and one under that of the Misses Mulloy, of Oakport. A dispensary is maintained by Lord Lorton for the benefit of his tenantry; and another has been lately established at Cootehall, by the exertions of the Messrs. Mulloy, by whom and the other principal landed proprietors it is supported.

ARDCATH, a parish, in the barony of UPPER DULEEK, county of MEATH, and province of LEINSTER, $6\frac{3}{4}$ miles (S. by W.) from Drogheda, on the road from Dublin to Drogheda; containing 1774 inhabitants. About one-half is under an improved system of tillage, and the remainder is excellent pasture land; the principal corn crop is wheat. There are about 300 acres of bog, which is being gradually reclaimed and brought into cultivation. On the townland of Cloghan is a quarry of excellent slate, but it has not been worked for some years. The weaving of linen was formerly carried on to a considerable extent: about 200 looms are at present employed in weaving cotton for the Dublin and Drogheda manufacturers; and there are two oatmeal-mills, one worked by wind and the other by water. A fair is held on May 8th principally for cattle. The parish is in the diocese of Meath; the rectory is impropriate in the Marquess of Drogheda, and the vicarage forms part of the union of Duleek. The tithes amount to £265, of which £195 is payable to the impropriator and £70 to the vicar. In the R. C. divisions the parish is the head of a union or district which comprises also the parish of Clonalvy and part of Piercetown, and contains two chapels, situated respectively at Ardcath and Clonalvy: the former is a neat building, erected about 80 years since, and recently much enlarged; the additional part stands upon the glebe land, by permission of the vicar of Duleek. A school at Cloghantown, of 48 boys and 16 girls, is aided by a donation of £5 per annum from the Rev. M. Langan, P.P.; and there is an evening pay school at Yellowford. The Rev. John Leonard, late P.P., bequeathed the ground on which the residence of the R. C. clergyman is built, and fifteen additional acres of land, to be vested in trustees for the use of all future pastors; £10 per annum for the joint use of the three parishes of the R. C. union, and one ton of oatmeal to be distributed annually in the same district. The ruins of the ancient church are extensive, but void of interesting details; the belfry remains, and a bell has been preserved in it from time immemorial, at the joint expense of the Protestant and R. C. inhabitants, and is used at funerals, and by the latter to assemble their congregations.

ARDCAVAN, a parish, in the barony of SHELMALIER, county of WEXFORD, and province of LEINSTER, adjoining the town of Wexford, (with which it is connected by the bridge), and containing 878 inhabitants. It is situated on the eastern shore of the estuary of the Slaney, and comprises 2370 statute acres, as applotted under the tithe act. Ely House, the property of the Marquess of Ely, is situated near the bridge, at the southern extremity of the parish, and is the residence of R. Hughes, Esq. The parish is in the diocese of Ferns, and is an impropriate cure, forming part of the union of Ardcolme; the rectory is impropriate in the Earl of Portsmouth. The tithes amount to £139. 18. $1\frac{3}{4}$., of which £73. 1. $10\frac{3}{4}$. is payable to the impropriator, and £66. 16. 3. to the curate. In the R. C. divisions it is included in the union or district of Castlebridge, where the chapel is situated, and the greater part of which village is within its limits. Near the shore of Wexford harbour are the ruins of the old church; and at Ballytramont there are considerable remains of the ancient castle of that name. An extensive coppice wood, comprising about 65 statute acres, stretches along the estuary from the latter place.

ARDCLARE, or CLONIGORMICAN, a parish, in the half-barony of BALLYMOE, county of ROSCOMMON, and province of CONNAUGHT, $5\frac{1}{4}$ miles (N. N. W.) from Roscommon, on the road to Castlerea; containing 2633 inhabitants. It comprises 8066 statute acres, principally under pasture; there is no waste land, and only a small quantity of bog, sufficient for supplying the inhabitants with fuel. Limestone of the best description abounds, but the quarries are not worked for any particular purpose. The principal gentlemen's seats are Runnymead, that of J. Balfe, Esq.; Ballymacurly, of M. Nolan, Esq.; Briarfield, of C. Hawkes, Esq.; and Faragher Lodge, of the Rev. Lewis Hawkes. Manorial courts are held in the townland of Farragher three times in the year. The living is a vicarage, in the diocese of Elphin, to which the vicarages of Kilcooley, Creeve, Killuken, Shankill, Kilmacumsy, and Tumna were episcopally united in 1809, which seven parishes constitute the union of Ardclare, in the patronage of the Bishop; the rectory is impropriate in the Earl of Essex and Lord De Roos. The tithes amount to £176. 12., one-half of which is payable to the impropriators (the Earl of Essex receiving £73. 11. 8. and Lord De Roos, £14. 14. 4.) and the other half to the vicar; and the gross amount of the tithes of the union payable to the incumbent is £491. 11. $10\frac{1}{2}$. The church was originally built by Chas. Hawkes, Esq., of Briarfield, as a chapel of ease, about the year 1720, and subsequently became the parochial church; it is a plain edifice in good repair. There is neither glebe-house nor glebe. In the R. C. divisions the parish forms part of the union or district of Glinsk and Ballymoe; the chapel, a neat edifice recently erected, is situated on the townland of Ballymacurly. There are three pay schools, in which are about 100 boys and 40 girls.

ARDCLARE, a village, in the parish of KILMACTEIGUE, barony of LENEY, county of SLIGO, and province of CONNAUGHT, 9 miles (N. E.) from Foxford, on the road to Ballymote; containing about 20 houses and 110 inhabitants. It has a market on Saturday, and is a station of the constabulary police.

ARDCLINIS, a parish, in the Lower half-barony of GLENARM, county of ANTRIM, and province of ULSTER, 6 miles (N. by W.) from Glenarm; containing 1617 inhabitants. This parish is situated on Red bay in the North Channel, and comprises, according to the Ordnance survey, 15,691 statute acres, of which 15,144 are applotted under the tithe act and valued at £2055 per annum. The surface is hilly and irregular, but the land in cultivation is fertile, and the system of agriculture is in a very improving state. Much of the waste land has been planted, especially the hills, imparting to the coast an interesting and cheerful aspect. The arable and inhabited portion of the parish consists of one long strip extending from the village of Carnlough along the sea-coast into Red bay, and up one side of the beautiful glen of Glenariff. On the land side it is enclosed by a steep and lofty mountain, ascended only by narrow paths traversing its acclivities, by which the inhabitants convey their fuel in slide carts. The river Acre rises in the neighbouring mountains, and forms a boundary between this parish and that of Layde; it abounds with excellent trout, and where it empties itself into the sea is a salmon fishery. The highest part of the mountains is called Carnealapt-Aura, and near Broughshane they are mostly covered with heath and abound with moor game. Glenariff, one of the seven great glens, is flat in the centre; the river winds through the whole extent of it in a serpentine course, and being on a level with the sea, whenever a high tide meets a flood, it overflows its banks and inundates the glen; the rise on each side towards the rocks assumes an appearance of circular rising ground. Three-fourths of the superficial extent of the parish are composed of mountainous, marshy, boggy, and unprofitable land. Limestone and basalt are found in great abundance. The scenery is enlivened with several gentlemen's seats, among which are Drumnasole, the residence of F. Turnley, Esq.; Knappan, of Major Higginson; and Bay Lodge, of Major Williams. Several of the inhabitants are engaged in the fishery carried on in the bay, where there is a small but commodious harbour, and vessels from 14 to 20 tons' burden can enter the river Acre at high water. Fairs are held at Carnlough. The royal military road passes through this parish, the most mountainous of all the parishes on the coast, notwithstanding which the road preserves a perfect level throughout, at an elevation of a few feet above high water mark; the excavations round Garron Point will be 360 feet in depth. Garron Point is one of the eight coast-guard stations, in the district of Carrickfergus.

The parish is in the diocese of Connor, and the rectory forms part of the union of Agherton and corps of the treasurership in the cathedral church of Connor, in the patronage of the Bishop: the tithes amount to £150. The church has for many years been in ruins, and divine service is performed in the school-room at Drumnasole, near the centre of the parish. In the R. C. divisions it is in the union or district of Layde, or Cushendall; the chapel at Glenariff is a spacious building, in which divine service is performed every alternate Sunday. There is a place of worship for Methodists, open every alternate Thursday. A large school-house was erected at Drumnasole, at an expense of £1000, by F. Turnley, Esq., and entirely supported by that gentleman till the year 1833, when it was placed under the management of the National Board of Education: there are also other schools, the whole affording instruction to about 230 boys and 170 girls. On the summit of a headland, near Garron Point, are the remains of a large Danish camp, called Dunmaul or Doonmul, which, according to tradition, was occupied by the Danes during their continuance in Ireland, and from which they set sail when they finally quitted the country.

ARDCOLLUM.—See KILMURRY, county of Tipperary.

ARDCOLME, a parish, in the barony of Shelmalier, county of Wexford, and province of Leinster, 2½ miles (N. E. by N.) from Wexford; containing 790 inhabitants. This parish is situated on the north side of Wexford harbour, and on the road leading from Wexford, by way of Oulart, to Dublin: it comprises 2070 statute acres, as applotted under the tithe act, and contains a small part of the village of Castlebridge and the island of Beg Erin in Wexford harbour, on which are the remains of a very ancient church. The living is an impropriate curacy, in the diocese of Ferns, to which the rectories of St. Margaret and Artramont, the vicarages of Tickillen and Kilpatrick, and the impropriate cures of Ardcavan, Ballyvalloo, Skreen, and St. Nicholas were united by act of council in 1764, and formed the union of Ardcolme, which is in the patronage of the Bishop; but by an act of council in 1829, the parish of Kilpatrick and eight townlands, constituting the greater portion of the adjoining parish of Tickillen, were separated from this union and erected into a distinct benefice: the rectory of Ardcolme is impropriate in the Earl of Portsmouth. The tithes amount to £125. 16. 9., of which £71. 4. 10. is payable to the impropriator, and £54. 11. 11. to the incumbent; and the gross tithes of the benefice payable to the incumbent amount to £676. 5. 7. The parochial church is situated in the village of Castlebridge, and was erected in 1764 on the site of an ancient castle, which, with an acre of land, was given for that purpose by the Bishop; the expense was defrayed partly by subscription and partly by the parishioners, aided by a gift of £150 from the late Board of First Fruits; the Ecclesiastical Commissioners have lately granted £310 for its repair. It is a neat plain edifice surrounded by some fine old elm trees, and contains a neat tablet to Lieut.-Col. Jones Watson, who was killed in the disturbances of 1798, and interred in the churchyard at Carrick; and another to Edward Turner, Esq., who, with others, fell a victim to popular fury on the bridge at Wexford, on the 20th of June in the same year. The glebe-house is a neat and substantial building, towards the erection of which the same Board gave £100, in 1806: there are three glebes in the present union, comprising together about 71 acres, of which 32 are in this parish. In the R. C. divisions the parish forms part of the union or district of Castlebridge, where the chapel is situated. The parochial school was established under the auspices of the incumbent, the Rev. J. W. Stokes, who pays the master £20 per annum; and the school-house, a neat building lately erected at his expense, will accommodate from 50 to 60 children. The ruins of the old church still remain, situated about a mile from the present church.

ARDCRONEY, a parish, in the barony of Lower Ormond, county of Tipperary, and province of Munster, 2 miles (S. by W.) from Burris-o-kane, on the road to Nenagh; containing 1681 inhabitants. It comprises 5810 statute acres, as applotted under the tithe act. The soil is mostly light; there are several small bogs in the parish, which abounds also with limestone. The water of a lake covering about 172 plantation acres was drained off by the late Rev. R. Falkiner, of Mount Falcon, in 1800, and the land is now highly productive. The principal seats are Mount Falcon, the property and residence of Mrs. Falkiner; Beechwood, the property of Col. Toler Osborne, but in the occupation of D. Falkiner, Esq.; Conger House, the residence of F. Falkiner, Esq.; Willsborough, the property and residence of J. Falkiner,

Esq.; Ballinderry, the property of T. Sadleir, jun., Esq., on which a house is about to be erected; Ballyrickard, the residence of N. Falkiner, Esq.; Woodlands, of R. Falkiner, Esq.; and Whitstone, the property of Elias Bowler, Esq. Beechwood was once the residence of the late Earl of Norbury, and was originally a castle, of which the present house is a part; on a stone is the date 1594, with the initials O. H. The living is a vicarage, in the diocese of Killaloe, and in the patronage of the Bishop, to whose mensal the rectory is appropriate: the tithes amount to £307. 11. 6¾., of which £205. 1. 0½. is payable to the Bishop, and £102. 10. 6¼. to the vicar. The church is a very neat structure, built in 1824. There is a glebe of three acres, but no glebe-house. In the R. C. divisions this parish forms part of the union or district of Modreeny, or Cloghjordan: the chapel is a small building on the townland of Ardcroney. There is a parochial school, also a private pay school. On an eminence near the high road are the remains of the old church, forming a conspicuous ruin; and on the townland of Ballyluskey is an ancient castle, consisting of one square tower. At the rear of Beechwood House, on an eminence, is a large fort or rath, planted with trees, the summit of which is encircled by a stone wall.

ARDEE, an incorporated market and post-town, and a parish, in the barony of Ardee, county of Louth, and province of Leinster, 10 miles (S. W. by S.) from Dundalk, and 34½ miles (N. N. W.) from Dublin; containing 6181 inhabitants, of which number, 3975 are in the town. This place, anciently called *Atherdee* or *Athirdee*, derives its name from its situation on the river Dee. Though a town of great antiquity, it was chiefly indebted for its former prosperity and importance to Roger de Pippart, one of the English adventurers, who became lord of the surrounding territory, and erected a strong castle here, about the beginning of the thirteenth century. In the year 1207 he also founded an hospital for Crouched friars of the order of St. Augustine, dedicated to St. John, and endowed it with a caracute of land, to which he afterwards added two more, and other gifts. Eugene, Archbishop of Armagh, who died in 1215, confirmed the charter of this establishment, and granted it the privilege of electing its own prior, and it attained an eminent degree of wealth and importance. A Carmelite friary was also founded at an early period, to which Ralph de Pippart, in the reign of Edw. I., granted certain endowments out of his manor of Ardee, and its revenues were further augmented by several of the inhabitants. During the invasion of Edward Bruce, who laid waste much of the surrounding country, many of the inhabitants assembled for protection in this friary, which was attacked by a party of Scots and Irish under his command, and reduced to ashes. John de Bermingham, after repelling these invaders, was created Earl of Louth, and had a grant of the manor, but was soon afterwards killed in an insurrection of his own people. In 1538, the town was burnt by O'Nial and his associates; and in the following year George Dowdall, the last prior of the Augustine monastery, surrendered that house with all its possessions in lands and advowsons, and was allowed a pension of £20 sterling until he should obtain some ecclesiastical preferment. Having been appointed to the archbishoprick of Armagh, he received a grant for life of the monastery and its appurtenances, in 1554; and in 1612 its possessions in and near the town were granted, by Jas. I., to Sir Garret Moore, who also subsequently received a grant of the remainder. On the breaking out of hostilities in 1641, Sir Phelim O'Nial obtained possession of the town, which thence became the head-quarters of the Irish army; but Sir Henry Tichborne advanced against it in the same year, with his small force from Drogheda, and retook the town and castle, in which a garrison was then placed. At a subsequent period the Marquess of Ormonde issued orders to the garrison to destroy the town, which, from their neglect or disobedience of his commands, afterwards fell into the hands of Cromwell. Jas. II., after leaving Dundalk, retired with his army to this place; but on the approach of William's forces, previously to the battle of the Boyne, retreated to Drogheda.

The town is situated in a very fertile corn district, and consists of one principal street, with lanes branching from it; many of the houses are of respectable appearance. Turf is brought for the supply of the inhabitants from a large bog about 1½ mile to the west, by means of a branch of the river Dee, which has been made navigable for boats. Malting is extensively carried on; and there are a corn-mill and a corn and flour-mill. The market is held on Tuesday and is well supplied: a meat market, or shambles, was erected by the corporation in 1796, which cost about £600; and a corn market about the year 1710, at an expense of nearly £2000, for each of which they pay a ground rent of about £10 per annum. Fairs, of which four are held under the charter of Queen Anne (in confirmation and extension of a patent of Chas. II. in 1681), and three were granted by patent of Geo. III. in 1819, are held on March 1st, April 10th, June 6th, July 8th, Aug. 20th, Oct. 23rd (a large fair for sheep), and Dec. 17th, principally for live stock, on a plot of ground which has been enclosed at a considerable expense by the corporation. The tolls were granted by charter to the corporation, who, previously to 1823, claimed the right of levying toll not only at the market and fairs, but also toll thorough and pontage; but after considerable resistance, accompanied by riot and disorder, their claim to the latter was negatived at the Dundalk assizes in that year; and the payment of the former has been since also resisted, but their right has been confirmed by the assistant barrister for the county. Here is a chief station of the constabulary police.

A corporation is first mentioned in a charter of the 51st of Edw. III. (1377), as set forth in a charter of inspeximus and confirmation of the 3rd of Rich. II., under the style of "the Provosts (or Portreeves) and Commonalty of the town of Athirde;" and certain customs on goods for sale were granted to them for a term of ten years, and confirmed by succeeding monarchs, in aid of enclosing the town with a stone wall and paving the streets. A charter of the 1st of Hen. V. (1414), granted cognizance of all pleas, real and personal, and jurisdiction of assize, with return of writs and other important privileges, within the town and precincts; and by a statute in the 33rd of Hen. VI., confirmed by another in the following year, it was enacted that the portreeves should be justices of the peace. The present governing charter was granted in the 11th of Queen Anne, 1713; under it the corporation is styled "the Portreeve, Burgesses, and Commons of the Corporation of Atherdee;" and consists of the portreeve, 23 other burgesses, and an unlimited number of freemen, assisted by a town-clerk, constable, two serjeants-at-mace, and other inferior officers: there is also a select body composed of the portreeve, six burgesses, and six common council freemen. The portreeve is elected annually out of the burgesses on the 23rd of April, by the portreeve, burgesses, and freemen, and is sworn in on Sept. 29th; the burgesses are elected for life out of the freemen, by the corporation at large; the freemen are created by nomination of the common council and subsequent election of the corporation at large; and the members of the common council are created for life in the same manner as the burgesses. The borough returned to the Irish parliament two members, elected by the burgesses and freemen, until the Union, when, of the £15,000 awarded as compensation for the abolition of the elective franchise, one-half was paid to Wm. Ruxton, Esq., and the remainder to Chas. and Wm. Parkinson Ruxton, Esqrs. The portreeve under the charter is a justice of the peace, coroner, and clerk of the market; but, being usually a justice of peace for the county, and the local courts having fallen into disuse, these peculiar functions are little exercised, and the corporation is now little more than nominal. The county quarter sessions for the division of Ardee are held here in January and June; and petty sessions are held every Wednesday, at which the portreeve and county magistrates preside. The old castle is now used as a court-house; and attached to it is a well-regulated county bridewell of modern erection. The revenue of the corporation is derived from rents of lands and tolls, and amounts to about £135 per annum.

The parish comprises, according to the Ordnance survey, 4884½ statute acres. With the exception of about 300 acres of bog, it is principally under tillage; the soil is very fertile, and the system of agriculture much improved. It contains several quarries of limestone and greenstone. The surrounding scenery has been much improved by extensive planting. Ardee House is the seat of Mrs. Ruxton, and Red House, that of W. Parkinson Ruxton, Esq.; a handsome demesne is attached to each. The living is a vicarage, in the diocese of Armagh, to which the rectory of Kildemock was united by act of council in 1700, and subsequently the vicarages of Shenlis, Smarmore, and Stickillen episcopally, forming the union of Ardee, in the patronage of the Lord-Primate: the rectory is impropriate in Viscount Ferrard. The tithes amount to £392. 13. 11., the whole of which is payable to the impropriator, who allows a stipend to the incumbent, who, besides a glebe-house and 40 plantation acres of glebe, valued at £120 per ann., at Kildemock (nearly in the centre of the union), has a glebe in this parish comprising 104 plantation acres and valued at £391. 11. 5. per ann., fifteen tenements in the town let for £107. 2. 2. per ann., and half an acre in Stickillen of the annual value of £1. 10. The gross annual value of the benefice, tithe and glebe inclusive, is £842. 13. 7. The church, which was formerly that of the Augustine monastery, is an ancient and spacious structure, supposed to have been built in 1208, and still in good repair. The R. C. district comprises the Protestant union and the parish of Maplestown in addition, and contains two chapels, situated at Ardee and Kildemock: the former stands at the entrance to the town from the south, and was built in 1829; it is a handsome and commodious edifice faced with hewn stone, 100 feet long by 56 broad, with a gallery extending round three sides of it.

There are two schools for both sexes on the foundation of Erasmus Smith: the boys' school-room was built in 1806, and the girls' in 1817, at a total expense of £600, of which the corporation contributed £450 and about three roods of the fair green as a site, and W. P. Ruxton, Esq., £150. There are seven private pay schools, also a dispensary and a savings' bank. Of the Augustine monastery, with the exception of the church, only the eastern wall of the belfry at the west end, and an adjoining cell on the north are remaining; and of the Carmelite friary there are no vestiges. Near the church are the remains of an old college, which have been converted into a thatched dwelling. The ancient castle, situated in the middle of the town, and now used as a court-house and gaol, is of quadrangular form, with a high roof and a rudely pointed gateway; the east and west fronts are defended by projecting towers, which rise above the rest of the building. In the centre of the town is also another ancient castle, which has long been in the possession of the Hatch family; it was granted by Cromwell to Williams, one of their ancestors, and has been recently fitted up as a handsome dwelling by W. Hatch, Esq., the present proprietor; it is defended by embrasures and a tower on the east side, on which have been placed two four-pounders, by permission of the lord-lieutenant and council in 1828. Close to the town is a fortified mount of great magnitude, anciently called *Cnuc na Scanghaim*, and the seat of the chiefs of the district. The Earl of Meath enjoys the inferior title of Baron Brabazon, of Ardee, by which his ancestor, Sir Edward Brabazon, was elevated to the peerage of Ireland, in 1616.

ARDERA, a townland, in the barony of IVERK, county of KILKENNY, and province of LEINSTER, 3½ miles (W. N. W.) from Waterford; containing 334 inhabitants. This townland, which anciently was part of the possessions of the abbey of Jerpoint, is bounded on the north by the parish of Ullid, and on the south by that of Rathkyran, of which latter it is, in the civil divisions, considered to form a part, and comprises 804 statute acres. It is in the diocese of Ossory, and is one of eighteen denominations constituting the union of Burnchurch: the tithes amount to £69. In the R. C. divisions it forms part of the union or district of Moncoin.

ARDFERT, a decayed borough and market-town, and a parish, in the barony of CLANMAURICE, county of KERRY, and province of MUNSTER, 5 miles (N.N.W.) from Tralee, and 144½ (S. W. by W.) from Dublin; containing 3585 inhabitants, of which number, 717 are in the town. The name of this place, sometimes written *Ardart*, signifies, according to Sir James Ware, "a wonderful place on an eminence," or, as some interpret it, "the hill of miracles." *Ardart* has also been considered

Arms.

a corruption of *Ard Ert*, "the high place of Ert." Matthew Paris calls it *Hertfert*, "the place of miracles of Hert or Ert;" and in the Annals of Innisfallen it is mentioned under the name of *Hyferte*, which denotes "the territory of miracles, or of Ert." It is thought to have been made by St. Ert, in the fifth century, the seat of a bishop's see, which comprehended the northern part of the county. St. Brendan erected a sumptuous monastery here in the sixth century, which, with the town, was destroyed by fire in 1089: it was again reduced to ashes by Cormac O'Culen, in 1151, and, with the town, suffered a like fate in 1179, on which occasion it is supposed to have been entirely demolished. In 1253, Thomas, Lord of Kerry, founded a monastery for conventual Franciscans, probably on the site of the former, which was held in high estimation on account of numerous miracles said to have been performed in it: the founder and several other lords of Kerry, with many of their respective families, were interred in this monastery. A leper-house was founded about 1312 by Nicholas Fitz-Maurice, who also erected a castle, of which little is recorded until the reign of Elizabeth, when the town was destroyed by a party of the royal forces under Maurice Stack, in 1599; and in the following year the castle was besieged by Sir Charles Wilmot, and, after a vigorous defence for nine days, was surrendered by the garrison, on some small pieces of ordnance being brought against it from an English vessel; the constable was hanged, but the lives of the rest were spared. The castle was rebuilt by Patrick, lord of Kerry, in 1637, but was demolished by an Irish leader named Lawler, in 1641, and there are now no remains. In the same year the cathedral was also destroyed, and the south transept was afterwards fitted up for divine service.

This is a declining town, without either trade or manufacture, and presents only the appearance of a village. The market, which was held on Thursday, was granted, with a fair on the festival of St. Peter and St. Paul and the following day, and a court of pie poudre and the usual tolls, by letters patent bearing date July 6th, 10th of Jas. I. (1612), to Thomas, lord of Kerry, then principal owner of the district. Fairs are held on Whit-Monday, July 9th, and Aug. 15th. The collection of tolls is not confined to sales made in the public fair; every person selling in his own house, on the fair day, is compelled to pay toll to the collector. A penny post from Tralee has been lately established; and here is a station of the constabulary police.

It has always been considered a borough by prescription, there being no charter of incorporation on record. The corporation, under the title of "The Portreeve, Burgesses, and Freemen of the Borough of Ardfert, in the county of Kerry," consisted of a portreeve, twelve burgesses, and an unlimited number of freemen. The borough returned two members to the Irish parliament in 1639, and continued to exercise the franchise till the Union, when the £15,000 awarded as compensation for the loss of that privilege was paid to the trustees of the marriage settlement of the late Earl of Glandore: the right of election was vested in the corporation. For some years after the Union, corporate meetings took place for the election of a portreeve and filling up vacancies among the burgesses, principally with a view to preserve the corporate property in the commons from encroachment; but the corporation was little more than nominal, and its meetings have fallen into total disuse. The borough extends towards the east and west a considerable distance from the town, but on the south-west a portion of the town itself is outside the limits, which are not accurately defined: it is entirely within the parish, and is said to include the Sheep Walk, Grague, Killarane, Brandon Well, Kilquane, Laragh, Gortaspidale, and the commons. The above grant of Jas. I., in 1612, conferred on Thomas, lord of Kerry, the privilege of holding courts baron and courts leet, with other manorial rights. The Earl of Listowel is now lord of the manor, and appoints a seneschal, who holds, in what was probably the old borough bridewell, a manor court once in three weeks, for the trial of actions of debt amounting to 40*s*. late currency, of which the jurisdiction extends about 2½ miles round the town; all trials are by jury, the jurors being summoned from the tenants of the manor, who are bound by their leases to serve, or are otherwise liable to a fine; but the business in this court is decreasing, from the holding of petty sessions in the town every alternate week, and of the county quarter sessions before the assistant barrister at Tralee. The only property now admitted to belong to the corporation is the commons adjoining the town, comprising about 200 acres, and valued at £70 per annum, on which the inhabitants exercise a right of commonage; they were formerly very extensive, but encroachments have been made from time to time, which have been a source of constant disputes, and there are now on them about 100 houses or cabins, valued with the land at about £200 per annum; the occupants are free from rent, and formerly escaped all county rates, but the latter have of late been levied.

The Diocese of Ardfert and Aghadoe consists of a union of two ancient sees, which from time immemorial have been incorporated. The see of Ardfert, or Ardart, was anciently called *Kiaragi* or *Kerrigia*, also the bishoprick of *Iar-Muan*, or West Munster; and from history and public records it appears that the bishops of Ardfert were likewise denominated bishops of Kerry, which title is still retained in the R. C. divisions. On the translation of Thomas Fulwar (the last bishop of Ardfert) to Cashel, in 1660, this see was held *in commendam* with that of Limerick, of which latter Edward Singe was in that year consecrated bishop; and on his translation to Cork, in 1663, Ardfert was permanently united to Limerick, under the prelacy of Wm. Fuller. The ancient diocese of Aghadoe can now only be traced in its archdeaconry, which is annexed to the chapter of Ardfert, and in the remains of its ancient cathedral. The diocese is one of the eleven constituting the ecclesiastical province of Cashel, and comprehends the entire county of Kerry and a small portion of that of Cork: it extends about 66 British miles in length and 61 in breadth, and comprises by estimation a superficial area of 676,450 plantation acres, of which 647,650 are in Kerry, and 28,800 in Cork. The chapter consists of the dean, chancellor, treasurer, precentor, and archdeacon: there are no prebendaries or vicars choral attached to the cathedral; the only other endowed office is a minor canonry, which does not exist in connection with any other cathedral in Ireland, except that of St. Patrick, Dublin. The see lands and gross annual revenue of the diocese are included in the return for the diocese of Limerick. Of the cathedral, dedicated to St. Brendan, a portion of the remains has been fitted up as the parochial church, which was repaired in 1831 by subscription of the bishop and dignitaries: there is no economy fund. The consistorial court consists of a vicar-general, surrogate, registrar, deputy-registrar, and proctor: there is also a diocesan schoolmaster. The diocese comprehends 89 parishes, forming 51 benefices, of which 9, including the deanery, are in the gift of the crown; 21, including the other dignities, are in the patronage of the bishop, and the remaining 21 in lay patronage. The number of churches is 35, besides 8 other buildings in which divine service is performed; and of glebe-houses, 20. In the R. C. divisions the diocese (which retains its ancient name of Kerry) extends, with the exception of a small part of one of the northern parishes, over the whole of that of the Established Church, and also includes the parishes of Kilcaskin, Kilcatern, Kilaconenagh, and Kilnamanagh, in the Protestant diocese of Ross, and is suffragan to that of Cashel. It comprehends 43 parochial unions or districts, and contains 88 chapels, served by 43 parish priests and 34 coadjutors or curates: the bishop's district is that of Killarney.

The parish lies on the western coast, and contains 6013 statute acres, as applotted under the tithe act, exclusively of a considerable extent of sand-hills, marsh, and bog. Within its limits is the creek or harbour of Barra, where a pier was some years since constructed by the late Fishery Board, which from its position has hitherto been of no avail: the entrance is flanked by rocks rising to the height of nearly 100 feet, and was formerly defended by a castle, of which a considerable part remains, and from which, according to tradition, a chain was thrown across to the opposite rock, to prevent the sudden entry of hostile vessels; further in, on the Fenit side, are the remains of another old castle. The pasture farms are extensive; the tillage farms average from 20 to 30 acres. The principal seat is Ardfert Abbey, subsequently noticed. About a mile to the east of the town is Tubrid, a seat belonging to J. O'Connell, Esq. Sackville House, lately in the occupation of the Rev. R. Maunsell, is the property of the Crosbie family; and Barra, on the north shore of the creek of that name, is the residence of T. Collis, Esq. Within a short distance of the town are the ruins of a castle, called Rahanane, formerly the residence of the Bishops of Ardfert, and still attached to the see, but held on lease by Capt. Willow. The living is a rectory, in the diocese of Ardfert and Aghadoe, and is divided into five equal portions, held respectively by the dean, precentor, chancellor, treasurer, and perpetual curate: the portion attached to the deanery was united, at a period prior to any existing records, to the rectories of Ratass and Killanear, constituting the corps of the deanery of Ardfert, in the patronage of the Crown: the tithes of the parish amount to £253. 16. 11., and of the decanal union to £479. 19. 8½., to which being added the value of the glebe-lands, lying in Ardfert and Ratass, the gross income of the dean, according to the Commissioners of Ecclesiastical Inquiry, is £549. 9. The church consists of the south transept of the old cathedral: it is served by a perpetual curate, whose stipend, payable by the dignitaries, has been recently augmented by one-fifth of the rectory, and a portion of the glebe, which formerly constituted part of the endowment of the archdeaconry. There is no glebe-house: the glebe lands comprise 280*a.* 1*r.* 20*p.*, plantation measure, of which 37*a.* 1*r.* 8*p.* belong to the dean, 71*a.* 0*r.* 12*p.* to the precentor, 45*a.* to the treasurer, 15*a.* to the perpetual curate, and 112*a.* to the minor canon, who has also other lands, amounting in the whole to about 180 acres, let on lease at an aggregate rental of £205. 12. In the R. C. divisions this place is the head of a union or district, which comprises the parishes of Ardfert, Kilmoiley, Ballynahaglish, and Fenit, and contains three chapels, situated respectively at Ardfert, Chapeltown, and Lerrigs: the first, erected in 1783, at an expense of £300, is a neat slated building, with a sacristy, and over the altar is a painting of the Crucifixion. There are two free schools; one, a thatched stone building adapted to the reception of 140 children, but in which at present about 45 are taught, was erected by Mrs. Crosbie, at an expense of £120, and is supported by her and the dignitaries of the cathedral; the other, in which are 150 boys and 90 girls, is a slated building near the R. C. chapel, erected at an expense of £90 by the Rev. J. O'Sullivan, P. P., by whom it is chiefly supported. Here is also a dispensary.

The cathedral, dedicated to St. Brandon or Brendan, occupied an eminence on the north side of the town, and is said to have been destroyed in the war of 1641. The remains consist of the walls of the nave and choir, which are perfect: the east window has three lofty lancet-shaped compartments, ornamented internally with light and elegant clustered pilaster columns; on each side is a niche, in one of which stands the figure of a bishop, rudely sculptured, but in excellent preservation, lately found in sinking a vault, and called and venerated as the effigy of St. Brandon; near it, in the choir, is another of much superior workmanship. On the south side, near the altar, are nine windows ornamented with pilaster columns terminating in a trefoil arch; at the west end, on the north side, are two square windows, opposite which are three bold arches resting on square pillars, which led from the cathedral probably into a chapel, and there were also two other entrances into this part of the building, the principal at the north-west corner. Four rude Norman arches still remain, of which the centre is the largest and was the doorway. A doorway at the north-west led into a later addition, part of which only remains, and in 1668 was purchased for her tomb by the Dowager Countess of Kerry, and has since been the family vault of the Crosbies. To the west of the cathedral are two detached buildings, one having the Norman and the other the pointed arch. An ancient round tower, which formerly stood near the cathedral, fell about 60 years since. Within half a mile to the east, in a beautiful park of the late Earl of Glandore's, are the cruciform ruins of the Franciscan abbey, consisting of the nave and choir, with a lofty tower on the west, a chapel on the south, and the refectory on the north, adjoining which are two sides of the cloisters, the whole principally in the pointed style. The great east window has five divisions, and is of bold design. On the south side the choir was lighted by nine windows, under which are five arches in the wall, differing in style and elevation, and probably intended as monumental recesses for abbots; in the second is an altar-tomb of the last Earl and Countess of Glandore. The south chapel, of which the great window is perfect and its details handsome, was connected with the nave by three noble pointed arches resting on massive, but peculiarly elegant, circular columns. A stone in the buttress of the arch nearest the tower bears a rude inscription, which, from the difficulty of decyphering it, has given rise to various opinions, but, on lately removing the moss and dirt, proves to be in Latin, and purports that Donald Fitz Bohen, who sleeps here, caused this work (probably the chapel) to be done in 1453. In the choir are several very ancient tombstones, one bearing the effigy of an abbot. Near these ruins stands Ardfert Abbey, the mansion of the Crosbie family, who have resided here since the reign of Elizabeth, when Dr. John Crosbie, of Maryborough, Queen's county, was preferred to the bishoprick, and his descendants successively attained the honours of Baron Branden, Viscount Crosbie, and Earl of Glandore, now extinct. Col. David Crosbie, son of the bishop, who distinguished himself in the service of Chas. I., mentions, in his claims to Cromwell in 1653, that the Irish had burnt his house at Ardfert, which had cost him more than £1000 in building; (it appears, from an inscription still remaining, to have been completed in 1635;) and the original order by Col. Fitz Morice, for its destruction, is among the MSS. in the library. The succeeding mansion was modernised by the first Lord Branden in 1720, and has been greatly improved by its present occupant, Mrs. Crosbie: it contains an extensive library of choice works and numerous family MSS., and in the dining and drawing-rooms is a variety of paintings, mostly family portraits. The park is well stocked with deer; the gardens are extensive, and open into several fine avenues of elm, lime, and beech trees.

ARDFIELD, a parish, in the barony of IBANE and BARRYROE, county of CORK, and province of MUNSTER, 5 miles (S. by E.) from Clonakilty, containing 2023 inhabitants. This parish is situated on the south coast, and is bounded on the east by the bay of Clonakilty; it comprises 2313 statute acres, as applotted under the tithe act, and valued at £2053 per annum. About four-fifths are under cultivation: there is very little waste land and no bog; the poor bring the turf from Clonakilty. The soil, though light and in some places very stony, generally produces good crops. There are about 800 acres of land, called the commons, wholly in the occupation of poor people who have enclosed it; some of it is remarkably good, and the whole is under cultivation. Indications of copper ore appear at Duneen, and many excellent specimens have been found: attempts to raise it were made several years since, but the design was abandoned. There are several large and handsome houses in the parish: the principal are Dunmore, the seat of J. Beamish, Esq.; Dunowen House, of G. Sandes, Esq.; the Tower, of Lieut. Speck, R. N.; Greenfield, of H. Galway, Esq.; and Balliva, of M. Galway, Esq. At its southern extremity is Dunowen Head, off which lie the Shanbuee rocks; and in the parish is Dunny Cove, where is stationed the western coast-guard detachment within the district of Kinsale. The living is a vicarage, in the diocese of Ross, and in the patronage of the Bishop: the rectory is impropriate in M. Roberts and T. W. Foot, Esqrs. The tithes amount to £203. 1. 6½., of which £110. 15. 4¾. is payable to the impropriators, and the remainder to the vicar. The church is in ruins; but divine service is performed in a house fitted up for that purpose at Dunny Cove. The glebe comprises eleven acres of excellent land, but there is no glebe-house. In the R. C. divisions this parish is the head of a union or district, comprising the parishes of Ardfield and Rathbarry, in each of which is a chapel; that of Ardfield is a low, plain, but commodious edifice, situated on the commons. There are schools in which 140 boys and 170 girls are taught, also a school at Dunny Cove, a Sunday school under the superintendence of the vicar, and one or two hedge schools. The ruins of the old church are situated on the highest point of land in the parish; and near them is a building which during the war was used as a signal tower, but is now the residence of Lieut. Speck, who commands the coast-guard at Dunny Cove. Close to the Cove are the ruins of a castle.

ARDFINNAN, a parish, in the barony of IFFA and OFFA WEST, county of TIPPERARY, and province of MUNSTER, 4 miles (S. S. E.) from Cahir; containing 878 inhabitants. The village extends into the parish of Ballybacon, and contains 316 inhabitants. The place derives its name, signifying "the hill of Finian," from an eminence on which its castle was built, and from St. Finian the Leper, who flourished in the latter part of the sixth century, and founded here an abbey of Regular Canons, to which, about the year 903, Cormac Mac Cuillenan, the celebrated monarch and archbishop of Munster, bequeathed one ounce of gold and one of silver, with his horse and arms: it was plundered and burnt by the English forces, in 1178. Here was also at an early period a monastery for Conventual Franciscans, concerning which there are no particulars on record. The village is situated on both banks of the river Suir, which is here crossed by a bridge of fourteen arches, and on the mail coach road from Dublin to Cork, by way of Clonmel. Within half a mile above the bridge, according to M'Curtin's annals, Terlogh O'Brien, King of Munster, routed Terlogh O'Connor, Monarch of Ireland, in 1150, when O'Hyne, Prince of Fiachra, and O'Fflahertie, Prince of West Connaught, were slain, with the greater part of the monarch's army. The castle was erected by King John, when Earl of Morton and Lord of Ireland, in 1184: it was a large rectangular pile strengthened by square towers at the corners, and belonged to the Knights Templars, on the suppression of which order it was granted to the Knights of St. John of Jerusalem, and subsequently to the Bishop of Waterford; its ruins occupy a picturesque and elevated site on a rock overlooking the river, and consist of the gateway and greater part of the walls. From public records it appears that this place had anciently a corporation: in 1311, 4th o. Edw. II., a grant of "pontage for three years" was made to "the Bailiffs and good men of Ardfynan," at the request of the Bishop of Limerick. In 1399, John, Earl of Desmond, was drowned in crossing the ford here with his followers, on returning from an incursion into the territory of the Earl of Ormonde. The parish comprises 1081 statute acres, as applotted under the tithe act: there are some limestone quarries, the produce of which is chiefly burnt for manure. A fair, chiefly for the sale of pigs, is held at the village on Feb. 2nd, and it has a patent for two other fairs on May 17th and Nov. 19th. Petty sessions are held once a fortnight, and a manorial court six times in the year; and here is a station of the constabulary police. The living is a rectory, in the diocese of Lismore, with the vicarage of Neddins and the rectory of Rochestown episcopally united, forming the union of Ardfinnan, in the patronage of the Archbishop of Cashel: the tithes are £1701, and the gross tithes of the benefice amount to £345. The church is a plain modern edifice. The glebe-house was built by a gift of £100 and a loan of £1200, from the late Board of First Fruits, in 1818; the glebe comprises 20*a.* 2*r.* 11*p.* In the R. C. divisions this parish is the head of a district, which comprises also Neddins, Rochestown, Ballybacon, and Tulloghmelan, and contains three chapels, at Ardfinnan, Ballybacon, and Grange. There are two private schools. Dr. Downes bequeathed £8. 6. 8. per ann., late currency, for apprenticing Protestant children.

ARDGLASS, a sea-port, post-town, and parish, in the barony of LECALE, county of DOWN, and province of ULSTER, 5½ miles (S. E. by E.) from Downpatrick, and 80¾ miles (N. N. E.) from Dublin; containing 2300 inhabitants, of which number, 1162 are in the town. This place derives its name, signifying in the Irish language "the High Green," from a lofty green hill of conical form, called the Ward, and situated to the west of the town: from the remains of several castles it appears to have been formerly a place of some importance. Jordan's Castle is memorable for the gallant and protracted defence that it made during the insurrection of the Earl of Tyrone, in the reign of Elizabeth, and derived its present name from its loyal and intrepid proprietor, Simon Jordan, who for three years sustained the continued assaults of the besiegers, till he was at length relieved by the Lord-Deputy Mountjoy, who sailed with a fleet from Dublin and landed here on the 17th of June, 1611; and after relieving the garrison, pursued the insurgents to Dunsford, where a battle took place, in which they were nearly annihilated; and Jordan was rewarded for his services by a concordatum from the Queen. The port of Ardglass appears to have been in a flourishing condition from a very early period; a trading company from London settled here in the reign of Hen. IV., and in the reign of Hen. VI. it had an extensive foreign trade and was superior to any other port in the province of Ulster. At that time the town had received a charter of incorporation, was governed by a mayor, and had a port-admiral and revenue officers. Hen. VIII. granted the customs of the port, then worth £5000 per annum, to Gerald Fitzgerald, Earl of Kildare, in whose family they remained till 1637, when, with certain privileges enjoyed by the port of Carrickfergus, they were purchased by the crown, and the whole was transferred to Newry and Belfast, from which time the trade of Ardglass began to decline and the town ultimately became only a residence for fishermen. It was formerly the property of a branch of the Leinster family, of whom the last resident, Lord Lecale, sold the manor to W. Ogilvie, Esq., who had married the Dowager Duchess of Leinster, and under whose auspices the town recovered its former importance; at his decease it descended to his heir, Major Aubrey W. Beauclerc, its present proprietor.

The town is pleasantly and advantageously situated on the eastern coast, and on the side of a hill overlooking the sea, and is well known to mariners by two conspicuous hills, one on the west, called the Ward of Ardglass, and the other on the east, called the Ward of Ardtole. Mr. Ogilvie, on its coming into his possession in the year 1812, built entire streets, a church and school-house, and an elegant hotel; he also constructed hot, cold, and vapour baths; built and furnished lodging-houses for the accommodation of visiters, and rendered it one of the most fashionable watering-places in the North of Ireland. The town in its present state consists of one long street, nearly of semicircular form, from which several smaller streets branch off: in front of the inner bay is a range of excellent houses, called the Crescent; and there are many good houses in front of the harbour, adjoining which is a long range of building in the castellated style, called the New Works, although they are so old that nothing is known either of the time or the purpose of their erection. They form together a line of fortifications, 250 feet in length from east to west, and 24 feet in breadth, close to the shore; the walls are three feet in thickness and strengthened with three towers, one in the centre and one at each extremity. These buildings were originally divided into thirty-six apartments, eighteen on the ground floor and eighteen above, with a staircase in the centre; each of the lower apartments had a small arched door and a large square window, which renders it probable that they had been shops occupied by merchants at some very early period, possibly by the company of traders that settled here in the reign of Hen. IV. About the year 1789, Lord Chas. Fitzgerald, son of the Duke of Leinster, who was then proprietor, caused that portion of the building between the central and the western tower to be enlarged in the rear, and raised to the height of three stories in the castellated style; and from that time it has been called Ardglass Castle, and has been the residence of the proprietor of the estate. It was formerly called Horn Castle, either from a great quantity of horns found on the spot, or from a high pillar which stood on its summit previously to its being roofed; and near it is another castle, called Cow'd Castle, signifying the want of horns, from a word in the Scottish dialect, of which many phrases are still in use in the province. In a direct line with Ardglass Castle, and due west of it, are Cow'd Castle above noticed, and Margaret's Castle, both square ancient structures having the lower stories arched with stone; and on the north-west side of the town, on a considerable elevation, are two other castles, about 20 feet distant from each other, the larger of which is called King's Castle and the smaller the Tower; they have been partly rebuilt and connected with a handsome pile of building in the castellated style. Jordan's Castle, previously noticed, is an elegant building, 70 feet high, standing in the centre of the town, and having at the entrance a well of excellent water. The surrounding scenery is beautiful, and the air salubrious; the green banks of Ardtole and Ringfad, on the north and south sides of the bay, overhang the sea, where ships of the largest burden can approach within an oar's length of the bold and precipitous rocks that line the coast. From the Ward of Ardglass is a delightful prospect extending from 30 to 40 miles over a fertile country: on the south-west, beyond Killough and the beautiful bay of Dundrum, are seen the lofty mountains of Mourne rising in sublime grandeur; on the east, the Isle of Man, and on the north-east, the Ayrshire mountains of Scotland, in distant perspective, appearing to rise from the ocean, and embracing with their extended arch more than one half of the horizon. During the fishing season the view of the sea from this place is rendered peculiarly striking and animated by the daily arrival and departure of vessels, and the numerous shoals of mackarel, pollock, and other fish visible on the surface of the water for miles. There are no manufactures; the labouring classes being wholly employed in the fisheries off the north-east coast, of which this place is the common centre. During the season there are frequently in the harbour, at one time, from 300 to 400 vessels from Donaghadee, Carlingford, Skerries, Dublin, Arklow, and the Isle of Man, but principally from Penzance, on the coast of Cornwall. The boats come regularly into the harbour to dispose of their fish, which is quickly purchased by carriers, who take it into the interior of the country, and by merchants who cure it; but chiefly by masters of sloops and small craft, who wait in the harbour for the arrival of the fishing boats, and proceed directly to Dublin or Liverpool to dispose of the herrings fresh. These sloops usually perform two trips in the week, and the masters frequently make from £20 to £50 by each cargo. The harbour is admirably adapted for trade and steam navigation; and, since the erection of the new pier, is sufficient to accommodate steamers of any tonnage, and there is sufficient depth of water for vessels of 500 tons burden, which can enter at any state of the tide. There is an inner harbour, where a quay and pier have been erected for the accommodation of the fishing vessels; it is called Kimmersport, and is capable of accommodating a great number of fishing-boats, exclusively of other vessels of 100 tons burden; but the sea recedes from it at low water. On the quay are capacious stores for corn, in which an extensive trade is carried on. Adjoining the outer harbour a pier was completed, in 1814, at an expense of £14,000. The new pier was constructed in 1834, at an expense of £25,000, by Mr. Ogilvie, under the superintendence of Sir John Rennie: it extends 300 feet from the extremity of the old pier into deep water, and is 20 feet broad; it is built of large blocks of stone from the Isle of Man, hewn and dressed, forming a breakwater, and affording a beautiful promenade embracing fine views of the Isle and Calf of Man. A handsome lighthouse is now being erected on the pier, which is connected with the land by a very capacious wharf covering nearly an acre of ground, with a basin of semicircular form, beyond which are the quays for the colliers. The harbour is situated in lat. 54° 15′ 20″ (N.), and lon. 5° 35′ 20″ (W.); and the trade of the port is rapidly increasing. There is a patent for a market and four fairs. A constabulary police force, and a coast-guard station, forming one of the seven that constitute the district of Newcastle, have been established here. A manorial court is held for debts and pleas to the amount of £100.

By an order in council, dated Oct. 19th, 1834, the townlands of Jordan's Crew and Kildare's Crew, formerly belonging to the parish of Ballee, and the townland of Ross, formerly in the parish of Kilclief, were permanently united to this parish, which now comprises 1137¼ statute acres, according to the Ordnance survey. The lands, which are all arable, are very fertile and in a profitable state of cultivation; there is not a rood of waste land or bog. At a short distance from the town, and near the shore, are extensive quarries of good rubble stone, from which were raised the materials used in the construction of the numerous buildings lately erected in the parish, and partly in the building of the pier, for the easier conveyance of which a rail-road, a quarter of a mile in length, was laid down. The living was formerly a perpetual curacy, and the rectory formed part of the union of Ballyphilip and corps of the chancellorship of Down, which union was lately dissolved on the recommendation of the Ecclesiastical Commissioners, and Ardglass is now an independent rectory and benefice, in the diocese of Down, and in the patronage of the Bishop; the tithes amount to £130. The church was built on the site of an ancient edifice, the late Board of First Fruits having granted £800 as a gift and £400 as a loan, in 1813: it is a handsome edifice, with a tower and spire 90 feet high. In digging the foundation, an oblong stone, broader at the top than at the bottom, was found near the place of the ancient altar, and is still in the churchyard: it has at the top a dove sculptured in relief; in the centre the crucifixion; and on each side a shield of arms. Underneath are some lines in curiously raised letters of the old English character, from which, though rendered almost unintelligible by intricate literal combinations, it appears to have been dedicated to the memory of Mrs. Jane O'Birne, in 1573. The Ecclesiastical Commissioners have lately granted £130 for the repair of this church. The glebe-house was built in 1815, a quarter of a mile from the church, at an expense of £500, of which £450 was a gift and £50 a loan from the late Board of First Fruits. The glebe contains three plantation acres. In the R. C. divisions this parish is united with Dunsford, by which latter name the union is generally known. Each has a chapel; that of Ardglass is a very neat edifice, built in 1829 on a spacious site given by Mr. Ogilvie. There is a school under the Trustees of Erasmus Smith's Charity, in which are about 90 boys and 80 girls; also four private schools, in which are about 60 boys and 50 girls, and a dispensary.

About half a mile to the north-east of the town, on a hill in the townland of Ardtole, are the ruins of an ancient place of worship, called the old church of Ardtole, of which the eastern gable, with a large arched opening, and the two side walls, more than three feet in thickness, are remaining, and are of strong but very rude masonry. In Ardtole creek, on the north-east side of the bay, is a natural cavern with a large entrance, which gradually contracts into a narrow fissure in the rock, scarcely admitting one person to creep through it; the elevation is very great, from which circumstance the townland probably derived its name Ardtole, signifying "high hole:" some persons have penetrated a considerable way into this cavern, but no one has explored it fully. Ardglass formerly gave the title of Earl to the family of Cromwell, and subsequently that of Viscount to the Barringtons.

ARDGUIN, or ARDQUIN, a parish, in the barony of Ardes, county of Down, and province of Ulster, on Lough Strangford, and on the road from Portaferry to Belfast; containing, with part of the post-town of Portaferry, 994 inhabitants. There appears to have been a monastery at this place, founded at a very early period: according to Harris' History of Down it was the priory of Eynes, which, on the authority of a patent roll among the public records, was seized by the crown during the war between England and France, and was granted, in 1411, by Hen. IV. to Thomas Cherele. It afterwards became the chief residence of the bishops of Down, of whom the last that resided here was Dr. Echlin, who was consecrated to the see in 1614. According to the Ordnance survey the parish comprises 3043 statute acres, of which 80 are under water. The soil, though in some parts interspersed with rocks which rise above the surface, is in general fertile; the lands are in a good state of cultivation; there is neither waste nor bog. Clay-slate is raised for building, and for mending the roads. Portaferry House, the splendid mansion of Col. A. Nugent, is situated in a richly planted demesne, with an extensive park ornamented with stately timber. Here are several mills for flour and oatmeal, and for dressing flax; the situation of the parish on Strangford Lough affords great facility of conveyance by water. A manorial court is held for the recovery of debts not exceeding five marks, with jurisdiction over the whole of the parish. The living is a rectory, in the diocese of Down, held by the bishop, who appoints a curate, for whose stipend he has set apart certain lands belonging to the see. No church appears to have existed here from a period long prior to the Reformation till the year 1829, when the present edifice was erected by Dr. Mant, the present bishop; it is a neat small building with a square tower, and occupies a picturesque situation on an eminence between Lough Strangford and Lough Cowie, which latter is a fresh-water lake of considerable extent. There is neither glebe nor glebe-house; the lands appear to have been granted as mensal lands to the see, and consequently to have been tithe-free; but their exemption is at present a subject of dispute, and the tithes are returned under the composition act as amounting to £289. 19. 7½., payable to the bishop. In the R. C. divisions the parish forms part of the union or district of Upper Ardes. There is a Sunday school; also a pay school, in which are about 42 boys and 32 girls. There are considerable remains of the monastery and episcopal palace, which shew that the buildings were originally of very great extent.—See PORTAFERRY.

ARDKEEN, a parish, in the barony of ARDES, county of DOWN, and province of ULSTER, 3 miles (N. by E.) from Portaferry; containing 2176 inhabitants. This place derives its name, originally *Ard-Coyne*, from its situation on the shores of a lake, which was formerly called Lough Coyne. It was one of the most important strong holds of the ancient Irish, who made it a place of refuge from the violence and rapacity of the Danes, and had a large and well-fortified camp protected on three sides by the sea, with extensive pastures in the rear for their cattle. On this point of land, jutting into the lough and forming a fertile peninsula nearly surrounded by every tide, Raymond Savage, one of the followers of De Courcy, erected a strong castle in 1196, which became the chief residence of that family, whose descendants throughout the whole of the insurrection remained firmly attached to the English monarchs. In 1567, Shane O'Nial, who had overrun and destroyed the neighbouring country on every side, besieged this castle, but was so vigorously repulsed that he retreated with great loss and never penetrated farther southward into the Ardes. The parish comprises, according to the Ordnance survey, 4800½ statute acres, of which 169 are islands, and 114 are covered with water. The living was formerly a perpetual curacy, in the diocese of Down, and the rectory formed part of the union of Inch and the corps of the prebend of St. Andrew's in the cathedral of Down; but the Ecclesiastical Commissioners having recommended the dissolution of the union on the next avoidance of the prebend, Ardkeen and the northern part of Witter were constituted a distinct rectory, in the patronage of the Bishop, in 1834, by consent of the prebendary, and the perpetual curate was made rector: the tithes amount to £464. 18. 9. The church is situated on the peninsula and at the extreme western boundary of the parish; it is a small ancient edifice, and contains several monuments to the family of Savage, its original founders. The glebe-house was built at an expense of £500, of which £450 was a gift and £50 a loan from the late Board of First Fruits, in 1816: the glebe comprises 12½ Cunningham acres, valued at £1 per acre and subject to a rent of £4 per annum. In the R. C. divisions this parish is included within the unions or districts of Upper and Lower Ardes: the chapel at Lisbawn is connected with that of Ballygelgat, in the parish of Witter. A school of 76 boys and 84 girls is supported by Col. and Lady H. Forde, who contribute £50 per annum; there are also a Sunday school and a private school. The only remains of the castle are the foundations; the fosses are tolerably perfect, and some of the gardens and orchards may be traced.

ARDKILL, a parish, in the barony of CARBERY, county of KILDARE, and province of LEINSTER, 4 miles (E.) from Edenderry, on the road from Mullingar to Naas and Kildare; containing 864 inhabitants. It is a rectory, in the diocese of Kildare, wholly impropriate in the Marquess of Downshire; the tithes amount to £168. 17. 5½. In the R. C. divisions it forms part of the union of Carbery. At Dimtura is a school under the patronage of Viscount Harberton.

ARDMAYLE, a parish, in the barony of MIDDLETHIRD, county of TIPPERARY, and province of MUNSTER, 3 miles (N.) from Cashel; containing 1914 inhabitants. This appears to have been formerly a place of some importance; in many parts foundations of ancient houses have been discovered, and there are also remains of several castles. Of the latter, the castle of Sinone, consisting of a circular tower, is the most ancient; it is called in the Irish language *Farrin-a-Urrigh*, and it is said that many of Strongbow's forces, on their retreat from Cashel, were slain and interred here: human bones are frequently dug up near the spot, and within the last few years a very large helmet was discovered. The castle at Castlemoyle, at present consisting only of a square tower, was anciently the residence of the Butlers, and subsequently of the Cootes. Cromwell is said to have attacked it, and after gaining possession, to have hanged the proprietor: it still retains vestiges of its original extent, and appears to have been handsomely built. There are also some remains of another castle near the bridge. The parish is situated near the main road from Cashel to Thurles, and on the river Suir, over which is a bridge of stone; it comprises 4772 statute acres, as applotted under the tithe act, and valued at £6225 per annum. The land is principally under an improved system of tillage; there is neither bog nor waste land. Limestone abounds and is quarried for building, and for burning into lime. Ardmayle House is the residence of T. Price, Esq.; Longfield, situated in a well-planted demesne, of R. Long, Esq.; Fort Edward, of E. Long, Esq.; and Noddstown, of R. Armstrong, Esq., closely adjoining to which is a square tower. Here is a station of the constabulary police. The living is a perpetual curacy, in the diocese of Cashel, and in the patronage of the Archbishop; the rectory is impropriate in the Rev. W. Sutton and the vicars choral of the cathedral of Cashel: the tithes amount to £312. 9. 2., the whole payable to the impropriators, who pay the perpetual curate a stipend of £30, to which the Ecclesiastical Commissioners add £70. The church, with the exception of the old tower crowned with an embattled turret, was rebuilt by aid of a gift of £800 and a loan of £150 from the late Board of First Fruits, in 1815. The glebe-house was erected by aid of a gift of £450 and a loan of £50 from the same Board. In the R. C. divisions this parish is the head of a union or district, called Bohirlahan, comprising Ardmayle and Ballysheehan, each of which has a chapel; the chapel for Ardmayle is situated at Bohirlahan, and is of recent erection. A school of 56 boys and 22 girls is aided by Mr. Beasley, who erected the school-house, and the Rev. Wm. Kirwan, P. P., who supplies books and stationery.

ARDMORE, a parish, in the barony of DECIES-within-DRUM, county of WATERFORD, and province of MUNSTER, 5 miles (E. N. E.) from Youghal; containing 7318 inhabitants, of which number, 414 are in the village. This place, which is situated on the bay of Ardmore in St. George's channel, derived its name, signifying "a great promontory or eminence," from the Drumfineen mountain, an extensive and elevated range forming its northern barrier, and of which Slieve Grine constitutes a very considerable portion. In the infancy of Christianity in Ireland, St. Declan, a native of this country and a member of the tribe of the Decii, founded a religious establishment here, which became an episcopal see, over which he was confirmed bishop by St. Patrick in 448. The see of Ardmore continued to flourish as a separate bishoprick under a succession of prelates, of whom the next after the founder was St. Ultan, till the time of the English invasion, soon after which it was incorporated with the diocese of Lismore. The parish, which includes the principal portion of the barony, comprises 28,135 statute acres, as applotted under the tithe act; the mountainous portion affords tolerable pasturage and is well stocked with black cattle; and the lands between the mountains and the sea are fertile and in a good state of cultivation. Crushea, the seat of Mrs. Gun Paul, is a handsome modern residence pleasantly situated on the north side of the bay, and commanding a fine view of the sea. Ards, the residence of P. Lawlor, Esq., is a castellated mansion situated about a mile from the village, near the sea, and commanding an extensive and interesting prospect. Loscairne, the extremely neat modern residence of W. J. Carew, Esq., is pleasantly situated at the eastern verge of the parish, adjoining the new public road from Dungarvan to Youghal, by way of Ring. Glenanna Cottage, the marine residence of H. Winston Barron, Esq., is situated near Ballymacart. A new line of road has been made within the last few years from Dungarvan, through Ring, to Youghal, by which the distance to the Ferry point is 17 miles, and the construction of which has given a great impulse to agricultural improvement, by providing a convenient outlet for the produce of the district. It intersects the parish from N. E. to S. W.; and another road, in a N. W. direction, commencing at the upper bridge of Killongford, is now in progress, which will pass through the townlands of Ballyharrahan and Killongford, and over Slieve Grine mountain, and in its course will be shorter, by $2\frac{3}{4}$ miles, than the old road: the Slieve Grine mountain is principally the property of H. Villiers Stuart, Esq., of Dromana. The village is situated on the shore of a bay open to the east and protected on the south by Ardmore Head; the beach is of great extent and smoothness, and there is an interesting view of St. George's channel. Its situation, and the beauty of the surrounding scenery, make it a desirable place of resort for sea-bathing. Copper and lead mines were formerly worked, and, from the specimens still found, the ores appear to have been of rich quality. At Minehead, so called from the adjacent works, and near the village, iron ore of very good quality was also procured. A constabulary police force, and one of the five coast-guard stations which constitute the district of Youghal, have been established here.

The living is a vicarage, with that of Ballymacart united, in the diocese of Lismore, and in the patronage of the Bishop; the rectory constitutes the corps of the precentorship in the cathedral of Lismore. The tithes amount to £650, of which £433. 6. 8. is payable to the precentor, and £216. 13. 4. to the vicar; and the gross tithes of the benefice amount to £258. The church and glebe-house are annexed to the vicarage: the glebe belonging to the precentor consists of the lands of Ardocharty, in this parish, comprising 68*a.* 5*p.*, and $48\frac{1}{2}$*a.* in the parish of Lismore; and the vicarial glebe comprises 20*a.* 1*r.* 9*p.* In the R. C. divisions this parish is the head of a union or district, comprising the parishes of Ardmore, Ballymacart, and Lisginan, in each of which is a chapel; the chapel of Ardmore is situated in the village, and is a commodious edifice of recent erection. There are a Sunday school and five pay schools, in the latter of which are about 240 children. Some remains exist of the ancient church, consisting chiefly of the chancel, part of which, till the recent erection of the present edifice, was used as the parish church; it was a fine building, richly decorated with sculpture, and still displays traces of its former magnificence. To the south-east of the church is a small, low, and plain building, called the Dormitory of St. Declan, and held in great veneration by the inhabitants of the neighbourhood; it was repaired and roofed about a century since by Bishop Willis. In the churchyard is one of the ancient round towers, a fine specimen of those monuments of remote antiquity. On Ardmore Head are some slight remains of an ancient church, but in a state of such dilapidation that few traces either of its original architecture or embellishment can be distinguished. Near it is St. Declan's well, which is held in veneration by the people of the neighbourhood; and on the beach is St. Declan's stone, resting on a ledge of rock, by which it is raised a little from the ground, and at which, on July 24th, the festival of the saint, numbers of people assemble for devotional purposes. Several circular intrenchments may be traced in various parts of the parish. Near Ardmore Head is a large and curious cavern, called the "Parlour;" and on the coast, which is precipitously rocky, are several other caverns.

ARDMORE, county of ARMAGH.—See MOYNTAGHS.

ARDMOY.—See ARMOY.

ARDMULCHAN, a parish, in the barony of SKREEN, county of MEATH, and province of LEINSTER, $2\frac{1}{2}$ miles (N. E.) from Navan; containing 1061 inhabitants. This parish is situated on the high road from Navan to Drogheda, and the new road from Trim to Duleek runs through the southern part of it: its northern part is intersected by the Boyne navigation. It comprises 3347 statute acres, as applotted under the tithe act: about two-thirds are under tillage, and the remainder is good grazing land; there is no waste or bog. Limestone abounds, and there is a good quarry of stone for building. Ardmulchan House is the seat of R. Taaffe, Esq.; and Hayes, a handsome residence, of R. Bourke, Esq. The parish is in the diocese of Meath, and the rectory is united to Painstown: the tithes amount to £253. 16. 10½. In the R. C. divisions also it is part of the union or district of Black Lion or Painstown. There is a free school for boys and girls at Hayes, under the patronage of R. Bourke, Esq., who built the school-house, gave an acre of land rent-free, and allows £24 per ann. for its support; the girls' school is principally supported by Mrs. Bourke.

ARDNAGEEHY, a parish, in the barony of BARRYMORE, county of CORK, and province of MUNSTER, 5 miles (S. W.) from Rathcormac, on the mail coach road from Cork to that place; containing 3715 inhabitants. It comprises 15,546 statute acres, as applotted under the tithe act, and valued at £5708 per annum. The Nagle mountains and Leppers Hill form a tract of nearly 6000 acres, and on the south side of the river Bride are nearly 2000 acres of waste land: these lands are generally rough pasture, affording but a very scanty supply of herbage for cattle. Of the lands under cultivation, the greater portion is in tillage, and the system of agriculture is improving. There are about 400 acres of bog, but it is not worked. The substratum of the soil is clay-slate; a coarse heavy kind of slate is quarried for roofing, and flag-stones are found in abundance, but neither are worked to any extent. There are several large and handsome houses in the parish, the principal of which are Bridestown, the residence of E. Morgan, Esq.; Mount Pleasant, of the Rev. E. G. Hudson; Kiluntin, of R. Roche, Esq.; Glanassack, of Mrs. Wallis; and Westmount, of M. Westropp, Esq. A small paper-mill is worked at Glenville, where fairs for cattle, sheep, and pigs are held on the 4th of May and the 3rd of November. There are constabulary police stations at Glenville and Watergrass-hill. Petty sessions are held at the latter place every alternate Tuesday. The living is a rectory and vicarage, in the diocese of Cork, and in the patronage of the Bishop; the tithes amount to £438. 9. 3. The church is a neat modern edifice, situated at Glenville, for the erection of which the late Board of First Fruits gave £500 in 1798. There is no glebe-house; and the glebe, comprising 40 acres purchased by the same Board, has been lost through some defect in the title. In the R. C. divisions the parish is the head of a union or district, also called Watergrass-hill, which comprises the parishes of Ardnageehy and Ballynaultig, and parts of those of Dunbollogue and Kilquane; there are chapels at Glenville and Watergrass-hill, both small plain buildings. The parochial male and female schools at Glenville are supported chiefly by the rector, and there is another school for boys and girls on the demesne of Glenville, for which the proprietor built a school-house in 1821: about 200 children are taught in these schools, and there are six hedge schools, in which are about 300 children, and a Sunday school. About two miles to the south of the church are the ruins of the old parish church, romantically situated among the hills.

ARDNAREE, a village, in that part of the parish of KILMOREMOY which is in the barony of TYRERAGH, county of SLIGO, and province of CONNAUGHT, adjacent to Ballina, and containing 2482 inhabitants. This place, which may be considered as a suburb to Ballina, is connected with that town by a bridge over the river Moy; and consists of one principal street, from which several lanes diverge, containing altogether 312 houses. In 1427 a monastery for Eremites of the order of St. Augustine was founded here, but by whom is not known; there are some slight remains, consisting of a beautiful arched doorway and several windows. The environs are remarkably pleasant, and a new bridge of four arches has been recently erected. Fairs are held on June 20th, Oct. 10th, and Dec. 13th; and here is a constabulary police station. The parish church, a plain edifice with a tower and spire, is situated in the village; and a R. C. chapel, a handsome structure in the later English style, and ornamented with minarets, has been erected at an expense of £9000, and to which it is contemplated to add a tower and spire; when completed, it will be a great ornament to the town and suburb of Ballina; it is the cathedral church of the R. C. see of Killala, the bishop of which resides here.—See KILMOREMOY.

ARDNORCHER, otherwise HORSELEAP, a parish, partly in the barony of KILCOURSEY, KING'S county, but chiefly in that of MOYCASHEL, county of WESTMEATH, and province of LEINSTER, 3 miles (W. N. W.) from Kilbeggan, on the river Brosna, and on the mail coach road from Dublin to Galway; containing 3701 inhabitants. It contains 10,826 statute acres, of which 10,673 are applotted under the tithe act; there is a considerable tract of bog, but no mountain or waste land. The principal proprietor is Lord Maryborough. Limestone abounds in the parish, but there are no quarries of note. The principal seats are Bracca Castle, the residence of S. Handy, Esq.; Gageborough, of J. C. Judge, Esq.; Ballard, of R. Bolger, Esq.; and Temple-Macateer, of M. Kelly, Esq. The living is a vicarage, in the diocese of Meath, with the vicarages of Kilcumreagh, Kilmanaghan, Kilbride-Langan, and Rahue, and in the patronage of the Crown; the rectory is impropriate in the Marquess of Downshire. The tithes amount to £327. 13. 9½., of which £189. 4. 7. is payable to the impropriator, and the remainder to the vicar; and the gross annual value of the five parishes which constitute the union of Ardnorcher, including tithe and glebe, is £827. 0. 9., out of which the vicar pays the perpetual curate of Kilmanaghan and Kilbride-Langan £60 per ann., to which is added £40 per ann. from the augmentation fund. The church, to which a spire was added in 1822, is an ancient building in good repair: it stands on an eminence above the village of Horseleap. The glebe house was built by aid of a gift of £100 and a loan of £1150, in 1815, from the late Board of First Fruits; the glebe comprises 45 plantation acres, valued at £94 per annum. In the R. C. divisions this parish is the head of a union or district called Clara, comprising the parishes of Ardnorcher and Kilbride-Langan, in both of which are chapels; that of Ardnorcher is a large building in the village of Horseleap, erected in 1809. Besides the parochial school, in which ten boys and fifteen girls are taught, there are seven private pay schools, in which are about 120 boys and 60 girls. The lands of Moycashel, which give name to the barony, are situated in this parish. Anciently here were several castles, now mostly in ruins; that of Donour is still preserved in good repair by Sir Richard Nagle, Bart., and there is another at Bracca. The fort of Ardnorcher, or *Ard-an-orchor*, literally translated "the fort of slaughter," was one of the frontier forts of the English pale, and for some centuries past has been vulgarly called "Horseleap," on account of an extraordinary leap which is said to have been formerly made into it over the drawbridge by an English knight, in escaping from a close pursuit: this ancient doon or moat formed a strong link in the chain of forts and castles constructed along that part of the county of Meath which was within the English pale, to protect the new settlers and check the inroads of the Irish. At Temple-Maccateer are the remains of a monastery, said to have been founded in 440 by St. Kiaran; and at Gageborough was a nunnery, founded by Matilda de Lacey in the 13th century; many coins have been dug up at the former place. A holy well, dedicated to St. David, was formerly much resorted to on the patron day, the 27th of June, but the custom has nearly fallen into disuse.

ARDPATRICK, formerly a parish, now forming part of the parish of Kilquane, in the barony of Costlea, county of Limerick, and province of Munster, 4½ miles (S. E.) from Kilmallock; containing, with Kilquane and the parish of Particles, 2735 inhabitants. An abbey is said to have been founded here by St. Patrick, of which circumstance, though no historical record exists, there is yet sufficient evidence that a religious foundation was established here in the earliest ages of Christianity. By an inquisition of the 39th of Elizabeth, it was found that the hill of Ardpatrick was anciently granted to the corbeship founded in the church of Ardpatrick, a small sum out of the proceeds being paid annually to the bishop; and that the office of corbe had from time immemorial been continued by succession in the sept of the Langanes, by one of whom it was then held. Near the confines of this townland is Sunville, the ancient residence of the Godsall family. In the ecclesiastical divisions it is unknown as a parish, and in ancient records was supposed to be part of that of Donoughmore, in the county of Clare, forming a portion of the estate belonging to the see, and held under lease from the Bishop of Limerick; but for many years it has been united to the parish of Kilquane. The tithes amount to £33. 13. 10. In the R. C. divisions it forms part of the union or district of Kilfinnan; a large and handsome chapel has been lately erected at the foot of Ardpatrick hill. On the summit of this hill are the ruins of the ancient monastery; and near the north-west angle are the remains of an ancient round tower, the greater portion of which fell down a few years since. Gold ore has been found here, also the fossil remains of an elk, or moose deer, which are now in the possession of G. Russell, Esq., of Charleville.—See Kilquane.

ARDQUIN.—See ARDGUIN.

ARDRAHAN, a parish and post-town, partly in the barony of Kiltartan and partly in that of Loughrea, but chiefly in the barony of Dunkellin, county of Galway, and province of Connaught, 15 miles (S. E. by E.) from Galway, and 97 (W. by S.) from Dublin, on the road from Limerick to Galway; containing 3805 inhabitants. It comprises 12,950 statute acres, as applotted under the tithe act, a large portion of which is irreclaimable waste, though at the eastern extremity of the parish is a range of peat mountain, which is profitable as affording pasture for numerous black cattle. Flannel is rather extensively made by hand-spinning, for which a ready sale is found at Oranmore market, 12 miles distant. The principal residences are Cregclare, that of J. S. Lambert, Esq.; Castle Taylor, of Gen. Sir J. Taylor; Tillyra, of J. Martyn, Esq.; Castle Daly, of J. Daly, Esq.; and Rahenc, of J. O'Hara, Esq. A constabulary police force is stationed here, and petty sessions are held once a fortnight.

The living is a vicarage with a portion of the rectory, and with the rectory of Beagh forms the union of Ardrahan, in the diocese of Kilmacduagh, and in the patronage of the Marquess of Clanricarde. The tithes amount to £463, of which £84 is payable to the bishop, £23 to the archdeacon, and £356 to the incumbent; and the gross tithes of the benefice amount to £535. 6. 1½. The church was erected about 30 years since, by aid of a loan from the late Board of First Fruits, but was so indifferently built as to require a new roof, and has recently been repaired by the Ecclesiastical Commissioners. The glebe-house was also erected by a gift of £400 and a loan of £400 from the Board of First Fruits. The glebe comprises twelve acres. The R. C. parish is co-extensive with that of the Established Church, and there is a chapel at Labane; divine service is also performed occasionally by the parish priest at Tyllira castle. A national school is about to be established, and there are several pay schools in the parish. Here is a dispensary for Ardrahan and Gort. Along the mountain's side are several mineral springs, and where there are strong indications of iron ore.

ARDRESS, a village, in the parish of Killaghton, barony of Kilconnell, county of Galway, and province of Connaught, 5½ miles (S. W.) from Ballinasloe; containing 136 inhabitants.

ARDREVAN, county of Carlow.—See FENNAGH.

ARDRIE, (LITTLE) a parish, in the barony of Kilkea and Moone, county of Kildare, and province of Leinster, ½ a mile (S. by E.) from Athy; containing 302 inhabitants. This place, which is situated on the road from Athy to Carlow, and comprises only 295 statute acres, anciently belonged to the monastery of St. Thomas, near Dublin, and was assigned to the precentorship in the cathedral church of St. Patrick, Dublin, on the institution of that dignity in 1219. It is a rectory, in the diocese of Dublin, partly appropriate to the precentorship, partly impropriate in Michael Goold Adams, Esq., and partly forming a portion of the union of St. Michael's Athy. The tithes amount to £24, of which £16 is payable to the impropriator, and £8 to the incumbent of St. Michael's; the portion appropriated to the precentorship is 154*a.* 2*r.* 8*p.*, let on lease at an annual rent of £12.

ARDRISTIN, a parish, in the barony of Rathvilly, county of Carlow, and province of Leinster, 1¾ mile (S. W. by W.) from Tullow, on the road to Clonegal; containing 543 inhabitants. It comprises 1525 statute acres, as applotted under the tithe act; and within its limits is a part of the suburbs of the town of Tullow, called the Green and Tullow-beg. Except one townland entirely surrounded by the parish of Aghade, it is bounded on the east and south-east by the river Slaney. More than one-half of its surface consists of meadow and pasture land; the rest, with the exception of a small tract of bog, is arable. It formerly constituted part of the union of Aghade: the living is now a distinct impropriate curacy, in the diocese of Leighlin, and in the patronage of the Bishop; the tithes amount to £145. The ruins of the church, situated on the townland of Ardristin, are divided by a pointed arch and are 63 feet in length. In the R. C. divisions it forms part of the union or district of Tullow.

ARDSALLAGH, a parish, in the barony of LOWER NAVAN, county of MEATH, and province of LEINSTER, 2½ miles (S. S. E.) from Navan; containing 289 inhabitants. It is bounded on the east by the river Boyne, and comprises 1032 statute acres, principally under tillage, as applotted under the tithe act, and has neither waste land nor bog: the prevailing substratum is limestone. The banks of the river are adorned with the mansion and demesne of Ardsallagh, the property of Earl Ludlow, whose ancestor, in 1755, was raised to the peerage of Ireland by the title of Baron Ludlow, of Ardsallagh, and in 1760 advanced to the dignities of Viscount Preston, of Ardsallagh, and Earl Ludlow. It is a rectory, in the diocese of Meath, and forms part of the union of Navan: the tithes amount to £150. In the R. C. divisions also it is included in the union or district of Navan. At Cannistown is a public school for boys and girls. There are some remains of the walls of the old church, with a burial-ground attached. According to Archdall, St. Finian of Clonard founded a monastery here near the river, of which no vestiges can be traced.

ARDSALLIS, a village, in the parish of TOMFINLOUGH, barony of BUNRATTY, county of CLARE, and province of MUNSTER, 5½ miles (N.W.) from Six-mile-bridge, on the road from Newmarket-on-Fergus to Quin: the population is returned with the parish. Nearly adjoining it is a good race-course, which was formerly much frequented, but the races have been for many years discontinued. Fairs are held on the 12th of May and the 12th of August, chiefly for cattle, and were formerly well attended.

ARDSKEAGH, a parish, in the barony of CONDONS and CLONGIBBONS, county of CORK, and province of MUNSTER, 2 miles (S. by E.) from Charleville; containing 302 inhabitants. This parish, called also Ardskreagh, is separated from the main body of the barony in which it is included by the intervention of the northern part of the barony of Fermoy. It comprises 1993½ statute acres, as applotted for the county cess, and valued at £1420 per annum. The land under tillage is tolerably fertile, but a large portion of the parish is mountain pasture; the system of agriculture is gradually improving. The living is a rectory, in the diocese of Cloyne, and in the patronage of the Bishop: the tithes amount to £88. 11. 9. There is neither church nor glebe-house; the occasional duties are performed by the clergyman of the adjoining parish. The glebe, near the site of the old church (some remains of which still exist in the burial-ground), comprises four acres. In the R. C. divisions the parish is partly in the union or district of Charleville, but chiefly in that of Ballyhea. A school is held in the old chapel at Newtown.

ARDSTRAW, or ARDSRATH, a parish, partly in the barony of OMAGH, but chiefly in that of STRABANE, county of TYRONE, and province of ULSTER; containing, with the post-town of Newtown-Stewart, 21,212 inhabitants. This place was distinguished, under the name of Ardsrath, as the seat of an ancient bishoprick, over which St. Eugene, or Oen, presided about the year 540. At a very early period a small stone church or chapel existed here; and the names are recorded of several bishops who presided over the see, which, in 597, was removed to Maghera, and finally to Derry, in 1158. This place suffered repeatedly by fire, and appears to have been destroyed about the close of the twelfth century. The parish, which is situated on the road from Dublin to Londonderry, comprises, according to the Ordnance survey, 44,974¼ statute acres, of which 537¼ are covered with water. The surface is pleasingly diversified with hill and dale, and enlivened by the rivers Struell, Glenelly, and Derg, which, after flowing through the parish, unite in forming the river Morne, which abounds with trout and salmon; and also with several large and beautiful lakes, of which three are within the demesne of Baron's Court. The land is chiefly arable, with pasture intermixed; and the soil in the valleys is fertile; but there are considerable tracts of mountain and several extensive bogs. Limestone is found in several places at the base of the mountain called Bessy Bell, the whole of the upper portion of which is clay-slate; on the summit of another mountain, called Mary Gray, it is found with clay-slate at the base; and round the southern base of the former are detached blocks of freestone scattered in every direction. There are also some quarries of limestone at Cavandaragh; the stone is raised in blocks, or *laminæ*, from a quarter of an inch to three feet in thickness. The mountains within and forming a portion of the boundary of the parish are Bessy Bell, Douglas, and Mary Gray, which present beautiful and romantic scenery, particularly in the neighbourhood of Newtown-Stewart; and the view from the high grounds, including the lakes and rivers by which the parish is diversified, is truly picturesque. There are five bridges; one at Moyle, of three elliptic arches; a very ancient bridge at Newtown-Stewart, of six arches; another of six arches at Ardstraw, and a modern bridge of three arches on the Derry road. The principal seats are Baron's Court, the residence of the Marquess of Abercorn; Castlemoyle, of the Rev. R. H. Nash, D.D.; Woodbrook, of R. M. Tagert, Esq.; Newtown-Stewart Castle, of Major Crawford; Coosh, of A. Colhoun, Esq.; and Spa Mount, of E. Sproule, Esq. There were formerly several bleach-greens in the parish, but at present there is only one in operation, which is at Spa Mount, on the river Derg, and in which about 16,000 pieces are annually bleached and finished, principally for the London market.

The living is a rectory, in the diocese of Derry, and in the patronage of the Provost and Fellows of Trinity College, Dublin: the tithes amount to £1094. The church is a large and beautiful edifice with a handsome spire, and is situated in the town of Newtown-Stewart; a grant of £478 for its repair has been lately made by the Ecclesiastical Commissioners. A new church, or chapel of ease, is about to be built at Baron's Court, or Magheracreegan, for which the late Board of First Fruits granted £600, now in the hands of the Ecclesiastical

Commissioners. The glebe-house has a glebe of 681 acres attached to it, of which 461$\frac{3}{4}$ are in a state of cultivation. The R. C. parish is co-extensive with that of the Established Church, but is divided into East and West Ardstraw; there are chapels at Newtown-Stewart, Dragish, and Cairncorn. There are five places of worship for Presbyterians in connection with the Synod of Ulster, at Ardstraw, Newtown-Stewart, Douglas Bridge, Clady, and Garvetagh; that of Ardstraw is aided by a second class grant, and those of Newtown-Stewart, Douglas-Bridge, and Clady have each a third class grant. There are also two places of worship for Presbyterians of the Seceding Synod, one at Drumligagh of the first class, and the other at Newtown-Stewart of the second class; and there are a meeting-house for Primitive and two for Wesleyan Methodists. The parochial school at Newtown-Stewart is aided by an annual donation from the rector; and there are fifteen other public schools in different parts of the parish, and seventeen private schools; in the former are 1600, and in the latter about 780, children: and thirty-five Sunday schools. The poor are supported by voluntary contributions, aided by the interest of £100 in the 3$\frac{1}{2}$ per cents., being a sum due to the parish, which was recovered about twenty years since by process of law, and by act of vestry added to the poor fund. There are numerous interesting remains of antiquity in the parish, the most ancient of which are those of the monastery and cathedral of Ardsrath, near the village, consisting chiefly of the foundations of that part of the building which was formerly used as the parish church, the remains of some very beautiful crosses of elaborate workmanship, and several upright stones and columns richly fluted; but the churchyard, which was very extensive, has been contracted by the passing of the public road, in the formation of which many remains of antiquity were destroyed. Nearly adjoining is a ruin which tradition points out as the bishop's palace, and which was occupied as an inn when the Dublin road passed this way. About three miles above Ardstraw Bridge, and situated on a gentle eminence, are the picturesque ruins of Scarvaherin abbey, founded by Turloch Mac Dolagh, in 1456, for Franciscan friars of the third order, and on its dissolution granted by Queen Elizabeth to Sir Henry Piers; and near Newtown-Stewart is the site of the friary of Pubble, which appears to have been an appendage to Scarvaherin, and was granted at the same time to Sir Henry Piers; of the latter, nothing but the cemetery remains. In Newtown-Stewart are the extensive and beautiful remains of the castle built by Sir Robert Newcomen, in 1619; it is in the Elizabethan style, with gables and clustered chimneys. Jas. II. lodged in this castle, on his return from Lifford in 1589, and by his orders it was dismantled on the day following; with the exception of the roof, it is nearly perfect. At the foot of the mountain called Bessy Bell are the ruins of an ancient building called Harry Ouree's Castle, concerning which some remarkable legends are preserved by the country people; they consist of two circular towers, with a gateway between them, and some side walls, which overhang their base more than 8 feet. Near the end of the bridge at Newtown-Stewart is a large mound of earth, evidently thrown up to protect the ford, which in early times must have been of importance as the only pass through the vast range of the Munterlony mountains. There was a similar fort on the ford of Glenelly, near Moyle Castle, and another at the old ford at the village of Ardstraw. On the summit of Bessy Bell, or *Boase-Baal,* on which in pagan times sacrifice is supposed to have been offered to Baal or Bel, is a large and curious cairn; there are also cairns on the summit of Mary Gray, and more than thirty forts in the parish, nearly in a line from east to west, which were designed to guard the passes on the rivers of Glenelly and Derg. About a mile below Newtown-Stewart, in the bed of the river, is a single upright stone, called the "Giant's Finger," and lately "Flinn's rock," respecting which many strange traditions are preserved in the neighbourhood.—See NEWTOWN-STEWART.

ARDSTRAW-BRIDGE, a village, in the parish of ARDSTRAW, barony of STRABANE, county of TYRONE, and province of ULSTER, 3 miles (W. N. W.) from Newtown-Stewart: the population is returned with the parish. This place, formerly Ardsrath, is of high antiquity, and was distinguished for its ancient and greatly celebrated abbey, noticed in the preceding description of the parish of Ardstraw. The village is situated on the river Derg, which is here wide and rapid, and is crossed by an ancient stone bridge of six arches, over which the old road from Londonderry to Dublin formerly passed: it contains 32 houses, some of which are well built, but several of them are old and in a neglected state. There were formerly six fairs held in the village, which were large and well attended, but they have been discontinued for some time. There is a place of worship for Presbyterians in connection with the Synod of Ulster, and a public school.

ARDTRAMONT.—See ARTRAMONT.

ARDTREA, or ARTREA, a parish, partly in the barony of DUNGANNON, county of TYRONE, and partly in the barony of LOUGHINSHOLIN, county of LONDONDERRY, and province of ULSTER; containing, with the district or perpetual curacy of Woods-chapel, and the greater part of the market and post-town of Moneymore, 12,390 inhabitants, of which number, 7471 are in the district of Woods-chapel. During the rebellion of the Earl of Tyrone, in the reign of Elizabeth, this place was the scene of numerous conflicts; and in the parliamentary war, in 1641, it was involved in many of the military transactions of that period. In 1688-9, a sanguinary battle took place here between the adherents of Jas. II., who were in possession of the forts of Charlemont and Mountjoy, and the forces of Wm. III., commanded by Lord Blayney, who, having possession of Armagh, was desirous of assisting the garrisons of Inniskillen and Derry, and for this purpose determined to force a passage to Coleraine, which he accomplished, after defeating a detachment of the enemy's forces at the bridge of Ardtrea. The parish, which is also called Ardtragh, is situated partly on Lough Beg, but chiefly on Lough Neagh, and is intersected by the Ballinderry river and by numerous roads, of which the principal are those leading respectively from Armagh to Coleraine, from Omagh to Belfast, and from Stewarts-town to Moneymore. It contains, according to the Ordnance survey, 20,962$\frac{3}{4}$ statute acres, of which 18,679$\frac{1}{4}$ are in the county of Londonderry, including 2181$\frac{1}{2}$ in Lough Neagh, 317$\frac{1}{2}$ in Lough Beg, and 26$\frac{1}{2}$ in the river Bann. The soil is very various; the land is chiefly arable, and is fertile and well cultivated, especially around Moneymore, on the estate belonging to the Drapers' Company, and on that belonging to the Salters' Company round Ballyronan. There are several extensive tracts of bog in various parts, amounting in the whole to nearly 3000 acres, and affording an ample supply of fuel. Freestone of every variety, colour and quality, is found here in abundance; and there is plenty of limestone. At a short distance from the church, on the road to Cookstown, is an extraordinary whin-dyke, which rises near Ballycastle in the county of Antrim, passes under Lough Neagh, and on emerging thence near Stewart Hall, passes through this parish and into the mountain of Slievegallion, near Moneymore. Spring Hill, the pleasant seat of W. Lenox Conyngham, Esq., is an elegant and antique mansion, situated in a rich and highly improved demesne, embellished with some of the finest timber in the country. The other principal seats are Lakeview, the residence of D. Gaussen, Esq.; Warwick Lodge, of W. Bell, Esq.; and Ardtrea House, of the Rev. J. Kennedy Bailie, D.D. The farm-houses are generally large and well built; and most of the farmers, in addition to their agricultural pursuits, carry on the weaving of linen cloth for the adjoining markets. There is an extensive bleach-green, which, after having been discontinued for some years, has been repaired and is now in operation. The primate's court for the manor of Ardtrea is held at Cookstown monthly, for the recovery of debts under £5; and its jurisdiction extends over such lands in the parishes of Lissan, Derryloran, Kildress, Arboe, Desertcreight, Ardtrea, Clonoe, Tamlaght, Ballinderry, and Donaghendrie, as are held under the see.

The living is a rectory, in the diocese of Armagh, and in the patronage of the Provost and Fellows of Trinity College, Dublin: the tithes amount to £738. 9. 3¾. The church, an elegant edifice in the later English style, was erected in 1830, near the site of the ancient church; the principal entrance is a composition of very elegant design, and, from its elevated site, the church forms a very pleasing object in the landscape. The glebe-house is a large and handsome residence, built of hewn freestone by the late Dr. Elrington, then rector of the parish and subsequently Bishop of Ferns, aided by a gift of £100, and a loan of £1050, from the late Board of First Fruits: the glebe comprises 115¼ acres. The district church, called Woods-chapel, is situated at a distance of 10 miles from the mother church: the living is a perpetual curacy, in the patronage of the Rector. In the R. C. divisions the parish is the head of a union or district, called Moneymore, which comprises this parish and part of that of Desertlyn, and contains three chapels, one at Moneymore, one at Ballynenagh, and a third at Derrygaroe. There are two places of worship for Presbyterians at Moneymore, one for those in connection with the Synod of Ulster, of the first class, built by the Drapers' Company at an expense of £4000; and one for those in connection with the Seceding Synod, of the second class, built by subscription on a site given by the Drapers' Company, who also contributed £250 towards its erection. There are three schools aided by the Drapers' Company, and one at Ballymulderg, the whole affording instruction to about 170 boys and 170 girls; and there are also two pay schools. An ancient urn very elaborately ornamented was found in a kistvaen, on opening a tumulus in the townland of Knockarron, in 1800, and is now in the possession of John Lindesay, Esq., of Loughry.—See MONEYMORE, and WOODS-CHAPEL.

ARKLOW, a sea-port, market and post-town, and a parish, in the barony of ARKLOW, county of WICKLOW, and province of LEINSTER, 12 miles (S.) from Wicklow, and 40 miles (S. by E.) from Dublin; containing 6309 inhabitants, of which number, 4383 are in the town. This place, formerly called *Arclogh* and *Alercomshed*, appears to have been occupied as a fishing station from time immemorial. It was included in one of those grants of territory for which Hen. II., in 1172, caused service to be done at Wexford; and by an original charter, preserved among the rolls of Kilkenny Castle, it appears that John, Lord of Ireland, granted and confirmed the castle and town of Arclogh, with all their appurtenances, to Theobald Fitzwalter, hereditary lord-butler of Ireland. Fitzwalter founded here a monastery, which he dedicated to the Blessed Virgin, for monks of the Cistertian order, whom he brought from the abbey of Furness, in Lancashire. The barony, which with the chief butlery always descended to the next heir male, was inherited by Theobald, the third of that name, who died here on the 26th of September, 1285, and was buried in the abbey church, under a tomb ornamented with his effigy. In 1281, a battle was fought near this place between the English and the Irish, in which the latter were totally defeated by Stephen de Fulborne, Bishop of Waterford and Lord Justiciary of Ireland; and in 1316, the O'Tooles and O'Byrnes, who had risen in arms and burnt Arklow, Bray, and Newcastle, with all the neighbouring villages, were defeated on the 16th of April by Edward le Boteler. In 1331, the castle was taken by the O'Tooles, but was retaken by Lord de Birmingham; and in the year following it was again taken by the Irish, who were finally repulsed by Sir Anthony Lucy, who repaired the fortifications and strengthened the garrison. In 1641, the castle was surprised by a party of insurgents, and the garrison put to the sword; and being afterwards held for the royalists, it was, in 1649, assaulted by Oliver Cromwell in his victorious march southward, and on its surrender was totally demolished. During the disturbances of 1798, a battle was fought near Arklow bridge, between the king's troops, under the command of Gen. Needham, and the insurgents, in which the latter were defeated and their leader shot; among the slain on the side of the royal forces was Thomas Grogan Knox, Esq., of Castletown, cornet of the 5th dragoon guards, to whose memory a neat marble tablet has been placed in the church.

The town is situated on the acclivity of a hill extending along the right bank of the river Ovoca, and on the mail coach road from Dublin to Wexford. The Ovoca, after winding through the beautiful and romantic vale to which it gives name, passes under a bridge of nineteen arches at this place, and discharges itself into the sea, about 500 yards below the town. It is divided into the Upper and Lower Towns, which latter is called the "Fishery;" and in 1831 it contained 702 houses. The houses in the Upper Town, which consists of one principal street, are neatly built; those in the Lower Town, which is chiefly inhabited by fishermen, are mostly thatched cabins. The inhabitants are amply supplied with water from numerous excellent springs, but no works have been established to convey it to their houses; and the only improvement that has recently taken place is the Macadamising of the principal street, and the laying down of foot pavements. On the site of the ancient castle are barracks for two companies of infantry. The principal trade is the fishery, which was formerly very lucrative, having two seasons in the year; one in May, which has lately ceased; and the other in November, which, though still continued, has become so unproductive as scarcely to remunerate the persons employed in it. The fishery, in 1835, employed about 200 boats in the herring fishery and in dredging for oysters, of the latter of which great quantities are taken off the coast in some years, and sent to different parts of Ireland and to England. Formerly much of the copper ore from the Wicklow mines, which are situated nearly midway between this town and Rathdrum, was shipped from this port during the summer season; and some trade is still carried on in the importation of coal. The want of a safe harbour in which the fishermen might shelter during bad weather, which for two or three seasons has prevailed on this coast, has been severely felt, there being no port between Kingstown and Waterford into which they can run for shelter, and many lives are annually lost. The harbour is accessible only for small boats, as the passage is sinuous and subject to shifting sands. The market is on Thursday; and fairs are held on Jan. 11th, March 22nd, April 19th, May 14th, June 28th, Aug. 9th, Sep. 25th, and Nov. 15th, chiefly for the sale of woollen cloth, cattle, sheep, and pigs. A constabulary police station has been established here; and on the north side of the river, in the parish of Kilbride, is a coast-guard station belonging to the Gorey district. The petty sessions for the barony of Arklow are held every Thursday, in a neat court-house rented by the magistrates for that purpose, and of which the lower part is appropriated to the use of the savings' bank.

The parish, which is situated at the south-eastern extremity of the county, and intersected by the river Ovoca, comprises 5851 statute acres, as applotted under the tithe act. The surface is broken, abrupt, and mountainous; the soil towards the coast, and in the inlets between the hills is rich, and abounds with excellent marl, which, together with lime, is used for manure. The system of agriculture has been greatly improved, under the auspices of the Agricultural Society; the drill husbandry is practised where the soil will admit of it, and green crops have been partially introduced. The mountain of Croghan Kinshela, towards the close of the last century, became an object of intense interest from its supposed production of native gold; a peasant fishing in one of the streams which descended from it discovered, at different times, small particles of gold, which for about 12 years he continued to sell privately to a goldsmith, till, in September 1796, the discovery became known, and thousands of persons engaged in the search for this precious metal. Several masses of extraordinary size were found, one of which weighed nine, another eighteen, and a third twenty-two ounces; and so great was the number of the peasantry allured to the spot by the hope of enriching themselves, that in the short space of six or seven weeks, during which the washing of the sands was continued, not less than 2666 ounces of pure gold were obtained, which were sold for £10,000. After the people had continued their searches for a little more than six weeks, Government took possession of the mine, and stationed a party of the Kildare militia to prevent further encroachment; an act of parliament was passed for working it, and Messrs. Weaver, Mills, and King were appointed directors of the operations. Steam-works were established on several rivulets which descended from the mountain; and from this time till May 1798, when the works were destroyed in the insurrection of that disturbed period, the total quantity of gold found was 944 oz., 4 dwts., and 15 grs., which was sold for £3675. 8. 0. In 1801 the mining operations were resumed, and on the representation of the directors, Government was induced to extend the search upon a more systematic principle: the stream-works were continued to the heads of the several streams, and the solid mass of the mountain was more minutely examined, by cutting trenches in every direction down to the firm rock. The veins already known, and such as were afterwards discovered by the process of trenching, were more extensively explored and their depth minutely ascertained, by means of a gallery, or level, driven into the mountain at right angles to the general range of their direction. The mineral substances thus obtained were subjected to a rigid chymical analysis, but in no instance was a single particle of gold discovered; the result of these operations convinced Government that no gold existed as an inherent ingredient in any of the veins which traversed the mountain, and the works were consequently abandoned.

The environs of Arklow are much admired for the beauty, richness, and variety of their scenery; the banks of the Ovoca are embellished with handsome seats, and the sides of the vale with woods of luxuriant growth. Shelton Abbey, the seat of the Earl of Wicklow, though in the parish of Kilbride, forms a conspicuous and interesting feature in the scenery of this parish; it is beautifully situated on the north bank of the river, and at the base of a range of hills of gentle elevation, richly wooded with oak and birch. The mansion, which was remodelled some years since by the Messrs. Morrison, is a low quadrilateral edifice with two principal fronts, richly embellished with decorated pinnacles, and resembling an ecclesiastical structure of the 14th century, converted into a baronial residence at a subsequent period; the entrance-hall is wainscoted with carved oak, and the ceiling delicately enriched with fan tracery, of which the pendants are gilt; the great hall, gallery, and state apartments, are all in a style of corresponding richness and elegance; the library contains an exceedingly valuable collection of works made by a learned member of the family; and the cloisters are in a style of appropriate beauty. The demesne, which comprises more than 1000 statute acres, is ornamented with some of the most stately beech and chestnut trees in the island; and the whole forms one of the most delightful retreats in this romantic part of the country. During the temporary sequestration of the family estates at the time of the Revolution, Jas. II., on his flight to Waterford, after the battle of the Boyne, was entertained at Shelton Abbey by the party then in possession; and there is still a road within the demesne which is called King James's road. Glenart, a castellated mansion belonging to the Earl of Carysfort, and at present occupied by his lordship's brother, the Hon. Capt. Proby,

R. N., is situated on the south bank of the Ovoca, nearly opposite to the abbey, on a gentle slope in a very retired spot, commanding from the high grounds some fine views of the sea and of the richly wooded hills of Shelton Abbey and Bally-Arthur. Ballyrane, the seat of the Rev. T. Quin, is a handsome modern house, pleasantly situated within a mile of the town, of which it commands a fine view, and also of the sea. Lambarton, the seat of Capt. Hore, R.N., is beautifully situated in the midst of fine plantations, and commands delightful views of the sea and the demesnes of Shelton and Bally-Arthur, terminating in the magnificent range of mountains in the neighbourhood of Lugna-quilla. Emma Vale, the seat of D. Wright, Esq., is situated about a mile to the south-west of the town; the house has been enlarged and improved, the plantations are tastefully laid out, and the prospect comprehends a fine view of Glenart woods and mansion, Bally Arthur and the distant part of Shelton demesne, and an extensive range of mountain scenery. Elton, about half a mile to the south, is a commodious house occupying a healthful situation.

The living is a vicarage, in the diocese of Dublin and Glendalough, to which the greater portion of the rectory, which formerly belonged to the abbey of Voney, was united in the year 1673, subject to a reserved rent of £3. 12.; and to which also the vicarage of Enorily and the perpetual curacies of Killahurler, Kilbride, and Templemichael, and part of the rectory of Kilgorman, were united from time immemorial till 1833, when they were, with the exception of Killahurler and Kilgorman, separated from it by act of council and made a distinct benefice; leaving only Arklow and Killahurler, with part of Kilgorman, to constitute the vicarial union, which is in the patronage of the Archbishop. The other portion of the rectory is impropriate in W. Johnson and D. Howell, Esqrs. The tithes amount to £230. 15. 4¾., of which £46. 8. 7½. is payable to the lay impropriators, and the remainder to the incumbent; and the gross tithes of the union payable to the incumbent amount to £250. 8. 8. The church, situated in the principal street of the town, was erected in 1823, at an expense of £2000, of which sum £1100 was granted on loan by the late Board of First Fruits; and in 1829 it was enlarged, at an expense of £1200, granted by the same Board, in consideration of which grant the additional sittings are free. It was built after a design by Mr. Johnson, and is in the later English style, with a square tower. A grant of £249 has been lately made by the Ecclesiastical Commissioners for its repair. In the R. C. divisions this parish is the head of a union or district, which comprehends the parishes of Arklow, Killahurler, and Ballintemple, in the county of Wicklow, and of Inch and Kilgorman in the county of Wexford. The chapel is a handsome modern structure, situated opposite to the remains of the ancient castle; and there are chapels also at Johnstown, Castletown, and Ballycowgue, to all of which schools are attached. There is a small place of worship for Wesleyan Methodists. About 320 children are instructed in the several public schools, of which a boys' school is supported by the Trustees of Erasmus Smith's charity, two for girls are aided by Mrs. Proby, and an infants' school is maintained by voluntary contributions; and there are six private schools, in which are about 240 children, and two Sunday schools. A fever hospital and dispensary was erected in 1821, at an expense of £550, of which sum, £400 was presented by the grand jury, and the remainder was raised by subscription: it is a neat square building, in a healthy situation just without the town. The only relic of the ancient castle is a small fragment mantled with ivy, situated on an eminence above the river and adjoining the barracks. The cemetery of the Cistertian abbey is still used as a burying-place by the Roman Catholics. Arklow gives the title of baron, in the peerage of Ireland, by creation, to his Royal Highness the Duke of Sussex, and by tenure to the noble family of Butler, Marquesses of Ormonde.

ARLES, a village, in that part of the parish of Killeban which is in the barony of Slieumargue, Queen's county, and province of Leinster, 5 miles (N. W. by N.) from Carlow; containing 205 inhabitants. This place, which contains about 40 houses, is situated on the road from Carlow to Maryborough, and is of neat and pleasing appearance. The manufacture of tiles of excellent quality for roofing and flooring, and which were sent to Dublin and other places, where they were in much request, has been in a great degree superseded by the use of slates, and is now nearly extinct; the manufacture of yarn and linen is carried on to a small extent. The principal object of interest is the mausoleum of the Grace family, occupying the site of the south wing of the parish church, which was called Grace's chapel; it is 21 feet in length and 16 feet in breadth, with a lofty gabled roof, terminating at each extremity in crooked pinnacles 31 feet in height; the lower story consists of a vault with a circular roof, designed for the reception of the remains of the deceased members of the family, above which is a vaulted apartment of the same dimensions with a groined roof, in which are placed monumental inscriptions; in blank windows on the exterior are also large tablets, formerly within the building that previously occupied the site of the present mausoleum; the whole was erected in 1818, and the prevailing character is that of the later English style.

ARMAGH (County of), an inland county, in the province of Ulster, bounded on the north by Lough Neagh, on the east by the county of Down, on the south-east by that of Louth, on the south-west by Monaghan, and on the west and north-west by Tyrone: it is situated between 54° 3′ and 54° 31′ (N. Lat.), and between 6° 14′ and 6° 45′ (W. Lon.); and comprises, according to the Ordnance survey, 328,076 statute acres, of which 267,317 acres are tillable, 17,941 are covered with water, and the remainder is mountain and bog. The population, in 1821, was 197,427; and, in 1831, 220,134.

This tract is supposed to have been part of that named by Ptolemy as the territories of the *Vinderii* and *Voluntii*: it afterwards formed part of the district called Orgial, which also comprised the counties of Louth and Monaghan. The formation of this part of Ireland into a separate dominion is said to have taken place so early as the year 332, after the battle of *Achaighleth-derg*, in Fermoy, in which, as recorded by Tigernach, abbot of Clonmacnois, who died in 1068, Fergus Feagha, son of Froechair the Brave, the last of the Ultonian kings who resided in Eamania, was killed by the three Collas, who then expelled the Ultonians from that part of the province to the south of Lough Neagh, and formed it into an independent state, to which they gave the name of *Orgial*, afterwards corrupted into *Oriel* or *Uriel*, names by which it was distinguished to the beginning of the seventeenth century.

The county was made shire ground, under its present name, in 1586, by the lord-deputy, Sir John Perrott, who, not relying with confidence on the vigilance and care of Henry O'Nial and Sir Henry Bagnell, to whom the government of Ulster had been entrusted, projected the division of the greater part of that province into seven counties, of which Armagh was one, and took its name from the chief town in it. For each of these counties he appointed sheriffs, commissioners of the peace, coroners, and other officers. Previously to this arrangement, the chief part of the property of the county had centred in the families of the O'Nials, the Mac Cahans, and the O'Hanlons. At the commencement of the seventeenth century, it was principally vested in those of Mac Henry, Acheson, O'Nial, Brownlow, and O'Hanlon, exclusively of the great territories settled on Moharty, which the Mac Cahans had forfeited in rebellion, and a large tract of country called Oirther, afterwards Orior, a district in the southern part, which also escheated to the crown by rebellion of a branch of the O'Hanlons. According to a project for planting, by Jas. I., the whole of the arable and pasture land, amounting to 77,580 acres, was to be allotted in 61 proportions of three classes of 2000, 1500, and 1000 acres each, among the English and Scottish undertakers, the servitors, and the Irish natives. A portion was also assigned to the primate, another for glebes for the incumbents (of whom there was to be one for each proportion), another for the four corporate towns of Armagh, Mountnorris, Charlemont, and Tanderagee, and a fourth for a free grammar school. The native Irish were to be distributed among a few of the several proportions, with the exception of the swordsmen, who were to migrate into waste lands in Connaught and Munster. The project, which was but partially effected, was not acted upon until 1609, when a royal commission was issued to inquire into the king's title to the escheated and forfeited lands in Ulster, with a view to the plantation there. Inquisitions were consequently held, the return of which for Armagh, made in August of the same year, states that the county was then divided into the five baronies of Armaghe, Toaghriny, Orier, Fuighes, and Onylane or O'Nealane, and enumerates with great particularity the names and tenures of the proprietors. In 1618, a second commission was issued to Captain Pynnar and others, to ascertain how far the settlers located there in the intervening period had fulfilled the terms of their agreement. It is somewhat remarkable that, although the inquisition names five baronies, three only are noticed in Pynnar's survey; those of Armaghe and Toaghriny being omitted, probably because they contained no forfeited property. The number of the proportions specified in the survey are but 22, eleven of which, situated in O'Neylan, were in the hands of English undertakers; five in the Fuighes, in those of Scottish undertakers; and seven in Orier were allotted to servitors and natives. The number of tenants and men capable of bearing arms in the two first proportions amounted to 319 of the former, and 679 of the latter; the number in Orier is not given.

The county is partly in the diocese of Dromore, but chiefly in that of Armagh. For civil purposes i is now divided into the baronies of Armagh, Turaney O'Neilland East, O'Neilland West, Upper Fews, Lowe Fews, Upper Orior, and Lower Orior. It contains th city and borough of Armagh; part of the borough, sea port, and market-town of Newry; the market and post towns of Lurgan, Portadown, Tanderagee, Market-hil and Newtown-Hamilton; the disfranchised borough c Charlemont; the post-towns of Richhill, Keady, Black watertown, Loughgall, Tynan, Forkhill, and Flurry Bridge; and the market-towns of Middleton and Cross meglan, which, with Killylea, have each a penny post Prior to the Union it sent six members to the Iris parliament, two for the county at large, and two for eac of the boroughs; but at present its representation con sists of three members in the Imperial parliament, tw for the county at large, and one for the borough of Ar magh. The election takes place at Armagh; and th constituency, as registered in Oct. 1836, consisted o 384 £50, 324 £20, and 2384 £10 freeholders; 5 £5 and 19 £20 rent-chargers; and 122 £20 and 573 £1 leaseholders; making a total of 3811. It is in th north-east circuit: the assizes are held at Armagh where the county court-house and gaol are situated; an quarter sessions at Armagh, Lurgan, Market-hill, an Ballybott, of which the three last have each a court house and bridewell. The number of persons charge with criminal offences and committed to the county gao in 1835, was 385, and of civil bill commitments, 111 The local government is vested in a lieutenant, vice lieutenant, 13 deputy-lieutenants, and 63 other magis trates; besides whom there are the usual county officers including three coroners. There are 17 constabular police stations, having in the whole a force of a stipen diary magistrate, sub-inspector, paymaster, 5 chief an 19 subordinate constables, and 99 men, with 5 horses maintained equally by Grand Jury presentments and b Government. The amount of Grand Jury presentments for 1835, was £27,259. 2. $3\frac{1}{2}$., of which £4704. 0. 3 was for the public roads of the county at large £9974. 1. $7\frac{1}{2}$. for the public roads, being the baronia charge; £1475. 11. 4. in repayment of loans advance by Government; £2279. 10. 7. for the police, an £8825. 18. 6. for public establishments, officers' salaries buildings, &c. The public charitable institutions are district lunatic asylum, and the county infirmary an fever hospital at Armagh; and dispensaries at Cross meglin, Forkhill, Market-hill, Jonesborough, Keady Blackwatertown, Seagoe, Loughgall, Richhill, Lurga Newtown-Hamilton, Poyntz-Pass, Tynan, Portadown Tanderagee and Ballybott, supported by equal Gran Jury presentments and private subscriptions. Ther are also dispensaries at Tanderagee, Portadown, an Tullyhappy, built and supported by the Earl an Countess of Mandeville; and a fever hospital at Mid dleton, built and supported by the Trustees of Bisho Sterne's munificent bequest. In the military arrange ments this county is within the northern district, o which Armagh is the head-quarters, where there ar an ordnance-depôt and an infantry barrack constructe to accommodate 12 officers, 174 men, and 5 horses at Charlemont there is a fort, with an artillery barrac for 5 officers, 151 men, and 79 horses, to which is at tached an hospital for 22 patients.

The northern verge of the county, near Lough Neagh

the north-western adjoining Tyrone, and the neighbourhoods of Armagh, Market-hill, and Tanderagee, are level; the remainder is hilly, rising in the southern parts into mountains of considerable elevation. The highest is Slieve Gullion, rising, according to the Ordnance survey, 1893 feet above the level of the sea; it is about seven miles from the southern border, and is considered to be the loftiest point of land in Ulster, except Slieve Donard, in the neighbouring county of Down. Slieve Gullion sinks on the east into the Fathom Hills, which skirt the Newry water. One of the finest and most extensive prospects in Ulster is obtained from its summit, which commands the bay of Dundalk; and the bold and picturesque features of mountain scenery are confined to this immediate vicinity, including the Doobrin mountains and the neighbourhood of Forkhill. Westward to the Fews the country exhibits a chain of abrupt hills, the greater part of which can never be reduced to a state of profitable cultivation. Further west are the Fews mountains, a subordinate range, lying in a direction from south-east to north-west. The fertility of the more level districts towards the eastern, northern, and north-western confines is very remarkable, especially in the views from Richhill, the numerous demesnes being sufficiently wooded to ornament the whole country, and the surface generally varied by pleasing undulations. From the shores of Lough Neagh, however, extend considerable tracts of low, marshy, and boggy land. The other lakes are few and small: that of Camlough, romantically situated on the northern verge of Slieve Gullion, is the largest. Lough Clay, in the western part of the county, which gives rise to one of the branches of the Callen river, is the next in size; but neither of them would be noticed for extent or beauty if situated in some of the neighbouring counties. A chain of small lakes occupying the south-western boundary of the county is valuable from the supply of water afforded by them to the mills in their neighbourhood. Coney Island, near the southern shore of Lough Neagh, and between the mouths of the Blackwater and Bann rivers, is the only island in the county; it is uninhabited. The climate is more genial than most of the other counties in Ulster, as is evinced by the greater forwardness of the harvests: this advantage has been attributed to the nature of the soil and subsoil, the gentle undulation of the surface, the absence of moor or marshy land, and the protection by mountains from the cooling breezes of the sea.

The soil is generally very fertile, especially in the northern part, the surface of which is a rich brown loam, tolerably deep, on a substratum of clay or gravel. There is an abundance of limestone in the vicinity of Armagh, and in Kilmore and other places; and there are quarries near Lough Neagh, but the stone lies so deep, and they are subject to such a flow of water, as to be of little practical use. Towards Charlemont there is much bog, which yields red ashes, and is easily reclaimable; the substratum of this is a rich limestone. The eastern part of the county consists of a light friable soil. In the south the country is rocky and barren: huge rocks of granite are found on the surface promiscuously mixed with blocks of limestone, as if thrown together by some convulsion of nature. All the limestone districts make good tillage and meadow ground: the natural meadow found on the banks of the rivers, and formed of a very deep brown loam, yields great crops without manure. The hilly district is generally of a deep retentive soil on a gravelly but not calcareous substratum: a decayed freestone gravel, highly tinged with ferruginous ore, is partially found here: the subsoil is sometimes clay-slate. In these districts heath is peculiarly vigorous, except where the judicious application of lime has compelled it to give place to a more productive vegetation. Except near Newtown-Hamilton, there is but little bog among these hills. The valleys which lie between them have a rich and loamy soil, which yields much grain, and does not abound in aquatic plants, although the *poa fluitans* grows in them in great luxuriance. The general inequality of surface which pervades the county affords great facilities for drainage.

In consequence of the dense population the farms are generally very small, and much land is tilled with the spade. Wheat is a very general crop in the baronies of Armagh, the O'Neillands, and Turaney; the main crops in the other baronies are oats, flax, and potatoes. In the smaller farms potatoes constitute the first and second crops, sometimes even a third; and afterwards flax occupies a portion of the potatoe plot, and barley the remainder, if the soil be dry and fine, but if otherwise, crops of oats are taken in succession. The treatment of the wheat crop consists of one harrowing and one ploughing, to level the potatoe furrows; if two crops of potatoes have preceded, a small quantity of ashes is scattered over the surface. The seed most in use is the red Lammas wheat, and the quantity sown is about three bushels to the acre. Potatoe oats are commonly sown on the best lands; black oats, and sometimes white oats, on land manured with lime, in the mountainous districts; this latter species, when sown on mountain land not previously manured and drained, will degenerate into a black grain in two or three seasons. Flax is invariably sown on potatoe ground, the plot being tilled with the spade, but not rolled: Dutch seed is sown on heavy soils, American on light soils. The seed is not saved, and therefore the plant is pulled just before it changes colour, from an opinion that when thus prepared it makes finer yarn. More seed was sown in 1835 than was ever before known, in consequence of the increased demand from the spinners in England and Ireland. The pasturage is abundant and nutritious; and though there are no extensive dairies, cows are kept by all the small farmers of the rich northern districts, whence much butter is sent to the Belfast market a considerable quantity of butter, generally made up in small firkins, is also sent to Armagh and Newry for exportation. The state of agriculture in modern times has very much improved; gentlemen and large farmers have introduced all the improved agricultural implements, with the practice of drainage, irrigation, and rotation crops. Mangel-wurzel, turnips, clover, and all other green crops are now generally cultivated even upon the smallest farms, particularly around Market-hill, Tanderagee, Banagher, and other places, where the greatest encouragement is given by Lords Gosford, Mandeville, and Charlemont, and by Col. Close and other resident gentlemen, who have established farming societies and expend large sums annually in premiums. The Durham, Hereford, North Devon, Leicester, Ayrshire, and other breeds of cattle have been introduced, and by judicious crosses a very superior stock has been raised: some farmers on good soils have also brought over the Alderney breed, which thrives remarkably well; but in some of the mountain districts the old long-horned breed of the country is still preferred, and a cross between it and the old Leicester appears to suit both soil and climate, as they grow to a large size, give great quantities of milk, and fatten rapidly. The breed of sheep and horses has also been greatly improved, the former kind of stock is chiefly in the possession of gentlemen and large farmers. The horses used in farming are mostly a light active kind; but the best hunters and saddle horses are brought hither by dealers from other counties. Numerous herds of young cattle are reared on the Fews mountains, which are the only part of the county where grass farms are extensive. Goats are numerous, and are allowed to graze at liberty in the mountainous districts. Hogs are fattened in great numbers; the gentry prefer the Chinese breed, but the Berkshire is preferred by the country people, as being equally prolific and more profitable. Lime and dung are the general manures; the former is usually mixed with clay for the culture of potatoes, and is also applied to grass lands as a surface dressing preparatory to tillage, sometimes even three years before the sod is broken, as being deemed more effective than manuring the broken ground; the average quantity of lime laid on an acre is from 30 to 40 barrels. Thorn hedges well kept are the common fences in the richer districts, and with scattered timber trees and numerous orchards give them a rich woody appearance. In the mountainous district, too, the same fences are rising in every direction. Many parts of the county, particularly in the barony of Armagh, are decorated with both old and new timber: and in comparison with neighbouring districts it has a well-wooded appearance; but there are no extensive woodlands, although there is, near Armagh, a large public nursery of forest trees.

The geological features of the county are various and interesting. The mountain of Slieve Gullion, in its south-eastern extremity, is an offset of the granite district of Down, and is remarkable for the varieties of which it is composed. It is in the form of a truncated cone, and presents on some sides mural precipices several hundred feet in height, from which it acquires an appearance of greater elevation than it really attains: the summit is flat, and on it is a lake of considerable extent. The granite of this mountain, particularly that procured near the summit, is frequently used for millstones, being extremely hard and fine-grained, and composed of quartz, feldspar, mica, and hornblende. This, indeed, is here the common composition of this primitive rock, the feldspar being grey and the mica black. Sometimes the hornblende is absent, in which case the rock is found to be a pure granite; and at others it graduates into a beautiful sienite composed of flesh-coloured feldspar and hornblende. Flesh-coloured veins of quartz are also found to variegate the granite, in a beautiful manner, in several places. On the south, towards Jonesborough, the sienite succeeds to the granite, and afterwards passes into porphyry, which is succeeded by silicious slate. The Newry mountains and the Fathom hills are composed of granite. Around Camlough mica slate is found in vast beds. Westward the granite district of Slieve Gullion extends to the hill above Larkin-mill, on the western declivity of which the granite basis is covered by almost vertical strata, composed first of an aggregation of quartz and mica with steatite, which in the distance of about a quarter of a mile is occasionally interstratified with greenish grey clay-slate, of which the strata still further west are wholly composed. Several slate quarries have here been opened and partially worked, but none with spirit or skill: the principal are at Dorcy, Newtown-Hamilton, Cregan-Duff, and in the vicinity of Crossmeglan. Further distant this becomes grauwacke slate, by being interstratified with grauwacke. In the neighbourhood of Market-hill the strata comprise also hornblende slate and greenstone porphyry. Sandstone is also connected with this district; there is a quarry of remarkably fine freestone at Grange; and on the surface of the southern confines is seen the intermixture of grit and limestone rocks above noticed. Trap rocks, forming a hard stone varying in hue between dark green and blue, here called whin, are found in various places in huge blocks and boulders, or long narrow stones. The substratum of the eastern portion of the county varies between a silicious schistus and an argillaceous deposit, forming a grauwacke district, which extends across to the western confines of the county. The west and middle of the county is limestone, which is generally white, except in the vicinity of the city of Armagh, where it assumes a red tinge, exhibiting that colour more distinctly as it approaches the town, improving also in quality, and increasing in the varieties of its shades. The minerals, as connected with metallurgy, are so few as scarcely to deserve notice, lead only excepted, a mine of which was worked in the vicinity of Keady, on a property held by the Earl of Farnham, under Dublin College; but after much expenditure the operations were discontinued in consequence of the loss incurred, which, however, has been attributed to the want of skilful or honest superintendence. Lead ore has also been found near Market-hill, in several places near Newtown-Hamilton, on the demesne of Ballymoyer, near Hockley, in Slieve Cross, near Forkhill, and in the parish of Middleton. Some indications of iron, imperfect lead, regulus of manganese, and antimony, have been found in a few spots. The other mineral substances found here are potters' clay and a variety of ochres. Various kinds of timber, particularly oak, pine, and yew, have been raised out of the bogs; petrified wood is found on the shores of Lough Neagh; and fern, spleenwort, and mosses have been discovered in the heart of slaty stones.

The woollen trade flourished extensively in this county until interrupted by the legislative measures enacted by William III., and cloth of every description was manufactured. The linen manufacture is now pursued in all its branches, the finest goods being produced in the northern parts. The extent of the manufacture cannot easily be ascertained, because much comes in from the outskirts of the neighbouring counties, though the excess thus arising is most probably counterbalanced by the goods sent out of Armagh to the markets in the adjoining counties. At the commencement of the present century, the value of its produce annually was estimated at £300,000, and at present exceeds £500,000. Large capitals are employed by bleachers, who purchase linen and bleach it on their own account; the principal district is on the river Callan, at Keady. Considerable sums are also employed in the purchase of yarn, which is given out to the weaver to manufacture. Woollen goods are made solely for home consumption, and in only small quantities. Manufactories for the necessaries of life in greatest demand, such as candles, leather, soap, beer, &c. are numerous; and there are mills for dressing flax and spinning linen yarn, and numerous large flour-mills.

The two principal rivers are the Blackwater and the Bann, which chiefly flow along the north-eastern and north-western boundaries of the county, the former discharging itself into the western side of Lough Neagh, and the latter into the southern part of the same lake, at Bann-foot ferry. The Newry water, after flowing through a narrow valley between the counties of Down and Armagh, empties itself into the bay of Carlingford, below Newry. The Callan joins the Blackwater below Charlemont: the Cusheir falls into the Bann at its junction with the Newry canal; and the Camlough, flowing from the lake of the same name, discharges itself into the Newry water. This last named river, during its short course of five miles, supplies numerous bleach-works, and corn, flour, and flax mills: its falls are so rapid that the tail race of the higher mill forms the head water of the next lower. The Newtown-Hamilton river is joined by the Tara, and flows into Dundalk bay, into which also the Flurry or Fleury, and the Fane, empty themselves. The total number of main and branch streams is eighteen, and the combined lengths of all are 165 miles. The mouths of those which flow into Lough Neagh have a fine kind of salmon trout, frequently 30lb. in weight: the common trout is abundant and large, as are also pike, eels, bream, and roach. An inland navigation along the border of the counties of Armagh and Down, from Newry to Lough Neagh, by the aid of the Bann and the Newry water, was the first line of canal executed in Ireland. Commencing at the tideway at Fathom, it proceeds to Newry, and admits vessels drawing nine or ten feet of water, having at each end a sea lock. From Newry to the point where the Bann is navigable, a distance of fifteen miles, is a canal for barges of from 40 to 60 tons, chiefly fed from Lough Brickland and Lough Shark, in the county of Down. The river Bann, from its junction with the canal to Lough Neagh, a distance of eleven miles and a half, completes the navigation, opening a communication with Belfast by the Lagan navigation, and with the Tyrone collieries by the Coal Island or Blackwater navigation. The chief trade on this canal arises from the import of bleaching materials, flax-seed, iron, timber, coal, and foreign produce from Newry; and from the export of agricultural produce, yarn, linen, fire-bricks, pottery, &c. The canal from Lough Erne to Lough Neagh, now in progress, enters this county near Tynan, and passes by Caledon, Blackwatertown, and Charlemont to its junction with the river Blackwater above Verner's bridge, and finally with Lough Neagh. A line of railway from Dublin to Armagh, and thence to Belfast, and another from Armagh to Coleraine, have been projected. The roads are generally well laid out, and many of them of late have been much improved.

Among the relics of antiquity are the remains of the fortress of Eamania, near Armagh, once the royal seat of the kings of Ulster. The Danes' Cast is an extensive line of fortification in the south-eastern part of the county, and stretching into the county of Down. The tumulus said to mark the burial-place of "Nial of the hundred battles" is still visible on the banks of the Callan. The Vicar's Cairn, or Cairn-na-Managhan, is situated near the city of Armagh. Cairn Bann is in Orior barony, near Newry. A tumulus in Killevy parish contains an artificial cavern. Two ancient brazen weapons were found in a bog near Carrick, where a battle is said to have been fought in 941. Spears, battle-axes, skeyns, swords, the golden torques, and collars, rings, amulets, and medals of gold, also various ornaments of silver, jet, amber, &c., have been found in different places, and are mostly preserved. Near Hamilton's Bawn, in 1816, was found the entire skeleton of an elk, of which the head and horns were placed in the hall of the Infirmary at Armagh; and in the same year also the body of a trooper was discovered in a bog near Charlemont, of which the dress and armour appeared to be of the reign of Elizabeth. The religious houses, besides those of the city of Armagh, of which any memorial has been handed down to us were Clonfeacle, Killevey or Kilsleve, Kilmore, Stradhailloyse, and Tahellen. The most remarkable military remains are Tyrone's ditches, near Poyntz Pass, Navan fort, the castles of Criff-Keirn and Argonell, the castle in the pass of Moyrath, and Castle Roe.

The peasantry are in possession of superior comforts in their habitations as well as in food and clothing, which cannot be attributed solely to the linen manufacture, as their neighbours of the same trade in the adjoining counties of Cavan and Monaghan are far behind them in this respect. The county possesses sufficient fuel for domestic consumption; but coal is imported from England by the Newry canal, and from the county of Tyrone by the Blackwater. In no other county do the working classes consume so much animal food. The general diffusion of the population is neither the result of a predetermined plan, nor of mere accident: it arises from the nature of the linen manufacture, which does not require those employed in it to be collected into overgrown cities, or congregated in crowded factories. Engaged alternately at their loom and in their farm, they derive both health and recreation from the alternation. Green lawns, clear streams, pure springs, and the open atmosphere, are necessary for bleaching: hence it is that so many eminent bleachers reside in the country, and hence also the towns are small, and every hill and valley abounds with rural and comfortable habitations.

In the mountainous districts are several springs slightly impregnated with sulphur and iron. The borders of the bogs sometimes also exhibit ferruginous oozings, one of which in the Fews mountains is said to be useful in scrofulous complaints. The same effect was also formerly attributed to the waters of Lough Neagh, in the north-western limits of this county. Boate states, in addition to this, that the temperature of the sand at the bottom of the bay in which this sanative quality is perceived, alternates frequently between cold and warmth. A petrifying quality, such as that said to exist in some parts of Lough Neagh, has been discovered at Rose-brook, near Armagh, the mansion-house of which was built, in a great measure, of petrifactions raised from a small lake there. Petrified branches of hawthorn have been found near the city of Armagh; and fossil remains of several animals have also been discovered in the limestone rocks in the same vicinity. Petrifactions of the muscle, oyster, leech, together with dendrites, belemnites, and madreporites, are also found; and in the mountain streams are pure quartz crystals, of which a valuable specimen, found near Keady, is in the possession of Dr. Colvan, of Armagh.

Seal.

ARMAGH, a city, market and post-town and a parish, partly in the barony of O'Neilland West, but chiefly in that of Armagh, county of Armagh (of which it is the capital), and province of Ulster, 31 miles (S. W. by W.) from Belfast, and 65¾ (N. N. W.) from Dublin; containing 10,518 inhabitants, of which number, 9470 are within the limits of the borough.

The past importance of this ancient city is noticed by several early historians, who describe it as the chief city in Ireland. St. Fiech, who flourished in the sixth century, calls it the seat of empire; Giraldus Cambrensis, the metropolis; and, even so lately as 1580, Cluverius styles it the head of the kingdom, adding that Dublin was then next in rank to it. The original name was *Druim-sailech*, "the hill of sallows," which was afterwards changed to *Ard-sailech*, "the height of sallows," and, still later, to *Ard-macha*, either from *Eamhuin-macha*, the regal residence of the kings of Ulster, which stood in its vicinity, or, as is more probable, from its characteristic situation, *Ard-macha*, signifying "the high place or field."

Armagh is the head of the primacy of all Ireland, and is indebted for its origin, and ecclesiastical pre-eminence, to St. Patrick, by whom it was built, in 445. He also founded, near his own mansion, the monastery of St. Peter and St. Paul, for Canons Regular of the order of St. Augustine, which was rebuilt by Imar O'Hoedegan, and was the most distinguished of the religious establishments which existed here, having materially contributed to the early importance of the place. This institution received numerous grants of endowment from the native kings, the last of whom, Roderick O'Connor, made a grant to its professors, in 1169; insomuch that its landed possessions became very extensive, as appears from an inquisition taken on its suppression. Attached to it was a school or college, which long continued one of the most celebrated seminaries in Europe, and from which many learned men, not only of the Irish nation, but from all parts of Christendom, were despatched to diffuse knowledge throughout Europe. It is said that 7000 students were congregated in it, in the pursuit of learning, at one period; and the annals of Ulster relate that, at a synod held by Gelasius at Claonadh, in 1162, it was decreed that no person should lecture publicly on theology, except such as had studied at Armagh. The city was destroyed by accidental conflagrations in the year 670, 687, and 770, and also sustained considerable injury in the last-mentioned year by lightning. In subsequent periods it suffered severely and repeatedly from the Danes, a band of whom having landed at Newry, in 830, penetrated into the interior, and having stormed Armagh established their head-quarters in it for one month, and on being driven out, plundered and reduced it to ashes. In 836, Tergesius or Thorgis, a Danish chieftain, equally celebrated for his courage and ferocity, after having laid waste Connaught and a great part of Meath and Leinster, turned his arms against Ulster, which he devastated as far as Lough Neagh, and then advancing against Armagh, took it with little difficulty. His first act, after securing possession of the place, was the expulsion of the Bishop Farannan, with all the students of the college, and the whole body of the religious, of whom the bishop and clergy sought refuge in Cashel. The numerous atrocities perpetrated by the invaders at length excited a combined effort against them. Nial the Third collected a large army, and after having defeated the Danes in a pitched battle in Tyrconnel, advanced upon Armagh, where, after a second successful engagement, and while preparing to force his victorious way into the city, the main position of the enemy in these parts, he was drowned in the river Callan, in an attempt to save the life of one of his followers. Malachy, his successor, obtained possession of the city, in which a public assembly of the princes and chieftains of Ireland was held, in 849, to devise the means of driving their ferocious enemies out of the island. In their first efforts the Danes suffered several defeats; but, having concentrated their forces, and being supported by a reinforcement of their countrymen, they again marched against Armagh, and took and plundered it about the year 852.

The subsequent annals of Armagh, to the commencement of the 11th century, are little more than a reiteration of invasions and conquests by the Danes, and of successful but brief insurrections of the natives, in all of which this devoted city became in turn the prize of each contending army, and suffered all the horrors of savage warfare. In 1004, the celebrated Brian Boru entered Armagh, where he presented at the great altar of the church a collar of gold weighing 20 ounces; and after his death at the battle of Clontarf, in 1014, his remains were deposited here, according to his dying request, with those of his son Murchard, who fell in the same battle. From this period to the English invasion the history of Armagh exhibits a series of calamitous incidents either by hostile inroads or accidental fires. Its annals, however, evince no further relation to the events of that momentous period than the fact of a synod of the Irish clergy having been held in it by Gelasius, in 1170, in which that assembly came to the conclusion that the foreign invasion and internal distractions of the country were a visitation of divine retribution, as a punishment for the inhuman practice of purchasing Englishmen from pirates and selling them as slaves; and it was therefore decreed that every English captive should be liberated. The city suffered severely from the calamities consequent on the invasion of Edward Bruce, in 1315, during which the entire see was lamentably wasted, and the archbishop was reduced to a state of extreme destitution, by the reiterated incursions of the Scottish army.

During the local wars in Ulster, at the close of the 15th and the beginning of the 16th centuries, this city was reduced to a state of great wretchedness; and in the insurrection of Shane O'Nial or O'Neal, Lord Sussex, then lord-lieutenant, marched into Ulster to oppose him; and having attacked him successfully at Dundalk, forced him to retire upon Armagh, which the lord-lieutenant entered in Oct. 1557, and wasted with fire and sword, sparing only the cathedral. In 1566, O'Nial, to revenge himself on Archbishop Loftus, who had transmitted information of his hostile intentions to Government, even before the Irish chieftains and the lord-deputy had preferred their complaint against him, resolved on a special expedition against this city, and on this occasion committed dreadful havoc, not even sparing the cathedral. In the year 1575, Sydney, the lord-deputy, marched into Ulster against Turlogh O'Nial, and fixed his head-quarters at Armagh, whither that chieftain, after some ineffectual negociations through the agency of his wife, proceeded, and having surrendered himself, was permitted to return home without molestation. In the short but sanguinary war carried on between the English Government and Hugh O'Nial, Earl of Tyrone, towards the close of the reign of Elizabeth, the earl obtained possession of this place by stratagem; but unfavourable events in other parts soon obliged him to evacuate the place. In the course of the same war, Armagh was again invested, in 1598, by this chieftain, who hoped to reduce it a second time by famine, but was baffled by the treachery of his illegitimate son, Con O'Nial, who, having deserted to the English, discovered a private road by which Sir Henry Bagnall, the British commander, was enabled to send in such a supply of men and provisions as completely frustrated the earl's efforts. Soon after, the English were utterly defeated, and their commander killed, in a desperate attempt to force O'Nial's intrenchments, the immediate consequence of which was their evacuation of Armagh, which, however, was retaken in 1601, by Lord Mountjoy, who made it one of his principal positions in his Ulster expedition, and occupied it with a garrison of 900 men. In the early part of the 17th century, a colony of Scottish Presbyterians settled here, from which it is supposed Scotch-street, near the eastern entrance of the town, took its name.

At the commencement of the war in 1641, Armagh fell into the hands of Sir Phelim O'Nial, who, on being soon after forced to evacuate it, set fire to the cathedral, and put to death many of the inhabitants. On the breaking out of the war between James II. and William, Prince of Orange, the Earl of Tyrconnel, then lord-lieutenant under the former sovereign, took the charter from the corporation, and placed a strong body of troops in the town; but they were surprised and disarmed by the people of the surrounding country, who had risen in favour of the new dynasty: the garrison was permitted to retreat without further injury to Louth, and Lord Blayney, having taken possession of the town, immediately proclaimed King William. This nobleman, however, was soon afterwards compelled to evacuate it, and retreat with his forces to Londonderry, at that period the last refuge of the Protestants. James, in his progress through the north to and from the siege of Derry, rested for a few days at Armagh, which he describes as having been pillaged by the enemy, and very inconvenient both for himself and his suite. In 1690, Duke Schomberg took possession of it, and formed a depôt of provisions here. No important event occurred after the Revolution until the year 1769, when this city furnished a well-appointed troop of cavalry to oppose Thurot at Carrickfergus. In 1778, on the apprehension of an invasion from France and of civil disturbances, several of the inhabitants again formed themselves into a volunteer company, and offered the command to the Earl of Charlemont, by whom, after some deliberation, it was accepted. In 1781, an artillery company was formed; and in the following year, a troop of volunteer cavalry, of which the Earl of Charlemont was also captain. In 1796, this nobleman, in pursuance of the wishes of Government, formed an infantry company and a cavalry troop of yeomanry in the town, whose numbers were afterwards augmented to 200: they were serviceable in performing garrison duty during the temporary absence of the regular troops in the disturbances of 1798, but in 1812 were disbanded by order of the lord-lieutenant.

The city, which is large, handsome, and well built, is delightfully situated on the declivity of a lofty eminence, round the western base of which the river Callan winds in its progress to the Blackwater. It is chiefly indebted for its present high state of improvement to the attention bestowed on it by several primates since the Reformation, especially by Primate Boulter, and, still more so, by Primate Robinson, all of whom have made it their place of residence. The approaches on every side embrace interesting objects. On the east are the rural village and post-town of Rich-hill, and the demesne of Castle-Dillon, in which the late proprietor erected an obelisk on a lofty hill in memory of the volunteers of Ireland. The western approach exhibits the demesnes of Caledon, Glasslough, Woodpark, Elm Park, and Knappagh; those fromDungannon and Loughgall pass through a rich and well-wooded country; that from the south, descending through the fertile, well-cultivated, and busy vale of the Callan, the banks of which are adorned with several seats and extensive plantations, interspersed with numerous bleach-greens and mills, is extremely pleasing; and that from the south-east, though less attractive, is marked by the classical feature of Hamilton's Bawn, immortalised by the sarcastic pen of Swift. Many of the streets converge towards the cathedral, the most central point and the most conspicuous object in the city, and are connected by cross streets winding around the declivity; they have flagged pathways, are Macadamised, and are lighted with oil gas from works erected in Callan-street, by a joint stock company, in the year 1827, but will shortly be lighted with coal gas, the gasometer for which is now in progress of erection; and since 1833 have been also cleansed and watched under the provisions of the general act of the 9th of Geo. IV., cap. 82, by which a cess is applotted and levied on the inhabitants. A copious supply of fresh water has been procured under the authority of two general acts passed in 1789 and 1794. Metal pipes have been carried through all the main streets, by which a plentiful supply of good water is brought from a small lake or basin nearly midway between Armagh and Hamilton's Bawn, in consideration of a small rate on each house; and fountains have also been erected in different parts of the town occupied by the poorer class of the inhabitants. The city is plentifully supplied with turf, and coal of good quality is brought from the Drumglass and Coal Island collieries, 11 miles distant. A public walk, called the Mall, has been formed by subscription, out of ground granted on lease to the corporation, originally in 1797, by the primate, being a part of the town commons, which were vested in the latter for useful purposes by an act of the 13th and 14th of Geo. III.: the enclosed area, on the eastern side of which are many superior houses, comprehends nearly eight acres, kept in excellent condition. In addition to this, the primate's demesne is open to respectable persons; and his laudable example has been followed by two opulent citizens, who have thrown open their grounds in the vicinity for the recreation of the inhabitants. The Tontine Buildings, erected as a private speculation by a few individuals, contain a large assembly-room having a suite of apartments connected with it, a public news'-room, and a savings' bank. Dramatic performances occasionally take place in this edifice, from the want of a special building for their exhibition. The public library was founded by Primate Robinson, who bequeathed for the free use of the public his valuable collection of books, and endowed it with lands at Knockhamill and houses in Armagh yielding a clear rental of £339. He also erected the building, which is a handsome edifice in the Grecian style, situated to the north-west of the cathedral, and completed in 1771, as appears by the date in front, above which is the appropriate inscription "ΤΟ ΤΗΣ ΨΥΧΗΣ ΙΑΤΡΕΙΟΝ." The room in which the books are deposited is light, airy and commodious, and has a gallery: there are also apartments for a resident librarian. In 1820, an additional staircase was erected, as an entrance at the west end, which has in a great measure destroyed the uniformity and impaired the beauty of the building. The collection consists of about 20,000 volumes, and comprises many valuable works on theology, the classics, and antiquities, to which have been added several modern publications. In the record-room of the diocesan registry are writings and books bequeathed by Primate Robinson to the governors and librarian, in trust, for the sole use of the primate for the time being. The primate, and the dean and chapter, by an act of the 13th and 14th of Geo. III., are trustees of the library, with liberal powers. The observatory, beautifully situated on a gentle eminence a little to the north-east of the city, was also erected by Primate Robinson, about the year 1788, on a plot of 15 acres of land: the building is of hewn limestone, and has on its front the inscription, "The Heavens declare the glory of God;" it comprises two lofty domes for the observatory, and a good house for the residence of the astronomer. The munificent founder also provided for the maintenance of the astronomer, and gave the impropriate tithes of Carlingford for the support of an assistant astronomer and the maintenance of the observatory, vesting the management in the primate for the time being and twelve governors, of whom the chapter are eight, and the remaining four are elected by them as vacancies occur. Primate Robinson dying before the internal arrangements were completed, the establishment remained in an unfinished state till 1825, when the Right Hon. and Most Rev. Lord J. G. De La Poer Beresford, D.D., the present primate, furnished the necessary instruments, &c., at a cost of nearly £3000. This city is usually the station of a regiment of infantry: the barracks occupy an elevated and healthy situation, and are capable of accommodating 800 men. In the immediate vicinity is the archiepiscopal palace, erected in 1770 by Primate Robinson, who also, in 1781, built a beautiful chapel of Grecian architecture nearly adjacent, and embellished the grounds, which comprise about 800 acres, with plantations tastefully arranged.

Though an increasing place, Armagh has now no manufactures, and but little trade, except in grain, of which a great quantity is sent to Portadown and Newry for exportation: much of the flour made in the neighbourhood is conveyed to the county of Tyrone. After the introduction of the linen manufacture into the North of Ireland, Armagh became the grand mart for the sale of cloth produced in the surrounding district. From a return of six market days in the spring of 1835, the average number of brown webs sold in the open market was 4292, and in private warehouses 3412, making a total of 7704 webs weekly, the value of which, at £1. 11. each, amounts to £620,942. 8. per annum. But this does not afford a just criterion of the present state of the trade, in which a great change has taken place within the last 20 years; the quantity now bleached annually in this neighbourhood is nearly double that of any former period, but only a portion of it is brought into the market of Armagh. The linen-hall is a large and commodious building, erected by Leonard Dobbin, Esq., M.P. for the borough: it is open for the sale of webs from ten to eleven o'clock every Tuesday. A yarn market is held, in which the weekly sales amount to £3450, or £179,400 per annum. There are two extensive distilleries, in which upwards of 25,000 tons of grain are annually consumed; an ale brewery, consuming 3800 barrels of malt annually; several extensive tanneries; and numerous flour and corn mills, some of which are worked by steam. The amount of excise duties collected within the district for the year 1835 was £69,076. 5. 8½. The Blackwater, within four miles of the city, affords a navigable communication with Lough Neagh, from which, by the Lagan canal, the line of navigation is extended to Belfast; and to the east is the navigable river Bann, which is connected with the Newry canal. A canal is also in progress of formation from the Blackwater, to continue inland navigation from Lough Neagh to Lough Erne, which will pass within one mile of the city. The markets are abundantly supplied; they are held on Tuesday, for linen cloth and yarn, pigs, horned cattle, provisions of all kinds, vast quantities of flax, and flax-seed during the season; and on Saturday, for grain and provisions. Fairs are held on the Tuesday after Michaelmas, and a week before Christmas, and a large cattle market has been established on the first Saturday in every month. By a local act obtained in 1774, a parcel of waste land adjoining the city, and containing about 9½ plantation acres, was vested in the archbishop and his successors, to be parcelled into divisions for holding the fairs and markets, but only the fairs are now held on it. The market-house, an elegant and commodious building of hewn stone, erected by Archbishop Stuart, at an expense of £3000, occupies a central situation at the lower extremity of Market-street; the old shambles, built previously by Primate Robinson, have been taken down, and a more extensive and convenient range, with markets for grain, stores, weigh-house, &c., attached, was erected in 1829 by the committee of tolls: the supply of butchers' meat of very good quality is abundant, and the veal of Armagh is held in high estimation: there is also a plentiful supply of sea and fresh-water fish. Several of the inhabitants, in 1821, raised a subscription, by shares (on debentures or receipts) of £25 each, amounting to £1700, and purchased the lessee's interest in the tolls, of which a renewal for 21 years was obtained in 1829: eight resident shareholders, elected annually, and called the "Armagh Toll Committee," have now the entire regulation and management of the tolls and customs of the borough, consisting of market-house, street, and shambles' customs, in which they have made considerable reductions, and the proceeds of which, after deducting the expenses of management and five per cent. interest for the proprietors of the debentures, are applied partly as a sinking fund for liquidating the principal sum of £1700, and partly towards the improvement of the city and the places for holding the fairs and markets. The Bank of Ireland and the Provincial Bank have each a branch establishment here; and there are also branches of the Northern and Belfast banking companies. The post is daily: the post-office revenue, according to the last return to Parliament, amounted to £1418. 4. 0½.

The inhabitants were incorporated under the title of the "Sovereign, Free Burgesses, and Commonalty of the Borough of Ardmagh," in 1613, by charter of Jas. I., which was taken from them by Jas. II., who granted one conferring more extensive privileges; but Wm. III. restored the original charter, under which the corporation consists of a sovereign, twelve free burgesses, and an unlimited number of freemen, of whom there are at present only two; a town-clerk and registrar, and two serjeants-at-mace are also appointed. The sovereign is, by the charter, eligible by the free burgesses from among themselves, annually on the festival of the Nativity of St. John the Baptist (June 24th); the power of filling a vacancy in the number of free burgesses is vested in the sovereign and remaining free burgesses; the freemen are admitted by the sovereign and free burgesses; and the appointment of the inferior officers is vested in the corporation at large. By charter of King James, the borough was empowered to send two representatives to the Irish parliament, but the right of election was confined to the sovereign and twelve burgesses, who continued to return two members till the union, when the number was reduced to one. The nature of the franchise continued the same until the 2nd of Wm. IV., when the free burgesses not resident within seven miles of the borough were disfranchised, and the privilege of election was extended to the £10 householders; and as the limits of the district called "the corporation" comprehend 1147 statute acres unconnected with the franchise, a new electoral boundary (which is minutely described in the Appendix) was formed close round the town, comprising only 277 acres: the number of voters registered, according to the latest classified general return made to Parliament, amounted to 454, of whom 443 were £10 householders and 11 burgesses; the number of electors qualified to vote at the last election was 541, of whom 360 polled; the sovereign is the returning officer. The seneschal of the manor of Armagh, who is appointed by the primate, holds his court here, and exercises jurisdiction, both by attachment of goods and by civil bill process, in all causes of action arising within the manor and not exceeding £10: the greater part of the city is comprised within this manor, the remainder being in that of Mountnorris adjoining. The assizes and general quarter sessions are held twice a year; a court for the relief of insolvent debtors is held three times in the year; and the county magistrates resident in the city and its neighbourhood hold a petty session every Saturday. The corporation grand jury consisted of a foreman and other jurors, usually not exceeding 23 in number, chosen from among the most respectable inhabitants by the sovereign, generally within a month after entering upon his office, and continued to act until the ensuing 29th of September; but its dissolution took place at the close of the year 1832, when a new grand jury having been formed amidst much political excitement, they determined, under an impression that the inhabitants would resist any assessment which they might make, to abrogate their functions, and the system appears to be abandoned. The inconvenience which resulted from the dissolution of the corporation grand jury induced the inhabitants to adopt measures for carrying into effect the provisions of the act of the 9th of Geo. IV., cap. 82, previously noticed. The sessions-house, built in 1809, is situated at the northern extremity of the Mall: it has an elegant portico in front, and affords every accommodation necessary for holding the courts, &c. At the opposite end of the Mall stands the county gaol, a neat and substantial building, with two enclosed yards in which the prisoners may take exercise, and an infirmary containing two wards for males and two for females: there is also a tread-wheel. It is constructed on the old plan, and does not afford convenience for the classification of prisoners, but is well ventilated, clean, and healthy. The females are instructed by the matron in spelling and reading. In 1835, the average daily number of prisoners was 85; and the total net expense amounted to £1564. 14. 6. Armagh is a chief or baronial constabulary police station, of which the force consists of one chief officer, four constables, and twelve men.

Arms of the Archbishoprick.

The See of Armagh, according to the common opinion of native historians, was founded by St. Patrick, who in that city built the cathedral and some other religious edifices, in 445. Three years after, he held a synod there, the canons of which are still in existence; and in 454 he resigned the charge of the see (to which, on his recommendation, St. Binen was appointed), and spent the remainder of a life protracted to the patriarchal period of 120 years, in visiting and confirming the various churches which he had founded, and in forming others. Prior to the year 799, the bishop of Armagh and his suffragan bishops were obliged to attend the royal army during the military expeditions of the king of Ireland; but on a remonstrance made by Conmach, then archbishop, the custom was discontinued. A tumult which broke out in the city, during the celebration of the feast of Pentecost, in 889, between the septs of Cinel-Eoghain, of Tyrone, and Ulidia, of Down, affords an instance of the great power exercised by the archbishops at this period. Moelbrigid, having succeeded in quelling the disturbance, mulcted each of the offending parties in a fine of 200 oxen, exacted hostages for their future good conduct, and caused six of the ringleaders on each side to be executed on a gallows. The commencement of the twelfth century was marked by a contest as to the right of the primacy, which had been monopolised during fifteen episcopal successions by a single princely tribe, as an hereditary right. "Eight married men," says St. Bernard, "literate indeed, but not ordained, had been predecessors to Celsus, on whose demise the election of Malachy O'Morgair to the primatial dignity, by the united voice of the clergy and people, put an end to the contest, though not without some struggles." Malachy resigned the primacy in 1137, and in lieu of it accepted the bishoprick of Down, which see he afterwards divided into two, reserving one to himself. His object seems to have resulted from a wish to procure leisure for a journey to Rome, with a view to prevail upon the pope to grant palls to the archbishops of Armagh and Cashel; but in this he was, on his first journey, disappointed, by being informed that so important a measure could only be conceded in pursuance of the suffrage of an Irish council. On making a second journey for the same purpose, he fell sick on the road, and died at the abbey of Clarevall, in the arms of his friend, St. Bernard. Nevertheless, this object was soon after accomplished, even to a greater extent than he had proposed. In 1152, Cardinal Paparo arrived in Ireland as legate from Pope Eugene III., with four palls for the four archbishops, to whom the other Irish bishops were subjected as suffragans. The following sees, several of which are now unknown even by name, were then placed under the provincial jurisdiction of the archbishop of Armagh; viz., Connor, Dumdaleghlas (now Down), Lugud, Cluainiard or Clonard, Connanas, Ardachad, (now Ardagh), Rathboth (now Raphoe), Rathlurig or Rathlure, Damliag, and Darrick (now Derry).

The origin of a dispute between the Archbishops of Armagh and Dublin, regarding their respective claims to the primatial authority of Ireland, may be traced to this period, in consequence of a papal bull of 1182, which ordained that no archbishop or bishop should hold any assembly or hear ecclesiastical causes in the diocese of Dublin, unless authorised by the pope or his legate: but it was not until the following century that this dispute acquired a character of importance. The rank of the former of the e prelates among the bishops of Christendom was determined at the council of Lyons, where, in the order of subscription to the acts, the name "Albertus Armachanus" preceded those of all the bishops of France, Italy, and Spain. In 1247, Archbishop Reginald or Rayner separated the county of Louth from the diocese of Clogher, and annexed it to Armagh. Indeed, before this act, the inadequacy of the revenue to maintain the dignity of the see occasioned Hen. III. to issue a mandate to the lord justice of Ireland, to cause liberty of seisin to be given to the Archbishop of Armagh of all the lands belonging to the see of Clogher: but this writ was not carried into effect. In 1263, Pope Urban addressed a bull to Archbishop O'Scanlain, confirming him in the dignity of primate of all Ireland; but the authenticity of the document has been disputed. This bull did not put an end to the contest about precedency with the Archbishop of Dublin, which was renewed between Lech, Archbishop of Dublin, and Walter Jorse or Joyce, then primate, whose brother and successor, Rowland, persevering in the claim, was resisted by Bicknor, Archbishop of Dublin, and violently driven out of Leinster, in 1313. Again, in 1337, Primate David O'Hiraghty was obstructed in his attendance on parliament by Bicknor and his clergy, who would not permit him to have his crosier borne erect before him in the diocese of Dublin, although the king had expressly forbidden Bicknor to offer him any opposition. In 1349 Bicknor once more contested the point with Fitz-Ralph, Archbishop of Armagh; and, notwithstanding the king's confirmation of the right of the latter to erect his crosier in any part of Ireland, the lord justice and the prior of Kilmainham, being bribed, as is supposed, by Bicknor, combined with that prelate in opposing the claims of the primate, who thereupon excommunicated the resisting parties. Shortly after both Bicknor and the prior died; and the latter, on his death-bed, solicited Fitz-Ralph's forgiveness through a special messenger. After his decease, his body was refused Christian burial, until absolved by the primate in consequence of his contrition. In 1350, the king, through partiality to John de St. Paul, then Archbishop of Dublin, revoked his letter to Fitz-Ralph, and prohibited him from exercising his episcopal functions in the province of Dublin; and, in 1353, Pope Innocent VI. decided that Armagh and Dublin should be both primatial sees; the occupant of the former to be styled Primate of all Ireland, and of the latter, Primate of Ireland. In 1365, the Archbishops Milo Sweetman and Thomas Minot renewed the controversy, which, after that period, was suffered to lie dormant till Richard Talbot, Archbishop of Dublin, prevented Primate Swain from attending his duty in five successive parliaments held in 1429, 1435, and the three following years. Primates Mey and Prene experienced similar opposition; but after the decease of Talbot, in 1449, their successors enjoyed their rights undisturbed till 1533, when John Alen, Archbishop of Dublin, revived the contest with Primate Cromer, but seemingly without success. Edw. VI. divested Archbishop Dowdall of the primacy, in 1551, in order to confer it on George Browne, Archbishop of Dublin, as a reward for his advocacy of the Reformation; but on the same principle the right was restored to Dowdall on the accession of Mary. In 1623, Launcelot Bulkeley revived the contest with Primate Hampton, and continued it against his successor, the distinguished Ussher, in whose favour it was decided by the Earl of Strafford, then lord-deputy, in 1634.

At the commencement of the Reformation, Primate Cromer was inflexible in his determination to oppose its introduction into the Irish church; and on his death, in 1542, his example was followed by his successor, Dowdall, who, after the accession of Edw. VI., maintained a controversy on the disputed points with Staples, Bishop of Meath, in which both parties claimed the victory. The English government, finding him determined in his opposition to the new arrangements, issued a mandate rendering his see subordinate to that of Dublin, which caused Dowdall to quit the country and take refuge on the continent. The king, deeming this act a virtual resignation of the see, appointed Hugh Goodacre his successor; but Dowdall was restored by Queen Mary, and held the see till his death in 1558, the year in which his protectress also died. Notwithstanding the ecclesiastical superiority of the see of Armagh over that of Dublin, the income of the latter was so much greater, that Adam Loftus, who had been appointed Archbishop of Armagh on the death of Dowdall, was removed a few years after to Dublin, as being more lucrative: he was only 28 years of age on his first elevation, being the youngest primate of all Ireland upon record, except Celsus. In 1614-15, a regrant of the episcopal property of Armagh, together with a large additional tract of land, accruing from the forfeited estates of the Earls of Tyrone and Tyrconnel, was made to Primate Hampton. His immediate successor was the celebrated James Ussher, during whose primacy Chas. I. endowed anew the college of vicars choral in the cathedral, by patent granted in 1635, by which he bestowed on them various tracts of land, the property of the dissolved Culdean priory. Ussher was succeeded by Dr. Bramhall, a man also of great learning and mental powers, who was appointed by Chas. II. immediately after the Restoration. Dr. Lindsay, who was enthroned in 1713, endowed the vicars choral and singing boys with £200 per annum out of lands in the county of Down, and also procured for them a new charter, in 1720. Dr. Boulter, who was translated from the see of Bristol to that of Armagh, on the death of Lindsay in 1724, is known only as a political character; a collection of his letters is extant. He was succeeded by Dr. Hoadly, translated from Dublin, who published some sermons and other works; and the latter by Dr. Stone, also an active participator in the political events of the time. His successor was Dr. Robinson, Bishop of Kildare, and after his translation created Baron Rokeby, of Armagh, whose history may be best learned in the contemplation of the city over which he presided, raised by his continued munificence from extreme decay to a state of opulence and respectability, and embellished with various useful public institutions, worthy of its position among the principal cities of Ireland; and from the pastoral care evinced by him in an eminent degree in the erection of numerous parochial and district churches for new parishes and incumbencies, to which he annexed glebes and glebe-houses, and in promoting the spiritual concerns of his diocese.

Of the R. C. archbishops, since the Reformation, but little connected with the localities of the see is known. Robert Wauchope, a Scotchman, who had been appointed by the pope during the lifetime of Dowdall, may rightly be considered the first; for Dowdall, though a zealous adherent to the doctrines of the Church of Rome, had been appointed solely by the authority of Hen. VIII. Peter Lombard, who was appointed in 1594, is known in the literary and political circles by his commentary on Ireland, for which a prosecution was instituted against him by Lord Strafford, but was terminated by Lombard's death at Rome, in 1625, or the year following. Hugh M[c]Caghwell, his successor, was a man of singular piety and learning, an acute metaphysician, and profoundly skilled in every branch of scholastic philosophy: a monument was erected to his memory by the Earl of Tyrone. Oliver Plunket, appointed in 1669, obtained distinction by his defence of the primatial rights against Talbot, Archbishop of Dublin; but his prosecution and death for high treason, on a charge of favouring a plot for betraying Ireland to France, have rendered his name still more known. Hugh M[c]Mahon, of the Monaghan family of that name, was appointed in 1708: his great work is the defence of the primatial rights, entitled "*Jus Primitiale Armacanum*," in which he is said to have exhausted the subject.

The *Archbishoprick*, or *Ecclesiastical Province of Armagh* comprehends the ten dioceses of Armagh, Clogher, Meath, Down, Connor, Derry, Raphoe, Kilmore, Dromore, and Ardagh, which are estimated to contain a superficies of 4,319,250 acres, and comprises within its limits the whole of the civil province of Ulster; the counties of Longford, Louth, Meath, and Westmeath, and parts of the King's and Queen's counties, in the province of Leinster; and parts of the counties of Leitrim, Roscommon, and Sligo, in the province of Connaught. The archbishop, who is primate and metropolitan of all Ireland, presides over the province, and exercises all episcopal jurisdiction within his own diocese; and the see of Down being united to that of Connor, and that of Ardagh to the archiepiscopal see of Tuam, seven bishops preside over the respective dioceses, and are suffragan to the Lord-Primate. Under the Church Temporalities' Act of the 3rd of Wm. IV., the archiepiscopal jurisdiction of the province of Tuam will become extinct on the death of the present archbishop, and the dioceses now included in it will be suffragan to Armagh.

The *diocese of Armagh* comprehends the greater part of that county, and parts of those of Meath, Louth, Tyrone, and Londonderry: it comprises by computation a superficial area of 468,550 acres, of which 1300 are in Meath, 108,900 in Louth, 162,500 in Tyrone, and 25,000 in Londonderry, It was anciently divided into two parts, the English and the Irish, now known as the Upper and Lower parts: the English or Upper part embraces that portion which extends into the counties of Louth and Meath, and is subdivided into the rural deaneries of Drogheda, Atherdee or Ardee, and Dundalk; and the Irish or Lower part comprehends the remaining portion of the diocese in the counties of Armagh, Tyrone, and Londonderry, and is subdivided into the rural deaneries of Creggan, Aghaloe, Dungannon, and Tullahog. In all ancient synods and visitations the clergy of the English and Irish parts were congregated separately, which practice is still observed, the clergy of the Upper part assembling for visitation at Drogheda, and those of the Lower at Armagh. The see of Clogher, on the first avoidance by death or translation, will, under the Church Temporalities' Act, become united to that of Armagh, and its temporalities will be vested in the Ecclesiastical Commissioners for Ireland. There are 100,563 statute acres belonging to the see of Armagh, of which 87,809 are profitable land, the remainder being bog or mountain; and the gross amount of its yearly revenue on an average is about £17,670, arising from chief rents, fee farms, and copyhold leases. On the death of the present primate the sum of £4500 is, under the above act, to be paid out of the revenue annually to the Ecclesiastical Commissioners. The chapter consists of a dean, precentor, chancellor, treasurer, archdeacon, and the four prebendaries of Mullaghbrack, Ballymore, Loughgall, and Tynan, with eight vicars choral, and an organist and choir. The dean and precentor are the only dignitaries for whom houses are provided; five houses are assigned for the vicars choral and organist. Each dignity and prebend has cure of souls annexed, as regards the benefice forming its corps. The economy estate of the cathedral yields an annual rental of £180. 1. 5., which is expended in the payment of salaries to the officers of the cathedral, and in defraying other charges incident to the building. The diocese comprises 88 benefices, of which, 14 are unions consisting of 45 parishes, and 74 consist of single parishes or portions thereof. Of these, 4 are in the gift of the Crown, 51 in that of the Lord-Primate, 12 are in lay and corporation patronage, and 21 in clerical or alternate patronage. The total number of parishes or districts is 122, of which 91 are rectories or vicarages, 23 perpetual cures, 1 impropriate, and 7 parishes or districts without cure of souls; there are 22 lay impropriations. The number of churches is 88, besides 11 other buildings in which divine service is performed, and of glebe-houses, 74.

In the R. C. Church the archbishoprick of Armagh, as originally founded, is the head or primacy of all Ireland; and the same bishopricks are suffragan to it as in the Protestant Church. The R. C. diocese comprises 51 parochial benefices or unions, containing 120 places of worship, served by 51 parish priests and 65 coadjutors or curates. The parochial benefice of St. Peter, Drogheda, is held by the archbishop; and the union of Armagh, Eglish, and Grange is annexed to the deanery. There are 68 Presbyterian meeting-houses, and 44 belonging to other Protestant dissenters, making in the whole 331 places of worship in the diocese.

The parish of Armagh comprises, according to the Ordnance survey, 4606¾ statute acres, of which 1051¼ are in the barony of O'Neilland West, and 3555½ in that of Armagh. The rural district is only of small extent: the system of agriculture has very much improved of late; the land is excellent, and yields abundant crops. Limestone prevails, and is mostly used in building and in repairing the roads; in some places it is beautifully variegated, and is wrought into chimney-pieces. The principal seats are the Primate's palace; Ballynahone, that of Miss Lodge; Beech Hill, of T. Simpson, Esq.; Tullamore, of J. Oliver, Esq.; and those of J. Simpson, Esq., and J. Mackey, Esq., at Ballyards. The living consists of a rectory and vicarage, in the diocese of Armagh, consolidated by letters patent of the 11th and 12th of Jas. I., and united, in the reign of Chas. I., to the parishes of Eglish, Lisnadell, and Ballymoyer, in the patronage of the Lord-Primate. These parishes, having been so long consolidated, are not specifically set forth in the incumbents' titles, so that Armagh has practically ceased to be, and is no longer designated a union in the instruments of collation. The deanery is in the gift of the Crown, and is usually held with the rectory, but they are not statutably united, and the former has neither tithes nor cure of souls: it is endowed with five tenements and a small plot of land within the city, the deanery-house and farm of 90 acres, and five townlands in the parish of Lisnadill, comprising in all 1142 statute acres, valued at £274. 13. 7½. per annum. The deanery-house, situated about a quarter of a mile from the cathedral, was built in 1774. The rectorial glebe-lands comprise about 380 acres, valued in 1831 at £368. 6. 9. per annum. The tithes of Armagh and Grange amount to £500; and the gross value of the deanery and union of Armagh, tithe and glebe inclusive, amounts to £2462. 1. 2½. There are six perpetual cures within the union, namely, Grange, Eglish, Killylea, Lisnadill, Armaghbreague, and Ballymoyer, the endowments of which amount to £440 per annum, paid by the rector out of the tithes. The Ecclesiastical Commissioners have recommended that the union, on the next avoidance of the benefice, be partially dissolved, and the district of Ballymoyer erected into a new parish; and that the deanery and consolidated rectory and vicarage, now belonging to different patrons, be united and consolidated, the respective patrons presenting and collating alternately, agreeably to the Irish act of the 10th and 11th of Chas. I., cap. 2,—or that the advowson of the deanery be vested solely in the patron of the rectory and vicarage, which are of much greater value than the deanery, the patron of which to be compensated by being allowed the right of presentation to the new parish of Ballymoyer.

The cathedral church, originally founded by St. Patrick in 445, was burnt by the Danes of Ulster, under Turgesius, who, in 836, destroyed the city. At what time the present building was erected is not accurately known; the crypt appears to be of the 11th or 12th century, but there are several portions of a much earlier date, which were probably part of a former, or perhaps of the original, structure. It appears from an existing record that the roof, which for 130 years had been only partially repaired, was, in 1125, covered with tiles; and in 1262 the church was repaired by Archbishop O'Scanlain, who is supposed to have built the nave and the elegant western entrance. The cathedral was partially burnt in 1404 and 1566, after which it was repaired by Primate Hampton, who in 1612 rebuilt the tower; it was again burnt in 1642 by Sir Phelim O'Nial, but was restored by Archbishop Margetson, at his own expense, in 1675, and was further repaired in 1729 by the Dean and Chapter, aided by Archbishop Boulter. Primate Robinson, in 1766, roofed the nave with slate, and fitted it up for divine service; the same prelate commenced the erection of a tower, but when it was raised to the height of 60 feet, one of the piers, with the arch springing from it, yielded to the pressure from above, and it was consequently taken down even with the roof of the building. The tower was again raised to its present height and surmounted by a spire, which, from a fear of overpowering the foundation, was necessarily curtailed in its proportion. Primate Beresford, on his translation to the see, employed Mr. Cottingham, architect of London, and the restorer of the abbey of St. Alban's, to survey the cathedral with a view to its perfect restoration, and the report being favourable, the undertaking, towards which His Grace subscribed £8000, was commenced under that gentleman's superintendence in 1834. The piers of the tower have been removed and replaced by others resting upon a more solid foundation, in the execution of which the whole weight of the tower was sustained without the slightest crack or settlement, till the new work was brought into contact with the old, by a skilful and ingenious contrivance of which a model has been preserved. The prevailing character of the architecture is the early English style, with portions of the later Norman, and many of the details are rich and elegant, though long obscured and concealed by injudicious management in repairing the building, and, when the present work now in progress is completed, will add much to the beauty of this venerable and interesting structure. The series of elegantly clustered columns separating the aisles from the nave, which had declined from the perpendicular and will be restored to their original position, was concealed by a rude encasement, with a view to strengthen them; and many of the corbels, enriched with emblematical sculpture, were covered with thick coats of plaister. Among other ancient details that had been long hidden is a sculpture of St. Patrick with his crosier, in a compartment surmounted with shamrocks, which is perhaps the earliest existing record of that national emblem; and another of St. Peter, with the keys, surmounted by a cock, discovered in the wall under the rafters of the choir. There are several splendid monuments, of which the principal are those of Dean Drelincourt, by Rysbrach; of Primate Robinson, with a bust, by Bacon; of Lord Charlemont, who died in 1671, and of his father, Baron Caulfield. The ancient monuments of Brian Boru or Boroimhe, his son Murchard, and his nephew Conard, who were slain in the battle of Clontarf and interred in this cathedral, have long since perished. The church, which was made parochial by act of the 15th and 16th of Geo. III., cap. 17th, occupies a commanding site; it is 183½ feet in length, and 119 in breadth along the transepts.

To the east of the cathedral and Mall, on an eminence in front of the city, is a new church, dedicated to St. Mark: it is a handsome edifice in the later English style; the interior is elegantly finished; the aisles are separated from the nave by a row of arches resting on clustered columns, from the capitals of which spring numerous ribs supporting a handsome groined roof. This church, which is indebted for much of its decorations to the munificence of the present primate, was built at an expense of £3600, and contains about 1500 sittings, of which 800 are free. There are also six other churches within the union. In the R. C. divisions this parish is the head of a union or district, which comprises also the parishes of Eglish and Grange, and forms one of the benefices of the primate: the union contains three chapels, situated at Armagh, Annacramp, and Tullysaren. The first was built about the year 1750, on ground held under different titles, the proprietors having successively devised a permanent interest therein to the congregation at a nominal rent; the building has of late been much enlarged and improved, but is still too small for the R. C. population; it is triple-roofed, as if intended for three distinct buildings, yet has a good effect. The places of worship for dissenters are, one built in 1722 with part of the ruins of the church and monastery of St. Peter and St. Paul, and having a substantial manse in front, for a congregation of Presbyterians in connection with the Synod of Ulster, who settled here about the year 1670, and endowed with a first class grant of royal bounty; one for Seceders, built about the year 1785, and endowed with a second class grant; one for the Evangelical or Independent congregational union; one for Wesleyan Methodists, built in 1786, with a comfortable house for the minister attached, and situated near the spot where Mr. Wesley, in 1767, frequently preached; and one near it for Primitive Wesleyan Methodists.

The free grammar-school, to the south of the observatory, is endowed with seven townlands in the parish of Loughgilly, comprising 1514 acres, and producing a clear rental of £1377, granted in trust to the primate and his successors in 1627, for the support of a grammar school at Mountnorris: part of the income is applied to the maintenance of several exhibitions at Trinity College, Dublin. The buildings occupy the four sides of a quadrangle, the front of which is formed by a covered passage communicating on each side with the apartments of the head-master and pupils; on the fourth side is the school-room, 56 feet long by 28 broad, behind which is a large area enclosed by a wall and serving as a play-ground. They were completed in 1774, at an expense of £5000, defrayed by Primate Robinson, and are capable of conveniently accommodating 100 resident pupils. A school for the instruction of the choir boys has been established by the present primate, the master of which receives a stipend of £75 per annum, and is allowed to take private pupils. The charter school was founded in 1738, and endowed with £90 per ann. by Mrs. Drelincourt, widow of Dean Drelincourt, for the maintenance and education of 20 boys and 20 girls, who were also to be instructed in the linen manufacture, housewifery, and husbandry. In that year the corporation granted certain commons or waste lands, called the "Irish-Street commons," comprising upwards of 8 statute acres, on which the school premises, including separate residences for the master and mistress, were erected, and to which Primate Boulter annexed 13 statute acres adjoining. The endowment was further augmented with the lands of Legumin, in the county of Tyrone, comprising about 107 acres, and held under a renewable lease granted in trust by Primate Robinson to the dean and chapter: the present annual income is £249. 8. 2. The primate and rector are trustees, and the officiating curate is superintendent of the school, in which only ten girls are now instructed in the general branches of useful education; the surplus funds have been allowed to accumulate for the erection of premises on a more eligible site, and it is in contemplation to convert the establishment into a day school for boys and girls. In 1819, Primate Stuart built and endowed a large and handsome edifice, in which 105 boys and 84 girls are at present taught on the Lancasterian plan, and about 160 of them are clothed, fifteen by the dean, and the remainder principally by Wm. Stuart, Esq., son of the founder. The income is about £100 per annum; £31. 10. is given annually by the present primate and Mr. Stuart. The building is situated on the east side of the Mall, and consists of a centre and two wings, the former occupied as residences by the master and mistress, and the latter as school-rooms. There is a national school for boys and girls, aided by a grant of £50 per ann. from the National Board of Education and by private subscriptions, for which a handsome building is now in course of erection by subscription, to the east of the Mall, with a portico in front. In Callan-street is a large building erected for a Sunday school by the present primate, who has presented it to the committee of an infants' school established in 1835, and supported by voluntary contributions. At Killurney is a National school for boys and girls, built and supported by the Hon. Mrs. Caulfeild; and there are other schools in the rural part of the parish. The total number of children on the books of these schools is 653, of whom 285 are boys and 368 are girls; and in the different private schools are 270 boys and 200 girls.

The county hospital or infirmary is situated on the north-western declivity of the hill which is crowned by the cathedral, at the top of Abbey-street, Callan-street,

ARM

and Dawson-street, which branching off in different directions leave an open triangular space in front. It is a fine old building of unhewn limestone, completed in 1774, at an expense of £2150, and consisting of a centre and two wings; one-half is occupied as the surgeon's residence, the other is open for the reception of patients; there are two wards for males and one for females. The domestic offices are commodious and well arranged, and there are separate gardens for the infirmary and for the surgeon. The entire number of patients relieved in 1834 was 3044, of whom 563 were admitted into the hospital, and 71 children were vaccinated: the expenditure in that year amounted to £1145. 8. 8., of which £500 was granted by the grand jury, and the remainder was defrayed by private subscription. Prior to the establishment of the present county infirmary by act of parliament, the inhabitants had erected and maintained by private contributions an hospital called the "Charitable Infirmary," situated in Scotch-street, which they liberally assigned over to the lord primate and governors of the new establishment, and it was used as the county hospital until the erection of the present edifice. The fever hospital, situated about a furlong from the city, on the Caledon road, was erected in 1825, at an entire cost, including the purchase and laying out of the grounds, &c., of about £3500, defrayed by the present primate, by whose munificence it is solely supported. It is a chaste and handsome building of hewn limestone, 50 feet in length and 30 in width, with a projection rearward containing on the ground floor a physician's room, a warm bath and washing-room, and on the other floors, male and female nurses' rooms and slop-rooms, in the latter of which are shower baths. On the ground floor of the front building are the entrance hall, the matron's sitting and sleeping-rooms, and a kitchen and pantry: the first and second floors are respectively appropriated to the use of male and female patients, each floor containing two wards, a fever and a recovery ward, the former having ten beds and the latter five, making in all thirty beds. The subordinate buildings and offices are well calculated to promote the object of the institution: there is a good garden, with walks in the grounds open to convalescents; and with regard to cleanliness, economy, and suitable accommodation for its suffering inmates, this hospital is entitled to rank among the first in the province. The Armagh district asylum for lunatic poor of the counties of Armagh, Monaghan, Fermanagh, and Cavan, was erected pursuant to act of parliament by a grant from the consolidated fund, at an expense, including purchase of site, furniture, &c., of £20,900, to be repaid by instalments by the respective counties comprising the district, each of which sends patients in proportion to the amount of its population, but is only charged for the number admitted. It has accommodation for 122 patients, who are admitted on an affidavit of poverty, a medical certificate of insanity, and a certificate from the minister and churchwardens of their respective parishes. The establishment is under the superintendence of a board of directors, a resident manager and matron, and a physician. Thirteen acres of ground are attached to the asylum, and are devoted to gardening and husbandry. The male patients weave all the linen cloth used in the establishment, and the clothing for the females; gymnastic exercises and a tennis-court have been lately established. From the 14th of July, 1825, when the asylum was first opened, to the 1st of Jan., 1835, 710 patients were admitted, of whom 400 were males and 310 females: of this number, 305 recovered and were discharged; 121 were discharged relieved; 70 unrelieved and restored to their relations; 89 died, and 16 were transferred to the asylum at Londonderry; leaving in this asylum 109. The average annual expense for the above period amounted to about £1900, and the average cost of each patient, including clothing and all other charges, was about £17 per annum.

Among the voluntary institutions for the improvement of the city the most remarkable is the association for the suppression of mendicity, under the superintendence of a committee, who meet weekly. For this purpose the city is divided into six districts, and eight resident visiters are appointed to each, one of whom collects the subscriptions of the contributors on Wednesday, and distributes them among the paupers on the ensuing Monday. The paupers are divided into three classes, *viz.*, those wholly incapacitated from industrious exertion; orphans and destitute children; and paupers with large families, who are able in some measure, though not wholly, to provide for their subsistence. The visiters personally inspect the habitations of those whom they relieve, and report to the general committee. The paupers are employed in sweeping the streets and lanes, by which means the public thoroughfares are kept in a state of great cleanliness; and itinerant mendicants are prevented from begging in the streets by two authorised beadles. "The Robinson Loan Fund" consists of an accumulated bequest of £200 by Primate Robinson, in 1794, held in trust by the corporation, and lent free of interest, under an order of the Court of Chancery made in Feb. 1834, in sums of from £10 to £30, to tradesmen and artificers resident or about to settle in the city, and repayable by instalments at or within 12 months; and there is another fund for supplying distressed tradesmen with small loans to be repaid monthly. A bequest was made by the late Arthur Jacob Macan, who died in India in 1819, to the sovereign and burgesses and other inhabitants of Armagh, for the erection and endowment of an asylum for the blind, on the plan of that at Liverpool, but open indiscriminately to all religious persuasions, and, if the funds should allow of it, for the admission also of deaf and dumb children, with preference to the county of Armagh. The benefits derivable under the will are prospective, and are principally contingent on the death of certain legatees.

Basilica Vetus Concionaria, "the old preaching church," was probably used in later times as the parish church: a small fragment still remains contiguous to the cathedral, where the rectors of Armagh were formerly inducted. The priory of the Culdees, who were secular priests serving in the choir of the cathedral, where their president officiated as precentor, was situated in Castle-street, and had been totally forsaken for some time prior to 1625, at which period the rents were received by the archbishop's seneschal, and the whole of its endowment in lands, &c., was granted to the vicars choral. Temple Bridget, built by St. Patrick, stood near the spot now occupied by the R. C. chapel. He also founded *Temple-na-Fearta*, or "the church of the miracles," without the city, for his sister Lupita, who was interred there, and whose body was discovered at the commencement of the 17th century in an upright posture, deeply buried under the rubbish, with a cross before and behind it. The site of the monastery of St. Columba was that now occupied by the Provincial Bank, at the north-east corner of Abbey-street; the two Methodist chapels stand on part of its gardens. There are many other vestiges of antiquity in the city and its vicinity. The most ancient and remarkable is *Eamhuin Macha* or *Eamania*, the chief residence of the Kings of Ulster, situated two miles to the west, near which several celts, brazen spear heads, and other military weapons have been found. *Crieve Roe*, adjoining it, is said to have been the seat of the only order of knighthood among the ancient Irish; its members were called "Knights of the Red Branch," and hence the name of the place. In the same neighbourhood is the Navan Fort, where also numerous ornaments, military weapons, horse accoutrements, &c., are frequently found; and on the estate of Mr. John Mackey, in the townland of Kennedy, are the remains of two forts, where petrified wood and other fossils have been found. In the primate's demesne are extensive and picturesque ruins of an abbey; near the asylum are the walls of Bishop's Court, once the residence of the primates; and on the banks of the Callan are the remains of the tumulus of "Nial of the hundred battles." On a lofty eminence four miles to the south-east is *Cairnamnhanaghan*, now called the "Vicar's Cairn," commanding an extensive and pleasing prospect over several adjacent counties. It is a vast conical heap of stones in the parish of Mullaghbrack, covering a circular area 44 yards in diameter, and thrown together without any regularity, except the encircling stones, which were placed close to each other, in order to contain the smaller stones of which the cairn is composed. Its size has been much diminished by the peasantry, who have carried away the large stones for building; but the proprietor, the Earl of Charlemont, has prohibited this destruction. Coins of Anlaff the Dane, Athelstan, Alfred, and Edgar have been found in and around the city. Armagh gives the title of Earl to his Royal Highness Prince Ernest Augustus, Duke of Cumberland.

ARMAGH-BREAGUE, a district parish, partly in the barony of Armagh, and partly in the barony of Lower Fews, county of Armagh, and province of Ulster, 7 miles (S.) from Armagh, on the road from Keady to Newtown-Hamilton; containing 3632 inhabitants. It was formed into a parish under the provisions of an act of the 7th and 8th of Geo. III., cap. 43, by taking three townlands from the parish of Lisnadill, and three from that of Keady, the former principally heath and mountain, and the latter tithe-free; and comprises 9113 statute acres, of which 5000 are arable, and the remainder waste and bog. The mountains abound with clay-slate; and there are also indications of lead and copper ores, but no attempt has yet been made to work either. About two miles from the village is Mountain Lodge, the residence of Hugh Garmany, Esq. At Linen Vale there is an extensive bleach-green, where 20,000 pieces of linen are annually finished for the English markets. The inhabitants are chiefly employed in the weaving of linen and in agricultural pursuits. The living is a perpetual curacy, in the diocese of Armagh, and in the alternate patronage of the Rectors of Armagh and Keady, the former of whom contributes £60 and the latter £40 per annum as a stipend for the curate; there is neither glebe-house nor glebe. The church, situated on the summit of one of the Fews mountains, is a small neat edifice, in the early English style; it was built in 1831, at an expense of £600, a gift from the late Board of First Fruits. In the R. C. divisions this parish is one of three that form the union or district of Lisnadill or Ballymacnab, and contains a small chapel at Granemore. In the parochial school are 80 boys and 40 girls; the master has a house and three roods of land rent-free. The school-room, a large and commodious building, was erected by subscription in 1826. There are also a Sunday school for gratuitous instruction, and a hedge school. Lough Aughnagurgan, the source of the river Callan, is in this district; and on the summit of one of the mountains stands the South Meridian Arch belonging to the observatory of Armagh.

ARMOY, or ARDMOY, a parish, partly in the barony of Upper Dunluce, but chiefly in that of Carey, county of Antrim, and province of Ulster, 4 miles (S. S. W.) from Ballycastle; containing 2622 inhabitants, of which number, 129 are in the village. St. Patrick is said to have had a cell at this place, where, in attempting to convert the natives to Christianity, his disciple Uhda was killed. The parish is situated on the river Bush, and is intersected by a small river called the Wellwater, which rises in a bog on the eastern side, and, with its tributary streams, flows through the parish into the river Bush on the western side. The road from Ballycastle to Ballymena passes through it, and is intersected by one from east to west, and by another from north-east to south-west. It comprises, according to the Ordnance survey, 9349 statute acres, of which $826\frac{3}{4}$ are in Upper Dunluce and $8522\frac{1}{4}$ in Carey; about seven-tenths are arable, pasture, and meadow land. The surface is broken by a ridge of mountains which take their names from the townlands to which they are contiguous, and of which the north side affords good pasturage for cattle, and the summits are heathy and barren; about nine-tenths of the great hill of Knocklayd, the highest in the county, is good arable and pasture land. That portion of the parish which is under tillage is in a very high state of cultivation; the system of agriculture is rapidly improving, and composts of lime and earth, or moss, are used as manure for potatoes, by which the produce is greatly increased. There are three bogs, called respectively Ballyhenver, Breen, and Belaney, and the small bog of Moninacloygh; and turf may be had on the sides and summits of all the mountains. Several quarries of excellent white limestone and basalt afford good materials for building, and for repairing the roads. Turnarobert is the residence of the Rev. S. Hunter. The whole of the parish, with the exception of the townlands of Ballycanver, Park, Bunshanloney, and Mulaghduff, and part of the village of Armoy, belongs to the see of Connor. The village is very flourishing and has a penny post to Ballycastle: several handsome houses have been built, new roads have been opened, and bridges constructed over the river Wellwater. Fairs for horses, horned cattle, pigs, corn, and butter, are held on Jan. 25th, Feb. 25th, March 29th, May 25th, Aug. 16th, Nov. 14th, and Dec. 26th.

The living was formerly a vicarage, the rectory being appropriate to the archdeaconry of Connor, from the year 1609 till 1831, when, upon the decease of Dr. Trail, the last archdeacon, it became a rectory under the provisions of Bishop Mant's act; it is in the diocese of Connor, and in the patronage of the Bishop; the tithes amount to £225. The church, situated in the centre of the parish, was rebuilt in 1820, for which a loan of £415 was obtained from the late Board of First Fruits: it is a neat plain edifice, and has been lately repaired by a grant of £128 from the Ecclesiastical Commissioners. The glebe-house was built in 1807, at an expense of £376. 10. 4.: the glebe comprises 23 acres, valued at £30 per annum. In the R. C. divisions this parish is united with that of Ballintoy, in each of which there is a chapel: that in Armoy is a small edifice. There is also a place of worship for Presbyterians in connection with the Synod of Ulster, of the third class. The parochial school is in the townland of Doonan; there are national schools at Breene and in the village of Armoy, and another school at Mulaghduff. In the churchyard are the remains of an ancient round tower, 47½ feet in circumference and 36 feet high; the present rector has enclosed the upper part with a dome of wood and stone, in which is placed the church bell. Some beautifully clear crystals, called Irish Diamonds, are found on Knocklayd; and fragments of gneiss, porphyry and mica slate are found in various parts of the parish.

ARRAN ISLANDS, a barony, in the county of Galway, and province of Connaught, 30 miles (W. S. W.) from Galway; containing 3191 inhabitants. This barony consists of a group of islands called the South Arran Isles, situated in the centre of the mouth of Galway bay, stretching south-east and north-west from 52° to 53° (N. Lat.), and from 9° 30′ to 9° 42′ (W. Lon.); and comprising Arranmore or the Great Arran to the west, Ennismain or Innismain (called also the Middle Island), and Innishere or the Eastern island, which are thickly inhabited; also the small rocky isles called Straw Island, the Branach Isles, and Illane-Earhach or the Western Isle. They are supposed to be the remains of a high barrier of land separated at some remote period by the violence of the sea; and from evident appearances of their having been anciently overspread with wood, their retired situation, and the existence of druidical remains, to have been appropriated to the celebration of the religious rites of the early Irish, prior to the introduction of Christianity. The Firbolg tribes had possession of these islands at a very early period; and in the third century they were held, it is said, by the sept of Eogan More, King of Thomond. They subsequently became the residence of St. Ibar, one of the missionaries sent to Ireland before the time of St. Patrick; and in the 5th century the Great Island was given by Ængus, King of Cashel, to St. Endeus or St. Enda, who founded several monasteries, and built several churches, of which the principal was named after him Kill-Enda, now called Killeany. This island soon became celebrated for its number of holy men, and such was the fame of Enda for sanctity, that it was visited during his lifetime by St. Kieran, St. Brendan, and the celebrated Columbkill; it still bears the name of "Arran of the Saints." In 546 it was agreed between the kings of Munster and Connaught, whose territories were separated by the bay of Galway, that these islands should be independent of both, and pay tribute to neither. In 1081 the Great Island was ravaged by the Danes. The sept of Mac Tiege O'Brien were temporal lords of the islands from a very remote period, and the inhabitants of the English part of the town of Galway entered early into strict alliance and friendship with them; but this compact did not save the islands from being plundered and burnt by Sir John D'Arcy, Lord-Justice of Ireland, who, in 1334, sailed round the western coast with a fleet of 56 vessels. In 1485 a monastery for Franciscans was founded in the Great Island, in which was also erected a famous abbey for Canons Regular. In the reign of Elizabeth the O'Briens were expelled by the sept of O'Flaherty, of the neighbouring mainland of Connaught; on which occasion the mayor and sheriffs of Galway sent a petition to the Queen in favour of the former, to whom, they state, they paid an additional tribute of wine, in consideration of their protection, and of their expenses in guarding the bay and harbour of Galway against pirates and coast plunderers. In consequence of this petition, a commission was issued, under which it appeared that the islands belonged of right to the crown; and in 1587 letters patent were granted, by which the Queen, instead of restoring them to the ancient proprietors, gave them to John Rawson, of Athlone, on condition of his keeping constantly on them 20 foot soldiers of the English nation. This property afterwards became vested in Sir Robert Lynch, of Galway; but the Clan Tieges still claimed it as their patrimony, and taking advantage of the troubles of 1641, prepared, with the assistance of Boetius Clanchy, the younger, a man of great property and influence in the county of Clare, to invade the islands; but the execution of their design was prevented by the timely interference of the Marquess of Clanricarde and the Earl of Thomond. In 1651, when the royal authority was fast declining, the Marquess of Clanricarde placed 200 musqueteers on these islands, under the command of Sir Robert Lynch; the fort of Ardkyn, in the Great Island, was soon after repaired and mounted with cannon; and by these means they held out against the parliamentary forces for nearly twelve months after the surrender of Galway. In December of that year, the Irish, defeated in every other quarter, landed here 700 men in boats from Iar Connaught and Inis Bophin; and on the 9th of the following January, 1300 of the parliamentary infantry were shipped from the bay of Galway to attack them, and 600 more marched from the town to Iar Connaught, to be sent thence, if necessary, to their aid; but on the 13th the islands surrendered, on condition that quarter should be given to all within the fort, and that they should have six weeks allowed them to retire to Spain, or any other country then at peace with England. Sir Robert Lynch, the late proprietor, being declared a traitor, the property was forfeited and granted to Erasmus Smith, Esq., one of the most considerable of the London adventurers, from whom it was purchased by Richard Butler, fifth son of James, first Duke of Ormonde, who was created Earl of Arran in 1662, and to whom it was confirmed by royal patent under the Act of Settlement. On the surrender of Galway to the forces of Wm. III., in 1691, Arran was again garrisoned and a barrack was erected, in which soldiers were quartered for many years. In 1693, the title of Earl of the Isles of Arran was conferred on Charles, brother of the second Duke of Ormonde, with whom it became extinct in 1758; it was revived in favour of Sir Arthur

Gore, Bart., in 1762, and from him the title has descended to the present Earl. The islands are now the property of the Digby family, of whom the present head is the Rev. John Digby, of Landerstown, in the county of Kildare.

Their appearance, on approaching, is awfully impressive; the dark cliffs opposing to the billows that roll impetuously against them a perpendicular barrier, several hundred feet high, of rugged masses shelving abruptly towards the base, and perforated with various winding cavities worn by the violence of the waves. *Arranmore*, or the *Great Island*, which is the most northern of the three, is about 11 miles in length, and about 1¾ mile at its greatest breadth; and comprises the villages of Killeany, Kilmurvey, and Onought, and the hamlets of Icirarn, Ballyneerega, Mannister, Cowruagh, Gortnagopple, Furnakurk, Cregacarean, Shran, and Bungowla. In the centre is a signal tower; and at Oaghill, on the summit, is a lighthouse, elevated 498 feet above the level of the sea at high water, and exhibiting a bright revolving light from 21 reflectors, which attains its greatest magnitude every three minutes, and may be seen from all points at a distance of 28 nautical miles, in clear weather. The island is bounded on the south and west by rocky cliffs, from 300 to 400 feet high; but on the north are low shelving rocks and sandy beaches; and the passage to the northward is called the North Sound, or entrance to the bay of Galway. There is only one safe harbour, called Killeaney or Arran bay: in the upper part of the bay is a small pier, erected by order of the late Fishery Board in 1822, which has eight feet of water. *Ennismain*, or the *Middle Island*, is separated from Arranmore by Gregory Sound, which is about four miles broad and navigable from shore to shore: it is of irregular form and about eight miles in circumference; and comprises the village of Maher and the hamlets of Moneenarouga, Lissheen, Ballindoon, and Kinavalla. The inhabitants are chiefly engaged in fishing and making kelp; they have a few row-boats and a number of canoes, or corachs, made of osiers and covered with pitched canvas. The northern point of this island is lofty and rugged, but terminates in a low sandy beach, and on several sides it is boldly perpendicular. *Innishere*, or the *Eastern Island*, is separated from Ennismain by a rocky and dangerous passage, called Foul Sound, which is about a league broad, with a ledge of rocks having on it six feet of water. It is about a mile and a half in length, three quarters of a mile in breadth, and four miles in circumference; and comprises the village of Temore, and the hamlets of Forumna, Castle, and Cleganough. The tillage is chiefly for potatoes, with a little rye; but the inhabitants live principally by fishing and making kelp, which is said to be the best brought to the Galway market. There is a signal tower on the island, and near it an old castle. To the west of Arranmore are the *Branach Isles*, two of which, about eight acres in extent, afford good pasturage, and the third is a perpendicular and barren rock of about two acres.

The surface of all the islands is barren rock, interspersed with numerous verdant and fertile spots. There are many springs and rivulets, but these afford in dry seasons a very inadequate supply of water, which is either brought from the main land for the use of the cattle, or the cattle are removed thither during the continuance of the drought. The best soils are near the shore and are sandy, with a mixture of rich loam: the prevailing crops are potatoes, rye, and a small kind of black oats; the inhabitants raise also small quantities of barley and wheat, for which they apply an additional portion of sea-weed, their only manure; and they grow small quantities of flax; but the produce of their harvests seldom exceeds what is required for their own consumption. The pasture land is appropriated to sheep and goats, and a few cows and horses, for which they also reserve some meadow: the mutton is of fine flavour and superior quality; but the most profitable stock is their breed of calves, which are reputed to be the best in Ireland, and are much sought after by the Connaught graziers. The grasses are intermingled with a variety of medicinal and sweet herbs, among which the wild garlick is so abundant as to give a flavour to the butter. The plant called *Rineen*, or "fairy flax," is much relied on for its medicinal virtues in almost all cases; the tormentil root serves in place of bark for tanning; and there is another plant which gives a fine blue dye, and is used in colouring the woollen cloth which the islanders manufacture for their own wear. The fisheries are a great source of profit, and in the whole employ about 120 boats; of these, 30 or 40 have sails and are from five to ten tons' burden; the rest are small row-boats and canoes, or corachs. The spring and beginning of the summer are the season for the spillard fishery; immense quantities of cod, ling, haddock, turbot, gurnet, mackerel, glassin, bream, and herring are taken here; and lobsters, crabs, cockles, and muscles are also found in abundance. The inhabitants rely chiefly on the herring fishery, which is very productive; and in April and May, many of them are employed in spearing the sun-fish, or basking shark, from the liver of which they extract considerable quantities of oil. Hares and rabbits abound in these islands, which are also frequented by plovers, gannets, pigeons, ducks, and other wild fowl; and the cliffs are the resort of numerous puffins, which are taken for the sake of their feathers by cragmen, who descend the cliffs at night by means of a rope fastened round the body, and are lowered by four or five of their companions. In one of the islands a very fine stratum of dove-coloured and black marble has been discovered; and from the various natural resources of this apparently barren district, the inhabitants are enabled to pay a rental of from £2000 to £3000 per annum to the proprietor. The most remarkable of the natural curiosities are the three caverns called the Puffing Holes, at the southern extremity of Arranmore; they communicate with the sea and have apertures in the surface of the cliff, about 20 perches from its brink, from which, during the prevalence of strong westerly winds, prodigious columns of water are projected to the height of a ship's mast.

The three islands form three parishes in the diocese of Tuam, and, in respect to their vicarages, are part of the union of Ballynakill, from the church of which they are 28 miles distant; the rectories are impropriate in the Digby family. The tithes amount to £47. 19. 10¾., of which £38. 8. is payable to the impropriator, and £9. 11. 10¾. to the incumbent. In the R. C. divisions they form one parish, which is served by a clergyman resident at Oaghill, where a chapel, a neat slated building, has been recently erected. About 400 children are educated in four pay schools at Arranmore. There are still some very interesting remains not only of druidical antiquity, but also of the ancient churches and monasteries. The ruins of the old abbey of Kill-Enda are situated nearly at the eastern extremity of the largest island; and in the opposite direction are the ruins of seven churches, one of which, called Tempeil-Brecain, was probably dedicated to that saint. Near it is a holy well, and throughout the island are various others, and also numerous ancient crosses. In Ennismain are the ruins o two churches, dedicated to the Blessed Virgin; and in Innishere, anciently called Arran Coemhain, were three, namely, St. Coemhain's or Kevin's, St. Paul's, and Kill-i-Gradhandomhain, with the first of which was connected a monastery founded by St. Fechin. The most remarkable of the primitive fortifications is Dun-Ængus, situated on the summit of a great precipice overhanging the sea: it consists of three enclosures, the largest of which is encircled by a rampart of large stones standing on end; and there are one of similar size and others smaller. From the secluded situation of these islands, the language, manners, customs, and dress of the natives are peculiarly primitive; instances of longevity are remarkable. The shoes worn are simply a piece of raw cow hide, rather longer than the foot, and stitched close at the toes and heel with a piece of fishing line. The Irish language is commonly spoken, and being replete with primitive words, varies from the dialect of the natives of the mainland, but not so as to be unintelligible; a great portion of the inhabitants, however, speak good English. In the Great Island is a place called the Field of Skulls, from the number of human bones found in it, and thence supposed to have been the site of a battle fought during some intestine quarrel of the O'Briens.

ARRANMORE, an island, in the parish of Templecroan, barony of Boylagh, county of Donegal, and province of Ulster, 3 miles (W. N. W.) from Rutland; containing, in 1834, 1141 inhabitants. This is the largest of a group of islands called the Rosses, lying off the north-west coast, about two miles from the shore, in lat. 54° 51′ 45″ (N.), and lon. 8° 31′ 45″ (W.): it is three miles in length and three in breadth, and is about nine miles distant from the mainland; comprising, according to the Ordnance survey, 4355 statute acres, of which about 650 only are under cultivation and in pasture, and the remainder is rugged mountain. In 1784 a large herring fishery was carried on successfully on this part of the coast, in which 400 sail of vessels and about 1000 small boats were employed; but within the last thirty or forty years it has been entirely discontinued. On the north point of the island, which is a large rock of granite, was formerly a lighthouse, fitted up with an improved apparatus in 1817 by the corporation for the improvements of the port of Dublin, which has since been removed to Tory Island; the house remains, but is not lighted. There is good anchorage on the east side of the island in an open roadstead. In the R. C. divisions this place forms part of the parish of Templenane or Templecroder, in which is the chapel, where divine service is performed every third Sunday.

ARTAGH.—See TAUGHBOYNE.

ARTANE, otherwise ARTAINE, a parish, in the barony of Coolock, county of Dublin, and province of Leinster, 2½ miles (N.) from the Post-office, Dublin; containing 583 inhabitants. The village is situated on the road from Dublin to Malahide, and has a penny post. Artane castle was long the property of the Donellans of Ravensdale, and is said to have been the scene of the death of John Alen or Alan, Archbishop of Dublin, who, in endeavouring to escape from the vengeance of the house of Kildare, which he had provoked by his adherence to the will and measures of Cardinal Wolsey, was shipwrecked near Clontarf; and being made prisoner by some followers of that family, was brought before Lord Thos. Fitzgerald, then posted here with the insurgent army, whom he earnestly entreated to spare his life; but, either failing in his supplications, or from the wilful misconstruction of a contemptuous expression by Fitzgerald into a sentence of death on the part of those around him, as variously alleged by different writers, he was instantly slain in the great hall of the castle, on the 28th of July, 1534. On the breaking out of hostilities in 1641, it was taken by Luke Netterville, one of the R. C. leaders, at the head of a body of royalists, and garrisoned. The parish comprises 946 statute acres, of which about 20, including roads, are untitheable and of no value. The old castle was pulled down in 1825, and on its site and with its materials was erected, by the late Matthew Boyle, Esq., uncle of the present proprietor, M. Callaghan, Esq., a handsome house, which commands a splendid view of the islands of Lambay and Ireland's Eye, the hill of Howth, and the Dublin and Wicklow mountains. The other seats are Elm Park, the residence of T. Hutton, Esq.; Thorndale, of D. H. Sherrard, Esq.; Woodville, of J. Cornwall, Esq.; Artaine House, of T. Alley, Esq.; Mount Dillon, of H. Cooper, Esq.; Kilmore House, of H. Hutton, Esq.; Belfield, of Capt. Cottingham; Artaine Cottage, of J. Cusack, Esq.; Pozzodigotto, of Mrs. Atkinson; and Stella Lodge, of M. Curwen, Esq. In its ecclesiastical concerns this is a chapelry, in the diocese of Dublin, and one of three which, with the rectory of Finglas and the curacy of St. Werburgh's, Dublin, constitute the corps of the chancellorship in the cathedral church of St. Patrick, Dublin, which is in the patronage of the Archbishop. The church is a picturesque ruin, partly covered with ivy: in the burial-ground is a tombstone to the Hollywood family, to which the manor belonged for many ages, and of which John Hollywood, a distinguished mathematician and philosopher of the 13th century, was a member. In the R. C. divisions it is in the union or district of Clontarf, Coolock, and Santry. A neat school-house for boys and girls, with apartments for the master and mistress, was built near the old church by the late M. Boyle, Esq., in 1832, at an expense of more than £600, of which £150 was repaid by the National Board, which contributes £25 per annum towards the support of the school, and, in 1833, Mr. Boyle bequeathed £10 per annum for the same purpose: the number of boys on the books is 116, and of girls, 107.

ARTHURSTOWN, or KING'S-BAY, a post-town, in the parish of St. James, barony of Shelburne, county of Wexford, and province of Leinster, 9¼ miles (S. E. by S.) from New Ross, and 80 (S. by W.) from Dublin; containing 170 inhabitants. This place is situated on Waterford harbour, three miles below the junction of the rivers Barrow, Suir, and Nore, and derives its origin and name from its proprietor, Arthur, first and present Lord Templemore, whose seat is here, and by whom it has been mostly built within the last few years. The trade consists principally in the importation of coal and culm from South Wales, and slates from Bangor; and the exportation to Waterford of corn, pigs, butter, eggs, honey, and poultry. It has a commodious quay, with a gravelly strand open to Waterford harbour; and a pier of millstone grit found in the quarries here, 306 feet in length, and originally intended for the accommodation of the boats employed in the fishery, has been constructed at an expense of £3000, of which £700 was granted by the late Fishery Board, and the remainder was defrayed by Lord Templemore. Vessels of 100 tons' burden can come up close to the pier, but the entrance has lately become partially choked with an accumulation of mud, which requires speedy removal, and the adoption of some plan calculated to prevent a recurrence of the obstruction. The bay is subject to a heavy sea during the prevalence of south, south-west, and north-west winds. This place is a chief constabulary police station, and a station of the coast-guard. There is a dispensary, and a fever hospital was also built, but the Grand Jury, on application being made for its support, deemed it unnecessary.—See JAMES (ST.)

ARTRAMONT, or ARDTRAMONT, a parish, in the barony of SHELMALIER, county of WEXFORD, and province of LEINSTER, 4 miles (N.) from Wexford; containing 661 inhabitants. It is situated on the north-western side of the estuary of the Slaney, and comprises 2384 statute acres, as applotted under the tithe act, of which 129 are woodland. A kind of red sandstone adapted for building is quarried in the parish. The surrounding scenery is pleasingly diversified, and in some parts highly picturesque. Artramont, the elegant seat of G. le Hunte, Esq., is beautifully situated on an eminence surrounded by a fine plantation, and commanding an extensive view of Wexford harbour and the country adjacent: the demesne is separated from the parish of Tickillen, on the north, by a romantic glen called Eden Vale, the steep sides of which are covered from the water's edge to their summits with young and thriving plantations; and from one point of view are seen three picturesque cascades, formed by the precipitation of the little river Sow from a rocky height of 50 or 60 feet. St. Edmond's, the residence of J. Lane, Esq., is also in the parish. The parish is in the diocese of Ferns, and is a rectory, forming part of the union of Ardcolme: the tithes amount to £184. 12. 3¾. The church has long been in ruins. In the R. C. divisions it is in the union or district of Crossabeg, where the chapel is situated. A school for children of both sexes was established in 1818; the school-house, a handsome building in the rustic style, was erected at the expense of Sir Francis le Hunte, by whom the school is chiefly supported; it affords accommodation, including a girls' work-room, for about 100 children; the master has apartments and two acres of land, with £20 per annum, and six tons of coal yearly. Within the demesne are the ruins of Artramont castle; and there are also vestiges of a Danish fort, with a square moat, in the parish.

ARTREA.—See ARDTREA.

ARVAGH, a market and post-town, and a parish, in the barony of TULLOGHONOHO, county of CAVAN, and province of ULSTER, 10¾ miles (S.W.) from Cavan, and, by way of that town, 66 miles (N. W. by W.) from Dublin; containing 4580 inhabitants, of which number, 422 are in the town. This parish is situated on the road from Killesandra to Scrabby, near the point of junction of the three counties of Cavan, Leitrim, and Longford, and was formed by the disunion of thirty townlands from the parish of Killesandra. Near the town is the lake of Scraba, one of the sources of the river Erne, which, with the lakes through which it runs, is commonly called in its entire extent Lough Erne. The market is on Friday, and is well supplied with provisions: the market-house, situated in the centre of the town, was built by the Earl of Gosford, to whom the town belongs. Fairs are held on Jan. 28th, March 25th, April 1st, May 2nd, June 8th, Aug. 8th, Sept. 23rd, Nov. 1st, and Dec. 23rd. Here is a station of the constabulary police. The living is a perpetual cure, in the diocese of Kilmore, and in the patronage of the Vicar of Killesandra: the perpetual curate has a fixed income of £75 per annum late currency, of which £50 is paid by the incumbent of Killesandra, and £25 from the funds of the Ecclesiastical Commissioners. The church was built by aid of a gift of £900 and a loan of £100, in 1819, from the late Board of First Fruits. The glebe-house is small but conveniently built; and the glebe comprises 21 acres. In the R. C. divisions this parish remains included in the union or district of Killesandra, and has a chapel, situated at Corronee. There is a place of worship for Wesleyan methodists. There are two public schools, one in the town and the other at Corronary, and other private and Sunday schools in the parish.

ASHBOURNE, a post-town, in the parish of KILLEGLAND, barony of RATOATH, county of MEATH, and province of LEINSTER, 12½ miles (S. by E.) from Drogheda, and 10¼ (N. by W.) from Dublin, on the mail coach road to Londonderry and Belfast; containing 60 houses and 473 inhabitants. It is a constabulary police station, and has fairs on Jan. 6th, April 16th, May 21st, July 29th, and Oct. 31st. Here is a R. C. chapel, a neat modern building; and a dispensary is principally supported by the rector and curate, assisted by some of the parishioners.—See KILLEGLAND.

ASHFIELD, a parish, in the barony of TULLAGH-GARVEY, county of CAVAN, and province of ULSTER, ½ a mile (S. W.) from Cootehill, on the road to Belturbet; containing 3013 inhabitants. It formerly constituted part of the parish of Killersherdiny, from which it was separated in 1799; and comprises 4426 acres, as applotted under the tithe act, and valued at about £4006 per annum. The land is in general good, and there is very little waste; the system of agriculture is slowly improving. The manufacture of linen for broad sheeting is carried on to a considerable extent. Ashfield Lodge, the seat of Col. Clements, is beautifully situated on an eminence within view of the church, beneath which swiftly flows the Cootehill river, a tributary to Lough Erne, and is surrounded with extensive plantations. Fort Henry, formerly a seat of the Clements family, is now that of the Rev. J. Thompson. The living is a perpetual curacy, in the diocese of Kilmore, and in the patronage of the Vicar of Killersherdiny, with which parish the tithes are included and are payable to the vicar: the perpetual curate has a fixed annual income of £100, of which £50 is payable by the Ecclesiastical Commissioners. The church is a handsome edifice, with a lofty spire, occupying a very elevated site; it was built by aid of a gift of £500 from the late Board of First Fruits, in 1795, and, in 1818, the Board also granted £500, of which one half was a gift and the other a loan. The glebe-house was built by a gift of £450 and a loan of £50 from the same Board, in 1812; the glebe comprises 20 acres. In the R. C. divisions this parish forms part of the union or district of Killersherdiny: the chapel is situated at Drummurry. Besides the parochial school, there is one at Doohurrick under the patronage of Mrs. Clements; also three private pay schools.

ASHFORD, a village and post-town, in the parish of RATHNEW, barony of NEWCASTLE, county of WICKLOW, and province of LEINSTER, 3 miles (W. N. W.) from Wicklow, and 21¾ (S. by E.) from Dublin: the population is returned with the parish. This place, which is situated on the south side of the river Vartrey, and on the mail coach road from Dublin, consists of several neat cottages, and is pleasantly situated in the centre of a rich agricultural district; it has a small but well-conducted posting-house and hotel. Fairs are held on April 27th, June 24th, Sept. 8th, and Dec. 16th.—See RATHNEW.

ASHFORD.—See KILLEEDY.

ASKEATON, a market and post-town, and a parish (formerly a parliamentary borough), in the barony of LOWER CONNELLO EAST, county of LIMERICK, and province of MUNSTER, 16 miles (W. S. W.) from Limerick, and 113 miles (S. W. by W.) from Dublin; containing 2799 inhabitants, of which number, 1515 are in the town. This place is indebted for its foundation and early importance to the Fitzgeralds, who had a magnificent castle here, and of whom James, seventh Earl of Desmond, founded a monastery in 1420, for Conventual Franciscans, which was reformed, in 1490, by the Observantine friars, and ranked among the finest ecclesiastical structures in Ireland. In 1558, James Fitzgerald, fifteenth Earl of Desmond, and High Treasurer of Ireland, died here and was buried in the monastery. He was succeeded by his son Garret, called by way of distinction the Great Earl, who forfeited his life and his large estates by his participation in the insurrection during the reign of Elizabeth. In 1564 a provincial chapter of the Franciscan order was held in the monastery; but in the hostilities which broke out soon after, the monks were expelled and some of them put to death by the English forces. The Earl of Desmond, who, in 1573, had been in the custody of the mayor of Dublin, made his escape to the castle of this place, which, in 1579, he garrisoned against the Queen's forces under Sir Nicholas Malby. In April of the following year it was attacked by Sir George Carew; but the garrison retired during the night, leaving a train of gunpowder which blew up part of the fortress, and the English took possession of the remainder of the castle, which was the last that held out for this powerful earl. In 1642, Lord Broghill sent 200 men to defend the town, which was then walled, and to prevent the inhabitants from revolting to the insurgents; it was for some time bravely defended by this force, but was at length compelled to surrender. In 1648 the Confederate Catholics took possession of the abbey, and commenced repairing and restoring it.

The town is pleasantly situated on the road from Limerick to Tarbert, and on the banks of the river Deel, which discharges itself into the Shannon about two miles below, and is here crossed by an ancient bridge of five arches connecting the opposite portions of the town: it contains about 260 houses, of very indifferent appearance. The Deel runs through the demesne of Inchirourk-More, and has a waterfall, or salmon leap, the scenery of which is wild and romantic; there is a beautiful view of it from the town. The fishery belongs to Mr. Hunt, and was formerly of considerable value, but it has been much injured by the erection of the Scotch weirs on the Shannon, which the proprietors are taking steps to remove. The trade consists principally in grain and flour, which have been exported direct to the foreign markets. There are two large flour-mills; one near the castle, the property of Mr. Hewson, is very extensive. The town is advantageously situated for trade, from its vicinity to the Shannon, and having a good river up which the tide flows, capable of admitting vessels of 60 tons' burden, and which might be deepened at a trifling expense, so as to admit vessels drawing 15 feet of water to the bridge: the quays are spacious. In the spring, considerable quantities of sea-weed and sand are landed for manure. The market day is Tuesday, and a market-house is about to be erected on ground given by R. Hunt, Esq. Fairs are held on July 30th and Oct. 9th, for horses, cattle, and sheep. Here is a station of the constabulary police. The borough was incorporated by charter of the 11th of Jas. I. (1613), under the style of "the Sovereign, Free Burgesses, and Community of the Borough of Askeaton;" and the corporation was made to consist of a sovereign and 12 free burgesses, who, amongst other privileges, were empowered to have a court of record, to be held every Monday, for the trial of all actions personal to the extent of five marks. It returned two members to the Irish parliament until the Union, when it was deprived of the franchise; and of the £15,000 awarded in compensation for the loss of that privilege, £6850 was paid to Henry Thomas, Earl of Carrick, £6850 to the Trustees of the will of Hugh, Lord Massey, £1100 to Sir Vere Hunt, Bart., and £200 to Sir Joseph Hoare, Bart. The corporation has since become extinct. A court of petty sessions is held before the county magistrates every alternate Tuesday. A manorial court, with jurisdiction to the amount of £10 late currency, was formerly held every month before the seneschal, who was appointed by Sir Matthew Blakiston, Bart., lord of the manor; but it has been discontinued in consequence of the establishment of the petty sessions, and no seneschal has been appointed since the death of the last, in 1834.

The parish comprises 6138 statute acres, as applotted under the tithe act. The surface is very undulating, and numerous rocky knolls rise considerably above the ordinary level. The lands are arable and pasture; the soil is everywhere light; but the system of agriculture, though advancing, is still capable of further improvement. Limestone of good quality is obtained in great abundance; and copper ore has been discovered in several places, but no attempt has been hitherto made to work it. The scenery is pleasantly diversified and enlivened with numerous gentlemen's seats, of which the principal are Inchirourk-More, the residence of R. Hunt, Esq.; Shannon View, of J. Browne, Esq.; Mantle Hill, of J. Hunt, Esq.; Castle Hewson, of W. Hewson, Esq.; and the Abbey, of the Rev. M.

Fitzgerald, P.P. The living is a vicarage, in the diocese of Limerick, with the rectory of Lismakeery and the vicarage of Iverus united, forming the union of Askeaton, in the patronage of Sir Matthew Blakiston, Bart.; the rectory is impropriate in R. Hunt, Esq. The tithes amount to £450, of which £300 is payable to the impropriator, and £150 to the vicar; and the tithes of the benefice amount to £410. The church, situated in the town, is in a very dilapidated condition, and has been condemned by the ecclesiastical provincial architect. The glebe-house, a large and handsome residence, was built in 1827: the glebe comprises 17¼ acres. In the R. C. divisions the parish is the head of a union or district, comprising the parishes of Askeaton, Iverus, Lismakeery, and Tomdeely; there are two chapels, one in the town, and one at Ballystean, both thatched buildings. Adjoining the church is a parochial school for boys and girls; four public schools afford instruction to about 190 children; and there are three pay schools, in which are about 150 boys and 50 girls. There is also a dispensary. The present parochial church was that of the commandery of Knights Templars, founded in 1298; on the south side is a transept, now in ruins, and separated from the church by two lofty arches which have been rudely closed up; and near the east end are the remains of an ancient tower, square at the base and octangular above. This tower and also the church and transept are precisely in the state in which they are described in the "Pacata Hibernica," published more than 200 years since. To the west of the church are the remains of the once stately castle, boldly situated on a rock of limestone in the river Deel; and near it are those of the banqueting-house, a very spacious and elegant building, and, with the exception of the roof, still in a very perfect state; the arched vaults beneath are very extensive, and the windows of the great hall are lofty and of beautiful design. On the eastern bank of the river, and at a short distance to the north, are the venerable ruins of the Franciscan abbey: it is built entirely of the dark grey marble which is found here in great abundance; the cloisters are nearly entire, and of beautiful character; on each side of the enclosed quadrangle are twelve lofty pointed arches supported by cylindrical columns with richly moulded capitals; and in the centre of the square is an ancient thorn of stately growth. The church, with the exception of the roof, is partly standing; the eastern gable, with its lofty window, has some beautiful details in the later English style; the other portions are much decayed, and large masses of the walls lie scattered around, as if detached by the force of gunpowder; these ruins are close to the bank of the river, and are almost washed by every tide. Two miles north of the town are the ruins of Court Browne castle, seated on an eminence overlooking the Shannon. In 1834 two very splendid fibulæ of pure gold were found near the town; and, in the following year, several ancient gold coins were discovered in sinking the foundation of a wall on the west side of the river. Silver chalices, crosiers, and a great number of coins have been found near the abbey and the castle.

ASSEY, or ATHSY, a parish, in the barony of LOWER DEECE, county of MEATH, and province of LEINSTER, 4 miles (S.) from Navan, on the river Boyne; containing 108 inhabitants. The land, though not rich, is tolerably productive; a considerable portion is under tillage, and the remainder is good grazing land. Bellinter, the seat of the Rev. J. Preston, is situated in a well-wooded demesne of more than 800 acres, stretching into the adjoining parish of Balsoon. The living is a rectory, in the diocese of Meath, to which the rectory of Balsoon was united by diocesan authority in 1826, together forming the union of Assey, in the patronage of the Crown: the tithes amount to £62. 15. 4½., and the gross amount of tithes of the benefice is £132. There is neither church nor glebe-house in the union, the occasional duties of which are performed by the incumbent of Kilmessan, who receives £24 per annum, besides the glebe, which consists of three acres, valued at £6 per annum. The Commissioners of Ecclesiastical Inquiry, in 1831, have recommended that the two parishes be formed into one, to be called the parish of Athsy, and that a church and glebe-house for a resident minister be erected. In the R. C. divisions this parish forms part of the union or district of Dunsany and Kilmessan.

ATHASSEL, a parish, in the barony of CLANWILLIAM, county of TIPPERARY, and province of MUNSTER, 3½ miles (W.) from Cashel; containing, with the parish of Relickmurry, 5498 inhabitants. This place, which is situated on the river Suir, was distinguished for its priory, founded towards the close of the 12th century by William Fitz Aldelm de Burgho, for Canons Regular of the order of St. Augustine, and dedicated to St. Edmund the King and Martyr. In 1319 the town was set on fire by Lord John, brother of Lord Maurice Fitz-Thomas; and, in 1329, Bryan O'Brien burned it to the ground: there are still some slight traces of its site. The priory, which was amply endowed, and of which the abbot sat in parliament, continued to flourish till the reign of Edw. VI., when it was dissolved; and in that of Philip and Mary it was, with other possessions, granted to Thomas, Earl of Ormonde. The remains are extensive and highly interesting, and shew the buildings to have been distinguished for elegance and magnificence, and equal, if not superior, to any monastic structure in the kingdom. In this monastery was interred Richard de Burgho, second Earl of Ulster, called, from his complexion, the Red, who, after giving a splendid entertainment to the nobles and his friends at Kilkenny, in 1326, retired hither and soon after died. Castle Park, the seat of R. Creaghe, Esq., is a spacious and well-built mansion, pleasantly situated in a richly planted demesne, in which are some remains of an ancient castle; Ballycarron, the seat of T. Butler, Esq., is situated in an extensive and finely planted demesne; Golden Hills is the castellated residence of H. White, Esq.; and Springmount, that of J. White, Esq. Suir Castle, the residence of J. Robbins, Esq., is situated on the banks of the Suir, and within the demesne are the ruins of a castle with a square tower. The other seats are Gaulty View, the residence of F. Massey, Esq.; Ballyslatteen, of R. Butler, Esq.; and Hymenstown, of R. Scully, Esq. The parish is in the diocese of Cashel, and is a rectory, forming part of the union of Relickmurry: the tithes, including those of the parish of Relickmurry, amount to £550. In the R. C. divisions it forms part of the union or district of Golden.

ATHBOY, a market and post-town, and a parish (formerly a borough), in the barony of LUNE, county of MEATH, and province of LEINSTER, 5 miles (N. W.)

from Trim, and 28 (N. W. by W.) from Dublin; containing 5317 inhabitants, of which number, 1959 are in the town. This place derives its name, signifying in the Irish language "the yellow ford," from its situation on a stream which falls into the river Boyne near Trim. The town, in 1831, contained 346 houses, and is at present a place of very little trade: the road from Oldcastle to Dublin runs through it; there is a very large flour-mill. The market is on Thursday, and is well supplied with corn and provisions. The principal fairs are held on the Thursday before Jan. 28th, May 4th, Aug. 4th, and Nov. 7th, and there are others on March 3rd and 10th, June 22nd and 30th, and Sept. 22nd and 29th, but they are very inconsiderable. Here is a chief station of the constabulary police.

In the 9th of Hen. IV. (1407), a charter was granted on petition from the provost and commonalty, which, after setting forth that the town had been from time immemorial an ancient borough, confirmed all existing privileges, and granted a guild mercatory, freedom from tolls and customs throughout the king's dominions, and other immunities. Hen VI., in 1446, gave a confirmatory charter, by which additional customs were also conferred for a term of 60 years. These charters were also confirmed in the 9th of Hen. VII.; and in the 9th of Jas. I. (1612), on a surrender of the corporation property, a charter of inspection and confirmation was granted, under which the corporation was entitled "the Provost, Free Burgesses, and Commonalty of the Town of Athboy." This charter vested the right of electing the provost in the burgesses and freemen, and the burgesses and all inferior officers in the corporation at large; it ordained that the provost should be a justice of the peace, and prohibited all other justices from acting within the borough, which comprised an extent of one mile beyond the town in every direction: it also granted a court of record, with jurisdiction to the amount of £10. From the second of Elizabeth the borough returned two representatives to the Irish parliament, who were exclusively elected by the members of the corporation; but it was disfranchised at the Union, when the £15,000 compensation money for the loss of this privilege was awarded to the trustees under the will of John, then late Earl of Darnley, to be applied to the trusts of the will. The corporation then fell into disuse, and is now extinct. By patent granted in 1694 to Thomas Bligh, Esq., "the town's lands and commons," and several other denominations of land, were erected into a manor, and power was given to him and his heirs to hold a court leet twice in the year, and a court baron every three weeks, or not so often, before a seneschal; but no manor court has been held, or seneschal appointed, since the beginning of the present century. Petty sessions are held every alternate Thursday by the county magistrates.

The parish extends five Irish miles in length and four in breadth: the land is mostly of very good quality, and is principally under grass; there is an abundance of limestone, used both for building and manure. The principal seats are Ballyfallon, the residence of J. Martley, Esq.; Mitchelstown, of F. Hopkins, Esq.; Athboy Lodge, of J. Noble, Esq.; Frayne, of W. Hopkins, Esq.; Grenanstown, of P. Barnewall, Esq.; Frankville, of F. Welsh, Esq.; Dance's Court, of H. Biddulph Warner, Esq.; and Causestown, of — Thunder, Esq. The living is a vicarage, in the diocese of Meath, to which the rectory and vicarage of Girly, and the rectories of Moyagher, Rathmore, and Kildalky were united by act of council in 1678, now forming the union of Athboy, in the patronage of the Crown, the Lord-Primate, and the Bishop of Meath: the rectory is appropriate to the Lord-Primate. The tithes of this parish amount to £560, of which £360 is paid to the lord-primate, and £200 to the vicar; and the tithes of the entire union are £486. 3. 4½. The church has an ancient tower, but the body of the building is somewhat modern; the Ecclesiastical Commissioners have lately granted £102 for its repair. The glebe-house, situated near the town, was built in 1818, at an expense of £1700, principally defrayed by a gift of £100 and a loan of £1050 from the late Board of First Fruits: the glebe comprises six acres in Athboy and 1½ in Girly, valued at £2 per acre. In the R. C. divisions the parish is the head of a union or district, comprising the parishes of Athboy and Rathmore: the chapel is now in course of re-erection, and when completed will be a handsome and commodious edifice in the ancient style of architecture, with a steeple 90 feet high; it will be lighted by five windows of considerable dimensions on each side, and three at each end, and will have three entrances in front. The parochial school, held in the market-house, is supported under the patronage of the Earl of Darnley: and there is an infants' school. At Frayne is a school for boys and girls under the patronage of Lady Chapman, of Killua Castle. About 150 boys and 90 girls are instructed in these schools; and in the other private pay schools there are 112 boys and 54 girls. There is a dispensary; and three almshouses were founded by the late Earl of Darnley, containing apartments for twelve poor widows, who have each an annual allowance of £5. 5., with a garden and ten kishes of turf: about 43 poor out-pensioners also receive weekly allowances from his lordship's successor. A monastery of Carmelite friars was founded here early in the 14th century, which, with its possessions, was granted in the 34th of Hen. VIII. to Thomas Casey. There are some picturesque remains of the ancient church, and at Frayne are considerable ruins of two ancient castles, and of a third at Causestown. This town confers the inferior title of Viscount on the Earl of Darnley.

ATHEA, or TEMPLE-ATTEA.—See RATHRONAN.

ATHENEASY.—See ATHNASSY.

ATHENRY, an incorporated market and post-town, and a parish, partly in the baronies of CLARE, DUNKELLIN, KILCONNELL, and TYAQUIN, but chiefly in the barony of ATHENRY, county of GALWAY, and province of CONNAUGHT, 11 miles (E.) from Galway, and 95½ (W. by S.) from Dublin; containing 12,185 inhabitants, of which number, 1319 are in the town, which is wholly within the barony of Athenry. This place, anciently called Athnere, is said to have derived its name from *Ath-na-Riagh*, "the King's ford," or "the abode of a King." Sir James Ware considers it to have been the chief town of the *Anteri*, who, ac-

Seal.

cording to Ptolemy, were the ancient inhabitants of this part of the country. It was the first town established by the De Burgos and Berminghams, the Anglo-Norman invaders of Connaught, and at a remote period was surrounded with walls and became a place of importance. In the reign of John, Meyler de Bermingham granted a site of land here for the foundation of a Dominican monastery, and contributed towards the erection of the buildings, which were completed in 1261. Florence O'Flin, Archbishop of Tuam, and the Earls of Ulster and many others were munificent benefactors to this establishment, which became very extensive and wealthy, and the chief burial-place of the Earls of Ulster and all the principal families of this part of Ireland. Indulgences for the benefit of the monastery were granted by the Pope in 1400, and in 1423 its church was burned down; in 1427, some of the monks obtained licence from the Pope to found two subordinate establishments; and in 1445 Pope Eugene IV. renewed the bull of Pope Martin for repairing the church, at which time there were 30 brethren in the monastery. A Franciscan friary was founded here by Thomas, Earl of Kildare, in 1464, and chapels were successively erected by his wife, the Earl of Desmond, and O'Tully. In 1577, the two sons of the Earl of Clanricarde, called the "Mac-an-Earlas," renouncing the submission which they had recently made to Queen Elizabeth, assembled their partisans in considerable force and sacked the town, destroyed the few houses that had recently been built, set fire to the new gates, and drove away the workmen employed in repairing the fortifications and in erecting other buildings, which had been undertaken by the chief governor, Sir Henry Sidney. From this period the town remained in a deserted condition till 1584, when Robert Foyle, John Browne, and other of its former inhabitants petitioned the queen's council in England for such encouragement as would enable them to bring over English artisans and tradesmen to settle in the town, to rebuild and improve it, and to support a sufficient force for its future protection. The queen, in 1585, directed the lord-deputy to grant their request forthwith; and although no record exists of any such grant having passed the seal, several buildings were erected and numerous improvements were made. In 1596 the northern Irish invested the town, burned the gates, and forced an entrance; but they were repulsed in an attack on the castle, which was bravely defended, and having failed in an attempt to scale the battlements, they took possession of all the wall towers, and made prisoners of the inhabitants who guarded them; they afterwards set fire to the town, which, with the exception only of the castle, the abbey, and the church, was again reduced to ashes, and from this time seems to have been entirely neglected except by its immediate proprietors. In 1644 the Dominican establishment was revived and converted into a university; and in 1662 a writ of privy seal was issued on behalf of the inhabitants; but the town, which formerly held the second rank in the county, never recovered its ancient importance. It is situated on the road from Oranmore to Monivae, and also from Loughrea to Tuam, and contains about 250 houses. The market, with a fair in October, was granted to Sir Wm. Parsons, Bart., in 1629, and is on Friday, but is only indifferently attended; and fairs for sheep and cattle are held on May 5th, July 2nd, and Oct. 20th, of which that in July is the largest. A constabulary police force is stationed here.

The borough is very ancient and probably exists by prescription. From a murage grant made to the "bailiffs and honest men of Athenry," in the 4th of Edw. II. (1310), it would appear that a corporation previously existed; and writs of the first and some subsequent years of the reign of Rich. II. shew that it then returned representatives to parliament. Queen Elizabeth, by letters patent dated at Greenwich in the 16th of her reign, granted to the portreeve and burgesses divers extensive privileges, and in the same year gave them the site and precincts of the Dominican monastery. In 1578 she conferred upon them various rectories and tithes; but all these privileges and possessions appear to have become forfeited during the civil dissensions which soon afterwards ensued, as Chas. II., by his letters under the privy seal in 1662, after reciting the petition of "the ancient inhabitants, natives, and freemen of the old corporation of Athenry," and other particulars referring to the borough, ordered that they should be forthwith reinvested with the said town and corporation, with all their rights, interests, and estates, and all privileges and immunities, excepting such inhabitants as had been disloyal and disobedient to his government. A charter was granted in the 4th of Jas. II., on a seizure of the franchises, but it does not appear to have been accepted or acted upon. The grant of Elizabeth is that under which the borough is governed: the corporation is styled "the Portreeve, Burgesses, and Freemen of the Corporation of the Town and Liberties of Athenry," and consists of a portreeve and an unlimited number of burgesses and freemen: the above grant empowers them to appoint a common clerk and "all such other necessary servants as Trim used," but the only inferior officers are a serjeant-at-mace, craner, pound-keeper, two appraisers, and a bellman, who are appointed by the portreeve. The portreeve is annually elected on the 14th of Sept. by the portreeve and burgesses, from three burgesses nominated on the preceding day by the same body, and is sworn in on the 29th: the burgesses are nominated on one day, elected on the next, and sworn on the 29th of Sept., and are now about twenty in number. The borough returned two members to the Irish parliament till the Union, who were elected by the portreeve and burgesses; the £15,000 awarded as compensation for the abolition of its franchise was paid to the trustees of the marriage settlement of Theophilus Blakeney, Esq. The limits of the borough comprehend the town and a surrounding agricultural district, called "the liberties." The portreeve, who has power to appoint a deputy, is a justice of the peace within the borough and its liberties, clerk of the market, and sole judge in the borough court. The town or portreeve's court is held for all pleas, real and personal, to an unlimited amount, as often as business requires, which of late has been but seldom, and generally on a Monday, not in any fixed court-house or place, but in different parts of the town; the ordinary process is by attachment against the debtor's goods, on affidavit made by the plaintiff. Petty sessions are held in the town every Friday, at which three of the county magistrates usually attend.

The parish comprises 1954 statute acres, as applotted under the tithe act: the system of agriculture is somewhat improved; there is a considerable extent of unreclaimed bog. A coal-pit was opened some years since at Castle Lambert, and a considerable quantity of coal was found, but it was soon discontinued; the present proprietor, however, contemplates reopening it. The principal seats are Castle Lambert, that of W. Lambert, Esq., and Athenry House, the property of J. Lopdell, Esq. The living is a rectory and vicarage, in the diocese of Tuam; the rectory is partly appropriate to the prebend of Taghsaxon, but is principally consolidated with the vicarage (to which are united the chapelries of Abbert and Dunmacloughy), and in the patronage of the Crown for two turns, and the Bishop for one: the tithes amount to £1075, of which £7. 10. is payable to the prebendary, and £1067. 10. to the incumbent. The church is a very neat edifice, built about the year 1828, by aid of a gift of £1500 from the late Board of First Fruits; and there is also a church at Monivae, served by a perpetual curate. There is neither glebe nor glebe-house. The R. C. parish is co-extensive with that of the Established Church; the chapel is a plain slated building in the town. In addition to the parochial school, in which about 55 boys and 35 girls are taught, there are four private pay schools, in which are about 240 children. There is also at Monivae a school of about 30 boys and 30 girls; and at Monivae and Newcastle are two private schools, in which are about 70 boys and 40 girls. Some remains exist of the ancient town walls and of one of the gates. The ruins of the Dominican monastery evince its ancient extent and grandeur; the tower of the church still remains, and the east window is of good design. On Mr. Lopdell's estate is a chalybeate spring, which is much resorted to. Athenry formerly gave the title of Baron to the family of Bermingham, and was the premier barony of Ireland, being created in 1178; this title is now claimed by Edmund Bermingham, Esq., of Dalgan, and also by — St. George, Esq., of Tyrone, in the county of Galway, and the matter is under investigation by the House of Peers.

ATHGLASSON, a village, in the parish of Kilskyre, barony of Upper Kells, county of Meath, and province of Leinster; containing 19 houses and 114 inhabitants.

ATHLACCA, or ATHLATRICHE, a parish, in the barony of Coshma, county of Limerick, and province of Munster, 3 miles (S. W. by W.) from Bruff; containing 1381 inhabitants. The place was anciently the residence of the powerful family of De Lacy, who were proprietors of the surrounding territory, and had two very strong castles, one near the present village, and the other at Tullerbuoy, now Castle Ivers. In 1691, a sanguinary battle was fought here between the Irish adherents of Jas. II. and a force of militia and dragoons commanded by Capt. O'Dell on the part of Wm. III., in which the latter were defeated with great slaughter. The parish is situated on the road from Croom to Kilmallock, and is intersected by a beautiful little river called the Morning Star, which falls into the Maigue about a mile below the village. It comprises 5453½ statute acres, as applotted under the tithe act; the land is very fertile, resting on a substratum of limestone, and around Rathcannon it is exceedingly productive. About one-half is under tillage; the remainder is rich meadow and pasture land, on which a great number of cattle are fed; there is not an acre of waste land or turbary. A great want of timber prevails throughout this district; scarcely a tree or shrub, or even a hedge-row is to be seen, except around the houses of the principal inhabitants. Castle Ivers, the residence of R. Ivers, Esq., is about a mile from the village, and is pleasantly situated in a well-planted demesne. A constabulary police force has been stationed in the village. The parish is in the diocese of Limerick, and is a rectory, united to Dromin: the tithes amount to £306. 12. 7½. The church, built by aid of a loan of £560 from the late Board of First Fruits, in 1813, was burnt by the Rockites in 1822; and the present church, a small but neat edifice, with a tower and lofty spire, was erected in the following year by a cess levied on the parish. The glebe-house, built by aid of a gift of £400 and a loan of £360 from the Board, in the same year, is a handsome residence situated on a glebe of 14 acres, the whole of which is tastefully laid out. In the R. C. divisions the parish also forms part of the union or district of Dromin, and has a chapel. A school of about 60 boys and 20 girls is aided by the Rev. J. O'Regan, P.P. Adjoining Castle Ivers are the ruins of Tullerbuoy castle; and near the village are those of Old Court, also the ancient residence of the De Lacy family. On the summit of a fertile eminence are the extensive remains of the castle of Rathcannon, built by the O'Casey family in the 16th century, on the site of a very ancient fortress. Near Castle Ivers are the ruins of Kilbroney church, built on a gentle eminence by the Knights Templars, in 1289, in view of their extensive manor of Ross-Temple. In the churchyard are some ancient and very curious tombs of the De Lacy family, who were great benefactors to the church and parish, and presented a valuable service of communion plate. Near the castle of Rathcannon a very perfect specimen of the elk or moose deer was discovered by Archdeacon Maunsell, who presented it to the Royal Society of Dublin: the body, from the nose to the tail, is 11 feet in length; the antlers measure 12 feet from tip to tip, and the highest point is 10 feet from the ground.

ATHLEAGUE, a post-town and parish, partly in the barony of Killian, county of Galway, but chiefly in that of Athlone, county of Roscommon, and in the province of Connaught, 4½ miles (S. W.) from Roscommon, and 79¼ (W.) from Dublin; containing 5361 inhabitants, of which number, 488 are in the town. This parish is situated on the river Suck, and on the road from Roscommon to Mount-Talbot and Loughrea: it contains 7601 statute acres, as applotted under the tithe act; the state of agriculture is improving. There are large tracts of bog, now being reclaimed, but not on an extensive scale; more than half of the Galway portion of the parish consists of this species of land. Limestone and freestone of excellent quality abound; and mines of iron were formerly worked, but were discontinued from the scarcity of fuel. Over the Suck is a long winding causeway bridge of ten arches carried from one islet to another, and forming a communication between the two counties; from one end of it the houses stretch along the right bank of the river, with a street or road ascending a hill at right angles; the number of houses in the town, in 1831, was 84. The principal seats in the parish are Rookwood, the handsome residence of E. Kelly, Esq.; Castle Kelly, the seat of D. H. Kelly, Esq., originally built as a castle in the 14th century, and of which the modern portion is castellated and part of the ancient structure still remains; Fortwilliam, the seats of N. J. Ffrench, Esq.; Curramore, of Christopher Balfe, Esq.; and Thornfield, of J. Mahon, Esq. Near the river are some large insulated mills. Fairs are held on July 11th and Sept. 24th. The living is a vicarage, with the vicarages of Fuerty and Kilbegnet episcopally united in 1809, in the diocese of Elphin, and in the patronage of the Bishop: the rectory is impropriate in the Incorporated Society for Protestant Charter Schools, by deed of request from Lord Ranelagh. The tithes amount to £226. 3. 1., of which £90. 9. 2½. is payable to the impropriator, and the remainder to the vicar: the gross amount of tithes in the union payable to the incumbent is £288. There are two churches in the union: that of Athleague, formerly a domestic chapel of the family of Lystre, is an old building in bad repair. The glebe-house was built by a gift of £400 and a loan of £214 from the late Board of First Fruits, in 1815: the glebe annexed to it comprises 23 acres, besides 20 acres in the parish of Fuerty. The R. C. parish is co-extensive with that of the Established Church: the chapel is situated in the town, and is in bad repair. The parochial school is supported by subscription; and there are several hedge schools, on the books of which are 290 boys and 130 girls. Between Castle Kelly and Rookwood is a rath, in which stood an abbey of Grey friars, where Maylesa O'Hanayn, abbot of Roscommon, died in 1266: and near it was a cell in which, according to tradition, four bishops were interred. In 1819, some labourers digging for gravel under a bog that had been cut away, on the estate of Castle Kelly, found a gold fibula weighing 17½ oz., now in the possession of the Very Rev. H. R. Dawson, Dean of St. Patrick's, Dublin. A chalybeate spring issues from the hill of Mount-Mary.

Seal.

ATHLONE, a borough, market and post-town, and an important military station, partly in the barony of Brawney, county of Westmeath, and province of Leinster, and partly in the barony of Athlone, county of Roscommon, and province of Connaught, 12 miles (N. E. by E.) from Ballinasloe, 15¼ (S. E. by S.) from Roscommon, and 59½ (W.) from Dublin; containing 11,406 inhabitants. This place derives its name from the words *Ath Luain*, signifying in the Irish language "the ford of the moon," of which, previously to the introduction of Christianity, the ancient inhabitants were worshippers; or, according to some, from *Ath-Luan*, in reference to the rapids at the bridge over the Shannon. After the erection of a town at this ford it obtained the name of *Bail-ath-Luain*, or "the town of the ford of the moon," by which, now contracted into *Blahluin*, it is generally called by the Irish inhabitants of the neighbourhood. The town is situated on the river Shannon, by which it is divided into two parts, and on the great western road from Dublin to Galway through Ballinasloe. An abbey for Cistertian monks, dedicated to St. Peter, was founded, according to Ware, in 1216, on the western or Connaught side of the Shannon, to which in that year King John gave certain lands in exchange for the site on which was erected the Castle of Athlone, besides one-tenth part of the expenses of the castle, which afterwards become one of the principal military stations in the country. The castle was progressively increased in strength, and so important was it regarded by the English monarchs, that when Hen. III. granted the dominion of Ireland to his son Prince Edward, this town was expressly reserved with other principal cities; and when the same monarch granted the whole of Connaught to Richard de Burgo, he retained for himself five cantreds contiguous to the castle. In this reign another monastery was founded on the eastern side of the Shannon, by Cathal Croibh-Dearg O'Connor, Prince of Connaught, and completed by Sir Henry Dillon, who was interred in it in 1244. In the reign of Elizabeth this place was greatly improved, the fortifications were strengthened, and the castle was for some time occupied by the Earl of Essex. The castle became the seat of the presidency of Connaught, and when the insurrection broke out in 1641, it was occupied by Viscount Ranelagh, then lord-president, with the usual ward of a royal castle. Independently of its several defences, the town was strong in itself, being built of stone; and the inhabitants having given assurances of their determination to defend it against all enemies, the president entrusted it entirely to their custody; but in a few weeks they secretly formed a design of enabling the insurgents to seize the president and his family, and to surprise the castle. For this purpose they admitted Sir James Dillon's forces within the walls on the night of Saturday, in the hope of surprising Lord Ranelagh on his way to church in the English town on the following day; but by some mistake in the appointed signal the design miscarried. The Irish forces laid close siege to the castle for twenty-two weeks, when it was relieved by some troops sent from Dublin by the Duke of Ormonde, who strengthened the garrison; but with this reinforcement the president effected nothing more than an unimportant defeat of the Connaught men near Ballintobber. During the president's absence on this expedition, the insurgents of Westmeath under Sir James Dillon attacked the English town in such numbers that the garrison were compelled to abandon the walls, but they defended the houses till Captain St. George, making a sally from the castle, compelled the assailants to withdraw. By occupying the pass of Ballykeran, however, Dillon's forces cut off all communication with the metropolis, and reduced the town to a state of extreme distress for want of supplies, which an entire troop had to cut its way through his forces to Dublin to solicit. At length, all hope of assistance being extinct, the president negotiated with the enemy for a safe conduct for his wife and family to Trim, which was honourably granted; and so forcibly did Lady Ranelagh, at Dublin, urge the necessities of the deserted English in this town, that a convoy was sent to bring the inhabitants away. This convoy, which consisted of 1100 foot and a few horse, summoned from the garrisons around Dublin, under the command of Sir Richard Grenville, arrived at Athlone in the latter part of February, 1642, and found the English there so much reduced in numbers as scarcely to muster more than 450 men, and many of these so wasted by famine and disease as to be unable to march. They fought their way home through the pass of Rochonell, and the custody of the castle was assumed by Viscount Dillon of Costelloe. After the victories obtained by Cromwell, the castle was taken on a second attack by Sir Charles Coote for the parliament; and during the fury of the war the town was burned; though restored, it never recovered its former strength or appearance; and in the reign of Charles II. the eastern portion of it was destroyed by an accidental fire.

During the war of the Revolution, the town was held for James II. by Col. Richard Grace, an experienced officer, and a garrison, consisting of three regiments of foot, with nine troops of dragoons and two troops of horse in and around it. Immediately after the battle of the Boyne, Lieutenant-General Douglas was sent by William III. to assault the town. Colonel Grace, doubtful of his ability to defend the whole, burnt the eastern portion of it, and breaking down some of the arches of the bridge, fortified himself in the other part; and Douglas, after battering the castle for eight days without success, withdrew his forces in the middle of the night. Towards the midsummer of 1691, the main body of William's army was led to the assault by De Ginkell, who first made himself master of the eastern portion of the town, of which, after the retreat of Douglas, the Irish had taken possession, and had fortified it with additional works. From the 20th till the 30th of June, a destructive cannonade was kept up across the river by both parties from batteries successively erected; during this period, after expending 12,000 cannon balls, many tons of stone shot, 600 shells, and more than 50 tons of powder, De Ginkell destroyed not only the castle but every house on the Roscommon side of the river. New works, however, were constantly thrown up by the garrison, assisted by the Irish army under St. Ruth, which had encamped at a short distance for the especial defence of the bridge, the passage of which was perseveringly contested with frequent destructive losses to William's army. On the last day of the siege a council of war was held, when it was resolved to storm the town, and the ringing of the bell of St. Mary's church was appointed as a signal for crossing the river. This was accordingly effected the same evening by the army in three divisions, and such was the simultaneous velocity of their movements, that after half an hour's sanguinary conflict the assailants became masters of the town, which was immediately evacuated by the garrison. A detachment, which had been sent by St. Ruth to oppose them, was repulsed by the victorious army, who turned the guns of the garrison against them; and St. Ruth, on their taking possession of the place, decamped with his forces to Aughrim, fifteen miles distant. During this siege the loss of the defenders amounted to 1200; and their brave commander, Col. Grace, who had been chamberlain to James II., while Duke of York, and one of his most faithful adherents, was killed in the action. The English, on taking possession of the town, immediately directed their attention to its restoration and to the repair of its fortifications and works; and it soon became one of the principal military depôts for arms, stores, and ammunition. On the 27th of October, 1697, the castle was, during one of the severest storms ever known here, struck by the electric fluid, which set fire to the magazine, in which were 260 barrels of gunpowder, 10,000 hand grenades charged, and a great quantity of match and other combustible stores, the whole of which exploded with so violent a concussion that all the houses in the town, except a few cottages without the gates, were shattered or destroyed: the loss of life, however, was comparatively small, only 7 persons being killed and 36 wounded.

The town, though at present the largest on the Shannon next to Limerick, still retains much of its character as a military station. On the Leinster side, one of the principal entrances near the river is through a gateway in one of the old square towers; and the ancient walls, though in a great measure concealed by buildings, extend for a considerable distance in that direction. On the Connaught side there are scarcely any traces of the walls or gates; but in this quarter are situated all the present military defences of the place. These consist principally of the castle, which forms a *tête du pont*, and of advanced forts and redoubts on the outside of the town to defend the main approaches along the great road from Galway by Ballinasloe, the most important line of communication with that part of the country which is most exposed to invasion. A short canal on this side of the river enables boats navigating the Shannon to avoid the rapids at the bridge of Athlone, and adds materially to the strength of the works: it is crossed by three bridges, one of which is falling into decay, and of which two are defended by palisades, those of the third having been taken down to facilitate the passing of the mail coaches. The bogs along the river are a sufficient protection to the town on the south side. The oldest of the works is a tower of decagonal form, which, from the massive structure of the walls, was probably the keep of the ancient castle, though having a new exterior; it is situated on a lofty mound supported on the side next the river by a stupendous wall, but overlooked on the opposite side by the houses in the upper part of the town. The platform on which this tower, now used as a barrack, is situated, is bounded on the side next the lower town by dwellings for the officers, and walls of imposing appearance; and on the others by modern works mounted with cannon, commanding not only the approach on the Connaught side of the river but also the bridge itself; and the strong circular towers at irregular intervals, with the carefully fortified entrance, give to the whole place a very formidable appearance. To the north of the castle are the barracks, calculated for the accommodation of 267 artillery, 592 infantry, and 187 horses; a pontoon establishment is also attached, and there are two magazines, an extensive ordnance depôt, and an hospital. The buildings occupy an elevated situation on the banks of the river, and comprise an area of about 15 statute acres, including spacious squares for exercise; besides the barracks for the men, there are within the enclosure detached houses for the officers of the different departments, store-houses, and an armoury. The armoury, a detached building, usually contains 15,000 stand of arms, including the muskets of eight regiments of militia of the central counties; and the hospital is situated on the high ground a short distance from the river, and is calculated for the reception of 96 patients. This place is the head-quarters of the western district, and the residence of the major-general and staff of the district. The town is divided into two nearly equal portions by the river Shannon, over which is a bridge erected in the reign of Elizabeth, which, though 100 yards in length, is only twelve feet wide; the passage, therefore, is often attended with difficulty, and on market-days and at the fairs with danger; it is further obstructed by the traffick of three flour-mills, one at each end and the other on the bridge; the narrowness of the arches, which are ten in number, and the width of the piers between them, prevent the free course of the water, and in time of floods cause an inundation on the shores of Lough Ree. On the south side are various sculptured tablets inserted in a wall, about nine feet broad, rising above the parapet and surmounted by a pediment ornamented with mouldings; their various inscriptions afford a curious history of its erection. It is in contemplation to build a new bridge by a loan from Government, which, on the recommendation of the Shannon Navigation Committee, it is expected, will be granted for the improvement of that river from Lough Allen to Limerick. The total number of houses within the limits of the town is 1027, of which 546 are slated and the remainder thatched; they are built chiefly of limestone, though bricks of excellent quality are made in great quantities a little below the town. A regatta is annually held on Lough Ree in August, and continues for four days; and races take place occasionally at Ballykeran. About a mile and a half from Athlone, on the Leinster side of the Shannon, is Moydrum Castle, the handsome residence of Viscount Castlemaine, a solid castellated mansion with square turrets at each angle, beautifully situated on the edge of a small lake, and surrounded by an extensive and richly wooded demesne. The other gentlemen's seats near the town, and also on the same side of the river, are the Cottage, the seat of W. Cooke, Esq.; the Retreat, of F. E. Moony, Esq.; the moorings, of Capt. James Caulfield, R. N; Spring Park, of P. Cusack, Esq.; Lissevolan, of H. Malone, Esq.; Auburn, of W. F. Bruce, Esq.; Bonahenley, of S. Longworth, Esq.; and Creggan Castle, the property of F. Longworth, Esq. On the Connaught side are Shamrock Lodge, the seat of J. Robinson, Esq.; and Handsfield, of A. Robinson, Esq. At Burnbrook are some corn-mills with a good residence, belonging to E. Burne, Esq.

The manufacture of felt hats was formerly carried on here to a great extent, but only a few are now made for the supply of the immediate neighbourhood. There are two extensive distilleries, each producing from 40,000 to 50,000 gallons of whiskey annually; two tanneries, two soap and candle manufactories, two public breweries on a large scale, and several corn-mills. The amount of excise duties collected within the district, in 1835, was £37,927. 3. 10. A communication by steam-boat between this place and Limerick has been lately established, and passage boats meet the steamers at Shannon harbour and proceed to Dublin by the grand canal. The market is held on Tuesday and Saturday, of which the latter is the principal, when sheep, swine, and great quantities of grain are exposed for sale: it is held in an open space under the wall supporting the castle mound, but the principal meat market is at the shambles near the river, and is abundantly supplied with provisions of all kinds; fish is procured in the lake and the river Shannon, and salt-water fish is brought from Galway. The fairs, to which is attached a court of pie poudre, are on the Monday after Epiphany, March 10th, Holy Thursday, and Aug. 24th, each by the charters ordained to last three days. A branch of the Provincial Bank of Ireland has been established here for the last eight years; and there is a constabulary police station.

The town was incorporated by charter dated Dec. 16th, 4th of Jas. I. (1606), which was seized by Jas. II. on a judgment of forfeiture obtained in the court of exchequer, and a new charter was granted in the 3rd of that monarch's reign; but the judgment being subsequently declared void, the former has since been and still is the governing charter, and the latter has not been acted upon since the accession of Wm. III. Other charters confirming and extending the privileges of the corporation were granted on the 16th of Jas. I. and 17th of Chas. II.; and the "New Rules" made by the lord-lieutenant and privy council, in the 25th of Chas. II., provided that the appointment of the sovereign, recorder, and town-clerk should be subject to their approval. The style of the corporation is "The Sovereign, Bailiffs, Burgesses, and Freemen of the Town of Athlone;" and the officers are a sovereign, two bailiffs, thirteen burgesses (including the constable of the castle, Viscount Castlemaine), a recorder, town-clerk, serjeant-at-mace, and billet-master; and there is a select body called the common council. The sovereign is elected by the common council from among the burgesses, annually on the 29th of June, and has the privilege of appointing a vice-sovereign with the approbation of the bailiffs and a majority of the burgesses; the bailiffs are elected from the freemen by the common council, on the same day as the sovereign, and are *ex officio* members of the council; the burgesses are elected for life from among the freemen, and the freemen also for life, by the common council, of which body, according to the practice of the corporation, twelve must be present to constitute an election; the recorder and town-clerk (who is also deputy-recorder) are appointed by the common council; and the serjeant-at-mace and billet-master, of whom the former acts as constable in the borough, are appointed by the sovereign. The common council are unlimited in number, but usually consist of not more than twenty persons, including the sovereign and vice-sovereign and two bailiffs; they hold their office for life, and vacancies are filled up by themselves from among the burgesses and freemen. The borough sent two representatives to the Irish parliament prior to the Union, since which period it has sent one to the imperial parliament. The right of election was formerly vested in the burgesses and freemen, amounting, in April 1831, to 71; but by the act of the 2nd of Wm. IV., cap. 88, the non-resident freemen, except within seven miles, have been disfranchised, and the privilege has been extended to the £10 householders. The limits of the borough comprehend under the charter a circle of a mile and a half radius from the centre of the bridge, but, as regards electoral purposes, were diminished by the late enactments and now include only the town and a very small surrounding district, comprising 485 statute acres; they are minutely described in the Appendix. The number of voters registered at the last general election amounted to 274, of whom 179 polled: the sovereign is the returning officer. The sovereign or vice-sovereign and the recorder are justices of the peace within the borough, having exclusive jurisdiction under the charter; the sovereign is also coroner, escheator, and clerk of the market. The civil court of the borough, which has jurisdiction in pleas not exceeding £5 late currency, was held under the sovereign every third Thursday, but has been discontinued for more than fourteen years. The sovereign, or his deputy, sits thrice a week to hear complaints on matters arising within the borough. Quarter sessions for the Athlone division of the county of Roscommon are held here in March and October, and at Roscommon in June and December. The portion of the borough on the Westmeath side of the river is in the Moat division of that county, where the quarter sessions are held regularly four times a year. Petty sessions for the adjacent rural districts are held within the limits of the borough on both sides of the river, on alternate Saturdays, at which the county magistrates respectively preside. By letters patent in the 27th of Chas. II. the half-quarter of land of Athlone, otherwise Beallagh, with the manor, castle, &c., was granted to Richard, Lord Ranelagh, with power to hold courts leet and baron, which courts are not now held; but the seneschal of the manor of Twyford, who holds his courts at Moat, claims jurisdiction over that part of the borough which is in the county of Westmeath. The court-house, or Tholsel, was built in 1703: it was partly occupied as a guard-room, and partly for holding the sovereign's court, but has been taken down. There is a borough prison, to which, from its unfitness, offenders are only committed for a few hours prior to their removal; and within the corporation district is a prison belonging to the county of Roscommon, to which the sovereign commits offenders.

The town comprises the parishes of St. Peter and St. Mary, the former in the western and the latter in the eastern portion. The living of St. Peter's is a perpetual curacy, in the diocese of Elphin, and in the patronage of the Bishop. The church, which is situated on the site of the ancient monastery of St. Peter, was built in 1804, by aid of a gift of £500, and a loan of £300, from the late Board of First Fruits, and has been recently repaired by a grant of £344 from the Ecclesiastical Commissioners. The glebe-house was built at the same time by a loan of £312 and a gift of £100 from the same Board; the glebe comprises six acres, in three lots near the church. The living of St. Mary's is a rectory and vicarage, in the diocese of Meath, and in the patronage of the Bishop; the tithes amount to £304. 12. 3½. The rectory was granted by Chas. I., in 1636, to Richard Linguard, together with a portion of the tithes of the parish of Ratoath, in the county of Meath, for the augmentation of the vicarage, which was then stated to be worth only £40 per annum; these tithes now amount to £100. The church was rebuilt in 1826, by a grant of £2300 from the late Board of First Fruits: it is a neat edifice, with a square embattled tower; the tower of the old church is still standing, and contains the bell which gave the signal for William's army to cross the river at the siege of Athlone. The glebe-house was built in 1812, by a gift of £100 and a loan of £500 from the late Board of First Fruits, and has been lately enlarged and beautified, the incumbent having received permission from the bishop to expend £600 upon it, to be repaid to him or his heirs; the glebe comprises eight acres. In the R. C. divisions the parish of St. Peter is united with that of Drum, and contains three chapels, besides a small religious house of the Augustinian order, now falling into decay; and the R. C. parish of St. Mary is co-extensive with that of the Established Church, but in the diocese of Ardagh, and contains a spacious chapel, erected in 1794, and also a chapel attached to a religious house of the Franciscan order, rebuilt in 1825. There are places of worship for Baptists and Wesleyan and Primitive Methodists.

"The Ranelagh school" was founded pursuant to a grant, in 1708, by Richard, Lord Ranelagh, of the castle, manor, town, and lands of Athlone, with the customs, &c., belonging thereto, together with the lands of Clonarke, stated to contain 427 acres, and of Gortnanghan or Gortecorson, containing 43 acres, in trust for the erection, contingent on the death of his daughter, Lady Catherine Jones, without issue, of two schools at Athlone for 20 boys and 20 girls, and two at Roscommon, with chapels attached; and also for the payment of £20 per annum to the minister of Athlone. Lady Jones dying without issue in 1740, the estates were, about 20 years after, vested by act in the Incorporated Society for promoting charter schools; and a school for the maintenance, instruction, clothing, and apprenticing of boys was founded in the parish of St. Peter. The number of boys was limited to 40, with each of whom, on being apprenticed, a premium of £10 was paid; but from a considerable diminution of the income the school has been for some years declining, and there are now not more than 15 boys, with whom only £7 is paid as an apprentice fee. In the same parish also are a school for boys, another for girls, and a Sunday school. St. Mary's has also a parochial school for boys and girls, and a Sunday school. The abbey school, for the sons of Roman Catholics, is aided by subscriptions; and there is a school for boys and girls aided by a grant of £10 and a premium of £2 per ann. from the Baptist Society. The number of children on the books of these schools, excepting the Sunday schools, is 371, of whom 218 are boys and 153 girls; and in the different private pay schools about 550 children are taught. There is a dispensary in the parish of St. Peter, and another in that of St. Mary. Robert Sherwood bequeathed the interest of £50 to the poor; and William Handcock, Esq., ancestor of Lord Castlemaine, by deed in 1705, gave lands now producing a rental of £46. 2. 3. per annum, to be distributed by his representatives among the poor of both parishes on the recommendation of the ministers and churchwardens; he also bequeathed £20 per annum for the support of a schoolmaster, who must have taken the degree of A. B. The sum of £8 late currency, called the Dodwell grant, is annually distributed among a number of poor women; and £13 per annum, paid by a Mr. Evans, of Dublin, to the rector, is divided among old men. At Courson, about a mile from Athlone, in the parish of St. Mary, are some small vestiges of an ancient castle formerly belonging to the O'Briens; on opening the ground near the ruins, a gold chain was found some years since. At Cloonakilla, in the parish of St. Peter, are the remains of an old chapel; and at Cloonow, on the banks of the Shannon, about three miles below the town, is a more considerable ruin with a cemetery attached. There are numerous chalybeate springs in the neighbourhood. Athlone gave the title of Viscount to the Earl of Ranelagh, and at present gives that of Earl to the family of De Ginkell.

ATHLUMNEY, a parish, in the barony of SKREEN, county of MEATH, and province of LEINSTER, ¼ of a mile (S. by E.) from Navan; containing 1148 inhabitants. This parish is situated on the river Boyne, by which it is separated from the parish of Navan, and over which are two bridges of stone; it is intersected by the roads leading respectively from Navan and Trim to Drogheda, and is skirted on the south by the mail coach road from Dublin to Enniskillen. An old castle, situated on the right bank of the river, was formerly the property of the Dowdell family, by whom it was destroyed, to prevent its falling into the hands of Cromwell. The remains consist of an extensive and irregular pile of building of an oblong form, with two projecting square towers apparently of more ancient foundation than the remainder, which, with its gabled windows, appears to be in the Elizabethan style. The parish comprises 2398 statute acres, as applotted under the tithe act. The land is of excellent quality and mostly under tillage; and limestone abounds and is quarried to a considerable extent. Athlumney, the seat of P. Ponsonby Metge, Esq., is beautifully situated on the banks of the Boyne, commanding some pleasing views, and the demesne is well planted and tastefully embellished. There are extensive flour and oatmeal-mills on the river, and a flax-mill in which upon the average 260 men are employed. The Boyne navigation from Navan to Drogheda passes through the parish. The living is a vicarage, in the diocese of Meath, and in the patronage of P. P. Metge, Esq., in whom the rectory is impropriate; the tithes amount to £270, of which £180 is payable to the impropriator, and £90 to the vicar. The church is in ruins, and there is neither glebe-house nor glebe: divine service is performed by the vicar, every Sunday evening, in a private house. In the R. C. divisions this parish is the head of a union or district, called Johnstown, comprising the parishes of Athlumney, Kilcarn, Follistown, Gerrardstown and Staffordstown, and containing two chapels, situated at Johnstown and Walterstown; the chapel at Johnstown is a very old edifice, and it is in contemplation to rebuild it. There are two schools; one at Johnstown of 79 boys and 59 girls, and the other in Mr. Blundell's factory, towards the support of which that gentleman gives £18 per annum.

ATHNASSEY, or ATHENEASY, a parish, in the barony of COSTLEA, county of LIMERICK, and province of MUNSTER, 3 miles (E. N. E.) from Kilmallock; containing 549 inhabitants. It is situated on the road from Kilmallock to Hospital, and comprises 2799 statute acres, as applotted under the tithe act. The land is good; about one-half is under tillage, and the remainder is meadow, chiefly attached to dairy farms, except a small tract of very valuable bog, which is rapidly diminishing. Nearly in the centre of the parish is Martinstown, the residence of M. Walsh, Esq. The parish is in the diocese of Limerick, and is a rectory forming part of the union of Kilmallock belonging to the Dean and Chapter of Limerick; the tithes amount to £225. 1*l*. 2½., forming part of the economy fund of the cathedral; the glebe comprises 27 acres of profitable land. In the R. C. divisions it is the head of a union or district, also called Ballinvana, comprising the parishes of Athnassey, Bulgadine, Emly-Grenan, Kilbreedy-Major, and Ballinvana; the chapel, built in 1834, is near the verge of the Red bog. The only school is a pay school of about 15 boys and 12 girls. Some fragments of the old church are still remaining in the burial-ground attached to it: it is supposed to have been founded in the 7th century, and was dedicated to St. Athanasius, from which circumstance probably the parish may have derived its name. There are several traces of ancient military works within the parish, and several military weapons of rude workmanship have been found; also the ruins of a small religious house called Adam's Church, and fragments of castles or buildings at Fauntstown, Gormanstown, and Stephenson, near the first of which are a ruined chapel and a celebrated holy well.

ATHNETT.—See ANHID.

ATHNOWEN (ST. MARY), or OVENS, a parish, partly in the barony of BARRETTS, but chiefly in that of EAST MUSKERRY, county of CORK, and province of MUNSTER, 1½ mile (W.) from Ballincollig; containing 1953 inhabitants. This parish, which is generally called Ovens, is situated on the south line of road from Cork to Macroom, and is bounded on the north by the river Lee, and intersected by the Bride. It comprises 4660 statute acres, as applotted under the tithe act, and valued at £7594 per annum: the soil in the northern or hilly part is rather poor and stony, but in the vales extremely rich, lying on a substratum of limestone forming part of the great limestone district extending to Castlemore on the west, and to Blackrock on the east. The limestone is quarried to some extent for burning into lime for the supply of the hilly districts to the north and south for a a distance of several miles. The principal seats are Grange, the residence of J. Hawkes, Esq., which occupies the site of Grange abbey (said to have been founded by St. Cera, who died in 679), and includes part of the ancient walls; Sirmount, of G. Hawkes, Esq., which occupies an elevated site commanding an extensive prospect over a highly interesting and richly cultivated tract of country; Spring Mount, of S. McCarthy, Esq.; Clashenure, of Kyrle Allen, Esq.; and the glebe-house, of the Rev. W. Harvey. There are two boulting-mills on the river Bride; one at Killumney belonging to Mr. D. Donovan, jun.; and the other at Ovens, belonging to Messrs. R. Donovan and Sons. The petty sessions for the district are held every alternate week at Carroghally. The living is a rectory and vicarage, in the diocese of Cork, united by diocesan authority, in 1785, to the prebend of Kilnaglory in the cathedral church of St. Finbarr, Cork: the tithes amount to £425. The church is a neat ancient structure, with a square tower crowned with pinnacles. There is a glebe-house, with a glebe of 20*a*. 2*r*. 17*p*. In the R. C. divisions this parish is the head of a union or district called Ovens, which includes also the parishes of Desertmore and Aglish, and the ploughlands of Millane and Killumney, in the parish of St. Finbarr, Cork: the chapel, erected in 1835, is a handsome edifice of hewn limestone, in the mixed Gothic and Grecian styles of architecture. The male and female parochial schools are supported principally at the expense of the rector. There is also a national school, in which are 140 children, under the patronage of the Roman Catholic clergy, for which a spacious school-room has been built near the chapel. A dispensary has been established for the relief of sick poor. Near the bridge of Ovens over the river Bride is the entrance to the celebrated limestone caves, which Smith, in his history of Cork, describes as 18 feet in height; but from the accumulation of rubbish they are now not more than three feet high, and are nearly filled with water. They branch off into several ramifications, and from the roofs of some of them depend stalactites of various forms: their dimensions have never been satisfactorily ascertained. There are some remains of the ancient castle, called Castle Inchy.

Seal.

ATHY, an incorporated market and post-town, in the barony of WEST NARRAGH and RHEBAN, county of KILDARE, and province of LEINSTER, 17¾ miles (S. W. by S.) from Naas, and 32 (S. W.) from Dublin; containing 4494 inhabitants. This place derives its name from an ancient ford called *Athelehac*, or anciently *Athlegar*, the "ford towards the west," which led from the territory of Leix to that of Calleagh or Caellan, and near which a great battle was fought between the people of Munster and those of Leix, under Lavisegh Cean Mordha, in the 3rd century. Donough O'Brien and his forces crossed the river Barrow at this ford, on their retreat from the battle of Clontarf. The town appears to have originated in the foundation of two monasteries, soon after the English invasion; one on the west bank of the Barrow, by Richard de St. Michael, Lord of Rheban, in 1253, for Crouched friars; and the other on the east bank, by the families of Boisle or Boyle and Hogan, some time in the 13th century, for Dominican or Preaching friars. It was frequently exposed to the assaults of the neighbouring septs, especially of the O'Kellys, whose territories, then called Caellan, are included in the modern county of Kildare. In 1308 the town was burnt by the Irish, and in 1315 was plundered by the Scots under Robert Bruce, who gained the battle of Ardscull, in which were killed, on the side of the English, Raymond le Gros and Sir William Prendergast, and on the side of the Scots, Sir Fergus Andressan and Sir Walter Murray, all of whom were buried in the Dominican monastery. In 1422, the Lord Justice of Ireland, considering Athy, from its situation on the Irish frontier, to be one of the keys of the Marches of Kildare, and necessary to be maintained for the defence of those parts, placed it in the custody of a military governor; and about the year 1506, a castle was built on the eastern side of the river, by Gerald, eighth Earl of Kildare for the protection of the town, which being enlarged in 1575, by one of the family of White, has since obtained the name of White's Castle, and in 1648 was held by the Irish under O'Nial, but was taken in 1650 by the parliamentary forces under Cols. Hewson and Reynolds.

The town is pleasantly situated on the river Barrow, and on the mail coach road from Dublin, through Cashel, to Cork; and the surrounding country is remarkably open and healthy. In 1831 it comprised 733 houses, and consists chiefly of one long street divided into two parts by the river, over which is a neat stone bridge of five arches, built in 1796. On the east side of the bridge the road from Monastereven to Carlow intersects the main street at right angles, forming, on the Carlow side, a neat square called the Market-square. The only trade is in corn, of which a very considerable quantity is sold in the market, for the supply of some extensive mills on the Barrow, and of the Dublin market, the proportion destined for which is sent thither by the Grand Canal in boats and barges; there is also a daily fly-boat, for the conveyance of passengers to the metropolis. Its situation in the midst of an exhaustless turbary, affording fuel at a low price, is advantageous for the establishment of manufactures; and its facility of communication by water with Dublin and other parts of the kingdom admirably adapts it for carrying on an extensive inland trade. The market is on Tuesday and Saturday, and, in addition to an ample supply of corn, is well furnished with meat, poultry, butter, and other provisions. Fairs are held on the 25th of April and July, under patent granted August 17th, 1756, by Geo. II.; also on March 17th, June 9th, Oct. 10th, and Dec. 11th, for cattle, sheep, and pigs. There is a chief station of the constabulary police, also a barrack capable of accommodating a troop of cavalry.

The inhabitants were incorporated in 1613, at the instance of Sir Robert Digby, Knt., by a charter, in which the corporation is entitled "the Sovereign, Bailiffs, Free Burgesses, and Commonalty of the Borough of Athy." The officers of the corporation are a sovereign (who is a justice of the peace), 2 bailiffs, 12 free burgesses, a recorder, and several inferior officers. The sovereign and bailiffs are elected annually, on June 24th, by the sovereign, bailiffs, and burgesses, out of the body of burgesses, and are sworn into office on Sept. 29th; the burgesses are elected for life, out of the body of the freemen; the latter, in recent instances, have been nominated by the sovereign. The governing body consists of the sovereign, bailiffs, and burgesses: the recorder, treasurer, and inferior officers are appointed either by the sovereign or the governing body. The borough returned to the Irish parliament two members until the Union, when, of the £15,000 awarded as compensation for the abolition of the elective franchise, £13,800 was paid to the Duke of Leinster, as proprietor of the borough, and £1200 to Lord Ennismore. A court of record was held here until 1827, for determining pleas to any amount arising within the borough and its liberties, which extend half a mile in every direction from White's Tower. A curl court, for the recovery of debts under 40*s*., late currency, is held on the 1st Monday in every month, at which the sovereign presides. The summer assizes for the county, and the Epiphany and Midsummer quarter sessions for the division, and also a weekly petty session on Tuesday, are held in the court-house, which is a neat and commodious building in the market-square. A court, called a "presenting court," is held annually in the month of October, to make presentments for the ensuing year; and a market jury of 12 persons is also chosen as inspectors of the markets, weights, and measures. The county gaol is situated outside the town, on the road to Carlow: it was completed in 1830, at an expense of £6000, of which £2000 was given by the Duke of Leinster, in addition to the site, and the remainder was paid by the county; it is a well-arranged building on the radiating principle, the governor's house being in the centre, and comprises 6 airing-yards, 6 day-rooms, 2 work-rooms, and 32 sleeping and 3 solitary cells, with a matron's room, 2 hospitals, and a chapel.

The town comprises the greater part of the parishes of St. John and St. Michael, which, together with the rural parishes of Ardrie and Churchtown, constitute the vicarage of St. Nicholas, or Nicholastown, united by act of council, in 1804, to the rectory and vicarage of Tankardstown, in the diocese of Dublin, and in the alternate patronage of the Crown and the Archbishop; the tithes of the several parishes amount to £544. 2. 6. The church of the union, a plain edifice, is in the parish of St. Michael; and a new church is about to be built on a site given by the Duke of Leinster. The glebe contains seven acres. In the R. C. divisions this town is the head of a union or district, comprising the same parishes as the Protestant union, together with that of Kilberry, and containing two chapels, one in St. Michael's and the other at Tankardstown; the former is a spacious and handsome edifice, built in 1796, principally by a donation from the late Maurice Keating, Esq., of Narraghmore, on an acre of land given by the Duke of Leinster, who also contributed towards its erection. There are places of worship for Calvinists and Wesleyan Methodists. The parochial school, in which 120 children are instructed, is held in a room behind the court-house. Contiguous to the R. C. chapel are two large school-rooms, one for 400 boys, built in 1826 by voluntary subscription, aided by a donation of £100 from the Duke of Leinster, who also gave the site and erected a convenient residence for the parish priest, at a nominal rent; the other, capable of containing 100 girls, was built by a donation from the late Mrs. Dooley. Here is a dispensary; and a charitable association for relieving the aged and distressed, without regard to religious distinctions, is maintained by subscriptions, aided by annual donations of £50 from the Duke of Leinster, £30 from the Rev. F. S. Trench, and £5 from Lord Downes. There are several remains of antiquity; but of the ancient monasteries little is left besides a gateway on the Carlow road, which, when seen in connection with the plantations intervening between it and the river, forms a picturesque and interesting feature in the landscape. Near the entrance from the Dublin road is a modern building occupied by two Dominican friars, with a small domestic chapel, near which is the ancient burial-ground of St. Michael's. The remains of White's castle, which is situated close to the bridge, consist only of a massive square and embattled tower, now used as the police barrack. On the western bank of the river stand the remains of Woodstock castle: the date of its erection is unknown, but it is supposed to have been built, about 1290, by a descendant of the Earl of Pembroke, or more probably at a later period by Thomas Fitzgerald, seventh Earl of Kildare, who, on marrying Dorothea, daughter of Anthony O'Moore, of Leix, in 1424, received the manors of Woodstock and Rheban as her dower. The walls are very thick and in moderately good preservation, and the mullioned windows are much admired for the elegance of their execution; a fine arched gateway and part of the outer court yet remain. The castle was taken from the insurgents, in 1642, by the Marquess of Ormonde, who made it a halting-place for his troops; and, in 1647, Owen Roe O'Nial surprised it and put the garrison to the sword, but Lord Inchiquin compelled him soon afterwards to surrender both it and Athy. Rheban castle is on the west bank of the Barrow, above two miles from the town. In the 2nd century, Rheban was one of the inland towns, and is found in Ptolemy's map. The castle was built, or greatly enlarged, in the 13th century, by Richard de St. Michael, when it and an adjoining district named Dunamase were erected into a barony, of which he was created baron. The first English settlers strengthened and repaired this castle, as also the opposite one of Kilberry. Its name was formerly *Raiba* or *Righban*, "the habitation of the King," and though now in ruins, its massive walls, mullioned windows, and imposing position, show that it was intended to awe the surrounding country. In 1325, Rheban, Dunamase, and all their dependencies, were taken by O'Moore, whose descendant, Anthony O'Moore, gave it in dower to the Earl of Kildare, through whom it has descended to the Dukes of Leinster. About three miles from the town, on the Dublin road, and in a most commanding position, is a rude but very extensive ancient fortification constructed entirely of earth raised so high as to command all the adjacent country: it is called the Moat of Ardscull, and if not raised on the occasion of the battle, was probably the scene of it; it was enclosed and planted about ten years since by the Duke of Leinster, and is a conspicuous landmark.

ATTANAGH, a parish, partly in the barony of Upper Ossory, Queen's county, but chiefly in that of Fassadining, county of Kilkenny, and province of Leinster, 1¾ mile (E. S. E.) from Durrow; containing 750 inhabitants. This parish, formerly called *Rathanna* and *Attier*, is situated on the river Nore, and comprises 2445 statute acres, as applotted under the tithe act. The living is a rectory and vicarage, in the diocese of Ossory; the rectory is united to that of Aharney, and in the patronage of the Crown; the vicarage is united by act of council to the vicarage of Aharney and the rectories of Kilmenan and Rossconnell, in the patronage of the Bishop. The tithes amount to £138. 9. 2¾., of which £92. 6. 1¾. is payable to the rector, and the remainder to the vicar; and the gross tithes payable to the vicar amount to £362. 11. 3½. The tithes of the rectorial union amount to £318. 19. 5¾. The church, a plain neat edifice, was erected by aid of a loan of £850 from the late Board of First Fruits, in 1821. The glebe-house is situated on a glebe of 40 acres, on which also the church is built, and there is another glebe of 100 acres in Rossconnell. In the R. C. divisions this parish is one of the nine denominations that form the union or district of Ballyragget. The parochial school, in which are 25 children, is supported by the rector and vicar; and there is a private pay school.

ATTYMASS, a parish, in the barony of Gallen, county of Mayo, and province of Connaught, 3½ miles (N.) from Foxford; containing 3276 inhabitants. This parish is bounded on the south by the river Moy, and on the east by the Ox mountains. The lands are chiefly under tillage, but the system of agriculture is not in a very improved state; there are large tracts of waste land, which are chiefly irreclaimable bog and mountain. Freestone abounds, but limestone is rather scarce, being found only in some parts of the parish. The surface is interspersed with several lakes, which being surrounded with mountains have a beautifully picturesque appearance. Fairs are held at Bonnefinglass on May 24th, July 7th, Nov. 15th, and Dec. 15th. The living is a vicarage, in the diocese of Killala, and forms part of the union of Ardagh; the rectory is impropriate in Sir W. H. Palmer, Bart. The tithes amount to £180. 7. 6., which is equally divided between the impropriator and the vicar. The R. C. parish is co-extensive with that of the Established Church; the chapel is a neat slated building. There are three hedge schools, in which are about 150 boys and 100 girls. On the edge of a lake at Kildermot is a picturesque ruin of an ancient convent.

AUBURN, a village, in the parish and barony of KILKENNY WEST, county of WESTMEATH, and province of LEINSTER, 5½ miles (N. E.) from Athlone: the population is returned with the parish. It is a very small place, but is celebrated as being the spot from which, from real life, Oliver Goldsmith drew his enchanting description of rural scenery in the "Deserted Village:" the house in which the poet resided is now in ruins; and the hawthorn tree, round which a wall was built to preserve it, has been carried away piecemeal as relics. Near the village is Lissoy, which is described in his tale of the "Vicar of Wakefield" as "the modest mansion," in which it is known he gave an accurate picture of his sister, and brother-in-law, Daniel Hodson, Esq., who resided there.—See KILKENNY WEST.

AUGHA.—See AGHA.

AUGHACREW.—See AGHACREW.

AUGHADOWN, or AGHADOWN, a parish, in the East Division of the barony of WEST CARBERY, county of CORK, and province of MUNSTER, 3¼ miles (W. S. W.) from Skibbereen; containing, with several inhabited islands, 5419 inhabitants. This parish is situated on the north bank of the river Ilen, and comprises 7063 statute acres, as applotted under the tithe act, and valued at £5400 per annum. Its surface is very uneven; in some parts, especially towards the north, it is rocky and unproductive; but near its southern boundary, towards the Ilen, the land is good and produces excellent crops. About two-thirds of it are under cultivation; the remainder is rocky ground and bog, of which latter there is a considerable extent near Newcourt. The state of agriculture is not much improved; the old heavy wooden plough is still used, and some of the land is cultivated by spade labour; the fences are everywhere much neglected. Several good roads intersect the parish, one of which is a new line from Skibbereen to Crookhaven, likely to be of considerable advantage. The Ilen is navigable for vessels of 200 tons' burden nearly to its eastern extremity: a quay and storehouses have been constructed at Newcourt, but are entirely neglected, and the harbour is only frequented by a few sand boats, which discharge their cargoes there for the convenience of the farmers. The principal seats are Aughadown House, that of H. Becher, Esq., occupying an elevated site in the midst of flourishing plantations, and commanding a fine view of the western coast; Lake Marsh, of Hugh Lawton, Esq.; Whitehall, of S. Townsend, Esq.; Newcourt, of Becher Fleming, Esq.; the glebe-house, the residence of the Rev. T. D. Moore; and Holly Hill, of the Rev. J. Coppinger, P.P. Fairs for the sale of cattle, sheep, pigs, &c., are held on May 6th and Oct. 2nd. A manor court is held monthly by a seneschal appointed by Lord Carbery, for the recovery of debts under 40*s.*; and here is a constabulary police station. The living is a vicarage, in the diocese of Ross, and in the patronage of the Bishop; the rectory is partly impropriate in Lord Audley and partly forms the corps of the archdeaconry of Ross. The tithes amount to £600, of which £300 is payable to the impropriator and appropriator, and £300 to the vicar. The church, situated on the margin of the river, is a small neat edifice with a square tower, and was built by aid of a loan of £500, in 1812, from the late Board of First Fruits. The glebe-house is handsome and commodious, and is situated on a glebe of 45½ acres. In the R. C. divisions this parish is the head of a union or district, which comprises also the parish of Kilcoe and part of Abbeystrowry, and contains two chapels, situated at Aughadown and Kilcoe, the former of which is a large and handsome edifice, occupying an elevated site near Currabeg. In addition to the parochial schools, there are schools at Whitehall and near Newcourt, also a pay school. In the demesne of Whitehall are the ruins of Kincoe or Kincolisky castle, built by the O'Driscols in 1495; and on the grounds of Lake View are some picturesque remains of an ecclesiastical edifice, called by the people of the neighbourhood the Abbey of Our Lady.

AUGHAGOWER, a parish, partly in the barony of MURRISK, but chiefly in that of BURRISHOOLE, county of MAYO, and province of CONNAUGHT, 4 miles (S. E. by S.) from Westport; containing 12,045 inhabitants. It is situated on the confines of the county of Galway, and on the road from Westport to Ballinrobe: the greater portion is mountain, about one-tenth only being under tillage; about 100 acres are woodland, and there are large tracts of bog. The system of agriculture is in a very rude and unimproved state, spade husbandry being still prevalent to a considerable extent. Lead mines have been opened in the mountains, which are the property of the Marquess of Sligo, but they are not worked at present; and there is a large quarry of slate of a very heavy quality, which is not now in operation. Mount Browne House, now the seat of J. Browne, Esq., was, during the disturbances of 1798, the seat of the Right Hon. Denis Browne, brother of the Marquess of Sligo, and was for some time in the possession of the insurgents. The linen manufacture is partially carried on, but is diminishing every year, and at present affords employment only to a small number of persons. Fairs are held on June 24th, July 21st, Aug. 6th, and Sept. 29th. The parish is in the diocese of Tuam; the rectory is appropriate to the archdeaconry, and also to the prebends of Faldown and Killabeggs in the cathedral of Tuam; the vicarage forms part of the union of Westport. The tithes amount to £450, of which £355 is payable to the vicar. The church, a modern edifice with a square tower, was erected at an expense of £1200. The R. C. parish is co-extensive with that of the Established Church: the chapel is a small thatched building, and there is also a chapel at Erriff of similar character, both inadequate to the accommodation of their respective congregations. There are six schools, situated respectively at Ayle, Ardygommon, Cushinkeel, Aughagower, Triangle, and Lanmore, in which about 700 children are taught; and there is also a hedge school at

Carranmore of 50 boys and 40 girls. The only antiquities are a round tower in the village, and the remains of an old castle at Doone. St. Patrick founded here the monastery of Achadfobhair, and placed St. Senach over it: it afterwards became the parish church.

AUGHALOO, or AUGHLOE, a parish, in the barony of DUNGANNON, county of TYRONE, and province of ULSTER; containing, with the post-town of Caledon, 10,140 inhabitants. This parish, which is the most easterly in the county, is bounded on the east by the river Blackwater, and is situated on the mail coach road from Armagh to Aughnacloy; it contains, according to the Ordnance survey, 19,583¾ statute acres, of which 140 are under water. The surface is pleasingly undulated and well planted and watered; the lands are in a high state of cultivation, the system of agriculture is greatly improved, and there is little waste land and only a small portion of bog. There are several gentlemen's seats, of which the principal are Caledon Hill, the seat of the Earl of Caledon; Crilly, of R. Pettigrew, Esq; Rahaghy, of N. Mayne, Esq.; and Drummond, or Cottage Hill, of H. Moore, Esq. It is in the diocese of Armagh, and is a rectory and vicarage, forming part of the corps of the archdeaconry of Armagh and the union of Carrenteel; the tithes amount to £609. 4. 7. The church is situated in the town of Caledon. A perpetual curacy was founded here in 1807, by the archdeacon, who endowed it with £50 per annum and 26½ acres of glebe; it has also an augmentation from Primate Boulter's fund, and is in the gift of the Archdeacon. In the R. C. divisions this parish is the head of a union or district, comprising the parishes of Aughaloo and Carrenteel; the chapel is at Caledon. There are three places of worship for Presbyterians, at Minterburn, Crillig, and Caledon, the last in connection with the Seceding Synod and of the second class: there is also an Independent meeting-house, but no regular service is performed in it. The parochial school is at Caledon; there are male and female schools at Ramakit, Curlough, Minterburn, and Dyan, built and chiefly supported by the Earl of Caledon; a school near the demesne was built and is supported by the Countess of Caledon, in which 40 girls are clothed and educated; and a school at Rahaghy is under the National Board. These schools afford instruction to about 580 boys and 370 girls; and there are also five private schools, in which are about 100 boys and 150 girls, and 14 Sunday schools. Close to a stream that separates the union of Carrenteel from the parish of Errigal-Kerogue is a sulphuric spring, resembling in its properties the Harrogate waters, but wanting their purgative quality: it has been enclosed in a small house erected over it by an individual who had received benefit from the use of the water. At Glenarb are the remains of a monastery with a burial-ground, and numerous stone crosses have been discovered.—See CALEDON.

AUGHAMACART, or AGHAMACART, a parish, in the barony of UPPER OSSORY, QUEEN'S county, and province of LEINSTER, 4½ miles (W. S. W.) from Durrow; containing 2222 inhabitants. This place is situated on the confines of the county of Kilkenny, and on the road from Durrow to Johnstown and from Dublin to Cork. A priory of Augustine canons was founded here in 550 by O'Dempsey, under the invocation of St. Tighernach, which soon afterwards became the burial-place of the Fitzpatricks, princes of Ossory, who were its patrons. In the 43rd of Elizabeth it was granted to the descendants of that family, then barons of Upper Ossory, who erected a castle at Culla Hill, which now forms a picturesque ruin: the principal remains are a lofty rectangular tower very much broken, and fragments of various outer walls surrounded by a moat. The parish comprises 9135 statute acres, as applotted under the tithe act: the lands are in general fertile and in a good state of cultivation; the system of agriculture is much improving; the waste land consists of mountain. The principal seats are Phillipsboro', the residence of Mrs. Phillips; Belmont, of J. Roe, Esq.; Edmundsbury, of Capt. Thompson; Old Town, of — Delany, Esq.; and Lodgefield, of Lodge Phillips, Esq. Fairs are held at Culla Hill on May 27th and Oct. 2nd, of which the latter is a large sheep fair. The living is a vicarage, in the diocese of Ossory, with the vicarages of Cahir and Killeen united episcopally and by act of council, and in the patronage of Ladies G. and F. Fitzpatrick, in whom the rectory is impropriate: the tithes of the union amount to £466. 13. 4., of which £300 is payable to the impropriators, and the remainder to the vicar. The church is old but in tolerable repair. There is no glebe-house; the glebe comprises 29*a.* 1*r.* 3*p.* In the R. C. divisions this parish forms part of the union or district of Durrow; the chapel is at Culla Hill. A Sunday school is supplied with books by the Sunday School Society of Dublin; and there are three pay schools, in which are about 100 boys and 86 girls. Of the ancient priory, only portions of the chapel walls and of the belfry remain, the latter having an arched doorway of good design. In the vicinity are the remains of an ancient castle, situated in the demesne of the La Touche family, at the foot of a hill on the margin of a spacious lake, and environed with woods; they consist of a large low round tower with walls of great thickness, surmounted with battlements and turrets, forming a picturesque object in the landscape.

AUGHANAGH, or AGHANAGH, a parish, in the barony of TIRAGHRILL, county of SLIGO, and province of CONNAUGHT, 5 miles (N. W.) from Boyle, on Lough Arrow, and on the road from Boyle to Sligo; containing 2393 inhabitants. It is bounded on the south by the Curlew mountains, and comprises 5412 statute acres, as applotted under the tithe act, with a considerable extent of mountain and bog. There are quarries of excellent limestone resembling marble, and much used for building. Hollybrook, the residence of J. Folliott, Esq., is beautifully situated on the shore of Lough Arrow; the grounds are well planted, and contribute in a pleasing manner to embellish the scenery of the lake. It is a vicarage, in the diocese of Elphin, forming part of the union of Boyle: the tithes amount to £110. 15. 4½., of which £62. 6. 1½. is payable to the impropriators, and £48. 9. 3. to the vicar. In the R. C. divisions it is included in the union or district of Riverstown: the chapel at Greyfort is a good slated building. At Currydora there is a school under the patronage of Wm. Phibbs, Esq.; and there is a private pay school in the parish. On the lands of Aughada are the remains of an abbey.

AUGHANUNCHON, or AGHANINSHON, a parish, in the barony of KILMACRENAN, county of DONEGAL, and province of ULSTER, 1½ mile (N. E.) from

Letterkenny; containing 1848 inhabitants. This parish, which is situated on Lough Swilly, and on the road from Letterkenny to Ramelton, comprises, according to the Ordnance survey, 4011½ statute acres, including 184¼ acres of tideway. The living is a rectory and vicarage, in the diocese of Raphoe, and in the patronage of the Bishop: the tithes amount to £147. The church is in a very dilapidated state. The glebe-house, a comfortable residence, was built in 1782, by aid of a gift of £100 from the late Board of First Fruits; the glebe comprises 300 acres. In the R. C. divisions it forms part of the union or district of Aughnish. The parochial school is supported by an endowment from Col. Robertson's fund, aided by the rector; and there are two other schools.

AUGHAVAL, or OUGHAVAL, a parish, in the barony of MURRISK, county of MAYO, and province of CONNAUGHT; containing, with the market and post-town of Westport, 13,921 inhabitants. This parish is situated on the bay of Westport, and on the road from Castlebar to Lewisburgh; it is partly bounded by the celebrated mountain of Croagh Patrick, and comprises 26,748 statute acres, as applotted under the tithe act, and valued at £7017 per annum. The land is chiefly under tillage; the system of agriculture is improving; there are large tracts of bog, which, lying on an inclined plane, might be easily reclaimed and rendered productive. Limestone of good quality abounds and is quarried for building, for mending the roads, and for burning into lime. Lead mines were formerly worked, but are now disused; and in the mountain of Sheffrey a copper mine was opened, but has long been discontinued. The principal seats are Westport House, the mansion of the Marquess of Sligo; Murrisk Abbey, of J. Garvine, Esq.; Trafalgar Lodge, of C. Higgins, Esq.; Marino, of J. Cuff, Esq.; Holdhead, of the Rev. F. L. Rutledge; and Boathaven, of the Rev. J. D'Arcy Sirr. Besides the market at Westport, fairs are also held there and at Murrisk. The living is a vicarage, in the diocese of Tuam, with the vicarages of Aughagower, Kilmaclasser, and Kilgavower united by act of council, constituting the union of Aughaval, otherwise Westport, in the patronage of the Archbishop; the rectory is appropriate to the archdeaconry of Tuam and prebend of Killabeggs. The tithes amount to £300, of which £225 is payable to the incumbent, and the remainder to the archdeacon and prebendary; and the tithes of the entire benefice amount to £884. 10. The church, an old building in the demesne of the Marquess of Sligo, was erected by aid of a gift of £500 from the late Board of First Fruits, in 1797, and was lately repaired by a grant of £166 from the Ecclesiastical Commissioners. The glebe-house was built by a gift of £300 and a loan of £500 from the same Board, in 1815; the glebe comprises seven acres. The R. C. parish is co-extensive with that of the Established Church: there are three chapels, one in Westport, which is spacious and ornamented with a handsome front; the other two are at Thornhill and Drummin, and are new slated buildings, but quite inadequate to the accommodation of their respective congregations. There are places of worship at Westport for Presbyterians and Wesleyan Methodists, the former in connection with the Synod of Ulster and of the third class. At Westport are four free schools and an infants' school, in which about 330 boys and 200 girls are taught; and there are also 17 private schools, in which are about 860 children. There are some remains of an ancient abbey at Murrisk, and in the parish are some chalybeate springs. A large patron is held annually at Murrisk on the 28th of August.—See WESTPORT.

AUGHAVEA, or AGHAVEAGH, a parish, in the barony of MAGHERASTEPHENA, county of FERMANAGH, and province of ULSTER, on the road from Lisnaskea to Five-mile-town; containing, with the post-town of Brookborough, 6281 inhabitants. It comprises, according to the Ordnance survey, 17,142 statute acres, of which 10,096 are applotted under the tithe act. About 17½ acres are water, and nearly one-fourth of the land is bog or mountain, the former affording good fuel, and the latter pasturage for cattle; there is no waste land but what may occur from neglect or from a bad system of cultivation. The greater portion of the land is under tillage, and the system of agriculture is improving. There are some excellent quarries of freestone, which is raised for building and for other uses. The principal seats are Nutfield, the residence of Lady Brook; Abbey Lodge, of J. Macartney, Esq.; Greenhill, of Major Irvine; Whitepark, of A. Bailey, Esq.; and Gola, of Major Dundas. The living is a rectory and vicarage, in the diocese of Clogher, and in the patronage of the Bishop; the tithes amount to £300; there are 14 townlands in the parish, the tithes of which are annexed to the old abbey of Lisdoune, in the possession of the Leonard family, and are not included in the applotment under the tithe act. The church is a plain edifice, erected by aid of a gift of £200 and a loan of £300 from the late Board of First Fruits, in 1813; and divine service is also performed every Sunday in the school-house at Brookborough. The glebe-house is a handsome modern building; the glebe comprises 43 acres. In the R. C. divisions the parish forms part of the union or district of Aughalurcher, and has a chapel. There is a place of worship for Wesleyan Methodists at Brookborough, where is the parochial school, supported under the patronage of Sir A. H. Brooke, Bart. There are also five other schools in the parish.—See BROOKBOROUGH.

AUGHAVILLER, or AGHAVILLER, a parish, in the barony of KNOCKTOPHER, county of KILKENNY, and province of LEINSTER, 3 miles (S. W.) from Knocktopher, on the road from Kilkenny to Carrick-on-Suir; containing 1887 inhabitants. The farm-houses, being well built and slated, present a neat and comfortable appearance; there is a good freestone quarry in the parish. Castle Morres, the splendid mansion of Harvey de Montmorency, Esq., occupies an elevated site, and has been recently much enlarged and improved. The estate confers the titles of Baron and Viscount Mountmorres in the peerage of Ireland, which are now held by a relation of the present proprietor. Three fairs, called "the fairs of Harvey," are held at Hugginstown. The parish is in the diocese of Ossory, and is a rectory and vicarage, forming part of the union of Knocktopher: the tithes amount to £200. In the R. C. divisions also it is included within the union of Knocktopher, or Ballyhale: it contains two chapels, situated respectively at Newmarket and Hugginstown; in the former is held a Sunday school. Near Castle Morres, within a few yards of the site of the old church, is the lower part of an ancient round tower of breccia, measuring 50 feet in circumference above the base.

AUGHER, a market-town (formerly a parliamentary borough), in the parish and barony of CLOGHER, county of TYRONE, and province of ULSTER, 2 miles (N. E. by E.) from Clogher, and 75¼ (N. N. W.) from Dublin; containing 726 inhabitants. Of the origin and early history of this place but very little is known. In the reign of Elizabeth, Lord-Deputy Mountjoy placed in it a powerful garrison to defend the pass through the valley in which it is situated, that retained possession for some time, constantly harassing the army of the Earl of Tyrone till his final surrender at Mellifont. From this place the queen's army marched when it crossed the mountains to give battle to the earl at Magheralowney, where that chieftain's principal magazine was taken, in June 1602. At the time of the English settlement of Ulster, by virtue of a decree by James I. in 1611, Sir Thomas Ridgway, Knt., Treasurer at War for Ireland, received, in 1613, a grant of 315 acres of land in the barony of Clogher, under an agreement that he should, within four years, settle on a parcel of land called Agher twenty Englishmen or Scots, chiefly artificers and tradesmen, to be incorporated as burgesses and made a body politic within the said four years; and should set apart convenient places for the site of the town, churchyard, market-place, and public school; he was likewise to assign to the burgesses houses and lands and 30 acres of commons. Sir Thomas received also, in 1611, the grant of a market and two fairs to be held here; and in 1613, the town and precincts, with the exception of a fort and bawn called Spur Royal castle, which had been erected, were created a borough. Besides the 315 acres of land on which he was to found the borough, Sir Thomas received a grant of 2000 acres called Portclare; and according to Pynnar's report in 1619, it appears that, besides the fort and bawn, he had built 16 houses of stone in the town, which were inhabited by English artificers who were burgesses, and had each two acres of land, and commons for their cattle. In 1630, Sir James Erskine, Knt., then proprietor of the manor, received a grant of two additional fairs. On the breaking out of the war in 1641, a garrison was stationed here by Col. Chichester and Sir Arthur Tyringham, and the castle was gallantly defended against the insurgent forces, who, in an attempt to take it by storm, were repulsed. This defeat so exasperated their leader, Sir Phelim O'Nial, that in revenge he ordered his agent, Mac Donnel, to massacre all the English Protestants in three adjacent parishes. Sir James Erskine dying without male issue, the extensive manor of Portclare, which in 1665 was confirmed in the family by Chas. II., under its present name of Favour Royal, was divided between his two daughters, who married into the families of Richardson and Moutray, and the respective portions are still in the possession of their descendants, of whom the present proprietor of Augher castle has assumed the additional surname and arms of Bunbury. The castle was finally dismantled by order of parliament, and continued in a state of dilapidation and neglect till 1832, when it was restored and a large and handsome mansion built adjoining it by Sir J. M. Richardson Bunbury, Bart. The ancient building consisted of a pentagonal tower surrounded by a wall 12 feet high and flanked by four circular towers: the wall has been removed, but one of the round towers has been restored; and the entrance gateway has also been removed and rebuilt on an elevated situation commanding some fine views, in which the remains of the old castle form an interesting object: the mansion is situated in a well-wooded demesne of 220 acres, and upon the margin of a beautiful lake.

The town is situated on the river Blackwater, over which is a bridge adjoining it, and in a fertile valley between two ridges of lofty mountains clothed with verdure to the summit, of which the highest, Knockmany, is covered on its south side with thriving plantations. It consists of one principal street, from which another branches at right angles on the south leading to Clogher; and has a penny post to Aughnacloy. Several new roads have been lately formed; and not far distant is an excellent bog. The lands in the neighbourhood are well cultivated. Besides Augher Castle, there are several gentlemen's seats near the town, described in the article on the parish of Clogher, *which see*. The market is on Monday, and has lately become a good market for oats; and fairs for the sale of cattle, sheep, pigs, and other commodities, are held on the last Monday in every month, in the market-place set apart under the original grant at the bottom of Clogher-street; the market-house is the only public building in the town. The collection of tolls and customs has been discontinued by the proprietors of the manor. Here is a chief station of the constabulary police.

The charter granted in 1613 incorporated the inhabitants under the style of "The Burgomaster, Free Burgesses, and Commonalty of the Borough of Agher," with the privilege of holding a civil court of record with jurisdiction to the extent of five marks, and of returning two members to the Irish parliament, which they continued to exercise till the Union, when the £15,000 compensation money for the abolition of its franchise was awarded to James, Marquess of Abercorn. Since that period no corporate officers have been appointed, and the town is now entirely within the jurisdiction of the county magistrates, who hold petty sessions irregularly. The seneschal of the manor holds a court here every third Monday, for the recovery of debts to the amount of 40*s*., the jurisdiction of which extends into the parishes of Errigal-Kerogue, Errigal-Trough, Ballygawley, and Clogher; and a manorial court leet is held once in the year. Divine service is performed in the market-house every Sunday by the officiating clergyman of Clogher. A school for boys was built on part of the Commons Hill, or Fair Green, granted by the proprietors of the manor to the deans of Clogher, in trust for a school-house, and with funds provided from the "Lord-Lieutenant's School Fund:" it is supported by private subscriptions and by a weekly payment of 1*d*. from each pupil; and a school for girls is supported in a similar manner.

AUGHNACLOY, a market and post-town, in the parish of CARRENTEEL, barony of DUNGANNON, county of TYRONE, and province of ULSTER, 16 miles (S. E.) from Omagh, and 75½ (N. N. W.) from Dublin; containing 1742 inhabitants. This place, which is on the confines of the county of Monaghan, is situated on the river Blackwater, and on the mail coach road from Dublin to Londonderry. The town was built by Acheson Moore, Esq., who also erected the parish church, and it is now the property of R. Montgomery Moore, Esq., his descendant: it consists of one principal street of considerable length, from which three smaller streets branch off, and contains 365 houses, of which the greater number are thatched buildings, although there are several good houses of brick roofed with slate, and in the immediate neighbourhood are several gentlemen's seats, which are described in the articles on their respective parishes. The market is on Wednesday, and is very well attended; and fairs for live stock are held on the first Wednesday in every month. There is a convenient market-house. A constabulary police station has been established here; and petty sessions are held every alternate Monday. The church, a spacious and handsome edifice, was erected in 1736. There are a R. C. chapel, and places of worship for Presbyterians in connection with the Synod of Ulster, and for Primitive and Wesleyan Methodists. The parochial school is supported by the archdeacon, and there are three other schools. At Garvey, one mile distant, is a very valuable mineral spring, which has been found efficacious in dyspeptic and cutaneous diseases; it is enclosed within a large building, and near it is a house affording excellent accommodation to those who frequent it for the benefit of their health. Dr. Thomas Campbell, author of Strictures on the History of Ireland, was a native of this place.

AUGHNAMULLEN, a parish, in the barony of Cremorne, county of Monaghan, and province of Ulster, 3 miles (S. by W.) from Ballibay, on the road to Dublin; containing 18,032 inhabitants. It comprises, according to the Ordnance survey, 30,710 statute acres (including 1643¼ under water), of which 26,468 are applotted under the tithe act and valued at £19,323 per annum: there are large tracts of mountain and bog. The mountain of Bunnanimma is an isolated mass about six miles in circumference, and its summit, which, according to the above survey, rises 886 feet above the level of the sea, is the highest point of land in the county: the waters flow from this mountain on the south-east to the sea at Dundalk, and on the west-north-west to Ballyshannon. On the south-east part of it is Lough Eagish, or Crieve Lough, partly supplied by springs and partly by rain water, which descends from the heights by which it is flanked on the east and west. A stream issuing from it presents by its rapid fall and constant supply, together with the abundance of fuel furnished by the bogs in the neighbourhood, such favourable sites for bleaching-mills that not less than fourteen mills are situated on its short course northward to Ballibay water, the tail race of one serving as the head of the next below it: the lake is under the care of an engineer, or waterman, to regulate the flow of water, so that a deficiency is seldom experienced even in the driest seasons. There are many other lakes in the parish, the principal of which are Lough Avean, Lough Chantinee, and Lough Ballytrain, besides several of smaller size. A battle is said to have been fought on an island in the lough opposite the glebe-house, where many large bridles and battle-axes have been found: this island comprises several acres of very excellent land, mostly in pasture. Of the entire extent of the parish, 25,008 acres are arable and pasture, and 1503 are bog and waste land. The soil is of an average quality, and the system of agriculture is capable of great improvement: flax of good quality is cultivated to a great extent, and wheat, oats, barley, and rye are also grown. There are very extensive bleach-greens at Crieve, near Ballibay, the property of Messrs. S. Cuningham and brothers; also similar establishments at Drumfaldra and Cremorne, respectively belonging to Messrs. Cuningham and Mr. Jackson; and at Chantinee, to Mr. Forbes. There are flax-mills at Crieve and Laragh, the latter, in which machinery for spinning has been recently erected, the property of Messrs. Davison, and, with a weaving factory and bleach-green, affording employment to more than 300 persons; a large corn-mill at Rea, and two others at Derrygooney, all well supplied with water from the lakes. Some slate quarries of an inferior description, and a lead mine, were formerly worked, but have been discontinued. The principal seats are Mountain Lodge, situated in a beautiful demesne, that of Lieut.-Col. Ker; Lough Bawn, of W. Tenison, Esq.; Chantinee, in the demesne of which are some fine waterfalls, of J. Tilly Forbes, Esq.; the glebe-house, the residence of the Rev. R. Loftus Tottenham; Cremorne Green, of J. Jackson, Esq.; Crieve House, of S. Cuningham, Esq.; Drumfaldre, of John Cuningham, Esq.; Carnaveagh, of Jos. Cuningham, Esq.; Derrygooney, of R. A. Minnitt, Esq.; Laragh, of A. Davison, Esq.; Bushford, of R. Thompson, Esq.; Corfada, of J. McCullagh, Esq.; and Milmore, of the late T. Brunker, Esq.

The living is a rectory and vicarage, in the diocese of Clogher, and in the patronage of the Bishop: the tithes amount to £900. The church is a plain neat edifice, with a tower surmounted by four turrets, and occupies a picturesque situation: a grant of £185 has been recently made by the Ecclesiastical Commissioners for its repair. Near Ballytrain is a chapel of ease, a very neat modern structure, for the eastern division of the parish. The glebe-house is handsome and commodious, and the glebe comprises 40 acres. In the R. C. divisions this parish is divided into two districts, east and west, having separate parochial clergy: there are five chapels, of which one at Luttin, to which is attached a burial-ground, was built in 1822, at an expense of £800; and another at Loughbawn, a spacious slated edifice, was built in 1833 at an expense of £1000. There are two places of worship for Presbyterians; one at Ballytrain, in connection with the Synod of Ulster, and of the third class; and the other at Crieve, in connection with the Seceding Synod, of the second class. There are four public schools, in which about 360 boys and 180 girls are taught; and there are fifteen hedge schools, in which are about 600 boys and 360 girls; and five Sunday schools. On the summit of a hill overlooking Lough Eagish, about 25 years since, an urn was found in a rude tomb covered with a stone which weighed about two tons, supposed to be the burial-place of some prince or chief. The townland of Cremorne gives the title of Baron to the family of Dawson, of Dawson's Grove, in this county.

AUGHNISH, a village, in a detached portion of the parish of Oughtmanna, barony of Burren, county of Clare, and province of Munster, 5 miles (N. W.) from Burren; containing 46 houses and 304 inhabitants. This village, like others on this part of the coast, is frequented during the summer for sea-bathing; it is situated on the bay of Galway and near Aughnish Point, a headland on the north side of the harbour of New Quay, projecting into the bay from the peninsula formed by the parish of Duras, in the county of Galway, and forming the northern extremity of the county of Clare. On this point is a martello tower, and there is also one on Finvarra Point, to the south-west, in another detached portion of the parish.

AUGHNISH, a parish, in the barony of KILMACRENAN, county of DONEGAL, and province of ULSTER, containing, with part of the post-town of Ramelton, 4937 inhabitants. This parish is situated on Lough Swilly, and on the road from Letterkenny to Rathmullen: it comprises, according to the Ordnance survey, 9194½ statute acres, of which 8146 are applotted under the tithe act, and valued at £3954 per annum. The land is principally arable and pasture, with a small quantity of bog; agriculture is improving, and the waste lands are being reclaimed. There are extensive bleach-greens and flour-mills belonging to Mr. Watts; and the parish is benefited by its vicinity to the river Lannon, which is navigable for vessels of 150 tons burden to Ramelton. Fairs are held on the Tuesday after May 20th and Dec. 11th, and on the 17th of July; and petty sessions are held every alternate Thursday at Ramelton. The gentlemen's seats are Fort Stewart, the residence of Sir J. Stewart, Bart., and Shellfield, of N. Stewart, Esq. The living is a rectory, in the diocese of Raphoe, united subsequently to the 15th of Jas. I. to the rectory of Tully or Tullaferne, together forming the union of Aughnish or Tullyaughnish, which is in the patronage of the Provost and Fellows of Trinity College, Dublin. The tithes amount to £509. 7. 4., and the entire tithes of the benefice to £1100. The church, which is at Ramelton, is a plain structure, rebuilt by aid of a gift of £200 and a loan of £800, in 1826, from the late Board of First Fruits, and a donation of £800 from the late Dr. Usher. The glebe-house, in the centre of the parish, one mile from the church, was built in 1828, at an expense of £6000, of which £1384. 12. was a loan from the same Board, and the remainder was either charged on the revenues of the living or contributed by the incumbent. The glebe lands in Aughnish consist of 389*a.* 3*r.*, and in Tullaferne, of 512*a.* 0*r.* 15*p.*, each portion valued at 10*s.* per acre. The R. C. parish is co-extensive with that of the Established Church, and is one of those held by the Bishop of Raphoe; the chapel is a spacious building. There is a place of worship for Presbyterians of the Synod of Ulster, of the first class, also for Seceders and Wesleyan Methodists. The parochial school is aided by Col. Robertson's fund; and there are four other public schools: about 200 boys and 250 girls are taught in these schools, besides which there are about 150 boys and 60 girls educated in private schools, and there is a Sunday school at Glenlary. A school-house is in course of erection by the Synod of Ulster. There are also a dispensary, a loan fund, a fund for supplying flax, and a Ladies' Society.—See RAMELTON.

AUGHOURE.—See FRESHFORD.

AUGHRIM, a post-town and parish, partly in the barony of CLONMACNOON, but chiefly in that of KILCONNELL, county of GALWAY, and province of CONNAUGHT, 29 miles (E.) from Galway, and 75½ miles (W. by S.) from Dublin; containing 2205 inhabitants, of which number, 587 are in the town. This place is celebrated for the memorable and decisive battle fought in its immediate vicinity on the 12th of July, 1691, between the forces of Wm. III., consisting of 18,000 men under the command of Gen. de Ginkell, and the Irish army of Jas. II., consisting of 25,000 men under General St. Ruth. Each general having taken up his position, of which that of St. Ruth, on Kilcommodon hill, was very strong, the action commenced at noon by a detachment from the English lines forcing, after a very sharp skirmish, the pass on the right of the Irish camp. About five o'clock the left wing of the English, both infantry and cavalry, advanced against the Irish; and after the engagement had continued more than an hour and a half with varied success, St. Ruth detached a considerable part of the cavalry of his left wing to the support of the right, which was severely pressed. Gen. Mackay, availing himself of this opportunity, and while the cavalry were forcing the pass of Aughrim castle, ordered several regiments of infantry to pass the bog and to wheel from the right to sustain them. Hurried on by their impetuosity, these regiments approached almost to the main body of the Irish army, and being encountered by the enemy's horse and foot were, after a severe conflict, partly driven back to the bog; but Gen. Talmash, who commanded the English cavalry of the left wing, assisted by Gens. Mackay and Rouvigny from the right, advancing to their support, bore down all opposition, and enabled the infantry of the centre to rally and repossess themselves of their former ground. St. Ruth, seeing that the result of the battle depended on his making a powerful impression on the English cavalry, advanced against them with a body of the Irish cavalry, but being killed by a cannon ball, his whole army was thrown into confusion and retreated with precipitation. The pursuit was continued for three miles with the greatest activity; and the Irish lost 7000 men slain and 450 taken prisoners, besides their cannon, ammunition, and baggage; while, on the side of the English, only 700 were killed and 1000 wounded. Gen. de Ginkell, after his victory, remained here for a few days to refresh his forces.

The town, which is situated on the road from Ballinasloe to Galway, and contains about 100 houses, was anciently called *Eachraim*, or *Aghrim O'Many*, and was the site of a priory of Canons Regular of the order of St. Augustine, said to have been founded in the 13th century and dedicated to St. Catherine, by Theobald, first Butler of Ireland; the establishment continued to flourish till the dissolution, when it was given to Richard, Earl of Clanrickarde. The market has fallen into disuse: fairs are held on June 21st and Oct. 14th. The October fair is noted for the number of turkeys which are sold, in general not less than 20,000; they are smaller than those of other parts of Ireland. A constabulary police force is stationed in the town. The Grand Canal comes up to Ballinasloe, within three miles of it.

The parish comprises 6700 statute acres, as applotted under the tithe act: about half a mile from the town, on the Ballinasloe road, there is an extensive bog. The gentlemen's seats are Aughrim Castle, the residence of R. Stanford, Esq.; Northbrook, of J. North, Esq.; Aughrim glebe, of the Rev. H. Martin; Eastwell, of J. Ussher, Esq.; Ballydonnellan, of A. Donnellan, Esq.; Castron, of Mrs. Lynch; Fahy, of Capt. Davys; Oatfield, of Major Lynch; Fairfield, of T. Wade, Esq.; Ballieghter, of P. Donnellan, Esq.; and Lissevahane, of F. K. Egan, Esq. The living is a vicarage, in the diocese of Clonfert, with part of the rectory united, and to which also the rectories and vicarages of Killaghton, Kilgerrill, and Killimore-daly were episcopally united in 1735, together constituting the union of Aughrim, which is in the patronage of the Bishop; the rectory is also partly appropriate to the see and partly to the deanery. The tithes amount to £147. 15. 9., of which £32. 8. 0¾. is payable to the Ecclesiastical Commissioners, £9. 4. 7½. to the dean, and £106. 3. 0¾. to the vicar; and the tithes for the whole benefice amount to £408. 9. 2½. The church is a neat edifice, erected by aid of a loan of £1500 from the late Board of First Fruits, in 1817. The glebe-house was built by aid of a gift of £400 and a loan of £340 from the same Board, in 1826: the glebe comprises 20*a.* 1*r.* 4*p.* In the R. C. divisions the parish forms part of the union or district of Kilconnell; the chapel here is a neat building. There are places of worship for Primitive and Wesleyan Methodists. The parochial school for boys and girls is aided by the vicar; and there are two other schools, in which about 120 children are educated. Some remains yet exist of the castle of Aughrim, which, about the time of the battle, was the residence of the family of O'Kelly. Swords, spear heads, and cannon balls, with numerous coins of Jas. II., are frequently dug up. Aughrim gives the title of Viscount to the family of De Ginkell, descendants of Gen. De Ginkell, on whom it was conferred by Wm. III., together with that of Earl of Athlone, March 4th, 1692, for his important services here and at Athlone, and to whom he subsequently granted all the forfeited estates of William Dongan, the attainted Earl of Limerick, comprising 26,480 acres of profitable land.

AUGHRIM, a parish, in the barony and county of ROSCOMMON, and province of CONNAUGHT, 3½ miles (S.) from Carrick-on-Shannon; containing 4537 inhabitants. This parish, anciently called *Tirebrine*, is situated on the road from Drumsna to Elphin, and on the river Shannon: it comprises, by the county books, 5535 statute acres, of which 5316 are applotted under the tithe act and are principally under tillage; there are about 130 acres of woodland, besides some small detached tracts of bog and several inferior lakes. There are quarries of excellent limestone for building. The principal seats are Rockville, the residence of W. Lloyd, Esq.; Lisadurn, of J. Balfe, Esq.; Rushhill, of J. Devenish, Esq.; and Cloonfad, of Martin Brown, Esq. Petty sessions are held here on alternate Thursdays; and there is a fair at Ardsallagh on the 21st of December. The living is a vicarage, with the rectory and vicarage of Cloonaff and the vicarage of Killumod episcopally united in 1811, in the diocese of Elphin; the rectory forms the corps of the prebend of Tirebrine in the cathedral church of Elphin; both are in the patronage of the Bishop. The tithes amount to £190, payable in moieties to the prebendary and the vicar; and the gross amount of tithes payable to the incumbent is £237. The church is a neat plain building with a small spire, erected in 1744, and has been lately repaired by a grant of £154 from the Ecclesiastical Commissioners. There is no glebe-house: the glebe comprises 18*a.* 2*r.* 25*p.*, and is subject to a rent of £15. The R. C. parish is co-extensive with that of the Established Church; the chapel is situated on the townland of Rodeen. There are three public schools, in which are 150 boys and 80 girls; and in various other hedge schools are about 270 boys and 130 girls. The ruins of the old church, in which some of the Earls of Roscommon were interred, yet exist. On the summit of a high hill on the estate of Rockville, which commands extensive views of the surrounding country, is a very large fort, containing in the middle a heap of stones, said to be the place of interment of some native chief.

B

BADONY (LOWER), a parish, in the barony of STRABANE, county of TYRONE, and province of ULSTER, 8 miles (N. N. E.) from Armagh; containing 7024 inhabitants. This place is situated on the Munterlowney Water, and is bounded on the north by the Spereen mountains, which are the highest in the county, and among which the mountain of Mullaghcairn rises to a very considerable height above the rest; its summit, according to the Ordnance survey, being 1778 feet above the level of the sea. The base of this mountain is a vast accumulation of sand and water-worn stones, rising to an elevation of 900 feet, and in it is an extraordinary fissure called Gortin Gap, through which the road from Omagh leads to the village of Gortin. The parish, according to the same survey, comprises 47,921¾ statute acres (including 178½ under water), of which the greater portion is mountain and bog, but the former affords good pasturage and the latter an abundance of fuel: the vale of Gortin is fertile and well cultivated. Through the range of mountains opposite to Mullaghcairn is a pass called Barnes Gap, in which various indications of copper ore have been discovered. In these mountains is Beltrim, the handsome residence of A. W. C. Hamilton, Esq., proprietor of the principal part of the parish; and in a large bog is the ancient fortress of Loughnacranagh, where the Earl of Tyrone sheltered himself from the British troops under Lord-Deputy Mountjoy, who despatched Sir Henry Dockwra from Omagh, in June 1602, to give battle to the Irish prince, whom he defeated. The inhabitants are principally employed in agriculture and in the breeding of cattle; and the weaving of linen cloth is carried on in several of the farm-houses. The living is a rectory, in the diocese of Derry, separated from Upper Badony by order of council in 1706, and in the patronage of the Bishop: the tithes amount to £750. The church, situated in the village of Gortin, is a small neat edifice with a campanile turret at the west end. There is neither glebe nor glebe-house at present, but a house is about to be built on a glebe of 30 acres of land granted for that purpose by Mr. Hamilton. The R. C. parish is co-extensive with that of the Established Church, and contains two chapels, one at Ruskey, the other at Greencastle. There is a place of worship for Presbyterians in connection with the Synod of Ulster. The parochial school is supported by the rector and Mr. Hamilton; and there is a school at Ruskey under the trustees of Erasmus Smith's charity, and others at Liscable, Winneyduff, Caronhustion, and Broughderg. These schools afford instruction to about 180 boys and 120 girls: there are also eleven private schools, in which are about 450 children; and eight Sunday schools.

BADONY (UPPER), a parish, in the barony of STRABANE, county of TYRONE, and province of ULSTER, 4 miles (N. N. E.) from Newtownstewart; containing

5715 inhabitants. A monastery for Franciscans of the third order was founded at Corrick about the year 1465; it continued to flourish till the dissolution, and in the reign of Jas. I. was given, with all its possessions, to Sir Henry Piers, who soon after sold it to Sir Arthur Chichester; it was subsequently granted to the Hamilton family, whose descendant is the present proprietor. There are some highly picturesque remains of this abbey, affording an idea of the original extent and elegance of the buildings. Here was also a strong castle or fortress, of which there are some remains. The district appears to have been distinguished at an early period as the scene of various important battles, and in the fastnesses of its mountains the lawless and daring found a secure asylum. In the reign of Elizabeth O'Nial was defeated here with the loss of all his baggage, plate, and treasures, and compelled to make his escape across the river Bann to his castle of Roe. The parish comprises, according to the Ordnance survey, 38,208¼ statute acres, including 150½ under water: nearly three-fourths are mountain and bog, and the remainder, with the exception of a small portion of woodland, is arable. The state of agriculture is progressively improving; extensive tracts of mountain have been recently enclosed and brought into cultivation, and great portions of bog and mountain may still be reclaimed. Part of the Sawel mountain is within its limits, and, according to the Ordnance survey, rises to an elevation of 2235 feet above the level of the sea. Most of the farmers and cottagers unite with agricultural pursuits the weaving of linen; and great numbers of cattle and horses are bred and pastured in the extensive mountain tracts. Fairs are held on the 16th of every month for the sale of cattle, horses, and pigs, and are in general numerously attended. A constabulary police force has been stationed here. A manorial court is held monthly, at which debts under £2 are recoverable; and a court of petty sessions is held every alternate week at Gortin.

This parish was formerly much more extensive than it is at present; an act of council was obtained, by which it was divided into the parishes of Upper and Lower Badony, and a church was soon afterwards built for the latter at Gortin. The living is a rectory, in the diocese of Derry, and in the patronage of the Bishop: the tithes amount to £396. 18. 6. The church is an ancient structure, in the early English style: for the repair of which a grant of £108 has been lately made by the Ecclesiastical Commissioners. The glebe-house, a handsome residence, was built in 1821, by aid of a loan of £225 from the late Board of First Fruits; the glebe comprises 195 acres, of which 86 are mountain. The R. C. parish is co-extensive with that of the Established Church; there are two chapels, of which one, near the foot of the mountain, is a spacious building. There are places of worship for Presbyterians of the Synod of Ulster and of the Seceding Synod; the minister of the former officiates also in the adjoining parish of Lower Badony. The parochial male and female school is aided by a small annual payment bequeathed by the late C. Hamilton, Esq., but is chiefly supported by the rector. There are two schools situated respectively at Castledamp and Clogherney; a school at Corrick, supported by — Gardiner, Esq.; a male and female school at Glenroan, built and supported by Major Humphreys; and a school at Plumb Bridge, supported by subscription: there are also four pay schools, and two Sunday schools.

BAGNALSTOWN, a post-town, in the parish of Dunleckney, barony of Idrone East, county of Carlow, and province of Leinster, 8 miles (S.) from Carlow, and 49 miles (S. S. W.) from Dublin; containing 1315 inhabitants. This town is beautifully situated on the river Barrow, and on one of the mail coach roads from Dublin to Kilkenny; it is a place of considerable trade, and is rapidly rising into importance; there are some extensive corn-mills. It has a patent for two fairs, and ten other fairs have been lately established by the proprietors. Quarter sessions are held here in Jan., April, July, and October. Petty sessions are held every Monday; and there is a manorial court, but no seneschal is at present appointed. Here is a station of the constabulary police. The court-house is a handsome building in the Grecian style, in front of which is a portico with four Doric pillars. There is also a large and handsome R. C. chapel, and a dispensary.

BAILIEBOROUGH, or MOYBOLOGUE, a market and post-town, and a parish, partly in the barony of Lower Kells, county of Meath, and province of Leinster, and partly in that of Castlerahan, but chiefly in that of Clonkee, county of Cavan, and province of Ulster, 11½ miles (N. W. by N.) from Kells, and 42¼ miles (N. W.) from Dublin; containing 10,480 inhabitants, of which number, 1085 are in the town. This town is situated on the road from Cootehill to Kells, and consists of only one street, containing 165 houses. The market is the largest in the county, and is on Monday. Fairs are held on Feb. 17th, May 17th, June 15th, Aug. 14th, Oct. 14th, and Nov. 17th. The Hilary and Midsummer general quarter sessions are held here: the court-house was enlarged and improved in 1834. The bridewell was built in that year, and contains five cells and two yards, with separate day-rooms and yards for female prisoners. A manorial court is held yearly; and here is a station of the constabulary police.

In the incumbent's title this parish is denominated Moybologue, otherwise Bailieborough: it was formed by act of council in 1778, by separating from the parish of Killan, now called Shercock, 29 townlands, including the town of Bailieborough, and uniting them to the parish of Moybologue. It comprises 17,152 statute acres, as applotted under the tithe act. The land is generally of good quality: that part of the parish which is in the county of Meath is cultivated for all kinds of grain. Several small bogs are scattered over its surface, which are diminishing in extent either by draining or digging for fuel. There are some quarries of an inferior kind of stone, chiefly used for building, and about a mile from the town is an extensive bleach-green, with a comfortable house and small demesne, the residence of W. Spear, Esq. Bailieborough Castle, the seat of Sir Wm. Young, Bart., is situated in a fine demesne, and occupies the site of an ancient fortress described in Pynnar's Survey, under the head of Tonregie, as a vaulted castle, with a bawn 90 feet square, and two flanking towers, attached to which were 1000 acres of land: this ancient castle remained standing till within a few years, when it was pulled down to make room for additions and improvements in the present house. Near the town also are Bexcourt, the seat of the Rev.

E. Mahaffy; and the glebe-house, the residence of the Rev. J. Gumley. The living is a united rectory and vicarage, in the diocese of Kilmore, and in the patronage of the Bishop. The tithes amount to £553. 1., of which £314. 1. is payable by the Moybologue portion of the parish, and £239 by the townlands added to it. The old church being a dilapidated building, a new one is in course of erection. The glebe-house was built by a gift of £100 and a loan of £900, in 1811, from the late Board of First Fruits; the glebe consists of two farms near the church, comprising 117 acres, and 43 acres of bog. In the R. C. divisions the parish is partly in the union or district of Killan or Shercock, and partly in that of Kilmainham and Tivorcher: the chapel of the former is situated in the town of Bailieborough; and that of the latter, which is in the county and diocese of Meath, at Tivorcher. There are two meeting-houses for Presbyterians; one in connection with the Synod of Ulster, of the third class; and the other in connection with the Seceding Synod, of the first class. The Wesleyan Methodists have also a place of worship, in which divine service is performed every alternate Sunday. The parochial school, at Lisnalea, is supported by the incumbent; and there are three other public schools, in which 180 boys and 110 girls are taught, and a school is in progress at Kellan. There are 13 private schools, in which are about 500 boys and 250 girls. A dispensary was established in 1822.

BALBRIGGAN, a sea-port, market, and post-town, and a chapelry, in the parish and barony of BALROTHERY, county of DUBLIN, and province of LEINSTER, 15 miles (N. by E.) from Dublin; containing 3016 inhabitants. According to Ware, a sanguinary conflict took place here on Whitsun-eve, 1329, between John de Bermingham, Earl of Louth, who had been elevated to the palatine dignity of that county, Richard, Lord De Malahide, and several of their kindred, in array against the partisans of the Verduns, Gernons, and Savages, who were opposed to the elevation of the earl to the palatinate of their county; and in which the former, with 60 of their English followers, were killed. After the battle of the Boyne, Wm. III. encamped at this place on the 3rd of July, 1690. The town, which is situated on the eastern coast and on the road from Dublin to the North of Ireland, owes its rise, from a small fishing village to a place of manufacturing and commercial importance, to the late Baron Hamilton, who, in 1780, introduced the cotton manufacture, for which he erected factories, and who may justly be regarded as its founder. It contains at present about 600 houses, many of which are well built; hot baths have been constructed for visiters who frequent this place during the bathing season. In the environs are several gentlemen's seats, of which the principal is Hampton Hall, the residence of G. A. Hamilton, Esq. The inhabitants are partly employed in the fishery, but principally in the cotton manufacture; there are two large factories, the machinery of which is worked by steam-engines and water-wheels of the aggregate power of 84 horses, giving motion to 7500 spindles, and spinning upon the average about 7400 lb. of cotton yarn per week. More than 300 persons are employed in these factories, to which are attached blue dye-works; and in the town and neighbourhood are 942 hand-looms employed in the weaving department. The principal articles made at present are checks, jeans, calicoes, and fustians. The town is also celebrated for the manufacture of the finest cotton stockings, which has been carried on successfully since its first establishment about 40 years since; there are 60 frames employed in this trade, and the average produce is about 60 dozen per week. There are on the quay a large corn store belonging to Messrs. Frost & Co., of Chester, and some extensive salt-works; and in the town is a tanyard. The fishery, since the withdrawing of the bounty, has very much diminished: there are at present only 10 wherries or small fishing boats belonging to the port. The town carries on a tolerably brisk coasting trade: in 1833, 134 coal vessels, of the aggregate burden of 11,566 tons, and 29 coasting vessels of 1795 tons, entered inwards, and 17 coasters of 1034 tons cleared outwards, from and to ports in Great Britain. The harbour is rendered safe for vessels of 150 tons' burden by an excellent pier, completed in 1763, principally by Baron Hamilton, aided by a parliamentary grant, and is a place of refuge for vessels of that burden at ¾ tide. A jetty or pier, 420 feet long from the N. W. part of the harbour, with a curve of 105 feet in a western direction, forming an inner harbour in which at high tide is 14 feet of water, and affording complete shelter from all winds, was commenced in 1826 and completed in 1829, at an expense of £2912. 7. 9., of which the late Fishery Board gave £1569, the Marquess of Lansdowne £100, and the remainder was subscribed by the late Rev. Geo. Hamilton, proprietor of the town. At the end of the old pier there is a lighthouse. The Drogheda or Grand Northern Trunk railway from Dublin, for which an act has been obtained, is intended to pass along the shore close to the town and to the east of the church. The market is on Monday, and is abundantly supplied with corn, of which great quantities are sent to Dublin and to Liverpool; and there is a market for provisions on Saturday. Fairs are held on the 29th of April and September, chiefly for cattle. A market-house was erected in 1811, partly by subscription and partly at the expense of the Hamilton family. The town is the head-quarters of the constabulary police force of the county; and near it is a martello tower with a coast-guard station, which is one of the nine stations within the district of Swords. Petty sessions for the north-east division of the county are held here every alternate Tuesday.

The chapelry of St. George, Balbriggan, was founded by the late Rev. G. Hamilton, of Hampton Hall, who in 1813 granted some land and settled an endowment, under the 11th and 12th of Geo. III., for the establishment of a perpetual curacy; and an augmentation of £25 per annum has been recently granted by the Ecclesiastical Commissioners from Primate Boulter's fund. In 1816 a chapel was completed, at an expense of £3018. 2. 2., of which £1400 was given by the late Board of First Fruits, £478. 15. 2. was raised by voluntary subscriptions of the inhabitants, and £1139. 7. was given by the founder and his family. This chapel, which was a handsome edifice with a square embattled tower, and contained monuments to the memory of R. Hamilton, Esq., and the Rev. G. Hamilton, was burned by accident in 1835, and the congregation assemble for divine service in a school-room till it shall be restored, for which purpose the Ecclesiastical Commissioners have lately granted £480. The living is in the patronage of G. A. Hamilton, Esq. There is a chapel belonging to the R. C. union or district of Balrothery and Balbriggan, also a place of worship for Wesleyan Methodists. The parochial school and a dispensary are in the town.—See BALROTHERY.

BALDOYLE, a parish, in the barony of COOLOCK, county of DUBLIN, and province of LEINSTER, 6 miles (N. E.) from Dublin; containing 1208 inhabitants, of which number, 1009 are in the village. The village is pleasantly situated on an inlet or creek of the Irish Sea, to the north of the low isthmus that connects Howth with the mainland: it comprises about 200 houses, and is much frequented in summer for sea-bathing. Some of the inhabitants are engaged in the fishery, which at the commencement of the present century employed nine wherries belonging to this place, averaging seven or eight men each; at present nearly 100 men are so engaged. Sir W. de Windsor, lord-justice of Ireland, held a parliament here in 1369. The creek is formed between the mainland and the long tract of sand on the north of Howth, at the point of which, near that port, a white buoy is placed; it is fit only for small craft. The manor was granted to the priory of All Saints, Dublin, by Diarmit, the son of Murchard, King of Leinster, who founded that house in 1166. The corporation of Dublin owns the entire parish, about two-thirds of which are arable: the system of agriculture is improving, and the general routine of crops is pursued with success. Donaghmede, the seat of Mrs. King; Talavera, of Capt. N. Furnace; and Grange Lodge, of W. Allen, Esq., are the principal seats. The village is a chief station of the constabulary police, and also a coast-guard station, forming one of the nine which constitute the district of Swords. The Drogheda or Grand Northern Trunk railway from Dublin to that town, for which an act has been obtained, is intended to pass through the grange of Baldoyle. The parish is in the diocese of Dublin, and is a curacy forming part of the union of Howth: it is tithe-free. In the R. C. divisions it is included in the union or district of Baldoyle and Howth, which comprises also the parishes of Kinsealy and Kilbarrack, and contains three chapels, situated respectively at Howth, Kinsealy, and Baldoyle, which last has been lately rebuilt by subscription, and has a portico of four Tuscan pillars surmounted by a pediment, above which rises a turret supporting a dome and cross: attached to the chapel are school-rooms, in which about 60 boys and 60 girls are taught. The parochial school-house is in the village, and there is also a hedge school in the parish, in which are 12 children. At the Grange are the picturesque ruins of the ancient church, surrounded by horse-chestnut, lime, and sycamore trees; and in the grounds of Donaghmede is a holy well, which is resorted to on St. John's eve by the peasantry.

BALDUNGAN, a parish, in the barony of BALROTHERY, county of DUBLIN, and province of LEINSTER, 14 miles (N. N. E.) from Dublin; containing 88 inhabitants. A strong fortress was erected here, in the 13th century, by the Barnewall family, which subsequently became the property of the Lords of Howth, and in the civil war of 1641 was defended for the parliament by Col. Fitzwilliam, but was ultimately surrendered to the royalists, by whom it was dismantled and a great portion of the building destroyed; the remains, which were very extensive, have, within the last few years, been almost wholly taken down by the tenant. Near its site are still some remains of a church, more than 80 feet in length, with a tower of ten sides, of durable materials and excellent workmanship. According to Archdall, here was a commandery of Knights Templars, dedicated to the Blessed Virgin, of which this was probably the church. The prevailing substratum of the parish is limestone; but the hill of Baldungan is chiefly composed of Lydian stone and flinty slate. The living is a rectory, in the diocese of Dublin, and in the patronage of the Earl of Howth: the tithes amount to £52. 4. The church is in ruins, and there is neither glebe-house nor glebe. In the R. C. divisions the parish forms part of the union or district of Skerries.

BALDWINSTOWN, a village, in the parish of GARRISTOWN, barony of BALROTHERY, county of DUBLIN, and province of LEINSTER, 4 miles (N. W.) from Ashbourne; containing 35 houses and 218 inhabitants.

BALEEK, or BELLEEK, a parish, partly in the baronies of UPPER and LOWER FEWS, and partly in that of LOWER ORIOR, county of ARMAGH, and province of ULSTER, 6 miles (S. E.) from Market-Hill; containing 3396 inhabitants, of which number, 129 are in the village. In the reign of Elizabeth an English garrison was stationed at this place; but it was besieged and taken by O'Donnell, of Tyrconnell, who put every individual to the sword. The village is situated on the road from Newry to Newtown-Hamilton, and contains about 20 houses. The parish was constituted in 1826, by the separation of twelve townlands, comprising 5509 statute acres, from the parish of Loughgilly, of which eight pay tithes to the perpetual curate, and four to the rector of Loughgilly. The living is a perpetual curacy, in the diocese of Armagh, and in the patronage of the Rector of Loughgilly: the tithes amount to £331. 3., of which £179. 3. is payable to the curate, and the remainder to the patron. The church, built in 1827, is a plain small edifice in the ancient style, with a lofty square tower. There is no glebe-house: the glebe comprises 20 acres in the townland of Lisnalee. In the R. C. divisions the parish is one of three forming the union or district of Loughgilly, and contains a chapel. There is a place of worship for Presbyterians. Two schools afford instruction to about 160 boys and 110 girls; and there are also two hedge schools, in which are about 50 children, and three Sunday schools.

BALFEIGHAN, a parish, in the barony of UPPER DEECE, county of MEATH, and province of LEINSTER, 1 mile (N.) from Kilcock; containing 155 inhabitants. It is situated on the road from Kilcock to Summerhill, and is one mile and a half in length and one mile in breadth. Piercetown, the residence of T. Cullen, Esq., is within its limits; and the Royal Canal runs through the southern verge of the parish. It is a rectory, in the diocese of Meath, and forms part of the union of Raddonstown: the tithes amount to £87. 13. 9½. In the R. C. divisions it is part of the district of Batterstown. There are some remains of the old church.

BALGREE, a hamlet, in the parish of KILSKYRE, barony of UPPER KELLS, county of MEATH, and province of LEINSTER; containing 12 houses and 77 inhabitants.

BALGRIFFIN.—See BELGRIFFIN.

BALLAGH, or BAL, a market-town and parish, in the barony of CLANMORRIS, county of MAYO, and province of CONNAUGHT, 6 miles (S. E. by E.) from Castlebar; containing 1586 inhabitants, of which number, 343 are in the town. This town is situated on the road from Castlebar to Claremorris, and is intersected by a small river, which has its source in the vicinity: it consists of one long street containing 75 houses, all of modern erection, and has a cheerful and pleasing appearance. The market is on Tuesday; and fairs are held on June 11th, Aug. 12th, Sept. 26th, and Oct. 15th, which are among the largest in the county for cattle and sheep; there are two smaller fairs on the 1st of May and 7th of October. A penny post has been established between this town and Ballyglass. Here is a constabulary police station; and petty sessions for the district are held every Tuesday in the court-house, a neat building of modern erection. The lands are partly under tillage and partly in pasture, and for fertility are thought equal, if not superior, to any in the county. Limestone abounds in the parish, and is quarried for building and agricultural purposes. Athevalla, the seat of the Rev. Sir F. Lynch Blosse, Bart., is a handsome mansion nearly adjoining the town; and Ballagh Lodge, the seat of H. Waldron, Esq., and Logatiorn, of W. M. Fitzmorris, Esq , are also in the parish. The living is a vicarage, in the diocese of Tuam, with the rectories and vicarages of Rosslee and Minola episcopally united, forming the union of Ballagh, in the patronage of the Bishop: the rectory constitutes the corps of the prebend of Ballagh in the cathedral church of St. Mary, Tuam: the tithes amount to £175, and the prebend is returned as of the value of £190 per annum; and the tithes of the whole, both rectorial and vicarial, amount to £395, which is received by the prebendary, who is also rector of the union. There is neither church, glebe-house, nor glebe. Divine service is occasionally performed in the court-house. In the R. C. divisions the parish is the head of a union or district, comprising also the parishes of Drum, Rosslee, and Minola, and containing two chapels, one in the town, a good slated building, and the other at Balcarra. A school-room has been erected, at an expense of £200, in which about 200 boys and 100 girls are instructed; and there are two hedge schools in the parish, in which are about 68 boys and 22 girls. St. Mochuo, or Cronan, who died in 637, founded a monastery here, of which he became the first abbot. This place is at present distinguished for the remains of an ancient round tower, which, though the upper part is wanting, is still about 50 feet high. Near it are the ruins of a small church, of the same kind of stone, and apparently of similar workmanship, in one of the walls of which is a monumental inscription of great antiquity. There are two small chapels, built on arches over the river that runs through the town, and great numbers of people resort thither annually to perform special devotions. A well, dedicated to the Blessed Virgin, with a small chapel attached, is attended by great numbers of the peasantry at patrons held on the 15th of August and 8th of September. About two miles from the town is Castle Derowil, and about three miles distant is Brieze Castle, both square buildings of the ordinary character.

BALLAGHADIREEN, a market and post-town, in the parish of KILCOLEMAN, barony of COSTELLO, county of MAYO, and province of CONNAUGHT, 12 miles (W.S.W.) from Boyle, and 97¾ miles (W. by N.) from Dublin; containing 1147 inhabitants. This town is situated on the new mail coach road from Ballina to Longford, and consists of three principal streets, containing about 200 houses, of which nearly all are neatly built and slated. Here are infantry barracks, adapted to the accommodation of 4 officers and 92 non-commissioned officers and privates. Many improvements have recently taken place in the town, which is rapidly rising into importance. The market is on Friday; and fairs are held on March 25th and 26th, May 1st, June 25th, Aug. 1st, Sept. 8th, Nov. 1st, and Dec. 22nd. The market-house is a commodious building; and a court-house has been erected, in which petty sessions are held every Tuesday. A chief constabulary police and coast-guard stations have been established here, and there is a R. C. chapel. Within a mile of the town are the ruins of Castlemore.—See KILCOLEMAN.

BALLAGHMEIHAN.—See ROSSINVER.

BALLAGHMOON, a parish, in the barony of KILKEA and MOONE, county of KILDARE, and province of LEINSTER, 3 miles (S. W. by S.) from Castledermot; containing 311 inhabitants. This parish is situated on the confines of the county of Carlow, and comprises 2042 statute acres, as applotted under the tithe act. It is a rectory and vicarage, in the diocese of Dublin, and forms part of the union of Castledermot: the tithes amount to £110. In the R. C. divisions also it forms part of the union or district of Castledermot.

BALLAGHTOBIN.—See BALLYTOBIN.

BALLEE, or BALLY, a parish, in the barony of LECALE, county of DOWN, and province of ULSTER, 3 miles (S. E. by E.) from Downpatrick, on the road to Ardglass; containing 2598 inhabitants. It formerly comprised, according to the Ordnance survey, 6427¾ statute acres, of which 6282 acres were applotted under the tithe act; but the townlands of Jordan's Crew and Kildare's Crew have been severed from it under the Church Temporalities Act, and united to the parish of Ardglass, and Ballystokes has been annexed to Saul, with their tithes and cure of souls; the tithes of Ballyhosit have been also appropriated to the incumbent of Ardglass, but the cure of souls remains to the rector of Ballee. It is wholly under cultivation; the land is very good, and there is neither waste land nor bog. Ballyhosit House, the residence of T. Gracy, Esq., is a large and handsome edifice; Ballee House is in the occupation of R. Stitt, Esq.; the glebe-house is commodious and well built, and there are many other good houses, principally occupied by wealthy farmers. Until lately it formed part of the corps of the deanery of Down, but the union was dissolved under the provisions of the Church Temporalities Act, which came into operation on the 1st of Nov., 1834, and after the preferment of the late dean, when a new arrangement was effected by act of council. The living is now an independent rectory, in the diocese of Down, and in the gift of the Crown. The entire tithes of the parish amounted to £598. 14. 3., of which, under the new arrangements, £340. 13. is payable to the rector of Ballee, subject to a deduction of £25. 3. appropriated to the economy fund of the cathedral; and of the remainder, £146 is payable to the dean, £97 to the rector of Ardglass, and £14 to the rector of Saul. The church is a large plain edifice without a tower, built on the foundations of a former structure in 1749. The glebe-house was built at an expense of £500, of which

£450 was a gift and £50 a loan from the late Board of First Fruits, in 1816; and there is a glebe of seven acres. In the R. C. divisions it is the head of a union or district, which also comprises the parish of Ballyculter, and contains three chapels, situated respectively at Ballycrottle, in Ballee, and at Strangford and Cargagh, in Ballyculter. There is a large meeting-house for Presbyterians in connection with the Remonstrant Synod, of the second class. The parochial school, in which 40 boys and 28 girls are taught, is supported conjointly by the rector and Hugh Johnson, Esq., of London, and there are two others. There are also four private schools, in which are 113 boys and 90 girls. J. Dunn, an eccentric itinerant dealer, by will in 1798, gave £100 in trust to A. Gracy, Esq., who purchased with it a chief-rent at Ballymote, in the parish of Downpatrick, which is divided annually between the Presbyterian poor of Down and Ballee. R. Glenny left £100, the interest to be equally divided among the poor Catholics, Protestants, and Presbyterians of the parish, but it is not now available; and Mrs. Kelly, of Loughkeland, by will in 1805, gave £100 in trust to Mr. Gracy, with which he purchased a house in Downpatrick, now let on lease at an annual rent of £10, which is distributed among the poor at Christmas. Near the mountain of Slieve-na-Gridel, which, according to the Ordnance survey, rises 414 feet above the level of the sea, is a remarkable druidical altar, the table stone of which is 11 feet long and 9 broad; and on the townland of Ballyalton is an ancient burial-ground, in which are some curiously inscribed stones. A splendid golden torques, richly ornamented and set with gems, was found near the glebe in 1834.

BALLEEN, a parish, in the barony of GALMOY, county of KILKENNY, and province of LEINSTER, 2 miles (W. N. W.) from Freshford: the population is returned with the parishes of Coolcashin and Sheffin. It comprises about 1409 statute acres, and is a vicarage, in the diocese of Ossory, forming part of the union of Freshford and prebend of Aghoure; the rectory is appropriate to the Dean and Chapter of St. Canice, Kilkenny. The tithes amount to £101. 7. 4., of which £67. 11. 6½. is payable to the appropriators, and £33. 15. 9½. to the vicar. In the R. C. divisions it is included in the union or district of Lisdowney. Here are the picturesque ruins of a castle, on a stone of which is inscribed the date 1455.

BALLIBAY, a market and post-town, and a parish, partly in the barony of MONAGHAN, but chiefly in that of CREMORNE, county of MONAGHAN, and province of ULSTER, 8 miles (S. by E.) from Monaghan, and 50 miles (N. W. by N.) from Dublin; containing 6685 inhabitants, of which number, 1947 are in the town. This place, which is situated at the intersection of the roads from Castle-Blayney to Cootehill and Clones, and from Carrickmacross to Monaghan, derives its name from a pass between the lakes at the southern extremity of the town. A battle was fought in the vicinity, at a place called Ballydian, between De Courcy, first Earl of Ulster, and the Mac Mahons and O'Carrols. Prior to the introduction of the linen manufacture the town was of very little importance; but since the establishment of its linen market about the middle of the last century, it has rapidly advanced, and now contains about 400 houses, many of which are respectable and comfortably built, and has become the principal mart for the inhabitants of the surrounding country. The manufacture of linen, of a texture from nine to fourteen hundreds, is extensively carried on throughout the parish. The market is on Saturday, and is amply supplied; great quantities of butter are sold, and from October to February inclusive not less than from 8000 to 12,000 stone of flax is sold weekly: there are also extensive markets for grain on Tuesday and Friday. Fairs are held on the third Saturday in every month, and are remarkable for large sales of horses, horned cattle, and pigs. A reading society was established in 1816, and is supported by a proprietary of annual subscribers; the library contains nearly 1000 volumes. Petty sessions are held in the market-house irregularly: and here is a constabulary police station.

The parish comprises, according to the Ordnance survey, 8741¼ statute acres, of which 181 are in the barony of Monaghan, and 8560¼ in that of Cremorne; 180 acres are under water. It was formed by act of council in 1796, by separating from the parishes of Tullycorbet and Aughnamullen several townlands, applotted under the tithe act and valued at £6957 per annum. Its surface is studded with lakes and boldly diversified with hills and dales. About four miles from the town is the mountain of Bunnanimma, at the base of which are bleach-greens and mills. The approach to the town opens upon an extremely beautiful and picturesque tract of country. To the east are seen, at the distance of 20 miles, the deep blue summits of the lofty Slievegullion, with the village, about a quarter of a mile beneath, apparently embosomed in hills and situated on the margin of a lake a mile in diameter, which forms its boundary on the east and south, and is itself bounded by a rich amphitheatre of woods. The soil is of a fair average quality, but agriculture is not in a very forward state: the growth of flax has been much encouraged, and large quantities of very good quality are raised. There is no waste land. Very extensive tracts of bog supply the inhabitants and the various works with abundance of fuel; so great is the quantity consumed that many of the manufacturers employ from 60 to 100 persons for three months every year to dig and prepare it. The draining of these bogs, and the numerous population around the works, have caused a great change in the climate of the Bunnanimma mountain, which formerly was liable to be enveloped in thick fogs for ten or twelve days successively; but now the drying of the turf is seldom interrupted for a single day. The mountain lands, though naturally very poor, have on this side been nearly reclaimed. The prevailing substratum is whinstone; slate also exists, and was formerly quarried for roofing; and there are extensive quarries of greenstone, called "Ribbil," of which the town is built. A lead mine was opened at Laragh, about half a mile from the town, but it has not been worked since 1826; it is very rich in ore, and from silver found in it has been manufactured some plate in the possession of Col. C. A, Leslie. About half a mile from the town is Ballibay House, the seat of that gentleman, on whose estate the town is built; it is a handsome and spacious mansion beautifully situated on the border of a lake, and backed by some extensive plantations. The other principal residences in the parish are Derry Valley, the seat of T. McCullagh, Esq.; Aghralane, of T. Lucas, Esq.; and Lake View, the residence of the Rev. Hercules Langrishe, the incumbent.

The living is a rectory and vicarage, in the diocese of Clogher, and in the patronage of the Bishop: the tithes amount to £383. 5. The church is a neat edifice occupying a romantic situation on an eminence rising abruptly from the lake; the east window is embellished with stained glass, and there are some tablets to the memory of the Leslie family. The glebe-house is a handsome residence, towards the erection of which the late Board of First Fruits gave £100: the glebe comprises 25 acres. In the R. C. divisions this parish forms part of the union or district of Tullycorbet: the chapel is situated at Ballintra, about a mile and a half from the town; and there is a small chapel of ease in the town, connected with the clergyman's residence. There are two places of worship for Presbyterians in connection with the Synod of Ulster; one of which, in the town, is a handsome building in the later English style, and is of the second class; the other is about a mile distant, and nearly adjoining it is a place of worship for Seceders. About 150 boys and 110 girls are taught in four public schools; and there are also six hedge schools, in which are about 140 boys and 70 girls; and two Sunday schools. A dispensary is open two days in the week for the gratuitous aid of the poor.

BALLIBOPHAY, a village, in the parish of STRANORLAR, barony of RAPHOE, county of DONEGAL, and province of ULSTER, 10½ miles (W. by S.) from Lifford, and 118 miles (N. W. by N.) from Dublin; containing 168 houses and 874 inhabitants. It is situated on the river Finn, and on the road from Donegal to Strabane, and consists principally of one street. A market for grain and provisions is held in a market-house every Thursday; and cattle fairs are held on May 21st and Dec. 20th. Here is a chief station of the constabulary police.—See STRANORLAR.

BALLICKMOYLER, a village, in the parish of KILLEBAN, barony of SLIEUMARGUE, QUEEN'S county, and province of LEINSTER, 5 miles (S. S. W.) from Athy, on the road from Maryborough to Carlow; containing 249 inhabitants. This place was, previously to the disturbances in 1798, rapidly increasing in extent and prosperity, and had obtained a patent for holding a weekly market; but during that calamitous period more than half of it was laid in ruins and its market abandoned. The village contains about 40 houses; and there are some gentlemen's seats in the vicinity, which are described in the article on the parish. Fairs are held on March 16th and Nov. 11th, and petty sessions every Wednesday. The village is the chief constabulary police station for the barony, and contains a dispensary.—See KILLEBAN.

BALLINA, a sea-port, market, and post-town, in the parish of KILMOREMOY, barony of TYRAWLEY, county of MAYO, and province of CONNAUGHT, 17¼ (N. N. E.) from Castlebar, and 125 miles (W. N. W.) from Dublin; containing 5510 inhabitants. This town, originally called *Belleek*, or the "Ford of the Flags," owes its origin to O'Hara, Lord Tyrawley, who built the first street, of which some houses are still remaining; and is indebted for the commencement of its commercial importance to the establishment of a cotton-factory here, in 1729, by that nobleman, who also obtained for the inhabitants the privilege of a weekly market and a fair. During the disturbances of 1798 the town was attacked by the French under Gen. Humbert, who, having landed on the 22nd of August in Kilcummin bay, and made themselves masters of that town, sent forward on the day following a detachment to assault this place, which on its approach to the town, affecting to retreat from a reconnoitring party that had been sent out by the garrison, led it into an ambuscade, where the Rev. G. Fortescue, nephew of Lord Clermont and rector of the parish, who had volunteered his services, was shot by a party of the French that had concealed themselves under a bridge. On the day following, the main body of Gen. Humbert's forces advanced to the town, of which they took possession on the evening of the 24th, when the garrison, under Col. Sir T. Chapman and Major Keir of the Carbineers, retreated to Foxford, a village about eight miles distant.

The town is beautifully situated on the river Moy, by which it is separated from the county of Sligo, and on the mail coach road from Sligo to Castlebar; it consists of several streets, and contains about 1200 houses, most of which are regular and well built. The river Moy, over which are two stone bridges, is navigable from the sea, about six miles distant, for vessels not drawing more than 11 feet of water, to within a mile and a half of the town. Barracks have been erected, and have lately undergone considerable repair. Races are held at Mount Falcon, generally in May, on a fine course, the property of J. F. Knox, Esq. Within the last ten years great improvements have taken place in the town; many new houses have been built, and are inhabited by merchants and others engaged in trade and commerce. A new line of road leading to Killala, and continued to Foxford and Swinford, with the intention of completing it to Longford, has been constructed by aid of £8000 from Government, and, when completed, will shorten the distance between Ballina and Dublin at least 10 miles. A new line of road along the bank of the river, leading to the quay at Ardnaree, has also been made, at an expense of £1500, one-half of which was paid by the merchants of this place and the other by the county of Sligo; and another line of road on the Ballina side of the river, intended to communicate with the quay at Belleek, has been formed, at an expense of £700 raised by subscription, towards which Messrs. Armstrong and West largely contributed. A new bridge communicating with the lower part of the town, at a short distance from the present bridge, is now being erected, at an estimated expense of £1200, to be defrayed by subscription, towards which the Earl of Arran, proprietor of a large portion of the town, has contributed £100, and in compliment to whom it will be called Arran Bridge. Other improvements are also in progress and in contemplation; the grand juries of the counties of Mayo and Sligo have presented £3000 towards the erection of a handsome bridge on the site of the present old bridge, which is inconveniently narrow. A ship canal was formerly commenced by Government, under the superintendence of Mr. Nimmo, for bringing vessels up to the town, instead of landing their cargoes at the present quay; but after £1000 had been expended, the works were discontinued and have been since falling into decay. A communication by canal to Lough Conn, and thence to Galway, has been projected by Mr. Bald, the county surveyor, which would open an abundant source of industry and wealth to the inhabitants of these mountain districts, at present inaccessible from want of roads, and greatly increase the commercial interests of the town. The environs are pleasingly diversified; and near the town are numerous gentlemen's seats, which are enumerated in the articles on their respective parishes.

A very extensive tobacco and snuff manufactory was established in 1801, by Mr. Malley, who first persevered in opening the navigation of the river Moy, and thus gave a powerful impulse to the commercial prosperity of the town: the manufacture continued to flourish, and in 1809 the duties paid to Government amounted to £8000. In 1834, Mr. J. Brennan, a merchant from Belfast, introduced the provision trade, which was previously unknown in this neighbourhood, and erected spacious premises adjoining the river, and commodious stores 350 feet long and 140 feet wide, with complete apparatus adapted to a peculiar method of curing: in this concern 10,000 pigs are annually killed, and after being cured are sent to London; and there are also others which carry on an extensive provision trade. There are two large ale and porter breweries, and two large oatmeal and flour-mills. The weaving of linen is carried on to a small extent by weavers who work in their own houses. This is the principal port in the county: in 1829 there were 119 vessels, of the aggregate burden of 11,097 tons, employed in the exportation of grain to the extent, in the course of that year, of 10,831 tons of oats, 130 tons of wheat, 106 tons of barley, and 30 tons of meal; and during the same period, 66 vessels, of the aggregate burden of 5479 tons, were employed in the importation of British and foreign goods. The fishery is carried on with great success; at the falls of the river are salmon weirs, which have been rebuilt by Messrs. Little, at an expense of £1500, and in which great quantities of fish are taken and shipped for Dublin and Liverpool. Farther down the river, near the quay, are placed drafting nets, in which great numbers are taken; the fishery is rented at £1500 per annum. The market is on Monday; and fairs are held on the 12th of May and the 12th of August. Commodious shambles have been erected in Mill-street for the use of the market. The Provincial Bank and the Agricultural and Commercial Bank have each established a branch here. This is a chief station of the constabulary police. Courts of petty sessions are held every Tuesday; and a quarter session is held here in July every year. The court-house, a neat plain building, was erected at an expense of £1000, paid by the county. There are places of worship for Baptists and Wesleyan Methodists, and a dispensary. On the eastern bank of the river are the remains of an abbey, founded by St. Olcan or Bolcan, a disciple of St. Patrick; they have a large ancient doorway of beautiful design.—See KILMOREMOY and ARDNAREE.

BALLINA, a village, in the parish of TEMPLEICHALLY, barony of OWNEY and ARRA, county of TIPPERARY, and province of MUNSTER; containing 832 inhabitants. This place is situated on the road from Killaloe to Newport, and on the river Shannon, over which is a bridge of nineteen arches connecting it with the town of Killaloe, in the county of Clare. It contains about 110 houses, has a fair on the 24th of March (chiefly for pigs), and is a constabulary police station. One of the chapels belonging to the R. C. union or district of Templeichally and Kilmastulla, otherwise called the union of Ballina and Boher, is situated in the village, Near the bridge are some remains of an ancient castle, probably erected to defend the passage of the river.—See TEMPLEICHALLY.

BALLINABOY, a parish, partly in the county of the city of CORK, and partly in the baronies of EAST MUSKERRY and KERRYCURRIHY, but chiefly in the barony of KINNALEA, county of CORK, and province of MUNSTER, 6 miles (S. S. W.) from Cork, on the road to Kinsale; containing 2887 inhabitants. This place, which is situated on the river Awinbuoy, formerly belonged to the abbey of St. Finbarr, and, in 1582, was, with other lands, granted by Queen Elizabeth to Henry Davells; it subsequently became part of the estate of the first Earl of Cork, from whom the property descended to the Earl of Shannon, the present owner. In 1600, Florence McCarthy assembled here 2000 of his followers, and made a desperate attack on the English, whom he compelled to take refuge behind the walls of an old castle. During their retreat a party of English musqueteers, having concealed themselves behind the bank of a ditch, fired upon the Irish forces, and the English cavalry charging them at the same time, put them completely to the rout.

The parish comprises about 8219 statute acres, as applotted under the tithe act, of which 6903 are arable, 1000 pasture, 300 waste, and 16 woodland. The land on the north side of the river is cold and mountainous, and 500 or 600 acres are covered principally with heath; the system of agriculture is in a very unimproved state. There being no bog, fuel is obtained from the bog of Annagh, in the adjoining parish. Ballinaboy House, the seat of J. Molony, Esq., is a handsome modern mansion surrounded with young and thriving plantations: the other seats are Tuligmore House, the residence of D. Keller, Esq.; Mount-Mary, of W. Fortune, Esq.; Barretts Hill, of James Donagan, Esq.; and Glenview, of the Rev. T. Beamish. There is a flour-mill at Five-mile-bridge belonging to Mr. Herrick; and there is also another in the village of Ballinahassig. At a short distance from the latter place a fine arch, 50 feet in height and nearly of the same span, has been thrown over the glen, at the back of Mount-Mary, over which the high road passes from Ballinahassig to Innishannon. A new road now forming from Cork to Kinsale will contribute to the improvement of this place. At the Half-way House is a constabulary police station. The living is a perpetual curacy, in the diocese of Cork, and in the patronage of the Earl of Shannon, the impropriator, who contributes £25 per ann. towards the curate's stipend, which is augmented to £75 from Primate Boulter's fund: the tithes are estimated at £500, and have long since merged into the rent. The church is a small dilapidated building, said to have been new-roofed about 60 years since. There is neither glebe-house nor glebe. In the R. C. divisions the parish forms part of the union of Ballinahassig, in which there are two chapels. There is a pay school, in which are 50 boys and 20 girls.—See BALLINAHASSIG.

BALLINACALLY, a village, in the parish of KILCHRIST, barony of CLONDERLAW, county of CLARE, and province of MUNSTER, 3 miles (N. N. E.) from Kildysart; the population is returned with the parish. It is situated on the road from Kildysart to Ennis, and near the river Fergus, on the banks of which is a small quay of rude construction, from which corn, butter, pork, and other agricultural produce are sent to Limerick, in boats of 10 or 12 tons burden, and where limestone and sea manure are landed for the supply of the neighbourhood. It has a daily penny post to Ennis and Kilrush, and a public dispensary: and fairs are held on June 14th, Sept. 16th, and Nov. 8th, chiefly for cattle. A little to the north of the village is the ruined tower or castle of Dangan, the upper part of which is supported only by the winding stone staircase.—See KILCHRIST.

BALLINACARGY, or BALNACARRIG, a market and post-town, in the parish of KILBIXY, barony of MOYGOISH, county of WESTMEATH, and province of LEINSTER, 7½ miles (W. by N.) from Mullingar, and 45¾ miles (W. by N.) from Dublin; containing 308 inhabitants. This town is situated on the road from Mullingar to Colehill, in the county of Longford, and near the right bank of the Royal Canal; it contains about 60 houses, neatly built and roofed with slate. Nearly adjoining it is an extensive deer-park belonging to Mrs. O'Connor Malone, in whom the fee of the town is vested. The markets are held on Wednesday for corn and butter, and on Saturday for provisions; and fairs are held on the 9th of May and Oct. 20th. It is a constabulary police station; and petty sessions are held every Wednesday. The R. C. parochial chapel for the union or district of Kilbixy is situated in the town. A large school-house was built by Lord Sunderlin, open to children of all denominations; the master's salary is paid by Mrs. Malone. Here is a dispensary.—See KILBIXY.

BALLINACARRIG, otherwise STAPLESTOWN, a parish, partly in the barony of RATHVILLY, but chiefly in that of CARLOW, county of CARLOW, and province of LEINSTER, 1 mile (E. N. E.) from Carlow; containing 615 inhabitants. This parish, which is situated on the river Burren, and on the road from Carlow to Tullow, comprises 2576 statute acres, as applotted under the tithe act, and valued at £2200 per annum. Two-thirds of the land are arable, and nearly one-third pasture or wet grazing land; there is little waste or unprofitable bog; the state of agriculture is improving. There are some quarries of excellent granite for building; and mills at which about 10,000 barrels of flour are annually made. The principal gentlemen's seats are Kilmany, the residence of S. Elliott, Esq.; Staplestown Lodge, of H. Waters, Esq.; and Staplestown Mills, of — Mason, Esq. The living is an impropriate curacy, in the diocese of Leighlin, united by act of council in 1804 to the rectories of Tullowmagrinagh and Ballycrogue, constituting the union of Staplestown, in the gift of the Bishop; the rectory is appropriate to the Dean and Chapter of Leighlin. The tithes amount to £170, of which £100 is payable to the dean and chapter, and £70 to the impropriate curate: the entire tithes of the benefice payable to the incumbent amount to £411. 17. 6. The church, situated in Staplestown, is a small neat edifice, erected in 1821; it contains a tablet to the memory of Walter Bagenal, the last male representative of that ancient family. There is a glebe-house but no glebe. In the R. C. divisions the parish is in the union or district of Tullowmagrinagh, also called Tinriland. There are two schools, in which are about 40 children. Some remains of the old church yet exist. Sir Wm. Temple resided at Staplestown, from which many of his letters are dated; there are still some remains of the house in which he lived.

BALLINACLASH, a district parish, in the barony of BALLINACOR, county of WICKLOW, and province of LEINSTER, 2¾ miles (S. W. by S.) from Rathdrum; containing 3855 inhabitants. This district is situated on the river Avonbeg, over which there is a bridge, and on the road from Rathdrum to Glenmalur. It is of recent creation as a parish, and comprehends the constablewicks of Ballykine and Ballinacor, forming a perpetual curacy, in the diocese of Dublin and Glendalough, and in the patronage of the Rector of Rathdrum, who pays the curate's stipend. The church, on the townland of Ballinaton, is a neat building with a square tower, in the later English style of architecture, erected in 1834, at an expense of £900, granted by the Church Temporalities Commission. There is no glebe-house or glebe. There are two schools in the village, one a daily school and the other a Sunday school.—See BALLYKINE and BALLINACOR.

BALLINACLOUGH.—See BALLYNACLOUGH.

BALLINACOR, a constablewick or sub-denomination of the parish of RATHDRUM, barony of BALLINACOR, county of WICKLOW, and province of LEINSTER, 2½ miles (W.) from Rathdrum; containing 1221 inhabitants. This place is situated in the mountain district leading to Glenmalur, and comprises 27,225 statute acres, of which 20,473 are mountain, and 6752 are arable and pasture land, and of which also 16,619 acres are applotted under the tithe act. Ballinacor, the seat of W. Kemmis, Esq., is beautifully situated on the side of a hill commanding an extensive view of the vale towards the Cormorce copper mines. The military road intersects the constablewick, in which are the barracks of Drumgoff and Aughavanah. Fairs are held on Feb. 4th, May 1st, Aug. 4th, and Nov. 4th. As regards its tithes, which amount to £103. 17. 6¾., this is one of the denominations that constitute the union or benefice of Rathdrum; it also forms, with the constablewick of Ballykine, the perpetual cure of Ballinaclash, in the diocese of Dublin and Glendalough, and in the patronage of the Incumbent of Rathdrum. A school is supported by Mr. Kemmis, in the village of Grenane.

BALLINACOURTY, a parish, in the barony of DUNKELLIN, county of GALWAY, and province of CONNAUGHT, 3 miles (S. by W.) from Oranmore; containing 3250 inhabitants. This parish is situated on the eastern shore of the bay of Galway, and on the road from Oranmore to an inlet of the bay forming the approach to Claren-Bridge. The inlet of Tyrone or Ballinacourty is well sheltered, and has good anchorage for vessels drawing not more than ten feet of water, which, however, must not venture in when it comes within two hours of low water of spring tides, as there are then only nine feet in the channel. Westerly winds occasion a great swell at the entrance, in which case it should not be attempted before half flood, nor after half ebb. On the south side of the haven there is a small pier called St. Kitt's, built by the Fishery Board, but adapted only for boats, the strand being dry at low water; it was never properly finished, and is now in a ruinous condition. Small craft sail up this inlet three miles further, to a point near Claren-Bridge and Kilcolgan. In the parish is the Cottage, the residence of J. Ryan, Esq. The living consists of a rectory and a perpetual curacy, in the diocese of Tuam; the former is part of the union of St. Nicholas and corps of the wardenship of Galway; and the latter is one of four which constitute the union of Kilcummin. The tithes amount to £240, of which £180 is payable to the warden, and £60 to the perpetual curate. In the R. C. divisions the parish is in the diocese of Galway, and forms part of the union or district of Oranmore: the chapel is a large thatched building, capable of accommodating 1000 persons. There is a school at Gurrane, in which about 70 boys and 50 girls are taught; and there are three private pay schools, in which are about 120 children. At the village of Ballinacourty are the remains of an old church.

BALLINACOURTY, a parish, in the barony of CORKAGUINEY, county of KERRY, and province of MUNSTER, 8½ miles (E. by N.) from Dingle, on the road to Tralee; containing 1884 inhabitants. It comprises 2973 statute acres, as applotted under the tithe act. A considerable portion is rough mountain pasture, with some bog, but mostly reclaimable; the remainder is under cultivation. A few boats are employed in fishing in the bay of Dingle, but for want of proper shelter the fishery is very limited. The construction of a small pier on this side of the bay would be of great advantage. Fairs are held at Ballinclare on the 1st of May and 4th of October, for black cattle and pigs. At Annascall is a constabulary police station; and petty sessions are also held there. A seneschal's court for the barony is held at Ballintarmin, generally on the last Wednesday in the month, at which debts not exceeding £10 late currency are recoverable. The living is a vicarage, in the diocese of Ardfert and Aghadoe, and about the year 1750 was episcopally united to six other vicarages, constituting the union of Kilflyn; the rectory is impropriate in the Earl of Cork. The tithes amount to £161. 10. 9. The church, situated at Annascall, was erected by aid of a loan of £600 from the late Board of First Fruits, in 1816. The glebe-house of the union is situated here, and was built by aid of a gift of £450 and a loan of £200 from the same Board, in 1821: there is also another at Kilflyn. The glebe comprises 14 plantation acres; and there is also an old glebe of four acres about a mile distant. In the R. C. divisions this parish forms part of the district of Ballinvohir; a chapel is now in course of erection at Annascall, at which place is a school, principally supported by the Earl of Cork. There are still some remains of the old church in the burial-ground.

BALLINACURRA, a village, in the parish of MIDLETON, barony of IMOKILLY, county of CORK, and province of MUNSTER, 1 mile (S.) from Midleton; containing 527 inhabitants. This place is pleasantly situated on the banks of the Midleton river, and contains 144 houses. It is well situated for trade; and several large grain stores and malt-houses have been recently built, and some excellent quays have been constructed. A bridge has been thrown across the creek, over which passes the road to Rostellan; and several other improvements are in contemplation. A considerable trade is carried on in the exportation of grain, which is chiefly sent to Liverpool, Bristol, and London; and in the importation of coal, timber, iron, slate, and other heavy goods for the supply of the flourishing town of Midleton, to which place the navigation might be extended at a small expense. Limestone is very abundant throughout the neighbourhood, and great quantities are quarried for building, and burnt for agricultural purposes. The harbour communicates with that of Cove by a passage called the East Ferry; the tide rises here from eight to twelve feet, and brigs of 300 tons burden can safely sail up to the quay. There are in the neighbourhood several handsome houses, occupied by wealthy individuals; and nearly adjoining the village are the ruins of the ancient parish church.—See MIDLETON.

BALLINADEE, a parish, in the East Division of the barony of EAST CARBERY, county of CORK, and province of MUNSTER, 4 miles (S. E.) from Bandon; containing, with the merged parish of Kilgoban, 2800 inhabitants, of which number, 228 are in the village. It comprises 7558 statute acres, as applotted under the tithe act, and valued at £4265 per annum. Nearly the whole is under tillage: the land is generally good, and the system of agriculture has very much improved; the cultivation of turnips, vetches, and other green crops, has been lately introduced with much advantage. Slate quarries in different parts are worked, but not to a great extent, for the supply of the neighbourhood and the town of Bandon, and the produce is sent down the river Bandon to be shipped to Cork and other ports. The village consists of 42 houses, most of which are small but well built, and it contains a large flour-mill of great power, which was much improved in 1836. A new line of road has been constructed, within the last two years, to Ballinspittle, a distance of three miles and a half. There are several small quays on the river, at which great quantities of sea sand for manure are landed for the supply of the adjacent parishes: more than 100 boats are engaged in raising it, of which about 20 belong to this parish. Here are also several weirs on the river for taking salmon. The gentlemen's seats are Rock House, that of J. Gillman, Esq., situated on the side of a romantic glen, in the centre of some highly improved grounds; Rock Castle, of E. Becher, Esq.; Peafield, of George H. Rawlins, Esq.; Peafield House, of J. Minton, Esq.; Ballyvolan, of Walter Tresillian, Esq.; Knocknacurra, of Benjamin Gillman, Esq.; and the Glebe-house, the residence of the Rev. R. N. Perry. Kilgoban Castle, at present untenanted, is situated at the side of the river Bandon, and is in good preservation, forming a striking feature in the surrounding scenery, which in many parts is picturesque and very interesting, particularly in the vicinity of Rock House, Kilgoban, and the glens near the village of Ballinadee. The living is a rectory, in the diocese of Cork, united at a period prior to any existing record with the denominations of Kilgoban, Rathdowlan, and Mackloneigh, which constitute the corps of the treasurership in the cathedral church of St. Finbarr, Cork, in the patronage of the Bishop: the tithes amount to £616. 10. 8½., and the gross income of the treasurer is returned at £644 per annum. The church is a large edifice, built in 1759, and a square tower has been recently added. The glebe comprises 5*a.* 2*r.* 12*p.* In the R. C. divisions the parish forms part of the union or district of Courceys, and contains a chapel, a large plain edifice, rebuilt within the last five years, at an expense of £400. The male and female parochial schools are aided by an annual donation of £10 from the rector: there are also a Sunday school and a daily pay school. On the lands of Kilgoban is the ruined tower of an ancient castle, which belonged to the family of McCarthy, beneath which, by the river's side, a great quantity of gold and silver coins, with numerous gold rings, was dug up in 1824.

BALLINAFAD, a village, in the parish of AUGHANAGH, barony of TIRAGHRILL, county of SLIGO, and province of CONNAUGHT, 2½ miles (N. N. W.) from Boyle, on the road to Sligo; containing 20 houses and 140 inhabitants. A fair is held on the 29th of August; and here is a station of the constabulary police.—See AUGHANAGH.

BALLINAFAGH.—See BALLYNEFAGH.

BALLINAGAR, a village, in the parish and barony of GEASHILL, KING'S county, and province of LEINSTER, 2½ miles (S. W.) from Philipstown, on the road from Edenderry to Tullamore; containing 32 houses and 153 inhabitants. A large and handsome R. C. chapel for the union or district of Ballykean is in course of erection, in the ancient English style of architecture. —See GEASHILL.

BALLINAGERAGH, a village, in the parish of KILCARRAGH, barony of CLANMAURICE, county of KERRY, and province of MUNSTER, 7 miles (S. W. by S.) from Listowel, on the road to Tralee; containing 35 houses and 230 inhabitants. A patron fair, one of the largest in the county, is held here on Sept. 29th, and is numerously attended.—See KILCARRAGH.

BALLINAGH, a market-town, partly in the parish of BALLINTEMPLE, but chiefly in that of KILMORE, barony of CLONMAHON, county of CAVAN, and province of ULSTER, 4 miles (S. W.) from Cavan, on the road to Granard; containing 702 inhabitants. This town was entirely destroyed by fire in a disturbance which took place in 1794; it consists at present of two streets crossing each other at right angles, and in 1831 contained 135 houses, the greater part of which are thatched, and of which three only are in the parish of Ballintemple. The market is on Saturday, and is held in a neat plain market-house. Fairs are held on March 31st, June 6th, August 5th, Oct. 3rd, and Dec. 21st. This is a station of the constabulary police; and petty sessions are held every alternate Wednesday. There is a R. C. chapel; also a good slated school-house, containing on the ground floor a school-room for boys, and on the upper story, one for girls.—See KILMORE.

BALLINAGLERAGH.—See DRUMREILLY.

BALLINAGORE, a village, in the parish of NEWTOWN, barony of MOYCASHEL, county of WESTMEATH, and province of LEINSTER, 2½ miles (N. E.) from Kilbeggan, on the road to Mullingar; containing 35 houses and 182 inhabitants. The river Brusna flows through the village, and is crossed by a bridge of four arches. On its banks is an extensive bleach-green, with a fulling-mill, the property of W. H. Mulock, Esq. There are also some large flour-mills, capable of grinding 40,000 barrels of wheat annually, and affording employment to 70 men. Here is a station of the constabulary police.—See NEWTOWN.

BALLINAHAGLISH.—See BALLYNAHAGLISH.

BALLINAHASSIG, a village, in that part of the parish of BALLINABOY, which is in the barony of KERRICURRIHY, county of CORK, and province of MUNSTER, 6 miles (S.) from Cork, on the road to Kinsale; containing 147 inhabitants. It was distinguished as the scene of a battle which took place in 1600, between a party of English and the insurgent forces under the command of Florence McCarthy. Here are mills belonging to Mr. D. Keller, capable of making 7000 barrels of flour annually, which, together with three or four houses and about twice as many cabins, constitute the village. Fairs are held on May 2nd, June 29th, Aug. 10th, and Sept. 29th; and here is a dispensary. It is the head of a R. C. union or district, comprising the parishes of Ballinaboy, Dunderrow, and Templemichael-de-Duagh, and containing chapels at Ballyheedy and Killeedy Hill.—See BALLINABOY.

BALLINAHINCH, a market and post-town, in the parish of MAGHERADROLL, barony of KINELEARTY, county of DOWN, and province of ULSTER, 8 miles (E.) from Dromore, and 74½ (N. by E.) from Dublin; containing 970 inhabitants. This town was founded by Sir George Rawdon, Bart., after the insurrection of 1641, as appears by the patent of Chas. II. granting the manor of Kinelearty to the Rawdon family, which, after reciting that Sir George had built a town and two mills, and had repaired the church, and that a large space had been appropriated for holding markets and fairs, created that manor, with a demesne of 1000 acres and courts leet and baron, and granted the privilege of a market to be held on Thursday, and two fairs annually. During the disturbances of 1798, the main body of the insurgents, after being repulsed near Saintfield, took post here on Windmill-hill and on some high ground in the demesne of the Earl of Moira, a descendant of Sir G. Rawdon. On the 12th of June, Gen. Nugent marched against them from Belfast with the Monaghan regiment of militia, part of the 22nd dragoons, and some yeomanry infantry and cavalry; and was joined near this place by Lieut.-Col. Stewart with his party from Downpatrick, making in all about 1500 men. The insurgents were soon driven from their post on the Windmill-hill, and the king's troops set fire to the town. Both parties spent the night in preparations for a general action, which took place at an early hour on the following morning, and was maintained about three hours with artillery, but with little effect. At length the Monaghan regiment of militia, posted with two field-pieces at Lord Moira's gate, was attacked with such determined fury by the pikemen of the insurgents that it fell back in confusion on the Hillsborough cavalry, which retreated in disorder; but these troops having rallied, while the Argyleshire fencibles entering the demesne, were making their attack on another side, the insurgents retired to a kind of fortification on the top of the hill, which for some time they defended with great courage, but at length gave way and dispersed in all directions; the main body fled to the mountains of Slieve Croob, where they soon surrendered or retired to their several homes, and thus was the insurrection terminated in this quarter.

The town is situated on the road from Dromore to Saintfield, and consists of a square and four streets, comprising, in 1831, 171 houses, many of which are well built. The market is on Thursday, and is well supplied; and fairs are held on the first Thursday in January, Feb. 12th, March 3rd, April 5th, May 19th, July 10th, Aug. 18th, Oct. 6th, and Nov. 17th. A linen-hall was built by the Earl of Moira, but it has fallen into ruins. Here is a station of the constabulary police. A court for the manor of Kinelearty was formerly held, in which debts to the amount of £10 were recoverable, but it has fallen into disuse. There is a large court-house in the square, built by Lord Moira in

1795, but now in a dilapidated state. The same nobleman also built a church in 1772, which having fallen into decay was taken down in 1829, and a new edifice was erected on its site, towards which £850 was granted by the late Board of First Fruits; the tower and spire of the old building remain on the west side of the present church. Opposite to it is a spacious R. C. chapel; and there are three places of worship for Presbyterians, one in connection with the Synod of Ulster, and the others in connection with the Seceding Synod. A school for girls is supported by voluntary contributions. In a picturesque and fertile valley, two miles south of the town, is a powerful sulphureous chalybeate spring, which is much resorted to during summer, and has been highly efficacious in scrophulous disorders: there are two wells, one for drinking and the other for bathing, but sufficient accommodation is not provided for the numbers that repair to the spot.—See MAGHERADROLL.

BALLINAKILL.—See BALLYNAKILL.

BALLINAKILL, a market and post-town (formerly a parliamentary borough), in the parish of DYSARTGALLEN, barony of CULLINAGH, QUEEN'S county, and province of LEINSTER, 10 miles (S. S. E.) from Maryborough, and 50 miles (S. W.) from Dublin; containing 1927 inhabitants. This is a place of some antiquity, but was not made a market-town till the year 1606, when a grant of a market and fair was made to Sir T. Coatch, proprietor of the manor of Galline. In 1612 it was incorporated by Jas. I., and was invested with considerable privileges, to foster the plantation made here by Sir T. Ridgway, Bart. The castle, of which there are still some remains, fell into the possession of the R. C. party during the insurrection of 1641, and when Cromwell's troops overran the island, being bravely defended by its garrison, it was cannonaded from the Warren-Hill, adjoining Heywood demesne, by Gen. Fairfax, and the garrison was at length compelled to surrender. The town is situated in a fertile district, the soil of which is principally composed of a deep clay adapted both for the dairy and for tillage. To the east is Heywood, the seat of the Trench family, in a richly varied demesne ornamented with plantations and artificial sheets of water. The manufacture of woollen stuffs, formerly more extensive, is still carried on to a limited degree, and there is a brewery. The market is on Saturday, and has somewhat declined since the establishment of a market on the same day at Abbeyleix, a few years since: the market-house is kept in repair by Earl Stanhope, the lord of the manor. Fairs are held on the 16th of Jan. and Feb., 22nd of March and April, 13th of May, first Thursday after Whit-Sunday, 13th of June and July, 12th of Aug., and 16th of Sept., Oct., Nov., and Dec.; that in Nov. is a large fair for bullocks. Here is a station of the constabulary police.

Under the charter of Jas. I. the corporation was styled "The Sovereign, Burgesses, and Freemen of the Borough of Ballinakill;" and consisted of a sovereign, twelve burgesses, and an unlimited number of freemen, but is now extinct. The corporation returned two members to the Irish parliament until the Union, when the £15,000 awarded as compensation for the loss of that privilege was paid to Charles, Marquess of Drogheda. Quarter and petty sessions were formerly held in the town, but have been removed to Abbeyleix, about three miles distant. The parish church, a handsome edifice with a tower and spire, is situated in the town; and there is a R. C. chapel. Here is a national school, in which about 330 boys and 350 girls are taught; also a dispensary. The R. C. poor of the town derive benefit from a bequest of £500 by a Mr. Dillon.—See DYSARTGALLEN.

BALLINAKILLY, or BALLYNAKILTY, a parish, in the barony of KILLIAN, county of GALWAY, and province of CONNAUGHT, 5¼ miles (W. by S.) from Ballinamore, on the road from Tuam to Ballinasloe; containing, with the parish of Aghiart, 1630 inhabitants. It is a rectory and vicarage, in the diocese of Tuam, and forms part of the union of Moylough; the tithes, including those of Aghiart, amount to £148. 10. 8¼. In the R. C. divisions it is part of the union or district of Mount-Bellew. There is a hedge school, in which about 40 boys and 16 girls are taught.

BALLINALACK, a village, in the parish of LENEY, barony of CORKAREE, county of WESTMEATH, and province of LEINSTER, 8 miles (N. W. by N.) from Mullingar; containing 51 houses and 334 inhabitants. This place is situated on the banks of the river Inny, over which is a bridge of five arches, and on the road from Mullingar to Longford. It is a chief constabulary police station, and contains the parochial school, which is under the patronage of J. Gibbons, Esq.

BALLINAMAGHERY, a hamlet, in the parish of CARLINGFORD, barony of LOWER DUNDALK, county of LOUTH, and province of LEINSTER; containing 16 houses and 94 inhabitants.

BALLINAMARA.—See BALLYNEMARA.

BALLINAMONA.—See MOURNE.

BALLINAMORE, co. GALWAY.—See KILLIAN.

BALLINAMORE, a market and post-town, in the parish of OUTRAGH, barony of CARRIGALLEN, county of LEITRIM, and province of CONNAUGHT, 19½ miles (W.) from Cavan, and 77½ miles (N. W. by W.) from Dublin; containing 312 inhabitants. This town, which is situated on the road from Killyshandra, and intersected by a small river, consists of 63 neatly built houses, and a considerable number of straggling cottages. It was formerly the seat of the iron manufacture, and works were established for smelting the ore found in the vicinity. The market, which is on Tuesday, is one of the largest in the county for grain and provisions; and fairs are held on the 15th of February, May 12th, Aug. 16th, and Nov. 12th. It is a constabulary police station; petty sessions are held irregularly; and the quarter sessions for the southern division of the county are held here in April and October. A court-house has been recently erected, to which is attached a bridewell containing four cells, with apartments for the keeper; the cost of the building was £2200, of which £1200 was lent by Government, to be repaid by instalments: it is also in contemplation to build a market-house. The parish church, a R. C. chapel, and a place of worship for Methodists, are situated in the town. Near it is Garadise Lough, a considerable sheet of water, on the shore of which is Garradice, the seat of W. C. Percy, Esq.; and there are several other lakes in the vicinity.—See OUTRAGH.

BALLINAMUCK, a village, in that part of the parish of KILLOE, which is in the barony and county of LONGFORD, in the province of LEINSTER, 8 miles (N.) from Longford, on the road from Newtown-Forbes to Arvagh; containing 30 houses and 163 inhabitants. The remainder of the French army under Gen. Humbert, which had landed in Kilcummin bay on the 22d of August, 1798, for the assistance of the insurgent forces, made a final stand in the neighbourhood, where, being surrounded by the English army under Lord Cornwallis, they were compelled to surrender on the 9th of the following month. Having arrived on the preceding evening, the French forces were closely pursued by Col. Crawford and Gen. Lake; while Lord Cornwallis, with the grand army, crossing the river at Carrick-on-Shannon, advanced to St. Johnstown to intercept their progress to Granard. Col. Crawford having attacked their rear, about 200 of the infantry surrendered themselves prisoners; the remainder continued to defend themselves for about half an hour, when, on the appearance of the main body of the army under Gen. Lake, they also surrendered. The number of Gen. Humbert's army at the time of their surrender was reduced to 96 officers and 748 privates. Here is a station of the constabulary police, also a quarry of fine freestone.—See KILLOE.

BALLINARD.—See BALLYNARD.

BALLINASAGGART. — See ERRIGALL - KEROGUE.

BALLINASLOE, a market and post-town, partly in the parish of CREAGH, barony of MOYCARNON, county of ROSCOMMON, but chiefly in the parish of KILCLOONY, barony of CLONMACNOON, county of GALWAY, and province of CONNAUGHT, 12 miles (W. by S.) from Athlone, and 71¾ miles (W. by S.) from Dublin, on the road to Galway; containing 4615 inhabitants. This town is situated on the river Suck, which divides it into two unequal parts, of which the larger is in the county of Galway. It appears to have arisen under the protection of its castle, which in the reign of Elizabeth was one of the strongest fortresses in Connaught, and the ruins of which are situated on the Roscommon side of the river, and is now one of the most flourishing towns in the south and west of Ireland. In 1831 it comprised 632 houses, nearly all slated, of which 265 were built during the ten years preceding. The two portions are connected by a line of two bridges and causeways crossing some small islands, and about 500 yards in length, in which are 16 arches. Here are three tanyards, a flour and three oatmeal-mills, a manufactory for felt hats, a coach-manufactory, two breweries, and a large establishment for curing bacon; and in the vicinity are some quarries of excellent limestone. An extension of the Grand Canal has been formed within the last few years from Shannon harbour to this town, through the bogs on the south side of the river Suck, which not only affords a regular conveyance for passengers to Dublin and other places, but greatly facilitates the trade of the town. The Ballinasloe Horticultural Society for the province of Connaught was founded in 1833, under the patronage of the Earl of Clancarty, and holds its annual meetings on the first Monday in March; three public shows take place in the year, when prizes are awarded for the best specimens of various kinds of fruit, flowers, and vegetables. The annual meetings of an Agricultural Society are also held here in October. Garbally Park, in the immediate vicinity, is the seat of the Earl of Clancarty, the proprietor of the town: the mansion is situated in a well-wooded demesne, and was rebuilt in 1819; it contains a good collection of paintings, and the public are allowed free access both to the house and grounds. Near the town, also, is Mackna, the seat of his lordship's brother, the Hon. and Ven. Chas. le Poer Trench, D.D., Archdeacon of Ardagh. The market is on Saturday, and is well supplied with corn. The celebrated fair of Ballinasloe is the greatest cattle mart in the kingdom; it is held on the Galway side of the river, from the 5th to the 9th of October. The black or horned cattle are exhibited in an extensive area set apart for the fair outside the town; and a plot of ground in Garbally Park is appropriated to the show of sheep on the day before the fair, when very extensive purchases are made, and those that remain unsold are driven to the fair green. Great quantities of wool were formerly sold, but the establishment of factors in Dublin and other large towns has altered the channel of this branch of trade. The number and variety of goods exhibited for sale render the fair a great resort for all classes of dealers. The number of sheep exhibited in 1835 was 61,632, of which 54,974 were sold; and of cattle, 7443, of which 6827 were sold. Fairs for live stock are also held on May 7th and July 4th; and on the 6th of July there is a large fair for wool, which has been lately revived, and lasts four days: the wool fairs formerly continued from two to five weeks. Petty sessions are held every Wednesday and Saturday in a court-house attached to the bridewell, an old house not adapted either for confinement or security. This is the head-quarters of the Galway constabulary police; and a company of infantry, for whose accommodation there is a barrack for 56 men, and two companies of cavalry are occasionally stationed here.

The church of the union of Creagh occupies an elevated site in the town. In the R. C. divisions this place is the head of a union or district, comprising the parishes of Kilcloony and Creagh, and containing a chapel in each; that of Kilcloony is situated at the extremity of the market-square. There are places of worship for Primitive and Wesleyan Methodists. Three schools for boys and girls, one for girls only, and an infants' school, are chiefly supported by the Earl of Clancarty, and from other sources, at an expense of about £150 per annum; and there is a national school for both sexes, under the patronage of the R. C. clergyman. The lunatic asylum for the province of Connaught, situated here, was opened in 1833, and is capable of accommodating 150 inmates; it is built of limestone, in the form of the letter X, with a handsome cupola, and the ground attached to it comprises 14 plantation acres enclosed by a wall; the entire expenditure, including cost of building and purchase of site and furniture, was £27,130. 4. 6. Here is also a dispensary, and a Benevolent Society has been formed. The remains of the castle consist of the outer walls only, enclosing a square area, with a round tower in one angle, which has been converted into a neat residence called Ivy Castle, the seat of J. T. Maher, Esq.; the most picturesque portion is a bridge across the fosse to a gateway. The townland of Dunlo, on which the Galway portion of the town is built, gives the inferior title of Viscount to the Earl of Clancarty.—See KILCLOONY and CREAGH.

BALLINAVOREN, a hamlet, partly in the parish of ARDAGH, barony of MORGALLION, and partly in that of DRUMCONDRA, barony of LOWER SLANE, county of

MEATH, and province of LEINSTER, 4 miles (N.) from Nobber; containing 14 houses and 83 inhabitants. Here is a plain R. C. chapel, which it is in contemplation to rebuild.

BALLINCALLA, or BALLINCHOLLA, a parish, partly in the barony of Ross, county of GALWAY, but chiefly in that of KILMAINE, county of MAYO, and province of CONNAUGHT, 2 miles (S. W.) from Ballinrobe, on the road to Cong; containing 3031 inhabitants. It comprises 7102 statute acres, as applotted under the tithe act: about one-half of the land is under tillage, one-fourth is pasture, and the remainder waste mountain and bog. A fair is held at Lough Mask, on the 20th of September. It is a rectory and vicarage, in the diocese of Tuam, and forms part of the union of Kilmolara: the tithes amount to £328. The glebe-house of the union is situated here, and was erected by aid of a gift of £400 and a loan of £398 from the late Board of First Fruits, in 1819: the glebe comprises 20 acres. In the R. C. divisions it is part of the union or district called the Neale. There is one pay-school, in which are about 30 males and 15 females. On the borders of Lough Mask are some remains of an old castle.

BALLINCLARE, a small hamlet, in the parish of BALLINACOURTY, barony of CORKAGUINEY, county of KERRY, and province of MUNSTER, 8 miles (E. by N.) from Dingle, on the road to Tralee; containing 13 houses and 88 inhabitants. Fairs are held on May 1st and Oct. 4th, chiefly for cattle and pigs.

BALLINCOLLIG, a post-town, in the parish of CARRIGROHANE, barony of BARRETTS, county of CORK, and province of MUNSTER, 5¼ miles (W.) from Cork, and 130½ miles (S. W.) from Dublin, on the road from Cork to Macroom; containing 875 inhabitants. This place is chiefly distinguished as a military depôt, and for its extensive gunpowder-mills, formerly carried on under the superintendence of Government, but, after having been for some years discontinued, recently purchased by the present proprietors, and now in full operation. The artillery barracks form an extensive quadrangular pile of buildings, having in the eastern range the officers' apartments, and on the western side an hospital and a neat church, built in 1814, in which divine service is regularly performed by a resident chaplain. The buildings contain accommodation for 18 officers and 242 non-commissioned officers and privates, and are adapted to receive eight field batteries, though at present only one is stationed here, to which are attached 95 men and 44 horses: in the centre of the quadrangle eight gun sheds are placed in two parallel lines, and near them are the stables and offices; within the walls is a large and commodious school-room. Immediately adjoining the barracks, and occupying a space of nearly four miles in extent, are the gunpowder-mills, 16 in number. At convenient distances are placed the different establishments for granulating and drying the gunpowder, making charcoal, refining sulphur and saltpetre, making casks and hoops and the various machinery connected with the works; the whole communicating with each other, and with the mills, by means of small canals constructed for facility of carriage, and for preventing such accidents as might occur from other modes of conveyance. In appropriate situations, and adjoining these establishments, are the residences of the different persons superintending the works; and at the eastern extremity of the ground, but at a considerable distance from the mills, are two ranges of comfortable cottages for a portion of the work-people, now tenanted by 54 families, which obtain a comfortable livelihood. The number of persons employed is about 200, and the quantity of gunpowder manufactured annually is about 16,000 barrels. The police depôt for the province of Munster is situated here; the men are drilled till they become efficient, and then drafted off to the different stations in the province. There is a R. C. chapel, to which is attached a school. To the south of the town, and on a limestone rock rising abruptly from the surrounding meadows, are the remains of Ballincollig castle, of which one of the towers is in tolerable preservation. —See CARRIGROHANE.

BALLINCUSLANE, a parish, in the barony of TRUGHENACKMY, county of KERRY, aud province of MUNSTER, 4½ miles (S. E. by S.) from Castleisland; containing 4700 inhabitants. The parish, which is situated on the west bank of the river Blackwater, and on the confines of the county of Cork, is intersected by the old and new roads from Castleisland into that county, the latter being the road to King-William's-Town, now in progress at the expense of Government. It comprises 37,118 statute acres, as applotted under the tithe act, a large portion of which consists of rough mountain pasture and bog, which is mostly reclaimable: the arable land is of good quality, and limestone is found in abundance near Ardnagragh, and is used principally for manure. The only gentlemen's seats are Derreen, a lodge belonging to J. Bateman, Esq., and Mount-Eagle, the sporting residence of C. G. Fairfield, Esq., who, with Col. Drummond, are proprietors of one-sixth of the seigniory of Castleisland, and have made considerable improvements by planting, draining, and the construction of new roads. The living is a rectory, in the diocese of Ardfert and Aghadoe, and till lately was one of the four that constituted the union of Castleisland, in the patronage of the Proprietors of that seigniory; but the union has been divided into three separate livings, confirmed by act of council in 1836: the tithes amount to £460. 12. 7. Divine service is regularly performed at Derreen; but it is expected that a church will be built in the parish. In the R. C. divisions the parish, with the exception of a small portion attached to Knocknagashel, forms part of the union or district of Castleisland; the chapel, a plain but commodious building, is situated at Cordel, near Ardnagragh. A school-house has been lately built near Mount-Eagle, for 120 children; and there are six private schools, in which about 100 boys and 50 girls are educated. At Ardnagragh are the ruins of Desmond's chapel, with a burial-ground attached, now called Kilnananima; here the remains of "The Great" Earl of Desmond (who was slain in 1583) were interred. Near this spot are the ruins of Kilmurry castle, which was taken by Col. Phaire, of Cork, in 1650: this and the castles of Kilcushnan and Bally-Mac-Adam, situated within half a mile of each other, were inhabited by three brothers named Fitzgerald, of the Desmond family, between whom such enmity subsisted that none of them would suffer the others to pass unmolested through his lands.

BALLINDANGAN.—See CROSSBOYNE.

BALLINDERRY, a parish, in the barony of UPPER MASSAREENE, county of ANTRIM, and province of ULSTER, $3\frac{1}{2}$ miles (N.) from Moira; containing 5356 inhabitants. At Portmore, an extensive castle was erected by Lord Conway, in 1664, on the site of a more ancient fortress: it contained accommodation for two troops of horse, with a range of stabling 140 feet in length, 35 feet in breadth, and 40 feet in height; the remains consist only of the ancient garden wall, part of the stables, and the ruins of one of the bastions. During the Protectorate the learned Jeremy Taylor retired to this place, and remained at the seat of Lord Conway till the Restoration, when he was promoted to the bishoprick of Down and Connor. On a small island in the lough are still some remains of a summer-house, in which he is said to have written some of the most important of his works, and in the neighbourhood his memory is still held in great respect. The parish is situated on the road from Antrim to Dublin, and is intersected by the mail coach road from Lurgan to Antrim: it comprises, according to the Ordnance survey, 10,891 statute acres, of which $283\frac{1}{2}$ are in Portmore Lough. The land is almost all arable and in a good state of cultivation; the system of tillage is improving. There is little or no waste land; in the north-east and south-west parts of the parish are some valuable bogs. The weaving of linen and cotton affords employment to a considerable number of persons, but the greater number of the inhabitants are engaged in agriculture. The Lagan canal from Lough Neagh, on the north-west, to Belfast passes within the distance of a mile. The parish is within the jurisdiction of the manorial court of Killultagh, held at Lisburn.

The living is a vicarage, in the diocese of Connor, and in the patronage of the Marquess of Hertford, in whom the rectory is impropriate: the tithes amount to £480, of which £400 is paid to the vicar, and £80 to the impropriator. The church was erected in 1827, through the exertions of Dean Stannus, at an expense of £2200, of which the Marquess of Hertford gave £1000, and the late Board of First Fruits the remainder; it is a handsome edifice, in the later style of English architecture, with a tower and spire 128 feet in height, and is beautifully situated on rising ground near the small village of Upper Ballinderry. There is a glebe of eight acres, but no glebe-house. In the R. C. divisions the parish forms part of the union or district of Aughagallon and Ballinderry: the chapel is a small building. There is a place of worship for Presbyterians in connection with the Synod of Ulster, of the third class; also a Moravian meeting house. In addition to the parochial school, there are schools at Lower Ballinderry, Killultagh, and Legartariffe; all, except the last, were built within the last ten years, chiefly through the benevolent exertions of Dean Stannus, at an expense of £600; they are well conducted, and will accommodate 300 children: there are also several private pay schools. —Murray, Esq., bequeathed £100 British; J. Moore Johnston, Esq., £83. 6. 8.; and Hugh Casement, Esq., £25 Irish currency, to the poor of the parish. The old parish church, which was built after the Restoration of Chas. II., still remains; and on the eastern side of it is a burial-place, called Templecormack, in the centre of which the foundations of a small building may be traced. There are also some remains of an ancient church close to Portmore Lough, at the western extremity of the parish. The manor of Killultagh gives the title of Baron Conway of Killultagh to the Seymour family.

BALLINDERRY, or BALLYDERRY, a parish, partly in the barony of DUNGANNON, county of TYRONE, but chiefly in the barony of LOUGHINSHOLIN, county of LONDONDERRY, and province of ULSTER, 7 miles (S. E. by E.) from Moneymore; containing 3163 inhabitants. This parish is situated on the Ballinderry river, which here separates the above-named baronies and counties, and falls into the north-western portion of Lough Neagh. It comprises, according to the Ordnance survey, 8177 statute acres, of which $2268\frac{1}{2}$ are in the county of Tyrone, and $5908\frac{1}{2}$ are in Londonderry; 2978 acres form a portion of Lough Neagh. The greater part belongs to the Salters' Company, of London; part belongs to the see of Derry; and some of the lands are held under Cromwellian debentures, and are the only lands in the county of Londonderry, west of the river Bann, that are held by that tenure. A castle was built by the Salters' Company at Salterstown, in 1615, soon after they had obtained the grant of those lands from Jas. I.; and in the insurrection of 1641 it was surprised by Sir Phelim O'Nial, who put all the inmates to death, with the exception of the keeper, who, with his wife and family, effected their escape to Carrickfergus, where, taking refuge in the church, they were finally starved to death. It continued for some time in the possession of the insurgents, who, being ultimately driven from their post, destroyed it, together with the church adjoining. Nearly the whole of the land is arable and under an excellent system of cultivation; a valuable tract of bog produces excellent fuel, and there is no waste land. There are several large and well-built houses in the parish; but the only seat is Ballyronan, that of J. Gaussen, Esq. The inhabitants combine with agricultural pursuits the weaving of linen and cotton cloth; and at Ballyronan an extensive distillery has been lately established by Messrs. Gaussen, situated on the shore of Lough Neagh, close to the little port of Ballyronan. The living is a rectory, in the diocese of Armagh, and in the patronage of the Lord-Primate: the tithes amount to £192. 6. 2. The church, a large edifice in the later English style of architecture, was erected in 1707. The glebe-house, nearly adjoining, was built at an expense of £980, of which £100 was a gift from the late Board of First Fruits, in 1795: the glebe comprises 413 acres of well-cultivated arable land. The R. C. parish is co-extensive with that of the Established Church; there is a chapel at Ballylifford, and at Derryaghrin is an altar in the open air. Near the church is a place of worship for Wesleyan Methodists. The parochial school, in which are about 40 boys and 20 girls, is aided by a donation of £10 per annum from the rector; and there are three Sunday schools, one of which is held in the R. C. chapel, and three daily pay schools, in which are about 80 children. The ruins of the castle at Salterstown, situated on the margin of the lake, present a picturesque and interesting appearance, but are fast mouldering away. Adjoining the bridge over the river are the remains of an ancient iron forge, erected by the Salters' Company in 1626, but which soon after fell into disuse. At Salterstown, near the site of the old church and close to the shore of Lough Neagh, is a chalybeate spring, which has been found efficacious in cutaneous disorders, and was formerly much resorted to; bnt having become mixed with other water, its efficacy is greatly diminished. At Ballyronan is a large ancient fortress in good preservation.

BALLINDERRY, a hamlet, in the parish of TERRYGLASS, barony of LOWER ORMOND, county of TIPPERARY, and province of MUNSTER, 5 miles (N. W.) from Burrisokane, on the river Shannon; containing 7 houses and 54 inhabitants.

BALLINDERRY, county of WICKLOW.—See RATHDRUM.

BALLINDOON, a parish, in the barony of BALLINAHINCH, county of GALWAY, and province of CONNAUGHT, 6 miles (S. W.) from Clifden; containing 4943 inhabitants. This parish is situated on the Connemara or western coast, and within its limits are the bays of Mannin and Bunowen, Slyne Head, and the islands of Innisdanrow, Innisdoogan, Innisinan, Lyin, Carrigaroon, Doonglass, Immul, Duck, Horse, Islannora, and Fox. In the famine that prevailed on this part of the coast, in 1831, the inhabitants were reduced to extreme want and destitution, and but for the timely aid of the London Relief Committee, it would have been, in the words of the parish priest, "a desert and uninhabited country." The manufacture of kelp was formerly carried on to a very great extent, and was a source of lucrative employment, till the alteration in the duties took place, since which time it has been altogether discontinued. At present agriculture and fishing are the chief occupations of the inhabitants, of whom almost all have portions of land; the females make a red flannel for domestic use, and many are employed in knitting woollen stockings, which are celebrated as the Connemara hose, but the price is so low as scarcely to repay their labour, they being unable to earn more than three-halfpence daily. In Bunowen bay a vessel may ride in moderate weather; the entrance is on either side of a rock called Carrigascoilty. From Ross point, on the main land, to Islannora a range of rocks extends to Slyne Head, which is situated in latitude 53° 24′ 30″ (N.), and longitude 10° 7′ 40″ (W.), and runs off to the westward in five or six small islets, the outermost of which is Island Immul, which has deep water close in shore: there are two sounds among these isles that may be passed with boats. On this point the commissioners for improving the port of Dublin have erected a lighthouse. Rounding Slyne Head are Mannin bay and the harbour of Ardbear or Clifden. The living is a rectory and vicarage, in the diocese of Tuam, and forms part of the union of Ballynakill: the tithes amount to £40. In the R. C. divisions the parish is included in the union or district of Clifden; the chapel is a neat building. There are four pay schools, situated respectively at Errislannin, Ballindoon, Aldbrack, and Ballyconnelly, in which are about 250 children.

BALLINEA, a village, in the parish of MULLINGAR, barony of MOYCASHEL and MAGHERADERNAN, county of WESTMEATH, and province of LEINSTER, 2¾ miles (W. by S.) from Mullingar, on the road to Athlone; containing 18 houses and 109 inhabitants. It is a constabulary police station.

BALLINECARGY, a village, in the parish of DRUNG, barony of TULLAGHGARVEY, county of CAVAN, and province of ULSTER, 6 miles (S. W.) from Cootehill, on the road to Cavan; containing 25 houses and 150 inhabitants.

BALLINGADDY, a parish, in the barony of COSTLEA, county of LIMERICK, and province of MUNSTER, 2¼ miles (S.) from Kilmallock, on the road to Kilfinnan; containing 1031 inhabitants. It comprises 5615 statute acres, as applotted under the tithe act, of which about 400 are mountain, and the remainder is generally in a good state of cultivation. Mount-Russel, the residence of J. Russell, Esq., is beautifully situated at the foot of the mountain range, commanding an extensive view over a very rich vale. It is a rectory and vicarage, in the diocese of Limerick, and forms part of the union of Kilmallock: the tithes amount to £280. The ruins of the old church are situated near Riverfield; and adjoining the churchyard are 24 acres of excellent glebe. In the R. C. divisions it forms part of the union or district of Kilmallock; the chapel is a small thatched building. There is a pay school, in which are about 40 boys and 30 girls.

BALLINGARRY, a parish, in the barony of COSTLEA, county of LIMERICK, and province of MUNSTER, 3 miles (E. N. E.) from Kilfinnan, on the road to Galbally; containing 2497 inhabitants. The land is generally good, and some recent improvements in tillage have been introduced by Mr. Gabbet, who has an excellent farm managed upon the most approved principles of modern agriculture. The surface is varied, and there are some hills of considerable elevation, of which the Black mountain and Slieve-Reagh are the principal, stretching westward towards Kilfinnan, and every where affording excellent pasture for numerous herds of young cattle and flocks of sheep. Near Grierston, on the border of the parish, is a very extensive and valuable bog; in the midst of it rises a copious stream flowing southward towards Mitchelstown, and also another flowing northward and forming part of the Daun. Fairs are held at Ballinvreena, also on the border of the parish, on April 21st, June 21st, Aug. 31st, and Nov. 19th, for horses, cattle, and pigs. There are several large and handsome houses, the principal of which are Annagurra, the residence of Thos. T. Adams, Esq., and Grierston, the fine old family mansion of the Masseys. It is a rectory, in the diocese of Emly, and forms part of the union and corps of the prebend of Killenellick in the cathedral church of Emly: the tithes amount to £250. The church is a ruin situated on a gentle elevation, and forming a conspicuous object. The glebe comprises six plantation acres. The R. C. parish is co-extensive with that of the Established Church; the chapel is a large modern edifice in the village of Glenbrohane. There are two pay schools, in which are about 160 children.

BALLINGARRY, a market and post-town, and a parish, in the barony of UPPER CONNELLO, county of LIMERICK, and province of MUNSTER, 16 miles (S. W. by S.) from Limerick, and 111½ miles (S. W. by W.) from Dublin; containing 8651 inhabitants, of which number, 1685 are in the town. Several religious houses appear to have been founded here at a very early period, and have been greatly confounded with each other by various writers. The earliest of which any account is preserved is one founded by Donough Carbrae O'Brien, for Conventual Franciscans, a little eastward of the town, but generally attributed to Fitzgerald, Lord of Clenlis; the walls, which are tolerably perfect, and a beautiful square tower, are still remaining. A preceptory of Knights Templars was founded in 1172, which, after the suppression of that order in 1304, was granted to the Knights Hospitallers; and in the immediate vicinity was a Cistertian abbey, founded by the Fitzgeralds, in 1198, and dedicated to the Blessed Virgin, which afterwards became a cell to the abbey of Corcomroe; it was also called Kilson, and from the similarity of the name has often been mistaken for the abbey of Kilsane. There was also a convent for sisters of the order of St. Augustine, of which no vestiges can be traced. The town is situated on the road from Rathkeale to Charleville, and in a pleasing and sheltered valley which opens towards the west; it consists of one long irregular street and several smaller, and contains 276 houses, of which the greater number are small but tolerably well built. A building called the Turret was erected by a branch of the De Lacy family, and repaired by Col. O'Dell in 1683, as appears by a stone in the chimney; it was lately the residence of Major O'Dell. Near the town are the Fort-William flour-mills, the property of Mrs. Graves; and three miles to the east are the Kilmore flour-mills, the property of John Tuthill, Esq., of Kilmore House, adjacent to which is a good bridge, built by his grandfather. The markets are on Tuesday and Friday, chiefly for the sale of vegetables; there is no market-house, and the public scales are in the open street. Fairs are held on Easter-Monday, Whit-Monday, July 4th, and Dec. 5th, chiefly for the sale of horses, horned cattle, and pigs. Here is a station of the constabulary police; and petty sessions are held every Saturday.

The parish comprises 16,219½ statute acres, as applotted under the tithe act, and valued at £16,013 per annum. About 100 acres are common lands; and of the remainder, a large proportion is good arable land under an improved state of agriculture, but the greater portion is pasture; there is scarcely any bog or waste land. The soil is very variable, in some parts remarkably fertile, and in others rocky, sterile, and cold; it is for the greater part based on a substratum of silicious grit rising from the limestone vales into hills of considerable elevation in three different parts of the parish. To the south-west of the town rises the hill of Kilnamona, on which is a lake, supposed to have been formed by the excavation of a coal mine, and called Lough-na-Gual, or "the lake of coal." Directly opposite is Knockfiernha, which commands a most extensive prospect. The principal seats are Ballyno Cox, the handsome residence of W. Cox, Esq.; Glenwilliam Castle, of W. H. Massy, Esq.; Ballino Kane, of W. Scanlan, Esq.; the Grove, of Major O'Dell; Odell Ville, of T. A. O'Dell, Esq.; Rossmore, of Capt. J. W. Shelton; Mount Brown, of J. S. Brown, Esq.; Heathfield, of E. Lloyd, Esq.; Fort-William, of T. O'Dell, Esq.; Liskennett, of R. K. Sheehy, Esq.; Woodstock, of Rich. D. Graves, Esq.; Ash Grove, of D. D. Power, Esq.; Frankfort of R. Standish, Esq.; the Glebe, of the Rev. T. Gibbings; Ballynail, of J. Cox, Esq.; Kilbeg, of H. Scanlan, Esq.; and Spring Mount, of E. Fitzgerald, Esq. There are also many neat villas in the parish. The living is a rectory and vicarage, in the diocese of Limerick, and in the patronage of the Earl of Cork: the tithes amount to £900. The church, a small but very neat edifice in the early English style, with a lofty square tower, was built in 1820. The glebe-house was built by aid of a loan of £500 from the late Board of First Fruits, in 1822. The R. C. parish is co-extensive with that of the Established Church; there are three chapels, one in the town, one near Knockfiernha, and one near the south-eastern extremity of the parish. The parochial school for male and female children is aided by the rector, who provides the school-house rent-free; and there are eight pay schools, in which are about 420 children. A dispensary is supported by subscriptions. Adjoining the town are the remains of a very beautiful castle, of which the original name and the history are unknown; it is now called Parson's Castle, having been, previously to the erection of the glebe-house, the residence of the rector. About a mile to the north are the ruins of Lisamoota castle, and in the Grove demesne are those of Bonistoe (now commonly called Woodstock) castle. Within the limits of the parish are slight traces of other castles and of two small churches; on the summit of Lisduan hill are the remains of Jackson's Turret; and on Knockfiernha is a conical pile raised on the spot where stood the ancient temple of Stuadhraicin.

BALLINGARRY, a parish, in the barony of Lower Ormond, county of Tipperary, and province of Munster, 4 miles (E. by N.) from Burrisokane; containing 1767 inhabitants, of which number, 85 are in the hamlet, which consists of 13 houses. This parish is situated on the high roads from Roscrea to Portumna and from Nenagh to Parsonstown, and comprises 3498 plantation acres, divided into nearly equal portions of tillage and pasturage; the state of agriculture is much improved, and green crops are partially cultivated. There is a considerable extent of bog; and limestone of good quality abounds and is used for building. Knockshagowna, or "the Hill of the Fairies;" connected with which are some interesting legends, rises to a considerable height in the parish, and is an excellent landmark to the surrounding country; its summit, on which is a small tower, commands a very extensive view into several adjacent counties; on the east and west sides it is well planted, and the land on its north-eastern declivity is of excellent quality. A lake, surrounded by a large bog, and called Lough-na-Inch, is said to be very deep; near the centre is a small island formed artificially by piles of wood, but for what purpose is matter of conjecture. The principal seats are Lisbryen, situated in a well-planted demesne, that of T. Bunbury, Esq.; South Park, of C. Atkinson, Esq.; Ballymona, which is extensively planted, of Ralph Smith, Esq.; Fairy Hill, also well planted, of W. H. Cox, Esq.; Ballingarry Castle, of Marmaduke Thompson, Esq.; Clifton and White Hall, the former the seat and the latter the property of Capt. Shepherd; and Fairy Mount, the residence of the Rev. J. H. Saunderson, the vicar. Lismacrory, the ancient residence of the family of Smith, is now the property of Mr. Bunbury. Here is a station of the constabulary police.

The living is a vicarage, in the diocese of Killaloe, to which the vicarage of Uskeane was episcopally united in 1772 and 1809, and in the patronage of the Bishop; the rectory is impropriate in M. Thompson, Esq. The tithes amount to £263. 2. 6., of which £159 is payable to the impropriator, and £104. 2. 6. to the vicar; and the entire tithes of the benefice, payable to the vicar, are £208. The church is an ancient edifice with a spire and minarets, for the repair of which the Ecclesiastical Commissioners have lately granted £157. There is neither glebe-house nor glebe. In the R. C. divisions this parish forms part of the union of Burris-o-kane: the chapel is situated at the Pike, and is of recent erection. A school was established in 1834 by the vicar, by whom, aided by a few private subscriptions, it is supported. There are some remains of the ancient castle of Ballingarry, from which it appears to have been of great strength and magnitude.

BALLINGARRY, or GARE, a parish, in the barony of SLIEVARDAGH county of TIPPERARY, and province of MUNSTER, 5 miles (E. by N.) from Killenaule; containing 5872 inhabitants. This parish, which is situated on the southern portion of the great coal field of Slievardagh, and is the property of Matthew Pennefather, Esq., comprises 13,325 statute acres, as applotted under the tithe act, and chiefly in pasture; there is neither bog nor waste land. The village has arisen within the last 20 years, and consists of nearly 100 neatly built houses inhabited principally by persons connected with the adjacent collieries. Fairs are held on Whit-Monday, July 23rd, Nov. 11th, and Dec. 12th, and are well supplied with cattle and pigs. There is a constabulary police station in the village. The principal seats are Coal Brook, that of H. Langley, Esq., a handsome residence; Harley Park, of J. P. Poe, Esq., pleasantly situated in a richly planted demesne; and Ballyphilip, of Ambrose Going, Esq., the demesne of which is tastefully laid out. The living is a vicarage, in the diocese of Cashel, and in the patronage of the Bishop; the rectory is impropriate in the Rev. — Hayden; the tithes amount to £738. 9. $2\frac{3}{4}$., of which £492. 6. $1\frac{3}{4}$. is payable to the impropriator, and the remainder to the vicar. The church, a neat plain edifice with a tower, was erected by aid of a gift of £470 from the late Board of First Fruits, in 1811. The glebe-house was built by a gift of £350 and a loan of £450 from the same Board, in 1814: the glebe comprises $17\frac{1}{2}$ acres, subject to a rent. The R. C. parish is co-extensive with that of the Established Church: the chapel, which is situated in the village, is a handsome and spacious edifice, erected in 1828 on a site of about two acres of land given by the late Col. Pennefather; in the chapelyard is a school-house. A school-house under the trustees of Erasmus Smith's foundation was erected at an expense of £300, and two acres of land were assigned to it by the late Col. Pennefather; and there are three other schools, supported by private subscription. These schools afford instruction to about 250 boys, and 120 girls; and there are also six pay schools, in which are about 270 boys and 170 girls.

The coal field, of which a considerable portion is within this parish, extends 7 miles in length and 3 miles in breadth: the coal is found in three distinct seams of 12, 18, and 24 inches in thickness, lying above each other at intervening distances varying from 90 to 140 feet, dipping to a common centre, and appearing at the surface on all sides: the extreme depth of the lowest seam is about 700 feet. The coal beds lie about 1800 feet over a mass of limestone rock of great thickness, which shews itself at the surface all round on an average within two miles of the pits. The coal field is divided among various proprietors in portions varying from 1000 to 1500 acres, each of whom is the owner of the coal upon his own land. Some of the mines have been drained and worked by the proprietors, by means of day levels or adits, for which the undulation of the surface is extremely favourable; and of late years several of the collieries have been let on lease to the Mining Company of Ireland, who have erected steam-engines for raising the water from the deeper parts of the mines, and made various other improvements for working them to greater advantage. The collieries on the estate of Coalbrook had been worked upon a judicious plan and with great success by the late proprietor, Charles Langley, Esq., for the last 30 years, and are still carried on in a similar manner by the present proprietor. On the estate of Kilballygalavin, also in this parish, and the property of the Earl of Carrick, are mines under lease to the Mining Company, which are now being opened; and on the estate of Boulintlea, belonging to Edward Cooke, Esq., are others under lease to the same Company, which are now in operation, and for working which, on a more extensive scale, preparations are now in progress. The mines on the estate of Ballyphilip are very extensive, and the coal is of good quality; they have not latterly been worked to advantage, but arrangements are now in progress for opening them to a greater extent and working them upon a more improved plan. The average price of large coal at the pit is 15*s*. per ton, and of culm, 7*s*. The coal, which is of the non-flaming kind, is in great request with malsters and millers for drying corn; and is also esteemed very profitable for culinary uses, for which it is carried to a great distance. About three-fourths of the produce of the mines is culm, which is used chiefly for burning lime. The entire produce of the coal field at present is valued at about £25,000 per annum; but the returns are likely to be much augmented by the more extensive working of the mines and the increased demand arising from the progressive improvements in agriculture.

BALLINGLEY.—See BALLYINGLEY.

BALLINLOGHY, or BALLINLOUGH, a parish, in the barony of SMALL COUNTY, county of LIMERICK, and province of MUNSTER, 6 miles (E. N. E.) from Bruff; containing 1286 inhabitants. This parish, which is situated on the road from Pallas-Greine to Bruff, comprises 2007 statute acres, as applotted under the tithe act, and is the joint property of the Earls of Sandwich and Aldborough. The land is in general good, and is subdivided into a great number of small farms; the inhabitants are amply supplied with fuel from three bogs in the neighbourhood. It is a vicarage, in the diocese of Emly, and forms part of the union of Aney: the rectory is impropriate in the Earl of Limerick. The tithes amount to £243. 16. 10., of which two-thirds are payable to the impropriator and the remainder to the vicar. There is neither church nor glebe-house: the glebe comprises 12 acres of excellent land, which are wholly claimed by the Earl of Kenmare. In the R. C. divisions it is part of the union or district of Hospital and Herbertstown. Here are two eminences, one called Cromwell's Hill and the other Cromwell's Moat; both have traces of works on them, but apparently of much greater antiquity than the time of Cromwell.

BALLINLONDRY, or BALLINLANDERS, a parish, in the barony of COSTLEA, county of LIMERICK, and province of MUNSTER, 3 miles (N. W.) from Galbally, on the road to Kilfinane; containing 2999 inhabitants, of which number, 281 are in the village, which is large and of modern erection, consisting of good houses built of stone and roofed with slate; it is a constabulary police station. The parish is the property of the Earl of Kingston. The land is generally good and is mostly under tillage, producing abundant crops: there is a considerable tract of bog, in the centre of which rises a very copious spring supplying two streams, one flowing to the north and the other to the south, and both forming a boundary between this parish and that of Ballingarry. It is a rectory and vicarage, in the diocese of Emly, and forms part of the union of Duntrileague, and the corps of the prebend of Killenellick in the cathedral of Emly: the tithes amount to £250. The old church has long since fallen into decay, and is now a picturesque and venerable ruin near the village; in the churchyard is a remarkably fine ash tree. The glebe comprises three acres of excellent land. The R. C. parish is co-extensive with that of the Established Church; the chapel, a large handsome building, is situated in the village. There are three pay schools, in which are about 150 children; and a dispensary is supported in the usual way.

BALLINLOUGH, a village, in the parish of KILSKYRE, barony of UPPER KELLS, county of MEATH, and province of LEINSTER, 1 mile (N.) from Crossakeel; containing 117 inhabitants. It is situated on one of the roads from Kells to Oldcastle, and comprises about 20 houses, besides the R. C. chapel of the district.

BALLINLOUGH, a village, in the parish of KILTULLAGH, barony of BALLINTOBBER, county of ROSCOMMON, and province of CONNAUGHT, 5 miles (W. by S.) from Castlerea; containing 130 inhabitants. It is situated about half a mile from Lough Aelwyn, and consists of about 45 small houses and cabins built in detached groups and upon uneven ground. It has rather a picturesque appearance, and derives a considerable degree of interest from the parish church, a new and handsome edifice, situated upon an eminence immediately behind it. A fair is held on Sept. 29th. Ballinlough House is the residence of the Rev. J. Le Poer Trench; and between the village and the lake is Willsborough House, a small ancient mansion, formerly the seat of the Wills family. A constabulary police force has been established here. There are two schools.

BALLINODE, a village, in the parish of TYDAVNET, barony and county of MONAGHAN, and province of ULSTER, 3 miles (N. W.) from Monaghan; its population is included in the return for the parish. This place is situated on the road from Monaghan to Enniskillen, by way of Brookborough, and on a small river, over which there is a good stone bridge; and contains the parochial church and school, the former of which is a neat edifice with a steeple, and a dispensary. It has a patent for a fair for cattle on the first Saturday in every month, but no fairs are now held.

BALLINODE, a village, in the parish of CALRY, barony of UPPER CARBERY, county of SLIGO, and province of CONNAUGHT, 2 furlongs (E.) from Sligo, on the road to Manor-Hamilton; containing 17 houses and 85 inhabitants.

BALLINONTY, a hamlet, in the parish of KILCOOLEY, barony of SLIEVARDAGH, county of TIPPERARY, and province of MUNSTER, 1½ mile (N.) from Killenaule; containing 171 inhabitants. This place, which is the property of W. Going, Esq., is situated on the north-west confines of the Slievardagh coal field, and contains 12 houses, or cabins, inhabited by persons employed in the coal-works. There is a good sessions-house in the hamlet, in which the road sessions for the barony of Slievardagh, and the petty sessions for the division are held, the former, as occasion requires, and the latter weekly. There is also a dispensary.

BALLINROBE, a market and post-town, and a parish, in the barony of KILMAINE, county of MAYO, and province of CONNAUGHT, 14 miles (S. by E.) from Castlebar, and 116½ miles (W. by N.) from Dublin; containing 8923 inhabitants, of which number, 2604 are in the town. A monastery for friars of the order of St. Augustine was founded here some time prior to 1337, in which year it is mentioned in the registry of the Dominican friary of Athenry, under the name of the monastery *de Roba*. The town is situated on the river Robe, from which it derives its name, and on the road from Hollymount to Cong; it consists of one principal street, from which two others diverge, and, in 1831, contained 441 houses, of which nearly all are well built and slated, and several are of handsome appearance. There are barracks for cavalry and infantry; the former adapted to the accommodation of 8 officers and 106 non-commissioned officers and privates, with stabling for 84 horses; the latter for 6 officers and 96 non-commissioned officers and men, with an hospital for 20 patients. A considerable trade is carried on in corn; and large quantities of wheat and potatoes, the latter of excellent quality, are sold in the town. There are a large flour-mill, an extensive brewery and malting establishment, and a tanyard, all in full operation. The market is on Monday, and is well supplied with corn and provisions; and fairs are held on Whit-Tuesday and the 5th of December, chiefly for sheep and cattle. A chief constabulary police station has been established here. There is a patent for a manorial court, but none is held; petty sessions are held every Monday, and general sessions take place in June and December. The court-house is a neat building well adapted to the purpose, and affording also accommodation for the market. The bridewell contains four cells, three day-rooms, and two airing-yards, with other requisite accommodation.

The parish, which is situated on the loughs Mask and Carra, comprises 13,504 statute acres, as applotted under the tithe act, of which 7290 are arable, 3888 pasture, 324 woodland, 1120 bog, and 882 acres waste land. The land under cultivation has been greatly impoverished by burning and other defective modes of management, and the pastures might be much improved by draining; the system of agriculture, however, is gradually improving. The plantations are mostly on rushy land; and of the waste, about 400 acres are a limestone rock. Limestone of very good quality is quarried for building and for agricultural purposes. The surrounding scenery, particularly towards Lough Mask, is very pleasing; the mountains of Joyce's country, rising in the distance on the west side of the lake, and the east side being embellished with numerous handsome demesnes. Among the gentlemen's seats are Curramore, the residence of Jeffrey Martin, Esq., pleasantly situated on Lough Mask; and on the same lake,

Cuslough House, formerly the seat of Lord Tyrawley, and now of R. Livesey Esq.; and Creagh, that of J. Cuff, Esq. On Lough Carra is Lakeview, the residence of Mrs. Blake. Robe Villa is the seat of Courtney Kenny, Esq., in the demesne of which, and on the bank of the river, are the remains of the abbey; Lavally House, of R. Fair, Esq.; Springvale, of Henry Joseph Blake, Esq.; and Cluna Castle, the residence of J. Gildea, Esq. The living is a rectory and vicarage, in the diocese of Tuam, and in the patronage of the Archbishop; the tithes amount to £480. The church, a neat plain building, was repaired in 1815, towards which the late Board of First Fruits granted a loan of £300; and the Ecclesiastical Commissioners have lately granted £251 for its further repair. The glebe-house, a handsome residence, was built by aid of a gift of £100 and a loan of £1050 from the late Board; the glebe comprises 10 acres. The R. C. parish is co-extensive with that of the Established Church: the chapel, a large slated building with a lofty square tower, was erected in 1815 by subscription, towards which the late Lord Tyrawley gave £50 and one acre of land. There is a place of worship for Baptists. Two schools in the town are aided by donations from C. N. Knox, Esq., and afford instruction to about 200 children; and there are seven private pay schools in the parish, in which are about 320 children, and a Sunday school. There is also a dispensary. Numerous remains of ancient forts may be traced; and on the grounds of Mr. Clendinning and Mr. Rycroft are chalybeate springs.

BALLINSPITTLE, a village, in the parish of Ringrone, barony of Courceys, county of Cork, and province of Munster, 4 miles (W. S. W.) from Kinsale, on the road to Kilbritain: containing 105 inhabitants. It has recently been much improved by J. B. Gibbons, Esq., who has erected a square of slated houses. There is a court-house, in which petty sessions are held on alternate Tuesdays; and it is a constabulary police station. Fairs are held on May 14th and September 25th, and a large fair for pigs commences on St. Stephen's day, and is held every Monday for about a month. A road is being formed from the village to the ferry of Kinsale. The R. C. chapel for the union or district of Courceys is situated here, and has been recently repaired by a bequest of £200 from the late T. Rochford, Esq., of Garretstown. Near it is a large school, built in 1833 by a gift of £200 from Mr. Rochford, on land given by Mr. Gibbons. A dispensary has been erected for the parishes of Ringrone, Kilbritain, Ballinadee, and the remainder of the barony of Courceys. Ballinspittle House is the residence of J. Barry Gibbons, Esq., and around the village are several other handsome houses, which are noticed in the article on Ringrone.

BALLINTAMPLE, a village, in the parish of Ahamplish, barony of Lower Carbery, county of Sligo, and province of Connaught, 13 miles (N.) from Sligo; containing 20 houses and 110 inhabitants. It is situated on the peninsula of Mullaghmore, and is a station of the coast-guard.

BALLINTEMPLE, a parish, in the barony of Clonmahon, county of Cavan, and province of Ulster, $6\frac{3}{4}$ miles (S. by W.) from Cavan, containing, with part of the town of Ballinagh, 4982 inhabitants. This parish is situated on the road from Virginia to Killyshandra, and comprises, according to the Ordnance survey, including $54\frac{1}{4}$ under water, $10,657\frac{3}{4}$ statute acres, of which 8074 are applotted under the tithe act. It is a vicarage, in the diocese of Kilmore, and forms part of the union and corps of the deanery of Kilmore; the rectory is impropriate in the representatives of Richard, Earl of Westmeath. The tithes amount to £259, of which £104 is payable to the impropriators, and the remainder to the vicar. The church was erected in 1821 by aid of a loan of £1200 from the late Board of First Fruits. The glebe comprises 103*a.* 1*r.* 29*p.* of profitable land, valued at £87. 13. 10. per annum. The R. C. parish is co-extensive with that of the Established Church; there are three chapels, called respectively the upper and lower chapels and the chapel of ease. The parochial school and two others afford instruction to about 180 boys and 60 girls; and there are also three private pay schools, in which are about 170 boys and 50 girls.—See Ballinagh.

BALLINTEMPLE, a parish, in the barony of Kilnemanagh, county of Tipperary, and province of Munster, 6 miles (N. E.) from Tipperary, on the road to Thurles; containing 786 inhabitants. It comprises about 3600 statute acres, principally under an improved system of tillage. Dundrum, the handsome seat of Viscount Hawarden, who is proprietor in fee of the barony, is beautifully situated in a fine demesne, comprising more than 2400 statute acres, of which nearly 800 are well planted; the grounds are tastefully laid out, and there is a profusion of fine old timber on the estate. A new line of road from Dundrum to Cappaghmore is in progress, which will there unite with a road to Limerick, and thus open a more direct line of communication with that city, by which a saving of about five miles will be effected in the distance. At the junction of this road with that from Thurles to Tipperary, and at the base of the Kilnemanagh hills, is situated the modern village of Dundrum or Newtown-Dundrum. Fairs are held here at Whitsuntide, and on the second Tuesday in October; and it is a station of the constabulary police. The living is a rectory and vicarage, in the diocese of Cashel, to which the rectories and vicarages of Rathlynan, Oughterleague, and Kilpatrick were united by act of council in 1795, forming the union of Ballintemple, in the patronage of the Bishop. The tithes of the parish amount to £240, and of the benefice to £726. 9. $2\frac{3}{4}$. The church is a plain modern edifice, situated nearly in the centre of the union. There is a glebe-house, with a glebe of 20 acres. Here is a R. C. chapel. Near Dundrum is a school for both sexes, supported by Viscount Hawarden, with a house and garden; and there is another school aided by private subscriptions, together affording instruction to about 220 children: also a dispensary.

BALLINTEMPLE, a parish, in the barony of Arklow, county of Wicklow, and province of Leinster, $4\frac{1}{2}$ miles (N. W. by W.) from Arklow; containing 1021 inhabitants. This parish is situated on the road from Arklow to Carlow, and on the river Derry, which meets the Ovoca at the Wooden Bridge hotel in the village, thence called the second "Meeting of the Waters." The soil is fertile, and the system of agriculture improving. Some of the streams descending from the mountain Croghan-Kinshela, which towards the close of the last century was explored for gold, run through this parish; and shafts have been sunk for copper, with a prospect of success, though they are stopped at present from a disputed claim to the royalty between the Earl of Carysfort and the Marquess of Ormonde. The living is a rectory, in the diocese of Dublin and Glendalough, and in the patronage of William Brian, Esq.: the tithes amount to £103. 16. 11. The church, built by aid of a gift of £800 and a loan of £50 from the late Board of First Fruits, in 1816, is in a state of dilapidation from the dry rot. The glebe-house commands a beautifully picturesque view of the woods of Ballyarthur and Knockname, and from the upper grounds is an extensive and pleasing prospect over the Vale of Ovoca: the glebe comprises 2½ acres. In the R. C. divisions the parish is included in the union or district of Arklow; the chapel is at Ballycowgue, and attached to it is a school. The parochial school is supported by weekly payments from the children. There is also a hedge school. In the centre of the parish is an ancient cemetery.

BALLINTOBBER, a parish, in the barony of CARRA, county of MAYO, and province of CONNAUGHT, 8 miles (N. N. W.) from Ballinrobe; containing 6212 inhabitants. This parish, the name of which signifies in the Irish language the "town of the well," probably derived that appellation from a spring which descends from a natural arch in a rock, with such force as to act like a shower bath, and near which is no other stream whatever. Cathol O'Conogher, King of Connaught, in 1216, founded an abbey here for Canons Regular of the order of St. Augustine, which he dedicated to the Holy Trinity; it was burned in 1263, but was restored, and continued to flourish till the dissolution; in 1605 a lease of it was granted in reversion for 50 years to Sir John King, Knt. This abbey is said to have been erected on the site of an ancient castle, in which were buried the former lords of Mayo; and part of its remains are now converted into a R. C. chapel. The buildings appear to have been truly magnificent, and many of the ruined portions are still entire in their principal features; though the principal tower has fallen, the lofty arch on which it was supported is still remaining, and nearly 50 feet high; the doorway is a beautiful specimen of the pointed receding arch, supported on each side by a range of five columns. The parish is situated on the road from Castlebar to Ballinrobe. There is a wide extent of mountain, exclusively of which the land is nearly equally divided between arable and pasture; and there is a considerable tract of wood and flooded lands. The living is a rectory, in the diocese of Tuam, entirely appropriate to the vicars choral of the cathedral of Christ Church, Dublin; the tithes amount to £240. In the R. C. divisions the parish is united to those of Burriscarra and Towaghty: the chapel is at Killavalla. There are three daily pay schools, in which are about 170 boys and 40 girls.

BALLINTOBBER, a parish, partly in the half-barony of BALLYMOE, but chiefly in the barony of BALLINTOBBER, county of ROSCOMMON, and province of CONNAUGHT, 4 miles (S. E. by S.) from Castlerea; containing 2480 inhabitants. This place is supposed to derive its name, signifying "the town of the wells," from some fine springs near the village. It is uncertain at what period the castle, now in ruins, was built: tradition ascribes its erection to Cathol Creudfarag O'Conor, in the 13th century; but Ledwich attributes it to Sir John King, to whom the property was granted in 1605. The same writer asserts that the place had its origin in an abbey founded in 1216 by O'Conor, King of Connaught. In 1590, Hugh O'Conor Don or Dun, having incurred the hatred of his sept by accepting an English knighthood and remaining in allegiance to Queen Elizabeth, was besieged in the ancient castle by Hugh Roe O'Donnell, and was taken prisoner and deprived of his chieftaincy. In the war of 1641, Lord Ranelagh, Lord-President of Connaught, led a force of 900 foot and two or three troops of horse against the castle, then the principal strong hold of the O'Conor Don, near which were assembled 3000 horse and foot of the Mayo forces under Butler, and the insurgents of this county under O'Conor himself. The lord-president, to draw them into the plain ground, feigned a retreat for about three miles, and was pursued by the enemy; but turning round, he charged and routed them. The parish is situated on the river Suck, and on the road from Roscommon to Castlerea; and comprises 4274 statute acres, as applotted under the tithe act. Considerable tracts of bog are spread over its surface; and there is a quarry of excellent limestone. The village contains about twenty-six dwellings, all cabins except three; and behind it to the west, at the extremity of a limestone ridge, are the grand and picturesque ruins of the castle. The principal seats are Willsgrove, the property of W. R. Wills, Esq.; Enfield, the seat of P. O'Connor, Esq.; French-dawn, of Mrs. French; Fortwilliam, the residence of P. Teighe, Esq.; Willsbrook, of —— O'Connor, Esq.; and Tenny Park, the seat of T. T. Byrne, Esq. A large fair for horses, formerly much resorted to for the sale of yarn, is held on Aug. 25th. Petty sessions are also held here, generally monthly. The living is a rectory and vicarage, in the diocese of Elphin, forming the corps of the prebend of Ballintobber in the cathedral church of Elphin, and united by act of parliament of the 9th of Queen Anne to the vicarages of Baslick and Kilkeevan, which three parishes constitute the union of Ballintobber or Kilkeevan, in the patronage of the Bishop: the tithes amount to £200; and the gross tithes of the benefice to £625. The church of the union is in Kilkeevan: it is a neat edifice of ancient English architecture, built in 1818 by a loan of £2500 from the late Board of First Fruits. The glebe-house, also situated in that parish, was built by aid of a gift of £100 and a loan of £825 from the same Board: the glebe comprises 14*a.* 3*r.* 30*p.* The R. C. parish is co-extensive with that of the Established Church: the chapel is situated in the village. There is a school at Willsgrove under the patronage of W. R. Wills, Esq., by whom the school-house was built, in which about 80 boys and 40 girls are taught; and there are two hedge schools, in which are about 130 boys and 40 girls. The remains of the castle consist of a quadrangular enclosure, 270 feet in length and 237 in breadth, defended by strong polygonal towers at each angle, and by two others, one on each side of the principal gateway, facing an esplanade at the end of the limestone ridge on which they are situated; they are surrounded by a deep fosse, over which was a drawbridge from a postern. The towers much resemble those of Caernarvon castle, and that on the south-west is very imposing and picturesque.

BALLINTOGHER, a village, in the parish of KILLERY, barony of TIRAGHRILL, county of SLIGO, and province of CONNAUGHT, 3½ miles (S.W.) from Dromohair; containing 201 inhabitants. This place, which is situated on the road from Dromohair to Collooney, comprises about 40 thatched dwellings, and contains the parish church, a small plain building, and the parochial Roman Catholic chapel, a large and commodious edifice. Fairs are held on Jan. 22nd, June 8th, July 28th, Oct. 17th, and Dec. 8th; and here is a station of the constabulary police. Near it is Oldcastle, the residence of E. Loftus Neynoe, Esq.; occupying the site of the ancient castle of Kingsfort. Iron ore has been found in the vicinity; and in the mountains of West Lough Gill are indications of coal, manganese, iron, and copper, besides a great variety of clays.—See KILLERY.

BALLINTOY, a parish, in the barony of CAREY, county of ANTRIM, and province of ULSTER, 4 miles (N.W.) from Ballycastle; containing 4061 inhabitants, of which number, 278 are in the village. This parish is situated on the most northern part of the coast of Antrim, which is here diversified with creeks and bays, and with cliffs and headlands of singular and romantic appearance. It lies opposite to the north-west point of the island of Rathlin, and comprises, according to the Ordnance survey, 12,753¾ acres (including Sheep and Carrickarede islands), of which about one-half is arable, one-third pasture, and the remainder bog. The surface is boldly varied: immediately above the village rises the lofty hill of Knocksoghy, covered with rock and furze; there is also another hill called Croaghmore, which rises to a great height, and may be seen at a great distance; its sides are arable, and on the summit, which is fine pasture, without any heath, are a cairn of stones and some graves. The land about the village and near White Park bay is in a high state of cultivation. Seaweed, of which some is made into kelp, and shell sand and lime are the chief manures. The village contains about 60 houses: the road from Ballycastle to Bushmills passes through the parish, and commands some pleasantly diversified scenery and some highly romantic views, among which are White Park bay and the beautiful windings of the shore studded with detached masses of basaltic rock and limestone. Near it is Mount Druid, the residence of the Rev. Robert Trail, a handsome mansion deriving its name from the Druidical relic on the hill above it. In the hills are found mines of wood-coal, which seems to be peculiar to this part of the coast: it is found in strata generally under basalt, varying from two inches to two feet in thickness, and displays the grain, knots, roots, and branches of timber; it is generally used as domestic fuel, but its disagreeable smell renders it very ineligible for that purpose. These mines belong of right to the Antrim family, who are lords in fee; but their claim has never been asserted to prevent the tenants raising as much coal as they might require. There are extensive quarries of good stone, which is obtained for building and also for repairing the roads; and limestone abounds in the parish. Some of the inhabitants are employed in spinning yarn and weaving, but the greater number are engaged in agriculture. There are salmon fisheries at Portbraddon, Carrickarede, and Laryban, on the coast. The insulated rock of Carrickarede is separated from the main land by a chasm 60 feet wide and more than 80 feet deep; at this place the salmon are intercepted in their retreat to the rivers. The fishing commences early in spring and continues till August: a rude bridge of ropes is every year thrown across the chasm, which remains during the season, and a singular kind of fishery is carried on, which is generally very productive. The other fish taken off this coast are glassen, grey gurnet, cod, lythe, ling, sea trout, mackerel, and turbot: a species of red cod, and a small thick red fish of indifferent quality, called murranroe, are also found here. About 30 boats are employed in the fishery, which are drawn up in the several creeks along the shore; there are also several bays, into one of which, called Port Camply, vessels of light tonnage occasionally sail from the Scottish coast. At Port Ballintoy there is a coast-guard station, which is one of the eight stations that form the district of Ballycastle. Fairs are held in the village for horses, Scotch ponies, cattle, pigs, and pedlery, on June 3rd, Sept. 4th, and Oct. 14th. The parish is within the jurisdiction of the manorial court of Ballycastle, which is held there every month.

The living is a rectory, in the diocese of Connor, and in the patronage of the Bishop: the tithes amount to £415. 7. 8. The church, a plain edifice with a spire, was rebuilt on the site of the ancient structure, in 1813, by aid of a gift of £800 from the late Board of First Fruits; it is romantically situated on a plain on the sea-shore, backed by lofty hills. The glebe-house was built by the present incumbent in 1791, and is situated on a glebe of 40 acres, subject to a rent of £25. 5. late currency. In the R. C. divisions this parish is united to that of Armoy, and contains a small chapel. There is a place of worship for Presbyterians in connection with the Synod of Ulster. A parochial school was founded and endowed by Mrs. Jane Stewart, under whose will the master is appointed by the vestry held at Easter, and has a salary of £15 per annum. At Prollisk and Island Macallen are two schools, supported by a society of which the late Dr. Adams was the originator, which, with the parochial school, afford instruction to about 240 boys and 80 girls; and there are also three private schools, in which are about 90 boys and 30 girls. The splendid ruins of Dunseverick castle, one of the earliest Scottish fortresses, situated on a bold and isolated rock projecting into the sea, at the north-west extremity of the parish, and formerly the seat of the O'Cahans, form an interesting feature on the coast; traces of the outworks are still visible, and the remains of the keep, consisting only of part of the shell crowning the summit of the rock, which has been rendered more inaccessible by clearing away immense masses from the base, in order to make it the more precipitous, derive much interest from the singularity of their situation. At Port Coan, near the Giants' Causeway, is a singular cavern, the sides and roof of which are formed of round pebbles imbedded in a matrix of basalt of great hardness. At the other extremity of the parish, on the sea-coast to the east of the village, and about a mile from the road leading to Ballycastle, are the ruins of Mac Allister's castle, a small fortress erected by the native chieftain whose name it bears, but at what precise period is not known; it is situated on the verge of a frightful chasm, on the lower extremity of an abrupt headland connected with the shore by a narrow isthmus, which is perforated at its base by several caverns, in one of which are some basaltic columns. There are some remains of the ancient church of Templeastragh, the burial-ground of which is still in use.

BALLINTRA, a village, in the parish of DRUMHOLM, barony of TYRHUGH, county of DONEGAL, and province of MUNSTER, 4½ miles (N. N. E.) from Ballyshannon; containing 439 inhabitants. This village, which is situated on the road from Ballyshannon to Donegal, and at an equal distance from both those towns, consists of one street containing about 90 houses, and has a daily penny post to Donegal and Ballyshannon. Within a mile is Brown Hall, the seat of the Rev. Edward Hamilton, a handsome mansion in a beautifully picturesque demesne, through the groves of which winds a river that in some parts rushes down thickly wooded precipices, and within view of the house is a small lake. This scenery, which is called the *Pullins*, is strongly contrasted with the dreary tracts of country that surround it, especially on the south and east. Fairs are held on the 1st of February, March 25th, May 20th, June 24th, Aug. 1st, Oct. 3rd, and Nov. 30th, for general farming stock. This is a station of the constabulary police; petty sessions are held on alternate Mondays: and in the village are situated the parish church, a place of worship for Wesleyan Methodists, and a dispensary.—See DRUMHOLM.

BALLINTUBBER, or FONSTOWN, a parish, in the barony of BALLYADAMS, QUEEN'S county, and province of LEINSTER, 3¼ miles (W. by S.) from Athy: the population is returned with the parish of Ballyadams. This parish is situated on the road from Maryborough to Carlow; agriculture is improving, there is a small quantity of bog, and limestone is quarried for building. Kellyville, the residence of the late Judge Kelly, is now the property of Thos. Kelly, Esq. It is a rectory and vicarage, in the diocese of Leighlin, united to that of Ballyadams, and its tithes are included in the composition for that parish. The church of the union, a neat small edifice in good repair, is situated here, and adds greatly to the pleasing appearance of the village. In the R. C. divisions also it forms part of the union or district of Ballyadams. The schools are noticed in the description of that parish.

BALLINURE.—See BALLYNURE.

BALLINVANA, a parish, in the barony of COSTLEA, county of LIMERICK, and province of MUNSTER, 3 miles (S .E.) from Kilmallock, on the road to Knocklong; containing 2710 inhabitants. In ecclesiastical concerns this place is not known as a parish, but is considered as forming part of the parishes of Emly Grenan, Kilbreedy, and Athnassey, and is annexed to the union of Kilmallock. In the R. C. divisions it forms part of the union of Athnassey. On the summit of a gentle eminence are the ruins of Fauntstown castle, erected by the Faunt family in the reign of Jas. I.; and not far distant are the remains of an old church, near which is a holy well, much frequented on the 25th of March, the patron day: close to the well is an ash tree, of which the branches are weighed down by the numerous offerings placed on them by the votaries.

BALLINVARRY.—See BALLYVARY.

BALLINVOHIR, a parish, in the barony of CORKAGUINEY, county of KERRY, and province of MUNSTER, 12 miles (E.) from Dingle; containing 2924 inhabitants. This parish, which is situated on the bay of Dingle, and on the road from Dingle to Tralee, comprises 13,190 statute acres, as applotted under the tithe act, a large portion of which consists of coarse mountain pasture, with some patches of bog. The mountain of Lack, from the summit of which is obtained a panoramic view of the various mountains on this side of the bay, and of the Iveragh mountains on the opposite shore, is within its limits; and at the foot of Acres mountain is a small portion of the parish, which is entirely detached from the rest. A new road, about three English miles in length, is about to be constructed from Inchbridge, in this parish, through Glaunaheera, to the mail coach road from Dingle to Tralee, by which travellers from Dingle to Cork may pass through Killarney, instead of the more indirect way through Tralee, now in use. The system of agriculture is gradually improving; and from the abundance of sea manure on the shores of the bay, for the conveyance of which this new road will afford greater facility, there is every prospect that the greater portion of the waste land will be brought into cultivation. Some of the inhabitants are employed in the fishery. The living is a rectory, in the diocese of Ardfert and Aghadoe, constituting the corps of the archdeaconry of Ardfert, in the patronage of the Bishop. The tithes of the parish amount to £203. 1. 6., and of the entire benefice to £253. 18. 11.: the Blasquet Islands are included in the payment of tithes for this parish. There is neither church nor glebe-house, but there is a glebe of 22*a.* 3*r.* 14*p.* The Protestant parishioners attend the church of Ballinacourty, and the occasional duties are performed by the curate of that parish. In the R. C. divisions the parish partly forms the head of a union or district, in which is also included the parish of Ballinacourty, and is partly in the union of Cappaclough or Kilgobbin: there is a chapel at Lack, and a new chapel is in course of erection at Annescall, in the former parish. A school is held in the chapel at Lack, and other children of the parish attend the school at Annescall; there are also three pay schools in the parish. At Inch are the ruins of a church, or chapel, overshadowed by a white thorn tree of large size; there are no remains of the parish church, but the old burial-ground near Annescall lake is still used.

BALLISAKEERY, a parish, in the barony of TYRAWLEY, county of MAYO, and province of CONNAUGHT, 2½ miles (S. E.) from Killala; containing 5730 inhabitants. This parish, which is situated on the river Moy, and on the mail coach road from Ballina to Killala, comprises 11,281 statute acres, as applotted under the tithe act, and valued at £4705 per annum. The lands are principally under tillage; the system of agriculture is very much improved, and there is little waste land but what is very deep and irreclaimable bog, of which there are very large tracts. Limestone is found in some parts of the parish. There are several gentlemen's seats, of which the principal are Reserk, the residence of Cowen Green, Esq.; Broadlands Park, of P. C. Howley, Esq.; Netley Park, of H. W. Knox, Esq.; Ballybrooney, of J. Perkins, Esq.; and Farrow, of T. Waldron, Esq. The river Moy, which is celebrated for the abundance and quality of its salmon, is navigable on the border of the parish, and forms the pool of Ballisakeery, which is accessible to vessels of small burden. The living is a vicarage, in the diocese of Killala, to which the vicarage of Rathrea was united by act of council in 1807, and in the patronage of the Bishop; the rectory is appropriate to the deanery and archdeaconry of Killala. The tithes amount to £368. 11. 8½., of which £175. 7. 8½. is paid to the impropriators, and the remainder to the vicar; the entire tithes of the benefice amount to £273. 4. The church is a neat plain edifice, erected by a loan of £1025 from the late Board of First Fruits, in 1810; the Ecclesiastical Commissioners have lately granted £131 for its repair. The glebe-house, a handsome residence, was built by aid of a gift of 400 and a loan of £400 from the same Board, in 1820: the glebe comprises 29 acres. The R. C. parish is co-extensive with that of the Established Church; a chapel is now in process of erection in the village of Cooncal, and will be completed in a short time. There are places of worship for Presbyterians, Wesleyan Methodists, and Baptists. There are five public schools, of which a female school is supported by the Misses Knox, of Rappa, and in which about 200 boys and 200 girls are taught; also two hedge schools, in which are about 100 boys and 30 girls. There are some remains of the ancient abbey of Rosserick or Reserk, near the river Moy, founded by one of the sept of Joyce, for friars of the Franciscan order; they consist of the ruins of the church and a burial-ground; in the centre of the gable end is a square tower, and in the monastery is a closet of hewn stone for two confessors.

BALLON, a parish, in the barony of Forth, county of Carlow, and province of Leinster, 3½ miles (S. E.) from Tullow; containing 1439 inhabitants, of which number, 161 are in the village. This parish is situated on the road from Newtown-Barry to Carlow, and comprises 3520 statute acres, as applotted under the tithe act: it is principally grazing land; the state of agriculture is much improved; and in Ballon hill is a quarry of fine granite. The gentlemen's seats are Larogh, the residence of J. O'Brien, Esq.; and Altamount, of Nelson St. George, Esq. Fairs are held here on March 28th, and Aug. 12th. It is a vicarage, in the diocese of Leighlin, and is part of the union of Aghade: the rectory is impropriate in Lord Cloncurry. The tithes amount to £220 of which £140 is payable to the impropriator, and £80 to the incumbent. In the R. C. divisions, this parish forms part of the union or district of Gilbertstown, called also Ballon and Ratoe: the chapel, situated in the village of Ballon, is in good repair. In the village is also a school for boys and girls, for which the school-house was built by R. Marshall, Esq.; and there is another at Conaberry. These schools afford instruction to about 160 boys and 160 girls; and there are two hedge schools, in which are about 190 boys and 130 girls.

BALL'S-BRIDGE, a village, in that part of the parish of St. Mary, Donnybrook, which is within the county of the city of Dublin, in the province of Leinster, 1½ mile (S. E.) from the Post-office, Dublin: the population is returned with the parish. This place derives its name from a bridge of three arches erected here over the Dodder, in 1791, and rebuilt in 1835. It is pleasantly situated on the high road from Dublin to Kingstown and Bray, and on the left or west bank of the river, which issues from the mountains near Rockbrook, and falls into the Liffey near Ringsend. In the immediate vicinity, and on the right of the road from Dublin, stood Baggot-rath Castle, which was seized during the night by the forces of the Marquess of Ormonde, on his meditated investiture of the city, in 1649; but soon after daybreak on the following morning, the assailants were driven out by the garrison of Dublin and pursued and completely defeated. In 1651 the castle was taken by storm by Oliver Cromwell. All remains of it have long since disappeared; and within the last few years several handsome houses have been erected on its site. Adjoining the village, on the south, and along the banks of the Dodder, are works for printing linen, calico, and cotton, established about the year 1740, and since greatly extended and improved by Messrs. Duffy and Co., who for more than 40 years have been the sole proprietors. They are at present capable of finishing 100,000 pieces annually, are worked by the water of the Dodder and by steam-engines of 40-horse power, and afford constant employment to more than 400 persons. Near the village are the Hammersmith iron-works, established in 1834 by Mr. R. Turner: the front of this extensive establishment is 200 feet long, presenting a handsome façade towards the road; and at the back are numerous dwelling-houses for the workmen, which are called the Hammersmith cottages. The road on which these works are situated has been greatly improved; wide footpaths have been formed, and the whole is lighted with gas. Nearly adjoining the works are the botanical gardens belonging to Trinity College. The village is within the jurisdiction of the Dublin Court of Conscience for the recovery of small debts, and for all criminal matters within that of the metropolitan police. In the post-office arrangements it is within the limits of the twopenny-post delivery. An infants' school, a neat building with apartments for a master and mistress, was erected chiefly at the expense of Mr. and Mrs. Patten: here is also a dispensary.—See Donnybrook (St. Mary).

BALLY.—See BALLEE.

BALLYADAMS, a parish, partly in the barony of Stradbally, but chiefly in that of Ballyadams, Queen's county, and province of Leinster, 3½ miles (S. W.) from Athy; containing, with the parish of Baltintubber, 2165 inhabitants. This parish, which gives name to the barony within which it is chiefly included, and is also called *Kilmakedy*, is situated on the road from Carlow to Maryborough; and comprises 6811 statute acres, as applotted under the tithe act, of which about 30 are woodland, 260 bog, and the remainder good arable land. The state of agriculture is improving; limestone is quarried for building and burning; there are some quarries of good flag-stone, and coal is found in the parish. Ballyadams Castle is the seat of Capt. Butler; Gracefield, of Mrs. Kavanagh; and Popefield, of Capt. Pope. To the north of the old castle is Southville, formerly a residence of the late Richard Grace, of Boley, Esq. The living is a rectory and vicarage, in the diocese of Leighlin, with the rectory and vicarage of Ballintubber united from time immemorial; the patronage is disputed, and in the mean time the Bishop presents. The tithes of the united parishes amount to £553. 16. 11. The church of the union is at Ballintubber; the old parish church is a ruin situated on an eminence, and containing a monument with the recumbent effigies of Sir Robert Bowen, of Ballyadams Castle, and his lady, and one to the memory of the late Major-Gen. Sir Edward Butler. There is neither glebe nor glebe-house.

In the R. C. divisions the parish is the head of a union or district which comprises also the parishes of Ballintubber, Tullowmoy, Kilclonbrook, Rathaspeck, and Tecolme, and contains three chapels, one of which is in this parish. There is a school of about 80 boys and 50 girls. A school at Ballintubber was founded towards the close of the last century by Bowen Southwell, Esq., who endowed it with £20 per annum; and there are three pay schools. On a hill opposite to that on which are the remains of the church, are the ruins of the old castle of Ballyadams, which was besieged in 1641; they consist of embattled walls with projecting towers, and a lofty keep, and present a very interesting appearance. Near the castle are two very ancient wells sunk a few feet in the solid limestone rock, the water of which is supposed to have had medicinal properties imparted to it by St. Patrick. Cobler's Castle, bordering on the barony of Stradbally, was built on the summit of a lofty hill, to give employment to the neighbouring poor in a season of scarcity.

BALLYAGHRAN.—See AGHERTON.

BALLYANE, or BALLYANNE, a parish, in the barony of BANTRY, county of WEXFORD, and province of LEINSTER, 2 miles (N. E. by N.) from New Ross; containing 1096 inhabitants. This place is memorable for a battle which took place at Ballanveigga, in 1643, between the king's troops commanded by the Marquess of Ormonde, after their retreat from New Ross, and the insurgent forces under Gen. Preston, in which the latter were defeated and compelled to effect their escape across the river Barrow. The parish is situated on the high road from New Ross to Newtown-Barry, and is bounded on the west by the Barrow, from which a small creek navigable for lighters affords a facility of conveyance for limestone for the supply of the neighbouring country. It comprises 6480 statute acres, consisting of nearly equal proportions of arable and pasture land; there is a very little woodland, no waste, and only about 40 acres of bog at Gobbinstown. The soil is generally light and on the higher grounds shingly, but fertile; the system of agriculture has been greatly improved. Ballyane, the handsome seat of Victor O'Farrell, Esq., is finely situated on the brow of a richly wooded eminence, from which there is an extensive prospect; and Berkeley, the seat of J. Berkeley Deane, Esq., is a good mansion embosomed in thriving plantations, and commanding a distant view of the White mountains. It is a rectory, in the diocese of Ferns, and is part of the union of St. Mary's, New Ross; the tithes amount to £243. 3. 6½. The church is in ruins; In the R. C. divisions it forms part of the union or district of Cushinstown, or Carnagh; the chapel is a neat building, and attached to it is a residence for the clergyman. There is a school at Rathganogue, founded by the late Henry Houghton, Esq., who endowed it with £15 per annum charged on the demesne of Ballyane; the school-house, a handsome building, was erected on a site given by Edmund Sweetman, of Sweetmount, Esq., and about 100 children are educated in the school.

BALLYBACON, a parish, in the barony of IFFA and OFFA WEST, county of TIPPERARY, and province of MUNSTER, 4 miles (E. by S.) from Clogheen: containing 2970 inhabitants. This parish is situated on the mail coach road from Cork to Dublin, and near the river Suir; and comprises 4158 statute acres, as applotted under the tithe act. The river Tarr flows through it; and within its limits is Kilgrogy, the residence of S. Clutterbuck, Esq. The living is a rectory and vicarage, in the diocese of Lismore; the rectory is part of the union of Kilrush and corps of the archdeaconry of Lismore, and the vicarage is united to that of Tubrid. The tithes amount to £461. 10. 1., of which £283. 0. 10. is payable to the archdeacon, and £178. 9. 3. to the vicar. There is no church; the glebe, which belongs to the archdeacon, comprises 17¾ acres. In the R. C. divisions this parish forms part of the union of Ardfinnan: two chapels are now being erected. There are two pay schools, in which are about 100 boys and 80 girls. Here is a well, called *Poul-a-Tarr*, 48 feet in depth, from which there is a constant and copious flow of water.

BALLYBARRACK, a parish, in the barony of UPPER DUNDALK, county of LOUTH, and province of LEINSTER, 1¼ mile (S. S. W.) from Dundalk, on the road to Ardee; containing 444 inhabitants. It comprises, according to the Ordnance survey, 1018¼ statute acres; the lands are principally under tillage, and there is neither bog nor waste. It is a rectory, in the diocese of Armagh, and wholly impropriate in P. Coleman, Esq: the tithes amount to £186. 2. 6. There is no church nor any provision for the cure of souls. In the R. C. divisions it is in the union or district of Kilcurley, or Haggardstown, where the chapels are situated. There is a hedge school, in which are about 50 boys and 20 girls.

BALLYBEG, or BALLYBEGSHANAGH, a parish, in the barony of ORRERY and KILMORE, county of CORK, and province of MUNSTER, 1 mile (S.) from Buttevant, with which parish its population is returned. This place, which appears to have merged into the parish of Buttevant, is situated on the river Awbeg, and on the mail coach road from Cork to Limerick, which towards Mallow winds for some distance through a rocky glen recently embellished with plantations, and at the northern opening of which are situated the venerable remains of the abbey of St. Thomas. This establishment was a priory for Canons Regular of the order of St. Augustine, founded by Philip de Barry, who, in 1229, endowed it with ample revenues, in remembrance of which his equestrian statue of brass was erected in the church. The endowment was subsequently augmented, in 1235, by Sir David de Barry, who founded the friary of Buttevant. The priory and its possessions were, in the 10th of Jas. I., granted to Sir. J. Jephson, whose descendant, C. D. O. Jephson, Esq., is the present proprietor of the parish. The parish comprises 2045 statute acres, as applotted under the tithe act, and valued at £1693 per annum. The only seat is Springfield, the residence of J. Norcott, Esq. The living is an impropriate rectory, in the diocese of Cloyne; the tithes, being wholly the property of Mr. Jephson, are not under composition; the occasional duties of the parish devolve on the incumbent of Buttevant. In the R. C. divisions it is included in the union or district of Buttevant. The remains of the abbey consist of the steeple, part of the chancel with the east window, and a lofty tower detached from the rest of the building, of which it originally formed a part, and which shews the whole to have been an extensive pile. Close to the abbey are the vestiges of an ancient round tower. Many years since a stone coffin was excavated from the ruins of the abbey, containing a skeleton ornamented with a cross and chains of gold.

BALLYBENARD.—See FENNAGH.

BALLYBOFEY.—See BALLIBOPHAY.

BALLYBOG. — See KILCROHANE, county of KERRY.

BALLYBOGGAN, or DE-LAUDE-DEI, a parish, in the barony of UPPER MOYFENRAGH, county of MEATH, and province of LEINSTER, 2½ miles (S. W.) from Clonard, on the river Boyne, and on the road from Kinnegad to Edenderry; containing 1477 inhabitants. A priory for Augustine Canons was founded here in the 12th century by Jordan Comin, and dedicated to the Holy Trinity; it was consumed by fire in the beginning of 1446, and in the following year its prior died of the plague. In the 33rd of Hen. VIII. it was granted with various other possessions, to Sir William Bermingham, afterwards created Lord Carbrey, *in capite*, at an annual rent of £4. 3. 4.; and the reversion was, in the 41st of Elizabeth, granted to Edward Fitzgerald and his heirs: there are some remains of the buildings on the north-west bank of the river Boyne. There is a small quantity of bog in the parish. New Park is the property of the Rev. J. Digby. A fair for cattle is held on the 25th of September. It is a perpetual curacy, in the diocese of Meath, episcopally united to that of Castlejordan; the rectory is impropriate in the Gifford family. The tithes amount to £220, the whole payable to the impropriator, who allows the perpetual curate £30 per annum. In the R. C. divisions the parish also forms part of the union or district of Castlejordan. There are two pay schools, in which are 80 boys and 11 girls; and a dispensary.

BALLYBOGHILL, a parish, in the barony of BALROTHERY, county of DUBLIN, and province of LEINSTER, 4 miles (N. W. by N.) from Swords, on the road from Dublin, by Naul, to Drogheda; containing 664 inhabitants, of which number, 144 are in the village, in which is a station of the constabulary police. It is a vicarage, in the diocese of Dublin, and forms part of the union and corps of the prebend of Clonmethan in the cathedral of St. Patrick, Dublin; the rectory is impropriate in the Crown. The tithes amount to £275. 15. of which £141 is payable to the crown, and £134. 15. to the vicar. The church is in ruins. In the R. C. divisions it is in the union or district of Naul, also called Damastown; the chapel is a neat building. A school-house was erected in the village by subscription, and there are two private schools in the parish.

BALLYBOUGHT, a parish, in the barony of UPPERCROSS, county of DUBLIN, and province of LEINSTER, 2 miles (S. W.) from Ballymore-Eustace; containing 207 inhabitants. This parish is situated on the road from Ballymore to Hollywood, and is chiefly under an improving system of tillage and pasturage; it forms part of the lordship and manor of Ballymore. White Lays is the seat of J. M. Lynch, Esq. It is a vicarage, in the diocese of Dublin, and is one of four which constitute the union of Ballymore; the rectory is appropriate to the treasurership in the cathedral of St. Patrick, Dublin. The tithes amount to £41. 3. 1., of which £11. 18. 9. is payable to the treasurer, and £29. 4. 4. to the vicar. The church is in ruins; and there is neither glebe nor glebe-house. In the R. C. divisions also it is included in the union or district of Ballymore. Near Broad Lays is a rath or moat, in which, on its being opened a few years since, was discovered, about twenty feet from the surface, a large circular flagstone placed over several compartments, each having a small flag at the top and containing ashes and burnt bones. Near White Lays there is a circle of large blocks of granite, which must have been brought hither, as there is no granite in the parish; in the centre were several upright stones, which have been removed; it is supposed to be a druidical relic.

BALLYBOY, a parish, in the barony of BALLYBOY, KING'S county, and province of LEINSTER, comprising the market and post-town of Frankford, and containing 4182 inhabitants. This parish is situated on the road from Tullamore to Parsonstown, adjacent to the Silver river, and comprises 8861 statute acres, as applotted under the tithe act. It gives name to the barony, and had formerly a castle of some note, which, in 1690, being garrisoned by six companies of Lord Drogheda's regiment of foot, was attacked by a detachment of Gen. Sarsfield's army encamped between Limerick and Athlone; but after a sharp conflict, in which the garrison sustained great loss, the assailants were at length compelled to retreat. On the north and south are very extensive bogs, of which 3000 acres are within the parish: with the exception of a small portion of pasture and meadow, the remainder of the land is arable, and though of inferior quality, is under an improved system of cultivation; the only woodland is Ballinacrig, containing 13¾ acres. There are a distillery and brewery, and a flour-mill; and in addition to the market and fairs at Frankford, fairs are held at the village of Ballyboy on May 4th and Dec. 6th. Petty sessions are held every alternate Saturday. The gentlemen's seats are Castlewood, that of N. Fitzsimon, Esq.; Greenhills, of T. Hobbs, Esq.; Ridgemount, of R. J. Drought, Esq.; Temora, of T. L'Estrange, Esq.; Barnaboy, of R. Chadwick, Esq.; Derrinboy, of A. Gamble, Esq.; and Williamfort, of W. Whitfield, Esq. It is a vicarage, in the diocese of Meath, and forms part of the union of Fircall; the rectory is impropriate in the Marquess of Downshire: the tithes amount to £227. 8. 10¾., of which £146. 4. 3½. is payable to the impropriator, and the remainder to the vicar. The church, situated in the centre of the parish, was built by a loan of £900 from the late Board of First Fruits, in 1815, and has been lately repaired by a grant of £279 from the Ecclesiastical Commissioners: it is served by a stipendiary curate. There is no glebe-house; but there is a glebe comprising 367 acres of profitable land, valued at £321. 1. 7. per annum. In the R. C. divisions the parish is the head of a union or district, called Frankford, comprising the parishes of Ballyboy and Killaughy, each containing a chapel; that of Ballyboy is situated in the town of Frankford. The parochial school is aided by an annual donation of £10 from the vicar: there is a national school, aided by a donation of £6 per annum from the Marquess of Lansdowne; and a school at Castlewood is supported for the benefit of his own tenants by Mr. Fitzsimon, who allows the master £25 per annum. About 170 children are taught in these schools; and there are also six private pay schools, in which are about 150 children. An almshouse for five widows was founded by Mrs. Stoney; and there is a dispensary. On the lands of Barnaboy is a mineral spa.—See FRANKFORD.

BALLYBOYS, in the barony of LOWER DUNDALK, county of LOUTH, and province of LEINSTER, on the north side of the bay of Dundalk; the population is returned with Ballymascanlan. It comprises, according to the Ordnance survey, 1435¾ statute acres, and contains within its limits Bellurgan Park, the seat of E. Tipping, Esq., in which is a picturesque eminence commanding views of a bold and striking character. In the R. C. divisions it forms a separate district, called "The Lordship;" the chapel is situated near the bay, on the road to Riverstown.

BALLYBRACK, a hamlet, in that part of the parish of ROSSMERE which is within the barony of DECIES-without-DRUM, county of WATERFORD, and province of MUNSTER, 2 miles (S. E.) from Kilmacthomas; containing 28 dwellings and 165 inhabitants.

BALLYBRAZILL, a parish, in the barony of SHELBURNE, county of WEXFORD, and provinee of LEINSTER, 5 miles (S. E.) from New Ross; containing 384 inhabitants. This small parish is situated on the road from Wexford, by Ballinlaw Ferry, to Waterford, and was, during the disturbances of 1798, visited by the insurgent army, which, after the battle of New Ross, encamped at Slieve Keiltre, which is partly within its limits, and took possession of Ballysop, now the seat of the Rev. W. Gifford, which they made the head-quarters of the commander in chief. The lands are principally in tillage, and the system of agriculture is generally improving. A small domestic manufacture of woollen cloth is carried on, affording employment to a few persons. It is an impropriate curacy, in the diocese of Ferns, and is part of the union of St. Mary's, New Ross; the rectory is impropriate in the Marquess of Ely: the tithes amount to £100, payable to the impropriator, who pays annually to the curate £2 late currency. The church is in ruins. In the R. C. divisions it is included in the union or district of Suttons, of which the chapel is at Horeswood, in the parish of Kilmokea.

BALLYBRENNAN, a parish, in the barony of FORTH, county of WEXFORD, and province of LEINSTER, 5 miles (S. S. E.) from Wexford; containing 260 inhabitants. This parish is situated on the southern channel of Wexford haven, and on the road from Wexford to Rosslare Fort. It comprises 1030 statute acres; the system of agriculture has much improved, principally through the exertions of Messrs. H. and R. Jones, the latter of whom has reclaimed from the harbour about five acres of land, now forming a thriving plantation. A few of the inhabitants, during the season, are employed in the herring fishery. Ballybrennan Castle is the property of the Earl of Rathdown, and is occupied by Mr. R. Jones, who has a large corn store here, and has lately erected a windmill. The remains of the ancient castle, except a wall incorporated in the modern dwelling-house, have been taken down by the present tenant; several human bones were recently found near its site. The living is a rectory and vicarage, formerly included in the Wexford union, from which it was separated in 1831, in the diocese of Ferns, and in the patronage of the Bishop: the tithes amount to £57. 15. 6¾., in addition to which the incumbent receives £14. 1. 5½. out of the tithes of Killinick. The church is in ruins. In the R. C. divisions the parish is within the union or district of Tagoat.

BALLYBRICKEN.—See CAHIRELLY.

BALLYBRITTAS, a village and post-town, in the parish of LEA, barony of PORTNAHINCH, QUEEN'S county, and province of LEINSTER, 7¼ miles (N. E.) from Maryborough, and 33 miles (S. W. by W.) from Dublin; containing 168 inhabitants. This place is celebrated for a battle which was fought here, in the reign of Elizabeth, between a part of the army of the Earl of Essex and the Irish, led by the chieftains O'Dempsey and O'Moore, in which the former was defeated; and from the circumstance of the latter cutting off the high plumes worn by the English, the scene of the conflict was called "the Pass of Plumes." The village, which is situated on the high road from Dublin to Maryborough, consists of about 30 houses neatly built, and has a pleasing appearance. In the vicinity are Bellegrove, the residence of G. Adair, Esq.; Glenmalire, of Mrs. Trench; Rath, of T. Trench, Esq., the Derries, of R. M. Alloway, Esq.; and Ashfield, of H. Birch, Esq. Fairs are held on March 25th, May 12th, and Aug. 15th; petty sessions are held once a fortnight; and here is a station of the constabulary police. Near the village were formerly the remains of an ancient castle, which belonged to the O'Dempseys, Lords of Clanmalire, and was destroyed in the time of Cromwell.—See LEA.

BALLYBROOD, a parish, in the barony of CLANWILLIAM, county of LIMERICK, and province of MUNSTER, 3 miles (S.) from Cahirconlish; containing 1520 inhabitants. This parish, which is situated on the road from Cahirconlish to Herbertstown, comprises 2224 statute acres, as applotted under the tithe act: about one-half is arable, and the remainder is meadow and pasture, with a small quantity of valuable bog. The soil is mostly fertile, and the system of agriculture improved; the principal crops are wheat, barley, oats, and potatoes. Basalt forms the principal substratum, and rises to a considerable elevation, forming the hill of Ballybrood: it assumes in some places a shivery slaty appearance, and in others is tabular and compact, but is suddenly terminated by a small rivulet between the church and the glebe-house, where the limestone formation commences. The limestone is of good quality, and great quantities are quarried and burnt upon the spot for manure. The principal residences are Ballybrood House, that of S. Maunsell, Esq.; Mount Minute, of W. Gabbet, Esq.; and Caherline House, now occupied by a farmer: there are also several large and well-built farm-houses. Fairs are held here on June 12th and Oct. 11th; two others named in the charter are discontinued. A constabulary police force is stationed here; the barrack has a small castellated tower. The living is a rectory and vicarage, in the diocese of Emly, with the vicarage of Isertlaurence, the rectories and vicarages of Kilteely, or Listeely, and Rathjordan, and the entire rectory of Aglishcormick united at a period prior to any known record, which five parishes constitute the union of Ballybrood, and the corps of the precentorship of the cathedral of Emly, in the patronage of the Archbishop of Cashel: the tithes amount to £150, and of the whole benefice to £689. 6. 9¼. The parish church, built by aid of a gift of £500 from the late Board of First Fruits, in 1807, was burnt by the Rockites in 1822; and the present handsome edifice, in the early English style, with a tower surmounted with an octagonal spire, was erected in the following year. The glebe-house was built by aid of a gift of £100 and a loan of £1500 from the same Board, in 1818: the glebe comprises 26 acres, of which 12 were procured in exchange for 12 acres of glebe at Isertlaurence, in 1815, when 14 more were added, subject to a rent of £4. 4. per acre. Independently of the glebe lands of the union, there are 221*a*. 3*r*. 26*p*. of land at Emly belonging to the precentorship, and let on lease at a rent of £31. 12. 4. per annum, making the entire value of the dignity, as returned by the Ecclesiastical Commissioners, £821. In the R. C. divisions this parish forms part of the union or district of Cahirconlish. A large school-house is now being built.

BALLYBUNNIAN, or BALLYBUNYAN, a village, in the parish of KILLEHENY, barony of IRAGHTICONNOR, county of KERRY, and province of MUNSTER, 8 miles (W. N. W.) from Listowel: the population is returned with the parish. This village, which is situated on a small bay, to which it gives name, in the mouth of the Shannon, has recently become a place of resort for sea-bathing, and is also much frequented on account of the highly interesting and romantic caverns with which its cliffs are indented. The bay is about 500 paces in breadth, and from it to Kilconly Point stretches a fine range of cliffs, presenting a line of coast of the most picturesque character: on the summit of one of the loftiest are vestiges of the old castle of Ballybunnian, with subterranean passages. The cliffs in many places are pierced with extensive caverns and rocky inlets of singular form and variety; those immediately contiguous to the bay, extend in numerous intricate passages, through which a boat may pass for a considerable distance parallel with the coast, without entering the open sea. Beyond these are others of greater depth and height, in one of which pyrites of copper abound; one of the insulated rocks is perforated with an arch, through which is a passage for boats; another extreme point is penetrated by a still loftier arch, and near it is a vast pillar of rock, rising out of the sea from a narrow base, and called the "Devil's Castle," or the "Eagle's Nest." One of the caverns is about 60 feet high in the interior; and there are several beautiful waterfalls from the summit of the cliffs, on one of which are the remains of Doon castle. These caverns and the geological formation of the coast were the subject of a treatise by W. Ainsworth, Esq., of Dublin, in 1834. Some of the mineral substances of part of the cliffs ignited spontaneously in 1753, and burnt for a considerable time, leaving curious traces of the action of the fire. Ballybunnian House, the property of the Gun family, is occasionally fitted up as an hotel; and there are several lodging-houses for the accommodation of visiters during the bathing season. A very profitable salmon fishery, the property of Christopher Julian, Esq., is carried on: the fish is of very fine quality, and great quantities are cured and sent to London in kits weighing about 40lb. each. Vessels of 50 tons' burden may enter the river at high water and sail up nearly a mile from the beach: and lighters pass up the Cashen a distance of eight miles, with the tide, with sand and sea-weed for manure.—See KILLEHENNY.

BALLYBUR, a parish, in the barony of SHILLELOGHER, county of KILKENNY, and province of LEINSTER, 4 miles (S. W.) from Kilkenny; containing 237 inhabitants. It is situated on the road from Kilkenny to Callan, and comprises 655 statute acres, as applotted under the tithe act. During the prelacy of David Hacket, who presided over the see of Ossory from 1460 to 1478, this place, which at that time had its own church, was annexed to the cathedral of St. Canice, Kilkenny, at the instance of its patron, R. Vole, Esq. It is a vicarage, in the diocese of Ossory, and forms part of the union of St. Canice, which is served by the vicars choral of the cathedral, to whom the rectory is appropriate. The tithes amount to £43. 8. 4. In the R. C. divisions it is partly in the union or district of St. Canice, and partly in that of Danesfort.

BALLYBURLEY, or PRIMULT, a parish, partly in the barony of LOWER PHILIPSTOWN, but chiefly in that of WARRENSTOWN, KING'S county, and province of LEINSTER, 3¼ miles (W. S. W.) from Edenderry; containing, with the parish of Coolcor, 1672 inhabitants. This parish is situated near the road from Edenderry to Philipstown, and comprises 5291 statute acres, as applotted under the tithe act. The arable land is excellent, and in a very high state of cultivation: the Scottish system of agriculture, including a rotation of corn and green crops, with drill husbandry, was extensively and successfully introduced about twenty years since by G. and S. Rait, Esqrs. Limestone abounds, and is chiefly used for building and for making roads; a portion is burnt for lime. The parish is bounded on one side by the Yellow river, a stream deriving its name from the quantity of oxyde of iron with which the water is impregnated; on the north passes the Grand Canal, in its course to Tullamore. The principal seats are Ballyburley, that of J. Wakely, Esq., a fine old mansion in the Elizabethan style; Green Hill, of F. Longworth Dames, Esq.; Rathmoyle, of G. Rait, Esq.; Clonin, of S. Rait, Esq.; and Coolville, of T. Grattan, Esq. Petty sessions are held every alternate Wednesday at Fahy, near the village of Rhode. The living is a rectory, in the diocese of Kildare, to which the rectory of Coolcor was united by act of council, forming by prescription one benefice in the patronage of J. Wakely, Esq.: the tithes amount to £285. The church is a small neat building, erected in 1686 by J. Wakely, as appears from a stone over the doorway, bearing a rude sculpture of the founder's arms and a Latin inscription; the Ecclesiastical Commissioners have lately granted £136 for its repair. Within is a curious ancient monument representing in rude relief the family arms and the effigy of a warrior dressed in the full military costume of the age, with an inscription underneath, purporting that it was erected by T. Wakely, Esq., of this place, in memory of his wife Maud, daughter of Alderman W. Handcock, of Dublin, who died May 3rd, 1617, and also to the memory of himself and Catherine Cusack, sister of Maud: it further states that Thomas was the son of John Wakely, Esq., captain of 100 horse and 100 foot in the beginning of Queen Elizabeth's reign, which he governed to the advancement of her highness' service. There is neither glebe nor glebe-house. In the R. C. divisions this parish forms part of the union or district of Castropetre, or Edenderry: the chapel, which is situated at Rhode, is a large and well-built edifice in the form of a T. There is a school in connection with the Established Church, supported by subscription, to which children of all denominations are admissible.

BALLYCAHANE, a parish, partly in the barony of Small County, but chiefly in that of Pubblebrien, county of Limerick, and province of Munster, 3 miles (N. by E.) from Croom; containing 1242 inhabitants. It is situated on the road from Limerick to Charleville, by way of Manister; and comprises 2103 statute acres, of which 1140 are under tillage, and about 800 are meadow and pasture; the remainder is bog or marshy land near Garran and on the boundary of the parish, near Tory hill, much of which is dug out, and the whole may be drained and cultivated at a trifling expense, as there is an ample fall to the Maigue river. The entire parish is based on a substratum of limestone, and several quarries are worked extensively. There are several handsome houses and cottages, the principal of which are Maryville, the residence of Hugh F. Finch, Esq.; Fort Elizabeth, of the Rev. J. Croker; and Ballycahane House, of Capt. Scanlon. The living is a rectory, in the diocese of Limerick, forming the corps of the prebend of Ballycahane in the cathedral church of St. Mary, Limerick, in the patronage of the Bishop; the tithes amount to £166. 3. 0¾. The church is a large edifice, in the early English style, with a tower, built in 1823 by aid of a loan from the late Board of First Fruits. There is no glebe-house: the glebe comprises five acres of excellent land. In the R. C. divisions the parish is included within the union or district of Fedamore: the chapel is a large plain edifice situated at Caherduff. The male and female parochial schools are principally supported by subscriptions from the rector, curate, and Mr. Finch, of whom the last-named gentleman gave the land on which the school-house was built by subscription. There are also two private schools in the parish. Not far from the church are the ruins of the ancient castle of Ballycahane, built by the family of O'Grady in 1496, near which numerous ancient silver and copper coins have been found; and near Tory hill are the remains of a church once belonging to the Knights Templars, and subsequently to the abbey of Nenagh. Near these is a lake, respecting which some strange traditions are extant.

BALLYCAHILL, a parish, in the barony of Eliogarty, county of Tipperary, and province of Munster, 4 miles (W.) from Thurles, on the road from Nenagh to Cashel; containing 1818 inhabitants, of which number, 39 are in the hamlet. It comprises 3884 statute acres, as applotted under the tithe act: the lands are principally under tillage; part of the bog of Ballynahow is within its limits; and there is abundance of limestone, which is quarried for building and burning. Castle Fogarty, the ancient seat of the O'Fogarty family, from whom it descended to its present proprietor, J. Lanigan, Esq., is a square castellated mansion, with embattled towers at the angles, and is situated in a fine demesne, comprising 450 statute acres, and richly embellished with wood. Prior Lodge, the property and residence of the Rev. Dr. Prior, is situated in a small but tastefully disposed demesne; and Montalt, the property of J. Lanigan, Esq., is now in the occupation of William Ryan, Esq. The hamlet is a constabulary police station. It is a rectory, in the diocese of Cashel, entirely impropriate in Mrs. Carrol and Mr. Fogarty. The tithes amount to £246. 6. 10½., payable to the impropriators, who allow a stipend of £7 per annum to the curate of Holycross for the performance of the clerical duties. The church is in ruins; the Protestant inhabitants attend divine service at the churches of Holycross and Moyaliffe. In the R. C. divisions it is united with Holycross; the chapel is a spacious and neat structure with a tower. There are three pay schools, in which are about 150 children. The remains of the castle of Ballynahow consist chiefly of a circular tower.

BALLYCALLAN, a parish, in the barony of Cranagh, county of Kilkenny, and province of Leinster, 4¼ miles (W. by S.) from Kilkenny, on the road to Killenaule; containing 1807 inhabitants, and 5278 statute acres. An attempt was some years since made to discover coal, and a little culm was raised, but the undertaking was ultimately relinquished. Bellevan, now in the occupation of J. Waring, Esq., was the residence of the late J. Evans, Esq., who bequeathed about 1100 acres of land here, and a very large sum of money in trust for the benefit of the different charities and public institutions of Kilkenny. Here is a station of the constabulary police. It is a rectory and vicarage, in the diocese of Ossory, and forms part of the union of Callan: the tithes amount to £413. 3. 1. The church serves as a chapel of ease to that at Callan, and is in bad repair. Contiguous to it there is a glebe of two acres. In the R. C. divisions it is the head of a union or district, which comprises also the parishes of Kilmanagh and Killaloe, and part of Callan, and contains three chapels, situated respectively at Ballycallan, Kilmanagh, and Killaloe. There are two private pay schools, in which about 340 boys and 230 girls are taught.

BALLYCANNEW, a parish, in the barony of Gorey, county of Wexford, and province of Leinster, 4 miles (S.) from Gorey, on the road to Ferns, and near the river Owen-a-varra; containing 1167 inhabitants, of which number, 345 are in the village. It comprises 3600 statute acres. The village contains about 60 houses, and fairs are held on April 23rd, July 25th, Sept. 21st, Oct. 2nd, and Nov. 30th, for cattle. It is a rectory, in the diocese of Ferns, and is part of the union of Leskinfere, or Clough, and the corps of the treasurership in the cathedral of Ferns; the tithes amount to £192. The church is served by a curate appointed by the rector of Leskinfere; the Ecclesiastical Commissioners have lately granted £208 for its repair. There is a glebe of 4½ acres, on which is a small house. In the R. C. divisions it forms part of the union or district of Camolin, a considerable village in the parish of Tomb, where the chapel is situated. There is a place of worship for Primitive Wesleyan Methodists in the village, built a few years since. The parochial school is aided by a donation of £5 per annum from the rector: the school-house, with apartments for the master, was built at an expense of £80, defrayed partly by subscription and partly by a grant from the lord-lieutenant's fund; the master has in addition an acre of ground rent-free. The rector also contributes to the support of another school in the parish. A bequest of £3 per annum, late currency, by Mr. Windass, chargeable on the lands of Mangan, in the parish of Kiltrisk, is distributed annually among the poor. On clearing away a Danish fort, on a farm in this parish, two urns of unbaked clay were discovered, containing ashes and burnt bones.

BALLYCARANEY, or BALLYCRANA, a parish, in the barony of Barrymore, county of Cork, and province of MUNSTER, 8 miles (S. S. E.) from Rathcormac; containing 1036 inhabitants. It comprises 6461 statute acres, as applotted under the tithe act, and valued at £3240 per annum: a very small portion is in pasture, and the remainder is under tillage. The gentlemen's seats are Lemlara House, that of Garrett Standish Barry, Esq., situated in a well-cultivated and highly improved demesne; Ballinaclashy, of the Rev. G. E. Cotter; and Ballycrana, of Jos. Wilson, Esq. It is a rectory, in the diocese of Cloyne, and forms part of the union of Lisgoold and corps of the precentorship in the cathedral of Cloyne: the tithes amount to £184. 12. 3¾. In the R. C. divisions also it is included in the union or district of Lisgoold.

BALLYCARNEY, a district parish, in the barony of SCARAWALSH, county of WEXFORD, and province of MUNSTER, 3 miles (W. by S.) from Ferns: the population is returned with the parishes of Ferns, Templeshambo, and Monart, out of which this district parish has been recently formed. The village, which is in the parish of Ferns, is situated on the eastern bank of the Slaney, over which is a neat stone bridge, and on the road from Enniscorthy to Newtownbarry: it has a penny post from Ferns, and is a constabulary police station. The district church is a handsome structure in the later English style of architecture, recently erected: the living is a perpetual curacy, in the diocese of Ferns, and in the patronage of the Rectors of Ferns and Templeshambo.

BALLYCARRY, a village, in the parish of TEMPLECORRAN, barony of LOWER BELFAST, county of ANTRIM, and province of ULSTER, 4½ miles (N. E.) from Carrickfergus; containing 247 inhabitants. This village is pleasantly situated about a mile from the shore of Lough Larne, opposite to Island Magee, and on the road from Carrickfergus to Larne: it comprises about 50 houses, and the inhabitants are partly employed in the spinning of yarn and weaving of linen cloth, and partly in agriculture. There is a penny post to Carrickfergus and Larne; and fairs are held on June 21st, Aug. 19th, and Oct. 31st. Here are the ruins of the ancient parish church, formerly a spacious and handsome cruciform structure.

BALLYCASTLE, a sea-port, market and post-town, in the parish of RAMOAN, barony of CAREY, county of ANTRIM, and province of ULSTER, 9¼ miles (N. E. by E.) from Dervock, and 132 miles (N.) from Dublin: containing 1683 inhabitants. This place, in the Irish language called *Ballycashlain*, or "Castletown," derived that name from a castle built here in 1609 by Randolph, Earl of Antrim, who was directed by Jas. I. to raise "faire castels" at reasonable distances on his vast estates, that the country might be the more speedily civilized and reduced to obedience. The town is advantageously situated on the northern coast, at the head of the fine bay to which it gives name, and in a beautiful valley at the foot of Knocklayd, opposite to the island of Rathlin. It consists of the Upper and Lower Town, of which the latter, called the Quay, is separated from the former by a road bordered with fine trees, which, sheltered by the hills intervening between them and the coast, have attained a stately and luxuriant growth. The houses, amounting, in 1831, to 275 in number, are in general neatly built, and in both portions of the town are several of handsome appearance. Within the distance of half a mile from Ballycastle are the elegant seats of C. McGildowny, Esq., Capt. Boyd, A. and J. McNeale, Esqrs., and several others. It was formerly a place of great manufacturing and commercial importance, abounding with various works upon a large scale, among which were extensive breweries, glass-houses, salt-works, and spacious warehouses; and in the immediate neighbourhood were extensive collieries, the produce of which formed a material article in its trade. In 1730, endeavours were made in the Irish parliament to erect it into a place of import and export, but were successfully opposed by the Irish Society and the corporation of Londonderry. It had a spacious harbour, in which 74-gun ships could anchor in safety in any weather, and upon the improvement of which £130,000 had been expended; also a pier and quay, the construction of which cost £30,000. But this high degree of prosperity, which the town attained under the auspices of Hugh Boyd, Esq., began to decline soon after that gentleman's decease, and all that at present remains of its trade is a small fishery carried on by a few boats in the bay. The harbour is now completely choked up; the pier and quay are a heap of ruins; the custom-house has been converted into a whiskey shop, the breweries are untenanted, the glass-houses have been converted into a carpenter's shops, and the mansion-house is a parish school. The collieries, which extended nearly a mile in length along the coast, and from which from 10,000 to 15,000 tons were annually exported, subsequently declined; the estate is now in chancery, and the works, which had been conducted with success from a very remote period, are discontinued. They were situated in the adjoining parish of Culfeightrin, but were always called the Ballycastle collieries, and occupied the northern face of Cross Hill, an eminence nearly 500 feet in height, of which about 150 feet are formed by a cap of columnar basalt resting on alternating of strata sandstone and clay-slate, extending 150 feet in depth, immediately under which is the bed of coal, at an elevation of 200 feet above the level of the beach. No manufactures are carried on at present, with the exception of a few webs of linen, which are woven in the houses of some of the farmers; a little fishing is carried on in the bay, but the inhabitants are principally employed in agriculture. The market is on Tuesday, and a great market is held on the first Tuesday in every month; the fairs are on Easter-Tuesday, the last Tuesdays in May, July, and August, Oct. 25th, and Nov. 22nd, for Raghery ponies, horses, cattle, sheep, pigs, linen yarn, and pedlery. Here is a station of the constabulary police; also a coast-guard station, which is the head of a district comprising also the stations of Port Rush, Port Ballintrae, Port Ballintoy, Rathlin Island, Tor Head, Cushendun, and Cushendall, and under the charge of a resident inspecting commander. A manorial court is held by the seneschal every month, for the recovery of debts and the determination of pleas to the amount of £20 by attachment and civil bill process; its jurisdiction extends over the entire barony of Carey, with the exception of Armoy. A court baron is also held in April and October; and petty sessions are held every alternate Tuesday. There is a very good market-house, and a commodious court-house, in which the courts and petty sessions are held.

A handsome church, in the Grecian style of architecture, with a lofty octagonal spire, was erected in 1756, at the sole expense of H. Boyd, Esq.: the stone for building it was procured from the quarries in the parish, which were then worked on that gentleman's estate. It is a chapelry, in the diocese of Connor, endowed with £60 per ann., of which £20 per ann. is paid by the trustees of Primate Boulter's augmentation fund, and the remainder by the patron, H. Boyd, Esq., descendant of the founder. There is neither glebe-house nor glebe. The R. C. chapel is a small building; and there are places of worship for Presbyterians and Wesleyan Methodists the former in connection with the Synod of Ulster and of the third class. There are several schools in the town, principally supported by the resident gentry. H. Boyd, Esq., in 1762, built and endowed with the rental of the townlands of Carnside and Ballylinney, reserving only £40 for the incumbency of Ballycastle, 20 almshouses near the church, for poor men, or the widows of poor men who had worked eight years in the collieries or other works on his estate; they are still maintained, and are tenanted by the deserving poor of the town under the superintendance of the Primate, the Bishop, and the Chancellor of Connor for the time being, whom he appointed trustees for the management of the lands. There are some ruins of the castle from which the town derived its name; also some ruins of Bona Margy, a religious house founded in 1509 by Charles Mac Donnell, for monks of the Franciscan order, and one of the latest of those establishments which were founded in Ireland; the remains of the chapel are the most perfect. This is the burial-place of the Antrim family, who have put a new roof upon a small oratory erected over the ashes of their ancestors, over the window of which is a Latin inscription scarcely legible, importing that it was built in 1621 by Randolph Mac Donnell, Earl of Antrim. In 1811 was found, by the side of a rivulet near the town, a flexible rod of gold composed of twisted bars 38 inches long, hooked at each end, and weighing 20 ounces and a half; it was undoubtedly a Roman torques, and probably brought hither by some of the Danish or Scottish ravagers of Roman Britain. There is a strong chalybeate spring near the town; and on the shores are found chalcedony, opal, jasper, and dentrites.

BALLYCASTLE, a village, in the parish of DUNFEENY, barony of TYRAWLEY, county of MAYO, and province of CONNAUGHT, 15 miles (N. W.) from Ballina: the population is returned with the parish. This place is situated on the north-west coast, and commands a fine view of Downpatrick Head: the beach affords excellent accommodation for sea-bathing, and by the outlay of a little capital it might be made a delightful watering-place. Several improvements have already been made; many new houses have been built, a market-place is in course of erection, and a new line of road is now being constructed through the mountains to Belmullet, which will materially add to the advantages of the place. Petty sessions are held every Wednesday; it is a constabulary and chief revenue-police station, and has six fairs in the year, and a penny post to Killala.

BALLYCLARE, a market and post-town, partly in the parish of BALLYNURE, but chiefly in that of BALLYEASTON, barony of LOWER BELFAST, county of ANTRIM, and province of ULSTER, 93½ miles (N.) from Dublin; containing 824 inhabitants. This place is situated close to the Six-mile-water, and at the extremity of the mail coach road, which branches off from that between Belfast and Antrim. The town, which is neatly built, contains about 180 houses, and is noted for its monthly linen market, and for its horse fairs, which are held on May 24th, July 19th, Aug. 23rd, and Nov. 22nd. There are places of worship for Presbyterians and Wesleyan Methodists, the former in connection with the presbytery of Antrim, and of the second class.

BALLYCLERAHAN, a parish, in the barony of IFFA and OFFA EAST, county of TIPPERARY, and province of MUNSTER, 4 miles (S. W.) from Fethard; containing 568 inhabitants. This parish, which forms part of the lands belonging to the see of Cashel, is situated on the road from Cashel to Clonmel, and is chiefly remarkable for its castle of great strength, said to have been built by Mocklerough More, or the "great Mockler," whose territories extended from this place to Nine-mile House, or, as it was then called, Mockler's Grange. This castle, opposite to which the Butler family erected a strong fortress on their own estate, was besieged by Cromwell, who in vain attempted to make any impression upon it, from an eminence since called *Crugg Denial Noi*, or the "Rock of the Nine Soldiers," from the loss of nine of his men who were killed by a discharge from the castle; but changing his position during the night, he assaulted it in the morning and obtained possession of it after an obstinate resistance. Mockler and his second son fell bravely defending the castle, and his eldest son, being taken prisoner, was hanged at the gate; another of his sons with a few of the family, escaped to France, but the rest of the garrison were put to the sword. The remains consist of a lofty square tower in one of the angles of the court, which is enclosed with very strong and high walls of stone; also part of a dwelling-house within the area, and, on the outside, the ruins of a chapel near the gateway. The parish comprises 1038 statute acres, as applotted under the tithe act. It is a rectory, in the diocese of Cashel, and forms part of the union and corps of the deanery of Cashel; the tithes amount to £75. 0. 8. There is no church; the inhabitants attend divine service in the adjoining parish of Newchapel. The glebe comprises 11 acres. The R. C. parish is co-extensive with that of the Established Church; the chapel is a spacious building. There are two pay schools, in which are about 70 boys and 20 girls.

BALLYCLOG, or BALLYNECLOG, a parish, in the barony of DUNGANNON, county of TYRONE, and province of ULSTER, 2 miles (N.) from Stewarts-town, on the road to Moneymore; containing 2786 inhabitants. This place formed part of the lands granted by Jas. I. to Sir Andrew Stewart, and with the exception of the lands belonging to the primate, which are in the manor of Cookstown, is wholly included within the manor of Stewarts-town. The parish is situated on Lough Neagh, and comprises, according to the Ordnance survey, 7796¾ statute acres, of which 3092¼ are in the lough. The lands are chiefly under tillage; there are about 15 acres of woodland and 20 of bog; the system of agriculture is in a highly improved state, and there is not a single acre of waste land in the parish. Coal, limestone, freestone, basalt, and quartz prevail; and many rare plants grow here, which are not found in any other part of the country. Among the gentlemen's seats the principal are Steuart Hall, the residence of the Earl of Castlesteuart; Belmont, of A. T. Bell, Esq.; and Drumkirn, of E. H. Caulfield, Esq. The lands of Belmont are an original freehold held by the Bells and Darraghs for more than three hundred years by allodial tenure, being the only lands in the country held by that title. The living is a rectory, in the diocese of Armagh, and in the patronage of the Lord-Primate; the tithes amount to £184. 12. 3¾. The church is a small plain ancient structure with a tower and spire; and in the churchyard are the family vaults of the Steuarts of Steuart Hall, and the Bells of Belmont, to whom some handsome monuments of freestone have been erected. The glebe-house was built by aid of a gift of £100 from the late Board of First Fruits, in 1792: the glebe comprises 97 acres, of which 7 are exhausted bog and altogether unprofitable. In the R. C. divisions this parish forms part of the union or district of Steuart's-town: the chapel is situated at the northern extremity of the parish. The Presbyterians have a place of worship at Brae. There is a school under the Trustees of Erasmus Smith's Charity; also three schools, situated respectively at Upper Back, Eirey, and Ochill, aided by annual donations from the Countess of Castlesteuart; and a school at Drumkirn supported by Mrs. Caulfield. These schools afford instruction to about 230 boys and 200 girls; and there is also a private school of about 30 children at Drumbanaway. A considerable rivulet in this townland disappears beneath a hill and appears again on the shore of Lough Neagh, at a distance of three miles; and in the townland of Brae is a spring of excellent water issuing from between the basalt, freestone, and limestone strata, producing 290 gallons per minute, and ebbing and flowing at the new moon.

BALLYCLOGHY.—See MONEMOINTER.

BALLYCLOUGH, or LAVAN, a parish, partly in the barony of Duhallow, but chiefly in that of Orrery and Kilmore, county of Cork, and province of Munster, 3½ miles (W. N. W.) from Mallow; containing 3853 inhabitants. In March, 1691, a body of native forces in the interest of Jas. II. posted themselves at this place and began to throw up entrenchments; but on the approach of Major Culliford from Cork, with a detachment of 400 men, they were compelled to abandon their works. The village is situated on a gentle eminence at the opening of a vale, through which flows the river Finnow, formed by a collection of various springs, in its course to the Blackwater. Adjoining are the extensive boulting-mills of Messrs. Haines and Smith, driven by the Finnow, and generally giving employment to 25 persons. Fairs are held on Easter Monday, June 21st, Aug. 5th, and Sept. 19th, chiefly for cattle and pigs. A constabulary police force is stationed here. The new line of road from Mallow to Kanturk and Newmarket, runs through the parish, which comprises 9641 statute acres, as applotted under the tithe act, and valued at £7905 per annum: the lands are chiefly arable, and there is neither mountain nor bog. Limestone abounds, and forms the substratum of the eminence on which the village is situated; and on the estate of Col. Longfield are indications of culm, but it has not yet been worked. The principal seat is Longueville, the noble mansion of Col. Longfield, representative of the late Viscount Longueville, who derived his title from this place: the house, consisting of a centre and two spacious wings, is beautifully situated on the northern bank of the Blackwater, in the midst of some very rich and varied scenery. Near the village is Blossomfort, the neat residence of J. Smith, Esq.; and in the parish are Waterloo, the residence of H. Longfield, Esq.; Summerville, of J. N. Wrixon, Esq.; Kilpatrick, of W. J. McCormick, Esq., M.D.; and Ballythomas, of R. Bullen, Esq.

The living is a vicarage, in the diocese of Cloyne, with that of Drumdowney episcopally united, and in the patronage of the Bishop; the rectory is impropriate in Col. Longfield. The tithes amount to £781. 10., of which £381. 10. is payable to the impropriator, and £400 to the vicar, and the tithes of the whole benefice amount to £430. The church, a neat edifice with a square embattled tower crowned with pinnacles, was erected in 1830, partly by subscription, towards which the late Lord Lisle contributed £100 and Lord Arden and Col. Longfield £50 each, partly by a loan of £730 from the late Board of First Fruits, and partly by the sale of the pews. The glebe-house, a handsome and commodious residence, was built by the Rev. John Chester, the present incumbent: the old glebe, comprising only half an acre, has been enlarged by the addition of 13*a.* 3*r.* 13*p.*, plantation measure, in reduction of the rent of which, at six per cent., a fine of £200 was paid by the late Board of First Fruits. In the R. C. divisions this is one of the four parishes that constitute the union or district of Kilbrin, also called Ballyclough; the chapel, a thatched building in the village, is about to be converted into a school, and a new chapel erected. A school of about 20 boys and 40 girls is supported by subscription; a Sunday school of 10 boys and 20 girls is supported by the vicar, and there are four pay schools, in which are about 180 boys and 116 girls. A bequest of £4 per ann. late currency, from Nicholas Lysaght, Esq., is regularly paid by Lord Lisle and distributed among the poor. A lofty square tower in excellent preservation, and inhabited by the steward of R. E. P. Coote, Esq., formed part of Ballyclough Castle, built by a branch of the family of Barry, called Mac Roberts or Mac Robert-Barry: it is situated in a well-planted demesne, which has been laid out with a view to building, and was completely repaired about 30 years since, and a range of substantial out-offices has been subsequently added. Mount North, a fine old mansion of the Lysaght family, has been deserted for many years, and is now in a very dilapidated state. Near the high road was an obelisk, erected on four arches by the first Lord Lisle, which was destroyed by lightning in the winter of 1834, and the stones were thrown to a great distance. Near the village is a strong chalybeate spring, partly overflowed by a brook; and at Kilpatrick is another. At Kilgubbin is a planted Danish rath, which has been from time immemorial used as a cemetery for still-born children; the numerous graves of diminutive length, with proportionably small tombstones, have a very interesting appearance. The churchyard is the burial-place of the family of Lysaght, of Mount North, ennobled in the person of John, created Baron Lisle, of Mount North, Sept. 18th, 1758, and also of the Longfields of Longueville.

BALLYCLUG, a parish, in the barony of Lower Antrim, county of Antrim, and province of Ulster;

containing, with part of the post-town of Ballymena, called the village of Henryville, 3692 inhabitants. This place, with a district extending many miles around it, was the property of the ancient and princely sept of the O'Haras, who settled here during the reign of Hen. II., and whose ancient mansion still occupies the summit of a gently rising eminence near the village of Crebilly. During the insurrection in 1641, Cromwell wrested from them a considerable portion of the manor of Crebilly, or the "Kearte," which he divided among several of his adherents. Some of the timber about Crebilly is of very ancient growth; and there are several traces of the former splendour, and many traditions of the princely hospitality of the chiefs of the O'Hara sept. The parish comprises, according to the Ordnance survey, 8268¾ statute acres, about one-fifth of which is brush-wood and mountain, which is gradually being brought into cultivation; 150 acres are bog, 30 acres are woodland, and the remainder is arable and pasture. The soil is fertile, and the system of agriculture is greatly improved; the cultivation of wheat, for which the land is well adapted, has been recently introduced with success. Fairs are held at Crebilly on the 26th of June and 21st of August, for horses, black cattle, sheep, and pigs; they were formerly the largest in the province, but are now indifferently attended. Courts leet and baron are held annually; and a manorial court for the district of Kearte is held monthly by the seneschal, for the recovery of debts, with jurisdiction over the whole of this parish and parts of the parishes of Connor and Rathcaven. The living is a rectory and vicarage, in the diocese of Connor, formerly belonging to the chancellorship, but episcopally united to the impropriate curacy of Kirkinriola on the death of the late Dr. Trail; the tithes amount to £129. 4. 7½. In the R. C. divisions this parish is united to Ballymena: the chapel, situated at Crebilly, was erected in 1810, near the ancient seat of the O'Haras. A school was built at Caugherty in 1829, one at Ballavaddan in 1800, and a parochial school is now being built under the management and patronage of the rector: there are also two other public schools, and a private and three Sunday schools. Col. O'Hara, in 1759, bequeathed £20 per annum to the poor of this parish, which is regularly distributed according to the will of the testator. There are some remains of the ancient parish church, also of Dunavaddan chapel; besides numerous remains of forts, intrenchments, and Druidical altars, and several moats and tumuli, scattered over the surface of this parish.

BALLYCOLLON.—See COOLBANAGHER.

BALLYCOLLONBEG.—See MOUNTMELLICK.

BALLYCOMMON, a parish, in the barony of LOWER PHILIPSTOWN, KING'S county, and province of LEINSTER, 3½ miles, (W.) from Philipstown, on the road from Dublin to Tullamore, containing 1226 inhabitants. It comprises about 6730 statute acres, of which 4244 are applotted under the tithe act: about 2503 acres are pasture, and 1743 arable land; and there are 2430 acres of bog, 50 of waste, and 5 or 6 of woodland. The living is a rectory, in the diocese of Kildare, and in the patronage of the Crown; the tithes amount to £138. 9. 2¾. The church has been lately repaired by a grant of £335 from the Ecclesiastical Commissioners. The glebe-house was built by aid of a gift of £450 and a loan of £160, in 1817, from the late Board of First Fruits; the glebe comprises 3*a.* 1*r.* 15*p.* In the R. C. divisions the parish forms part of the union or district of Philipstown. There is a school aided by private subscriptions, also a hedge school, in each of which are about 40 children.

BALLYCONNELL, a market and post-town, in the parish of TOMREGAN, barony of TULLAGHAGH, county of CAVAN, and province of ULSTER, 12½ miles (N. W. by W.) from Cavan, and 68 miles (N. W. by W.) from Dublin; containing 453 inhabitants. This place had its origin in the English settlement in the time of Jas. I., when Capt. Culme and Walter Talbot received 1500 acres, on which, at the time of Pynnar's survey in 1619, was a strong bawn 100 feet square and 12 feet high, with two flanking towers and a strong castle, three stories high, the whole occupying a site well adapted for the defence of the surrounding country. The town is situated on the road from Belturbet to Swanlinbar, and consists of two streets, together containing about 80 houses. The market is on Friday, and is well supplied with corn and provisions; and fairs are held on Jan. 3rd, Feb. 13th, March 17th, April 18th, May 16th, June 24th, July 29th, Aug. 29th, Sept. 26th, Oct. 25th, and Dec. 3rd, chiefly for cattle, pigs, and corn. It is a constabulary police station; the Easter and October sessions for the county are held here, and petty sessions every alternate Monday. The court-house is a handsome stone building; and attached to it is a bridewell containing three cells, with separate day-rooms and airing-yards for male and female prisoners. Here is the parish church, which has been lately repaired by a grant of £106 from the Ecclesiastical Commissioners. A school-house has been built at an expense of £227, defrayed partly by the incumbent, partly by the proprietor of the Ballyconnell estate, and partly by Government. Ballyconnell House, the residence of J. Enery, Esq., is beautifully situated in a fine demesne on the Woodford river, which winds through the extensive and well-wooded grounds in its course to Lake Annagh and Lough Erne; the house was erected in 1764, by the late G. Montgomery, Esq., on the site of the castle of Ballyconnell, which was entirely destroyed by an accidental fire. There is a chalybeate spring in the demesne.

BALLYCONNICK, a parish, in the barony of BARGY, county of WEXFORD, and province of LEINSTER, 7½ miles (S. W.) from Wexford, on the road to Bannow; containing 510 inhabitants. In a return to a royal visitation held in 1615, it was designated Ballycormick, and returned as a chapel to the prebend of Taghmon. The parish comprises 1445 statute acres, as applotted under the tithe act, and is chiefly in tillage. It is a rectory, in the diocese of Ferns, and is part of the union and corps of the prebend of Taghmon, in the cathedral of Ferns: the tithes amount to £95. 1. 7. In the R. C. divisions it is included in the union or district of Rathangan and Clarestown. A parochial school, in which are about 30 boys and 20 girls, is supported by subscription.

BALLYCONREE, a hamlet, in the parish of DROMCREHY, barony of BURREN, county of CLARE, and province of MUNSTER; containing 9 houses and 60 inhabitants.

BALLYCONRY, a parish, in the barony of IRAGHTICONNOR, county of KERRY, and province of MUNSTER 3½ miles (N. W. by W.) from Listowel: the population is returned with the parish of Lisseltin. This small parish, which is also called *Ballyconry-derico*, is situated on the road from Listowel to Ballybunnian; and comprises 1118 statute acres, of which 233¾ are arable, 540¼ are pasture, and 343¾ are bog. Some improvement has taken place in agriculture by the introduction of sand and sea-weed as a manure, brought in large quantities from Ballybunnian bay. Ballyconry House is the seat of Eyre W. Stack, Esq. In ecclesiastical matters this is a distinct parish, but in civil affairs it is considered as forming part of the parish of Lisseltin. The living is a vicarage, in the diocese of Ardfert and Aghadoe, with the vicarage of Kilfeighny and one-fifth part of the rectory of Ardfert united, together constituting the corps of the precentorship of Ardfert, in the patronage of the Bishop; the rectory is impropriate in Anthony Stoughton, Esq. The tithes amount to £36, payable in moieties to the incumbent and the impropriator; £2 per annum is payable to the curate of Lisseltin, who discharges the clerical duties: the tithes of the benefice payable to the incumbent are £179. 18. 8. The glebe lands of the precentorship lie in Ardfert, and comprise 115*a.* 0*r.* 1*p.*, statute measure, let on lease at an annual rent of £27. 13. 10. In the R. C. divisions it is included in the union or district of Lisseltin.

BALLYCOOLANE, or CLOGHRAN-HIDART, a parish, in the barony of CASTLEKNOCK, county of DUBLIN, and province of LEINSTER, 4 miles (N.) from Dublin; containing 72 inhabitants. This place, which originally belonged to the priory of All Saints, passed, on the dissolution of that house, with its other possessions, to the mayor and corporation of Dublin. The gentlemen's seats are Haighfield, the residence of J. Martin, Esq., and Yellow Walls, that of W. Finn, Esq., both commanding fine views of the Dublin and Wicklow mountains, with the country adjacent. Here is a constabulary police station. The living is an impropriate curacy, in the diocese of Dublin, held with the vicarage of Finglass, and in the patronage of the Archbishop; the rectory is impropriate in the corporation of Dublin. There is no church, but the churchyard is still used as a burial-place. In the R. C. divisions the parish forms part of the union or district of Castleknock. There are two pay schools, in which are about 50 children.

BALLYCOR, a parish, in the barony of UPPER ANTRIM, county of ANTRIM, and province of ULSTER, 1 mile (N. by E.) from Ballyclare: the population is returned with the parish of Ballyeaston. This parish, which is situated on the road from Broughshane to Larne, and is bounded on the north and east by the Six-mile-water, comprises 7330 statute acres, according to the Ordnance survey. It is a rectory, in the diocese of Connor, and is partly one of the five parishes which constitute the union and corps of the prebend of Carncastle in the cathedral of Connor, and partly one of the two which form the perpetual curacy of Ballyeaston.

BALLYCOTTON, a village and ploughland, in the parish of CLOYNE, barony of IMOKILLY, county of CORK, and province of MUNSTER, 4 miles (S. E.) from Cloyne; containing 856 inhabitants. This is an isolated portion of the parish, situated on the shore of a bay of the same name in St. George's channel, six miles from Poor Head, and consists of a scattered village comprising about 150 small houses: it is much frequented in the summer for sea-bathing. At the entrance of the bay are two isles called the Ballycotton islands, situated five miles (W. by S.) from Capell or Cable Island, and about one mile from the main land. This is one of the five stations of the coast-guard that are comprised within the district of Youghal. A new district church for the accommodation of the inhabitants of Ballycotton and Churchtown was built not far from the village, in 1835, at an expense of £330, raised by subscription. The living is a perpetual curacy, in the patronage of the Bishop; and the curate's stipend is paid partly by the dean and chapter and the vicars choral of the cathedral church of Cloyne, to whom the tithes of the parish belong, and partly by the precentor, as rector of Churchtown. The male and female parochial schools for Ballycotton, Churchtown, and Kilmahon are situated at Ballybraher.

BALLYCROGUE, a parish, in the barony and county of CARLOW, and province of LEINSTER, 3 miles (S. E. by E.) from Carlow; containing 72 inhabitants. This small parish is situated on the river Burren, and consists of only one townland, comprising 385 statute acres. In civil matters it is considered as forming part of Ballinacarrig, and is one of the three parishes which constitute the union of Ballinacarrig or Staplestown, in the diocese of Leighlin: the tithes amount to £21. 2. 6. In the R. C. divisions it is in the district of Tullowmagrinagh.

BALLYCROY, a district, in the parish of KILCOMMON, barony of ERRIS, county of MAYO, and province of CONNAUGHT, 16 miles (S. E. E.) from Belmullet; containing 2925 inhabitants. This place is situated on Blacksod bay, and is deeply indented by the bay of Tulloghane, which, stretching far into the land, receives the waters of the river Owenmore. It consists of a large tract of bog, enclosed by an extensive range of mountains on the south and east, but exposed to the western storms, by which the crops, chiefly potatoes, are frequently destroyed, and the cultivators, who depend chiefly on the produce of their land, are reduced to a state of famine. Fish is abundant in the bay, but the inhabitants derive little benefit from this circumstance, being too poor to provide themselves with nets, lines, and boats to carry on the fishing with any profit. This is one of the three R. C. districts into which the parish is divided: the chapel at Cross Hill is an old thatched house appropriated to that purpose, the scanty means of the inhabitants being insufficient for the erection of a better.—See KILCOMMON.

BALLYCULTER, a parish, in the barony of LECALE, county of DOWN, and province of ULSTER; containing, with the post-town of Strangford, 2221 inhabitants. It is situated on Lough Strangford, and comprises, according to the Ordnance survey, (including islands and detached portions) 5177½ statute acres, of which 1753 are applotted under the tithe act; about four-fifths are arable and pasture, and the remainder, excepting about 70 acres of woodland and 40 of water, is waste land and bog. The soil is very fertile, and the land is in a state of excellent cultivation; a considerable quantity of corn is sent to Liverpool and Glasgow. At Tallyratty are some lead mines, which were worked in 1827, and found very productive; the ore is considered to be of superior quality, but they are not now worked. Castle Ward, the splendid seat of

Lord Bangor; Strangford House, the residence of the Hon. Harriet Ward; and Strangford Lodge, that of J. Blackwood, Esq., are situated in the parish. The village is neatly built, and is one of the most pleasant in the county. A manor court is held at Strangford every three weeks by the seneschal of the lord of the manor, in whom are vested very extensive privileges; its jurisdiction extends over the parish and the river of Strangford. The living is a rectory, in the diocese of Down, and was formerly annexed to the deanery of Down, from which it was separated in 1834, and made a distinct rectory, in the patronage of the Crown; the tithes amount to £387. 15. 7. The church, a spacious and handsome structure, was erected in 1723, and a tower and spire were added to it in 1770: the Ecclesiastical Commissioners have lately granted £295 for its repair. There is a chapel at Strangford, the private property of Lord De Roos, of which the rector is chaplain. The glebe-house was built by aid of a gift of £450 and a loan of £50 from the late Board of First Fruits, in 1817: there is a glebe at Strangford, comprising 6*a.* 2*r.* 37*p.* Lord Bangor is about to build a glebe-house in or near the village for the residence of the rector. In the R. C. divisions the parish forms part of the union or district of Ballee; there are two chapels, one at Strangford and the other at Cargagh; and there are two places of worship for Wesleyan Methodists. In the village is a handsome school-house, with residences for a master and mistress, built in 1824, and supported by an annual donation of £50 from Lord Bangor, and a small donation from the rector. An infants' school is supported entirely by the Hon. Harriet Ward. These schools afford instruction to about 94 boys and 84 girls; and there are also two pay schools, in which are about 82 boys and 48 girls, and four Sunday schools. Near the church are four handsome alms-houses, built in 1832 at the expense of Lady Sophia Ward, who endowed them with £40 per annum, payable out of the estate of Lord Bangor for ever; the management is vested in three trustees, of whom the rector for the time being is one. Within the parish are three castles erected by De Courcy and his followers after the conquest of Ulster; one is situated close to the quay at Strangford, one on the creek below Castle Ward, and the third is Audley Castle on a rock opposite to Portaferry.

BALLYCUMBER, a hamlet, in the parish of LEMANAGHAN, barony of GARRYCASTLE, KING'S county and province of LEINSTER, 3 miles (W. S. W.) from Clara: the population is returned with the parish. This is a neat village, comprising 13 houses, pleasantly situated on the river Brosna, over which there is a good stone bridge, and on the road from Clara to Ferbane: it has a penny post from Clara. Ballycumber House is the handsome residence of J. Warnford Armstrong, Esq.; and about two miles distant is Castle Armstrong. Fairs for black cattle, sheep, and pigs are held on May 2nd and Dec. 1st.

BALLYCUSLANE.—See BALLINCUSLANE.

BALLYDAIGH.—See BALTEAGH.

BALLYDEHOB, a village, in the parish of SKULL, Western Division of the barony of WEST CARBERY, county of CORK, and province of MUNSTER, 8 miles (W. S. W.) from Skibbereen; containing 601 inhabitants. The village is situated on a new line of road formed by the Board of Works from Skibbereen to Rock island; and derives its name from its position at the confluence of three streams, whose united waters are crossed by a handsome stone bridge, below which they expand into a small but secure haven, near the termination of Roaring Water bay. It consists of a long and irregular street containing about 100 houses, some of which are large and well built; and is rapidly increasing in size and importance, particularly since the formation of the new road, which has made it a considerable thoroughfare, aided by its propinquity to the copper mines of Cappach and the slate quarries of Audley's Cove and Filemuck, which renders it well adapted for business. Fairs for horses, cattle, sheep, pigs, and pedlery are held on Jan. 1st, Feb. 2nd, March 12th, Easter Tuesday, Whit-Tuesday, June 29th, July 15th, Aug. 15th, Sept. 8th, Oct. 10th, Nov. 1st, and Dec. 8th. A penny post to Skibbereen has been recently established; and here is a station of the constabulary police. A chapel of ease was built in 1829 by the late Board of First Fruits, at an expense of £600; it is a small handsome edifice, in the early English style of architecture, without a tower. A large and handsome R. C. chapel was also erected in 1826; and there is a place of worship for Wesleyan Methodists. A school, in connection with the Kildare-Place Society, and another at Liskeencreagh, are supported by the Cork Diocesan Association: and adjoining the R. C. chapel is a large school for boys and girls, built in 1835 by the Rev. J. Barry. Here is a dispensary, a branch to that at Skull, *which see.*

BALLYDELOHER, or BALLYLOOHERA, a parish, in the barony of BARRYMORE, county of CORK, and province of MUNSTER, 5 miles (N. E. by E.) from Cork; containing 1145 inhabitants. This parish, which is sometimes called Kilroan, but is more generally known by the name of Brooklodge, is situated on the road from Cork to Tallow. The hilly portions of this district, like most others in its vicinity, are shallow and stony, but are tolerably well cultivated, particularly near that branch of the Glanmire river which separates this parish from that of Caherlog. At Butlerstown are some very extensive paper-mills; there are also a spade and shovel manufactory and a small tuck-mill. Riverstown House, the beautiful residence of J. Browne, Esq., and formerly of Dr. Peter Browne, the celebrated Bishop of Cork and Ross in the early part of the last century, and also of Dr. Jemmett Browne, Bishop of Cloyne, is in this parish. It is a rectory, in the diocese of Cork, and forms part of the union and corps of the prebend of Killaspigmullane in the cathedral of St. Finbarr, Cork: the tithes amount to £177. 10. The church of the union was formerly at Ballyvinny, but was suffered to fall to decay on the erection of a new church in this parish, a neat small edifice, built in 1829, in aid of which £625 was granted by the late Board of First Fruits. It is also in contemplation to erect another church or chapel near Watergrass hill. There is no glebe-house; but the entire glebe of the union, consisting of ten acres, is in this parish. In the R. C. divisions the parish is included in the union or district of Glauntane or New Glanmore. The parochial school is situated at Riverstown, half a mile from the church, and is principally supported by local subscriptions.

BALLYDELOUGHY, or BALLYLOUGH, a parish, in the barony of FERMOY, county of CORK, and province of MUNSTER, 1½ mile (E. by N.) from Doneraile; containing 718 inhabitants. This parish, which is situated near the river Funcheon, and on the south of the road from Doneraile to Mitchelstown, comprises 1200 statute acres, as applotted under the tithe act, and valued at £1891 per ann.: the soil is good, and limestone exists in abundance. It is a vicarage, in the diocese of Cloyne, and forms part of the union and corps of the prebend of Glanworth in the cathedral of Cloyne; the rectory is impropriate in the Earl of Donoughmore. The tithes amount to £159. 16. 0½. of which £69. 19. 5½. is payable to the impropriator, and the remainder to the vicar. The ruins of the church still remain in the burial-ground. In the R. C. divisions also it is included in the union or district of Glanworth: the chapel is at Ballyndangan. About 50 children are educated in a private school. The late Rev. John Kelleher, P. P. of Glanworth, bequeathed £50 towards the erection of a school-house at Ballyndangan, in aid of which an application will be made to the National Board. About a quarter of a mile to the north of the ruins of the church are those of the ancient castle of Ballylough. Ballyndangan the ancient seat of the family of Terry, is now occupied as a farm-house.

BALLYDONNELL, a parish, in the barony of ARKLOW, county of WICKLOW, and province of LEINSTER, 4½ miles (S. E.) from Rathdrum; containing 645 inhabitants. This parish, which is situated on the lower road from Arklow to Wicklow, comprises 2803 statute acres. It is a rectory and vicarage, in the diocese of Dublin and Glendalough, and forms part of the union of Castlemacadam: the ecclesiastical duties were separated from that union by act of council in 1830, by which Ballydonnell was included in the newly erected district parish of Redcross, the church of which is situated in that village.

BALLYDRASHANE. — See BALLYRASHANE.

BALLYDUFF, county of KERRY.—See BENMORE.

BALLYDUFF, a parish, in the barony of CORKAGUINEY, county of KERRY, and province of MUNSTER, 7½ miles (N. E.) from Dingle; containing 420 inhabitants, of which number, 92 are in the village. This parish, which is situated near the road from Dingle to Tralee, comprises 9825 statute acres, as applotted under the tithe act. Nearly one-half is mountain and bog, partly reclaimable; that portion of the land which is under tillage is of good quality. The only seat is Liscarney, the property of T. B. Hussey, Esq. The village contains 15 houses, and is a constabulary police station. The living is an impropriate curacy, in the diocese of Ardfert and Aghadoe, the rectory being wholly impropriate in the Earl of Cork; the tithes amount to £55, payable to the impropriator, out of which £10 per annum is allowed for the discharge of the clerical duties. There are some ruins of the church in the ancient burial-ground, near which is a small glebe. In the R. C. divisions this parish is included in the union or district of Castlegregory. On the border of the parish is a romantic glen, called Maharabo, where it is said the last wolf in this part of the country was killed; the particular spot is still called Wolf Step.

BALLYEASTON, a district parish, in the barony of UPPER ANTRIM, county of ANTRIM, and province of ULSTER, on the road from Ballyclare to Larne; containing with the post-town of Ballyclare and the grange of Doagh, 5892 inhabitants. It consists of the ancient parishes of Ballycor and Rashee, comprising, according to the Ordnance survey, 13,790½ statute acres; about one-half of which are arable. The village, which is 1½ Irish mile (N.) from Ballyclare, is situated at the junction of several roads, near the Six-mile-water, and in 1831 contained 61 houses. The living is a perpetual curacy, in the diocese of Connor, and in the patronage of the Prebendary of Carncastle: the income of the curate is £103. 1. 6½. per ann., of which £69. 4. 7½. arises from tithe, £13. 6. 11. is added by the prebendary, and £20 from Primate Boulter's fund. The church was erected in 1786. There is neither glebe-house nor glebe. In the R. C. divisions it forms part of the union or district of Carrickfergus and Larne. There are four places of worship for Presbyterians; one in connection with the Synod of Ulster, of the first class; one with the Presbytery of Antrim, of the second class; one with the Seceding Synod, also of the second class; and one for Covenanters, which is open every alternate Sunday. There are four schools, in which are about 140 boys and 90 girls; also nine pay schools, in which are about 160 boys and 110 girls. —See BALLYCLARE and DOAGH.

BALLYEGRAN, a village, in the parish of CASTLETOWN-CONYERS, barony of UPPER CONNELLO EAST, county of LIMERICK, and province of MUNSTER, 5 miles (N. W.) from Charleville; containing 172 inhabitants. This small village, consisting only of a few thatched cabins, is situated on the road from Charleville to Ballingarry, and gives name to the R. C. union or district, comprising the parishes of Castletown-Conyers, Kilmeedy and Drumcollogher; the chapel is a small building. Not far distant are the remains of a heathen temple.—See CASTLETOWN-CONYERS.

BALLYELLIN, a parish, partly in the barony of ST. MULLIN'S, but chiefly in that of IDRONE EAST, county of CARLOW, and province of LEINSTER, adjacent to Graigue and Goresbridge; containing 1760 inhabitants. This parish consists of two detached portions separated by the parish of Slyguff, one of which contains five townlands, and the other, two: it is bounded on the north by the river Barrow, which separates it from the county of Kilkenny, and over which there is a bridge at Goresbridge; and comprises 5266 statute acres, of which 4754 are applotted under the tithe act and valued at £4052 per annum. Here is a quarry of black marble, used for tombstones and chimney-pieces. Ballyellin House is the residence of Walter Blackney, Esq. It is a rectory, in the diocese of Leighlin, and forms part of the union of Lorum: the tithes amount to £413. 1. 6½. The ruins of the church are situated within a burial-ground near the road from Borris to Goresbridge. In the R. C. divisions it is in the union or district of Bagnalstown or Dunleckney. On the lands of Clowater are the ruins of a castle.

BALLYFARNON, a village, in the parish of KILRONAN, barony of BOYLE, county of ROSCOMMON, and province of CONNAUGHT, 3 miles (N. W.) from Keadue; containing 150 inhabitants. This is an improving place, and promises to increase in importance from the contemplated new mail coach road from Carrick-on-Shannon to Sligo, which is intended to pass through the village. A customary weekly market has been established; and fairs are held on Feb. 9th, April 16th, May 19th, July 6th, Aug. 20th, Sept. 21st, Oct. 21st, and Dec. 17th. A constabulary police force and a revenue station have been established here; and there is a school of about 90 boys and 40 girls.—See KILRONAN.

BALLYFEARD, a parish, in the barony of KINNALEA, county of CORK, and province of MUNSTER, 4½ miles (N. E. by E.) from Kinsale; containing 1337 inhabitants. This parish comprises 4500 statute acres, of which 3576 are applotted under the tithe act and valued at £2460 per annum: about 3500 acres are arable and pasture, and 1000 waste and bog. The land is in general very good and principally under tillage; but agriculture, as a system, is comparatively unknown; the chief manure is sea-sand, which is brought from Menane Bridge, three British miles distant. It has been proposed to cut a canal from Belgooley to the river Menane, and application has been made to Government for that purpose, but nothing has been yet decided. The village contains 24 houses indifferently built; it is a constabulary police station, and petty sessions are held every alternate Wednesday. The living is a vicarage, in the diocese of Cork, and in the patronage of the Bishop; the rectory is impropriate in the Earl of Shannon; the tithes amount to £260, of which one-half is payable to the impropriator, and the other to the vicar. There is no church, but divine service is regularly performed in the parochial school-house, which is licensed for that purpose. The glebe comprises five acres, but there is no glebe-house. In the R. C. divisions this is one of the three parishes that constitute the union or district of Clontead; the chapel at Ballingarry is a plain thatched building. The parochial school and a Sunday school are under the superintendence of the vicar: there are also two pay schools in the parish.

BALLYFERMOT, a parish, in the barony of NEWCASTLE, county of DUBLIN, and province of LEINSTER, 3 miles (W. by S.) from Dublin; containing 402 inhabitants. It is intersected on the south side by the Grand Canal, and comprises 1178 statute acres, as applotted under the tithe act, and valued at £3214 per annum. Ballyfermot Castle, an ancient building, is now the residence of Capt. Lamplin; the other seats are Johnstown, the residence of T. Daly, Esq., and Johnstown Lodge, of — Place, Esq. An extensive paper-manufactory, belonging to Messrs McDonnel and Sons, in which from 70 to 80 persons are generally employed, is carried on at Killeen: the principal kinds made are bank-note paper for the Bank of Ireland, and printing paper for the Dublin newspapers. Within the enclosure of this establishment, which resembles a small town, are dwelling-houses for the workmen and their families: the house of the proprietor is pleasantly situated in some tastefully ornamented grounds. There is also in the parish a small manufacture of glue and parchment. It is a rectory, in the diocese of Dublin, and is part of the union of Chapelizod: the tithes amount to £130. The church is in ruins. In the R. C. divisions it is included in the union or district of Lucan, Palmerstown, and Clondalkin.

BALLYFOIL, a parish, in the barony of KINNALEA, county of CORK, and province of MUNSTER, 10 miles (E. by N.) from Kinsale; containing 1291 inhabitants. This parish, which is called also *Bealfoyl* and *Poliplicke*, was formerly part of the possessions of Tracton Abbey, and from time immemorial was reputed free from tithes, till brought within the operation of the tithe composition act. It is situated on the southern coast, and comprises 1304 statute acres, as applotted under the tithe act. The soil is fertile, and about one-half of the land is under tillage; the remainder is in dairy farms. The system of agriculture is improved; the only manure is sea-sand, which is brought into Rocky bay and Roberts' Cove, two small coves in the parish, in large boats, of which several are employed in this trade. At Roberts' Cove is a valuable slate quarry, belonging to Sir Thomas Roberts, Bart., but it is not worked to any considerable extent. Britfieldstown, the seat of Sir Thomas Roberts, Bart., is pleasantly situated in a secluded spot above Roberts' Cove. On the same estate is Fort Richard, the residence of J. Galwey, Esq. The Cove affords a commodious shelter for vessels of 200 tons' burden, which occasionally arrive laden with coal, and return with cargoes of slate. The coast-guard station here is the most westerly of the eight stations that constitute the district of Cove. A little to the west, on the summit of Roberts' Head, is a ruined signal tower, from which is an interesting and extensive prospect. It is an impropriate curacy, in the diocese of Cork, and is part of the union of Tracton, where the Protestant inhabitants attend divine worship; the rectory is impropriate in the Earl of Shannon. The tithes amount to £109. 4. 6. the whole of which is payable to the impropriator. The church has long been a ruin. In the R. C. divisions it forms part of the union or district of Kinnalee or Tracton. The parochial male and female schools are supported by the Cork Diocesan Society; there is also a hedge school in the parish.

BALLYGARTH, a parish, in the barony of LOWER DULEEK, county of MEATH, and province of LEINSTER, 4 miles (N. W.) from Balbriggan; containing 96 inhabitants. This parish is situated on the Nanny water, on the eastern coast, and is skirted on the west by the mail coach road from Dublin, by Balbriggan, to Drogheda. It comprises 810 statute acres, of which 758 are applotted under the tithe act: the lands are principally under grass, and the parish is remarkably well planted; the hedge-rows abound with thriving trees, and the scenery is generally pleasing. Ballygarth Castle, the seat of Lieut.-Col. T. Pepper, is picturesquely situated on the banks of the Nanny water; the demesne, which is well wooded, comprises 486 statute acres, and contains the ruins of the ancient parish church. Corballis House, the seat of J. Smith Taylor, Esq., is pleasantly situated in a demesne of 372 statute acres of fertile land. At the mouth of the Nanny water is a coast-guard station, which is one of the nine that constitute the district of Swords. The living is a rectory, in the diocese of Meath, and in the patronage of the Crown; the tithes amount to £62. There is neither church nor glebe-house; near the ruins of the old church are two acres of glebe, and there are other detached portions, amounting in the whole to four acres. In the R. C. divisions the parish forms part of the union or district of Stamullen.

BALLYGARUFF, a village, in the parish of TEMPLETOGHER, barony of BALLYMOE, county of GALWAY, and province of CONNAUGHT, 2½ miles (W. S. W.) from Ballymoe, on the road from Dunmore to Castlerea; containing 15 dwellings and 72 inhabitants.

BALLYGAWLEY, a market and post-town, and a parish, partly in the barony of CLOGHER, and partly in that of DUNGANNON, county of TYRONE, and province of ULSTER, 13 miles (S. E.) from Omagh, and 74 miles (N. W. by N.) from Dublin; containing 4428 inhabitants, of which number, 972 are in the town. The lands and manor of Moyenner and Balegalle were granted by Jas. I. to Capt. William Turvin, but he neglecting to comply with the conditions of the grant, they were afterwards granted, in 1614, to Sir Gerard Lowther, who erected on the bank of a small river a very extensive castle, which he enclosed within a bawn of stone and lime and made a place of great strength. This castle was destroyed, in 1642, by the insurgents under Sir Phelim O'Nial: the walls and two towers of the bawn, with part of the castle walls, are still remaining; and a modern house has been recently erected on the site. The town is situated on the mail coach road from Dublin to Londonderry, and consists of three streets and a market-place; it contains about 250 houses, some of which are large and well built, and is the property of Sir Hugh Stewart, Bart., whose handsome mansion, Ballygawley House, is about two miles distant from the town. Innismagh, the seat of Col. Verner; Anahoe, of H. Crossle, Esq.; and Martray, of Mervyn Stewart, Esq., are within the parish. A small manufacture of gloves is carried on in the town, which, from the goodness of the materials and the neatness of the workmanship, are in general demand. There is an extensive brewery, that has acquired celebrity for the quality of its ale, and a large distillery of malt whiskey has been established. The market is on Friday; it is amply supplied with provisions of all kinds, and every alternate week a large quantity of linen cloth is exposed for sale. Fairs are held on the second Friday in every month, principally for the sale of cattle, sheep, and pigs. A constabulary police force has been stationed here; petty sessions are held once a fortnight; and as the head of the manor of Moyenner or Ballygawley, manorial courts are held in the town for the recovery of debts not exceeding 40*s.* This district was constituted a parish in 1830, by an order of council under the provisions of an act of the 7th and 8th of Geo. IV., when eighteen townlands were separated from the parish of Errigal-Kerogue, in the barony of Clogher, and twelve from that of Carrenteel, in the barony of Dungannon, and formed into the parish of Ballygawley. These townlands are situated near the mountains and contain some good land, particularly on the north-east, where the soil is good and well cultivated. The living is a perpetual curacy, in the diocese of Armagh, and in the alternate patronage of the Rectors of Errigal-Kerogue and Carrenteel. The curate's income is £70 per annum, contributed in moieties by the rector of Errigal-Kerogue and the archdeacon of Armagh, as incumbent of Carrenteel. The church is a small but handsome edifice, in the later English style, erected at an expense of £1000, of which sum, £900 was a gift from the late Board of First Fruits. There is a place of worship in the town for Presbyterians in connection with the Synod of Ulster, of the third class; also a Baptist meeting-house in the parish. A boys' school is supported by Sir Hugh Stewart, and there is a school at Knockany, together affording instruction to about 130 boys and 130 girls; there is also a private school at Lisgonnell of about 70 boys and 30 girls.

BALLYGERVIN.—See CARRIGALINE.

BALLYGIBBON, a parish, in the barony of UPPER ORMOND, county of TIPPERARY, and province of MUNSTER, 4 miles (E.) from Nenagh; containing 1074 inhabitants. It is situated on the turnpike road from Nenagh to Cloghjordan, and comprises about 650 acres, as applotted under the tithe act. There is a considerable tract of bog, and limestone abounds in the parish. Ballygibbon, the residence of D. E. Young, Esq., and Glanahilty Castle, the property of J. C. Fitzgerald, Esq., and now in the occupation of W. Kennedy, Esq., are the principal gentlemen's seats. A brewery at Bantis is conducted on an extensive scale by Edward Kennedy, Esq., who has also an extensive distillery at Cloghjordan. It is a rectory and vicarage, in the diocese of Killaloe, and is part of the union of Ballymackey: the tithes amount to £101. 10. 9¼. There are some remains of the ancient church. In the R. C. divisions it forms part of the union or district of Toomavarra or Aghnameadle; the chapel is situated in the parish of Ballymackey.

BALLYGLASS, a village and post-town, in the parish of TOWAGHTY, barony of CARRA, county of MAYO, and province of CONNAUGHT, 8¾ miles (S. E. by S.) from Castlebar, and 116 miles (W. by N.) from Dublin, on the road from Hollymount to Castlebar: the population is returned with the parish. Petty sessions are held every alternate Friday in a small court-house; and it is a station of the constabulary police. In the vicinity are several gentlemen's seats, which are noticed in the account of the parish.

BALLYGORMAN, a village, in the parish of CLONCHA, barony of ENNISHOWEN, county of DONEGAL, and province of ULSTER, 4 miles (N. W. by N.) from Malin; containing 227 inhabitants. It is situated at the extremity of the promontory of Malin Head, and is the most northern village in Ireland. A signal tower has been erected by order of the Board of Admiralty; and, not far distant, a small pier and harbour are in course of formation, by excavating the solid rock. There are two coast-guard stations, one at the Head and another at Glengad. On a ledge of rock near the Head a small basin has been scooped out, where, at every tide, is deposited a small quantity of water, which the country people consider efficacious for sores.—See CLONCHA.

BALLYGRIFFIN, a parish, in the barony of CLANWILLIAM, county of TIPPERARY, and province of MUNSTER, 3½ miles (W. N. W.) from Cashel; containing 1383 inhabitants. It is situated on the river Suir, which is here crossed by a bridge, and comprises 2778 statute acres, as applotted under the tithe act, of which 960 acres are bog. Lisheen, the seat of Sir J. J. Fitzgerald, Bart., is pleasantly situated in a well-planted demesne. It is a rectory, in the diocese of Cashel, and is part of the union of Relickmurry or Athassel; the tithes amount to £191. 8. 7. In the R. C. divisions it forms part of the union or district of Annacarthy. There is a pay school, in which are about 50 boys and 30 girls. There are some remains of a castle, near which are the ruins of an ancient church or chapel.

BALLYGUNNER, a parish, in the barony of GAULTIER, county of WATERFORD, and province of MUNSTER, 3 miles (E. S. E.) from Waterford; containing 709 inhabitants. This parish is situated on the road from Waterford, which here divides into two branches leading respectively to Passage and Tramore; it comprises 1369 statute acres, as applotted under the tithe act. Near the point where the road divides is a stone which is supposed to have been part of an ancient cromlech, from which circumstance the adjacent house, belonging to Mr. Reynett, derived its appellation Mount Druid. A constabulary police station has been established, and petty sessions for the division are held every fortnight, at Callaghan, in this parish. It is a vicarage, in the diocese of Waterford, and is part of the union of Ballynakill; the rectory is appropriate to the Dean and Chapter of the cathedral church of Waterford. The tithes amount to £157. 7. 4. of which £92. 19. 3. is payable to the dean and chapter, and £64. 8. 1. to the vicar. In the R. C. divisions it forms part of the union or district of Trinity Within and St. John, Waterford, and contains a chapel. A school is supported by an annual donation of £21 from — Fitzgerald, Esq.

BALLYGURRUM, or BALLYGORUM, a parish, in the barony of IDA, county of KILKENNY, and province of LEINSTER, 4¼ miles (W. S. W.) from New Ross; containing 693 inhabitants. This parish is situated on the river Barrow, and comprises 1827 statute acres, as applotted under the tithe act, and valued at £1655 per annum. The village is pleasantly situated near the confluence of the Suir and Barrow. Here is a square tower or castle, built at an early period by the Fforstall or Forestall family, which afterwards belonged to the Aylwards, whose name is perpetuated in that of Aylwardstown, the adjacent property of the Earl of Besborough, and now the seat of the family of Strange. The scenery of the immediate neighbourhood is highly interesting, and is embellished with Ringville, the seat of Lady Esmonde, and Rochestown, that of — Forestall, Esq. It is a vicarage, in the diocese of Ossory, and forms part of the union of Rossbercon; the rectory is impropriate in the Corporation of Waterford. The tithes amount to £165, of which £110 is payable to the corporation, and £55 to the vicar. In the R. C. divisions it forms part of the union or district of Slieruagh. There is a pay school, in which are about 50 children.

BALLYGURTEEN.—See KILMEEN, county of CORK.

BALLYHACK, a village, in the parish of ST. JAMES, barony of SHELBURNE, county of WEXFORD, and province of LEINSTER, 6½ miles (N. W.) from Fethard; containing 258 inhabitants. This place is situated at the outlet of the rivers Barrow, Suir, and Nore, in Waterford harbour, and is chiefly supported by the shipping that anchor in the estuary, where, both at the quay and in the anchorage grounds, large vessels may ride securely in all states of the weather: the decrease in the amount of its population, within the last seven years, is attributable to the growth of Arthurstown, in the same parish. It is a fishing station; and a small trade is carried on in corn and pigs for the Waterford market. Fairs are held on the Thursday after Trinity Sunday, March 25th, June 17th, 24th, and 29th, July 26th, Aug. 24th, and Sept. 29th. Here are the ruins of a castle; and there was anciently a commandery, which belonged to the grand priory of Kilmainham, and was subordinate to that of Kilcloghan.—See JAMES (ST.).

BALLYHAISE, a market and post-town, in the parish of CASTLETERRA, barony of UPPER LOUGHTEE, county of CAVAN, and province of ULSTER, 3½ miles (N. W.) from Cavan, and 59 miles (N. W.) from Dublin, on the road from Cavan to Cootehill; containing 142 houses and 761 inhabitants. Ballyhaise House, the seat of W. Humphreys, Esq., is a spacious mansion, with an elevated front curiously ornamented with arches. The linen trade was formerly carried on here to a very considerable extent, but is now extinct. There is a tanyard, employing 7 or 8 persons; and near the town are some extensive flour and oatmeal-mills. The market is on Saturday; and fairs are held on the 1st of March, April 11th, May 18th, June 20th July 3th, Aug. 30th, Oct. 3rd, Nov. 6th, and Dec. 13th, chiefly for horses, cattle, and pigs. The market-house is an arched edifice built of brick, and of singular appearance. Here is a station of the constabulary police. The parochial church, a remarkably neat edifice in excellent repair, is situated just without the town; and there is also a R. C. chapel.—See CASTLETERRA.

BALLYHALBERT, a parish, in the barony of ARDES, county of DOWN, and province of ULSTER, 3 miles (N. E.) from Kirkcubbin: the population is returned with the union of St. Andrew's. It comprises, according to the Ordnance survey (including islands), 4012 statute acres. The village, which in 1831 contained 322 inhabitants, is situated on the eastern coast, and on the road from Portaferry to Donaghadee: it contains about 70 houses, and is a coast-guard station, forming one of the twelve which constitute the district of Donaghadee. Off the coast is Burr Island, the most eastern point of land in Ireland. The parish is in the diocese of Down, and is one of the three of which the vicarages were consolidated by the 2nd of Queen Anne into the union of Ballywalter, or vicarage of St. Andrew's; the rectory is appropriate to the Lord-Primate. The tithes amount to £388. 2. 6., of which £258. 15. is payable to the appropriator, and £129. 7. 6. to the incumbent. On the next avoidance of the benefice of St. Andrew's, this parish will become a separate living, in the patronage of the Lord-Primate. There are some remains of the old church near the village. In the R. C. divisions it forms part of the union or district of Lower Ardes or Ballygelget. There is a place of worship for Presbyterians in connection with the Synod of Ulster; also a school.

BALLYHALE, a village, in the parish of DERRYNAHINCH, barony of KNOCKTOPHER, county of KILKENNY, and province of LEINSTER, 1 mile (S. by E.) from Knocktopher, on the road from Kilkenny to Waterford; containing 69 houses and 369 inhabitants. Fairs are held on Jan. 5th, March 28th, May 10th, July 9th, Sept. 21st, Nov. 11th, and Dec. 8th. The parochial R. C. chapel, a neat building with an ancient tower, is situated at this place, which gives name to the union or district, comprising the parishes of Derrynahinch, Knocktopher, Aughavillar, and Killeasy, and parts of those of Burnchurch, Jerpoint, and Kells, and containing four other chapels, besides a friary chapel.—See DERRYNAHINCH.

BALLYHANE, or BALLYHEAN, a parish, in the barony of CARRA, county of MAYO, and province of CONNAUGHT, 4½ miles (S. by W.) from Castlebar; containing 3734 inhabitants. This parish is situated on the road from Castlebar to Ballinrobe, and is principally under tillage; it contains Kilboyne House, the residence of Sir S. O'Malley, Bart. Fairs are held on July 4th, and

Aug. 20th. It is a rectory and vicarage, in the diocese of Tuam, and forms part of the union of Burriscarra, the church of which, a neat plain edifice, is situated in this parish, and has been lately repaired by a grant of £269 from the Ecclesiastical Commissioners: the tithes amount to £165. In the R. C. divisions it is part of the union or district of Castlebar: the chapel is a good slated building. At Drumrathcahil is a school of 76 boys and 40 girls; and there are two pay schools. At Kinturk are the ruins a fine old castle, formerly one of the residences of Grace O'Malley.

BALLYHAUNIS, a market-town, in the parish of ANNAGH, barony of COSTELLO, county of MAYO, and province of CONNAUGHT, 9 miles (W. by N.) from Castlerea, and $97\frac{1}{2}$ miles (W. by N.) from Dublin, on the road from Castlerea to Castlebar: the population is returned with the parish. A monastery was founded here for friars of the order of St. Augustine, and largely endowed by the family of Nangle, who afterwards took the name of Costello: it subsisted till the reign of Jas. I., and at the commencement of the insurrection in 1641 was restored by some friars of the same order. The remains of the ancient buildings consist only of the walls of a church, with two small wings connected with it by arches; on the site of the conventual buildings a modern house has been erected, which is at present occupied by Augustinian friars. The market is on Tuesday; and fairs are held on June 1st, July 2nd, September 22nd, and October 29th, chiefly for horses and cattle. The town contains a constabulary police station, and has a penny post to Clare and Frenchpark.— See ANNAGH.

BALLYHEA, a parish, partly in the barony of ORRERY and KILMORE, but chiefly in that of FERMOY, county of CORK, and province of MUNSTER, 2 miles (S. S. E.) from Charleville; containing 1591 inhabitants. At this place was an ancient castle belonging to the Fitzgerald family, called Castle Dod, which was taken in 1642 by Lord Inchiquin, on which occasion 200 of the Irish were slain. The parish is situated on the river Awbeg, and is intersected by the mail coach road from Cork to Limerick. It comprises 5235 statute acres, as applotted under the tithe act, and valued at £5151 per ann.: the greater portion is under tillage, held in large farms; the land is generally good, and there is some good grazing land, on which store cattle are fattened for the Cork market. Limestone gravel is found in abundance, and burnt for manure. The only seat is Castle Harrison, the residence of Standish Harrison, Esq., erected on the site of Castle Dod. It is a vicarage, in the diocese of Cloyne, forming the corps of the prebend of Ballyhea in the cathedral of Cloyne, and united also to the vicarage of Rathgoggan; the rectory is appropriate to the vicars choral of the cathedral of Christchurch, Dublin; the tithes amount to £400. The church has been long in ruin, and, from its extent and its ornamental details, appears to have been a spacious and handsome edifice. The glebe comprises $2\frac{1}{2}$ acres. In the R. C. divisions the greater portion of the parish is united with the parishes of Ardskeagh, Cooline, Emerick or Imphrick, Aglishdrinagh, and part of the parish of Shandrum: the chapel, a spacious building on the border of Aglishdrinagh, was erected in 1831, on a site given by Mr. Harrison. There are two pay schools, in which are about 50 children.

BALLYHEIGUE. or BALLYHEIGH, a parish, in the barony of CLANMAURICE, county of KERRY, and province of MUNSTER, 10 miles (N. N. W.) from Tralee; containing 3766 inhabitants. This parish is situated on a bay of the same name on the western coast, and includes within its limits the promontory of Kerry Head; it comprises 8100 statute acres, the greater portion of which is mountain, bog, and waste. With the exception of two farms only, the whole parish is the property of Col. J. Crosbie, who is resident; the farms are large and are held on old leases immediately from the head landlord. The lands under tillage are rendered fertile by the abundance of sea manure which is procured upon the coast: several of the low boggy tracts are defended only by sand hills from the irruption of the sea. From its exposed situation, being open to the Atlantic on the north, south, and west, timber attains little growth. Good brown-stone for building is found near the shore. Ballyheigue Castle, the seat of Col. J. Crosbie, is a superb structure, in the later English style of architecture, erected after a design by Mr. R. Morrison, and situated in an extensive demesne tastefully disposed and highly embellished. Ballyheigue has been made a penny post to Tralee; and a patent has been obtained for holding fairs, but none have been yet established. A seneschal's court is occasionally held for the manor; and the petty sessions for the district are also held here. The living is a rectory and vicarage, in the diocese of Ardfert and Aghadoe, and in the patronage of the Bishop: the tithes amount to £290. 15. 4. The church is a small but neat edifice, erected on the site of the former structure by aid of a gift of £800 from the late Board of First Fruits, in 1814. The glebe-house was built by aid of a gift of £350 and a loan of £450 from the same Board, in 1820: the glebe comprises 20 acres. In the R. C. divisions the parish forms part of the union of Killury or Causeway, and contains a chapel. In the parochial school are about 20 boys and 20 girls; and there are four pay schools, in which are about 480 children.

The coast, for the greater part, is a long, low, and sandy strand, and very dangerous to vessels embayed near it. The bay of Ballyheigue lies between Tralee bay and Ballyheigue or Kerry Head, which latter is situated in lat. 52° 24′ 40″ (N.), and lon. 9° 54′ (W.); it affords no shelter for vessels, and has been frequently mistaken for the Shannon, in consequence of the latitude of Loop Head being inaccurately laid down in the charts. A coast-guard station is placed here, forming one of the five which constitute the district of Listowel; and there is also a constabulary police station. The scenery along the coast is bold and in some places strikingly grand; the bay is frequented during the summer months for sea-bathing; and in the neighbourhood is a remarkably fine spa. About two miles to the north of Ballyheigue are the remains of the small castle of Ballingarry, built by Col. D. Crosbie in the war of 1641, for the defence of a narrow isthmus leading to a small peninsula in which he had sheltered his English tenantry from the attacks of the native insurgents; they received supplies here from the opposite side of the Shannon, sent by the friends of Lord Inchiquin, but the place was at length taken through the treachery of a servant. About two miles to the north of Ballyheigue castle are the remains of a small chapel, dedicated to Saint McIda. Very fine amethysts and Kerry diamonds are found in the cliffs of

Kerry Head; they are procured by persons suspended by ropes from the cliffs, and detach them with hammers from the crevices of the rocks. Near the ruins of Ballingarry castle is Minegahane, near which the swell that precedes stormy weather produces a sound among the rocks resembling the discharges of cannon.

BALLYHEOGUE, a parish, partly in the barony of BANTRY, and partly in that of SHELMALIER, county of WEXFORD, and province of LEINSTER, 6 miles (S.) from Enniscorthy; containing 928 inhabitants. This parish, which is situated on the road leading along the west bank of the river Slaney from Wexford to Enniscorthy, comprises 4240 statute acres, as applotted under the tithe act, and in the cultivation of which the improved system has been adopted: there are about 60 acres of underwood, and the remainder is principally arable. Bellevue, formerly the residence of the late Rt. Hon. G. Ogle, and now the seat of Anthony Cliffe, Esq., is an elegant mansion, with conservatories and every appendage, beautifully situated in an extensive demesne on the banks of the Slaney; the principal front is towards the river, and consists of a centre with a noble portico of eight Ionic columns, and two boldly projecting wings: the grounds are tastefully laid out, and the whole forms an interesting feature in a landscape of great beauty. Birchgrove, the seat of Admiral Wilson; and McMines, that of P. King, Esq., consisting of the ancient castle of that name, with some later additions, are also in this parish, and are both finely situated on the banks of the Slaney. The Slaney is navigable to Pool-Darragh (which part of the river separates this parish from that of Ballinaslaney) for the largest ships that can cross the bar of Wexford harbour, and to Enniscorthy for vessels of smaller burden. The contemplated canal for completing the navigation for vessels of large burden between Wexford and Enniscorthy will, according to the proposed plan, commence opposite Bellevue, at the townland of Pool-Darragh, in the parish of Ballinaslaney, and continue along the east bank of the river to within half a mile of the bridge at Enniscorthy, a distance of 6½ English miles. During the season an extensive salmon fishery is carried on in the river. It is an impropriate curacy, in the diocese of Ferns, and is part of the union of Killurin: the tithes, amounting to £135. 13. 10¼., are appropriate to the curacy, except those of the townland of Ballyheogue, which are merged in the rent. In the R. C. divisions it forms part of the union or district of Bree; the chapel, situated at Galbally, is a handsome building with a residence for the priest, erected at an expense of £2000 by J. H. Talbot, Esq., of Talbot Hall, who also endowed it with 15 acres of land for the use of the priest. Attached to the chapel is a school, partly supported by subscription; and there are three pay schools, in which are about 70 children. The late Rt. Hon. G. Ogle, who resided at Bellevue, was a great promoter of the improved system of agriculture in this country, and author of the popular ballad of "Molly Asthore," and several other admired productions.

BALLYHOE, a hamlet, in the parish of DRUMCONDRA, barony of MORGALLION, county of MEATH, and province of LEINSTER, 3½ miles (N.) from Drumcondra; containing 8 houses and 52 inhabitants. It is situated on the old road from Drumcondra to Carrickmacross, and is a station of the constabulary police.

BALLYHOOLEY, or AGHULTIE, a parish, in the barony of FERMOY, county of CORK, and province of MUNSTER, 4 miles (W. by N.) from Fermoy, on the road to Mallow; containing 2297 inhabitants, of which number 533 are in the village. It extends on both sides of the river Blackwater, and comprises 5185 statute acres, as applotted under the tithe act, and valued at £4616 per annum. The land on the south side of the river is chiefly mountain pasture, forming part of the Nagle mountains, and based on a substratum of brown-stone; and that on the north side has a good limestone soil. The system of agriculture is improved, but is still very imperfect; lime is almost exclusively used for manure. There is an abundance of turf, which is drawn from the south of the Blackwater at a distance of two miles from the village; limestone abounds, and great quantities are procured for building and burning. Convamore, the seat of Viscount Ennismore, is a handsome modern mansion, beautifully situated in a fine demesne stretching along the banks of the Blackwater, and commanding an interesting view of the windings of that river through rich masses of wood to the picturesque ruins of the ancient castle of Ballyhooley, situated on a rocky eminence over the Blackwater, and, with the present church and the ruins of the former, both closely adjoining, presenting a highly picturesque and romantic group. Gurteen House, the residence of Luke G. Campion, Esq., is finely situated on an eminence overlooking the river and commanding an extensive and richly diversified view of this truly picturesque country, combining a wide range of mountain, wood, and water, with the fine ruins of Creg and Ballyhooley castles; the house has been greatly enlarged and improved. Upper Convamore, the residence of J. Delany, Esq., is also in the parish. The village is situated near the river, over which is a stone bridge: it contains 85 houses, the greater number of which are thatched, and is a constabulary police station. At Millvale is an extensive corn-mill. The river Blackwater, from its numerous shoals and rapids, is not navigable in this part of its course.

The living is a rectory and vicarage, in the diocese of Cloyne, united by act of council to the vicarage of Killathy, and with it forming the corps of the prebend of Aghultie in the cathedral of Cloyne, and in the patronage of the Bishop; the tithes amount to £468, and of the whole benefice to £618. The church, a small plain building without a tower, was erected about 60 years since, near the site of the old church, of which there are still some remains. There is no glebe-house, and only one acre of glebe. In the R. C. divisions the parish is one of the five that constitute the union or district of Castletown-Roche; the chapel, situated in the village, is a spacious and commodious building recently erected. There are two schools, one of 134 boys, the other of 56 girls; the latter, which is in the chapel-yard, was built at the expense of the late Rev. J. Kirby, P. P.; both are under the superintendence of the National Board, and towards their support Lord and Lady Ennismore, and D. Callaghan, Esq., are liberal contributors. Ballyhooley castle was formerly one of the principal fortresses of the Roches, and on its forfeiture was granted with the adjoining lands to Sir Richard Aldworth: it was taken in 1645 by Lord Castlehaven, who commanded the royal forces in this district. In the demesne of Convamore is a spring impregnated with carbonate of lime; and there is also a similar spring on the new line of road to Cork. There are several raths or forts in the parish.

BALLYHUSKARD, a parish, in the barony of BALLAGHKEEN, county of WEXFORD, and province of LEINSTER, 3 miles (S. E. by E.) from Enniscorthy; containing 2487 inhabitants. It is situated on the road from Enniscorthy to Oulart, and contains Oulartleigh, the seat of Arthur Murphy, Esq.; and Ballycoursey, of Anthony Hawkins, Esq. The living consists of a rectory and perpetual curacy, in the diocese of Ferns; the former constitutes part of the union of St. Mary's, Enniscorthy, and the latter is in the patronage of the Rector; the tithes amount to £547. 13. 5.; the curate's stipend is £75 per annum. The church is a neat edifice with a tower, built in 1829. There is a glebe of 20 acres, but no glebe-house. In the R. C. divisions the parish is partly in the union or district of Edermine, and partly in that of Oulart: the former portion contains the chapel of Glanbryan; and the latter, that of Ballincurry. There is a place of worship for the Society of Friends. A parochial school is about to be established; and there are five hedge schools, in which are about 160 children, and a Sunday school. A specimen of the gigantic horned fossil deer of Ireland *(cervus megaceros)* was discovered near the bog of Itty, in this parish, in 1835; prior to which, portions of several others of the same species had been dug up near the same spot. This skeleton is in the possession of Dr. Macartney, of Enniscorthy, at whose expense it was dug out, and by whom it has been set up in an out-house adjoining his residence: its dimensions exceed those of the skeleton in the museum of Trinity College, Dublin.

BALLYINGLEY, a parish, in the barony of SHELMALIER, county of WEXFORD, and province of LEINSTER, 5 miles (S. W. by S.) from Taghmon; containing 204 inhabitants. This parish is situated on the east bank of the Scar river, and contains 746 statute acres, as applotted under the tithe act. By a return to a regal visitation, in 1615, it appears to have been one of the mensals of the bishop of Ferns, which it still continues to be. It is one of the six parishes that constitute the union of Horetown, in the diocese of Ferns: the tithes amount to £31. 16. 11¼., of which £21. 4. 7½. is paid to the Ecclesiastical Commissioners, and £10. 12. 3¾. to the incumbent. The church is in ruins. The parish is within the R. C. district of Ballymitty.

BALLYJAMESDUFF, a market and post-town, and a district parish, in the barony of CASTLERAHAN, county of CAVAN, and province of ULSTER, 8½ miles (S. E.) from Cavan, and 44¾ miles (N. W. by W.) from Dublin; containing 3227 inhabitants, of which number, 863 are in the town. The town is situated on the old mail coach road from Virginia to Cavan, and consists of five streets, containing together 150 houses. The market is on Tuesday, and is amply supplied; and fairs are held on Feb. 4th, March 8th, April 16th, May 7th, June 10th, July 17th, Aug. 15th, Sept. 2nd, Oct. 26th, Nov. 29th, and Dec. 23rd. Here is a constabulary police station, and petty sessions are held. The parish was created in 1831, by disuniting nine townlands from the parish of Castleraghan, five from that of Denn, two from Lurgan, and four from the parish of Kildrumferton. The living is a perpetual curacy, in the diocese of Kilmore, and in the patronage of the several Incumbents of the above parishes, who present in rotation: the stipend of the perpetual curate is £80 per annum, towards which £30 is contributed by the incumbent of Castleraghan, £20 by the incumbent of Kildrumferton, and £15 each by the incumbents of Denn and Lurgan. The church is a plain edifice, erected in 1834 by aid of a grant of £900 from the Ecclesiastical Commissioners, and subscriptions amounting to £200. In the R. C. divisions the parish forms part of the union or district of Castleraghan and Munterconnaught; the chapel is a spacious building. There is a place of worship for Presbyterians in connection with the Synod of Ulster, and of the third class; also two for Wesleyan Methodists. A school at Remonan is supported by Lord Farnham, and another at Ballyjamesduff is aided by private subscriptions: about 140 boys and 150 girls are instructed in these schools; and there are three pay schools, situated respectively at Rawson, Lackenmore, and Lackenduff, in which are about 180 boys and 90 girls.

BALLYKEANE, or KILLEIGHY, a parish, partly in the barony of GEASHILL, but chiefly in that of UPPER PHILIPSTOWN, KING'S county, and province of LEINSTER, 3½ miles (N. N. W.) from Portarlington; containing 2415 inhabitants. It is situated on the road from Portarlington to Tullamore, and comprises 8069 statute acres, as applotted under the tithe act. The living is a rectory and vicarage, in the diocese of Kildare; the former is united to that of Killaderry, and the latter is a distinct benefice, in the patronage of the Bishop: the tithes amount to £304. 12. 3¾., of which £203. 1. 6½. is payable to the rector, and the remainder to the vicar. The church is a handsome building, erected in 1827, by aid of a grant of £900 from the late Board of First Fruits. The glebe-house was built by aid of a gift of £450 and a loan of £120 from the same Board: the glebe comprises 7½ acres. In the R. C. divisions the parish is united with part of that of Geashill, in which union are three chapels, one at Ballykeane, and the others at Killeigh and Ballynegar in Geashill. A school, in which 17 boys and 16 girls are taught, is aided by subscriptions; and there are three private schools, in which are 90 boys and 55 girls, and four Sunday schools.

BALLYKELLY, a village, in the parish of TAMLAGHT-FINLAGAN, barony of KENAUGHT, county of LONDONDERRY, and province of ULSTER, 3 miles (W. by S.) from Newtownlimavady; containing 290 inhabitants. This place, with the lands around it, was granted by Jas. I., on the plantation of Ulster, to the Fishmongers' Company of London, who, in 1619, erected a large and handsome castle, the custody of which was entrusted to James Higgins, Esq., who had a garrison of 40 able men, with arms for its defence. The estate was held under lease from the company, by the Hamiltons and Beresfords, from the year 1628 till the death of Geo. III., when it reverted to the company, who immediately commenced improvements on an extensive scale. The village is situated on the road from Londonderry to Coleraine, and contains 67 houses, of which the greater number are handsomely built. The proprietors have built in it several very neat cottages; a large and handsome meeting-house, in the Grecian style of architecture, for Presbyterians in connection with the Synod of Ulster; an excellent dispensary, with a very good house for a resident surgeon; and large and substantial school-rooms, with residences for the master and mistress; and various other improvements are in progress in and around the village. Nearly adjoining are several large and handsome houses, the principal of which are Walworth, the residence of the Rev. G. V. Sampson; Walworth Cottage, of Major Stirling; Drummond, of A. Sampson, Esq.; and Finlagan, of the Rev. O. M[c]Causland. Walworth was built by the Beresfords in 1705, and occupied by that family till the death of Geo. III.; the woods around it contain some of the finest timber in the county, and are among the most extensive in the north of Ireland. Corn stores have been built; and a market for grain is occasionally held. A penny post from Londonderry to this place has been established. Close to the village is the parish church of Tamlaght-Finlagan, a small but handsome edifice, with a large square tower surmounted by a lofty octagonal spire; and here is a Presbyterian meeting-house, a spacious and handsome edifice, of the first class. Near the church are the ruins of Walworth castle, erected by the company in 1619; and adjoining are the ruins of a church, built by the Hamilton family in 1629.—See TAMLAGHT-FINLAGAN.

BALLYKENNEDY, or GRACE-HILL, a village, in the parish of AHOGHILL, barony of LOWER TOOME, county of ANTRIM, and province of ULSTER, 1½ mile (W. S. W.) from Ballymena; containing 326 inhabitants. This place is situated on the river Maine, over which is a bridge of four arches, connecting it with the village of Galgorim. It owes its origin to the Rev. John Cennick, who, in 1746, founded here an establishment of Moravians, or United Brethren, who hold under Lord O'Neill, on lease renewable in perpetuity, about 200 plantation acres of land, which are divided in small portions among the brethren. The village consists of 39 family residences, of which the greater number are small cottages, exclusively of the chapel, and the two principal houses for unmarried brethren and sisters respectively, which occupy three sides of a quadrangle, of which the area is ornamented with shrubs. The sisters support themselves by various kinds of needlework, particularly tambour and embroidery, which are much admired, and also superintend an extensive boarding-school for young ladies. The inhabitants of the brethren's house having greatly diminished in number, the greater part of the building has been appropriated as a boarding-school for young gentlemen, conducted by the minister of the establishment and several assistants, and a daily school for boys and girls of the surrounding country. A small linen manufacture and several other trades are carried on. Each family has land sufficient for the keep of a cow and the raising of potatoes. The chapel is a neat and commodious building; the burial-place is on the summit of a rising ground, at a distance from the village. In a bog in this townland is a curious artificial mount; and within its limits may be yet seen the ruins of an ancient church.—See AHOGHILL.

BALLYKINDLAR, a parish, in the barony of LECALE, county of DOWN, and province of ULSTER, 3 miles (N. E.) from Clough; the population is returned with the parish of Tyrella. This parish derives its name, signifying the "Town of the Candlestick," from the appropriation of its tithes to furnish lights for the cathedral of Christchurch, Dublin. It is situated on the bay of Dundrum, on the eastern coast, and on the road from Newry to Ardglass, and comprises, according to the Ordnance survey, 2038½ statute acres, the property of the Marquess of Downshire. A considerable portion of the surface consists of sand hills, and the land is in general very indifferent. There was formerly an extensive tract of bog, which was drained in 1819, and is now wholly under cultivation. It is a rectory, in the diocese of Down, entirely appropriate to the economy funds of the cathedral of Christchurch, Dublin: the tithes amount to £54. 5. 6½. There has been neither church nor incumbent in the parish since the Reformation. On the shore of the inner bay of Dundrum, or Clough bay, are some ruins of the ancient parish church. In the R. C. divisions it is the head of a union or district, also called Tyrella, comprising the parishes of Ballykindlar and Tyrella, and part of Loughin-island, and containing chapels at Ballykindlar and Dromaroad. Near the former is a school-house.

BALLYKINE, a constablewick or sub-denomination of the parish of RATHDRUM, barony of BALLINACOR, county of WICKLOW, and province of LEINSTER, 2¾ miles (S. W.) from Rathdrum; containing 2634 inhabitants. This place, which is situated in the mountain district leading from Arklow to Donard, was anciently celebrated for its monastery, which, according to Archdall, was founded by the brother of St. Kevin. It includes the villages of Ballinaclash, Sheanna, Cappagh, Aghrim, and the old borough of Carysfort, and comprises 9904 statute acres, as applotted under the tithe act, of which 6952 acres are arable and pasture land, and the remainder mountain. Whaley Abbey, the seat of R. W. Whaley, Esq., occupies the site of the ancient monastery; and within the constablewick are also Ballard Park, the residence of D. Lawrence, Esq., and Clash Cottage, of E. Johnson, Esq. By an inquisition, taken in 1604, this is denominated a rectory, which, with those of Rathdrum and Moycredyne or Moycreddin, was found to have belonged to the priory or monastery of All Saints, and was granted for ever, on the 4th of February, 30th of Hen. VIII., to the mayor, bailiffs, and commons of the city of Dublin, at an annual rent of £4. It now forms one of the denominations constituting the union or benefice of Rathdrum, in the diocese of Dublin and Glendalough; and also, together with the constablewick of Ballinacor, constitutes, as regards the cure of souls, the new district parish of Ballinaclash, of which the living is a perpetual curacy, in the patronage of the Rector of Rathdrum, who receives the whole of the tithes, amounting to £181. 8. 6½. In the R.C. divisions it is in the union or district of Rathdrum. At Ballinaclash is a school, supported by the rector of Rathdrum; also a Sunday school.

BALLYLANEEN, a parish, in the barony of UPPER-THIRD, county of WATERFORD, and province of MUNSTER, 3 miles (S.) from Kilmacthomas; containing 3575 inhabitants. This parish is situated on the river Mahon and on St. George's channel, and comprises 6194 statute acres, as applotted under the tithe act. Carrig Castle, the residence of H. Power, Esq., and Seafield, of P. Barron, Esq., both pleasantly situated, are within its limits. It is a vicarage, in the diocese of Lismore, and is part of the union of Stradbally; the rectory is impropriate in the Duke of Devonshire. The tithes amount to £378. 10., of which £78. 10. is payable to the impropriator, and £300 to the vicar. In the R. C. divisions also it forms part of the union or district of Stradbally, and contains a chapel. There are five pay schools, in which are about 270 boys and 97 girls. There are some considerable remains of Ballynaclash castle, situated on an eminence; and at Temple-Bric is a vast insulated rock, about 40 yards from the shore, on which are traces of an ancient building supposed to have been the residence of O'Bric, chief of the southern Decies. A species of hawk, remarkable for great strength and courage, formerly frequented this rock, and is still occasionally seen.

BALLYLARKIN, a parish, in the barony of CRANAGH, county of KILKENNY, and province of LEINSTER, 1¾ mile (S. W.) from Freshford; containing 243 inhabitants. It is situated on the road from Freshford to Johnstown, and comprises 4733 statute acres, of which £1370 are applotted under the tithe act and valued at £1090 per annum: the lands are arable and pasture in nearly equal portions. The living is a vicarage, in the diocese of Ossory, and in the patronage of the Dean and Chapter of St. Canice, Kilkenny, to whom the rectory is appropriate. The tithes amount to £92. 6. 1¾., of which £61. 10. 9¼. is payable to the appropriators, and the remainder to the vicar. There is neither church, glebe-house, nor glebe: the Protestant inhabitants attend divine service at Freshford church. In the R. C. divisions the parish forms part of the union or district of Freshford. Here are the ruins of a castle, once the seat of the Shortall family, which for a long time was of great note in this county.

BALLYLENNAN, a parish, in the barony of SHELMALIER, county of WEXFORD, and province of LEINSTER, 5 miles (S. W. by S.) from Taghmon; containing 733 inhabitants. This parish is situated on the high road from Wexford to Duncannon Fort, and is separated on the east from the barony of Bargy, and on the south-east from the barony of Shelburne, by a navigable stream called indifferently the Bannow or Scar river. It comprises 2460 statute acres, as applotted under the tithe act, of which about 60 acres are woodland, and the remainder chiefly under tillage. The soil is generally light, with the exception of some very rich land near the Scar river, the mud of which supplies abundance of manure; the system of agriculture is good, and still improving; and the dwellings of the peasantry, which are cleanly and cheerful, afford striking indications of industry and comfort. At the mouth of the Scar river, in Bannow bay, is a small quay for landing limestone and manure, which are brought from the peninsula of Hook, on the other side of the bay of Fethard, in boats of about 15 tons burden. Rosegarland, the elegant seat of F. Leigh, jun., Esq., though to all appearance a modern mansion, is incorporated with some of the walls, and occupies part of the site of an Anglo-Norman fortress, originally quadrangular and flanked at the opposite angles with massive square and round embattled towers, of which latter, one has been raised by the present proprietor to the height of 60 feet, commanding a luxuriant and extensive prospect over the numerous rich demesnes with which this part of the country is ornamented. The gardens and pleasure grounds are tastefully laid out; in the former, which comprise seven acres, are four Portugal laurels of extraordinary growth, planted in the form of a square at the distance of 1¾ yard asunder, and extending their foliage over an area of 65 yards in circumference; the latter are adorned with some fine timber, and a branch of the Scar winds through them, adding much to the beauty and fertility of the demesne. This is an impropriate curacy, endowed with the small tithes, in the diocese of Ferns, and forms part of the union of Horetown; the rectory is impropriate in the Earl of Portsmouth. The tithes amount to £174. 6. 6½., of which £114. 6. 6½. is payable to the impropriator, and £60 to the rector of Horetown. The remains of the church have been converted into a mausoleum for the family of Leigh. In the R. C. divisions it is within the liberty of Tintern, and with Clongeen is known as the parish of Rosegarland.

BALLYLINAN, a village, in the parish of KILLEBAN, barony of BALLYADAMS, QUEEN'S county, and province of LEINSTER, 3 miles (S. W.) from Athy, on the road to Castlecomer; containing 94 houses and 533 inhabitants. In the strata of the neighbouring lands are numerous marine *exuviæ;* and some valuable coal mines, called the Wolf-Hill and Mordulah collieries, are worked by steam-engines recently erected. Great quantities of fine flag-stones were formerly raised on the adjoining townland of Boley; but on the discovery of similar quarries near Carlow, more conveniently situated for conveyance by canal, they were abandoned. Stones containing a large proportion of iron are found on the lands called Iron Park; but no works have been yet established. The village is a constabulary police station, and has a penny post to Athy. Fairs are held in it on Jan. 11th, Feb. 10th, May 10th, Sept. 2nd, and Nov. 26th; and petty sessions every Saturday. To the north is Rahin, the seat of Lieut.-Col. Weldon, a handsome mansion surrounded by thriving plantations; and at a short distance are the luxuriant woods of Gracefield Lodge, the seat of the ancient family of Grace, whose old mansion has been taken down and replaced by an elegant villa in the later English style, from a design by Mr. Nash, completed in 1817; the grounds have been tastefully embellished, and the approach from the Kilkenny side presents some beautiful and interesting mountain scenery. In the village are the ruins of an old church, near which some ancient coins have been dug up; and on the Marquess of Lansdowne's estate of Luggaghcurran, in the vicinity, are the remains of a cromlech, consisting of five upright pillars about 4½ feet high, and a table stone 8½ feet long, 7 wide, and 2½ feet in thickness. On the highest point of the Boley hills, and near the woods of Gracefield, is Dundrom, an extensive earthwork consisting of a vast mound, the summit of which is 130 yards in diameter, enclosed by a high bank, and surrounded at the base by a fosse 30 feet wide at the bottom. Within the enclosure is a well of fine water, and from the mound is a view of uncommon extent. This post was occupied by a party of the insurgents in 1798.—See KILLEBAN.

BALLYLINCH, a parish, in the barony of GOWRAN, county of KILKENNY, and province of LEINSTER, 1 mile (N.) from Thomastown; containing 298 inhabitants. It forms part of the estate of Mount Juliet, and comprises 165 statute acres. It is a vicarage, in the diocese of Ossory, and is included in the union of Burnchurch; the rectory is a sub-denomination forming part of the Mount Juliet demesne. The tithes amount to £96, and are payable to the incumbent. In the R. C. divisions it is comprehended in the union or district of Thomastown.

BALLYLINNEY, a parish, in the barony of LOWER BELFAST, county of ANTRIM, and province of ULSTER, 1½ mile (S. S. E.) from Ballyclare, on the road from Belfast to Doagh; containing 2412 inhabitants. It comprises, according to the Ordnance survey, 5684 statute acres (including 320½ in Ballywalter grange), which are generally in a good state of cultivation. The living is a vicarage, in the diocese of Connor, united from time immemorial to the vicarage of Carnmoney and the rectory of Ballymartin; the rectory is impropriate in the Marquess of Donegal. The tithes amount to £300, of which £200 is payable to the impropriator, and £100 to the vicar. The church was destroyed by the insurgents under the Earl of Tyrone, and has not been rebuilt; the churchyard is still used as a burial-ground by the parishioners. In the R. C. divisions the parish forms part of the union or district of Larne and Carrickfergus. There are three schools situated respectively at Bruslie, Palentine, and Ballylinney, in which are 114 boys and 95 girls; also two pay schools, in which are 58 boys and 77 girls.

BALLYLONGFORD, a town, in the parish of AGHAVALLIN, barony of IRAGHTICONNOR, county of KERRY, and province of MUNSTER, 4 miles (W. by S.) from Tarbert; containing 1300 inhabitants. This town is situated on the road from Tarbert to Ballybunnian, at the head of an estuary or creek of the river Shannon, and contains about 300 houses. Its position is favourable for the export trade, the creek forming a port for lighters which carry corn and turf to Limerick; the trade in turf is very considerable from the vast supply afforded by the extensive tracts of bog in the vicinity, forming part of the possessions of Trinity College, Dublin. The harbour has 16 feet of water at high tides, and is capable of being made one of the best on the Shannon; but that of Tarbert being considered to possess superior advantages, is more likely to be improved. A fair or market is held every alternate Thursday, chiefly for pigs and cattle. This place has a penny post dependent on Tarbert. Petty sessions are held every Monday, and, once in three weeks, a baronial court for the manor of Carrig-a-foile; and here is a station of the constabulary police. There are several gentlemen's seats in the vicinity, enumerated in the article on Aghavallin, *which see*. The parochial church is situated about ¼ of a mile to the north of the town, but having been condemned by the provincial architect as unworthy of repair, it is expected that a new church will be shortly built by the Ecclesiastical Board, at an estimated expense of about £650. The R. C. chapel in the town is a spacious slated building with two galleries, erected in 1806 at an expense of £2000; and near it a large building for a school has been lately erected, at a cost of £350. Here is also a dispensary. In the vicinity of the town, but in Kilnaughten parish, are the extensive and picturesque ruins of Lislaghtin abbey.

BALLYLOUGH.—See BALLYDELOUGHY.

BALLYLOUGHLOE, a parish, in the barony of CLONLONAN, county of WESTMEATH, and province of LEINSTER, 4 miles (E. N. E.) from Athlone, on the road to Mullingar; containing 4739 inhabitants. In 1795 a skirmish took place at the Five-mile House between the peasantry and the yeomanry, in consequence of an attempt to enforce the ballot for the militia. The parish comprises 6194 acres, as applotted under the tithe act: the lands are generally in a good state of cultivation, and under an improved system of agriculture; there are about 70 acres of bog, but no waste land. Limestone abounds, and lead ore has been found, but no vein has hitherto been discovered. Moydrum Castle, the seat of Viscount Castlemaine, is a handsome castellated mansion, erected in 1814, and beautifully situated in an extensive demesne, on one side of which is a small lake. The other seats are Glynwood House, that of John Longworth, Esq., a handsome modern residence near the road from Dublin to Athlone; Belvill, of Gustavus Jones, Esq.; Twyford, of E. Hodson, Esq.; Ballinalack, of Christopher Adamson, Esq.; Cairn Park, of W. G. Adamson, Esq.; and Coolvock, of F. Dillon, Esq.; and on the eastern confines, near Moate, is Shurock, the property of Sir W. Jackson Homan, Bart. A manorial court is held alternately at Moate and Baylin on the first Monday in every month. The living is a rectory and vicarage, in the diocese of Meath, with the rectory and vicarage of Drumraney united by act of council in 1804, and in the patronage of the Bishop; the tithes of the parish amount to £360, and the gross tithes of the benefice to £650. 15. 4½. The church, a neat edifice of stone and in good repair, was erected in 1812, by aid of a loan of £400 from the late Board of First Fruits; and the glebe-house was built by a gift of £100 and a loan of £675 from the same Board, in 1809. The glebe comprises 32 acres of profitable land, valued at £2. 15. 4½. per acre; and there is a glebe in Drumraney of 33 acres, valued at £87. 9. per annum. In the R. C. divisions the parish, also called Caulry, is in the diocese of Ardagh, and is co-extensive with that of the Established Church; the chapel is a large building at Mount-Temple, attached to which is a school under the National Board. A school at Baylin is supported by Lord Castlemaine, and another at the same place, for girls, by Lady Castlemaine; and a school at Ballinagarbery is supported by a bequest from the late Dr. Maxwell. In these schools about 150 boys and 190 girls receive instruction: and there are also three pay schools, in which are about 200 children. There are several remains of ancient castles and Danish raths; near the church is a remarkable moat, similar to that at Castle-Kindelane; and there are also two mineral springsin the parish. There was anciently a friary at Farrenemanagh, near this place, which was in ruins at the time of issuing an inquisition in the 3rd of Jas. I., but no vestiges of it can now be traced.

BALLYLOUGHNANE, a village, in the parish of LOCKEEN, barony of LOWER ORMOND, county of TIPPERARY, and province of MUNSTER, 4 miles (S. W. by S.) from Parsonstown; containing 28 houses and 143 inhabitants. It is situated on the verge of the county, and is separated from the King's county by the river Brosna.—See LOCKEEN.

BALLYMACALENNY.—See KILLESHANDRA.

BALLYMACARRETT, a town and parish, forming part of the suburbs of BELFAST, in the barony of UPPER CASTLEREAGH, county of DOWN, and province of ULSTER; containing 5168 inhabitants. This place, previously to 1825, was simply a townland in the parish of Knockbreda, or Bredagh, and in the history of the county, published in 1744, is described as containing only two buildings, Mount Pottinger and a mill. It is now become a populous and flourishing town, occupying a site formerly covered by every tide, but which has been reclaimed by an extensive embankment stretching from Conswater westward to the river Lagan, opposite to the quays of Belfast, and thence on the shore of that river to Ormeau, the splendid residence of the Marquess of Donegal. The town, which in 1831 contained 257 houses, forms an appendage to Belfast, from which it is separated only by the river Lagan, which here separates the counties of Down and Antrim, and over which is a stone bridge of 21 arches: it is irregularly built, but has been greatly improved by the formation of several new streets; and a handsome bridge of five arches, about 400 yards above the long bridge, and opening a more direct communication with the southern part of Belfast, has been lately erected under an act obtained in 1831, at an expense of £6000, raised in transferable shares of £25 each. The first manufacture established here was that of glass; and since the first glass-house was built, in 1776, two other extensive establishments have been erected, though at present only one is in operation. A pottery upon a very large scale was soon afterwards established; and previously to the removal of the duty on salt, there were two extensive works for the manufacture of that article from rock salt brought from England, for exportation, which are now discontinued. The Lagan foundry, for the manufacture of steam-engines and other machinery on the most improved principles, affords employment to 140 persons: and in 1832 the first patent machine for making paper ever introduced into Ireland was made at these works. A very extensive rope-yard and sail-cloth manufactory, affording employment to 130 persons, are carried on; and two large vitriol works, of which one, established in 1799, was the second erected in the kingdom, are in full operation for supplying the bleachers, dyers, and calico printers in the neighbourhood. There are also extensive starch-manufactories, and meal and flour-mills driven by steam and water; and two large mills for spinning linen yarn were erected in 1834, and employ more than 300 persons. The manufacture of calico and muslin is carried on upon a very extensive scale, affording employment to several hundred persons. Here is a constabulary police station. This place was erected into a parish by an act of the 12th of Geo. III., and comprises 575 statute acres, which are exempt from tithes; about 28½ acres are under water, and the remainder are arable and pasture. The living is a perpetual curacy, in the diocese of Down, and in the patronage of the Rector of Knockbreda: it is endowed with the tithes of Ballynafeigh, an adjoining townland, amounting to £50, which is augmented from Primate Boulter's fund. The church, a neat building, was erected in 1826 by aid of a grant of £800 from the late Board of First Fruits and by subscription. In the R. C. divisions the parish forms part of the union or district of Belfast, in the diocese of Connor; the chapel was built in 1829. There are places of worship for Presbyterians in connection with the Synod of Ulster and the Seceding Synod, and for Covenanters and Wesleyan Methodists. There are five schools in which about 298 boys and 182 girls are instructed; also three pay schools, in which are about 90 boys and 50 girls.

BALLYMACART, a parish, in the barony of Decies-within-Drum, county of Waterford, and province of Munster, 6 miles (S. S. E.) from Dungarvan; containing 984 inhabitants. This parish, also called *Aglishvenan*, is situated on the shore of St. George's channel, and comprises 2966 statute acres, as applotted under the tithe act. On the south-east is the cape or promontory of Mine Head, forming the northern point of the entrance to Ardmore bay. Here is Glenanne Cottage, the marine villa of H. Winston Barron, Esq. It is a vicarage, in the diocese of Lismore, united to that of Ardmore; the rectory is impropriate in the Duke of Devonshire. The tithes amount to £124, of which £82. 13. 4. is payable to the impropriator, and £41. 6. 8. to the vicar. In the R. C. divisions also it forms part of the union or district of Ardmore: the chapel is a large building. At Mount Barron there is a school under the patronage of H. W. Barron, Esq., who gave the school-house and four acres of land: it is attended by about 200 boys and 54 girls.

BALLYMACARTHY, a village, in the parish of Kilmaloda, Eastern Division of the barony of East Carbery, county of Cork, and province of Munster, 3 miles (E.) from Clonakilty; containing 167 inhabitants. During the disturbances of 1798 this place was the scene of an obstinate engagement between a party of the insurgent forces and some companies of the Westmeath militia, which would have terminated in the defeat of the latter, but for the arrival of the Caithness legion from Bandon, which came very opportunely to their aid. The village is situated on the road from Bandon to Clonakilty, and consists of 32 houses, some of which are large and well built: the new road connecting these two towns here crosses the old line. Close adjoining are the extensive mills of Messrs. Swete and Co., in which more than 8000 barrels of wheat are annually ground into flour for the supply of the neighbouring towns.—See Kilmaloda.

BALLYMACELLIGOTT, a parish, in the barony of Trughenackmy, county of Kerry, and province of Munster, 4¾ miles (S. E.) from Tralee; containing 3535 inhabitants. This parish, which is situated on the high roads leading from Tralee to Castle-Island and Killarney, comprises 11,552 statute acres, as applotted under the tithe act: about 2300 acres are bog and coarse mountain pasture, which, from the abundance of limestone and turf, might be easily reclaimed. The great limestone quarry of Ballymacelligott is situated on the estate of A. Blennerhassett, Esq., of Ballyseedy, and about half-way on the old road from Tralee to Castle-Island. A quarry was first opened here in 1811, for building the barracks at Tralee, but was afterwards discontinued; and near that spot is the present quarry, which was first opened to procure materials for enlarging Ballyseedy House, since which time it has been constantly worked and the stone used for the county gaol and the new court-house at Tralee, and latterly for the ship canal from Tralee to Blennerville, and affords constant employment to about 30 men. Stones of the largest size required for public works are detached with great facility by wedges, on account of the regularity of the strata, and the produce of the quarry being of very superior quality, is in general request for the ornamental parts of public buildings: the average quantity raised weekly is about 50 tons. Several curious caverns are formed in the strata by a stream forcing its subterraneous course for nearly two miles, and, when explored by torch light, exhibit many beautiful and highly grotesque appearances; the entrance to the principal cavern is within the border of the adjoining parish of O'Brennan. The most remarkable of these caverns is one which in appearance resembles the interior of a cathedral, with a pulpit and kneeling figures formed by the stalactites; the discharge of a pistol produces a report like thunder. The principal seats are Spring Hill, that of Capt. Chute; Chute Hall, of R. Chute, Esq.; Arabella, of F. Peet, Esq.; Maug House, of W. Sealy, Esq.; Rathanay, of Mrs. Rowan; and Maglass, of W. Ledmond, Esq. In the northern part of the parish is a romantic glen, called *Gloun-na-geentha*, memorable as the scene of the discovery and death of the great Earl of Desmond by Kelly, an Irish soldier, in 1583; his head was sent to London, and ordered by Queen Elizabeth to be fixed on London bridge, and his body, after being concealed for some weeks, was interred at Ardnagrath, in a small chapel which still bears his name. This glen has lately been planted by Mr. Blennerhassett, and improvements have been made by Capt. Chute and Mr. Sealy, and orchard planting by J. O'Connell, Esq., for his tenantry at Maglass.

The living is a rectory, in the diocese of Ardfert and Aghadoe, to which the rectories of Nohoval-Kerry and a portion of the rectory of Currens have been episcopally united from a period prior to any existing record, forming the union of Ballymacelligott, in the patronage of the Crosbie family; the tithes of this parish amount to £336. 18. 5., and of the whole benefice to £463. 11. 4., including the rectorial tithes of that part of the parish of Currens which lies to the north of the river Maine (amounting to £58. 3. 1.), which is a portion of this union, but the ecclesiastical duties of the whole parish devolve on the incumbent of Currens, or union of Kiltalla. The church is a spacious and substantial building with an embattled tower crowned with pinnacles; it was erected on the site of the old parish church, by aid of a gift of £466 and a loan of £466 from the late Board of First Fruits, in 1820. There is no glebe-house: the two glebes in the union comprise about 23 statute acres. In the R. C. divisions this parish is the head of a union or district, comprising also the parishes of Nohoval-Kerry, Ballyseedy, and O'Brennan, and small parts of the parishes of Annagh and Ratass: the chapel here is a large slated building; and there is also one at Clohers adjoining the parish of O'Brennan, a thatched building. Near Arabella are two places of worship for Wesleyan Methodists, one of which is of the Primitive class. There is a school under the superintendence of the incumbent, and another under the direction of the parish priest is partly supported by subscription. In these schools about 90 children are instructed; and there are also three pay schools, in which are about 150 children. A shop is occasionally opened for the sale of blanketing and clothing at reduced prices to the poor. At Ballingrilough are the remains of an old castle which belonged to the Mac Elligotts; and there are several old forts in the parish, in some of which excavations have been discovered regularly walled and floored.

BALLYMACHUGH, a parish, in the barony of CLONMAHON, county of CAVAN, and province of ULSTER, 6¼ miles (E. N. E.) from Granard; containing 3428 inhabitants. This parish is situated on the borders of Lough Sheelan, on the confines of the counties of Longford and Meath, and comprises, according to the Ordnance survey, 7728½ statute acres, of which 1827¾ are water. The system of agriculture is improving; oats and potatoes are the principal crops. The gentlemen's seats are Arley Cottage, that of Lord Farnham, and Fortland, of W. Gosling, Esq. Petty sessions for the district are held in the school-house every third Saturday. It is a vicarage, in the diocese of Ardagh, and is part of the union of Granard; the rectory is impropriate in the Misses Blundell: the tithes amount to £265. 16. 11., of which £118. 3. 1. is payable to the impropriators, and £147. 13. 10. to the vicar. The church, a plain building, has been recently enlarged at an expense of £800. The glebe comprises 11 acres, valued at £1. 16. per acre. The R. C. parish is co-extensive with that of the Established Church; the chapel is a large plain building recently erected. The parochial school for boys and girls is aided by donations from Lord Farnham and the incumbent; at Ballynany there is a school, and one at Orley is supported by Lord Farnham, by whom the school-house was built; in these schools are about 280 boys and 230 girls. There is also a Sunday school at Orley. A dispensary is also supported in the customary manner. On an island in the lake are the ruins of Crover castle, and on another, those of an old church covered with ivy.

BALLYMACKEY, a parish, in the barony of UPPER ORMOND, county of TIPPERARY, and province of MUNSTER, 5 miles (E.) from Nenagh; containing 3066 inhabitants. This parish is situated on the mail coach road from Dublin to Limerick, and is intersected by the river Olitrin. There are about 2000 acres of bog, and of the remainder the greater portion is under tillage; the system of agriculture is much improved, and there is abundance of limestone in the parish. Castle Willington, the seat of J. Willington, Esq., which takes its name from a lofty and very perfect square tower near the mansion, is situated in a well planted demesne watered by the river Olitrin. Woodville, the residence of Humphrey Minchin, Esq., and Besborough, of T. Sadlier, jun., Esq., are both pleasantly situated in grounds tastefully laid out and kept in fine order: Mount Pleasant, the residence of Captain Jackson, is a handsome mansion pleasantly situated; as is also Donnybrook, the property of W. Poe, Esq., but at present in the occupation of a tenant. There are several other gentlemen's residences in the parish, of which the principal are Lissanisca, that of R. Smithwick, Esq.; Shanbally, of P. Smithwick, Esq.; Hermitage, of W. Jackson, Esq.; Elmhill, of W. Middleton, Esq.; Camira, of the Rev. P. Bolton; and Falleen, of G. Riall, Esq. Here is a constabulary police station. The living is a rectory and vicarage, in the diocese of Killaloe; the vicarage is episcopally united to the entire rectory of Templedowney or Toomavarra, constituting the union of Ballymackey, and the corps of the chancellorship of Killaloe, with which are held episcopally the rectory of this parish and the rectory and vicarage of Ballygibbon, in the patronage of the Bishop. The tithes amount to £424. 12. 3¾., and of the union to £609. 4. 7½. The church is a neat modern edifice, erected by aid of a loan of £1000 from the late Board of First Fruits, in 1815. The glebe-house, one mile and a half distant from the church, was built by aid of a gift of £300 and a loan of £500 from the same Board, in 1814: the glebe comprises 15*a.* 0*r.* 5*p.* In the

R. C. divisions this parish forms part of the union or district of Toomavarra or Aghnameadle, and contains a chapel. A parochial school of 20 boys and 20 girls is supported by an endowment of £6 per annum and an annual donation from the rector; and there are seven pay schools, in which are about 200 children; also a dispensary.

BALLYMACNAB.—See LISNADIL.

BALLYMACODA.—See KILMACDONOUGH.

BALLYMACORMICK, a parish, partly in the barony of ARDAGH, but chiefly in that of MOYDOW, county of LONGFORD, and province of LEINSTER, 1½ mile (S.) from Longford; containing 3935 inhabitants. This parish, which is situated on the road from Longford to Ballymahon, comprises 9641 statute acres, of which more than 3000 are bog and waste land: the cultivable lands are chiefly in tillage. On the lands of Mullaghavorneen coal is said to exist, but the vein has never been explored; and limestone and sandstone are found in all directions lying very near the surface. The Royal Canal runs through the parish, affording a facility of communication with Dublin. The only gentleman's seat is Rockspring House, the residence of W. Coates, Esq. It is a rectory and vicarage, in the diocese of Ardagh, and is part of the union of Templemichael: the tithes amount to £200. The church, a neat building with a square tower, situated nearly in the centre of the parish, was erected in 1826, by a gift of £900 from the late Board of First Fruits. The glebe comprises 34*a.* 1*r.* 10*p.* valued at £70. 12. 6. per annum. In the R. C. divisions it is included in the union or district of Templemichael, the chapel of which is situated at Shrand. The parochial school is supported by local subscriptions and an annual grant from the Ardagh Diocesan Society, and there are three other schools, altogether affording instruction to 170 boys and 170 girls; there are also nine private schools, in which are about 280 boys and 140 girls, and a Sunday school. There are some remains of the old church; and on the lands of Ballinamore are the ruins of an old church and of an ancient fortress.

BALLYMACWARD, a parish, partly in the barony of TYAQUIN, and partly in that of KILCONNELL, county of GALWAY, and province of CONNAUGHT, 4 miles (S.) from Castle-Blakeney, on the road to Kilconnell; containing 4995 inhabitants. It comprises 8909 statute acres, as applotted under the tithe act; there is also a considerable tract of waste land and bog. The gentlemen's seats are Mount Hazle, that of A. Browne, Esq.; Mount Bernard, of Bernard Browne, Esq.; Hampstead, of F. Davis, Esq.; Carrana, of J. Fitzsimons, Esq.; Crayon, of M. O'Kelly, Esq.; Greenhills, of S. Barrett, Esq.; Keave House, of W. Woods, Esq.; and Keave Lodge, of A. Lynch, Esq. Here is a station of the constabulary police. The living is a vicarage, in the diocese of Clonfert, united, with part of the rectory, to the rectory and vicarage of Clonkeen; the other portion of the rectory is partly appropriate to the see and partly to the deanery. The tithes amount to £279. 13. 10½., of which £55. 7. 8¼. is payable to the Ecclesiastical Commissioners, £16. 12. 3¾. to the dean, and £207. 13. 10¼. to the incumbent; and the entire tithes of the benefice amount to £267. 13. 10¼. The church is a neat building, erected in 1820. The R. C. union or district is co-extensive with that of the Established Church; there is a chapel in each parish. The parochial school, in which are about 90 boys and 100 girls, is aided by annual donations from the Earl and Countess of Clancarty and the incumbent; and a plot of ground has been laid out for the erection of a national school, towards which the greater portion of the funds has been subscribed. There are also two private pay schools, in which are about 120 boys and 30 girls.

BALLYMACWILLIAM, a parish, in the barony of WARRENSTOWN, KING'S county, and province of LEINSTER, 2½ miles (N. N. W.) from Edenderry, on the road to Mullingar; containing 1156 inhabitants. It comprises 4192 statute acres, about two-thirds of which are pasture, and one-third under tillage. The land is of very superior quality, and the state of agriculture is excellent: there are considerable tracts of bog, much of which has been exhausted and brought under cultivation. The gentlemen's seats are Jonestown, that of J. Houghton, Esq.; Mount Wilson, of R. Newsome, Esq.; and Ballybritton, of J. Hynes, Esq. The living is a rectory, in the diocese of Kildare, and in the patronage of the Crown: the tithes amount to £232. 16. 8. The church is in ruins, and there is neither glebe nor glebe-house; the Protestant inhabitants attend divine service at the churches of Ballyburley and Monasteroris. In the R. C. divisions the parish forms part of the union or district of Castropetre. There is a school in which about 80 boys and 30 girls are taught; the school-house was built by Lord Trimlestown, who also endowed it with an acre of land. Some ruins exist of the ancient castles of Ballybritton and Ballyhassil.

BALLYMADUN, or BALLYMODUM, a parish, in the barony of BALROTHERY, county of DUBLIN, and province of LEINSTER, 1½ mile (N.) from Ashbourne; containing 795 inhabitants, of which number, 73 are in the village. This parish is situated on the road from Balbriggan to Ratoath: it was anciently the residence of a hermitess, who had a cell here, and claimed a small rent-charge from the prioress of Grace-Dieu at Lusk; the ruins of an ancient church may still be traced. Part of the bog of Corragh is within its limits, and white marl is found in great abundance; there is also a very fine quarry of calp in the village. Borranstown, the residence of W. P. Segrave, Esq., is a handsome mansion with an elegant Ionic portico of four columns supporting a cornice and pediment in the principal front; it occupies an elevated site commanding extensive views of the surrounding country. Nutstown, the residence of M. Curtis, Esq., is also in the parish. It is a vicarage, in the diocese of Dublin, and is part of the union and corps of the prebend of Clonmethan in the cathedral of St. Patrick, Dublin; the rectory is impropriate in Robert William Netterville, Esq. The tithes amount to £162. 9. 3., the whole of which is payable to the impropriator. The church is in ruins. The glebe comprises 31*a.* 3*r.*, statute measure. In the R. C. divisions it is included in the union or district of Garristown and Ballymadun; the chapel is a neat building, and was enlarged by the addition of a gallery in 1833. The horns of an elk, measuring 11f. 8in. from tip to tip, were dug up in 1823, and are now in the possession of F. Savage, Esq., one of the principal proprietors of the parish.

BALLYMAGARVEY, a parish, in the barony of UPPER DULEEK, county of MEATH, and province of LEINSTER, 6 miles (S.) from Slane; containing 401 inhabitants. This parish is situated on the Nanny-water; the soil is fertile, the land in a high state of cultivation, and there are several flourishing plantations, which add to the pleasing character of the surrounding scenery. Ballymagarvey, the seat of Mrs. Osborne; Balrath, of Mrs. G. Tandy; Snugborough, of Lawrence Cruise Smyth, Esq.; and Mullafin, the property of H. Smith, Esq., are in the parish. There is a flour and corn-mill. It is a vicarage, in the diocese of Meath, and is part of the union of Kentstown; the rectory is impropriate in the heirs of Sir Andrew Aylmer. The tithes amount to £140, of which £90 is payable to the impropriators, and £50 to the vicar. The glebe comprises $4\frac{1}{4}$ acres of profitable land, valued at £2. 10. per acre. In the R. C. divisions it is the head of a union or district called Blacklion, comprising the parishes of Ballymagarvey, Painstown, Ardmulchan, Brownstown, Kentstown, and Tymole, and containing two chapels, at Blacklion and Yellow Furze; the former is a plain thatched building. There is a pay school, in which are about 20 children.

BALLYMAGAURAN, a village, in the parish of TEMPLEPORT, barony of TALLAGHAGH, county of CAVAN, and province of ULSTER, 4 miles (N. E.) from Ballinamore, on the road to Killesandra; containing 20 houses and 89 inhabitants. Fairs are held on May 23rd, Aug. 12th, and Nov. 23rd, of which the last is a good fair for cattle. Some remains of the old castle, which was destroyed by Cromwell, yet exist.—See TEMPLEPORT.

BALLYMAGLASSON, a parish, in the barony of RATOATH, county of MEATH, and province of LEINSTER, 4 miles (S. by W.) from Dunshaughlin; containing 613 inhabitants. This parish, which is situated on the road from Dublin to Summerhill, comprises 3381 statute acres, as applotted under the tithe act. Prior to the year 1824, it formed part of the union of Kilmore: the living is a rectory, in the diocese of Meath, and in the patronage of the Crown; the tithes amount to £193. 16. $10\frac{3}{4}$. The church, a neat edifice at a considerable distance from the high road, was built by aid of a gift of £600 from the late Board of First Fruits, in 1800. In the R. C. divisions it forms part of the union or district of Batterstown, in the parish of Rathregan. Ballymaglasson House is the property and occasional residence of W. Murphy, Esq.

BALLYMAGOOLY, a village, in the parish of RAHAN, barony of FERMOY, county of CORK, and province of MUNSTER, 2 miles (E.) from Mallow; the population is returned with the parish. This place, which is pleasantly situated on the south bank of the river Blackwater, and on the road from Mallow to Fermoy, consists chiefly of a range of small houses stretching along the south side of the road; and between it and the Blackwater is Ballymagooly, the handsome seat of J. Courtenay, Esq., commanding a fine view of the beautiful scenery on the banks of the river: it was the site of the ancient castle of that name, which was garrisoned by the English in 1691, and its relief in that year gave rise to the battle of Bottle Hill. The parish church, at a short distance from the village, towards the river, with its churchyard surrounded with trees, is a pleasing object. The parochial school-house, a neat building, is situated towards the east end of the village.—See RAHAN.

BALLYMAHON, a market and post-town, in the parish of SHRUEL, barony of RATHCLINE, county of LONGFORD, and province of LEINSTER, $16\frac{1}{2}$ miles (W.) from Mullingar, and 55 miles (W.) from Dublin; containing 1081 inhabitants. This place is supposed to have derived its name from Mahon, King of Thomond, who, according to O'Halloran and other writers, defeated Fergal, son of Ruarc, in a great battle which took place here in 960. There was formerly a castle of considerable strength, but nothing now remains except some of the arches, upon which a dwelling-house has been erected. The town is pleasantly situated on the river Inney, over which is a bridge of five arches and on the road from Longford to Athlone; and though possessing no features of attraction in itself, derives much interest from the beauty of the scenery in its environs. Weaving was formerly carried on to some extent, but has for some time been discontinued, and at present its trade is principally with the neighbouring towns of Longford, Mullingar, Edgeworth's-town, Athlone, Moate, and Lanesborough, with respect to all of which it is conveniently situated. The Royal Canal passes near the town in its course from Dublin to Tarmonbarry, and a boat for the conveyance of passengers and goods to Dublin passes daily. The market is on Thursday, chiefly for the sale of provisions; and fairs are held on the Thursday before Ash-Wednesday, May 11th, Aug. 11th, and Nov. 21st: the May fair is much resorted to by graziers, and is considered one of the best in the province for cattle. The market-house, a commodious building, is situated in the centre of the town; and over it is a large room in which the sessions are held. A chief constabulary police force is stationed in the town; and the quarter sessions for the county are held here, alternately with Longford, four times in the year, for the trial of civil bills only. Petty sessions for the division are also held every Monday. The parish church is situated in the town; in which are also a spacious R. C. chapel, and the residence of the R. C. Bishop of Ardagh, who officiates as parish priest; and a dispensary under the superintendence of a resident physician. Goldsmith, the poet, who was born at Pallice, in the adjoining parish of Forgney, passed several years of his childhood in this town, where he lived with his widowed mother; and some years since a meeting was held here to make arrangements for erecting a monument to his memory near the place of his nativity.—See SHRUEL.

BALLYMAKENNY, a parish, partly in the barony of FERRARD, county of LOUTH, but chiefly in the county of the town of DROGHEDA, and province of LEINSTER, $2\frac{1}{2}$ miles (N.) from Drogheda; containing 563 inhabitants. This parish is situated on the road from Drogheda to Annagasson, and comprises, according to the Ordnance survey, $1592\frac{1}{4}$ statute acres, of which $848\frac{1}{4}$ are in the county of the town of Drogheda; 860 acres are applotted under the tithe act. Listoke, the residence of Lieut.-Col. Battersby, is a handsome mansion pleasantly situated. The living is a perpetual curacy, in the diocese of Armagh, erected in 1785, and in the patronage of the Lord Primate; the rectory is appropriate to the see. The tithes amount to £131. 5., which is wholly payable to the perpetual curate, the Primate being only nominally rector, and deriving no emolument from the appropriation. The church is a handsome modern edifice with a spire, for the repair of which the Ecclesiastical Commissioners have lately granted £123. 12. 10. The glebe-house is situated near the church: the glebe comprises 22*a.* 3*r.* 2*p.* In the R. C. divisions the parish is one of the three that constitute the union or district of Moylary, also called Ballymakenny. There is a school affording instruction to about 45 boys and 12 girls.

BALLYMAKILL.—See BALLYNAKILL.

BALLYMANNY, a parish, partly in the barony of South Naas, and partly in that of East Ophaly, county of Kildare, and province of Leinster, 4 miles (E.) from Kildare, on the road to Naas; containing 185 inhabitants. It is a rectory, in the diocese of Kildare, and is part of the union of Killishy: the tithes amount to £36. 18. 5. In the R. C. divisions it forms part of the union or district of Newbridge.

BALLYMARTIN, a parish, in the barony of Upper Belfast, county of Antrim, and province of Ulster, 8 miles (N. N. W.) from Belfast; containing 721 inhabitants. This parish is situated on the Six-mile river, by which it is bounded on the north, and comprises, according to the Ordnance survey, 2421¼ statute acres, including a detached portion of 560 acres: the soil is fertile, and the system of agriculture is improving. It is a rectory, in the diocese of Connor, and is part of the union of Carmoney: the tithes amount to £150. There is neither church nor any place of worship in the parish; the inhabitants are chiefly Presbyterians, and attend the places of worship of that denomination in the neighbourhood. There is a school of 25 boys and 15 girls. The ruins of the ancient church still remain, and the churchyard is used as a burial-ground by most of the inhabitants.

BALLYMARTLE, a parish, in the barony of Kinnalea, county of Cork, and province of Munster, 4 miles (N. by E.) from Kinsale; containing 1706 inhabitants. This parish derives its name from the ancient family of Martel, to whom it formerly belonged; it is situated on the old road from Cork to Kinsale, and contains 5452 statute acres, as applotted under the tithe act and valued at £3994 per ann. About 40 or 50 acres are woodland; 100 acres, young plantations; and the remainder, except a very small portion of bog at Scart, is arable and pasture. The soil, though generally light, is tolerably fertile; in that part of the parish bordering on Templemichael, on the west, it is of a very superior quality, being a yellow loam of some depth and bearing excellent crops. About three-fourths of the land are under tillage, and the remainder generally in large dairy farms. Sand and other marine manures are brought up within a mile of the parish, and are extensively applied by the farmers, affording employment to a considerable number of persons. There is a small oatmeal-mill, and in the southern part of the parish is a flour-mill. The principal seats are Ballintober, the residence of the Rev. J. Meade; Ballymartle, of W. R. Meade, Esq.; Coolkirky, of T. Herrick, Esq.; Glendoneen, of the Rev. J. Stoyle. They are all finely wooded; the proprietor of the last has planted 180,000 trees on his demesne, which are in a very flourishing state, and the whole forms a very interesting and beautiful feature in the view of a country so generally destitute of wood. Near the church is a constabulary police station; and petty sessions are held in the village every alternate Monday. The living is a rectory, in the diocese of Cork, and in the patronage of the Crown: the tithes amount to £424. 12. 4. The church is a small, plain ancient structure, and contains a monument to Sir John Meade, Bart., grandfather of the first Lord Clanwilliam, and judge of the palatine court of the county of Tipperary, who was buried there. The glebe comprises 5¾ acres, but there is no glebe-house. In the R. C. divisions the parish is the head of a union or district, comprising also that of Cullen; the chapel, near the village, is a plain modern edifice. A Sunday school is supported by the rector; and there are two pay schools, in which are 30 boys and 11 girls.

BALLYMARTYR.—See BALLYOUTERA or CASTLEMARTYR.

BALLYMASCANLON, a parish, in the barony of Lower Dundalk, county of Louth, and province of Leinster, 2 miles (N. E.) from Dundalk; containing 6339 inhabitants. This parish derives its name from the sept of the Scanlons, its ancient proprietors: it is situated on the northern shore of the bay of Dundalk, and on the high road from Dublin to Belfast; a good road from Carlingford to Newry also passes through it. The lordship formerly belonged to Mellifont abbey, on the dissolution of which it was granted to the Moores, ancestors of the Marquess of Drogheda, by whom it was sold to the family of Fortescue, and is now the property of T. Fortescue, Esq. It comprises, according to the Ordnance survey, 15,997½ statute acres, including 177¼ in the detached townland of Kilcurry. In the eastern part of the parish is a range of heathy mountains not designated by any general name, but of which one is called Carriquit, extending 7½ miles in a direction nearly from north to south; in summer they afford tolerable pasturage, and from the chalybeate properties of the springs which issue from them are supposed to contain iron ore. The western part is much improved by extensive plantations, and the scenery throughout is highly picturesque. The south and east portions form part of the shore of the bay, off which are taken fish of all kinds, more especially flat fish. Agriculture is in an advanced state; the land in some parts yields fine crops of wheat, barley, oats, and potatoes. Limestone abounds and is quarried for building and also to be burnt into lime for manure. The manufacture of linen is carried on to a limited extent: there are some bleaching establishments on the banks of the Flurry, the principal of which belong to R. Benison, Esq., who has also recently erected a flax-mill, and R. Thomson, Esq. At Ballymascanlon are corn-mills, the property of J. W. Mac Neale, Esq.; and there are other oatmeal and flour-mills, and a manufactory for edge tools, at Ravensdale. The principal seats are Ravensdale Park, the residence of T. Fortescue, Esq., a handsome mansion situated in an extensive and beautiful demesne, with a well-stocked deer park; and Ballymascanlon House, of J. Wolfe Mac Neale, Esq. There are also many other genteel residences, namely, Annaverna, the seat of the late Baron McClelland, and now the residence of his widow; Strandfield, of J. Moore, Esq.; Mount Pleasant, of J. Mac Neale, Esq.; in Ravensdale, the residences of R. Benison, R. Thomson, A. H. Rutherford, and B. Thomson, Esqrs.; Aughnaskeagh, of J. Black, Esq.; Claret Rock, of T. McGrath, Esq.; the Cottage, of Mrs. Rogers; the Villa, of Mrs. Skelton; Brohatna Lodge, the property of

H. R. Brush, Esq.; and the glebe-house, the residence of the Rev. H. T. Hobson, the incumbent.

The living is an impropriate curacy, in the diocese of Armagh, and in the patronage of T. Fortescue, Esq., impropriator of the rectory. The parish, having formerly been abbey land, is tithe-free, and the lord of the manor pays to the incumbent out of the impropriation an annual stipend of £20, which is augmented with a grant of £73. 12. per ann. from Primate Boulter's fund. The church is a plain structure with a tower, partially built in 1819 by a loan of £550 from the late Board of First Fruits, and repaired in 1836 by a grant of £256 from the Ecclesiastical Commissioners: it contains three handsome monuments, one to the memory of the late Baron McClelland, and the others to the Rev. Dennis Magrath and the Rev. Owen Ormsby, late incumbents; that to the latter was erected by subscription among the Protestant parishioners. The glebe-house is situated on a glebe of 20 acres, about 2¼ miles from the church. In the R. C. divisions this parish is included in the union or district of Faughart, and has three chapels, of which one, situated at Rock Marshall, is a neat and spacious edifice, built on ground given by Mr. Fortescue. There is a place of worship for Presbyterians in connection with the Synod of Ulster. The parochial school is aided by an annual donation from the impropriator; there are two other schools aided by private subscriptions. and two R. C. schools are about to be placed under the National Board of Education: there are also six private pay schools in the parish, and a dispensary. Here is a cromlech of three upright stones supporting a massive tabular stone, about 12 feet long and 9 broad, and computed to weigh more than 30 tons: it is vulgarly called the *Giant's Load*, from a tradition that it was brought to the place by a giant named Porrah Baugh Mac Shaggcan. Near it, in the same field, is a rath called *Chillo Ca Larc*, said to be the burial-place of Mac Scanlon, chief of that sept in the tenth century. There are some remains of the ancient castle of Ballymascanlon; also of an old church on Faughart Hill, with a cemetery adjoining, in which is a large stone said by tradition to point out the grave of Edward Bruce, brother to the Scottish king: there are likewise several Danish raths on this hill. Mount Bagnall, at the eastern extremity of the parish, is an artificial eminence occupying a very romantic situation near the precipitous banks of the river, and is supposed to be of Danish origin. In the same vicinity is the old mansion of Piedmont, formerly the residence of the Balfours.

BALLYMENA, or BALLYMANIA, a market and post-town, in the parish of KIRKINRIOLA, barony of LOWER TOOME, county of ANTRIM, and province of ULSTER, 24¾ miles (N. W.) from Belfast, and 105 miles (N.) from Dublin; containing 4067 inhabitants. In the disturbances of 1798 this place was the scene of an obstinate battle between the yeomanry and the United Irishmen of the surrounding district, who, on the 7th of June, entered the town and proceeded to attack the market-house, which was defended by a party of the yeomanry aided by a few of the military and some of the loyal inhabitants; the insurgents having gained possession of the lower part of the market-house, the yeomanry surrendered themselves prisoners of war; but while a party of them was marching out of the market-house, those who were within being instigated by a person named Davis to give the United Irishmen another volley, the fire was returned from the street, and several of the loyalists were killed while descending the steps. Some straggling parties of the enemy brought into the town Captain Ellis, of Innisrush, and Thomas Jones, Esq., of Moneyglass, with a number of the yeomanry, whom they took prisoners at Straid, in this parish, and lodged them in the market-house; and on the day following, several of the yeomanry were marched into the town as prisoners. Great divisions took place in the committee of the United Irishmen, on the propriety of marching direct to Antrim, which they had been informed was in the possession of the king's troops; but on hearing of the royal proclamation, offering a free pardon to all, with the exception of officers, who should lay down their arms and disperse, almost all the men from Route were disposed to accept the terms; some, who were determined on making a stand, joined the united camp at Donegore, while others departed homewards, leaving the town to be taken possession of by Col. Clavering and the military, who, after the recapture of Antrim, had encamped at Shanescastle, in the neighbourhood.

The town is pleasantly situated on the river Braid, over which is a large bridge of stone: it owes its rapid rise and present importance to the linen manufacture, which was introduced into the neighbourhood by the Adairs and Dickeys about the year 1732, since which time it has greatly increased in extent, wealth, and importance. It comprises more than 700 houses, in general large and well-built, among which are a few of very ancient character, with gabled fronts. The linen trade is carried on extensively in the neighbourhood, and within a circuit of 5 miles round the town are 14 bleach-greens, at each of which, on an average, about 15,000 pieces are annually bleached, exclusively of considerable quantities of brown and black goods, which are also finished here, and for the manufacture of which there are several large establishments. Several linen merchants unconnected with the bleaching department reside in the town. There is a mill for spinning linen yarn by machinery; and an extensive ale brewery, originally established in 1729, continued in operation for more than a century, and was afterwards purchased by Clotworthy Walkinshaw, Esq., who, in 1831, converted it into a distillery, in which great quantities of barley, grown in the neighbourhood, are annually consumed. Branches of the Provincial Bank of Ireland and of the Belfast and Northern Banking Companies have been established here. The market is on Saturday for the sale of linens, of which 4000 pieces are on an average sold every market-day; there are two weekly markets for grain, pork, and other provisions, of which great quantities are bought and sent to Belfast either for home consumption or for exportation; great numbers of horses, cattle, and pigs are also sold on the market-days. Fairs for every description of live stock are annually held on July 26th and Oct. 21st; but the sales on the market days preceding and following these dates are frequently greater than at the fairs. The market-house is a commodious edifice in the centre of the town, with a steeple 60 feet high. Here is a chief constabulary police station. Courts leet and baron are annually held for the manor; a court under the seneschal is held every month for the recovery of debts; and petty sessions are held every alternate Tuesday. The quarter sessions for the county are held in January and June, alternately with Ballymoney. There is a secure and well-built bridewell, containing seven cells. The parish church, a large plain structure with an embattled tower crowned with pinnacles, is situated in the town; and there are also a R. C. chapel, built in 1820; two places of worship for Presbyterians in connection with the Synod of Ulster, one for Seceders, and one for Wesleyan Methodists. The diocesan school, originally established at Carrickfergus in the reign of Elizabeth, was removed to this place in 1829, when an acre of land was given by William Adair, Esq., on which the building was erected, at an expense of £900: the master, who is appointed by the Lord-Primate and the Bishop of Connor alternately, derives his stipend from the beneficed clergy of the dioceses of Armagh and Connor, and is allowed to receive private boarders. A free school was founded here in 1813, by John Guy or Guay, who bequeathed £24 per annum to the master, and £50 towards the erection of a school-house, which, with a house for the master, was built in 1818: there are 200 children in the school, who are gratuitously taught reading, writing, and arithmetic, and supplied with books and stationery. In connection with this establishment a female school is now being built, for the instruction of the girls in needlework. A parochial school was established in 1832, in which 170 children are instructed and occasionally clothed by subscription. The Parade school, to which is attached an adult school, was rebuilt in 1833, and is in connection with the London Hibernian Society. The only remains of antiquity are some terraces and foundations of walls of a castle built in the reign of Jas. I.—See KIRKINRIOLA.

BALLYMITTY, a parish, in the barony of SHELMALIER, county of WEXFORD, and province of LEINSTER, 4 miles (S. S. W.) from Taghmon; containing 404 inhabitants. This parish is intersected by the new road from Bannow to Wexford: it is chiefly under tillage, and there is no waste land: the drill system of husbandry prevails, and much general improvement has taken place. Stone for building is quarried in the parish: and a stream which falls into Bannow bay is navigable to Coolcliffe for lighters, which come up with the tide from the peninsula of Hook, laden with limestone for burning. Coolcliffe is the seat of Lieut.-Col. Sir W. Cox, Knt. The living is a rectory and vicarage, in the diocese of Ferns, united to the rectory of Taghmon; the impropriate rectorial tithes were granted to the incumbent by an instrument dated March 9th, 1670; the entire tithes amount to £82. 9. 10. In the R. C. divisions the parish is the head of a union or district, also called Bannow, which comprises the parishes of Ballymitty, Bannow, Carrig, and Kilcavan, and the greater part of Ambrosetown; and contains a chapel at Ballymitty, a neat building with a residence for the clergyman, and another at Danes-castle, in the parish of Carrig. A school is about to be established under the superintendence of the R. C. clergyman; and there is a private pay school, in which are about 20 boys and 10 girls. On the grounds of Hill Town are the remains of an ancient castle, consisting of a square tower now converted into a barn.

BALLYMODAN, a parish, partly in the Eastern Division of the barony of EAST CARBERY, but chiefly in that of KINNALMEAKY, county of CORK, and province of MUNSTER; containing, with the greater part of the borough of Bandon, 9969 inhabitants. It is bounded on the north by the river Bandon, and comprises 7408 statute acres, as applotted under the tithe act, and valued at £4670 per annum. The land in general is tolerably good, and the system of agriculture has been greatly improved by the encouragement and example of the Bernard family and the resident gentry of the neighbourhood. The surrounding scenery is richly diversified and embellished with several gentlemen's seats, among which the principal is Castle Bernard, formerly Castle Mahon, the elegant seat of the Earl of Bandon. It is a stately mansion, erected in 1806 near the site of the former castle, which originally belonged to the O'Mahony family and was subsequently the residence of Judge Bernard, by whom it was greatly improved in 1715. The park, which is on the south bank of the river and about a mile from Bandon, extends into the parish of Kilbrogan, and is justly celebrated for the beauty and variety of its scenery and the extent and rich luxuriance of its woods. At no great distance from the present house is the ancient fortress of the family of O'Mahony, of whom the last chieftain of that sept, Connogher O'Mahony, proprietor of the seigniory of Kinnalmeaky, fell fighting in the rebellion of the Earl of Desmond, whose cause he had embraced; it forms a striking and an interesting feature in the widely extended and highly beautiful demesne. The other seats are the Farm, a handsome house in the Elizabethan style, the residence of the Hon W. S. Bernard; Mayfield, of T. Poole, Esq.; Hare Hill, of J. Beamish, Esq.; Mount Prospect, of Mrs. Bradshaw; Overton, of Col. Clerke; Richmount, of J. Sealy, Esq.; and Clancoole, of Mrs. Gillman. The living is a vicarage, in the diocese of Cork, and in the patronage of the Bishop; the rectory is impropriate in the Duke of Devonshire. The tithes amount to £800, payable in moieties to the impropriator and the vicar. The church, a plain neat edifice, situated in the town of Bandon, was erected at the expense of the first Earl of Cork, in 1618, and the Ecclesiastical Commissioners have lately granted £441 for its repair. The glebe contains $9\frac{1}{4}$ acres, but there is no glebe-house. In the R. C. divisions the parish is united with that of Kilbrogan and part of Desertserges, forming the union or district of Bandon. There is a place of worship for Presbyterians in connection with the Synod of Munster, of the second class, and there are also places of worship for Primitive and Wesleyan Methodists. The parochial school is at Bandon; and a large and commodious school-house, with a residence for the master, has been erected by the Duke of Devonshire on Cavendish quay; another parochial school at Curravarrahane is endowed with a house for the master and two acres of land by the vicar, by whom also it is supported. There are also several other schools in Bandon, which see. Of the ancient church, situated to the east of the town, only the cemetery remains.

BALLYMOE, a village, in that part of the parish of DRIMTEMPLE which is in the barony of HALF BALLYMOE, county of GALWAY, and province of CONNAUGHT, $3\frac{1}{2}$ miles (S. E.) from Castlerea . the population is included in the return for the parish. It is situated on the river Suck, and on the road from Roscommon to Castlerea, to both of which it has a penny post. Fairs are held on Feb. 1st, March 16th, May 21st, June 24th, Aug. 22nd, and Oct. 25th.—See DRIMTEMPLE.

BALLYMONEY, a market and post-town, and a parish, partly in the north-east liberties of COLERAINE, county of LONDONDERRY, and partly in the barony of KILCONWAY, but chiefly in that of UPPER DUNLUCE, county of ANTRIM, and province of ULSTER, 35 miles (N. W.) from Belfast, and 119 miles (N. by W.) from Dublin; containing 11,579 inhabitants, of which number, 2222 are in the town. This place was anciently the head of one of those Irish districts called Tuoghs, which were similar to the present baronies; and in a grant from the crown, by which it was given to Alexander Mac Donnel, it was designated *Tuogh Ballymoney*, that is, "the district of the town in the bog," part of it at present being situated on a bog several feet in depth. The parish is bounded on the west by the river Bann, which passes within three miles of the town, and is intersected by the road from Belfast to Derry. The town is built upon an eminence, and from its situation is considered healthy: a new line of mail coach road is now being constructed to pass through it, and in every respect it is rapidly improving. A new road has been opened across the Garry bog leading to Ballycastle and the Giant's Causeway, and a bridge has been lately erected over the river Bann at Agivey, about three miles distant, opening a direct communication with the county and city of Derry, Tyrone, and other places. Races were formerly held here and were in high repute; but they have been discontinued for some years, and a steeple chace for a gold cup has been substituted, which takes place in the middle of December. The trade consists principally in the sale of linens manufactured in the neighbourhood, for which this town is, next to Ballymena, the chief depôt. The linen market has long been established, and is eminent for the superior quality of the goods sold here. Though much less extensive than it was, it is still very considerable: from 15,000 to 20,000 double pieces are annually sold, and on the first Thursday in every month large quantities of seven-eighths linen, of various qualities, are sold here, principally for the London market, under the name of "Coleraines," being purchased and bleached by the persons engaged in that trade. Some years since, the finer pieces sold at very high prices, generally from 7*s.* to 8*s.* per yard, and some of the finest webs at 10*s.* 6*d.* per yard. There are two markets every month for low-priced brown linens, three quarters of a yard wide, which are sent to England and America: but the demand for these latter goods have decreased. A very extensive trade is carried on in grain, butter, pork, and general provisions. The market for grain was first established in 1820; but for want of encouragement it languished for a time and was discontinued; in 1831 it was revived, and the new market-place was appropriated to its use, and stores were built by Messrs. McEldeny & Co., for the use of which and for weighing they are entitled to one penny per sack; a considerable quantity of oats is sent to Liverpool, London, and other English markets, and some are consumed in a distillery near the town. The market for provisions was established about the year 1790, and has since been gradually increasing and is now largely supplied: about 4000 carcases of pigs are generally sold during the season, which are principally cured at home for the Liverpool and other English markets; they were formerly all sent to Belfast, and a considerable number are still purchased by the curers of that place. A public crane was established under the provisions of an act of the 52nd of Geo. III. In the market for butter about 10,000 casks are generally disposed of during the season, the greater part of which is shipped off from Portrush, about 9 miles distant, for Liverpool. There are a soap and candle and a tobacco manufactory, a tanyard, and a large brewery in the town; and at Moore Fort, about 3 miles distant, is a very extensive distillery belonging to James Moore, Esq., in which from 50,000 to 60,000 gallons of whiskey are annually made: there is also a mill for spinning flax, and a very extensive flour-mill. A branch of the Belfast banking company has been established here. The trade of the town is susceptible of great increase, from its favourable situation in the centre of a rich tract of country, without any markets nearer to it than Ballymena on the one side, and Coleraine on the other. There is, however, but little facility of water carriage, the river Bann not being navigable above Coleraine, nor below Portna. The general market is on Thursday; and fairs are held annually on May 6th, July 10th, and Oct. 10th. A chief constabulary police station has been fixed here. The manorial court for the barony of Dunluce is held in the town on the first Friday in every month; petty sessions are held every alternate Thursday; and the quarter sessions for the county are held here and at Ballymena alternately. The court-house or town-hall, the property of Lord Mark Kerr, is situated in the centre of the town; and the bridewell, recently built, contains seven cells, with day-rooms and airing-yards adapted to the classification of prisoners, and apartments for the keeper.

The parish comprises, according to the Ordnance survey, 23,108$\frac{3}{4}$ statute acres, of which 21,736$\frac{1}{2}$ are in Upper Dunluce, and 753$\frac{1}{4}$ in Kilconway; 18,367 are applotted under the tithe act; about 500 acres are woodland, 2225 bog, 59$\frac{1}{2}$ water, and the remainder principally arable land. The soil is fertile, and the system of agriculture greatly improving: the principal crops, till within the last few years, were barley and oats, of which last great quantities are still grown in the neighbourhood; but the cultivation of wheat has been recently introduced, and is rapidly increasing; abundant crops are now raised and begin to form a material portion of the corn trade. Coal and iron-stone are found in abundance at O'Hara Brook; and there are medicinal springs on several parts of the estate. The principal seats are O'Hara Brook, that of C. O'Hara, Esq.; Leslie Hill, of J. Leslie, Esq.; Ballynacree, of Sampson Moore, Esq.; Moore Fort, of J. Moore, Esq.; Greenville, of J. R. Moore, Esq.; Stranocum, of J. Hutchinson, Esq.; and Vine Cottage, of J. Thompson, Esq. The parish comprises the ancient parishes of Ballymoney, Dunlap, Kilmoil, and Tullagore; it is a rectory, in the diocese of Connor, and is the corps of the precentorship in the cathedral of Connor, which is in the patronage of the Bishop: the tithes amount to £1015. 7. 7$\frac{1}{2}$., and the gross income of the precentorship is returned by the Commissioners of Ecclesiastical Inquiry at £1073. 10. 8. per annum. The church, a large plain edifice with a tower and cupola, was built in 1782, near the site of an ancient church, of which there are still some remains. The glebe-house is situated on a glebe of 20 acres. In the R. C. divisions the parish is the head of a union or district, comprising also that of Dunluce, in both of which are chapels in which the parish priest officiates. There are places of worship for Presbyterians in connection with the Synod of Ulster, for those of the Remonstrant Synod, Seceders, and Covenanters; the first is a first class congregation, and that of the Seceding Synod a second class. A school was established in 1813 by the trustees of Erasmus Smith's fund. Sampson Moore, Esq., J. Leslie, Esq., and C. O'Hara, Esq., have each built and endowed schools on their own estates, for the education of the poor; and there are also other schools in different parts of the parish. In these schools are about 200 boys and 100 girls; and there are 13 private schools, in which are about 300 boys and 200 girls, and 11 Sunday schools. A mendicity association for suppressing vagrant mendicity, by giving employment and relief to the poor at their own dwellings, was established in 1821, and a dispensary in 1827. On the estate of Major Rowan is a fine moat, commanding a very extensive view; there is also another at Moore Fort, and one in the townland of Cross. A double patera of gold, weighing 19 ounces and 10 drachms, of elegant form and curious workmanship, was discovered in this parish by a peasant a few years since.

BALLYMONEY, a parish, in the Eastern Division of the barony of EAST CARBERY, county of CORK, and province of MUNSTER, 10 miles (W. by S.) from Bandon; containing 3802 inhabitants. This parish, which is intersected by the river Bandon, and skirted on the north by the mail coach road from Bandon to Dunmanway, comprises 7056 statute acres, as applotted under the tithe act and valued at £4017 per annum. The land is of good quality; about two-thirds of the parish are under cultivation, and the remainder is chiefly mountain and bog. The old heavy wooden plough is generally in use, and, except on the lands of the resident gentry, agriculture as a system is unknown. The opening of a new line of road through the parish to Clonakilty, whence sea manure is obtained in abundance, has afforded the means of bringing much poor land into cultivation. Great quantities of fuel are raised from the bogs, which supply turf and bog wood for the neighbourhood to the south. Near Ballyneen is Phale House, the residence of E. H. Good, Esq.: a mile to the west is Kilcascan, the seat of W. J. O'Neill Daunt, Esq., a handsome castellated mansion embosomed in young and thriving plantations; and at Ballincarrig is the neat residence of J. Heazle, Esq. A domestic manufacture of coarse linen is carried on for home consumption. At Ballincarrig are Rockcastle mills, the property of Mr. Heazle, capable of grinding 5000 bags of wheat annually, and affording constant employment to 20 persons; and at Ballyneen a few persons are engaged in weaving cotton cord, but the principal pursuit is agriculture. Ballyneen is a constabulary police station, and petty sessions are held there every alternate Monday. The living is a rectory, in the diocese of Cork, and in the patronage of the Bishop: the tithes amount to £785. The church is an old but a very neat edifice. The glebe-house, pleasantly situated in the centre of some extensive improvements, was built by aid of a gift of £100 from the late Board of First Fruits, in 1789: the glebe comprises 43 acres. In the R. C. divisions, one-half of the parish is included in the union or district of Dunmanway, and the other half in that of Kinneigh or Enniskean: the chapel at Ballincarrig, belonging to the former, is a small neat edifice recently erected. There is a place of worship for Wesleyan Methodists at Ballyneen. The parochial male and female school is aided by annual donations from the rector and his lady; and another school is supported by the rector. These schools afford instruction to about 60 boys and 40 girls; and there are also three hedge schools, in which are about 150 children, and a Sunday school. There are some remains of Ballincarrig castle, originally built to command a very important pass in the valley; it is a lofty square pile of building, 96 feet high, the walls of which are 6 feet in thickness; a spiral stone staircase, still in tolerable preservation, leads to the battlements; the platform and one of the gables are entire, but the roof has been long destroyed. The upper apartment is lighted by circular arched windows in the Norman style, with mouldings enriched with curious devices, and various scriptural emblems, among which is Our Saviour on the cross between the two thieves, and on two sides of the room are seats: there are also the initials R.M.—C.C., and the date 1585, above which is an angel with expanded wings. This inscription is supposed to commemorate the founder, Randal M^c^Carty, and his wife Catherine Collins. Below this apartment is a lofty vaulted hall, which, from the brackets and small windows still remaining, is supposed to have been originally divided into three different stories. At a short distance to the south-east is a circular keep or watch tower; to the south is a lake; and to the north is a bog of considerable extent terminated by a low ridge of rugged rocks. Though the date of the castle is supposed to be 1585, the original tower is evidently of much greater antiquity, and probably of the 12th or 13th century. Near the castle have been found several silver coins.

BALLYMORAN.—See ALMORITIA.

BALLYMORE, or TANDERAGEE, a parish, in the barony of LOWER ORIOR, county of ARMAGH, and province of ULSTER: containing, with the town of Tanderagee, the village of Clare, and the greater part of the village of Poyntz-Pass (all which are separately described) 7963 inhabitants. This parish is situated on the road from Newry to Portadown, and comprises, according to the Ordnance survey, 14,158¾ statute acres, of which 13,958 are applotted under the tithe act and valued at £10,052 per annum: about 100 acres are under plantation, 300 are bog, and 60 waste and water; the remainder is all arable land, remarkably good and in a high state of cultivation, producing abundant crops. There are veins of potters' clay and fullers' earth, both of excellent quality and lying near the surface close to the town; but neither have been worked. Several quarries in the parish yield excellent building stone; that at Tullyhue is now being worked for building the splendid castle of Tanderagee, and produces stone of very superior quality. This castle, which is now being rebuilt by its proprietor Viscount Mandeville, is situated near the town, and forms a conspicuous and highly interesting feature in the view. The other seats are Dromenargoole House, that of Davis Lucas, Esq.; Acton House, of Conway R. Dobbs, Esq.; Harrybrook, of R. Harden, Esq.; Cooley Hill, of R. Hardy, Esq.; Orange Hill, of J. Creery, Esq.; and Derryallen, of J. Behan. Esq.. Fairs are held in the town on July 5th and Nov. 5th, and on the first Wednesday in every month; and at Clare on

May 12th, for horses, cattle, and sheep. Courts leet and baron are also held, the former twice in the year, and the latter on the third Thursday in every month, for the recovery of debts under 40*s*. Petty sessions are held in the town every Tuesday. The living is a rectory, in the diocese of Armagh, and the corps of the prebend of Ballymore in the cathedral church of St. Patrick, Armagh, in the patronage of the Lord-Primate: the tithes amount to £1000. The church is a spacious and handsome structure, in the early English style, with an embattled tower crowned with pinnacles, and was erected in 1812, at an expense of £2200, of which £1500 was a loan from the late Board of First Fruits, and £700 a gift from Lady Mandeville; the Ecclesiastical Commissioners have lately granted £144 for its repair. The glebe-house is a handsome residence, and the glebe comprises 520 acres. In the R. C. divisions the parish is the head of a union or district, called Tanderagee, which comprises also the parishes of Acton and Mullaghbrack, and contains three chapels, one in each parish; that of Ballymore is situated at Poyntz Pass. There are meeting-houses at Tanderagee and Clare for Presbyterians in connection with the Synod of Ulster, the former of the third and the latter of the first class; another at Clare in connection with the Seceding Synod, and of the first class; and places of worship for Primitive and Wesleyan Methodists. The parochial school is supported by the rector, the Dean of Tuam; five schools are supported by Lord Mandeville, two are aided by annual donations from Lord Gosford and the Rev. Mr. Bell, and there are three others, altogether affording instruction to about 580 boys and 440 girls; there are also three pay schools, in which are about 80 boys and 180 girls, and four Sunday schools. The interest of a bequest of £100 by some member of the Montagu family is divided in equal shares among the poor of the parishes of Ballymore and Seagoe. There are some very slight remains of the ancient church, where are two extensive cemeteries nearly adjoining each other, one exclusively for Protestants, and the other for Roman Catholics; in the latter is interred the noted Redmond O'Hanlon, the Irish rapparee. Near Ballynaback are two chalybeate springs, which have been found efficacious in scorbutic diseases.—See TANDERAGEE and CLARE.

BALLYMORE, or BALLYMORE-EUSTACE, a market-town and parish, in the barony of UPPERCROSS, county of DUBLIN, and province of LEINSTER, 18 miles (S. W.) from Dublin; containing 2085 inhabitants, of which number, 841 are in the town. This town derives its name, signifying "the great town of Eustace," from its foundation by that family, a branch of the Fitzgeralds, who also erected here a castle of great strength, the ruins of which have been lately entirely removed. It is situated on the river Liffey, over which is a handsome stone bridge of six arches, and consists of one principal and three smaller streets: there is a penny post to Naas. The great southern road formerly passed through it, but has been diverted through the village of Kilcullen by the construction of a new line, and the town has since considerably decayed. A large manufactory, in which every description of cloth is made, was erected in the vicinity by Mr. Christopher Dromgoole, in 1802 and, when in full work, employs about 700 persons. The market, granted by Jas. I. to the Archbishop of Dublin, having fallen into disuse, was revived about seven years since; it is held on Wednesday and is well supplied with grain. Fairs are held on Easter-Monday, June 24th, Aug. 26th, Oct. 28th, and Dec. 21st, principally for cattle, pigs, and sheep. Here is a station of the constabulary police. The parish is the head of a lordship and manor belonging to the Archbishop of Dublin, and comprising the parishes of Ballymore, Ballybought, Cotlandstown, Yagoe, Tipperkevin, and Tubber, in the county of Dublin, and of Milltown and Tornant, and part of Rathsallagh, in the county of Wicklow. The system of agriculture is improving. Mount-Cashell Lodge, the property of the Earl of Mount-Cashell, is pleasantly situated, and is in the occupation of Mr. Dromgoole. The other principal residences are Ardenode, that of E. Homan, Esq.; Season, of Mrs. O'Brien; and Willfield, of R. Doyle, Esq. The living is a vicarage, in the diocese of Dublin and Glendalough, with those of Ballybought, Cotlandstown, and Yagoe episcopally united time immemorially, forming the union of Ballymore, in the patronage of the Archbishop: the rectory is partly appropriate to the economy estate of the cathedral of St. Patrick, Dublin, and partly united to those of Boystown and Luske, which together constitute the corps of the treasurership in that cathedral. The tithes amount to £145. 11. 1., of which £27. 10. 7. is payable to the lessee of the dean and chapter, £39. 2. 7. to the lessee of the treasurer, and £78. 17. 11. to the vicar; and the gross tithes of the benefice amount to £137. 2. 3. The church is a plain building with an embattled tower surmounted with pinnacles, erected in 1820 by the late Board of First Fruits, at a cost of £900: the churchyard is of great extent, and contains the remains of the old church, and numerous ancient tombstones. There is neither glebe nor glebe-house. In the R. C. divisions this parish is the head of a union or district, which comprises also the parishes of Ballybought, Cotlandstown, and Tipperkevin, in the county of Dublin, and the parish of Hollywood and part of Blessington, in that of Wicklow: the chapel at Ballymore is a substantial and commodious building, and there is another at Hollywood. The parochial school is supported by subscription; and there is another school, for which a school-house was erected by subscription in 1835, at an expense of about £400: there are also two private schools in the parish. About a mile from the town the river Liffey forms the celebrated cascade of Poul-a-Phuca, or the Demon's Hole, consisting of three successive waterfalls 150 feet in height. The chasm is only 40 feet wide, and is skirted on each side by perpendicular masses of grauwacke rock; and when the river is swollen by heavy rains the water rushes down with tumultuous impetuosity into a circular basin of the rock, worn quite smooth and of great depth, the form of which imparts to it the motion of a whirlpool, and from which the cascade derives its name. It then dashes through narrow openings in the rocks, and forms two more falls, the lowest being about 50 feet high. Immediately over the basin, on the line of the new turnpike road from Blessington to Baltinglass, is a picturesque bridge of one pointed arch springing from rock to rock, built in an antique style from a design by the late Alex. Nimmo, Esq., at an expense, including the land arches and approaches, of £4074. 15.; the span of the arch is 65 feet, the altitude of the chord above the upper fall is 47 feet, and the height of the keystone of the arch above the bed of the river is 150 feet. The late Earl of Miltown took a lively interest in this picturesque spot, which he embellished by planting one side of the glen forming part of his estate, making walks, and erecting rustic buildings in various places, besides a banqueting-room, 45 feet long by 25 wide, from which there is a delightful view of the falls and the bridge, with the perpendicular rocks partly planted, and the upper moss seat appearing through the arch; but owing to the disturbances of 1798 he went abroad, and some time after sold it to Col. Aylmer, who is now the proprietor, and has appointed a person to take proper care of it, by whom accommodation has been prepared for the numerous visiters that resort hither from Dublin and elsewhere, and seats have been placed in the most advantageous situations for obtaining different views of the fall; a rustic seat above the head of the fall commands an excellent view of the cataract, bridge, lower rustic seat, and banqueting-hall, with the windings of the river.

BALLYMORE, or ST. OWEN'S of LOUGHSEUDY, a post-town and parish, in the barony of RATHCONRATH, county of WESTMEATH, and province of LEINSTER, 12 miles (W. by S.) from Mullingar, and 57½ miles (W.) from Dublin; containing 3494 inhabitants. An abbey is said to have been founded here in the year 700; but the only religious establishment of which there are any authentic records was a monastery founded by the De Lacy family in 1218, and dedicated to the Blessed Virgin, for Premonstratensian canons and Benedictine nuns, who occupied distinct portions of the same building. Hen. VIII. made the church of this monastery the cathedral church for the diocese of Meath, which it continued to be for a short time. In the parliamentary war of 1641, this was the principal military station of the English in this part of the country; the garrison had possession of a strong fortress on the shore of Lough Shodie, or Loughseudy, which was accessible from the land only by a drawbridge across a wide and deep moat. In the war of the Revolution, when part of the English army had fortified themselves at Mullingar, this place was strengthened by a party of the Irish forces from their head-quarters at Athlone, with the view of acting against Mullingar; but they were soon attacked by Gen. De Ginkell, and pursued with loss to Moat-a-Grenogue. The fort of Ballymore, on the island in the lake, was still in the possession of James's forces, and garrisoned with 1000 chosen men; but the forces of William advancing from Athlone to besiege it, the garrison, on seeing some armed boats launched to act against it from the lake, on which side it was defenceless, surrendered themselves prisoners of war after only one day's defence, and the fort was taken by Gen. De Ginkell, who repaired the fortifications and placed in it a strong English garrison. The town, which is situated on the mail coach road from Moate, extends partly into the parish of Killare, and contains 663 inhabitants, of which number, 510 are in that part of it which is in the parish of Ballymore; it consists chiefly of small houses and cabins, and the only public buildings are the parish church and R. C. chapel. It had formerly a market, which has been discontinued; but fairs are held on Whit-Monday and Oct. 14th. Here is a chief constabulary police station; and petty sessions are held every alternate Friday.

The parish, which is called St. Owen's of Loughseudy, comprises 9189 statute acres, as applotted under the tithe act: about three-fifths of its entire extent are arable, and the remainder is pasture, with some waste land and bog. Agriculture, which had been long in a very neglected state, has within the last five or six years shewn some slight indications of improvement. There are some fine limestone quarries, which are worked for building and for burning into lime, but only for private use. The lake of Shodie, or Loughseudy, is studded with some pleasing islets towards the north. Beyond it is Shinlas, formerly the residence of the Malones, but now in ruins: Emoe, the seat of F. Magan, Esq., and Moyvoughly, that of C. Arabin, Esq., are pleasantly situated about two miles south-west of the town. The living is a perpetual curacy, in the diocese of Meath, united to the impropriate curacy of Killare, and in the patronage of the Bishop to whom the rectory is appropriate: the tithes amount to £323. 1. 6¼., payable to the bishop. The church, a neat edifice with a square tower, was erected by aid of a loan of £1200 from the late Board of First Fruits, in 1827. The glebe-house was built by a gift of £450 and a loan of £50 from the same Board, in 1813: the glebe comprises 30 acres. In the R. C. divisions this parish is the head of a union or district, which comprises also the parish of Killare, each of which contains a chapel. There are seven pay schools, in which are about 330 children. Near the town are the remains of an ancient castle, said to have belonged to the De Lacy family; the only portion standing is a round tower, about 20 feet in height.

BALLYMORE, a parish, in the barony of FORTH, county of WEXFORD, and province of LEINSTER, 2¼ miles (W.) from Broadway; containing 522 inhabitants. This parish is situated near Lough Ta, and comprises 2520 statute acres, as applotted under the tithe act. It is a rectory, in the diocese of Ferns, and forms part of the union of Kilscoran, also called Tacumshane, which constitutes the corps of the chancellorship in the cathedral of Ferns: the tithes amount to £203. 17. 11½., payable to the chancellor. In 1832 the parishes of Ballymore and Tacumshane were formed into an ecclesiastical district under the name of Churchtown, and a perpetual curacy was instituted. The new church is situated in the parish of Tacumshane, but close to the border of this parish, and was built by aid of a grant from the Ecclesiastical Commissioners. In the R. C. divisions it is in the union or district of Maglass; a chapel has been lately erected. There is a school at Moonfield Cross.

BALLYMOREEN, a parish, in the barony of ELIOGARTY, county of TIPPERARY, and province of MUNSTER, 4 miles (S. S. E.) from Thurles, on the mail coach road from Dublin to Cork; containing 1237 inhabitants. It comprises 2870 statute acres, as applotted under the tithe act; there are about 500 acres of bog, and of the remainder of the land, the greater portion is under tillage. Parkstown is the residence of J. P. Lanphier, Esq.; and at Liskevin are the residences of R. Beere, T. Millet, and J. Going, Esqrs. The living is a vicarage, in the diocese of Cashel, and in the patronage of the Archbishop; the rectory is impropriate in the Marquess of Ormonde. The tithes amount to £200, of which £60 is payable to the impropriator, and £140 to the vicar. There is no church, glebe-house, or glebe; the members of the Established Church attend divine service at Littleton, about 2½ miles distant. There are two pay schools, in which are about 100 boys and 60 girls.

BALLYMOTE, a market and post-town, in the parish of EMLYFAD, barony of CORRAN, county of SLIGO, and province of CONNAUGHT, 11 miles (S. by W.) from Sligo, and 94½ miles (W. N. W.) from Dublin; containing 875 inhabitants. This place appears to have derived its origin from a castle built in 1300 by Richard de Burgo, Earl of Ulster, which, after its seizure by the native Irish during the insurrection of 1641, was found to be of such strength as to offer a serious obstacle to the complete subjugation of Connaught; it was at length taken, in 1652, by the united forces of Ireton and Sir C. Coote. A small monastery for Franciscan friars of the third order was founded here by the sept of Mac Donogh, and at the suppression was granted to Sir H. Broncard, who assigned it to Sir W. Taaffe, Knt.: an inquisition of the 27th of Elizabeth records that it belonged to the castle, and had been totally destroyed by the insurgents. The town is situated at the junction of six roads, but has not one principal road passing through it: it consists of one main street, and contains 140 houses. The surrounding country is well cultivated, and its surface agreeably undulates; and there is a good view from an obelisk erected by Lady Arabella Denny on a small hill near the town. In the immediate vicinity is Earl's Field, the property of Sir R. Gore Booth, Bart., to whom the town belongs; and in a delightful situation, within a quarter of a mile, is the glebe-house, which commands a fine prospect of the surrounding mountains and the distant hill of Knocknaree. About 2½ miles from the town is Temple House, the handsome residence of Col. A. Perceval, beautifully situated on the banks of a lake of that name, and in a fine demesne containing some good old timber; on the edge of the lake are the ruins of the old house, which was built by the O'Hara family in 1303, and was afterwards given to the Knights Hospitallers. The linen manufacture was formerly carried on here to a great extent, under the encouragement of the Rt. Hon. Thos. Fitzmorris, but is now nearly extinct. The market is held on Friday for provisions; and fairs are held on the last Monday in January, May 11th, first Monday (O. S.) in June, Sept. 3rd, first Monday (O. S.) in November, and second Monday (O. S.) in December. Quarter sessions are held here in a sessions-house in January, April, July, and October; and petty sessions on alternate Tuesdays. The bridewell is the only one in the county: it affords the requisite statutable accommodation, and there are a day-room and airing-yard for prisoners of each sex. This is a chief station of the constabulary police. The parish church is situated in the town; and there are a R. C. chapel, a meeting-house for Wesleyan Methodists, and a dispensary. The remains of the ancient castle, built by Richard de Burgo, occupy an area 150 feet square, with towers at the angles, and sufficiently denote its former strength. At the southern extremity of the main street are the ruins of the Franciscan friary; over the principal entrance is the figure of a pope carved in stone, but somewhat mutilated. A book, called the Book or Psalter of Ballymote, was written in Irish by the monks of this place, and is yet extant. There is a fort of rather unusual elevation about one mile from the town.—See EMLYFAD.

BALLYMOYER, a parish, in the barony of UPPER FEWS, county of ARMAGH, and province of ULSTER, 3 miles (N. E.) from Newtown-Hamilton; containing 2729 inhabitants. This place, formerly called Tahellen, was the site of a religious establishment founded by St. Patrick, who appointed St. Killian to preside over it, and of which the church was destroyed by fire in 670; the ancient cemetery may still be traced in the demesne of Ballymoyer Lodge. The parish is situated on the road from Newtown-Hamilton to Newry, and comprises, according to the Ordnance survey, 7381¼ statute acres, of which about 40 acres are underwood, about 2605 are bog and waste land, and the remainder arable and pasture. The lands were heathy and barren previously to 1778, when Sir Walter Synnot erected a house and became a resident landlord; scarcely a tree or shrub was to be seen, and the agricultural implements were of the rudest kind. He constructed good roads in the vicinity, planted forest trees to a considerable extent, and by his example and liberal encouragement of every improvement both as to their habitations and system of agriculture, effected a great change in the habits of the peasantry, and in the appearance of the country, which is now in an excellent state of cultivation, yielding abundant produce; the cultivation of green crops has been introduced, and is practised with success. There are some good quarries of stone; and in the demesne of Ballymoyer Lodge are some lead mines, the ore of which is very pure and lies conveniently for working. The river Cusher has one of its sources within the parish. Among the gentlemen's seats are Ballymoyer Lodge, the residence of Marcus Synnot, Esq., proprietor of the parish under the see of Armagh, pleasantly situated in a demesne of 300 acres, embellished with thriving plantations and forest timber of excellent growth, planted by the owner; Ballintate, of Capt. Synnot; and Ballymoyer Cottage, of W. Reed, Esq. Petty sessions are held here every Wednesday. The living is a rectory and perpetual curacy, in the diocese of Armagh; the rectory is part of the union of Armagh; and the perpetual curacy was instituted under the provisions of an act of the 7th of Geo. III., cap. 17, and is in the patronage of the Rector of Armagh: the tithes amount to £200, the whole of which is payable to the rector of Armagh: the income of the curate arises from a stipend of £50 from the rector, £12. 6. from the augmentation fund, and £50 from the glebe, amounting in all to £112. 6. per annum. In the report of the Ecclesiastical Commissioners, in 1831, it is recommended to separate this parish from the union, and make it a distinct benefice. The walls of the original church were erected in the reign of Chas. I., but the clergyman appointed having been murdered, it remained unroofed until 1775, when Primate Robinson caused the work to be finished. The present church, a large and handsome edifice with a lofty square tower, was built in 1822, by aid of a gift of £900 from the late Board of First Fruits. The glebe-house, within a few perches of the church, was built in 1825, at an expense of £500, of which £450 was a gift and £50 a loan from the same Board; the glebe comprises 32*a.* 2*r.* 28*p.* In the R. C. divisions the parish is one of the three forming the union or district of Loughgilly, and contains a chapel. There are male and female parochial schools, aided by subscriptions from the ladies of the neighbourhood, and two other schools, supported by subscription, in which are about 200 boys and 100 girls; and there are also two Sunday schools. The remains of the former church, with the exception of the roof, are in good preservation, and form a picturesque and interesting object. Near the eastern end is a remarkably large ash tree, beneath the shade of which are deposited the remains of Florence Mac Moyer, otherwise Mac Wire or Mac Guire, a Franciscan friar, upon whose evidence Primate Plunket was executed at Tyburn in 1680. Some years since, a cairn was opened here and found to contain two separate tombs, in one of which were two urns of elegant form and workmanship containing ashes; one of them is in the possession of Mr. Synnot, of Ballymoyer Lodge, who has also a variety of ancient coins found in the neighbourhood, and some curiously marked stones, found in the large cairn of Mullyash, in the county of Monaghan.

BALLYMURRY, a village, in the parish of KILMEAN, barony of ATHLONE, county of ROSCOMMON, and province of CONNAUGHT, 3 miles (S. S. E.) from Roscommon: the population is returned with the parish. This village is situated on the road from Roscommon to Athlone, and consists of a few neatly built houses and about 20 cabins. It has a neat and improving appearance, and is kept remarkably clean; the manufacture of pottery is carried on to a moderate extent. The parish R. C. chapel, a thatched building in good repair, and a place of worship for the Society of Friends, are situated in the village; here is also the parochial school, under the patronage of Lord Crofton.—See KILMEAN.

BALLYNACLOGH, or DOLLARDSTOWN, a parish, in the barony of COONAGH, county of LIMERICK, and province of MUNSTER, 1½ mile (N. by W.) from Pallas-Greine, on the road from Limerick to Tipperary; containing 211 inhabitants. The land is everywhere of good quality, being mostly based on limestone. It is a rectory, in the diocese of Emly, forming the corps of the prebend of Ballynaclogh in the cathedral of Emly, and one of the rectories that constitute the union of Dromkeen and corps of the archdeaconry of Emly: the tithes amount to £46. In the R. C. divisions it is within the union of Greine, or Pallas-Greine; the chapel is situated in the little village of Nicker.

BALLYNACLOUGH, a parish, in the barony of UPPER ORMOND, county of TIPPERARY, and province of MUNSTER, 3 miles (S. E.) from Nenagh; containing 1149 inhabitants. This parish is situated on the river Arra, which falls into the Shannon at Drominear, and comprises 3701 statute acres, as applotted under the tithe act: the land is all arable and pasture, the soil fertile, and the system of agriculture much improved. Limestone abounds, and a marble quarry has recently been reopened on the demesnes of Debsborough and Ballynaclough, with a prospect of its being extensively worked; the marble is both of red and grey colour, and of very fine quality. There is a small corn-mill. Debsborough, the seat of J. Bayly, Esq., is pleasantly situated in a demesne tastefully laid out and well planted: the other seats are Ballynaclough, that of R. N. Bayly, Esq., and Bayly Farm, of Mrs. Bayly. A constabulary police force has been stationed in the parish. The living is a vicarage, in the diocese of Killaloe, united, since the foundation of the deanery, to the entire rectories of Drominear and Kilkeary, and the vicarage of Terryglass, which four parishes constitute the union of Ballynaclough and the corps of the deanery of Killaloe, in the patronage of the Crown: the rectory is impropriate in the Rev. Daniel and Mrs. Wall, and the Misses Elizabeth and Harriet Hardy: the tithes amount to £235, of which £156. 13. 4. is payable to the impropriators, and £78. 6. 8. to the dean; and the tithes of the whole benefice amount to £408. 6. 8. The church, a neat modern edifice, was erected by aid of a gift of £500 from the late Board of First Fruits, in 1815. The glebe-house is situated on a glebe of *7a. 1r. 18½p.*, and there is also a glebe of 15 acres in Terryglass. In the R.C. divisions this parish forms part of the union or district of Kilmore; the chapel is a modern building, situated on the townland of Ballyquiveane. There is a parochial school of about 20 boys and 20 girls, supported by the dean and John Bayly, Esq.,; and there are two pay schools, in which are about 80 boys and 10 girls. The poor have the benefit of the dispensaries at Nenagh and Silvermines. There are some remains of the old church adjoining the present structure, and also of the castle of Ballynaclough, which have a picturesque effect.

BALLYNACRAGGY, a hamlet, in the parish of DROMCREEHY, barony of BURREN, county of CLARE, and province of MUNSTER, 3 miles (W.) from Burren; containing 19 houses and 123 inhabitants. This place, which derives its name from an ancient castle, of which there are some remains, is situated on the road from Burren to Ballyvaughan. A school is about to be established, for which purpose Captain Kirwan has given the site and £10 towards the erection of the building.—See DROMCREEHY.

BALLYNACURRA.—See MIDLETON.

BALLYNADRIMNA, a parish, in the barony of CARBERY, county of KILDARE, and province of LEINSTER, 3 miles (W.) from Enfield; containing 1503 inhabitants. This parish is situated on the road from Kilcock to Kinnegad, and contains Garriska House, the property of C. Nangle, Esq. It is a vicarage, in the diocese of Kildare, and is part of the union of Castle-Carbery; the rectory is impropriate in the Marquess of Downshire: the tithes amount to £92. 6. 10¼. In the R. C. divisions it forms part of the union or district of Ballyna or Johnstown; the chapel, a neat building, is at Garriska. There is a school at Broadford, in which are 60 boys and 60 girls.

BALLYNAHAGLISH, a parish, in the barony of TRUGHENACKMY, county of KERRY, and province of MUNSTER, 5½ miles (W.) from Tralee; containing 2883 inhabitants. This parish is situated on the bay of Tralee, and comprises 2875 statute acres, as applotted under the tithe act; the land is chiefly under tillage, producing excellent crops, and the system of agriculture has been greatly improved within the last few years; sea-weed and sand are extensively used as manure, and good limestone, of a kind approaching to grey marble, is also obtained. The seats are Oyster Hall, that of Barry Collins, Esq., and Oyster Lodge, of — Nelligan, Esq. The village of Taulert, or Chapeltown, lies on the south-eastern shore of the creek or harbour of Barra, and is partly inhabited by fishermen. On account of the fine bathing strand in Tralee bay, and a chalybeate spring of great power on the border of the parish and adjoining Clogherbrien, it is much frequented during the summer by visiters from Tralee and other places, for whose accommodation some neat bathing-lodges have been erected. There is a coast-guard station at Kilfinura, on Tralee bay. The living is a vicarage, in the diocese of Ardfert and Aghadoe, with the entire rectory of Annagh and the rectory and vicarage of Clogherbrien episcopally united from a period prior to any known record, forming the union of Ballynahaglish, in the patronage of Sir Edward Denny, Bart.: the rectory is impropriate in the Denny family: the tithes amount to £230. 15. 4., and of the whole benefice to £733. 16. 10. The church, an ancient structure built in 1619, is situated on an eminence thence called Church-hill, a little to the east of Chapeltown; it was repaired by aid of a gift of £900 from the late Board of First Fruits, in 1820, and the Ecclesiastical Commissioners have recently granted £127 for its further repair. The glebe-house was erected by aid of a gift of £100 from the same Board, in 1741; it adjoins the church, and commands fine views of the bays of Tralee and Brandon, and the Dingle mountains. The glebe comprises 34 statute acres. In the R. C. divisions this parish forms part of the union or district of Ardfert; the chapel, situated in the village of Chapeltown, is in a very dilapidated condition. There are three private schools, in which about 120 children are educated.—See Kilfinura.

BALLYNAHAGLISH, a parish, in the barony of Tyrawley, county of Mayo, and province of Connaught, 2½ miles (S. by E.) from Ballina; containing 5103 inhabitants. This place derived its name, signifying in the Irish language "the Town of the Church," from an ancient abbey or religious establishment, of which there are some slight remains, though nothing of its history is recorded. The parish is situated on the west bank of the river Moy, which is navigable here and is celebrated for its salmon; and comprises 11,559 statute acres, as applotted under the tithe act and valued at £4620 per annum. The system of agriculture is improved; there is a very extensive tract of bog, of which a great portion is reclaimable, also abundance of limestone, sandstone, and granite quarried for building and for mending the roads. The gentlemen's seats are Mount Falcon, that of J. F. Knox, Esq., on the demesne of which is a good race-course; and Rehins, of W. Atkinson, Esq. It is a vicarage, in the diocese of Killala, and is part of the union of Ardagh; the rectory is impropriate in the vicars choral of the cathedral of Christ-Church, Dublin. The tithes amount to £300, payable in moieties to the impropriators and the vicar. The church is in ruins. The glebe comprises 15 acres; there is no glebe-house. In the R. C. divisions it is the head of a union or district, called Backs, which comprises also the parish of Kilbelfad, and contains two chapels, one in each parish; that of Ballynahaglish is not yet completed. There is an ancient burial-ground in the townland of Ballynahaglish, and another at Killeen, which is unconsecrated and is appropriated to the interment of infants dying before baptism. There are two schools, situated respectively at Mount Falcon and Lisaniska, under the National Board, the former aided by an annual donation from J. F. Knox, Esq.; two schools under the Baptist Society, and one at Rehins Lodge, supported by Mrs. Atkinson and her daughters. In these are about 230 boys and 130 girls: there is also a hedge school of about 20 boys and 20 girls. There are the remains of an ancient castle called Castle-Mac Andrew, also several cromlechs and numerous encampments, in the parish; and at Gortnaderra is a curious cave.

BALLYNAHOWN, a village, in the parish of Killaleagh, barony of Clonlonan, county of Westmeath, and province of Leinster, 5 miles (S.) from Athlone, on the road to Parsonstown: the population is returned with the parish. It was for more than nine centuries the residence of the Malone family, whose ancient mansion, built on the site of an old castle and now unoccupied, is the principal object of interest. The estate, together with the old family mansion, called Ballynahown House, has at length passed into other hands. Here is a constabulary police station.—See Killaleagh.

BALLYNAKILL, a parish, in the barony of Ballynahinch, county of Galway, and province of Connaught, 4 miles (N.) from Clifden; containing 7183 inhabitants. This parish is situated on the bay of the same name on the western coast, and comprehends within its limits Claggin bay, and one side of Killery harbour, with the islands of Ilane-a-green or Crump, Innisbruin, Bradilan, and Freachillan; it comprises 5142 statute acres, as applotted under the tithe act. The male inhabitants are principally employed in agriculture, and occasionally in the herring fishery; and the females in spinning woollen yarn and knitting stockings. During the famine that prevailed on this part of the coast in 1831, the inhabitants of this parish were reduced to the greatest distress, and 1500 families must have perished but for the prompt relief afforded. At Derry-Inver, within the bay of Ballynakill, a small pier has been erected by Government, which has proved very useful for trade and the fisheries, and has contributed much to the improvement of the surrounding district. The entrance to Claggin bay is easy, the ground clean and good, and the shelter tolerable, with depth of water sufficient for any ship. On the south side the Board of Fisheries has constructed a small pier opposite to the anchorage ground, which has been found to be very beneficial. The living is a rectory and vicarage, in the diocese of Tuam, with the rectories and vicarages of Omey or Umma, Moyrus, and Ballindoon, and the six vicarages of Ennisboffin, Killanin, Arranmore, Arranbeg, Ennismain, and Ennishere, episcopally united in 1667, forming altogether the union of Ballynakill, in the patronage of the Bishop: the tithes amount to £64. 12. 3¾., and of the whole union to £270. 6. 11¾. The church of the union is situated in the parish of Omey, and was built by aid of a gift of £600 from the late Board of First Fruits, in 1812. The glebe-house was built by aid of a gift of £337 and a loan of £75 from the same Board, in 1816: the glebe, which is also situated in the parish of Omey, comprises 40 acres. In the R. C. divisions this parish is the head of a union or district, comprising also Ennisboffin, and containing three chapels, situated respectively at Ballynakill, Coilmore, and Ennisboffin; and in this parish divine service is also performed at a house in Tully. There is a school at Tully under the Tuam Diocesan and the Dublin Ladies' Irish Societies, in which 13 boys and 7 girls are instructed; and there are three pay schools, situated respectively at Tully, Ballynakill, and Rossroe, in which are about 80 children.

BALLYNAKILL, a parish, in the barony of HALF-BALLYMOE, county of GALWAY, and province of CONNAUGHT, 6¼ miles (W.) from Roscommon; containing 4315 inhabitants. This parish is situated near the road from Roscommon to Dunmore, and comprises about 3000 acres of arable land, about 20,000 acres of mountain pasture, and nearly the same quantity of waste, mountain, and bog. It is a vicarage, in the diocese of Elphin, and forms part of the union of Donamon; the rectory is impropriate in Viscount Ranelagh. The tithes amount to £230. 10., payable in moieties to the impropriator and the vicar. In the R. C. divisions it is the head of a union or district, called Glinsk and Kilcroan, which comprises the parishes of Ballynakill, Clonigormican, Ardclare, Oran, and Kilcroan, and contains two chapels, one of which is situated at Glinsk, in this parish. There are five hedge schools, in which are about 270 boys and 70 girls.

BALLYNAKILL, a parish, in the barony of LEITRIM, county of GALWAY, and province of CONNAUGHT, 7½ miles (W. S. W.) from Portumna; containing, with the town of Woodford, 13,103 inhabitants. This parish is situated on the road from Portumna to Gort, and comprises 12,006 statute acres, as applotted under the tithe act; about 800 acres are woodland, and the remainder arable and pasture. Marble Hill, formerly Gortenacuppogue, the seat of Sir J. Burke, Bart., is finely situated in a demesne extensively wooded, commanding several interesting views, and distinguished by its great variety of surface; in the grounds is a spring called Macduff's well, within a few yards of which are vestiges of a stone altar. The other seats are Shannon Hill, the residence of M. Conolly, Esq.; Ballinagar, of the Hon. A. Nugent; Cloncoe, of Ulick Burke, Esq.; Moyglass, of J. Burke, Esq.; Eagle Hill, of Capt. H. Pigott, J. P.; Brook Ville, of Martin White, Esq.; Ballycorban, of Matthew White, Esq.; and Carroroe Lodge, of H. Clarke, Esq. Fairs are held on the 1st of June and 26th of October. It is a rectory, in the diocese of Clonfert, partly appropriate to the see and deanery, and partly forming a portion of the union of Lickmolassy: the tithes amount to £299. 15. 1., of which £50. 15. 4½. is payable to the Ecclesiastical Commissioners, £13. 18. 11¼. to the dean, and the remainder to the incumbent. The church is at Woodford, and the Ecclesiastical Commissioners have recently granted £213 for its repair; the glebe at Ballynakill comprises 6*a.* 3*r.* In the R. C. divisions the greater part of the parish is divided into two entire benefices, called Ballynakill and Woodford, and the remainder forms part of a third: there are chapels at Cloncoe, Loughtorick, Marble Hill, Knockadrian, and Woodford; the last erected in 1837, at a cost of £400. A National school has been recently built, and there are nine pay schools, in which are 178 boys and 363 girls. There are the ruins of an old castle, which appears to have been of great strength; and numerous forts. In the demesne of Marble Hill is a subterranean passage, now so choked up with reeds and other obstructions as to render it difficult to ascertain its extent; and there are numerous vestiges of antiquity in the grounds. At Ballinagar, about a mile and a half from the village, are Mullins Wells, formerly much visited during the summer, the grounds around them being tastefully laid out.—See WOODFORD.

BALLYNAKILL, a parish, in the barony of COOLESTOWN, KING'S county, and province of LEINSTER, 3 miles (S. by W.) from Edenderry, on the road to Tullamore; containing 947 inhabitants. It comprises 3668 statute acres, as applotted under the tithe act: about one-fourth part of the profitable land is arable, and the remainder is partly meadow and partly pasture; there are large tracts of bog, besides a considerable quantity that is exhausted; the state of agriculture is good. The Grand Canal passes through the parish, and there are limestone quarries within its limits. The gentlemen's seats are Ballymorin, that of D. Odlim, Esq.; and Ballylekin, of F. Lee, Esq. The living is a vicarage, in the diocese of Kildare, united to the rectory of Clonsast; the rectory is impropriate in Richard Garden, Esq., of Bath. The tithes amount to £157. 16. 11., of which £92. 6. 1¾. is payable to the impropriator, and the remainder to the vicar. In the R. C. divisions the parish is partly in the union or district of Edenderry, and partly in that of Clonsast or Clonbollogue. There is a private pay school, in which about 25 boys and 20 girls are taught. Here are the ruins of the ancient castle of Purefoy, one of the numerous small square buildings erected in this part of the country to protect the English pale.

BALLYNAKILL, a parish, in the barony of TIRAGHRILL, county of SLIGO, and province of CONNAUGHT, 9 miles (S. S. E.) from Sligo; containing 1767 inhabitants. This parish is situated on the road from Sligo to Ballyfarnon, and is intersected by the small river Dubhglass, which at Rockbrook forms several small cascades, and passes under a natural bridge of one arch, 6 feet high and 20 feet in the span. It comprises 2679 statute acres, as applotted under the tithe act: the land is good, and is chiefly under the old unimproved system of tillage; there is a large extent of bog, and limestone abounds in the parish. Rockbrook is the residence of E. H. Cogan, Esq., and Moorfield, of T. Irwin, Esq. Petty sessions are held at Sowey every third Tuesday. It is a vicarage, in the diocese of Elphin, and forms part of the union of Boyle; the rectory is appropriate to the prebend of Kilmacallane in the cathedral of Elphin. The tithes amount to £83. 1. 6½., payable in moieties to the prebendary and the vicar. The Protestant inhabitants resort to the church in the parish of Ballysumaghon. In the R. C. divisions it is the head of a union or district, called Sowey, which comprises also the parishes of Ballysumaghan and Kilross: the chapel is a thatched building in very indifferent repair, situated at Sowey. Two schools, in which about 50 boys and 30 girls are taught, are supported by private subscriptions. At Carrickcoolla there are some inconsiderable remains of an old castle. On the lands of Ballynakill is a holy well, dedicated to the Blessed Virgin, to which the peasantry resort on Sept. 8th to perform certain devotions; and near it is a large rock, in which there are several natural caverns of very small dimensions.

BALLYNAKILL, a parish, in the barony of GAULTIER, county of WATERFORD, and province of MUNSTER, 2 miles (E. S. E.) from Waterford; containing, with Little Island in the river Suir, 609 inhabitants. This parish is pleasantly situated on the road from Waterford to Passage and Dunmore, commanding a beautiful view of the city, with the vessels on the river Suir, which encircles Little Island with a wide but shallow channel on the north, and a narrow winding stream of greater depth on the south. It comprises about 1800 statute acres, of which the island contains about 290 acres, forming a delightful spot commanding a fine view of the city of Waterford, the course of the Suir, and the adjacent counties of Kilkenny and Wexford, terminated by the lofty and picturesque mountains of Ury and Slieve Kielta. On the island is a comfortable farm-house, near which is an old castle, supposed to have been erected in the sixteenth century; it is a strong square building with lofty battlements, having a small pointed entrance archway, above which is an oriel window with some rude sculpture; a staircase, faintly lighted by loopholes, leads to the summit, from which the view is singularly grand and extensive: it is the property and occasional residence of J. Fitzgerald, Esq. In the parish are several gentlemen's seats, of which the principal are May Park, the residence of George Meara, Esq., pleasantly situated near the banks of the Suir, and commanding some fine views; Mount Pleasant, the handsome residence of S. King, Esq., near the high road; Belmont, the seat of J. Roberts, Esq., situated near the river; and Ballynakill House, the property of N. Power, Esq., now occupied by a tenant. The living is a vicarage, in the diocese of Waterford, with the vicarages of Ballygunner, Kilmacleague, and Kilmacomb episcopally united, together forming the union of Ballynakill, in the patronage of the Bishop; the rectory is impropriate to the Dean and Chapter of Waterford. The tithes amount to £139. 3. 6. of which £84. 1. 9. is payable to the dean and chapter, and £55. 1. 9. to the vicar; and the tithes of the whole benefice amount to £245. 0. 10. The church, a neat edifice with a spire, was built by aid of a gift of £900 from the late Board of First Fruits, in 1816. There is no glebe-house: the glebe, situated in another part of the union, comprises 10 acres. In the R. C. divisions this parish forms part of the union or district of St. John's, Waterford. A Protestant school, endowed with lands by Bishop Foy, and in which 47 boys are boarded and educated, and at a proper age apprenticed, is supported under the control of the Bishop, Dean, and Mayor of Waterford.

BALLYNAMALLARD, a village, in the parish of Magheracross, barony of Tyrkennedy, county of Fermanagh, and province of Ulster, $5\frac{1}{4}$ miles (N. by E.) from Enniskillen, on the road to Omagh; containing 72 houses and 323 inhabitants. It is a constabulary police station; and has fairs on Feb. 12th, Aug. 5th, and Nov. 28th, of which only the first is kept and is a good fair for horses. There is a penny post to Enniskillen and Omagh. The parish church is in the village; and there are also places of worship for Wesleyan and Primitive Methodists, and a dispensary.—See Magheracross.

BALLYNAMONA, or MOORTOWN, a parish, in the barony of Small County, county of Limerick, and province of Munster, 5 miles (N. E) from Bruff; containing 513 inhabitants. This parish is situated on the road from Hospital to Pallas-Greine, and comprises 1317 statute acres; the land is in general remarkably good, resting upon a substratum of limestone, through which appear some small rocks of basalt. About one-fourth is under tillage, and the remainder is meadow and pasture, with more than 100 acres of turbary, which affords excellent fuel; the system of agriculture is improved. It is a vicarage, in the diocese of Emly, and is part of the union of Aney; the rectory is impropriate in Edward Deane Freeman, Esq. The tithes amount to £131, of which two-thirds are payable to the impropriator and the remainder to the vicar. In the R. C. divisions it forms part of the union or district of Hospital and Herbertstown. On the banks of a small stream, close to the road, are the remains of the castle built by the Raleighs in the reign of Elizabeth; and not far from it are the ruins of the old parish church.

BALLYNARD, or CAHIRFOSSORGE, a parish, in the barony of Small County, county of Limerick, and province of Munster, 6 miles (N. E. by N.) from Bruff, on the road from Limerick to Hospital; containing 867 inhabitants. This parish comprises 1366 statute acres, as applotted under the tithe act: the land is in general good, resting on a substratum of limestone, except in some few places where the basalt rises in gentle knolls. It is a vicarage, in the diocese of Emly, and is part of the union of Aney; the rectory is impropriate in Edward Deane Freeman, Esq. The tithes amount to £148. 18., of which two-thirds are payable to the impropriator and the remainder to the vicar. In the R. C. divisions the parish forms part of the union or district of Hospital and Herbertstown, in which latter is the chapel for this parish. There are two pay schools, in which are about 60 boys and 30 girls. Not far from the chapel are the ruins of the old church; and on the hill are the remains of Ballynard castle, built by the Geraldines in the fifteenth century, and for many years the residence of the Ballynard branch of that powerful family. At Eaglestown are some remains of the old family mansion of the Powels.

BALLYNASCREEN, a parish, in the barony of Loughinsholin, county of Londonderry, and province of Ulster; containing, with the market and post-town of Draperstown, 7854 inhabitants. This appears to have been a place of importance at a very early period; frequent notice of it occurs in the Trias Thaumaturga and other ancient records, though it is neither mentioned in the Monasticon nor in the Visitation of 1622, which includes every other parish in the neighbourhood. The original church, the ruins of which are situated in a romantic and sequestered glen among the mountains, is said to have been founded by St. Patrick, and subsequently consecrated by St. Columb as a parochial church. The parish is intersected by the river Moyola, which has its sources amidst the mountain regions of Slieve Gullion, Moneymeeney, and Slieve Dovin, which extend into the county of Tyrone, where they meet the Munterloney range. It comprises, according to the Ordnance survey, 32,492 statute acres, of which about 200 acres are mountain, waste, and bog. Part of the parish belongs to the Drapers' Company, of London, part to the representative of the Skinners' Company, and part to the see of Derry. The soil is various: around Draperstown and on the banks of the Moyola it is a deep gravel and sand, and in an excellent state of cultivation, producing good crops of wheat, flax, oats, and potatoes, and some barley, but on the higher grounds the chief crops are flax, oats, and potatoes. The freestone is of superior quality and is extensively worked for building. Manganese has been found in detached nodules in several of the mountain streams:

and Boate, in his Natural History, states that gold has been also discovered here. Derrynoyd Lodge is the residence of the Rt. Hon. Judge Torrens. The inhabitants are principally employed in agriculture, with which they combine the weaving of linen and dealing in cattle, great numbers of which are bred on the mountains and exported to England and Scotland.

The living is a rectory, in the diocese of Derry, and in the patronage of the Bishop: the tithes amount to £623. 1. 6½. The church, a large handsome edifice in the early English style, is situated at Draperstown, and was erected in 1760, principally through means of the Earl of Bristol, then Bishop of Derry; and the tower and a handsome octagonal spire were added in 1792, aided by contributions from Sir Wm. Rowley, Bart., and the Drapers' Company, the latter of whom are proprietors of the estate and contributed £50. The glebe-house, a handsome residence, is situated on a glebe of 161*a.* 3*r.* 12*p.*; and there is another glebe in the townland of Bancran, containing 750*a.* 1*r.* 7*p.*, much of which is mountain and pasture land. The R. C. parish is co-extensive with that of the Established Church; there are chapels at Moneymeeny and Straw. Two male and female schools are supported by the rector; two, situated at Black Hill and Carnamony, are supported by the Drapers' Company; and there are seven schools, situated respectively at Draperstown, Derrynoyd, Brackragh-Dysart, Drumard, Labby, Altyaskey, and Straw, under the National Board. In these schools are about 700 boys and 520 girls; and there are also two private schools, in which are about 100 children; and five Sunday schools. The ruins of the old church are highly interesting. There are numerous relics of antiquity, particularly cromlechs, of which there were formerly five within the limits of the parish. — See DRAPERSTOWN.

BALLYNASLANEY, a parish, partly in the barony of SHELMALIER, but chiefly in that of BALLAGHKEEN, county of WEXFORD, and province of LEINSTER, 4¾ miles (S. by E.) from Enniscorthy; containing 916 inhabitants. This parish is situated on the eastern bank of the river Slaney, and on the mail coach road from Wexford to Enniscorthy; it comprises 2608 statute acres, as applotted under the tithe act. A small portion is marshy, but by far the greater portion is good arable and pasture land. The river is navigable for vessels of large burden as far as Pooldarragh, in this parish, at which place the contemplated canal to Enniscorthy, a distance of 6½ British miles, will commence, according to the proposed plan. It is an impropriate curacy, in the diocese of Ferns, annexed to the rectory of Edermine by act of council in 1806; the rectory is impropriate partly in the Earl of Portsmouth and partly in the Representatives of Walter Redmond, Esq. The tithes amount to £161. 10. 9., of which £106. 3. 0¾. is payable to the impropriators, and the remainder to the curate. The church, of which even the ruins have been removed, must have been originally a handsome structure; a very fine Norman doorway, formerly a part of it, has been inserted in the church of Kilpatrick at Saunders-court. In the R. C. divisions the parish forms part of the union or district of Oylgate, in the parish of Edermine, where stands the chapel. There is a pay school in which about 40 children are educated.

BALLYNAULTIG, or KILSHANNAH, a parish, in the barony of BARRYMORE, county of CORK, and province of MUNSTER, adjacent to Rathcormac; containing 1270 inhabitants. This parish, which is also called Kilshanahan, is situated on the road from Cork to Rathcormac, and comprises 2791 statute acres, as applotted under the tithe act, and valued at £2454 per annum: the soil is for the greater part strong and shallow, but is more fertile near the river Bride, which abounds with excellent trout. The gentlemen's seats are Scartbarry, that of E. Wilson, Esq., and Bushy Park, of R. Gifford Campion, Esq. It is a rectory, in the diocese of Cork, forming part of the union and corps of the prebend of Killaspigmullane in the cathedral of St. Finbarr, Cork: the tithes are included in the composition for Killaspigmullane. There is no church, but there is an old burial-ground within or near which the ancient church is supposed to have been situated. In the R. C. divisions it forms part of the union or district of Ardnageehy or Watergrass-Hill.

BALLYNEEN, a village, in the parish of BALLYMONEY, Eastern Division of the barony of EAST CARBERY, county of CORK, and province of MUNSTER, 10 miles (W. S. W.) from Bandon; containing 691 inhabitants. This village is situated on the mail coach road from Bandon to Dunmanway, and on the north bank of the river Bandon, over which is a spacious bridge of ten arches: it consists of one principal street, with a shorter street branching from it towards the bridge, and in 1831 contained 121 houses, the greater number of which are tolerably well built. A few of the inhabitants are employed in the weaving of coarse linens for home consumption, and in the manufacture of cotton cord; but the greater number are engaged in agriculture. A constabulary police force has been stationed here; and district petty sessions are held in a court-house generally every alternate Monday. There is a place of worship for Wesleyan Methodists; also a dispensary, which annually affords medical relief to more than 5000 patients of the surrounding neighbourhood.—See BALLYMONEY.

BALLYNEFAGH, or BALLINAFEAGH, a parish, in the barony of CLARE, county of KILDARE, and province of LEINSTER, 4 miles (W. N. W.) from Clare, on the road to Edenderry; containing 614 inhabitants. It is nearly surrounded by the bog of Clashaghbane, and contains 2184 statute acres, as applotted under the tithe act. The living is a vicarage, in the diocese of Kildare, and in the patronage of the Crown; the rectory is impropriate in Lord Cloncurry. The tithes amount to £105. A church and glebe-house have been lately erected; and there is a glebe of 14 acres, in five parcels. There is a school of about 130 children.

BALLYNEMARA, or BALLINAMARA, a parish, in the barony of CRANAGH, county of KILKENNY, and province of LEINSTER, 2½ miles (S. S. E.) from Freshford, on the road from Kilkenny to Johnstown; containing 867 inhabitants. It comprises 3755 statute acres of tolerably good land, of which about two-thirds consist of pasture land, and one-third is under tillage. The living is a vicarage, in the diocese of Ossory, and in the patronage of the Dean and Chapter of St. Canice, Kilkenny, to whom the rectory is appropriate: the tithes amount to £240, of which £160 is payable to the appropriators, and £80 to the vicar. The church is a plain modern building. There is neither glebe-house nor glebe. In the R. C. divisions the parish forms part of the union or district of Freshford. The parochial school is held in the vestry-room of the church; and there is a private pay school, in which are about 70 boys and 20 girls. The late Robt. Lanigan, Esq., bequeathed £100 for the erection of two houses for two poor widows, who are to have a small annual allowance, and preparations are in progress for carrying his intentions into effect.

BALLYNOCHEN.—See WELLS.

BALLYNOCKEN, a village, in the parish of FENNAGH, barony of IDRONE EAST, county of CARLOW, and province of LEINSTER, 3 miles (S. W. by W.) from Myshall; containing 28 houses and 169 inhabitants.—See FENNAGH.

BALLYNOE, a parish, in the barony of KINNATALOON, county of CORK, and province of MUNSTER, 6 miles (W. by S.) from Tallow; containing 2692 inhabitants. This parish is situated on the old road from Castlemartyr to Fermoy, and comprises 10,271 statute acres, of which 50 are woodland, 1500 bog, and 8721 arable and pasture land; 7514 acres are applotted under the tithe act, of which the gross rental is estimated at £4222 per annum. The land consists of a light soil resting on clay-slate, but is in general tolerably fertile: the principal manure is lime brought from the vale of the Bride. Not far from the village is Ballynoe House, the residence of A. Hargrave, Esq.; and there are several commodious houses occupied by respectable farmers. It is a rectory and vicarage, in the diocese of Cloyne, the former united from time immemorial to the rectory of Ahern, and the latter united to the vicarage of Knockmourne: the tithes amount to £915. 3., of which two-thirds are payable to the rector and one-third to the vicar. There is a glebe of 2½ acres, but no glebe-house. In the R. C. divisions it forms part of the union or district of Knockmourne, also called Ballynoe: the chapel, situated in the village, is a large plain building, erected in 1835, and is also appropriated to a national school. A little to the south-east of the village are the ruins of the parish church; and near them are other extensive ruins, supposed to be the remains of an establishment founded by the Knights Hospitallers, to whom the rectory anciently belonged.

BALLYNURE, a parish, in the barony of LOWER BELFAST, county of ANTRIM, and province of ULSTER, 6 miles (N. W.) from Carrickfergus; containing, with part of the town of Ballyclare, 3549 inhabitants, of which number, 415 are in the village. This parish, which is situated on the Six-mile-water, and on the road from Carrickfergus to Antrim, comprises, according to the Ordnance survey, 8540¾ statute acres. The soil is fertile, and the lands are generally in a good state of cultivation; the system of agriculture is improving; there is some waste land, and a considerable tract of bog. A kind of basaltic stone is quarried and used for building and for repairing the roads. There is an extensive bleach-green; also a large paper-mill, in which the most improved machinery is used for the manufacture of the finer kinds of paper. Fairs for cattle, pigs, and pedlery are held on the 16th of May, Sept. 5th, and Oct. 25th; there are large horse fairs in May and Nov., and also on Christmas-day, at Reagh Hill; and fairs are also held at Ballyclare, *which see.* In the village is a constabulary police station; and a manorial court is held every third week by the seneschal, for the recovery of debts to the amount of £10. The living is a rectory, in the diocese of Connor, united by charter of the 7th of Jas. I. to the vicarages of Kilroot and Templecorran, together constituting the corps of the prebend of Kilroot in the cathedral of Connor: the tithes amount to £330. The church, a plain small edifice, built about the year 1602, is situated near the western extremity of the parish. There is neither glebe nor glebe-house. In the R. C. divisions the parish forms part of the union or district of Larne and Carrickfergus. There is a place of worship in the village for Presbyterians in connection with the Synod of Ulster, of the second class. There are three schools, which afford instruction to about 240 children; and four pay schools, in which are about 90 boys and 70 girls. The late Mr. Dobbs, of Castle Dobbs, bequeathed £100 for winter clothing for the poor.

BALLYNURE, a parish, in the barony of UPPER TALBOTSTOWN, county of WICKLOW, and province of LEINSTER, 3 miles (S. W.) from Dunlavin, on the road from Baltinglass to Ballitore; containing 1874 inhabitants. It comprises 6932 statute acres, nearly all arable land; the soil is fertile, and the system of agriculture improving. There is neither bog nor waste land; fuel is consequently scarce, and the inhabitants are supplied only from the bog of Narraghmore, which is five miles distant. Ballynure, the seat of H. Carroll, Esq., is an elegant mansion situated in a rich demesne. Grange-Con, formerly the grange of the abbey of Baltinglass (which, together with this estate, was granted by Queen Elizabeth to Sir J. Harrington), was till lately the residence of H. Harrington, Esq., who erected two spacious galleries for the reception of paintings and curiosities, of which he was an indefatigable collector. The other seats are Knockrigg, the residence of J. Wall, Esq.; Bessina, of H. Harrington Wall, Esq.; Barronstown, of J. Wilson, Esq.; and Griffinstown, of W. Cooke, Esq. A constabulary police force has been stationed at the small village of Bumboa Hall. It is a rectory, annexed to that of Baltinglass, in the diocese of Leighlin: the tithes amount to £300. The church, a small neat edifice with a square tower crowned with pinnacles, was erected by aid of a gift of £800 from the late Board of First Fruits, in 1814. In the R. C. divisions also it is included in the union or district of Baltinglass; the chapel is at Bumboa Hall, and adjoining it is a school of 84 boys and 50 girls. In the grounds of Grange-Con are the remains of an ancient castle; there are a rath and an ancient cemetery on the grounds of Knockrigg, and several other raths in different parts of the parish.

BALLYORGAN, a village, in the parish of KILFLYN, barony of COSTLEA, county of LIMERICK, and province of MUNSTER, 8 miles (S. E.) from Kilmallock, on the road to Kildorrery; containing 61 houses and 369 inhabitants. The parochial R. C. chapel is situated here; and not far distant are the parish church, the glebe-house, and the parochial schools.—See KILFLYN.

BALLYOUGHTERA, a parish, in the barony of IMOKILLY, county of CORK, and province of MUNSTER; containing, with part of the market and post-town of Castlemartyr, 1509 inhabitants. This parish comprises, with Cahirultan, 4215 statute acres, as applotted under the tithe act, and valued at £3142 per annum: the state of agriculture is on some farms improved, but on others it is very backward. A considerable portion is comprised within the park of Castlemartyr, and is either laid out in woods and ornamental grounds or devoted to pasture. The eastern part, including a portion of the town of Castlemartyr, is richly adorned with wood and in a good state of cultivation; and contains several elegant seats, of which the principal are Castlemartyr, that of the Earl of Shannon, which is described under the head of that town: Dromadda, of G. W. Courtenay, Esq.; Kilbree, of S. W. Adams, Esq.; and Ballyhickady, of Capt. Leach. The living is a rectory and vicarage, in the diocese of Cloyne, consolidated with the rectory of Cahirultan and united by act of the 9th of Anne, cap. 12, to the vicarage of Imogeely or Mogeely, which together constitute the union of Castlemartyr and corps of the prebend of Cahirultan, in the patronage of the Bishop: the tithes, embracing the entire union, amount to £435. 12. 7., and the entire value of the prebend is returned at £523. 15. The church, situated in the town of Castlemartyr, is a neat building in a spacious spot of ground surrounded by lofty elms. The glebe-house, in Imogeely, was erected by aid of a gift of £100 and a loan of £1350, in 1815, from the late Board of First Fruits: the glebe comprises 22 acres lying partly in Castlemartyr, partly in Cahirultan, but chiefly in Imogeely. In the R. C. divisions the parish forms part of the union or district of Imogeely or Castlemartyr, at the former of which is the chapel; and there is another chapel on the border of the parish, near Ballintowlas, adjoining which is the national school. In the demesne of Castlemartyr, and near its south-eastern boundary, are the ruins of the old parish church, which was built in 1549, and destroyed in the war of 1641. The ruins of the ancient castle of Imokilly, from which the barony derives its name, afterwards called Ballymartyr castle, and now Castlemartyr, are in this parish, as are also the ruins of the castle of Ballintowlas; and near the latter there is an extensive lake.

BALLYOVEY, a parish, in the barony of Carra, county of Mayo, and province of Connaught, $6\frac{1}{4}$ miles (N. by W.) from Ballinrobe; containing 4025 inhabitants. This parish, which is pleasantly situated on the borders of Loughs Mask and Carra, and on the high road from Castlebar to Ballinrobe, comprises 19,823 statute acres, as applotted under the tithe act. The surface is mountainous, and there are extensive tracts of bog: the lands now in cultivation are principally under tillage. The scenery is boldly varied: in the bosom of the mountains is Tarmacady, the summer lodge of Dean Plunket; and Partree, the seat of J. Lynch, Esq., is beautifully situated on Lough Carra. It is a rectory and vicarage, in the diocese of Tuam, partly appropriate to the prebend of Killabegs in the cathedral church of St. Mary, Tuam, and partly included in the union of Burriscarra: the tithes amount to £162, of which £23. 5. $2\frac{3}{4}$. is payable to the prebendary of Killabegs, and the remainder to the incumbent. There is neither church, glebe-house, nor glebe. In the R. C. divisions it forms a separate benefice, called Partree; there are two chapels, one at Partree, a small thatched building, and the other in the mountains at Ballybannon, a spacious slated edifice. There are six pay schools, in which are about 340 children.

BALLYPATRICK.—See RATHPATRICK.

BALLYPHILIP, a parish, in the barony of Ardes, county of Down, and province of Ulster; containing, with the post-town of Portaferry, 3090 inhabitants. This parish is situated between Strangford Lough and the eastern coast, and comprises, according to the Ordnance survey, 2430 statute acres, of which 1839 are applotted under the tithe act. The land is fertile, and, with the exception of about 30 acres of bog, called Ballygaroegan Moss, which supplies the inhabitants with fuel, is in a good state of cultivation. Within its limits is Carney or Kerney Point, off which are two dangerous shoals, called Carney Pladdy and Butter Pladdy. The living is a rectory, in the diocese of Down, with the vicarage of Ballytrustin and the rectories of Slanes and Ardglass united by charter in the 7th of Jas. I., which four parishes constitute the union of Ballyphilip and the corps of the chancellorship of Down, in the patronage of the Bishop: the tithes amount to £208. 16. 9; and the gross income, including tithe and glebe, is £490. 10. per annum. The church, situated in the town of Portaferry, is a neat modern edifice, erected in 1787, and has been lately repaired by a grant of £343 from the Ecclesiastical Commissioners. The glebe-house was built in 1818, at an expense of £1090, of which £825 was a loan from the late Board of First Fruits, and £265 was added by the present incumbent, and is chargeable on his successors. The glebe comprises 15 Cunningham acres, valued at £45 per annum. It was recommended by the Commissioners of Ecclesiastical Inquiry, in 1831, that the parish of Ardglass, being seven miles distant, and in which a perpetual curacy of small value has been erected, should be severed from the union, and an equivalent given to the chancellor. In the R. C. divisions the parish forms part of the unions or districts of Lower and Upper Ardes, which latter is united to part of Ardkeen, Witter, Ballytrustin, Slanes, and Ardguin; there are two chapels, one near Portaferry, a spacious and handsome edifice, and the other at Witter, three miles distant. There are places of worship at Portaferry for Presbyterians in connection with the Synod of Ulster, of the second class, and for Wesleyan Methodists. A parochial school of 70 boys and 70 girls, at Portaferry, is aided by an annual donation of £30 late currency from Andrew Nugent, Esq., who built the school-house, and by a smaller from the rector; there are also seven pay schools in the parish, in which are about 60 boys and 60 girls. A bequest of £3 per annum to the poor, by one of the Bangor family, is charged on the Castle-Ward estate. An ancient church, which, according to tradition, belonged to a wealthy abbey, formerly occupied the site of the present glebe-house, near which human bones, tombs, and extensive foundations are frequently dug up. Bankmore, a large and perfect rath, and a smaller fort at Ballytrustin, are within the parish. The late Marquess of Londonderry received the rudiments of his education in the glebe-house, under Dr. Sturrock, then chancellor of Down, and incumbent of this parish.—See Portaferry.

BALLYPOREEN, a village, in the parish of Templetenny, barony of Iffa and Offa West, county of Tipperary, and province of Munster, 4 miles (W. S. W.) from Clogheen, on the road from Cork to Dublin; containing 113 houses and 513 inhabitants. It is the residence of M. Burke, Esq.; and Ballywilliam is the residence of the agent of Cæsar Sutton, Esq. Fairs are held on May 12th, Aug. 21st, and Dec. 17th. It is a constabulary police station; and a court is held for the manor, which is the property of the Earl of Kingston, since whose accession the village has been much improved. The parish church, recently erected; the R. C. chapel; and a dispensary, are situated here. There is a mineral spring of some repute.

BALLYRAGGET, or DONOUGHMORE, a post-town and parish, in the barony of FASSADINING, county of KILKENNY, and province of LEINSTER, 8 miles (N. by W.) from Kilkenny, and 53¾ (S. W. by S.) from Dublin; containing 2609 inhabitants, of which number, 1629 are in the town. This place appears to have derived its origin from a castle belonging to the Butler family, which in 1600 was garrisoned by the forces of Sir George Carew, Lord-President of Munster, when the sons of Lord Mountgarret, to whom it then belonged, were in rebellion against the crown, and had engaged with O'More to arrest the Earl of Ormonde. Previously to this period it had been a favourite residence of the celebrated Lady Margaret Fitzgerald, Countess of Ormonde, who is said to have frequently issued from the castle at the head of her armed retainers, to ravage the property of such of the neighbouring families as she deemed to be her enemies. In 1619, Jas. I. constituted this place a manor, and granted to its lord, Richard, third Viscount Mountgarret, the privilege of holding two fairs. During the Whiteboy disturbances, the castle was appropriated as a barrack for the use of the military stationed in the district. The town is situated on the road from Kilkenny to Durrow, and on the river Nore, over which is a good stone bridge of 10 arches; it consists of one principal street, with several smaller streets diverging from it, and contains about 300 houses. Fairs are held on Feb. 20th, April 20th, June 22nd, Sept. 4th, Oct. 20th, and Dec. 10th; and additional fairs, recently established, are held on Jan. 11th, March 14th, May 9th, and July 22nd. Here is a station of the constabulary police; a manor court is held occasionally, and petty sessions irregularly. The parish comprises 5268 statute acres, as applotted under the tithe act; there is a quarry of hard black limestone. In the immediate vicinity of the town is Ballyragget Lodge, formerly the seat of the Butlers of Ballyragget, which family became extinct on the demise of the late Rt. Rev. Dr. J. Butler, R. C. Archbishop of Cashel. The mansion is a fine building, and in the demesne are the remains of Ballyragget castle, in a good state of preservation. The parish is in the diocese of Ossory; the rectory is impropriate in the Marquess of Ormonde, and the vicarage is part of the union of Odogh. The tithes amount to £190, of which £120 is payable to the impropriator, and £70 to the vicar. In the R. C. divisions it is the head of a union or district, which comprises the parishes of Ballyragget, Ballyouskill, Rosconnel, and Attanagh, and parts of those of Durrow, Abbeyleix, Freshford, Burnchurch, and Kilmocar; and contains two chapels, one at Ballyragget and one at Attanagh. There are eight pay schools and a Sunday school in the parish.

BALLYRASHANE, or ST. JOHN'S-TOWN, a parish, partly in the barony of LOWER DUNLUCE, county of ANTRIM, but chiefly in the north-east liberties of COLERAINE, county of LONDONDERRY, and province of ULSTER, 3 miles (N. E.) from Coleraine; containing 2851 inhabitants. This parish is situated on the road from Coleraine to Ballycastle, and comprises, according to the Ordnance survey, 6360¾ statute acres, of which 2689 are in the county of Antrim, and the remainder in the county of Londonderry. The greater portion of the land is fertile and in a high state of cultivation; wheat and barley have been introduced since the year 1829, and are raised with great success. There are detached portions of bog, affording a good supply of fuel. Vast quantities of basalt are raised; and in a geological point of view the parish is very interesting, containing beautiful specimens of amorphous, columnar, and divaricated basalt, which are found here in all their varieties, accompanied with chalcedony, opal, zeolite, and other fossils; it abounds also with botanical specimens of considerable interest. Brookhall, the seat of S. Boyce, Esq., is in this parish. The inhabitants are principally employed in the weaving of linen cloth; and there are some paper-mills for brown and fancy papers, affording employment to about 30 persons. The living is a rectory, in the diocese of Connor, and in the patronage of the Bishop: the tithes amount to £350. The church is a plain small edifice, in the later English style, erected by aid of a grant of £900 from the late Board of First Fruits, in 1826. The glebe-house, nearly adjoining it, was built in 1828: there is no glebe. In the R. C. divisions the parish forms part of the union or district of Coleraine. There are two places of worship for Presbyterians in connection with the Synod of Ulster; one at Kirkstown of the first class, and the other at Ballywatt of the third class. The male and female parochial schools at Lisnarick are supported by the rector, who also contributes annually to the support of a school at Ballyrack; at Ballyvelton is also a school, and there are two private pay schools and two Sunday schools. At Revellagh are the ruins of a castle and fort. There are also some extensive artificial caverns at Ballyvarten, Island Effrick, and Ballynock; the first has four rooms or cells, 5 feet high and 2½ feet wide, having the sides formed of unhewn stones and the roof of large flat stones.

BALLYROAN, a parish, in the barony of CULLINAGH, QUEEN'S county, and province of LEINSTER, 2½ miles (N. E.) from Abbeyleix, on the road from Monastereven to Durrow; containing 3544 inhabitants, of which number, 714 are in the village. It comprises 8625 statute acres, as applotted under the tithe act, and contains several high hills, the largest of which, Cullinagh, gives name to the barony. The village, which lies low, contains 132 houses; it is a constabulary police station, and has a patent for a market, but no market is held. Fairs are held on Jan. 6th, April 2nd, May 15th, the first Wednesday in July (O. S.), Aug. 15th, and the second Wednesday in Nov. (O. S.), chiefly for cattle and pigs. At Cullinagh are some cotton-mills and a boulting-mill, both badly supplied with water; in the former about 50 persons are employed, of whom two-thirds are children. But the inhabitants are chiefly engaged in agriculture: the soil consists of a rich loam and a deep black earth, and is equally productive under tillage and in dairy husbandry. The system of agriculture is improving; there is but a small tract of bog, not more than sufficient to supply the inhabitants with fuel. The dairy lands are sometimes appropriated to the fattening of black cattle. Limestone is quarried principally for burning; and grit flagstone is found in the mountains. A thin stratum of coal has been discovered, but has not been worked, though there is near it a mineral vein; much of the same kind of coal is found in the mountain of Cullinagh, where works were commenced but have been discontinued some years. The chief seats are Blandsfort, the residence of J. T. Bland, Esq., in whose family it has continued since 1715; and Rockbrook, of L. Flood, Esq. The living is a rectory and vicarage, in the diocese of Leighlin, and in the patronage of the Crown: the tithes amount to £415. 7. 8½. The church is a neat plain edifice in good repair. There is neither glebe-house nor glebe. In the R. C. divisions the parish is in the union or district of Abbeyleix; the chapel is a spacious edifice. In the village is a school endowed with lands in Cappaloughlan, bequeathed by Alderman Preston: the school-house is a large slated building, erected at an expense of £500; about 20 boys receive a classical and English education under a master, whose stipend is £55 per annum, each boy paying £4 yearly in addition. There are also a scriptural and a national school, in which are about 80 boys and 50 girls. Sir Jonah Barrington, late Judge of the High Court of Admiralty, and author of "Personal Sketches of His Own Times," and other works relating to Ireland, resided at Cullinagh.

BALLYROBERT, a grange, in the parish of TEMPLEPATRICK, barony of LOWER BELFAST, county of ANTRIM, and province of ULSTER, 2 miles (S.) from Ballyclare: the population is returned with the parish. It is situated on the roads from Carrickfergus to Ballywater and Doagh, and comprises, according to the Ordnance survey, 883½ statute acres.

BALLYRONAN, or PORTBALLYRON, a village, in the district of Wood's-chapel, barony of LOUGHINSHOLIN, county of LONDONDERRY, and province of ULSTER, 3 miles (S. E.) from Magherafelt, on the western shore of Lough Neagh. This village was founded by the late D. Gaussen, who, in 1788, built a forge here for manufacturing spades, &c., and soon afterwards erected stores, which led to the building of quays and the formation of a port, which has greatly benefited the surrounding country. A large distillery was erected in 1824, and a brewery in 1830, by Messrs. Gaussen and Sons. Vessels of about 50 tons' burden ply regularly between this port and Belfast and Newry, exporting wheat, fruit, spirits, ale, and freestone, and bringing back barley, timber, slate, iron, wine, groceries, &c. This village is well situated for trade, as, besides being on Lough Neagh, several roads diverge from it, and the projected railroad from Coleraine to Armagh will pass near it. It is on the estate of the Salters' Company, of London, which is held by the Marquess of Londonderry and Sir Robert Bateson, Bart., under a lease which will expire about 1852, when the company intend to make extensive improvements. Here is a public school, principally supported by the lessees of the estate, Mrs. Gaussen, sen., and D. Gaussen, Esq., one of the proprietors of the village. Near it are the ruins of Salterstown castle and a cromlech.

BALLYSADERE, or BALLASODARE, a parish, partly in the barony of LENEY, but chiefly in that of TIRAGHRILL, county of SLIGO, and province of CONNAUGHT, comprising the post-town of Collooney and the villages of Ballydryhed and Tubberscanavin (all of which are separately described); and containing 7562 inhabitants, of which number, 546 are in the village. It is situated on the road from Boyle to Sligo, and on the Unshion or Ballysadere river, which issues from Lough Arrow, near Boyle, and is here joined by the Coolaney river; and after falling over several ledges of rocks, the last of which is ten feet in height, empties itself into an arm of the sea, called Ballysadere channel. St. Fechin founded a monastery here towards the middle of the seventh century, which was richly endowed: in 1179 it was burnt by the men of Moylisha and Moylterary, and in 1188 was again destroyed by fire, but was restored and existed until the general dissolution, when a lease of it was granted, in the 30th of Eliz., for 21 years, to Bryan Fitz-William, at an annual rent of £2. 13. 4.: the remains are situated above the waterfalls, and consist merely of the outer walls, which are richly clothed with ivy. St. Fechin also founded an abbey at Kilnemanagh, which existed till the general suppression, when it was granted to Richard, Earl of Clanricarde; there are yet some remains. The parish comprises 9999 statute acres, as applotted under the tithe act: between one-third and one-half of it is waste land and bog; there is little woodland, except from 600 to 700 acres on the Markree estate. The land under cultivation is generally good, but the old system of tillage, though gradually improving, is still mostly practised. There are quarries of excellent limestone, much used for building, and some of it is also hewn into mantel-pieces and other ornamental parts of masonry; and a lead mine, yielding also a considerable proportion of silver, was worked a few years since, but has been abandoned. Near it are some chalybeate springs, not used. The village of Ballysadere, which comprises about 45 houses, is a place of some little business, and has a penny post. The falls on the river afford favourable sites, and a never-failing supply of water for mills: there is a large corn-mill, belonging to Mr. Sim, worked by two wheels of 36-horse power, and employing 25 persons; and another on a large scale, with the most approved machinery, was built by Mr. Culbertson in 1835, having two water-wheels of 70-horse power, and employing 20 persons; there are also some smaller corn-mills, and a large bleach-mill and green. Vessels of about 100 tons' burden come up the channel for the exportation of corn and meal: a small pier has been built, and it is in contemplation to erect one on a more extensive scale. Fairs are held at the village on Feb. 8th, May 30th, July 11th, Aug. 4th, Oct. 24th, Nov. 12th, and Dec. 15th; and besides those held at Collooney and Tubberscanavin (which are enumerated in the accounts of those places), the largest fair for horses in the county is held at Carricknagatt, on Feb. 1st. Here is a station of the constabulary police. Petty sessions are held every alternate Thursday at Collooney; and a manorial court is occasionally held there, under the seneschal. Markree, the seat of E. J. Cooper, Esq., is a handsome and modern castellated building, situated in the centre of an extensive demesne clothed with wood and spreading into verdant lawns, through which the Unshion pursues a winding course: the gateways leading into the demesne are handsome structures, of ancient English architecture, and in the grounds there is a very excellent observatory. The other seats are Cloonamahon, that of J. Meredith, Esq.; the Cottage, of R. Culbertson, jun., Esq.; Ballysadere House, of J. Reed, Esq.; and Ballysadere Villa, of A. Sim, Esq.

The living is a vicarage, in the diocese of Achonry, constituting the corps of the prebend of Ballysadere, in the patronage of the Bishop: the rectory is impropriate in Matthew Baker, Esq.: the tithes amount to £461. 10. 9½., payable in moieties to the impropriator and the incumbent. The church, situated at Collooney, is a handsome building, in the ancient English style of architecture, and contains some good monuments, of which one to the memory of the late Mrs. Cooper, executed at Florence, is a fine piece of sculpture; it was enlarged in 1834, by aid of a gift of £700 from the Ecclesiastical Commissioners, and donations of £800 from Mr. Cooper and £50 from Major O'Hara. The glebe-house was built by aid of a gift of £400 and a loan of £400, in 1819, from the late Board of First Fruits: the glebe comprises 20 acres. In the R. C. divisions this parish is the head of a union or district, called Collooney, comprising also the parish of Kilvarnet, and containing three chapels, situated respectively at Collooney and Currownagh, in Ballysadere, and the third in Kilvarnet. There are seven schools, two of which, at Ballysadere and Collooney, were built and are supported by Mr. Cooper; also five private pay schools and Sunday schools. On an eminence immediately over the harbour is an ancient burial-ground of considerable extent, still used, in which are the remains of a church.

BALLYSAX, a parish, partly in the barony of West Ophaly, but chiefly in that of East Ophaly, county of Kildare, and province of Leinster, 2¾ miles (S. W. by W.) from Kilcullen-Bridge; containing 996 inhabitants. This parish is situated within a mile of the great southern road from Dublin to Cork, and comprises 4995 statute acres, as applotted under the tithe act, and valued at £2817 per annum. The greater portion is under tillage, and the remainder, with the exception of a large tract of bog and waste, is meadow and pasture; the soil is fertile, and the system of agriculture improved. Adjoining the parish is the celebrated race-course called the Curragh; and within its limits is Ballysax House, the elegant seat of G. O'Kelly, Esq. On the Curragh are also Cobourg Lodge, the residence of J. Maher, Esq.; Brownstone House, of G. Knox, Esq.; Ballyfair House, occupied during the races by His Excellency the Lord-Lieutenant; Lark Lodge, of W. Disney, Esq.; Maddenstown House, of W. Kelly, Esq.; Turf Lodge, of R. Hunter, Esq.; Jockey Hall, of G. Watts, Esq.; Athgarvon Lodge, of the Hon. F. Ponsonby; and Maddenstown, of Terence Kelly, Esq. A fair is held at the French Furze on July 26th. The living is a rectory and vicarage, in the diocese of Kildare, and in the patronage of the Crown: the tithes amount to £186. The church, a neat edifice, with a square embattled tower crowned with pinnacles, was erected by aid of a loan from the late Board of First Fruits, in 1826; and the Ecclesiastical Commissioners have lately granted £249 for its repair. There is a glebe-house, with a glebe comprising 19*a.* 2*r.* In the R. C. divisions the parish forms part of the union or district of Sancroft. A school is supported by local subscription, aided by an endowment bequeathed by the late Rev. William Tew; and there is also a school in connection with the National Board. In these about 60 boys and 40 girls are instructed; and there is a pay school, in which are 20 boys and 20 girls. The Rev. W. Tew also bequeathed £50 in the 3½ per cent. for the benefit of the poor.

BALLYSCADANE, a parish, in the barony of Costlea, county of Limerick, and province of Munster, 4 miles (S. E. by S.) from Hospital. It is situated on the road from Galbally to Hospital, and comprises 893 statute acres, as applotted under the tithe act: the land is in general of good quality, and chiefly in pasture. Nearly in the centre of the parish is Ryves Castle, the residence of P. Ryan, Esq.; and at no great distance is Scarteen, the property also of Mr. Ryan, but at present unoccupied. It is a rectory, in the diocese of Emly, united from time immemorial to the entire rectory of Glanbane, together constituting the corps of the deanery of Emly, in the patronage of the Crown: the tithes amount to £40. 12. 6., and of the whole union to £88. 4. The lands of the deanery, called the mensal lands of Gurteen, comprise 179*a.* 2*r.* 15*p.*, statute measure, let on lease at £92. 6. 1½. per annum, with an annual renewal fine of £27. 13. 10¼.: the entire income of the deanery, as returned by the Commissioners of Ecclesiastical Inquiry, amounts to £225. 16. 10. per annum. The church has long since fallen into decay: in the churchyard, which is within the demesne of Ryves Castle, is a handsome monumental obelisk to the family of Ryan. There is no glebe-house in either parish; the glebe comprises 4*a.* 2*r.* 36*p.*, and there is also a glebe of 7 acres in the adjoining parish of Galbally. In the R. C. divisions this parish forms part of the union or district of Emly.

BALLYSCULLION, a grange, in the barony of Toome, county of Antrim, and province of Ulster, 4 miles (N. W.) from Randalstown; containing 3351 inhabitants. This place, which is an extra-parochial district, never having paid either church cess or tithe, is situated on the road from Portglenone to Antrim, and is bounded on the north-west by the river Bann; it comprises, according to the Ordnance survey, 4279¼ statute acres. There is no provision for the cure of souls; the members of the Established Church attend divine service in the contiguous parish of Duneane, in the diocese of Connor. In the R. C. divisions it forms part of the union or district of Ballyscullion, in the diocese of Derry; the chapel is a small plain building; there is also a place of worship for Presbyterians.

BALLYSCULLION, a parish, partly in the barony of Upper Toome, county of Antrim, but chiefly in that of Loughinsholin, county of Londonderry, and province of Ulster; containing, with the post-town of Bellaghy, 6453 inhabitants. This parish, which is intersected by the roads leading respectively from Castle-Dawson to Portglenone, and from Maghera to Bellaghy, comprises, according to the Ordnance survey, 12,750¼ statute acres, of which 10,617¼ are in the county of Londonderry, 2406 are part of Lough Beg, and 72¾ part of the river Bann, which here forms the boundary of the parish, barony, and county. On the plantation of Ulster, these lands were granted by Jas. I. to the Irish Society, and by them transferred to the Vintners' Company of London, who founded the castle and town of Bellaghy, described under its own head. At a very early period a monastery was founded on an island in Lough Beg, about two miles from the shore, then called Ynis Teda, but now Church island, from the parish church having been subsequently erected there: this establishment continued to flourish till the dissolution, and some of the lands which belonged to it are still tithe-free. Two townlands in the parish belong to the see of Derry, and the remainder has been leased in perpetuity by the Vintners' Company to the Marquess of Lothian, the Earl of Clancarty, Lord Strafford, and Sir Thomas Pakenham. There are from 400 to 450 acres of bog, part of which in summer affords coarse pasturage for cattle; a portion of it lying remote from the Bann is of a blackish colour, and capable of cultivation for rye and potatoes; the other part, which from its white colour is called "flour bog," is quite incapable of cultivation till it has been cut away for fuel, when the subsoil appears, varying from 5 to 10 feet in depth. The land is fertile, and under the auspices of the North-West Agricultural Society, of which a branch has been established here, is generally in an excellent state of cultivation; mangel-wurzel, rape, turnips, and other green crops, are being introduced with success. There are indications of coal in several parts, particularly on the Castle-Dawson estate; but there is no prospect of their being explored or worked while the extensive bogs afford so plentiful a supply of fuel. Of the numerous seats the principal are Castle-Dawson, the seat of the Right Hon. G. R. Dawson; Bellaghy Castle, the residence of J. Hill, Esq.; Bellaghy House, of H. B. Hunter, Esq.; Fairview, of R. Henry, Esq.; and Rowensgift, of A. Leckey, Esq. The splendid palace built here by the Earl of Bristol, when Bishop of Derry, one of the most magnificent in the country, was scarcely finished at his Lordship's decease, and was soon after taken down and the materials sold: the only entire portion that has been preserved is the beautiful portico, which was purchased by Dr. Alexander, Bishop of Down and Connor, who presented it to the parish of St. George, Belfast, as an ornament to that church. A small portion of the domestics' apartments and a fragment of one of the picture galleries are all that remain. There are some extensive cotton-mills at Castle-Dawson, also flour, corn, and flax-mills; and about a mile above the town is a small bleach-green. Fairs for cattle, sheep, and pigs are held at Bellaghy on the first Monday in every month; and a manorial court is held monthly, for the recovery of debts not exceeding £2.

The living is a rectory, in the diocese of Derry, and in the patronage of the Bishop: the tithes amount to £350. The church, situated in Bellaghy, is a large and handsome edifice, erected in 1794 on the site of a former church built in 1625: it is in the early English style, with a lofty and beautiful octagonal spire erected at the expense of the Earl of Bristol, and is about to be enlarged by the addition of a north aisle. There is a chapel at Castle-Dawson belonging to the Dawson family, by whom it was built and endowed; it is open to the inhabitants. The glebe-house is about a quarter of a mile from the town on a glebe comprising 70 acres; and there is also a glebe of 84 acres at Moneystachan, in the parish of Tamlaght-O'Crilly, all arable land. In the R. C. divisions this parish comprehends the grange of Ballyscullion, in the diocese of Connor, in which union are two chapels, one at Bellaghy and the other in the grange. At Ballaghy are places of worship for Presbyterians in connection with the Synod of Ulster, Methodists, and Seceders. There is a male and female parochial school, aided by annual donations from the rector and the proprietors of the Bellaghy estate, who built the school-house; and there are five other schools, which afford instruction to about 300 boys and 240 girls; also three private schools, in which are about 100 boys and 20 girls. Here is a dispensary conducted on the most approved plan; and the proprietors of the Bellaghy estate annually distribute blankets and clothes among the poor. The ruins of the old church on Ynis Teda, or Church island, are extensive and highly interesting; and close to them a square tower surmounted by a lofty octangular spire of hewn freestone was erected by the Earl of Bristol, which is a beautiful object in the landscape. A large mis-shapen stone, called Clogh O'Neill, is pointed out as an object of interest; and not far distant is a rock basin, or holy stone, to which numbers annually resort in the hope of deriving benefit from the efficacy of the water in healing diseases.

BALLYSCULLOGUE.—See HORTLAND.

BALLYSEEDY, a parish, in the barony of TRUGHENACKMY, county of KERRY, and province of MUNSTER, 4½ miles (S. E. by S.) from Tralee; containing 1164 inhabitants. This parish is situated on the river Mang or Maine, and on the mail coach road from Tralee to Killarney; it comprises 3509 statute acres, as applotted under the tithe act, and valued at £2640 per annum, and there are 92 acres exempt from tithe. The land is mostly under tillage; the principal crop is oats. Towards the west the parish includes a portion of the Slievemish mountains; the land there is chiefly coarse mountain pasture, and there is a considerable portion of light bog; about 500 acres of bog and mountain have been planted within the last two or three years. Limestone abounds and is extensively used for manure. Ballyseedy House, the handsome residence of Sir E. Denny, Bart., is situated in an extensive and richly wooded demesne; and at Ballyseedy is the residence of the Rev. Mr. Nash, pleasantly situated on an eminence commanding a fine view of the country towards the south and east. The river Mang or Maine has its rise in the neighbouring mountains, and empties itself into Castlemaine bay; it abounds with excellent trout. On the banks of a small river that flows through the parish and falls into Tralee bay is a large flour-mill. The living is a vicarage, in the diocese of Ardfert and Aghadoe, and in the patronage of Arthur Blennerhasset, Esq., in whom the rectory is impropriate: the tithes amount to £120, and are payable in equal portions to the impropriator and the vicar. There is neither church, glebe-house, nor glebe, but divine service is performed in the school-house at Farmer's-Bridge. The ruins of the old church, to which a burial-ground is attached, are in the demesne of Ballyseedy. In the R. C. divisions this parish forms part of the union or district of Ballymac-Elligott. The Wesleyan Methodists assemble for divine worship in a private house. A neat school-house has been lately erected at the village of Farmer's-Bridge, under the auspices of the Rev. A. B. Rowan, of Belmont; it was built and is supported by subscription: there is also a school under the superintendence of the R. C. clergyman; in these schools about 100 children are educated.

BALLYSHANNON, a sea-port, market, and post-town (formerly a parliamentary borough), partly in the parish of INNISMACSAINT, but chiefly in that of KILBARRON, barony of TYRHUGH, county of DONEGAL, and province of ULSTER, 35 miles (S. W.) from Lifford, and 102 miles (N. W.) from Dublin; containing 3775 inhabitants, of which number, 1390 are in the Purt. In remote ages this town was called *Athseanaigh*, and the chieftains of Tyrconnell had a castle, here in which Hugh O'Donnell, prince of Tyrconnell, received his son, Hugh Roe, after his escape from the castle of Dublin, in 1592. In 1597 the neighbourhood was the scene of the most important military operations of that period. An English force, consisting of 22 regiments of infantry and 10 of cavalry, under the command of Sir Conyers Clifford, crossed the Erne by a ford, although vigorously opposed by O'Donnell's troops, and succeeded in establishing their head-quarters at the monastery of Asharouagh. Here they received heavy ordnance from Galway by sea, and laid close siege to the castle of Ballyshannon, but met with an unexpectedly strong resistance, and many of their best officers and men were killed or wounded. After continuing the siege for five days, the English were compelled to make a precipitate retreat, closely pursued by O'Donnell and his allies, and being unable to cross the Erne at the ford by which they advanced, they tried another that was seldom attempted, where many were killed or drowned, and thus one of the first expeditions into this long independent territory terminated very disastrously. On the grant by Jas. I. of the earldom and territory of Tyrconnell to Rory O'Donnell, in 1603, he reserved the castle of Ballyshannon and 1000 circumjacent acres. The castle was taken in 1652 by the Earl of Clanricarde.

This town is situated at the head of the harbour of the same name, at the mouth of the river Erne, which is here crossed by a bridge of fourteen arches, and divides the town into two parts; that on the south side, in the parish of Innismacsaint, being called the Purt of Ballyshannon. It comprises three streets and the suburb of the Purt, and in 1831 contained 689 houses, of which 287 were in the parish of Innismacsaint. Here is an artillery barrack for about 40 men, with stabling for 40 horses. A distillery is carried on, manufacturing above 100,000 gallons of whiskey annually, and which increased its trade one-third in 1835; and there is a large brewery. The imports are timber, coal, slate, rock salt, bark, iron, earthenware, and grocery; and the exports are grain, and fresh, salted and pickled salmon. There is a fine salmon fishery in the river Erne, which produces from 60 to 80 tons annually. Here is a small custom-house. The town is favourably situated for commerce and manufacturers, having a large population, and a fertile country around it: it is within four miles of Lough Erne, which embraces an inland navigation of more than fifty miles through the richest part of Ireland, and for purposes of manufacture the river Erne, in a course of four miles, affords numerous sites for mills, having a succession of falls amounting to 140 feet. The surrounding country contains much mineral wealth; a rich mine of zinc has been lately discovered at the Abbey, a lead mine near Bandoran, and rich specimens of copper in the vicinity. The harbour, the entrance to which was formerly obstructed by a bar, has been rendered accessible to vessels of 250 tons' burden. This great improvement, which will probably render the place a respectable port, was made at the sole expense of Col. Conolly, who has formally resigned any claim on the loan of £5000 sanctioned by the Commissioners of Public Works in furtherance of the undertaking, and in an exemplary manner has promoted to a great extent the making of roads and other improvements throughout the entire district. The navigation of the river is stopped abruptly by a grand cascade called the Fall, where the whole body of water descending from Lough Erne, in a stream about 150 yards wide, falls about 16 feet with a tremendous roar down a steep cliff into a basin forming the head of the harbour. This cascade is seen to most advantage in winter, when the river is swollen by rains, and at the recess of the tide the noise of the descending water may be heard many miles off. Plans have been suggested for opening a communication with Lough Erne; among others it has been lately proposed to avoid the falls, not by cutting a canal, but by forming a rail-road to Belleek, which, however, has not been yet carried into effect. The market is held in the market-house on Tuesday and Saturday, for potatoes, pigs, oats, oatmeal, &c.; and fairs are held on the 2nd of every month, except September, when it is held on the 18th. A branch of the Provincial Bank of Ireland has been established, and a chief constabulary police force stationed here.

The town was incorporated by a charter of Jas. I., dated March 23rd, 1613; and the corporation was entitled "the Portreeve, Free Burgesses, and Commonalty of the Town of Ballyshannon." From the time of its incorporation till the Union, when it was disfranchised, it returned two members to the Irish parliament, and the £15,000 compensation was paid to the Earl of Belmore. A court of record was created under the charter, but has fallen into disuse. A seneschal's court is held once in three weeks under the lord of the manor, having jurisdiction to the amount of 40*s.*; it was established by charter of Jas. I., dated April 9th, 1622, granting large possessions to Henry Folliott, Baron of Ballyshannon. Petty sessions also are held generally once a fortnight. The gentlemen's seats in the vicinity are enumerated in the articles on Kilbarron and Innismacsaint, *which see.* On an eminence called Mullinashee, adjoining the town, stands the parish church of Kilbarron; and there are two R. C. chapels, two places of worship for Methodists, and one for Presbyterians. There are also three public schools, and a dispensary. A small portion of the ruins of the once celebrated castle of the O'Donnells, Earls of Tyrconnell, is in the town; and near to it, on the road to Belleek, are a few vestiges of the ancient church of Sminver.

BALLYSHEEHAN, a parish, in the barony of MIDDLETHIRD, county of TIPPERARY, and province of MUNSTER, 3 miles (N.) from Cashel; containing 3034 inhabitants. It is situated on the mail coach road from Dublin, by way of Cashel, to Cork, and comprises 8678 statute acres, of which 3657 are applotted under the tithe act and valued at £7118 per annum. There are about 150 acres of bog, producing a valuable supply of fuel, and 50 acres of woodland; the remainder is arable and pasture. New Park, the handsome seat of Matthew Pennefather, Esq., is pleasantly situated in a well-planted demesne of 960 statute acres; and Dually is the seat of J. Scully, Esq. Fairs are held on May 6th, Aug. 15th, and Dec. 5th; and a constabulary police force is stationed here. The living is a vicarage, in the diocese of Cashel, and in the patronage of the Archbishop; the rectory is impropriate in S. Cooper, Esq. The tithes amount to £415. 7. 8¼., of which £265. 7. 8¼. is payable to the impropriator, and £150 to the vicar. There is neither church, glebe-house, nor glebe; the members of the Established Church attend divine service at Cashel and Ardmoyle. In the R. C. divisions this parish forms part of the union or district of Boherlahan; the chapel is a neat modern building. There are three pay schools, in which are about 140 boys and 90 girls. Ballytarsney Castle, a lofty square tower, is said to have been built by a person named Hacket, who, according to tradition, was hanged by one of Cromwell's generals, who had gained possession of it by treachery.

BALLYSHONBOY.—See KILQUANE, county of LIMERICK.

BALLYSONAN, a parish, partly in the barony of EAST OPHALY, but chiefly in that of WEST OPHALY, county of KILDARE, and province of LEINSTER, 4½ miles (S. W.) from Kilcullen; containing 472 inhabitants. It is situated on the mail coach road from Dublin, by way of Cashel, to Cork, and comprises 2602 statute acres, as applotted under the tithe act, and principally under tillage. Ballysonan House is the residence of T. Kennedy, Esq. The living is a rectory and vicarage, in the diocese of Kildare, constituting the corps of the prebend of Ballysonan in the cathedral of Kildare, and united by act of council, in 1795, to the rectory of Kilrush, forming the union of Ballysonan, in the alternate patronage of the Crown and the Bishop; the tithes amount to £209, and of the entire benefice to £430. 9. 10. The church, a plain structure, was built in 1796 by aid of a gift of £500 from the late Board of First Fruits, and the Ecclesiastical Commissioners have lately granted £196 for its repair. The glebe contains 25*a.* 2*r.* 20*p.*, but there is no glebe-house. In the R. C. divisions this parish forms part of the union or district of Sancroft. There is a school of 30 boys and 30 girls. Dame Annesley bequeathed the lands of Carrighill, in this parish, for the purpose of establishing and supporting a school, but the bequest has not been appropriated to that use; the rector is now making efforts to render it available.

BALLYSPILLANE, a parish, in the barony of BARRYMORE, county of CORK, and province of MUNSTER, 2 miles (N. W.) from Midleton; containing 577 inhabitants. This parish comprises 2076 statute acres, as applotted under the tithe act and valued at £1263 per annum: it is chiefly under tillage, with but little waste land; the northern part is mountainous, and the soil shallow and but indifferently productive. The living is a vicarage, in the diocese of Cloyne, and prior to the collation of the present incumbent was part of the union of Midleton and corps of the treasurership in the cathedral of Cloyne, but is now a distinct benefice, in the patronage of the Bishop; the rectory is impropriate in G. Lukey, Esq., of Midleton. The tithes amount to £228, payable in moieties to the impropriator and the vicar. There is neither church, glebe, nor glebe-house. In the R. C. divisions the parish forms part of the union or district of Midleton. There are some ruins of the parochial church.

BALLYSUMAGHAN, a parish, in the barony of TIRAGHRILL, county of SLIGO, and province of CONNAUGHT, 4 miles (E. by S.) from Collooney; containing 1815 inhabitants. This parish is situated on the road from Sligo to Drumsna, by way of Ballyfarnon, on the confines of the county; and comprises 2829 statute acres, as applotted under the tithe act. The soil is principally a good deep loam, but the state of agriculture, though much improved within the last twenty years, is still very low; there is not much waste land, but a large tract of bog affording a good supply of fuel. There are several quarries of stone, principally limestone of a very fine description, used for building and for burning into lime. The gentlemen's seats are Castle Neynoe, that of Col. W. B. Neynoe, and Doomalla, of Owen Phibbs, Esq. The French army, after the battle of Collooney, passed close to this place, and encamped the same night within a quarter of a mile from it. It is a vicarage, in the diocese of Elphin, and forms part of the union of Boyle; the rectory is partly impropriate in Viscount Lorton, and partly appropriate to the prebend of Kilmacallane in the cathedral church of Elphin. The tithes amount to £73. 16. 11., of which one-half is payable to the prebendary. The church is a neat building, erected about six years since on a site in the demesne of Castle Neynoe, given by Col. Neynoe; and the Ecclesiastical Commissioners have lately granted £181 for its repair: it is resorted to by the inhabitants of Ballysumaghan, Kilróss, and Ballynakill, three of the parishes which form the union. Near to it is the glebe, but there is no glebe-house at present. In the R. C. divisions it is included in the union or district of Sowey. There is a school in the village of Castle Neynoe, and another at Bloomfield, in which about 100 boys and 90 girls are taught. A Sunday school is held in the church, and it is in contemplation to establish a parochial school: there is also a hedge school, in which are about 40 boys and 30 girls. Within the parish are several Danish forts; and in the burial-ground of Culticloghan are the remains of an old church. Numerous fossils are found in the limestone quarries.

BALLYTANKARD.—See TANKARDSTOWN.

BALLYTARSNEY, a parish, in the barony of IVERK, county of KILKENNY, and province of LEINSTER, 6½ miles (E. S. E.) from Carrick-on-Suir: the population is returned with the parish of Poleroan. This parish is situated on the road from Waterford to Limerick, and is about five British furlongs in length and breadth, comprising 1116 statute acres. It is a rectory and vicarage, in the diocese of Ossory, and forms part of the union of Clonmore: the tithes amount to £81. 14. 8½. In the R. C. divisions it forms part of the union or district of Moncoin. Here are the remains of a square fort, which appears to have been of considerable strength.

BALLYTOBIN, a parish, in the barony of KELLS, county of KILKENNY, and province of LEINSTER, 4 miles (S. E.) from Callan; containing 759 inhabitants. It is situated on the road from Callan to Carrick-on-Suir, and comprises 2364 statute acres, as applotted under the tithe act. Ballytobin House, the seat of Abraham Whyte Baker, Esq., is a place of considerable antiquity, and is situated in a fine demesne abounding with timber of aged growth, with a deer park attached; there is a sycamore tree of very large dimensions near the house. On this estate also is Wellington (formerly called Cahirliske), occupied by J. W. Pope, Esq. Here is a station of the constabulary police. It is a rectory and vicarage, in the diocese of Ossory, and forms part of the union of Kells: the tithes amount to £150. The church is a neat modern edifice with a spire, built by aid of a gift of £300 from the late Board of First Fruits, in 1829, and of £400 from A. W. Baker, Esq., who also allows £10 per ann. to the parish clerk. In the R. C.

divisions it is part of the union or district of Donemagan. There are two private schools, in which are about 40 boys and 20 girls.

BALLYTORE, a post-town, in the parish of TIMOLIN, barony of NARRAGH and RHEBAN EAST, county of KILDARE, and province of LEINSTER, 13 miles (S. S. W.) from Naas, and 28½ miles (S. W. by S.) from Dublin; containing 141 houses and 933 inhabitants. This town, which is situated on the river Griese and on the mail coach road from Dublin to Carlow, was, in 1798, taken by the insurgents, in whose possession it remained two days, and by whom it was set on fire. It is conspicuous for the neatness and regularity of its appearance, and is principally inhabited by members of the Society of Friends; it has obtained considerable celebrity from its school, originally established in 1726, by Abraham Shackleton, a member of that society, and in which the celebrated Edmund Burke received the rudiments of his education. Ballytore House is the residence of T. R. Whitty, Esq. Fairs are held on March 10th, Aug. 15th, and Nov. 30th. A constabulary police force has been stationed in the town. There is a place of worship for the Society of Friends, established in 1707; a Lancasterian school is supported partly by subscription and partly by weekly payments from the children; and here are a dispensary and a savings' bank. Mary Leadbeater, daughter of Mr. Richard Shackleton, and author of "Cottage Dialogues" and other works calculated to improve the social condition of the Irish peasantry, was a native of this place.—See TIMOLIN.

BALLYTRAIN, a village, in the parish of AUGHNAMULLEN, barony of CREMORNE, county of MONAGHAN, and province of ULSTER, 5 miles (S.) from Ballibay, on the old road to Shercock; containing 44 houses and 220 inhabitants. It is a station of the constabulary police; and fairs, chiefly for pigs, cattle, and sheep, are held on Feb. 1st, March 17th, May 1st, June 11th, Aug. 1st, Sept. 29th, Nov. 1st, and Dec. 23rd. In 1834, a R. C. chapel was built, at an expense of £100. The lake of Ballytrain is an extensive sheet of water supplying several mills, particularly one belonging to R. A. Minnett, Esq. Near the village is Lake View, the residence of the Rev. E. Mayne. In the vicinity are several forts, one of which is of great extent and commands a view of some picturesque scenery, embracing twelve lakes.—See AUGHNAMULLEN.

BALLYTRUSTIN, a parish, in the barony of ARDES, county of DOWN, and province of ULSTER, 1 mile (S. E.) from Portaferry; containing 735 inhabitants. This parish, which is not noticed in the Down survey, is situated on the eastern coast; it comprises, according to the Ordnance survey, including detached portions, 1681¾ statute acres. The soil is fertile, and the lands are all in an excellent state of cultivation, producing abundant crops. It is a vicarage, in the diocese of Down, and is part of the union of Ballyphilip and corps of the chancellorship of Down; the rectory is impropriate in John Echlin, Esq. The tithes amount to £190. 4. 2½. of which £117. 14. 5. is payable to the impropriator, and £72. 9. 9½. to the vicar. There are some remains of the ancient church, and the churchyard is the chief burial-place of the R. C. parishioners. In the R. C. divisions it forms part of each of the unions or districts of Lower and Upper Ardes. At Kerney is a school of 100 boys and 80 girls, aided by subscription and an annual donation of £8 from Dr. Blacker, on whose estate the school-house was erected by a grant of £100 from the Lord-Lieutenant's fund. At Ballyfounder is a very large rath, nearly perfect.

BALLYVALDEN, a parish, in the barony of BALLAGHKEEN, county of WEXFORD, and province of LEINSTER, 12½ miles (S. by W.) from Gorey; containing 1379 inhabitants. It is situated near the eastern coast, and comprises 2338 statute acres, as applotted under the tithe act. The living is a vicarage, in the diocese of Ferns, held with the impropriate curacies of Kilmuckridge and Millenagh; and in the patronage of the Bishop; the rectory is impropriate in the Earl of Portsmouth. The tithes amount to £179. 7. 9., of which £112. 6. 2½. is payable to the impropriator, and £67. 1. 6½. to the vicar. The church of the union is at Kilmuckridge. In the R. C. divisions the parish forms part of the union or district of Blackwater. There are three hedge schools, in which about 170 children are educated.

BALLYVALLOO, a parish, in the barony of BALLAGHKEEN, county of WEXFORD, and province of LEINSTER, 6½ miles (N. E. by N.) from Wexford; containing 809 inhabitants. This parish is situated on the coast of St. George's channel, and on the old road from Wexford to Dublin; and comprises 1725 statute acres, as applotted under the tithe act. It is an impropriate curacy endowed with the vicarial tithes, in the diocese of Ferns, and forms part of the union of Ardcolme; the rectorial tithes belong to the almshouse at Enniscorthy. The entire tithes amount to £115. 8. 3½., of which £59. 13. 3½. is the portion belonging to the almshouse, and £55. 15. is payable to the incumbent; the glebe comprises 20 acres. In the R. C. divisions it is included in the Blackwater union or district. It is not recognised as a parish in civil matters, but is considered as forming part of the parish of Killely.

BALLYVARY, a market-town, in the parish of KILDECAMOGUE, barony of GALLEN, county of MAYO, and province of CONNAUGHT, 5½ miles (N. E. by E.) from Castlebar: the population is returned with the parish. It is situated on the road from Castlebar to Swinford, and near a small river issuing from Lough Cullen. The market is on Wednesday; and fairs are held on May 29th, Aug. 18th, and Nov. 14th. Here is a station of the constabulary police. In the town is a R. C. chapel, erected on a site given by the Rev. L. Rutledge, of Bloomfield. In the immediate vicinity are Ballyvary House, the seat of C. Goodwin, Esq.; and Currangowan, of E. Deane, Esq.—See KILDECAMOGUE.

BALLYVAUGHAN, a village, in the parish of DROMCREEHY, barony of BURREN, county of CLARE, and province of MUNSTER, 6 miles (W.) from Burren; containing 151 inhabitants. This place is situated on a small bay to which it gives name on the western coast, and opening into the bay of Galway. The village, in 1831, contained 23 houses, since which time several new houses have been built, and it is progressively improving. Some of the inhabitants are employed in the herring fishery, which is carried on successfully on this coast. The bay is very shallow and in general fit only for boats; but small vessels may anchor in 2½ fathoms of water on good holding ground, about two or three cables' length south of Finvarra Point. There are some remains of an old quay, which is now of little use; a new quay would add greatly to the prosperity of the place, as, independently of the fishery, turf is landed here in great quantities from Connemara for the supply of the neighbouring country. A market for corn and pigs is held weekly on Thursday; and fairs have been lately established on the 24th of June and 23rd of September. Here is a station of the constabulary police; also a coast-guard station, which is one of the seven that constitute the district of Galway. A court for the manor of Burren is held by the seneschal about once in six weeks, at which small debts are recoverable; and the road sessions for the district are also held in the village. At a small distance to the east, and near the shore, are some vestiges of the old castle of Ballyvaughan.—See DROMCREEHY.

BALLYVINNY.—See KILLASPIGMULLANE.

BALLYVOURNEY, a parish, in the barony of WEST MUSKERRY, county of CORK, and province of MUNSTER, 8 miles (W. by N.) from Macroom; containing 3681 inhabitants. St. Abban, who lived to a very advanced age and died in 650, founded a nunnery at this place, which he gave to St. Gobnata, who was descended from O'Connor the Great, Monarch of Ireland. Smith, in his history of Cork, notices the church of this establishment, but it has since fallen into decay. The parish, of which the name signifies "the Town of the Beloved," is chiefly the property of Sir Nicholas C. Colthurst, Bart.; it is situated on the river Sullane, and on the road from Cork to Killarney, and comprises 26,525 statute acres, as applotted under the tithe act, and valued at £6073. 15. per annum. The surface is very uneven, in some parts rising into mountains of considerable elevation, the highest of which is Mullaghanish: about one-half is arable and pasture land, with 70 acres of woodland. Much of the land has been brought into a state of cultivation by means of a new line of road from Macroom, which passes through the vale of the Sullane, and is now a considerable thoroughfare; and great facilities of improvement have been afforded by other new lines of road which have been made through the parish; but there are still about 16,000 acres of rough pasture and moorland, which might be drained and brought into a state of profitable cultivation. The river Sullane has its source in the parish, in the mountains bordering on the county of Kerry, and after intersecting it longitudinally pursues an eastern course through the parish of Clondrohid to the town of Macroom, to the east of which, at the distance of a mile, it discharges itself into the river Lee; there is also a lake called Lough Ivoig. Fairs are held on the 10th of May, July, Sept., and Nov.; and there is a constabulary police station. The living is a rectory and a vicarage, in the diocese of Cloyne; part of the rectory is comprehended in the union of Clenore and corps of the chancellorship of the cathedral of St. Colman, Cloyne, and part is united to the vicarage, forming the benefice of Ballyvourney, in the patronage of the Bishop. The tithes amount to £731. 14. 7., of which £231. 14. 7. is payable to the chancellor of Cloyne, and £500 to the incumbent. The church is a very neat edifice, in the early English style, erected in 1824 by aid of a gift of £600 from the late Board of First Fruits. The glebe-house was built at the same time, partly by gift and partly by a loan from the same Board. In the R. C. divisions the parish is one of the three that constitute the union or district of Kilnemartry; the chapel, a plain and spacious edifice, was built in 1830. There are three daily pay schools, in which are about 70 boys and 20 girls. The ruins of the conventual church are very extensive and interesting; in one of the walls is a head carved in stone, which is regarded with much veneration. Near these ruins is a holy well, much resorted to on the 11th of February, the festival of St. Gobnata, the patroness, and also on Whit-Monday; and near the well is a large stone with a circular basin or font rudely excavated, the water from which is held sacred.

BALLYWALTER, a grange, in the parish of BALLYLINNY, barony of LOWER BELFAST, county of ANTRIM, and province of ULSTER: the population is returned with the parish. It is situated on the road from Carrickfergus to Doagh, and comprises, according to the Ordnance survey, 320½ statute acres.

BALLYWALTER, or WHITECHURCH, a parish, in the barony of ARDES, county of DOWN, and province of ULSTER, 4 miles (N. E.) from Kirkcubbin: the population is returned with tbe the union of St. Andrew's. This parish is situated on the eastern coast, and with a detached portion comprises, according to the Ordnance survey, 3379 statute acres. The village, which in 1831 contained 664 inhabitants, is situated in lat. 54° 32′ 20″ (N.), and lon. 5° 28′ (W.), and is a coast-guard station, forming one of the twelve that constitute the district of Donaghadee. It is a vicarage, in the diocese of Down, and is part of the union of Ballywalter or St. Andrew's; the rectory is appropriate to the Lord-Primate. The tithes amount to £339. 18. 1., of which £226. 12. 1. is payable to the Lord-Primate, and £113. 6. to the incumbent. On the next avoidance of the benefice of St. Andrew's, this parish will become a separate living, in the patronage of the Lord-Primate. In the R. C. divisions it forms part of the union or district of Lower Ardes. There are two places of worship for Presbyterians in connection with the Synod of Ulster. Some ruins of the old church yet exist.

BALLYWILLIAM.—See ROCHESTOWN.

BALLYWILLIN, or MILLTOWN, a parish, partly in the barony of LOWER DUNLUCE, county of ANTRIM, but chiefly in the North-East liberties of COLERAINE, county of LONDONDERRY, and province of ULSTER, 3½ miles (N. by E.) from Coleraine, on the road to Portrush; containing 2219 inhabitants. This parish is bounded on the north by the Atlantic ocean, and comprises, according to the Ordnance survey, 4673¼ statute acres, of which 1617 are in the county of Antrim: about 300 are sand and 150 bog; the remainder is arable and pasture. The entire district abounds with fossils and minerals of great variety, and with features of high geological interest. The soil, though various, is generally good; and the lands are in an excellent state of cultivation, particularly where not exposed to the drifting of the sand, which accumulates on the coast near Portrush. There is no waste land, except the sand hills near Portrush, which, from the constant blowing of the north and north-west winds, have overspread a large tract of excellent land, which it has been found impossible to reclaim. Much of the bog has been exhausted and brought under cultivation, and there is now barely sufficient for the supply of fuel. There are vast quantities of ironstone; in some places the ore is found nearly in a metallic state, and in nodules of stone used for making the roads have been found nuclei of almost pure metal.

Limestone is very abundant, but is not worked; the extensive quarries in the adjoining parish of Dunluce being held under a lease which prohibits the opening of any other upon the estate. Basalt in every variety is found here in a confused mixture of amorphous basalt with veins of red ochre, chert, soap-stone, and zeolite. In other parts there are magnificent columnar masses, the prisms of which are more perfect and more beautiful than those of the Causeway. These columns form part of a bold ridge of hills lying north and south, and displaying some of the finest features of basaltic formation in the island. Beardiville, the seat of Sir F. Macnaghten, Bart., a spacious and handsome mansion, is pleasantly situated and surrounded with extensive and thriving plantations; and at Portrush are several elegant lodges and pleasing villas, which are occupied by their respective proprietors during the bathing season, and one of which belongs to the Bishop of Derry. The Skerries, a cluster of islands about a mile from the shore, and containing, according to the Ordnance survey, 24*a.* 1*r.* 9*p.*, belong to this parish. Behind the middle of the largest of them a vessel may ride well sheltered in from 5 to 7 fathoms of water, and on good holding ground.

The living is a rectory, in the diocese of Connor, and in the patronage of the Bishop: it was formerly an appendage to the chancellorship of that see, under a grant by Jas. I., at which time a vicarage was instituted; but it again became a rectory under the provisions of Dr. Mant's act, on the death of Dr. Trail in 1831. The tithes amount to £263. The church is an ancient, spacious, and handsome edifice, in the early English style, and is said to be the only one in the diocese or county, built prior to the Reformation, in which divine service is now performed; it has neither tower nor spire, but being situated on an eminence it is visible at the distance of several leagues at sea. There is a glebe-house, for the erection of which the late Board of First Fruits, in 1828, gave £450 and lent £140. In the R. C. divisions this parish forms part of the union or district of Coleraine. There is a place of worship at Magherabuoy for Presbyterians in connection with the Synod of Ulster, and of the second class, and at Portrush is one for Wesleyan Methodists. The male and female school at Portrush is aided by an annual donation from Miss Rice; the school-house was erected in 1832 by Dr. Adam Clarke. A male and female school is aided by an annual donation from Mr. Lyle. In these schools are about 80 boys and 60 girls; and there are also a pay school, in which are about 40 boys and 10 girls, and a Sunday school. Here are the remains of Ballyreagh, or "the Royal Castle," situated on a promontory having a bold façade of rock rising to the height of 296 feet, the base of which is washed by the Atlantic. Dunmull, originally a druidical circle, afterwards a Danish fort, and now a pasture for sheep, is one of the most curious and extensive vestiges of antiquity in the country; and about half a mile to the north-west of the church are the remains of a druidical circle and altar, with an extensive and well-arranged cave; there is also a druidical altar near Beardiville, in a very perfect state. Fine impressions of the cornua ammonis are found in the chert at Portrush; the cornua and the echenite are found also in the limestone, and every variety of the zeolite and opal in the basaltic or trap formation, with chalcedony, strontium, agate, rock tallow, and veins of fullers earth.

BALNABRACKNEY, a village, in that part of the parish of Castle-Jordan which is in the barony of Upper Moyfenragh, county of Meath, and province of Leinster; containing 14 houses and 86 inhabitants.

BALNACARRIG.—See BALLINACARGY.

BALRAHAN, or BALRAHEEN, a parish, in the barony of Ikeathy and Oughterany, county of Kildare, and province of Leinster, 3 miles (S. W.) from Maynooth; containing 615 inhabitants. It is situated on the road from Kilcock to Naas, and is generally divided into small holdings and chiefly under tillage. The soil is productive, and the system of agriculture improved; there is some good pasture land, producing excellent clover, and fuel is plentiful and cheap. The seats are Rathcoffey House, the property of the late Archibald Hamilton Rowan, Esq., now comparatively deserted; and Painstown, that of Gerald Aylmer, Esq. It is a rectory and vicarage, in the diocese of Kildare, and is part of the union and corps of the prebend of Donadea in the cathedral of Kildare: the tithes amount to £161. In the R. C. divisions it forms part of the union or district of Clane: the chapel, situated at Rathcoffey, is a neat building. There is a private school, in which about 70 boys and 30 girls are educated. The ancient castle of Rathcoffey was besieged and taken by Col. Monk, in 1642, when 70 of the garrison were made prisoners, most of whom were executed in Dublin: the only remains are the gateway of the fortress; all the rest was taken down by Mr. Rowan, when he erected the present mansion.

BALRODDAN.—See RADDONSTOWN.

BALROTHERY, a parish and village, in the barony of Balrothery, county of Dublin, and province of Leinster; containing, with the post-town of Balbriggan, 5078 inhabitants, of which number, 375 are in the village. This place, which gives name to the barony, was anciently annexed to that part of the church of Lusk which in the earlier ages belonged to the archdeaconry of Dublin, and was separated from it about the year 1220 by Archbishop Henry. The village is situated on the road from Dublin to Balbriggan, from which latter it is distant about a mile, and in 1831 contained 84 houses. According to tradition, Jas. II. is said to have slept at the White Hart Inn here, before the battle of the Boyne: and the same distinction is claimed by another ancient house in the village, which was formerly an extensive inn. Fairs are held on the 6th of May and 12th of August. The parish comprises 8767 statute acres, as applotted under the tithe act: about 320 acres are woodland, principally in the demesne of G. A. Hamilton, Esq., and about 80 are bog or waste land; the remainder is arable and pasture, but is principally under tillage, and is very fertile in corn, which is the chief produce. A small portion of the bog of Ring is within the parish; and near the glebe is a reservoir of 22 acres, called the Knock, which supplies the mills of Balbriggan with water. At Curtlagh is a very fine stone quarry, and good stone for building is also obtained from the cliffs. The coast is composed of strata of transition rocks of grauwacke, grauwacke slate, clay-slate, and greenstone, with spar in small portions. The Drogheda, or Grand Northern Trunk, railway from Dublin to that town will pass through the parish, close to the shore. Hampton Hall, the seat of G. A. Hamilton, Esq., is an elegant mansion situated in a rich demesne of 500 acres, finely wooded and pleasingly diversified with hill and dale: the grounds command extensive sea views alternated with luxuriant woods, with the isles of Skerries in the foreground, and the Mourne mountains in the distance, stretching far into the sea towards the north. Ardgillan Castle, the seat of the Hon. and Rev. E. Taylor, is a handsome building in the castellated style, beautifully situated in a park finely wooded and commanding some interesting views of the sea. The other seats are Lowther Lodge, that of G. Macartney, Esq., in the grounds of which is an ancient rath; Inch House, of J. Madden, Esq., having also a rath within the demesne; Knockingin, of W. O'Reilly, Esq.; and Tankerville, of T. Swan Croker, Esq.

The living is a vicarage, in the diocese of Dublin, and in the patronage of the Rev. Fras. Baker, the present incumbent; the rectory is impropriate in the trustees of Wilson's hospital, in the county of Westmeath. The tithes amount to £530, of which £250 is payable to the impropriators, and £280 to the vicar. The church, with the exception of the tower, which is embattled and surmounted at the north-west angle with a circular turret, and at the others with small turrets, was taken down and rebuilt, by aid of a loan of £1000 from the late Board of First Fruits, in 1816. The glebe-house was built by aid of a gift of £250 and a loan of £550 from the same Board, in 1815; the glebe comprises 29¾ acres. There is a chapel of ease at Balbriggan, the living of which is a perpetual curacy, endowed by the late Rev. George Hamilton. In the R. C. divisions this parish is the head of a union or district, called the union of Balrothery and Balbriggan, and comprising also the parish of Balscadden: there are three chapels in the union, one at the village of Balrothery, another at Balbriggan, and a third in the parish of Balscadden. There is also at Balbriggan a place of worship for Wesleyan Methodists. There are three schools, in which about 205 boys and 110 girls receive instruction; also three pay schools, and a dispensary, in the town. Near the church are the remains of Balrothery castle, the date of which is unknown; the roof is covered with flag-stones of great thickness, and the general style of the building refers it to a period of considerable antiquity. Within a quarter of a mile of the town are the ruins of Bremore castle, the ancient seat of a branch of the Barnewall family, consisting of some of the out-buildings and part of a chapel, with a burial-ground, which is still used by some of the inhabitants. The skeletons of four moose deer were dug up on the glebe by the Rev. Mr. Baker. At Curtlagh there is a chalybeate spring.—See BALBRIGGAN.

BALSCADDEN, a parish, in the barony of Balrothery, county of Dublin, and province of Leinster, 2 miles (W.) from Balbriggan; containing 1011 inhabitants. This parish borders on the county of Meath, from which it is separated by the Naul river: it contains two commons, called the common of Balscadden and the bog of the Ring; and there is a quarry of good building stone on the lands of Milestown. Part of the demesne of Gormanston Castle is within its limits, but the castle itself is in the adjoining county. Winter Lodge, the residence of the late J. Woods, Esq., is not now inhabited. The living is a vicarage, in the diocese of Dublin and in the patronage of the Dean and Chapter of Christ-Church, Dublin; the rectory forms the corps of the treasurership in the cathedral of Christ-Church, in the gift of the Crown. The tithes amount to £180, of which £120 is payable to the treasurer, and £60 to the vicar. There is neither church nor glebe-house, but in a burial-ground in the village are the ruins of a church: the glebe consists of 4½ acres of profitable land. In the R. C. divisions this parish forms part of the union or district of Balrothery and Balbriggan: the chapel, situated in the village, is a neat structure, built by subscription in 1819, at an expense of more than £500. There is a school on the common of Balscadden, in which about 80 boys and 70 girls are taught: the school-house was built in 1832, when 3½ acres of the common were enclosed and attached to it; and it is in contemplation to erect a house for the master and mistress. There are also two private pay schools in the parish. Local tradition states that a battle was fought near the village, at a place called Cross Malin, where a small mound has been raised and a wooden cross erected on its summit; and it is said that there was an encampment on the common. The well of Tubbersoole was formerly resorted to from an opinion of its efficacy in healing diseases of the eye.

BALSOON, a parish, in the barony of Lower Deece, county of Meath, and province of Leinster, 4½ miles (E. by N.) from Trim; containing 311 inhabitants. This parish is situated on the river Boyne, and on the road from Athboy, by Bective Bridge, to Dunshaughlin. The land is principally under tillage; the soil is fertile, and the system of agriculture is improved. Fairs are held at Bective Bridge, near the boundary of the parish. It is a rectory, in the diocese of Meath, and is part of the union of Assey: the tithes amount to £69. 4. 7½. In the R. C. divisions it forms part of the union or district of Dunsany and Kilmessan, at which latter place is the chapel for this part of the union.

BALTEAGH, or BALLYDAIGH, a parish, in the barony of Kenaught, county of Londonderry, and province of Ulster, 2 miles (S. E.) from Newtownlimavady; containing 3326 inhabitants. This parish, which is situated on the Balteagh water and bounded on the west by the river Roe, is intersected by the roads leading respectively from Dungiven and Garvagh to Newtownlimavady, and by the road from Coleraine to Londonderry. It comprises, according to the Ordnance survey, 11,505¾ statute acres, and, except a small portion belonging to the see of Derry, is the property of the Marquess of Waterford, being part of the grant made by Jas. I. to the Haberdashers' Company, of London, who have long since alienated it in perpetuity. About one-fourth part of the land forms a portion of the mountains of Cedy and Donaldshill, which latter is the highest ground in the parish, and, according to the Ordnance survey, has an elevation of 1315 feet above the sea at low water. Much of the mountainous land affords excellent pasture for cattle, and might easily be reclaimed; and the remainder, extending from the bases of these mountains towards the river Roe, is rich and fertile, and in a good state of cultivation, producing abundant crops. In the front of the Cedy mountain is a large quarry of white limestone, which is there topped by the lofty mountains of basalt extending on the east to Coleraine, on the south-east to Garvagh, and on the north-east to Magilligan. In the bed of the Balteagh water, freestone, calcareous sand-stone, and thin layers of coal are found alternating. The principal seats are Ballyquin House, the residence of Capt. Tedlie, and Drumagoscar, of the Rev. R. Henderson. The weaving of linen is carried on in some of the farm-houses; and there are a flour and two oatmeal-mills, and two flax-mills in the parish. The living is a rectory, in the diocese of Derry, and in the patronage of the Bishop: the tithes amount to £373. 18. 6. The church, a small edifice with a square tower crowned with pinnacles, was erected in 1815, on a site near the ruins of the old church at the base of Donaldshill, at an expense of £700, a gift from the late Board of First Fruits, which also granted a loan of £277 for its repair in 1828. The glebe-house, situated about a quarter of a mile to the north of it, is a good residence; the glebe comprises 135*a.* 0*r.* 33*p.*, lying on both sides of the Balteagh water. In the R. C. divisions this parish forms part of the union or district of Newtown-limavady, and contains a chapel. There is a place of worship at Lislane for Presbyterians in connection with the Synod of Ulster, of the second class. The parochial schools are at Ardmore: there are other schools at Terrydrummond and Carrick, aided by the rector and W. Campbell, Esq.; and the Marquess of Waterford is about to establish schools at Lisbane and Drumsurn. The number of children at present taught in these schools is, on the average, 250, of which about one-third are girls: there are also four Sunday schools (one of which is held in the Presbyterian meeting-house), and a private school in which about 30 children are educated. There are remains of an extensive cromlech; and the walls of the ancient church form an interesting ruin. There are sulphureous and chalybeate springs in several parts of the parish. Numerous fossils are imbedded in the limestone of Cedy, particularly belemnites, trilobites, and dendrites.

BALTIBOYS.—See BOYSTOWN.

BALTIMORE, a village and sea-port (formerly an incorporated and parliamentary borough), in the parish of TULLAGH, Eastern Division of the barony of WEST CARBERY, county of CORK, and province of MUNSTER, 7 miles (S. W.) from Skibbereen; containing 459 inhabitants. This place is situated on a fine harbour to which it gives name in St. George's channel, and was anciently called *Dunashad*. It is supposed to have been a sanctuary of the Druids and one of the principal seats of the idolatrous worship of Baal, whence its present name, *Beal-ti-mor*, signifying, in the Irish language, "The Great Habitation of Beal," is probably derived. In 1537, the men of Waterford, in revenge for an attack made by Fineen O'Driscoll and his son on some merchant vessels consigned to that port, fitted out three armed ships with 400 men on board, which arriving in the harbour anchored under the castle: the garrison fled on their approach, and this force, after having laid waste the adjacent island of Innisherkin, landed here and set fire to the castle and town of Baltimore. So great was the resort of foreign fishermen to this coast, that, in 1552, Edw. VI. was advised by his parliament to erect a fort on the harbour, and compel them to pay a tribute; but the proposal was not carried into effect. In 1602, Sir Fineen O'Driscoll surrendered the castle to the Spaniards, and supplies of artillery and ammunition were conveyed into it for its defence by the Spanish commander, Don Jean D'Aquila, on whose capitulation soon after at Kinsale, it was delivered up according to the terms of the treaty. The town was, in 1629, reduced to great distress by Sir Walter Coppinger, who claimed and took possession of the castle, with the manor and town of Baltimore, upon which last the English inhabitants had expended more than £2000. Sir Walter was summoned before the Lords-Justices, but in the mean time sold the property to Mr. Becher, who dispossessed the English colonists, and they never afterwards recovered their property. About two years after, the Algerines made a descent upon this coast, attacked the castle, plundered the town, and carried away with them more than 200 prisoners to Algiers, most of whom were English settlers. After these two calamities the town never regained its former prosperity, and in a short time dwindled into an insignificant village; and in 1645 the castle, which was well fortified, and amply supplied with ordnance and ammunition, was taken by Captain Bennet and held for the parliament.

The inhabitants received a charter of incorporation from Jas. I., dated March 25th, 1613, by which the government was vested in a sovereign, twelve burgesses, and a commonalty: the sovereign was empowered to hold a court of record in personal actions not exceeding five marks, and the privilege of returning members to parliament was granted. In 1689, Jas. II. granted another charter, dated subsequently to the accession of Wm. III., which recites that the provost, free burgesses, and commonalty had enjoyed many privileges which had been seized into the King's hands by a judgment of the Exchequer. From the time of its first incorporation the borough continued to return two members to the Irish parliament till the legislative union, when it was disfranchised, and the £15,000 awarded as compensation for the abolition of the franchise was paid to Sir John Evans Freke, Bart., who in 1807 succeeded to the title of Lord Carbery, and is the present proprietor; the right of voting was vested in the householders, and the seneschal of the manor was the returning officer. The limits of the old borough cannot now be well defined by any marked boundaries; they included part of the manor, and extended for about a quarter of a mile round the town by land. The corporation is extinct, and the only official person remaining is a water-bailiff now appointed by the proprietor and lord of the manor, by whose authority he collects certain dues from all vessels not belonging to the port which enter it, whether they discharge their cargoes or not.

The village is situated on the eastern shore of the harbour, and immediately around the ruins of the ancient castle; and, though small, is rapidly increasing in size and importance. Several large and handsome houses have been recently erected, and others are in progress; and in 1833 a substantial pier was constructed at the joint expense of the Fishery Board and Lord Carbery. The trade of the port consists chiefly in the export of slate, copper-ore, flax, wheat, oats, and potatoes; and in the import of timber, iron, coal, salt, and general merchandise. In 1835, nine vessels of the aggregate burden of 2030 tons entered inwards, and the same number cleared outwards either with passengers or ballast, as connected with the foreign trade; and vessels of the aggregate burden of 10,300 tons entered inwards, and 299 of the aggregate burden of 17,643 tons cleared out, as connected with the coasting trade. The amount of duties paid at the custom-house for that year was £2059. 18. 6.; but much of the timber being imported for the use of the copper mines, the greater part of the duty was returned. The number of vessels registered as belonging to the port is 99, of the aggregate burden of 6426 tons. The custom-house is at Castle-Townsend, a distance of 10 miles from this place. The jurisdiction of the port extends from Galley Head, on the east, to Mill Cove on the west, and includes the creeks or harbours of Bearhaven, Bantry, Crookhaven, Baltimore, and Castle-Townsend, together with all rivers, bays, and creeks within its limits. The harbour is situated about seven miles (E. by N.) from the south-west point of Cape Clear, and is convenient for shipping bound either eastward or westward. The pier, though small, is a great accommodation to the fishermen as a landing-place on the mainland, for the fishery of Cape Clear; and a small quayage is collected for keeping it in repair. There are neither fairs nor markets. A coast-guard station has been established here, which is one of the nine that constitute the district of Skibbereen. The parish church, a new and handsome building with a lofty square tower, is situated in the village: it was erected in 1819, and forms a very conspicuous and beautiful feature in the landscape, as seen from the harbour. A school-house for male and female children was built at the expense of Lord Carbery in 1832: and there is a dispensary for the benefit of the inhabitants of the numerous islands in the bay. The ruins of the castle, on the summit of a lofty rock over the pier, and commanding every part of the harbour, are extensive and beautifully picturesque.—See TULLAGH.

BALTINGLASS, an ancient borough, market, and post-town, and a parish, in the barony of UPPER TALBOTSTOWN, county of WICKLOW, and province of LEINSTER, 32 miles (W. S. W.) from Wicklow, and 28 miles (S. S. W.) from Dublin; containing, with the town of Stratford-on-Slaney, 4110 inhabitants, of which number, 1670 are in the town of Baltinglass. This place, according to most antiquaries, derives its name from *Baal-Tin-Glas*, signifying, according to common acceptation, "the pure fire of Baal," and is thence supposed to have been one of the principal seats of druidical worship. At the time of the English invasion it formed part of the inheritance of the Kings of Leinster; and about the year 1148, or 1151, Diarmit Mac Murchad O'Cavanagh, the reigning monarch, founded here a monastery for Cistertian monks, in the church of which he was afterwards interred. Among the most distinguished benefactors to this establishment, which became a mitred abbey, was John, Earl of Morton, afterwards King of England; and among its abbots was Albin O'Molloy, one of the most zealous advocates of the Irish clergy, in opposition to the overbearing allegations of Giraldus Cambrensis. The monastery was frequently plundered by the mountain septs of the O'Byrnes and the O'Tooles; and in 1314 the abbot obtained from the English government permission to hold a conference with the chiefs of those formidable septs, who in the deed for this purpose are designated "Irish Felons," in order to recover "the goods and chattels of which he had been robbed, or a full equivalent for the same." The monastery was suppressed in 1537, and with its extensive possessions, including the castle and manor of Baltinglass, was granted, in 1541, to Thomas Eustace, Lord Kilcullen, whom Hen. VIII. created Viscount Baltinglass. In the reign of Elizabeth a parliament was held here, in which was passed an act rendering every kind of inheritance forfeitable for high treason, emphatically called the statute of Baltinglass. James, the third Viscount Baltinglass, and his four brothers, having joined in the great Desmond insurrection, were convicted of high treason; and their estates being confiscated under this statute, were granted by Queen Elizabeth to Sir John Harrington. The manor is now the property of Henry Carroll, Esq., of Ballynure; and the castle, with the town and other considerable property in the neighbourhood, is in the possession of the Earl of Aldborough. During the disturbances of 1798, the insurgents, after their defeat in the county of Wexford, stationed themselves in the mountains of this neighbourhood, and continued for some time to commit outrages on the peaceable inhabitants of the surrounding country.

The town is pleasantly situated in a romantic vale watered by the Slaney, over which is a stone bridge of three arches connecting those parts of it which are on the opposite banks of the river. It consists of four principal streets, with two or three others of less importance, and in 1831 contained 256 houses: it is amply supplied with water from springs, and, from its situation on the great road from Dublin, by Tullow, to Wexford, enjoys a considerable traffic. There are infantry barracks for one officer, and 25 non-commissioned officers and privates: and a constabulary police and a peace preservation force are stationed in the town. The manufacture of linen, woollen, and diaper was formerly carried on here extensively; there are two bleach-greens in the town in full operation, and an extensive flour-mill. There are also some extensive cotton and calico-printing works at Stratford-on-Slaney. A market and fairs were granted, in 1617, to Sir Thomas Willmott by Jas. I. Chas. II., in 1663, granted by charter a market, to be held on Friday, and two fairs for three days each in May and September, to Sir Maurice Eustace, with the tolls thereof; and four more fairs were granted, in 1763, to John, Lord Baltinglass, by a patent which also contains a grant of a market on Tuesday, not held, and of the tolls and customs of the markets and fairs to his lordship. The market is on Friday; and the fairs are held on Feb. 2nd, March 17th, May 12th, July 1st, Sept. 12th, and Dec. 8th. Until within the last few years the tolls and customs were received by the corporation, but the collecting of them has been discontinued.

The town was incorporated by charter of Chas. II. in the 15th year of his reign (1663), under the designation of the "Sovereign, Burgesses, and Free Commons of the Borough of Baltinglass." The corporation consists of a sovereign, twelve burgesses, a recorder and town-clerk, a serjeant-at-mace, and a clerk of the market. The sovereign is elected annually by and from the burgesses, on the Monday next after the feast of St. John the Baptist, and sworn into office on the Monday after Michaelmas-day; he has power to appoint a deputy from among the resident burgesses, by consent of a majority of that body; the sovereign or deputy is a justice of the peace within the borough during the year of office, and the former for one year after; the sovereign is also coroner. Burgesses are elected for life, but have no functions to perform. The power of appointing the recorder and town-clerk during pleasure, and also the clerk of the market, was vested by the charter in Sir Maurice Eustace, his heirs and assigns; and the serjeant-at-mace is appointed by the sovereign and burgesses. The freedom of the borough is obtained only by gift of the corporation; the freemen are exempted from serving upon juries without the limits of the borough, which, according to the charter, extend beyond the town, and comprise 300 acres lying on the west and south sides. The corporation had nearly become extinct, there being only two burgesses and not one freeman in 1832, when ten burgesses were chosen. The borough returned two members to the Irish parliament till the Union, when it was disfranchised, and the sum of £15,000 awarded as compensation was paid to the trustees of the Earl of Aldborough: the sovereign was the returning officer. The borough is included in the manor of Baltinglass, and the manor court was constituted a court of record, in which the seneschal presided, with jurisdiction to the amount of £10, but has been long discontinued. The quarter sessions for the western division of the county are held here; as are also the petty sessions for the upper division of the barony of Talbotstown, every alternate Friday, before the county magistrates. The court-house is situated at the extremity of the principal street, on the eastern bank of the river. The district bridewell, situated in the town, contains ten cells, three day-rooms, and three airing-yards, in one of which is a tread-wheel; and though badly planned and inconveniently situated, it affords sufficient facility for the classification of the prisoners usually confined within its walls.

The parish comprises 11,691 statute acres, as applotted under the tithe act. The lands are in a good state of cultivation; the soil is fertile, and the system of agriculture is improved; there is very little bog or waste land. Stratford Lodge, the seat of Lady Elizabeth Stratford, is a spacious mansion pleasantly situated in a demesne of 100 acres tastefully laid out and planted, ornamented with several sheets of water, and commanding from the house some extensive views, including the town, the valley, and a magnificent range of mountain scenery. Saunders Grove, the seat of R. F. Saunders, Esq., is a spacious and handsome mansion of hewn stone lined with brick, beautifully situated in a rich demesne adorned by the windings of the Slaney. Golden Fort, situated on an eminence over the Slaney, opposite the demesne of Saunders Grove, is the seat of Lieut.-Gen. Saunders, who has very much improved the estate, by the introduction of an improved system of agriculture and a superior breed of cattle. The lands of Golden Fort and Rathbran, both in this parish, are subject to a charge of double county cess, an error which will probably be rectified by the general survey now in progress. Slaney Park, the residence of the Rev. W. Grogan, and Whitehall, that of W. Butler, Esq., are in the parish; and on the townland of Ladytown, which is part of this parish, but detached and completely surrounded by the county of Carlow, is Mount Lucas, the residence of Capt. Jackson, commanding extensive mountain views and the scenery of the valley. The living is a rectory, annexed to that of Ballynure, in the diocese of Leighlin, and in the patronage of Henry Carroll, Esq.: the tithes amount to £618. 9. 2¾. The church, which occupies the site of the chancel of the ancient abbey, was repaired, and a square tower added to it, in 1815, at an expense of £500, and a grant of £252 has been lately made by the Ecclesiastical Commissioners for its further repair. The churchyard is the burial-place of the Aldborough family, and over the remains of his deceased ancestors the present earl, in 1832, erected a massive mausoleum of granite, terminating in a pyramidal spire. There is a chapel of ease at Stratford-on-Slaney. In the R. C. divisions this parish is the head of a union or district, which comprises also the parishes of Ballynure and those parts of the parishes of Timolin and Moon which are in the county of Wicklow, and that part of Kineagh which is in the county of Kildare; the chapel near the town is a neat edifice with a tower, and there is also a chapel at Stratford-on-Slaney. In the town of Baltinglass is a place of worship for Wesleyan Methodists, and at Stratford is one for Presbyterians. At Stratford Lodge are two schools, one an infants' school, and both supported by Lady Elizabeth Stratford; and there are two other schools, altogether affording instruction to about 260 boys and 190 girls. A second infirmary for the county of Wicklow, containing four wards, in which are 20 beds, with a dispensary annexed to it, has been established in the town; there is also a savings' bank. Within the demesne of Stratford Lodge is a shop for supplying the poor with goods at cost price. There are some considerable remains of the Cistertian abbey, chiefly consisting of a series of seven pointed arches springing from alternated round and square pillars with curiously carved capitals, which formerly separated the south aisle from the nave; the church appears to have been a spacious cruciform structure, and the west end, which is still standing, has the remains of a lancet-shaped window of three lights; the walls enclose a large area, which appears to have been surrounded with monastic buildings. Of the ancient castle, now converted into a farm-house, two Norman doorways leading into a court-yard are still remaining; and formerly many fragments of stone highly wrought lay scattered in all directions. Near the town is a cromlech, and numerous other relics of antiquity are said to have been lately existing there. On the eminence on which Golden Fort is built are two circular intrenchments or raths, surrounded by moats, in one of which the proprietor of the estate discovered, a few years since, a number of gold coins, from which circumstance the seat derived its name; and in the other, which is of larger dimensions and in a much more perfect state, was found a kistvaen containing an urn of rude pottery, in which were ashes, with a number of human bones scattered around: in the same demesne is an ancient cemetery. Baltinglass gives the title of Baron to the noble family of Stratford, Earls of Aldborough.—See STRATFORD-ON-SLANEY.

BALTRAY, a village, in the parish of TERMONFECKAN, barony of FERRARD, county of LOUTH, and province of LEINSTER, 2½ miles (E.) from Drogheda; containing 428 inhabitants. It is situated at the estuary of the river Boyne, on the eastern coast, and in 1831 contained 81 dwellings, of which the greater number are thatched cabins.

BANADA, a village, in the parish of KILMACTIGUE, barony of LENEY, county of SLIGO, and province of CON-

NAUGHT, 3 miles (W. by S.) from Tubbercurry: the population is returned with the parish. It comprises about 30 cabins, and is beautifully situated on the banks of the river Moy, which winds through it in a broad deep stream, and on the road from Tubbercurry to Foxford. A friary of Eremites, following the rule of St. Augustine, was founded here in 1423, through the industry of a brother of the order, and was dedicated to Corpus Christi. The modern seat, called the Abbey, is the residence of D. Jones, Esq., and from a plantation rises the lofty steeple of the ancient monastery, built of hewn stone and still entire. Fairs are held on Jan. 17th, May 19th, and Aug. 7th; and here is a station of the constabulary police.—See KILMACTIGUE.

BANAGHER, a market and post-town (formerly a parliamentary borough), in the parish of RYNAGH, barony of GARRYCASTLE, KING'S county, and province of LEINSTER, 6 miles (N. W. by N.) from Parsonstown, and 64 miles (W. S. W.) from Dublin; containing 2636 inhabitants. This town is situated on the side of a hill, on the south bank of the Shannon, just above the influx of the little Brosna river, and at the junction of the roads from Parsonstown to Cloghan and Eyrecourt. The bridge, connecting it with the Galway shore, is one of the oldest across the Shannon: it consists of several small arches with projecting piers, and is very narrow and inconvenient, but of great strength and solidity. Latterly, however, this bridge, which is supposed to have stood between 400 and 500 years, has shown numerous symptoms of decay: it completely obstructs the navigation of the river, to remedy which a canal with a swing-bridge over it has been formed on the Galway side. Its military defences are very strong: on the King's county or Banagher side is a *tête-du-pont* mounting three pieces of heavy ordnance, and about a ¼ of a mile lower down the river is a circular field work with six pieces of ordnance; on the Galway side to the right is a Martello tower, and on the left a small battery. The town comprises about 500 houses, mostly well built; the streets are Macadamised. It has a reading-room; and close to the bridge are infantry barracks for 3 officers and 63 men. There are a distillery, brewery, malt-house, and tanyards; and the town has a good general trade with the rural population of the surrounding district. It is well situated for trade, having the advantages of steam navigation to Limerick and the sea, and of water communication with Athlone, Ballinasloe, and Dublin: the introduction of steam navigation on the Shannon, has greatly benefited the general trade of this place, and in the autumn of 1836 extensive surveys were made by order of Government, with a view to improve the navigation of this noble river. The market, originally granted in 1612 to Sir John McCoghlan, Knt., to be held on Thursday,—and to the corporation in 1628 on Monday,—is now held on Friday, and is a considerable corn market. Fairs are held on May 1st, Sept. 15th and three following days, Oct. 28th, and Nov. 8th; that held in September is a large fair for live stock, inferior only to that of Ballinasloe. Here is a station of the constabulary police.

The inhabitants were incorporated in 1628 by charter of Chas. I., by which it was ordained that certain lands, altogether comprising 200 acres of arable and pasture land, and 70 acres of wood and moor, should be a free borough; 1-13th of these lands was granted to Sir Arthur Blundell and his heirs, 1-13th to Sir Matthew Derenzie and his heirs, and 1-13th to each of the other burgesses named in the charter, to be held in free burgage at a rent of 3*s.* 1*d.* respectively. It further granted to the corporation 222 acres of arable and pasture land, and 7 acres of wood and moor, for the support of a resident preaching minister, whom they were to appoint; and 200 acres of arable and pasture, and 85 acres of wood and moor, for the maintenance of a schoolmaster in the town, to be appointed by the viceroy, or, in default, by a majority of the burgesses. It also contained a grant of a court with jurisdiction to the amount of £20; and constituted the sovereign, or his deputy, a justice of the peace within the borough, and coroner and clerk of the market, and empowered the corporation at large to send two members to the Irish parliament. The corporation was styled "The Sovereign, Burgesses, and Free Commons of the Borough and Town of Bannacher *alias* Bannagher;" and consisted of a sovereign and twelve burgesses, with power to admit freemen and appoint a recorder and other officers; but the corporate offices have not been filled up since the year 1800, when the borough was deprived of its right of parliamentary representation, and the £15,000 awarded as compensation was paid to the Rt. Hon. Wm. Brabazon Ponsonby. The sovereign formerly held, under the charter, a court for the recovery of debts to the amount of £20 late currency, which was discontinued about forty years since: the only court now held is a court of petty sessions every alternate Monday. The lands granted by the charter for a preaching minister are said to have been formerly held by a clergyman appointed by the corporation, who officiated in a church now fallen into decay in the town; but they have for many years become united to the rectory, and are now held by the incumbent of the parish. At the entrance to the town is the parish church, a handsome edifice in the ancient English style of architecture, with a tower and spire, built in 1829 at an expense of £2286, of which £2030 was granted on loan by the late Board of First Fruits. There is also a R. C. chapel, a large plain building in good repair. A school was established by the corporation pursuant to the charter granting lands for its endowment: by an act of the 53rd of Geo. III., cap. 107, these lands, which according to a survey made in 1817 comprised about 370 acres, of which about 233 acres are arable and pasture, were vested in the Commissioners of Education, and the schools placed under their control. The lands were formerly let at a rent of £300, but are now held by the master at a rent of £148. 17. 10. per annum, and the Board has recently proposed to allow him a salary of £200 on the condition of his surrendering all interest in them, with a view to their being placed under the superintendence of a local qualified agent. The school is held very near the town, and was suspended from 1798 to 1807: there are no free scholars on the establishment, which in no respect differs from an ordinary classical school, except that it is under the control of the Board. The parochial school in the town is aided by an annual donation from the incumbent; and there is a national school for boys and girls, aided by voluntary contributions, also a dispensary. In the vicinity is Cloghan Castle, the seat of Garrett O'Moore, Esq., and one of the oldest inhabited castles in Ireland; and a short distance to the south of the town, near the banks of the Little Brosna river, are the ruins of Garry castle, which gave name to the barony.—See RYNAGH.

BANAGHER, a parish, partly in the barony of TIRKEERAN, but chiefly in that of KENAUGHT, county of LONDONDERRY, and province of ULSTER, 2 miles (W. by S.) from Dungiven; containing 4086 inhabitants. This parish, which for extent is the second in the county, is situated on the road from Toome to Londonderry, and is nine miles in length from east to west and seven miles in breadth from north to south. It contains 27 townlands, of which 16 are in the barony of Tirkeeran and 11 in that of Kenaught, and comprises, according to the Ordnance survey, 32,475 statute acres, of which 17,748¼ are in the latter barony. The apparent decrease in its population, since 1821, is attributable to the separation of nine townlands, which, together with nine from the parishes of Upper and Lower Cumber, were taken, in 1831, to form the district curacy of Learmount. The early history of this place is involved in great obscurity; by some writers it is said that St. Patrick, when he crossed the Foyle, visited it and founded the church, the ruins of which are still remaining, and on a stone is inscribed, in modern capitals, "This church was built in the year of God 474." The style of the building is evidently of a much later period, and corresponds with a local tradition that the church was built by St. O'Heney, and with the style of the tomb erected to his memory in the adjoining cemetery. It is also said that a monastery, of which St. O'Heney was abbot, formerly existed here; but though there are, near the church, the remains of a small square building of more recent erection and evidently used for domestic purposes, which is called the abbey, no mention occurs in historic records of any religious establishment, nor are there any monastic lands in the parish, except such as belonged to the abbey of Dungiven.

The parish is divided among several proprietors; seven townlands belong to the see of Derry, six to the Skinners' and three to the Fishmongers' Companies; ten are freeholds, of which nine pay a chief rent to the Skinners' and one to the Fishmongers' Companies; and one, on which are the church, glebe-house, and parochial schools, belongs to the rector. The land in many places is well drained and in a good state of cultivation, but not less than 13,432 acres are mountain land, though affording good pasturage; and there are 546 acres of flow bog, which is being rapidly reclaimed and brought into cultivation. In the mountains, particularly in Finglen, are found very large and beautiful specimens of rock crystals, or Irish diamonds, generally truncated pentagonal prisms, with facets often of the clearest lustre, and sometimes of the colour and brilliancy of the beryl. These crystals vary, however, in colour and lustre, and are found of all sizes. The largest ever discovered was found in Finglen water, in 1796; it weighs 84½ lb., and is in the possession of Michael Ross, Esq., of Banagher Cottage; it is called the Dungiven Crystal, and has been noticed by several writers as an object of admiration. Freestone is found in great quantities, and is of a bright fawn colour and very durable, as appears from the old churches of Banagher and Dungiven; limestone is also abundant. There are several handsome seats in the parish, and most of them are embosomed in rich and flourishing plantations; the principal are Ashpark, the residence of J. Stevenson, Esq.; Knockan, of I. Stevenson, Esq.; Drumcovatt, now occupied as a farm-house; Banagher Cottage, the residence of Michael Ross, Esq.; Kilcreen, of I. Beresford, Esq.; and Straid Lodge, of the Rev. J. Hunter. There is a large bleach-green at Knockan, where 8000 pieces of linen are annually bleached and finished for the English markets; some linen cloth is also woven by the farmers in their own houses, but the greater number of the inhabitants are employed in agriculture.

The living is a rectory, in the diocese of Derry, episcopally united to the vicarage of Dungiven, which two parishes form the union of Banagher, in the patronage of Robert Ogilby, Esq., as lessee under the Skinners' Company: the tithes amount to £650, and the gross value of the benefice, including tithe and glebe, is £1201. There is a church in each of the parishes: the church of Banagher, a large and handsome edifice, with a tower surmounted by a beautiful octagonal spire, is situated on elevated ground about a mile west of the old church, and was built in 1782; the spire was added at the expense of the Earl of Bristol, then Bishop of Derry. The glebe-house, nearly adjoining the church, is a large and handsome residence, built in 1819 by the Rev. Alexander Ross, the present incumbent, at an expense of £2350, upon the glebe townland of Rallagh, which comprises 422*a.* 0*r.* 39*p.* of arable land. The Ecclesiastical Commissioners, in their report for 1831, have recommended the dissolution of the union, and that each parish shall become a separate benefice on the next avoidance. In the R. C. divisions this parish is the head of a union or district, which comprises also the parishes of Bovevagh and Learmount, and contains three chapels, one at Feeny, one at Altinure in the mountain district, and one at Foreglen. There is a place of worship at Ballyhenedein for Presbyterians in connection with the Synod of Ulster, of the second class; it is a handsome building, in the Grecian style of architecture, erected in 1825 at the expense of the Fishmongers' Company. There are male and female parochial schools at Ballagh, aided by an annual donation from the rector; the school-house is a large and handsome building, erected by subscription. At Tyrglassen is a male and female school, supported by the Fishmongers' Company; and at Fincarn is a male and female school supported by R. Ogilby, Esq. In these schools are about 120 boys and 100 girls; and there are also three private schools, in which are about 200 children, and three Sunday schools, one of which at Tyrglassen is supported by the Fishmongers' Company.

The ruins of the old church are situated on the summit of a sandy ridge on the south side of the river Owenreagh, in a retired and beautiful valley, and are very interesting; they consist of the church and a small square building, sometimes called the abbey. The church consisted of a nave and chancel, but the partition wall, the arch, and the eastern gable have disappeared; the side walls and the west front are remaining and tolerably entire; the nave and chancel appear each to have been lighted by a very narrow lancet window on the south side, ornamented externally with curious circular mouldings; the only entrance appears to have been from the west, through a square-headed doorway with a bold architrave, and on one of the stones on the north side is the inscription in modern capitals before noticed. There are also the ruins of an ancient church at Straid, said by the country people to have been the second founded by St. Patrick in this part of the kingdom; but the style of the building is of much less remote antiquity. There are also the foundations of a third church in the townland of Templemoile, but no part of the building is remaining, nor is there any history or tradition of it extant. On the glebe is a curious vitrified fort, on which the Midsummer fires are made; and near the church is an extensive artificial cave. In the cemetery of the old church is a curious monument to the memory of St. O'Heney, the supposed founder of the church and of the small building near it which is called the abbey; it is of a square form, with sharp pointed gables and a roof of stone; and on the western side is an effigy of the saint in tolerable preservation. Here is a very curious ancient cross, with the fragments of a second, which, with three others, marked out the consecrated ground around this venerable pile.

BANBRIDGE, a market and post-town, in the parish of SEAPATRICK, barony of UPPER IVEAGH, county of DOWN, and province of ULSTER, 10 miles (N. N. E.) from Newry, and 60 miles (N.) from Dublin; containing 2469 inhabitants, but since the last census the population has much increased. This flourishing town was anciently called Ballyvally, and acquired its present name from the erection of a bridge over the Bann in 1712, on the formation of a new line of road from Dublin to Belfast. The old road passed a little to the north of it, and crossed the Bann at Huntley Glen by a ford, through which the army of Wm. III. passed on the 11th of June, 1690, on its march to the Boyne. It is situated on both sides of the river, and in 1831 contained 446 houses, many of which are handsome and well built; the larger portion is on the western side, on an eminence sloping to the river, and communicating with the smaller by the bridge, which is a handsome structure of hewn granite: the streets are wide, and the entire town wears an aspect of neatness and comfort surpassed by few places in this part of the country. In the centre of the principal street to the west of the river formerly stood the market-house, a large and inconvenient building, which was taken down in 1832 to make way for a series of improvements. Prior to that period the street was very steep and difficult of access; but an excavation, 200 yards long and 15 feet deep, has been made along its centre, crossed by a handsome viaduct of one elliptic arch of hewn granite, under which the mail coaches and other vehicles pass. The street being very wide, a carriage road was left on each side of the excavation, running parallel with it and on a level with the ground floors of the houses, shops, and public buildings: these side roads are protected throughout their entire length by a stone wall rising from the bottom of the excavation to the height of three feet above their level. The excavation interrupts the communication between the houses on the opposite sides of the street; but the viaduct being placed at the intersection of the streets obviates that inconvenience. This great undertaking was completed in 1834, at an expense, including the erection of the viaduct and the formation of its approaches, of £19,000.

The town is comparatively of modern origin, and has risen with uncommon rapidity to an eminent degree of commercial importance as the head of the principal district of the linen manufacture. Even when almost every port was closed against the introduction of Irish linens, and the trade was nearly lost to the country, those of Banbridge found a ready market; and when the energies of the linen merchant on the old system were nearly paralysed by foreign competition, the merchants of this place created a new trade, by commencing as manufacturers on an extensive scale, and opening an intercourse with America and other parts. The numerous falls on the river and the uniform supply of water appear to have attracted the attention of the manufacturers soon after bleaching became a separate branch of the trade; and shortly after the application of machinery to this department, several mills were erected on its banks, mostly on a small scale, as the process at that time was very tedious and every web of considerable value. Although a formidable barrier to enterprise resulted from the unsettled state of the country, and the system of selling only through the factors in Dublin restricted the operations of the trade and regulated the prices, the linen merchants of this district seem to have gradually prospered, as, in 1772, there were no less than 26 bleach-greens on the Bann river. At that time, however, the trade was principally carried on at Gilford, and the webs were mostly marked as "Gilford linens," and, after the introduction of linen seals, were nearly all sealed there. The Dromore merchants also transacted an important business; the finer fabrics had even acquired the name of "Dromores," and a great quantity of the higher numbers is still woven in and around that town, but principally for the Banbridge manufacturers. At present comparatively very little business is done at either of those places, the entire trade of this part of the country having concentrated itself in the vicinity of Banbridge, which has thus become one of the most important inland manufacturing towns in Ireland. Linen of every description is manufactured and bleached in the neighbourhood: at Brookfield, Huntly Glen, Seapatrick, Millmount, Ballydown, and Ashfield are manufacturers on a large scale, for whom more than 66,000 webs are annually finished, comprising linens of various quality, sheeting, diapers, damasks, drills, cambrics, &c., by a vast number of weavers, who work in their own dwellings and are dispersed over the surrounding parishes. There are very extensive bleach-greens at Ballievey, Ballydown, Clibborn Vale, Millmount, Milltown, Springvale, Mill-Park, Hazelbank, Banford, and Mountpleasant, where 185,710 webs were bleached and finished in 1834, being nearly equal to the entire quantity bleached in this county at the end of the last century. At Seapatrick is an extensive establishment for weaving union cloths by machinery, in which are employed 100 power-looms impelled by a water-wheel 15 feet in diameter and 22 feet broad on the face. There are also very large thread manufactories for home consumption and exportation at Huntley Glen, Milltown, and Banbridge; a mill for spinning linen yarn at Coose, and adjoining it, chymical works for the supply of the bleachers. These different establishments provide employment for more than 2000 persons connected with this branch of the linen trade alone. Branches of the Provincial Bank of Ireland and of the Northern and Belfast banking companies have been established here. The situation of the town on the great north road to Belfast, and in the centre of a fertile and highly cultivated district watered by the Bann, is very advantageous to its interests. It is within three miles of the Newry and Lough Neagh canal, to which a branch may be formed at little expense; this improvement appears to have been at one period contemplated, from an excavation which is still traceable from Millmount down the valley on the south side of the Bann. Within an extent of four miles there are six good stone bridges over the Bann, besides several of wood: in 1690 there was not one bridge over this river throughout its entire course of 36 miles, from the mountains of Mourne to Lough Neagh. The Marquess of Downshire is proprietor of the town and a large tract of land in its vicinity. The principal seats in the neighbourhood are Ballievey House, the residence of G. Crawford, Esq.; Ballyvalley, of the Rev. J. Davis; Millmount, of R. Hayes, Esq.; Brookfield, of Brice Smyth, Esq.; Huntley Glen, of Hugh Dunbar, Esq.; the glebe-house, of the Rev. D. Dickinson; Edenderry, of W. A. Stewart, Esq.; Seapatrick House, of F. W. Hayes, Esq.; Lenaderg Cottage, of T. Weir, Esq.; and Banview, of G. Little, Esq. There are also several large and handsome houses in the town, the residences of wealthy merchants and professional gentlemen; and the farm-houses in the vicinity are built in a superior style of convenience and comfort. The market is on Monday, and is abundantly supplied with all kinds of provisions, and with pedlery and other commodities: the sale of yarn and brown linens, formerly very extensive, has declined since the new system of spinning and manufacturing was established, but considerable quantities of both are still disposed of. The market-house, situated in the centre of the town, close to the viaduct, is a large and handsome edifice surmounted by a dome, and was built by the Marquess of Downshire in 1834, at an expense of £2000: a brown linen hall was also erected by him in 1817, and a market-place for meal and grain in 1815. Fairs are held on the first Monday in every month; and fairs for horses, cattle, sheep, pigs, and manufactured goods are held on Jan. 12th, first Saturday in March, June 9th, August 26th, and Nov. 16th; the last is a very noted fair for horses. Petty sessions are held once a fortnight, and here is a chief station of the constabulary police.

The parochial church, situated in this town, is a handsome cruciform edifice, with a tower surmounted by a spire, recently built at an expense of about £3000, which was chiefly raised by subscriptions among the more wealthy parishioners. Near it is a large and handsome meeting-house, recently completed for Presbyterians in connection with the Remonstrant Synod, and of the first class, in lieu of an old one erected in 1720: and there are also one for Presbyterians in connection with the Synod of Ulster, of the third class, and, at a short distance from the town, one for Seceders; besides a place of worship each for Wesleyan and Primitive Methodists. A school, in which about 60 boys and 50 girls are taught, is endowed with £50 per ann. and $1\frac{1}{2}$ acre of land: the school premises, including residences for the master and mistress, were built by subscription, towards which the Marquess of Downshire contributed £90. Here is also a dispensary. Within half a mile from the town, on the Dromore road, a sulphureous chalybeate spring has been lately discovered, the water of which having been analysed is found to equal that of Aix la Chapelle, and is efficacious in scorbutic complaints. This is the birth-place of the late Baron McClelland, third baron of the Exchequer; and near the town was born Dr. Dickson, Bishop of Down and Connor.—See SEAPATRICK.

Seal.

BANDON, or BANDON-BRIDGE, a borough, market, and post-town, partly in the parish of KILBROGAN, barony of KINALMEAKY, but chiefly in that of BALLYMODAN, partly in the barony of KINALMEAKY, and partly in the East Division of the barony of EAST CARBERY, county of CORK, and province of MUNSTER, $15\frac{1}{2}$ miles (S. W.) from Cork, and $141\frac{1}{2}$ (S. W. by S.) from Dublin; containing 9917 inhabitants. This place derives its name from the erection of a bridge over the river Bandon, and owes its origin to the English planters on the great Desmond forfeitures in the reign of Elizabeth. It is first noticed in 1609, when Jas. I. granted to Henry Becher, Esq., the privilege of a Saturday's market and two fairs at the town lately built on the south side of the river Bandon, near the bridge; and in the grant made to Becher, in 1612, of a moiety of the territory of Kinalmeaky, which was erected into the manor of "Castle Mahowne," power was given to him and his heirs to appoint a clerk of the market in the newly erected town called Bandon-Bridge, or in any other town within the said territory, with the privilege of licensing all tradesmen and artisans settling therein. These grants were shortly afterwards purchased by the first Earl of Cork, whose exertions in promoting its growth and prosperity entitle him to be regarded as the founder of the town, which he peopled with a colony of Protestants from Bristol, and which in a few years, from a mere waste of bog and wood, became a spacious, handsome, and well fortified place, continuing to flourish and to increase in extent and importance. At the commencement of the civil war in 1641, the town was placed under the government of Lord Kinalmeaky, son of the Earl of Cork, who took possession of it in January 1642, and mustering all the inhabitants put it into an excellent state of defence. As it was the only walled town in this part of the country, it became an asylum for the English of the surrounding district, and by its own resources maintained four companies of foot, raised a corps of volunteers, and made every preparation both for offensive and defensive warfare. On the 18th of February a party of Irish under McCarty Reagh approached, when Lord Kinalmeaky sallying out with 200 foot and 60 horse, a severe conflict ensued, in which, without the loss of a single townsman, more than 100 of the assailants were killed. The inhabitants soon afterwards, in conjunction with a troop from Kinsale, defeated another party that had lain in ambush to surprise them, and in a short time took several forts in the adjacent territory which had been held by the Irish; they also killed fifty who had made an attempt to carry off their cattle; but on Cromwell's approach in 1649, they declared for the parliament. In 1688, hearing that the Earl of Clancarty was advancing with six companies of foot of the army of Jas. II., to reinforce the two companies of foot and the troop of horse already stationed here, the inhabitants disarmed the garrison, killed several of the soldiers, took possession of their arms and horses, and shut the gates against the Earl. At length, however, they were obliged to yield for want of provisions, but refused to give up any of their leaders, and consented to pay £1000 as the price of their pardon; on their submission the walls were razed to the ground and have never been rebuilt.

The town is situated on the river Bandon, and on the mail coach road from Cork to Bantry; the principal part lies in a valley environed with lofty hills and watered by the river, which separates the parishes of Ballymodan and Kilbrogan, the former on the south and the latter on the north bank, and near the bridge receives a tributary stream called the Bridewell. Under the various names of Boyle-street, Shannon-street, and Main-street it extends on the south side for about 1½ mile parallel with the river, and on the north for about half that distance; it is also built partly on the acclivities of the hills on both sides of the river, which are agreeably wooded and are ornamented with several mansions, villas, and cottages, that give to the environs a pleasing and picturesque appearance. The old town is built on the estate of the Duke of Devonshire, who repairs its streets and is reimbursed by a poundage of five per cent. on the rent reserved in all leases of houses in this part; what is called the Irish town, including Boyle, Shannon, and Main streets, with an estate adjoining, belongs to the Earl of Shannon; and the western portion is the property of the Earls of Cork and Bandon. The total number of houses, in 1831, was 1580, of which about 1170 were slated and the remainder thatched: many respectable private houses have been built in the more elevated parts of the town, chiefly of a durable freestone of a light brown colour found in the neighbourhood. The streets are very indifferently paved and only partially flagged: the inhabitants are supplied with water principally from wells and public pumps, the latter erected and kept in repair by the Duke of Devonshire and the Earl of Shannon on their respective estates; and in 1835 a company was formed for lighting the town with gas, which, under the provisions of the general paving act, has likewise power to watch and cleanse the town, and for these purposes has appointed watchmen and scavengers and commenced the erection of gas-works. A public library was established in 1825 by a proprietary of £5 shareholders, who pay a subscription of 10*s.* annually, and annual subscribers of £1 are admitted by ballot: it contains several hundred volumes, including a copy of Rees's Encyclopœdia presented by the Duke of Devonshire, and one of Rymer's Fœdera presented by the Government in 1835. The parochial library, under the management of the Protestant clergy, was established in 1823, and contains several hundred volumes on divinity and other subjects; and a similar library was formed by the Wesleyan Methodists in 1830. There are also two reading-rooms supported by annual subscribers; and a third has been recently opened for poor Protestants, who pay a penny per month and are supplied with newspapers a day or two after their arrival by gift or loan from the neighbouring gentry. Assemblies are held at the Devonshire Arms hotel, a large and well-conducted inn and posting-house, containing a spacious ball-room, in which also concerts and music meetings occasionally take place. The barracks, a neat and commodious building on the north side of the town, afford accommodation for 8 officers and 119 non-commissioned officers and men, with stabling for 61 horses, and are under the inspection of the barrack-master at Kinsale. Near the town is Castle Bernard, the seat of the Earl of Bandon, also many other gentlemen's seats, which are noticed in their respective parishes. These, with their extensive woods and plantations, particularly the hanging woods to the east of the town and extending two miles beyond Innishannon (noticed by Spenser), impart to the scenery of the neighbourhood a high degree of richness and luxuriance of character.

The manufacture of camlets, stuffs, and other woollen goods prevailed here to a great extent at the close of the last and beginning of the present centuries, and was succeeded by the spinning and weaving of cotton, which continued to flourish till 1825; spinning-mills were erected on a large scale, and more than 1000 persons were employed in weaving, but both branches have fallen off, insomuch that the mills are in ruins and not more than 100 weavers are employed. A manufacture of fine stuffs was introduced in 1835 by Mr. Scott, who has erected a steam-engine for preparing the wool and spinning the yarn: this establishment affords employment to nearly 100 persons, exclusively of 100 weavers in the town and neighbourhood, and its produce has already obtained considerable celebrity for its superior texture. Here are five ale and porter breweries, three of which are extensive and produce 25,000 barrels annually: also two very large distilleries, one of which, the property of Messrs. Allman and Co., is capable of producing 200,000 gallons of whiskey annually; the other was built by Maurice Fitzgerald, Esq., in 1835, and consumes annually 1400 barrels of malt and 5800 barrels of oats and barley, yielding 60,000 gallons of whiskey. Connected with the latter is a large flour-mill, and there is also another on an extensive scale. This place has long been noted for the tanning of leather, which is in great demand: there are nine tanyards in active operation, employing more than 100 men. From the great consumption of the breweries, distilleries, and mills, very little grain is exported: the imports are coal, culm, timber (in which a considerable trade is carried on direct with St. John's, New Brunswick, and Quebec), and iron, which are brought in sloops to Colliers' Quay, three miles from the town, and thence by land carriage; articles of domestic consumption are brought by land carriage principally from Cork. A canal from Colliers' Quay to Dunmanway has been at different times contemplated, and surveys have been made, but the design has not yet been carried into effect; and a railway has been lately projected from Rockpoint, four miles to the east, which, if brought through the town, would be of great benefit to its trade. Branches of the Provincial Bank of Ireland and of the Agricultural and Commercial Banking Company have been established here. The markets are on Wednesday and Saturday, of which the latter is the principal, and is abundantly supplied with provisions of all kinds; and fairs are held on May 6th, Holy Thursday, Oct. 29th, and Nov. 8th, for live stock and general merchandise. There are three convenient market-places, built at the expense of the Duke of Devonshire: the meat and fish markets, on the north side of the river, are held in a commodious building in the form of a polygon, surrounded by stalls and forming a piazza for the market people: the potatoe, corn, and egg markets, on the south side, are held in an oblong edifice conveniently fitted up and well adapted to its several uses; more than 20,000 eggs are sold here every week during the spring, and are conveyed to Cork to be shipped for England. The tolls of the town belong to the Duke of Devonshire, and, after the determination of a demise of them to the corporation in 1806, were paid until 1830, when His Grace suspended the collection of them until some arrangement should be effected by the legislature. A regular and extensive intercourse is maintained between this town and Cork, for which city several stage coaches leave daily and return the same evening; the Cork and Bantry mail passes and re-passes daily, and every alternate day a stage coach from Skibbereen to Cork passes through the town: there are also mail coaches every day to Kinsale, Dunmanway, and Timoleague. Here is a chief station of the constabulary police.

The inhabitants were incorporated by charter of the 11th of Jas. I. (1614), and, by letters patent of the 19th of Chas. II. (1667) received a grant of lands in the baronies of Ibane and Barryroe. Jas. II., in the 4th of his reign, granted a new charter founded on a seizure of the franchises, which soon became inoperative. The corporation is styled "The Provost, Free Burgesses, and Commonalty of the Borough of Bandon-Bridge;" and consists of a provost, 12 burgesses, and an unlimited number of freemen, assisted by a town-clerk and two serjeants-at-mace. The common council is a body not mentioned in the charter, but constituted by a by-law of the corporation made in 1621: it consists of twelve members, who are elected from the freemen by the corporation at large, as vacancies occur. The burgesses are chosen from the common council, on vacancies occurring, by the provost and burgesses; and the provost is elected annually from and by the burgesses at Midsummer, and enters upon his office at Michaelmas: the provost and burgesses also appoint the town-clerk and serjeants-at-mace. The freedom is at present acquired by grace, birth for the eldest son of a freeman, and nomination of the provost, who during the year of his office has the privilege of naming one; the freemen are elected by a majority of the body at large assembled in a court of D'Oyer Hundred; neither residence nor any other qualification is considered necessary. The borough sent two members to the Irish parliament prior to the Union, since which period it has returned one to the Imperial parliament: the right of election was formerly vested in the provost and burgesses only, but by the act of the 2nd of Wm. IV., cap. 88, has been extended to the £10 householders; and a new boundary was formed for electoral purposes closely encircling the town, and comprising an area of 439 acres, which is minutely described in the Appendix. The number of voters registered in March 1836 was 367, of whom 355 were £10 householders and 12 burgesses: the provost is the returning officer. He is also by charter a justice of the peace within the borough, and is named in all commissions of the peace for the county. A court of record was formerly held every Thursday, with jurisdiction to the amount of £3. 6. 8., but has been discontinued of late years. The quarter sessions for the West Riding are held here in October; and petty sessions for the division are also held here every Monday by the county magistrates, who by courtesy have concurrent jurisdiction with the provost within the borough. The court-house is a neat substantial building; and not far from it is a commodious county bridewell. Manorial courts for the recovery of debts under 40*s*. are held once in three weeks respectively by the seneschals of the different manors: the manor of Castle Mahon or Castle Bernard belongs to the Earl of Bandon; Coolfadda, to the Duke of Devonshire; and Claugh McSimon, to the Earl of Shannon. The corporation formerly possessed lands under the patent of Chas. II. amounting to about 1340 statute acres, which having mortgaged at different periods, they finally disposed of with a view to pay certain debts in 1809, since which period they have had no income or property of any kind.

The parish churches of Ballymodan and Kilbrogan are both in the town: the former is not distinguished by any architectural details of importance; it contains a handsome monument to Fras. Bernard, Esq., one of the justices of the court of common pleas, and an ancestor of the Earl of Bandon. The church of Kilbrogan, commonly called Christchurch, was begun in 1610 by Henry Becher, Esq., and finished by the first Earl of Cork in 1625, as appears by a date on a stone in the south wall: it is a cruciform structure, and occupies the site of a Danish encampment; in the churchyard are the graves of three of Clancarty's soldiers, who were slain in the attempt to take the town for Jas. II. In the R. C. divisions this place is the head of a union or district which comprises the parishes of Ballymodan and Kilbrogan, and part of that of Desertserges: the chapel is a spacious and handsome edifice, built by subscription in 1796, and situated on an eminence in the south part of the town: there is also a chapel at Agrohil in Kilbrogan. On an elevated site in the north part of the town is a convent of the Presentation order, established in 1829, to which are attached a domestic chapel and a spacious school-room, in which, according to the season, from 200 to 400 poor female children are gratuitously instructed. There is a meeting-house for Presbyterians in connection with the Synod of Munster; also places of worship for Primitive and Wesleyan Methodists, of which that for the latter is a large and handsome edifice. The classical school was founded by the Earl of Burlington: the master has a commodious residence, with suitable offices and a large play-ground attached, and receives a salary of £40 per ann. from the Duke of Devonshire. A suitable building in the old Cork road, comprising separate school-rooms for boys and girls, an infants' school, and apartments for the master and mistress, was erected at the expense of the Duke of Devonshire: the former, containing about 100 children, is supported by the trustees of Erasmus Smith's foundation; and the latter, in which are 90 infants, is supported by the joint contributions of the Duke and the rector of the parish. A large and handsome school in Shannon-street, in which 120 girls and 100 infants are gratuitously taught, was built in 1814 by the proceeds of a repository and by contributions, and is supported by subscriptions of the Duke of Devonshire and others. His Grace has also built a handsome school on Cavendish quay, towards the support of which he subscribes £50 per ann., and the remainder of the expenses are defrayed by local contributions; about 100 children are gratuitously taught in this school. Adjoining the R. C. chapel is a school aided by a subscription of £30 per ann. from the Duke, in which 200 boys are taught. The Wesleyan Methodists have three schools, in which 70 boys, 65 girls, and 80 infants receive instruction; one for boys is supported by H. Cornwall, Esq. An infirmary, fever hospital, and a dispensary are maintained in the customary manner. A savings' bank was established in 1817, and a handsome building was erected from the surplus funds in 1835: the deposits, in 1836, amounted to more than £22,000. Several bequests have been made for the benefit of the poor. Sir Richard Cox, an eminent statesman and historian, born in 1650; Dr. Nicholas Brady, who assisted Tate in composing a new version of the Psalms, born in 1659; and Sir William Jumper, a distinguished naval officer, were natives of this place. The town gives the titles of Earl, Viscount, and Baron to the family of Bernard, Earls of Bandon; and the inferior title of Baron of Bandon-Bridge to the family of Boyle, Earls of Cork and Orrery.—See BALLYMODAN and KILBROGAN.

BANGOR, a sea-port, incorporated market and post-town, and a parish, partly in the barony of LOWER CASTLEREAGH, but chiefly in that of ARDES, county of DOWN, and province of ULSTER, 11½ miles (N. E. by E.) from Belfast, 21 miles (N.) from Downpatrick, and 91½ miles (N. by E.) from Dublin; containing 9355 inhabitants, of which number, 2741 are in the town. The origin and early history of this ancient town are involved in some obscurity, and have been variously described by different writers. The most authentic records concur in stating that, about the year 555, St. Comgall founded here an abbey of Regular Canons, which may have led to the formation of a town, if one did not exist previously, and over which he presided fifty years, and died and was enshrined in it. Some time subsequently to the foundation of the abbey, a school was established here under the personal direction of St. Carthagus, which in progress of time became one of the most eminent seminaries in Europe, and was resorted to by numbers of young persons of distinction from various parts; and, according to some writers, when Alfred founded or restored the university of Oxford, he sent to the great school at Bangor for professors. In 613 the town was destroyed by fire, and in 674 the abbey was burnt. In the beginning of the ninth century they suffered severely from the predatory incursions of the Danes, in one of which, about the year 818, these merciless marauders massacred the abbot and about 900 monks. In 1125 it was rebuilt by Malachy O'Morgair, then abbot, with the addition of an oratory of stone, said by St. Bernard to have been the first building of stone and lime in Ireland; and from which this place, anciently called the "Vale of Angels," derived the name of *Beanchoir*, now Bangor, signifying the "White Church," or "Fair Choir." Malachy was soon afterwards appointed to the see of Connor, and held with it the abbacy of Bangor till his preferment to the archbishoprick of Armagh. The abbey continued to flourish and was endowed with extensive possessions, which after the conquest were considerably augmented by the kings of England: amongst its lands was a townland in the Isle of Man, called Clenanoy, which the abbot held on the singular condition of attending the king of that island at certain times. In 1469, the buildings having fallen into decay through the abbot's neglect, Pope Paul II. transferred the possession of the abbey from the Regular Canons to the Franciscans, who continued to hold it till the dissolution. After that period, a great part of its lands was either granted to or seized by the O'Nials, who kept possession till the rebellion of Con O'Nial in the reign of Elizabeth, when it was forfeited to the Crown. Jas. I., on his accession to the throne, found the northern part of Ireland in a deplorable condition, and almost depopulated; and in the third year of his reign, resolving to plant English and Scottish colonies in Ulster, granted the site of the abbey, with all its former possessions in this county, to Sir James Hamilton, afterwards created Viscount Claneboye, who brought over a large number of Scots from Dunlop in Ayrshire, accompanied by their own minister, Robert Blair, who, although a Presbyterian, was presented to the church living of Bangor, and ordained in 1623 according to the Presbyterian form, the Bishop of Down officiating as a presbyter: he was afterwards appointed Scottish chaplain to Chas. I. From him were descended Robert Blair, of Athelstoneford, author of a poem called "The Grave;" and the celebrated Hugh Blair, D.D., of Edinburgh, the former his grandson and the latter his great-grandson. From Sir J. Hamilton are descended, either lineally or collaterally, the families of Bangor, Dufferin, Killileigh, and some others of principal note in Ulster. In 1689, the advanced army of Wm. III. arrived here in seventy sail of transports under the command of Duke Schomberg, and disembarked at Groomsport, a fishing village about a mile from the town, where they encamped for the night; being well received and finding plenty of provisions, the transports, which had been furnished with supplies, sailed back to Chester for a reinforcement of troops.

The town is advantageously situated on the south side of Belfast Lough or Carrickfergus bay, and on the direct sea coast road from Belfast to Donaghadee; in 1831 it contained 563 houses, most of which are indifferently built, and is much frequented for sea-bathing during the summer. The streets are neither paved nor lighted, but are kept very clean; and the inhabitants are but indifferently supplied with water. There is a public library; and an Historical Society has been recently formed in connection with it. The cotton manufacture is carried on to a considerable extent in the town and neighbourhood, and affords employment to a great number of the inhabitants of both sexes in the weaving, sewing, and ornamental branches. It was first established here in the finer branches between the years 1783 and 1786, by the late George Hannay, who, if not the first, was at least one of the first persons who introduced that department of the manufacture into the North of Ireland. Two spinning factories were subsequently erected under the patronage of the late Rt. Hon. Col. R. Ward, who constantly resided here and took an active interest in the improvement of the town; one was built by two gentlemen from Scotland in 1800: who conducted it till 1813, when it was purchased by a company, who kept the concern in full work till 1826, when it became the property of one of the partners, who now retains it: the other, in which Col. Ward held a share, and of which, on the dissolution of the partnership by the death of Mr. Hannay, he became sole proprietor, was built in 1804. The number of persons of both sexes constantly employed in these two factories varies from 260 to 280: those engaged in the weaving and sewing branches of the trade being dispersed over the parish, as well as resident in and immediately around the town, cannot so easily be enumerated. Many operatives from Belfast find employment; and agents have been commissioned by the Glasgow merchants to get goods manufactured here, from the superior manner in which the weaving and sewing are executed. The linen trade is also carried on to a limited extent, chiefly for home consumption. The trade of the port is inconsiderable: black cattle, horses, grain, and flax are exported: the only imports are coal and timber. The bay is well sheltered, and affords good anchorage in deep water for vessels detained by an unfavourable wind; and the harbour is capable of great improvement, although attempts made at the expense of individuals have failed. A small pier was built about the year 1760, by means of a parliamentary grant of £500 to the corporation for promoting and carrying on the inland navigation of Ireland. The market is on Tuesday, but is not well attended: the market-house was built of late years by the lords of the manor. Fairs for black cattle, horses, and pedlery are held on Jan. 12th, May 1st, Aug. 1st, and Nov. 22nd. The only toll or custom which appears to have been ever paid was that of the "tongues" of cattle slaughtered in the market, which was claimed by the provost, but has been relinquished. The mail coach runs daily to and from Belfast. A constabulary police force, and an establishment of the coast-guard in connection with the Donaghadee district, are stationed here.

The inhabitants were incorporated by charter of the 10th of Jas. I. (1613), under the style of "The Provost, Free Burgesses, and Commonalty of the Borough of Bangor:" the corporation under the charter consists of a provost, 12 other free burgesses, and an unlimited number of freemen, with two serjeants-at-mace, but of whom only one town-serjeant is now appointed. The provost is elected from and by the free burgesses annually on the Feast of St. John (June 24th), and is sworn into office at Michaelmas; and the free burgesses are appointed during good behaviour, as vacancies occur, by a majority of the provost and remaining free burgesses: there is no separate class of freemen distinct from the free burgesses. The borough returned two members to the Irish parliament until the Union, when the £15,000 granted in compensation for the abolition of its franchise was awarded in moieties to Henry Thomas, Earl of Carrick, and the trustees of the estate of Nicholas, Viscount Bangor: the right of election was confined to the provost and free burgesses, and the provost was the returning officer. The charter constituted the provost clerk of the market and judge of a borough court of record, to be held every Saturday, with jurisdiction in personal actions to the amount of five marks; but it does not appear that this court has ever been held. Petty sessions are held once a fortnight, and a manorial court every third Thursday before the seneschal, with jurisdiction to the amount of £20, late currency: the proceedings are by attachment or civil bill. A court leet is held by the seneschal once a year, at which constables for the several townlands in the manor are appointed. The manor is held in moieties by Viscount Bangor and a member of the same family, Mr. Ward, a minor, who is the representative of the Earl of Carrick, a former proprietor. The property of the corporation consists of several plots of ground lying in various directions around the town, and containing altogether 59*a.* 1*r.* and 18*p.*, now occupied in very small lots and at low rents by 43 tenants, and producing a gross rental of £52. 13. 2. per annum, which is generally applied to public and useful objects. The limits of the borough include the town and a small surrounding district, locally termed "the corporation," the exact boundaries of which are uncertain.

The parish is bounded on the north by the bay of Belfast, on the east by the Northern channel, on the south by the parishes of Donaghadee and Newtownardes, and on the west by that of Hollywood. It contains the Copeland islands, including which it comprises, according to the Ordnance survey, 17,027 statute acres, of which 12,597¼ are in the barony of Ardes; the greater part is good arable and pasture land, mostly in excellent cultivation, especially the extensive estate of Portavo, and there are several others in the parish little inferior to it in point of husbandry; the farm-buildings are neat and comfortable, and the peasantry are of moral and very industrious habits. The first Parochial Ploughing Society in Ireland was established here in 1816, by the exertions and under the patronage of J. Rose Cleland, Esq., from which may be dated the origin of the North-east Farming Society and the commencement of agricultural improvement in the North of Ireland. Bangor moss is now nearly exhausted, and is gradually being brought into cultivation; but there is a large extent of bog called Cotton, and in the townland of Ballow is a small bog, in which were found the skeletons of several elks, the head of one of which, with the antlers, measuring nine feet from tip to tip, is preserved in the Royal Institution at Belfast. Several streams on which are corn and flax-mills intersect the parish, and there are three windmills for corn. The neighbouring bays produce a variety of fish; oysters of large size are taken in abundance. The surrounding scenery is pleasingly diversified, and enriched in some parts with stately timber, chiefly fir and oak; and in the vicinity of the several gentlemen's seats are thriving plantations of beech, sycamore, ash and poplar, of comparatively modern growth. The principal seats are Ballyleidy, that of Lord Dufferin, a handsome and spacious mansion pleasantly situated in a rich and extensive demesne; Bangor Castle, late the seat of the Rt. Hon. Col. Ward, surrounded with extensive grounds tastefully laid out; Crawfordsburn, of W. Sharman Crawford, Esq., M.P., pleasantly situated on the shore; Portavo, of D. Kerr, Esq., in a well-planted and richly cultivated demesne; and Ballow, of W. Steele Nicholson, Esq., and Rath-Gael House, of J. Rose Cleland, Esq., both embellished with thriving plantations. Slate is found in several parts, but has been only procured in one quarry, which has not been worked sufficiently deep to produce a quality capable of resisting the action of the atmosphere. There are also mines of coal, especially on the estate of Lord

Dufferin, whose father opened and worked them on a small scale, since which time they have been abandoned; and a lead mine was worked here to some extent about thirty years since, in which copper ore and manganese were also found.

The living is an impropriate curacy, in the diocese of Down, and in the alternate patronage of Viscount Bangor and — Ward, Esq., in whom the rectory is impropriate. The parish is tithe-free, except two townlands, the property of Lord Dufferin, which pay tithe amounting to £52. 6. 9.; the curacy is endowed with a money payment of £55.7.8. per ann. by the impropriators. The church was built near the site of the old abbey, in 1623, and a very neat tower and spire were subsequently added to it by a bequest of the late A. Moore, Esq., of Tyrone. In attempting to enlarge it, in 1832, the foundation was so much disturbed by injudicious excavations that it was found necessary to take it down, with the exception of the tower; and a spacious and handsome structure, in the later style of English architecture, was erected in the following year, at an expense of £935, which was defrayed by the parishioners, aided by subscriptions to a considerable amount from some of the landed proprietors. There is a very good glebe-house, with a glebe of 12 Cunningham acres. In the R. C. divisions this parish forms part of the union or district of Newtownardes; but there is no chapel within its limits. There are two meeting-houses for Presbyterians, the first was built originally about the year 1650, by a congregation which began the erection of a new and beautiful building in 1831, and the other was built in 1829 by a new congregation: they are both in connection with the Synod of Ulster, and one is of the first and the other of the third class. The Primitive and Wesleyan Methodists have also each a place of worship. A school for girls and an infants' school are supported by the executors of the late Col. Ward; an infants' school is also supported by Mrs. Trench; at Ballyleidy is a school for girls, founded and supported by Lady Dufferin; a school for boys and girls at Crawfordsburn built in 1832, by the late Lord Dufferin, is supported with a bequest by the late Mr. John McGowan and other contributors; and there are two national schools at Crawfordsburn and Conlig, besides six other schools in the parish, aided by subscriptions. In these schools are about 460 boys and 340 girls, many of the latter of whom are clothed in each under the benevolent patronage of Lady Dufferin; and there are also eight private pay schools, in which are about 120 boys and 50 girls, and eleven Sunday schools. The first Sunday school in Ireland was formed at Rath-Gael in 1788, by J. R. Cleland, Esq. Here is a dispensary; a mendicity society is supported by subscription, and there are a friendly society and a savings' bank. Adjoining the town is a property called "Charity Lands," let for £42. 11. 1. per annum, which is applied towards the support of some of the above institutions and other charitable purposes. Of the ancient abbey there is only a small fragment remaining in part of the garden wall of the glebe-house. Near the quay is an old building supposed to have been used as a custom-house, the tower of which has been converted into dwelling-houses. Vestiges of 25 raths and forts may be traced in the parish; the largest was Rath Gael, or "fort of the strangers," which extended over more than two acres and was encompassed by a double vallum; part of it is now occupied by the plantations and house of that name. Druidical relics have been frequently found in various parts of the parish. Christian O'Conarchy, the first abbot of Mellifont, was born at or near this place; he was consecrated Bishop of Lismore about the year 1150, and was constituted the pope's legate in Ireland; he died in 1186. William Hamilton, a very ingenious poet, was also born here in 1704; his works were printed in 12mo. at Edinburgh, in 1760, eight years after his death. Bangor gives the titles of Viscount and Baron to the family of Ward, to whom the town and a considerable portion of the parish belong.

BANGOR, a village, in the parish of KILCOMMON, barony of ERRIS, county of MAYO, and province of CONNAUGHT, 10 miles (E. S. E.) from Belmullet: the population is returned with the parish. It is situated on the road from Castlebar to Belmullet, and contains two comfortable inns. Fairs are held on the 20th of Jan., Feb., March, and April, May 10th, June 11th, July 20th, Aug. 11th, Sept. 8th, Oct. 16th, Nov. 16th, and Dec. 11th; and here is a station of the constabulary police. The parochial R. C. chapel of East Kilcommon is situated in the village. In the immediate vicinity is the shooting-lodge of W. Bingham, Esq.: the surrounding country is mountainous, and grouse is abundant during the season. Near the village is the lake of Carramore, celebrated for its salmon and trout: it communicates with the bay of Tulloghane by the rivers Munning and Owenmore.—See KILCOMMON.

BANNOW, a parish, formerly a corporate town and parliamentary borough, in the barony of BARGY, county of WEXFORD, and province of LEINSTER, 1½ mile (N. E. by E.) from Fethard; containing 2185 inhabitants. This parish is of a peninsular form, being bounded on the south-east by Ballyteigue bay, in St. George's channel, and on the west by the bay or harbour of Bannow, which forms the estuary of the Scar river; and is situated near the new line of road along the east side of the mountain of Forth to Wexford. It formed part of the territory originally granted by Dermod Mac Murrough, last king of Leinster, to Hervey, who accompanied Robert Fitz-Stephen in his expedition, which landed at Bag-and-bun bay, within sight of this place. From an early period after the English settlement here was a town of some note, it being mentioned in the earliest charter of New Ross, by which, in the reign of Edw. I., Roger Bigod granted to the burgesses of that town "as extensive privileges as were enjoyed by the men of Bannow, Kilkenny, or any other town in Leinster." The old town has long since disappeared: part of its site is covered with sand drifted from the sea, in some places to the depth of many feet; and the inequalities of the surface immediately adjoining the churchyard are supposed by some to be occasioned by the ruins of the town lying at a considerable depth, from which circumstance it has obtained the appellation of the Irish Herculaneum. It does not appear that there is any charter of the borough on record; but there are extant numerous inquisitions, *post mortem*, of the reigns of Jas. I and Chas. I., finding the seisin of certain parties in premises and rents in the town and burgages, which appear to have been held in burgage tenure, but they make no mention of a corporation. Notwithstanding the decay, if not the total annihilation of the town, it continued to send two representatives to the Irish parliament until the Union, when the £15,000 awarded in compensation for the abolition of the franchise was paid to Charles, Marquess of Ely, and Charles Tottenham, Esq., of Ballycurry, in the county of Wicklow. The names of St. Mary's, St. Tullock's, and St. Benedict's streets are retained on the quit-rent books of the Crown, but their sites are merely conjectural. The only perceptible remains of antiquity are the ruins of its venerable church, situated within a walled enclosure at a short distance from the shore, and at an elevation of about 30 feet from the level of the sea: they are of considerable extent, and consist of the walls of the nave and chancel, surmounted by embattled parapets, and having two small chapels attached, the whole being unroofed; the east window of the chancel appears to have been in the decorated English style, and still retains some fragments of flowing tracery; the ancient font was removed some years since to the R. C. chapel at Danescastle, where it is preserved with great care. There are many ancient tombstones in the churchyard, one of which records the death of a person named French at the advanced age of 140.

The parish comprises by estimation about 2980 statute acres, as rated for the county cess, exclusively of Carrig, which is ecclesiastically incorporated with it. The soil, though light, is fertile and in a high state of cultivation, the system of husbandry having greatly improved; the land is well adapted to the growth of corn, and produces excellent crops; the situation is favourable for an abundant supply of sea manure, and has the advantages of navigation on both sides of the parish. The neighbourhood is thickly studded with comfortable farm-houses, decent cabins, and cottages of a superior description let to numerous families that resort hither during summer for the benefit of sea-bathing; and the roads throughout the parish are kept in excellent order. The principal seats are Grange, that of S. Boyse, Esq., who is the chief proprietor of land in the parish; Graige House, the residence of R. Boyse Osborne, Esq.; Kiltra, of W. Marchant, Esq.; and Barrystown, the property of the Rev. R. King. A lead mine was worked to some extent by the late celebrated George Ogle, Esq., but since his death the works have been discontinued, as it is said from the vein being exhausted; and, according to Mr. Frazer, in his statistical survey of the county, silver was anciently procured on the lands of Barrystown; but this silver mine was probably the lead mine worked by Mr. Ogle, which might have contained more than the usual proportion of silver, and have thence derived its denomination of silver mine. The small farmers and the peasantry are comfortable in their circumstances and highly exemplary in their manners: in the whole parish there is not one resident mendicant, all who are able to work finding full employment. This desirable state of society is attributable to the active exertions of T. Boyse, Esq., and to the beneficial effects of an agricultural school established some years since by the Rev. W. Hickey, then vicar, under the auspices of S. Boyse, Esq., father of the above, who granted 40 acres of improvable land for that purpose: the pupils divided their time between the pursuits of study and agricultural labour; the best practical treatises on agriculture were adopted, and the most improved agricultural implements were in use: the school-house was built partly by a grant from the fund at the disposal of the lord-lieutenant, and is now occupied as a farm-house, and the school was conducted by Mr. Hickey until his removal to another benefice. This gentleman has distinguished himself by many popular writings on agriculture and gardening, and gave evidence of the efficiency of the establishment before a parliamentary committee in 1830.

Bannow bay produces an abundance of various kinds of fish. The harbour is navigable for vessels of 120 tons' burden: one side of the entrance to it is called the Isle of Bannow, it being connected with the mainland only by an isthmus of sand; from this there is a ferry to the barony of Shelburne, and between it and the little port of Fethard or Feathard, is Bag-and-bun bay, where Robert Fitz-Stephen landed his troops for the conquest of Ireland. The harbour or creek is an out-port of Wexford, and the business of the customs here, and of the bar of Lough at the south-eastern extremity of the parish, is transacted by an officer residing at Cullenstown, near the latter place. At Newtown is a quay where coal, culm, and Welsh slate are landed and stored; timber is also brought hither from Waterford, and corn is occasionally shipped here, though mostly sent to Wexford by land; limestone from Slade, on the eastern side of Hook peninsula, is brought up the bay in boats averaging from 14 to 20 tons' burden. An agent from Lloyd's resides at this place. At the bar of Lough is a coast-guard station, being one of the five comprised in the Wexford district, and there is a small detachment at the Isle of Bannow. Off this bar, and about ½ a mile from the shore, are two small islands, called the Keroe islands, on the larger of which a house was built a few years since by Mr. Boyse, as a temporary shelter for shipwrecked persons. The coast on both sides of the parish is much frequented for the purpose of sea-bathing; accommodation is afforded by most of the farmers, who let their houses during the season. Some of the inhabitants are engaged in the herring and cod fishery At Cullenstown are the remains of a castle, which about 70 years since was converted into a dwelling-house; the parapet and upper story have been taken down, and it has now the appearance of a modern building.

It is a vicarage, in the diocese of Ferns, and forms part of the union of Kilcavan or Kilkevan; the rectory is impropriate in Cæsar Colclough, Esq. The tithes amount to £364. 17. 5¾., of which £212. 6. 2. is payable to the impropriator, and the remainder to the vicar. The church of the union is within the border of the parish of Kilcavan: the glebe-house, in this parish, about 2½ miles distant from it, was built by aid of a gift of £400 and a loan of £330 from the late Board of First Fruits, in 1821. In the R. C. divisions this parish forms part of the union or district of Ballymitty, also called Bannow: the chapel is at Danescastle, in the parish of Carrig. On the decline of the agricultural school, which took place after the removal of Mr. Hickey, a private school, called the Bannow grammar school, for the preparation of young men for the Irish University, was established here by the Rev. H. Newland, D.D., author of the "Apology for the Church in Ireland," and other works connected with the state of religion in this country. The parochial school, for children of both sexes, is partly supported by subscription: the school-house was built at an expense of £150, of which £60 was a grant from the lord-lieutenant's fund: there is a national school at Danescastle, in which about 50 boys and 20 girls are taught, and there are three hedge schools in the parish. A dispensary is supported in the usual manner. About a mile from Danescastle there is a small convent of Augustine Friars, who are reputed to be the representatives of the more sumptuous monastery of that order, of which the ruins are among others in the neighbourhood of Clonmines: attached to it is a small but elegant chapel erected in 1829.—See CARRIG.

BANSHA, or TEMPLENEIRY, a parish, in the barony of CLANWILLIAM, county of TIPPERARY, and province of MUNSTER, 4 miles (S. S. E.) from Tipperary; containing 2975 inhabitants, of which number, 281 are in the village. The village is pleasantly situated on the mail coach road from Limerick, through Cahir, Clonmel, and Carrick-on-Suir, to Waterford, and in 1831 contained 45 houses. A mill is worked by a stream from the river Arra, which runs through the village. A penny post to Clonmel has recently been established; and it is a station of the constabulary police. The parish is bounded on the south by the summit of part of the Galtee mountains; on the west by Trinity College lands and a stream which separates it from part of the parish of Kilshane; on the north, by the parish of Clonfinglass and the river Arra; and on the east, by the parish of Clonbullogue. It comprises 11,443 statute acres, as applotted under the tithe act, and valued at £4516 per annum; more than one-half is arable and pasture land, and the remainder mountain. The rivers Arra and Aherlow flow through the parish: the Arra is remarkable for its excellent trout, which are of a rich pink colour, and in season throughout the year; and the Aherlow abounds with trout and eels, and frequently has salmon. A considerable portion of the Galtee mountains extends through the parish from east to west, and is partly pasturable for sheep and goats and a few mountain cattle, producing various kinds of heath and fern, and abounding with grouse, hares, and rabbits. A portion of the Tipperary hills on the estates of E. O'Ryan and J. A. Butler, Esqrs., is also in the parish; these hills stretch in a direction parallel with the Galtees, and are much frequented by woodcocks and foxes. The intervening valley is very fertile and in a high state of cultivation. In the bogs near the base of the hills have been found several large black oaks lying horizontally near the surface. The parish is well wooded throughout; on the Galtees is Ballydavid, an extensive wood of oak, beech, birch, larch, fir, and Weymouth pine; and on the Tipperary hills is Bansha Wood, abounding with thick-set, beech, birch, fir, and oak; there are also several plantations, and nearly adjoining the village is a good nursery. Limestone is the prevailing substratum, and is quarried for building, repairing the roads, and burning into lime for manure. A road from Cashel to Mitchelstown intersects the parish, and there are numerous other roads, which are kept in excellent repair. Lismacue, the seat of Hugh Baker, Esq., is a handsome castellated mansion, pleasantly situated in a highly cultivated demesne embellished with stately avenues of lime and beech trees, which latter are considered to be the finest in the kingdom. Bansha Castle, the seat of E. O'Ryan, Esq., an elegant building in the castellated style, and Aherlow Castle, of J. A. Butler, Esq., are also prettily situated. Ash-Grove Castle, or Castle-Mary, the seat of the Rev. Trevor Lloyd Ashe, lord of the manor of Bansha, is a castellated mansion in the Italian style of architecture, situated at the base of the Galtee mountains, 4000 acres of which are attached to the estate: the mountain scenery is exceedingly wild and romantic, and the rich and well-wooded vale beneath presents a pleasing contrast with the grandeur of the adjacent heights. On the estate is an ancient well, dedicated to St. Berryhearth, which is much frequented by the peasantry; and in the demesne is a small temple, in the Grecian style, with pleasure grounds attached, dedicated to the Virgin. About halfway to the summit of the mountains is Lake Musgrave, an extensive sheet of water, imbedded within rocks, whose frowning summits afford secure eyries to eagles, and retreats to other birds of prey. The other seats are Ballydavid House, that of G. Baker, Esq.; Ashgrove, of S. Moore, Esq.; Barnalough House, of P. Smithwicke, Esq.; and Ruan Lodge, of T. S. Manning, Esq.

The living is a rectory and vicarage, in the diocese of Cashel, united from time immemorial to the rectory and vicarage of Graystown and the vicarage of Donohill, together constituting the corps of the precentorship of Cashel, and in the patronage of the Bishop. The tithes amount to £230. 15. $4\frac{1}{2}$., and the tithes of the benefice to £675. 7. $8\frac{1}{4}$.: the entire value of the precentorship, including glebe, is returned at £723. 7. 4. The church is a neat building, to which a handsome spire was added in 1813; it contains a marble monument to the late William Baker, Esq., of Lismacue. The glebe-house, near the church, is a commodious residence: the glebe contains nine acres, and there are also two pieces of ground in the parish of Donohill, containing 58*a.* 2*r.* 6*p.*, belonging to the precentor and let on lease at £7 rent and a renewal fine of £14 annually. The R. C. parish is co-extensive with that of the Established Church; the chapel, adjoining the churchyard, is a neat building. There are four pay schools, in which are about 160 boys and 60 girls. In the marsh lands have been found heads, horns, and skeletons of the moose deer, one of which, of large dimensions, was found some few years since. The only relic of antiquity is a ruined wall, said to have formed part of the ancient castle of Bansha, but its history is quite unknown.

BANTRY, a sea-port, market and post-town, in the parish of KILMACOMOGUE, barony of BANTRY, county of CORK, and province of MUNSTER, $47\frac{1}{2}$ miles (W. S. W.) from Cork, and $173\frac{1}{2}$ (S. W.) from Dublin; containing 4275 inhabitants. This place, called anciently Kilgoban, derived that name from St. Goban, its original founder or patron, and its present appellation, Bantry, from Beant-Mac-Farriola, a descendant of the O'Donovans and Mahonys, chieftains of the western portion of this country. During the insurrection of the Earl of Desmond, in 1581, Lord Barry and Goran Mac Swiney attacked the garrison of this place, but were repulsed with the loss of many of their men. In 1689, a French fleet entered the bay, and being pursued by the English fleet under Admiral Herbert, bore down upon the latter in a line of 28 ships of war and 5 fire-ships, when a brisk action ensued, in which the English stood to sea in order to gain some advantage by manœuvring, and which terminated by the French Admiral's returning into the bay. In 1691, a Dutch ship was captured in the bay by the native Irish in the interest of Jas. II., but was retaken by Col. Becher, with the loss, on the part of the Irish, of 36 men drowned and as many taken prisoners. In March of the same year, Sir David Collier with 300 men advanced to this place, where he encamped, and defeated a party of the Irish forces, of whom 70 were killed and 15 made prisoners: in the following May, some smaller skirmishes took place here; and in June, Col. Townsend, with his forces, killed 100 of the rapparees or insurgent marauders, and brought away a quantity of plunder. In 1697, a body of troops in the service of Wm. III. arrived from Flanders, and landed in the harbour; and in 1796, a French fleet with 15,000 men intended for the invasion of Ireland appeared in the bay; but being dispersed by a storm, in which one-fourth of their ships were lost, returned without attempting to make a descent upon the coast. In 1800, while the main body of the Channel fleet was at rendezvous here, the crew of his Majesty's ship Tremeraire mutinied; but by the spirited firmness of the captain, the late Admiral Eyles, 20 of the ringleaders were seized, taken to Portsmouth and tried, and thirteen of them were executed at Spithead.

The town is situated at the northern extremity of the bay to which it gives name, in a small valley encircled by lofty mountains, which attracting the clouds in their passage over the Atlantic, involve it in almost continual rains. It consists of two parallel streets leading towards the bay, on opposite sides of the river, over which are two bridges, and a cross street, affording communication between them: the streets are indifferently paved, and not lighted; the inhabitants are supplied with water from numerous springs. The approaches, with the exception of the new mail coach road along the margin of the bay, are steep and incommodious, and are lined with cabins of very inferior description. Little improvement has been made in the town, except by the erection of some very extensive stores by Mr. O'Connell and Mr. Corkery, merchants of the place, and the enlargement of the principal hotel, which now affords ample accommodation to the numerous tourists who, during the summer season, frequent this place on their way to Glengariff and the lakes. A new and important line of road is in progress from Kenmare to Bantry, through Glengariff; it will afford a view of some of the most beautiful scenery in this part of the kingdom, embracing Glengariff and Bantry bay, of which latter it will command an extensive prospect, and is a continuation of the new line from Killarney to Kenmare. New roads have been opened from this town to Skibbereen, which will be highly advantageous to the neighbourhood, and other roads from Glengariff to Cork are also in contemplation. Nearly adjoining the town is Sea Court, the seat of the Earl of Bantry, situated on a gentle eminence commanding a magnificent view of the noble harbour and bay, with the lofty mountains on the opposite shore: the mansion is a spacious square edifice, containing a fine collection of paintings and some pieces of armour brought from the east by Viscount Bearhaven; and immediately in front of it is the undulating and fertile island of Whiddy, formerly a deer park, but now converted into valuable farms, the picturesque appearance of which is heightened by the ruins of an ancient castle, built by the O'Sullivans in the reign of Hen. VI.; the eminence behind the house is finely planted, and the demesne, including an extensive deer park, is tastefully laid out, and forms an interesting feature in the landscape. The trade of the port was formerly very considerable, and the town had attained a high degree of commercial importance. Previously to the withdrawing of the protecting duties, the manufacture of coarse linen and cotton began to thrive here and afforded employment to several hundred persons; these linens, here called "Vitries," were striped pieces chiefly used for bagging; and the sales frequently exceeded £4000 per annum. Butter, pork, and beef were formerly shipped from the port in great quantities, and, about the year 1775, several cargoes of butter were sent annually to Portugal. The only manufacture at present is that of flour, of which the Bantry Mills, belonging to Messrs. Kingston and Co., are capable of producing 12,000 bags annually. A small porter brewery is carried on in the town by Mr. L. Young; and at Donemark are the brewery and mills of Mr. Michael Murphy. A considerable trade prevails in corn raised in the neighbouring parishes, and since 1815 has been rapidly increasing; in 1835, not less than 10,000 barrels of wheat and 3000 barrels of oats were shipped from this port to the English markets. A very lucrative pilchard fishery was for many years conducted, but has long been discontinued, that fish having left the shores. The present fishery is principally confined to hake, in which 24 hookers are engaged, each carrying 15 men; but mackarel, herrings, and sprats are also taken. The fish are cured in houses formerly called fish palaces, and of late the sales of the three last kinds have produced more than £2000 per annum; they find a ready market within a circuit of 50 miles. The shores of the bay abound with a calcareous deposit which forms a valuable manure, and which, about Glengariff and in other parts of the bay, is so thickly impregnated with coral as to be considered little inferior in strength to pure lime: a considerable number of men are employed in procuring it, and the quantity raised produces on the average more than £4000 per annum. In the year ending Jan. 5th, 1836, 31 vessels of the aggregate burden of 1010 tons, principally laden with corn, cleared outwards from this port, and 26 vessels of the aggregate burden of 814 tons entered inwards, of which, two were foreign ships laden with timber from America, and the remainder coasters with cargoes of salt, coal, earthenware, and iron. The bay is spacious, safe, and commodious for ships of any burden. The principal market is on Saturday, and is amply supplied with provisions of all kinds; and there is also a market for provisions daily. Fairs are held on March 19th, May 1st, June 9th, July 15th, Aug. 21st, Oct. 15th, and Dec. 1st. Here is a chief constabulary police station. Petty sessions are held on alternate Fridays; and the quarter sessions for the West Riding of the county are also held here in February. The court-house is a neat building ornamented with a cornice and pediment supported by two broad pilasters, between which is a handsome window; and behind it is the bridewell for the barony. The parish church, a neat edifice in the early English style, with a lofty tower, is situated on the bank of the river, at the western extremity of the town; and on an eminence at the eastern extremity is a large R. C. chapel, erected at an expense of £2500. There is also a place of worship for Wesleyan Methodists. There are two school-houses in the town, one erected by subscription, and the other by a bequest of £200 from the Rev. D. Crowley, late parish priest of Bantry; and a dispensary. Bantry gives the titles of Earl, Viscount, and Baron, in the Irish peerage, to the ancient family of White, of whom the present Earl was created Baron in 1797, Viscount in 1800, and Earl of Bantry and Viscount Bearhaven in 1816.

BAPTIST GRANGE.—See GRANGE ST. JOHN.

BARNA, a village, in the parish of RAHOON, county of the town of GALWAY, and province of CONNAUGHT, 3 miles (W.) from Galway: the population is returned with the parish. It is situated on the coast of Galway bay, and is chiefly noted for the quality of its butter, with which it supplies the town of Galway. A pier was originally built by a private individual in 1799, and rebuilt by Mr. Nimmo in 1822, but being only indifferently constructed, it was destroyed in 1830, and partially rebuilt in the following year by the officer of the coast-guard and collector of Galway, with the aid of charitable funds at their disposal, and has been found very useful for the fishery; it is sheltered from the south and south-west gales, and is the only safety harbour for small craft in an extent of 27 miles of coast. Barna is the seat of Nicholas Lynch, Esq. Here are a constabulary police station and a coast-guard station, the latter forming one of the seven stations that constitute the district of Galway. The R. C. chapel for the parish, a small thatched building, is situated here.—See RAHOON.

BARNA, a hamlet, in the parish of DUNKERRIN, barony of CLONLISK, KING'S county, and province of LEINSTER, 3 miles (N. E.) from Moneygall; containing 81 inhabitants.

BARNAHELY, a parish, in the barony of KERRICURRIHY, county of CORK, and province of MUNSTER, 2 miles (N. E. by E.) from Carrigaline: containing 1022 inhabitants. This parish is situated on the south-west shore of Cork harbour, and was anciently part of the possessions of Gill abbey: it comprises 882¾ statute acres, as applotted under the tithe act, and valued at £1025 per annum, and is almost entirely under tillage, which is gradually improving. There is no waste land: a tract of marshy land on the estate of Castle-Warren has been lately reclaimed and is now applied to grazing. There are some valuable limestone quarries, which are worked chiefly for burning. Ringaskiddy, or Ring, a small village on the shore, is resorted to in summer for sea-bathing: the building of boats and yachts is carried on here to some extent, and during the winter season a considerable number of yawls are engaged in fishing. Ballybricken, the elegant mansion and demesne of D. Conner, Esq., is delightfully situated on the margin of the harbour, of which it commands a most beautiful view, and from which the grounds rise with a gentle acclivity, and are embellished with a profusion of fine timber. Prospect Villa, the elegant residence of Lieut.-Col. Burke, is situated a little to the east of it; the grounds are well planted, and these two seats form prominent and attractive objects in every view of the harbour. Castle-Warren, the seat of R. Warren, Esq., is a spacious mansion erected in 1796, and incorporated with the ancient castle of Barnahely, said to have been built by Milo de Cogan, one of the early Norman settlers, who obtained extensive grants in this county, and is represented by local tradition to have been interred in the churchyard of this parish: the castle, of which a portion remains, belonged to the archdeacons of Monkstown in the middle of the 17th century. Raffeen is the seat of T. Dorman, Esq.; and there are several ornamental cottages which contribute to embellish the scenery of this beautiful district. The parish is in the diocese of Cork: the entire tithes, amounting to £100, are impropriate in the Earl of Shannon. The Protestant inhabitants attend divine service at the church of Carrigaline. In the R. C. divisions it forms part of the union or district of Passage; the nearest chapel is that of Shanbally, in the parish of Carrigaline. The only school is a hedge school, in which 90 children are taught. There is a Danish fort in good preservation on the lands of Prospect Villa; and as some labourers employed in the construction of a new line of road were cutting through a limestone rock, a short time since, they discovered in its cavities a number of marine shells, at a distance of at least two miles from the nearest part of the strand. There is a chalybeate spa at Raffeen, which has been found efficacious in cases of dyspepsia, and is exceedingly valuable as a tonic diuretic.

BARNANE, or BARNANELY, a parish, in the barony of IKERRIN, county of TIPPERARY, and province of MUNSTER, 2¼ miles (W. N. W.) from Templemore; containing 775 inhabitants. This parish is situated on the road from Burris-o-leigh to Dunkerrin, and comprises 2015 statute acres, as applotted under the tithe act, and valued at £1842 per annum: about 100 acres are common, 46 woodland, and the remainder is principally arable. It includes the "Devil's Bit Mountain," so called from its form, which appears as if a bit had been taken out of it. At the foot of this mountain lies the demesne of Barnane, the seat of R. Carden, Esq., which is tastefully laid out and well planted; and within it are the ruins of the old parish church. It is a rectory and vicarage, in the diocese of Cashel, and is part of the union of Fithmone: the tithes amount to £105. There is a pay school of 25 boys and 20 girls in the parish.

BARONSTOWN, a parish, in the barony of UPPER DUNDALK, county of LOUTH, and province of LEINSTER, 4 miles (W. N. W.) from Dundalk; containing 1012 inhabitants. It is situated on the turnpike road from Dundalk, by Castle-Blayney, to Monaghan, and comprises, according to the Ordnance survey, 2208½ statute acres. The lands are nearly all arable and pasture; the soil is fertile, and the system of agriculture has been greatly improved; there is very little waste land, and not more bog than is sufficient to supply the inhabitants with fuel. Derefalone, the seat of G. McGusty, Esq., is in this parish. The living is a rectory, in the diocese of Armagh, with the curacies of Philipstown-Nugent, Kene, and Roche, united by act of council in 1785, forming the union of Baronstown, in the patronage of the Lord-Primate for three turns, and of the Dean and Chapter of Christ-Church, Dublin, for one: the tithes amount to £219. 10. 11½., and of the entire benefice to £414. 7. 9½. The church of the union, a neat edifice with a tower, and in good repair, is situated on an eminence at Philipstown-Nugent, nearly in the centre of the union; and almost adjoining it is the glebe-house, to which are attached 17 acres of profitable land. In the R. C. divisions the parish is partly united with Philipstown-Nugent and Dunbin, forming the union or district of Baronstown, and partly included in that of Haggardstown; the chapel, called the chapel of Kilcurly, is close on the confines of this parish and of that of Dunbin. There is a school at Kilcurly of about 80 boys and 40 girls. At Belrobin was an ancient castle, formerly the residence of a branch of the Bellew family; its site is now occupied by the residence and offices of Mr. Owen McKone, one of the most extensive occupiers of land in the county. There is also a rath or ancient fort at the same place, which has been planted, and another on the townland of Milltown.

BARRAGH, a parish, partly in the barony of St. Mullins, but chiefly in that of Forth, county of Carlow, and province of Leinster; containing, with a part of the post-town of Newtown-Barry, 4713 inhabitants. It is situated upon the river Slaney, and on the roads from Myshall to Clonegal, and from Enniscorthy to Carlow; and comprises, with the parish of Pubbledrum, 17,602 statute acres, as applotted under the tithe act, and valued at £1030 per annum. About 1600 acres are mountain and bog, 789 woodland, and the remainder arable and pasture; the state of agriculture is improving. Fine granite for building is found in the parish. The gentlemen's seats are Kilbride, the residence of J. R. Keogh, Esq.; and Ballynoe, of the Rev. G. Dawson. The living is a vicarage, in the diocese of Leighlin, and in the patronage of the Bishop: the rectory is appropriate to the vicars choral of the cathedral of Christ-Church, Dublin: the tithes amount to £692. 6. 2., of which £461. 10. 9¼. is payable to the lessee of the appropriators, and £230. 15. 4¾. to the vicar. The church, situated at Kildavin, is a small edifice, built by aid of a gift of £800 from the late Board of First Fruits, in 1812; the Ecclesiastical Commissioners have lately granted £123 for its repair. There is neither glebe nor glebe-house. In the R. C. divisions this parish is, with the exception of one townland, included in the union or district of Clonegal or Moyacomb: there is a chapel at Kildavin. A national school, in which about 120 boys and 100 girls are taught, is aided by a grant of £20 per annum from the new Board of Education; and another school is supported by Mr. Keogh. There are also three hedge schools in the parish, in which are about 130 boys and 100 girls. The estate of Clonmullen formerly belonged to the Kavanaghs, but was forfeited in the war of 1641; it is said to have been the residence of Ellen Kavanagh, the heroine of the celebrated Irish ballad of Aileen Aroon. There are some remains of the old church, clad with ivy; the burial-ground is separated from them by a rivulet.—See Newtown-Barry.

BARRETTS-GRANGE, a parish, in the barony of Middlethird, county of Tipperary, and province of Munster, 1 mile (S. E.) from Fethard; containing 233 inhabitants. This small parish was, until recently, considered as having merged into that of Coolmundry. It is in the diocese of Cashel, and is one of the parishes which constitute the union of Killenaule, to which the rectory is annexed: the tithes amount to £49.

BARRINGTON'S BRIDGE, a village, in the parish of Clonkeen, barony of Clanwilliam, county of Limerick, and province of Munster, 6 miles (E.) from Limerick: the population is returned with the parish. This place is situated on the road from Limerick to Abington, and on the river Mulkern, over which is an elegant bridge of one arch of cast iron, from which the village derives its name. The surrounding country is fertile, and the scenery agreeably diversified and embellished with modern and elegant cottages and substantial farm-houses, mostly with gardens and orchards attached to them. Though small, it has a pleasing and cheerful aspect; there is a neat and commodious hotel; a penny post has been established from Limerick, and it is a chief station of the constabulary police. A neat school-house has been built for a school in connection with the National Board, with separate apartments for the master and mistress. At a short distance from the village is the ancient parish church, in the Norman style, the western entrance of which presents some very beautiful details.—See Clonkeen.

BARRY, a village, in the parish of Tashinny, barony of Abbeyshruel, county of Longford, and province of Leinster; 3¼ miles (W. S. W.) from Colehill: the population is returned with the parish. It is situated on the road to Ballymahon, and is a station of the constabulary police. Fairs are held on January 27th, April 28th, July 28th, and October 27th. A school for poor children is maintained by the Dowager Countess of Rosse. Near the village was formerly an ancient castle, of which only some trifling vestiges can be traced; and in the immediate vicinity is a high moat. —See Tashinny.

BARTRA, or BARTRACH, an island, in the parish of Killala, barony of Tyrawley, county of Mayo, and province of Connaught, 2 miles (S. E.) from Killala: the population is returned with the parish. It is situated at the mouth of the river Moy, forming part of the coast of the harbour of Killala, and is the residence of Capt. Kirkwood. At the south-east end is the bar of Moy, on which there is only three feet of water.

BASLICK, a parish, in the barony of Ballintobber, county of Roscommon, and province of Connaught, 5 miles (N. E.) from Castlerea; containing 3574 inhabitants. This parish, which was anciently called *Baisleac-mor*, is situated on the road from Elphin to Castlerea, and comprises 6560 statute acres. According to the Annals of the Four Masters and other authorities, here was an abbey in the time of St. Patrick, of which St. Sacell was abbot or bishop; and in the year 800, St. Cormac, its abbot, died here. The state of agriculture is almost wholly unimproved; there is little woodland, except in the demesnes of the several seats; of the remainder of the parish, about three-fourths are arable and one-fourth pasture, or what is called "Bottom" land. There are several quarries of limestone, used only in constructing the fences. The gentlemen's seats are Rathmile House, that of Rich. Irwin, Esq.; Milton, of Roderic O'Connor, Esq.; Emla, of Rob. Irwin, Esq.; Heathfield, of Nicholas Balfe, Esq.; and Ballyglass, of R. Kelly, Esq. Fairs are held at Castle-Plunkett on the first Thursday in May (O. S.) and on Aug. 13th and Oct. 11th. It is a vicarage, in the diocese of Elphin, and forms part of the union of Ballintobber; the rectory is impropriate in the Earl of Essex: the tithes amount to £350, payable in moieties to the impropriator and the vicar. The R. C. parish is co-extensive with that of the Established Church; the chapel is a small building on the townland of Kilmurry. The remains of the old parish church are situated within a cemetery enclosed by iron railings and still used for interment.

BATTERJOHN, a hamlet, in the parish of DERRYPATRICK, barony of LOWER DEECE, county of MEATH, and province of LEINSTER; containing 15 dwellings and 93 inhabitants.

BATTERSTOWN.—See RATHREGAN.

BAULICK.—See BUOLICK.

BAWN, or BLACKNOW, a grange, in the barony of GALMOY, county of KILKENNY, and province of LEINSTER. It is also called *Baunrichen*, and is said to have been part of the possessions of the monastery of Fertagh. In ecclesiastical matters it is one of the denominations which constitute the union of Burnchurch, in the diocese of Ossory. Fairs are held on Ascension-day, July 8th, Sept. 8th, and Oct. 29th.

BAWNBOY.—See KILSUB.

BAYLIN, a village, in the parish of BALLYLOUGHLOE, barony of CLONLONAN, county of WESTMEATH, and province of LEINSTER, 3 miles (E.) from Athlone, on the road to Mullingar; containing 39 houses and 225 inhabitants. It is a constabulary police station; and a manorial court is held on the first Monday in every month. A school-house was built here by Lord Castlemaine, who endowed it with an acre of land, and the school is supported by his Lordship and Lady Castlemaine. There is a mineral spring in the village, strongly impregnated with iron.—See BALLYLOUGHLOE.

BEAGH, or ST. ANNE'S, a parish, in the barony of KILTARTAN, county of GALWAY, and province of CONNAUGHT, containing, with part of the post-town of Gort, 5343 inhabitants. This parish is situated on the confines of the county of Clare, and on the road from Galway and Loughrea to Ennis. A monastery of the third order of Franciscans was founded here about the year 1441, but by whom is unknown: in an inquisition of the 28th of Elizabeth it is denominated a cell or chapel, and its possessions appear to have consisted of half a quarter of land, with its appurtenances and tithes, which had been long under concealment. The parish comprises 12,331 statute acres, as applotted under the tithe act, and there is some bog; agriculture is improved, and there is good limestone. The seats are Loughcooter Castle, that of Viscount Gort; Cregg House, of F. Butler, Esq.; Ballygaagen, of W. Butler, Esq.; Ashfield, of D. McNevin, Esq.; Castle Lodge, of C. Lopdell, Esq.; River View, of Mrs. Lopdell; Sallymount, of J. Butler, Esq.; Prospect, of Mrs. Nolan; Rhyndifin, of E. Blaquiere, Esq.; Rose Park, of — Hugo, Esq.; and Rose Hill, of A. Keeley, Esq. Large fairs for cattle, sheep, and pigs are held at the village of Tobberindony, on July 12th, and Sept. 20th. It is a vicarage, in the diocese of Kilmacduagh, united with part of the rectory, and forming part of the union of Ardrahan; the remaining portion of the rectory is appropriate to the see. The tithes amount to £218. 1. 6., of which £38. 15. 4½. is payable to the Ecclesiastical Commissioners, and £179. 6. 1½. to the incumbent. The R. C. parish is co-extensive with that of the Established Church: the chapel is a plain building, but a new one is about to be erected on a site given by D. McNevin, Esq. There are six hedge schools in the parish, in which are about 340 children. Here are the remains of the ancient castles of Fidane and Arddameilivan; those of the former are in good preservation and very massive. At a place called the Punch-bowl the Gurtnamackin river first disappears underground.

BEAMORE, or BEMOOR, a village, in the parish of COLPE, barony of LOWER DULEEK, county of MEATH, and province of LEINSTER, 1¼ mile (S.) from Drogheda, on the road to Naule; containing 23 houses and 123 inhabitants.

BEATÆ-MARIÆ-DE-FORE.—See FEIGHAN of FORE (ST.).

BEAULIEU, county of KILKENNY.—See OWNING.

BEAULIEU, a parish, in the barony of FERRARD, county of LOUTH, and province of LEINSTER, 2 miles (E. by N.) from Drogheda; containing 535 inhabitants. This place was occupied by Sir Phelim O'Nial and the insurgent forces during the siege of Drogheda, which was defended by Sir Henry Tichborne, one of the lords justices of Ireland, who, on the forfeiture of the estate by the Plunkett family, purchased and obtained a grant of it from Chas. II.; the Rev. Alexander Johnson Montgomery, his descendant by the female line, is the present proprietor. The parish is situated at the estuary of the river Boyne, on the eastern coast, and comprises, according to the Ordnance survey, 1228 statute acres, including 218¾ of tideway of the Boyne. Beaulieu House, the seat of the Rev. A. J. Montgomery, was built by the lady of Sir H. Tichborne: it is a stately mansion, situated in an extensive and finely planted demesne, bounded on the south by the Boyne, and contains an ornamental sheet of water; a very handsome entrance lodge has been recently erected. The living is a rectory, in the diocese of Armagh, and in the patronage of the Lord-Primate: the tithes amount to £105. The church, a neat structure with a tower, was built by aid of a gift of £600 from the late Board of First Fruits, in 1807; and contains some handsome marble monuments to the Montgomery family, and one to the Donagh family of Newtown; in the churchyard is a curious stone with the figure of a skeleton in high relief and the date, apparently 1117. There is neither glebe nor glebe-house. In the R. C. divisions the parish forms part of the union or district of Termonfeckan. The parochial school of 10 boys and 10 girls is aided by an annual donation from the rector, and the master has a house and land from the Rev. A. J. Montgomery; there is also a pay school, in which are about 20 boys and 10 girls.

BEAUMONT, a village, in the parish of KILSHARVAN, barony of LOWER DULEEK, county of MEATH, and province of LEINSTER, 2 miles (E.) from Duleek; containing 77 inhabitants. This village, which comprises only 12 houses, is situated on the road from Duleek to Laytown, and on the Nanny water, which is here crossed by a stone bridge. Here is an extensive flour and oatmeal-mill, with six pairs of millstones and a steam-engine of 20-horse power, which has been recently erected and fitted up with the most improved machinery. It is the property of J. McCann, Esq., whose residence adjoins the mill.—See KILSHARVAN.

BECAN, or BEKAN, a parish, in the barony of COSTELLO, county of MAYO, and province of CONNAUGHT, 4 miles (W. by N.) from Ballyhaunis; containing 5659 inhabitants. It is situated on the road from Claremorris to Frenchpark, and is principally under tillage, with the exception of a few grazing farms. Becan is the residence of J. Bourke, Esq., and Ballenville, of J. Crean, Esq. The river Robe has its source within the limits of the parish. It is a rectory and vicarage, in the diocese of Tuam, and is part of the union of Kiltullagh: the tithes amount to £127. 8. 5¼. The R. C. parish is co-extensive with that of the Established Church: the chapel is a plain thatched building. At Brackloon is a school of about 60 boys and 50 girls; and there are five private schools in the parish, in which are about 300 boys and 100 girls. There are some ruins of the old church, with a burial-place annexed, which is still used.

BECTIVE, a parish, in the barony of UPPER NAVAN, county of MEATH, and province of LEINSTER, 3 miles (S. W.) from Navan; containing 671 inhabitants. This parish, called also *De Beatitudine*, was granted by Chas. I. to Sir Richard Bolton, Lord Chancellor of Ireland, in 1639, and is now the property of his descendant, Richard Bolton, Esq. It derived considerable celebrity from a Cistertian monastery founded here, in 1146 or 1152, by Murchard O'Melaghlin, King of Meath, which was dedicated to the Blessed Virgin, and richly endowed: this establishment, of which the abbot was a lord in parliament, continued to flourish, and in 1195, by order of Matthew, Archbishop of Cashel, at that time apostolic legate, and John, Archbishop of Dublin, the body of Hugh de Lacy, which had been for a long time undiscovered, was interred here with great solemnity, but his head was placed in the abbey of St. Thomas, Dublin. In the same year, the Bishop of Meath, and his Archdeacon, with the Prior of the abbey of Duleek, were appointed by Pope Innocent III. to decide a controversy between the monks of this abbey and the canons of St. Thomas, Dublin, respecting their right to the body of De Lacy, which was decided in favour of the latter. Hugh de Lacy, who was one of the English barons that accompanied Hen. II. on his expedition for the invasion of Ireland, received from that monarch a grant of the entire territory of Meath, and was subsequently appointed chief governor of the country. He erected numerous forts within his territory, encouraging and directing the workmen by his own presence, and often labouring in the trenches with his own hands. One of these forts he was proceeding to erect at Durrow, in the King's county, in 1186, on the site of an abbey, which profanation of one of their most ancient and venerable seats of devotion so incensed the native Irish and inflamed their existing hatred, that whilst De Lacy was employed in the trenches, stooping to explain his orders, a workman drew out his battle-axe, which had been concealed under his long mantle, and at one blow smote off his head. The abbey and its possessions, including the rectory of Bective, were surrendered in the 34th of Hen. VIII., and were subsequently granted to Alexander Fitton.

The parish, which is situated on the river Boyne, and on the road from Trim to Navan, comprises 3726 statute acres, chiefly under tillage; the system of agriculture is improved, and there is neither waste land nor bog. Limestone of very good quality is abundant, and is quarried both for building and for burning into lime, which is the principal manure. Bective House, the seat of R. Bolton, Esq., is a handsome modern residence, pleasantly situated on the banks of the river Boyne. The parish is in the diocese of Meath, and, being abbey land, is wholly tithe-free: the rectory is impropriate in Mr. Bolton. There is no church; the Protestant parishioners attend divine service in the neighbouring parishes of Kilmessan and Trim. In the R. C. divisions it is included in the union or district of Navan; the chapel at Robinstown is a neat modern edifice. There is a school near the R. C. chapel, for which it is intended to build a new school-room; and there is also a hedge school of 21 boys and 19 girls. The ruins of the ancient abbey occupy a conspicuous site on the west bank of the river, and have a very picturesque appearance: they consist chiefly of a lofty square pile of building, the front of which is flanked by a square tower on each side; the walls and chimneys of the spacious hall, and part of the cloisters, are remaining; the latter present a beautiful range of pointed arches resting on clustered columns enriched with sculpture, and displaying some interesting details. There are also some picturesque remains of an ancient chapel in the vicinity. Bective gives the inferior title of Earl to the Marquess of Headfort.

BECTIVE-BRIDGE, a village, in the parish of BALSOON, barony of LOWER DEECE, county of MEATH, and province of LEINSTER, 3¾ miles (E. N. E.) from Trim; containing 142 inhabitants. This place is situated on the road from Dunshaughlin to Athboy, and on the river Boyne, over which is a stone bridge connecting it with the parish of Bective, from which circumstance it has derived its name. It contains about 30 dwellings, and has two annual fairs; one on the 16th of May, principally for dry cows and young heifers, which is well attended, and the other on the 1st of November, chiefly for cattle and pigs.—See BALSOON.

BEG-ERIN, or BEGRIN, a small island in Wexford harbour, in the parish of ARDCOLME, barony of SHELMALIER, county of WEXFORD, and province of LEINSTER, 2½ miles (N. E.) from Wexford. This island, of which the name signifies in the Irish language "Little Ireland," is situated in the northern part of Wexford harbour, and was, at a very early period, distinguished as the residence of St. Ibar, or Ivore, who, according to Ware and Archdall, founded here, in 420, a celebrated monastery for Canons Regular of the order of St. Augustine, over which he presided till his death. He established a school here, in which he instructed numerous scholars in sacred literature and various sciences, and was in such reputation for learning, as well as for the sanctity of his life, that he obtained the appellation of *Doctor Begerensis*; he died on the 23d of April, in the year 500, and was interred in the monastery. St. Ængus, in his litany, invokes 150 saints, all of whom were disciples of St. Ibar. Of the monastery there are no vestiges, unless the ruins of a small chapel, of which the rudeness of the masonry indicates a very remote antiquity, may be regarded as such. In 1171, Robert Fitz-Stephen, after having been deceived into the surrender of his castle of Ferry-Carrig, and such of his garrison as were not perfidiously put to death, were brought to this place, where they were detained prisoners till the landing of Hen. II. at Waterford, soon after which they were liberated by that monarch. The island was, in 1549, alienated by a fee-farm lease, at a rent of seven shillings, to James Devereux, and is now occupied by Henry Cooper, Esq., who has built a handsome rustic cottage for his residence, which is surrounded with thriving shrubberies and plantations. Mr. Cooper has made several improvements in farming and embanking; and his family, with one or two of his workmen, constitute the whole of the population of the island.

BEGGARSBRIDGE.—See ROCHFORT-BRIDGE.

BEG-INNIS or BEGNERS ISLAND, in the parish of CAHIR, barony of IVERAGH, county of KERRY, and province of MUNSTER, lying near the north-east end of the island and post-town of Valencia: the population is returned with the parish. It is situated nearly in the centre of the chief entrance to the harbour of Valencia, on the western coast, from which island it is separated by a channel varying in breadth from one-eighth to one-half of a mile; and comprises about 330 statute acres of land, held by J. Primrose, Esq., of Hill Grove. The opening to the north, called Lough Kay, has deep water, but is much exposed to the great ocean swell. The south-eastern shore is covered with a fine shell sand, which forms a valuable manure, and is conveyed in boats to a considerable distance. There is a quarry of slate on the island, in the working of which the greater portion of the inhabitants are employed. Nearly in the centre of it is a remarkable conical hill, called the Sugar Loaf.

BEHAGH, or BEAGH, a hamlet, in the parish of ABBEY, barony of BURREN, county of CLARE, and province of MUNSTER; containing 14 dwellings and 101 inhabitants. The parochial R. C. chapel, a small thatched building, is situated here.

BELAN, a parish, in the barony of KILKEA and MOONE, county of KILDARE, and province of LEINSTER, 3 miles (S. S. W.) from Ballytore: the population is returned with the parish of Timolin. It is situated on the road from Dublin to Castledermot, and comprises 1176 statute acres, as applotted under the tithe act, and valued at £865 per annum. Belan House, the seat of the Earl of Aldborough, is an extensive pile of building, situated at the foot of Bolton hill and occupying the site of an ancient castle which formerly belonged to a branch of the Fitzgerald family, and was destroyed by Cromwell in the parliamentary war; in the house is preserved an ancient bed, in which Jas. II. and Wm. III. successively slept in the year 1690. It is a rectory and vicarage, in the diocese of Dublin, and is part of the union of Timolin: the tithes amount to £102. 10. In the R. C. divisions it is included in the union or district of Castledermot.

BELANAGARE, a village, in the parish of KILCORKEY, barony of BALLINTUBBER, county of ROSCOMMON, and province of CONNAUGHT, 2 miles (S. by E.) from Frenchpark: the population is returned with the parish. This place is situated on the mail coach road from Longford to Ballina, and consists of about 30 houses, of which several are neatly built. It was formerly the residence of the O'Conor Don, who has lately removed to a new lodge in the immediate neighbourhood, since which the village has been neglected and is falling into decay. The old mansion, now in ruins, was an irregular building with numerous gables and tall chimneys, and is surrounded with stately trees. The surrounding scenery is interesting, and the roads leading to the village are shaded by trees growing in the hedge-rows. Fairs are held on Jan. 6th, and the first Wednesdays in March, Aug. and Nov.; the January fair is noted for young horses and pigs. Petty sessions are held here irregularly. The R. C. parochial chapel is situated in the village, and was built by the late O'Conor Don, in 1819; the roof is covered with sandstone slate found in the neighbourhood. A large school is held in the chapel.—See KILCORKEY.

BELCARRA, a village, in the parish of DRUM, barony of CARRA, county of MAYO, and province of CONNAUGHT, 4 miles (S.) from Castlebar: the population is returned with the parish. This place, which is situated on the road from Castlebar to Hollymount, and comprises about 35 houses, is a constabulary police station, and has fairs on Feb. 2nd, June 4th, and Nov. 10th. It contains the parish church and R. C. chapel. In the immediate vicinity is Elm Hall, once the seat of Lord Tyrawley, but now in ruins.—See DRUM.

BELCLARE, or BELCLARE-TUAM, a parish, in the barony of CLARE, county of GALWAY, and province of CONNAUGHT, 3½ miles (S. S. W.) from Tuam, on the road to Headfort; containing 2371 inhabitants. A monastery of Franciscan friars was founded here in 1291, and at an early period had acquired very ample possessions, but little more of its history is recorded. The celebrated hill of Knockman, or Knockma, from which is an extensive and delightful view, is situated in the parish; and there are several extensive tracts of bog, and a flour-mill. The gentlemen's seats are Thomastown, the residence of Capt. Kirwan, and New-Garden, of Roderick O'Connor, Esq. It is a vicarage, in the diocese of Tuam, and, with a portion of the rectory, forms part of the union of Tuam; the other portion of the rectory is appropriate to the deanery of Tuam. The tithes amount to £235, of which one-half is payable to the dean and the other to the incumbent. In the R. C. divisions it is the head of a union or district, called Clare-Tuam, comprising the parishes of Belclare, Kilmoylan, and Kilmacrean, and containing two chapels, situated respectively in Belclare and Kilmacrean; the former is a good slated building recently erected. A school for Protestant females is wholly supported by Mrs. Kirwan, of Castle Hackett; and there are two pay schools, situated respectively at Wood's quay and Carabeg, in which are 148 boys and 21 girls.

BELCOE, a village, in the parish of BOHOE, barony of GLENAWLEY, county of FERMANAGH, and province of ULSTER, 9 miles (W. S. W.) from Enniskillen: the population is returned with the parish. It is situated near Lough Macneau, on the confines of the county of Cavan, and has fairs on April 5th, June 5th, Aug. 5th, Oct. 6th, and Nov. 26th. Here is a noted well, called Darugh Phadric.—See BOHOE.

Arms.

BELFAST, a sea-port, borough, market-town, and parish, partly in the barony of LOWER, but chiefly in that of UPPER, BELFAST, county of ANTRIM, and province of ULSTER, 8 miles (S. by W.) from Carrickfergus, 13¼ (S. E. by E.) from Antrim, and 80 (N.) from Dublin; containing, in 1821, 44,177, and in 1831, 60,388 inhabitants, of which latter number, 53,287 were in the town and suburbs, and 48,224 in the borough; and within three years after the latter census the population of the parish had increased nearly 7000 more. At a very early period this place obtained, according to some writers, the appellation of *Beala-farsad*, which has been supposed to signify "Hurdles-ford town," and according to others that of *Bela-fearsad*, "the town at the mouth of the river;" which latter is accurately descriptive of its situation on the river Lagan, near its influx into the lough or bay of Belfast. But, perhaps, a still more probable conjecture is that which ascribes its etymology to the Irish *Ball-Fosaght*, signifying "the town with a ditch or foss," which, from its low situation, were anciently constructed round the town, to protect it from the tide. Previously to the English conquests in the province of Ulster, it appears to have been a fortified station commanding the passage of the river, which is here fordable at low water, and important also from its position on the line between the ancient stations of Carrickfergus and Ardes, respectively in the counties of Antrim and Down, between which the Lagan has ever been regarded as the boundary. The original fort, of which the site is now occupied by St. George's church, was taken and destroyed about the year 1178, by John de Courcy, who soon after erected a noble castle on a more eligible spot. King John marched his army to this place, in 1210; but no notice of any town occurs till the year 1316, when the destruction of the town and castle by Edward Bruce is recorded. The Irish chieftains, having by his aid recovered their ancient possessions, rebuilt the castle, of which, through the intestine divisions in England and their union with the English settlers in Ulster, they kept uninterrupted possession for nearly two centuries, till the reign of Hen. VII., when the Earl of Kildare, at the head of a large army, in 1503, took and destroyed the town and castle; but the latter was soon afterwards repaired by the native chieftains, from which, however, their forces were again driven by the earl, in 1512, and compelled to retire to the mountains. From this period Belfast remained in a ruined and neglected state, till the year 1552, when Sir James Crofts, lord-deputy, repaired and garrisoned the castle; and during the same year the Irish of Ulster again appeared in arms, under the command of Hugh Mac Nial Oge, but the English government offered terms of accommodation which that chieftain accepted, and, swearing allegiance to Hen. VIII., he obtained a grant of the castle and town of Belfast, with other extensive possessions. After the death of Hugh, who was killed in 1555 by a party of Scottish marauders, his possessions passed to other branches of his family, with the exception of the castle, which was placed in the custody of Randolph Lane, an English governor; in the 13th of Elizabeth it was granted, with its extensive dependencies, to Sir Thomas Smythe and his son, on condition of their keeping a certain number of horse and foot in readiness to meet at Antrim after a brief notice, to attend upon the lord-deputy. In 1573 the Earl of Essex visited the fortress, which the Irish had previously, on different occasions, frequently attempted to take by surprise; and in 1575 the Lord-Deputy Sydney encountered the Irish forces at the ford of this place. About that period, Belfast is said to have had a forest and woods, of which all traces have long since disappeared. After the death of Elizabeth, the garrison, influenced by Hugh O'Nial, Earl of Tyrone, refused submission to the English crown; but, on the defeat of that powerful leader and his adherents, the English gained the ascendency, and Sir Arthur Chichester, lord-deputy in the reign of Jas. I., issued his summons requiring the supplies of horse and foot, according to the tenure by which the castle was held; and no one appearing in answer to this requisition, the castle and demesne became forfeited to the crown, and were given to Sir Arthur in 1612.

Prior to the civil war in 1641, the town had attained a considerable degree of commercial importance, and was the residence of many merchants and men of note; but the inhabitants, being chiefly Presbyterians, suffered severely for refusing to conform to the Established Church; many of them left the kingdom, and those who remained embraced the parliamentarian interest. The immediate local effect of this rebellion was the suspension of all improvements, but the town was saved from assault by the defeat of the rebels near Lisburn; and, while the insurgents were overpowering nearly all the surrounding country, Belfast was maintained in security by the judicious arrangements of Sir Arthur Tyringham, who, according to the records of the corporation, cleared the water-courses, opened the sluices, erected a draw-bridge, and mustered the inhabitants in military array. In 1643 Chas. I. appointed Col. Chichester governor of the castle, and granted £1000 for the better fortification of the town, which, while the people of the surrounding country were joining the Scottish covenanters, alone retained its firm adherence to the royal interest. The royalists in Ulster, anticipating an order from the parliament for a forcible imposition of the Scottish covenant, assembled here to deliberate upon the answer to be returned to Gen. Monroe, commander of the Scottish forces in Ireland, when required to submit to that demand; but the latter, being treacherously informed of their purpose, and favoured by the darkness of the night, marched to Belfast with 2000 men, surprised the town, and compelled them to retire to Lisburn. The inhabitants were now reduced to the greatest distress; Col. Hume, who was made governor of the castle for the parliament, imposed upon them heavy and grievous taxes, and the most daring of the Irish insurgents were constantly harassing them from without. After the decapitation of Chas. I., the presbytery of this place, having strongly expressed their abhorrence of that atrocity, were reproachfully answered by the poet Milton; and the Scottish forces of Ulster having, in common with the covenanters of their native country, embraced the royal cause, the garrison kept possession of it for the king. But Gen. Monk, in 1648, seized their commander, Gen. Monroe, whom he sent prisoner to England, and having assaulted Belfast, soon reduced it under the control of the parliament, who appointed Col. Maxwell governor. In 1649, the town was taken by a manœuvre of Lord Montgomery; but Cromwell, on his arrival in Ireland, despatched Col. Venables, after the massacre of Drogheda, to reduce it, in which enterprise he succeeded.

On the abdication of Jas. II., the inhabitants fitted out a vessel, and despatched a congratulatory address to the Prince of Orange, whom they afterwards proclaimed king; but, within a few days, James's troops having obtained possession of the place, many of the inhabitants fled to Scotland and elsewhere for safety, and several of the principal families were placed under attainder. On the landing of Duke Schomberg at Bangor, on Oct. 13th, 1689, with an army of 10,000 men, the Irish forces evacuated the town, of which Col. Wharton took possession in the name of King William: a reinforcement of 7000 well-appointed troops from Denmark shortly after joined the forces of Schomberg, which had encamped under the walls; and on June 14th, 1690, the king arrived in person, and issued from this town a proclamation to the army forbidding them to lay waste the country. The king remained here for five days, whence he proceeded to the Boyne by way of Hillsborough, and on his march issued an order to the collector of the customs of Belfast, to pay £1200 per annum to the Presbyterian ministers of Ulster, which grant formed the origin of the more extensive royal bounty at present paid to that body. The castle was destroyed by an accidental fire in 1708, and has not been rebuilt. In 1715, on the threatened invasion of the Pretender, the inhabitants of the town and neighbourhood formed themselves into volunteer corps for the better defence of the country; in 1745 they again had recourse to arms; and in 1760, by their prompt muster, in conjunction with the people of the surrounding country, they saved their town from the French under Thurot, who had landed at Carrickfergus, intending to surprise Belfast; but, overawed by the muster of 12,000 men, posted within two miles of Carrickfergus on the road to Belfast, he hastily re-embarked, after having obtained a considerable supply of brandy, wine, and provisions from the merchants of that town. The formation of the Irish volunteers, induced all the principal young men of Belfast again to accoutre themselves, and they assumed a formidable political attitude, until suppressed with the rest of that body. Notwithstanding the powerful excitement which prevailed towards the close of the 18th century, Belfast, although the centre of motion to the northern union, was preserved in peaceable subjection by the precaution of Government in placing in it a strong military force: but the spirit of disaffection had diffused itself considerably, and seven individuals were executed here for treason. With the exception of commercial difficulties, from which, however, this town suffered less than any other of equal importance in the kingdom, few circumstances have occurred in modern times to retard its progress; and it is now the most flourishing in the island, celebrated alike for its manufactures and commerce, and for the public spirit of its inhabitants in the pursuit of literature and science, and in the support of charitable and other benevolent institutions.

The town is advantageously situated on the western bank of the river Lagan, a long narrow bridge of 21 arches, erected in 1686, connecting it with the suburb of Ballymacarrett, in the county of Down, below which the river expands into the noble estuary called Belfast or Carrickfergus Lough; another bridge over the Lagan into the county of Down has been lately erected, and there is a third at some distance to the south. Its general appearance is cheerful and prepossessing; the principal streets and squares, which are well formed and spacious, are Macadamised, and the footpaths flagged with excellent freestone. The houses are handsomely built of brick and slated, and several new squares, terraces, and ranges of building have been recently erected, making the total number of houses 8022. The town is lighted with gas from works belonging to a company established by act of parliament in 1822. The inhabitants, previously to 1795, were but scantily supplied with water; but the late Marquess of Donegal granted to the trustees of the Incorporated Charitable Society a lease, for 61 years, of all the springs of water on his estate; and in 1805 the Malone springs were purchased, and the water was brought to the town at an expense of £3650. In 1817 an act was obtained, under the authority of which the trustees appointed water applotters, who took upon themselves the whole management, and now receive the rates, paying to the Society £750 per annum.

The town, though situated little more than six feet above high water mark of spring tides, is considered healthy, the air being pure and salubrious; and the surrounding scenery is richly diversified and, in many parts, picturesque. An extended range of mountains, 1100 feet in height, rises at the distance of two miles to the north-west; and within the limits of the parish is Divis mountain, 1567 feet above the level of the sea at low water. The views down the lough in a north-eastern direction are strikingly beautiful, the shores on both sides being decorated with elegant country seats and plantations. The inhabitants have long been distinguished for their zealous encouragement of literary pursuits, and the first edition of the Bible ever published in Ireland was printed at Belfast in the year 1704. In this town also was established, in 1737, the Belfast News Letter, the first newspaper ever printed in the North of Ireland: there are now several others, also a Mercantile Register and monthly periodicals. The Belfast Society for Promoting Knowledge, established in 1788, is supported by annual subscriptions of one guinea; the library contains more than 8000 volumes, and there are a cabinet of minerals, and a valuable philosophical apparatus. The Literary Society, for improvement in literature, science, antiquities, and the arts, was established in 1801; and the Historic Society, for the study of general history, the British laws and constitution, and the cultivation of oratory, in 1811. The Natural History Society, established in 1821, has recently erected a very handsome building: the lower story is an imitation of the Choragic monuments of Thrasyllus, with a portico, which is an exact copy of that of the octagon tower of Andronicus at Athens; and the upper portions are designed after the model of the temple of Minerva: the interior comprises several spacious, lofty, and elegant apartments, with lecture-rooms, an observatory, and a very valuable museum. The Botanic Gardens were formed in connection with the Natural History Society, by some of the members, who, in 1827, purchased for that purpose about 16 acres of land, on the banks of the Lagan, about a mile from the town, on the Malone road: they are under the direction of a committee of 21, elected from the holders of 500 shares of five guineas each, of whom those holding less than four shares pay also a subscription annually; the society has expended more than £4000 on these gardens, to which persons may subscribe without being shareholders. A spacious and handsome news-room, to which respectable strangers have free access, on entering their names in a book kept for the purpose, occupies the lower story of the Commercial Buildings: there is another large news-room in one of the wings of the White Linen Hall; a third has been recently opened in connection with the office of the Northern Whig newspaper, and a fourth under the patronage of the Belfast Society. Over the exchange is an elegant suite of assembly-rooms; there are also others in the Commercial Buildings, and there is a neat theatre in Arthur-street. On the north-eastern side of the town are artillery and infantry barracks; and a town-major is regularly appointed, this being nominally a garrison town: it is also a chief constabulary police station for the county.

Belfast owes much of its importance to the increase of the linen trade of Ulster, of which it is now become the grand depôt. In 1830 a very extensive mill was erected for spinning linen yarn upon the same principle as in the chief houses at Leeds, in order to meet the increasing demand of the manufacturers; and, in 1832, a large cotton-mill was adapted to the spinning of the refuse flax of the linen-mill, for the use of the canvas weavers. In these two mills more than 700 persons are employed, and, since their erection, a linen cloth manufactory has been established on a very large scale at Ligoneil, two miles distant, which is the first of the kind in this part of the country. Seven more spinning mills, containing 48,000 spindles, and affording employment to more than 5000 persons, were built in 1834, and several others have been erected since; they are all of brick, roofed with slate, and are mostly five stories high. The celebrated Ardoyne damask manufactory was established in 1825; and the elegance of the fabric soon extended its reputation, and obtained royal patronage, an extensive order for his Majesty being at present under execution. Linens and sheetings of the stoutest fabric, for the London market, are likewise manufactured in this establishment, the proprietor of which, Michael Andrews, Esq., obtained the gold medal of the Royal Dublin Society for specimens of his productions, shewn at their exhibition of national manufactures, held in Dublin, in May 1835. The business of the linen trade of the whole kingdom was for a long time transacted solely in Dublin, by agents resident there; but the serious inconvenience experienced by the numerous bleachers in the province of Ulster, in consequence of the remoteness of the principal mart, prompted them to the establishment of a linen-hall at Belfast, and in 1785 a spacious and handsome quadrangular building was erected in the centre of Donegal-square, by public subscription, and called the White Linen Hall, which affords great facility for making up assorted cargoes for foreign countries; great quantities are exported to America, the West Indies, and various other places, and nearly all the London merchants are supplied by factors resident here. The Brown Linen Hall, erected about the same time, is an enclosed space on the south side of Donegal-street, containing several detached platforms, where the merchants attend every Friday for the purchase of brown webs from the weavers, who assembled here from the surrounding districts. The webs brought to this mart are principally one yard in width, and of the finest quality; and so great is the quantity purchased by the merchants, who are also bleachers, that in the Belfast district, situated within a distance of six miles of the town to the west and south west and containing in all fourteen bleaching-greens (of which eleven are within the parish of Belfast), 260,000 pieces are annually bleached, exceeding by 87,000 the number of pieces bleached in the same district in the year 1822; the value of the goods finished annually in these establishments is little less than one million sterling.

The cotton manufacture, of which Belfast is the centre and principal seat, was originally introduced here in 1777, by Mr. Robert Joy, father of Chief Baron Joy, and at that time one of the proprietors of the Belfast News Letter. That gentleman had been chiefly instrumental in establishing the incorporated poor-house, which under his auspices became the nursery of this important branch of manufacture, at that time unknown in any other part of Ireland, and which, after struggling with various difficulties, at length attained such rapidity of progress that, in 1800, it afforded employment to 27,000 persons within a circuit of ten miles round Belfast, and is still carried on here to a vast extent in all its branches, more especially in the spinning department, for which alone there are, in the town and neighbourhood, no less than 21 factories. The machinery used in these works is partly impelled by steam, but chiefly by water, for which the streams in the neighbourhood are particularly favourable, by reason of the rapidity of their currents and their numerous falls; and gives motion to about 982,000 spindles and 640 power-looms, which latter are of very recent introduction. The buildings are of very large dimensions, in general from six to eight stories in height, and in some of them from 800 to 2000 persons are employed. The principal articles manufactured are velvets, fustians, jeans, ticking, checks, ginghams, quiltings, calico muslins, and muslinets. There are also very extensive print-fields, bleach-greens, dye-works, and establishments for every department of the manufacture, which in the aggregate affords employment to 36,225 persons; but is at present in a declining state, several of the works having been recently suspended, and others applied to different purposes. Connected with these establishments are various manufactories for machinery, iron-forges, and works for the preparation of oil of vitriol and other chymical products used in bleaching, dyeing, and printing, together employing about 1000 persons; engraving also, as connected with the printing of cotton goods, is carried on extensively. An iron-foundry was first established here in 1792; in 1798 the Lagan foundry, in Ballymacarrett, was erected, where steam-engines are now made; and in 1811 the Belfast foundry, in Donegal-street, was built, in which the patent rotatory steam-engines, originally invented by one of the proprietors, have been manufactured. In 1834 the manufacture of machinery for spinning flax was first successfully introduced into Ireland, by the proprietors of the Belfast foundry; two other foundries have been since established,—the Phœnix, in York-street, and the Soho foundry, in Townsend-street, where spinning machinery is made; there are also several other foundries on a smaller scale, the whole affording employment to about 600 persons. The making of vitriol was introduced in 1799; at present there are two establishments, in which about 180 persons are employed. The manufacture of flint glass was commenced in 1776, and in a few years several extensive glass-houses were erected; at present there are only two in operation, employing together about 90 persons. There are two distilleries, which annually produce 311,000 gallons of spirits, nearly the whole of which is for home consumption: about 150 men are employed in the process; and at Brookfield, adjoining the town, is another upon an extensive scale. There are twelve extensive ale and porter breweries, from which many thousand barrels are annually exported; some large flour and meal-mills, worked by steam and water; and extensive manufactories for tobacco, soap, candles, starch, glue, and paper, both for home consumption and for exportation. The tanning of leather for exportation was formerly carried on to a great extent, and at the commencement of the present century there were 36 tanyards in the town and neighbourhood; but it has much declined, and is at present chiefly confined to the home market. The manufacture of ropes and canvas was originally introduced in 1758, to which were added, in 1784, the making of sail-cloth, and, in 1820, the making of sails, which has since grown into celebrity and affords employment to a great number of persons of both sexes. Ship-building was commenced in the year 1791, prior to which time all vessels belonging to the port were built and repaired in England and Scotland; there are now two extensive yards, with graving docks and every requisite appendage, in which more than 200 men are constantly employed, and from which four or five brigs of the first class, and schooners of from 100 to 360 tons' registered burden, are annually launched. Several ships have also been lately built, among which is the Hindoo, of 400 tons' register, for the East India trade.

The trade of the port, comparatively of modern origin, has been rapid in its growth and uniformly increasing in its progress: it originally rose into importance on the purchase by the Crown, in 1637, of the privileges possessed by the corporation of Carrickfergus (of which port Belfast was formerly only a dependency), of importing merchandise at a far lower rate of duty than was paid at any other port. After the completion of this purchase, the custom-house of that place was removed to Belfast, which, however, arose into distinguished notice only with the linen trade, as, at the commencement of the last century, there were only five vessels, of the aggregate burden of 109 tons, belonging to the port; and the amount of custom-house duties, in 1709, was not more than £1215. In 1740 it had not only become well known on the continent as a place of considerable trade, but was in equal repute with the most celebrated commercial towns in Europe; and in 1785 it became the principal depot of the linen trade, from which time its commerce rapidly increased. During the fluctuations of trade by which other places suffered so severely, Belfast experienced comparatively but little diminution of its commerce, and in 1825 derived a considerable addition to its trade in the increase of the cross-channel intercourse, from the introduction of steam navigation. In 1833, the number of vessels which entered inwards at the port was 2445, and which cleared outwards, 1391; and the amount of duties paid at the custom-house exceeded £412,000. The trade has been rapidly and uniformly increasing every year; and in that ending on Jan. 5th, 1836, the number of vessels that entered inwards was 2730, and that cleared outwards, 2047; and the amount of duties paid at the custom-house, was £357,645. 2. 10., and of quayage dues at the ballast-office, £9289. 19. 11. The commerce of the port consists of various branches, of which the most important at present is the cross-channel trade, which in 1747 employed only three vessels, collectively of 198 tons' burden; from that time it appears to have rapidly increased, and, since the more direct and expeditious intercourse with the principal ports of Great Britain, afforded by the introduction of steam navigation, has absorbed a considerable portion of the foreign and colonial trade. The principal exports connected with this branch are linen cloth, manufactured cotton goods, and agricultural produce. Its extensive trade in provisions is of very recent introduction, and affords a striking demonstration of the great improvements in the system of agriculture which have taken place since the commencement of the present century, previously to which considerable quantities of corn were annually imported, and in 1789 the only articles shipped from this port were beef and butter, in very limited quantities. The chief imports by the cross-channel trade are tea, sugar, cotton, wool, and various articles for the use of the manufacturers, bleachers, and dyers; also British manufactured goods, and articles of general merchandise. The number of vessels that entered inwards from British ports during the year 1835 was 2949, and the number that cleared outwards, 1534; of these there were nine steam-boats, of which four were employed in the Glasgow, three in the Liverpool, and two in the London trade. The first steam-boat that crossed the channel to this port was from Liverpool, in 1819, but it was not till 1824 that steam-boats were employed in the transmission of merchandise: the passage by steam navigation to Liverpool is performed, on the average, in 14 hours, to London in 132 hours, to Glasgow in 14 hours, and to Dublin in 14 hours.

The trade with the United States and with British North America is also very considerable: the chief exports are linen cloth, manufactured cotton goods, blue, starch, and whiskey; the imports are timber and staves, tobacco, cotton, wool, ashes, and flax and clover seeds. In 1835, the number of vessels in this trade which entered inwards was 78, and of those that cleared outwards 76, the latter taking out 2675 emigrants, of whom 1824 were destined for the British American colonies, and 851 for the United States. The trade with the West Indies commenced in 1740, and, of late, several first-class vessels have been built expressly for it; 9 vessels entered inwards, and 15 cleared outwards, in 1835, in connection with the British West India islands only. The trade with the Baltic, which is on the increase, consists in the importation of tallow, timber, ashes, flax, and hemp. Tallow and hides are also imported from Odessa; mats, pitch, tar, flax, and flax seed from Archangel; and wine, fruit, lemon and lime juice, olive and other oils, brimstone, and barilla, from the Mediterranean and the Levant. The total number of vessels employed in the foreign trade, which entered inwards in 1835, was 184, and of those that cleared outwards, 145. The coasting trade is also of great importance; exclusively of ordinary vessels of different classes, and of the regular steam-packets for goods and passengers to Liverpool, London, Dublin, Greenock, Glasgow, and Stranraer, it employs packets, in the summer season, to the Isle of Man, Whitehaven, North Wales, Port Stewart, Derry, and to several other places on the Irish and Scottish coasts. There is also engaged in this trade a regular establishment of vessels of different classes to London, Maryport, Workington, and Whitehaven, those to the last three ports being chiefly employed in the coal trade; the imports supply the greater part of the North of Ireland. The number of vessels belonging to the port is 219, of an aggregate burden of 23,681 tons; but they are very inadequate to the extent of its commerce, of which a very large portion is carried on in ships belonging to other countries.

The port is very advantageously situated for trade at the mouth of the Lagan in Belfast Lough, sometimes called Carrickfergus bay, a noble arm of the sea forming a safe and commodious harbour, well sheltered and easy of access; the entrance is about six miles in breadth from the point between Groomsport and Ballyholm bay, in the county of Down, and White Head in the county of Antrim; the length from the latter point to the quays at Belfast is 12 miles, decreasing gradually in breadth towards the bridge, where it is very much contracted by the different quays and landing-places, and the embankments of Ballymacarrett. The preservation and improvement of the port and harbour were vested in the Ballast Corporation, constituted by act of parliament in 1785, which was repealed by an act obtained in 1831, and a new "Corporation for Preserving and Improving the Port and Harbour of Belfast" was created, consisting of "the lord of the castle" and "the sovereign," the parliamentary representatives for the counties of Antrim and Down, and the boroughs of Belfast, Carrickfergus, and Downpatrick, and sixteen other commissioners, of whom four go out of office annually, and their successors are elected subject to the approbation of the lord-lieutenant and privy council. Their annual income, arising from pilotage, tonnage, quayage rates on imports and exports, ballastage, &c., on an average of five years, ending Jan. 5th, 1836, amounted to £8868. 18. 8., and the expenditure to £8789 8. 4. The objects of obtaining the new act, in 1831, were to enable the commissioners to purchase quays and grounds for the improvement of the harbour, and to render the enactments suitable to the present state of the trade of the town, which had increased nearly tenfold since the passing of the former act. Below the bridge a fine range of quays extends along the north-west bank of the river, with two graving docks, which were constructed soon after the port was frequented by large vessels; three of these wet docks extend into the principal streets of the town. A spacious graving dock was completed in the year 1826, at an expense of £26,000, by the Ballast Corporation; and several extensive wet docks, quays, and warehouses are now being constructed below the town, under an act of parliament obtained in 1829, by Messrs. Holmes and Dunbar, who have already expended £35,000 in this undertaking: the first of these docks, completed in 1832, is 400 yards in length and 100 yards in breadth, and is intended for the large ships in the timber trade, and for those in the coal trade till the other docks are constructed. The harbour commissioners, under the act of 1831, contemplate the deepening and enlarging of the harbour, the formation of a new channel from the quays to the Mile-water river, the construction of floating docks with entrance locks, additional quays, and other improvements; but these works are at present delayed. The custom-house, a very indifferent building, is situated on Hanover-quay. The Lagan navigation, extending in a line of 22 miles from the port to Lough Neagh, by way of Lisburn, was constructed under an act of the 27th of Geo. III., confirmed by others to the 54th of the same reign, by which the proprietors were invested with a small duty on beer and spirits in the excise district of Lisburn, since commuted for an annual money payment out of the consolidated fund: the number of debentures issued from 1785 to 1793 was sixty-two, amounting to £62,000. The navigation is continued partly in the bed of the river, and partly by collateral cuts to a mile above Lisburn; but, from its circuitous course and the high rate of the tolls, goods are conveyed by land with greater expedition and at less expense. Divers new roads have been formed in the immediate neighbourhood of the town; and, under an act of parliament obtained in 1832, a railway from the harbour to Cave Hill is now being constructed, in a double line, which is the first work of the kind in the North of Ireland.

The Chamber of Commerce was originally established in 1783; its meetings were suspended from 1794 to 1802, since which time they have been resumed without interruption, greatly to the benefit of trade and the interests of the town. The Old Exchange, situated nearly in the centre of the town, at the end of Donegal-street, is the private property of the Marquess of Donegal; it was formerly the place of public resort for the merchants, but, since the erection of the Commercial Buildings, has been used only for the election of the chief magistrate. The Commercial Buildings were erected in 1822, opposite to the Exchange, at an expense of £20,000, by a proprietary of 200 shareholders incorporated by act of parliament in 1823, and by a committee of whom, annually elected, the affairs of the institution are conducted: the buildings comprise an excellent commercial hotel, a spacious and handsome news-room, over which is an elegant assembly-room, and behind these an area with a piazza for the use of the merchants; and in connection with them are numerous offices principally occupied by professional men. The north front, of Irish granite, is decorated with eight lofty Ionic columns, and the west front is principally occupied by shops: the merchants assemble in the news-room and hold 'Change on Monday, Wednesday, and Friday. The revenue derived by Government from the post-office, in 1835, was £10,073. The banking establishments are the Northern Banking Company, established in 1824; the Belfast Banking Company, in 1826; and the Ulster Banking Company, in 1836: all have branches in the different large towns throughout the province. There are also branches of the Bank of Ireland, the Provincial Bank, and the Agricultural and Commercial Bank of Ireland.

Jas. I., in 1605, 1608, and 1611, made grants of markets and fairs, which were all included in one grant to Arthur, Lord Chichester, in 1621, of a market to be held on Friday, and fairs annually on Aug. 1st and 2nd, and Oct. 28th and 29th; this grant was also confirmed by Charles II. to Arthur, Earl of Donegal, in 1668. Though the markets are open daily, the principal market day is Friday: the two fairs are now held on Aug. 12th and Nov. 8th. There are in Smithfield two market-places for meat, two for fish, and one for hay, straw, and hides, besides several others for meat and vegetables in various parts of the town, all of which are well supplied: the market for pork and butter is in the weigh-house and buildings adjoining; the sale of poultry of all kinds, collected from a great distance, forms a regular trade; and the fish market is well supplied with turbot and salmon from the coasts of Antrim and Derry.

Belfast is in some measure indebted for its incorporation to the favour shewn to the Chichester family by Jas. I., who, in 1612, granted to Sir Arthur Chichester, who had previously established a number of Devonshire men in the townland of Malone, the castle and an extensive surrounding territory; and in the following year incorporated the inhabitants by charter. In the 4th of Jas. II., on a seizure of the franchises, a charter, the provisions of which were in most respects similar to those of the former, was granted, but is now considered void. Geo. II., in the 33rd year of his reign, also granted a charter, which, however, is only an inspeximus of the charter of Jas. I. The corporation is styled "The Sovereign, Free Burgesses, and Commonalty of the Borough of Belfast;" and consists of a sovereign, lord of the castle, constable of the castle, twelve other free burgesses, and an unlimited number of freemen, assisted by a town-clerk and two serjeants-at-mace. The sovereign is chosen annually on the 24th of June by the free burgesses, from three of their own body nominated by the lord of the castle (or, in default of such nomination, which seldom occurs, elected by themselves), and is sworn into office before the lord, or in his absence before the constable of the castle, on Michaelmas-day. The lord of the castle is a member of the corporation by tenure of the castle of Belfast; the office is held by the Marquess of Donegal, in whose family it has continued since the date of the charter; the constable is appointed by instrument under seal of the lord of the castle, and becomes a free burgess. The other free burgesses are chosen, as vacancies occur, by the sovereign and the remainder of their body; the town-clerk is elected by the sovereign and burgesses; and the serjeants-at-mace are chosen by the corporation at large. The freedom of the borough is acquired only by gift of the sovereign and free burgesses; at present there are no freemen. The borough returned two representatives to the Irish parliament from the date of its incorporation till the Union, after which it sent one to the Imperial parliament, but its original number was restored by the act of the 2nd of William IV., cap. 88, passed to amend the representation. The right of election was formerly vested exclusively in the free burgesses, but by the act above-named has been extended to the £10 householders: the number of voters registered at the close of 1835 was about 1600: the sovereign is the returning officer. The jurisdiction of the corporation and of the town police is supposed to extend on the north to the Mile-water, and on the south to the Blackstaff, both of which streams fall into the Lagan, which forms its boundary on the east; and on the west is also a boundary, but so imperfectly defined that disputes are constantly arising with respect to the county cess, which within it is levied on the houses, and without it only on the acre. Under the act now regulating the harbour a jurisdiction is given to the judges of assize, justices of the peace for Antrim, and the sovereign of Belfast, over all offences committed within the limits of the port and harbour, or within 500 yards of the quays in the county of Down, as if such offences had been committed within the county of Antrim. The act of the 2nd and 3rd of Wm. IV., cap. 89, assigns a new boundary for elective purposes, which is minutely described in the Appendix. The sovereign is a justice of the peace for the borough, and usually holds the commissions of the peace for the counties of Antrim and Down; he is also clerk of the market, and, *ex officio*, a member of different bodies incorporated under local acts for the improvement of the town and port. The charter granted a court of record for the recovery of debts not exceeding £20, arising within the borough or its liberty, to be held every Thursday before the sovereign, but it has long since fallen into disuse. The manor court, held every third Thursday before the seneschal (who is appointed by the Marquess of Donegal, as lord of the manor of Belfast, within which the borough is situated), has jurisdiction over the entire parish, and over the townland of Ballynafeigh, in the county of Down, to the amount of £20 present currency, by process of attachment or arrest: the seneschal also proceeds by civil bill under the manor court acts: the prison of the court was abolished in 1828, and defaulters are now sent to the county gaol. Courts leet for the manor are also held by the seneschal; at that held in May, constables, applotters, and appraisers are appointed for the ensuing year. The sovereign holds petty sessions every Monday and Wednesday at the sessions-house, at which county magistrates may also attend. The stipendiary police magistrate, appointed in 1816, holds a court of petty session at the sessions-house every Thursday, at which other justices attend; a magistrate's court at the police-office every Tuesday and Saturday, where he disposes of cases respecting servants' wages, and other matters not requiring the attendance of two justices; and also sits daily at the office of the nightly watch establishment. The county quarter sessions are held in this town, in conjunction with other places, four times in the year; and the assistant barrister then determines causes by civil bill under his statutable jurisdiction, for the division of Belfast. The house of correction, adjoining the quarter sessions court-house, is a good building of brick, erected in 1817, but is not sufficiently adapted for the classification of prisoners, who are chiefly employed in breaking stones for the streets of the town: it contains good schools, for both sexes, to which two hours in the day are devoted. Commissioners of police were appointed by an act of parliament passed in 1800, and amended in 1816, under which a police tax, amounting on an average of five years, ending with 1835, to £9000 per annum, is levied for the maintenance of patrols by night and by day, and for lighting, cleansing, and paving the town and precincts.

The parish, according to the Ordnance survey, contains 19,559 statute acres, and was anciently called Shankill, but no church having existed at the latter place for more than two centuries, it is now generally designated the parish of Belfast. The living is a vicarage, in the diocese of Connor, and province of Armagh, and in the patronage of the Marquess of Donegal, to whom the impropriate rectory belongs: the entire parish is under the tithe composition act, and, with the exception of a portion, called the Upper Falls, pays £950 per annum, of which £600 belongs to the lay impropriator, and the remainder to the vicar, who has also a glebe-house near the church, and 20 acres of land. The parochial church, dedicated to St. Anne, was erected in 1778, at the expense of the late Marquess of Donegal: it consists of a nave and chancel, with a lofty Ionic tower surmounted by a Corinthian cupola covered with copper, forming an interesting and conspicuous object for many miles round; the portico, which was inferior in character to the rest of the building, has been replaced by one of loftier elevation. About 1830 the late Board of First Fruits gave £666 for the repair, and the Ecclesiastical Commissioners have recently granted £375 for the improvement, of the church. *St. George's* church, or chapel of ease, was erected in 1812, on the site of a former edifice, called the corporation church, which had been built on the ruins of the ancient castle: it is a splendid structure, consisting of a nave and chancel, with a magnificent and highly enriched portico of six noble columns and four fluted pilasters, supporting a cornice and pediment, in the tympanum of which are the arms of the united sees of Down and Connor, and of the town, in alto relievo; this splendid specimen of Corinthian architecture was removed from the front of a palace built by the late Earl of Bristol, when Bishop of Derry, on the shore of Lough Beg, the materials for which were quarried from the Derry mountains, and worked by Irish artists, and after that noble prelate's decease purchased, on the demolition of the palace, by Dr. Alexander, then Bishop of Down and Connor, and now of Meath, and by him presented to this church: the Ecclesiastical Commissioners have recently granted £123. 6. 7. for the repair of the building. The living is a perpetual curacy, in the patronage of the Vicar, and was endowed by the late Board of First Fruits with £3000, laid out in the purchase of the tithes of Naas, in the county of Kildare, producing under the composition act £126 per ann., and further endowed by the vicar with a portion of the tithes of the Upper Falls, now producing to the curate, under the same act, £50 per annum. *Christchurch*, containing 1000 free sittings, and situated near the Royal Institution, was erected by the late Board of First Fruits, aided by subscription, and was opened for divine service in 1833: the living is a perpetual curacy, endowed with £50 per ann. by the Board, together with the rents of the pews, and in the patronage of the Vicar. It is also in contemplation to erect a church, or chapel, in the townland of Upper Malone, in this parish, about three miles south of the town.

Belfast is the seat of the R. C. see of Down and Connor, and the residence of the Bishop; there are two spacious chapels in the town, one of which, erected in 1811, and considered as the cathedral, is an elegant edifice, in the later style of English architecture: there are also other chapels at Ballymacarrett, Hollywood, Green Castle, and Ballyclare, all in the R. C. parish of Belfast. There are seven places of worship for Presbyterians, of which that for the third congregation (so called from the order of its formation), built in 1831 at an expense of £10,000. by Mr. Millar, a native and resident architect, is perhaps the most elegant edifice of its kind in the three kingdoms. The front is enriched with a stately Grecian-Doric portico of ten lofty columns resting on a basement of twenty steps, and surmounted by a beautiful attic balustrade, composed of a series of pedestals and light pierced work, having a novel and pleasing effect; the other portions of the building are noble and elegant in design, and beautiful in detail, especially the grand staircase leading to the gallery, from which may best be observed that agreeable harmony of design and unity of effect which are strikingly characteristic of this chaste and beautiful edifice. The meeting-house for the fifth congregation, in Fisherwick-place, erected in 1827 at an expense of £7000; and that for the sixth, in May-street, built in 1829 at an expense of £9000, are also spacious and elegant structures. There are three places of worship for the Seceders (sometimes called Burghers or Antiburghers), two for Covenanters or Reformed Presbyterians, two each for Primitive and Wesleyan Methodists, and one each for General Baptists, the Society of Friends, and Independents. Five of the Presbyterian meeting-houses are in connection with the Synod of Ulster, namely, those of the third, fourth, fifth, sixth, and seventh congregations; the fifth and sixth are of the first class and the fourth and seventh of the second class. Two are in connection with the Presbytery of Antrim, namely, those of the first and second congregations, the first being a collegiate charge, and each of the first class; and two more in connection with the Seceding Synod are of the first class.

The "Royal Belfast Academical Institution," which reflects so much honour on its founders, was projected in 1807; and, within a few weeks from the first promulgation of the design, subscriptions to the amount of £16,000 were raised for carrying it into effect: this sum was further increased by subscriptions from other parts of Ireland, and from England; and, under the patronage of the Marquess of Hastings, and by the unwearied exertions of several gentlemen, nearly £5000 was subscribed in India: making the total amount £25,000. In 1810, the patrons and principal subscribers were by act of parliament incorporated a body politic, to consist of the Lord-Primate, the Marquess of Donegal, the Bishop of Down and Connor, the Bishop of Dromore, and more than 70 of the principal subscribers, including all who should subscribe and pay 20 guineas, with power to elect a president, vice-presidents, treasurer, secretary, managers, visitors, and auditors, of whom 21 should be competent to form a board, to transact all business relative to the institution, with license to take lands not exceeding £2500 per annum, and other privileges. The buildings were completed at an expense, including furniture and apparatus, of £28,954. 3. 8., leaving no provision for the endowment of professorships; for which object the managers applied to government, and in the year 1814 received from parliament a grant of £1500, which was continued during the years 1815 and 1816; after which it ceased till 1824, when it was renewed on the recommendation of the Commissioners of Education, and in the year 1834 was increased to £3500; of which sum £2000 was for additional buildings, and £1500 for general expenditure. The institution comprehends a collegiate and a school department, the former under the direction of seven professors of natural philosophy, moral philosophy, logic and the belles lettres, mathematics, Latin and Greek, Hebrew, and anatomy, respectively; there are also two professors of divinity, one appointed by the general Synod of Ulster, and the other by the Seceding Presbyterian Synod of Ireland. The professors were, in 1818, constituted a board of faculty for superintending the courses of instruction and discipline observed in the institution, as were also the masters of the school department for that branch of it. The collegiate department is conducted on a plan similar, in most respects, to that of the university of Glasgow; the session commences in November and ends in May, when public examinations take place; the mathematical class is generally very numerous, and is considered equal to any in the United Kingdom; the classical course is also extensive; the moral philosophy class has no prescribed course of reading, but lectures are given and examinations are held; the course of anatomy is pursued rather as a branch of general education than as a medical study, though admirably calculated as a first course for medical students, for whom it is in contemplation to establish a distinct class. The school department comprises the mercantile, English, classical, mathematical, Italian, French, and drawing schools, each superintended by a separate master. There are at present about 200 students in the collegiate, and 210 pupils in the school department of the institution, to which is attached a good library, a museum, and a valuable philosophical apparatus. Nearly all the candidates for the Presbyterian ministry in Ireland are educated here; and the Synod of Ulster, and the Seceding Synod of Ireland, by whom the institution is cordially patronised, consider the general certificate of the faculty equivalent to the degree of M. A. in any of the Scottish universities, or to that of B. A. in Trinity College, Dublin, or either of the English universities: the total receipts of this establishment, for 1835, were £3646. 8. 5., and the expenditure was £3735. 19. 5. The number of children educated in the various charity and other free schools, excepting the Sunday schools, is about 2850, of whom 1480 are boys and 1370 girls; one on the Lancasterian plan was formerly a Sunday school, and was converted into a day school in the year 1811, when a spacious school-house of brick, with a residence for the master, was built at an expense of £2000, raised by lottery and by local subscriptions; the school in Brown-street was established in the year 1812, under the patronage of the Marquess of Donegal, and a large and handsome brick building, with houses for the master and mistress adjoining, was erected by subscription, at an expense of £1500; the school in Donegal-street, which was the first in the North of Ireland, that placed itself in connection with the National Board, was founded in 1829, under the patronage of the Right Rev. Dr. Crolley, R. C. Bishop of Down and Connor, and two large school-houses were built adjoining the R. C. cathedral; and in the townland of Malone the late Marquess of Donegal, in 1765, built a very large school-house on the demesne of Willmount, and endowed it with the rent of an adjoining farm, now let for £40 per annum, which appears to have been originally a charter school, but is now open to all children of the neighbourhood, of whom those attending it are educated gratuitously, and supplied with books. The number of private schools is 74, in which are 3630 boys and 2820 girls.

The Incorporated Poor-house, for the reception of the aged and infirm poor, and the support of their children during infancy, was built at an expense of £7000, raised by a lottery and by public subscription, on an elevated site at the upper end of Donegal-street, granted in 1771 by the Marquess of Donegal; and the founders of this humane institution were incorporated by act of parliament in 1774, under the title of "the President and Assistants of the Belfast Charitable Society." The funds, which from the improvement in property are likely to increase, at present exceed £2500 per annum, arising from an annuity of £750 paid by the commissioners of water, the surplus of the revenue of the harbour commissioners after paying the necessary expenses of improving and maintaining the harbour, rents of land and houses, annual subscriptions and donations, and from collections at the churches and principal chapels. There are at present more than 480 individuals who are lodged, clothed, and fed in the house, of whom the aged, both male and female, are employed in some useful occupation, or in its domestic management; and the children, for whose instruction a master and a mistress are appointed with salaries respectively of £25 and £20 per annum, are also taught some business in the house, or apprenticed to trades, or to the sea service: each is at liberty to attend his own place of worship on Sunday; and ministers of all denominations are allowed to officiate in the house during the week. The House of Industry, for the suppression of mendicity and the promotion of industry among the poor, was established in Smithfield in 1809; it is principally supported by voluntary contributions, and affords employment in weaving, spinning, knitting, net-making, and other branches of industry, to the unemployed poor, making up any deficiency in their earnings by donations of food and clothing; it assists poor housekeepers, relieves strangers and forwards them to their destination, supplies deserving mendicants with food and punishes the refractory, accommodates industrious families with small loans or occasional grants, and has diffused great benefit over this populous town, in which it has entirely abolished mendicity. The Fever Hospital was established in 1817, and a dispensary, instituted in 1792, has been incorporated with it: the buildings, situated in Frederick-street, are handsome and commodious, with a spacious area in front, and are adapted to the reception of 226 patients; it is supported by donations, bequests, and subscriptions, also by fines levied by magistrates and grand jury presentments, of which the last alone amount to about £400 per annum, and its annual income is about £1000: it is open to patients not only of the town, but from the county at large, of whom a great number are annually relieved. The Lying-in Hospital was originally established in Donegal-street, in 1794, but in 1830 removed to a more spacious and handsome building erected for it on the new road; it is liberally supported by subscription. The Belfast District Lunatic Asylum, for the reception of pauper patients from the counties of Antrim and Down, and from the county of the town of Carrickfergus, was erected on an eminence one mile from the town, near the Falls road, in 1829, at an expense, including furniture and other contingencies, of £25,319. 13., defrayed by Government under an act of the 1st and 2nd of Geo. IV.: the buildings, which are handsome, were originally adapted for 104 patients, and consist of a centre comprising the house of the governor and the committee-rooms, and two wings, in which are eight corridors containing each thirteen cells for patients, and two others of smaller size containing six cells each, for those of more violent derangement; each corridor has a day-room for the patients, and one also for the keeper: the grounds surrounding the house comprise an area of more than 21 acres, to which the patients have free access, and the whole is enclosed with a stone wall fourteen feet high, with a porter's lodge at the entrance: the males are employed in weaving linen and cotton, gardening, and cultivating the land; and the females in spinning, knitting, and domestic occupations. The management of the asylum is vested in a committee appointed by the general board in Dublin; the medical department is superintended by a physician, governor, and matron, assisted by 26 keepers and others: the annual expenditure, about £2000, is advanced by Government, but repaid by the grand juries of the respective counties. Many extraordinary cures have been effected, and upon an average nearly one-half of the patients have been restored to sanity by the skilful and humane system of treatment introduced and successfully practised by the governor. A savings' bank was established in 1816, for which a handsome edifice was erected in 1830, at an expense of £1400, raised from a fund which had accumulated from the gratuitous superintendence of the committee for the fourteen years preceding; the amount of deposits at present is nearly £90,000. There are also several minor establishments for the benefit of the poor, among which may be noticed the female penitentiary; the society for the relief of the destitute sick, established in 1826; the society for clothing the poor, in 1827; the society for discountenancing vice and promoting the Christian religion, also in 1827; the association for the protection of the rights of conscience, in 1830; the society for the religious improvement of the poor, also in 1830; a Bible society, tract societies, and a library of religious books for the use of the poor.

There are no remains of antiquity in the town, though some are scattered over the parish: near Stranmillis, on the Lagan, was an ancient chapel, called *Capella de Kilpatrick;* on the summit of a hill in Upper Malone was the *Capella de Crookmuck;* near Callender's Fort, on the Falls road, about two miles from the town, was that of *Cranock,* of which traces of the foundations and a large cemetery are still remaining; and on the same road, the chapel of *Kilwee,* where numerous elegantly carved crosses and other sepulchral monuments have been found. About three miles on the Carrickfergus road is a small fragment of an ancient fortress, called Greencastle; in Upper Malone was an extensive fort called Castle Cam, or Freeston Castle, on the site of which the elegant mansion of Malone House has been erected; at a small distance on the left of the road to Shaw's-bridge are seen the foundations of a third fort; in the grounds of Malone, near Lismoine, are the remains of a fourth; and in the R. C. burial-ground at Friar's Bush are the remains of a fifth. Among the most curious relics of antiquity are the caves in various places formed in the earth and in the hard limestone rock; of the former, three were discovered in 1792 at Wolf Hill, the largest of which is eight yards long and one yard wide, with four small chambers diverging from it; on the side of a small hill in the townland of Ballymargy is one of larger dimensions, and in a more perfect state, with two entrances; and near Hannahstown is one still larger, which since 1798 has been closed, having at that time been a place of concealment for arms. Three large caves, which give name to the mountain called Cave Hill, are all formed in the perpendicular face of an immense range of basaltic rock; the lowest is 21 feet long, 18 wide, and from 7 to 10 feet in height; above this is another, 10 feet long, 7 wide, and 6 in height; and above that is a third, said to be divided into two unequal parts, each of which is more extensive than the largest of the other caves; but the ascent is so dangerous that few venture to visit it. The large ramparts of earth, called raths, or forts, are also numerous: of these the most extensive is Mac Art's fort, on the summit of Cave hill, protected on one side by a precipice, and on the others by a single ditch of great depth and a vallum of large dimensions; the enclosed area is nearly level, and, from the height of the mountain, which is 1140 feet, commands a view of vast extent, variety, and beauty, including the Isle of Man, the Shores and mountains of Scotland, and a large portion of the counties of Antrim, Down, Armagh, Derry, and Donegal. Near the base of Squires hill are many smaller raths, and two of large dimensions almost at the summit of the Black mountain; and near the shore, at Fort William, is an encampment, 70 feet square, surrounded by a deep fosse and defended by a bastion at each angle, and said to have been thrown up by King William in 1690; near it is another intrenchment of ruder construction. There are two large cairns on the Black mountain, in one of which, in 1829, was found a large urn filled with calcined human bones, a spear head, and two ornaments of brass; there is also a cairn on Cave hill, and one on Squires hill. Great numbers of stone and flint hatchets, and arrow heads of flint, have been discovered; and brazen celts and querns, or hand mill-stones, are occasionally found.

Among the gentlemen's seats in the parish the most conspicuous for their elegance are Ardoyne, the residence of M. Andrews, Esq.; Ballydrain, of H. Montgomery, Esq.; Ballysillen, of J. F. Ferguson, Esq.; Beech Park, of Arbuthnot Emerson, Esq.; Beech Mount, of Lewis Reford, Esq.; Brookfield, of T. Tripp, Esq.; Cromac, of T. Garret, Esq.; Duncairn, of A. J. Macrorey, Esq.; the Falls, of J. Sinclaire, Esq.; Fortfield, of W. Johnson, Esq.; Fort-William, of G. Langtry, Esq.; Glenbank of T. Mackay, Esq.; Glennalena, of W. Orr, Esq.; Glenville, of Mrs. McCance; the Grove, of W. Simms, Esq.; Jennymount, of R. Thomson, Esq.; Larkfield, of Henderson Black, Esq.; Ligoneil, of A. Stewart, Esq.; Lismoine, of R. Callwell, Esq.; the Lodge, of J. Emerson Tennent, Esq., M.P. for Belfast; Low-Wood, of J. Thomson, Esq.; Malone House, of W. Wallace Legge, Esq.; Mount Collier, of A. Mulholland, Esq.; Mount Vernon, of Hill Hamilton, Esq.; New Forge, of J. Ferguson, Esq.; Park-Mount, of J. McNeile, Esq.; Old Park, of H. Lyons, Esq.; Sea-view, of J. Boomer, Esq.; Springfield, of J. Stevenson, Esq.; Strandmillis, of G. Black, Esq.; Suffolk, of W. McCance, Esq.; Wheatfield, of J. Blair, Esq.; Willmount, of J. Stewart, Esq.; Wolf Hill, of Mrs. Thompson; Woodburn, of M. Charley, Esq.; Finaghy, of J. Charley, Esq.; and Strigoniel, of J. Steen, jun., Esq. The mineral productions are coal, iron, manganese, marble, limestone, freestone, gypsum, and fullers' earth, of which only the limestone is worked; the coal seams are seen in the Collin and Dunmurry water, and under the lands of Willmount, near which place also, and at New Forge, is the iron; the manganese, at the foot of the Black mountain, near which is a fine stratum of grey marble; and the gypsum, in the Collin and Forth water. Among the eminent natives of this place may be noticed, Dr. Black, the celebrated chymist; the Rev. T. Romney Robinson, author of an able mathematical work, and principal astronomer in the observatory at Armagh; J. Templeton, Esq., who left in manuscript the Botany and Natural History of Ireland, now in preparation for the press by his son; and J. Emerson Tennent, Esq., author of the History of Modern Greece, &c. Among the distinguished persons who have resided here may be mentioned the late Dr. R. Tennent, the philanthropist; Dr. Abernethy, author of the Attributes; Edward Bunting, a celebrated professor of music and collector of the ancient melodies of Ireland; Dr. J. L. Drummond, author of various scientific treatises and botanical works; Dr. Bruce, author of a life of Homer and other works; and Dr. W. H. Drummond, author of various poetical, religious, and political works. Belfast gives the titles of Earl and Baron to the ancient family of Chichester, Marquesses of Donegal.

BELGRIFFIN, or BALGRIFFIN, a parish, in the barony of Coolock, county of Dublin, and province of Leinster, 5 miles (N. E.) from Dublin; containing 259 inhabitants. This place formerly belonged to the ancient family of the De Burgos, who held the manor in the 14th century, and by whom the castle was erected. It afterwards became the property of the O'Neills and De Bathes, and the castle was for some time the residence of Richard, Duke of Tyrconnel, Lord-Deputy of Ireland under Jas. II. The parish is situated on the turnpike road from Dublin to Malahide: the lands are chiefly under tillage; the system of agriculture is improving, and the parish generally is noted as a corn district. Belgriffin Park, the seat of the Rev. T. F. Walker, is pleasantly situated; the mansion is built with the materials of the ancient castle, of which there are now no remains. The other seats are Bellcamp, the property of J. J. Baggot, Esq.; Clare Grove, of General Cuppage; Airfield, of Alderman Sir Edmund Nugent; and Sea View, of T. Franklyn, Esq. The living is a rectory and vicarage, in the diocese of Dublin; the rectory is united to that of Drumshallen and to the half rectories of Kilcullen and Glasnevin, together forming the corps of the precentorship in the cathedral of Christ-Church, Dublin, in the patronage of the Crown; and the vicarage is part of the union of St. Doulogh's, in the patronage of the Precentor. The lands in this parish belonging to the precentor comprise 29*a.* 2*r.* 3*p.*, let on lease for £3. 13. 4. per annum, and an annual renewal fine of £18. 9. 2¾.; and the lands of the union comprise altogether 680*a.* 3*r.* 21*p.*, let on lease for £95. 19. 5. per annum, and annual renewal fines of £114. 9. 2.; making the gross income of the precentorship, including the tithes, £484. 19. 6¾. per annum. In the R. C. divisions the parish forms part of the union or district of Baldoyle and Howth. In 1580, Mr. John Bathe left a piece of land at Chapelizod for the support of an hospital for four poor men of this parish. There are some remains of the old church.

BELLAGAN, a village, in the parish of Carlingford, barony of Lower Dundalk, county of Louth, and province of Leinster, 2½ miles (S.) from Carlingford; containing 155 inhabitants. It is situated on the south-west side of the entrance into the bay of Carlingford, and consists of about 25 houses, which are mostly inhabited by small farmers and agricultural labourers.—See Carlingford.

BELLAGHY, a village and post-town, in the parish of Ballyscullion, barony of Loughinsholin, county of Londonderry, and province of Ulster, 9½ miles (S.) from Kilrea, and 100¼ (N.) from Dublin: the population is returned with the parish. This place became the head of a district granted in the reign of Jas. I. to the Vintners' Company, of London, who, in 1619, founded the village, and erected a strong and spacious castle, the custody of which they entrusted to Baptist Jones, Esq., who had a well-armed garrison of 76 men for its defence. In the war of 1641 the castle was besieged and taken by a party of insurgents under the command of one of the Mac Donnells, and in the following year burned to the ground. It occupied a gentle eminence on the north-west side of the village, but no portion of it is remaining; the very site has been cultivated as gardens, and the only traces are some of the arched cellars beneath the roots of some large trees. The village is situated on the western shore of Lough Beg, and on the roads leading respectively from Castle Dawson to Portglenone and from Kilrea to Toome; it consists of one long street intersected at right angles by two shorter streets; the houses are generally small, but well built; and the environs are remarkably pleasant, and are embellished with gentlemen's seats, of which the principal near the village are Bellaghy Castle, the residence of J. Hill, Esq., and Bellaghy House, of H. B. Hunter, Esq. Fairs are held on the first Monday in every month, for the sale of cattle, sheep, and pigs, and are well attended. A court for the Vintners' manor is held once every month, for the recovery of debts under £2: its jurisdiction extends over the parishes of Ballyscullion, Kilrea, Tamlaght-O'Crilly, Termoneeny, Maghera, Desertmartin, Kilcronaghan, Magherafelt, and Killelagh. Adjoining the village is the parish church of Ballyscullion, a large and handsome building; and at a short distance is a small R. C. chapel. Here is also a place of worship for Wesleyan Methodists; and a meeting-house is now being built for Presbyterians in connection with the Synod of Ulster. The parochial school for boys and girls, a large and handsome building, was erected at the joint expense of the Marquess of Lothian, Earl of Clancarty, Lord Strafford, and the Hon. T. Pakenham, G.C.B., proprietors of the estate by purchase from the Vintners' Company, who have also endowed it with £5 per annum, and a like sum is granted by the rector: and there is a school for girls, supported by subscription, also a school built and supported by the Methodists.—See Ballyscullion.

BELLAGHY, a village, in the parish of Achonry, barony of Leney, county of Sligo, and province of Connaught, 10 miles (S. W.) from Ballymote, on the road to Swinford; containing 34 houses and 170 inhabitants. A market for provisions is held on Wednesday, and a fair is held every month: the market-house is situated in the centre of the village. Here is a station of the constabulary police.—See Achonry.

BELLAIR, a hamlet, in the parish of Lemanaghan, barony of Garrycastle, King's county, and province of Leinster, 6 miles from Clara; containing 81 inhabitants. The village, which is of modern origin, is situated on the road from Clara to Moat, and was founded by the family of Mullock: it has a neat and orderly appearance; the houses are built of stone and slated. Contiguous to it is the residence of Thos. H. Mulock, Esq., sheltered by plantations raised with great care. Mount Mulock, in the vicinity, is another seat of this family. Petty sessions are held here and at Doone every alternate Friday.—See LEMANAGHAN.

BELLEEK, county of ARMAGH.—See BALEEK.

BELLEEK, a parish, in the barony of LURG, county of FERMANAGH, and province of ULSTER, 3 miles (E.) from Ballyshannon; containing 2702 inhabitants, of which number, 260 are in the village. This place is situated on Lough Erne, and on the road from Enniskillen to Ballyshannon, and was erected into a parish in 1792, by disuniting 36 townlands from the parish of Templecarn; it comprises, according to the Ordnance survey, 12,848½ statute acres, of which 9706 are applotted under the tithe act, and 2576 are water. The land is principally heathy mountain, but that which is under tillage is of very superior quality; the state of agriculture, though very backward, is gradually improving; there is a large tract of bog, and abundance of limestone. The seats are Castle Caldwell, the residence of J. C. Bloomfield, Esq., and Maghramena, of W. Johnston, Esq. The village contains 47 houses, and has a penny post to Ballyshannon and Enniskillen. It is a station of the constabulary police; fairs are held on Feb. 3rd, March 17th, May 17th, June 20th, and Oct. 10th, and petty sessions every alternate Thursday. The living is a rectory and vicarage, in the diocese of Clogher, and in the patronage of the Bishop: the tithes amount to £110. The church, a neat plain edifice, was erected in 1790, and the Ecclesiastical Commissioners have recently granted £267. 9. 2. for its repair. The glebe-house is a handsome residence: the glebe comprises 660 statute acres. In the R. C. divisions the parish forms part of the union or district of Templecairn or Pettigo; the chapel is a spacious and well-built edifice, with a slated roof. There are schools at Belleek and Tullynabehogue, partly supported by the rector; and at Castle Caldwell is a school supported by Mrs. Bloomfield. In these schools are about 60 boys and 80 girls; and there are also three pay schools, in which are about 180 boys and 70 girls, and a Sunday school. There are some ruins of the old church; on the shore of Lough Keenaghan are those of an abbey; and there are remains of several Danish forts in the parish.

BELLEWSTOWN, a village, in the parish of DULEEK, barony of UPPER DULEEK, county of MEATH, and province of LEINSTER, 1 mile (E.) from Duleek; containing 13 houses and 77 inhabitants. It is situated on the road from Duleek to Laytown, and on the Nanny water. Races are held in June on the hill of Bellewstown, and are well attended; the days vary, but on the last Thursday in the month the king's cup is run for. The view from this hill is very extensive, embracing the Carlingford and Mourne mountains, and the bays of Dundalk and Carlingford.—See DULEEK.

BELLOUGH, a village, in the parish of CLONOULTY, barony of KILNEMANAGH, county of TIPPERARY, and province of MUNSTER, 6 miles (S. E.) from Cashel, on the high road from Tipperary to Thurles; containing about 60 houses and 400 inhabitants.

BELMULLET, a small sea-port, in the parish of KILCOMMON, barony of ERRIS, county of MAYO, and province of CONNAUGHT, 32¼ miles (W. by N.) from Ballina: the population is returned with the parish. This place is beautifully and advantageously situated on an isthmus to which it gives name, on the western coast, and which separates the bay of Blacksod from that of Broadhaven. It is a rapidly improving town: the surrounding district, about 20 years since, was scarcely accessible; but since that period, by the construction of several lines of road by Messrs. Nimmo, Knight, and Bald, the engineers, and more especially those from the county town of Castlebar and Ballina, the whole barony has been thrown open, and a great improvement has taken place in the agriculture of the district and the commerce of the port. In 1822 the land in the barony produced only about 80 tons of oats and barley; but in 1834 and 1835, the annual produce was 1800 tons. This great improvement has resulted from the reclaiming of the adjacent lands, and from Belmullet having become a very considerable mart, where the neighbouring farmers can readily find immediate purchasers for all their produce. The town owes its origin to the establishment of the head-quarters of the commander of the coast-guard here, in 1822. It is uniformly built, and contains 117 houses; it has a penny post to Ballina, and its general appearance, as seen from Blacksod bay, is pleasing and prepossessing. A new line of road has been constructed along the coast, from Ballycastle to Belmullet and thence to Westport, a distance of 57 miles, forming a most interesting drive. The trade consists chiefly in the export of grain, especially of oats and barley; and several spacious warehouses have been built for the deposit of corn. A commodious quay was constructed in 1826, at an expense of £700, of which sum, £300 was given by the late Fishery Board, and £300 by Mr. Carter. The harbour is capable of very great improvement, and by cutting through the narrow part of the isthmus, a canal might be made, at an estimated expense of £2000, which would enable vessels of 150 tons' burden to pass from Broadhaven into Blacksod bay, and in all winds at full tide into the Atlantic ocean, without being detained for months, as is now frequently the case. Fairs are held on the 15th of every month, except when it falls on Sunday, in which case the fair is held on the following Monday. Here is a chief constabulary police station; and the coast-guard district comprises the stations of Belmullet, Dugurth, Duhooma, Ballycovy, Blacksod, Ballyglass, and Renown Tower, and is under the superintendence of Capt. Nugent, resident inspecting commander, and a county magistrate. Petty sessions are held every Saturday: the court-house was built in 1833, at an expense of £200, by Mr. Ivers. There is also a dispensary. In the vicinity are several gentlemen's seats, noticed in Kilcommon and Kilmore-Erris, *which see.*

BELTURBET, an incorporated market and post-town, partly in the parish of DRUMLANE, but chiefly in that of ANNAGH, barony of LOWER LOUGHTEE, county of CAVAN, and province of ULSTER, 12 miles (N. N. W.) from Cavan, and 67 (N. W.) from Dublin; containing 2026 inhabitants. It is pleasantly situated on the river Erne, on the road from Cavan to Ballyconnell, and owes its origin to the Lanesborough family, whose patronage has also contributed materially to its prosperity. In 1610, certain conditions were proposed by the lords of the council in England to Sir Stephen Butler, of *Bealetirbirt*, Knt., for establishing a market here and erecting a corporation; and in 1613 it received its first charter, whereby the king, on petition of the inhabitants, and for the purpose of furthering the plantation of Ulster, incorporated the village and its precincts into a borough. By an indenture in 1618 Sir Stephen Butler, in fulfilment of the conditions of the lords of the council, granted and confirmed to the corporation certain parcels of land amounting altogether to 284 acres, also a weekly market and two annual fairs, and a weekly court of record, the whole to be held of him or his successors in the fee, in fee-farm for ever, at the rent of 30*s.* yearly. This indenture contains a covenant on the part of the corporation that all the inhabitants should be ready at all times to be mustered and trained to arms whenever required by Sir Stephen, or his heirs or assigns, or by the Muster-master General of Ulster, or any of the king's officers duly authorised; and that they should grind their corn at Sir Stephen's mill. By Pynnar's survey, made in 1619, it appears that the newly erected houses were built of "cage work," and all inhabited by English tradesmen, who had each a garden, four acres of land, and commonage for a certain number of cows and horses. In 1690, the town, being garrisoned by a body of the forces of Jas. II., was taken by surprise by the Enniskilleners, who fortified it for their own party. It contains several neat houses, but the greater number are indifferently built and thatched. The wide expanse of Lough Erne to the north, and the varied character of the surrounding scenery, impart to the environs an interesting and highly picturesque appearance. A handsome bridge of three arches is in course of erection over the Erne, for which the Board of Works has consented to grant a loan of £1700, and has already advanced £500 on account. There is a cavalry barrack for 7 officers, 156 non-commissioned officers and men, and 101 horses. A very extensive distillery belonging to Messrs. Dickson, Dunlop, and Co., was erected in 1825 at an expense of £21,000, and enlarged and improved in 1830, at an additional cost of £6000: it is wrought by never-failing water power, and the quantity of whiskey made annually is from 90,000 to 100,000 gallons; about 100 persons are usually employed. There are also some malting establishments. The river Erne opens a communication through Lough Erne to within three miles of Ballyshannon; but in dry weather the navigation is interrupted by shoals, which might be removed, to the great improvement of the trade of the town. The market is on Thursday, and is principally for butter, oatmeal, potatoes, and yarn, of which last there is a good supply. Fairs are held on Ash-Wednesday, Sept. 4th, and the first Thursday in every other month. Here is a station of the constabulary police.

The charter of Jas. I., granted in 1613, after incorporating the inhabitants, empowered them to return two representatives to the Irish parliament, and to hold a court of record every Tuesday, before the provost, with jurisdiction to the extent of five marks, besides conferring other privileges, which were confirmed by the indenture made between Sir Stephen Butler and the corporation, by which the jurisdiction of the court of record in all actions, personal or mixed, was extended to £6. 13. 4., and it was ordered to be held before the bailiff and stewards of the corporation every Saturday. The corporation is styled "the Provost, Burgesses, Freemen, and Inhabitants of the borough of Belturbet," which in some degree differs from the style prescribed by the charter of Jas. I. and the indenture. The officers named in the charter are a provost, twelve free burgesses, and two serjeants-at-mace; the other officers are a treasurer, town-clerk, herd, marshal-keeper or corporation gaoler, pound-keeper, foreman of the market jury, and weigh-master. The provost is by the charter to be elected by the provost and free burgesses from among the latter annually on the 24th of June, and sworn in upon Sept. 29th. The burgesses are chosen from among the inhabitants by the provost and free burgesses, and by the usage of the corporation must be freemen prior to their election; there are at present only nine or ten, all non-resident, and they were formerly entitled to certain privileges and emoluments now lost. No recognised right to the freedom at present exists, nor does it appear that any freemen have been admitted by the provost and burgesses for many years, except for the purpose of qualifying persons immediately after elected burgesses. The town-clerk and other officers of the corporation, whose offices have not fallen into desuetude, are appointed by the provost. The municipal affairs are regulated by the inhabitants assembled by the provost at what are termed "Town Courts," which are held before the provost generally eight or ten times in the year, and in which are made by-laws for the government of the town, the corporation property is regulated, and complaints of trespass respecting commonage and upon the private lands within the district are referred for investigation and adjustment to the market jury. This jury consists of not less than twelve members appointed from the inhabitants by the provost, and sworn in at the town court; its duties are not only to inspect the meat brought to market, of which the foreman is appointed clerk by the provost, but to superintend the property of the corporation generally, forming, in fact, a court of arbitration, and exercising a jurisdiction highly beneficial to the inhabitants. The borough returned two members to the Irish parliament until the Union, when the £15,000 awarded as compensation for the abolition of its franchise was paid to Armar, Earl of Belmore, who had a short time previously purchased the borough for that amount from the Earl of Lanesborough. It comprises the town and precincts, forming a district termed "the corporation," the boundaries of which are clearly defined. The provost is chief magistrate, and is by usage the first magistrate named upon the commission in the county, and next in rank to the lieutenant; he formerly sat with the judges at the county assizes, but has not for many years exercised this privilege. The court of record, in which he presided, has fallen into disuse for nearly 30 years. Petty sessions are held by the county magistrates every Saturday in the market-house, of which the upper part is appropriated to that use and the lower to the purpose of the market. Beneath this building was the corporation gaol, a damp and unhealthy prison, which was prohibited to be used as a place of confinement after the passing of the act of the 7th of Geo. IV., c. 74. The commons in possession of the corporation comprise about 120 acres; the right of commonage enjoyed by the inhabitants is regulated by the possession of the whole or a portion of a homestead, to which also a proportionate quantity of bog is annexed: these homesteads include certain portions of the front of streets, defined and granted to individuals on the original foundation of the town, and subsequently divided among different tenants, and the right to commonage was by usage similarly apportioned. The lands allotted for the private occupation of the burgesses are said to have been granted to them and their heirs, instead of their successors, and, under the name of "burgess acres," are divided and separately enclosed as private properties. The only revenue which the corporation now possesses is derivable from some nominal reservations on fee-farm grants made, within the last few years, of small portions of the commons, the fines on which, amounting to £175, were applied to the repairs of the market-house.

The parish church of Annagh, a neat edifice with a tower surmounted by a spire, is situated in the town; it was rebuilt by a loan of £923 from the late Board of First Fruits in 1828, and of £800 in 1829. It is in contemplation to erect a handsome R. C. chapel. The parochial school for boys is on the foundation of Erasmus Smith, and was built on an acre of ground granted by the corporation, who also gave a site for the erection of a school for girls on the same establishment, which is supported by subscription; and there is an infants' school, also a dispensary. Six alms-houses for poor widows were built on a site granted by the corporation in 1733, the inmates of which are supported by a legacy bequeathed by a Mr. Maunsell, of Dublin, and distributed by the rector. He also distributes the interest of £100 paid by the Earl of Lanesborough's agent, £3 per ann. derived from a charity called Fellor's List, and £6 per ann. accruing from another charity; and there is a house in the town bequeathed by Benjamin Johnson for the benefit of the poor, and let for £1. 16. 11. per annum. In the church-yard are vestiges of a strong fortification enclosing an extensive area, with bastions and salient angles of great strength; about two miles distant are some venerable ecclesiastical ruins, with others at Clinosy; and in the vicinity are the remains of an ancient castle.—See ANNAGH and DRUMLANE.

BENBURB, or BINBURB, a small village, in the parish of CLONFEACLE, barony of DUNGANNON, county of TYRONE, and province of ULSTER, 5¾ miles (N. N. W.) from Armagh: the population is returned with the parish. The first notice of this place under its present name occurs during the rebellion of the Earl of Tyrone, when the Lord-Deputy Boroughs crossed the river Blackwater at *Bean-Bhorb*, at the head of the English forces, in June 1597; and being seized with a sickness of which he died a few days after at Newry, was succeeded in the command of the army by the Earl of Kildare, between whom and the Earl of Tyrone a severe engagement took place, in which the English were defeated, the Earl of Kildare mortally wounded, and his two foster brothers slain; many of the English were killed in battle, and numbers perished in the river. Sir Henry Bagnall, with 4500 foot and 400 horse, marched against the Earl of Tyrone's army, with which he had a severe conflict; many of the English cavalry were dreadfully mangled by falling into pits dug by the enemy and covered with branches of trees; but after surmounting these and other obstacles, Bagnall made a vigorous attack upon the right wing of the Irish army commanded by the earl himself, and on the left under O'Donnell of Tyrconnell; a dreadful carnage ensued, the two armies being wholly engaged; but just when victory seemed to incline towards the English forces, Bagnall was shot by a musket ball in the forehead and fell dead on the field. The English, thrown into confusion by the loss of their leader, were defeated, and in their retreat to Armagh, many were trodden down by the Irish cavalry. This triumph of Tyrone was but of short duration; the Lord-Deputy Mountjoy defeated him in several battles, and had driven him back to the camp at *Bean-Bhorb*, where, on the 15th of July, 1601, a battle was fought, in which Tyrone was totally defeated and his army compelled to retreat in confusion to his chief fortress at Dungannon.

On the plantation of Ulster, Sir Robert Wingfield received from James I. a grant of 1000 acres of land at Benburb, by a deed dated Dec. 3rd, in the 8th year of that monarch's reign; and previously to the year 1619 he had erected a castle on these lands, built the present church, and founded the village, which at that time contained 20 houses. This new establishment continued to flourish till the breaking out of the war in 1641, when the castle was surprised by order of Sir Phelim O'Nial, on the night of the 22nd of October, and the whole of the inmates put to death. On the 5th of June, 1646, this place became the scene of a battle between Sir Phelim O'Nial and Gen. Monroe; the former, with a large body of men, took up a position between two hills, with a wood in his rear and the river Blackwater, at that time difficult to pass, on his right. Monroe, with 6000 foot and 800 horse, marched from Armagh and approached by the opposite bank of the river, where, finding a ford, now called Battleford Bridge, he crossed and advanced to meet O'Nial. Both armies were drawn up in order of battle, but instead of coming to a general engagement, the day was spent in skirmishing, till the sun, which had been favourable to the British, was declining, when, just as Monroe was beginning to retreat, he was attacked by the Irish, who made a furious onset. An English regiment commanded by Lord Blayney fought with undaunted resolution till they were cut to pieces and their leader slain; the Scottish horse next gave way, and the infantry being thrown into disorder, a general rout ensued. More than 3000 of the British forces were slain and their artillery and stores taken, while, on the part of O'Nial, not more than 70 were killed. The castle was soon after dismantled, and has ever since remained in ruins; it was the largest in the county, and, though weakly built, occupies a remarkably strong position on the summit of a limestone rock rising perpendicularly from the river Blackwater to the height of 120 feet. In the village is a small ancient out-post strongly built and probably forming an entrance to the castle, which on every other side was defended by natural barriers. Near the village are Tullydoey, the seat of J. Eyre Jackson, Esq., where also is the residence of T. Eyre, Esq.; and Castle Cottage, of Capt. Cranfield. There were formerly very extensive bleach-greens near the village, and the mills and engines are still remaining; but the principal part of the business is carried on at Tullydoey, where large quantities of linen are finished for the English markets; the weaving of linen is also carried on to some extent. The Ulster canal, now in progress, passes on the eastern side of the river and village, and is here carried through a hill of limestone, which has been excavated to the depth of 80 feet, and is conducted longitudinally over the mill-race by an aqueduct of considerable length. A court is held on the first Friday in every month for the manor of Benburb, which extends over 47 townlands and comprises 9210 acres, for the recovery of debts not exceeding £2. The parish church is situated close to the village, in which is also a place of worship for Presbyterians in connection with the Synod of Ulster. The ruins of the castle are extensive and highly picturesque; and near the walls was found a signet ring bearing the arms and initials of Turlogh O'Nial, which is now in the possession of Mr. Bell, of Dungannon. The O'Nials had a strong hold here of greater antiquity than the castle erected by Sir R. Wingfield.—See CLONFEACLE.

BENDENSTOWN.—See GILBERTSTOWN.

BENEKERRY, otherwise BUSHERSTOWN, a parish, in the barony of RATHVILLY (but locally in that of Carlow), county of CARLOW, and province of LEINSTER, $2\frac{1}{2}$ miles (E. N. E.) from Carlow; containing 135 inhabitants. This parish is situated on the road from Carlow to Tullow, and is bounded on the south-west and east by the river Burren: more than four-fifths consists of meadow and pasture land, and the remainder is arable, with a few acres of woodland. In the ecclesiastical divisions it is not regarded as a parish, but as forming part of that of Urglin, the incumbent of which receives the tithes, except of about ten acres, which pay tithe to the incumbent of Ballinacarrig or Staplestown.

BENMORE, or BALLYDUFF, a village, in that part of the parish of RATTOO which is in the barony of CLANMAURICE, county of KERRY, and province of MUNSTER, 12 miles (N. N. W.) from Tralee; containing 448 inhabitants. It is situated on the road from Tralee to Ballybunnian, by the Cashen ferry, and contains 71 houses, which are mostly thatched, and form one street. Fairs are held on the 1st of June and Sept., Nov. 10th, and Dec. 21st. It is a police station, and petty sessions are held every alternate week. The R. C. chapel, a slated building, is in the centre of the village. Ballyeagh, near it, was the scene of a desperate affray, in the summer of 1834, between the rival factions of the Cooleens and Lawlors, when sixteen of the former were killed or drowned, while endeavouring to cross the Cashen ferry, in their retreat. Ballyhorgan, the ancient seat of the Stoughton family, is in the neighbourhood.—See RATTOO.

BENNETTS-BRIDGE, a village, partly in the parish of KILLARNEY, barony of GOWRAN, and partly in that of DANESFORT, barony of SHILLELOGHER, county of KILKENNY, and province of LEINSTER, 5 miles (W. S. W.) from Gowran; containing 426 inhabitants. This place is situated on the river Nore, which is here crossed by a good stone bridge on the road from Kilkenny to Thomastown, and contains 85 houses. There are some flour-mills in the immediate vicinity. Fairs are held on Feb. 24th, Aug. 26th, Sept. 19th, and Dec. 21st; and it is a station of the constabulary police. There is a R. C. chapel of ease to Danesfort, with a national school adjoining it.—See KILLARNEY and DANESFORT.

BENOWEN, or BUNNOWN, a parish, in the barony of KILKENNY WEST, county of WESTMEATH, and province of LEINSTER, $2\frac{3}{4}$ miles (N. by E.) from Athlone; containing 1418 inhabitants. This parish forms the north-eastern bank of an arm of Lough Ree, called the Inner Lake, and, near the village of Glasson, touches for a few perches on the road from Athlone to Ballymahon. It was the retreat of Sir James Dillon, when driven from Athlone, which he had taken, in 1641, by one of the boldest military manœuvres on record. In his retreat from that place Sir James at first took up his quarters at Bally-Kieran, and afterwards retired to the castle of Killinure, in this parish, whence, in about three weeks, he recaptured Athlone, which, after a short occupation, he was again compelled to abandon. The parish comprises 2937 statute acres, as applotted under the tithe act: about 160 acres are underwood and bog, and of the remainder, the principal portion is arable and pasture. Agriculture is in a state of slow but progressive improvement; the only waste lands are the rocky shores of the lake. Portlick Castle, the residence of Robert Smyth, Esq., is beautifully situated on the border of Lough Ree, and is one of the very few ancient feudal castles at present in good repair and inhabited. Killenmore, the residence of Capt. Fry, is also finely situated on the border of the lake. The other seats are St. Mark's, that of John Potts, Esq.; Lough Ree Lodge, of Gustavus H. Temple, Esq.; Killinure, of Major-Gen. Murray; Benowen, of Capt. Caulfield; and the beautiful cottage on Hare Island, in Lough Ree, belonging to Viscount Castlemaine. The living is a perpetual curacy, in the diocese of Meath, and in the patronage of the Bishop, to whom the rectory is appropriate, as a mensal: the tithes amount to £92. 6. $1\frac{3}{4}$., payable to the lessee of the bishop. The church, a neat plain structure, was erected in 1822, by aid of a gift of £600 from the late Board of First Fruits in 1818. The glebe-house was built by aid of a gift of £415 and a loan of £46 from the same Board, in 1829. In the R. C. divisions this parish forms part of the union or district of Noughoval. A school of 6 boys and 18 girls is aided by Lord Castlemaine and an annual donation from the rector; and there is a pay school, in which are about 12 children. The ruins of the ancient church, in which are some monuments to the Dillon family, are romantically situated on the verdant bank and at the very extremity of the Inner Lake; and a little higher up are the ruins of the ancient castle of Benowen. A small portion of Killinure castle still remains, occupying a site on a bold and picturesque eminence over the Inner Lake, and adjoining Killinure House; and on Hare Island are the ruins of a religious house, founded by the family of Dillon, some of whose descendants still live in the neighbourhood. There is also a well dedicated to the Blessed Virgin.—See GLASSON.

BERE, or BEAR ISLAND. This island forms part of the parish of KILACONENAGH, in the barony of BERE, county of CORK, and province of MUNSTER: it is situated on the north side of the bay of Bantry, 21 miles (W. by. S.) from Bantry, and contains 1898 inhabitants. It comprises 2849 acres, of which about one-fourth is under tillage, and the remainder consists of mountain, bog, and pasture land, and is the property of R. H. Eyre, Esq. The inhabitants are principally occupied in fishing and agriculture, but the system of husbandry is rude and unimproved. A pier has been built at Lawrence Cove, which is very useful to the fishery, affording protection to 16 hookers of 12 tons and 90 yawls of 3 or 4 tons each, belonging to the island, and employing about 1000 persons exclusively in the fishery. The southern shore is bold and rocky, but on the north the land slopes gently to the water's edge: there is a small lake on the south side. The whole island is of the clay-slate formation, and excellent stone for flagging is obtained in some of the quarries: copper ore has been found in several places, but no attempt has yet been made to search for mines. The chief communication is by boats from Castletown, and there are also boats from the Bank and other places on the mainland. After the arrival of the French fleet in the bay, in 1796, Government erected five Martello towers, a signal tower, a large and commodious barrack for two officers and 150 men, a quay, storehouses, and other public works, all of which are now in a neglected condition; the barrack has been taken down, and the rest of the works are under the care of a resident lieutenant. In the R. C. divisions this island forms part of the union of Castletown, in the diocese of Kerry: the chapel is a low thatched building of mean appearance, occupying the site of an ancient church. A school for boys and girls was established in 1825. Divine service is regularly performed in the school-house by the vicar. The sites of three churches are indicated by the burial-grounds, which are still used for interment. There are the remains of a Danish fort or rath on the island. Between the island and the mainland is Bere haven, capacious and well sheltered, and affording good anchorage in water sufficiently deep for the largest ships in the navy: it has two entrances, one at the west and the other at the east end of the island, both rendered somewhat dangerous by rocks. Bere-haven gives the inferior title of Viscount to the Earl of Bantry.

BEREGH, or LOWRYSTOWN, a market-town, in the parish of CLOGHERNEY, barony of OMAGH, county of TYRONE, and province of ULSTER, 7 miles (S. E.) from Omagh: the population is returned with the parish. It is situated on the road from Omagh to Dungannon, and consists of one long wide street containing about 70 houses, most of which are well built, though rapidly falling into decay. The former residence of the Belmore family, proprietors of the town, an elegant and spacious mansion, is now in ruins; and the town exhibits every appearance of neglect. The inhabitants are principally employed in agriculture, with which they combine the weaving of linen cloth. The patent for the market and fairs was granted under the name of Lowrystown; the market is on Wednesday, and fairs are held regularly on the first Monday in every month for cattle, sheep, and pigs. A constabulary police force is stationed here; and petty sessions are held every alternate week. One of the chapels for the R. C. parish of Clogherney is situated in the town.—See CLOGHERNEY.

BETAGHSTOWN, or BETTYSTOWN, a village, in the parish of COLPE, barony of LOWER DULEEK, county of MEATH, and province of LEINSTER, 3½ miles (E. S. E.) from Drogheda; containing 214 inhabitants. This place is situated on the eastern coast, and contains 26 houses, chiefly thatched cabins; it is the property of R. Shepheard, Esq., whose seat is in the neighbourhood. The coast is here a shallow strand, and, from the extent of fine sandy beach, the village has become a place of some resort for sea-bathing, and would be much more numerously frequented if suitable accommodations were provided. The surrounding scenery is pleasingly diversified, and in the immediate vicinity are many handsome private residences.—See COLPE.

BEWLEY.—See OWNING.

BILLY, a parish, partly in the barony of CAREY, but chiefly in that of LOWER DUNLUCE, county of ANTRIM, and province of ULSTER; containing, with the post-town of Bushmills, 5845 inhabitants. This parish is bounded on the west by the river Bush, and on the south-east by the sea; it is also intersected for nearly three miles by the road from Ballymoney, through Bushmills, to the Giants' Causeway, which is within its limits. Including eight townlands which now form part of the parish of Dunseverick, it comprises, according to the Ordnance survey, 17,329¾ statute acres, of which 16,860 are applotted under the tithe act, and valued at £8139 per annum. The land is generally in a good state of cultivation; the system of agriculture is considerably advanced, and is still improving; there is very little waste land, except moss and bog, which together form nearly one-third of the surface. Whinstone abounds, and is quarried for building and for the roads; limestone is found in great quantity and occasionally burned for manure, and wood-coal is obtained near the Causeway. Among the principal seats are Bushmills House, the residence of Sir F. W. Macnaghten, Bart.; Ballylough, of W. Trail, Esq.; Ballydivity, of J. Stewart Moore, Esq.; Black Rock House, the property of Miss Wray, and now in the occupation of Hugh Lecky, Esq.; and Bentfield, formerly the residence of Col. Wray, but at present uninhabited. There are some weirs on the river Bush, near its influx into the sea, for taking salmon, of which great quantities are sent to Liverpool and London. A market on Tuesday, and five fairs are held at Bushmills (*which see*); and on the day after Dervock fair, which is generally on Aug. 12th (except that day falls on the Saturday or Sunday, on which occasions it is held on the Monday following), a pleasure fair, called the Causeway fair, is held at the Rock Head, above the Giants' Causeway, and is numerously attended by persons for many miles round, for whose accommodation tents are pitched. This parish was formerly the head of a union, which comprised also the parishes of Armoy, Ballyclug, Donegore, and Kilbride, together forming the corps of the archdeaconry of Connor; but by the act of the 5th of Geo. IV., obtained by Dr. Mant, the union has been dissolved, the parishes disappropriated from the archdeaconry, and the rectorial tithes annexed to their respective vicarages, with the exception only of this parish, of which the rectory and vicarage alone now constitute the corps of the archdeaconry, with the cure of souls, the former archdeacons having no cure of souls: it is in the diocese of Connor, and patronage of the Bishop. The late Archdeacon Trail, then rector of this parish, in 1830, separated nine townlands from it, giving the tithes of four; and his brother, the Rev. Robt. Trail, rector of Ballintoy, seven townlands from that parish, giving the tithes of three, for the formation and endowment of the perpetual curacy of Dunseverick, the patronage of which is vested alternately in the respective incumbents: the new church is a very neat building in a central situation. The tithes of the parish amount to £489. 4. 7½., of which £37. 9. 3. is paid to the perpetual curate, and the remainder to the archdeacon. The church, a plain substantial building, was erected on the site of a former structure, by aid of a gift of £800 and a loan of £500, in 1815, from the late Board of First Fruits. The glebe-house was built in 1810, by the Rev. T. Babington, vicar, aided by a gift of £350 and a loan of £450 from the same Board. In the R. C. divisions it forms part of the union or district of Coleraine. There are two meeting houses for Presbyterians in connection with the Synod of Ulster, one of which is of the third class, and there are places of worship for Seceders, Covenanters, and Wesleyan Methodists. At Eagry is a school under the trustees of Erasmus Smith's charity, for which a good school-house has been erected, with a residence for the master, who has two acres of land; a school is held in a house hired for that purpose at Bushmills, and is supported by subscription; there is a parochial school for girls, for which a house was built, in 1832, by William Trail, Esq.; also schools at Moycraig, Carnbore, Straidbilly, and Dromiarran, and another is held in the Methodist meeting-house at Castle-Cat, which was endowed with £20 by the late Dr. Adam Clarke. The Rev. Archdeacon Trail, in 1831, bequeathed £50 for the use of the poor of the parish, which has been invested in Government securities, and the interest is annually distributed by his son, W. Trail, Esq. There are some remains of the ancient castle of Ballylough, which was of much importance; the lake on which it was situated has been drained, and is now under cultivation.

The Giants' Causeway, probably the most extensive and curious assemblage of basaltic columns in the world, is situated between Port-na-Grange and Port Noffer, in N. Lat. 55° 20′ and W. Lon. 6° 50′; and derives its name from a popular tradition that it was erected by giants, as the commencement of a causeway across the ocean to Scotland. This very interesting natural curiosity forms part of a large promontory, of which Bengore Head, about a mile distant, is the most northern point in Ireland. The only access to it by land is down a winding path, cut at the expense of the late Earl of Bristol, while Bishop of Derry, on the western side of a verdant headland called Aird Snout, to two detached hills called the Stookans, whence the first view of this stupendous work of nature is obtained. This view is one of the most magnificent imaginable, embracing an immense bay broken with capes and headlands, rising abruptly to the height of 400 feet above the level of the sea, and consisting of lofty colonnades of the most symmetrically-formed basaltic pillars, inserted in the cliffs like artificial supporters, standing in groups like gigantic honeycombs, or scattered in pleasing disorder like the ruins of a city of temples and palaces. From the Stookans the road leads to the base of the causeway, which extends in a northerly direction from the promontory into the sea. This splendid natural pier is somewhat triangular in form; the base beneath the cliff being 135, the eastern side 220, and the western 300, yards long; while the breadth in the centre is about 60. The view of the causeway from the footpath suggests the idea of an immense unfinished embankment, forming an inclined plane, in some places rising by successive steps, in others presenting a nearly level pavement, formed by the tops of the closely united columns, with some chasms exhibiting the admirable arrangement of this wonderful structure. The causeway is divided into three unequal parts. The little, or western, causeway is 386 feet long, but only 16 high, and is separated from the central compartment by an enormous whin dyke, extending from the cliff to the sea. The middle section, which is the shortest, contains a magnificent group of lofty pillars, called "the honeycomb," and is also bounded on the east by a whin dyke. Beyond this is the grand causeway, which is 706 feet long by 109 wide in the middle: in that part of this compartment which is called "the loom" it attains an elevation of 34 feet, from which it diminishes in height gradually as it approaches the sea, into which it enters for some distance beyond low water mark. In the western and central compartments all the columns are perpendicular, but in the grand causeway they are vertical towards the east, inclining eastward as they approach the sea, and westward near the base of the cliff. The three divisions of the causeway comprise 37,426 distinct and perfect columns, besides many that are broken and scattered about in its vicinity. The columns consist of prisms of equal dimensions through their whole height, which ranges from 15 to 36 feet, with diameters of from 15 to 28 inches, and varying in their number of sides from 3 to 9, although the greater number are pentagons and hexagons. Each of the pillars is perfectly distinct, and almost invariably differs in size, number of sides, and points of articulation from the adjacent columns, to which, however, it is so close that not even water can pass between them. Almost every column is composed of several pieces, the joints of which are articulated with the greatest exactness, and in a strictly horizontal direction. Generally the upper part of the section is concave and the lower convex, but this arrangement is sometimes reversed. The cavity or socket is perfectly circular, from two to four inches deep, and in a few instances its rim is divided, covers two or three articulations, and terminates in sharp points. In a few of the columns no joints are visible; in some, three, four, or more may be traced; and, in "the loom," columns are found which are divisible into as many as 38 pieces. The basalt of which these columns is composed is of a very dark colour, approaching to black; its weight is three times as great as that of water; and of 100 of its constituent parts, 50 are silicious earth, 25 iron, 15 argillaceous earth, and 10 calcareous earth and magnesia. About 300 yards east of the causeway is the Giants' Organ, about 120 feet long, consisting of 60 columns, of which those in the centre are 40 feet high, but those on the sides are lower. At the eastern extremity of Port Noffer are four lofty and massive basaltic columns, rising to the height of 315 feet; they are hexagonal and jointed, and from their height and isolated position are called the Chimney Tops. Near these is the Theatre, consisting of three distinct colonnades, the successive tiers of which are separated by horizontal strata of amorphous basalt, red and grey ochre, and fossil coal, the alternations of which with the columnar basalt produce a very extraordinary and pleasing appearance. A little eastward of Port-na-Spagna is a perpendicular cliff, 326 feet high, composed of alternate layers of columnar and horizontal basalt, arranged with surprising regularity; but the most picturesque cliff is Pleaskin, which rises from the sea in a gentle acclivity for more than 300 feet, and then ascends perpendicularly 70 feet more to its summit. This beautiful headland is 382 feet in height, and strikingly exhibits the geological formation of this district, as it consists of numerous clearly distinguishable strata, which rise above each other in the following order; at the base is a bright red ochreous rock, on which are placed tabular basalt, grey ochreous rock, amorphous basalt, clear red basalt, irregular basalt with cracks, iron ore, imperfectly formed basaltic pillars, argillaceous rock, fossil coal, and the lower range of basaltic columns, which is 45 feet high. Imposed on this colonnade are grey rock containing nodules of iron, slightly columnar basalt, grey ochreous rock, amorphous basalt, and then the upper range of basaltic pillars, which forms a magnificent colonnade 64 feet high, and has broken basalt for a superstratum, above which is vegetable mould covered with green sod. This splendid headland, which is unrivalled for beauty of arrangement and variety of colouring, is seen to most advantage from the sea, from which also some of the grandest views of the causeway and its adjacent scenery are obtained. Fossil wood, as black and compact as coal, and fossil oysters and muscles are found in the limestone rock that forms the substratum of the causeway and its neighbouring promontories; and large opals, chalcedony, agates, &c., are collected here. Specimens of these fossils and minerals, and a wooden model of the causeway, are in the museum of Trinity College, Dublin.

BINGHAMSTOWN, or SALEEN, a village, in the parish of KILMORE-ERRIS, barony of ERRIS, county of MAYO, and province of CONNAUGHT, 3 miles (S. E.) from Bellmullet: the population is returned with the parish. This place is situated on the eastern shore of the peninsula called the Mullet, and consists of one long street indifferently built: it commands a good view of Saleen bay, in which a landing pier has been erected by the late Fishery Board, where considerable quantities of corn and potatoes are shipped for Westport, and various articles of merchandise are brought back. A fair is held on the first day of every month throughout the year; there is a market-house. Petty sessions are held in a court-house every Thursday; and here is a constabulary police station. The parish church, a neat plain edifice, is situated in the village, in which is also a R. C. chapel.—See KILMORE-ERRIS.

BIRMINGHAM (NEW), a village and post-town, in the parish of KILCOOLEY, barony of SLIEVEARDAGH, county of TIPPERARY, and province of MUNSTER, 11½ miles (E. N. E.) from Cashel, and 82 (S. W. by S.) from Dublin; containing 298 inhabitants. This place, which is situated at the termination of the mail coach road branching from Littleton, contains about 50 houses, and is indebted for its origin and name to the late Sir Vere Hunt, Bart., who, struck with its favourable situation contiguous to the coal mines of the Killenaule district, used every effort to raise it into manufacturing importance. For this purpose he obtained patents for one or two weekly markets and twelve fairs, which are now discontinued; and the town, which was the residence of its founder, and is now the property of his son, Sir Aubrey de Vere, Bart., is at present comparatively deserted. It is a constabulary police station; and there is a small prison, to which offenders are committed occasionally by the county magistrates. The parochial R. C. chapel, a large and handsome structure in the later English style, and recently erected, is situated in the village; and there is a school of about 80 or 90 children.—See KILCOOLEY.

BIRR.—See PARSONSTOWN.

BLACKDITCHES.—See BOYSTOWN.

BLACKRATH, a parish, in the barony of GOWRAN, county of KILKENNY, and province of LEINSTER, 2 miles (N. E. by E.) from Kilkenny; containing 730 inhabitants. This parish is situated on the mail coach road from Dublin to Cork, and on the river Nore, on the banks of which there are two considerable flour-mills; and within its limits are the marble works described in the account of the city of Kilkenny. Lyrath, the seat of Sir J. D. W. Cuffe, Bart., is pleasantly situated on an eminence commanding a fine view of that city. It is a rectory, in the diocese of Ossory, forming the corps of the prebend of Blackrath in the cathedral of St. Canice, Kilkenny, and in the patronage of the Bishop: the tithes amount to £121. 1. 7½. There is neither church nor glebe-house, but there is a glebe of eight acres attached to the prebend. In the R. C. divisions it forms part of the union or district of Gowran. There is a private pay school, in which about 50 boys and 30 girls are taught. Some remains of the old church yet exist.

BLACKROCK, a chapelry, in the parish of ST. FINBARR, county of the city of CORK, and province of MUNSTER, 2¼ miles (E. S. E.) from Cork: the population is included in the return for the parish. This place is beautifully situated on a peninsula bounded on the north and east by the river Lee, and on the south by Lough Mahon and the Douglas channel. The castle was originally built in 1604 by the Lord-Deputy Mountjoy, to protect the passage up the river from the harbour to the city, and was subsequently vested in the corporation, who held their courts of admiralty in it, and by whom, having been some years since destroyed by an accidental fire, it was rebuilt in 1829, from a design by Messrs. Pain, and is now assigned to the mayor of Cork as an occasional residence during his year of office. It is situated on a limestone rock projecting into the river, and consists of one bold circular tower of hewn limestone, containing a small banqueting room, from which there is a fine view over the river: from this tower springs a small turret rising to a considerable elevation and displaying from the upper part of it two brilliant lights; and attached to it is a water gate, with some low embattled buildings in the rear, which harmonise well with the principal feature of the castle. Numerous advantages resulting from its proximity to Cork, the beauty of its situation, the salubrity of its climate, and the excellent accommodations for bathing, have rendered this one of the most desirable places of residence in the South of Ireland. It has a penny post to Cork, and the railroad from Cork to Passage will, if carried into effect, pass through the village. The scenery is of the most varied and pleasing character, exhibiting numerous elegant villas and cottages, with lawns, gardens, and plantations reaching down to the margin of the Lee, which is here a noble expanse of water more than a mile broad, constantly enlivened by steam-boats and other vessels. Among the principal seats are Dundanion Castle, that of Sir T. Deane, Knt.; Beaumont, of W. Beamish, Esq., a noble mansion consisting of a centre and two wings, with two conservatories, situated in tastefully arranged grounds; Lakelands, of W. Crawford, Esq.; Clifton, of J. Moore Travers, Esq.; Ring-Mahon Castle, of J. Murphy, Esq.; Besborough, of Ebenezer Pike, Esq.; Cleve Hill, of S. Perrott, Esq.; Castlemahon, of Sir W. A. Chatterton, Bart.; Ferney, of J. H. Manley, Esq.; Filtrim, of W. Fagan, Esq.; Ashton, of J. Cotter, Esq.; Prospect, of Carden Terry, Esq.; Rochelle, of R. W. Topp, Esq.; Carrigduve, of R. Notter, Esq.; Sans Souci, of R. B. Shaw,

Esq.; Carrigduve, of G. Sherlock, Esq.; Chiplee, of P. Maylor, Esq.; Ballinure House, of W. Crofts, Esq.; Lakeview House, of Miss Allen; Webbe Ville, of the Rev. C. Tuthill; Mary Ville, of J. Lindsay, Esq.; Lakeview, of P. Kearney, Esq., Templeville, of M. Murphy, Esq.; Rose Hill, of G. P. Rogers, Esq.; Lakeview, of W. Prettie Harris, Esq.; Temple Hill, of R. Hall, Esq.; Rosetta, of G. Frend, Esq.; Dean Ville, of J. Mac Mullen, Esq.; Knockrea, of A. W. Webb, Esq.; Barnstead, of the Rev. W. R. Nash; Midsummer Lodge, of Miss Jones; Clover Hill, of C. Connell, Esq.; North Cliffe, of J. Mac Donnell, Esq.; Prospect Lodge, of C. Terry Crofts, Esq.; Flower Lodge, of R. Mac Mullen, Esq.; Rockville Cottage, of J. Cogan, Esq.; Clifton Cottage, of F. C. Cole, Esq.; and Rock Cottage, of M. Smith, Esq. Besides these seats there are numerous villas which are let during the summer. The land is naturally very fertile, and is for the most part enclosed in lawns, gardens, and pleasure grounds; the rest, deriving from its contiguity to Cork an abundant supply of rich manures, and having the advantage of inexhaustible quarries of limestone and plenty of sea sand, is in a high state of cultivation, and supplies the Cork market with a large proportion of its vegetables. The substratum is limestone of excellent quality, which is extensively quarried for various purposes. Between the fissures of the rocks, near its junction with the clay-slate, are found numerous amethystine crystals, some of which are very large and clustery, and all are beautifully coloured; one specimen in the Cork Royal Institution weighs more than 40lb.

The church, dedicated to St. Michael, serves as a chapel of ease to the cathedral church of St. Finbarr, Cork, and was built in 1827, at an expense of £2100, of which £900 was given by the late Board of First Fruits, £100 by the corporation of Cork, and the remainder, with the exception of a few local subscriptions and the sale of pews, was defrayed by the dean and chapter, who appoint and pay the curate. It is a handsome edifice of hewn limestone, in the later style of architecture, with a tower crowned with battlements and pinnacles, and surmounted by a spire 60 feet high, which, with part of the tower and the western portion of the nave, was destroyed by lightning on Jan. 29th, 1836, but has been restored by aid of a grant of £310 from the Ecclesiastical Commissioners. The R. C. chapel, erected in 1821, is a large and handsome building, and is a chapel of ease to the parochial chapel of St. Finbarr, or the South chapel: it was begun at the private expense of the late Dean Collins, aided by a subscription of £300, and was completed and elegantly fitted up by means of a bequest of £1100 from the late T. Rochford, Esq., of Garretstown, part of which, in 1834, was expended in the erection of a house for the officiating priest near the chapel. An Ursuline convent was removed hither from Cork, in 1825: it was founded in 1771, by the late Miss Honora Nagle, whose portrait is in the visiting-room, and is the original of all the institutions of this class founded in Ireland. The community consists of 35 professed nuns and 6 lay sisters, and is governed by a superioress, her deputy, and a council of six. At this institution many of the daughters of the R. C. gentry are instructed; and in a separate building about 100 poor girls are gratuitously taught and partially clothed. The convent has a demesne of 42 acres, and is an ornamental building, consisting of a centre and two wings, with a frontage of 350 feet. The chapel, which is in the east wing, is fitted up with simple elegance and ornamented with four Ionic pilasters supporting a pediment, on the apex of which is a cross, and at each of the other angles a vase. It contains a neat monument to the Rev. Dr. Lyons, who was many years chaplain to the convent. A school-house connected with St. Michael's chapel was erected at Ballintemple in 1836; a school for boys was built in 1834, at an expense of £160, of which two-thirds were contributed by the National Board, and the remainder by J. Murphy, Esq., of Ring-Mahon Castle; and there is a school for girls, supported by subscription. Here is a dispensary, and near Ballintemple are two private lunatic asylums. Cittadella, belonging to Joshua Bull, Esq., was established by the late Dr. Hallaran, in 1798, and has secluded pleasure grounds for the use of the patients. Lindville belongs to Dr. Osborne, and is pleasantly situated in a demesne of 14 acres. A temperance society was established in 1835. At the village of Ballintemple, situated on this peninsula, the Knights Templars erected a large and handsome church in 1392, which, after the dissolution of that order, was granted, with its possessions, to Gill abbey. At what period it fell into decay is uncertain; the burial ground is still used. There are fragments of some ancient towers at Dundanion and Ring-Mahon, but nothing of their history is known.

BLACKROCK, a village, in the parish of Monkstown, half-barony of Rathdown, county of Dublin, and province of Leinster, 4 miles (S. E.) from Dublin Castle; containing 2050 inhabitants. This place, which is situated on the southern shore of Dublin bay, consists of one principal street extending along the road from Dublin to the head of the village, and continued along the two roads which meet there from Kingstown, also of several minor streets and avenues, containing altogether 308 houses irregularly built, of which some are in pleasant and retired situations. The village itself possesses few pleasing features, but the country around it is beautifully diversified, and the immediate vicinity is embellished with numerous detached villas surrounded with pleasure grounds disposed with much taste. Maritimo, the marine villa of Lord Cloncurry, and Blackrock House, the residence of the Rev. Sir Harcourt Lees, Bart., are beautifully situated; the Dublin and Kingstown railway passes through the grounds of both these seats. Carysfort House, the villa of the Right Hon. W. Saurin, commands a fine view of the sea and of the mountains in the neighbourhood; Newtown House, belonging to W. Hodgens, Esq., is finely situated, and from the rear is a noble view of the bay of Dublin. The other principal seats are Montpelier House, that of J. Duckett, Esq.; Mount Temple, of E. Brewster, Esq.; Frescati Lodge, of H. Cole, Esq.; Field Villa, of H. C. Field, Esq.; and Laurel Hill, of the Rev. Hugh White. Frescati, formerly the seat of the Fitzgerald family, a spacious mansion erected by the mother of Lord Thomas Fitzgerald, called "Silken Thomas," is now divided into four separate dwellings, and occupied by respectable families. The facilities for sea-bathing render this a place of great resort during the summer months; several respectable boarding-houses have been opened for the accommodation of visiters; and an excellent hotel, called Seapoint House, has been built and fitted up for the reception of families. Baths have been constructed by the Dublin and Kingstown Railway Company, on the side of the railway embankment, which passes along the sea-shore close to the village, and to these access is obtained by a handsome foot bridge from the high ground. An elegant bridge has been built over the railway, which passes close under Seapoint House, affording the inmates a facility of access to a boat pier on the opposite side. In the centre of the village is a large block of granite, on which are the remains of an ancient cross; to this spot, which is the southern extremity of the city of Dublin, the lord mayor, with the civic authorities, proceeds when perambulating the boundaries of his jurisdiction. The twopenny post has three deliveries daily from the metropolis; and in addition to the constant railway communication with the city, numerous cars are stationed here, plying in all directions. There is an Episcopal chapel in Carysfort avenue; it was formerly a dissenting place of worship, but was purchased a few years since, and endowed with £1000 from a fund bequeathed by Lord Powerscourt; the chaplain is appointed by the trustees. In the R. C. divisions this place forms part of the union of Booterstown; the chapel, situated in the village, was built in 1822, by subscription, at an expense of £750. A nunnery of Carmelite sisters was established in 1822, consisting of a superior, 20 professed nuns, and three lay sisters; the ladies of this convent support a school for the gratuitous instruction of 120 girls, who are also clothed annually at Christmas. A school for boys was built in 1822, by subscription, and is supported by collections at charity sermons; and a girls' school was erected in 1827, chiefly at the expense of the Rev. J. M^c^Cormick, R. C. clergyman, by whom it is partly supported. A savings' bank has been established.—See MONKSTOWN.

BLACKROCK, a village, in the parish of HAGGARDSTOWN, barony of UPPER DUNDALK, county of LOUTH, and province of LEINSTER, 2 miles (E.) from Dundalk; containing 434 inhabitants. This place is situated on the bay of Dundalk, and contains about 80 houses, which are neatly built. The beach is smooth and soft, and peculiarly adapted to sea-bathing; and, if due accommodation were provided for visiters, it might become a watering-place of general attraction. It is at present much frequented, during the summer season, by the farmers of the inland counties, both for the purposes of bathing and drinking the sea-water. Alexander Shekelton, Esq., of Dundalk, has a beautiful marine villa here. —See HAGGARDSTOWN.

BLACKWATER, a village, in the parish of KILCROHANE, barony of DUNKERRON, county of KERRY, and province of MUNSTER, 6 miles (W.) from Kenmare, on the road from that place to Sneem: the population is returned with the parish. This small village is romantically situated on the west bank of a river of the same name, that issues from Lough Brinn, situated among the mountains, and after separating the parishes of Kilcrohane and Templenoe, flows into the estuary of Kenmare river. The banks of the Blackwater are richly clothed with wood on each side, and are so steep and lofty that the bridge across is upwards of sixty feet above the water. The river immediately beneath and above the bridge is confined in a narrow channel, and rushes over rocks in numerous cascades, while below it expands to a considerable breadth, and forms a deep basin, in which vessels may lie in safety. The bridge of two narrow and lofty arches, the salmon-leap beneath, and the richly wooded banks on each side, form a highly picturesque and interesting scene. This place is a favourite resort for salmon fly-fishing, permission for which is always granted by the proprietor on a proper application; but there is no accommodation for the angler nearer than Kenmare, where, however, there is a very good and commodious hotel. At the mouth of the Blackwater is a salmon fishery, where more than 100 fine fish are sometimes taken at a haul: it is chiefly the property of the Rev. Denis Mahony, of Dromore Castle. Fairs are held here in July and December; and petty sessions for the Blackwater district are held monthly, at Clover Field, in the adjoining parish of Templenoe.—See KILCROHANE.

BLACKWATER, a village, partly in the parish of BALLYVALDEN, and partly in that of KILLELY or KILLILA, barony of BALLAGHKEEN, county of WEXFORD, and province of LEINSTER, 7 miles (N. E. by N.) from Wexford; containing 58 houses and 255 inhabitants. It is situated on the old coast road from Wexford to Dublin, about a mile from the shore of St. George's channel; there is also a direct road hence to Enniscorthy, about eight miles distant. Fairs are held on March 25th, May 12th, June 1st, Aug. 10th, and Nov. 10th. It is a station both of the constabulary police and the coast-guard: the latter, which is one of the eight comprised in the district of Gorey, has a detachment at Curracloe. The R. C. chapel of the district is situated in the village.

BLACKWATERTOWN, a post-town, in that part of the parish of CLONFEACLE which is in the barony of ARMAGH, county of ARMAGH, and province of ULSTER, 5 miles (N. N. W.) from Armagh, and 70 (N. N. W.) from Dublin; containing 103 houses and 528 inhabitants. This place is situated on the old road from Armagh to Dungannon, and on the river Blackwater, from which it takes its name; it is connected by a stone bridge of three arches with the old village of Clonfeacle, now forming part of the town. During the rebellion of the Earl of Tyrone, in the reign of Elizabeth, an English garrison was placed here to check the incursions of that chieftain, who, under a plea of some injuries done to his party by the English, in 1595, attacked and expelled the garrison, and obtained possession of the fortress, which he afterwards destroyed and abandoned on the approach of Sir John Norris. In 1596 the Earl covenanted to rebuild it, and to supply an English garrison to be then stationed in it with all necessaries, as one of the conditions upon which peace was granted to him by the queen. In the following year the English forces, under Lord-Deputy Borough, assaulted the place and easily took possession; but the insurgents soon reappeared, and commenced an attack; and though the further progress of the war was prevented by the death of the general, yet a strong English garrison was stationed here as a frontier post. Tyrone was once more compelled to agree to repair the fort and bridge, and to supply the garrison; but he shortly after attacked the former with the greatest vigour; and as the works were weak and imperfect, the assailants were repulsed only by the determined valour of the garrison. The earl afterwards attempted to reduce it by famine; and the besieged were driven to the last extremities, when Sir Henry Bagnall, with the English army of about 5000 infantry and cavalry, and some loyal Irish clans, marched to their relief. This force, however, suffered a total defeat between Armagh and the Blackwater, and the fortress was immediately surrendered to the enemy, though it was soon after recovered.

This town, from its situation on the Blackwater, carries on a considerable trade in the export of corn and potatoes, of which great quantities are annually shipped to Belfast and Newry, and in the importation of coal and timber. Sloops of 50 tons' burden can deliver their cargoes at the quay; and the Ulster Canal, which is now in progress, passes close to the town. There is an extensive bleach-green at Tullydoey, belonging to Messrs. Eyre; and the extensive spirit and corn stores of Mr. Hanna furnish an abundant supply for the neighbourhood. Fairs are held on the second Wednesday in every month throughout the year; and a constabulary police force is stationed here. Tullydoey, the seat of J. Eyre Jackson, Esq., and also the residence of T. Eyre, Esq., are within a short distance of the town. There is a place of worship for Wesleyan Methodists, also a dispensary. On the western side of the river is the ancient and extensive cemetery of Clonfeacle, the church of which being in ruins, another was erected at Benburb, which is now the parish church. Opposite to the town are vestiges of a fort, by some called the Blackwater fort, in the attempt to take which Sir Henry Bagnall lost his life; and by others supposed to have been the strong fortress of the Earl of Tyrone, and one of those for which he stipulated when he obtained a patent of favour from Queen Elizabeth.—See Clonfeacle.

BLANCHARDSTOWN, a village, in the parish and barony of Castleknock, county of Dublin, and province of Leinster, 4 miles (N. W.) from Dublin, on the road to Navan; containing 57 houses and 342 inhabitants. It is within the limits of the Dublin twopenny post delivery; and a constabulary police station has been established, in the barrack of which petty sessions for the district are held the second Monday in every month. The R. C. parochial chapel is situated here; also the Cabra nunnery, in which a school of 200 girls is maintained by the nuns, a few of the children paying a penny weekly merely to ensure their attendance; there is also a school for children of both sexes.—See Castleknock.

BLANCHFIELDSTOWN, or BLANCHVILLESKILL, a parish, in the barony of Gowran, county of Kilkenny, and province of Leinster, 2 miles (W. by S.) from Gowran; containing 224 inhabitants. This small parish is situated near the mail coach road from Dublin to Cork, by way of Kilkenny, and comprises 660 statute acres: the land is good and is principally under tillage, and there is plenty of limestone. Blanchvillestown, situated in a very neat demesne containing some fine timber, is the property of Major-Gen. Sir J. Kearney, and is held on lease by the Rev. Theobald Butler. It is a vicarage, in the diocese of Ossory, and forms part of the union of Kilfane and corps of the archdeaconry; the rectory is appropriate to the vicars choral of Christchurch, Dublin. The tithes amount to £69. 10. per annum, of which £46. 6. 8. is payable to the vicars choral, and £23. 3. 4. to the archdeacon. In the R. C. divisions it is included in the union or district of Gowran. There are some remains of the old church at Blanchvilleskill.

BLARIS.—See LISBURN.

BLARNEY, a village, in the parish of Garrycloyne, barony of East Muskerry, county of Cork, and province of Munster, 5 miles (N. W. by W.) from Cork; containing 417 inhabitants. It is situated on a river of the same name, over which is a handsome bridge of three arches, on the road from Cork to Kanturk, and comprises 57 houses, which are small but well built and slated. The noted castle of Blarney was built in 1446, by Cormac McCarthy, surnamed Laidir, who was descended in a direct line from the hereditary kings of Desmond or South Munster, and was equally distinguished by his extraordinary strength and feats of chivalry as by elegance and grace both of body and mind. It is situated on an isolated rock of limestone rising boldly over the junction of the rivers Blarney and Comane, and is the third castle occupying the site: the first was rather a hunting post of Dermot McCarthy, King of South Munster, and was built of timber; the second was built in the year 1200, and the present structure was raised on its foundations, which are still visible. In the reign of Elizabeth it was the strongest fortress in Munster, and at different periods withstood regular sieges, but was treacherously taken by Lord Broghill in 1646, and the army of King William demolished all the fortifications, leaving only the tower remaining. Donogh McCarthy, who commanded the forces of Munster, was first summoned to parliament in the reign of Elizabeth by the title of Baron of Blarney; and Chas. II., in 1658, conferred the title of Earl of Clancarthy on the head of this family, the last of whom was dispossessed after the siege of Limerick; and the estate, comprising all Muskerry, was forfeited to the crown for the earl's adherence to the cause of Jas. II. On the sale of the forfeited lands in 1692, the Hollow Sword Blade Company purchased all the land around this place, and more than 3000 acres in the parish were allotted to a member of the Company, and are now held by his descendant, George Putland, Esq., of Dublin. Justin McCarthy, of Carrignavar, the only lineal descendant of that family, holds a part of the ancient inheritance. The castle was purchased in 1701 by Sir James Jefferyes, governor of Cork, who soon after erected a large and handsome house in front of it, which was the family residence for many years, but is now a picturesque ruin. The top of the castle commands a very fine view over a rich undulating tract intersected by the rivers Blarney, Comane, and Scorthonac, and bounded on the north-west by the lofty chain of the Boggra mountains. On the east is the Comane bog, many years since an impenetrable wilderness, and the last receptacle for wolves in this part of the country: that river, which takes its name from its serpentine course, flows through the bog and joins the river Blarney under the walls of the castle; and their united waters receive a considerable accession from the Scorthonac, a rapid stream which rises in the Boggra mountains. The interest which both natives and strangers take in the castle arises more from a tradition connected with a stone in its north-eastern angle, about 20 feet from the top, than from any other circumstance: this stone, which bears an inscription in Latin recording the erection of the fortress, is called the "Blarney stone," and has given rise to the well known phrase of "Blarney," in reference to a notion that, if any one kisses it, he will ever after have a cajoling tongue and the art of flattery or of telling lies with unblushing effrontery. Few, however, venture upon this ceremony, from the danger in being lowered down to the stone by a rope from an insecure battlement 132 feet high. The "groves of Blarney" are of considerable extent and very interesting; and beneath the castle are some spacious natural caves, one of which was converted into a dungeon by some of its early proprietors: it is entered by a very strong door, near which is a solitary window scarcely admitting a ray of light, and there are several massive iron rings and bolts yet remaining. Stalactites and stalagmites of beautiful formation and very compact are found in these caves.

The village, though now of little importance, was once the most thriving in the county, and between the years 1765 and 1782, when the linen manufacture was carried on, had not less than 13 mills in operation, erected by St. John Jefferyes, Esq., at an expense of about £20,000. The cotton trade was afterwards introduced and flourished for a time, but has decayed; and the only establishments now in operation are a spinning-mill belonging to M. Mahony, Esq., in which about 120 persons are employed in spinning and dyeing woollen yarn for the extensive camlet manufactory in Cork; and a paper-mill, erected by G. Jenkins, Esq., which employs about 170 persons. St. John Jefferyes, Esq., the proprietor of the village, has it in contemplation to rebuild it on an enlarged and improved plan. Just above it stands the parish church, which was repaired and enlarged in 1835, and is a very neat edifice. Fairs are held on Sept. 18th and Nov. 11th; here is a station of the constabulary police; and petty sessions are held on alternate Tuesdays. A national school, capable of accommodating 500 children, was built in 1836, at an expense of £300, of which the Commissioners gave £90, the parishioners £11, and the Rev. M. Horgan, P.P., gave the remainder; and there is a dispensary.—See GARRYCLOYNE.

BLASQUET ISLANDS, also called BLASQUES or FERRITER'S ISLANDS, lying off the shore of the parish of DONQUIN, barony of CORKAGUINEY, county of KERRY, and province of MUNSTER, 10 miles (W.S. W.) from Dingle; the population is returned with Donquin. These islands were granted by the Earl of Desmond to the family of Ferriter, but were forfeited to the Crown by their joining in the rebellion of that nobleman, and in 1586 were granted, with other possessions, to George Stone and Cornelius Champion; they were afterwards purchased by Sir Richard Boyle, ancestor of the present proprietor, the Earl of Cork. They are rated for the county cess with the parish of Donquin, but for tithes with that of Ballinvohir, on the northern shore of Dingle bay. In September, 1588, part of the Spanish Armada, consisting of the admiral's ship the St. John, a large ship of 1000 tons called "Our Lady of the Rosary," and some smaller vessels, came into the Sound in distress. Our Lady of the Rosary struck on a rock and was wrecked, and of 500 persons on board, among whom were the Prince of Ascule and 100 gentlemen, only the pilot's son was saved: a violent storm soon after dispersed the rest of the ships. The islands, which are the most westerly on the coast of Ireland, are situated in Lat. 52° 6′ 40″ (N.), and Lon. 10° 33′ (W.), as taken from the southern point of the Great Blasquet; they are twelve in number, including those which are mere rocks, and extend 2½ miles W. by S. The largest is called the Great Blasquet or Innismore, and is nearly two miles from the main land: it is about three miles in length, and is elevated mountain ground, with some arable land towards the north-east extremity: ten families reside upon it at present, and there are the ruins of a very ancient church, with a burial-ground. The second in size, and the southernmost, is Innismackilane, which lies about seven miles W. by S. from Dunmore, and is low and bleak, but yields a very rich herbage: it is the abode of two families, and contains the ruins of an ancient chapel with a burial-ground, and a small stone-roofed cell or hermitage, with the remains of several others. The third is Innisnebroe or Quern Island, so called from its resemblance to the old mill-stones called "querns." The fourth and most northern, called Innistuskard, is about an Irish mile in length: only one family resides on it, and there is a stone cell similar to that above noticed. Near the Great Island are three smaller, one of which is called Innisbeg or the Little island, and consists of about 16 acres of rich grazing land; the other two are of the same character, but not so large. Most of them are stocked with sheep and black cattle, and abound with rabbits and sea-fowl, of which the last breed in vast numbers on the stupendous pyramidal rock forming the eighth island, and situated four miles W. N. W. from the Great island, and are taken for their feathers: near this rock is another of a similar form but inferior height. Here are also numbers of hawks and eagles, the former of which were once held in great esteem for sporting; and a small bird, called by the Irish *gourder*, and said to exceed the ortolan in deliciousness of flavour, appears to be peculiar to these islands. Smith, in his History of Cork, published in 1749, says that, for the space of 45 years before he visited the Great island, "neither man, woman, or child died on it."

BLENNERVILLE, a small sea-port town, in the parish of ANNAGH, barony of TRUGHENACKMY, county of KERRY, and province of MUNSTER, 1 mile (W.) from Tralee, containing 532 inhabitants. It is situated on the bay of Tralee, and consists chiefly of one street extending from a bridge over a small river which empties itself into the bay along the road to Dingle, and containing 88 houses, most of which are neatly built and roofed with slate. On the opposite side of the bay is an oyster bed, which with the fishery in the bay affords employment to a portion of the inhabitants. An extensive trade in corn is carried on with the port of Liverpool. Fairs are held on May 9th, Sept. 15th, Oct. 25th, and Dec. 19th; and there is a penny post daily between this place and Tralee. The Tralee ship canal, now in progress, will pass under the north end of the bridge and extend to the channel at a place called the Black rock; it is supposed that this work, when completed, will nearly annihilate the trade of Blennerville, which has hitherto been the port of Tralee. A portion of the slob on the east side of the bridge has been lately embanked by Mr. Blennerhasset, of this place. The parish church, a neat modern structure with a square tower, is situated in the town; as are also the Protestant and R. C. school-houses, and at Curragrague is a school under the trustees of Erasmus Smith's charity.—See ANNAGH.

BLESSINGTON (*St. Mary*), or BURGAGE, a market and post-town, and a parish, in the barony of Lower Talbotstown, county of Wicklow, and province of Leinster, 6¼ miles (E. S. E.) from Naas, and 14 (S. S. W.) from Dublin; containing, with Burgage, 2677 inhabitants, of which number, 426 are in the town. This place is situated on the river Liffey, and on the high road from Dublin, by Baltinglass, to Wexford, Carlow, and Waterford. The town occupies a rising ground on the north-western confines of the county, and was built by Archbishop Boyle in the reign of Chas. II.: it consists only of one street, and contains about 50 houses, which are mostly of respectable appearance, and a good inn or hotel. Considerable improvement has taken place since the construction of the new turnpike road from Dublin to Carlow, by way of Baltinglass, in 1829, by which the Waterford mail and the Kilkenny day mail, and several coaches and cars to the counties of Wexford and Carlow, have been brought through it. The celebrated waterfall called Poul-a-Phuca, about three miles distant on the road to Baltinglass, and described under the head of Ballymore-Eustace, is generally visited from this place. The market is on Thursday; and fairs are held on May 12th, July 5th, and Nov. 12th. Here is a station of the constabulary police; and the chief officer of the peace preservation force resides in the town. The inhabitants were incorporated by charter of the 21st of Chas. II. (1669), granted to Michael Boyle, Archbishop of Dublin and Chancellor of Ireland, and certain forfeited lands assigned to him were at the same time erected into a manor, to be called the manor of Blessington. This charter empowered the archbishop to hold before the seneschal of the manor a court leet with view of frankpledge twice in the year; a court baron every three weeks, or less frequently, for claims not exceeding 40*s.*; and a court of record when and where he should think proper, with jurisdiction not exceeding £10: and prescribed the style, constitution, and mode of electing the officers of the corporation. The corporation was styled "The Sovereign, Bailiffs, and Burgesses of the Borough and Town of Blessington;" and consisted of a sovereign, two bailiffs, and twelve burgesses, with power to a majority to admit freemen and choose inferior officers, and the archbishop was authorised to appoint a recorder and town-clerk. The borough returned two members to the Irish parliament till the Union, when the £15,000 awarded as compensation for the loss of the franchise was paid to Arthur, Marquess of Downshire; the right of election was vested in the corporation at large, which from that period has been extinct. Petty sessions are held on alternate Saturdays; and the Marquess of Downshire, as proprietor of the town, has power to hold a manorial court for the recovery of small debts.

The parish, which, previously to the erection of the town and church in 1683, was called Burgage, comprises 17,570 statute acres. The land is chiefly under tillage and pasturage, and there are some large tracts of mountain waste, on which are turf bogs; the state of agriculture has considerably improved. The subsoil is chiefly limestone gravel; and the mountains abound with granite, which is quarried and sent to Dublin for public buildings. The Marquess of Downshire had a handsome mansion and demesne of 410 statute acres, with a deer park of 340 acres, all surrounded by a wall, and situated on the right of the road from Dublin: the mansion was originally built by Primate Boyle, the last ecclesiastical chancellor of Ireland, who held his court of chancery here, and built houses for the six clerks, two of which yet remain; the interior was burnt by the insurgents in 1798 and has not been restored; the demesne is richly embellished with fine timber. About two miles from the town, on the road to Baltinglass, is Russborough, the elegant seat of the Earl of Miltown: the mansion, erected after a design by Mr. Cassels, architect of the Bank of Ireland, is in the Grecian style, and consists of a centre and two wings, connected by semicircular colonnades of alternated Ionic and Corinthian pillars, and presenting a noble façade of hewn stone 700 feet in extent; the interior is fitted up in a style of sumptuous magnificence; the floors of the principal apartments are of polished mahogany, and there is an extensive and valuable collection of paintings, chiefly of the Italian school, arranged in seven apartments appropriated to its reception: the demesne comprises 405 statute acres tastefully laid out and planted. Russellstown, the seat of J. Hornidge, Esq., is also in the parish. The living is a vicarage with Burgage, in the diocese of Dublin and Glendalough, to which the vicarages of Boystown and Kilbride were united by act of council in 1833, forming the vicarial union of Blessington, in the patronage of the Archbishop; the rectory is united to those of St. Andrew's and Ardree, and part of Lusk, together constituting the corps of the precentorship in the cathedral church of St. Patrick, Dublin. The tithes, including those of Burgage, amount to £218. 10., of which £120 is payable to the precentor, and the remainder to the vicar, and the gross tithes of the benefice amount to £210. 19. 5. The lands of Great Burgage, comprising 670*a.* 3*r.* 10*p.* statute measure, let on lease at a rental of £64. 12. 3¾., form part of the endowment of the precentorship. The church, a neat edifice with a lofty square tower, was erected at the expense of Primate Boyle, who also gave a ring of bells: it is neatly fitted up, and an organ was erected by the grandfather of the present Marquess of Downshire, who allows the organist a salary of £40 per ann., to which £10 was formerly added by the parish, and now by the new Ecclesiastical Board: a monument to the memory of the founder records his benefactions to the town, and the inscription concludes with the motto, "Abi, et fac tu similiter." During the disturbances of 1798 the church was used as a barrack. Viscount Blessington, a descendant of Primate Boyle, in 1736, endowed the living of Blessington, otherwise Burgage, with 130 statute acres of land in the adjoining parish of Tipperkevin, subject to the payment of £5 per annum by the incumbent to the school: there is neither glebe-house nor glebe. In the R. C. divisions this parish is partly included in the union or district of Blessington, partly in that of Blackditches, and partly in that of Ballymore-Eustace: the first union comprises also the parishes of Rathmore, Kilbride, and Kilteel, and contains three chapels, situated at Cross and Eadestown, in Rathmore, and at Kilbride. A neat building, the upper part of which is used as a girls' school, and the lower as a court for holding the petty sessions, with a house for the master and mistress, has been erected at an expense of £800 by the Marquess of Downshire, who allows a salary of £20 to the master and £10 to the mistress, the latter of whom also receives the £5 payable by the incumbent: there are about 20 boys in the school, who are taught in a school-room a short distance from the building, and 30 girls. There are also five hedge schools in Blessington and Burgage, in which nearly 150 children are taught. A dispensary is supported in the customary manner. There are some ruins of the old church of Burgage, and in the churchyard are the remains of a castle, and on the outside is a very fine cross, hewn out of one large block of granite, and about 14 feet high. On the townland of Crosscool Harbour, near Liffey Cottage, are a burial-place and a holy well, the latter of which is much resorted to in June for its reputed efficacy in healing various diseases. On the townland of Three Castles are some remains of one of the ancient fortresses from which it has derived its name. Blessington gave the title of Earl to the family of Gardiner, now extinct; and Russborough gives the inferior titles of Viscount and Baron to the Earl of Miltown.

BODENSTOWN, or BOWDENSTOWN, a parish, in the barony of NORTH NAAS, county of KILDARE, and province of LEINSTER, 1½ mile (S. W.) from Clane; containing, with part of the village of Sallins, 458 inhabitants. It is bounded on the east by the river Liffey, over which is a very curious stone bridge of five arches, all differently shaped. About three-fourths of the land are pasture and appropriated to the fattening of stock for the Dublin and Liverpool markets, and the remainder is under tillage, producing good crops: there is no waste land or bog, yet the supply of fuel is abundant. The Grand Canal, which passes close to the parish, facilitates the conveyance of corn and potatoes to the metropolis, from which manure is also obtained in abundance. The gentlemen's seats are Blackhall, that of P. Wolfe, Esq.; Castlesize, of I. Manders, Esq.; Little Rath, of Mr. R. Hall, occupying the site of an ancient intrenchment; and Sallins Lodge, near which stood the old castle of Sallins, the residence of Mr. S. Holt. The living is a vicarage, in the diocese of Kildare, with the perpetual curacy of Sherlockstown episcopally united, forming the union of Bodenstown, in the patronage of the Bishop; the rectory is impropriate in the Earl of Mayo. The tithes amount to £90, of which £60 is payable to the impropriator and £30 to the vicar; and the tithes of the entire benefice amount to £65. There is no church, but a grant was made for the erection of one by the late Board of First Fruits; the Protestant parishioners attend the church of Clane. There is also no glebe-house: the glebe comprises 8 acres. In the R. C. divisions the parish forms part of the union or district of Kill. There is a pay school of about 10 children. The celebrated Theobald Wolfe Tone was a native of this parish, and lies in the same grave with his father in the churchyard.

BOHERBEE, or BOHERBUI, a village, in the parish of KILMEEN, barony of DUHALLOW, county of CORK and province of MUNSTER, 5 miles (W.) from Kanturk: the population is returned with the parish. This place is situated on the new line of road recently constructed by Government, and leading from Roskeen-Bridge, through King-William's-town, to Castle-island. The village, from its advantageous situation on the road above mentioned, and also near the junction of the roads from Kanturk and Newmarket to Millstreet, promises to become a place of some importance. A police barrack has been lately erected by Mr. W. Allen, for the accommodation of the constabulary force stationed here; and the R. C. parochial chapel, a large slated building recently erected, is situated in the village.—See KILMEEN.

BOHERLAHAN.—See ARDMAYLE.

BOHILLANE, or BOHOLANE, a parish, in the barony of IMOKILLY, county of CORK, and province of MUNSTER, 2¾ miles (E.) from Cloyne; containing 487 inhabitants. It is situated on the road from Ballycotton to Castlemartyr, and comprises 1848 statute acres, as applotted under the tithe act, and valued at £959 per annum. The land in general is tolerably good, and the greater part is under an improved system of tillage: in some places the soil is light, and rests on a substratum of clay-slate; in others, stiff and compact, occasionally abounding with springs; and in some, loose and shivery, absorbing great quantities of moisture. The living is a rectory, in the diocese of Cloyne, and in the patronage of the Bishop: the tithes amount to £191. 10. 3½. There is no church; the Protestant inhabitants resort for divine service either to Itermorrough or Cloyne. The ruins of the old church form a picturesque object: near them is a glebe of 12*a.* 2*r.* 36*p.*, but there is no glebe-house. In the R. C. divisions this parish forms part of the union or district of Ballymacoda in Kilmacdonough.

BOHOE, a parish, partly in the barony of MAGHERABOY, but chiefly in that of CLANAWLEY, county of FERMANAGH, and province of ULSTER, 5½ miles (W.) from Enniskillen; containing 2581 inhabitants. It is situated on the road from Enniskillen to Sligo, and comprises, according to the Ordnance survey, 15,058½ statute acres, of which 6151¼ are in the barony of Magheraboy, and 8907¼ in that of Clanawley. The living is a rectory and vicarage, in the diocese of Clogher, and in the patronage of the Bishop: the tithes amount to £120. The church, a plain edifice, was erected by aid of a gift of £200 from the late Board of First Fruits, in 1777, and the Ecclesiastical Commissioners have recently granted £157. 10. for its repair. There is no glebe-house; the glebe comprises 142 acres. In the R. C. divisions the parish forms part of the union or district of Devenish or Derrygonelly, and also part of that of Innismacsaint; the chapel, an indifferent building, belongs to the union of Devenish. The parochial school is supported by an annual donation from the incumbent, aided by subscription; and affords instruction to about 50 boys and 30 girls; and there are four pay schools, in which are about 150 boys and 70 girls. The mountain of Belmore, in this parish, has an elevation of 1312, and that of Glenkeel 1223, feet above the level of the sea.

BOHOLA, or BUCHOLLA, a parish, in the barony of GALLEN, county of MAYO, and province of CONNAUGHT, 6 miles (S. by E.) from Foxford; containing 3658 inhabitants. It is situated on the river Gustien, and on the road from Swinford to Castlebar, and is principally under tillage; the mountain of Slieve Conn, which is within its limits, is cultivated to the very summit; there is some bog. The principal seats are Barley Hill, the residence of Bernard McManus, Esq.; Carragawn, of E. Deane, Esq.; and Rosslevin Castle, of H. Jordan, Esq. It is a vicarage, in the diocese of Achonry, and is part of the union of Templemore; the rectory is impropriate in the representatives of the late Roger Palmer, Esq. The tithes amount to £374. 17. 8., of which one-half is payable to the impropriators, and the other to the vicar. The church is in ruins. The R. C. parish is co-extensive with that of the Established Church, and contains a chapel. There are two hedge schools, in which about 190 boys and 80 girls are educated.

BOLIES, a village, in the parish of DULEEK, barony of UPPER DULEEK, county of MEATH, and province of LEINSTER, 2 miles (S. W.) from Duleek, on the mail coach road from Dublin, through Duleek, to Belfast; containing 30 houses and 159 inhabitants.

BOLINALEA, or BONELEA, a village, in the parish of RATHNEW, barony of NEWCASTLE, county of WICKLOW, and province of LEINSTER, adjoining the post-town of Ashford, and containing about 80 houses and 476 inhabitants. It is situated on the old road from Newtown-Mount-Kennedy by Cronroe, to Rathdrum; and is a place of great resort during the summer season, from its contiguity to some of the most varied and luxuriant scenery through which the river Vartrey flows, and with which the neighbouring district abounds. The fairs of Ashford are held at this village.—See RATHNEW.

BOLY, or GALVOLY, a parish, in the barony of ELIOGARTY, county of TIPPERARY, and province of MUNSTER, 2¼ miles (S. S. E.) from Thurles; containing 426 inhabitants. This parish, which is also called Galbooly, and is situated on a branch of the river Suir, comprises 1268 statute acres, as applotted under the tithe act, and valued at £1012 per annum. It is a vicarage, in the diocese of Cashel, and is part of the union of Borrisleigh and corps of the treasurership in the cathedral of Cashel; the rectory is impropriate in John Bagwell, Esq., a minor. The tithes amount to £110, which is equally divided between the impropriator and the treasurer. There is a pay school, in which are about 70 boys and 30 girls.

BONAFOBLE.—See MOVILLE.

BONLAHEY, or BUNLAHEY, a village, in that part of the parish of GRANARD which is in the barony of GRANARD, county of LONGFORD, and province of LEINSTER, 3 miles (W. N. W.) from Granard, on the road to Ballinamuck; containing 65 dwellings and 299 inhabitants. Fairs are held on the 16th of May, July 26th, Oct. 15th, and Dec. 12th.—See GRANARD.

BONMAHON, a maritime village, in the parish of BALLYLANEEN, barony of UPPERTHIRD, county of WATERFORD, and province of MUNSTER, 3 miles (S.) from Kilmacthomas; containing 972 inhabitants. This place is situated on the coast of St. George's channel, and derives its name from the river Mahon, which rises in the Cummeragh mountains, and here falls into the sea. It is much frequented as a watering-place during the summer, and contains several neat private residences and convenient lodging-houses for the accommodation of visiters; and in the immediate vicinity are numerous houses built for persons employed in the mines. The beach is well adapted for bathing, and the village might be made a place of fashionable resort; but the land being principally the property of the College of Physicians, who cannot grant leases for more than 31 years, very little improvement has been made. The surrounding scenery is very pleasing, and a wooden bridge over the Mahon adds much to its picturesque character. A new church, with a school-house adjoining, has been recently erected on the eastern side of the river, in the parish of Kilbarrymeadan; the school is supported by Lady Osborne. The valuable mines of this place and in the neighbourhood produce copper and lead, with a portion of silver; they have been worked from an early period, and veins have been opened in several parts and worked to a considerable extent. In 1745 a Company rented these mines from Lord Ranelagh for a term of 31 years, under an agreement to give to his lordship one-eighth part of all the ore obtained; and the works were carried on with spirit for eight or ten years. They were subsequently worked by Mr. Wyse, who employed 300 men; and, in 1811, the Earl of Ormonde renewed the enterprise with every prospect of success, but, after a very large expenditure, was induced to desist; they are at present under the management of the Irish Mining Company. The veins are found in some parts of the rock within a few feet of the surface, and none have been worked to a greater depth than 25 yards. Copper ore is observed in many places along the beach. The principal mines are on the property of the Marquess of Ormonde, on the lands belonging to the see of Waterford, and on those of Lady Osborne and J. Power O'Shee, Esq.—See BALLYLANEEN.

BONNECONLAN.—See KILGARVEY.

BONOWEN.—See BENOWEN.

BOOTERSTOWN, a parish, in the half-barony of RATHDOWN, county of DUBLIN, and province of LEINSTER, 3¼ miles (S. E.) from Dublin; containing 2875 inhabitants. This place is situated on the road from Dublin to Kingstown and Bray, and on the southern coast of Dublin bay, the shores of which here assume a most interesting and beautifully picturesque appearance. On the opposite side are the finely wooded lands of Clontarf, the mountainous ridge of Howth connected with the main land by a low sandy isthmus, and the islands of Ireland's Eye and Lambay. Of the other side the land swells into the romantic hill of Mount Anville, with slopes richly wooded and embellished with numerous handsome seats, and to the east are the projecting high grounds of the Blackrock covered to the water's edge with trees. The parish comprises 450 statute acres, as applotted under the tithe act, and valued at £1589 per annum; the substratum is chiefly limestone and limestone gravel. Of the numerous handsome seats and villas, many of which are delightfully situated in highly embellished demesnes, commanding beautiful views of the bay of Dublin and of the mountains, the principal are Seamount, that of the Rt. Hon. J. Doherty, Chief Justice of the Court of Common Pleas; Sans Souci, of the late R. Roe, Esq.; Willow Park, of J. Ferrier, Esq.; Colognes, of I. M. D'Olier, Esq.; Rosemount, of C. Smith, Esq.; Rockville, of W. Murphy, Esq.; Sion Hill, of H. Lanauze, Esq.; Rockville House, of C. Hope, Esq.; Hermitage, of W. F. Mostyn, Esq.; Clareville, of Sir Ross Mahon, Bart.; Lota, of O'Gorman Mahon, Esq.; Chesterfield, of the Rev. W. Betty; Belleview, of J. Gillman, Esq.; Church View, of H. Higinbotham, Esq.; Arbutus Lodge, of W. Cullen, Esq.; South Hill, of A. Beytagh, Esq.; Mount Merrion, of H. Staines, Esq.; Woodview, of Lady Waller; Marino, of the Rev. R. H. Nixon; Brook Lawn, of J. McCullagh, Esq.; Graceville, of J. Woods, Esq.; Albion Cottage, of J. C. Bacon,

Esq.; Baymount, of Capt. Cockburn; Mereview, of T. Clinch, Esq.; Woodbine Cottage, of Capt. McNaghton; and Waltham, of A. Ormsby, Esq. The village, with those of Williamstown and Blackrock, nearly forms a continuous extent of town; and within the parish are the avenues of Merrion, Cross, Sydney and Williamstown, in each of which are rows of neat houses, with numerous detached villas. This place is much frequented during the summer season on account of its facilities for sea-bathing and its fine strand of smooth sand; numerous lodging-houses have been prepared for the accommodation of visiters; and a cross embankment communicating with the railway, which is carried on an embankment through the sea in front of the town, at a short distance from high water mark, has been constructed for their convenience. The twopenny post has three deliveries daily from the metropolis, and a constant and rapid communication with the city is maintained by the railway and by cars, which ply in both directions.

The living is a perpetual curacy, in the diocese of Dublin, erected out of the parish of Donnybrook by act of council in 1821, and in the patronage of the Archdeacon of Dublin; the rectory forms part of the corps of the archdeaconry. The tithes amount to £65. 0. 2., the whole of which is payable to the archdeacon, who allows the perpetual curate £16 per annum; the curacy was also endowed by the late Earl of Pembroke with £1000, since invested in ground rents now producing £73. 16. 10. The church is a handsome structure, in the later English style, with a square embattled tower with crocketed pinnacles at the angles, and surmounted by a lofty spire; the walls are strengthened with buttresses terminating in pinnacles, and crowned with an embattled parapet. It was erected in 1824, on a piece of ground given by the late Earl of Pembroke in Cross Avenue, at an expense of £5000, of which sum, £2700 was a gift from the late Board of First Fruits; and contains neat monuments to James Digges Latouche and Richard Verschoyle, Esqrs. In the R. C. divisions this parish forms the head of a union or district including also parts of the parishes of Donnybrook, Kill, Monkstown, Rathfarnham, Stillorgan, and Taney. The chapel is a spacious and handsome edifice, erected at the sole expense of the late Earl Fitzwilliam; there are also chapels at Blackrock and Dundrum. A neat parochial school-house, with apartments for a master and mistress, was built in 1826, near the church, at an expense of £600, defrayed by subscription; and an infants' school was built adjoining the former in 1833, in which is kept a parochial lending library; these schools are supported by subscription and collections at charity sermons. In connection with the R. C. chapel is a girls' school, to which Mrs. Verschoyle contributes £20 per annum. Here is a dispensary; and a Dorcas Society is supported by subscription and collections at charity sermons.

BORDWELL, a parish, in the barony of UPPER OSSORY, QUEEN'S county, and province of LEINSTER, $2\frac{3}{4}$ miles (N. E.) from Rathdowney; containing 869 inhabitants. It is situated on the road from Abbeyleix to Templemore, and comprises 2549 statute acres, as applotted under the tithe act. The state of agriculture is improving; there is a small quantity of bog; and limestone is quarried in the parish. The principal seats are Grantstown, the residence of R. Vicars, Esq.; Coolfin, of T. Roe, Esq.; and Fernville, of — Palmer, Esq. The living is a rectory and vicarage, in the diocese of Ossory, and in the patronage of the Bishop: the tithes amount to £137. 10. The church is in ruins, and divine service is performed in the school-house. There is neither glebe-house nor glebe. In the R. C. divisions the parish forms part of the union or district of Aghavoe; the chapel is a large building. The parochial school is supported by subscription, aided by annual donations from Lord Lorton, the rector, Mr. Roe, and others; and at Fox Rock is a National school; in these schools are about 50 boys and 30 girls. At Grantstown and at Kilbredy are the ruins of old castles.

BORRIS, or BORRIS-IDRONE, a village, in the parish of CLONAGOOSE, barony of IDRONE EAST, county of CARLOW, and province of LEINSTER, 3 miles (S. E.) from Goresbridge; containing 671 inhabitants. This place is situated near the river Barrow, on the road from Carlow to Ross: it has a patent for a market on Friday, which is not held, and a penny post to Goresbridge. Borris House, the noble seat of the late T. Kavanagh, Esq., is situated in an extensive and richly wooded demesne, and commands fine views terminated on the south-east by the imposing range of the Blackstairs mountains. This mansion, which externally exhibits the appearance of an English baronial residence of the 16th century, while every advantage of convenience and splendour is secured within, has been for ages the chief residence of the posterity of Donald Kavanagh, natural son of Mac Murrough, last King of Leinster, whose name and authority he subsequently assumed. In 1642, being garrisoned by the parliamentarians, it was besieged by the Irish, and with difficulty the garrison was relieved and reinforced by Sir C. Coote. In the disturbances of 1798 it sustained two attacks; first, on May 24th, when the insurgents were repulsed by Capt. Kavanagh's yeomanry corps, with the loss of 50 killed and wounded; and afterwards on June 12th, from a detachment sent against it from Vinegar Hill, on which occasion it was defended with great bravery by a party of the Donegal militia, who compelled the assailants, after burning the out-offices and destroying some houses in Borris, to retire with considerable loss. At Kilcamney, in the vicinity, an action was also fought, in which the insurgents were routed with the loss of their stores by the king's forces under Sir C. Asgill. Petty sessions are held here every alternate Thursday, and road sessions occasionally: the court-house was lately erected by Mr. Kavanagh. This is a chief constabulary police station; and there is a small barrack for the accommodation of about 30 men. Fairs for cattle, sheep, pigs, &c., are held on Jan. 1st, Feb. 5th, May 1st, July 2nd, Aug. 15th, Oct. 4th, and Nov. 14th, and four more fairs have been lately obtained; that in July is a considerable fair for wool. Attached to Borris House is a very handsome private chapel, erected by the late Mr. Kavanagh, and open to the inhabitants. In the R. C. divisions this place is the head of a union or district comprising parts of the parishes of Clonagoose, Ullard (county of Kilkenny), St. Mullins, and Ballyellin, and the whole of that of Kiltennel: the parochial chapel is a handsome edifice, lately built at an expense of £2000. There is a school, in which 150 boys and 90 girls are taught: the school-house is a commodious building, erected and fitted up by local contributions amounting to £274. 5. 6., and a grant of £97. 5. 6. from the National Board. A dispensary is maintained in the customary manner; and there is an institution called the Borris Benevolent Society, established about eight years, to which the payment of one shilling monthly entitles each member, in case of sickness, to a weekly allowance of 5*s.* for the first three months, and of 2*s.* 6*d.* afterwards so long as he shall continue sick. At Borris House is preserved the "*Figeen*," a curious ornament of silver and tin, found on the demesne; and an ancient horn and a casket, called the *Liath-Mersicith*, esteemed among the most valuable curiosities in the museum of Trinity College, Dublin, are relics which formerly belonged to the Kavanaghs.—See CLONAGOOSE.

BORRIS, QUEEN'S county. — See MARYBOROUGH.

BORRIS - IN - OSSORY. — See BURROS - IN - OSSORY.

BORRISLEIGH, or TWO-MILE BURRIS, a parish, in the barony of ELIOGARTY, county of TIPPERARY, and province of MUNSTER, 3½ miles (S. S. E.) from Thurles; containing, with the town of Littleton, 3020 inhabitants. This parish is situated at the junction of the roads leading respectively from Johnstown to Cashel, and from Killenaule and Thurles to New Birmingham; it comprises 7988 statute acres, as applotted under the tithe act, and valued at £5702 per annum. Within its limits is a small portion of the Bog of Allen, and the river Liscaveen forms a boundary between it and the parish of Ballymoreen. The village, which is small, is the property of Sir Hugh Nugent O'Reilly, and is only remarkable for the ruins of a church and castle, and the remains of a Danish fort, all within a few yards of each other. The living is a rectory, in the diocese of Cashel, united from a period prior to any known record to the vicarages of Boly or Galvoly and Drom, and to the chapelry of Leogh, together constituting the union of Borrisleigh and the corps of the treasurership in the cathedral of Cashel, in the patronage of the Archbishop: the tithes amount to £600, and of the benefice to £738. 1. 6½. The church is a handsome edifice, partly in the later English style, and was enlarged by aid of a loan of £1000 from the late Board of First Fruits, in 1820; and another loan of £923 was granted for its repair in 1828. There is a glebe-house, with a glebe of 30 acres, the latter subject to a rent; in the parish of Drom is also a glebe of 42*a.* 1*r.* 19*p.*, statute measure, leased at £30. 9. 3., with a renewal fine of £6. 10. per annum. In the R. C. divisions this parish forms part of the union or district of Moykarkey. The parochial school is supported by the rector, who contributes £20 per annum; and another school is maintained by private subscription. In these schools about 90 boys and 50 girls are instructed; and there are three pay schools, in which are about 100 boys and 80 girls.—See LITTLETON.

BORRISMORE, a townland, in the parish of URLINGFORD, barony of GALMOY, county of KILKENNY, and province of LEINSTER, 4 miles (W. by N.) from Freshford: the population is returned with the parish. This place anciently formed part of the possessions of the abbey of Jerpoint: it contains 2037 statute acres, as applotted under the tithe act, for which the composition amounts to £83. 2. 5. per annum, appropriate to the benefice of Burnchurch, in the diocese of Ossory.

BORRIS-O'-KANE.—See BURRIS-O'-KANE.

BOTHON.—See BUTTEVANT.

BOURNEY, or BOURCHIN, a parish, in the barony of IKERRIN, county of TIPPERARY, and province of MUNSTER, 4½ miles (S. E.) from Roscrea; containing 4061 inhabitants This parish is situated between the mail coach road from Dublin to Limerick, and the public road from Roscrea to Templemore; and comprises more than 9700 statute acres. The rivers Nore and Suir have their rise here in the side of the mountain of Benduff, their respective sources not being more than half a mile distant from each other; the Nore pursues nearly a direct course through this parish and Corbally into Burros-in-Ossory; the Suir forms the southern boundary of the parish. Dangan Lodge is the seat of J. Middleton, Esq.; Derrylahan, of J. Mason, Esq.; Mount Fresco, of Horatio Lloyd, Esq.; and Lorn Park, of G. Roe, Esq. Here is a station of the constabulary police. The living is a vicarage, in the diocese of Killaloe, to which the rectory and vicarage of Burrisnefarney were united by act of council, forming the union of Bourney, in the patronage of the Bishop; the rectory is impropriate in the Marquess of Ormonde. The tithes amount to £550, of which £350 is payable to the impropriator, and £200 to the vicar; and the gross tithes of the union payable to the incumbent amount to £384. 12. 4. The church is a plain building, for the repairs of which the Ecclesiastical Commissioners have recently granted £246. 8. 9. The glebe-house was built by aid of a gift of £350 and a loan of £450, in 1814, from the late Board of First Fruits: the glebe comprises about six acres in four detached portions in this parish. In the R. C. divisions the parish is the head of a union or district, which comprises also the parishes of Burrisnefarney and Corbally, and contains four chapels, all neat buildings, of which the principal is situated at Clonakenny, in this parish. There is a place of worship for the Society of Friends at Knockbally Meagher. The parochial schools afford instruction to about 40 boys and 40 girls; and there are also four private pay schools, in which are about 170 children. At Boulebane, Bawnmadrum, and Clonakenny are considerable remains of ancient castles; the first two are situated on an eminence very near each other.

BOVEVAGH, a parish, in the barony of KENAUGHT, county of LONDONDERRY, and province of ULSTER, 2 miles (N.) from Dungiven; containing 5552 inhabitants. At this place, anciently called *Boith-Medhbha*, a monastery was founded in 557 by St. Columb, of which Aidan, nephew of St. Patrick, was the first abbot. This establishment was situated on the western bank of the river Roe, and continued to flourish for some years, but was plundered and destroyed by the Danes, and was never afterwards rebuilt. The parish is intersected by two roads, one on each side of the river, leading from Dungiven to Newtownlimavady; and, according to the Ordnance survey, comprises 18,596 statute acres. The land is generally fertile, but the soil is very variable, passing through all the gradations from light sand to stiff clay and marl: on the banks of the river it is gravelly and remarkably productive. The system of agriculture is greatly improved; there is scarcely any mountain or waste land, and the bogs are mostly worked out and reclaimed. The geological features of the parish are highly interesting: the strata are laid open to view in the river and the several streams; the most valuable of those hitherto worked is the freestone, which is found in several parts, and of which the principal quarry is at Ballyhargan. From this quarry was procured the stone used in building the palace of Ballyscullion, the magnificent portico of which was removed to St. George's church, at Belfast; the stone found here is easily worked, but hardens by exposure to the air, and is of very good colour. Indications of manganese are also observable, and the beautiful pebbles called Dungiven crystals are frequently found. The weaving of linen cloth is carried on in many of the farm-houses and cottages. There are several seats, the principal of which are Streth House, the residence of Mrs. Edwards; Ballyhargan, of W. Osborne, Esq.; Ardenariff, of W. Douglas, Esq.; and Camnish House, of the Rev. Mr. Kidd.

The living is a rectory, in the diocese of Derry, and in the patronage of the Bishop: the tithes amount to £580. The church is a large and handsome edifice, in the later English style, with a lofty square tower crowned with pinnacles; it was erected in 1823, by aid of a gift of £300 from the late Board of First Fruits, and is situated on the west bank of the Roe, about a quarter of a mile from the site of the old church, which had fallen to decay some years previously. The glebe-house, a large and well-built residence, is situated on the east bank of the river: the glebe comprises 79 acres of fertile land. In the R. C. divisions this parish forms part of the union or district of Banagher, and contains two chapels, one at Derrylane, where service is performed every alternate Sunday, and the other at Ballymoney. There is a place of worship at Camnish for Presbyterians in connection with the Synod of Ulster, of the second class. The male and female parochial school at Burnfoot is aided by an annual donation from the rector, and was endowed with half an acre of land by Mr. Edwards; the school house, a good building of stone, was erected at an expense of £110, of which £50 was granted from the lord-lieutenant's fund, and the remainder raised by subscription. At Drumneesy is a male and female school, aided by the rector, who also contributes to the support of an infants' school at Bovevagh. In these schools are about 260 children; and there are six private schools, in which are about 280 children, and five Sunday schools. Near the old church is an artificial cave, 82 yards in length, with several galleries branching from it in different directions. About a mile north-east of the church is an upright stone, near which, according to tradition, a battle was fought, but which may probably be part of a cromlech, as there are other stones and vestiges of a druidical circle near the spot.

BOW, or BOA, ISLAND, partly in the parish of TEMPLECARNE, and partly in that of DRUMKEERAN, barony of LURG, county of FERMANAGH, and province of ULSTER, 2 miles (S.) from Pettigo; containing 382 inhabitants. This island, situated in the upper portion of the lower Lough Erne, comprises, according to the Ordnance survey, 1342 statute acres, of which nearly 787 are in Drumkeeran, and the remainder in the parish of Templecarne. The land is good, and the island is divided into a number of small farms varying from two to forty acres. There is a fine quarry of freestone. In the townland of Caldragh is a burial-ground.

BOYANAGH, a parish, partly in the barony of TYAQUIN, but chiefly in that of HALF-BALLYMOE, county of GALWAY, and province of CONNAUGHT, 6¾ miles (E. by N.) from Dunmore; containing 4861 inhabitants. It is situated on the road from Dunmore to Castlerea, and comprises 13,840 statute acres, a large extent of which is waste land and bog. Here are two oatmeal-mills, and limestone is abundant. Springfield is the seat of W. McDermot, Esq.; Ashfield, of I. Kelly, Esq.; Clondoyle, of B. Kelly, Esq.; and Lakeview, of I. O'Flyn, Esq. It is a vicarage, in the diocese of Tuam, and is part of the union of Kilkerrin; the rectory forms part of the union and corps of the deanery of Tuam: the tithes amount to £185, of which £120 is payable to the dean, and £65 to the incumbent. The church is in ruins, but the ground is still used for burials. In the R. C. divisions it is the head of a union or district, also called Glanamada, comprising the parishes of Boyanagh and Templetogher; there is a chapel in each, of which that of Boyanagh is situated at Kelnalag. A school, in which about 80 boys and 10 girls are taught, is supported by Lord Fitzgerald; and there are three private pay schools, in which are about 280 boys and 50 girls.

BOYLE, a corporate, market, and post-town, and a parish, in the barony of BOYLE, county of ROSCOMMON, and province of CONNAUGHT, 19¼ miles (S. S. E.) from Sligo, and 84½ miles (W. N. W.) from Dublin; containing 12,597 inhabitants, of which number, 3433 are in the town. This place had its origin in the foundation of a religious establishment, in 1148, at Grelacdinach, which, after several removals, was finally settled here in 1161, by Maurice O'Dubhay, the third in succession to Peter Mordha, its first abbot, who was promoted to the see of Clonfert, and was drowned in the Shannon in 1171. The abbey, which was dedicated to the Blessed Virgin, was founded for brethren of the Cistertian order of St. Bernard, and as a dependency of the great abbey of Mellifont, in the county of Louth. In 1197, Cornelius Mac Dermot, King of Moylurg (which included the greater part, if not the whole, of the barony of Boyle), died here in the habit of the order, and was interred within the precincts of the abbey. The English forces, commanded by the lords-justices Maurice Fitzgerald and Mac William, in 1235, encamped within the walls of the monastery, seized upon every thing belonging to it, and stripped the monks of their habits, to punish them for their endeavours to assist the King of Connaught. It was pillaged by Rory O'More, in 1315, but continued to flourish till the dissolution, and in 1569 was given by Queen Elizabeth to Patrick Cusacke, of Gerrardstown, in the county of Meath, by whom, or by a lay proprietor who afterwards succeeded him, it was forfeited. In 1589 it was granted to William Usher, on a lease of 21 years, at a rent of £14. 16. 4. per annum; and in 1595 it was besieged by the Earl of Tyrone with an army of 2300 Scottish Highlanders and Irish. In the 2nd, 4th, and 9th years of the reign of James I., inquisitions were made to ascertain its possessions; and in 1603 it was given to Sir John King, ancestor of the present Earl of Kingston and Viscount Lorton, which grant was, about 15 years afterwards, confirmed by another, which conferred also the privilege of holding courts leet and baron.

The town, which is the largest in the northern part of the county, and one of the principal within its limits, is situated on the river Boyle, which flows from Lough Gara into Lough Key, and on the mail coach road to Sligo. It is divided into two parts by the river, towards which the ground slopes precipitously on both sides; the older part extends up the acclivity on the north side, and the more modern portion stretches in a direction parallel with the north-west bank of the river, above the bridge; the most recent and improved part is on the south side of the bridge, ascending the hill and forming a crescent on its summit. The old bridge, an inconvenient structure, which connected these parts of the town, and on which was a statue of William III., has been taken down and replaced by a handsome structure of three arches, 100 feet long and 42 feet wide; the span of the principal arch is 30 feet, and the lightness and beauty of the design add greatly to the appearance of the town; it was erected at an expense of £500, one half of which was paid by the county and the other by Lord Lorton. Another bridge of a single arch, 50 feet in span, was thrown across the river in 1817; and below it there is a third, of five small arches. The old mansion of the Kingston family has been converted into infantry barracks for 12 officers and 260 non-commissioned officers and privates, with stabling for 5 horses and an hospital for 30 invalids. The principal street is on the line of approach from the new bridge to the barracks; the houses are built generally of limestone, but sandstone is used in some of the public buildings. On the erection of a new sessions-house, the old building was given up to Lord Lorton, and on the site of it a handsome lecture-room has been built, partly from a bequest by the late Rev. J. Gouldsbury, and partly by his lordship; in the back part of the building are the savings' bank, the charitable loan fund, the infants' school, and the dispensary. This town is the commercial centre of the extensive agricultural district which surrounds it, and carries on a considerable trade with Drumsna and Sligo. A market and fairs were granted to John Bingley and John King in 1604, prior to which date scarcely any notice occurs of the town. The staple articles are corn and butter: of the former very little is sold in the town, the greater part or nearly the whole being sent to Sligo; the butter market is on Monday, when great quantities are sold in firkins for exportation; yarn is also sold in large quantities to the purchasers who attend from the north for that purpose on the principal market day, which is Saturday; the sale of frieze and flannel has of late very much diminished. The market for provisions is held in an enclosure on the north west side of the bridge, formed at the expense of Lord Lorton about the year 1826, and is well supplied, not only with fish from the rivers and lakes, but also with sea-fish in abundance. Fairs are held on March 6th, April 3rd, May 9th and 30th, July 9th and 25th, Aug. 16th, Oct. 1st, and Nov. 25th. The only line of communication is the mail coach road from Dublin to Sligo, and all the trade of the town is conducted by land carriage. Here is a chief station of the constabulary police, for whose accommodation a barrack, with a handsome residence for the chief officer, has been erected near the abbey, at the expense of Lord Lorton.

The borough was incorporated by charter of the 11th of Jas. I. (1613), and a new charter was granted in the 4th of Jas. II., but as it was never acted on the former is the governing charter. The corporation is styled "the Borough-Master, Free Burgesses, and Commonalty of the Borough of Boyle," and consists of a borough-master, twelve other free burgesses, and an indefinite number of commonalty; of which the last-named body is not now recognised in practice. The borough-master is chosen annually from and by the free burgesses, but his duties are very limited, and he exercises little practical power; the free burgesses are also chosen, as vacancies occur, by the members of their own body, and hold office for life, but are removable for misconduct; and the charter empowers the corporation to appoint two serjeants-at-mace, but at present there is only a town-serjeant. They have also the power of creating a guild of merchants, of which there is now no trace, and of making by-laws. The borough, of which the limits include the town and a small district immediately surrounding it, returned two members to the Irish parliament, who were elected by the borough-master and free burgesses; and on its disfranchisement at the time of the Union, the £15,000 granted in compensation for the loss of that privilege was paid to Lord Lorton, as executor of his father, the late Earl of Kingston, to whom the borough belonged. The charter granted a court of record to be held every Tuesday, with civil jurisdiction to the amount of five marks, in which the borough-master is judge; but the business done being inconsiderable, it is not usually held oftener than about once in a month. According to practice the jurisdiction is exercised in cases of which the cause of action either arises within the borough, or where it arises without and there are goods of the defendant within the borough: the process is by attachment on oath made by the plaintiff. Quarter sessions are held here every nine months, for the Boyle division of the county, which comprises also the towns of Castlerea and Strokestown, where they are likewise held every nine months; and petty sessions are held by the county magistrates every Monday. A seneschal's court is held in the town, having no jurisdiction within the borough, but over several baronies within the county, extending to the distance of many miles round the town. The new sessions-house, towards the erection of which Lord Lorton contributed £500, is situated on the slope of the hill on the south side of the river fronting the main street, and is built of sandstone. Connected with it is the district bridewell, containing a keeper's house and eight cells upon the improved plan of construction: the entire expense, amounting to £2400, was advanced by government, to be repaid by the county in instalments.

The parish, which is also called Assylin, comprises 10,139 statute acres, as applotted under the tithe act. The lands are chiefly under tillage, and the system of agriculture is improved; there is little woodland, except on the demesnes of the resident gentry; about 1010 acres are bog and waste land. Limestone and freestone are found in abundance, and there are also some quarries of a species of marble; it is said that coal exists on the Curlew mountains, and that there were formerly iron-works on the river. Rockingham House, the superb residence of Viscount Lorton, is beautifully situated about two miles from the town, and on the south-east side of Lough Key: the building is of Grecian Ionic architecture, with a noble portico of six columns, on each side of which the façade is decorated with as many of the same order; on the north is a colonnade of six

Ionic columns, and on the east is an entrance through an orangery: the grounds are tastefully laid out, and there are four grand entrance lodges leading into the demesne, which comprises about 2000 statute acres, richly planted. On the northern bank of the river, close to the town, is Frybrook, the seat of H. Fry, Esq.; and near the abbey is Abbeyview, now occupied by the agent of Lord Lorton. On the south side of the river is Tangier, the seat of Capt. Caleb Robertson; and about two miles west of the town is Knockadoo, the handsome residence of Owen Lloyd, Esq. Near Knockadoo is Ballymore, the residence of the Rev. J. Elwood; and about a mile to the east is Mount Erris, the seat of Capt. Duckworth, commanding some fine views of Lough Key and the adjacent mountains. The living is a vicarage, in the diocese of Elphin, to which the vicarages of Taunagh, Kilmacallane, Drumcollum, Kilross, Aughanagh, Ballynakill, and Ballysumaghan, were episcopally united in 1802, which eight parishes constitute the union of Boyle, in the patronage of the Bishop; the rectory is impropriate in Viscount Lorton. The tithes amount to £313. 16. 10., of which £166. 3. is payable to the impropriator, and the remainder to the vicar; and the tithes for the whole benefice, including the rectorial tithes of four of the above-named parishes, which form the corps of a prebend held by the vicar, to £638. 6. 1½. There are three churches in the union, situated respectively at Boyle, Ballysumaghan, and Kilmacallane: the church at Boyle serves for the town and parish; that at Ballysumaghan serves also for the parishes of Kilross and Ballynakill; and that at Kilmacallane for the parishes of Taunagh and Drumcollum. The church of Boyle, situated near the old park, is a spacious building, for the repair of which the Ecclesiastical Commissioners have granted £182; it was erected by aid of a loan of £1000 from the late Board of First Fruits, in 1818. The glebe-house was built by aid of a gift of £100 from the same Board, in 1805. There are two glebes; one in this parish, comprising 20½ acres, and one in Kilmacallane of 18*a.* 3*r.* 34*p.* Arrangements have been made for forming this union into three benefices on its next avoidance. In the R. C. divisions the parish is the head of a union or district, comprising the parishes of Boyle and Kilbrine; there are two chapels in the town; and there are also places of worship for Wesleyan Methodists and Baptists. There are six public schools, of which a large girls' school and an infants' school are supported by Lady Lorton: in these about 350 boys and 330 girls receive instruction; there are also four Sunday schools and ten private schools, in which are 460 boys and 380 girls. A charitable loan society was established in 1824, under the patronage of Lord and Lady Lorton, by which about £90 is weekly distributed to the poor in small loans, to be repaid by instalments with a trifling interest; a dispensary is supported in the customary manner, and another is maintained by Lord Lorton, for the poor on the Rockingham estate and its vicinity.

The ivy-clad remains of the ancient abbey are situated near the river, and not far distant from the new bridge; they consist of vestiges of the conventual buildings, dispersed in the grounds of Capt. Robertson's seat, and of the principal part of the church, of which the nave, choir, and transepts, with the lofty and massive central tower, are in good preservation; the nave, 131 feet long and 25 feet wide, is separated from the aisles by a noble range of massive circular arches, supported partly by circular and clustered columns, with richly ornamented bases and capitals of various designs, between which are enriched corbels, from which sprang the arches of the groined roof; the wall of the south aisle is wanting, and the pillars stand exposed; some of the clerestory windows are partly remaining, though concealed by the thick ivy that crowns the irregular summit of the range; the central tower is supported on four massive columns, 48 feet high, of which the bases, formerly concealed by accumulated earth, have been cleared by Capt. Robertson, and are beautifully ornamented with various sculptured designs; of the arches, three are circular and the fourth pointed; the east window of the choir is of the triple lancet form; and the prevailing style of this once magnificent church is of the later Norman passing into the early English: within the walls is a tomb of the King family. To the north of the town is the low ridge of the Curlew mountains, over which are scattered numerous white cottages; and on which Sir Conyers Clifford, governor of Connaught in the reign of Elizabeth, was intercepted by O'Rourke, one of the petty chieftains of the district, his detachment routed, and himself slain. At Ardcarne, three miles to the east of the town, commence the plains of Boyle, extending ten miles in length and four in breadth, consisting of elevated limestone, with an undulating surface of rich pasture lands noted for fattening oxen and sheep. About a mile from the town, up the north bank of the river, on a knoll terminating abruptly, are the remains of the old church of Assylin, or Isselyn, which, from the extent of the ruined walls, appears to have been a very spacious building; around it is a large cemetery, which is still used as a place of sepulture by the inhabitants of the town. Below this spot the river rushes over the rocks with great impetuosity. At a small distance was a ford, formerly called Athdalaragh and now Ardagh, where was anciently an abbey of Canons Regular, which became the seat of a bishoprick, over which St. Comgallan presided in the time of St. Patrick; the abbey existed till 1201. On the right side of the road to Lough Gara is one of the largest cromlechs in Ireland; the table stone, which has a considerable inclination, is 15 feet long and 11 feet wide, and was formerly supported on five upright pillars, of which one has been removed.

BOYSTOWN, or BALTIBOYS, a parish, in the barony of LOWER TALBOTSTOWN, county of WICKLOW, and province of LEINSTER, 3 miles (S.) from Blessington; containing 3235 inhabitants. This parish is situated on the Liffey and King's rivers, and comprises, with the chapelries of Granabeg and Kilbeg, about 20,000 statute acres, of which nearly two-thirds are mountain, and the remainder is chiefly pasture land, with a small portion under tillage. The system of agriculture is improving; there is an extensive tract of bog, called Ballynahown, near Blackditches. At Baltiboys is a good quarry of slate, which was formerly worked to advantage, but is at present discontinued; and there are quarries of granite at Ballyknocken, which are still in operation. The surrounding scenery is bold and mountainous, and there are several gentlemen's seats, among which are Tulfarris, the seat of R. Hornidge, Esq., which was partly burnt by the insurgents in 1798; Baltiboys, of Lieut.-Col. Smith, who has recently erected a handsome mansion on the demesne, which commands some fine and extensive views; Humphreystown, of W. Cotton, Esq., the demesne of which is tastefully laid out and planted; Willmount, of W. Dunbavin, Esq., commanding an extensive view of the surrounding country; and Stormount, of W. Brown, Esq., from which also is a fine view, including the mansion and demesne of Russborough. There are also two shooting lodges, one at Kilbeg, belonging to W. Brady, Esq., and one at Marfield, the property of Robert La Touche, Esq. It is a vicarage, in the diocese of Dublin, and is part of the union of St. Mary Blessington, or Burgage; the rectory is appropriate to the corps of the treasurership in the cathedral church of St. Patrick, Dublin. The tithes amount to £181. 10., of which £110 is payable to the treasurer, and the remainder to the vicar. In the R. C. divisions it is included in the union or district of Blackditches, which comprises the whole of this parish and a part of Blessington; there are chapels at Blackditches and in the small village of Lacken, both of which are in this parish. A school-house, with apartments for a master and mistress, was built at the expense of Lieut.-Col. Smyth; there are eight hedge schools, in which are about 145 boys and 114 girls. There is an ancient cemetery at Baltiboys, and another at Templepooda.

BOYTONRATH, or LAGINSTOWN, a parish, in the barony of MIDDLETHIRD, county of TIPPERARY, and province of MUNSTER; containing 331 inhabitants. It comprises only 935 statute acres, as applotted under the tithe act; and is a rectory, in the diocese of Cashel, entirely appropriate to the vicars choral of the cathedral church of St. Patrick, Cashel, who pay a stipend of £2. 15. 4½. per ann. to the clergyman of the adjoining parish for the performance of occasional duties: the tithes amount to £35. There are two pay schools, in which about 80 boys and 40 girls are taught.

BRABAN.—See PREBAN.

BRACKHILL, a village, in the parish of KILCOLEMAN, barony of TRUGHENACKMY, county of KERRY, and province of MUNSTER, 1 mile (N. E.) from Milltown: the population is returned with the parish. It is situated on the road from Milltown to Castlemaine, of which latter it may be considered a suburb, being connected with it by Castlemaine bridge.

BRACKLINTOWN, a village, in the parish of CLONBERN, half-barony of BALLYMOE, county of GALWAY, and province of CONNAUGHT; containing 41 inhabitants.

BRANACH ISLES.—See ARRAN.

BRANDON.—See CLOGHANE.

BRANNICKSTOWN, a parish, in the barony of NAAS, county of KILDARE, and province of LEINSTER, adjoining the post-town of Kilcullen, and containing 272 inhabitants. This parish comprises 800 statute acres, 72 of which are plantations in gentlemen's demesnes, 19 are artificial water, about 10 are waste, 19 are bog, and the remainder arable and pasture land in nearly equal portions; the bog is well adapted for grazing in the summer and autumn. It forms part of the impropriate or perpetual curacy of Kilcullen, in the diocese of Dublin.

BRAY, a market and post-town, and a parish, in the half-barony of RATHDOWN, county of WICKLOW, and province of LEINSTER, 14 miles (N.) from Wicklow (by the sea road), and 10 (S. E. by S.) from Dublin; containing 3509 inhabitants, of which number, 2590 are in the town. This place derives its name, originally *Bré* or *Bree*, signifying a "hill" or "headland," from the precipitous promontory of clay slate and quartz, called Bray Head, which rises immediately on the south of the town to an elevation of 807 feet above the level of the sea, and from the singular indentation of its summit forms a well-known landmark to mariners. The manor, or lordship, of Bray, with all the territories of the O'Tooles, was granted, in 1173, by Richard de Clare, Earl of Pembroke, lord-deputy, to Walter de Riddlesford, one of the earliest of the Norman adventurers, to be held of the Crown by three knights' service, to be performed at Dublin. This grant, together with the seigniory of Castledermot and extensive privileges, was confirmed to him by John, Lord of Ireland, who subsequently granted him an annual fair to be held at Bray, with free warren and other privileges. Among the earliest notices of this place is the record of a grant of a burgage, with a portion of arable land, to the abbey of St. Thomas, near Dublin, by the same Walter de Riddlesford, whose estates, on failure of male issue, were at his death divided between two coheiresses; and in 1215 the abbot of St. Thomas obtained a grant of all the lands held by Walter de Riddlesford in fee, in the town of Bray, at a yearly rent of 3 and a fine of 60 marks. The town was frequently assailed by the mountain septs of the O'Byrnes and O'Tooles, to whose territories it was contiguous, and who, on the 16th of April, 1316, destroyed the castle; but they were on the same day attacked and defeated by Edmond Le Boteler. A fierce conflict took place near the town, in 1402, between these septs and the citizens of Dublin, headed by John Drake, their provost, on which occasion, according to Ware and Camden, 4000, but according to Hervey de Marlbrigge, 400 of the former were slain. At the dissolution of the religious houses, the possessions of the abbey of St. Thomas were granted to Sir Thomas Brabazon, whose descendant, the Earl of Meath, is the present proprietor in fee of the greater part of the town.

The town is situated on the Dargle or Bray river, which here forms a boundary between the counties of Dublin and Wicklow, and after passing under an old bridge of five arches, connecting the portions of the town which lie on different sides of it, falls into the sea a little below this place. That part of the town which is on the Wicklow side of the river consists of one long street of irregularly built houses, at the head of which are two smaller streets, one branching off on the left, from which the lower road to Wicklow is continued over the hill of Windgates; and the other on the right along the road to the glen of the Downs, and together containing about 450 houses. That part which is in the county of Dublin is called Little Bray; it forms part of the parish of Old Connaught, and contains about 230 houses and cottages, and 1168 inhabitants. The houses in both are in general neatly built, and the town has a cheerful and interesting appearance; it is neither paved nor lighted, but the road is kept in good order. The surrounding scenery is exceedingly romantic, and combines with its short distance from Dublin to render this place a favourite resort during the summer season for sea-bathing. A number of thatched cottages of great neatness, and containing, exclusively of offices, from three to eight rooms each, have been appropriated to the accommodation of visiters, to whom they are let furnished at rents varying from £40 to £50 and more for the season. The hotel and posting-house, conducted by Mr. Quin, jun., is fitted up with every regard to the superior accommodation of families and visiters of the highest respectability; hot and cold sea water baths may be had at all hours without delay, and the house has long been a favourite resort of parties on excursions of pleasure, and of wedding parties to spend the day in festivity and in the enjoyment of the beauties of the surrounding scenery. A spacious gravel walk, half a mile in length and perfectly straight, has been made from the rear of the hotel through the private grounds to the sea, forming a beautiful promenade, and commanding fine views. On the Dublin side of the river a race-course has been formed and races are held annually.

The trade, exclusively of what is requisite for the supply of the town, consists principally in the importation of coal, timber, slates, and limestone, in which two vessels of 70 tons each, one of 50 tons, and one of 25 tons, belonging to the place, are regularly employed. There is a very extensive brewery, with a malting store, capable of producing 300 barrels weekly; and near the brewery is a large flour-mill. The small haven is very incommodious, having a bar at the entrance, and only eight feet of water at spring and five feet at neap tides: from a change in the channel of the river, an outer beach has been formed, which breaks in some degree the violence of the sea. A plan for its improvement was suggested by the late Mr. Nimmo, who proposed to construct a pier of about 30 perches in length at the mouth of the river; but it has not been carried into effect. The river abounds with excellent trout, which are taken in great quantities and sent to Dublin and different parts of the country, and even to London. The market is on Tuesday and Saturday, and is abundantly supplied with provisions of every kind of the best quality. Fairs for friezes are held on Jan. 12th, May 4th, Aug. 5th, and Nov. 12th, and are attended by all the Dublin dealers; and fairs for cattle are held on the 1st of March, May, and July, Aug. 15th, Sept. 20th, and Dec. 14th. A constabulary police force has been stationed here, and also in Little Bray, the old castle in the latter having been fitted up as a barrack. A coast-guard station has also been fixed here, forming one of the five that constitute the district of Kingstown, to which use a martello tower near the mouth of the river, in which four guns are mounted, has been appropriated. There is also a martello tower on the strand near Bray Head, occupied by a private of the artillery. Petty sessions for the division are held in the school-house in Little Bray, every alternate Saturday; and the Earl of Meath, as lord of the manor of Kindlestown, holds a court here by his seneschal every month. By an inquisition taken in the reign of Chas. I. it appears, from various records, that the town had been in times past incorporated and endowed with many privileges.

The parish abounds with interesting and strikingly diversified scenery, and is embellished with numerous seats and pleasing villas. Kilruddery, the splendid mansion of the Earl of Meath, situated about one mile south of the town, was erected in 1820, on the site of the old family house, from a design by Mr. Morrison. It is an elegant structure, in the later English style of architecture; the entrance is under an octangular tower crowned with a cupola in the centre of the north front, opening into a spacious hall, in which are tastefully displayed several suits of armour and various warlike instruments brought from foreign countries; the saloon, drawing and dining rooms, and other apartments are richly and tastefully embellished and furnished in a style of costly magnificence. The demesne, which comprises more than 900 acres, is richly wooded, and is bounded on one side by the little Sugar Loaf mountain, and on the other by the rugged heights of Bray Head; in the pleasure grounds is a circular sheet of water surrounded with a fine hedge of beech, 20 feet high, through which are several entrances; and not far from it is the theatre, a quadrangular area enclosed on three sides by tiers of seats, and in which plays were formerly acted. Shanganagh, the residence of Gen. Sir G. Cockburn, is described in the article on Rathmichael. Bray Head, the seat of G. Putland, Esq., is finely situated near the foot of the promontory of that name, in a well-planted demesne of about 650 acres: the mansion is a chaste and elegant structure of the Tuscan order, with an embattled roof, from which are obtained extensive views of mountain scenery and of the sea; from the drawing-room antechamber is a noble conservatory of polygonal form, erected at an expense of £5000, and containing a fine collection of the most choice and rare exotics; the pleasure grounds and gardens are laid out with the greatest taste and kept in the finest order, presenting one of the principal attractions in this truly picturesque and much frequented part of the country. There are numerous handsome villas situated in grounds tastefully laid out and commanding very fine views: the principal are St. Valorie, the residence of the Hon. P. Cecil Crampton, third Justice of the Court of King's Bench; Springfield, of Alderman West; Fassarow House, of H. Crampton, Esq.; Old Court, of Major Edwards; Rich View, of Capt. Kettlewell; Fairy Hill, of P. W. Jackson, Esq.; Killarney Cottage, of — O'Reily, Esq.; Vevey, of the Misses Weldon; New-Court, of Mrs. McMahon; Fairy Hill (Bray), of J. Quin, Esq.; Prospect Cottage, of C. Tandy, Esq.; Riversdale, of C. La Grange, Esq.; Le Valle, of Miss Draper; Fassarow Cottage, of Capt. Sitwell; Navarra, of Mrs. Brady; and Glenbrook, of J. H. Brush, Esq.

The living consists of a rectory and vicarage, in the diocese of Dublin and Glendalough; the rectory is in the patronage of the Crown; and the vicarage, which has been from time immemorial united to the vicarage of Old Connaught, is in the patronage of the Archbishop. The tithes of this parish amount to £230, and of Bray, Old Connaught, and Rathmichael (which last was separated from the union in 1826), to £430. The church, a plain building with a small spire, situated on the verge of an eminence overhanging the river, was erected in 1609, and enlarged, by aid of a loan of £1020 from the late Board of First Fruits, in 1818. There is no glebe-house: the glebe comprises nine statute acres of excellent land. In the R. C. divisions this parish is the head of a union or district, comprising also the parishes of Powerscourt, Kilmacanogue, and part of the parish of Delgany, and containing three chapels, situated respectively at Bray, Kilmacanogue, and Castletown: the chapel at Bray is a spacious and handsome edifice, erected in 1833, and embellished with an altar-piece presented by Gen. Sir G. Cockburn. There is a place of worship for Presbyterians. There are two national schools; and a school, in which more than 100 children are clothed and educated, is supported by Mrs. Putland: in these schools are about 120 boys and 220 girls. An infants' school, held in a spacious building erected in 1829 by the late Viscount Powerscourt, is supported by private contributions; and there are also three pay schools, in which are about 57 boys and 25 girls, and a Sunday school. A building, originally intended for a barrack, has been converted into an hospital for cholera and fever patients, with a dispensary, erected by a grant from the Association for the Suppression of Vice and individual subscriptions. In Little Bray is a neat range of building, erected by subscription, part of which is used as school-rooms, and part as a savings' bank for the parishes of Bray, Delgany, and Powerscourt. A provident society was established in the town in 1832; a loan society has been lately instituted; and a manufactory of flax and wool is supported entirely by Mr. and Mrs. Putland, in which more than 40 poor women are employed; the materials, when wove into linens and linseys, are distributed gratuitously among the poor of the neighbourhood. One-third of the produce of an estate in the county of Longford, bequeathed to the parishes of Bray, Delgany, and Powerscourt by F. Adair, Esq., and amounting to about £60 per annum to each, is distributed among the poor.

Besides the remains of the castle at Little Bray, there are the ruins of two others in the parish; one in the grounds of Old Court, consisting of a tower, with some fragments of the walls. Near these is a rude pyramidal block of granite, on which are some faint traces of ancient sculpture, which, from a print taken before it was so much mutilated, appears to have represented the sacrifice of a ram; on the top of it is a cavity apparently designed for the reception of a cross. The remains of the other castle, at Fassarow, which was demolished by Cromwell, are not in any way remarkable; coins of William have been found near them, on the road to Old Connaught, where is an ancient cross with a rudely sculptured representation of the Crucifixion. Under Bray Head are the ruins of an ancient chapel, 40 feet long and 18 feet wide; it is built in a north and south direction, with a circular-headed window at each end, and the doorway on the east side; and near the glebe land is an ancient burial-ground. On levelling a bank of sand near the sea, in 1835, to make an approach to the demesne of Mr. Putland, several human skeletons of large dimensions were discovered, lying regularly east and west, with a stone at the head and another at the feet of each, but which crumbled into dust on exposure to the air; several Roman coins of the Emperor Adrian were found at the same time, and are now in Mr. Putland's possession. There are medicinal springs in the grounds of Kilruddery and Old Court.

BREAFY, or BREAGHWEE, a parish, in the barony of CARRA, county of MAYO, and province of CONNAUGHT, 2 miles (S. E.) from Castlebar; containing 2315 inhabitants. This place is situated on the road from Castlebar to Clare, and is bounded by a very considerable river, called the Minola, which by its frequent inundations does more injury to the surrounding districts than any other in the county or province. From its contiguity to Castlebar it was the scene of much skirmishing, foraging, and plundering, while the French troops under Gen. Humbert had possession of that town, in 1798. The parish comprises 5000 statute acres, as applotted under the tithe act: the land in cultivation is partly under tillage and partly in pasture, in nearly equal portions: there is a very considerable extent of bog, which might be reclaimed by draining. On the estate of Major Blake, of Fisher Hill, is a very fine quarry of stone, which is fit for buildings of the first order. Races are held generally in August, on a course within the parish. The principal gentlemen's seats are Breafy Lodge, the residence of Major Browne, who has made extensive improvements and plantations in the demesne; Windsor House, of Col. McAlpine; Fisher Hill, of Major Blake; Hawthorn Lodge, of C. O'Malley, Esq.; and Rocklands, of J. C. Larminie, Esq. It is a rectory and vicarage, in the diocese of Tuam, and is part of the union of Castlebar: the tithes amount to £57. 15. 11. In the R. C. divisions this is one of the three parishes that constitute the union or district of Aglish, or Castlebar; it contains a chapel, but no service is at present performed in it. A school at Lightfoot is supported by Mrs. O'Malley and J. Larminie, Esq.; and there are two others, in which are about 200 boys and 100 girls. There are some remains of a very ancient monastery.

BREDA.—See KNOCKBRIDE.

BREGOGUE, a parish, in the barony of ORRERY and KILMORE, county of CORK, and province of MUNSTER, 1 mile (N. N. W.) from Buttevant; containing 450 inhabitants. This place, which is situated on the road from Buttevant to Liscarrol, is not known in civil matters as a parish, having for all such purposes merged into that of Buttevant. It comprises 1314 statute acres, as applotted under the tithe act, which are of good quality, and mostly under tillage, producing ample crops: there is an abundant supply of limestone for manure and for other uses. The gentlemen's seats are Dunbarry, the residence of T. Heffernan, Esq.; Currymount, of J. O'Leary, Esq.; and Bregogue Castle, of J. Rogers. It is a vicarage, in the diocese of Cloyne, and is part of the union of Buttevant and Cahirduggan, formerly called the union of Bregogue; the rectory is impropriate in C. S. Oliver, Esq. The tithes amount to £150, payable in equal portions to the impropriator and the vicar. In the R. C. divisions it forms part of the union or district of Buttevant. There are some remains of the old castle incorporated into the dwelling-house of Mr. Rogers; also of the ancient church in the burial-ground.

BRICKENDOWN, a parish, in the barony of MIDDLETHIRD, county of TIPPERARY, and province of MUNSTER, 2½ miles (E.) from Cashel; containing 431 inhabitants. This parish is situated near the road from Cashel to Fethard, and contains a small village called Mocklershill: it comprises 1030 statute acres. Coleraine is the neat residence of — Price, Esq.; and Meldrum, situated in a well-planted demesne, is in the occupation of the Rev. R. Lloyd. The living is a rectory and vicarage, in the diocese of Cashel, and in the patronage of the Archbishop: the tithes amount to £64. 12. 3¾. There is neither church, glebe-house, nor glebe.

BRIDECHURCH, a parish, in the barony of CLANE, county of KILDARE, and province of LEINSTER, 1½ mile (N. W. by N.) from Naas; containing 376 inhabitants. This parish is bounded on the east by the river Liffey, over which the Grand Canal is carried by the Leinster aqueduct, a handsome building of five arches, with a parapet ornamented with balustrades of stone, erected in 1783. It comprises 2143 statute acres of good land, of which a considerable portion is woodland, and the remainder arable and pasture. The land being chiefly in the occupation of gentlemen, is in an excellent state of cultivation: there is neither waste land nor bog; but the Grand Canal passing through it, affords every facility for the supply of fuel, and for the conveyance of goods. Landerstown is the handsome seat of the Rev. J. Digby. It is a rectory, in the diocese of Kildare, and is part of the union of Caragh: the tithes amount to £92. 2. In the R. C. divisions it forms part of the union or district of Caragh and Downings. There are some ruins of the ancient church.

BRIDESWELL, a hamlet, in the parish of KILCLOAN, barony of UPPER DEECE, county of MEATH, and province of LEINSTER; containing 8 dwellings and 48 inhabitants.

BRIDESWELL, a village, in the parish of CAMMA, barony of ATHLONE, county of ROSCOMMON, and province of CONNAUGHT, 5½ miles (W. N. W.) from Athlone; containing 130 inhabitants. This place derives its name from a copious spring of very pure water, close to which is an ancient building, formerly a chapel, from which a doorway leads to the well, now converted into a bath. Over the doorway are an inscription and a coat of arms, from which it appears that this alteration was made by Sir Randal Mac Donnell, the first Earl of Antrim, in 1625. The village is built around a level green, on which was formerly kept one of the most celebrated patron festivals, but, on account of its immoral tendency, it has been suppressed by the exertions of the R. C. clergy. A constabulary police force has been stationed here; and there is also a dispensary.—See CAMMA.

BRIDGETOWN, a parish, in the barony of FERMOY, county of CORK, and province of MUNSTER, 1 mile (S.) from Castletown-Roche; containing 970 inhabitants. This place is situated on the river Blackwater, and near the road from Mallow to Fermoy: it derived its name from a bridge that formerly existed here, which is said to have been destroyed by Cromwell. A priory for canons of the congregation of St. Victor was founded here in the reign of John, by Alexander Fitz-Hugh Roche, and dedicated to the Blessed Virgin: it was liberally endowed by the founder, and supplied with monks from the priory of Newtown, in the county of Meath, and from the abbey of St. Thomas, near Dublin. Edw. I. confirmed the original endowment, which was greatly augmented by the Roche family; and in 1375, when Edw. III. issued his writ to the Bishops and commons, to elect persons to assist him and his council in the government of the kingdom, and in the prosecution of the war in which he was then engaged, Thomas, the prior of this house, was one of those deputed for that purpose. The extensive remains of the abbey are pleasantly situated at the confluence of the rivers Awbeg and Blackwater, here flowing through a rocky glen; they consist principally of parts of the church, and the refectory and cloisters may still be traced. On the south side of a chapel, near the site of the altar, under an arch of irregular construction, is a monument, supposed to be that of the founder, from an inverted armorial shield charged with one fish, but without any inscription; the present arms of the Roche family are three fishes. In a small chapel adjoining is a tomb, inscribed "Theobald Roche," with the date 1634; and in both chapels are several ancient and curiously sculptured gravestones. The parish comprises 3022 statute acres, as applotted under the tithe act, and valued at £2071 per annum: about one-third of the land is coarse mountain pasture, forming part of the range called the Nagle mountains, on the south side of the river; the land under tillage is good, and produces abundant crops. The only seat is Clifford, the residence of T. Lloyd, Esq., pleasantly situated on the north bank of the Blackwater. Prior to the year 1835, the parish formed part of the union of Castletown-Roche, from which it was then separated and made a distinct benefice: it is a rectory and vicarage, in the diocese of Cloyne, and in the patronage of the Bishop; the tithes amount to £180. In the R. C. divisions it still forms part of the union or district of Castletown-Roche.

BRIDGETOWN, a village, in the parish of MULRANKIN, barony of BARGY, county of WEXFORD, and province of LEINSTER, 7 miles (S. S. W.) from Wexford; containing 21 houses and 113 inhabitants. It is situated on a small river of the same name, which runs into the lough formed by the Burrow of Ballyteigue, and has a penny post to Wexford. Here are a constabulary police station, and a dispensary. The glebe-house of the union is situated within a short distance of the village.—See MULRANKIN.

BRIGHT, a parish, in the barony of LECALE, county of DOWN, and province of ULSTER, 3 miles (S. by E.) from Downpatrick; containing 2030 inhabitants. This parish is situated on the road from Downpatrick to Killough, and comprises, according to the Ordnance survey, 5544¼ statute acres, of which 5503 are applotted under the tithe act. The land, with a trifling exception, is all in an excellent state of cultivation, and there is neither waste land nor bog. Oakley, the handsome residence of J. Birney, Esq., is situated in a fertile demesne of 168 acres, tastefully disposed and embellished with some of the finest timber in the county. The parish was formerly one of the six which constituted the union and the corps of the deanery of Down, from which it was separated by act of council in 1834, when, with the townland of Carradressy, which formerly belonged to Kilclief but was annexed to Bright by the same act, it was constituted a separate and distinct parish. The living is a rectory, in the diocese of Down, and in the patronage of the Crown: the tithes amount to £583.18. 9. The church, a small edifice in the Grecian style, erected in 1745, is situated on the summit of an eminence, and is an excellent landmark for mariners: it contains an elegant monument to the memory of Lord Lecale. There is neither glebe-house nor glebe. In the R. C. divisions it is the head of a union or district, comprising also the parish of Rathmullen, and containing three chapels, situated respectively at Conierstown in Bright, and at Killough and Rossglass in Rathmullen. Here is a school of about 80 boys and 50 girls, for which a school-house in the churchyard was built by subscription; also a pay school, in which are about 20 boys and 20 girls. Near the church are the ruins of Bright castle; and about a mile and a quarter to the west are those of Castle Screen, built within the area of a Danish rath, near which are the remains of the ancient abbey of Erynagh, founded by Magnell Makenlefe, King of Ulster, Sept. 8th, 1126 or 1127. This abbey was garrisoned against De Courcy in 1177, who, for that reason, levelled it with the ground and transferred its possessions to the abbey of Inch, which he subsequently founded in the Isle of Inis Courcy, on the ruins of a pagan temple. A circle of upright stones and other Druidical remains are still existing near the spot.

BRIGOWN, a parish, in the barony of CONDONS and CLONGIBBONS, county of CORK, and province of MUNSTER, on the road from Fermoy to Cahir; containing, with the market and post-town of Mitchelstown, 9169 inhabitants. It comprises 14,502 statute acres, as applotted under the tithe act, and valued at £12,101 per annum; 104 acres are woodland, 2726 mountain and bog, 83 roads and waste, and the remainder good arable and pasture land, principally under tillage. The soil is mostly a heavy loam; and the system of agriculture is in a state of progressive improvement. Limestone abounds in the parish: on the lands of Kilshanna are some fine quarries, which are worked for various purposes; some of this stone is susceptible of a high polish, and several handsome mantel-pieces have been made of it for Mitchelstown Castle, the spacious and superb castellated mansion of the Earl of Kingston, which adjoins Mitchelstown and is described under that head. A new line of road between Mitchelstown and Lismore, was opened in 1835, at the expense of the county. Ballinvillin, the property of the Earl of Kingston, and occasionally the residence of his lordship's agent, is pleasantly situated near the river Gradogue, commanding a fine view of the castle and demesne. The glebe-house, the residence of the Rev. R. H. Graves, D. D., is a handsome and commodious mansion, situated on a gentle eminence near the town.

The living is a rectory, in the diocese of Cloyne, constituting the corps of the prebend of Brigown in the cathedral of Cloyne, and in the patronage of the Bishop: the tithes amount to £1000. The church was originally built in 1801 at the sole expense of the late Countess of Kingston; it fell down in the year following, and was rebuilt by her ladyship in 1803; it again fell down in 1804, and was rebuilt in the following year. It was enlarged in 1830, by aid of a loan of £1300 from the late Board of First Fruits, and a gift of £500 from the Earl of Kingston towards the erection of the tower and spire, which are much admired for their beautiful proportions and elegant design. The glebe-house was completed by a gift of £100 and a loan of £1000, in 1807, from the same Board, in addition to an outlay of £1300 by the then incumbent, chargeable on his successor. The original glebe comprised 9 Irish acres, to which 12 more were added under a lease for ever from the late Countess of Kingston, at a rent of £4. 4. per acre. In the R. C. divisions the parish is the head of a union or district, which is also called Mitchelstown, and comprises the parishes of Brigown and Marshalstown, and the hamlet of Ballinamona, in the parish of Kilbehenny. The chapel, a spacious and handsome cruciform structure, is situated in the town; the first stone was laid by the Earl of Kingston, who contributed £500 towards the expense of its erection. The parochial school occupies a site given by the noble family of King; and was built in 1827 by a grant from the lord-lieutenant's school fund. All children that apply for instruction are taught gratuitously, without distinction of religion; the master and mistress are supported by annual donations of £25 from that family and £15 from the rector, who also supplies coal and other requisites. A school kept in the old R. C. chapel is aided by a grant of £30 per annum from the National Board and collections at the chapel. In these are about 500 children; and there are also five pay schools, in which are about 190 children. The late Robert Crone, Esq., bequeathed £15 per annum to be distributed by the rector among the poor of the parish. On the lands of Kilshanna is a chalybeate spring, but not used for medicinal purposes. The college chapel is the burial-place of the Kingston family. The ruins of the old parish church are situated in the Mitchelstown demesne; and there are vestiges of a more ancient one near the glebe, said to have been founded by St. Finnahan. Here was also an ancient round tower, which is supposed to have fallen about the year 1720.—See MITCHELSTOWN.

BRINNY, a parish, partly in the Eastern Division of the barony of EAST CARBERY, and partly in the barony of KINNALEA, but chiefly in that of KINNALMEAKY, county of CORK, and province of MUNSTER, 3 miles (N. E.) from Bandon; containing 1949 inhabitants. In the civil war of 1641 a running fight took place between a part of the garrison of Bandon and a body of insurgents, which terminated at Brinny bridge in the defeat of the latter, of whom 50 were killed. The parish is situated on the north road from Cork to Bandon, and comprises 7200 statute acres, as applotted under the tithe act. About two-thirds of the land are under tillage, and the remainder in pasture; the soil is good, and the system of agriculture is greatly improved; there is neither waste land nor bog. Good building stone, of which there are several quarries, and flags of excellent quality abound in the parish. The surrounding scenery is pleasingly diversified, and there are several handsome gentlemen's seats, the principal of which are Upton, the residence of the Rev. Somers Payne; Brinny House, of J. Nash, Esq.; Garryhankard, of T. Biggs, Esq.; Beechmount, of T. Hornebrook, Esq.; Brothersfort, of W. Whiting, Esq.; and Kilmore, of W. Popham, Esq. There are some extensive flour-mills near the bridge, and in the demesne of Upton is a police barrack. The living is a rectory and vicarage, in the diocese of Cork, with the rectory and vicarage of Knockavilly episcopally united in 1810, forming the union of Brinny, in the patronage of the Bishop: the tithes amount to £405, of which £5 is payable to the dean of Cork and £400 to the rector; and the gross amount of tithe is £1025. The church was wholly rebuilt by aid of a loan of £300 from the late Board of First Fruits, in 1813; it is a neat edifice with a tower. Divine service is also performed in a licensed house at Knockavilly, and in a school-house in the summer evenings. The glebe contains only eight acres, and there is no glebe-house. In the R. C. divisions this is one of the five parishes constituting the union or district of Innishannon. The parochial school, in which are 27 boys and 18 girls, is supported principally by the rector, who also superintends a Sunday school; and a school of 58 boys and 30 girls is supported by subscription, aided by an annual donation of £3 from the parish priest.

BRITWAY, a parish, partly in the barony of KINNATALOON, but chiefly in that of BARRYMORE, county of CORK, and province of MUNSTER, $5\frac{1}{2}$ miles (E. S. E.) from Rathcormac; containing 1098 inhabitants. It is bounded on the north by the river Bride, and comprises 3712 statute acres, of which 3568 are applotted under the tithe act, and valued at £2206 per annum. Of its entire surface there are 646 acres of mountain, capable of great improvement, and 380 acres of marshy land and exhausted bog, the whole of which is reclaimable. The land in cultivation consists of a light shallow soil, and the greater part is under tillage. Ballyvolane, the seat of Capt. Pyne, is a neat residence, situated in a well-wooded demesne. It is a rectory, in the diocese of Cloyne, and is part of the union of Ahern: the tithes amount to £281. 8. $0\frac{1}{4}$. In the R. C. divisions it forms part of the union or district of Castlelyons. The male and female schools for Britway and Ahern are near the latter place; and there is a hedge school in this parish, in which are about 50 boys and 20 girls.

BROADFORD, a post-town, in the parish of KILSEILY, barony of TULLA, county of CLARE, and province of MUNSTER, 8 miles (N.) from Limerick, and 94 miles (S. W. by W.) from Dublin; containing 71 houses and 383 inhabitants. It is picturesquely situated on the road from Killaloe to Ennis, at the foot of a range of hills extending to Lough Derg on the Shannon, and has a post-office dependent on that of Limerick; a constabulary police force is stationed here, and fairs are held on the 21st of June and the 21st of November. The parish church, a neat building with a square tower, is situated in the town; and a large and handsome R. C. chapel is now in course of erection on an eminence overlooking it. Here are the parochial school, (chiefly supported by the minister) and a public dispensary. This place is much visited by anglers and sportsmen: the neighbourhood affords excellent grouse shooting, and about a mile to the west is Doon lake, remarkable for the size of its pike, and abounding also with bream. In the vicinity are several gentlemen's seats and shooting-lodges, which are more particularly noticed in the article on Kilseily. There are some excellent quarries near the village, producing slate of superior quality.—See KILSEILY.

BROADISLAND.—See TEMPLECORRAN.

BROADWAY, a village, in the parish of ST. IBERIUS, barony of FORTH, county of WEXFORD, and province of LEINSTER, 8 miles (S. S. E.) from Wexford; containing 160 inhabitants. It is situated at the northern extremity of Lady's Island lake, on the high road from Wexford to Carne, and till lately was a regular post town, but it is now only a sub-office to Wexford. Fairs are held on the Thursday after Trinity Sunday and on Oct. 18th. Here is a public dispensary. At Doyle's Cross, near the village, is a place of worship for Wesleyan Methodists; and near it is Broadway Cottage, the residence of Dr. Lindsay.—See IBERIUS (ST.).

BROOKBOROUGH, a post-town, in the parish of AUGHAVEA, barony of MAGHERASTEPHANA, county of FERMANAGH, and province of ULSTER, 13 miles (E.) from Enniskillen, and $75\frac{1}{4}$ miles (N. W.) from Dublin; containing 83 houses and 480 inhabitants. This town is situated on the road from Lisnaskea to Five-mile-town, and is a chief constabulary police station. Fairs are held on the third Tuesday in every month, for the sale of cattle, sheep, and pigs, and of butter, cloth, and yarn; premiums are given every fair day to the largest purchasers and sellers, by a committee who have the management of the fairs. A manorial court is held occasionally, at which small debts are recoverable; and petty sessions are held every alternate Tuesday. Divine service, according to the form of the Established Church, is performed in a parochial school-house every Sunday evening; and there is a place of worship for Wesleyan Methodists. Here is also a dispensary.

BROOKLODGE.—See BALLYLOOHERA.

BROSNA, a parish, in the barony of TRUGHENACKMY, county of KERRY, and province of MUNSTER, 10 miles (N. by E.) from Castleisland; containing 2168 inhabitants. It is situated on the small river Clydagh, and on the confines of the counties of Limerick and Cork, and comprises 18,013 statute acres, as applotted under the tithe act, and valued at £2180 per annum. A large portion of the land consists of coarse mountain pasture and bog, the greater part of which might be reclaimed. A new line of road, about eight miles in length, is now in progress, at the expense of Col. Drummond and C. Fairfield, Esq., extending from the bridge over the Clydagh (an arch of 60 feet span), on the new road from Listowel to Newmarket, and passing through this and the adjoining parish of Ballincuslane to the village of Ardnagrath, on the old mountain road from Castleisland to Millstreet. It is in contemplation to extend this road to Scortaglin, to form a junction with the new Government road from Castleisland to King-William's-town, by which the surrounding country will be greatly improved. This place was occasionally the head-quarters of the Whiteboys, during the disturbances of 1822; but since the opening of the road from Listowel to Newmarket, the neighbourhood has enjoyed perfect tranquillity. In that part of the parish which borders on the counties of Limerick and Cork is a constabulary police station. The living is a rectory and vicarage, in the diocese of Ardfert and Aghadoe, and in the patronage of the Bishop: the tithes amount to £175. There is neither church nor glebe-house; the glebe comprises $2\frac{1}{4}$ acres. In the R. C. divisions this parish is the head of the union or district of Brosna or Knocknagashel, which comprises also parts of the adjoining parishes of Castleisland and Ballincuslane; the chapel is a thatched but commodious building, and during the summer months a school is held in it, under the superintendence of the parish priest; there is also a chapel at Knocknagashel, in the parish of Castleisland. There are two private schools, in which about 120 children are educated. Some slight vestiges of the ancient parish church may still be traced in the burial-ground.

BROUGHSHANE, a market and post-town, in the parish of RACAVAN, barony of LOWER ANTRIM, county of ANTRIM, and province of ULSTER, $28\frac{3}{4}$ miles (N. N. W.) from Belfast, and 109 miles (N.) from Dublin; containing 828 inhabitants. This town is pleasantly situated on the river Braid, at the termination of the mail coach road from Ballymena, to which it has a sub-post-office, and consists of one long street, containing about 180 houses indifferently built. In the neighbourhood are several gentlemen's seats; and at no great distance is Tullymore Lodge, finely situated on a stream tributary to the Braid. The market is on Tuesday, and is principally for butter and pork: fairs are held on June 17th and Sept. 3rd. A constabulary police force has been stationed here; and the manorial court of Buckna is held here every month, for the recovery of debts amounting to £20. The church of the union of Skerry, or the Braid, a neat edifice with a spire, is situated in the town; in which are also a place of worship for Presbyterians in connection with the Synod of Ulster, and a dispensary. At Dumfare, in the vicinity, is a large mount of very imposing aspect.—See RACAVAN.

BROWN-MOUNTAIN, an extra-parochial district, in the barony of KELLS, county of KILKENNY, and province of LEINSTER; containing 25 inhabitants. This place is Crown land, and has never paid tithes; it is united with the impropriation of Tullahought, and the spiritual duties are performed by the curate of Kilmoganny.

BROWNSTOWN, a parish, in the barony of UPPER DULEEK, county of MEATH, and province of LEINSTER, 4 miles (E. by S.) from Navan; containing 487 inhabitants. It is situated on the road from Navan, through Ashbourne, to Dublin, and comprises 864 statute acres of arable and pasture land, with the exception of about 32 acres of waste and bog: the land is fertile and principally under tillage, and the system of agriculture is improving. There is a good limestone quarry; a valuable stratum of potters' clay has been discovered; and there are strong indications of the existence of copper ore, but no attempt to work it has hitherto been made. The only seat is Brownstown House, the property and formerly the residence of the Somerville family, and now being put into a state of repair. It is a rectory, in the diocese of Meath, entirely impropriate in Sir W. Meredyth Somerville, Bart.: the tithes amount to £73. There is no church or chapel, only an ancient burial-ground: the clerical duties of the parish are performed by the incumbent of the adjoining parishes forming the union of Kentstown. In the R. C. divisions it forms part of the union or district of Blacklion. There are two hedge schools, in which are about 34 boys and 24 girls.

BRUFF, a market and post-town, and a parish, in the barony of COSHMA, county of LIMERICK, and province of MUNSTER, 11½ miles (S. S. E.) from Limerick, and 105¼ (S. W.) from Dublin; containing 2932 inhabitants, of which number, 1772 are in the town. This appears to have been a place of importance at a very early period; a castle was built in the town and another at no great distance from it by the De Lacy family, in the reign of Hen. III. This family subsequently became tributary to the Fitzgeralds, and held the castle under the princes of Desmond, in all whose misfortunes they largely participated, especially during the reign of Elizabeth. On the 4th of April, 1600, a severe engagement took place here between Pierce De Lacy, governor of the castle, and some troops from the garrison of Kilmallock, under the command of Capt. Slingsby, in which the former was defeated with the loss of 300 men; and on the 18th of the same month the lord-president obtained possession of the castle, in which he placed a garrison of 140 men. In 1641 this place was the scene of a sanguinary battle between the English forces and the insurgents, in which the latter were victorious, and committed acts of great cruelty. In 1762 the Whiteboys assembled here in great numbers and committed outrages; and in 1786 they again visited the town, and on the 15th of July in that year, they burnt several houses and destroyed much valuable property. In 1793 a large body of the Defenders made a desperate effort to seize the town, but were repulsed by the 34th regiment of foot and many slain on both sides. In 1822 the Rockites assembled here in great numbers, and made an attempt to burn the church and several private houses, but were frustrated by the active and judicious exertions of the neighbouring gentry, aided by a large body of the military stationed in the town. The town, which, with the surrounding neighbourhood, was formerly the property of the Hartstonge family, and now forms part of the estate of the Earl of Limerick, is situated on the river Dawn, or Morning Star, and on the road from Limerick to Cork: it consists of one principal street and several smaller streets and lanes, and contains 314 houses. The market is on Friday; and fairs are held on May 24th, July 23rd, Oct. 18th, and Nov. 28th. A stipendiary magistrate resides at this place, which is a chief constabulary police station; and the quarter sessions are held here in January and June, and petty sessions every alternate Wednesday. The court-house is a large commodious building, and there is also a small but well-regulated bridewell.

The parish comprises 1264 statute acres, as applotted under the tithe composition act: the land is of the best quality, producing abundant crops, though the system of agriculture is by no means good; the greater portion is meadow and pasture land, all resting upon limestone, which is extensively quarried for building, repairing the roads, and for agricultural uses. The principal seats are Rockbarton, the elegant residence of Lord Guillamore, near the town; Caher, of Lieut.-Col. O'Grady; Kilballyowen, of the De Courcy O'Grady; Uregare House, of Mrs. Gubbins; Green Park, of R. Ivers, Esq.; and Miltown, of G. Gubbins, Esq. The living is a vicarage, in the diocese of Limerick, and in the patronage of the Bishop; the rectory is impropriate in the Earl of Kenmare. The tithes amount to £180, of which £120 is payable to the impropriator and £60 to the vicar. The church, a large edifice in the early English style, with a tower surmounted by a lofty octagonal spire of stone, contains an ancient monument of the Hartstonge family rather in a neglected condition: the chalice bears a curious inscription in Latin, recording its formation and the changes which it has undergone. The glebe-house, a neat little residence about half a mile from the town, is situated on an excellent glebe of 8½ acres, for which the vicar pays a rent of £25. 6. 11. per annum. In the R. C. divisions this parish is the head of a union or district, comprising also the parishes of Tullybracky, Grange, Meanas, Manister, and part of the parishes of Uregare, Glenogra, and Dromin; and containing three chapels, situated respectively at Bruff, Grange, and Meanas. The first is a handsome building, in the early English style, erected in 1833; the interior is well arranged, and the altar, of scagliola marble, is embellished with a very beautiful painting of the three Marys, by J. Haverty, Esq., a native artist; the building was commenced by the late R. C. incumbent, the Very Rev. Dr. Ryan, and completed by the R. C. dean of Limerick, the present parish priest. The male and female parochial school, in which are 20 boys and 20 girls, is chiefly supported by the vicar, by whom it was instituted in 1831. There are two pay schools, in which are about 200 children, and a school for adults. A few fragments of the ancient castle are still remaining; and not far distant are the foundations of an ancient friary. To the north-west of the town are some traces of Templebodeen, or Templeen, said to have been erected by the Knights Templars in 1284; foundations of buildings are frequently discovered.

BRUHENNY.—See CHURCHTOWN, barony of ORRERY, county of CORK.

BRUIS, a parish, in the barony of CLANWILLIAM, county of TIPPERARY, and province of MUNSTER, 3 miles (S. W.) from Tipperary; containing 1350 inhabitants. This parish contains Mount Bruis, the pleasant residence of Mrs. Doherty. It is a rectory, in the diocese of Emly, and forms part of the union and corps of the prebend of Lattin in the cathedral of Emly: the tithes amount to £150. In the R. C. divisions also the parish is included in the union or district of Lattin.

BRUMBRUSNA, a hamlet, in the parish of LENEY, barony of CORKAREE, county of WESTMEATH, and province of LEINSTER, 6 miles (N. N. W.) from Mullingar; containing 16 houses and 94 inhabitants. It is situated on Lough Hoyle, and on the mail coach road from Mullingar to Longford, and is surrounded by three lofty hills.

BRUREE, or BRUGHRIGH, a parish, partly in the barony of SMALL COUNTY, but chiefly in that of UPPER CONNELLO, county of LIMERICK, and province of MUNSTER, 4 miles (N. W.) from Charleville, on the direct line of road to Limerick; containing 4364 inhabitants, of which number, 451 are in the village. This place was distinguished at a very early period for a half-yearly meeting of the Irish bards, which, according to O'Halloran, was continued till the year 1746. The parish comprises 8530 statute acres, as applotted under the tithe act, of which the greater portion is pasture and meadow land connected with extensive dairy farms, and the remainder under tillage: the land is remarkably good, and the system of agriculture is improving. The river Maigue winds through a beautiful valley, of which the rich meadows on its banks slope gently to its margin: the meadows in the southern part of the parish are subject to frequent inundations from the overflowing of this river. The eastern portion of the parish consists entirely of limestone, which is extensively quarried for agricultural purposes and for the roads; but the grit is generally worked for building. The scenery is pleasingly varied, and in the parish are several handsome houses, of which the principal are Harding Grove, the residence of H. Harding, Esq.; Rockhill, of J. Cushin, Esq.; Bruree House, of R. Fetherston, Esq., J.P.; and Bruree Lodge, of J. Langton, Esq., J.P. The village, containing, in 1831, 87 houses, is a constabulary police station, and is much improving; several good houses have lately been built; here are also a boulting-mill, a grist-mill (used chiefly for oatmeal), and a manufactory for combing, carding, and spinning wool, and for napping and tucking the cloth, which is of great advantage to the population for many miles round. Fairs are held on May 9th, June 25th, Sept. 14th, and Nov. 25th, for cattle, sheep, pigs, and pedlery. A new road has recently been formed from Croom to Charleville through the western part of the parish, which will become the principal road between Limerick and Cork.

It is a rectory and vicarage, in the diocese of Limerick; the rectory forms part of the union and corps of the deanery of Limerick, and the vicarage is in the patronage of the Dean. The tithes amount to £600. 4., of which two-thirds are payable to the dean and the remainder to the vicar. The church is a neat edifice, in the early English style, with a square tower and octangular spire of hewn stone; it was built near the site of the old church, by aid of a gift of £800 from the late Board of First Fruits, in 1812. The glebe-house, which belongs to the vicarage, was built by a gift of £400 and a loan of £380 from the same Board, in 1813. Attached to the rectory is a glebe of *7a. 1r. 8p.*; the glebe belonging to the vicarage comprises 15 acres. In the R. C. divisions this parish is the head of a union or district, called also Rockhill, which comprises the parishes of Bruree and Colemans-well, and contains three chapels, situated respectively in the village of Bruree, at Rockhill, and at Colemans-well. The parochial schools are situated on the rector's glebe, and endowed by the present dean with half an acre of land; and there are two pay schools, in which are about 100 boys and 60 girls. In the village are a dispensary, and a good building erected during the prevalence of the cholera, in 1832, and now used as a fever hospital. Here are the ruins of a strong fortress erected by the De Lacys, who formerly possessed the surrounding country: it consisted of three strong castles enclosed by a wall and ramparts more than 120 yards in circumference; two of the castles are remaining. Adjoining the church is a large and strong castle in a tolerably perfect state, erected by the Knights Templars in the 12th century. There are some remains of the small church of Cooleen, or Temple-Colman, now called Howardstown, built by the Knights Templars in 1287, and on the suppression of that order annexed to this parish.

BRUSNA, a village, in the parish of KILMURRY-ELY, barony of CLONLISK, KING'S county, and province of LEINSTER, 1¾ mile (E.) from Shinrone; containing 134 inhabitants. It is situated on the river of the same name, and is a station of the constabulary police. Here is a R. C. chapel.—See KILMURRY-ELY.

BRYANSFORD, a village, in the parish of KILCOO, barony of UPPER IVEAGH, county of DOWN, and province of ULSTER, 2½ miles (S.) from Castlewellan; containing 185 inhabitants. This village, which is situated on the road from Newry to Newcastle, contains about 30 houses neatly built, chiefly in the Elizabethan style, the gardens in front of which give it a comfortable and rural appearance, and the surrounding scenery is agreeably diversified. Tollymore Park, the seat of the Earl of Roden, is a beautiful residence situated in extensive grounds embellished with some of the finest larch trees in the country; it is approached by three noble entrances, called respectively the barbican, the central, and the hilltown; the central entrance from the village is through a very lofty archway, and in the lodge is kept a book for entering the names of visiters; the grounds are always open to the public. There is a good inn and posting-house, with every accommodation for families. The parish church of Kilcoo, a spacious edifice with a lofty embattled tower, is situated in the village; and at a short distance to the north of it is a R. C. chapel, belonging to the union of Bryansford or Lower Kilcoo; it is a neat edifice in the later English style, erected in 1831 at an expense of £900, on a site given by the Earl of Roden. A school for boys, built in 1826, is supported by the same nobleman; and adjoining it is a circulating library also maintained by the Earl and gratuitously open to all the people of the village: there is a female school, built in 1822 and supported wholly by the Countess of Roden.—See KILCOO.

BUCHOLLA.—See BOHOLA.

BULGADINE, a parish, in the barony of COSTLEA, county of LIMERICK, and province of MUNSTER, 3 miles (N.) from Kilmallock; containing 1152 inhabitants. In the ecclesiastical divisions this is not known as a separate parish, being regarded as forming part of the parishes of Uregare, Kilbreedy-Major, and Athnassey: it comprises 3395 statute acres, as applotted under the tithe act. The occupiers of land in this neighbourhood are subjected to a penalty of £10 per acre if more than two acres out of every twenty are tilled; hence the meadows and pastures are very extensive, and are considered as the most fertile in the county. Near the village, which is very small, consisting only of a few thatched houses, is the ancient and neglected mansion of the family of Evans, now the property of Lord Carbery, which, though at present in a state of miserable dilapidation, was formerly one of the most magnificent residences in the province. In the R. C. divisions this place is partly in the union or district of Kilmallock; and partly in that of Athnassey or Ballinvana; it contains a chapel for this part of the union.

BULLANE, a parish, in the barony of ATHENRY, county of GALWAY, and province of CONNAUGHT, 4½ miles (N.) from Loughrea; containing 551 inhabitants. This parish is situated on the road from Loughrea to Castle-Blakeney, and comprises 1283 statute acres, as applotted under the tithe act. It is a rectory and vicarage, in the diocese of Clonfert, partly appropriate to the prebend of Annacalla, partly to the sacristy of the cathedral of Clonfert, and partly included in the union of Kilcolgan, in the diocese of Kilmacduagh. The tithes amount to £46, of which £23 is payable to the prebendary of Annacalla, £12 to the sacristan, and £11 to the incumbent of Kilcolgan. In the R. C. divisions it is part of the union or district of New Inn, and contains a chapel.

BULLOCK, BLOYKE, or BULLOG, a village, in the parish of MONKSTOWN, half-barony of RATHDOWN, county of DUBLIN, and province of LEINSTER, 6¾ miles (S. E.) from Dublin: the population is returned with the parish. This place, which is now only a small fishing village, situated close to the southern shore of Dublin bay, was formerly defended by a castle of considerable extent. The period of its erection is unknown, though it is supposed to be co-eval with those of Dalkey; it is an octangular building, having but few windows and surmounted by a graduated parapet. Near it is a neat residence occupied by Capt. Hutchinson; and in the vicinity is Perrin Castle, the residence of Alderman Perrin, a handsome building in the castellated style, beautifully situated in grounds tastefully laid out and commanding some fine mountain and sea views. The Ballast Board of Dublin have a small quay here for shipping granite, with which this neighbourhood abounds. On blasting the rocks, a large quantity of silver coins was found a few years since. The fishery, at the commencement of the present century, employed several yawls in taking whiting, pollock, and herrings; at present there are about ten yawls belonging to the village.—See MONKSTOWN.

BUMBOA HALL, a small village, in the parish of BALLYNURE, barony of UPPER TALBOTSTOWN, county of WICKLOW, and province of LEINSTER, 3 miles (N.) from Baltinglass; containing 81 inhabitants. It is situated on the road from Baltinglass to Ballitore, and contains a good house called the Hall, the residence of Stephen Wilson, Esq. Near it are Ballynure and Grange-Con, the former the seat of H. Carroll, Esq., and the latter, till of late, the residence of H. Harrington, Esq. A peace preservation force is stationed in the village; and there is a neat R. C. chapel belonging to the union or district of Baltinglass, with a school adjoining it.—See BALLYNURE.

BUMLIN, or STROKESTOWN, a parish, in the barony and county of ROSCOMMON, and province of CONNAUGHT; containing, with the market and post-town of Strokestown, 4913 inhabitants. This parish is situated on the new mail coach road from Dublin to the West of Ireland, and comprises 4399 statute acres, as applotted under the tithe act and valued at £4038 per annum. Part of Slievebawn mountain is situated within its limits, the summit of which towards the east commands a most extensive view. The land is chiefly under tillage; limestone abounds, and there are considerable tracts of bog. Castlenode is the seat of J. Morton, Esq. The living is a vicarage, in the diocese of Elphin, to which the vicarages of Kiltrustan and Lissonuffy were episcopally united in 1811, which three parishes form the union of Bumlin, in the patronage of the Bishop: the rectory is partly appropriate to the prebendary of Kilgoghlin in the cathedral church of Elphin, but chiefly impropriate in C. and R. Armstrong, Esqrs. The tithes amount to £285. 3. 9., of which £100. 3. 5. is payable to the impropriators, £21 to the prebendary, and £164. 0. 4. to the vicar; and the gross vicarial tithes of the benefice amount to £533. 14. 7½.; the annual income of the prebendary of Kilgoghlin is £310. 14. 2. The church, situated at Strokestown, is a handsome edifice with a spire, built in 1814 by aid of a loan of £2700 from the late Board of First Fruits. The glebe-house was also built by a gift of £337 and a loan of £150 from the same Board: the glebe comprises ten acres. In the R. C. divisions this parish is the head of a union or district, comprising also the parish of Kiltrustan, and containing three chapels, situated at Strokestown, Scramogue, and Kiltrustan, the two former in the parish of Bumlin. The parochial school, in which are about 50 children, is chiefly supported by the vicar and by private subscriptions; there are also seven hedge schools, in which about 100 boys and 90 girls are taught. The late B. Mahon, Esq., bequeathed £800 late currency for the benefit of the poor of the three parishes forming the union.—See STROKESTOWN.

BUNCLOADY.—See NEWTOWN-BARRY.

BUNCRANA, a market and post-town, in the parish of LOWER FAHAN, barony of ENNISHOWEN, county of DONEGAL, and province of ULSTER, 11 miles (N. N. W.) from Londonderry, and 129½ miles (N. W. by N.) from Dublin; containing 1059 inhabitants. Though of some importance in the reign of Elizabeth, this place subsequently fell into great decay, but was restored and laid out in its present form by Sir John Vaughan, in 1717. The town is beautifully situated on the eastern shore of Lough Swilly, at the foot of the mountains of Ennishowen, and, from the romantic and picturesque beauty and salubrity of its position, has of late years become a bathing-place of considerable resort. It consists of three principal and several smaller streets, remarkably clean, and contains 248 houses, of which the greater number are large and well built of stone; the environs are adorned with several handsome houses, villas, and bathing-lodges. Buncrana Castle, close to the town, was the residence of the O'Donnells and O'Doghertys; but after the flight of O'Nial, O'Donnell, and other northern chieftains, in 1607, the territory escheated to the Crown. In the following year, Sir Cahir O'Dogherty, having rebelled against the English authority and carried on a sanguinary war for nearly six months, was defeated and taken prisoner by Sir Arthur Chichester, and was closely confined in this castle, which was shortly after granted to Sir Arthur: one of the towers, with the staircase of stone and the dungeon beneath, remains tolerably entire. A new castle, now the property and residence of Mrs. Todd, was built by Sir John Vaughan in 1717; it is approached by a very handsome bridge over the river, and in front are extensive gardens and terraces, all in excellent preservation. Lough Swilly here expands into an arm of the sea, bounded by mountains and rocks of majestic character, and forming a capacious haven of easy access, suitable for vessels of any burden. On the south side of the entrance are the Swilly Rocks, about half a mile from the shore; on the west side, at Fannet Point, there is a lighthouse, with a fixed light of nine lamps, showing a deep red colour seaward and a bright light towards the lough. Two rivers empty themselves into the lough, one on each side of the town, after falling over several ledges of rock in their channels: in the northern, or, as it is commonly called, the Castle river, is an extensive and valuable salmon fishery; on the southern river are flax, oatmeal, and flour-mills. From its central situation the town has been chosen as the head-quarters of the artillery forces attached to the batteries on the Foyle and Swilly. At Naiads' Point is a battery, which is one of six erected on the threatened invasion of the French, with accommodation for one officer and 27 men, now under the care of a master-gunner and five men; and at Ballynary there is a coast-guard station. Considerable portions of the adjacent mountain district are being brought into cultivation: copper and lead ores are found, and slate of excellent quality abounds in these mountains, but has never been worked. In 1745 the linen manufacture was introduced by Col. Vaughan, and flourished for some time, and, in 1784, various branches of the cotton trade, particularly the weaving of velvets, fustians, corduroys, and plain cloth, to which the printing of cotton was added, but, although carried on with much spirit, it declined after his death. A manufactory for sail-cloth and ducking was afterwards established, and continued to flourish till the year 1830, when the premises were destroyed by fire. There are now in course of erection extensive mills and factories for weaving fine and coarse linens for the Manchester market, also a large flour-mill and fulling-mill nearly adjoining. Several vessels are engaged in fishing for soles, plaice, and turbot, which are taken off these shores in large quantities and of a superior kind, carried over land to Derry, and sent from that port by steam to Liverpool. Oysters of large size and good flavour are also taken in the lough. The markets are on Tuesday and Saturday, and in the winter season there is a large market on the last Friday in every month. Fairs are held on May 9th, July 27th, Sept. 8th, and Nov. 15th. General quarter sessions are held once, and road sessions six times, in the year; and petty sessions are held every alternate week. The court-house, a large and handsome building in the centre of the town, was erected at an expense of £1300 by the late Wm. Todd, Esq., and presented to the county on this being made a town for holding quarter sessions. A court for the manor of Buncrana is held on the first Monday in every month, for the recovery of debts under 40*s*. Here is a station of the constabulary police. The parochial church, situated in the town, is a neat edifice: it was built in 1804, considerably enlarged and improved in 1816, and, being still too small, is again about to be enlarged, for which the Ecclesiastical Commissioners have recently granted £370. 6. 8. There are places of worship for Presbyterians in connection with the Synod of Ulster, and for Primitive and Wesleyan Methodists. A large and handsome building for a school was erected by the trustees of Erasmus Smith's charity, by whom and the incumbent the school is supported; and at Cock Hill there is a national school. A dispensary is maintained in the customary manner.—See Fahan (Lower).

BUNDORAN, a village, in the parish of Innismacsaint, barony of Tyrhugh, county of Donegal, and province of Ulster, 4 miles (S. W.) from Ballyshannon: the population is returned with the parish. This village, which consists of one street on the road from Ballyshannon to Sligo, is situated on Ballyshannon harbour, on the western coast, and on the confines of the county of Sligo: the coast is bold and rocky. It is a favourite place of resort for sea-bathing during the summer; several small but respectable houses have been built for the accommodation of visiters; and extensive hot and cold sea-water baths have been fitted up. There is a daily penny post to Ballyshannon and Sligo.

BUNGOWLA, a hamlet, in the parish and island of Arranmore, barony of Arran, county of Galway, and province of Connaught: the population is returned with the parish. It is situated at the western extremity of the island of Arranmore, in the entrance of the bay of Galway. Off the shore of this part of the island are the Branach Isles, six in number, three of which are rocks.

BUNNAWN, or BONANE, a parish, in the barony of Glanerough, county of Kerry, and province of Munster, 6 miles (S.) from Kenmare; containing 1158 inhabitants. This place, which is situated on the confines of the county of Cork, is not in the ecclesiastical divisions known as a separate parish, but considered as forming part of the parish of Kilcaskin, in the adjoining barony of Bere, county of Cork, and diocese of Ross. It is the property of the Marquess of Lansdowne, and consists chiefly of rocky mountain and bog; it is intersected by two old roads, both impassable for carriages; one running direct, by a wild rocky pass called the "Priest's Leap," to Bantry bay, and the other to Glengariff. A new road from Kenmare to Glengariff is now in progress, under the Board of Public Works, which will pass through the parish, over the range of mountains separating the counties of Cork and Kerry, and will in some places be carried to an elevation of 1000 feet above the level of the sea,affording great facilities for the improvement of this wild and mountainous district. At Dromfeaghny is an ancient burial-ground, in which are the ruins of an old church. In the R. C. divisions the parish forms part of the union or district of Kilcaskin, in the county of Cork, and diocese of Kerry; the chapel is at Deelis. A school-house is about to be built at Tulloha, at the joint expense of the Marquess of Lansdowne and the National Board of Education.

BUNRATTY, a post-town, and parish, in the barony of BUNRATTY, county of CLARE, and province of MUNSTER, 6 miles (W. by N.) from Limerick, and 100 miles (W. S. W.) from Dublin; containing 1300 inhabitants. This place is situated on the mail coach road from Limerick to Ennis, and on the northern shore of the river Shannon. The castle was erected in 1277, by the De Clares, and was subsequently the residence of the Earls of Thomond; it was besieged in 1305, but not taken; and the small town adjacent to it was burned in 1314. The castle was either enlarged or rebuilt by Sir Thomas de Clare, in 1597, and is still the largest in the county. Till within the last few years it was the residence of T. de Clare Studdert, Esq., who has erected a handsome modern mansion in the demesne, and the old castle is now used as a constabulary police barrack. It is a lofty and massive quadrangular structure, with a tower at each angle; the upper parts of the towers at each end of the quadrangle are connected by an arch; it still retains its old baronial hall unaltered, and, till deserted by the family, displayed a spacious and lofty banqueting-room; the outworks and appendages were of great extent, as is evident from the vestiges that may still be traced. A handsome bridge of one arch was built over the river Ougarnee, by Mr. Studdert, who also constructed near it a commodious quay, which is about to be enlarged; boats of large size can come up to it. Considerable quantities of sea manure are landed here for the supply of the neighbourhood, and turf is brought from Kilrush. In the Shannon near this place are several islands, one of which, called Quay Island, is inhabited by only one family: the anchorage off this island, called Bunratty Roads, is considered to be the best in the Shannon, and here the West India vessels discharge their cargoes for Limerick. Off Clonmoney is another island, called Saints' Island, containing about 50 statute acres of the richest land, and inhabited by two families. Fairs are held here on Feb. 3rd, the second Tuesday before Easter, June 3rd, July 19th, and Oct. 20th, for cattle, pigs, and sheep. A seneschal's court for the manor of Bunratty is occasionally held, in which debts not exceeding £10 late currency may be recovered.

The parish comprises 2649 statute acres, as applotted under the tithe act, and mostly in pasture; those parts bordering on the Shannon afford rich grazing land. Bunratty Castle, the seat of T. de Clare Studdert, Esq., is pleasantly situated within the ancient demesne, and commands fine views of the Shannon and of an extensive tract of country: the mansion is spacious and of modern design, and the demesne is embellished with fine timber of stately growth. Immediately adjoining the village is Bunratty, the residence of Mrs. Paliser, in the rear of which are the ruins of an old church, the walls of which are in good preservation. The other seats are Clonmoney, that of D. Canny, Esq., and Woodpark, of M. Dalton, Esq. It is a rectory and vicarage, in the diocese of Killaloe; the rectory forms part of the union of Tomfinlogh or Traddery, in the patronage of the Earl of Egremont; and the vicarage part of the union of Kilfinaghty. The tithes amount to £150, of which £100 is payable to the rector, and £50 to the vicar. The church of the union is at Six-mile-bridge, in that parish. The glebe-house is situated on a glebe of 11 acres in this parish, subject to a rent of £21. 10. per annum late currency. In the R. C. divisions it forms part of the union or district of Newmarket, and is held with several others by the administrator of the R. C. Bishop of Killaloe; the chapel is a commodious modern building. There is a small school under the superintendence of the vicar, in which are about 20 children; and at Clonmoney is a school under the direction of the R. C. clergyman. There is also a private school, in which about 65 children are educated.

BUOLICK, or BAOLICK, a parish, in the barony of SLIEVARDAGH, county of TIPPERARY, and province of MUNSTER, $2\frac{1}{2}$ miles (N. E.) from New Birmingham; containing 2271 inhabitants. This parish is situated on the confines of the county of Kilkenny, and on the road from Johnstown to Killenaule: it is skirted on the west by the bog of Allen, and comprises 6355 statute acres, as applotted under the tithe act, and valued at £5120 per annum. A considerable quantity of coal is obtained here, and works are now being opened on the estate of Mark Byrne, Esq. Littlefield is the property of E. Cooke, Esq., who occasionally resides here. The living is a rectory, in the diocese of Cashel, and in the patronage of the Archbishop: it is at present held by the treasurer of the cathedral church of St. Patrick, Cashel, but forms no part of the endowment of that dignity: the tithes amount to £420. There is neither church, glebe, nor glebe-house; some remains of the old church yet exist, covered with ivy; the inhabitants resort to Burris church. In the R. C. divisions the parish is the head of a union or district, called Gurtnahoe, comprising also the parishes of Kilcooley and Fennor, and containing two chapels, situated at Gurtnahoe in Buolick, and at New Birmingham in Kilcooley: the former is a spacious building, in digging the foundations for which many human bones were discovered, supposed to be those of the slain in a battle said to have been fought at Ballysloe by the kings of Leinster and Munster. Three national schools are situated at Ballysloe, Clonimiclan, and Gurtnahoe, in which are about 180 boys and 100 girls. There are considerable remains of an old castle, which appears to have been of great strength; it was the residence of the family of Butler, Viscounts Ikerrin, and is now the property of R. La Touche, Esq., who has a considerable estate in the parish. Here are also two large Danish forts.

BURGAGE.—See BLESSINGTON.

BURGESS, or BURGESS-BEG, a parish, in the barony of OWNEY and ARRA, county of TIPPERARY, and province of MUNSTER, $5\frac{1}{2}$ miles (S. W.) from Nenagh; containing 3570 inhabitants. It is situated on the mail coach road from Dublin to Limerick, and comprises 4749 statute acres, as applotted under the tithe act, and valued at £4002 per annum. About 97 acres are mountain and bog; the remainder is good arable land. It is a rectory and vicarage, in the diocese of Killaloe, and forms part of the union of Castletown-Arra: the tithes amount to £276. 18. 5½. In the R. C. divisions it is included in the union or district of Youghal-Arra, and contains a modern chapel on the townland of Ballywilliam. There are three private pay schools, in which about 160 boys and 90 girls are taught. Some remains of the church yet exist, with a monument on which is inscribed "*Donato O'Brien de Gortmore.*"

BURNCHURCH, or KILTRANEEN, a parish, partly in the barony of Galmoy, but chiefly in that of Shillelogher, county of Kilkenny, and province of Leinster, 4 miles (S. S. W.) from Kilkenny; containing 1450 inhabitants. This parish is situated on the road from Kilkenny to Carrick-on-Suir, and comprises 5373 statute acres: it is principally under an improved system of tillage; there is plenty of limestone, used chiefly for burning into lime. Farmley, the seat of R. Flood, Esq., is situated in a well-planted demesne, and was the residence of the Rt. Hon. Henry Flood, one of the most distinguished members of the Irish House of Commons, who died here in 1791, and was interred in the parish church. This place has a patent for fairs, but none are held. The living is a vicarage, in the diocese of Ossory, to which the vicarages of Danesfort, Kilfeara, Abbey-Jerpoint, West-Jerpoint, Ballylinch, and Grangeleggan or Grangeclovan, and the denominations of Dunbell, Grange-Kilree, Woollen-Grange, Blackrath-Grange, Garran, Mocktown or Rathbin, Ardera, Lismatigue, and Plebestown have been immemorially united and were consolidated by act of council in 1678, forming the union of Burnchurch, which is in the alternate patronage of the Crown and the Bishop; the rectory is appropriate to the vicars choral of the cathedral of Christchurch, Dublin: the tithes of the parish amount to £320. 12. 6. payable in moieties to the vicars choral and the vicar. The church is a neat edifice with a steeple, built by aid of a loan of £600, in 1810, from the late Board of First Fruits. The glebe-house was built by a gift of £100 and a loan of £1500, in 1815, from the same Board: the glebe comprises 20 acres. In the R. C. divisions the parish is included in the four several unions or districts of Danesfort, Freshford, Moncoin, and Ballyhale. The parochial school is supported by the incumbent; and there is a private school, in which are about 70 boys and 30 girls; also a Sunday school. Near the church is a fine old castle in a good state of preservation.

BURREN, or BURRIN, a village and post-town, in the parish of Abbey, barony of Burren, county of Clare, and province of Munster, 18 miles (N. by W.) from Ennis, and 115¾ miles (W. by S.) from Dublin: containing 23 houses and 147 inhabitants. This place is situated on the road from Ballyvaughan to Curranroe Bridge, and about a quarter of a mile from the small harbour of Burren, now called New Quay, from the construction of a quay within the last few years, a little to the east of the former, of which there are still some remains: it is a constabulary police station. A court is held every six weeks by the seneschal of the manor, in which small debts are recoverable. The harbour is frequented by 30 hookers of about 12 tons' and 150 yawls of 3 tons' burden each, engaged in the fishery, which affords employment to about 500 men. Large quantities of corn, butter, sheep, and pigs, are shipped here; and such is the convenience of the harbour, that in hard weather 100 sail of small craft have taken refuge in it at a time. The coast is noted for its oysters, which are in high repute for their superior flavour and quality; the great oyster bed, called the Burren Red bank, and the harbour, are more particularly described in the account of the parish of Abbey, *which see.*

BURRISCARRA, a parish, in the barony of Carra, county of Mayo, and province of Connaught, 5¾ miles (N. N. W.) from Hollymount; containing 1535 inhabitants. This place was distinguished at a very early period for its monastery of Carmelites or White friars, which Pope John XXIII. gave to Eremites of the Augustinian order in 1412; it existed till the general dissolution, and there are still some small remains of the ancient buildings, which appear to have been extensive and of elegant character. The parish is situated upon Lough Carra, and within a mile and a half of the road from Castlebar to Dublin: it comprises 4510 statute acres, as applotted under the tithe act; the land is of a light sandy quality; there is but a small quantity of bog. The principal seats are Moore Hall, that of G. Moore, Esq., beautifully situated on Lough Carra, in an extensive demesne richly planted; Tower Hill, of Major Blake; Carnacon, of J. McDonnell, Esq.; Clogher, of Crean Lynch, Esq.; and Castlecarra, of T. Lynch, Esq. The living is a rectory and vicarage, in the diocese of Tuam, episcopally united for more than 65 years to the rectories and vicarages of Ballyhane and Ballyovey, together forming the union of Burriscarra, in the patronage of the Archbishop: the tithes amount to £65, and of the whole benefice to £368. 14. 9½. The church of the union is in Ballyhane; there is neither glebe-house nor glebe. In the R. C. divisions this parish forms part of the union or district of Ballintobber: the chapel, a good cruciform building, erected in 1835 at an expense of £2000, and decorated with a painting of the crucifixion, is situated at Carnacon. A school of 60 boys and 20 girls is held in the chapel. There are some remains of a nunnery, and a very fine mineral spring.

BURRISHOOLE, a parish, in the barony of Burrishoole, county of Mayo, and province of Connaught; containing, with the market and post-town of Newport-Pratt, 11,761 inhabitants. This place, from a bull of Pope Innocent VIII., dated February 9th, 1486, appears to have been distinguished as the seat of a monastery for friars of the Dominican order, founded by Richard de Bourke, Lord Mac William Oughter, head of the Turlough family, and dedicated to the Blessed Virgin. The monastery was granted to Nicholas Weston, who assigned it to Theobald, Viscount Costello-Galen; there are still some remains. The parish is situated on the north-east shore of Clew bay, and on the high road from Castlebar to Achill island: it comprises 12,550 statute acres, as applotted under the tithe act. The lands are chiefly under tillage; and many of the islands in Clew bay, which are within the parish, afford good pasturage for sheep. There is a large tract of mountain and bog, about two-thirds of which are reclaimable. Salt-works were formerly carried on here. The principal inhabited islands are Mynishmore, Inishna-crusna, Inish-cougha, Inishurken, Inishtubride, and Inishturk. There are two large lakes in the parish, called Lough Feagh and Lough Furnace; and on the narrow neck of land between these are the ruins of an old smelting furnace; there is also another at the old abbey. The river of Burrishoole, on which is an excellent salmon fishery, has its source in these lakes. The principal seats are Newport House, that of Sir R. Annesley O'Donell, Bart.; Newfield, of J. McLoughlin, Esq.; Seamount, of Connell O'Donnell, Esq.; Tymore, of J. T. S. Stuart, Esq.; Newfort, of J. Hilles, Esq.; and Abbeyville, of J. McDonnell, Esq. The living is a rectory and vicarage, in the diocese of Tuam, and in the patronage of the Archbishop: the tithes amount to £350. The church is a neat plain structure, for the repairs of which the Ecclesiastical Commissioners have recently granted £338. 9. 3. The glebe-house was built by aid of a gift of £400 and a loan of £360, in 1819, from the late Board of First Fruits: the glebe comprises 51*a*. 3*r*. 26*p*. The R. C. parish is co-extensive with that of the Established Church, and contains two chapels, one at Newport-Pratt and the other at Newfield, both good slated buildings. There is a place of worship for Primitive Methodists, open each alternate Wednesday and Friday; and a Presbyterian minister attends occasionally and performs divine service in the parish school-house. There are twelve public schools in the parish; that at Trienbeg is aided by an annual donation from the Marquess of Sligo, and a school-house at Newport-Pratt was erected at the expense of the Rev. Jas. Hughes, P. P. In these schools are about 1300 children; and in a hedge school at Carrig-a-neady are about 20 children. There are the remains of a castle, formerly belonging to the O'Malley family; also several Druidical caves, many of which contain large rooms arched over with flags. A patron is held here on St. Dominick's day, the 4th of August. —See Newport-Pratt.

BURRISNEFARNEY, a parish, partly in the barony of Ikerrin, county of Tipperary, and province of Munster, but chiefly in the barony of Clonlisk, King's county, and province of Leinster, 1½ mile (W.) from Moneygall; containing 269 inhabitants. This parish is situated near the high road from Dublin to Limerick, which runs on the north-west, and is bounded on the south-east by the Devil's Bit range of mountains, near which the little river Allitrim has its source, which separates the parish from that of Aghnameadle on the west, and abounds with fine trout. It comprises 4138 statute acres, as applotted under the tithe act, and valued at £3438 per annum, exclusive of waste. The land is good, and, being chiefly in the hands of gentlemen, is much improved and in grass; there is very little bog, not more than sufficient to supply the inhabitants with fuel. The gentlemen's seats are Loughton, formerly the residence of T. Ryder Pepper, Esq., and now of Lieut.-Gen. Lord Bloomfield, who is making extensive additions and improvements to the house and demesne; Thorn Vale, of George Garvey, Esq.; Barnagrotty, of J. Tydd Abbott, Esq.; White Ville, of R. White, Esq.; and Larch Vale, the neat residence of the Rev. W. Gresson. It is a rectory and vicarage, in the diocese of Killaloe, united by act of council to the vicarage of Bourney or Bourchin: the tithes amount to £184. 12. 3½. The church is a neat modern building, with a metal roof, situated contiguous to the Loughton demesne, and erected under the patronage of T. R. Pepper, Esq., to whose memory it contains a handsome marble tablet. In the R. C. divisions, also, it forms part of the union or district of Bourney. The parochial school, on the Laughton demesne, was founded and is partly supported by a donation of £20 per annum from Mrs. Pepper, sister of Lord Bloomfield and widow of T. R. Pepper, Esq.; about 50 girls are taught in it. The Rev. Kennedy O'Kennedy, late rector of the union, bequeathed £500 to the poor of this parish and Bourney, to be disposed of for their benefit at the discretion of the rector and churchwardens; but no part of it has yet been received. A parochial relief fund now exists, founded on the plan of the Rev. Dr. Chalmers. There are some remains of an old castle on the Loughton demesne.

BURRIS-O'-KANE, or BURROS-O'-KEANE, a post-town and parish, in the barony of Lower Ormond, county of Tipperary, and province of Munster, 12¾ miles (W. by N.) from Roscrea, and 71¾ miles (W. S. W.) from Dublin; containing 2635 inhabitants. This town is situated on the road from Nenagh to Portumna and Banagher, and of late years has undergone much improvement; many new houses have been built, and others are in contemplation. Fairs are held on the 26th of April, June, and September, and on Dec. 15th. Petty sessions are held every Saturday; and here is a chief station of the constabulary police. There is a bridewell, comprising two small cells, a day room, and a cell for females, but it is on a confined plan and in a bad situation. The land is principally under an improving system of tillage: there is a considerable extent of bog, in detached portions. In the townland of Tumbricane is a quarry of limestone of superior quality, which is mostly used for tombstones and building. The principal seats are Arran Hill, the property of the Marquess of Ormonde, but in the occupation of T. G. Stoney, Esq.; Greyfort, the property of — Saunders, Esq.; Killavalla, the seat of R. Johnston Stoney, Esq.; and Bushey Park, of T. Towers, Esq. The living is a rectory and vicarage, in the diocese of Killaloe, and in the patronage of the Bishop: the tithes amount to £185. 2. 4¾. The church is a plain structure, built by aid of a loan of £500 from the late Board of First Fruits, in 1812, and for the repairs of which the Ecclesiastical Commissioners have recently granted £631. 17. 2. The glebe-house was built at the same time, by a gift of £400 and a loan of £300 from the Board: the glebe comprises 11¾ acres. In the R. C. divisions the parish is the head of a union or district, which comprises also the parishes of Eglish and Ballingarry, and contains a chapel in each parish; that of Burris-O'Kane, now in course of erection, will be a commodious and handsome building. The parochial schools are aided by the rector; and there are a free school and two schools aided by private subscription. About 140 boys and 90 girls are taught in these schools; and there are two private pay schools, in which are about 30 of each sex. A fever hospital and dispensary are maintained in the usual manner. There are considerable remains of a square tower castle, called Tumbricane, which appears to have been of great strength.

BURRIS-O'-LEAGH, a post-town, in the parish of Glankeen, barony of Kilnemanagh, county of Tipperary, and province of Munster, 36¼ miles (N. N. W.) from Clonmel, and 72¾ miles (S. W.) from Dublin; containing 1340 inhabitants. This is a place of considerable antiquity; it is situated on the road from Thurles to Nenagh, and comprises 237 houses. An extensive distillery was formerly carried on here; there is a brewery; and at Fantane, in the vicinity, is another, both on a small scale. Fairs are held on June 9th, Aug. 6th, and Nov. 27th, which is a large fair for pigs. Petty sessions are held once a fortnight; and here is a chief station of the constabulary police. The parish church and a R. C. chapel are situated in the town. A school for the children of Roman Catholics is aided by a donation of £10 per annum from the parish priest; and there is a dispensary.—See GLANKEEN.

BURROS-in-OSSORY, a market and post-town, in the parish of AGHABOE, barony of UPPER OSSORY, QUEEN'S county, and province of LEINSTER, 13 miles (S. W. by W.) from Maryborough, and 53 miles (S. W. by W.) from Dublin; containing 770 inhabitants. This place was formerly of some importance: being bounded on the north by the river Nore, and encompassed on every other side by bogs, it formed the great pass to Munster; and for its defence the Fitzpatricks, proprietors of the district, at an early period built a castle, of which, as appears by his will, Sir Barnaby Fitzpatrick, second baron of Upper Ossory, was in possession in 1582. In 1600, Queen Elizabeth granted this place, among other possessions, to Florence Fitzpatrick and his son, which grant was confirmed by Jas. I. in 1611. The castle was, in 1641, besieged by Florence; and the garrison, consisting of Protestants of Upper Ossory, though enduring the greatest sufferings from want of provisions, refused to surrender, and kept possession of it till they were relieved by Sir C. Coote. In 1642, Bryan, the sixth baron, accompanied the insurgents to besiege this castle, which was subsequently granted to the Duke of Ormonde, and, with the townland of Burros, comprising 600 acres, is now part of the estate of the Duke of Buckingham. The town is situated on the mail coach road from Dublin to Limerick, and consists of one long street containing about 130 houses. It has a market; and fairs are held on Jan. 25th, March 21st, May 31st, June 24th, Aug. 15th, Oct. 11th, Nov. 21st, and Dec. 20th. A constabulary police force is stationed in the town; and the quarter sessions for the county are held in April and October, and petty sessions irregularly. Here is also a dispensary. Near the town, on the estate of the Earl of Mountrath, are some remains of the old castle of Ballaghmore, built by the Fitzpatricks, which, in 1647, was attacked by Capt. Hedges and the garrison of Burros, to whom it surrendered, and was partly dismantled; the captain, on his return, was intercepted, and before he reached his quarters lost several of his men. On Kyle hill, about two miles from the town, is a rude stone chair, called by the peasantry the "Fairy Chair," which was probably in former times a seat of judgment of the Brehons.—See AGHABOE.

BURRY, a parish, in the barony of UPPER KELLS, county of MEATH, and province of LEINSTER, 1¾ mile (S. W.) from Kells; containing 1027 inhabitants. This parish is situated on the road from Mullingar to Kells and Drogheda, and comprises 3339 statute acres, as applotted under the tithe act. The land, which is of great fertility, is almost equally divided between tillage and pasture, and the system of agriculture is in a highly improved state. There is a considerable tract of bog, which partly supplies the town of Kells with turf; and there are some quarries of limestone and greenstone. Balrath, the seat of C. A. Nicholson, Esq., is a handsome residence, pleasantly situated in an extensive and well-wooded demesne, with a park well stocked with deer, and in which are some remains of the old church, with a burial-ground attached. The other seats are Springville, the residence of P. O'Reilly, Esq.; and Berford, of J. Dyas, Esq. It is a rectory, in the diocese of Meath, and is part of the union of Kells and corps of the archdeaconry of Meath: the tithes amount to £150 The glebe comprises 2*r.* 19*p.*, valued at £1. 10. per annum. In the R. C. divisions, also, it forms part of the union or district of Kells. There are two daily pay schools, one at Drumbarrow and the other at Scurlogstown, in which are about 100 boys and 60 girls.

BURT, a parish, in the barony of ENNISHOWEN, county of DONEGAL, and province of ULSTER, 6 miles (N. W.) from Londonderry; containing 3765 inhabitants. This parish, which anciently formed part of the parish of Templemore, is situated on Lough Swilly, and comprises, according to the Ordnance survey, 10,672½ statute acres. The living is a perpetual curacy, in the diocese of Derry, and in the patronage of the Dean, to whom the tithes are payable: the curate's stipend is £100 per annum late currency, of which £75 is paid by the dean, and the remainder is advanced from the augmentation funds of the Ecclesiastical Commissioners. The church, a neat small edifice, was built about a century since. There is no glebe-house. In the R. C. divisions the parish forms part of the union or district of Iskahan, Burt, and Inch, and contains a chapel. There is also a place of worship for Presbyterians in connection with the Synod of Ulster, of the first class. A parochial school, in which are about 40 boys and 4 girls, is supported by the Dean of Derry; and there are three pay schools, in which are about 80 boys and 30 girls, and three Sunday schools. On the shore of Lough Swilly are the ruins of the castle of Burt, or Birt, erected by Sir Cahir O'Dogherty in the 15th century, consisting of a single tower, situated on a commanding eminence.

BUSHMILLS, a market and post-town, in that part of the parish of BILLY which is in the barony of CAREY, county of ANTRIM, and province of ULSTER, 6¼ miles (N. E. by N.) from Coleraine, and 125½ (N.) from Dublin; containing 108 houses and 507 inhabitants. This place is pleasantly situated near the mouth of the river Bush, from which it derives its name: it is neatly built, and is the general place of resort for parties visiting the Giant's Causeway, about two miles distant, for whose accommodation a large and handsome hotel has been erected by Sir F. W. Macnaghten, Bart., who, in 1827, established a weekly market here. A distillery is carried on, and is much celebrated for the quality of its whiskey, of which about 12,000 gallons are annually made and principally sent to England, Scotland, the West Indies, and America. There is a manufactory of spades, shovels, scythes, and sickles upon the river Bush; extensive paper-mills have been erected by F. D. Ward, Esq., for the supply of the home and Scottish markets, and near them are mills for flour and for dressing flax. The market is on Tuesday, and is well supplied with grain, linen yarn, pork, and provisions of all kinds; and fairs are held on Jan. 28th, March 28th, June 28th, July 21st, Oct. 21st, and Dec. 12th. Here is a constabulary police station; and the petty sessions for the district are held every fortnight. The court-house, a large and handsome building, recently erected by Sir F. W. Macnaghten, contains also apartments for the police, and some cells for the confinement of prisoners. The parish church of Dunluce is situated in the town; and there are also a place of worship for Presbyterians in connection with the Synod of Ulster, and one for Methodists. A school has been established by the trustees of Erasmus Smith's charity, for the instruction of the children of parishioners, the master of which has a good house and two acres of land; there are also several schools in various parts of the parish. In the immediate neighbourhood is Bushmills House, the seat of Sir F. W. Macnaghten, Bart., who has made numerous improvements on his estate: the mansion is at present being rebuilt in a very splendid style, and with the grounds will form an interesting ornament to the place. In the bed of the river, near the bridge, are some small but beautiful basaltic columns fantastically curved.

BUTLERSBRIDGE, a village, in the parish of CASTLETERRA, barony of UPPER LOUGHTEE, county of CAVAN, and province of ULSTER, 3 miles (N. N. W.) from Cavan; containing about 40 houses and 211 inhabitants. It is pleasantly situated on the river Ballyhaise, and on the road from Cavan to Enniskillen, and has a fair on the second Monday in every month throughout the year. Here is a R. C. chapel of ease to those of Castleterra and Ballyhaise; and a daily penny post to Cavan and Belturbet has been established.

BUTLERSTOWN.—See KILRONAN, county of WATERFORD.

BUTTEVANT, a post-town and parish (formerly an incorporated market-town), in the barony of ORRERY and KILMORE, county of CORK, and province of MUNSTER, 22 miles (N. by W.) from Cork, and 121¾ (S. W.) from Dublin; containing 5535 inhabitants, of which number, 1536 are in the town. This parish, which is situated on the river Awbeg and on the road from Mallow to Charleville, was anciently called *Bothon*, and is said to have derived its present name from the exclamation *Boutcz en avant*, "Push forward," used by David de Barry, its proprietor, to animate his men in a contest with the McCarthys, which was subsequently adopted as the family motto of the Earls of Barrymore, who derived their title of Viscount from this place. It appears to have attained considerable importance at an early period after the first invasion, from the notices of it which occur in ancient records still existing. On the 26th of September, 1234, a grant was made by Hen. III. to David de Barry of a market on Sunday, and a fair on the vigil and day of St. Luke the Evangelist and for six following days. In the 11th of Edw. II. (1317), a grant of release of £105 required of the commonalty of the town of "Botavant" by the exchequer, to be applied in enclosing it with walls, was made at the request of John Fitz-David de Barry, to whom the town belonged, and who was required to see that the money was duly employed in the same. In the 49th of Edw. III., another grant, dated Aug. 6th, 1375, was made to the "Provost and Commonalty of Botavaunt," ratifying a former grant of part of the "waste" of the town, with the north gate and customs there. A priory and a nunnery were founded here at an early period; the priory was restored in 1290, by David Oge Barry, Lord Buttevant, for Conventual Franciscans, and dedicated to St. Thomas the martyr; the nunnery was under the invocation of St. Owen, or St. John the Baptist, but there are no particulars of its foundation or order. During the war between the houses of York and Lancaster, the town suffered considerable devastation; and in 1568 the castle was taken by the Lord-Deputy Sydney. In 1641 the Irish army of the south assembled here under the command of Lord Mountgarret, and proceeded to Mallow: and early in the year 1643, Lord Inchiquin assembled his forces here, consisting of 4000 foot and 400 horse. The manor of Buttevant continued in the possession of the Barrymore family, and was sold by Richard, the last Earl, to the late John Anderson, Esq., of Fermoy: it was purchased, in 1831, by Lord Doneraile, the present proprietor.

The town is situated on the western bank of the river Awbeg, over which are two bridges, one on the old and the other on the modern road from Cork to Limerick: it consists principally of one main street extending along the mail coach road, and in 1831 contained 204 houses. Immediately adjoining, on the north-west, are the barracks, an extensive range of buildings, occupying a spacious enclosed area of nearly 23 statute acres, divided into two quadrangles by the central range, in which is an archway surmounted by a cupola and affording communication between them. Near Buttevant Castle is an extensive and substantial flour-mill, erected by Sir James Anderson and furnished with machinery of superior construction; it is capable of manufacturing 20,000 barrels of flour annually, but at present is not in operation. The market has been long discontinued; but fairs are held on March 27th, July 20th, Oct. 14th, and Nov. 20th, chiefly for cattle. The market-house is situated on the west side of an open square at the southern extremity of the town; the upper part is used as the court-house. A constabulary police force is stationed here; a seneschal's court for the manor of Buttevant is occasionally held, in which debts, not exceeding 40*s*. late currency, are recoverable; and petty sessions are held every alternate Wednesday. Including Lisgriffin, the parish comprises 7543 statute acres: the land is of very good quality and principally under tillage; there is neither woodland nor waste, and but a small quantity of bog. Limestone abounds, and there is one quarry near the town of very superior quality, of a light grey colour and very fine grain, from which the stone for building the new R. C. chapel has been taken. Buttevant Castle, the residence of Sir J. Caleb Anderson, Bart., was originally called King John's Castle, and formed one of the angles of the ancient fortifications of the town; it was considerably enlarged and modernised by the late Mr. Anderson, and has lost much of its antique appearance; it is beautifully situated on a rocky eminence on the margin of the river, of which it commands a fine view; within the demesne is the church, the spire of which combining with other features of the scenery adds much to the beauty of the landscape. The other seats are Castle View, that of Barry Gregg, Esq.; Velvetstown, of T. Lucas Croft, Esq.; and Temple Mary, of J. O'Leary, Esq.: there are also several neat cottage residences. The river Awbeg, celebrated by Spenser under the appellation of the "Gentle Mulla," abounds with fine white trout.

The living is a perpetual curacy, in the diocese of Cloyne, episcopally united, at a period prior to any existing record, to the vicarages of Bregogue and Kilbroney, and to the perpetual curacy of Cahirduggan, together forming the union of Buttevant and Cahirduggan, formerly called the union of Bregogue, in the patronage of the Bishop; the rectory is impropriate in C. Silver Oliver, Esq. The tithes, amounting to £926. 10., are wholly payable to the impropriator. The curate is also chaplain of the barracks; and the tithes of the benefice amount to £139. 4. The church is a handsome structure in the later English style, with a square embattled tower surmounted by a finely proportioned spire: it is situated near the river and within the castle demesne, and was built in 1826, near the site of an ancient church, of which there are still some remains, and on the site of another of more recent date; the late Board of First Fruits granted a loan of £1600 for its erection: a handsome mural monument has been erected to the Rev. T. Walker, late minister of the parish. There is neither glebe-house nor glebe. In the R. C. divisions the parish forms the head of a union or district, which comprises also the parishes of Ballybeg, Bregogue, and Kilbroney, and contains the chapels of Buttevant and Lisgriffin, both in this parish. The new chapel at Buttevant, commenced in 1831, is now nearly completed; the estimated expense was £3000, of which £600 was granted on loan by the Board of Public Works, and the remainder raised by subscription, through the unwearied exertions of the Rev. C. Buckley, P.P., towards which Lord Doneraile contributed £30, and also presented the site. It is a very handsome structure of hewn limestone, in the later English style, consisting of a nave and transept, between which, on each side, rises a square embattled tower crowned with richly crocketed pinnacles; the walls are strengthened with buttresses at the angles and between the windows of the nave, terminating in crocketed pinnacles above an embattled parapet carried round the building; and the gables of the transept are surmounted by Maltese crosses, beneath which, on each side, is a cinquefoiled niche resting on a projecting corbel. The nave is lighted by a range of three windows of two lights ornamented in cinquefoil, with a quatrefoiled circle in the crown of the arch; and the transept is lighted at each end by a noble window of five lights, 26 feet high, and elaborately enriched with tracery: the tower on the east side was a detached watch-tower belonging to the abbey, erected by one of the Earls of Desmond for the protection of the brethren in times of violence, and incorporated with the present building. A parochial house will be built near it for the priest's residence; and part of the old chapel has been converted into a national school, in which are 240 boys. The parochial school, in which are 40 boys and 30 girls, is kept in a house rented by the Rev. Dr. Cotter and Col. Hill, and is supported by subscription, aided by an annual donation of £10 each from Lords Doneraile and Arden; there are also six private schools, in which are about 340 children. The fever hospital, which contains also a dispensary, is a substantial stone building near the river, capable of receiving 30 patients.

The ruins of the abbey are finely situated on the steep bank of the river Awbeg, and consist chiefly of the walls of the nave, chancel, and some portions of the domestic buildings; the upper part of the central tower, supported on arches of light and graceful elevation, fell down in 1814; the tomb of the founder, David de Barry, is supposed to be in the centre of the chancel, but is marked only by some broken stones which appear to have formed an enclosure. On the south side of the nave are the remains of a finely proportioned chapel, in which, and also in the nave and chancel, are numerous tombs and inscriptions to the memory of the Barrys, Fitzgeralds, Lombards, and others. Near the abbey are some vestiges of an ancient building supposed to have been the nunnery. Nearly in the centre of the town are the remains of Lombards' castle, a quadrangular building flanked at each angle by a square tower, one of which is nearly in a perfect state, and, with a portion of the castle, has been converted into a dwelling-house. At Lisgriffin are the ruins of an ancient castle of the family of Barry. Some remains of the old town walls may yet be traced; and in a burial-ground at Templemary are the ruins of an ancient church or chapel. The title of Viscount Buttevant, conferred on the Barry family in 1406, has been dormant since the death of the last Earl of Barrymore, but is now claimed by James Redmond Barry, Esq., of Glandore, in the county of Cork.

C

CABINTEELY, a village, partly in the parish of KILLINEY, but chiefly in that of TULLY, half-barony of RATHDOWN, county of DUBLIN, and province of LEINSTER, 6¼ miles (S. S. E.) from Dublin: the population is returned with the respective parishes. This place, which is situated on the road from Dublin to Bray, is a constabulary police station, and has a two-penny post to Dublin: it comprises a number of small irregularly built houses, and a R. C. chapel for the union or district of Kingstown. In the vicinity are several handsome seats, the principal of which is Cabinteely House, the residence of the Misses Byrne, descended from the O'Byrne dynasty of Wicklow: the house forms three sides of a square, commanding extensive views of the bays of Dublin and Killiney, with the beautiful adjacent country; and the demesne is adorned with thriving plantations and presents many natural beauties. Among the other seats are Brenanstown House, the admired residence of G. Pim, Esq.; and Glen-Druid, of Mrs. Barrington. Near Loughlinstown, on the right of the road leading to Bray, is the site of an extensive encampment, held there in 1797 and for several years after the disturbances in 1798. At Glen-Druid there is a very perfect cromlech, consisting of six upright stones supporting one of 14 feet by 12, which is supposed to weigh about 25 tons.

CABLE ISLAND.—See CAPELL ISLAND.

CADAMSTOWN, or CADMANSTOWN, a parish, in the barony of CARBERY, county of KILDARE, and province of LEINSTER, 6 miles (W. by N.) from Kilcock; containing 1205 inhabitants. It is situated on the road from Kilcock to Kinnegad, and comprises 3637 statute acres, as applotted under the tithe act Balyna House is the seat of R. More O'Ferrall, Esq. The living is a rectory, in the diocese of Kildare, and is annexed to the union of Castle-Carbery; the whole of the tithes, which amount to £118. 8. 10¼., are impropriate in the Marquess of Downshire. In the R. C. divisions it is the head of a union or district, called Balyna or Johnstown, comprising also the parishes of Mylerstown, Ballynadrimna, Nurney, Kilrenny, and Carrick: there are three chapels in the union, situated respectively at Johnstown-Bridge, Garrisker, and Nurney; the first is a handsome edifice recently erected in the later English style, with a tower and spire of hewn stone. A school at Balyna, chiefly supported by R. M. O'Ferrall, Esq., affords instruction to about 100 boys and 60 girls; and there is a private school, in which are about 20 boys and 20 girls. At Johnstown-Bridge are the ruins of the old church.

CADAMSTOWN, a village, in the parish of LETTERLUNA, barony of BALLYBRITT, KING'S county, and province of LEINSTER, 3 miles (S. E.) from Kinitty, on the road from Parsonstown to Clonaslie; containing 18 houses and 108 inhabitants. Here is an extensive boulting-mill and malting establishment.

CAHER.—See CAHIR, county of TIPPERARY.

CAHERA, or CAHARAGH, a parish, in the Western Division of the barony of WEST CARBERY, county of CORK, and province of MUNSTER, 4 miles (N.) from Skibbereen; containing 6999 inhabitants. This parish is situated on the roads from Skibbereen and Dunmanway, which meet at Dromore, near its centre, and proceed northward to Bantry; and is intersected by the river Ilen, on which, near Dromore, are some beautiful cascades. It contains 27,380 statute acres, of which 17,284 are arable, 5211 pasture, 155 woodland, and the remainder waste or bog; 20,054 acres are applotted under the tithe act, and valued at £7227 per annum. The surface is uneven, but in many places very productive, although it consists chiefly of small fields interspersed among rocks, and is cultivated by spade labour; and although the roads are excellent, the farmers continue to carry manure to their land on the backs of horses. The principal seats are Mount Music, the residence of the Rev. R. F. Webb, the rector; Gurtnascree, of A. O'Driscoll, Esq.; Woodville, of T. Wood, Esq.; and that occupied by the Rev. D. Dore, P. P. The living is a rectory and vicarage, in the diocese of Cork, and in the patronage of the Bishop: the tithes amount to £650. The church is a small, neat, cruciform edifice, without tower, spire, or bell: it was built in 1829, at an expense of £650 given by the late Board of First Fruits. There is neither glebe-house nor glebe. In the R. C. divisions this is the head of a union or district, comprising the parish of Cahera and part of Abbeystrowry: there are two chapels, one a large and handsome building at Killeenagh, on a lofty eminence near the church; the other, a small plain edifice at Dromore. The male and female parochial schools are supported by the Cork Diocesan Association, aided by the rector and Mr. Newman; and near the chapel at Killeenlagh is a school, containing about 100 boys and 70 girls. There are also a private school, in which are about 90 boys and 60 girls, and a Sunday school. Near Lisnagle are the ruins of a strong castle, once the residence of McCarthy, King of Cork. The ruins of the old church also remain, which the people here call the Abbey of Cahir.

CAHIR, a parish, in the barony of IVERAGH, county of KERRY, and province of MUNSTER; containing, with the market and post-town of Cahirciveen, 5653 inhabitants. This parish is situated on the harbour of Valencia, on the south-western coast; and is intersected by the high road from Tralee to Valencia; it includes within its limits Beg-innis or Begnis island, which, however, is situated nearer to the island and parish of Valencia, and between which and Dowlas Head is the northern entrance to the harbour. It comprises 20,452 statute acres, of which about 7000 are arable, 6500 mountain pasture, 6932 waste land and bog, and about 20 acres woodland. The soil is in general light; and the system of agriculture, though still in a backward state, has improved considerably since the construction of the new line of road through this and the neighbouring parishes, and along the coast of Castlemaine bay, as projected by the late Mr. Nimmo about 20 years since, by the completion of which great benefit has been conferred upon a district depending upon sea-weed and sea sand chiefly for manure, and for the conveyance of which from the coast to the interior it affords great facility. Shell sand of superior quality is brought from Begnis island and is extensively used for manure. There is no limestone nearer than Killorglin, a distance of 28 miles; and probably on account of the steepness of the hills, and the imperfect drainage of the lowlands, the spade is much more in use than the plough. The seats are Castlequin, that of Kean Mahony, Esq.; Bahoss, the newly erected mansion of Charles O'Connell, Esq., situated nearly in the centre of a reclaimed bog, and commanding a fine view of the amphitheatre of mountains by which it is encircled; and Hillgrove, the residence of J. Primrose, Esq., surrounded by a finely wooded demesne, a feature of rare occurrence in this wild district. Near the foot of Hillgrove is Cashen, the old mansion of the O'Connell family, and the birthplace of Daniel O'Connell, Esq., who holds the greater portion of a large estate in this parish under the Provost and Fellows of Trinity College, Dublin, besides a large tract his own estate. The prevailing rocks are of the slate formation, and slates of a good quality have been quarried on Cahirciveen mountain, and used for roofing the houses in the town. A few boats belonging to the parish are employed in the fishery, and several others are engaged in the conveyance of shell sand from Begnis island.

The living is a rectory and vicarage, in the diocese of Ardfert and Aghadoe, episcopally united, prior to the date of any existing record, to the rectory and vicarage of Glenbegh and the rectory of Killinane, together constituting the union of Cahir, in the patronage of the Crown: the tithes amount to £226. 16. 10., and of the whole benefice to £517. 13. 10. The church is a neat plain edifice, built in the year 1815 by aid of a loan of £540 from the late Board of First Fruits. There is a glebe-house; and the glebe lands, in four separate parcels, comprise 107½ acres. In the R. C. divisions the parish forms part of the union or district of Cahirciveen, which also comprises the parish of Killinane: there are two chapels, situated at Cahirciveen and Fielmore; the former is a spacious building with a handsome belfry of hewn stone surmounted by a cross; the latter is a chapel of ease in the parish of Killinane. There is a national school endowed with the interest of a bequest of £500 from the late Gen. Count O'Connell, aided by annual donations from the Marquess of Lansdowne and Daniel and Maurice O'Connell, Esqrs.; also a free school supported by subscription, in which together about 650 children are educated. A fever hospital was established in 1834, for the reception of 25 patients; and there is a dispensary. Nearly opposite to the town are the extensive ruins of the ancient castle of Bally-Carbery; and at a small distance from them are the remains of one of those remarkable circular buildings, similar to Staig Fort, which are found only in Kerry, and which are generally supposed to have been built as places of security against the incursions of pirates on this wild and remote coast. Opposite to the north-east coast of Valencia island is the lofty cliff called Dowlas Head, near which is a spacious cavern; the entrance is low, but the interior is lofty, and bears a slight resemblance to a cathedral.—See CAHIRCIVEEN.

CAHIR, a parish, in the barony of UPPER OSSORY, QUEEN'S county, and province of LEINSTER; containing 519 inhabitants. It is situated on the road from Durrow to Kilkenny, and forms part of the union of Aughamacart, in the diocese of Ossory, in which the vicarage is included: the rectory is impropriate in Ladies G. and F. Fitzpatrick. In the R. C. divisions it is part of the union or district of Durrow.

CAHIR, or CAHER, a market and post-town, and a parish, in the barony of IFFA and OFFA WEST, county of TIPPERARY, and province of MUNSTER, 7¾ miles (W. N. W.) from Clonmel, and 87½ (S. W. by S.) from Dublin; containing 8462 inhabitants, of which number, 3408 are in the town. This place is situated on the river Suir, and at the junction of the mail coach roads leading respectively from Waterford to Limerick, and from Cork, by way of Cashel, to Dublin. The town is of remote antiquity, and appears to have attained a considerable degree of importance at a very early period. A castle was built here prior to the year 1142, by Connor, King of Thomond and Monarch of Ireland; and, in the reign of John, Geoffry de Camvill founded a priory to the honour of the Blessed Virgin, for Canons Regular of the order of St. Augustin, which continued to flourish till 1540, when it was surrendered to the Crown; there are still some remains of the buildings. The manor was one of those belonging to the Butler family; and in the reign of Elizabeth the castle was besieged by the Earl of Essex, with the whole of his army, when the garrison, encouraged by the hostilities then waged by the Earl of Desmond, held out for ten days, but was compelled to surrender. In 1647, this fortress was invested by Lord Inchiquin, and, notwithstanding its great strength, surrendered in a few hours, after some of its outworks had been gained by the assailants.

The present town owes its rise to the late Earl of Glengall, and has been enlarged and greatly improved by the present Earl, whose seat is within its limits; it is pleasantly situated on the river Suir, and is well built and of handsome appearance. About a mile distant are extensive cavalry barracks, adapted for 23 officers and 346 non-commissioned officers and privates, with stabling for 292 horses, and an hospital attached; and the staff of the Tipperary militia is also stationed in the town. At Scartana, in the vicinity, races are held annually in September or October, and are generally well attended. A linen factory was established under the Cahir Local Association, formed originally in 1809, which laid the foundation of a spinning school, and in 1823 established a market for the sale of linen and yarn. Diapers and fine linens were at first the principal articles manufactured, but coarser fabrics have latterly been produced. For want of an advantageous market the whole of this trade declined; and in 1822, the London Relief Committee, under the immediate patronage of the Earl and Countess Dowager of Glengall, established the present Leghorn, Tuscan, British, and fancy straw plat manufactory; it was projected by Mr. John Parry, of London, who first introduced the manufacture of Italian straws into England, for which he received a medal from the Society of Arts. The produce of this manufacture, in which a large number of females is employed, is chiefly disposed of to the wholesale houses in London. By a failure of one of those houses in 1828, the business of the factory was greatly impeded; but the pecuniary assistance afforded by the Earl of Glengall has enabled the present proprietor, Mr. Richard Butler, to carry it on as extensively as before. The articles manufactured are of superior quality, and find a ready sale in the English market. Weaving-looms for fancy plats of Italian straw with silk, of very ingenious workmanship, have been recently established, and at present afford employment to 68 females, and arrangements are in progress for considerably extending this branch of the trade. There are five very extensive flour-mills in the town and its immediate neighbourhood; the mill at Cahir Abbey, the property of Mr. Grubb, is on a very large scale and is worked by an engine of 80-horse power. The market, which is chiefly for agricultural produce, is on Friday; the market-house is a neat and commodious building. Fairs are held on Feb. 8th, April 12th, May 26th and 27th, July 20th, Sept. 18th and 19th, Oct. 20th, and Dec. 7th. A constabulary police force is stationed in the town. A manorial court, in which debts to the amount of £10 are recoverable, is held every six weeks by the seneschal; and petty sessions are held weekly. The bridewell, a handsome castellated building, contains five cells, one day-room, and two airing-yards. The trade of this place and neighbourhood will be much improved by the construction of the contemplated railway from Tipperary to Carrick-on-Suir, for which an act has been obtained, and towards the completion of which the Commissioners of Public Works in Ireland have agreed to advance a loan, on condition that there be an equal subscription, which latter at present amounts to £60,000. It is to have a branch from Tipperary to Killaloe, to communicate with the Upper Shannon, and the estimated expense does not exceed £150,000.

The parish comprises 13,923 statute acres, as applotted under the tithe act, of which about 890 are woodland, 9560 arable, 1764 pasture, and 1709 waste land, bog, and mountain: the land is in general of good quality, and the system of agriculture is in a very improved state. The Galtee range of mountains commences here, and the scenery in the neighbourhood is of a highly picturesque character. Cahir House, the seat of the Earl of Glengall, is situated in the town, and the demesne extends for more than two miles on both sides of the river. The park, which is finely planted and well stocked with deer, comprises 560 acres; and in a secluded part of it is a picturesque retreat of modern erection, called the Cottage, which is greatly admired for the extreme beauty of its situation. The river Suir winds gently through the demesne, and contributes to the interest and diversity of the landscape. Cahir Abbey, the residence of Richard Grubb, Esq., is a handsome house recently erected by the proprietor, and pleasantly situated in grounds tastefully disposed and commanding some fine views. The other seats are Garnavella, the handsome residence of J. Archer Butler, Esq.; Altavilla, of W. Going, Esq.; Ballybrado, of J. Wm. Fennell, Esq.; and Killemley Hall, beautifully situated on the river Suir and commanding some highly picturesque views, the property of H. Hughes, Esq., but in the occupation of L. Clutterbuck, Esq. The living is a vicarage, in the diocese of Lismore, episcopally united, in 1803, to that of Grange St. John, forming the union of Cahir, in the patronage of the Crown; the rectory is appropriate to the Archbishop of Cashel. The tithes amount to £900, of which £500 is payable to the archbishop, and £400 to the vicar; and the gross tithes of the benefice, payable to the vicar, amount to £460. The church was rebuilt, in 1817, by aid of a loan of £2500 from the late Board of First Fruits: it is a spacious structure of stone, in the later English style, with an embattled tower surmounted by a finely proportioned spire, the whole after a design by Mr. Nash, of London. The glebe-house, a handsome residence, was built by aid of a gift of £100 and a loan of £750 from the same Board, in 1809: the glebe comprises 10*a.* 2*r.* 22*p.* In the R. C. divisions this parish is the head of a union or district, comprising the parishes of Cahir and Mortlestown; the chapel, lately rebuilt, is a spacious and handsome cruciform edifice, in the later English style, with a lofty and well-proportioned spire. There is a place of worship for the Society of Friends. The parochial schools are under the trustees of Erasmus Smith's charity; the school-house was built at an expense of £1034, of which £600 was defrayed from the funds of that charity, and £434 by the late Earl of Glengall, who also gave two acres of land; and there is a national school, aided by subscription. In these schools about 180 boys and 170 girls are instructed; there are also twelve private schools, in which are about 580 children. A dispensary and fever hospital were founded by the local London Relief Committee. The ruins of the old castle are situated on an island in the river, and present a very interesting and highly picturesque appearance. This is the burial-place of the Butler family, Earls of Glengall, to whom it gives the inferior titles of Viscount and Baron.

CAHIRCIVEEN, a market and post-town, in the parish of Cahir, barony of Iveragh, county of Kerry, and province of Munster, 36 miles (S. W.) from Tralee, and 183 (S. W. by W.) from Dublin; containing 1192 inhabitants. This town, of which the greater portion has arisen since the formation of the new line of road along the coast of Castlemaine bay and through the Iveragh mountains to Valencia, is pleasantly situated at the base of the Cahirciveen mountain, and on the high road from Tralee to Valencia. In 1815 there were only five houses in the entire village, but within the last ten years it has rapidly increased, and consists of one principal street stretching along the main road, and of two smaller streets branching from it at right angles, one of which leads down to the quay, and the other to the upper road or old village of Cahir, which consists only of mud cabins. The houses on the new road are neatly built and roofed with slate; the town has a lively and cheerful appearance; the approaches are all by good roads kept in excellent order, and great improvements have been made in the neighbourhood. A subscription news-room upon a small scale has been established, also an agency for transacting business with the National Bank of Ireland. The chief trade carried on is the importation of timber, salt, and iron; oats and flour from some mills to the east of the town are occasionally exported. The flour-mills were erected at an expense exceeding £4000, and from the increasing cultivation of wheat in this district, are now extensively worked. A pier and a small quay were constructed in 1822, which are much used, but would have been more beneficial to the town had they been built a little below the present site; the quay is accessible to vessels of considerable burden. About 400 persons are employed in the fishery, but being also engaged in agriculture they neglect the best seasons for fishing. At Renard Point, immediately opposite to the "foot" of Valencia island, is a small quay, from which is a ferry to Valencia. It is supposed that Renard, which is about 2½ miles to the west of Cahirciveen, will be the commencement of the great western railway, should that work be carried into execution. The market is on Saturday; and fairs are held on the 1st of September and 13th of December, besides which, several others have been recently established. A constabulary police force has been stationed here; and petty sessions are held in the town every alternate week. The bridewell is a neat and well-arranged building. The parish church and the R. C. chapel (the latter a handsome building), and a fever hospital and dispensary, are situated in the town. Here is also a national school.—See Cahir.

CAHIRCONLISH, a post-town and parish (formerly incorporated), in the barony of Clanwilliam, county of Limerick, and province of Munster, 7 miles (E. S. E.) from Limerick, and 116 (S. W. by W.) from Dublin; containing 3964 inhabitants, of which number, 703 are in the town. It is situated one mile west of the new line of road from Limerick to Clonmel, and was formerly a walled town, containing four castles and an extensive and celebrated college, every vestige of which has long since disappeared, and its site is only known from a field still retaining the name of the College Field. The town was formerly incorporated, as appears by a grant made in the 32nd of Edw. III., and dated Nov. 9th, 1358, conferring "murage for 20 years" on "the Provost, Bailiff, and Commonalty of the town of Catherkenlyshe." On Aug. 7th, 1690, Wm. III. encamped here on his march to the siege of Limerick, as did also Gen. de Ginkell in the following year. The town contains about 120 houses, of which several are large and well built, but in a dilapidated state: it is a constabulary police station, and fairs are held on May 16th, Aug. 20th, Oct. 17th, and Dec. 5th.

The parish contains 4777 statute acres: the soil is variable, but in general very productive; about one-third is under tillage; the remainder is meadow, pasture, or demesne, with about 120 acres of bog, which is here valuable. Near the town stands Cahirconlish House, a handsome modern residence, erected near the site of the old family mansion, by the proprietor, Major Wm. Wilson; it is surrounded by fine plantations and ornamental grounds. The old mansion, which stood on a rock, was one of the castles above noticed, and, though previously exhibiting no extraordinary marks of decay, suddenly split from top to bottom, one half falling into a heap of ruins, and the other left standing; the gateway, on which are the arms of the Wilson family, yet remains. Not far distant are Baskill, the residence of B. Friend, Esq., and the glebe-house, of the Rev. M. Moore. The living is a vicarage, in the diocese of Emly, united in 1791, by act of council, to the vicarage of Luddenbeg and the rectory and vicarage of Carrigparson, together forming the union of Cahirconlish, in the patronage of the Archbishop of Cashel: the rectory is appropriate to the vicars choral of the cathedral of Christ-Church, Dublin. The tithes amount to £581. 11. 1., of which £369. 4. 7. is payable to the vicars choral, and the remainder to the vicar; the gross tithes payable to the incumbent amount to £362. 1. 6½. The church is a spacious edifice, in the early English style, with a lofty square tower surmounted by an octagonal spire of hewn stone. The glebe-house was built by aid of a gift of £100, in 1796, from the late Board of First Fruits. The glebe, which is attached to the glebe-house, is tastefully planted and contains 14½ statute acres; besides this there are two other glebes, one of 5 statute acres, opposite the entrance to Cahirconlish House, and the other in the townland of Grenane, of 2 acres. In the R. C. divisions this parish is the head of a union or district, comprising the parishes of Cahirconlish, Isert-Lawrence, Carrigparson, and Ballybrood, and part of Dromkeen, and containing two chapels, one at Kilmurry in Cahirconlish, and the other at Isert-Lawrence. The male and female parochial schools afford instruction to about 90 boys and 90 girls; the school-house is a large and handsome building, erected by the Wilson family, who also contribute liberally towards the support of the schools. There is also a school at Inch-St. Lawrence. Near the glebe-house, about a mile from the town, is the castle of *Carrigifariogla*, now called Carrigoreely, or "O'Farrell's rock", built by the Bourkes, but last occupied by the O'Dalys. There are also near the town the scattered fragments of what appears to have been an outer wall of an old fortress, called *Croc-a-Ysenachuis-leann*, or "the old Hill of the Castle;" and on the banks of the Mulchair are the ruins of Castle Brittas, built by the Bourkes, Lords of Brittas.

CAHIRCORNEY, a parish, in the barony of Small County, county of Limerick, and province of Munster, 8 miles (S. S. E.) from Limerick; containing 880 inhabitants. This parish is situated on the river Comogue, and on the high road from Limerick to Hospital; it contains 2872 statute acres, as applotted under the tithe act, three-fourths of which are meadow and pasture, and the remainder under tillage. The soil is fertile, and the land under tillage produces abundant crops; but the system of agriculture is in a very backward state, the farmers directing their chief attention to the produce of the dairy. The Comogue or "crooked" river has its source near the ancient cathedral of Emly, and taking a westerly course passes through the parish, near the ruins of Glenogra castle and church, the castle of Rathmore, and the splendid remains of Monisternenagh, and falls into the river Maigue at Croom. On the south-west the parish is bounded by a small portion of Lough Gur, which is surrounded by limestone hills of gentle elevation covered with luxuriant verdure. In this lake are two islands, from one of which, strongly fortified, the English troops were much annoyed, on their march between Cork and Limerick during the war in the reign of Elizabeth. At Ballingoola there is a paper-mill, affording employment to 20 persons. The living is a vicarage, in the diocese of Emly, episcopally united, in 1681, to the vicarage of Kilkellane, together forming the union of Cahircorney, in the patronage of the Earl of Kenmare, during whose legal incapacity the presentation is in the Crown; the rectory is impropriate in John Croker, Esq. The tithes amount to £150, of which £100 is payable to the impropriator and £50 to the vicar; and the gross tithes of the benefice payable to the incumbent amount to £95. The church is an ancient structure, and contains a handsome monument to the Croker family, erected in 1723. The glebe-house was built by aid of a gift of £450 and a loan of £120 from the late Board of First Fruits; it is the residence of the Rev. Patrick Fitzgerald, vicar, and author of the History of the county of Limerick. The glebe comprises 7*a*. 4*p*., subject to a rent of £14 per annum, payable to the Croker family, proprietors of the whole parish. In the R. C. divisions the parish forms part of the union or district of Herbertstown and Hospital. There is a pay school, in which are about 40 boys and 30 girls. At Raleighstown are the remains of an ancient building, enclosed with a bawn defended at the angles by four small towers; it was erected in the reign of Jas. I. by Thomas Raleigh, Esq., uncle to the celebrated Sir Walter Raleigh, and afterwards became the property of the Croker family, who built a splendid house here, now in ruins. On the summit of a hill above Raleighstown is an extraordinary circular building of huge blocks of stone, curiously fitted into each other without mortar; it is of great strength, and evidently of remote antiquity. Near the shore of Lough Gur are the remains of two concentric circles of upright stones; but they are so much broken that the form can scarcely be determined.

CAHIRDUGGAN, a parish, in the barony of Fermoy, county of Cork, and province of Munster, 3 miles (S. W.) from Doneraile; containing 1801 inhabitants. This parish is situated on the river Awbeg, by which it is bounded on the north, and on the mail coach road from Mallow to Buttevant and Charleville: it comprises 6148 statute acres, as applotted under the tithe act, and valued at £5216 per annum. The land, in general of excellent quality, is chiefly under tillage, with some good pasture, and the system of agriculture is improving. At Drumcree there is a common of about 262 acres, tithe free, which is used by the inhabitants for grazing cattle. The parish contains abundance of limestone, which is extensively worked for building and for agricultural purposes. Culm has been found in the lands of Baltindaniel, but is not worked at present. There is a patent for holding several fairs, but the only one held is that of Cahirmee, on July 12th, which is one of the largest horse fairs in the South of Ireland. The principal seats are Cloheen, the residence of Lieut.-Col. A. Hill; Hazlewood, of W. Lysaght, Esq.; Springfort, of J. Foot, Esq.; Elmvale, of J. Duggan, Esq.; Danville, of W. Nash, Esq.; and Monte Video, of H. D. Spratt, Esq. It is a perpetual curacy, in the diocese of Cloyne, and forms part of the union of Buttevant; the rectory is impropriate in C. D. O. Jephson, Esq., and Major Crone. The tithes amount to £340. 11., the whole payable to the impropriators, who allow a stipend for the discharge of the clerical duties: the tithes of five townlands in the eastern part of the parish, comprising 1058 acres, are in dispute between the impropriators, but are at present payable to the lessee of Mr. Jephson. The church, which is in ruins, was built on its present site in the reign of Charles II. In 1717 the roof was taken off and service discontinued, by order of Bishop Crewe, and the parish was united to Doneraile, from which it was separated in 1758, and continued to be a distinct benefice till 1806, when it was united to Buttevant. In the R. C. divisions it is one of the three that form the union or district of Doneraile. Several Danish raths are found here in excellent preservation and generally surrounded by a single rampart and ditch. The site of an ancient castle, formerly belonging to the Roches, is still visible about a mile from Doneraile. Near it stood a considerable village, which tradition says was nearly depopulated by a plague and subsequently deserted.

CAHIRELLY, or BALLYBRICKEN, a parish, in the barony of CLANWILLIAM, county of LIMERICK, and province of MUNSTER, 8 miles (S. S. E.) from Limerick; containing 1346 inhabitants. This place appears to be of considerable antiquity, and its church is said to have been founded by St. Ailbe, Bishop of Emly, in the time of St. Patrick; it would also appear to have attained an early degree of importance, as three castles were erected within its limits. The parish is situated on the river Comogue, by which it is bounded on the south; the mail coach road from Limerick to Cork passes within a quarter of a mile of its western extremity; and it is intersected from north to south by the road from Limerick to Hospital. It comprises 2636 statute acres, as applotted under the tithe act, of which 33 acres are roads and waste, and the remainder arable, pasture, and meadow land, of which last a great portion is frequently overflowed by the river: the western portion is rich grazing land, mostly belonging to large dairy farms, and the greater part of the eastern portion is in the occupation of small farmers, and is generally cultivated by spade labour. A patent for a market and four fairs on May 14th, Aug. 26th, Nov. 6th, and Dec. 21st, was granted to Michael Furnell, Esq. On Mr. Furnell's estate are quarries of very excellent limestone, worked at present chiefly for the proprietor and his tenantry. On this estate are West Cahir Elly castle, and the residence of Mr. Furnell, a neat building in the cottage style, with tastefully disposed grounds, situated near Longford bridge (an ancient structure of nine arches), where are some fine specimens of the moose deer and coins, dug up on the estate; also the residence of Mr. Hannan, in well-planted grounds ornamented with shrubs and evergreens. The living is a vicarage, in the diocese of Emly, and in the patronage of the Archbishop of Cashel; the rectory is appropriate to the vicars choral of the cathedral of Christ-Church, Dublin. The tithes amount to £140, of which £90 is payable to the appropriators, and £50 to the vicar. The glebe, in two detached portions, comprises 9¼ acres, but there is no glebe-house. In the R. C. divisions the parish is the head of the union or district of Ballybricken, which also comprises the parish of Carrigparson; the chapel is a substantial and handsome edifice, recently erected on the site of a former chapel in the townland of Ballybricken. There is a pay school, in which are about 50 boys and 20 girls; and Mr. Furnell has given a site for a national school. Of the three ancient castles, one, called the Black castle, has lately fallen to the ground; West Cahir Elly castle is in perfect and substantial repair; and Ballybricken castle is in ruins. Here are also the ruins of Cahirelly abbey, the burial-ground of which is enclosed and planted, and contains the ancient tomb of the Furnell family.

CAHIRFOSSORGE.—See BALLYNARD.

CAHIRLAG, a parish, in the barony of BARRYMORE, county of CORK, and province of MUNSTER, 6 miles (E. by N.) from Cork; containing 1840 inhabitants. It is situated on the road from Cork to Youghal, and comprises 3530 statute acres, as applotted under the tithe act: nearly one-third is held by private gentlemen, and laid out in lawns, plantations, and pleasure grounds; the remaining two-thirds are almost equally divided between pasture and tillage. The dairy farms furnish Cork and its neighbourhood with a great quantity of butter, which is celebrated for its flavour The tillage is conducted on an improved plan, the Scottish system being generally prevalent; and, from the vicinity of Cork and the sea, an abundance of various kinds of manure is easily obtained. The river Glanmire turns several valuable mills, of which the Glanmire boulting-mill is the property of R. Shaw, Esq.; a steam-engine is being erected for this mill, which will enable it to manufacture more than 25,000 barrels of flour annually. The river is navigable, at spring tides, to the bridge at Lower Glanmire for vessels of 40 tons' burden, which bring up coal, culm, and sea sand, for the supply of the neighbourhood. At Riverstown is a distillery belonging to Messrs. Lyons and Co., which is capable of making 180,000 gallons of spirits annually. The scenery of the parish and its vicinity is pleasingly diversified, and embellished with numerous gentlemen's houses, among which are Dunkettle, the seat of A. Morris, Esq.; Richmond, of R. Mannix, Esq.; Factory Hill, of W. Letchfield, Esq.; Glenville, of E. Newsom, Esq.; Glentown, of Mrs. McCall; Maryborough, of J. Wallis, Esq.; Rockgrove, of Simon Dring, Esq.; Glenburn, of A. Lewis, Esq.; Annmount, of the Rev. Dr. Coghlan; Killora Lodge, of the Rev. R. Berry; Woodville, of N. W. Cummins, Esq.; Killahora, of J. Martin, Esq.; Richmond, of the Rev. W. L. Beaufort; Northesk, of J. Carnegie, Esq.; New Glanmire Lodge, of the Rev. Dr. Collins; and Combermere Cottage, of J. Keane, Esq. The living is a rectory, in the diocese of Cork, united by act of council, in 1785, to the rectories and vicarages of Little Island and Rathcooney, together forming the union and corps of the prebend of Rathcooney, formerly Cahirlag, in the cathedral church of St. Finbarr, Cork the tithes amount to £300. There is a glebe comprising *7a. 3r. 3p.* In the R. C. divisions this parish is the head of a union or district, also called Glauntane or New Glanmire, comprising the parishes of Cahirlag, Little Island, and Kilquane, and containing two chapels, one in the village of New Glanmire, the other in Kilquane. The rents of two farms, one on the lands of Rockgrove, the other on those of Rusgrane, left by the late Rev. Murtagh Keene, formerly P.P. of Glauntane, in trust to the R. C. Bishop of the diocese, and James Cantillon, Esq., of Little Island, are appropriated to the education of poor children of this division, without regard to religious distinction; and a school-house has been built at Glauntane, adjoining the chapel. On a lofty eminence stand the picturesque ruins of the old parish church; and not far distant are the remains of a pagan judgment seat, druids' circle and altar.

CAHIRNARRY, a parish, partly in the barony of CLANWILLIAM, county of LIMERICK, but chiefly in the county of the city of LIMERICK, and province of MUNSTER, 4 miles (S. E.) from Limerick; containing 1939 inhabitants. This parish is situated on the road from Limerick to Charleville, and comprises 1832 statute acres. About one-fourth of the land, which is in general remarkably good, is under tillage; the remainder is rich meadow and pasture land, chiefly grazed by milch cows, whose milk is daily sent to Limerick. Limestone quarries are numerous, all furnishing good stone, which is raised for agricultural purposes. At one of the extremities of the parish is a valuable bog of about 70 acres. A new line of road leading from Limerick to Charleville, and avoiding the hill, has been recently opened. In the village of Ballyneedy is a constabulary police station. The principal seats are Ballyneguard, the residence of J. Croker, Esq.; Cahirnarry House, of J. Cripps, Esq.; Ballyneedy, of J. Fitzgerald, Esq.; and the glebe-house, of the Rev. J. Gabbett: there are also several other excellent houses. The living is a perpetual curacy, in the diocese of Limerick, and in the gift of the Dean; the rectory is part of the union and corps of the deanery of Limerick. The tithes amount to £173. 7. 8., payable to the dean. The curate's income is £75 per annum, paid by the dean; he has also the glebe-house and glebe, for which he pays a nominal rent. The church is a small plain building, with a tower and spire of hewn stone, erected by aid of a gift of £350, in 1810, from the late Board of First Fruits. The glebe-house was erected by aid of a gift of £450, and a loan of £50, from the same Board, in 1813: the glebe comprises five acres. In the R. C. divisions this parish forms part of the union or district of Donoughmore or Knockea. There are two private schools, in which are about 130 children. On the summit of the hill, east of the church, is a small turret, erected by the late John Howley, Esq., in 1821, to commemorate the election of Thomas Spring Rice, Esq., the present Chancellor of the Exchequer, as a member of parliament for the city of Limerick. In the churchyard is a very splendid monument covering a large vault, also erected by Mr. Howley, and in which his remains are interred. From the summit of the hill are some very extensive views; and not far distant from it are the ruined castles of Rathsiward, Drombanny, and Liccadoen.

CAHIRULTAN, a parish, in the barony of IMOKILLY, county of CORK, and province of MUNSTER, contiguous to the town and within the demesne of Castlemartyr. This parish, at a very early period, belonged to the Knights Templars, and subsequently to the Knights Hospitallers; it afterwards merged into the parish of Ballyoughtera, and both appear to have formed the ancient parish of Ballymartyr. It is a rectory, in the diocese of Cloyne, united by an act of the 9th of Anne, cap. 12, with Ballymartyr and Mogeely or Imogeely, under the name of Castlemartyr, and constituting the corps of the prebend of Cahirultan in the cathedral church of St. Colman, Cloyne, in the patronage of the Bishop: the tithes for the whole amount to £435. 12. 7½. The ruins of the old church are in the park of Castlemartyr. The glebe-house and glebe are in the parish of Imogeely; the glebe of the union comprises 22*a.* 3*r.* In the R. C. divisions it forms part of the union of Imogeely, or Castlemartyr.

CAHIRVALLY, or CAHIRVALLAGH, a parish, partly in the barony of CLANWILLIAM, county of LIMERICK, but chiefly in the county of the city of LIMERICK, and province of MUNSTER, 4 miles (S. by E.) from Limerick; containing 1463 inhabitants. This parish is situated on the road from Limerick to Fedamore, and contains 3517 statute acres, as applotted under the tithe act, and valued at £4802 per annum. The land is remarkably good; part of it is under tillage, and the remainder is rich meadow, pasture, and demesne land. There are several large and handsome houses in the neighbourhood, the principal of which are Roxborough, the fine mansion and demesne of the Hon. J. P. Vereker, and Friarstown, the highly improved residence of Vere Hunt, Esq. It is a rectory, in the diocese of Limerick, and is part of the union and corps of the treasurership of the cathedral of Limerick: the tithes amount to £211. 18. The church has long been in ruins and the parishioners resort to that at Kilpeacon. In the R. C. divisions it forms part of the union or district of Donoughmore or Knockea; the chapel is a large and handsome edifice. There is a private school, in which are about 40 children. At Liccadoen is a very good spa, the water of which is strongly impregnated with iron and sulphur, but it is much neglected, and other waters are allowed to mingle with it.

CALARY, a district parish, in the several baronies of BALLINACOR, HALF-RATHDOWN, and NEWCASTLE, county of WICKLOW, and province of LEINSTER, 5 miles (S. S. W.) from Bray; containing 2533 inhabitants. This parish was formed out of the several parishes of Kilmacanogue, Kilcoole, Derralossory, Newcastle, and Powerscourt, in 1831, under the provisions of an act of the 7th and 8th of Geo. IV. It is situated in the rugged table lands which extend southward from the great Sugar Loaf mountain to the vicinity of Roundwood; and lies embosomed between the lower range of hills among which the Downs hill claim pre-eminence, and the more elevated chain of heights above which the lofty Djouce rises in towering grandeur. It comprehends a dreary tract of poor elevated land, bog, and barren mountain, extending on the east to the glen of the Downs, and on the west to Luggelaw, comprising more than 9720 statute acres of productive land, with a large tract of unprofitable waste. The Sugar Loaf mountain rises to the height of 2000 feet above the level of the sea; on the western side its height is apparently diminished by the low range called the Long Hill, which conceals its base. The Djouce mountain has an elevation of 2392 feet, and is conspicuous in every extended view in the north part of the country. The easiest ascent to the summit of this stupendous mass is from the waterfall at Powerscourt; and the view obtained from it is of the most magnificent character. To the west of the Djouce mountain is Luggelaw, a richly verdant vale, beautifully contrasting with the rugged severity and dreary barrenness of the other parts of this wild and romantic district. This delightful place is commonly visited from Roundwood, and has, under the auspices and by the taste of the La Touche family, been rendered one of the most interesting scenes in the county. The approach to it is over the southern shoulder of the Djouce mountain; and on passing the summit of a ridge which previously presented only bold undulations of dark heath clad mountains, a sudden turn of the road presents a fine view of Lough Tay, overshadowed by the vast granite precipice of Carrigemann on the opposite side, rising in rugged cliffs perpendicularly to the height of 1000 feet. A little further, on the opposite side of the road, an opening discloses a fine view of an extensive glen in the mountain, the precipitous sides of which are richly planted to a certain height, above which they are thinly clad with heath. At the head of the glen are some meadows of beautiful verdure, and a fine lawn shaded by overhanging woods, on which is a handsome lodge in the early English style, built by the late David La Touche, Esq., and now the residence of Robert D. La Touche, Esq. The lodge, which is open to visiters by permission of the family, is approached by a road through the wood, near the margin of the lake, a fine sheet of water comprising 72 Irish acres, and abounding with trout and char. On the side above the house a new hanging walk has been constructed among the plantations, commanding a view of the glen and lake below, and a splendid mountain vista across the lower extremity of Lough Dan, terminating in a prospect of the unrivalled mountain of Lugnaquilla. The other seats in the parish are Ballinastoe, that of G. Bentley, Esq.; Mullinavigne, of — Smith, Esq.; Tittour, of J. Nuttal, Esq.; and Whitehall, of Capt. Whitmore. The new line of road from Bray to Roundwood, and the Long hill road from Enniskerry to the same place, pass through the parish; but the latter is little used, as there is a branch communicating with the former, on which Major Beresford has built a very neat hotel. The river Liffey has its source near the War hill, in this parish.

The living is a perpetual curacy, in the diocese of Dublin and Glendalough, instituted by diocesan authority, and in the patronage of the Incumbents of the several parishes of Kilmacanogue and Derralossory, each of whom pays one-third of the curate's stipend of £50 per annum, and has two presentations; and of the Incumbents of Powerscourt and Newcastle, each of whom pays one-sixth, and has one presentation. The church, a neat edifice in the later English style, with a square embattled tower crowned with pinnacles, was built in 1834, on a site near the new line of road, presented by the Earl of Rathdown, and the late Board of First Fruits granted £900 towards its erection; the lower part of the tower is appropriated as a vestry-room. In the R. C. divisions the parish is comprised respectively in the unions or districts of Bray and Powerscourt, Glendalough, and Kilquade. The parochial school is aided by the Earl of Rathdown, who allows a few acres of land rent-free for its support: there is another school at Ballinastoe. In these schools are about 50 boys and 70 girls, and there is also a Sunday school. A dispensary has been lately built at Ballinastoe.

CALEDON, a market and post-town, in the parish of Aughaloo, barony of Dungannon, county of Tyrone, and province of Ulster, 7 miles (W.) from Armagh, and 70 miles (N. N. W.) from Dublin; containing 1079 inhabitants. This town, which was formerly named Kennard, as it is still frequently called by old people, although its manor, markets, and fairs, are all known by the modern name of Caledon, appears to have been more anciently called Aghaloo, it being the head of the parish of that name, and the site of its venerable church, which was destroyed in the insurrection of 1641. It appears to have been an important military post from a very early period, having been the property and principal residence of one of the princely sept of O'Nial. The first direct mention of it is in 1498, when the Lord-Deputy Kildare marched against Mac Art O'Nial, and having defeated and driven him from his strong hold in Kennard, presented the fortress and territory to the British ally, Tirlagh O'Nial, whose descendants seem never to have been found in arms against England, until Sir Phelim O'Nial headed the insurgents in 1641; for, in the settlement under Jas. I., Tirlagh O'Nial had a grant of Kennard, with 4000 acres. Tirlagh built here a bawn of lime and stone, some time prior to 1619, near which he erected a castle. This was afterwards the residence of Sir Phelim, from which he sallied on the evening of the 22nd of October, 1641, having invited himself to supper with Lord Caulfield, at Charlemont. While at the supper table he made Lord Caulfield a prisoner, and having separated his lordship's family and the garrison, carried them prisoners to Kennard, in the castle of which he put his lordship to death. Sir Phelim, who had been educated as a Protestant in England, soon found himself at the head of 30,000 men, and waged a sanguinary warfare against the English. The whole of the county of Tyrone remained in the possession of the insurgents till 1646, when Gen. Munroe, at the head of 6000 foot and 800 horse, marched against the Irish under Owen Roe O'Nial. Having passed through Armagh, Munroe, on the 6th of June, crossed the Blackwater at the ford near Kennard, and fought the battle of Benburb, or, as it is here called, Batterford Bridge, in which he was defeated and many British officers and men were slain.

This town, which is situated on the river Blackwater, and on the road from Armagh to Omagh, was, before 1816, a mean village, but is now, through the exertions of the Earl of Caledon, one of the best built towns in the North of Ireland: it contains 226 houses, nearly all of which are built of stone. The neighbourhood presents gentle swells and fertile vales, producing abundant crops. Close to the town are extensive flour-mills, erected by Lord Caledon in 1823, where above 9000 tons of wheat are ground annually, all of which is grown in the vicinity, where scarcely an acre of wheat was sown at the beginning of the century. The Ulster canal, now in the course of formation, passes through the Earl of Caledon's demesne, a little to the westward of the town. The market is on Saturday, and is well attended; and a fair is held on the second Saturday in every month. A constabulary police force has been stationed here; and there are barracks for the militia. A court for the recovery of debts under 40*s.* is held in the market-house, on the first Monday in each month, for the manor of Caledon, which extends into the parishes of Aughaloo and Clonfeacle, in the county of Tyrone, and of Tynan, in that of Armagh; and petty sessions are held in the town once a fortnight. There are several large and elegant houses in the neighbourhood, the principal of which is Caledon Hill, the seat of the Earl of Caledon, which stands in a richly ornamented demesne of 650 Irish acres, extending beyond the Blackwater into the county of Armagh. Not far distant are Tynan Abbey, the residence of Sir James Stronge, Bart.; Glasslough, of Mrs. Wynne Leslie; Crilley, of R. Pettigrew, Esq.; Rahaghy, of N. Mayne, Esq.; Annagh, of C. Richardson, Esq.; Drummond, of H. Moore, Esq.; and the glebe-house, of the Rev. E. A. Stopford; besides several large and good houses in the town.

The living was made a perpetual curacy in 1807, and 20 acres were then added to the old glebe, which consisted only of 6½ acres: it is in the diocese of Armagh, and patronage of the Archdeacon. The income is £100 per annum, arising from a salary of £50 paid by the archdeacon; £15, the estimated value of 26½ acres of glebe land; and £35. 2., paid by the trustees of Primate Boulter's augmentation fund. The present church occupies the site of the ancient building, and is the parish church of Aughaloo: it was erected by Primate Robinson, in 1767, during the incumbency of the Rev. C. W. Congreave; the spire was built by the present Lord Caledon, by means of a bequest by his late father; and the church was enlarged and otherwise improved by his lordship. It is a large and handsome edifice, in the later English style of architecture, comprising a nave, chancel, and south transept, and for repairing it the Ecclesiastical Commissioners recently granted £175. 8. 11. There are a R. C. chapel and a place of worship for Wesleyan Methodists. The parochial school is situated near the church: it was built in 1776 by Mr. Congreave, and is endowed with 3 acres of land and 3 tenements given by Primate Robinson, and also with £8 per annum by Lord Caledon. Schools at Ramakit, Curlough, Dyan, and Minterburn, are principally supported by Lord Caledon; there are national schools at Rahaghy and Mullinahorn; and near the demesne is a female school built and supported by the Countess of Caledon, in which 40 girls are clothed and educated. Here is a dispensary; and a mendicity association was established in 1829, to which Lord Caledon subscribes £100 per annum. Among the charitable bequests is £100 left by Alex. Pringle, Esq., and vested in the funds, in the name of Lord Caledon; the interest, with that of several smaller sums, is applied to the relief of the poor. Two extensive lakes existed here formerly, one on the north and the other on the south side of the town, with an island in the centre of each; that on the south has been drained and brought into cultivation; the north lake remains, and the island in it, which borders on the glebe is beautifully planted. Almost the last vestiges of the ancient castle of the O'Nials were removed a few years since, and a clump of trees planted to mark the entrance into the courtyard: some of the flooring of the castle was subsequently discovered, about four feet beneath the surface of the ground, in forming the new road to Aughnacloy. Some old swords and other military instruments have been found in the neighbourhood, and are preserved at Caledon Hill. Caledon gives the titles of Baron, Viscount, and Earl to the family of Alexander, in which the proprietorship of the town is vested.—See AUGHALOO.

CALLABEG, or KILNASEAR, also called LOUGHMOE-EAST, a parish, in the barony of ELIOGARTY, county of TIPPERARY, and province of MUNSTER, 2½ miles (S. E.) from Templemore; containing 1600 inhabitants. This parish is situated on the river Suir, which separates it from Loughmoe-West, and on the road from Templemore to Thurles, and comprises 3417 statute acres, as applotted under the tithe act. On the townland of Killahara is a very fine old castle, which formerly belonged to the Purcells, and is now the property of Mr. Trant. It is a rectory and vicarage, in the diocese of Cashel, and is part of the union of Templetuohy and corps of the prebend of Kilbragh in the cathedral of Cashel: the tithes amount to £249. 17. 9. There is a pay school, in which are about 30 boys and 20 girls.

CALLAGHAN'S MILLS, a village, in the parish of KILLURANE, barony of TULLA, county of CLARE, and province of MUNSTER, 3 miles (S. W.) from Tulla: the population is returned with the parish. It is situated on the high road from Six-mile-bridge to Scariff, and about midway on the road from Tulla to Broadford. Fairs are held on May 8th, June 27th, and Nov. 14th. Here is a R. C. chapel of ease to the parochial chapel of Kilkishen, in which a school is also held under the superintendence of the curate.

CALLAN, an incorporated market and post-town, and a parish (formerly a parliamentary borough), partly in the barony of SHILLELOGHER, but chiefly in that of KELLS, county of KILKENNY, and province of LEINSTER, 8 miles (S. by W.) from Kilkenny, and 65½ (S. W. by S.) from Dublin; containing 6112 inhabitants. This is a place of considerable antiquity, and was the territory or ancient inheritance of the O'Glohernys and the O'Coillys or O'Callans: the Fforstalls or Forestalls, Butlers, and Comerfords had fortified castles here, the ruins of some of which yet exist. It was a walled town, as appears from divers grants of murage to the local authorities. In the year 1261, the native sept of McCarty took up arms and here attacked by surprise John Fitzgerald, whom they slew, together with his son Maurice and several knights and other gentlemen of that family: but from the dissensions which subsequently arose among the Irish themselves, the Fitzgeralds recovered their power and possessions here. The Earl of Desmond, in 1345, summoned a parliament to meet at this place, in opposition to that convened by the English deputy; but the vigorous measures enforced by the latter prevented its assembling. In 1405 a battle was fought near the town between James, Earl of Ormonde, lord-deputy, and the Irish under O'Carroll, aided by the sept of the Burkeens, of the county of Tipperary, in which O'Carroll was slain. James, Earl of Ormonde, founded here an Augustinian friary, the origin of which has by some writers been attributed to Hugh De Mapilton, Bishop of Ossory, about the year 1256: the founder died in 1487, and was interred in it; and at the dissolution it was granted, with its possessions, to Thomas, Earl of Ormonde. In the reign of Elizabeth, the celebrated James Fitz-Maurice of Desmond took this town; and in 1650 it fell into the hands of Cromwell, who, aided by Ireton, besieged it for a few days with great loss of life to the inhabitants.

The town is situated on the King's river, and on the mail coach road from Dublin, by way of Clonmel, to Cork: it is chiefly the property of Viscount Clifden, and consists of four streets meeting in the centre, and in point of size ranks the second in the county, but is very indifferently built; the thoroughfares were formerly very bad, but have been improved in the town, though the roads in the vicinity are still much in need of repair. Many years ago, the late Lord Callan introduced some weavers from Carrick-on-Suir, but the project of establishing the manufacture was soon abandoned. There are a large flour and two grist-mills, but the want of employment for the excessive population is very great. The market is held in a small market-house on Tuesday and Saturday; and a large market for pigs is held every Monday from January to May, attended by buyers from Waterford, Kilkenny, Clonmel, and Carrick-on-Suir, and the sales are very extensive. Fairs for the sale of live stock, wool, and, in autumn, considerable quantities of poultry, are held on May 4th, June 13th, July 10th, Aug. 21st, Oct. 10th, Nov. 4th, and Dec. 14th; the May, June, July, and October fairs are the principal. Here is a chief station of the constabulary police.

This appears to be a corporation by prescription; and it is recorded that Wm. Mareschal, or Marshall, granted a charter to it in 1217. A writ of the 4th of Rich. II. (1380) recites that the towns of Callan and Kilkenny were part of the lordship of the Earl of Gloucester, and that all merchants and others within that lordship ought to be free of customs and murage, which immunities the sovereigns and commonalties had enjoyed since the foundation of those towns; and commands that they should not be molested against the tenour of such liberties. Other grants were made in the 19th of Rich. II., 4th of Hen. IV., 11th of Eliz., 7th of Chas. I., and 30th of Geo. III. The corporation is styled "the Sovereign, Burgesses, and Freemen of Callan," and consists of a sovereign and an undefined number of burgesses and freemen, with two bailiffs and a town-clerk. The sovereign is elected annually by the burgesses and freemen: the latter are about 20 in number, and are admitted for life by the corporation at large. The borough sent representatives to the Irish parliament of the 27th of Elizabeth, and thenceforth without intermission until the Union, when it was disfranchised, and the £15,000 awarded in compensation for the abolition of its electoral rights was paid to George, Lord Callan. The town court is held before the sovereign or his deputy generally every Monday, but sometimes on other days, for the recovery of debts not exceeding 40*s.* late currency. The limits of the borough include the entire town and a considerable space round it, but extend unequally in different directions, from half a mile to nearly two miles. The corporation has a small property in lands and houses, let for about £15 per annum, but derives its principal revenue from the customs, which on an average yield about £50 per annum.

The parish comprises 4700 statute acres, as applotted under the tithe act, and valued at £5798 per annum; about 600 acres were enclosed under an act in 1831. The whole is capable of tillage, and, with very trifling exceptions, is in cultivation; vast quantities of limestone are procured and burnt for manure. West Court, situated in a very neat demesne and surrounded by trees of stately growth, is the residence of the Rev. C. Butler Stephenson, the rector; it formerly belonged to Lord Callan, and prior to that was the property of the Earl of Desart. The living is a rectory and vicarage, in the diocese of Ossory, united by act of council, in 1763, to the rectories and vicarages of Tullaroan, Tullamain, Coolaghmore, Killaloe, and Ballycallan, together forming the union of Callan, in the alternate patronage of the Crown and the Marquess of Ormonde. The tithes amount to £550, and of the entire benefice to £2338. 19. 10. There are two churches in the union, one at Callan, and the other at Ballycallan. The parish church, which was very extensive, was formerly occupied by Canons Regular of the order of St. Augustine, under an abbot: the ante-chapel is in ruins, but displays two windows of beautiful design and in good preservation, and there are several tombstones of considerable antiquity, some of which are elaborately carved, with a handsome monument to the Comerfords; the Ecclesiastical Commissioners have recently granted £393 for the repairs of this church. The church at Ballycallan, distant about four miles, is a small edifice, built about 60 years since at the request of several of the inhabitants. There is no glebe-house: the glebe lands of the union are in divers places, and comprise 32 acres. In the ante-chapel at Callan was a shrine under the invocation of the Holy Trinity and St. Catherine, for the purpose of saying mass for the repose of the noble family of Desart: this foundation still exists as a chaplaincy, in the gift of the Earl of Desart; it has no cure of souls, but the chaplain is required to attend visitations. In the R. C. divisions this parish is partly in the union or district of Ballycallan; and the remainder forms the head of a union, comprising also the parishes of Coolaghmore, Tullamain, Earlstown, and part of that of Kells, called Mallardstown. The latter union or district contains three parochial chapels, situated respectively at Callan, Newtown, and Coologh. The chapel at Callan is a spacious edifice, not quite finished, in the southern part of the town; the interior is very neat, and the ceiling is chastely and handsomely carved. The chapel or (as it is called) church of the Augustinian friary was erected through the exertions of the very Rev. John Rice, at an expense of £4000: the building, which was commenced in 1810 and completed in a few years, is of hewn stone, in the ancient English style of architecture, and has a beautifully groined ceiling: the altar-piece is the copy of a design by Dominichini, by an Italian artist; and on each side of the altar is a niche, in which it is intended to place two marble statues, now in progress of execution at Rome by Mr. Hogan. The chapel is situated on the declivity of a hill; and in the basement story are apartments for the clergymen, harmonising with the general design of the building, and fronting a small lawn environed by gravel walks enclosed between fences of beech trees, and bounded by the King's river, which is crossed by a neat wooden bridge leading into the abbey field, in which are situated the venerable ruins of the ancient friary, consisting principally of a tower 90 feet high. The friary is occupied by three Augustinian friars of a different order from the Canons Regular previously noticed. The Protestant parochial school, in which are about 20 boys and 20 girls, is aided by donations from Lord Clifden and the incumbent, who also contribute to the support of a sewing school. A national school, in which on an average 212 boys daily attend, is endowed with 25 acres, parcel of the late commons, by the act of 1831; and another has been lately opened for girls, of whom 167 daily attend on an average. There are also several private schools in the parish. A dispensary is maintained in the customary manner; and a loan fund has been lately established. Callan gives the title of Viscount in the peerage of Ireland to the family of Feilding, Earls of Denbigh, in right of their superior title of Earl of Desmond.

CALLIAGHSTOWN, a parish, in the barony of NEWCASTLE, county of DUBLIN, and province of LEIN-

STER, contiguous to the post-town of Rathcoole; containing 67 inhabitants. It is situated on the road from Dublin to Naas, and comprises about 972 statute acres of arable and pasture land. For all civil purposes it is considered a townland in the parish of Rathcoole, and even in ecclesiastical affairs is regarded only as a chapelry in that parish. It is a rectory and vicarage, in the diocese of Dublin, forming part of the union of Rathcoole, in which its tithes are included.

CALRY, or COLRY, a parish, in the barony of UPPER CARBERY, county of SLIGO, and province of CONNAUGHT; containing, with a part of the borough and sea-port town of Sligo, 6247 inhabitants, of which number 3741 are within the borough of Sligo. This parish is situated on the river Garvogue, which separates it from the parish of St. John, in its course from Lough Gill to the sea, and on the roads from Ballyshannon and Enniskillen to Sligo. It contains 4383 statute acres, as applotted under the tithe act: the land is generally light, with a small quantity of bog and some mountain wastes, and is principally under tillage; the state of agriculture is improving; there is an abundance of limestone, which is used for building. The manufacture of linen was formerly carried on extensively, but few are now employed in it. Lough Gill, part of which is in the parish, is an extensive and beautiful sheet of water, about a mile and a half from Sligo, with which it is connected by the river Garvogue, that is navigable for large boats seven or eight miles. The scenery is very romantic, and is greatly embellished with the highly cultivated demesne of Hazlewood, the handsome residence of Owen Wynne, Esq. The lough is studded with islands, of which Church and Cottage islands are the largest. At Hollywell is another demesne belonging to Mr. Wynne, from which mountains covered with wood, the lake with its numerous islands, and the road sometimes running under stupendous rocks and sometimes through small planted glens, present scenes of great beauty. The other seats are Percy Mount, that of Sir Percy Gethin, Bart; Colga House, of T. Homan, Esq.; Ballyglass, of Gowan Gilmore, Esq.; Faught's Cottage, of R. Christian, Esq.; Willsboro', of W. Fausset, Esq.; Willybrook, of the Ormsby family; Barroe House, of Holles Clarke, Esq.; Rathbracken Cottage, of W. Christian, Esq.; Mount Shannon, of H. H. Slade, Esq.; Shannon, of Edward Patterson, Esq.; the Cottage, of J. Gethin, Esq.; Ballyternin House, of Mrs. Griffiths; and Ellenville, of H. Irwin, Esq., M.D.

The living consists of a vicarage and perpetual curacy, in the diocese of Elphin, the former being part of the union of St. John's, Sligo, and the latter in the patronage of the Incumbent of St. John's; the rectory is appropriate to the vicars choral of the cathedral of Christ-Church, Dublin. The tithes amount to £353. 11. 7., payable in moieties to the vicars choral and the vicar. The income of the perpetual curacy amounts to £73. 1. 6., arising from £23. 1. 6. paid by the Ecclesiastical Commissioners, and £50 from the vicars choral. The church, belonging to the perpetual cure, is a handsome structure in the later English style, with a beautiful spire: it was built by aid of a gift and loan from the late Board of First Fruits, in 1823. The glebe-house was also built by aid of a gift of £112 and a loan of £37, in 1821, from the same Board. In the R. C. divisions this parish forms part of the union or district of Sligo; the chapel is at Colga. Here are a school established and supported by the trustees of Erasmus Smith's charity; a female parochial school at Calry; and a school at Ballin, which was built by John Wynne, Esq., at an expense of £250, and supported by that gentleman. About 120 boys and 70 girls are educated in these schools; and there are also a private school of about 50 boys and 30 girls, and five Sunday schools. The part of the parish that is within the town of Sligo contains the county infirmary, fever hospital, and dispensary. The remains of antiquity consist of the Sod fort, which was defended by Sir Teague O'Regan against Wm. III., the ruins of some churches in Church and Cottage islands, and what are supposed to be druidical remains in Mr. Wynne's park at Hazlewood.

CALTRA, or CALTRAGH, a village, in the parish of CASTLE-BLAKENEY, barony of KILCONNELL, county of GALWAY, and province of CONNAUGHT, 1 mile (E.) from Castle-Blakeney; containing 200 inhabitants. It is situated on the road from Tuam to Ballinasloe, and has four fairs, which are held on May 14th, July 16th, Sept. 21st, and Dec. 14th.

CALVERSTOWN, a village, in the parish of DAVIDSTOWN, barony of NARRAGH and RHEBAN EAST, county of KILDARE, and province of LEINSTER, 1 mile (N.) from Ballytore; containing 22 houses and 150 inhabitants. It is situated on the road from Dublin to Carlow, and has two fairs on May 1st and Sept. 21st.

CALVES ISLANDS, in the parishes of KILCOE and SKULL, barony of WEST CARBERY, county of CORK, and province of MUNSTER, 6 miles (S. W.) from Ballydehob; containing 86 inhabitants. They are three in number, and are situated at the entrance to Roaringwater bay, off the harbour of Skull: the largest, called the Middle Calf, contains 78 statute acres; the second in size, called the East Calf, contains 75 acres; and the third, called Leacrer, or the West Calf, 65 acres. There are two families in West Calf, and six in Middle Calf, which belong to the parish of Skull, and five families in East Calf, which forms part of the parish of Kilcoe. The islands are contiguous, lying in a line nearly east and west, about midway between Cape Clear and Long island, and about 5 Irish or 6¼ British miles from the mainland. A school was established in 1835 on the Middle island, in which all the children and adults of these islands may receive gratuitous education; 18 children and 14 adults were in this school at the commencement of 1836.

CAMLIN, or CRUMLIN, a parish, in the barony of UPPER MASSAREENE, county of ANTRIM, and province of ULSTER; containing, with the post-town of Crumlin, 1274 inhabitants. This parish is situated on Lough Neagh, by which it is bounded on the west, and on the road from Antrim to Lurgan; it comprises, according to the Ordnance survey, 6417¼ statute acres, of which 5455 are applotted under the tithe act, and 708¼ form part of the lake. About three-fourths of the parish are good arable land, and the remainder is pasture. The system of agriculture is greatly improved, and the whole of the parish is in an excellent state of cultivation, and is well fenced, drained, and planted: wheat, which was scarcely raised in the district, has, since the establishment of large flour-mills at Crumlin, been extensively cultivated, and now forms the principal feature in its agriculture. Limestone is extensively quarried for agricultural and other purposes. The principal seats are Thistleborough, that of James Whittle, Esq.; Gobrana, of J. Whitla, Esq.; and Cherry Valley, of C. W. Armstrong, Esq. Independently of agricultural pursuits, several hundreds of the population are employed in weaving linens and cottons for the manufacturers of Belfast and its neighbourhood; here are also a flax and a flour-mill. Fairs are held monthly for cattle and pigs, and of late very valuable horses have been sold. It is a vicarage, in the diocese of Connor, and is part of the union of Glenavy; the rectory is impropriate in the Marquess of Hertford. The tithes amount to £195, of which £43. 5. is payable to the impropriator, and £151. 15. to the incumbent. The church is a fine ruin; it was destroyed by the army of Jas. II., who had its depôt here in 1689: in the north and south walls are series of sepulchral arches continued the entire length of the building, and nearly in a perfect state. In the R. C. divisions also it forms part of the union or district of Glenavy. There is a place of worship for Presbyterians in connection with the Remonstrant Synod, of the second class. The parochial school is supported by the vicar; and a school is supported by the Hon. Col. Pakenham, who erected for it a large and handsome school-house, and occasionally provides clothing for the scholars. In these schools are about 90 boys and 60 girls; and there are also three pay schools, in which are about 60 boys and 50 girls, and three Sunday schools. Dr. William Crawford, author of " Remarks on Chesterfield's Letters," " History of Ireland," and other works; and Adam Crawford, Esq., M.D., author of an " Experimental Essay on Animal Heat," and compiler of the transactions of the Royal Society, were natives of Crumlin, *which see.*

CAMLOUGH, an ecclesiastical district, in the barony of UPPER ORIOR, county of ARMAGH, and province of ULSTER, 3 miles (W.) from Newry; containing 5822 inhabitants. This was anciently part of the O'Hanlons' country, and at the general plantation of Ulster, 1000 acres, or 12 townlands, with the manor of Maghernahely, were granted to Henry Mac Shane O'Nial for life, and after his death to Sir Toby Caulfield, who built an extensive bawn of stone and lime at Maghernahely, on the site of an ancient church. At Corrinchigo, in this district, Sir John Davis had at the same time a grant of 500 acres; but neglecting to plant or tenant the allotment, it was resumed and granted to Sir Oliver St. John, and is now the property of Viscount Mandeville. Camlough was formerly part of the extensive parish of Killevey, which, for ecclesiastical purposes, was divided into two parts in 1773. It is situated on the road from Newry to Newtown-Hamilton, and on a lake called Camlough, or " the Crooked Lough;" and comprises 10,176 statute acres, of which 2415 are mountain and bog, and 144 lake and water. The greater portion of the land is remarkably good, and in an excellent state of cultivation. Much of the mountain land cannot be brought into cultivation, although in many places there is sufficient depth of soil for the growth of forest trees. Near the village is the lake from which it derives its name, a fine sheet of water comprising 90 acres, a stream issuing from which flows in a northern direction to the Newry water, and gives motion to the machinery of several corn and flour, flax, spinning, and scutch-mills, besides beetling-engines, spade manufactories, and bleach-greens. At Bessbrook are very extensive mills for spinning linen yarn, worked by steam and water, and furnishing employment to 180 persons. Here are also two spade-forges, and two extensive bleach-greens but only the beetling-engines of the last are at present employed. A fair is held on the third Monday in each month; and a constabulary police force has been stationed here. There are several large and handsome houses in the district, the chief of which are Divernagh House, the residence of J. White, Esq., and Bessbrook, of J. Nicholson, Esq.

The living is a perpetual curacy, in the diocese of Armagh, and in the patronage of the Precentor of the cathedral church of St. Patrick, Armagh: the curate's income is derived from the tithes of five-townlands, amounting to £146. 2. 10. The church is a small edifice, with a tower and low spire, and is one of the numerous churches built by Primate Robinson; it was erected in 1774, but not consecrated till 1785, and the Ecclesiastical Commissioners have recently granted £150. 5. 9. for its repair. The glebe-house is situated at Ballintemple, three miles from the church, on a glebe of 80 statute acres: it was built in 1805, for which the late Board of First Fruits granted £150. In the R. C. divisions this is the head of a union or district, also called Carrickcruppin, comprising Camlough and part of the parish of Killevey, and containing three chapels, two in Camlough, situated respectively at Carrickcruppin and Lisslea, and the third at Killevey. A school at Sturgan, under the trustees of Erasmus Smith's charity, is endowed with £30 per ann., and with two acres of land and a residence for the master. There are a school of 65 children at Maghernahely, and one of 80 at Divernagh; a school at Corrinchigo was built and is supported by Lord Mandeville; and a handsome school-house has been lately built in the village, in connection with the National Board, aided by the noble proprietor, the Earl of Charlemont. In the townland of Aughnacloghmullan there is an extraordinary cairn, 44 yards in length by 22 in breadth: it contains a chamber, 19 yards long, and divided into four compartments, and is formed of upright stones, about seven feet high, surmounted by very large stone slabs, the whole covered with loose stones and earth. The walls of the bawn erected by Sir Toby Caulfield remain almost entire, and exhibit many of the hewn stones of the ancient abbey of Killevey. A little eastward of these walls stands the shaft of an elegant cross, of which the rest lies in a ditch. Some of the mullions of the windows of the abbey are seen in the walls at Divernagh; and an elegant silver medal was found near its site, and is now in the possession of W. W. Algeo, Esq. The Rev. H. Boyd, translator of Dante's " Divina Comedia," was perpetual curate of this parish.

CAMMA, a parish, in the barony of ATHLONE, county of ROSCOMMON, and province of CONNAUGHT, 8 miles (W. N. W.) from Athlone; containing 4115 inhabitants. It is situated on the road from Athlone to Mount-Talbot, and comprises 10,114 statute acres, as applotted under the tithe act. The land is chiefly under tillage; there are about 648 acres of bog, but no waste land; the system of agriculture is improving; limestone is quarried for agriculture and other uses. The principal seats are Lysterfield, that of J. Lyster, Esq.; Curraboy House, of J. Byrne, Esq.; and Milltown, of G. King,

Esq. It is a vicarage, in the diocese of Elphin, and is part of the union of Kiltoom; the rectory is impropriate in Lord Kingsland. The tithes amount to £195, of which £85 is payable to the impropriator, and £110 to the incumbent. In the R. C. divisions it is the head of a union or district, including also the parish of Kiltoom; there is a chapel at Curraboy, and also one in the parish of Kiltoom. At Carrick is a national school, in which are about 80 boys and 30 girls; and there are four pay schools, in which are about 160 boys and 70 girls. Only the ruins of the old parish church, with a burial-ground, remain; and there are some ruins of the old castle of Curraboy, built by the Dillons, near which are several raths or forts.

CAMOLIN, a post-town, in the parish of TOMB, barony of SCARAWALSH, county of WEXFORD, and province of LEINSTER, 20¾ miles (N.) from Wexford, and 53¾ (S.) from Dublin; containing 639 inhabitants. This place derives its name from a religious house founded, according to Alban Butler, by St. Molin, second Bishop of Ferns, who died in the 7th century, and of which there are still some remains on the Mountnorris estate. It is situated on the river Bann, on the mail coach road from Gorey to Wexford, and contains 112 houses. Immediately adjoining is Park View, the residence of H. Parke, Esq. A constabulary police force is stationed here; and fairs for cattle and pigs are held on Feb. 9th, April 4th, June 9th (which is the principal fair), Aug. 9th, Sept. 28th, and Nov. 9th. The parish church of Tomb, and the R. C. chapel of the district of Camolin, are situated in the village; and there is a dispensary.—See TOMB.

CAMUS-juxta-BANN.—See MACOSQUIN.

CAMUS-juxta-MORNE, a parish, in the barony of STRABANE, county of TYRONE, and province of ULSTER; containing, with part of the town of Strabane, 6570 inhabitants. This parish, which is situated on the old road from Dublin to Londonderry, and on the river Morne, comprises, according to the Ordnance survey (including 20¾ acres in Lyons island), 7505¾ statute acres, of which 103¾ are water, about 4540 are arable and pasture land, and the remainder mountain and bog; 6743 acres are applotted under the tithe act, and valued at £3078 per annum. The land, although in some places rocky, is generally very fertile, producing abundant crops, particularly in the vale of Morne. The inhabitants combine the weaving of linen with their agricultural pursuits. The principal houses are Milltown Lodge, the residence of Major Humphries, and the glebe-house, of the Rev. J. Smith. The living is a rectory, in the diocese of Derry, and in the patronage of the Bishop: the tithes amount to £468. The church is in the town of Strabane, and is a large and handsome edifice, for the repairs of which the Ecclesiastical Commissioners have recently granted £184. 4. 2.: it was originally built as a chapel for the new town of Strabane, by the Earl of Abercorn, in 1619, and has been used as the parish church since the destruction of the mother church, about the middle of the 17th century. The glebe-house was built by aid of a gift of £100 and a loan of £800 from the late Board of First Fruits, in 1832, upon the townland of Bierney, which constitutes the glebe, comprising 300 acres, and is more than three miles from the church. In the R. C. divisions the parish is the head of a union or district called Clonleigh and Camus, and comprising both those parishes: there are two chapels in the union, of which that of Camus, in the town of Strabane, is a large plain edifice. There is a large meeting-house for Presbyterians in connection with the Synod of Ulster, of the first class; and there are places of worship for Wesleyan and Primitive Methodists. The parochial school, on the glebe of Bierney, is supported by the trustees of Erasmus Smith's charity, and the master has a rent-free residence and two acres of land. At Milltown is a school for boys and girls, erected by the Marquess of Abercorn, a large and handsome building, with a separate residence for the master and mistress, each of whom receives £20 a year from the Marquess, who also aids a school established at Edymon; and there is a national school at Strabane. About 160 boys and 100 girls are educated in these schools. Prior to 1829 a blue-coat school existed here, with an income of £30 per annum, which sum is now applied to clothing 12 boys. Near Milltown school are the dispensary and fever hospital belonging to Strabane; they are large and well ventilated buildings, admirably arranged for their purposes. The ruins of the old parish church are situated on the banks of the Mourne: it was founded by St. Colgan in 586, and destroyed during the insurrection of 1641.—See STRABANE.

CANICE (ST.).—See KILKENNY.

CANNAWAY, or CANNABOY, a parish, in the barony of EAST MUSKERRY, county of CORK, and province of MUNSTER; containing, with the village and post-town of Killinardrish, 1518 inhabitants. This parish is situated on the south side of the river Lee, and is connected with the parish of Macroom by a noble bridge at Coolcour, and with that of Magourne by the ancient bridge of Carrigadrohid. It contains 5414 statute acres, as applotted under the tithe act, and valued at £4274 per annum. There are about 300 acres of woodland, 100 of bog, and a good deal of rocky waste; the remainder is almost equally divided between pasture and arable land, the latter producing good crops; there are also some dairy farms, the butter from which is sent to Cork market. At Barnateampul is a tract of bog, which supplies the inhabitants with fuel. The river Lee here flows with great rapidity, particularly after heavy rains, when it inundates the adjacent country to a considerable distance. The scenery presents an alternation of rock and meadow, the latter receding into small deep glens covered with wood, which produce a very pleasing effect. The principal seats are Killinardrish House, the residence of R. Crooke, Esq.; Nettleville Hall, of R. Neville Nettles, Esq.; Llandangan, of S. Penrose, Esq.; Rockbridge Cottage, of Lieut.-Col. White; Forest, of T. Gollock, Esq.; Oak Grove, of J. Bowen, Esq.; Coolalta, of W. Furlong, Esq.; and an elegant Italian lodge, lately built by R. J. O'Donoghue, Esq. Petty sessions are held at Shandangan every alternate Wednesday.

The living is a vicarage, in the diocese of Cork, and in the patronage of the Bishop; the rectory is part of the union of Kilcoan and corps of the prebend of Killaspigmullane, in the cathedral church of St. Finbarr, Cork. The tithes amount to £267. 6. 1¾., of which £55 is payable to the prebendary, and the remainder to the vicar. The church is a plain building, with a lofty square tower, on a high hill about a mile and a half west of Killinardrish; its erection was aided by a gift of £600 from the late Board of First Fruits, in 1814. There is no glebe-house, but a glebe of about five acres. In the R. C. divisions this parish forms part of the union or district of Kilmurry; there is a neat chapel at Barnateampul. The male and female parochial school is chiefly supported by the vicar, as is also the Sunday school.—See KILLINARDRISH.

CANON ISLAND, or INNISNEGANANAGH, an island, in the parish of KILDYSART, barony of CLONDERLAW, county of CLARE, and province of MUNSTER, about 1½ mile (E.) from Kildysart: the population is returned with the parish. It is situated at the confluence of the Shannon and Fergus, about ¾ of a mile from the shore, and contains 207 acres of excellent land, partly under tillage, the sea-weed collected on its shores being used as manure. It was anciently called *Elanagranoch;* and here Donald O'Brien, king of Limerick, in the 12th century, founded or rebuilt a priory for Canons Regular of the order of St. Augustine. A moiety of the priory, with the various lands, tithes, profits, and demesne lands thereof, was granted in fee, in 1605, to Donogh, Earl of Thomond, and was afterwards granted in fee, or confirmed, to his successor, Henry, in 1661. The ruins, which are situated at the north-eastern extremity of the island, consist of a square tower and a considerable portion of the body of the building, which is said to have covered a quarter of an acre.

CAPE CLEAR ISLAND, a parish, in the Eastern Division of the barony of WEST CARBERY, county of CORK, and province of MUNSTER, 16 miles (S. by W.) from Skibbereen; containing 1059 inhabitants. This island, called by the Irish *Innish Dharnley*, and in ecclesiastical records *Insula Sanctæ Claræ*, though at a much greater distance from the mainland, may be regarded as the principal of a large cluster of islands in the Atlantic ocean, lying off the coast of Carbery, and situated between Dundedy Head and Brow Head, which latter was the *Notium* of Ptolemy. It is separated from the mainland by the sound of Gaskenane, in which is always a strong tide, and in high winds a very heavy sea; and having, consequently, less intercourse with it than the islands nearer the coast, the native inhabitants have retained more of their original manners, language, and customs. The island, which is now the property of Sir William Wrixon Becher, Bart., is three miles in length and one mile and a half in breadth, and comprehends 17 town-lands comprising 1400 acres, of which 649 are subdivided into 137 small farms of about 5 acres each, and about 200 acres are arable and the remainder rough pasture land. The soil is shallow and would be unproductive, but for a careful system of cultivation, entirely performed by the women, and wholly with the spade. The chief crops are oats and potatoes; the quantities raised in some seasons are inadequate to the supply of the inhabitants: the manure is sand and seaweed, which the women collect upon the strand, and carry on their backs up the steep and dangerous cliffs that surround the island, which is accessible only by two small harbours by which it is nearly intersected from north to south. The chief supply of fuel is brought from the mainland, as the island itself affords none, except what is made of a black mud found near the western lake, and baked during the summer; the inhabitants suffer extreme privations in winter from the scarcity of fuel. Flax is grown in some parts and spun into yarn, and coarse woollen cloths are manufactured, for domestic use which, instead of being thickened by mills, are put into pools of water and trampled by the younger and more active females. All the more elevated parts of the island are of the schistus formation, but in several parts, near the level of the sea, good freestone is found in abundance.

The scenery is extremely wild and romantic, particularly on the south side of the island, where it presents to the Atlantic a steep and inaccessible cliff. At the south-west point of the island, overhanging the sea, and accessible only by a narrow and dangerous pathway, not more than three feet in breadth, are the ruins of Dunanore castle, or the "Golden Fort," which, from its distance from all the landing places, would appear to have been built more for the purpose of a safe retreat in case of invasion, than for the defence of the shores: the view from the battlements is very extensive, and embraces a great variety of objects of a bold and imposing character. In the south-western part are three fresh water lakes, one called Lough Erral, the water of which has a saponaceous and powerfully detersive quality, cleansing in a short time any vessel that may be thrown into it; this water, which is used for washing and for cleaning flax, has been analysed by Dr. Rutty and found to contain a portion of natron, to which he attributes its cleansing properties. There is also a lake near the western coast, remarkable for the number and size of its eels; and there are numerous springs of excellent fresh water in several parts. The men are wholly employed in fishing, for which the island is admirably adapted: they leave home every Monday or Tuesday morning during the summer season, and return on Friday evening or Saturday morning. Their fishing craft and tackle have been much improved since the establishment of the late Fishery Board: they now go out to sea in hookers, or half-decked vessels, to the distance of 20 or 30 leagues. On their return, the fish are given to the women to cure, and the men generally spend their time in leisure and recreation till the day of their departure next. The fish, when cured, is sold to retail merchants who visit the island for that purpose; and should any remain unsold, it is sent to the Cork market. The men are expert and resolute seamen, and the best pilots on the coast; they are remarkable for discerning land at a distance in snowy or foggy weather, possess an uncommon sagacity in discovering the approach of bad weather, and are exceedingly skilful in the management of their vessels. The inhabitants seldom leave home unless to sell their fish, or to supply themselves with necessaries from the mainland. The cattle and sheep are very small, and there are only four horses on the island. The wool is exceedingly fine, which is attributable to the pasturage, as sheep brought in from the mainland produce in a short time a fleece of excellent quality. A good harbour has been formed, and a neat pier constructed on the south side of the island, at the joint expense of Sir W. W. Becher, Bart., and the late Fishery Board.

Cape Clear is well known to mariners as a conspicuous landmark. On the south side of the island is a lighthouse, erected by the corporation for improving the port of Dublin; it exhibits a bright revolving light of 21 lamps, of which, seven become visible every two minutes; the lantern has an elevation of 480 feet above the level of the sea, and in clear weather the light may be seen from all points at a distance of 28 nautical miles. Adjoining the lighthouse is the signal tower, erected after the attempt of the French to land at Bantry bay, and purchased by the above corporation. On the north side of the island, and about a quarter of a mile from the shore, vessels may anchor in moderate weather. About four miles (W.) from Cape Clear is Fastnet rock, famous for the quantities of ling, hake, &c., taken near it. According to the census of 1831, there were 206 houses occupied by 200 families; the houses are mostly built of stone and thatched; and from the unsheltered situation of the island, exposed to every raging blast; the inhabitants are obliged to secure the thatch on the roofs by an interwoven covering of netting or matting kept down by heavy stones. There is a coast-guard station on the island.

It is a vicarage, in the diocese of Ross, and is part of the union of Kilcoe; the rectory is impropriate in Sir W. W. Becher, Bart. The tithes amount to £34, of which one-half is payable to the impropriator, and one-half to the vicar. There is neither church nor glebe-house; divine service is occasionally performed in the tower of the lighthouse. The glebe, on which are the ruins of an ancient church, comprises 25*a.* 3*r.* 26*p.* In the R. C. divisions this island is the head of a union or district, comprising also the island of Innisherkin, and containing in each a chapel, of which the chapel here is a small thatched building. There is a national school, in which are about 40 boys and 20 girls. Not far from the harbour are the ruins of St. Kiaran s church; on the shore is an ancient stone with a cross rudely sculptured on it, and at a short distance a holy well. Till about the year 1710, the islanders had a resident king chosen by and from among themselves, and an ancient code of laws handed down by tradition, which it was his duty to administer; and though the king had neither funds for the maintenance of his dignity, nor officers to enforce his authority, the people generally submitted voluntarily to these laws, and were always ready to carry his judgments into execution. The greater number of the laws are become obsolete, but some still remain and are enforced with rigour. The island was formerly remarkable for a race of men of extraordinary stature and strength, whose feats are the subject of many interesting narratives. The O'Driscolls, several of whom were kings of the island, were the most celebrated; they had large possessions and held five or six castles in different parts of the country, which were all forfeited in the insurrection of 1601, after which they emigrated to Spain, leaving behind them only their dependents, whose posterity have long since mingled with the peasantry.

CAPELL, or CABLE ISLAND, in the parish of Kilmacdonough, barony of Imokilly, county of Cork, and province of Munster, 5 miles (S.) from Youghal. This island, which is uninhabited, lies at the entrance to Youghal bay, off Ring Point, in lat. 51° 53′ 30″, and lon. 7° 51′ 30″. Being high and precipitous, it is difficult of access, except in calm weather; its south-western side has been much excavated by the waves, and at the base of some of the cliffs are huge detached masses of rock. It is the property of the Marquess of Thomond, and contains about 30 acres of excellent pasturage for sheep. Its elevation and central position point it out as an admirable situation for a lighthouse, which would be of great benefit to vessels entering Youghal bay and to the trade of Cork harbour. On this island the Capells, or Supples, as they are called in Irish, are said to have landed at the period of the first English invasion, and from them it takes its name, although it is laid down in most charts and maps as Cable Island; but so early as the reign of Rich. III., and frequently since, it is mentioned in the charters of Youghal as Capell Island, having been made one of the boundaries of the admiralty jurisdiction and port of Youghal, as well by land as by water.

CAPPACLOUGH, a village, in the parish of Kilgobbin, barony of Corkaguiney, county of Kerry, and province of Munster, about 9 miles (W. S. W.) from Tralee; containing 419 inhabitants. It is situated on the old road from Tralee to Dingle, and contains the ruins of the old R. C. chapel, which gives name to the parochial district; a new chapel has been built near the village, at Camp, where are the ruins of an old castle.

CAPPAGH, or CAPPA, a parish, in the Shanid Division of the barony of Lower Connello, county of Limerick, and province of Munster, 4 miles (W.) from Adare; containing 694 inhabitants. This parish is situated on the road from Adare to Shanagolden, and comprises 1124 statute acres, as applotted under the tithe act. The soil in some parts is good, but a great proportion of the parish is stony, and in some places the limestone rock rises above the surface; on its border, next to Rathkeale, are some exhausted bogs. The village is a station of the constabulary police; and not far from it is Cappagh House, the residence of R. Peppard, Esq. It is a rectory and vicarage, in the diocese of Limerick, and is part of the union of St. Mary and corps of the deanery of Limerick: the tithes amount to £95. The church is in ruins, and there is no glebe-house, but a glebe comprising above eight acres. In the R. C. divisions it forms part of the union or district of Stonehall and Cappagh; the chapel is a large plain thatched edifice. There is a private school of 50 children in the parish. Near Cappagh House are the ruins of Cappagh castle, built by Dermod Mac Einery in the reign of King John, and having fallen into the hands of the Geraldines it shared the fate of their numerous other castles, being confiscated for their rebellion against Queen Elizabeth; it stands on an artificial mound, and the ruins are 90 feet high and form an interesting feature of the landscape.

CAPPAGH, a parish, partly in the barony of Omagh, but chiefly in that of Strabane, county of Tyrone, and province of Ulster, 2 miles (N.) from Omagh; containing, with the district parish of Mountfield, 13,589 inhabitants. This parish, according to the Ordnance survey, comprises 37,670½ statute acres, of which 34,626¾ are in Strabane, and 3043¾ in Omagh; the applotment under the tithe act embraces 16,097 acres, and 266¾ are water. The greater part of the land is reclaimed bog or mountain, and about 1500 acres are woodland: in some places the land is remarkably good, particularly in the eastern part of the parish, but not more than one-fourth is cultivated. Part of the mountains of Bessy Bell, Mary Gray, and Mullaghcairn are in this parish, and afford good pasturage for cattle to their very summits. The inhabitants combine with agricultural pursuits the spinning of flax and weaving of linen. There is abundance of freestone, with limestone of inferior quality, and several indications of coal are met with. Gortin gap, through which a road runs from Omagh to Gortin, is a deep ravine stretching in a northern and southern direction through Mullaghcairn or Cairntogher, which is the highest mountain in the county. There are several handsome houses in the parish, the principal of which are Mountjoy Cottage, the residence of C. J. Gardiner, Esq.; Mount Pleasant, of the Rev. C. Cregan; Facary Lodge, of Sir W. McMahon, Bart.; Mountfield Lodge, of the Rev. Mr. Stack; Lislimanahan, of Capt. Hill; Lisanally, of G. Norris, Esq.; Millbank, of H. Peebles, Esq.; Mullaghmore, of R. Burges, Esq; and Ergennagh glebe-house, of the Rev. H. H. Harte. The improvements made during the last 50 years are very extensive; the late Lord Mountjoy commenced planting the demesne of Rash, now called Mountjoy Forest, in 1780, and much of the timber is large and very promising. The late Sir W. McMahon built a very handsome house, surrounded by extensive plantations, at Facary, and also laid out a town at Mountfield, where markets and fairs will be held. A new road has been opened through the parish, direct from Omagh to Belfast.

The living is a rectory, in the diocese of Derry, and in the patronage of the Provost and Fellows of Trinity College, Dublin: the tithes amount to £1000. The church is a large and handsome edifice, in the Grecian style, with a lofty and beautiful octagonal spire: it was erected in Mountjoy Forest, in 1768, at the sole expense of Dr. Gibson, then rector. The glebe-house is being rebuilt upon an enlarged scale: the glebe consists of 573 acres, about half a mile from the church, and of two other portions containing 999 acres, making a total of 1572 acres, only 410 of which are under cultivation. There is a chapel of ease at Mountfield, four miles from the church; it is a small but very beautiful edifice, with a lofty spire, standing on the south side of a high mountain, and was built at an expense of £1000 by the late Board of First Fruits, in 1828: the living is a perpetual curacy, endowed with £25 per ann. from Primate Boulter's fund, and in the gift of the Rector. Divine service is also performed, every second Sunday, in the school-houses of Calkill, Carrigan, Castletown, Taercur, and Mayne. The R. C. parish is co-extensive with that of the Established Church, and has two chapels, one at Knockmoyle, the other at Killyclogher. There are places of worship for Baptists and Presbyterians of the Synod of Ulster, the latter of the third class. The male and female parochial schools are situated on the glebe, and are supported by the rector, who has given the master a house and three acres of land. Mountfield male and female schools were supported by the late Sir W. McMahon; a school at Knockmoyle was founded under the will of John McEvoy, who endowed it with £16 per annum, for the gratuitous education of the poor children in Mountjoy Forest, and vested its management in the Rector for ever. There are also schools at Carrigan, Taercur, Killynure, Common, Crevenagh, and Lislap; six under the National Board, at Castlerody, Killyclogher, Carrigan, Tetraconaght, Beltony, and Rathcarsan; and other schools at Edenderry, Calkill, and Drummullard. In these schools are about 770 boys and 450 girls; and there are also four private schools, containing about 90 boys and 40 girls, and six Sunday schools. The ruins of the old church are scarcely discernible, but the cemetery is much used. There are several forts on Mary Gray mountain, close to each other.

CAPPAGHWHITE, a village, in the parish of Toom, barony of Kilnemanagh, county of Tipperary, and province of Munster, 6½ miles (N.) from Tipperary; containing 695 inhabitants. This place, which has been much improved within the last forty years, and contains 115 houses, is situated on the new line of road from Tipperary to Nenagh, to the former of which it has a penny post. It is a constabulary police station; fairs are held on June 4th, July 27th, Sept. 29th, Nov. 16th, and Dec. 21st; and there are a R. C. chapel and a dispensary. Cappagh House is the residence of Mrs. Fitzmaurice Hunt. Five hundred acres of land near the village were, about seven years since, leased by Col. Purefoy to the Mining Company of Ireland, who after incurring some expense in searching for copper, relinquished the enterprise.

CAPPAMORE, or TUORAGH, a village, partly in the parish of Doon, and partly in that of Tuoragh, barony of Owneybeg, county of Limerick, and province of Munster, 10 miles (S. E.) from Limerick; containing 711 inhabitants. This village is situated near the banks of the small river Mulcairn, over which is a handsome stone bridge, and on the road from Limerick to Templemore; it consists chiefly of two irregularly built streets. Fairs are held on April 20th, July 1st, Sept. 20th, and Dec. 12th, for cattle and pigs. A spacious chapel is now in progress of erection for the R. C. district of Cappamore, which includes the parish of Tuoragh and part of the parishes of Doon and Abington.

CAPPANACOSS, or CAPPANACUSH, the chief of a group of islands of that name, in the parish of Templenoe, barony of Dunkerron, county of Kerry, and province of Munster, about 3 miles (S. W. by W.) from Kenmare: the population is included in the return for the parish. It is situated in the river Kenmare, and consists entirely of limestone rock, in some places approaching to a grey marble, and said to have been formerly worked by Sir William Petty, ancestor of the Marquess of Lansdowne. About a British mile west of the island are the Roancarrig rocks, so called from the number of seals that frequent them.

CAPPOG, or KIPPOGUE, a parish, in the barony of Ardee, county of Louth, and province of Leinster, 1 mile (N.) from Dunleer; containing 542 inhabitants, of which number, 128 are in the village. This parish is situated on the road from Drogheda to Dundalk, and comprises, according to the Ordnance survey, 1283½ statute acres, partly pasture but chiefly arable land. It is a rectory, in the diocese of Armagh, and constitutes part of the union of Dunleer: the tithes amount to £127. 11. In the R. C. divisions it is also part of the union or district of Dunleer.

CAPPOQUIN, a post-town, in the parish of Lismore, barony of Coshmore, county of Waterford, and province of Munster, 30¾ miles (W. S. W.) from Waterford, and 106½ (S. W. by S.) from Dublin; containing 2289 inhabitants. This place is of considerable antiquity, and had anciently a castle supposed to have been erected by the Fitzgerald family, but at what period is unknown. In the war of 1641, this castle was garrisoned by the Earl of Cork; and in 1642, Lord Broghill, on his return from the relief of Knockmoane with about 60 horse and

140 foot, defeated a party of the insurgents who were strongly posted in its vicinity, and, with the loss of only one man of his party, killed 200 of them and two of their captains. In July, 1643, Gen. Purcell, having assembled his army at this place to besiege Lismore, ravaged the surrounding country; and, in 1645, the castle was taken by Lord Castlehaven after an obstinate defence. The Earl of Cork built a bridge over the river at this place, and in the 17th and 18th of Chas. II., an act was passed for building a new bridge. The town is pleasantly situated on the northern bank of the river Blackwater, in the angle from which it takes its course southerly to Youghal, and on the mail coach road from Waterford, through Youghal, to Cork. The navigation is continued by a canal to Lismore, and several new roads have been formed on the best levels diverging from the town, opening an improved communication with the adjoining counties. A road has also been constructed along the western bank of the river to Youghal; and it is intended to take down the present bridge, which is a light structure of wood, and replace it with a substantial building of stone. The surrounding country is finely diversified, and abounds with highly picturesque scenery. Near the town is the seat of Sir R. Keane, Bart., a handsome mansion of hewn stone, situated in a richly improved, and well planted demesne, commanding a fine view of Dromana and the river Blackwater. Fairs are held in the town on March 17th, May 31st, July 5th, Sept. 20th, and Oct. 29th. A constabulary police force has been stationed here, and petty sessions are held once a fortnight.

The church, which is a chapel of ease to the church of Lismore, from which it is 2½ miles distant, is a neat edifice with a spire; and near it is a R. C. chapel. There is a school under the Cork Society for supporting Schools in Munster, for which a neat school-house of stone has been erected, at an expense of £250; and a dispensary is supported. At Mount Melleray, near the town, is the abbey of St. Bernard la Trappe, recently erected in the midst of a large mountainous tract, previously a barren wild, granted for that purpose to the society on very liberal terms by Sir R. Keane, Bart. The monastery encloses a quadrangular area, on three sides of which are ranges of building, 162 feet in length, 30 feet broad, and 32 feet high, containing a dormitory, kitchen, chapter-room, sacristy, and other apartments; and on the fourth side is the church of the monastery, 185 feet in length, 30 feet wide in the nave, 52 feet in the transept, and 50 feet high, with a tower surmounted by a spire of wood sheeted with copper painted to imitate stone, 140 feet high from the ground. Great improvements have been made in the land; 120 acres of the mountain have been reclaimed, and fencing, draining, and the making of roads have been extensively carried on; about eight acres have been enclosed for a kitchen garden, producing excellent vegetables; and more than 30,000 trees have been planted, most of which are flourishing. The monks have opened a school for the poor of the neighbourhood, and intend also to establish an agricultural school.

CARAGH, or CAROGH, a parish, in the barony of CLANE, county of KILDARE, and province of LEINSTER, 3 miles (N. W.) from Naas; containing 1031 inhabitants. This parish, of which the name is sometimes written Kerogh, is situated on the river Liffey, and on the turnpike-road from Naas to Edenderry. The soil is fertile; the land is chiefly in the occupation of private gentlemen, and is in a state of excellent cultivation. Clover, turnips, and other green crops are raised with success, and the potatoes are all drilled; there is neither waste land nor bog in the parish, but fuel is obtained in abundance from bogs in the immediate vicinity. Donore, the spacious mansion of W. Hussey Burgh, Esq., was built by the late Walter Hussey, Esq., grandfather of the present proprietor, who afterwards took the name of Burgh, and was appointed chief baron of the Irish Exchequer. Yeomanstown, the seat of W. H. Mansfield, Esq., is also in this parish. On the river Liffey are the Yeomanstown mills, capable of manufacturing from 6000 to 7000 barrels of flour annually. The living consists of a rectory and vicarage, in the diocese of Kildare; the rectory is united to the vicarage of Naas; and the vicarage was episcopally united, in 1764, to the entire rectory of Bridechurch and the vicarage of Downings, together forming the union of Caragh, in the patronage of the Bishop. The tithes amount to £205, of which £136. 13. 4. is payable to the rector, and £68. 6. 8. to the vicar. There is at present no church in the union; but a grant of £900 was made by the late Board of First Fruits for the erection of one; in the mean time, divine service is performed in a house at Downings, licensed by the Bishop. There is neither glebe-house nor glebe. In the R. C. divisions this parish is the head of a union or district, including also the parishes of Downings and Ladytown: the chapel is a neat modern edifice, near the site of the old parish church; there is also a chapel at Prosperous. A school-house has been built by subscription, on a site presented by A. Mansfield, Esq., for a school in connection with the National Board, in which are about 120 boys and 90 girls.

CARBERY, an island, in the parish of SKULL, Western Division of the barony of WEST CARBERY, county of CORK, and province of MUNSTER, 16 miles (S. W.) from Bantry; containing 4 inhabitants. This small island is situated in Dunmanus bay, and comprises only six acres of land: it is very little frequented, although large ships may ride in summer on good ground any where above it, and there is excellent anchorage to the west of the island.

CARBERY, or CASTLE-CARBERY, a parish, in the barony of CARBERY, county of KILDARE, and province of LEINSTER, 3¼ miles (E. N. E.) from Edenderry; containing 1476 inhabitants, of which number, 159 are in the village. This place derives its name from an ancient castle, of which there are some remains, situated on a lofty isolated hill, and which was, early in the 14th century, a seat of the Bermingham family, of whom Sir William Bermingham, Knt., was created Baron of Carbery, in 1541. It was afterwards the property of the family of Colley or Cowley, ancestors of the present noble family of Wellesley; and in 1783, Arthur Pomeroy, Esq., having married an heiress of that house, obtained the title of Lord Harberton, of Carbery, and was afterwards created Viscount Harberton. The parish is situated at the north-western extremity of the county, on the confines of the King's county, near the source of the river Boyne, and on the verge of the Bog of Allen, which is here bounded by abrupt eminences of limestone: the greater portion of the land is arable, and some of the farms wholly under tillage. Newberry, the seat of Viscount Harberton, is in the immediate vicinity of the village. The other seats in the parish are Drummin House, the residence of R. Grattan, Esq., M.D.; Ballyhagan, of Miss Palmer; and Newberry House, of E. Wolstenholme, Esq. The village consists of 27 dwellings; it is a constabulary police station; and fairs are held on May 26th and Oct. 2nd. The living is a vicarage, in the diocese of Kildare, united to those of Nurney, Ballynadrimna, Cadamstown, Dunfert, Mylerstown, Ardkill, and Carrick, together forming the union of Carbery, in the patronage of Lord Harberton; the rectory is impropriate in the Marquess of Downshire. The tithes amount to £133. 19. 4¾., of which £89. 6. 3¼. is payable to the impropriator, and £44. 13. 1½. to the vicar; and the gross tithes of the benefice amount to £303. 13. 5½. The church is a neat plain edifice, with a square tower. There is no glebe-house; the glebe comprises 3¾ acres in several detached portions. In the R. C. divisions this parish is partly in the union or district of Ballina, and partly the head of a union, comprising also the parishes of Dunfert, Ardkill, and Kilmore, in which are two chapels, one here and one at Dunfert; the former is a plain building in good repair. The parochial school, in which are about 40 boys and 20 girls, is supported by subscription; and there are two pay schools, in which are about 60 boys and 30 girls. The ruins of the castle consist chiefly of a square pile of building with tall chimneys, apparently of the time of Hen. VIII.

CARDANGAN, or CURDANGAN, a parish, in the barony of Clanwilliam, county of Tipperary, and province of Munster; containing, with part of the town of Tipperary, 2345 inhabitants. This parish is situated on the road from Tipperary to the glen of Aherlow, and extends into a plain which for its fertility and beauty is called the Golden Vale: it contains some of the richest land in Ireland, although occasionally alternated with heathy mountain. The principal seats are Brookville, that of J. Sadleir, Esq., and Ballyglass, of Mrs. Slattery. It is a vicarage, in the diocese of Emly, and is part of the union and corps of the prebend of Lattin in the cathedral of Emly; the rectory is impropriate in Wm. Moore, Esq. The tithes amount to £153. 15., of which £102. 10. is payable to the impropriator, and £51. 5. to the vicar. In the R. C. divisions also it is part of the union or district of Lattin. Here is a free school under the trustees of Erasmus Smith's charity, which is more particularly noticed in the article on Tipperary, also a pay school, in which are about 30 boys and 10 girls.

CARGAN, or CARRIGIN, a parish, in the barony of Clare, county of Galway, and province of Connaught, 3¼ miles (S. W.) from Headford, on the eastern shore of Lough Corrib; containing 1214 inhabitants. It is a rectory and vicarage, in the diocese of Tuam, and is part of the union of Headford: the tithes amount to £103. 10. 7. In the R. C. divisions also it forms part of the union or district of Headford. At Ballyconlaght there is a daily pay school of 60 boys and 14 girls.

CARGINS, or CARRAGANS, an extra-parochial district, in the barony of Upper Orior, county of Armagh, and province of Ulster, 6 miles (N. W.) from Dundalk; containing 355 inhabitants. This place is situated on the road from Newtown-Hamilton to Dundalk, and in the midst of a mountainous district: it comprises 503 acres, of which more than 100 are mountain, half of which is barren rock; the land in cultivation is of a light friable nature, producing good crops. The Irish language only is spoken. There is a pay school, in which are about 35 children.

CARLANSTOWN, a village, in the parish of Kilbeg, barony of Lower Kells, county of Meath, and province of Leinster, 2½ miles (N.E.) from Kells; containing 293 inhabitants. It is situated on the road from Bailieborough to Dublin, by Navan, and in 1833 comprised 53 houses. Fairs are held on March 12th, May 1st, Aug. 6th, and Nov. 19th; the last is for fat cattle, and is considered the largest and best of the kind in the county. Sir H. Meredyth, Bart., the proprietor, intends making considerable improvements in the village. The R. C. parochial chapel is situated here.—See Kilbeg.

Arms.

CARLINGFORD, a seaport, market and post-town, and a parish (formerly a parliamentary borough), in the barony of Lower Dundalk, county of Louth, and province of Leinster, 11½ miles (E. by N.) from Dundalk, and 59¾ (N.) from Dublin; containing 12,185 inhabitants, of which number, 1319 are in the town. This town appears to have originated in the erection of a castle, either by De Lacy or De Courcy, by order of King John, in 1210, but is mentioned by some authorities as the place where St. Patrick, in 432, effected his second landing; and the ferry of Carlingford was granted by Sir John de Courcy, in the year 1184, to the abbey of Downpatrick. The town, which gradually rose in the neighbourhood of the castle, appears to have consisted chiefly of castellated buildings, arising from its situation on the frontier of the pale.. In 1301, Matilda de Lacy, widow of David, Baron of Naas, granted the advowson of the church to the priory of Kilmainham; and in 1305, Richard de Burgo, Earl of Ulster, founded a monastery for Dominicans here, dedicated to St. Malachy. Edw. II., in 1358, granted to his son, Lionel, Earl of Ulster, licence to hold a weekly market on Thursday, and a yearly fair here for six days. In 1404, the manor of Carlingford and town of Irish-Grange, which had previously belonged to the abbey and convent of Newry, vested by forfeiture in the king, who granted them in fee to Richard Sedgrave. A mint was established here in 1467, by act of parliament; and in 1495 it was enacted that Englishmen only should be constables of the castle. In 1596, Henry Oge, son-in-law of the Earl of Tyrone, notwithstanding the submission made and pledges given by that nobleman to Queen Elizabeth, made an attempt to surprise the castle, but was defeated. Sir Henry Tichbourne took possession of the town in 1642, not, however, before it had suffered much injury by fire, from the adherents of Sir Phelim O'Nial. In 1649, Lord Inchiquin, after taking Dundalk, marched to this place, and compelled the castle, with other neighbouring fortresses, to surrender; but in the following year it was delivered up to Sir Charles Coote and Col. Venables. A party of the forces of Jas. II., in 1689, set fire to the town, in their retreat before the army of Duke Schomberg, who, in consequence, issued a proclamation threatening that, if such conduct were repeated, he should give no quarter. During the duke's encampment at Dundalk, and while disease was spreading through his forces, the sick were removed into Carlingford, until they became too numerous to be accommodated.

The town is beautifully situated on the south-west side of the spacious lough or bay to which it gives name, and immediately at the base of an extensive range of mountains which terminates at this point. It consists of 288 houses, and, though small, has an interesting appearance, from the venerable ruins of its castle and abbey; it has a sub-post-office to Newry. The scenery of the bay is remarkably fine: the Mourne mountains, on the opposite side, are beautifully varied with rocks, woods, heath, and verdure; and in the foreground the shores are enlivened with neat cottages and numerous bathing-lodges. Carlingford mountain, which overhangs the castle, attains, according to the Ordnance survey, an elevation of 1935 feet above the level of the sea: from its height and position it intercepts, during a great part of the summer, the direct rays of the sun, for several hours before sunset. The oysters found in the bay are highly esteemed, and are sent in great quantities to Dublin, Liverpool, and other places. There is some trade in grain, great quantities of herrings are caught during the season, and fishing nets are made. The port has also some trade with Dublin, to which it sends large quantities of potatoes; and coal is imported from Scotland and Whitehaven. The bay, one of the finest natural havens on the coast, is eight miles in length and about four in breadth, extending inland, in a north-western direction, to Warren Point. The tide flows past the town to the port of Newry, and the harbour is accessible to large vessels at spring tides, but near the mouth the navigation is rendered rather hazardous by shoals and sunken rocks. A lighthouse at Cranfield Point on the northern side of the bay has been removed, and one, showing a bright fixed light, has been erected in its stead on Hawlbowling rock; at half-tide it shows, at night, an additional light halfway up the building; in the day, a black ball is hoisted on the top of a pole, 10 or 12 feet above the lantern, and in thick or foggy weather a bell is kept continually tolling by clock-work. On Greenore Point also a small lighthouse with a revolving light has been erected. The harbour dues are collected in the name of the Marquess of Anglesey, as lord of the manor, and admiral of Carlingford bay; they are leased for £20 per annum. The market is on Saturday; fairs are held on the first Saturday in each month, and there is also one on Sept. 29th. There are a coast-guard and a chief constabulary police station in the town, also three coast-guard stations at Cooley Point, Greenore Point, and O'Meath.

This is a borough of very great antiquity, probably by prescription. A corporation is recognised so early as 1326, when the king granted to the bailiffs of "Karlyngford" a charter for levying murage for six years, to enclose the town with a stone wall. By patent dated the 13th of March, 1409, Hen. IV., on the petition of the corporation, representing that the town had been often burned and wasted by the Irish and Scotch, acquitted them of all subsidies, tollages, &c., for several years; and for the same reasons, customs were granted to them, for 24 years from 1501, towards fortifying the town with a stone wall. Queen Elizabeth granted by charter, in 1571, extensive privileges and immunities. The governing charter, dated the 9th of August, 17th of Jas. I. (1619), creates a sovereign, 12 burgesses, and a commonalty of six, giving them authority over the whole of Carlingford and its liberties, with the exception of the castle of Arthur Bagenal, lord of the manor and its appurtenances. This charter declared that the corporation should be styled the "Sovereign, Burgesses, and Commonalty of the Town and Borough of Carlingford;" and should consist of a sovereign, twelve burgesses, and an unlimited number of freemen; two serjeants-at-mace and a coroner, a clerk of the market, and clerk of the entries, were also to be appointed. The sovereign is elected by and from among the burgesses, on Sept. 29th, and is a justice of the peace within the borough; he has the power of appointing a deputy, subject to the approbation of the burgesses. The burgesses are elected out of the commonalty for life, by the existing burgesses, and in conjunction with the sovereign possess the power of admitting freemen and appointing the corporation officers. As the admission of freemen was optional with them, none have been admitted since 1754. The sovereign and burgesses returned two members to the Irish Parliament prior to the Union, when the £15,000 paid as compensation for the loss of the franchise was divided equally between the Marquess of Downshire and the guardians of Mr. Ross Balfour Moore. The limits of the borough are reputed to extend about 2 miles on the north, and $1\frac{3}{4}$ mile on the south, side of the town, along the sea shore, and from the top of a ridge of mountains rising immediately behind it to the shore of the bay. A borough and manor court, formerly held here, have been discontinued; and the borough gaol, called "the blackhole," under the tholsel, has been disused for many years. Petty sessions are held on alternate Saturdays. The corporation has no property, except what they may be entitled to in commons belonging to the town, which, according to the Down survey, contained 1231 acres; and the only officer now appointed is the sovereign.

The parish comprises, according to the Ordnance survey, $20,049\frac{3}{4}$ statute acres, of which $65\frac{1}{4}$ are water. The commonage extends along the side of a mountain, some part of which is enclosed, and on which the poor of the neighbourhood graze their cattle. The land in Cooley is of very superior quality and under a good system of tillage, particularly the farms of R. De Verdon, Esq., and those of Wilville and Ballug; there is no bog, and fuel is consequently scarce. Near the town are some extensive limestone quarries, the produce of which is principally sent northward. Nootka Lodge is the residence of Hugh Moore, Esq., and commands a fine view of the sea and the Mourne mountains. Among the other seats are Grange, the residence of T. Gernon, Esq.; Monksland House, of R. De Vernon, Esq.; Wilville House, of J. Gernon, Esq.; Castleview, of W. Moore, Esq.; Balley Castle, of John Parks, Esq.; and O'Meath, of John Bell, Esq. The living is a vicarage, in the diocese of Armagh, and in the patronage of the Archbishop, to whom the rectorial tithes are appropriate: the tithes amount to £457, of which £152. 6. 8. is paid to the archbishop, and £304. 13. 4. to the vicar. The church is a modern building, with the exception of the tower. A new glebe-house was built by aid of a loan of £750 from the late Board of First Fruits, in

1813: the glebe, in its immediate vicinity, comprises about 21 acres. In the R. C. divisions this parish forms the two unions or districts of Carlingford and Cooley, comprising four chapels, those of Carlingford and O'Meath in the former, and of Grange and Mullabay in the latter; the chapels of Carlingford and Grange are neat buildings, and that at O'Meath was built on a plot of ground given by the Marquess of Anglesey, who also contributed £30 towards the expense. There is also, in the town, a place of worship for Presbyterians of the Remonstrant Synod, of the third class. The parochial school for boys and girls is aided by an annual donation from the vicar; and there are two schools for the children of Roman Catholics on the estate of the Marquess of Anglesey at O'Meath, which are partly supported by him. These schools afford instruction to about 100 boys and 60 girls; and there are also twelve hedge schools, in which are 340 boys and 160 girls. A considerable sum has been contributed by Alex. Hamilton, Esq., towards the erection of a school-house, which has been built on a piece of ground belonging to the lord-primate, and is under the superintendence of the curate. It is also in contemplation to establish a school in the vicinity of the R. C. chapel at Carlingford, and another at O'Meath, in connection with the National Board of Education. Here is a dispensary.

The remains of the Dominican monastery consist principally of the walls of the conventual church, with a square tower supported on lofty pointed arches, and separating the nave from the chancel; at the west end of the nave are two turrets, connected by a battlement, and on the south is a small detached ruin, probably a chapel. These ruins, which are situated at the extremity of the town farthest from the castle, being overgrown with ivy, have a very interesting and romantic appearance. On the summit of a neighbouring hill, at Ruskey, are small remains of a church, or chapel, with traces of a burial-ground, but no monuments or even graves: it is thought to have been a rural residence of the abbot. About halfway between the abbey and the castle are the ruins of a square building, with windows of an ecclesiastical character, curiously ornamented with sculptures of animals, human heads, and foliage. The remains of the castle, called King John's castle, shew it to have been an irregular pile of building, nearly in the form of a horse-shoe: the walls in some parts are eleven feet thick, and some of the salient points are defended by loophole abutments; it is washed by the sea on the eastern side, and on the land side is a narrow pass overhung by wild and lofty mountains. The castle seems to have been erected to command this pass, and it enclosed various baronial halls and apartments, and a courtyard surrounded with galleries: the chief entrance is on the side next the sea, from a platform on which was apparently a battery for the defence of the harbour. The pass is only wide enough to allow a very small number of men to walk abreast: on one side of it the mountain rises abruptly, and on the other are dangerous precipices with the sea below. At Templetown are the ruins of an ancient church, with a burial-ground attached; near which are the remains of the castle of Ballug, a square pile of building with very thick walls, defended at the opposite angles by square turrets; the lower part has been converted into stables, and the upper into corn-lofts. Carlingford formerly gave the title of Earl to the family of Taaffe, which becoming extinct on the death of Theobald, the 4th Earl, in 1738, Geo. III., in 1761, conferred the title of Viscount Carlingford on the family of Carpenter, together with that of Earl of Tyrconnel.

CARLOW, an inland county of the province of LEINSTER, bounded on the east by the counties of Wicklow and Wexford, on the north by those of Kildare and Wicklow, on the west by the Queen's county and Kilkenny, and on the south by that of Wexford. It extends from 52° 26′ to 52° 54′ (N. Lat.), and from 6° 30′ to 7° 12′ (W. Lon.); and comprises an area, according to the Ordnance survey, of 219,863 acres, of which 196,833 are cultivated land, and 23,030 mountain and bog. The population, in 1821, was 78,952, and in 1831, 81,988.

This district, so far as can be collected from Ptolemy, was the habitation of the *Brigantes* and *Cauci*; or, according to Whitaker, of the *Coriundi*. Afterwards it formed the northern part of the principality of *Hy Kinselagh*, and was distinguished by the name of *Hy Cabanagh* and *Hy Drone*: in later times it was called *Catherlough*. It is noticed in the earliest period of Irish history as the scene of contention between Conmal, son of Heber, and grandson of Milesius, and a descendant of Heremon, the latter of whom was defeated at Leighlin. When Con of the Hundred Battles, who reigned about the middle of the second century, divided the island into two jurisdictions, Dinrigh or Dewa Slaney, between Carlow and Leighlin, and Naas in Kildare, were made the sites of the royal palaces of the kingdom of Leinster. No traces of ruins, however, now exist to confirm the truth of this traditionary record, with respect to the former of those places. The synod of the clergy held about the year 630, to decide on the proper time for the celebration of Easter, met at St. Gobhan's abbey, in Old Leighlin; and about the same time the bishoprick, which takes its name from that place, was founded. That the county shared with the other parts of the island in the devastations committed by the Danes, during the ninth and tenth centuries, appears from the fact that the rich abbey of Achadfinglas was plundered by them in 864. The year 908 was distinguished by a decisive battle between the people of Leinster and those of Munster, the latter headed by Cormac Mac-Cuillenan, better known as the writer of the Psalter of Cashel than by his political or military acts: the scene of this battle was at Moyalbe, supposed by O'Halloran and Lanigan to be somewhere in the vicinity of Ballymoon, in this county; the Munster men were defeated, and Cormac, with many of his nobles and officers, and six thousand of his best soldiers, slain. In the same century, the monastery of St. Mullins was plundered by the Danes, and Leighlin was three times taken by the people of Ossory. After the arrival of the English, it appears that some of the petty chieftains of the district refused to join in the alliance formed by Dermot Mac Murrough, their king, with the Welsh invaders. For, when Strongbow, after having dispersed the numerous army with which Roderic, King of Ireland, had invested Dublin, marched southward to relieve Fitz-Stephen, then blocked up in Carrig castle, near Wexford, he was assailed during his passage through Hy Drone by O'Ryan, the lord of the country, with such impetuosity that victory remained doubtful, until the death of the Irish leader turned the scale in favour of the invaders. It was in this battle that Strongbow is said to have hewn his son, a youth about fifteen years of age, in two, for deserting his post during the engagement. The importance attached by the conquerors to the possession of the territory thus acquired is evident from the fact that, within a few years after, the castles of Carlow, Leighlin, and Tullow, were erected by Hugh de Lacy, then lord-deputy. After the death of William, Earl-Marshal, to whom nearly the whole of Leinster belonged in right of his wife Isabel, daughter of Strongbow by Eva, princess of Leinster and heiress of Dermot Mac Murrough, this vast estate was divided among his five daughters; and the palatinate of Carlow, which had been previously made one of the twelve counties into which King John divided all those parts of Ireland that acknowledged his government devolved by marriage on Hugh le Bigod, Earl of Norfolk, who thus became earl-marshal and lord of Carlow, in right of his wife Maud, eldest daughter of the deceased. For many subsequent years the English kept possession of these border districts by a very frail tenure. At the close of the thirteenth century, Old Leighlin was burnt in an incursion of the people of the neighbouring territory of Slieumargy, which was then considered to be part of the county; and, at the commencement of the next century, it appears that the owners of this princely estate, the palatinate of Carlow, having also large possessions in England, paid but little attention to its interests. Residing in another country, and finding their income from this quarter diminishing, in consequence of the mismanagement of their deputies and the disturbed state of the country, they had recourse to a remedy, which, however effectual at first, ultimately proved destructive to their interests in this quarter. They retained one of the Kavanaghs, the descendants of Mac Murrough, and, though illegitimate, the inheritor of his hereditary rights, as a kind of military agent, to supply by the sword the deficiencies of the law. Kavanagh, thus placed in a situation peculiarly tempting to a turbulent and ambitious character, soon broke the connection, and seized upon a great portion of Carlow and Wexford, as belonging to him of right: he further assumed the regal title of Mac Murrough, and strengthened his newly acquired power by an alliance with the O'Byrnes and O'Tooles of the neighbouring mountainous district of Wicklow. In 1316, Sir Edmund Butler, lord-justice, defeated Mac Murrough near Ballylethan; and the same year was marked by the incursion of Edward Bruce into the southern counties. But though the invader passed through Castledermot and Tullow, in his progress southward, he made no impression on this county; and, that it still continued subject in a great degree to the sway of the Kavanaghs may be inferred from the circumstance that, in 1323, Donnell Mac Arthur Mac Murrough, "a slip of the royal family," as Campion calls him, raised forces and displayed his banner within two miles of the city of Dublin. He paid dearly, however, for his temerity, being defeated by a party of the garrison. O'Nolan, dynast of Forth barony, and twenty-five of his followers were killed; and Mac Murrough's life was spared only on payment of £200, a large sum in those days; after remaining six years immured in Dublin castle, he at length contrived to effect his escape through the connivance of his keeper.

After this the Irish enjoyed the ascendancy for some time; they plundered the English and burnt their churches. One outrage was marked with features of peculiar atrocity. The church of Freineston, or Friarstown, was attacked during the time of divine service, the building fired, and the priest and congregation, while attempting to escape, driven back into the flames. The spiritual as well as temporal power was called into action to inflict punishment for this horrid act. It was visited by a sentence of excommunication from the pope; and the burghers of Wexford, aided by others of the English, having attacked the perpetrators when preparing to advance upon the English settlement there, routed them with considerable loss both in the field and in crossing the Slaney. The depredations of the Irish borderers at this period called for the most decisive measures, as a preliminary for which it was deemed expedient to summon the most distinguished nobles and prelates to a council in England. But such was the reduced state of the county, from the long continuance of deeds of outrage, that the return to the writ of summons states that, "by reason of poverty, from the frequent robberies and depredations of the Irish enemies, there was no layman able to attend the king in the English council." It appears further that a temporary protection from the predatory assaults of the borders could only be procured by the degrading payment of a tribute called the Black Rent. In 1332, the castle of Clonmore was taken by the English, yet, notwithstanding the advantage thus gained, Sir John D'Arcy, the lord-justice, could devise no more effective means for repressing the spirit of insubordination than by calling in the assistance of Maurice Fitzgerald, afterwards Earl of Desmond, whose services were purchased by a promise of remuneration from the treasury, and whose compliance changed the aspect of affairs. Advancing against the Mac Murroughs and O'Nolans, he ravaged their district, compelled their submission, and exacted hostages for its continuance. But the most disastrous effects were produced by this connection; the lord-justice, unable to fulfil his pecuniary engagements, was forced to connive at the extortion of coyn and livery, now first practised by the English; a grievance the more intolerable, as it was limited neither in place nor time. Every lord of a castle, or warden of the marches, made war at his pleasure, until the desolation became universal and threatened to be perpetual. Still, however, the Irish, though worsted on most occasions, were in arms. In 1339, the Earl of Kildare pursued the O'Dempseys across the Barrow; and the greatest booty ever seized in the country was carried from Idrone, by the Bishop of Hereford, then lord-justice. In 1346, the county of Carlow, with all its appurtenances, was granted *in capite* to Thomas de Brotherton, Earl of Norfolk and Marshal of England. The next year, Donald Mac Murrough, styled Prince of Leinster, was murdered by his own followers: some years after, the castles of Kilbelle, Galbarstown, and Rathlyn were taken and dismantled by the O'Nolans, the Mac Murroughs, and the O'Birnes. In 1361, Lionel, the king's son, arrived in Ireland as lord-lieutenant. The importance attached by him to the possession of this district is shown by his causing the king's exchequer to be removed to Carlow town, and by his expending the large sum of £500 on the repairs of its fortifications. But the neglect of the English Government and the intestine feuds of the natives had been suffered to ferment too long to admit of an effectual remedy by the exertions of any single governor. To such a height had the power of the Irish chieftains increased that, within a very few years, the boundary of the pale was transferred from Carlow to the immediate vicinity of Dublin. The system of ravage and desolation continued. The annals of the time state that the priory of Old Leighlin, being situated in a depopulated and wasted country, obtained a grant of public money to enable it to give refuge and succour to the king's subjects; and that the bishop of the diocese was plundered of all his goods, in 1376, by the insurgents; also that, in 1389, he obtained a grant of Galroestown, near the O'Tooles' country, as a residence in lieu of his own, which had been rendered uninhabitable.

When Richard II. first visited Ireland, in 1394, the place selected by him to receive the homage and oaths of fidelity of the Irish was in an open field at Ballygorey, near Carlow, when Malachias and Arthur Mac Murrough, Gerald O'Birne, Donald O'Nolan, and others, swore fealty before the earl-marshal on bended knees, and without girdle, skein, or cap. Pensions on this occasion were granted to several of them, especially to Art Mac Murrough, chief of the Kavanaghs, whose grant was continued to his family till the time of Henry VIII. Yet hardly had the king quitted the country, when the Irish again asserted the independence they had so long struggled to maintain; and Richard, determined to effect the complete subjugation of the country, returned thither in 1399. He marched from Waterford to Dublin through the districts of the Mac Murroughs, Kavanaghs, O'Tooles, and O'Byrnes; but, in consequence of the severe pressure on his men from want of provisions, he performed no action worthy of notice beyond that of felling considerable quantities of timber, and clearing the highways through his line of march. The state of affairs in England compelled his speedy departure. In 1420, in order to make up a subsidy of 1000 marks voted to the king, the county of Carlow was assessed at four marks, one shilling and fourpence; while that of Louth, nearly of the same area, was charged with twenty-five marks, twelve shillings and fivepence; a convincing proof of the low ebb to which the former had been reduced by its internal distractions. In 1494, the brother of the Earl of Kildare, then strongly suspected of treasonable intentions, seized on Carlow castle, but was compelled by the lord-deputy to surrender it, after sustaining a siege of ten days. Lord Thomas Fitzgerald, better known by the name of "the Silken Knight," who broke out into rebellion against Henry VIII. in 1534, was in possession of six of the chief castles of the kingdom, of which Carlow was one. Three years afterwards, the act of Absentees was passed, in consequence of which the Duke of Norfolk was deprived of this county, which he inherited from Thomas de Brotherton, and a great part of it was afterwards bestowed upon the Ormonde family. In the same year, the lord-deputy defeated the Kavanaghs, and compelled their chief to submit and give hostages. The act for the suppression of religious houses, in 1537, caused the dissolution of three only in this county, being the preceptory of Killarge, the Carmelite monastery of Leighlin-Bridge, and the Augustinian friary of Tullow. In the same reign a fierce contest for their territorial possessions took place between two branches of the Kavanagh family, in which, after a pitched battle, wherein upwards of one hundred were killed on each side, Cahir Mac Art, of Polmonty, prevailed over Gerald Mac Cahir, of Garryhill, and secured possession of the disputed property. During the succeeding reign of Edward VI., this family was perpetually harassed by Sir William Brabazon, lord-deputy, who ravaged the country, and ultimately compelled the chieftain of it to make a formal submission, renounce the name of Mac Murrough, and surrender his jurisdiction and territory. A change of fortune attended it in the ensuing reign. Charles Mac Art Kavanagh was created Baron of Balian, and after his death, his brother Dermot had the same title; but these honours were insufficient to secure their attachment to the Government; for, in 1555, they invaded the county of Dublin, but were ultimately driven by a sortie of the armed citizens into Powerscourt castle, where, on the appearance of a regular military force, they surrendered at discretion, and were taken to Dublin, where seventy-five of them were hanged and the rest pardoned. During this and the preceding period, the barony of Idrone was considered to be a distinct jurisdiction from the county of Carlow. By an inquisition taken in the reign of Richard II. it appears, that Sir John Carew, who came into the country in the train of Lionel, Duke of Clarence, was in possession of it, and that it devolved, at his death, on Sir Leonard Carew, upon whose decease the Kavanaghs seized on it and held it by force of arms. Sir Peter Carew revived and established the family claim to it before the privy council of Ireland, in 1567; and the next year he was employed by the lord-deputy to put down Sir Edmund Butler, who had joined the great Earl of Desmond in his rebellion, and succeeded not only in taking Sir Edmund's castle of Cloughgrenan, but in routing a large body of the earl's friends in Kilkenny, and in compelling the Kavanaghs, who had taken up arms in the same cause, to throw themselves upon the queen's mercy, and give hostages. Still, the restless spirit of the natives of this district seems to have been indomitable; for, in 1571, they "began again," as Hooker quaintly expresses it, "to play their pageants." A quarrel having taken place between one of the Kavanaghs and a proprietor of the name of Browne, recourse was had to arms, and Browne was killed; but the strife was not thus terminated. The Wexford people joined the weaker party, and the quarrel was still carried on for some time in petty but sanguinary conflicts, in which the superior generalship of the leader of the Kavanaghs finally prevailed. The strife, however, led to no remarkable changes.

During the attempts made by the court of Spain to excite insurrections in Ireland, in the latter part of Elizabeth's reign, the county was harassed by a new disturber. Rory Oge O'More, a chieftain of the Queen's county, attacked and burnt part of the town of Leighlin-Bridge: he did not, however, remain unmolested. Sir George Carew, a relative of Sir Peter, attacked him unexpectedly by night and routed his party; but the fugitives having discovered the great inferiority of numbers that pursued them, rallied and drove the English back to Leighlin castle, which they very nearly succeeded in taking. O'More afterwards made an attack on the town of Carlow, but with as little success; he was finally taken and executed as a rebel. The same spirit of turbulence continued to the close of Elizabeth's reign. Donell Kavanagh, usually called Spaniagh or the Spaniard, made himself peculiarly formidable by his prowess and activity. In 1590, having procured the aid of the mountain tribes of Wicklow, he plundered the whole country from the border of Wexford to the gates of Dublin. At length Lord Mountjoy undertook the subjugation of the district, which he effected after ravaging Donell Spaniagh's country, whence he carried off an immense booty of cattle, and secured his conquest by placing garrisons in the strong posts of Wicklow and Tullow. So effectually did he succeed, that the leaders of those districts served under his standard in his subsequent operations for tranquillising Munster, in effecting which he made Carlow his head-quarters, "as being, as things stood, the place best to give directions to all parts and to secure the most dangerous." It was not until the ninth year of his reign that James I. found sufficient leisure to put in practice his pacific project for the settlement, or plantation, as it was called, of Carlow, Wexford, and Wicklow counties. In that year a king's letter was issued on the subject, but it does not appear to have been followed up, with respect to the first of these counties, by further measures. On the breaking out of the civil war in 1641, the people of Carlow and Wexford, together with those of the Wicklow mountains, took up arms against the Government; and not content with overrunning these counties, they marched into Waterford, where they were defeated by Sir William St. Leger, president of Munster. The next year, the Earl of Ormonde having entered the county with a large force, the Irish, who were in possession of the town of Carlow, and had blocked up the English garrison in the castle, broke up the siege and retreated with some loss; and the garrison, consisting of 500 men, was thus saved from destruction. When the confederate Catholics afterwards resolved to levy a force of 31,700 men, this county was assessed at 2400, of which 40 cavalry and 400 infantry were to serve in the general army, and the remainder to act in the county. The county was not exempt from its share in the sufferings of 1798: the amount of money claimed by the loyalists within it, in compensation for their loss of property during the disturbances, was £24,854. 14. 7.

This county is entirely within the diocese of Leighlin. For purposes of civil jurisdiction it is divided into the baronies of Carlow, Idrone East, Idrone West, St. Mullins North, St. Mullins South, Rathvilly, and Forth. Idrone was divided into East and West, and made two distinct baronies, in 1802, under the provisions of an act passed in 1799; and by an order in council, dated June 2nd, 1834, St. Mullins was also divided, pursuant to the same act, into North and South, or Upper and Lower St. Mullins, now constituting distinct baronies. The county contains the borough, market, and assize town of Carlow; the market and post-towns of Tullow, Bagnalstown, and Leighlin-Bridge; the market-town of Hacketstown, which has a penny post; the post-town of Clonegal, and part of that of Newtownbarry; and the ancient disfranchised borough of Old Leighlin, now a small and deserted village. The largest villages are Borris, Rathvilly, and the Royal Oak. Prior to the Union it sent six members to the Irish parliament; namely, two knights of the shire, and two representatives for each of the boroughs of Carlow and Old Leighlin; but since that period its representatives in the Imperial parliament have been limited to two members for the county at large, and one for the borough of Carlow. The county constituency, as registered at the close of 1835, consists of 273 £50, 134 £20, and 846 £10, freeholders; 1 £50, 15 £20, and 108 £10 leaseholders; and 9 £50, and 49 £20, rent-chargers; making a total of 1435 registered voters. The county is included in the home circuit: the assizes and general quarter sessions are held at Carlow, where are the court-house and county gaol; and quarter sessions are also held at Tullow and Bagnalstown, at the former of which and at Moneybeg are bridewells. The number of persons charged with offences and committed, in 1835, was 363, and of civil bill commitments, 23. The local government is vested in a lieutenant, 6 deputy-lieutenants, and 50 other magistrates, besides whom there are the usual county officers, including two coroners. There are 19 constabulary police stations, with a force of 5 chief and 20 subordinate constables, and 105 men, with 3 horses; the cost of maintenance is defrayed equally by Grand Jury presentments and by Government. There are a district lunatic asylum, and a county infirmary and fever hospital, at Carlow, also fever hospitals at Tullow and Bagnalstown; and dispensaries, supported by equal subscriptions and Grand Jury presentments, at Carlow, Tullow, Leighlin-Bridge, Borris, Hacketstown, Bagnalstown, Myshall, and Clonegal. The amount of Grand Jury presentments, for 1835, was £15,162. 13. 10½. of which £87. 11. 2. was for the public roads and buildings of the county at large; £4905. 8. 9. for the baronial roads; £4817. 0. 6. for public buildings, charities, officers' salaries, &c.; £2483. 10. 7½. for police, and £2869. 2. 10. in repayment of an advance made by Government. In the military arrangements the county is included in the eastern district, and contains one barrack station for cavalry at Carlow, affording accommodation for 8 officers, 112 non-commissioned officers and men, and 90 horses.

This county presents a considerable variety of surface: the ground is generally undulating, particularly in its northern parts, where the rivers Barrow and Slaney form broad valleys of great fertility and beauty, rising into low hills clothed to the summits with a rich herbage varied by fine plantations. To the south and west the character changes. In the south the land rises into a very elevated ridge, which runs along the whole of the south-eastern verge of the county, separating it by a strongly marked natural barrier from that of Wexford. The northern portion of this ridge, which commences from the valley of the Slaney at Newtownbarry, is called Mount Leinster, and is separated at its southern extremity from the Blackstairs mountain by Sculloge gap, the only passage through which a communication can be kept up between the two counties. Blackstairs extends in the same direction till it is interrupted by the Barrow, where its rugged and precipitous termination, together with the peculiarly sombre tints of its appearance throughout its whole extent, has fixed upon it the name just mentioned. This part of the country is comparatively barren and of discouraging aspect. To the west of the Barrow there is also a tract of elevated land, called the Ridge of Old Leighlin, which, however, being cultivated to the very summit, does not strictly merit the name of mountain. This latter district is deficient in the natural beauties which gratify the eye in the northern and eastern parts; but their absence is considered to be amply compensated by the treasures concealed beneath the surface, as this part of the county forms the commencement of the great coal field of Leinster, and bears all the external marks of diminished fertility which usually characterise such tracts. Though the country is well watered, there is nothing in it entitled to the name of lake, although the more ancient name of its chief town, Catherlough, "the city on the lake," would lead to such an inference. The climate is mild and salubrious, subject neither to the extremes of heat and cold, nor of excessive moisture, to which regions in the neighbourhood of lofty mountains, or near the shores of the Atlantic, are liable. The soil is rich and generally of a calcareous nature, except in the more mountainous parts, and, even there, cultivation has been carried to a considerable height on the acclivities. Agriculture is in as highly improved a state here as in any other part of Ireland. So far back as 1779, the vicinity of Carlow town was noticed by Young as one of the few places in which green crops formed part of the system of rural economy, turnips being at that time extensively planted there; though it does not appear that they became a general farm crop till many years after. Since 1817, agriculture, as a system, has been extending its beneficial effects with rapid progress under the fostering care and spirited example of some of the resident gentry. Wheat of a superior quality is grown in every part, barley only on some of the most favoured soils, whilst oats and potatoes are universal; the barley has long been celebrated and in great demand, and large quantities are annually shipped to England; the potatoes also, particularly those grown on the calcareous soils, are much esteemed. Turnips are every where cultivated with success by the gentry and large farmers; but the small farmers are generally averse to the culture of green crops, notwithstanding the inducement held out by several landlords of releasing them from the payment of rent for land tilled for turnips or mangel-wurzel. Clover seed is sometimes sown on the larger farms, and the sowing of grass seeds in laying down exhausted land is now pretty general, although the old and pernicious system of allowing the land to recover by a natural process is still too prevalent; flax, hemp, rape, vetches, &c., are occasionally sown. The pastures are remarkably good, and although the land is not so rich as in some parts of Tipperary and Limerick, the cattle attain a larger size here than in either of those counties. Dairies are numerous, and the dairy farms extensive and profitable; butter, generally of very superior quality and much esteemed in the English and foreign markets, is the chief produce; cheese is made only for domestic consumption. The dairy farmers pay great attention to the selection and breed of milch cows. Limerick heifers were much in demand, but a cross between the Durham breed and the old country cow is now the favourite: some of the Durham breed are, nevertheless, highly prized for the dairy, but they neither fatten so soon nor weigh so profitably as those crossed with the Limerick, Devon, or Teeswater breeds. Sheep of the New Leicester breed have been introduced at considerable expense by some of the most spirited agriculturists, and are now become pretty general and in high repute; they appear to be well adapted to the soil and climate, and bear an excellent fleece. In the hilly districts the sheep are smaller; those in highest repute are a cross between the new Leicester and the Kerry. Pigs are not so generally kept here as in some of the adjoining counties, and are mostly of an inferior kind. Draining has been introduced by some of the gentry, but irrigation is very little practised. The fences are far superior to those of the adjoining counties, though in many cases the large old ditches or mounds of earth, with a deep shough on one or both sides, are to be seen. A kind of fence common here is formed out of the blocks of white granite which lie scattered over a great part of the county or are procured from the quarries; these blocks being cloven with great regularity, the larger slabs are fixed upright in the ground, and the lighter and longer pieces ranged transversely along the top, in the manner of posts and rails, forming an unique and very durable fence. Agricultural implements on the most approved principles are generally used in every part, except the hilly districts, where the old heavy implements may still be partially seen: the iron plough and light harrow have been in use some years by gentlemen, and are now in the possession of almost every farmer. The old heavy wooden car has given place generally to one of lighter form, with iron-bound spoke wheels, but having very short shafts. Carts nearly similar to those of England, with narrow wheels, are every where used by the wealthy farmers, but the old clumsy low-backed car is common upon the road. The whole of the county, with the exception of the mountainous parts already noticed, is well wooded: trees thrive well, but not every species; an oak wood is rarely met with, although oaks flourish in the soil. The spruce and silver fir, after having been tried for some time, were extirpated on account of their unhealthy appearance; the soil was thought not suitable to them. The weeping, or Hertfordshire, elm is frequently to be seen: the elm in general germinates earlier here then elsewhere. But the most beautiful and ornamental trees are the sycamore, chesnut, lime, birch, and white thorn, the last of which attains a large size: the entire level part of the county presents much the appearance of some of the English counties. Lime is plentiful, and the facilities of its conveyance for agricultural purposes abundant. Fuel is equally so: coal is brought from the collieries of Kilkenny and the Queen's county by land carriage, and turf is procured from the small bogs in this and the adjoining counties. Horticulture is in an advanced state; few farm-houses are without a vegetable garden, and the scarcer kind of esculents, and likewise flowers, are generally cultivated.

The county lies between the great eastern granite district of the county of Wicklow and the coal formation of the Queen's county and Kilkenny. The granite shews itself along the south-eastern verge, in the mountainous range of Mount Leinster and Blackstairs, where it is interrupted by the precipitous valley of St. Mullins, but it appears again at Brandon hill, in the southern part of Kilkenny. The coal country is surrounded by and rests upon limestone, the strata of which, wherever examined, present appearances extremely similar. The description of the limestone valley between the granite country, two miles east of the town of Carlow, and the coal field as far westward, may serve to give a clear idea of the general nature of this part of the country. At the base of Browne's hill, two miles east of Carlow, the granite is covered with stratified silicious limestone, dipping 60° west of north at an angle of 10° from the horizon: the colour is light greyish blue, with numerous petrifactions, chiefly bivalve shells; it is calcined with great difficulty, and gives, on analysis, of carbonate of lime, 95.00; of silica, with a tinge of iron, 4.50; and of carbon, 0.50. The stratification is quite regular between the granite country and Carlow, but with a change of colour and character as it recedes from the mass of granite. At first it changes to a dark blue, and madrepores are visible in it. The beds are extremely vesicular, and their numerous cavities are coated with a series of different fossils. On approaching Carlow, the limestone becomes more silicious and of a deeper colour: at the town the colour is dark or iron grey, and the texture fine-grained, and it is sometimes polished and used for chimney-pieces: to the west of the town the limestone is lighter in colour and much purer. Here the Lydian stone begins to appear in quantity, both in irregular beds and round nodules. The stone becomes still lighter in colour and finer in quality as it approaches the west. Some specimens from the higher quarries were found to contain solely carbonate of lime, with a small residuum of carbon, not amounting to a quarter per cent. The number of petrifactions in the upper quarry is immense, comprehending a great variety of fossil productions. On approaching the point where the coal strata join the limestone, the stratification is generally disturbed; the rock becomes shivery and breaks into indeterminately angular small fragments. The quantity of Lydian stone is greatly increased; the actual point of contact between the limestone and coal being scarcely visible, on account of the disturbance of the strata. The Lydian stone appears to pass into slate clay, no division existing between them. The succession of rocks visible at Old Leighlin, is as follows, commencing from the bottom: dark blueish grey limestone, 10 feet; irregular black Lydian stone, with silicious petrifactions, 2 feet; light grey limestone, 20 feet; Lydian stone, with numerous silicious petrifactions, 3 feet; flinty slate, in very thin beds, the uppermost of which graduate into slate clay, and contain balls of clay ironstone of a dark blue colour, 30 feet; and sandstone flag, 200 feet. This stone continues to the summit of the hill, where it varies very much in quality, and passes from soft sandstone into soft micaceous slag, which divides into thin laminæ from one-tenth of an inch to an inch in thickness. Besides the irregularities above described, beds of brown spar rock are met with near the point of junction of the two formations; but they are more frequent on the southern and western boundaries than on the northern and eastern. The limestone field abounds with rolled calcareous masses, pebbles, gravel, sand and marl, forming escars of considerable elevation, in which the calcareous gravel and sand frequently exhibit a stratified disposition with layers very distinct from each other.

Carlow is almost exclusively an agricultural district. An inland trade, particularly in grain, is carried on by the Barrow to Waterford, and by the Slaney to Wexford. But though the county is much indebted to both these rivers for the increase of its agricultural prosperity, neither has any claim to be considered as belonging to it exclusively. The former has been rendered navigable from Athy bridge, in the county of Kildare, to the tideway at the rocks called the Scars, below St. Mullins, a distance of about 43 miles: the total fall is 172 feet. The navigation is chiefly in the bed of the river, except near the several mills, where there are artificial cuts and locks: the total extent of the new cuts is five miles; their breadth, 27 feet at the bottom and 42 at the surface of the water. The Derry and Derreen, branches of the Slaney, and the Burren, a branch of the Barrow, are insignificant streams. The roads are numerous, and in general well constructed.

Among the more remarkable relics of antiquity are a large cromlech at Browne's hill, near Carlow, and another, still larger, at Tobinstown; also a rath near Leighlin-Bridge and, near Tullow, a pillar, perforated at the top and thence called *Clogh a' Phoill*, "the stone with the hole." The Kavanagh family were in possession of several curious relics of antiquity, of which the most remarkable was an ivory horn mounted and ornamented with gilt brass, supposed to have been the tenure by which they held the estate: it has been deposited in the museum of Trinity College, Dublin. Another of these is the *Figeen*, a kind of ring, composed of a mixture of silver and tin; it was found in a ditch in the demesne of Borris. A third is the *Liath Meisicith*, being a brass box encased with silver, and containing extracts from the gospels written on vellum in Latin, but in the Irish character: it is also deposited in Dublin College. Near Cloghgrenan some brazen swords and arrow-heads were raised out of a ford in the Barrow. Several remains of monastic buildings still exist. The most remarkable are those of Achadfinglass near Leighlin, Athade, Ballymoon (or, as it is called by Archdall, Bally-Mac-William-roe), Killarge, Kilfortchean, Old Leighlin, Leighlin-Bridge, St. Mullins, and Tullow. The remains of a round tower were visible near the church of Kellystown, until the year 1807, when they were cleared away to make room for a belfry. Around Old Leighlin are numerous remains of ancient buildings, among the most conspicuous of which are those of the venerable cathedral; and in several parts are ruins of churches, some of remote origin, close to which the modern churches have in many instances been built, tending to heighten the picturesque effect. The most remarkable of the military antiquities is Carlow castle, built on the banks of the Barrow. In Idrone East are Ballylaughan, called also Ballylorgan castle, whose remains retain many traces of its former strength and importance; and Ballymoon castle, a structure of the Knights Templars, the walls of which are of great thickness, and sheep graze peaceably within its enclosure. Black castle, built on the eastern side of Leighlin-Bridge, retains its walls: near it was another fortress, built by one of the Fitzgeralds, and named for distinction White castle. The castles of Gilbertstown, Rathlin, Lorum, and Rathnegeragh, were in the same barony. Clonmore castle, in Rathvilly, is in tolerable preservation. There are no remains of the castle of Tullow: it is supposed to have stood near the site of the present church. The ruins of Castle Grace are near Tullow. Clonmullen castle, of which some traces were in existence about fifty years since, though now obliterated by the plough, was anciently remarkable as the residence of Donell Spaniagh, and perhaps not less so, at a more modern period, for possessing as an inmate Ellen Kavanagh, immortalised by Carolan in his affecting melody of Aileen a Roon, and recently made the subject of an interesting poem by Mr. R. Garrett, of Janeville, in this county. The habitations of the peasantry are of a better description than in many other parts of the country, the general appearance and habits of both sexes much improved, and the interior of their dwellings neat and comfortable. At Garrowhill, or Knockdrimagh, near the bottom of Mount Leinster, is a chalybeate spring; but its efficacy is little known except in its immediate vicinity.

Seal.

CARLOW, an incorporated borough, market, and post-town, and a parish, in the barony and county of CARLOW, and province of LEINSTER, 18¼ miles (N. E.) from Kilkenny, and 39¼ (S. W. by S.) from Dublin; containing 9597 inhabitants, of which number, 9114 are in the borough. This town, called, till within a comparatively recent period, *Catherlough*, or *Catherlagh*, is supposed to have derived that name, signifying in the Irish language "the city on the lake," from its proximity to a large sheet of water which formerly existed here. The erection of the castle has been variously attributed to Eva, daughter of Dermot Mac Murrough; to Isabel, daughter of Strongbow, and to King John; but with more probability to Hugh de Lacy, about the year 1180. In the reign of Edw. II., the castle belonged to the crown, and was made the head-quarters of the seneschalship of the counties of Carlow and Kildare, instituted on account of the disturbed state of those districts. About the year 1361, Lionel, Duke of Clarence, established the exchequer of the kingdom at this place, and expended £500 in fortifying the town with walls, of which at present there is not a vestige. James Fitzgerald, brother of the Earl of Kildare, seized the castle in 1494; but it was soon afterwards invested by the lord-deputy, Sir Edward Poynings, to whom, after a siege of ten days, it was surrendered. In 1534 it was taken by Lord Thomas Fitzgerald, during his insurrection; and in 1577 the town was assaulted by Rory Oge O'More. Jas. I. granted the manor to Donogh, Earl of Thomond, whom he also made constable of the castle. In 1641, the whole county was overrun by the insurgents, and the castle of Carlow was invested by a strong party and reduced to great extremity; a number of Protestants had taken refuge within its walls, and the garrison was about to surrender, when it was relieved by a detachment of the Earl of Ormonde's forces under the command of Sir Patrick Wemys. On his approach the insurgents raised the siege, and, after burning the town, took flight, but 50 of them were killed in the pursuit. This place was constantly exposed to the assaults of the insurgents; and the castle, after sustaining a siege for nearly a month, ultimately surrendered in May, 1647. It was, in 1650, closely invested by Ireton and the republican army; and after a severe cannonade which greatly injured the castle, the garrison surrendered on conditions to Sir Hardress Waller, whom Ireton had left to conduct the siege. After the battle of the Boyne, in 1690, Wm. III. led his army southward through this town; and during the disturbances of 1798, it was assaulted by the insurgents on the morning of the 25th of May. The garrison, consisting partly of regular troops and partly of yeomanry, amounting in the whole to 450, repulsed the assailants, though 2000 in number, with the loss of 600 of their men, on which occasion they were obliged to burn several of the houses, in order to compel the insurgents to abandon them.

The town is pleasantly and advantageously situated on the eastern bank of the river Barrow, over which is a bridge of four arches connecting it with the extensive suburban village of Graigue, in Queen's county: it is surrounded by a rich agricultural district, and sheltered by some ranges of hills well cultivated to their summits. It is of considerable extent, and contains more than fourteen good streets, of which the two principal, intersecting each other at right angles and continued through its whole length and breadth, divide the town into four nearly equal portions, which are again divided and subdivided by smaller streets into 42 portions; it is rapidly increasing in all directions, and a new street, chiefly for private residence, is now in progress, which, when completed, will be one of its greatest ornaments. Though a place of such high antiquity, it has an air of modern neatness: the streets are paved and kept in repair by county presentments, the two principal by the county at large, and the others by the barony in which the town is situated; and the inhabitants are supplied with water from public pumps. On the south side of the town is a stream called the Burren, which flows into the Barrow; and on a rising ground above its influx are the stately remains of the ancient castle, towering to the height of 60 feet above the roofs of the houses. There are two subscription reading-rooms; and to the south-east of the town are cavalry barracks for 8 officers and 112 non-commissioned officers and privates, with stabling for 90 horses, and an hospital for 20 patients. From its advantageous situation on the Barrow, affording a facility of communication with the ports of Ross, Waterford, and Dublin, the town has become the principal mart for the agricultural produce of the well-cultivated districts around it, and carries on an extensive trade in corn and butter; the latter is of a very superior quality, and meets with a ready sale in the London market. The trade down the river has, within the last 14 years, greatly increased, while that upwards has diminished, in consequence of the heavy tolls demanded on the canal conveyance to the metropolis. The quantity of corn and flour sent hence to Waterford and other ports for exportation has, within that period, advanced from 2000 to 15,000 quarters; and the quantity of butter weighed in the market and in private stores is at present not less than 35,000 firkins. The river Barrow is navigable from Athy, where the Grand Canal from Dublin joins it, and thence to its confluence with the river Suir below Waterford; boats consequently pass from this place to Dublin, Ross, and Waterford; there is a lock on the river, and good quays have been constructed for the accommodation of vessels employed in the trade. This is the head-quarters of the southern district of the revenue police, and there are sub-stations at Newtownbarry, Freshford, and Gore's-bridge: there is also a chief constabulary police station in the town. The market-days are Monday and Thursday; and fairs are held on May 4th, June 22nd, Aug. 26th, and Nov. 8th. The revenue of the post-office, according to the latest return to Parliament, amounted to £1395. 1. 6.

The earliest charter on record relating to the borough is that of Wm. Marshall, Earl of Pembroke, granted about the close of the 13th century. It created an open community of burgesses endowed with considerable privileges, including a guild mercatory and other guilds, with exemption from tolls and customs throughout the earl's whole lands, except the towns of Pembroke and Wexford; it also mentions a hundred court as being then in existence in the town, and ordained that it should be held only once in the week. Jas. I., in 1613, granted a charter of incorporation, conferring, among other privileges, a right to return two members to Parliament; and the present governing charter was obtained on petition from Chas. II., in 1674. Jas. II. granted a charter founded on a seizure of the franchises by a decree of the exchequer, which being declared void, it soon became inoperative. Under the charter of Chas. II. the corporation is styled "The Sovereign, Free Burgesses, and Commonalty of the Borough of Catherlagh;" and consists of a sovereign, twelve free burgesses, and a commonalty, assisted by a town-clerk, two serjeants-at-mace, a weighmaster of butter, and a bellman. The sovereign is annually elected by the sovereign for the time being and a majority of the burgesses from their own body, on the 24th of June, and enters upon his office on the 29th of September: he is *ex officio* a justice of the peace for the borough and the county, and clerk of the market, and with the approbation of the burgesses may appoint one of them to be his deputy. The burgesses are elected from the freemen by a majority of the sovereign and burgesses; the town-clerk and serjeants-at-mace are chosen by the sovereign and burgesses, and the weighmaster of butter is appointed by the sovereign. The freemen are elected by the sovereign and burgesses. The borough returned two members to the Irish parliament till the Union, since which period it has sent only one to the Imperial parliament. The right of election, previously confined to the sovereign and burgesses, was, by the act of the 2nd of Wm IV., for amending the representation, extended to the resident freemen and £10 householders, of whom, including the suburb of Graigue, which has been comprised within the new electoral boundary (of which the limits are minutely described in the Appendix), the number is 383, of which 380 are householders, and three freemen resident within seven miles; the sovereign is the returning officer. By the charter the corporation had power to hold a court of record for pleas to the amount of five marks; but they at present exercise no jurisdiction whatever, either civil or criminal. The assizes, and also the quarter sessions for the county, are held here; and petty sessions are held every Thursday before the sovereign and county magistrates. The manor court has jurisdiction to the amount of £10 late currency over the entire town and an extensive rural district; it had fallen into disuse prior to 1833, when the lord of the manor, B. Hamilton, Esq., appointed a seneschal, and the court was revived, but few cases have been since determined in it. The court-house, a newly erected building at the junction of the Castledermot and Athy roads, near the entrance of the town, is a handsome octagonal edifice with a fine Doric portico, in imitation of the Acropolis at Athens, resting upon a platform to which is an ascent by a broad flight of steps; the whole is of hewn granite of chaste design and execution, and forms a striking ornament to the town. Near it is the county gaol, well adapted for the classification and employment of prisoners, who are engaged in useful labour and are taught trades, to qualify them on their discharge for a life of useful industry; the female prisoners are carefully instructed and employed under a duly qualified matron; a school has been established, and the sick are carefully attended by the medical officer; but the hospital is not yet sufficiently prepared for the reception of patients. There is a tread-wheel, which is worked for raising water to supply the gaol.

The parish comprises 1955 statute acres, of which about 648 are plantations, a few acres bog, and the remainder good arable and pasture land. The surrounding scenery is pleasingly varied and in many parts beautifully picturesque; and there are several handsome seats in the parish. Oak Park, formerly called Paynestown, and now the residence of Col. Bruen, is a handsome spacious building, consisting of a centre and two wings, situated to the north of the town in a fine demesne embellished with stately groves of full-grown oak. To the east of it are Browne Hill, the seat of W. Browne, Esq.; and Viewmount House, formerly the seat of Sir E. Crosbie, Bart., and now the residence of R. C. Browne, Esq., pleasantly situated and commanding a beautiful prospect of the neighbouring country. On the opposite side of the river, below the town, is Clogrennan, the seat of J. S. Rochford, Esq., beautifully situated in a highly improved demesne. The living is a rectory, in the diocese of Leighlin, and in the patronage of the Crown for two presentations, and of the Bishop for one: the tithes amount to £400. The church is a modern structure, with a beautiful spire terminating at an elevation of 195 feet, having a massive gilt cross presented by the ladies of Carlow: the Ecclesiastical Commissioners have recently granted £488. 4. 10. for its repair. Near the river, to the north of the town, is an ancient burial-ground, called "The Graves," said to have been granted to the parish by the Earl of Thomond. There is no glebe-house; the glebe comprises 3½ acres. The R. C. parish is co-extensive with that of the Established Church, and is the benefice of the Bishop of Kildare and Leighlin. The R. C. cathedral is an elegant cruciform structure, in the later English style, with a lofty tower at the southern extremity of the transept, surmounted by a lantern of beautiful design terminating at a height of 151 feet from the base: it occupies the site of the old chapel, and is a rich ornament to the town. At the foot of the altar are interred the remains of the Rt. Rev. Dr. James Doyle, late bishop, distinguished by his letters under the signature of J. K. L., and his important evidence before both houses of parliament. He entered the college of Carlow, as professor of rhetoric, in 1809, and was soon afterwards appointed professor of theology; in 1819 he was raised to the R. C. see of Kildare and Leighlin, and died of a lingering decline on the 10th of June, 1834. Braganza House, the residence of the R. C. bishop, is situated in the immediate vicinity of the town. There are places of worship for Presbyterians, the Society of Friends, and Wesleyan Methodists.

The R. C. college of St. Patrick, for the education of youth and of the R. C. clergy, was founded by the late Rev. Dr. Keefe, and opened in the year 1795 under the direction of the late Dean Staunton: the system of education comprises the Hebrew, Greek, Latin, Italian, French, and English languages, sacred and profane history, rhetoric, geography, arithmetic and the mathematics, to which are added natural and moral philosophy, humanity, and theology, under the superintendence of professors and assistants, who are members of the house and are resident. The building, which consists of a spacious centre connected with two wings by corridors, is situated in a park comprising an area of 34 acres, nearly in the centre of the town, and enclosed with high walls and well planted, affording ample opportunities of healthful recreation and undisturbed retirement. The institution is under the direction of a president, vice-president, and prefect of the lay college, dean of the ecclesiastical college, and other officers: the fees are £31. 10. per annum for lay, and £25 for ecclesiastical students. Connected with it is a neat chapel, with a burial-ground attached. The Diocesan school of Leighlin and Ossory is supported by a grant of £120 per annum from the Diocesan fund, and is open also to boarders paying £31. 10., and to day scholars paying £6. 6. A parochial school is aided by an annual donation of £10 from the rector; and there are two national schools and an infants' school. In these are about 370 boys and 485 girls; and there are several private schools, in which are about 500 boys and 258 girls. The district lunatic asylum for the counties of Carlow, Kilkenny, Wexford, and Kildare, and the county of the city of Kilkenny, is situated in this town, and was built in 1831, at an expense, including the cost of erection and purchase of land and furniture, of £22,552. 10. 4.: it is under excellent regulation, is calculated to accommodate 104 lunatics, and attached to it are 15¼ acres of land; the number of inmates in the summer of 1836 was 99. The county infirmary is supported by grand jury presentments and local subscriptions, aided by a parliamentary grant; a fever hospital, opened for the reception of patients in 1829, is supported by grand jury presentments alone; a dispensary is maintained in the usual way, and a Magdalene asylum is supported wholly by subscriptions. The remains of the old castle consist only of one side of the quadrangle, at each end of which is one of the massive round towers that flanked its angles; the remainder having been undermined in an injudicious attempt to convert it into a private lunatic asylum, fell down in 1814; the length of the side from tower to tower is 105 feet. The walls are of very great thickness, and shew that it must have been a fortress of much strength; and from the loftiness of its elevation and the commanding position which it occupies, it has a striking appearance of majestic grandeur. Near Oak Park was a small Franciscan friary, founded by the Cooke family, formerly proprietors of that estate. Browne Hill and Viewmount both occupy the site of an ancient religious establishment, called St. Kieran's abbey; and in the vicinity are the remains of a cromlech, of which the table stone is 23 feet in length, 19 in breadth, and at the upper end nearly 4½ feet thick; it is supported at the east end on three upright stones, 15 feet 8 inches high, and at a distance is another upright stone standing by itself. Carlow gives the inferior title of Viscount to the family of Dawson, Earls of Portarlington.

CARMAVY, a grange, in the parish of KILLEAD, barony of LOWER MASSAREENE, county of ANTRIM, and province of ULSTER, 6 miles (S. E.) from Antrim; the population is returned with the parish. This grange is situated upon the road from Belfast to Antrim: and comprises, according to the Ordnance survey, 789¼ statute acres.

CARMONEY.—See CARNMONEY.

CARN, or CARNDONAGH, a market and post-town, in the parish of DONAGH, barony of ENNISHOWEN, county of DONEGAL, and province of ULSTER, 17 miles (N.) from Londonderry, and 135½ (N. N. W.) from Dublin; containing 618 inhabitants. This place, which is pleasantly situated on an eminence near the head of the bay of Straghbregagh, or Strabeagy, and on the road from Londonderry to Malin, consists of a small square and four good streets, and contains 198 houses, many of which are large and well built; a river runs through it, and another has its course a little to the north. The market is on Monday; and fairs are held on the 21st of Feb., May, Aug., and Nov. Here is a chief constabulary station, with barracks for the police; and it is the head of a coast-guard district, comprising also the stations of Dunree Fort, Dunaff Head, Malin Head, Port Redford, and Green Castle. In the vicinity are many excellent houses, the principal of which are, Tunalague, the residence of R. Cary, Esq., proprietor of the town; the glebe-house, of the Rev. G. Marshall; Fairview, of J. Magill, Esq.; and Bridge House, of M. Rankin, Esq. The parish church, near which is an ancient and curious stone cross, and the R. C. parochial chapel, a large and handsome edifice, erected in 1826, are situated in the town. There are also a meeting-house for Presbyterians in connection with the Synod of Ulster, male and female parochial schools, a large and handsome national school, and a dispensary.—See DONAGH.

CARNAGH, a parish, in the barony of BANTRY, county of WEXFORD, and province of LEINSTER, 3 miles (S. E. by S.) from New Ross; containing 319 inhabitants. This parish is situated on the road from Enniscorthy, by Ballinlaw Ferry, to Waterford; and thence through New Ross to Wexford. It comprises 1842 statute acres, as applotted under the tithe act: the lands are principally under tillage; an exhausted bog has been reclaimed and is now under cultivation, and there is no waste land. The system of agriculture is progressively improving, and the industry and comfort of the farmers and the peasantry are evident from the external appearance of their dwellings. There are some quarries of building stone, which, although of inferior quality, is still used for that purpose in the neighbourhood. Carnagh, the family seat of H. Lambert, Esq., is situated in a pleasant demesne. At Ballinabooley is a constabulary police station. It is a rectory, in the diocese of Ferns, and is part of the union of St. Mary, New Ross: the tithes amount to £80. The church is in ruins. In the R. C. divisions the parish, with the exception of the townland of Ballymacar, is the head of a union or district called Cushinstown, comprising the parishes of Carnagh, Ballyane, Tallerath, and Old Ross; the chapel is at Cushinstown. Two school-rooms, with apartments for a master and mistress, are about to be erected by the Lambert family. Near Ballinabooley is a rath, underneath which was discovered a subterraneous apartment, approached by a passage of upright flag-stones, and capable of receiving from 20 to 25 persons; it is supposed to have been constructed by the Danes, for the concealment of plunder in cases of emergency. The streams in various parts of the parish are of a chalybeate nature, but the water is seldom used medicinally.

CARNALLOWAY, or CARNALWAY, a parish, in the barony of SOUTH NAAS, county of KILDARE, and province of LEINSTER, $4\frac{1}{2}$ miles (S. by W.) from Naas; containing 1291 inhabitants. It is bounded on the south by the river Liffey, which separates it from the parish of Old Kilcullen, and is on the turnpike road from Naas to Dunlavin. During the disturbances of 1798, a battle was fought at Nineteen-mile-House, in this parish, between a party of the insurgents and a detachment of cavalry. The parish comprises 3408 statute acres, as applotted under the tithe act: the lands are chiefly under tillage; the soil is good, and the system of agriculture much improved; there is no waste land, but a large quantity of bog. The living is a rectory and vicarage, in the diocese of Kildare, and in the patronage of the Bishop and of Robert La Touche, Esq.; the former having one, and the latter three turns: the tithes amount to £226. 3. 1. The church, a very neat edifice with a tower and spire, was built by the late John La Touche, Esq., and contains a tablet to the memory of Capt. Cooke, who fell while charging the insurgents at Kilcullen bridge, in 1798. The late Board of First Fruits granted £100, in 1810, towards the erection of a glebe-house, attached to which are 10 acres of glebe. In the R. C. divisions this parish forms part of the union or district of Newbridge. There is a parochial school, built by the late John La Touche, Esq., and supported by R. La Touche, Esq., affording instruction to about 80 children; and a school, in which are about 50 boys and 40 girls, is aided by an annual donation from the R. C. clergyman. There are also a private school, in which are about 10 boys and 10 girls, and a Sunday school. In that part of Kilcullen which is in this parish are a fever hospital and a dispensary.

CARNCASTLE, or CASTLE-CAIRN, a parish, in the barony of UPPER GLENARM, county of ANTRIM, and province of ULSTER, 3 miles (N. W. by N.) from Larne; containing 2167 inhabitants. This parish is situated on the shore of the North channel, which forms its eastern boundary, and upon the road from Larne to Glenarm, and the royal military road from Belfast to the Giant's Causeway; it contains, according to the Ordnance survey, 9725 statute acres, and is in an excellent state of cultivation. The soil is very fertile, producing excellent crops: there are only 15 acres of bog. Basalt is quarried for building and repairing the roads; limestone is abundant, and coal is known to exist in great quantities. At Ballygally is a coast-guard station, which is one of eight that are included in the district of Carrickfergus. About five miles from the coast are the Hulin or Maiden rocks, two of which are always visible above water. On these lighthouses have been built by the corporation for the improvement of the port of Dublin, which are called the North and South Maiden Rock Lights, and are 1920 feet apart. The northern light is 84 feet above high water level, and the southern, 94 feet; both are fixed and bright lights.

The living is a rectory and perpetual curacy, in the diocese of Connor, of which the rectory was united, by charter of the 7th of Jas. I., to the rectories of Kilwaughter, Ballycor, Rashee, and Derrykeighan, together constituting the corps of the prebend of Carncastle in the cathedral church of St. Saviour, Connor, and in the patronage of the Bishop; the perpetual curacy is in the gift of the rector. The tithes of the parish amount to £174. 4. 6., and the gross value of the tithes and glebe of the union is £751. 5. 4. per annum, of which £55 is paid by the prebendary to the perpetual curate, whose stipend is augmented to £96 per ann. out of Primate Boulter's fund. The church, a small plain edifice with a lofty spire, was built on the site of a former church, by aid of a loan of £350, granted in 1815 by the late Board of First Fruits; and a house was purchased for a glebe-house with a gift of £450, and a loan of £50, from the same Board: the glebe comprises five acres. In the R. C. divisions this parish forms part of the union or district of Larne and Carrickfergus; the chapel is a small building. There are two places of worship for Presbyterians, one connected with the Synod of Ulster, of the third class; the other connected with the Remonstrant Synod, of the second class. Near the church is the parochial school, endowed with £3 per annum by the late Mr. Wilson; a school of 43 boys and 9 girls is in connection with the National Board; and there are a private school of 12 boys and 25 girls, and two Sunday schools. On an insulated rock in the sea are the remains of Ballygally or Cairn castle, from which the parish takes its name. There are also some remains of the ancient manor-house, built in 1625, in the Elizabethan style; and of an old church. In the parish are a curious perforation in a mass of basalt, called the Black Cave, and a very pure vein of feldspar, capable of being worked to advantage.

CARNE, or CARNA, a parish, in the barony of EAST OPHALY, county of KILDARE, and province of LEINSTER, 4 miles (S. E.) from Kildare; containing 550 inhabitants. It is situated on the road from Athy to Newbridge, and is in the diocese of Kildare. The rectory is appropriate to the dean and chapter of Kildare, who possess 178 statute acres of land in the parish; and the vicarage forms the corps of the precentorship of that cathedral, in the patronage of the Bishop, but is at present sequestrated in the Ecclesiastical Commissioners. The tithes amount to £90, of which £81. 9. 6. are payable to the dean and chapter, and £8. 10. 6. to the precentor. There is no church or glebe-house, but a glebe of ten acres. In the R. C. divisions this parish is the head of a union or district called Sancroft, comprising the parishes of Carne, Ballysonan, Killrush, and Ballysax; the chapel at Sancroft is a large building, and there is a national school there in which about 40 boys and 30 girls are educated.

CARNE, a parish, in the barony of FORTH, county of WEXFORD, and province of LEINSTER, $2\frac{1}{2}$ miles (S. E. by S.) from Broadway; containing 828 inhabitants. This place, of which the present name in the Irish language signifies a stone, was anciently called *Salanga*, afterwards *Slieve Domangaird*, and in the time of Ptolemy, *Hieron*, or "the Sacred Promontory." According to Archdall, St. Domangart founded a monastery here at the foot of the mountain, but no traces of it can be discerned: near the spot, however, is a burial-ground with the ruins of a chapel, called St. Vaugh's, the rude architecture of which denotes its remote origin. The parish is situated on the shore of St. George's channel, and terminates in Carnsore Point, the south-eastern extremity of Ireland, in lat. 52° 10′ (N.) and lon. 6° 16′ 45″ (W.); it is bounded on the south and east by the sea, and on the west by the lough of Lady's Island, and comprises 1739 statute acres, as applotted under the tithe act, nearly the whole of which is arable and pasture. With the exception of a small eminence called the hill of Chour, at the south-west point, the surface is flat, and being destitute of timber has a very naked aspect: the soil, though naturally poor, is, from the extensive use of sea-weed and marl as manure, rendered very productive. Little improvement has taken place in the system of agriculture, except the practice of drilling potatoes, which has been lately introduced; the arable lands in many parts are so interspersed with large stones as greatly to obstruct the progress of the plough. Beans, which form one of the principal crops, find a ready market at Wexford for exportation. The farm buildings are neat, and the dwellings of the peasantry have an appearance of cleanliness and comfort. The principal articles of fuel are furze and bean-stalks; some sea coal is brought from Wexford. The road from Carnsore Point to that town divides the parish into two nearly equal parts. Castletown, situated in the centre of the parish, about a quarter of a mile to the west of the main road, was formerly the ancient mansion of the Pallisers. Castle Palliser was erected by the late Capt. Pierce Harvey, and is now in the occupation of Sir Hugh Palliser, Bart. On the beach is Carna House, the seat of J. Howlin, Esq. Some coarse linen and linsey woolsey are manufactured for home consumption; and during the season about twelve boats are employed in the herring and lobster fisheries carried on off the coast, on which are two small but convenient creeks, one at Carne and the other at Nethertown. At Carne bay is a coast-guard station, which is one of the six stations comprehended within the Wexford district, and has a detachment at Tacumshane. The living is a rectory and vicarage, in the diocese of Ferns, and in the patronage of the Bishop: the tithes amount to £280. The church is a plain edifice of great antiquity, without tower or spire, for the repairs of which the Ecclesiastical Commissioners have recently granted £114. The glebe-house, a neat substantial building with suitable out-offices, was erected in the year 1802 by the present incumbent, the Rev. R. Bevan, at an expense of £1039, of which £100 was granted by the late Board of First Fruits: the glebe comprises nine acres. In the R. C. divisions the parish is in the district of Lady's island, attached to which is a school attended by the children of this parish. On the estate of the Waddy family are the remains of the ancient castle of Cloest, built by the earliest English settlers in the reign of Hen. II., and consisting of a tower between 70 and 80 feet high in good preservation.

CARNEARNEY, a hamlet, in the parish of Ahoghill, barony of Lower Toome, county of Antrim, and province of Ulster, on the river Maine; containing 12 houses and 60 inhabitants.

CARNEW, a market and post-town, and a parish, partly in the baronies of Scarewalsh and Gorey, county of Wexford, but chiefly in the barony of Shillelagh, county of Wicklow, and province of Leinster, 23 miles (S. W. by S.) from Wicklow, and 47 (S. by W.) from Dublin; containing 6865 inhabitants, of which number, 826 are in the town. During the disturbances of 1798, Col. Walpole, who had been ordered to collect what forces he could and place them under the command of Gen. Loftus, then at Gorey, arrived at this place on the evening of June 2nd, with 500 men, two six-pounders, and a howitzer, which he stationed here as the best point from which to attack the insurgents, who were encamped at Ballymore Hill. On the following day, leaving two companies in the town, he marched with the remainder to Gorey, where, in conjunction with Gen. Loftus, he concerted a plan for attacking the enemy by two different routes on the following day. But unfortunately disregarding the arrangement he had made, and rashly assuming the entire command, he led his men into a defile, where a great number were slaughtered, and he was killed in the first onset. The insurgents, after spending several days in plundering the town and neighbourhood of Gorey, advanced to Carnew, which they destroyed, with the exception of a malt-house, in which the garrison had retired; and after several ineffectual attacks, in which they sustained considerable loss, pursued their march to Kilcavan Hill. Near Ballyellis, also, while a troop of the ancient Britons, under the command of Capt. Erskine, was on its march to attack the insurgents, they blocked up the way with cars, carts, &c., hemmed in the little party on all sides, and killed every one of the troop, who were all buried in the vicinity. The town is situated on the road from Gorey to Tullow and Carlow, and on the side of a mountainous eminence that overlooks a fertile valley. It consists principally of one street, containing 131 houses, and has, during the last three or four years, been greatly improved by Earl Fitzwilliam, who has, besides other buildings, erected two rows of neat houses. The air is salubrious, and there is a good supply of water, but peat is obtained only from a bog at the distance of seven miles. Two snuff and tobacco manufactories, and a small brewery, are carried on. The market is on Thursday, chiefly for potatoes, pigs, and poultry; and horse and cattle fairs, which are frequently attended by English dealers, are held by patent on the first Thursday after the 12th of Feb., May, Aug., and Nov. Four other fairs have been recently established, and are held on the 1st of April, July, and Oct., and Dec. 22nd. Petty sessions are held on alternate Saturdays, in a neat building erected by Earl Fitzwilliam, over which is the constabulary police barrack, this town being the residence of the chief constable of the Tinahely district.

The parish comprises 23,137 statute acres, as applotted under the tithe act, of which 15,084 are in Wicklow, and 8053 in Wexford: about one-fifteenth is waste land, and there are 500 acres of woodland; the remainder is arable and pasture. The soil is in general fertile, and the lands chiefly under tillage; and the system of agriculture has been greatly improved since the institution of the Shillelagh and Casha Farming Society at Coolattin, by the late Earl Fitzwilliam, in 1830. At Kilcavan are quarries of building stone and slate, the latter of which is sent into the counties of Carlow and Wexford. Detached granite is also worked in the parish. Besides Coolattin Park, the property of Earl Fitzwilliam, and residence of his agent, R. Chaloner, Esq., there are in the parish, or its vicinity, Tombreen, the seat of T. Swan, Esq.; Upper Bullingate, of H. Braddell, Esq.; Lower Bullingate, of W. Braddell, Esq.; Hillbrooke, of J. Symes, Esq.; Croney Horn, of Dr. De Rinzy; Ballyellis, of R. H. Dowse, Esq.; Umrigar, of R. Blayney, Esq.; Donishall, of R. Bookey, Esq.; Coolboy House, of J. Chamney, Esq.; Barracks, of R. Nickson Sherwood, Esq.; Kilcavan, of R. Taylor, Esq.; Buckstone, formerly occupied as barracks, but now the residence of E. Smith, Esq.; and Carnew Castle, of the Rev. H. Moore, the rector. This castle is popularly said to have been battered and unroofed by the army of Cromwell from a rock above the town, still called Cromwell's rock, on his march from Dublin to Wexford. It was newly roofed and thoroughly repaired, about 20 years since, by the late Earl Fitzwilliam. The living is a rectory and vicarage, in the diocese of Ferns, and in the patronage of the Bishop: the tithes amount to £830. 15. 4½. In 1833, a portion of the parish was detached and erected into the perpetual curacy of Shillelagh, which is in the gift of the rector. The church, which was enlarged in 1813, is a handsome building with an embattled tower crowned with pinnacles and surmounted by a spire, which was added in 1831; and the Rev. C. Cope, who was 33 years rector of this parish, bequeathed £100 for the purchase of a bell. It contains three handsome marble monuments; one in memory of J. Chamney, Esq., Captain of the Coolattin Yeomanry Infantry (who, with his nephew, an officer in that corps, was killed in the insurrection of 1798, in an action at Ballyrahine, in the adjoining parish of Mullinacuff), was erected by the late Earl Fitzwilliam; the second to the memory of W. Wainwright, Esq., J. P., and for above 30 years agent and sole manager of his lordship's estates in the counties of Wicklow, Wexford, and Kildare; and the third in memory of T. Bookey, Esq., of Mount Garnet, in the county of Kilkenny. The body of the church has been condemned by the Ecclesiastical Commissioners, and is about to be rebuilt. There is neither glebe-house nor glebe. In the R. C. divisions that part of the parish which is in Wicklow is included in the union or district of Carnew and Crosspatrick, also called Tomacork, where the chapel is situated; and that part which is in Wexford is in the union or district of Kilrush, and has a chapel at Askeymore. There is a place of worship in the town for Wesleyan Methodists. A parochial library has been established; and there are schools at Montabower, Askeymore, and Carnew, principally supported by Earl Fitzwilliam, in which are educated about 460 Protestant and Roman Catholic children; also a school connected with Tomacork chapel, and two hedge schools. A dispensary is supported in the customary manner; there is an association for employing the poor in spinning and weaving, superintended by the ladies of the town and neighbourhood; and a loan fund was established in 1834. This last institution is conducted by a committee of gentlemen, and has been highly beneficial; the loans have been returned without the loss of a single penny, although, in Dec. 1836, they amounted to about £200 weekly, which is repaid by weekly instalments of one shilling per pound; a fourth part of the profits of this admirable institution (which are considerable) is applied to charitable purposes. On the townland of Umrigar are five raths or moats, in one of which, a few years since, an urn of coarse pottery containing bones and ashes was discovered. Francis Sandford, a celebrated writer on heraldry, was born here in 1630.—See SHILLELAGH.

CARNEY, a village, in the parish of DRUMCLIFF, barony of LOWER CARBERY, county of SLIGO, and province of CONNAUGHT, 5 miles (N. W.) from Sligo; containing 45 houses and 220 inhabitants. It is situated on the bay of Drumcliff, about half a mile to the left of the road from Sligo to Ballyshannon; and has a market on Thursday and fairs on May 26th and June 24th, chiefly for cattle and sheep. A constabulary police force is stationed here; and a dispensary is supported principally by Sir R. G. Booth, Bart.—See DRUMCLIFF.

CARNLOUGH, or CARNALLOCK, a maritime village, in the parish of ARDCLINIS, barony of LOWER GLENARM, county of ANTRIM, and province of ULSTER, 2¾ miles (N. by W.) from Glenarm; containing 213 inhabitants. This place, originally a small fishing village, is pleasantly and advantageously situated between the bays of Cushendall and Glenarm, and from the fineness of its strand is much frequented during the summer months for sea-bathing. It consists of 47 houses, and many elegant villas and sea-bathing lodges have been erected in the valley of Glencule, forming an interesting and highly ornamental feature in that secluded vale. The surrounding scenery possesses great natural beauty, and in some parts assumes a character of majestic grandeur. A very extensive deer park, forming part of the demesne of Glenarm castle, and some richly wooded tracts and thriving plantations add greatly to its beauty. The bay of Carnlough is small but very commodious; and a quay for shipping, erected at an expense of £1200 by the late P. Gibbons, Esq., will contribute greatly to promote the prosperity of the place.—See ARDCLINIS.

CARNMONEY, a parish, in the barony of LOWER BELFAST, county of ANTRIM, and province of ULSTER, 3 miles (N. by E.) from Belfast; containing 5423 inhabitants. This place was anciently called *Coole*, and according to tradition there was a town of that name of considerable extent near the present church, on the decay of which the parish took its modern name from an adjoining hill with a large cairn on its summit. It is situated on Carrickfergus bay, and on the road from Belfast to Londonderry; and, according to the Ordnance survey, comprises 8937¼ statute acres, of which about 230 are too mountainous to be cultivated, and the remainder is arable or pasture land, excepting about 70 acres of bog. The land is generally in a high state of cultivation, especially near the shore, where several gentlemen, who are practical agriculturists, till their own estates, and their improved methods are almost generally followed by the farmers. Great quantities of limestone are raised in the parish, and are shipped to Scotland and other places. The village of Whitehouse (*which see*) has considerable manufactures: there are a cotton and flax-spinning manufactory, and extensive works for printing cloths, which are made here exclusively for the Manchester market; and at

White Abbey also is a cotton and flax-spinning manufactory. These establishments together employ about 670 persons. The scenery is embellished with several gentlemen's seats, the principal of which are Merville, the residence of J. Rowan, Esq.; Macedon, of J. Cunningham, Esq.; White Abbey, of — Getty, Esq.; Claremont, of Mrs. Clewlow; Abbey Lands, of H. McCalmont, Esq.; Whitehouse, of — Shaw, Esq.; and the glebe-house, of the Rev. S. Smythe, the vicar.

The living is a vicarage, in the diocese of Connor, united, it is supposed in 1614, to the vicarage of Ballylinney and the rectory of Ballymartin, together constituting the union of Carmoney, in the patronage of the Marquess of Donegal, in whom the rectory is impropriate. The vicarial tithes amount to £210; and according to the report of the Ecclesiastical Commissioners, the gross value of the union, including tithes and glebe, is £575 per annum. The rectorial tithes were placed under composition in 1835. The church, a modern and spacious edifice in good repair, is built on an eminence near the site of a former church, and is intended for the three parishes of the union. The glebe-house is a handsome building, erected by aid of a gift of £300 and a loan of £500 from the late Board of First Fruits, in 1814: the glebe comprises 80 statute acres, valued at £115 per annum. In the R. C. divisions the parish forms part of the union or district of Belfast. There are two meeting-houses for Presbyterians in connection with the Synod of Ulster, of the first and second classes: charitable bequests to the amount of £260 have been left, the interest of which is divided annually among poor Presbyterians. There are also places of worship for Covenanters, or members of the Reformed Synod, and Independents. Near the church is the parochial school, principally supported by the vicar. A very large school-house was built at Whitehouse by the Messrs. Grimshaw, and the school is now in connection with the National Board; one has also been built and is supported by the proprietors of the White Abbey cotton works; the Presbyterians have built and support a school at Ballyduff; and there is also a school at Ballycraigy, built and supported by Francis Turnley, Esq. About 400 children receive education in these schools, and about 200 more in private schools. About a mile north from the church, near the shore, are the picturesque ruins of a large religious house, called White Abbey, from which the townland takes its name, and which was probably the original establishment that was removed to Woodburn: the principal remains are an elegant chapel, in the later Norman or early English style. On the verge of the parish, near Carrickfergus, are the remains of another religious house, called Monkstown, adjoining which is an ancient cemetery, where, according to tradition, Fergus, King of Scotland, who was shipwrecked in the adjacent bay, was interred.

CARRENTEEL, a parish, in the barony of DUNGANNON, county of TYRONE, and province of ULSTER; containing, with the post-town of Aughnacloy, 7459 inhabitants. This place formed part of the manor of Portclare, a very extensive district granted to Sir Thomas Ridgeway, in 1611, by Jas. I., by whose order a fortress called Lismore Bawn was erected here in 1619, of which there are extensive ruins. During the war in 1641, this parish was visited by the contending parties and the church was destroyed; some vestiges of it may still be traced in the ancient cemetery adjoining the village. The parish is situated on the river Blackwater, and on the mail coach road from Dublin to Londonderry · including twelve townlands forming part of the district parish of Ballygawley, it comprises, according to the Ordnance survey, 13,431¾ statute acres, of which 13,080 acres are applotted under the tithe act, and 61 are water; the land is chiefly under an excellent system of cultivation, and produces good crops. The northern side of the parish is mountainous, and contains a tract of bog; and there are extensive quarries of limestone and freestone of very good quality. The seats are Storm Hill, that of R. Montgomery Moore, Esq.; the Bawn, of E. Moore, Esq.; Millview, of S. Simpson, Esq.; and the glebe-house, the residence of the Rev. Archdeacon Stopford. The inhabitants, in addition to their agricultural pursuits, employ themselves at home in weaving linen and cotton. Fairs are held in the village on the first Wednesday in every month, chiefly for cattle and horses. By order of council under the provisions of an act of the 7th and 8th of Geo. IV., twelve townlands were separated from this parish, in 1830, to form part of the district parish of Ballygawley. The living is a rectory and vicarage, in the diocese of Armagh, united by charter in 1637 to the rectory and vicarage of Aghaloo, together constituting the union of Carrenteel and corps of the archdeaconry of Armagh, in the patronage of the Lord-Primate. The tithes amount to £406. 3. 1., and of the union to £1015. 7. 8. It is recommended by the Ecclesiastical Commissioners to dissolve this union on the next avoidance, and to make each parish a separate benefice. After the destruction of the church of Carrenteel, in 1641, a church was erected at Aghaloo, but it was taken down after the erection of the present church at Aughnacloy, which was built in 1736, at the sole expense of the late Acheson Moore, Esq., to which, in 1796, his daughter and heiress, Mrs. Malone, added a tower surmounted by a lofty octagonal spire; and to the repairs of which the Ecclesiastical Commissioners have recently granted £190. 18. The glebe-house, about half a mile from the church, was erected in 1790, and £2000 has been expended on its repair and improvement; the glebe comprises 1046 statute acres, valued at £969 per annum. The R. C. parish is co-extensive with that of the Established Church, and is called Aughby; there are chapels at Aughnacloy, Caledon, and Killin. There are two meeting-houses for Presbyterians, one in connection with the Synod of Ulster, of the second class, and the other with the Seceding Synod; and places of worship for Wesleyan and Primitive Methodists. The parochial male and female school is wholly supported by Archdeacon Stopford, and there are four other schools; in these about 240 boys and 150 girls are instructed, and there are also a private school of 60 boys and 20 girls, and five Sunday schools. At Garvey are the ruins of an extensive and elegant castle, erected by the late Col. Moore, which, very soon after its completion, was suffered to fall into decay; they are situated near those of Lismore Bawn. In this townland, which is about a mile from Aughnacloy, is a very valuable mineral spring; the water contains sulphur, nitre, magnesia, and steel held in solution with carbonic acid; it has been found efficacious in cutaneous diseases and in dyspeptic complaints; a large room has been erected over the spring, and the water issues from a fountain of marble in the centre. Near it is a good house for the accommodation of persons frequenting the spa.—See AUGHNACLOY.

CARRICK, a parish, in the barony of CARBERY, county of KILDARE, and province of LEINSTER, 2¼ miles (N.) from Edenderry; containing 604 inhabitants. This parish is situated on the road from Edenderry to Kinnegad, and on the banks of the river Boyne; the land is in a good state of cultivation, and the system of husbandry greatly improved; there is a considerable tract of bog. There are some excellent limestone quarries, and at Ballindolan is a quarry of black flag-stone. The seats are Rahan, that of the Rev. C. Palmer; Ballindolan, of Humphrey Borr, Esq.; and Grange Castle, of — Tyrrell, Esq. A fair is held at Russel Wood on the 28th of August. It is a vicarage, in the diocese of Kildare, and is part of the union of Carbery; the rectory is impropriate in the Marquess of Downshire. The tithes amount to £149. 16. 1½. In the R. C. divisions the parish forms part of the union or district of Cadamstown. A male and female parochial school at Rahan, in which are 30 boys and 30 girls, is supported by the vicar, aided by subscriptions. There are some remains of the old castle of Carrig, the residence of the Bermingham family, and of the old church, their burial-place; and also the ruins of Kinnefad, another residence of that family.

CARRICK, or CARRICKBAGGOT, a parish, in the barony of FERRARD, county of LOUTH, and province of LEINSTER, 2½ miles (S. S. E.) from Dunleer; containing 340 inhabitants. This parish, which is situated on the coast road from Drogheda to Dundalk, contains 826¼ statute acres, chiefly arable land, and includes part of the demesne of Rokeby Hall. It is a rectory, in the diocese of Armagh, and is part of the union of Rathdrummin: the tithes amount to £57. 8. 6. In the R. C. divisions it forms part of the union or district of Clogher. There are some remains of the old church.

CARRICK, a parish, in the barony of FARTULLAGH, county of WESTMEATH, and province of LEINSTER, 5¼ miles (S. by W.) from Mullingar; containing 576 inhabitants. This parish is situated upon Lough Ennel, by which it is bounded on the north and west, and contains 2115 statute acres, principally under tillage, with very little bog: there is a considerable and sudden elevation of the land above the lough. The seats are Carrick, the residence of W. Fetherston H., Esq.; and Robinstown, of W. D'Arcy Irwin, Esq. It is a rectory, in the diocese of Meath, and is part of the union of Moylisker: the tithes amount to £76. In the R. C. divisions, part of the parish is in the union or district of Fartullagh, and the remainder in that of Mullingar. There is a hedge school, in which about 30 children are taught. Numerous raths are scattered over the parish; near Carrick are the remains of an old church, and near Robinstown those of an old castle.

CARRICK, or CARRIG, a parish, in the barony of BARGY, county of WEXFORD, and province of LEINSTER, 6 miles (S. S. W.) from Taghmon; containing 707 inhabitants. This place, which is situated near the southern coast, is also called St. Imock's, and by the country people *Shamogues.* It is only known as a parish in the civil divisions, having been long since ecclesiastically incorporated with the parish of Bannow, in the diocese of Ferns, and both united to the parish of Kilcavan. The village of Danescastle, from its proximity to the coast, is much frequented during the summer season for sea-bathing; and a car running through Taghmon to Wexford leaves this place three mornings in the week and returns in the afternoon. The parish comprises 2997 statute acres, as assessed to the county rate; the land is chiefly under tillage; and the system of agriculture has been greatly improved within the last few years. Limestone brought from Slade up the bay of Bannow is the principal manure. At Barrystown are vestiges of ancient lead mines, the ore of which is said to have contained a very large proportion of silver, whence probably they have been traditionally called silver mines. In the R. C. divisions this place forms part of the union or district of Ballymitty; the chapel, a neat edifice, is at Danescastle; and in the chapel-yard is a comfortable residence for the R. C. clergyman, adjoining which is a national school. At a short distance from the village of Danescastle is a lofty square tower, the erection of which is attributed to the earliest of the Norman settlers; it has much of the gloomy character of that period.

CARRICK-A-REDE.—See BALLINTOY.

CARRICK-BEG, a suburb to the town of Carrick-on-Suir (formerly an incorporated town), in the parish of KILMOLERAN, barony of UPPERTHIRD, county of WATERFORD, and province of MUNSTER; containing 2704 inhabitants. This place, of which the name signifies Little Carrick, was formerly called *Carrick-mac-Griffin;* it is situated on the south side of the river Suir, over which is an ancient stone bridge connecting it with Carrick-on-Suir. From a grant of restoration of murage and pontage to the provost and commonalty of the Town of Carrick-mac-Griffin, made in the 18th of Edw. III., dated 12th July 1344, it would appear to have been a borough. A friary for Conventual Franciscans, dedicated to St. Michael, was founded here in the year 1336, by James Butler, Earl of Ormonde, to whose great grandfather, Theobald, the lands of Carrick-mac-Griffin had been granted. The first warden was John Clyn, a Franciscan friar of Kilkenny; he wrote short annals from the birth of Christ to the year 1315, and from that year continued them more copiously and carefully to the year 1349, when he died of the plague. This establishment flourished till the dissolution, when it was granted with all its possessions to the Earl of Ormonde. Of the ancient buildings, the tower of the church is almost the only remaining portion; it is square and nearly perfect, projecting considerably beyond the foundation on which it rests, and is based on a single stone, from which it rises in the form of a truncated pyramid inverted; a fine flight of spiral steps in the wall leads to the summit. The monastery, which was a large and very irregular structure, has been taken down; and a modern chapel, now the parish chapel, has been erected on the site; the principal entrance is under an arch of very elegant design, which had been preserved from the ruins of the ancient building. A Franciscan friary was erected near the site of the former in 1822, by the Rev. Michael Fleming, now R. C. Bishop of Newfoundland: the friary chapel is in the later English style, faced with hewn stone; the principal entrance is of handsome design; above it is a well-sculptured figure of a saint, and at the opposite extremity, a tower erected in imitation of that of the old abbey; the ceilings of both chapels are richly and delicately groined. The woollen manufacture was formerly carried on here very extensively, affording employment to a great number of the population; but within the last 30 years it has gradually been falling to decay. Fairs are held on Jan. 26th, Feb. 26th, March 25th, April 28th, June 15th, July 15th, Sept. 27th, Nov. 7th, and Dec. 5th. A constabulary police force is stationed here.

CARRICKBOY, a hamlet, in the parish of KILGLASS, barony of ABBEYSHRUEL, county of LONGFORD, and province of LEINSTER, 5 miles (S.) from Edgeworthstown: the population is returned with the parish. This place is situated on the road from Edgeworthstown to Ballymahon; it contains Richmont, the seat of J. Huggins, Esq., M. D., and is a constabulary police station.

Arms.

CARRICKFERGUS, a sea-port, borough, market- and post-town, and parish, and a county of itself, locally in the county of ANTRIM, of which it was the ancient capital and is still the county town, 88 miles (N.) from Dublin; containing 8706 inhabitants. This place, which is of great antiquity, is by some writers identified with the ancient *Dun-Sobarky* or *Dun-Sobairchia*, according to Dr. Charles O'Conor from a prince named Sobairchius, who made it his residence; but the correctness of this supposition is doubted by others. It is thought to have derived its present name, signifying "The Rock of Fergus," early in the 4th century, from Fergus Mac Erch, a chieftain of Dalaradia, who established the first Irish settlement on the opposite coast of Caledonia. An ancient triad quoted by Dr. O'Conor records that St. Patrick blessed a tower or strong hold of the Dalaradians, in which was a well of miraculous efficacy, called *Tipra Phadruic*, "The well of St. Patrick." It is uncertain at what period the castle was originally erected; the present structure, from the style of its architecture, was evidently built soon after the arrival of the English. John, Earl of Morton and Lord of Ireland, was here in the lifetime of his father, Hen. II. (from whom John De Courcy received the grant of all the lands he might conquer in Ulster); and his despatch to the king, dated at Carrickfergus, in which he mentions his having taken the castle, is still extant among the MSS. in the library of Trinity College, Dublin, and is written in Latin. This castle, with subsequent additions, is still remaining, and is justly considered one of the noblest fortresses of that time now existing in Ireland. De Courcy having fallen into disgrace with the succeeding English monarchs, his castles and possessions in this county fell into the hands of the De Lacy family, who, becoming tyrannical and oppressive, incurred the anger of King John. During the contentions which arose among the English settlers, after they had established themselves in the country, this place suffered so much that Hugh de Lacy the younger, who, on the restoration of his family to the royal favour, repaired the town and strengthened it by the introduction of new settlers, has even been regarded as its founder. In 1234 Carrickfergus is mentioned as one of the haven towns of Ulster; but from that period till shortly after the commencement of the 14th century, little of its history is known. The De Lacys, again becoming obnoxious to the English monarch, and the Lord-Justice Mortimer being sent against them with a considerable force, they made their escape into Scotland, and invited Edward Bruce, the brother of the Scottish monarch, to invade the country, and become their king. Accordingly, in 1315, Bruce embarked 6000 men at Ayr, and, accompanied by the De Lacys and several of the Scottish nobility, landed at Wolderfirth, now Olderfleet, where, being joined by numbers of the Irish chieftains, he routed Richard de Burgo, now Earl of Ulster, who had been sent against him; and having slain several of the English nobles and taken many of them prisoners, advanced to lay siege to the castle of this place. During the siege, Thomas, Lord Mandeville, who commanded the garrison, made a sally on the assailants, whom he repulsed at the first onset; but, being recognised by the richness of his armour, he was felled to the ground by the blow of a battle-axe and instantly killed. The garrison, disheartened by the loss of their commander, agreed to surrender the castle within a limited time, and on the appointed day, 30 of the Scottish forces advancing to take possession, were seized as prisoners, the garrison declaring that they would defend the place to the last; but for want of provisions they were soon obliged to surrender. Bruce, having secured Carrickfergus, advanced to Dublin, and arrived at Castleknock, within four miles of the city; but finding the citizens prepared for his reception, he entered the county of Kildare, and advanced towards Limerick, laying waste the country with fire and sword; on his retreating towards the north, he was attacked near Dundalk by Sir John Bermingham, who defeated the Scottish forces and killed their leader. King Robert Bruce arrived soon after with a strong reinforcement, but on learning the fate of his brother, returned to his own dominions, and thus terminated an enterprise which had thrown the country into a state of unprecedented desolation.

After the evacuation of the country by the Scots, Carrickfergus again reverted to its former possessors; but the desultory warfare carried on at intervals for successive ages in the north of Ireland, during which its strength and situation rendered it the centre of operations, subjected it to many severe calamities. In 1333, William, Earl of Ulster, was assassinated here by his own servants; and his countess, with her infant daughter, fleeing into England, the O'Nials, the original lords of the soil, immediately succeeded in expelling the English settlers, and for a time retained possession of the place. In 1386 the town was burned by the Scots; and in 1400 it was again destroyed by the combined forces of the Scots and Irish. In 1481 a commission was granted to the mayor and others, to enter into a league with the Earl of Ross, Lord of the Isles, who had usurped the sovereignty of the Hebrides from the Scottish crown. In 1497 the town and neighbourhood were visited by famine; and in 1504 it was resolved that none but an Englishman should be entrusted with the custody of its castle, or with that of Green Castle, in the county of Down. The town continued for many years to be a strong hold of the English, and even when the English Government was so reduced as to be scarcely able to maintain a standing army of 140 horse within the English pale, the castle still remained in their possession. In 1573 the corporation addressed a remonstrance to the Lord-Deputy Fitzwilliam, representing that one-third of the town was then in ruins; and, in the summer of the same year, it was still further desolated by fire. In this state it remained for many years, though the Earl of Essex landed here with his train, on taking possession of the government of Ulster, to which he had been appointed; and though Sir Henry Sidney, the succeeding lord-deputy, gave the English council a forcible representation of its deplorable condition, in the account of his northern expedition, two years afterwards. The particular events by which it was reduced to this state of desolation are detailed in a "Discourse of Knockfergus," preserved among the Cottonian manuscripts in the British Museum, in which its calamities are ascribed to an early quarrel with Bryan Balloughe, chieftain of the adjoining territory of Claneboy, whose son and successor continued to harass the inhabitants till they were compelled to purchase peace by consenting to pay an annual tribute; to the repeated devastating incursions of the Scots; to the continued depredations of the O'Nials and Mac Donnels, and to various other causes. The Lord-Deputy, Sir Henry Sidney, made great efforts for the improvement and security of the town, but so greatly were the resources of the townsmen reduced that, in 1581, Lord Grey, then deputy, found it necessary to issue an express edict prohibiting them from paying to the Irish lord of the country the tribute hitherto paid to the successors of Bryan Balloughe, and called, in that document, "Breyne Balaf's Eric."

The extensive privileges enjoyed by the inhabitants of this place, and the protection afforded by new fortifications, soon caused an increase in its population and importance. On the breaking out of the war in 1641, Sir Henry Mac Neill was to have surprised the town, but was defeated by the vigilance of Col. Arthur Chichester, the governor; and it now became one of the principal places of refuge for the Protestants of the neighbouring counties. In 1642, the town and castle were, according to agreement, delivered up to General Monroe, who, having landed with 2500 Scottish auxiliaries, to carry on the war against the Irish, made this place his head-quarters till 1648, when he was taken by surprise in the castle, and sent prisoner to England by General Monk, who was, by the parliament, appointed governor in his place, and rewarded with a gratuity of £500; and in the year following, the castle, which had been surrendered to the Earl of Inchiquin, was reduced for Cromwell by Sir Charles Coote. In 1666, the garrison mutinied, seized the castle and the town, and acted with such desperate resolution that the Government, alarmed at their excesses, sent the Earl of Arran, son of the Duke of Ormonde, by sea, to reduce them; and the latter nobleman marching also against them with the few forces on whose fidelity he could rely, the mutineers, after some resistance, surrendered; 110 of them were tried by a court martial, of whom nine were executed, and the companies to which they belonged were disbanded. In the early part of 1689, an attempt was made by the Protestant inhabitants of the neighbourhood to take this fortress, which was then held by the troops of James II., but without success; in the course of the year, however, Schomberg, William's general, invested it with a large force, and the garrison, after having exhausted all their ammunition, surrendered. In 1690 William III. landed here to take the command of his army; and from this time the town was undistinguished by any historical event till the year 1760, when it was attacked by the French, under the command of Thurot. The gates were quickly closed, and though General Flobert, who led the assault, was wounded, the garrison, consisting only of one hundred men, was soon obliged to capitulate for want of ammunition. The country people, however, supported by reinforcements from the interior, rose on all sides to repel the assailants; and on the approach of an English squadron, which had been despatched on the first intelligence of the projected invasion, the French, after supplying themselves with provisions and water, hastily re-embarked, taking with them three of the principal inhabitants, who were afterwards found on board the commander's ship, when she struck to the English off the Isle of Man. In 1778, the celebrated Paul Jones appeared off the town, but did not land, contenting himself with the capture of an armed vessel that had been sent to attack him. In 1785, His present Majesty, when lieutenant on board the ship of Commodore Gower, arrived in the bay; on which occasion the Carrickfergus volunteers solicited the honour of forming a body guard for his Royal Highness, which was courteously declined.

The town is situated on the north-western shore of Carrickfergus bay, or Belfast Lough, along which it extends for nearly a mile, comprising three portions, the town within the walls, and two suburbs, called respectively the Irish and the Scottish quarters; the former situated to the west, along the road leading to Belfast; and the latter to the north-east, along the road to Larne and Island Magee, and inhabited by the descendants of a colony of fishermen from Argyle and Galloway, who took refuge here from the persecutions of 1665. The town within the walls was formerly entered by four gates, of which only the remains of the North or Spittal gate now exist; of the walls there is yet a considerable portion on the north and west sides in a very perfect state. The town contains about 800 houses, built chiefly of stone and roofed with slate; several of superior character have been built within the last forty years, during which period considerable improvements have taken place. The castle, which is in good preservation, and during the disturbances of 1798 was used as a state prison, is situated on a rock projecting boldly into the sea, by which it is surrounded on three sides at high water; this rock is 30 feet in height at its southern extremity, and declines considerably towards the land; the outer walls of the castle are adapted to the irregularities of its surface; and the entrance is defended by two semicircular towers, with a portcullis and machicolation above. In the interior are barracks for the reception of two companies of foot and a few artillerymen. The keep is a square tower 90 feet high, the lower part of which is bomb-proof, and is used as a magazine: in the third story is an apartment 40 feet long, 38 feet wide, and 26 feet high, called Fergus's dining-room. The well in this tower, anciently celebrated for its miraculous efficacy, is now nearly filled up; a quantity of old iron was taken out of it many years since, from which it may have derived its medicinal properties. The castle was formerly governed by a constable, who had very extensive powers; the present establishment consists only of a governor and a master-gunner. Musical societies formerly existed and occasional assemblies were held in the town, but the only source of public amusement at present is a sporting club. Though formerly celebrated for its trade and commerce, this place has never been distinguished for the extent of its manufactures: the linen manufacture, which was the staple, has, within the last fifty years, been superseded by that of cotton, for which there are at present two spinning factories; and many persons are engaged in weaving checks, ginghams, and other cotton goods for the manufacturers of Belfast and Glasgow. There are also two mills for spinning linen yarn, and an extensive distillery, producing annually about 90,000 gallons of whiskey, with mills, malt-kilns, and other conveniences on an improved system; the tanning of leather, which was introduced here at an early period, is still carried on to a great extent. The vicinity affords numerous advantageous sites for the establishment of manufactories: a considerable water power is supplied by the Woodburn and Sulla-tober rivers, and by the water of Lough Morne; there are 1070 feet of waterfalls, calculated at 676-horse power, of which by far the greater part is unoccupied.

The fishery in the bay constitutes the chief employment of the poorer inhabitants of the suburbs, and the boats fitted out from the two quarters differ in their construction and the mode of working them: those from the Irish quarter, of which there are about seven or eight, with four men each, are smack-rigged and work by trawling or dredging; the fish generally taken is plaice, but skate, sole, and lythe or pollock are occasionally caught, and lobsters and oysters of very large size and good flavour are also dredged. The boats from the Scottish quarter are small and without decks, of not more than two or three tons' burden, rigged with a fore and main lug sail, and are occasionally worked with oars to the number of six in winter and four in summer: in the latter season from 16 to 20 boats, carrying four or six persons each, are generally employed, and both lines and nets are used; but in the former, when lines are principally used, the number of hands is increased to nine or ten: the fish chiefly taken by these boats are cod, ling, hake, lythe, and herring; lobsters are also caught and kept in traps or baskets. The town derives also an accession of trade from its being frequented as a bathing-place during summer, and from the assizes, sessions, and parliamentary elections for the county of Antrim being held in it. From the privilege of importing merchandise at lower duties than were paid throughout the rest of the country, its commerce was formerly very extensive, and its returns were greater than those of any other port in Ireland; but this privilege was sold to the crown in 1637, and the trade was immediately transferred to Belfast, to which place even the produce of its cotton manufacture is sent for exportation. It is now a member of the port of Belfast, under which head the registry of its vessels and the duties paid at the custom-house are included. The trade consists principally of the importation of coal and the exportation of cattle and occasionally of grain.

The harbour is situated in latitude 54° 42′ 45″ (N.), and longitude 5° 47′ (W.), 9½ miles (N. W. by W.) from the Copeland islands' lighthouse. It is formed by a pier extending from the old castle, in a western direction, to a distance of 460 feet, and within about 400 feet of low water mark at spring tides; at high water it affords only a depth of from six to nine feet, so that vessels of more than 100 tons cannot approach the quay; it is also subject to the accumulation of mud and sand. A handsome pier was erected for the use of the fishermen, in 1834, at an expense of £2600, defrayed by a grant from Government and by local subscriptions. The port is sheltered by land from the prevailing south and west winds; and though winds from the other points produce a certain degree of swell in the offing, yet, from the situation of the Copeland islands and Kilroot point, it is so protected as not to be open seaward more than 2½ points of the compass. But the imperfections of the harbour greatly restrict the trade of the port: a plan and report were drawn up by Sir John Rennie for constructing a new harbour outside the present, so as to insure a depth of 15 feet at low water of spring tides, the estimate for which, including the construction of works for protecting it against the accumulation of sand, and for the requisite accommodation of the shipping, was £55,150; these improvements, from a variety of causes, would render the port one of the most thriving and convenient in the North of Ireland, and a useful auxiliary to the flourishing town of Belfast. A new road leading to Doagh, Templepatrick, and Antrim is in progress, which, when completed, will afford the means of a direct conveyance of grain from an extensive tract to this port, and open a market for the consumption of coal, groceries, and other commodities imported. The market is on Saturday; and fairs are held on May 12th and Nov. 1st. The market-house, built by subscription in 1755, is also used for the meetings of the "Assembly," or aldermen and burgesses of the corporation.

The incorporation of the town as a county of itself is ascribed by tradition to King John; the shrievalty was held jointly with that of the county of Antrim. But although it existed as a separate county long prior to the time of Elizabeth, the charter of the 11th of her reign is the earliest on record containing such incorporation. Its boundaries are described in this charter and in one of the 7th of Jas. I., with a reservation of the castle and its precincts, together with the ancient liberties and royalties appertaining to it, and of sites for a sessions-house and prison for the county of Antrim; but the latter charter excluded from the county of the town certain lands which had been granted and confirmed to the corporation by charter of the 44th of Elizabeth. The franchise now acknowledged is stated to differ from both, and to be in conformity with a riding of the franchises made by the corporation in 1785. In 1810 it was decided, on an issue tried at the assizes, that the lands of Straid and Little Ballymena, described by the charter of Elizabeth as being within the boundary, but not within that marked out by the charter of James, though still belonging to the corporation, are not within the franchise. This is probably a borough by prescription: the earliest notice of the existence of a corporation is in the record of a commission dated 1274, in which year the Scots landed on the neighbouring coast to assist the O'Neills against the English. Hen. IV., in 1402, on the petition of the mayor and three burgesses released them, for one year, from the payment of the annual rent of 100*s.* for the customs, to aid them in rebuilding the town, which had been burned by his enemies. Queen Elizabeth, in the 11th of her reign (1569), on a representation of the inhabitants that they had lost their letters patent in the disturbances and persecutions of rebels and enemies, by which they were deprived of the enjoyment of their franchises, granted a charter of incorporation conferring on them, besides several special immunities, all such other privileges and jurisdictions as the corporation of Drogheda possessed; and ordaining that they should hold the borough of the king, as of his castle of Knockfergus, at an annual rent of 10*s.*, payable half-yearly, until the fortifications should be repaired and a grant of lands made, and then at a rent of £40 per annum. The grant of lands was conferred by charter of the 44th of Elizabeth, founded on an inquisition issued to ascertain the quantity which had previously belonged to the corporation. James I., in addition to the charter of the 7th of his reign, before noticed, granted others in the 10th and 20th, the former of which is now the governing charter, and the latter created fourteen persons and their successors a corporation, by the style of the "Mayor, Constables, and Society of the Merchants of the Staple." In the "new rules" of the 25th of Chas. II., for regulating corporations in Ireland, it was ordained that the appointment of the mayor, recorder, sheriffs, and town-clerk should be subject to the approbation of the lord-lieutenant and privy council.

The corporation, under the style of "the Mayor, Sheriffs, Burgesses, and Commonalty of the Town of Carrickfergus," consists of the mayor (who is an alderman), 16 other aldermen, two sheriffs (who are burgesses), 22 other burgesses, and an indefinite number of freemen, assisted by a recorder and town-clerk (who is also clerk of the peace), two coroners, three town-serjeants, a water-bailiff, sword-bearer, and other officers. The charter of the 10th of Jas. I. granted a guild merchant within the town, and ordained that all the merchants should be a corporation, by the name of the "Two Masters and Fellows of the Guild Merchant of the Town of Knockfergus," the masters to be elected annually from and by the merchants of the guild, on the Monday after the feast of St. Michael, with power to make by-laws and impose fines. The guilds now remaining are those of the Hammermen, Weavers, Carters, Taylors and Glovers, Butchers, Trawlers and Dredgers, Hookers, and Shoemakers or Cordwainers, incorporated at different periods; but their restrictive privileges in trade have been abandoned as impolitic or useless, and they are now kept up only in form. The mayor is elected annually from among the aldermen, at an assembly of the corporation at large, on the 24th of June, and by the charter must be sworn before the constable of the castle, or, in his absence, before the vice-constable, and in the presence of the mayor for the preceding year, on Michaelmas-day; he has power, with the assent of a majority of the aldermen, to depute one of that body to be vice-mayor in his absence. The aldermen, who may be from 8 to 16 in number, are chosen, on vacancies occurring, from the 24 burgesses by the remaining aldermen, and are removable for misbehaviour by a majority of the body. The sheriffs are eligible from the free burgesses by the mayor, sheriffs, burgesses, and commonalty, annually on the 24th of June: they are sworn on the feast of St. Michael before the mayor and burgesses, and are removable for cause. The burgesses, who are not mentioned by any of the charters as a definite class in the corporation, and were formerly unlimited in number, have been restricted to 24, and, according to practice, are elected in an assembly of the mayor, sheriffs, and remaining burgesses, neither freedom nor residence being requisite as a qualification, and are supposed, like the aldermen, to hold during good behaviour. The freemen are admissible, in courts of the whole corporation held by the mayor, by the right of birth extending to all the sons of freemen, also by marriage, apprenticeship to a freeman within the county of the town, and by gift of the corporation: among other privileges granted by charter to the freemen, of which most have been long disused, it was ordained that no person should be attached or arrested in the house of a freeman, except for treason or felony. The recorder is eligible by the mayor, sheriffs, burgesses, and commonalty, to hold his office either for life, for a term of years, or at the will of the corporation, as may be deemed expedient, but is usually elected for life: he may, with the consent of the mayor and a majority of the aldermen, appoint a deputy to execute the office. The town-clerk is eligible by the whole body, and holds his office during pleasure; and the coroners, by the charter, are eligible by the mayor, sheriffs, burgesses, and commonalty, from the inhabitants, annually on the same day with the mayor and sheriffs, or any other deemed more expedient, and are removable for cause; but in practice it is considered that they ought to be elected from the freemen, and they appear to hold office for life or good behaviour. A treasurer, who was formerly the mayor for the time being, is now appointed by the assembly, and is usually an alderman. The "assembly" is composed of the mayor, aldermen, sheriffs, and burgesses, who manage all the affairs of the corporation; they assume the power of making by-laws, and of demising the property of the corporation. The charters of Elizabeth and James confirmed to this borough the right of sending two representatives to the Irish parliament, which it continued to exercise till the Union, since which period it has returned one to the Imperial parliament. The elective franchise was vested in the mayor, aldermen, burgesses, and freemen of the town, and in the freeholders to the amount of 40*s.* per annum and upwards in the county of the town, amounting, in Jan., 1832, to about 850; but by the act of the 2nd of Wm. IV., cap. 88, the non-resident freemen, except within seven miles, have been disfranchised, and the privilege has been extended to the £10 householders and the £20 and £10 leaseholders for the respective terms of 14 and 20 years; by this act the 40*s.* freeholders retain the franchise for life only. The number of voters registered at the close of 1835 was about 1200: the sheriffs are the returning officers.

The mayor (as also his deputy or vice-mayor) is a justice of the peace within the town, and is further (without mention of the vice-mayor) constituted a justice of the peace throughout the county of the town, being empowered, with the recorder, to hold courts of session and gaol delivery: he is admiral of the liberties, which extend northward to Fair Head and southward to Beerlooms, about 40 miles in each direction, with the exception only of Bangor and the Pool of Garmoyle; and may issue attachments against ships and cargoes, or against persons on board, for the recovery of debts wherever contracted: he is also a magistrate for the county of Antrim, and he or his deputy is judge of the Tholsel court; he is appointed *custos rotulorum* of the county of the town, and is escheator, master of the assays, and clerk of the market; and the charter empowers him to grant licences for ships coming to the port, upon entering, to buy or forestall merchandise, and also for the salting of hides, fish, &c. The recorder is a justice of the peace within the county and county of the town; he is the assessor of the mayor in the Tholsel court, and he or his deputy is judge of the court leet and view of frank-pledge to be held in the town twice a year, within a month after Easter and Michaelmas. In 1828, on the petition of the inhabitants, two additional justices were appointed by the lord-lieutenant, under the powers of the act of the 7th of Geo. IV., cap. 61. The corporation has not any exclusive jurisdiction over matters arising within the borough, except that which results from its forming a county of itself: the courts are those of assize and quarter and petty sessions, also a Tholsel court, a sheriffs' or county court, a court leet with view of frankpledge, and a court of pie-poudre. The assizes for the county of the town are held at the usual periods before the mayor, with whom the other judges of assize are associated in commission; since 1817 they have been held in the county of Antrim court-house, under the act of the 28th of Geo. III., cap. 38, confirmed by several succeeding statutes. The quarter sessions are held before the mayor, recorder, and the two additional justices, in the market-house, which has been appropriated for that purpose since the building called the Tholsel was taken down: the court has jurisdiction over all felonies and minor offences committed within the county of the town, with power to inflict capital punishment, which, however, is not exercised, offences of a more serious kind being referred to the judges of assize. The Tholsel court, which is a court of record, having jurisdiction over the county of the town to an unlimited amount of pleas in personal actions, is by the charter to be held every Monday and Friday, but is now held on the former day; and is empowered to proceed by summons, attachment (which is the usual form), *distringas*, or any other process, on affidavit before the mayor, whose presence is only deemed necessary in the event of a trial, which seldom takes place. Petty sessions are held once a week, usually before the two additional justices. The assistant barrister for the county of Antrim holds his courts here for trying causes by civil bill; and the assizes and two of the quarter sessions for the county of Antrim are held here. The local police consists of three constables, appointed and paid by the grand jury of assize, and of twelve unpaid constables appointed at the court leet.

The charter granted one-third part of the customs' dues of the port to the corporation, who enjoyed considerable advantages under this privilege, which, in the year 1637, they surrendered to the Crown in consideration of a sum of £3000, to be paid to trustees and invested in land, but from its non-investment the town has been deprived of all benefit accruing from this grant. The charter of the 10th of Jas. I. also granted the right of fishery in the river and a ferry over it, with various fines, waifs, wrecks of the sea, forfeitures, &c., arising within their liberties, from which they derive no advantage at present. Their revenue arises exclusively from rents reserved out of their property in lands, amounting to about £359 late currency. The corporation court-house and gaol were at "Castle Worraigh" previously to 1776, in which year the county of Antrim grand jury exchanged their gaol and court-house in the vicinity of the castle of Carrickfergus for "Castle Worraigh," on the site of which part of the present court-house for that county was built, and the corporation continued to use the old gaol of the county of Antrim until 1827, when prisoners under criminal charges were removed from it to the new gaol; and after the passing of an act for regulating prisons, the old Tholsel having become ruinous, a new arrangement was entered into between the respective grand juries of Carrickfergus and Antrim, by which the former pay, in lieu of all charges, "£13 for every 365 days of a prisoner confined in the county of Antrim gaol." The court-house for the county of Antrim is a neat building, fronted with hewn stone, situated at the east end of the main street; and adjoining it, on the north side, is the gaol, which, though capable of containing 340 prisoners, is but ill adapted for their classification or for the preservation of strict discipline.

The county of the town extends about five statute miles along the shore, and its mean length and breadth are nearly equal; it contains, according to the Ordnance survey, 16,700*a.* 1*r.* 34*p.*, including Lough Morne, which comprises 89*a.* 3*r.* 22*p.* The amount of Grand Jury presentments, for 1835, was £839. 5. 7½., of which £186. 8. 9. was for repairing the roads, bridges, &c.; £386. 10. 3. for public establishments, charities, officers' salaries, &c.; and £266. 6. 7½. for the repayment of a loan advanced by Government. Lough Morne, or More, about three miles north of the town, is said to be the largest in Ireland at the same elevation, which is 556 feet above the level of the sea; it has a powerful spring near the centre, and is well stored with eels and pike. The principal streams, all of which take a nearly direct course into the bay, are the Woodburn, which is formed by the union of two rivulets about two miles above the town (on each of which is a picturesque cascade), and supplies two large cotton mills, a flour and corn-mill, and a large mill for spinning linen yarn near the town; the Orland Water, which descends from Lough Morne, and falls into the bay at the eastern suburb of the town; the Sulla-Tober, which falls into the bay near the same place; the Copeland Water, which forms the eastern boundary of the county; the Silver Stream, which bounds it on the south-west; and the Red River: in all of these are found black and white trout, eels, and stickleback. The surface is studded with the villages of Eden or Edengrenny, Clipperstown, Woodburn, and Bonnybefore; with several hamlets, numerous gentlemen's seats scattered along the shore, and surrounded with ornamental plantations; and several farm-houses of comfortable appearance interspersed throughout. The principal gentlemen's seats are Thornfield, the residence of P. Kirk, Esq., M. P.; Oakfield, of W. D. D. Wilson, Esq.; St. Catherine's, of Col. Walsh; Glen Park, of Capt. Skinner; Barn Cottage, of J. Cowan, Esq.; Prospect, of — Vance, Esq.; Woodford, of the Rev. J. Gwynn; Sea Park, of the Rev. J. Chaine; and Scout Bush, of Edw. Bruce, Esq.

The parish is co-extensive with the county of the town; the living is a rectory, in the diocese of Conner, united, by charter of the 7th of Jas. I., with the rectories of Island Magee and Ralloo, the vicarage of Inver, and the grange of Moylusk or Moblusk, which union constitutes the corps of the deanery of Connor, in the patronage of the Crown: the tithes of the parish amount to £400; and the gross annual income of the deanery, tithe and glebe inclusive, is £1004. 7. The church, dedicated to St. Nicholas, is an ancient cruciform structure, with a tower, surmounted by a lofty spire; it is said to have been erected on the site of a pagan temple, and appears to have been attached to the Franciscan monastery formerly existing here; the chancel window is embellished with a representation of the baptism of Christ, in painted glass. The north aisle was the property and burial-place of the family of Chichester; having fallen into a ruinous condition, it was parted by a wall from the rest of the church, but in 1830 was given to the parishioners by the present Marquess of Donegal, the head of that family, and is now fitted up as free sittings for the poor: it contains a large mural monument, with effigies of several of the Chichesters; and round the walls were formerly armorial bearings and trophies, of which only a few fragments are remaining. The subterraneous passage under the altar, which communicated with the ancient monastery, may still be traced. The Ecclesiastical Commissioners have lately granted £141 for the repair of this church. There is no deanery-house: the glebe lands are let for £32. 7. per annum. In the R. C. divisions the parish forms part of the union or district of Larne and Carrickfergus; the chapel, in the western suburbs, was erected in 1826. There are places of worship for Presbyterians in connection with the Synod of Ulster, of the first class (a large and handsome edifice), Wesleyan Methodists, Independents, and a small congregation of Covenanters; one for Unitarians is in course of erection.

The Diocesan free grammar school, founded here by Queen Elizabeth, was discontinued about 35 years since. A free school for boys and girls is supported by a bequest of £42 per annum by the late E. D. Wilson, Esq., arising from lands in the borough, to which the rector adds £2 annually: by the testator's will, the children are required to attend every Sunday in the Established Church. There are two public schools in the town, and others at Woodburn, Duncrew, Loughmorne, and Ballylaggin. In 1811 a Sunday school was opened in the town, which for several years was the only one, and was attended by 400 children and 30 gratuitous teachers; but it has partially declined, from the institution of other schools in the town and neighbourhood, in connection with the Established Church and the several dissenting congregations. The number of children on the books of the day schools amounts to more than 400 boys and 300 girls; and in the private pay schools are about 60 boys and 40 girls. In 1761, Henry Gill, Esq., bequeathed £10 per annum each, arising from property in the borough, "to fourteen aged men decayed in their circumstances," and also houses and gardens to such of them as might not have residences: this sum, by an increase in the value of the property, has been augmented to £14 each, late Irish currency, or to £12. 18. 6. sterling, which is annually received by fourteen aged men of whom ten have also houses. In 1782, William Adair, Esq., of Westminster, gave £2000 three per cent. stock, in trust to the Adairs, proprietors of the Ballymena estate, the interest to be distributed among the poorer freemen, of whom nineteen received annually £3. 3. each; but at present the sums distributed to each vary in proportion to the necessities of their several families; there are also several minor charitable bequests. In 1826 a mendicity association was established, which is supported by subscription; and there are societies for the distribution of clothing among the poor, and for other benevolent purposes.

The Franciscan monastery above noticed, as connected with the parish church, was founded in 1232, and became of so much importance that, in 1282, a general chapter of the whole order was convoked here: it stood within the walls of the town, and its site is at present occupied by the gaol for the county of Antrim. Immediately to the west of the town was the Premonstratensian priory of Goodburn or Woodburn, on the western bank of that stream; it was dedicated to the Holy Cross, and its foundation is attributed to a member of the family of Bisset, which quitted Scotland about the year 1242, in consequence of the murder of the Duke of Athol. Adjoining the eastern suburb was the hospital of St. Bridget, said to have been founded for the reception of lepers; the lands adjoining the site are still called the Spital parks. To the north of the town a well, now called Bride-well, marks the site of another hospital dedicated to St. Bridget. Several silver coins, of the reign of Hen. II., have been found about the castle. There are numerous barrows or tumuli scattered over the face of the county of the town, of which some have been opened and found to contain rude urns, ashes, and human bones; the largest of these, which are chiefly sepulchral, is called *Duncrue*, or the "fortress of blood." At Slieve-True is a cairn, 77 yards in circumference and 20 feet high; a little towards the west of the same mountain is another, of nearly equal dimensions; and about a mile to the north-east is a third, exactly similar. In several places are artificial caves, probably intended as places of concealment. At a place called the Friars' Rock are traces of small circular buildings, supposed to have been friars' cells; and about two miles north-west of the town are the ruins of two churches, called respectively Killyan, or Anne's Church, and Carnrawsy. The mineral springs, though not very numerous, are of various qualities: one of these, in the bed of a stream in the eastern part of the town, is a nitrous purgative water; another, about a mile to the east of it, is a fine saline spring; and the waters of another, near the western bank of Lough Morne, are sulphureous and chalybeate, and were once in great repute for their efficacy. Among the distinguished persons born here may be noticed Bishop Tennison, and Richard Kane, a general in the army of Wm. III. The women of the Scottish quarter and the county adjacent commonly retain their maiden surnames after marriage.

CARRICK-M^cQUIGLEY, a village, in the parish of UPPER MOVILLE, barony of ENNISHOWEN, county of DONEGAL, and province of ULSTER, 2½ miles (S.) from Moville: the population is returned with the parish. It is situated near Lough Foyle, on the road from Derry to Moville. A grant of a market and four fairs was made to the inhabitants in the reign of Chas. I.; the market has long been discontinued, and the fairs are very indifferently attended. Near the village are several handsome gentlemen's seats, which are noticed more particularly in the article on Upper Moville.

CARRICKMACROSS, a market and post-town, and a parish, in the barony of FARNEY, county of MONAGHAN, and province of ULSTER, 20 miles (S. E. by S.) from Monaghan, and 40 (N. W. by N.) from Dublin; containing 12,610 inhabitants, of which number, 2970 are in the town. This place derives its name from its situation on a rock and from one of its early proprietors, and is the only town in the barony. The barony was granted by Queen Elizabeth to the Earl of Essex, who resided in the castle here, part of the walls of which are still standing in the garden of W. Daniel, Esq. It was leased by the earl to Mr. Barton, whose wife and children were burnt, with the castle, by the insurgents of 1641, while he was attending his parliamentary duties in Dublin, as representative of the county of Monaghan. The town is situated on the mail coach road from Dublin to Londonderry, and consists of one principal street, with some smaller streets or lanes branching from it; and contains about 560 houses, many of which are of respectable appearance. A considerable retail trade is carried on with the surrounding country; and soap, candles, brogues, and coarse hats, are manufactured in the town, in which there are also a tanyard, a brewery (employing 100 men), and a distillery. Distillation was carried on here to a considerable extent before the Union, for 20 years, after which it very much declined; but, in 1823, a large distillery was erected, which makes 200,000 gallons of spirits annually, consuming in the manufacture about 25,000 barrels of grain, including malt, which is made in the town. The general market is held on Thursday, and one for corn on Wednesday and Saturday: the number of pigs exposed for sale at the market, during the season, is very great; they are principally purchased by dealers from Dundalk, Newry, and Belfast, for exportation. Fairs are held on May 27th, July 10th, Sept. 27th, Nov. 9th, and Dec. 10th; those in May and December, the latter of which is for fat cattle, are the largest. The market-house stands in the centre of the main street, and was built out of the ruins of the castle. Petty sessions are held every alternate week; and here are a constabulary police station and a county bridewell on a small scale, but containing the necessary accommodation for the separation of prisoners.

The parish, which is also called Magheross, contains, according to the Ordnance survey, 16,702$\frac{1}{4}$ statute acres, including 299 of water; 15,068 acres are applotted under the tithe act, and there is a great quantity of bog. In the vicinity of the town are several lime-kilns, and the land has been greatly improved by the extensive use of lime as a manure. Mr. Shirley supplies his tenants at about half the usual price from his kilns, in which about 8000 barrels were burnt in 1835. The principal lakes are Loch Mac-na-ree, Lisdronturk, Corvalley, and Chantinee Loch, only part of which is in this parish. Coal exists, but is not worked at present; but good limestone and freestone are quarried for building. Lisinisk, the seat of Adam Gibson, Esq., is in this parish, which also includes part of the demesne of Loch Fea Castle, the seat of E. J. Shirley, Esq., although the castle is in Magheracloony. The living is a vicarage, in the diocese of Clogher, and in the patronage of the Bishop; the rectory is impropriate in Col. Willcox: the tithes amount to £969. 4. 7$\frac{1}{2}$., of which £323. 1. 6$\frac{1}{2}$. is payable to the impropriator, and £646. 3. 1. to the vicar. The church is a neat stone edifice with a tower and spire, having a good clock with four dials. The remains of the old church are still standing: it was built in 1682, to replace the one that was destroyed by fire in 1641. There is a glebe-house, with a glebe of 112 acres. The R. C. parish is co-extensive with that of the Established Church, and is the benefice of the Bishop of Clogher, who resides in the town: there are three chapels, situated at Corduff mountain, Corcreagh, and Carrickmacross, the last of which is a handsome building, erected in 1783. There is also a Presbyterian meeting-house. A free grammar school was founded here by Lord Weymouth in 1711, and endowed with £70 per annum: it has been disused for some years, but the school-house is being rebuilt by the Marquess of Bath, a descendant of the founder. There are two national schools at Carrickmacross; six schools, situated at Mullaghcrogery, Cornasassinagh, Carrickmaclim, Corraghery, Corduffkelly, and Cargamore, aided by annual donations from E. J. Shirley, Esq.; a school supported by subscriptions, and two other schools, in which the pupils are taught gratuitously. About 780 boys and 670 girls are taught in these schools, and about 470 boys and 230 girls in 13 private and hedge schools; there are also three Sunday schools. A dispensary was established in 1823; here is also a mendicity society; and a savings' bank was instituted in 1831 by the Marquess of Bath and Mr. Shirley: the amount of deposits, in November, 1835, was £1503. 14. 3., belonging to 81 depositors, the number of whom is rapidly increasing.

CARRICKMINES, a village, in the parish of TULLY, half-barony of RATHDOWN, county of DUBLIN, and province of LEINSTER, 7 miles (S. S. E.) from Dublin. Fairs are held on Jan. 12th, April 14th, June 24th, and Oct. 14th; and here are the remains of an old castle.

CARRICK-on-SHANNON, a market and post-town, (formerly a parliamentary borough), partly in the parish of KILLUKEN, barony of BOYLE, county of ROSCOMMON, but chiefly in the parish of KILTOGHART, barony and county of LEITRIM, and in the province of CONNAUGHT, 27 miles (S. E. by S.) from Sligo, and 77 (W. N. W) from Dublin; containing 1870 inhabitants. This town is situated on the mail coach road from Dublin to Sligo, and on the north-eastern bank of the Shannon, over which is a bridge to a small suburb in the county of Roscommon, the tolls of which were granted, in 1684, to Sir George St. George, on condition of his keeping it in repair: the present structure, consisting of eleven arches, was built in 1718. It contains 321 houses, and is badly paved and not lighted. A small trade is carried on in coarse linen, druggets, frieze, and coarse flannel; and it is the chief market for grain and provisions in Leitrim, but is principally supplied from Roscommon. Great quantities of butter are sent to the Dublin and Newry markets, and a considerable quantity of yarn is sold. The market is on Thursday; and fairs are held on Jan. 18th, March 20th, May 12th, June 6th, Aug. 11th, Sept. 14th, Oct. 22nd, Nov. 21st, and Dec. 16th, and are the principal fairs in Leitrim for cattle. An enclosed market-place, with considerable accommodation, was erected by Mr. St. George, who is the owner in fee of the site of the town, but it is not much frequented. Great facilities for trade are afforded by the Shannon, which has lately been rendered navigable up to Lough Allen, by which this town is placed on one of the most important lines of communication in the island. A constabulary police force has been stationed here; and there are infantry barracks, which are unoccupied, although this is the only military station in the county.

This place was incorporated by Jas. I., in 1613, under the title of "The Provost, Free Burgesses, and Commonalty of the Borough of Carrigdrumruske;" and the corporation was composed of a provost, 12 free burgesses, and an indefinite number of freemen. The provost was elected on the 24th of June by the provost and burgesses, and was sworn in on the 29th of September. The free burgesses were elected by the provost and burgesses; no freemen have existed for a very long period, and the only officer appointed by the corporation was the weighmaster, who receives a compensation under the butter act, 10th of Geo. IV., c. 41. The borough sent two members to the Irish parliament, elected under the charter by the provost and free burgesses. On the abolition of its franchise, at the time of the Union, the £15,000 awarded as compensation was given to the Earl of Leitrim. No provost has been elected since 1826, and the corporation is virtually extinct. Under the charter a court of record was established, but it has not been held for many years; and there is no manor court within the borough, but a petty session is held every alternate Monday. This town being the capital of the county of Leitrim, the assizes are held here, as also the quarter sessions for the southern division of the county in January and July. The county court-house, bridewell, and gaol are situated in the town; the gaol is built in a polygonal form, having 10 wards with separate sleeping-cells for each prisoner, and a good tread-mill: the prisoners are taught reading and writing by the master and matron. The parish church of Kiltoghart, which, prior to 1698, was at a distance, was removed in that year by act of parliament into the town, and was erected on a plot of ground given by Sir George St. George, Bart.: it was rebuilt in 1829, by a loan of £2000 from the late Board of First Fruits, and is a handsome structure with a spire and a clock, which was given by C. Manners St. George, Esq.: this gentleman also presented, in 1837, a fine painting of the Nativity, by Plagemann. The R. C. chapel occupies a site given, with a plot of ground in the rear, in 1807, by Mr. St. George, who expended a considerable sum in finishing the interior, and built a gallery at his own expense. There are also places of worship for Wesleyan and Primitive Methodists, and parochial schools. The county infirmary situated here is a good building, erected in 1800: attached to it is a dispensary. The number of infirmary patients is about 300, and of dispensary patients about 4000, annually. A loan fund has also been established, with a capital amounting to £2000.—See Killuken and Kiltoghart.

CARRICK-on-SUIR, a market and post-town, and a parish, in the barony of Iffa and Offa East, county of Tipperary, and province of Munster, 13 miles (W. N. W.) from Waterford, and 78¼ (S. W. by S.) from Dublin; containing 7445 inhabitants, of which number, 6922 are in the town. This place formed part of the possessions of Theobald Butler, to whom were granted also the lands of Carrig-mac-Griffin, now Carrick-Beg, and whose grandson, Edmond, founded a castle here about the year 1309. The castle was, in 1336, granted by his son, James Butler, created Earl of Ormonde in 1328, to the Franciscan friary of Carrick-Beg, which he had founded; and continued to form part of the endowment of that house till about the year 1445, when, the brethren having suffered it to fall into ruin, a re-grant of it was purchased from them by Sir Edmond Butler Mac Richard, grandson of James, third Earl of Ormonde, who rebuilt both the castle and the bridge. A priory, dedicated to St. John the Evangelist, was founded here at the end of the 12th or beginning of the 13th century, for Canons Regular of the order of St. Augustine, by William de Cantell and Dionisia his wife, daughter of Thomas Fitz-Anthony; it was afterwards subject to the hospital of St. John de Acon, at London, and after the dissolution was granted to Thomas, Earl of Ormonde, in 1557, which grant was confirmed in 1562 by Queen Elizabeth, who also remitted the reserved rent. A castle was erected on the site of the priory by Thomas Duff, called Black Thomas, Earl of Ormonde. Here was also a nunnery for poor Clares, of which nothing more has been recorded. In 1500, the Earl granted a charter to the burgesses of the town, dated at Waterford.

The town is pleasantly situated on the north bank of the river Suir, which here forms a boundary between the counties of Tipperary and Waterford, and is connected by an ancient stone bridge with the suburb of Carrick-Beg, on the opposite side, in the county of Waterford. It consists of one long street extending in a direction from east to west, from which three smaller streets diverge on the north to the fair green, a spacious area surrounded by houses, and one on the south side to the river: the total number of houses, in 1831, was 1292. There are cavalry barracks for 8 officers and 148 non-commissioned officers and privates, with stabling for 52 horses; but they are now occupied by infantry. In 1670, the great Duke of Ormonde established the woollen manufacture here, which flourished till towards the close of the last century, but has since declined: at present there is only a very limited trade in ratteens of superior quality, which are made in the town and vicinity. There are some tanneries and breweries; but the chief trade is the sale of agricultural produce and of provisions, which are sent to Waterford for exportation, and to Clonmel for the supply of that town and neighbourhood. The trade in corn and butter, the produce of the surrounding district, is stated in a petition to parliament, presented by the inhabitants in 1832, and praying for the privilege of sending a representative to the Imperial parliament, to amount at that time to £240,000, and previously to have exceeded £360,000 per annum. The river is not navigable for vessels of considerable burden farther than Fiddown, a few miles below the town, whence lighters are used for conveying the produce. The rail-road from Waterford to Limerick, if completed, will pass through the town. The market is on Saturday; and fairs are held on the first Thursday in every month for cattle and pigs. A constabulary police force is stationed in the town; and petty sessions are held here every alternate week: the manor court formerly held in the castle is discontinued.

The parish, which is exempt from county rates by grant of Wm. III., comprises about 1600 statute acres, which, with the exception of about 32 acres of common, called Carrick green, where the fairs are held, are chiefly arable. The surrounding country is peculiarly beautiful, being part of the district or plain which, for its singular fertility, is called the "Golden Vale," throughout enlivened by the river Suir, the banks of which are embellished with the richest variety of scenery. The chief seats within the parish are Tinvane, the handsome residence of H. W. Briscoe, Esq.; the Cottage, of W. O'Donnell, Esq.; Deerpark Lodge, of — Haliday, Esq.; and Mount Richard, of J. Power, Esq.: and within a range of three or four miles are Curraghmore, the seat of the Marquess of Waterford; Besborough, of the Earl of Besborough; Coolnamuck, of Charles W. Wall, Esq.; and Castletown, of R. Cox, Esq. The living is a vicarage, in the diocese of Lismore, and in the patronage of the Marquess of Ormonde; the rectory is impropriate in W. H. Bradshaw, Esq. The tithes amount to £193. 16. 11., of which £129. 4. 7½. is payable to the impropriator, and £64. 12. 3½. to the vicar. The church is in ruins. The glebe-house was built by aid of a gift of £400 and a loan of £270 from the late Board of First Fruits: the glebe contains 3*r*. 3*p*. In the R. C. divisions the parish is the head of a union or district, comprising the parishes of St. Nicholas in Carrick-on-Suir, and Newtownlenan, in each of which there is a chapel. The chapel of this parish is a spacious and handsome building; the interior is well arranged, and the altar is embellished with a painting of the Crucifixion by a native artist. There are a monastery of the order of the Christian Brotherhood, and a convent of sisters of the order of the Presentation; to the former is attached a school of 250 boys and to the latter a school of 500 girls, aided by subscription; there are also seven private schools, in which are about 200 boys and 100 girls. Here are a fever hospital and a dispensary. A poor-house for destitute persons of the R. C. religion is supported with a bequest of £2000 by Thomas and Richard Wadden, augmented with £30 per annum by James Sause, Esq., and a bequest of £400 by Mr. Kennedy: a few acres of land have also been bequeathed to it. A rent-charge of £10 was bequeathed to the Protestant poor by Mrs. Cook, about a century since. The castle is still a stately building, though much of it is in ruins; it was for many years the residence of the Ormonde family, and part of it has been converted into a private residence. There are some small remains of the ancient town walls. Carrick gives the title of Earl to a branch of the Butler family.

CARRIG, or CARRIGLEAMLEARY, a parish, in the barony of Fermoy, county of Cork, and province of Munster, 2¼ miles (N. E.) from Mallow; containing 1133 inhabitants. This parish is situated on the north bank of the river Blackwater, and on the north road from Mallow to Fermoy; it comprises 3238 statute acres, as applotted under the tithe act, and valued at £3462 per annum. The land is good and mostly under an improved system of tillage, with the exception of Mount Nagle, which affords good pasturage; there is no bog. Limestone abounds, and is quarried for agricultural and other uses. Carrig Park, the seat of W. H. Franks, Esq., is beautifully situated on the banks of the Blackwater, which are here richly wooded: the ruins of Carrig castle, on the summit of a rock overhanging the river, form an interesting and picturesque object as seen from the opposite bank; and the whole demesne, in which are the vestiges of an ancient burial-ground, abounds with richly varied scenery. This parish was formerly united to that of Rahan, and on its separation about 30 years since, part of it was added to Rahan, to make the divisions more equal. The living is a vicarage, in the diocese of Cloyne, and in the patronage of the Bishop; the rectory is appropriate to the vicars choral of the cathedral of Christ Church, Dublin. The tithes amount to £270, and are equally divided between the vicars choral and the vicar. A neat small church, in the later English style, but without a tower, is now in progress of erection on the site of the old parish church, part of the walls of which will be incorporated in the new building; the estimated expense is £222. 10., towards defraying which the Ecclesiastical Commissioners have granted £192. 10. 8. Divine service is in the mean time performed in a private house. There is neither glebe-house nor glebe. In the R. C. divisions this parish forms part of the union or district of Killavullane or Kealavullen, at which place, and also at Annakissy, is a chapel. There are two private schools, in which about 50 children are educated.

CARRIGAHOLT, a small port and village, in the parish and barony of Moyarta, county of Clare, and province of Munster, 11¾ miles (W.) from Kilrush: the population is returned with the parish. It is situated on the harbour and road-stead of the same name, within the estuary of the river Shannon. The castle, now in ruins, was formerly the fortified residence of the Mac Mahons, the chiefs of that part of this country which forms the peninsula called the "Western Corkavaskin," still denominated "the west." The last siege to which it was exposed was in 1649, when it was taken by Gen. Ludlow, and Teigue Keigh was the last of the Mac Mahons to whom it belonged. On his attainder it passed by grant from Queen Elizabeth to Henry O'Brien, brother to the Earl of Thomond, whose unfortunate grandson, Lord Clare, resided in it when he raised a regiment of horse, called the "Yellow Dragoons," which in 1689 was the flower of King James's army. The town now belongs to Lady Burton, whose ancestor was an officer in the army of King William. The ruins of the castle occupy a bold situation on the verge of a cliff overhanging the sea, enclosed by a court-yard and high walls on one side, and by rocks and the bay on the other. A small quay or pier was constructed partly by the late Fishery Board and partly by grand jury presentments: it is of considerable service to agriculture and the fisheries, and is frequented by six hookers, of seven tons each, and upwards of 500 corrachs, which give employment to about 400 persons, particularly in the herring fishery, which commences in July. This is the principal place in the neighbourhood for the shipment of agricultural produce; 900 tons of grain, 700 firkins of butter, and 3000 pigs, having lately been shipped here in one year, by three individuals: it also exports hides to Limerick. The bay of Carrigaholt lies opposite that part of the Kerry shore, within the mouth of the Shannon, which is called the Bale bar. It has good and secure anchorage with the wind to the northward of west, but being entirely exposed to the ocean swell, the sea, which sets in with southerly or westerly winds, renders it unsafe to lie there. The inner harbour, however, is better protected from those winds, but is shallow, having no more than 2½ or 3 fathoms of water within the line from Carrigaholt Castle to the opposite side of the bay. Capt. Manby, who was employed by the Irish Government to survey the Shannon, recommended that a small pier should be extended from the spot called Lord Clare's pier, (which was formed in 1608 but has gone to decay,) at nearly a right angle to the shore, sufficiently to afford shelter to the one that already exists, and that this should be carried out farther, so as to permit boats to sail from it till almost low water. The roads in the immediate vicinity of the village are in bad condition, and must be repaired before the port can be easily accessible by land. The valley on the north side of Kilkadrane Hill having been often mistaken by night for the proper channel for entering the Shannon, a light has been placed on the top of the hill, red to seaward, and a fixed bright light as seen descending the river. In the village is a public dispensary, and near it is the R. C. chapel.—See MOYARTA.

CARRIGALINE, a parish, partly in the county of the city of CORK, and partly in the barony of KINNALEA, but chiefly in that of KERRICURRIHY, county of CORK, and province of MUNSTER, 7 miles (S. E.) from Cork; containing 7375 inhabitants. This place was in early times called *Beavor*, or *Bebhor*, and derived its name from the abrupt rocky cliff on which are the remains of the ancient castle, built by Milo de Cogan in the reign of King John, and for nearly two centuries occupied by the Earls of Desmond, by whom it was forfeited, in the reign of Queen Elizabeth. The castle, together with the lands of Carrigaline and Ballinrea, was then granted by the queen to Sir Anthony St. Leger, who demised them to Stephen Golding, from whom they were purchased by Sir Richard Boyle, afterwards Earl of Cork, and from him descended to the present proprietor, the Earl of Shannon. In 1568, the Lord-Deputy Sidney, after relieving the Lady St. Leger in Cork, advanced against this fortress, which he took from James Fitzmaurice after an obstinate resistance, and from this time during the entire reign of Elizabeth it had the reputation of being impregnable. In 1589, Sir Francis Drake, with a squadron of five ships, being chased by a Spanish fleet of superior force, ran into Cork harbour; and sailing up Crosshaven, moored his squadron in a safe basin, sheltered by Corribiny Hill, close under Coolmore. The Spaniards pursued, but, being unacquainted with the harbour, sailed round the shores without discovering the English fleet, and giving up the search, left it here in perfect security. The basin in which Sir Francis lay has since been called Drake's pool.

The parish is situated on the road from Cork to Tracton, and contains 14,254 statute acres, as applotted under the tithe act, and valued at £16,606 per annum; the surface is pleasingly undulated, and the soil is fertile; a considerable part is under an improved system of tillage, and the remainder is in demesne, meadow, or pasture land. There is neither waste land nor bog; coal, which is landed at several small quays here, is the chief fuel. A light brown and purplish clay-slate is found; and limestone of very superior quality is raised at Shanbally, in large blocks, and after being hewn into columns, tombstones, &c., is shipped to Cork and other places. The appearance of the country is beautifully varied: the views from the high grounds are extensive and picturesque, commanding the course of the Awenbwuy, with its capacious estuary, called Crosshaven, and embellished with numerous gentlemen's seats. The principal are Maryborough, the residence of W. H. Worth Newenham, Esq., situated in a beautiful demesne of 545 acres, with a lofty square tower a little to the east of the house, which commands a magnificent prospect of the town and harbour of Cove, and the rich scenery of the river; Mount-Rivers, of M. Roberts, Esq.; and Ballybricken, of D. Conner, Esq. The village has a very pleasing appearance; it consists of several good houses and a number of decent cottages, extending into the parish of Kilmoney, on the south side of the river, over which is a bridge of three arches. There are two large boulting-mills, the property of Messrs. Michael Roberts and Co., which grind 12,000 sacks of flour annually, of which the greater part is shipped for England from Cork. The trade consists chiefly in the export of corn, flour, and potatoes, and the import of coal and culm. The channel of the river has been lately deepened six feet, and vessels can now deliver their cargoes at the bridge. A creek runs up to Shanbally, and another forms the channel of Douglas, both of which are navigable for vessels of 70 tons' burden, which bring up lime, sand, and manure, and take away limestone and bricks, the latter of which are made near Douglas. Salmon, white trout, sole, plaice, and oysters of superior quality, are obtained in these inlets, and, in the latter part of the summer, herrings are occasionally taken in great quantities. The river Awenbwuy, winding through a rich corn country, is well situated for commerce, and several large mills are in course of erection on its banks. Fairs are held in Carrigaline on Easter-Monday, Whit-Monday, Aug. 12th, and Nov. 8th, for cattle, sheep, and pigs. There is a penny post to Cork; and a chief constabulary police force has been stationed here. Petty sessions are held in the court-house every Tuesday, and a manorial court once in three weeks.

The living is a rectory, in the diocese of Cork, and in the patronage of the Earl of Shannon: the tithes amount to £1080. The church is a very handsome edifice of hewn limestone, in the later English style of architecture, with a massive square tower crowned with pinnacles and surmounted by an elegant and lofty octagonal spire pierced with lights: it was erected in 1823, near the site of the former church, and enlarged in 1835, by the addition of a north transept; the windows are very light, chaste, and beautiful, particularly the eastern one, the upper part of which is ornamented with stained glass. Near the west front is a lofty arch, beneath which is an altar-tomb of grey marble, with a recumbent leaden figure, now much mutilated, of Lady Susanna Newenham, who died in 1754. A chapel of ease has been built at the village of Douglas, in the northern division of the parish, within the liberties of the city of Cork. There is no glebe-house, but a glebe of 6*a.* 3*r.* 9*p.* In the R. C. divisions the parish partly forms the head of a union or district, comprising the four ploughlands called Carrigaline and the parishes of Templebready and Kilmoney, and is partly in the union of Douglas or Ballygervin, and partly in that of Passage: the chapel is in that part of the village of Carrigaline which is on the south side of the river. The male and female parochial schools are supported by subscription; the school-rooms were built in 1834. At Raheens are schools for boys and girls, the former supported by a donation of £50 per ann. from W. H. W. Newenham, Esq., and the latter by Mrs. Newenham; a school is aided by annual subscriptions, amounting to £4, and there are other hedge schools in the parish, altogether affording instruction to about 450 children, and a Sunday school. Here is also a dispensary. At Ballinrea there is a mineral spring, which is considered to be of the same kind as that of Tunbridge Wells, and has been found efficacious in cases of debility; and near it is a holy well, dedicated to St. Renogue, which is resorted to by the country people on the 24th of June.

CARRIGALLEN, or CLINCORICK, a parish, in the barony of CARRIGALLEN, county of LEITRIM, and province of CONNAUGHT, 5 miles (S. W. by W.) from Killesandra, on the road to Drumsna; containing 7809 inhabitants, of which number, 492 are in the village. The parish contains 15,000 statute acres, including a great quantity of bog: the cultivation is principally by spade labour; limestone of the best kind is quarried at Newtown-Gore. The village comprises about 100 houses: it has a market for grain and provisions on Monday; and fairs are held on April 4th, May 7th, Aug. 9th, Oct. 8th, and the last Friday in Dec. Fairs are also held at Longfield on May 17th, Oct. 10th, and Dec. 29th. There is a penny post to Killesandra and Ballinamore; and a constabulary police force has been stationed here. Petty sessions are held every alternate Saturday, but the manor court has been discontinued since the institution of the assistant barrister's court. The principal seats are Killigar, the residence of John Godley, Esq., situated in a richly wooded demesne, embellished with three fine sheets of water; Drumsilla, of Acheson O'Brien, Esq.; and Cloncorrick Castle, the property of Pierce Simpson, Esq., by purchase from Major W. Irwin. This castle was built by the O'Rourkes, and here resided John O'Rourke, son of Thady, the last of the family who lived in any degree of splendour, until, in the reign of Queen Elizabeth, at a Court of Claims held at Carrigallen, he was deprived of his estate and declared illegitimate, on the evidence of Abbot Macaward. The castle has received such additions and alterations as scarcely to leave a feature of its original character. Woodford House, which is half a mile north of Newtown-Gore, is built on the ruins of another of the O'Rourkes' castles: the estate was formerly well wooded, and remarkable for its oaks, and there are still two fine walled gardens of considerable extent. It was a place of great splendour, and belonged to the ancestors of W. Ormsby Gore, Esq., of Porkington, Shropshire.

The living is a vicarage, in the diocese of Kilmore, and in the patronage of the Bishop, to whom the rectory is appropriate: the tithes amount to £450, of which £151. 1. 6. is payable to the bishop, and £298. 18. 6. to the incumbent. The church, a good building with a square tower, and in excellent repair, was erected in 1814, by aid of a loan of £1500 from the late Board of First Fruits. The glebe-house was built by a gift of £100, and a loan of £1350, from the same Board, in 1819: the glebe comprises 590 acres. There is also a church at Killigar, with a small parsonage-house adjoining, built and endowed by John Godley, Esq., at an expense of £1100. The R. C. parish is co-extensive with that of the Established Church, and contains two chapels, one at Mullinadaragh, and the other, called the Lower Chapel, at Aughal: there is also a place of worship for Wesleyan Methodists at Newtown-Gore. At Drumshangour are two schools, aided by annual donations from Mr. and Mrs. Godley, who at their own expense support two at Killigar: there are also schools at Carrigallen, Newtown-Gore, Corglass, Corneagh, and Kievy. In these schools are educated 480 boys and 400 girls; and there are also three private schools, in which are about 100 boys and 60 girls, and two Sunday schools, one of which is supported by Mr. Godley.

CARRIGANS.—See KILLEA, county of DONEGAL.

CARRIGDOWNANE, or CARRIGDOWNIG, a parish, in the barony of FERMOY, county of CORK, and province of MUNSTER, 5 miles (S. W.) from Mitchelstown; containing 219 inhabitants. This small parish, which is situated on the river Funcheon, and on the road from Kildorrery to Fermoy, comprises 785 statute acres, as assessed to the county rate, and valued at £687 per annum. The land is in general of good quality and chiefly under tillage, but the system of agriculture is in a backward state. Limestone is plentiful, and is quarried for burning into lime, which is the principal manure. Stannard's Grove, the property of the Cotter family, is at present uninhabited. The living is a rectory and vicarage, in the diocese of Cloyne, and in the patronage of the Bishop: the tithes amount to £90. The church is in ruins; and the Protestant parishioners attend the church of Nathlash, a mile distant. There is no glebe-house; the glebe comprises 10 Irish acres. In the R. C. divisions this parish forms part of the union or district of Kildorrery. There are some remains of the ancient parish church.

CARRIGG, a parish, in the barony of SHELMALIER, county of WEXFORD, and province of LEINSTER, 2 miles (W.) from Wexford; containing 1054 inhabitants. This place is situated on the road to New Ross, and on the river Slaney, at its influx into the haven at Wexford. In the townland of Ferry-Carrigg, and near the bridge over the Slaney, Robert Fitz-Stephen, in 1171, built a strong castle, in which he was soon afterwards besieged by the Irish under Donald of Limerick, natural son of Dermod Mac Murrough, the last King of Leinster. Donald, finding himself unable to reduce it by force, had recourse to stratagem, and by a feigned account that Strongbow and his friends in Dublin had been put to the sword by the victorious army, who were on their march to this place, prevailed upon Fitz-Stephen, by the promise of a safe passport into Wales, to surrender himself and the garrison into his hands. Many of the men were instantly put to death; and Fitz-Stephen and the remainder were conveyed in chains to a small island called Beg Erin, in the north part of Wexford haven, where they were confined till the landing of Hen. II. at Waterford, when, being removed to that town, they were placed in Ragnal's or

Reginald's tower, from which they were soon afterwards liberated by the English monarch.

The parish is bounded on the north by the river Slaney, over which is a handsome bridge of American oak, built by the architect of the old Wexford bridge, under an act passed in 1794, which empowered subscribers to raise £7000 for that purpose, who, on payment of one-fifth of that sum, were to be constituted a corporate body, under the designation of the "Commissioners of Carrigg Bridge," and to have a common seal. The northern part is intersected by the mail coach road from Wexford to Dublin, and the road from Wexford to New Ross also passes through it. It comprises 2538 statute acres, as applotted under the tithe act, of which the greater portion is in pasture and the remainder under tillage; the system of agriculture is progressively improving. Here are some quarries of good building stone, from which the works now in progress at St. Peter's College, Wexford, are supplied. The scenery is pleasingly varied, including the richly wooded banks of the Slaney and the Forth mountains, by which the parish is bounded on the west. Belmont, the residence of Charles Arthur Walker, Esq., is finely situated on a commanding eminence above the Slaney, and embraces some beautiful views of that river above Wexford bridge, and especially of that side of it which is ornamented by the elegant mansions and richly wooded demesnes of Saunders Court, Artramont, and other gentlemen's seats. The other seats are Barntown House, the newly erected residence of Major Perceval; Cullentra, of G. Little, Esq.; Park House, of Capt. J. W. Harvey; Janeville, of D. Jones, Esq.; and Bettyville, of Mrs. Redmond: there are also several other villas. The Slaney affords every facility of water conveyance for the supply of the neighbourhood.

Seal.

This is one of the 16 parishes that constitute the union of St. Patrick's, Wexford. The living is an impropriate curacy, in the diocese of Ferns, and in the patronage of the Bishop; the rectory is impropriate in the Earl of Portsmouth. The tithes amount to £185. 1. 5., of which £62. 3. 5½. is payable to the impropriator, and £122. 17. 11½. to the curate. There are some remains of the old parish church below Belmont; and in the churchyard, under an altar-tomb, are deposited the remains of Lieut.-Col. Jones Watson, who fell on the 30th of May, 1798, while leading the yeomanry of this county to attack the insurgents, who had encamped at the Three Rocks on the mountain of Forth. In the R. C. divisions this parish forms part of the union or district of Glynn; the chapel is at Barntown, and adjoining it is the national school, in which about 150 children of both sexes are gratuitously instructed, under the superintendence of the R. C. clergyman. The remains of the castle of Ferry-Carrigg, in the parish of Tickillen, are romantically situated on a pinnacle of rock commanding the pass of the river, and consist principally of a lofty square tower. On the opposite side of the river, and in the parish of Carrigg, was a castle called Shan-a-Court, or John's Court, supposed to have been built in the reign of John, and in which that monarch is said to have held a court. The remains consist only of the trenches; many of the stones were used in building the more ancient part of Belmont house. In this parish is also Barntown Castle, which appears to have been built about the same time as that of Ferry-Carrigg, and by some writers is attributed to the same founder; it consists of a lofty square tower still nearly entire; Barntown formed a portion of the lands granted by Cromwell to Col. Le Hunt, whose descendants still reside at Artramont, in the neighbourhood.

CARRIGLEAMLEARY.—See CARRIG, county of Cork.

CARRIGNAVAR, a village, in the parish of DUNBOLLOGE, barony of BARRYMORE, county of CORK, and province of MUNSTER, 5 miles (N.) from Cork; containing 282 inhabitants. It is situated on the road from Cork to Mallow, in a fine fertile country, and has lately been much improved by its proprietors, Lord Midleton and J. McCarthy, Esq. The castle, of which little more than a square tower remains, is said to have been the last fortress in Munster which came into Cromwell's possession. It stood on the banks of the river Glanmire, and was built by Daniel, second son of Lord Muskerry, who died in 1616, and was one of the dependencies of the manor of Blarney. The village contains a neat R. C. chapel and a school.—See DUNBOLLOGE.

CARRIGPARSON, or WILLESTOWN, a parish, partly in the barony of CLANWILLIAM, county of LIMERICK, but chiefly in the county of the city of LIMERICK, and province of MUNSTER, 4½ miles (S. E.) from Limerick; containing 487 inhabitants. This parish is situated on the road from Limerick to Cashel, and contains 828 statute acres, about one-half of which is in tillage, producing good crops of wheat, oats, and potatoes, and the other is mostly meadow. Basalt and limestone are found here, the former mostly in a state of decomposition; and between the north-western extremity of the parish and Cahirnarry is an extensive and valuable bog. The living is a rectory and vicarage, in the diocese of Emly, and is part of the union of Cahirconlish: the tithes amount to £95. 15. 4½. There is neither church nor glebe-house, but a glebe of five acres near the remains of the old church. In the R. C. divisions this parish forms part of the district or union of Ballybricken; the chapel is at Bohermora. There is a private school of 30 boys and 10 girls.

CARRIGROHANBEG, or KILGROHANBEG, a parish, in the barony of BARRETTS, county of CORK, and province of MUNSTER, 3 miles (W.) from Cork; containing 659 inhabitants. This parish, which is situated in a very fertile district adjoining the western boundary of the county of the city of Cork, is bounded on the south by the river Lee, and on the east by the Awenbeg, or Shawnagh, a small river which flows from Blarney and falls into the Lee opposite to the beautiful ruins of Carrigrohane castle. It contains 1513 statute acres, as applotted under the tithe act, and valued at £1936 per annum: the surface is pleasingly diversified, and the soil, resting on a substratum of clay-slate, is extremely fertile. The land is chiefly in pasture, and the farmers attend almost exclusively to the dairy, for supplying the city of Cork with milk and butter. The vale of Awenbeg is beautifully romantic, and on the banks of that river were formerly some mills for manufacturing paper and some iron forges; the vale of the Lee is exceedingly fertile, and the meadows are occasionally irrigated by the overflowing of the river. The gentlemen's seats are Woodside, the residence of the Rev. E. M. Carleton, commanding a fine view down the vale, with an excellent farm adjoining it belonging to the proprietor of the estate, who has done much towards improving the agriculture of the surrounding district; Rock Lodge, of R. Carleton, Esq.; Beechmount, of the Rev. R. Cahill; and Temple Hill, of Russell Fitton, Esq. The living is a rectory, in the diocese of Cloyne, and in the patronage of the Bishop: the tithes amount to £156. 11. 7. There is no church, but divine service is regularly performed by the rector in his own house; the ruins of the old parish church, covered with ivy, and presenting a very picturesque appearance, are situated between the high road and the river Lee, near its junction with the Awenbeg. There is neither glebe-house nor glebe. In the R. C. divisions this parish forms part of the union or district of Inniscarra. The male and female parochial schools are supported by the rector, in connection with the Cloyne Diocesan Association.

CARRIGROHANE, or KILGROHANMORE, a parish, partly in the county of the city of CORK, but chiefly in the barony of BARRETTS, county of CORK, and province of MUNSTER, 4 miles (W. by S.) from Cork; containing 1921 inhabitants. This parish is situated on the south bank of the river Lee, over which is a stone bridge connecting it with the parish of Inniscarra, and on the new line of road through Magourney to Macroom. The whole comprises 2578 acres, as applotted under the tithe act, and valued at £4655 per annum; and that part of it which is included within the barony of Barretts contains 1556 acres, valued at £2136, according to the county estimate. The land is of excellent quality, and the farms, being in the occupation of persons of capital, are in an excellent state of cultivation. From the low price of grain, the produce of the dairy and the grazing of cattle have been found more profitable than growing corn; the lands are therefore being converted into dairy farms. The parish forms part of the limestone district that extends from near the source of the river Bride, along its southern bank, across the vale to the west of the city of Cork, and passing through its southern suburbs, terminates at Blackrock. The quarrying of limestone and manufacture of gunpowder at Ballincollig encourage that industry among the people of which the fruits are seen in their comfortable appearance and the improved state of their habitations. On the river Lee are some extensive mills, capable of manufacturing from 350 to 400 sacks of flour weekly. About a mile and a half from the church are several very handsome houses, occupied by the officers connected with the garrison of Ballincollig.

The living is a rectory, in the diocese of Cork, united from time immemorial to the rectories of Curricuppane and Corbally, and to one-fourth of the rectory of Kinneagh, which four parishes constitute the corps of the precentorship of the cathedral of St. Finbarr, Cork: the tithes of the parish amount to £330, and of the whole union to £943. The church is a small plain edifice, situated near the river Lee, to the repairs of which the Ecclesiastical Commissioners have recently made a grant of £143. There is no glebe-house in the union, but a glebe of 22 acres and 38 perches. In the R. C. divisions this parish, together with the parishes of Kilnaglory and Inniskenny, and a small part of that of Ballinaboy, form the union or district of Ballincollig, where there is a chapel. There are male and female parochial schools supported by subscriptions; a national school at Ballincollig, in which are about 100 boys and 70 girls; a public and two private schools, one of which is for infants, in which are about 60 boys and 40 girls; and a Sunday school supported by the rector. Behind the church are considerable remains of the ancient castle, and the fine ruins of a more modern house, of great strength, of which nearly the whole of the outer walls are remaining. The turrets, pierced with loop-holes, which project from the upper story of the latter building, indicate that it was built about the reign of Queen Elizabeth, but the castle is evidently much older and both were ruined in the war of 1641. At Ballincollig are the ruins of an extensive castle, situated on an isolated rock which rises in the midst of a fertile plain. This castle was built by the Barrett family, in the reign of Edw. III. William Barrett joined in the insurrection of the Earl of Desmond against Elizabeth, but was pardoned by Her Majesty and received into favour. In the war of 1641 it was in the possession of the insurgents, who were dispossessed by Cromwell in 1645: it was garrisoned for Jas. II. in 1689, but after his flight fell into decay, and is now a stately ruin, with a very strong and lofty square tower still nearly perfect.

CARRIGTOHILL, a parish, in the barony of BARRYMORE, county of CORK, and province of MUNSTER, 3 miles (W.) from Midleton; containing 3666 inhabitants. This parish is situated on the road from Cork to Waterford, and comprises 10,025 statute acres, as applotted under the tithe act, and valued at £8270 per annum: about 800 acres are woodland and nearly 500 waste; and of the remainder, 6600 are arable and 2600 pasture. The soil is in some places very light, and in others deep and rich, producing excellent crops: the system of agriculture has been extensively improved by the example and encouragement of the late Mr. Smith Barry and other resident proprietors. Great quantities of limestone are quarried and burnt into lime for manure. The scenery in almost every part is exceedingly interesting, particularly near Foaty, around which the rich woods and thriving plantations are beautifully diversified with water. Several extensive plantations have been made in other parts of the parish, which in a few years will add greatly to the appearance of the country. The principal gentlemen's seats are Foaty, the elegant residence of the late J. Smith Barry, Esq.; Ann Grove, of F. Wise, Esq.; Tulligreen, of Hughes Martin, Esq.; Spring Hill, of W. J. Wakeham, Esq.; Rockville, of T. Barry, Esq.; Green View, of R. Barry, Esq.; Barry's Lodge, of D. Barry, Esq.; Union Lodge, of the Rev. W. Gifford; Water Rock, of W. Wakeham, Esq.; and Johnstown, of Mrs. Palmer. The village consists principally of one long irregular street, and contains 98 small houses indifferently built. It is a constabulary police station; and fairs are held on the 12th of March and May, Aug. 26th, Sept. 19th, and Nov. 8th, chiefly for horses, cattle, pigs, and pedlery, and, from the central situation of the place, are in general well attended. A new line of road from this place to Cove has been recently opened through Foaty, and a very handsome bridge has been erected over the arm of the sea.

The living is a vicarage, in the diocese of Cloyne, united by act of council from a very early period to the particle of Kilcurfin, and in the alternate patronage of the Bishop and the representatives of the late John Anderson, Esq.; the rectory is impropriate in the representatives of George Lukey, of Midleton, Esq. The tithes amount to £1035. 4., of which £690. 2. 8. is payable to the impropriator, and £345. 1. 4. to the vicar. The church, a small but venerable structure, was repaired and much improved in 1835, by a grant of £144. 8. from the Ecclesiastical Commissioners. The glebe-house was built in 1825, by aid of a gift of £300 and a loan of £450 from the late Board of First Fruits. The glebe comprises 15 acres, of which 5 are a rock of limestone. In the R. C. divisions this parish is the head of a union or district, comprising the parishes of Carrigtohill and Mogeeshy; the chapel is situated on the site of an old abbey near the churchyard, and near it is a parochial house for the priest. There is a school at Foaty for boys and girls, founded by the late J. Smith Barry, Esq.; the boys are under the superintendence of the Protestant curate, and the girls under the direction of Mrs. Smith Barry; adjoining the school-rooms are houses for the master and mistress, and there are also two pay schools. Nearly adjoining the village are the ruins of a Franciscan abbey, founded and endowed by the Barry family: one of its towers still serves as a steeple for the present parish church, which and the R. C. chapel have been erected on its site; there are also several detached portions of the buildings remaining, but they are rapidly falling to decay. In the northern part of the parish are the ruins of the ancient parish church of Kilcurfin; and near the old entrance to Foaty are the remains of Castle Cloydubh, now called Barry's Court, from which the Barrymore family takes the title of Baron; it derives its name from Philip de Barry, whose uncle Fitz-Stephen granted him three cantreds here, where he built the castle in the beginning of the 13th century. During the insurrection of the great Earl of Desmond, in 1580, Capt., afterwards Sir Walter, Raleigh received a commission to seize this castle; but Lord Barry, the proprietor, having received intelligence of his design, previously set fire to it; it was an extensive and very strong pile, and one of the earliest erected in this part of the kingdom. In various parts of the parish are caverns which penetrate for a considerable distance into the limestone rocks, and in some of them are very large and beautiful stalactites.

CARRIGUE, or CARRIG, an island, in the parish of Aghavallin, barony of Iraghticonnor, county of Kerry, and province of Munster, 1½ mile (N. W.) from Ballylongford: the population is included in the return for the parish. This small island is situated in the river Shannon, nearly opposite to the island of Inniscattery, but on the Kerry side, and is about a mile and a half in circumference, containing 120 statute acres, of which 100 are arable; it belongs to Trinity College, Dublin, and is farmed by the Rev. S. B. Lennard, of Adare, and in a high state of cultivation. It is pleasantly situated for bathing, and abounds with a variety of water-fowl. There are a battery and bomb-proof barrack for 20 men; and it is a station of the coast-guard. The north shore is the only place where ships of heavy burden can ride in safety; the south, west, and east being very shallow at low water: and about a mile from the northern part of the island is a shoal, which has only a boat passage at ebb tide. Here is an extensive ruin, which was formerly a monastery, subject to the O'Connors, from whom the barony is named, and who owned the castle of Carrigafoyle, known as "the impregnable castle," from its long resistance to the attacks of Cromwell; it was one of the last taken by him, and the 12 people found in it were hanged. Off the island is an excellent oyster bed, also a good plaice and mullet fishery.

CARRIGVISTAIL, a village, in the parish of Templetenny, barony of Iffa and Offa West, county of Tipperary, and province of Munster; containing 58 inhabitants.

CARRIKIPPANE.—See CURRICUPPANE.

CARRUNE, CARRON, or CARNE, a parish, in the barony of Burren, county of Clare, and province of Munster, 6 miles (N. N. W.) from Curofin; containing 1045 inhabitants. It is situated on the road from Ennis and Curofin to Burren and New Quay, and is chiefly rocky pasture well adapted for sheep, of which the farmers' stock principally consists; a very small proportion is under tillage, which is slowly improving. Limestone abounds, and some copper mines were formerly worked, but are now discontinued. Columbkill Cottage, the neat residence of Terence O'Brien, Esq., and Tarmon parsonage, recently erected for the R. C. clergyman, are the only seats of importance. The living is a rectory and vicarage, in the diocese of Kilfenora; the rectory constitutes part of the sinecure union of Killielagh, in the patronage of the Marquess of Thomond; and the vicarage is part of the union of Noughaval, and the corps of the precentorship of the cathedral church of St. Fachnan, Kilfenora, in the patronage of the Bishop. The tithes amount to £70 per annum, of which one-half is payable to the rector, and the other to the Ecclesiastical Commissioners, in whom the benefice is sequestrated. There is neither church, glebe-house, nor glebe. In the R. C. divisions the parish forms the head of a union or district, comprising the parishes of Carrune, Noughaval, and Kilcorney; there are two chapels, one at Crughville, in this parish, and one in the village of Noughaval. There are two pay schools, in which are about 90 boys and 60 girls. The parochial church is in ruins, and there are the remains of two other old churches at Crunane and Glanculmkil; the burial-ground of each is still used. St. Columb is said to have founded an abbey at Glanculmkil, which subsequently became the parish church; the bed of the saint, formed of stones, is still preserved as a relic. Some brass coins have been dug up here. Near St. Columb's bed is one of the finest springs in the country, but the water possesses no medicinal properties.

CARYSFORT, MOYCREDDIN, or MOYCREDYNE, a borough, in the parish of Rathdrum, barony of Ballinacor, county of Wicklow, and province of Leinster, 5 miles (S. W.) from Rathdrum: the population is returned with the parish. This place, which is situated on the road from Rathdrum to Carnew, was formerly appropriated to the priory of All Saints,

Dublin; and in the reign of Hen. VIII. was granted to the mayor, bailiffs, and commons of that city. During the lieutenancy of Lord Falkland, between the years 1625 and 1629, a castle was erected here in order to check the turbulent septs of O'Toole and O'Byrne: but in 1641, the garrison being withdrawn to Dublin on a case of emergency, and the castle being left in the custody of a few unarmed English, it was surprised and taken by the O'Byrnes, who had intercepted a supply of arms and ammunition sent for its defence. By a charter of Charles I., in 1628, this place was erected into a small military depôt, and constituted a borough, under the control of a sovereign and twelve free burgesses. The corporation was endowed with lands not only for their own support, but also for maintaining the garrison of the castle; and the sovereign was made a justice of the peace, and for a year after the expiration of his office presided in a court for the recovery of debts not exceeding £20. The same charter also conferred upon the sovereign and free burgesses the privilege of returning two representatives to the Irish parliament, which they continued to exercise till the Union, when the borough was disfranchised, and the £15,000 granted as compensation was awarded to John, Earl of Carysfort. This town has dwindled into a small village, consisting only of a few houses of the humblest class, situated in a mountainous district. The corporation appear to have scarcely exercised any of their rights, except that of returning members to parliament, and at present it seems totally extinct as a borough. Fairs are held on Whit-Monday, Nov. 12th, and Dec. 26th. Here is a chapel, which was formerly endowed by the charter of Chas. I. with 130 acres of land, for the maintenance of a chaplain, whose appointment was vested in the sovereign and burgesses, or, on their failing to appoint, the income from the endowment was to be paid to any minister officiating in the town. From the extinction of the corporation, the endowment is lost, but the service of the chapel is performed by the rector of Rathdrum, or his curate. There is a R. C. chapel, which is the parochial chapel of Rathdrum. The Royal chartered school was founded by Chas. I., who granted to the sovereign and burgesses 200 acres of arable land and 97 acres of mountain and bog, for the sole use of such schoolmaster as the deputy or other chief governor of Ireland should appoint to reside and teach in the borough. This endowment had been for many years comparatively unavailing; a school was kept in a miserable cabin, and under an inefficient teacher; but a large and commodious school-house, with comfortable apartments for the master and his family, was recently built by the Board of Education, and there are now more than 100 children in the school. The income arising from the endowment, about £160 per annum, is received by the Board, who pay the master's salary, provide all school requisites, and keep the buildings in repair. Carysfort gives the titles of Earl and Baron to the family of Proby.—See Rathdrum.

CASHCARRIGAN, a village, in the parish of Kiltubrid, barony and county of Leitrim, and province of Connaught, 6¾ miles (N. E.) from Carrick-on-Shannon, on the road to Ballinamore; containing 18 houses and 94 inhabitants. It is a constabulary police station, and has a penny post to Carrick-on-Shannon, and a dispensary. Fairs are held on Feb. 1st, March 17th, May 1st and 28th, June 29th, Aug. 1st, Sept. 21st, Oct. 8th, Nov. 1st, and Dec. 21st.—See Kiltubrid.

CASHEL, a parish, in the barony of Rathcline, county of Longford, and province of Leinster, 4½ miles (S.) from Lanesborough; containing 5087 inhabitants. This parish is situated on the river Shannon, and on the road from Lanesborough to Ballymahon, and contains 10,420 statute acres, as applotted under the tithe act: the land is principally under tillage, but there is some marsh land and several thousand acres of bog in the northern and eastern parts of the parish. The substratum is limestone, of which there are some good quarries. The seats are Newpark, the residence of Capt. W. J. Davys, and a small seat belonging to Sir G. R. Fetherston, Bart., of Ardagh. The living is a vicarage, in the diocese of Ardagh, and in the patronage of the Archbishop of Tuam, as diocesan: the rectory is impropriate in Messrs. Armstrong, lessees of Lord Fauconberg: the tithes amount to £664. 13. 11., of which £443. 3. 2. is payable to the impropriators, and £221. 10. 9. to the incumbent. The church is a plain structure, with a square tower, built in 1816 by aid of a gift of £800 from the late Board of First Fruits. The glebe-house was erected in 1817, by aid of a gift of £400 and a loan of £400 from the same Board: the glebe consists of 35 acres. The R. C. parish is co-extensive with that of the Established Church; the chapel, at Newtown, is a handsome cruciform building, ornamented with minarets, and of recent erection; near it is a national school; and there are seven private schools in the parish, in which 220 boys and 154 girls receive instruction. Near the church are the ruins of an abbey, said to have been a dependency of the Augustinian abbey on Quaker island: they are covered with ivy, and a low arched doorway and lancet-shaped window still remain. At Cashel nearly the whole extent of Lough Ree is visible: this lake, of which the name signifies "the king of lakes," extends from Lanesborough to Athlone, and is nearly 20 miles in length, and in some parts 9 in breadth. A regatta generally takes place in August, which is attended by many pleasure-boats from Limerick. Its shores are studded with handsome residences, and it contains many picturesque islands, the largest of which are Hare Island (still thickly covered with its original woods, and on which Lord Castlemaine has a fishing-lodge), Inchmore, Inchturk, Inchboffin, All Saints' Island, Inisclothrann, or Quaker island, and Inchyana. Killenure, or the inner lake, is a picturesque portion of Lough Ree, branching eastward into the county of Westmeath, and containing Temple and Friars' islands, the former of which is the property of R. H. Temple, Esq., who has a neat lodge on it; the latter of G. Jones, Esq., who has also erected a lodge. In Inisclothrann, which is also called Seven Church island, and Quaker island, are the remains of seven churches. An abbey was founded here in 540, by St. Diarmuit Naoimh, or "the Just," which was pillaged by the men of Munster, in 1010, 1016, 1050, and 1087; in 1155 it was burnt, and in 1193 plundered by Gilbert de Nangle. The abbey of Inisboffin, founded about 530, by St. Rioch, nephew of St. Patrick; and the abbey founded on the island of All Saints, by St. Kieran, in 544, were also ravaged by the men of Munster on the same occasions; and in 1089 all three were plundered and destroyed by Muircheartach O'Brien, aided by a large fleet of Danes. It is said that a descendant of Sir Henry Dillon, of Drumrany, who came into Ireland with John, Earl of Morton, erected an abbey on the island of All Saints, probably on the site of the ancient abbey of St. Kieran, which was granted at the suppression to Sir Patrick Barnwall. Augustin Mac Graidin, who was a canon and died here in 1405, wrote the lives of the Irish Saints, and continued the annals of this abbey to his own time; the work is still preserved in the Bodleian Library at Oxford.

Seal.

CASHEL, a city (being the seat of an archbishoprick and diocese), borough, market, and post-town, in the barony of MIDDLETHIRD, county of TIPPERARY, and province of MUNSTER, 12 miles (N. N. W.) from Clonmel, and 75 (S. W.) from Dublin; containing, within the corporate lands, 12,582 inhabitants, of which number, 6971 are in the city. This place was the residence of the kings of Munster; and a synod was held in it by St. Patrick, St. Ailbe, and St. Declan, in the reign of Ængus, who, after his conversion to the Christian faith by St. Patrick, is said to have founded a church here. It is uncertain at what period Cashel first became the head of a bishoprick; indeed, its early history is involved in much obscurity, and has been a fertile source of hypothetical inquiry. Some writers assert that Cormac Mac-Culinan, King and Bishop of Cashel, who was killed in his retreat from battle in 908, either founded or restored the cathedral, by building on the rock of Cashel an edifice now called Cormac's chapel, one of the most interesting architectural remains in the kingdom; but its erection is, with greater probability, ascribed by others to Cormac Mac Carthy, the pious King of Desmond. In 990, this place was fortified by Brian Boru, who rebuilt thirteen royal houses and palaces in Munster, one of which is still pointed out at the corner of Old Chapel-lane, in this town. Until the year 1101, the buildings on the rock of Cashel were merely such as composed the *Dun*, or royal residence, or the *Carsoil*, or habitation on the rock of the kings of Munster; the cathedral probably occupied some other site. In that year, according to the Annals of Innisfallen, Murtogh O'Brien convened a great Assembly of the clergy and people of Cashel, in which he assigned over to the bishops that "hitherto royal seat" of the kings of Munster, and dedicated it to God, St. Patrick, and St. Ailbe. The same annals record that, in 1127, Cormac Mac Carthy, King of Desmond, erected a church here (the chapel above noticed), called from him *Teampul Chormaic*, which in 1134 was consecrated by the archbishop and bishops of Munster, in the presence of the nobility and clergy. A new church was built in 1169, on the site of the present cathedral, by Donald O'Brien, King of Limerick, who endowed it with lands, and converted the church founded by Cormac into a chapel or chapter-house on the south side of the choir of the new edifice.

Hen. II., on landing at Waterford in 1172, marched to Cashel, where he received the homage of the above-named Donald O'Brien; and in November of that year he summoned a general synod of the Irish clergy, which was also attended by those Irish lords who submitted to his sway, and at which Christian, Bishop of Lismore, the pope's legate, presided. This assembly acknowledged the sovereignty of Henry; and of the ordinances enacted by it, one exempted the persons of the clergy from the jurisdiction of civil courts in criminal cases, and their lands from all secular taxes; and another enjoined a perfect conformity of the church of Ireland with that of England. Henry, during his stay here, bestowed on the archbishop and chapter the city of Cashel, with a large tract of the adjoining country. After his departure, Richard Strongbow led an army to this place against the native princes of the west, and encamped here, awaiting the arrival of reinforcements from Dublin, which being defeated at Thurles, he was compelled to retreat precipitately to Waterford. In 1179 the town was burnt; after its restoration, Donat or Donchad O'Lonargan, who succeeded to the see in 1216, erected it into a borough. Hen. III., in 1228, remitted to Archbishop Marian and his successors the new town of Cashel, to be held of him and his heirs in free, pure, and perpetual alms, discharged from all exactions and secular services. Sir David le Latimer, seneschal to Archbishop Marian, founded an hospital for sick and infirm poor, in honour of St. Nicholas, which was afterwards given to a society of Cistertians introduced by Archbishop David Mac Carvill. In 1243 a Dominican friary was founded by Archbishop David Mac Kelly, which being destroyed by an accidental fire, was rebuilt by Archbishop Cantwell, who was constituted both patron and founder by an instrument dated at Limerick about the year 1480; and in 1250 Archbishop Hacket founded the Franciscan friary. Hore Abbey, called also "St. Mary's Abbey of the Rock of Cashel," was originally founded for Benedictines; but Archbishop Mac Carvill, having dreamt that the monks had made an attempt to cut off his head, forcibly dispossessed them of their house and lands, and gave the whole of their possessions to a body of Cistertian monks, whom he brought from the Abbey of Mellifont, in the county of Louth.

In 1316, on Palm-Sunday, Edward Bruce came hither with his army from Limerick, and proceeded to Nenagh; and in 1372 a parliament was held at this place. In 1495, during the baronial feuds, Gerald, Earl of Kildare, influenced by hostile feelings towards David Creaghe, then archbishop, set fire to the cathedral, and in the presence of the king subsequently defended this outrage, in answer to the accusations of his persecutors, on the ground that he would not have destroyed the building had he not thought that the archbishop was in it at the time. On the termination of the insurrection headed by the Earl of Tyrone, this place, with others, surrendered at discretion, in 1603, to the lord-deputy Mountjoy. Lord Inchiquin advanced against it from the siege of Cahir, in 1647: the inhabitants took refuge in their church on the rock, which was well fortified and garrisoned. Inchiquin proposed to leave them unmolested, on condition of their contributing £3000 and a month's pay for his army: this offer being rejected, he took the place by storm, with great slaughter both of the soldiery and citizens, among whom 20 of the R. C. clergy were involved; and after having secured the immense booty of which he obtained possession, dispersed his forces into garrison. In 1690 the adherents of King William who had been wounded in the attack on Limerick were hospitably received by the inhabitants of Cashel, whose humane attention induced the king, on the bridge of Golden, about four miles distant, to renew their charter by letter, which is still in the possession of the corporation.

The town is situated on the mail coach road from Dublin to Cork, about two miles from the river Suir, in a fine open country; it consists of one principal street, from which several others diverge irregularly, and contains 1059 houses. The inhabitants are very inadequately supplied with water, partly by pumps, which in summer afford only a scanty supply of hard water unfit for many culinary and domestic purposes, and partly with soft water conveyed by pipes from a distance of two miles. A small stream from the same source was brought into the town some years since, through the exertions of Archdeacon Cotton, at an expense of above £200, which was defrayed by subscription and an annual grant of £50 from the grand jury of the county, under the authority of an act of parliament called Lee's Act; but in a very short time it proved useless. Subsequently, W. B. Upton, Esq., an inhabitant, suggested a plan for bringing such a supply from a distance of 17 miles as would admit of the passage of boats also, by which turf from the bog of Allen, about 4½ miles distant, and coal from the Killenaule collieries, about 14 miles distant, might be conveyed to the town: the estimated cost was £9000, to advance which sum an application was made to Government, but the plan failed in obtaining the sanction of Government, and no steps have been since taken towards accomplishing so desirable an object. The archbishop's palace was formerly situated at Cammas, about two miles distant: the present, which stands within the city and was erected about the middle of the last century, is a large and well-built mansion, with extensive gardens attached, from which the ruins of the cathedral on the rock appear strikingly grand and conspicuous. Attached to the palace is a building in which is deposited a library of nearly 9000 volumes, chiefly bequeathed by Archbishop Bolton in 1741, for the use of the clergy of the diocese, and preserved by the archbishop, but there is no special fund for its support; some of the clergy have of late contributed to its augmentation by subscriptions for the purchase of a few valuable modern works. The infantry barracks are a handsome range of building, occupying three sides of a quadrangle, and are adapted to the accommodation of one field officer, six other officers, and 146 non-commissioned officers and privates, with stabling for three horses and an hospital for 21 patients. The markets are on Wednesday and Saturday: the market-house, situated in the centre of the Main-street, is not now open for the use of the public, except for the purpose of weighing butter and other articles. Fairs are held on March 26th and Aug. 7th; and in 1826 a grant of a fair on the third Tuesday in every month was made to Richard Pennefather, Esq., with a court of piepoudre. This is the residence of the chief magistrate of police (Capt. Nangle), and a chief constabulary police station for the district.

The town, as previously noticed, was erected into a borough about 1216, by Archbishop Donat, who gave burgage tenements to the burgesses, and is said to have also conferred on them the same privileges as were enjoyed by the burgesses of Bristol, reserving to the see a yearly rent of 12*d.* out of each burgage. Archbishop Marian, in 1230, granted the town to the provost and twelve burgesses, except only the shambles, then situated behind the present shambles, and the great bakehouse in John-Street, subsequently called Cunningham's Hall: he also granted them free pasture in all his lands (except meadows, corn, and manors), and empowered them to hold a hundred court and a court baron for hearing and determining pleas, reserving out of these grants only small chief-rents. Rich. II., in 1378, confirmed all the privileges of the corporation; and other charters, chiefly confirmatory, were granted by Archbishop Roland in 1557, and by Queen Elizabeth, in reward of their dutiful conduct, in 1584. Chas. I., in 1637, granted a new charter, ordaining that the town or borough should be called the "City of Cashel;" and two years after, another, which is now the governing charter. Jas. II. seized the franchises into his own hands, pursuant to a decree of the exchequer, and subsequently granted a charter which is now considered void: their ancient rights and privileges were restored to the corporation by King William, as before stated. In the "New Rules" of the 25th of Chas. II., for regulating corporations in Ireland, it was ordained that the appointment of the mayor, recorder, and town-clerk should be subject to the approbation of the lord-lieutenant and privy council. The corporation, under the style of the "Mayor, Aldermen, Bailiffs, Citizens, and Commons of the City of Cashel," consists of a mayor, aldermen (limited by the charter to 17 in number), two bailiffs, and an unlimited number of commons, aided by a recorder, town-clerk, two serjeants-at-mace, a sword-bearer, and a crier; a treasurer is also appointed. The mayor is elected annually on June 29th, by the court of common hall, and is one of three persons nominated by the aldermen from among themselves, but the choice may be extended to the citizens and commons, at the discretion of the aldermen; he is sworn into office on Sept. 29th, and, with the concurrence of three aldermen, has power to appoint a deputy during illness or absence. The aldermen, on vacancies occurring, are chosen from among the freemen by the remaining aldermen, and hold office for life. The recorder, according to practice, is elected by the mayor and aldermen, but the charter gives the power to the entire body; he holds his office during good behaviour, and may appoint a deputy. The bailiffs, by the charter, are eligible from among the citizens, one by the mayor and aldermen and one by the corporation at large; according to practice they are elected annually on June 29th in the common hall from among the freemen, on the recommendation of the aldermen. The town-clerk is elected annually with the mayor and bailiffs; the sword-bearer is eligible by the whole body, and holds his office during good behaviour; and the serjeant-at-mace and the crier are appointed by the mayor. The freedom is obtained only by gift of the mayor and aldermen, who are the ruling body of the corporation, and have the entire management of its affairs. The city returned two members to the Irish parliament until the Union, since which it has sent one to the Imperial parliament. The right of election was vested solely in the corporation, but by the act of the 2nd of Wm. IV., cap. 88, has been extended to the £10 householders of an enlarged district, comprising an area of 3974 acres, which has been constituted the new electoral borough, and the limits of which are minutely described in the Appendix: the number of electors registered at the close of 1835 was 277, of whom 8 were freemen; the mayor is the returning officer.

The mayor, deputy mayor, and recorder are justices of the peace for the city of Cashel and the county of Tipperary; and they are judges of the Tholsel court, the attachments and other process of which are executed by the bailiffs. This court, which by the charter is to be held weekly, and of which Thursday is the court day, has jurisdiction (not exclusive) in causes not exceeding the amount of £20 late currency; arising within the ancient bounds of the city and its liberties; and suits may be commenced in it either by action or attachment, on affidavit made before the mayor or his deputy of the amount and cause of action. Very few causes are now tried in this court, attributable to the expense of the proceedings, and to the facility for recovering debts afforded by the assistant barrister's court. In addition to this jurisdiction, the charter gives it a further jurisdiction to the extent of 40*s.* in causes arising without the city and liberties; but this power is in some degree limited by the 36th of Geo. III., cap. 39, which requires that the cause of action shall have arisen, or that the defendant be resident, within the city and liberties. The charter granted a court baron to be held before the mayor every three weeks; and a court leet with view of frankpledge, to be held within a month after Easter and Michaelmas, before the mayor and recorder, or before one of them and the deputy of the other. Quarter sessions for the county are held here in January and July, and generally continue ten days; petty sessions for the division are held every Wednesday by the county magistrates; and similar sessions are held for the city, at which both the county and city magistrates preside. The county court-house and prison, erected in 1818, on the south side of the city fronting the green, form a neat and substantial pile of building of stone: the former is sufficiently adapted to the transaction of business; and the latter, to which the city magistrates also commit prisoners, contains eight cells, three dayrooms, and two airing-yards. The corporation estates comprise 2024 Irish acres, let on lease for 99 years to various tenants, and producing an income of about £220 per annum.

Arms of the Bishoprick.

The first bishop of Cashel of whom any authentic notice occurs is Cormac Mac-Culinan, King of Munster, who, as was not uncommon at that period, exercised also spiritual jurisdiction over his subjects. He was descended from Ængus, and succeeded to the throne of Munster and to the see of Cashel, in 901, but was killed on his retreat from battle in 908, and interred in the abbey of Castledermot, where he was educated. From this period till 1152 only four of his successors are noticed, who, with the exception of one, are all styled archbishops of Cashel. Donat O'Lonargan, who then succeeded to the bishoprick, received from Cardinal Paparo, the legate of Pope Eugene III., one of the four palls which had been sent by him to Ireland, and of which the other three were conferred on Gelasius of Armagh, Gregory of Dublin, and Edan of Tuam. During the prelacy of Donald O'Hullucan, who succeeded in 1158, a synod was held here by command of Hen. II., at which all the archbishops and bishops of Ireland, except the archbishop of Armagh, assisted, and at which Christian O'Conarchy, the pope's legate, and the bishop of Lismore presided. At this synod Henry received from the archbishops and bishops charters, with their seals appended, by which they confirmed the kingdom of Ireland to him and his heirs, and constituted them kings and lords of Ireland for ever; transcripts of these charters were sent by the king to Pope Alexander, who by his apostolical authority gave his confirmation to them. Pope Innocent III., in 1210, confirmed to Donat O'Lonargan II., who had been promoted to the see in 1206, all the revenues and possessions of the archbishoprick, and subjected to his metropolitan jurisdiction the cathedrals of the suffragan bishopricks of Limerick, Killaloe, Fennabore, Waterford, Ardmore, Lismore, Cloyne, Cork, Ross, Ardfert, and Emly. Donald O'Brien, King of Limerick, about the time of the English invasion, built a new cathedral church, and converted the structure previously existing into a chapel or chapter-house; he also made large grants of land to the see, which was further endowed by his son Donat, surnamed Carbrac, with other grants of land in Thomond, and with the islands of Sulleith and Kismacayl, all which grants were confirmed by King John in 1215. The see of Emly was united with the archbishoprick of Cashel by act of parliament in 1568, during the prelacy of James Mac-Caghwell, who succeeded to the dignity in 1567, and was the first archbishop of the united sees of Cashel and Emly. Miler Magragh, who was elevated to the united sees in 1570, was in high favour with Queen Elizabeth, from whom he held in commendam the sees of Lismore and Waterford, on his resignation of which he obtained a commendam of the two bishopricks of Killala and Achonry, in Connaught, which he held with the see of Cashel till his death. The grant of these sees appears to have been made to him and his heirs for ever, in the way of union to the see of Cashel. After the death of Archbishop Thomas Price, in 1684, the see remained vacant for a long period, during which the revenues were received by collectors appointed by the Crown, and distributed by Jas. II., among the Roman Catholic bishops, no successor being appointed till 1690, when Narcissus Marsh became archbishop. By the Church Temporalities act (3rd of Wm. IV.) it was specially provided that the see of Waterford and Lismore, then vacant by the death of Dr. Bourke, should be annexed to Cashel, which accordingly took place on the passing of that act, when the Temporalities of both dioceses, with the episcopal palace, became vested in the Ecclesiastical Commissioners.

The archbishoprick, or ecclesiastical province, of Cashel comprehends the eleven dioceses of Cashel, Emly, Limerick, Ardfert and Aghadoe, Waterford, Lismore, Cork, Ross, Cloyne, Killaloe, and Kilfenora. It contains a superficies of 3,439,750 acres, and comprises within its limits the whole of the civil province of Munster, parts of the county of Kilkenny, and King's county, in the province of Leinster, and part of the county of Galway, in the province of Connaught. The archbishop is primate and metropolitan of Munster; he presides over the whole province, and exercises all episcopal jurisdiction within the united dioceses of Cashel, Emly, Waterford, and Lismore, and, in consequence of the union of the see of Limerick with the consolidated sees of Ardfert and Aghadoe, also of the sees of Cork, Ross, and Cloyne, and of those of Killaloe and Kilfenora, which are united to the sees of Clonfert and Kilmacduagh; three bishops only preside over the dioceses of the province, and are suffragan to the archbishop of Cashel. Under the provisions of the Church Temporalities act all archiepiscopal jurisdiction will cease on the next avoidance of the archbishoprick; Cashel, with the united dioceses of Emly, Waterford, and Lismore, will be made a bishoprick, and with the other sees of the province become suffragan to the archbishop of Dublin.

The diocese of Cashel comprehends the greater part of the county of Tipperary and small portions of the counties of Kilkenny and Limerick; it is 35 British miles in length and 29 in breadth, comprehending an estimated superficies of 278,000 acres, of which 600 are in Kilkenny, 850 in Limerick, and the remainder in the county of Tipperary. There are belonging to the archiepiscopal see, or united dioceses of Cashel and Emly, 20,046½ statute acres; and the gross amount of its yearly revenue, including the prebends of Glankyne and Isertlaurence, on an average of three years, ending December, 1831, was by the Ecclesiastical Commissioners returned at £7354. 2. The chapter consists of a dean, precentor, chancellor, treasurer, and archdeacon, and the five prebendaries of Glankeen, Killaldriffe or Killaldry, Fennor, Newchapel, and Kilbragh; the prebend of Glankeen belongs to the archbishop in right of his see. The vicars choral are a separate corporate body, anciently consisting of eight, but now of five only; they are endowed with various lands and tithes, the former comprising 644 statute acres, and both let on lease at £690. 10. 7¼. per annum. The economy estate of the cathedral consists of the rectorial tithes of the parish of St. Patrick's Rock, and the interest of £1000 in the new three and a half per cent. stock, together with a small sum in the old 3½ per cents., amounting to £399. 9. per annum. The diocese comprises 49 benefices, of which 22 are unions, and 27 single parishes or portions of parishes; three are in the gift of the Crown, three in lay patronage, and the remainder in the patronage of the archbishop. The total number of parishes or districts is 103, of which 92 are rectories and vicarages, and the remainder perpetual or impropriate curacies, or parishes without provision for the cure of souls. There are 31 churches, and two other buildings in which divine service is performed; and 27 glebe-houses.

In the R. C. divisions the archbishop of Cashel is primate and metropolitan of Munster; his dioceses are Cashel and Emly, to which the six bishopricks of Cloyne and Ross, Cork, Kerry, Killaloe, Limerick, and Waterford and Lismore, are suffragan. The diocese of Kilfenora, which is united to Kilmacduagh, in the province of Connaught, is alternately suffragan to the archbishopricks of Cashel and Tuam. The united R. C. dioceses of Cashel and Emly comprise 47 parochial unions or districts, containing 88 chapels served by 46 parish priests and 63 coadjutors or curates. The parochial benefices of Thurles and Moykarky are held by the archbishop: the cathedral, situated in the town of Thurles, is a very fine structure. There are one Presbyterian and four other dissenting places of worship.

The city is comprised within the parishes of St. John the Baptist and St. Patrick's Rock; the former containing 5207, and the latter 9454, statute acres, as applotted under the tithe act. The living of St. John's is a rectory entire, united time immemorially to the entire rectory of Ballyclerihan and the rectory and vicarage of Coleman, together constituting the corps of the deanery of Cashel, in the diocese of Cashel, and in the patronage of the Crown. The tithes of the parish amount to £341. 5. 10., and of the union to £483. 9. 4.; the glebe comprises 100 acres at Deansgrove, and there is also a glebe of 11 acres in Ballyclerihan, but no deanery or glebe-house. Besides several tenements, the lands belonging to the dean comprise 203½ acres, let on lease at a rent of £58 and annual renewal fines of £40; the gross annual revenue of the deanery, including tithes and lands, as returned by the Commissioners, amounts to £625. The church, erected on the site of a former edifice and completed in the year 1783, is a handsome and spacious structure of stone, with a lofty spire of good proportions, and serves both for the cathedral and the parochial church: the result of a survey made by Archbishop Agar having proved the old cathedral church to be incapable of restoration, the two were consolidated by act of council in 1749, and a portion of the economy fund of the cathedral was appropriated to the erection of this church, and lately towards keeping it in repair; and the Ecclesiastical Commissioners have also recently made a grant of £138. 18. 6. for repairing it. The living of St. Patrick's Rock is a rectory and vicarage, the rectory appropriate to the economy fund of the cathedral church, and the vicarage to that of the vicars choral; the tithes amount to £701. 5. 9., of which £362. 5. 8. belongs to the former, and £339. 0. 1. to the latter. In the R. C. divisions the two parishes form the union or district called Cashel, which is the union or parish of the Dean. The chapel of St. John's, situated in Friar-street, is a spacious and elegant structure, now undergoing extensive alteration and repair, including the erection of a spire; it is faced with hewn stone, and, when completed, will be very ornamental to the city. Behind it is a convent of nuns of the order of the Presentation; and there is another chapel at Rosegreen, in the parish of St. Patrick's Rock. There is a place of worship for Wesleyan Methodists, a neat building situated in the Main-street, and erected by subscription on a site granted at a nominal rent by W. Pennefather, Esq., in which part of the old prison built by Edw. I. was incorporated; it was opened for divine service on the 2nd of July, 1833. At the entrance to the city from Dublin are the buildings of the charter school, founded in 1751, and towards the support of which Archbishop Price contributed £50 per annum during his lifetime, and at his death bequeathed £300; it was also endowed with £600 by Archbishop Palliser, and, in 1746, with a lease for 99 years of 27 acres of land by the corporation: for many years 83 boys were supported and educated in this establishment, but since the withdrawal of parliamentary aid from the society at Dublin, the school has been discontinued. A parochial school is supported by annual grants of £21 from the archbishop and £10 late currency from the dean, in addition to which the dean and chapter provide a school-house and books. A national school was established by the late Rev. Dr. Wright, parish priest, which is aided by a grant of £25 per ann. from the Board of Education, and by collections at the Roman Catholic chapel: the school-house is a good slated building erected by Dr. Wright at an expense of £332. A national school is also conducted by the Presentation nuns, and is aided by an annual grant of £32 from the Board, and a donation of £60 per annum from the parish priest: there is also a Sunday school well attended. The total number of children on the books of the day schools, which are in the parish of St. John, is 584, of whom 206 are boys and 378 girls; and in the different private pay schools there are, in the same parish, 400 boys and 180 girls, and in that of St. Patrick's Rock, 65 boys and 55 girls. The county infirmary is a handsome and commodious building, situated on the green: it contains 40 beds, and is now being enlarged for the reception of a greater number of patients: in 1835, the number admitted into the house was 325, and of out-patients 4386; the total expenditure for that year amounted to £1043. 14. 9½. A charitable loan society has been recently established for advancing sums of money on security to necessitous tradesmen, who repay it by weekly instalments in the proportion of one shilling in the guinea.

The principal gentlemen's seats in the immediate vicinity are Newpark, the residence of M. Pennefather, Esq., D. L.; Richmond, of R. Butler H. Lowe, Esq., D. L.; Longfield, of R. Long, Esq., D. L.; Rockview, of S. Cooper, Esq.; Dualla, of J. Scully, Esq.; Ballinamona, of W. Murphy, Esq.; Deer Park, of J. Hare, Esq.; and Race-Course Lodge, of Avary Jordan, Esq. The rock of Cashel is an extraordinary mass rising on every side with a precipitous and rugged elevation, and consisting of concentric strata of limestone; the remains of the ancient structures by which it is crowned have an imposing and highly romantic appearance. Among these, *Cormac's chapel*, standing in a line parallel with the south side of the choir of the cathedral, is one of the best-preserved buildings of that age in the kingdom; the walls and roof are of stone, the latter finely groined. The entrance doorway is a Norman arch richly moulded and ornamented with zig-zag and bead-work; above it is a device in bas relief of a centaur shooting at an animal with a bow and arrow; the groining of the roof springs from low pillars with capitals variously ornamented. At the eastern end is a large recess, separated from the western part by a circular arch highly enriched and ornamented with grotesque heads of men and animals: within this recess is another of smaller dimensions, probably intended for the altar. The walls of each portion of the building are relieved with blank arches, and the pilasters from which they spring have been richly ornamented with various devices. A window has been recently opened by the Rev. Archdeacon Cotton, which has rendered visible some very ancient painting in fresco in the recesses of the walls; fourteen stone figures, representing the twelve Apostles and others, have also been discovered. The exterior walls of the chapel are, on the south side, ornamented with blank arches supported by pillars with grotesque heads; and attached to the building is a square tower, strengthened with bands of masonry and similarly ornamented. *The ancient cathedral*, now in ruins, was a spacious cruciform structure, with a central tower supported on pointed arches, and generally in the early English style of architecture; it is in several parts embattled, and with other features of a military character presents a venerable and singularly picturesque appearance. But it is more striking as a grand and well broken mass, than remarkable either for the elegance or richness of its details. The only monument worthy of notice is that of Archbishop Magrath, who is represented in a recumbent posture; it bears the date 1621, and was erected by himself about one year before his death. On the south side of the cathedral is the vicars' hall; and at the eastern angle of the north transept is an ancient round tower, in a very perfect state of preservation, its stone roof being still entire; the several stages were lighted by windows, of which the ledges are still remaining; the original doorway has been walled up, and another opened leading into the cathedral. The Dominican friary, situated in Moorlane, was, after its dissolution, granted in perpetuity by Henry VIII. to Walter Fleming, *in capite*, at the annual rent of 2*s.* 6*d.*: this was one of the noblest buildings of the order in Ireland, and considerable remains of its spacious cruciform church may yet be seen between the rock and the Main-street. At a short distance from the town are the remains of Hore abbey, which are noticed in the description of the parish of that name. At the back of Friar-street formerly were the remains of the Franciscan monastery, the site of which is partly occupied by the R. C. chapel; after its dissolution it was granted, in the 31st of Hen. VIII., to Edmund Butler, Archbishop of Cashel, to be held by him *in capite* at an annual rent of 2*s.* 10*d.* On the ascent to the cathedral is a stone, on which, according to tradition, the Kings of Munster were annually inaugurated. This place gives the titles of Viscount and Earl to the family of Moore, Earls of Mountcashel.

CASTLANE.—See WHITECHURCH.

CASTLEBAR, a market and post-town, and a parish (formerly a parliamentary borough), in the barony of CARRA, county of MAYO, and province of CONNAUGHT, 44 miles (S. W.) from Sligo, and 125¼ (W. by N.) from Dublin; containing 11,805 inhabitants, of which number, 6373 are in the town. This place owes its rise and importance to the ancestor of its present proprietor, Sir John Bingham, who, in 1609, obtained for it the grant of a market and fair. In 1613, Jas. I. granted the inhabitants a charter of incorporation, under which the government of the town was vested in a portreeve, fifteen free burgesses and a commonalty, with power to hold a court of record every Monday for the recovery of debts not exceeding five marks. The charter also conferred upon the portreeve and free burgesses the right of returning two members to the Irish parliament; and in 1620, the inhabitants received a grant of a second annual fair. After the quelling of the disturbances of 1798, in the autumn of that year the French, under the command of Gen. Humbert, having landed in the bay of Kilcummin on the 22nd of August, made themselves masters of that town, and proceeded to Ballina, of which they took possession on the 24th. On the following day, Gen. Hutchinson arrived at this place from Galway, and being joined on the evening of the 26th by Lieut.-Gen. Lake, every disposition was made for the reception of the invaders, who, after an obstinate contest, made themselves masters of the town, of which they kept possession for some days; but learning that the Marquess Cornwallis was approaching with his army, Gen. Humbert abandoned the place, and retreated with his forces towards Sligo.

The town is situated on the river of Castlebar, which has its source in Lough Lanark, and on the mail coach road from Ballinasloe to Westport: it consists of one principal street nearly a mile in length, from which diverge several smaller streets and lanes; and in 1831 contained 909 houses, some of the best of which are built round the green, which forms a pleasant promenade; the streets are paved and kept in repair at the expense of the county. The barracks, a fine range of building recently erected, and commodiously adapted for artillery and infantry, are arranged for 60 men of the former, and for 24 officers and 565 non-commissioned officers and privates of the latter. The linen manufacture, which was formerly much more extensive, is still carried on here; and a considerable quantity of linen and linen yarn is sold in the linen-hall, a neat building at the entrance of the town from Ballina. There are a tobacco and snuff and a soap and candle manufactory, a brewery, and a tannery; and the general trade of the town, with the exception only of the linen trade, is gradually improving. The market is on Saturday; and fairs are held on May 11th, July 9th, Sept. 16th, and Nov. 18th. A branch of the Agricultural and Commercial Bank of Ireland has been established in the town, in which are also a chief constabulary and a revenue police station. Under the charter of Jas. I. the corporation continued to return two members to the Irish parliament till the Union, when the borough was disfranchised, and the sum of £15,000 awarded as compensation was paid to Richard, Earl of Lucan. From that period till 1824 the corporation occasionally elected officers, but exercised little or no magisterial jurisdiction; for the last ten years it has been virtually extinct; and the court of record has been consequently discontinued. The assizes for the county are held here, and also the quarter sessions in January and October; petty sessions are also held every Saturday. The court-house is an extensive and well-arranged building. The new county gaol, situated at the southern extremity of the town, is a spacious and handsome building with a castellated front, erected in 1834, at an expense of £23,000: the arrangement is on the radiating principle, with the governor's house in the centre; it is well adapted for due classification, and contains 140 cells, with day and work rooms and airing-yards, in one of which is a treadmill applied to the raising of water; in the upper part of the governor's house is the chapel, accessible to the prisoners by corridors communicating with it by neat iron bridges; the female prisoners are divided into two classes, under the care of a matron and assistant, and an excellent school has been established; the average number of prisoners (which in 1835 was 181) will allow a separate cell to each at night, and during the day they are employed chiefly in breaking stones. The total expense for 1835 was £2083. 1. 3½.

The parish, which is also called Aglish, comprises 13,342 statute acres, as applotted under the tithe act; about 1400 are bog and waste, and the remainder arable and pasture. The lands are principally under tillage; the soil is good, and the system of agriculture much improved. The surrounding scenery is beautifully picturesque and finely varied, terminating in a distant view of the mountains by which the landscape is nearly surrounded. Castlebar, the seat of the Earl of Lucan, is romantically situated on the brow of a steep eminence overhanging the river, and attached to it is an extensive and well-wooded demesne, affording a pleasant promenade to the inhabitants of the town. The other seats are Spencer Park, that of Major O'Malley, D. L.; Mount Gordon, of Patrick Boyd, Esq; Ballynew, of the Rev. H. Pasley, J. P.; and Rocklands, of John C. Larminie, Esq. Many of the inhabitants are employed in quarrying excellent limestone used for building; and turf is carried by water for several miles to the town through the lake and the Castlebar river. A manorial court, at which debts to any amount were recoverable, was formerly held by a seneschal appointed by Lord Lucan; it has been discontinued for some years, but is about to be revived. The living is a rectory and vicarage, in the diocese of Tuam, united by act of parliament, in 1711, to the rectories and vicarages of Breafy, Turlough, and Kildecamoge, and the vicarage of Islandedin, forming the union of Castlebar, in the patronage of the Archbishop. The church, a handsome structure in the later English style, with a lofty square embattled tower, was erected in 1828, by aid of a gift of £2000 from the late Board of First Fruits; there is also a church in the parish of Turlough. There is no glebe-house: the glebe of the union comprises four acres; and the tithes of the parish amount to £190. In the R. C. divisions the parish is the head of a union or district, including also Ballyhane and Breafy, and comprising two chapels, at Castlebar and Ballyhane; the former is a spacious slated edifice. There is a place of worship for Wesleyan Methodists. A handsome building has been erected in the town for the parochial school, at an expense of £220, of which £90 was granted from the rector's school funds; the rector principally supports the boys' school, and contributes also to that of the girls, and both are aided by local subscriptions. At Castlebar and Clonkeen are national schools, to one of which Lord Lucan gives an annual donation of £10. In these schools are about 370 boys and 300 girls; and there are also eight pay schools, in which are about 200 boys and 70 girls. The county infirmary, a large building, is situated at the south end of the town; there are also a dispensary for the barony of Carra, and one for the town. At the head of Lough Lanark, near the town, is an ancient burial-place, commanding a fine view of the distant mountains; and on the other side of the lake are the ruins of a fortified residence. The Earl of Lucan enjoys the inferior title of Baron Lucan, of Castlebar.

CASTLE-BELLINGHAM, a post-town, in the parish of Gernonstown, barony of Ardee, county of Louth, and province of Leinster, 6 miles (S. S. E.) from Dundalk, and 34 (N. by W.) from Dublin; containing 115 houses and 611 inhabitants. This town, which is situated on the river Glyde, and on the mail coach road from Dublin to Belfast, takes its name from a castle belonging to the Bellingham family, which was burnt by the forces of Jas. II. in their retreat before the army of King William, previously to the battle of the

Boyne. The neighbourhood is embellished with several handsome seats, of which those of Lady Bellingham, Miss Bellingham, Major Sweeny, and Mrs. Filgate are the chief. An extensive brewery, in which the celebrated Castle-Bellingham ale is made, and a large malt-house, both belonging to J. Woolsey, Esq., give employment to about 70 persons. Fairs are held on Easter-Tuesday and Oct. 10th, for cattle, linen, &c. Here is a constabulary police station. The parish church, remarkable for its neatness, is situated in the town, and contains a fine font and some handsome monuments. There is a school supported by subscriptions; and a dispensary. Near the church, and at the entrance to the castle demesne, some neat cottages in the Elizabethan style have been erected for four widows, and endowed with £64 per ann., in 1826, by Sir W. Bellingham, Bart. There are some remains of the ancient castle near the river; and in a small bog adjoining, several perfect heads, with part of the horns, of the elk or moose deer have been found.—See GERNONSTOWN and GREENMOUNT.

CASTLE-BLAKENEY, called also GALLAGH, or KILLASOLAN, a post-town and parish, partly in the barony of KILCONNELL, but chiefly in that of TYAQUIN, county of GALWAY, and province of CONNAUGHT, 25 miles (E. N. E.) from Galway, and 86 (W.) from Dublin; containing 4305 inhabitants. This parish is situated on the road from Ballinasloe to Tuam, and comprises about 3000 acres of arable and pasture land, and 1000 of waste land and bog. The principal seats are Castle Ffrench, that of Lord Ffrench; Caltra Lodge, of P. J. Joyce, Esq.; Caltra House, of J. Kelly, Esq., J. P.; Cruise Lawn, of W. Cruise, Esq.; Greenville, of P. Cruise, Esq.; and Tycooly, of C. J. O'Kelly, Esq., J.P. Here are two mills for grinding oatmeal, and limestone is abundant. There is a constabulary police station, and fairs are held in the town on Jan. 2nd, March 17th, Whit-Tuesday, July 26th, and Oct. 2nd; fairs are also held at Caltra, in this parish, *which see.* The living is a rectory, in the diocese of Elphin, and in the alternate patronage of the Crown and the Bishop: the tithes amount to £300. The church is a neat building, erected by a gift of £200, and a loan of £200, in 1812, from the late Board of First Fruits. There is a glebe-house with a glebe of 80 acres and two detached glebes of four acres. The R. C. parish is co-extensive with that of the Established Church, and is also called Caltra, from the chapel being situated there, which is about to be rebuilt. A school is aided by annual donations from the Archbishop of Tuam and Mr. and Mrs. Blakeney; and there are a school aided by Lord Clonbrock, and another by Lord Ffrench. About 200 boys and 160 girls are taught in these schools, and about 50 boys and 30 girls attend a hedge school.

CASTLE-BLAYNEY, a market and post-town, in the parish of MUCKNOE, barony of CREMORNE, county of MONAGHAN, and province of ULSTER, 11 miles (S.E. by E.) from Monaghan, and 49 (N. N. W.) from Dublin; containing 1828 inhabitants. It derives its name and origin from Sir Edward Blayney, governor of the county of Monaghan in the reign of Jas. I., who, in consideration of the dependence of his garrison at Monaghan and Newry for a supply of provisions, which was rendered precarious by the hostility of the intervening country, received a grant of two ballybetaghs of land here, on condition of his erecting a fort between Monaghan and Newry; Castle-Blayney was accordingly erected, as a secure halting-place for the royal troops, and Sir Edward received this extensive estate, which his descendants still enjoy. The collection of habitations formed in the vicinity never, however, assumed the appearance of a town until the establishment of the linen market, and the rebuilding of the houses with stone, in the latter part of the last century, by the late noble proprietor. It is situated on the mail coach road from Dublin to Londonderry, and comprises 341 houses; is lighted by subscription, and has a respectable appearance. It consists of three streets meeting in the market-place, which is of a triangular form; and in the centre, on an elevated spot commanding every avenue, is the market-house, a very neat and ornamental building, with a spacious room on the second story, and a neat bell turret above the roof. Near the market-house are convenient shambles. The manufacture of linen, though not so extensive as formerly, furnishes employment to many persons in the surrounding districts; and there are three tanyards in the town. The principal market is on Wednesday, when considerable quantities of yarn and flax are sold: there are also markets for corn and butter on Tuesday and Friday; and fairs for live stock are held on the first Wednesday in every month. Here is a constabulary police station; also a neat sessions'-house, in which the quarter sessions for the county are held four times in the year, and petty sessions every alternate week; and a county bridewell, which affords the necessary accommodation for the classification of prisoners. The mansion of Castle Blayney, the seat of Lord Blayney, is closely adjoining, and is encompassed by a demesne of great extent and beauty, which includes the Lake of Mucknoe and some fine woodland scenery: it is a handsome modern edifice, built near the site of the old castle. The ruins of an ancient fortress in Cornero wood, on the shore of the lake, are also within the demesne. The parish church of Mucknoe is in the town; it is very neat, with a handsome spire, and the interior has been comfortably fitted up by Lord Blayney, who has also planted the churchyard with trees and evergreens. There are also places of worship for Roman Catholics, Presbyterians, and Wesleyan Methodists. The parochial school, situated here, has an average attendance of 35 children; and there is a school for girls, supported by Lady Blayney, with an average attendance of 70 children. Here is also a fever hospital. —See CLONTIBRET and MUCKNOE.

CASTLEBRACK, a parish, in the barony of TINNEHINCH, QUEEN'S county, and province of LEINSTER, 6 miles (W. N. W.) from Portarlington; containing 1855 inhabitants. This parish, which is situated in the north-east angle of the county, where it joins King's county, and on the river Oweness, derives its name from the castle, now in ruins, which was built by the Dunne family and was formerly a strong place surrounded by a moat. Fairs are held on May 16th and Aug. 12th. It is a vicarage, in the diocese of Kildare, and is part of the union of Rosinallis or Oregan; the rectory is impropriate in Gen. Dunne. The tithes amount to £210. 2. 6., of which £140. 1. 8. is payable to the impropriator, and the remainder to the vicar. In the R. C. divisions it forms part of the union or district of Mountmellick; the chadel is on the otwnland of Clonaghedor, where there is a national school, in which are about 30 boys and 40 girls, and a hedge school, in which are about 30 boys and 20 girls.

CASTLEBRIDGE, a village, partly in the parish of Tickillen, partly in Ardcolme, but chiefly in Ardcavan, barony of Shelmalier, county of Wexford, and province of Leinster, 2½ miles (N.) from Wexford; containing 416 inhabitants. This place, which derives its name from the ancient castle that formerly stood here, is situated on the north side of Wexford harbour, at the confluence of the Castlebridge river with the river Sow, and on the road from Wexford to Oulart, at the junction of the parishes of Ardcavan, Ardcolme, and the detached part of Tickillen. It consists of a few neat dwellings on both sides of the Castlebridge river, and is chiefly remarkable for its extensive trade in corn, for which its situation, commanding the whole extent of county to the south of Arklow, and its proximity to Wexford, are peculiarly favourable. Nearly the whole produce of that district is, in order to avoid the tolls at Wexford bridge, deposited in this village, where are very extensive stores, mills, and malt-houses belonging to Mr. Patrick Breen, from which a canal was cut by his predecessor, in 1810, opening a communication with the river Slaney. The stores are capable of containing about 40,000 barrels of corn, and about 65,000 barrels are exported annually. It is sent by boats of 15 or 20 tons' burden to Wexford harbour, where it is shipped, without any extra charge, on board the vessels that convey it to the various channel ports between Glasgow and London. About 3000 barrels of malt are also made here annually. Fairs have been long held on April 11th and Dec. 26th, and two others have been lately established and are held on June 10th and Sept. 25th. A constabulary police force is stationed here. The parish church of Ardcolme, built on the site of the ancient castle, is in that part of the village which is in the parish of Ardcavan, and the Ecclesiastical Commissioners have recently granted £310. 18. 6. for its repair. The R. C. chapel for the union or district of Castlebridge, which includes the parishes of Ardcavan, Ardcolme, St. Margaret, St. Nicholas, Skreen, and part of Killesk, is also in the village, where a residence is about to be built for the parish priest. A large school for children of both sexes is in course of erection by subscription; and a branch of the Skreen and Ardcolme dispensary has been established here.

CASTLEBUOY, or ST. JOHNSTOWN, an extra-parochial liberty, in the barony of Ardes, county of Down, and province of Ulster, 3 miles (N.E.) from Portaferry; containing 744 inhabitants. This place is situated on Cloghy bay, and, according to the Ordnance survey, comprises 1358¼ statute acres. A commandery or preceptory of St. John the Baptist of Jerusalem, dependent on the priory of Kilmainham, was founded here by Hugh de Lacy, in 1189, which continued till the commencement of the fifteenth century; the building is now in ruins, and the family of Echlin possesses several townlands in freehold which have always enjoyed exemption from tithe and church cess, and also a manor which belonged to the commandery, the court of which is now held once in three weeks. The manor is called Cloghy, and the court has jurisdiction over the liberty of Castlebuoy, the parishes of Slanes and Ballytrustin, and part of Witter, and any sum not exceeding £5 is recoverable in it, either by attachment or civil bill process. The lofty tower of the castle and ruins of the church are situated in one of the most secluded and fertile vales in the Ardes. On a chain of rock in the channel, three miles east from the shore, is the South Rock or Kilwarlin light-house. There is a private school, in which are about 70 boys and 60 girls.

CASTLE-CAULFIELD, a village, in the parish of Donaghmore, barony of Dungannon, county of Tyrone, and province of Ulster, 3 miles (W.) from Dungannon; containing 212 inhabitants. This town was founded by Sir Toby Caulfield, afterwards Lord Charlemont, to whom Jas. I. granted the lands called Ballydonnell, or the town of O'Donnell, in 1610. Sir Toby, in 1614, began building a mansion-house in the Elizabethan style, which afterwards acquired the name of Castle-Caulfield, and around which he located 41 British families, and mustered 30 men at arms. The second Lord Charlemont added a large gatehouse with towers, and a keep or donjon. In Pynnar's Survey it is described as "the fairest house in all these parts;" it is now a stately ruin, the gables and clustered chimneys producing a fine effect. The village is situated in a fertile valley, on the road from Dungannon to Omagh, and consists of one small street containing about 50 houses; the inhabitants are generally engaged in agriculture and the weaving of linen; a daily penny post to Dungannon has been established. Limestone and coal are found in the neighbourhood; and fairs, held on the second Monday in every month, for the sale of live stock, are numerously attended. A court for the manor of Castle-Caulfield is held by the seneschal; and petty sessions are held every alternate Saturday. Besides Castle-Caulfield, the seat of the Earl of Charlemont, here are several elegant houses, enumerated in the article on Donaghmore, *which see*. The parish church is in this village, and was built in 1685: it is a large and handsome edifice, in the Grecian style of architecture, except the south windows, which are in the later English style, and were brought from the old church of Donaghmore, which was destroyed in the war of 1641. A neat mural monument, in memory of the Rev. G. Walker, was erected on the south side of the altar, by his widow, in 1703. This distinguished man, while residing here in 1688, raised a regiment of infantry at his own expense, to act against the adherents of Jas. II., and proceeded to Londonderry, in the defence of which he had the principal share, and subsequently, on the death of Major Baker, became sole governor of the city. After the siege was raised, he resigned the command of the garrison, came to England, where he was most graciously received by their Majesties, and in Nov., 1689, received the thanks of the House of Commons, having just before published an account of the siege. A letter, written by Archbishop Tillotson, is extant, in which he says, "the king, besides his first bounty to Mr. Walker, hath made him bishop of Londonderry, that so he may receive the reward of that great service in the place where he did it." He returned to Ireland with King William, and having resolved to serve a campaign before he took possession of his bishoprick, was killed at the head of his regiment at the battle of the Boyne, on the 1st of July, 1690. In the village is a chapel belonging to the Seceding Synod, of the first class. Near the church is the male and female parochial school, capable of accommodating 300 children; it is endowed with two acres of land and £5 per annum from the rector, and was built in 1823 at an expense of £253, with apartments for the master and mistress. The ruins of the castle, and a very large and perfect fort near Parkanour, are the only vestiges of antiquity; but tradition points out the site of a friary, near the latter, although no remains are visible.

CASTLECOMER, a market and post-town, and a parish, in the barony of FASSADINING, county of KILKENNY, and province of LEINSTER, 9½ miles (N.) from Kilkenny, and 46 (S. W.) from Dublin; containing 13,242 inhabitants, of which number, 2436 are in the town. This town is situated on the river Deen, and on the road from Kilkenny, by Athy, to Dublin. It suffered greatly in the disturbances of 1798, from the violence of a party of the insurgents, by whom a considerable portion of the town was destroyed. It was, however, soon restored, and at present consists of one wide main street and several smaller, containing, in 1831, 455 houses, chiefly inhabited by persons engaged in the extensive collieries in the parish and neighbourhood. The infantry barracks, a neat range of buildings, are adapted for 8 officers and 126 non-commissioned officers and privates, with suitable offices. The market is chiefly for provisions, and some neat shambles have been erected. Fairs are held on March 27th, May 3rd, June 21st, Aug. 10th, Sept. 14th, Oct. 28th, and Dec. 14th. A constabulary police force is stationed here; the quarter sessions for the county once in the year (in June), and petty sessions every Friday, are held in the town; and a court for the recovery of small debts is held by the seneschal of the manor.

The parish comprises 21,708 statute acres, and contains the principal portion of the extensive coal field of the district. The coal is of the kind commonly called Kilkenny coal, which, containing no bitumen, burns without blaze or smoke; the larger pieces alone are applied to domestic purposes, the smaller fragments being chiefly used for burning lime. These collieries have been worked for more than a century: the regular strata were first discovered in digging for iron-ore in that part of the territory of Ida which belonged to the Brenans, and which was purchased from that sept, in the reign of Chas. I., by Sir Christopher Wandesford, and erected into a lordship by charter of the same monarch. Its extent at that time was estimated at 13,400 plantation acres; and the father of the last Lord Wandesford was the first who worked the pits to any advantage. The principal workings are all between the small river Deen, which flows by the town, and the hills to the east and north-east, extending towards Donane. The substratum on which the coal rests is remarkable for withstanding the agency of fire, and has been used with great success in the making of fire-bricks; the depth of the pits varies from 31 to 39 yards. The chief property in these mines was vested in the Wandesford family, to whom this place gave the title of Earl, now extinct, and whose representative, the Hon. Charles Butler Wandesford, brother of the Marquess of Ormonde, inherited in right of his mother, the sister of the late Lord Wandesford, and has a handsome modern residence adjoining the town. A great portion of the coal is conveyed through the southern counties by the rivers Suir and Barrow, and by the Grand Canal to Dublin. There are also some collieries at Pherodagh, or Firoda, about a mile and a half to the north-west of Castlecomer, from which a fine black glossy culm is raised with greater facility than from the mines here. There are a bleach-green and a grist-mill in the parish.

The living is a rectory and vicarage, in the diocese of Ossory, and in the patronage of the Crown: the tithes amount to £969. 4. 7½. The church, situated in the town, is a neat edifice with a tower; and there is a chapel of ease at Mooneenroe, in the collieries, built by subscription aided by a grant from the late Board of First Fruits, in 1818. Lectures on religious subjects are delivered also in the school-rooms adjoining the church and chapel of ease. The glebe-house was built by aid of a gift of £100 and a loan of £1500 from the same Board, in 1819. In the R. C. divisions the parish forms part of the three several unions or districts of Castlecomer, Clough, and Muckalee, the first of which comprises about one-half of it: there are four chapels belonging to these unions, one of which is in the town. There is also a place of worship for Wesleyan Methodists. Near the R. C. chapel is a convent, and adjoining it a school under the care of the nuns. The schools adjoining the parish church and chapel of ease are supported by an annual donation of £100 from the Hon. C. B. Wandesford, and £34 from the rector; an infants' school is also supported by subscription. In these schools about 380 children receive gratuitous instruction; and there are also eight pay schools, in which are about 330 children, and three Sunday schools. A dispensary was erected by the Countess of Ormonde, and an auxiliary branch of the Hibernian Bible Society has been established in the town.

CASTLE-CONNEL, or STRADBALLY, a post-town and parish, partly in the barony of OWNEY and ARRA, county of TIPPERARY, and partly in that of CLANWILLIAM, county of LIMERICK, but chiefly in the county of the city of LIMERICK, and province of MUNSTER, 5¾ miles (N. E.) from Limerick, and 88 (S. W. by W.) from Dublin; containing 5616 inhabitants, of which number, 1313 are in the town. This place, which was anciently called *Carrig-Cnuil*, derives its name from an ancient fortress, originally a seat of the O'Briens, Kings of Thomond, and in which a grandson of Brian Boroihme is said to have been treacherously murdered by the reigning prince. At the period of the English invasion this was a fortress of some eminence. In 1199 King John granted five knights' fees to William de Burgh, a baron of the family of Fitz-Aldelm, in which was included this parish, with a condition that he should erect a castle therein. This and the adjoining parishes were the first places in Limerick of which the English obtained possession. In 1578 Queen Elizabeth wrote letters of condolence to William de Burgh for the loss of his eldest son, who was slain in a skirmish with the Earl of Desmond, and the same year created him Baron of Castle-Connel, and gave him a yearly pension of 100 marks. In the war of 1641 Lord Castle-Connel forfeited his estate and title, which were restored on the accession of Jas. II.; the title became extinct in 1691, but the estate continues in the De Burgh family. In 1651 a strong garrison was placed in the castle by Gen. Ireton, while on his march to blockade Limerick. It was strongly garrisoned by the troops of Jas. II. in

1690, but on the 12th of August, in that year, was surrendered at discretion by Capt. Barnwell to Brigadier Steuart. On the retreat of the English army, it was again garrisoned by James's troops, which in the following year defended it for two days against the Prince of Hesse Darmstadt, and after its surrender it was blown up by order of Gen. De Ginkell.

The town, which is pleasantly situated on the eastern bank of the Shannon, which separates Limerick from Clare, lies a mile and a half west of the Dublin road, and in 1831 contained 178 houses, many of which are handsome villas and cottages of modern erection. It is resorted to during the summer, for the benefit of its spa, the waters of which resemble those of Spa in Germany. The soil around it is of a calcareous nature, and the sediment of the water has been successfully applied for the cure of ulcers, while the waters have proved very efficacious in scorbutic affections, bilious complaints, obstructions in the liver, jaundice, and worms; they are a strong chalybeate, having a mixture of absorbent earth and marine salt. Treatises have been written on their nature, and many persons are stated to have been cured by them, after ineffectually trying the continental spas. The waters rise from between limestone and basalt, filtering through a thin layer of blue unctuous earth, and yielding a constant supply. The spring is enclosed in a mean building, and the surplus water flows into the Shannon. There are two good hotels and a number of commodious lodging-houses in the town; a coach runs daily to Limerick, and there is a daily post. A constabulary police force has been stationed here, and petty sessions are held every alternate Monday. There is a patent for fairs on Easter-Monday, June 1st, July 16th, and Oct. 4th, of which only the first is now held.

The parish comprises 5850 statute acres, as applotted under the tithe act, about three-fourths of which are arable and pasture land, and the remainder is common pasture and reclaimable bog on the bank of the Shannon: it contains also a large undefined portion of the bog of Allen. The lands are principally under tillage; the soil is fertile, and the system of agriculture rapidly improving by the introduction of green crops; limestone is abundant. The bulk of the inhabitants are agriculturists, or dependent on the visiters to the spa; but many obtain employment in cutting turf and conveying it to Limerick, particularly for its large distillery; River Lawn, a mile below the town, is an extensive bleach-green and mill; and at Annacotty, near Mount Shannon, one of the first paper-mills established in Ireland was erected by Mr. Joseph Sexton. The parish is connected with the county of Clare by an ancient structure called O'Brien's Bridge, originally built by one of the royal line of Thomond, and in later times often strongly contested by the various parties who strove to obtain possession either of the important fortress of Castle-Connel, or the wealthy city of Limerick. It was partially destroyed by the Earl of Ormonde, in 1556, but was soon afterwards restored. The Shannon is not navigable here until within about a mile of the bridge, where the canal from the Clare side joins the river, there being many shoals, rocks, and cascades in its channel. It abounds with trout and salmon, of which latter there is a valuable fishery at the waterfall called the Leap. The falls here are numerous, there being a descent of 50 feet in less than three miles, and add greatly to the beauty of the scenery, which is embellished with the mansions and parks of the neighbouring gentry, and the ruins of three ancient castles, that of Castle-Connel being in the parish, and those of Newcastle and Castle-Troy being distinctly visible from its higher parts, while the Keeper mountains form a noble background on the north-east. The climate is good, the air remarkably pure, and great improvements have recently been made by reclaiming bog, &c., particularly by the proprietors of the Limerick distillery. Among the seats, the most distinguished is Mount Shannon, the residence of the Earl of Clare, and one of the finest mansions in the South of Ireland: the hall and library are particularly entitled to notice, and the grounds are laid out with great taste. Not far distant is Hermitage, the beautiful seat of Lord Massy; Caherline, of W. H. Gabbett, Esq.; Prospect, of Godfrey Massy, Esq; New Garden, of Massy Ryves, Esq.; Shannon View, of W. White, Esq.; Belmont, of Capt. Stackpoole; Woodlands, of J. Tuthill, Esq.; Castle-Connel House, of H. O. Callaghan, Esq.; Stormont, of Mrs. Kelly; Doonass, of Sir Hugh Dillon Massy, Bart.; Fairy Hall, of H. O. Bridgeman, Esq.; and Mulcaher, of the Rev. J. Crampton. A handsome range of well-built houses, called the Tontine, three stories high, with projecting roofs, was erected here in 1812, by the late W. Gabbett, Esq., from a fund raised by subscription; but not answering the expectation of the subscribers, they have been sold. Opposite these buildings is an island of about four acres, connected with the main land by a causeway 23 feet wide. About two miles north of Castle-Connel is the small but pretty village of Montpelier, which has a sulphureous spa of great virtue in ulcerous and cutaneous diseases; but in consequence of other water being allowed to mingle with it, its efficacy has been diminished and few resort to it.

The living is a rectory and vicarage, in the diocese of Killaloe, episcopally united, in 1803, to the rectory and vicarage of Kilnegaruff, and in the patronage of the Bishop: the tithes amount to £244. 12. $3\frac{3}{4}$., and of the benefice to £516. 7. $1\frac{1}{2}$. The church, erected in 1809, by aid of a grant of £250 from the late Board of First Fruits, was greatly enlarged in 1830, and is now a beautiful cruciform edifice with a lofty octagonal spire. There is no glebe-house, but a glebe of 2*a.* 0*r.* 14*p.* The R. C. union is co-extensive with that of the Established Church; the chapel is a large plain edifice. The parochial schools are chiefly supported by the rector; and there are a female school near Mount Shannon, supported by Lady Isabella Fitzgibbon, and an infants' school supported by voluntary contributions. In these schools are about 90 boys and 180 girls; and there are four private schools, in which are about 260 children. A dispensary was established in 1819. The only remains of the ancient and strong fortress of Castle-Connel are part of the tower and fragments of some other parts, situated on an isolated limestone rock, having an area of 42 yards by $27\frac{1}{2}$. The only other vestige of antiquity is on the island opposite the Tontine, which was formerly called Inis-cluan; it consists of the remains of a friary, founded in 1291 by Renald de Burgh, for Franciscans, and has lately been converted into out-houses to a handsome newly erected cottage.

CASTLE-CONNOR, a parish, in the barony of TYRERAGH, county of SLIGO, and province of CONNAUGHT, 4 miles (N. by E.) from Ballina; containing 4507 inhabitants. This place derives its name from an ancient castle, of which the ruins are still visible; and is situated on the river Moy and on the road from Ballina to Sligo. The parish comprises 16,223 statute acres, as applotted under the tithe act; the greater portion is under an improving system of tillage, and there are some large stock farms; there is a considerable extent of bog, and abundance of limestone is quarried for agricultural and other purposes. The principal seats are Moyview, that of the Hon. Col. Wingfield; Cottlestown, of S. Kirkwood, Esq.; Knockroe House, of G. Ruttledge, Esq.; Seaville, of P. I. Howly, Esq.; and Kinnaird, of J. Paget, Esq. The living is a vicarage, in the diocese of Killala, united by act of council, in 1806, to the vicarage of Kilglass; the rectory, formerly appropriate to the see, is now sequestrated in the Ecclesiastical Commissioners. The tithes amount to £476. 6. 1., one-half of which is payable to the Ecclesiastical Commissioners, and the other to the vicar. The church was built by aid of a gift of £900 from the late Board of First Fruits, in 1818. The glebe-house was built in 1820, by aid of a gift of £100 and a loan of £675 from the same Board: the glebe of the union comprises 50 acres. The R. C. parish is co-extensive with that of the Established Church; the chapel is at Castletown. A school is supported at Doorneen; and there are three pay schools, in which are about 240 children. Here is also a dispensary. There are some remains of the old castle on the bank of the Moy, and of the old church of Kilvanley with a burial-ground. There are also some Danish raths.

CASTLE-CONWAY.—See KILLORGLIN.

CASTLECORR.—See KILBRIDE.

CASTLE-DAWSON, or DAWSON'S-BRIDGE, a market and post-town, partly in the parish of BALLYSCULLION, but chiefly in that of MAGHERAFELT, barony of LOUGHINSHOLIN, county of LONDONDERRY, and province of ULSTER, 28 miles (N. W.) from Belfast, and 97 (N.) from Dublin; containing 674 inhabitants. This place derives its name from its proprietors, the Dawson family. On the plantation of Ulster, the eight townlands of Mayola were granted by Jas. I. to Sir Thomas Philips, whose sons sold them, in 1633, to Thomas Dawson, Esq., from whom they have descended to the Right Hon. G. R. Dawson. The town appears to have assumed its present form and name in the year 1710, during the proprietorship of Joshua Dawson, Esq., chief secretary for Ireland, and for many years member of parliament for the borough of Wicklow. It is delightfully situated on the two sides of the Mayola, over which is a handsome stone arch, erected by the Dawson family, and from this circumstance the town derived its former name of Dawson's Bridge: it consists of two principal and some smaller streets, containing, in 1831, 129 houses, many of which are large and well built. Here are extensive cotton twist mills, built in 1803, and furnishing employment to about 100 persons in the buildings and about 800 in the adjoining parishes. Near the town are large flour and oatmeal-mills; and in several places in the neighbourhood are manufactories of coarse earthenware, bricks, &c., and a bleach-green in which 800 pieces of linen are annually prepared for the London market. The market is on Saturday, and is well supplied with every kind of provisions; and in the season great quantities of grain, pork, and butter are purchased here, principally for the Belfast merchants: the market-house and grain stores are extensive and well built. Fairs are held on the last Saturday in each month, for the sale of linen cloth, yarn, cattle, pigs, sheep, and pedlery. The eight townlands of Mayola were, by letters patent, in 1712, erected into the manor of Castle-Dawson, with extensive privileges; and a manorial court is held monthly by the seneschal, in which debts to the amount of £20 are recoverable. Petty sessions are held every alternate week; and there is a constabulary police station. The soil in every part of the neighbourhood is fertile, and under an excellent system of cultivation. Coal is found, but no attempt has been made to work it, the seams being too thin to pay the expense, while turf is abundant. Nearly adjoining the town is The House, the residence of the Right Hon. G. R. Dawson, situated in a beautiful demesne, in which is an ancient avenue three miles in length, opening to a magnificent view of Lough Neagh, to which it extends. On an eminence close adjoining the town stands a beautiful and lofty obelisk, erected by the Earl of Bristol, to commemorate the virtues and benevolence of the Dawson family. There are several other handsome houses in the town and neighbourhood, the principal of which are Fairview, the seat of R. Henry, Esq.; Rowens Gift, of Capt. Crofton; Millbrook, of A. Spotswood, Esq.; Mount Aeriel, of S. J. Cassidy, Esq.; with those of Capt. Bouverie, W. Graves, Esq., and others. The church is small, but very neat; it stands on the western side of the Mayola, in the parish of Ballyscullion. The former edifice was built in 1710, by Joshua Dawson, Esq., and having fallen into ruin some years since, the present structure was erected by the Right Hon. G. R. Dawson, by whom it has been beautifully ornamented; on a brass tablet in an ancient carved oak frame is inscribed the genealogy of the Dawson family; it has also a beautiful window of stained glass. There is a large meeting-house for Presbyterians in connection with the Synod of Ulster, of the second class. A school for boys and girls is supported by subscriptions; and at Hill Head is a school supported by the London Hibernian Society. Of the castle built by Thomas Dawson, Esq., who was deputy-commissary in the reign of Chas. I., and which stood in the demesne near the church, little now remains, but the foundations of the walls and terraces are still traceable. The castle built by Joshua Dawson, Esq., in the year 1713, is now in ruins; and The House, built in 1768 by Arthur Dawson, Esq., who was member of parliament for the county of Londonderry, and chief baron of the exchequer, is now the family mansion. The present proprietor has made some extensive plantations around it and on other parts of his estate which flourish luxuriantly, and greatly embellish the surrounding scenery: Shillgray wood is very ancient, and contains some remarkably fine oak and beech trees. Ancient urns, ornaments of gold, spears, celts, and other relics have been found here. In the neighbourhood are some bogs, 30 feet deep, in which four separate layers of timber are imbedded: the lowest is principally oak, in a very sound and perfect state; the next chiefly yew, the third fir, and the uppermost birch, hazel, hawthorn, &c. Nuts, acorns, and the cones of fir are frequently found in these bogs, in very perfect condition.—See BALLYSCULLION and MAGHERAFELT.

CASTLEDERG, or DERG-BRIDGE, a market and post-town, in the parish of SKIRTS, barony of OMAGH, county of TYRONE, and province of ULSTER, 8 miles (S.) from Strabane, and 107¼ (N.) from Dublin; containing 575 inhabitants. The town is indebted for its origin to Sir John Davis, attorney-general for Ireland to Jas. I., to whom a grant of 2000 acres of land, then called Gartagh, was made in 1609, on which Sir John, prior to 1619, built a castle and established 16 British families; he also erected a stone bridge over the river Derg, adjoining the castle, which, being the first built over that river, gave the town the name of Derg-Bridge, by which it is still frequently called. Sir John had another grant of land at Claraghmore, upon which he built a castle, called Kerlis, and constructed a causeway, seven miles long and eight feet wide, in a straight line over mountains and through bogs, from one castle to the other. Several parts of this road are still traceable, but others have been broken up to make the road from this town to Drumquin. In the war of 1641, Sir Phelim O'Nial besieged the castle of Derg; and although he was driven away with disgrace and considerable loss of men, horses, and ammunition, yet he so greatly injured it that it was never afterwards repaired, and remains a noble pile of ruins on the northern bank of the river. The bridge erected by Sir John Davis remained till 1835, when it was taken down, and a handsome bridge of hewn stone, of four arches, has been erected.

The town, which is also called Castle-Derrick and Churchtown, is situated on the road from Newtown-Stewart to Pettigo, and on the new line of road from Londonderry to Enniskillen, betweeu which places two coaches running daily pass through it. It consists of one principal and two smaller streets, containing 105 houses, many of which are large and well built, and has much improved under the patronage of Sir R. A. Ferguson, Bart., its proprietor, who has lately built a very handsome inn. The market is on Friday, and is large and well attended; a fair is held on the first Friday in every month. A constabulary police force has been stationed here; petty sessions are held on alternate Saturdays; a court for the manor of Hastings every third Saturday, in which debts under 40*s*. are recoverable; and a monthly court for the manor of Ardstraw, for debts to a similar amount. There was anciently a church in the town, which was in ruins in 1619, when it was rebuilt by Sir John Davis; but being destroyed by Sir Phelim O'Nial in 1641, there was no church till 1731, when the present neat edifice was built by Hugh Edwards, Esq., of Castle-Gore, and was much improved in 1828. There is a national school for boys and girls, and a dispensary. Hugh Edwards, Esq., in 1735, bequeathed an acre of land on which to build a school-house, and £24 annually for the support of a master, to teach eight poor boys, but the school was not built; it is now, however, about to be erected and endowed. Not far from the town are the ruins of Castle-Gore, formerly the residence of the proprietors of the Manor-Hastings estate.—See SKIRTS.

CASTLE-DERMOT, a post-town and parish (formerly a market-town), in the barony of KILKEA and MOONE, county of KILDARE, and province of LEINSTER, 7¼ miles (S. E. by E.) from Athy, and 34 (S. W. by S.) from Dublin; containing 3634 inhabitants, of which number, 1385 are in the town. This place, called anciently *Diseart-Diarmuda*, and afterwards *Tristle-Dermot*, appears to have derived its origin from an abbey founded here for Canons Regular, about the year 500, by St. Diermit, which was plundered by the Danes in 843, and again in 1040. Cormac Mac-Culinan, the celebrated Archbishop of Cashel and King of Munster, was educated in this abbey under the abbot Snedgus, and at his death, in 907 or 908, was interred here. It was the chief residence of the O'Tooles, and on the English invasion was, with other territories of that sept, given to Walter de Riddlesford, who here erected a castle and founded a priory for Crouched Friars, which, with its possessions, was granted at the dissolution to Sir Henry Harrington, Knt. In 1264 a conference was held in the town, and was attended by Richard de Rupella, lord chief justice, to deliberate on the sanguinary feuds between the Geraldines and the De Burghs, when the governor and several other persons of distinction were seized by Maurice Fitz-gerald and his party, and carried prisoners to the castle of Ley. In 1302 a Franciscan monastery was founded here by Thomas Lord Offaly, which, in 1316, was plundered by the Scots under Edward Bruce, who also destroyed the town, but were soon afterwards defeated by Lord Edmond Butler, in a battle fought in the immediate vicinity. In the reign of Hen. IV. a parliament was held here to deliberate upon the best means of repressing the Ulster insurgents and expelling the Scottish invaders; and in 1499 another parliament was held in the town, and some curious sumptuary laws were passed. During the time of a fair, in 1532, the town was attacked by the insurgents under the Earl of Kildare; and it appears to have been finally ruined in the war which broke out in 1641. It was taken for Cromwell by Cols. Hewson and Reynolds, in 1650, since which time its extensive ecclesiastical buildings have been in ruins, and its former prosperity has never revived. In the disturbances of 1798, it was attacked by a party of the Kildare and Wicklow insurgents, on their march to assault the town of Carlow; but the assailants were vigorously repulsed by a body of regular infantry, and pursued in their retreat by the yeomanry.

The town is situated on the small river Lyrr, or Lane, and on the road from Dublin, by Carlow, to Cork, in the centre of an extensive plain, scarcely relieved by a single tree, and presents a striking contrast of venerable towers and stately ruins intermingled with humble cabins and houses generally of the poorest character. Large masses of detached rock are scattered on the banks and in the channel of the river, obstructing the current of an otherwise peaceful stream, and every thing around wears an appearance of continued decay. There is neither trade nor manufacture; the place is wholly dependent upon agriculture, and on the traffic resulting from its situation on a public thoroughfare, several coaches to and from Dublin passing daily through the town. The market has been long discontinued; but fairs are still held on Feb. 24th, Tuesday after Easter, May 24th, Aug. 4th and 5th, Sept. 29th, and Dec. 19th, chiefly for horses, cattle, and sheep, but also for general merchandize; the chief horse fair is in August. A constabulary force is stationed here; and petty sessions are held every alternate Wednesday.

The parish comprises 8735 statute acres, as applotted under the tithe act, and valued at £6207 per annum: the soil is good, and the system of agriculture improving. There is no bog; the nearest place from which turf can be obtained is 13 miles distant. Coal is brought from Carlow or Athy, where is the nearest communication by canal; large quantities of grey granite are quarried in the parish. The principal gentlemen's seats are Levitstown, the residence of W. Caulfield, Esq.; Barn Hills, of — Hill, Esq.; Bellview, of Jonas Duckett, Esq.; Ballinacarrig, of G. Paine, Esq.; Coltstown, of John Moffit, Esq.; and Marshalstown, of — Duckett, Esq. The living is a vicarage, in the diocese of Dublin, episcopally united from time immemorial to the vicarages of Ballaghmoon, Graney, Grangerosnolvin, and Kilkea, and to the half rectory and entire vicarage of Monmohennock or Dunmanogue, together constituting the union of Castledermot, and the corps of the prebend of Monmohennock or Dunmanogue in the cathedral church of St. Patrick, Dublin, in the patronage of the Archbishop; the rectory is appropriate to the see of Kildare. The tithes amount to £553. 16. 11., of which £369. 4. 7½. is payable to the bishop of Kildare, and £184. 12. 3½. to the vicar; and the aggregate tithes of the benefice amount to £941. 18. 5½. The church, a remarkably neat edifice, was repaired in 1831, by aid of a grant of £300 from the late Board of First Fruits, and a donation from the bishop of Kildare. In the R. C. divisions this parish is the head of a union or district, comprising the parishes of Castledermot, Moone, Timolin, Kilkea, Killelan, Dunmanogue, Grangerosnolvin, and Kinneagh, and part of the parish of Graney; there are three chapels in the union, one in this parish, a spacious edifice combining various styles of architecture, and one each at Moone and Levitstown. A school-house was built by the Earl of Kildare, who endowed it with £500, and bequeathed to it the same sum at his decease; the school was opened in 1734, and further endowed with 20 acres of land by his son James, Marquess of Kildare: it has, however, been discontinued since 1832. A parochial school, in which are 20 boys and 8 girls, is supported by the incumbent; and national schools are about to be erected on part of the site of the ancient Franciscan convent, given by Richard Farrell, Esq. Here is a dispensary. The remains of antiquity, though rapidly passing away, are yet highly interesting. In the churchyard, and still used as a belfry, is an ancient slender circular tower, not so high as the round towers of Kildare and other places; at a small distance from its base it is covered with ivy, and has a very picturesque appearance. There are also two crosses, sculptured with several curious emblematical figures and groups, and with certain characters, of which translations were published in the Irish Magazine for 1814. These crosses, apparently of the same date, are traditionally said to have been erected by Abbot Carpreus, in the 9th century, to whom is also attributed the erection of the round tower, and are supposed to point out the burial-places of different saints; they are divided into compartments, each embellished with a group of figures representing probably some scriptural subject; and of that which is still standing erect, the central compartment contains a rudely sculptured representation of the Crucifixion; on one of the arms is a figure in a sitting posture, playing upon a stringed instrument; and on the other are two figures, of which one is apparently in the act of paying homage to the other. Near the crosses is a fine Norman arch, decorated with the toothed ornament, the only remains of a church built by the first English settlers, most probably to replace that to which the round tower and the crosses were appendages. In another part of the town are the extensive and beautiful remains of the Franciscan convent, consisting at present chiefly of the abbey church and the chapel of St. Mary, the former a long building, lighted at the west end by two lofty lancet-shaped windows, and at the east end by a window which, though now greatly mutilated, appears to have been of elegant design; on the south side, and attached to the church, is a low square tower with a circular staircase turret; and on the north side, opening into the church by a lofty pointed arch, was the chapel of the Blessed Virgin, distinguished for the elegance and richness of its windows, of which the principal was a very magnificent window of four lights, with a large cinque-foiled circle in the crown of the arch, having the spandrils ornamented in trefoil. Of the monastery of the Crouched Friars nothing remains but a single tower; the foundations of the conventual buildings have disappeared, and the ground has been ploughed to their very base.

CASTLE-DILLON, a parish, in the barony of South Salt, county of Kildare, and province of Leinster, 2½ miles (S. W.) from Celbridge, on the river Liffey; containing 136 inhabitants. It is a rectory, in the diocese of Dublin, and one of the seven denominations that constitute the union of Kildrought or Celbridge. In the R. C. divisions it also forms part of the union or district of Celbridge.

CASTLE-DURROW.—See DURROW.

CASTLE-ELLIS, a parish, in the barony of Ballaghkeen, county of Wexford, and province of Leinster, 2 miles (S.) from Oulart; containing 1750 inhabitants. This parish is situated on the road from Wexford to Gorey, and comprises 5312 statute acres, principally under tillage, with some good pasture land: the soil is in general fertile, the only poor land being a sandy tract, and the system of agriculture is improving. The parish abounds with limestone gravel, containing a large proportion of marine shells, and with white and blue marl; and at Ballybuie, or Ballyboy, are some quarries of good granite used for building. The only seat is Newfort, the property of Lord Kilmaine, and now occupied by E. Turner, Esq. The living is an impropriate curacy, in the diocese of Ferns, to which the vicarage of Kilmalog and the impropriate curacies of Killesk and Killely were united by act of council in 1798, forming the union of Castle-Ellis, or Kilmalog, in the patronage of the Bishop: the tithes, amounting to £288. 3. 6½., are impropriate in Capt. Villiers Hatton, who allows a stipend for the performance of the clerical duties; and the entire tithes of the benefice, payable to the incumbent, amount to £197. 5. 7. The church was built by aid of a loan of £600 granted in 1813, by the late Board of First Fruits. The glebe-house was also built by aid of a gift of £100 from the same Board, in 1810: the glebe consists of four detached portions comprising in all 73 acres, and lying near the sites of the old churches. In the R. C. divisions this parish is partly in the union or district of Oulart, and partly in that of Blackwater, where the parochial chapels are respectively situated. A commodious school-house was erected at Ballybog, a few years since, by Mrs. Jessop, of Dowry Hall, who has endowed it with £40 per annum and about two acres of land, and also allows yearly six tons of coal: the school is open to all children from the surrounding parishes, who are provided with books and stationery, and there is a separate school-room for girls.

CASTLEFINN, a post-town, in the parish of DONAGHMORE, barony of RAPHOE, county of DONEGAL, and province of ULSTER, 4½ miles (W. by S.) from Lifford, and 111¾ (N. W. by N.) from Dublin: the population is returned with the parish. This place, which was anciently called Castle-Fynyn, belonged about the close of Elizabeth's reign to Sir Neill Garbh O'Donnell. It is situated on the river Finn, which is navigable to the Foyle for vessels of 14 tons' burden, and is on the road from Strabane to Stranorlar; it consists of a single street. Here is a R. C. chapel.—See DONAGHMORE.

CASTLE-GREGORY, a town, in the parish of KILLEINY, barony of CORKAGUINEY, county of KERRY, and province of MUNSTER, 12 miles (W.) from Tralee; containing 970 inhabitants. This town, which is situated on the Connor Hill road from Tralee to Dingle, and on the southern coast of Tralee bay, derives its name from an ancient castle founded by Gregory Hussey, which, in the war of 1641, was garrisoned for the king by its then proprietor, Walter Hussey. After sustaining a protracted assault from Cromwell's forces, the garrison, with their commander, escaped by night to Minard Castle, in the neighbourhood, in which they were besieged by Cols. Le Hunt and Sadler, and blown up by gunpowder laid under the vaults of the castle; there are no remains of this fortress. The town contains 160 houses, the greater number of which are thatched. A patron fair is held on Aug. 15th, which is also a fair for cattle. It is in contemplation to establish a penny post from Tralee and Dingle. A constabulary police force and a coast-guard have been stationed here; the latter has a detachment at Magharee, and is one of the five stations that constitute the district of Tralee. Petty sessions are held irregularly. The R. C. chapel, a substantial cruciform structure, was erected in 1831; and a school-room is about to be built, the late Rev. T. Fitzgerald, P. P. having bequeathed £30 per annum for educating poor children of the parish.—See KILLEINY.

CASTLEHAVEN, a parish, in the East Division of the barony of WEST CARBERY, county of CORK, and province of MUNSTER, 4½ miles (W.) from Skibbereen; containing 5619 inhabitants. This parish, anciently called *Glanbarrahane*, derived that name from a deep rocky glen dedicated to St. Barrahane, and its modern appellation from the castle that protected the haven. In the war of 1601, Castlehaven was a place of great importance, for it was here that six Spanish ships landed about 2000 men, with stores, ordnance, and ammunition, in consequence of which the disaffected septs cast off the mask of submission, all the country from Kinsale westward declared for the invaders, and O'Driscoll, lord of a fort at Castlehaven, which commanded the harbour, delivered it to his foreign friends. The forts at Baltimore, Innisherkin, and Dunboy, were also placed in the hands of Don Juan d'Aquila, the Spanish commander, who immediately garrisoned them, lavished gold upon their former proprietors, to whom he gave Spanish commissions, and took their followers into his pay. Admiral Leveson, who was sent here with a fleet, after sinking and destroying some of the Spanish vessels in the haven, was, by contrary winds, exposed to a battery erected by the enemy on shore, which was principally directed against his ship, and did considerable execution, so that he was obliged to return to Kinsale in a very shattered condition. The army of Tyrone and O'Donnel having been completely routed by the Lord-Deputy Mountjoy, the Spanish general agreed to evacuate Castlehaven, and in Feb., 1602, it was surrendered to Capt. Harvey for Queen Elizabeth, under the capitulation of Kinsale, after some unavailing opposition on the part of O'Driscoll, its proprietor. In 1645, the castle, well supplied with ordnance, was held for the parliament by William Salmon.

This parish is situated on the harbour of the same name, on the southern coast, and contains 10,421 statute acres, as applotted under the tithe act, and valued at £6336 per annum. About two-thirds of the land are cultivated; the remainder is waste, consisting of high barren rocky ridges, or bog. Cultivation is principally performed by the spade, or the heavy old wooden plough. The harbour is more than half a mile in width, and is very secure and well sheltered: it is adapted for vessels drawing 10 feet of water, which can lie about a quarter of a mile above Reen Head, with the rocks called the Stags in sight. The coast here is bold and picturesque, with several small islands lying off it, the principal of which are Horse Island and one called Blackrock. The Stags are three very conspicuous rocks lying four miles (S. W. ½ W.) from the entrance of the harbour; and Toe head is a broad promontory, between which and Gocaun point is a small but well sheltered bay. The principal seats are Castle Townsend, the residence of Col. Townsend; Point House, of R. B. Townsend, Esq.; Drishane, of T. Somerville, Esq.; Smithville, of T. Townsend, Esq.; and Shepperton, of M. Townsend, Esq. The living is a rectory and vicarage, in the diocese of Ross, and in the alternate patronage of the Crown and the Bishop: the tithes amount to £600. The church is a large and very handsome edifice, with a lofty square tower supported by buttresses and crowned with pinnacles: it stands in the demesne of Castle Townsend, and was built in 1827, of hewn fawn-coloured freestone obtained from the quarries on Horse Island, at an expense of £1500, of which £1250 was granted by the late Board of First Fruits, and £250 was contributed by Col. Townsend. There is an elegant glebe-house, standing on a glebe of 15 acres. In the R. C. divisions the parish is the head of a union or district, comprising the parishes of Castlehaven and Myross. The chapel is a large and commodious edifice, erected by subscription in 1834, on the lands of Raheens, about a mile from Castle Townsend. The male and female parochial schools are in Castle Townsend, and are aided by the rector and Col. Townsend. An infants' school was established there in 1835, and is supported by subscription. There are also four hedge schools and a Sunday school in the parish. The ancient castle, the walls of which are still visible near the mouth of the harbour, was built by the O'Driscolls, and subsequently belonged to the family of Touchet, of which George Touchet, Lord Audley, who had been governor of Utrecht, and was wounded at Kinsale in 1602, was created Earl of Castlehaven, in 1616: this title was enjoyed through five generations, but became extinct in 1777. Not far distant from the castle are the remains of the old church of Glanbarrahane; and near it is a well, dedicated to St. Barrahane, still frequented.

CASTLEHYDE.—See LITTER.

CASTLE-ISLAND, an island, in the parish of SKULL, in the Western Division of the barony of WEST CARBERY, county of CORK, and province of MUNSTER, 4 miles (E. by N.) from Skull; containing 89 inhabitants. This island, which is situated in Roaring Water bay on the southern coast, comprises 141 statute acres of land, which is mostly under tillage and cultivated by the spade, producing good crops of wheat, oats, and potatoes: the surface is gently undulating, and the substratum a compact schistus. Though tolerably fertile, it produces no plant higher than the creeping furze. It is about a mile and a quarter distant from the mainland, between Long island and Horse island, and contains only 15 small cabins indifferently built. On the coast of a small bay near its eastern extremity are the ruins of a castle, erected by O'Donovan More, in the beginning of the 14th century.

CASTLE-ISLAND, a town and parish, in the barony of TRUGHENACKMY, county of KERRY, and province of MUNSTER, 8 miles (S. E. by E.) from Tralee; containing 6161 inhabitants, of which number, 1570 are in the town. This place derives its name from the "Castle of the Island of Kerry," erected by Geoffrey de Marisco in 1226, and which, in 1345, was taken by Sir Ralph Ufford, lord-justiciary of Ireland, from Sir Eustace de la Poer and other knights, who held it for the Earl of Desmond, and on being captured were immediately executed. In 1397, Gerald, the fourth Earl of Desmond, commonly called "the poet," having gone out of his camp here, was privately assassinated. Queen Elizabeth granted the town and lands adjoining to the Herbert family, under the designation of "the manor of Mount Eagle Loyal," which, by a survey made by Hogan, in 1729, was found to comprise 36,920 plantation acres, valued at £3169. 12. 10. per annum. In 1733, a fee farm lease, subject to a reserved rent of £1900 per ann. for ever, was made of this property to five of the principal gentlemen of the county, who subsequently admitted a sixth; and hence it acquired the title of "the seignory of Castle-island." The proprietors afterwards made a division of the property, with the exception of the town and about 600 acres around it. The castle, of which there are still some remains, was destroyed by the Irish in 1600. The town is situated on the river Maine, and at the junction of the mail coach roads from Tralee and Killarney to Limerick; and on the completion of the new Government road from King-William's-town, it will be also on the direct road from Tralee to Cork. It consists chiefly of one long and wide street extending nearly east and west, with a market-house at the western extremity, from which the road to Tralee branches off on the north-west, and that to Killarney on the south-west: it had formerly a market and daily post. The new Government road has opened a line for a new street, which will diverge at right angles from the south side of the main street towards King-William's-town. In 1825, an act was obtained for dividing the town and undivided lands, which was carried into effect, and under it various improvements were made in the town. The total number of houses, in 1831, was 266, several of which are neatly built of limestone; and since the construction of the Government road, several additional houses have been erected. The river Maine rises suddenly from a well, called *Tubbermang*, about three quarters of a mile to the south-east of the town, and flowing by the south side of it, is crossed by three bridges at a very small distance from each other. This was once the capital of the county, and the assizes were formerly held here; but since Tralee became the county town, the place has declined very much, and its market has been discontinued. Fairs are still held on the first Monday in January and February, March 17th, April 20th, Easter-Monday, May 20th, June 24th, Aug. 1st (which is a great horse fair), and Oct. 1st, and there are two in November and two in December. There is a penny post to Tralee, Newcastle, and Killarney; a constabulary police force has been stationed here, and petty sessions are held at the court-house every alternate Wednesday. A manor court for the seigniory was formerly held, in which small debts were recoverable; a weighmaster and other petty officers are still appointed by Lord Headley, one of the proprietors, to whom the tolls of the fairs are payable. The court-house is a neat and substantial building at the western extremity of the main street; and there is a small but neat bridewell near the old barracks; it is one of the eight in the county, and contains, besides the rooms for the keeper, six cells, two day-rooms, and two airing-yards.

The parish comprises 32,577 statute acres, as applotted under the tithe act; the soil is various. Part of it is within that portion of the seigniory of Castle-island which belongs to Lord Headley, and consequently participates in the extensive and beneficial improvements which his lordship commenced in 1823 in this previously barren and unprofitable district. Among these are branch roads constructed at his expense from the new Government road between Castle-island and Abfeale, extending nearly 10 miles, and affording a facility of communication with every farm. Great improvements have been accomplished by a more efficient system of draining and fencing; upwards of fifty substantial farm-houses and cottages have been erected, Lord Headley having made stipulated allowances for that purpose; plantations to the extent of 350 acres have been made, and the appearance of the country has now an air of cheerfulness and comparative fertility. Limestone abounds, and is extensively used for manure; and there are considerable tracts of bog. The living is a rectory entire, in the diocese of Ardfert and Aghadoe, and in the patronage of Lord Headley, H. A. Herbert, Esq., Col. Drummond, and W. Meredith, Esq., as proprietors of the seigniory of Castle-island, also of Col. Townsend and W. T. Crosbie, Esq., who sold their respective shares to Lord Ventry and F. Chute, Esq., but retained their right of advowson. The tithes amount to £638. 18. 6. Previously to the decease of the late incumbent, the parish was united with those of Ballincuslane, Dysert, and Killintierna; but in consequence of the proprietors of the seigniory having omitted to nominate an incumbent within the limited time, the presentation for that turn lapsed to the bishop, who dissolved the union, and divided it into the three separate and distinct benefices of Castle-island, Ballincuslane, and Dysert with Killintierna, which separation was confirmed by act of council dated Jan. 4th, 1836. The church consists of the nave of a former structure, with the belfry thickly covered with ivy; and contains a neat mural monument to some of the Merediths of Dicksgrove, and on the south side of the exterior is a small sculptured head supposed to represent that of St. Nicholas, probably the patron saint; it is about to be thoroughly repaired, for which purpose the Ecclesiastical Commissioners have granted £290. The glebe-house, at Kilbannevan, was built in 1818, by aid of a gift of £100 and a loan of £1200 from the late Board of First Fruits; the glebe comprises 32 acres, valued at £48 per annum. In the R. C. divisions the parish for the greater part is the head of a union or district, comprising also the greater portion of the parish of Ballincuslane, and the remaining portions of both are included in the district of Brosna. The chapel at Castle-island is a spacious cruciform structure, and has recently been repaired and newly fronted with hewn limestone; adjoining it is a dwelling-house for the parish priest, recently erected. There is also a chapel at Knocknagashel, in the north part of the parish, which is attached to the Brosna district; it was erected in 1834, on a site given by Lord Headley, who also paid one-half of the expense of its erection, the other half being defrayed by his lordship's tenants in that district. There is a third chapel at Scartaglin, in the south part of the parish, which belongs to the district of Castle-island. Male and female schools are supported by the proprietors of the seigniory and the rector; and there are two schools under the superintendence of the R. C. clergyman. In these schools about 190 children are instructed; and there are also eight private schools. A dispensary has been established at the court-house. Between the western and the central bridges, on the banks of the Maine, are the ruins of the castle, consisting of several detached masses, two of which are of lofty elevation, and the whole show the original structure to have been of considerable extent. At Kilbannevan, adjoining the glebe-house, are the remains of an old church with a burial-ground; and there is still remaining a portion of the old court-house, in the rear of the present building.

CASTLE-JORDAN, or GUNGEDAH, a parish, partly in the barony of Upper Moyfenragh, county of Meath, and partly in the barony of Coolestown, but chiefly in that of Warrenstown, King's county, and province of Leinster, 3¼ miles (S. W.) from Kinnegad; containing 3967 inhabitants. This parish is situated on the road from Trim to Philipstown, and on the river Boyne, which separates it from the county of Kildare. There is a very large extent of bog; and gritstone used for building is procured from some quarries in the parish. The gentlemen's seats are Kildangan, the residence of E. Haughton, Esq.; and Tubberdaly, of J. Downing Nesbitt, Esq. The living is an impropriate cure, in the diocese of Meath, united by diocesan authority to that of Ballyboggan; the rectory is wholly impropriate in the heirs of the late Sir Duke Gifford, to whom the tithes, amounting to £380, are payable. The annual income of the curate is £100 late currency, of which £30 is paid by the impropriators and £70 by the Trustees of Primate Boulter's augmentation fund. The church, which is in the county of Meath, was built in 1826, at an expense of £664. 12. 1., defrayed by aid of a loan from the late Board of First Fruits. There is neither glebe-house nor glebe. In the R. C. divisions this parish is the head of a union or district, also called Boughilnebracnay, comprising Castle-Jordan and Ballyboggan, and containing two chapels. There are five private schools, in which about 190 children are educated. Here are the ruins of a castle, formerly occupied by the Giffords.

CASTLEKEIRAN, a village, in the parish of Loghan, barony of Upper Kells, county of Meath, and province of Leinster, 2½ miles (W. N. W.) from Kells; containing 24 houses and 162 inhabitants.

CASTLEKNOCK, a parish, in the barony of Castleknock, county of Dublin, and province of Leinster, 3¾ miles (N. W.) from Dublin; containing 4251 inhabitants, of which number, 188 are in the village. Tradition says that this was a royal residence of the Danes, and that, in 1167, Roderick O'Connor encamped here with his Connaught forces, when he led a numerous army to Dublin, where he was solemnly inaugurated King of Ireland, and engaged the Danish residents in his pay. The castle was given by Earl Strongbow to his friend, Hugh de Tyrrell, who was styled Baron of Castleknock. It was taken by Edward Bruce in 1316, and Hugh de Tyrrell and his lady made prisoners, but released on the payment of a large ransom. In June, 1642, the castle was taken for the parliament by Col. Monk, afterwards Duke of Albemarle, who slew in the assault 80 of its defenders, and subsequently hanged many more; but in November, 1647, Owen Roe O'Nial, and Sir Thomas Esmonde, Bart., at the head of a royalist force, retook it. The Marquess of Ormonde encamped here in 1649, when he threatened to besiege Dublin; and after the Restoration it fell into decay.

The parish is situated on the road from Dublin to Navan, and is intersected by the Royal Canal: it contains 6627 statute acres, the whole of which is arable land. Here are extensive limestone quarries, in which fossil remains are frequently found. On the Liffey are three woollen mills, where friezes, kerseys, lambskins, and Petershams, are manufactured; they have been established nearly a century, and employ above 60 persons during the winter. A factory for worsted and worsted yarn has been recently established at Blanchardstown, which employs between 80 and 100 persons; there are also on the Liffey a mustard and two flour-mills, and at Cardiff Bridge is a small iron-foundry. The parish is within the Dublin twopenny post delivery. Petty sessions are held every alternate Monday at Blanchardstown, where there is a constabulary police station. The scenery on the banks of the Liffey, towards Lucan, is very beautiful, and the northern side of the valley is celebrated for strawberries. In addition to the viceregal lodge, and the chief and under secretaries' residences, the parish contains many seats commanding delightful views: the principal seats are Sheep-hill, the residence of J. H. Hamilton, Esq., situated in a demesne of 500 acres; Farmley, of Charles Trench, Esq.; Knockmaroon, of Col. Colby; Park View, of A. Ferrier, Esq.; Mountsackville, of J. Hawkins, Esq.; Diswellstown, of C. O'Keeffe, Esq.; Airfield, of R. Manders, Esq.; Hybla, of the Rev. G. O'Connor; Scripplestown, of W. Rathborne, Esq.; Dunsinea, of H. Rathborne, Esq.; Scribblestown, of A. Holmes, Esq.; Ashtown, of J. Dunne, Esq.; Elm Green, of F. Dwyer, Esq.; Oatlands, of J. Godley, Esq.; Haymount, of Dr. Marsh; Bellville, of J. Murphy, Esq.;

Ashfield, of W. Oldham, Esq.; Cabra, of J. Plunkett, Esq.; and Huntstown, of O. Coghlan, Esq

The parish is divided into the northern and southern portions, each of which is subdivided into smaller parts: the prebendal or northern part furnishes an endowment for the two prebends of Mullahidart, or "*Castrum Knoc ex parte decani*," and Castleknock, or "*Castrum Knoc ex parte precentoris*," in the cathedral church of St. Patrick, Dublin. In 1219, the great tithes were appropriated by Archbishop Henry to the priory of Malvern, in Worcestershire, on condition that they should add five monks to their number; and in 1225 the prior and monks granted to the uses of the economy fund of St. Patrick's cathedral a moiety of the tithes of the manor of Castleknock, renouncing to the archbishop all right to the vicarage and its small tithes and oblations. During the prelacy of Archbishop Luke, a new division of the tithes was made, by which, of the four parts into which they were divided, one was assigned to the prebendary of Mullahidart, one to the prebendary of Castleknock, one to the economy estate of St. Patrick's cathedral, and one to the priory of Malvern, which transferred its interest to the abbot and convent of St. Mary, near Dublin, in 1468. This last portion having become impropriate on the dissolution of the religious houses, and forfeited by the rebellion of the impropriator, was granted as an augmentation of the vicar's means: and this division of the tithes still exists. The living is consequently a vicarage, in the diocese of Dublin, endowed with a portion of the great tithes, and united to the prebend of Castleknock and the rectory of Clonsillagh and curacy of Mullahidart, with cure of souls: it is in the patronage of the Bishop. The tithes amount to £560, of which £220 is payable to the economy estate, £140 to the prebendary of Mullahidart, and £200 to the prebendary of Castleknock. There are two churches in the vicarial union, one at Castleknock, the other at Clonsillagh; the former was rebuilt by a loan of £1000 from the late Board of First Fruits, and large subscriptions, in 1810, replacing one that had been built, in 1609, on the site of an Augustinian abbey for Canons Regular, founded in the 13th century by Richard Tyrrell, and dedicated to St. Bridget. There is a glebe-house; and the glebe, in two parcels, comprises 19*a.* 1*r.* 5*p.*, besides 8 acres which have been taken into the Phœnix Park, and for which, and also for the tithes of the park, the vicar receives £50. 15. per ann. late currency, from Government. In the R. C. divisions this parish is the head of a union or district, comprising the parishes of Castleknock, Chapelizod, Clonsillagh, Cloghranhidart, and Mullahidart; and containing three chapels, one at Blanchardstown, one at Porterstown (in Clonsillagh), and one at Chapelizod. At Cabra is a nunnery of the order of St. Dominick: the society removed hither from Clontarf about 1820, and consists of a chaplain, prioress, and nuns, besides lay-sisters; it is a respectable ladies' school, and the sisterhood also instruct from 150 to 200 poor children, who are partly clothed. The nunnery is surrounded with grounds tastefully laid out, and has a neat chapel and dwelling-house for the chaplain. There is another nunnery at Blanchardstown, in which more than 200 poor children are taught. In addition to the parochial school, there are two by the side of the canal, one for boys, maintained by a bequest from the late Mr. Morgan; and the other supported out of the produce of lands devised by a lady named Mercer, and yielding a rent of more than £750 per ann., vested in trustees, by whom 50 girls are maintained, clothed, and educated. A school for boys and girls at Abbotstown is supported solely by J. H. Hamilton, Esq., of Sheep-hill, by whom the children are also partly clothed; at Blanchardstown is a national school for both sexes; and a free school was built by Luke White, Esq. The late Mr. Tisdal bequeathed a large sum to the parochial schools, which is to be paid after his widow's death. There are a savings' bank and a dispensary. The remains of the ancient fortress of Castleknock occupy the summit of a lofty hill. In Knockbrush Hill, which is situated near the Ashbourne road, are occasionally found bones of men and horses, military weapons, and coins. Part of this hill is evidently artificial, and tradition says that it was raised over those who fell on this spot, in 1014, in the widely extended battle of Clontarf. Ancient horse-shoes, spurs, and other relics, have been dug up at Scripplestown. At Abbotstown are some remains of the abbey; and there is also a well dedicated to St. Bridget.

CASTLELOST, a parish, in the barony of FARTULLAGH, county of WESTMEATH, and province of LEINSTER; containing, with the post-town of Rochford-Bridge, 1909 inhabitants. This place was celebrated at a very early period for an extensive monastery, founded at Rathyne, or Rathenin, by St. Carthag or Mochuda, in which he presided for more than 40 years over 867 monks, who supported themselves and the neighbouring poor by their labour. There was also a very eminent school under the direction of St. Carthag, in connection with the monastery; but, in the Easter holidays of 630, he and his monks were driven from the abbey by King Blathmac, and the saint took refuge at Lismore, in the county of Waterford, where he died in 636. He is said to have been succeeded by St. Constantine, King of Britain, who resigned his crown; and the names of succeeding abbots are preserved till the year 783, from which date there are no further records of the monastery. The parish is situated on the road from Dublin to Athlone, and is bounded on the south by part of the bog of Allen: comprising 10,794 statute acres, of which 5932 are applotted under the tithe act. The surface is gently undulating, with few hills of considerable elevation, the highest of which is Gnewbane: the lands are principally under tillage, and the system of agriculture is improving. In Gnewbane are some quarries of a species of marble, and also of black-stone; and at the foot of the hill is an extensive tract of bog separating this parish from King's county. The principal seats are Sidebrook, that of J. Rochfort, Esq.; Heathfield, of Dr. Fergusson; Farview, of D. North, Esq.; Gortumloe, J. H. Shiel, Esq.; Cottage, of Mrs. Shiel; and Drummond Lodge, of T. M. Carew, Esq. The living is a rectory, in the diocese of Meath, and in the patronage of Lord Kilmaine: the tithes amount to £221. 10. 8¾. The rector also receives tithes from the townlands of High and Low Baskin, in the parish of Drumraney. The church, a neat modern edifice, was erected in 1815, by aid of a gift of £800 from the late Board of First Fruits. The glebe-house was built by aid of a gift of £400 and a loan of £400 from the same Board, in 1810: the glebe comprises 22 acres, subject to a rent of £24 per annum. In the R. C.

divisions this parish forms the district of Miden and Milltown. The parochial school is aided by an annual donation from the incumbent; there are about 24 boys and 13 girls in this school. A national school at Rochford-Bridge is also in progress; and there are three pay schools, in which are about 128 children. There are still remaining some ruins of the old castle, and of an ancient mansion-house, which were for successive ages the residences of the Tyrrell family, whose possessions were forfeited in the war of 1641. There are also, on the castle lands, the remains of the ancient parish church; it contains vestiges of various monuments to that family, among which is an altar-tomb with the recumbent figure of a knight in armour. After the decay of the old church, another was erected on the demesne of Gaulstown by one of the Rochfort family; it was used for more than 100 years previously to the erection of the present church, and is now a venerable ruin, forming an interesting and picturesque feature in the scenery of Gaulstown, the seat of Lord Kilmaine, in the adjoining parish of Kilbride-Pilate. There are several Danish forts, one of the largest of which is in the townland of Gortumloe, the estate of J. H. Shiel, Esq., whose labourers, in 1836, discovered in the adjoining field four perfect human skeletons.

CASTLE-LYONS, a market-town and parish, partly in the barony of CONDONS and CLONGIBBONS, but chiefly in the barony of BARRYMORE, county of CORK, and province of MUNSTER, 2 miles (E. by N.) from Rathcormac; containing 5647 inhabitants, of which number, 689 are in the town. It was originally called Castle Lehane, or Castle O'Lehan, from the castle belonging to the sept of Lehan being situated here; and it is stated that three cantreds here, which were unjustly detained from Robert Fitz-Stephen by his son Ralph, were subsequently granted by King John to William de Barry, who erected a castle here in 1204, and his descendants for some ages were called the Lords Barry of Castle Lehane. In 1307, John de Barry founded an abbey here, which at the dissolution was granted to Richard, first Earl of Cork, who assigned it to his daughter, wife to David, first Earl of Barrymore, "to buy her gloves and pins." Another of the De Barrys founded a monastery here for Carmelites or White friars. In 1645, Lord Broghill, being posted here with the royal cavalry to cover the army under Lord Inchiquin, that was besieging Castlemartyr, drew the Irish cavalry under Gen. Purcel into an action, commonly called the battle of Castle-lyons, in which he gained a decisive victory. The castle, nevertheless, fell into Lord Castlehaven's hands soon afterwards.

The town is situated on the river Bride, and on the road from Dublin to Rathcormac, and contains 116 houses. Here are a woollen-manufactory and dye-house, a corn-store, and flour-mills, the last built in 1808, worked by the river Bride, and manufacturing 10,000 bags of flour annually. The market is on Thursday, and great quantities of poultry are sold. Fairs are held on New Year's day, Easter and Whit-Mondays, Aug. 28th, Sept. 29th, and Nov. 16th, for cattle and general merchandise. A constabulary police force has been stationed in the town; and there is a penny post to Rathcormac. A manorial court is held once in every three weeks, for debts not exceeding 40*s.* by a seneschal, under S. Perrot, Esq., of Cork, who has recently purchased the manor.

The parish comprises 12,326 statute acres, as applotted under the tithe act, and valued at £11,726 per annum: three-fourths of the land are arable, and the rest pasture; considerable improvements have recently been made both in agricultural implements and the breed of cattle. There is no waste land, and very little bog, but abundance of limestone, which is used for building, repairing the roads, and burning. The river Bride abounds with very fine trout. The gentlemen's seats are Castle-lyons House, the residence of the Rev. J. Brown Ryder, A.M.; Kilcor Castle, of Cornelius O'Brien, Esq; Bally-Roberts Castle, of Michael Mackay, Esq.; Towermore House, of Mrs. Oliver; Coole Abbey, of H. Hawke Peard, Esq.; Mohera House, of J. O'Sullivan, Esq.; Bachelor's Hall, of the Rev. P. Berry, M.A., vicar; Ballyclough, of E. Creed, Esq.; and Kilbarry, of E. Wigmore, Esq. The living is a vicarage, in the diocese of Cloyne, and in the patronage of the Bishop; the rectory is impropriate in the Rev. J. B. Ryder. The tithes amount to £1713. 11. 1½. of which £1142. 7. 5. is payable to the impropriator, and £571. 3. 8½. to the vicar. The church is an old building, erected on the site of one more ancient. Connected with it is a mausoleum of the Barry family, which contains a sumptuous marble monument, consisting of two Corinthian columns supporting a pediment surmounted by a coronet, and bearing a latin inscription to the memory of James Barry, Earl of Barrymore, who died Jan. 5th, 1747. There is no glebe-house, but a glebe of two acres. In the R. C. divisions this parish is the head of a union or district, comprising Castle-lyons, Coole, and Britway; the chapel is at Bridgelane, a quarter of a mile from the town. There is a school supported by Mr. Corbett, in which are about 80 boys and 40 girls; and there are also two private schools, in which are about 100 boys and 50 girls, and a Sunday school superintended by the vicar. Samuel Perrot, Esq., erected a school at an expense of £300, and contributed £20 yearly towards its support, which has been discontinued. A bequest of £500 late currency was made by the late Rev. Mr. Harrison, formerly vicar of this parish, in trust to the dean and chapter of Cloyne, the interest of which, now amounting to £27. 17. 9. annually, is distributed among the Protestant poor of the parish. Part of the abbey, erected in 1307, is still standing connected with the parish church. Of the castle of the Lehans there are no remains, but on taking down some of the walls, to make room for the castle of the Lords Barrymore, a stone was found with the inscription, LEHAN O'CVLLANE HOC FECIT MCIIII. Nothing now remains of the castle of the De Barrys, but part of the arches on which it stood, and some of the partition walls: several coins of the Henrys, Mary, Elizabeth, Jas. II., and Wm. III., have been found among the ruins, and are in the possession of the Rev. J. B. Ryder. On the banks of the river Bride is Bally-Roberts castle, a high square tower, built by Robert de Barry as a defence against the Fitz-Geralds of Coshbride; and on the confines of this parish and those of Fermoy and Rathcormac is the mountain Corran Tierna, or Carn hill, a remarkable eminence, on the summit of which were discovered, after removing an immense heap of stones and a large flagstone, two antique urns, containing ashes; one was broken by the workmen, to ascertain whether it contained money; the other is in the possession of the Rev. J. B. Ryder, and is nearly globular, neatly marked, and has apparently been baked.

CASTLEMACADAM, a parish, in the barony of ARKLOW, county of WICKLOW, and province of LEINSTER, 5 miles (N. W.) from Arklow; containing 5155 inhabitants. This place derives its name from an ancient castle, which was destroyed in the frequent incursions of the O'Byrnes, and rebuilt in 1308, by Piers Gaveston, during his lieutenancy of Ireland. The parish is situated on the mail coach road from Dublin to Wexford, and on both sides of the beautiful Vale of Ovoca; it contains 12,360 statute acres, and although abounding in mineral wealth, is poor for agricultural purposes. The scenery is unequalled for its variety of beautiful and sublime views, in which the most pleasingly picturesque is combined with the most strikingly romantic. The enchanting valley of Ovoca, which is the scene of Moore's exquisite ballad, "The Meeting of the Waters," is principally within its limits, and contains a most admirable mixture of mountain, forest, lawn, and river scenery. After the conflux of the Avonmore and Avonbeg, at "the Meeting of the Waters," near Castle-Howard, the united stream takes the name of the Ovoca. The banks are about a quarter of a mile distant from each other, and for nearly eight miles are thickly wooded. The mail coach road from Dublin to Wexford, by way of Arklow, winds through this picturesque vale, which is adorned by the woods of Castle-Howard, Ballyarthur, Castlemacadam, Shelton Abbey, and Glenart, the hills containing the copper mines of Cronebane, Trigon, Ballymurtagh, and Ballygahan, and the village of Newbridge. The most splendid view of the valley is obtained from Ballyarthur, the seat of E. Symes Bayly, Esq. It is a plain house, but the demesne, which contains above 1600 statute acres, is richly wooded, and extremely varied in surface. The avenue leading to the house, which is through a turreted archway, near the village of Newbridge, is about two British miles in length, and with a gentle ascent winds through a wood of luxuriant growth. This road terminates at the lawn in front of the house, which contains above 60 British acres of undulating ground, on the top of the hill. A path behind the house leads to a terrace on the uppermost ridge of the northern bank of the Ovoca, which commands a prospect of the union of the Ovoca and Aughrim rivers, called the "Second Meeting," and of Croghan-Kinshela, which contains the Wicklow gold mines. But the most delightful view is from the spot where stood an octagonal temple, about half a mile from the terrace, the path to which is through a walk so thickly planted as to exclude the prospect of the surrounding country. This privation increases the gratification derived from the magnificent view which suddenly bursts on the eye. This enchanting demesne is open to all respectable persons, and during the summer is visited by very great numbers, being considered, from the exquisite beauty of its prospects, one of the most delightful spots in Wicklow. Near the head of the vale stands Castle-Howard, the magnificent seat of the late Col. Robert Howard, which crowns the summit of an almost precipitous cliff, rising from the east bank of the Ovoca and overlooking the confluence of the Avonmore and Avonbeg: the demesne is tastefully laid out, and ornamented with rustic buildings. Besides these seats, there are Cherrymount, the residence of the Rev. T. Webber, and Mine View, of J. Kilbee, Esq., from which there is an extensive prospect.

Mining operations were commenced here in 1787, by a company afterwards incorporated in 1798, under the name of the Irish Mining Company. The aggregate produce of Cronebane, up to 1811, was 26,875 tons of ore, which produced 1717 tons of copper. Above £12,000 worth of copper had also been obtained from the waters of the mine, by keeping them in tanks with old iron, which caused the copper to precipitate itself. The mines of Ballymurtagh were worked with eminent success by Mr. Whaley, of Whaley Abbey, so early as 1755. From the low price of copper, these mines were in a languishing state for several years; but in 1834, the Board of Public Works advanced £1000 for the erection of machinery in Cronebane, and a similar sum for Ballymurtagh both to be repaid by instalments, with interest. In 1835, four of the mines were in operation; of these, Cronebane and Tigrony, leased from the Irish Mining Company to the Cornish firm of Williams, Brothers, & Co., affords employment to above 600 persons. These mines are entirely worked by water; there are 8 water wheels, one of which is 50 feet, and two are 40 feet, in diameter; they produce about 90 tons of ore weekly, which yield from 5½ to 7½ per cent. of pure copper. In the middle of the last century, Mr. Weaver, superintendent of the Irish Mining Company's mines, discovered a brown indurated oxyde of iron, containing minute particles of silver to the amount of 6¼ per cent.; the communion plate for the parish church is made of this silver. The Connaree mines, worked by Messrs. Kempston and Tilly, are said to produce the richest copper ore at present known in Ireland, yielding an average from 9½ to 15 per cent., and in some instances even 35 per cent., of pure metal: 150 people are employed in these mines, raising about 1000 tons of ore annually. A steam-engine of 50-horse power has been erected to drain the mine, and is said to have been the first introduced into Wicklow. The Ballymurtagh mines are held by the Wicklow Copper Mining Company, on a lease which will expire about 1850, at a rent of one-tenth of the produce: about 380 persons are employed, who raise about 400 tons of ore monthly, which yields 5½ per cent. of copper. More than 20 veins have been discovered, extending nearly a mile and a half in length, and varying from a few perches to nearly half a mile in breadth. Four principal shafts have been sunk, the deepest of which is 120 fathoms; and a steam-engine of 50-horse power, and one of 45 are used for draining them. The working of Ballygahan mine, belonging to Viscount Powerscourt, was re-commenced by the Royal Irish Mining Company, in 1833, who raise from 40 to 50 tons per month, but intend working it on a larger scale. The shipping-place for all these mines is the port of Wicklow, to which their produce is conveyed by a difficult land carriage. There are some quarries of clay-slate in the parish, which is used for building, and also some detached masses of granite.

The living is a rectory, in the diocese of Dublin and Glendalough, united by act of council to part of the vicarage of Ballydonnel and the vicarage of Kilmacoo, forming the union of Castlemacadam, in the patronage of the Archbishop: a very small portion is impropriate in Charles Cooper, Esq. The tithes amount to £246. 7. 7., of which £230. 15. 4¾. is payable to the incumbent, and £15. 12. 2¼. to Mr. Cooper. The church is a neat edifice, standing on an elevated ridge which projects into the western side of the vale, midway between the two "Meetings of the Waters." A portion of the ruins of the castle, erected in the 14th century, is incorporated in the walls of this church, the erection of which was aided by a loan of £1000 from the late Board of First Fruits, in 1819; the Ecclesiastical Commissioners have lately granted £291 for its repair. There is a glebe-house; the glebe comprises about 30 acres. In the R. C. divisions this parish is partly in the union or district of Danganstown, but chiefly forms the head of a union, called Newbridge and Barrenisky, comprising also the parishes of Kilbride and Redcross, and part of that of Templemichael; and containing two chapels, one at Barrenisky and one at Newbridge; attached to the latter is a national school. There are three parochial schools under the direction of the rector, which are supported partly by subscriptions and partly by the proprietors of land granting small portions to the schools rent-free. There is also a school supported by the proprietors of the copper mines, principally for the miners' children. The interest of a bequest of £100 is divided among the poor; and a savings' bank was established here in 1834.

CASTLE-MAGNER, a parish, partly in the barony of ORRERY and KILMORE, but chiefly in that of DUHALLOW, county of CORK, and province of MUNSTER, 3½ miles (E. by N.) from Kanturk; containing 2853 inhabitants. It derives its name from the family of Magner, to whom this part of the country formerly belonged, and who erected a castle here, which was forfeited during the protectorate. This castle and lands were granted to the family of Bretridge, from whom they passed to the Hartstonges; the remains now form part of a farmer's residence. Not far from Castle-Magner, in the parish of Subulter, is Knockninoss, where, on the 13th of November, 1647, a battle was fought between the English, under Lord Inchiquin, and the Irish army commanded by Lord Taaffe, in which the English obtained a complete victory: a detailed account of the battle is given under the head of Subulter. During the same war, Loghort castle, in this parish, was garrisoned with 150 men by Sir Philip Perceval, ancestor of Lord Arden, but was taken by the Irish, who held it till May, 1650, when Sir Hardress Waller, with a battery of cannon, captured it, and in his letter to the parliament describes it as a place of great strength. This castle, which was built in the reign of John, remained in a state of ruin for many years after the protectorate, but was repaired in the early part of the 18th century by Lord Egmont. It is 80 feet high, with walls 10 feet thick at the base, but gradually diminishing to 6, and encompassed with a deep moat or trench passed by a drawbridge. Here was formerly an armoury for 100 cavalry, well furnished with broadswords, bayonets, pistols, carbines, and other weapons, among which was the sword of Sir Alex. Mac Donald, who was treacherously killed by a soldier, after the battle of Knockninoss: these arms have been deposited at Charlesfort for security.

The parish is situated on the new line of road from Mallow to Kanturk, and is partly bounded on the south by the river Blackwater, and contains about 7760 statute acres, consisting of nearly equal portions of arable and pasture land; there is some woodland, and a considerable quantity of wet rushy ground, but no bog or waste. The soil is generally fertile, producing excellent crops, and there are several large dairy farms. On the lands of Coolnamagh are some pits of culm, forming part of the Dromagh vein, but not worked at present. Limestone abounds, and is quarried for building, repairing roads, and making lime. The new Government line of road to King-William's-town passes through the extremity of the parish for about a mile and a half. Four fairs were formerly held at Cecilstown, at which is a constabulary police station, and petty sessions are held there every Monday. Ballygiblin, the seat of Sir W. W. Becher, Bart., is an elegant mansion of some antiquity, but recently modernised with great taste. In its beautiful demesne are the ivy-clad ruins of a church, which tradition states was intended to be the parish church, but was not completed. The other residences are Bettyville, the seat of J. Therry, Esq.; Ramaher, of C. Purcell, Esq.; the glebe-house, of the Rev. J. D. Penrose,; Cecilstown Lodge, of W. Wrixon, Esq.; and Assolas, belonging to Sir W. W. Becher.

The living is a vicarage, in the diocese of Cloyne, and in the patronage of the Bishop; the rectory is impropriate in John Longfield, Esq. The tithes amount to £809. 5. 1., of which half is payable to the impropriator and half to the vicar. The church, which stands on an eminence, and is a plain neat structure, was erected in 1816, by aid of a loan of £500 from the late Board of First Fruits; but the spire was built at the expense of Lord Arden. The glebe-house was erected by aid of a loan of £300, and a gift of £500, in 1813, from the same Board: the glebe consists of only two roods of land. In the R. C. divisions this parish is the head of a union or district, comprising Castle-Magner, Rosskeen, and Subulter, and has a small chapel here. A school of 50 boys and 30 girls, under the National Board, is aided by Sir W. W. Becher, Bart.,who allows 20 guineas per annum; and a school for boys and girls is supported by the trustees of Erasmus Smith's foundation, who allow £20 per annum to the master, with a contingent gratuity of £10, and £14 per annum to the mistress, with a like gratuity of £8. The school-house, which contains apartments for the teachers, is a neat building in the rustic style, erected by the late Hon. John Perceval, and is kept in repair by Lord Arden.

CASTLEMAINE, formerly a market-town, in the parish of KILTALLAGH, barony of TRUGHENACKMY, county of KERRY, and province of MUNSTER, 1¼ mile (N. by E.) from Milltown; containing 387 inhabitants. This place, which is situated on the harbour of Castlemaine, on the south-west coast, takes its name from a castle erected on the bridge over the river Maine by McCarthy More and the Earl of Desmond, as a defence to their frontiers. Each of these chiefs was to garrison it alternately for their joint protection; but when the earl received possession of it from McCarthy, he retained it in his own power, and on the expiration of the term for which his garrison was to remain, refused to admit McCarthy, and kept entire possession of the castle, which remained in his family till the reign of Elizabeth. The garrison under Thomas Oge defended it for a considerable time against the Queen, but it was ultimately taken by the English forces. During the war in 1641, it was in the hands of the Irish, till it was taken and demolished by Cromwell's troops under Gen. Ludlow. After the Restoration, though the castle was in ruins, a constable continued to be regularly appointed, and the clerk of the Crown was generally selected for that office. The constable had 10*s.* per day and the fishery above the river; but on the death of the last constable the income was reduced, and the present constable receives £50 per annum for the ground rent, with the privileges of the two fairs and the fishery. The royalty extends to high water mark on the south side of the river; and the crown lands, which are on the north side, comprise about seven plantation acres, which are called the King's acres.

The town, which is situated on the north side of the river Maine, and on the road from Castle-island to Dingle, contains only 62 houses. The Maine flows into the harbour of Castlemaine, which is a continuation of the bay of Dingle; the bridge is supposed to be coeval with the old Thomond bridge at Limerick. The castle stood over it, and projected considerably on the east side; the buttresses of the arch by which it was supported are remaining, and the stone socket on which the pivot of the castle gate turned is still to be seen. The trade consists principally in the exportation of corn, and the importation of coal, salt, and other necessaries; but since the erection of a quay and warehouses at Callanafercy, between the mouths of the Maine and Laune, it has very much decreased. Vessels of 100 tons' burden can come up to the bridge; but from the circuitous course of the river, they require two tides, which creates a delay very injurious to trade. On both sides of it are level tracts of ground, formerly swamps, but now wholly embanked and reclaimed. The late Mr. Nimmo reported that, if cuts were made across the winding parts of the river, vessels drawing 12 feet of water might discharge their cargoes at the town, and barges navigate four miles above the bridge, to which distance the tide extends. The expense of this improvement, and also of laying down proper marks to direct the navigation, would not exceed £1500; and the advantage derivable from it to the agriculture and the trade of the district would be very great. The erection of a pier would be a great improvement, there being scarcely any portion of the old pier remaining. Fairs are held on September 3rd and November 21st, for cattle, and two others have been recently established. Three miles to the west of the town are the ruins of Castledrum, erected by the sept of Moriarty; and on the lands of Farnass is a good chalybeate spa.—See KILTALLAGH.

CASTLEMARTYR, a post-town (formerly a parliamentary borough), partly in the parishes of ITERMORROUGH, BALLYOUGHTERA, and MOGEELY, barony of IMOKILLY, county of CORK, and province of MUNSTER, 19 miles (E. by N.) from Cork, and 127 (S. W. by S.) from Dublin; containing 830 inhabitants. This place is situated on the road from Youghal to Midleton, and on the mail coach road from Dublin, by Waterford to Cork; it appears to have risen into importance at a very early period. At the time of the English invasion, the castle, then called the castle of Imokilly, was resolutely defended by one of the Geraldines; but the English at length reduced it and kept in it a powerful garrison, till 1196, when Donald McCarthy besieged and destroyed it by fire, burying the garrison in its ruins. and putting to death all who escaped from the flames, The castle was afterwards rebuilt and became a very important fortress, commanding the pass between Cork and Youghal, and was strongly fortified and garrisoned by the English. In 1575, this castle, then called the castle of Ballymartyr, was garrisoned by Fitzgerald, seneschal of Imokilly, but was attacked by the Lord-Deputy Sidney and his forces, aided by 200 of the citizens of Cork, who, after a protracted and vigorous defence, compelled the garrison to surrender, and Fitzgerald narrowly escaped by flight. In 1645 it was besieged by Lord Inchiquin, to whom it was given up on honourable terms; and during the whole period of the parliamentary war, the town was the scene of violence and depredation, and was frequently plundered and partially destroyed. In 1688 it was plundered by Lieut.-Gen. McCarthy and the Irish forces, on their retreat from Cork; and in 1690, after the battle of the Boyne and the surrender of Youghal, a detachment of 36 dragoons and 42 infantry of King William's forces charged a body of 300 Irish at this place; the cavalry pursued them to the castle, in which they took refuge, and being joined by the infantry, they compelled the fortress to surrender, and the garrison to march out without either horses or arms: in this skirmish the Irish lost 60 men killed and 16 prisoners. In 1691, after the surrender of Limerick, the Irish under Gen. McCarthy obtained possession of the town by stratagem, but were shortly after driven out by a party of the garrison from Youghal, since which time the castle has been in ruins.

The town consists of one wide street, at one end of which is the demesne of the Earl of Shannon, and at the other a bridge, beyond which a cross road leads on the right to the villages on the sea coast, and on the left to Imogeely, Fermoy, and Tallow. On the right side of this cross road, which is lined with fine ash trees, some neat houses have been recently built, forming a suburb to the town. The total number of houses is 129, most of which are large and well built, and the whole being whitewashed gives the town a very cheerful appearance. The approach from Midleton is by a magnificent avenue of lofty elms, one mile in length, and terminating at the eastern gate of Lord Shannon's demesne. About two miles from the town are Ballynona flour-mills, the property of Mr. W. Jackson, who has a neat cottage residence adjoining; the mills are propelled by a mountain stream, and produce about 12,000 bags of flour annually. Fairs are held on the 2nd of May and October; a constabulary police force is stationed here; and petty sessions are held every alternate Wednesday.

The inhabitants were incorporated by charter of Chas. II., dated July 28th, 1675, granted to Roger, Earl of Orrery, by which the castle and lands forming his estate were erected into a lordship, called the manor of Castlemartyr, with courts leet and baron, and a court of record with jurisdiction extending to £200, under a seneschal to be appointed by his lordship. The charter also granted that the castle, town, and lands of "Ballymartyr," part of the said manor, should be a free borough, under the designation of the "Borough and Town of Castlemartyr," and should extend into the county of Cork in every direction from the centre of the town, so as to comprise in the whole an area of 100 acres. The corporation was styled "The Portreeve,

Bailiffs, and Burgesses," and consisted of a portreeve, two bailiffs, and twelve burgesses, who had power to admit freemen at their discretion, and to send two members to the Irish parliament; the former privilege was never exercised, nor have the limits of the borough been defined. The portreeve and bailiffs are annually elected on the Monday after St. John's day; and the burgesses, as vacancies occur, are chosen by the corporation. The portreeve has power to appoint a deputy; both are justices of the peace and coroners for the borough, during their year of office, and the portreeve for one year after. The corporation continued to return two members to the Irish parliament till the Union, when the borough was disfranchised, and the £15,000 awarded as compensation was paid to Richard, Earl of Shannon. The charter gave power to appoint a recorder and town-clerk, who were never appointed, and the only officer elected is a serjeant-at-mace, who also acts as a peace officer. A manorial court is held on the second Monday in every month, or oftener if required, by the seneschal, in which debts under £2 late currency are recoverable. The charter granted two weekly markets, but none are held; a market-house was erected in 1757, by the Hon. Henry Boyle, and a beam and scales are kept in it by the serjeant-at-mace, who receives small fees for weighing grain and other articles. There is a small bridewell belonging to the borough, chiefly used for the temporary confinement of disorderly persons. The parish church of Ballyoughtera is situated on a gentle eminence on the north side of the town; the Ecclesiastical Commissioners have lately granted £225 for its repair. A dispensary has been established, and a fever hospital is entirely supported by the Earl of Shannon. Twelve almshouses were built for six aged men and six aged women of the borough, under a provision of the charter, authorising the lord of the manor to endow them with such lands as he might think proper. These almshouses are not kept up, and the Earl of Shannon, in lieu of them, allows £5 per annum each to 12 aged persons of the borough.

Immediately adjoining the town is Castlemartyr, the seat of the Earl of Shannon, a spacious mansion erected by the Rt. Hon. Henry Boyle, Speaker of the Irish House of Commons. It is a substantial structure, consisting of a centre with a handsome portico and two extensive wings, and is situated in a demesne of 1000 acres tastefully laid out in lawns and shrubberies, embellished with woods of stately growth, diversified with some beautiful sheets of water, and intersected with numerous walks and rides commanding fine views of the richly varied and highly picturesque scenery with which the demesne abounds. Near the house is a large and beautiful lake, and there are two of smaller dimensions within the grounds; also two canals, over one of which is an elegant bridge. The shrubberies are exceedingly luxuriant, and the flower garden contains a great number of rare and hardy exotics, which, from the mildness of the climate, attain an extraordinary size. The ruins of the old castle of Imokilly, or Castlemartyr, the ancient seat of the Fitzgeralds, mantled with ivy to the very summit, and surrounded at the base with trees of stately growth, form a strikingly interesting feature in the landscape; and within the demesne are also the ruins of the ancient parish churches of Ballyoughtera and Cahirultan. The deer park is about two miles distant; it contains some of the finest timber in the country. In the neighbourhood are numerous other seats, among which are Dromadda, the residence of G. W. Courtenay, Esq.; Kilbree, of S. W. Adams, Esq.; Kilmountain, of J. Boles, Esq.; Carew's Wood, of the Rev. J. Leslie; Ballyhickaday, of Capt. Leach; Springfield, of the Rev. W. Boles; and Castletown, of Norman Uniacke, Esq. The ruins of the ancient castle shew it to have been a place of great strength, and from the variety of its architecture it appears to have been built at different times. Richard Alfred Millikin, a gentleman distinguished for his talents and benevolence, author of a poem called "The River side" and other productions, including the well-known song of the "Groves of Blarney," was born here in 1767. The Earl of Shannon enjoys the inferior title of Baron Boyle of Castlemartyr, in the peerage of Ireland.

CASTLEMORE, a parish, in the barony of Costello, county of Mayo, and province of Connaught, 2 miles (N. W.) from Ballaghadireen; containing 3094 inhabitants. This parish, which is situated on the new line of mail coach road from Ballaghadireen to Ballina, is four miles in length, and comprises 8342 statute acres, as applotted under the tithe act. About 2780 acres are bog and waste land; and of the remainder, the greater portion is under tillage. The land is cold and unproductive; the system of agriculture is very backward. The principal seats are Castlemore, the residence of J. Plunkett, Esq.; and Brooklawn, of the Rt. Rev. Dr. McNicholas, R. C. Bishop of Achonry. The living is a vicarage, in the diocese of Achonry, episcopally united to those of Kilcolman and Kilmovee, forming the union of Castlemore, in the patronage of the Bishop; the rectory is impropriate in Lord Dillon. The tithes amount to £150, of which one-half is payable to the impropriator, and the remainder to the vicar; and the gross tithes of the benefice amount to £270. 4. 5. The church of the union is at Ballaghadireen. There is a glebe-house: the glebe of the union comprises 20 acres. In the R. C. divisions this parish forms part of the union or district of Kilcoleman; the chapel is in the town of Ballaghadireen. There are two national schools, situated respectively at Brusna and Aughalustra, the former of which is endowed with four acres of land given by Lord Dillon: about 100 boys and 100 girls are instructed in these schools; and there is also a pay school, in which are about 50 boys and 30 girls.

CASTLE-PLUNKETT, a village, in the parish of Baslick, barony of Ballintobber, county of Roscommon, and province of Connaught, 5½ miles (E. by S.) from Castlerea: the population is returned with the parish. It is situated on the road from Strokestown to Castlerea, and comprises about 40 cabins. The vicinity is bare of trees, with the exception of Millton, the seat of Roderic O'Connor, Esq., where the woods extend down a gentle slope to a turlough of near 200 acres, and have a rich appearance. Fairs are held here on the 1st Thursday (O. S.) in May, Aug. 13th, and Oct 11th.—See Baslick.

CASTLE-POLLARD, a market and post-town, in the parish of Rathgraff, barony of Demifore, county of Westmeath, and province of Leinster, 10 miles (N. by E.) from Mullingar, and 42 (W. N. W.) from Dublin; containing 1618 inhabitants. This place is situated about a mile and a half to the west of Lough

 Rr

Lane, and about two miles to the north-east of Lough Derveragh, in a fertile valley, and is surrounded by a richly varied country embellished with numerous gentlemen's seats. It consists of several streets and a small detached suburb, and in the centre is a square, in which stands the market-house. The market is on Wednesday; and fairs are held on May 21st, Aug. 1st, Oct. 10th, and Dec. 10th. A chief constabulary force is stationed here; a manorial court is held four times in the year, by a seneschal appointed by W. Dutton Pollard, Esq., who is proprietor of the town; and petty sessions are held every Wednesday.

The parish church was built in 1820, on a new site adjoining the Kinturk demesne; the tower and part of the old church remain, and the churchyard, in which stands the school-house, is still used as a burial-ground. There are also a R. C. chapel, a dispensary and fever hospital, and a parochial school in the town. A savings' bank has been established, in which the deposits amount to more than £20,000. Immediately adjoining is Kinturk, the seat of W. D. Pollard, Esq., a handsome residence situated in a fine demesne embellished with extensive plantations; within the grounds is a lofty hill, in a grave on the summit of which was found the skeleton of a man, and near it a very large iron spur. Pakenham Hall, the seat of the Earl of Longford, to the west of Kinturk, is a handsome castellated mansion in a demesne embellished with timber of stately growth, and tastefully laid out: the gardens are remarkably fine, and kept in excellent order. Near the town are also Turbotstown, the residence of Gerald Dease, Esq.; Galstown, of Hubert de Bourgh, Esq.; Lough Park, of N. Evans, Esq., beautifully situated on the shore of Lough Lane; Benison Lodge, of the Rev. T. Smyth; Coolure, of the Hon. Sir T. Pakenham, G.C.B., on the shore of Lough Derveragh; and Lake View, of W. Smyth, Esq. The old castle of Kinturk, from which the town took its name, was situated in the centre of it, but there are no remains.

CASTLE-POLLARD.—See RATHGRAFF.

CASTLERAHAN, a parish, in the barony of CASTLERAHAN, county of CAVAN, and province of ULSTER; containing, with the post-town of Ballyjamesduff, 6960 inhabitants. This parish is situated on the road from Virginia to Mount-Nugent, and comprises, according to the Ordnance survey, 10,315 statute acres (including 102½ in Lough Ramor), of which 9722 are applotted under the tithe act. Contiguous to the town is a small lake, near which a shaft was sunk some few years since, and indications of coal were discovered. The gentlemen's seats are Fort Frederick, the residence of R. Scott, Esq., and Mount Prospect, of T. Nugent, Esq. Since the census of 1831, nine townlands have been separated from this parish to form, with portions of other parishes, the district parish of Ballyjamesduff, *which see.* The living is a rectory and vicarage, in the diocese of Kilmore, and in the patronage of the Bishop: the tithes amount to £304. 1. 10½. The church, a small ancient building, is in very indifferent repair. The glebe-house, a handsome residence, was rebuilt in 1818, by aid of a gift of £100 and a loan of £1500 from the late Board of First Fruits: the glebe comprises 350 acres. In the R. C. divisions this parish is the head of a union or district, comprising also the parishes of Muntercon-naught and Ballyjamesduff. The chapel, a large handsome edifice, erected in 1834, at an expense of £2000, is situated in the townland of Cormeen. There is a place of worship for Presbyterians in connection with the Synod of Ulster, of the third class. The parochial school is supported by subscription aided by an annual donation of £10 from the rector; a school at Clonkuffe has an endowment of two acres of land by the Bishop, and is aided by subscription; and there is a school at Ennagh, supported by Miss Sankee. In these schools about 160 boys and 60 girls are instructed; and there are four pay schools, in which are about 220 boys and 100 girls. Near Ballyjamesduff (*which see*) are two Danish raths.

CASTLEREA, a market and post-town, in the parish of KILKEEVAN, barony of BALLINTOBBER, county of ROSCOMMON, and province of CONNAUGHT, 13¾ miles (N. W.) from Roscommon and 88½ (W. by N.) from Dublin; containing 1172 inhabitants. This place appears to have arisen under the protection of the proprietor's castle, the site of which is now occupied by the seat of Lord Mount-Sandford, into whose demesne a gate opens directly from the market-place. The town consists of one long street extending from the market-place, and continued by bridges over the river Suck and a small river that runs through the demesne of Lord Mount-Sandford and unites with the Suck immediately below the town. The total number of houses is 162, of which the greater number are built of sandstone; clusters of cabins extend along the roads, and there are several pretty cottages and small houses surrounded with trees, which, being neatly white-washed, give the neighbourhood a very cheerful appearance. There are several springs of excellent water, and the place is considered remarkably healthy. A very extensive distillery, producing annually more than 20,000 gallons of whiskey, is conducted with success; and there are also a brewery and a tannery. The market for corn is on Wednesday, and has lately been rapidly increasing; and there is a market on Saturday for provisions, which is amply supplied; large quantities of butter, both fresh and in firkins, are sold here for the supply of distant markets, and cattle of every description and great quantities of yarn are brought for sale; the markets are held by patent of Lord Mount-Sandford, who has erected convenient shambles, which will be of great benefit to the town. Fairs are held on May 23rd, June 21st, Aug. 23rd, and Nov. 7th, and are well attended. A chief constabulary force has been stationed here, the sub-inspector for the county being resident in the town. The quarter sessions for the western division of the county are held here every nine months; and petty sessions are held every Wednesday. The sessions-house is a commodious building in the market-place, and attached to it is a bridewell containing the requisite accommodation. Castlerea House is the seat of Lord Mount-Sandford, and near it is a handsome house fitted up by his lordship for the residence of his chaplain.

The parish church is a neat edifice with a square embattled tower; the R. C. chapel is a spacious structure, but being in indifferent repair, it is in contemplatiion to rebuild it; there is also a place of worship for Wesleyan Methodists. A school-house for a school on Erasmus Smith's foundation was erected here by the late Rev. William Sandford, who endowed it with the interest of £200; and a handsome school-house, with apartments for a master and mistress, was erected by Lord Mount-Sandford, for a male, female, and infants' school, supported by his lordship; there is also a national school. A dispensary has been established; and a building, with wards attached for the reception of patients, is about to be erected on an improved principle by Lord Mount-Sandford. A loan fund has existed for some years with great benefit to the poor; the capital at present is £600. Dr. Young, Bishop of Clonfert, an eminent natural philosopher and mathematician, was a native of this place.—See KILKEEVAN.

CASTLEREAGH.—See KNOCKBREDA.

CASTLE-RICHARD, a village, in that part of the parish of LISMORE, which is in the barony of COSHMORE, county of WATERFORD, and province of MUNSTER, 3 miles (S. W.) from Lismore: the population is returned with the parish. This pleasant village consists of remarkably neat cottages with gardens in front, and is situated on the south side of the river Blackwater. The surrounding scenery is pleasingly varied, and among its more prominent features is Glencairne, the handsome seat of Gervaise Bushe, Esq., commanding some fine views of the vale of the Blackwater and of the country adjacent.

CASTLE-RICKARD, a parish, partly in the barony of CARBERY, county of KILDARE, but chiefly in the barony of UPPER MOYFENRAGH, county of MEATH, and province of LEINSTER $4\frac{3}{4}$ miles (N. E.) from Clonard; containing 554 inhabitants. This parish, which derives its name from an ancient castle, of which there are no remains, is situated on the river Boyne, and on the road from Edenderry to Trim. The seats are Castle-Rickard, the residence of G. Lucas Nugent, Esq.; and Lion's Den, of Godwin Swift, Esq. The living is a rectory, in the diocese of Meath, and in the patronage of the Bishop: the tithes amount to £170. The church is a plain edifice in good repair. The glebe-house was built in 1790, by aid of a gift of £100, from the late Board of First Fruits; and there are two glebes, comprising 10 acres. In the R. C. divisions this parish forms part of the union or district of Kildalkey. There is a hedge school at Inchmore of about 50 boys and 40 girls.

CASTLE-ROBERT.—See ROBERTSTOWN.

CASTLETERRA, a parish, in the barony of UPPER LOUGHTEE, county of CAVAN, and province of ULSTER; containing, with the post-town of Ballyhaise, 6502 inhabitants. This parish is situated on the road from Cavan to Cootehill, and comprises, according to the Ordnance survey, $9980\frac{3}{4}$ statute acres (including $151\frac{1}{2}$ under water), of which 9526 are applotted under the tithe act; about 900 acres are woodland, mountain, or bog, and the remainder is arable or pasture. There is an iron mine, which has never been worked; and a new road is being made through the parish from Ballyhaise to Cavan. The principal seats are Ballyhaise House, the residence of W. Humphreys, Esq.: Lisnagowan, of Mrs. Humphreys; and the glebe-house, of the Rev. G. Knox. The living is a rectory and vicarage, in the diocese of Kilmore, and in the patronage of the Bishop: the tithes amount to £288. 10. The church is a handsome building, repaired in 1819 by aid of a loan of £1200 from the late Board of First Fruits. There is a glebe-house, with a glebe of 195 acres. The R. C. parish is co-extensive with that of the Established Church, and has chapels at Ballyhaise, Castleterra, and Butler's-bridge, of which Ballyhaise chapel, built in 1810, cost £400; and Castleterra, built in 1829' cost £650. The parochial school-house is built of stone, and cost £270, one-half of which was paid out of the lord-lieutenant's school fund, the other half by subscriptions. It is under the patronage of W. Humphreys, Esq., and is aided by an annual donation from the incumbent, who also partially maintains three other schools: there are national schools at Ballyhaise and Butlerstown. About 260 boys and 240 girls are educated in these schools; and about 60 boys and 100 girls are educated in private schools. In 1777, Brockhill Newburgh, Esq., bequeathed £10 annually, charged on his estate at Ballyhaise, for the repair of the church; also £10 annually out of the Redhills estate, for bread to be distributed weekly among the poor of the parish. About two miles from Ballyhaise there is a chalybeate spring.—See BALLYHAISE.

CASTLETOWN, or CASTLETOWN-BEARHAVEN, a post-town, in the parish of KILACONENAGH, barony of BERE, county of CORK, and province of MUNSTER, 31 miles (W.) from Bantry, and 202 (S. W.) from Dublin; containing 1468 inhabitants. This town takes its name from an ancient castle that stood here, and is celebrated as being the place where the only part of Gen. Hoche's army that landed was made prisoners, in 1796. It is situated on an inner bay, on the northern side of the harbour of Bearhaven, and comprises one long street of newly built houses, running along the margin of the bay of Castletown, opposite the north-western point of Bear island. The town has grown up since the discovery of the Allihais copper mines, in 1812, as, prior to that time, it consisted of only a few fishermen's cabins, but now it contains more than 300 houses, with several large shops, and is rapidly increasing. It is the only town in the barony, and there is none nearer than Bantry, which is 31 Irish miles distant. It is encircled by lofty mountains, except towards the south-east, where, on the opposite side of the bay, rise the lofty hills of Bear island, crowned by signal and martello towers. The trade consists principally in supplying the miners in Kilcateerin. Fairs are held on Jan. 1st, Easter-Tuesday, May 12th, and Sept. 4th, principally for the sale of cattle, pigs, sheep, and pedlery. A constabulary police force has been stationed here, for which there is an excellent barrack. It is also the residence of the district inspecting commander of the coast-guard, whose district includes Garnish, Colaris, and Castletown. Petty sessions are held irregularly, and a manorial court once a month, for the recovery of debts under 40*s*. A bridewell with separate cells has been recently erected for the temporary confinement of prisoners. The little bay of Castletown is advantageously situated, and vessels of 400 tons' burden may anchor in safety: it opens by a deep channel into the northern branch of Bantry or Bearhaven bay. The pier affords great protection to the fisheries, and is much used for trading purposes; the timber, iron, and other articles for the supply of the neighbourhood being landed here; but the roads connected with it are still in a bad state. Belonging to this port are four decked boats of 20 tons' burden each, 12 hookers of 12 tons, and 51 yawls of 4 tons, which furnish employment to about 400 fishermen. A little westward from the town is the church of Kilaconenagh; and there is a large cruciform Roman Catholic chapel, built in the year 1822, at an expense of £1000.

The male and female parochial schools, built in 1825, are supported by the Cork Diocesan Association and the vicar: there is also a large national school recently built, and a dispensary. There are some remains of Dhermod's castle, and the residence of the inspector of the coast-guard occupies part of its site. Many silver coins have been found at Ross McOwen, including one of Cromwell's; and near Mill cove is a very beautiful cascade.

The harbour of Bearhaven is very large, well sheltered, and sufficiently deep for the largest ships, with a good bottom. There are two entrances; the western, which is the most direct and readiest for vessels arriving from the west or south; and the eastern, which is the safest for strangers. On this bay was situated the castle of Dunboy, which was surrendered to the Spaniards, on their invasion of Ireland in 1601 by its owner, Daniel O'Sullivan. Early in the following year, however, when it should have been given up to the English, in execution of the treaty of Kinsale, O'Sullivan, provoked at the capitulation of the Spaniards, and disdaining to acknowledge their right to divest him of his ancient property, took possession of the castle by surprise and seized the arms and ammunition the Spaniards had deposited there. In April, the English army marched against the O'Sullivans to Bantry, where they embarked, and on the 6th of June landed on the opposite side of the bay, in spite of attempts to oppose their descent. Dunboy was defended for O'Sullivan by a garrison of 143 chosen men, under the command of Richard McGeoghegan, who made one of the most obstinate defences ever known in the kingdom; notwithstanding which the castle ultimately fell into the hands of the English, and was demolished. Bearhaven gives the title of Viscount to the ancient family of White, Earls of Bantry, which was ennobled for its zeal and activity against the French fleet, in 1796.—See KILACONENAGH.

CASTLETOWN, a village, in the parish of KINNEIGH, Western Division of the barony of EAST CARBERY, county of CORK, and province of MUNSTER; containing 314 inhabitants. It is situated in the heart of a wild mountainous district, and for some time after the English settlement in the reign of Jas. I. was a flourishing town, but being sacked in the war of 1641 it never revived. It now contains 57 small cabins indifferently built, and has fairs for cattle, sheep, and pigs on Jan. 1st, Easter-Tuesday, May 12th, and Sept. 4th. Here is a R. C. chapel.—See KINNEIGH.

CASTLETOWN, a parish, in the barony of COONAGH, county of LIMERICK, and province of MUNSTER, 7¼ miles (N. N. W.) from Tipperary; containing 1055 inhabitants. This place derives its name from an ancient castle built by one of the O'Hurleys towards the close of the 14th century, and of which there are still some very interesting ruins. The parish is situated on the road from Doon to Tipperary, on the confines of the county, and comprises 6896 statute acres, as applotted under the tithe act. The soil is tolerably fertile, and the land chiefly under tillage; there is an extensive tract of very valuable bog, which in some part lets at the high rate of 18*s.* per perch. It is a rectory, in the diocese of Cashel, and is appropriate to the mensal of the Archbishop: the tithes amount to £67. 2. 10. There is neither church nor chapel. In the R. C. divisions it is part of the union of Doon. A little to the south of the castle ruins are the remains of the old parish church, and not far distant are those of the small church of Templebuie.

CASTLETOWN, a parish, partly in the barony of LOWER, but chiefly in that of UPPER DUNDALK, county of LOUTH, and province of LEINSTER, 1 mile (N. W.) from Dundalk; containing 838 inhabitants. This place is situated on the bay of Dundalk, and on the roads leading respectively to Castle-Blayney and Armagh, which branch off near the village. It derived its name and most probably its origin from the erection of an ancient castle, which in 1318 was assaulted and partly destroyed by Edward Bruce, and which, after sustaining great injury during the parliamentary war, was finally surrendered to Cromwell. The castle occupies an eminence about a mile from Dundalk: the remains, which are nearly in a perfect state, consist of a large quadrangular massive pile, defended at two of the angles by small projecting square towers, and at the two opposite angles by similar towers of larger dimensions, all rising above the high pointed roof of the main building, and crowned with battlements, forming an object of very imposing character. Tradition says that it was a residence of Fingal: it subsequently belonged to the lords Bellew, whom the Boyne family succeeded; and the present proprietor derives his title from a fee-farm grant made by Mr. Sibthorpe, trustee to the late Lord Boyne. The buildings are at present occupied only as offices of the modern mansion adjoining, which is the residence of J. Eastwood, Esq., who intends immediately to convert the castle into a residence. Near the demesne is the residence of Jacob C. Murphy, Esq. The parish comprises, according to the Ordnance survey, 2610¾ statute acres, of which 2047¾ are in Upper and 563 in Lower Dundalk. The system of agriculture, though better than it was, is still capable of great improvement; the gentlemen who cultivate their own lands have adopted the improved system, but many of the working farmers adhere to the ancient mode. There are some good quarries at Greenfield, from which stone is raised for building and mending the roads. The mountain streams of Philipstown, Dungooley, and Forkhill, unite in this parish, a little before their influx into the sea, forming the river of Castletown, up which the tide flows nearly a mile, affording every facility of navigation.

It is a rectory and vicarage, in the diocese of Armagh, and forms part of the union of Dundalk: the tithes amount to £200. 6. 5¼. In the churchyard are the ruins of an old chapel, which, from an inscription over the altar, appears to have been erected in 1631, by Sir Walter Bellew, Priest, in honour of St. John the Baptist. In the R. C. divisions it is part of the union or district of Dundalk. A national school has been built in the churchyard, and an infants' school is supported under the patronage of the rector, Mr. and Mrs. Eastwood, and Mr. Murphy. On the summit of the hill, on the brow of which the castle is situated, is a remarkable fort, forming a conspicuous object from the plains round Dundalk: in the centre is an extensive circular mount, having on the top a depressed surface, 460 feet in circumference, surrounded by an intrenchment with a high counterscarp on the outside. Adjoining this, on the east, is a quadrangular intrenchment, with a rampart, fosse, and counterscarp; and on the west is a semicircular intrenchment similarly formed, but of smaller dimensions. These fortifications occupy the entire summit of the hill, and are prominently conspicuous for many miles around. Various lines of circumvallation may be traced around the castle; and on the plains below are the remains of a fort, little inferior to that on the summit of the hill, and the ruins of the old church or chapel, covered with ivy and presenting a picturesque object, in the cemetery, which is still used as a burial-ground. About a mile from the castle are the ruins of Balrichen castle, within half a mile of which are the remains of a singular fort, called Mount, or Moat Albani, situated near the small river Carrickasticken. The castle of Balrichen, or Balbriggan, which formerly belonged to one of the chiefs of the English pale, is situated on a gradual ascent between two winding rivers: it consisted of a lofty quadrangular tower, with a walled court-yard capable of containing a numerous retinue. Beyond this castle is the pleasant little promontory of Balrichen, between the rivers of Balrichen and Philipstown, which unite near this place. Various druidical remains are scattered over this promontory, the chief of which are a circle of five large upright stones on the summit of a hill, a cairn and several pillars, some detached, and some in groups. On an elevated piece of ground, called Carrickedmond, at no great distance from Balrichen, and near the Carrickasticken river, are numerous druidical relics, consisting of a temple of two concentric circles of large stones, with two smaller stones in the centre, two cairns, the foundations of a circular building, several small circles in which rude earthen kistvaens and human bones have been found, and detached upright stones, some of large size and probably monumental.

CASTLETOWN, a village, in the parish of Lackan, barony of Tyrawley, county of Mayo, and province of Connaught, 8 miles (N.N.W.) from Killala: the population is returned with the parish. This village, which consists of about 60 houses, is pleasantly situated on the bay of Killala, and has two fairs, one on June 15th, and the other on Sept. 29th.

CASTLETOWN, a village, in the parish of Offerlane, barony of Upper Ossory, Queen's county, and province of Leinster, 1¾ mile (S. by W.) from Mountrath; containing 367 inhabitants. This place takes its name from an ancient castle, occupying a commanding situation on the bank of the river Nore, and which, in the early part of the 16th century, was garrisoned by Sir Oliver Norris, son-in-law of the Earl of Ormonde, with a view to curb the power of the Fitzpatricks, to whom it was afterwards relinquished, and of whom Barnaby Fitzpatrick was, in 1541, created Baron of Upper Ossory. The village is pleasantly situated on the river Nore, and on the road from Dublin to Limerick; it contains 59 houses, many of which are good residences, and the whole has an appearance of neatness and respectability. Near it are some large flour and oatmeal-mills. A fair is held on June 29th; and there were formerly fairs on May 2nd and Oct. 18th. A constabulary police force is stationed here, and petty sessions are held on alternate Saturdays. There is a R. C. chapel in the village.—See Offerlane.

CASTLETOWN-ARRA, a parish, in the barony of Owney and Arra, county of Tipperary, and province of Munster, 8 miles (W.N.W.) from Nenagh; containing 4110 inhabitants. This parish is situated on the river Shannon, and on the road from Nenagh to Killaloe; it comprises 6697 statute acres, as applotted under the tithe act, and valued at £5110 per annum: about 720 acres are mountain, and the remainder is good arable and pasture land. At Garry-Kennedy are some very extensive slate quarries belonging to the Mining Company of Ireland, from which great quantities of slate are raised and shipped from a quay which has been constructed there, for which the steam navigation on the Shannon, and the canal, afford every facility. The scenery is strikingly diversified; it includes a large portion of Lough Derg, and the mountains of Clare and Galway. Castlelough, the seat of Anthony Parker, Esq., is finely situated in a richly cultivated demesne of 640 acres, embellished with timber of stately growth and with young and thriving plantations; the deer park is extensive and well stocked. The other seats within the parish are Lansdowne, the residence of Mrs. Parker, and those of G. Watson and — Kent, Esqrs., at Garry-Kennedy. A constabulary police force has been stationed here; and fairs, chiefly for cattle, sheep, and pigs, are held at Portroe on March 22nd, May 14th, July 23rd, and Nov. 11th. The living is a rectory and vicarage, in the diocese of Killaloe, episcopally united, in 1781, to the rectories and vicarages of Youghal-Arra and Burgess-Beg, forming the union of Castletown-Arra, in the patronage of the Bishop: the tithes amount to £304. 12. 3¾., and of the whole benefice to £997. 16. 11¼. The church, an ancient structure of simple style, is pleasingly situated on the margin of Lough Derg. The glebe-house was built by aid of a gift of £250 and a loan of £550 from the late Board of First Fruits, in 1820. The glebe comprises 3 acres, and there are other glebe lands in the union, comprising together 4*a.* 3*r.*, making in the whole 7*a.* 3*r.* The R. C. parish is co-extensive with that of the Established Church; the chapel is at Portroe. A parochial school, in which about 50 boys and 30 girls are instructed, is supported by the rector; and there is a pay school, in which are about 120 boys and 70 girls. The old castle from which this place derived its name was formerly the residence of the Parkers, but is now in ruins; the demesne skirts the Shannon for a considerable distance, commanding some beautiful and extensive views.

CASTLETOWN-CONYERS, a parish, in the barony of Upper Connello East, county of Limerick, and province of Munster, 3 miles (S.) from Ballingarry: the population is returned with the union or parish of Corcomohide. This place, called anciently *Kilmoodan*, took the name of Castletown-Mac-Eineiry from a castle erected here, in 1349, by a chieftain of that name, who possessed a large extent of territory in this part of the country, which was forfeited by the adherence of his descendant to the cause of Jas. II., and granted by Wm. III. to Capt. George Conyers, from whom it derives its present appellation. Archdall notices an abbey of great splendour and extent, founded here by the Mac Eineiry family; but nothing further is recorded of its history, nor are there any remains of it. The parish is situated on the road from Rathkeale to Charleville, and comprises 10,086 statute acres, as applotted under the tithe act: about one-eighth of the land is under tillage, producing good crops; the remainder is in demesnes, and in meadow and pasture land belonging to large dairy farms; there is a large tract of turbary, which is very valuable as fuel. The whole of the substratum is limestone, of which several very fine quarries are extensively worked. The surrounding country is highly improved, and abounds with interesting scenery and with numerous handsome seats, of which the principal within the parish are Castletown-Conyers, the residence of C. Conyers, Esq.; Rossmore, of J. W. Shelton, Esq.; Capanishane, of R. Mason, Esq.; Glenbrook, of M. Mason, Esq.; Fort Elizabeth, of E. Nash, Esq.; Ballyegran Cottage, of A. Odell, Esq.; Gortroe Cottage, of H. Hart, Esq.; and Drew's Court, the property of the Drew family, but at present unoccupied. Fairs are held on Feb. 11th, April 17th, Nov. 3rd, and Dec. 1st, chiefly for cattle, sheep, pigs, and pedlery.

The living is a vicarage, in the diocese of Limerick, united to the vicarages of Kilmeedy and Drumcolloher, together forming the union of Corcomohide, in the patronage of the Vicars Choral of the cathedral church of St. Mary, Limerick, to whom the rectory is appropriate. The tithes are included in the gross amount for the union of Corcomohide. The church has been long in ruins, and there is neither glebe-house nor glebe. In the R. C. divisions this parish is the head of the union or district of Ballyegran, comprising also the parishes of Kilmeedy and Drumcollogher; the chapel, a large plain edifice, is situated in the village of Ballyegran, in this parish; and there is also a chapel in the parish of Kilmeedy. There is a dispensary in the village of Castletown-Conyers. The ruins of the old church are situated near the village; and there are some small fragments of the ancient castle, but they are inadequate to convey a distinct idea of the original extent or character of the buildings.

CASTLETOWN-DELVIN, a market and post-town, and a parish, in the barony of DELVIN, county of WESTMEATH, and province of LEINSTER, 10 miles (N. E. by E.) from Mullingar, and 39¼ (N. N. W.) from Dublin; containing 4513 inhabitants, of which number, 419 are in the town. The castle was built by Hugh de Lacy, Lord of Meath, for his brother-in-law, Sir Gilbert de Nugent, who resided in it for some time, and then built the neighbouring castle of Clonyn, which was burnt at Cromwell's approach during the parliamentary war. The town contains 77 houses: the market is on Friday, and fairs are held on the 17th of March and 1st of May and December, for cattle. Petty sessions are held every alternate Monday, and here is a station of the constabulary police. The parish is situated on the road from Athboy to Drumcree, and contains 15,659 statute acres, as applotted under the tithe act, besides a considerable quantity of waste land. There are tracts of bog and small lakes; and limestone is abundant, but is not worked. The land which is generally good, is principally under tillage and pasture. Clonyn, the residence of the Marquess of Westmeath, a descendant of Sir Gilbert de Nugent, is close to the town, and is surrounded by extensive grounds richly ornamented with timber. The other seats are South Hill, the residence of W. Chapman, Esq.; Mitchelstown, of G. Hinds, Esq.; Rossmead, of H. W. Wood, Esq., surrounded by fine plantations; Ballyhealy, of P. Batty, Esq.; Clonmaskill, of Laurence Loyd Henry, Esq.; and Archerstown, the property of R. Smyth, Esq.

The living is a vicarage, in the diocese of Meath; the rectory is partly impropriate in Nicholas Ogle, Esq., and partly appropriate to the vicarage, which was united by diocesan authority, in 1821, to the entire rectory of Clonarney or Clonarvey, and is in the patronage of the Crown and the Marquess of Drogheda. The tithes amount to £449. 18., of which £276. 18. 5. is payable to the impropriator and the remainder to the vicar; and the gross tithes of the benefice amount to £258. 9. 2¼. The church is a plain building of ancient date, but in excellent repair. The glebe-house was built in 1815, by aid of a gift of £400, and a loan of £320, from the late Board of First Fruits: the glebe consists of 13¾ acres of land valued at £18. 9. 2. per annum. In the R. C. divisions the parish forms the head of a union or district, comprising also the parishes of Kilweilagh and Killagh, and containing two chapels, one at Castletown-Delvin, the other at Killulagh. There is a school at Ballyhealy under the patronage of Mrs. Batty, and one at Moortown supported by the Marquess of Westmeath; there is also a national school at Ballinvalley. In these schools are 96 boys and 121 girls; and 170 boys and 110 girls are educated in five private schools. A dispensary is supported in the usual way. The ruins of the old castle built by De Lacy occupy the sides of a quadrangle, with a round tower at each corner; and on eminences near Archerstown are the ruins of two ancient castles, and on a hill further west stands a very conspicuous tower. There is also a round tower on a hill to the south-west of the town and another near Ballyhealy. The remains of a large fortress occupy the summit of an abrupt eminence on the eastern side of the parish; and there are remains of other strong buildings at Cullydougran, on the opposite border. The Marquess of Westmeath enjoys the inferior title of Baron Delvin, in the peerage of Ireland.

CASTLETOWN-ELY, a parish, in the barony of CLONLISK, KING'S county, and province of LEINSTER, 1 mile (S. E.) from Moneygall; containing 391 inhabitants. It is situated on the confines of the county of Tipperary, and comprises 1563 statute acres, as applotted under the tithe act, of which about 150 acres are bog. Bushenstown, the residence of G. Minchin, Esq., is situated in a large demesne highly enriched with fine timber, and ornamented with varied and picturesque scenery; some hills rise boldly to the south-west of the demesne, and within it is a modern round tower, which forms a conspicuous land-mark. It is a rectory and vicarage, in the diocese of Killaloe, and is part of the union of Dunkerrin: the tithes amount to £122. 15. 10. In the R. C. divisions it forms part of the union of Moneygall or Dunkerrin. There are two pay schools, in which are about 40 boys and 40 girls. There are some remains of the old parish church.

CASTLETOWN-KILPATRICK, a parish, in the barony of MORGALLION, county of MEATH, and province of LEINSTER, 3 miles (S. S. E.) from Nobber; containing 1211 inhabitants. This parish is situated on the roads from Slane to Nobber, and from Kells to Ardee, and contains 3895 statute acres, as applotted under the tithe act. The land is of very good quality; about three-fourths are in pasture, and there is no bog. The principal seats are Rathhood, the residence of R. Cruise, Esq.; Stephenstown, of H. Owens, Esq.; Headstown, of Lieut.-Col. Gerrard; and Legga, of A. Kieran, Esq. The living is a rectory, in the diocese of Meath, united by act of council to the rectories of Knock and Drakestown, and in the alternate patronage of the Crown and the Bishop: the tithes of the parish amount to £278. 1. 2.; and the gross value of the benefice, including tithe and glebe, is £690. 8. 7. The church is a neat edifice, with a tower, and was rebuilt in 1823, at an expense of £467. 12. 4. The glebe-house, which is close to the church, was erected in 1824, by aid of a loan of £1107. 13. 10. from the late Board of First Fruits. The glebe comprises 43 plantation acres, valued at £119. 18. 10. per annum; and there are also a glebe in Knock of 3½ acres, and one in Drakestown of 4 acres, together valued at £36 per annum. In the R. C. divisions this parish is the head of a union or district, comprising also the parishes of Knock, Drakestown, Kilshine, and Clongill, and containing two chapels, one at Castletown and the other at Fletcherstown. There is a school at Castletown-Cross, aided by the incumbent, in which are about 6 boys and 3 girls.

CASTLETOWN-KINDELANE, or VASTINA, a parish, in the barony of Moycashel, county of Westmeath, and province of Leinster, 4¾ miles (N.) from Kilbeggan; containing 4052 inhabitants, of which number, 191 are in the village. This place is called also Castletown-Geoghegan, from its earliest proprietors, the McGeoghegans, chiefs of Moycashel, of whose ancient castle there are still some remains, and is principally the property of Sir Richard Nagle, Bart., the representative of that ancient family, who is resident. The parish is situated on the road from Kilbeggan to Mullingar, and comprises 10,116 statute acres, as applotted under the tithe act. The land is almost equally divided between arable and pasture; there is a considerable tract of red bog, but no waste land, and the system of agriculture is improving. Limestone abounds, but no quarries are worked. Jamestown, the seat of Sir R. Nagle, Bart., is a spacious and handsome castellated mansion of modern erection, containing an interesting collection of ancient portraits and some curious relics of antiquity; in the vicinity is preserved McGeoghegan's Chair, in which the chiefs of Moycashel were anciently inaugurated. Middleton, the property of J. Middleton Berry, Esq., and now occupied by W. Hodson, Esq., is also in the parish. The village consists of 36 houses; it is a constabulary police station, and there is a patent for fairs, but none are held at present. The living is a rectory, in the diocese of Meath, and in the patronage of the Crown; the tithes of 50 acres are impropriate in Sir Wm. Lambart Cromie, Bart. The entire tithes amount to £495. 13. 10., of which £15. 13. 10. is payable to the rector of Churchtown for a townland in this parish, which is impropriate in that union, and the remainder to the vicar; that part of the rectory which is impropriate in Sir W. L. Cromie, is not under composition. The church, a modern building in good repair, was erected in 1808, by aid of a gift of £500 from the late Board of First Fruits. The glebe-house was built in 1813, by aid of a gift of £100 and a loan of £900 from the same Board: the glebe comprises 20 acres, subject to an annual rent of £2. 2. per acre. In the R. C. divisions the parish is the head of a union or district, comprising also the parish of Newtown; there are two chapels, one in Castletown village and one at Raheenmoore. The parochial school, on the glebe land, is supported by subscription and an annual donation from the rector; and there is a national school endowed with two acres of land by the late Richard Malone, Esq., of Baronstown. In these schools about 55 boys and 40 girls are instructed; and there are also six pay schools, in which are about 134 children.

CASTLETOWN-ROCHE, a post-town and parish, in the barony of Fermoy, county of Cork, and province of Munster, 18 miles (N. by E.) from Cork, and 116 (S. W.) from Dublin; containing 3648 inhabitants, of which number, 1095 are in the town. This place derives its name from a castle erected here by the family of Roche, lords of Fermoy. In 1580 it was suddenly visited by Capt. (afterwards Sir Walter) Raleigh, who conveyed both Lord Roche and his lady to Cork on suspicion of disloyalty; his lordship, however, proved his innocence and was honourably acquitted. During the parliamentary war the castle sustained many sieges, and in 1649 was defended for several days by Lady Roche against a detachment of the parliamentarian army, who had raised a battery against it on the opposite field, since called Camp Hill. On the refusal of the owner to compound with Cromwell for its restoration, it was confiscated; but it had sustained so much damage during the siege, that its new proprietor found it necessary to rebuild it from the foundation, with the exception of the keep, which is a fine specimen of the architecture of the middle ages. The town is pleasantly situated on the declivity of a steep hill rising from the west bank of the river Awbeg, over which is a neat bridge of five arches, and on the high road from Fermoy to Doneraile; and with the castle and the church has a highly picturesque appearance, on the approach from the east bank of the river. It contains 165 houses, of which some are neatly built, and a small barrack, in which an officer and one company of infantry are generally stationed. Below the bridge are two large flour-mills, and near Annsgrove the making of bricks is carried on to a small extent. The market, granted, together with two fairs, to the Rev. Thomas Widenham in the reign of Geo. II., is discontinued; the fairs are held on May 25th and Sept. 29th, and two additional fairs on July 28th and Dec. 12th have greatly declined. A constabulary police force is stationed here; and petty sessions are held in the town every alternate Tuesday.

The parish comprises 6333 statute acres, as applotted under the tithe act, and valued at £6378 per annum. The lands are chiefly under tillage; there is neither waste land nor bog. The soil is fertile, and well adapted to the growth of corn; the wheat raised here is of the best quality, and the system of agriculture is greatly improved. In many of the farms belonging to the gentry, the Scottish system of husbandry has been introduced with success. Great numbers of sheep and cattle are fattened here for the neighbouring markets: the cattle are in general stall-fed. Limestone is found in great abundance and of excellent quality, and is extensively quarried both for building and for burning into lime; and the clay for bricks is found on the banks of the river, on the estate of Annsgrove. The surrounding country is beautifully picturesque; and the river Awbeg, the "gentle Mulla" of Spenser, is celebrated for the richness and variety of its scenery. Castle Widenham, the noble mansion of H. Mitchel Smith, Esq., is situated on the summit of a rocky eminence overhanging the river, the banks of which are here richly wooded, and commands extensive and varied prospects over the surrounding country, itself forming a conspicuous and beautiful object from every point of view. The tower or keep of the ancient fortress has been incorporated in the present structure, which is in a style of corresponding character, and rises majestically above the woods in which it is embosomed, forming a strikingly romantic feature in the landscape. The castle, with its outworks, occupied a considerable extent of ground surrounded by a strong rampart with parapets and turrets, of which a large portion is still remaining; there is a descent to the river of 100 steps cut in the solid rock, for supplying the castle with water. Annsgrove, the elegant seat of Lieut.-Gen. the Hon. Arthur Grove Annesley, is a handsome mansion recently built by the proprietor, on the verge of a precipitous cliff rising from the river Awbeg, which flows through the demesne: the grounds are laid out with great taste and surrounded by thriving plantations. Glenamore, the seat of the representatives of the late Rev. T. Hoare, is beautifully situated in the midst of picturesque and romantic scenery. The living is a rectory and vicarage, in the diocese of Cloyne, formerly united to the rectories and vicarages of Bridgetown and Kilcummer, from which, on the death of the late incumbent in 1835, it was separated, and is at present a distinct benefice, in the patronage of the Bishop: the tithes amount to £518. 15. 5. The church is a remarkably handsome structure, with a tower surmounted by a finely proportioned octagonal spire; the lower stage is pierced with a window on every face, the copings of which form a zigzag ornament continued all round; it was erected on the site of the old church, in 1825, by aid of a loan of £1250 from the late Board of First Fruits, and the Ecclesiastical Commissioners have recently made a grant of £100 for its repair. It occupies the summit of a rocky eminence, the base of which is washed by the Awbeg, forming a conspicuous and picturesque feature in the view of the place. There is neither glebe-house nor glebe. In the R. C. divisions this parish is the head of a union or district, comprising also the parishes of Killathy, Ballyhooley, Kilcummer, and Bridgetown; the chapel is a spacious but plain building, on which the chapel at Ballyhooley is dependent. There are four private schools, in which about 220 children are educated. Walter Croker, Esq., about 80 years since, bequeathed £100, the interest to be annually divided by the minister and churchwardens among the Protestant poor of the parish: in the town is a dispensary. Below the castle, and near the margin of the river, is a holy well, dedicated to St. Patrick, on whose anniversary a patron is held here: the water is remarkably pure, and is much esteemed by the peasantry for its supposed virtues.

CASTLE-TOWNSEND, a village, in the parish of CASTLEHAVEN, East Division of the barony of WEST CARBERY, county of CORK, and province of MUNSTER, 4½ miles (E.) from Skibbereen; containing 901 inhabitants. This village, which derives its name from Castle-Townsend, the seat of Col. Townsend, is situated on the north side of the harbour of Castlehaven, and consists of one long street, with a shorter one diverging from it, comprising 150 houses, which are mostly small but well built. It contains the custom-house for the port of Baltimore, and is a coast-guard station in the district of Skibbereen, and a constabulary police station. It occupies a gentle declivity, which descends to the bay, and is well adapted for an extensive trade, but has none, except a little in fish. The harbour, which is half a mile wide, is well sheltered, and vessels of 500 tons' burden can anchor within the haven. There is a ferry to the opposite parish of Mycross, affording a ready communication with the village of Union-Hall, on the harbour of Glandore. The fine seat of Castle-Townsend was attacked, in 1690, by about 500 Irish troops in the interest of Jas. II., under young O'Driscoll, who were so warmly received by the proprietor and a garrison of 35 men, that in two assaults they lost 40 of their number, with their commander and two other officers. It was attacked again, soon afterwards, by Mac Fineen O'Driscoll, at the head of 400 men, who, having slain five of its garrison of 30 dragoons, compelled the rest to surrender. Col. Culliford subsequently retook the castle, after killing ten and capturing five of the Irish garrison. The elegant church of Castlehaven stands on a bold eminence above the village; and the parochial and infants' schools are also situated here. —See CASTLEHAVEN.

CASTLEVENTRY, a parish, partly in the barony of IBANE and BARRYROE, but chiefly in the Western Division of the barony of EAST CARBERY, county of CORK, and province of MUNSTER, 5 miles (W.) from Clonakilty; containing 2474 inhabitants. This parish is situated a little to the north of the road from Cork to Skibbereen, between Clonakilty and Ross, and comprises 4663 statute acres, as applotted under the tithe act. About one-half of the land is under tillage, producing good crops; the remainder is chiefly rough hilly pasture, with some small portions of bog, which is very valuable for fuel. Much of the rough and unprofitable land is capable of being reclaimed; but although new and excellent lines of road have been recently opened, very little improvement has yet been made in the system of agriculture. It is a vicarage, in the diocese of Ross, and is part of the union of Kilkeranmore; the rectory is impropriate in — Foot and — Roberts, Esqrs. The tithes amount to £524, of which one-half is payable to the impropriators, and the other to the vicar. The church is a large edifice, in the early English style, with a lofty square tower, and was built by aid of a gift of £900 from the late Board of First Fruits. There is neither glebe-house nor glebe. In the R. C. divisions it forms part of the union or district of Kilmeen. The parochial male and female schools, at Saroo, are supported by the Cork Diocesan Association, the vicar, and J. S. Townsend, Esq., who has endowed the schools with an acre of land. On the summit of a lofty hill are the ruins of the old church, situated in a very strong fortress, called *Templum Ventrie*, built in 1298 by the Knights Templars, on the site of a heathen temple; and near it are the remains of another, called *Bealad*. In the neighbourhood have been found several ancient ornaments and some celts of stone and bronze.

CASTLEWELLAN, a market and post town, in that part of the parish of KILMEGAN which is in the barony of UPPER IVEAGH, county of DOWN, and province of ULSTER, 9 miles (W. S. W.) from Downpatrick, and 64¾ (N. by E.) from Dublin; containing 729 inhabitants. This place is situated on the mail coach road from Newry to Downpatrick, on the side of a small lake, and though partly surrounded by mountains, occupies rather a conspicuous site. The town is well built, and consists principally of an upper and lower square connected by a street, containing 122 houses, most of which are neat structures. There are barracks for two companies of infantry, a detachment from the military depôt at Newry, usually stationed here. The bleaching of linen, which is the principal trade of the place, was first introduced here by Mr. Moffat, in 1749, since which time it has greatly increased, and several large bleach-greens have been established. Those of Messrs. Murland are capable of bleaching and finishing 20,000 pieces annually, and those of Mr. Steel, 8000; a large proportion of the linen is sent to the American and West India markets, the remainder to England and Scotland. There is an extensive mill for spinning linen-yarn, erected in 1829, and the first for fine yarns ever established in Ireland; it is worked by steam and water power, and lighted with gas made on the premises; another is in course of erection on a very large scale, to be propelled by a water wheel 50 feet in diameter and 10 feet on the face. In these several establishments more than 500 persons are constantly employed. The manufacture of linen is also extensively carried on by Mr. J. Murland and Mr. Steel, the former employing 450 and the latter 300 persons. There are also some large corn-mills, and mills for dressing flax. The market is on Monday, and is amply supplied with provisions and pedlery, and large quantities of brown linen and linen-yarn are brought for sale every market day. Fairs are held on the first of February, May, June, and September, the 13th of November, and the Tuesday before Christmas. The market-house, situated in the centre of the upper square, is a neat building, with a belfry and clock, surmounted by a spire. A constabulary police force is stationed here; a manorial court, having jurisdiction over nine townlands in this parish and that of Drumgooland, is held every three weeks, in which debts to the amount of £10 are recoverable; and petty sessions are also held in the market-house every alternate Tuesday. Divine service, according to the rites of the Church of England, is performed every Sunday in the market-house. There are also in the town a R. C. chapel and places of worship for Presbyterians and Wesleyan Methodists. A school-house was built and endowed by J. Murland, Esq., for the gratuitous instruction of children of both sexes; and a school is supported by Earl Annesley. At the foot of Slieve-na-lat, and on the border of the lake, is an elegant cottage, built by Earl Annesley, and ornamented with gardens and pleasure grounds tastefully laid out, in which is a temple, commanding a fine view of the surrounding scenery. Earl Annesley enjoys the inferior title of Baron of Castlewellan, in the peerage of Ireland. —See KILMEGAN.

CASTROPETRE, or MONASTERORIS, a parish, in the barony of COOLESTOWN, KING'S county, and province of LEINSTER; containing, with the market and post-town of Edenderry and the village of Conabury, 4009 inhabitants. This parish derived its name, Monasteroris, from Sir John de Bermingham, Earl of Louth, who founded an abbey here, in 1325, for conventual Franciscans, which was called, from his Irish name, Monasterfeoris, or the monastery of Mac Feoris. In 1511, Cahir O'Connor, Lord of Offaley, was slain near this monastery by his own countrymen; and in 1521, the abbey was held for a considerable time against the Earl of Surrey, then lord-lieutenant, who afterwards took and kept possession of it. At the general suppression it was granted to Nicholas Herbert, who died in 1581, possessed of the abbey and townland of Monasteroris. The parish is situated on the line of the Grand Canal, and at the source of the river Boyne, and is bounded on the north-west, north, and east by the bog of Allen, through which the navigation to Tullamore is cut. It contains 8401 acres, as applotted under the tithe act, exclusively of about 1000 acres of unreclaimed bog. There are some limestone quarries, and a vein of silver and lead ore, which has been worked twice, but relinquished on account of its poverty. The chief seats are Leitrim House, the residence of W. Purefoy Lumm, Esq.; Monasteroris House, of the Rev. W. G. Wakeley; and Lummville, the property of Mr. Lumm, but occupied by a respectable farmer. The living is a vicarage, in the diocese of Kildare, and in the patronage of the Crown; the rectory constitutes the corps of the prebend of Castropetre in the cathedral of Kildare. The tithes amount to £415. 7. 8½., of which £276. 18. 5½. is paid to the prebendary, and the remainder to the vicar. The church is at Edenderry, and is a plain but neat edifice, to the repairs of which the Ecclesiastical Commissioners have recently made a grant of £374. 2. 9. There is neither glebe-house nor glebe. In the R. C. divisions this parish is the head of a union or district, also called Edenderry and Killane, comprising the parishes of Castropetre, Ballymacwilliam, Ballyburley, and Croghan, and parts of those of Ballynakill and Castle-Jordan; and containing three chapels, situated at Edenderry, Rhode, and Kranghan. There are also places of worship for the Society of Friends and Primitive Methodists. Here are two schools, aided by subscriptions from the rector, the Marchioness of Downshire, and Mrs. Murray, in which are 30 boys and 47 girls; and about 100 boys and 60 girls are taught in five private schools. A few remains of the abbey of Monasteroris still exist; and at Ballykillinfort, in the neighbourhood, is a celebrated rath, with a vault in the centre, in which were found, some years since, several relics, and some ancient coins, in high preservation. It was defended by strong ramparts, and was very difficult of access. There is a chalybeate spring in the parish.—See EDENDERRY.

CAUSEWAY, a village, in the parish of KILLURY, barony of CLANMAURICE, county of KERRY, and province of MUNSTER, 10 miles (N.) from Tralee: the population is returned with the parish. This place, which is situated at the junction of the roads leading respectively from Ardfert and Ballyheigue to Cashen-ferry, derives its name from a paved highway carried over the bogs to the mountain district on the north, and which in its progress intersects the village. Fairs are held on the 2nd of April and May, July 16th, and Nov. 15th, chiefly for cattle; and a constabulary police force is stationed here. About half a mile to the west are the parish church and glebe-house; and the R. C. chapel, a large slated cruciform edifice, is in the village. A national school has been built, and is chiefly supported by a bequest of £1000 from the late Rev. Dr. Nealan, P. P., a native of the parish, who, both as a magistrate and as parish priest, contributed greatly to preserve the peace of this district during the disturbances of 1798.

CAVAN (County of), an inland county of the province of Ulster, bounded on the north by the county of Fermanagh; on the west, by that of Leitrim; on the south, by those of Longford, Westmeath, and Meath; and on the east and north-east, by that of Monaghan. It extends from 53° 43′ to 54° 7′ (N. Lat.); and from 6° 45′ to 7° 47′ (W. Lon.); and comprises, according to the Ordnance survey, 477,360 statute acres, of which 421,462 are cultivated land, 30,000 unimproved mountain and bog, and 22,141 are under water The population, in 1821, was 195,076; and in 1831, 228,050.

According to Ptolemy, this tract, with the districts included in the adjacent counties of Leitrim and Fermanagh, was occupied by the *Erdini*, designated in the Irish language *Ernaigh*, traces of which name are yet preserved in that of Lough *Erne* and the river *Erne*, upon which and their tributaries these districts border. This district, exclusively of the greater part of the present county of Fermanagh, formed also the ancient principality of *Breghne*, *Brefine*, *Breifne*, *Breffny*, or *Brenny*, as it has been variously spelt, which had recognised limits from time immemorial, and was divided into the two principalities of Upper or East Breifne and Lower or West Breifne, the former composed almost entirely of the present county of Cavan, and the latter of that of Leitrim. East Breifne was often called Breifne O'Reilly, from its princes or chiefs having from remote ages borne that name: they were tributary to the O'Nial of Tiroen long before the arrival of the English, although Camden says that in his time they represented themselves as descended from the English family of Ridley, but were entirely Irish in manners. The county is celebrated in the history of the wars in Ireland for the fastnesses formed by its woods, lakes, and bogs, which long secured the independence of its native possessors. Cavan was one of the counties formed in Ulster, in 1584, by Sir John Perrott, lord-deputy of Ireland, and derived its name from the principal seat of its ancient rulers, which is still the provincial capital: in the following year it was represented in a parliament held in Dublin by two loyal members of the family of O'Reilly. Both Breffnys anciently formed part of Connaught, but the new county was incorporated with Ulster. The O'Reillys were at this time a warlike sept, particularly distinguished for their cavalry, and not living in towns, but in small castles scattered over the country. In order to lessen their influence by partitioning it among different leaders, and thus reduce them to the English law, it was resolved to divide the country into baronies and settle the proprietorship of each exclusively on a separate branch of the families of the former proprietors. Sir John O'Reilly, then chief lord of the country, had covenanted to surrender the whole to Queen Elizabeth, and on the other part Sir John Perrott had covenanted that letters patent should be granted to him of the whole; but this mutual agreement led to no result, and commissioners were sent down to carry the division into effect. By them the whole territory was partitioned into seven baronies, of which, two were assigned to Sir John O'Reilly free of all contributions; a third was allotted to his brother, Philip O'Reilly; a fourth to his uncle Edmond; and a fifth to the sons of Hugh O'Reilly, surnamed the Prior. The other two baronies, possessed by the septs of Mac Kernon and Mac Gauran, and remotely situated in the mountains and on the border of O'Rorke's country, were left to their ancient tenures and the Irish exactions of their chief lord, Sir John, whose chief-rent out of the other three baronies not immediately possessed by him was fixed at 10*s*. per annum for every pole, a subdivision of land peculiar to the county and containing about 25 acres: the entire county was supposed to contain 1620 of these poles.

But these measures did not lead to the settlement of the country; the tenures remained undetermined by any written title; and Sir John, his brother, and his uncle, as successive tanists, according to the ancient custom of the country, were all slain while in rebellion. After the death of the last, no successor was elected under the distinguishing title of O'Reilly, the country being broken by defeat, although wholly unamenable to the English law. Early in the reign of James I., the lord-deputy came to Cavan, and issued a commission of inquiry to the judges then holding the assize there concerning all lands escheated to the Crown by attainder, outlawry, or actual death in rebellion; and a jury of the best knights and gentlemen that were present, and of whom some were chiefs of Irish septs, found an inquisition, first, concerning the possessions of various freeholders slain in the late rebellion under the Earl of Tyrone, and secondly, concerning those of the late chiefs of the country who had shared the same fate; though the latter finding was obtained with some difficulty, the jurors fearing that their own tenures might be invalidated in consequence. Nor was this apprehension without foundation; for, by that inquisition, the greater part, if not the whole, of the county was deemed to be vested in the Crown, and the exact state of its property was thereupon carefully investigated. This being completed, the king resolved on the new plantation of Ulster, in which the plan for the division of this county was as follows:—the termon, or church lands, in the ancient division, were 140 poles, or about 3500 acres, which the king reserved for the bishop of Kilmore; for the glebes of the incumbents of the parishes to be erected were allotted 100 poles, or 2500 acres; and the monastery land was found to consist of 20 poles, or 500 acres. There then remained to be distributed to undertakers 1360 poles, or 34,000 acres, which were divided into 26 proportions, 17 of 1000 acres each, 5 of 1500, and 4 of 2000, each of which was to be a parish, to have a church erected upon it, with a glebe of 60 acres for the minister in the smallest proportions, of 90 in the next, and of 120 in the largest. To British planters were to be granted six proportions, *viz.*, three of the least, two of the next, and one of the largest, and in these were to be allowed only English and Scottish tenants; to servitors were to be given six other proportions, three of the least, two of the middle, and one of the largest, to be allowed to have English or Irish tenants at choice; and to natives, the remaining fourteen, being eleven of the least, one of the middle, and two of the greatest size. There then remained 60 poles or 1500 acres, of which 30 poles, or 750 acres, were to be allotted to three corporate towns or boroughs, which the king ordered should be endowed with reasonable liberties, and send burgesses to parliament, and each to receive a third of this quantity; 10 other poles, or 250 acres, were to be appendant to the castle of Cavan; 6 to that of Cloughoughter; and the remaining 14 poles, or 346 acres, to be for the maintenance of a free school to be erected in Cavan. Two of the boroughs that were created and received these grants were Cavan and Belturbet, and the other 250 acres were to be given to a third town, to be erected about midway between Kells and Cavan, on a site to be chosen by the commissioners appointed to settle the plantation; this place was Virginia, which, however, never was incorporated. The native inhabitants were awed into acquiescence in these arrangements, and such as were not freeholders under the above grants, were to be settled within the county, or removed by order of the commissioners. The lands thus divided were the then profitable portions, and to each division a sufficient quantity of bog and wood was superadded. A considerable deviation from this project took place in regard to tithes, glebes, and parish churches. A curious record of the progress made by the undertakers in erecting fortified houses, &c., up to the year 1618-19, is preserved in Pynnar's Survey; the number of acres enumerated in this document amounts to 52,324, English measure, and the number of British families planted on them was 386, who could muster 711 armed men. Such was the foundation of the rights of property and of civil society in the county of Cavan, as existing at the present day, though not without subsequent disturbance; for both O'Reilly, representative of the county in parliament, and the sheriff his brother, were deeply engaged in the rebellion of 1641. The latter summoned the R. C. inhabitants to arms; they marched under his command with the appearance of discipline; forts, towns, and castles were surrendered to them; and Bedel, Bishop of Kilmore, was compelled to draw up their remonstrance of grievances, to be presented to the chief governors and council.

Cavan is partly in the diocese of Meath, and partly in that of Ardagh, but chiefly in that of Kilmore, and wholly in the ecclesiastical province of Armagh. For civil purposes it is divided into the eight baronies of Castleraghan, Clonmahon, Clonkee, Upper Loughtee, Lower Loughtee, Tullaghgarvey or Tullygarvey, Tullaghonoho, or Tullyhunco, and Tullaghagh or Tullyhaw. It contains the disfranchised borough and market-towns of Cavan and Belturbet; the market and post-towns of Arvagh, Bailieborough, Ballyconnell, Ballyhaise, Ballyjamesduff, Cootehill, Killesandra, Kingscourt, Stradone, and Virginia; the market-towns of Ballinagh and Shercock; the post-towns of Crossdoney, Mount-Nugent, and Scrabby; the modern and flourishing town of Mullagh; and the villages of Butlersbridge and Swanlinbar, each of which has a penny post. Prior to the Union it sent six members to the Irish parliament, two for the county at large, and two for each of the boroughs of Cavan and Belturbet; but since that period its only representatives have been the county members returned to the Imperial parliament and elected at Cavan. The constituency, as registered under the act of the 2nd and 3rd of Wm. IV., cap. 89, amounted, on the 1st of February, 1836, to 2434 electors, of whom 317 were £50, 236 £20, and 1652 £10 freeholders; 17 were £20 rent-chargers; 6 were clergymen registering out of benefices of £50; and 27 were £20, and 179 £10 leaseholders. It is in the north-west circuit: the assizes are held at Cavan, in which are the county court-house and gaol. Quarter sessions are held in rotation at Cavan, Bailieborough, Ballyconnell, and Cootehill; and there are a sessions-house and bridewell at each of the three last-named towns. The number of persons charged with criminal offences and committed to prison, in 1835, was 478, of whom 62 were females; and of civil bill commitments, 112. The local government is vested in a lieutenant, 10 deputy-lieutenants, and 85 other magistrates, including the provost of Belturbet, who is a magistrate of the county *ex officio*. There are 23 constabulary police stations, having in the whole a force of 8 chief and 22 sub-constables, and 151 men, with 8 horses, maintained equally by Grand Jury presentments and by Government. The county infirmary and fever hospital are situated at Cavan; and there are 18 dispensaries, situated respectively at Arvagh, Bailieborough, Ballyjamesduff, Ballyconnell, Belturbet, Ballymacue, Ballinagh, Ballyhaise, Cootehill, Crossdoney, Cavan, Killesandra, Kingscourt, Mullagh, Shercock, Swanlinbar, Stradone, and Virginia; all of which are maintained partly by Grand Jury presentments and partly by voluntary contributions in equal portions. The amount of Grand Jury presentments for 1835, was £22,525. 4. 9., of which £1860. 8. 9. was for the public roads of the county at large; £7287. 19. 8. for the public roads, being the baronial charge; £6792. 15. 9. for public buildings and charities, officers' salaries, &c.; £4033. 5. for police; and £2550. 15. 7. in repayment of a loan advanced by Government. Cavan, in military arrangements, is included in the northern district, and contains the stations of Belturbet and Cavan, the former for cavalry and the latter for infantry, which afford unitedly accommodation for 13 officers, 286 men, and 101 horses.

The county lies about midway in the island between the Atlantic Ocean and the Irish sea, its two extreme points being about 20 miles distant from each. The surface is very irregular, being every where varied with undulations of hill and dale, occasionally rocky, with scarcely a level spot intervening; but the only mountainous elevations are situated in its northern extremity. To the north-west the prospect is bleak, dreary, and much exposed; but in other parts it is not only well sheltered and woody, but the scenery is highly picturesque and attractive; numerous lakes of great extent and beauty adorn the interior; and, generally, the features of the country are strikingly disposed for landscape decoration. Yet these natural advantages are but partially improved, though in no part of Ireland are there demesnes of more magnificence and beauty. The scenery of the lakes is varied by numerous beautiful islands, and lofty woods overhang the river Erne, which flows into the celebrated lake of that name in the neighbouring county of Fermanagh. Bruce hill forms a striking object in the southern extremity of the county; the Leitrim mountains overlook its western confines; while towards the north-west rises the bleak, barren, and lofty range of the Slieve Russell mountains. But the chief mountains are those which separate this county and province from Connaught, encircling Glangavlin, namely, the Lurganculliagh, the Cuilagh, Slievenakilla, and the Mullahuna, the highest of which is 2185 feet above the level of the sea Some of the lakes cover many hundred acres, several of the smaller are nearly dry in summer, and might be effectually drained; all abound with fish, and their waters are remarkably clear. The streams issuing from some of them flow through the vales with much rapidity; their final destination is Lough Erne or Lough Ramor. A ridge of hills crosses

CAV

the county nearly from north to south, dividing it into two unequal portions: on the summit, near Lavy chapel, is a spring, a stream descending from which takes an easterly course towards Lough Ramor and into the Boyne, which empties itself into the Irish sea in Drogheda harbour; another stream flows westward through Lough Erne into the Atlantic, on the coast of Donegal. From the elevation and exposure of the surface, the climate is chilly, though at the same time salubrious; the exhalations from its numerous lakes being dispelled by the force of the gales. The soil in its primitive state is not fertile, being cold, in many places spongy, and inclined to produce rushes and a spiry aquatic grass: it commonly consists of a thick stratum of stiff brown clay over an argillaceous substratum; but when improved by draining and the application of gravel or lime, it affords a grateful return of produce. In the vales is found a deep brown clay, forming excellent land for the dairy.

Agriculture is very little improved: the chief crops are oats and potatoes; in some districts a considerable quantity of flax is cultivated, and wheat, within the last two or three years, has become a more common crop. Green crops are seldom or ever grown, except by some of the nobility and gentry. Lord Farnham has in cultivation a large and excellent farm, and around Virginia are evidences of a superior system of husbandry. The chief proprietors afford by example and encouragement every inducement to agricultural improvement, but with little success, except in the introduction of the iron plough, which has been generally substituted for spade labour, by which the land was formerly almost exclusively cultivated. Into the mountain districts, however, neither the plough nor wheel car has yet found its way; the spade, sickle, and flail are there the chief agricultural implements, cattle and pigs the common farm stock, and oats and potatoes the prevailing crops. The sides of the mountains are generally cultivated for oats to a considerable height, and their summits are grazed by herds of small young cattle. This practice more especially prevails in the barony of Tullaghagh, in the mountain district between the counties of Fermanagh and Leitrim, generally known as "the kingdom of Glan," but more properly called Glangavlin, or the country of the Mac Gaurans. To this isolated district there is no public road, and only one difficult pass; in some places a trackway is seen by which the cattle are driven out to the fairs of the adjacent country. It is about 16 miles in length by 7 in breadth, and is densely inhabited by a primitive race of Mac Gaurans and Dolans, who intermarry and observe some peculiar customs; they elect their own king and queen from the ancient race of the Mac Gaurans, to whom they pay implicit obedience. Tilling the land and attending the cattle constitute their sole occupation; potatoes and milk, with, sometimes, oaten bread, their chief food; and the want of a road by which the produce of the district might be taken to the neighbouring markets operates as a discouragement to industry and an incentive to the illicit application of their surplus corn. Wheat might be advantageously cultivated in most of the southern parts of the county, by draining and properly ploughing the land; a great defect consists in not ploughing sufficiently deep, from which cause the grain receives but little nourishment, and the land soon becomes exhausted, and is allowed to recover its productiveness by natural means. Hay seeds are scarcely ever sown. The farms are mostly small; and in many parts the farmer has looms in his house for weaving linen, on which he mainly depends for support, and hence neglects his land. Weaving, however, has of late somewhat declined, but tillage has not improved in proportion. Barley is sometimes sown, and the crop is generally good. In consequence of the system here practised of shallow ploughing and the unchecked growth of weeds, flax does not flourish in this so well as in some of the other northern counties, but it is still an amply remunerative crop. The fences in most parts are bad, consisting chiefly of a slight ridge of earth loosely thrown up. Draining and irrigation are wholly unpractised, although the country offers great facility for both; the gentle elevations are generally dry, and afford, beneath the surface, stones for draining; and the low grounds abound with springs, whose waters might be applied to the beneficial purposes of irrigation. Large allotments in the occupation of one individual are found only in the mountainous districts, and are applied to the grazing of young cattle during the summer months. In the demesnes of the gentry some sheep are fattened; but there are no good sheepwalks of any extent, except in the neighbourhood of Cavan, which district, indeed, is so superior to any other part of the county for fattening, that oxen are fed to as great size as in any part of Ireland. Dairy farms are by no means numerous, although the butter of Cavan is equal to that of any other part of the kingdom. The breed of cattle varies in almost every barony: that best adapted to the soil is a cross between the Durham and the Kerry, but the long-horned attains the greatest size. In the mountain districts the Kerry cow is the favourite; and in the lower or central parts, around Cavan, are some very fine Durham cattle and good crosses with the Dutch. The sheep are mostly a cross between the New Leicester and the old sheep of the country; the fleece, though mostly light, is good, and the mutton of excellent flavour. The horses are a light, hardy, active breed, well adapted to the country. The breed of pigs has been much improved, and although they do not attain a large size, they are profitable and readily fatten. Lime is the general manure, although in some parts the farmer has to draw it many miles; and calcareous sand and gravel, procured from the escars in the baronies of Tullaghonoho and Loughtee, are conveyed for that use to every part of the county where the roads permit, and sometimes even into the hilly districts, by means of two boxes, called "bardocs," slung across the back of a horse, which is the only means of conveyance the inhabitants of those parts possess. The woods were formerly very considerable, and the timber of uncommon size, as is evinced by the immense trees found in the bogs; but demesne grounds only are now distinguished by this valuable ornament. There are, however, numerous and extensive plantations in several parts, which in a few years will greatly enrich the scenery, particulary around the lakes of Ramor and Shellin, also near Stradone, Ballyhaise, Ballymacue, Fort Frederic, Farnham, Killesandra, and other places. The county contains bogs of sufficient extent for supplying its own fuel, and of a depth every where varying, but generally extremely great: they commonly lie favourably for draining, and the peat yields the strong red ashes which form an excellent manure. There is likewise a small proportion of moor, having a boggy surface, and resting on partial argillaceous strata: in these a marl, highly calcareous and easily raised, most commonly abounds. The fuel in universal use is peat.

The minerals are iron, lead, silver, coal, ochres, marl, fullers' earth, potters' clay, brick clay, manganese, sulphur, and a species of jasper. Limestone and various kinds of good building stone are also procured, especially in the north-western extremity of the county, which comprises the eastern part of the great Connaught coal field. A very valuable white freestone, soft to work but exceedingly durable, is found near Ballyconnell and at Lart, one mile from Cavan. The substratum around the former place is mostly mountain limestone, which dips rapidly to the west, and appears to pass under the Slieve Russell range of mountains, which are composed of the new red sandstone formation, with some curious amalgamations of greenstone. To the west of Swanlinbar rises the Bealbally mountains, through which is the Gap of Beal, the only entrance to Glangavlin; and beyond, at the furthest extremity of the county, is Lurganculliagh, forming the boundary between Ulster and Connaught. The base of this mountain range is clay-slate; the upper part consists entirely of sandstone, and near the summit is a stratum of mountain coal, ten feet thick, in the centre of which is a vein of remarkably good coal, but only about eight inches in thickness. The coal is visible on the eastern face of the mountain, at Meneack, in this county, where some trifling workings have been made, to which there is not even a practicable road; its superficial extent is supposed to be about 600 acres. The sandstone of these mountains, in many parts, forms perpendicular cliffs of great height; and the summit of Cuilagh, which is entirely composed of it, resembles an immense pavement, traversed in every direction by great fissures. Frequently, at the distance of from 80 to 100 yards from the edge of the precipice, are huge chasms, from twelve to twenty feet wide, extending from the surface of the mountain to the bottom of the sandstone. Some of the calcareous hills to the west of the valley of Swanlinbar rise to a height of 1500 feet, and are overspread with large rolled masses of sandstone, so as to make the entire elevation appear at first sight as if composed of the same. Iron ore abounds among the mountains of this part of the county, and was formerly worked. A lead mine was worked some years ago near Cootehill, and lead and silver ore are found in the stream descending from the mountain of Ortnacullagh, near Ballyconnell. In the district of Glan is found pure native sulphur in great quantities, particularly near Legnagrove and Dowra; and fullers' earth and pipe clay of superior quality exist in many parts. Proceeding towards the Fermanagh mountains, beautiful white and red transparent spars are found within a spade's depth of the surface; and here are two quarries of rough slate. Potters' clay, in this part of the county, occurs in every townland, and some of it is of the best and purest kind; patches of brick clay of the most durable quality are also common.

The chief manufacture is that of linen, upon which the prosperity of the inhabitants entirely depends, as it is carried on in almost every family. The average quantity of linen annually manufactured, and sold in the county, was estimated, at the commencement of the present century, to amount in value to £70,000; and pieces to the value of above £20,000 more are carried to markets beyond its limits. The number of bleaching establishments at the same period was twelve, in which about 91,000 pieces were annually finished. The quantity made at present is much greater, but the article is considerably reduced in price. Some of the bleach-greens are out of work, but, from the improvement of the process, a far greater number of webs is now bleached than was formerly; in 1835, nearly 150,000 pieces were finished, mostly for the English market. These establishments, around which improvements are being made every year, and which diffuse employment and comfort among a numerous population, are principally in the neighbourhoods of Cootehill, Tacken, Cloggy, Bailieborough, Scrabby, and Killiwilly. Frieze is made for home use, especially in the thinly peopled barony of Tullaghagh. The commerce of the county is limited and of little variety: its markets are remarkable only for the sale of yarn, flax, and brown linen; the principal are those of Cootehill and Killesandra.

The chief river is the Erne, which has its source in Lough Granny, near the foot of Bruce hill, on the south-western confines of the county, whence it pursues a northern course into Lough Oughter, and hence winds in the same direction by Belturbet into Lough Erne, which, at its head, forms the northern limit of the county. In most other parts the waters consisting of numerous lakes and their connecting streams, are with few exceptions tributary to the Erne. The Shannon has its source in a very copious spring, called the Shannon Pot, at the foot of the Cuilagh mountain in Glangavlin, in the townland of Derrylaghan, four miles south of the mountain road leading from Enniskillen to Manor-Hamilton, and nine miles north of Lough Allen: from this place to Kerry Head, where it falls into the sea, it pursues a course of 243 miles, of which it is navigable 234 miles, and during that distance has a fall of not more than 148 feet. The Blackwater has its source in a lake at Bailieborough Castle, and flows on by Virginia into Lough Ramor, whence it enters the county of Meath, and becomes a tributary to the Boyne. A line of artificial navigation has been proposed from Belturbet by Cootehill into the county of Monaghan. The old lines of roads are injudiciously formed, so as to encounter the most formidable hills. Although the new lines are made to wind through the valleys, yet, with the exception of those very recently made, they are of inferior construction. The material formerly used was clay-slate, which pulverised in a short time; but, since the recent grand jury act came into operation, the newest lines have been well laid out, and the only material now used is limestone or greenstone. Several new and important lines have been formed, and others are in progress or contemplated: among the roads which promise to be of the greatest advantage are those through the wild district of Glangavlin; they are all made and kept in repair by grand jury presentments.

The remains of antiquity are comparatively few and uninteresting. The most common are cairns and raths, of which the latter are particularly numerous in the north-eastern part of the county, and near

Kingscourt: in one at Rathkenny, near Cootehill, was found a considerable treasure, together with a gold fibula. There are remains of a round tower of inferior size at Drumlane. The number of abbeys and priories was eight, the remains of none of which, except that of the Holy Trinity, now exist, so that their sites can only be conjectured. Few also of the numerous castles remain, and all, except that of Cloughoughter, are very small. Though there are many good residences surrounded with ornamented demesnes, the seats of the nobility and gentry are not distinguished by any character of magnificence; they are noticed under the heads of the parishes in which they are respectively situated. The more substantial farmers have good family houses; but the dwellings of the peasantry are extremely poor, and their food consists almost entirely of oatmeal, milk, and potatoes. The English language is generally spoken, except in the mountain districts towards the north and west, and even there it is spoken by the younger part of the population, but the aged people all speak Irish, particularly in the district of Glan. With regard to fish, the lakes afford an abundance of pike, eels, and trout; and cod, salmon, and herrings, are brought in abundance by hawkers. The chief natural curiosities are the mineral springs, of which the most remarkable are those at Swanlinbar and Derrylyster, the waters of which are alterative and diaphoretic; those at Legnagrove and Dowra, containing sulphur and purging salt, and used in nervous diseases; the well at Owen Breun, which has similar medicinal properties; and the purgative and diuretic waters of Carrickmore, which are impregnated with fixed air and fossil alkali. The mineral properties of a pool in the mountains of Loughlinlea, between Bailieborough and Kingscourt, are also very remarkable. In 1617, Sir Oliver Lambart was created baron of Cavan, and this title was raised to an earldom in favour of his son Charles, by whose lineal descendants it is still enjoyed.

Seal.

CAVAN, an incorporated market and post-town, (formerly a parliamentary borough) in the parish of URNEY, barony of UPPER LOUGHTEE, county of CAVAN (of which it is the chief town), and province of ULSTER, 25½ miles (S. E. by S.) from Enniskillen, and 55 (N. W. by W.) from Dublin; containing 2931 inhabitants. This town was, from a period of remote antiquity, the seat of the O'Reillys, tanists of the district now forming the county to which it gives name, and who had a castle here, of which there are no other remains than some vaults and part of the foundation. A monastery for friars of the order of St. Dominick was founded here in 1300, and dedicated to the Blessed Virgin, by Giolla-Jisoa-Ruadh O'Reilly, dynast of Breffny; but about the year 1393, the monks were expelled by the same sept, and others of the Franciscan order substituted in their place. In 1468 the monastery, and Bally-Reilly, the castle above noticed, were burnt by the English under the Lord-Deputy Tiptoft, Earl of Worcester; but the former appears to have been restored previously to the year 1499, and to have been occupied by friars of the order of the Strict Observance. It was again reformed by John, son of Cahal O'Reilly, in 1502, and provincial chapters of the order were held in it in 1521, 1539, and 1556. Owen O'Nial, the celebrated general of the Irish army, who died by poison, as is supposed, at Cloughoughter, was buried in this abbey, in 1649. There are no remains of the establishment, which was commonly called Keadue; the tithes now belong to the Dean of Kilmore, and in his title are described as "the rectory of Keadue." In the early part of the reign of Jas. I., the lord-deputy pitched his tent to the south of the town, which is described as being a very unimportant place, for the purpose of reducing this part of the country to the observance of English laws and customs. Under the partition of lands made pursuant to an inquisition as stated in the article on the county, ten poles were allotted to the town of Cavan, which the king proposed to incorporate; ten poles to the castle, and 14 to the maintenance of a free school to be erected in the town. In 1610, Jas. I. granted the inhabitants a charter of incorporation, in the preamble of which it is stated that the town was the only place of trade in the county, and the only town where the justices could conveniently meet for their assize and gaol delivery, and that the inhabitants during the late insurrection, had supplied the garrison and performed good and acceptable service to Queen Elizabeth, from time to time, according to their best abilities. The commissioners for the plantation of Ulster reserved and set out eight poles of land, adjoining the town, to be granted to the new corporation; and the charter constituted the town and all lands within the compass of one mile from the stone house or castle in which Walter Bradie then dwelt, with the exception of the castle of "the Cavan," or O'Reilly's castle, and the two poles of land called Rosgolyan, the Borough of Cavan. This place was the scene of some skirmishing in the time of Cromwell, and till very lately a house was standing in the principal street, in which he is said to have resided for several weeks. In 1690, some of the forces of Jas. II., having assembled here for the purpose of attacking Belturbet, the Enniskilleners, under their victorious leader Wolsey, marched hither with a view to take them by surprise; but the Duke of Berwick having arrived with a considerable reinforcement, they had, with a force of only 1000 men, to contend with 4000 of the enemy. Wolsey, however, attacking them with spirit, the native forces of James fled at the first onset, when the Enniskilleners burst into the town and began to plunder it; those who had fled to the fort now sallied out to renew the engagement. Wolsey, as the only means of recalling his men, set fire to the town, and having rallied his forces, completed the victory with great slaughter. Human bones have been found in great numbers on the side of the hill overhanging the town, where the battle took place.

The town is situated on the road from Dublin to Enniskillen, and consists of several streets, of which the principal contains some well-built houses; there are infantry barracks capable of accommodating six officers and 130 non-commissioned officers and privates. A large garden, handsomely laid out in walks and planted, was left by the will of the late Lady Farnham, under certain restrictions, as a promenade for the inhabitants. Though in the midst of a manufacturing district, there is little trade carried on. The market, originally granted in the 1st of Jas. I. to John Binglie, gent., and subsequently by the charter of the 8th of Jas. I. to the corporation, is on Tuesday, but is chiefly for potatoes and meal; a very small quantity of yarn is brought for sale. Fairs, chiefly for young cattle and horses, are held on Feb. 1st, April 4th, May 14th, June 30th, Aug. 14th, Sept. 25th, and Nov. 12th, and a chief constabulary police force has been established here. Farnham, the seat of Lord Farnham, is one of the noblest ornaments of the county, for though the house does not possess much exterior magnificence, it is surrounded by a demesne of nearly 3000 acres, comprising the richest pastures and the greatest variety of scenery, adorned with wood and water, and every where improved by art. Lough Oughter, on one side of it, spreads out from under the woods of Killy, and encircles many beautiful islands crowned with the finest timber. One of these, named Cloughoughter, was the place of confinement of the venerable Bishop Bedell, when in the hands of the insurgents, in the war of 1641: the tower in which he was imprisoned is now a fine ruin. Nearly adjoining the demesne is Castle Saunderson, the seat of A. Saunderson, Esq., surrounded by a luxuriant demesne commanding the most beautiful views of Lough Erne. Clover Hill, an excellent mansion, the seat of J. Sanderson, Esq., has also a very beautiful demesne, richly adorned, and bordered by a spacious lake.

Under the charter of Jas. I., the corporation consists of a sovereign, two portreeves, twelve burgesses, and an indefinite number of freemen, assisted by a recorder, town-clerk, and other officers. But the regular appointment of these officers has been discontinued for several years; the sovereign and deputy are stationary in office, and are now the only representatives of the corporation. The town and the lands enumerated in the charter are held at a fee-farm rent of £1 English currency per annum. The same charter conferred the privilege of returning two members to the Irish parliament, which was exercised till the period of the Union, when £15,000 awarded as compensation for the abolition of the franchise was paid in moieties to Theophilus Clements and T. Nesbitt, Esqrs. The charter granted to the corporation a borough court of record, to be held before the sovereign and two or more burgesses, every three weeks; but this court has not been held since 1796. The assizes, and the Hilary and Midsummer quarter sessions, are held here; petty sessions are also held every week. The county court-house is a fine spacious building, with a portico in front. The county gaol is a very spacious building, to which additions have been recently made on the radiating principle; it contains in the whole 68 cells, 8 day-rooms, and 10 airing-yards, in one of which is a tread-mill, and is well adapted for the classification of prisoners; a good school has been established in it. The average number of prisoners is 120; and the whole expense of the gaol, for 1835, was £1190. 3. 5½.

The parish church of Urney is situated in the town. The R. C. chapel, erected in 1824, at an expense of £1000, is a neat building; over the altar is a painting of the Descent from the Cross. On the confines of the town is a classical school of royal foundation, under the charter of the 2nd of Chas. I., which vested several townlands in the counties of Armagh, Cavan, Fermanagh, Donegal, and Tyrone, in the primate and his successors in trust for the endowment of schools in each of those counties. By a late act of parliament the management has been transferred to a Board of Commissioners of Education: the nomination of master rests with the lord-lieutenant. The school-house, erected in 1819, at an expense of £800, is a spacious building, calculated for the reception of 100 pupils, and beautifully situated on a lawn bounded by a branch of the Erne, and surrounded with an amphitheatre of hills. The income arising from the endowment is £641. 13. 5. per annum, out of which the master receives a salary of £400, and the remainder is appropriated to the repayment of a loan from Government for the buildings. Several parochial and Sunday schools are supported by subscriptions; and a handsome school-house has been erected in the town, in which a school is supported by Lord Farnham. The county infirmary is a plain building capable of receiving 52 patients. There is an almshouse for a poor widow, supported by private subscription. In Swellan lake, about a quarter of a mile from the town, have been found, at different times, some of the largest horns of the elk that have been discovered in Ireland. The celebrated Dr. Sheridan, the friend and correspondent of Dean Swift, was for many years master of the royal school of this place, and was frequently honoured with visits from the dean; a bower in the garden, called Swift's bower, is still in existence.—See Urney.

CECILSTOWN, a village, in that part of the parish of Castlemagner, which is within the barony of Duhallow, county of Cork, and province of Munster, 5½ miles (W. N. W.) from Mallow; containing 331 inhabitants. It is situated on the road from Mallow to Kanturk, and consists of 46 houses, of which the greater number are thatched. Here is a national school, and a penny post to Mallow has been established. A constabulary police force is stationed here; and petty sessions are held in the school-house every Monday. Cecilstown has a patent for four fairs annually, but they are not now held.—See Castlemagner.

CELBRIDGE, or KILDROUGHT, a market and post-town, and a parish, partly in the barony of South Salt, but chiefly in that of North Salt, county of Kildare, and province of Leinster, 4¼ miles (N. N.E.) from Naas, and 11 (W. by S.) from Dublin; containing 2421 inhabitants, of which number, 1647 are in the town. This town, pleasantly situated on the left bank of the river Liffey, over which is a handsome stone bridge, and on the turnpike road from Dublin to Prosperous, is indebted for its origin to the Limerick family, from whom it was purchased by the Rt. Hon. W. Conolly, speaker of the Irish House of Commons, whose representative, Col. E. M. Conolly, is the present proprietor. It consists principally of one street; the houses, about 270 in number, are in general well built; the inhabitants are amply supplied with water. The woollen manufacture was carried on to a considerable extent, and a very large range of building was erected in 1805, comprising all the requisite machinery for that manufacture in its various branches; the works were put in motion by a water wheel of 200-horse power, and when in full operation afforded employment to 600 persons; but they are not at present in work. Adjoining the town, though in the parish of Donocomper, is a cotton-spinning and power-loom weaving factory, employing, when in full work, about 100 persons. The market is on Saturday, chiefly for provisions and hardware; fairs are held on the last Tuesday in April, Sept. 8th, and Nov. 7th; and a constabulary police station has been established here. Petty sessions are held every Monday.

The parish comprises 1758 acres, as applotted under the tithe act. The environs are justly celebrated for their great beauty, and are ornamented with several gentlemen's seats. Castletown, the splendid mansion of Col. Conolly, is a noble structure of hewn stone, consisting of a centre connected with two wings by semicircular colonnades of the Ionic and Corinthian orders; it is situated in an extensive park, intersected with numerous avenues of stately timber and sloping gently to the Liffey, which flows through the demesne, and separates the parishes of Celbridge and Donocomper. Oakly Park, the handsome seat of R. Maunsel, Esq., is in this parish; and contiguous to it is Celbridge Abbey, built by the late Dr. Marley, Bishop of Clonfert, and now the residence of J. Ashworth, Esq., proprietor of the woollen manufactory in the town. The house is associated with the memory of Dean Swift, who is said to have spent much of his time here in the society of the lady whom he has celebrated under the name of Vanessa; and a rustic seat on the bank of the Liffey, which passes through the demesne, and over which is a spacious bridge of stone, is said to have been planned by him. The living is a rectory and vicarage, in the diocese of Dublin, episcopally united, in 1801, to the rectory and vicarage of Killadoon, the vicarage of Straffan, the rectory of Castledillon, the half rectories of Donoghmore and Donocomper, and the chapelry of Simonstown, together forming the union of Celbridge, in the patronage of the Crown: the tithes of the parish amount to £145. The church, situated in the lower extremity of the town, is a neat edifice, erected in 1813, by a loan of £1500 from the late Board of First Fruits; it has a tower and spire, and within it is the mausoleum of the Conolly family. There is a neat glebe-house: the glebe for the whole union comprises 48 acres. In the R. C. divisions this parish is the head of a union or district, comprising the parishes of Celbridge and Straffan, in each of which is a chapel. About half a mile from the town is a handsome school-house, built by the Rt. Hon. William Conolly, in 1740, and endowed by him with 50 acres of land and a rent-charge of £309 per annum out of the estate of Castletown; this endowment has been transferred to the funds of the Incorporated Society, who have the appointment of the master and mistress; the school-house has been greatly enlarged since its connection with the society, and is now capable of receiving 150 children; there are at present about 100 girls on the foundation, 30 of whom are nominated by the Conolly family. A parochial school-house, built by the same family, is entirely supported by the founders; there are also four private schools in the parish. There is a fever hospital and dispensary, a neat building erected in 1813, and containing six wards with four beds in each. In the old churchyard was a sumptuous monument to the memory of the Right Hon. W. Conolly, the founder of the Castletown property, which has lately been closed up; and just without the demesne are the ruins of a chapel belonging formerly to the Earl of Limerick.

CHAPEL-CHARON, a parish, in the barony of Shelmalier, county of Wexford, and province of Leinster, 5 miles (N. W.) from Wexford: the population is returned with the parish of Killurin into which it has merged. It consists of only two small townlands, and is not recognised as a parish in any civil or modern ecclesiastical divisions. It is situated on the river Slaney, and on the road from Wexford to Enniscorthy, and is presumed to have been, prior to the Reformation, an appendage to Carrigmannon, the ancient seat of the family of Devereux, who had a chapel here. It is a rectory, in the diocese of Ferns, and is part of the union of Killurin. In the R. C. divisions it is included in the union or district of Glynn.

CHAPEL-IN-THE-WOODS.— See WOODSCHAPEL and ARDTREA.

CHAPEL-ISLAND, an extra-parochial liberty, in the barony of Bantry, county of Cork, and province of Munster, 2 miles (N. W.) from Bantry; containing 5 inhabitants. This island, which is situated in the bay of Bantry, derived its name from a chapel founded on it, of which there are no vestiges except the burial-ground. It comprises about 24 statute acres of extremely fertile land, which is in a high state of cultivation, and as part of the Bandon estate, in which parish it is locally included, is the property of the Duke of Devonshire. There is only one house on the island, which is occupied by the farmer who manages the land. Though nearly adjoining Hog and Horse islands, which also belong to the duke, it is more than 30 miles from any other portion of the Bandon estate.

CHAPELIZOD, a parish, in the barony of Castleknock, county of Dublin, and province of Leinster, 3 miles (W.) from Dublin; containing 2181 inhabitants, of which number 1632 are in the village. This place is supposed to have derived its name from *La Belle Isode* a daughter of one of the ancient Irish kings, who had a chapel here. The lands belonging to it were granted by Hugh de Lacy, in 1173, to Hugh Tyrrell, which grant was afterwards confirmed by Hen. II. In 1176, they were given by the Tyrrells to the hospital of the Knights Templars of Kilmainham, and after the suppression of that order remained in possession of their successors, the Knights of St. John of Jerusalem, till the dissolution of the monasteries, in the reign of Hen. VIII. They subsequently passed through various hands till 1665, when the Duke of Ormonde, by command of the king, purchased the entire manor, with the mansion, from Sir Maurice Eustace, for the purpose of enclosing the Phœnix park, and the old mansion-house became the occasional residence of the Lord-Lieutenant. In 1671, Col. Lawrence obtained a grant of several houses and about 15 acres of land adjacent to the village for 41 years, at an annual rent of £42, for the purpose of establishing the linen manufacture, under the auspices of the Duke of Ormonde, who, with a view to promote its success, invited over numerous families from Brabant, Rochelle, the Isle of Rhé, and other places, who were skilled in the art of manufacturing linens, diapers, tickens, sail-cloth, and cordage, and established those manufactures here in the greatest perfection. In 1690, Gen. Douglas, on his march to Athlone, encamped for one night at this place; and soon after, King William himself, subsequently to his expedition to the south, passed several days here in issuing various orders and redressing grievances. In 1696, Lord Capel, Lord-Deputy of Ireland, died at the vice-regal residence here after a long illness, during which several important meetings of the council took place; and though the house was repaired by Primate Boulter, when Lord-Justice of Ireland, in 1726, it has never since been occupied by the lord-lieutenants: a house near the village, called the King's, is said to be that occasionally used as the vice-regal lodge. The village, which is of considerable size, and extends into the parish of Palmerstown, in the barony of Newcastle, is situated on the south-western verge of the Phœnix park, and contains 200 houses, of which 103 are in that part of it which is in the parish of Palmerstown. It is within the delivery of the Dublin twopenny post, and is chiefly remarkable for the beautiful scenery in its vicinity, especially along the banks of the Liffey, towards Lucan, and for the extensive strawberry beds which are spread over the northern side of the vale. The woollen manufacture was formerly carried on very extensively, and continued to flourish till the commencement of the present century, when there was a large factory, two fulling-mills, and an extensive corn and wash mill, which have been succeeded by a flax-mill on a very large scale, erected by Messrs. Crosthwaite, the present proprietors, and affording constant employment to more than 600 persons. There are also a bleach-green and several mills.

The living is a rectory and vicarage, in the diocese of Dublin, united at a period unknown to the rectories of Palmerstown and Ballyfermot, together forming the union of Chapelizod, in the patronage of the Archbishop: the tithes amount to £1. 19. 5½., and the gross amount for the whole benefice is £301. 19. 5½. The church is a small plain edifice, erected in the reign of Anne, and remarkable only for its tower covered with ivy, from the summit of which is an extensive and highly interesting prospect over the surrounding country. There is neither glebe-house nor glebe. In the R. C. divisions this parish forms part of the union or district of Castleknock. There is a chapel in the village; and near it is a school-room, erected in 1834 for a school to be placed in connection with the National Board. A school is supported by subscription, in which about 18 boys and 54 girls are instructed; and there are also a pay school, in which are 60 boys and 40 girls, and two Sunday schools. A dispensary in the village is supported in the usual way. Col. Lawrence, the founder of the manufactures of this place, was the author of a well-known pamphlet, published in 1682, and entitled "The Interest of Ireland in its Trade and Wealth." The Hibernian school in the Phœnix park, described in the article on Dublin, is in this parish.

CHAPELMIDWAY, a parish, in the barony of Castleknock, county of Dublin, and province of Leinster, 7 miles (N.) from Dublin; containing 335 inhabitants. The principal seats are Corrstown, the residence of H. Cosgrave, Esq., and Kilcorkin, of J. Litton, Esq. It is a rectory and vicarage, in the diocese of Dublin, forming part of the union of Kilsallaghan, with which the tithes are included. In the R. C. divisions it is part of the union or district of Finglas. The ruins of the church are situated on the old road from Dublin to the Naul.

CHAPEL-RUSSELL, a parish, in the barony of Kenry, county of Limerick, and province of Munster; containing, with the post-town of Pallas-Kenry, 1204 inhabitants. It was formerly called *Kilelura* or *Cillenalotar*, and was created a parish, under its present name, by the late Dr. Elrington, while Bishop of Limerick. It is situated on the road from Limerick to the quay of Ringmoileau, and within a mile of the river Shannon; and contains 587 statute acres, as applotted under the tithe act, of which nearly the whole is arable. Prior to 1785, the whole was an open field, on which a great number of cattle depastured, but it has been enclosed. The land is tolerably fertile, and the soil is everywhere based on limestone, which in some places rises above the surface. Near the town of Pallas-Kenry are two small lakes, which appear to have been formed by cutting turf. The living is a rectory and vicarage, in the diocese of Limerick, and in the patronage of the Bishop; it was formerly part of the bishop's mensal, but on its being erected into a rectory by Dr. Elrington, he endowed it with all the tithes, which amount to £55. 7. 8½. The parish appears formerly to have been part of the parish of Ardcanny, or to have been held by the same incumbent; and the church of that parish being in a ruinous state, and situated at the southern extremity of the parish, it is the intention of the bishop to unite the two parishes, when the church of Chapel-Russell, which is a large and handsome edifice, will become the church of the union. It was built in 1822, by aid of a gift of £900 from the late Board of First Fruits, and £100 from the Incorporated Society, for the erection of a gallery for the children of the Shannon Grove charter school; but as this school was suppressed soon afterwards, the gallery is now open to the parishioners. The Ecclesiastical Commissioners have lately granted £116 for repairing the church. There is neither glebe-house nor glebe. In the R. C. divisions this parish forms part of the union or district of Kildimo: the chapel, which is a neat building, is at White Forge. There is also a chapel for Wesleyan Methodists. The parochial schools, in which are about 100 children, are aided by subscriptions from Lord Charleville and the rector: about the same number also receive instruction in two private schools. There were formerly two charter schools, one of which long since fell into decay, but the other existed till within the last few years, under the patronage of the Charleville family. The school, which cost £5000, is large and well built, and is now occupied in separate tenements; and the land is held by a farmer. A loan fund has been established. Within the parish are the ruins of the castle of Pallas-Kenry, originally built by the O'Donovans, but subsequently occupied by the Fitzgeralds, Knights of the Valley, who greatly enlarged and strengthened it at various periods: a great part of the walls fell down in the winter of 1834, but it is still a picturesque and beautiful ruin. Not far distant from it is the curious little church of Killenalotar, only twelve feet long and eight broad; the walls, the west door, and the east window are quite perfect.—See Pallas-Kenry.

CHAPPLE (or the Chapel of St. Clement), a parish, in the barony of Bantry, county of Wexford, and province of LEINSTER, 6 miles (S. S. W.) from Enniscorthy; containing 827 inhabitants. It is situated on the little river Boro, and on the mail car road from New Ross to Enniscorthy, and contains 3747 statute acres, which are chiefly under tillage. The soil is in general light and poor, and the state of agriculture has undergone but little improvement. At Boro Hill is the seat of Jeremiah Fitzhenry, Esq. The living is an impropriate curacy, in the diocese of Ferns, and is part of the union of Killegney; the rectory is appropriate to the bishoprick. There is a glebe of 16 acres, and the tithes amount to £173. 10. 9. In the R. C. divisions this parish forms part of the union or district of Templeudigan, also called Killegney: the chapel, a neat building, is at Clogbawn or Cloughbawn, in this parish, and was erected soon after 1798, partly by a loan from Government. Near it is the national school, built in 1816 by Lord Carew, who has endowed it with four acres of land, and allows £15 per annum to the master. No less than 84 young men, who have been educated at this school, have subsequently become schoolmasters. About 120 boys and 30 girls are taught in the school, and about 70 more children in three private schools.

Seal.

CHARLEMONT, an incorporated market-town and district parish (formerly a parliamentary borough), in the barony and county of ARMAGH, and province of ULSTER, 5 miles (N. by W.) from Armagh, and 68 miles (N. by W.) from Dublin; containing 3642 inhabitants, of which number, 523 are in the town. This place derives its name from Charles, Lord Mountjoy, who, while Lord-Deputy of Ireland in 1602, erected a castle here, and called it Charlemont, partly after his name, and partly after his title. It was built to prevent the incursions of the O'Nials into the English pale, and to guard the wooden bridge which then afforded the only passage over the Blackwater. In 1641 it was deemed a place of considerable importance, and was taken by stratagem by Sir Phelim O'Nial, on the 22nd of October. Lord Caulfeild, a brave officer, grown old in the royal service, had been made governor, and lived with his Irish neighbours in unsuspecting confidence, when Sir Phelim invited himself to sup with his lordship, and he and his followers being received, on a pre-arranged signal seized the family, made the garrison prisoners, ransacked the castle, and afterwards killed Lord Caulfeild in one of O'Nial's houses. That chieftain subsequently retiring before the English forces, made this castle his head-quarters for a short time. Owen O'Nial, expecting to be besieged here, strengthened the defences; and when the Scottish General Monroe attempted to surprise it, he was repulsed with loss, but the castle was at length captured by Sir Charles Coote. In 1665 it was sold to Chas. II. for £3500, since which time it has been vested in the Crown. It was garrisoned by the Irish for Jas. II., in 1690, under Sir Teague O'Regan, and invested by Duke Schomberg. Caillemote, a French officer, being posted on the Blackwater, and harassing the garrison, after some time the governor was summoned to surrender. O'Regan, a courageous Irish officer, determined to hold out to the last extremity, but the distresses of the garrison becoming intolerable, the governor proposed terms of capitulation on the 13th of May, and on the 14th the garrison marched out with the honours of war, to the number of 800 men. On taking possession of the castle, the duke found in it 17 pieces of cannon, one large mortar, 83 barrels of gunpowder, and various munitions of war.

The town is situated near the confluence of the rivers Blackwater and Callen, and on the road from Armagh to Dungannon and Coleraine. In 1833 it contained 111 houses, and is connected with the post-town of Moy by a recently erected stone bridge. Charlemont castle is still a place of great strength, fortified with bastions, a dry ditch, and escarp and counterscarp; and there are two ravelins, one in front, the other in rear of the works, surrounded by a glacis which runs along the side of the Blackwater. It is the ordnance depôt for the North of Ireland, and the head-quarters of the artillery for the district of Ulster. Formerly it had a military governor, but on the death of Gen. Sir John Doyle, Bart., in 1835, the office was abolished, as being a sinecure. The barracks, which are occupied by two companies of the Royal Artillery, are constructed to accommodate 5 officers, 151 non-commissioned officers and privates, and 79 horses, with an hospital attached for 22 patients. The town is well situated for trade, the river Blackwater being navigable for vessels of 90 tons' burden to Lough Neagh; it is connected with Belfast by the Lagan canal, and with Newry by the canal of that name, and the great Ulster canal now in progress to Lough Erne will open a communication with the West of Ireland. The linen manufacture is carried on to a considerable extent. There is a good market held on Saturday; and fairs are held on the 12th of May, Aug. 16th, and Nov. 12th, for cattle, linen yarn, and provisions. The charter granted to the corporation a market on Tuesday and a fair on the 1st and 2nd of May, with the tolls; and a subsequent patent to Sir Toby Caulfeild, dated March 1st, 1622, granted to him a market on Wednesday and a fair on the 5th and 6th of August, with the tolls; but these charter and patent fairs and markets have long been discontinued.

The borough, which comprises the townland of Charlemont, containing above 200 acres, and the liberties, containing 20 acres, was incorporated by charter of Jas. I., dated April 29th, 1613. The corporation consists of a portreeve, 12 burgesses, and an unlimited number of freemen. The portreeve was to be elected annually, on St. John's day, by the portreeve and free burgesses, the latter of whom were to be elected for life out of the inhabitants; and the freemen were to consist of all the inhabitants, and as many other persons as the corporation might elect. The charter also conferred on the portreeve and free burgesses the right of returning two members to parliament, which was exercised until the Union, when Francis William, Earl of Charlemont received £15,000, as patron of the borough, for the abolition of its franchise. Since the Union, the regularly elected burgesses have not acted; but Mr. Livingstone, the last portreeve, some time before his death, summoned in his official capacity a " corporation jury," similar to that which existed in Armagh; and in the year 1821 the surviving members of that jury elected a portreeve. From that time meetings have been held annually, at which a portreeve, town-clerk, and other officers have been elected, and burgesses and freemen admitted; and since 1827, the lord-lieutenant has ratified the portreeve's election. The borough court, granted by the charter to be held weekly, under the presidency of the portreeve, with jurisdiction in personal actions not exceeding five marks, having fallen into disuse, has been renewed by the new corporation. Courts leet and baron for the manor of Charlemont are held by the seneschal in the town of Moy, in May and November, and their jurisdiction extends over a wide district.

The agriculture of the surrounding district is in a progressive state of improvement: there is some good peat bog, and coal also is said to exist. The principal seats in the vicinity are Church Hill, the residence of Col. Verner; the Argory, of W. McGeough Bond, Esq.; and Clonfeacle glebe-house and demesne, occupied by the Rev. H. Griffin, all of which can be seen from the town. The living, which was created in 1830, is a perpetual curacy, in the diocese of Armagh, and in the patronage of the Rector of Loughgall. The new parish or district comprises the townlands of Charlemont, Corr, and Donavally, with Anagh McManus, Keenahan, Ahinlig, Lishloshly, Kinnego, Mullaghmore, Termacrannon, Anasamery, and Clenmaine. The church is a handsome structure, resembling in front one of the grand altars of York Minster; it was built and consecrated in 1833, by His Grace the Lord-Primate, and contains a handsome monument to the late Mrs. Jackson. Divine service is performed in two school-houses in the district, and on every alternate Sunday in the barrack for the military, by the perpetual curate. There is neither glebe-house nor glebe; the income of the perpetual curate is an annual money payment from the rector of Loughgall. The Wesleyan Methodists have a chapel in the town. The male and female parochial school was built in 1821, near the church, by the Board of Ordnance and the inhabitants; it is supported by subscription. Summer Island male and female school, with a residence for the master, has an endowment of £7. 10. from Col. Verner. Clenmaine school is supported by subscriptions; and Kinnego school, built and supported by W. Parnell, Esq., is situated on the College lands. About 100 boys and 90 girls are educated in these schools, besides which there are a barrack and a hedge school, in which are about 80 boys and 40 girls, and three Sunday schools. There are some remains of the fortifications at Legerhill, from which Duke Schomberg bombarded the town, and of a Danish rath. A curious gold ring, and a gold cross, studded with gems, and said to have belonged to Sir Teague O'Regan, have been discovered here; also, a few years since, a body almost in a complete state of preservation, with the clothes and spurs perfect. In the museum of Messrs. W. & J. Jackson there is a rare collection of minerals, petrifactions, coins, and other relics found in and near the town. Charlemont gives the title of Earl to the family of Caulfeild.

CHARLESTOWN, a village, in the parish of KILBRIDE-LANGAN, barony of KILCOURSEY, KING'S county, and province of LEINSTER, adjoining the town of Clara: the population is returned with the parish. This place is situated on the road from Farbane to Kilbeggan, and was formerly the seat of an extensive linen trade, for the management of which a linen-hall was established. The village consists of about 40 houses, and had a patent for two annual fairs and a linen market weekly on Monday. Adjoining it is the castle of Kilcoursey, once a place of great strength, which gave name to the barony. In the vicinity are also Cloghatana, the old residence of the Fox family; Ballynamintan and Marshbrook, the ancient seats of the Mars family; and Kilfylan, the residence of an ancient branch of the De Berminghams.

CHARLESTOWN, a parish, in the barony of ARDEE, county of LOUTH, and province of LEINSTER, 2 miles (N. by W.) from Ardee; containing 1407 inhabitants. This parish is situated on the road from Ardee to Monaghan; and comprises, according to the Ordnance survey, 2699½ statute acres, of which 1797 acres are applotted under the tithe act and valued at £2870 per annum. The land is very fertile, and the system of agriculture much improved: there is some bog, which supplies the inhabitants with fuel, but very little waste land in the parish. A few individuals are employed in weaving linen; but the principal part of the population are engaged in agricultural pursuits. There are some quarries of stone fit for building, but none of limestone. Rahanna, the seat of Clarges Ruxton, Esq., is in this parish. The living is a vicarage, in the diocese of Armagh, united by acts of council, in 1737 and 1754, to the vicarage of Tallanstown, and the rectories of Philipstown, Maplestown, and Clonkeehan, which five parishes constitute the union of Charlestown or Philipstown, in the patronage of the Lord-Primate; the rectory is impropriate in the Hon. Baron Foster. The tithes of the parish amount to £271. 17. 6., of which £234. 17. 6. is payable to the impropriator, and £37 to the vicar: the amount of tithes for the union, including glebe, payable to the incumbent, is £476. 15. 4. The church, a handsome edifice in the later English style, with a tower and spire, together 108 feet high, was erected in 1827, at an expense, exclusively of the spire, of £1385, a loan from the late Board of First Fruits: the spire was added at an expense of £220, defrayed by the Rev. R. Olpherts, the present incumbent, and several of the resident gentry. The churchyard is enclosed with a handsome iron palisade resting on a low wall of hewn stone, towards the expense of which the lord-primate contributed £50. The glebe-house, a handsome residence within a quarter of a mile from the church, was built by a gift of £250 and a loan of £550 from the late Board of First Fruits: the glebe comprises seven acres of land, valued at £3 per acre, but subject to a rent of £11. 10. 9. per annum, payable to the representatives of the late Alexander Dawson, Esq. In the R. C. divisions the parish forms part of the union or district of Tallanstown. Adjoining the church is the parochial school-house, containing two large school-rooms, each for 60 boys and girls respectively, with suitable apartments for the master and his family; it was built in 1827, chiefly at the expense of the Rev. R. Olpherts, aided by a grant from Government and some charitable donations: the master, in addition to other contributions, receives £10 per annum from the incumbent. There are some remains of the ancient parish church.

Seal.

CHARLEVILLE, an incorporated market and post-town (formerly a parliamentary borough), in the parish of RATHGOGAN, barony of ORRERY and KILMORE, county of CORK, and province of MUNSTER, 29 miles (N. by W.) from Cork, and 114¼ miles (S. W.) from Dublin; containing 4766 inhabitants. This town, so named in honour of Chas. II., is of comparatively recent origin, having been founded by Roger, first Earl of Orrery and Lord-President of Munster, in the year 1661. That nobleman erected a magnificent mansion here for his own residence, in which he kept his court of presidency, and by his influence obtained for the inhabitants a charter of incorporation from Chas. II., dated May 29th, 1671. Charleville House was burnt by the Irish under the command of the Duke of Berwick, in 1690, and by his order, after he had dined in it. In 1691, Col. Lumley came to this place on the 18th of August, with a party of soldiers, when the enemy posted here fled, leaving many of their men killed and wounded. Captain Massey, who had been left behind, fired his pistols at the soldiers of William's army; and he and a cornet, being taken prisoners with protections in their pockets, were hanged as deserters. The town is situated on the mail coach road from Cork to Limerick, near the border of the latter county, and on the north-east side of an elevated tract, from which stretches an extensive plain of rather cheerless aspect. The land to the south is of superior quality, producing abundant crops. At the western end of the town the plantations of Sanders Park, the demesne of C. Sanders, Esq., have a pleasing appearance. It consists principally of two parallel streets communicating by two others crossing them at right angles; one of which is a wide and spacious thoroughfare, the chief place of traffic, particularly on market days. It is neither paved nor lighted, but the inhabitants are well supplied with water from springs and a public pump. Nothing appears to have been done for the improvement of this place for some years; but the lord of the manor, the Earl of Cork and Orrery, is now renewing upon advantageous terms a number of long leases that have recently fallen in, which has given an impulse to its improvement, and several new houses have in consequence been lately erected: the number of houses, in 1831, was 741. A new road, eight Irish miles in length, has been just completed from Charleville to Croom, that will shorten the distance to Limerick. There are three tanyards and a small blanket-manufactory in the town; and immediately adjoining it are two large flour-mills. The market is on Saturday, and is well supplied with provisions. Fairs are held on the 10th of January, March 16th, May 12th, Aug. 15th, Oct. 10th, and Nov. 12th, for fat cattle, pigs, hardware, and other merchandise; the last two are held by patent, the others are of recent establishment. The shambles for butchers' meat are in a small enclosed area at the back of the court-house. A sub-branch of the National Bank of Ireland has been recently established here, in connection with the Branch Bank of Limerick. A military force of two officers and 40 men is stationed here, but there is no permanent barrack; and a constabulary police station has been also established in the town.

By charter granted in the 23rd of Chas. II. to Roger, Earl of Orrery, erecting his lands into a manor, this town was made a free borough, and the inhabitants were incorporated under the designation of the "Sovereign, Bailiffs, and Burgesses of the Borough of Charleville." The corporation consists of a sovereign, two bailiffs, twelve burgesses, and an indefinite number of freemen. The sovereign and bailiffs are elected annually from the burgesses, by the corporation, on the Monday after St. John's day, and sworn into office on the Monday after Michaelmas-day. The burgesses are elected by the corporation as vacancies occur by death or otherwise, and the persons proposed are at the same time made freemen of the borough. The sovereign is a justice of the peace within the borough, and acts occasionally in that capacity; he is also coroner and billet-master. The corporation was some years since nearly extinct, the members being reduced to the sovereign and one bailiff only. In 1826 the sovereign and the remaining bailiff re-elected themselves, and also filled up all the vacancies; and the corporation at present consists of a sovereign, two bailiffs, and twelve burgesses, as originally constituted. The charter conferred upon the corporation the privilege of returning two members to the Irish parliament, which was regularly exercised till the Union, when the borough was disfranchised, and the £15,000 awarded as compensation was paid in moieties to the Earls of Shannon and Cork. The sovereign, or his deputy, is usually appointed seneschal of the manor, the greater portion of which extends into the county of Limerick; and as such he holds a court of record, the jurisdiction of which extends to the determination of pleas not exceeding £200 late currency: the proceedings are according to the usual course of common law, and actions are commenced either by arrest of the person, attachment of the goods, or serviceable writ; and under the act of the 7th and 8th of Geo. IV., cap. 59, he has also a civil bill jurisdiction. Petty sessions are held in the town every alternate Monday, by the county magistrates. The court and market-house is a small plain building on the north side of the main street.

The ancient parish church of Rathgogan has been for a long time in ruins, and the present church, erected by the founder of the town, is situated on the south side of the main street: it is a plain building without either tower or spire; the walls have been lately embattled with hewn limestone. The Roman Catholic chapel, a neat and spacious edifice, erected by subscription in 1812, is ornamented with quoins, cornices, and window mouldings of hewn stone; the altar is large and remarkably elegant, and is embellished with several paintings of superior execution; a handsome cupola was added to the chapel in 1829, and adjoining it is a parochial house for the priest. An edifice has been lately erected for the meetings of Bible and other similar associations, also as a place of preaching for occasional preachers. There are several schools, the minuter details of which will be found in the article on the parish of Rathgogan. Among these is a national school recently established, for which a remarkably neat building of hewn limestone has been erected, at an expense of £800, of which £600 was raised by subscription, and the remainder granted by the new National Board. A classical school was founded by the first Earl of Cork and Orrery, who endowed it with £40 per annum, continued by the present earl, who appoints the master: the celebrated Barry Yelverton, Attorney-General for Ireland, subsequently Chief Baron of the Exchequer, and afterwards created Viscount Avonmore, was educated here. A dispensary is supported, and a fever hospital is about to be erected, towards which the Earl of Cork has subscribed £100. Near the town was formerly a charter school for female foundlings, which has been discontinued for many years: the buildings are at present occupied as a dwelling-house by the incumbent, the Rev. J. R. Cotter, the inventor of a new and very powerful bass wind instrument, called the Basso Hibernico, which obtained the patronage of Geo. IV., and was introduced into his band. The interest of a bequest of £100 by the late Mr. Ryan is to be applied towards the support of the national school; and a further bequest of £50 in clothing to the poor of Charleville. At Belfort, near the town, is a spring of remarkably pure water, with a slight mineral tinge; it is held in great veneration by the peasantry, who resort to it in great numbers. John Macdonald, commonly called *Shaun Claraugh*, an Irish poet, resided here for several years, and was buried at Ballysally, near the town.

CHEEKPOINT, or BOLTON, a village, in the parish of Faithlegg, barony of Gaultier, county of Waterford, and province of Munster, 1½ mile (N.) from Passage: the population returned with the parish. This place, which was formerly part of the estate of the late Mr. Bolton, and is now the property of Nicholas Power, Esq., of Faithlegg House, is situated on Waterford harbour, at the confluence of the rivers Suir and Barrow, the latter of which is navigable for ships to the town of New Ross. It was formerly the Waterford post-office packet station, and the seat of a hosiery and cotton manufacture, but the station has been removed to Dunmore, and the manufacture has failed. Rope-making was also carried on to a limited extent; but since the removal of the packet station, the place has fallen into decay.

CHURCH-HILL, a post-town, in the parish of Inismacsaint, barony of Magheraboy, county of Fermanagh, and province of Ulster, 9 miles (N. W.) from Enniskillen, and 89½ miles (N. W.) from Dublin: the population is returned with the parish. This place is situated near the mail coach road from Dublin to Ballyshannon, and has a sub-post-office to the latter place and Enniskillen. Fairs are held on the 14th of May, 30th of August, and 30th of November. There is a place of worship for Wesleyan Methodists; and a dispensary.

CHURCH ISLAND, or INNISMORE ISLAND, in the parish of Calry, Upper half-barony of Carbery, county of Sligo, and province of Connaught, 3½ miles (E.) from Sligo; containing, in 1821, 9 inhabitants. It is situated in Lough Gill, and contains 180 acres, the property of Owen Wynne, Esq. St. Lemon founded a church here in the time of St. Columb, the ruins of which still exist at the east end of the island, overgrown with ivy. The abbey was accidentally destroyed by fire in 1416, in which the valuable manuscripts of O'Curnin, together with the short book of that family, and many other rare curiosities, perished. In former ages it was the burial-place of the parishioners.

CHURCH - JERPOINT. — See JERPOINT-CHURCH.

CHURCHTOWN, or BALLINTEMPLE, a parish, in the barony of Imokilly, county of Cork, and province of Munster, 4 miles (S. E.) from Cloyne; containing 1756 inhabitants. This parish, called also Ballygourney, is situated on St. George's channel, and comprises 4730 statute acres, as applotted under the tithe act and valued at £2123. 19. 8. per annum. The greater part of the surface is hilly; the soil generally is light and shallow, resting wholly on a substratum of clay-slate, and the lands are principally under tillage. The village consists of 35 dwellings, most of which are small mud cabins roofed with thatch. Between this parish and that of Kilmahon is a detached portion of the parish of Ballyoughtra, called Snugborough, containing 92 acres, and more than two miles distant from the main body of that parish. The living is a rectory and vicarage, in the diocese of Cloyne, and is part of the union of Lisgoold, and the corps of the precentorship in the cathedral church of St. Colman, Cloyne. The tithes amount to £500. 5. The old parish church has long been in ruins; but a district church for this parish and that of Ballycotton was erected in 1835, at an expense of £330. raised by subscription. The glebe comprises seven acres in two portions. In the R. C. divisions the parish forms part of the union of Cloyne; the chapel is a small neat edifice. The male and female parochial school for this parish and those of Kilmahon and Ballycotton is situated at Ballybraher, and is supported by subscription; and there are two pay schools. There are two coast-guard stations, situated respectively at Ballyandrein and Ballycotton, within the Youghal district.

CHURCHTOWN, or BRUHENNY, a parish, in the barony of Orrery, county of Cork, and province of Munster, 3½ miles (N. by W.) from Buttevant; containing 2795 inhabitants. This parish is situated on the road from Buttevant to Liscarrol, and contains 7029½ statute acres rated to the county cess, and valued at £6334. 16. 11. per annum. The land is generally good, and mostly in pasture; and agriculture is improving. Some bog, limestone, and a reddish-coloured marble are found here. The principal seats are Burton House, originally built by Sir Philip Perceval, destroyed in the war of 1641, rebuilt by the late Earl of Egmont, and now the residence of the Rev. Matthew Purcell; and Churchtown House, the residence of the Rev. F. W. Crofts. The village contains several neat slated houses, a good inn, and a constabulary police station. A court for the manor of Burton, which includes several parishes, is held once in three weeks, in which debts not exceeding 40*s.* late currency are recoverable. The greater part of the parish is the property of the Earl of Egmont, who takes his title from the townland of Egmont, within its limits. The living is a rectory, in the diocese of Cloyne, and in the patronage of the Bishop: the tithes amount to £550. The church is a plain building with a square tower; and the spire, which was thrown down about three years since, has been rebuilt by a grant of £258 from the Ecclesiastical Commissioners. There is no glebe-house, but a glebe of 12 acres. In the R. C. divisions this parish forms part of the union or district of Liscarrol: the chapel is a neat cruciform building, and is about to be improved. There are two private schools, in which are about 80 boys and 30 girls; and the Earl of Egmont intends to build one at Churchtown, capable of accommodating 700 children, which will be placed under the National Board.

CHURCHTOWN, county of DUBLIN.—See TANEY.

CHURCHTOWN, or RHEBAN, a parish, in the barony of WEST NARRAGH and RHEBAN, county of KILDARE, and province of LEINSTER; containing, with part of the post-town of Athy, 2009 inhabitants, of which number, 706 are in the town. This parish is situated on the river Barrow, and on the road from Athy to Monastereven, and contains 7245 statute acres, as applotted under the tithe act. It is the site of the ancient city and castle of Rheban, noticed in Ptolemy's map as one of the principal inland cities, the only remains of which are a deep quadrangular intrenchment, with a high conical mount at its western extremity. A fair was formerly held here on St. Michael's day, but has long since been removed to Athy. It is an impropriate curacy, in the diocese of Dublin, and is one of the nine denominations which constitute the union of Athy or Nicholastown; the rectory is impropriate. The tithes amount to £390, of which £260 is paid to the impropriator, and £130 to the incumbent. In the R. C. divisions also the parish forms part of the union or district of Athy.

CHURCHTOWN, a parish, in the barony of LOWER NAVAN, county of MEATH, and province of LEINSTER, 3 miles (N. N E.) from Trim; containing 448 inhabitants. This parish is situated on the road from Ardbraccan to Trim, and on that from Athboy to Navan, and is separated from Clonmacduff by a small river: the land is principally under tillage, and has a substratum of limestone. The principal seats are Philpotstown, the residence of John T. Young, Esq.; and Churchtown, of Mrs. Kellett. It is in the diocese of Meath, and is one of the six parishes which constitute the union of Ardbraccan; the rectory is impropriate in the representatives of Miss Reynell, of Killynan. The tithes amount to £53. 1. 6½. per ann., of which £43. 6. 11. is payable to the impropriator, and the remainder to the incumbent. In the R. C. divisions the parish is united to those of Clonmacduff, Moymet, Tullyhanogue, Rataine, and Kilcooly, called the union of Dunderry, or of Churchtown and Moymet, in each of which latter places are chapels; that of Churchtown is situated at Dunderry bridge. There is a school at Dunderry, aided by annual donations from the Earl of Fingall and Earl Ludlow. Some small remains of the old church exist, with a burial-ground attached.

CHURCHTOWN, a parish, in the barony of RATHCONRATH, county of WESTMEATH, and province of LEINSTER, 4¾ miles (W. by S.) from Mullingar; containing 980 inhabitants. This parish is situated on the road from Mullingar to Athlone, and on Lough Ennel, by which it is bounded on the south; it comprises 966 statute acres, as applotted under the tithe act. The land is chiefly in pasture; that which is under tillage produces good crops, and the system of agriculture is gradually improving: there is a small portion of bog, and abundance of limestone. The Royal Canal nearly touches the northern extremity of the parish. The living is a rectory, in the diocese of Meath, united by act of council, in 1809, to the rectory of Dysart and the chapelry of Conragh, and in the alternate patronage of the Crown and the Bishop: the tithes amount to £180. 8. 3., and of the whole union to £373. 8. 3. The church is a neat modern building with a square tower, erected in 1811, by aid of a gift of £600 from the late Board of First Fruits; it is nearly in the centre of the union. The glebe-house near it was built in 1814, by aid of a gift of £400 and a loan of £210 from the same Board. There are two glebes, comprising together 24 acres, valued at £2 per acre. In the R. C. divisions the parish is also the head of a union, co-extensive with that of the Established Church; there are chapels at Dysart and Conragh. A school is supported by subscription, aided by the rector, in which are about 30 children. There are some remains of the old church, with a cemetery; and at Teaghboyan are the remains of a monastery, of which St. Baithen was abbot, and probably the founder; no records of it since the year 1229 are extant.

CHURCHTOWN, a district parish, in the barony of FORTH, county of WEXFORD, and province of LEINSTER, 2½ miles (S. W.) from Broadway; containing 1429 inhabitants. It is situated on the Lough of Tacumshane, and was constituted an ecclesiastical district, comprising the parishes of Ballymore and Tacumshane, in 1834. The living is a perpetual curacy, in the diocese of Ferns, and in the patronage of the Chancellor of the diocese for the first three turns, after which the right of presentation will vest in the Bishop. The tithes of five townlands comprising 693 statute acres, amounting to £70. 10. 1½., and a glebe of more than four statute acres were allotted for the support of the curate. The church, a neat building, was finished in 1835, at an expense of £800, granted by the late Board of First Fruits. In the R. C. divisions it is partly in the district of Maglass, and partly in that of Lady's Island, in which respectively are the chapels of Ballymore and Tacumshane. A parochial school has been established under the superintendence of the perpetual curate. The only remains of antiquity are the ruins of the old parish church of Tacumshane.

CLADDAGH, a village, and suburb of the town of GALWAY, in that part of the parish of RAHOON which is within the county of the town of GALWAY, and in the province of CONNAUGHT: the population is returned with the parish. This place is situated on the coast of the bay of Galway, and from that circumstance its name, which in the Irish language signifies "the sea shore," is said to be derived. It is a large and populous village, consisting almost entirely of thatched cottages and inhabited chiefly by fishermen engaged in the extensive fishery carried on in the bay. Though within the jurisdiction of the town of Galway, and separated from it only by the mouth of the river, it forms a kind of colony, remarkable for the primitive peculiarity of its inhabitants, who differ not only in habits and character, but also in dialect from those of Galway. The whole estate is the property of Mr. Whalley, whose ancestor was a colonel in Cromwell's army. The inhabitants pay no direct taxes, nor do they suffer strangers, whom they call "transplanters," to live among them. They seldom marry out of their own village, and generally at a very early age; the parents contriving to give as a dower either a boat or a share in a boat, which is sufficient to secure a maintenance for the families. They depend entirely on the fishery; on returning from sea, the fish is consigned entirely to the women, who dispose of it to hawkers and to those who have standings in the market-place of Galway. About 140 sail boats, each from 12 to 14 tons' burden, and about 50 row boats are engaged in the fishery, which affords employment to nearly 2200 persons, but is carried on without much enterprise, and might under better regulations be very much increased. The fishermen elect from among themselves, annually on St. John's day, officers whom they call a mayor and sheriffs, when they march in procession through the town of Galway, preceded by men carrying bundles of reeds fastened to the ends of poles, to which at night they set fire from numerous bonfires kindled in various parts of the town. To these officers they pay implicit obedience, and in all things submit to their authority; the only official distinction used by the mayor is the white sail of his boat and a flag at the mast head. The time of fishing is indicated by the approach of sea fowl and other unfailing signs; the fleet then assemble, and stand out to sea by signal from the mayor, who also regulates the time for setting the nets, which at first is done simultaneously, after which each boat is allowed to fish at pleasure. The fishermen claim and exercise an exclusive right to fish in the bay, according to their own laws, any infringement of which is punished by the destruction of the nets, or even the boats, of the offending party. For the protection of those who attempted to fish against the regulations of the Claddagh fishermen, a gun-brig was stationed in the bay some few years since, during which time the object was obtained; but on its removal, the fishermen again enforced their authority, and now exercise an uncontrolled power of preventing others from fishing in the bay in opposition to their peculiar regulations. The bay abounds with fish of every kind; but the Claddagh boats are principally engaged in the herring fishery; shell fish of every kind is abundant, and few places are better supplied with oysters. The boats, since the increase of their tonnage, navigate to Limerick, Westport, Sligo, and other places. A very convenient pier has been constructed for the boats belonging to this place, and the Commissioners of Public Works have advanced £300 on loan towards continuing the quay wall. With the exception of two Protestant families that settled among them during the last century, the inhabitants are all Roman Catholics; and their chapel is attached to a Dominican friary nearly in the centre of the village. This friary occupies the site of the ancient convent of St. Mary of the Hill, founded by the O'Hallorans for Premonstratensian nuns, on whose retirement it was granted, in 1488, by Pope Innocent VIII. to the Dominican friary of Athenry. It was richly endowed by various inhabitants, but was dispossessed of its revenues at the dissolution; and in 1642, Lord Forbes, on his landing here, took possession of the house, and converted it into a battery for the reduction of the town of Galway; but failing in that object, he defaced the church and committed other outrages. In 1652 the whole of the buildings were levelled with the ground by the corporation, to prevent their conversion by Cromwell's soldiers into a station for assaulting the town. The present friary was built upon the site, and the chapel was completed in 1800: the latter is a neat edifice, 100 feet in length and 28 feet in breadth; the high altar is richly decorated, and a spacious gallery with a good organ has been erected. The residence of the friars, adjacent to the chapel, commands some beautiful and extensive views, including a pleasing prospect over the bay, terminated by the opposite shores of Oranmore, Renville, and Ardfry, and the Clare mountains, with the new lighthouse and part of the town quay and shipping.

CLADY.—See CLAUDY.

CLAHANE.—See CLOHANE.

CLANDUFF.—See CLONDUFF.

CLANE, a post-town and parish (formerly a market-town), in the barony of CLANE, county of KILDARE, and province of LEINSTER, 4 miles (N. N. W.) from Naas, and 14 miles (W. S. W.) from Dublin; containing 2121 inhabitants, of which number, 1031 are in the town. This place, which gives name to the barony, is of very great antiquity, and appears to have derived its present appellation from *Cluaine*, in the Irish language signifying a "sanctuary," or "sacred retreat." The town most probably owes its origin to the foundation of an abbey in the sixth century, by St. Ailbe, who made St. Senchell the elder its first abbot; and in which a great synod was held in 1162, under Gelasius, Archbishop of Armagh, assisted by 26 bishops and a great number of abbots, when a decree was passed that no person should be admitted Professor of Divinity in any college in Ireland, who had not studied at Armagh. In 1272, a Franciscan convent was founded here by Sir Gerald Fitzmaurice, the third Lord Ophaley. This establishment flourished till the dissolution, and was, with all its appurtenances, assigned, in the 24th of Hen. VIII., to Robert Eustace, John Trevor, and others *in capite*. A castle was built here, but at what time or by whom does not appear; it added greatly to the importance of the town, but has long been in ruins. The town, in which a few houses were burned by the king's troops during the disturbances of 1798, is pleasantly situated on the river Liffey, over which is a bridge of six arches, and in 1831 comprised 225 houses neatly built. The woollen manufacture is carried on to a small extent. The market, from its vicinity to that of Naas, has fallen into disuse; but fairs, chiefly for the sale of cattle, sheep, and pigs, are held on March 28th, April 28th, July 25th, and Oct. 15th. A constabulary police station has been established in the town; and petty sessions are held by the county magistrates every alternate Saturday.

The parish comprises 2380 statute acres, as applotted under the tithe act; the greater portion is under tillage, the soil is fertile, and the system of agriculture improved. There are quarries of good limestone, which are worked with success; and limestone, lime, and sand are sent to Dublin by the Grand Canal, which passes within two miles of the town. The living is a vicarage, in the diocese of Kildare, episcopally united to the vicarages of Mainham and Clonshamboe, and to the rectory of Killybegs, together forming the union of Clane, the patronage of which is disputed by Lord Kingsland: the rectory is impropriate in the representatives of Lord Falconberg. The tithes of the parish amount to £188. 11. 10½. of which £99. 2. 11½. is payable to the impropriators, and £89. 8. 11. to the vicar. The church, an ancient structure, has been lately modernised; it is a neat edifice with a tower and spire, and is kept in repair by a small estate called Economy Lands, now producing about £60 per annum. The glebe-house is a handsome building: the glebe lands for the union comprise 29 acres

In the R. C. divisions this parish is the head of a union or district, comprising also the parishes of Clane, Balrahan, Ballynefagh, Timahoe, and Mainham, and containing three chapels, situated respectively in the three first-named parishes; that of Clane is a plain cruciform building in good repair. The parochial school is maintained by subscription among the Protestant inhabitants; the school-house is a building of stone, erected at an expense of £300. A Roman Catholic free school, formerly supported by the Dublin Patrician Society, is now under the National Board of Education; the school-house was built in 1819, at an expense of £300; and there are two schools supported by subscription. In these schools are about 200 children; and there is also a pay school, in which are 52 children. At Betaghstown is an endowed school, which was suspended for several years, but, in 1824, the Court of Chancery passed a decree for its revival. A dispensary is supported in the usual way. Of the Franciscan convent, founded by Sir Gerald Fitzmaurice, the skeleton of the conventual church is standing; in the body of the church, and serving as the headstone of a modern grave, is the lower half of the effigy of a crusader, probably part of the monument of the founder previously noticed.

About a mile from Clane, but in the parish of Mainham, is Clongowes Wood College, formerly Castle Browne, the seat of Wogan Browne, Esq., by whom it was greatly enlarged and beautified in 1788, and from whose brother and heir, Gen. Browne, it was purchased and opened as a college for the education of the sons of the Catholic nobility and gentry, in 1814. The building, to which large additions have been made for the accommodation of the students, is a spacious quadrangular structure, flanked at the angles by four lofty towers, and is pleasantly situated in the centre of an ample and richly wooded demesne. The principal corridor is more than 300 feet in length; the hall for study is above 80 feet long and 38 feet wide, and is lighted by a double range of windows on each side; the refectory is of the same dimensions, and the apartments of the students are spacious and lofty. The college chapel is 80 feet in length, and is divided into a nave and aisles by two ranges of Ionic columns; it has a fine organ, and the tabernacle on the high altar is wholly of marble and agate. The college contains an extensive library and museum, with a theatre for lectures in natural philosophy and experiments in chymistry, for public exercises in declamation, and musical concerts of the pupils. The institution is under the direction of a president, a minister or dean of the college, a procurator or bursar, and a prefect or general director of studies; there are six professors in the classical department, a professor of mathematics, and a professor of natural philosophy and chymistry. There are also three prefects, whose duty is to superintend the conduct of the pupils during the hours of study and recreation.

CLARA, a market and post-town, and ecclesiastical district in the barony of KILCOURSEY, KING'S county, and province of LEINSTER, 6 miles (N. N. W.) from Tullamore, and 48½ miles (W. by S.) from Dublin; containing 7743 inhabitants, of which number, 1149 are in the town. This place is situated on the river Brosna, near the Grand Canal, and on the road from Tullamore to Athlone. The town contains 228 houses, most of which are neatly built, and the inhabitants are amply supplied with timber, fuel, and water. It had formerly a considerable trade, and an extensive market for grain; not less than eleven distilleries were conducted with success; but since the completion of the canal it has been deprived of most of its trade. The weaving of cotton and linen employs about 260 persons; the manufacture of tobacco, soap, and candles, is carried on; there are a brewery, a tanyard, and four corn and flour-mills, the produce of two being exclusively for the English market; also an extensive bleach-green. The market is on Wednesday, and is amply supplied with grain; and fairs are held on Jan. 6th, Feb. 1st, March 25th, May 12th, June 29th, July 25th, Sept. 26th and 27th, and Nov. 1st, for cattle, horses, sheep, and pigs. It is a constabulary police station; and petty sessions are held every Wednesday. The gentlemen's seats are Clara House, the residence of Edw. Cox, Esq., proprietor of the town; Woodfield, of A. Fuller, Esq.; and Kilclare, of John Armstrong, Esq.

The district, which forms part of the union of Ardnorcher, comprises the parishes of Kilmanaghan and Kilbride-Langan, forming the perpetual curacy of Clara, in the diocese of Meath, and in the patronage of the Incumbent of Ardnorcher. The church, a handsome edifice, was built about 60 years since; the Ecclesiastical Commissioners lately granted £212 for its repair. The glebe-house was built in 1812, by aid of a gift of £450 and a loan of £50 from the late Board of First Fruits. The income of the perpetual curate is £92. 6. 11. per annum, arising from 10 acres of glebe, a stipend of £55. 7. 8½. per annum paid by the incumbent of Ardnorcher, and £18 per annum from Primate Boulter's augmentation fund. In the R. C. divisions the district forms part of the unions of Kilmanaghan and Clara; the latter also comprising the parishes of Ardnorcher and Kilbride-Langan, and containing two chapels, one at Horseleap, and the other at Clara, where preparations are in progress for erecting, in a handsome style, St. Bridget's Abbey, as a new R. C. church, on an eminence overhanging the town. There are places of worship for Primitive and Wesleyan Methodists, and one for Baptists; also a dispensary. About two miles north from Clara is the extensive bog of Kilmaleady, which in 1821 burst its bounds and flowed for nearly a mile and a half down an adjoining valley. Its further progress was arrested by judicious measures, but not till after it had covered about 150 acres, of which from 60 to 80 were buried under a superincumbent stratum of bog from six to ten feet in depth.

CLARA, county of MAYO.—See CLARE-ISLAND.

CLARAH, or CLARA, a parish, in the barony of GOWRAN, county of KILKENNY, and province of LEINSTER, 3¼ miles (E. by N.) from Kilkenny; containing 657 inhabitants. This parish is situated on the mail coach road from Dublin to Kilkenny, and contains 3165 statute acres. The principal seats are Clifden, the property of Viscount Clifden (to whom it gives title), but occupied by R. Blanchfield, Esq.; Kilmagan, the residence of James Butler, Esq.; and Clara Castle, of A. Byron, Esq. The living is a vicarage, in the diocese of Ossory, and is part of the union of St. John's; the rectory is impropriate in the corporation of Kilkenny. The tithes amount to £270, of which £180 is payable to the impropriators, and £90 to the vicar. The parochial church is in ruins: there is a glebe of 15 acres. In the R. C. divisions the parish forms part of the union or district of Gowran, and has a neat chapel. There are two private schools, in which are 100 boys and 40 girls.

CLARAN-BRIDGE, a village, in the parish of STRADBALLY, barony of DUNKELLIN, county of GALWAY, and province of CONNAUGHT, 3½ miles (S.) from Oranmore, on the mail coach road from Galway to Gort; containing, in 1836, 450 inhabitants. A patent was granted in 1820 for a market, which is held on Tuesday, principally for oats and wheat. Fairs, chiefly for pigs and horses, are held on the first Thursday after the 11th of Feb. May, Aug., and Nov. The inlet of Ballinacourty runs up to the bridge at this place, and great benefit would result from the erection of a small pier, considerable quantities of sea-weed being landed here for manure, and peat for fuel. The village is the property of T. N. Redington, Esq., whose mansion of Kilcornan, in the vicinity, is about to be partially rebuilt, with additions. In the demesne are the ruins of an ancient castle, stated to have been the residence of Norah Burke, a cruel chieftainess of the Clanricarde family. Near it is Kilcolgan Castle, the seat of M. St. George, Esq. At the eastern entrance to the village are the R. C. chapel and the monastery of St. Patrick, built by the present proprietor's grandfather and father, who endowed the monastery with seven acres of land, on condition that the monks should gratuitously educate the poor children on the Kilcornan estate. The late C. Redington, Esq., also gave the site, and his widow is about to erect a house for the Sisters of Charity, at the northern entrance to the village.—See STRADBALLY.

CLARE, an ancient village, in the parish of BALLYMORE, barony of LOWER ORIOR, county of ARMAGH, and province of ULSTER, 2 miles (W. S. W.) from Tanderagee; the population is returned with the parish. It originally formed part of the extensive possessions of the O'Nials; after the attainder of Hugh, Earl of Tyrone, it was granted by Jas. I. to Michael Harrison, from whom it passed to Henry Boucher, Esq., who, in 1619, erected a bawn of stone and lime, 100 feet long by 80 wide, and subsequently built a large stone edifice, which was the origin of Clare castle, and located many English and Scottish families here. These settlers soon afterwards erected a meeting-house, which was destroyed, together with the whole village, in the war of 1641. A patent for a weekly market on Tuesday, and a fair on the 12th of May and two following days, was obtained in the reign of Jas. I. The market has not been held for many years, but the fair still exists, and is well supplied with horses, cattle, and pigs. The village is situated on the river Cusher, over which is an ancient stone bridge; and on the river are very extensive flour, meal, and flax-mills. Several important privileges were formerly exercised as belonging to the manor, but the estate having been sold by the Earl of Sandwich, in 1807, no manorial court has since been held. In the village is a meeting-house for Presbyterians in connection with the Synod of Ulster, occupying the site of that destroyed in 1641; and near it is one in connection with the Seceding Synod. There are also male and female schools. In the vicinity are the ruins of Clare castle, standing on an eminence which commands extensive prospects over one of the best cultivated districts in the North of Ireland: the castle is the property of Robt. Harden, Esq., of Harrybrook, who intends to rebuild it in the ancient style.—See BALLYMORE.

CLARE (County of), a maritime county of the province of MUNSTER, bounded on the east and south by Lough Derg and the river Shannon, which successively separate it from the counties of Tipperary, Limerick, and Kerry; on the west by the Atlantic Ocean, and on the north-west by Galway bay; while on the north and north-east an imaginary boundary separates it from the county of Galway. It extends from 52° 30′ to 53° (N. Lat.), and from 8° 15′ to 9° 30′ (W. Lon.); and comprises, according to the Ordnance survey, 802,352 statute acres, of which 524,113 are cultivated land, 259,584 unimproved mountain and bog, and 18,655 are occupied by rivers and lakes. The population, in 1821, was 208,089; and in 1831, 258,262.

The inhabitants of this tract, in the time of Ptolemy, are designated by him *Gangani*, and represented as inhabiting also some of the southern parts of the present county of Galway: in the Irish language their appellation was *Siol Gangain*, and they are stated, both by Camden and Dr. Charles O'Conor, to have been descended from the *Concani* of Spain. The present county formed from a very early period a native principality, designated *Tuath-Mumhan*, or *Thomond*, signifying "North Munster;" and contained the six cantreds of Hy Lochlean, Corcumruadh, Ibh Caisin, Hy Garman, Clan Cuilean, and Dal Gaes. In *Hy Lochlean*, or *Bhurrin*, the present barony of Burren, the O'Loghlins or O'Laghlins were chiefs; in *Corcumruadh*, the modern Corcomroe, the O'Garbhs, although that portion is stated by Ware to have been occupied by the septs of O'Connor and O'Loghlin; in *Ibh Caisin*, the present Ibrickane, the Cumhead-mor O'Briens, this being the hereditary patrimony of the O'Briens or O'Bricheans; in *Hy Garman*, the modern Moyarta, the O'Briens Arta; and in *Clan Cuilean*, the present Clonderlaw, the Mac Namaras; *Dal Gaes* comprised the more extensive districts included in the baronies of Inchiquin, Bunratty, and Tulla, forming the entire eastern half of the present county, and was ruled by the O'Briens, who exercised a supreme authority over the whole, and who preserved their ascendancy here from the date of the earliest records to a late period. Few have more honourably distinguished themselves in the annals of their country than these chiefs and their brave Dalcassian followers, especially in the wars against the Danes, who long oppressed this country with their devastations, and formed permanent stations on the Shannon, at Limerick and Inniscattery. From these and from the entire district they were, however, finally expelled, early in the 11th century, by the well-directed efforts of the great Brien Boroihme, the head of this sept, and monarch of all Ireland, whose residence, and that of his immediate successors, was at Kinkora, near Killaloe. About the year 1290, the Anglo-Norman invaders penetrated into the very heart of Thomond, and in their progress inflicted the most barbarous cruelties, especially upon the family of O'Brien; but they were compelled to make a precipitate retreat on the advance of Cathal, prince of Connaught. De Burgo, in the year 1200, also harrassed this province from Limerick; and William de Braos received from King John extensive grants here, from which, however, he derived but little advantage. Donald O'Brien, amid the storms of war and rapine which laid waste the surrounding parts of Ireland, was solicitous for the security of his own territories, and, as the most effectual method, petitioned for, and obtained from Hen. III., a grant of the kingdom of Thomond, as it was called, to be held of the king during his minority, at a yearly rent of £100, and a fine of 1000 marks. Nevertheless, Edw. I., by letters patent dated Jan. 26th, 1275, granted the whole land of Thomond to Thomas de Clare, son of the Earl of Gloucester, who placed himself at the head of a formidable force to support his claim. The O'Briens protested loudly against the encroachments of this new colony of invaders, and in a contest which speedily ensued, the natives were defeated, and the chief of the O'Briens slain; but with such fury was the war maintained by his two sons, that the new settlers were totally overthrown, with the loss of many of their bravest knights: De Clare and his father-in-law were compelled to surrender, after first taking shelter in the fastnesses of an inaccessible mountain; and the O'Briens were acknowledged sovereigns of Thomond, and acquired various other advantages. De Clare afterwards attempted with some success, to profit by the internal dissensions of the native septs. He died in 1287, at Bunratty, seized, according to the English law, of the province of Thomond, which descended to his son and heir, Gilbert de Clare, and, on the death of the latter without issue, to his brother, Richard de Clare. The O'Briens being subdued by Piers Gaveston, the latter greatly extended his power in this province, where, in 1311, he defeated the Earl of Ulster, who had commenced hostilities against him. Shortly after, the English again received a defeat from the O'Briens, and Richard de Clare, who died in 1317, had no English successor in these territories. Of the settlements made by these leaders, the principal were Bunratty and Clare, long the chief towns of the district; and the English colonists still maintained a separate political existence here; for so late as 1445, we find the O'Briens making war upon those not yet expelled. All of them, however, were eventually put to the sword, driven out, or compelled to adopt the manners of the country; the entire authority reverting to the ancient septs, among whom the Mac Mahons rose into some consideration. In the reign of Hen. VIII., Murchard or Murrough O'Brien was created Earl of Thomond for life, with remainder to his nephew Donogh, whose rights he had usurped, and who was at the same time elevated to the dignity of Baron Ibrakin. Murrough was also created Baron Inchiquin, with remainder to the heirs of his body, and from him the present Marquess of Thomond traces his descent. On the division of Connaught into six counties by Sir Henry Sidney, then lord-deputy, in 1565, Thomond, sometimes called O'Brien's country, was also made shire ground, and called Clare, after its chief town and its ancient Anglo-Norman possessors. In 1599 and 1600, Hugh O'Donell plundered and laid waste the whole county: Teg O'Brien entered into rebellion, but was shortly after slain. In accordance with its natural position, the county, on its first erection, was added to Connaught; but subsequently, in 1602, it was re-annexed to Munster, on petition of the Earl of Thomond.

With the exception of three parishes in the diocese of Limerick, it is included in the dioceses of Killaloe and Kilfenora, the whole of the latter being comprised within its limits: it is wholly in the province of Cashel. For purposes of civil jurisdiction it is divided into the nine baronies of Bunratty, Burren, Clonderlaw, Corcomroe, Ibrickane, Inchiquin, Islands, Moyarta, and Tulla. It contains the borough and market-town of Ennis; the sea-port and market-town of Kilrush; the market and post-towns of Curofin and Ennistymon; the post-towns of Newmarket-on-Fergus, Six-mile-Bridge, Scariff, Killaloe, Kildysert, Miltown-Malbay, Burren, Knock, Broadford, and Bunratty; the town and port of Clare; and the smaller towns of Kilkee and Liscanor, the latter of which has a small harbour. The election of the two members returned by this county to the Imperial parliament takes place at Ennis; the constituency registered under the late act consists of 300 £50 freeholders, 271 £20 freeholders, 1888 £10 freeholders, and 12 £20 and 47 £10 leaseholders; making a total of 2518. The number of electors that polled at the last general election was 686. It never had more than one parliamentary borough, that of Ennis, which sent two members to the Irish parliament, and still sends one to that of the United Kingdom. Clare is included in the Munster circuit: the assizes are held at Ennis, and the quarter sessions at Ennis, Six-mile-Bridge, Kilrush, Ennistymon, and Miltown-Malbay. The county gaol is at Ennis, and there are bridewells at Kilrush, Tulla, Six-mile-Bridge, and Ennistymon. The number of persons charged with criminal offences and committed to the county gaol, in 1835, was 733, and of civil bill commitments, 182. The local government is vested in a lieutenant, 12 deputy-lieutenants, and 102 other magistrates, with the usual county officers, including three coroners. The number of constabulary police stations is 54, having in the whole a force of 8 chief and 62 subordinate constables, and 235 men, with 8 horses, maintained equally by Grand Jury presentments and by Government. The peace preservation police consists of 1 magistrate, 3 chief and 18 subordinate constables, and 82 men, the total expense of whose support amounted, in 1835, to £5340. 0. 2. Parties of the revenue police are stationed at Ennis and Killaloe. At Ennis are situated the county house of industry, and the county infirmary and fever hospital, besides which there are eleven dispensaries, situated respectively at Curofin, Doonass, Ballyvaughan, Six-mile-Bridge, Carrigaholt, Kilrush, Ennistymon, Tomgrany, Kildysert, Newmarket, and Killaloe, all maintained by Grand Jury presentments and voluntary contributions in equal portions. The total amount of Grand Jury presentments, for 1835, was £44,290. 8. 11., of which £4568. 14. 7¼., was for the public roads of the county at large; £11,452. 9. 10. for the public roads, being the baronial charge; £16,291. 18. 5½. for public buildings and charities, officers' salaries, &c.; £6699. 18. 9¼. for police; and £5277. 7. 3. in repayment of loans advanced by Government. In military arrangements this county is included in the south-western district, and contains the three barrack stations of Clare Castle, Killaloe, and Kilrush, affording in the whole accommodation for 19 officers and 325 men; and there are small parties stationed at the respective forts or batteries of Kilkerin, Scattery Island, Dunaha, and Kilcredane, erected during the continental war to protect the trade of Limerick, and each affording barrack accommodation to 16 artillerymen; and also at Aughnish Point and Finvarra Point, on the southern shore of the bay of Galway.

The county possesses every diversity of surface, and great natural advantages, which require only the hand of improvement to heighten into beauty. Of the barony of Tulla, forming its entire eastern part, the northern portion is mountainous and moory, though capable of improvement; and the eastern and southern portions are intersected by a range of lofty hills, and are studded with numerous demesnes in a high state of cultivation; and there is a chain of lakes extending through this and the adjoining barony of Bunratty, which might easily be converted into a direct navigable line of communication between Broadford, Six-mile-Bridge, and the river Shannon. Bunratty barony, which includes the tract between this and the river Fergus, has in the north a large proportion of rocky ground, which is nevertheless tolerably productive, very luxuriant herbage springing up among the rocks, and affording pasturage for large flocks of sheep. The southern portion of this barony, adjoining the rivers Fergus and Shannon, contains some of the richest land in the county, both for tillage and pasturage; the uplands of this district are also of a superior quality. Inchiquin barony, lying to the north-west of Bunratty, has in its eastern part chiefly a level surface, with a calcareous, rocky, and light soil; the western consists for the most part of moory hills, with some valleys of great fertility: the part adjoining the barony of Corcomroe is highly improvable, limestone being every where obtained. The barony of Islands, which joins Inchiquin on the south and Bunratty on the west, is chiefly composed on the western side of low moory mountain, but towards the east, approaching the town of Ennis and the river Fergus, it greatly improves, partaking of the same qualities of soil as Bunratty, and containing a portion of the corcasses. Between this last and the Shannon is the barony of Clonderlaw, very much encumbered with bog and moory mountain, but highly improvable, from the facility of obtaining lime and sea manure. The four remaining baronies stretch along the western coast. That of Moyarta constitutes the long peninsula between the Shannon and the Atlantic, forming the south-western extremity of the county, and terminating at Cape Lean or Loop Head, where there is a lighthouse: this also abounds with bog and moory hills, capable of great improvement. The southern part of Ibrickane, which lies north of Moyarta, is nearly all bog, and the northern is composed of a mixture of improvable moory hills and a clay soil. Corcomroe, the next maritime barony on the north, is of the same character as the last-mentioned lands, having a fertile clay soil on whinstone rock, here called cold stone, to distinguish it from limestone: the land about Kilfenora and Doolan is some of the richest in the county. Burren, forming the most northern extremity of the county, is very rocky, but produces a short sweet herbage excellently adapted for the sheep of middle size and short clothing wool, of which immense numbers are raised upon it, together with some store cattle. Besides the numerous picturesque islands in the Shannon and Fergus rivers, there are various small islets on the coast, in the bay of Galway, and in the great recess extending from Dunbeg to Liscanor, called Malbay, an iron-bound coast rendered exceedingly dangerous by the prevalence of westerly winds: the principal of these is Mutton Island, besides which there are Goat Island and Enniskerry Island, the three forming the group of the latter name. The coast at Moher presents a magnificent range of precipitous cliffs, varying from 600 to nearly 1000 feet in height above the sea at low water, on the summit of which a banqueting-house in the castellated style has been lately erected by Cornelius O'Brien, Esq., for the use of the public. The lakes are very numerous, upwards of 100 having names: the majority are small, though some are of large extent, namely, Lough Graney, Lough O'Grady, Lough Tedane, and Lough Inchiquin; the last is remarkable for its picturesque beauty and for its fine trout. Turloughs, called in other places Loghans, are frequent; they are tracts of water either forced under ground from a higher level, or surface water mostly collected on low grounds, where it has no outlet, and remains until evaporated in summer: there is a very large one at Turloghmore, two near Kilfenora, and more in other places. Although the water usually remains on the surface for several months, yet on its subsiding, a fine grass springs up, that supports great numbers of cattle and sheep.

The climate is cool, humid, and occasionally subject to boisterous winds, but remarkably conducive to health; frost or snow are seldom of long continuance. So powerful are the gales from the Atlantic, that trees upwards of fifty miles from the shore, if not sheltered, incline to the east. On the rocky parts of the coast these gales cause the sea, by its incessant attrition, to gain on the land, but where sand forms the barrier, the land is increasing. The soil of the mountainous district, extending from Doolan southward towards Loop Head, and thence along the Shannon to Kilrush, and even still further in the same direction, together with that of the mountains of Slieveboghta, which separate the county from Galway, is generally composed of moor or bog of different depths, from two inches to many feet, over a ferruginous or aluminous clay or sandstone rock, highly capable of improvement by the application of lime, which may be procured either by land carriage or by the Shannon. A large portion of the level districts is occupied by bogs, particularly in the baronies of Moyarta and Ibrickane, where there is a tract of this character extending from Kilrush towards Dunbeg about five miles in length and of nearly equal breadth. On the boundaries of the calcareous and schistose regions the soils gradually intermingle, and form some of the best land in the county, as at Lemenagh, Shally, Applevale, Riverstown, &c. A piece of ground of remarkable fertility also extends from Kilnoe to Tomgraney, for about a mile in breadth. But the best soil is that of the rich low grounds called corcasses, which extend along the rivers Shannon and Fergus, from a place called Paradise to Limerick, a distance of more than 20 miles, and are computed to contain upwards of 20,000 acres. They are of various breadth, indenting the adjacent country in a great diversity of form. From 18 to 20 crops have been taken successively from them without any application of manure: they are adapted to the fattening of the largest oxen, and furnish vast numbers of cattle to the merchants of Cork and Limerick for exportation. The part called Tradree, or Tradruihe, is proverbially rich. These corcasses are called black or blue, according to the nature of the substratum : the black is most valuable for tillage, as it does not retain the wet so long as the blue, which latter consists of a tenacious clay. The soil in the neighbourhood of Quinn Abbey is a light limestone, and there is a large tract of fine arable country where the parishes of Quinn, Clonlea, and Kilmurry-Negaul unite.

The arable parts of the county produce abundant crops of potatoes, oats, wheat, barley, flax, &c. A large portion of the tillage is executed with the spade, especially on the sides of the mountains and on rocky ground, partly owing to the unevenness of the surface and partly to the poverty of the cultivators. The system of cropping too often adopted is the impoverishing mode of first burning or manuring for potatoes, set two or three years successively; then taking one crop of wheat, and lastly repeated crops of oats, until the soil is completely exhausted: but it is gradually giving place to a better system. Fallowing is practised to some little extent; and many farms are cultivated on an improved system, one important part of which is an alternation of green crops. An improved system of spade husbandry (trenching or Scotch drilling) has been lately introduced, and if generally adopted would be productive of great advantages. Vast quantities of potatoes, usually boiled and sometimes mixed with bran, are used to feed cows and other cattle in winter. Beans were formerly sown to a great extent in the rich lands near the rivers Shannon and Fergus, but this practice has greatly declined. Red clover and rye-grass are the only artificial grasses generally sown. The corcasses yield six tons of hay per Irish acre, and even eight tons are sometimes obtained. Except near the town of Ennis, there is but a very small number of regular dairies, a few farmers and cottagers supplying the neighbouring villages with milk and butter. A considerable quantity of butter is sent to Limerick from Ennis, being chiefly the produce of the pastures near Clare and Barntick; and it is also now made by the small farmers in most parts, and sent to Limerick for exportation to London. The pastures of Clare are of sufficient variety for rearing and fattening stock of every kind. A totally opposite character is presented by the limestone crags of Burren, and the eastern part of the baronies of Corcomroe and Inchiquin, which are, with few exceptions, devoted to the pasturage of young cattle and sheep, though in some places so rugged that four acres would not support one of the latter. Intermixed with these rocks, however, are found lands of a good fattening quality, producing mutton of the finest flavour, arising from the sweetness of the herbage, though to a stranger it might appear that a sheep could scarcely exist upon them; the parishes of Kilmoon and Killeiny contain some of the best fattening land in the county. Large tracts of these mountains are let by the bulk and not by the acre. The other baronies likewise present every variety, from the rich corcass to mountains producing scarcely any thing but heath and carex of various sorts, barely sufficient for keeping young cattle alive. The enclosed pastures are often of very inferior quality, from the ground having been exhausted with corn crops, and never laid down with grass seeds, but allowed to recover its native herbage; a gradual improvement, however, is taking place, but the great defect consists in not properly clearing the ground. In the eastern and western extremities of the county the pasture land usually consists of reclaimed mountain or bog, having a coarse sour herbage, intermixed with carex, and capable of sustaining only a small number of young cattle. The herbage between Poulanishery and Carrigaholt is remarkable for producing good milk and butter; and that of the sand hills opposite Liscanor bay, and along the shore from Miltown to Dunbeg, is also of a peculiar kind: these elevations consist entirely of sands blown in by the westerly winds, and accumulated into immense hills by the growth of various plants, of which the first, and now one of the most common, was perhaps sea reed or mat weed. Besides the home manures, some farmers apply (though not to a sufficient extent) limestone gravel, which is found in different parts; limestone, now used very extensively; marl, of which the bed of the Shannon produces inexhaustible quantities, and by the use of which astonishing improvements have been effected in the neighbourhood of Killaloe; other species of marl of less fertilising powers, dug at Kilnoe, and between Feacle and Lough Graney, in the barony of Tulla; near the coast, sea-sand and seaweed, with which the potatoe ground is plentifully manured, and which is frequently brought up the Fergus by boats to Ennis, and thence into the country, a distance of four miles. Ashes, procured by burning the surface of the land, until lately formed a very large portion of the manure used here, but the use of them is now much condemned, especially for light soils. Great improvements have been made upon the old rude implements of agriculture; the Scotch plough is generally used. In the rocky regions the only fences are, of necessity, stone walls, generally built without mortar: walls ten feet thick, made by clearing the land of stones, are not uncommon in these districts. The cattle are nearly all long-horned, generally well-shaped about the head, and tolerably fine in the limb, good milkers and thrifty. A few of the old native breed are still found, chiefly in mountainous situations: they are usually black or of a rusty brown, have black turned horns and large bodies, and are also good milkers and very hardy. The improved Leicester breed has been introduced to a great extent and of late years the short-horned Durham and Ayrshire cattle have been in request and are becoming general. Oxen are not often used in the labours of husbandry. The short and fine staple of the wool of the native sheep has been much deteriorated by the introduction of the Leicester breed, but the encouragement of the South Down may in a great measure restore it. The breed of swine has been highly improved, the small short-eared pig being now universal. The breed of horses has also undergone great improvement; the horse fair of Spancel Hill is attended by dealers from all parts of Ireland. The chief markets for fat cattle are Cork and Limerick; great numbers of heifers are sent to the fair of Ballinasloe. Formerly there were extensive orchards in this county, especially near Six-mile-Bridge, and a few still remain. Very fine cider is made from apples of various kinds, mixed in the press, and it is in such repute that it is generally bought for the consumption of private families, principally resident.

Few counties present a greater deficiency of wood, yet few afford more favourable situations for the growth of timber where sheltered from the cold winds of the Atlantic: the practice of planting, however, is gaining ground, but the general surface of the county is still comparatively bare. The most valuable timber is that found in the bogs; it consists of fir, oak, and yew, but chiefly the two former: in red bogs, fir is generally found; in black bogs, oak. The fir is frequently of very large dimensions, and most of the farmers' houses near places where it can be procured are roofed with it. The manner of finding these trees is somewhat curious: very early in the morning, before the dew evaporates, a man takes with him to the bog a long, slender, sharp spear, and as the dew never lies on the part over the trees, he can ascertain their situation and length, and thrusting down his spear, can easily discover whether they are sound or decayed: if sound, he marks with a spade the spot where they lie, and at his leisure proceeds to extricate them from their bed. Along the coast of Malbay, where not even a furze bush will now grow, large bog trees are frequently found. The extensive boggy wastes are susceptible of great improvement: the only part not containing large tracts of this kind is the barony of Burren, the inhabitants of the maritime parts of which bring turf in boats from the opposite coast of Connemara. On the other hand, a considerable quantity of turf is carried from Poulanishery to Limerick bay, a water carriage of upwards of forty miles, for the supply of which trade immense ricks are always ready on the shore; and sometimes the boats return laden with limestone from Askeaton and Aughnish. Although large tracts formerly waste, including all the corcasses, have been gained from the Fergus and the Shannon, yet a large portion of the marshes on their banks still remains subject to the overflow of these rivers. The fuel chiefly used is turf, but a considerable quantity of coal is now consumed by respectable families.

The principal minerals are lead, iron, manganese, coal, slate, limestone, and various kinds of building stone. Very rich lead-ore has been found near Glendree, near Tulla, at Lemenagh, and at Glenvaan in the barony of Burren; a vein of lead was discovered, in 1834, at Ballylicky, near Quinn, the ore of which is of superior quality and very productive; it is shipped at Clare for Wales. There are strong indications of iron in many parts, especially near the western coast; but it cannot be rendered available until a sufficient vein of coal shall have been found in its vicinity. Manganese occurs at Kilcredane Point near Carrigaholt Castle, near Newhall, on the edge of a bog near Ennistymon, and at the spa well of Fierd, on the sea shore near Cross, where it is formed by the water on the rocks. Coal has been found in many places, particularly near the coast of the Atlantic, but few efforts have been made to pursue the search with a view to work it. The best slates are those of Broadford and Killaloe, of which the former have long been celebrated, though the latter are superior, and both are nearly equal to the finest Welsh slates; the Killaloe quarry is worked to a greater depth than those of Broadford. Near Ennistymon are raised thin flags, used for many miles around for covering houses, but requiring strong timbers to support them. The Ballagh slates are however preferred for roofing, as being thinner than most of the same kind. There is another quarry of nearly the same sort near Kilrush, one near Glenomera, and others in the western part of the county. At Money Point, on the Shannon, a few miles from Kilrush, are raised very fine flags, which are easily quarried in large masses. Limestone occupies all the central and northern parts of the county, in a vast tract bounded on the south by the Shannon, on the east by a line running parallel with the Ougarnee river to Scariff bay, on the north by the mountains in the north of Tulla and the confines of Galway, and on the west by Galway bay and a line including Kilfenora, Curofin, and Ennis, and meeting the Shannon at the mouth of the Fergus. The limestone rises above the surface in Burren and in the eastern parts of Corcomroe and Inchiquin, and in some places presents a smooth and unbroken plane of several square yards; the calcareous hills extending in a chain from Curofin present a very curious aspect, being generally isolated, flat on the summit, and descending to the intervening valleys by successive ledges. Detached limestone rocks of considerable magnitude frequently occur in the grit soils; and large blocks have been discovered in Liscanor bay, seven or eight miles from the limestone district: in a bank near the harbour of Liscanor, water-worn pebbles of limestone are found and burned. At Craggleith, near Ennis, a fine black marble, susceptible of a very high polish, is procured. The shores of Lough Graney, in the north-eastern extremity of the county, produce a sand chiefly composed of crystals, which is sought for by the country people for upwards of 20 miles around, and is used for scythe boards, which are much superior to those brought from England: sand of similar quality is likewise procured from Lough Coutra, in the same mountains. Copper pyrites occur in several parts of Burren. An unsuccessful attempt to raise copper ore was made at Glenvaan. In the time of James I., as appears from a manuscript in the Harleian collection, there was a silver mine adjacent to O'Loughlin's castle in Burren; and an old interpolator of Nennius mentions that precious metals abounded here. Antimony, valuable ochres, clays for potteries, and beautiful fluor spar, have likewise been discovered in small quantities.

Linen, generally of coarse quality, is manufactured by the inhabitants in their own dwellings, but entirely for home consumption. A small quantity of coarse diaper for towels is also made, and generally sold at the fairs and markets, as is also canvas for sacks and bags; but this trade is now very limited. Frieze is made, chiefly for home use; and at Curofin and Ennistymon, coarse woollen stockings, the manufacture of the adjacent country, are sold every market day, but the trade has considerably declined; they are not so fine as the stockings made in Connemara, but are much stronger. The only mills besides those for corn are a few tuck-mills scattered over the country. The river Ougarnee, from its copiousness and rapidity, is well adapted for supplying manufactories of any extent, and runs through a populous country. Though the numerous bays and creeks on the Shannon, from Loop Head to Kilrush, are excellently adapted for the fitting out and harbourage of fishing boats, yet the business is pursued with little spirit. The boats that are used are not considered safe to be rowed within five miles of the mouth of the Shannon, and from their small size, the fish caught is not more than sufficient for supplying the markets of Limerick, Kilrush, and Miltown, and the southern and western parts of the county; the northern and eastern being chiefly supplied from Galway. In the herring season from 100 to 200 boats are fitted out in this river for the fishery, which, however, is very uncertain. It is thought that a productive turbot fishery might be carried on in the mouth of the river, but there are no vessels or tackling adapted for it: the boats are chiefly such as have been used from the remotest ages, being made of wicker-work, and formerly covered with horse or cow hides, but latterly with canvas; they are generally about 30 feet long, and only three broad, and are well adapted to encounter the surf, above which they rise on every wave. Kilrush has some larger boats. In Liscanor bay a considerable quantity of small turbot is sometimes caught. Fine mullet and bass are sometimes caught at the mouths of the rivers, and many kinds of flat fish, together with mackarel and whiting, are taken in abundance in their respective seasons. Oysters are procured on many parts of the coast; those taken at Pouldoody, on the coast of Burren, have long been in high repute for their fine flavour. The bed is of small extent, and the property of a private gentleman, and they are not publicly sold. Near Pouldoody is the great Burren oyster bed, called the Red Bank, where a large establishment is maintained, and from which a constant supply is furnished for the Dublin and other large markets. Oysters are also taken at Scattery island and on the shores of the Shannon, particularly at Querin and Poulanishery, where the beds are small but the oysters good, and almost the whole of their produce is sent to Limerick. Crabs and lobsters are caught in abundance on the shores of the bay of Galway, in every creek from Black-head to Ardfry; and are procured in smaller quantities on the coast of the Atlantic, from Black-head to Loop-head. The salmon fishery of the Shannon is very considerable, and a few are taken in every river. Eels are abundant, and weirs for taking them are extremely numerous. The commerce of the county consists entirely in the exportation of agricultural produce, and the importation of various foreign articles for home consumption: of this trade Limerick is the centre, although Kilrush likewise participates in it. The only harbours between the mouth of the Shannon and Galway bay, an extent of upwards of 40 miles, are Dunmore, which is rendered dangerous by the rocks at its entrance, and Liscanor, which is capable of properly sheltering only fishing-boats. The fine river Fergus is made but little available for the purposes of commerce, the trade with Limerick being chiefly by an expensive land carriage. The only corn markets are those of Ennis, Clare, and Kilrush, which are very abundantly supplied, and much grain is purchased at them for the Limerick exporters; corn is also shipped for Galway at Ballyvaughan and New Quay, on the north coast.

The most important river is the Shannon, which first touches the county on its eastern confines as part of Lough Derg, and thence sweeps round by Killaloe (where it forms the celebrated falls) to Limerick, from which city to the sea, a distance of 60 miles, it forms a magnificent estuary, nine miles wide at its mouth, where it opens into the Atlantic, and is diversified by many picturesque islands, bays, and promontories. This noble river, which washes no less than 97 British miles of its coast, is the great channel of the trade of the county, and besides its maritime advantages, affords a navigable access to all the central parts of the kingdom and to Dublin: the navigation, however, was incomplete until, through the exertions of the Board of Inland Navigation, the obstacles at Killaloe were avoided by the construction of an artificial line for some distance. The numerous bays and creeks on both its sides render it, in every wind, perfectly safe to the vessels navigating to Limerick, the quays of which place are accessible to ships of 400 tons' burden. Very important projected improvements of the navigation of this noble river, involving an enormous expenditure, are detailed in the account of the city of Limerick. The Fergus, a river of this county exclusively, has its source in the barony of Corcomroe, and running through the lakes of Inchiquin, Tedane, Dromore, Ballyally, and several others, and receiving the waters of various smaller streams, pursues a southern course to the town of Ennis, where it is augmented by the waters of the Clareen; whence, flowing by Clare, it spreads below the latter place into a wide and beautiful estuary, studded with picturesque islands, and opening into that of the Shannon: from this river it is navigable up to Clare, a distance of eight miles, for vessels of nearly 500 tons' burden, and up to Ennis for small craft. Its banks in many places present a rich muddy strand, capable of being enclosed so as to form an important addition to the corcass lands: it receives many mountain streams, and after heavy rains rises so rapidly, that large tracts of low meadow are occasionally overflowed and the hay destroyed. From Lough Feroig, situated on the top of the mountain of Slieveboghta, in the barony of Tulla, and on the confines of Galway, issues a stream which runs southward into the beautiful Lough Graney, and winding hence eastward collects the superfluous waters of Annalow Lough and Lough O'Grady, and, about two miles below the latter, falls into Scariff bay, a picturesque part of Lough Derg. The fine stream of Ougarnee rises near and flows through Lough Breedy, communicates with Lough Doon, receives the waters of Lough Clonlea, and, after forming of itself a small lake near Mountcashel, pursues its southerly course by Six-mile-Bridge, and falls into the Shannon near Bunratty castle, about nine miles below Limerick; the tide flows nearly to Six-mile-Bridge. The other considerable streams are the Ardsallas, Blackwater, and Clareen, and the Ennistymon river: the smaller streams are almost innumerable, except in the barony of Burren, which is scantily supplied. Except the canal between Limerick and Killaloe, there is no artificial line of navigation, although it has been proposed to construct a canal from Poulanishery harbour, about twelve miles from Loop-head, across the peninsula to Dunbeg, and another from the Shannon, at Scariff bay, through Lough Graney, to Galway bay. The roads are numerous and generally in good repair: the principal have been much improved within the last few years, and many hills have been lowered. Soon after the famine and distress of 1822, a new road was made near the coast between Liscanor, Miltown-Malbay, and Kilrush, and another between the last-named place and Ennis. The roads recently completed or now in progress, in aid of which grants have been made by the Board of Public Works, are, a direct road leading from the newly erected Wellesley bridge at Limerick to Cratloe, partly at the expense of the Marquess of Lansdowne; a road from Knockbreda to the boundary of the county towards

Loughrea, extending along the eastern side of Lough Graney, and proposed to be continued to Kiltannan, towards Tulla and Ennis; and a road along the shore of Lough Derg, between Killaloe and Scariff. A road has also been lately made, at the expense of the county, from Scariff bay along the northern side of Lough O'Grady and the western side of Lough Graney, to the boundary of the county towards Gort, with a branch to the south towards O'Callaghan's mills. The bridges are generally good: a handsome new bridge has been lately built, under the superintendence of the Board of Public Works, over the Fergus at Ennis, and another of large dimensions and elegant structure is now in progress over the Inagh near Liscanor.

The remains of antiquity are numerous and diversified. There are cromlechs at Ballygannor, Lemenagh, Kilnaboy, Tullynaglashin, Mount Callan and Ballykishen: near the last-named are two smaller, and the remains of a cairn. Raths abound in every part, and many have been planted with fir trees. One occupies the spot near Killaloe, where formerly stood King Brien Boroihme's palace, or castle, called Kinkora. Pillar stones occur only in a few places: some may be seen on the road between Spancel Hill and Tulla. Of the ancient round towers, this county contains five, *viz.*, those of Scattery Island, Drumcleeve, Dysert, Kilnaboy, and Inniscalthra, in Lough Derg. Near the cathedral of Killaloe is the oratory of St. Moluah, supposed to be one of the most ancient buildings in Ireland. Thirty religious houses were founded in this county, but at present there are remains only of those of Corcomroe, Ennis, Quinn, Inniscalthra, and Inniscattery. At Kilfenora several ancient crosses of great curiosity are to be seen; a very remarkable one is fixed in a rock near the church of Kilnaboy; and near the church and round tower of Dysert a very curious one lies on the ground. The castles still existing entire or in ruins amount in number to 120, of which the family of Mac Namara, it is traditionally said, built 57. There are 25 in the barony of Bunratty, of which those of Bunratty and Knopoge are inhabited; 13 in Burren, of which those of Castletown and Glaninagh are inhabited, and Newtown castle is a round fortress on a square base; 8 in Clonderlaw, of which that of Donogrogue is inhabited; 14 in Corcomroe, of which that of Smithstown is inhabited; 6 in Ibrickane; 22 in Inchiquin, of which those of Mahre and Dysert are inhabited: 3 in Islands; 4 in Moyarta, of which that of Carrigaholt is inhabited; and 25 in Tulla. Many of them are insignificant places, built by the proprietors in times of lawless turbulence; others, small castellated houses erected by English settlers. Bunratty castle, however, is of considerable extent, and was once considered a place of great strength. The modern seats are described under the heads of the parishes in which they are respectively situated. The better class of farmers and graziers have generally comfortable dwelling-houses and convenient offices, with roofs of slate or flags. The poorer classes are usually badly lodged in houses built of stone without mortar, the walls of which are consequently pervious to the wind and rain. The cottages are always thatched, either with straw, sedges, rushes, heath, or potatoe stalks: a want of cleanliness is universally prevalent. Few cottages are without sallow trees, for kishes or baskets, which many of the labourers know how to make; and almost all have small potatoe gardens. The Irish yet spoken in the remote parts of the county is chiefly a jargon of Irish with English intermixed, and is rapidly falling into disuse. Hurling matches are a favourite sport of the peasantry, and chairs, or meetings of both sexes at night in some public-house, constitute another source of amusement. Mineral waters are found in many places, and are chiefly chalybeate: that at Lisdounvarna has long been celebrated for its efficacy in visceral complaints; at Scool and Kilkishen are others well known; and two more are situated near Cloneen, about a mile north-west of Lemenagh Castle, and at Cassino, near Miltown-Malbay. Many holy wells, remarkable naturally only for the purity of their waters, exist in different parts, but are little regarded, except by the peasantry. The great falls in the Shannon, near Killaloe, are worthy of especial notice. The title of Earl of Thomond, derived from this county, was raised to a Marquesate in 1800, in favour of the family of O'Brien, which also derives from the extensive territory of Inchiquin the titles of Earl and Baron, and from the district of Burren also that of Baron. The title of Earl of Clare is borne by the family of Fitzgibbon.

CLARE, a town, in the parish of Clare-Abbey, barony of Islands, county of Clare, and province of Munster, 2 miles (S.) from Ennis; containing 1021 inhabitants. It is situated on the river Fergus, about 12 miles from its confluence with the Shannon, is of great antiquity, and was formerly the capital of the county. In 1278 a great battle was fought here between Donell O'Brien and Mahon O'Brien, in which the latter was defeated. According to the annals of the Mac Brodies, the castle was built by Donogh O'Brien, surnamed Cairbreach, King of Thomond, and in 1641 was surprised and burnt by Murrough O'Brien, who took possession of the lands. Although the town contains some good slated houses, the greater number are thatched, and on the commons to the west, poor cottiers from various parts have located themselves and erected wretched cabins, which gives to this suburb an air of extreme poverty. On the site of the castle are cavalry barracks, affording accommodation for 17 officers and 234 men; and, from its central situation, the town is well adapted for a military depôt. Fairs are held on May 21st, Aug. 17th, and Nov. 11th. A great quantity of salmon is taken in the Fergus, and occasionally sold at the low price of 3*d.* per lb. The parochial church, a Roman Catholic chapel, the parochial school, and a dispensary, are in the town. This is one of the principal ports of the county for the export of grain, by means of the Fergus. The entrance to the river lies between Rinana Point, on the east, and Innismurry on the west, and is about 5 miles wide, but the ship channel does not exceed three-fourths of a mile in width, and is not adapted for vessels drawing more than 16 feet of water. The quay, although only 80 feet long, and therefore accommodating but one vessel at a time, is yet of considerable service, as before its erection in 1815 there were no means of shipping or discharging a cargo, and vessels of any kind very rarely visited the town. At present, one or two come every month, bringing coal and taking back grain to Liverpool, where, in 1831, it was sold at a higher rate than any other grain in the market. About 600 feet above the quay there is a bridge, the abutments of which rest on a solid bed of rock, forming an obstruction that separates the Upper from the Lower Fergus; this bridge leads to an island, on which stand the remains of the castle. A second and smaller bridge, leading to the mail coach road to Limerick, crosses the arm of the river that runs round Castle Island. The main branch of the river, from the bridge to the quay, is about 250 feet wide. From Clare to Ennis by the Upper Fergus is three miles: this is a fine piece of water, about 150 feet wide, wearing much the appearance of a large canal. It sometimes overflows its banks, and greatly fertilises the adjacent country. To form a communication between the Upper and Lower Fergus, it is proposed to place a dam and lock at the falls, about a furlong above the bridge, and to deepen the bed of the river between those places from three to six feet, and between the quay and the bridge about four feet.

CLARE, or CLARA, an island, in the parish of KILGAVOWER, barony of MURRISK, county of MAYO, and province of CONNAUGHT, 15 miles (W.) from Westport; containing 1616 inhabitants. It is situated in the middle of the entrance of Clew bay, off the western coast, and is the property of Sir Samuel O'Malley, Bart., a descendant of that ancient sept, of which name there were 67 families resident in 1821. A cell of Carmelite friars was founded here in 1224, under the Invocation of the Blessed Virgin, which was afterwards annexed to the abbey of Knockmoy, in the county of Galway. Grace O'Malley, better known by the name of *Graa Uile*, and whose exploits in the 16th century are traditionally preserved in the island, made this place her strong hold, built a castle here, and had all her large vessels moored in the bay. This extraordinary woman was the daughter of Owen O'Malley, and widow of O'Flahertie, two chiefs in this part of Connaught. After the death of O'Flahertie, she married Sir Richard Bourke, called Mac William Oughter, who died in 1585. She was high spirited, bold, and adventurous, and at an early age became fond of a maritime life; she was ever foremost in danger, and her fame for intrepidity was such that Lord-Deputy Sydney, writing to the English council in 1576, observes, "O'Malley is powerful in galleys and seamen." The island is about four miles in length, and comprises about 3000 acres of cultivable and mountain land, which is undivided and held by the inhabitants in common; the agriculture is improving, and large quantities of grain are shipped here for Westport; the soil is fertile, but the crops are sometimes seriously injured by storms. In the R. C. divisions the islands of Clare and Innisturk form a parish, in which are places of worship, but no regular chapel; the inhabitants are all Roman Catholics. There are some remains of the old castle and of a telegraph; the highest point of land is 1520 feet above the level of the sea. About 340 persons, who are also farmers, are occasionally employed in the fishery; and a pier has been constructed, which is also used for the landing of sea manure. On the north-east point of the island a lighthouse was erected in 1818, by the corporation for improving the port of Dublin; it is situated in lat. 53° 49′ 30″ (N.), and lon. 9° 55′ 30″ (W.), and shews a steady bright light from 21 lamps, at an elevation of 487 feet above the level of the sea, which may be seen at a distance of 29 nautical miles in clear weather. Clew bay is from 10 to 12 miles in length and about 6 miles in breadth; about one-third of the breadth at the entrance is occupied by Clare Island, and in the upper part are numerous small islands, which, with the adjoining creeks and inlets of the mainland, form a variety of safe roadsteads and harbours for vessels of every class. The islands and channels on the Westport side of the bay are protected from the sea by a very singular breakwater of shingle and boulder stones, running with little interruption from the entrance of Newport harbour, at Innishugh island, to the southern shore, under Croaghpatrick mountain. Within this line of beach are six navigable openings, of which the most important is Beulascrona, nearly in the centre, forming the ordinary channel up to Westport, and marked by a small lighthouse on the northern beach.

CLARE, or CLAREMORRIS, a market and post-town, in the parish of KILCOLEMAN, barony of CLANMORRIS, county of MAYO, and province of CONNAUGHT, 14 miles (S. E. by S.) from Castlebar, and 117½ (W. by N.) from Dublin; containing 1476 inhabitants. It is situated on the road from Ballinrobe to Castlerea, and consists of one long street, containing about 300 houses, principally slated. The market is on Wednesday; and fairs are held on May 24th, June 22nd, Aug. 17th, Sept. 27th, and Nov. 23rd. It is a chief station of the constabulary and revenue police, the latter having subordinate stations at Castlebar, Newport-Pratt, and Oughterard. Quarter sessions are held twice in the year at the court-house, which is a large building, about a quarter of a mile from the town, and petty sessions every Wednesday. The parochial church, a handsome building of ancient English architecture, with a light steeple, was erected by aid of a gift, in 1828, of £831, and a loan of £923 from the Ecclesiastical Commissioners. The R. C. chapel, a spacious slated building is in the town, and there is a place of worship for Wesleyan Methodists. About two miles from the town are the ruins of the castle of Marneen.—See KILCOLEMAN.

CLARE-ABBEY, a parish, in the barony of ISLANDS, county of CLARE, and province of MUNSTER, 2 miles (S.) from Ennis; containing, with the town and commons of Clare, 3881 inhabitants. This parish is situated on the river Fergus, and on the road from Ennis to Limerick, and was the seat of a richly endowed abbey, founded in 1195, for Augustinian friars, by Donald O'Brien, King of Limerick. At the suppression, in 1543, it was granted to the Barons of Ibrackan by Hen. VIII., and in 1620 was given in fee to Donough, Earl of Thomond, which grant was confirmed, in 1661, to Henry, Earl of Thomond. The parish contains 6694 statute acres; there are about 200 acres of bog, and the rest is principally in pasture; sea-weed is procured for manure on the shores of the Fergus, and limestone exists in abundance. Two fairs are held annually at Clare; and a seneschal's court for the recovery of small debts is held there monthly for the manor of Clonroad. The principal seats are Buncraggy, finely situated on the banks of the Fergus, and surrounded by a richly wooded demesne, the property of the Marquess of Conyngham, but now occupied by J. James, Esq.; Carnelly, the seat of the representatives of the late Col. Stamer; and Barntick, of D. Roche, Esq. The living is an impropriate cure, in the diocese of Killaloe, and in the patronage of the Bishop; the rectory is impropriate in the Earl of Egremont, the representatives of Giles Daxon, Esq., and the Rev. F. Blood. Of the 6694 acres, the tithes of 1153, amounting to £35. 1. 6., are paid to the incumbent alone; of 1005, amounting to £27. 13. 10., to the impropriators alone; and of 1904, amounting to £54. 9. 9., in equal shares to the incumbent and impropriators: the remaining 2632 acres being unprofitable land, pay no tithes. The church is a neat structure with a square tower, erected in 1813, by aid of a gift of £800 from the late Board of First Fruits, and repaired recently by a grant of £162. 4. 7. from the Ecclesiastical Commissioners. The glebe-house was built in 1822, by aid of a gift of £450 and a loan of £50 from the former Board. The glebe comprises 15 acres, subject to a rent of 10*s.* per acre, as £450 was paid by the late Board of First Fruits to reduce the rent. In the R. C. divisions this parish is the head of a union or district, called Clare, comprising the parishes of Clare-Abbey and Killone, in each of which is a chapel; that at Clare is a thatched building, which it is intended shortly to re-erect on a larger scale. There is a school under the care of the incumbent, in which are about 50 children; and there are two hedge schools, containing about 80; also a school under the superintendence of the parish priest. The remains of the abbey consist of a tower in tolerable preservation, surmounted by graduated battlements, and the ivy clad walls of the abbey church, which together form a very picturesque object when viewed from a distance.

CLARE-GALWAY, a parish, partly in the barony of CLARE, and partly in that of DUNKELLIN, county of GALWAY, and province of CONNAUGHT, 5 miles (N. E.) from Galway; containing 3588 inhabitants. This parish is situated on the river Clare, about four miles from its influx into Lough Corrib, and comprises 10,025 statute acres, as applotted under the tithe act. A monastery for Franciscan friars was founded at Clare-Yndowl about the year 1290, by John de Cogan, who erected the buildings in a very elegant style and at a great expense. During the vacancy of the see of Enachdune, the pontificalia were deposited in this monastery till the appointment of a bishop; but were forcibly carried off, in 1296, by Philip de Blund, archdeacon of Tuam, by order of the Archbishop, who was desirous of annexing the see of Enachdune to that of Tuam. The monastery was further endowed, in 1368, by Thomas, Lord Athenry, and subsisted till the dissolution, when, with other possessions, it was granted to Richard, Earl of Clanricarde. The ruins are highly interesting, and give an adequate idea of the original extent and character of the building. The tower of the church still remains; it is supported on a pointed arch of beautiful symmetry, and, being close to the road from Galway to Tuam, is an object of great attraction to travellers. A portion of the ruins has been converted into a residence for Franciscan friars, and a small chapel has been built adjoining it, forming a strong contrast with the elegant grandeur of the ancient monastery. The river Clare is navigable for boats to Lough Corrib during the winter, and at a moderate expense might be rendered so at all seasons. A penny post to Galway and Tuam has been established. A castle was erected here by one of the family of De Burgo; it was strongly garrisoned by the Earl of Clanricarde on the breaking out of the war of 1641, and in 1643 was seized for the Irish by Capt. Burke, but was retaken by Sir Charles Coote in 1651. The remains, which are in good preservation, prove it to have been a fortress of great strength. The living is a vicarage, in the diocese of Tuam, and in the patronage of the Archbishop; the rectory is appropriate to the Warden of Galway: the tithes amount to £240. There is neither church, glebe house, nor glebe. The R. C. parish is co-extensive with that of the Established Church: the chapel is a small slated building. There are two pay schools, situated respectively at Clare-Galway and Clash, in which are about 80 boys and 50 girls.

CLARE-TUAM.—See BELCLARE.

CLASHACROW, or DE-GLAISHCROE, a parish, in the barony of CRANAGH, county of KILKENNY, and province of LEINSTER, 1¼ mile (S. S. E.) from Freshford; containing 250 inhabitants. This parish is situated on the river Nore, and on the road from Kilkenny to Freshford, and comprises 979 statute acres, as applotted under the tithe act. It is a rectory, in the diocese of Ossory, and forms part of the union of Freshford: the tithes amount to £73. 16. 11. In the R. C. divisions it is also part of the union or district of Freshford.

CLASHMORE, a post-town and parish, in the barony of DECIES-within-DRUM, county of WATERFORD and province of MUNSTER, 12 miles (S. W.) from Dungarvan; containing 3772 inhabitants, of which number, 387 are in the town. Glaismhor abbey was founded here, according to Archdall, by Caunchear, at the command of St. Mochuda of Lismore, who died in the year 655; it subsisted till the general suppression, when its possessions were granted to Sir Walter Raleigh. The town is situated on the mail coach road from Waterford through Youghal to Cork (to each of which a sub-post-office has been lately established), and near the navigable river Blackwater, from which a navigable pill runs up within half a mile of the town, and in its course receives the waters of the Greague rivulet; it is navigable for lighters of 20 tons burden, and might be greatly improved at a trifling expense. Over the river Blackwater is a handsome and very long wooden bridge, which leads towards Youghal. The total number of houses, in 1831, was 50. A distillery is carried on, producing nearly 20,000 gallons of whiskey annually; and there is a large boulting-mill. Fairs are held on Feb. 8th, May 20th, Aug. 20th, and Dec. 16th. A constabulary police force is stationed here; and petty sessions are held every alternate week. The small village of Ballinamultina, in this parish, is about half a mile to the north-east of the town, on the road to Dungarvan, and contains the handsome residence of F. Kennedy, Esq. The parish is bounded on the west by the river Blackwater, and comprises 7068 statute acres, as applotted under the tithe act; the lands near the river are fertile, but towards the east are mountainous and of inferior quality. About one-half of the parish is under tillage, and the remainder in pasture. Clashmore House, the seat of R. Power, Esq., is pleasantly situated in a fine demesne, near the confluence of the Greague stream with the Blackwater; the grounds are embellished with some remarkably fine trees; and near the mansion is a well of excellent water, called St Mochuda's well. The living is a rectory and vicarage, in the diocese of Lismore, partly impropriate in the Duke of Devonshire, and partly constituting the corps of the prebend of Clashmore in the cathedral of Lismore, to which the vicarage, with cure of souls, is united, and in the patronage of the Archbishop of Cashel. The tithes amount to £705. 2. 8., of which £382. 16. 8. is payable to the impropriator, and £322. 6. to the prebendary. The church is a neat modern edifice with a spire. The glebe-house, the residence of the prebendary, is pleasantly situated; the glebe comprises 10 acres, subject to a rent of £3 per acre. In the R. C. divisions this parish is the head of a union or district, including also the parish of Kinsalebeg, in each of which is a chapel; that of Clashmore is a neat and commodious edifice, recently erected. A school-house was built by the Kildare-Place Society, but it is not now used as such. There are two pay schools, in which are about 220 children, and a dispensary.

CLAUDY, a village, in the parish of Upper Cumber, barony of Tirkeran, county of Londonderry, and province of Ulster, 7½ miles (E. N. E.) from Londonderry; containing 180 inhabitants. It is situated on the road from Belfast to Londonderry, to the latter of which it has a penny post. Eight fairs are held for cattle, horses, and pigs; a constabulary police force has been stationed in the village, and petty sessions are held on the first Friday in every month. In the vicinity are some handsome seats and extensive woods and plantations, which are described in the article on the parish; and there are some large bleach-greens, not now in use. In the village are a R. C. chapel, a place of worship for Presbyterians in connection with the Synod of Ulster, and a national school.

CLAUDY, a village, in the parish of Urney, barony of Strabane, county of Tyrone, and province of Ulster, 3 miles (S. S. W.) from Strabane; containing 176 inhabitants. It is situated on the road from Londonderry to Sligo, and on the river Finn, comprising one irregularly built street containing 44 houses, most of which are old. Fairs for the sale of cattle, sheep, and pigs, are held on Aug. 1st and Nov. 16th. Close to the village is a handsome bridge of seven arches over the Finn, connecting Claudy with the county of Donegal. Prior to the erection of this bridge, there was an important ford here, which was contested with great slaughter by the partisans of William and James, in 1688; and at the time of the siege of Londonderry it was a strong post under Col. Skeffington, who was driven from it by the Duke of Berwick, a short time before Jas. II. crossed the Finn at this place.—See Urney.

CLEENISH, a parish, partly in the baronies of Magherastephana and Tyrkennedy, but chiefly in the barony of Clanawley, county of Fermanagh, and province of Ulster; containing, with the post-town of Lisbellaw (*which see*), 10,557 inhabitants. This place derived its name, originally *Cluan Innis*, from an island in Lough Erne, where was a monastery, of which St. Synell was abbot about the middle of the 6th century, and with whom St. Fintan resided for more than 18 years. The parish, which is situated on the shores of Lough Erne, and on the road from Dublin to Enniskillen, comprises, according to the Ordnance survey, 36,531 statute acres (including islands), of which 996¼ are in the barony of Magherastephana, 4898¼ in that of Tyrkennedy, and 30,636½ in the barony of Clanawley: 3804¼ acres are under water, including 1051 in Upper, and 492½ in Lower Lough Mac Mean, 1448½ in Upper Lough Erne, and 811¼ in the river Erne and small loughs. In Upper Lough Erne are several islands, of which those of Bellisle, Killygowan, and several smaller ones, are within the limits of this parish. There is little wood, except on gentlemen's demesnes, and there are several bogs and a large tract of mountain. The land is of good quality, and the system of agriculture is improving; a large portion is in meadow and pasture, and that which is under tillage produces good crops. Limestone and freestone are abundant and are quarried for agricultural and for building purposes; and in the mountainous parts of the parish good flags are obtained. The gentlemen's seats are Fairwood Park, the residence of J. Denham, Esq.; Skea, of G. Hassard, Esq.; Garden Hill, of W. Hassard, Esq.; Bellisle, of the Rev. J. G. Porter; Snow Hill, of J. D. Johnstone, Esq.; Russian, of Capt. Jones; Ballanaleck, of A. Nixon, Esq.; Lisbofin House, of C. Fausset, Esq. Corrard House, the property of Sir A. B. King, Bart.; and Cliniharnon Cottage, the residence of the Rev. J. O'Reilly, commanding fine lake and mountain views. Near it is a holy well, overspread by the branches of a large thorn. Fairs are held at Holywell and Lisbellaw, for cattle and pigs. A manorial court is held on the estate of Gen. Archdall; and petty sessions are held at Shanmullagh and Lisbellaw every fortnight.

The living is a rectory and vicarage, in the diocese of Clogher, and in the patronage of the Provost and Fellows of Trinity College, Dublin: the tithes amount to £568. 15. 4. The church is a neat edifice, built in 1818 by aid of a gift of £900 from the late Board of First Fruits, and is surrounded by plantations. There are also chapels of ease at Lisbellaw and Mullaghdan, both neat buildings, to the latter of which the Ecclesiastical Commissioners have recently made a grant of £134. 9. 11. for repairs. The glebe-house is a good residence, built in 1825; the glebe comprises 840 statute acres. In the R. C. divisions the parish forms part of the union or district of Enniskillen, and is partly a parish of itself; there are four chapels, one of which, at Lisbellaw, belongs to the union of Enniskillen, and the other three to this parish; the latter are situated respectively at Mullaghdan, Mullymeisker, and Holywell, and are all neat edifices; that at Holywell was built in 1829, at an expense of £400. There are two places of worship for Presbyterians of the Seceding Synod, one of the second class at Lisbellaw, and the other at Corrard. There is also at Lisbellaw a place of worship for Wesleyan Methodists. There are two schools aided by subscription, and a national school at Mullymeisker, in which together about 200 boys and 130 girls are instructed. There are also 16 pay schools, in which are about 560 boys and 300 girls, and seven Sunday schools. Several mineral springs exist in different parts of the parish, but they are not used medicinally.

CLEMENTSTOWN, a village, in the parish of Ashfield, barony of Tullaghgarvey, county of Cavan, and province of Ulster, ¾ of a mile (N. N. W.) from Cootehill; containing 182 inhabitants. This place derived its name from its proprietor, Col. Clements: it is situated on the road from Cootehill to Red hills and Belturbet, and contains 44 houses. Here is a good stone bridge of four arches, crossing the Cootehill river from Bellamont forest to Lough Erne.

CLENORE, a parish, in the barony of FERMOY, county of CORK, and province of MUNSTER, 2½ miles (S.) from Doneraile; containing 1303 inhabitants. This parish is situated on the north side of the river Blackwater, and on the road from Mallow to Castletown-Roche, and contains 4163 statute acres, as applotted under the tithe act, about two-thirds of which are arable and the remainder pasture. The land is in general of superior quality, and by the exertions of Pierce Nagle, Esq., irrigation and other improvements in agriculture have been extensively introduced. There is a small quantity of wet bog, and abundance of limestone, which is worked for building and agricultural purposes. Culm exists, and a shaft has been sunk, from which some fine specimens have been obtained. The principal seats are Anakissy, the residence of Pierce Nagle, Esq.; Killura, of Cornelius Linihan, Esq.; and Castle-Kevin, of E. Badham Thornhill, Esq. The ancient castle was the property of the Roches, and the present extensive castellated mansion was rebuilt by Mr. Thornhill after designs by Mr. Flood, in the Elizabethan style. It consists of a regular front flanked by semicircular towers with embattled parapets: at the back is an octangular tower, from which the light is thrown into the grand hall through a window of stained glass, exhibiting the family arms, &c. The entrance is through a porch of hewn limestone, and a skreen of the same material extends along the front of the building.

The living is a rectory and vicarage, in the diocese of Cloyne, united from the earliest period with the rectories of Ahacross and Templemolloghy, part of the rectory of Ballyvourney, and the nominal vicarage of Rogeri Calvi, which only exists in the incumbent's titles and the diocesan records: these parishes constitute the corps of the chancellorship of the cathedral of Cloyne, in the patronage of the Bishop. The tithes of this parish amount to £350, and the entire tithes of the union payable to the incumbent amount to £791. 14. 5. The church is a neat modern edifice with a square tower, built in 1811, near the ruins of one of ancient date, by aid of a gift of £800 from the late Board of First Fruits. There is no glebe-house; but a glebe of about 6½ acres. In the R. C. divisions this parish is one of the three that form the union or district of Monanimy, which has chapels at Kealavullen, in the parish of Monanimy, and at Anakissy, in Mr. Nagle's demesne. There is a private school, in which are about 24 children.

CLERIHAN, a village, in the parish of NEWCHAPEL, barony of IFFA and OFFA EAST, county of TIPPERARY, and province of MUNSTER, 4 miles (N. W.) from Clonmel; containing 230 inhabitants. This place is situated on the road from Clonmel to Cashel, and contains 37 houses; it has a fair on Sept. 30th, and is a constabulary police station. There is a neat R. C. chapel in the village.—See NEWCHAPEL.

CLIFDEN, a sea-port, in the parish of OMEY, barony of BALLYNAHINCH, county of GALWAY, and province of CONNAUGHT, 39½ miles (W. by N.) from Galway, and 144 miles (W.) from Dublin; containing 1257 inhabitants. It is situated on an eminence on the shore of a winding estuary that falls into Ardbear, or Clifden, harbour, on the Connemara or western coast; and is quite of modern origin, as it contained only one house in 1815, when John D'Arcy, Esq., settled here, principally through whose exertions 300 had been erected previously to 1835, including a commodious hotel for the accommodation of visiters; and although Clifden and a large tract of country did not yield 1*s.* of revenue in 1814, it yielded a revenue of £7000 in 1835. In that year also 800 tons of oats were exported to London and Liverpool, when, so recently as 1822, scarcely a stone of oats could be procured. It has a daily post to Galway. A chief constabulary police force is stationed in the town; and it is the residence of the inspecting commander of the Clifden district of coast-guard stations, which comprises Innislaken, Mannin bay, Claggan, and the Killeries. Markets are held in a neat market-house on Wednesday and Saturday; and fairs on June 25th, Sept. 1st, Oct. 15th, and Dec. 17th. This is a quarter sessions town, and petty sessions are held every second Thursday. There is a bridewell, containing three day-rooms and several cells, with keepers' apartments; and a handsome sessions-house is in course of erection. An elegant church and school have been erected, principally at Mr. D'Arcy's expense; and there are a R. C. chapel, national school, dispensary, and fever hospital in the town. At a short distance, on the northern side of the town, is Clifden Castle, the delightful residence of John D'Arcy, Esq., the proprietor of the district, by whom it was erected. It is a castellated house standing on the verge of a fine lawn sloping down to the bay, and sheltered behind by woods and a range of mountain; the view to the right embraces a wide expanse of ocean. The pleasure grounds comprise about fifteen acres, and are adorned with a grotto of considerable extent, through which passes a stream, and with a shell-house or marine temple, composed of shells, spar, ore, &c.; though on the shore of the Atlantic, the trees and shrubs flourish luxuriantly. Two copper mines were worked here for a short period, and some coal has been found in the neighbourhood. Green and white marble are met with near Clifden Castle, of which the former has been worked, but not extensively.

The surrounding country is mountainous: much of it has been brought into cultivation by Mr. D'Arcy. It is generally a boggy soil, from three to four feet deep; sea sand has been principally employed in reclaiming the bog, which produces particularly fine oats, that have borne a higher price in London than any other in the market. In 1822, roads were commenced by Government from Oughterard to Clifden, from Galway to Clifden, and from Clifden to Westport, the completion of which and the formation of new ones in Connemara would prove highly beneficial to the district. There is a quay at Clifden, where vessels of 200 tons burden can lie, and part of the funds for the relief of the distressed Irish were expended in lengthening it. Corn and butter are shipped here for Liverpool, and large quantities of sea manure landed. This quay was commenced by Mr. Nimmo, in 1822, and its completion would be of great benefit, as it is the only place from which corn and fish are exported, and at which salt, iron, pitch, tar, hemp, timber, groceries, and manufactured goods, are imported. There is a great quantity of fish on this coast, and vessels from the Skerries and other places often fish here. At the head of Ardbear harbour is a good salmon fishery, into which falls the mountain stream or river of Owen-Glan. The shores of the bay of Clifden, which is also called Ardbear, are high; the entrance to the harbour would be greatly benefited by the erection of a lighthouse on Caragrone rock. Mackenzie, in his chart of the western coast, lays this down as the safest and best harbour for large vessels: it is a rendezvous for vessels of war on this coast, which can ride in the greatest storms secure from all gales. Stores for salt and other necessaries for the fishery, or for ships in distress, have been erected near the harbour. Within a mile of the town are the remains of a druids' altar; and at Clifden Castle is an excellent chalybeate spring.—See Omey.

CLODY.—See CLOYDAGH.

CLOGH, or CLOUGH, a village, in the parish of Dunaghy, barony of Kilconway, county of Antrim, and province of Ulster, 6 miles (N. W. by N.) from Broughshane; containing 121 inhabitants. This place is situated at the junction of several roads, on the acclivity of a hill near the Ravel water, and comprises 20 houses. It is the head of the manor of Old Stone, and contains the manorial court-house, in which the court was formerly held once in three weeks; but the court leet only is now held there. The court-room is large and of good proportions; adjoining it is a jury-room, and underneath are two rooms for debtors, against whom decrees have been issued out of the manor court: it is maintained by the barony. On a high rock which overlooks the village and surrounding country to a considerable distance formerly stood a castle, of which the principal remains are part of a gateway of great strength. Within it there appears to have been a draw well, and beyond it a fosse, which divides the surface of the rock into two equal parts: the foundations of various buildings may yet be perceived. It is stated by tradition to have belonged originally to the Mac Quillans, until taken from them by the Mac Donnells, the result of a great battle fought on the mountain of Ora or Slievenahera. At an early period a nunnery is also said to have stood on this rock. Fairs are held on Feb. 8th, April 4th, May 27th, Aug. 5th, Nov. 8th, and Dec. 9th, chiefly for the sale of cattle, and a great number of ponies are brought to them from the highlands of Scotland.—See Dunaghy.

CLOGHAN, a village and post-town, in the parish of Gallen, barony of Garrycastle, King's county, and province of Leinster, 4½ miles (N. E.) from Banagher, and 60 (S. W. by W.) from Dublin; containing 460 inhabitants. This place, which is situated on the road from Ferbane to Banagher, and near the river Shannon and the grand canal, contains 84 dwellings, which are chiefly thatched and neatly whitewashed cottages. Fairs are held on Jan. 1st, May 16th, and Oct. 29th; and a constabulary police force is stationed in the village. Numerous ruined castles of the O'Coghlan sept are scattered over the surrounding country, of which the most remarkable is that of Streamstown, near Castle-Iver, where are also some boulting-mills; and about a mile from the village was the ancient manorial mansion of the family.—See Gallen.

CLOGHANE, or CLAHANE, a parish, in the barony of Corkaguiney, county of Kerry, and province of Munster, 6 miles (N. N. E.) from Dingle; containing 2772 inhabitants, of which number, 222 are in the village. This place is situated on St. Brandon's bay on the western coast; and the parish is divided by part of the Connor range of hills into the northern and southern portions. In the former is St. Brandon's Hill, a mountain of considerable elevation, near the summit of which are the remains of an oratory or chapel, dedicated to St. Brandon, and a remarkably fine spring of water. This mountain, of which, from its proximity to the sea, the summit is rarely seen unclouded, is terminated on the north by the promontory of Brandon Head, 8½ nautical miles (E. ¾ N.) from Smerwick, between which and Magharee Head, on the east, is Brandon bay. This bay, from the number of sunken rocks and the frequent squalls from the mountains, is extremely dangerous; and vessels can only anchor in safety on the western side, and there only in fair weather. A small pier was erected by the late Fishery Board. The fishery is chiefly carried on in yawls and canoes; it affords employment during the season to 250 persons, who at other times are engaged in agriculture. A considerable quantity of sea manure is landed at the pier; great quantities of butter are sent hence in hookers to Limerick; and there is a flour-mill and also a tucking-mill in the parish, both worked by water. At Ballyguin is a coast-guard station, being one of those which constitute the district of Dingle. The village, which is near the shore of the bay, contains 43 houses, mostly thatched; and in it are situated the parochial church, a R. C. chapel, and a school.

The parish, including a detached portion called Lateeves, a very fertile tract of 889 acres, locally in the parish of Kilmelchedor, comprises 27,740 statute acres, as applotted under the tithe act, of which a large tract consists of mountain and bog; a small portion of the land is under tillage, producing excellent and early crops; the chief manure is sea-weed, which is obtained in great abundance. The principal seats are Brandon Lodge, the residence of Mrs. Hussey; Fermoyle, of J. Hillyard, Esq.; and Keelmore, of P. B. Hussey, Esq. The living is a rectory and vicarage, in the diocese of Ardfert and Aghadoe, and in the patronage of the Bishop: the tithes amount to £184. 12. 3¾. The church, a neat edifice with a square tower, situated in the village of Cloghane, was erected in 1828, by aid of a gift of £830 from the late Board of First Fruits. There is neither glebe-house nor glebe. In the R. C. divisions the north portion of the parish forms part of the union or district of Killeiny, or Castle-Gregory; the south portion, with the exception of Lateeves, is included in the district of Dingle; and the detached portion of Lateeves forms part of the district of Kilmelchedor. The chapel in the village, a commodious slated building, erected in 1824, is dependent on that of Killeiny, or Castle-Gregory. The parochial school at Ballyguin is chiefly supported by an annual donation from the incumbent; and a school in the village is supported under the patronage of the R. C. clergyman. The ruins of the old parish church are still remaining; and on the sea shore are some remains of an ancient castle, of which no account is extant. At Coomainaire, or "the Valley of Slaughter," numerous ancient arrows have been found at various times, from which circumstance and the traditional name of the place it would appear that a battle had been fought here at a very remote period. A patron is held on the last Sunday in July, in honour of St. Brandon.

CLOGHBRACK, a village, in the parish and barony of Ross, county of Galway, and province of Connaught, 7 miles (W. by N.) from Cong, on the road to the Partry mountains; containing 191 inhabitants.

CLOGHEEN, a market and post-town, partly in the parish of TULLAGHORTON, but chiefly in that of SHANRAHAN, barony of IFFA and OFFA WEST, county of TIPPERARY, and province of MUNSTER, 11½ miles (S. W.) from Clonmel, and 94 (S. W. by S.) from Dublin; containing 1928 inhabitants. This place is situated on the river Tar, and on the mail coach road from Clonmel to Cork, near the foot of the steep northern ascent of the mountain of Knockmeladown. A large trade in agricultural produce is carried on, chiefly for exportation, and more than 80,000 barrels of wheat are annually purchased in its market and in the neighbourhood, which is made into flour of very superior quality and sent by land to Clonmel, whence it is conveyed down the Suir. For this purpose there are seven flour-mills in the town and neighbourhood, which are worked by fourteen water wheels; there is also an extensive brewery. A new road has lately been made from Clogheen to Lismore, with a branch to Cappoquin, the greatest rise on which is one in 30 feet. The neighbouring mountains abound with iron-stone, and iron ore was formerly smelted here. At Castle-Grace, near the town, a lead mine was worked about 40 years since, the ore of which contained a large proportion of silver. The environs abound with varied scenery. In the immediate vicinity is Bay loch, about three quarters of a mile in circumference, and its depth in the centre is about 33 yards; a mountain rises over it with nearly a perpendicular ascent to an elevation of about 600 feet, and eagles are sometimes seen hovering over the lake. On the north side of Knockshannacoolen, Lord Lismore planted about 100 acres of trees, which thrive well and form a pleasing contrast with the ruggedness of the neighbouring mountains. Shanbally Castle, the splendid seat of his lordship, is about 2½ miles from the town. The market is on Saturday; and fairs are held on Whit-Monday, Aug. 1st, Oct. 28th, and Dec. 12th. The market-house is a commodious building. At the entrance of the town are barracks for the accommodation of two troops of cavalry. A constabulary police force has been stationed here; a manor court is held before the seneschal of the manor of Everard's castle, in which the town is included, for the recovery of debts not exceeding £10; and petty sessions are held on alternate Thursdays. There is a small bridewell, comprising four cells, two day-rooms, and two airing-yards; also a dispensary and fever hospital. At a short distance from the church are the ruins of the parish church of Shanrahan, near which are the remains of St. Mary's abbey; and on the summit of Knockmeladown were interred the remains of Henry Eeles, who published many papers on electricity. Adjoining the town are Cooleville, the residence of S. Grubb, Esq., and Claishleigh, of S. Grubb, Esq. A few miles distant, at Skiheenarinky, on the estate of the Earl of Kingston, is a very remarkable cavern in the limestone strata. The entrance is by a descent of 15 or 20 feet, in a narrow cleft of the rock, into a vault 100 feet in length and 60 or 70 feet high; a winding passage on the left leads for about half a mile through a variety of chasms, some of which are so extensive that, when lighted up, they have the appearance of a vaulted cathedral supported by massive columns; the walls, ceiling, and pillars often presenting highly fantastic forms, and are incrusted with spar of great brilliancy. The stalactites in some places form entire columns, and in others have the appearance of drapery hanging from the ceiling in graceful forms; the angles between the walls appear as if fringed with icicles, and in one part of the caverns is a deep pool of water, the passage of which has not been yet explored. About a quarter of a mile to the east of this cavern is the entrance to another that was discovered in 1833.—See SHANRAHAN and TULLAGHORTON.

CLOGHER, or KILCLOGHER, a parish, in the barony of FERRARD, county of LOUTH, and province of LEINSTER, 6¼ miles (N. E.) from Drogheda; containing 1392 inhabitants. This place, which was anciently called *Kilfinnabhoir*, was distinguished, in the earliest ages of Christianity in Ireland, by the foundation of a religious establishment, of which St. Nectan, nephew of St. Patrick, was abbot or bishop. It is situated on the eastern coast; and the village, which is about half a mile to the west of Clogher Head, contains about 80 houses and 592 inhabitants, who are chiefly engaged in the fishery, which employs seven smacks from 25 to 40 tons burden each, and 20 row boats. On the north side of Clogher Head is a small cove or dock, partly natural and partly excavated, to which a passage for boats has been cut through the beach. It is much frequented by fishing vessels, on account of its affording shelter from all winds but the north-east; it was much improved by the late Wallop Brabazon, Esq., and might be made one of the best safety harbours in the kingdom. On the south side of the promontory a broad strand extends four miles to the mouth of the Boyne; and to the north of the village, stretching to Dunany Point, is a sandy bay with low reefs, of which one, nearly in the centre, called Cargee, is covered at high water. At Clogher Head is a coast-guard station, one of the six that constitute the Dundalk district. The parish contains, according to the Ordnance survey, 1861¼ statute acres, and is principally under tillage; and there is no waste land. The principal seat is Glaspistole House, the residence of J. Markey, Esq. It is a rectory and vicarage, in the diocese of Armagh, and is part of the union of Termonfeckan: the tithes amount to £98. In the R. C. divisions it forms part of the union or district of Rathdrummin, and has a neat chapel at Hackett's Cross, with a national school adjoining. There are also a school aided by Capt. Hanfield, and a small hedge school. Near Mr. Markey's seat are the ruins of an ancient castle, consisting principally of a square tower, and at the village of Clogher are the ruins of the old church.

CLOGHER, a parish, in the barony of KILNEMANAGH, county of TIPPERARY, and province of MUNSTER, 6 miles (S. W.) from Thurles; containing, with the parish of Rathkenan, 2062 inhabitants. This parish is situated on the high road from Tipperary to Thurles, and comprises 6997 statute acres, as applotted under the tithe act, and valued at £4935 per annum. About one-half is good arable and pasture land, and the remainder, with the exception of a small portion of underwood, is mostly mountainous, with some bog. The living is a vicarage, in the diocese of Cashel, united at a period unknown to the vicarages of Inshyanly and Dovea, and the rectory and vicarage of Moykarkey, together forming the corps of the chancellorship of Cashel, in the patronage of the Archbishop; the rectory is impropriate in W. Moore, Esq. The tithes amount to £276. 18. $5\frac{1}{2}$. of which two-thirds are payable to the impropriator, and the remainder to the incumbent; and the amount of tithes for the union, payable to the chancellor, is £452. 6. $1\frac{3}{4}$. There is neither church nor glebe-house; the Protestant parishioners attend the church of Clonoulty; those of Inshyanly, the churches of Thurles and Templemore; and those of Moykarkey, that of Holy Cross. The glebe comprises 27 acres. In the R. C. divisions the parish forms part of the union or district of Clonoulty. There is a pay school, in which are about 140 children.

CLOGHER, an incorporated market and post-town, a parish, and the head of a diocese (formerly a parliamentary borough), in the barony of CLOGHER, county of TYRONE, and province of ULSTER, 7 miles (W.) from Aughnacloy, and $82\frac{1}{2}$ (N. W. by N.) from Dublin; containing, with the towns of Augher and Five-mile-town, and the village of Newtown-Saville (all separately described) 17,996 inhabitants, of which number, 523 are in the town. This place is said to have derived its name from a stone covered with gold, which in pagan times is reported to have made oracular responses. The *Clogh-or*, or "golden stone," was preserved long after the abolition of paganism; for McGuire, canon of Armagh, who wrote a commentary on the registry of Clogher, in 1490, says "that this sacred stone is preserved at Clogher, on the right of the entrance into the church, and that traces of the gold with which it had been formerly covered by the worshippers of the idol called Cermaed Celsetacht are still visible." There is still a very ancient stone lying on the south side of the cathedral tower, which many believe to be the real Clogh-or. It appears to have some very ancient characters engraved on it, but is evidently nothing more than the shaft of an antique cross of rude workmanship, of which there are several in the ancient cemetery. Clogher is called by Ptolemy *Rhigia* or *Regia*; and according to some authors, St. Patrick founded and presided over a monastery here, which he resigned to St. Kertenn when he went to Armagh, to establish his famous abbey there; but according to others, it was built at the command of St. Patrick in the street before the royal palace of Ergal, by St. Macartin, who died in 506, and from its vicinity to this palace both the abbey and the town appear anciently to have been called Uriel or Ergal. In 841, the abbot Moran Mac Inrachty was slain by the Danes. In 1041 the church was rebuilt and dedicated to St. Macartin. In 1126 the Archdeacon Muireadhach O'Cuillen was killed by the people of Fermanagh. Moelisa O'Carrol, Bishop of Clogher, in 1183, on his translation of the archbishoprick of Armagh, presented to this abbey a priest's vestments and a mitre, and promised a pastoral staff; he also consecrated the abbey church. Bishop Michael Mac Antsair, in 1279, exchanged with the abbot the episcopal residence that had been built near the abbey by Bishop Donat O'Fidabra, between 1218 and 1227, for a piece of land outside the town, called Disert-na-cusiac, on which he erected another episcopal palace. His immediate successor, Matthew Mac Catasaid, erected a chapel over the sepulchre of St. Macartin. In 1361 the plague miserably afflicted Ireland, particularly the city of Clogher, and caused the death of the bishop. In April 1395, while Bishop Arthur Mac Camaeil was employed in rebuilding the chapel of St. Macartin, the abbey, the cathedral, two chapels, the episcopal residence, and 32 other houses, were destroyed by fire; but the bishop applied himself with unwearied diligence to the rebuilding of his cathedral and palace. In 1504, another plague ravaged Clogher and caused the death of the bishop. Jas. I., in 1610, annexed the abbey and its revenues to the see of Clogher, by which it was made one of the richest in the kingdom. Between 1690 and 1697, Bishop Tennison repaired and beautified the episcopal palace; and his successor, Bishop St. George Ash, expended £900 in repairing and improving the palace and lands, two-thirds of which was repaid by his successor. Bishop Sterne, in 1720, laid out £3000 in building and other improvements of the episcopal residence, £2000 of which was charged on the revenues of the see.

The town is situated on the river Blackwater, the source of which is in the parish, and consists of one row of 90 houses, the northern side only being built upon. Some of the houses are large, handsome, and well built with hewn stone, and slated. The episcopal palace is a large and handsome edifice close to the cathedral, on the south side of the town, and consists of a centre with two wings: the entrance is in the north front by an enclosed portico, supported by lofty fluted columns. It is built throughout of hewn freestone, and standing on elevated ground commands extensive views over a richly planted undulating country. Its erection was commenced by Lord John George Beresford, Primate of Armagh, while Bishop of Clogher, and completed by Lord Robert Tottenham, the present bishop, in 1823. Attached to the palace is a large and well-planted demesne of 566 acres, encircled by a stone wall; and within it are the remains of the royal dwelling-place of the princes of Ergallia, a lofty earthwork or fortress, protected on the west and south by a deep fosse; beyond this, to the south, is a camp surrounded by a single fosse, and still further southward is a tumulus or cairn, encircled by a raised earthwork. The market is on Saturday; the market-house was built by Bishop Garnett. Fairs for live stock are held on the third Saturday in every month. The market was granted to the bishop by letters patent dated April 20th, 1629: he was also authorised to appoint two fairs and receive the profits of the market and fairs. The old fairs, which are supposed to have been granted by the charter, are held on May 6th and July 26th.

At the solicitation of Bishop Spottiswood, Chas. I., in 1629, directed that, "for the better civilizing and strengthening of these remote parts with English and British tenants, and for the better propagation of the true religion, the lord-lieutenant should by letters patent make the town of Clogher a corporation." This was to consist of a portreeve and 12 burgesses, to be at first nominated by the bishop; the portreeve was afterwards to be elected on Michaelmas-day, by and from among the burgesses. No freemen were created, and the bishops appear to have connected a burgess-ship with each of the stalls in the cathedral. Prior to March 29th, 1800, the bishops had nominated the members of parliament for the borough without opposition, and the seneschal of their manor had been the returning officer; but at that time the Irish House of Commons resolved that the limits of the borough were co-extensive with the manor, and as the freeholders of the manor had tendered their votes in favour of two candidates, they were declared by the Irish parliament to be duly elected, and the bishop's nominees were unseated. At the Union, the £15,000 granted as compensation for abolishing the elective franchise was claimed by the bishop, the dean and chapter, and prebendaries of the cathedral, and the Rev. Hugh Nevan, seneschal of the manor; but their claim was disallowed and the money paid to the Board of First Fruits. By the charter a grant was to be made to the corporation by the bishop of 700 Irish acres near the town, for which a rent of 8*d.* per acre was to be paid. Out of the profits of 200 acres of this land the corporation was, within two years, to erect a school-house and maintain a schoolmaster, with a servant, for a grammar school. English was to be taught by the master, who was always to be appointed by the bishop. The portreeve was to have 200 acres of the grant assigned for his support while holding the office, and for the payment of a steward and serjeant or bailiff; and the profits of the remaining 300 acres were to be divided among the burgesses. This grant appears not to have been made. The charter granted a civil court of record to the corporation, with a jurisdiction extending to a circle of three miles in every direction round the cathedral, and to the amount of £5 English, with a prison for debtors. Since the death of the last seneschal, about 1823, this court has not been held. Quarter sessions are held here twice a year in the sessions-house, alternately with Dungannon, for the baronies of Dungannon and Clogher; and there is a bridewell.

The See of Clogher is one of the most ancient in Ireland, and had its origin in the religious foundation instituted by St. Patrick, or his friend St. Macartin, a descendant of Fiachus Araidh, King of Ulster, who was succeeded in the mingled abbacy and prelacy by St. Tigernach, St. Laserian, St. Aidan (who converted the Northumbrians to Christianity, and was the first bishop of Lindisfarne), and other celebrated ecclesiastics of the early ages. So late as the 12th century, Edan O'Killedy, bishop of this see, subscribed his name as Bishop of Uriel to the great charter of Newry. The equally ancient see of Clones was at a remote period annexed to it, as also were those of Ardsrath and Louth. About 1240, Hen. III. sent a mandatory letter to Maurice Fitzgerald, Lord-Justice of Ireland, commanding him to unite the bishoprick of Clogher to the archiepiscopal see of Armagh, on account of the poverty of both. This union was not then effected, but under the Church Temporalities act it will take place on the death of the present bishop. About 1266, the bishoprick of Ardsrath was taken possession of by the Bishop of Derry, and Louth by the Archbishop of Armagh; and on the death of Bishop Arthur Mac Camaeil, the archbishop claimed his best horse, ring, and cup as an heriot. Clogher being situated in a part of the island to which the English arms or laws had scarcely ever extended, had not a bishop of English extraction before the time of Edmund Courcey, who was consecrated in 1485. The last bishop who held the

Arms of the Bishoprick.

see and its temporalities from the court of Rome was Hugh or Odo O'Cervallan, promoted by Paul III., and confirmed by Hen. VIII., in 1542. The first Protestant bishop was Miler Magragh, who had been a Franciscan friar and was made Bishop of Down by Pope Pius V., but afterwards becoming a Protestant, was placed in this see by Queen Elizabeth in 1570, and soon afterwards was made Archbishop of Cashel. From the time of his translation, owing to the disturbances in this part of the country, there was no bishop till 1605, when George Montgomery, a native of Scotland, was made bishop by Jas. I., and held the see with those of Derry and Raphoe, and afterwards with that of Meath. On the death of Bishop Boyle, in 1687, the episcopal revenues were paid into the exchequer, and the see continued vacant about three years, when King William translated Dr. Tennison to it. This diocese is one of the ten which constitute the ecclesiastical province of Armagh: it comprises a small portion of the county of Louth and parts of the counties of Donegal and Tyrone, the greater part of Fermanagh, and the whole of Monaghan; and is 76 British miles long and 25 broad, comprehending a superficies of about 528,700 plantation acres, of which 1850 are in Louth, 25,000 in Donegal, 68,100 in Tyrone, 254,150 in Fermanagh, and 179,600 in Monaghan. The chapter consists of a dean, archdeacon, precentor, chancellor, and the five prebendaries of Kilskerry, Findonagh, Tullycorbet, Tyhallon, and Devenish. According to the registry, the ancient chapter consisted of twelve canons, of which the dean and archdeacon were two: this was altered by Bishop Montgomery, and the offices of precentor and chancellor were added; and hence it is that the archdeacon of this diocese, as the more ancient officer, ranks next the dean. The lands belonging to the see amount to 22,591 statute acres, of which 18,851 are profitable land; and the gross average annual income, as returned by the Commissioners of Ecclesiastical Inquiry, is £10,371, and the net revenue, £8686. 11. 6. There is no economy fund connected with the cathedral; it was for many years kept in repair out of a fund bequeathed for charitable purposes by Bishop Sterne, but the trustees have lately withdrawn the grant. The consistorial court of the diocese is held at Monaghan: its officers are a vicar-general, a surrogate, two registrars and a deputy, and two proctors; the registrars are keepers of the records, which consist of copies of wills from 1659 to the present time, documents relating to inductions to benefices, &c. The diocesan school is at Monaghan, and is described in the article on that place; and there are free schools connected with the diocese at Carrickmacross and Enniskillen. The total number of parishes in the diocese is 45, which are either rectories and vicarages, or vicarages, the rectorial tithes of which are partly appropriate to the see, and partly impropriate in lay persons. The benefices are also 45, of which, one is in the gift of the Crown, 37 in that of the Bishop, four in that of Trinity College, Dublin, one in that of the Marquess of Ely, and one in that of Sir Thomas B. Lennard, Bart.; the remaining one is a perpetual curacy, in the gift of the prebendary of Devenish. The only union is that of Currin and Drumkrin, which will be dissolved on the next avoidance. The number of churches is 61, and of glebe-houses, 38. In the R. C. divisions this diocese, as originally constituted, forms a distinct bishoprick, and is one of the eight suffragan to Armagh: it comprises 37 parochial unions or districts, containing 81 chapels served by 37 parish priests and 51 coadjutors or curates. The bishop's parish is Carrickmacross, where he resides; and the dean's, Monaghan.

The parish is of great extent, and comprehends the manors of Augher, in which is the town of that name; Clogher (granted by Chas. I. to the bishop), in which is the town of Clogher; Blessingburne, in which is the town of Five-mile-Town; Mount-Stewart; and part of the manor of Killyfaddy, granted to Sir Wm. Cope, and the rest of which is in the adjoining parish of Donagheavy: there are eight townlands of the manor of Clogher, called abbey lands, which are tithe-free. It contains 49,761 statute acres, according to the Ordnance survey, of which 30,000 are good arable and pasture land, 213¼ are water, and 19,761 are waste heath and bog, the greater part of which is, however, highly improvable; of its entire surface, 43,754 acres are applotted under the tithe act. The land in the vicinity of the town is remarkably fertile and well cultivated; freestone and limestone are abundant, and there are indications of coal and lead ore. Clogher is situated on a lofty eminence, in the midst of a rich and diversified country encircled by mountains, which on the south approach within one mile, and on the north within two miles of the town, and the highest of which is Knockmany. Slieve Beagh, on the southern border of the parish, rises to an elevation of 1254 feet above the level of the sea. Besides the episcopal palace, the parish contains several fine residences. The deanery or glebe-house, which is about a quarter of a mile west of the cathedral, is a handsome house in a fertile and well-planted glebe. Not far distant from it is Augher Castle, the splendid residence of Sir J. M. Richardson Bunbury, Bart.; Cecil, the seat of the Rev. Francis Gervais; Corick, of the Rev. Dr. Story; Killyfaddy, of R. W. Maxwell, Esq.; Blessingburne Cottage, of Col. Montgomery; Daisy-hill, of A. Millar, Esq.; Fardross, the ancient seat of A. Upton Gledstanes, Esq.; Ballimagowan, of A. Newton, Esq.; Waring Bank, of J. M^c^Lannahan, Esq.; and Corcreevy House, of Lieut.-Col. Dickson.

The living is a rectory and vicarage, in the diocese of Clogher, constituting the corps of the deanery of Clogher, in the patronage of the Crown: the tithes amount to £850, and the income of the dean, including tithes and glebe, is £1374. 17. 3. The cathedral, which is dedicated to St. Macartin, and from time immemorial has been used as the parish church, was built in the ancient style of English architecture by Bishop Sterne, in 1744, at his own expense, but was remodelled in the Grecian style by Dean Bagwell, in 1818, who erected stalls for the dignitaries and a gallery for the organist and choir, also galleries in the two transepts; and about the same time the whole was newly roofed and ceiled. The Ecclesiastical Commissioners have recently made a grant of £197 for repairs. It is a large and handsome cruciform structure, with a lofty square tower rising from the west front, in which is the principal entrance: the throne, which is very beautiful, occupies the western angle of the south transept, and the whole of the interior is handsomely fitted up. There are several elegant monuments, among which are Bishop Garnett's, who died in the year 1783, and Bishop Porter's, who died in 1819. The chapter-house is near the entrance, on the right. There are two chapels of ease in the parish, one at Five-mile-Town, or Blessingburne, and one at Newtown-Saville; and divine service is regularly performed every Sunday in the market-house at Augher, in several of the school-houses in distant parts of the parish, and also at Lislie during the summer. The glebe-house, or deanery, is about a quarter of a mile from the cathedral. The glebe comprises 556*a.* 1*r.* 24*p.* statute measure, of which 100*a.* 1*r.* 28*p.* are annexed to the deanery, and 455*a.* 3*r.* 36*p.* are leased, at a rent of £337. 15. 6½. and renewal fines amounting to £20. 7. per annum. The R. C. parish is co-extensive with that of the Established Church, and there are chapels at Aghadrummond, Escragh, and Aghentine; there are also places of worship for Presbyterians at Longridge and Aghentine. The free school in the town is under the patronage of the Bishop: the master's salary is derived from the proceeds of a bequest of £420 by Bishop Garnett, which the existing bishop augments to £40 per annum. The school-house was built in 1780, by Bishop Garnett, at an expense of £300. At Beltany there is a male and female school, on Erasmus Smith's foundation, endowed with two acres of land by the Rev. F. Gervais, who, in conjunction with the trustees of that charity, built the school-house, at an expense of £658. 19. 6. There are a female school at Cecil, built and supported by Mrs. Gervais; and schools for both sexes at Escragh, supported by Capt. Maxwell at Five-mile-Town, supported by Col. Montgomery, and at Ballyscally, supported by J. Trimble, Esq., all under the National Board; there are also four other schools. In these schools are about 490 boys and 330 girls; and there are seventeen private schools, in which are about 540 boys and 350 girls, and thirteen Sunday schools. A dispensary is maintained in the customary manner. At Lumford Glen is a deep ravine, in which a small stream of water flows through a cleft in the rock and forms a beautiful cascade. A carriage drive, edged with fine plantations, has been made to this waterfall.

CLOGHERBRIEN, a parish, in the barony of TRUGHENACKMY, county of KERRY, and province of MUNSTER, 1½ mile (W. N. W.) from Tralee, containing 1330 inhabitants. This parish is situated on the road from Tralee to the Spa, and near the bay of Tralee, and contains 3345 statute acres, as applotted under the tithe act. The land is generally good and mostly under tillage: the system of agriculture is gradually improving, and sea-weed is much used as manure. There is no bog, but turf is supplied from Castle-Gregory, on the south-west side of the bay. It is a rectory and vicarage, in the diocese of Ardfert and Aghadoe, and is part of the union of Ballynahaglish: the tithes amount to £332. 6. 1. In the R. C. divisions it is chiefly included in the union or district of Tralee, but a small part is in the union of Ardfert. The church is in ruins, but the burial-ground by the road side is much used and contains several neat tombs. There is a hedge school of about 25 children.

CLOGHEREEN, a village, in the parish of KILLARNEY, barony of MAGONIHY, county of KERRY, and province of MUNSTER, 2 miles (S.) from Killarney; containing 145 inhabitants. It is situated on the new road from Killarney to Kenmare, and comprises about 30 houses, some of which are of recent erection, neatly built, and slated. From its proximity to the enchanting demesne of Muckross, to the interesting and highly picturesque ruins of the abbey of that name, and to the shores of the great lower lake of Killarney, it has of late years been very much frequented during the season by visiters to the lakes, for whom several neat lodging-houses have been erected, and it is in contemplation to build a spacious hotel, with coach-houses and other suitable accommodations. The small river that runs from the village into the Lower Lake is about to be made navigable for boats, and a bason formed within the gate of Muckross demesne, the seat of H. A. Herbert, Esq., who has it in contemplation to erect a church and school-house, and to endow the former with £100 per annum for the support of a curate. This is usually the starting point for those who ascend Mangerton mountain. The road hence to Killarney is skirted with gentlemen's seats; and the new road towards Kenmare winds round the richly wooded base of Torc mountain, and along the shores of the middle and upper lakes, embracing a succession of grand and sublime scenery, constantly varying in character.

CLOGHERNY, or CLOUGHENRY, a parish, in the barony of Omagh, county of Tyrone, and province of Ulster, 6 miles (S. E.) from Omagh; containing 6785 inhabitants. This parish, anciently Donaghaneigh, is situated on the road from Dungannon to Omagh, and contains, according to the Ordnance survey, 17,791½ statute acres (including a detached portion of 2368½ acres), about 8000 of which are arable, mostly under a good system of cultivation. There is a market at Beregh on Wednesday, and a fair on the first Monday in every month; and fairs are also held at Seskinore, on the second Monday in every month, for live stock. The principal seats are Gortmore, the residence of J. Galbraith, Esq.; Mullaghmore, of R. Burges, Esq.; Seskinore, of Mrs. Perry; and Somerset, of the Rev. J. Lowry. The living is a rectory, in the diocese of Armagh, and in the patronage of the Provost and Fellows of Trinity College, Dublin, who purchased the advowson in 1830: the tithes amount to £692. The church is a large and handsome edifice, built about 1746, and enlarged and much improved in 1773. The glebe-house was built in 1774, about which time the parish was disunited from Termon: it is large and handsome, and is on a glebe of 154 acres; there is also a glebe at Upper Clogherny, comprising 422 acres, and another called Mullaghollin, in the parish of Termon, comprising 508 acres, making a total of 1084 acres of arable land, besides about 850 acres of mountain and bog. The R. C. parish is co-extensive with that of the Established Church, and is called Beregh; there are chapels at Beregh, Liskmore, and Brackey. At Dervethroy is a meeting-house for Presbyterians in connection with the Synod of Ulster, of the third class; and at Seskinore is one in connection with the Associate Synod. The parochial school, situated near the church, is a large and handsome edifice, built by the inhabitants, at a cost of £800, and is supported by the rector; and there are 11 other schools in the parish, also four Sunday schools. About a mile from the church are the ruins of the old church of Donaghaneigh, in a large townland, which is extra-parochial, and belongs to the Bishop of Clogher.

CLOGHJORDAN, a post-town and district parish, in the barony of Lower Ormond, county of Tipperary, and province of Munster, 9½ miles (W.) from Roscrea, and 70¼ (S. W.) from Dublin; containing 2770 inhabitants, of which number, 824 are in the town. This town is situated on the road from Nenagh to Parsonstown, and consists principally of one main street; it contains 129 houses, and has a neat and cheerful appearance. A large distillery is carried on, in which from 40,000 to 60,000 gallons of whiskey are annually made. A patent for a market exists, but no market has been yet established, though much desired by the inhabitants. Fairs are held on May 12th, Aug. 12th, and Dec. 1st; and a police force is stationed in the town. The living is a perpetual curacy, in the diocese of Killaloe, erected out of the parish of Modreeny in 1826, and in the patronage of the Incumbent of that parish: the stipend of the curate is £76. 3. 1., of which £46. 3. 1. is paid by the incumbent of Modreeny, and £30 from the augmentation fund under the management of the Ecclesiastical Commissioners. The church, a handsome light edifice, in the later English style, with an elegant spire, was built by a gift of £900 and a loan of £923 from the late Board of First Fruits, in 1830. There is neither glebe-house nor glebe. In the R. C. divisions it is the head of a union or district, comprising also the parishes of Modreeny, Ardcrony, and Kilruan, in which are three chapels; the chapel at Cloghjordan is a neat plain building. There are places of worship for Baptists and Wesleyan and Primitive Methodists, also a dispensary and fever hospital. A plan for the relief and diminution of pauperism originated in the town with William French, Esq., of Cangort Park, who, in 1823, established the "Deacon's Poor Fund," at first limited to the parish of Modreeny, and subsequently extended to many other parishes, particularly to those of Dolla, Kilmore, and Ballynaclogh, in which it has been attended with the most beneficial results.

CLOGHPRIOR, a parish, in the barony of Lower Ormond, county of Tipperary, and province of Munster, 4 miles (S. W.) from Burrisokane; containing 1452 inhabitants. This parish is situated near the river Shannon, and on the high road from Nenagh to Burrisokane, and comprises 3532 statute acres, as applotted under the tithe act, and valued at £3083 per annum. About 480 acres are common; there is a very small portion of bog, and of the remainder, by far the greater portion is arable and under tillage; the soil is light and rests on a substratum of limestone. The gentlemen's seats are Ashley Park, the residence of G. Atkinson, Esq., and Prior Park, of W. Waller, Esq., both richly planted demesnes; East Prospect, of J. S. Handcock, Esq.; and Carney Castle, of A. French, Esq. The last is a handsome modern house on part of the site of the ancient castle, now in ruins, and formerly for many years the residence of the Grace family; it was attacked by Cromwell, and becoming forfeited, was re-purchased by the same family, and has descended by inheritance to its present proprietor. The parish is in the diocese of Killaloe, and is a rectory and vicarage, forming part of the union of Finnoe: the tithes amount to £212. 6. 2. In the R. C. divisions it is part of the union or district of Cloghjordan. There is a pay school, in which are about 80 boys and 40 girls. There are some slight remains of a religious foundation, probably of a priory, from which the parish may have taken its name, but no record of it is extant.

CLOGHRAN, or CLOGHRAN-SWORDS, a parish, in the barony of Coolock, county of Dublin, and province of Leinster, 1½ mile (S.) from Swords; containing 613 inhabitants. This parish, which takes the adjunct of Swords to distinguish it from another parish of the same name south-west from Dublin, is situated on the road from Dublin to Swords. Limestone abounds, and near the church is a quarry in which various fossils are found; under this quarry are copper and lead ores, but neither has yet been profitably worked. Baskin Hill, the seat of J. Tymons, Esq., was built by the present Bishop of Dromore, who resided there while rector of St. Doulough's; and Castle Moat, the seat of J. Mac Owen, Esq., takes its name from an extensive moat, or rath, within the demesne, from which is a fine view of the country towards the village of the Man-of-War and the sea, including Lambay Island, Ireland's Eye, Howth, and the Dublin and Wicklow mountains. In 1822, some ancient silver and copper coins, Danish pipes, pikes, and musket bullets were ploughed up near the spot. The living is a rectory, in the diocese of Dublin, and in the patronage of the Crown: the tithes amount to £184. 12. 3¾. The church is a very plain and simple edifice. The glebe-house was rebuilt in 1812, by aid of a gift of £400 and a loan of £392 from the late Board of First Fruits: the glebe comprises seven acres of cultivated land. In the R. C. divisions the parish forms part of the union or district of Swords.

CLOGHRAN-HIDART.—See BALLYCOOLANE.

CLOHAMON.—See KILRUSH, county of Wexford.

CLOMANTO, or CLOGHMANTAGH, a parish, in the barony of Cranagh, county of Kilkenny, and province of Leinster, 3½ miles (W.) from Freshford, on the road from Kilkenny to Thurles; containing 889 inhabitants. It comprises 3597 statute acres, as applotted under the tithe act, and valued at £2413 per annum; about 480 acres are mountain and woodland, and the remainder arable and pasture. The system of agriculture is very much improved; and there is abundance of limestone, which is quarried for building, but chiefly for burning into lime, which is the chief manure. The principal seats are Woodsgift, the residence of Sir R. B. St. George, Bart., adjoining the demesne of which are temporary loughs, called Loghans, formed by springs which burst forth at the commencement of the wet season, but discontinue in the spring; and Balief Castle, the handsome residence of R. St. George, Esq., in the demesne of which are the remains of the ancient castle, a round tower in a good state of preservation. The Clomanto flour-mills, capable of manufacturing about 12,000 barrels annually, are impelled by a small river that intersects the parish; and attached to them is a large starch-manufactory, both belonging to Mr. W. Lyster. The living consists of a rectory and vicarage united, and a perpetual curacy, in the diocese of Ossory; the rectory and vicarage form part of the union of Freshford and of the corps of the prebend of Aghoure in the cathedral of St. Canice, Kilkenny; the perpetual curacy was instituted by act of council, in 1828, by detaching five townlands from this parish, and uniting them with the parishes of Urlingford and Tubrid, and portions of the parishes of Burnchurch and Tullaroan, together forming the perpetual curacy of Clomanto, which is in the patronage of the incumbents of the several parishes out of which it was formed, each of whom contributes to the curate's stipend. The tithes amount to £184. 12. 5. The old parish church is in ruins, and there is neither glebe-house nor glebe. A church has been recently erected for the district curacy; it is a handsome edifice, situated on the verge of the parish. In the R. C. divisions the parish is partly in the union or district of Urlingford, and partly in that of Freshford. There are two pay schools, in which are about 100 children. The remains of the old castle of Clomanto consist of a square tower in good preservation; both it and Balief castle belonged anciently to the Shortall family. On the summit of Clomanto hill is a circular mound of stones, 87 paces in circumference, enclosed by a circular barrier of stones including several acres, approaching nearest to the mound on the east. Part of this circle has been destroyed; the name *Cloghman-Ta,* signifying in the Irish language the "stone of God," is sufficiently indicative of the use to which this place was applied.

CLONABRENY, or RUSSAGH, a parish, in the barony of Demifore, county of Meath, and province of Leinster, 1½ mile (W. by N.) from Crossakeel; containing 139 inhabitants. This parish, which is situated on the road from Killesandra, by Athboy, to Dublin, contains 1668 statute acres, as applotted under the tithe act. The lands are generally in a good state of cultivation, and the system of agriculture has of late been very much improved. The gentlemen's seats are Clonebrany, the residence of W. Blayney Wade, Esq., a handsome mansion in a highly cultivated and richly planted demesne of 615 statute acres; and Bobsville, the pleasant residence of Lieut.-Col. Battersby. There is a patent for a manorial court, but none is held. It is a rectory, in the diocese of Meath, and is part of the union of Loughcrew: the tithes amount to £32. In the R. C. divisions it forms part of the union or district of Kilskyre. There are some small remains of the old church, with a burial-ground.

CLONAGHEEN, a parish, in the barony of Maryborough West, Queen's county, and province of Leinster, 3¼ miles (S. E. by S.) from Mountrath: the population is returned with the parish of Clonenagh. It is situated on the road from Dublin to Limerick, and is bounded on the south-west by the river Nore, over which is a neat bridge, here called the Poor Man's Bridge. There is a large tract of valuable bog. It is a rectory, in the diocese of Leighlin, and is part of the union of Clonenagh, for which and Clonagheen there is but one composition of tithes. The schools are also noticed under the head of that parish. In the R. C. divisions the parish forms part of the union or district of Mountrath.

CLONAGOOSE, a parish, in the barony of Idrone East, county of Carlow, and province of Leinster; comprising the village of Borris, which has a penny post to Goresbridge; and containing 2394 inhabitants. This parish, which is also called *Clonegford,* is bounded on the south-west by the river Barrow, the navigation of which extends to New Ross and Waterford, and up the river to Athy, where the canal to Dublin commences. It comprises 5392 statute acres in a high state of cultivation, as applotted under the tithe act; there are about 325 acres of woodland and 460 of waste. The principal seats are Borris House, the residence of the ancient family of Kavanagh, for a description of which see Borris; and Kilcoltrim, of Luke Hagarty, Esq. The living is a vicarage, in the diocese of Leighlin, episcopally united, in 1714, to that of Kiltennel, but recently separated from it, and in the patronage of the Bishop; the rectory is impropriate in Lord Cloncurry. The tithes amount to £255, of which £165 is payable to the impropriator, and £90 to the vicar, whose income has been lately augmented by the Ecclesiastical Commissioners with a grant of £20 per ann., from Primate Boulter's fund. A parochial church is in progress of erection, prior to which the only place of worship in connection with the Protestant establishment was a beautiful private chapel attached to Borris House, built by the late Mr. Kavanagh. In the R. C. divisions this parish is partly attached to the union or district of Borris, and partly to that of Dunleckney; at the former is a handsome chapel, lately built at an expense of £2000. A parochial school for boys and girls, and an infants' and a Sunday school, are supported by subscription; and at Borris, Ballymartin, and Ballymurphy are national schools for both sexes: the day schools afford instruction to about 400 boys and 320 girls. A charitable loan fund of £60 is conducted for the benefit of the poor of all denominations. The remains of the old church are situated in a burial-ground about a mile from Borris.

CLONAKILTY, or CLOUGHNAKILTY, an incorporated sea-port, market and post-town (formerly a parliamentary borough), in the parish of KILGARRIFFE, East Division of the barony of EAST CARBERY, county of CORK, and province of MUNSTER, $25\frac{1}{2}$ miles (S. W. by S.) from Cork, and $151\frac{1}{2}$ miles (S. W.) from Dublin; containing 3807 inhabitants. This town, anciently called *Tuogh Mc Cilti*, appears to have had a corporation at an early period, for, in the records of the city of Cork, there is a petition from the portreeve and corporation of Clonakilty, dated July 5th, 1605: it, however, owes its importance to the family of Boyle. Sir Richard Boyle, first Earl of Cork, obtained for the inhabitants, in 1613, a charter of incorporation from Jas. I. On the breaking out of the war in 1641, the English settlers in the town were compelled to flee for refuge to Bandon, carrying with them the charter and muniments of the borough. In the following year, Lord Forbes, with his English regiment from Kinsale and some companies from Bandon, arrived here, and leaving two companies of Scottish troops and one of the Bandon companies to secure the place till his return, proceeded on his expedition towards the west. This force was, soon after his departure, attacked by multitudes on all sides; and the Scottish troops refusing to retreat, were cut to pieces. The Bandon company defended themselves, with great difficulty, in an old Danish fort on the road to Ross, till a reinforcement came to their relief, when they unitedly attacked the Irish, and forced them into the island of Inchidony, when, the tide coming in, upwards of 600 of them were drowned. The troops then returned to the town, to relieve a great number of their friends who had been taken prisoners, and were confined in the market-house. In 1691, the town was attacked by 800 Irish troops in the service of Jas. II., but they were quickly repulsed by the garrison, consisting of 50 dragoons and 25 foot. During the disturbances of 1798, a skirmish took place here between the king's forces and the insurgents, in which many of the latter were killed and the remainder dispersed.

The town is situated on the Gorar or Farla river, which falls into the bay close to the principal street, and in a pleasant fertile valley environed by hills of moderate elevation, which descend to the harbour. It consists of four principal streets diverging at right angles from the centre, and is well supplied with water from two public pumps erected by the Earl of Shannon. It has been much improved recently by the erection of several good houses and a spacious square, the centre of which is planted and laid out in walks, so as to form an agreeable promenade. Some excellent roads have also been made in the neighbourhood. A public library was established by a body of shareholders, in 1825: there are also three news-rooms and a lending library for the poor. Balls are occasionally given in the rooms over the market-house, during the sessions week. There are commodious infantry barracks for 4 officers and 68 privates. The staple trade of the town is the linen manufacture, which furnishes employment to 400 looms and 1000 persons, who manufacture to the amount of £250 or £300 weekly, but when the trade was in the height of its prosperity, the weekly sales were frequently £1000. The cotton-manufacture also employs about 40 looms. A spacious linen-hall was built some years since by the Earl of Shannon: it is attended by a sworn salesman and three deputies, by whom all the cloth brought to the hall is measured and marked. The corn trade is carried on chiefly by agents for the Cork merchants, who ship it here and receive coal as a return cargo. There are 14 lighters of 17 tons burden each regularly employed in raising and conveying sand to be used in the neighbourhood as manure. The harbour is only fit for small vessels, the channel being extremely narrow and dangerous, and having at the entrance a bar, over which vessels above 100 tons can only pass at high spring tides: large vessels, therefore, discharge their cargoes at Ring, about a mile below the town. It is much used as a safety harbour by the small craft for several miles along the coast. The market is held on Friday, and is amply supplied with good and cheap provisions; and three fairs are held under the charter on April 5th, Oct. 10th, and Nov. 12th, and two subsequently established on June 1st and Aug. 1st, all for cattle, sheep, and pigs; the Oct. and Nov. fairs are noted for a large supply of turkeys and fowls. A spacious market-house has been built, at an expense of £600; and shambles were erected in 1833, by the corporation, on ground let rent-free by the Earl of Shannon, who is proprietor of the borough. A chief constabulary police force has been stationed here.

By the charter of Jas. I. the inhabitants were incorporated under the designation of the "Sovereign, Free Burgesses, and Commonalty of the Borough of Cloughnakilty;" and Sir Richard Boyle was constituted lord of the town, with power to appoint several of the officers, and to a certain extent to superintend the affairs of the corporation, which was to consist of a sovereign and not less than 13 nor more than 24 burgesses, assisted by a serjeant-at-mace, three constables, a toll-collector, and weighmaster. The sovereign is annually elected by the lord of the town out of three burgesses chosen by the corporation, and the recorder is also appointed by him. Vacancies among the burgesses are filled up by themselves from among the freemen, who are admitted solely by favour of the corporation. The sovereign and recorder are justices of the peace within the borough, the limits of which extend for a mile and a half in every direction from a point nearly in the centre of the town, called the Old Chapel. The charter conferred the right of sending two members to the Irish parliament, which it continued to exercise till the Union, when the £15,000 awarded as compensation for its disfranchisement was paid to the Earl of Shannon, a descendant of Sir Richard Boyle. The sovereign and recorder were empowered to hold a court of record, for the recovery of debts and the determination of all pleas to the amount of £20 late currency; but since the passing of the act limiting the power of arrest to sums exceeding £20, it has been discontinued. A manorial court is held every third Wednesday by a seneschal appointed by the Earl of Shannon, which takes cognizance of debts and pleas not exceeding 40*s.*; and the sovereign and recorder hold courts of petty session in the market-house, every Monday. Petty sessions are also held every Thursday by the county magistrates; and the general quarter sessions for the West Riding of the county are held here in July. The county court-house is a neat edifice of hewn stone, ornamented with a pediment and cornice supported by two broad pilasters, between which is a handsome Venetian window. Connected with it is a bridewell, and both were erected at the expense of the county.

The parish church of Kilgarriffe is situated in the town, on an eminence to the north of the main street: it is a plain edifice, with a square tower at the west end, and was rebuilt in 1818, at an expense of £1300, of which £500 was a loan from the late Board of First Fruits, and the remainder was contributed by the Earl of Shannon and the Rev. H. Townsend. In the R. C. divisions this place gives name to a union or district, comprising the parishes of Kilgarriffe, Kilnagross, Templeomalus, Carrigrohanemore, Desart, Templebryan, and parts of the parishes of Kilkerranmore and Inchidony: the chapel is a spacious building, and there is a place of worship for Wesleyan Methodists. A classical school was established in 1808, under the patronage of the Earl of Shannon, who has assigned a large and handsome house, with land, for the residence of the master: there are more than 60 boys on the establishment. A dispensary, a house of industry, and a benevolent society have been established, which have been found highly beneficial, and are liberally supported by the Earl of Shannon and the inhabitants generally. The late Michael Collins, D. D., R. C. Bishop of Cloyne and Ross, who was author of several tracts on the state of Ireland, and was examined before a committee of the House of Commons, in 1825, was a native of this place. About a mile north of the town is a tolerably perfect druidical temple, some of the stones of which are nearly as large as those of Stonehenge; the centre stone of the circle is very large, and is composed of one mass of white quartz.

CLONALLON, a parish, in the barony of Upper Iveagh, county of Down, and province of Ulster, 6 miles (S. S. E.) from Newry; containing, with the town and district parish of Warrenspoint, 8630 inhabitants. This parish is situated on the bay of Carlingford, by which it is bounded on the south and west, and on the road from Newry to Rosstrevor, and comprises, according to the Ordnance survey, 11,658¼ statute acres, of which about 200 acres are woodland, 150 bog, 200 mountain (including about 100 acres of bog on the summit), and 173½ under water; of the remainder, nearly two-thirds are arable and one-third pasture. A very extensive and lucrative oyster fishery is carried on, employing a great number of boats, and herrings are occasionally taken in large quantities. The gentlemen's seats are Narrow Water House, the residence of R. Hall, Esq., a splendid mansion of hewn granite quarried upon the estate, and built in the Elizabethan style; Drumaul Lodge, that of James Robinson, Esq.; and Clonallon House, that of the Rev. J. Davis. The living is a rectory and vicarage, in the diocese of Dromore, united by charter of the 7th of Jas. I. to the rectory of Drumgath, together constituting the union of Clonallon and the corps of the chancellorship of Dromore, in the patronage of the Bishop: the tithes amount to £450, and the gross annual value of the benefice, tithe, and glebe included, is £961. 10. The parish church is a very ancient edifice in good repair, and a church has been recently erected at Warrenspoint, which has been made a district curacy. The glebe-house is situated on a glebe of 190 acres of profitable land, valued at £339. 10. per annum. The Ecclesiastical Commissioners have recommended the dissolution of the union on the next avoidance, leaving Clonallon alone as the corps of the chancellorship. The R. C. parish is co-extensive with that of the Established Church; there are three chapels, situated respectively at Mayo, Burn, and Warrenspoint. There are a handsome new meeting-house for Presbyterians in connection with the Synod of Ulster, one for those in connection with the Remonstrant Synod, and one each for Wesleyan and Primitive Methodists. The parochial school is aided by the rector; and at Mayo is a national school, in which together are about 140 boys and 80 girls; and there is an infants' school of 30 boys and 40 girls. Here are the ruins of a square castle. Close to the ferry of Narrow Water, Hugh de Lacy, Earl of Ulster and lord-deputy of Ireland, built a castle in 1212, which remained entire till 1641; but the present remains are more probably those of a castle erected by the Duke of Ormonde in 1663. Not far distant was a small spot surrounded by the sea, called Nuns' Island, on which were formerly considerable ruins; but the embankment now in progress for defending the channel has obliterated every vestige of them; they were probably the ruins of a religious establishment, which gave name to the island, or perhaps those of the castle of De Lacy.

CLONALVEY, a parish, in the barony of Upper Duleek, county of Meath, and province of Leinster, 8 miles (S.) from Drogheda, on the road from Naul to Navan; containing 1055 inhabitants. It comprises 4928 statute acres, of which 1661 are applotted under the tithe act: the land is in a high state of cultivation, being almost equally divided between arable and pasture. Part of the bog of Garristown is in this parish, but has been reclaimed; and there is a very good quarry of flag-stones near the ruins of the church. About 50 cotton-looms are employed by the Dublin and Drogheda manufacturers. It is a vicarage, in the diocese of Meath, and is part of the union of Julianstown; the rectory is impropriate in the Rev. Mr. Beaufort. The tithes amount to £155, of which £100 is payable to the impropriator, and £55 to the vicar. There is a glebe of 20 acres, valued at

£43. 15. 10½. In the R. C. divisions it is part of the union or district of Ardcath; the chapel is a neat modern building. There is a national school, aided by £5 per ann., from the parish priest, in which 50 boys and 30 girls are taught. There are some remains of the old church, also of a large rath at Grange.

CLONANA, a village, in the parish of GALLEN, barony of GARRYCASTLE, KING'S county, and province of LEINSTER, 1½ mile (N. W.) from Clogher; containing 79 dwellings and 385 inhabitants. It is situated near the river Shannon: the surrounding scenery is pleasingly varied, and the old castle of Clonana, now the residence of — Molony, Esq., forms a romantic feature in the landscape. It is a quadrangular structure, built on a rock, on the road side between the river Brosna and the canal, and is in a state of excellent preservation.

CLONARD, a post-town and parish, in the barony of UPPER MOYFENRAGH, county of MEATH, and province of LEINSTER, 11½ miles (W.) from Kilcock, and 26 (W. by N.) from Dublin; containing 4353 inhabitants, of which number, 66 are in the town or village. A religious establishment was founded here about the year 520, by St. Finian, and became the seat of a small diocese, to which, before 1152, were added the bishopricks of Trim, Ardbraccan, Dunshaughlin, and Slane, and their common see was fixed at Clonard. St. Finian, the first bishop, was tutor to St. Columbkill, and many other eminent scholars and saints; he died of the plague about 548. On the death of Ethri O'Miadachain, in 1174, his successor, Eugene, substituted the title of Meath for that of Clonard; but the bishop's see remained at the latter place till 1206, when Simon Rochfort, an Englishman, forsaking the old cathedral of Clonard, made the abbey at Newtown near Trim his cathedral. A great part of the abbey erected by St. Finian was burnt in 764; and the abbey was destroyed and its clergy put to the sword by the Danes in 838. In 939, Ceallachan, King of Cashel, assisted by the Danes of Waterford, plundered the abbey. In 947, King Congalagh exempted the abbey from payment of cess, &c. In 970, Donell, son of Murcha, pillaged and burnt Clonard. Sitric, the son of Ablaoimh, with the Danes of Dublin, in 1016, pillaged and destroyed the abbey. In 1045, the town, together with its churches, was wholly consumed, being thrice set on fire in one week. In 1085, Engus O'Candelbain, prince of Hy Loegaire, while a monk in this abbey, was killed by Mac Coirthen O'Muobruain, Lord of Delbna. The abbey was twice plundered in 1131, by the people of Carbrey and Teaffia. In 1113, Connor, King of Munster, plundered Meath and forcibly carried off the riches of the whole province, which had been lodged for safety in the abbey church. In 1136, the inhabitants of the Brenny, now Leitrim and Cavan, plundered and sacked the town, maltreated Constantine O'Daly, then chief poet of Ireland, and took from the abbey a sword which had belonged to St. Finian. The town and abbey were plundered and burnt by Mac Murcha and Earl Strongbow, in 1170, but both were rebuilt by the inhabitants; they were, however, again destroyed in 1175. Besides the calamities above enumerated, the town and abbey were frequently burnt or pillaged in the 11th and 12th centuries. About 1175, Walter, son of Hugh de Lacy, erected, probably on the ruins of the ancient abbey, an Augustinian monastery. In 1200, the English of Clonard slew Mathghamhain, the son of Fitzpatrick O'Ciardha, who in revenge burnt the town. Prior to the arrival of the English, O'Melaghlin, King of Meath, had founded a nunnery here, which afterwards became a cell to that of St. Bridget of Odder. In the war of 1641, this place acquired considerable celebrity from the gallant defence of the castle of Tycroghan, made by Lady Fitz-gerald. During the disturbances of 1798, a party of 3000 insurgents, under the command of William Aylmer, marched to this place, but met with so obstinate a resistance from Lieut. Tyrrell with 27 yeomanry, in a fortified house, that they were detained till succours arrived from Kinnegad and Mullingar, and were then obliged to retire.

This place, which was formerly called *Cluainioraid*, and more anciently *Rossfinnchuill*, is situated on the river Boyne, and on the mail coach road from Dublin to Galway. The town, or village, contains only 10 houses; it is a constabulary police station. The parish comprises 10,584 statute acres, as applotted under the tithe act, nearly the whole of which is arable or pasture land; the soil is generally light and tolerably productive; besides bog, there are several hundred acres rendered useless for half the year by the overflowing of the Boyne and five small rivers which fall into it. The Royal Canal enters the parish from the county of Kildare by a noble aqueduct over the Boyne, and, after passing through it for four miles, enters Westmeath. The great western road also enters from Kildare by Leinster bridge, which was erected in 1831, and is very handsome.

The living is a vicarage, in the diocese of Meath, united by act of council, in 1782, to the vicarage of Killyon or Killeighlan, together forming the union of Clonard, in the patronage of the Bishop: the rectory is impropriate in Joseph Ash, Esq., of Drogheda. The tithes amount to £484. 12. 3¼., of which £323. 1. 6¼. is payable to the impropriator, and the remainder to the vicar: the gross value of the benefice, including tithes and glebe, is £327. 13. 10½. The church, which stands about half a mile from the village, is in the early English style of architecture, with a lofty square tower, and was built on the site of the former edifice by aid of a loan of £400, in 1810, from the late Board of First Fruits. The Ecclesiastical Commissioners have recently granted £222. 13. 10. for its repair. The glebe-house, near the church, is large and convenient, and is situated on a very good glebe of 40 acres, valued at £120 per annum. In the R. C. divisions the parish is partly in the union or district of Kinnegad, and partly the head of a union or district called Longwood, and comprising part of Clonard and the whole of Killyon, in which union are two chapels, one at Longwood, the other at Killyon; the chapel in the town of Clonard, which is a large plain edifice, belongs to the union of Kinnegad. The parochial school is aided by donations from Lord Sherborne and the rector, and a bequest by the late Lady Jane Loftus; and there is also a national school, in which together are about 100 boys and 80 girls, and about 120 more are educated in three hedge schools. Among the vestiges of antiquity is a rath near the church, with a very fine conical mound, the summit of which is crowned with a flourishing ash tree; and at the distance of 500 paces is a spacious square fort. Many spears, celts, querns, and other relics have been dug up near the banks of the Blind river, in the neighbourhood of this rath and fort. Near the former have been found great quantities of scoriæ and charcoal, being the refuse of ancient and extensive iron works. The castle of Tycroghan has been taken down, and its materials used in the erection of modern houses on its site. In the vicinity is a part of the walls of an ancient friary, or church, in a burial-ground. In the church is a very old baptismal font, ornamented with figures in high relief.

CLONARNEY, a parish, in the barony of DELVIN, county of WESTMEATH, and province of LEINSTER, 1 mile (N. by W.) from Castletown-Delvin, on the road to Crossakeel; containing 848 inhabitants. This parish comprises 2168 statute acres, as applotted under the tithe act; the land is principally arable and pasture, with about 50 acres of waste or bog; here is abundance of limestone. It is a rectory, in the diocese of Meath, and is part of the union of Castletown-Delvin: the tithes amount to £92. 6. 1¾. per ann. In the R. C. divisions it forms part of the union or district of Clonmellon. Here is a hedge school, in which 23 boys and 18 girls are educated. There are some remains of the old church, with a cemetery attached.

CLONASLEE, an ecclesiastical district, in the barony of TINNEHINCH, QUEEN'S county, and province of LEINSTER, 7¼ miles (W. N. W.) from Mountmellick, and 47¾ (W. S. W.) from Dublin; containing 514 inhabitants, and in the village 79 houses. This place is situated on the river Barradois, over which is a good bridge, and has a penny post to Mountmellick. There is a boulting-mill in the parish, and fairs are held on May 3rd and Nov. 7th, and petty sessions weekly. Adjoining the village is the fine demesne of Brittas, the property of Gen. Dunne. The district was formerly part of the parish of Kilmanman, in the union of Rosinallis, from which it was separated some years since and erected into a district parish. It is a perpetual curacy, in the diocese of Kildare, and in the patronage of the Incumbent of Rosinallis. The church is a handsome edifice, with a well-proportioned spire, erected in 1814, under the direction and auspices of Gen. Dunne, aided by a gift of £800 and a loan of £300 from the late Board of First Fruits, and for the repairs of which the Ecclesiastical Commissioners have recently granted £377. 5. 6. The glebe-house was built by a gift of £450 and a loan of £50 from the late Board of First Fruits, in 1830. In the R. C. divisions it is the head of a union or district, comprising also parts of the parishes of Rery and Kilmanman; the chapel is a spacious building. There is a parochial school, and also a school in connection with the trustees of Erasmus Smith's charity; the school-house, a large slated building, was erected at an expense of £300. At Clara Hill, about a mile from the village, are the ruins of an old castle, which was formerly the residence of a younger branch of the Dunne family; and near the east bank of the Barradois or Clodiagh river are the ruins of a castle, called Ballinakill, built in 1680 by Col. Dunne. To the south of this is Coolamona, once a place of considerable strength, forming an outpost of Tinnehinch, but now nearly demolished. In the neighbourhood are some raths, in one of which was found, in 1734, a rude kistvaen of unhewn flags, covered by a tumulus of earth and stones.

CLONBEG, a parish, in the barony of CLANWILLIAM, county of TIPPERARY, and province of MUNSTER, 4 miles (S. by W.) from Tipperary; containing 3662 inhabitants. This parish is situated in the glen of Aherlow, through which runs the river of that name, and is intersected in the south-western portion by the new road from Tipperary to Mitchelstown; it comprises 10,616 statute acres, as applotted under the tithe act, of which about 250 are woodland, and nearly one-third of the remainder are incapable of tillage, though part might be improved. The lands in the valley are generally of good quality; there is a large tract of bog on the mountains, and slate abounds, but is not quarried. The scenery of the glen is of highly picturesque character. The north side of the Galtee mountains is within the parish, and within the last thirty-five years abounded with red and fallow deer; but from the improvements that have taken place in agriculture, and the increase of the population, they have totally disappeared. On the top of Galtimore is a large flat stone, called "Kingston" or "Dawson's Table," which is seen from a great distance; and near it is a remarkably fine spring of water, a circumstance unusual at such an elevation; there are also three small lakes in the vicinity of that mountain and within the parish. The gentlemen's seats are Ballinacourty, the residence of J. H. Massy Dawson, Esq., commanding a fine view of Galtimore and of the glen of Aherlow; Ballywire, of J. Bolton Massy, Esq.; and Woodville, of Matthew Gibbons, Esq. A constabulary police force is stationed here. The living is a rectory, in the diocese of Cashel, and in the patronage of the Archbishop: the tithes amount to £369. 4. 7½. The church is small and out of repair, and it is in contemplation to rebuild it. The glebe-house is a handsome residence; the glebe comprises 18 acres. In the R. C. divisions the parish forms part of the union or district of Galbally; the chapel is a neat plain building. The parochial schools, in which are about 30 boys and 20 girls, are aided by annual donations from the rector, Capt. Dawson, and Mr. Hill. There are also two pay schools, in which are about 50 boys and 20 girls. There are some remains of Moore abbey, and several Danish raths in the parish; and on the hill is a good chalybeate spring.

CLONBERN, a parish, in the half-barony of BALLYMOE, county of GALWAY, and province of CONNAUGHT, 10 miles (W. N. W.) from Ballynamore, on the road to Tuam; containing 2374 inhabitants. It is a vicarage, in the diocese of Tuam, and is part of the union of Kilkerrin; the rectory is appropriate partly to the see, and partly to the provostship of Tuam, the latter portion forming part of the corps of the deanery of Tuam, in the patronage of the Crown. The tithes amount to £160, of which £120 is payable to the appropriators, and the remainder to the vicar. In the R. C. divisions it forms part of the union or district of Kilkerrin; the chapel at Lerbir is a small thatched building. There are two pay schools, situated respectively at Lerhir and Mohanagh in which are about 120 boys and 40 girls.

CLONBRONEY, or CLONEBRONE, a parish, partly in the barony of ARDAGH, but chiefly in that of GRANARD, county of LONGFORD, and province of LEINSTER, 6½ (W.) from Granard, on the road to Longford; containing 4819 inhabitants. Here was a nunnery, said to have been founded by St. Patrick, which was destroyed by fire in 778, but was soon restored, and existed at least till the 12th century. In 1798, Lord Cornwallis encamped here before the battle of Ballinamuck. The parish contains 12,101 statute acres, as applotted under the tithe act, of which 51 are woodland, 9892 arable and pasture, 1382 bog, 444 grazing bog and 332 curragh or fen. Excellent limestone is found here. Fairs are held on May 9th and Nov. 18th. The principal seats are Kilshruly, the residence of T. N. Edgeworth, Esq.; Curraghgrane, of W. L. Galbraith, Esq.; Whitehill, of H. B. Slator, Esq.; Lissard, of J. L. O'Ferrall, Esq.; and Lakeview, of R. Grier, Esq. The living is a vicarage, in the diocese of Ardagh, and in the patronage of the Bishop; the rectory is partly impropriate in Michael Nelligan, Esq., and partly appropriate to the see of Ardagh. The tithes amount to £406. 5. 11., of which £115. 7. 11½. is paid to the impropriator, £124. 13. 8¼. to the Archbishop of Tuam (as Bishop of Ardagh), and £166. 4. 2½. to the vicar. The church is a handsome structure, in the ancient style of English architecture, built in 1825, by aid of a gift of £1100 from the late Board of First Fruits, and enlarged in 1830, by a loan of £300 from the same Board, and a donation of £100 from the Countess Dowager of Rosse. The glebe-house was built in 1822, by aid of a gift of £200 and a loan of £255 from the Board: the glebe comprises 38 acres. The R. C. parish is co-extensive with that of the Established Church; there is a chapel at Ballinalee, or St. Johnstown, and one in Drumeel. At Drumeel is a national school, and there is another in course of erection in the village. There are also a school for boys at St. Johnstown, a male and female school at Drumderrig, and one in Ballinascroaw; a female school in the village is aided by the vicar and curate, and an infants' school is supported by Col. Palliser. The school-house in the village is a good building. Sir James Ware left a tract of land called Scolands, for the instruction of children, but his bequest has been a considerable time under litigation. Mr. Charlton left the lands of Moate Ferrall, the profits to be distributed among male and female servants, on their marriage. Near White Hill is a remarkable moat, which is said to have been the residence of the head of the O'Ferralls, the ancient proprietors of the soil. There are some remains of the ancient church of Clonbrone, with a cemetery attached. The small lake of Gurteen discharges its superfluous waters into the river Camlin by a subterraneous passage, extending a quarter of a mile in length. At Firmount was born the Abbé Edgeworth, who attended Louis XVI. on the scaffold, as his confessor.

CLONBULLOGE, or PUREFOY'S PLACE, a village, in the parish of Clonsast, barony of Coolestown, King's county, and province of Leinster, 5½ miles (S. by W.) from Edenderry: the population is returned with the parish. This village is situated on the small river Barrow, and is surrounded by the bog of Allen; it consists only of a few small and indifferent dwellings, the larger houses having been burned in the disturbances of 1798, during which period it was the only place in this part of the country that suffered from actual violence. Fairs are held on July 11th and Oct. 29th; and a constabulary police force is stationed here. The parish church, which was built about the year 1670, is situated in the village, and the Ecclesiastical Commissioners have recently granted £243. 8. for its repair.—See Clonsast.

CLONBULLOGE, or CLONBOLOGUE, a parish, in the barony of Clanwilliam, county of Tipperary, and province of Munster, 4½ miles (S. E.) from Tipperary, containing 1457 inhabitants. This parish is situated near the mail coach road from Limerick to Waterford, and is intersected by the river Arra; it comprises 3192 statute acres, as applotted under the tithe act, and valued at £2518 per annum. Lismacue, the residence of H. Baker, Esq., is a handsome mansion, the demesne of which extends into the parish of Templeneira. It is a rectory, in the diocese of Cashel, and is part of the union of Tipperary: the tithes amount to £136. 12. 3¾., and the glebe comprises 46 statute acres. There are two pay schools, in which are 70 children.

CLONCA.—See CLONCHA.

CLONCAGH, or CLOUNCAGH, a parish, in the barony of Upper Connello, county of Limerick, and province of Munster, 3½ miles (N. E.) from Newcastle, on the road to Ballingarry; containing 1397 inhabitants. It comprises 4331½ statute acres, as applotted under the tithe act. To the north is a lofty ridge of silicious grit formation, but the remainder of the parish is low and chiefly in meadow and pasture. The land under tillage produces excellent crops; around the old church it is remarkably fertile. Balliahill, the residence of W. Odell, Esq., is situated in a plain of great fertility; and not far from it is Brook Lodge, the occasional residence of H. Massey, Esq., of Mount Massey, in the county of Cork. It is a vicarage, in the diocese of Limerick, and is part of the union of Clonelty; the rectory is appropriate to the vicars choral of the cathedral church of St. Mary, Limerick. The tithes amount to £255, of which £170 is paid to the lessees of the vicars choral, and the remainder to the vicar. In the R. C. divisions it forms part of the union or district of Knockaderry, in which are two chapels, one at Knockaderry and the other at this place, both plain buildings. There is a pay school, in which are 30 boys and 10 girls. The ruins of the old parish church are very extensive, and are said to occupy the site of an abbey founded here by St. Madoc in the sixth century, and of which little is known but the name; it afforded shelter to some of the distressed Irish after the disastrous battle of Monasternenagh, which took place during the Earl of Desmond's insurrection.

CLONCALL.—See FORGNEY.

CLONCAST.—See CLONSAST.

CLONCAT, a village, in the parish of Girley, barony of Upper Kells, county of Meath, and province of Leinster, containing 22 houses and 128 inhabitants.

CLONCHA, or CLONCA, a parish, in the barony of Ennishowen, county of Donegal, and province of Ulster, 5 miles (N.) from Carn; containing 6654 inhabitants. This parish is bounded on the north by the Atlantic ocean, and the west by Strabregagh bay, and comprises, according to the Ordnance survey, 19,643 statute acres. The land is much diversified, but generally cold, wet, and barren: the higher grounds form the mountains of Knockamany and Knockbrack, whose summits and sides are covered with heath, coarse herbage, and bog. These mountains are principally composed of schist, or clay-slate, but in the lower districts there are considerable deposits of coarse blue limestone, and granite and porphyry are sometimes found in detached masses. Coral, jasper, chalcedony, opal, agate, and cornelian, are sometimes found in small masses on the shores, and are called in the neighbourhood Malin pebbles; some of them are of considerable value, and are set in seals, rings, necklaces, and other ornaments. Here is the lough or harbour of Strabregagh, which separates the parish from those of Donagh and Clonmany: it is unfit for vessels that draw much water, though small vessels can find shelter any where along the Runevad Point, and is often mistaken for Lough Swilly, which has caused many shipwrecks. The coast on each side of the entrance is very rocky, and the tides rapid. From Strabregagh to Coolort, and from Malin to Glengad, it presents a series of picturesque precipices, among which is Malin Head, the most northern point of the mainland of Ireland, being in N. Lat. 55° 20′ 40″, and W. Lon. 7° 24′. Eight miles east of the Head, and five from the shore, is the island of Ennistrahul, on which is a light-house, exhibiting a bright revolving light, visible only once in two minutes. To the east of the Head, and a mile and a half from the shore, are several small isles, called the Garve Islands. In the townland of Ballyhillian, at Malin Head, there is an admiralty signal tower; and at Malin Head and Glengad are coast-guard stations. Strabregagh abounds with salmon, and seals are sometimes found in it. At Portmore, near Slieve Ban, a pier and harbour are being constructed, at the expense of Capt. Hart, to whom the property of Malin Head belongs. The principal seats are Malin Hall, the residence of J. Harvey, jun., Esq., situated in a beautiful demesne embellished with flourishing plantations, which are highly ornamental in this bleak and exposed district; Rockville, of the Rev. J. Canning; and Goorey Lodge, of J. Harvey, sen., Esq.

The living is a rectory and vicarage, in the diocese of Derry, and in the patronage of the Marquess of Donegal: the tithes amount to £555; the glebe comprises 370 acres, of which 110 are barren. The church is at Malin, and was built in 1827, by aid of a loan of £200 from the late Board of First Fruits, and a gift of £100 each from Bishop Knox and Mr. Harvey, of Malin Hall: it is a neat plain building, with a handsome square tower. In the R. C. divisions part of this parish is united to part of Culdaff, forming the union or district of Cloncha; the remaining portions of the two parishes are also united and form the district of Culdaff. There are chapels at Lag and Aughacloy, in the former district, and at Bogan in the latter, all in this parish. At Goorey is a large Presbyterian meeting-house connected with the Synod of Ulster, of the third class. The parochial schools, which are in the town of Malin, are principally supported by the Harvey family. There is a female working school at Malin, also schools at Keenagh and Tully, both built on the estate of Mr. Harvey, of Malin Hall, who is the principal landed proprietor in the parish; and one near Malin Head. In these schools about 400 boys and 230 girls are educated; and there are also five private schools, in which are about 190 children, and three Sunday schools. At Larachrill are ten upright and two prostrate stones, about six feet high, so disposed as to form part of a druidical circle of 60 feet in diameter. At Umgal is shewn what is called Ossian's grave, and near it are places bearing the names of many of the events recorded in his poems. There are likewise traces of a monastery, and several churches or cells, whose names are unknown. Both history and tradition mention a conventual church at Malin, of which the only vestiges are a heap of stones. Pilgrimages are still performed to this place, which terminate by bathing in a small hollow in the rocks at Malin Head, which is filled at every tide and is reputed to possess the power of curing diseases. The old church of Cloncha, which has been disused since 1827 and is falling into ruin, appears to have been an abbey or priory. Near it is a stone pillar, 18 feet high, which was apparently the shaft of a cross, and is ornamented with scrolls and emblems; the upper part is broken off, and lies at some distance. At Ballyahillon is a natural cave in the rocks, of considerable extent: it is here known as "Hell's hole," and is the subject of many extraordinary tales.—See Malin.

CLONCLARE, or CLOONCLARE, a parish, partly in the barony of Rossclogher, but chiefly in that of Dromahaire, county of Leitrim, and province of Connaught; containing, with part of the post-town of Manorhamilton, 9128 inhabitants. This parish is situated on the road from Enniskillen to Sligo, and comprises 33,241 statute acres, as applotted under the tithe act, besides a great extent of waste land, much of which is reclaimable, and a large quantity of bog. Coal exists, but is not worked; and there is abundance of limestone, some of which is used for building. Large veins of iron ore of the best quality exist in the mountains of Doon and Glenfarne, which also furnish freestone equal to that of Portland. There is a bleach-green at Glenboy. Glenfarne Hall, the residence of C. H. Tottenham, Esq., is situated in a very extensive demesne on Lough MacNean, which communicates with Lough Erne. The other seats are Hollymount, the residence of Simon Armstrong, Esq.; Glenboy, of Lewis Algeo, Esq.; and Fortland Cottage, of G. Gledstanes, Esq.

The living is a vicarage, in the diocese of Kilmore, united from time immemorial to the vicarages of Clonlogher and Killasnett, together forming the union of Manorhamilton, in the patronage of the Bishop, to whom the rectory is appropriate. The tithes amount to £300, of which £200 is paid to the bishop, and £100 to the vicar; and the gross tithes of the benefice amount to £421. 6. 8. The church is a plain building with a handsome spire, erected in 1804, and for its repair the Ecclesiastical Commissioners have recently granted £115. The R. C. parish is co-extensive with that of the Established Church, and is also called Glenfarne; there are two chapels, one at Glenfarne, the other in the town of Manorhamilton; a third is in course of erection at Kilticlogher. At Manorhamilton are two places of worship for Methodists. There are six schools in the parish; that at Manorhamilton is supported by a bequest, in 1819, from the late James John Masterson, Esq., of £26. 6. 6. per annum. In these schools about 170 boys and 230 girls receive instruction, and 14 boys and 25 girls are taught in a private school.—See Manorhamilton and Kilticlogher.

CLONCURRY, a parish, partly in the barony of East Ophaly, but chiefly in that of Ikeathy and Oughterany, county of Kildare, and province of Leinster, 4 miles (W. N. W.) from Kilcock; containing 2299 inhabitants. A Carmelite friary, dedicated to the Blessed Virgin, was founded here by John Roche, in 1347, which, together with the village, was burnt by some of the Irish septs in 1405; it appears, however, to have been restored, and continued to exist till the Reformation, when it was granted to William Dixon in the 35th of Hen. VIII. The manor became the property of the Aylmer family, whose ancient seat, the castle, was defended for the parliament, in 1643, by Col. Monk, who was at length obliged to abandon it for want of provisions. From the Aylmer family the estate was afterwards purchased by Sir Nicholas Lawless, subsequently created Baron Cloncurry. During the disturbances of 1798, a skirmish took place at the foot of Ovidstown Hill, in this parish, between the king's troops and a party of the insurgents who had effected their escape from the county of Wexford. The parish, which is situated on the road from Dublin to Galway, and on the line of the Royal Canal, comprises 2449 statute acres, as applotted under the tithe act. The land is chiefly in pasture, and great numbers of cattle are fattened for the Dublin and English markets; in that portion of it which is under tillage the improved system of agriculture is adopted; there are about 400 acres of good bog. Ballinakill, the seat of T. Kearney, Esq., is a handsome modern house. It is a vicarage, in the diocese of Kildare, and is part of the union of Kilcock; the rectory is partly impropriate in the representatives of the late Michael Aylmer, Esq., and the remainder forms the corps of the deanery of the cathedral church of St. Bridget, Kildare, the appointment to which is elective by the chapter. The tithes amount to £476. 8. 2¾., of which £161. 8. 3. is payable to the dean, £105 to the vicar, and the remainder to the impropriators. The church is in ruins. In the R. C. divisions the parish also forms part of the union or district of Kilcock. There is a private school, in which are about 30 boys and 20 girls. There are some inconsiderable remains of the ancient Carmelite friary. The title of Baron Cloncurry was first conferred on Sir Nicholas Lawless, in 1789 and his descendant, the present Lord Cloncurry, was raised to the English peerage in 1831.

CLONDAGAD, or CLONDEGAD, a parish, in the barony of ISLANDS, county of CLARE, and province of MUNSTER, 7¼ miles (S. S. W.) from Ennis; containing 4650 inhabitants. This parish is situated on the west bank of the river Fergus, and contains 16,436 statute acres, of which 4711 are good arable and pasture land, and 11,725 are improvable bog and mountain. The arable land is good, and produces excellent crops of grain, which, with butter, pork, &c., are sent to Limerick from a small rudely constructed quay at Ballycorig. Good building stone abounds. A seneschal's court is held occasionally at Ballycorig for the manor of Clonroad, in which small debts are recoverable. The living is a vicarage, in the diocese of Killaloe, forming, with part of the rectory, the corps of the prebend of Clondagad in the cathedral of Killaloe, and in the patronage of the Bishop; the other portion of the rectory is impropriate in John Scott, Esq. The tithes amount to £415. 7. 8½., of which £230. 15. 4¾. is payable to the impropriator, and £184. 12. 3¾. to the vicar. The glebe-house was erected in 1812, by a gift of £400 and a loan of £296 from the late Board of First Fruits: the glebe comprises 3*a.* 3*r.* 22*p.* The church is a small plain building with a square tower, and was erected on the site of a former one by aid of a gift of £600, in 1808, from the same Board. In the R. C. divisions the parish is the head of a union or district, comprising also the parish of Kilchrist, and containing two chapels; that for Clondagad is at Launa. There are five private schools, in which about 420 children are educated. At Ballycorig are some remains of the castle of that name.

CLONDALKIN, a parish, in the barony of UPPERCROSS, county of DUBLIN, and province of LEINSTER, 5 miles (S. W.) from Dublin; containing 2976 inhabitants, of which number, 374 are in the village. This place, anciently called *Cluain-Dolcan*, and by the Danes *Dun-Awley*, appears, from the evidence of its ancient round tower, still in good preservation, to have had a very remote origin. A monastery was founded here, of which St. Cronan Mochua was the first abbot; and a palace here belonging to Anlaff, or Auliffe, the Danish king of Dublin, was, in 806, destroyed by the Irish under Ciaran, the son of Ronan. The monastery was plundered and burnt in 832, 1071, and 1076, since which last date there is no further record of its history. In 1171, Roderic O'Connor, King of Leinster, with the forces of O'Ruarc and O'Carrol, Prince of Argial, marched to this place against Earl Strongbow, who was then besieging Dublin; but in order to oppose his further progress, Strongbow advanced to give him battle, and after some days' skirmishing compelled him to retreat, leaving Dublin to the mercy of the English. The village, near the entrance of which are the remains of a fortified castle, consists chiefly of one irregular street, and in 1831 contained 150 houses neatly built, though small, and some neatly ornamented cottages appropriated to the uses of charitable and benevolent institutions. It is situated on the small river Camma, and the road from Dublin to Newcastle, and is a constabulary police station. In common with the parish, it is within the jurisdiction of the manor court of St. Sepulchre's Dublin. The greater portion of the parish is arable land; the soil is fertile, and the system of agriculture very much improved under the auspices of many resident gentlemen, who farm their own estates, and have established ploughing matches for prizes, which are annually distributed. There are quarries of good limestone, which is raised in abundance for agricultural and other uses. The gentlemen's seats are Newlands, the residence of P. Crotty, Esq., a handsome modern mansion, previously occupied by the late Lord Kilwarden, Chief-Justice of the King's Bench; Collinstown, of M. Mills, Esq.; Larkfield, of J. Hamilton, Esq., in the grounds of which are the ruins of an old castle covered with ivy; Corkagh, of W. Stockley, Esq.; Little Corkagh, of H. Arabin, Esq.; Moyle Park, of W. Caldbeck, Esq.; Neilstown House, of L. Rorke, Esq.; Nanger, of P. C. Rorke, Esq., formerly an old embattled castle, now modernised; Clondalkin, of Mrs. Anne Connolly; Kilcarbery, of H. Phillips, Esq.; St. Mark's, of Capt. Foss; Neilstown Lodge, of C. Brabazon, Esq.; Flora-ville, of F. Smith, Esq.; Rosebank, of W. Bayly, Esq.; Clonburrows, of M. Pearson, Esq.; Collinstown Cottage, of the Rev. Mr. O'Callaghan; and Clover Hill, of D. Kinalson, Esq. There is an oil-mill in the parish, and in the demesne of Little Corkagh are some gunpowder-mills, established a century since, but not used since 1815; one of them has been converted into a thrashing and cleaning mill, capable of preparing 100 barrels daily. The Grand

Canal passes through the parish, and the Royal Canal through the northern part of the union, near the Duke of Leinster's demesne.

The living is a rectory and a vicarage, in the diocese of Dublin; the rectory is united to those of Rathcool, Esker, Kilberry, and Tallagh, together constituting the corps of the deanery of St. Patrick's Dublin, in the patronage of the Chapter; and the vicarage is united to the rectory of Kilmactalway, the vicarage of Kilbride, the curacies of Drimnagh and Kilmacrudery, and the half rectories of Donoghmore and Donocomper, together constituting the union of Clondalkin, in the patronage of the Archbishop. The tithes of Clondalkin amount to £473. 18. 11., of which £428. 2. 5¼. is payable to the dean, and £43. 0. 9¾. to the vicar. The glebe-house, a good residence in the village, was built in 1810, by aid of a gift of £100 and a loan of £450 from the late Board of First Fruits: the glebe comprises 17*a*. 2*r*. 5*p*. of profitable land. The church is a small modern edifice in good repair, and requires to be enlarged. In the R. C. divisions the parish forms part of the union or district of Palmerstown, Clondalkin, and Lucan; the chapel at the village of Clondalkin is a neat building. There is also a chapel attached to the monastery of Mount Joseph, which is pleasantly situated on high ground commanding extensive views, at no great distance from the mail coach road from Dublin to Naas: this establishment was founded in 1813, and consists of a prior and several brethren, with a chaplain, who support themselves by their own industry. Some of them conduct a day and boarding school for such as can afford to pay; and in connection with the monastery is a school of about 200 boys, supported by a grant of £16 per annum from the National Board, and collections at an annual charity sermon. There is another national school, and there are two others and a Sunday school, for which school-rooms have been erected at an expense of £240, towards which the Rev. Dr. Reade, the present incumbent, contributed £140, and also assigned in perpetuity to the parish the ground on which they are built; the total number in these schools is about 216 boys and 305 girls. There is also a school in the village, in which about 130 girls are instructed and 40 annually clothed; it is under the management of Mrs. Caldbeck, and supported by her, aided by collections at the R. C. chapel and the sale of the children's work. The school-room was built by subscription, in 1831, on land given by Wm. Caldbeck, Esq., who also, in 1833, gave land for the erection of a house for the R. C. clergyman, and for a dispensary. The Rev. Dr. Reade has also established almshouses for destitute widows, a poor shop, repository, Dorcas institution, and a lying-in hospital. Nearly adjacent to the present church are the almost shapeless ruins of the old conventual church of the monastery, which was afterwards the parochial church, and among them is an ancient cross of granite, nine feet high; it appears to have been a spacious structure, about 120 feet long and from 50 to 60 feet wide; and near it is the ancient round tower previously noticed. This tower is about 100 feet high and 15 feet in diameter, and is covered with a conical roof of stone; its style is of the plainest order, and it is in good preservation; the entrance is about 10 feet from the ground, and the base of the column to that height was, about 60 years since, cased with strong masonry. There are four openings looking towards the cardinal points in the upper story, in which a room has been formed by its proprietor, R. Caldbeck, Esq., having an ascent by ladders from within, and commanding a most extensive and interesting prospect over the surrounding country. At Ballymount are extensive remains of a once strong castle, consisting principally of the enclosing walls and the keep: within the walls is a respectable farm-house, evidently built with the old materials.

CLONDEHORKY, a parish, in the barony of Kilmacrenan, county of Donegal, and province of Ulster; containing, with the post-town of Dunfanaghy, 6477 inhabitants. This parish is situated on the bay of Sheep Haven, on the north-western coast, and comprises, according to the Ordnance survey, 29,632¾ statute acres, of which 26,859 are applotted under the tithe act, and 421½ are water. A small portion is woodland, a considerable portion arable and rough pasture, and there is a large tract of waste land and bog, of which much might be easily reclaimed. Near Rough Point is an extensive rabbit-warren. There are quarries producing slates of tolerable quality, and an inferior kind of marble is also found in the parish. Silicious sand of excellent quality is obtained from Muckish mountain, where iron ore is found: this mountain rises to an elevation of 2190 feet above the level of the sea. The gentlemen's seats are Horn Head, the residence of W. Stewart, Esq.; Marble Hill, of G. Barclay, Esq.; Ards, of A. Stewart, Esq., attached to which is a beautiful demesne; and Castle Doe, of Capt. Hart, formerly the residence of the Sandford family, and described as a very strong castle surrounded by a bawn 40 feet square and 16 feet high. Fairs are held on the 10th of every month at Creaslough, and there are others at Dunfanaghy *which see*. A manor court is occasionally held, at which small debts are recoverable. At Sheep Haven is a coast-guard station, one of the seven constituting the district of Dunfanaghy. Within the limits of the parish is the point called Horn Head, in latitude 55° 12′ 50″ (N.), and longitude 7° 58′ 20″ (W.); and between it and the peninsula of Rossgull, or Rosguill is Sheep Haven, off the eastern side of which are several rocks above water, the outermost of which, nearly two miles west of Melmor Point, is called Carrickavrank rock.

The living is a rectory and vicarage, in the diocese of Raphoe, forming the corps of the prebend of Clondehorky, in the cathedral church of Raphoe, and in the patronage of the Provost and Fellows of Trinity College, Dublin. The tithes amount to £280. There is no glebe-house; the glebe comprises 400 acres, of which 200 are a barren sandy tract. The church is a neat plain structure, built by aid of a gift of £300 from the late Board of First Fruits. The R. C. parish is co-extensive with that of the Established Church: the chapel, a spacious building, was erected in 1830, at an expense of £600, and there is a place of worship for Presbyterians in connection with the Synod of Ulster, of the third class. The parochial school is supported partly from Col. Robertson's fund and by annual donations, and a school at Cashelmore is supported by Mr. Stewart, of Ards. In these schools about 120 boys and 70 girls are instructed; and there are three pay schools, in which are about 170 boys and 90 girls. At Ballymacswiney are some ruins of a monastery for Franciscans, founded by McSwine; and near the coast is "McSwine's Gun," a perforation in the rock, through which the sea is forced, during or immediately after a storm from the north-west, to a height of between 200 and 300 feet, with so great a noise as to be heard for 10 miles.—See DUNFANAGHY.

CLONDERMOT.—See GLENDERMOTT.

CLONDEVADOCK, or CLONDEVADOGUE, a parish, in the barony of KILMACRENAN, county of DONEGAL, and province of ULSTER, 15½ miles (N. by E.) from Letterkenny; containing 9595 inhabitants. This parish, which comprises, according to the Ordnance survey, 27,367¼ statute acres, of which 627¾ are water, is situated on the north-western coast; it comprehends the greater part of the peninsular district of Fannet, or Fanad, extending northward into the ocean, and terminating in the points called Maheranguna and Pollacheeny. The surface is for the most part occupied by mountains of considerable altitude, among which Knockalla is 1196 feet above the level of the sea: these are separated by deep and narrow vales, of which the soil is tolerably good, consisting of a brown gravelly mould, sometimes inclining to clay, on a basis of white gravel, brownish or reddish clay, slate of various colours, and sometimes soft freestone rock. The parish contains about 60 quarter lands of good arable and bad pasture, with much waste and barren land: many acres have been covered and destroyed by the shifting sands. The point of Fannet is in lat. 55° 15′ 50″ (N.) and lon. 7° 39′ (W.): it is on the western side of the entrance of Lough Swilly, and a lighthouse has been erected on it, of which the lantern has an elevation of 90 feet above the level of the sea at high water; it consists of nine lamps, displaying a deep red light towards the sea, and a bright fixed light towards the lough or harbour, and may be seen in clear weather from a distance of 14 nautical miles. The seats are Croohan House, the residence of R. H. Patton, Esq.; Greenfort, of H. Babington, Esq.; and Springfield, of M. Dill, Esq.

The living is a rectory and vicarage, in the diocese of Raphoe, and in the patronage of the Provost and Fellows of Trinity College, Dublin: the tithes amount to £463. 5. 4½. The glebe-house was built by aid of a loan of £100 from the late Board of First Fruits, in 1795; the glebe comprises 240 acres, of which 160 are uncultivated. The church is a plain structure, towards the repairs of which the Ecclesiastical Commissioners have recently granted £371. 10. 3. The R. C. parish is co-extensive with that of the Established Church, and contains two large chapels. There are five schools, one of which, the parochial school, is partly supported by annual donations from the rector and the late Col. Robertson's school fund. In these about 250 boys and 130 girls are instructed; and there are two pay schools, in which are about 70 boys and 11 girls, and five Sunday schools.

CLONDRA.—See RICHMOND HARBOUR.

CLONDROHID, a parish, in the barony of WEST MUSKERRY, county of CORK, and province of MUNSTER, 2 miles (N. W.) from Macroom; containing 5293 inhabitants. This parish is situated on the road from Cork to Killarney, and is intersected by the river Foherish, which, rising in the mountains of Glaundave, runs nearly through its centre, and joins the Sullane near Carrig-a-Phouca. It contains 25,276 statute acres, as applotted under the tithe act, and valued at £8070 per annum: of these, 50 acres are woodland, 8748 arable, 8898 pasture, 491 bog, and the remainder mountain and waste land. The waste land consists of rocky ground, which is adapted to the growth of timber, there being a natural growth of oak, birch, mountain ash, holly, and willow in the rocky districts. The bog is the most valuable portion of the parish, as it principally supplies the town of Macroom with fuel, besides furnishing the parishioners with firing for domestic purposes and burning lime. Great quantities of land have been brought into cultivation since 1812, but the state of agriculture has undergone little improvement; the old heavy wooden plough, or the spade, is still used. Towards the southern boundary, round Carrig-a-Phouca, are large masses of bare rock, with small patches of cultivable land interspersed. The mountains of Muskerrymore, on the north, and of Mullaghanish, which form the boundary between Cork and Kerry on the west, notwithstanding their elevation, afford excellent pasture. At Prohus and Glauntane are extensive slate quarries, the latter producing slate of very superior quality; and veins of copper ore are numerous in the neighbourhood of the former. In the rivulet of Bawnmore are strata of excellent freestone, dipping almost vertically. The old and new roads from Cork to Killarney, the former of which is the mail coach road; pass through the parish, and it is also intersected by a third road leading from Macroom to the Muskerry mountains. Within its limits are scenes of great variety and beauty, particularly near Carrig-a-Phouca and Cushkeen-morrohy, the latter of which vies with the romantic scenery of Killarney or Glengariff, but being at a distance from the road is little known. The vale of the Sullane, with the lofty mountains and craggy rocks in its vicinity, presents a wild and romantic scene. The principal seats in the parish are Ash Grove, the residence of R. Ashe, Esq.; Yew Hill, of J. Williams, Esq.; Mount Cross, of Mrs. Pearson; Hanover Hall, of J. Bowen, Esq.; and the glebe-house, of the Rev. R. Kirchhoffer.

The living is a rectory and vicarage, in the diocese of Cloyne, and in the patronage of the Bishop: the tithes amount to £1034, of which £58. 9. 6. is payable to the economy estate of the cathedral, and £975. 10. 6. to the incumbent. The glebe-house was erected by aid of a gift of £100, and a loan of £1500, from the late Board of First Fruits, in 1813: the glebe comprises 80 acres, of which 56*a.* 1*r.* 24*p.* belong to the economy estate of the cathedral of St. Colman, Cloyne. The church is a large plain edifice, erected in 1774, and rebuilt in 1829, chiefly at the expense of the rector. In the R. C. divisions this parish, with the exception of a small portion united to Kilnemartry, is a benefice in itself, in which are two chapels, one at Carriganimy, a small plain building; the other at Gurraneacopple, a large substantial edifice. The male and female parochial schools are situated on the glebe, and are supported by the rector. A national school is connected with the chapel at Gurraneacopple; and there is a Sunday school under the superintendence of the rector, besides two hedge schools. The castle of Carrig-a-Phouca is in this parish: it was built by the McCartys of Drishane, on an isolated rock in the vale of the Sullane, and consists of a square tower, still nearly entire, and one of the most perfect specimens of early castle architecture in the kingdom. The entrance is by a high craggy rock, up which not more than one person at a time can climb. In the mountains at Clashmaguire is a large heathen temple, many of the stones of which are nearly as large as those of Stonehenge. At Gurtavannir are two upright stones, and near them is a druidical circle. Not far distant is the table stone of a cromlech, besides many single upright stones of large size, called Gollanes by the peasantry. In the vicinity of the glebe is a rock called the Giant's Table, surrounded by stone seats. In 1822, there were some disturbances at Carriganimy, during which the Tralee mail was plundered, and many of the peasantry were killed.

CLONDUFF, or CLANDUFF, a parish, in the barony of UPPER IVEAGH, county of DOWN, and province of ULSTER, 2¾ miles (S.) from Rathfriland; containing, with the village of Hilltown, 7916 inhabitants. This parish is situated on the river Bann, and on one of the roads leading from Newry to Downpatrick; and comprises, according to the Ordnance survey, 21,241¾ statute acres, of which 889 are mountain, with a portion of bog, and the remainder good arable and pasture land, the former producing excellent crops. Eagle mountain, at the southern extremity of the parish, is 1084 feet above the level of the sea. The gentlemen's seats are King's Hill, the residence of W. Barron, Esq.; Cabra, the property of A. McMullan, Esq., recently erected on the site of the ancient residence of the Mac Gennis family; and Hilltown Parsonage, the residence of the Rev J. A. Beers. About a mile from the village of Hilltown, and on the river Bann, is a bleach-green, the first or uppermost on that river, which in its course becomes a most important stream to bleachers and manufacturers of linen. The parish anciently formed part of the possessions of the abbey of Bangor, and by an inquisition in 1605 was found to comprise 22 townlands, now increased to 25, which, with the exception of four within the bishop's court at Dromore, are within the jurisdiction of the manorial court of Rathfriland. The living is a vicarage, in the diocese of Dromore, and in the patronage of the Bishop; the rectory, with the exception of the tithes of four townlands, which belong to the vicar, is impropriate in the Earl of Clanwilliam. The tithes amount to £364. 1. 7., of which £164. 4. 3. is payable to the impropriator, and the remainder to the incumbent. The glebe-house is a handsome residence at Hilltown: the glebe comprises 21 acres of very good land. The church is also at Hilltown, *which see.*. The R. C. parish is co-extensive with that of the Established Church; there are two chapels, one at Cabra, and one in the village of Hilltown, where is also a place of worship for Presbyterians in connection with the Synod of Ulster, of the third class. Besides the parochial school at Hilltown, there are schools at Tamrye, Drumnascamph, Ballycashone, and Ballynagrapog, and a national school near Hilltown; and there are two pay schools, in which are about 100 children. About a mile to the east of Hilltown are the ruins of the old parish church, in a large and very ancient burial-ground, in which were interred, in 1809, John and Felix O'Neill, supposed to have been the last male descendants of the once powerful sept of Tir-Oen. A very handsome antique chalice, now in the possession of A. Murphy, Esq., of Rathfriland, and also a quern, in the possession of the Rev. J. A. Beers, were dug up in the churchyard in 1832.

CLONDULANE, a parish, partly in the barony of FERMOY, but chiefly in that of CONDONS and CLONGIBBONS, county of CORK, and province of MUNSTER, 2 miles (E. by S.) from Fermoy; containing 1585 inhabitants. In Jan., 1642, David Barry, Earl of Barrymore, took Careysville castle, formerly called Ballymacpatrick castle, in this parish, after an obstinate resistance, and in view of the Irish army on the other side of the Blackwater. The garrison, consisting of 51 men, were all made prisoners and afterwards executed. Carrickabrick, at the western extremity of the parish, is said to have been besieged by Cromwell; the effects of cannon are still visible on the walls. This parish lies on both sides of the river Blackwater, and on the road from Fermoy to Lismore, and contains 4736 acres, as applotted under the tithe act, and valued at £6437. 10. per annum. The land is chiefly under tillage, but there is a considerable quantity of meadow and excellent pasture on the banks of the Blackwater, and also about 200 acres of woodland. There is no bog, which renders fuel scarce and dear, it being chiefly obtained from Youghal, whence it is brought in lighters to Tallow, and thence by land carriage. The state of agriculture is progressively improving; the Scottish system prevails on several estates. A continuous substratum of limestone runs along the north side of the river, and some patches are found on the south side, which are worked for building or repairing the roads. At Glendullane are extensive flour-mills, built by the late Earl of Mountcashell, who constructed a mill-dam across that part of the Blackwater called Poul-Shane, where there is water enough for a vessel of several tons' burden, although the river is not navigable higher than Cappoquin: these mills, which are worked by Mr. R. Briscoe, of Fermoy, furnish employment to about 30 persons, and are capable of producing above 20,000 bags of flour annually. The principal seats are Careysville, the residence of E. K. Carey, Esq., the handsome modern mansion built on the site of Careysville castle; Mount Rivers, of Matthias Hendley, Esq.,; Bellevue, of Thomas Dennehy, Esq.; Straw Hall, of J. Carey, Esq.; Rockville, of the Rev. J. Mockler; Lukeyville, of Mrs. Lukey; Rathealy, of J. Lucas, Esq.; and Bettyville, of R. Nason, Esq.

The living is a vicarage, in the diocese of Cloyne, and in the patronage of the Bishop; the rectory is impropriate in the Norcott family. The tithes amount to £740 which is equally divided between the impropriators and the vicar. There is no glebe-house, but a glebe of 12 acres near the church. The church is a small plain building, erected in 1811, by aid of a gift of £800 from the late Board of First Fruits; and the Ecclesiastical Commissioners have recently granted £176. 17. 4., for its repairs. In the R. C. divisions this parish forms part of the union or district of Fermoy. A school-house has been lately built and placed under the National Board. A short distance eastward from the bridge of Fermoy are the ruins of the castles of Carrickabrick and Liclash, both reduced to solitary towers; the former, one side of which is nearly battered down, stands on the south bank of the Blackwater; the latter, which stands on the north bank, is a low square tower mantled with ivy. Near Liclash castle are two curious caverns in the limestone rock; also a large rath or fort.

CLONE, county of LEITRIM.—See CLOON.

CLONE, a parish, partly in the barony of GOREY, but chiefly in that of SCARAWALSH, county of WEXFORD, and province of LEINSTER, 4 miles (N. E. by N.) from Enniscorthy; containing 1270 inhabitants. This parish, which is situated on the eastern road from Enniscorthy to Ferns, comprises 6348 statute acres, as applotted under the tithe act, and valued at £3099 per annum; the land is principally under an improving system of tillage, and drill husbandry is in general use; there are only a few patches of bog, and no waste land. There are some quarries of excellent building stone, from which has been raised the stone for the new church; and a slate quarry has lately been opened on the Portsmouth estate at Killibeg, about three miles distant from the town of Enniscorthy, yielding slates not inferior to those generally in use. Solsborough, the seat of the Rev. Solomon Richards, is a handsome mansion, situated in a finely wooded demesne, and commanding a pleasing view of the town of Enniscorthy and the river Slaney. The other seats are Killibeg, the residence of Mrs. Sparrow, and Tomsollagh, of Mr. Rudd. This was formerly one of the three parishes constituting the union of Ferns, from which it has been recently separated, and is now an independent rectory, in the diocese of Ferns, forming the corps of the prebend of Clone in the cathedral of Ferns, and in the patronage of the Bishop. The tithes amount to £332. 6. 1¾. The church, a neat edifice in the later English style, was erected in 1833, by aid of a grant of £900 from the late Board of First Fruits, on a site given by the Rev. Solomon Richards. The ruins of the old church are near Ferns, and attached to them is a burial-ground. The glebe comprises 21*a.* 0*r.* 9*p.* In the R. C. divisions the parish is the head of the union or district of Monageer, comprising also part of the parish of Monimolin, and those parts of the parishes of Ballyhuskard, Templeshannon, and Kilcormuck, which lie on the north-west side of the river Blackwater; the chapel at Monageer is a neat edifice. The parochial school, in which about 40 children are instructed, is supported by the rector, and it is in contemplation to build a school-house near the church, on a site to be given by the rector; there is also a private school, in which are about 50 children. In removing a tumulus, or, as it is frequently called, a moat, on the demesne of Mr. Richards, some time since, an ancient urn of unbaked clay, rudely carved and containing calcined bones, enclosed by flags, was discovered.

CLONEA, a parish, in the barony of DECIES-without-DRUM, county of WATERFORD, and province of MUNSTER, 4½ miles (E. by N.) from Dungarvan; containing 773 inhabitants. This parish is situated on the bay of Clonea in St. George's channel, and comprises 3338 statute acres, as applotted under the tithe act. Clonea Castle, the residence of Walter McGwire, Esq., is pleasantly situated near the cliffs, and commands a fine view of the sea. It is a vicarage, in the diocese of Lismore, and is part of the union of Stradbally; the rectory is impropriate in the Duke of Devonshire. The tithes amount to £199. 8., of which £132. 18. 8. is payable to the impropriator, and the remainder to the incumbent: the glebe comprises 1*a.* 3*r.* 31*p.* In the R. C. divisions the parish forms part of the union or district of Kilgobinet; the chapel is a plain building. There is a pay school, in which are about 25 boys and 5 girls.

CLONEAMERY, or CLOWEN, a parish, in the barony of IDA, county of KILKENNY, and province of LEINSTER, 1 mile (S. E.) from Innistiogue; containing 777 inhabitants. This parish, which is situated on the left bank of the river Nore, and on the mail coach road from Dublin to New Ross, by way of Thomastown, comprises 3277 statute acres, of which 170 are woodland, 648 mountain and waste, 129 bog, and the remainder arable and pasture land. It is a rectory and vicarage, in the diocese of Ossory, forming the corps of the prebend of Cloneamery in the cathedral of St. Canice, Kilkenny, and part of the union of Innistiogue, in the patronage of the Bishop. The tithes amount to £135. In the R. C. divisions also it forms part of the union or district of Innistiogue; the chapel is at Clediagh. Here is a private school, in which about 60 boys and 30 girls are educated. Bishop Pococke bequeathed 116 plantation acres of mountain land, called Bishop's Hill, and worth about £50 per annum, for the instruction of children, which is held by the Incorporated School Society. On a steep mound near the river stand the ruins of Clowen castle, belonging to the Fitzgeralds, and singularly divided into two parts. There are also some remains of an old church. In a romantic glen up a creek of the Nore is Clodagh waterfall; it is a cascade of great beauty falling down a rugged precipice of about 60 feet, and from the fissures of the overhanging rocks on both sides spring a great variety of trees and shrubs.

CLONEE, a post-town, in the parish and barony of DUNBOYNE, county of MEATH, and province of LEINSTER, 7 miles (N. W.) from Dublin; containing 217 inhabitants. It is situated on the road from Dublin to Navan, and on the confines of the county of Dublin; and has a constabulary police station.—See DUNBOYNE.

CLONEEN.—See CLONYNE.

CLONEGAL, a post-town, in that part of the parish of MOYACOMB which is in the barony of ST. MULLINS NORTH, county of CARLOW, and province of LEINSTER, 14¼ miles (S. E. by E.) from Carlow, and 53½ (S. S. W.) from Dublin; containing 446 inhabitants. It is situated on the road from Tullow to Newtownbarry, and on the river Derry, which divides it into two parts, and in 1831 comprised 76 houses. Fairs are held on July 31st, Nov. 12th and 22nd, and the first Wednesday in and the 11th of December, for cattle: fairs for the sale of frieze were formerly held on the first Wednesdays in February, March, and May, and on Ascension-day, but have been discontinued. Here is a constabulary police station. The parish church, a good modern building, is situated in the town; and there are a R. C. chapel, a place of worship for Methodists, and a handsome school-house in connection with the National Board, lately built. Here is also a castellated mansion built by the family of Esmonde, in 1625.—See MOYACOMB.

CLONEGAM, a parish, in the barony of UPPER-THIRD, county of WATERFORD, and province of MUNSTER, 4½ miles (S. E. by S.) from Carrick-on-Suir; containing 2220 inhabitants. This parish, which is situated near the river Suir, comprises 4800 statute acres, as applotted under the tithe act, and is chiefly demesne land attached to Curraghmore, the splendid seat of the Marquess of Waterford. The ancient castle of Curraghmore, which now forms part of the present mansion, was attacked by Cromwell in his retreat from Waterford, in 1649, and surrendered on honourable terms. Curraghmore is situated about two miles south of the river Suir, and in the vale of the Clodagh, a small stream that descends from the mountains; and is approached between two extensive ranges of offices connected by the ancient castle front, on the parapet of which is a large figure of a stag, the crest of the Beresford family. The ancient castle has been in the lower part converted into a magnificent hall, and in the upper into a stately and superb apartment, called the castle room. In the rear of it is the more modern and spacious mansion, erected by the great-grandfather of the present marquess, commanding a rich and extensive view, in the foreground of which, at the extremity of the town, is a large artificial lake; and in the distance, the stupendous and rugged mountains of Moanewollagh. The private pleasure grounds between the house and the river Clodagh are extensive and beautifully laid out; and a broad gravel walk leading from them is continued along the bank of the river, to which the gardens extend. The demesne, which comprises 4000 acres, is richly ornamented with stately timber in such profusion, as in some parts to form woods of very great extent and luxuriant growth. This magnificent seat is pre-eminently distinguished for the natural grandeur of its scenery, diversified with lofty hills, rich vales, and dense woods, combining every variety of rural beauty with features of romantic and picturesque character. The other seats are Rocketts Castle, the residence of the Rev. J. T. Medlycott; Mayfield, of J. Malcomson, Esq.; Milford, of A. Labertouche, Esq.; and Mount Bolton, of J. Bolton, Esq. The river Clodagh, which separates the parish from those of Kilmeadon and Guilcagh, is navigable for boats of any size for three miles from its junction with the Suir, and at a short distance from Curraghmore forms a considerable picturesque waterfall and salmon leap.

The living is a rectory, in the diocese of Lismore, episcopally united, in 1801, to that of Newtown-Lennan, together forming the union of Clonegam, in the patronage of the Crown: the tithes of the parish amount to £300 and the entire tithes of the benefice to £741. 9. 5. There is neither glebe-house nor glebe. The church, situated on the side of a hill, was rebuilt by the grandfather of the present marquess, in 1794: it is an elegant small edifice; the windows are of stained glass, and the west window is particularly fine, representing in its various compartments some of the most interesting subjects of sacred history. The churchyard is the burial-place of this noble family; and on the summit of the hill above the church is a round tower, erected by the grandfather of the present marquess, in memory of his eldest son, who was killed at the age of thirteen: it was intended to raise it to the height of 120 feet, but it was left unfinished at an elevation of 70 feet. Near the tower lies the great west window of the old cathedral of Waterford which it was intended to incorporate in an artificial ecclesiastical ruin, to form a characteristic group with the round tower. In the R. C. divisions this parish forms part of the union or district of Carrick-on-Suir. At the gate-house of Curraghmore is a handsome modern building, erected by the Marchioness of Waterford as a school for the children of the neighbouring peasantry, and supported by the Marquess; there is a school established and partly supported by Messrs. Malcomson, in which are 60 boys and 20 girls; and there are two private schools, in which are about 90 boys and 30 girls. On an eminence commanding a fine view of the Earl of Besborough's improvements, on the opposite side of the river Suir, is an erect stone of large dimensions, concerning which many strange traditions are prevalent in the neighbourhood; and about 40 yards distant are three subterranean apartments, which were discovered in 1810.

CLONEHORKE, a parish, in the barony of UPPER PHILIPSTOWN, KING'S county, and province of LEINSTER; containing, with part of the borough and market-town of Portarlington, 2988 inhabitants. This parish is situated on the left bank of the river Barrow, and on the road from Portarlington to Mount-Mellick. It is a rectory, in the diocese of Kildare, entirely appropriate to the rector of Geashill, of which parish it is considered to form part. There is a church, or chapel of ease, for the repairs of which the Ecclesiastical Commissioners have recently granted £213. 9. In the R. C. divisions it is part of the union or district of Portarlington.

CLONELTY, or CLONITA, a parish, in the GLENQUIN Division of the barony of UPPER CONNELLO, county of LIMERICK, and province of MUNSTER, 3 miles (N. E.) from Newcastle; containing 1327 inhabitants. This parish is situated on the road from Ballingarry to Newcastle, and contains 3541 statute acres. The land is generally good: about one-half is under tillage, producing abundant crops of wheat, oats, and potatoes; the remainder is meadow and pasture, the latter of which includes the high grounds of Knockaderry, which are of silicious formation, and are being gradually brought into cultivation. Within the parish is the village of Knockaderry, *which see.* Near the village is Knockaderry House, the ancient seat of the D'Arcy family, and present residence of T. D'Arcy Evans, Esq., situated amidst extensive plantations. The living is a vicarage, in the diocese of Limerick, episcopally united, in 1744, to the vicarage of Cloncah, and in the patronage of the Vicars Choral of the cathedral church of St. Mary, Limerick, to whom the rectory is appropriate. The tithes amount to £285, of which £195 is payable to the vicars choral, and the remainder to the vicar; the entire tithes of the benefice amount to £180. There is neither church, glebe-house, nor glebe. In the R. C. divisions this parish is united to Cloncah and Grange, and is the head of a union or district called Knockaderry, in which there is a small plain chapel. At Knockaderry is a national school, in which are about 50 boys and 20 girls; and there is a private school of about 30 boys and 20 girls. The old church is supposed to have been founded by St. Ita or Ittai, early in the 7th century; its ruins form a picturesque object. Near it are the remains of Ballynoe castle, which was built by the Knights Templars.

CLONENAGH, a parish, partly in the baronies of CULLINAGH and MARYBOROUGH EAST, but chiefly in that of MARYBOROUGH WEST, QUEEN'S county, and province of LEINSTER; containing, with the parish of Clonagheen and the post-town of Mountrath, 18,136 inhabitants. This place, originally called *Cluain-aith-chin* and *Cluain-ædnach*, is of very remote antiquity. A monastery was founded here, at an early period, by St. Fintan, who became its first abbot, and was succeeded by St. Columba, who died in 548. This abbey was destroyed in 838, by the Danes, who, in 843, carried its venerable abbot, Aid, who was also abbot of Tirdaglass, into Munster, where, on the 8th of July, he suffered martyrdom. After being frequently plundered and destroyed by the Danes, it continued to flourish for a considerable period, but little is known of its history subsequently to the English invasion. At Gutney Cloy, in this parish, a battle took place between the forces of Brian Boroimhe, on their return from Clontarf, and those of Fitzpatrick, Prince of Ossory. The parish is situated on the road from Maryborough to Roscrea, and comprises, with Clonagheen, 34,855 statute acres, as applotted under the tithe act. Of these, from 9000 to 12,000 are bog, and about half that number is mountain and waste; the remainder is arable and pasture land, nearly in equal portions. The system of agriculture is greatly improved, and green crops have been generally introduced. Ballyfin House, the elegant mansion of Sir C. H. Coote, Premier Baronet of Ireland, is a modern structure in the Grecian style of architecture, and is fitted up in a style of costly splendour; it is situated on a very elevated site on the side of a mountain, and commands extensive views of the surrounding country. The other seats are Springmount, that of Sir E. J. Walshe, Bart.; Forest, of J. Hawkesworth, Esq.; Ann Grove Abbey, of J. E. Scott, Esq.; and Scotch Rath, of R. White, Esq. An extensive cotton manufactory is carried on at Mountrath, where fairs are held on Jan. 6th, Feb. 17th, April 20th, May 7th, June 20th, Aug. 10th, Sept. 29th, and Nov. 5th, for general farming stock. Petty sessions are held at Mountrath every Thursday, and at Ann Grove every alternate Wednesday.

The living is a rectory, in the diocese of Leighlin, episcopally united, in 1661, to the rectory and vicarage of Clonagheen, and in the alternate patronage of the Crown, which has two presentations, and of the Bishop, who has one: the tithes for both parishes amount to £1500; there is neither glebe-house nor glebe. There are two churches, one at Mountrath, a spacious and handsome edifice, erected in 1800, by aid of a gift of £900 and a loan of £500, and enlarged in 1830, by aid of a loan of £1500, from the late Board of First Fruits, and towards the repair of which the Ecclesiastical Commissioners have recently granted £246. 18. 7.; and one at Roskelton, a neat small edifice, for the repair of which the Commissioners have also granted £254. 12. 3. At Ballyfin is a chapel, endowed by the Hon. William Pole, the chaplain of which is paid by Lord Maryborough; towards the repairs of this chapel, the Ecclesiastical Commissioners have also recently granted £368. 8. 4. In the R. C. divisions the parish is styled an abbacy, and constitutes the three benefices of Ballyfin, Mountrath and Clondacasey, and Raheen and Shanahoe. There are five chapels, all neat plain buildings, situated respectively at Mountrath, Ballyfin, Raheen, Shanahoe, and Clondacasey; also places of worship for the Society of Friends and Wesleyan and Primitive Methodists. There are a monastery and convent of St. Patrick's and St. Bridget's confraternity, to which a school is attached; the school-house was built by the late Dr. Delany. At Oak, Cootestreet, Ballyfin, Mountrath, Trummera, Raheen, and Ballyeagle, are national schools; and there are five schools supported by subscription. In these schools about 680 boys and 450 girls are instructed; and there are also five pay schools, in which are about 170 boys and 250 girls. The late Rt. Hon. W. Pole bequeathed £100 per annum late currency for the endowment of the chapel at Ballyfin, and £20 per annum for a schoolmaster and clerk. At Forest is a chalybeate spring.—See MOUNTRATH.

CLONES, a market and post-town, and a parish, partly in the barony of CLONKELLY, county of FERMANAGH, and partly in the baronies of MONAGHAN and DARTRY, county of MONAGHAN, and province of ULSTER, 10 miles (W. S. W.) from Monaghan, and 62 (N. W. by N.) from Dublin; containing 22,254 inhabitants. The ancient name of this place was *Cluan Innis*, "the Island of Retreat," it having formerly been nearly surrounded by water; and more recently it was called *Cloanish* or Clounish. An abbey, dedicated to St. Peter and St. Paul, was founded here in the early part of the 6th century, by St. Tigernach or Tierney, who, becoming Bishop of Clogher, removed that see to Clones, where he died of the plague in 550. The abbot was the *Primus Abbas*, or first mitred abbot of Ireland. In 836, the abbey was burnt; and in 929, Ceanfoile, comarb of Clones and Clogher, died here. The abbey was destroyed by fire in 1095, and, in 1184, the abbot Gilla Christ O'Macturan was elected Bishop of Clogher. In 1207, Hugh de Lacy destroyed the abbey and town; but five years after they were rebuilt by the English, who also erected a castle here. In 1316, and again in 1504, the abbot of Clones was elected Bishop of Clogher. In 1486 died the abbot Philip Mac Mahon, and, in 1502, the abbot James Mac Mahon, both relations of the Lords of Ergal. The abbey was dissolved by the act of Hen. VIII., and in the 29th of Elizabeth an inquisition was taken of its possessions. The manor of this abbey is still called "St. Tierney," and at the suppression was granted, together with the abbey, to Sir Henry Duke. The corbeship, or comorbanship, of Clones seems to have been held by the sept of Mac Mahon, the head of which, during the rebellion in Queen Elizabeth's reign, procured from the pope a grant of it for his eldest son, who was then a boy, with one of whose daughters it was conveyed in marriage to Sir Francis Rushe, whose daughter Elinor, in 1629, again conveyed it in marriage to Sir Robt. Loftus, eldest son of Adam, Lord Loftus, Primate and Chancellor of Ireland, and first Chancellor of Trinity College, Dublin. In 1640, Sir Robert and his son Henry died, and the manor came to Anne, only daughter of the former, who married the Hon. Richard Lennard Barrett, whose son, Dacre Barrett, Esq., represented the county of Monaghan in the Irish parliament in 1692: it has since continued in this family, and is now the estate of Sir Thomas Barrett Lennard, Bart. In the settlement of Ulster, to assimilate the Irish to the English church, corbeships were abolished, and their possessions, commonly called termon lands, granted to the bishops. At the time of the dissolution of monasteries, there were three ecclesiastical estates belonging to Clones; *viz.*, the abbey lands, now the property of Sir T. B. Lennard, which are tithe-free; the estate of the great church of Clones, belonging to the same proprietor, which pays one-third of the tithes to the incumbent; and the lands of the corbe, or the termon lands, the property of the Bishop of Clogher, which pay the entire tithes to the incumbent.

The town is situated on the road from Monaghan to Belturbet, and contains 429 houses, of which those recently erected are slated, and the more ancient are thatched. There is a brewery in the town; and at Stonebridge is an extensive foundry for spades, ploughs, and other agricultural implements, established about ten years since; also large flour-mills at Analoar, on the river Finn. The Agricultural and Commercial Bank has a branch establishment in the town. A yarn market is held on Thursday, at which linen cloth to the value of £150 is sold weekly; and there is a fair on the last Thursday in each month, for cattle, pigs, horses, &c., which is well supplied; and a fair is held at Roslea, in this parish, on the 8th of each month. The market-place of Clones is of a triangular form, with a market-house in it, and a pump, also a very ancient stone cross, the shaft of which is about 12 feet high; it stands at the top of a flight of steps, and both the shaft and top are ornamented with figures in relief; the upper part is circular, and the whole has a very antique appearance. Here is a chief constabulary police station. A manorial court, called "St. Tierney's Manor Court," is held in the town monthly by the seneschal, for the recovery of debts under £2; and petty sessions are held every alternate Friday. Courts are also held in the parish for the manors of Roslea and Shannick.

The parish is of great extent, comprising, according to the Ordnance Survey, 42,877¾ statute acres, of which 27,581½ are in Fermanagh, and 15,296¼ in Monaghan. About one-twentieth of the land is bog, 616¾ acres are water, and the mountainous tracts afford good pasture. Agriculture is in an improved state, and much of the land is of a superior quality; tillage is conducted on an extensive scale. Limestone of good quality is found in various places, and on the summit of Carnmore mountain is a quarry of fine white freestone, which is much used for building. A vein of coal was found near this mountain, but is not worked. That part of the parish which is in Dartry barony has no fewer than 32 lakes, of which, Loughs Oonagh, Camm, and Lisnaroe, and the lake near Smithsborough, are the largest. In that part of it which is in the barony of Monaghan is an extensive lake, near Watts-bridge, besides five smaller lakes, the waters of which unite in their course towards Newbliss. The principal seats are Summerhill, of the Rev. J. Richardson; Lisnaroe, of Nicholas Ellis, Esq.; Lough Oonagh, of Mrs. Murray; Spring Grove, of E. Madden, Esq.; Johnstown, of C. P. Irvine, Esq.; Scottsborough, of W. Scott, Esq.; Island Cottage, of Captain Ross; Carrowbarrow, of the Rev. M. F. Dudgeon; and the glebe-house, of the Very Rev. H. Roper, rector of the parish, and Dean of Clonmacnois.

The living is a rectory and vicarage, in the diocese of Clogher, and in the patronage of Sir T. B. Lennard, Bart.: the tithes amount to £950. 3. 11¾. The glebe-house was rebuilt in 1816, and towards defraying the expense, a gift of £100 and a loan of £1500 were granted by the same Board: the glebe comprises 700 acres. The parochial or mother church stands on the hill of Clones, at the upper end of the market-place, and has a handsome steeple, with a clock and bell: it was built at an expense of about £3500, of which £1022 was a loan and £900 a gift, in 1822, from the late Board of First Fruits. There are also two chapels of ease on the townlands of Clough and Aughadrumsee; the former was built by a loan of £1015 from the late Board of First Fruits, in 1828; to the repairs of the latter the Ecclesiastical Commissioners lately granted £136. 2. 11. In the R. C. divisions this parish forms two benefices, Clones East and Clones West: there are chapels at Clones and Drumswords for the former, and at Roslea and Magherarney for the latter; the chapel at Roslea is a spacious building, erected in 1834, with a bell tower and beautiful altar. There is a Presbyterian meeting-house at Stonebridge, in connection with the Synod of Ulster, and of the third class: at Smithsborough is one of the second class, connected with the Seceding Synod; and there are places of worship for Wesleyan and Primitive Methodists. There are male and female parochial schools at Cluigh, also schools at Clones, Carra-street, Smithsborough, Rossbrick, Larg, Granshaw, Magherarney, Aughnashalvey, Bruskena, Greaghawarren, Deer-Park, Clonkeen, Clononacken, Ahadrumsee, Clones, Spring-grove, Magheravilly, Gortnawing, Patenbar, and Knockavaddy. Each of these schools is aided by subscriptions, and at Salloo is one supported by J. Whittsit, Esq. The whole afford instruction to about 1200 boys and 700 girls; and in 11 private schools are about 180 boys and 90 girls, besides a considerable number in 12 Sunday schools. There are two dispensaries, one at Clones, the other near Roslea; a savings' bank, the deposits in which, belonging to 133 depositors, amounted to £3241. 9. 6. on the 20th of November, 1835; and a charitable loan fund.

On the south side of the town are the ruins of the ancient abbey to which it owes its early fame, and through which the road from Cootehill now passes. The walls of a small chapel still remain on one side of the road, and are built of square hewn freestone on the outside, and of limestone within; it is encompassed by an ancient burial-ground, enclosed by a strong wall. On the other side of the road is another burial-ground, similarly enclosed, in which are many curiously decorated tombstones, and where there is yet standing one of the ancient round towers. The walls of this tower are four feet thick, and very rough on the outside, but composed of smooth limestone within. The internal diameter is 10 feet, and there are resting-places for the joists of five successive floors. The thickness of the walls diminishes towards the top, and there is a doorway about four feet above the ground; at the top were large embrasures. On the surface, in this burial-ground, is a large stone coffin: the lid is very heavy, and of an angular shape, like the roof of a house, with two small pillars rising from the ends, and an ancient inscription on each side, but so much defaced as to be illegible. It is supposed to be the coffin of a Mac Mahon. Near these cemeteries is an extensive artificial mound of earth, very steep and rather difficult of access, being on the summit of a considerable hill. In the parish are two wells, much celebrated among the peasantry for curing the jaundice; one, about three miles from Clones, on the road leading to Monaghan, is called the Grailabuy Well; the other, about a mile from Clones, on the road to Enniskillen, is called Clintiveran Jaundice Well. Near the fort is an excellent spring, called Tubber Tierney.

CLONEY, or CLONIE, a parish, in the barony of BUNRATTY, county of CLARE, and province of MUNSTER, 4½ miles (E. by N.) from Ennis; containing 3531 inhabitants. This parish is situated on the road from Ennis to Tulla, and contains about 7695 statute acres, which are mostly in tillage, and agriculture is improving: there are about 2260 acres of bog. At Ballylisky a lead mine was discovered in 1834, yielding ore of superior quality, which is shipped for Wales at Clare. Fairs for live stock are held at Spancel hill on Jan. 1st, May 3rd, June 24th, Aug. 20th, and Dec. 3rd. In Clonie, the demesne of Burton Bindon, Esq., are a small lake, and the ruins of the old church and castle of Clonie. The living is a vicarage, in the diocese of Killaloe, and is part of the union of Quinn: the rectory is partly appropriate to the prebend of Tullagh in the cathedral of St. Flannan, Killaloe, and partly constitutes a portion of the sinecure union of Ogashin. The tithes amount to £221. 10. 9¼., of which £92. 6. 1¾. is payable to the rector, £106. 3. 1. to the vicar, and £23. 1. 6½. to the prebendary of Tullagh. In the R. C. divisions the parish forms part of the union or district of Quinn, in which the parochial chapel is situated, and there is a chapel of ease in the demesne of Clonie. At Spancel Hill is a school under the patronage of A. Hogan, Esq.; and in the parish are two hedge schools, in which are about 130 boys and 60 girls.

CLONEYGOWN, a village, in the parish of BALLYKEANE, barony of UPPER PHILIPSTOWN, KING'S county, and province of LEINSTER, 3½ miles (N.W.) from Portarlington; containing 158 inhabitants. This small village is situated on the road from Portarlington to Tullamore; it consists of about 30 tenements, and has a constabulary police station. Here are the mansion and demesne of Cloneygown, the seat of William Newcombe, Esq.

CLONFAD, or CLONFADFORAN, a parish, in the barony of FARTULLAGH, county of WESTMEATH, and province of LEINSTER; containing, with part of the post-town of Tyrrell's-Pass, 1369 inhabitants. This parish is situated on the road from Mullingar to Tyrrell's-Pass, and is intersected in the southern part by the mail coach road from Dublin to Athlone. It comprises 3264 statute acres, as applotted under the tithe act, of which about one-fifth is land of the best, three-fifths of middling, and the remainder of very inferior, quality. The land is principally in pasture; the soil is light, and the substratum generally limestone, of which there are quarries at Calverstown; and at Gnewbaron Hill, part of which is in this parish, is a fine quarry of grey limestone, which bears a high polish and is manufactured into handsome mantel-pieces: lime is the principal manure. The gentlemen's seats are Calverstown, the residence of J. Hornidge, Esq.; Guilford, of F. Usher, Esq.; Templeoran, of Mrs. Johnson; Newcastle, of C. Coffey, Esq.; and Dalystown, of C. Pilkington, Esq. The living is a rectory, in the diocese of Meath, and in the patronage of the Bishop: the tithes amount to £156. 18. 5½. The glebe-house was built by aid of a gift of £400 and a loan of £300 from the late Board of First Fruits, in 1810: the glebe comprises 20 acres. The church is a handsome edifice in the later English style, with a tower surmounted by a well-proportioned spire, and is situated at Tyrrell's-Pass; the late Board of First Fruits lent £250, in 1828, and the Ecclesiastical Commissioners have recently granted £147 towards its repair. In the R. C. divisions the parish forms part of the union or district of Fartullagh or Rochford-Bridge; the chapel is a plain edifice, situated at Meedeen. The parochial school-house was built at an expense of £400, of which £240 was given by the Countess of Belvedere, £112 from the lord-lieutenant's fund, and £48 by the rector, who allows the master an annual donation; in this school about 70 boys and 70 girls are instructed; and there is a pay school at Meedeen, in which are about 20 boys and 10 girls. There are some remains of an old church in the village of Clonfad; and at Newcastle are the ruins of an old fortification, said to have belonged to the Tyrrells.—See TYRRELL'S-PASS.

CLONFEACLE, a parish, partly in the barony of ARMAGH, and partly in that of O'NEILLAND WEST, county of ARMAGH, but chiefly in the barony of DUNGANNON, county of TYRONE, and province of ULSTER, 5½ miles (N. N. W.) from Armagh; containing, with the districts of Derrygortrevy, Moy, and Blackwater-town, (each of which is separately described) 19,547 inhabitants. This place was distinguished at a very remote period as the seat of a religious establishment of great reputation, of which St. Lugud, or Lugaid, was abbot about the year 580. It was soon after vested in the Culdean monks, whose chief establishment in Ireland was at Armagh, and with it this house became united about the middle of the 10th century. The Culdees kept possession of the church, and several large tracts of land in the parish, till the Reformation, when the whole became forfeited to the Crown, and were granted by Jas. I., on the 13th of May, 1614, to Primate Hampton, and his successors for ever, under the denomination of the "Termon, or Erenach lands of Clonfeicle," together with the church and rectory, which latter has since passed from the Primate, and is now vested in the Provost and Fellows of Trinity College, Dublin. During the Irish wars, and more especially in the rebellion of the Earl of Tyrone, this district was the scene of numerous sanguinary battles, the details of which are given in the article on Benburb. The parish is intersected by the river Blackwater, over which are several large and handsome stone bridges; and comprises, according to the Ordnance survey, 26,218 statute acres, of which 21,582 are in Tyrone, and 4636 in Armagh. The surface is diversified by several small and beautiful lakes, the principal of which is Lough Curran, on an artificial island in which have been discovered the remains of buildings and warlike and domestic implements; and near it is the old camp of the O'Nials, now Fort Magarrett. The land is chiefly arable: the soil is light but generally fertile, producing excellent crops; the system of agriculture is improved, and there is no waste land, except a tract of bog or marsh, about 400 acres in extent. Limestone and freestone abound in the parish: there are extensive and valuable limestone quarries at Benburb. The Ulster canal passes for three miles through the parish, on the Armagh or eastern side of the Blackwater. At Benburb a rock has been excavated to the depth of 86 feet, and the canal carried longitudinally over a mill-race for a very considerable distance, by a handsome aqueduct. The scenery is pleasingly diversified and beautifully picturesque; the glen through which the Blackwater flows is highly romantic, and the canal, when completed will add to the interest of the landscape. The principal seats are Dartrey Lodge, the residence of W. Olpherts, Esq.; the Argory, of W. McGeough Bond, Esq.; and Tullydoey, of J. Eyre Jackson, Esq., at which place is also the residence of T. Eyre, Esq. The weaving of linen is carried on extensively by the farmers and cottiers at their own dwellings; and at Tullydoey is an extensive bleach-green.

The living is a rectory and vicarage, in the diocese of Armagh, and in the patronage of the Provost and Fellows of Trinity College, Dublin: the tithes amount to £1030. The glebe-house is a good building; the glebe comprises 532*a.* 3*r.* 17*p.* of good arable land. The church was destroyed during the rebellion of Tyrone, since which time the village of Clonfeacle has been neglected and now forms part of Blackwater-town; and, in the same rebellion, the church of Eglish was destroyed, and that parish has ever since been included in the parish of Clonfeacle. The present parish church is situated close to the village of Benburb, on the confines of the counties of Armagh and Tyrone; it was built by Sir R. Wingfield, in 1619, and repaired and enlarged in 1815, by a gift of £800 from the late Board of First Fruits; the Ecclesiastical Commissioners have recently granted £526. 11. towards its further repair. There are also a church at Moy and one at Derrygortrevy; the latter stands near the site of the old church of Eglish. In the R. C. divisions the parish is called Upper and Lower Clonfeacle, and includes the whole parish of Eglish; there are chapels at Eglish, Moy, and Blackwater-town. There is a place of worship at Benburb for Presbyterians in connection with the Synod of Ulster of the second class; and one at Crew in connection with the Associate Synod: and at Blackwater-town is a place of worship for Wesleyan Methodists. The parochial school, near the church at Benburb, was built in 1832, by the Rev. Henry Griffin, the present rector, by whom it is principally supported; there are also schools at Blackwater-town and Derrycrevy, and near the old churchyard at Clonfeacle is a national school. At Benburb, Gorestown, Drummond, Mullycarnan, and Carrowcolman, schools were built and are supported by funds arising from a bequest, by Lord Powerscourt, of £2000 for charitable uses, and are conducted under the moral agency system. The sum of £4 per annum is paid to the poor of this parish from Drelincourt's charity, and two children are eligible to the Drelincourt school at Armagh. A bequest of £100 was made to the poor by a person whose name is now unknown. The ruins of Benburb castle, situated on the summit of a limestone rock overhanging the river, have a very picturesque appearance; and near them was found a silver signet ring, bearing the arms and initials of Turlogh O'Nial, which is now in the possession of Mr. Bell, of Dungannon. Several interesting relics of antiquity have been found in various parts; a large well-formed canoe was found in the bed of the river at Blackwater-town, in 1826, and is now in the garden of C. Magee, Esq.; it is scooped out of an oak tree, and is in good preservation. The same gentleman has also some very perfect querns, an altar of rude construction, several stone hatchets, and the horns of an elk, which were found a few years since at Drumlee. At Tullydoey are some inconsiderable vestiges of an ancient fort.

CLONFERT, a parish, in the barony of Duhallow, county of Cork, and province of Munster; containing, with the post-towns of Kanturk and Newmarket, 14,145 inhabitants. This parish, which is also called "Trinity Christ Church Newmarket," is situated on the rivers Allua and Dallua, which meet at Kanturk, in their course to the Blackwater; and on the road from Cork, through the Bogra mountains, to Abbeyfeale, in the county of Limerick, and Listowel, in the county of Kerry. It extends 16 Irish miles from north-west to south-east, and contains 64,871 acres, valued for the county cess at £19,677 per annum. About half the parish consists of bog and mountain; the other half of arable and pasture land of inferior quality. There are extensive beds of culm, some of which, near Newmarket, have been but are not now worked. This district has been much benefited by the road from Cork to Abbeyfeale, which was constructed soon after the distress in 1822; and much further benefit would be produced by connecting that road with the new Government road from Roskeen bridge, through King-William's-Town, to Castle Island, by a short road of about five Irish miles, passing the valuable but hitherto isolated, limestone quarry at Tour. This parish comprehends the extensive manor of Newmarket, and portions of those of Kanturk and Castle Mac Auliffe; the remainder of the latter manor is in Kilmeen, and of Kanturk, in Kilmeen and Kilbrin.

The living is a vicarage, in the diocese of Cloyne, and in the patronage of the Bishop; the rectory is impropriate in Col. Longfield, of Longueville: the tithes amount to £1163. 1. 6., of which half is paid to the impropriator and half to the vicar. A glebe-house was erected in 1811, near Newmarket, aided by a loan of £1125 from the late Board of First Fruits, but, having become dilapidated, has been taken down: the glebe comprises 9 statute acres, one having been lately annexed to the old burial-ground of Clonfert, by permission of the bishop. The parish church, in the town of Newmarket, is a handsome edifice, in the later style of English architecture, built in 1826, at an expense of £2200, of which £2000 was a loan from the late Board of First Fruits; it has a square tower, embattled and pinnacled, and surmounted by a lofty spire, the whole formed of hewn limestone. The church at Kanturk, which is annexed to the perpetual cure of that place, is a neat building, with a square tower, embattled and pinnacled. In the R. C. divisions this parish contains two parochial districts, Kanturk and Newmarket, *which see.* Besides the schools at those places, the Irish Society has four circulating schools in the parish; and there are several private schools. Of Mac Auliffe's castle, which was situated near Newmarket, and was a chief seat of the sept of that name, only the foundation exists; but of the castle of Carrigacashel, near Priory, the ruins still remain. There was formerly a castle on the Mount, near Mr. Aldworth's lodge, in Newmarket, and another at Curragh, which also belonged to the Mac Auliffes; both have been demolished, and on the site of the latter is a handsome modern house, the residence of Neptune Blood, Esq. In Mr. Aldworth's demesne many trinkets and military implements have been found. Here are some chalybeate springs.

CLONFERT, a parish, and the seat of a diocese, in the barony of Longford, county of Galway, and province of CONNAUGHT, 3 miles (N. N. E.) from Eyrecourt; containing 5915 inhabitants. This place, in the Irish language *Cluain-Fearth*, signifying "a retired spot," owes its origin and early importance to St. Brendan, son of Finloga, who, in 558, founded here an abbey, which afterwards became the cathedral church of the see of Clonfert. In 744 this place was destroyed by fire, and four years after again suffered a similar calamity; in 839 the Danes burned the abbey and killed the abbot, and, in 841, entirely reduced the place to ashes. Four years after it was again destroyed by fire, and in 949 the abbey was plundered; in 1031 the town was plundered by O'Ruark, and in 1045 it was again destroyed by fire. In 1065 Hugh O'Ruark, King of Breifné, and Thady O'Kelly, King of Maine, plundered the abbey; but on the day following they were defeated by Hugh O'Connor, King of Connaught, who overthrew their armies aud sank or dispersed their fleet in the Shannon. The subsequent history of this place is little more than a repetition of similar disasters, notwithstanding which it continued to flourish as the head of the diocese. During the prelacy of Bishop John, the cathedral was enlarged and beautified; the episcopal palace was rebuilt by Bishop Dawson; and in the reign of Chas. II. the cathedral, which had suffered from violence and dilapidation, was wholly restored. The ancient monastery existed independently of the bishoprick till the Reformation, when Hen. VIII., in the 35th of his reign, united it to the prelacy. The parish is situated on the road from Eyrecourt to Ballinasloe; it is bounded on the east by the river Shannon, and is intersected by the Grand Canal, in cutting for which through the bog an ancient wooden causeway was discovered, that, soon after exposure to the air, crumbled to dust. It comprises 12,335 statute acres, as applotted under the tithe act, a very large portion of which is bog; the remainder is good arable and pasture or meadow land, of which last there are large tracts bordering on the river. There are two constabulary police stations in the parish, one at Clonfert and the other at Clonfert bridge. It also contains the village of Isker or Esker.

Arms of the Bishoprick.

The DIOCESE of CLONFERT originated in the monastery founded by St. Brendan, who was its first abbot, and in whose time the church, previously famous for its seven altars, became a cathedral. St. Brendan, as are indeed many of his successors, is by various writers styled indifferently abbot or bishop, though some contend that St. Moena, whom St. Brendan, on his abdication, appointed his successor, and whom he survived, was the first to whom the latter title was given. St. Moena died in 571; and St. Brendan, who was the founder of many other abbeys, and is said to have presided over 3000 monks, died in 577, at Enachdune, whence his remains were removed to Clonfert and interred in the abbey. Of the successors of St. Moena, till after the arrival of the English in the reign of Hen. II., very little is recorded. The abbey was frequently plundered and burned by the Danes; and in 845, Turgesius, at the head of a party of those ravagers, not only burned and destroyed the houses in the town, but reduced the churches and conventual buildings to ashes. After the death of Bishop Thomas O'Kelley, in 1263, the see remained vacant till 1266, when John, the pope's nuncio, and an Italian, was appointed bishop; and on his translation to the archbishoprick of Benevento, in Italy, the temporalities were seized by the escheator of the Crown, but were restored the same year to Robert, a monk of Christchurch, Canterbury, who was made bishop by the provision of Pope Clement IV. John was a great benefactor to the cathedral, and is supposed to have erected and embellished the west front, which has been erroneously referred to a much later period. Roland Linch, who succeeded to the see of Kilmacduagh in 1587, received the see of Clonfert, vacant by the death of Stephen Kerovan, to hold in commendam; since which time the two dioceses have constantly remained united under one bishop. This bishop, however, greatly diminished the revenues of the united sees, by granting the possessions of Kilmacduagh at a nominal rent. Bishop Robert Dawson, who succeeded to the prelacy in 1627, repaired or rather rebuilt and beautified the episcopal palace of Clonfert. Bishop Wolley succeeded in 1664, and during his prelacy repaired the cathedral of Clonfert; but after his death, in 1684, the episcopal revenues were seized into the hands of Jas. II. and paid over to the Roman Catholic prelates, and the see remained vacant till after the Revolution, when William Fitzgerald was advanced to the prelacy by letters patent of William and Mary, dated July 1st, 1691. From this time a regular succession of bishops has been invariably maintained in the see, which, with the united see of Kilmacduagh, continued to form one diocese, suffragan to the archbishop of Tuam, till December, 1833, when, on the death of the bishop of Killaloe, it was, under the provisions of the Church Temporalities act of the 3rd of Wm. IV., united to those of Killaloe and Kilfenora, and the estates of the diocese became vested in the Ecclesiastical Commissioners. It is one of the six dioceses that constitute the episcopal province of Tuam, and comprehends part of the county of Roscommon, a large portion of the county of Galway, and one parish on the east side of the Shannon, in King's county. It is 37 Irish miles in length and 32 in breadth, and comprises an estimated superficies of 250,000 acres, of which 17,500 are in Roscommon, 193,100 in Galway, and 4400 in King's county. The lands belonging to the see comprise 7794 statute acres, of which 3844 are profitable and the remainder unprofitable land; and the gross amount of its annual revenue, on an average of three years ending with 1831, was £2385. 8. 9¾. The chapter consists of a dean; an archdeacon; the eight prebendaries of Fenore, Annacalla, Kilconnell, Killaspicmoylan, Kilteskill, Droughta, Ballynoulter, and Kilquane; and a sacrist. There are neither canons nor vicars choral, and no member of the chapter has either cure of souls or official residence. The income of the chapter, with the exception of that of the dean, arises entirely from portions of tithes in various parishes; the dean's income is £457. 12. 7., arising from portions of tithes in 23 parishes, and lands adjoining the village of Kilconnell, containing 30*a.* 1*r.* 19*p.*, let on lease at £20 per annum, with renewal fines of £10 every three years. There is no economy fund at the disposal of the chapter: the repairs of the cathedral consequently devolve upon the Ecclesiastical Commissioners, who have recently granted £484. 15. for that purpose. The consistorial court of the united dioceses of Clonfert and Kilmacduagh is held at Loughrea; its officers are a vicar-general, a registrar, and a proctor; the registrar is also keeper of the records, consisting of copies of leases of the see lands from 1724 to the present time, wills, and deeds of administration. The total number of parishes in the diocese is 38, included in 11 unions, which are either rectories and vicarages, or vicarages of which the rectorial tithes are partly appropriate to the see or to members of the chapter. The total number of benefices, including dignities, is 22, of which one is in the gift of the Crown, 18 in the patronage of the Bishop, and 3 in that of the Marquess of Clanricarde; the number of churches is 13, and of glebe-houses, 8. In the R. C. divisions this diocese is one of the seven suffragan to Tuam, and comprises 23 parochial unions or districts, containing 44 chapels served by 23 parish priests and 11 coadjutors or curates. The bishop's parish is Loughrea.

The living is a vicarage, in the diocese of Clonfert, and the head of a union, including also Clontuskert and Kilmalinoge, in the patronage of the Bishop; the rectory is appropriate to the see, the deanery, the prebends of Kilconnell, Kilteskill, Fenore, and Annacalla, and to the sacristy of Clonfert. The tithes of the parish amount to £309. 4., and of the benefice to £367. 10. The glebe lands of the union comprise 55¾ acres. The church, which is both capitular and parochial, is an ancient and spacious structure, to which a gift of £500 was made in 1793, and a like sum in 1813, by the late Board of First Fruits; the service is performed in the chancel, which is too small for the accommodation of the parishioners; the nave, which is very spacious, is therefore about to be adapted to their use, for which purpose, and for general repairs, the Ecclesiastical Commissioners have recently granted £484. 15. The episcopal palace is situated very near the church. The glebe-house was built in 1817, by aid of a gift of £400 and a loan of £400 from the late Board of First Fruits. There is also a church at Clontuskert, a neat and substantial edifice. In the R. C. divisions this parish is partly in the union or district of Kiltormer, but chiefly the head of a union, including also the parishes of Dononaughta and Meelick, and called also the union of Eyrecourt, in which are three chapels, situated respectively at Brackloon, in this parish (a large slated building), at Eyrecourt, in the parish of Dononaughta, and at Meelick. There are two free schools in which are about 80 boys and 70 girls; and there are also five pay schools, in which are about 200 children, and a Sunday school. At Brackloon are the ruins of an old castle; and between Clonfert and Laurencetown is a chalybeate spring, the water of which is efficacious in complaints of the liver.

CLONFERT-MULLOE.—See KYLE.

CLONFINGLASS.—See KILALDRIFF.

CLONFINLOGH, a parish, in the barony and county of Roscommon, and province of Connaught, 3 miles (S. by W.) from Strokestown, on the road to Roscommon; containing 4540 inhabitants. This parish comprises 6283 statute acres, as applotted under the tithe act, and valued at £4029 per ann.: the land is equally divided between arable and pasture, except about 300 acres of bog. Limestone is found of excellent quality. On the eastern side of the parish is part of the isolated ridge of Slievebawn, and at its base is the race-course of Ballynafad, near which a fair for horses and sheep is held on Aug. 27th. It is a vicarage, in the diocese of Elphin, and is part of the union of Clontuskert; the rectory is partly impropriate in the representatives of Lord Kingsland, and partly forms a portion of the corps of the prebend of Kilgoghlin in the cathedral of Elphin. The tithes amount to £184. 12. 3½. In the R. C. divisions it is part of the union or district of Carraghroe, also called Lissonuffy; the chapel is on the townland of Carrowniscagh. There are four hedge schools, in which about 100 boys and 60 girls are educated. The ruins of Ballynafad castle still remain: it belonged to a branch of the O'Connors, and was placed under Queen Elizabeth's authority by Charles O'Connor Roe.

CLONGEEN, a parish, in the barony of Shelmalier, county of Wexford, and province of Leinster, 4½ miles (S. W. by W.) from Taghmon; containing 1716 inhabitants. It is situated on the road from New Ross to Bannow, and comprises 5343 statute acres, chiefly under tillage; the system of agriculture is slowly improving. Long Grage, the handsome residence of Cæsar Sutton, Esq., was the scene of a sharp action during the disturbances of 1798, which took place on the 20th of June between the insurgents and the forces under General (afterwards the celebrated Sir John) Moore, who fell at Corunna, and who on the preceding day had taken up a position in the demesne, in order to intercept their retreat from Vinegar Hill by way of Clonmines. Fairs are held at Rathgorey on Holy Thursday and Oct. 28th. The living is an impropriate curacy, in the diocese of Ferns, and in the patronage of Francis Leigh, Esq., in whom the tithes, amounting to £200, are impropriate, and who contributes towards the performance of the clerical duties of Clongeen and Kilcowanmore, both of which are at present annexed to the impropriate union of Tintern. There are no remains of the church. In the R. C. divisions this parish forms part of the union or district of Tintern: the chapel, situated in the village, is a neat building, with a house for the priest adjoining. A school for the children of Roman Catholics is supported by subscription; and there are two hedge schools in the parish. There is a dispensary in the village. A house called Abbey Braney, the property of Mr. Cliffe, of Bellevue, is said to occupy the site of a religious establishment, of which there are no particulars on record.

CLONGESH, or CLOONGISH, a parish, in the barony and county of Longford, and province of Leinster; containing, with the post-town of Newtown-Forbes, 6736 inhabitants. This parish is situated on the road from Longford to Carrick-on-Shannon, and on the rivers Camlin and Shannon; it contains 9616 statute acres, of which about 900 are woodland, 6800 arable and pasture, and the remainder waste and bog. Limestone quarries are worked for building and burning. A court for the manor of Castle-Forbes is held occasionally; and petty sessions are held at Newtown-Forbes every alternate Tuesday. The principal seats in the parish are Castle-Forbes, the residence of the Earl of Granard; Brianstown, of Thomas Gordon Auchmuty, Esq., representative of that Ilk, in Fife, North Britain; Lismoy, of the Rev. J. Mitchell; Lisbrack Cottage, of Verschoyle Crawford, Esq.; Monalagan Cottage of Dr. Forbes Crawford; and Hermitage, of T. H. Ellis, Esq. Castle-Forbes was besieged by the Irish troops for some weeks, in the parliamentary war of 1641, and its defenders were obliged to capitulate for want of supplies.

The living is a rectory and vicarage, in the diocese of Ardagh, united to part of the vicarage of Killoe, and in the patronage of the Bishop: the tithes amount to £461. 10. 9. The glebe-house was built in 1810, by aid of a gift of £100, and a loan of £650, from the late Board of First Fruits: the glebe comprises 50 acres, and is contiguous to the church. The church, situated at Newtown-Forbes, is supposed to have been originally built by the British settlers, about 1694; it has been rebuilt by aid of a gift of £830 from the late Board of First Fruits, in 1829. There is also a church on St. Ann's Hill, in that part of Killoe which is united with this parish. The R. C. parish is co-extensive with that of the Established Church: the chapel is at Newtown-Forbes, where there is also a place of worship for Methodists. At Lisnabo is a free school for both sexes, founded and endowed by the Rev. J. Mitchell, of Lismoy, who has charged his estate with an annuity of £50 for its support; the school-house is an excellent slated building, with apartments for the master and mistress, and cost £700. A school is aided by the rector and diocesan fund, and there are four pay schools: in these about 600 children are educated. There are a few Danish raths, and the ruins of two churches. Part of the parish is called the Scots' Quarter, a Scottish colony having settled here in the beginning of the reign of Jas. I.—See NEWTOWN-FORBES.

CLONGILL, a parish, in the barony of MORGALLION, county of MEATH, and province of LEINSTER, 5 miles (N. W.) from Navan, on the road from Kells to Drogheda, contain 260 inhabitants. This parish comprises 2225 statute acres, of which 1667 are applotted under the tithe act. The farms are in general large, and several are occupied by the proprietors: the lands are principally in pasture and of very excellent quality, and grazing is carried on extensively. A stream called the Yellow river intersects the parish near Arch Hall, the seat of J. Paine Garnett, Esq., a handsome mansion pleasantly situated in a well-wooded demesne, comprising about 350 statute acres. It is a rectory, in the diocese of Meath, and is part of the union of Kilshine: the tithes amount to £100. The glebe-house was built by aid of a gift of £400 and a loan of £350 from the late Board of First Fruits, in 1811: there are four glebes, comprising together 21 acres. In the R. C. divisions the parish is part of the union or district of Castletown-Kilpatrick; the chapel is at Fletcherstown. The parochial school, in which are about 20 boys and 20 girls, is supported by subscription. Here is an ancient castle in a tolerably good state of preservation.

CLONIE.—See CLONEY.

CLONIGORMICAN.—See ARDCLARE.

CLONKEEHAN, a parish, in the barony and county of LOUTH, and province of LEINSTER, 3 miles (N. E.) from Ardee; containing 333 inhabitants. The river Glyde separates this parish from those of Tallanstown and Maplestown, but it is connected with the latter by a bridge on the road from Ardee to Dundalk. The parish comprises, according to the Ordnance survey, 605 statute acres, two-thirds of which are included within the demesne of Corballis, the seat of T. Lee Norman, Esq. It is a rectory, in the diocese of Armagh, and is part of the union of Charlestown, or Philipstown: the tithes amount to £46. 3. 1. The church is in ruins. In the R. C. divisions the parish forms part of the union or district of Tallanstown.

CLONKEEN, or CLOONKEEN, also CLONKEEN-KERILY, a parish, in the barony of TYAQUIN, county of GALWAY, and province of CONNAUGHT, 7 miles (N. E.) from Athenry; containing 1806 inhabitants. Thomas O'Kelly, Bishop of Clonfert, and afterwards Archbishop of Tuam, about 1435, erected the parish church of Clonkeen, or Clonkeen-kernill, into a convent of Franciscans of the Third Penitential order, at the instance of David and John Mull-Kerrill, and Pope Eugene IV. confirmed this donation in 1441. This monastery existed till 1618, when its possessions were held by Conor Duffe O'Naghten, and Conor Oge O'Naghten, both of Galway. The parish is situated on the road from Kilconnell to Tuam, and contains 3132 statute acres. It is a vicarage, in the diocese of Clonfert, and is part of the union of Ballymacward; the rectory is partly appropriate to the vicars choral of the cathedral of Christ-Church, Dublin, and partly to the see and deanery of Clonfert. The tithes amount to £82. 10. 6. of which £11. 1. 6½. is payable to the Ecclesiastical Commissioners, £11. 1. 6½. to the dean, and the remainder, except *7s. 6d.* to the vicars choral, to the incumbent. In the R. C. divisions it is part of the union or district of Ballymacward, or Gurteen; the chapel is at the latter place.

CLONKEEN, a village, in the parish and barony of KILLIAN, county of GALWAY, and province of CONNAUGHT, 4 miles (S. W.) from Ballinamore; containing, in 1836, 250 inhabitants. It is situated on the road from Ballinamore to Dunmore, and is the joint property of the Hon. Martin Ffrench and D. H. Kelly, Esq.

CLONKEEN, a parish, in the barony of CLANWILLIAM, county of LIMERICK, and province of MUNSTER, 5½ miles (E. by S.) from Limerick; containing 628 inhabitants. This parish is situated on the road from Limerick to Abington, and contains 2496 statute acres, as applotted under the tithe act. The soil is fertile, and the land is well cultivated, producing abundant crops. The houses are generally good, and mostly surrounded with gardens and orchards, particularly near Barrington Bridge, where several neat cottages, and an hotel and post-office have been recently erected, a police station established, and numerous other improvements made. The parish is in the diocese of Emly, and the rectory is appropriate to the Archbishop of Cashel's mensal. The church, which is of Saxon or early Norman architecture, of which the western doorway is a very fine specimen, was much injured by the Whiteboys, in 1762, and has not been repaired; that at Abington is used by the parishioners. In the R. C. divisions the parish forms part of the union or district of Murroe. There is a school, in which about 100 boys and 40 girls are taught.

CLONKEEN, a parish, in the barony of ARDEE, county of LOUTH, and province of LEINSTER, 3 miles (N. W.) from Ardee, on the road to Monaghan; containing 1981 inhabitants. It comprises 4321½ statute acres, according to the Ordnance survey, valued at

£4582 per annum: the soil is fertile, and the land is mostly under cultivation; the system of agriculture is in a highly improved state. There are some quarries of greenstone, which is raised for building and for repairing the roads. The principal seats are Rogerstown, the residence of Miss Young; Cardistown, of J. Caraher, Esq.; Glach, of R. Shegog, Esq.; and Cromartin, belonging to the Clement family. The living is a rectory and vicarage in the diocese of Armagh, and in the patronage of the Lord-Primate: the tithes amount to £300. The glebe-house is a good residence, built by the present rector, the Rev. W. Lee, and has attached to it 12*a.* 1*r.* 17*p.* of glebe. The church is an ancient structure, and contains a neat monument to the Caraher family. In the R. C. divisions the parish forms part of the union or district of Tallanstown. There are two hedge schools, in which are about 80 boys and 30 girls. Near Lagan bridge are the ruins of an ancient castle.

CLONKYNE.—See ABBEYLEIX.

CLONLARA.—See KILTONANLEA.

CLONLEA, or CLONLEIGH, a parish, in the barony of TULLAGH, county of CLARE, and province of MUNSTER, 4½ miles (N.) from Six-mile-bridge; containing 3105 inhabitants. It comprises, exclusively of a large quantity of mountain and bog, 5355 statute acres, as applotted under the tithe act: the surface is partly occupied by lakes. The land is mostly in tillage, and some improvements have been made in the system of agriculture, from the judicious example of D. Wilson, Esq., and T. Studdert, Esq., the former of whom has planted to the extent of nearly 50 Irish acres within a few years. Limestone is abundant, and is extensively used for manure, there being 60 limekilns within this district. Two fairs are held annually at Enagh, and three at Kilkishen. A new road is in progress from Tulla to Limerick, through Kilkishen and by the Glonagruss mountain. The principal seats are Belvoir, the residence of D. Wilson, Esq.; Glenwood, of Basil Davoren, Esq.; Mount Bayley of H. Bayley, Esq.; and Sion Ville, the property of T. Studdert, Esq. The living is a rectory and vicarage, in the diocese of Killaloe; the rectory, with those of Kilfinaghty, Kilseily, Killurane, Killokennedy, Kinloe, Feacle, and the half rectory of Ogonilloe, constitutes the union of Omullod, in the patronage of the Earl of Egremont; the vicarage is in the patronage of the Bishop, who has the ploughland of Clonlea as part of his mensal. The tithes amount to £171. 18. 1½. The glebe-house was erected by aid of a gift of £450, and a loan of £100, in 1815, from the late Board of First Fruits. The glebe comprises 10¼ acres, subject to a rent of £3 late currency per acre. The church at Kilkishen is a small neat structure, with a square tower, built by a gift of £800, in 1811, from the late Board of First Fruits, and repaired in 1834, by a grant from the Ecclesiastical Commissioners. In the R. C. divisions the parish is the head of a union or district, called Kilkishen, comprising the parishes of Clonlea and Killuran: there are three chapels, situated respectively at Kilkishen, at Oatfield, and at Callaghan's Mills in the parish of Killuran. A new school-house has lately been erected at Belvoir, to which is attached a model farm; the cost of the building was £190, of which £76 was paid by D. Wilson, Esq., and the remainder by the National Board. There are also five other schools in the parish, one of which at Kilkishen is under the patronage of the parish priest. At Scart is a chalybeate spring. On the south-west bank of Clonlea lake are the ruins of the old parish church and the burial-ground. The old ruin of Stackpoole, formerly the seat of a family of that name, is beautifully situated in this parish, overlooking the lakes of Pollagh and Mount Cashel; it is now the property of the Earl of Limerick, on whom it confers the title of Baron Foxford.

CLONLEIGH, county of DONEGAL.—See LIFFORD.

CLONLEIGH, a parish, in the barony of BANTRY, county of WEXFORD, and province of LEINSTER, 5 miles (N. E.) from New Ross; containing 661 inhabitants. This parish is situated on the high road from Ross to Newtownbarry, and contains 2679 statute acres, principally under tillage. The rectory is part of the union of St. Mary's New Ross, in the diocese of Ferns; for the clerical duties it forms part of the perpetual cure of Templeudigan. The tithes amount to £101. 15. 8¼. In the R. C. divisions it is included in the union or district of Templeudigan, where the chapel is situated. There is a hedge school of about 10 children: and a school is about to be built by subscription, near the chapel of Poulpeasty, on two acres of land granted by C. R. Frizell, Esq., of Stapolin.

CLONLOGHAN, a parish, in the barony of BUNRATTY, county of CLARE, and province of MUNSTER, 5 miles (W. by S.) from Six-Mile-Bridge; containing 763 inhabitants. This parish is situated on the river Shannon, and contains 2711 statute acres as applotted under the tithe act, which are mostly in pasture: it includes part of the rich corcasses on the banks of the Shannon. Knockhane is the residence of P. McMahon, Esq. The living is a rectory and vicarage in the diocese of Killaloe; the rectory is part of the rectorial union of Tomfinlogh; the vicarage is part of the vicarial union of Kilfinaghty. The tithes amount to £105. In the R. C. divisions the parish forms part of the union or district of Newmarket.

CLONLOGHER, or CLOONLOGHER, a parish, in the barony of DROMOHAIRE, county of LEITRIM, and province of CONNAUGHT, 1½ mile (N. E.) from Manorhamilton; containing 1245 inhabitants. This parish, which is situated on the road from Carrich-on-Shannon to Manorhamilton, contains 6029 acres, as applotted under the tithe act. It consists principally of mountain land, on which some successful attempts at irrigation have been made; there is a small bog, and limestone abounds. The principal seat is Larkfield, the residence of J. O'Donnell, Esq. It is a vicarage, in the diocese of Kilmore, and is part of the union of Clonclare or Manor-Hamilton; the rectory is partly appropriate to the see of Kilmore, and impropriate in Owen Wynne, Esq. The tithes amount to £64, of which £33. 6. 8. is payable to the bishop, £16. 13. 4. to the vicar, and £14 to Owen Wynne, Esq. A corbeship appears to have existed here in ancient times, as, in 1663, the termon or Erenagh lands in Clonlogher were granted to the bishop of Kilmore and his successors; and Mr. Owen Wynne is called Abbot of Clonclare in the Report of the Ecclesiastical Commissioners in the year 1830, and holds ten acres of glebe. In the R. C. divisions the parish is partly in the union or district of Drumlease, and partly in that of Killargy. At Larkfield is a school of 100 boys and 79 girls.

CLONMACDUFF, a parish, in the barony of UPPER NAVAN, county of MEATH, and province of LEINSTER, 3 miles (N.) from Trim; containing 716 inhabitants. This parish, of which the name signifies "Mac Duff's Retreat," is situated on the road from Navan to Athboy. The land is chiefly under tillage; and there is a considerable tract of bog, affording abundance of turf for fuel. Meadstown is the residence of Christopher Barnwall, Esq. It is a rectory, in the diocese of Meath, forming part of the union of Ardbraccan; the tithes amount to £136. 5. 4. In the R. C. divisions it forms part of the district of Churchtown and Moymet. At Dunderry is a small school, supported by subscription.

CLONMACNOIS, or CLUANMACNOIS, a parish, in the barony of GARRYCASTLE, KING'S county, and province of LEINSTER, 8 miles (S. by W.) from Athlone; containing, with the town of Shannon-Bridge, 4446 inhabitants. This place, also called "Seven Churches," is conspicuously distinguished in the earlier periods of Irish ecclesiastical history for the number and opulence of its religious establishments, its schools for instruction in the liberal arts, and the veneration in which it was held as a place of sepulture for the royal families of Ireland. It was originally called *Druim Tipraid*, but from its schools, which were attended by the children of the neighbouring princes, it obtained the appellation of *Cluain-Mac-Nois*, signifying in the Irish language the "Retreat of the Sons of the Noble." St. Keiran, or Kiaran, the younger, founded an abbey here, in 548, on ground given by Dermod Mac Cervail, King of Ireland, which obtained the episcopal authority usually attached to such establishments. In 1199, this place was attacked by the forces of William de Burgo, Fitz-Andelm, and several of the Irish chieftains; in 1200, it was plundered by the English under Miler Fitz-Henry, and in 1201 was completely sacked by the same assailants. The churches, the town, and the cathedral suffered the greatest violence and depredation; the vestments of the priests, the books, the chalices, the plate, and the provisions and cattle of the monks, were carried off and their grounds laid waste. The abbey was again plundered by William de Burgo, in 1204, and in the year following the town was partly destroyed by an accidental fire. A castle was erected here by the English in 1214, and in 1227 the town was three times set on fire by the son of Donnell Bregagh O'Melaghlin. The see continued to flourish under a regular succession of prelates till the time of Elizabeth, when the English garrison of Athlone plundered the cathedral, destroyed the altars, and mutilated and defaced the ornaments with which it was decorated. On the death of Peter Wall, the last bishop, in 1568, the see was united to that of Meath by act of parliament, and at present this place ranks only as a parish, the very name of the ancient diocese having merged in that of Meath.

The parish formed part of the county of Westmeath until 1688, when, through the influence of the bishop of Meath, it was separated from the barony of Clonlonan, in that county. It is situated on the east bank of the river Shannon; nearly two-thirds of the surface are bog, part of it being a continuation of the bog of Allen; there are many hills, the upper portions of which afford tolerable pasture; on the banks of the river is some good meadow land; and the valleys, which are mostly in tillage, afford excellent crops of corn, although the soil is rather light, and in some parts sandy. Nearly in the centre is a lake of about 90 acres, called Clonfanlagh, encompassed on the north and east by hills, and on the opposite sides by an extensive bog, and abounding with pike and perch. The substratum is limestone, which is quarried both for building and for agricultural purposes. The river Shannon is navigable hence to Limerick and Athlone. The living is a vicarage, in the diocese of Meath, and in the patronage of the Bishop: the tithes amount to £264. 2. 2., payable to the incumbent. The present income of the deanery arises solely from the lands of Kilgarvin, comprising three cartrons, in this parish, let on lease at an annual rent of £36. 18. 5½., and an annual renewal fine of equal amount. The church is one of the ancient structures that were built around the cathedral, and contains some very singular and interesting old monuments; the Ecclesiastical Commissioners have recently granted £220 towards its repair. In the R. C. divisions the parish is in the diocese of Ardagh, and is partly a distinct benefice, called Seven Churches, and partly united to Lemanaghan. There are two chapels, one at Shannon-Bridge and one at Clonfanlagh. The parochial school is aided by an annual donation from the vicar; there is also a school at Shannon-Bridge, under the patronage of the parish priest, and one at Clonlyon supported by subscription. In these schools about 80 boys and 50 girls are instructed; and there are about 200 children in the several pay schools.

The ecclesiastical ruins are very extensive: the most conspicuous objects are the ruined gables of the numerous small churches that surround the cathedral, and two of those round towers that are found almost exclusively near the sites of the earliest religious establishments. The cathedral is said to have been built by the O'Melaghlins, princes of Meath; and within the cemetery, comprising about two Irish acres, were ten dependent churches, built by the kings and petty princes of the circumjacent territories, one of which, Temple-Doulin, has been restored, and is now the parish church. A nunnery was founded here at a very early period, but was destroyed by fire in 1180, and one circular arch is all that remains of it. About a furlong from the ruins of the cathedral are the remains of the episcopal palace, a strong but rude castle surrounded by a moat and counterscarp. The cemetery was a favourite place of sepulture with the neighbouring chieftains, many of whom were buried here, and many ancient inscriptions in Irish, Hebrew, and Latin, have been discovered among the ruins. It is still venerated as a place of interment throughout the neighbouring country; and the 9th of September is kept as a patron day, in honour of St. Kieran, when from 3000 to 4000 persons annually assemble here and remain for two days; huts and booths are erected for their accommodation, and such is the veneration in which the place is held, that many persons come from distant parts of the country, and even from the county of Donegal.—See SHANNON-BRIDGE.

CLONMANY, or CLUINMANAGH, a parish, in the barony of ENNISHOWEN, county of DONEGAL, and province of ULSTER, 5 miles (W. by N.) from Carne; containing 6450 inhabitants. According to Archdall, a very rich monastery existed here, built by St. Columb in the 6th century, of which there is now no trace, but the festival of that saint is observed on the 9th of June. The parish, which is bounded on the north by the Atlantic ocean, comprises 23 divisions, called quarter lands, and, according to the Ordnance survey, 23,376 statute acres, two-thirds of which are irreclaimable mountain land, and 127¼ are water. The shore forms a semicircle of nearly nine miles, and abounds with sea-weed, which is used as manure. The mountains, of which the largest is Raghtin, rising to an elevation of 1656 feet above the level of the sea, are chiefly composed of whinstone and clay-slate, and near the pass to Desertegney a valuable deposit of limestone has been recently discovered. In the mountain of Ardagh are veins of lead ore, which have not yet been worked. The land is not generally favourable for cultivation. There are three corn-mills. Fairs are held on Jan. 1st, March 24th, June 29th, and Oct. 10th, for horses, cattle, sheep, flax, yarn, &c. Within its limits are the rivers Clonmany and Ballyhallon: the former has its rise in Meendoran lough, and the latter from a small spring in the western part of the parish; they contain trout and eels, and in autumn, salmon. Within the parish also is Dunaff Head, between which and Fanet Point, in the parish of Clondevadock, is the entrance to Lough Swilly. On Dunree Point an artillery station was erected in 1812, in which a small garrison is still maintained. At Rockstown is a coast-guard station, and at Strand, or Clonmany, one for the constabulary police. The principal seats are Dresden, the residence of T. L. Metcalfe, Esq.; Glen House, of M. Doherty, Esq.; and the glebe-house, of the Rev. Mr. Molloy.

The living is a rectory and vicarage, in the diocese of Derry, and in the patronage of the Marquess of Donegal: the tithes amount to £400. The glebe-house, which is on a glebe of five acres, was built in 1819, by aid of a gift of £100, and a loan of £675, from the late Board of First Fruits: the glebe at Cherbury comprises 365 acres, of which 300 are uncultivated. The church is a neat structure, with a low square tower: it is situated in the vale of Tallaght, and the Ecclesiastical Commissioners lately granted £368. 4. 3. for its repair. The R. C. parish is co-extensive with that of the Established Church, and has a large and well-built chapel. The parochial school is aided by an annual donation from the incumbent; and at Garryduff is a very large and handsome school-house, built in 1835. There is a school at Urras, aided by an annual donation from Mrs. Merrick, in which are educated 35 boys and 17 girls; and there are four pay schools, in which are 170 boys and 30 girls. On the north-east of the parish are the ruins of a castle, called Carrick-a-Brakey, consisting of a circular tower, 25 feet high and 8 feet in diameter, and a square building, 30 feet high and 10 feet in diameter. A mile south-east of this is another castle, called in Irish *Caislean na Stucah;* it stands on a pyramidal rock, insulated by spring tides, the top of which is 80 perches above the level of the sea, and is inaccessible except by long ladders. Tradition states that it was built by Phelemy Brasselah O'Doherty. At Magheramore is a very perfect cromlech, consisting of a table stone of above 20 tons, supported by three upright pillars: it is called Fion McCuil's finger stone. Among the natural curiosities is a chink in a rock at Tallaght, under which is a cavern: and at Leenan Head is a beautiful cave, 70 yards long and 5 or 6 broad, excavated by the sea, through which boats can pass; besides a waterfall dashing over a perpendicular rock 50 feet high, and several caves. Here are also some chalybeate springs; and on the lofty mountains eagles still build their nests, and are very destructive, particularly in the lambing season.

CLONMEEN, or CLOONMEEN, a parish, in the barony of DUHALLOW, county of CORK, and province of MUNSTER, 2 miles (S. S. E.) from Kanturk; containing 5344 inhabitants. A monastery for Augustine Friars was founded here by the O'Callaghans, ancestors of Lord Lismore; and a castle existed here, which was destroyed in the war of 1641. On the 26th of July, 1652, a body of the parliamentary forces under Lord Broghill, having during the night repulsed the cavalry of Lord Muskerry, who was endeavouring with his Irish forces to advance to the relief of Limerick, crossed the Blackwater, about half a mile east of Bantyre bridge, came up with Lord Muskerry's troops, posted on the elevated ground of Knockbrack or Knockiclashy, and made so resolute an attack that they were routed with great slaughter. After the Restoration, Sir Richard Kyrle settled here, erected iron-works, cut down woods, and considerably improved the neighbourhood; and when the French threatened to invade Ireland, in 1666, Sir Richard offered to raise a troop of 60 horse. The parish is situated on both sides of the river Blackwater, and on the new Bogra road from Kanturk to Cork: the new Government road to King-William's-Town and Castle Island passes through that part of Clonmeen which lies to the north of the Blackwater. It comprises 20,815 statute acres, as applotted under the tithe act, and valued for the county cess at £7632 per annum. The land consists partly of reclaimable mountain pasture and bog, and partly of arable land, which latter produces wheat of a superior quality. Culm exists at Drumcummer, but is not worked; and there is a valuable limestone quarry near Rosskeen bridge. Gurtmore rock, on the south side of the Blackwater, rises to a considerable height, and contains several large caverns. The seats are Gurtmore House, the residence of the Rev. P. Townsend, and Gurtmore, of E. Foote, Esq.

The living is a vicarage, in the diocese of Cloyne, and with part of the rectory is episcopally united to the vicarage of Rosskeen, forming the union of Clonmeen, in the patronage of the Bishop; the other portion of the rectory is appropriate to the economy estate of the cathedral of St. Colman, Cloyne. The tithes amount to £415. 9. 3.; and the gross value of the tithes of the benefice is £369. 4. 7½. The church is an old dilapidated building, without a tower, and was the burial-place of the O'Callaghans: it has been recently condemned, and it is expected that a new one will shortly be erected. In the R. C. divisions that portion of the parish lying north of the Blackwater forms part of the union or district of Castle-Magner; the remainder is the head of a union or district, comprising also the parish of Kilcorney, and containing two chapels, one in each parish; the chapel of Clonmeen, at Bantyre Cross, is a large edifice lately built, and adjoining it is a commodious house, erected by the late Rev. Myles Bourke, parish priest, who bequeathed it for the benefit of his successors. A parochial school has been recently built and is supported by subscription; and there are several private schools, in which are about 250 children. On one of the Gurtmore rocks, on the south side of the Blackwater, stand the remains of the castle of Clonmeen, near which several cannon balls have been lately discovered.

CLONMEL, county of CORK.—See GREAT ISLAND and COVE.

Seal.

CLONMEL, a borough, market and assize town, and a parish, partly in the barony of UPPERTHIRD, county of WATERFORD, but chiefly in that of IFFA and OFFA EAST, county of TIPPERARY, and province of MUNSTER, 23 miles (W. by N.) from Waterford, and 82½ miles (S. W. by S.) from Dublin; containing 20,035 inhabitants, of which number, 17,838 are in the town. This place, of which the origin is ascribed to a period prior to the invasion of the Danes, is supposed to have derived its name from *Cluain-Meala*, signifying in the Irish language the "plain of honey," in allusion either to the character of its situation and the peculiar richness of the soil, or to the valley in which it stands being bounded by picturesque mountains that afford honey of fine flavour. It appears to have been the capital of the palatine liberty, as it now is of the county of Tipperary; and is probably indebted for its early importance to the patronage of the Butler family. According to Archdall, a Dominican friary was founded here in 1269, but by whom is not known; and the same author states that the Franciscan friary was also founded in that year by Otho de Grandison, though the date inscribed upon it is 1265: this friary was reformed in 1536, by the friars of the Strict Observance, and having been surrendered to the Crown in 1540, was, with its possessions, three years after, granted in moieties to the sovereign and commonalty of Clonmel and the Earl of Ormonde; its church was esteemed one of the most magnificent ecclesiastical structures in the country. In 1516, the town, which was surrounded with walls and strongly fortified, was besieged and taken by the Earl of Kildare; and during the civil war of the 17th century, having been garrisoned for the king by the Marquess of Ormonde, it was attacked by Cromwell in 1650, with his army from Kilkenny, but was bravely defended by Hugh O'Nial, a northern officer, who, with 1200 of his provincial forces, maintained it with such valour that, in the first assault, not less than 2000 of the besieging army were slain, and the siege was turned into a blockade. After a resolute defence for two months, the garrison, being without any prospect of obtaining relief, secretly withdrew to Waterford, and the inhabitants surrendered upon honourable terms: the town remained in the possession of the parliamentarians till a short time prior to the Restoration, when it was retaken by the royalists. At the Revolution, the town, which was held by the partisans of Jas. II., was abandoned on the approach of William's army to besiege Waterford.

It is situated on the banks of the river Suir, in a beautiful and fertile valley bounded by picturesque mountains, and on one of the two main roads from Dublin to Cork, and that from Waterford to Limerick. With the exception of that portion which is built on islands in the river, it is wholly on the northern or Tipperary side of the Suir, and is connected with the Waterford portion by three bridges of stone. The principal street is spacious, and extends from east to west, under different names, for more than a mile in a direction nearly parallel with the river; the total number of houses, in 1831, was 1532. The town is lighted with gas from works erected, in 1824, by Messrs. Barton and Robinson, of London, who sold them, before they were completed, for about £8000 to the British Gas-Light Company of London, under whom they are now held on lease. The provisions of the act of the 9th of George IV., for lighting and watching towns in Ireland, have been adopted here: the inhabitants are amply supplied with water by public pumps in the various streets. Several newspapers are published, and there are four news-rooms, one of which is a handsome building lately erected at the eastern end of the town, and called the County Club House. At the eastern entrance into the town are extensive barracks for artillery, cavalry, and infantry; behind them, on an elevated and healthy spot, is a small military hospital, capable of receiving 40 patients.

In 1667, the plan of Sir Peter Pett for introducing the woollen manufacture into Ireland was carried into effect by the Duke of Ormonde, then Lord-Lieutenant; and, in order to provide a sufficient number of workmen, 500 families of the Walloons were invited over from Canterbury to settle here. The manufacture continued to flourish for some time, but at length fell into decay, in consequence of the prohibitory statutes passed by the English parliament soon after the Revolution, and is at present nearly extinct. A factory for weaving cotton has been established by Mr. Malcomson, which at present affords employment to 150 girls; he has also an extensive cotton-factory at Portlaw, in the county of Waterford. A very extensive trade is carried on in grain and other agricultural produce of the district, principally with the Liverpool and Manchester markets; great quantities of bacon are also cured and sent to London and the channel ports. There are two very large ale and porter breweries in the town; and at Marlfield, about a mile distant, is a distillery for whiskey upon a very extensive scale. The Excise duties collected within this district, in 1835, amounted to £75,520. 16. The only mineral production in the neighbourhood which forms an article of commerce is slate, of good quality, found at Glenpatrick and worked by the Irish Mining Company. Though not a sea-port, the town, from its situation at the head of the Suir navigation, is the medium through which the corn and provision export trade is carried on between the southern and eastern portions of this large county and England. There are generally about 120 lighters, of from 20 to 50 tons burden, employed in the trade of this place; and several hundred carriers are engaged during winter on the roads communicating with Clonmel and the principal towns within 40 miles round: a considerable portion of the trade of Waterford also passes through the town. In the year ending April 30th, 1832, not less than 230,543 cwt. of flour,

28,678 barrels of wheat, 19,445 barrels of oats, 3878 barrels of barley, 21,559 cwt. of butter, 2769 cwt. of lard, and 63,751 flitches of bacon, besides smaller quantities not enumerated, were sent for exportation. The navigation of the Suir was formerly very imperfect: in 1765, a parliamentary grant was obtained to form a towing-path, by which the passage of the boats has been greatly accelerated. The river is still in many places so shallow that, in dry seasons, the navigation is much impeded. An act has recently been obtained for its improvement; and it is proposed to form a railroad between Carrick, where a basin is intended to be formed, and Limerick, thereby opening a communication between the Suir and the Shannon. There is a salmon fishery in the river, the quays of which are spacious and commodious, extending from the central bridge along the north side. The Bank of Ireland, the Provincial Bank, the Agricultural and Commercial Bank, and the National Bank of Ireland, have branch establishments here. The market days, under the charter of the 6th of Jas. I., are Tuesday and Saturday; and fairs are held on May 5th and Nov. 5th, and also on the first Wednesday in every month (except May and November), for the sale of cattle, sheep, horses, and pigs, and on the preceding day for pigs only. The butter market is a spacious building, provided with suitable offices for the inspector and others; all butter, whether for home consumption or exportation must be weighed and duly entered: there are also convenient shambles and a large potatoe market. The post is daily; the revenue of which, for 1835, was about £3000. The royal mail and day car establishment, under the direction of its proprietor, Mr. Bianconi (to whose enterprising exertions the south of Ireland is so much indebted for the establishment of public cars), is in this town. A chief constabulary police station has been established here.

The corporation is of great antiquity, and probably exists by prescription. Numerous charters have at various times been granted since the reign of Edw. I.; that under which the borough is now governed was granted in the 6th of Jas. I. (1608), and, under the title of "The Mayor, Bailiffs, Free Burgesses, and Commonalty of the Town or Borough of Clonmel," ordains that the corporation shall consist of a mayor, two bailiffs, twenty free burgesses (including the mayor and bailiffs), and a commonalty, with a recorder, chamberlain, town-clerk, and other officers. The freedom was formerly obtained by nomination of a burgess to the common council, a majority of whom decided on the admission; but at present the rights of birth, extending only to the eldest son, apprenticeship to a freeman within the borough, and marriage with a freeman's daughter, are recognised as titles to it. The borough returned two members to the Irish Parliament till the Union, since which time it has sent one to the Imperial Parliament. The elective franchise was vested in the freemen at large, amounting, in the year 1832, to 94 in number; but by the act of the 2nd of Wm. IV., cap. 88, it has extended to the £10 householders: the number of voters registered at the close of 1835 was 805; the mayor is the returning officer. The electoral boundary, under the act of the 2nd and 3rd of Wm. IV., cap. 89, is confined to the town, including Long Island on the south and a space on the north side of the river for buildings contemplated in that quarter, and comprises an area of 361 statute acres, the limits of which are minutely described in the Appendix. The jurisdiction of the corporation extends over a large rural district comprising about 4800 statute acres, of which 3800 are in the county of Waterford, and 1000 in Tipperary: the mayor and recorder are justices of the peace. The Tholsel court, for determining pleas to any amount within the town and liberties, in which the cause of action must arise or the defendant reside, is held every Wednesday, before the mayor and bailiffs. The mayor's court, in which he presides, is held every Wednesday, for the recovery of debts not exceeding 10*s.* late currency; and the mayor and bailiffs hold a court leet twice in the year. Petty sessions are held every alternate Friday. The elections for parliamentary representatives, and the assizes and quarter sessions for the county of Tipperary are held here, the last in April and October. The old court-house, which was built after a design by Sir Christopher Wren, was some years since converted into shops; the new court-house is a light and handsome structure. The county gaol is a large stone building; but prior to the erection of the house of correction, which was completed in the year 1834, it was too small for the number of prisoners generally confined in it; it is now adapted to their classification, contains schools for both sexes and a tread-mill, which is applied to the raising of water for the supply of the prison.

The parish extends beyond the Suir a considerable distance into the county of Waterford, and comprises 8907 statute acres, of which 5922 are applotted under the tithe act. The principal seats are Knocklofty, that of the Earl of Donoughmore; Kilmanahan Castle, of Lieut.-Col. Nuttall Greene; Marlfield, of J. Bagwell, Esq.; Barn, of S. Moore, Esq.; Woodrooff, of W. Perry, Esq.; Rathronan, of Major-Gen. Sir H. Gough, K.C.B.; Kiltinane Castle, of R. Cooke, Esq.; Darling Hill, of the Hon. Baron Pennefather; and Newtown-Anner, of Lady Osborne: there are also many other handsome residences. The views from the demesnes of Knocklofty and Kilmanahan Castle abound with interest and variety, and are not surpassed by any in this part of the country. At Kiltinane Castle a very rapid stream issuing from a rock forms a remarkable natural curiosity. The living is an entire rectory, in the diocese of Lismore, and in the gift of the Corporation: the tithes amount to £300. The glebe-house was built by aid of a gift of £100 and a loan of £650 from the late Board of First Fruits, in 1810; the glebe, dispersed in small parcels in the town and suburbs, comprises 2*a.* 1*r.* 2*p.* The church, dedicated to St. Mary, is an ancient structure, with a handsome octangular embattled tower, 84 feet high, at the eastern extremity of the south side; it was formerly a good specimen of the early English style of architecture, but on its repair, in 1805, it was modernised and retains but little of its original character; a grant of £1019. 12. was made by the Ecclesiastical Commissioners for its repair. In the chancel is a beautiful monument, by Taylor of York, to the memory of Mary, wife of J. Bagwell, Esq., and recording also the death of that gentleman and his eldest son, the late Rt. Hon. Wm. Bagwell, uncle of the present proprietor of Marlfield. There is also a monument erected by the parishioners, in the year 1795, as a tribute of respect to the memory of Dr. J. Moore, who was rector of this parish for 66 years. In the porch are slabs with inscriptions and armorial bearings of the noble family of Hutchinson, Lord Donoughmore, and in one of the shields are impaled the arms of Moore, of Barn. The R. C. parish is co-extensive with that of the Established Church, and is the benefice of the vicar-general of the united dioceses of Waterford and Lismore, and contains two chapels, one in Irishtown, and the other a large and neat modern building in Johnston-street; also a Franciscan friary in Warren-street, lately rebuilt, and a Presentation convent situated beyond the western bridge. There are places of worship for Presbyterians in connection with the Synod of Munster, the Society of Friends, Baptists, Unitarians, and Primitive and Wesleyan Methodists. The grammar school was founded in 1685, by R. and S. Moore, Esqrs., ancestors of the Mount-Cashel family, who endowed it with the lands of Lissenure and Clonbough, in the county of Tipperary, producing a rental of £369, for the gratuitous instruction of the sons of freemen in Latin. The old school-house having fallen into decay, a large and substantial building has been erected within the last few years at the western extremity of the town, on a site granted at a nominal rent by the late Col. Bagwell, and at an expense of nearly £5000, of which £4000 was advanced out of the consolidated fund, for the repayment of which £240 per annum is appropriated from the proceeds of the endowment: there are at present, including boarders, about 90 boys in the school. A parochial school for boys is partly supported by a joint bequest from Dr. Ladyman and Mrs. Pomeroy, amounting to £7 per annum, late currency, and £2 per annum from the rector; and there are a parochial school for girls and an infants' school, both supported by voluntary contributions: a handsome and commodious building has been lately erected for these schools, containing three school-rooms, each capable of accommodating 100 scholars. Two schools for girls are superintended by two ladies, who teach the children gratuitously; a school for boys is supported by collections at the R. C. chapels, which are partly appropriated in paying the master's salary, and partly in providing clothing for the children; and there are Sunday schools in connection with the Established Church and the Presbyterian and Methodists' congregations. The number of children in attendance daily is, on an average, 580; and in the private pay schools are about 650 children.

The fever hospital and dispensary adjacent to it, both handsome and commodious buildings on the north side of the town, are liberally supported. The house of industry for the county of Tipperary, for the reception and support of 50 male and 50 female aged and infirm poor persons of good character, and for the restraint of male and female vagrants, is an extensive building in an airy situation at the foot of the western bridge, opened in 1811: it is supported by grand jury presentments, and is under the government of a corporation by act of parliament; it has a department for orphan children, who, when of proper age, are apprenticed to different trades; the receipts last year were £1543. 5., and the expenditure, £1335. 16. A district lunatic asylum for the county of Tipperary was opened in 1835: the building is capable of accommodating 60 patients, and was erected at an expense, including the purchase of land, furniture, &c., of £16,588. A savings' bank has been established; and there are also a mendicity society and a clothing society, the latter established in 1833. A society has lately been formed for the maintenance and education of the orphan children of Protestant parents, and within the first year, 33 were so provided for. Several charitable bequests to a considerable amount have been left to the parish by different individuals.

Of the town walls, which encompassed only what is now the central part of the town, on the northern bank of the river, there are only very imperfect remains; the entrance was by four principal gates, of which only the west gate, which has been lately very substantially repaired and forms an ornament to the town, is now standing; and of the various towers by which they were defended, there are three remaining near the church-yard. Near the western end of the town are the ruins of the church of St. Stephen, and in the southern suburb are those of the church of St. Nicholas. Some trifling remains of the ancient castle may still be traced in what is now the office of the Tipperary Free Press. In the neighbourhood are the ruins of several castles, and traces of encampments or Danish forts; at Gurteen is a cairn or druids' altar; and near Oakland is a holy well, called St. Patrick's well; also the ruins of an ancient chapel, in which are several large stones bearing inscriptions. About half a mile to the south-east is a chalybeate spring, resorted to medicinally; and near the south suburb is another of similar kind, but not much used. The Rev. Laurence Sterne was born here in 1713; and Bonaventura Baro, or Baron, who wrote numerous works during a long residence at Rome, where he died in 1696, was also born here. Clonmel gives the titles of Earl and Viscount to the family of Scott; the father of the present Earl was the Rt. Hon. John Scott, the celebrated chief justice of the King's Bench in Ireland, who was created Baron Earlsfort in 1784, and was advanced to the Viscounty of Clonmel in 1789, and to the earldom in 1793.

CLONMELLON, a market and post-town, in the parish of Killua, barony of Delvin, county of Westmeath, and province of Leinster, 4¾ miles (W. N. W.) from Athboy, on the road to Oldcastle; containing 960 inhabitants. This is a neat little town, consisting of 183 houses, the market is on Tuesday: and fairs are held on Jan. 28th, May 2nd, July 25th, and Sept. 29th. Petty sessions are held once a fortnight, and here is a station of the constabulary police. The parish church, dedicated to St. Lucy, and situated close to the town, is a good building, with a spire. The parochial school, which is under the National Board, but was built by Sir T. Chapman, is also here; and there is a dispensary.—See Killua.

CLONMETHAN, a parish, in the barony of Nethercross, county of Dublin, and province of Leinster, 4 miles (E.) from Ashbourne; containing 677 inhabitants. A great quantity of corn is grown in this parish, and it contains a limestone quarry. A cattle fair is held in the demesne of Fieldstown on Whit-Monday. The principal seats are the glebe-house, the residence of the Rev. T. Radcliff, from which is a fine view of the surrounding country; Fieldstown, the seat of P. Bourne, Esq.; Brown's Cross, of W. L. Galbraith, Esq.; and Wyanstown, of R. Rooney, Esq. The parish is in the diocese of Dublin, and with the vicarages of Ballyboghill, Ballymadun, Palmerstown, and Westpalstown, perpetually united to it by act of council in 1675, constitutes the prebend of Clonmethan in the cathedral of St. Patrick, and in the patronage of the Archbishop: the tithes amount to £270. The glebe-house was erected in 1817, by aid of a gift of £100, and a loan of £1350, from the late Board: there is a glebe of 35 acres in this parish, and one of 19 acres and 2 roods in Ballymadun; and the gross revenue of the prebend, according to the report of the Commissioners of Ecclesiastical Inquiry, is £638. A neat church was erected in 1818, by £250 parish cess, and a loan of £500 from the late Board of First Fruits, and the Ecclesiastical Commissioners have lately granted £175. 4. 11. towards its repair. The mother church of Clonmethan was dedicated to St. Mary, and the chapel of Fieldstown, which was dedicated to St. Catharine, was subordinate to it. In the R. C. divisions the parish forms part of the union or district of Rollestown, and has a chapel at Old Town, which was erected in 1827, by subscription, and cost nearly £300. Here is a private school, in which are 50 children; and at Old Town is a dispensary.

CLONMINES, an ancient disfranchised parliamentary borough, and a parish, in the barony of SHELBURNE, county of WEXFORD, and province of LEINSTER, on the high road from Wexford to Duncannon and Fethard, near the upper extremity of a small bay, 5 miles (N. E. by N.) from Fethard; containing 360 inhabitants. This parish comprises 1359 statute acres, and is the property of A. Annesley, Esq., of Blechingdon Park, in the county of Oxford. The town, which was of great antiquity but is now only distinguished by its ruins, occupied an area of about 20 acres, and was surrounded by a vallum and fosse. According to Mr. Fraser it had, in the time of the Danes, a mint for coining silver, which was found on the opposite side of the Scar, at a place called Barry's-town, in the parish of Bannow. A convent for Eremites of the order of St. Augustine was founded here at a very early period by the family of Kavanagh or Cavenagh, which was considerably enlarged and beautified by Nicholas Fitz-Nicholas, in 1385, and was subsequently occupied by friars of the order of St. Dominick. A castle was also built by one of the family of Roger de Sutton, who accompanied Fitz-Stephen to Ireland, which has been converted into a farm-house, and is now in the occupation of Mr. Richard Sutton, a descendant of the founder, whose family is now the only one residing within the limits of the ancient town. Ships formerly came up to the town, but the port has been blocked up by a shifting bar at the entrance. The borough seems to have been held of the king in free burgage: several inquisitions *post mortem*, in the reigns of Jas. I. and Chas. I., mention the seisin of certain persons in burgages, but contain no allusion to a corporation or charter, which it appears the borough never had. It returned two members to the Irish parliament prior to the Union, when the £15,000 awarded as compensation for the abolition of its franchise was granted to Chas., Marquess of Ely, and Chas. Tottenham, of Ballycurry, in the county of Wicklow, Esq. This is an impropriate curacy, in the diocese of Ferns, and forms part of the union of Tintern; the tithes, amounting to £80, are impropriate in Cæsar Colclough, Esq. In the R. C. divisions also it is in the union or district of Tintern. A parochial school-house was built by Mr. Annesley, by whom the school and a dispensary are supported. The ruins of the ancient town are very interesting: they are commonly called "Clonmines Castles," and consist chiefly of the tower and walls of the parish church, and a fragment of the wall which enclosed the monastery, with one of the flanking towers. Embosomed in trees, and forming a strikingly picturesque feature in these ruins, is a small chapel surmounted by two turrets leading by spiral staircases within to a parapet: it is said to have been built by a person that had risen from the humble station of a cowherd to great opulence, over the remains of his mother, and was endowed by him with a stipend for a priest to say masses for her soul; it is still called the Cowboy's Chapel.

CLONMORE, a parish, in the barony of RATHVILLY, county of CARLOW, and province of LEINSTER, 2½ miles (S. S. W.) from Hacketstown, on the road from Tullow to Hacketstown and Tinahely; containing 2244 inhabitants. It comprises 26,210 statute acres, of which about 2430 are covered with heath and furze, 130 are woodland, and 1500 bog, and of the remainder, one-fifth is arable and the rest a kind of pasture and meadow: of its entire surface, 5855 acres are applotted under the tithe act. There are some indications of agricultural improvement, although a considerable quantity of unprofitable land might be reclaimed and brought under tillage. Clonmore Lodge is the residence of Lieut.-Col. Whelan; Castle View, of the Rev. R. A. Martin; and the glebe-house, of the Hon. and Rev. Archdeacon Stopford. The living is a rectory, in the diocese of Leighlin, and constitutes the corps of the archdeaconry of Leighlin, in the patronage of the Bishop: the tithes amount to £304. 12. 3¾. The glebe-house was built about 1812, by aid of a gift of £100 and a loan of £450 from the late Board of First Fruits: the glebe comprises ten acres. The church, a plain decent edifice. was built about the same period, by aid of a gift of £600 from the Board. In the R. C. divisions this parish is the head of a union or district, comprising the parishes of Clonmore, Liscoleman, and Mullinacuffe, and parts of those of Haroldstown, Aghold, Crecrim, and Fennagh: the chapel at Clonmore is a plain slated building, not in very good repair; and there are two others in the union, situated at Knockballastine and Kilquiggan, in the parishes of Liscoleman and Aghold. There are a parochial and a national school, affording instruction to about 180 children, including several sent hither from the Foundling Hospital in Dublin. At a short distance from the church are the venerable ruins of the castle,the origin of which, though not satisfactorily ascertained, is with some degree of probability attributed to the Earl of Ormonde, to whom the place was granted in the reign of Hen. VIII., although the castle of Clonmore is recorded to have been taken by the English in 1332. The ruins form three sides of a quadrangle, 170 feet square, of which the fourth has been demolished; at the angles are towers, and the whole was surrounded by a deep fosse, now filled up; several cabins have been built within the walls. Clonmore gives the inferior title of Baron to the Earl of Wicklow.

CLONMORE, a parish, in the barony of IVERK, county of KILKENNY, and province of LEINSTER, 2½ miles (S. S. E.) from Piltown, on the mail coach road from Limerick to Waterford; containing 702 inhabitants. Agriculture is in an improved state, and there is no waste land; the bog on the estate of Cloncunny has been drained and reclaimed by its proprietor, Henry H. Briscoe, Esq. Limestone is quarried for manure and for building and repairing the roads; town manure and culm are brought by the river Suir. The principal seats are Silverspring, the residence of D. Osborne, Esq., and Cloncunny, of Henry H. Briscoe, Esq. The living is a rectory and vicarage, in the diocese of Ossory, united to those of Ballytarsney, and in the patronage of the Bishop: the tithes amount to £173. 3. 7., and of the whole benefice, to £254. 18. 3½. The glebe-house was built by aid of a gift of £400, and a loan of £386, from the late Board of First Fruits, in 1817: the glebe comprises 11*a*. 19*p*. The church was erected by aid of a gift of £900 from the late Board, in 1818; and the Ecclesiastical Commissioners have recently granted £151. 11. 8. towards its repair. In the R. C. divisions this parish is in the union or district of Moncoin. A well at Greagavine was formerly much resorted to by pilgrims on Ascension-day; the water was said to cure ague by immersion. There are some slight remains of an old church. Part of the ancient residence of the bishops of Ossory is still remaining.

CLONMORE, a parish, in the barony of FERRARD, county of LOUTH, and province of LEINSTER, 2½ miles (E. by N.) from Dunleer; containing 769 inhabitants, of which number, 74 are in the hamlet. It comprises, according to the Ordnance survey, 1905 statute acres, two-thirds of which are under tillage. The land is of superior quality and highly cultivated, producing excellent crops of wheat and barley; the farms and farm-houses are of a superior description. There is a constabulary police station in the hamlet. The living is a rectory, in the diocese of Armagh, and in the patronage of the Lord-Primate. The tithes amount to £170. The glebe-house, which is a handsome building, was erected in 1782, on a glebe of 17 acres. The church is a small but handsome edifice, built in 1794, at the sole expense of Primate Robinson. In the R. C. divisions the parish forms part of the union or district of Dysart, and has a chapel at Wyanstown. There is a parochial school, established and supported by the rector, in which about 20 children are educated. Here are the ruins of a castle, said to have been the residence of the De Verduns, also the walls of an ancient church, where a patron is held annually on the 9th of June, in honour of St. Columbkill, the reputed founder.

CLONMORE, county of TIPPERARY.—See KILLAVENOGH.

CLONMORE, a parish, partly in the barony of SHELMALIER, but chiefly in that of BANTRY, county of WEXFORD, and province of LEINSTER, 4 miles (S. S. W.) from Enniscorthy; containing 1371 inhabitants. This place, anciently called *Cluain dicholla gairbhir*, is of great antiquity; St. Maidoc having founded a monastery here in the 6th century, for canons of the order of St. Augustine, which, in 740, was burnt. In 832 it was plundered by the Danes, and in 833 they burnt the abbey on Christmas night, killed many of the monks, and carried others into captivity. Dermot Mac Moilnambo, Lord of Kennselach, plundered and destroyed Clonmore in 1040, and in 1041 it met a similar fate from Donogh, the son of Bryan. It is situated on the river Slaney, which is navigable for flat-bottomed lighters to Enniscorthy. The parish comprises 6987 statute acres of arable and pasture land. Good building stone is abundant in different places. Wilton, the residence of H. Alcock, Esq., occupies the site of one of the ancient castles of the Furlongs, and is being remodelled, in the castellated style, considerably enlarged, and faced with fine white granite from Mount Leinster: in the park is a fine sheet of water, abounding with wild fowl, which has lately been much enlarged and rendered ornamental. The other seats are Macmine Castle, the residence of Pierce Newton King, Esq., an ancient castellated mansion on the banks of the Slaney; Merton, the property of T. A. Whitney, Esq.; Kilgibbon, of H. Alcock, Esq.; Birmount, a deserted mansion of the Leeson family; Clonmore, the seat of W. Woodcock, Esq.; and Birmount Cottage, the neat residence of J. Gethings, Esq. It is a vicarage, in the diocese of Ferns, and is part of the union of St. Mary, Enniscorthy; the rectory is appropriate to the see. The tithes amount to £458. 18. 7½., of which £305. 19. 1. is payable to the bishop, and £152. 19. 6½. to the vicar. A neat church, in the later English style of architecture, with an embattled tower, was erected at Bree, in the year 1827, on a site given by H. Alcock, Esq., by aid of a grant from the late Board of First Fruits; and the Ecclesiastical Commissioners have recently granted £128. 2. 4. towards its repair. It forms a perpetual curacy, with a stipend of £100, in the patronage of the Rector of Enniscorthy. In the R. C. divisions, part of the parish is in the union or district of Davidstown, also called Clough; and the remainder is the head of a district, called Bree, comprising the greater portion of the parishes of Clonmore and Ballyheogue, in each of which is a chapel; that of Clonmore is situated at Bree. A parochial school was established about five years since, to which the bishop subscribes £10 per annum; about 12 children are educated in it, and about 100 in three pay schools. There is also a Sunday school, under the superintendence of the perpetual curate. Some vestiges of the old church still exist in the burial-ground; and on a hill are the remains of a cromlech, in a state of tolerable preservation. At Dononore, on Mr. Alcock's estate, is a waterfall, formed by the river Boro; and near it is an ancient rath or fort.

CLONMULSH, a parish, in the barony and county of CARLOW, and province of LEINSTER, 4½ miles (S.) from Carlow, on the road to Bagnalstown; containing 711 inhabitants. It comprises 3102 statute acres, as applotted under the tithe act, and valued at £2458 per annum. Garryhundon, the seat of Sir R. Butler, Bart., is situated on the townland of that name, which, by an inquisition of Jas. I., in 1607, was found to be in the possession of Theobald, Lord Butler; and by a similar inquisition, in 1623, the townlands of Ballybar and Clonmulsh are recorded to have been held by Peter Carew, Baron of Idrone. The living is a rectory, in the diocese of Leighlin, and in the patronage of the Bishop: the tithes amount to £330. 15. 4¾. The church is a small plain building, situated near the road. In the R. C. divisions this parish is in the union or district of Leighlin-Bridge. On the townland of Powerstown there is a school, in which about 30 children are taught, aided by an annual donation of £6 late currency from the rector.

CLONMULT, a parish, partly in the baronies of IMOKILLY, and KINNATALOON, but chiefly in that of

Barrymore, county of Cork, and province of Munster, $5\frac{1}{2}$ miles (S. W.) from Tallow, on the road to Castle-Martyr; containing 1128 inhabitants. It comprises 3850 statute acres, as applotted under the tithe act, and valued at £2491 per annum. The surface is generally mountainous and wild, and agriculture is in an imperfect state. The village contains about 20 cabins. The living is a rectory and vicarage, in the diocese of Cloyne, and in the patronage of the Bishop: the tithes amount to £225. In the R. C. divisions the parish forms part of the union or district of Castle-Martyr, and has a chapel in the village of Clonmult. There is a private school of about 20 children.

CLONNEARL, a village, in the parish and barony of Kiltartan, county of Galway, and province of Connaught, $2\frac{1}{2}$ miles (W.) from Gort; containing 203 inhabitants.

CLONODONNELL, a parish, in the barony and county of Longford, and province of Leinster, 4 miles (W.) from Longford, on the road to Strokestown; the population is returned with the parish of Killashee. It contains 1889 acres of arable and pasture land, and 3372 of bog. Good limestone is found, much of which is burnt in the vicinity of Richmond harbour, which place has a penny post to Longford, and a distillery manufacturing 80,000 gallons of whiskey annually, and employing about 70 men. The Royal Canal terminates there, and enters the Camlin, which joins the Shannon. The principal seats are Springfield, the residence of Capt. V. Skipton; and Rhynnmount, of W. D'Arcy, Esq. It is a vicarage, in the diocese of Ardagh, united, with part of the rectory, by act of council in 1781, to the rectory and vicarage of Killashee; the other portion of the rectory is appropriate to the see: the tithes amount to £77. 11. 2., of which £26. 6. 11. is payable to the archbishop of Tuam, and £51. 4. 3. to the vicar. There is a glebe of 19*a.* 2*r.* 25*p.* In the R. C. divisions it forms part of the union of Killashee (*which see*), and has a chapel at Richmond harbour, where a school is supported by the incumbent, who built the school-house on the glebe, and uses it as a lecture-room. On the island of Clondra are the remains of a very ancient church; and near it are the ruins of Clonleman castle.

CLONOE, a parish, in the barony of Dungannon, county of Tyrone, and province of Ulster, 2 miles (S. by E.) from Stewartstown, on the road to Lurgan; containing 5555 inhabitants, and comprising, according to the Ordnance survey, $12,070\frac{3}{4}$ statute acres, of which $29\frac{1}{2}$ are part of the Blackwater, and $2940\frac{3}{4}$ are part of Lough Neagh (called Washing bay), by which the parish is bounded on the east. A large tract of marshy ground and bog extends from the shore of the lough to the Blackwater, and the remainder is good arable and pasture land. Near the north-western extremity of the parish are the extensive ruins of Mountjoy castle, built by the Earl of Mountjoy, when lord-deputy of Ireland, in 1601, to check the Earl of Tyrone. This castle, which was built of brick made on the spot, is situated on a gentle eminence close to the shore of the lake, and was thought of so much importance, on the plantation of Ulster, that Jas. I. made this place a corporate borough, and granted 300 acres of land for its support, and 300 acres more to maintain a garrison. In the war of 1641 it was taken by Turlogh O'Nial, who kept possession of it till his total defeat by Gen. Monroe, in 1643; it was dismantled by order of parliament in 1648, since which time it has been in ruins. The Earl of Tyrone built a strong castle on the shore of Lough Neagh, towards the close of the 16th century, and called it *Fuith-na-gael*, or the "Abomination of the Stranger;" but it was soon after taken by the English, and no traces of it remain.

The living is a rectory, in the diocese of Armagh, and in the patronage of the Provost and Fellows of Trinity College, Dublin: the tithes amount to £461. 10. $9\frac{1}{4}$. The glebe-house was built by aid of a gift of £200 and a loan of £550 from the late Board of First Fruits: the glebe comprises 78 acres. The church is a small ancient edifice; it was repaired in 1699, and the Ecclesiastical Commissioners have recently granted £197. 6. for its further repair. The R. C. parish is co-extensive with that of the Established Church; there are two chapels, one at Clonoe and one at Mountjoy; the latter was built in 1835. The parochial school is aided by the rector; a manor school is supported by A. Annesley, Esq., lord of the manor, at whose expense a large and handsome school-house was erected; there is also a school at Aughamullan. In these schools are about 170 children; and there is a pay school, in which are about 70 children. The late Dr. E. Sill bequeathed his estate, called Barn Hill, at Stewartstown, together with all his real and personal property, to build and support an hospital in this parish, at Washing bay, near the influx of a stream called the "Holy River" into Lough Neagh; the funded property exceeded £3000, and the lands produce more than £100 per annum, but no hospital has yet been built.

CLONOGHILL.—See CLOONOGHILL.

CLONOULTY, a parish, in the barony of Kilnemanagh, county of Tipperary, and province of Munster, near the river Suir, 6 miles (N. N. W.) from Cashel, on the high road from Tipperary to Thurles; containing 3600 inhabitants, and comprising 9720 statute acres, as applotted under the tithe act; about 80 acres are underwood, 480 bog, and the remainder are good arable and pasture land; the substratum is limestone. The gentlemen's seats are Cappamorrough, the residence of J. Green, Esq., and Woodford, of J. Murphy, Esq. Fairs are held on July 5th and Nov. 12th, and petty sessions every alternate week. The living is a vicarage, in the diocese of Cashel, and in the patronage of the Archbishop: the tithes amount to £461. 10. $9\frac{1}{4}$. The glebe-house was built by aid of a gift of £150 from the late Board of First Fruits, in 1789: the glebe comprises 15*a.* 0*r.* 22*p.* The church is in bad repair, and application has been made to the Commissioners for the erection of another. In the R. C. divisions this parish is the head of a union or district, comprising the parishes of Clonoulty and Clogher, in the former of which are two chapels, situated respectively at Clonoulty and Rossmore. The parochial schools are supported by the incumbent; there is a school for R. C. children, for which a house was built at Clonoulty, at an expense of £114, by Mr. W. Reilly, of Cashel, who also contributes £10 per annum towards its support, and a school at Rossmore; about 230 children are instructed; and there is also a pay school, in which are about 30 children.

CLONPET, a parish, in the barony of Clanwilliam, county of Tipperary, and province of Munster, situated in the heart of a mountainous district, $2\frac{1}{4}$ miles

(S.) from Tipperary; containing 907 inhabitants. It is a vicarage, in the diocese of Emly, and is part of the union of Lattin; the rectory is impropriate in William Moore, Esq.: the tithes amount to £92, of which £58 is payable to the impropriator, and £34 to the vicar. In the R. C. divisions it also forms part of the union or district of Lattin. There is a small pay school of seven boys.

CLONPRIEST, a parish, in the barony of IMOKILLY, county of CORK, and province of MUNSTER, 2½ miles (S. W.) from Youghal, on the road to Cork; containing 3417 inhabitants. It comprises 6935 statute acres, as applotted under the tithe act, and valued at £6334 per annum. A large portion of the land lies very low, but forms a valuable marsh, on which a great number of cattle are fed; and the remainder is in tillage, and produces excellent crops. Several of the farm-houses are handsomely and substantially built, and there is an extensive tract of bog, which affords abundance of fuel. A large quantity of butter is made here for the Cork market. There are some quarries of limestone and brown building stone, also a quarry of slate, of very indifferent quality. The tide comes up the Fanisk to Inchiquin Castle, admitting large boats and lighters. The living is a rectory, in the diocese of Cloyne, and in the patronage of the Crown: the tithes amount to £869. 2. 4½., and the glebe comprises 30 acres. The church is a very old and inconvenient building, situated at one extremity of the parish, and inaccessible during a portion of the winter; it is in contemplation to erect another on a more eligible site. In the R. C. divisions the parish forms part of the union or district of Youghal; the chapel is at Gartrough or Yurtroe. There is a school, aided by an annual donation from Lord Ponsonby, in which about 140 children are instructed; also a private pay school, in which are about 80 children. On the bank of the river Fanisk are the ruins of Inchiquin Castle, now called Inchiquin Tower, consisting of a round tower 9 yards in diameter, of which the walls are more than 12 feet thick: it is the property of Lord Ponsonby, and was formerly the head of a barony called Inchicoigne; it is still the head of a manor, for which courts are held at Killeagh, in the adjoining parish of that name.

CLONROAD.—See ENNIS.

CLONROCHE, a village, in the parish of CHAPPLE, barony of BANTRY, county of WEXFORD, and province of LEINSTER, formerly called Stonepound, 6 miles (S. W.) from Enniscorthy on the road to New Ross: the population is returned with the parish. It is a thriving village; a reading and news-room, on a small scale, has been established and is supported by subscription. Here is a constabulary police station; fairs are held on Jan. 26th, Feb. 13th, March 13th, May 14th, July 14th, Sept. 25th, Oct. 24th, Nov. 24th, and Dec. 26th, chiefly for cattle; and petty sessions are held at irregular intervals.—See CHAPPLE.

CLONRUSH, a parish, in the barony of LEITRIM, county of GALWAY, and province of CONNAUGHT, situated on Lough Derg, 10½ miles (S. by W.) from Portumna; containing 3084 inhabitants. It comprises 11,201 statute acres, as applotted under the tithe act, and valued at £2890 per annum: a great part is annually flooded by the Shannon, and it contains a large tract of poor marsh land. Iron mines exist in the mountains, and Lough Derg furnishes means of communication with Limerick and Dublin. At Tintrim is the seat of J. Burke, Esq., on which is a chalybeate spring; and beautifully situated on the banks of the Shannon is Meelick, the ancient seat of the Burke family, but now uninhabited. It is a vicarage, in the diocese of Killaloe, and is part of the union of Inniscalthra; the rectory is appropriate to the economy fund of the cathedral of Killaloe: the tithes amount to £130, of which £70 is payable to the economy fund and £60 to the vicar. In the R. C. divisions it is the head of a union or district, comprising the parishes of Clonrush and Inniscalthra, in each of which is a chapel. There are two public schools, one at Furness and one at Dromane.

CLONSAST, or CLONCAST, also called CLONBOLLOGUE, a parish, in the barony of COOLESTOWN, KING'S county, and province of LEINSTER, 6¼ miles (N. E. by E.) from Portarlington; containing 3914 inhabitants, and comprising about 25,000 statute acres, of which about 14,000 are cultivable, the remainder bog. The living is a rectory, in the diocese of Kildare, united in 1796, by act of council, to the vicarage of Ballynakill, forming the union of Clonsast, in the alternate patronage of the Duke of Leinster and the Bishop: the tithes amount to £628. 12. 3½., and of the union to £694. 3. 0¾. The church is a plain building, to the repairs of which the Ecclesiastical Commissioners have recently granted £243. In the R. C. divisions the parish is the head of a union or district, called Clonbollogue, comprising this parish and parts of those of Geashill and Ballynakill, in which are chapels at Clonbollogue and Brackna, and the Island chapel. The parochial school is aided by an annual donation from the incumbent; and there is a school at Clonbollogue. In these schools about 250 children are educated; there are also four private schools, in which are about 110 children.

CLONSHAMBOE, a parish, in the barony of IKEATHY and OUGHTERANY, county of KILDARE, and province of LEINSTER, 3½ miles (S. S. W.) from Kilcock, on the road to Naas; containing 297 inhabitants. It is a vicarage, in the diocese of Kildare, and is part of the union of Clane; the rectory is impropriate in the representatives of Lord Falconberg: the tithes amount to £98. 12. 6½., of which £30. 8. 9½. is payable to the impropriator, and the remainder to the vicar. In the R. C. divisions it forms part of the union or district of Kilcock.

CLONSHIRE.—See CLOUNSHIRE.

CLONSILLAGH, a parish, in the barony of CASTLEKNOCK, county of DUBLIN, and province of LEINSTER, 7 miles (N. W.) from Dublin; containing 954 inhabitants, and comprising 2943 statute acres, the whole of which is arable land. There are limestone quarries in the parish, and an extensive flour-mill on the Liffey, erected on the site of a very ancient one, called "the Devil's Mill," from its having been erected, according to tradition, in one night. The Royal Canal passes through the parish. Woodlands, formerly called Luttrell's Town, and the seat of the Earls of Carhampton, is now the property and residence of Col. T. White. The demesne includes above 648 statute acres, exceedingly picturesque; the mansion is a noble building, in the castellated style, and is said to contain a room in which king John slept: that monarch granted the estate to the Luttrell family. In a glen, a stream, which is supplied from a beautiful lake in the park, of 20 acres, rolls over a rocky bed and forms a cascade about 30 feet high. The other seats are Coolmine, the residence of A. Fitzpatrick, Esq.; Clonsillagh, of R. H. French, Esq.; Broomfield, of the Rev. S. Thompson; Clonsillagh, of Ignatius Callaghan, Esq.; Hansfield, of T. Willan, Esq.; and Phibblestown, of Capt. H. Reid, R. N. The parish formerly belonged to the priory of Malvern, in Worcestershire. It is a rectory, in the diocese of Dublin, and is part of the union of Castleknock: the tithes amount to £240. The church is a small neat building. In the R. C. divisions it also forms part of the union or district of Castleknock, and has a neat chapel at Porterstown, built by the late L. White, Esq., who also built a school-house, with apartments for the master and mistress: the school is supported by subscription, and there is one on the lower road, near the Liffey; they afford instruction to about 90 children.

CLONSKEA, anciently CLONSKEAGH, a small village, in that part of the parish of St. Mary, Donnybrook, which is in the half-barony of Rathdown, county of Dublin, and province of Leinster, 2 miles (S.) from the Post-Office, Dublin, on the road to Enniskerry, by way of Roebuck; the population is included in the return for the parish. It contains a dye stuff factory and iron-works; and is within the jurisdiction of the city of Dublin court of requests. ClonskeaCastlegh, the handsome residence of G. Thompson, Esq., affords fine views of the city and bay of Dublin, with the adjacent mountains; it was built by H. Jackson, who acted a prominent part in the disturbances of 1798. On digging in front of the mansion, a few years since, a layer of muscle shells, about three feet thick, and imbedded in clay, was found about eight feet below the surface. The other seats are Rich View, the residence of M. Powell, Esq., and Virge Mount, of the Rev. J. C. Crosthwaite.

CLONTARF, a parish, in the barony of Coolock, county of Dublin, and province of Leinster, on the northern shore of Dublin bay, 2½ miles (E. N. E.) from the Post-Office, Dublin; containing 3314 inhabitants, of which number, 1309 are in the village. Clontarf stands in a very richly wooded and finely cultivated country, and is distinguished in Irish history as the scene of a sanguinary battle, which put a final period to the Danish power in Ireland. But although this memorable battle takes its distinguishing name from this parish, it is probable, from the numbers of human bones discovered in excavating the ground for streets on the north side of Dublin, and at Knockbrush Hill near Finglass, that the scene of action embraced a much more extended tract of country. On the first invasion of Ireland by the English, O'Brian and O'Carrol, who came to the assistance of Roderic, the last king of all Ireland, at the siege of Dublin, took post in this vicinity. The principal lands in the parish appear to have been vested in a religious house founded here in 550, and erected into a commandery of Knights Templars in the reign of Hen. II., which, on the suppression of that order, became a preceptory of Knights Hospitallers of St. John of Jerusalem, and was one of the chief appendages of the grand priory of Kilmainham. Sir J. Rawson, the last prior, after the surrender of this house and its revenues, was created, by Hen. VIII., Viscount Clontarf, with a pension of 500 marks per annum. Since that period, the possessions of the establishment, after passing through various hands, were erected into a manor and conferred by the Crown on Admiral Vernon, whose descendant, J. E. Venables Vernon, Esq., is the present proprietor. This place was burned in 1641, by the parliamentarian general, Sir C. Coote, on the 15th of December.

The present village is of considerable extent, and is much frequented for sea-bathing by visiters from the north of Dublin; and the scenery in many parts is highly interesting. It was formerly a fishing town of some importance, and along the water's edge are still many wooden buildings, called the Clontarf sheds, formerly used for the purpose of curing the fish taken here. Several neat lodging-houses have been erected and numerous pleasant villas and ornamented cottages have been built in detached situations. Near the strand was formerly the Royal Marine charter school; the buildings now belong to Mr. Brierly, who has erected large hot and cold sea-water baths. Opposite to Dollymount is an extensive causeway stretching into the sea, erected by the Ballast Board to deepen the channel between Poolbeg, or the south wall lighthouse and the north wall light. From this causeway is a long strip of sandy ground, called the North Bull, which is partly green, extending towards the hill of Howth, and surrounded on all sides by the sea; and off the sheds is a profitable oyster bank. The parish comprises 1039 statute acres, as applotted under the tithe act, and valued at £5283 per annum. On the shore is the shaft of a lead mine, which has been opened at different times since the reign of Jas. I., and although it afforded a considerable quantity of rich ore, both of the common sulphate and cubicular kinds, the operations have invariably been unsuccessful from the influx of sea water. The Drogheda, or Grand Northern Trunk railway from Dublin to Drogheda will, when completed, pass through this parish; and there is a constabulary police station. Clontarf Castle, the seat of J. E. V. Vernon, Esq., was one of the most ancient castles within the English pale, and is supposed to have been erected either by Hugh de Lacy or by Adam de Frepo, one of his knights, to whom he granted the lordship; the old castle was taken down in 1835, and a handsome mansion in the later English style, with a tower of Norman character, is now in progress of erection, from a design by Mr. W. Morrison. There are many handsome seats and pleasant villas: the principal are Furry Park, the residence of T. Bushe, Esq.; Sybil Hill, of J. Barlow, Esq.; Clontarf House, of Mrs. Colvill; Elm View, of W. C. Colvill, Esq., formerly the seat of Lords Shannon and Southwell; Verville, of C. A. Nicholson, Esq., Convent House, of the Hon. Arthur Moore, second justice of the court of common pleas; Dollymount, of T. and L. Crosthwaite, Esqrs.; Prospect, of R. Warren, Esq.; Bellgrove, of R. Simpson, Esq.; Beachfield, of J. Tudor, Esq.; Clontarf, of B. Mitford, Esq.; Ivy House, of R. Ellis, Esq.; Danesfield, of J. Campbell, Esq.; Seafield House, of T. Gresham, Esq.; Merchamp, of E. Shaw, Esq.; Thornhill, of H. O'Reilly, Esq.; Bay View, of F. L'Estrange, Esq.; Baymount House, of J. Keily, Esq., formerly for some years the residence of Dr. Trail, Bishop of Down and Connor; Bedford Lodge, of W. I. Moore, Esq.; Rose Vale, of Sir E. Stanley, Knt.; Strandville, of Alderman Tyndall; Strandville House, of W. Minchiner, Esq.; Merville, of

R. Peter, Esq.; Moira Lodge, of W. Taylor, Esq.; Fort View, of S. Morris, Esq.; Sea View, of Capt. Dundas; and Crab-lake, of W. Leckie, Esq.

The living is a rectory, in the diocese of Dublin, and in the patronage of the Crown: the tithes amount to £220. By a clause in the act of Explanation in 1680, the tithes and altarages were settled on the incumbent and his successors, at a rent of £6. 2. 6¼. per ann. The church, dedicated to St. John the Baptist, occupies the site of the ancient monastery, and was rebuilt in 1609: it is a small neat edifice, with an elevation above the western entrance perforated for a bell, and contains several ancient monuments in good preservation. In the R. C. divisions the parish is the head of a union or district, comprising the parishes of Artane, Clontarf, Clonturk, Coolock, Glasnevin, Killester, Raheny, and Santry; there are chapels at Clontarf, Coolock, Ballyman near Santry, and at Annesley bridge. Clontarf chapel was built after a design by P. Byrne and Son, on a site near the sheds, presented by Mr. Vernon; and M. Carey, Esq., bequeathed £1000 towards its erection. It is a spacious and elegant structure, in the later style of English architecture, 152 feet in length and 63 feet 6 inches in breadth, and forms a striking ornament to the place. In the village is a Carmelite monastery, consisting of five laymen, who carry on their respective trades as a means of supporting the institution; among these is an extensive bakery, which supplies the neighbourhood and part of Dublin with excellent bread; attached to the establishment is a neat chapel. There was formerly a nunnery, the inmates of which removed to Cabragh about 12 years since, and the house is now occupied by the Hon. Judge Moore. In the old chapel is a male and female school, supported by the interest of accumulated receipts at charity sermons, amounting to £700, and of a bequest of £500 by M. Carey, Esq.: the average number of children is about 100. The parochial school, to which Mr. Vernon has given a house rent-free, is supported by subscription; an almshouse for 12 widows is supported by Sunday collections and charity sermons; and a loan fund was established in 1835. In making some alterations at Elm View, silver coins of Hen. II. and brass coins of Jas. I. were found; and at Danesfield a Danish sword was dug up in the garden, in 1830.

CLONTEAD, or CLOUNTADE, a parish, in the barony of KINSALE, county of CORK, and province of MUNSTER, 2 miles (N. W.) from Kinsale, on the mail coach road to Cork; containing 1337 inhabitants. Knock-Robbin, in this parish, was the scene of a repulse of part of the Spanish army in 1601; and during the war of 1641, the royal forces were frequently encamped here. The parish extends from the western termination of Oyster haven, in a southerly direction, till it meets the River Bandon at White Castle cove: it is intersected by the little river Belgooley, and bounded on the south by the Bandon river. It contains 1727 statute acres, as applotted under the tithe act, and valued at £946 per ann.; and was anciently part of the possessions of Tracton abbey. The land is generally good and in an excellent state of cultivation, being chiefly under tillage, and producing abundant crops of wheat, barley, oats, and potatoes: the manure used is principally sea sand, which is brought in barges from the bay of Kinsale to the village of Brownsmills. There are some good dairy farms. At Mullanadee is a flour-mill, called the Kinsale mill, which produces 8000 barrels of flour annually. The gentlemen's seats are Palacetown, the residence of S. P. Townsend, Esq., and Knock-Robbin, of Captain E. Bolton. It is an impropriate curacy, in the diocese of Cork, and is part of the union of Tracton; the rectory is entirely impropriate in the Earl of Shannon. The tithes amount to £73. 17. In the R. C. divisions it is the head of a union or district, comprising also the parishes of Ballyfeard and Kilmonogue; the chapel is a large plain edifice, built on an eminence. A school is supported by Mr. Townsend; and there is a small pay school. Near the new road are the ruins of the church; and about two miles from Kinsale are the remains of an old circular fort defended by a rampart and fosse, called Liscrally, which gives name to the surrounding lands: it contains subterraneous passages, which extend all round the mound.

CLONTIBRET, a parish, in the barony of CREMORNE, county of MONAGHAN, and province of ULSTER, on the confines of the county of Armagh, 6 miles (N. by W.) from Castle-Blayney, on the road to Monaghan; containing 15,941 inhabitants, and comprising, according to the Ordnance survey, 26,553¼ statute acres, of which 334 are part of Mucknoe lake, 198¾ are in small loughs, 3920 bog, and the remainder, with the exception of a small portion of rough rocky pasture, good arable land, and all under tillage. Agriculture is improving; and the bog affords abundance of good fuel. Grauwacke slate is found in abundance, and is quarried for building and for repairing the roads. A mine of antimony was discovered on Lord Middleton's property, and was worked for some time, but not paying, it was discontinued. A lead mine has been recently opened in Carriganure, on the estate of E. Lucas, Esq. M.P., of Castleshane; and lead ore is also found in the townland of Killicrum. Millmount, the handsome residence of A. Swanzy, Esq., and Rockfield House, of H. Swanzy, Esq., are within the parish. The living is a rectory and vicarage, in the diocese of Clogher, constituting the corps of the archdeaconry of Clogher, and in the patronage of the Bishop. The tithes amount to £800; and the gross revenue of the dignity, including tithes, glebe, and lands, is returned at £852. The glebe-house was erected in 1752, by aid of a gift of £100 from the late Board of First Fruits; the glebe comprises 40 acres, besides which the lands of the archdeaconry, called the "Archdeacon's Hill," situated in the parish of Clogher, contain 9*a.* 2*r.* 12*p.*, let on lease at a rent of £16. 16. per annum. The church is a plain old structure, with an ancient square tower surmounted by a spire; it is in a very dilapidated condition, and it is in contemplation to erect a new church. Divine service is also occasionally performed in a school-house at the southern extremity of the parish. In the R. C. divisions, part of the parish is included in the union or district of Mucknoe or Macrey, and the remainder forms a district of itself; the chapel is at Anyallow. There is a place of worship for Presbyterians in connection with the Synod of Ulster, and also one in connection with the Seceding Synod on the confines of the parish; and there is also a place of worship for Primitive Wesleyan Methodists. There are parochial and other schools aided by private subscription; in which about 520 children are instructed; and there are two pay schools, in which are about 120 children. There is a dispensary at Castleshane, close to the parish, in the benefits of which it partakes. Charitable donations to the amount of £500, and £15 per ann., have been bequeathed by various benefactors for the relief of the poor. Much pine or fir, with the roots frequently upright, and the mark of fire on them, and much black and grey oak, are found in the boggy lands. In Cornero wood, on the shore of Mucknoe lake, are the ruins of an ancient castle.

CLONTUBRID, a parish, in the barony of CRANAGH, county of KILKENNY, and province of LEINSTER, 1½ mile (N. W.) from Freshford, on the road to Durrow; containing 157 inhabitants. It is a vicarage, in the diocese of Ossory, and is part of the union of Freshford; the rectory is appropriate to the economy estate of the cathedral of St. Canice, Kilkenny. The tithes are included with those of Balleen. In the R. C. divisions it forms part of the union or district of Lisdowney, and has a small chapel. Here is a singular cell, supposed to have been a hermitage, built over a spring called *Tubbrid na Draoith*, or "the druids' well:" it measures seven feet by two feet six inches, and is raised a little above the ground and entered by a pointed arch.

CLONTURK, or DRUMCONDRA, a parish, in the barony of COOLOCK, county of DUBLIN, and province of LEINSTER, 1 mile (N.) from Dublin, on the roads to Howth, Malahide, and Swords; containing 2713 inhabitants. The river Tolka bounds the parish on the south, a woollen mill on which was washed away in 1834 by a flood, but was rebuilt in 1836; there is also a brass foundry. The city police have a station on the strand. There are many beautiful seats, the chief of which is Marino, that of the Earl of Charlemont; it is entered from the Strand road, near Fair View, by an elegant semicircular gateway of hewn granite, which attracted the notice of his late Majesty, Geo. IV., who pronounced it to be the most perfect structure of the kind in his dominions. The demesne contains above 100 acres, and is well wooded. The mansion, which contains some elegant apartments, is of plain and unpretending exterior; but this want of embellishment is fully compensated by the Temple or Casino. This fine imitation of Grecian architecture crowns the summit of a gentle eminence in the centre of the demesne. It rises from a square platform, ascended on the north and south sides by broad flights of marble steps. Contiguous to the Casino, which was erected by the late Lord Charlemont, from a design by Sir W. Chambers, is an extensive pleasure ground surrounding a small but beautiful sheet of water, supplied from a copious fountain gushing from a rock-work grotto. The other residences are Belvidere House, that of Sir J. C. Coghill, Bart.; Drumcondra House, of Gen. Sir Guy Campbell, K.C.B., in whose grounds are the remains of an ancient building; Drumcondra Castle, of R. Williams, Esq.; Hampton Lodge, of Mrs. A. Williams; High Park, of G. Gray, Esq.; Hartfield, of P. Twigg, Esq.; Donnycarney, of Abel Labertouche, Esq.; Richmond Castle, of A. Williams, Esq.; Annadale, of W. Hone, Esq.; Union Lodge, of J. English, Esq.; Well Park, of W. Kirwan, Esq.; Woodbine Lodge, of H. Yeo, Esq.; Richmond House, of P. Birch, Esq.; Tokay Lodge, of M. Kerr, Esq.; Mary Ville, of J. J. Finn, Esq.; Rosemount, of W. Butler, Esq.; and Sally Park, of W. Mathews, Esq.

The living is a perpetual curacy, in the diocese of Dublin, and in the patronage of the Corporation of Dublin, in which the rectory is impropriate. The church is a small plain building, erected in the early part of the last century by the Coghill family, and was repaired and decorated by the corporation in 1833, at an expense of £500. On its north side is a large tomb, erected to the memory of Marmaduke Coghill, Chancellor of the Exchequer for Ireland, on which reclines his effigy in his official robes, with figures of Minerva and Religion below. On the south side of the churchyard are interred the remains of F. Grose, Esq., the distinguished antiquary, who died in Dublin, in May 1791; and T. Furlong, a native poet, was buried here in 1827. In the R. C. divisions the parish is in the union or district of Clontarf, and has a chapel near Annesley bridge. The parochial school is in the village of Drumcondra; and an infants' school was established in 1829, at Philipsburgh strand; there is also a girls' school at the Richmond convent. This nunnery is of the Presentation order, and is surrounded with grounds tastefully laid out, and has a chapel annexed. In the village of Drumcondra is an asylum for poor women, called the Retreat. Annesley bridge, and the causeway connected with it, were erected by act of parliament in 1796 and 1797, at an expense of about £6000: they cross a portion of ground overflowed by the tide, at the confluence of the Tolka with the Liffey. Higher up, on the left, the Tolka is crossed by the old bridge of Ballybough. Philipsburgh strand extends from one bridge to the other. To the east of Annesley bridge is a cluster of buildings, called Fair View; and beyond them, between the Malahide and Howth roads, is Marino Crescent, consisting of large handsome houses, with an enclosed lawn in front, which extends to the road bounding the strand; it commands fine views, and is very convenient for sea-bathing.

CLONTUSKERT, or CLONTHUSKERT, a parish, partly in the barony of LONGFORD, but chiefly in that of CLONMACNOON, county of GALWAY, and province of CONNAUGHT, 5 miles (N. N. W.) from Eyrecourt, on the road to Ballinasloe; containing 4002 inhabitants, and comprising 11,837 statute acres. Boadan, or Broadan, founded a monastery here for Augustinian canons, in the early part of the 9th century, and was the first abbot; at the suppression it was granted to Richard, Earl of Clanricarde. Gurteemona is the seat of J. Blake, Esq. The living is a vicarage, in the diocese of Clonfert, and, with the greater portion of the rectory united, is part of the union of Clonfert: the other portion of the rectory is appropriate to the see: the tithes amount to £304. 12. 3¾., of which £46. 3. 1. is payable to the Ecclesiastical Commissioners, and £258. 9. 2¾. to the incumbent. The glebe-house was built in 1820, by aid of a gift of £250, and a loan of £450 from the same Board. The church, which is at Glanlahan, is a very neat building, with a spire of hewn stone; it was erected in 1818, by aid of a gift of £900 from the late Board of First Fruits. The R. C. parish is co-extensive with that of the Established Church, and has a chapel. There is a school at Glanlahan, aided by annual donations from the Earl of Clancarty and the rector; and at Bonla is another school: together they instruct about 270 boys and 180 girls, besides whom, about 100 children are taught in three hedge schools. The ruins of the abbey are in good preservation: the gateway is still perfect, and the east window is very fine; and there are several ancient inscriptions, still very legible, the principal of which are those of the O'Kellys.

CLONTUSKERT, or CLONTHUSKERT, a parish, in the barony of BALLINTOBBER, county of ROSCOMMON, and province of CONNAUGHT, on the river Shannon, and at the head of Lough Ree, by which it is bounded on the east and south, 1¾ mile (N. W.) from Lanesborough; containing 2975 inhabitants. This parish is also called Cloonturskan; within its limits are extensive tracts of bog. The abbey is said to have been founded by St. Faithleg, for Augustinian canons; and, at the dissolution, a lease of its possessions was granted for 21 years to Fryall O'Farrell, at the yearly rent of £11. 9. 8. Very little of the buildings remains, but the cemetery, which is still used, contains the tombs of several families of distinction. The living is a vicarage, in the diocese of Elphin, and is part of the union of Clonfinlogh; the rectory is impropriate in the representatives of Lord Kingsland. The tithes amount to £229. 18. 3¾., of which £186. 7. 4¾. is payable to the impropriators, and the remainder to the incumbent. In the R. C. divisions this parish forms part of the union or district of Kilgeffin or Kilbride. Here are three pay schools, in which about 160 children are educated.

CLONYNE, or CLONEEN, a parish, partly in the barony of SLIEVARDAGH, but chiefly in that of MIDDLETHIRD, county of TIPPERARY, and province of MUNSTER, 4 miles (E.) from Fethard; containing 1680 inhabitants, and comprising 12,078 statute acres. Fairs are held on May 30th, June 29th, and Nov. 1st. It is a rectory and vicarage, in the diocese of Cashel, and is part of the union of Fethard: the tithes amount to £300. In the R. C. divisions it is the head of a union or district, including the parishes of Clonyne and Drangan, in each of which is a chapel. There is a school in which are about 130 children.

CLOON, or CLONE, a parish and village, partly in the barony of CARRIGALLEN, but chiefly in that of MOHILL, county of LEITRIM, and province of CONNAUGHT, 3 miles (E. N. E.) from Mohill; containing 19,589 inhabitants. An abbey was founded here about the year 570, by St. Fraech or Froech, which was then called *Cluain-cholluing*, and the site of it *Cluain-Conmacne*, in the territory of *Muntereoluis*, now part of the county of Leitrim; it was subsequently dedicated to its founder, and was formerly of very great repute; it afterwards took the name of Clone, and became a parish church. The land is chiefly under tillage; limestone is quarried for agricultural and other uses. Lead ore has been found near Aughavas, but has not been worked to any extent. The principal seats are, Rhynn, the residence of Lord Clements, pleasantly situated on the well-planted shore of Rhynn lake, an extensive sheet of water abounding with fish; Lakefield, of Duke Crofton, Esq.; Drumdarkin, of G. B. West, Esq.; and Brook Lawn, of Mrs. O'Brien. The village is a constabulary police station, and fairs are held on Feb. 12th, April 5th, May 26th, June 13th, July 10th, Aug. 26th, Sept. 29th, Nov. 2nd, and Dec. 20th; they are well attended, and are among the principal in the county for cattle. Petty sessions are held every alternate Wednesday. The living is a rectory and vicarage, in the diocese of Ardagh, and in the patronage of the Bishop: the tithes amount to £1009. 18. 8. The glebe-house is not in a habitable state: the glebe, in five separate portions, comprises 323 acres. The church, a plain edifice in the early English style, was erected by aid of a loan of £1500 from the late Board of First Fruits, in 1821; the former church had several portions of the old abbey incorporated with it; but it has been entirely removed to make room for the present structure. In the R. C. divisions this parish forms three parochial unions or districts, the chapels of which are situated respectively at Cloon, Aughavas, and Gortlitera. There are six public schools, one of which is supported by the rector, and two by S. White, Esq. In these schools about 340 boys and 200 girls are instructed; and there are 25 pay schools, in which are about 1440 children; and two Sunday schools. There is a loan fund, with a capital of £300. At Rhynn are the remains of an old castle, built by the Reynolds family, near which Lord Clements has erected a handsome residence; and there are two chalybeate springs in the parish.

CLOONAFF, or CLONCRAFF, a parish, in the barony and county of ROSCOMMON, and province of CONNAUGHT, 5 miles (N. N. E.) from Strokestown, on the shore of Lough Baffin; containing 2524 inhabitants, and comprising 9471 statute acres, as applotted under the tithe act. The lands are principally under tillage, producing good crops, and there is a proportionate quantity of bog, affording a sufficient supply of fuel. Moss Hill, the seat of Capt. Conry, is pleasantly situated; and there are three lakes in the parish. The rectory and vicarage form part of the union of Aughrim, in the diocese of Elphin: the tithes amount to £100. The ancient parish church was part of a monastery said to have been founded by St. Patrick, and which was in existence in the 12th century. The R. C. parish is co-extensive with that of the Established Church; there are two chapels, one in the townland of Cloonaff, and one in that of Drummamullan. There is a school of about 120 children aided by £2. 2. per ann. from Mrs. Conry.

CLOONOGHILL, a parish, in the barony of CORRAN, county of SLIGO, and province of CONNAUGHT, 3½ miles (W. S. W.) from Ballymote, on the road from Boyle to Ballina; containing 2241 inhabitants. This place was formerly called Clonymeaghan, and was the seat of a Dominican monastery, founded about 1488, by the sept of Mac Donogh, which afterwards became a cell to that of Sligo: at the dissolution its possessions were granted to Richard Kyndelinshe. The parish contains 4551 statute acres, as applotted under the tithe act: the land is generally good, and there is not much bog. Limestone quarries are worked here. Fairs are held at Buninadan on Jan. 14th, June 2nd, Aug. 6th, Sept. 10th, Oct. 7th, and Nov. 27th. The principal seats are Ballinaclough, the residence of J. West, Esq.; Grayfort, of J. Rea, Esq.; Roadstown, of D. O'Connor, Esq.; Drumrahan, of J. Taffe, Esq.; and Old Rock, of J. Trumble, Esq. It is a rectory and vicarage, in the diocese of Achonry; the rectory is partly impropriate in J. Baker, Esq., and partly, with the vicarage, forms a portion of the union and corps of the deanery of Achonry. The tithes amount to £170 per annum, of which £90 is payable to the impropriator, and the remainder to the dean. In the R. C. divisions it is the head of a union or district, called

Buninadan, comprising the parishes of Cloonoghill, Kilturra, and Killowshalway; and containing two chapels, of which that of Cloonoghill, at Buninadan, is a large slated building. There is a school at Ballinaclough, under the patronage of J. West, Esq., in which are about 110 children; and there is also a hedge school of about 50 children. On the banks of the river are the remains of an old castle, built by the Mac Donoghs; and on the lands of Church Hill is a large cromlech, consisting of a horizontal and three upright stones.

CLOUGH, a post-town, in the parish of LOUGHIN-ISLAND, barony of KINELEARTY, county of DOWN, and province of ULSTER, 5 miles (S. W.) from Downpatrick, on the road to Newry, and 68¾ miles (N. by E.) from Dublin; containing 309 inhabitants. Here is a constabulary police station, and fairs are held on May 27th, July 5th, Oct. 21st, Nov. 22nd, and Dec. 23rd. In the vicinity are Seaforde House, the splendid mansion of M. Forde Esq.; Mount Panther, the beautiful seat of J. Reed Allen, Esq.; and Ardilea, that of the Rev. W. Annesley. Here is a large Presbyterian meeting-house in connection with the Synod of Ulster, but it has been closed several years.—See LOUGHIN-ISLAND.

CLOUGH, a village, in the parish of CASTLECOMER, barony of FASSADINING, county of KILKENNY, and province of LEINSTER, 1 mile (N. N. E.) from Castlecomer on the road to Athy; containing 116 houses and 582 inhabitants, who are chiefly employed in the neighbouring collieries. It is a constabulary police station; and the R. C. chapel of the district of Clough, which comprises parts of the parishes of Castlecomer and Rathaspeck, is situated here.

CLOUGH, county of LONGFORD.—See KILCOMMICK.

CLOUGH, county of WEXFORD.—See LESKINFERE.

CLOUGHENRY.—See CLOGHERNEY.

CLOUGHMILLS, a village, in the parish of KILLAGAN, barony of KILCONWAY, county of ANTRIM, and province of ULSTER, 8 miles (S. E. by E.) from Ballymoney, on the road to Ballymena; containing 15 houses and 101 inhabitants.

CLOUNAGH, a parish, in the barony of LOWER CONNELLO EAST, county of LIMERICK, and province of MUNSTER, 2 miles (W.) from Rathkeale; containing 648 inhabitants. It comprises 2313 statute acres, as applotted under the tithe act, and valued at £2434 per annum. About one-third of the land is under tillage, and the remainder, with the exception of a few acres of rough and marshy ground, is fine pasture and meadow land. the soil is fertile, producing abundant crops. The substratum is limestone, which is quarried for agricultural and other purposes. Waterfield, a good old mansion, is the residence of J. Creagh, Esq. The living is a rectory and vicarage, in the diocese of Limerick, and forms part of the corps of the chancellorship in Limerick cathedral: the tithes amount to £138. 9. 2½. There is no glebe-house, and only one acre of glebe. In the R. C. divisions the parish is the head of a union or district, called Coolcappa, comprising the parishes of Clounagh, Dundonnell, Dunmoylan, Kilbroderan, and Kilcoleman; the chapel, a large plain building, is at Coolcappa, in this parish. There is a pay school of about 30 children. Some remains of the old church exist; and not far distant are the beautiful ruins of Lisnacille Castle, built by the Mac Sheehys about 1445.

CLOUNCORAGH.—See COLEMAN'S-WELL.

CLOUNCREW, or CLUINCINNO, a parish, in the barony of UPPER CONNELLO EAST, county of LIMERICK, and province of MUNSTER, 3 miles (N. E.) from Drumcolloher, on the road to Ballyegran; containing 270 inhabitants. It comprises 1663 statute acres, as applotted under the tithe act, part of which is under tillage, producing good crops, and the remainder pasture and meadow. The living is a rectory, in the diocese of Limerick, and is held in commendam by the bishop: the tithes amount to £72. There is neither church, chapel, glebe-house, nor glebe. The Protestant parishioners attend the parish church of Kilmeedy. In the R. C. divisions it is united to Drumcolloher. On the bank of the river are some remains of the old church, which was destroyed in the war of 1641.

CLOUNEY, or CLONEY, a parish, in the barony of CORCOMROE, county of CLARE, and province of MUNSTER, 3 miles (E. by S.) from Ennistymon, on the road to Ennis; containing 3371 inhabitants. This parish comprises 9741 statute acres, which are mostly in tillage; the land is good and the system of agriculture gradually improving; there is a considerable quantity of bog. It is in the diocese of Kilfenora; the rectory is part of the union and corps of the deanery of Kilfenora, and the vicarage forms part of the union of Kiltoraght. The tithes amount to £160, of which two-thirds are payable to the rector and the remainder to the vicar. Divine service is performed in the glebe-house of Kiltoraght. In the R. C. divisions it forms part of the union or district of Ennistymon, and contains a chapel at Tierlahan, near Kilthomas, in which a school is held; and there are also two private schools, in which altogether are about 250 children.

CLOUNSHIRE, or CLONSHERE, a parish, in the barony of LOWER CONNELLO EAST, county of LIMERICK, and province of MUNSTER, on the road from Limerick to Rathkeale, 1½ mile (W.) from Adare; containing 542 inhabitants, and comprising 1124 statute acres, as applotted under the tithe act, about half of which is under cultivation, and the remainder is cold, dry, strong pasture. Limestone abounds. Here are two flour-mills, worked by excellent machinery, the produce of which is chiefly sent to Limerick. Clounshire House, the residence of J. Dickson, Esq., is pleasantly situated amid flourishing plantations. The rectory and vicarage form part of the union of Rathkeale and corps of the chancellorship in the cathedral of Limerick: the tithes amount to £90: there is a glebe of seven acres of good land. In the R. C. divisions the parish forms part of the district of Adare. The parochial schools, in which are 60 boys and 30 girls, were built and are supported by J. Dickson, Esq. The ruins of the ancient castle of Gurran Buidhe form a conspicuous object; and the ruins of Clounshire, or Clonshere, castle are in the valley, near the mill. Some remains of the old church also exist, and in the churchyard are the shafts of two very ancient crosses.

CLOYDAGH, or CLODY, also called CLOGRENNAN, a parish, partly in the barony of SLIEUMARGY, QUEEN'S county, and partly in the barony of CARLOW, but chiefly in that of IDRONE WEST, county of CARLOW, and province of LEINSTER, on the river Barrow, which is navigable to Waterford, 2½ miles (S. W. by S.) from Carlow on the road to Leighlin-Bridge; containing 1422 inhabitants, and comprising 4737 statute acres, of which 290 are woodland, and 324 bog; the remainder is arable and pasture; 3764 acres are applotted under the tithe act, and valued at £3774 per annum. The state of agriculture is very good. Limestone abounds, and is applied both as manure and for building: there are limekilns on a large scale, the produce of which is chiefly conveyed into the counties of Wicklow and Wexford. Coal also abounds, and is worked extensively. Sessions are held quarterly at Milford. Here are extensive corn-mills and malt-kilns, in which about 100 persons are employed. The principal seats are Clogrennan Castle, the residence of Col. Rochfort; Milford, of J. Alexander, Esq.; Font-hill, of W. Fishbourne, Esq.; and Lenham Lodge, of Capt. Butler. Clogrennan was formerly an estate of the Dukes of Ormonde, and gave the title of baron in the Irish peerage to the Earls of Arran. The castle was taken by Sir P. Carew, in 1568, from Sir E. Butler, who was then in rebellion: in 1642 it was besieged by the Irish, but was relieved by Col. Sir P. Wemys; and here the Marquess of Ormonde mustered his forces prior to the battle of Rathmines. The ruins, overgrown with ivy and forming a remarkably picturesque object, yet exist, together with the remains of an old church, near the present house, which is approached through one of its gateways. The grounds, which are very beautiful, are bordered on the west by the mountains of the Queen's county, the sides of which are clothed with wood to a considerable height, and on the east by the course of the Barrow, adorned by several well-wooded islets. On Bawn-Ree, Jas. II. encamped after his defeat at the battle of the Boyne. Some curious relics of antiquity, including brazen swords and arrow-heads, were found in a ford across the Barrow, about 1¼ mile distant, in 1819. The living is a vicarage, in the diocese of Leighlin, and in the patronage of the Bishop; the rectory is impropriate in Col. Bruen and W. Fishbourne, Esq. The tithes amount to £276. 18. 5½., of which £92. 6. 1. is payable to the vicar, and the remainder to the lay impropriators. The glebe-house was built by a gift of £400 and a loan of £360 from the late Board of First Fruits, in 1813; the glebe comprises six acres, subject to a rent of £4. 4. per acre. The church, a plain neat edifice in good repair, was built by aid of a gift of £500 from the same Board in 1803, and to the repairs of it the Ecclesiastical Commissioners have recently made a grant of £167. 5. 11. In the R. C. divisions this parish is in the union or district of Old Leighlin, and has a chapel. Besides the parochial school, there is one in the chapel-yard at Ballinabranna; the number of children in these schools is about 150; and in a hedge school are taught about 90 children. The ruins of the old church are in the demesne of Clogrennan; the cemetery is still used.

CLOYNE, a market and post-town, a parish, and the seat of a diocese, in the barony of IMOKILLY, county of CORK, and province of MUNSTER, 14 miles (E. by S.) from Cork, and 126 (S. W. by S.) from Dublin, on the road from Midleton to the sea; containing 6410 inhabitants, of which number, 2227 are in the town. It originated in the foundation of the see of Cloyne by St. Colman, who died in 604. In 707, an abbey was erected on the west side of the cathedral, which was plundered in 978 by the people of Ossory, and again, in 1089, by Dermot, the son of Fiordhealbhach O'Brien. The town is pleasantly situated in a level or slightly undulating plain, and is well sheltered by rising grounds and plantations, which give great amenity to the climate. It comprises two streets intersecting each other at right angles, and contains 330 houses, most of which are small and irregularly built. The bishop's palace is a large edifice, built by Bishop Crow, in 1718, and enlarged by several of the succeeding prelates. The grounds are well arranged, and near the house is a noble terrace, extending the whole length of the garden. The palace and demesne were leased, in 1836, by the Ecclesiastical Commissioners, to H. Allen, Esq., for 999 years, at a rent of £450 per annum, a fine of £2000, and £1300 for the timber: Mr. Allen intends to take down all the old part of the palace. The only manufacture is that of brogues and hats, which employs about 100 persons. The market is held on Thursday, and is well attended by buyers from Cove and Cork. Fairs are held on Feb. 24th, Easter and Whit-Tuesdays, Aug. 1st, Sept. 12th, and Dec. 5th, for the sale of horses, cattle, sheep, pigs, and implements of husbandry. It is a constabulary police station. The bishop, who is lord of the manor, appoints a seneschal, who holds a court-leet annually, and a manor court once in three weeks. Petty sessions are held every second Wednesday. The parish comprises 10,324 acres, of which 9552 are subject to tithe; the remainder consists of the bishop's lands, or those belonging to an ancient hospital, upon which part of the town is built. The soil is good, particularly in the valley, where it rests on a substratum of limestone. At Carrigacrump is a quarry of fine marble, somewhat similar to the Italian dove-coloured marble; it is the property of Col. Hooden. The parish is intersected by that of Kilmahon, which entirely separates from it the village and ploughland of Ballycotton, forming the extreme western point of the coast in Ballycotton bay. Besides the Episcopal palace, the principal seats are Kilboy House, the residence of F. Rowland, Esq.; Kilcrone, of J. Hanning, Esq.; Barnabrow, of J. R. Wilkinson, Esq; the Residentiary-house, of the Rev. W. Welland; Cloyne House, the seat of H. Allen, Esq.; the residence of the Rev. Dr. Hingston, Vicar-General of the diocese; Jamesbrook Hall, of R. W. G. Adams, Esq.; and Ballybane, of T. Gaggin, Esq. Not far from the town are Rostellan, the seat of the Marquess of Thomond, and Castle-Mary, of the Rev. R. Longfield.

Arms of the Bishoprick.

The DIOCESE of CLOYNE is called, in the ancient Roman Provincial, *Cluain-Vanian*, and by the Irish historians *Cluain-Vama*. Of the successors of St. Colman little is recorded till after the arrival of the English in the reign of Hen. II.; the only names that have been preserved from the foundation of the see till that period are those of O'Malvain, who died in 1094; Nehemiah O'Moriertach, who presided from 1140 till 1149; and of his successors, O'Dubery and

O'Flanagan, of whom the former died in 1159, and the latter in 1167. At the time of the English invasion, Matthew, whose surname is supposed to have been O'Mongagh, presided over the see; he died in 1192, and from that time till 1430 there was, with very little intermission, a regular succession of prelates, though few particulars of their history are recorded. Upon the election of Daniel, a Franciscan friar, in 1249, the dean and chapter refused to present him to the king for his approbation, and proceeded by apostolic mandate to the archbishop of Cashel and the bishops of Killaloe and Lismore, to have him consecrated. The king (Hen. III.) consequently refused to invest him with the temporalities, but ultimately consented upon the condition that the dean and chapter should give security by patent not to make any election for the future, without first obtaining licence, nor to proceed to consecration without previously presenting the person elected to the king for his approbation. During the prelacy of Maurice O'Solehan, who succeeded to the prelacy in 1320, Edw. III. wrote to Pope John XXII., stating that, in consequence of the poverty of the bishopricks of Cork and Cloyne, he designed to unite them into one see, to which the pope readily consented, and issued his apostolic bull, dated Aug. 2nd, in the 11th year of his pontificate, for that purpose, which was to take place on the death or avoidance of the present bishops. Walter Le Reed was translated from the see of Cork to the archbishoprick of Cashel, in 1330, but the bull having been lost in the mean time, the union was not effected. John de Swafham, who succeeded in 1363, was sent by the parliament, in commission with the bishop of Meath and others, in 1373, to represent to Edw. III. the state of the kingdom of Ireland, the result of which was the mission of the Earl of March into Ireland. This prelate was distinguished for his writings against the Wickliffites, for which, in 1376, he was promoted to the see of Bangor by Pope Gregory XI. In 1377, his successor, Bishop Wye, applied to Pope Gregory to remedy the loss of the bull, and an exemplification of it was sent to him from Rome, which had equal validity; but Wye being deprived for misconduct, nothing was done till the accession of Bishop Pay, in 1421, when he referred the matter to the parliament in Dublin, but they refused to interfere, and Milo Fitz-John, then Bishop of Cork, refusing his sanction to the union, the case was referred to the court of Rome. Bishop Pay died in 1430, and the see of Cork being also vacant by the death of Milo Fitz-John, who died in the same year, the two vacant sees were both canonically united and conferred by Pope Martin V. upon Jordan, Chancellor of Limerick, who succeeded in 1431. From this time the sees continued to be united for more than 200 years, till 1638, when George Synge was consecrated Bishop of Cloyne, and William Chappel, Bishop of Cork and Ross, which two sees were united on the separation of that of Cloyne. In 1639, the wardenship of the collegiate church of Youghal was united in perpetuity to this see, and so continues; but the late Bishop Brinkley obtained an act for separating the rectory from the wardenship, and it is now presented to as an ordinary benefice. From the death of Bishop Synge, in 1653, the see remained vacant till the Restoration, when it was united to those of Cork and Ross, and continued so during the prelacies of Michael Boyle and Edward Synge; but on the death of the latter, in 1678, it was again separated, and continued to be a distinct see till September, 1835, when, on the death of the last bishop, Dr. John Brinkley, it was, by the provisions of the Church Temporalities Act of the 3rd of Wm. IV., re-annexed to the see of Cork and Ross.

The diocese is one of the eleven that constitute the province of Cashel; it is wholly within the county of Cork, and comprehends an estimated superficies of 539,700 acres. The lands belonging to the see comprise 12,482 statute acres, much of which is rough unprofitable mountain; and the gross yearly revenue amounted, on an average of three years ending on the 31st of December, 1831, to £3402. The gross revenue, including the union of Ahada, which was formerly annexed to the see, but which has been separated by the provisions of that act, was previously £5008. The chapter consists of a dean, precentor, chancellor, treasurer, archdeacon, and the 14 prebendaries of Donaghmore, Aghultie, Inniscarra, Brigown, Kilmacdonough, Cahirultan, Killenemer, Glenore or Glanworth, Cooliney, Ballyhay, Coole, Kilmaclenan, Subulter, and Lackeen; there are also five vicars choral not members of the chapter. The economy fund, on an average of three years ending with 1831, amounted to £559. 10. 8. per annum, arising from rents of land, tithes and glebes reserved by lease, and one sixth-part of the tithes of the parish of Cloyne; it is appropriated to the payment of officers' salaries, and to the maintenance of the cathedral in repair. The consistorial court, held in the chapter-house, on the north side of the cathedral, every third Tuesday, consists of a vicar-general, a surrogate, two advocates, two registrars, four proctors, and an apparitor. The total number of the parishes in the diocese is 125, of which 22 are unions, the whole comprising 91 benefices, of which 13 are in the patronage of the Crown, 69 in that of the Bishop, 2 in that of the Incumbents, 6 in lay patronage, and one in the alternate patronage of the Bishop and a layman. The number of churches is 64, and there are 21 school and other houses in which divine service is performed till churches can be built; the number of glebe-houses is 29. In the R. C. divisions this diocese is united with that of Ross, forming the bishoprick of Cloyne and Ross, and comprising 42 parochial benefices, or unions, containing 89 chapels, which are served by 90 clergymen, 42 of whom, including the bishop, or parish priests, and 58 coadjutors or curates. The parochial benefice of the bishop is the Great Island, including the parish of Clonmel, and that part of the parish of Temple Robin which is on that island. There is no cathedral belonging to either of the sees; the bishop resides in his parish, near Cove.

The rectory of Cloyne is appropriate to the economy estate and the vicars choral of the cathedral, and two curates are appointed to discharge the duties of the parish: the parochial tithes amount to £1317, of which one-sixth is payable to the economy estate, and five-sixths to the vicars choral. The cathedral, which is dedicated to St. Colman, and is used as the parish church, is a large cruciform edifice, in the later English style of architecture, and is supposed to have been erected so early as the 14th century. The principal entrance is from the west, beneath a lofty pointed arch, and on the north side is a small, low, pointed doorway.

The interior is remarkably neat, and kept in a good state of repair: the choir is tastefully fitted up, and is used as the parish church, but being found too small for that purpose, the organ was removed, in 1780, to the junction of the nave and transepts, by which the choir has been lengthened 21 feet. In 1829, galleries were built to accommodate the increasing congregation, and pews were erected, in 1836, round the communion table. On the north side of the choir is the entrance to the chapter-house, which is evidently much more modern than the cathedral. In the north transept is a handsome monument erected to the memory of Dr. Woodward, and in the south transept, one for Dr. Warburton, both formerly bishops of this see. The transepts also contain some elegant monuments of the Longfields, Lumleys, and other families of note. At the village of Ballycotton, four miles from Cloyne, a new district church was built in 1835, by subscription, at an expense of £330: the curate is paid by the dean and chapter and vicars choral of Cloyne, as appropriators of this parish, and by the precentor, as rector of Churchtown, the district church being for the accommodation of both these parishes. This parish is the head of a R. C. union or district, comprising the parishes of Cloyne, Churchtown, Kilmahon, and part of Kilteskin; the chapel at Cloyne is a large, plain, old edifice.

The diocesan school is united to that of Cork. The Cloyne free school and charity were founded by Bishop Crow, by will dated Oct. 4th, 1726, in which he bequeathed the farm of Bohermore, and the small burgage of Cloyne, for the maintenance of poor Protestant boys, after paying £8 per ann. to the widows and orphans of clergymen of the diocese. The present income exceeds £200 per annum, and ten boys are maintained, clothed, and educated for three years, at the expiration of which they are apprenticed, with a premium of £4 each. Six chorister boys are also educated, supported, and clothed by the dean and chapter, and 14 free boys of the town are educated at this establishment. The school-house was erected in 1814, out of the accumulated funds of the charity, on land given by Bishop Bennett. There are also two national schools, in which are 550 boys and 366 girls. A fund for lending sums not exceeding £2 has long existed in the town, to which Bishop Brinkley contributed £70, and which circulates about £600 annually. A benevolent society for the relief of sick and indigent room-keepers is supported partly by voluntary contributions, and partly by the profits and tolls of the fairs and market, which were transferred to this charity, in 1833, by the late Bishop Brinkley, and are continued by the present Bishop of Cork and Cloyne. A fund for relieving the widows of the clergy of the diocese was established in 1828, which, in June 1835, had accumulated to £953. Here is also a parochial Protestant almshouse for poor persons, who receive a weekly allowance from the Sunday collections in the cathedral; also a fever hospital and dispensary.

Opposite the western entrance to the cathedral is one of the ancient round towers, which, in 1835, was surrounded with an iron railing, at the expense of the dean and chapter, by whom it is kept in repair. This ancient structure is perfect, except the top: the original building is 92 feet high, and a modern castellated addition has made the entire height 102 feet; it is quite cylindrical from top to bottom, its uniform diameter being 9 feet, and the walls being 33 inches thick. The tower is divided into five floors or stages, which are nearly perfect; the upper story contains a bell, which was presented to the cathedral by Dean Davies in 1683, and hung here, the cathedral having no bell tower. At that time the top of the tower was open, and the bell attracted the lightning, by which it was cracked; the castellated part was therefore added for its protection. Of the ancient abbey founded in 707, or the hospital founded in 1326, there are no vestiges except the lands of the latter, which are still called the Spital fields. A small castle was erected here in the 14th century, by Bishop John de Cumba, but was destroyed by the Fitz-Edmunds after the Reformation. At Ballymaloe is a curious old house, built by the Fitzgeralds, who forfeited it in the war of 1641, and now the property of Mr. Forster; in the hall are two very large pair of elks' horns. In the neighbourhood are several very extensive natural caves in the limestone district, in some of which are very pure and beautiful stalactites.

CLUIN.—See CLONEAMERY.

COACHFORD.—See MAGOURNEY.

COAGH, a village, in that part of the parish of Tamlaght which is in the barony of Dungannon, county of Tyrone, and province of Ulster, 3 miles (S. by E.) from Moneymore; containing 393 inhabitants. This place formed part of the estate granted to the Hon. Andrew Stewart by Jas. I., in 1612, and confirmed by Chas. I. in 1630. A battle took place here at the ford of the river, in 1641, when the chapel of Tamlaght was destroyed by the parliamentarians; and, in 1688, Jas. II. crossed the river at this place, on his march to the siege of Derry. The village, which in 1831 consisted of 76 well-built houses, is pleasantly situated on the road from Magherafelt to Stewartstown, in a fertile vale, about two miles from Lough Neagh, and on the river Coagh or Ballinderry, over which is an ancient narrow bridge of stone of six arches. It is the property of William Lenox Conyngham, Esq., in whose family the estate has remained since the year 1663; and was erected about the year 1728, by George Conyngham, Esq., who obtained for it a charter for a market and four fairs, which have been changed to a market held on the first Friday in every month, for the sale of linens and provisions, and to 12 fairs held on the second Friday in every month, for horses, cattle, and agricultural produce. The market-house, a spacious and commodious building, was erected in 1828, by the present proprietor, who also built a good school-house and supports a school for male and female children. The linen market is very considerable; and the fairs, which are toll-free, are numerously attended. It is a constabulary police station, and has a penny post to Moneymore. There is a place of worship for Presbyterians in connection with the Synod of Ulster.—See Tamlaght.

COAL ISLAND, a post-town, partly in the parishes of Donoghenry and Clonoe, but chiefly in that of Tullyniskan, barony of Dungannon, county of Tyrone, and province of Ulster, 3 miles (N. E.) from Dungannon: the population is returned with the respective parishes. This flourishing trading village is situated in the centre of the Tyrone coal field, on the roads from Dungannon to Ballinderry, and from Lurgan to Stewartstown: it comprises 184 houses, which are generally well built with stone and covered with slate, and has a sub-post-office to Dungannon. The coal district extends from Mullaghmoyle, on the north, to Dungannon on the south, a distance of six miles, with an average breadth of two. Great difficulty is found in working it, owing to the softness of the bed on which it rests, and the dangerous state of the roof, unless expensively propped. At present the mining operations are confined to Drumglass, in the neighbourhood of Dungannon, and the vicinity of Coal Island: the collieries at the latter place are on a small scale, and principally worked by manual labour, but are moderately profitable. Coal Island originated in the formation of the Tyrone canal, which was begun by Government in 1744, and was intended to intersect the entire coal field of Tyrone, but was not carried beyond this place. The canal is not more than three miles in length from the river Blackwater, which it joins near Lough Neagh, to Coal Island, but it has been commenced and partially completed in several places westward; bridges have been erected over the line; an aqueduct of three large arches was to have conveyed it over the Terren; and a rail-road was to have connected it with some of the minor collieries, for which purpose a viaduct, here called "the Dry Hurry," was thrown over the Cookstown road, two miles from Dungannon. All these edifices are of hewn freestone, handsomely finished and in good preservation; but in many places the canal is filled up and cultivated, so that in a few years the line will not be traceable. This is now a place of considerable trade, and has 35 large lighters, or barges, which frequently make coasting voyages to Dublin, and sometimes across the channel to Scotland. Extensive ironworks, forges, and plating-mills were erected here in 1831, and there are others at Oghran and New Mills for the manufacture of spades, edge-tools, &c. Here is also an extensive establishment for the manufacture of fire-bricks and crucibles, commenced in 1834 by two gentlemen from Stourbridge, in Worcestershire. Most of the manufactured articles are sent to London or Liverpool. Near this is a pottery, and there is also a flour-mill, where 2000 tons of wheat are annually ground for the Belfast market. Bleach-greens have been established at Derryvale, Terren Hill, and New Mills, where 20,000 pieces of linen are annually finished for the English market. Several warehouses, granaries, yards, and other conveniences for carrying on an extensive trade are placed round a small but convenient basin, and in the village and its vicinity are the residences of several wealthy merchants. The exports are coal, spades, shovels, fire-bricks, fire-clay, crucibles, earthenware, linen cloth, wheat, oats, flour, &c.: the imports are timber, deals, iron, salt, slates, glass, &c. The village being in three parishes, has three churches within two miles of it, and a district church is about to be erected for its use. The R. C. chapel for the parish of Donoghenry is not far distant.

COGLANSTOWN.—See TULLY.

COLE-HILL, a post-town, in the parish of Teighshinod, barony of Moydow, county of Longford, and province of Leinster, 12½ miles (W. by N.) from Mullingar, and 51 miles (W. by N.) from Dublin: the population is returned with the parish. It is situated on the road from Dublin to Ballymahon, and has a sub-post-office to the latter town and to Ballinacargy.

COLEMAN, or COCKMAN, a parish, in the barony of Middlethird, county of Tipperary, and province of Munster, 2 miles (S. W.) from Fethard; containing 561 inhabitants. It is situated on the road from Fethard to Clonmel, and contains 2663 statute acres, as applotted under the tithe act. It is a rectory and vicarage, in the diocese of Cashel, forming part of the union of St. John, and of the corps of the deanery of Cashel: the tithes amount to £140. In the R. C. divisions it forms part of the district of Clerihan.

COLEMAN'S WELL, or CLOUNCORAGH, a parish, in the barony of Upper Connello East, county of Limerick, and province of Munster, 2 miles (N. N. W.) from Charleville, on the road to Ballingarry; containing 821 inhabitants. This parish comprises 4506 statute acres, as applotted under the tithe act. It is watered by the river Maigue, which here forms a boundary between the counties of Cork and Limerick. The land in every part is moderately good, and in the neighbourhood of Foxall and Drewscourt, where it is well farmed and planted, it is very fertile; the meadow land is considered equal to any in the county. The living is a rectory, in the diocese of Limerick, and held in commendam by the Bishop, or, according to some writers, forms part of the mensal of the see: the tithes amount to £110. 0. 10. The church has long since fallen into decay, and the Protestant parishioners attend divine service in the parish church of Bruree. In the R. C. divisions the parish forms part of the union or district of Bruree, which is also called Rockhill, and contains a chapel. The water of St. Colman's well is reputed to possess great efficacy, and is held in high veneration by the peasantry of the surrounding country who assemble here in great numbers on the anniversary of the saint, and at other times.

Seal.

COLERAINE, a sea-port, borough, market and post-town, and a parish, in the barony or district called the town and liberties of Coleraine, county of Londonderry, and province of Ulster, 24½ miles (E. N. E.) from Londonderry, and 118¼ (N.) from Dublin; containing 7646 inhabitants, of which number, 1978 are in the parish of Killowen, and 5668 in the town. This place derives its present name from *Cuil-Rathuin*, descriptive of the numerous forts in the vicinity, and is by some writers identified with the *Rath-mor-Muighe-line*, the royal seat of the kings of Dalnaruidhe. The original town, now called Killowen, on the western bank of the river Bann, and which subsequently became the chief or shire town of the county of Coleraine, is of very remote antiquity; and in 540 had a priory of Canons Regular, of which St. Carbreus, a disciple of St. Finian, and first bishop of Coleraine, was abbot. This establishment continued to flourish till the year 930, when Ardmedius, or Armedacius, was put to death by the Danes; it was, together with several other churches, plundered in 1171 by Manus Mac Dunleve, since which period no notice of it occurs till the year 1213, when, with the exception of the church, it was destroyed to furnish materials for a castle which was erected here by Thomas Mac Uchtry and the Gaels of Ulster. The county of Coleraine is described as having extended from the river Bann, on the east, to Lough Foyle on the west, and as having formed part of the possessions of O'Cahan, from whose participation in the rebellion of the Earl of Tyrone, in the reign of Elizabeth, it became, with the whole province of Ulster, forfeited to the crown. Jas. I., in 1613, granted this district to a number of London merchants, who were in that year incorporated by charter, under the designation of the "Governor and Assistants of the New Plantation in Ulster," and from that period the name of the county was changed into Londonderry. The Governor and Assistants, generally called the Irish Society, were by their charter bound to build the town of Coleraine, to people it, to enclose it with a wall, and to establish a market, within seven years from the date of their charter, by which were granted to them the entire abbey of St. Mary, its site, and the lands belonging to it, together with the old town, now Killowen, and all its appurtenances. But this condition appears to have been very much neglected, for Pynnar, in his first survey, in 1619, says, "that part of the town which is unbuilt is so dirty that no man is able to go into it, especially what is called, and should be, the market-place." The same writer, in his second survey, dated 1625, says,—"The town of Coleraine is in the same state as at the last survey; only three houses are added, which are built by private individuals, the society allowing them £20 a piece. The walls and ramparts are built of sods; they do begin to decay, on account of their narrowness; the bulwarks are exceedingly little, and the town is so poorly inhabited that there are not men enough to man the sixth part of the wall." So unpromising was the condition of this settlement that, in addition to the sum of £20, large portions of land were allotted for each tenement, and long leases at nominal rents were offered to all who would undertake to build houses.

A conspiracy of the natives having been formed to seize the place, in 1615, military stores were sent hither from London; and by a vote of the common council, a citadel was built for its defence in the following year; it was a strong fortress, commanding the ferry, and was kept in repair and well garrisoned by the Irish Society, till the erection of the bridge in 1716. The bridge, which was wholly of wood, was so much injured by floods that it fell in 1739; and in 1743 a new bridge was built, with pillars and buttresses of stone, towards the erection of which the Irish Society gave the timber and £2050 in money; in 1806 it was widened, at the expense of the county, by transverse beams supporting a foot-path of four feet on each side. The growth of the place was exceedingly slow, and so little had its trade advanced that, in 1633, the customs of the port, for the half year ending on Lady-day in that year, amounted only to £18. 9. 8½. On the breaking out of the war in 1641, the town was attacked by a body of 1000 insurgents, but was vigorously defended by the garrison and inhabitants, amounting to 200, who defeated the assailants. It was taken by Gen. Monk for the parliament, in 1648, but was afterwards given up to Sir C. Coote. On the advance of the forces of Jas. II. into the north, in order to repress the Protestant party, Mount-Alexander, Rawdon, and other leaders, stationed themselves with a force of about 4000 men at Coleraine, which they fortified and kept possession of with a view to prevent the Irish from passing the Bann. They were here joined by Lord Blaney with his party from Armagh; and though for a time they repulsed the enemy, yet the Irish, after a successful skirmish, passed the river in boats, and the party stationed here finding the place no longer tenable, fled by various routes to Derry, in order to take possession of it, before the Irish should cut them off from their last place of refuge. The subsequent history of the town consists of little more than a succession of disputes in the corporation, and between that body and the Irish Society, relative to their respective rights, privileges, and possessions: the Society enclosed the quay and made the port duty free, in 1741.

The town, which is the second in the county in importance, and is rapidly increasing, is situated on the east bank of the river Bann, about three miles from its influx into the sea, and is connected by a handsome bridge with the village of Killowen, or Waterside, a considerable suburb on the opposite bank of the river. It is large and handsomely built, consisting of five principal streets, a spacious square called the Diamond, and several smaller streets; the houses in the Diamond, New-row, Church-street, and Bridge-street, are large and well-built, especially those of later erection; in the Diamond and in Church-street are some ancient houses of timber cage-work, said to have been framed in London and sent over by the Irish Society to be erected here. A Board of Commissioners has been appointed under the act of the 9th of Geo. IV., for lighting and cleansing the town, which is paved at the expense of the county; and the inhabitants are supplied with excellent water from numerous springs at the outlets of the town and from pumps. It is a very great thoroughfare, and is the principal passage over the river Bann, connecting the counties of Antrim and Derry, and opening a communication with all the ports on the north and north-western coasts. The neighbourhood is remarkable for the pleasing diversity of its scenery, enlivened by the fine stream of the Bann, and embellished with the grounds of some handsome seats. On the west side of the river, immediately below Killowen, is Jackson Hall, the residence of Mrs. Maxwell, an elegant mansion situated in extensive grounds tastefully laid out; and there are various others, among which are Down Hill, built by the Earl of Bristol, when Bishop of Derry, and now the property and residence of Sir James R. Bruce, Bart.; Somerset, the residence of the Rev. Thomas Richardson; Knockintern, of Hugh Lyle, Esq.; Ballysally, of W. Galt, Esq.; Castleroe, of Lieut.-Col. Cairnes; Millburn House, of Stewart C. Bruce, Esq.; Cromore, of J. M. Cromore, Esq.; and Ballyness, of Capt. Hannay. The air is extremely salubrious, and during the prevalence of typhus fever in 1817, and of the cholera in 1832, the number of deaths in proportion to the population was very small. The town is abundantly supplied with all the necessaries and luxuries of life at a moderate charge, which renders it desirable as a place of residence for persons of limited income. There is a public library, supported by annual subscriptions of a guinea; also a subscription news-room, and an amateur concert, which is held weekly

This place has long been celebrated for its trade in

the finer linens, known as "Coleraines," but at what time it was first established here is not precisely known. The first bleach-green ever known in this part of the country was established at Ballybrittan, by Mr. John Orr, in 1734, for the bleaching of fine 7-8th and 4-4th linens. That gentleman having succeeded in establishing a very lucrative trade, other bleach-greens were soon afterwards formed at Gortin, Ballydivitt, Macosquin, Drumcroom, Mullamore, Keeley, Aghadowey, Rusbrook, Collans, Mullycarrie, Island Effrick, Castle Roe, Greenfield, and other places. The quantity now bleached annually exceeds 200,000 pieces; they are of the finest quality, and four-fifths of them are sent to the English markets. These linens are woven at the farm-houses throughout the country; the webs, when finished, are brought to market in the brown state, and sold to the bleachers, who assemble on their stands every Saturday from 10 till 11 o'clock, during which hour more than 1000 webs are generally purchased. This is one of the very few towns of which the market has not been materially injured by the recent changes that have taken place in the linen trade. The bleachers of the neighbourhood also attend the markets of Ballymoney, Dungannon, Fintona, Stewartstown, Armagh, Newtownstewart, Strabane, and Derry, for the purchase of brown webs; but the best markets in Ireland for these goods are Coleraine and Ballymoney. At Mullamore is a large establishment for the preparation of warps and yarn for linen webs, commenced in 1832, by Alexander Barklie, Esq.; there are at present more than 800 looms in constant operation; the weaving is not done on the premises, but is given out as task work to men who weave it at their own houses. The only manufactures carried on are those of linen, cotton, hard and soft soap, bleaching salts, leather, and paper. A brewery and malt-house was originally established by Messrs I. and C. Galt, in 1770, and after passing through various hands was purchased by Messrs. O'Kane and Mitchell, the present proprietors, who annually consume 200 tons of malt in the production of 2000 barrels of strong and common ale.

The town, from its situation on the river Bann, only four miles from the Atlantic, enjoys important advantages for commerce, but at present its trade is limited. Its chief imports are timber, iron, barilla, ashes, coal, and salt; and its exports are linen cloth, pork, butter, salmon, wheat, barley, oats, potatoes, and whiskey, and since the construction of the harbour of Portrush, there has been a considerable trade in live stock, poultry, eggs, and fruit. The number of vessels trading annually to the port, including the outer harbour of Portrush, is about 160, having an aggregate burden of about 13,000 tons. From the 1st of September, 1831, to the 31st of August, 1832, 36,888 sacks (or 5533 tons 4 cwt.), of grain and 3491 pigs were shipped from this place. During the following year, the quantity of grain decreased to 27,132 sacks, the cause of which may be attributed to the establishment of markets at Garvagh, Bushmills, and Ballymoney; the number of pigs shipped during the latter period increased to 6340, notwithstanding the establishment of those markets. The quantity of butter exported varies considerably; since the passing of the recent act it has decreased from 11,000 to 9000 firkins, from the same cause. The port immediately adjoins the town; the entrance to the river is obstructed by a bar of shifting sand, over which vessels drawing more than five feet of water at neap tides, or nine feet at spring tides, cannot pass; the current of the tide runs past the mouth of the river, and the rise in Lough Foyle is nearly twice as great as in the Bann. During winter the navigation of the river is in a manner stopped, the spring tides occurring too early and too late, before and after daylight,and a heavy swell of the sea generally setting in from October till April. To remedy this inconvenience, a new harbour was constructed at Portrush, about 4½ miles distant from the town, at an expense of £16,225. 17. 11., raised under an act of parliament in shares of £100 each: the entrance is 27 feet deep at low water of spring tides, and vessels drawing 17 feet can enter and ride in perfect safety. A steam-boat, built for this station, commenced plying between Portrush and Liverpool in August 1835; and another has since been established from the port to Glasgow, each of which makes a passage every week. There is a custom-house with the usual officers; and there are bonding stores and a timber-yard. An extensive and lucrative salmon fishery is carried on at Crannagh, on the Bann, under lease from the Irish Society; there is but one season during the year, beginning in May and ending on the 12th of August. The quantity taken is generally about 190 tons the whole of which is packed in ice and conveyed by smacks and steam-boats to Liverpool and other distant markets, where they are in high estimation for their size and flavour. There is also another salmon fishery on the Bann, at a part called the Cutts, where the river makes a rapid fall of 12 feet over a ledge of rocks which the fish cannot ascend, except when there is a strong fresh in the river, and where a weir has been placed to intercept them; about 80 tons are annually taken here; both stations belong to the same Company. There is also an eel fishery, which commences in September, when the fish are returning from Lough Neagh and the rivers, to the sea; they are taken by means of pales and wattling, constructed so as to converge in the direction of the current, and having a net attached; this fishery is worth £800 per annum. Great quantities of eels are taken and sold fresh in the neighbouring markets, or salted for winter use.

The market is on Saturday, and is well supplied with provisions of all kinds. The grain market was first established in 1819, since which time it has rapidly increased: it is held on Monday, Wednesday, and Friday, and on an average 3000 tons of grain, principally oats, are annually sold, of which the greater part is sent to Liverpool, and some to London, Bristol, and Glasgow. An additional market for pork and butter is held on Wednesday. The market-place is situated on the eastern side of the town, on ground belonging to the corporation, by whom it was built at an expense of £2744, and to whom belong the tolls, customs, pickage, and stallage, amounting to about £300 per annum: it is commodiously fitted up, with separate apartments for the sale of butter, pork, and meal, sheds for tallow, hides, and flax, stores and offices for provision merchants, keepers' houses and every accommodation; and was opened on the 25th of March, 1830. There are fairs on the 12th of May, 5th of July, and 1st of November; the principal is on the 12th of May, for black cattle, horses, and sheep. A branch of the Northern Banking Company, one of the Belfast Banking Company, and one of the

Provincial Bank of Ireland have been established here.

The inhabitants received a charter of incorporation from Jas. I., in 1613, by which the government was vested in a portreeve, free burgesses, and commonalty, and by another charter granted in the same year, which latter is the governing charter, in a mayor, recorder, chamberlain, coroner, twelve aldermen (including the mayor), and 24 principal burgesses, assisted by a town-clerk, prothonotary, serjeants-at-mace, and other officers. The mayor is elected by the common council from the body of aldermen, on the 1st of October, and is sworn into office on the 25th of March following. The aldermen are elected from the burgesses, and the burgesses from the freemen, though in general the burgess is made a freeman to qualify him for election: the freedom is obtained only by gift of the corporation. The mayor, recorder, and four of the senior aldermen are justices of the peace within the borough and liberties; and the county magistrates, of whom, by virtue of his office, the mayor is always senior and sits on the right hand of the judge at the assizes, have concurrent jurisdiction. The corporation hold courts of record for the recovery of debts and the determination of pleas to any amount within the town and liberties, of which, according to their charter, the jurisdiction extends to the distance of three miles in every direction from the centre of the town; they are also empowered to hold courts of session for the borough, but do not exercise that privilege. Previously to the Union, the borough returned two members to the Irish parliament; the right of election was vested in the mayor, aldermen, and burgesses alone, but by the decision of a parliamentary committee it was declared to be vested also in the freemen. Since the Union it has returned one member to the Imperial parliament; and since the passing of the act of the 2nd of William IV., cap. 88, the right of election is in the corporation, freemen, and £10 householders. A new boundary has been drawn round the borough, the details of which are minutely described in the Appendix. The number of electors is 214, of whom 26 are burgesses and freemen, whose rights are reserved for life, 184 £10 householders, and 4 occupiers of houses and lands of the yearly value of £10; of these, 185 polled at the late election for the borough, in 1835: the mayor is the returning officer. The quarter sessions for the county are held here in April and October; the assistant barrister presides with the magistrates, for the trial of offences against persons and property, and alone in civil actions not exceeding £20. By the original grant each of the twelve proprietors of the county was empowered to hold a manorial court, but the business of these courts is generally transferred to the quarter sessions. Petty sessions are held on alternate Thursdays. The town-hall is situated in the centre of the square called the Diamond; it was originally erected in 1743, and has been more than once enlarged, and is now undergoing a thorough repair at the expense of the corporation: it is a lofty square building surmounted by a cupola, in which a clock was placed in 1830, at the expense of the Marquess of Waterford: the hall contains courts for the quarter sessions, apartments for transacting the corporation business and the election of members, a newsroom, library, ballast-office, and a savings' bank.

The borough comprises, independently of several others within its liberties, the parishes of Coleraine and Killowen (described under its own head), the former comprising the town on the eastern side, and the latter the suburb of that name on the western side, of the Bann. The parish contains, according to the Ordnance survey, 4846¼ statute acres. The living is a rectory, in the diocese of Connor, and in the patronage of the Irish Society: the tithes amount to £450: the glebe-house was built by aid of a loan of £692 and a gift of £92, in 1828, from the late Board of First Fruits: the glebe comprises 45 acres. The church, a large plain edifice, was erected in the year 1614, by the Irish Society, and in 1684 a south aisle was added to it, at the expense of the corporation; a very handsome spire was built at the expense of the Society in 1719, but it stood for a short time only. The church contains many ancient and some very elegant monuments, and the Ecclesiastical Commissioners have recently granted £282. 19. 6. towards its repair. In the R. C. divisions this place is partly in the diocese of Connor, and partly in that of Derry, and forms part of the union or district of Killowen or Coleraine; the chapel is a spacious and handsome edifice, situated at Killowen. There are two places of worship for Presbyterians in connection with the Synod of Ulster, one of the first class, and one of the second class; one for Seceders, of the first class, and one each for Independents and Methodists. A school for the gratuitous instruction of 130 boys and 130 girls was founded and endowed, in 1705, by the Irish Society, but from mismanagement it fell into disuse about the year 1739, and was altogether discontinued till 1820, when a new school, with houses for the master and mistress, was built by the Society, who, in 1828, transferred their interest in it to trustees chosen from the most respectable inhabitants of the town, since which time it has been productive of the greatest benefit; the salaries of the master and mistress are paid by the Society. There is a very excellent female work school, where the children are taught sewing and other domestic accomplishments, which is supported by Miss Rippingham, by whom it was established many years since; there are also, at Killowen, a school which was founded and endowed by the late Mr. Kyle, and a parochial school held in the old church and supported by the Clothworkers' Company. There are also four other schools, two of which, situated respectively at Gateside and Ballyclaber, are under the National Board; and seven pay and four Sunday schools. A dispensary is supported in the usual way. A loan fund was established in 1764, for lending two guineas each to industrious workmen, to be repaid by monthly instalments of 3*s.* 6*d.*; out of this establishment arose a poor-house fund, which was laid out in fitting up a house for the reception of old and decayed inhabitants: it was supported by subscription and the earnings of the inmates, who were employed in the spinning of cotton. This establishment was discontinued in the year 1790, and the house was given to a few poor aged persons, who occupied it rent-free till 1803, when a portion of it was fitted up as a private dwelling, and the rent paid to the actuary of the loan fund. It was subsequently rebuilt, at an expense of £800, by the Marquess of Waterford, who presented it to the town, and in 1830 it was opened for the reception of the poor, who are maintained and clothed by subscription and annual donations from the Marquess of

Waterford and the Irish Society, and a bequest of £20 per annum by the late Griffin Curtis, Esq. The house will accommodate 40 persons. A mendicity society was also formed here in 1825; the committee, who are subscribers of £1. 1. per annum, meet every Tuesday, when claims for relief are examined, and two members appointed to administer relief to the poor at their own dwellings. The priory of St. John, or *Kil-Eoin*, from which the suburb on the western side of the Bann, now Killowen, took its name, has altogether disappeared; a part of that establishment formed the old parish church, on the site of which another was subsequently erected, the remains of which have been converted into a school-room. Not far distant was the monastery for Canons Regular, founded by Carbreus in 540, and the site of the castle which was built on the ruins is now occupied by Jackson Hall. In sinking for foundations in the part of the town of Coleraine which occupies the site of the ancient abbey of St. Mary, stone coffins, human bones, and other relics of antiquity, together with foundations of some of the conventual buildings, are frequently discovered. One mile south of the town is Mount Sandel, one of the largest and most perfect raths in the kingdom; it is 200 feet high, surrounded by a deep dry fosse, and encircled near its summit by a magnificent terrace; in the centre is a deep oblong cavity, called the Giant's Grave, formed apparently for the purpose of concealment. There is also a very high and perfect rath a little west of the Cranagh; another close to the church of Killowen; and a very curious fort near Ballysally. This place has been celebrated from the earliest annals of Irish history, and has produced many eminent lawyers, senators, and divines: among the latter was Dr. John Vesey, born here in March, 1632, and successively Archdeacon of Armagh, Dean of Cork, Bishop of Limerick. and Archbishop of Tuam. From this last dignity he was driven by the harsh conduct of Lord Tyrconnell, and remained in London in great poverty till he was restored to his see, on the accession of William III.; he was three times after his restoration made Lord-Justice of Ireland, and died in 1716, aged 84. John Abernethy, an eminent Presbyterian divine, was born here in 1680. Coleraine has given title to many noblemen; the last was that of baron to the family of Hanger.

COLLIGAN, a parish, in the barony of DECIES-without-DRUM, county of WATERFORD, and province of MUNSTER, 3½ miles (N. N. W.) from Dungarvan; containing 1009 inhabitants. It is situated on the road from Dungarvan to Clonmel, and contains 3679 statute acres, as applotted under the tithe act. The high grounds are well planted, and here is a neat house and grounds, which is the occasional residence of Walter McGwire, Esq. The living is a vicarage, in the diocese of Lismore, and in the patronage of the Duke of Devonshire, in whom the rectory is impropriate: the tithes amount to £135, of which £90 is paid to the impropriator, and the remainder to the vicar. In the R. C. divisions the parish forms part of the union or district of Kilgobinet, and contains a chapel. Here is a cavern of considerable extent in the limestone rock.

COLLINSTOWN, a market-town, in the parish of ST. FEIGHAN of FORE, barony of DEMIFORE, county of WESTMEATH, and province of LEINSTER, 3 miles (S. E.) from Castle-Pollard; containing 145 inhabitants. It is situated on the road from Dublin to Granard, and on the southern bank of Lough Lane, and contains 25 houses, of which nine are slated. The market is held on Saturday, in a market-house in the centre of the town; and fairs are held on May 8th and Oct. 30th. It is a constabulary police station, and petty sessions are held every Saturday. Near the market-house is a R. C. chapel. The vicinity is diversified with hills and woodlands, and embellished with the scenery of the lake and the seats and demesnes of Barbavilla, Drumcree, and Ralphsdale.—See FEIGHAN of FORE (ST.).

COLLON, a post-town and parish, partly in the barony of LOWER SLANE, county of MEATH, but chiefly in that of FERRARD, county of LOUTH, and province of LEINSTER, 6 miles (W. N. W.) from Drogheda, on the road to Ardee, and 28 (N. by W.) from Dublin; containing 3217 inhabitants, of which number, 1153 are in the town. This place formerly belonged to the celebrated abbey of Mellifont, and was confirmed to the abbot by Hen. II., at the close of the 12th century. The town has a remarkably neat appearance, and consists of two streets intersecting near the church, and contains 215 houses, of which the greater number are slated. It owes its present prosperity to its proprietors, the Fosters, who established a cotton-manufactory here, which for some time employed more than 600 looms. Linen was previously made here, and its manufacture has been resumed, but the cotton manufacture has entirely ceased. There is a bleach-green, employing more than 50 persons, with a steam-engine of 10-horse power; also a flax-mill, and in the town and its vicinity are three corn-mills, worked by steam and water power. It is a chief constabulary police station. On the 20th of Sept., 1229, Hen. II. granted to the abbot and convent of Mellifont a market on Tuesday in their town of Collon: there is a market-house and an open area at the north end of the town for holding a market, but, except for butchers' meat, none has been held lately. Fairs are held on May 10th, June 29th, Oct. 20th, and Nov. 24th. Petty sessions are held every alternate Thursday.

The parish contains about 8600 statute acres, which are mostly under tillage; there is no waste or bog, but 513 acres of woodland. Here is Oriel Temple, the seat of Viscount Ferrard, whose predecessor was the Rt. Hon. John Foster, the last speaker of the Irish House of Commons, who, in 1821, was created Lord Oriel: it is distinguished by the beauty of its surrounding grounds, and the richness of its extensive plantations. The demesne contains about 1000 acres: in it is a grotto, of which the interior is lined with shells, stained glass, coloured stones, &c., said to be the work of Lady Ferrard; there is also a beautiful rustic cottage. The house contains some good pictures, among which is a full-length portrait of the first Lord Oriel, by Sir Thos. Lawrence. In the vicinity of the town is a nursery of forest trees, consisting of seven acres, which is the property of Lord Ferrard. About a mile from it is Mount Oriel, from which there is an extensive and magnificent view, including the Bay of Carlingford and the grand chain of the Mourne mountains. Belpatrick mountain, which, according to the Ordnance survey, rises 789 feet above the level of the sea, is also within the parish.

The living is a vicarage, in the diocese of Armagh, united by act of council, in 1769, to the rectory and vicarage of Mosstown, and in 1782 the rectory of Dromin was added to the union, which is in the patronage of the Lord-Primate and Viscount Ferrard, in the latter of whom the rectory is impropriate, and by whom the land is let tithe-free. About 1769, the late Chief Baron Foster gave a glebe of ten acres, and built the glebe-house, on condition that an augmentation of £50 should be granted from Primate Boulter's fund, and that he should have the patronage of the endowed vicarage two turns out of three. The living was subsequently augmented by the impropriate tithes of Mosstown, which were purchased for the purpose by the Trustees of Primate Boulter's fund, and now produce £248. 14. 11. Besides the glebe at Collon, there is one of three acres at Mosstown, and another at Dromin of nearly 10 acres; and the gross tithes of the benefice amount to £453. 4. 6. The church, an elegant structure of hewn limestone, in the ancient style of English architecture, was built in 1813, during the incumbency of Dr. Beaufort, author of the "Ecclesiastical Map and Memoir of Ireland:" the cost was about £8000, of which £3800 was a gift and £700 a loan from the late Board of First Fruits; the members of the Foster family contributed bountifully towards its erection; the Ecclesiastical Commissioners have lately granted £368. 6. 9. for its repair. The interior is 90 feet by 40, the ceiling beautifully groined, and it has five windows on the south side, besides a large east window over the altar. All the side windows are of stained glass, the gift of the present Baron Foster; the east window is in course of preparation, being the gift of the impropriator. Under the church is the burial-place of that family, and in it is a marble monument to the memory of Catherine Letitia Foster, widow of William, Lord Bishop of Clogher, which was erected by her daughter, the Countess de Salis. The ecclesiastical duties of Collon were formerly performed by a monk from Mellifont abbey. The R. C. parish is co-extensive with that of the Established Church; the chapel is a neat structure. There is also a place of worship for Wesleyan Methodists. A male and female school, under the trustees of Erasmus Smith's charity, is aided by a donation from Lord Ferrard; and there are two others aided by the vicar. Besides these, there are an infants' school, supported by Mrs. Green, and two private schools. At Belpatrick is a school principally supported by Edward and James Singleton, Esqrs. There is also a dispensary in the town.

COLLOONEY, a post-town, in that part of the parish of Ballysadere which is in the barony of Tiraghrill, county of Sligo, and province of Connaught, 5¼ miles (S.) from Sligo, on the road to Dublin, and 98¾ (N. W.) from Dublin; containing 553 inhabitants. It consists of one long street, containing 90 houses, of which 13 are slated, and the remainder thatched. At Carricknagatt the French, after quitting Castlebar, were attacked on the 5th of Sept., 1798, by Col. Vereker, with a detachment of the city of Limerick militia, some yeomanry, and the 24th light dragoons; but after a smart action of about an hour and a half, the Colonel was nearly surrounded, and obliged to retreat, with the loss of his artillery, to Sligo, whence he withdrew to Ballyshannon. The assault was sufficient, as it is supposed, to deter the French from attacking Sligo, and they marched to Dromahaire. The market is on Thursday; and fairs were formerly held on May 3rd, June 1st, Aug. 9th, Sept. 5th, Nov. 21st, and Dec. 16th, but that of Nov. 21st is the only one now held. Here are a large bleaching establishment and an oatmeal-mill. Near the town are Onnachmore, the residence of C. R. O'Hara, Esq.; and Camp Hill, of A. Kelly, Esq. In the town are the parish church and a R. C. chapel, a linen-hall, a dispensary, and two schools. It is a station of the constabulary police.—See Ballysadere.

COLLUMBKILL, a parish, in the barony of Gowran, county of Kilkenny, and province of Leinster, 1½ mile (N. E.) from Thomastown; containing 779 inhabitants. This parish is situated on the road from Thomastown to Greig, and contains 7113 statute acres. Kilmurry is the seat of Lord Chief Justice Bushe. It is a rectory and vicarage, in the diocese of Ossory, and is part of the union of Thomastown: the tithes amount to £278. In the R. C. divisions also it forms part of the union or district of Thomastown; the chapel is at Murg. There are two private schools in which are about 60 boys and 50 girls.

COLMOLYN, or CULMULLEN, a parish, in the barony of Upper Deece, county of Meath, and province of Leinster, 3¼ miles (W. by S.) from Dunshaughlin; containing 934 inhabitants, of which number, 51 are in the hamlet. This parish is situated on the cross road from Kilcock to Warrenstown, and contains 2091 statute acres, as applotted under the tithe act. Colmolyn House is the elegant residence of A. J. Dopping, Esq. It is a vicarage, in the diocese of Meath, and is part of the union of Knockmark; the rectory is impropriate in the Provost and Fellows of Trinity College, Dublin The tithes amount to £280, one-half of which is payable to the Provost and Fellows, the other to the vicar. In the R. C. divisions it forms part of the union or district of Dunshaughlin, and has a large and handsome chapel. There is a school of 18 boys and 5 girls, for which Mr. Dopping allows a house and garden rent-free. Near Colmolyn House are the remains of an ancient church, and on the eastern side of the parish is an extensive rath.

COLPE, or COLPE-cum-MORNINGTON, a parish, in the barony of Duleek, county of Meath, and province of Leinster, 2¼ miles (E. by S.) from Drogheda; containing 1970 inhabitants, of which number, 71 are in the hamlet. This parish is situated on the eastern coast, at the mouth of the river Boyne. It is said to have derived its name from Colpa, one of the sons of Milesius, who is stated to have been drowned at the mouth of the Boyne, while attempting to land for the invasion of the country. Here St. Patrick landed when on his way to Taragh, then the seat of the kings of Ireland. In 1182, Hugh de Lacy founded an abbey for Augustinian canons, and made it dependent on the abbey of Lanthony, in Monmouthshire, afterwards translated to the vicinity of Gloucester. In 1300, Roger, the prior, was attached and fined 20*s.* for stopping some Dominican friars in Drogheda, and robbing them of the body of Roger Wetherell, and a bier and pall. At the suppression, this abbey, besides other possessions, had the tithes of Weisle's Farm, in Mornington, which place was the original seat of the family of Wellesley, the head of which has successively been created Earl of Mornington and Marquess Wellesley, and which includes among its members, at present, the Marquess Wellesley, the Duke of Wellington, and Lords Cowley and Maryborough. No part of the abbey now exists, but a chapel to the south of its site is the burial-place of the Bellew family. The parish contains 4793 statute acres, principally under tillage, and of moderately good quality; there is no bog or waste land. At Pilltown are some quarries containing indications of copper, and in which some fossils have been found. The branch of the great northern road through Balbriggan runs through the parish, which will also be intersected by the Dublin and Drogheda Grand Northern Trunk railway. The principal seats are, Bettystown, the residence of R. Shepheard, Esq.; Eastham, of F. Anderson, Esq., Pilltown, of T. Brodigan, Esq.; Mornington House, of G. F. Blackburne, Esq.; Beabeg, of H. Smith, Esq.; Mornington, of Burton Tandy, Esq.; Beamore, of J. Cooper, Esq.; Farm Hill, of W. Walsh, Esq.; Triton Lodge, of C. Segrave, Esq.; and Cowslip Lodge, the property of G. H. Pentland, Esq.

The living is a vicarage, in the diocese of Meath, united by episcopal authority, in 1826, to the vicarage of Kilsharvan, and in the patronage of the Marquess of Drogheda; the rectory is partly impropriate in W. Dutton Pollard, Esq., of Castle-Pollard, and partly appropriate to the vicarage of St. Peter's, Drogheda, as part of the tithes were purchased by the late Board of First Fruits as an endowment for that vicarage. The tithes amount to £165, the whole of which is payable to the impropriators: the union is also called Mariners' town, and the gross value of the benefice, including tithes and glebe, is £81. 4. 6. The glebe-house was erected about twenty years since by J. Brabazon, Esq., who presented it to the parish, with £1000 to pay the rent to the heirs after his decease. He also granted a glebe, comprising 10 acres of profitable land, which, with the glebe-house, is valued at £35 per annum; and there is a glebe of $3\frac{1}{2}$ acres at Kilsharvan, valued at £12 per annum. The church is a neat structure in good repair, built in 1809, by aid of a gift of £600 from the late Board of First Fruits. In the R. C. divisions the parish forms part of the union or district of St. Mary, Drogheda; and there is a small chapel at Mornington, in which is a school of about 20 children. There is also a pay school at Beamore, of about 30 children. On the beach at the mouth of the Boyne, which is a level strand, is an ancient building, called the "Maiden Tower," with a small obelisk near it, called the "Lady's finger;" it serves as a landmark for vessels bound to Drogheda. From the records of the corporation of Dublin, it appears to have been erected in the reign of Elizabeth, and was probably so called in compliment to Her Majesty. At the Maiden Tower is a pool called the Long Reach, which extends a quarter of a mile inland, where vessels may lie at low water. A little north of the church is an ancient rath, where Colpa is said to have been interred; and the church of Rath-Colpa is alluded to in the ancient Irish records. The mouth of the Boyne, anciently called "Inver-Colpa," was frequented by foreign merchants at a remote period; and some are of opinion that St. Patrick, on escaping from his captivity, here found a vessel to convey him to the continent.

COLRY.—See CALRY.

COLUMBKILL.—See CULLUMKILL.

COMBER, or CUMBER, a post-town and parish, partly in the barony of UPPER, but chiefly in that of LOWER CASTLEREAGH, county of DOWN, and province of ULSTER, 14 miles (N. by W.) from Downpatrick, and 91 (N. by E.) from Dublin; containing 8276 inhabitants, of which number, 1377 are in the town. St. Patrick founded an abbey here, of which nothing is now known. Brien Catha Dun, from whom the O'Nials of Clandeboy descended, and who fell by the sword of Sir John de Courcey, about 1201, also founded an abbey to the honour of the Blessed Virgin, and supplied it with monks of the Cistertian order from the abbey of Albalanda, in Carmarthenshire. John O'Mullegan was the last abbot, and voluntarily resigned the abbacy in 1543. The site and lands were granted, in the 3rd of Jas. I., to Sir James Hamilton, afterwards Lord Clandeboy, whose successors used the greater part of the materials in erecting a mansion near the town, called Mount Alexander, which is now a heap of ruins, and the parish church occupies the site of the abbey. This place derives its name from the river on which it is situated, and which flows into Strangford Lough, on the east side of the parish. The town, which is tolerably well built, forms three streets and a large square, on the road from Belfast to Downpatrick. Messrs. Andrews and Sons have an extensive bleach-green here, where 20,000 pieces of linen are finished annually, principally for the London market; they have also large flour-mills and corn stores. There are two distilleries; one of them, which is the property of Messrs Millar & Co., is among the oldest in the North of Ireland, having been erected in 1765. The tide from Strangford Lough flows to within half a mile of the town, and at a trifling expense might be made very beneficial to it. Great advantages would also result from the erection of a pier near Comber water foot; vessels of 200 tons might then come in with every tide. Coal is at present brought up in small lighters, but the principal fuel is peat; there is a very extensive bog, called Moneyreagh, or the Royal Bog, from which great quantities are sent to Belfast and other places. Fairs are held on Jan. 5th, the second Monday in April, June 19th, and Oct. 28th, principally for farming horses and cattle. Here is a constabulary police station. A manorial court is held here every third Thursday, for the manor of Comber, or Mount Alexander, which has jurisdiction in debts not exceeding £2 over 30 townlands in the parish of Comber, Barnemagarry, in the parish of Kilmud, and Ballycloghan, in that of Saintfield. There is also a court for the recovery of debts not exceeding £20 late currency.

The parish, which includes the ancient parish of Ballyricard, comprises, according to the Ordnance survey, 17,420 statute acres, of which 16,134 are in Lower Castlereagh; about 20 are common, 117 water, and 150 or 200 bog; the remainder is arable and pasture land, of which three-fourths are under tillage. Agriculture is in a very improved state, and the soil is very productive. There are some good quarries of freestone, equal in fineness and durability to the Portland stone; and coal has been found in three places, but no mines have been opened. There are several gentlemen's seats, the principal of which are Ballybeen, the residence of J. Birch, Esq.; Ballyalloly, at present unoccupied; Killynether House, the residence of T. McLeroth, Esq.; and Maxwell Court, of J. Cairns, Esq. The living is an impropriate curacy, in the diocese of Down, and in the patronage of the Marquess of Londonderry, in whom the rectory is impropriate. The parish is tithe-free, with the exception of the townlands of Ballyanwood, Ballycreely, and Ballyhenry, the tithes of which are paid to the Marquess of Londonderry, who pays the curate's stipend. A glebe-house was built in 1738, towards the erection of which the late Board of First Fruits gave £100: the glebe consists of eleven acres. The church is a small ancient building, in the later style of English architecture, and contains some neat marble monuments, particularly those to the memory of the Rev. Robert Mortimer, Capt. Chetwynd, Lieut. Unet, and Ensign Sparks, of the York fencible infantry, who fell in the battle of Saintfield, during the disturbances of 1798,—and of the Rev. Messrs. Birch, father and son, the former of whom died in 1827, the latter in 1830, whose monument was erected by the subscriptions of 520 of their parishioners. Some fragments of the abbey are incorporated in its walls. There are a meeting-house at Comber for Presbyterians in connection with the Synod of Ulster, of the first class; another at Moneyreagh, connected with the Remonstrant Synod, of the same class; and a third at Gransha, connected with the Seceding Synod, of the second class: there is also a place of worship for Wesleyan Methodists. The parochial school, in which about 100 boys and 70 girls are taught, was built in 1813, at the joint expense of the Marchioness of Londonderry and the trustees of Erasmus Smith's charity; the building is kept in repair by the Marchioness, who, in 1832, erected a house for the master. There are also national schools at Ballymaglaff, Tullygiven, and Ballystockart More than 300 children are educated in these schools, besides which, 740 are taught in 12 private schools. A house of industry was founded in 1824, by the Marquess of Londonderry, who subscribes £25 annually towards its support: it affords an asylum for 12 of the aged poor, and also distributes meal, potatoes, &c., to 60 families at their own dwellings. There is a large druidical altar in Ballygraphan, the table stone of which, now lying on the ground, measures 19 feet by 6 and is 4 feet thick: the five upright stones are in an adjoining hedge-row. Numerous forts and raths are scattered over the parish.

COMER.—See CASTLECOMER.

COMMER.—See KILMACREAN.

CONABURY, a village, in the parish of CASTROPETRE, barony of COOLESTOWN, KING's county, and province of LEINSTER, adjoining the town of Edenderry, and containing 24 houses and 143 inhabitants. This village is situated on the road from Dublin to Tullamore, and is divided into Upper and Lower Conabury.

CONEY ISLAND, county of Clare.—See INNISDADROM.

CONEY ISLAND, an island, in the parish of KILLASPICBROWN, barony of CARBERY, county of SLIGO, and province of CONNAUGHT: the population is returned with the parish. This island, which is situated in the bay of Sligo, was anciently called *Inishmulclogby*, and is enumerated among the territories settled on the Earl of Strafford and Sir Thomas Radcliffe, in 1663. It is at present the property of J. Meredith, Esq., and near it is a small island called Church island, on which are the ruins of the ancient parish church of Killaspicbrown, nearly covered with sand.

CONFOY, a parish, in the barony of NORTH SALT, county of KILDARE, and province of LEINSTER, 1½ mile (N. W.) from Leixlip; on the road from Dublin to Maynooth; containing 165 inhabitants. It is intersected by the Royal Canal, and had formerly a town and a castle of some importance, which are noticed by Camden. Of the latter there are some considerable remains, consisting of a massive square tower of five stages, with turrets at the north and west angles; that at the north angle contains a winding staircase opening through pointed arches into each story; both are lighted by loopholes; the principal entrance was under a semicircular archway. In the war of 1688 the castle is said to have been strongly garrisoned, and to have sustained an attack. It is a rectory and vicarage, in the diocese of Dublin, forming part of the union of Leixlip, with which the amount of its tithes is returned. In the R. C. divisions also it is part of the union or district of Leixlip.

CONG, a post-town and parish, partly in the barony of Ross, county of GALWAY, but chiefly in that of KILMAINE, county of MAYO, and province of CONNAUGHT, 19 miles (S.) from Castlebar, and 121 (W.) from Dublin; containing 8378 inhabitants. This place, though now only an inconsiderable village, was formerly a town of some importance, and the ancient residence of the kings of Connaught. A monastery, dedicated to the Blessed Virgin, was founded here by St. Fechan, who died in 664; though by some writers its foundation is ascribed to Donald, son of Æd, nephew of Amirach, King of Ireland, who is said to have made St. Fechan its first abbot. Little further is recorded of its history till 1134, when a great part of the town was burnt and the abbey plundered by the people of Munster. Roderic O'Connor, the last native king of all Ireland, spent the last 15 years of his life in seclusion within this monastery, where he died on the 29th of November, 1198, in the 82nd year of his age; he was interred at Clonmacnois. In 1201 the town and monastery were plundered by William de Burgo, who repeated his ravages in 1204; and in 1310, the town was plundered by Hugh Breifneach. The family of De Burgo afterwards became munificent benefactors to the abbey, to which they gave ample endowments in land, and it continued to flourish till the dissolution. Queen Elizabeth granted part of its possessions to the Provost and Fellows of Trinity College, Dublin; and Jas. I. granted a lease of the abbey to Sir John King, Knt., ancestor of the present Earl of Kingston.

The town is situated on an island formed by the several openings of a subterraneous river that flows from Lough Mask into Lough Corrib; the principal of these openings rises in a great body from a depth of 73 feet, forming a powerful eddy which turns two large mills, and the approaches are over three bridges. It consists of two streets of small houses, of which the greater number are thatched, and has a sub-post-office to Ballinrobe. There are two large mills, the property Mr. John Thompson, erected about 40 years since, and each grinding on an average 300 tons of wheat annually. Fairs are held at Funshinough in May and September; and petty sessions are held every Saturday alternately for Mayo and Galway.

The parish comprises 17,622 acres, as applotted under the tithe act, of which about 240 are woodland, 480 mountain and bog, and, with the exception of about one-fifth, which is waste, the remainder is good arable and pasture land, chiefly under tillage, and producing excellent crops; that which is in pasture, lying upon a substratum of limestone, feeds a large number of sheep and goats. Limestone is everywhere found, rising in many places above the surface; and there are quarries of the finest description of building stone, which is sent to most parts of the adjacent counties, for which Lough Corrib, navigable for 20 miles to Galway for boats of 10 tons' burden, affords a facility of conveyance. The gentlemen's seats are Strand Hill, the residence of T. Elwood, Esq.; Garracloone, of R. Blake, Esq.; Ballymagibbon, of J. Fynn, Esq.; Blake Hill, of Mrs. Blake; Ashford, of Lord Oranmore; Royal Rock, of the Rev. M. Waldron; Houndswood, of Martin D'Arcy, Esq.; and the glebe-house, of the Rev. E. L. Moore. The living is a rectory and vicarage, in the diocese of Tuam, and in the patronage of the Archbishop: the rectory is partly impropriate in Sir R. A. O'Donel, Bart., as representative of the abbot of Cong, and partly appropriate to the prebend of Killabegs in the cathedral of Tuam. The tithes amount to £489. 4. 7½., of which £18. 9. 2¾. is payable to the prebendary, and the remainder to the incumbent: the impropriate tithes are not under composition. The glebe-house was built by aid of a gift of £400 and a loan of £380 from the same Board, in 1817: the glebe comprises 25½ acres. The church, a neat edifice with a small square tower, and in good repair, was erected by aid of a loan of £640 from the late Board of First Fruits, in 1811. The R. C. parish is co-extensive with that of the Established Church; the chapel is a handsome edifice, in the later English style, with a square tower surmounted with a cross. The parochial school is under the Tuam Diocesan Society, aided by an annual donation from the incumbent; a school at Ballymagibbon is supported by John Fynn, Esq.; one at Funshinough is aided by Martin D'Arcy, Esq.; and there is a national school at Carrokeel. About 430 children are instructed in these schools; and there are also four pay schools, in which are about 150 children; and a dispensary. There is an ancient cross in the centre of the town, and the ruins of several churches are still to be seen here. Spars of various colours are found, and the neighbourhood abounds with natural curiosities. Lough Mask, which is on much higher ground than Lough Corrib, discharges its superfluous waters into the latter by subterraneous channels, which, from the openings in the limestone, may in several places be seen flowing at a great depth below the surface. The most remarkable of these openings is the Pigeon Hole, which is of great depth; a descent to it is formed by 68 steps, and at the bottom the water rushes with great violence and noise till it is again lost in the dark recesses of the cavern, which extends to a considerable distance; in the middle of the stream is a small eel weir. There are several other caverns in the limestone range, of which Kelly's Cave and the Lady's Buttery have their roofs fantastically encrusted. In Lough Corrib is the island of Innisduras, containing 29 acres and about 20 inhabitants. Near the glebe-house are the ruins of four druidical circles.

CONNA, or CONNOUGH, a village, in the parish of KNOCKMOURNE, barony of KINNATALOON, county of CORK, and province of MUNSTER, 4¾ miles (N. W.) from Tallow: the population is returned with the parish. This place, which is situated on the river Bride, is a constabulary police station, and has fairs on May 12th, June 20th, October 3rd, and Nov. 21st. The R. C. chapel is situated here. Conna castle is said to have been built by one of the Earls of Desmond, and was taken by storm, in 1645, by the Earl of Castlehaven. In 1653 it was burnt, and Avis, Joanna, and Jane German, daughters of Edward German, perished in the flames, as appears by a monument with an inscription recording this calamity in Knockmourne church. The castle, of which only a high square tower remains, stood on an isolated limestone rock on the south side of the river Bride. Excellent salmon and trout are caught in this river.

CONNAUGHT (OLD), a parish, in the half-barony of RATHDOWN, county of DUBLIN, and province of LEINSTER; containing, with part of the town of Bray, 1947 inhabitants. This parish, which is commonly called Old Conna or Connagh, is situated on the mail coach road from Dublin to Bray and Newtown-Mount-Kennedy. Besides the village of Old Connaught, it contains Little Bray, which forms the northern portion of the town of Bray, within the manor of which this parish is included. It is bounded on the east by the sea, and on the south by the Dargle river, over which there is a bridge that connects the counties of Wicklow and Dublin, and near which is a common of about 14 acres, that is used as a race-course. The parish, most of which belongs to Miss Roberts, contains 4050 statute acres, and is remarkable for salubrity of climate, beauty of sea and mountain prospect, and convenience of sea-bathing. The land is chiefly laid out in villas and ornamental plantations, and the part that is under tillage is occupied by substantial farmers. From its proximity to the sea, the Wicklow mountains, and the metropolis, with other natural advantages, this is a favourite place of residence. The principal seats are Old Connaught, the residence of the Rt. Hon. Lord Plunket; Palermo, of the Rev. Sir S. S. Hutchinson, Bart.; Cork Abbey, of the Hon. Col. Wingfield; Woodbrook, of Sir J. Ribton, Bart.; Old Connagh Hill, of Miss Roberts; Thornhill, of F. Leigh, Esq.; Jubilee, of Miss Ryan; Oaklawn, of W. Garde, Esq.; Ravenswell, of I. Weld, Esq.; Beauchamp, of Capt. Lovelace Stamer; Woodlawn, of W. Magan, Esq.; Moatfield Cottage, of Capt. C. Johnstone; Bray Lodge, of W. C. W. Newberry, Esq.; Crinlin Lodge, of J. Cahill, Esq.; and Wilfort, of Messrs. Toole. At the entrance to Little Bray, through which the coaches from Dublin to Wexford pass, are three handsome houses, occupied by the physician to the dispensary, the Rev. W. Purcell, and Mrs Galway. The village of Old Connaught is small and pleasant, having a flourishing plantation of horse chestnut trees in its centre: it contains several neat cottages, and the handsome residence of R. Morrison, Esq. the architect.

It is a rectory and vicarage, in the diocese of Dublin, and forms part of the union of Bray: the tithes amount to £240. Prior to 1728, the rectorial tithes formed part of the Archbishop of Dublin's mensal, but in that year, the tithes of this parish and of several others were annexed to their respective incumbencies having cure of souls. In the R. C. divisions this parish forms part of the union or district of Kingstown, and has a chapel at Crinkin. There are two schools, one for boys, aided by a collection at the church, and the other for girls, supported by voluntary subscriptions, in which are educated 100 girls and 87 boys. The poor enjoy a share of the rents of an estate in the county of Longford, bequeathed by F. Adair, Esq., to the unions of Delgany and Bray, and the parish of Powerscourt. In the grounds of Moatfield, or Wilfort, is an old rath; and in those of Ballyman are the ruins of a church, in a curiously detached churchyard. The ruins of the parish church also form a picturesque object.

CONNELL (GREAT), a parish, in the barony of Connell, county of Kildare, and province of Leinster, containing, with the post-town of Newbridge, 1911 inhabitants. In 1202, a priory was founded here, under the invocation of the Blessed Virgin and St. David, by Meyler Fitz Henry, who placed in it Regular Canons from the monastery of Lanthony, in Monmouthshire. It subsisted till the Reformation, when it was granted to Edward Randolfe, with reversion to Sir Edw. Butler; it was re-granted in the 3rd of Elizabeth to Sir Nicholas White, and is now the property of Thos. Eyre Powell, Esq. The parish is situated on the mail coach road from Dublin to Limerick, and comprises 4738 statute acres, as applotted under the tithe act, and valued at £2337 per annum. The land is chiefly under tillage, and the improved system of agriculture is making gradual progress. At Athgarvan ford, on the Liffey, are the extensive boulting-mills of Messrs. Tuthill and Reeves, in which 15,000 bags of flour are made annually. The principal seats are, Great Connell Lodge, the property of T. E. Powell, Esq., but occupied by E. Butler, Esq.; Rosetown, the seat of E. Bateman, Esq.; and Hillsborough, of G. Higgins, Esq. The living is a perpetual curacy, in the diocese of Kildare, to which that of Ladytown is annexed, and in the patronage of the Bishop; the rectory is impropriate in T. E. Powell, Esq. The tithes amount to £171. 5. 2. The church is a small plain edifice, erected about 50 years since; and the Ecclesiastical Commissioners have recently made a grant of £187 towards its repair. In the R. C. divisions this parish is the head of a union or district, comprising Great and Old Connell, Killishy, and Morristown-Biller, with parts of Carnalloway and Kill: the chapel is near Newbridge, *which see.* There are three private and two pay schools, in which about 60 boys and 60 girls are educated; and a national school is about to be erected. The remains of the priory consist chiefly of the east gable of the church, with a great extent of ruinous walls, and many fragments of masonry, among which is the mutilated tomb of Prior Wellesley, Bishop of Kildare. Over the gateway, on one side, is a small sculpture of the Crucifixion, and on the other, Our Saviour crowned with thorns, and a mitred ecclesiastic; and on another fragment is the figure of St. Peter, bearing the keys. It is said that, within the memory of persons still living, a round tower, 75 feet high, was destroyed during the minority of the present proprietor's father.

CONNELL (OLD), a parish, in the barony of Connell, county of Kildare, and province of Leinster, 4½ miles (S. W.) from Naas; containing 958 inhabitants. This parish, which is situated on the mail coach road from Dublin to Limerick, comprises 2900 acres, as applotted under the tithe act, which are chiefly under tillage. The improved system of agriculture has been introduced, and the practice of drilling generally adopted; fuel is plentifully supplied from an extensive bog in the immediate neighbourhood. Morristown-Lattin, the ancient family seat of Patrick Lattin, Esq., the translator of Voltaire's Henriade into English verse, whose family has been settled here since the reign of John, is situated in a very retired demesne, ornamented with a profusion of stately timber, chiefly fine oak, ash, elm, and beech of uncommon size. Old Connell House is the seat of E. J. Odlum, Esq.; within the demesne is a fine Danish rath. It is a rectory, in the diocese of Kildare, forming part of the union of Morristown-Biller; the tithes amount to £140. The church was built by a gift of £900 and a loan of £300 from the late Board of First Fruits, in 1828. In the R. C. divisions it is part of the union or district of Newbridge: the chapel is at Two-mile-house. There is also a small neat chapel, with a spire, belonging to a Dominican friary on the bank of the Liffey, in which only three brethren reside. There are two hedge schools, in which are about 60 boys and 30 girls. In the gardens of Old Connell House are some ruins of the ancient church.

CONNELLS, a village, in the parish of Kilmacduagh, barony of Kiltartan, county of Galway, and province of Connaught, 3 miles (W.) from Gort, on the road to Ennis; containing 12 houses and 87 inhabitants.

CONNOR, a parish, and the head of a diocese, in the barony of Lower Antrim, county of Antrim, and province of Ulster, 4 miles (S. S. E.) from Ballymena; containing 8682 inhabitants, of which number, 289 are in the village. A religious establishment was founded here at an early period, of which little beyond the names of some of its abbots is now known. It was made the head of the diocese of Connor, and the first bishop was Ængus Macnisius, commonly called St. Macnise, who died soon after the commencement of the sixth century: he is said to have been a disciple of St. Olcan, who was one of St. Patrick's pupils. Connor appears anciently to have been called *Dailnaraigh,* from its cathedral being in the territory of Dalaradia. In 1124, Malachy O'Morgair was consecrated bishop. At this time, according to St. Bernard, the inhabitants of the diocese were very uncivilised; but by a few years' residence among them, St. Malachy wrought as great a change in their morals as was effected by St. Patrick in the fifth century. By the solicitations of John, Bishop of Connor, Pope Eugene IV. was prevailed upon, in 1442, to unite the bishopricks of Down and Connor, the former being then vacant by the deprivation of John Cely. This union had been approved by letters patent of Hen. IV., in 1438, when the bishops of the two sees were desirous that the survivor should have both; but when it was effected the union was strongly opposed by John Prene, Archbishop of Armagh, who wished the pope to appoint William Bassett, a Benedictine monk, to the bishoprick of Down. The union has, however, continued without interruption since that period, and the subsequent history of the diocese of Connor is included in that of Down and Connor. By the Church Temporalities Act (3rd of Wm. IV.) the see of Dromore is to be united with Down and Connor, on the death or translation of either of the bishops; and the title of the united sees is to be the Bishoprick of Down, Connor, and Dromore.

The diocese is one of the ten which constitute the

ecclesiastical province of Armagh: it comprehends parts of the counties of Down and Londonderry, and the greater part of that of Antrim, containing an estimated superficies of 395,500 acres of which 3700 are in Down, 9400 in Londonderry, and 382,400 in Antrim. The cathedral establishment appears to have been refounded by patents of the 7th of Jas. I. (1610), which ordained that the church should be called the church of St. Saviour, Connor, and that the chapter should consist of a dean, archdeacon, chancellor, precentor, and treasurer, and the four prebendaries of Connor, Cairn-Castle, Rasharkin, and Kilroot. There are no canons or vicars choral, and neither the dignitaries nor prebendaries have any ecclesiastical duties to perform in respect of their offices. Chas. II., by letters patent in 1663, constituted the church of Lisburn the cathedral for the united dioceses, both the old cathedrals being then in ruins; but, in 1790, an act was passed for the restoration of Down cathedral at Downpatrick. Lisburn church, however, is still used as the cathedral for the bishoprick of Connor: there is no economy fund connected with it, but the building is in a good and sound state, and has hitherto been kept in repair by the parishioners. The extent of see lands is 6411 profitable acres, and the gross yearly income of the bishoprick, on an average of three years ending Dec. 31st, 1831, amounted to £3065. 3. 4¾. The consistorial court is the same as for that of Down, and is held at Lisburn, where the records of the united dioceses are preserved. The diocesan school, which was originally established at Carrickfergus, was removed to Ballymena in 1829, when a consolidation was made of part of the diocese of Armagh and the whole of that of Connor, under the act of the 3rd of Geo. IV.; and an acre of land was given by William Adair, Esq., on which the school-house was erected, in 1830, at an expense of £900. The master, who is allowed to receive boarders, is nominated alternately by the Archbishop of Armagh and the Bishop of Down and Connor: the emoluments, which are small, are contributed by the bishops and beneficed clergy of both dioceses. The number of parishes in the diocese is 72, exclusively of 6 without cure of souls; they are included in 47 benefices, of which, 2 are in the patronage of the Crown, 1 in that of the Lord-Primate, 21 in that of the Bishop, and 15 in lay patronage; the remainder are perpetual or district curacies, in the gift of the respective incumbents of benefices out of which they were formed. The number of churches is 57, besides eight other places of worship, and of glebe-houses, 30.

In the R. C. divisions this diocese is united as in the Established Church, forming the bishoprick of Down and Connor, in which are 21 parochial unions or districts, containing 45 chapels served by 31 clergymen, 21 of whom are parish priests, and 10 coadjutors or curates. The cathedral is an elegant edifice in the town of Belfast, and is used as one of the parochial chapels. Belfast is also the residence of the R. C. Bishop.

The village consists of about 50 houses, and contains a dispensary. Fairs are held on Feb. 1st, May 2nd, Aug. 2nd, and Oct. 28th. The parish, which is situated on the river Glenwherry, comprises, with Kells, according to the Ordnance Survey, 17,135¾ statute acres, about one third of which is arable, one-half pasture, and one-sixth bog. The living is a vicarage, in the diocese of Connor, united, with part of the rectory, by charter of the 7th of Jas. I., to the rectories of Killagan and Killyglen, and the vicarage of Solar, which constitute the union and corps of the prebend of Connor in the cathedral of St. Saviour, at Lisburn, in the patronage of the Bishop; the remainder of the rectory is impropriate in Viscount Ferrard. The tithes of the parish amount to £151, of which £86 is payable to the impropriator, and £65 to the vicar; and the gross tithes of the benefice amount to £279. 12. The glebe-house was built by a gift of £400 and a loan of £400, in 1820, from the late Board of First Fruits; the glebe comprises 40 acres, valued at £40 per annum. The church was erected by aid of a gift, in 1815, from the same Board. In the R. C. divisions this parish is united with those of Drummaul and Antrim, forming the union or district of Drummaul; there is a chapel in each. There are two places of worship for Presbyterians, the largest of which is in connection with the Synod of Ulster, and of the first class. There are national schools at Tannybrack, in which are 47 boys and 14 girls, and at Tamnaghmore, of 80 boys and 54 girls; two schools, in which are about 200 children, are partly maintained by Lord Ferrard, who subscribes £15. 15. annually; and there are several private pay schools, and some Sunday schools. In the vicinity is an artificial mount with outworks.

CONRAGH, or CONRY, a parish, in the barony of Rathconrath, county of Westmeath, and province of Leinster, 4 miles (E.) from Ballymore, on the road from Mullingar to Athlone, containing 930 inhabitants. The land is principally under tillage, and there is much bog and limestone. Here are Charleville, the seat of C. Kelly, Esq., and Tozerstown, of W. T. Dillon, Esq. At Loughnavally is a police station, and a patron or fair is held there on the 15th of August. This is a chapelry, in the diocese of Meath, and is part of the union of Churchtown; the rectory is impropriate in the Marquess of Downshire. The tithes amount to £65, of which £40 is paid to the impropriator, and the remainder to the incumbent. In the R. C. divisions also the parish forms part of the union or district of Churchtown, and has a chapel at Loughnavally. There is a pay school at Carna, in which are about 25 children. There are the remains of an old church at Conragh, and of old castles at Tozerstown and Cronghill. On the celebrated hill of Knockusneach are two large rocks, said to have been St. Patrick's bed; and some of the Irish kings resided in the neighbourhood.

CONVOY, a parish and village, in the barony of Raphoe, county of Donegal, and province of Ulster, 3 miles (W. S. W.) from Raphoe; containing 5380 inhabitants, of which number, 356 are in the village. It is situated on the river Dale, and on the road from Stranorlar to Raphoe, from which latter parish it was separated in 1825, and formed into a distinct parish, comprising, according to the Ordnance survey, 20,082 statute acres. At its north-western extremity is the mountain of Cark, 1198 feet above the level of the sea. The village consists of one long street, comprising 73 houses; and has fairs on May 17th, Oct. 26th, and Nov. 3rd. The village of Cornagillagh is also in this parish. Convoy House is the residence of R. Montgomery, Esq. The living is a perpetual curacy, in the diocese of Raphoe, and in the gift of the Dean of

Raphoe: the curate's income consists of £75 paid by the dean, and £25 from Primate Boulter's augmentation fund. The church is a handsome structure, in the ancient English style of architecture, and was erected by aid of a gift of £420, and a loan of £300, from the late Board of First Fruits, in 1822. In the R. C. divisions the parish forms part of the union or district of Raphoe, and has a large plain chapel near the village. There is a meeting-house for Presbyterians, in connection with the Synod of Ulster, of the second class; also one for Covenanters. The parochial school is aided by a grant from Col. Robertson's fund; and there are seven other public schools in the parish, in all of which more than 500 children are taught; also four Sunday schools.

CONWALL, a parish, partly in the barony of RAPHOE, but chiefly in that of KILMACRENAN, county of DONEGAL, and province of ULSTER; containing, with the post-town of Letterkenny, 12,978 inhabitants. This parish is situated on the road from Lifford to Dunfanaghy, and contains, according to the Ordnance survey, 45,270 statute acres, of which 32,715 are in the barony of Kilmacrenan; there is much waste land and bog. Among the seats are Ballymacool, the residence of J. Boyd, Esq.; and Gortlee, of J. Cochran, Esq. The living is a rectory and vicarage, in the diocese of Raphoe, and in the patronage of the Provost and Fellows of Trinity College, Dublin. The tithes amount to £800. The glebe-house was built in 1816, by aid of a gift of £100 and a loan of £1500 from the late Board of First Fruits: the glebe comprises 868 acres, of which 328 are arable. The church, to the repairs of which the Ecclesiastical Commissioners have recently granted £273. 11. 7., is a small plain structure with a spire, in the town of Letterkenny. In the R. C. divisions this parish forms part of the district of Aughnish, and has chapels at Letterkenny and Glen-Swilly. There are two Presbyterian meeting-houses in Letterkenny, one in connection with the Synod of Ulster, of the first class, the other is connected with the Seceding Synod, and is of the second class. There are also places of worship for Covenanters and Methodists. The parish school is aided by £12 per annum from the late Col. Robertson's school fund, and an annual donation from the rector; and there are a Presbyterian free school and eight other public schools in the parish, in all of which about 850 children are taught; also eight Sunday schools. An abbey existed here so early as the 6th century, and continued at least till the 13th. There are still some ruins of the old parish church.—See LETTERKENNY.

COOKSTOWN, a parish, in the barony of RATOATH, county of MEATH, and province of LEINSTER, 12 miles (N. N. W.) from Dublin; containing 98 inhabitants. This parish is situated on the confines of the county of Dublin, and on the road from Ratoath, and contains 1947 statute acres. It is in the diocese of Meath, and is held as a chapelry with the union of Ratoath: the rectory is impropriate in Mr. James Kennedy and Mr. Abraham Sandys. The tithes amount to £68. 1. 3., of which £47. 15. is payable to the impropriators, and £20. 6. 3. to the incumbent. In the R. C. divisions also it forms part of the district of Ratoath.

COOKSTOWN, a market and post-town, in that part of the parish of DERRYLORAN which is in the barony of DUNGANNON, county of TYRONE, and province of ULSTER, 20 miles (E. N. E.) from Omagh, and 86½ (N. N. W.) from Dublin, by the mail road, but only 79 by the direct road; containing 2883 inhabitants. This place derives its name from its founder, Allan Cook, who had a lease for years renewable under the see of Armagh, upon whose land the old town was built, about the year 1609. It is situated on the mail coach road from Dungannon to Coleraine, and consists of one wide street more than a mile and a quarter long, with another street intersecting it at right angles, containing 570 houses, many of which are large, well built with stone, and slated. The present town was built about the year 1750, by Mr. Stewart, its then proprietor, and is advantageously situated in a fine and fertile district, which is well wooded and watered, and abundantly supplied with limestone. A patent for a market and fairs was granted to Allan Cook, Aug. 3rd, 1628. The market is on Tuesday for grain, and on Saturday for linen cloth, flax, yarn, cattle, pigs, and provisions. Fairs are held on the first Saturday in every month, for general farming stock. The market-place consists chiefly of merchants' stores and shops. At Greenvale is a large establishment for bleaching, dyeing, and finishing linens for the English markets; there are others at Wellbrook and at Ardtrea, besides two large ones at Tullylaggan. A constabulary police force has been stationed in the town. A manorial court for the primate's manor of Ardtrea is held here once a month, for the recovery of debts under £5: its jurisdiction extends into the parishes of Lissan, Derryloran, Kildress, Desertcreight, Arboe, Ardtrea, Clonoe, Ballyclog, Tamlaght, Ballinderry, and Donoghenry. Petty sessions are held on alternate Fridays. Close adjoining the town is Killymoon, the residence of W. Stewart, Esq., proprietor of the town and of the land immediately adjacent; it was built from a design by Mr. Nash, in the pure Saxon style, and is situated in an extensive demesne, containing some uncommonly fine timber. Not far distant are Loughry, the residence of J. Lindesay, Esq., and Lissan, the seat of Sir T. Staples, Bart. The former is in a demesne of about 200 acres, finely wooded, and watered by the river Loughry: the estate was granted, in 1604, by Jas. I. to Sir Robert Lyndesay, his chief harbinger, and has ever since been the residence of the senior branch of that ancient family, which is among the claimants of the earldom of Craufurd and Lyndesay. The other seats in the vicinity are Oaklands, the residence of Capt. Richardson; the glebe-house, of the Rev. C. Bardin, D. D.; and Greenvale, of T. Adair, Esq.; besides several other handsome houses in and near the town. The parish church of Derryloran, in the southern part of the town, is a large and handsome cruciform edifice, built of hewn freestone from a design by Mr. Nash, in the early English style of architecture: it has a tower and lofty octagonal spire, and the interior is fitted up in the Saxon style. Near the centre of the town is a large and handsome Presbyterian meeting-house, in connection with the Synod of Ulster, and also one in connection with the Associate Synod, each of which is of the first class and has a manse for the clergyman. A second meeting-house in connection with the Synod of Ulster was built in 1835, and there are places of worship for Wesleyan and Primitive Methodists, and, at a short distance from the town, a large R. C. chapel. An infants' school was established in 1834, by Mrs. Hassard and other ladies, for which a house is now being built; and a parochial school-house is also being erected, on land given by Mr. Stewart: near the town are several other schools. Here are also a news-room and a dispensary. Close to the town are the ruins of the old church of Derryloran, and not far distant are two large forts, one circular, the other square. In Killymoon demesne are the ruins of an old meeting-house; at Drumcraw is the site of a church, and at Loughry a fine cromlech.—See DERRYLORAN.

COOLAGHMORE, a parish, in the barony of KELLS, county of KILKENNY, and province of LEINSTER, 3 miles (S. S. E.) from Callan, on the road to Clonmel; containing 1417 inhabitants. This parish comprises 5332 statute acres, as applotted under the tithe act, and valued at £4196 per annum. It is a rectory and vicarage, in the diocese of Ossory, and forms part of the union of Callan: the tithes amount to £383. 10. per annum. In the R. C. divisions also it forms part of the union or district of Callan, and has a chapel at Coolagh.

COOLANEY, a small market-town, in the parish of KILLORAN, barony of LINEY, county of SLIGO, and province of CONNAUGHT, 4 miles (W.) from Collooney; containing 326 inhabitants. This place is situated on the road from Sligo to Tubbercurry; it contains about 70 houses, and has a penny post to Collooney. Here are a dispensary and a Baptist meeting-house; and it is a station of the constabulary police. In the centre of the village is the court-house, where petty sessions are held on alternate Wednesdays. The market is on Friday, and fairs are held on the 29th of May and 5th of December: it is in contemplation to erect a market-house. —See KILLORAN.

COOLBANAGHER, or COOLBENGER, a parish, in the barony of PORTNEHINCH, QUEEN'S county, and province of LEINSTER; containing, with the parish of Ardea, or Ardrea, the post-town of Emo, and part of that of Mountmellick, 7456 inhabitants. It comprises 8623 statute acres, as applotted under the tithe act. The soil is generally fertile, and there is a considerable tract of waste land, which is mostly exhausted bog, also a large tract of valuable bog; the system of agriculture is daily improving. Limestone abounds, and is quarried for building, repairing the roads, and burning into lime for manure. The principal seats are Emo Park, the residence of the Earl of Portarlington; Woodbrook, of Major Chetwood; Lauragh, of the Rev. Sir Erasmus Dixon Borrowes, Bart.; Knightstown, of Joseph Kemmis, Esq.; and Shane Castle, of Thomas Kemmis, Esq. From a desire to introduce manufactures and trade into this part of the country, for the employment of the population, Mr. Kemmis has established, on his estate at Shane, an iron-foundry and manufactory. The Dublin Grand Canal passes through the parish to Mountmellick; also a tributary stream which, running northward, falls into the Barrow at Portnehinch bridge. Petty sessions are held at Lauragh.

The living is a rectory, in the diocese of Kildare, episcopally united, in 1804, to the rectory of Ardea or Ardrea, together forming the union of Coolbanagher, in the patronage of the Crown: the tithes amount to £276. 18. 5½. per annum. The extent of the union, as applotted under the tithe act, is 15,763 statute acres; and the tithes for the whole amount to £536. 6. 1¾. per annum. The glebe-house, in Ardea, is a handsome residence, built in 1790: the glebe comprises 26½ acres. The church, also in Ardea, is a handsome edifice, erected at the expense of the late Lord Portarlington, on the summit of an eminence not far from the southern extremity of the union. In the R. C. divisions this parish forms part of the union or district of Portarlington; the chapel, at Emo, is a very neat edifice. There is a place of worship for Wesleyan Methodists. The parochial school is at Moret, and there are about six other schools at that and other places in the parish: a spacious slated building was erected for one under the trustees of Erasmus Smith's charity, at an expense of £500, chiefly defrayed by I. C. Chetwood, Esq.; and the school at Emo is endowed with 20 acres of land by the Hon. Lionel Dawson. There are about 700 children in these schools. The ruins of the ancient church are still visible, and also those of the castle of Moret, in the vicinity of which are the venerable remains of Shane Castle, formerly called "Sion" or "Shehan Castle," which was the head of a manor, when in the possession of Sir Robert Preston, in 1397, but it has shared the fate of the other castles of Leix. During the parliamentary war it was seized by the insurgents, in 1641; taken from them the year following by Sir Charles Coote, retaken by Owen Roe O'Nial in 1646, and finally surrendered, in 1650, to Cols. Hewson and Reynolds, who demolished the outworks, and left nothing but the present building remaining. It is situated on a high conical hill, and was fitted up in the last century by Dean Coote, who converted it into a very pleasant residence.—See EMO and MOUNTMELLICK.

COOLBOY, or CASTLE-BOY, a village, in the new district parish of SHILLELAGH, barony of SHILLELAGH, county of WICKLOW, and province of LEINSTER, 2¼ miles (S.) from Tinahely; containing 105 inhabitants. It is situated on the road from Carnew to Rathdrum, and has eight fairs, which are held on the last Wednesday in January, first Wednesday (O. S.) in March, the last Wednesday in April, the first Wednesday (O. S.) in June, the last Wednesday in July, Sept., and Oct., and the Wednesday in Ember week. Adjoining the village is Coolboy House, a respectable mansion, the residence of John Chamney, Esq.

COOLCAPPAGH.—See KILBRODERAN.

COOLCASHIN, a parish, in the barony of GALMOY, county of KILKENNY, and province of LEINSTER, 3½ miles (N. W.) from Freshford; containing 564 inhabitants. This parish comprises 2792 statute acres, as applotted under the tithe act, and valued at £2793 per annum. It is in the diocese of Ossory, and the vicarage forms part of the union of Freshford, and the corps of the prebend of Aghoure in the cathedral church of St. Canice, Kilkenny; the rectory is appropriate to the dean and chapter. The tithes amount to £164. 10., of which £109. 13. 4. is payable to the appropriators, and £54. 16. 8. to the vicar. In the R. C. divisions it is part of the union or district of Lisdowney; the chapel is at Whitegate.

COOLCOR, a parish, in the barony of LOWER PHILIPSTOWN, KING'S county, and province of LEINSTER, 6 miles (W.) from Edenderry, on the road to Philipstown: the population is returned with the parish of Ballyburley. It was formerly a rectory, in the diocese of Kildare, but is now united and consolidated with Ballyburley, *which see.*

COOLCRAHEEN, or COOLCRAGHIN, a parish, in the barony of FASSADINING, county of KILKENNY, and province of LEINSTER, 3 miles (N. N. E.) from Freshford; containing 668 inhabitants. This parish is situated on the road from Kilkenny to Castle-Durrow, and contains 2768 statute acres, mostly under tillage. Limestone is abundant, and is used for building and burning for manure. Foulksrath Castle is of some antiquity, but has been converted into a comfortable dwelling by T. Wright, Esq., an eminent agriculturist and grazier. It is a rectory and vicarage, in the diocese of Ossory, and is part of the union of Odogh: the tithes amount to £200. In the R. C. divisions it forms part of the unions or districts of Conahy and Muckalee. The ruins of Inchmore castle, opposite Inchmore island in the Nore, are in this parish: it consisted of a strong square keep of considerable antiquity, united to a splendid mansion in the Elizabethan style, and was erected by Robert Grace, baron of Courtstown, and member of parliament for the county of Kilkenny, who died about the year 1640.

COOLE, a parish, forming a detached portion of the barony of KINNATALOON, county of CORK, and province of MUNSTER, 3 miles (S. E.) from Fermoy; containing 338 inhabitants. This parish, which is nearly surrounded by Castle-Lyons, is situated on the road from Fermoy to Tallow, and comprises 1200 statute acres, as applotted under the tithe act, and valued at £1265 per annum; about 20 acres are woodland, 900 arable, and the remainder pasture; there is no bog or waste land. The higher grounds are finely wooded, and visible from a considerable distance. Coole Abbey is a large and handsome mansion, the residence of H. H. Peard, Esq., situated in an extensive and well-planted demesne; near it is High Park, the residence of the Rev. J. W. Edgar. The parish is in the diocese of Cloyne, and the rectory forms the corps of the prebend of Coole, in the cathedral of Cloyne, in the patronage of the Bishop: the tithes amount to £150. There is no church, but divine service is regularly performed in Coole Abbey mansion. In the R. C. divisions the parish forms part of the union or district of Castle-Lyons, and has a small plain chapel at Coolagaun. In the demesne of Coole Abbey are some ruins of the ancient abbey, which gave name to the parish. It was founded in 1296, by the Barry family, by whom it was given to the Knights Templars, and was formerly the summer residence of the bishops of Cloyne. Near these ruins are some beautiful arches belonging to the old church, which are covered with evergreens. On the more elevated part of the demesne are some vestiges of the ancient castle of Coole, formerly belonging to the Earls of Desmond. In 1642 this fortress was surrendered to Condon of Ballydorgan, an insurgent leader, on his promising a safe conduct to the garrison, which consisted of thirty of Lord Barrymore's troopers; but they were all killed except one.

COOLE, a village, in the parish of MAYNE, barony of DEMIFORE, county of WESTMEATH, and province of LEINSTER, 3 miles (W.) from Castle-Pollard; containing 341 inhabitants. It is situated on the road from Castle-Pollard to Granard, and near the shore of Lough Derveragh, and comprises about 70 houses. Two small fairs are held on the 20th of May and November.—See MAYNE.

COOLEAGH, a parish, in the barony of SLIEVARDAGH, county of TIPPERARY, and province of MUNSTER, 3 miles (S.) from Killenaule, on the road to Fethard; containing 714 inhabitants. It comprises 2486 statute acres, as applotted under the tithe act, and is a rectory and vicarage, in the diocese of Cashel, forming part of the union of Killenaule: the tithes amount to £150.

COOLGRANEY, a village, in that part of the parish of INCH which is in the barony of GOREY, county of WEXFORD, and province of LEINSTER, 3 miles (S. S. W.) from Arklow, on the road to Gorey; containing 274 inhabitants. Fairs for cattle and pigs are held on Jan. 24th, May 11th, June 11th, Aug. 3rd, Oct. 15th, and Dec. 10th. Here is a station of the constabulary police force, also a dispensary. The vicinity was the scene of the last pitched battle between the insurgent and royalist forces during the disturbances of 1798.—See INCH.

COOLINE, a parish, in the barony of ORRERY and KILMORE, county of CORK, and province of MUNSTER, 1½ mile (S. W.) from Charleville; containing 455 inhabitants. This small parish is situated on the road from Charleville to Liscarrol, and contains 1130 statute acres, as applotted under the tithe act, and valued at £1539 per annum for the county cess. The land, which is extremely rich, is partly in pasture, and the portion under tillage produces excellent crops; the system of agriculture is slowly improving. A stratum of limestone gravel extends into the parish, and is chiefly used for repairing the roads; and there are indications of culm at Milltown. The principal seats are Cooline House, the residence of R. Weldon, Esq.; and Milltown Castle, of G. Bruce, Esq., a handsome castellated mansion in the later English style. It is in the diocese of Cloyne, and is a rectory, constituting the corps of the prebend of Cooline in the cathedral of Cloyne, in the gift of the Bishop: the tithes amount to £70. In the R. C. divisions the parish forms part of the union or district of Ballyhea. The ruins of the church still remain in the ancient burial-ground.

COOLKERRY, a parish, in the barony of UPPER OSSORY, QUEEN'S county, and province of LEINSTER, 1 mile (E. by S.) from Rathdowney, on the road to Castledurrow; containing 375 inhabitants. This parish comprises 1720 statute acres, as applotted under the tithe act. It is a rectory and vicarage, in the diocese of Ossory, entirely impropriate in the Ladies G. and A. Fitzpatrick: the tithes amount to £110, wholly payable to the impropriators, who allow an annual stipend of £10. 10. to the vicar of Aughmacart for performing the clerical duties. The church is in ruins, and the Protestant parishioners attend the church at Rathdowney. In the R. C. divisions the parish forms part of the union or district of Aghavoe.

COOLLATTIN, a village, in the new district parish of SHILLELAGH, barony of SHILLELAGH, county of WICKLOW, and province of LEINSTER, 3¼ miles (S. by W.) from Tinahely, on the road to Carnew; containing 21 houses and 108 inhabitants. It derives its name from the contiguous seat and demesne of Coollattin, the property of Earl Fitzwilliam, and the residence of R. Chaloner, Esq. Fairs are held on the 26th of Feb., May, Aug., and Nov. The Shillelagh Farming Society was established here in 1830, by the late Earl Fitzwilliam.

COOLMUNDRY, a parish, in the barony of MIDDLETHIRD, county of TIPPERARY, and province of

MUNSTER, 1 mile (S. E.) from Fethard; containing 380 inhabitants. This parish comprises, according to the county assessment, 1984 statute acres, and contains part of the extensive demesne of Grove, the seat of W. Barton, Esq., of Fethard. It is a rectory, in the diocese of Cashel, entirely impropriate in Cæsar Sutton, Esq.: the tithes amount to £72. 19.

COOLOCK, a parish, in the barony of COOLOCK, county of DUBLIN, and province of LEINSTER, 3¾ miles (N. N. E.) from Dublin, on the road to Malahide; containing 914 inhabitants, of which number, 190 are in the village, which contains 26 houses, and is a constabulary police station. The parish comprises 1691 statute acres, as applotted under the tithe act: the soil is fertile, and well adapted for corn. Limestone abounds, and a quarry near the glebe-house is worked for agricultural and other purposes. There are numerous handsome seats and pleasant villas, from most of which are fine views of the bay and city of Dublin, with the adjacent country. Of these the principal are Beaumont, the residence of A. Guinness, Esq.; Newbrook, of E. H. Casey, Esq.; Belcamp, of Sir H. M. J. W. Jervis, Bart.; Brookeville, of R. Law, Esq.; Coolock House, of H. Brooke, Esq.; Coolock Lodge, of T. Sherrard, Esq.; Shrubs, of W. White, Esq.; Bonnybrook, of T. W. White, Esq.; Newbery Hill, of A. Ong, Esq.; Priors Wood, of T. Cosgrave, Esq.; Gracefield, of R. Eames, Esq.; Lark Hill, of E. Hickson, Esq.; Moatfield, of M. Staunton, Esq.; Darendale, of F. Gogarty, Esq.; Clare Grove, of Gen. A. Cuppage; Airfield, of Alderman Sir E. Nugent, Knt.; and Cameron Lodge, of H. Jones, Esq.

The living is a vicarage, in the diocese of Dublin, and in the patronage of the Marquess of Drogheda, in whom the rectory is impropriate: the vicarial tithes amount to £249. 4. 7½. There is a glebe-house, with a glebe comprising 17*a.* 2*r.* 25*p.* The church, dedicated to St. Brandon, a neat edifice, was partly rebuilt and enlarged, by aid of a loan of £500 from the late Board of First Fruits, in 1818. In the R. C. divisions the parish forms part of the union or district of Clontarf. The chapel was erected in 1831, at an expense of £800, raised by subscription: it is a very neat edifice, in the later English style, with a belfry over the principal entrance; the interior is very well arranged and neatly decorated. The parochial school, for which a house was built at an expense of £300, the gift of Sir Compton Domville, Bart., is supported by subscription, and attended by 30 or 40 children. A school of 30 children, for which a handsome cottage has been built in the grounds of Beaumont, and an infants' school in connection with it, are wholly supported by Mrs. Guinness; and in connection with the R. C. chapel is a school to which W. Sweetman, Esq., gives £20 per annum. On a common near the church, which is now enclosed, a great concourse of persons connected with Emmet's insurrection was assembled, ready to march into Dublin at the appointed signal. In the grounds of Newbrook, through which flows a small stream, are the walls of a holy well, dedicated to St. Donagh; the spot is much resorted to, on St. John's Eve, by poor sick people, who, after rubbing themselves against the walls, wash in a well in the adjoining grounds of Donaghmede. In the grounds of Shrubs was anciently a nunnery, and human bones are frequently dug up there. There are ancient raths in the grounds of Bonnybrook and Moatfield.

COOLRAINE, a village, in the parish of OFFERLANE, barony of UPPER OSSORY, QUEEN'S county, and province of LEINSTER, 4 miles (N. W.) from Mountrath, on the road to Roscrea; containing 53 houses and 324 inhabitants. It is a constabulary police station. A boulting-mill has been erected, and there is a dispensary in the village, near which is the parochial school-house, a neat stone building.—See OFFERLANE.

COOLSTUFFE, a parish, in the barony of SHELMALIER, county of WEXFORD, and province of LEINSTER, 1½ mile (E.) from Taghmon; containing 577 inhabitants. This parish is situated on the high road from Wexford, through Taghmon, to New Ross; and contains 3320 statute acres, of which nearly one-half is in pasture, and the remainder under an improving system of tillage. It is a rectory, in the diocese of Ferns, and forms the corps of the prebend of Coolstuffe in the cathedral of Ferns, in the gift of the Bishop: the tithes amount to £200. The glebe-house was erected in 1806, by aid of a gift of £100 from the late Board of First Fruits; and there is a glebe of 4½ acres of good land. There is no church; the inhabitants resort to that of the adjoining parish of Taghmon, of which the incumbent of this parish is curate. In the R. C. divisions the parish is chiefly within the union or district of Taghmon, and partly in that of Glyn. A parochial school-house was erected in 1829, on the glebe, by the present incumbent, who contributes £5 per ann. towards the support of the school. A school, chiefly for females, is patronised by the Hon. Mrs. Hoare, who provides the school-house, and allows £2 per annum to the mistress. At Sygansaggard are the remains of an old castle, consisting of a square tower of considerable strength, said to have been built by the Hearne family, but of which no particulars are recorded.

COOTEHILL, a market and post-town, in the parish of DRUMGOON, barony of TULLAGHGARVEY, county of CAVAN, and province of ULSTER, 12 miles (N. E.) from Cavan, and 57 (N. W. by W.) from Dublin; containing 2239 inhabitants. This town is situated on the road from Kingscourt to Clones, and consists of four wide streets, containing 438 houses, nearly all of which are slated. It is on the borders of a lake, which is navigable for the greater part of the distance of seven miles between this place and Ballybay, in Monaghan; and is a considerable market for linen. The webs are principally broad sheetings of superior quality, and the number of pieces sold annually to be bleached is about 40,000. The trade, which had considerably declined, has for the last two or three years been improving. The general market is on Friday, and the corn market on Saturday, in the market-house. Fairs are held on the second Friday in each month for cattle, flax, and yarn. Here is a chief constabulary police station. Petty sessions are held every Wednesday, and quarter sessions at Easter and in October in a very neat sessions-house. The bridewell contains three cells, with separate day-rooms and yards for males and females, and apartments for the keeper. The seats in the neighbourhood are very beautiful, especially Bellamont Forest, the residence of C. Coote, Esq., which derived its name from the title of Earl of Bellamont enjoyed, until the year 1800, by the ancient family of Coote. The house is of brick, two stories high, with a noble Doric portico of stone, and the rooms of the lower story are strikingly grand; it contains some fine paintings, among which is the death of Dido, by Guercino, also full-length portraits of the late Earl and Countess of Bellamont by Sir Joshua Reynolds, the former in the full costume of a Knight of the Bath, a fine painting in excellent preservation. The demesne comprises above 1000 plantation acres, of which nearly one-half is occupied with woods; it includes several lakes and a spa, and commands beautiful views from Dismond Hill and its several eminences. The other principal seats are Ashfield Lodge, the residence of H. J. Clements, Esq.; Annilea, of M. Murphy, Esq.; Bellgreen, of T. Brunker, Esq.; and Rakenny, of T. L. Clements, Esq. The town contains the parish church, a R. C. chapel, and two places of worship for Presbyterians, one for the Society of Friends, one for Moravians, and one for Wesleyan Methodists. There are three schools, including an infants' school, also a Sunday school in the old church and at each of the Presbyterian chapels, a dispensary, and a Ladies' Society for selling blankets and clothing at half-price. In an ancient fort at Rakenny a considerable quantity of gold, with a large golden fibula, was found in an iron pot.—See DRUMGOON.

COPELAND ISLANDS, a cluster of three islands, situated at the south entrance of Belfast Lough, and in that part of the parish of BANGOR which is in the barony of ARDES, county of DOWN, and province of ULSTER, called respectively Copeland, Lighthouse and Mew islands. They derived their common name from the family of the Copelands, who settled here in the time of John de Courcey, in the 12th century, and of whose descendants, some are still to be found in the tract called Ballycopeland, on the mainland. Copeland island, the largest of the three, called also Big island and Neddrum, is 2 miles (N. N. E.) from Donaghadee, and about one mile from the mainland; it comprises about 200 acres, and contains 15 houses; near a small inlet, called Chapel bay, are the ruins of a church, with a burial-ground. About halfway between this island and the mainland is a rock, called the Deputy, on which a buoy is placed; and at the west end of the island is the Katikern rock, always above water, from which run two ledges about a cable's length, and on which a stone beacon has been erected. There is good anchorage on the west side of the island, and in Chapel bay on the south of Katikern, in from two to three fathoms of water, in all winds but those from the south-east. Lighthouse, or, as it is also called, Cross island, is about 1 mile (N. E.) from Copeland island, and is one furlong in length and about half a furlong in breadth, comprising about 24 acres. The Lighthouse from which it takes its name is a square tower, 70 feet high to the lantern, which displays a light to the south-east, to guide vessels from the north and south rocks, which are $3\frac{1}{2}$ leagues distant, and to the north-west, to guard them from the Hulin or Maiden rocks lying between the mouths of Larne and Glenarm. The lighthouse is situated in lat. 54° 41′ 15″ (N.), and lon. 5° 31′ (W.), and the light is plainly seen at Portpatrick and the Mull of Galway, in Scotland, from the latter of which it is 10 leagues distant. Mew island is a quarter of a furlong (E.) from Lighthouse island, and comprises about 10 acres of rocky pasture; it lies very low, and is extremely dangerous to mariners; in the sound between it and Copeland island is a flat rock with only three feet of water on it, called the Pladdens; and a rapid tide sets through the sound. Off this island the Enterprise, of Liverpool, a homeward-bound vessel from the coast of Guinea, was totally wrecked in 1801; she is said to have had on board £40,000 in dollars, which, with all her cargo, lay buried in the sea, till 1833, when Mr. Bell, by means of a diving apparatus, succeeded in recovering about 25,000 of the dollars, five brass guns, and other valuable property.

CORBALLIS, a village, in the parish of DULEEK, barony of LOWER DULEEK, county of MEATH, and province of LEINSTER, 4 miles (W.) from Drogheda; containing 23 houses and 127 inhabitants.

CORBALLY, a parish, in the barony of BARRETTS, county of CORK, and province of MUNSTER, $5\frac{1}{4}$ miles (S.W.) from Cork. It is situated on the road from Cork to Bandon, and is a rectory, in the diocese of Cork, two-third parts of which are appropriate to the vicars choral of the cathedral of St. Finbarr, Cork, the remaining third forming part of the union of Carrigrohane and of the corps of the precentorship of Cork. The tithes amount to £70, of which £46. 13. 4. is payable to the vicars choral, and £23. 6. 8. to the precentor.

CORBALLY, a parish, in the barony of IKERRIN, county of TIPPERARY, and province of MUNSTER, 3 miles (S.E.) from Roscrea; containing 3090 inhabitants. This place derived an early degree of celebrity from a very ancient abbey founded about the 7th century for Culdean monks, on an island in the parish, called Mona Incha, and dedicated to St. Columba. This island, which comprised little more than two acres of firm ground encompassed by a soft morass, recently drained by its proprietor and brought into cultivation, is noticed by Giraldus Cambrensis, who came into Ireland as preceptor of John, Earl of Morton, afterwards King of England, who says that there a few Culdees or Colidei "did devoutly serve God." An opinion even in his time prevailed that no person, however severe might be his malady, could die in this island, from which tradition it obtained the appellation of *Insula Viventium*, or "the Isle of the Living." This legendary celebrity made it the resort of numerous pilgrims from the remotest parts of the country, but did not prevent the brethren from emigrating to the more healthy shores of the neighbouring village of Corbally, where they fixed their residence, and where there are still the remains of a small neat cruciform chapel, with narrow lancet-shaped windows. The abbey continued to flourish till the dissolution, and, in the 28th of Elizabeth, the site and possessions were granted to Sir Lucas Dillon. Of the abbey on the island there are still the remains of the church, which, though raised on a spot scarcely accessible, exhibits a beauty of style and costliness of materials scarcely to be expected in so retired and isolated a spot. The abbey church appears to have been 44 feet in length and 18 feet in width; the arches of the choir, and of the western entrance, are of the Norman semicircular character, and decorated with rich and varied mouldings embellished with highly wrought ornaments. To the north of the church is a small oratory, and the abbey and a separate room for the abbot were formerly to be traced. Attached to the church is a burial-ground, in which are the remains of a fine cross. There was also on this island an ancient building called the "Woman's Church."

The parish consists of three detached portions intersected by the parish of Roscrea, and comprises 10,125 statute acres, as applotted under the tithe act, of which about 400 are woodland, 3200 bog, and the remainder good arable and pasture land. The system of agriculture is improved, and there is no waste land except the bog, which affords abundance of fuel. There are numerous quarries of grit-stone, which forms the basis of the principal hills, and is used in all kinds of building; there are very few quarries of limestone, but limestone gravel and pebbles, which make the whitest lime, are found in abundance. Mount Heaton, the property of the Misses Taylor, but now occupied by Mrs. Hutchinson, a handsome mansion with a castellated front, flanked at the principal entrance with two stately towers, and containing spacious and elegant apartments, is beautifully situated in a richly wooded and highly embellished demesne of 400 acres, watered by a branch of the river Brosna, and finely diversified; the gardens are spacious and kept in excellent order, and in the grounds are some white thorn trees of the growth of more than two centuries. Corville, the seat of the Hon. F. A. Prittie, is a handsome structure in the Grecian style, and is seen to great advantage terminating a long avenue from the entrance gate; the demesne is ample and tastefully embellished, and in the grounds are the ruins of an old church and a square tower on an eminence. Timoney, the seat of J. D. Hutchinson, Esq., is situated on a rising ground surrounded by hills finely wooded, and by plantations covering 100 acres; the grounds are embellished with timber of stately growth, and contain some of the largest spruce and Scottish fir trees in the country. Great improvements have been made on this estate by the proprietor, and much rocky mountainous waste land has been reclaimed. Rockforest, the seat of W. H. Hutchinson, Esq., was a castle occupied by the family of Hutchinson, whose ancestor came to Ireland as a captain in Cromwell's army, and subsequently settled here in 1660, and has since been the seat of the eldest branch of that family. This castle sustained several sieges, and repeated injuries from the rapparees, who, on one occasion, surprised the garrison and carried off the proprietor into Connaught, where he was detained a prisoner; the present house, which is incorporated with the old castle, is situated on a bold eminence and surrounded by extensive plantations, which, rising abruptly from the plain, forms one of the most striking and beautiful prospects between Dublin and Limerick: there is some fine old timber on the grounds. It was anciently called Knockballymaher, which was changed for its present name by its late proprietor, T. Hutchinson, Esq., who at considerable expense excavated a handsome lake in the demesne, and made great improvements on the estate; the lake is well stocked with fish, and on it is a canoe of considerable dimensions, hollowed out from a single tree by the American Indians; it was picked up off the banks of Newfoundland, and presented to Mr. Hutchinson. Dungar, the seat of J. Hutchinson, Esq., is beautifully situated in a highly cultivated demesne, and the gardens are very extensive; in the grounds is an old castle covered with ivy, having a commodious staircase leading to the summit, from which is an extensive and beautiful view of the surrounding country. Birch Grove, the seat of J. Birch, Esq., is a handsome residence pleasantly situated; some additions were made to the house by the late Mr. Elsam; the principal staircase winds through a round tower with a richly gilded dome; the east window of the old abbey at Roscrea is preserved and placed in a very picturesque situation in the grounds, and the ancient carved door of the "Woman's Church" at Mona Incha forms the entrance to the gardens. Mona Incha, the residence of G. Birch, Esq., is an elegant villa in the Italian style. Mount Butler, the residence of Capt. Smith, is a very pleasing villa; the grounds are tastefully laid out and kept in excellent order. Derryvale, the residence of W. Smith, Esq., and Tenderry, of Charles Hart, Esq., are also in the parish. Spruce Hill is the handsomely planted demesne of Lord Norbury, but contains no residence. An extensive distillery at Birch Grove, and a large brewery at Racket Hall, are carried on by Messrs. Birch and Co., and afford employment to 100 persons. Fairs are held at Williamstown on March 11th and Nov. 27th, chiefly for pigs. A private canal, about four miles in length, has been constructed, from which are several branches, one for conveying turf to the distillery at Birch Grove, and another to the Rathdowney road leading to Roscrea, and partly supplying the latter town; all run into the bog of Corbally, in which is a lake about one Irish mile in circumference. A considerable portion of the bog has been reclaimed by Messrs. Birch, and is now in a high state of cultivation.

It is a rectory, in the diocese of Killaloe, entirely impropriate in the Earl of Portarlington, by whom the tithes, amounting to £403. 1. 6¾., are leased to several persons. There is no church, but divine service is performed in a private building on the Timoney estate, every Sunday and holiday, and evening service every Wednesday during the summer, by a clergyman principally supported by J. D. Hutchinson, Esq. In the R. C. divisions the parish forms part of the union or district of Bourney; there are two chapels, one at Williamstown, and one at Camlin. There is a meeting-house for the Society of Friends on the Rockforest estate, endowed by the family of Hutchinson. A school is supported by J. D. Hutchinson, Esq., in which about 80 children are instructed. There are two chalybeate springs on the demesne of Rockforest, considered as strong as that of Ballyspellan, in the county of Kilkenny; also a petrifying stream.

CORBALLY, a parish, in the barony of GAULTIER, county of WATERFORD, and province of MUNSTER, 6½ miles (S. S. E.) from Waterford; containing 285 inhabitants. This parish is situated on Tramore bay, and contains 698 statute acres, as applotted under the tithe act, chiefly arable land. It is a rectory, in the diocese of Waterford, and forms part of the union of Killure: the tithes amount to £55. In the R. C. divisions it is part of the union or district of Tramore, and contains a chapel. At Summerville is a public school of about 20 girls.

CORCLONE, a parish, in the barony of STRADBALLY, QUEEN'S county, and province of LEINSTER, 2 miles (N. E.) from Stradbally, on the road to Athy; containing 650 inhabitants. This parish comprises about 2400 statute acres, as applotted under the tithe act. The Grand Canal passes through it. The gentlemen's seats are Ballykilcavan, the residence of Sir E. H. Walsh, Bart.; and Brockley Park, of — Finer, Esq. The living, formerly united to that of Killeny, from which it has been recently separated, is a rectory, in the diocese of Leighlin, and in the patronage of the Bishop: the tithes amount to £233. There is no glebe-house; the glebe comprises 2*a*. 39*p*. The church is a neat small edifice in good repair. In the R. C. divisions the parish forms part of the union or district of Stradbally; there is no chapel at present, but it is in contemplation to build one at Vickerstown.

CORCOMOHIDE, an ecclesiastical union, including the civil parishes of Castletown-Conyers, Drumcolloher, and Kilmeedy, in the barony of Upper Connello East, county of Limerick, and province of Munster; containing 10,742 inhabitants. These parishes, each of which is described under its own head, are all contiguous, and together comprise 14,370¼ statute acres, as severally applotted under the tithe act; the tithes for the whole amount to £900, of which £570 is payable to the Countess of Ormonde, as lessee under the vicars choral of the cathedral church of St. Mary, Limerick, and £330 to the incumbent. There are two public schools, to one of which Mr. Stevelly contributes £10 annually, and to the other Col. White subscribes 10 guineas and has given a house and garden: about 150 children are educated in these schools, and about 750 in 12 private schools.

CORCOMROE.—See ABBEY.

CORK (County of), a maritime county of the province of Munster, and the largest in Ireland, bounded on the east by the counties of Tipperary and Waterford, on the north by that of Limerick, on the west by that of Kerry, and on the south-west, south, and south-east by St. George's Channel: it extends from 51° 12′ to 52° 13′ (N. Lat.), and from 9° 45′ to 10° 3′ (W. Lon.); and comprises, according to the Ordnance survey, 1,725,100 statute acres, of which 1,024,340 are cultivated, and 700,760 are occupied by mountains, bogs, &c. The population, in 1821, was 629,786, and in 1831, 700,359, of which latter number, 407,935 were in the East, and 292,424 in the West, Riding.

The earliest inhabitants of the south-western part of this extensive territory are designated by Ptolemy *Uterni* or *Uterini*, and by other writers *Iberni, Iberi*, and *Juerni*. They occupied most of the southern part of the country subsequently called Desmond: their name and situation prove them to have been of Spanish Iberian origin, and the former, as well as that of the tribes from which they sprung, and the designation *Ibernia* or *Hibernia*, applied to the whole island even by Ptolemy, was derived from the western situation of the country which they inhabited. From Ptolemy's map it appears that the most eastern maritime part of the county in the south of Cork was, in the same age, inhabited by a people whom he called *Vodiæ* or *Vodii*, but who are unnoticed both by Sir James Ware and Dr. Charles O'Conor. The *Coriondi*, whose name still bears some affinity to the Irish appellation of this tract, were, according to Smith, the inhabitants of the middle and northern parts, particularly near the present city of Cork, and are said to have sprung from the *Coritani*, a British tribe occupying a tract in the eastern part of England. The ancient divisions of the country prior to the English settlements, were intricate, and at present can with difficulty be ascertained. The whole formed the southern and most important part of the petty kingdom of Cork or Desmond, which comprised also the western portion of the present county of Waterford, and all Kerry. *Desmond*, signifying "South Munster," was more properly the name of only the south-western part of the principality, which was divided into three portions, of which the whole of that called Ivelagh or Evaugh, including the country between Bantry and Baltimore, and also that called Bear, lying between Bantry and the Kenmare river, are included in the modern county of Cork. Bear still partly retains its ancient name, being divided into the baronies of Bear and Bantry; but Evaugh is included in the barony of West Carbery, which, with East Carbery, Kinalmeaky, and Ibawn or Ibane and Barryroe, anciently formed an extensive territory, deriving its name from its chieftain, Carbry Riada, and in which are said to have been settled four of the eight families of royal extraction in Munster, the head of one of which was McCarty Reagh, sometimes styled prince of Carbery. Kerrycurrihy was anciently called Muskerry Ilane, and comprised also the barony of Imokilly, on the north side of Cork harbour: the only maritime territory remaining unnoticed, *viz*. Kinnalea, was formerly called Insovenagh. Besides Kerrycurrihy and Imokilly, the entire central part of the county, between the rivers Lee and Blackwater, formed a portion of the ancient territory of Muskerry, which name the western portion of it still retains. The north-western extremity of the county, forming the present barony of Duhallow, is in some old writings called Alla and Dubh Alla; and its chief, who, to a very late period, enjoyed almost regal authority, was sometimes styled prince of Duhallow. The remainder, to the north of the Blackwater, formed, before the English conquests, a principality of the O'Keefes, called Fearmuigh.

Henry II., about the year 1177, granted to Robert Fitz-Stephen and Milo de Cogan the whole kingdom of Cork, except the city and the cantred belonging to the Ostmen settled there, which he retained in his own hands; but they were unable to take possession of more than seven cantreds lying nearest the city, receiving tribute from the other twenty-four. They introduced other Anglo-Norman families and their retainers; and the military colony thus established was never completely uprooted. Cork was one of the districts erected into a county by King John, and the English power was gradually extended by the divisions arising from female inheritance and inferior grants; large tracts of country were successively held by the Carews, De Courcys, and other families, of whom the former, who were styled Marquesses of Cork, built the castle of Donemark, in the western part of the county, and others in Imokilly, for protection against the natives. The chief men of this family, with many other English settled here, removed into England on the breaking out of the civil war between the houses of York and Lancaster; while De Courcy, who remained, besides divesting himself of some of his possessions, which he gave in marriage with his daughters, lost a considerable portion by the superior power of the natives. The English were thus greatly reduced both in numbers and power, and were subsequently further weakened by the usurping measures of the Earls of Desmond, to whom Robert Fitz-Geoffry Cogan granted all his lands in Ireland, including one-half of Cork; but the whole was forfeited by the attainder of the last Earl, in 1582. This induced the settlement of new colonies of the English; for although a considerable portion was regranted to the Fitz-Geralds and other resident families, the rest of the forfeitures was divided in seigniories and granted by letters patent to several English gentlemen, who were called undertakers, from being bound to perform the conditions mentioned in the articles for the plantation of this province with English, who were consequently settled here in great numbers, especially by Sir Richard Boyle, afterwards created Earl of Cork. In the Spanish invasion of 1600, this county was wholly the scene of operations, particularly in the vicinity of Kinsale. During the civil war which broke out in 1641, the bands of trained English contributed much to the maintenance of British interests here, which, however, were greatly weakened by these commotions, until in a great measure renewed towards the period of the Restoration by the settlement of republican officers, soldiers, and adventurers; and the Protestant inhabitants of English descent again proved their strength by the most active and important services in 1691.

This large county contains the whole of the united dioceses of Cork, Ross, and Cloyne, and about 28,800 plantation acres of that of Ardfert and Aghadoe. By the statute of the 4th of Geo. IV., cap. 93, it was divided, for the more frequent holding of general sessions of the peace, into two districts, called the East and West Ridings: the former comprises the baronies of Duhallow, Orrery and Kilmore, Condons and Clongibbons, Fermoy, Kinnatalloon, Imokilly, Kerrycurrihy, Kinnalea, Barrymore, Barretts, and East Muskerry (with the exception of the parishes of Ahinagh and Aghabologue), together with the liberties of the city of Cork and of Kinsale: the West Riding is composed of the baronies of Ibane and Barryroe, Beer or Bear, Bantry, West Muskerry, Kinalmeaky, Courcies, East Carbery (east and west divisions), and West Carbery (east and west divisions), with the two parishes of Ahinagh and Aghabologue, in the barony of East Muskerry. Besides the city of Cork, which, with an extensive surrounding district forms a county of itself, it contains the borough, market, and sea-port towns of Youghal and Kinsale; the borough and market-towns of Bandon and Mallow; the sea-port and market-towns of Cove and Bantry; the market and post-towns of Fermoy, Skibbereen, Macroom, and Dunmanway; the ancient disfranchised boroughs of Baltimore, Castlemartyr, Charleville, Clonakilty, Doneraile, Midleton, and Rathcormac, all of which, except the first, are post-towns; the post-towns of Ballincollig, Buttevant, Castletown-Bearhaven, Castletown-Roche, Cloyne, Innishannon, Kanturk, Kildorrery, Kilworth, West Millstreet, Mitchelstown, Passage, and Rosscarbery; and the small towns of Castle-Lyons, Crookhaven, Liscarrol, and Timoleague. Prior to the Union it sent twenty-four members to the Irish parliament, being two for the county at large, and two for each of the boroughs, besides the two for the county of the city of Cork. At present it sends to the Imperial parliament two representatives for the county at large, two for the city of Cork, and one each for the boroughs of Bandon, Kinsale, Mallow, and Youghal. The recent enactments have made no alteration in the number of representatives, but have constituted each riding a separate jurisdiction for the purposes of registry: the county members are elected at the court-house in the city of Cork. The total number of voters registered up to March, 1836, was 4394, of which 1179 were £50, 532 £20, and 1828 £10 freeholders; 158 £20, and 639 £10 leaseholders, and 23 £50, and 35 £20 rent-chargers. The county is included in the Munster circuit: the assizes are held in the city of Cork; and by the act of the 4th of Geo. IV., it is enacted that five general sessions of the peace shall be holden in alternate months in each of the two ridings, so that in the county at large a session is held every month, except the two in which the general sessions are holden for the entire county: the sessions for each division are directed to be holden, for the East Riding, alternately in the city of Cork, and at Midleton, Fermoy, Mallow, and Kanturk; and for the West Riding, alternately at Bandon, Macroom, Bantry, Skibbereen, and Clonakilty; the precise days to be settled by the high sheriff, the two assistant barristers, and the clerk of the peace. In all processes connected with these sessions, the several divisions are to be carefully distinguished as Cork County East Riding, and Cork County West Riding; but with the exception of the power given to the lord-lieutenant to appoint an assistant barrister for each, with a salary equal to that of similar officers in entire counties, the officers and jurisdictions of the county are not in any manner altered from those which are customary. In the city of Cork are the county gaol and house of correction, rules for the management of which were drawn up by a committee of the magistrates in 1816, which were afterwards embodied in the general act for the prisons of Ireland. There are, besides, seventeen bridewells, situated respectively at Midleton, Bandon, Clonakilty, Skibbereen, Bantry, Dunmanway, Macroom, Mitchelstown, Fermoy, Mallow, Cove, Kinsale, Rosscarbery, Millstreet, Kanturk, Youghal, and Charleville. The number of persons charged with criminal offences and committed to the county prison in 1835, was 740. The local government is vested in a lord-lieutenant, 16 deputy-lieutenants, and 282 other magistrates; besides whom there are the usual county officers, including four coroners. The constabulary force consists of 16 chief and 85 subordinate constables, and 426 men, with 17 horses, the expense of maintaining which is defrayed equally by Grand Jury presentments and by Government. The coast-guard districts are those of Youghal, containing the stations of Helwick Head, Ardmore, Youghal, Knockadoon, and Ballycotton; Cove, containing the stations of Ballycroneen, Poor Head, Lighthouse, East Ferry, Cove, Cork, Crosshaven, and Robert's Cove; Kinsale, containing the stations of Upper Cove, Oyster Haven, Old Head, Howshand, Courtmasherry, Barry's Cove, Dunny Cove, and Dirk Cove; Skibbereen, containing the stations of Milk Cove, Glandore, Castle-Townsend, Barlogue, Baltimore, Long Island, Crook Haven, Dunmanus, and Whithorse; and Castletown, containing the stations of Colaris, Garnish, and Castletown: the entire force consists of 5 inspecting commanders, 32 chief officers, and 251 men. The public charitable institutions are the lunatic asylum, house of industry and infirmary at Cork, an infirmary at Mallow, 12 fever hospitals, and 48 local dispensaries, maintained partly by subscription and partly by grand jury presentments: the dispensaries are situated respectively at Mitchelstown, Millstreet, Castletown-Roche, Bandon,

Ovens, Ballyneen, Newmarket, Kanturk, Cloyne, Rosscarbery, Timoleague, Charleville, Buttevant, Kildorrery, Dunbullogue, Whitechurch, Kinsale, Glanworth, Fermoy, Glenville, Midleton, Bantry, Ballyclough, Skibbereen, Rathcormac, Glandore, Innishannon, Donoughmore, Doneraile, Glanmire, Carrigaline, Clonakilty, Dunmanway, Cove, Kilworth, Ballydehob, Passage, Macroom, Castletown-Bearhaven, Inniscarra, Conna, Castlemartyr, Magourney, Crookstown, Ballymacoda, Blarney, Glauntain, and Water-grass Hill. The total amount of the county Grand Jury presentments, for 1835, was £62,645. 15. 8¾., of which £6978. 19. 0¾. was for the public roads and bridges of the county at large; £17,629. 16. 5. for public roads, being the baronial charge; £21,026. 19. 5. for public establishments, officers' salaries, and buildings; £9864. 16. 6. for police, and £7145. 4. 4. for repayment of advances made by the Government. In the military arrangements the county is in the Southern District; it contains sixteen military stations, situated respectively at Ballincollig, Buttevant, Charles Fort, Clonakilty, Fermoy, (which is the principal, and the military depôt of the district,) Kinsale, Mallow, Millstreet, Mitchelstown, Youghal, Skibbereen, and, in Cork Harbour, at Spike Island, Camden Fort, Carlisle Fort, Rocky Island, and Hawlbowling Island; and affording barrack accommodation in the whole, for 352 officers and 6799 men.

The surface of the county is of considerable variety and much natural beauty, but exhibits a very great deficiency of timber, and of hedge rows and plantations. The western part is bold, rocky, and mountainous; while the northern and eastern portions are distinguished for their richness and fertility. But even in this irregularity some order is perceived, the ranges of high land stretching nearly in the direction of east and west, though several ranges of hills branch off in transverse directions. The principal deviation from this general character is seen in the Bogra mountains, forming a high and barren tract in the centre of the county, between the rivers Lee and Blackwater, and which, instead of rising into narrow summits, spread out into an ample area, having in some places a deep boggy surface. The great longitudinal ranges of high ground are likewise often intersected by deep glens and gullies, through which numerous small streams find a rapid descent, and, after heavy rains, form beautiful waterfalls. The western mountains differ from the rest in form and aspect, being far more rocky, bold, and sterile, and abruptly parted by gaps and fissures. The entire south and south-western portions of the county are composed of stupendous masses of schistose rock, standing as barriers against the waves of the Atlantic, which, for the greater part of the year, are driven with fury against them by the force of the prevailing winds. Of low grounds, the most extensive tracts are those in which limestone is found: the largest is in the northern part of the county, lying north of the Blackwater, and extending upwards of twenty miles in length from east to west, varying in breadth from five to nine. This rich and beautiful expanse of country, though comparatively flat, is, however, agreeably diversified with gentle elevations, and contains but little land forming a dead level. By far the greater part of the county, excepting its western portion, has a similar undulating character; even the mountains are little more irregular in their outlines than the lower grounds, and the transition from one to the other is by very gentle degrees. The limestone vale, in which part of the city of Cork is situated, commences at Castlemore, about 10 miles to the west of it; and though at first of inconsiderable breadth, on crossing Cork harbour and reaching Imokilly, it takes a wider range, and throughout its course to the sea presents a fine tract of the best cultivated ground in the county. The line of coast presents a series of magnificent headlands, separated from each other by numerous inlets forming safe and commodious harbours, of which the most noted are those of Youghal, Cork, Kinsale, Baltimore, Crookhaven, Dunmanus, and Bantry, in the last of which, surrounded by the majestic scenery of the western mountains, whole navies may ride in safety. The numerous estuaries, disclose at low water, rich banks of calcareous sand for manure, and afford access to the interior of the country by navigation. On the south-western coast are various small, rocky islands, of which the principal are Cape Clear and Innisherkin, near the harbour of Baltimore; Bear island and Whiddy island, in Bantry bay; and Dursey island, off the extremity of Bearhaven promontory, forming the most western extremity of the county. In the mountainous parts of the district are several small lakes, among which are those of Cahir, near Glengariffe; others on Three-Castle Head: that of Loughbofinny, near Bantry; and those of Shepperton; three between Bantry and Dunmanway, and the interesting lake of Googane-Barra, with smaller sheets of water at Rathbarry, Macloneigh, Ballintowlus, Drinagh, and in other parts.

The climate is remarkable for the mildness of its temperature, never reaching those extremes of heat and cold to which the same degree of latitude is subject even in England. This arises from its proximity to the Atlantic, across which the prevailing winds come loaded with vapours, seldom objectionable in winter, but often intercepting the maturing rays of the summer's sun; which circumstance renders the corn raised here, though good, generally inferior to that of a drier climate. The county, however, suffers much less in this respect than the neighbouring more western counties; and its climate has been decidedly improved by the draining of bogs and swamps. The soils present no great variety, and may be distributed into four classes, each comprising several species differing in degrees of fertility, but united by a general resemblance of component parts. These are,—1st. The calcareous soils, or those found in the limestone tracts, which exceed all the rest in richness and fertility, producing the finest herbage and best wheat, and having always a crumbling and mellow surface.—2nd. The loamy soils not calcareous, comprising the deep and mellow loams remote from limestone, occurring in several of the less elevated parts, especially towards the south, where they constitute the best lands: they are next in quality to the former, to which some of the best bear a close affinity both in texture and fertility; they generally rest on clay-slate.—3rd. The light and shallow soils resting upon an absorbent bottom, as gravel, or rubbly stone, which have a much shallower and less vigorous arable surface than the preceding, but commonly afford a short sweet herbage peculiarly adapted for sheep, and produce the best corn in wet seasons.—4th. The moorland or peat soil, the usual substratum of which is a hard rock or coarse retentive clay, and is of greater extent than any of the preceding classes, occupying both bog and mountain, and even several tracts of elevated land, which, though improved by culture, still exhibit sufficient traces of their origin: though inferior in fertility, some portions of this class may be rendered productive of good crops of grass, oats, and potatoes; but the most elevated portions can never afford any thing better than coarse summer pasturage. Sands occur only on the sea-shore, and are most extensive in the bays of Courtmasherry, Bantry, Kinsale, Clonakilty, and Ross.

The tillage, except on the demesnes of resident gentlemen, presents rather unfavourable features, owing in a great measure to the want of skill and adequate capital, the too minute subdivision of farms, and the superabundant population of the arable districts. The crop of the greatest importance, and cultivated with the greatest care, is that of potatoes, which constitute the staple food of the small farmers and the labourers: it is succeeded in the more fertile districts by wheat, for which the ground is not unfrequently manured with lime, and this is followed by one or two crops of oats. The ground is rarely levelled, properly cleared, or sown with artificial grasses, except by a few of the more opulent farmers on calcareous soils in the west and south parts of the county; barley and oats are more generally cultivated. The land held by the small farmers, or cottiers, presents an impoverished appearance, and is rarely left to recruit its productive powers by means of rest, until first exhausted by over-cropping. The cabins occupied by this class of tenants are for the most part of a wretched description. A considerable portion of the northern part of the county is appropriated to dairy farms, and is but thinly inhabited; but the land there is in good condition, and the farm-houses more comfortable than in the tillage districts. Some of the principal landowners have corrected the abuses of the cottier system, and adopted for the improvement of their estates, and the amelioration of their tenantry, the practice of letting sufficiently large farms to occupying and working tenants, and providing them with comfortable dwelling-houses and farm-offices suitable to the extent of land and the condition of the holder. The substances generally employed as manure are, common dung, lime, earth collected from the ditches, sea-sand, and sea-weed. As the beds of limestone are situated in the northern and eastern parts of the county, the farmers in the south-west are precluded from using this material, but find an abundant substitute in the calcareous sea-sand driven upon the shore, which is partly composed of pulverised marine shells in various proportions, and of which the coral sand of Bantry bay, being wholly calcareous, is most esteemed: some kinds of a red colour are also in great esteem; those of a dark blue colour seem to be composed chiefly of the fragments of muscle shells. Spade labour is generally preferred to the use of the plough, of which the prevailing kind is of very rude construction, having short and thick handles, a low beam, and the coulter and sock placed obliquely, so that in working, the mould-board is raised out of the ground; the Scotch swing plough has been introduced by the gentry and wealthy farmers in the neighbourhood of Cork and other places. Formerly hay and corn were brought from the fields on slide cars or crooks, both of which are still used in the west; but the general improvement of the roads has introduced the wheel car, which, however, is of very rude construction, consisting of little more than a pair of shafts connected by a few cross bars, and resting upon a wooden axletree fixed into small solid wheels of ash plank, and turning with them; in all the low districts the cart, or "butt," has become general. The fences contribute to the general naked appearance of the surface, being commonly formed of banks of earth dug from trenches on each side, and faced with sods or stones; they are frequently planted with furze, and occasionally with white thorn and forest trees. The cattle of the south and south-west are small, seldom weighing more than $3\frac{1}{2}$ cwt.; formerly they were all black, but at present the breed is mixed, and of various colours; they generally yield abundance of milk. In the baronies of Duhallow, and Orrery and Kilmore, forming the north-western portion of the county, the Leicester breed, or, as they are here commonly called, the Limerick heifers, form the stock of some of the rich dairy farms; lands of inferior quality are stocked with a mixed breed of these and the old native black cattle. Indeed the cattle of the great northern vale are altogether superior in size and form to those of the more southern and western districts; and the same may be observed of all other kinds of live stock. The Holderness, Devon, Durham, and Ayrshire breeds have also been partially introduced. There are no large flocks of sheep, except in gentlemen's demesnes; the Leicester is the prevailing breed on good soils, and the common and half-bred Irish on inferior soils. Horses, mostly black, are, in the northern portion of the county, universally employed by the common farmers: in other parts are kept great numbers of mules of a small size, which are occasionally employed in draught, but chiefly for back loads; and being easily fed, very long lived, and able to endure great fatigue, are well adapted to the purposes of a poor peasantry in a rough country. Of the extensive woods with which this county was once adorned, numerous vestiges are found both above and beneath the surface. Although now so denuded, the oak, birch, alder, fir, and yew, and even the ash and poplar, appear to be indigenous, and of shrubs and underwoods there seems to have been a still greater variety. The former growth of firs in this part of the island is also traced by their existence in the bogs, in which they greatly exceed in number all the rest. The mountain lands, covered with little but heath and sedgy grass, form extensive tracts of comparative waste: the bogs and marshes are chiefly confined to these elevated regions, being elsewhere of very small extent. The scarcity and dearness of fuel are in many parts very disadvantageous; the maritime towns and the richer inhabitants generally obtain coal from England; while the mass of the people are compelled to seek for peat, which in many places has been exhausted; furze is often planted to supply this grievous deficiency.

The crown lands of *Pobble O'Keefe* are in the centre of a wild district on the confines of the counties of Limerick, Kerry, and Cork, which, until within these few years, had been neglected and deserted, and was nearly inaccessible for want of roads. They are estimated to contain about 9000 statute acres of undulating hilly country, the soil of which varies from a strong clay to a loamy gravel and sand on the higher grounds, with tracts of alluvial land and peat bog in the valleys and along the bottoms. The Crown is at present in actual possession of 5000 acres only; the remainder being withheld by the adjacent proprietors who claim to be entitled to the inheritance. When these lands were surrendered to the Crown they were inhabited by about 70 families residing in miserable mud cabins, the only buildings then on the property, subsisting almost entirely on the deteriorated produce of a few acres of potatoe tillage, and depending on the produce of a few cows and their harvest labour in the adjoining district for the payment of their rent. With every local facility for drainage, the lands were saturated with water, and covered with thick matted beds of moss, rushes, and heath, the growth of ages. Under these circumstances, Mr. Weale, who was deputed to survey the estate, suggested to the Commissioners of Woods and Forests that the Crown, instead of reletting or selling, should retain possession of the property, render this wild district accessible by the construction of proper roads, and cause its natural resources to be made available for ameliorating the condition of its inhabitants; and thus foster a numerous body of loyal, contented, and prosperous peasantry. Mr. Weale's benevolent suggestions have been acted upon, and under the superintendence of Mr. Griffith, the government engineer, an excellent road has been constructed from Roskeen Bridge on the Blackwater, about seven British miles above Mallow, by the collieries of Coolclough, Dromagh, and Clonbanin through the village of Boherbee, and the centre of the Crown estate, and, crossing the Blackwater near its source, it extends to Castleisland in the county of Kerry; another branching off from Clonbanin also crosses the Blackwater and extends to Shanogh Cross in the same county, where it forms the mail road from Cork to Killarney. The former line is 33½ British miles in length, and forms a direct communication between Tralee and Cork; the latter measures 9¾ miles, and forms an equally direct communication between Killarney and Mallow. These roads have been executed chiefly at the expense of Government, who advanced £17,000 of the gross estimate of £24,987; the remainder, £7937, was presented by the Grand Juries of Cork and Kerry. The roads are completed, with the exception of a portion of the line between Castleisland and King-William's-Town, which is expected to be speedily finished. The general improvement of this district already affords a striking contrast to its utterly neglected state previously to their formation. The new village, called "*King-William's-Town*," on the east bank of the Blackwater, on the road to Castleisland, with the various improvements made by Government in its vicinity, is described under that head.

The geological divisions may be classed under four principal heads. The calcareous districts comprise the greater part of the vale to the north of the Blackwater, and of the vale south-west of Cork, the vale of Imokilly extending from Midleton to Killeagh, and the vale of the Bride from Rathcormac to Tallow. Detached beds of this formation are to be met with at Moylan and Taur, near Newmarket, at Blarney, near Macroom, near Bantry, at Timoleague, at Skibbereen, and near Cloyne. It also forms the Barrel rocks on the coast near Youghal. The marble presents a great variety of colours, and is for the most part close-grained and susceptible of a good polish. That raised near Cork is grey, with white veins; that near Castle Hyde is of a darker hue, embellished with various shades and a rich display of shells. A very beautiful species is found near Castlemartyr. The district bordering on Kerry and Limerick forms a portion of the great southern coal field, many parts of which contain valuable beds of non-flaming coal, similar to that of Kilkenny, and of culm much used for burning lime. It extends from the north-western boundary of the county to the river Awbeg, running west of that river and north of the Blackwater, and lying chiefly between the limestone district and the last named river. The principal collieries, and the most important in the south of Ireland, are in the valley of the Blackwater, where beds of coal and culm are found running parallel with each other. The largest now worked is that of Dromagh, in the barony of Duhallow, 22 miles from Cork, and the property of Nicholas Leader, Esq. This colliery has been worked uninterruptedly for nearly a century; a large capital has been expended in useful works connected with it within the last fifteen years, and it is now in excellent order and capable of supplying any demand. The second division includes the mountains on the western confines of the county, and the two extensive ranges enclosing the great calcareous vale on the north side of the Blackwater, one on the north and the other on the south. The northern range is of the grauwacke formation, and is composed of various beds of red, green, and grey schist and sandstone. The mountains which separate Bantry bay from the Kenmare estuary are composed of beds of schist and sandstone of various colours, but similar in their composition to the grauwacke formations of other parts of the county. The eastern mountains have generally a thick covering of clay mixed with small stones, while those of the west are more bare and rocky: indications of iron are more or less visible in all. The third great district is that of the clay-slate, locally known as the brown and red stone, which prevails in all the middle and northern parts of the county not included in either of the above-named divisions, and which first occurs on the south on a line forming the southern boundary of the limestone district of Cork, from the western mountains eastward. To the north of the city, this stone occupies the whole of the great elevated tract between the vale of Cork and the Blackwater: though commonly of shades of red, it has some other varieties of colour as well as of texture: it affords good building stone and flags, but will not split into laminæ sufficiently thin for roofing. The last division is that of the clay-slate, called also grey-stone, the epithet grey being indicative of the prevailing hue of the rocks, the colours of which really vary considerably. It comprehends by far the greater portion of the remainder of the county, lying to the south of the vale of Cork, and contains several kinds of argillite, some of grit, a few strata of calcareous schist and a large proportion of slate. The numerous quarries along the southern coast supply Cork and most parts of the northern districts with slates for roofing, some of a good kind, but the best of a quality inferior to those imported from Wales. Extensive quarries of excellent slate have, however, been lately opened near Skull, and others at Nohaval, Ringabella, and some other places. Large pieces of quartz, generally of a circular form, and sometimes weighing three or four cwt., are frequently found lying on the surface of the ground; and near Ross there is a very curious and remarkable rock composed entirely of white quartz. Vast numbers of grit stones, often of large size, are likewise scattered over the surface, above which the rocks in the south-western parts are seen projecting in almost every field. The dip of the strata throughout the county is in most places very rapid, and everywhere very irregular. Freestone is found on Horse island near Castle-Townsend, and in small veins in several places along the coast: extensive quarries of it are worked on the Duke of Devonshire's estate, near Bandon, and on Capt. Herrick's, near Innishannon, on which latter appear also some rocks of greenstone. Of the metallic ores, that of iron is the most abundant, and appears to have been formerly smelted to a considerable extent. Lead ore has been found in many places in small veins, generally combined with quartz; in some parts it is very productive, particularly at Annacarriga and Ringabella; the latter mines are worked on a considerable scale. Copper has also been found in abundance; the whole barony of Bear produces it more or less, and near Castletown are extensive and valuable mines worked with much spirit. There are large deposits of this ore in the parish of Skull: valuable mines are now in operation on Horse island, and on the mainland, adjoining the slate quarries at Ballydehob, from which an abundance of excellent ore is obtained. Veins of copper ore are likewise found in Kilmoe, near Crookhaven, and in several other places, but are not elsewhere worked with spirit or advantage. Manganese is abundant and very pure, particularly in the neighbourhood of Ross, the Leap, Nohaval, Castleventry, and other places, but is only worked with any degree of spirit in the parish of Kilfaughnabeg, near Leap, where it is obtained very good and in large quantities. The impregnation of two small turf bogs near Rosscarbery with particles of copper, by the agency of springs, has led to an opinion that the neighbouring mountains contain abundance of it: the turf of one of these bogs was burned, and the ashes sent to Swansea where good copper was procured from them. In Whiddy island, in Bantry bay, is found a peculiar kind of black chalk.

The manufactures are various, but of trifling importance. Flannel and frieze are made in most places, some for sale, but the greater part for home use: the dyeing of the latter, chiefly of a blue colour, is carried on to a considerable extent in Carbery, and at Bandon, where a large number of hands are likewise employed in woolcombing, in the camlet and stuff trade, and in the cotton manufacture. The spinning of woollen yarn and the manufacture of camlets, stuffs, valentias, and woollen cloth of various kinds, are carried on at Blarney and Glanmire; and there is an extensive manufacture of stuffs at Cork, of calicoes at Templemartin, and of paper near Blarney, at Dripsey, and on the Bandon river near Morah: there are also iron-works near Blarney. The manufactures more immediately connected with the trade of the city of Cork, which, however, are unimportant as compared with its commerce, are described in the account of the city. The inhabitants of the maritime districts derive a principal means of support from fishing, frequently procuring not only enough for their own families, but a surplus for sale: the principal fish is hake, the season for taking which is from July to November. A singular kind of fishery is carried on during the months of Sept. and Oct. in the strands of Ross and Castlefreke, where the inhabitants of the neighbourhood assemble, when the tide is low, and dig out of the sand great numbers of a choice and peculiar kind of small eel, which are sold in the markets of Clonakilty and Ross. Clonakilty and Courtmasherry strands also supply this fish, but less plentifully; and likewise afford great quantities of cockles and muscles. The commerce of the county consists in the exportation of a great portion of its agricultural produce, and the importation of coal and other commodities for the ordinary supply of the inhabitants.

The principal river is the Blackwater, which, rising in the mountains on the confines of Kerry, runs southward along the western border of this county to the vicinity of Millstreet, where it suddenly turns eastward, and after a course of many miles, passing Mallow, Fermoy, &c., enters the county of Waterford, after a short course through which it returns to that of Cork at its most eastern extremity, where it forms the harbour of Youghal. Owing to the rapidity of its current this noble river is navigable scarcely higher than the reach of the tide; but few others present a greater variety of beautiful scenery, having on one side a range of lofty mountains, and on the other a wide tract of fertile country, both adorned by fine plantations and forming a striking and agreeable contrast. The river Lee also has its source on the confines of Kerry, in a lake called Gougane-Barra, encompassed by wild and rocky mountains: after a course of about thirty miles eastward it reaches Cork, through which city it flows in two channels, and becomes navigable for vessels of considerable burden on meeting the tide: below Cork it soon expands into a wide estuary, in which are several considerable islands, on the largest of which stands the modern town of Cove. The course of this river until it reaches the vale of Carrigdrohid, is very irregular, through hills exhibiting much variety, but no scenery approaching in luxuriance to that of the Blackwater; but here and below Cork it rivals the most celebrated rivers, in the winding variety of its channel and the cultivated richness of its shores. The Bandon has its source in the Owen mountain above Dunmanway and runs eastward through the town of Bandon, and by the beautiful village of Innishannon to Kinsale, of which place it forms the harbour. The Ilen also rises in the same mountains, and runs nearly southward to the town of Skibbereen, where it increases in size on meeting the tide, and forms the harbour of Baltimore. Among the small streams, which are exceedingly numerous, may be noticed the Awbeg, tributary to the Blackwater, and celebrated under the poetic name of "the gentle Mulla," by Spenser, who resided at Kilcolman castle in its vicinity. The only valuable fish in the rivers is salmon, of which the Blackwater affords the greatest abundance, while those of the Lee are distinguished for their superior quality, and are always in season: eels and trout are found in all, pike and perch only in a few. Their general rapidity renders the number of advantageous sites for the erection of mills very great; and boulting-mills are particularly numerous on their banks. This county has no canals; some have been proposed, but none executed, and only one begun, *viz.*, that designed to extend from Mallow to the Duhallow coal-pits, but which has long been abandoned. The roads, which were in a very bad state, have been much improved since the commencement of the present century by sums originally furnished for the most part by Government, but ultimately repaid by Grand Jury presentments, and several new lines have been constructed. The turnpike trusts, which are very few, are partly vested in trustees, and partly in the hands of contractors.

Stone circles, cromlechs (commonly called Druids' altars), raths or circular mounds of earth, caves, and stone pillars, are numerous, particularly raths. Near Clonakilty is a remarkable stone circle: close to the church is an ancient pillar, formed of a single stone, and in the vicinity an artificial cave. In the neighbourhood of Ross is an imperfect circle of smaller diameter than the preceding, and near it a cromlech, and an upright stone of the same kind as those composing the circle. In the mountains of Clondrohid is a spacious circle; at Ring, near Clonakilty, the remains of another; and fragments of several may be seen in different parts of the county. Near Glanworth is a monument of extraordinary size and form, called in Irish *Labacolly*, or the "witches' bed." In the demesne of Castlemary, near Cloyne, are the remains of a similar monument. At Rosscarbery are caves of much greater extent than that near Clonakilty. Another subterraneous vault has been discovered in the Great island in Cork harbour, between Cove and Cuskinny. There are also large caves at the Ovens, about seven miles westward from the city of Cork. Many of the raths have vaults or caves, the entrances to which lie on the eastern side, and which, after winding for some distance, terminate in a small square room in the centre. A very large rath of stone may be seen on the hill of Knockdrummon, above Castletown; and there are several of similar construction in the rocky parish of Ballyvourney. The cairns and barrows are commonly met with near waters or bogs. Of ancient round towers there are two, one at Cloyne, the other at Kineth: the former is 102 feet high, with floors and ladders perfect from bottom to top; the latter is divided into six stories, each 11 feet 9 inches high. At various places urns have been found in tumuli; and several brass trumpets were discovered in a bog between Cork and Mallow. Divers ancient remains of minor importance are still occasionally found.

The number of religious houses, of the existence of which in ancient times evidences are still found in records or in ruins, was very great. Archdall enumerates no less than sixty-nine, and states that the sites of nine of these were unknown. Most of those mentioned by him were built subsequently to the first English invasion, and owed their foundation to the descendants of the English adventurers. Those of which some vestiges still exist are at Rosscarbery, Buttevant, Ballybeg, Monanimy, Timoleague, Innisharkan, Bantry, Abbey-Mahon, Abbeystrowry, Ballyvourney, Mourne, Bridgetown, Glanworth, Ballymacadam, Red Abbey in Cork, Tracton, Coole, and Youghal. Of the ancient fortresses erected by the early English invaders and their descendants the remains are very numerous, owing to their massy strength and durability: some are of a superior description, and deficient neither in magnificence nor accommodation; but by far the greater number are composed merely of a square tower or keep usually very high, to compensate for the small size of the area by the number of stories, and containing only cold and gloomy apartments: they generally occupy bold and commanding situations, and many had an enclosed area attached, flanked by smaller towers; in size there is a great disparity, some being very small and rudely built. The castle of Kanturk is of the greatest extent and magnificence: the other principal fortresses of which there are extensive remains are those of Blarney, Macroom, and Lohort, of which the first is one of the finest edifices of the kind in the kingdom. Donneen castle, though a very small structure, deserves notice for its remarkable situation in Ross bay, on a point of land forming part of the mainland at the time of its erection, but now isolated by the force of the waves. Of fortified residences of a later age, bearing some resemblance to the English mansion-houses in the Elizabethan style, there are yet remaining three, built about the year 1638, one at Monkstown, near Cork harbour; one called Castle-Long, on Oyster haven, and the third at Ballyvireen, a little to the west of Ross. The modern residences of the nobility and gentry, among which Mitchelstown Castle, the splendid mansion of the Earl of Kingston, is pre-eminently distinguished for its extent and grandeur, are noticed in the description of the parishes in which they are respectively situated. The appearance of the farm-houses seldom affords matter for commendation; though varying in size, according to the circumstances of the occupier, they are all built on the same plan, with an open chimney at one end, and at the other a small room separated by a partition and serving both as a bed-chamber and a store-room. Few farm-yards are attached to the houses, and these are very small and confined: the corn being frequently stacked on circular stages supported by upright cap-stones: barns are never used for any other purpose than thrashing, and are consequently built very small: the common farmer, indeed, is often unprovided with either stage or barn, and thrashes his grain in the open air. The cabins of the poor have no glass windows and only one door, which is almost always left open to admit the light, and by which the smoke mostly escapes; an arrangement which, in bad weather, makes them very cold and uncomfortable. The general condition of the labouring poor is very wretched; a cabin and an acre of ground to plant potatoes in, generally held at forty or fifty shillings per annum, and under an obligation of working for the farmer at an extremely low rate, forms their chief means of subsistence. Almost their sole food throughout the year is potatoes, except that on the sea-coast they obtain fish, and boil different kinds of sea-weed. The peasantry are nevertheless hardy, active, and lively, and generally, except in the mountain districts, speak the English language. A striking similarity in some of their customs in husbandry, and some of their agricultural terms, is observed between them and the inhabitants of the south-western English counties. The most remarkable ancient customs still preserved are, the wailing over deceased persons, the waking, and the lighting of fires on Midsummer's Eve. Among the entire population there is a considerable intermixture of English blood and English surnames; but the names of the old Irish families also remain. There are several chalybeate springs, but none of medicinal celebrity except those of Mallow, which resemble the Bristol waters in taste and temperature, and are reputed to possess the same properties.

Seal.

CORK, a sea-port, city, and a county of itself, and the head of a diocese, locally in the county of CORK, of which it is the capital, and in the province of MUNSTER 51 miles (S.W. by W.) from Waterford, and 126 (S.W. by S.) from Dublin; containing 107,007 inhabitants, of which number, 84,000 are in the city and suburbs.

This place, which in extent and importance is the second city in Ireland, and is distinguished for its fine harbour, derived its ancient names *Corcach* and *Corcach-Bascoin,* signifying in the Irish language "a marshy place," from its situation on the navigable river Lee. The earliest authentic account of its origin occurs in Colgan's life of St. Nessan, to whose preceptor, St. Barr or Finbarr, is attributed the foundation of a cathedral church, to which, as the abode of that saint, such numbers of disciples resorted from all parts, that the desert in which it stood soon became the site of a considerable city. St. Nessan, according to the annals of the four masters, died in 551: if this be correct, he could not be a disciple of St. Finbarr, unless the latter flourished at a period much earlier than that stated by Sir James Ware, namely, about the year 630. The original city was built on a limestone rock, on the margin of the south branch of the river, and appears to have grown up around the cathedral and westward as far as the monastery called Gill Abbey; but what from a very early period has been more especially regarded as the city was erected on the island formed by the Lee, and its origin is ascribed to the Danes, who, after repeatedly plundering the old city and its religious establishments for more than 300 years, settled here in 1020, but did not long retain possession, being eighteen years afterwards defeated with great slaughter, and the whole of their property destroyed by fire. In 1080 the city is said to have been destroyed by lightning; and eight years afterwards the Danes of Dublin, Waterford, and Wicklow united their forces to recover possession of it, but were defeated by a large body of the natives of Oneachach, now forming the district of West Carbery. According to other accounts, Dermot, the son of Foird-healbhach O'Brien, in the same year, laid waste and plundered the town, and carried away the relics of St. Finbarr.

At the time of the English invasion, the city and the adjacent country were in the undisturbed possession of the Danes, who held them under Dermot Mac Carthy or Mac Carty, prince of Desmond, of which extensive territory this place was the capital. On the landing of Hen. II., in 1172, that chieftain was the first to acknowledge his sovereignty: attending his court on the day after his arrival, he resigned to the English monarch his city of Cork, and did him homage, and paid tribute for the rest of his possessions. The king immediately appointed an English governor, with a garrison, which being soon after obliged, from the small number of his forces, to withdraw, Mac Carty resumed possession; and the inhabitants, in 1174, fitted out 30 barques, and, proceeding to Dungarvan, fell with all their force upon Strongbow's army under Raymond le Gros, who had been plundering the neighbouring country, and had just shipped his booty for Wexford; they were, however, repulsed, and Gilbert their commander was slain. In 1177, Henry granted the surrounding territory to Milo de Cogan and Robert Fitz-Stephen, with the exception of the city and adjacent cantreds occupied by the Ostmen, which he kept in his own possession. In 1185 the city was besieged by the Irish forces under Mac Carty; Fitz-Stephen, being closely shut up within the walls, sent for assistance to Raymond le Gros, then at Wexford, and that nobleman coming promptly by sea with a reinforcement of 20 knights and 100 archers, the garrison made a sally and routed the Irish at the first onset. In the following year Dermot Mac Carty, while holding a conference with some other Irish chiefs near the city, was slain by a party of English under Theobald Fitz-Walter, the founder of the noble house of Ormonde; but, shortly after, the success which crowned the military efforts of the native Irish left this the only considerable place of strength in Munster in the possession of the English. The city was now surrounded by the troops of Desmond, and a force detached to its relief was totally defeated; but from the secret jealousies that prevailed in the Irish camp, Daniel Mac Carty, one of the principal chieftains, abandoned the siege, and the garrison was saved from destruction. The English, however, being without succour or provisions, cut off from all intercourse with their countrymen, and perpetually harassed by their enemies, were in a short time obliged to capitulate to the Prince of Desmond; but in a few years they recovered possession of the city, and strengthened it by the erection of an additional fort, which kept the men of Desmond in subjection. Shandon Castle is said to have been built by Philip de Barry, nephew of Fitz-Stephen; and in 1199, John Despenser, the first civic magistrate upon record, was made provost of Cork. From this period a great chasm occurs in the history of the place, which does not appear to have experienced any important changes, or to have been distinguished by any remarkable event, till the death here, in 1381, of the lord-deputy, Edmund Mortimer, Earl of March and Ulster, when John Colton, Dean of St. Patrick's, Dublin, was immediately appointed to that office. In 1492, Perkin Warbeck, in his assumed character of Richard duke of York, arrived here from Lisbon, and was kindly received by the citizens; after a short stay, he embarked for France, whence he returned to this city in 1495, and soon after departed for Scotland; he once more visited this place, and having enlisted a small force, set sail for Cornwall. After the disastrous termination of Warbeck's expedition, the mayor of Cork was hanged for countenancing that impostor; and in 1498, on account of the disloyalty of the citizens, the Earl of Kildare placed a strong garrison here, and compelled the principal inhabitants to swear allegiance to Hen. VII., and give bonds and pledges for their future obedience. In 1541, the mayor was one of four commissioners, appointed in lieu of the Irish brehons or judges, to hear and determine all controversies among the natives of this province. In 1568, the lady of Sir Warham St. Leger, lord-president of Munster, was, during the absence of her husband, besieged by the insurgents in the city, but was relieved by the lord-deputy, Sir Henry Sidney, with 400 men from England;

and in 1575 the lord-deputy again came hither with his forces, and remained six weeks. During this period Queen Elizabeth presented Maurice Roche, mayor of Cork, for his able services against the insurgents, with a silver collar of the order of St. Simplicius, which is still preserved by his descendant, Thos. C. Kearney, Esq., at Garrettstown.

At the commencement of the great Desmond insurrection, the city became the head-quarters of the English forces, and Sir John Perrot arrived with six ships of war for the protection of the port against the threatened assault of the Spaniards. In 1598 Sir Thomas Norris, vice-president of Munster, was obliged to shut himself up here for security against the insurgents sent from Ulster by O'Neill; and in 1601 the lord-deputy assembled at this place the army destined to expel the Spaniards from Kinsale, which was soon after reinforced with 2000 men from England. At this period the city is described by Camden as "of an oval figure surrounded by walls, environed and intersected by the river, which is passable only by bridges, and consisting of one straight street continued by a bridge; it is, however, a little trading town of great resort, but so beset by rebellious neighbours as to require as constant watch as if continually besieged." On the death of Queen Elizabeth, in 1602, the mayor and corporation refused at first to proclaim the accession of James; the citizens took arms, and set guards upon the gates to prevent any soldiers from entering the town, disarmed the Protestants, refused to admit Sir Charles Wilmot, who came with his army to quell the disturbance, and determined to acknowledge no authority but that of the mayor; they then proceeded to organize a plan of defence, and, among other outrages, fired upon Shandon Castle, then the residence of Lady Carew, and upon the bishop's palace, where were assembled the commissioners to whom the government of the province had been entrusted. The commissioners sent to Halbowling Fort, in the harbour, for a supply of artillery; but the citizens manned some boats to take that fort, and, if possible, to intercept the supply; and though the attempt was frustrated, several men were killed on both sides; and they succeeded, after some difficulty, in demolishing the Queen's Fort, on the south side of the city. On the 11th of May the lord-lieutenant marched with all his forces into the city, and after condemning some of the leaders to punishment, and leaving a strong garrison, proceeded to Limerick, where similar disturbances had taken place. On this occasion the Queen's Fort was rebuilt as a citadel, to keep the citizens in subjection; and further, to prevent a recurrence of these outrages, the city and liberties were, in 1608, constituted a distinct and independent county. In 1613, James I., in a letter to Sir Arthur Chichester, proposed that Cork should be divided into two counties; but the scheme was opposed by the Earl of Cork, who had lent the lord-president Villiers £500 towards repairing the forts of Cork and Waterford, by which means they were put into a state of defence. In 1636 the Algerines, who had infested this coast five years previously, reappeared, and, aided by the French, spread terror among the inhabitants. The Earl of Strafford, in a letter dated Sept. 15th of that year, states that "the Turks still annoy this coast; they came of late into Cork harbour, took a boat with eight fishermen, and gave chase to two others that saved themselves among the rocks, the townsmen looking on without the power or means to assist them." In March, 1642, the city was blockaded by the insurgents under Gen. Barry and Lord Muskerry; but part of the garrison, making a sally, pursued a detachment of them to their camp at Rochfortstown, where, without the loss of a single man, they killed 200 of the enemy, put their whole army to flight, and took all their baggage and carriages. In 1644 two conspiracies to betray the city to the insurgents, at the head of one of which was the mayor, were discovered and suppressed. On the approach of Cromwell, in 1649, the inhabitants embraced the cause of the parliament. In 1688 a large party of Irish horse and foot, under Lieut.-Gen. Mac Carty, entered the city at midnight, disarmed the Protestant inhabitants, plundered the houses of the most wealthy, and committed similar excesses in all the neighbouring villages. James II. arrived here shortly after; and in the autumn of 1689 the Protestant inhabitants were seized and imprisoned by Lord Clare, the governor, and many of them were sent to the neighbouring castles of Blarney and Macroom. In September, 1690, the city was besieged by the army of Wm. III., under the command of the Earl of Marlborough and the Duke of Wirtemberg; and on this occasion, notwithstanding an agreement with the inhabitants to the contrary, the suburbs were burnt by the governor Mac Elligott; the fortresses called the Catt and Shandon Castle were taken without resistance; and from both these, as well as from a battery near the Red Abbey, and from the steeple of the cathedral church, the south fort and the city were assailed. A breach being made by the cannon at Red Abbey, the troops advanced to the assault; on which the garrison, after a siege of five days, surrendered prisoners of war to the number of 4500, of whom many afterwards made their escape, and 160 were blown up in the Breda man of war, then lying in the harbour. In marching to the assault, the Duke of Grafton, who had entered as a volunteer in William's army, was killed. The royal troops took possession of the city on the 29th of September; and the magistrates, resuming their offices, proclaimed King William and Queen Mary. The annals of the city during the period subsequent to the Revolution, record little deserving of special notice. In 1746, the militia of Cork consisted of 3000 foot and 200 horse, together with a well-appointed company of 100 gentlemen, commanded by Col. H. Cavendish. In 1787 the city was honoured by the presence of the king, then Prince William Henry, commander of the ship Pegasus, which lay at Cove: two years after, a flood, occasioned by a heavy fall of rain, immediately following a storm of snow, which had continued for several days, laid the whole of the streets under water, to the height of five feet, and in some places of seven; several houses were washed away, many injured, and immense damage inflicted on property. The first mail coach arrived in Cork from Dublin in 1789.

About the commencement of the 17th century the city consisted of only one principal street, now called North and South Main-street, and it appears to have undergone but little extension or improvement till the reign of Wm. III., when the corporation began to form new streets and erect public buildings. In 1701 it had only two entrances, the north, leading from Dublin, and the south, from Kinsale; and two bridges, the north and the south, built of wood, and which, by an act of the 1st of Geo. I., cap. 19, the corporation were empowered to rebuild of stone. From the records of the corporation and a plan of the city it appears that, about the middle of the last century, a navigable branch of the river ran down the centre of the South Mall, and that the ground on which the houses forming the south side of that street now stand was an island, beyond which was another small tract called Goose island, now occupied by Charlotte quay; and for many years subsequently another branch ran through Patrick-street, up which vessels sailed at every tide. A map published in 1766 shows that the fields then reached down to the north branch of the river; and the neighbourhood of Ballynamocht, to the east of the Dublin road, was under cultivation. Its rapid advancement may be attributed to the great capabilities of its almost matchless haven, which renders it the emporium of commerce for this part of the country; and the numerous improvements that have since taken place are fully commensurate with its increased importance. It is generally regarded as consisting of the city, the suburbs, and the liberties, all which constitute the county of the city. One mile west of the cathedral the river Lee divides into two branches, insulating a tract about two English miles in length and half a mile in breadth, on which the ancient city was built; and uniting again at its eastern extremity, expands into a noble estuary a mile broad, forming the commencement of the harbour. But that which is now considered as the city includes a district stretching to a considerable distance north and south of these two branches, in which numerous elegant streets have been recently formed, and its limits are progressively extending. The smaller channels which ran through the streets presented at low water a mass of mud, but being some years since arched over by the corporation, the most spacious and elegant streets have been formed above them. Across the two main branches of the river, within the city, are nine stone bridges communicating with the district which, in 1813, was defined for the purpose of local taxation, under the provisions of an act of the 53rd of Geo. III., and is marked out by stones set up in various directions, separating it from the liberties: this district comprises an area of 2379 statute acres, the whole is generally called "the city," and 10,263 houses, of which 8212 are dwelling-houses, and 2051 are warehouses, stores, and other buildings.

The general appearance of the city, particularly since its recent extensive improvements, is picturesque and cheerful; the principal streets are spacious and well paved; most of the houses are large and well built, chiefly of clay-slate fronted with roofing slate, which gives them a clean though sombre appearance; others are built of the beautiful grey limestone of the neighbourhood, and some are faced with cement; those in the new streets are principally of red brick. The streets are now made and repaired under the directions of the commissioners of wide streets, originally constituted a body corporate by an act of the 5th of Geo. III., cap. 24, with extensive powers conferred by that and subsequent acts; and nearly £6000 is annually expended in paving, cleansing, and improving them. The privilege of licensing vehicles of every description plying for hire within the city is vested in these commissioners, who have framed a code of by-laws and a table of rates for regulating them. The city is lighted with gas by the General United Gas Company of London, who in 1825 contracted with the commissioners of wide streets to supply the city and suburbs with coal gas for 21 years, at £3130. 13. 4. per annum: the works are situated on the south branch of the river, and afford an excellent supply. The inhabitants are provided with water from the river Lee, raised by two large water wheels into a capacious reservoir, and thence distributed by metal pipes through all the lower parts of the city: it is conveyed into each house on payment of £2. 2. per annum, but application is about to be made to parliament for an act to empower the Company to regulate the rate according to the value of the houses, as provided by the English and Scottish acts. The works, situated on the north side of Wellington bridge, one mile above the town, were originally constructed by the corporation; but the undertaking was some years since divided into 100 shares, of which 25 were retained by that body, and the remainder purchased by private individuals: it is intended to construct a reservoir on a higher level, from which the water may be conveyed into every house in the city. Until the general establishment of the constabulary system this city had no regularly constituted police; but a force consisting of one officer and 80 men was introduced, for whose accommodation the guard-houses in Tucky-street and Shandon have been fitted up: there is not yet any public nightly watch, but private watchmen are appointed.

Of the bridges over the Lee several are modern and elegant structures. Patrick's bridge, the last over the northern branch, and to which vessels sail up, was erected in 1789 from a design by Mr. M. Shanahan, by a company of shareholders, and was a pay bridge, with a portcullis, which was removed by the commissioners of wide streets in 1823: it consists of three elliptic arches surmounted by an open balustrade, built entirely of hewn limestone, and connects the noble line of quays extending on both sides of the river through the principal part of the city. North bridge, over the same branch, was built of stone early in the last century, at the expense of the corporation, on the site of an ancient wooden bridge, which, with another of the same kind at the southern extremity of the main street, formed for ages the only accessible communication between the town and country: it was thoroughly repaired and widened by the corporation in 1831, when two foot-paths of cast iron were formed, and it now opens a ready communication between the North Main-street, the butter markets, and the populous districts of Shandon. Wellington bridge, at the western extremity of the city, near the termination of the Mardyke, and close to the division of the main channel of the Lee, is a noble structure of hewn limestone, erected by Messrs. Pain, from a design by Richard Griffiths, Esq.: it consists of a centre arch of 50 feet and two side arches each of 45 feet span, with solid parapets, the piers of the arches sunk in caissons; and opens a fine communication with the new western road, near George the Fourth's bridge, which here crosses the south branch of the river. This latter bridge is a plain structure of one arch, built in 1820 entirely of hewn limestone. Midway between it and the Lee mills is a handsome bridge of one arch of 50 feet span, which by a raised causeway leads from the new western road to the county gaol and house of correction. Clarke's bridge, built by the corporation in 1726, is an ancient structure of red clay-slate, communicating between Great George's-street and the cathedral. South bridge, built also by the corporation a few years previously, on the site of the ancient wooden bridge, is a neat structure of three segmental arches of hewn limestone, and has been widened at their expense by the addition of two foot-paths. Parliament bridge, a handsome edifice of one lofty arch, with open parapets, built of hewn limestone, connects the South Mall with Sullivan's quay, to which vessels of considerable burden sail up. Anglesey bridge, erected in 1830 by Sir Thos. Deane, from a design by Mr. Griffiths, is a very handsome structure of hewn limestone, with parapets of cast iron; and consists of two elliptic arches 44 feet in span, with a rise of eleven feet, having between them a waterway of 32 feet crossed by two parallel drawbridges of cast iron, which are raised to admit vessels above it, and are designed to prevent the confusion resulting from the numerous cars and other vehicles which pass over it, by compelling each to keep its proper side. This bridge, which is the last on the southern branch of the river, was built at an expense of more than £9000, defrayed by the commissioners of the new corn market: it is the thoroughfare to Blackrock, Douglas, and Passage, and opens an approach from Warren's-place and the eastern end of the South Mall, on the north, to the new corn market on the south side of the river.

The scenery around the city is exceedingly beautiful, particularly on the east, where two lines of road, called Upper and Lower Glanmire roads, have been formed along the north bank of the river, one on the elevated ground and the other close to the strand; and a variety of new streets, terraces, crescents, and detached villas, have been erected on the sides and summits of the gentle acclivities, commanding magnificent views of the river Lee, the city, Blackrock, and the beautiful and fertile district bounded by the hills of Carrigaline. The scenery on the south side of the river, from Anglesey bridge to Blackrock and Passage, is pleasingly undulating and diversified; elegant houses, with lawns, gardens, and plantations sloping to the water's edge, and commanding delightful views over the noble expanse of water to the lofty and verdant hills of Rathcoony, have been built throughout the entire space. The beauty of the scenery, the mildness and salubrity of the climate, the abundance and purity of the water, the fertility of the soil, and the excellence of the markets, have induced many wealthy families from distant parts to settle here, who have erected very elegant villas and cottages in fanciful situations and in every variety of architectural style. Besides those named under the respective heads of Blackrock, Douglas, Glanmire, and other places in the vicinity of the city, the following are worthy of notice; Woodville, the residence of Gen. Sir Thos. Arbuthenott; Tivoli House, of J. Morgan, Esq.; Eastview, of J. Leycester, Esq., a very pretty villa in the cottage style, commanding a splendid view down the river towards Passage, and containing many valuable paintings and other specimens of virtû; Summerhill, of G. Newenham, Esq.; Belleview, of J. W. Topp, Esq.; Shanakill, of D. Leahy, Esq.; Silver Spring, of J. Cummins, Esq.; Hyde Park, of J. S. Murphy, Esq.; Clifton, of N. Murphy, Esq.; Wilton, of C. H. Leslie, Esq.; Hyde Park House, of J. Morrow, Esq.; Temple Ville, of D. Murphy, Esq.; Carolina, of Mrs. Carroll; Trafalgar, of T. Lyons, Esq.; Beach Hill, of M. Salmon, Esq.; Vostersberg, of W. M. Reeves, Esq.; Ballynamote, of J. Chatterton, Esq.; Woodview, of D. Hamblin, Esq.; Doughcloyne House, of D. Sarsfield, Esq.; Lehannah, of T. Curtis, Esq.; Lehannah, of C. Matthews, Esq.; Somerstown, of J. Swiney, Esq.; Doughcloyne, of J. Simpson, Esq.; Chetwind, of J. Forrest, Esq.; Strawberry Hill, of W. R. Westropp, Esq.; Bruin Lodge, of R. Beare, Esq.; Woodhill, of W. Fitzgibbon, Esq.; Glanmire Rock, of W. Adams, Esq.; The Castle, of Ald. Gibbings; Cottage, of Kieffe O'Kieffe, Esq.; Mount Vernon, of E. Ronayne, Esq.; Castle White, of J. Cope, Esq.; Snugborough, of T. Nelson, Esq.; and Ardmanning, of W. D. White, Esq. The entrance from Dublin, by Patrick's bridge, is remarkably striking and picturesque: the road winds through the beautiful vale of Glanmire and enters that of the Lee opposite the castle of Blackrock, where it joins that from Waterford, Youghal, Midleton, and Cove, and continues westward beneath the plantations of Lota Beg and the lofty and fertile hills of Rathcoony, studded with numerous detached villas commanding the most delightful views of the noble estuary. The approach from Limerick is by a new line of road carried through a fine undulating country; at a short distance from Blackpool it crosses a pleasant valley by a viaduct supported by six lofty arches. The entrance from the west and south is by the new western road parallel with the Mardyke, and midway between the two main branches of the Lee; it crosses George the Fourth's bridge, and is one of the best improvements in or around the city. The approach from Cove, by way of Passage, is through the village of Douglas, passing numerous elegant villas and cottages, and entering the city by Anglesey bridge.

The principal promenade is the Mardyke, a fine raised walk a mile long, extending through the meadows midway between two branches of the river, and shaded by a double row of lofty flourishing elms, from which are extensive and varied views. The Botanic Garden, for some time a favourite place of resort, was sold in 1826, and has been converted by its proprietor, the Very Rev. Theobald Matthews, Provincial of the Capuchins or Reformed Franciscans, into a cemetery laid out in the style of the Père la Chaise, at Paris: the graves are distributed over the greater part amid the shrubs, plants, and flowers brought hither at a very great expense by the original proprietors; the ground is intersected by broad gravel walks, and there are several handsome monuments. Among these, one of the most remarkable is that erected over a vault belonging to Messrs. Murphy and O'Connor: it consists of a sarcophagus of Portland stone resting on a base of limestone. On the sarcophagus is the figure of a mourning angel, as large as life, of white Italian marble, wrought in Rome by Mr. John Hogan, a native of Cork. At the bottom of the Grand Parade close to the south branch of the river, is a handsome equestrian statue of Geo. II. On a commanding eminence to the north-east of the city are the barracks for infantry and cavalry, erected in 1806 by the late Abraham Hargrave, Esq., and conveniently adapted to the accommodation of 156 officers and 1994 men, with stabling for 232 horses; the grounds for parade and exercise are spacious, and there is an hospital capable of receiving 120 patients. In the south suburb is also a military hospital for about 130 invalids, affording the advantage of change of air for convalescents, but kept up by Government principally as a *point d'appui* to the surrounding hills; it was by a ball from a battery on this spot that the Duke of Grafton was killed during the siege in 1695. In the South Mall is an elegant house for the county club, built in 1826 by Messrs. Pain, at an expense of about £4000; the front consists of a rustic basement, from which rise three engaged columns of the composite order supporting an entablature and cornice; on the ground floor are a public dining-room 40 feet long by 20 wide, a private dining-room of smaller dimensions, and several apartments for the secretary and steward; and on the first floor are reading, billiard, and card rooms, above which are bed-chambers. The club consists of about 300 members, each of whom pays £5 on admission and a subscription of £5 per annum; naval and military officers are admitted on payment of the annual subscription only. There are also two other club-houses, namely, Daly's, in the Grand Parade, and the Tucky-street club-house, at the corner of that street and the Grand Parade. The theatre, a well-arranged edifice erected in 1759 by S. Barry and H. Woodward, both celebrated actors in their day, is opened annually for a few months; and balls, concerts, races, and regattas occasionally take place.

The Cork county and city Horticultural Society, established under the patronage of the Duchess of Kent, published its first report in January 1835, by which it appears that, during the three first exhibitions, 233 prizes were awarded to successful candidates for the best specimens of vegetables, fruits, flowers, and herbaceous plants; and according to the 2nd report published Jan. 1836, 274 were awarded: the society is liberally supported by subscription, and promises to be eminently conducive to the horticultural and agricultural improvement of the district. An agricultural society was formed in 1836. The Cork Library Society, in the South Mall, was founded in 1790, and the library contains a valuable collection of more than 10,000 volumes in the various departments of science, art, and general literature; it is managed by a committee who meet every alternate week for the selection of books, the admission of members by ballot, and the transaction of ordinary business. The Cork Royal Institution was founded in 1803 by subscription among private gentlemen of the city and county, for diffusing the knowledge and facilitating the introduction of all improvements in the arts and manufactures, and for teaching by lectures the application of science to the common purposes of life. The obvious usefulness of such an institution recommended it to the favourable consideration of Government, and in 1807 the proprietors obtained a royal charter of incorporation and a parliamentary grant of £2000 per annum. For several years lectures were annually given on Natural Philosophy, Natural History, Chemistry, Mineralogy, Botany, and other useful branches of Science; but in 1830 the grant was withdrawn, and the lectures have been since discontinued. On withholding the grant, Government presented to the proprietary the old custom-house, a fine spacious building in Nelson-place, subject to a rent of £65 per ann., to which the Crown was previously liable. There are at present, belonging to the institution, museums of natural history and mineralogy, a scientific and medical library containing more than 5000 volumes, philosophical and chemical apparatus, and a splendid series of casts from the antique. Several efforts have been made to convert this institution into a collegiate establishment, which the situation of Cork in a populous district remote from the metropolis and surrounded by numerous large towns, and the opportunities of practical study afforded by its Medical and Surgical Charitable Institutions and the existence of a School of Physic and Surgery, render peculiarly desirable, and would compensate for the loss which the inhabitants of the city and surrounding districts have sustained by the withdrawal of the parliamentary grant. The Cork Scientific and Literary Society was founded or revived in 1834, after the dissolution of a former society about ten years previously, and consists of about 90 members and 15 subscribers who pay 10*s*. per ann.; the former are required to produce in rotation an essay at each meeting of the society, which is read on that evening and discussed at the next meeting, in which discussions the subscribers are permitted to take part: the meetings are held in the lecture-room of the Cork Royal Institution. The meetings of the Cuvierian society, formed in 1835, are held in the same place. The object of this society is the promotion of a friendly intercourse among those who wish to cultivate science, literature, and the fine arts, so as, by personal communication and occasional courses of lectures, to diffuse more generally the advantages of intellectual and scientific pursuits. The Society of Arts was established about the year 1815 for the advancement of painting and sculpture, and was at first liberally encouraged; George IV., when Prince Regent, presented to the society, in 1820, a very valuable collection of casts from the antique; the students were numerous, and were instructed in drawing, and a course of lectures on Anatomy as connected with the art of design was regularly delivered; but the funds becoming in a few years insufficient to defray the expenses, the casts presented by the King were transferred to the Royal Institution. The society, however, still exists, and affords patronage and assistance to youthful genius; Dr. Woodroffe continues to give lectures on the Anatomy of expression, the Philosophy of the human body, and on Phrenology. The Mechanics' Institute was founded in 1824, and has a library of 1500 volumes, a reading-room, and two schools, one for instruction in the arts and sciences, and one for design; there are 210 members, and lectures on scientific subjects are occasionally delivered. The school of Physic and Surgery was founded by Dr. Woodroffe in 1811, and continues to flourish; lectures on Anatomy, Physiology, the theory and practice of Surgery and Midwifery, Materia-Medica, practice of Physic and Clinical Surgery are delivered during the winter half-year: this School is connected with the South Infirmary and the Hospital of the House of Industry, and, being duly recognised by the Royal College of Surgeons in London, the Apothecaries' Hall, Dublin, and the Army and Navy Medical Boards, has been of great benefit to medical students of the south of Ireland. Certificates of attendance at Dr. Cesar's lectures on Anatomy and Materia-Medica, delivered at the Royal Institution, are recognised by the Royal College of Surgeons, London, at Apothecaries' Hall, by the Army and Navy Boards, the Faculty of Physicians and Surgeons of Glasgow, and many continental universities.

The trade of Cork, previously to the late war with France, consisted chiefly in the exportation of butter and beef for the supply of the British navy, to the West Indies, and to the ports of France, Spain, and the Mediterranean; and of hides and tallow chiefly to England. At that time the surrounding districts were nearly all under pasturage and scarcely produced sufficient corn for the supply of their inhabitants; the lands were grazed by vast herds of cattle, and the quantity of beef cured for exportation was perhaps ten times as great as at present; but from the impetus since given to agriculture, a considerable portion of the land has been brought under tillage, and an extensive trade in corn and flour consequently established. This was one of the first places in which the interests of trade and commerce were taken under the protection of the merchants themselves, who established a committee consisting of fourteen merchants who export butter, seven butter merchants who collect it from the various farms, and three tanners, elected annually by their respective trades: this body, under the simple designation of the "Committee of Merchants," is in all respects similar to the Chamber of Commerce in other parts; it has existed as the accredited organ of the trading community and been recognised as such in several local acts since the year 1729, and communicates with the public authorities on subjects connected with the trade of Ireland. The butter trade, which is considered as the most important in the province of Munster, and is carried on in this city to a greater extent than in any other part of the united kingdom, is conducted by two distinct classes of merchants, of whom the one, called the butter merchants, purchase the butter from the dairy farmers, or receive it at the current price for a certain per centage, taking their chance of a rise or fall in the market; and the other, called the export merchants, ship it either on order or on their own account. This trade was formerly regulated by local acts emanating from the Committee of Merchants, under whose superintendence the Cork butter obtained a preference in all foreign markets; and though by representations to parliament from other parts of Ireland all restrictions have been removed, the old regulations are still retained by a compact among the merchants; and the butter is brought to the same weigh-house, where, after its quality has been ascertained by sworn inspectors annually appointed, it is weighed and the firkins are each branded with the quality and weight and with the private mark of the inspector. The weigh-house is capable of receiving 4000 firkins for examination at one time; and the quantity which passed through it annually on an average of four years ending April 30th, 1835, was 263,765 firkins; in the last of these years it exceeded 279,000 firkins, and the trade is gradually increasing. The business of the weigh-house is conducted under the superintendence of a general weigh-master and a sub-committee of export and butter merchants, who appoint inspectors, scalesmen, and other officers. At present there are engaged in this branch of trade between 60 and 70 merchants: the butter is made principally in the counties of Cork, Kerry, and Limerick, particularly Kerry; the best in quality, in proportion to the quantity, comes from the counties of Cork and Limerick, especially the latter and the northern part of the former, where the dairy farmers are more wealthy, their farms more extensive, and the quality of the soil better than in Kerry or the southern part of Cork. Butter made in Kerry is considered more suitable for warm climates than that of the same quality made in Limerick, from the inferior fertility of the soil and the numerous springs of soft water with which the former county abounds. The carriers employed in conveying the butter from the remote dairy districts take back grocery and other articles of domestic consumption; and this important branch of trade also furnishes constant employment to a numerous body of coopers, not only in the manufacture of firkins, but in what is called trimming or preparing the article for exportation, that which is intended for warm climates requiring the cooperage to be so tight as to exclude the air and confine the pickle. The corn trade of Cork may now be classed among the more important branches of its commerce: the quantity exported annually on an average of four years ending Dec. 25th, 1835, was 72,654 barrels of wheat, 126,519 barrels of oats, and 1749 barrels of barley; and very large quantities of barley and oats are consumed in the distilleries and breweries of the city. A new corn-market was built in 1833 by trustees appointed under an act of the 3rd of Geo. IV., cap. 79: it is a quadrangular enclosure, 460 feet in length and 330 in breadth, situated beyond the south branch of the river near Anglesey bridge; the area, which is enclosed with a high stone wall, is divided into twelve covered walks for the purchasers and thirteen carriage ways for unloading the corn, which is protected from rain by the projecting roofs of the walks; at right angles with these, and extending the whole breadth of the area, is a covered space for weighing; and there are appropriate offices for the collector and the clerks. The expense of its erection, with that of the bridge leading to it, amounted to £17,460, of which the government advanced £4615 towards building the bridge, and the commissioners of parliamentary loans lent £10,000; two individual proprietors of ground in its vicinity, besides giving the site rent-free, contributed £2500 towards the building, which, with the erection of the bridge, is calculated to augment the value of the residue of their property. The quantity of agricultural produce brought to the market is rapidly increasing: in the year ending Aug. 31st, 1835, 83,938 barrels of wheat, 91,743 barrels of barley, 120,597 barrels of oats, and 23,483 carcasses of pork, were weighed here. The increase of tillage before noticed naturally diminished the curing of beef, but it greatly increased that of pork: the provision trade, though diminished, may yet be regarded as the next in importance to that of corn: the government contracts for the navy are still for the greater part executed by the merchants of Cork, though a large portion of the beef is frequently supplied from Dublin; and the provisions for the East India and other trading ships are also chiefly supplied by them. The curing of hams and bacon, formerly confined to Belfast and Waterford, has within the last few years been extensively carried on both here and at Limerick, the breed of hogs being now quite as good in the southern as in the northern and midland counties. The supply of plantation stores for the West Indian proprietors, which was formerly very extensive, has much decreased; and the shipments of provisions to the West Indies as merchandise have dwindled into insignificance, and will now scarcely remunerate the adventurer. The provision trade of the port has also sustained considerable diminution from throwing open to foreigners the supplies of Newfoundland, to which colony upwards of 30,000 barrels of pork were exported annually, chiefly from Cork and Waterford, besides flour, oatmeal, butter, bacon, candles, leather, boots and shoes, and other commodities, and returns were made in fish and oil; this branch of commerce has been almost entirely usurped by the ports of Hamburgh, Copenhagen, and the United States, to which the English schooners previously freighted with the above cargoes either here or at Waterford now go. The quantity of provisions sent from this port on an average of three years ending with 1835 was 16,469 tierces, 19,216 barrels and 5604 half-barrels of beef and pork, and 23,492 bales of bacon annually. The introduction of steam navigation has much increased the exportation of flour to London, Bristol, and Liverpool, the quantity of flour exported on an average of four years ending with 1835 was 79,119 sacks annually. The trade in live stock (chiefly black cattle, sheep, and pigs), in poultry and eggs, and the produce of the river fisheries, has also been greatly promoted by the same means, and is now very extensive. On an average 1200 pigs and half a million of eggs are sent off weekly; and not only is the salmon of the Blackwater, the Bride, the Lee, and the Bandon sent to England by steamers, but that of the rivers in the most remote parts of Kerry is sent hither cured in kits for exportation. The salmon fishery of the Lee has long been celebrated both for the quantity and quality of the fish, which are in season during the whole year, and are distinguished for the superior excellence of their flavour; but the indiscriminate method of taking them with weirs, traps, and nets has nearly destroyed the fishery.

The trade with the Mediterranean consists principally in the importation of bark, valonia, shumac, brimstone, sweet oil, liquorice, raisins, currants and other fruit, marble, and various small articles. The importation of wine is steady and considerable, but not so extensive as formerly, in consequence of the increased consumption of home-distilled spirits: the quantity imported on an average of three years ending with 1835 was 398 pipes, 74 butts, 701 hogsheads, 517 quarter-casks, and 246 cases annually. From 5000 to 6000 tons of salt are annually imported from St. Ubes, exclusively of a large quantity brought from Liverpool. The trade with St. Petersburgh, Riga, Archangel, and occasionally with Odessa, is chiefly in tallow, hemp, flax, linseed, iron, hides, bristles, and isinglass, but is not very extensive: and as a considerable portion of the tallow and part of the hemp comes indirectly through London and Liverpool, the returns of these articles and others imported in a similar manner are necessarily imperfect: the estimated importations of tallow average about 1580 hogsheads, and of hemp 400 tons, annually. The Baltic trade in timber was gradually declining until the practice of bringing it in through Halifax at the colonial duty of 10*s.* per load was resorted to. Large quantities of timber are brought from Canada, the trade with which is flourishing: the staves and potashes formerly brought from New York and Baltimore now come mostly from Quebec, though several cargoes of staves have been recently imported from the United States viâ St. John's (New Brunswick) and Nova Scotia. Flax seed, formerly imported to a considerable extent direct from New York, is now brought from the Baltic and Odessa, and is derived indirectly from England; the quantity of tobacco that paid duty at the custom-house, on an average of three years ending with 1835, was 647,000 lb. annually. The decline of the outward West India trade, and the facility of procuring supplies from the English ports by steamers, have considerably diminished the direct importation of sugar and other articles of West Indian produce: the quantity of raw sugar annually imported, on an average of three years ending with 1835, amounted to 3109 hhds., 468 tierces, 596 barrels, and 5654 bags; and of refined sugar, to 546 hhds. and 486 tierces. The quantity of herrings now imported, almost exclusively for home consumption, is on an average of three years 17,904 barrels annually. Vast quantities were formerly imported from Scotland and Gottenburgh, and after being repacked here, were shipped off to the West Indies, being found to keep good in that climate better than those from any other port; but the Scots sending for men from Cork soon learned the peculiar mode of packing them, and the trade from this port was discontinued. Fish is imported from Newfoundland, Labrador, and Gaspe in considerable quantities, amounting on the average to 500 tons annually. Many of the merchants are of opinion that the deep sea line fishery on the Nymph Bank, and that in the bay of Galway, if properly conducted, would not only furnish a sufficient supply for home consumption, but even a surplus for exportation. The direct foreign trade of the port having been very much diminished since the introduction of steam navigation, the wholesale dealer in almost every article has been greatly injured; the retailer can now, without holding stock, ensure a weekly supply by steam from Liverpool or Bristol, and, both as regards foreign produce and articles of British growth or manufacture, has thus become an importer; even if he could purchase equally as cheap from the Cork merchant, he prefers announcing his importations in the daily newspapers, by which his own trade is benefited in proportion as that of the wholesale dealer is injured. This diversion of the channel of trade has consequently caused a depression in the value of large warehouses, formerly used as stores for merchandise. But notwithstanding the introduction of steam navigation, the tonnage of sailing vessels belonging to the port has, within the last 25 years, greatly increased; and a manifest improvement has taken place in the principle of their construction. Formerly the vessels built here were considered so inferior that underwriters were reluctant to insure them, and even the Cork merchants preferred shipping valuable cargoes in others; now the London traders of the highest class, which are insured at Lloyd's for a less premium than other vessels, have been built in the river of Cork. By far the greater portion of the tonnage is, however, employed in the Canadian timber and Welsh coal trades, the latter of which was formerly for the most part carried on in Welsh vessels. The coal trade is very considerable: a local duty of one shilling per ton late currency is levied for the support of the Foundling Hospital on all coal brought into the port, amounting to about 120,000 tons annually. The number of registered vessels belonging to the port, in Jan. 1836, was 302, of the aggregate burden of 21,514 tons, and employing 1684 men: this enumeration includes vessels trading from Kinsale and Youghal, which are now registered as belonging to Cork. There are two ship-building yards, each having a patent slip in which vessels of 500 tons can be hauled up and repaired: vessels of every size to 400 tons have been built in these yards. At Passage there are two ship-building yards, one of them having a very fine dry dock: these establishments employ about 200 hands. During the year ending Jan. 5th, 1836, 164 British ships of the aggregate burden of 29,124 tons, and 27 foreign ships of 2912 tons aggregate burden, employed in the foreign trade, entered inwards; and 69 British and 20 foreign ships, of the aggregate burden of 10,098 tons, cleared outwards: in the trade with Great Britain, 2246 vessels of all kinds, of 226,318 tons aggregate burden, entered inwards, and 1384 of 166,516 tons aggregate, cleared outwards: and in the intercourse with Irish ports, 406 vessels, of 18,564 tons aggregate burden, entered inwards; and 596 of 20,384 tons aggregate cleared outwards. The amount of duties paid at the custom-house for the same year was £216,446. 1. 7. and of Excise for the same period £252,452. 14. 6½. The superior facilities afforded by steam navigation have given an extraordinary impulse to the trade of this port: the agricultural produce of all the western parts of the country south of Limerick is brought hither for exportation, in return for which, groceries, woollen and cotton goods, and other commodities are received. The completion of the great Western railway from Bristol to London will tend to a still further extension of this profitable system of interchange, by expediting the conveyance of live stock, provisions, and other Irish produce to London. In 1821, two steam-boats were employed by a Scottish Company to trade between Cork and Bristol, but, from drawing too much water, did not remain on this station more than six months, after which the boats of the Bristol Company traded for some time, and in 1825 the St. George's Company introduced a line of packets between Cork and Liverpool, and afterwards between Cork and Bristol, which have been ever since continued, and have engrossed the entire carrying trade of the port by steam. The capital of this company amounts to £300,000, subscribed in shares, of which one-third are held by Cork proprietors. It now employs seven vessels of about 500 tons' burden and 250-horse power each; two of these ply to Bristol, one to Liverpool, three to London, and one to Dublin: all carry passengers, goods, and cattle. The company's office, built on Penrose's quay in 1832, is a neat building with an entrance porch of the Doric order surmounted by a pediment on four Ionic columns, above which is a sculpture of St. George and the Dragon. Four smaller steam-boats ply daily between Cork and Cove. The American Steam-Packet Company's vessels will touch here on their way to and from Liverpool. Rail-roads to Cove, Passage, and Limerick, are in contemplation.

The noble harbour of Cork, which gave rise to the motto of the city, "*Statio bene fida carinis*," is admirably adapted to all the purposes of the most extended commerce; and from its convenient situation, the perfect security with which numerous fleets may winter in a land-locked basin, and its excellent anchorage at all times, it became in time of war the rendezvous of large fleets and convoys, and the port from which the British navy was supplied with all kinds of provisions cured and prepared in a superior manner. The number of small craft on the coast, and of fishing hookers, pilot boats, lighters, and pleasure yachts in the river; the dense population of its shores, inured to hardships and privations, and other considerations, tended to render Cork in the estimation of British statesmen one of the most important places in the empire: and the vast expenditure of public money for supplies during the war; the detention at Cove, sometimes for months together, of large fleets of war, and powerful expeditions, with vast numbers of merchant vessels; the sums laid out on public works in the harbour, the barracks at Cork, Ballincollig, and Fermoy, the powder-mills at Ballincollig, and various other works, for many years gave an extraordinary impulse to its commercial prosperity. What is considered more peculiarly the harbour is situated nine miles below the city, opposite the town of Cove, where ships of any burden may ride in safety; the best anchorage for large ships is off Cove fort, now dismantled and occupied as a naval hospital, where there are from 5 to 8 fathoms of water; vessels of great draught can pass up the river as far as Passage, within five miles and a half of the city, where they discharge and load by means of lighters; and vessels drawing only 14 or 15 feet of water can proceed to the town quays. On the east side of the entrance from the sea to the harbour is Roche's Tower lighthouse, having ten lamps which exhibit a steady deep red light towards the sea, and a bright light towards the harbour. The only naval depôt and victualling-yard in Ireland were at Cove, but the establishment now consists merely of an agent and two clerks, and is maintained at an expense of £225 per annum. During the war and for several years after this was the port station of an admiral having a large fleet under his command; but the admiral's flag and the navy have been withdrawn, and at present, the King's flag is seldom seen on the Irish coast, except on the Lord-Lieutenant's yacht. On Halbowling island are the spacious and admirably designed naval storehouses, tank, and other requisites, now abandoned; on Spike island are powerful batteries commanding the entrance of the harbour, and on Rocky island is the depôt for gunpowder. The ballast office, situated on Lapp's island, was established by act of the 1st of Geo. IV., cap. 52, which also provided for the regulation of pilots and the improvement of the port and harbour, by a Board of Harbour Commissioners consisting of the mayor, two sheriffs, the parliamentary representatives of the city, five members of the common council, and 25 merchants, of whom the five senior members go out annually in rotation. Among the various improvements made by this board is the line of quays extending on both sides of the river from the North bridge on the north channel, round the eastern extremity of the island, to Parliament bridge on the south, a distance of one statute mile and a half. From the end of Penrose's quay a new line extending eastward is now nearly completed, and the marsh lying between it and the lower Glanmire road is in course of drainage: when this is accomplished the main central portion of the city will be encompassed with a noble line of quays, 18 feet high and nearly four statute miles in extent, built and coped with limestone principally from the quarries on the Little island and Rostellan. From 1827 to 1834 not less than £34,389 was expended on new quays from the proceeds of the harbour dues. The commissioners have also made an important improvement by deepening the bed of the river, which formerly admitted only vessels of 120 tons, but is now navigable to the quays for vessels of 250 tons; shoals and dangerous banks have been removed by a steam-dredging machine, and buoys laid down to mark the limits of the channel; excellent regulations have been adopted for the conduct of the pilots; lights have been placed on the castle of Blackrock, and various other measures calculated to promote the prosperity of the port have been carried into effect. The average receipts of the commissioners, arising from duties on imports and exports, tonnage duty, and the sale of ballast, for six years to 1835 inclusive amounted to £7549. 16. 8., and the expenditure to £7762. 12. 0. A navigation wall, commencing nearly opposite to the custom-house and extending about an Irish mile along the south shore of the river, was commenced in 1763, to prevent the channel from being choked with the mud which is washed up at every tide; and it is in contemplation to reclaim the extensive slab on the south of it, and render it available to the increase and improvement of the city. The custom-house, completed in 1818, and in which also the business of the excise is transacted, is a plain edifice situated at the eastern extremity of Lapp's island: the central front is ornamented with a pediment, in the tympanum of which are the royal arms, and connected with it are very extensive and appropriate buildings; the long room is spacious and well adapted to the purpose; the commercial buildings, on the South Mall, were erected in 1813, from a design by Sir Thomas Deane, by a proprietary of 129 £100 shareholders incorporated by charter in the 48th of Geo. III., for the accommodation of merchants, for which purpose they are much better adapted than the old exchange: they are fronted with cement, and ornamented with Ionic columns between the windows; the coffee-room, on the first floor, in which the merchants meet, is 60 feet long, 35 feet wide, and 20 feet high, with a coved ceiling chastely embellished, and is well supplied with the English and Irish newspapers and periodicals. Communicating with the commercial buildings, and belonging to the same proprietary, is the Imperial Clarence hotel, well conducted by Mr. McDowel: attached to it is a ball-room, 70 feet long and 36 feet wide, elegantly fitted up, with a refreshment room adjoining, 50 feet long and 36 feet wide; and there are twelve drawing-rooms for private families, and a commercial room for travellers, with every accommodation requisite in a first-rate hotel: all the principal mails start from it. The chamber of commerce, a neat building in Patrick-street, was erected by a body of seceders from the proprietary of the commercial buildings, who, within the last few years, in consequence of a dispute, associated under the above designation, but not, as the name implies, with any reference to the commercial interests of the port, which are under the superintendence of the committee of merchants: the large room is well supplied with newspapers and periodicals, and, like that of the commercial buildings, is open to naval and military officers and to all strangers; the lower and other parts of the building are appropriated to the purposes of a commercial hotel. The post-office is a small but convenient building near the centre of the city: its revenue, in 1835, was £13,022. 4. 11. The first mail coach that entered the city was established between Dublin and Cork, on the 8th of July, 1789: there are now day and night mails from Dublin, and one from Waterford every morning, each carrying the English letters, but letters from London come through Dublin, unless ordered viâ Waterford; and there are several other mail-coaches from Limerick, Bantry, Tralee, and other places, which arrive in the evening before the departure of the Dublin night mail.

The manufactures of the town, though in some branches rather extensive, are generally of little importance compared with its commerce. Formerly Blackpool, a large and populous portion of the suburbs, was principally inhabited by persons engaged in the manufacture of coarse woollens, linens, cottons, thread camlets, stuffs, woollen yarn, and hats, and in wool-combing, dyeing, and other similar occupations; but in 1812, the protecting duty of 10 per cent. on British manufactures, which fostered those of Ireland, being removed, vast numbers were thrown out of employment, who, having in vain remonstrated and petitioned for a more gradual alteration of the system, were ultimately compelled to seek employment in England. The principal branch of manufacture now carried on is the tanning of leather, which article was formerly imported from London and Bristol, but since the assimilation of the duties has become a great source of export; there are 46 tanyards in various parts of the suburbs, of which 25 are very extensive; and in 1835 there were 615 tanners and curriers in constant employment. The average number of hides tanned annually is about 110,000, of which the greater portion were till lately purchased in Liverpool and London, but in 1835, a new branch of commerce was opened by the importation of hides direct from Montevideo and Gibraltar: the number of native hides annually weighed at the crane, on an average of three years ending April 30th, 1835, was 32,068, and of calf skins, 73,416; and the quantity of leather exported on an average of five years ending with 1835 was 5624 bales and 214 crates annually. The quantity of bark imported from foreign countries and from England and Wales for the use of the tanneries, from 1830 to 1835 inclusive, amounted on an average to 6948 tons annually, and of valonia from Smyrna, to more than 2000 tons annually. The encouragement afforded to tillage and the increased production of corn, to supply the demand during the late continental war, gave rise to the establishment of corn-mills, breweries, and distilleries on a large scale, of which the first-named are numerous in the vicinity; the largest breweries are those of Messrs. Beamish and Crawford, and Messrs. Lane; the former is exclusively confined to the manufacture of porter. These breweries employ a great number of hands, and conduce much to the improvement of agriculture. There are seven distilleries in the city and its vicinity; those in the former produce annually 1,400,000 gallons of whiskey, and in the latter, 600,000; the whole consume 268,000 barrels of corn, and employ about 1000 men: the quantity of whiskey shipped at the port in 1835 was 1279 puncheons. There are seven iron-foundries, affording employment to upwards of 300 workmen; and five manufactories in which spades, shovels, &c., are made, also two manufactories of steel, and an extensive establishment for coppersmith's work chiefly for the distilleries and breweries. The quantity of iron imported annually is upwards of 6000 tons; and in the various departments of the iron trade within the city and liberties, including smithies, nearly 1000 men are employed. The paper-mills are numerous and extensive, and their produce is in great demand: the number of persons employed exceeds 400. In the city are two large glass-houses for the manufacture of flint glass for the home and foreign markets, with extensive premises for cutting, engraving, &c., attached to each, affording employment to 246 persons. The manufacture of woollen cloth was introduced prior to 1732, and flourished for many years: the principal manufacturers were Messrs. Lane, who for more than twenty years after the union furnished the entire clothing for the Irish army; their mills were situated at Riverstown, but are now applied to other purposes. At Glanmire are the extensive mills of Messrs. Lyons and Hanly, for the manufacture of fine cloth; and at Blarney are mills for spinning yarn for the supply of Mr. Mahony's stuff and camlet manufactory in Cork. There are still a few wool-combing and dyeing establishments, besides mills at Douglas and Glanmire, where linens and cottons are bleached and finished, and several rope-walks established for the manufacture of patent cordage. Many of the poor are employed in weaving coarse cotton checks, which are sold at a very low price by Messrs. Todd and Co., who have a very large establishment on the plan of those in London, furnished with goods of every kind. Cutlery of superior quality is extensively manufactured, and bears a higher price than that brought from England. The trade in gloves is very flourishing, and employs a great number of people; those made here are always sold as Limerick gloves. Acids, mineral waters, and vinegar of superior quality are also extensively made. The manufacture of canvas was formerly extensive, but is now declining, the article being imported cheaper from Liverpool, Glasgow, Greenock, and East Cocker. The soap manufacture has been much diminished by the increase of tillage and the decrease in the slaughtering of cattle; and the manufacture of candles, with which this place once almost exclusively supplied the West Indian market, in which it still enjoys a preference, has been affected by the same cause. The Bank of Ireland and the Provincial Bank, about the year 1825, opened branch establishments here, which have afforded liberal accommodation to trade; and two new joint stock companies, the National, and the Agricultural and Commercial, have since established branch banks in the city. The savings' bank is a large and handsome edifice; the deposits, at the close of 1836, exceeded £240,000: it was established in 1817, from which period to the end of 1836, the number of depositors was 24,000, of whom 7066 are now on the books. The principal market days are Wednesday and Saturday but all the markets are open daily. Fairs under the charter are held on Trinity-Monday and Oct. 1st, in an open area called Fair-field, half a mile to the north-west of the town. The city market, for meat, fish, poultry, fresh butter, vegetables, and fruit, was opened in 1788: it is conveniently situated near the centre of the city, with spacious entrances from Patrick-street, Prince's-street, and the Grand Parade, and comprises several detached buildings suitably arranged; it is divided into separate departments, and is abundantly supplied daily with every kind of provisions. The cattle market is held near the Shandon markets: the number of horned cattle annually sold here for the provision merchants formerly exceeded 50,000, but the average of three years ending Dec. 25th, 1835, was less than 6000 annually: the number of pigs sold alive in this market to the provision merchants is on an average 90,000 annually, exclusively of the carcases sold in the new corn market.

The corporation is very ancient, and exists probably by prescription. A charter was granted by John, Earl of Morton, while viceroy of Ireland, in the reign of his father Hen. II., in the preamble of which it is stated—"I have granted and given, and by this my charter confirm, to the citizens of Cork all the fields held of my city of Cork and the ground on which the city is, now for my benefit to increase the strength of the citizens. This is to them and their heirs to hold of me and my heirs, and to remain in frank burgage, by such custom and rent as the burgesses of Bristol, in England pay yearly for their burgages; and to secure my city of Cork I grant this to the same my citizens of Cork all the laws, franchises, and customs or freight which are in Bristol on whatsoever sails. And firmly commanding that the aforesaid my citizens of Cork and their heirs and their successors have the aforesaid city of Cork of me and my successors as is aforesaid, and have all the laws and franchises and frank customs of Bristol; and as those were wont to be used and written in my court and in my hundred of Cork, and in all business. And I forbid that any wrong or hindrance be given to the aforesaid laws and franchises, which gift from us are given and granted, &c." A copy of this charter is preserved amongst the Harleian MSS. in the British Museum, but the original is lost. The earliest charter extant is one of the 26th of Hen. III., which granted the city and its appurtenances in fee farm at an annual rent of 80 marks, with prisage of wine, custom, and cocket within the jurisdiction of the port, and certain personal privileges to the citizens, among which was an exemption from toll and all other customs throughout his dominions: under this charter the chief officer of the corporation was called "provost." Edw. I. granted two charters, in the 19th and 31st of his reign, the latter of which authorised the bailiffs and men of Cork to have murage, as in other towns in Ireland, for six years. The charter of the 11th of Edw. II. is the first in which the office of mayor is named: the same monarch, in the following year, confirmed the charter of the 19th of Edw. I., and gave to the mayor elect the privilege of being sworn before his predecessor in office, instead of going to Dublin to take the oaths before the barons of the exchequer; charters were also granted in the 4th and 5th of Edw. III., 5th of Rich. II., and 2nd of Edw. IV., the last of which, after reciting that the mayor and commonalty had eleven parish churches within the city, with suburbs extending one mile in every direction, that had been for 50 years preceding destroyed by Irish enemies and English rebels, on which account they were unable to pay the fee farm rent, remitted all arrears, and granted them the cocket of the city for the construction of the walls, to be held until they should be able to travel peaceably one mile beyond them. In the 15th of Edw. IV. all former charters were confirmed, and the mayor and citizens were allowed to enjoy all their franchises both within the city and suburbs and through the entire port, "as far as the shore, point, or strand called Rewrawne, on the western part of the said port, and as far as to the shore, point, or strand of the sea, called Benowdran, on the eastern part of the same port, and so far as the castle of Carrigrohan, on the western side of the said city, and in all towns, pills, creeks, burgs, and strands in and to which the sea ebbs and flows in length and breadth within the aforesaid two points, called Rewrawne and Benowdran:" it then releases during pleasure all arrears of the rent of 80 marks, and grants that the corporation, in lieu thereof, shall in future render at the exchequer 20lb. of wax. Hen. VII. granted a charter of inspeximus; and Hen. VIII., in the 1st of his reign, gave a confirmatory charter, and in the 28th another, which also conferred upon the mayor the privilege of having a sword carried before him, the sword-bearer to wear "a remarkable cap" (which ceremony is still observed), and granted him the custody of the castle. Edw. VI., in the 3rd of his reign, granted a charter of confirmation; and in the 18th of Eliz. the mayor, recorder, and bailiffs, and the four senior aldermen who had served the office of mayor, were constituted keepers of the peace within the city both by land and by water; and they, or three of them, of whom the mayor and recorder were to be two, were appointed justices of oyer and terminer and general gaol delivery, with power to enquire into all felonies, trespasses, &c., within the city and liberties; this charter also contained a grant to the corporation of all fines and amercements. The charter of the 6th of Jas. I., after granting that Cork should be a free city, and changing the style of the corporation to that of mayor, sheriffs, and commonalty, with power to make by-laws for the regulation of the municipality, constituted the city and a surrounding district to be marked out by commissioners a distinct county, over which the powers of the justices of the peace for the city were extended, and released the corporation from their annual payment of 20lb. of wax: this charter also granted permission to hold two fairs with all tolls, &c., and created a corporation of the staple with privileges equal to those of London or Dublin. In the 7th of Chas. I. a confirmatory charter was granted, which, after declaring that justices of the county of Cork should have no jurisdiction within the city, further directs that each mayor, on retiring from office, shall be an alderman, and that all the aldermen shall be members of the common council, provided the number do not exceed 24: it also empowers the corporation to elect a town-clerk, clerk of the Crown, and public notary; and likewise six aldermen of the ward, who should have power to determine all causes not exceeding 40*s.* arising within their respective wards. By the charter granted in the 9th of Geo. II. all the aldermen, immediately on retiring from the office of mayor, were made justices of the peace within the county of the city: the same monarch, in the 21st of his reign, granted another charter, which is the last given to the corporation, authorising them to hold two fairs annually at a place called the Lough, within the liberties, and to take the usual tolls. Under the authority of these charters a series of by-laws passed in 1721, for electing the officers and otherwise regulating the affairs of the corporation, the different classes in which are the mayor, sheriffs, aldermen, burgesses, and commonalty or freemen. The mayor is chosen on the first Monday in July, nominally by a majority of the freemen, according to a form expressed in one of the by-laws, from among the resident burgesses or persons who have served the office of sheriff, of whom five, whose names have been drawn from a hat containing the names of all entitled to be elected, are put in nomination; but this right of the freemen to choose the mayor is rendered almost nugatory by an association called the "Friendly Club," consisting of about 500 of the freemen, of whom more than 300 are resident, by one of whose rules the members are bound to vote for one of the two senior burgesses of the five whose names are drawn. The sheriffs are elected on the same day as the mayor, by and from the freemen; but the interposition of the Friendly Club operates in like manner as in the election of mayor. The aldermen are such members of the corporation as have served the office of mayor, and are unlimited in number; six of them, elected by the freemen at large in a court of D'Oyer hundred held for the purpose on a vacancy occurring, are called "Aldermen of the Ward." The burgesses are those who have served the office of sheriff, and are also unlimited in number; and the common council is composed of the mayor, recorder, two sheriffs, and aldermen, not exceeding in all 24, and should they not amount to that number, the deficiency is made up by election from among the burgesses. All by-laws, and orders for the payment of money, letting and disposing of the corporate property, and the admission of freemen, must originate in the common council, and are afterwards confirmed in the court of D'Oyer hundred. Besides the recorder, the assistant officers of the corporation are a common speaker (who represents the commonalty and attends the meetings of the council, where he is permitted to sit and hear the deliberations, but has no vote), town-clerk, chamberlain, clerks of the Crown, peace, and council, a water and deputy water bailiffs, sword-bearer, two serjeants-at-mace, assay-master, weighmasters, two coroners, and other inferior officers; the principal of these are elected by the freemen at large, in a court of D'Oyer hundred. The appointment of the mayor, sheriffs, recorder, and town-clerk is subject to the approbation of the lord-lieutenant and privy council. The freedom is inherited by the first-born sons of freemen, and obtained by apprenticeship of seven years to a freeman and by grace especial of the common council, subject, in the last case, to the approval of the court of D'Oyer hundred, except as regards persons of distinction who may happen to be in the city, and to whom the council think fit to present the freedom. The city first sent members to the Irish parliament in 1374, but representatives who appear to have served in London were chosen previously. The right of election was vested in the freemen of the city, and in the 40*s.* freeholders and £50 leaseholders of the county of the city, of whom the freemen, in 1831, amounted in number to 2331, and the freeholders to 1545, making a total of 3876; but by the act of the 2nd of Wm. IV., cap. 88 (under which the city, from its distinguished importance, retains its privilege of returning two representatives to the Imperial parliament, and the limits of the franchise, comprising the entire county of the city, remain unaltered), the non-resident freemen, except within seven miles, have been disfranchised, and the privilege of voting at elections has been extended to the £10 householders, and the £20 and £10 leaseholders for the respective terms of 14 and 20 years. The number of voters registered up to Jan. 2nd, 1836, amounted to 4791, of whom 1065 were freemen; 2727 £10 householders; 105 £50, 152 £20, and 608 forty-shilling freeholders; 3 £50, 7 £20, and 2 £10 rent-chargers; and 1 £50, 26 £20, and 95 £10 leaseholders: the sheriffs are the returning officers. The mayor, recorder, and all the aldermen are justices of the peace for the county of the city; and the mayor is also a judge of assize, justice of the peace for the county at large, a judge of the courts of record and conscience, and president of the council and of the court of D'Oyer hundred. Under the new Police bill, there are a chief constable, a head constable, 11 constables and 62 sub-constables. The courts of the corporation are the mayor and sheriffs' court, the courts of city sessions and conscience, and the police office or magistrates' court. The mayor and sheriffs' court, held weekly, has jurisdiction in all personal and mixed actions, except replevin and ejectment, in pleas to any amount; and is a court of record, in which the pleadings are similar to those of the superior courts. Suits may be commenced either by serviceable writ, bailable writ, or attachment against goods, in which last mode the debt sought to be recovered must amount to at least 40*s*. Irish. The mayor and sheriffs originally presided as judges; but by the 11th and 12th of Geo. III., cap. 18, the recorder, or his deputy, being a barrister of three years' standing, was made judge, and authorised to sit alone; in his absence the mayor and one of the sheriffs are necessary to constitute a court. The city sessions court is held quarterly before the justices, but by the act above noticed the recorder is empowered to hold the court alone, and in general is the only judge presiding; a grand jury is returned by the sheriff to serve for the entire quarter, and the court sits weekly by adjournment. The number of prisoners tried at these sessions in 1835 was 401, of whom 110 were for felonies and 291 for misdemeanours. The court of conscience was constituted by act of the 3rd of Geo. IV., cap. 85, for the recovery of debts not exceeding 40*s*. arising within the county of the city: the act appoints the mayor and aldermen of the ward judges, not less than three of them to be sufficient to hold the court. The police-office, or magistrates' court, adjoins the court of conscience, and was constituted by the same act. The revenue of the corporation, exclusively of the expense of collecting the tolls, amounts to about £6237 per annum, arising from various sources.

The city is within the Munster circuit: the assizes for the county at large are held here, and, at the same time, those for the county of the city. It is also one of the places at which, in September, the assistant barrister holds his courts for the East Riding. The present city court-house, or guildhall, is situated on the south side of the exchange, and contains on the first floor a council-chamber, in which the mayor and council assemble to transact business and hold the courts of D'Oyer hundred. The exchange, situated at the angle of Castle-street and the north Main-street, a small regular structure of hewn stone, erected by Twiss Jones in 1709, at the expense of the corporation, has been taken down, and is to be re-erected in front of the market on the Grand Parade. The old county court-house, anciently called "the King's Castle," being too small and inconvenient, a county and city court-house was erected in 1835 by Messrs. Pain: it is a large and handsome edifice, in the Grecian style of architecture, with a boldly projecting portico of eight columns supporting an entablature and cornice surmounted by a pediment, on the apex of which is a group of figures representing Justice between Law and Mercy: the interior contains two semicircular courts, and the various offices in the back part of the building are so arranged as to afford the public and the officers facility of access without collision; the judges and barristers can go from one court to the other by private passages; and the entire building, which was erected at an expense of about £20,000, reflects equal credit on the taste and judgment of the architects. The mansion-house, beautifully situated on the bank of the river, near the entrance to the Mardyke Walk, is a large and handsome edifice, built in 1767 by the celebrated Ducart, at an expense of £3793. The entrance-hall and staircase are spacious; on the first landing-place is a well-sculptured bust of George IV., and in a niche in the first lobby is a full-length marble effigy of the first Rt. Hon. Wm. Pitt, in his robes of office and holding a scroll in his right hand, placed there in 1766. The dining and drawing-rooms are large and fitted up in a costly manner: in the former is a full length figure of Wm. III. in armour, with a scroll in the right hand and the head encircled by a wreath of laurel, standing on a pedestal bearing an inscription recording its erection by the corporation and citizens in 1759. In the entrance-hall are the ancient "nail" or "nail head" of the city, and the ancient standard brass yard; also a curious representation of the city arms cut in stone, which was found some years since on taking down the old custom-house. The city gaol is a castellated building, situated on an eminence near Sunday-well. It was at first divided into two equal compartments, one for males and the other for females; but the original arrangement has been altered, and the prison is now divided into 32 wards, 8 for male and 1 for female debtors, 9 for male and 8 for female culprits; the remaining 6 are hospital wards. There are 54 cells, affording accommodation for 162 male culprits; and 48 for females, accommodating 96. Each ward has a day room and airing-yard, and in one of these is a tread-mill used to raise water for the supply of the prison. Separate places of worship are fitted up for Protestants and Roman Catholics: the number of prisoners committed, in 1835, was 263 male and 153 female criminals; 245 male and 99 female misdemeanants; 29 soldiers; 314 male and 31 female debtors, making a total of 851 males and 283 females. The expenditure for that year was £2557. 3. 6. The city bridewell is for the temporary confinement of prisoners under examination before final committal, and of disorderly persons taken up in the night until brought before the magistrates; eight cells with fire-places in each were recently added to it for solitary confinement. The gaol and house of correction for the county are situated at a short distance from the town on the south side of the new western road. The entrance was originally from the south; but the new approach to the city, between the north and south branches of the river, afforded the architects an opportunity of forming an entrance on the north side, for which purpose a bridge of one arch was built over the south channel communicating with a causeway raised about six feet across the adjacent meadows. Along the north side of the prison is an esplanade, about 40 feet broad, in the centre of which, and directly opposite to the bridge is an entrance portico of four Doric columns surmounted by a pediment; the design is taken from the Temple of Bacchus, at Athens. The gaol has been enlarged at different periods, and is now very commodious and well-arranged. It is under the direction of a governor and deputy-governor; and is divided into 8 wards, 2 for male debtors, 5 for male offenders, and 1 for females of every description, which is subdivided into three sections appropriated respectively to debtors, untried and convicts. The male wards contain 95 cells, capable of accommodating 425 inmates; that of the females has accommodations for 66; each ward has a day-room and a spacious airing-yard: there are four solitary cells. The gaol and the surrounding extensive enclosed ground are kept in the highest order; the prisoners, who on their admission are clothed in a distinguishing prison dress, are fully occupied either on the tread-wheel or in the duties of whitewashing and cleansing the floors, yards, and passages. The number of prisoners committed in 1835 was 978, of whom 740, including 203 females, were charged with criminal offences; 200, of whom 12 were females, were debtors; 20 were soldiers, and 18, of whom one was a female, were committed under process of the exchequer. The House of Correction, built by Messrs. Pain on the north side of the gaol, is a well-arranged edifice, consisting of a centre and two detached wings towards the gaol, and of three other ranges of building, radiating from the centre northward. The centre contains the governor's apartments on the ground floor, a chapel both for Protestants and Roman Catholics on the second, and an infirmary on the third. The radiating buildings contain 78 cells, with washing-rooms in each range; on the ground floor are day and work rooms, having airing-yards attached to them. The number of convicts committed, in 1835, was 567. The prison is under the management of a governor. The classification and regulations, both of the gaol and house of correction, are highly conducive to the reformation of the prisoners. Those in the latter establishment are employed in manufacturing their own clothing and other necessary articles of consumption: attached to it is a tread-mill, used for supplying both prisons with water. A sum of £1600 was presented by the Grand Jury, at the last autumn assizes, for an hospital for the use of the prisoners, to be erected on the adjoining ground: it is to extend 100 feet in front, the centre to be two stories high, with wings; the interior is to be divided into six wards, three for each sex. The Female Penitentiary or Convict Depôt, occupies the site of the old fort erected in the southern suburb, in the reign of Elizabeth. It is capable of containing 250 inmates, who are brought hither from all parts of Ireland, and remain until the arrival of vessels to convey them to their final place of destination. During their residence here they are employed in needle-work, washing and knitting, so as to supply not only themselves but all the convicts sent out of Ireland with clothing: the number of suits thus made annually is about 1000. The number committed to this prison, in 1835, was 457, of whom 315 were transported to New South Wales. Schools have been established in all the prisons. The hulk is no longer used as a place of confinement.

Arms of the Bishoprick.

The foundation of the See of Cork is generally ascribed to St. Barr or Finbarr, in the early part of the 7th century: his relics, which were enclosed in a silver shrine, were carried away from the cathedral, in 1089, by Dermot, the son of Turlough O'Brian, when he pillaged Cork. St. Finbarr is said to have been succeeded by St. Nessan. In 1292, Bishop Robert Mac Donagh was twice fined £130 for presuming to hold pleas in the ecclesiastical courts for matters belonging to the Crown; and these two fines were paid, with the exception of £84. 14. 2., which was remitted. In 1324 Philip of Slane was sent in embassy to the pope by Edw. II., and discharged his commission with such address that he was made one of the privy council of Ireland. On his return, an assembly of bishops, noblemen, and others was held, at which it was resolved that all disturbers of the public peace should be excommunicated; that the small and poor bishopricks not exceeding £20, £40, or £60 per annum, and which were governed by the mere Irish, should be united with the more eminent bishopricks; and that the Irish abbots and priors should receive Englishmen into lay brotherhoods, as in England. In 1430, the sees of Cork and Cloyne being both vacant, Pope Martin V. united them, and appointed Jordan, chancellor of Limerick, bishop of the united diocese. The last Roman Catholic bishop before the Reformation was John Fitz-Edmund, of the noble family of the Geraldines, who was appointed bishop by the pope in 1499. After his death his powerful relatives seized the revenues of Cloyne and part of those of Cork. In 1536, Dominic Tirrey, who was reckoned favourable to the Reformation, was appointed bishop by mandate of Hen. VIII., and held the see 20 years, during which period the pope appointed two ecclesiastics to the united see, neither of whom took possession. Matthew Sheyn, who was appointed bishop by Elizabeth in 1572, was a great enemy to the veneration paid to images, and, in October, 1578, burnt that of St. Dominick at the high cross of Cork, to the great grief of the people. William Lyon was consecrated bishop of Ross in 1582, and on the 17th of May, 1586, Elizabeth annexed the sees of Cork and Cloyne to Ross, in favour of this prelate, who, in a return to a regal visitation held about the year 1613, states "that the bishoprick of Cloyne was granted by his predecessor, in fee farm, at five marks rent; that Cork and Ross, when he came into possession, were worth only £70 per annum, but that he had improved them to £200 per annum; that he built a mansion-house at Ross, at an expense of at least £300, which, in a little more than three years after, was burnt down by the rebel O'Donovan; that he found no episcopal house at Cork, but that he built one, which cost him at least £1000; and that he never was in possession of the house belonging to the bishoprick of Cloyne, which was withheld from him by Sir John Fitz-Edmund Fitz-Gerald in his lifetime, and since his death by his heir." After Bishop Lyon's decease, the see was successively occupied by John and Richard Boyle, relatives of the

Earls of Cork: the latter, who was afterwards archbishop of Tuam, died at Cork in 1644, and was buried in the cathedral, in a vault he had prepared during his prelacy. While he occupied this see, he is stated to have repaired more ruinous churches and consecrated more new ones than any other bishop in that age. This prelate was succeeded by Dr. Chappel, provost of Trinity College, Dublin, whose successor was Michael Boyle, son of Dr. Chappel's predecessor. Bishop Boyle was succeeded by Dr. Synge, who, by will dated May 23rd, 1677, left several legacies to the poor of St. Finbarr's (Cork), Youghal, Cloyne, and Innishowen. From the death of this prelate, the see of Cloyne was held separately from the united see of Cork and Ross until 1835. Dr. Wetenhall, who was the first Bishop of Cork and Ross, "suffered great cruelties and oppressions from the year 1688 to the settlement under King William," and at his own expense repaired the episcopal palace at Cork. Dr. Brown, Provost of Trinity College, was promoted to this bishoprick in 1709, and held it till his death, in 1735. By his encouragement several churches were rebuilt or repaired, and glebe-houses erected; and a handsome public library, with a large room for a charity-school, was built near the cathedral. He expended more than £2000 on a country house, built in a demesne of 118 acres belonging to the see, at Ballinaspick or Bishopstown, near Cork, which he occupied as a summer residence, and left to his successors free from any charge. By will he left £300 contingently, of which one-third of the interest was to be paid to the librarian of the library recently erected near the cathedral (to which he also bequeathed some of his books), one-third for the purchase of books for its use, and the remainder for the widows and children of poor clergymen; he also left £20 to the poor of St. Finbarr's parish, and £100 for clothing and apprenticing poor children. On the death of Dr. Brinkley, bishop of Cloyne, in 1835, that bishoprick was added to Cork and Ross by the Church Temporalities Act of the 3rd of Wm. IV., and the united see is called the bishoprick of Cork, Ross, and Cloyne. By the act for amending the Church Temporalities Act, £1500 per annum, commencing Sept. 14th, 1835, has been granted out of the funds at the disposal of the Ecclesiastical Commissioners, to compensate Dr. Kyle, the present bishop, for the loss he has sustained in exchanging the temporalities of Cork and Ross for those of Cloyne. The diocese is one of the eleven which constitute the ecclesiastical province of Cashel; it is entirely within the county of Cork, extending about 74 miles in length and 16 in breadth, and contains an estimated superficies of 356,300 acres. The chapter of Cork consists of a dean, precentor, chancellor, treasurer, archdeacon, and the twelve prebendaries of Kilbrogan, Kilbritain, Killaspigmullane, Cahirlog, Liscleary, Killanully, Inniskenny, Kilnaglory, Holy Trinity, St. Michael, Desertmore, and Dromdaleague. The see lands comprise 3306 acres, about one-half of which is profitable land; and its gross annual revenue, on an average of three years ending Dec. 31st, 1831, was £2630. 1.; the whole is now vested in the Ecclesiastical Commissioners, under the Church Temporalities Act. To the dean belong, as the corps of the deanery, the rectory and vicarage of Templebready, and the rectories of Cullen and Templemartin, the tithes of which amount to £921. 4. per annum; besides which he has a residence, or deanery, and the right of nomination to the perpetual cure of Templebready, of the annual value of £56. 6. 7., and to the curacy of St. Finbarr's of the annual value of £100. To the precentor belong the rectories of Carrigrohane, Curricuppane, a third of Corbally, and a fourth of Kinneigh, the tithes of which amount to £858. 6. 8. per annum; to the chancellor belongs the consolidated rectory of St. Nicholas, the tithes of which amount to £315; to the treasurer belong the rectory entire of Ballinadee, and the tithes of the townlands of Kilgoban, Rathdowlan, and Mackloneigh, amounting altogether to £651. 10. 8½.; to the archdeacon belong the rectories of St. Peter, in the city of Cork, and those of Nohoval, Kilmanogue, Dunbollogue, and Dunisky, the tithes of which amount to £856. 4. 7., and about £200 of which is paid as minister's money, in lieu of tithes, for St. Peter's parish. The endowments of the prebends will be found in the accounts of the parishes after which they are named. The cathedral is also the parish church of St. Finbarr's, and is described in the account of that parish in a subsequent part of this article. The annual income of the economy estate, on an average of three years ending Aug. 30th, 1831, was £786. 3. 6., principally arising from the tithes of two-thirds of that part of the parish of St. Finbarr which is in the city, and of the whole of that part which is in the county, of Cork. The expenditure consists of repairs of the cathedral, and payments to its officers, &c., but principally in the building and support of St. Michael's chapel at Blackrock, from which, in 1831, the economy estate was in debt £1400. This is the only fund under the control of the dean and chapter in their corporate capacity, and the only benefices in their patronage are the perpetual cure of Marmullane and the chapelry of St. Michael. The four vicars choral possess a net annual income of more than £1200, arising from the tithes of several parishes and the rents of some houses in Cork, and yielding to each above £300 per annum. The palace is the only portion of the property of the see, except the mensal and demesne lands, that is not vested in the Ecclesiastical Commissioners. The consistorial court of the dioceses of Cork and Ross is held in the chapter-house at Cork; its officers are a vicar-general, registrar, and proctors; the registrar is keeper of the records of the see, which consist of original wills, oaths, declarations, canons, and records of the proceedings of the bishops, the oldest of which commences in 1521. The total number of parishes in the diocese is 84, of which 11 are unions; they are comprised in 65 benefices, 6 of which are in the patronage of the Crown, 2 in the alternate patronage of the Crown and the Bishop, 41 in the gift of the Bishop, 5 in the gift of incumbents, and the remaining 11 in the patronage of laymen. There are 58 churches and 26 school buildings, besides which are other houses licensed by the bishop, in which divine worship is regularly performed. The glebe-houses are 25 in number.

In the R. C. divisions Cork forms a separate bishoprick, comprising 35 parochial districts, containing 81 chapels: of these, 71 are parochial, 3 annexed to presentation convents, and one to each of the Dominican, Capuchin, Augustinian, Carmelite, and Franciscan friaries; one to an Ursuline convent, and one to the Magdalen Asylum, Cork. The total number of the R. C. clergy, in 1835, including the bishop, was 74, of which

35 were parish priests and 39 coadjutors or curates. The parochial benefice of the bishop, who resides in Cork, is the union of Shandon, called the North Parish.

The county of the city comprises a populous rural district of great beauty and fertility, watered by several small rivulets and intersected by the river Lee and its noble estuary: it is bounded on the north by the barony of Fermoy, on the east by that of Barrymore, on the south by Kerricurrihy, and on the west by Muskerry: it comprehends the parishes of St. Finbarr, Christ-Church or the Holy Trinity, St. Peter, St. Mary Shandon, St. Anne Shandon, St. Paul and St. Nicholas, all, except part of St. Finbarr's, within the city and suburbs, and those of Curricuppane, Carrigrohanemore, Kilcully, and Rathcoony, together with parts of the parishes of Killanully or Killingly, Carrigaline, Dunbullogue or Carrignavar, Ballinaboy, Inniskenny, Kilnaglory, Whitechurch, and Templemichael, without those limits; and contains, according to the Ordnance survey, an area of 44,463 statute acres, of which, 2396 are occupied by the city and suburbs. The Grand Jury presentments for 1835 were as follow: new roads, bridges, &c., £611. 19. 7.; repairs of roads, bridges, &c., £2641. 14. 0½.; public buildings, charities, officers' salaries, and miscellaneous expenses, £14,592. 1. 1.; police establishment, £1148. 14. 3.; repayment of advances by Government, £1254. 19. 6.; wide street commissioners for lighting, paving, &c., £8800; making a total of £29,049. 8. 5½.

The parish of *St. Finbarr* is a rectory, appropriate to the dean and chapter and vicars choral. The tithes under the composition act amount to £990 per annum, of which £690 constitute the greater portion of the economy fund of the cathedral under the control and management of the dean and chapter, and £300 are payable to the vicars choral: a residentiary preacher with a stipend of £100, of which £50 is from the economy fund, and £50 from the respective members for discharging their turns of preaching; a reader, with a stipend of £75 paid by the vicars choral out of their estates, and a curate, who also acts as librarian, with a fixed stipend of £21 from the economy fund, are appointed for the ordinary performance of the ecclesiastical duties. The parish church, which is also the cathedral of the see of Cork, and is dedicated to the saint whose name it bears, was rebuilt between the years 1725 and 1735, and for defraying the expense a duty of 1*s*. per ton was imposed by act on all coal and culm imported into Cork for five years, from May 1st, 1736: it was newly roofed in 1817 at an expense of £617 from the economy fund. The new structure is of the Doric order, except the tower, supposed to be part of the ancient building, erected by Gilla-Aeda O'Mugin, in the 12th century, and is surmounted by a lofty octangular spire of hewn stone under which is the principal entrance; on the south is the chapter hall, where the consistorial court is held, on the north the vestry room; the choir is lighted by a fine Venetian window; the bishop's throne, of black Irish oak, and the prebendal stalls, are handsomely finished, and well arranged: a beautiful monument of white marble, erected to the memory of Chief Baron Tracton, whose body is interred in the cathedral, has been recently transferred from St. Nicholas' church to a conspicuous position in it. Near the cathedral is the bishop's palace, built between 1772 and 1789, during the prelacy of Dr. Mann, a large and well-constructed edifice, on the southern bank of the river Lee, surrounded by pleasure grounds and gardens, and containing some fine paintings, among which is a portrait of Dr. Lyons, concerning whose preferment to the see a traditionary story, but wholly unsupported by documentary evidence, relates, that having received a promise from Queen Elizabeth to be promoted to the first vacancy in her gift, in consequence of his gallant conduct as captain of a ship in several actions with the Spaniards, he applied for the bishoprick of Cork on the death of the bishop, and notwithstanding the objections made in consequence of his former profession, by urging his reliance on the royal promise, he was appointed to the see. On the south side of the cathedral is Dean's Court, a good modern house, the residence of the Dean. A chapel of ease to this parish has been erected at Blackrock, for the description of which, see Blackrock. The living of the parish of *Christ-Church* is a vicarage, in the patronage of the Bishop; the rectory constitutes the corps of the prebend of the same name in the cathedral church, and is in the gift of the Crown: the prebendary derives his income from lands at Blackrock, averaging in rent and renewal fines, £396. 18. 5¾ per annum; the endowment of the vicarage, arising solely from houses assessed to minister's money, amounts to about £650 per annum: it has neither glebe nor glebe-house. The old church was taken down in 1716, and rebuilt in 1720 by a tax of 1*s*. per ton on coal imported for 15 years: the steeple having afterwards sunk on one side so as to swerve 3½ feet from the perpendicular, though without any fissures, thus presenting a very singular appearance, was lowered to the level of the roof and ultimately wholly removed, and the church rebuilt by the Messrs. Pain. The new structure is 97 feet by 57, its richly panelled ceiling rests on ranges of Ionic pillars of scagliola continued across the eastern end; along the northern and southern walls are galleries supported by Doric pilasters. Several of the lower columns, with parts of the floor, having been destroyed by the dry rot, Richard Beamish, Esq., civil engineer, in 1831, replaced the whole lower range of columns with pillars of cast iron without the smallest derangement of the upper columns, thus effectually securing the stability of the entire edifice. Several gravestones, some of the 16th century, and bearing emblematic devices, were discovered during the progress of the alterations. The living of *St. Peter's* is a rectory, united from time immemorial with the entire rectories of Nohoval, Kilmonogue, Dunbullogue, and Dunisky, together constituting the union and corps of the archdeaconry, in the patronage of the Bishop. The archdeacon's gross income is about £1000, arising from minister's money assessed on St. Peter's parish, from the tithes of the four rural parishes, and from reserved rents of houses, out of which he pays a perpetual and four stipendiary curates. The church, one of the most ancient in the city, formerly had as a steeple a tower detached from it considerably to the west, which once defended the city wall; its site is now occupied by an alms-house: the altar is ornamented with fluted Corinthian pilasters, and on its south side was a monument to the memory of Sir Matthew Deane and his lady, of the date of 1710, now removed to the further end of the church. The living of *St. Mary's Shandon* is a rectory and vicarage, with the rectory of St. Catharine, near Shandon, which has merged into it, united from time immemorial, and in the alternate patronage of the Duke of Leinster, and the Rev. Robert Longfield. There is neither glebe nor glebe-house: the tithes amount to £25, under the composition act, and the minister's money to £40 per ann., in addition to which the rector receives a rental of £95. 10. 9., from 7 houses in Shandon-street. This income is charged with the stipend of £75 per annum to a licensed curate. The church of the ancient parish of Shandon, which comprised the present parishes of St. Mary, St. Anne, and St. Paul, occupied the site of St. Anne's church, and from its proximity to Shandon castle, was several times damaged by contending factions and ultimately destroyed by the Irish about 1690: the present church, a neat edifice, was built in 1696, on a new site, and the Ecclesiastical Commissioners have lately granted £198. 19. 4. for its repairs. *St. Anne's Shandon* is a rectory, in the alternate patronage of the Duke of Leinster, and the Rev. Robert Longfield. It has neither glebe nor glebe-house. The tithes under the composition act amount to £240. 3. 5½., and the minister's money is about £370 per annum. The church, a large and handsome edifice, with a tower of several stories, 120 feet high, was built by subscription in 1772, on the site of the old church of Shandon, and being erected on an eminence, is prominently conspicuous from most parts of the city: the Ecclesiastical Commissioners have granted £259. 9. 10. for its repairs. A chapel of ease to this parish was erected in 1836, near the Brickfields, in the later English style of architecture, from a design of Messrs. Pain, with a western tower surmounted by a light and elegant spire and two lofty pinnacles at the east end; capacious school-rooms have been formed below the level of the floor at the same end where the ground declines rapidly; the late Board of First Fruits granted £1000, and an equal sum was raised by subscription for the erection of this building. The living of *St. Paul's* is a rectory, in the alternate patronage of the Duke of Leinster, and the Rev. Robert Longfield. The parish was formed, in 1726, out of the districts of the East Marsh, in the parish of St. Mary Shandon, and Dunscombe's Marsh, in that of Christ-Church: the income, amounting to about £200 per ann., is derived solely from assessments of minister's money: there is neither glebe nor glebe-house. The church is a neat edifice in the Grecian style, built by subscription on the formation of the parish, and on ground granted by the corporation. The living of *St. Nicholas'* is a rectory, united by act of council in 1752 with those of St. Bridget, St. John of Jerusalem, St. Stephen, St. Mary de Narde, St. Dominic, and St. Magdalene, which together constitute the corps of the chancellorship, in the patronage of the Bishop. The income of the union is £293. 18. 0., arising from houses assessed to minister's money, the tithes of St. Magdalene amounting to £21, the tithes of St. Nicholas and houses producing £5. 18. 0. per ann. The church, formerly a chapel of ease to St. Finbarr's, was built in 1723 by contributions from Bishop Browne and others, and is a small neat edifice, situate in the southern part of the city. A free church, near the South Infirmary, is now nearly completed, and above St. Patrick's bridge the hulk of an old vessel forms the Bethel or Mariner's church. The church of St. Brandon, which was situate on the north side of the river, on the road to Youghal, has been entirely destroyed, but the cemetery is still in use.

The principal schools in connection with the Established Church are the following. St. Stephen's Blue Coat Hospital was founded pursuant to a grant of lands and tenements in the north and south liberties by the Honourable William Worth, by deed dated Sept. 2nd, 1699, now producing a rental of £443. 4. 4. which, with the interest of £500 saved by the trustees, is expended in the maintenance, clothing, and education of 22 boys, the sons of reduced Protestant citizens, and in aid of the support of four students at Trinity College, Dublin: it is under the superintendence of the mayor and council, who nominate the boys. The school premises are situated on an eminence in the parish of St. Nicholas, and comprise a good school-room, dining-hall, apartments for the governor, and suitable offices, with an enclosed playground in front. The Green Coat Hospital, in the churchyard of St. Anne's Shandon, was founded about 1715, chiefly through the exertions of some military gentlemen and others to the number of 25, who by an act passed in 1717 were incorporated trustees, for the instruction of 20 children of each sex in the rudiments of useful knowledge and the principles of the Protestant religion, and for apprenticing them at a proper age, with a preference to the children of military men who had served their country. No regular system appears to have been introduced prior to 1751, but subsequently 40 children were clothed and educated till 1812; the number has since been increased by aid of a parliamentary grant, and at present there are 40 boys and 28 girls in the school. The income amounts to £96. 7. 11¼. per annum, of which £83. 15. 11¼. arises from donations and bequests, and the remainder from annual subscriptions: the chief benefactors were Daniel Thresher, who devised the lands of Rickenhead, in the county of Dublin, now let for £26 per annum on lease, which will expire in 1844, when they will probably produce at least £100 per annum; and Francis Edwards, of London, who devised eleven ploughlands in the parish of Ballyvourney, let permanently for £11 per annum: a librarian and treasurer, chosen from among the trustees, act gratuitously. The building consists of a centre and two wings, the former containing two school-rooms and apartments for the master; in the west wing are a library and board-room, with apartments for the mistress; and the other wing contains lodging-rooms for about 38 poor parishioners. Deane's charity schools were founded under the will, dated in 1726, of Moses Deane, Esq., of this city, who devised the rents of certain premises held for a term of years in trust to the corporation, to accumulate until they should yield a sum of £1200 for the parishes of St. Peter, St. Nicholas, St. Mary Shandon, and Christ-Church respectively, which sums were to be invested in lands in the county of Cork, and the rents applied to the instruction and clothing of 20 boys and 20 girls of each parish. The portion of the bequest assigned to the parish of St. Peter having been paid, the school was re-opened in 1817, and now affords instruction to 30 boys and 35 girls, of whom 20 of each sex are clothed: the endowment produces £66. 17. per annum, and an additional sum of about £50 is raised annually by subscriptions and the proceeds of an annual sermon: these form the parochial schools of St. Peter's. The portion assigned to the parish of St. Nicholas was obtained by the Rev. Archdeacon Austin, and was afterwards vested in the hands of the commissioners for charitable bequests by the Rev. Dr. Quarry. In 1822 a grant was obtained, and a plain and commodious building containing two school-rooms was erected in Cove-street, to which, in 1831, the Rev. J. N. Lombard, the present rector, added a school-room for infants: there are now in these schools 76 boys and 99 girls, of whom 30 boys and 25 girls are clothed out of the funds, which now amount to £189. 14. 10. per annum, and the children receive a daily supply of bread. The portion belonging to St. Mary Shandon's was lost for many years, but by the exertions of Dr. Quarry, the present rector, £800 was recovered, which, by a legacy of £100 and accumulated interest, has been augmented to £2000 three and a half per cent. reduced annuities: a commodious building of red brick ornamented with hewn limestone, and containing apartments for the master and three spacious school-rooms with a covered play-ground for the children, was erected in 1833 under the superintendence of Dr. Quarry, at the cost of £743. 2. 6. collected by him for that purpose: the pupils amount to 64 boys and 46 girls. An infants' school affords instruction to 100 children: the entire average of attendance may be averaged at 200. A Sunday and an adult school are also held in the same building. The boys' and girls' schools are supported by a portion of the dividends arising from the funded property, and by local subscriptions, and a collection after a charity sermon; and the infants' school by a portion of the same dividends and subscriptions. The parish of Christ-Church obtained no portion of Deane's bequest, the lease of the premises from which it was payable having expired. The diocesan schools for the sees of Cork, Ross, and Cloyne, are situated in Prince's-street, and are attended by 60 pupils, of whom 14 are taught gratuitously. On the eastern side of the cathedral is a free school founded by Archdeacon Pomeroy for the instruction in reading, writing, and arithmetic, of ten boys, to be nominated by the bishop; the master's original salary of £10 having been augmented by the dean and chapter, and by a bequest by the late Mrs. Shearman, to £30, twenty boys are now instructed gratuitously and are also taught the mathematics. Attached to the school is a library, founded also by the archdeacon, and much enlarged by a bequest of the late Bishop Stopford: it contains more than 4000 volumes, chiefly valuable editions of the classics and works on Divinity, and is open gratuitously to the clergy of the diocese and the parishioners of St. Finbarr's.

According to the R. C. divisions, the city with the suburbs is divided into three unions or parishes, St. Mary's and St. Anne's, St. Peter's and St. Paul's, and St. Finbarr's. St. Mary's and St. Anne's comprises nearly the whole of the Protestant parishes of St. Mary, St. Anne, and St. Catherine: the duties are performed by the parish priest, who is the Bishop, six curates, and two chaplains. The parochial chapel, which is also the cathedral, is a spacious structure, with a plain exterior: the eastern end having been destroyed by an accidental fire, it was rebuilt, and, with the rest of the interior, decorated by the Messrs. Pain in the later English style of architecture: the altar-piece is extremely rich and similar to that of the abbey of St. Albans, in England. There are chapels of ease at Brickfields and Clogheen: the former, dedicated to St. Patrick, is a handsome edifice in the Grecian style by the Messrs. Pain: the principal front is ornamented by a lofty and elegant portico of eight columns of grey marble, not yet finished, and approached by a flight of steps, extending along the entire front: from the centre of the roof rises a cupola, supported by eight Corinthian columns, surmounted by figures representing as many of the Apostles; the whole topped by a pedestal and cross. This chapel was opened for divine service, October 18th, 1836. St. Peter's and Paul's, comprising the Protestant parishes of the same name, with portions of those of Christ-Church, St. Anne's, and St. Finbarr's, is a mensal of the Bishop: the duties are performed by an administrator and two curates. The parochial chapel, a plain edifice, built in 1786, has an elegant altar in the Corinthian style, with a fine painting of the Crucifixion. St. Finbarr's comprises the Protestant parish of St. Nicholas, most part of St. Finbarr's, and a small portion of that of Christ-Church: the duties are performed by a parish priest and four curates, one of whom resides near Blackrock, and officiates at the chapel of ease there, which is noticed under the article descriptive of that village. The parochial chapel is in Dunbar-street, a spacious building, erected in 1776, in form of a T: under the altar is a figure of a "dead Christ," of a single block of white marble, executed at Rome, at an expense of £500, by Hogan, a native or Cork. In the chapel is also a monument to the memory of the Rev. Dr. McCarthy, coadjutor bishop, in which he is represented in the act of administering the sacrament to a person labouring under malignant fever, thus expressing in the most lively manner the cause of his premature death. There are four friaries belonging severally to the Augustinians, Franciscans, Dominicans, and Capuchins; two monasteries for monks, one of the Presentation order, the other of the Christian Brotherhood; and two convents for nuns of the Presentation order, one in the southern and the other in the northern part of the city. The Augustinians had an institution, called Gill Abbey, founded by St. Finbarr, for canons regular of the order, largely endowed by Cormac Mac Carthy, King of Cork, and shortly afterwards completed by Gilla Aeda, bishop of the see, from whom it derived its name; it anciently formed the cathedral establishment. The present state of this and the other decayed monastic buildings in the city is described in the subsequent part of this article, which treats of its antiquities. The institution at present is situated in Brunswick-street, and consists of a prior and four priests: the chapel, erected in 1780, was much enlarged in 1827; over the altar is a good painting of the Crucifixion. The Franciscan monastery was founded in 1214, on the north side of the city, by Dermot Mac Carthy Reagh, and rebuilt in 1240 by Lord Philip Prendergast. The present institution, situated in Grattan-street, consists of a guardian and four priests: the chapel, a neat building, was erected in 1830 by subscription, at an expense of £4500. The Dominican friary was founded in 1229, by the Barry family, on an island on the south side of the city, whence it acquired the name of the Abbey of the Island. The institution is now situated in Dominic-street, on the site of

Shandon castle, and consists of a prior and six priests. A new chapel, dedicated to St. Mary, is being erected on Pope's quay from a design gratuitously furnished by Kearnes Deane, Esq, who superintends its erection on a principle of similar liberality. When finished, it will consist of a portico of six Ionic columns with a triangular pediment surmounted by sculptured figures, with a stately portico, enriched with Corinthian pillars on each side, and topped by a dome with an octangular tambour. The interior, 112½ by 100 feet, will be also enriched by ranges of Corinthian pillars; the cost will be defrayed both by voluntary subscriptions collected in the usual manner and by a weekly penny collection from the industrious and poorer classes. A Sunday school with about 500 pupils is attached to this body. The Capuchins' or Reformed Franciscans' institution, situated in Blackman's-lane, consists of a provincial, guardian, and three priests. The chapel was built by the celebrated Arthur O'Leary, who was a priest of this order. A new chapel has been commenced in 1823, on Charlotte's-quay, by the present provincial, the Very Rev. Theobald Matthews, who has contributed liberally to its expense, which has already amounted to £10,000; the remainder is derived from subscriptions and weekly collections. The structure, from a design and under the superintendence of Messrs. Pain, is built of a light grey limestone, and is already carried up as high as the roof; when finished, it will present a splendid specimen of the later English style, with a tower and spire, 200 feet high: the front has a portico of three lofty arches resting on octagonal piers; between the centre piers is a rich screen, forming a kind of porch to the doorway. The piers, ten in number, are continued at the angles of the building, those not connected with the tower terminating like those of Hen. VII.'s chapel at Westminster, from which spring the exterior flying buttresses. Similar buttresses are introduced in connection with the turrets at the angles of the tower, which rise from a base just above the arches before mentioned. The tower will consist of two stories, having an open parapet of tracery passing round it, above which will rise the spire: the upper story of the tower and the lower portion of the spire will be open, so managed as to combine strength and variety with airy lightness. The contract for the building was nearly £12,000, but it is estimated that the entire cost will exceed £20,000. The Sunday schools, under the care of the Josephian Society (the Very Rev.T. Matthews, patron), are composed of religious and well-educated young men who instruct 500 boys: the day schools are under the superintendence of 50 Ladies Governesses, five of whom attend every day and are assisted by a matron and instruct 500 girls; an infants' school for 350 children is under the direction of the same ladies, aided by a matron from the London parent institution. Evening schools for the instruction of apprentices and labouring boys are under the care of the same society. The Presentation Monastery, situated in Douglas-street, was established in 1827 in buildings previously occupied by the Nuns of the Presentation order. The community consists of a superior and ten brothers, who devote themselves to the instruction of the poor on a system embracing every branch of useful education. Attached to the dwelling is a spacious building, divided into four large apartments capable of accommodating 1000 boys; about 600 receive instruction and are apprenticed when at a proper age. The funds are derived from subscriptions and the proceeds of an annual sermon. The school owes its origin to the late Very Rev. Dean Collins, priest of the parish, who contributed liberally towards the erection of the building, and also to its support. The Lancasterian school, at the end of Great George's-street, is conducted by this community; it is 80 feet by 60, and capable of accommodating 1000 pupils; it is attended by the same number, and supported in the same manner as the school previously described. The Christian Brotherhood was instituted in 1811; the present buildings, situated in Peacock-lane, were erected in 1815. The community consists of a superior and eight brothers, who devote themselves to the instruction of the poor in two schools, one in Peacock lane, the other on Sullivan's-quay: the former of these, two stories high and divided into six apartments, each 45 feet by 25, affords accommodation for 800 boys; in the latter about 300 attend. The schools are conducted and supported in the same manner as those of the Presentation Monastery. The community's dwelling-house is at a short distance from the former of these schools, on an elevated and commanding situation. The Presentation Convent, in Douglas-street, owes its origin to the late Miss Honora Nagle, who in 1777 erected a small building for that purpose; which being soon found too small for the increasing number of its inmates, the building now occupied by the parochial clergymen and by the monks of the Presentation order, was erected by the ladies and their friends, under the superintendence of the Very Rev. Dean Collins: the establishment has since become the parent house of the Presentation Institute in Ireland. After the decease of this lady, the new order was approved of by Pope Pius VI. and confirmed by Pius VII., under the title of "the Presentation of the Blessed Virgin Mary." Dean Collins, then the parish priest, purchased, in 1825, the interest of the present buildings (partly erected by Miss Nagle) from the Ursuline Nuns, who had removed to their present abode in Blackrock; and the present community of the Presentation Institute removed into them on Oct. 1st, 1827, from the buildings now occupied by the Parochial Clergy and the Monks of the Presentation order. The community consists of a superioress, 17 professed and 2 lay nuns, who devote their whole time to the gratuitous instruction of poor female children; the average attendance of pupils is about 500. The buildings, with the chapel, form a very respectable pile in an elevated situation. The remains of the foundress are interred in the cemetery within the grounds, and those of Dean Collins within the chapel, in which there is a neat marble slab erected to his memory. There is an almshouse for 20 poor old women in connection with it, chiefly supported by the ladies. The North Presentation convent was founded in Chapel-street in 1799, and removed to the present house in Clarence-street in 1808. The community consists of a superioress, 14 professed nuns and two lay sisters, who devote their time to the same purpose as those in Douglas-street already described: the average attendance of children at the school is 600, one-third of whom are clothed annually by a subscription of the citizens: the buildings with the chapel form a handsome pile. A branch of the Sisters of Charity, Stanhope-street, Dublin, was established near the cathedral 10 years since; the community consists of six inmates, who go out to relieve the sick poor and to instruct them in the duties of religion.

The Presbyterians have two places of worship, one in connection with the Synod of Munster, and the other in connection with that of Ulster; each is of the first class. There are also two places of worship for Wesleyan Methodists, and one each for the Baptists, the Society of Friends, the Independents and the Primitive Methodists. The congregation belonging to the Synod of Munster is a Cromwellian establishment, and one of the oldest dissenting congregations in Cork: the place of worship, a commodious and well-arranged edifice, is in Princes's-street: a boys' and girls' school in connection with it, the pupils of which are clothed and apprenticed at a proper age, is supported by subscription and the proceeds of an annual sermon: there is also an alms'-house, with accommodation for 15 inmates, but having only 9 at present in it; also a loan fund and a lending library. J. Pedder, Esq., bequeathed to the congregation £600, one half for the ministers, and the other for the poor; S. McCarthy also bequeathed £300 for the same purpose. Dr. Hincks, Greek professor in the Royal Belfast Academical Institution, and author of a Greek and English Lexicon and other works connected with classical literature, was minister of this congregation for many years. The congregation of the Synod of Ulster holds its devotional meetings in a large room in Tuckey-street, formerly the assembly-room belonging to Daly's Club-house. The Wesleyan Methodists' places of worship, both neat and commodious edifices, are in Henry-street and Patrick-street; attached to the former are a female day school and an infants' school; each has a Sunday school; all are supported by subscription. The Baptist place of worship is a plain building in Marlborough-street. The meeting-house belonging to the Society of Friends consists of a large and convenient range of buildings lately erected in Grattan-street, on the site of the old meeting-house, and comprising an apartment for public worship, with committee-rooms attached to it, and, fronting the street, a commodious dwelling-house for the resident care-taker and for reduced aged and infirm members: the expense, amounting to £4200, was defrayed by a subscription of its own members. The Independent meeting-house, in Old George's-street, was built by Messrs. Pain in 1829, at an expense of about £3000; it is an oblong edifice, 80 feet by 40, with two semicircular appendages; and in front is a small portico of four fanciful columns resembling the Corinthian order; the ceiling is arched and richly pannelled. The Primitive Methodists have their place of worship in French Church-street.

In addition to the schools already noticed are many more in the different parishes of the city and suburbs, supported principally by annual grants, local subscriptions, and collections after charity sermons. In Christ-Church parish are the male and female parochial schools, of which the boys' school has an endowment of £15 late currency bequeathed by Mrs. Shearman; an infants' school, and several Sunday schools. In the parish of St. Anne Shandon are the male and female parochial schools; the parochial infants' school; the Brickfields' National schools, aided by grants from the National Board, and several Sunday schools. A school in George's-street was established in 1822, principally by the exertions of Dr. P. Kehoe, for the instruction of deaf and dumb children, into which, since its foundation, 60 children have been admitted; of these, 30 have been withdrawn by their parents from time to time; 15 have been apprenticed; 4 died, and 11 are at present in attendance. Here is a branch of the Juvenile Auxiliary Society to the National Institution for the deaf and dumb at Claremont, near Dublin. In the parish of St. Finbarr are the parochial male school, aided by an annual subscription of £20 from the dean and chapter, and a bequest of £10 per annum late currency from Mrs. Shearman; the parochial female school, a National school for boys at Blackrock, a school supported by subscriptions, and several Sunday schools. In the parish of St. Mary Shandon are a National school for boys and girls in Blarney-lane, and another at Sunday's Well: the latter was erected in 1835, at an expense of £340, of which the National Board of Education contributed £186, and the remainder was defrayed by subscription; it is a neat building of two apartments each 52 feet by 24, and affords instruction to about 350 of each sex. In the parish of St. Nicholas the Masonic Female Orphan Asylum, Cove-street, was founded in 1820, in which the children are maintained, clothed, educated, and apprenticed to trades or other useful occupations: from its commencement to July 31st, 1836, 60 children have been admitted, of whom 40 have been apprenticed: the expense for that year was about £300: the parish also contains a friary school for girls, and an infants' school adjoining the chapel of the Capuchins, a friary and Sunday and evening school for girls, and a Sunday school in connection with the Established Church. In the parish of St. Paul are a Protestant free school for boys and girls, several of whom are clothed, and, under the same roof, an infants' school; a free school for girls, endowed with the dividends on £450 three and a half per cent. consol. bank annuities; and two Sunday schools. In the parish of St. Peter are a school for girls adjoining the chapel of St. Peter and St. Paul, under the superintendence of a committee of ladies, and aided by the interest of a bequest from the late Mr. Rochford; St. Patrick's asylum for orphans, under the superintendence of the R. C. clergyman, in which 20 boys and 20 girls are boarded, lodged, clothed, and educated, and at a proper age apprenticed, and which is supported by subscriptions and a collection after a charity sermon, amounting to about £220 per annum; a school for girls, and an infants' school in connection with the Wesleyan Methodists; and several Sunday schools. These schools altogether, exclusively of the Sunday schools, afford instruction to about 3750 boys and 3250 girls; there are also 45 private pay schools, in which about 1150 boys and 740 girls are taught.

The Foundling Hospital, in Leitrim-street, was opened in 1747. It is governed by an incorporated board, consisting of the diocesan, the mayor, recorder, aldermen, sheriffs, common-councilmen and common-speaker, with 26 of the commonalty, elected by the D'Oyer Hundred, and is maintained by a local tax on coal and culm, weigh-house fines, carriage licenses and penalties on car drivers, amounting to about £5500 annually. The infants, received periodically from the churchwardens, are placed out at nurse till they are six or seven years old, when they become inmates until of an age to be apprenticed. The average number of the former class is 1000 and of the latter 400. They are educated as Protestants and bound to Protestant masters. Good conduct during apprenticeship is rewarded by a gratuity of three guineas. The building is a small quadrangle, of which the chapel forms one side; the other three are appropriated to school-rooms (two for the boys and two for the girls), dormitories, and other necessary apartments. A resident chaplain superintends the details of the institution. The North Infirmary, adjoining the churchyard of St. Anne's, Shandon, was formed in 1744 by the members of a musical society, who appropriated their surplus funds for its support, and by individual subscriptions, and was established by an act passed in 1752; it is supported by a Grand Jury presentment of £250, a grant of £50 from Government, and voluntary subscriptions, all which together, with funded property arising from bequests, amounts to about £500 per annum. In 1829 Mr. Sampayo, a native of the city, but resident in London, contributed £1000 for the enlargement of the hospital accommodation, which having been increased by a bequest of £500 from Mr. Rochford and by other subscriptions, amounting in all to £3200, the trustees determined to erect a new building capable of containing 100 beds, on the ground belonging to the old infirmary. The building, erected by Mr. Hill, a resident architect, consists of a plain structure, of three stories, forming three sides of a quadrangle, 100 feet in front, with lateral returns of 75 feet each. The ground floor is appropriated to the dispensary department and to accommodation for officers; the two upper stories are laid out in wards. The expense of its erection was £3760. 13. 6. Its affairs are conducted by a board of trustees partly official and partly elected annually. The number of patients during 1835 was, interns, cured 227, relieved 30, died 8, remaining at the close of the year 30; total, 295 · externs, cured or relieved, 14,606; general total, 14,901. The income for the same year was £1703. 12. 2., and the expenditure, £1559. 4. 6., from which latter item is to be deducted £800 paid to the architect on account of the building, leaving £759. 4. 6. for the current annual expenses of the institution. The South Infirmary was established under the 11th and 12th of Geo. III., and is supported by a similar presentment of £250 late currency from the Grand Jury, an annual grant of £50 by the Government, and subscriptions amounting to about £200 per annum. The building contains about 32 beds, and is well adapted to its purpose; the wards are large and well ventilated. The number admitted in 1835 was 381, of whom 243 were discharged cured, 76 relieved, 25 died, 6 absconded, and 30 remained on Jan. 1st, 1836; during the same year, 14,354 externs were cured or relieved. An attempt was some time since made by the trustees to unite these infirmaries and constitute them a general hospital both for the county and the county of the city of Cork, and to erect a large building sufficient for the purpose; this arrangement being subsequently limited to the union of the infirmaries only, an act was procured in the 2nd and 3rd of Wm. IV., but from some difficulty which arose the design was ultimately abandoned. The Fever Hospital and House of Recovery, established in 1802, and supported by annual subscriptions and Grand Jury presentments, is situated in an airy part of the north suburbs; and from its opening to the 31st of Oct., 1836, not less than 51,085 patients have been admitted. In 1816 a detached building, capable of containing 80 beds, was added to it, into which, during the prevalence of cholera, 775 patients of that class were admitted. The building is spacious, well arranged, and thoroughly ventilated, and contains 200 beds: the total expenditure for the year 1835 amounted to £1295. 17. 10. The Lying-in Hospital, on the Mardyke parade, was established in 1798, and is supported by subscription under the superintendence of a committee of ladies; it contains 12 beds, and, in 1835, 368 poor women participated in the benefits of the establishment. The Cork Midwifery Dispensary and Institution for Diseases of Women and Children was opened in Brown-street in 1834, and is supported by subscription. The Cork General Dispensary, Humane Society, and Cow-pock Institution was established in 1787, and is supported by Grand Jury presentments, donations, and subscriptions: in the year ending April 1st, 1836, not less than 11,198 patients received medical and surgical relief from this establishment, of whom 5066 were relieved in their own dwellings. The Lunatic Asylum for the county and city is situated on the Blackrock road, and is connected with the House of Industry adjoining, and under the direction of the same board of governors; the house, though spacious, is not adapted for complete classification; a considerable piece of ground in front enclosed with a high wall is used as a place of recreation for the patients, and is cultivated by them; the number in 1836 was 370, which is 70 more than can be properly accommodated; the institution is supported by presentments on the county and county of the city, apportioned by sharing equally certain fixed expenses, and by contributing to the maintenance of the inmates according to the number sent from each: the annual average expenditure amounts to £4000. The asylum is under the medical superintendence of Dr. Osburne, and of a moral governor, the former of whom has a private establishment at Lindville for the reception of insane patients, beautifully situated on a limestone rock gently sloping to the river, of which it commands a pleasing view; and attached to it is an enclosed demesne of 14 acres, affording extensive walks and ample means of recreation to the patients under his care. The House of Industry is an extensive building, affording accommodation to 1200 inmates, who are always under its roof, and of whom two-thirds are women; these are employed in household work, washing, spinning, plain work, weaving, and platting straw; and the males in picking oakum, weaving, quarrying and breaking stones for the roads, and in cleaning the streets. The establishment contains two medical and surgical hospitals, in which are 150 beds; and there are three schools for boys and girls, each under a separate teacher. It is supported by Grand Jury presentments, the labour of the inmates, collections at charity sermons, and by subscriptions and donations; and is conducted with the greatest regard to the comfort and moral improvement of the inmates. The Magdalene Asylum, in Peacock-lane, was founded in 1809 by Nicholas Therry, Esq., for the protection and reformation of penitent females of dissolute habits, who now contribute to their own maintenance by honest industry. The County and City of Cork Refuge, in Deane-street, instituted in 1825 for destitute females, and more especially for female liberated prisoners, is supported by subscription; there are at present 30 inmates in this institution. There are various almshouses, principally of parochial character, among which the chief are the corporation almshouses, and those of the parishes of St. Finbarr, St. Nicholas, Christ-Church, and St. Peter and St. Paul; the almshouses in connection with the South Presentation convent, founded by Miss Nagle for aged women; and St. John's Asylum, in Douglas-street, for aged men, the two latter of Roman Catholic origin. Capt. Bretridge, in 1683, devised the lands of East Drumcummer to the corporation for ever, in trust for the payment of 10*s.* 6*d.* weekly to seven poor old Protestant men that had been soldiers, the surplus to be applied in apprenticing the children of poor soldiers of the Protestant religion in the city and liberties, or in default of such, the children of other poor Protestant parents; the present income is £258 per annum. In 1584, Stephen Skiddy bequeathed to the mayor and aldermen £24 per annum, to be paid by the Vintners' Company of London, and to be distributed among ten poor, honest, and aged persons of the city. Almshouses were built for each of these charities, and in 1718 a new house was erected for both near the Green Coat Hospital, at an expense of £1150, arising from the sale of the former site; the piazzas were subsequently added at the expense of some benevolent individuals: the annual income of Skiddy's charity, arising from the original bequest and the rents of certain premises granted by the corporation in 1702, is now £235. 18., and is expended in the support of 41 aged widows and five aged men, who have apartments in the almshouse. Mr. William Masterson bequeathed £30 per annum to the poor of the parish of St. Mary, of which sum, £16 is distributed in sums of £2 to poor Protestant tradesmen, £10 is given as marriage portions to two Protestant female servants married to Protestant tradesmen, and the remaining £4 to the Green Coat Hospital. In 1832, W. Lapp, Esq., bequeathed £30,000 for the support of poor old Protestants in the city; but the will not being properly attested to pass freehold estates, the heir resists payment; it, is, however, thought that the personal property will be sufficient to pay nearly the whole of the bequest. There are various societies for the diffusion of religious knowledge. The charitable loan fund originated in the establishment of a society for the relief of poor confined debtors by Henry Shears, in 1774; by a deed dated March 30th, 1785, trustees were empowered by the Musical Society of Dublin to lend money, at first free of interest, to industrious tradesmen in sums from £2 to £5, but subsequently with a charge of 1*s.* interest on each loan of £3 under the authority of the act of the 4th of Geo. IV. cap. 32. The funds are now entirely appropriated to the purposes of the loan society, and are lent in sums of £3, the borrower giving security for repayment by weekly instalments of 2*s.* 6*d.*: the number of families repaying the loan in 1834 was 1150.

Among the remains of antiquity one of the most ancient was Gill Abbey, which, after standing 980 years, fell down in 1738; no vestiges of it can now be traced, but near the site is a cave, anciently called the cave of St. Finbarr, and several fragments of stone pillars and other sculptured ornaments have been lately turned up on the spot. An Augustinian monastery, also on the south side of the town, is the only one of which there are any remains: it is stated by various writers to have been founded at different periods, by some in the reign of Edw. I., by others in that of Hen. V. or VI., and by some even so late as 1472 or 1475; the remains consist of the tower, which is 64 feet high, and is called the Red abbey. The Franciscan monastery had a stately church in which many illustrious persons were interred, but it is now entirely demolished, and Hebert's-square is built on its site. On digging the foundations of the buildings in this square in 1836, a stone curiously sculptured with the date 1567 marked on it was discovered, also a plate of metal 34 inches by 30, now in Mr. Hebert's possession, on which is represented the Nativity, accompanied by a long description, apparently in Dutch. The site of the Dominican friary, called the Abbey of St. Mary of the Island, is now occupied by Mr. O'Keefe's distillery. A nunnery, dedicated to St. John the Baptist, and from which St. John's-street took its name, was founded early in the 14th century; the site was discovered a few years since, when several tombstones were dug up near the spot. St. Stephen's priory for lepers was founded in the south suburbs, at a very early period, on the site now occupied by the Blue Coat Hospital; and a Benedictine priory is said to have been founded by King John on the south side of the city, and made a cell to the English abbey at Bath. Bourke mentions a house of White friars and a preceptory of Knights Templars, of which not the slightest vestiges can be traced. Of the ancient walls of the city, with their circular towers, there are considerable remains near the North bridge, and in the rear of the foundry the wall is perfect: of the fortifications in and near it, the last, which was called from its founder Skiddy's castle, was taken down in 1785. A mint was established in the city after the English settlement, but the specimens of coinage are extremely scarce; the earliest extant are silver pennies and halfpennies of the reign of Edw. I., which have on the obverse the king's head within a triangle, with the inscription EDW: R: ANGL: DUX: HYB:. Among the writers who have contributed to elevate the literary character of the city, exclusively of professional writers, are Arthur Murphy, the translator of Tacitus, and author of several successful tragedies and comedies; O'Keefe, the writer of comedies; Edw. Murphy, editor of Lucian; the celebrated Arthur O'Leary, equally distinguished for his wit, learning, and eloquence, and his biographer the Rev. Thos. England; Thos. Crofton Croker, author of "Fairy Legends" and other works illustrative of Irish customs and superstitions; James Roche, author of several articles on the history and descent of the principal commoners of the empire; Dr. Wood, a writer on natural history and on the antiquities of Ireland; John O'Driscol, late judge of Dominica, who published a work in two volumes on the state of Ireland; the Rev. Thos. Townsend, author of the statistical survey of the county of Cork; Dr. Maginn, a principal contributor to Fraser's Magazine; the Rev. Dr. Hincks, already noticed as a former minister of the Presbyterian congregation in connection with the Synod of Munster; Henry Uppington, a writer on various scientific subjects; the writer of the articles in Fraser's Magazine, under the fictitious name of Father Prout, is a native of this city; Richard Milliken, both a poet and a painter; Miss Milliken, writer of several novels. Of eminent painters, Cork is the native place of the celebrated Barry, professor of Painting in the Royal Academy of London, a man equally memorable for his genius, his eccentricities, and his spirit of independence; also Butt, Grogan, Ford, and McAlise: Hogan the sculptor is a native of this city. Cork gives the title of Earl to the senior branch of the noble family of Boyle.

CORKBEG, a parish, in the barony of IMOKILLY, county of CORK, and province of MUNSTER, 5 miles (S. W.) from Cloyne; containing 2221 inhabitants. This parish is situated on the southern coast, at the entrance to Cork harbour, by which it is bounded on the west. In 1690, the fortress, erected in 1596, to protect the entrance to the harbour, was garrisoned for Jas. II., but his troops were driven out by the Earl of Marlborough, on the 21st of September, and this was the first strong hold he took in Ireland. After this it was suffered to fall into decay, the platform or gun batteries being all that now remains. The parish contains 3319 statute acres, as applotted under the tithe act, and 100 acres within the walls of Carlisle fort, which are uncultivated and nominally tithe-free. About three-fourths of the land are under tillage, and clover and green crops are grown in small quantities. The principal seats are Rochemount, the residence of J. W. Roche, Esq.; Trabolgan, of E. Roche, Esq., surrounded by a finely varied and well-planted demesne of 400 acres: the mansion has an extensive front facing the sea, and includes two conservatories containing a fine collection of exotics. On the north-west side of the parish, projecting into the harbour, is Corkbeg House, the elegant residence of R. U. Penrose Fitzgerald, Esq.; the lawn and shrubbery are connected by a narrow slip with the main land, where the remainder of the demesne, comprising 350 acres of some of the best cultivated land in the barony is situated. Carlisle fort and Roche's tower lighthouse are within the limits of the parish: the former, which is situated near the mouth of Cork harbour, is a large fortress, erected at a great expense soon after the entrance of the French fleet into Bantry bay, and was garrisoned till 1828; the barrack will accommodate 7 officers and 155 artillery men, but is at present occupied only by a master-gunner and six men. Roche's tower lighthouse, which was rebuilt in 1835, is on the eastern side of the entrance to the harbour, and occupies the site of an old castle, called Roche's tower: the lantern is elevated 139 feet above high water mark, and consists of 10 lamps giving a steady fixed light, which may be seen 14 nautical miles in clear weather. As seen from the harbour and from Cove, the light is bright, and from the sea it is a deep red. Large vessels entering the harbour at nearly low water should be careful to avoid the rocks called the Stags, which are on the east side of the entrance, and the harbour rock, which is within them, and bears N. N. W. ¾ W. from Roche's tower nearly half a mile, and has 15 feet of water at low spring tides.

The living is a rectory and vicarage, in the diocese of Cloyne, and was formerly part of the union of Ahada, but, on the death of Dr. Brinkley, in 1835, who held it as Bishop of Cloyne, the union was dissolved, and it now forms a separate living, in the gift of the Crown. The tithes amount to £517. 12. 3. The glebe comprises 22 acres, and it is intended to erect a glebe-house. The old church of this parish being in ruins, a new one will be built at the same time partly by private subscriptions, and partly by an expected grant from the Ecclesiastical Commissioners. In the R. C. divisions this parish is part of the district of Ahada. The parochial school for boys is in the village of Whitegate: it was built and endowed in 1831, by Col. Fitzgerald. The female and infants' schools are altogether supported by Mrs. Blakeney Fitzgerald. A free school was founded in 1818 by the late John Roche, Esq., who endowed it with £10 per annum: it is now under the National Board. There are also two private schools. The number of children receiving education in 1835, was 179. The ruins of the old church, which is supposed to have been built in 1587, are in the midst of a large wood. On the north side of them is a mausoleum belonging to the family of Roche, of Trabolgan; and on the south-west side is a large enclosed space belonging to the ancient family of Fitzgerald. Between the lighthouse and Carlisle fort are the remains of Prince Rupert's tower; and near Corkbeg House are the ruins of the old castle, built by the Condons in 1369, and for a long period the residence of that family. In the middle of a large field at Finnure are extensive ruins, supposed to have belonged to a religious establishment.

COROFIN.—See CUROFIN.

CORRICK, or CORRIG-BRIDGE, a village, in the parish of KILCOMMON, barony of ERRIS, county of MAYO, and province of CONNAUGHT, 16 miles (E.) from Belmullet: the population is returned with the parish. This village is situated on the road from Crossmolina and Castlebar to Belmullet, and on the river Corrig or Owenmore, over which is a bridge of four arches, from which it takes its name; it is a constabulary police station.

CORROFIN.—See KILMOCRENAN.

CORROGE, a parish, in the barony of CLANWILLIAM, county of TIPPERARY, and province of MUNSTER, 1 mile (E. S. E.) from Tipperary: the population is returned with the parish of Kilshane. This parish comprises only 753 statute acres. It is a vicarage, in the diocese of Emly, and forms part of the union and corps of the prebend of Lattin in the cathedral of Emly: the rectory is impropriate in the representatives of the Rev. Robt. Watts. The tithes amount to £45 per annum, payable in equal moieties to the impropriator and the incumbent. The burial-ground is still used.

COSCORY, or ENNIS-CORKER, an island, in the parish of KILDYSART, barony of CLONDERLAW, county of CLARE, and province of MUNSTER, 1 mile (E. by S.) from Kildysart. This island, which is inhabited by one family only, is situated near the western shore of the river Fergus, at its junction with the Shannon, and contains about 165 statute acres of excellent land, which is mostly in pasture; the portion under tillage is manured with sea-weed, and produces good crops of grain and potatoes.

COTLANDSTOWN, a parish, partly in the barony of UPPERCROSS, county of DUBLIN, and partly in that of UPPER NAAS, county of KILDARE, and province of LEINSTER, 1¼ mile (E. by N.) from Ballymore-Eustace; containing 459 inhabitants. This parish is situated on the river Liffey, and on the road from Ballymore-Eustace to Kilcullen. It comprises 1490 statute acres, partly in pasture and partly under tillage; the system of agriculture is improving, and the principal crops are barley, oats, and potatoes. The gentlemen's seats are

Stonebrook, the residence of O'Connor Henehy, Esq., in whose demesne is the ancient parochial burial-ground; and Mullaboden, of the Rev. H. Johnston. The Dublin part of the parish is within the jurisdiction of St. Sepulchre's Court, Dublin. The parish is partly in the diocese of Dublin, and partly in that of Kildare: the rectory of the Kildare portion is appropriate to the see, and that of the Dublin portion forms part of the corps of the treasurership of St. Patrick's cathedral; the vicarage forms part of the union of Ballymore-Eustace. The tithes amount to £69. 15. 5¼., of which £49. 7. 6¼. is payable to the Bishop of Kildare, £4. 7. 11. to the lessee of the treasurer of St. Patrick's, Dublin, and the remaining £8 to the vicar. In the R. C. divisions the parish forms part of the union or district of Ballymore-Eustace. In the Kildare part of the parish is a private school of about 20 boys and 20 girls.

COUMDEEHY, a village, in the parish of BALLYHEIGUE, barony of CLANMAURICE, county of KERRY, and province of MUNSTER, 10 miles (N. N. W.) from Tralee; containing 378 inhabitants. It is situated on the road from Tralee to Kerry Head, and near the western coast, and comprises about 50 houses, which are mostly thatched. Here are stations of the constabulary police and coast-guard. Races are annually held on the beach in September, and a patent for a fair on the 8th and 9th of that month exists, but is not acted upon. A considerable quantity of sea-weed is collected on the beach and used as manure. The coast here is extremely dangerous; the bay, which is shallow and has a foul bottom, has often been mistaken for the mouth of the Shannon, in consequence of an error in marking the latitude of Loop Head on the charts, which has occasioned many fatal shipwrecks. The parochial church and glebe-house are within a quarter of a mile of the village; near the latter is a school, supported by the incumbent, the Rev. J. P. Chute.

COURTMACSHERRY, a maritime village, in the parish of LISLEE, barony of IBANE and BARRYROE, county of CORK, and province of MUNSTER, 2½ miles (S. E.) from Timoleague; containing 680 inhabitants. This village is pleasantly situated on the harbour of the same name on the southern coast, and contains about 140 houses, which form one long street extending along the south side of the bay. Its eastern part consists of small mean cabins, but in the western are numerous large and handsome houses, recently erected for the accommodation of visiters during the bathing season. It possesses many local advantages for trade and commerce, and is well situated for carrying on an extensive fishery; for which, and the general improvement of the place, great encouragement has been lately afforded by the Earl of Shannon. Several small vessels of different classes are engaged in the coal and corn trade, in the fishery, and in the conveyance of sand for manure. Of these, seven are colliers trading with Newport, eight are hookers, engaged in conveying corn, potatoes, &c., to Cork, and bringing back timber, iron, and other merchandize; four are lighters, chiefly employed in conveying sand; and about 20 vessels are exclusively engaged in the fisheries: the value of the fish taken in 1835 was estimated at £2460. A small but convenient pier, constructed chiefly at the expense of the Earl of Shannon, has proved a great protection to the fisheries and very beneficial to trade. Several new lines of road have been lately opened, and other improvements are in contemplation, which, together with its beautiful and sheltered situation, the salubrity of its atmosphere, and the abundant supply of fish and all other kinds of provision, have rendered this village one of the most fashionable bathing-places on the southern coast. Small vessels may lie in safety, in two fathoms of water, near the quay in this harbour; and about a quarter of a mile to the east, in a very small creek formed by a perpendicular clay cliff, a vessel may lie in 1½ or 2 fathoms; but as the channel is narrow and the tide rapid, one anchor must lie on the shore: near the middle of the bay are two rocks, called the Barrels; the southernmost is small, and dry at low water, and the other, which is larger, is about ½ a mile to the north of the former, and is seldom seen above water. At the southernmost Barrel rock the extremity of the old head of Kinsale bears S. E. by E., and the Horse rock, which is always above water, W. To avoid the Barrel rocks on the west side, vessels should keep within a mile and a half of the shore, on the west side of the bay. The best anchorage, in westerly winds, is on the same side of the bay, in 10 or 12 fathoms, or on the north side of the Horse rock, in 4 or 5 fathoms. At the village is a station of the coast-guard, being one of the eight comprised in the district of Kinsale. Here are also male, female, and infants' schools, built and supported by Mr. and the Misses Leslie; and a clothing establishment, under the management of the vicar, is supported by subscription, and, together with a loan fund, has proved very beneficial to the poor. Adjoining the village is the beautiful demesne and summer residence of the Earl of Shannon; in the immediate neighbourhood are the ruins of Abbey Mahon; and at the distance of two miles are the extensive and picturesque ruins of the abbey and castle of Timoleague.

COVE, commonly called the COVE of CORK, a sea-port, market, and post-town, partly in the parish of CLONMELL, but chiefly in that of TEMPLEROBIN, in the Great Island, barony of BARRYMORE, county of CORK, and province of MUNSTER; containing 6996 inhabitants. By way of Passage, crossing the ferry, it is only 9½ miles (E. S. E.) from Cork; but overland, by way of Foaty, it is 14¼ miles from that city, and 133 miles (S. W. by S.) from Dublin. It is situated on the north side of Cork harbour, in lat. 54° 51′, and lon. 8° 18′ 45″. The progress of Cove has been very rapid. So recently as 1786 it was a small village, consisting of a few scattered houses inhabited by the tide-waiters and pilots of Cork, and some miserable cabins occupied by fishermen; at present it is a large and handsome town, comprising nine large and several smaller streets. The great increase of its population principally arose from its convenient situation for the shipping in Cork harbour, in which, during the French war, 600 sail of merchant vessels have been at anchor at one time, and 400 sail have left the harbour under convoy in one day. These great fleets always lay immediately in front of the present town, and many of them within half a cable's length of the shore. It has also been greatly benefited by the erection of Carlisle and Camden forts; martello towers on Great Island, Hawlbowling, and Ringskiddy; and by the bomb-proof artillery barracks on Spike Island. In addition to this, Hawlbowling was fortified and made the ordnance depôt, and the Lords of the Admiralty made it the only naval victualling depôt in Ireland; and Rocky island was excavated and made the chief gunpowder magazine for the southern part of the kingdom. It was also the place of embarkation for troops ordered on foreign service, and the station of an admiral. The great expenditure of money for these works, and for the supply of provisions and other requisites for the shipping in the harbour, caused many persons to settle here, and the number was increased by the visits of invalids and persons of fortune, who were attracted by the salubrity of its climate and the beauty of its situation in the finest harbour in Europe. Cove is built on the side of a clay-slate hill, on the south shore of Great Island, which rises from the water's edge, and being very steep, the streets, which are parallel to the shore, rise tier above tier, and being backed by the high grounds of the island, present a very picturesque view from the entrance to the harbour. The principal streets are nearly level, and those that connect them wind so gradually as greatly to diminish the apparent steepness of their ascent. The houses in the main streets are mostly large and well built of stone, and many of them faced with slate; the streets are all wide, clean, well paved, and abundantly supplied with water from springs in the clay-slate. The principal market is on Saturday, but there is one held daily, which is abundantly supplied with fish, vegetables, meat, &c. A large and handsome market-house, consisting of a centre and wings, was erected by the late J. Smith Barry, Esq., in 1806: the centre is appropriated to the sale of fish and vegetables, the west wing to the storing and sale of potatoes, and the east wing is fitted up as shambles. The post is daily, and yielded a revenue of £977 when the last return was made to parliament. There is a constabulary police barrack; and a chief coast-guard station, the head of the district, which includes Cove, Ballycroneen, Poor Head, the lighthouse, East Ferry, Cork, Crosshaven, and Robert's Cove. Petty sessions are held every week; and there is a small prison of two cells for the temporary confinement of offenders. Near the western entrance to the town is a large and handsome pier, erected in 1805, at a cost of £20,000, and connected with it are very capacious quays. Here is a building called the Boarding Station, occupied by tide-waiters and other custom-house officers of Cork.

The views round Cove are extremely beautiful. Beyond the harbour, on the east, are Rostellan, Castle-Mary, and the vale of Cloyne, with its ancient cathedral and round tower; to the south is the capacious bay, with its numerous ships, noble entrance, lighthouse, and forts; on the west is Ringskiddy with its martello tower, Carrigaline with its noble estuary, and the broad entrance to the Lee; and on the north are the high lands of Great Island, which shelter the town of Cove in that direction. Near the town are several elegant mansions, marine villas, &c., which are more particularly noticed in the article on Great Island. The celebrated regatta of Cove takes place in July or August: the prizes are numerous and valuable, and many of the best yachts in Ireland, with some from England and Scotland, attend its celebration. Near the custom-house quay is a splendid edifice in the Italian style, built by the Yacht Club and occupied by its members during the regatta season. The parish church of the union of Clonmell and Templerobin is on an elevated site in the centre of the town: it is a large and elegant edifice, in the early English style of architecture, with stained glass windows, aad was built in 1810, by aid of a loan of £2000 from the late Board of First Fruits. Near it is a R. C. chapel, which was enlarged in 1835. There is also a small place of worship for Wesleyan Methodists. The parochial schools are large neat buildings, erected by subscription on land given by Lord Midleton, who is an occasional donor; they are under the Kildare-place Society, but are supported by subscription. An infants' school has existed here about three years, and is supported by subscription: a school-house is being built for it near the parochial schools; and a very large building for a national school is also in progress of erection, partly at the expense of the National Board, and partly by a bequest of £25 per annum left by W. Lynch, Esq., in 1831. There are a fever hospital and a dispensary, and a military bathing hospital for the province of Munster. There is a parochial alms-house for twelve poor Protestants, each of whom receives 2*s.* 6*d.* weekly from the Sunday collections in the church, with coal and clothing during the winter, from a bequest of £100 by the late Miss Spratt. A Benevolent Society, and a loan fund for poor mechanics, have also been established.

COVE, or SUMMERCOVE, a village, in the parish of Rincurran, barony of Kinsale, county of Cork, and province of Munster, 1 mile (E.) from Kinsale; containing 446 inhabitants. This village is beautifully situated on the harbour of Kinsale, and consists of neatly built houses, among which are several commodious villas and lodges for the accommodation of the numerous visiters from various parts of the country that frequent this place during the summer for the benefit of sea-bathing. An extensive fishery is carried on, and affords employment to a large portion of the inhabitants. An annual regatta is held in July or August, and a race-course has been formed in the vicinity by subscription, where races are held after the regatta. In the village are the male and female parochial schools, established by the rector in 1829, in connection with the Kildare-place Society, but now supported by him in connection with the Cork Diocesan Association: the rector also provides a house, rent-free, for the master. Above the village is the church of Rincurran, a beautiful and conspicuous object; and in the vicinity is the extensive garrison of Charlesfort.

CRANFIELD, a parish, in the barony of Upper Toome, county of Antrim, and province of Ulster, 1 mile (S. W. by S.) from Randalstown; containing 386 inhabitants. This parish is situated on the road from Randalstown to Toome, and on the western shore of Lough Neagh, of which, according to the Ordnance survey, it comprises 2691½ statute acres, besides 834½ acres of land in a good state of cultivation, agriculture having greatly improved; there is neither bog nor waste land: the spinning and weaving of linen cloth is carried on. It is within the jurisdiction of the manorial court of Mullaghgane, held every month at Toome. The living is a rectory, in the diocese of Down and Connor, partly impropriate in William Cranstone, Esq., of Belfast, and partly episcopally united, from time immemorial, to the vicarage of Duneane, to the church of which the Protestant inhabitants of this parish resort. The tithes amount to £35. 11. 11. The ancient parish church is now a noble pile of ruins, situated on the verge of Cranfield Point, overlooking Lough Neagh. Near them is a celebrated well, to which the peasantry resort in great numbers on June 26th, 27th, and 28th, and booths are erected for their accommodation; they perform "stations" round the ruins of the church, and drink and wash in the waters of the well, which is supposed to have been endued with healing properties by St. Olcan, who is traditionally recorded to have been buried here in earth brought from Rome; and in which are found beautiful yellow crystals, very scarce and held in high estimation. A curiously carved cross of wood, marking the limit of what is considered holy ground, stands a mile from the well.

CRAUGHWELL, a post-town, in the parish of Killora, barony of Dunkellin, county of Galway, and province of Connaught, 12 miles (S. E. by E.) from Galway, and 92 (W. by S.) from Dublin: the population is returned with the parish. Petty sessions are held every Monday, and a constabulary police force is stationed here. The town is intersected by a mountain stream, and in the neighbourhood are several gentlemen's seats, among which are Ballimore, the residence of R. Rathborne, Esq.; Rockfield, of Mark Browne, Esq.; Aggard, of John Lambert, Esq.; and Moyode Castle, of Burton Persse, Esq. The church for the union of Kilinane, and the Roman Catholic chapel, are situated here.

CREAGH, a parish, in the Eastern Division of the barony of West Carbery, county of Cork, and province of Munster; containing, with the greater part of the post-town of Skibbereen, 5914 inhabitants. It is situated on the southern coast, and comprises 6897 statute acres, as applotted under the tithe act, and valued at £4849 per annum, of which about 80 are woodland. The surface is very uneven, rising into mountains of considerable elevation, and of the schistus formation, extending over about one-third of the parish; they are mostly rocky and bare, but in some places afford excellent pasturage. There are few fields where the rock does not appear, but there is scarcely an acre which does not afford some pasture or tillage, which is carried even to the top of the hills. There are about 20 acres of bog. The land under cultivation yields tolerable crops, mostly produced by spade labour. The parish is bounded on the north by the river Ilen, along the banks of which the land is very good and in many places richly planted. The whole of the corn exported from Skibbereen is shipped at an excellent quay at Oldcourt, on this river, to which vessels of 200 tons' burden can come up at high water, being conveyed thither in small four-oared boats. A manor court is held every three weeks, for the recovery of debts under 40*s.*; and here are the ruins of an ancient castle, now converted into corn-stores. Near the southern boundary of the parish, which opens upon the Atlantic, is Lough Hyne, a curious and extensive gulph, penetrating nearly two miles inland, and the passage from the sea being very narrow, and between craggy cliffs, the water rushes through it with great violence on the ebb and flow of every tide. The best oysters and several kinds of sea fish are found in it; and in its centre is a small island, containing the ruins of Cloghan castle, one of the castles of the O'Driscolls. The surrounding scenery is very beautiful, the mountain sides being clothed with young and thriving plantations. A new road has lately been formed, and other improvements are in progress. Good slate is obtained in many places. The principal seats in the parish are Creagh House, the residence of Sir W. W. Becher, Bart.; Killeena, of the Rev. John Wright; the glebe-house, of the Rev. H. B. Macartney; Lough Hyne Cottage, of D. McCarty, Esq.; Inane, of H. Marmion, Esq.; Glenview, of S. Lewis, Esq.; Green Park, of John Gallwey, Esq.; and there are some large and substantial farm-houses.

The living is a rectory in the diocese of Ross, and in the patronage of the Bishop: the tithes amount to £500, and there is a glebe of 15 acres. The church is a small neat edifice, with a square tower ornamented with pinnacles: it was erected by aid of a gift of £600, and a loan of £400, in 1810, from the late Board of First Fruits. In the R. C. divisions this parish forms part of the union of Skibbereen. The parochial school was built on the glebe in 1834; it is in connection with the Cork Diocesan Association, but is principally supported by the rector; and there is a national school in Skibbereen. In these about 150 boys and 60 girls are taught; and there is also a private school of about 50 children. The ruins of the old church adjoin the present edifice; on the glebe is a holy well.

CREAGH, a parish, in the half-barony of Moycarnon, county of Roscommon, and province of Connaught; containing, with a part of the post-town of Ballinasloe, 2864 inhabitants. This parish is situated on the river Suck, which is here 116 feet above the level of the sea, and on the road from Athlone to Galway; it comprises 4775 statute acres, as applotted under the tithe act; the agriculture is greatly improving, limestone abounds, and there is a considerable portion of bog. The principal seats are Fort-William, the residence of T. Lancaster, Esq.; Ardcarn, of Capt. J. Bell; Lancaster Park, of J. Lynch, Esq.; Castle Park, of W. D. Kelly, Esq.; Birchgrove, of J. O'Shaughnessy, Esq.; and Woodmount, of Hugh Kelly, Esq. The living is a vicarage, in the diocese of Clonfert, united episcopally, with a portion of the rectory, about 1739, to the rectory of Taghmaconnell and the rectory and vicarage of Kilcloony, together forming the union of Creagh, in the patronage of the Bishop; the other portion of the rectory is partly appropriate to the see, and partly to the deanery, of Clonfert. The tithes amount to £135, and of the union to £279. 19. 0½.: there is no glebe-house, but there are two glebes, containing 6*a.* 2*r.* 6*p.* The church is in Ballinasloe, a neat cruciform edifice with a small spire, and was built by aid of a loan of £962, in 1818, from the late Board of First Fruits. In the R. C. divisions the parish forms the head of the union or district of Kilcloony or Ballinasloe, and contains a chapel. About 50 boys and 20 girls are taught in the parochial free school, under the London Hibernian Societies, aided by donations from Lady Clancarty and the incumbent; and about 170 boys and 70 girls are educated in five private schools. The burial-ground is attached to the ruins of the old parish church. In the grounds of Thomas Lancaster, Esq., is a mineral spring, not at present resorted to.

CRECORA, a parish, partly in the county of the city of Limerick, partly in the barony of Coshma, but chiefly in the barony of Pubblebrien, county of Limerick, and province of Munster, 5 miles (S. W.) from Limerick; containing 1928 inhabitants. It is situated on the road from Patrick's Well to Bruff, and contains 3010 statute acres, as applotted under the tithe act, of which 194 are in the townland of Kilgobban, which is near Adare, and detached from the main body of the parish, forming one estate, generally called Adare Farm. The land is every where good, being based on a substratum of limestone, and about two-thirds are under tillage, the chief crops being wheat and potatoes: but on the Ashfort estate, consisting of 200 acres, the farmer is subject to a heavy penalty should more than 3 acres be at one time under tillage. Here are four detached bogs, comprising about 300 acres, which are become very valuable and could be let at a very high rent. The surface of the country is generally interesting, and ornamented by several handsome houses, the principal of which are Richmond Villa, the neat residence of Mrs. Wallace; Jockey Hall, now occupied by a farmer; Greenmount, the residence of John Green, Esq.; Doneen, of Villiers Peacock, Esq.; Ballymurphy, of Eyre Powell, Esq.; and Ashfort, of the Rev. Joseph Jones. The living is a vicarage, in the diocese of Limerick, and in the patronage of the Vicars Choral of the cathedral of Limerick, to whom the rectory is appropriate: the tithes amount to £210, of which £135 is payable to the lessee of the appropriators, and £75 to the vicar. There is neither church nor glebe-house, but a glebe of 17¼ Irish acres, 10 of which belong to the appropriators, and 7¼ to the vicar. In the R. C. divisions this parish is the head of a union or district, also called Loughmore, comprising the parishes of Crecora, Mungret, Knocknagaul, and part of Kilpeacon, and containing two chapels, situated respectively at Crecora and Mungret; the former is a large modern edifice. From the interesting ruins of the old church, which was destroyed in the war of 1641, it seems to have been well built and capacious: many of the wealthy families of the neighbourhood have vaults in the cemetery. About 100 boys and 60 girls are educated in three private schools here.

CRECRIM.—See CRYCRIM.

CREEKSTOWN, or CRIKSTOWN, a parish, in the barony of RATOATH, county of MEATH, and province of LEINSTER, 13 miles (N. N. W.) from Dublin, on the road to Belfast; containing 209 inhabitants. This parish comprises 1380 statute acres, as applotted under the tithe act, and valued at £1399 per annum. Sothern, the neat residence of E. H. W. Roney, Esq., is situated here. It is a vicarage, in the diocese of Meath, and is part of the union of Ratoath: the tithes amount to £90. In the R. C. divisions it is the head of a union or district, comprising the parishes of Creekstown, Kilmoon, Kilbrew, Donaghmore, and Grenogue, and containing two chapels, one at Curraha and one at Donaghmore, both plain buildings and the former now being rebuilt. About 30 children are taught in a school held in the chapel. The parish formerly belonged to the Barnewall family, of whose ancient residence there are some remains, as there are also of the parish church.

CREEVE, a parish, partly in the barony of ROSCOMMON, but chiefly in that of BOYLE, county of ROSCOMMON, and province of CONNAUGHT, 3 miles (N.) from Elphin, on the road to Boyle; containing 3159 inhabitants. It comprises 2716 statute acres, as applotted under the tithe act. The surface is varied with low elevations of limestone and limestone gravel; there is very little bog. Portobello, the residence of T. Stafford, Esq.; and Ryefield, of N. Cummins, Esq., are in this parish. It is a vicarage, in the diocese of Elphin, and is part of the union of Ardclare; the rectory forms part of the union and corps of the precentorship of Elphin. The tithes amount to £92. 6. 2., which is equally divided between the precentor and vicar. The R. C. parish is co-extensive with that of the Established Church, and contains two chapels, one at Ryefield, the other at Caighy. There are two schools under the Elphin Diocesan Society, which are aided by annual donations from Viscount Lorton, the rector, the curate, and the Rev. Mr. Lloyd, and afford instruction to about 70 children. There are also two hedge schools, in which about 80 children are taught. A friary of the third order of Franciscans was founded here, of which scarcely any remains are visible; a lease of its possessions was granted by Queen Elizabeth, in 1582, to Bryan Mac Dermot.

CREGGAN, a parish, partly in the barony of UPPER DUNDALK, county of LOUTH, and province of LEINSTER, but chiefly in the barony of UPPER FEWS, county of ARMAGH, and province of ULSTER, 8 miles (W. N. W.) from Dundalk, on the road to Newtown-Hamilton; containing 14,261 inhabitants, of which number, 1674 are in that part of the parish which is in the county of Louth. This parish comprises, according to the Ordnance survey, 24,815¼ statute acres, of which 21,823½, including 419½ of water, are in Armagh, and 2991¾ in Louth. Of these, 21,640 acres are applotted under the tithe act, and valued at £19,708 per ann.; and 1088 are mountain, bog, and lakes. The surface is irregularly broken and the general aspect bold: the soil is generally good, and the system of cultivation improving. Linen cloth and yarn are manufactured to a small extent by the farmers, whose principal dependence has been the breeding of cattle, but now most of the grazing land has been converted into arable, and even much of the mountainous district has been brought into cultivation. The river Creggan, which divides this parish into two nearly equal parts, turns several mills and contains fine trout. Near the village are several hundred acres of bog or moorland used for fuel; and here is a coarse kind of granite and also a coarse slate, which is very hard and durable: the quarries, however, are not much worked, except by the neighbouring farmers, who use the stone for building. The village is pleasantly situated, and the surrounding scenery is picturesque. A market is held on Friday at Crossmaglen, for provisions, and fairs on the first Friday in every month for farming stock. Cullyhanna, also a village in this parish, is an improving place. Fairs are held in it on the second Tuesday in January, April, July, and October; and there are two at Ball's-Mills. There is a penny post to Dundalk; and petty sessions for the Crossmaglen district are held in the school-room at Creggan, on alternate Saturdays, or weekly if requisite. The principal seats in the parish are Urker Lodge, the property of T. P. Ball, Esq., to whom the parish principally belongs; Crossmaglen, of Capt. Ball; and Clohog Lodge, of R. G. Wallace, Esq.

The living is a rectory and vicarage, in the diocese of Armagh, and forms the corps of the treasurership in the cathedral of St. Patrick, Armagh, in the patronage of the Lord-Primate. The tithes amount to £1050: the glebe-house, which is near the church, is romantically situated on the river Creggan, which flows through a deep glen abounding with picturesque scenery, and ornamented with evergreens, rustic seats, and walks cut out of the solid rock: the surrounding grounds have been greatly improved by the Rev. Dr. Atkinson, the rector. The glebe, comprising 300 Irish acres, consists of the whole townland of Cregganban except 40 acres appropriated as a glebe for Newtown-Hamilton, when that parish was severed from Creggan. The church is a spacious and handsome edifice in the centre of the parish, built in 1758, and to which a lofty square tower was added in 1799. In the R. C. divisions the parish is the head of two unions or districts, called Upper and Lower Creggan; the former contains four chapels, situated at Crossmaglen, Glasdrummond, Mowbane, and Shela, of which that at Crossmaglen was built in 1834, on a site given by T. P. Ball, Esq., at an expense of £750; and the one at Glasdrummond is a large and handsome building. The part called Lower Creggan is united with the parish of Newtown-Hamilton, and contains a chapel at Cullyhanna and one in Newtown-Hamilton, both in that parish. At Freeduff is a meeting-house for Presbyterians in connection with the Synod of Ulster of the second class; and there is a place of worship for Wesleyan Methodists at Ball's-Mills. The parochial schools, in which are about 50 boys and 40 girls, are supported by the rector, who gives the house, which was built in 1822, and a garden and two acres of land rent-free for the master, besides books for the children. There is a female working school in the church-yard, and an infants' school superintended by Mrs. Atkinson; also schools at Tullynavale and Anavachavarkey, built by the rector, aided by some subscriptions, and chiefly supported by him; in the former, which is a large and handsome edifice, divine service is performed by the rector, or his curate, on Sunday evenings. At Darsey is a national school; and there are thirteen private schools in the parish, in which about 460 children are educated. A dispensary was established at Crossmaglen in 1830. In the northern part of the parish are vestiges of an ancient intrenchment, which extended more than a mile in length and about one third of a mile in breadth; it is now intersected by roads.

CREHELP, or CRYHELP, a parish, in the barony of LOWER TALBOTSTOWN, county of WICKLOW, and province of LEINSTER, 2½ miles (E.) from Dunlavin; containing 760 inhabitants. This parish, which is situated on the western boundary of the county, and on the confines of the county of Dublin, is intersected by the old road from Blessington to Baltinglass, by Stratford-on-Slaney. The lands are mostly under an improved system of tillage. There are some quarries of good slate, and a little bog. A peace preservation force has been stationed here. It is a rectory and curacy, in the diocese of Dublin and Glendalough; the rectory is appropriate to the incumbency, and the curacy forms part of the union of Donard. The tithes amount to £87. 3. 7. In the R. C. divisions the parish is in the union or district of Dunlavin. There are two private schools, in which are about 30 boys and 30 girls.

CREMORGAN.—See KILCLONBROOK.

CREVAGH.—See CRUAGH.

CREVENISH, an island, in the parish of KILMINA, barony of BURRISHOOLE, county of MAYO, and province of CONNAUGHT, 6 miles (S. W.) from Newport-Pratt; containing about 20 inhabitants. It is situated on Clew bay, and is the property of the Marquess of Sligo.

CRINKLE, a village, in the parish of BIRR, barony of BALLYBRITT, KING'S county, and province of LEINSTER; containing 86 houses and 531 inhabitants. It immediately adjoins the post-town of Parsonstown, and is situated on the road thence to Roscrea.

CROAGH, a parish, in the barony of LOWER CONNELLO EAST, county of LIMERICK, and province of MUNSTER, 3 miles (N. E. by N.) from Rathkeale, on the road to Adare; containing 3394 inhabitants, of which number, 274 are in the village. This place appears to have been anciently of considerable importance; so early as the year 1109, it had a very rich abbey, a corporation, and two castles. Jas. II., after his defeat at the Boyne, is reported to have slept one night at Amigan castle, now in ruins; but it is not certain that he came farther south than Waterford. Near it is a small stream, supposed to be efficacious in cutaneous disorders. The parish is divided into two parts by a portion of that of Adare, which separates the townlands of Ballinvira, Ballinagoold, Ballinacurra, and Lisnamuck from the rest of the parish; it comprises 8100 statute acres, as applotted under the tithe act, almost all of which is under an improving system of tillage. The greater part of the land is good, though light, and rests on a substratum of limestone; the remainder is meadow and pasture, there being no waste land, and but little turbary. Superior lead ore is often found amidst the limestone rocks, and large masses are sometimes turned up by the plough at Ardnaprehane, but no search has ever been made for it. The village consists of one irregular street, containing 46 small houses, and has fairs on March 1st, May 1st, Aug. 3rd, and Nov. 1st. Within the parish are several large and handsome houses, the principal of which are Ballylin, the residence of R. Smith, Esq.; Hollywood, of J. Hewson, Esq.; Smithfield, of R. Smith, Esq.; Ballinvira, of Gerald Browne Fitzgerald, Esq.; Newpark, of Gerald Evans Fitzgerald, Esq.; and the glebe-house, the residence of the Rev. W. Ashe, rector and prebendary.

The living is a rectory in the diocese of Limerick, being the corps of the prebend of Croagh in the cathedral of Limerick, and in the patronage of Matthew Barrington, Esq.: the tithes amount to £553. 6. 11. The glebe-house, a handsome residence, was erected in 1831, by a gift of £100, and a loan of £900, from the late Board of First Fruits, and is situated about half a mile from the village, on a glebe of 10 acres purchased by the Board; and near the church is a small glebe of 1*r.* 14*p.* The church, formerly a large cruciform edifice, is nearly in ruins; the eastern portion, or chancel, is the only part now roofed; there are considerable remains of the old walls. In the R. C. divisions the parish is the head of a union or district, comprising also that of Kilfinney; the chapel, a large plain edifice, is near the village of Croagh. There is a school under the Baptist Society in that village in which upwards of 300 boys and girls are taught, also one at Lisnamuck under the National Board, in which are about 100 boys and 100 girls; and about 70 children are taught in a private school. The late John Walcott, Esq., of Clifton, near Bristol, but originally of Croagh House, built in his lifetime three almshouses at Ballylin for six poor widows of this parish, and endowed each with half an acre of land for a garden, and a weekly allowance of 1*s.* to each inmate, and 10*s.* each at Easter and Christmas, payable for ever out of his estate at Croagh. Mount Aylmer, in this parish, was the birthplace of William Butler Odell, author of several poetical pieces of considerable merit.

CROGHAN, a parish, in the barony of LOWER PHILIPSTOWN, KING'S county, and province of LEINSTER, 3 miles (N.) from Philipstown; containing 842 inhabitants. It is situated on the road from Edenderry to Tyrrel's-Pass; the surface is flat and overspread with bogs. The only eminence is Croghan Hill, on the confines of the county of Westmeath, which is celebrated by Spenser, in his Fairy Queen; it is clothed with verdure, and forms a striking object in so flat a district. The land is principally in pasture and appropriated to the feeding of store sheep and cattle; and part of the female population are employed in spinning worsted. Near it is Clonerle, the beautiful seat of W. Magan, Esq., the demesne of which is embellished with rich plantations. The living is a rectory and vicarage, in the diocese of Kildare, and is sequestrated in the Ecclesiastical Commissioners: the tithes amount to £82, payable to the Commissioners, and the occasional duties of the parish are performed by the vicar of the adjoining parish of Kilclonfert. There is neither church nor glebe-house. A school is supported by local subscriptions, affording instruction to about 160 boys and 130 girls. At the base of Croghan Hill are the remains of the church, which was formerly a chapel belonging to the ancestors of Lord Tullamore, on whose estate it is situated.

CROGHAN, a village, in the parish of KILLUKEN, barony of BOYLE, county of ROSCOMMON, and province of CONNAUGHT, 4 miles (N. by W.) from Elphin, on the road to Boyle. It is an improving village, containing about 20 houses and cabins, the property of Guy Lloyd, Esq. Drugget, frieze, and flannel are manufactured here; petty sessions are held every Tuesday, and fairs on the Wednesday after Trinity-Sunday and the 28th of October, for fat cattle, for which the October-fair is considered to be one of the largest in this district. Here is a constabulary police station, and a dispensary; and a loan fund was established by Mr. Lloyd, in 1833, with a capital of £500. In the village is the R. C. parochial chapel, a spacious and well-built structure; and in the immediate vicinity is Croghan House, the handsome residence of Guy Lloyd, Esq., who has effected considerable improvements in the neighbourhood.

CROGHANE, or CROHANE, a parish, in the barony of SLIEVARDAGH, county of TIPPERARY, and province of MUNSTER, 2¼ miles (E.) from Killenaule; containing 1393 inhabitants. This parish, which is situated on the confines of the county of Limerick, comprises 5524 statute acres, as applotted under the tithe act, and valued at £4460 per annum. It is a prebend and vicarage, in the diocese of Cashel, forming part of the union and corps of the archdeaconry: the tithes amount to £300. The parochial school is aided by the rector; and there is a R. C. pay school, in which are about 70 boys and 50 girls.

CROGRONE, formerly a parish, in the Eastern Division of the barony of EAST CARBERY, county of CORK, and province of MUNSTER, 6 miles (W. S. W.) from Kinsale; containing 63 inhabitants. This parish, situated in the midst of a fertile tract of country, has merged into the several parishes of Kilbritain, Ringrone, and Templetrine, by which it is surrounded. In 1498 it was given by De Courcy to the abbey of Timoleague, from which the cure was served till the Reformation, since which period it has invariably been regarded as part of the several parishes above named: the ruins of the ancient church yet exist.

CRONROE, or CRONROW, a village, in the parish of RATHNEW, barony of NEWCASTLE, county of WICKLOW, and province of LEINSTER, 1 mile (S. S. W.) from Ashford, on the road to Rathdrum: the population is returned with the parish. This village takes its name from the adjoining seat of Isaac A. Eccles, Esq., a large plain mansion, occupying an elevated situation, backed by an enormous rocky eminence called the great rock of Cronroe, whence there is a delightful and extensive view. Cronroe has long been the residence of the present family, and was the seat of the late Ambrose Eccles, Esq., a gentleman of some literary celebrity. Fairs are here on May 12th and Oct. 2nd.

CROOK, a parish, in the barony of GAULTIER, county of WATERFORD, and province of MUNSTER, 6 miles (E. by S.) from Waterford; containing 976 inhabitants. A castle was founded here in the 13th century by the Baron of Curraghmore, which subsequently became a preceptory of the Knights of St. John of Jerusalem, with whom it remained till the Reformation. The site and the lands belonging to it were granted by Queen Elizabeth, in the 27th of her reign, on lease for 60 years to Anthony Power, at an annual rent of £12. 11. 10.; and in 1638 they were granted by Chas. I. to Sir Peter Aylward. A village in the parish derived the name of New Geneva from the proposed establishment at this place of a colony of Genevese, who were compelled to leave their own country in 1785. For this purpose the parliament granted £50,000, but in consequence of their requiring certain privileges and immunities which it was not thought proper to concede, the projected settlement was abandoned. The parish is situated on Waterford harbour, and comprises 1831 statute acres, as applotted under the tithe act. A military barrack was erected in the village, in which were stationed one or two regiments generally during the war; but the establishment was afterwards abandoned, and the buildings have been taken down. Kilcop House is the seat of John Coghlan, Esq. The living is a rectory, in the diocese of Waterford, and in the patronage of the Crown: the tithes amount to £190. 5. 3. There is neither church nor glebe-house; the glebe comprises three acres. In the R. C. divisions the parish forms part of the union or district of Passage.

CROOKHAVEN, a village, in the parish of KILMOE, Western Division of the barony of WEST CARBERY, county of CORK, and province of MUNSTER, 19 miles (S.W.) from Skibbereen; containing 424 inhabitants. It is situated upon the harbour of Crookhaven, and consists of a long irregular street, at one end of which stands the parochial church, erected in 1700, at the expense of Dr. Brown, Bishop of Cork, for the accommodation of sailors frequenting the port. It was formerly a place of considerable importance, many foreign vessels having resorted hither for provisions, and during the last war was much frequented by ships of the navy. The harbour being very spacious and well sheltered, renders it a desirable haven, and particularly convenient for vessels bound eastward. A considerable trade is carried on in the exportation of wheat, oats, pork, and butter, and timber and coal are occasionally imported. Here are a constabulary police and a coast-guard station, which latter is one of the nine included in the Skibbereen district. The parochial and Sunday schools are under the superintendence of the rector, and a school is chiefly supported by the Rev. L. O'Sullivan, P.P. Not far from the town are the ruins of Castle Mehan, which was built by the Mehans or O'Heas in 1540.

CROOKSTOWN.—See MOVIDDY.

CROOM, a post-town and parish, partly in the barony of PUBBLEBRIEN, but chiefly in that of COSHMA, county of LIMERICK, and province of MUNSTER, 9 miles (S. by W.) from Limerick, and 105¼ (S. W.) from Dublin; containing 6978 inhabitants, of which number, 1268 are in the town. The origin of the town is involved in mystery: it is supposed to have been a place of considerable importance from a very remote period, but the earliest intimation of it is the erection of a castle by Dermot O'Donovan, in the reign of King John, to protect the ford or pass of the river, and also to secure that portion of the present barony of Coshma which the O'Donovans had then lately taken from the Mac Eneirys, and which King John, when Earl of Morton, is said to have confirmed to O'Donovan. The O'Donovans having been driven hence into the western district of the county of Cork, this castle became the property of the Earl of Kildare, who rebuilt it in a superior manner, and flanked it by four circular towers, making it his chief seat and strong hold; and from it is derived the war cry of "Crom-a-boo," which is still the motto of the Dukes of Leinster, the descendants of the Earls of Kildare. During successive wars, it was several times attacked by the English. In the reign of Elizabeth, the Geraldines were three times besieged in the castle of Croom; the last time was in 1600, when the Lord-President Carew, at the head of 1500 men, attacked the castle, which had a powerful garrison under its constable, the celebrated Pierce Lacy, who made his escape in the night, and in the morning the fortress was surrendered. In 1610, the castle and manor of Croom were restored by James I. to the Fitzgeralds, who, however, again forfeited it by joining in the insurrection of 1641; in 1678, Chas. II. granted both to the Duke of Richmond, who resided in the castle for several years. In 1691, it was garrisoned by the adherents of Jas. II., but on the approach of the forces of Wm. III. they abandoned the fortress, and took refuge in Limerick: after which it remained unoccupied till recently rebuilt by John Croker, Esq., its present proprietor. The town is situated on the eastern bank of the river Maigue over which is a handsome bridge of six arches, and on the new road from Limerick to Charleville, which, when completed, will be the most advantageous line from Limerick to Cork: it comprises two principal streets with smaller ones branching from them, and contains 213 houses. This is a constabulary police station; petty sessions are held in the town every Monday; and fairs on May 3rd, June 22nd, Sept. 1st, and Dec. 8th.

The parish contains 13,003 statute acres, as applotted under the tithe act, the estimated rental being £15,872: the land is in general remarkably good, and under excellent cultivation. The soil is based on a substratum of limestone, and Tory hill affords one of the best specimens of disintegration to be found in Ireland. At Carass, on the river Maigue, is a very powerful flour-mill, fitted up in a superior style, with machinery of the most improved construction, the property of D. Roche, Esq.; and close adjoining the bridge of Croom is another large mill, belonging to H. Lyons, Esq. In addition to the interesting castle, the residences of the gentry in the parish are Carass, of D. Roche, Esq.; Toureen, of J. D. Lyons, Esq., D. L.; Croom House, the property of Mr. Lyons, Carass Court, of Jeffrey Browning, Esq.; Glen-Bevan, of J. Bevan, Esq.; Cherry Grove, of J. Barry, Esq.; Bellevue, of Massy Yielding, Esq.; Clorane, a fine old house belonging to the Hunt family; Newborough, of C. Wilson, Esq.; the glebe-house, of the Rev. E. Croker, rector of the parish; and Tory Hill, of the Rev. L. Harnett; besides several villas, cottages, and substantial farm-houses.

The living is a rectory and vicarage, in the diocese of Limerick, and in the patronage of J. Croker, Esq., of Ballynagard. It is called one parish, but appears to embrace the old parishes of Croom, Dunaman, Dunkip, and Dullas, all of which are contiguous to Croom and near Patrick's well: five miles distant are the townlands of Clonana, Clonduff, Lorriga, Ballycurrane, and Lisaleen, which anciently formed the parish of Clonana, though now considered part of that of Croom. The tithes amount to £1200. The glebe-house is a handsome edifice, erected on the new glebe, in 1813, by aid of a gift of £100 and a loan of £800 from the late Board of First Fruits. The glebe comprises 10 acres of excellent land, half a mile from the church; it was given by Mr. Lyons in lieu of the old glebe adjoining the church, now part of the demesne of Croom House. The church stands on the western bank of the river Maigue, and is a small neat edifice, in the early English style of architecture, with a square tower: it appears to have been erected on the site of a larger building, and the Ecclesiastical Commissioners have recently granted £151. 2. 1. for its repair. In the R. C. divisions the parish is the head of a union or district, comprising the parishes of Croom, Anhid, Dunaman, Carrigran, and Dysert; and containing two chapels, one at Croom, the other at Ballynabannogue; the former, situated near the church, is a spacious plain cruciform edifice. There is a small place of worship for Wesleyan Methodists; also a dispensary. There are four private schools, in which about 280 boys and 120 girls are educated. Close to the town are extensive remains of the castle of the O'Donovans; and not far distant are fragments of the old church. Within the parish are ruins of the churches of Dunaman, Dunkip, and Clonana, also of the castle of Tullyvin; besides the ruins of a chapel in the grounds of Carass, built by Lord Carbery as a domestic place of worship, and situated close on the bank of the river, at the foot of a rustic bridge. The beautiful round tower of Carrigreen is a mile north-west from Croom, in the parish of Dysert; and the ruins of the abbey of Nenagh or Maig, generally called *Monaster Nenagh*, stand two miles eastward: a more detailed description of each will be found in the articles on those places.

CROSSAKEEL, a post-town, in the parish of KILSKYRE, barony of UPPER KELLS, county of MEATH, and province of LEINSTER, 5 miles (S. W. by S.) from

Kells, and 36 miles (N. W.) from Dublin; containing 290 inhabitants. This village is situated on the road from Kells to Oldcastle, and consists of about 60 houses: it has a sub-post-office to Kells. Fairs are held on May 9th, Aug. 16th, and Dec. 15th. A constabulary police force is stationed here; and petty sessions are held every alternate week. The parochial church, a handsome structure with a lofty spire, and a dispensary, are situated in the village; and there is a school under the trustees of Erasmus Smith's charity, and a Sunday school.—See KILSKYRE.

CROSSBOYNE, a parish, in the barony of CLANMORRIS, county of MAYO, and province of CONNAUGHT, 2 miles (S. E.) from Claremorris, on the road to Tuam; containing 5765 inhabitants. This parish comprises 9277 statute acres, as applotted under the tithe act, and valued at £6058 per annum. The land is good, and agriculture is gradually improving on the lands of the gentry, although modern implements are not generally adopted by the farmers; there is plenty of bog for fuel, and limestone is also found here. The surrounding scenery is richly diversified with wood and water; there are several delightful demesnes, of which the principal are Castlemagarett, the seat of Lord Oranmore, situated in a noble domain enriched with excellent timber; Brookhill, the residence of J. Lambert, Esq.; Farmhill, of E. D. Gonne Bell, Esq.; Prospect, of F. Crean, Esq.; and the residence of the Rev. W. Crofton, rector. The village of Ballindine, or Ballindangan, in this parish, is described under its own head.

The living is a vicarage, in the diocese of Tuam, and in the patronage of the Archbishop; the rectory is partly appropriate to the dean of Tuam and the prebendary of Killabegs in the cathedral of Tuam, and partly impropriate in S. Lindsey Bucknall, Esq. The tithes amount to £307. 1. 5½., of which £62. 6. 1½. is payable to the impropriator, £209. 18. 4¾. to the incumbent, and the remainder to the dean and prebendary. The glebe-house was erected by aid of a gift of £100, and a loan of £300, in 1822, from the late Board of First Fruits: the glebe comprises four acres. The church is a plain old building with a chancel and a new tower, which was erected by aid of a loan of £350 in 1819, from the same Board; the Ecclesiastical Commissioners have recently granted £268 for its repair. In the R. C. divisions this parish is the head of two unions or districts, called Crossboyne and Ballindangan; the former comprises part of the parish of Crossboyne and the entire of that of Taugheen, and contains three chapels, one of which is a large slated building at Crossboyne; in the Ballindangan district are two chapels, one in the village of that name, and the other at Drymills. Lord Oranmore gives £10 per ann. towards the support of a grammar school; and his lady has a school at Ballindangan, towards which she allows £15 per annum, where the children are taught needlework and the manufacture of straw-plat. The Rev. Mr. Crofton also supports a school in connection with the Tuam Diocesan Society. The old fortress of Castlemagarrett is in ruins; in the demesne of Brookhill are several Druidical or Danish remains, and a choice collection of plants. In Crossboyne churchyard there are many ancient monuments of a rude character; and near Prospect House is a chalybeate spring, the water of which is valuable as a tonic.

CROSSDONEY, a village and post-town, in the parish of KILMORE, barony of CLONMAHON, county of CAVAN, and province of ULSTER, 4 miles (S. W.) from Cavan, and 59¼ (N. W.) from Dublin; the population is returned with the parish. This small neat village, containing only 12 houses, is situated on the road from Killesandra to Cavan, and is surrounded by several gentlemen's seats. Fairs are held on April 5th, May 27th, Aug. 26th, and Nov. 17th. Near it is a good bleaching establishment; and at its entrance is Lismore, the seat of Col. Nesbitt, one of the oldest in the county.

CROSSERLOUGH.—See KILDRUMFERTON.

CROSSGAR, a village, in that part of the parish of KILMORE which is in the barony of UPPER CASTLEREAGH, county of DOWN, and province of ULSTER, 5 miles (N.) from Downpatrick, on the road to Belfast; containing 474 inhabitants and about 125 houses, mostly very small. It is noted only for its fairs, which are held on the second Wednesday in every month, and are well attended, particularly for the sale of horned cattle and pigs. It has a penny post to Downpatrick, and in the vicinity is Crossgar House, the residence of — Hamilton, Esq., also that of the late E. S. Ruthven, Esq., and the handsome house and demesne of Redemon.—See KILMORE.

CROSSHAVEN, a village, in the parish of TEMPLEBREADY, barony of KERRYCURRIHY, county of CORK, and province of MUNSTER, 5 miles (E. S. E.) from Carrigaline; containing 513 inhabitants. It is situated on the noble estuary to which it gives name, but which is more generally known as the river Carrigaline, within the harbour of Cork, opposite to Dog's nose Point, and a little west from Ram Head; it comprises about 100 houses, which are small, but well built; and is one of the eight coast-guard stations in the district of Cove. In the creek a vessel may ride in 10 or 12 feet of water. Crosshaven House, the residence of T. Hayes, Esq.; Camden Fort (described in the account of Templebready), and several handsome villas and lodges, the summer residences of those who visit the coast for sea-bathing, closely adjoin the village. An extensive fishery was formerly carried on, but it has so much declined that only five small vessels remain, and these are occasionally employed in the grain and coal trade.

CROSS ISLAND.—See COPELAND ISLANDS.

CROSSMAGLEN, a village, in that part of the parish of CREGGAN which is in the barony of UPPER FEWS, county of ARMAGH, and province of ULSTER, 8 miles (N. W.) from Dundalk, on the road to Newtown-Hamilton; containing 545 inhabitants. It comprises about 100 houses, of which several are large and well built, and has a penny post to Dundalk: the surrounding scenery is strikingly diversified. In the vicinity is a small lake, called Lough Maglen, or Magherlin; and there are numerous others in the surrounding district. The slate quarires here were formerly worked to some extent, but they are now in a declining state. A market for provisions is held on Friday; and there are fairs on the last Friday in every month for black cattle, horses, sheep, and pigs. A constabulary police station has been established in the village; and a spacious and handsome R. C. chapel has been recently erected, which is the parochial chapel of a very extensive district, called Lower Creggan. A dispensary was built by subscription in 1830.—See CREGGAN.

CROSSMOLINA, a market and post-town, and a parish, in the barony of TYRAWLEY, county of MAYO, and province of CONNAUGHT, 6½ miles (W. by S.) from Ballina, and 131¼ (W. N. W.) from Dublin; containing 11,479 inhabitants, of which number, 1481 are in the town. It stands on the river Deel, over which is a large stone bridge, on the direct road to the barony of Erris from Castlebar, and consists of a good main street and two converging ones, containing 310 houses. The market is on Thursday; and fairs are held on May 23rd, Sept. 12th, Oct. 26th, and Dec. 17th; and at Rakestreet on Feb. 2nd, March 25th, Aug. 23rd, and Dec. 8th. Petty sessions are held weekly, and here are also revenue and constabulary police stations. The parish contains a portion of the stupendous mountain of Nephin, 2840 feet above the level of the sea, on the western extremity of Lough Conn, a grand sheet of water, extending 10 miles in length, and in some places 4 in breadth. It comprises about 24,300 statute acres, one-third of which is arable land; the remainder is bog and mountain, the greater part reclaimable, but little improvement has taken place in agriculture. About a mile from the town, on the bank of the river Deel, are quarries of very fine stone; and limestone and free-stone abound. There are several gentlemen's seats in the vicinity: the principal are Eniscoe, the residence of M. Pratt, Esq.; Gurtner Abbey, of G. Ormsby, Esq.; Abbeytown, of W. Orme, Esq.; Knockglass, of T. Paget, Esq.; Fortland, of Major Jackson; Glenmore, of W. Orme, Esq.; Greenwood Park, of Capt. J. Knox; Belleville, of W. Orme, Esq.; Millbrook, of W. Orme, sen., Esq; Netley Park, of H. Knox, Esq.; Castle Hill, of Major McCormick; Ballycorroon, of E. Orme, Esq.; Stone Hall, of T. Knox, Esq.; Fahy, of Ernest A. Knox, Esq.; Cottage, of W. Ormsby, Esq.; Rappa Castle, of Annesley Gore Knox, Esq. (See Kilfyan); and the Vicarage-house, the residence of the Rev. — St. George, rector. Deel castle, on the banks of the river of the same name, now a fine modern residence, surrounded with much old timber, stands on the site of a very ancient structure.

The living is a vicarage, in the diocese of Killala, united to the vicarages of Addergoole, Kilfyan, and Magaunagh, together forming the union of Crossmolina, in the patronage of the Bishop: the rectory is partly appropriate to the vicars choral of the cathedral of Christ-Church, Dublin, and partly to the prebend of Errew in the cathedral of Killala. The tithes amount to £460, of which £17 is payable to the vicars choral, £213 to the appropriators, and £230 to the vicar: the gross amount of the tithes of the union is £550. The glebe-house was built by a gift of £100, and a loan of £825, in 1814, from the late Board of First Fruits: the glebe comprises 35 acres. The church is a neat plain edifice, with a square tower and spire, erected in 1810, by aid of a loan of £1000, in 1809, from the late Board of First Fruits; and the Ecclesiastical Commissioners have recently granted £197 for its repair. In the R. C. divisions the parish forms part of the union or district of Glanbest, and partly a district or parish in itself, in which are two chapels, one at Kilmurra and one at Crossmolina; the former was built in 1785, at an expense of £50, and the latter in 1806, and cost £200. A painting of the Madonna over the altar was brought from Rome by Archbishop McHale. There is a place of worship for Wesleyan Methodists at Crossmolina. There are seven schools, one of which is aided by a donation of £10 per annum from Mrs. Palmer, and a house and two acres of ground, valued at £10 per annum, given by the late Mrs. Palmer; also six hedge schools and a Sunday school. The total nnmber of children on the books of these schools is upwards of 1000. A dispensary has been established. At Errew, a peninsula stretching from the barony of Tyrawley into Lough Conn, are the ruins of a friary, which was dedicated to the Blessed Virgin, having a beautiful east window. There is also a ruin at Abbeytown; at Kildavarrogue are the remains of the old church, with a burial-place; and near the church are the ruins of an old castle.

CROSSNA, a village, in the parish of ARDCARNE, barony of BOYLE, county of ROSCOMMON, and province of CONNAUGHT, 6 miles (N. E.) from Boyle: the population is returned with the parish. It occupies, with Mount Prospect, the crest of a hill commanding a fine view of the rich lower country around Lough Key; the ridge is of sandstone. The village and neighbourhood are improving in appearance: the pastures, though generally rough, have been subjected to partial irrigation in the lower grounds, and the arable lands produce good crops of oats and potatoes. The superb house and demesne of Rockingham (described in the article on Ardcarne) stands here; and there is a large R. C. chapel in the village.

CROSSPATRICK, a parish, partly in the half-barony of SHILLELAGH, county of WICKLOW, and partly in the barony of GOREY, county of WEXFORD, and province of LEINSTER, 3½ miles (E.) from Tinahely; containing 1119 inhabitants. It is situated on the road from Rathdrum to Carnew, and comprises 4058 statute acres, which are chiefly under tillage. The soil is fertile, and agriculture has greatly improved under the auspices of the Agricultural Society established at Coollattin and patronised by Earl Fitzwilliam; there is a bog at Cammar, and another at Coolafancy. The principal seats are Hill View, the residence of Sandham Symes, Esq., and Coolafancy, of Christmas Johnston, Esq., both commanding extensive mountain views; and there are several respectable farm-houses. The living is a rectory, in the diocese of Ferns, united prior to any known record to the rectory of Kilcommon, which two parishes constitute the union and corps of the prebend of Crosspatrick in the cathedral of Ferns, and in the patronage of the Bishop. The tithes of the parish amount to £217. 16. 11¼.; and the gross tithes of the benefice to £674. 15. 5. There are two churches in the union; that of Crosspatrick was erected in 1828 by a grant of £900 from the late Board of First Fruits: it is in the later English style of architecture, with a square tower surmounted with pinnacles, and the Ecclesiastical Commissioners have recently granted £203 for its repair. In the R. C. divisions this parish forms part of the union or district of Tomacork, also called the union of Carnew and Crosspatrick; there is a chapel at Coolafancy. There is also a place of worship for Wesleyan Methodists. The parochial school, at Cootroe, is supported by the prebendary, and has an endowment in land valued at £10 per annum by the late Earl Fitzwilliam, who also built the school-house. Near Coolboy is a substantial school-house, which was erected and supported by the same nobleman. A school-house was also erected, in 1835, at Logan, by Lord Powerscourt. Some remains of the old church are visible near the new building, adjoining which is the burial-ground, used by the Roman Catholics.

CROSSPLATTEN, a hamlet, in the parish of Duleek, barony of Lower Duleek, county of Meath, and province of Leinster, 2 miles (N. E.) from Duleek, on the road to Drogheda; containing 9 houses and 79 inhabitants.

CRUAGH, or CREVAGH, a parish, in the barony of Newcastle, county of Dublin, and province of Leinster, 6 miles (S.) from Dublin; containing 1216 inhabitants. This parish is situated on the river Owendugher, a branch of the Dugher or Dodder river, by which it is separated from the parish of Whitechurch; and comprises 4762½ statute acres, of which 2400 are mountain, including about 400 acres of good bog. Killakee, the residence of S. White, Esq., is a spacious mansion, situated in a tastefully embellished demesne, with a well-wooded glen through which a mountain stream rushes with great force over its rocky bed; and surrounded by a winding road, several miles in circuit, commanding some magnificent views of the city and bay of Dublin, with the hill of Howth, Ireland's Eye, Lambay Island; of the mountains of Mourne in the distance, which are distinctly visible in clear weather, and of a beautiful country in the foreground. There are numerous handsome villas, with tastefully disposed grounds, commanding fine views of the city and bay of Dublin and the country adjacent. Among these are, Woodtown House, the residence of the Hon. Chief Baron Joy; Orlagh, of N. Callwell, Esq.; Rockbrook, of Mrs. Fry; Tibradon, of J. Jones, Esq.; Cloragh, of C. Davis, Esq.; Woodbine Lodge, of T. B. Smithson, Esq.; Springfield, of R. Jones, Esq.; Woodtown, of Mrs. Collins; Air Park, of J. Delaney, Esq.; Spring Vale, of R. Sherlock, Esq.; Mount Venus House, of H. R. Armstrong, Esq.; Mount Michael, of M. Walsh, Esq.; Laurel Hill, of W. Bourk, Esq.; Summerville, of J. T. Moran, Esq.; Woodtown, of J. Dodd, Esq.; Hayfield, of W. Scott, Esq.; and Prospect Hill, of J. Dodd, Esq. There are four paper-mills, only one of which is at present at work, and employs about 60 persons. Two woollen-manufactories have been established; the chief articles are friezes, flannels, kersey, coating, and blankets, and the number of persons employed at present is 100, though a few years since, when in full work, more than 600 were engaged. The great military road commences in this parish, taking a course of 37 miles through a wild mountainous district previously deemed incapable of improvement, and opening a communication with Wicklow and with the south and west parts of the country. It is a rectory, in the diocese of Dublin, forming part of the union of Tallaght: the tithes amount to £181. 17. 6. In the R. C. divisions it forms part of the union or district of Rathfarnham. On the grounds of Mount Venus are the remains of a cromlech, the table stone of which has fallen; and of the upright stones on which it was supported, one only is standing, the others lying near it. The whole is of granite; the table stone is 19 feet long, 10 feet broad, and 5 feet thick; and the pillars are about 10 feet in height. The burial ground of the old church, now a ruin, is still much used.

CRUISETOWN, a parish, in the barony of Lower Kells, county of Meath, and province of Leinster, 1¾ mile (S. W.) from Nobber, on the road to Kells; containing 427 inhabitants. It comprises about 2430 statute acres, two-thirds of which are under tillage; there are some quarries of black stone. Cruisetown, formerly the property of the ancient family of Cruise, now belongs to Mr. Shaw, who contemplates building a new house here: in the demesne are two lakes. The living is a rectory, in the diocese of Meath, and in the alternate patronage of the Crown and the Bishop: the tithes amount to £100. Here is neither church, glebe-house, nor glebe. In the R. C. divisions the parish forms part of the union or district of Nobber: the chapel is a plain building. About 30 boys and 12 girls are educated at a hedge school at Altamont. There are some small remains of the ancient church, with a burial-ground attached, in which are some very ancient monuments of the Cruise family.

CRUMLIN, a post-town, in the parish of Camlin, barony of Upper Massareene, county of Antrim, and province of Ulster, 5½ miles (S.) from Antrim, and 79 (N.) from Dublin; containing 128 houses and 641 inhabitants. This town is situated on the river Camlin, of which its name is a corruption, and on the road from Lurgan to Antrim; it consists of one long wide street, from which branches one of smaller dimensions leading to the Antrim road, and has a neat and cheerful appearance. At one extremity is the beautiful cottage and highly embellished grounds of Glendarragh, the seat of Col. Heyland, through which flows the river Camlin, noted for the petrifying quality of its waters: among the many fine specimens of petrified substances which it has afforded is the entire root of a tree, of five cubic feet. Adjoining the town are the most extensive and complete flour-mills in the country; they were originally built in 1765, by Rowley Heyland, Esq., and were the first that were erected in the north of Ireland. These mills were considered of so much importance that Government erected very extensive warehouses for storing wheat and other grain, and encouraged by every means the growth of wheat in the surrounding district. There are several other mills belonging to the same concern, but as all purchases and sales are made at this place, they all come under the denomination of the Crumlin mills. They are now the property of Messrs. Robert Macaulay and Son; the machinery, which is of very superior construction, is impelled by the water of the Camlin river, and the quantity of grain annually consumed is on the average 3000 tons of wheat and the same quantity of oats. A large portion of the flour is shipped for the Clyde, and the several ports of the north of England; and during the year 1833, 2000 tons of flour and oatmeal were sent from this establishment to Liverpool and Manchester alone. A flax-mill has been erected by the Messrs. Macaulay, and several hundred persons in the town and neighbourhood are constantly employed in weaving linens and cottons for the manufacturers of Belfast and other places. From its situation on Lough Neagh, this place derives every possible facility of communication by water with Belfast, Newry, Antrim, and other towns. Fairs are held on the first Monday in every month, for horses, cattle, and pigs; and a constabulary police force is stationed in the town. Petty sessions are held once a fortnight. There is a place of worship for Presbyterians in connection with the Synod of Ulster.—See Camlin.

CRUMLIN, or CROMLIN, a parish, in the barony of NEWCASTLE, county of DUBLIN, and province of LEINSTER, 2¾ miles (S. W.) from the post-office, Dublin; containing 958 inhabitants, of which number, 544 are in the village, which consists of 115 houses. It is one of the four manors of the county anciently annexed to the Crown, and governed by a seneschal, who receives £300 per annum. In 1594 the village was burned by Gerald Fitzgerald, at the head of the Wicklow insurgents. In 1690, after the victory of the Boyne, a part of William's army encamped here; and it is said to have been at this place that the king himself settled the method of granting protection, which was accordingly made public. On July 10th, he also issued hence his proclamation for stopping the currency of the brass money coined by Jas. II., except at reduced rates of valuation. It is a police station connected with the city of Dublin police. Here are extensive quarries of limestone, from which Dublin is chiefly supplied; and large flour-mills have for many years been in operation at Kimmage. The principal gentlemen's residences are Crumlin House, that of W. Collins, Esq.; Crumlin Lodge, of G. Oakley, Esq.; Crumlin, of R. Smith, Esq.; and the Glebe-house, of the Rev. J. Elliott: in the grounds of Mr. Smith is a moat or rath, from which is an extensive view of the beautiful scenery in the neighbourhood. The living is an impropriate curacy, in the diocese of Dublin, and in the patronage of the Dean and Chapter of St. Patrick's, to whom the rectory is appropriate. The tithes amount to £250: the glebe comprises only 1*a.* 36*p.* The church, which is a neat structure, was rebuilt, in 1816, by aid of a loan of £1000 from the late Board of First Fruits, but the old tower was preserved. In the R. C. divisions the parish forms part of the union or district of Rathfarnham: the chapel in the village is a neat building. There is a school in connection with the church, and one under the National Board of Education, in which together about 120 boys and 80 girls are educated. About £70 per annum, arising from land bequeathed at a very remote period, is applied to the relief of the poor of this parish.

CRUMP, or ILANE-A-GREEN, an island, in the parish of BALLYNAKILL, barony of BALLYNAHINCH, county of GALWAY, and province of CONNAUGHT, 10 miles (N. E.) from Clifden. This island, which is inhabited by only one family, is situated near the entrance of Ballynakill harbour on the western coast, and contains about 70 statute acres of arable land.

CRUSHEEN, a village, in the parish of INCHICRONANE, barony of BUNRATTY, county of CLARE, and province of MUNSTER, about 6½ miles (N. N. E.) from Ennis, on the road to Gort; containing 57 houses and 316 inhabitants. Fairs are held on the lands of "Brodagh by Crusheen" on Jan. 17th, May 20th, Aug. 15th, and Nov. 19th, for general farming stock. It is a constabulary police station, and has a dispensary. Petty sessions once a fortnight, and the road sessions for the district, are held here; also a seneschal's court occasionally for the manor of Bunratty, in which small debts are recoverable. The old R. C. chapel stands here, and a new one is now nearly completed: in the ancient burial-ground, Sir Theobald Butler, who framed the articles of the Treaty of Limerick, lies interred.—See INCHICRONANE.

CRYCRIM, or CRECRIM, a parish, partly in the barony of RATHVILLY, county of CARLOW, but chiefly in the half-barony of SHILLELAGH, county of WICKLOW, and province of LEINSTER, 4½ miles (E. N. E.) from Tullow; containing 510 inhabitants. It comprises 2431 statute acres, as applotted under the tithe act, and is an impropriate cure, in the diocese of Leighlin, forming part of the union of Aghold; the rectory is appropriate to the dean and chapter of Leighlin. The tithes amount to £144. 15. 1. of which £96. 10. 1. is payable to the dean and chapter, and £48. 5. to the appropriate curate. In the R. C. divisions it forms part of the union or district of Clonmore. At Ballyconnel there is a R. C. chapel, also a national school.

CULDAFF, or COOLDABH, a parish, in the barony of ENNISHOWEN, county of DONEGAL, and province of ULSTER, 6 miles (N. W.) from Moville; containing 5995 inhabitants. It is bounded on the north-east by the Atlantic ocean, and contains, according to the Ordnance survey, including detached portions, 20,089½ statute acres, about two-thirds of which are mountain and bog, and 55½ acres are water including the tideway of Culdaff river. The surface is generally mountainous, intersected with occasional districts of cultivated land. The mountains of Crucknanionan, Clonkeen, Carthage, and Glengad, the highest summit of which is called Croagh, are covered with black heath, intermixed with coarse grass and bog; that called Squire Carn, on the southern boundary of the parish, is 1058 feet above the level of the sea. The land is generally cold, and cultivation is not in an advanced state, except in the neighbourhood of Culdaff House, where an improved practical system of agriculture has been advantageously introduced, as also near Carthage House, the residence of the Rev. James Knox. Limestone abounds, and is carried hence to a considerable distance. Prior to the year 1812, large quantities of cod were taken off this coast, but that species of fish has since almost wholly disappeared. Salmon of excellent flavour is, during the summer months, taken in the river and for several miles along the coast, but it also is now scarce; in a small lake at Moneydarragh the char, or Alpine trout, is found in considerable numbers. In the several detached bogs of this parish great quantities of timber, chiefly fir and oak, are imbedded; the oak is generally black and in a good state of preservation. These bogs occupy a low tract of country, extending westward to Malin, with small elevated knolls of firm cultivated land rising from amid the bog, and known here as the "Isles of Grelagh:" it is supposed that the sea once flowed either over or around the whole, as marine exuviæ are every where found beneath the bog. The village of Culdaff, generally called Milltown, is situated on the eastern bank of the river, and contains about 30 houses. Fairs are held on the 10th of Feb., May, Aug., and Nov., for general farming stock. It enjoys an advantageous position for carrying on a considerable coasting trade, but very little business is done. Several good roads intersect the parish; and there is a penny post to Moville. Culdaff House, the residence of George Young, Esq., with an extensive and highly improved demesne, well fenced, planted, and cultivated, nearly adjoins the village; and not far distant is Redford, the residence of the Rev. R. Hamilton, by whose exertions a barren rocky district has been converted into a comparatively fertile plain.

The living is a rectory, in the diocese of Derry, and in the patronage of the Marquess of Donegal: the tithes amount to £482. The glebe-house stands a mile east of the village, on a glebe comprising 105 acres, of which 40 are uncultivated land. The church is a small neat edifice, in the early English style, with a square tower of modern erection. In the R. C. divisions part of this parish is united to part of Cloncha, forming the union or district of Culdaff, and the remainder forms part of the district of Cloncha: there is a large chapel at Bogan, in the latter parish, which serves for both. The parochial school for boys is principally supported by the rector, aided by local contributions. A school in the village of Culdaff was built and is principally supported by George Young, Esq., and his lady; and at Ballyharry is a school in connection with the National Board, and another at Caramora: in these schools about 140 boys and 100 girls are educated; and there are five private schools, in which are about 400 children, and three Sunday schools. On the summit of a steep rock, on the coast near Carthage are the remains of a circular fort, called Doonowen: it is nearly surrounded by the sea, and is supposed to have been the residence of the ancient proprietor of the barony of Ennishowen. At Cashel is a curious elevation, which appears to have been the site of a religious house; close adjoining are two perfect stone crosses of great antiquity, and near them the plinth of a third cross; at Baskil are two upright stones, supporting a horizontal one; and in several other parts of the parish are considerable remains of antiquity. The parish is said to have been the birth-place of the celebrated comedian Macklin.

CULFEIGHTRIN, or COOLFAYTON, a parish, in the barony of Carey, county of Antrim, and province of Ulster, ½ a mile (E.) from Ballycastle; containing 5012 inhabitants. This parish, which is also called Carey, from Castle Carey or Kerragh, which gave name to the barony, was the scene of a sanguinary conflict that took place between the forces of Mac Quellan and those of Sorley Boy Mac Donnell, who encamped on the plains of Bonamargy, on the 4th of July, 1569. This battle, by which the Mac Donnells obtained possession of the castles and estates of the Mac Quellans, is described as having continued throughout the whole vale of Glenshesk, of which every yard was fiercely contested, and nearly the entire surface strewed with the slain. The victory was at length determined in favour of the Mac Donnells, and the fate of Mac Quellan was finally decided on the mountains of Aura, on the 13th of the same month; Shane O'Dennis O'Nial fell in this battle, and his cairn or tumulus is still shewn near Cushendun. The parish, which is bounded on the north by the Atlantic ocean, comprises, according to the Ordnance survey, an area of 26,338 statute acres, including 49 acres under water. The surface is mountainous; the entire mountain of Carey, and the promontories of Fair Head, the most northern part of Ireland, and Tor Point being within the parish: the highest spot is Carnlea, which, according to the same survey, is 1253 feet above the sea. The system of agriculture is improving, but there are very large tracts of waste land, among which is the extensive mountain of Carey, covered with heath; the only profit from it is the peat or turf carried from its bogs for fuel: it is well stocked with grouse. The lower grounds are well cultivated, and the townland of Murloch, which is an inland continuation of the bold and craggy promontory of Fair Head, is extremely fertile, producing an abundance of corn and excellent pasturage. The collieries, generally known by the name of the Ballycastle mines, which were extensively worked about the middle of the last century, are in this parish, but were discontinued in 1833: it is supposed that the mines are exhausted, the workmen, on penetrating inland from the face of the promontory, for a distance of from a quarter to half a mile, having been stopped by a whin-dyke which here crosses the country, and though experimental shafts have been sunk on the other side of the dyke, lower than the levels previously wrought, no coal has been found: it is, however, conjectured that this mineral could be found by sinking under the former levels or beneath the surface of the sea. There are fine quarries of freestone, which are extensively worked, affording employment to a considerable number of persons; also valuable mines of coal under the promontory of Fair Head, and at Murloch; the former have never been worked, and the working of the latter has been discontinued for some years. The road from Belfast to the Giants' Causeway, along the shore, formerly led over the dreary mountain of Carey, where, for nearly ten miles, not a single habitation was to be seen. The royal military road is now in course of formation, by means of which that mountain will be avoided, or its difficulty obviated, and the baronies of Carey and Glenarm will be united by a splendid viaduct thrown across the romantic valley of Glendun. Great preparations have already been made by levelling the hills and the draining of bogs and lakes; the whole line of road for 8 miles through this parish is entirely new. The scenery is boldly diversified, including the stupendous rocks of Glendun, the lakes of Cranagh, and Tor Point and Fair Head, in the crags of which eagles build their nests. Within the limits of the parish are Churchfield, the residence of T. Casement, Esq.; Cushendun House, of Edm. A. McNeill, Esq.; Cottage, of Major McAulay; Glenmona, of M. Harrison, Esq.; and a cottage residence of Gen. O'Neill. At Tor Point and Cushendun are coast-guard stations, which are two of the eight that form the district of Ballycastle.

The living is a rectory and vicarage, in the diocese of Connor, and in the patronage of the Bishop; the rectory was attached to the Chancellorship of Connor from the year 1600 till 1831, when, on the death of Dr. Trail, the late chancellor, it became a separate consolidated rectory and vicarage under Bishop Mant's act. The tithes amount to £350: there is neither glebe-house nor glebe. The church, a neat edifice, in the later English style, was erected in 1830, on the site of the ancient structure, by a loan of £600 from the late Board of First Fruits. It is in contemplation to erect a chapel of ease at Cushendun, now a fashionable watering-place, at the eastern extremity of the parish, and seven miles distant from the mother church, which is situated at the opposite extremity. In the R. C. divisions the parish is the head of a union or district, comprising also the Grange of Innispollan, and containing two chapels; that in Culfeightrin is at Carey, near the church. An excellent school-house was built at Bonamargy, near the bridge, by Alexander McNeil, Esq.;

and there is also a school at Cushendun, chiefly supported by the resident gentry of the neighbourhood. About 180 children are educated in four private schools. On the bay of Cushendun are some fine remains of Castle Carey.

CULLEN, a parish, in the barony of DUHALLOW, county of CORK, and province of MUNSTER, $3\frac{1}{2}$ miles (N.) from Millstreet; containing 4385 inhabitants. It is situated on the Government new line of road from Killarney to Mallow (which will be of great benefit to the district in general), and on the north bank of the river Blackwater, and contains 13,409 statute acres, as applotted under the tithe act, and valued at £8478 per ann. The land, generally coarse, is occasionally good and under tillage; agriculture is gradually improving; there is a large portion of bog. Near Churchhill a culm mine has been worked for the last six years, which employs about 30 persons: brownstone, adapted for building, is found in the parish. The principal residences are Keale House, that of J. Leader, Jun., Esq.; Stake Hill, of Leonard Leader, Esq.; Church Hill, of Daniel McCartie, Esq.; Rathroe, of Denis McCarthy, Esq.; Derrigh, of Denis McCartie, Esq.; Knocknagehy, of J. Philpot, Esq.; Flintfield, of Denis O'Connell, Esq., M.D.; and Duaregill Castle, formerly belonging to the O'Keefes, the property and occasional residence of Dr. Justice, of Mallow. The living is a vicarage, in the diocese of Ardfert and Aghadoe, united since the year 1670, with those of Kilmeen and Droumtariffe; the rectory is partly appropriate to the deanery, and partly impropriate in the Earl of Donoughmore. The tithes amount to £328. 17. 4., of which £48. 17. 4. is payable to the lessee of the dean (being the rectorial tithes of 3162 acres), £130 to the lessee of the impropriator (being the rectorial tithes of 10,249 acres), and £150 to the vicar (being the vicarial tithes of the whole). The old church is in ruins; that of the union, and the glebe-house, are in Droumtariffe. In the R. C. divisions the parish is partly in the union or district of Droumtariffe, but chiefly in that of Millstreet: the chapel at Cullen is a modern slated building. There are four hedge schools, in which are about 230 children At Droumsicane, on the bank of the river Blackwater, are the picturesque ruins of an extensive square fortification, flanked by a round tower at each angle, the property of Sir Broderick Chinnery, Bart.: it had formerly a lofty square tower in the centre. Tradition says that at some remote period a battle was fought at Knockonard; and near Keale have been found spurs, spears, bronze battle-axes, and other relics. An ancient crescent of pure gold, weighing nearly $2\frac{1}{2}$oz., and valued at £9 British, was found near Knocknagehy in 1834. Adjoining the ruins of the church is a holy well, dedicated to St. Laserian, where a patron is held annually on July 24th.

CULLEN, a parish, in the barony of KINNALEA, county of CORK, and province of MUNSTER, 5 miles (N. N. E.) from Kinsale, on the road to Cork; containing 1251 inhabitants. It comprises 3940 statute acres, as applotted under the tithe act. The land is generally good, but the system of agriculture necessary for a succession of crops has not yet been introduced, although, from its vicinity to Carrigaline, and the facility of procuring sea-sand and sea-weed, cultivation is comparatively in a thriving state. Glynney is the seat of G. N. Dunne, Esq. It is a rectory, in the diocese of Cork, and is part of the union of Templebready, and corps of the deanery of Cork: the tithes amount to £253. 16. 10., and there is an excellent glebe-house, on a glebe of 21 acres. There are some ruins of the old church; the Protestant inhabitants attend divine worship at Ballymartle. In the R. C. divisions the parish forms part of the union or district of Ballymartle. There is a day school of about 20 children.

CULLEN, a parish, partly in the barony of CLANWILLIAM, county of TIPPERARY, and partly in that of COONAGH, county of LIMERICK, and province of MUNSTER, 4 miles (N. W.) from Tipperary; containing 1412 inhabitants, of which number, 498 are in the village, which was formerly a market-town, but is now an inconsiderable place. Here is a constabulary police station; and two fairs are held, one moveable, either in May or June, the other on Oct. 29th. The living is a rectory, in the diocese of Emly, united from time immemorial to the rectories of Solloghodmore and Solloghodbeg, and the vicarage of Toughcluggin, together forming the union of Cullen, in the patronage of the Archbishop of Cashel. The tithes of the parish amount to £122. 7. $6\frac{1}{2}$., and of the union, to £591. 5. $7\frac{1}{4}$. The glebe-house was built by aid of a gift of £100 and a loan of £900, in 1819, from the late Board of First Fruits: there are three glebes in the union, comprising together $45\frac{1}{4}$ acres. The church is a plain building. In the R. C. divisions the parish forms part of the union or district of Lattin: the chapel is a small building. The parochial schools, in which about 20 boys and 10 girls are educated, are supported by the incumbent, and about 120 children are taught in two hedge schools. In a small bog has been found a great number of interesting relics of remote antiquity, an account of which was furnished to the Society of Antiquaries, in 1774, by Governor Pownall, and which is inserted in their Archæologia.

CULLENWAYNE, a parish, in the barony of CLONLISK, KING'S county, and province of LEINSTER, containing, with the post-town of Moneygall, 1653 inhabitants, of which number, 379 are in the town. This parish is situated on the road from Dublin to Limerick, and contains 3550 statute acres, of which about 1100 are reclaimable bog. The principal residences are Rathenney House, that of Maunsell Andrews, Esq., situated in a handsome demesne; Green Hills, of the Rev. W. Minchin; Silver Hills, of Mrs. Smith; and Rathenney Cottage, of J. Andrews, Esq. It is a rectory and vicarage, in the diocese of Killaloe, and is part of the union of Templeharry: the tithes amount to £227. 9. $10\frac{1}{4}$. In the R. C. divisions the parish forms part of the union or district of Dunkerrin; the chapel is at Moneygall. The parochial school is aided by the incumbent and other contributors; a school in the village is supported by the parish priest, and there are two others. There is also a private school, in which are about 30 boys and 10 girls.

CULLINSTOWN, a parish, in the barony of SKREEN, county of MEATH, and province of LEINSTER, 4 miles (S.) from Duleek; containing 298 inhabitants. This parish is situated on the confines of the county of Dublin, near the great north road from Dublin to Belfast, by Ashbourne: it is a rectory, in the diocese of Meath, entirely impropriate, and annexed to the union of Duleek. In the R. C. divisions also it forms part of the union or district of Duleek. There is a hedge school, aided by local subscriptions, in which are about 30 children.

CULLOHILL, a village, in the parish of AGHAMACART, barony of UPPER OSSORY, QUEEN'S county, and province of LEINSTER, 3 miles (W.) from Durrow, on the road to Kilkenny; the population is returned with the parish. Fairs are held on May 27th and Oct. 2nd, for farming stock in general, but particularly sheep. A constabulary police force is stationed here; and the parochial chapel of the district of Durrow is situated in the village.—See AGHAMACART.

CULLUMKILL, or COLUMBKILL, a parish, in the barony of GRANARD, county of LONGFORD, and province of LEINSTER, 3 miles (W.) from Granard, on the road to Arvagh; containing 8543 inhabitants. This parish is situated on Lough Gawnagh, commonly called Ernehead lake, which divides it into two parts, and is embellished with some very beautiful scenery. It contains 13,646 statute acres, of which several thousand are bog, and about 120 woodland. This is a mountain district, having large tracts of waste land; the crops are principally oats and potatoes. Near Derrycross is a slate quarry, which has never been worked; and there are quarries yielding limestone of the best kind. Ernehead, the handsome seat of J. Dopping, Esq., stands delightfully on the edge of the lake, in a demesne well planted with fine timber; and about two miles off, nearly surrounded by the lake, is Woodville, the seat of R. Lambert, Esq., commanding rich and extensive views of the lake and surrounding country; here is also Frankfort, the seat of J. McEvoy, Esq. It is a vicarage, in the diocese of Ardagh, and is part of the union of Granard; the rectory is impropriate in W. Fulke Greville, Esq. The tithes amount to £664. 12. 2¼., which is equally divided between the impropriator and the vicar. The church stands nearly in the centre of the parish, and is in good repair, and ornamented with minarets: it was erected in 1829, by aid of a gift of £830 from the late Board of First Fruits. In the R. C. divisions the parish is the head of a union or district, comprising also the western part of the parish of Abbeylaragh, and containing three chapels, one on the townland of Aughnacliffe, one on that of Ballinnulty, and one on that of Mullinloughto. A school is about to be established in connection with the Ardagh Diocesan Society; and about 600 boys and 260 girls are educated in ten private schools. A monastery of Canons Regular, founded about the middle of the fifth century by St. Columb, stood on Inchmore, or the Great Island, in Lough Gawnagh, on the confines of Cavan and Longford, partly in Abbeylaragh, and partly in Columbkill: the island consists of 20 or 30 acres, and is now uninhabited. This monastery was destroyed by the Danes in 804, but was restored, and continued to exist until the 15th century. On the borders of the lake are the remains of the castle of Rossduff: and near Dunbeggan are two druidical altars, one supported by two, and the other by three, upright stones. Near the church of Cullumkill is a beautiful specimen of jasper.

CULLYBACKEY, a village, in the parish of AHOGHILL, barony of LOWER TOOME, county of ANTRIM, and province of ULSTER, 3 miles (N. W.) from Ballymena; containing 235 inhabitants. This village, which is situated on the river Maine, contains about 50 houses, including a place of worship for Presbyterians. The manufacture of linen is extensively carried on, and a fair was formerly held for its sale. Cullybackey House was formerly the residence of John Dickey, Esq., by whom, in 1778, a corps was raised, called the Cullybackey volunteers; it is now the seat of John Dickey, Esq. Iron-works are said to have formerly existed here, and vitrified substances have been found.

CULMORE.—See TEMPLEMORE.

CULMULLEN.—See COLMOLYN.

CULTYMOUGH.—See KILLEDAN.

CUMBER, county of DOWN.—See COMBER.

CUMBER, LOWER, a parish, in the barony of TIRKEERAN, county of LONDONDERRY, and province of ULSTER, 6 miles (S. E. by S.) from Londonderry, on the road to Dungiven; containing 4584 inhabitants. This parish was separated from the original parish of Cumber in 1794, when this portion of it, comprising, according to the Ordnance survey, 14,909 statute acres, was constituted a parish of itself. The land under cultivation is very fertile, particularly that portion which lies in the vale of the Faughan; good pasturage is obtained on the mountains, which compose about one-third of its surface. Several mountain streams run through the parish, of which the Burntallaght is the most interesting; on this water is a beautiful cascade, called the Neiss, which falls over a ridge of clay-slate nearly 80 feet. Considerable portions of the parish are the property of some of the London chartered companies, by whom great improvements have been effected. In the vale of the Faughan, which extends through the parish and is pleasingly wooded, stand several elegant houses, surrounded by grounds of singular beauty. The inhabitants combine with their agricultural pursuits the weaving of linen cloth; and there is an extensive bleach-green, where 16,000 pieces are annually finished, principally for the English market. There are several handsome bridges both of wood and stone, and between the Oaks and Oaks Lodge is a suspension bridge, which, as seen from the road, has a very pleasing effect. The principal residences are the Oaks, that of Acheson Lyle, Esq.; Oaks Lodge, of Hugh Lyle, Esq.; the Cross, of James Smith, Esq.; and the Glebe-house, of the Rev. Wm. Hayden.

The living is a rectory, in the diocese of Derry, and in the patronage of the Bishop: the tithes amount to £560. The glebe-house was erected in 1800, by a gift of £100 from the late Board of First Fruits: the glebe comprises 106 acres, of which about 30 are uncultivated. The church is a convenient and substantial edifice, built in 1795, by aid of a gift of £500 from the Board. The rector has every fifth presentation to the perpetual cure of Learmount, a district formed out of the original parish of Cumber, in 1831. In the R. C. divisions the parish is partly in the union or district of Glendermot, and partly in that of Cumber Claudy; the chapel, which belongs to the former, is a small edifice, situated at Mullaghbuoy, in the mountain district. The Presbyterians have a large meeting-house at Breakfield, in connection with the Synod of Ulster, of the first class. The male and female parochial schools at Aughill are supported by the rector; and there are large schools at Ervey, Tamnamore, and Ballinamore; the first was built and is supported by the Grocers' Company. The remains of antiquity are numerous; at Slaght Manus is a very large cromlech, the table stone of which is 10 feet long, and is supported by four pillars; and at Mullaghbuoy are the remains of another, but less perfect. In the townland of Listress is a large artificial cave, with five chambers, all built of field stones, covered with broad flag-stones, over which is a covering of earth two feet thick.

CUMBER, UPPER, a parish, partly in the barony of STRABANE, county of TYRONE, but chiefly in that of TIRKEERAN, county of DERRY, and province of ULSTER, 7½ miles (N. E.) from Londonderry; containing, with Claudy (which has a daily penny post), 5430 inhabitants. The early history of this parish cannot be satisfactorily traced, further than that St. Patrick, having crossed the Foyle, founded several churches in this district, one of which occupied the site of the present church of Cumber. The original name is variously written by early historians; the present is modern, and acquired since the taxation of Pope Nicholas in 1291. At the Reformation the rectory belonged to the abbey of Derry, and was given by Jas. I. to the bishop, as part of the abbey lands. In 1622, it appears, by the Ulster Visitation book, to have been held with Banagher. The ancient parish of Cumber was the most extensive in the diocese, until 1794, when it was divided into Upper and Lower Cumber, by order in council: the parish of Upper Cumber, according to the Ordnance survey, comprising 26,202¼ statute acres, of which 23,072¾ are in Derry, and 3129½ in Tyrone; the latter form a hilly district amid the Mounterloney mountains. In some parts, particularly on the Walworth estate, and on that of Learmont, the land, though hilly, is well cultivated; the extensive bogs are being worked out, and brought into cultivation. The inhabitants combine the weaving of linen cloth, with agricultural pursuits; there are several commodious and excellent bleach-greens on the Faughan water, none of which, however, are now at work. The southern parts of the parish consist chiefly of mountains, the principal of which is Sawel, the highest in the county, being 2236 feet above the level of the sea; its summit is on the boundary between two counties. These mountains afford excellent pasturage on every side; and the rivers Faughan, Glenrandle, and Dungorthin have their sources in them. There are large woods and much valuable timber in the demesne of Park-Learmont; and the plantations of Cumber, Alla, and Kilcatton greatly embellish the surrounding scenery. There are several large and elegant houses, of which the principal are Learmont, the seat of Barre Beresford, Esq.; Cumber House, of John H. Browne, Esq.; Kilcatton Hall, of Alexander Ogilby, Esq.; and Alla, of the Rev. Francis Brownlow.

The living is a rectory, in the diocese of Derry, and forms the corps of a prebend in the cathedral of Derry, in the patronage of the Bishop: the tithes amount to £740. The glebe, situated in Glenrandle, half a mile from the church, consists of the townlands of Alla, Gilky Hill, and Tullentraim, containing 1508 statute acres. The church is a large modern edifice, with a small bell turret on the western gable, erected in 1757, on the site of an ancient building. In 1831, eight townlands were separated from the parish, to form part of the new district or parish of Learmont, and the rector of Upper Cumber has the alternate presentation to that perpetual cure. In the R. C. divisions the parish is partly included in the union or district of Banagher, and partly forms the head of a district, comprising also a part of that of Lower Cumber; there are chapels at Claudy and Gortscreagan. The Presbyterians have a meeting-house at Claudy, in connection with the Synod of Ulster. The parochial school, situated on the glebe lands of Alla, is well built and convenient; it is supported by the trustees of Erasmus Smith's charity, and is under the management of the rector, who has endowed it with two acres of land. Male and female schools were built and are supported by the Fishmongers' Company; and they have also excellent male and female schools at Gortilea and Killycor. There are also schools at Ballyarton, Craig, Kilcatton, and Claudy. A female school at Claudy is principally supported by Lady Catherine Brownlow, who likewise contributes to some others. A female work school at Cumber was built and is supported by Mrs. Browne and other ladies of the parish. A male and female school at Learmont is principally supported by the Beresford family. There are also Sunday schools and a private day school. At Mulderg is a large dispensary, built and supported by the Fishmongers' Company. There are the remains of a druidical altar at Baltibrecan; and at Altaghoney were discovered, in the summer of 1835, three stone coffins, each covered with three flag stones, and in each an urn containing ashes, calcined bones, &c. The graves were two feet deep in the gravel, where 8 feet of bog had been cut off the surface; and near the coffins were two idols, carved out of solid oak, which, with the urns, are now in good preservation, in the museum of Alex. Ogilby, Esq., of Kilcatton, who has also a good collection of landscapes, groups, &c., more than 200 of which are from his own pencil.

CURDANGAN.—See CARDANGAN.

CURNASASE, a village, in the parish of DULEEN, barony of UPPER KELLS, county of MEATH, and province of LEINSTER; containing 21 thatched houses and 108 inhabitants.

CURNASEER, a village, in the parish of KILTOOM, barony of ATHLONE, county of ROSCOMMON, and province of CONNAUGHT, 3 miles (N. W.) from Athlone, on the road to Roscommon; the population is returned with the parish. It has a station of the constabulary police. A large R. C. chapel is in course of erection near it, also a school-house, which is to be in connection with the National Board.

CUROFIN, or COROFIN, a small market and post-town, in the parish of KILNEBOY, barony of INCHIQUIN, county of CLARE, and province of MUNSTER, 7 miles (N. N. W.) from Ennis, on the road to Kilfenora, and 118 miles (W. S. W.) from Dublin; containing 900 inhabitants. This town is situated about three-quarters of a mile south-east of Inchiquin lake, and near the western extremity of Lough Tadane: these loughs are connected by a river flowing through them, which is here crossed by a stone bridge. It comprises about 140 houses, mostly thatched, and consists of one main street, commencing near the bridge, and a shorter one branching off, towards the east, at the end of which stands the church, and on the south side of it the R. C. chapel. Considerable quantities of yarn stockings, the manufacture of the surrounding country, were formerly brought to this place for sale, but the trade has long been on the decline. Adjoining the bridge is Richmond, the residence of the Rev. S. Walsh, P. P.; and about three-quarters of a mile west of the town, and near the shore of Inchiquin lake, is Riverstown, the old mansion of the Burton family, now converted into a chief constabulary police station. A boat race has lately been established on the lake of Inchiquin (which is remarkable for the beauty of its scenery and for its fine trout), and is likely to become annual. Lough Tadane is said to abound with roach and very large pike. A small market is held on Wednesday; and there are two fairs, one on the day before Ascension-day, and one on Nov. 22nd. The market-house is an old building, supported by slanting buttresses, and is at present almost disused, the corn being chiefly sent to Ennis. Petty sessions are held on alternate Wednesdays; and road sessions for the district are also held here. A seneschal's court for the manor of Inchiquin is occasionally held, in which small debts are recoverable. The church is a small neat edifice. The R. C. chapel is a spacious slated building, erected by subscription about ten years since. The parochial school is chiefly supported by the Rev. Mr. Blood and Edward Synge, Esq. Here is also a large school, under the patronage of the parish priest. Hugh McCurtin, the learned antiquary, grammarian, and poet, author of an Irish dictionary, died here about 1720, and was interred at Kilvedane, in the neighbourhood.—See Kilneboy.

CURRAGH, a hamlet, in the parish of Duleen, barony of Upper Kells, county of Meath, and province of Leinster; containing 78 inhabitants.

CURRAGHALEEN, a village, in the parish of Drum, barony of Athlone, county of Roscommon, and province of Connaught, 4 miles (W. by S.) from Athlone: the population is returned with the parish.

CURRAGRANEMORE, a parish, in the barony of Ibane and Barryroe, county of Cork, and province of Munster, 2¾ miles (S. E.) from Clonakilty; containing 63 inhabitants. This place is locally situated within the parish of Templeomalus, of which it is considered to form a part: it comprises only 120 acres, which are tithe free, and constitutes a prebend in the cathedral of Ross, in the patronage of the Bishop. The income of the prebendary arises solely from the rent of lands leased to Mr. John Barret for £55. 7. 8. per annum.

CURRAN, a village, in the detached portion of the parish of Maghera, barony of Loughinsholin, county of Londonderry, and province of Ulster, 3 miles (N. E.) from Maghera; containing 34 houses and 174 inhabitants. This village is situated on the road from Tobbermore to Castledawson, and on the river Moyola, which is here crossed by a handsome bridge. Fairs are held on June 23rd and November 22nd, for cattle and pigs; and there is a large flour-mill in the village. Here are a male and female school under the National Board. The land around the village, except on the banks of the Moyola, is poor; there are large and valuable bogs extending hence to Tobbermore.—See Maghera.

CURRANROE, a village, in the parish of Abbey, barony of Burren, county of Clare, and province of Munster, 2 miles (E.) from Burren; containing 92 inhabitants. This village is situated at the extremity of an inlet from the bay of Galway, which forms the harbour of Burren, or New Quay, into which the sea rushes with considerable force for nearly four miles, and up to Curranroe bridge, which forms the boundary of the counties of Clare and Galway. It is a neat and improving place, several slated houses having been erected within the last few years; and is a station of the constabulary police. Here is a small quay, at which turf and sea manure are landed; but in consequence of the new road lately made towards the interior, it is about to be removed, and a more commodious one constructed by Burton Bindon, Esq., who employs a considerable number of labourers in clearing the ground of stones, and placing them on the slab in the bay, to promote the growth of sea weed, in which a great trade is here carried on. Curranroe, the neat cottage residence and farming establishment of Mr. Bindon, is in the village, and in the vicinity is the great oyster bed called the Red Bank, which is described in the article on the parish of Abbey.

CURRENS, a parish, partly in the barony of Magonihy, and partly in that of Trughenackmy, county of Kerry, and province of Munster, 6¼ miles (N. E.) from Milltown; containing 1565 inhabitants. This parish is situated on the road from Castle Island to Dingle, and on the rivers Mang, or Maine, and the Brown Flesk; it comprises 4456½ statute acres, as applotted under the tithe act, of which about three-fifths lie on the south of the Maine, and in the barony of Magonihy. The soil is light, and agriculture is improving; the substratum on the north of the Maine consists of limestone, which is much used for manure, and there is a quarry of good stone adapted for building; there are some patches of bog. Riverville is the seat of Richard Marshall, Esq. A large cattle fair is held on May 6th; two other fairs formerly held have been discontinued. It is a rectory and vicarage, in the diocese of Ardfert and Aghadoe, and is part of the union of Kiltallagh: the tithes amount to £162. 3. 1., of which £58. 3. 1. is payable to the rector of Ballymacelligott, for the rectorial tithes of that part of the parish which lies north of the Maine; £47 to the incumbent, for his vicarial tithes of the same portion; and £57 to the same for the entire tithes of that portion which lies south of the Maine. In the R. C. divisions the greater part of this parish is in the union or district of Ballymacelligott; the remainder forms the head of a district, comprising also the parishes of Dysart and Killentierna: the parochial chapel is in the village of Currens, and there is a chapel of ease in Killentierna. About 40 children are educated in a hedge school.

CURRICUPPANE, or CURRIKIPPANE, a parish, in the county of the city of Cork, and province of Munster, 2¼ miles (W.) from Cork; containing 1042 inhabitants. This parish is bounded on the south by the river Lee, and on the west by the Shawnagh or Awnbeg, which is also the boundary between the dioceses of Cork and Cloyne. It comprises 2094 statute acres, as applotted under the tithe act, and valued at £4482 per annum. The surface is undulating, rising in some parts into very considerable eminences immediately from the banks of the Lee, and commanding a fine view of the course of that river through a beautiful and rich tract of country, with the fertile district of Carrigrohane and Ovens to the west, and of the city of Cork and its suburbs to the east, beyond which is the noble expanse of the Lee to Blackrock. The lands are chiefly meadow and pasture, and what is under tillage is in an excellent state of cultivation; the soil is fertile, and the supply of manure abundant. The elevated districts are all of the clay-slate formation; some are richly planted, and have a picturesque and beautiful appearance. The principal gentlemen's seats are Leemount, the residence of Capt. Thos. Otho Travers; Kitsborough, of William Wagget, Esq.; Prospect, of A. Morgan, Esq.; Mount Desert, of N. Dunscombe, Esq.; West Hill, of the Rev. J. Webb, LL.D; Mount Desert, of T. J. Wise, Esq.; Lee Bank, of R. Hatton, Esq.; and Hillsborough, of C. W. Dunscombe, Esq. It is a rectory, in the diocese of Cork, and forms part of the union of Carrigrohane and corps of the precentorship in the cathedral church of St. Finbarr, Cork: the tithes amount to £280. The church has been for many years in ruins, and the Protestant parishioners attend the church of Carrigrohane; there is neither glebe-house nor glebe. In the R. C. divisions it forms part of the union or district of North Parish, Cork; the chapel is a plain building.

CURRIGLASS, a village, in the parish of MOGEALY, barony of KINNATALOON, county of CORK, and province of MUNSTER, $1\frac{3}{4}$ mile (W.) from Tallow, on the road to Fermoy; containing 514 inhabitants. This village is situated in the fertile vale of the Bride, and near the confines of the counties of Cork and Waterford: it consists of a short street extending nearly east and west, with another branching from it towards the south. The parochial church, a small but neat structure with a square tower, is near the east end of the village. Here is a station of the constabulary police; also a male and female school in connection with the National Board. In the vicinity are numerous gentlemen's seats, embosomed in finely wooded demesnes. Adjoining the village are three trees, an oak, a cedar, and a holly, remarkable for their size and vigour; and some of the pleasure-grounds contain a variety of valuable exotics of great size and beauty, particularly the Verbena, which flourishes here in the open air.—See MOGEALY.

CURRIN, a parish, partly in the barony of COOLE, county of FERMANAGH, but chiefly in the barony of DARTRY, county of MONAGHAN, and province of ULSTER, 3 miles (S. W.) from Clones, on the road to Ballyhaise and Stradone; containing, with the town of Drum and the village of Scotshouse (each of which is separately described), 7180 inhabitants. This parish comprises, according to the Ordnance survey, 11,372 statute acres, of which 10,987 are in Monaghan, and 385 in Fermanagh. The land is chiefly arable; there are about 200 acres of woodland, but little bog, and fuel is very scarce. There are several lakes in the parish, of which those contiguous to Drum, and to the Hilton demesne, are the most extensive. In addition to agricultural labour, the chief occupation of the inhabitants is the linen manufacture. Hilton Lodge, the beautiful residence of Col. Madden, is situated on the confines of Fermanagh, and commands a fine view of the neighbouring mountains; the demesne, which is several hundred acres in extent, is well furnished with fine timber, and has a well stocked deer park. The other seats are Minore, that of Captain Cottnam; and Laurel Hill, the property of George Moore, Esq.

The living is a rectory and vicarage, in the diocese of Clogher, united by episcopal authority to part of the rectory and vicarage of Drumkrin, together forming the union of Currin, in the patronage of the Bishop. The tithes amount to £400, and the gross tithes of the benefice to £584. The glebe, which was erected by a gift of £380. 15. from the late Board of First Fruits, in 1828, comprises 60 acres of profitable land, valued at £100 per annum. The parochial church, at Scotshouse, is a neat modern structure in good repair; there is also a chapel of ease at Drum. On the next avoidance it is provided by acts of council, dated Jan. 7th, 1804, and March 6th, 1806, that the union be dissolved, when the part of Drumkrin will be attached to the parish of Drummully. The R. C. parish is co-extensive with that of the Established Church: the chapel is at Scotshouse. There are two Presbyterian meeting-houses in Drum, one in connection with the Synod of Ulster, of the third class; and one for Seceders, of the second class. There are schools at Scotshouse, Tattenaghcake, Carnagarry, Aghrea, Mockla, Carne, Laurel Hill, Killefargy, and Drum, in which are about 530 boys and 330 girls. There are also three private schools, in which are about 40 boys and 20 girls; and six Sunday schools.

CURROHILL and MENTAUGHS, an extra-parochial district, in the barony of ENNISHOWEN, county of DONEGAL, and province of ULSTER; containing 311 inhabitants. This district was formerly part of the lands appertaining to the abbey of Derry, or Templemore, and is locally situated in the parish of Clonmany.

CURRY, a village, in the parish of ACHONRY, barony of LINEY, county of SLIGO, and province of CONNAUGHT, 9 miles (S. W.) from Ballymote, on the road to Swinford, containing about 40 houses and 167 inhabitants. It gives name to the R. C. district, the parochial chapel of which stands here. Fairs are held on Ascension-day, Corpus Christi, and Aug. 9th.

CUSHENDALL, or NEWTOWN-GLENNS, a post-town, in the parish of LAYDE, barony of LOWER GLENARM, county of ANTRIM, and province of ULSTER, 10 miles (N. W.) from Glenarm, and 116 miles (N.) from Dublin; containing 481 inhabitants. This place is beautifully situated within a quarter of a mile from the sea, on the Glenagan stream, which falls into Cushendall bay immediately below the town; it is also intersected by the river Dall, over which a handsome stone bridge has been erected. The surrounding country is strikingly romantic; and the coast, independently of the picturesque scenery it affords, is highly interesting to the geologist, from the diversity of its strata and the numerous caverns with which it abounds. The town, which is neatly built, contains about 90 houses, and is much frequented by persons visiting the Giants' Causeway, to which the new military road along the coast passes through it, and a handsome and commodious hotel has been built for their accommodation. The parish church of Layde, a small neat edifice at the western end of the town, was built in 1832, by a gift of £900 from the late Board of First Fruits. Cushendall bay affords good anchorage for vessels in from 3 to 9 fathoms of water. Fairs, chiefly for Raghery ponies, cattle, sheep, and provisions, are held on Feb. 14th, March 17th, May 14th, Aug. 15th, Sept. 29th, Nov. 14th, and Dec. 22nd. The market-house is a convenient building. A constabulary police station has been established here; also a coast-guard station, which is one of the eight constituting the district of Ballycastle. Petty sessions are held every alternate week; and there is a house of correction in the town. On a mount in it is a castle, which is attributed to the Danes. —See LAYDE.

CUSHENDUN, a small sea-port, partly in the parish of CULFEIGHTRIN, in the barony of CAREY, and partly in that of LAYDE, barony of LOWER GLENARM, county of ANTRIM, and province of ULSTER, 3 miles (N. N. E.) from Cushendall; the population is returned with the respective parishes. This place is situated on a small bay of that name, at the mouth of the river Dun or Glendun, and has recently been much frequented as a watering-place during the summer season. It appears to have derived its name from its situation near the mouth of the Dun, and carries on some trade in cattle and pigs with the opposite coast of Cantire, in Scotland. Here are extensive quarries of freestone. The harbour, which has been formed by the construction of a pier, partly at the expense of Government, affords good shelter to a number of small vessels, which remain here all the winter; it has good anchorage in winds blowing from the shore, and vessels of 50 tons' burden can cross the bar. There are a few small vessels from 14 to 20 tons' burden belonging to the port, and several boats are employed in the herring fishery in the bay. Here is a coast-guard station, forming one of the eight which constitute the district of Ballycastle. On the coast are some spacious caverns of singular construction.

CUSHINGTOWN.—See CARNAGH.

D

DALKEY, a parish, in the barony of UPPERCROSS, county of DUBLIN, and province of LEINSTER, 6¾ miles (S. E.) from Dublin; containing 1402 inhabitants, of which number, 544 are in the village. This place, which is situated at the eastern extremity of the bay of Dublin, was formerly a town of considerable importance, and appears to have had a charter of incorporation at an early period, as, from an enrolment in the 33rd of Edw. III., dated Feb. 8th, 1358, "the provost and bailiffs in the town of Dalkey, the sheriff of Dublin, and the bailiff of Senkyl, were commanded to allow the master of a Spanish ship arrested by them to depart." In 1414, Sir John Talbot, Lord Furneval, afterwards the celebrated Earl of Shrewsbury, landed here to take upon him the viceregal government; and, in 1558, the Earl of Sussex embarked his forces at this port to oppose the Scottish invaders at the isle of Rathlin, on the coast of Antrim. Fairs and markets were established in 1480, for the encouragement of foreigners, who resorted hither to trade with the inhabitants; and seven strong castles were erected for their protection and the security of their merchandise. The harbour was extremely favourable to the commerce of the town; vessels could lie in safety under shelter of the neighbouring island, by which they were protected from the north-east winds, and from the depth of water they could sail at any hour. The tolls of the fairs and markets were appropriated to the paving and improvement of the town, which, till the latter part of the 17th century, continued to be a place of great commercial resort, especially for the merchants of Dublin; but since that period its harbour has been abandoned for others of greater convenience, and the town has dwindled into an insignificant village. It is situated at the base of a high hill, commanding extensive views over the bay of Dublin, and in a neighbourhood abounding with picturesque and diversified scenery. Four of its ancient castles have been entirely destroyed, and the remains of three others, which have been long dismantled, convey striking indications of their former importance; one has been converted into a private dwelling-house, another is used as a store, and the third as a carpenter's shop. A twopenny post has been established, and there is a constabulary police station in the village. Here is also a station of the coast-guard, the limits of which extend from Dalkey Head to Irishtown, within which are batteries at Dalkey island, Sandy Cove, and Kingstown, and nine martello towers.

The parish comprises 444 statute acres, as applotted under the tithe act, and valued at £703. 6. 6½. per ann. A great portion of the land is open common, an extensive tract of which, adjoining the village, has, during the continuance of the public works at Kingstown harbour, been allowed to remain in the occupation of many who put themselves in possession of it, and have sold their assumed portions of it to others. At the farthest extremity of the common, on the coast opposite Dalkey island, are lead mines, which were formerly worked to some extent, but are now discontinued. On the common are the government quarries, which are worked by Messrs. Henry, Mullins and McMahon, under a contract for the completion of Kingstown Harbour. The largest blocks of granite blasted by gunpowder are lowered to the long level of the railway by three inclined planes. Dalkey common is celebrated in the old ballad of the "Kilruddery Hunt," written in 1774, by Mr. Fleming, and of which a copy was presented by the Earl of Meath to Geo. IV., on his visit to Dublin in 1821. The marine views are exceedingly beautiful, and the general scenery of the neighbourhood, which is richly diversified, is enlivened by numerous pleasing villas; the principal are Sorrento, the seat of the Rev. R. Mac Donnell, F.T.C.D., commanding a beautiful view of the sea, with Wicklow and Bray Head, the Sugar Loaves, Djouce, Shankill, part of the Dublin mountains, and the beautiful bay of Killiney; Braganza Lodge, of — Armstrong, Esq.; Barn Hill, of Mrs. Johnston; Shamrock Lodge, of T. O'Reilly, Esq.; Charleville, of C. Brabazon, Esq.; and Coolamore, of Jeremiah Hanks, Esq., from which is an extensive view of the bay of Dublin. There are also numerous pleasant cottages, commanding fine views of the sea, which are let during the summer to respectable families. It is a perpetual curacy, in the diocese of Dublin, and is part of the union of Monkstown; the rectory forms part of the corps of the deanery of Christchurch, Dublin. The tithes amount to £21. 9. 8., of which two-thirds are payable to the dean, and the remainder to the curate. The church is in ruins: it was situated in the village, and appears to have been originally a very spacious structure. In the R. C. divisions the parish forms part of the union or district of Kingstown. A national school is maintained by subscription, for which a good school-house was erected by subscription, in 1824; and there is also a school on the common, supported by small payments from the children aided by subscription; in these are about 190 boys and 150 girls. About the commencement of the present century, a circle of granite blocks enclosing a cromlech was standing on the common; but the cromlech and the stones surrounding it were blasted with gunpowder and carried away, to furnish materials for the erection of a martello tower on the coast. About five years since, in ploughing the grounds of Quatrebras, a stone grave was discovered, in which was a perfect skeleton; the proprietor of the estate, Capt. Nicholson, would not suffer it to be disturbed, and it still remains in the same state as when first found. Numerous ancient copper coins have been discovered in the same field.

DALKEY ISLAND, in the parish of Dalkey, barony of Uppercross, county of Dublin, and province of Leinster. This island is situated in 53° 16′ 40″ (N. Lat.), and 6° 5′ 20″ (W. Lon.), and forms the south-eastern extremity of the bay of Dublin. Tradition states that the citizens of Dublin retired to it when that place was visited by the great plague, in 1575; and in modern times they have occasionally resorted hither for convivial purposes. Prior to 1798, it was the custom annually in the month of June to elect a mock king of Dalkey, with various officers of state, whose proceedings were recorded in a newspaper called the "Dalkey Gazette." The island is separated from the mainland of the parish by a channel called Dalkey Sound, about 1200 yards long, and 330 wide at its S. E., and 230 at its N. W. entrance. It was formerly considered a very safe and convenient harbour, and was the principal anchorage for ships resorting to the ancient sea-port of Dalkey. In 1815, it was surveyed as a site for an asylum harbour for the bay, and disapproved. The island contains about 25 statute acres of land, one-half of which affords good pasturage for cattle. The only inhabitants are a few artillerymen stationed at the battery, which mounts three 24 pounders, and has on its summit a martello tower, which is entered from the top. Here are the ruins of a church, dedicated to St. Benedict; and kistvaens, or stone coffins, of rude workmanship and great antiquity have been found near the shore. Near the church is a well, said to be efficacious in ophthalmic complaints; and some medicinal plants are found on the island. To the N. W. of Dalkey are the Clara, Lamb, and Maiden rocks, in the cavities of which an abundance of shell fish is found; and to the N. E. are the small islands called the Muglins.

DALYSTOWN, a village, in the parish of Trim, barony of Lower Moyfenragh, county of Meath, and province of Leinster; containing about 20 houses and 118 inhabitants.

DANESCASTLE, a village, in the parish of Carrick, barony of Bargy, county of Wexford, and province of Leinster, 6 miles (S. S. W.) from Taghmon, on the road to Bannow; containing 123 inhabitants. This village, which derives its name from an ancient castle in its vicinity, is, from its proximity to the sea, much frequented during the summer season for bathing; and a facility of communication is afforded by a public car running hence through Taghmon to Wexford. The R. C. chapel of the district, a neat and spacious edifice, stands in the village; and in the chapel yard is a comfortable residence for the priest, adjoining which is a good school-house in connection with the National Board. Here is a dispensary, and a penny post to Taghmon has been established. At a short distance from the village are the ruins of Danes Castle, consisting of a lofty square tower, the erection of which is attributed to the earliest of the Norman settlers, and partakes much of the gloomy character of that period.—See Carrick.

DANESFORT, or DUNFORT, a parish, in the barony of Shillelogher, county of Kilkenny, and province of Leinster, 3 miles (S.) from Kilkenny, on the road to Thomastown; containing, with the parish of Annamult, and part of that of Tradingetown or Ballyreddin, 1263 inhabitants. This parish, which is also called Dunfert and Dunsert, comprises 5832 statute acres, as applotted under the tithe act: the land is principally under tillage, the soil fertile, and the system of agriculture improved; limestone is found in abundance, and is quarried both for building and burning into lime for manure. Danesfort, the seat of Major Henry Wemys, is pleasantly situated; in the demesne are the ruins of an ancient church. It is a vicarage, in the diocese of Ossory, and is part of the union of Burnchurch; the rectory is impropriate in the mayor, aldermen, and burgesses of the city of Kilkenny. The tithes amount to £250 of which one-half is payable to the corporation, and the other half to the vicar. In the R. C. divisions it is the head of a union or district, comprising also the parishes of Ennisnag, Killahane and Grove, Grange Abbey, and Annamult, and parts of the parishes of Ballyreddin, Burnchurch, Kells, and Ballybar: there are five chapels, situated respectively at Danesfort, Lady's-well, Grange, Bennet's-bridge, and Kells-grange. There is a school at Bennet's-bridge under the National Board, in which are about 80 children; and there are two pay schools, in which about 100 are educated. Here was anciently a castle, built by William, Earl Mareschal; and there are several Danish forts in the parish.

DANGAN, a post-town, in that part of the parish of Killereran which is in the barony of Tyaquin, county of Galway, and province of Connaught, 23¼ miles (N. E.) from Galway, and 91½ (W. by S.) from Dublin: the population is returned with the parish. This small town, which contains only about 30 houses, is situated on the road from Tuam to Ballinasloe.—See Killereran.

DANGAN, OLD, a village, in the parish of Kilmacow, barony of Iverk, county of Kilkenny, and province of Leinster, 3 miles (N. by W.) from Waterford; containing about 40 houses and 192 inhabitants.

DANGANDARGAN, a parish, in the barony of Clanwilliam, county of Tipperary, and province of Munster, 2½ miles (S. W.) from Cashel, on the road from Golden to Clonmel; containing 323 inhabitants, and comprising 1077 statute acres, as applotted under the tithe act. It is a rectory, in the diocese of Cashel, and forms part of the union of Athassel and Relickmurry: the tithes amount to £105. In the R. C. divisions it is part of the union or district of Golden.

DANION.—See DINGINDONOVAN.

DANISTOWN, a parish, in the barony of Skreen, county of Meath, and province of Leinster, 6½ miles (S.) from Slane; containing 145 inhabitants. This parish is situated on the river Nannywater, and on the road from Navan, by Blacklion, to Duleek, comprising 1144 statute acres, as applotted under the tithe act: the system of agriculture is improved; there is neither waste land nor bog. It is a rectory and vicarage, in the diocese of Meath, and forms part of the union of Kentstown: the tithes amount to £80; the glebe comprises 1*a.* 2*r.* In the R. C. divisions it is part of the union or district of Blacklion; the chapel is a neat plain building.

DARAGH, or GLENROE, a parish, in the barony of Costlea, county of Limerick, and province of Munster, 4 miles (S. E.) from Kilfinane; containing 1856 inhabitants. This place, generally called *Daragh-Glenroe,* signifying "the Oaks of the red valley," is situated on the road from Limerick to Mitchelstown, and derives its name from an ancient and extensive forest of oaks, in the vale of Glenroe, extending from the hills of Glenasheen to the river at Towerlegan. Towards its north-west boundary are still some woods of oak, the remains of the ancient forest. Near its south-western extremity the road to Ballingarry crosses a small river, near the confluence of two streams, forming a boundary between the dioceses of Cork and Emly, and between this parish and the adjacent parishes of Ballylander and Ballingarry. The parish, which adjoins the county of Cork, comprises 6635 statute acres, as applotted under the tithe act, and valued at £4197 per annum. The land is every where of excellent quality, and generally under a good system of cultivation. Daragh House, the seat of F. Bevan, Esq., is pleasantly situated, and extensive improvements are in progress around it. Ballynacorty House is the seat of M. Bourke, Esq. Near Daragh House are some extensive slate quarries, but they have not been worked to a sufficient depth to procure slates equal to those of the counties of Waterford and Cork. A new line of road from Limerick to Mitchelstown is in course of formation, which, when completed, will become the principal road from Limerick to Cork. The living is a vicarage, in the diocese of Limerick, united by act of council to that of Kilfinane, together forming the union of Daragh, in the patronage of the Earl of Cork, in whom the rectory is impropriate: the tithes amount to £240, of which £105 is payable to the impropriator, and the remainder to the vicar; and the tithes for the whole benefice amount to £300. There is neither church, glebe-house, nor glebe. In the R. C. divisions the parish is the head of a union or district called Glenroe, comprising also the parish of Kilflyn, in each of which is a chapel; the chapel of Daragh, in Glenroe, is a spacious and handsome edifice, erected in 1834, at an expense of £750. There is a pay school of about 20 boys and 20 girls. There are the ruins of a churchyard. Near the road leading from Mitchelstown to Kilflyn are the remains of the old hospital of Daragh.

DARGLE.—See POWERSCOURT.

DARGLE, LITTLE.—See WHITECHURCH, county of Dublin.

DARVER, a parish, in the barony and county of Louth, and province of Leinster, 3½ miles (N. W.) from Castle-Bellingham; containing 631 inhabitants. It comprises, according to the Ordnance survey, 1992 statute acres of good arable and pasture land, of which 1935 are applotted under the tithe act. Darver Castle is the seat of J. Booth, Esq. The living is a rectory, in the diocese of Armagh, separated on the death of the last incumbent from the parish of Dromiskin, pursuant to the recommendation of the Ecclesiastical Commissioners in 1831, and in the patronage of the Lord-Primate. The tithes amount to £230: the glebe comprises 1¾ acres, valued at £8 per annum. The ruins of the church are near Darver Castle: there is no glebe-house. In the R. C. divisions it is the head of a union or district, comprising Darver and Dromiskin, in each of which is a chapel. There is a school under the National Board, in which are about 190 boys and 150 girls.

DAVIDSTOWN, a parish, in the barony of Narragh and Rheban, county of Kildare, and province of Leinster, 4½ miles (S. S. W.) from Kilcullen, on the road from Dublin to Athy; containing 1464 inhabitants. It is principally under tillage. The rectory is appropriate to the see of Kildare, and the parish, which is in the diocese of Dublin, forms part of the impropriate curacy of Kilcullen: the tithes amount to £199. 7. 4. In the R. C. divisions it is within the union or district of Crookstown, called also Narraghmore. There is a school at Calverstown under the Trustees of Erasmus Smith's charity, in which are about 30 boys and 40 girls.

DEER ISLAND, or INNISMORE, an island, in the parish of Kilchrist, barony of Clonderlaw, county of Clare, and province of Munster, 3½ miles (N. E.) from Kildysart; the population is returned with the parish. This island is situated near the western bank of the river Fergus, about a quarter of a mile from the shore of Kildysart parish, and contains 493 statute acres, which are nearly equally divided between pasture and tillage. It is the property of the Earl of Egremont, and is also called Inchmore, or the "Great Island," being the largest of those by which the Fergus is adorned, and is remarkable for the fertility of its soil. Flax was formerly cultivated here to a considerable extent, and afforded employment to the female population, but it is now only partially grown. There are some vestiges of an abbey still remaining, founded (according to Archdall) at a very early period, by St. Senan of Inniscattery, who appointed St. Liberius, one of his disciples, to preside over it.

DELGANY, a post-town and parish, in the half-barony of Rathdown, county of Wicklow, and province of Leinster, 9½ miles (N.) from Wicklow, and 15¼ (S. S. E.) from Dublin; containing 2268 inhabitants, of which number, 188 are in the village. Towards the close of the fifth century a religious cell was founded by St. Mogoroc, brother of St. Canoc, at this place, which was anciently called Dergne, or Delgne; and in 1022 a great battle was fought here between Ugain, King of Leinster, and Sitric, the Danish King of Dublin, in which the latter was defeated. The parish, which is situated on the mail coach road from Dublin to Wexford, and on the lower road from Bray to Wicklow, and is bounded on the east by the sea, comprises 3782 statute acres, as applotted under the tithe act, and valued at £4965. 12. 2. per annum. The land is fertile, the system of agriculture much improved, and there is scarcely any waste land and but very little bog. The village is beautifully situated in a sequestered spot on the banks of the stream that waters the Glen of the Downs, and consists of about 30 houses and cottages, which are built in a very pleasing style. A small manufacture of straw plat and nets is carried on; and about three miles to the south of Bray Head, on a low rocky point, is the small fishing hamlet called the Greystones, where is a coast-guard station, which is one of those that form the district of Kingstown. This point, which is a headland of slate projecting into deep water, has been considered by Mr. Nimmo to afford a suitable site for the construction of a harbour, and his estimate for erecting a serviceable pier is £4000. This would enclose an area of two acres for an outer harbour, and of one for an inner harbour, with a depth of ten feet at low water. The scenery is richly diversified, and the neighbourhood is embellished with numerous seats, of which Bellview is the chief. It is situated in the Glen of the Downs, which is a deep ravine formed by a disruption of the mountain, apparently by some convulsion of nature, with precipitous sides, richly clothed with wood. Near its northern entrance stands Mrs. Peter La Touche's rustic cottage, on the margin of a fine lawn. The eastern part of the glen is included in the beautiful demesne of Bellview, the seat of Mrs. Peter La Touche. The stately mansion, to which extensive offices are attached, was built at an expense of £30,000 by the late David La Touche, Esq., who, in 1753, purchased the lands of Ballydonagh, now called Bellview, and in 1754 erected the house, which has been subsequently enlarged by the addition of wings. Behind it is a conservatory 264 feet in length, furnished with many rare exotics; it cost £4000. An elegant domestic chapel is in its immediate vicinity. The demesne, containing above 600 acres, commands a variety of magnificent prospects. There are several walks leading to the Octagon House, Banqueting-room, and Turkish Tent; and within it is a park of 55 acres, well stocked with deer. These beautiful grounds are open to the public on Mondays and by special application on other days. Besides Bellview, there are several other fine seats affording delightful mountain and marine views, the chief of which are Templecarrig, the residence of Major Beresford; Glencarrig, of the Rev. H. Madden; Coolagad, of R. Fox, Esq.; Rathdown, of W. Morris, Esq.; Kindlestown House, of Capt. Morris; and Kindlestown Lodge, of J. Evans, Esq.

The living is a rectory, in the diocese of Dublin and Glendalough, united by act of council, prior to the year 1700, to the vicarage of Kilcoole and Kilmacanogue, together forming the union of Delgany, in the patronage of the Archbishop. This union also comprehends the ancient chapelries of Killossory, Doran or Hartain, Kilbride, Carrick, Kilmacbur, Glasmollen, and Grangenowal, which are now only known as townlands. The tithes amount to £206. 2. 3¾., and of the union to £594. 19. 4. The glebe-house stands on a glebe of more than two acres near the church. The church, which was erected in 1789, after a design by Whitmore Davis, and at the sole expense of Peter La Touche, Esq., is a spacious and handsome structure, enlarged in 1832, by a loan of £1200 from the late Board of First Fruits: it is in the later English style, with a lofty embattled tower surmounted with pinnacles; the altar is on the north side, and the font of black marble was presented by Chalworth Brabazon, Esq. At the east end is a handsome monument to David La Touche, Esq., finely executed by Noah Hickey, a native artist, consisting of a full length figure of the deceased in a standing posture, surrounded by several members of his family. In the R. C. divisions the parish is partly in the union or district of Kilquade, and partly in that of Bray. The parochial school, and a school at Greystones, are supported by subscription; and at Windgates is a school on the foundation of Erasmus Smith; all are under the superintendence of the Protestant clergyman. Here is a dispensary in connection with that at Newtown-Mount-Kennedy, also a parochial library and a poor-shop for supplying the necessitous with goods at cost price; and two legacies, amounting to £67. 10., have been bequeathed to the poor. On the farm of Mr. W. W. Ireland is the picturesque ruin of the chapel, or cell, of St. Crispin; and at a short distance from it, in a deep ravine towards the sea, stand the ruins of the castle of Rathdown, the ground plan of which may be traced, and the basement story of a tower, the walls of which are four feet thick, are still visible. On the townland of Kindlestown are extensive remains of Kindlestown castle. The remains of the former church are in a burial ground at a short distance from the present building; and in the small hamlet of Windgates is a very large cairn.—See Kilcarrig.

DELVIN.—See CASTLETOWN-DELVIN.

DENN, a parish, partly in the barony of Castlerahan, and partly in that of Clonmahon, but chiefly in the barony of Upper Loughtee, county of Cavan, and province of Ulster, 5¼ miles (S. by E.) from Cavan, on the road to Ballyjamesduff; containing 5915 inhabitants. It comprises, according to the Ordnance survey, 11,600¼ statute acres (including 125½ acres under water), of which 7774½ are in Upper Loughtee, 2113¾ in Clonmahon, and 1712 in Castlerahan; 11,237 are applotted under the tithe act. Within the last few years, five townlands have been separated from it, forming, together with portions of three other parishes, the benefice and perpetual curacy of Ballyjamesduff. There are about 20 acres of woodland, and 500 of bog; the remainder is good arable and pasture land. In the northern part of the parish is the mountain of Slieve Glagh, 1050 feet above the level of the sea; and in the south-western part is that of Ardkilmore, 878 feet high. Fairs are held at Cross-keys, on Jan. 12th and March 17th, for general farming stock. The living is a vicarage, in the diocese of Kilmore, and in the patronage of the Bishop; the rectory is impropriate in the Marquess of Westmeath. The tithes amount to £375, of which £150 is payable to the impropriator, and the remainder to the vicar. The glebe-house was erected by aid of a loan of £618 from the late Board of First Fruits, in 1817: the glebe comprises 151 acres. The church, a neat small edifice, was rebuilt by aid of a loan of £600 from the same Board, in 1812. The R. C. parish is co-extensive with that of the Established Church; there are two chapels, one in the townland of Drumavaddey, and one at Cross-keys, both small buildings, and the latter old and dilapidated. In the parochial school are about 50 boys and 20 girls; and there are five pay schools, in which are about 220 boys and 70 girls.

DERENNISH, or DOURINCH, an island, in the parish of Kilmina, barony of Burrishoole, county of Mayo, and province of Connaught, 5 miles (S. W.) from Newport-Pratt: the population is returned with the parish. It is situated in Clew bay, and contains 52 statute acres, the property of the Marquess of Sligo.

DERG.—See SKIRTS.

DERNISH, or DERRINISH, an island, in the parish of AHAMPLISH, barony of LOWER CARBERY, county of SLIGO, and province of CONNAUGHT, 10 miles (N. N. E.) from Sligo: the population is returned with the parish. This island is situated near the entrance of Milk-haven, on the north-west coast, and contains about 76 statute acres of land, the property of Lord Palmerston. On its south-west side is safe anchorage in all weather in two fathoms. About ½ a mile north of it is Carrignaspanach rock, which lies off the entrance of the haven, and the Tyrconnell rock is about ¼ of a mile from the shore Milkhaven is situated about three leagues east of the point of Ballyconnell; the entrance is difficult, and only adapted for vessels drawing from 6 to 8 feet of water.

DERRALOSSORY, or DERRYLOSSORY, a parish, partly in the barony of NEWCASTLE, but chiefly in that of BALLYNACOR, county of WICKLOW, and province of LEINSTER, 9 miles (N. W.) from Wicklow; containing 4412 inhabitants. This parish, which is situated in the mountain district of Glendalough, and on the road from Dublin, by way of the Seven Churches, to Rathdrum, is intersected by the river Avonmore, and comprises 54,865 statute acres, as applotted under the tithe act, and valued at £5894 per ann. A very considerable portion is rough mountain, affording tolerable pasturage for sheep and cattle; about 700 acres are woodland, and 16,000 good arable and pasture land; the quantity of waste and bog has been greatly reduced. The military road also passes through the parish. The soil is various, and the system of agriculture improved; the principal crops are potatoes and oats, the cultivation of which has been gradually extended far up the mountains. In the vale of the Avonmore, and in the more western mountains, are large tracts of bog, of which those in the lower grounds have been nearly cut out for fuel. At Glendascene are some very extensive lead mines, worked by the Irish Mining Company, and affording employment to 180 persons. Though generally characterised by dreariness of aspect, the heights in some parts present features of grandeur and sublimity; and extensive plantations have been made on several of the demesnes, which materially improve the scenery of the parish. The principal seats are Derrybane, the residence of W. Truelock Bookey, Esq., situated in a tastefully disposed demesne under the hill of the same name, which is richly clothed with timber, and commands a fine view of the picturesque vales of Clara and Glendalough, with the distant mountains, and containing within the grounds the venerable remains of the ancient abbey church of Glendalough; Roundwood Park, the seat of J. Gower, Esq.; Castle Kevin, of — Frizell, Esq., M.D., who has planted with rich and ornamental timber the various hills around the demesne, commanding extensive views of Lough Dan and the wild scenery of that neighbourhood; Lake Park, the admired residence of Gerard Macklin, Esq., situated on the side of Carrigroe, formerly a wild and barren spot, which has been reclaimed and formed into a handsome demesne commanding fine views of Lough Dan and the adjacent mountains; Dromeen, of Capt. Hugo, which, in the disturbances of 1798, was partly destroyed by the insurgents, who were repulsed with great loss by a detachment of military sent for its protection; Glenwood, of H. Grattan, Esq., who is now erecting a school-house in the demesne, and has covered the hills on his property with thriving plantations; and Cronybyrne, of L. Byrne, Esq. Fairs are held at Togher on Jan. 3rd, for cattle, March 8th, for frieze, and 14th, for cattle, May 19th, July 26th, Aug. 1st, Sept. 5th and 19th, Nov. 8th, and Dec. 5th, for frieze.

The living, though denominated a perpetual curacy, is endowed with the rectorial tithes; it is in the diocese of Dublin and Glendalough, and in the patronage of the Archbishop of Dublin. The tithes amount to £456. 10. The glebe-house, which is situated close to the village of Annamoe, was built by aid of a gift of £250 and a loan of £550 from the late Board of First Fruits, in 1816, together with a considerable sum from the incumbent. The glebe comprises 60 acres, of which 20 are barren and unprofitable land. The church, situated in a wild and uncultivated tract between Roundwood and Annamoe, and remote from any dwelling, was enlarged in 1820, by aid of a loan of £450 from the same Board, together with large contributions from the parishioners. In the R. C. divisions the parish is called Glendalough, and is co-extensive with that of the Established Church; there are chapels at Roundwood and Annamoe. The parochial school at Raheen is supported by subscription, and there is a national school at Glendalough; in these about 100 children are instructed, and there are also two pay schools, in which are about 80 children. At Castle Kevin are the ruins of the old castle of the O'Tooles, which was reduced by Cromwell, between whom and the royalists a battle took place also at the ford over the river, between this place and the Seven Churches.—See GLENDALOUGH.

DERRILIN.—See KINAWLEY.

DERRY.—See LONDONDERRY.

DERRY, a village, in that part of the parish of BALLINCHALLA which is within the barony of ROSS, county of GALWAY, and province of CONNAUGHT, 7½ miles (N. W.) from Cong; containing 95 inhabitants. It is situated on Lough Mask, and contains about 20 houses.

DERRYAGHY, or DERRIAGHY, a parish, partly in the barony of UPPER BELFAST, but chiefly in that of UPPER MASSEREENE, county of ANTRIM, and province of ULSTER, 2 miles (N.) from Lisburn; containing 5325 inhabitants. In 1648, a severe battle was fought near the church, between the royalist forces commanded by Col. Venables and Sir Charles Coote, and the Scots under Monroe, in which the latter were defeated. The parish, which is bounded on the southeast by the Lagan Canal, and situated on the road from Belfast to Dublin and Armagh, comprises, according to the Ordnance survey, 12,479¾ statute acres, of which 6857¾ are in Upper Massereene; about one-third is under tillage, and two-thirds are in pasture. The surface is in many parts mountainous; the soil in the lower part is fertile, producing excellent crops of wheat and barley in the plains, and of oats and potatoes in the mountainous districts; the system of agriculture is rapidly improving; there is a considerable tract of bog, and a large extent of uncultivated land in the mountains, which affords excellent pasturage for cattle. Coal and iron-stone abound in the parish, and attempts have been made to work mines, but the adventurers abandoned their enterprise before they had penetrated to a sufficient depth. There is an extensive limestone district, which is worked for building and for manure. The parish is rich in mineral productions, but none of the mines are worked to any extent, though the Lagan Canal affords every facility of water conveyance. The surrounding scenery is boldly varied and enlivened with several gentlemen's seats, among which are Ballymacash, the elegant mansion of E. Johnson, Esq., J. P.; Seymour Hill, of W. Charley, Esq.; Ingram Lodge, of Jonathan Richardson, Esq.; and Collin, of Walter Roberts, Esq. There are three extensive bleach-greens, the property of Messrs. Charley, Richardson, and Roberts, in which, upon the average, more than 50,000 pieces of linen, lawn, and damask of the finest quality are annually bleached and finished for the English markets. A manorial court is held here every three weeks, for the manor of Derryvolgie, for the recovery of debts under £2; and a court of record is held occasionally, for the recovery of debts and determination of pleas under £200.

The living is a vicarage, in the diocese of Connor, and in the patronage of the Lord-Primate, to whom the rectory is appropriate: the rectorial tithes, which belonged to Black Abbey in Ardes, previously to the Reformation, are now held under the Lord-Primate, on a lease which will expire in 1841, when the living, by his lordship's munificence, will become a rectory: the tithes amount to £450, of which £300 is paid to the lessee of the Lord-Primate, and £150 to the vicar. The church, which was nearly destroyed in the battle previously mentioned, was shortly after rebuilt, and was enlarged and beautified in 1813. In the R. C. divisions the parish forms the head of a union or district, comprising also a small portion of that of Belfast, or Shankill, and containing three chapels, one near the village of Milltown, the Rock chapel in the mountains, and one at Hannah's town, in the Belfast portion of the union. A parochial school was established here previously to 1750, and endowed by Mrs. Hamill with £50 for the instruction of 12 children; it has been rebuilt, and is now well attended. A school was built at Ballymacash, in 1790, by the Rev. Philip Johnson, and handsomely rebuilt in 1833, by E. Johnson, Esq., by whom it is supported: a school was also built at Stonyford by the Marquess of Hertford, and other subscribers; and there are schools at Collin and Rushy Hill, in connection with the National Board, also six pay schools. In the mountain district are the interesting ruins of Castle Robin, once the residence of Shane O'Nial, and subsequently rebuilt by Sir Robert Norton, in 1579. On the mountain of Collin is a large cairn, and there are several raths and forts scattered throughout the parish. Bishop Jeremy Taylor resided for some time at Magharalave House, now in ruins; Dr. William Smith, Bishop of Raphoe, was born at Ballymacash; Philip Skelton, author of some valuable works on divinity, was born here in 1707; and the Rev. Philip Johnson, for 61 years vicar, was also a native of this parish. He distinguished himself during the disturbances of 1798; wrote a reply to Plowden, who had made mention of him in his History of Ireland, and died in 1833.

DERRYBRIEN, an extra-parochial place, in the barony of LOUGHREA, county of GALWAY, and province of CONNAUGHT, about 9 miles (S.) of Loughrea; containing 907 inhabitants. It consists of a range of mountains of the same name, extending from Gort to Woodford, and partly separating the southern part of the county from Clare: there is a good road over them from Woodford to Gort. Here is a R. C. chapel, dependent on that of Killeenadeema.

DERRYBRUSK, a parish, partly in the barony of MAGHERASTEPHENA, but chiefly in that of TYRKENNEDY, county of FERMANAGH, and province of ULSTER, 4 miles (N. E.) from Enniskillen; containing 1329 inhabitants. It comprises, according to the Ordnance survey, 4656¼ statute acres, of which 4372¼ are in the barony of Tyrkennedy; 241½ are water, and 2298 are applotted under the tithe act. Adjoining Lough Erne a monastery for Dominican friars was founded, and dedicated to the Blessed Virgin, by Mac Manus, lord of the place, of which there are still some remains, also traces of the village of Gola, in which it was situated. Derrybrusk House is the seat of J. Deering, Esq. The living is a rectory and vicarage, in the diocese of Clogher, and in the patronage of the Bishop: the tithes amount to £77. 10. 9¼.; the glebe comprises 40 acres. There has been no church from time immemorial in this parish; the Protestant inhabitants of the central and southern portions attend the churches of the neighbouring parishes, and divine service is performed in a school-house once on the first Sunday in every month. There is a school at Ballyreague, in which are about 50 children.

DERRYGALVIN, a parish, in the county of the city of LIMERICK, and province of MUNSTER, 3 miles (S. E.) from Limerick, on the road to Tipperary; containing 722 inhabitants. It comprises 1592 statute acres, of which 18 are bog: the land is remarkably good, about one-half under tillage, the remainder excellent meadow land attached to the large dairy farms which supply the city of Limerick with milk and butter. The principal seats are Coolanave, the residence of J. Shine, Esq.; Ballyclough House, of H. Rose, Esq.; and Killonan House, of F. O'Brien, Esq. It is a rectory, in the diocese of Limerick, and is part of the union of Kilmurry: the tithes amount to £128. The glebe lands comprise six acres, and are subject to a rent of £6 per annum. In the R. C. divisions it forms part of the union or district of St. Patrick's, Limerick. The dioceses of Limerick, Killaloe, and Cashel meet in the townland of Scart. There are ruins of the old church. The basaltic formations here have a very curious appearance, and seem to indicate a volcanic origin.

DERRYGONNELLY, a market-town, partly in the parish of DEVENISH, and partly in that of INNISMACSAINT, barony of MAGHERABOY, county of FERMANAGH, and province of ULSTER, 7 miles (N. W.) from Enniskillen, on the road to Sligo; the population is returned with the respective parishes. This town, which is the property of Gen. Archdall, consists of one main street of newly built houses, and a market-house: it has a penny post to Enniskillen. The market is on Saturday; and fairs are held on the 24th of each month for general farming stock. A constabulary police force is stationed here, and petty sessions are held every alternate week: a manorial court also is occasionally held. It contains a R. C. chapel dependent on that of Devenish, which union or district is also called Derrygonnelly, and a place of worship for Wesleyan Methodists. Near the town are the ruins of an old church, originally a chapel of ease to the parochial church, built by the Dunbar family.

DERRYGORTREVY, a district parish, in the barony of DUNGANNON, county of TYRONE, and province of ULSTER, 3 miles (S. W. by S.) from Dungannon, on the road to Aughnacloy; containing 5282 inhabitants. This district was formed in 1819, by setting off 36 townlands of the parish of Clonfeacle, or rather from the ancient parish of Eglish, which was united to Clonfeacle in the 15th of Chas. II., and thence the whole was called Clonfeacle. The land is generally good, and in an unimproved state of cultivation. There are rocks of excellent limestone, abundance of freestone, and indications of coal, but none of these have ever been worked. The living is a perpetual curacy, in the diocese of Armagh, and in the patronage of the Rector of Clonfeacle, to whom the entire tithes are paid, and who allows the curate annually £93. 9. 3. The glebe-house was erected by aid of a gift of £450, and a loan of £50, in 1822, from the late Board of First Fruits; the glebe comprises 20 acres. The church is a small neat edifice, with a lofty square tower, erected in 1815, at a cost of £800 by the same Board; it is situated on an eminence, half a mile west from the ancient church of Eglish. In the R. C. divisions this district is called Eglish, at which place there is a chapel. The parochial school, near the church, was built in 1825, and is aided by an annual donation from Lord Ranfurly. A school at Gort is partly supported by Lord Caledon; and there are others at Clogherney, Cormullan, and Mullicar. About 40 boys and 20 girls are educated in a private school: there is also a Sunday school.

DERRYGRATH, a parish, in the barony of IFFA and OFFA WEST, county of TIPPERARY, and province of MUNSTER, 2¼ miles (E. by S.) from Cahir; containing 1299 inhabitants. It is situated on the road from Clonmel to Cahir, and comprises 3764 acres, of which about 30 are woodland, 2430 arable, 1088 pasture and 16 bog. Woodrooff, the seat of William Perry, Esq., is in a handsome and well-planted demesne, which extends into the adjoining parishes. The living is a vicarage, in the diocese of Lismore, and in the patronage of the Bishop; the rectory constitutes the corps of the chancellorship of the cathedral of St. Carthage, Lismore. The tithes amount to £230. 6., of which £120 is payable to the appropriator, and £110. 6. to the vicar: the glebe comprises 16*a*. 3*r*. 24*p*. The church is a plain neat building erected by aid of a gift of £800, and a loan of £400, in 1816, from the late Board of First Fruits. The parochial schools are supported by the incumbent, and there is a female school under the patronage of Mr. Perry, also a hedge school of about 100 children.

DERRYHEEN, an ecclesiastical district, in the barony of UPPER LOUGHTEE, county of CAVAN, and province of ULSTER, 3 miles (N. W.) from Cavan, on the road to Enniskillen; containing 1771 inhabitants. This place was erected into an ecclesiastical district in 1834, by disuniting nine townlands from the parish of Urney, three from that of Kilmore, three from Castleterra, and a portion of the parish of Drumlane. It is situated on the river Derryheen, and contains some good arable and pasture land in a state of improved cultivation, though partially subject to occasional inundation from the surrounding lakes, and a moderate portion of valuable bog. The living is a perpetual curacy, in the diocese of Kilmore, and in the patronage of the incumbents of the parishes out of which it was formed: the income of the curate arises from a money payment contributed by each of the patrons. There is neither glebe-house nor glebe. The church is a neat and well-built edifice. A school at Dedris is supported by Lord Farnham, and there is one at Inishmore, together affording instruction to about 100 boys and 60 girls. Here are the ruins of some ancient buildings, called Church Urney, supposed to have been monastic: they form apicturesque object, with a burial-ground attached, used by the R. C. inhabitants.

DERRYKEIGHAN, a parish, partly in the barony of LOWER DUNLUCE, and partly in that of CAREY, county of ANTRIM, and province of ULSTER; containing, with the Grange of Drumtullagh, and post-town of Dervock, 5134 inhabitants. This parish is situated on the river Bush, and is intersected by the roads from Coleraine to Ballycastle, and from Ballymoney to the Giants' Causeway: according to the Ordnance surveys it comprises 11,396½ statute acres. Great improvement has been made in the system of agriculture since the commencement of the present century, by the exertions of gentlemen residing on their own estates, in which they have been greatly assisted by G. Macartney, Esq., of Lisanour Castle, and J. Montgomery, Esq., of Benvarden. The bogs have been drained and partly reclaimed; the crops are excellent, and the wheat, though only cultivated since 1827, is inferior in quality and produce to none in the county; there is still some bog remaining, which produces excellent fuel, and of which part is being brought into cultivation every year. The scenery is pleasingly diversified, and enriched with the flourishing plantations with which, notwithstanding their elevated situation and proximity to the sea, the neighbouring gentlemen's seats are surrounded. Of these the principal are Ballydivity, the residence of J. Stewart Moore, Esq.; Lisconnan, of J. Allen, Esq.; Grace Hill, of H. Irwin Stuart, Esq.; and Knockmore, of Hugh Mackay, Esq. Bush Bank, the seat of Capt. Pottinger, was destroyed by an accidental fire in 1833, but is about to be rebuilt. At Mosside is a manufactory of ropes and cordage made from the bog fir, which is found in large quantities and prepared for that purpose; it affords employment to a great number of persons. The whole of the parish is within the Bushmills district, where courts and petty sessions are held every alternate Monday. It is a rectory, in the diocese of Connor, and is part of the union and corps of the prebend of Cairncastle in the cathedral of Connor: the tithes amount to £430. The glebe-house was built in 1826, by a loan of £1107. 13. 10. from the late Board of First Fruits: the glebe comprises 28½ acres valued at £25 per annum. The Ecclesiastical Commissioners have recommended that on the next avoidance of the union this parish be severed from the rest, and constituted a separate and distinct benefice. The original church was a very small and incommodious building; but in 1831 G. Macartney, Esq., gave an Irish acre of land, which he enclosed with a stone wall, close to the town of Dervock, as a site for the erection of a new church, towards the building of which he contributed also £150; a sum was raised by subscription in the neighbourhood, and the late Board of First Fruits granted a loan of £600, and with these sums the present church was completed. It is a spacious and handsome structure, in the later English style of architecture, with a lofty square embattled tower crowned with pinnacles; being too small for the congregation it is about to be enlarged by the addition of transepts, which will give it a cruciform character. There are two places of worship for Presbyterians, one near the town of Dervock, in connection with the Synod of Ulster, of the second class; the other for Seceders, at Mosside, also of the second class. There are six public schools, one of which is aided by Mrs. Macartney; five private pay schools, and three Sunday schools. Attached to this parish are the 13 quarters called the Grange of Drumtullagh, which was probably an appendage to a monastery at some remote period. There are some large caves at Ballylusk and Idderoan, which were first discovered in 1788; and there are several large forts and tumuli at Cairncullough, Cairncarn, and other places in the parish.—See DERVOCK.

DERRYLORAN, a parish, partly in the barony of LOUGHINSHOLIN, county of LONDONDERRY, but chiefly in that of DUNGANNON, county of TYRONE, and province of ULSTER, on the road from Armagh to Coleraine, and from Omagh to Belfast; containing, with the post-town of Cookstown, 8406 inhabitants. It comprises, according to the Ordnance survey, 12,100¼ statute acres, of which 9656½ are in Tyrone, and 2443¾ in Londonderry. There are 400 acres of woodland and 100 of bog; the remainder is arable and pasture land: the Drapers' Company of London are the chief proprietors. The soil is fertile and well cultivated, and the bog is very valuable as fuel. The parish is well fenced and watered by the river Ballinderry, and ornamented with the plantations of Killymoon and Loughry, which, with the other seats, are more particularly noticed in the article on Cookstown, *which see.* The living is a rectory, in the diocese of Armagh, and in the patronage of the Lord-Primate: the tithes amount to £552. 8. The glebe-house was built in 1820, by aid of a gift of £100 and a loan of £1050 from the late Board of First Fruits. The glebe consists of 71 acres. The church, situated in Cookstown, was built in 1822, by aid of a loan of £3000 from the same Board, and the Ecclesiastical Commissioners have recently granted £283 for its repair. In the R. C. divisions the parish is united to that of Desertcreight, and contains a chapel at Cookstown, where are also four dissenting meeting-houses. Besides the schools in Cookstown, there are schools for both sexes at Ballygroogan, Tubberlane, Killycurragh, and Derrycrummy, aided by annual donations from Lord Castle-Steuart; two at Cloghoge; and one at Gortolery, aided by collections at the R. C. chapel.

DERRYLOSSORY.—See DERRALOSSORY.

DERRYNAHINCH, or DERRYNAHENSY, a parish, in the barony of KNOCKTOPHER, county of KILKENNY, and province of LEINSTER, 2¼ miles (S. E.) from Knocktopher, on the road from Kilkenny to Waterford; containing 1784 inhabitants, and comprising 8171 statute acres. It is a rectory and vicarage, in the diocese of Ossory, and is part of the union of Knocktopher: the tithes amount to £225. In the R. C. divisions it is the head of a union or district called Ballyhale, and comprising the parishes of Derrynahinch, Knocktopher, Aghaviller, Killeasy, and parts of Burnchurch, Jerpoint, and Kells, in which are five chapels, that of Derrynahinch being in the village of Ballyhale. There are four private schools, in which are about 180 children, and a Sunday school.

DERRYNANE.—See KILCROHANE.

DERRYNOOSE, DERRAGHNUSE, or MADDEN, a parish, partly in the barony of TURANY, but chiefly in that of ARMAGH, county of ARMAGH, and province of ULSTER, 2½ miles (N. N. W.) from Keady, on the road to Middleton; containing 8024 inhabitants. This parish was united to Tynan in 1663, and separated from it in 1709, when the first church was built at Madden, from which it is frequently called the parish of Madden. It comprises, according to the Ordnance survey, 15,049 statute acres, of which 9653¾ are in the barony of Armagh: about 716 are bog, and about 20 water. The land is light, but fertile, and in a high state of cultivation. Leslie Hill, the seat of David Leslie, Esq., is beautifully situated, and the avenue and plantations have been much improved of late years; there are also several good farm-houses in the parish. The living is a rectory and vicarage, in the diocese of Armagh, and in the patronage of the Archbishop: the tithes amount to £646. 10. 6. The glebe-house, which, as well as the church, is at Madden, was erected by the incumbent, the Rev. James Jones, and is large and handsome, and pleasantly situated on a fertile glebe of 460 acres. The church is a very commodious edifice, rebuilt in 1816, by aid of a loan of £1000 from the late Board of First Fruits, and recently repaired by aid of a grant of £157 from the Ecclesiastical Commissioners. In the R. C. divisions the parish is the head of a union or district, comprising also that of Keady, and containing three chapels, two in Keady and one at Derrynoose, near the ruins of the old church; it was built in 1824, at an expense of £500. There is a place of worship for Presbyterians in connection with the Synod of Ulster, which was rebuilt in 1834, at a cost of £800. Besides the parochial schools, there are others at Temple and Kilcreevy; a female school at Fargort, built by Capt. Singleton on two acres of land; and Derrynoose school, built by Lord Charlemont, and supported by his lordship, Col. Close, and Capt. Singleton; there are also five private schools. The old church is a picturesque object, situated in an extensive cemetery. Near Madden is a valuable chalybeate spring; and lead mines exist in the parish, but are not worked at present.

DERRYPATRICK, or DIRPATRICK, a parish, in the barony of LOWER DEECE, county of MEATH, and province of LEINSTER, 3 miles (N. E.) from Summerhill, on the road to Skryne; containing 435 inhabitants, of which number, 54 are in the hamlet; and comprising 1932 statute acres, as applotted under the tithe act. It is a rectory, in the diocese of Meath, entirely impropriate in Mrs. Reynell; the clerical duties are discharged by the rector of Knockmark: the tithes amount to £107. In the R. C. divisions it forms part of the union or district of Kilmore.

DERRYVILLANE, a parish, in the barony of CONDONS and CLONGIBBONS, county of CORK, and province of MUNSTER, 2 miles (S. E.) from Kildorrery, on the road from Castletown-Roche to Mitchelstown; containing 788 inhabitants. This small parish is situated on the eastern bank of the river Funcheon, and contains 1805 statute acres, as applotted under the tithe act, and valued at £1663 per annum. The land is generally good, and limestone abounds, which is burnt for manure. It is a vicarage, in the diocese of Cloyne, and forms part of the union and corps of the prebend of Glanworth in the cathedral of Cloyne; the rectory is impropriate in the Earl of Donoughmore: the tithes amount to £164. 7. 9¼., of which £97. 15. 5½. is payable to the impropriator, and the remainder to the vicar. The church is in ruins, but the burial-ground attached to it is still used. In the R. C. divisions, also, it is part of the union or district of Glanworth.

DERRYVULLEN, a parish, partly in the barony of TYRKENNEDY, but chiefly in that of LURG, county of FERMANAGH, and province of ULSTER, on the road from Enniskillen to Kesh; containing, with the post-town of Irvinestown, 10,646 inhabitants. This parish comprises, according to the Ordnance survey (including islands and detached portions), 23,645¾ statute acres, of which 15,070¾ are in the barony of Lurg, 2576¼ acres are in Lower Lough Erne, and 571 in small loughs. It is in six detached parts, which are severally on the roads from Enniskillen to Pettigoe, Lisnaskea, Tempo, Ballynamallard, and Irvinestown, and from Maguire's-bridge to Florence-Court: this last portion includes part of Ennismore island, half of which is in this parish and the remainder in Cleenish. The land is of middling quality, and the state of agriculture improving; the arable land is estimated to comprise 12,000 acres, and there are 500 acres of bog. The gentlemen's seats are Castle Archdall, the residence of Gen. Archdall; Rosfad, of J. Richardson, Esq.; Doraville, of Capt. H. Irvine; and Riverstown, of C. Archdall, Esq. The living is a rectory and vicarage, in the diocese of Clogher, and in the patronage of the Provost and Fellows of Trinity College, Dublin: the tithes amount to £606. 8. 9¾. There is a glebe-house, with a glebe of 600 acres. The church is at Irvinestown (*which see*), and there is a chapel of ease on the road from Enniskillen to Lisnaskea. In the R. C. divisions the parish is partly in the union or district of Enniskillen, and partly the head of a district, called Whitehill; it contains three plain chapels at Lisson, Whitehill, and Lissaroe. The Primitive and Wesleyan Methodists have each a place of worship. The parochial school-house was given by the Earl of Belmore; there are also eight other schools, in which about 460 boys and 300 girls are educated; about 270 boys and 140 girls are taught in nine private schools, and there are five Sunday schools.—See IRVINESTOWN.

DERVOCK, a post-town, in that part of the parish of DERRYKEIGHAN which is in the barony of LOWER DUNLUCE, county of ANTRIM, and province of ULSTER, 10 miles (E. N. E.) from Coleraine; and 123 (N. by W.) from Dublin, on the turnpike road from Ballycastle to Ballymoney; containing 362 inhabitants. This is a neat and well-built town, consisting of two streets, one on each side of the river Bush, and containing about 65 houses. It belongs entirely to G. Macartney, Esq., and has been greatly improved of late years. While in the possession of the late Lord Macartney, great encouragement was afforded to the linen manufacturers to settle here. There are some extensive corn and flour-mills on the banks of the river. Fairs are held for cattle and sheep, but chiefly for horses, on Jan. 12th, Feb. 23rd, May 14th, June 22nd, Aug. 12th, and Oct. 29th. A constabulary police force has been stationed here. The parish church, a handsome structure, is situated close to the town; as is also a R. C. chapel dependent on that of Ballymoney, and the Presbyterian meeting-house of the Synod of Ulster, which is a large building. A very handsome school-house was erected by G. Macartney, Esq., in 1829, and given by that gentleman for a parochial school; attached to it is a girls' school, established in 1832, and principally supported by Mrs. Macartney.—See DERRYKEIGHAN.

DESART, a parish, partly in the barony of IBANE and BARRYROE, and partly in the East Division of EAST CARBERY, county of CORK, and province of MUNSTER, 1 mile (E. by S.) from Clonakilty; containing 744 inhabitants. It is situated on the bay of Clonakilty, and comprises 582 statute acres, as applotted under the tithe act, and valued at £401 per annum. Although elevated, about half of it is under tillage, principally for wheat and potatoes; and the remainder is mountain pasture. It is a vicarage, in the diocese of Ross, and forms part of the union of Kilgarriffe; the rectory is appropriate to the Dean of Ross. The tithes amount to £75, of which £40 is payable to the appropriator, and £35 to the vicar. In the R. C. divisions it is part of the union or district of Clonakilty. On an elevated site near the shore are the ruins of a church, which measured only about 20 feet by 12.

DESERT, a parish, in the barony of BARRYMORE, county of CORK, and province of MUNSTER, 1½ mile (S. E.) from Rathcormac; containing 1141 inhabitants. It is a rectory and vicarage, in the diocese of Cloyne, forming part of the union of Gortroe, into which parish it has entirely merged, and with which the tithes are returned. In the R. C. divisions it is in the union or district of Rathcormac. The schools and further details are noticed under the head of Gortroe.

DESERT.—See DYSART, county of WATERFORD.

DESERTCREIGHT, a parish, in the barony of DUNGANNON, county of TYRONE, and province of ULSTER, 2¼ miles (S.) from Cookstown, on the road from Dungannon to Coleraine; containing 7516 inhabitants. This parish comprises, according to the Ordnance survey, 14,399½ statute acres, chiefly rich arable and pasture land in a high state of cultivation; in the southern part of it are about 1000 acres of mountain and bog. Here are slate quarries, but they are not now worked; and seams of coal may be distinguished in various parts, but no pits have ever been sunk: freestone and limestone are abundant. At Tullylaggan are two extensive bleach-greens, and near Desertcreight is a smaller, which annually bleach and finish upwards of 30,000 pieces for the London market; and a great quantity is woven by the country people in their own houses, the occupation of weaving being followed generally by the inhabitants, in addition to agricultural pursuits. In the upper part of the parish is the village of Rock, where fairs are held on the last Monday in every month, for cattle, sheep, pigs, &c.; and there are four during the year at Tullyhoge. The principal gentlemen's seats are Loughry, the elegant residence of J. Lindesay, Esq.; Desertcreight House, of J. Greer, Esq.; Rockdale, of J. Lowry, Esq.; New Hamburgh, of T. Greer, Esq.; Milton, of W. Greer, Esq.; Turniskea, of the Misses Bailie; Pomeroy House, of R. W. Lowry, Esq.; Elder Lodge, of Dr. Dickson; Rock Lodge, of Captain Daniell; Lime Park, of the Hon. And. Steuart; and the Glebe-house, of the Rev. A. G. Steuart.

The living is a rectory, in the diocese of Armagh, and in the patronage of the Provost and Fellows of Trinity College, Dublin: the tithes amount to £507. 13. 10., and the glebe comprises 177 acres. The church is a very ancient edifice, for the repairs of which the Ecclesiastical Commissioners have recently made a grant of £205. 14. 7.: it is situated in a deep and romantic valley. In the R. C. divisions this parish forms part of the union or district of Derryloran; there is a chapel at Tully O'Donnell, also an altar where divine service is performed on alternate Sundays. At Sandholes is a Presbyterian meeting-house in connection with the Seceding Synod, of the first class; and there is one at Grange for the Covenanters. A commodious school at Tullyhoge was built and is supported by J. Lindesay, Esq.; at Caddy is one built and supported by T. Greer, Esq.; others at Shevy, Sandholes, Drumbellahue, and Grange, are in connection with the Kildare-place Society; and there is one at the slate quarry, in connection with the National Board. There are also three private schools. At Donarisk stood the ancient priory of that name, founded by one of the O'Hagan family, in 1294, of which nothing exists but the cemetery, remarkable as the burial-place of the sept of O'Hagan, and more recently as that of the ancient family of Lyndsay and Crawford, of whom there are several tombs, but the most remarkable is that of Robert Lyndsay, chief harbinger to King James: this Robert obtained the grant of Tullyhoge, &c., from Jas. I., in 1604, where, and at Loughry, the family have ever since resided. Their house and documents were burnt during the civil war of 1641, and this tomb was also mutilated and covered over, in which condition it remained till 1819, when, in sinking a vault, it was discovered. Numerous ornaments of gold, silver, and copper, with various military weapons, have been found here; the latter seem connected with the camp and fortress of Tullyhoge, the chief residence of the sept of O'Haidhagine, or O'Hagan, where the kings of Ulster were inaugurated with the regal title and authority of the O'Nial from the most remote period. Of this important fortress nothing remains but large masses of stone lying scattered around, and the mound, surrounded by deep fosses and ramparts of earthwork.

DESERTEGNEY, a parish, in the barony of ENNISHOWEN, county of DONEGAL, and province of ULSTER, 13 miles (N. N. W.) from Londonderry; containing 1890 inhabitants. This parish is situated on the northern coast, amid the barren mountains of Ennishowen, and is bounded on the north by the Atlantic ocean, and on the west by Lough Swilly; it comprises, according to the Ordnance survey, 7577 statute acres, of which 5834 are applotted under the tithe act; the arable land includes 1794 acres; the remainder is mountain pasture. Some of the lower lands produce good crops of oats, flax, and potatoes; and wherever the mountains afford vegetation, they are depastured by numerous herds of small cattle and sheep. There are indications of copper and lead ore within the parish; and iron ore is abundant. The gentlemen's seats are Lensfort, the elegant residence of the Rev. W. Henry Hervey; and the glebe-house, of the Very Rev. Dean Blakeley. The living is a rectory, in the diocese of Derry, and in the patronage of the Marquess of Donegal: the tithes amount to £135; the glebe-house stands on a glebe of 166 acres, of which 88 are uncultivated. The church is a small neat edifice, with a square tower, situated close to the shore of Lough Swilly. In the R. C. divisions the parish forms part of the union or district of Upper and Lower Fahan and Desertegney; there is a small chapel, occupying the site of the old parish church. The parochial school, near the church, in which are about 30 boys and 15 girls, is a very neat edifice, erected in 1829 by the Rev. W. H. Hervey, and supported by him and a small donation from the rector. There are also two private schools, at Leaugin and Gortlick, in which are about 50 children; and a Sunday school. The gap of Mamore is a remarkable natural curiosity on the confines of this parish, opening to the Atlantic ocean, and most extensive and magnificent views are obtained from the mountains near it. In the Erwys and other lofty mountains of this district, the eagles continue to build, and they prove very destructive to the young lambs on the mountains.

DESERTLYN, or DYSERTLYN, a parish, in the barony of LOUGHINSHOLIN, county of LONDONDERRY, and province of ULSTER, on the road from Dublin to Coleraine; containing, with part of the post-town of Moneymore, 3318 inhabitants. It comprises, according to the Ordnance survey, 5561 statute acres, of which 4977 are applotted under the tithe act and valued at £3243 per annum. There are several bogs, and the soil is variable but generally good and well cultivated. The linen manufacture is connected with agriculture, and affords occasional occupation to the inhabitants. Coal and freestone are visible in several places, but the seams of coal are too thin to pay the expense of working, while turf is cheap. Limestone is also abundant and extensively worked. The principal seats are those of the Hon. and Rev. J. P. Hewitt, Rowley Miller, Esq., and James Smyth, Esq.

The living is a rectory, in the diocese of Armagh, and in the gift of the Lord-Primate: the tithes amount to £230. 15. 4½. The glebe-house was built in 1831, on a glebe of 200 acres. The church, which was built at Moneymore, in 1766, by aid of a gift of £424 from the late Board of First Fruits, is disused; and a beautiful church, in the Norman style of architecture, was erected by the Drapers' Company, in 1832, at an expense of £6000. In the R. C. divisions the parish is partly in the union or district of Lissan, and partly in that of Ardtrea. There is a place of worship for Baptists. In addition to the parochial schools, a large and handsome school-house at Larrycormick was erected and is chiefly supported by the Drapers' Company; there are two others within the parish. They afford instruction to about 320 children, exclusively of those in the Sunday school at Monemyore. The parish contains several raths, and a remarkable cairn on the top of Slieve Gallion.—See MONEYMORE.

DESERTMARTIN, a parish, in the barony of LOUGHINSHOLIN, county of LONDONDERRY, and province of ULSTER, 2 miles (W.) from Magherafelt, on the road from Armagh to Coleraine, containing 4934 inhabitants, of which number, 257 are in the village. This parish comprises, according to the Ordnance survey, 9580 statute acres, of which 6952 are applotted under the tithe act. Within its limits is Lough Insholin, which gives name to the barony; it contains several islands, and is nearly dry in summer. The soil is every where good, and the system of agriculture improved; the lands are chiefly in tillage, producing abundant crops; there are some valuable tracts of bog. A great portion of the mountain of Slieve Gallion, is within the parish; notwithstanding its great height, it affords excellent pasturage nearly to its summit. Limestone abounds, and some very valuable quarries are worked for building and for agricultural purposes. Freestone of excellent quality is also quarried for building; and numerous thin seams of coal have been discovered, but not of sufficient depth to pay the expense of working them. Dromore House is the residence of the Hon. and Rev. A. W. Pomeroy. The inhabitants combine with their agricultural pursuits the spinning of flax and the weaving of linen to some extent in the farm-houses. The village contains about 40 houses, most of which are well built, and, though small, it is remarkably clean and has a very neat and pleasing appearance. Fairs were formerly held here, but they have been for some time discontinued.

The living is a rectory, in the diocese of Derry, and in the patronage of the Bishop: the tithes amount to £400. The glebe comprises 326*a.* 1*r.* 17*p.*, of which, 105 are not cultivated; there is also another glebe belonging to the parish, called the townland of Lisgorgan, situated in Tamlaght-O'Crilly, and containing 179 acres. The church is a small edifice with a square tower, erected by aid of a loan of £800 from the late Board of First Fruits, in 1820; and is situated on the glebe, about a mile from the village. The R. C. parish is co-extensive with that of the Established Church; there are two chapels, situated respectively at Munsterlin and Cullion. There is a place of worship at Lecumpher for Presbyterians in connection with the Seceding Synod, and of the second class. The parochial school is chiefly supported by the rector, who also gives a house rent-free both to the master and mistress; the school-house, a handsome slated building, was erected in 1820. There are schools at Inniscarran and Cranny, founded and supported by the Drapers' Company, also three under the National Board. In these about 500 boys and 370 girls receive gratuitous instruction; and there are also a pay school, in which are about 30 boys and 20 girls, and five Sunday schools. Some remains of the old church exist on the bank of a small river near the village; and on the opposite bank are the remains of a fort, evidently raised to defend the pass of the river; a portion of the old church was taken down in 1820, to supply materials for building the parochial school-house.

DESERTMOON.—See DYSERTMOON.

DESERTMORE, a parish, partly in the barony of Barretts, but chiefly in that of East Muskerry, county of Cork, and province of Munster, 8 miles (S. W. by W.) from Cork; containing 1147 inhabitants. Here was a convent, of which St. Cyra, or St. Chera, was abbess, but when founded cannot be ascertained; it stood on the margin of a small stream, called the Bride, in honour of St. Bridget, to whom the convent was dedicated. Cormac McCarthy the Great founded here a Franciscan monastery, also in honour of St. Bridget. In the civil war of 1641, the castle of Kilcrea, in this parish, erected by the same McCarthy, was garrisoned by the Irish; it was subsequently cannonaded by Cromwell; a fissure in the wall, caused by the cannon, is still conspicuous. The parish is situated on the river Bride, and comprises 3844 statute acres, of which 480 are in the barony of Barretts, and are valued in the County Survey at £452 per annum; and 3422 are in East Muskerry, valued at £2599. 11. 10.: about seven-eighths are arable, the rest being waste and bog. The land is generally good, though the soil is light, the greater part to the south of the limestone valley being hilly, and the soil shallow, yet, under an improved system of agriculture, it produces excellent crops. An exhausted bog of great extent here is capable of being brought into cultivation; and an excellent limestone quarry is worked for the purposes of building and agriculture.

The living is a rectory, in the diocese of Cork, forming the corps of the prebend of Desertmore in the cathedral of St. Finbarr, Cork, and in the patronage of the Bishop: the tithes amount to £350. The glebe-house was built by aid of a gift of £100, and a loan of £600, from the late Board of First Fruits: the glebe comprises 60 acres. The church, a plain modern building, was erected by aid of a gift of £600, in 1814, from the same Board; and the Ecclesiastical Commissioners have recently granted £140. 13. 6. for its repair. In the R. C. divisions the parish forms part of the union or district of Ovens. The parochial schools, in which are about 20 children, are entirely supported by the rector, who provides the school-house and master's residence rent-free. The ruins of the Franciscan abbey are approached by an avenue of ash and sycamore trees, leading to the nave and choir of the church, which was a handsome structure, 150 feet in length, with a transept to the south 68 feet long, opening into an arcade or aisle, extending along both transepts and nave by five arches springing from circular pillars of hewn marble. The dormitories, refectory, kitchen, and other domestic buildings, are to the north. Between the nave and choir rises a light tower, 80 feet high. This venerable pile of ruins, shaded by the lofty trees of the avenue, and viewed together with an ivy-mantled bridge of eight arches, built by order of Cromwell, forms a very interesting feature in the landscape, the beauty of which is much increased by the remains of the castle of Kilcrea, consisting of a massive oblong tower, surrounded by a moat, and part of the barbican, with its towers and platforms in good preservation.

DESERTOGHILL, a parish, in the barony of Coleraine, county of Londonderry, and province of Ulster, 1 mile (S. E.) from Garvagh; containing 4701 inhabitants. This parish is intersected by the road from Dublin to Coleraine, and according to the Ordnance survey contains 11,469½ statute acres, of which about 6309 are arable, 2867 pasture, and 2293 bog, or waste land. The soil, though thin, is tolerably well cultivated, and produces abundant crops. The inhabitants combine with their agricultural pursuits the weaving of linen cloth in their own houses. The living is a rectory, in the diocese of Derry, and in the patronage of the Bishop: the tithes amount to £290. The glebe-house is a small old building on the glebe townland of Meettigan, in the parish of Errigal, which comprises 370 acres, 30 of which are on the southern side of the river, in the parish of Desertoghill, besides a plot of seven acres contiguous to the ruins of the old church. The present church is a large edifice, in the ancient style of English architecture, built in 1784, partly at the expense of Dr. Hervey, afterwards Earl of Bristol, and the Ecclesiastical Commissioners have recently granted £227. 4. 1. for its repair; it stands in the townland of Moyletra, one mile south of the old church. In the R. C. divisions the parish is the head of a union or district, also called Kilrea, comprising the parishes of Desertoghill, Tamlaght-O'Crilly, and Kilrea, and containing three chapels, one here and two in Tamlaght-O'Crilly. A large and handsome meeting-house is now being built at Moneydig for Presbyterians in connection with the Synod of Ulster. The parochial school at Ballyagan is supported by the rector; there are two schools under the Mercers' Company, two under the Ironmongers' Company, one under the National Board, and four others, also a private school. St. Columbkill here founded an abbey, which afterwards became parochial, but the old church, though now a picturesque ruin, does not bear evidence of such remote antiquity as some others in the neighbourhood; in 1622 it was one of the very few in the county that were in perfect repair. Not far distant from the old church is a small fortress; and in an adjoining field is an artificial cave of considerable extent, having three chambers or galleries. A curious stone, wherein are two small and rude founts, considered by the peasantry to be the impress of the knees of St. Columbkill while praying, stands in the churchyard. Half a mile above Garvagh is a curious encampment, called the Bonny Fort; and not far distant is a smaller one, called Roughfort: both appear to have been constructed to protect the mountain pass.

DESERTSERGES, a parish, partly in the barony of Kinalmeaky, but chiefly in the East Division of the barony of East Carbery, county of Cork, and province of Munster, 6 miles (S. W. by W.) from Bandon, on the old road from Cork to Dunmanway; containing 6629 inhabitants. It is situated on the south side of the river Bandon, and comprises 15,355 statute acres, as applotted under the tithe act, and valued at £9781 per annum. A great part consists of rough pasture and bog; the remainder is under tillage. The land is generally cold, but in some places moderately fertile; an inconsiderable tract, called Cashelmore, is common mountain. Quarries of good slate are extensively worked at Bracna. There is a large flour-mill on the river Bandon, erected in 1835, by Arthur B. Bernard, of Palace-Anne, Esq.; and not far distant a paper-mill. Fairs are held at Mount-Beamish on June 26th, Aug. 1st, Sept. 29th, and Dec. 16th, chiefly for cattle and pigs. The gentlemen's seats are Kilcoleman, the residence of Adderly Beamish, Esq., beautifully situated on the banks of the river Bandon, and surrounded by fine plantations; Cashel, of J. Beamish, Esq.; Mount Beamish, of John Beamish, Esq., M. D.; Kilrush, of A. Poole, Esq.; Kilcoleman-Beg, of W. Lamb, Esq.; Sun Lodge, of W. McCarty, Esq.; Church-Hill, of the Rev. Mountiford Longfield; and Kiel, of John Wren, Esq.

The living is a vicarage, in the diocese of Cork, and in the patronage of the Bishop; the rectory is appropriate to the vicars choral of the cathedral of St. Finbarr, Cork. The tithes of Desertserges amount to £1045, of which £315 is payable to the appropriators, and £730 to the vicar; the latter also receives the entire tithes of Garryvoe (a merged parish, to which Lord Kingsale presents), amounting to £315. There is an old glebe-house, with a glebe of 73*a.* 1*r.* 20*p.* The church is a good edifice, with a square tower, erected in 1802. The R. C. parish is co-extensive with that of the Established Church, except a small portion of the eastern district, which belongs to Bandon: the chapel, at Agheohil, is a large modern edifice. There are three Protestant parochial schools, in which are some R. C. children; one at Kilrush, supported principally by Capt. Poole, and the clergyman, and two by the Hon. and Rev. Chas. Bernard, the curate; one of these, at Moulnarogue, a handsome building, was erected by him in 1835; 180 boys and girls are instructed in these schools. There are also some pay schools, in connection with the R. C. chapel. Numerous forts are scattered over this parish; one, which is the most extensive and in the best preservation, surrounded by earthworks and fosses, stands on the lands of Kilmiran. In the north-eastern part of the parish are traces of the old church of Garryvoe. The remains of Derry castle form an interesting ruin; and several upright stones, called Golanes, seem to have been set up either to commemorate some important event, or to indicate the burial-place of some warrior. At Corron is a very powerful chalybeate spring, the waters of which contain large quantities of sulphur and iron, held in solution by carbonic acid gas.

DEVENISH, a parish, in the barony of Magheraboy, county of Fermanagh, and province of Ulster, 2½ miles (N. W.) from Enniskillen; containing 8219 inhabitants. This parish takes its name, signifying "Ox Island," from the island of Devenish in Lough Erne; and comprises, according to the Ordnance survey (including a detached portion and islands), 32,243¼ statute acres, of which 1436¼ are in Lower Lough Erne, 193¾ in Lough Melvin, and 312¾ in small lakes. More than half may be considered good arable land, and the remainder pasture and mountain; the system of agriculture improves very slowly. The river Scillies, rising in the mountains near Church hill, intersects the parish, and proceeding in a southward direction falls into Lough Erne, near Enniskillen; and several inconsiderable lakes are scattered over the parish. Over the Scillies are three bridges, each of three arches, and there is also a bridge over an arm of Lough Erne. The surface is very uneven, and in the centre is a chain of mountains of great breadth, extending four miles, and frequently interspersed with patches of arable and meadow land, the greater part affording pasture only in dry seasons. In that part of the parish near Enniskillen there is a scarcity of bog, but in other parts there is sufficient to supply the inhabitants with fuel. There are excellent quarries of limestone, and on the shore of Lough Erne is some of superior quality, which is quarried for manufacturing into chimney-pieces and for building, and for the conveyance of which the lake affords every facility. The village of Monea is wholly within the parish, and there are two others, Derrygonnelly and Garrison, of which the former is partly in Innismacsaint, in which also is situated an isolated portion of this parish, constituting the farm of Aughamuldoney. Of the gentlemen's seats, the principal are Ely Lodge, the property of the Marquess of Ely, situated on a picturesque island in Lough Erne, connected with the mainland by a bridge, and commanding an interesting view of wood and water in beautiful combination; Graan, the seat of A. Nixon, Esq.; Castletown, of J. Brien, Esq.; and Hall Craig, the property of J. Weir, Esq., an ancient and spacious mansion beautifully situated on the banks of the Scillies. The manufacture of linen is carried on by most of the farmers, who engage weavers to work at their own looms, and many of the women are employed in spinning flax. The river Scillies abounds with pike, bream, and perch, and salmon is occasionally taken in it; and in Lough Melvin, near the western boundary of the parish, is found the Gillaroo trout. Lough Erne is navigable from Belturbet to Belleek, a distance of 40 miles; and the river Scillies is also partly navigable but is very little used. Fairs are held at Monea on Feb. 7th, Whit-Monday, July 7th, Aug. 26th, Oct. 13th, and Nov. 12th, for cattle of all kinds, yarn, and turner's ware; fairs are also held at Garrison and Derrygonnelly.

The living is a rectory and vicarage, in the diocese of Clogher, constituting the corps of the prebend of Devenish in the cathedral of Clogher, and in the patronage of the Bishop: the tithes amount to £295. 7. 8¼. The glebe-house was erected in 1820, by aid of a loan of £843 from the late Board of First Fruits: the glebe comprises 400 acres. The parish church, for the repair of which the Ecclesiastical Commissioners have recently granted £205. 10. 10., is an ancient edifice without any remarkable architectural features, situated in the village of Monea. There is a chapel of ease at Garrison, erected by aid of a gift of £900 from the late Board of First Fruits, in 1828: it is served by a curate, and divine service is also performed in a farm-house on the mountains. In the R. C. divisions the parish is the head of a union or district, called also Derrygonnelly, and comprising also parts of the parishes of Innismacsaint and Bohoe; there are three chapels, one at Monea, one at Derrygonnelly, and one at Garrison, all plain structures. There are places of worship for Wesleyan Methodists, at Derrygonnelly and at Springfield, in each of which divine service is performed on alternate Sundays. Schools are supported by the rector at Monea and Levelly; a school for children of both sexes is supported at Moyglass, by the Marquess of Ely; one at Derrygonnelly, and another at Monea, by Mrs. Brien, of Castletown; and there is a school under the National Board at Knocknashannon, altogether affording gratuitous instruction to 450 children: there are two pay schools, in which are about 50 boys and 50 girls.

The island of Devenish appears to have derived its early importance from the foundation of a religious establishment, in honour of St. Mary, by St. Laserian, called also Molaisse and now Molush, who died in 563, and was succeeded by St. Natalis, son of Ængus, King of Connaught. This establishment was plundered by the Danes in 822, 834, and 961, and appears to have been refounded in 1130, and to have continued till the dissolution. The island, though not in itself very remarkable for picturesque beauty, forms a portion of the most interesting scenery in Lough Erne; it comprises about 70 or 80 Irish acres, and the land is so fertile as to require little or no manure; when viewed from the water, it presents an outline of oval form, but whether from neglect, or from the great value of the land, it is entirely destitute of timber. Of its ancient religious establishments there are some interesting remains: the lower church, dedicated to St. Molush, is 76 feet long and 21 feet wide, with a large aisle on the north; and near it is an ancient building, 30 feet long and 18 feet wide, with a roof entirely of hewn stone, called St. Molush's house. Near the summit of the hill are the remains of the abbey, of which the ruined church is 94 feet long and 24 feet wide, with a large aisle northward; near the centre is an arch of black marble, resting on four pillars and supporting a belfry tower, with a grand winding staircase leading to the summit, which commands an extensive prospect over the lake and the surrounding country. Within the abbey is a stone, bearing the inscription, in old Saxon characters, "*Matheus O'Dubagan hoc opus fecit, Bartholomeo O'Flannagan Priori de Daminis. A. D.* 1449." About 100 paces from the abbey is St. Nicholas' well to which great numbers formerly resorted. Near the church of the abbey is an ancient round tower in excellent preservation: it is 82 feet high and 49 in circumference, and formed of stones accurately hewn to the external and internal curve, and cemented with mortar in quantity so small that the joints of the stones are almost imperceptible; it is covered with a conical roof of hewn stones in diminishing series; under the cornice which encircles it at the top, and which is divided into four equal compartments, each containing a sculptured subject, are four windows facing the cardinal points, above each of which is a carved human head; below there are other windows at different distances, and about seven feet from the base is the entrance doorway, about four feet high. This beautiful monument of antiquity, which was beginning to show symptoms of partial dilapidation, was thoroughly repaired in 1835. There are some remains of an old castle at Monea, and of an ancient family residence at Tullycalter; several Danish forts are scattered over the parish; and in the bogs have been found querns or handmills for grinding corn, the stones of which were about two feet in diameter.—See DERRYGONNELLY and GARRISON.

DEVIL'S-GLEN.—See KILLESKY.

DEVLANE, or DAVILANE, an island, in the parish of KILMORE, barony of ERRIS, county of MAYO, and province of CONNAUGHT, 14 miles (S. W.) from Belmullet: the population is returned with the parish. This island is situated off Blacksod bay, on the western coast, about two miles from the extremity of the peninsula, called the Mullet: near it is a smaller island, called Devlane-beg.

DIAMORE, or DIAMOR, a parish, in the barony of DEMIFORE, county of MEATH, and province of LEINSTER, 1½ mile (W.) from Crossakeel, on the road from Oldcastle to Kells; containing 724 inhabitants. This parish comprises 4207 statute acres, as applotted under the tithe act. At Diamor is a quarry of good limestone, chiefly used for building; and at Bellvue is the neat residence of John Daniell, Esq. It is a vicarage, in the diocese of Meath, and forms part of the union of Loughcrew; the rectory is impropriate in E. Rotheram, of Hollymount, Esq. The tithes amount to £140, payable in equal portions to the impropriator and the vicar. In the R. C. divisions the parish forms part of the union or district of Kilskyre. There is a private school, in which are about 20 boys and 20 girls.

DINGINDONOVAN, or DANGAN, a parish, in the barony of IMOKILLY, county of CORK, and province of MUNSTER, 3 miles (N. N. W.) from Castle-Martyr; containing 1120 inhabitants. This parish, which by the country people is called Danion, comprises 5449 statute acres, as applotted under the tithe act. By draining, irrigating, and the introduction of modern farming implements, the state of agriculture has been greatly improved. A large supply of turf is procured from the mountain land, which constitutes about one-fourth of the parish. Fairs are held on Feb. 2nd, April 1st, and Aug. 5th, for the sale of cattle, sheep, pigs, pedlery, and agricultural and other implements. On the banks of a pretty glen is Ballyre, the residence of Crofton Uniacke, Esq.; and not far distant is Glengarra, of J. Uniacke, Esq.; these seats are surrounded by flourishing plantations, and are undergoing great improvements. The living is a rectory and vicarage, in the diocese of Cloyne, and in the patronage of the Bishop: the tithes amount to £155. There is neither church, glebe-house, nor glebe; the Protestant inhabitants attend divine service at Castlemartyr. In the R. C. divisions the parish forms part of the union or district of Killeagh, but there is no chapel here. There are two pay schools, in which are about 40 boys and 20 girls. The ruins of the old church form an interesting object; and near Glengarra are some remains of a castle, built by one of the Geraldines, in 1396; it was garrisoned by the Earl of Desmond against Queen Elizabeth, but was taken by Capt. Raleigh, and shortly afterwards was retaken by the Irish under McCarty, who, being obliged to abandon it, destroyed it by fire. It gave name to the whole district, called Old Castletown though now known as Glengarra.

DINGLE, or DINGLE-I-COUCH, an incorporated sea-port, market, and post-town, (formerly a parliamentary borough), and a parish, in the barony of CORKAGUINEY, county of KERRY, and province of MUNSTER, 22 miles (W.) from Tralee, and 173 miles (S. W. by W.) from Dublin; containing 6719 inhabitants, of which number, 4327 are in the town. This place was anciently called *Dangean-ni-Cushey*, or "the castle of Hussey," from a castle built here by an old English family of that name, to whom one of the Earls of Desmond had granted a considerable tract of land in the vicinity. On the rebellion and consequent forfeitures of the Desmond family and its adherents, it was, with divers lands, granted to the Earl of Ormonde, from whom it was purchased by Fitzgerald, Knight of Kerry, who had also a castle in this town. After the destruction of the Spaniards at Smerwick, in 1581, the lord-deputy rested here, where many of his men died from sickness, notwithstanding the supplies brought in by the Earl of Ormonde. Soon after this event, Queen Elizabeth granted £300 to the inhabitants to surround the town with walls; but in 1600, the *sugan* Earl of Desmond having been refused admittance into the Knight of Kerry's castle, revenged the affront by setting fire to the town; the Knight subsequently delivered up the castle to Sir Charles Wilmot, who for some time made it his head-quarters. Dingle is the most westerly town in Ireland; it is situated in lat. 52° 10′ 30″ and lon. 10° 15′ 45″, on the northern coast of the bay of the same name, an inlet from which forms the harbour; and may be called the capital of the extensive peninsula which comprises the entire barony of Corkaguiney. This district is generally supposed to have been colonised by the Spaniards, who formerly carried on an extensive fishery off the coast, and traded with the inhabitants, who still retain strong indications of their Spanish origin, and some of the old houses are evidently built in the Spanish fashion. The town occupies a hilly slope, and is surrounded by mountains on all sides except that towards the harbour, which here presents the appearance of a lake; the outlet being concealed by a projecting headland. The streets are irregularly disposed, but as there are more than the usual proportion of respectable slated houses, with gardens attached, the town has from a short distance a very pleasing appearance. The number of houses, in 1831, was 699, since which several others have been erected: the inhabitants are well supplied with excellent water; though not lighted, and but partially paved, it has been much improved within the last 20 years, is generally considered a very healthy place of residence, and has an excellent bathing strand. A news-room is supported by subscription. The manufacture of linen was formerly carried on to a considerable extent, and at one time exported to the amount of £60,000 annually; but since the great improvement of the cotton manufacture, it has gradually declined, and is now nearly extinct: a small quantity of coarse linen is still made in the town and neighbourhood, and sent to Cork. The present export trade, though not considerable, is increasing: it consists chiefly in corn and butter, of which about 10 cargoes, averaging 200 tons each, are annually sent to England, chiefly to Liverpool. The principal imports are iron, coal, salt, and earthenware. An extensive fishery is carried on in the bay and off the coast, in which about 100 boats, averaging six men in each, are exclusively employed; and which also affords employment to upwards of 1000 persons in curing and conveying the fish to various parts. The greater portion is sent by sea to Cork and Limerick, but a considerable supply is conveyed by land to Tralee and Killarney. The pier, originally built by the corporation, aided by a grant of £1000, in 1765, from the Irish Parliament, was enlarged by the late Fishery Board, and subsequently improved by the customs' department: it has been found beneficial for mercantile and agricultural purposes, as well as the fisheries: vessels of 300 tons' can come up to it. The harbour is well adapted for vessels of moderate burden, but not being discoverable from the sea, is what is nautically termed a "blind" one; it is, however, extremely difficult of access during a strong west wind, and vessels passing by it and running to the eastward are in danger of being lost on Castlemaine bar.

The market is on Saturday, and is well supplied with stock and provisions of every description; there are no fairs, the market being considered a sort of weekly fair for cattle and pigs: about 800 of the latter are sent annually to Cork. The market and court-house were erected by the late Knight of Kerry. There are two flour-mills, and an ale and porter brewery in the town, and branches of the National and Agricultural Banks have been lately established. Here are chief stations of the constabulary police and coast-guard; the latter being the head of the district, extending along the coast from the bay of Dingle to Brandon Head, and comprising the stations of Minard, Dingle, Ventry, Ferriter's-Cove, Ballydavid, and Brandon. Dingle is the residence of the inspecting commander. Queen Elizabeth, in the 28th year of her reign, (1585) signed a warrant for the grant of a charter of incorporation to the inhabitants of the town, with privileges similar to the borough of Drogheda, and with a superiority over the harbours of Smerwick, Ventry, and Ferriter's-Creek; but the charter was not actually granted until the 4th of Jas. I. This charter, which is the only one known, was granted to the "Sovereign, Burgesses, and Commonalty," from which it would appear that the corporation was then in existence, probably under the authority of the warrant of Elizabeth. The town, however, under the name of *Dingle-i-couch*, is found among those that sent members to Parliament in the 27th of Elizabeth. The style of the corporation is "The Sovereign, Burgesses, and Commonalty, of the Town of Dingle-i-Couch;" it consists of a sovereign, 12 burgesses (including the sovereign), and an indefinite number of freemen. The officers are a recorder, town-clerk, two serjeants-at-mace, weighmaster, and pound-keeper, none of whom are mentioned in the charter. The sovereign is elected from among the burgesses by the corporation at large, annually on the feast of St. James; but by the charter he may be also elected from the freemen. The charter does not contain any provisions as to the number of burgesses, or the mode of their election; but the number has always been limited to 12, who are elected for life by the corporation at large. No right of freedom has been recognised, and freemen are elected by the body corporate, without reference to qualification of residence or otherwise. The recorder is elected for life by the corporation; the town-clerk, formerly elected by the whole body, has of late been appointed by the sovereign alone; by whom also the serjeants-at-mace, weighmaster, and pound-keeper are appointed. The borough sent two representatives to the Irish Parliament until the Union, when it was disfranchised, and the entire compensation of £15,000 paid to Richard Boyle Townshend, Esq., several other claims having been disallowed. His representative, Lieut.-Col. John Townshend, and Lord Ventry are the principal proprietors of the town; the Earl of Cork has a small portion along the sea-shore. The jurisdiction of the corporation comprises a circle of two Irish miles radius by sea and land, measured from the parish church in the town, and includes the parishes of Dingle, Kildrum, Garfinagh, the south part of Cloghane and part of Kinnard; and the admiralty jurisdiction of the sovereign extends as far as an arrow will fly from the harbours of Dingle, Ventry, Smerwick, and Ferriter's-Creek. The sovereign is by the charter the sole justice of the peace within the borough, with power to try all but capital offences; he is also escheator and coroner, and has the exclusive return of writs: but these powers have not been strictly exercised, as the magistrates, coroner, and sheriffs of the county act by courtesy within the corporate limits. The civil court, called "The Tholsel Court of the Borough and Corporation of Dingle," is held every alternate Thursday by the recorder (who is always the sovereign, or deputy sovereign), and the jurisdiction is stated to extend to pleas of any amount: the mesne process is by service or attachment of the goods; but the latter process is only issued for debts exceeding 40*s.* late currency. The recorder also holds a court of conscience for demands under 5*s.* late currency: the process is by summons. Petty sessions are held by the county magistrates every alternate Friday, into which the criminal jurisdiction of the sovereign (who is also, but not *ex officio*, a magistrate for the county) has merged. Quarter sessions of the peace were in former times regularly held for the borough, when the vaults of Hussey's castle were used as the town gaol. Within the last half century these sessions have rarely been held; the last was in 1824, when a schedule of tolls and customs was settled by the grand jury. Under the new act, two sessions are to be holden annually here, in April and October. The new bridewell is a small but substantial building, containing two day-rooms, two yards, and six cells. Adjoining the town are some tracts of rocky and indifferent mountain land, called "The Commons," the boundaries of which are not defined; they are occupied indiscriminately by the poorer class of inhabitants, by whom some encroachments have been made in the erection of cabins, and the enclosure of small portions of ground for gardens: these are chiefly on the part called Milltown, where about 30 cabins have been built.

The parish contains 11,779 statute acres, as applotted under the tithe act, of which about one-fourth consists of coarse mountain pasture, partly reclaimable; there is a portion of bog, but not sufficient to supply the inhabitants with fuel. Sea-weed is extensively used for manure, and the state of agriculture is gradually improving. Good building stone is found in the parish. The principal seat in the vicinity is Burnham House, the property of Lord Ventry, and now the residence of his agent, D. P. Thompson, Esq., who has much improved the house and demesne. Burnham is situated on the S. W. side of the harbour (on the border of the adjoining parish of Kildrum), and commands a fine view of the town and harbour of Dingle, and the range of mountains at the foot of which they lie. The other seats are, the Grove, the former residence of the Knights of Kerry, now of J. Hickson, Esq., situated in a finely wooded demesne immediately adjoining the town; Monaree, of the Hon. R. Mullins; Farinikilla, the modern mansion of P. B. Hussey, Esq.; and Balintagart, of S. Murray Hickson, Esq. The living is an impropriate cure, in the diocese of Ardfert and Aghadoe, and in the patronage of Lord Ventry, in whom the rectory is impropriate: the tithes amount to £315, payable to the impropriator, who allows the curate £50 per annum (late currency), and has allotted him the vicarial tithes, amounting to £75, of the neighbouring parish, of which his Lordship has the nomination. Lord Ventry also maintains a chaplain, at a salary of £150 per annum, who is resident in the town, and assists in the performance of the clerical duties. The old church, which was dedicated to St. James, is said to have been built by the Spaniards: it was originally a very large structure. A part of it, called St. Mary's Chapel, was kept in repair until the erection of the present parish church, on the site of the ancient edifice, in 1807: the latter was built by a gift of £1100 from the late Board of First Fruits; it is a plain structure, and, having become too small for the increasing congregation, is about to be enlarged and thoroughly repaired; for which purpose a grant of £317. 17. 4. has been recently made by the Ecclesiastical Board. In the R. C. divisions the parish is the head of a union or district, which also comprises the parishes of Ventry, Kildrum, Garfinagh, the south part of Cloghane, Kinnard, and the greater part of Minard. The chapel at Dingle is a handsome and spacious modern edifice, and there are chapels at Ventry and Lispole. Adjoining the chapel at Dingle is a convent for nuns of the order of the Presentation, a branch from that of Tralee, established here in 1829; a neat chapel is attached, which contains a finely and well executed altar-piece of the crucifixion.

The parochial school is supported by subscription, and is under the superintendence of the curate. A school for boys, and a school at the convent for girls, have been hitherto chiefly supported by the parish priest; the girls are gratuitously instructed by the nuns, and are also taught plain and ornamental needlework. A new school-house, for the accommodation of about 500 boys, has been lately erected in connexion with the National Board, by whom two-thirds of the expense of its erection have been defrayed, and the remaining third by subscription: the total expense was about £300. Attached to Burnham House is a school for Protestant female orphans, originally established by Mrs. D. P. Thompson at Tralee, during the cholera (in consequence of the number of female orphans left destitute by that awful visitation), and recently removed to Burnham House. They are received on the recommendation of respectable parties, who guarantee the payment of £5 per annum for each towards the expense of their board, the deficiency being made up by the patrons: the number is at present limited to 16. The mistress receives from 25 to 30 guineas per annum, from Mr. Thompson, at whose expense, also, the school-house was fitted up and furnished, and who provides the children's clothing. The gross number of children educated in the parish, including three private schools, is 400, of which about 290 are boys and 110 girls. The late Matthew Moriarty, Esq., left a house in Dingle as a dwelling, rent-free, for eight poor widows; it is kept in repair by his representatives, but the inmates have no pecuniary allowance. Here is a dispensary. In the churchyard is a tomb of the Fitzgerald family, with an inscription in Gothic characters, bearing the date 1504. Of the ancient monastery which formerly existed here, as a cell to the abbey of Killagh, near Castlemaine, there are no remains. At Ballybeg, north-east of the town, is a strongly impregnated mineral spring, of a chalybeo-sulphureous nature, but not much used for medicinal purposes; and along the shore of the bay are several caves, in which are often found the beautiful crystallizations called "Kerry stones." From Connor Hill to the north-east of Dingle, on the road to Castle-Gregory, a splendid view, embracing both sides of the peninsula, is obtained. On one side is seen the bay of Dingle, as far as the island of Valentia, with the great Skellig rock in the distance, and the town and harbour of Dingle lying immediately beneath; and on the other side, Brandon bay and several bold headlands. On each side are mountains, with wide and deep valleys intervening, and numerous tarns or small lakes lying in the hollows of the hills.

DINISH ISLAND, in the parish of KILCROHANE, barony of DUNKERRON, county of KERRY, and province of MUNSTER, 2½ miles (S. S. W.) from Hogs Head, on the southern side of Ballinaskelligs bay, and about the same distance (W.) from Lambs Head, at the N. W. extremity of the Kenmare estuary, and on the western coast. It is the smaller of the two islands called the Hogs, and, together with the larger one called Scariff, is held by Daniel O'Connell, Esq., M. P., from the Earl of Cork. It is inhabited by three families, who are chiefly employed in the care of cattle grazed on the island. Close to these islands the depth of water is 28 fathoms; between them and Lambs Head are several smaller islands and rocks.

DISERT.—See DYSART, county of KERRY.

DISERT, or CARRIGEEN, a parish, in the barony of COSHMA, county of LIMERICK, and province of MUNSTER, 1½ mile (W.) from Croom; containing 180 inhabitants. It is situated on the western bank of the river Maigue, between the parishes of Croom and Adare, and contains 531 acres, as applotted under the tithe act. The living is a rectory, in the diocese of Limerick, forming the corps of the prebend of Disert in the cathedral of Limerick, and in the patronage of the Bishop: the tithes amount to £72. 10. The church having long since fallen to ruin, the parishioners attend divine service at Croom. In the R. C. divisions it forms part of the union or district of Croom. On the north side of the ruined church is a remarkable round tower, about 70 feet in height, standing on a rock of limestone: 14 feet from the foundation a circular-headed door opens to the north-east; on the opposite side is a pointed window, over which are three stories with square-headed lights, and at the top are four small slip windows. The mouldings round the door are in relief, and of superior workmanship in freestone, of which the window-frames are also composed; the remainder of the tower is constructed of limestone.

DISERT, or DYSART, a parish, in the barony of ATHLONE, county of ROSCOMMON, and province of CONNAUGHT, 10 miles (W. by N.) from Athlone, on the road to Ballinamore; containing 1661 inhabitants. This parish comprises 2972 statute acres, as applotted under the tithe act, and is principally under tillage; there is a considerable quantity of bog, and some limestone. It is a vicarage, in the diocese of Elphin, and is part of the union of Mount Talbot; the rectory is impropriate in Lord Ranelagh. The vicarial tithes amount to £18. 9. 3. In the R. C. divisions it is the head of a union or district, including also part of Taughboy; the chapel is a new and commodious building. The parochial school is supported by subscription; and Lord Mount-Sandford supports a school at Sandford. Lake Culleen is partly in this parish.

DOAGH, a grange and village, in the barony of UPPER ANTRIM, county of ANTRIM, and province of ULSTER, 1½ mile (S.W.) from Ballyclare; the population of the grange is returned with the parish of Ballyeaston; the village contains 49 houses and 195 inhabitants. This place comprises, according to the Ordnance survey, 2304½ statute acres, of which 9½ are under water, 48 woodland, 140 bog and marsh, and the remainder good arable land. The village is pleasantly situated near the Six-mile-water, and adjoining it is Fisherwick Lodge, a hunting seat belonging to the Marquess of Donegal, a very handsome house surrounded with thriving plantations, which add much to the beauty of the place. The tithes amount to £191. 3. 7½., of which £127. 7. 1. is payable to the impropriator, and the remainder to the vicar.

DOGGSTOWN, a parish, in the barony of MIDDLETHIRD, county of TIPPERARY, and province of MUNSTER, 2½ miles (S. S. W.) from Cashel; containing 94 inhabitants. This parish comprises 429 statute acres of good arable and pasture land, as applotted under the tithe act. It is a rectory, in the diocese of Cashel, forming part of the union of Knockgraffon: the tithes amount to

£27. 13. 10¼. In the R. C. divisions, also, it forms part of the union of Knockgraffon, and contains a chapel.

DOLLA, a parish, in the barony of UPPER ORMOND, county of TIPPERARY, and province of MUNSTER, 5 miles (S. S. E.) from Nenagh; containing 1041 inhabitants. This parish is situated at the termination of the Anglesey new road from Tipperary to Nenagh, and intersected by a small river: there is a large tract of mountain bog. Traverston, the seat of T. Going, Esq., is pleasingly situated in an extensive and well-planted demesne. It is a rectory, in the diocese of Killaloe, and is appropriate as a mensal to that see: the tithes amount to £161. 10. 9. There are some remains of the old church on the demesne of Kilboy. The poor's fund of Kilmore extends to this parish.

DOLLARDSTOWN.—See BALLYNACLOGH.

DOLPHIN'S BARN, a village, partly in the parish of ST. JAMES, barony of NEWCASTLE, and partly in that of ST. CATHERINE, barony of UPPERCROSS, county of DUBLIN, and province of LEINSTER. This village, forming a suburb of the city of Dublin, consists chiefly of a long street on the road to Crumlin, partly situated between the circular road and the Grand Canal, which latter intersects the village, and is here crossed by a stone bridge. There are several tanyards, and the extensive dye-works of Messrs. Pims, who have also dye stuff mills at Rudland; and on the Crumlin road are the dyeing and finishing works of Mr. P. Nevin. There is a R. C. chapel in the village, also a convent of nuns of the Carmelite order, who have a school for the gratuitous instruction of about 100 poor female children, and a select school for 12 young ladies.

DONABATE, or DONAGHBATE, a parish, in the barony of BALROTHERY, county of DUBLIN, and province of LEINSTER, 3 miles (N. by E.) from Swords; containing 386 inhabitants, of which number, 221 are in the village. This parish, which comprises 2366 statute acres, is situated on the eastern coast, near the inlets of Malahide and Rogerstown, and on the proposed line of the Grand Northern Trunk railway from Dublin to Drogheda, for which an act has been obtained. An extensive vein of green and white porphyry runs through it from east to west: the surrounding soil is limestone gravel and conglomerate grit. Contiguous to the village is Newbridge, the extensive demesne of Charles Cobbe, Esq. The house, which is a noble mansion, was erected by Archbishop Cobbe, about 1730, and contains several valuable paintings by the old masters, which were collected on the continent by the Rev. M. Pilkington, author of the Dictionary of Painters, who was vicar of this parish; the drawing-room contains several of the paintings described by him. Near this mansion is Turvey, the property of Lord Trimleston. There is a martello tower near the shore, and a constabulary police force is stationed in the village. The living is a vicarage, in the diocese of Dublin, episcopally united from time immemorial to the vicarage of Portrahan, or Portrane; the rectory is impropriate in the Rev. W. Hamilton and his heirs. The tithes amount to £220, of which £133. 6. 8. is payable to the impropriator, £66. 13. 4. to the vicar, and £20 to the economy estate of St. Patrick's cathedral, Dublin, as the rectorial tithes of the merged parish of Kilcreagh. The glebe-house was built in 1810, by aid of a gift of £100 and a loan of £320 from the late Board of First Fruits; and there is a glebe of nine acres, for which a rent of £29 per annum is paid. The church stands in a commanding situation, and contains a handsome marble monument to the memory of Dr. Cobbe, Archbishop of Dublin, who died in 1765: contiguous to the ancient tower is a ruined chapel, in which are several sepulchral monuments of the Barnewall family, the oldest of which is of the 16th century: the Ecclesiastical Commissioners have recently granted £184. 7. 6. for the repairs of the church. In the R. C. divisions this parish is the head of a union or district, comprising also Portrane, where the chapel is situated. On a commanding situation in the demesne of Newbridge are the remains of the ancient castle of Lanistown, and about a mile from the village are the ruins of Kilcreagh church.

DONADEA, a parish, in the barony of IKEATHY and OUGHTERANY, county of KILDARE, and province of LEINSTER, 4 miles (S. S. W.) from Kilcock; containing 400 inhabitants. This parish, which is situated on the western side of the bog of Allen, comprises 1976 statute acres, of which 120 are woodland, and of the remainder, nearly equal portions are under tillage and in pasture; the soil is good, and an improved system of agriculture prevails. There are excellent quarries of limestone, which is procured for building and burning; fuel is abundantly supplied from the bog of Allen. Donadea Castle is an ancient structure, belonging to the Aylmer family; in 1691 it was besieged by a party of forces in the interest of Jas. II., but was gallantly defended by Ellen, daughter of Thomas, Viscount Thurles, wife of Sir Andrew Aylmer; it has been lately modernised and improved, and is at present the residence of Sir Gerald George Aylmer, Bart. Woodside, a handsome villa, has lately been built by the Rev. W. J. Aylmer, the rector. The living is a rectory and vicarage, in the diocese of Kildare, episcopally united to that of Balrahan, which two parishes constitute the corps of the prebend of Donadea in the cathedral of Kildare, and in the alternate patronage of the Crown and Sir G. G. Aylmer: the tithes amount to £125. 4. 9½., and the tithes for the whole union amount to £286. 4. 9½. There is neither glebe-house nor glebe. The church, a neat edifice in the later English style, was erected in 1813, by a loan of £1000 from the late Board of First Fruits, and contains a curious monument to Sir Gerald Aylmer, the first baronet, and his lady. A neat school-house has been built of stone, at an expense of £340, of which £170 was granted from the lord-lieutenant's school fund, and the remainder raised by subscription and by the Kildare-Place Society; three acres of land were granted at a nominal rent by Sir G. G. Aylmer, on lease renewable for ever, and vested in the rector and churchwardens, for the master; the school is further supported by the Trustees of Erasmus Smith's charity; 30 boys and girls are educated in it. Here is a dispensary.

DONAGH, a parish, in the barony of ENNISHOWEN, county of DONEGAL, and province of ULSTER, containing, with the post-town of Carn, 5357 inhabitants. The ancient name given to Donagh by St. Patrick was *Domnach-Glinne-Tochuir*, "the Sabbath-House of the Glen with Fountains:" there is but a slight variation in the former portion of this title, and the latter is still the name of the valley where the silver mines were formerly worked. From the book of Armagh and other authorities it appears that a religious establishment was founded here, in 412, by St. Patrick, of which he appointed McCarthen, brother of the saint of Clogher, bishop, or abbot: of the several crosses which marked the limits of its sanctuary one only remains; the saint's penitential bed, and other relics, having been preserved here, this place was much resorted to by pilgrims on St. Patrick's day. The parish is situated on the shore of the bay of Straghbregagh, or Strabreagy, and is intersected by the roads leading from Londonderry to Malin and Malin Head, from Moville to Buncrana, and from Londonderry to Clonmany. It comprises, according to the Ordnance survey, 25,259¼ statute acres, the greater part of which are mountain and bog, incapable of being cultivated; small detached portions of land, under tillage, at the foot of the numerous mountains, extending from Glen Tocher to Strabreagy, yield oats, flax, potatoes, and some wheat and barley. Slieve Snaght, or the mountain of Snow, is the highest; according to the above survey, it rises 2019 feet above the level of the sea. From its northern side issues a small river, which runs through the town of Carn, and near the foot of this mountain is a pretty cascade, called Earmaceire. The mountains are mostly of schist, and slate and excellent flagstones are also found in them, besides extensive knolls and ranges of blue limestone. The limestone in Glen Tocher is remarkably good; the silver mines there were worked by an English company about 1790, but owing to the intimidation of the miners they were abandoned, and the attempt to work them has not been resumed. Two small tuck-mills employ about 12 people, but the greater part of the inhabitants are engaged in agricultural pursuits and in fishing. The parish contains numerous good houses, the principal of which are noticed under the head of Carn, *which see*.

The living is a rectory, in the diocese of Derry, and in the patronage of the Marquess of Donegal: the tithes amount to £365. The glebe-house is situated in the midst of a bog, one mile from the church, on the shore of the bay: sixty acres of good land were reserved, for the glebe of this parish, in the grant of the barony of Innishowen, by Jas. I., to Sir Arthur Chichester; the glebe now comprises 162 Cunningham acres, about 50 of which are under cultivation, and more are being reclaimed. The church is a small neat edifice, erected in 1769; the walls were newly raised, newly roofed, and otherwise improved in 1812. The R. C. parish is co-extensive with that of the Established Church, and is called Carndonagh; there is a large and handsome chapel in the town of Carn, built in 1826, at a cost of £1200. At Carn is also a large meeting-house for Presbyterians in connection with the Synod of Ulster. Besides the school at Carn, there are others under the National Board at Glen Tocher, Glengennan, and Glasalts; also one private and two Sunday schools, one of which is in connection with the Presbyterian meeting-house. A stone cross, six feet high, hewn out of a solid block, and ornamented with numerous scrolls and shamrocks, stands near the church; close adjoining which are the square shafts of two others, having on each side the figure of a human head. There are several forts in the parish.

DONAGH, a parish, in the barony of TROUGH, county of MONAGHAN, and province of ULSTER, containing, with the post-towns of Glasslough and Emyvale (which are separately described), 11,068 inhabitants. This parish is supposed to derive its name from St. Dimpna, the patron saint of the district, who is said to have conferred the virtue of preventing or curing almost all diseases (which many of the peasantry yet believe is retained) on the waters of the celebrated spring, Tubber-Phadric: her silver staff is in the possession of Owen Lamb, of Knockboy, near Monaghan. In March, 1688, about 3000 of the Irish being garrisoned in the fort of Charlemont, and attempting to plunder the Protestants of the neighbourhood of Armagh, Lord Blayney had frequent skirmishes with them, in which he constantly prevailed, until the 13th of the month, when, on being informed that his castle of Monaghan was taken by the Rapparees, and that all the Protestant forces in that quarter had retreated to Glasslough, where they were closely besieged by the enemy; and hearing that Sir Arthur Rawdon had quitted Loughbrickland, of which the Irish army, under Gen. Hamilton, had taken possession, he marched to join his friends at Glasslough, where they were relieved by the valour of Matthew Anketell, Esq., a gentleman of considerable property in the neighbourhood (which is now possessed by his immediate descendant, W. Anketell, Esq., of Anketell Grove), who had collected two troops of horse and three companies of foot. The Irish, commanded by Major McKenna, with a force of 600 men, intrenched themselves in an old Danish fort, called the fort of Drumbanagher, in a commanding situation, and from this eminence kept up a heavy fire on the Protestants who advanced against them: but Mr. Anketell, who was of undaunted courage, burst into the fort, at the head of his troops, routed and pursued the enemy with considerable slaughter, but was himself slain in the hour of victory. Major McKenna and his son were both taken prisoners, and the former was destroyed, in the moment of excitement, in revenge of the death of the spirited leader of the Protestant force. The body of Mr. Anketell was interred in the aisle of Glasslough church with great solemnity, and a plain stone with an inscription has been set up to his memory.

This parish is situated on the roads from Monaghan to Belfast, and from Dublin to Londonderry, on a small river called Scamegeragh, or the "sheep ford river," (from which a small village in the neighbourhood takes its name), which is tributary to that of the Blackwater, which also intersects the parish. According to the Ordnance survey, it comprises 16,202¼ statute acres, of which 241¾ are under water; the land is principally arable, with a small portion of pasture; there is a considerable tract of bog, with some woodland. Agriculture is much improved, under the auspices of a Farming Society, which holds its meetings at Glasslough. Besides the great lakes of Glasslough and Emy, there are two smaller ones. There are excellent quarries of marble, used for monuments and for the ornamental parts of architecture, which is largely exported to England and to the United States; freestone quarries also abound, whence large quantities, superior to Portland stone, are procured, and the great entrance to Caledon House was constructed of this stone; there is also an extensive quarry of grey basalt. The corn and flax-mills belonging to Mr. Young, called the New Mills, about 1½ mile from Glasslough, employ about 20 persons, and at Emyvale are mills belonging to William Murdock, Esq. In addition to agricultural and other pursuits, the linen manufacture is carried on to a considerable extent. Manor courts for Castle Leslie are held on the third Saturday of each month; and petty sessions are held at Emyvale on alternate Thursdays. The seats and demesnes are Glasslough Castle, the beautiful residence of Mrs. Leslie; Anketell Grove, of W. Anketell, Esq.; Fort Johnston, of T. Johnston, Esq.; and Castle Leslie, of C. Powell Leslie, Esq.

The living is a vicarage, in the diocese of Clogher, and in the patronage of the Bishop, to whom the rectory is appropriate: the tithes amount to £465, of which £310 is payable to the bishop, and £155 to the incumbent. There is a glebe-house, with a glebe of about 40 acres. The church is a plain edifice at Glasslough, built about 1775. The R. C. parish is co-extensive with that of the Established Church, and contains chapels at Glennin and Corraghrin. There is a Presbyterian meeting-house, in connection with the Synod of Ulster, of the third class; also a small place of worship for Wesleyan Methodists. Five schools, supported chiefly by subscription, afford instruction to about 570 children; there are also nine private pay schools and one Sunday school. The only remains of antiquity are the old church of Donagh, and the Danish rath of Drumbanagher, where the battle was fought. Very ancient coins have been found on the estate of Mrs. Leslie; and numerous silver ornaments, helmets of brass, steel swords, druidical relics, and Gothic figures, found in the parish, are now in the possession of the Rev. H. R. Dawson, Dean of St. Patrick's.

DONAGHADEE, a sea-port, and post-town, and a parish, in the barony of ARDES, county of DOWN, and province of ULSTER, 14¼ miles (N. E. by E.) from Belfast, and 94½ (N. N. E.) from Dublin; containing 7627 inhabitants, of which number, 2986 are in the town. It is situated on the coast in lat. 54° 38′ 20″ and lon. 5° 31′ 50″, and is one of the three principal stations for post-office packets. It anciently belonged to the monastery of Black Abbey, in the county of Down. The town comprises several streets, which are wide and well kept, and contains 671 houses. From being the point of communication between Ireland and Scotland, as it is only 22 miles distant from Portpatrick, it has been a packet station from a very early period. The voyage across the channel is generally made by steam vessels in about three hours. Its natural harbour is small, but has lately been greatly improved by the erection of two large stone piers carried out on ledges of rock to a depth of sixteen feet at low water, and enclosing a space of about 200 yards each way outside the original harbour. A great part of the interior has been excavated to the same depth as the entrance; the original estimate for the improvement of this harbour, which commenced in 1821, was £145,453, of which up to Jan. 5th, 1834, £143,704. 5. 8. had been expended. When finished, vessels drawing 16 feet of water may safely enter it at any period of the tide. The stone of which the piers, lighthouse, &c., are built, is the Anglesey marble. The lighthouse, at the extremity of the south pier, is a stationary red light. Donaghadee is a creek to the port of Belfast, and has a harbour master and one custom-house officer. Its principal imports are coal and timber, and its principal exports, live cattle and pigs. Nearly all the poor females are employed in embroidering muslin, chiefly for the Glasgow manufacturers: above £20,000 per ann. is paid as wages for this work, which was introduced in 1805. There are many wind and water mills, several of which are employed in dressing flax. There is no regular market; fairs are held on June 13th, Aug. 16th, Oct. 10th, and on the second Saturday in December. It is a constabulary police station, and the head of a coast-guard district, under the control of a resident inspecting commander, which comprises the twelve stations of Hollywood, Bangor, Crawfordsburn, Orlockhill, Groomsport, Donaghadee, Mill-isle, Ballywalter, Ballyhalbert, Cloghy, Taragh, and Strangford.

The parish comprises, according to the Ordnance survey, 9593 statute acres, which, with the exception of 32½ of water and about 1000 of bog, marsh, and waste land, are all arable: the land is in general well cultivated, producing very good crops. A considerable tract of bog, and part of Gransha moss, in this parish, are valuable as fuel, but are fast diminishing by cultivation. Slate of inferior value is obtained, and at a considerable depth is abundant and of excellent quality. Clay-slate is sometimes used for repairing the roads. A court of record is held by the seneschal of the manor, which has jurisdiction by attachment to the extent of £20, and by civil bill to the extent of 40s., over this parish, the district of Black Abbey, and the townland of Killyvalgen, in the parish of Ballywalter. It is held in the court-house once in three weeks, where also a court-leet is held annually in May, for the election of officers for the town and manor; and petty sessions are held every Wednesday. In the town are the handsome residences of D. Delacherois, Esq., its proprietor, and of S. Delacherois, Esq., Capt. Leslie, R. N., Mrs. G. Leslie, Mrs. Vaughan, and others; and near it are Carrodore Castle, the seat of N. D. Crommelin, Esq.; Ballywilliam Cottage, of Lady Charlotte Jocelyn; and the glebe-house, of the Rev. J. Hill. The living is a vicarage, in the diocese of Down, and in the patronage of the Lord Primate; at its institution it was endowed with all the alterages, and one-third of the tithes of corn and hay, and one-half of the townland of Mulletullenaghragh, as a glebe: the rectory is appropriate to the see of Armagh. The tithes amount to £720, of which £480 is paid to the lessee of the appropriator, and £240 to the vicar. The glebe-house was built in 1816; the glebe comprises 13 acres. The church is a large, ancient, cruciform structure, for the repair of which the Ecclesiastical Commissioners have recently granted £200. A lofty tower was built at its western end, in 1833, at the expense of D. Delacherois, Esq., aided by £50 bequeathed for that purpose by the late S. Delacherois, Esq. In the R. C. divisions the parish is in the union or district of Newtown-Ardes. There are two Presbyterian meeting-houses in the town, one of which is in connection with the Synod of Ulster, also one at Mill-isle of the third class. At Ballycopeland is one in connection with the Seceding Synod, of the second class, and one in the same connection at Carrodore, of the third class. The Primitive Methodists also have a meeting-house in the town. The parochial school was founded by Lady Mount-Alexander, for the education of 30 boys; there are two schools under the National Board at Carrodore, one of which is aided by an annual donation from Mrs. Crommelin; a school of 70 girls is supported by subscription, and there are three others in the town: there are also an infants' school and 10 private schools in the parish. A dispensary and infirmary are supported in the customary manner. Lady Mount-Alexander, by will dated 1769, bequeathed a perpetual annuity of £120 payable out of her estates in this parish to charitable purposes. Dr. Sempil bequeathed £20 per ann., and S. Delacherois, Esq., gave £100, the interest of which, with the former bequest, is annually distributed among the poor by the vicar. Close to the harbour is a rath, seventy feet high with a large platform on its summit commanding a fine view of the channel and surrounding country. A castellated powder magazine has been erected on its top which is approached by winding roads cut round the sides. Many smaller raths are scattered over the parish.

DONAGHCAVEY, or FINDONAGH, a parish, partly in the barony of OMAGH, but chiefly in that of CLOGHER, county of TYRONE, and province of ULSTER; containing, with the post-town of Fintona, 11,787 inhabitants. At the general plantation, this parish was known as the smaller portion of Fintona, and was granted by Jas. I., partly to Sir F. Willoughby, and afterwards to John Leigh, Esq., under the name of Fentonagh, and partly to Sir. W. Cope, under the name of Derrybard: it is now called the manor of Castlemaine. It is situated on the road from Omagh to Enniskillen, and contains, according to the Ordnance survey, 23,052¼ statute acres, of which 18,342¼ are in the barony of Clogher, and 4710¼ in that of Omagh; 9403 acres are applotted under the tithe act. Much of the mountainous land affords good pasturage for sheep and cattle, and is reclaimable; the bogs afford fuel, but they are fast being worked out. Great benefit has been derived from the improvements of the resident gentlemen in cultivation and planting, and by new lines of road. The country around Fintona is fertile and well planted; and the woods around Eccles are large and flourishing. Limestone is found within the parish, in which are some indications of coal and iron-ore. The inhabitants combine the weaving of linen cloth with their agricultural pursuits: there is a small forge, called a plating mill, for manufacturing spades, shovels, &c. At Fintona a court is held monthly for the manor of Castlemaine. The gentlemen's seats are, Ecclesville, the residence of C. Eccles, Esq.; Derrabard House, of S. Vesey, Esq.; Cavan House, of W. Dickson, Esq.; Cavan Lodge, of C. Lucas, Esq.; and the glebe-house, of the Rev. J. McCormick.

The living is a vicarage, in the diocese of Clogher, and in the patronage of the Bishop; the rectory forms the corps of the prebend of Findonagh in the cathedral of Clogher. The tithes amount to £600; there is a glebe-house, and two glebes comprising 400 acres. The gross annual value of the prebend is returned at £865. 17. 8. The church adjoins the town of Fintona, and was built after the civil war of 1641, during which the old one was destroyed; it is a large and venerable edifice, with a modern square tower, which was erected and the church much improved by aid of a loan of £400, in 1818, from the late Board of First Fruits. The R. C. parish is co-extensive with that of the Established Church; the chapel is near Fintona. There are two large meeting-houses for Presbyterians, and one for Wesleyan Methodists. Here are thirteen schools, in which about 580 boys and 300 girls are taught; and about 400 boys and 200 girls are educated in fifteen private schools: there are also six Sunday schools. On an eminence, in the midst of an extensive cemetery, the ruins of the old church form an interesting object; near the bridge are the remains of a very large cromlech. Nearly adjoining the glebe-house is a valuable sulphureous chalybeate spring.—See FINTONA.

DONAGHCLONEY, a parish, in the barony of LOWER IVEAGH, county of Down, and province of ULSTER, 2½ miles (S. by E.) from Lurgan, on the road to Banbridge; containing 5657 inhabitants. It comprises, according to the Ordnance survey, 6698 statute acres, of which 6384 are very fertile and principally under tillage: there is also a considerable tract of valuable bog. Waringstown House, the residence of the Rev. Holt Waring, is a spacious and handsome mansion, erected in 1667 by William Waring, Esq., and situated in an extensive and richly planted demesne embellished with stately timber. During the war of 1688, a party of the Irish adherents of Jas. II. took possession of this house, which they garrisoned and retained till the arrival of Duke Schomberg, in the following year, when they were driven out by that general, who slept here for two nights. There are several other seats, of which the principal are the Demesne, the residence of J. Brown, Esq.; Tullycarn, of H. Magill, Esq.; and Donaghcloney, of J. Brown, Esq.; and also several residences of merchants and manufacturers. The manufacture of linens, lawns, cambrics, diapers, sheetings, and other articles is carried on to a great extent. The weaving of diapers, on its introduction into Ireland, was first established in this parish by the spirited exertions of Samuel Waring, Esq., who brought over a colony from England, and with his own hands made the first spinning wheel and reel on improved principles, from drawings which he had procured while travelling in Holland, and similar wheels are now universally used throughout Ireland. There is a very extensive bleach-green at Donaghcloney, in which 8000 pieces are annually finished; and there is scarcely a house in the parish that is not, in some way, connected with this manufacture. The living is a rectory and vicarage, in the diocese of Dromore, formerly united by charter of Jas. I. to the rectories of Segoe and Moyntaghs, and part of the rectories of Magherally and Tullylish, together constituting the union of Donaghcloney and the corps of the archdeaconry of Dromore: but on the resignation of the Hon. and Rev. Pierce Meade, in 1832, the union was dissolved; Segoe alone became the corps of the archdeaconry, and this parish was constituted a separate and distinct benefice, in the patronage of the Bishop. The tithes amount to £261. 6.: there is neither glebe-house nor glebe. The church, situated in the neat village of Waringstown, near the mansion, is a very respectable edifice with a curious oak roof, and has been lately much enlarged at the joint expense of the Ecclesiastical Commissioners and the proprietor of the estate: it was originally built at the expense of Wm. Waring, Esq., who presented it to the parish, about the year 1680. Divine service is also performed in four school-houses in the parish, every Sunday evening and every alternate Thursday. In the R. C. divisions the parish forms part of the union or district of Tullylish. There is a place of worship for Presbyterians in connection with the Seceding Synod, of the first class. The parochial school is aided by an annual donation from the rector, and there are four other schools; in these together about 200 boys and 140 girls receive instruction: there are also five pay schools, in which are about 130 boys and 60 girls. The extensive cemetery of the parish is situated on the shore of the river Lagan; but there is not a vestige of the ancient church. A large bell was found in the bed of the river, and is now in the tower of Waringstown church; engraved upon it, in rude characters, is the inscription, "I belong to Donaghcloney."—See WARINGSTOWN.

DONAGHCUMPER, or DONOCOMPER, a parish, in the barony of SOUTH SALT, county of KILDARE, and province of LEINSTER, 2½ miles (S. W. by S.) from Leixlip; containing 1413 inhabitants. This place, which is also called Donocomfert, was distinguished at an early period by its priory for canons of the order of St. Victor, founded in 1202 by Adam de Hereford, in honour of St. Wolstan, Bishop of Worcester, then recently canonized. At the dissolution it was granted to Sir John Alen, the master of the rolls in Ireland, and afterwards lord chancellor, who was buried in the parish church, in which, till within a few years, was a monument bearing his effigy. The parish is situated on the road from Dublin to Celbridge, from which latter place it is separated only by the river Liffey, and comprises 4450 statute acres, as applotted under the tithe act. A bridge was erected over the Liffey, near the gate of St. Wolstan's priory, by John Ledleer, in 1308, which is still called New bridge, and consists of four irregular arches; it was in contemplation to rebuild it in 1794, but in that year a heavy flood having carried away nearly all the bridges on the river, this, which withstood its violence, was suffered to remain. A splendid mansion was erected here by Sir John Alen, on the priory lands, the site of which is now occupied by a handsome modern mansion, called St. Wolstan's, the seat of Richard Cane, Esq. The grounds, which are tastefully laid out and kept in the highest order, are watered by the Liffey, towards which they slope gently; and the demesne is embellished with several portions of the abbey, which have been carefully preserved by the proprietor, and have a beautifully picturesque appearance. At a short distance higher up the river is Donocomper, the seat of William Kirkpatrick, Esq.; the house has been recently enlarged, in the Tudor style of architecture, and the grounds are tastefully disposed. From both these seats the splendid mansion and noble demesne of Castletown are seen to great advantage, being separated only by the river. A cotton-spinning and weaving manufactory, in which power-ooms are employed, has been established here, which, when in full work, affords employment to 100 persons. The living is a rectory, in the diocese of Dublin; one-half is appropriate to the prebend of Kilmactalway, in the cathedral church of St. Patrick, Dublin, and the other half forms part of the union of Celbridge: the tithes amount to £190, one-half of which is payable to the prebendary, and the other to the incumbent of Celbridge. In the R. C. divisions the parish forms part of the union or district of Celbridge.

DONAGHEADY, a parish, in the barony of STRABANE, county of TYRONE, and province of ULSTER, on the road from Strabane to Cookstown; containing, with the post-town of Dunamanagh, 10,480 inhabitants. The greater part of this parish was granted by Jas. I. to Sir John Drummond, who founded the town of Dunamanagh, and built a bawn 109 feet square, no part of which remains, as the bawn was removed some years since, and the modern building called the Castle was erected on its site. It comprises, according to the Ordnance survey, 39,398½ statute acres, of which 28,728 are applotted under the tithe act, and valued at £10,271 per annum. There are about 154 acres of water, and 250 of bog; the remainder is arable and pasture land. There is abundance of excellent limestone, both for building and agricultural purposes, but the mountains are chiefly clay-slate. Many of the glens and banks of the rivers are covered with underwood, the remains of the extensive forests of Mounterlony. Formerly there were several bleach-greens in the parish, and a paper-mill near Dunamanagh, all of which are now unemployed; but the inhabitants unite linen-weaving at home with agricultural pursuits. The upper half of the parish, with the exception of the church lands, is in the manor of Eliston, the court for which is held at Gortin; and the lower half is in the manor of Donolonge, which was granted by Jas. I. to the Earl of Abercorn. A court is held at Donolonge monthly, for the recovery of debts under 40*s*. There are several handsome houses, the principal of which are Earl's Gift, the residence of the Rev. C. Douglas; Loughash, of Capt. Kennedy; Tullarton House, of R. Bond, Esq.; Glenville, of R. McRae, Esq.; Silver Brook, of J. Carey, Esq.; Black Park, of R. Ogilbye, Esq.; Thorn Hill, of A. C. D. L. Edie, Esq.; and the Grange, of T. Hutton, Esq.

The living is a rectory, in the diocese of Derry, and in the patronage of the Marquess of Abercorn: the tithes amount to £1350. The glebe-house was erected in 1792, by aid of a gift of £100 from the late Board of First Fruits: the glebe comprises 1192 acres. The church is a small neat edifice, half a mile west from the ruins of the old church; it is in the Grecian style, with a small cupola and a bell at the western end; and the Ecclesiastical Commissioners have recently granted £202 for its repair. In the R. C. divisions this parish is the head of a union or district, comprising Donagheady and Leckpatrick, and containing one chapel in the former and two in the latter: it is in the benefice of the dean of Derry. There are four Presbyterian meeting-houses, three of which are in connection with the Synod of Ulster, two being of the second class, and one with the Seceding Synod, also of the second class. The male and female parochial schools adjoin the church, and are supported by the Marquess of Abercorn and the incumbent. At Loughash is a large and handsome school-house, erected at an expense of £200: the school is under the National Board, as is another at Lisnarrow. There are also schools at Killeany, Rusky, Tamnaghbrady, Tyboe, Grange, and Ballyneuse; and an agricultural school at Loughash, supported by Capt. Kennedy. At Mount Castle, which gives the title of baron in the Irish peerage to the Marquess of Abercorn, are some fragments of a castle, built in 1619, by Sir Claude Hamilton, on an estate of 2000 acres, called Eden, which was granted to him by Jas. I.: it was the birth-place of Sir George Hamilton, who distinguished himself in the parliamentary war, and of his son, Gen. Hamilton, afterwards sixth Earl of Abercorn, who commanded the Protestant Irish army against Jas. II. at Londonderry and Enniskillen. Extensive ruins of the ancient church of Grange, which belonged to the abbey of Derry, exist on the banks of the Foyle. At Kildollagh are some large artificial caves, formed of loose stones, with flagstones over them covered with earth; they are about a quarter of a mile long, and contain several apartments; there is a less perfect one at Gortmaglen.—See DUNAMANAGH.

DONAGHENDRIE.—See DONAGHENRY.

DONAGHMORE, a parish, in the barony of RAPHOE, county of DONEGAL, and province of ULSTER; containing, with the post-town of Castlefin, 13,257 inhabitants. It is situated on the river Finn, and comprises, according to the Ordnance survey, 46,378 statute acres, of which 45,630 are applotted under the tithe act, and valued at £14,331 per annum, and 330 are water. More than one-third is mountainous and uninhabited; and, with the exception of a small portion of woodland, roads, and water, the remainder is good arable and pasture land. The living is a rectory and vicarage, in the diocese of Derry, and in the patronage of the Lighton family. The tithes amount to £1440. The glebe-house is a comfortable residence; the glebe comprises 750 acres. The church, situated near Castlefin, is a plain old edifice, towards the repairs of which the Ecclesiastical Commissioners have recently granted £273: there is also a chapel of ease opened for divine service in 1833. The R. C. parish is co-extensive with that of the Established Church; there are three chapels, situated respectively at Crossroads, Castlefin, and Sessaghoneel. The Presbyterians have three places of worship, two in connection with the Synod of Ulster, namely, one at Donaghmore of the first class, and the other at Raws; and one belonging to the Seceding Synod. There are eight schools, in which about 300 boys and 250 girls are instructed; and nine pay schools, in which are 620 boys and 220 girls, and 10 Sunday schools, with six classes of adults established by one of the curates, who instructs 180 males and 80 females.—See CASTLEFIN.

DONAGHMORE, a parish, in the barony of UPPER IVEAGH, county of DOWN, and province of ULSTER, 5¼ miles (N. by E.) from Newry; containing 4463 inhabitants. It is situated on the great road from Dublin to Belfast, and comprises, according to the Ordnance survey, 8396¼ statute acres; there are 110 acres of woodland, 499 of bog, 16 of waste, and 48 of water; the rest is arable and pasture land, generally good and in a high state of cultivation. Many of the inhabitants are employed in the weaving of linen for the merchants of Banbridge. Fairs are held on the first Friday in every month for cattle, sheep, and pigs, at Sheepbridge, which consists of only two houses, on the Newry road. Drummantine, the seat of the late Arthur Innis, Esq.; Beech Hill, of E. Curteis, Esq.; and the glebe-house, of the Rev. M. J. Mee, are the principal residences in the parish. The living is a vicarage, in the diocese of Dromore, and in the patronage of the Lord-Primate, to whom the rectory is appropriate: the tithes amount to £451, of which £251 is payable to the Lord-Primate, and £200 to the incumbent. The glebe-house, which is large and handsome, was erected in 1786, on a good glebe of 36 Irish acres, comprehending the townland of Tullagh, or Tullynacross. The church was built at the sole expense of Primate Boulter, in 1741: it is a small handsome edifice in good repair, with a lofty tower ornamented with buttresses, pinnacles, and finials, which was erected, in 1828, by voluntary contributions. The R. C. parish is co-extensive with that of the Established Church: a handsome chapel is now being built at Barr, and there is a small one at Ballyblaw. A meeting-house for Presbyterians, in connection with the Synod of Ulster, stands on the borders of this parish and that of Newry; and at the Rock is a large meeting-house for Seceders. There is a parochial school on the glebe, built in 1818, and principally supported by the vicar, who gives the master one acre of land rent-free; also a school at Derrycraw, built and supported by Trevor Corry, Esq.; and there are five private schools. In the churchyard is a remarkable old cross; beneath it is the entrance to an artificial cave, which extends a considerable distance, the sides being formed of loose stones, covered over with large flat stones: near the centre is a cross or transept, forming two distinct chambers; the cave is about 3 feet wide, 5 feet high, and 62 feet long, and, at the cross, nearly 30 feet broad. The Dowagh, or Danes' Cast, passes through the western extremity of the parish, and in some places forms the boundary between it and Drumbanagher, and between the counties of Armagh and Down.

DONAGHMORE, or DUNAGHMORE, a parish, in the barony of LOWER NAVAN, county of MEATH, and province of LEINSTER, 1½ mile (N.) from Navan; containing 2132 inhabitants. An abbey is said to have been founded here by St. Patrick, who placed St. Justin over it: its remote antiquity is corroborated by its round tower, which rises from a projecting plinth to a height of 70 feet, being 60 feet in circumference near the base; a portion of the stone roof remains, and the doorway on the east side is six feet from the ground; it is remarkable, in having on the key-stone of the entrance, a sculptured representation of Christ suffering on the cross. The parish is situated at the junction of the rivers Blackwater and Boyne, and comprises 3824 statute acres, as applotted under the tithe act: the land is generally good and under tillage; there is neither bog nor waste. Black Castle is the handsome residence of Richard Ruxton Fitzherbert, Esq.; the mansion is a spacious and modern structure, situated on the banks of the Boyne, which flows within sight of it; the demesne is extensive and well planted. Ratholdren Castle, the seat of the late — Cusack, Esq.; and Nevinstown, of Smith White, Esq.; are also within the parish. It is a rectory, in the diocese of Meath, and is part of the union of Navan: the tithes amount to £280 and there are about 8½ acres of glebe, valued at £17 per ann. In the R. C. divisions also it is part of the union or district of Navan. At Flower Hill there is a school-house built partly by Government, and partly by subscription, at an expense of £250: it is supported by annual donations from the Earl of Essex, Earl Ludlow, R. R. Fitzherbert, Esq., and the rector; about 40 boys and 30 girls are taught in it. Here are the ruins of a small church, with a high circular-headed arch, supporting part of a belfry.

DONAGHMORE, a parish, in the barony of RATOATH, county of MEATH, and province of LEINSTER, 9 miles (N. N. W.) from Dublin; containing 207 inhabitants, exclusively of the townland of Robertstown, which was omitted at the general census of 1831, and in 1834, contained 63 inhabitants. The parish is situated on the road from Dublin to Ashbourne, and comprises 3296 acres. It is a rectory and vicarage, in the diocese of Meath, forming part of the union of Ratoath, and is subject to a quit-rent of £29. 12.: the tithes amount to £178. 6. In the R. C. divisions it forms part of the union or district of Creekstown; the chapel is an ancient edifice, situated in the old burial-ground. A private school is held in it, in which about 23 boys and 15 girls are taught.

DONAGHMORE, or DOONAMOR, a parish, in the barony of DUNGANNON, county of TYRONE, and province of ULSTER, 2 miles (N. N. W.) from Dungannon; containing 12,144 inhabitants. At this place, anciently called *Domnach-mor*, "the great fortress," St. Patrick founded an abbey, where he placed St. Columb, which soon acquired extensive grants of land and other valuable possessions, and continued to flourish till after the conquest of Ireland by Hen. II. In the taxation of Pope Nicholas, in 1291, it is described as having contained many costly shrines. It appears to have been possessed by the Colidei, or Culdees, of Armagh, as by the inquisition of the 33rd of Hen. VIII. we find the Colidei had its rectory and tithes, which, with many townlands in the adjoining parishes, were granted to the Archbishop of Armagh after the Reformation. Though there are no vestiges, it is ascertained that it stood a little north-east of the present village; within its precincts was a large and elegant cross of freestone, on which were inscribed numerous hieroglyphics representing various passages in the Scriptures; having been thrown down and mutilated in the war of 1641, it remained in that condition till 1776, when Richard Vincent, Esq., caused it to be removed and placed where it now stands, at the head of the village; it consists of a plinth, a shaft, and a cross, and is 16 feet in height. Donaghmore was also an important military station, frequent mention being made of it in the successive wars of Ireland, particularly during the rebellions of the O'Nials and the O'Donnels.

The parish is situated on the road from Dungannon to Omagh, and comprises, according to the Ordnance survey, 18,410½ statute acres, of which, 146 are water; there are about 3000 acres of bog and mountain, but the greater part of the remainder is arable land. The present village has been built since the year 1796, under the direction, and by the spirited exertions, of A. Mackenzie, Esq., and is in a very flourishing state, comprising 88 well built and slated houses, mostly in one street. There is an extensive brewery of the celebrated Donaghmore ale, where upwards of 10,500 barrels of ale and beer are annually brewed; also soap and candle manufactories; much business is transacted in the spirit trade; and there are large brick-works adjoining the village. Near Castle-Caulfield is a small green for bleaching linen cloth, much of which is woven by the farmers and cottiers throughout the parish. A fair is held on the first Tuesday in every month, for cattle, sheep, pigs, &c.; and a manor court on the first Monday in every month in the Primate's manor of Donaghmore, for the recovery of debts under £5. There are some small lakes in the parish; in almost all of them are artificial islands, on which were castles, and where ancient implements of warfare, have been found. Among the principal seats are Fort Edward, that of Capt. Lindsay; Annaquinea, of J. Young, Esq.; Springfield, of R. Forster, Esq.; Beech Valley, of J. Wilcox, Esq.; Donaghmore Cottage, of J. King, Esq.; Parkanour, of J. Ynyr Burges, Esq.; Mullaghmore, of the Rev. T. Carpendale; Castle Caulfield, of H. King, Esq.; Tullynure Lodge, of the Rev. R. Fraser; and Mullagruen, of A. Mackenzie, Esq., which was built in 1683 by the celebrated Rev. G. Walker, defender of Londonderry, while he was rector of this parish, as appears by a shield bearing his arms and initials.

The living is a rectory and vicarage, in the diocese of Armagh, and in the patronage of the Lord-Primate: the tithes amount to £830. 15. 4½. There is a glebe-house, with a glebe comprising 459 acres of excellent arable land; and in this parish are also the glebes of Drumglass and Ardtrea. The church is a large plain edifice, situated at Castle-Caulfield: it is in contemplation to erect another church in the village of Donaghmore. In the R. C. divisions the parish forms the head of two unions or districts, being partly united with Pomeroy, and partly with that of Killeshill: there are chapels at Tullyallen and in the village of Donaghmore. There are three meeting-houses for Presbyterians; one in connection with the Synod of Ulster; and a school-house is used as a place of worship by the Independents. The parish school is at Castle-Caulfield: there are seven other schools, in which about 870 children are taught; and Mr. Mackenzie has lately built on his demesne, at the corner of the old churchyard, an infants' school, which is attended daily by more than 70 children, and which he entirely supports, intending to endow it at his death. About 50 boys and girls are educated in two private schools. In 1807, the Rev. George Evans bequeathed £200, two-thirds of the interest to be appropriated to support Sunday schools, of which there are six here, and one-third to the poor of the parish. Thomas Verner, Esq., made a similar bequest for the maintenance of these schools: and there is one supported by the Presbyterian minister. In the burial-ground are an ancient stone font and the plinth of a cross: the ruins of Castle-Caulfield form a beautifully picturesque object. There are several ancient forts in various parts of the parish.—See CASTLE-CAULFIELD.

DONAGHMORE, a parish, in the barony of BALLAGHKEEN, county of WEXFORD, and province of LEINSTER, 8½ miles (S. E. by S.) from Gorey, containing 2448 inhabitants. It is memorable as being the place where Dermod Mac Murrough, last King of Leinster, landed on his return from England, whither he had made a voyage to solicit aid against the confederate princes who had expelled him from his dominions. From this place he repaired privately to Ferns, which circumstance has given rise to a tradition that Glascarrig, in this parish, communicated with the castle of Ferns by a subterraneous passage, for which search has been made in vain. On the invasion by the English a considerable tract of land here was granted to Raymond le Gros, for which service was ordered by Hen. II. to be rendered at Wexford castle. According to Sir James Ware, a priory of Benedictine monks was founded at Glascarrig, in the 14th century, by Griffith Condon, Richard Roche, and others, and dedicated to the Blessed Virgin; it was, according to Archdall, subject to the monastery of St. Dogmael, in the county of Pembroke, whose abbot had the presentation of a monk when any vacancy occurred. At the dissolution it was granted to

Richard Boyle, first Earl of Cork; the remains, consisting only of part of the church, have been converted into farm-offices, and afford no indication of the original character of the building.

The parish is situated on the coast of St. George's channel, and comprises 5883 statute acres, as applotted under the tithe act, nearly the whole of which is under tillage; the system of agriculture is progressively improving. Limestone gravel is raised on the lands of Peppard's Castle, and quarries of an inferior kind of building stone are worked in other parts of the parish. A domestic manufacture of strong linen is carried on here, in which nearly all the female cottagers are employed; and there are oyster and herring fisheries along the coast. On the shore is Cahore Point, on which there is a telegraph: it is two leagues to the south of Courtown harbour, and about half a mile to the east of it is the northern extremity of the narrow sand bank called the Rusk and Ram, which extends thence S. by W. about 4 miles. At Cahore Point is a station of the coast-guard, being one of the eight comprised in the district of Gorey. Peppard's Castle, the seat of H. White, Esq., is a handsome modern mansion, in which have been incorporated some of the walls of the ancient castle; it is situated near the sea, about half a mile from the road to Wexford.

The living is an impropriate curacy, in the diocese of Ferns, and in the patronage of H. K. G. Morgan, Esq., in whom the rectory is impropriate: the tithes amount to £300, of which £23. 1. 6. is allotted by the impropriator to the curate, who receives a like sum out of the fund of the late Primate Boulter from the Ecclesiastical Commissioners. The church, which is situated on an eminence overlooking the sea, is a very ancient edifice, supposed to have been a cell to the abbey of Glascarrig, and is now in a dilapidated state. A new district church is about to be erected by subscription, on the border of the parish, near the adjoining parish of Kiltrisk, to which it has been united for the performance of clerical duties. In the R. C. divisions the parish forms part of the district of Ardamine, or River chapel, and contains a chapel at Ballygarret, to which a school is attached, and there are two or three others in the district. A Sunday school is held in the church; and a school-house has lately been built on the estate of J. George, Esq., towards which the late Rev. R. Jones Brewster, impropriate curate, bequeathed £100; the remainder was raised by subscription.

DONAGHMORE.—See DONOUGHMORE.

DONAGHMOYNE, a parish, in the barony of Farney (called also, from this parish, Donaghmoyne), county of Monaghan, and province of Ulster, 2½ miles (N. N. E.) from Carrickmacross; containing 14,070 inhabitants. It is situated on the mail coach road from Dublin to Londonderry, and comprises, according to the Ordnance survey, 25,604 statute acres, of which 102¼ are in Lough Muckno, and 258¼ in the smaller lakes with which the parish is interspersed. Nearly the whole of the land is in tillage; the soil is fertile and produces tolerably good crops, but the system of agriculture is in a very unimproved state. Limestone abounds in the southern part of the parish, and is quarried for building and for agricultural purposes; and coal has been discovered on the townland of Corlea, but has not been worked. At Thornford there is an extensive corn-mill. The principal gentlemen's seats are Longfield, the residence of J. Johnston, Esq.; Rahens, of J. Read, Esq.; Donaghmoyne, of J. Bashford, Esq.; Cabragh Lodge, of J. Boyle Kernan, Esq.; Rocksavage, of J. Plunkett, Esq.; Broomfield, of W. Henry, Esq.; Thornford, of Hamilton McMath, Esq.; and Longfield Cottage, of R. Banan, Esq.

The living is a vicarage, in the diocese of Clogher, and in the patronage of the Crown; the rectory is impropriate in J. B. Kernan, Esq. The tithes amount to £1430. 15. 4½., of which £476. 18. 5½. is payable to the impropriator, and £953. 16. 11. to the vicar. The glebe-house is a comfortable residence, with grounds containing seven acres; the glebe comprises 50½ acres. The church, a neat modern structure, was erected on a site presented by Jas. Bashford, Esq., by aid of a loan of £1250 from the late Board of First Fruits. In the R. C. divisions the parish is partly in the union or district of Inniskeen, and partly a benefice in itself; there are three chapels, situated respectively at Donaghmoyne, Lisdoonan, and Tapla, belonging to the parochial benefice, and one at Drumcatton belonging to the union of Inniskeen. There are schools at Lisdoonan and Donaghmoyne, supported by subscription, in which about 70 children are instructed; and 13 pay schools, in which are about 460 boys and 170 girls, also a Sunday school. At Fincairn, in the northern part of the parish, are several large stones, supposed to be a druidical monument. On the townland of Cabragh was formerly an abbey dependent on the abbey of Mellifont; and on the townland of Mannon are the remains of an ancient castle, or Danish fort, which, from its elevated situation, and the remains of the buildings on its summit, appears to have been a strong and very important post; it commands an extensive view of the surrounding country.

DONAGHPATRICK.—See DONOUGHPATRICK.

DONAGORE.—See DONEGORE.

DONAMON, a parish, partly in the half-barony of Ballymoe, county of Roscommon, but chiefly in that which is in the county of Galway, and province of Connaught, 4½ miles (S .W. by W.) from Roscommon; containing 1114 inhabitants. It is situated on the river Suck, on the road from Castlerea to Athleague, and contains 2500 statute acres, of which, 600 or 700 are bog, and 1526 arable and pasture, as applotted under the tithe act, except 100 of woodland. Agriculture is generally good, and still improving. There are quarries of limestone, which is used for building. The river Suck is here very deep and navigable, except at the bridge. The gentlemen's seats are Donamon Castle, the residence of St. George Caulfield, Esq.; and Emlaroy, of Oliver Armstrong, Esq. The living is a vicarage, in the diocese of Elphin, with those of Kilcroan and Ballinakill united, which three parishes form the union of Donamon, in the patronage of the Bishop; the rectory is partly impropriate in the Earl of Essex, and partly in St. George Caulfield, Esq. The tithes amount to £40. 2. 8., half of which is payable to the vicar, and half to the impropriators. There is neither glebe-house nor glebe. The church is an ancient building, in good repair; it was formerly a chapel of the Caulfield family, but when the church of Oran was blown down, it was given to the parishioners. In the R. C. divisions the parish forms part of the union or district of Kilbegnet. About 130 boys and 80 girls are taught in three schools, two of which are aided by the incumbent, and one by Mr. Caulfield, who contributes £20 per annum; and there is also a Sunday school. The Caulfield family has bequeathed £8 per annum, late currency, towards the repairs of the church, in which are some handsome monuments to the memory of its various members.

DONAMONA, a parish, in the barony of TULLAGH, county of CLARE, and province of MUNSTER, contiguous to the town of Killaloe, in which parish it has merged. It is a rectory, in the diocese of Killaloe, entirely appropriate to the economy estate of the cathedral of St. Flannan: the tithes amount to £42. 4. 3.

DONANEY, or DONENY, a parish, partly in the barony of UPPER PHILIPSTOWN, KING'S county, but chiefly in that of WEST OPHALY, county of KILDARE, and province of LEINSTER, 3 miles (S. W. by S.) from Kildare, on the road to Athy: containing 676 inhabitants. It is a vicarage, in the diocese of Kildare, and is part of the union of Lackagh; the rectory is appropriate to the bishop. The tithes amount to £130. 18., of which £87. 5. is payable to the bishop, and £43. 12. 8. to the vicar. There are three acres of glebe. In the R. C divisions it forms part of the union or district of Monasterevan. About 70 boys and 30 girls are educated in a private school. There are some remains of an ancient church: also the ruins of a castle, and a large mansion-house now gone to decay, which was once occupied by the family of Browne.

DONARD, a parish, in the barony of LOWER TALBOTSTOWN, county of WICKLOW, and province of LEINSTER, 4½ miles (E. by S.) from Dunlavin; containing, with the ancient chapelry of Dunbey, 1463 inhabitants, of which number, 717 are in the village. According to Archdall, St. Silvester, who accompanied St. Palladius into Ireland about the year 430, presided over a church here, in which he was interred and his relics were honoured, until they were removed to the monastery of St. Baithen, or Innisboyne. During the disturbances of 1798, the village was burnt by the insurgents, the inhabitants having been driven to seek refuge in Dunlavin: the church was garrisoned by the yeomanry, on this occasion, which greatly injured it, and it has since become dilapidated. The parish is situated on the Little Slaney, about a mile to the east of the main road from Dublin to Baltinglass and Tullow, and the road from Hollywood to Hacketstown runs through the village. The surrounding scenery is of a strikingly bold and romantic character. Donard House is the residence of Mrs. Heighington. A market and two fairs were formerly held here by patent, but both have been discontinued, though a pleasure fair is yet held on the 15th of Aug. This a constabulary police station. The living is a rectory and vicarage, in the diocese of Dublin and Glendalough, episcopally united, about 30 years since, to the curacy of Crehelp and the ancient chapelry of Dunbay, together forming the union of Donard, in the patronage of the Archbishop. The tithes amount to £220, and of the entire benefice, to £307. 3. 7. There is neither glebe-house nor glebe. The church is in the later style of architecture, with a square tower surmounted with pinnacles; the interior is very neatly fitted up, and on the north side there is a handsome white marble tablet to the memory of Charles Fauscett, Esq., who died in 1834: it was built on a new site in 1835, by aid of a grant of £850 by the late Board of First Fruits. In the R. C. divisions this parish forms part of the union or district of Dunlavin: there is a chapel in the village. The parochial school is aided by an annual donation from the vicar; and an infants' school for foundlings sent from the Foundling Hospital, Dublin, is supported by that institution. In these schools about 150 children are taught; and there is also a Sunday school. The remains of the church over which St. Silvester presided are on the summit of the mountain called Slieve Gadoe, or the Church-mountain, more than 2000 feet above the level of the sea, being the highest of the group that separates the King's river from the glen of Imail; it is the resort of numerous pilgrims, who are attracted by the supposed sanctity of a well close by the walls, the water of which, notwithstanding its great height, continues without any sensible increase or decrease throughout the year. Near the village is a moated rath, or Danish fort, and on the townland of Kilcough is another.

DONEGAL (County of), a maritime county of the province of ULSTER, bounded on the east and south-east by the counties of Londonderry, Tyrone, and Fermanagh, from the first-named of which it is separated by Lough Foyle; on the south, by the northern extremity of the county of Leitrim and by Donegal bay, and on the west and north by the Atlantic. It extends from 54° 28′ to 55° 20′ (N. Lat.), and from 6° 48′ to 8° 40′ (W. Lon.); comprising, according to the Ordnance survey, a surface of 1,165,107 statute acres, of which 520,736 are cultivated land, and 644,371 unimproved mountain and bog. The population, in 1821, was 248,270, and in 1831, 291,104.

In the time of Ptolemy it was inhabited by the *Vennicnii* and the *Rhobogdii*, the latter of whom also occupied part of the county of Londonderry. The *Promontorium Vennicnium* of this geographer appears to have been Ram's Head or Horn Head, near Dunfanaghy; and the *Promontorium Rhobogdium*, Malin Head, the most northern point of the peninsula of Innisoen or Ennishowen. The county afterwards formed the northern part of the district of Eircael or Eargal, which extended into the county of Fermanagh, and was known for several centuries as the country of the ancient and powerful sept of the O'Donells, descended, according to the Irish writers, from Conall Golban, son of Neil of the Nine Hostages, monarch of Ireland, who granted to his son the region now forming the county of Donegal. Hence it acquired the name of *Tyr-Conall*, modernised into *Tyrconnel* or *Tirconnel*, "the land of Conall," which it retained till the reign of Jas. I. The family was afterwards called Kinel Conall, or the descendants or tribe of Conall. Fergus Ceanfadda, the son of the founder, had a numerous progeny, among whom were Sedna, ancestor of the O'Donells, and Felin, father of St. Cohunt. Cinfaeladh, fourth in descent from Ceanfadda, had three sons, one of whom was Muldoon, the more immediate ancestor of the O'Donells; and another, Fiamhan, from whom the O'Dohertys, lords of Innisoen, derive their descent. A second Cinfaeladh, eighth in descent from Fergus Ceanfadda, was father of Dalagh, from whom the O'Donells are sometimes styled by the Irish annalists Siol na Dallagh, the sept of Daly, or the O'Dalys. Enoghaine, his eldest son, was father of Donell, from whom the ruling family took the surname it has borne ever since. His great grandson, Cathban, chief of the sept in the reign of Brian Boroimhe, first assumed the name of O'Donell as chief, which was adopted by all his subjects and followers. Besides the O'Dohertys, the septs of O'Boyle, Mac Sweeney, and several others were subordinate to the O'Donells of Tyrconnel.

The chieftaincy of Nial Garbh, who succeeded his father Turlogh an Fhiona in 1422, was the commencement of a sanguinary era of internal discord aggravated by external warfare. This chieftain, after having endured much opposition from his brother Neachtan, and maintained continual hostilities with the English, by whom he was at length taken prisoner, died in captivity.

The first effort of importance made by the English to subjugate this territory commenced by their seizure of the convent of Donegal and a castle of the O'Boyles, giving them a temporary command over the adjacent territory, from all which they were quickly expelled by the celebrated Hugh Roe, or Red Hugh, O'Donell, who succeeded to the chieftaincy in 1592. This powerful toparch, at an early period of his government, marched into Tir Owen against Tirlogh Luineagh O'Neil, chief of the sept of the same name and a partizan of the English, whom O'Donell, although he had recently entered into terms of amity with the Lord-Justice of Ireland, expelled from his principality in 1593, forced him to resign the title of O'Neil in favour of Hugh, Earl of Tyrone, and afterwards compelled the whole province of Ulster to acknowledge his superiority and pay him tribute. He then sent an embassy to the king of Spain to aid him in the total expulsion of the English, and having obtained a reinforcement of mercenaries from Scotland, carried on a successful war far beyond the limits of his own territory.

The English government, after various disasters, particularly the defeat of Sir Conyers Clifford in the Curlew mountains, resolved to transfer the seat of war into O'Donell's country, for which purpose a large fleet, having on board a force of six thousand well-appointed troops, was sent from Dublin under the command of Sir Henry Docwra. Having landed in Ennishowen in the summer of 1600, they possessed themselves of the forts of Culmore, Dunnalong, and Derry. Each of these fortresses was immediately invested by O'Donell, who, while his troops maintained the blockade, made two expeditions into Connaught and Munster. During his absence, his brother-in-law, Nial O'Donell, and his brothers were prevailed upon to join the English, and to give them possession of Lifford, which they fortified. Here also they were hemmed in by the Irish, as likewise at the monastery of Donegal, which they had afterwards gained. The landing of the Spaniards in the south caused a total suspension of arms in Ulster, and the subsequent defeat of the invaders at Kinsale compelled O'Donell to proceed to Spain in quest of further succours, where he died in September, 1602, being the last chief of the sept universally acknowledged as the O'Donell.

On the attainder in 1612 of Rory O'Donell, to whom Jas. I. had given the title of Earl of Tyrconnell and the greater part of the family possessions, the district, which had been erected into a county called Donegal, by Sir John Perrot, in 1584, was included by that king in his plan for the plantation of Ulster. By the survey then taken, the whole county was found to contain 110,700 acres of cultivable, or, as it was styled, profitable land. Of these, the termon lands, containing 9160 acres, were assigned to the bishoprick of Raphoe, to which they had previously belonged; 3680 acres were allotted for the bishop's mensal lands; 6600 acres for glebe to the incumbents of the 87 parishes into which the county was to be divided; 9224 acres of monastery lands to the college of Dublin; 300 acres to Culmore fort; 1000 acres to Ballyshannon, and 1024 acres, named the Inch, to Sir Ralph Bingley. The remainder, amounting to 79,074 acres, were to be divided among the settlers or undertakers, as they were called, in 62 portions, 40 of 1000 acres, 13 of 1500, and 9 of 2000 each, with a certain portion of wood, bog, and mountain, to constitute a parish. Of these portions, 38 were to be granted to English and Scotch undertakers, 9 to servitors, and 15 to natives. The 2204 acres still undisposed of were to be given to corporate towns to be erected and entitled to send burgesses to parliament, 800 to Derry, and 200 each to Killybegs, Donegal, and Rath: Lifford had 500 acres previously assigned to it. The residue of 604 acres was to be equally allotted to free schools at Derry and Donegal. All fisheries were reserved to the Crown. The distributive portions thus assigned do not correspond with the general total above stated, and the proposed provisions both as to distribution and regulation were far from being rigidly observed in practice.

The county is chiefly in the diocese of Raphoe, but parts of it extend into those of Derry and Clogher. For purposes of civil jurisdiction it is divided into the baronies of Raphoe, Kilmacrenan, Ennishowen, Tyrhugh, Bannagh and Boylagh. It contains the disfranchised borough, sea-port and market-towns of Ballyshannon, Donegal, and Killybegs; the disfranchised borough and market-town of Lifford; the disfranchised borough of St. Johnstown; the market and post-towns of Letterkenny, Ramelton, Raphoe, Carn, Stranorlar, Buncrana, and Moville Upper; the post-towns of Castlefin, Dunfanaghy, Ardara, Dungloe, and Narin, and several other small towns and villages, of which Bundoran, Mount-Charles, and Rathmullen have each a penny post. Prior to the union the county sent 12 members to parliament; two for the county at large, and two for each of the above-named boroughs, but, subsequently, it has been represented by the two county members only, who are elected at Lifford. The number of voters registered in January, 1836, was 1745; of whom 181 were freeholders of £50, 169 of £20, and 1159 of £10 per ann.; 33 clergymen of £50, and 1 of £20, being the freeholds of their respective benefices; 1 rent-charger of £50, and 10 of £20; and 48 leaseholders of £20, and 143 of £10. It is included in the north-western circuit. Lifford, where the county gaol and court-house are situated, is the assize town; quarter sessions are held four times in the year at Donegal, twice at Letterkenny, and once at Lifford and Buncrana. There are bridewells at Letterkenny and Donegal, and session-houses at each of those places and at Buncrana. The local government is vested in a lieutenant, 19 deputy-lieutenants, and 66 other magistrates, with the usual county officers. The number of persons charged with criminal offences and committed, in 1835, was 472, and of civil bill commitments, 49. There are 29 constabulary police stations, having a force of one stipendiary magistrate 7 chief and 30 subordinate constables and 116 men, with nine horses, the expense of whose maintenance is defrayed by equal Grand Jury presentments and by Government. The district lunatic asylum is in Londonderry and the county infirmary at Lifford. There are dispensaries at Lifford, Ballintra, Raphoe, Taughboyne, Killybegs, Moville, Clonmany, Killygarvan, Kilmacrenan, Kilcar, Letterkenny, Donegal, Muff, Culdaff, Stranorlar, Rutland, Donagh, Killygorden, Dunkaneely, Ramelton, Buncrana, Careygart, Ballyshannon, Dunfanaghy, and Mount-Charles, maintained by voluntary subscriptions and Grand Jury presentments in equal proportions. The amount of Grand Jury presentments for 1835 was £27,609. 1. 4., of which £163. 10. was for the public roads of the county at large; £14,799. 2. 4. for the public roads, being the baronial charge; £5301. 18. 11½. for public buildings and charities, officers' salaries, &c.; £3480. 10. 3. for police; and £3863. 19. 9½. in repayment of a loan advanced by Government. In the military arrangements the county is in the northern district. There are infantry barracks at Lifford and Ballyshannon, and artillery forts at Greencastle, Inch island, Rutland island, and at several places along the shores of Lough Swilly, each of which, except Greencastle, is garrisoned by a single gunner.

Donegal is the most western of the three northern counties of Ireland. The surface, which is much varied, may be arranged into two great divisions of mountain and champaign. The latter, which is subdivided into two portions by the Barnesmore mountains, comprises the barony of Raphoe and the maritime parts of that of Tyrhugh, round Ballyshannon and Donegal. The mountain region, comprehending all the remainder of the county, is interspersed with fertile valleys and tracts of good land, especially in the baronies of Kilmacrenan and Ennishowen. The most elevated mountains are Errigal, which, according to the Ordnance survey, rises 2463 feet above the level of the sea; Blue Stack, 2213 feet; Dooish West, 2143; Slieve Snaght, 2019; Silver Hill, 1967; Slieve League, 1964; and Aghla, 1958. There are also five others which have an elevation of more than 1500 feet, and twelve more exceeding 1000 feet in height. The most improved and populous district is that on the borders of the rivers Fin and Swilly, and the eastern confines near Lifford. In the western champaign district, between Ballintra and Ballyshannon, the surface is in many places moory, heathy and rocky, particularly near the south-east, where at a distance of three or four miles from the sea it rises into a tract of mountains ten or twelve miles broad, which sweeps round by Pettigo, Lough Derg, and the confines of Fermanagh; from these a range extends westward by Killybegs to Tellen Head, whence a vast expanse stretches by Rutland, the Rosses, and the shores of the Atlantic, across Loughs Swilly and Foyle, into the counties of Londonderry and Antrim. From Barnesmore to Donegal and Ballintra, the country is composed of bleak hills, many of which, though high, are covered with a sweet and profitable vegetation, while several points in the ascent from Killybegs into the mountains of the north present fine views of the bay and harbour of that port. Even amidst the wilds of Boylagh and Bannagh are cultivated and well-peopled valleys, but the district of the Rosses presents mostly a desolate waste. On its western side is a region of scattered rocks and hills, some on the mainland, others insulated: the larger of these rocks are thinly covered with peat and moss; a few admit of some degree of cultivation, while almost all the innumerable smaller rocks are entirely bare. Collectively, this group is known by the name of the islands of the Rosses. Arranmore, the largest, containing about 600 acres, is about two miles from the mainland; on Innis Mac Durn is the little town of Rutland; the largest of the rest are Irvan, Inniskeera, Inisfree, Owey and Gruit. Northward of the Rosses lies the district of Cloghanealy, in Kilmacrenan, entirely composed of disjointed rocks and dark heath, except where, at a lesser elevation near the sea, a stunted sward appears. On the northern coast, about five miles from the shore, is the island of Tory. The peninsula of Rossguill, formed by the bays of Sheephaven and Mulroy, and that of Fannet by Mulroy and Lough Swilly, are of similar character, except that in the latter the mountains attain a greater altitude, are separated by larger and more fertile valleys, and command prospects of such extent and variety as to attract visiters from distant parts. Lough Swilly, an arm of the sea penetrating far into the land, and receiving at its southern extremity the river from which it derives its name, has on its western shores a tract of rich arable soil losing itself gradually in the mountains, while its eastern side presents a tract of similar character extending towards Derry, under the general denominations of Blanket-nook and Laggan. To the north of the city of Londonderry lies the barony of Ennishowen, a large peninsula bounded on the east and west by the gulfs of Lough Foyle and Lough Swilly. It consists of a central group of mountains with a border of cultivation verging to the water's edge: in the mountains of Glentogher is an expanse of 4000 acres of peat and heath. Besides the great inlets on the northern coast already noticed, the shores are indented with numerous smaller recesses. The islands, except some of those of the Rosses, are very small, the principal being Rockiburn island, off Tellen Head; Inisbarnog, off Lochrusmore bay; Roanmish, off Iniskeel; Gold island, Inismanan, Inis-Irhir, Inisbeg, Inisduh, and Inis-bofin, off Kilmacrenan barony; and Seal island, Ennistrahull and the Garvilands, off Ennishowen. The lakes are numerous but small. The principal are Lough Derg, near the southern boundary of the county, celebrated for St. Patrick's Purgatory, a place of annual resort for numerous pilgrims, the particulars of which will be found in the account of Templecarne parish; and Lough Esk, near Donegal, a fine expanse of water environed with wild and romantic scenery. The others are Loughs Fin and Mourne (the head waters of rivers of the same name), Salt, Glen, Muck, Barra, Bee, Killeen, Broden, Veagh, Cartan, Dale, Kest, Fern, Golagh, and Nuire, with several others round the base of Slieve Snaght mountain; one near Dobeg, in Fannet; others in the Rosses, and others near Nairn, Ardara, Glenona, Glenleaghan, Lettermacaward, Brown Hall, Ballyshannon and elsewhere.

The climate was formerly cold and unhealthy, with an incessant humidity of atmosphere; but the drainage of some of the lakes and marshes, and the lowering of the levels and deepening of the beds of several rivers, during late years, have produced a very beneficial change, both as to the health of the inhabitants and the increase of arable land: the soils are very various: the richest are those of the champaign district in the south-east. Near Leitrim county it is deep, coarse, and sometimes incumbered with rushes, but in the vicinity of Ballyshannon it assumes a richer character. The change arises from the subsoil, here limestone, the bed of which extends to the neighbourhood of Donegal, supporting a light, gravelly, brown soil; thence to the mountains of Boylagh and Bannagh the soil gradually deteriorates, having a brown clay and rubbly substratum. From Dunkanealy to Killybegs and to Tellen Head the soil of the cultivable glens is a light gravelly till, resting on variously coloured earths and rocks; while that of the mountain region, with the exception of a few green spots, consists of a thin surface of peat on a substratum of coarse quartz gravel, under which are found variously coloured clays, based for the most part upon granite. The soil of the little dales in Fannet is a brown gravelly mould, or a kind of till based on gravel, soft freestone or clay-slate of various colours: but both here and at Horn head, to the west of Sheep Haven, the drifting sands, impelled by the gales from the Atlantic, have covered much good land. The soil of the arable lands of Ennishowen is mostly similar to that of those last described.

The chief tillage district is the barony of Raphoe, in which, besides potatoes, wheat, oats, and barley, flax is grown and manufactured largely. From Ballyshannon to Donegal and Killybegs tillage is general; and in Boylagh and Bannagh much land is now under cultivation, though formerly scarcely sufficient was tilled to supply the inhabitants with potatoes and grain. Oats and potatoes, the former chiefly for distillation, are the principal crops throughout the mountainous districts; but latterly the growth of barley and flax has been encouraged. Agriculture, as a system, however, is not much practised except among the resident gentry, by whom great improvements are annually made. They have formed and strenuously support farming societies, have awarded premiums, and recommended improved implements and a better rotation of crops. The effects of their exertions shew themselves in a very striking manner in the baronies of Raphoe and Tyrhugh, in each of which there is a farming society, which has been attended with very beneficial effects; wheat has been raised in both these baronies with the greatest success. Ballyshannon formerly imported flour to the amount of several thousand pounds annually; during the last two years, considerable quantities of wheat were exported. Turnips, vetches, mangel-wurzel and other green crops are common. In the two last-named baronies the fences, also, have been much improved: they are now generally formed of quickset hedges, while in most other parts, except the north of Ennishowen, they are sod ditches or dry stone walls. The iron plough is in general use among the gentry and larger farmers, but the old cumbrous wooden plough is still used in many parts. The angular harrow is becoming very general, and all other kinds of agricultural implements are gradually improving. A light one-horse cart, with iron-bound spoke wheels, has nearly superseded the old wooden wheel car, and the slide car is seldom seen out of the mountain districts, in which the implements are still rude in construction and few in number, consisting, on many farms, merely of the loy (a spade with a rest for the foot on one side only), the steveen (a pointed stake for setting potatoes), and the sickle. Good grasses of every species grow in the champaign tracts; but in the mountains they are coarse and bad. Cattle, which have been fed for twelve months on the latter, where the vegetation consists of aquatic grasses, rushes, and heath, are seized with a disorder called the *cruppan*, a sort of ague that is cured only by removal to better herbage; yet the change of pasture, if long continued, gives rise to another disease, called the *galar*, no less fatal, unless by a timely removal to the former soil. Even the pastures of the champaign parts are unfit for fattening and are therefore used only for grazing sheep, young cattle, and milch cows. A peculiar herbage, called sweet-grass, formed of joints from two to three yards in length, grows on the shores of Innisfree, several feet under the high water mark of spring tides, to which the cattle run instinctively at the time of ebb. In Raphoe, irrigation is general. Besides the composts usually collected for manure, lime is in universal demand. In the maritime district from Bally-shannon to Killybegs, sea-weed and shelly sand are the chief manures; throughout the mountains, sea-corac alone, except on the grounds of a few gentlemen where lime is used. The character of the cattle has been much improved by the introduction of the English and Scotch breeds, particularly the Durham, Leicester, and Ayrshire. A cross between the Durham and old Irish produces an animal very superior in appearance, but not found to thrive. The favourite at present is a cross between the old Leicester and the Limerick, which, being again crossed by the North Devon, or Hereford, grows to a large size and fattens rapidly. The breed of pigs has also been greatly improved; when fattened, they are by some sent to market alive, by others slaughtered at home and the carcases carried to Strabane or Londonderry for the provision merchants there. Fowl and eggs in large quantities are transmitted to the sea-ports for exportation. The county is very bare of wood, though there is some good ornamental timber in many of the demesnes, and young plantations, formed in several places, are very thriving. Well stocked orchards and gardens are to be met with round many of the farm-houses in Raphoe.

Granite forms the summit of all the mountains, and with the new red sandstone, rests on a substratum of limestone mostly of the primitive formation and containing no organic remains, although secondary limestone abounds in several parts. The limestone is found through all the level districts near the sea and elsewhere, and in the mountains forming the manors of Burleigh and Orwell. On the eastern shore of Lough Swilly, and in some other parts of Ennishowen, is found a species of calcareous argillite, having the appearance of grey limestone, but containing too much silex to burn freely. Round Carndonagh, in the same barony, is a dark blue limestone of superior quality. Many species of valuable marble have been discovered. One of these, of a pure white, free from flaws or discolouration, and capable of being raised in blocks of any dimension at a trifling expense, has been found in the Rosses; but the want of roads, though the quarries are at a short distance from the sea, prevents its exportation. Grey and black marble of very fine quality have also been found. Little advantage has hitherto been derived from any of the other mineral productions. Lead ore has been discovered in several places in the barony of Boylagh; in the river flowing from the mountain of Killybegs; on the surface near the western shore of Loughnabroden; at the foot of the Derryveagh mountains; in the Barra river; in Arran-more and other parts of the Rosses; and at Kieldrum, in the barony of Kilmacrenan, where there is a considerable deposit of ore collected for a lead-work which was carried on a few years since, but discontinued as being unprofitable from the want of experienced miners. Copper ore and iron pyrites may be traced in Errigal and Muckish mountains, and detached masses are found in several of the mountain streams and near Ballyshannon. Both these ores are abundant; and in several other parts the numerous vitriolic springs indicate larger deposits. Iron ore abounds in several parts. As long as fuel could be procured from the forests of Donegal, Derryveagh, Slievedoon and Kilmacrenan, the mines were wrought and the ore smelted. The remains of bloomeries are often met with in the mountains and the foundations of forges near some of the rivers. Manganese is also abundant. Coal appears in a thin seam at Dromore, on the shore of Lough Swilly, and indications of it are frequent in Innishowen, but no attempts have yet been made to raise it. The same remark applies to steatite or soap-stone, here called "camstone," though found in abundance in all the mountains of Kilmacrenan and Bannagh: it is mostly of a bright sea-green colour. At Drumarda, on the shores of Lough Swilly, on Tory island, and in the Rosses, are extensive beds of potter's clay, which is used in a small degree in manufacturing coarse pottery. Pipe clay and other kinds of useful clays are found frequently, but little used. Silicious sand of a very superior kind is abundant at Lough Salt, and in the Ards, whence considerable quantities are exported for the manufacture of glass. Excellent slates are raised near Letterkenny, Buncrana, and in some other places.

The manufacture of linen cloth of every kind of texture, chiefly from home-raised flax, is carried on to a considerable extent. Several bleach-greens are in full operation, and an extensive factory has been recently established at Buncrana. Cotton cords, velveteens, fustians, and checks are woven to a considerable extent for exportation, as are friezes for home consumption. Woollen stockings of excellent quality, manufactured in the barony of Boylagh, are in great demand. Whiskey is made very largely both in licensed and unlicensed distilleries: the latter are chiefly in the Rosses, Boylagh, and Ennishowen, which last place has long been celebrated for the quality of the spirit produced there. The north-western coast fisheries are chiefly confined to Donegal. They had declined greatly for many years in consequence of the herring, the chief object of capture, having deserted the coast. In 1830 it was ascertained that the shoals had returned, and the fishery consequently revived, insomuch that the value of the take in 1834 exceeded £50,000, and in the two succeeding seasons has been still greater. The coast every where affords the means of an abundant summer fishing; but the want of proper boats and tackle deters the fishermen from venturing to struggle against the stormy seas that break upon the shores during the winter. The white fishing for cod, ling, haddock, and glassen, and that of turbot and other flat fish, all of which are in inexhaustible abundance, is little attended to beyond the supply of the neighbourhood. The sun fish resorts hither and is sometimes taken. Seals are caught in large numbers in Strabreagy bay and near Malin. There are several salmon fisheries: the principal is that on the Erne at Ballyshannon; there are others in Loughs Foyle and Swilly and in some of the smaller bays. Eel and trout abound in all the lakes and rivers.

The bays and harbours are numerous, capacious, and safe. The principal are Lough Foyle, forming the entrance to the port of Londonderry and navigable for vessels of the largest draught to that city, and by lighters of 20 tons' burden to Lifford, and thence by the Fin-water to Castlefin; the small but secure bay of Strabreagy, well sheltered by Malin Head; Lough Swilly, the entrance to which is safe and easy; Mulroy; Sheephaven; the numerous inlets in the Rosses; Guibarra and Loughros bays, and the capacious bay of Donegal, containing within its scope the smaller harbour of Ballyshannon, on the improvement of which several thousand pounds have been expended by Col. Conolly.

The principal rivers are the Foyle, the Swilly, and the Erne. The first-named, and by far the most important in a commercial point of view, rises in Lough Fin, in the mountains of Branagh, and under the name of the Fin-water proceeds to Lifford, where, on its confluence with the Mourne from the east, the united stream takes the name of the Foyle, and flowing past the city of Londonderry, of which it forms the capacious port and harbour, opens out into Lough Foyle. The Swilly rises in the mountains of Glendore, and passing by Letterkenny forms a large estuary between Ramelton and Newtown-Conyngham, which at flood tide appears like a large arm of the sea, but at low water exhibits a dreary and muddy strand. Further on, and opposite to Rathmullen, is Inch island, beyond which the waters expand into a deep and spacious gulph, which was considered of such importance during the late war with France, as to be protected by numerous batteries and martello towers. The Erne, anciently called the Samaer, flows from Lough Erne, enters the county at Belleek, and after a rapid course of four miles forms the harbour of Ballyshannon, which, should a rail-road be formed between it and the Lough, would acquire a large accession of trade, and by the union of Loughs Erne and Neagh, so as to form a more speedy communication between the north and west of Ireland, become an important harbour. The Burndale river rises in Lough Dale in the mountains of Cork, and flowing eastward, joins the Foyle: it is navigable to Ballindrait for vessels of 12 tons. The other rivers are the Esk, Inver, Awen-Ea, Onea, Barra, Golanesk, Guidore, Clady, Hork, Awencharry, Lenan, Binnian, Awencranagh, Awenchillew, Sooley, and many smaller streams.

The roads, although, in consequence of the late Grand Jury act, considerably improved, and several new lines opened, require much to be done. They are, in general, badly constructed and not properly repaired, although the best materials are in abundance. Near the junction of the county with that of Fermanagh is a relic called "the Giant's Grave;" it is a cave, the side walls of which are formed of large blocks of unhewn stone, and the ceiling of flags of limestone. Another singular relic of antiquity connected with the O'Donell family is called "the Caah." It consists of a small box containing the Psalter of Columbkill, said to be written by the saint himself. Another, consisting of a flag-stone raised 18 inches from the ground on other stones, perfectly circular and regularly indented with holes half an inch deep and one inch in diameter, is in the deer-park of Castleforward. The ruins of seven religious houses still visible out of 41 are those of Astrath near Ballyshannon, Bally Mac Swiney, Donegal, Kilmacrenan, Lough Derg, Tory island, and Rathmullen. The principal castles yet remaining, wholly or in part, are Kilbarron, Killybegs, Donegal, Castle Mac Swiney, Dungloe, Ballyshannon, Fort Stewart, Burt, Doe and Green castle at the mouth of Lough Foyle. The modern seats, which are neither numerous nor peculiarly ornamental, are noticed in the accounts of their respective parishes. The farm-houses are comfortable, but defective in cleanliness. The cabins of the peasantry, especially near the coast, are wretched and extremely filthy, the cattle and swine generally associating with the family, a custom also observable at times in the champaign country. The fuel is turf: the food, potatoes, oaten bread, and fish. with some milk and butter; the clothing mostly frieze, though articles of cotton are common, especially for the women's wear. The English language, pronounced with a Scotch accent, is general in the flat country, but in the mountain region it is little spoken. The most extraordinary natural curiosity is a perpendicular orifice in one of the cliffs projecting over the sea near Dunfanaghy, which in certain states of the tide throws up a large jet of water with a tremendous noise: it is called Mac Swiney's Gun. Not far from Bundoran is a similar orifice, called the Fairy Gun, from which a perpetual mist issues in stormy weather, accompanied by a chaunting sound observable at a great distance. Near Brown hall is a subterraneous river with numerous caves, the water of which possesses a petrifying quality: reeds and pieces of boughs are very soon encrusted with the calcareous matter, and large deposits of sulphur are found on the banks. Natural caves are found on the shores near Bundoran, and numerous others in various parts. In Drumkellin bog, in Inver parish, a wooden house was found perfectly framed and fitted together, having a flat roof: its top was 16 feet below the present surface of the bog.

DONEGAL, a sea-port, market and post-town, and parish (formerly an incorporated parliamentary borough), in the barony of TYRHUGH, county of DONEGAL, and province of ULSTER, 24 miles (S. W.) from Lifford, and 113 (N. W.) from Dublin; containing 6260 inhabitants, of which number, 830 are in the town. In 1150 Murtogh O'Loghlen burnt this town and devastated the surrounding country. A castle was built here by the O'Donells about the 12th century; and a monastery for Franciscan friars of the Observantine order was founded in 1474, by Hugh Roe, son of O'Donell, Prince of Tyrconnell, and by his wife, Fiongala, daughter of O'Brien, Prince of Thomond. O'Donell, in 1587, bade defiance to the English government and refused to admit any sheriff into his district. The council at Dublin not having sufficient troops to compel his submission, Sir John Perrot, lord-deputy, proposed either to entrap him or his son. He accomplished his object by sending a ship freighted with Spanish wines to Donegal, the captain of which entertained all who would partake of his liberality. Young O'Donell and two of his companions accepted his invitation, and when intoxicated were made prisoners and conveyed to Dublin as hostages for the chief of Tyrconnell. After remaining a prisoner in the castle for a considerable time, he, in company with several other hostages, effected his escape and returned to Donegal, where he was invested with the chieftaincy of Tyrconnell, and married a daughter of O'Nial, chief of Tyrone. In 1592, an English force under Captains Willis and Convill took possession of the convent and the surrounding country, but were quickly expelled by the young Hugh Roe O'Donell, with the loss of their baggage. In 1600, O'Nial met O'Donell and the Spanish emissary, Oviedo, here, on the arrival of supplies from Spain at Killybegs, to concert the plan of a rebellion. Shortly after this, the English, taking advantage of O'Donell's absence in Connaught, marched a strong party to Donegal, and took possession of the monastery, which was unsuccessfully assaulted by O'Donell; and the debarkation of the Spaniards at Kinsale, about this time, occasioned him to go to their assistance, leaving the English in undisturbed possession. In 1631, the annals of Donegal, generally called the "Annals of the Four Masters," were compiled in the convent: the original of the first part of this work is in the Duke of Buckingham's library at Stowe, and of the second in the collection of the Royal Irish Academy; part of these interesting annals have been published by Dr. O'Conor, under the title of "*Rerum Hibernicarum Scriptores.*" The castle was taken, in 1651, by the Marquess of Clanricarde, who was, however, soon obliged to surrender it to a superior force. On the 15th of October, 1798, a French frigate of 30 guns anchored close to the town, and two more appeared in the bay; but the militia and inhabitants of the town and neighbourhood showing a determination to resist a landing, they left the harbour.

The town is pleasantly situated at the mouth of the river Esk, and consists of three streets, comprising 150 houses, and a large triangular market-place. The market is held on Saturday; and fairs on the 2nd Friday in each month. Here is a constabulary police station. The harbour is formed by a pool on the east side of the peninsula of Durin, where, at the distance of two miles below the town, small vessels may ride in two or three fathoms of water, about half a cable's length from the shore. There is a good herring fishery in the bay, in summer. The borough was incorporated by a charter of Jas. I., dated Feb. 27th, 1612, in pursuance of the plan of forming a new plantation in Ulster. The corporation consisted of a portreeve, twelve free burgesses, and an unlimited number of freemen; and the charter created a borough court, of which the portreeve was president, but it has long since been disused. From its incorporation till the Union the borough returned two members to the Irish Parliament, and on the abolition of its franchise, £15,000 was paid as compensation to the Earl of Arran and Viscount Dudley. Since that period the corporation has ceased to exist. By a grant to Henry Brook, in 1639, a manor was erected, comprehending the town of Donegal, with a court leet and a court baron, to be held before a seneschal appointed by the patentee, having a civil jurisdiction to the extent of 40*s*. The manorial court is still held monthly, on Mondays, except during the summer: petty sessions are held every alternate week; and the general quarter sessions for the county are held here in March, June, October, and December, in a small sessions-house. There is a small bridewell.

The parish comprises, according to the Ordnance survey, 23,260 statute acres, including 503¼ in Lough Esk and 214¾ in small lakes: 23,089 acres are applotted under the tithe act, besides which there are about 900 acres of bog and a large tract of mountain land, in which is the beautiful lake of Lough Esk, at the upper end of which is the romantic and picturesque place called Ardnamona, the property of G. C. Wray, Esq., and from which the river Esk descends southward to its estuary, in the inmost recess of the bay of Donegal. About a quarter of the cultivated land is arable, the remainder pasture. The living is a vicarage, in the diocese of Raphoe, and in the patronage of the Bishop; the rectory is impropriate in Col. Conolly. The tithes amount to £338. 9. 2½., of which £107. 13. 10¼. is payable to the impropriator, and the remainder to the vicar. The glebe-house was rebuilt by aid of a gift of £100, from the late Board of First Fruits in 1816; and there is a glebe of 38 acres. The church is a handsome structure, built in 1825, by aid of a donation of £100 from John Hamilton, Esq., and a loan of £1300 from the same Board. The R. C. parish is co-extensive with that of the Established Church, and has a chapel at Donegal and one at Townawilly. There is a meeting-house for Presbyterians in connection with the Synod of Ulster, of the third class, and one connected with the Seceding Synod, of the second class; also two places of worship for Independents and one for Wesleyan Methodists. The parochial school was built on land given by the Earl of Arran. There are also a school on Erasmus Smith's foundation, one supported by Mrs. Hamilton, and nine others aided by different Societies and subscriptions. In these are about 600 children, and there are three Sunday schools. About the close of the last century, Col. Robertson, son of a clergyman of this town, bequeathed a sum of money, out of the interest of which, £15 per annum was to be paid to each of the parishes in the diocese of Raphoe, for the support of a school-master to instruct children of all religious denominations. This fund has so much increased as to enable the trustees to grant £40 to each parish, for the erection of a school-house, provided an acre of land on a perpetually renewable lease be obtained for a site. There is a dispensary in the town, supported in the customary manner. Manganese is found in the demesne of Lough Esk, the residence of Thomas Brooke, Esq. Pearls, some of great beauty, have been found on the river Esk. The remains of the monastery are still visible at a short distance from the town: the cloister is composed of small arches supported by coupled pillars on a basement; in one part of it are two narrow passages, one over the other, about four feet wide, ten long, and seven high, which were probably intended as depositories for valuables in times of danger. A considerable part of the castle remains, and forms an interesting feature in the beautiful view of the bay; although it and the other property granted to the patentee, at a rent of 13*s.* 4*d.* per annum, have passed into other families, one of his descendants still pays a rent to the crown for it. Within three miles of the town is The Hall, the residence of the Conyngham family. Donegal gives the titles of Marquess and Earl to the Chichester family.

DONEGORE, a parish, in the barony of UPPER ANTRIM, county of ANTRIM, and province of ULSTER, 3½ miles (E. by N.) from Antrim; containing 2532 inhabitants. It comprises, according to the Ordnance survey, 6650 statute acres. The living is a rectory and vicarage, in the diocese of Connor, united to that of Kilbride, and the granges of Nalteen and Doagh, forming the union of Donegore, in the patronage of the Bishop. The tithes of the parish amount to £393. 7. 10½., and of the entire benefice, to £954. 5. 9.: there is a glebe-house. The church, which is nearly in the centre of the parish, was built in 1659. Divine service is also performed every Sunday in a private house at Kilbride. There is a meeting-house for Presbyterians in connection with the Synod of Ulster, of the first class, and one in connection with the Seceding Synod, of the second class. The parochial school, in which are about 60 children, is aided by the rector; and there are three Sunday schools.

DONEIRA, or DONIRY, a parish, in the barony of LEITRIM, county of GALWAY, and province of CONNAUGHT, 5¼ miles (W. N. W.) from Portumna; containing 2348 inhabitants. This parish is bounded on the west by the Slieve-Baughta mountains, and comprises 3963 statute acres, as applotted under the tithe act. It is in the diocese of Clonfert; the rectory is appropriate partly to the see and partly to the deanery of Clonfert, and partly with the vicarage forming part of the union of Tynagh. The tithes amount to £95. 13. 10½., of which £12. 17. 3. is payable to the Ecclesiastical Commissioners, £4. 12. 3¾. to the dean, and £78. 4. 3¾. to the incumbent. In the R. C. divisions it forms part of the union or district of Ballynakill, and contains a chapel.

DONEMAGAN, a parish, in the barony of KELLS, county of KILKENNY, and province of LEINSTER, 4 miles (E. by S.) from Callan, on the King's river; containing 1162 inhabitants. It comprises 3447 statute acres, as applotted under the tithe act; and is a rectory and vicarage, in the diocese of Ossory, forming part of the union of Knocktopher: the tithes amount to £184. 12. 3¾. In the R. C. divisions it is the head of a district, which also comprises the parishes of Kilree, Ballytobin, and Kilmoganny, and part of Kells; and contains the chapels of Donemagan and Kilmoganny. About 115 children are educated in two private schools, and a Sunday school is held in the R. C. chapel.

DONENY.—See DONANEY.

DONERAILE, a market and post-town, and a parish (formerly a parliamentary borough), in the barony of FERMOY, county of CORK, and province of MUNSTER, 21 miles (N. by W.) from Cork, and 132 (S. W.) from Dublin; containing 6940 inhabitants, of which number, 2652 are in the town. Sir William St. Leger, who was Lord-President of Munster in the reign of Chas. I., held his court here. He purchased the Doneraile estate of Sir Walter Welmond and John Spenser (son of the poet), which purchase was subsequently confirmed by the crown, and the estate created a manor. In the civil war of 1641, Sir William, both as a statesman and soldier, rendered important services; but his infirm health did not enable him long to sustain the hardships to which he was then exposed, and he died in the following year. In 1645, the Irish under Lord Castlehaven took the castle of Doneraile, and burned the greater part of the town.

It is pleasantly situated on the river Awbeg (the "Gentle Mulla" of Spenser), which is here crossed by a neat stone bridge of 3 arches, and on the mail road from Mallow to Mitchelstown; it consists chiefly of one wide main street, and a smaller one called Buttevant lane, and contains about 390 houses. The vicinity is extremely pleasing, the roads being shaded by fine fir and other trees, and the country studded with gentlemen's seats. By a charter of the 15th of Chas. I. (1639), constituting Sir William St. Leger lord of the manor, power was given to the seneschal to hold a court leet and court baron, with jurisdiction in personal actions to the amount of 40*s.*; also a market on Thursday, and two fairs annually on the feast of St. Magdalene and All Souls. The market is, however, now held on Saturday for provisions, but on account of its proximity to Mallow, it is but thinly attended; the fairs, which are held on the 12th of Aug. and Nov., have also much declined; and although the seneschal's court is still occasionally held, with the view of preserving the right, no business has been transacted in it for the last seven years. The market and court-house, a convenient building, is situated in the main street. Near the bridge is the extensive flour-mill of Messrs. Creagh & Stawell, and at Park is that of Messrs. Norcott & Co. This is a chief constabulary police station, and a small military force is also quartered in the town. By a second charter, granted in the 31st of Chas. II. (1660), the borough was empowered to return two members to the Irish parliament, and the elective franchise was vested in the freeholders made by the lord of the manor; but no corporation was created: the seneschal was the returning officer. From this period until the Union it continued to send two burgesses to parliament, when it was disfranchised and the compensation of £15,000 paid to the heirs of Hayes, Viscount Doneraile. His descendant, Hayes St. Leger, the third and present Viscount Doneraile, is lord of the manor, which extends over parts of this parish and that of Templeroan.

The parish, which extends to the Galtee mountains, on the confines of the county of Limerick, and includes the ancient subdivisions of Rossagh and Kilcoleman, contains 20,797 statute acres, as applotted under the tithe act, and valued at £9367 per annum. About 8800 acres are coarse mountain pasture: the arable land is in general good, and the state of agriculture is gradually improving, a considerable portion of the land being in the occupation of the resident gentry. Limestone abounds, and some good specimens of marble are occasionally obtained. Among the numerous seats, Doneraile Park, that of Viscount Doneraile, is distinguished for its extent and beauty: it is intersected by the river Awbeg, over which, and within the demesne are several neat stone and rustic bridges. The mansion is a handsome and substantial building, to which has been added, within the last few years, a large conservatory stored with the choicest plants; it is situated on an eminence gently sloping to the winding vale of the Awbeg. The other seats are Creagh Castle, that of G. W. B. Creagh, Esq.; Laurentinum, of the same family; Kilbrack, of Mrs. Stawell; Byblox, of Major Crone; all of which are on the Awbeg: and in the parish are also Donnybrook, the seat of W. Hill, Esq., Old Court, of J. Stawell, Esq.; Carker House, of N. G. Evans, Esq.; Lissa, of Capt. Croker; Hermitage, of J. Norcott, Esq.; Crobeg, of G. Stawell, Esq.; Cromore, of R. Campion, Esq. Park House, of A. Norcott, Esq.; Cottage, of J. Norcott, Esq., M. D.; Stream Hill, of G. Crofts, Esq.; Kilbrack Cottage, of the Very Rev. P. Sheehan, P.P.; and, in the town, the newly erected mansion of A. G. Creagh, Esq. The parish is in the diocese of Cloyne, and is a perpetual curacy, forming part of the union of Templeroan, or Doneraile, in the patronage of the Bishop; the rectory is impropriate in Edward Giles, Esq., of Park, near Youghal. The tithes (including Rossagh and Kilcoleman) amount to £1173. 7. 1., the whole of which is payable to the impropriator, subject to an allowance of £13. 6. 8., (late currency) to the officiating minister. The church, at the north end of the town, is a neat and commodious edifice with a tower, formerly surmounted by a spire which was blown down about 12 years since. It was erected in 1816, by aid of a loan of £2000 from the late Board of First Fruits, and contains an ancient font, and a mural monument to several members of the St. Leger family. The evening church service is performed in the court-house during the winter, and the Methodists also assemble there on alternate Fridays. Rossagh and Kilcoleman, which are said to have been formerly distinct parishes, have merged into this both for civil and ecclesiastical purposes. In the R. C. divisions the parish is united to those of Cahirduggan and Templeroan. The chapel is a handsome and spacious edifice, erected by subscription in 1827: it consists of a nave lighted on each side by lofty windows and surmounted by a cupola: the altar and other internal decorations correspond with its exterior. The site was given by Lord Doneraile, who also contributed £50 towards its erection. A convent for nuns of the order of the presentation has been established here for many years, and liberally endowed by Miss Goold. The chapel attached to it is open to the public on Sunday mornings, and the chaplaincy is endowed with £82 per ann., by Miss Goold, who has also appropriated £28 per ann. for clothing the children educated at the convent school, where about 400 girls are gratuitously instructed, and taught both plain and ornamental needlework. The parochial school of 25 children is aided by £10 per ann. from the incumbent, and a school at Ballinvonare of 110 children is aided by £12 per ann. from Harold Barry, Esq., who also provides the school-house. The Lancasterian free school of 300 boys is within the demesne of Lord Doneraile, by whom it is entirely supported, and a school of about 20 girls is supported by Lady Doneraile, who also pays a writing-master for attending it. A dispensary is supported here in the customary manner. At Ballyandree is a chalybeate spring, stated to be of much efficacy in complaints of the liver.

Of the remains of antiquity, Kilcoleman castle is the most interesting, from having been once the residence of the poet Spenser. It was originally a structure of some magnitude, the property of the Desmond family, and on their forfeiture was, with about 3000 acres of land, granted by Queen Elizabeth, in 1586, to Edmund Spenser, who resided here for about 12 years, during which period he composed his "Faery Queen." The ruins, situated on the margin of a small lake, have a very picturesque appearance, being richly clothed with ivy; the tower-staircase and the kitchen are still nearly entire, and one small closet and window in the tower quite perfect. The castle at Creagh is in good preservation, and about to be fitted up as an appendage to the family mansion. The ruins of Castle Pook still remain, but of Doneraile castle, which stood near the bridge, and in which Sir William St. Leger held his court of presidency, there is not a vestige. Doneraile gives the titles of Viscount and Baron to the family of St. Leger.

DONISLE.—See DUNHILL.

DONNYBROOK (ST. MARY), a parish, partly in the half-barony of RATHDOWN, county of DUBLIN, but chiefly within the county of the city of DUBLIN, 2 miles (S. by E.) from Dublin; containing 10,394 inhabitants. It includes the villages of Ballsbridge, Clonskea, Donnybrook, Old Merrion, Sandymount, and Ringsend with Irishtown, each of which is described under its own head. The village of Donnybrook is chiefly remarkable for its fair, the patent for which was granted by King John, to continue for 15 days, commencing on the Monday before the 26th of August. On the following day great numbers of horses, cattle, and sheep are sold; but the principal object is amusement and diversion. It is held in a spacious green belonging to Messrs. Maddens, who derive from it annually about £400. A twopenny post has been established here, since the erection of the Anglesey bridge over the Dodder. A hat manufacture was formerly carried on to a great extent, but it has greatly decreased; there are some saw-mills in the village, and a branch of the city police is stationed here. The parish is situated on the river Dodder, and comprises 1500 statute acres, as applotted under the tithe act; the lands are fertile and under good cultivation; and near the village is a quarry of excellent building stone, in which organic remains have been found. Exclusively of the gentlemen's seats described under the head of the several villages near which they are respectively situated, are Annfield, the residence of R. Percival, Esq., M. D.; Mount Errol, of Sir R. Baker, Knt.; Montrose, of J. Jameson, Esq., Swanbrook, of Alderman F. Darley; Gayfield, of T. P. Luscombe, Esq., Commissary-General; Priest House, of J. Robinson, Esq.; Stonehouse, of J. Barton, Esq.; Woodview, of E. J. Nolan, Esq.; Nutley, of G. Roe, Esq.; Thornfield, of W. Potts, Esq.; Airfield, of C. Hogan, Esq.; Simmons Court Hall, of G. Howell, Esq.; Belleville, of Alderman Morrison; Flora Ville, of M. Fitzgerald, Esq.; Donnybrook Cottage, of A. Colles, Esq., M. D.; Simmons Court, of P. Madden, Esq.; and Glenville, of J. O'Dwyer, Esq. Within the parish are iron-works, an extensive calico-printing establishment, a distillery, and salt works. The Dublin and Kingstown rail-road, the road from Dublin by Ballsbridge, and the road to Bray through Stillorgan, pass through it. That part of the parish which is in the county of the city is within the jurisdiction of the Dublin court of conscience. It is a chapelry, in the diocese of Dublin, and forms part of the corps of the archdeaconry of Dublin. The tithes amount to £166. 3. 0¾., to which is added about £300 collected as minister's money: there is no glebe-house, and the glebe comprises only about three-quarters of an acre. The church is a spacious and handsome edifice, in the early style of English architecture, with a tower surmounted by a well-proportioned spire; and was erected at Simmons Court (the old church in the village having fallen into decay), by a loan of £4154 from the late Board of First Fruits, in 1829. In the R. C. divisions the parish is united to those of St. Mark, Tawney, and St. Peter; there are chapels at Donnybrook and Irishtown, and a spacious chapel is now in progress near Cottage-terrace, Baggot-street. In the avenue leading to Sandymount is a convent of the Sisters of Charity, a branch from the establishment in Stanhope-street, Dublin; the sisters are employed in visiting the sick and in attending a school for girls; attached to the convent is a small neat chapel. There is a place of worship for Wesleyan Methodists close to the village of Donnybrook. A school for boys and another for girls are supported by subscription; and there is a dispensary at Ballsbridge. The hospital for incurables is in this parish, and is chiefly supported by Grand Jury presentments; and the Bloomfield retreat for lunatics was established by the Society of Friends. There are cemeteries at Donnybrook and Merrion; and at Simmons Court are the remains of an old castle, consisting of a massive pointed archway. In the grounds of Gayfield is a medicinal spring, the water of which is similar in its properties to that of Golden Bridge. Lord Chief Justice Downes was born in the castle of Donnybrook, now a boarding school.

DONNYCARNEY, or DONECARNEY, a village, in the parish of COLPE, barony of LOWER DULEEK, county of MEATH, and province of LEINSTER, 2½ miles (E.) from Drogheda; containing 25 houses and 108 inhabitants. This place is situated on the road from the sea, by way of Mornington, to Drogheda, and is said to have been the site of a nunnery, which at the suppression was granted to the Draycott family: the ruins are inconsiderable.

DONOGHENRY, or DONAGHENDRY, a parish, in the barony of DUNGANNON, county of TYRONE, and province of ULSTER, on the mail coach road from Dublin to Coleraine; containing, with the post-town of Stewartstown, 5364 inhabitants. It comprises, according to the Ordnance survey, 7154¾ statute acres, including 50¾ in Lough Roughan: 6889 acres are applotted under the tithe act, and valued at £5261 per annum, of which 426 are bog, and 6463 arable. The land is rich and well cultivated, and there are extensive quarries of limestone, freestone, and basalt. Near the glebe-house is an extensive deposit of new red sandstone; and in Annahone are valuable mines of coal, which, though discontinued in 1825, were formerly worked with great advantage: they are now leased by the owner to a spirited individual, who has recommenced them, with success, upon an extensive scale. Coal, clay, and other valuable deposits exist near Coal Island (see the article on that place). The manufacture of linen and union cloth is carried on to a considerable extent. Mullantean is the handsome residence of Miss Hall; Barnhill, of W. Holmes, Esq.; Donaghendry, of the Rev. F. L. Gore; Anketell Lodge, of Roger C. Anketell, Esq.; and Ardpatrick, of the Rev. W. J. Knox, near which are the remains of a Danish fort. The living is a rectory, in the diocese of Armagh, and in the alternate patronage of Sir Thomas Staples, Bart., and E. H. Caulfield, Esq.: the tithes amount to £315. The glebe-house is a large and handsome edifice, built (by aid of a gift of £100, and a loan of £825, in 1811, from the late Board of First Fruits) on a glebe comprising 30 acres of excellent land within the parish; the remainder of the glebe, 210 acres, being in the townland of Tamnavally, in the parish of Arboe. The church is situated in Stewartstown; it was built, in 1694, out of the forfeited impropriations by order of Wm. III., the old building at Donoghenry having been destroyed in the war of 1641; and a lofty square tower and side aisles have been recently added. There is a chapel of ease at Coal island, lately erected by subscription. In the R. C. divisions the parish is united to that of Ballyclog, and part of Clonoe, forming the union of Stewartstown, in which are two chapels, one at Stewartstown and one at Coal Island. Here are two Presbyterian meeting-houses, one in connection with the Synod of Ulster, and the other with the Seceding Synod, both of the second class. There are nine schools in the parish, including an infants' school lately established, all aided by subscription, and a school for girls supported by Mrs. Gore; about 550 children are taught. At Roughan are the ruins of an extensive castle, built by the Lord-Deputy Sidney, in the reign of Queen Elizabeth, and afterwards held by the Earl of Tyrone during his rebellion; and in the war of 1641, by Sir Phelim O'Nial, who placed a powerful garrison in it: it was afterwards dismantled, by order of parliament, and is now a picturesque ruin. At Donoghenry is the site of the old church and cemetery, which was the burial-place of the ancient family of Bailie, whose mansion-house adjoining is now in ruins. In a field contiguous is an upright stone, one of the supporters of a cromlech, and near it is another lying on the ground, in the upper side of which is a circular cavity, or artificial basin: about a quarter of a mile westward is a large and perfect cromlech, with a table stone, weighing more than 20 tons, placed within a circle of smaller stones. Near Stewartstown are the remains of a castle built by Sir Andrew Stewart, in the reign of Jas. I., to whom the monarch had granted extensive possessions in this neighbourhood. In 1823, a small cup, or chalice, was discovered in a bog at Dunaghy, full of silver coins of the Danish princes, many of which are preserved in the collection of R. C. Anketell, Esq. In the small lake of Ardpatrick is a floating island, and around its shores human bones, camp-poles, &c., have been discovered: in this lake many persons were drowned in the civil war of 1641; and around its shores the army of Jas. II. encamped on their march to Derry in 1689.—See Stewartstown.

DONOGHMORE, a parish, in the barony of North Salt, county of Kildare, and province of Leinster, 2 miles (E.) from Maynooth, on the road to Dublin, and on the banks of the Royal Canal, including part of the demesne of Carton, the seat of His Grace the Duke of Leinster. It is in the diocese of Dublin: one-half of the rectory is appropriate to the prebend of Kilmactalway in the cathedral church of St. Patrick, Dublin, and the other forms part of the union of Celbridge; the tithes amount to £17, payable in moieties to the prebendary and the incumbent. In the R. C. divisions it forms also part of the union or district of Celbridge. The ruins of the church are situated on the bank of the canal.

DONOHILL, a parish, partly in the barony of Clanwilliam, but chiefly in that of Kilnemanagh, county of Tipperary, and province of Munster, 3¾ miles (N.) from Tipperary, on the new line of road to Nenagh; containing 4308 inhabitants. This parish comprises 12,812 statute acres, as applotted under the tithe act. Greenfield, the residence of Col. W. Purefoy; and Philipstown, of H. B. Bradshaw, Esq., are the principal seats. A mountain stream, called the Anacarthy, runs through the parish, where is a small village of that name, in which are a constabulary police station, a chapel and a school. It is in the diocese of Cashel; the rectory is impropriate in the representatives of the Rev. R. Watts, and the vicarage forms part of the corps of the precentorship in the cathedral church of St. Patrick, Cashel. The tithes amount to £384. 12. 3¾., of which £200 is payable to the impropriators and the remainder to the vicar. The R. C. parish is co-extensive with that of the Established Church; there are two chapels, one at Anacarthy, and one at Donohill. There are five schools aided by subscriptions; in which about 500 children are taught. Some slight remains of the ancient church may be seen; there is a conical hill, supposed to be a Danish rath; and on an eminence near Anacarthy is a circular tower, called Ballysheedy Castle, forming a conspicuous object from a great distance.

DONONAUGHTA, a parish, in the barony of Longford, county of Galway, and province of Connaught; containing, with the post-town of Eyrecourt, 2277 inhabitants. This parish is situated on the river Shannon, and on the road from Banagher to Loughrea; and comprises 2423 statute acres, as applotted under the tithe act: a very small portion is woodland, and the remainder is principally under tillage. Among the gentlemen's seats are Eyrecourt Castle, that of J. Eyre, Esq., to which is attached a chapel of ease, built in 1677 by J. Eyre, Esq.; Eyreville, of T. S. Eyre, Esq.; Prospect, of C. A. O'Malley, Esq.; and Fahy, of T. Burke, Esq. It is in the diocese of Clonfert: the rectory is appropriate to the see, and the vicarage episcopally united, in 1813, to the vicarages of Meelick, Fahy, Tyrenascragh, Killimorbologue, Kilquane, and Lusmagh, forming the union of Dononaughta, in the patronage of the Bishop. The tithes amount to £71. 10. 9¼., of which £46. 3. 1. is payable to the Ecclesiastical Commissioners, and £25. 7. 8¼. to the vicar; and the tithes of the whole benefice amount to £299. 15. 4¼. The glebe-house was built by aid of a gift of £450, and a loan of £200, from the late Board of First Fruits, in 1822. The church, a plain building in Eyrecourt, was erected by aid of a loan of £307 from the same Board, in 1818: the Ecclesiastical Commissioners have lately granted £354 for its repair. Divine service is also performed in a school-house in the parish of Killimorbologue. In the R. C. divisions this parish is united to those of Clonfert and Meelik, forming the union of Eyrecourt, where the chapel is situated. A school for boys is supported by the interest of a bequest of £1000, and a house by the late Rev. J. Banks, to which Mr. Eyre has given an acre of land; and there is another school, aided by subscription, in which together are about 30 boys and 30 girls. —See Eyrecourt.

DONORE, a parish, in the barony of Lower Duleek, county of Meath, and province of Leinster, 2¼ miles (W. S. W.) from Drogheda, on the road to Navan; containing 1191 inhabitants, of which number, 124 are in the village. This parish anciently formed part of the possessions of the abbey of Mellifont. On July 1st, 1690, it was the position occupied by Jas II. during the battle of the Boyne, a detailed account of which is given in the article on Drogheda. The parish comprises 1954 acres: the ground under cultivation is naturally very productive, and there is neither waste land nor bog. Abundance of limestone is procured from an old and well-worked quarry at Sheephouse, and is much used for building; it is of a handsome light colour. By the canal, passing by Oldbridge, from Drogheda to Navan, timber, slates, stone, and coal are brought to Donore, and corn taken back to Drogheda. Old Bridge, the seat of H. B. Coddington, Esq., is situated in an extensive demesne, well planted, on the banks of the Boyne; a residence called Farm is also the property of this gentleman; and Stalleen is the property and occasional residence of William Sharman Crawford, Esq. The parish is in the diocese of Meath; the rectory is partly impropriate in the Marquess of Drogheda, but the greater part of the parish is tithe-free: the parishioners attend divine service at the churches of Duleek and Drogheda. In the R. C. divisions it is the head of a union or district, also called Rosnaree, comprising the parishes of Donore and Knockcomon, in each of which is a chapel. There is a school in which about 50 boys and 30 girls are taught. The ruins of the church consist of a gable and part of a side wall. In the lands of Old Bridge are several trenches and redoubts used at the battle of the Boyne; and at the foot of King William's glen is an obelisk in commemoration of the battle. Duke Schomberg is believed to have been buried within the gate of the grounds of H. B. Coddington, Esq.

DONORLIN.—See DUNORLIN.

DONOUGHMORE, a parish, in the barony of IBANE and BARRYROE, county of CORK, and province of MUNSTER, 5 miles (S. S. E.) from Clonakilty; containing 364 inhabitants. This parish is situated on the eastern side of the entrance to Clonakilty bay, on a very exposed and bold shore opening abruptly to the Atlantic. It comprises 306 statute acres, nearly all under tillage, and there is neither waste land nor bog. The principal manure is sand and sea-weed, which are found in abundance on the strand, and of which large quantities are sent to Clonakilty. There is a quarry of excellent slate, affording employment to a number of persons throughout the year. Along the coast are some beautiful small bays, but so much exposed that no use can be made of them, unless in very calm weather. A coast-guard station has been fixed at Rock Castle, near the village. Donoughmore is a prebend in the cathedral of Ross, and in the patronage of the Bishop: the tithes amount to £42. There is neither glebe-house, glebe, nor church; divine service is performed in the barrack of the coast-guard station every Sunday. In the R. C. divisions it forms part of the union or district of Lislee. The parochial school is supported by subscription under the patronage of the rector; and there is a pay school, in which are about 60 children. Here is a solitary square tower of very rude character; it has no windows, but two entrances, one from the ground and the other at some height above it, and appears to have been the tower of the ancient parish church. Around it is an ancient cemetery, now used chiefly for the interment of infants. Not far distant is a small but very perfect rath with a rampart 12 feet high.

DONOUGHMORE, a parish, partly in the barony of BARRETTS, but chiefly in that of EAST MUSKERRY, county of CORK, and province of MUNSTER, 12 miles (W. N. W.) from Cork, on the new line of road to Kanturk; containing 6794 inhabitants. This parish comprises 22,000 statute acres, of which 8000 acres, which had been forcibly withheld from the see of Cloyne (to which nearly half the parish belongs), since the year 1539, were, in 1709, recovered by Bishop Crow, and are now the property of that see, but in the hands of the Commissioners under the Church Temporalities act: about 2880 acres are bog and mountain, and the remainder is good arable and pasture land. The soil is generally cold and wet, except in the neighbourhood of Derry, where the lands are well cultivated and very productive. Not more than one-fourth of the land is under tillage; the remainder is mountain pasture and bog, especially in the northern part of the parish, where a vast tract of heathy bog and moorland extends to the summit of the Boggra mountain, on which numerous herds of cattle are pastured. The principal residences are Derry, that of J. B. Gibbs, Esq.; Derry Cottage, of the Rev. W. Meade; Kilcullen, of Jer. Lynch, Esq.; Firmount, of Horace Townsend, Esq.; and Fortnaght, of the Rev. Morgan O'Brien. The new line of road from Cork to Kanturk passes through this wild district, and will contribute greatly to its improvement: the rivers Dripsey and Awenbeg have their rise in it. Fairs are held on May 18th and Nov. 21st for general farming stock. Near the cross of Donoughmore is a constabulary police barrack. A manorial court is held under the Bishop of Cloyne, and petty sessions monthly. The rectory constitutes the corps of the prebend of Cloyne in the cathedral of St. Colman, and in the patronage of the Bishop: the tithes amount to £1100. The glebe-house is a very old building; the glebe comprises 14 acres of fertile land. The church is a small and very old edifice in a state of great dilapidation, and is about to be rebuilt by the Ecclesiastical Commissioners. The R. C. parish is co-extensive with that of the Established Church; there are two chapels, one near the cross of Donoughmore, and the other at Fortnaght, the former a spacious and neat edifice, the other a small plain building. A school is supported by the rector, in which about 20 children are educated; at Garrane is a school, in which about 30 boys and 20 girls are instructed, and for which a house was given by Mr. Stowell; and there are five pay schools, in which are about 300 boys and 160 girls. Between this parish and Kilshanig is the Pass of Redshard, where Lord-President St. Leger, in 1641, drew up such forces as he could raise to oppose the insurgents coming from the county of Limerick, and commanded by Lord Mountgarret, but on their messengers showing him their pretended commission from the king, he disbanded his forces and retired to Cork. This place gives the title of Earl to the family of Hutchinson.

DONOUGHMORE, county of KILKENNY.—See BALLYRAGGET.

DONOUGHMORE, a parish, in the county of the city of LIMERICK, and province of MUNSTER, $2\frac{1}{2}$ miles (S. E.) from Limerick; containing 729 inhabitants. This parish is situated on the road from Limerick to Bruff, and comprises 821 statute acres, as applotted under the tithe act, and about 97 acres of bog mostly cut out and reclaimed. The land is generally good, but, though so near the city of Limerick, the system of agriculture is in a very unimproved state; some of the land is depastured by milch cows and the produce sent daily to Limerick. There are several handsome residences in the neighbourhood, of which the principal are Ballyseeda, that of T. G. Fitzgibbon, Esq.; South Hill, of S. Evans, Esq.; and Clonlong, of J. Norris, Esq.; and there are several substantial houses, the occasional residences of some of the Limerick merchants, who have farms in the parish. Donoughmore is a prebend in the cathedral of Limerick, and in the patronage of the Bishop: the tithes amount to £92. 6. 1½. There is neither church, glebe-house, nor glebe. In the R. C. divisions the parish is the head of a union or district, comprising also the parishes of Cahirnarry and Cahirnavalla; the chapel is a small thatched building nearly in the centre of the parish. There is a pay school of about 100 children. The ruins of the ancient parish church are extensive and venerably picturesque, consisting of the walls and gables, which are tolerably entire and covered with ivy; within the area are the tombs and monuments of the ancient families of Roche, Kelly, Connell, and Fitzgerald.

DONOUGHMORE, a parish, in the barony of UPPER OSSORY, QUEEN'S county, and province of LEINSTER, 1¼ mile (N. W. by N.) from Rathdowney, on the road from Burros-in-Ossory to Kilkenny; containing 1211 inhabitants, of which number, 383 are in the village. This parish contains 3226 statute acres, as applotted under the tithe act. The village comprises about 70 houses, and contains extensive corn-mills and a large starch manufactory. Fairs are held in it on March 28th, June 12th and 13th, Aug. 31st, and Dec. 12th. The living is a rectory and vicarage, in the diocese of Ossory, and in the patronage of the Bishop: the tithes amount to £154. 9. 7½. There is a glebe-house, with a glebe of 193 acres. The church was rebuilt by aid of a loan of £500 from the late Board of First Fruits, in 1821. In the R. C. divisions the parish forms part of the union or district of Rathdowney, and contains a plain chapel. The parochial school is endowed with an acre of land by the rector, and there are two private schools, in all which about 100 children are educated.

DONOUGHMORE, a parish, in the barony of IFFA and OFFA EAST, county of TIPPERARY, and province of MUNSTER, 4½ miles (N.) from Clonmel, on the road to Thurles; containing 456 inhabitants. It comprises 1085 statute acres; there are some bogs and marshy land, and also some portions of uncultivated ground, which are susceptible of improvement and might be easily reclaimed. Limestone abounds in the parish, and is quarried exclusively for burning into lime, which is the principal manure. The living is a rectory, in the diocese of Lismore, united, by act of council in 1805, to the rectory of Kiltigan, together constituting the union and corps of the prebend of Donoughmore in the cathedral of Lismore, in the patronage of the Bishop: the tithes amount to £138. 9. 3., and the tithes of the union to £232. 3. 1. The glebe-house was built by aid of a gift of £350 and a loan of £450 from the late Board of First Fruits, in 1818: the glebe comprises 13*a.* 2*r.* 20*p.* The church has been in ruins from time immemorial, and the Protestant parishioners attend the church of Lisronagh, about two miles distant. In the R. C. divisions the parish forms part of the union or district of Powerstown. The remains of the church, which may possibly have been the church of a monastery said to have existed here at a very remote period, and of which St. Farannan was the first abbot, consist chiefly of an exterior and interior arch richly sculptured with mouldings and embellished with grotesque ornaments; they are of the later Norman style, and have sustained much injury from time and dilapidation.

DONOUGHMORE, a parish, in the barony of UPPER TALBOTSTOWN, county of WICKLOW, and province of LEINSTER, 5 miles (N. E.) from Baltinglass; containing 4130 inhabitants. This parish is situated on the river Slaney, and in the glen of Imail, which abounds with excellent pasturage: it comprises 25,202 statute acres, about 8100 of which form a large tract of mountain, having an extensive bog at its base. The land is in tillage and pasture, and great numbers of calves are fattened here, and large quantities of butter made for the Dublin market. The scenery is bold and rugged, contrasting strikingly with the milder character of the adjacent glen. At Knocknamunion is a factory for making blankets and frieze, and there is a granite quarry at Knockaderry. In this parish stand the Leitrim barracks, which were erected after the disturbances of 1798, at an expense of about £8000: they have been recently disposed of to a private individual. The seats are Coolmoney, the residence of Lady Louisa Hutchinson, a handsome and newly erected mansion, commanding fine views of the glen of Imail; and Ballinclea, of Richard Fenton, Esq. Donoughmore is a prebend in the cathedral church of St. Patrick, Dublin, in the patronage of the Archbishop: the tithes amount to £461. 10. 9¼. The glebe-house is situated about three-quarters of a mile from the church, on a glebe comprising 20 acres. The church was rebuilt in 1711, and the present tower added to it, in 1821, by aid of a loan of £400 from the late Board of First Fruits: it has been recently repaired. Evening service is also performed, during summer, in the school-house at Knockenargan. In the R. C. divisions the parish forms part of the union or district of Dunlavin and Donard; the chapel is at Davidstown. There are four schools, one of which is supported by the Trustees of Erasmus Smith's charity; the parochial school, near the church, was erected in 1821, by subscription; and one at Knockenargan was erected, in 1834, also by subscription, on half an acre of land given for the site by the Earl of Wicklow: in these schools about 120 boys and 70 girls are taught, and about 80 more boys and 60 girls in six private schools. A loan fund was established in 1824; Mrs. Caldwell left £20 per annum, late currency, to the Protestant poor; and the interest of £200 stock was left by the late Dr. Ryan, who was rector of this parish, in 1818, to five poor Protestants and five poor Roman Catholics.

On the townland of Castleruddery are several raths, or Danish mounds; the most conspicuous is one of considerable height on the grounds of Mr. J. Wilson, and on the same land is a druidical circle of about 120 feet in diameter, round which are numerous blocks of stone, some not of the district, and in the centre of the circle there was no doubt an altar. Adjoining the garden is a pond, in which skeletons of the elk, or moose deer, have been found. On the same townland a flint spear-head was found, on ploughing a field in 1829. At Knockenargan there are two raths, and another at Gibstown; at Knockendaragh is a very extensive one, which is surrounded by a rampart and fosse; there is another above Old Deer park, at Castleruddery, which is moated, besides several others in the parish. Near the little village of Knockendaragh is a cromlech. Eardestown and Brusselstown hills, the former 1314, and the latter 1305, feet above the level of the sea, are in this parish: the summit of the latter is encircled by three concentric mounds, the lowest of which is about half way down the declivity of the hill, and, with the next above it, is formed of rough loose stones; the uppermost is constructed of large unhewn blocks, piled up to a considerable height, forming round the summit of the hill a kind of mural crown, perceptible at a great distance. There is an old burial-place near Leitrim Barracks, used by the Roman Catholics; also slight remains of a seat called Seskin, and another called Snugborough, built by Col. Percy, about 1695; the former is now the property of the Earl of Wicklow, and the latter that of Harman Herring Cooper, of Shrewl Castle, Esq.

DONOUGHPATRICK, a parish, in the barony of Clare, county of Galway, and province of Connaught, $2\frac{3}{4}$ miles (E. by N.) from Headford; containing 3697 inhabitants. This parish is situated on the Black river, near Lough Corrib, and comprises 7719 statute acres, as applotted under the tithe act. It is a rectory and vicarage, in the diocese of Tuam, and is part of the union of Headford, or Kilkilvery. In the R. C. divisions it forms part of the union or district of Kilcooney and Donoughpatrick, which is also called Ballycolgan and contains a chapel. There are three pay schools, in which are 180 children.

DONOUGHPATRICK, a parish, partly in the barony of Lower Navan, but chiefly in that of Upper Kells, county of Meath, and province of Leinster, 4 miles (N. W.) from Navan; containing 931 inhabitants. St. Patrick is said to have founded an abbey here, to which Conal Mac Neill was a great benefactor; it was frequently plundered and burnt by the Danes prior to its final destruction by them in 994. The parish is situated on the road from Enniskillen to Drogheda, and on the river Blackwater: it comprises 3605 statute acres, as applotted under the tithe act. The land is about half under tillage and half pasturage, and of superior quality: there are quarries of limestone and brownstone. The gentlemen's seats are Gibbstown, that of J. N. Gerrard, Esq., situated in a well-planted demesne of about 1270 statute acres; and Randlestown, the property of Col. Everard, but the residence of Henry Meredith, Esq. The living is a vicarage, in the diocese of Meath, united, by act of council, in 1801, to the rectory of Kilberry, and in the patronage of Col. Everard, in whom the rectory is impropriate. The tithes amount to £280, of which £180 is payable to the impropriator, and £100 to the vicar; the gross value of the benefice, tithe and glebe inclusive, is £509. 9. 2. The glebe-house was erected in 1812, by aid of a gift of £200, and a loan of £600, from the late Board of First Fruits: the glebe comprises 18 acres, valued at £36 per annum. The church is a neat edifice; the body was rebuilt in 1805, and attached to an ancient tower; the Ecclesiastical Commissioners have recently granted £104. 3. 7. for its repair. In the R. C. divisions the parish forms part of the union of Kilberry and Telltown. The parochial school is aided by the incumbent, who has also given a house and garden, and in three private schools about 120 boys and 50 girls are educated. A large Danish fort at Gibbstown has been planted. A castle formerly existed here.

DONOWNEY, or DOWNONEY, a parish, in the barony of Bantry, county of Wexford, and province of Leinster, 5 miles (N. W.) from Taghmon; containing 208 inhabitants. This small parish is situated on the road from Enniscorthy to Duncannon Fort, and contains 1074 statute acres. It is in the diocese of Ferns; the rectory is appropriate to the see, and the vicarage forms part of the union of Horetown: the tithes amount to £38. 15. $4\frac{1}{2}$., of which two-thirds are payable to the bishop and the remainder to the vicar. In the R. C. divisions it is partly in the union or district of Taghmon, but chiefly in that of Newbawn or Adamstown. There are some remains of a cromlech.

DONQUIN, or DUNQUIN, a parish, in the barony of Corkaguiney, county of Kerry, and province of Munster, 7 miles (W. S. W.) from Dingle; containing, with the Blasquet or Ferriter's islands, 1363 inhabitants. This parish is situated at the south-western extremity of the peninsula of Dingle, and terminates in the promontory called Dunmore Head, the most westerly point of Ireland. The latter is called in Irish *Tig Vourney Geerane*, c. "Mary Geerane's House," in like manner as the extreme point of North Britain is called "John O'Groat's." Dunmore Head is in N. Lat. 52° 8′ 30″ and in W. Lon. 10° 27′ 30″: it lies about 5 Irish miles (W. by N.) from the entrance of Ventry harbour, and $3\frac{1}{2}$ miles (W. $\frac{1}{4}$ S.) from the west end of the island called the Great Blasquet. The parish contains 4937 statute acres, as applotted under the tithe act, of which nearly one half consists of coarse rocky mountain pasture, interspersed with patches of bog; the remainder is in tillage: sea-weed is extensively used for manure, and the state of agriculture is gradually improving. At Clohua is a small harbour for fishing boats employed during the season in taking mackerel, scad, and turbot; and at Ballyikeen is a station of the coast-guard. It is in the diocese of Ardfert and Aghadoe; the rectory is impropriate in Lord Ventry, and the vicarage forms part of the union of Marhyn. The tithes amount to £75, payable in moieties to the impropriator and the vicar: divine service is performed every Sunday at the coast-guard station. In the R. C. divisions the parish forms part of the union or district of Keel, or Terreter. A school has been recently built at Ballyikeen. On the rocky coast of this parish are often found the beautiful crystals called Kerry stones. The ruins of the church still remain in the burial-ground, where the Prince of Ascule was interred after the wreck of part of the Spanish Armada off this coast.—See Blasquet Islands.

DOOGH.—See KILKEE.

DOON, a parish, partly in the barony of Kilnemanagh, county of Tipperary, and partly in the barony of Owneybeg, but chiefly in that of Coonagh, county of Limerick, and province of Munster, 14 miles (S. E.) from Limerick, on the old road to Templemore; containing 5311 inhabitants, of which number, 178 are in the village. This parish comprises 27,734 statute acres, as applotted under the tithe act, of which more than 2000 acres are mountain and bog, about 4000 under tillage, and the remainder meadow and pasture. The soil in some places is remarkably rich, but the system of agriculture is in a very unimproved state, and a considerable portion of the meadow and pasture land is overflowed by the Dead and Mulcairn rivers. The bog in the lower parts of the parish is exceedingly valuable and lets at a very high rent; near the close of the last century more than 100 acres of bog moved from one townland into two others, destroying thirteen cabins, the inmates of five of which perished. Freestone of fine quality is quarried here for public buildings; much of it has been used in the city of Limerick and in other towns, and large quantities are shipped for England and other places. The principal seats are Castle Guard, the residence of the Hon. W. O'Grady, an ancient castle of the Earls of Desmond, enlarged and restored in the baronial style, with a lofty keep and ramparts; Toomaline House, of Mrs. Marshall, formerly a priory of Canons regular and a cell to the abbey of Inchenemeo, granted on its dissolution by Queen Elizabeth to Miler Magragh, Archbishop of Cashel, and of which there are still some remains; Bilboa House, now nearly in ruins, the property of the Earl of Stradbroke, and formerly the residence of Col. Wilson, built wholly of brick from Holland, situated in grounds formerly richly wooded but now going to decay, and commanding a fine view of the Bilboa mountains on the north, to which it has given name; and Glengare, of G. Hodges, Esq., situated on one of the 12 townlands of this parish which are in the county of Tipperary, and together comprise 4700 acres. Fairs are held at Bilboa on the 12th of August and May, and a constabulary force is stationed in the village. The living is a rectory, in the diocese of Emly, constituting the prebend of Doon in the cathedral of St. Ailbe, and in the patronage of the Archbishop of Cashel: the tithes amount to £830. 15. 4½. The glebe-house is a handsome residence, and the glebe comprises 35 acres, subject to a rent of £40 per annum payable to the trustees of Erasmus Smith's fund, who own much land in this parish. The church, rebuilt in 1800 by a gift of £500 from the late Board of First Fruits, is a small plain edifice with a low square tower; in the churchyard was interred the noted outlaw, Emun-a-Cnoc, or Edmund of the Hill. In the R. C. divisions this parish, with the exception of eight townlands in the union of Cappamore, is the head of a union or district, comprising also the parish of Castletown. Lord Stanley, who has an estate of about 600 acres in the parish, has given two acres, rent-free, to erect a chapel and school-house: the shell of the former edifice is nearly completed, at an expense of £1000 to the parishioners; it is situated on a small hill over the village, commanding a fine view of the Doon and Galtee mountains. There are five private schools, in which are 300 children.

DOONAS.—See KILTINANLEA.

DOONFEENY.—See DUNFEENY.

DORINCH, an island, in the parish of KILMINA, barony of BURRISHOOLE, county of MAYO, and province of CONNAUGHT, 5 miles (W.) from Westport; the population is returned with the parish. It is situated in Clew bay: in its vicinity is the smaller island called Dorinchbeg, and to the north is the bar at the entrance of Westport bay.

DORRAH, or DURROW, a parish, in the barony of LOWER ORMOND, county of TIPPERARY, and province of MUNSTER, 3 miles (W.) from Parsonstown, on the roads leading respectively from Portumna to Parsonstown and from Nenagh to Banagher; containing 3397 inhabitants. It is situated near the river Shannon, and is bounded on the north by the Brosna, comprising 10,829 statute acres, as applotted under the tithe act: about 3000 acres are bog, principally lying along the Shannon and the Brosna, and consequently capable of drainage from the fall of the land towards those rivers; and of the remainder the greatest portion is under tillage; a tract of about 200 acres of meadow, called the Inches, is of remarkably fine quality, and the parish generally is in a good state of cultivation. There is a quarry of good limestone, which is burnt for manure. The principal seats are Walsh Park, that of J. W. Walsh, Esq.; Sraduff, of T. Antisell, Esq.; Newgrove, of J. W. Bayly, Esq.; Rockview, of J. Lewis Corrigan, Esq.; Gurteen, of J. Lalor, Esq.; Arbour Hill, of J. Antisell, Esq.; Ross House, of R. Smith, Esq.; Clongowna, of the Rev. Mr. Troke; Ballyduff, of B. Walker, Esq.; and Redwood, the property of Major Bloomfield. There is a flour-mill at Derrinsallagh. The parish is in the diocese of Killaloe, and is a rectory and vicarage, forming part of the union of Lorrha and corps of the archdeaconry of Killaloe: the tithes amount to £415. 7. 8¼. It formerly consisted of three parishes, Bonahane, Pallas, and Ross, the remains of the churches of which are still visible, and the two former had glebes. At Ross there was a very extensive burial-ground, which has not been used as such within the memory of man. The church is a neat modern edifice, completed in 1832, for which a grant of £900 was made by the late Board of First Fruits: the old church has been occupied as a dwelling-house from time immemorial. In the R. C. divisions also the parish forms part of the union or district of Lorrha, called also Dorrha; the chapel, on the townland of Gurteen, has been lately fitted up in a neat manner. In the demesne of Walsh Park is a school-house built by the proprietor, who supports the school; and there is a school at Gurteen in connection with the National Board. At Redwood are the ruins of an old castle, and there are some remains of the ancient parish church.

DORSAKILE.—See KILPATRICK, county of WESTMEATH.

DOUGHBEG, a village, in the parish of CLONDEVADOCK, barony of KILMACRENAN, county of DONEGAL, and province of ULSTER; containing 55 houses and 284 inhabitants.

DOUGLAS, a chapelry, comprising that portion of the parish of CARRIGALINE which is in the county of the city of CORK, and in the province of MUNSTER, 1½ mile (S. E.) from Cork, on the road to Carrigaline; containing 816 inhabitants. This village, which is situated at the head of a small bay called Douglas channel, on the eastern side of Cork harbour, is irregularly built in two detached portions respectively on the upper and lower roads from Cork. Its origin is attributed to the settlement of a colony of linen weavers from Fermanagh, who in 1726 commenced here the manufacture of sail-cloth, which obtained such celebrity in the English market, that unlimited orders were received for all that could be made. This establishment continued to flourish till after the introduction of machinery into the English factories, which enabled the English manufacturers to undersell those of Ireland, and the trade consequently declined greatly, though the manufacture is still carried on. A very extensive rope-yard has long been established, and the patent cordage made here is in very great repute. There is a large boulting-mill belonging to Mr. G. White, capable of manufacturing 6000 barrels of flour annually, and which might be easily made to produce twice that quantity; there is also a mill on the road to Monkstown belonging to Mr. Power, of equal capability. A large quantity of bricks, of a bright ash colour, is made in the immediate vicinity of the village, and sent to a considerable distance inland; and great numbers are conveyed by small craft to the port of Cork. A penny post to Cork has been established, and a constabulary police force is stationed in the village. The environs of Douglas are exceedingly pleasant and the scenery richly diversified and embellished with numerous elegant seats and tasteful villas; the surface is undulated, rising in some places into considerable eminences and commanding extensive and interesting views. To the north and west are seen the course of the river Lee, the peninsula of Blackrock, the hills of Glanmire and Rathcooney, with others in the distance, the city of Cork, and the beautiful country towards Inniscarra. To the east and south are the mountains beyond Midleton and Youghal, the harbour of Cork with the town of Cove, the course of the Carrigaline river and the rich scenery on its banks. The principal seats are Maryborough, the residence of E. E. Newenham, Esq., a noble mansion in a spacious demesne embellished with stately timber; Old Court, of Sir Geo. Goold, Bart., an elegant residence beautifully situated on a commanding eminence embosomed in woods of luxuriant growth; Monsfieldtown, of T. C. Kearney, Esq.; the Hill, of A. O'Driscoll, Esq.; Vernon Mount, of O. Hayes, Esq.; Thornberry, of T. Townsend, Esq.; Belmont Cottage, of Capt. S. H. Lawrence; Windsor, of G. Cooke, Esq.; Rowan's Court, of Mrs. Evanson; Frankfield, of S. Lane, Esq.; Montpelier, of the Rev. M. O'Donovan; Alta Villa, of J. Woodroffe, Esq., M. D.; Charlemont, of C. Evanson, Esq.; Bloomfield, of W. Sheehy, Esq.; Shamrock Lawn, of W. P. Robinson, Esq.; Grange Erin, of W. E. Penrose, Esq.; Tramore, of T. S. Reeves, Esq.; Grange, of H. Conron, Esq.; Mount Conway, of H. Sharpe, Esq.; West Grove, of Mrs. S. Baylie; Ballybrack, of J. Heard, Esq.; Atkin Ville, of Mrs. Atkins; Mount Emla, of J. Barnes, Esq.; Garryduffe, of Mrs. Allen; Wilsfort, of Mrs. Dowman; Rose Hill, of W. Lane, Esq.; Douglas House, of T. Fitzgerald, Esq.; Castle Treasure, of C. Lloyd, Esq.; Ballinrea, of the Rev. J. Beesteed; Ballincurrig Cottage, of W. C. Logan, Esq.; Eglantine, of J. Leahy, Esq.; Villa Nova, of J. Lombard, Esq.; Knockreagh, of L. Nash, Esq.; Donnybrook, of L. Jones, Esq.; Factory Ville, of J. C. Bernard, Esq.; Hampstead, of Lieut. Boyle Hill; Bellevue, of E. Lucette, Esq.; Alton Ville, of A. C. McCarthy, Esq.; Bellair, of W. Perrier, Esq.; Garna Villa, of S. Harrison, Esq.; and Grange House, of J. R. Day, Esq. The chapel is a small neat edifice, and the Ecclesiastical Commissioners have lately granted £230 for its repair. In the R. C. division this place is the head of a union or district comprising also the parish of Ballygarvan; the chapel is a neat building, and there is also a chapel at Ballygarvan. The parochial male school is chiefly supported by the rector; a female school by Mrs. Reeves and a few ladies; and an infants' and female school are supported and superintended by Miss O'Donovan, of Montpelier: there is also a National school in the village, and a dispensary. There are raths at Old Court and Moneas, and some slight remains of Treasure castle.

DOULOUGH'S (ST.), a parish, in the barony of Coolock, county of Dublin, and province of Leinster, 5½ miles (N. E.) from Dublin, on the road to Malahide; containing 345 inhabitants. The land in this parish is of good quality and the soil favourable to the growth of corn, of which large crops are raised; the system of agriculture is improved, and there is abundance of limestone, which is quarried for agricultural and other uses, and in some of which varieties of fossils are found. The surrounding scenery is pleasingly and richly diversified, and from its elevation the parish commands extensive and beautiful views of the sea and the mountains in the neighbourhood. The principal seats, all of which command interesting prospects, are St. Doulough's Lodge, the residence of J. Rutherfoord, Esq.; St. Doulough's, of Mrs. Shaw; Lime Hill, of the Rev. P. Ryan, A. M.; and Spring Hill, of H. Parsons, Esq. It is a curacy, in the diocese of Dublin, and in the patronage of the Precentor of the cathedral of Christchurch, to whom the rectory is appropriate: the tithes amount to £160, payable to the incumbent. The church is a neat modern edifice, adjoining the ancient structure, which is still preserved as a singular and interesting relic of antiquity. In the R. C. divisions it forms part of the union or district of Baldoyle and Howth. About 60 children are taught in the parochial school, which is supported by subscription, aided by the incumbent. The ancient church of St. Doulough, which is still tolerably entire, is one of the oldest and most singular religious edifices in the country: it is situated on an eminence at the extremity of an avenue about 50 yards in length, at the entrance of which is a low granite cross supposed to have been originally placed over the south porch. The church is about 48 feet long and 18 feet wide, with a massive square embattled tower, and is built of the limestone found in the neighbourhood, with the exception of the mullions of the windows, the keystones of the arched roofs, and the more ornamental details, which are of oolite or fine freestone, probably imported in a previously finished state from Normandy or England. The south porch, which rises like a vast buttress at the south-eastern angle of the tower, contains a low and imperfectly pointed doorway leading into a crypt with a stone roof groined, and divided into two small apartments, one of which is almost entirely occupied with the altar-tomb of St. Doulough, the staircase leading to the tower, and the pillars supporting the roof. From this a low doorway leads into the eastern portion of the church, which is 22 feet long and 12 feet wide, lighted at the east end by a trefoiled window, and two smaller windows on the south and one on the north side. This part of the church and also the tower are evidently of much later date than the rest of the building, which is supposed to have been erected in the 10th century; the groining of the roof, the tracery of the windows, and other details contrasting strongly with the ruder portions of the structure. Between the south windows of the church, and projecting into its area, is the staircase leading through the upper portion of the porch to the tower, and opening into a small apartment with two pointed windows, beyond which is an apartment immediately under the roof, 36 feet in length and very narrow, having that portion of it which is under the tower rudely groined. In the south porch a staircase leads from the apartment in which is St. Doulough's tomb, to a very small apartment, called St. Doulough's bed, 5 feet long, 2 feet wide, and 2½ high, and lighted only by a loophole; the entrance is extremely low and narrow; the roof is vaulted, and in the floor is a small hole, through which a bell rope appears to have passed. The roof of the church forms a very acute angle, and the stones of which it is constructed are so firmly cemented that it is impervious to water, though it has been exposed to the weather for eight or nine centuries. This singular edifice comprises within its narrow limits seven different apartments, two staircases, and a great variety of windows of various designs, and door cases all differing in character. Near the church is a well, dedicated to St. Catharine, enclosed within an octagonal building with a groined roof of stone; of this building, with which a subterraneous passage communicated from the crypt in which is St. Doulough's tomb, the faces towards the cardinal points, in which are loopholes, are raised to a second story and crowned with a pediment, in which is a lancet-shaped window; the door is on the south side, and the whole is finished with a pyramidal dome, of which the upper part is wanting. The interior of the building is circular, and has three deep recesses in the walls, in which are stone seats. In the centre of the area is the well, encircled by a ring of stone two feet in depth and 5 inches thick on the edge. In each spandril of the arched ceiling, and over each recess in the walls, is a sunken panel, and the interior was formerly decorated with paintings of scriptural subjects.

DOVEA, a parish, in the barony of Eliogarty, county of Tipperary, and province of Munster, 4 miles (S. S. W.) from Templemore; the population is returned with the parish of Inch, of which, for all civil purposes, this is regarded as forming a part. A constabulary police force has been stationed here. It is in the diocese of Cashel; the rectory is impropriate in the Marquess of Ormonde, in trust for charitable uses at Kilkenny; and the vicarage forms part of the union of Clogher and corps of the chancellorship of Cashel.

DOWN (County of), a maritime county of the province of Ulster, bounded on the east and south by the Irish sea, on the north by the county of Antrim and Carrickfergus bay, and on the west by the county of Armagh. It extends from 54° 0′ to 54° 40′ (N. Lat.), and from 5° 18′ to 6° 20′ (W. Lon.); and comprises an area, according to the Ordnance survey, of 611,404 acres, of which, 502,677 are cultivated land, 108,569 are unprofitable bog and mountain, and 158 are under water. The population, in 1821, amounted to 325,410, and in 1831, to 352,012.

This county, together with a small part of that of Antrim, was anciently known by the name of *Ulagh* or *Ullagh*, in Latin *Ulidia* (said by some to be derived from a Norwegian of that name who flourished here long before the Christian era), which was finally extended to the whole province of Ulster. Ptolemy, the geographer, mentions the *Voluntii* or *Uluntii* as inhabiting this region; and the name, by some etymologists, is traced from them. At what period this tribe settled in Ireland is unknown: the name is not found in any other author who treats of the country, whence it may be inferred that the colony was soon incorporated with the natives, the principal families of whom were the O'Nials, the Mac Gennises, the Macartanes, the Slut-Kellys, and the Mac Gilmores. The county continued chiefly in the possession of the same families at the period of the settlement of the North of Ireland in the reign of King James, at the commencement of the seventeenth century, with the addition of the English families of Savage and White, the former of which settled in the peninsula of the Ardes, on the eastern side of Strangford Lough, and the latter in the barony of Dufferin, on the western side of the same gulf. It is not clearly ascertained at what precise period the county was made shire ground. The common opinion is that this arrangement, together with its division into baronies, occurred in the early part of the reign of Elizabeth. But from the ancient records of the country it appears that, previously to the 20th of Edw. II., here were two counties distinguished by the names of Down and Newtown. The barony of Ardes was also a separate jurisdiction, having sheriffs of its own at the same date; and the barony of Lecale was considered to be within the English pale from its first subjugation by that people; its communication with the metropolis being maintained chiefly by sea, as the Irish were in possession of the mountain passes between it and Louth. That the consolidation of these separate jurisdictions into one county took place previously to the settlement of Ulster by Sir John Perrott, during his government, which commenced in 1584, is evident from this settlement comprehending seven counties only, omitting those of Down and Antrim because they had previously been subjected to the English law.

The first settlement of the English in this part of Ulster took place in 1177, when John de Courcy, one of the British adventurers who accompanied Strongbow, marched from Dublin with 22 men-at-arms and 300 soldiers, and arrived at Downpatrick in four days without meeting an enemy. But when there he was immediately besieged by Dunleve, the toparch of the country, aided by several of the neighbouring chieftains, at the head of 10,000 men. De Courcy, however did not suffer himself to be blockaded, but sallied out at the head of his little troop, and routed the besiegers. Another army of the Ulidians having been soon after defeated with much slaughter in a great battle, he became undisputed master of the part of the county in the vicinity of Downpatrick, which town he made his chief residence, and founded several religious establishments in its neighbourhood. In 1200, Roderic Mac Dunleve, toparch of the country, was treacherously killed by De Courcy's servants, who were banished for the act by his order; but in 1203 he himself was seized, while doing penance unarmed in the burial-ground of the cathedral of Down, by order of De Lacy, the chief governor of Ireland, and was sent prisoner to King John in England. The territory then came into the possession of the family of De Lacy, by an heiress of which, about the middle of the same century, it was conveyed in marriage to Walter de Burgo. In 1315, Edward Bruce having landed in the northern part of Ulster, to assert his claim to the throne of Ireland, this part of the province suffered severely in consequence of the military movements attending his progress southwards and his return. Some years after,

William de Burgo, the representative of that powerful family, having been killed by his own servants at Carrickfergus, leaving an only daughter, the title and possessions were again transferred by marriage to Roger Mortimer, Earl of March, through whom they finally became vested in the kings of England.

It is partly in the diocese of Down, and partly in that of Dromore, with a small portion in that of Connor. For purposes of civil jurisdiction it is divided into the baronies of Ardes, Castlereagh, Dufferin, Iveagh Lower, Iveagh Upper, Kinelearty, Lecale, and Mourne, and the extra-episcopal lordship of Newry. It contains the borough, market, and assize town of Downpatrick; the greater part of the borough, market, and assize town, and sea-port of Newry; the ancient corporate, market, and post-towns of Bangor, Newtown-Ardes, Hillsborough, and Killyleagh; the sea-port, market, and post-towns of Portaferry and Donaghadee; the market and post-towns of Banbridge, Saintfield, Kirkcubbin, Rathfriland, Castlewellan, Ballinahinch, and Dromore; the sea-port and post-towns of Strangford, Warrenpoint, Rosstrevor, Ardglass, and Killough; the sea-port of Newcastle, which has a penny-post; the post-towns of Clough, Comber, Dromaragh, Hollywood, Moira, Loughbrickland, Kilkeel, and Gilford; and a part of the suburb of the town of Belfast, called Ballymacarret. Prior to the Union it sent fourteen members to the Irish parliament, namely, two for the county at large, and two for each of the boroughs of Newry, Downpatrick, Bangor, Hillsborough, Killyleagh, and Newtown-Ardes. It is at present represented by four members, namely, two for the county, and one for each of the boroughs of Newry and Downpatrick. The number of voters registered at the last general election was 3729. The election for the county takes place at Downpatrick. Down is included in the north-east circuit: the assizes are held at Downpatrick, where are the county gaol and court-house: quarter sessions are held at Newtown-Ardes, Hillsborough, Downpatrick, and Newry: the number of persons charged with criminal offences and committed to prison, in 1835, was 468, and of civil bill commitments, 87. The local government is vested in a lord-lieutenant, 19 deputy lieutenants, and 120 other magistrates, besides whom there are the usual county officers, including two coroners. There are 30 constabulary police stations, having in the whole a force of 5 chief and 30 subordinate constables and 114 men, with 6 horses, the expense of whose maintenance is defrayed equally by Grand Jury presentments and by Government. There are a county infirmary and a fever hospital at Downpatrick, and dispensaries situated respectively at Banbridge, Kilkeel, Rathfriland, Castlewellan, Dromore, Warrenspoint, Donaghadee, Newry, Newtownbreda, Hollywood, Hillsborough, Ardglass, and Bangor, maintained equally by private subscriptions and Grand Jury presentments. The amount of Grand Jury presentments for 1835 was £43,103. 7. 0¼., of which £5257. 6. 2. was for the public roads of the county at large; £17,226. 19. 2. was for the public roads, being the baronial charge; £11,923. 18. 4. for public buildings and charities, officers' salaries, &c.; £3429. 1. 5½. for police; and £5266. 1. 10¾. in repayment of a loan advanced by Government. In the military arrangements it is included in the northern district, and contains three barrack stations for infantry, namely, two at Newry and one at Downpatrick. On the coast there are nineteen coast-guard stations, under the command of two inspecting commanders, in the districts of Donaghadee and Newcastle, with a force of 15 chief officers and 127 men.

The county has a pleasing inequality of surface, and exhibits a variety of beautiful landscapes. The mountainous district is in the south, comprehending all the barony of Mourne, the lordship of Newry, and a considerable portion of the barony of Iveagh: these mountains rise gradually to a great elevation, terminating in the towering peak of Slieve Donard; and to the north of this main assemblage is the detached group of Slieve Croob, the summit of which is only 964 feet high. There are several lakes, but none of much extent: the principal are Aghry or Agher, and Erne, in Lower Iveagh; Ballyroney, Loughbrickland, and Shark, in Upper Iveagh; Ballinahinch, in Kinelearty; and Ballydowgan, in Lecale. The county touches upon Lough Neagh in a very small portion of its north-western extremity, near the place where the Lagan canal discharges itself into the lake. Its eastern boundary, including also a portion of the northern and southern limits, comprehends a long line of coast, commencing at Belfast with the mouth of the Lagan, which separates this county from that of Antrim, and proceeding thence along the southern side of Carrickfergus bay, where the shore rises in a gentle acclivity, richly studded with villas, to the Castlereagh hills, which form the back ground. Off Orlock Point, at the southern extremity of the bay, are the Copeland islands, to the south of which is the town and harbour of Donaghadee, a station for the mail packets between Ireland and Scotland. On the coast of the Ardes are Ballyhalbert bay, Cloughy bay, and Quintin bay, with the islets called Burr or Burial Island, Green Island, and Bard Island. South of Quintin bay is the channel, about a mile wide, to Strangford Lough, called also Lough Cone. The lough itself is a deep gulf stretching ten miles into the land in a northern direction, to Newtown-Ardes, and having a south-western offset, by which vessels of small burden can come within a mile of Downpatrick. The interior is studded with numerous islands, of which Boate says there are 260: Harris counts 54 with names, besides many smaller; a few are inhabited, but the others are mostly used for pasturage, and some are finely wooded. South of Strangford Lough are Gun's island, Ardglass harbour, and Killough bay Dundrum bay, to the south-west, forms an extended indentation on the coast, commencing at St. John's Point, south of Killough, and terminating at Cranfield Point, the southern extremity of the county, where the coast takes a north-western direction by Greencastle, Rosstrevor, and Warrenpoint, to Newry, forming the northern side of the romantic and much frequented bay of Carlingford.

The extent and varied surface of the county necessarily occasion a great diversity of soil: indeed there exists every gradation from a light sandy loam to a strong clay; but the predominant soil is a loam, not of great depth but good in quality, though in most places intermixed with a considerable quantity of stones of every size. When clay is the substratum of this loam, it is retentive of water and more difficult to improve; but when thoroughly cultivated, its produce is considerable and of superior quality. As the subsoil approaches to a hungry gravel, the loam diminishes considerably in fertility. Clay is mostly confined to the eastern coast of the Ardes and the northern portion of Castlereagh, in which district the soil is strong and of good quality. Of sandy ground, the quantity is still less, being confined to a few stripes scattered along the shores, of which the most considerable is that on the bay of Dundrum : part of this land is cultivated, part used as grazing land or rabbit-warren, and a small portion consists of shifting sands, which have hitherto baffled all attempts at improvement. There is a small tract of land south of the Lagan, between Moira and Lisburn, which is very productive, managed with less labour than any of the soils above mentioned, and earlier both in seed-time and harvest. Gravelly soils, or those intermixed with water-worn stones, are scattered over a great part of the county. Moory grounds are mostly confined to the skirts of the mountains; the bogs, though numerous, are now scarcely sufficient to afford a plentiful supply of fuel: in some parts they form the most lucrative portion of the property. The rich and deep loams on the sides of the larger rivers are also extremely valuable, as they produce luxuriant crops of grass annually without the assistance of manure.

The great attention paid to tillage has brought the land to a high state of agricultural improvement. The prevailing corn crop is oats, of which the favourite sorts are the Poland, Blantire, Lightfoot, and early Holland; wheat is sown in every part, and in Lecale is of excellent quality, and very good also in Castlereagh barony; barley is a favourite crop, mostly preceded by potatoes; rye is seldom sown, except on bog; much flax is cultivated; and turnips, mangel-wurzel, and other green crops are very general. Though, from the great unevenness of surface, considerable tracts of flat pasture land are very uncommon, yet on the sides of the rivers there are excellent and extensive meadows, annually enriched by the overflowing of the waters; and, in the valleys, the accumulation of the finer particles of mould washed down from the sides of the surrounding hills produces heavy crops of grass. Many of the finest and most productive meadows are those which lie on the skirts of turf bogs, at the junction of the peat and loam : the fertility of the compound soil is very great, the vegetation rapid, and the natural grasses of the best kind. Artificial grasses are general; clover in frequent cultivation, particularly the white. Draining is extensively and judiciously practised; and irrigation is successfully resorted to, especially upon turf bog, which, when reclaimed, is benefited by it in an extraordinary manner. In the management of the dairy, butter is the chief object: considerable quantities are sold fresh in the towns, but the greatest part is salted and sent to Belfast and Newry for exportation. Dung is principally applied as manure for raising potatoes, and great attention is paid by the farmers to collect it and to increase its quantity by additional substances, such as earth, bog soil, and clay. Lime, however, is the most general manure. At Ballinahinch, the most central part of the county, limestone of three kinds may be seen at a small distance from each other, the blue from Carlingford, the red from Castlespie, and the white from Moira, a distance of fourteen miles; the white is most esteemed. Limestone gravel is used in the neighbourhood of Moira, and found to be of powerful and lasting efficacy. Marling was introduced into Lecale about a century ago : the result of the first experiments was an immediate fourfold advance in the value of land, and the opening of a corn trade from Strangford; but the intemperate use of it brought it into discredit for some time, though it has latterly, under more judicious management, resumed its former character. Shell-sand is used to advantage on stiff clay lands; and sea-weed is frequently applied to land near the coast, but its efficacy is of short duration. Turf bog, both by itself and combined with clay, has been found useful. The system of burning and paring is practised only in the mountainous parts. In the neighbourhood of towns, coal-ashes and soot are employed: the ashes of bleach-greens, and soapers' waste, have been found to improve meadows and pastures considerably. The attention of the higher class of farmers has been for many years directed to the introduction of improved implements of husbandry, most of which have had their merits proved by fair trial: threshing machines are in general use. In no part of the country is the art of raising hedges better understood, although it has not yet been extended so universally as could be desired. In many parts the enclosure is formed of a ditch and a bank, from four to eight feet wide, and of the same depth, without any quicks; sometimes it is topped with furze, here called whins. In the mountainous parts the dry stone wall is common.

The cattle being generally procured more for the dairy than for feeding, special attention has not been paid to the improvement of the breed : hence there is a mixture of every kind. The most common and highly esteemed is a cross between the old native Irish stock and the old Leicester long-horned, which are considered the best milchers. But the anxiety of the principal resident landowners to improve every branch of agriculture having led them to select their stock of cattle at great expense, the most celebrated English breeds are imported, and the advantages are already widely diffusing themselves. The North Devon, Durham, Hereford, Leicester and Ayrshire breeds have been successively tried, and various crosses produced; that between the Durham and Leicester appears best adapted to the soil and climate, and on some estates there is a good cross between the Ayrshire and North Devon; but the long-horned is still the favourite breed of the small farmer. Great improvements have also been made in the breed of sheep, particularly around Hillsborough, Seaford, Downpatrick, Bangor, Cumber, Saintfield, and other places, where there are several fine flocks, mostly of the new Leicester breed. In other parts there is a good cross between the Leicester and old native sheep. The latter have undergone little or no change in the vicinity of the mountains; they are a small hardy race, with a long hairy fleece, black face and legs, some of them horned; they are prized for the delicacy and flavour of their mutton. The breed of pigs has of late been very much improved: the Berkshire and Hampshire mostly prevail; but the most profitable is a cross between the Dutch and Russian breeds, which grows to a good size, easily fattens, and weighs well; the greater number are fattened and slaughtered, and the carcases are conveyed either to Belfast or Newry for the supply of the provision merchants, where they are mostly cured for the English market. The breed of horses, in general, is very good. There are some remains of ancient woods near Downpatrick, Finnebrogue, Briansford, and Castlewellan; and the entire county is well wooded. The oak every where flourishes vigorously; in the parks and demesnes of the nobility and gentry there is a great quantity of full-grown timber, and extensive plantations are numerous in almost every part, particularly in the vale of the Lagan, from Belfast to Lisburn, and around Hollywood, and many of the hills have been successfully planted.

The Mourne mountains, extending from Dundrum bay to Carlingford bay, form a well-defined group, of which Slieve Donard is the summit, being, according to the Ordnance survey, 2796 feet above the level of the sea, and visible, in clear weather, from the mountains near Dublin: granite is its prevailing constituent. To the north of these mountains, Slieve Croob, composed of sienite, and Slieve Anisky, of hornblende, both in Lower Iveagh, constitute an elevated tract dependent upon, though at some distance from, the main group. Hornblende and primitive greenstone are abundant on the skirts of the granitic district. Mica slate has been noticed only in one instance. Exterior chains of transition rocks advance far to the west and north of this primitive tract, extending westward across Monaghan into Cavan, and on the north-east to the southern cape of Belfast Lough, and the peninsula of Ardes. The primitive nucleus bears but a very small proportion, in surface, to these exterior chains, which are principally occupied by grauwacke and grauwacke slate. In the Mourne Mountains and the adjoining districts an extensive formation of granite occurs, but without the varieties found in Wicklow, agreeing in character rather with the newer granite of the Wernerians: it constitutes nearly the whole mass of the Mourne mountains, whence it passes across Carlingford bay into the county of Louth. On the north-west of these mountains, where they slope gradually into the plain, the same rock reaches Rathfriland, a table land of inconsiderable elevation. Within the boundaries now assigned, the granite is spread over a surface of 324 square miles, comprehending the highest ground in the North of Ireland. Among the accidental ingredients of this formation are crystallised hornblende, chiefly abounding in the porphyritic variety, and small reddish garnets in the granular: both varieties occur mingled together on the top of Slieve Donard. Water-worn pebbles, of porphyritic sienite, occasionally containing red crystals of feldspar and iron pyrites, are very frequent at the base of the Mourne mountains, between Rosstrevor and Newcastle: they have probably been derived from the disintegration of neighbouring masses of that rock, since, on the shore at Glassdrummin, a ledge of porphyritic sienite, evidently connected with the granitic mass of the adjoining mountain, projects into the sea. Greenstone slate rests against the acclivities of the Mourne mountains, but the strata never rise high, seldom exceeding 500 feet. Attempts have been made to quarry it for roofing, which it is thought would be successful if carried on with spirit. Feldspar porphyry occurs in the bed of the Finish, north-west of Slieve Croob, near Dromara, and in a decomposing state at Ballyroany, north-east of Rathfriland. Slieve Croob seems formed, on its north-east and south-east sides, of different varieties of sienite, some of them porphyritic and very beautiful: this rock crops out at intervals from Bakaderry to the top of Slieve Croob, occupying an elevation of about 900 feet. Grauwacke and grauwacke slate constitute a great part of the baronies of Ardes, Castlereagh, and the two Iveaghs: it is worked for roofing at Ballyalwood, in the Ardes; and a variety of better quality still remains undisturbed at Cairn Garva, south-west of Conbigg Hill. Lead and copper ores have been found in this formation at Conbigg Hill, between Newtown-Ardes and Bangor, where a mine is now profitably and extensively worked. Two small limestone districts occur, one near Downpatrick on the south-west, and the other near Comber on the north-west, of Strangford Lough. The old red sandstone has been observed on the sides of Strangford Lough, particularly at Scrabo, which rises 483 feet above the lough, and is capped with greenstone about 150 feet thick; the remaining 330 feet are principally sandstone, which may be observed in the white quarry in distinct beds of very variable thickness, alternating with grauwacke. This formation has been bored to the depth of 500 feet on the eastern side of Strangford Lough, in the fruitless search for coal, which depth, added to the ascertained height above ground, gives from 800 to 900 feet as its thickness. The greatest length of this sandstone district is not more than seven miles; it appears to rest on grauwacke. Coal, in three seams, is found on the shores of Strangford, and two thin seams are found under the lands of Wilnmount, on the banks of the Lagan; there are also indications of coal in two places near Moira. Chalk appears at Magheralin, near Moira, proceeding thence towards the White mountains near Lisburn, and forming a low table land. The quarries chiefly worked for freestone are those of Scrabo and Kilwarlin, near Moira, from the latter of which flags are raised of great size and of different colours, from a clear stone-colour to a brownish red. Slates are quarried on the Ardes shore, between Bangor and Ballywalter, and near Hillsborough, Anahilt, and Ballinahinch: though inferior to those imported from Wales in lightness and colour, they exceed them in hardness and durability. In the limestone quarries near Moira, the stone is found lying in horizontal strata intermixed with flints, in some places stratified, and in others in detached pieces of various forms and sizes: it is common to see three of these large flints, like rollers, a yard long and twelve inches each in diameter, standing perpendicularly over each other, and joined by a narrow neck of limestone, funnel-shaped, as if they had been poured when in a liquid state into a cavity made to receive them. Shells of various kinds are also found in this stone.

The staple manufacture is that of linens, which has prevailed since the time of Wm. III., when legislative measures were enacted to substitute it for the woollen manufacture. Its establishment here is owing greatly to the settlement of a colony of French refugees, whom the revocation of the edict of Nantes had driven from their native country, and more especially to the exertions of one of them, named Crommelin, who, after having travelled through a considerable part of Ireland, to ascertain the fitness of the country for the manufacture, settled in Lisburn, where he established the damask manufacture, which has thriven there ever since. The branches now carried on are fine linen, cambrics, sheetings, drills, damasks, and every other description of household linen. Much of the wrought article, particularly the finer fabrics, is sent to Belfast and Lurgan for sale; the principal markets within the county are

Dromore (for finer linens), and Rathfriland, Kilkeel, Downpatrick, Castlewellan, Ballinahinch, Banbridge, Newry, Dromore, and Kirkcubbin, for those of inferior quality. The cotton manufacture has latterly made great progress here; but as the linen weavers can work at a cotton loom, and as the cotton weavers are unqualified to work at linen, the change has not been in any great degree prejudicial to the general mass of workmen, who can apply themselves to one kind when the demand for the other decreases. The woollen manufacture is confined to a coarse cloth made entirely for domestic consumption, with the exception of blanketing, which was carried on with much spirit and to a great extent, particularly near Lisburn. The weaving of stockings is pretty generally diffused, but not for exportation. Tanning of leather is carried on to a large extent: at Newry there is a considerable establishment for making spades, scythes, and other agricultural implements and tools; and there are extensive glass-works at Newry and Ballimacarett. Kelp is made in considerable quantities along the coast and on Strangford lough, but its estimation in the foreign market has been much lowered by its adulteration during the process.

There is a considerable fishery at Bangor, for flat fish of all kinds, and for cod and oysters; also at Ardglass for herrings, and at Killough for haddock, cod, and other round fish; the small towns on the coast are also engaged in the fishery, particularly that of herrings, of which large shoals are taken every year in Strangford lough, but they are much inferior in size and flavour to those caught in the main sea. Smelts are taken near Portaferry; mullet, at the mouth of the Quoile river, near Downpatrick; sand eels, at Newcastle; shell fish, about the Copeland islands; and oysters, at Ringhaddy and Carlingford.

The principal rivers are the Bann and the Lagan, neither of which is navigable within the limits of the county: the former has its source in two neighbouring springs in that part of the mountains of Mourne called the Deer's Meadow, and quits this county for Armagh, which it enters near Portadown, where it communicates with the Newry canal. The Lagan has also two sources, one in Slieve Croob, and the other in Slieve-na-boly, which unite near Waringsford: near the Maze it becomes the boundary between the counties of Down and Antrim, in its course to Carrickfergus bay. There are also the Newry river and the Ballinahinch river, the former of which rises near Rathfriland, and falls into Carlingford bay; and the latter derives its source from four small lakes, and empties itself into the south-western branch of Strangford lough. This county enjoys the benefit of two canals, *viz.*, the Newry navigation, along its western border, connecting Carlingford bay with Lough Neagh; and the Lagan navigation which extends from the tideway at Belfast along the northern boundary of the county, and enters Lough Neagh near that portion of the shore included within its limits. It originated in an act passed in the 27th of Geo. II.: its total length is 20 miles; but, from being partly carried through the bed of the Lagan, its passage is so much impeded by floods as to detract much from the benefits anticipated from its formation.

There are two remarkable cairns; one on the summit of Slieve Croob, which is 80 yards round at the base and 50 on the top, and is the largest monument of the kind in the county: on this platform several smaller cairns are raised, of various heights and dimensions. The other is near the village of Anadorn, and is more curious, from containing within its circumference, which is about 60 yards, a large square smooth stone supported by several others, so as to form a low chamber, in which were found ashes and some human bones. A solitary pillar stone stands on the summit of a hill near Saintfield, having about six feet of its length above the ground. Among the more remarkable cromlechs is that near Drumbo, called the Giant's Ring, also one on Slieve-na-Griddal, in Lecale; there is another near Sliddery ford, and a third is in the parish of Drumgooland; others less remarkable may be seen near Rathfriland and Comber. There are two round towers: one stands about 24 feet south-west of the ruins of the church of Drumbo, and the other is close to the ruins of the old church of Maghera: a third, distinguished for the symmetry of its proportions, stood near the cathedral at Downpatrick, but it was taken down in 1790, to make room for rebuilding part of that edifice. Of the relics of antiquity entirely composed of earth, every variety is to be met with. Raths surrounded by a slight single ditch are numerous, and so situated as to be generally within view of each other. Of the more artificially constructed mounds, some, as at Saintfield, are formed of a single rampart and foss; others with more than one, as at Downpatrick, which is about 895 yards in circuit at the base, and surrounded by three ramparts: a third kind, as at Dromore, has a circumference of 600 feet, with a perpendicular height of 40 feet; the whole being surrounded by a rampart and battlement, with a trench that has two branches, embracing a square fort, 100 feet in diameter: and there are others very lofty at Donaghadee and Dundonald, with caverns or chambers running entirely round their interior. A thin plate of gold, shaped like a half moon, was dug out of a bog in Castlereagh; the metal is remarkably pure, and the workmanship good though simple. Another relic of the same metal, consisting of three thick gold wires intertwined through each other, and conjectured to have formed part of the branch of a golden candlestick, was found near Dromore. Near the same town have been found a canoe of oak, about 13 feet long, and various other relics; another canoe was found at Loughbrickland, and a third in the bog of Moneyreagh. An earthen lamp of curious form was dug up near Moira, the figures on which were more remarkable for their indecency than their elegance.

There are numerous remains of monastic edifices, of which the principal are at Downpatrick, those of Grey abbey on the shore of Strangford lough, and at Moville near Newtown-Ardes, Inch or Innis-Courcy near Downpatrick, Newry, Black abbey near Ballyhalbert, and Castlebuoy, or Johnstown in the Ardes. The first military work which presents itself in the southern extremity of the county is Greencastle, on the shore of Carlingford bay, said to have been built by the De Burgos, and afterwards commanded by an English constable, who also had charge of Carlingford castle: these were considered as outworks of the pale, and therefore intrusted to none but those of English birth. The castle of Narrow-water is of modern date, being built by the Duke of Ormonde after the Restoration. Dundrum castle is finely situated upon a rock overlooking the whole bay to which it gives name: it was built by De Courcy for the Knights Templars, but afterwards fell into the hands of the Magennis family. Ardglass, though but a small village, has the remains of considerable fortifications: the ruins of four castles are still visible. Not far from it is Kilclief castle, once the residence of the bishops of Down; between Killough and Downpatrick are the ruins of Bright and Skreen castles, the latter built on a Danish rath, as is that of Clough; in Strangford lough are Strangford castle, Audley's castle, and Walsh's castle; Portaferry castle was the ancient seat of the Savages; in the Ardes are also the castles of Quintin, Newcastle, and Kirkestown; the barony of Castlereagh is so called from a castle of the same name, built on a Danish fort, the residence of Con O'Neill; near Drumbo is Hill Hall, a square fort with flanking towers; Killileagh Castle is now the residence of Hamilton Rowan, Esq.; and at Rathfriland are the ruins of another castle of the Magennises. General Monk erected forts on the passes of Scarva, Poyntz, and Tuscan, which connect this county with Armagh, the ruins of which still exist. At Hillsborough is a small castle, which is still maintained in its ancient state by the Marquess of Downshire, hereditary constable; and other castles in various parts have been taken down. The gentlemen's seats are numerous, and many of them are built in a very superior style of architecture; they are all noticed in their respective parishes.

Mineral springs, both chalybeate and sulphureous, abound, but the former are more numerous. Of these, the most remarkable are Ardmillan, on the borders of Strangford lough; Granshaw, in the Ardes; Dundonnell, three miles north-west of Newtown-Ardes; Magheralin, Dromore, Newry, Banbridge, and Tierkelly. Granshaw is the richest, being equal in efficacy to the strongest of the English spas. The principal sulphureous spa is near Ballinahinch: there is an alum spring near the town of Clough. The Struel springs, situated one mile south-east of Downpatrick, in a retired vale, are celebrated not only in the neighbourhood and throughout Ireland, but in many parts of the continent, for their healing qualities, arising not from their chymical but their miraculous properties: they are dedicated to St. Patrick, and are four in number, viz., the drinking well, the eye well, and two bathing wells, each enclosed with an ancient building of stone. The principal period for visiting them is at St. John's eve, on which occasion the water rises in the wells, supernaturally, according to the belief of those who visit them. Penances and other religious ceremonies, consisting chiefly of circuits made round the wells for a certain number of times, together with bathing, accompanied by specified forms of prayer, are said to have been efficacious in removing obstinate and chronic distempers. A priest formerly attended from Downpatrick, but this practice has been discontinued since the year 1804. Not far distant are the walls of a ruined chapel, standing north and south: the entrance was on the north, and the building was lighted by four windows in the western wall. St. Scorden's well, in the vicinity of Killough, is remarkable from the manner in which the water gushes out of a fissure in the perpendicular face of a rock, on an eminence close to the sea, in a stream which is never observed to diminish in the driest seasons.

Pearls have been found in the bed of the Bann river. Fossil remains of moose deer have been found at different places; and various kinds of trees are frequently discovered imbedded in the bogs. This county is remarkable as being the first place in Ireland in which frogs were seen: they appeared first near Moira, in a western and inland district, but the cause or manner of their introduction is wholly unknown. The Cornish chough and the king-fisher have been occasionally met with near Killough; the bittern is sometimes seen in the marshes on the sea-coast; the ousel and the eagle have been observed in the mountains of Mourne; and the cross-bill at Waringstown. Barnacles and widgeons frequent Strangford lough and Carrickfergus bay in immense numbers during winter; but they are extremely wary. A marten, as tall as a fox, but much longer, was killed several years since at Moira, and its skin preserved as a curiosity. Horse-racing is a favourite amusement with all classes, and is here sanctioned by royal authority; Jas. II. having granted a patent of incorporation to a society to be called the Royal Horsebreeders of the county of Down, which is still kept up by the resident gentry, and has produced a beneficial effect in improving the breed of race-horses. Downshire gives the title of Marquess to the family of Hill, the descendants of one of the military adventurers who came to Ireland in the reign of Elizabeth.

DOWN, Borough and Diocese of.—See DOWNPATRICK.

DOWNINGS, a parish, in the barony of Clane, county of Kildare, and province of Leinster, 5 miles (N. W.) from Naas, on the road to Edenderry; containing 1393 inhabitants. It is intersected by the Grand Canal, which passes through a large tract of bog extending into the parish, and has two bridges, called respectively Burgh's bridge and Bonner's bridge, where the summit level commences, which is estimated as having an elevation of 400 feet above the top of St. Patrick's steeple, Dublin, whence it proceeds to Ballyteague, a distance of four miles: there is a reservoir of 20 acres for the supply of the canal. The parish is mostly under tillage. The gentlemen's seats are Downings, the elegant residence of M. Bury, Esq., and Woodville, the seat of J. Bury, Esq. The living is a rectory and vicarage, in the diocese of Kildare, the rectory forming part of the union of Kilcock, and the vicarage part of the union of Bridechurch: the tithes amount to £132. Divine service is performed in a house appointed by the bishop, once every Sunday and holyday. In the R. C. divisions the parish forms part of the union or district of Carogh. There are some slight remains of the old parish church.

DOWNMAHON, or DUNMAHON, a parish, in the barony of Fermoy, county of Cork, and province of Munster, 3 miles (N. N. W.) from Fermoy; containing 927 inhabitants. It comprises 2263 statute acres, as applotted for the county cess, and valued at £2285. 8. 4. per annum; the land is chiefly in tillage and produces good crops. On the east bank of the Funcheon, near Glanworth bridge, is a large flour-mill, the produce of which is in high repute. The parish, which is said to have formerly belonged to the abbey of Fermoy, is an impropriate rectory, in the diocese of Cloyne: the tithes amount to £300, and are entirely payable to John Nason, Esq. In the R. C. divisions it forms part of the union or district of Glanworth. Here are the remains of a castle, consisting of a square tower.

DOWNPATRICK, an unincorporated borough, market, and post-town, and parish, in the barony of LECALE, county of DOWN, (of which it is the chief town), and province of ULSTER, 18 miles (S. E. by S.) from Belfast, and 74 (N.) from Dublin; containing 9203 inhabitants, of which number, 4784 are in the town.

This place, which was anciently the residence of the native kings of Ullagh or Ulidia, was originally named *Aras-Celtair* and *Rath-Keltair*, one signifying the house and the other the castle or fortification of Celtair, the son of Duach; by Ptolemy it was called *Dunum*. Its present name is derived from its situation on a hill, and from its having been the chosen residence of St. Patrick, who, on his arrival here in 432, founded in its vicinity the abbey of Saul, and, shortly after, an abbey of regular canons near the ancient *Doon* or fort, the site of which was granted to him by Dichu, son of Trichem, lord of the country, whom he had converted to the Christian faith. St. Patrick presided over these religious establishments till his death in 493, and was interred in the abbey here, in which also the remains of St. Bridget and St. Columbkill, the two other tutelar saints of Ireland, were subsequently deposited. The town was constantly exposed to the ravages of the Danes, by whom it was plundered and burnt six or seven times between the years 940 and 1111; and on all these occasions the cathedral was pillaged by them. In 1177, John de Courcy took possession of the town, then the residence of Mac Dunleve, Prince of Ullagh, who, unprepared for defence against an invasion so unexpected, fled precipitately. De Courcy fortified himself here, and maintained his position against all the efforts of Mac Dunleve, aided by the native chieftains, for its recovery. In 1183, he displaced the canons and substituted a society of Benedictine monks from the abbey of St. Werburgh at Chester. Both he and Bishop Malachy III., endowed the abbey with large revenues; and in 1186 they sent an embassy to Pope Urban III. to obtain a bull for translating into shrines the sacred reliques of the three saints above named, which was performed with great solemnity by the pope's nuncio in the same year. De Courcy having espoused the claims of Prince Arthur, Duke of Brittany, assumed, in common with other English barons who had obtained extensive settlements in Ireland, an independent state, and renounced his allegiance to King John, who summoned him to appear and do homage. His mandate being treated with contempt, the provoked monarch, in 1203, invested De Lacy and his brother Walter with a commission to enter Ulster and reduce the revolted baron. De Lacy advanced with his troops to Down, where an engagement took place in which he was signally defeated and obliged to retreat with considerable loss of men. De Courcy, however, was ultimately obliged to acknowledge his submission and consent to do homage. A romantic description of the issue of this contest is related by several writers, according to whom De Courcy, after the termination of the battle, challenged De Lacy to single combat, which the latter declined on the plea that his commission, as the King's representative, forbade him to enter the lists against a rebellious subject, and subsequently proclaimed a reward for De Courcy's apprehension, which proving ineffectual, he then prevailed upon his servants by bribes and promises to betray their master. This act of perfidy was carried into execution whilst De Courcy was performing his devotions unarmed in the burial-ground of the cathedral: the assailants rushed upon him and slew some of his retinue; De Courcy seized a large wooden cross, with which, being a man of great prowess, he killed thirteen of them, but was overpowered by the rest and bound and led captive to De Lacy, who delivered him a prisoner to the king. In 1205, Hugh de Lacy was made Earl of Ulster, and for a while fixed his residence at the castle erected here by De Courcy. In 1245, part of the abbey was thrown down and the walls of the cathedral much damaged by an earthquake. A desperate battle was fought in the streets of this town, in 1259, between Stephen de Longespee and the chief of the O'Neils, in which the latter and 352 of his men were slain. Edward Bruce, in his invasion of Ulster, in 1315, having marched hither, plundered and destroyed the abbey, and burnt part of the town: he again plundered the town three years afterwards, and on that occasion caused himself to be proclaimed King of Ireland at the cross near the cathedral. To subdue the opposition raised by the wealthy abbots of this district, under Primate Cromer, against the spiritual supremacy of Hen. VIII., Lord Grey, then lord-deputy, marched with a powerful army into Lecale, took Dundrum and seven other castles, and in May 1538, having defaced the monuments of the three patron saints and perpetrated other acts of sacrilege, set fire to the cathedral and the town; three years afterwards, this act was made one of the charges on which he was impeached and beheaded. On the surrender of the abbey in 1539, its possessions, with those of the other religious establishments in the town, were granted to Gerald, eleventh Earl of Kildare. In 1552, the town was plundered and partially destroyed by Con O'Neil, Earl of Tyrone; and two years afterwards it was assaulted by his son Shane, who destroyed its gates and ramparts. During the war of 1641, the Protestants of the surrounding district having fled hither for protection, the town was attacked by the Irish under the command of Col. Bryan O'Neil, who burnt a magnificent castle erected by Lord Okeham, and committed a great slaughter of the townsmen; many that escaped were afterwards massacred at Killyleagh.

The town is built upon a group of little hills, on the south shore of the western branch of Lough Cone or Strangford Lough, and consists of four principal streets rising with a steep ascent from the market-place in the centre, and intersected by several smaller streets and lanes: on the eastern side the hills rise abruptly behind it, commanding views of a fertile and well-cultivated tract abounding with richly diversified and picturesque scenery. It is divided according to ancient usage into three districts, called respectively the English, Irish, and Scottish quarters, and contains about 900 houses, most of which are well built: the streets are well paved, and were first lighted with oil in 1830; and the inhabitants are amply supplied with water. An ancient ferry across the western arm of Strangford lough connected this town with the neighbourhood to the north until a bridge was erected about one mile from the town, with a tower gate-house upon it, which was destroyed and the bridge itself greatly damaged in 1641. A public library and news-room was erected by subscription in 1825; and races are held in July alternately with Hillsborough, under charter of Jas. II., on an excellent course one mile south of the town. The members of the Down Hunt hold their annual meetings in a handsome building in English-street, called the County Rooms, which is also used for county meetings, &c. The barracks are an extensive and convenient range of buildings, formerly the old gaol, in which a detachment of two companies from the garrison at Belfast is placed. The only article of maufacture is that of linen, principally yard wide, for the West Indies and the English market, and drills for Scotland, in which about 700 weavers, are employed. There are two ale breweries in the town. On the banks of the Quoile, one mile distant, are excellent quays, where vessels of 100 tons' burden come in from Strangford lough: the principal imports are iron, coal, salt, timber, bark, and general merchandise: the exports are wheat, barley, oats, cattle, pigs, potatoes, and kelp. Formerly the tide flowed up close to the town, but in 1745 an embankment was constructed across the Quoile water, one mile distant, by the Rt. Hon. Edward Southwell, lord of the manor, which restrained it to that point, and about 500 acres of land were recovered: this embankment was swept away by a storm, and a second was formed by Lord de Clifford, with floodgates, &c., but after much rain a considerable portion of meadow land in the neighbourhood of the town is yet inundated. The market is on Saturday; it is large and well supplied with provisions of all kinds, and with pedlery. Brown linen webs were formerly sold on the market day in the linen hall, but the sale has of late much declined. The market-house is an old low building, containing some good upper rooms, in which the petty sessions are held and the public business of the town is transacted. Fairs are held annually on the second Thursday in January, March 17th, May 19th, June 22nd, Oct. 29th, and Nov. 19th. This is a chief constabulary police station, with a force consisting of one officer, one constable, and seven men.

Downpatrick had a corporation at an early period, the existence of which is recognised in 1403, when letters of protection were granted to it by Hen. IV., under the title of the "Mayor, Bailiffs, and Commonalty of the city of Down, in Ulster." The borough returned two members to the Irish parliament so early as 1585: this privilege was exercised till the union, since which they have returned one member to the Imperial parliament. The right of election was vested in the pot-wallopers, but under an act of the 35th of Geo. III. it was limited to the resident occupiers of houses of the annual value of £5 and upwards, who have registered twelve months before the election: the number of qualifying tenements under the old law was estimated at about 650. The act of the 2nd of Wm. IV., cap. 88, caused no alteration in the franchise or in the limits of the borough, which is co-extensive with the demesne of Down, containing 1486 statute acres: the number of voters registered, in 1835, was 525. The seneschal appointed by the lord of the manor is the returning officer. The manor, which is the property of David Ker, Esq., is very ancient, its existence being noticed in a record dated 1403. A patent of it was granted to Lord Cromwell by Jas. I., in 1617, whereby sundry monasteries, lands, and tenements, including the demesne of Down, were erected into the manor of Downpatrick: the manorial court, in which the process is either by attachment or civil bill, is held by the seneschal every third Tuesday, and has jurisdiction to the amount of £10 over 67 townlands in the parishes of Downpatrick, Saul, Ballee, Bright, Ballyculter, and Inch. The seneschal holds a court leet for the manor in spring and at Michaelmas. Petty sessions are held every Thursday: the assizes for the county are held alternately here and at Newry; and the county quarter sessions for the division of Downpatrick are held here in March and October. The county hall, or court-house, which was considerably enlarged and improved in 1834, occupies an elevated site in English-street; it is a large and handsome edifice, consisting of a centre and two wings, approached by a fine flight of stone steps; the centre is appropriated to the criminal court, the eastern wing to the civil court, and in the western are preserved the county records, &c.; it also contains a suite of assembly-rooms. The county gaol is a very commodious building, erected in 1830 at an expense of £60,000, and occupying an area of one acre and a half: the internal arrangements and management are calculated to carry into the best effect the improved system of prison discipline, and have been recommended as a model for similar establishments by the inspector-general of prisons.

Arms of the Bishoprick.

The SEE of DOWN is supposed to have originated in the abbey founded here by St. Patrick, but St. Carlan is said to have been the first bishop. Its early prelates are called Bishops of Dundalethglass, but it is probable that this see was generally included in the diocese of Connor, prior to the episcopacy of Malachy O'Morgair, who became bishop in 1137, and separated it from Connor; his immediate successors are called bishops of Ulster by some historians. John Cely was the last bishop who, in modern times, held the bishoprick of Down separate from that of Connor: he was deprived of it for his crimes and excesses in 1441. Archbishop Prene recommended William Bassett, a Benedictine monk, to the Pope, as a successor to Cely, but the pope added this see to that of Connor, and they have remained united to the present time. John, the first bishop of Down and Connor, was not, however, allowed to enjoy his united bishopricks in peace; for Thomas Pollard claimed to be Bishop of Down, and is supposed to have been supported by the archbishop, but lost his cause in 1449. John was fined shortly before his death for not appearing upon summons in Parliament. Bishop Tiberius, who is stated to have very much beautified the cathedral, was succeeded, about 1526, by Robert Blyth, abbot of Thorney, in Cambridgeshire, who held these bishopricks in commendam, and resided in England. The last bishop before the Reformation was Eugene Magenis, who was advanced to these sees by Pope Paul III.; and although John Merriman, chaplain to Queen Elizabeth, was consecrated bishop in 1568, the pope appointed Miler Magragh to the united see: he, however, never had possession of the temporalties, and subsequently becoming a Protestant was made Archbishop of Cashel. John Tod, who had been educated at Rome, but had renounced popery, was nominated bishop by Jas. I., in 1604, and held the see of Dromore in commendam: he was tried before the High Commission Court, which deprived him of the bishopricks, and afterwards poisoned himself in London. From 1660 to 1667 these sees were held by the celebrated Jeremy Taylor, who had also the administration of the see of Dromore, and was a privy counsellor and Vice Chancellor of the University of Dublin. Bishop Hutchinson, whose episcopacy commenced in 1720, hād the church catechism translated into Irish, and printed in English and Irish, primarily for the use of the inhabitants of Rathlin, and hence it is called the Rathlin Catechism. Under the Church Temporalities Act, when either the bishoprick of Down and Connor, or of Dromore, becomes vacant, Dromore is to be added to Down and Connor, and the surviving bishop is to take the title of Bishop of Down, Connor, and Dromore, and the temporalities of the see of Dromore are to be vested in the Ecclesiastical Commissioners. The diocese is one of the ten that constitute the ecclesiastical province of Armagh: it comprehends part of the county of Antrim, and the greater part of Down, extending 52 British miles in length by about 28 in breadth, and comprises an estimated area of 201,950 acres, of which, 800 are in Antrim and 201,150 in Down. The gross annual revenue of the see of Down, on an average of three years ending Dec. 31st, 1831, amounted to £2830. 16. 8½.; and there are 6411 acres of profitable land belonging to the diocese. The entire revenue of the united sees of Down and Connor averages £5896 per annum, and the see lands comprise 30,244 statute acres. The chapter consists of a dean, archdeacon, precentor, and treasurer, and the two prebendaries of St. Andrew's and Dunsford. The abbey founded by St. Patrick appears to have been the first cathedral of this see; it was several times plundered and burnt by the Danes. It was repaired by Malachy O'Morgair, in 1137, and by Malachy III., aided by John de Courcy, in 1176, and was burnt in 1315 by Lord Edward Bruce. Having been repaired or rebuilt, it was again burnt, in 1538, by Lord Leonard de Grey. In 1609, Jas. I. changed the name of the cathedral from St. Patrick's to the Holy Trinity, which was its original designation; and on account of its being in a ruinous condition, Chas. II., in 1663, erected the church of Lisburn into a cathedral and bishop's see for the diocese of Down and Connor. It continued in ruins till the year 1790, when it was restored by a grant of £1000 from Government and liberal subscriptions from the nobility and gentry of the county; and in the same year a rent-charge of £300 late currency on the tithes of the ancient union was appropriated by act of parliament for its repairs and for the support of an organist, three vicars choral, and six choristers. It is situated on an eminence to the west of the town, and is a stately embattled edifice chiefly of unhewn stone, supported externally by buttresses, and comprising a nave, choir, and aisles, with a lofty square tower at the west end, embattled and pinnacled, and smaller square towers at each corner of the east gable, in one of which is a spiral stone staircase leading to the roof. The aisles are separated from the nave by lofty elegant arches resting on massive piers, from the corbels of which spring ribs supporting the roof, which is richly groined and ornamented at the intersections with clusters of foliage. The lofty windows of the aisles are divided by a single mullion; the nave is lighted by a long range of clerestory windows, and the choir by a handsome east window divided by mullions into twelve compartments, which appears to be the only window remaining of the splendid edifice erected in 1412, and destroyed by Lord de Grey. Over the east window are three elegant niches with ogee pointed arches, containing on pedestals the remains of the mutilated effigies of St. Patrick, St. Bridget, and St. Columbkill. The choir is handsomely fitted up with stalls for the dignitaries. The cathedral was opened for the performance of divine service, after its restoration in 1817: the tower was completed in 1829, at an expense of £1900. It contains a monument to the memory of Edward Cromwell, Baron Okeham, who was proprietor of nearly all Lecale, and who died and was buried here in 1607; and another to his grandson Oliver, Earl of Ardglass, who was interred in 1668. The cathedral service is not performed, the building being used rather as a second parish church. The consistorial court of the united diocese is at Lisburn: it consists of a vicar-general, two surrogates, a registrar, deputy-registrar, and several proctors. The registrars are keepers of the records of the united diocese, which consist of the documents relating to the see lands, benefices, inductions, and wills, the earliest of which is dated 1650. The number of parishes in the diocese is 43, which are comprehended in 37 benefices, of which 6 are in the patronage of the Crown, 2 in that of the Lord-Primate, 12 in that of the Bishop, 1 in the gift of the Provost and Fellows of Trinity College, Dublin, 13 in lay patronage, and the remainder are perpetual curacies, in the gift of the incumbents of the parishes out of which they have been formed. The number of churches is 40, and there are 2 other episcopal places of worship, and 25 glebe-houses.

In the R. C. divisions this diocese is united as in the Established Church, forming the bishoprick of Down and Connor: in the Bishoprick of Down are 18 parochial districts, containing 37 chapels served by 28 clergymen, 18 of whom are parish priests and 10 coadjutors or curates. The cathedral of the united diocese is at Belfast, where the R. C. bishop resides.

The parish comprises, according to the Ordnance survey, 11,484½ statute acres, of which 125 are water, and there is neither waste land nor bog within its limits; the land is very fertile, and, with the exception of some marshes, is all arable, and in an improved state of cultivation. There are several quarries of rubble stone, which is used principally for building. The scenery is enriched with numerous gentlemen's seats, of which the principal are Hollymount, the beautiful residence of Col. Forde, situated in an extensive demesne, richly planted and well watered; Ballykilbeg House, the residence of J. Brett Johnston, Esq.; and Vianstown, of Mrs. Ward. About two miles from the town is the beautiful lake of Ballydugan; and near it is Ballydugan House, memorable as the residence of Col. White, who was murdered, and the mansion burnt in the war of 1641. The living is a rectory, in the diocese of Down, formerly united, by royal charter in the 7th of James I., to the rectories of Saul, Ballyculter, Ballee, Bright, and Tyrella, which together constituted the union and corps of the deanery of Down; but under the provisions of the Church Temporalities Act, the ancient union has been dissolved, and by act of council, in 1834, the rectories of Down and Tyrella, seven townlands in the parish of Ballee, one in that of Kilclief, and four in that of Bright, have been made to constitute the incumbency and corps of the deanery, which is in the patronage of the Crown. The gross income of the present deanery amounts to £1554. 15. 11½., of which £1078. 11. 3. is paid by the parish of Down, £164. 15. 9. by that of Tyrella; £6. 6. is the rental of a small glebe of 1*a.* 0*r.* 7*p.*; £146. 7. is received from the townlands of Ballee; £148. 2. 8½. from those of Bright, and £10. 13. 3. from that of Kilclief. Out of this income the dean pays £6 to the diocesan schoolmaster, £12. 16. for proxies, a quit-rent of £7. 9. 4½., £100 to a curate, &c., £100 for a residence (there being no deanery or glebe-house), and £127. 7. 10½. as a contribution to the cathedral. The parish church, a neat edifice in the Grecian style, was rebuilt on an enlarged scale in 1735, partly at the expense of Mr. Southwell, lord of the manor, and the Rev. — Daniel, then Dean of Down; it was repaired and newly roofed in 1760 and the Ecclesiastical Commissioners have lately granted £200 for its further repair. The R. C. parish is co-extensive with that of the Established Church, and contains two chapels, one in the town (built in 1790) and the other at Ballykilbeg, three miles distant. There are also two places of worship for Presbyterians, one in connection with the Synod of Ulster (completed in 1827, at an expense of £900, and now about to be enlarged), and of the second class; and the other with the presbytery of Antrim of the first class; and one each for Wesleyan Methodists, Methodists of the new connection, and Primitive Methodists.

The diocesan school, founded in the 12th of Elizabeth, appears to have fallen into decay until the year 1823, when it was united to that of Dromore, and an excellent school-room and residence for the master were erected at the end of Saul-street, in this town, in 1829, at an expense of £1000, defrayed by the county at large, on a site given by Lord de Clifford. It is free to all boys of both dioceses, and is endowed with £50 per annum from the diocese of Dromore, and £40 from that of Down, of which one-third is paid by the bishops and two-thirds by the clergymen, being a per centage on the net value of their livings; it is also further supported by a contribution of £10. 10. per ann. from the lay impropriators, a rent-charge of £20 on the estate of the late Lord de Clifford, and the rental of the land on which the school premises at Dromore were situated, amounting to £4. 4. The master is appointed by the lord-lieutenant, on the recommendation of the bishop. A parochial school conducted on the Lancasterian plan, and an infants' school, established in 1832, are supported by voluntary contributions; in connection with the Presbyterian meeting-house of the Synod of Ulster, is a large school-house for girls, and the trustees intend immediately to erect another for boys; at Hollymount are schools for boys and girls, supported by Lady Harriet Forde; and there are other day and Sunday schools supported by subscription. The number of children on the books of these day schools is 646, namely, 440 boys and 206 girls; and in the private pay schools are 340 boys and 200 girls. On a gentle eminence, a short distance southward from the town, stands the county infirmary, a large and handsome building erected in 1832, comprising a centre and two wings, which extend rearward, and containing 11 wards, in which are 40 beds, 20 for males and 20 for females. Near it is the fever hospital, also a large and well-arranged building, erected in the same year, and divided into 8 wards, containing 20 beds: these two buildings cost £6500. In English-street is an hospital founded in 1731 by the Rt. Hon. Edward Southwell, ancestor of the late Lord de Clifford, who endowed it with £237 per ann. payable out of the lands of Listonder and Ballydyan, in the parish of Kilmore, now the property of David Ker, Esq. The building, which is of brick, underwent a thorough repair in 1826, at an expense of £1000, defrayed by Lord de Clifford: it comprises a centre and two wings, the former occupied as an asylum for six aged men and six aged women, who have two rooms and a garden and £5 per ann. each; and the latter as schools for ten boys and ten girls, who are clothed and educated for four years, and receive £3 per ann. each towards their support, and on leaving the school at the age of 15 are apprenticed: the schoolmaster receives a salary of £15, with house, garden, and fuel, and the schoolmistress £12, with similar advantages. In the same street are four good houses for clergymen's widows of the diocese, of which two were founded in 1730 by the Rev. H. Leslie, Rev. J. Mathews, and Rev. J. Hamilton, who endowed them with £40 per annum from lands in Ballybranagh; and two in 1750, by the Rev. Edward Mathews, D. D., who endowed them with £42 per ann. from lands in Tubermony, Grangetown, and Ballywarren, all in this parish: the management is vested in the Dean and Chapter. John Brett, Esq., in 1810, bequeathed £300 in trust, the interest to be distributed annually among the poor of the town. A society for clothing the poor in winter, and a mendicity society for assisting the aged and infirm and preventing vagrancy, have been established. Besides the abbey founded by St. Patrick, there were, prior to the dissolution, a priory of regular canons, called the priory of the Irish, founded in honour of St. Thomas, in 1138, by Malachy O'Morgair, Bishop of Down; the priory of St. John the Baptist, called the priory of the English, founded by John de Courcy for crossbearers of the order of St. Augustine; an abbey of Cistercian monks, founded in the 12th century by — Bagnal, and a Cistercian nunnery, of both which no further particulars have been recorded; a Franciscan friary, founded about 1240 by Hugh de Lacy, or, according to some writers, by Africa, daughter of Godred, King of Man, and wife of John de Courcy; and an hospital for lepers, dedicated to St. Nicholas, which in 1413 was, with the hospital of St. Peter at Kilclief, granted in trust to certain individuals by royal charter: there are no remains of these ancient establishments, even their sites can scarcely be distinctly traced. There are several forts and raths in the parish; the most noted are the large rath or *doon* near the cathedral, which gave name to the town and county, and one at Ballykilbeg, finely planted by J. B. Johnston, Esq. In 1825, the head and horns of an elk of large size, the latter measuring 5 feet 11 inches between their extremities, and the head of a spear, were found in a marl-pit near the town. The celebrated Duns Scotus was born here in 1274: he was educated at Oxford, and in 1307 was appointed Regent of Divinity in the schools of Paris; his works are very voluminous. For a discription of the Struel wells, see the county article.

DOWNS, a village, in the parish of KILCOOLE, barony of NEWCASTLE, county of WICKLOW, and province of LEINSTER, 12 miles (N.) from Newtown-Mount-Kennedy; containing 171 inhabitants and 35 houses, the greater part of which are small thatched tenements. It has a station of the constabulary police; and fairs are held on Jan. 12th, May 4th, Aug. 5th, and Nov. 12th, chiefly for cattle and pigs. Here are the ruins of an old church. The "Glen of the Downs" is described under the head of Delgany.

DOWRY, or DOWRIE, a parish, in the barony of BUNRATTY, county of CLARE, and province of MUNSTER, 1¼ mile (E.) from Ennis, on the road from Clare to Spancel hill; containing 2099 inhabitants. It comprises 3684 statute acres, as applotted under the tithe act, and consists chiefly of arable and pasture land of second and third rate quality: there are about 800 acres of bog, and a considerable portion of limestone crag. Sea-weed and sand brought up the river Fergus are much used for manure. The seats are Moriesk, the finely wooded demesne of the Rt. Hon. Lord Fitzgerald and Vesci; Well-Park, that of the Rt. Rev. Dr. McMahon, R. C. Bishop of Killaloe; Castle Fergus, of W. Smith Blood, Esq., and Tuoreem, of W. O'Connell, Esq. The parish is in the diocese of Killaloe; the rectory is part of the union of Ogashin, and the vicarage of that of Quinn: the tithes amount to £217. 11. 6¼., of which, £102. 9. 3. is payable to the rector, £92. 6. 1¾. to the vicar, and £23. 1. 6½. to the prebendary of Tullagh. In the R. C. divisions it forms part of the union or district of Kilraghtis: the chapel is a small thatched building, but a new and very handsome structure is about to be erected on another site. A school supported by Mr. Howley having been lately discontinued, it is in contemplation to establish another on a more general plan.

DOWTH, a parish, in the barony of UPPER SLANE, county of MEATH, and province of LEINSTER, 3 miles (S. E.) from Slane, on the river Boyne; containing 362 inhabitants. This parish, which comprises about 1600 statute acres, was a principal scene of the battle of the Boyne, and is the residence of the Netterville family, the head of which was ennobled by Jas. I., with the title of Viscount Netterville of Dowth. The mansion called Dowth is in a demesne of more than 300 statute acres, in which is a large rath, also an extensive tumulus containing subterraneous passages in which a number of human and other bones have been found. The parish is in the diocese of Meath; the rectory is partly impropriate in W. D. Pollard, Esq., and partly appropriate to the vicarage of St. Mary, Drogheda; the vicarage forms part of the union of Duleek. The tithes amount to £92. 6. 2., and the glebe comprises 19½ acres, valued at £30 per annum. The late Lord Netterville left 60 acres of land for the support of six aged women and six orphan boys: the castle built by Hugh de Lacy has been altered and repaired for their accommodation, and also for a school supported out of the same bequest. A considerable part of the old church remains: it was the burial-place of the Netterville family, and contains a monument of the late lord. Here is a cromlech, consisting of four large upright stones, with several others lying near.

DOWTHSTOWN, or DOUTHSTOWN, also called DOWESTOWN, a parish, in the barony of SKREEN, county of MEATH, and province of LEINSTER, 3½ miles (S. by E.) from Navan, on the river Boyne and the mail coach road from Dublin to Enniskillen; containing 283 inhabitants. It is a vicarage, in the diocese of Meath, forming part of the union of Skreen; the rectory is impropriate in P. Metge, Esq. The tithes amount to £62, of which £41. 6. 8. is payable to the impropriator, and £20. 13. 4. to the vicar. The Hon. Gen. Taylor has a seat in the cottage style in a demesne of about 590 statute acres, of which about 240 are plantations.

DRAKESTOWN, a parish, in the barony of MORGALLION, county of MEATH, and province of LEINSTER, 3¾ miles (S.) from Nobber, on the road from Navan to Kingscourt; containing 982 inhabitants. It comprises 6582 statute acres, as applotted under the tithe act: the land is mostly in pasture, the surrounding country being generally good grazing land. It is a rectory, in the diocese of Meath, and is part of the union of Castletown-Kilpatrick: the tithes amount to £188. 3. 2., and there is a glebe of 4 acres, valued at £28 per annum. The R. C. parish is co-extensive with that of the Established Church. About 40 boys are educated in a private school.

DRANGAN, a parish, in the barony of MIDDLETHIRD, county of Tipperary, and province of MUNSTER, 4½ miles (N. E.) from Fethard; containing 1804 inhabitants. It comprises 5300 statute acres of tolerably good arable and pasture land, as applotted under the tithe act; and is a rectory and vicarage, in the diocese of Cashel, forming part of the union of Killenaule: the tithes amount to £325. In the R. C. divisions the parish forms part of the union or district of Cloneen; the chapel is a plain building. There are four pay schools, in which are about 150 boys and 170 girls; and in the village is a constabulary police station.

DRAPERSTOWN, or CROSS of BALLYNASCREEN, a market and post-town, in the parish of BALLYNASCREEN, barony of LOUGHINSHOLIN, county of LONDONDERRY, and province of ULSTER, 30 miles (S. E. by S.) from Londonderry, and 101 (N. by W.) from Dublin, on the road from Newtown-Stewart to Tubbermore; containing 412 inhabitants. In 1818, its name was changed from Cross to Draperstown, in consequence of its principally belonging to the Drapers' Company, under whose auspices a spacious market-house, hotel, and dispensary for their tenants, with surgeon's residence, are being built, chiefly in the Elizabethan style, and of freestone. The market is on Wednesday; and a fair for general farming stock is held on the first Friday in each month, and was established in 1792. The post-office is under Tubbermore, from which it is three miles distant; and here is a constabulary police station. The parochial church and school are situated in the town, and there is a general dispensary. — See BALLYNASCREEN.

DREENY.—See DRINAGH, county of CORK.

DREHIDTARSNA, or DREHEDHARSNIE, also called DROGHETARSNEY, a parish, in the barony of COSHMA, county of LIMERICK, and province of MUNSTER, 2 miles (S. W. by S.) from Adare; containing 358 inhabitants. This parish comprises 722 statute acres, as applotted under the tithe act, exclusively of the townland of Drehidtarsna, which is tithe-free: the land is of superior quality and well cultivated. It is a rectory and vicarage, in the diocese of Limerick; the rectory is part of the union and corps of the prebend of St. Munchin in the cathedral of St. Mary, Limerick: the vicarage is in the gift of the Prebendary. The tithes amount to £64. 12. 3½., of which £43. 1. 6. is payable to the prebendary, and the remainder to the vicar, who also receives £68 late currency from Primate Boulter's fund. The glebe-house was erected in 1828, on a glebe of 19 acres. The church is a small edifice with a tower; and on Sunday evenings a lecture is delivered in the glebe-house. In the R. C. divisions it is part of the union of Adare. The parochial schools are chiefly supported by the vicar and the Earl of Dunraven.

DRIMNAGH, or DRIMNA, formerly a parish, in the barony of Uppercross, county of Dublin, and province of Leinster, 2 miles (W. S. W.) from Dublin, on the road to Naas and on the Grand Canal. This ancient parish has merged into that of Clondalkin. There is a paper-mill at Lansdowne Valley; and near the Blue Bell is a woollen factory, at which coarse cloths are manufactured. In the direction of Crumlin stands Drimna Castle, formerly the head of a manor, of which the Barnewall family were lords from the time of John to that of Jas. I., and which was a place of some consequence in the reign of Chas. I. It is the property of the Marquess of Lansdowne, and is an irregular pile, occupied by Mr. E. Cavanagh. The church is in ruins. In the R. C. divisions it is part of the district of Lucan, Palmerstown, and Clondalkin.

DRIMOLEAGUE.—See DROMDALEAGUE.

DRIMTEMPLE, a parish, partly in the half-barony of Ballymoe, county of Galway, and partly in the other half-barony of Ballymoe, county of Roscommon, and province of Connaught, 4 miles (S. E. by S.) from Castlerea, on the road to Roscommon; containing 2383 inhabitants. It is surrounded by bog, and consists principally of pasture, although there is a considerable quantity of arable land. The seats are Dundermott, the residence of R. Blakeney, Esq.; Laragh, of Martin Connor, Esq.; Leabeg, of H. Browne, Esq.; Tenny Park, of T. T. Byrne, Esq.; Currisdoona, of F. T. Byrne, Esq.; and Bopeep Lodge, of H. French, Esq. In the village of Ballymoe are two mills, worked by Mr. Hurley, one grinding 100 tons of oatmeal, and the other 2000 barrels of wheat into flour annually. Petty sessions every Friday, and a fair on Feb, 1st, are held there. It is a vicarage, in the diocese of Elphin, forming part of the union of Oran; the rectory is impropriate in the Earl of Essex. The tithes amount to £133. 6. 8., of which £100 is payable to the impropriator and £33. 6. 8. to the vicar. The church for the union is at Ballymoe, and was built in 1832 by aid of a gift of £900 from the late Board of First Fruits. In the R. C. divisions it forms part of the union or district of Ballintobber, and has a chapel at Ballymoe, a good slated building which cost £500. There are two public schools, in which about 60, and four private schools, in which about 170, children are educated. At Cloonadera are a fine Danish fort and a chalybeate spa.

DRINAGH, or DREENY, a parish, partly in the Western Division of the barony of East Carbery, but chiefly in the Eastern Division of West Carbery, county of Cork, and province of Munster, 3 miles (S.) from Dunmanway, on the road from that place to Clonakilty; containing 4231 inhabitants.. This parish comprises 12,449½ statute acres, of which 5696 are applotted under the tithe act, and are valued at £4926 per ann.: there is about an equal portion of arable and pasture land, 4000 acres are reclaimable bog and mountain, and the remainder rocky mountain and irreclaimable bog. Great improvements have been recently made in agriculture by the opening of new lines of road. There are two lakes, the larger of which forms a boundary between the two baronies. The living is a vicarage, in the diocese of Cork, and in the patronage of the Bishop; the rectory is appropriate to the vicars choral of the cathedral of St. Finbarr, Cork. The tithes amount to £483, half of which is payable to the appropriators and half to the vicar. There is a glebe of 7 acres. The church is a small neat edifice, in the early English style, erected in 1818, by aid of a gift of £900 from the late Board of First Fruits. In the R. C. divisions the parish forms part of the union or district of Dromdaleague, and contains a chapel. In the parochial school, principally supported by the vicar, and in another school, which has a grant of £26 per annum, about 80 children are educated, and in five private schools about 330. At Kilronan are some valuable lands granted by Chas. II. to the see of Dublin. Here are the ruins of an old church, erected by the Knights Templars.

DRINAGH, a parish, in the barony of Forth, county of Wexford, and province of Leinster, 1½ mile (S. E.) from Wexford, on the southern shore of Wexford haven; containing 451 inhabitants. It comprises 1791 statute acres, chiefly under an improved system of tillage. Limestone is quarried near the shore of the harbour, and more than 20,000 tons are annually shipped. The seats are Somerset, that of G. Walker, Esq.; and Hermitage, of A. Meadows, Esq. It is in the diocese of Ferns, and is a rectory, forming part of the union of St. Patrick's, Wexford: the tithes amount to £90. 4. 0½. The ruins of the church exist in the ancient burial-ground. In the R. C. divisions it forms part of the district of Piercestown.

DRISHANE, a parish, partly in the detached portion of the barony of Magonihy, county of Kerry, and partly in the barony of Duhallow, but chiefly in that of West Muskerry, county of Cork, and province of Munster, on the road from Cork to Killarney, containing, with the town of Millstreet, 7036 inhabitants. It comprises 32,169 statute acres, as applotted under the tithe act, and valued at £12,635. 16. 9. per ann. About a seventh part of the land is fertile and well cultivated, but the greater part consists of mountain pasture and bog: much of the former, however, affords good herbage for large herds of cattle and goats; and a considerable part of the district of Kladach, containing about 2200 acres of rough moorland, might be reclaimed at a moderate expense. Slate is found in several places, also white clay of a tenacious quality; and near Drishane Castle is a bed of good limestone. The gentlemen's seats are Drishane Castle, the residence of H. Wallis, Esq.; Coole House, of H. O'Donnell, Esq.; Mount Leader, of H. Leader, Esq.; Rathduane, of J. E. McCarty, Esq.; Coomlagane, of J. McCarthy O'Leary, Esq.; Coole, of H. O'Donnell, Esq.; and the glebe-house, of the Rev. F. Cooper. The parish is in the diocese of Ardfert; the rectory is impropriate in the Earl of Donoughmore, and the vicarage was united, in 1760, to that of Nohoval-daly, together forming the union of Drishane, in the patronage of the Bishop. The tithes amount to £630, and are equally divided between the impropriator and the vicar; the tithes of the benefice amount to £455. There is a glebe-house with a glebe of 26 acres. The church, situated in Millstreet, is a large edifice with a square tower, in the Gothic style; A grant of £112. 17. 6. has been recently made by the Ecclesiastical Board for its repair. In the R. C. divisions it is the head of the union or district of Millstreet, which also comprises the greater part of the parish of Cullen: the chapel is at Millstreet, and there is also a chapel at Cullen. The parochial school, in Millstreet, is supported by H. Wallis, Esq., and the vicar. A school-house is about to be erected at Coomlegan, for which Mrs. McCarty, of Glyn, in 1811, bequeathed two acres of land and £40 per annum. There are also two private schools, and the number of children educated in the parish is about 150. Drishane Castle, which is in good repair, was erected by Dermot McCarty in 1436: his descendant, Donagh McCarty, was engaged in the war of 1641, by which he forfeited the estate: in the demesne are the ruins of the old parochial church. Of Kilmeedy castle, which was built by one of the McCarty family, in 1445, to command the wild mountain pass from Macroom to Killarney, the ruins still remain in the valley, near the mail coach road.—See MILLSTREET.

Seal.

DROGHEDA, a sea-port, borough, and market-town, and a county of itself, locally in the county of LOUTH, and province of LEINSTER, 57 miles (S by W.) from Belfast, and 23 (N.) from Dublin; containing 17,365 inhabitants, of which number, 15,138 are in the town. This place is said to have derived its name *Droighad Atha*, in the Irish language signifying "a bridge," from the erection of a bridge over the river Boyne, at a period prior to the English invasion; but no notice of any town of importance occurs till after that event. At a very early period, a monastery was founded here for canons of the order of St. Augustine. It was included in the original grant of Meath to Hugh de Lacy; but in 1220, when a new grant of that lordship was made to his son Walter, by Hen. III., the town and castle of Drogheda had become of so much importance, that the king retained them in his own possession, allowing to De Lacy £20 per ann. from the Exchequer, and the talliage of the town, as a compensation. At that time the Boyne, which now intersects the town, formed the boundary between the counties of Meath and Louth, and the two portions of the town on its opposite banks constituted separate boroughs. In 1229, Hen. III., by charter, gave to the town on the Louth side of the Boyne certain privileges and free customs similar to those of Dublin; and in 1247, the same monarch invested the burgesses of the town on the Meath side with similar privileges and inmunities, and granted them a weekly market and an annual fair for six days. A new charter was granted in 1253 to the burgesses of Drogheda in Louth, empowering them to elect a mayor, to exercise exclusive jurisdiction, and to hold an annual fair for 15 days: but the increase of the town was soon checked by the continued aggressions of the native inhabitants of the surrounding districts. In the 7th and 24th of Edw. I., the town received grants of toll for murage; and in 1316, the king granted 300 marks for the repair of the walls and turrets. In 1317, the burgesses of Drogheda in Meath obtained a new charter for a weekly market, with the grant of a piece of ground on which to hold the same, and the decision of all pleas except those of the crown. Mandates were issued, in 1319 and 1320, by the king to his justiciary in Ireland, to protect the mayor and burgesses of the town in Louth in the enjoyment of their liberties, and to grant remission of their fee farm rent of 60 marks per ann., to enable them to extend their fortifications. In 1375, a mayor of the staple was appointed for both towns; but the calamity of pestilence, added to that of almost incessant warfare with the Scots and native septs, had so reduced the burgesses that, in 1380, Rich. II., granted to them certain customs' duties for the repair of the fortifications and the general improvement of the town.

This place, from an early period was, in municipal privileges and political consequence, always considered as on an equality with the four royal cities of Dublin, Waterford, Limerick, and Cork; and of the numerous parliaments assembled by the lords-deputies, some of the most remarkable were held here. Rich. II., on the 16th of March, 1394, in the hall of the Dominican priory received the submission of O'Nial, O'Hanlon, O'Donel, Mac Mahon, and other native chieftains of Ulster. In 1407, the inhabitants united with those of Dublin in a predatory warfare against their commom enemies, which they extended even to the coast of Scotland. Hen. IV., towards the close of his reign, united the two boroughs into one body politic. In 1437, part of the fee-farm rent was remitted by Hen. VI., on account of the devastation of the town and the injury of its trade by the king's enemies. The Earl of Ormonde, on being removed from the office of chief governor, in 1444, assembled the nobility and gentry of the English pale at this place; and so strong were the testimonies in his favour, that he was reinstated in his office. A parliament was soon afterwards held here; another was also held in the 31st of Hen. VI., and, in 1467, a parliament assembled at Dublin was adjourned to this town, by which the Geraldines were attainted, and the Earl of Desmond appearing to justify himself, was instantly brought to the scaffold. In 1474, when the fraternity of arms was established, the goods of the men of Drogheda and Dublin were exempted from the tax for its support; and by the statute passed in Lord Grey's parliament, concerning the election of temporary chief governors, the mayors of Drogheda and Dublin were to have a voice in the council. In an engagement which took place at Malpas Bridge, during this reign, the mayor of Drogheda, at the head of 500 archers and 200 men armed with pole-axes, assisted in the defeat of O'Reilly and his confederates, who had committed great ravages in the county of Louth; in reward of which valiant conduct, the mayors are allowed to have a sword of state borne before them. In 1493, Lord Gormanston held a parliament here, but the validity of its proceedings was disputed; and in the 10th of Hen. VII., Sir Edward Poynings assembled another in this town, of which the acts relating to the adoption of the English statutes and other important matters have been more celebrated than those of any other parliament prior to the last century. In the succeeding reign, the importance of this place appears from the duties paid at the custom-house, which, in 1632, amounted to £1428. 15.

In 1641, it was attacked by the northern Irish in great numbers under Sir Phelim O'Nial, when a body of 600 foot and 50 horse, sent from Dublin for the relief of the garrison, was defeated at Julianstown bridge, about three miles from the town. Though Sir Henry Tichbourne, the governor, had an incompetent force, and the besieging army consisted of 20,000, yet from want of military skill, artillery, and ammunition, the latter were unable to form a regular encampment; and the siege was little more than a blockade. The town, however, was reduced to great distress from want of supplies, but the numerous assaults of the enemy were vigorously repulsed, and great numbers of their men, and several of their bravest officers were killed in the sallies of the garrison; and on intelligence of the approach of the Earl of Ormonde with a considerable force, the commander of the insurgent army raised the siege and retired towards the north. When Ormonde advanced towards Dublin against the parliamentarian governors, Col. Jones sent most of his cavalry to Drogheda, with a view to cut off Ormonde's supplies; but Lord Inchiquin coming immediately in pursuit of them, with a strong body of royalist cavalry, surprised and routed the party and laid siege to the town, which he soon obliged to surrender. After the battle of Rathmines, Col. Jones besieged the garrison placed here by the royalists, but suddenly retired on the approach of the Marquess of Ormonde with 300 men. The Marquess inspected and repaired the fortifications; and foreseeing the danger to which it would be exposed, committed the government of the town to Sir Arthur Aston, a gallant R. C. officer, with a garrison of 2000 foot and 300 horse, all chosen men and well supplied with ammunition and provisions. Cromwell, on landing at Dublin in 1649, marched with 10,000 men against Drogheda, as the most important town for opening a passage into the northern provinces; and after a siege of two days, his artillery having made a sufficient breach in the walls, the assault was commenced by his troops, who were twice repulsed; but in the third attack, headed by himself, he gained possession of the town, and in order to impress upon the Irish such a dread of his name as might prevent all opposition, gave orders to put the whole garrison to the sword: this barbarous execution was continued for five successive days, the governor and all his officers being included in the proscription, and even some ecclesiastics who were found within the town were butchered: a few of the garrison contrived to escape in disguise, and besides these only thirty were spared from the general massacre, who were instantly transported as slaves to Barbadoes.

In the war of the Revolution, this place was garrisoned by the forces of Jas. II., who had a magazine of military stores and ammunition here; and in the immediate vicinity was fought the celebrated battle of the Boyne. On the 30th of June, 1690, King William's army came within sight of the town and advanced in three columns towards the river. King James's camp extended westward from the town in two lines along its south bank. As his army was marching into camp, William advanced within cannon range of the ford at Oldbridge, to reconnoitre, and dismounted; while Berwick, Tyrconnel, Sarsfield, and some other of James's generals rode slowly along the opposite bank. On remounting, a ball from a field-piece concealed by a hedge grazed the bank of the river and taking a slanting direction struck his right shoulder, tearing his coat and slightly lacerating the flesh; but though a report of his death was quickly spread, William sustained no other injury than a difficulty in using his sword arm. A brisk cannonade was maintained from the opposite bank of the river till the approach of night; and on the following morning, William's right wing crossed the river at some fords below Slane, overpowering a regiment which had been stationed there to defend the passage, and made their way over a very unfavourable country to a morass through which the infantry passed with great difficulty, while the cavalry found a firmer passage on the right. The part of James's army stationed near the morass, astonished at their intrepidity, fled towards Duleek, suffering great loss in their flight. The central column of William's army now attempted to cross the river; the Dutch guards, followed by the Huguenots, Enniskilleners, Brandenburghers, and English, plunged into the stream near Oldbridge, in front of the enemy's lines and breastworks, checking the current by their numbers, and causing the water to rise so high that the infantry were obliged to carry their muskets above their heads. One squadron of the Brandenburghers was repulsed by General Hamilton's horse, and driven back through the river, and in their retreat threw the Huguenots into disorder; but the general's cavalry wheeling through Oldbridge were cut down by the Dutch and Enniskilleners, with the exception of a small party which encountered the Duke of Schomberg while rallying the Huguenots, wounded and made him prisoner, on which the French Protestants fired into the midst of the party and unhappily killed the Duke. The Rev. George Walker, who had so gallantly defended Londonderry, was also killed about the same time. After the conflict had continued about an hour, the Irish army retreated to Donore, where James had remained surrounded by his guards; and William, who had crossed the river, about a mile above Drogheda, with his left wing, placed himself at the head of his army; and when the enemy had advanced from Donore, almost within musket shot of his infantry, he was seen sword in hand animating his squadrons and preparing to fall on their flank. James's troops, however, halted and again retreated to Donore, but there charged with such success that the English cavalry, although commanded by William, were repulsed. The enemy was, however, bravely attacked by the Enniskilleners, supported by the Dutch, and ultimately by all the English army, and the battle was for some time maintained with equal bravery by both parties. But the Irish infantry being at last defeated, and the cavalry, after making a furious charge, routed, James and his troops retreated through the pass of Duleek. In this important battle James lost 1500 men, and William's army about one-third of that number. On the following day, King William sent Brigadier La Melloniere, with 1000 horse, a party of foot, and eight pieces of artillery, to summon Drogheda, which was defended by a garrison of 1300 men under Lord Iveagh, who, after a parley, accepted terms of capitulation, and marched out with their baggage, leaving behind them their arms, stores, and ammunition; and Col. Cutts' regiment immediately took possession of the place and preserved it from violence.

The town is advantageously situated on the great north road from Dublin to Belfast, and on the river Boyne, which discharges itself into the Irish sea about three miles below, and by which it is divided into two unequal portions, of which the larger, on the north side, is connected with the smaller by a bridge of three arches, erected in 1722. The streets are tolerably regular, and many of the houses are well built, especially those in the principal street, and on the quay, which extends along the north side of the river. The total number of houses is 2860, of which 1300 only are assessed to the rates for lighting and watching the town; for the former, which is done by a gas company established a few years since, the whole assessment amounts to £316, and for the latter to £239, per annum. The inhabitants are principally supplied with water from a well at the linen-hall; and the streets are paved and kept in repair, under the management of a committee, at the expense of the corporation, for which purpose about £230 is annually appropriated from the corporation funds. Of the ancient walls, beyond which the present town extends, the most curious and perfect portion is the gate of St. Lawrence, forming a handsome approach. A public reading and news-room has been fitted up in the Mayoralty-house, and a newspaper, called the Drogheda Journal, has been published since 1774. In Fair-street are infantry barracks, with an hospital for 20 patients; and there are similar barracks at Milmount. Adjoining the latter is Richmond Fort, erected about the year 1808, in which are two nine-pounders on a moveable platform, a guard-house, forming the entrance to the barracks, was built in 1831, and the mount on which the fort stands was at the same time further strengthened with palisades. The manufacture of coarse linen, calico, and stockings, formerly carried on to a very great extent, has, together with hand-loom weaving, very much declined. A very extensive mill for spinning flax has recently been erected by a company of proprietors, and is principally wrought by steam power. The tanning of leather was formerly carried on very extensively, and is still considerable; and the manufacture of soap and candles is also on a tolerably large scale. There are two iron foundries, several salt works, an extensive distillery, and three large breweries of ale and table beer, one of which, in James-street, belonging to Mr. Cairnes, produces ale which is in great repute, and is exported to England and the West Indies; attached to it is a very extensive malting establishment. There are several large flour and corn-mills, of which that belonging to Messrs. Smith and Smythe, with the adjoining stores, was erected at an expense of £20,000; the machinery is impelled by a steam-engine of 50-horse power, and is capable of grinding 40,000 barrels of wheat, and 60,000 barrels of oats annually.

The port carries on a very extensive trade chiefly with Canada, Nova Scotia, and New Brunswick, and also a very considerable cross-channel trade; the principal exports are corn, flour, oatmeal, cattle, butter, and linen cloth; and the chief imports are timber, slates, coal, rock-salt, iron, bark, herrings, and dried fish, with manufactured goods of all kinds. According to the returns for the year ending Jan. 5th, 1835, there were shipped from this port, 126,380 loads of meal, 42,500 bushels of wheat, 3000 barrels of peas, 37,000 sacks of flour, 2500 barrels of barley, 22,000 barrels of oats, 13,000 crates of eggs, 600 firkins of butter, 4100 cows, 12,000 sheep, 39,000 pigs, and 500 barrels of ale. The number of vessels in the foreign trade that entered inwards, during that year, was 14 British and 3 foreign, and two British vessels cleared outwards. In the trade with Great Britain and across the channel, 494 ships, including steam-vessels, entered inwards, and 462 cleared outwards; and in the trade with various ports in Ireland, 42 vessels entered inwards and 23 cleared outwards. The gross amount of the customs' duties, during the year 1835, was £9476. 19. 3., and for 1836, £13,382. 13. 2.; that of the excise duties collected in the district, in 1835, was £75,007. 19. 3½. The number of vessels registered as belonging to the port is 40, of an aggregate burden of 3763 tons. A considerable trade is carried on with Liverpool, between which place, Glasgow, and this port, five steam-packets, of about 350 tons each, are constantly plying. The harbour, for the improvement of which the Commissioners of Public Works have granted £10,000, has been rendered much more commodious, and is in a state of progressive improvement; a breakwater is about to be formed and a lighthouse erected. The river has been deepened four feet by a steam dredging vessel, calculated to raise 1000 tons hourly; it is navigable to the bridge for vessels of 200 tons', and above it for lighters of 70 tons', burden. A patent slip is also in progress of construction, and a large iron-foundry for steam machinery has been erected. The value of these improvements may be correctly estimated from the fact that, within the last seven years, the trade of the port has been more than doubled. The inland trade is also greatly facilitated by the Boyne navigation to Navan, which it is intended to extend to Lough Erne. The Grand Northern Trunk railway from Dublin, for which an act of parliament has been obtained, will enter the town at Pitcher Hill, in the parish of St. Mary. The markets are on Thursday and Saturday; and fairs for cattle of every kind, and especially for horses of superior breed, are held annually on May 12th, June 22nd, Aug. 26th, and Oct. 29th, by ancient charter; and by a recent patent also on March 10th, April 11th, Nov. 21st, and Dec. 19th, when large quantities of wool and various other articles of merchandise are exposed for sale. The corn market is a very neat and commodious building, erected after a design by the late Mr. F. Johnston. There are convenient shambles for butchers' meat, and adjacent is a fish market. The linen-hall is a spacious building of brick, containing five halls.

Besides the charters already noticed, many others were granted by different sovereigns. The two boroughs continued till the reign of Hen. IV. to be separately governed by their respective charters, and each had its separate corporate officers, from which circumstance the merchants frequenting the town were burdened with the payment of tolls and customs to both corporations, dissensions and debates were daily springing up between the two bodies, and in their contests blood was often shed and many lives were lost. To put an end to these evils, Hen. IV., by charter dated Nov. 1st, 1412, with the consent of the burgesses and commonalties, united both boroughs under one corporation, and erected the town, with the suburbs on both sides of the river, into a county of itself. Under this, which is the governing charter, the style of the corporation is the "Mayor, Sheriffs, Burgesses, and Commons of the County of the Town of Drogheda," and the government is vested in a mayor, two sheriffs, twenty-four aldermen (including the mayor), an indefinite number of common councilmen, a mayor of the staple, two coroners, recorder, town-clerk, sword-bearer, mace-bearer, water-bailiff, harbour-master, and subordinate officers. The freedom of the town is acquired by birth, or servitude of seven years' apprenticeship to a freeman of one of the seven trading guilds, and by especial grace, or gift of the corporation. The trading guilds are each under the government of a master and two wardens annually elected, and have each a common hall. The town sent members to the first Irish parliament ever held, and continued to return two members till the Union, since which time it has returned one member to the Imperial parliament. The right of election was vested in the freemen and freeholders, of whom there were about 936 previously to the passing of the act of the 2nd of Wm. IV., cap. 88, which disqualified the non-resident freemen except within seven miles, and extended the elective franchise to the £10 householders, and to £20 and £10 leaseholders, for the respective terms of 14 and 20 years. The borough is co-extensive with the county of the town, comprising an area of 5803 statute acres, of which, 844 are in a rural district in the parish of Ballymakenny, and the remainder in the parishes of St. Peter and St. Mary: the sheriffs are the returning officers. The mayor, recorder, and two senior aldermen who have served the office of mayor, are justices of the peace under the charter, and there are five additional justices appointed under the act of the 7th Geo. IV. The assizes for the county of the town are held twice in the year before the mayor and judges on the north-eastern circuit; and quarter sessions are held in Jan., April, June, and Oct., before the mayor and recorder. Petty sessions are held in the Tholsel court every alternate week; a court of record for pleas to any amount is held before the mayor and sheriffs; and a court of conscience, for the recovery of debts not exceeding £1. 3., is held every Tuesday and Friday before the mayor or his deputy. A mayoralty-house is provided in the town, as a residence for the mayor during his year of office, but it is seldom occupied. The Tholsel is a spacious and handsome building of hewn stone, well adapted to the holding of the assizes, quarter sessions, and other courts. The gaol on the north side of the town was erected in 1818; it is a neat and well-arranged building adapted to the classification of prisoners, and contains 6 wards, with day-rooms and airing-yards, apartments for debtors, and a chapel: the total expenditure, for 1835, was £379. 11. 11. The amount of Grand Jury presentments for 1835 was £1988. 4. 5¼., of which £171. 17. 11½. was for the repair of roads, bridges, &c.; £1390. 1. 1¾. for public buildings, charities, officers' salaries, and miscellaneous expenses; £8. 18. 6. for the police, and £417. 6. 10. for repayment of advances made by Government.

The town comprises the parishes of St. Peter, on the north side of the river, in the diocese of Armagh, comprising 3523 statute acres, as applotted under the tithe act; and St. Mary, on the south side, and in the diocese of Meath, containing 1435 acres, as applotted; with part of the parish of Ballymakenny. The living of each is a vicarage, in the patronage of the Marquess of Drogheda, in whom the rectories are impropriate. The tithes of St. Peter's amount to £300, payable to the impropriator: the annual income of the incumbent is £512. 2. 6., arising from certain lay tithes purchased by the late Board of First Fruits, minister's money, payment by the corporation, and rent of houses. the tithes of St. Mary's are £105, of which £31. 3. 1. is payable to the impropriator, and £73. 16. 11. to the vicar, who also receives a stipend of £30 from Evans's fund. St. Peter's church, which was rebuilt in 1753, is a handsome and substantial structure, in the Roman Doric style, with a tower surmounted by a spire, which wants a proportionate degree of elevation; it is the burial-place of the family of Moore, Marquesses of Drogheda, and contains also several handsome monuments to Lord Chief Justice Singleton, who resided in the town, John Ball, Esq., one of the king's serjeants, the Leigh and Ogle families, and others; the Ecclesiastical Commissioners have recently granted £463. 2. 3. towards its repair. The glebe-house adjoins the churchyard; there is a glebe of four acres in Drogheda, and one of 24 acres in Carlingford. St. Mary's church, a modern edifice, was erected in 1810, by a gift of £600 and a loan of £500 from the late Board of First Fruits, and the Ecclesiastical Commissioners have recently granted £175. 5. 7. towards its repair. The glebe-house, situated in the town, was purchased for the parish by the late Board in 1809, under the new acts, at a cost of £600, of which £461. 10. 9¼. was a gift, and £138. 9. 2¾. a loan: the glebe comprises five acres, valued at £20 per annum. The chapel of St. Mark, a handsome edifice, was erected as a chapel of ease to St. Peter's church; the corporation contributed £300 towards the expense, £900 was given in 1829 by the late Board of First Fruits, and the remainder was raised by local subscription: it is endowed with the rectorial tithes of Innismot, in the county of Meath, amounting to £65, by the corporation, who have transferred the patronage to the Lord-Primate, who adds £50 per annum. The R. C. parish of St. Peter is co-extensive with that of the Established Church, and is the benefice of the Archbishop; the chapel is a handsome and spacious structure, erected at an expense of more than £12,000, raised by subscription. St. Mary's is the head of a R. C. union, comprising also the parishes of Colpe and Kilsharvan, and containing two chapels, one at Drogheda, a large and handsome building, towards which Michael Duff, Esq., contributed between £4000 and £5000, and the other at Mornington, in the parish of Colpe. There are places of worship for Presbyterians and Wesleyan Methodists, the former in connection with the Seceding Synod, and of the second class: the building was erected in 1827, at an expense of £2000, towards which the corporation contributed £300. Here are three friaries, dedicated respectively to St. Francis, St. Augustine, and St. Dominick; also two convents of nuns, one dedicated to St. Dominick, and the other to the Blessed Virgin and of the order of the Presentation, both devoted to religious instruction. The Dominican or Sienna convent, beautifully situated in the environs, has a department for the instruction of young ladies, and a very elegant chapel. St. Peter's parochial school is supported by contributions, including an annual donation of £10. 10. from the corporation, and £10 from the vicar. In this parish are also one of the four classical schools under the trustees of Erasmus Smith's charity, who grant to it £280 per ann.; five other schools, one of which is in connection with the Presentation convent, a private school, and three Sunday schools; in the day schools together are about 1000 children. In the parish of St. Mary are a public school, in which are about 250, and a pay school of 70, children. An institution for the widows of Protestant clergymen was founded and endowed by Primate Boulter; and an almshouse, called the poor house of St. John, was founded by a grant from the corporation; it is a neat brick building, containing 12 apartments. An infirmary, with a dispensary, is supported by Grand Jury presentments and by corporation and parliamentary grants, at an annual cost of about £400; and a mendicity institution for which the corporation finds a house, is supported by voluntary contributions and the produce of the labour of its inmates. There is also a savings' bank. The amount of Grand Jury cess levied on the rural district of the county of the town is about £1080 per annum. The religious foundations of this place were anciently very numerous, and of several there are still some remains. On the north side of the river are those of the Augustinian priory, of which the steeple is standing; it is more generally called the old abbey, from its remote antiquity, having, it is supposed, been founded by St. Patrick, who it is said baptized his converts at a well within its precincts, which, previously to its late enclosure, bore his name; the old abbey experienced many injuries from its Irish and Danish assailants, but was rebuilt and endowed by the English in 1226. On the road leading to Collon, near the town, is a stone called Clough Patrick, or St. Patrick's stone, on which he prayed; in commemoration of which, the marks of his knees and staff were chiselled in the stone, and are yet to be traced. The hospital of St. Mary was founded early in the 13th century, for sick and infirm persons, by Ursus de Swemele, and was afterwards occupied by Crouched friars of the order of St. Augustine. The priory of St. Lawrence, near the gate of that name, is said to have been founded by the mayor and burgesses. The Dominican abbey, founded in 1224, by Lucas de Netterville, Archbishop of Armagh, afterwards became a house of great celebrity; it was proposed as the seat of an intended university, and after the dissolution was granted to Walter Dowdall and Edw. Becke. The Grey friary was founded in the 13th century, either by the family of D'Arcy or that of Plunket, and was, in 1518, reformed by the Observantine friars, and on its dissolution granted to Gerald Aylmer. The Augustine friary was founded in the reign of Edw. I., probably by the Brandon family; and there were two smaller foundations, known as the houses of St. James and St. Bennet. On the opposite side of the river was the priory or hospital of St. John, for Crouched friars, a cell to the priory of Kilmainham, supposed to have been founded by Walter de Lacy, a great part of the revenue of which was, after the dissolution, granted by Edw. VI. to James Sedgrave; and also the Carmelite friary, founded by the inhabitants, and which, with the houses of St. Mary, St. Lawrence, and the Augustinian friary, were, at the dissolution, given to the corporation. There was also a Franciscan monastery, of which the founder and history are not known. There are at present some remains of the old church of St. Mary, and of the Dominican abbey, in which was interred Patrick O'Scanlain, Archbishop of Armagh, in 1270. The abbey was dedicated to St. Mary Magdalene, and its majestic remains consist of a square tower, in the battlement of which is a breach, said to have been made by Cromwell's cannon. It was enacted by the Irish parliament, in 1465, that a university, enjoying the same privileges and immunities as that of Oxford, should be established at this place, but the design was not carried into execution. The Archbishops of Armagh formerly had a palace in the town for their accommodation while attending their parliamentary duties. Divers remains of earthworks, and traces of military operations, are still to be seen at several of the stations which were occupied by Cromwell during the parliamentary war. William of Drogheda, a writer on civil law in the 14th century, and James Miles, author of two works on religion and one on music, and who died a member of the Franciscan monastery at Naples, in 1639, were natives of this place. Drogheda gives the titles of Marquess, Earl, and Viscount, in the peerage of Ireland, to the family of Moore.

DROM, or DROMSPERANE, a parish, in the barony of ELIOGARTY, county of TIPPERARY, and province of MUNSTER, 2½ miles (S. W.) from Templemore, on the road from that place to Cashel; containing 1951 inhabitants. It comprises 4111 statute acres, and is in the diocese of Cashel; the rectory is impropriate in the Marquess of Ormonde; the vicarage forms part of the corps of the treasurership in the cathedral of St. Patrick, Cashel. The tithes amount to £221. 10. 9¼., of which £138. 9. 2¾. is payable to the impropriator, and the remainder to the vicar. In the R. C. divisions it is the head of a union or district, comprising this parish and Inch, in each of which is a chapel; that of Drom is a large handsome building, erected in 1829. There is a public school, in which about 180, and two private schools, in which about 170, children are educated. Here are some remains of the old church. A constabulary police force is stationed in the village.

DROMACOO, a parish, in the barony of DUNKELLIN, county of GALWAY, and province of CONNAUGHT, 8¾ miles (N. N. W.) from Gort, on the bay of Galway; containing 1044 inhabitants. It comprises 1723 statute acres, as applotted under the tithe act, and is in the diocese of Kilmacduagh; the rectory is partly appropriate to the see, partly to the vicars choral of Christchurch cathedral, Dublin, and partly to the prebendary of Islandeddy; the vicarage forms part of the union of Kilcolgan. The tithes amount to £53. 11., of which £12. 12. is payable to the Ecclesiastical Commissioners, £18. 18. to the vicars choral, £15. 15. to the vicar, and £6. 6. to the prebendary. In the R. C. divisions the parish, called Ballindirreen, from the place where the chapel is situated, is co-extensive with that of the Established Church. There are four private schools, in which are about 160 children. The ruins of the old church have been converted into a mausoleum for the family of

St. George, whose mansion stands in the adjoining parish of Stradbally, though part of the demesne is within the limits of this parish.

DROMAGH.—See DROUMTARIFFE.

DROMAHAIRE, a village, in the parish of DRUMLEASE, barony of DROMAHAIRE, county of LEITRIM, and province of CONNAUGHT, 8 miles (S. E. by E.) from Sligo, on the road from Collooney to Manor-Hamilton; containing 336 inhabitants. A castle was built here in early times by a chieftain of this district, called O'Rourke, and named after him, part of which still exists, but most of it was used by Sir William Villiers in the erection of the castle of Dromahaire, under a patent dated in 1626, by which 11,500 acres of land, with power to empark 2000 acres, and hold two markets, was granted to the Duke of Buckingham. Of this castle, seven massive and ornamented stacks of chimneys remain, and the lodge occupied by Mr. Stewart, agent to G. L. Fox, Esq., occupies part of its site. At Creevlea a monastery for Franciscans of the Observantine order was established, in 1508, by Margaret ny Brien, wife of O'Rourke. This building was never completed, but the walls, in which are some curious figures, are entire, and the altar is nearly so. The effigy of the great O'Rourke lies at full length on a tomb over the burial-place of his family, and there are also curious figures over the graves of the Morroghs, Cornins, and others. The village, which, together with the entire neighbourhood, has been greatly improved under the auspices of Mr. Lane Fox, contained, in 1831, 64 houses: it has a penny post to Collooney and is a constabulary police station. A market is held on Monday in a neat market-house, and a fair on the 13th of every month, and petty sessions are held on alternate Wednesdays. A dispensary is partly supported by a subscription of £20 per annum from Mr. Lane Fox. On the side of a hill are the ruins of an old church, consisting of a nave and chancel, divided by a heavy tower supported by elliptical arches. The conventual buildings, of which the foundation is attributed to St. Patrick, formed two squares contiguous to the church.

DROMARAGH, or ANNESBOROUGH, a post-town and parish, partly in the barony of KINELEARTY, partly in that of LOWER IVEAGH, but chiefly in that of UPPER IVEAGH, county of DOWN, and province of ULSTER; 5 miles (E. S. E.) from Dromore, and 72 miles (N. by E.) from Dublin, on the road from Banbridge to Ballynahinch; containing, with the district of Maghera hamlet, 10,129 inhabitants. It contains part of the lands granted by patent of Queen Elizabeth, in 1585, to Ever Mac Rorye Magennis, which were forfeited in the war of 1641, and afterwards granted by Chas. II. to Col. Hill; they are included in the manor of Kilwarlin. According to the Ordnance survey, it comprises 21,192¾ statute acres, of which 6027¼ are in Lower Iveagh, 7024½ are in Kinelearty, and 8141 are in Upper Iveagh. The greater part is arable land, and about 91¾ acres are under water; considerable improvement has been made in agriculture, and many even of the mountain tracts have been brought under tillage. The village, which is small, is called Annesborough, or Annesbury, in a patent which granted a weekly market on Thursday, and a fair for three days in Sept.; the market has been changed to Friday, and is held chiefly for the sale of butter and linen yarn; and the fairs are now held on the first Friday in Feb., May, Aug., and Nov., for farming stock and pedlery. Petty sessions are held in the village every fourth Monday: here is a sub-post-office to Dromore and Comber. Woodford, formerly the residence Jas. Black, Esq., has extensive bleach-works, and was once the seat of a flourishing branch of the linen manufacture. Dromaragh, with part of the rectory of Garvaghey, constitutes a union and the only prebend in the cathedral of Christ the Redeemer at Dromore, in the patronage of the Bishop: the tithes of the parish amount to £620. 17. 5., and of the union, to £937. 4. 3. The glebe-house was erected in 1821, for which a gift of £100 and a loan of £1125 was obtained from the late Board of First Fruits. The ancient glebe, consisting of one moiety of the townland of Dromaragh, which was granted to the rector in pure alms by Jas. I., is now in the possession of the Marquess of Downshire; 20 acres of the same, held at a rent of £42 per ann., constitutes the present glebe. The church is a small handsome edifice, with a tower and clock in good repair, built in 1811, at the expense of the parishioners. The Ecclesiastical Commissioners have recommended that this union be dissolved on the next avoidance of the prebend, and that Garvaghey be separated from it, and consolidated with its vicarage, and the 9½ townlands now forming the perpetual cure of Maghera hamlet be constituted a distinct parish, leaving the remainder of Dromaragh to form the corps of the prebend. The R. C. parish is co-extensive with that of the Established Church, with the exception of the district of Maghera hamlet, which is united to the R. C. parish of Magheradroll: the chapel is a large handsome edifice at Finnis, built in 1833. At Artana is a meeting-house for Presbyterians of the first class, in connection with the Synod of Ulster. Here are 10 public schools, two of which are aided by an annual donation from Capt. Maginnis; also 11 private and eight Sunday schools. On the mountain of Slieve Croob is a cairn, having a platform at the top, on which eleven smaller cairns are raised; and in the townland of Finnis is a remarkable artificial cave, 94 feet long, 6 feet wide, and upwards of 5 feet in height, with a transept near the centre, 30 feet long; the walls are rudely arched near the top, which is covered with slabs of granite: in 1833, the Rev. H. Elgee Boyd, rector of the parish, caused it to be cleared out and an iron door fixed up to protect it from injury.

DROMARD, a parish, in the barony of TYRERAGH, county of SLIGO, and province of CONNAUGHT, 5 miles (W.) from Collooney, on the road from Sligo to Ballina; containing 2560 inhabitants. Cromwell took this place, and burnt the old bawn of Tanragoe. In the reign of Wm. III., the castle of Longford successfully resisted two attacks of a detachment of the troops under Major Vaughan; numerous skeletons of men and horses are constantly being dug up in the demesne, where the battle was fought. The parish comprises 4923 statute acres, as applotted under the tithe act, and there is a considerable tract of unreclaimed mountain land. Here are quarries of limestone and granite of the best description. Fairs are held at Beltra on the Monday before Ash-Wednesday, May 21st, and August 20th. The principal seats are Tanragoe, the residence of Col. Irwin, a very old mansion which commands remarkably fine views of the bays of Sligo, Donegal, and Killybegs, and of Tellen Head, Benbullen, and Knocknaree; and the glebe-house, of the Rev. J. Stack: Longford House, the seat of Sir J. Crofton, Bart., was burnt in 1816. The living is a rectory and vicarage, in the diocese of Killala, and in the patronage of the Bishop: the tithes amount to £200. The glebe-house was built in 1833, by aid of a gift of £350 and a loan of £450 from the late Board of First Fruits; the glebe comprises 15½ acres. The church, a neat plain building with a square tower, was erected by the grandfather of Col. Irwin, and subsequently enlarged in 1818, by aid of a loan of £600 from the same board. The R. C. parish is co-extensive with that of the Established Church, and has a good slated chapel at Altnelvick. Here is a school of about 40 boys and 40 girls, under the trustees of Erasmus Smith's charity; the school-house is a stone slated building, erected at an expense of about £250, on an acre of land given by Col. Irwin. The Rev. Dr. Benton, late rector of the parish, left £200 late currency, which is now vested in the Commissioners of Charitable Bequests, and the interest distributed among the poor at Easter. Near the river of Ballinley are the ruins of an old religious house; and there are some remains of the old church, near which is a holy well, dedicated to St. Patrick. In the demesne of Longford is an old R. C. chapel, now disused; it was built by the O'Douds, from whom the Croftons inherit the estate.

DROMCLIFFE, or OGORMUCK, a parish, in the barony of ISLANDS, county of CLARE, and province of MUNSTER, on the river Fergus, and on the road from Limerick to Galway; containing, with the assize, market, and post-town of Ennis, 14.083 inhabitants. This parish, including Inch, comprises 8387 statute acres, as applotted under the tithe act. The land varies greatly in quality. There are about 240 acres of craggy pasture that might be easily converted into good arable land. At Cragleigh is some very fine close-grained black marble. The gentlemen's seats are Stamer Park, the residence of M. Finucane, Esq.; Abbeyville, of T. Crowe, jun., Esq.; Willow Bank, of E. J. Armstrong, Esq.; Greenlawn, of T. Mahon, Esq.; Hermitage, of W. Keane, Esq.; Cahircalla, of C. Mahon, Esq.; Beechpark, of R. Keane, Esq.; Ashline Park, of R. Mahon, Esq.; Cranaher, of B. Blood, Esq.; Brookville, of J. Mahon, Esq.; and Green Park, of the Rev. W. Adamson. The living is a vicarage, in the diocese of Killaloe, united in 1818, to those of Kilnemona, Kilraghtis, and Templemaly, forming the union of Dromcliffe, in the gift of the Bishop. The rectory is partly impropriate in R. Keane, Esq., and partly united, in 1803, to the rectories of Kilnemona and Kilmaly, in the patronage of the Marquess of Thomond. The tithes of the parish amount to £332. 6. 2½., of which, £101. 10. 9½. is payable to the impropriator, a similar sum to the rector, and the remaining £129. 4. 7¼. to the vicar; the tithes of the vicarial union are £285. 16. 10¾. The glebe contains four acres near the old church, which is in ruins: the present church at Ennis consists of part of the ancient Franciscan abbey. The site of the old glebe-house has been added to the church-yard, where, during the prevalence of the cholera, no less than 340 bodies were buried in one pit. In the R. C. divisions the greater part of the parish forms the union or district of Ennis, where the chapel is situated: the western part, called Inch, is the head of the district of that name, which also includes the parish of Kilmaly. A new chapel is now being built at Inch, and there is a chapel in Kilmaly. The number of children educated in the public schools, exclusively of the college, is 650; and there are seven private schools. Near the old church are the remains of one of the ancient round towers, of which about 50 feet are still standing. At Inch is a strongly impregnated chalybeate spring which is occasionally resorted to.—See ENNIS.

DROMCOLLOHER.—See DRUMCOLLOHER.

DROMCREHY, or DRUMCREELY, a parish, in the barony of BURREN, county of CLARE, and province of MUNSTER, 6 miles (W.) from Burren, on the bay of Ballyvaughan, and on the road from Burren to Kilfenora; containing 1758 inhabitants. It comprises 6186 statute acres, as applotted under the tithe act, of which a considerable portion is rocky mountain pasture, principally devoted to the grazing of sheep. The substratum is limestone, which in various places rises above the surface. Sea-weed, an abundance of which is procured in the bay, is the principal manure. The seats are Harbour Hill, the cottage residence of G. Mc Namara, Esq.: Sans Souci, of the Rev. J. Westropp; Ballyallaben, of J. O'Brien, Esq.; Mucknish, of J. S. Moran, Esq.; and Newtown Castle, of C. O'Loghlen, Esq. In the little creek of Pouldoody is a small oyster bed, the property of J. S. Moran, Esq., of Mucknish; the oysters taken there have long been celebrated for their delicious flavour, and are always disposed of by the proprietor in presents to his friends. The living is a rectory and vicarage, in the diocese of Kilfenora, united, in 1795, to the rectories and vicarages of Glaninagh, Rathbourney, and Killonoghan, together constituting the union of Dromcrehy and corps of the treasurership of Kilfenora, in the patronage of the Bishop. The tithes of the parish amount to £115, and of the entire benefice, to £330. The church is in ruins; that of the union is in the adjoining parish of Rathbourney. In the R. C. divisions the parish is part of the union or district of Glenarragha, or Glynn. A school is aided by the Duke of Buckingham, and another is about to be established. In this parish are the ruins of the castles of Mucknish and Ballynacraggy, and some vestiges of that of Ballyvaughan: at Newtown is a castle of unusual form, consisting of a round tower resting on a square base, and said to have been formerly the residence of the Prince of Burren; it is in good preservation and inhabited. On the lands called "The Bishop's Quarter" are the remains of a religious house, of which no particulars are recorded.—See BALLYVAUGHAN.

DROMDALEAGUE, or DRIMOLEAGUE, a parish, in the East Division of the barony of WEST CARBERY, county of CORK, and province of MUNSTER, 7 miles (S. W. by S.) from Dunmanway, on the river Ilen, and the road from Cork to Bantry; containing 4870 inhabitants. It comprises 17,565 statute acres, as applotted under the tithe act, and valued at £5150 per annum; of these 124 are woodland, 8152 arable, 2689 pasture, 4756 barren, and 1844 mountain, waste, and bog. The surface is very uneven, rising into hills of considerable elevation, particularly in the northern part of the parish, which is mostly rocky and bare, though in some places affording herbage for numerous herds of young cattle. Agriculture is in a very backward state. There is an excellent slate quarry, though but little used. Dromdaleague House is the residence of the rector, the Rev. T. Tuckey. Fairs are held on May 20th, September 25th, and October 27th, principally for cattle, sheep, and pigs; and there is a constabulary police station. The living is a rectory, in the diocese of Cork, united to part of the rectory of Fanlobbus, and constituting the corps of the prebend of Dromdaleague, in the cathedral of St. Finbarr, Cork, and in the patronage of the Bishop. The tithes amount to £450. The church is a small edifice built in 1790. In the R. C. divisions this parish is the head of a union or district comprising also the parish of Drinagh, in each of which is a chapel; that of Dromdaleague, a large cruciform edifice, is well built and roofed with slate. About 150 children are educated in the parochial and another school, the former aided by donations from Lord Carbery and the incumbent; and about 130 children are taught in three private schools: there is also a Sunday school. Near Dromdaleague House is a chalybeate spring, similar to that of Dunmanway. Two miles north from the church is Castle Donovan, erected by the head of the sept of that name in the reign of Henry IV.; a lofty square tower, with some other detached portions of the castle, rise in majestic grandeur in a pass between two lofty mountains.

DROMDEELY, or TOMDEELY, a parish, in the barony of Lower Connello East, county of Limerick, and province of Munster, 1½ mile (W. by S.) from Askeaton, on the south bank of the Shannon; containing 430 inhabitants. It comprises 1275 statute acres, as applotted under the tithe act: the land, which is nearly all arable, is generally light and much intermingled with limestone. The living is a vicarage, in the diocese of Limerick, and in the gift of the Precentor of St. Mary's cathedral, Limerick; the rectory forms part of the union of Nantinan, and the corps of the precentorship: the tithes amount to £75, of which £50 is payable to the precentor, and £25 to the vicar. In the R. C. divisions, the parish forms part of the union or district of Askeaton. Several islands in the Shannon belong to it; the largest is Greenish (*which see*), containing 45 acres. There are ruins of the old church, and, not far distant, of Dromdeely castle, a small square tower built by the Mahonys, and which, since the final expulsion of the Geraldines in 1580, has been gradually falling into decay.

DROMDOWNA.—See DRUMDOWNEY.

DROMIN, a parish, in the barony of Coshma, county of Limerick, and province of Munster, 2 miles (S.) from Bruff, on the roads from Limerick to Cork, and from Croom to Kilmallock; containing 1454 inhabitants. This parish comprises 4007 acres, as applotted under the tithe act, the whole of which is fertile and well cultivated: about one-half is in tillage, the remainder being rich meadow and pasture land, on which great numbers of cattle are annually fattened. There is neither waste land nor bog; fuel is consequently scarce, and the poor suffer greatly for want of it. The living is a rectory, in the diocese of Limerick, and in the patronage of John Croker, Esq., of Ballynaguard, being usually held with Athlacca; the tithes amount to £305. 9. 5., and the glebe comprises 24 acres. In the R. C. divisions the parish is the head of a union or district comprising also Athlacca, and parts of the parishes of Uregare and Glenogra, and containing two chapels, one in Dromin, and one in Athlacca. There is a private school, in which about 50 boys and 20 girls are taught. The ruins of Dromin church stand on an eminence near the middle of the parish, not far from which are the remains of Meadstown castle, built by the sept of O'Hanlon, in the 15th century, the walls of which are nearly entire; it was dismantled by order of Cromwell in 1654. A part of this castle is occupied by a farmer, and has acquired some modern celebrity by being the birth-place of Daniel Webb, Esq., author of the "Harmonies of Poetry and Music."

DROMIN, a parish, in the barony of Ardee, county of Louth, and province of Leinster, 1½ mile (N. W.) from Dunleer, near the road from Drogheda to Dundalk; containing 855 inhabitants, of which number, 141 are in the village. According to the Ordnance survey, it comprises 2042¼ statute acres. Rathcoole House, the seat of E. Tisdall, Esq., is situated in a neat demesne. It is a rectory, in the diocese of Armagh, and forms part of the union of Collon: the tithes amount to £204. 9. 7., and the glebe comprises 9¾ acres. In the R. C. divisions it forms part of the union or district of Dunleer: the chapel adjoins the village. About 180 children are taught in a school under the patronage of the Rev. W. H. Forster, the incumbent, who pays the master £10 per ann. Contiguous to the village are the remains of the old church, and a churchyard; and near the chapel is a large rath.

DROMINEER, a parish, in the barony of Lower Ormond, county of Tipperary, and province of Munster, 5 miles (N. W.) from Nenagh, containing 561 inhabitants. This parish, which is bounded on the east by Lough Derg, comprises 1672 statute acres of arable and pasture land. The principal seats are Annabeg, the residence of J. R. Minnitt, Esq.; Shannon Vale, of J. Odell, Esq.; and Hazle Point, of Lieut. P. Bayly, R. N. It is a rectory, in the diocese of Killaloe, and one of the parishes that constitute the union of Ballynaclough: the tithes amount to £110. In the R. C. divisions it forms part of the union or district of Monsea. A school, endowed by the Countess of Farnham with £30 per ann., and an acre and a half of land, affords instruction to about 40 children; and about 80 more are taught in a private school. One of the principal stations of the Inland Navigation Company on the Shannon has been established near the castle of Dromineer, which is much dilapidated. Here is a Danish fort, occupying more than two acres, in the ditch surrounding which brass battle-axes, coins, large human bones, &c., have been discovered.

DROMISKIN, a parish, in the barony and county of Louth, and province of Leinster, on the road from Drogheda to Dundalk; containing, with the post-town of Lurgan-green, 2621 inhabitants, of which number, 377 are in the village. According to the Ordnance survey it comprises 5312 statute acres, mostly of good quality and under an improved system of tillage; there is neither waste land nor bog. The principal seats are Dromisken House, the residence of the Brabazon family; the glebe-house, of the Rev. J. Smythe; and Miltown Grange, of Mrs. Fortescue. The living is a rectory and vicarage, recently separated from Darver, in the diocese of Armagh, and in the patronage of the Lord-Primate: the tithes amount to £573. 17. 7. The glebe-house was built in 1766, at an expense of £993. 10. The glebe comprises 21 acres, valued at £63 per annum. The church is a handsome structure, with a tower, rebuilt in 1823 by aid of a loan of £800 from the late Board of First Fruits. In the R. C. divisions the parish is part of the union or district of Darver; the chapel is a neat building, erected in 1823, at a cost of £800. About 400 children are educated in the parochial and another school; the former is aided by the incumbent. The castle of Miltown is a quadrangular building, defended at the angles by round towers, 45 feet high, surmounted by tall graduated battlements. Near the summit of a rising ground, two or three furlongs distant, is an arched subterraneous vault, extending for a considerable length, and supposed to have been a secret entrance to the castle. About 30 yards from the church is the lower part of an ancient round tower, which is surmounted by a modern pointed roof and used for a belfry.

DROMKEATH.—See GREENMOUNT.

DROMKEEN, a parish, in the barony of CLANWILLIAM, county of LIMERICK, and province of MUNSTER, 3 miles (N.) from Pallas-Greine, on the road from Limerick to Tipperary; containing 528 inhabitants. It comprises 831 statute acres; the land is in general of good quality; about one-half is under tillage, and the remainder is meadow and pasture. There are some quarries of limestone worked for building, and for agricultural purposes. The principal seats are Williamsfort, the residence of H. Croker, Esq.; and Dromkeen, formerly the residence of the Burgh family, now occupied by the Rev. M. Lloyd. The remains of the ancient mansion show it to have been an extensive and important establishment; and not far distant are the walls of an old church, in which is inserted a tablet recording its repair, in 1717, by the Rev. Richard Burgh, Lord Bishop of Ardagh, of which family it had been the burial-place from time immemorial. The living is a rectory and perpetual curacy, in the diocese of Emly, united at a period prior to any known record to the rectory of Kilcornan, and the rectory and prebend of Ballynaclough in the cathedral church of St. Ailbe, together constituting the archdeaconry of Emly, in the patronage of the Archbishop of Cashel; the perpetual curacy is in the patronage of the Archdeacon. The tithes amount to £36. The lands belonging to the archdeaconry consist of the townlands of Kilcornan and Garry-Phebole, in the parish of Kilcornan, and comprise 323*a*. 3*r*. 24*p*., let on lease at an annual rent of £355. 19. 1.; and the entire revenue is returned by the Ecclesiastical Commissioners at £547. 19. 1. There is no glebe-house. The church is a neat cruciform structure, with an octagonal tower embattled and crowned with pinnacles, erected by a gift of £900 from the late Board of First Fruits, in 1831. In the R. C. divisions the parish is partly in the union of Greine, or Pallas-Greine, but chiefly in that of Kilteely; in the latter portion is the chapel, a modern edifice near the parish church.

DROMLEAS.—See DRUMLEASE.

DROMLINE, a parish, in the barony of BUNRATTY, county of CLARE, and province of MUNSTER, 3 miles (S. E.) from Newmarket, on the river Shannon, and on the mail coach road from Limerick to Ennis; containing 1182 inhabitants. It comprises 2365 statute acres, as applotted under the tithe act, and contains a portion of the rich corcass lands on the banks of the Shannon, and about 370 acres of the Bishop's mensal lands. The land is partly in pasture, but chiefly in tillage, and the system of agriculture has been much improved. It is a vicarage, in the diocese of Killaloe, and forms the corps of the treasurership of the cathedral of Killaloe, and part of the union of Kilnasoolagh, in the gift of the bishop: the rectory is part of the sinecure union of Tradree, or Tomfinlogh, in the patronage of the Earl of Egremont. The tithes amount to £93. 8. 7¼., of which £55. 7. 8¼. is payable to the rector, and the remainder to the vicar. In the R. C. divisions this parish forms a portion of the union or district of Newmarket: the chapel for this part of the district is a large building of modern date, situated near Ballycunneen. At Smithstown are the remains of an old castle, of which no particulars are recorded.

DROMOD, a parish, in the barony of IVERAGH, county of KERRY, and province of MUNSTER, 7 miles (S. by E.) from Cahirciveen, on the river Inny, near its influx into Ballinaskelligs bay; containing 4600 inhabitants. It comprises about 270 "reduced acres," as applotted under the tithe act, consisting chiefly of mountain pasture, waste, and bog, with patches of arable land intermixed, and is principally the property of the Marquess of Lansdowne and the Provost and Fellows of Trinity College, Dublin. An abundance of sea-weed and sand is procured in Ballinaskelligs bay, and carried up the vale of the Inny for manure; and building stone is found in several places. Lough Currane, an extensive sheet of water about seven miles in circumference, contains several islands, and abounds with brown and white trout and salmon of superior quality. A considerable quantity of the latter is annually sent to London from the fish preserve at Waterville, the residence of James Butler, Esq., near the western extremity of the lake, at its outlet into the bay, and where salmon are sometimes kept for three months in the highest state of perfection. The lake is bounded on the south and east by ranges of lofty mountains, which are said to have been formerly covered with wood. At Kannagh is the seat of the Rev. George Hickson. At the village of Waterville are stations of the constabulary police and coast-guard, and petty sessions for the district are held there. The living is a rectory and vicarage, in the diocese of Ardfert and Aghadoe, episcopally united, previously to any existing record, to the rectory of Prior, and in the patronage of the Crown: the tithes amount to £226, and of the union to £346. 19. 9. The church is in ruins, but divine service is performed on Sundays in the parochial school-house. The R. C. parish is co-extensive with that of the Established Church: the chapel is at Mastergiehy. Nearly 160 children are taught in the parochial and another school; the former is aided by the incumbent; the latter has a large school-house, with residences for the master and mistress, erected partly by a bequest of the late Gen. Count O'Connell, but chiefly at the expense of J. O'Connell, Esq., by whom it is principally supported. There is a private school, in which are 50 children. Among the islands in the lake of Currane is one called Church island, on which are the ruins of an ancient church with a fine Norman arch at the entrance, said to be dedicated to St. Finian: there are also vestiges of some other buildings, and it is supposed that there were originally seven churches on the island, similar to those of Inniscattery in the Shannon and Inniscalthra in Lough Derg. Over the river Inny was formerly a foot-bridge, consisting of a single arch of about 24 feet span and only a yard wide, which from its peculiar form was called the Rainbow bridge: it was approached at each end by steps. There is no tradition as to the period of its erection, but about a century since the high-sheriff of the county held his court on it. At Waterville is a chalybeate spring, somewhat similar in its properties to that of Harrogate.

DROMORE, a market and post-town, a parish, and the seat of a diocese, in the barony of Lower Iveagh, county of Down, and province of Ulster, 16 miles (W. N. W.) from Downpatrick, and 66½ (N.) from Dublin, on the mail coach road to Belfast, from which it is 14 miles distant; containing 14,912 inhabitants, of which number, 1942 are in the town. Its name, anciently written *Druim-mor*, signifies "the Great Ridge," *Druim* being the term applied to a long ridge-shaped hill, such as that above Dromore. Its origin may be traced from St. Colman, who founded here an abbey for Canons Regular, which afterwards became the head of a see, of which he was made the first bishop. This abbey had acquired extensive possessions early in the 10th century, and was frequently plundered by the Danes; it also suffered materially from the continued feuds of the powerful septs of the O'Nials, Magennises, and Macartans. In the 14th century, Sir J. Holt and Sir R. Belknap, being convicted of treason against Rich. II., were condemned to death, but on the intercession of the clergy, were banished for life to the ville of Dromore, in Ireland. At the Reformation the cathedral was in ruins, and the town had greatly participated in the devastations of the preceding periods; in this situation it remained till 1610, when Jas. I. refounded the see by letters patent, rebuilt the cathedral, and gave to the bishop extensive landed possessions in this and several adjoining parishes, which he erected into a manor called "Bailonagalga," corrupted into Ballymaganles, a denomination or townland on which the town stands, with a court leet, twice in the year, a court baron every three weeks for pleas under £5, a free market every Saturday, and two fairs. An episcopal palace was commenced by Bishop Buckworth, but previously to its completion, the war of 1641 broke out, and the cathedral, the unfinished palace, and the town were entirely destroyed by the parliamentarian forces. From this time the town remained in ruins till the Restoration, when Chas. II. gave the see in commendam to the celebrated Jeremy Taylor, with Down and Connor, by whom the present church, which is also parochial, was built on the site of the ruined cathedral. In 1688, a skirmish took place near the town between a party of Protestants and some of the Irish adherents of Jas. II.

The town consists of a square and five principal streets, and contained, in 1831, 396 houses. There are two bridges over the Lagan; one, called the Regent's bridge, was built in 1811, and has a tablet inscribed to the late Bishop Percy, recording some of the leading traits of his character. Several bleach-greens were formerly in full work in the vicinity, and among others, that occupied by the late Mr. Stott, whose poetical effusions under the signature of Hafiz, in the provincial newspapers, attracted much attention; but all are now unemployed except one, in the occupation of Thos. McMurray and Co., connected with which is a manufacture of cambrics, and also a linen manufacture, established in 1832; another linen-factory was established at Ashfield, in 1828. The market is on Saturday, and is well supplied with all sorts of provisions, farming stock, and linen; and fairs are held on the first Saturday in March, May 12th, Aug. 6th, Oct. 10th, and Dec. 14th. A constabulary police force is stationed here; courts leet and baron are held for the manor, and petty sessions occasionally. In the bishop is vested, among other privileges, the power of appointing a coroner, escheator, and clerk of the market, and a bailiff.

Arms of the Bishoprick.

The Bishoprick of Dromore is supposed to have been included in that of Armagh till the 13th century, as the only bishops whose names are recorded prior to 1227 are St. Colman, the founder; Malbrigid Mac Cathesaige, and Rigan. About 1487, the Archbishop of Armagh, in a letter to Hen. VII., states that the revenues of this see did not exceed £40 per annum Irish, which was less by a third than sterling money, so that none would remain upon the bishoprick. Under the Church Temporalities Act, on this bishoprick or that of Down and Connor becoming vacant, they are to be united, and the remaining bishop is to be Bishop of Down, Connor, and Dromore; the temporalities of the see will then be vested in the Ecclesiastical Commissioners. It is one of the ten dioceses that form the ecclesiastical province of Armagh, and is 35½ English miles in length by 21½ in breadth, including an estimated area of 155,800 acres, of which 1500 are in Antrim, 10,600 in Armagh, and the remainder in Down. The Earl of Kilmorey claims exemption from the bishop's jurisdiction for his lordship of Newry, as having been extra-episcopal before the Reformation; it belonged to the monastery at Newry, which was granted by Edw. VI. to Sir Nicholas Bagnal, one of this nobleman's ancestors; yet in the Regal Visitation book of 1615, Nova Ripa *alias* Nieu Rie is among the parishes under the jurisdiction of the see of Dromore. In the ecclesiastical court at Newry, marriage licences, probates of wills, &c., are granted by Lord Kilmorey's authority under the ancient monastic seal. The bishop's lands comprise 18,424 statute acres; and the annual revenue of the bishoprick, on an average of three years ending Dec. 31st, 1833, was £4219. 12. The ancient chapter consisted of a dean, archdeacon, and prebendaries, but was remodelled by Jas. I., and made to consist of a dean, archdeacon, precentor, chancellor, treasurer, and the prebendary of Dromaragh, to which offices several rectories and vicarages were annexed. The consistorial court, held at Dromore, consists of a vicar-general, two surrogates, a registrar, apparitor, and two proctors. The diocesan school, which was united with that of Down in 1823, is described in the article on Downpatrick, where it is situated. The total number of parishes in the diocese is 26, exclusively of Newry, and of benefices 25, including 2 perpetual cures, of which the deanery is in the patronage of the Crown; the vicarage of Donaghmore is in the gift of the Lord Primate, and the vicarage of Aghalee in that of the Marquess of Hertford; the remainder are in the patronage of the Bishop. There is a church in each benefice, and two in Dromaragh and Clonallon; and five other places have been licensed for public worship by the bishop: the number of glebe-houses is 23. In the R. C. divisions the diocese is a separate bishoprick and one of the nine suffragan to Armagh. It comprises 17 parochial benefices, containing 34 chapels, which are served by 27 clergymen, 17 of whom, including the bishop, are parish priests, and 10 are coadjutors or curates. The bishop's parish is Newry, where he resides, and in which is a handsome cathedral.

The parish comprises, according to the Ordnance survey, 20,488¼ statute acres, of which 18,212 are applotted under the tithe act. The lands are generally of good quality, and almost all are either under tillage or in pasture, and in a tolerable state of cultivation, or enclosed within demesnes: there is not more bog than is requisite to furnish a supply of fuel. Not far from the town is the episcopal palace, the residence of the Lord Bishop, the grounds of which were richly planted by Bishop Percy, who also clothed the surrounding hills with the flourishing woods that now ornament them: Shenstone's celebrated seat at Leasowes was the model on which he designed his improvements: St. Colman's well is in the demesne. Near the town also is Gill Hall Castle, the mansion and demesne of the Earl of Clanwilliam. This extensive property was originally granted by Chas. II. to Alderman Hawkins, who, during the civil war, procured food, raiment, and lodging, in London, for 5000 Irish Protestants who had been driven from their country, and by his exertions £30,000, raised by subscription in England, was expended in clothing and provisions, which were sent over to Ireland for such as could not effect their escape. With the aid of four other gentlemen, he also raised a sum of £45,000 for the help of the distressed Irish both at home and in England; he afterwards resided for some time in Ireland, where he became possessed of the town of Rathfriland, forfeited with other property by the Magennisses, Lords of Iveagh, in the war of 1641. The other seats are Islanderry House, the residence of J. G. Waddell, Esq.; Altafort, of W. C. Heron, Esq.; Clanmurry, of W. McClelland, Esq.; the Villa, of J. Vaughan, Esq.; Quilly House, of R. Vaughan, Esq.; and Islanderry, of S. Fivey, Esq. The living is a rectory and vicarage, forming the corps of the treasurership in the cathedral church of Christ the Redeemer, Dromore, in the patronage of the Bishop. The tithes amount to £910; there is neither glebe-house nor glebe. The church, situated on the north bank of the Lagan, close to the town, is a plain neat edifice, and was constituted the cathedral church by act of the 21st of Geo. II.; it was thoroughly repaired, enlarged, and modernised in 1808, when the tower was taken down, and the original oaken roof replaced with one of slate, chiefly at the expense of Bishop Percy: the Ecclesiastical Commissioners have lately granted £145 for its repair. Beneath the communion table is a vault, in which Dr. Taylor and two of his successors are interred, but the only inscription is on a small mural tablet to Bishop Percy, author of the key to the New Testament, translator of the Northern Antiquities, and editor of the "Reliques of Ancient English Poetry," who presided over the see from 1782 to 1811: his remains are deposited in a vault in the transept added to the cathedral, where also are interred those of Mrs. Percy, the "Nancy," to whom his beautiful ballad is addressed. In the R. C. divisions the parish is the head of a union or district, comprising also the parish of Garvaghy, in each of which is a chapel. There are places of worship for Presbyterians in connection with the Synod of Ulster and the Remonstrant Synod, both of the first class, and for Wesleyan Methodists. Nearly 1500 children are educated in the public schools of the parish, of which one is chiefly supported by Mrs. Saurin, and one by Mr. Douglass; and there are also eight private schools, in which are about 430 children, and twelve Sunday schools. Near the church are two good houses for clergymen's widows, erected in 1729, and endowed by the bishop and clergy of the diocese. The Countess of Clanwilliam, who died in 1817, bequeathed to the poor a sum now producing £10. 3., and a further sum to the dispensary, producing £3. 7. per annum. Near the town are the remains of an ancient castle, built by William Worsley, son-in-law to Bishop Tod, for the bishop's protection, being one of the conditions on which a considerable extent of the see lands was alienated to Worsley, and which led to the act for restraining bishops from leasing lands beyond a term of 21 years. At the eastern extremity of the town is a remarkable earthwork, called the "Great Fort" (or "folkmote," as such works are called by Spenser,): it has a treble fosse on the north or land side, and a strong out-post to the south, continued in a regular glacis to the water's edge; and near Gill Hall is a fort of different character, and smaller, evidently erected to defend the pass of the river. In 1817 a cavern was discovered near the castle, hewn out of the solid rock, of rectangular form, and about 4½ feet high, 24 feet long, and 2½ feet wide; on the floor were several broken urns of coarse brown clay, charcoal, and calcined human bones. At Islanderry was found a canoe cut out of a solid oak, and near it a pair of oars. Celts, spear and arrow-heads of flint, with other ancient weapons of stone, brass, and bronze, have been found at Skeogh, among which were stone hatchets; many were in the museum of Bishop Percy, and many are now in the possession of Mr. Welsh, of Dromore. During the prelacy of Bishop Percy, a large and very perfect skeleton of an elk was found in one of the adjacent bogs; the distance between the tips of the horns was 10 feet 3 inches; it was placed in the bishop's palace, where it was carefully preserved. The valuable library belonging to Bishop Percy was purchased, after his death, by the Earl of Caledon, for £1000. Dromore formerly gave the title of Viscount to the Farnshaw family.

DROMORE, a parish, in the barony of OMAGH, county of TYRONE, and province of ULSTER, 8 miles (S. W.) from Omagh, on the road from that place to Enniskillen; containing 10,422 inhabitants. In the war of 1641 the insurgents were defeated in some skirmishes near this place, but revenged themselves by burning the church and killing many of the inhabitants, when the English were obliged to retire. According to the Ordnance survey, it contains 25,492½ statute acres, the greater part of which is productive, but there are more than 4000 acres of bog and mountain land. The canal, by which it is intended to connect Loughs Foyle and Erne, will pass through this parish. The village, which comprises about 100 thatched houses, is a constabulary police station, and has a penny post to Omagh, and a dispensary. Fairs are held for farming stock on Feb. 1st, March 17th, Easter-Monday, Whit-Monday, May 1st, June 24th, Aug. 1st, Sept. 29th, Nov. 1st and

26th, and Dec. 26th. The principal seats are Lakemount, the residence of J. Hamilton, Esq.; Fairy Hill, of A. Sproule, Esq.; and the Glebe-house, of the Rev. H. Lucas St. George. The living is a rectory and vicarage, in the diocese of Clogher, and in the patronage of the Bishop: the tithes amount to £694. 1. 4. The glebe-house has been lately erected, and the glebe comprises 589 acres. The church is a small plain building, erected in 1694. The R. C. parish is co-extensive with that of the Established Church, and has a chapel in the village. At Gardrum is a Presbyterian meeting-house in connection with the Synod of Ulster, of the first class; and at Toghardoo is a place of worship for Methodists. There are four public schools, in which about 450 children are educated; and sixteen private schools, in which are about 850 children; also a Sunday school. Here are some large and perfect forts; and it is stated that St. Patrick founded a nunnery here for St. Certumbria, the first Irish female who received the veil from his hands. At Kildrum was a religious house or church, which is supposed to have been the parochial church; but no vestige of the building can be traced, and the burial-ground is partially cultivated. The townlands of Shamragh and Agherdurlagh are called abbey lands, and are tithe-free.

DROMORE-WEST, a village and post-town, in the parish of Kilmacshalgan, barony of Tyreragh, county of Sligo, and province of Connaught, 18 miles (W. S. W.) from Sligo, and 113 (N. N. W.) from Dublin, on the mail coach road from Sligo to Ballina; containing 109 inhabitants. It consists of about 20 houses, and in the vicinity are several gentlemen's residences, of which Dromore House is the seat of John Fenton, Esq. Fairs are held on the first Thursday in Jan., June 6th, and Dec. 29th. A revenue police force has been stationed here, and there is a R. C. chapel.

DROMSPERANE.—See DROM.

DROMYN.—See DROMIN.

DROUMTARIFFE, or DRUMTARIFF, a parish, in the barony of Duhallow, county of Cork, and province of Munster, 2½ miles (S. W. by S.) from Kanturk, on the river Blackwater, and on the new government road from Roskeen bridge to Castle Island; containing 5926 inhabitants. It comprises 14,971 statute acres, as applotted under the tithe act, and valued at £9007. 17. 6½. per annum: of which about 3000 acres consist of coarse mountain pasture and bog. The arable land is of middling quality. Since the construction of the new government roads, lime has been extensively used as manure, and the state of agriculture greatly improved. The extensive and valuable collieries of Dromagh and Disert, the property of N. Leader, Esq., afford constant employment to a considerable number of persons. Dromagh colliery has been worked for nearly a century. Within the last fifteen years a large capital has been expended by the late N. P. Leader, Esq., on useful works connected with the collieries, which are now in excellent order, and capable of supplying an extensive demand. Among other improvements, he erected a large boulting-mill, near the new bridge over the river Allua, which, in compliment to him, has been named Leader's bridge. At Clonbanin, Dominagh, and Coolclough are other collieries worked by different proprietors. About forty years since, it was contemplated to open a navigable communication between these collieries and the sea at Youghal, by means of a canal cut through the vale of the Blackwater; and part of the line between this place and Mallow, to the extent of 3½ miles, was actually cut, and still remains visible. A railroad in the same direction has also been suggested, but no steps have yet been taken for accomplishing that object. Fairs are held at Dromagh on the 20th of May, Aug., and Nov., for general farming stock. The gentlemen's seats are Nashville, the residence of N. Leader, Esq.; Minchill, of J. C. Wallace, Esq.; and the Glebe-house, of the Rev. H. Bevan. Fort Grady, so called from an ancient rath or fort in its vicinity, and formerly the residence of the father of Viscount Guillamore, is now occupied as a farm-house. The parish is in the diocese of Ardfert and Aghadoe; the rectory is impropriate in Lord Lisle; the vicarage was united, in 1760, to those of Cullen and Kilmeen, forming the union of Droumtariffe, in the gift of the Bishop: the tithes amount to £384. 12. 3¾., of which £184. 12. 3¾. is payable to the impropriator, and the remainder to the vicar: the entire tithes of the benefice amount to £720. The glebe-house is a neat and commodious building, erected in 1825, by aid of a gift of £400 and a loan of £400 from the late Board of First Fruits; the glebe comprises about 24 statute acres. The old church was burnt by Lord Broghill's troops, in 1652; the present church, at Dromagh, is a neat edifice, of hewn stone, with a square pinnacled tower, erected in 1822, by aid of a gift of £300 and a loan of £300 from the same Board. In the R. C. divisions the parish forms the principal part of the district called Coolclough, which also includes parts of the parishes of Cullen and Kilmeen. The chapel, near Dromagh, is a spacious and handsome structure, originally built on a site presented by the late Mr. Leader, who also contributed £150 towards the building; it has been recently rebuilt, in the Gothic style, under the superintendence of the Rev. J. Barry, P. P., and has now a handsome front of hewn limestone, with a spire rising 80 feet from the ground. The chapel at Derrinagree is an old building. There are three private schools, in which about 200 children are educated. In the midst of the collieries is the ancient Castle of Dromagh, once the chief residence of the O'Keefes, consisting of a square enclosure flanked by four circular towers: it is now the property of Mr. Leader, by whose father one of the towers has been raised and fitted up, and part of the enclosure converted into offices. The battle fought, in 1652, at Knockbrack, in the vicinity, between the forces of Lord Broghill and those of Lord Muskerry, is described under the head of Clonmeen, and the geological features of the district under that of the county of Cork.

DRUM, or DRUMMONAHAN, a parish, in the barony of Carra, county of Mayo, and province of Connaught, 4 miles (S.) from Castlebar, on the mail coach road to Hollymount; containing 3497 inhabitants. A battle took place here, during the disturbances of 1798, between the English troops and a party of French who had landed at Kilcummin, and taken possession of the mansion and demesne of Ballinafad. The land is of good quality, and principally under tillage, but the system of agriculture is unimproved, and spade husbandry generally prevalent. There is a proportionate quantity of bog, and limestone is quarried both for building and for burning into lime. There are indications of iron ore.

but none has been worked. Great tracts of valuable grazing land might be obtained by draining the neighbouring bogs, and deepening the channel of the river. Ballinafad, the seat of Maurice Blake, Esq., is situated in a large and richly planted demesne; and Bridgemount, the residence of Joseph Acton, Esq., is also in the parish. Besides the fairs at Belcarra, others are held at Donomona on May 26th and Oct. 17th. The parish is in the diocese of Tuam, and is a rectory, entirely appropriate to the vicars choral of the cathedral of Christ-Church, Dublin: the tithes amount to £160. The glebe-house was built in 1821, by aid of a gift of £337 and a loan of £120 from the late Board of First Fruits; the glebe comprises 17 acres. The church, which serves also for the appropriate parishes of Towaghty and Ballintobber, is a handsome edifice, in the Grecian style, erected by a loan of £923 from the same Board in 1830. The duty is performed by the curate of the adjoining parish of Balla. In the R. C. divisions the parish forms part of the union or district of Balla: the chapel, a large slated building, is at Belcarra. A school at Belcarra, in which are about 40 boys and 40 girls, is endowed with a house and two acres of land, given to it by the late Col. Cuffe; and there are two private schools in that village, in which are about 130 boys and 40 girls. At Geesedon, on the river Miranda, which abounds with pike, are an ancient burial-ground and the ruins of an old castle; and at Donomona are the remains of a castle, which was the ancient family seat of the Blakes, now of Ballinafad.—See Belcarra.

DRUM, a market-town, in the parish of Currin, barony of Dartry, county of Monaghan, and province of Ulster, $2\frac{1}{2}$ miles (N.) from Cootehill, on the road to Clones, from both of which it has a penny-post: the population is returned with the parish. It occupies rather an elevated situation near Leysborough lake. In the vicinity is a quarry, from which the stone used in building the chapel of ease was obtained. It is a constabulary police station, and has fairs on the first Tuesday in every month. A chapel of ease to Currin church was built by a grant of £830 from the late Board of First Fruits, in 1828. Here are two Presbyterian meeting-houses, a school, and a dispensary.—See Currin.

DRUM, or EDARDDRUIM, a parish, in the barony of Athlone, county of Roscommon, and province of Connaught, 4 miles (S. W.) from Athlone, on the river Shannon, and on the road to Ballinasloe; containing 4957 inhabitants. An abbey was founded here by St. Diradius, or Deoradius, brother of St. Canoc, about the close of the fifth century: and in the retreat of the army of St. Ruth from Aughrim, this is thought to have been the spot where a battle was fought. The parish contains 8965 statute acres, as applotted under the tithe act: the land, in general very poor, is chiefly under tillage; there is still a considerable quantity of bog, though much has been reclaimed. The seats are Thomastown Park, the residence of Edmond H. Naghten, Esq.; Ardkenan, of Edw. Naghten, Esq.; Johnstown, of J. Dillon, Esq., now occupied by Mr. Kelly; Summer Hill, of J. Gaynor, Esq.; and White House, of Mrs. Reilly. There is a constabulary police station at Cranough. It is in the diocese of Tuam; the rectory is partly impropriate in the Incorporated Society; the vicarage is episcopally united to that of Moore. The tithes amount to £180, one-half payable to the impropriators, and the other to the vicar. There is no church. In the R. C. divisions the parish forms part of the union or district of St. Peter's, Athlone, in the diocese of Elphin: the chapel is in the old churchyard, in which are the ruins of a chapel, which was dedicated to St. Mary, and is said to have been erected by one of the O'Naghtens, in 550. About 200 children are taught in four private schools.

DRUMACHOSE, a parish, in the barony of Kenaught, county of Londonderry, and province of Ulster, on the river Roe, and on the road from Londonderry to Coleraine; containing, with the market and post-town of Newtown-Limavady, 5280 inhabitants. The greater part of this parish formed a portion of the grant made to the Haberdashers' Company, in the reign of Jas. I.; part of it was given by the same monarch to Sir T. Phillips, upon which he built a castle, and founded the town of Newtown-Limavady; and part was confirmed to the see of Derry. In the war of 1641 it was the scene of much calamitous hostility, and the inhabitants were at length driven to seek an asylum in Derry, under protection of Col. Mervyn, who finally routed the Irish. In 1688 the town was besieged, and the inhabitants again retired to Derry; and on the retreat of the army of Jas. II., in 1689, it was wasted with fire and sword. The parish, according to the Ordnance survey, comprises 11,683 statute acres (including $24\frac{3}{4}$ under water), of which 11,082 are applotted under the tithe act, and valued at £6032 per ann. Part of the land is very fertile and extremely well cultivated, particularly around Fruit Hill, Streeve, and other neighbouring places, and that portion towards the banks of the Roe is rich gravelly loam, well sheltered. On the mountain range of Cedy, the eastern limit of the parish, at the very summit, are about 1100 acres of mountain pasture. Here is abundance of excellent freestone and limestone, both of which are extensively worked, and there are indications of coal in several parts. The inhabitants combine the weaving of linen cloth with agricultural pursuits. There are two distilleries and a brewery, and two bleach-greens, one only of which is in full operation; there are also several corn, flour, and flax-mills. The scenery in various parts is highly interesting, the woods and plantations are thriving, and the country is ornamented with many handsome houses, of which the principal are Fruit Hill, the residence of Marcus M'Causland, Esq.; Streeve Hill, of Marcus Gage, Esq.; Roe House, of W. Moody, Esq.; the Lodge, of R. Conn, Esq; Bridge House, of D. Cather, Esq.; and the glebe-house, of the Rev. J. Olpherts. The living is a rectory, in the diocese of Derry, and in the patronage of the Bishop; the tithes amount to £424. 12. $3\frac{3}{4}$. The glebe-house was erected in 1816 on a glebe of $6\frac{1}{2}$ acres purchased by the late Board of First Fruits; the glebe, of which the greater part is at Gortygarn, 2 miles distant, comprises 112*a.* 2*r.* 15*p.* of arable land. The church, a handsome Grecian structure with a square tower, was erected, in 1750, upon the site of a former edifice at Newtown; and a north aisle was added in 1825 by aid of a loan of £200 from the late Board. In the R. C. divisions the parish is the head of a union or district, called Newtown-Limavady, comprising the parishes of Drumachose, Balteagh, Tamlaghtfinlagan, and parts of Aghanloo and Bovevagh, and containing three chapels, of which one is at Roe-mills, in this parish. There are places of worship for Presbyterians in connection with the Synod of Ulster, the Seceding Synod, and the Remonstrant Synod, all of the second class; and also for Covenanters, original Burghers, and Wesleyan Methodists. About 360 children are taught in eight public schools, of which one is supported by Erasmus Smith's trustees and endowed with three acres of glebe, one chiefly by the rector, a female school built and supported by Mrs. McCausland, a female work school built and supported by Mrs. Olpherts, and a school supported by Mr. McCausland: there are also seven private and four Sunday schools. Near Fruit Hill are the extensive and beautiful ruins of the ancient church; and at the Dog-Leap is the site of the ancient castle of the powerful sept of O'Cahan.

DRUMBALLYRONEY, a parish, in the barony of Upper Iveagh, county of Down, and province of Ulster; on the road from Newry to Downpatrick; containing, with a part of the market and post-town of Rathfriland, 8544 inhabitants. It comprises, according to the Ordnance survey, 12,338½ statute acres, of which 1896 are bog, 80 mountain and water, and 10,445 are applotted under the tithe act, all of which is arable or pasture land in excellent cultivation. Here is a lake, called Lough Ballyroney, in the centre of which is a small island. The manufacture of linen and drugget is extensively carried on. The living is a vicarage, in the diocese of Dromore, united from time immemorial to that of Drumgooland, and in the patronage of the Bishop; the rectory is part of the corps of the deanery of Dromore. The tithes amount to £482, of which £321. 6. 8. is payable to the dean, and the remainder to the vicar; the gross tithes of the benefice amount to £630. 9. 9. The church, a small neat edifice with a tower, was erected by aid of a gift of £500, in 1800, from the late Board of First Fruits. The glebe-house was built by aid of a gift of £200, and a loan of £300, in 1821, from the same Board: the glebe, given by the Countess of Clanwilliam in 1820, comprises 20 acres, subject to a rent of 15*s*. per acre. In the R. C. divisions the parish forms part of the union of Annaghlone, and has a small chapel near the Diamond. There is a place of worship for Presbyterians of the first class, in connection with the Synod of Ulster, and one for Covenanters. About 170 children are taught in two public schools, and there are eight private and four Sunday schools. The fine ruin of Seafin castle, which was for ages the strong hold of the Magennises, is situated on the Bann; and there are several other fortresses.

DRUMBANAGHER.—See KILLEVEY.

DRUMBEG, a parish, partly in the barony of Upper Belfast, county of Antrim, but chiefly in that of Upper Castlereagh, county of Down, and province of Ulster, ¾ of a mile (N. E.) from Lisburn, on the road to Belfast; containing 2883 inhabitants. According to the Ordnance survey it comprised 2704¾ statute acres, of which 1186¾ were in Down, and 1518 in Antrim; of these, 2627 were applotted under the tithe act, and valued at £3367 per ann.: but a portion of the parish of Drumboe having been lately added to it under the Church Temporalities' Act, it now comprises 6868 acres. The soil differs greatly in quality, from a sandy loam to a stiff clay, but is very fertile. The Lagan navigation from Belfast to Lough Neagh passes through the parish. The principal seats, besides those noticed under the head of Dunmurry (*which see*), are Glenburn, the residence of F. Crossley, Esq.; Wilmont, unoccupied; Finaghey, of J. Charley, Esq.; Larkfield, of Henderson Black, Esq.; Drumbeg Rectory, of the Rev. J. L. M. Scott; Drum House, of W. H. Smyth, Esq.; and Belvidere Cottage, a neat and commodious residence, lately built on the property of A. Durham, Esq. Ballydrain, the beautiful demesne of Hugh Montgomery, Esq., though not in this parish, is within 200 yards of the church, and with the adjoining grounds of Lakefield, the residence of Miss Richardson, and Lismoyne, of Mrs. Callwell, presents one of the finest landscapes in the neighbourhood of Belfast. A court leet and court baron are held every third week at Four Land Ends, for the manor of Drumbracklin, by a seneschal appointed by Narcissus Batt, Esq., lord of the manor, with jurisdiction for the recovery of debts under £20, extending over the townlands of Doneight and Lisnoe in the parish of Hillsborough, Ballyaulis in this parish, and Ballycairn, Ballylesson, Molough, and Knockbreccan in Drumboe. The living is a rectory, in the diocese of Down, and in the gift of the Bishop; a part of the rectorial tithes is impropriate in W. Charley, A. Durham, and Narcissus Batt, Esqrs., as lessees under the Marquess of Donegal. The tithes now amount to £336. 16. 6., of which £94. 13. 6½. is payable to the impropriators, and the remainder to the incumbent: the glebe-house was built in 1826, by a gift of £415 and a loan of £46 (British) from the late Board of First Fruits, exclusively of £450 expended by the incumbent in building and improvements; the glebe comprises eight statute acres. The church was rebuilt by subscription in 1795, by aid of a gift of £461 (British) from the same Board: it has a tower surmounted by a spire, which having been blown down in 1831, was rebuilt at the expense of J. Charley, Esq. About 300 children are educated in five public schools, two of which are on Erasmus Smith's foundation.

DRUMBOE, a parish, in the barony of Upper Castlereagh, county of Down, and province of Ulster, 4 miles (N. E.) from Lisburn, on the river Lagan, and on the old road to Belfast; containing 6429 inhabitants. Twelve townlands of the ancient parish having been lately annexed to Drumbeg, it now comprises 9629 statute acres, chiefly arable, with a very small proportion of woodland, and, except lands belonging to gentlemen who farm their own property, in a very indifferent state of cultivation, though lately much improved: there is a large tract of bog. The weaving of cotton is carried on for the manufacturers of Belfast; and at Edenderry is a bleachgreen. The Lagan opens a communication with Belfast, Lisburn, and Lough Neagh. The principal seats are Edenderry, the residence of W. Russel, Esq.; Edenderry House, of C. Dunlop, Esq.; Belvidere, of A. Durham, Esq.; New Grove, of J. Russel, Esq.; and the elegant lodge and greater part of the demesne of Purdysburn, the splendid residence of Narcissus Batt, Esq. The living is a rectory, in the diocese of Down, and in the patronage of the Bishop; the tithes amount to £517. The glebe-house was built in 1816, by a gift of £415 (British), and a loan of £46, from the late Board of First Fruits, exclusively of £200 expended by the incumbent: the glebe comprises 6½ acres. The church, a handsome Grecian edifice with a lofty tower surmounted by a copper dome, was erected, in 1788, by subscription, aided by a grant of £500 from the same Board, a donation of 150 guineas from Mr. Hull, of Belvidere, and of 100 guineas from the Marquess of Downshire. There are places of worship for Presbyterians, Independents, and Primitive and Wesleyan Methodists. Nearly 600 children are educated in the several public schools of the parish; that at Purdysurn was built at the expense of Mr. Batt, who supports the school and also provides residences for the master and mistress, who have about 150 pupils; and the master of a school at Ballymacbrennard receives £20 per annum from the trustees of Erasmus Smith's fund, and has an acre of land given by the Marquess of Downshire. There are also six private schools, in which are about 400 children. Not far from the church is the Giant's Ring, a circular entrenchment enclosing more than 8 plantation acres, perfectly level; in the centre of the enclosure is a large cromlech, or Druids' altar, consisting of seven upright stones supporting a table stone of nearly circular form and sloping towards the east: the land is now let, and the earth-work is being removed for the purpose of cultivation. In the burial-ground close to the supposed site of the ancient church was an abbey, said to have been founded by St. Patrick, and of which St. Mochumna was the first abbot; there is also an ancient round tower. In the parish are eight large raths, the most conspicuous of which, on the summit of Tullyard, is constructed of earth, loose stones, and vitrified substances, similar to the cairns of Scotland. It is supposed by some writers that there was anciently a fortified town here.

DRUMBOE.—See DUNBOE, county of LONDONDERRY.

DRUMCANNON, a parish, in the barony of MIDDLETHIRD, county of WATERFORD, and province of MUNSTER, on the high road from Waterford to Tramore; containing, with the post-town of Tramore, 4835 inhabitants. It is situated on the northern and western shores of the bay of Tramore, and comprises 7137 statute acres, as applotted under the tithe act. The surface is rather undulating, and rises into two hills of considerable elevation, called Carriglong and Pickardstown. The land, notwithstanding its exposure to the sea, is productive, and the system of agriculture is improving; there is a considerable portion of peat bog, and at Pickardstown is a quarry of flagstone, but not worked to any great extent. At the head of the bay of Tramore is a tract of about 1000 plantation acres, called the Back Strand; it is partly defended from the encroachment of the sea by a bar raised by the opposing influences of the tide and the land streams, and stretching from Newtown Head towards Brownstown Head, to the latter of which it is in contemplation to extend it by an artificial embankment. The living is a rectory, in the diocese of Waterford, partly impropriate in the Misses Hardy, and in the patronage of the Archbishop of Cashel: the tithes amount to £600, of which, £70 is payable to the impropriators and the remainder to the incumbent. The glebe-house was built at the same time, and both by aid of a gift of £250, and a loan of £938, from the late Board of First Fruits; the glebe comprises 10 acres. The church, situated in Tramore, was built in 1809; it is a small edifice, and application has been made for its enlargement. In the R. C. divisions the parish is the head of a union or district, called Tramore, and comprising also the parish of Corbally; the chapel is at Tramore, and there is another in Corbally. Here is a school endowed with £10 per ann. by the late Mrs. Quinn and £3 from R. P. Ronayne, Esq.; also a school supported by local subscriptions: in these are about 60 boys and 70 girls; and there are also three private schools, in which are about 80 boys and 20 girls, and a Sunday school. An alms-house for 12 poor men and 12 women has been founded at Tramore, under the will of the late Mrs. Catherine Walsh, of that town; and the late J. Power, Esq., of Newtown, bequeathed property amounting to about £3000 for charitable uses, which has not yet been rendered available.

DRUMCAR, a parish, in the barony of ARDEE, county of LOUTH, and province of LEINSTER, 1½ mile (N. by E.) from Dunleer, on the river Glyde, and near the high road from Dublin to Belfast; containing 1634 inhabitants. It comprises, according to the Ordnance survey, 4041½ statute acres, of which, 3712 are applotted under the tithe act, and 18½ are in the river Glyde. The soil is fertile and the lands are mostly under tillage; the system of agriculture is in a highly improved state; there is neither waste land nor bog. Two streams, abounding with salmon and trout, unite at a bridge, and form what is thence called the river of Drumcar. Drumcar, the seat of J. McClintock, Esq., is an elegant mansion, beautifully situated in an extensive and richly wooded demesne, commanding a fine view of the Carlingford and Mourne mountains and the sea; and at Annagasson is the residence of R. Thompson, Esq., pleasantly situated on the sea shore. Petty sessions are held every fortnight, near the seat of Drumcar. The parish is in the diocese of Armagh; the rectory is impropriate in the Lord-Primate, having been purchased by Primate Marsh, for the endowment of such clergyman as his lordship may appoint to it, and subject to the payment of £50 per annum to the perpetual curate of Moylary under certain provisions of the testator's will. The vicarage forms part of the union of Dunleer. The tithes amount to £343, of which £292 is payable to the lord-primate and £51 to the vicar; the glebe comprises 11 acres. The ruins of the parish church form an interesting relic on the demesne of Mr. McClintock; the Protestant parishioners attend the church at Dunleer, and divine service is performed every Sunday evening by the curate in the school-room at Drumcar; the old churchyard is still used as a burial-ground. In the R. C. divisions the parish forms part of the union or district of Dysart: there is no regular chapel, but a house has been given to the priest, in which he officiates. A school is supported by Mr. and Lady McClintock, who pay a master for teaching more than 100 children, and other expenses, amounting to £50 per annum. A school is also supported by Mr. Thompson, in which 40 children are instructed. A religious house appears to have existed here at a very early period.

DRUMCLIFFE, a parish, in the Lower half-barony of CARBERY, county of SLIGO, and province of CONNAUGHT, 3¼ miles (N. N. W.) from Sligo, on the mail coach road to Londonderry, through Ballyshannon; containing 13,956 inhabitants. This place anciently called *Cnoc na teagh*, was once a large town. A monastery was founded here, in 590, by St. Columba, who appointed his disciple, St. Thorian, or Mothorian, abbot, and to his office episcopal jurisdiction was united: the see was subsequently united to Elphin. St. Torannan, a succeeding abbot, who died in 921, was afterwards regarded as the patron saint of the place. A religious house was also founded at Cailleavinde by St. Fintan, a disciple of St. Columb. The parish comprises 17,038 statute acres, as applotted under the tithe act. The land is principally light and under tillage, and there is abundance of bog. On the north-west side of Magherow lies the Serpent Rock, so called from the great variety of its curious fossils, representing serpents, fishes, &c. Here are quarries of limestone; and at Glencar is a remarkable waterfall, 300 feet high; but when the wind is south, the water is prevented from descending. At Raughley is a good harbour, designed by Mr. Nimmo, and executed at the joint expense of the Government and Sir R. G. Booth, Bart. Petty sessions are held at Summerhill every Wednesday; and a manor court is held at Ardharman, under Sir R. G. Booth's patent. The principal seats are Lissadell, the residence of Sir R. Gore Booth, Bart.; Craig House, of the Hon. R. King; Dunally, of Col. Parke; Ellen-villa, of J. C. Martin, Esq.; Summerhill, of R. Irwin, Esq.; Elsinore, of R. Young, Esq.; Mount Shannon, of H. H. Slade, Esq.; Cottage, of J. Gethin, Esq.; Willoughbrook, of W. Ormsby Gore, Esq.; and Millbrook, of J. Simpson, Esq. The living is a vicarage, in the diocese of Elphin, and in the patronage of the Bishop; the rectory is impropriate in Owen Wynne, Esq. The tithes amount to £720, of which half is paid to the impropriator and half to the vicar. The glebe-house stands on a glebe of 40 acres. The church is a handsome building in the Gothic style, with a square tower ornamented with minarets, erected by aid of a loan of £800, in 1809, from the late Board of First Fruits, on part of the site of the ancient abbey: the church service is also performed every Sunday in the school-house at Lissadell. In the R. C. divisions this parish is divided into two parts, Drumcliffe and Rathcormac: and has three chapels. There is a place of worship for Wesleyan Methodists at Drum, and another at Ballinford; and also one for Primitive Methodists. Schools at Milltown and Castletown are supported by Sir R. G. Booth, Bart.; at Drum, by J. Wynne, Esq.; and there are two other public schools. In these about 500 children are educated, and in twelve private schools about 700 are taught; there are also four Sunday schools. There are some remains of the monastic buildings, and close to the shore are the ruins of the ancient castle of the Gore family, which settled here in the reign of Wm. III.: there is also a portion of an ancient round tower; and near the church are two remarkable crosses, one handsomely carved, the other mutilated. In the demesne of Summerhill is an extensive Danish fort, called Lisnalwray; and, near Lissadell demesne, a cromlech weighing several tons. There are also many ancient forts, one having a chamber under ground; and at Raughley are chalybeate springs. —See Carney.

DRUMCOLLOHER, a parish, in the barony of Upper Connello East, county of Limerick, and province of Munster, 9 miles (S.W.) from Charleville, on the road to Newcastle: the population of the village, in 1831, was 658; the remaining part of the parish is returned with Corcomohide. It comprises 2908¼ statute acres, as applotted under the tithe act; about one-fourth is under tillage, producing excellent crops, and the remainder is meadow and pasture land; the hills are cultivated nearly to their summits, and there is neither waste land nor bog: they are on the south side of the village, forming a natural boundary between the counties of Limerick and Cork, and are supposed to contain three several strata of coal, but no attempt has been yet made to work them. The general substratum of the parish is limestone, and several quarries have been opened in various parts for agricultural purposes and for building. The village is a constabulary police station, and has a daily penny post to Charleville. Fairs are held on March 15th, May 2nd, June 17th, Aug. 24th, Nov. 5th, and Dec. 3rd; they are in general large and well attended. The parish is in the diocese of Limerick; the rectory is appropriate to the vicars choral of the cathedral church of St. Mary, Limerick; and the vicarage forms part of the union or parish of Corcomohide, with which the tithes are returned. In the R. C. divisions the parish is the head of a union or district, comprising also the parishes of Killaliathan and Cloncrew, and part of Nonegay; the chapel is a small plain edifice. A male and female school are supported by L. White and R. J. Stevelly, Esqrs., under the superintendence of the vicar. Not far from the village are the ruins of the old parish church, which was a small and very ancient edifice.

DRUMCOLLUM, a parish, in the barony of Tiraghrill, county of Sligo, and province of Connaught, 10 miles (N. by W.) from Boyle, on the road to Sligo; containing 1652 inhabitants. It comprises 2807 statute acres, as applotted under the tithe act: the soil is generally good, but there is much marsh and bog. Here is Lisconney, the residence of B. O. Cogan, Esq. It is a vicarage, in the diocese of Elphin, forming part of the union of Boyle; the rectory is appropriate to the prebend of Kilmacallane in Elphin cathedral. The tithes amount to £83. 1. 6½., which are paid to the incumbent of Boyle, who is also prebendary of Kilmacallane. In the R. C. divisions it forms part of the union or district of Riverstown. About 50 children are educated in a public school. There is a burial-place, in which are the ruins of a church, said to have been founded by St. Columb.

DRUMCONDRA.—See CLONTURK.

DRUMCONRA, or DRUMCONRATH, a parish, in the barony of Lower Slane, county of Meath, and province of Leinster, 4 miles (W. S. W.) from Ardee, on the mail road from Dublin to Londonderry; containing 2967 inhabitants, of which number, 420 were in the village. This place was the scene of an action, in 1539, between the English of the Pale and the northern Irish under O'Nial. A considerable party of the latter, detached from the main army, had taken an advantageous position at Bellahoe, in order to oppose the passage of the river by the Lord-Deputy Grey and his forces, who were marching to attack the insurgents, but after an obstinate conflict, the English threw them into disorder; and their commander being killed, they retreated in dismay, and communicating the panic to the main body, the whole army of the Irish fled in every direction with so much precipitation, that 400 only of their forces fell in the pursuit. This victory broke up the northern confederacy, which had been raised to oppose the progress of the Reformation in Ireland. The parish comprises 7566 statute acres, as applotted under the tithe act: about 1500 are good grazing land, 300 bog, and the remainder, with the exception of a small quantity of waste land, is under tillage; the soil is fertile, the system of agriculture improved, and the parish generally in a good state of cultivation. There are several quarries of limestone, and a good quarry of building stone near the village; and on the townland of Kellystown, near Bellahoe, is a quarry of white marble, which is not worked at present. Aclare, the seat of H. Corbet Singleton, Esq., is pleasantly situated in a demesne comprising about 325 statute acres, one-fourth of which is underwood. Aclare Lodge is the neat residence of G. Moore Adams, Esq., and Newstone, the property of A. Forbes, Esq. A large portion of the lake of Bellahoe, which is a mile and a half in length and half a mile in breadth, and in which are two picturesque islands, is within the limits of the parish. The village is a constabulary police station, and has a penny post to Ardee.

The living is a rectory, in the diocese of Meath, and in the patronage of the Crown: the tithes amount to £507. 13. 10¼.; the glebe-house has seven acres of glebe attached to it. The church, a plain neat structure, was erected in 1766. The Ecclesiastical Commissioners have lately granted £261 for its repair. In the R. C. divisions the parish is the head of a union or district, comprising also Ardagh and Loughbraccan. The chapel, a spacious modern building, is situated near the village. In the parochial school are about 20 boys and 20 girls; and there are two private schools, in which are about 50 boys and 30 girls. Alderman W. Forbes bequeathed to the poor a rent-charge of £10 late currency, secured on the Newstone estate. Near the village is a large rath, commanding a very extensive view of the bay of Dundalk, with the several adjacent counties; it has been recently planted by H. C. Singleton, Esq., and forms a prominent and pleasing feature in the scenery of the place.

DRUMCREE, a parish, in the barony of O'NEILLAND WEST, county of ARMAGH, and province of ULSTER; containing, with the post-town and district parish of Portadown, 12,355 inhabitants. According to the Ordnance survey, it comprises 13,385¾ statute acres: there is a very large tract of bog, most of which is valuable. The weaving of linen and cotton is carried on to a great extent. The living is a rectory, in the diocese of Armagh, and in the patronage of the Lord-Primate: the tithes amount to £650. A large and handsome glebe-house was erected by the Rev. C. Alexander, in 1828, aided by a gift of £100 from the late Board of First Fruits: the glebe comprises 567 acres, of which 93 are bog. The parish church is a large ancient building, with a tower and spire; and a chapel of ease was built at Portadown, in 1826. The R. C. parish is co-extensive with that of the Established Church, and has a small chapel at Drumcree. There are places of worship for Wesleyan Methodists at Portadown and Scotch-street, and for Primitive Methodists at Derryanville, Scotch-street, and Drumnakelly. Two large and handsome schools have been erected and endowed by the Rev. C. Alexander, who also principally supports three others. The school at Mullantine was built and is supported by Lady Mandeville; and at Ballyworken, Sir F. W. Macnaghten, Bart., has endowed one with a house and four acres of land for the master. In these schools about 370 children are educated, and about 60 are educated in two private schools. Roger Marley, Esq., bequeathed £30 per annum to the poor, payable out of a farm at Drumanally; and Mrs. Johnston, in 1809, left for their use the interest of £100. At Battentaggart are considerable remains of an extensive mansion, erected by the Bolton family, in the reign of James I. A very ancient bell was found some years since in the churchyard of Drumcree.—See PORTADOWN.

DRUMCREE, a post-town, in the parish of KILCUMNEY, barony of DELVIN, county of WESTMEATH, and province of LEINSTER, 5 miles (S. E.) from Castle-Pollard, on the road to Athboy; containing 37 houses and 197 inhabitants. It has an improving appearance, and contains the parish church, (a neat plain edifice with a square tower), the parochial school-house, and a dispensary. The post is a sub-office to Castletown-Delvin and Castle-Pollard. A manorial court is held here twice a year by the seneschal of Robert Smyth, Esq.—See KILCUMNEY.

DRUMCULLIN, a parish, in the barony of EGLISH, or FIRCALL, KING'S county, and province of LEINSTER, 5 miles (S. W. by S.) from Frankford, on the road to Parsonstown; containing 3113 inhabitants. At a very early period, a religious establishment existed here, of which St. Barrindeus was abbot about the year 590. Nearly one-half of the parish is bog, but the land near Droughtville is considered some of the best pasture ground in the barony. A spacious lake covers an extensive flat at the foot of a range of thickly planted hills. Contiguous to it is a castle, which can at pleasure be insulated by its waters: it was reduced to its present state of ruin by Cromwell's forces. There are limestone quarries near, in which the fossil remains are abundant and nearly perfect. There are two fairs at Killion; and petty sessions are held at Thomastown every second Thursday. The seats are Droughtville, the principal residence of the Drought family, in a demesne comprising peculiar groups of conical hills, which form a picturesque and pleasing scene; Thomastown, of Capt. Bennett; Dove Grove, of J. Berry, Esq.; Dove Hill, of — Holmes, Esq.; Clonbela, of — Moloy, Esq.; and Killion, of R. Cassiday, Esq. The parish is in the diocese of Meath; the rectory is impropriate in the Marquess of Downshire, and the vicarage forms part of the union of Fircall. The tithes amount to £228. 18. 5., of which £147. 13. 10. is payable to the impropriator, and the remainder to the vicar: there is a glebe of 216*a.* 3*r.* 6*p.*, valued at £180. 1. per annum. In the R. C. divisions it forms part of the union or district of Eglish; the chapel, situated at Rath, is a large plain building. There is a school at Killion, which has a house and an acre of land, rent-free, from Mr. Cassiday, and in which are about 40 boys and 25 girls: Mrs. Holmes maintains one at Dove Hill: there are also four pay schools, one of which at Thomastown, has a house rent-free from Mr. Bennett, and in which about 130 children are educated. Adjoining Droughtville, are the remains of the old church of Drumcullin, having a fine entrance arch of curious workmanship. Near Pallis Inn, in this vicinity, are the ruins of a castle; and, towards Frankford, are four other fortified places in a similar state of decay. The plains around are supposed to have been the scene of different sanguinary encounters as within a spade's depth, vast quantities of human bones have been found: each surrounding height has vestiges of ancient fortifications; and on a very strong rath, which commands the whole district, there is an entire fort, most difficult of access, defended by a regular and double course of works, still in good preservation: this rath, being now planted, presents a very striking appearance, At Ballincar is a spa, of the same nature as that of Castleconnell, near Limerick; the water is of a yellow hue, and famous for healing scorbutic ulcers: another spa of the same kind is at Clonbela.

DRUMDOWNEY, or DRUMDOWNA, a parish, in the barony of ORRERY and KILMORE, county of CORK, and province of MUNSTER, 3 miles (W. by N.) from Mallow, near the road to Kanturk; containing 164 inhabitants. This parish, which comprises only 356 statute acres, as applotted under the tithe act, and valued at £489. 11. 11. per ann. was formerly more extensive; but the remainder has merged into the adjoining parish of Buttevant: a considerable portion of it is occupied by the wood of Drumdowney. The land is good and chiefly in tillage; limestone is in general use for manure, and the state of agriculture is improving. It is a vicarage, in the diocese of Cloyne, and forms part of the union of Ballyclough; the rectory is impropriate in Col. Longfield. The tithes amount to £58. 10., of which £28. 10. is payable to the impropriator, and the remainder to the vicar. In the R C. divisions it forms part of the union or district of Kilbrin, also called Ballyclough.

DRUMGATH, a parish, in the barony of UPPER IVEAGH, county of DOWN, and province of ULSTER, on the road from Downpatrick to Newry; containing, with the greater part of the post-town of Rathfriland (which is separately described), 4448 inhabitants. According to the Ordnance survey, it comprises 5330½ statute acres, of which about 100 are bog. It is a vicarage, in the diocese of Dromore, and patronage of the Bishop; the rectory forms part of the union of Clonallon, and corps of the chancellorship of Dromore cathedral. The tithes amount to £258, of which £168. 13. 4. is payable to the chancellor, and £89. 6. 8. to the vicar. There is a glebe-house, with a glebe of 150 acres. The church, which is in Rathfriland, is a neat building, for the repair of which the late Board of First Fruits lent £150, in 1829, and the Ecclesiastical Commissioners have recently given £119. The R. C. parish is co-extensive with that of the Established Church, and has chapels at Rathfriland, Barnmeen, and Drumgath. In Rathfriland is a large and handsome meeting-house for Presbyterians, in connection with the Synod of Ulster, of the first class, and a second is now being built; there is also one in connection with the Seceding Synod, of the second class, and one each for Covenanters, Wesleyan Methodists, and the Society of Friends. About 350 children are educated in two public and two private schools. Some ruins of the ancient church exist in a large burial-ground, and a curious antique bell was found in a bog in 1764.

DRUMGLASS, a parish, in the barony of DUNGANNON, county of TYRONE, and province of ULSTER, on the road from Armagh to Coleraine; containing, with the market and post-town of Dungannon (described under its own head), 5926 inhabitants. According to the Ordnance survey it comprises 3503¾ statute acres, of which 30 are waste land and the remainder arable and pasture, the greater part of which is fertile and well cultivated, particularly near the town. The surrounding country is ornamented with several gentlemen's seats, the principal of which are Northland Lodge, the residence of the Earl of Ranfurly, proprietor of the town and manor; Dungannon House, of E. Evans, Esq.; Millton, of J. Falls, Esq.; the Castle, of T. K. Hannington, Esq.; Killymeel, of J. Shiel, Esq.; and the seat of J. W. S. Murray, Esq. Here are extensive collieries worked by the Hibernian Mining Company under lease from the Lord-Primate. The upper and best seam is about a foot thick; under it is a thin stratum of iron-stone, and then a seam of coal two feet thick. About 180 persons are employed, who raise 500 tons weekly. A drift is being made from these works to coal beds on the Earl of Ranfurly's estate, about a mile distant; and a line of railway has been marked out from the collieries to the Tyrone canal at Coal Island. The living is a rectory, in the diocese of Armagh, and in the patronage of the Lord-Primate: the tithes amount to £200, and there is a glebe-house with a glebe of 59 acres near it, and one of 347 acres in the parish of Donaghmore. The church, which is in Dungannon, is a large and handsome edifice, for the repair of which the Ecclesiastical Commissioners have recently granted £307. In the R. C. divisions it is the head of a union or district, called Dungannon, comprising the parishes of Drumglass, Tullaniskin, and Killyman, and containing four chapels, one of which is at Dungannon. There are meeting-houses for Presbyterians, connected with the Synod of Ulster and the Seceding Synod, both of the second class, and one for Wesleyan Methodists. A royal free school was founded by Charles I. at Dungannon, at which place is the parochial school, endowed with £10 per ann. by the rector; and an infants' school was established in 1833. In these and two other public schools about 400 children are educated, besides about 280 in eleven private schools.

DRUMGOOLAND, a parish, in the barony of UPPER IVEAGH, county of DOWN, and province of ULSTER, 4 miles (N. E.) from Rathfriland, on the road from Castlewellan to Banbridge; containing 10,281 inhabitants. It comprises, according to the Ordnance survey, 19,653 statute acres, of which, 133¾ are under water, 3240 are mountain and bog, and the remainder is cultivated with great labour and expense, and in some parts is very productive: many of the inhabitants are employed in linen-weaving. Ballyward, a large handsome house, situated in a beautiful demesne, is the residence of C. F. Beers, Esq.; the Cottage, of Capt. Tighe; and Ballymacaveny, of the Rev. J. B. Grant. The parish is in the diocese of Dromore: the rectory is partly appropriate to the see and partly to the deanery of Dromore, and partly consolidated with the vicarage, which, from time immemorial, has been united to the vicarage of Drumballyroney, together forming the union of Drumgooland, in the patronage of the Bishop. The tithes amount to £495. 3. 0½., of which £380. 2. 8½. is payable to the incumbent, £59 to the bishop, and the remainder to the dean; and the gross value of the benefice, tithe and glebe inclusive, is £570. 16. 0½. The church is a large handsome edifice, in the early English style, erected, by aid of a gift of £900 from the late Board of First Fruits, in 1822; it contains a handsome monument erected by the parishioners to the memory of the Rev. T. Tighe, forty-two years rector of this parish. There is another church in Drumballyroney, where there is a good glebe-house, and a glebe of 20 plantation acres, valued at £30 per annum. In the R. C. divisions the parish forms two unions or districts, called Upper and Lower Drumgooland: the chapel for the former is at Leitrim; in the latter there are two, one at Gargary, the other at Dechamet. There are two meeting-houses for Presbyterians in connection with the Seceding Synod, one at Drumlee (of the first class), the other at Closkilt. There is a school for boys and girls at Ballyward, built and principally supported by C. F. Beers, Esq.; the parochial school, adjoining the ruins of the old church, is supported by the vicar and Miss Beers; and there are six other public, and five private, schools, also three Sunday schools. In this parish are several large and nearly perfect raths and forts; at Legananney is a large cromlech, of which the table stone is supported by three large upright stones; at Mullaslane are four large upright stones; a fifth, but smaller, stands not far off, and in the adjoining field is a single upright stone of enormous size. In the gable of the school-house at Drumgooland is a large, perfect, and ancient stone cross, which formerly stood in the churchyard, but, having been thrown down and broken, it was built into the wall by the late rector: the shaft and cross are of porphyry, and the plinth of granite.

DRUMGOOLSTOWN, a village, in the parish of Stabannon, barony of Ardee, county of Louth, and province of Leinster, 4 miles (E.) from Ardee, on the road to Castle-Bellingham; containing 117 inhabitants. It consists of 20 houses and is a constabulary police station.

DRUMGOON, a parish, partly in the barony of Tullaghgarvey, but chiefly in that of Clonkee, county of Cavan, and province of Ulster, on the road from Kingscourt to Clones; containing, with the post-town of Cootehill, 12,029 inhabitants. It comprises, according to the Ordnance survey, 15,475 statute acres, including 604 under water, of which 8122 are in Clonkee. Slate and lead ore abound here, but have been only partially worked; and the linen manufacture was formerly carried on to a great extent, but of late it has much declined: there is a large flour-mill and bakery. Bellamont Forest, the seat of C. Coote, Esq., stands in a forest on the banks of a beautiful lake adjoining the demesne of Lord Cremorne. The living is a rectory and vicarage, in the diocese of Kilmore, and in the patronage of the Rev. J. Hamilton; the tithes amount to £513. 9. 9. The glebe-house was built by aid of a gift of £375 from the late Board of First Fruits, in 1820, and was rebuilt by a loan of £1384. 12. and a gift of £92. 6. from that Board in 1831: the glebe comprises 343 acres. The church, situated in Cootehill, is a large handsome structure with a tower and spire, rebuilt by aid of a loan of £3200, in 1817, from the late Board. There is also a chapel of ease, a neat plain edifice, erected in 1834, about three miles distant from the church. The R. C. parish is co-extensive with that of the Established Church, and contains three chapels, one at Cootehill, another about a mile from it and a third at Muddabawn. There are two Presbyterian meeting-houses, one in connection with the Synod of Ulster, of the third class, and the other with the Seceding Synod, of the second class; also places of worship for the Society of Friends, Moravians, and Wesleyan Methodists. There are thirteen public schools, in which are about 1080, and fourteen private schools, in which are about 640, children; also an infants' school, and Sunday schools held in each meeting-house. A Society for the sale of blankets and clothing at half price is supported by ladies. The Bible Society has a repository here. Remains of an old encampment exist at Drumgoon; there are also several Danish raths, or forts. Large horns of the elk are often found, a pair of which ornament the porch of the glebe-house. The remains of the old parish church are on the townland of Drumgoon.—See Cootehill.

DRUMHOLM, DRIMHOLM, or DRUMHOME, a parish, in the barony of Tyrhugh, county of Donegal, and province of Ulster, 4 miles (N.) from Ballyshannon; containing 8502 inhabitants. St. Ernan, who died about 640, was abbot of a monastery here, where Flahertach O'Maldory, King of Tyrconnell, was buried in 1197. The parish is situated on Donegal bay, and, according to the Ordnance survey, comprises 35,433 statute acres, of which 15,482 are applotted under the tithe act. It is a vicarage, in the diocese of Raphoe, forming the corps of the prebend of Drumholm in Raphoe cathedral, and is in the patronage of the Bishop; the rectory is impropriate in Col. Conolly. The tithes amount to £735. 3. 6¾., of which £245. 1. 2¾. is payable to the impropriator, and the remainder to the vicar. The glebe-house was erected in 1792, by aid of a gift of £100 from the late Board of First Fruits. The glebe comprises 531 plantation acres, of which 400 are cultivated, and the remainder is a rabbit burrow. A church was built at Ballintra, in 1795, at an expense of £1098, of which £500 was a gift from the same Board, and the Ecclesiastical Commissioners have recently granted £252. 13. 9. for its repair. Another church was built at Rossnowlough, in 1830, by aid of a grant of £600 from the late Board of First Fruits, which also granted £350 towards building a chapel at Golard. The R. C. parish is co-extensive with that of the Established Church, and has a large plain chapel near Ballintra. There are places of worship for Presbyterians in connection with the Synod of Ulster, and for Wesleyan Methodists. About 690 children are educated in the public schools, and 20 in a private school; there are also eight Sunday schools.—See Ballintra.

DRUMKEEN, a village, in the parish of Killury, barony of Clanmaurice, county of Kerry, and province of Munster, 11 miles (W. S. W.) from Tralee; containing 70 houses and 386 inhabitants.

DRUMKEERAN, or DRUMCHEERAN, a parish, in the barony of Lurg, county of Fermanagh, and province of Ulster, ¼ of a mile (N.) from Kesh, on the road from Enniskillen, by Pettigo, to Donegal; containing 8522 inhabitants. This parish is bounded on the south-west by Lough Erne, and on the south-east by the river Ederny, which falls into the lough a little below the town of Kesh. It comprises, including islands, according to the Ordnance survey, 27,159 statute acres, of which 3498 are part of Lower Lough Erne; the land generally is of inferior quality and principally in pasture; but the system of agriculture is improving: there is no waste land, but a large extent of bog, which partly supplies the town of Enniskillen with fuel. There is abundance of limestone for agricultural purposes, and some good quarries of freestone for building. The gentlemen's seats are Clonelly, the residence of F. W. Barton, Esq., and Drumrush, of the Rev. J. Delap. The living is a rectory aud vicarage, in the diocese of Clogher, and in the patronage of the Bishop: the tithes amount to £415. The glebe-house is a large and handsome residence; the glebe comprises 270 acres. The church, a plain building with a tower, was formerly a chapel belonging to Vaughan's endowed school, the governors of which presented it to the parishioners, on the separation of Drumkeeran from the parish of Magheraculmony: the Ecclesiastical Commissioners have lately granted £105 for its repair. In the R. C. divisions the parish is the head of a union or district, called Blackbog, comprising also parts of the parishes of Magheraculmony and Templecarne, and containing three chapels, situated respectively at Edendycrummin, Blackbog, and Banna. There is a place of worship for Presbyterians, in connection with the Synod of Ulster, of the third class; also two places of worship for Wesleyan Methodists. The late George Vaughan, Esq., bequeathed, in 1758, an estate now producing £1000 per ann., for the foundation and endowment of a school for boarding, clothing, and educating Protestant children, under the direction of 13 trustees: there are 60 boys and 24 girls at present in the school, who, when of age, are apprenticed with a fee to the master, and a premium is given to each on the expiration of his indenture, on producing a certificate of good conduct. There is also a parochial school: a large school-house has been built in the Elizabethan style by the Rev. Mr. West, who as a landlord has done much for the improvement of husbandry; and about 450 children are taught in nine private schools. There are several raths, and some chalybeate and sulphureous springs, one of which issues from a rock in the centre of the river.

DRUMKERIN, a village, in the parish of Innismagrath, barony of Dromahaire, county of Leitrim, and province of Connaught, $5\frac{1}{4}$ miles (S. E.) from Dromahaire, on the road from Carrick-on-Shannon to Manor-Hamilton; containing 51 houses and 284 inhabitants. It has a penny post to Carrick-on-Shannon, a market on Wednesday, and twelve fairs on Jan. 27th, the second Wednesday in February, March 8th, April 4th, May 27th, June 24th, July 18th, Aug. 18th, Sept. 16th, Oct. 19th, Nov. 11th, and Dec. 9th. Petty sessions are held here every fortnight, on Wednesday.

DRUMKEY, a parish, in the barony of Newcastle, county of Wicklow, and province of Leinster, $\frac{1}{2}$ a mile (N. W.) from Wicklow, near the road from Dublin; containing 254 inhabitants. This parish is bounded on the east by the sea and part of the Murrough of Wicklow, and comprises 1679 statute acres, as applotted under the tithe act. It is in the diocese of Dublin and Glendalough, and is a rectory and vicarage, forming the corps of the prebend of Wicklow in the cathedral of St. Patrick: the tithes amount to £65. In the R. C. divisions it is part of the union or district of Wicklow. Here is a private school, in which are about 30 children.

DRUMKRIN, or ST. MARY'S DRUMCRIN, a parish, in the barony of Dartry, county of Monaghan, and province of Ulster, 10 miles (N.) from Cavan; containing 3751 inhabitants, and comprising 7469 statute acres. It is a rectory and vicarage, in the diocese of Clogher, partly united by act of council, in 1804, to the rectory and vicarage of Galloon, and partly to that of Currin; on the avoidance of the latter benefice, that part of the parish which is not united to Galloon will, with the exception of Hermitage and Lisnadish, which will remain annexed to Currin, be incorporated with the parish of Drummully. The tithes amount to £184. In the R. C. divisions it is in the union or district of Drummully, and has a chapel at Drumslow. About 130 children are educated in two public schools, and about 200 in five private schools.

DRUMLANE, a parish, in the barony of Lower Loughtee, county of Cavan, and province of Ulster, on the road from Clones to Ballyconnell; containing, with part of the post-town of Belturbet, 8547 inhabitants. A monastery was founded here in the 6th century, by St. Edan, Bishop of Ferns, which became subject to the abbey of St. Mary at Kells. The cemetery was formerly the place of interment of the chieftains of Breffny, and is still a favourite place of burial. Within its limits are the remains of an ancient round tower, built of limestone and red grit. According to the Ordnance survey, the parish comprises $20,066\frac{1}{4}$ statute acres, of which 3074 are water, and 16,583 are applotted under the tithe act. Of these, about 400 are bog, 50 woodland, and the remainder arable or pasture. The living is a vicarage, in the diocese of Kilmore, and in the patronage of the Bishop; the rectory is appropriate to the vicars choral of Christ-Church cathedral, Dublin. The tithes amount to £500, of which two-thirds are payable to the appropriators, and one-third to the vicar. There is a glebe-house, which was built by a loan of £675 from the late Board of First Fruits, in 1819, and a glebe of 340 statute acres. The church is a neat building with a square tower, erected in 1819 by a loan of £1500 from the late Board of First Fruits. In the R. C. divisions this parish forms the two unions or districts of Drumlane and Milltown, and has chapels at Staghell and Milltown. Here is a place of worship for Primitive Methodists. About 500 children are educated in seven public, and the same number in seven private, schools.

DRUMLARGAN, a parish, in the barony of Upper Deece, county of Meath, and province of Leinster, $1\frac{3}{4}$ mile (S. by E.) from Summerhill, on the road to Kilcock and Dublin; containing, in 1831, 148 inhabitants, but the population has since decreased. It is a rectory, in the diocese of Meath, and forms part of the union of Raddonstown: the tithes amount to £36. In the R. C. divisions it forms part of the union or district of Summerhill. There are remains of a rath, which seems to have connected the fortifications and religious houses surrounding Kilmore with the outposts of Lynch's castle, at Summerhill, the noble remains of which are yet standing in Lord Longford's demesne.

DRUMLEASE, a parish, in the barony of Dromahaire, county of Leitrim, and province of Connaught, on the road from Manor-Hamilton to Sligo; containing, with the village of Dromahaire (which is described under its own head), 3901 inhabitants. An abbey was erected here by St. Patrick, who placed St. Benignus over it; the site is said to have been that occupied by the parish church. The parish comprises 14,403 statute acres: there is a considerable quantity of bog. Limestone abounds, and at Dromahaire is a good marble quarry. Besides the fairs at Dromahaire, twelve monthly fairs are held at Newtown, where there are also fairs on the 25th of Feb., May, Aug., and November. The gentlemen's seats are Shriff Villa, the residence of Capt. H. Palmer; Bellvue, of P. Carter, Esq.; and Dromahaire Lodge, of D. Stewart, Esq., agent of G. L. Fox, Esq. The living is a vicarage, in the diocese of Kilmore, and in the patronage of the Bishop; the rectory is appropriate to the see. The tithes amount to £130, of which, £86. 13. 4. is payable to the bishop, and £43. 6. 8. to the vicar. The glebe-house was built by aid of a gift of £100, and a loan of £900, in 1834, from the Ecclesiastical Commissioners; the glebe comprises 577 acres. The church is a neat edifice, in a picturesque situation, rebuilt by aid of a loan of £1000 in 1817, from the late Board of First Fruits, and the Ecclesiastical Commissioners have recently granted £154. 19. 6. for its repair. In the R. C. divisions the parish is the head of a union or district, comprising also a small portion of Clonlogher; the chapel is in the townland of Luglustran. There is a place of worship for Primitive Methodists. About 420 children are taught in the four public schools of the parish, and there are five private schools, in which are about 450 children. Near the villa of Shriff is an ancient burial-ground, used by the Roman Catholics. By the side of Loughgill are the ruins of a fine old castle; and there are remains of religious houses near Dromahaire, and at the Lodge. There are a sulphureous and a chalybeate spring. Crystal spars abound in the rocks of the mountains.

DRUMLISH, a village, in the parish of Killoe, barony and county of Longford, and province of Leinster, 5½ miles (N.) from Longford, on the road from Mohill to Edgeworth's-town; containing 112 houses and 574 inhabitants. A customary market is held on Tuesday, principally for oats; and fairs are held on Jan. 6th, March 17th, May 14th, June 24th, Aug. 6th, Sept. 19th, Nov. 1st, and Dec. 2nd. Here is a constabulary police station; and the parish church and the R. C. chapel are situated in the village.

DRUMLOMAN, or DRUMLUMNUM, a parish, in the barony of Clonmahon, county of Cavan, and province of Ulster, 2½ miles (E. by N.) from Granard; containing 8007 inhabitants. It comprises, according to to the Ordnance survey, 17,147¾ statute acres, of which 1003 are water, including 541¼ in Lough Sheelin, 140¼ in Lough Gowna, and 121 in Lough Kinale. It is in the diocese of Ardagh, and is a vicarage, forming part of the union of Granard; the rectory is impropriate in the representatives of the late Dean Blundell. The tithes amount to £526. 3. 1., of which £221. 10. 9. is payable to the impropriators, and £304. 12. 3. to the incumbent. The Ecclesiastical Commissioners have lately granted £161 for repairing the church. The glebe comprises 150 acres, valued at £234. 8. per annum. There are four schools, one of which is supported by Lord Farnham, and in which about 900 children are taught; also two private schools, in which are about 170 children. Here was anciently an hospital, the endowments of which were granted by Jas. I. to Sir Edw. Moore.

DRUMMAUL, a parish, in the barony of Upper Toome, county of Antrim, and province of Ulster; containing, with the post-town of Randalstown (which is described under its own head), 9737 inhabitants. During the revolution of 1688, this parish was frequently the head-quarters of the Earl of Antrim's regiment, which marched hence to the attack of Londonderry; and in the disturbances of 1798, the insurgents were driven from Antrim into Randalstown, in this parish, by the king's troops. The parish is situated on the river Main, and on the northern shore of Lough Neagh; it is intersected by the road from Belfast to the eastern parts of the counties of Derry and Tyrone, and by the mail roads from Belfast to Coleraine, and from Antrim to Cookstown. It comprises, according to the Ordnance survey, 32,394 statute acres, of which, 11,472 are in Lough Neagh, and 171¼ in the river Main. The land, with the exception of a few farms, is in a very indifferent state of cultivation; the system of agriculture is, however, beginning to improve; there are bogs containing about 2800 acres. The beautiful demesne of Shane's Castle, which contains nearly 2000 acres, the property of Earl O'Neill, and for many years the principal seat of his family, is situated on the margin of Lough Neagh, and the grounds and plantations extend far on both sides of the river Main: the mansion was destroyed by fire in 1816, and is now in ruins; the park, which is well stocked with deer, is ornamented with fine timber. Millmount, the seat of G. Handcock, Esq., agent to Earl O'Neill; Hollybrook and Sharoogues are also in this parish. Coal and ironstone were formerly obtained here, and there are remains of extensive forges and smelting-furnaces at Randalstown. There are quarries of basaltic stone, from which materials are obtained in abundance both for building and for the roads. The spinning of cotton and weaving of calico were extensively carried on at Randalstown, there are excellent sites for bleach-greens and beetling-engines at Hollybrook, and a considerable quantity of linen is woven in various parts of the parish. The living is a vicarage, in the diocese of Connor, and in the gift of the Marquess of Donegal, in whom the rectory is impropriate: the tithes amount to £996. 6. 6., of which £546. 6. 6. is payable to the impropriator, and £450 to the vicar. The church, which is at Randalstown, is a neat edifice in the ancient English style, with an octagonal spire of freestone: it was built in 1832, on the site of a church erected in 1709, and cost £1800, of which, Earl O'Neill subscribed £300, besides giving a fine-toned organ; his lordship has also built a beautiful mausoleum for his family close to the church, the family burial-place having been at Edenduff-Carrick since 1722. In the R. C. divisions the parish is the head of a union or district, called Drummaul or Randalstown, comprising the parishes of Drummaul and Antrim, and parts of Connor, Templepatrick, Donegore, and Kilbride; there are three chapels, of which that of Drummaul is a large handsome building near Randalstown. In that town there is a Presbyterian meeting-house in connection with the Synod of Ulster, and one connected with the Seceding Synod, both of the first class; and the Covenanters have a meeting-house at Craigmore. There is a parochial school at Randalstown for children of both sexes, aided by a grant from Earl O'Neill, and six other schools in the parish; also another school at Randalstown. In these schools about 330 children are educated, besides which about 440 are taught in seven private schools, and there are also eight Sunday schools. There are some remains of the ancient church at Drummaul, and the site of an old church at Edenduff-Carrick, or Shane's-Castle. Adjoining the gardens of Shane's-Castle are some very fine columnar masses of basalt, similar to those of the Giant's Causeway, but less perfect in their form and less regular in their divisions; they descend into Lough Neagh, and disappear under the water. There are chalybeate springs in various parts of the parish.

DRUMMONAGHAN. — See DRUM, county of MAYO.

DRUMMULLY, a parish, partly in the barony of DARTRY, county of MONAGHAN, but chiefly in that of COOLE, county of FERMANAGH, and province of ULSTER, 4 miles (W. by S.) from Clones, on the road from Dublin to Enniskillen; containing 667 inhabitants. According to the Ordnance survey it comprises 7639 statute acres, including part of Drumkrin; of these, 2520 are in Monaghan and 5119 in Fermanagh. The soil is generally good, and there is no waste land, but abundance of bog and limestone; about 600 acres are under water. Among the seats are Cara, the residence of J. Hassard, Esq.; Lake View, of D. Smith, Esq.; and Farm Hill, of C. Crowe, Esq. The living is a rectory and vicarage, in the diocese of Clogher and patronage of the Bishop; on the demise of the incumbent of Currin, a considerable part of Drumkrin, which is now held with that parish, will be united to Drummully. The tithes amount to £19, and the glebe comprises 154 acres. The church is a small building. In the R. C. divisions it is the head of a district, including Drummully, Drumkrin, and Galloon, and has two chapels in the last-named parish: about 60 children are educated in a public and 100 in a private school.

DRUMOD, a village, in the parish of ANNADUFF, barony of MOHILL, county of LEITRIM, and province of CONNAUGHT, 5 miles (S.) from Drumsna, on the road from Dublin to Sligo; containing 29 houses and 162 inhabitants. This village originated in the establishment of works for smelting iron ore, which were carried on successfully till the supply of fuel failed in 1798, since which period the ore, which is reckoned of good quality, has been sent to England. It is a constabulary police station; petty sessions are held every Thursday, and cattle fairs on Jan. 3rd, March 28th, May 14th, June 29th, Aug. 13th, Oct. 10th, and Dec. 10th. Here is a chapel of ease, which was erected at the expense of F. Nesbitt, Esq.—See ANNADUFF.

DRUMPHEY.—See FENAGH.

DRUMQUIN, a market-town, in the parish of EAST LONGFIELD, barony of OMAGH, county of TYRONE, and province of ULSTER, 7 miles (W.N.W.) from Omagh, on the river Roe, and on the nearest road from Londonderry to Enniskillen; containing 406 inhabitants. It consists of one street and some detached houses, which, with the exception of a few of recent erection, are indifferently built and thatched; and was founded by Sir John Davis, about 1617, on a tract of 2000 acres of land granted to him by Jas. I. in 1611, under the name of Clonaghmore, on which he located 16 British families. He also built castles at Kerlis and at Gavelagh, on the Derg, at which latter place he had another grant of 2000 acres; and between the two castles constructed an excellent road, seven miles in a straight line over mountains and bogs, which in several places still remains perfect. There is a daily penny post to Omagh. The market, on Thursday, is well supplied with provisions and yarn; and fairs are held on Jan. 17th, March 21st, May 2nd, June 9th, Aug. 15th, Sept. 17th, Nov. 9th, and Dec. 12th, for general farming stock: those held in March and June are large and well attended. Here are a meeting-house for Presbyterians, in connection with the Synod of Ulster, a large male and female school, and a dispensary.

DRUMRAGH, a parish, in the barony of OMAGH, county of TYRONE, and province of ULSTER, on the mail coach road from Dublin to Londonderry; containing, with the post-town of Omagh, 11,289 inhabitants. It comprises, according to the Ordnance survey, 20,164 statute acres, of which 161¾ are under water, and 15,630 are applotted under the tithe act. About seven-eighths of the land are arable and pasture, and one-eighth waste and bog: the land in the middle portion of the parish is very good, and under a tolerable system of cultivation; but the higher grounds, approaching the mountains, are wet and cold, though capable of great improvement by draining. The inhabitants unite the spinning of linen yarn and the weaving of cloth with their agricultural pursuits. There are several large and handsome houses in and around Omagh: the principal in the rural portion of the parish are New Grove, the residence of Sam. Galbraith, Esq.; and Riverland, of the Rev. Robert Burrowes, D.D. A court baron is held at Ballynahatty, every third Wednesday, for the manor of Touchet (anciently called Fintonagh), for the recovery of debts under 40*s*. The living is a rectory, in the diocese of Derry, and in the patronage of the Provost and Fellows of Trinity College, Dublin. The tithes amount to £600. The glebe-house is situated five miles from the church, upon a glebe comprising 550 acres. The church, situated in Omagh, a large handsome edifice, with a tower and spire, which were added at the expense of Dr. Knox, Bishop of Derry, was erected in 1777 by the Mervyn family, and was greatly enlarged in 1820. The R. C. parish is co-extensive with that of the Established Church: there is a chapel at Omagh, and another at Drumragh. There are places of worship for Presbyterians, in connection with the Synod of Ulster, of the first and third classes, and of the second class, in connection with the Seceding Synod; also for Wesleyan and Primitive Methodists. About 400 children are taught in the seven public schools of the parish, of which one is endowed with a house and 2 acres of land, and one for girls is supported by Mrs. Spiller; there are also eleven private schools, in which are about 450 children, and eight Sunday schools. The old parish church is now a fine ruin, having the side walls and gables entire. —See OMAGH.

DRUMRANEY, or DRUMRATH, a parish, in the barony of KILKENNY WEST, county of WESTMEATH, and province of LEINSTER, 2¼ miles (W.) from Ballymore, on the road from Athlone to Mullingar; containing 3494 inhabitants. A monastery was founded here in 588, in honour of St. Enan, which was burnt by the Ostmen in 946, and by Brian McCinneide, in 995. The parish comprises 7290 statute acres, of which about 405 are bog, 3645 arable, and 3240 pasture; agriculture has much improved within the last few years. Limestone abounds, and lead ore is supposed to exist. The gentlemen's seats are Dorrington House, the residence of R. Jones, Esq.; Walterstown, of St. George Gray, Esq.; and Lissenode, of J. Russell, Esq. In the hamlet of Walterstown is a constabulary police station. The parish is in the diocese of Meath; the rectory and vicarage form part of the union of Ballyloughloe, the incumbent of which presents to the perpetual curacy of Drumraney. The tithes amount to £290. 15. 4½., payable to the incumbent of the union: the income of the perpetual curate is £100 per annum, of which £60 is paid by the incumbent, and £40 out of Primate Boulter's augmentation fund. Two townlands, called High and Low Baskin, pay tithes to the parish of Castlelost; they are impropriate in Lord Kilmaine, and extend over about 500 acres. The glebe-house was erected in 1814, by aid of a gift of £450, and a loan of £50 from the late Board of First Fruits; the glebe comprises 32 acres. The church, a neat building in good repair, was built in 1811, by aid of a gift of £500 from the same Board. In the R. C. divisions this parish is co-extensive with that of the Established Church: there is a chapel at Drumraney. About 100 children are taught in the three public schools of the parish, of which one was built by H. K. Digby, Esq.; and there are three private schools, in which are about 120 children. There are several raths; also remains of old forts and towers at High Baskin, Donomona, and near Dorrington; and at Killininny, Ballycloughdough, Ardnagard, and Walterstown, are remains of castles, formerly belonging to the Dillons, whose burial-place was anciently at Drumraney. Here is a holy well, dedicated to St. Enan; his festival is celebrated on the Sunday after Sept. 18th.

DRUMRATT, a parish, in the barony of CORRAN, county of SLIGO, and province of CONNAUGHT, 3 miles (S.) from Ballymote, on the road from Boyle to Ballymote; containing 1606 inhabitants. It is on the confines of the county of Roscommon, and comprises 3682 statute acres, as applotted under the tithe act. The lands are principally under tillage, and there is a due portion of good grazing land, with a sufficient tract of bog for fuel. Limestone is quarried for agricultural purposes. Abbeyville is the residence of J. Fleming, Esq. It is in the diocese of Achonry; the rectory is impropriate in Sir H. Montgomery, Bart., and the vicarage forms part of the union of Emlyfadd. The tithes amount to £204. 13. 11., of which £95. 3. 3. is payable to the impropriator, and £109. 10. 8. to the vicar. In the R. C. divisions the parish forms part of the union or district of Tumore; the chapel is at Culfader. There are two private schools, in which are about 90 boys and 40 girls. An abbey was founded here by St. Fechin, of which the last abbot of whom there is any record, died in 1016; it afterwards became the parish church, and there are still some remains.

DRUMREILLY, a parish, partly in the barony of TULLAGHAGH, county of CAVAN, and province of ULSTER, and partly in that of DROMAHAIRE, but chiefly in that of CARRIGALLEN, county of LEITRIM, and province of CONNAUGHT, 2½ miles (E. by N.) from Ballinamore, on the road to Killeshandra; containing 9278 inhabitants. This parish was separated from Templeport by act of council in 1835, and comprises 4373 statute acres, as applotted under the tithe act, besides a great portion of mountain. There are large grazing farms, and a vast quantity of bog. Limestone is found here. The parish is intersected by Lake Gorradise, on which stands Gorradise, the residence of W. C. Percy, Esq., and Bush Hill, of C. Gerard, Esq.; and in the vicinity is Corduff, the property of W. Penrose, Esq. There is a small island in the lake, called Robbers island. The living is a vicarage, in the diocese of Kilmore, and in the patronage of the Bishop: the rectory is appropriate to the see. The tithes amount to £300, of which £200 is payable to the bishop, and £100 to the vicar. There is no glebe-house: the glebe comprises 365 acres, of which 282 are profitable land, valued at £322. 15. 6½. per annum. The church is a plain structure, in good repair, built in 1737, by William Gore, Esq. In the R. C. divisions it is divided into three parochial benefices, Upper Drumreilly, Lower Drumreilly, and Ballinagleragh, containing three chapels, besides a fourth annexed to Lower Drumreilly, called the mountain chapel. About 500 children are educated in seven public, and 110 in two private schools; there is also a Sunday school.

DRUMSHALLON, a parish, in the barony of FERRARD, county of LOUTH, and province of LEINSTER, 4 miles (N.) from Drogheda, on the coast road to Dundalk; containing 1048 inhabitants. This parish was distinguished as the site of a monastery founded at *Druimineascluinn*, now Drumshallon, by St. Patrick, for Canons Regular, of which the abbot Tiarnach, who died in 876, and some of his successors were generally styled Bishops: in 969, being in the possession of the Danes, it was plundered by Muirceartagh, Prince of Oileach, and son of Donell, King of Ireland, on which occasion many of the Danish occupants were killed. The priory of the Holy Trinity, now Christ-Church, Dublin, had a cell of three canons at this place; but Albert, Archbishop of Armagh, desirous of reforming the state of religion, suppressed it, as preserving no regular order or discipline. The parish comprises, according to the Ordnance survey, 3585½ statute acres, including 372 acres in the detached townland of Labanstown on the sea coast, and 9¾ acres in Lough Kircock. Drumshallon is the residence of Gorges Henzill, Esq. The living is a rectory, in the diocese of Armagh, partly appropriate to the Dean and Chapter of Christ-Church, Dublin, and partly forming part of the corps of the precentorship in that cathedral, annexed to which are lands here comprising 494*a*. 1*r*. 29*p*. statute measure, let on lease to Mr. Henzill, at a rent of £46. 3. 1., with an annual renewal fine of £77. 10. 9¼.: the tithes amount to £178. 17. 4½., wholly payable to the precentor. The Protestant parishioners attend divine service in the church of Ballymakenny, the incumbent of which is paid £10. 10. per annum by the appropriators, for performing the occasional duties of this parish. In the R. C. divisions the parish is partly in the union or district of Termonfechin, and partly in that of Moylary; the chapel is at Fieldstown. The parochial school is under the patronage of the Countess de Salis, and aided with £12. 12. per annum, from the appropriators; and there is a private school, in which are about 40 boys and 20 girls.

DRUMSHAMBO, a village, in the parish of KILTOGHART, barony and county of LEITRIM, and province of CONNAUGHT; 6¾ miles (N. by E.) from Carrick-on-Shannon; containing 479 inhabitants. It is situated near the southern extremity of Lough Allen, not far from the point where the Shannon emerges from it, and close to that where the new line of navigation from Battle-bridge enters it. Works for smelting and manufacturing the iron ore found in the neighbourhood were formerly carried on here, and were continued in operation till 1765. The iron-stone was chiefly collected from the eastern shore of Lough Allen, and in the beds of the streams that descend from the Slieve-an-erin mountains to the lake, where small workings are also visible; vast woods, which formerly clothed the neighbouring valleys, supplied charcoal, and limestone as a flux was quarried close to the works, which appear to have consisted only of one small square blast furnace, from which the iron was carried to the neighbouring village, where it was forged into bars. The village is a constabulary police station, and has a penny post to Carrick-on-Shannon. Fairs are held on Feb. 15th, April 1st, May 16th, June 13th, July 18th, Aug. 16th, Oct. 6th, and Nov. 16th. The second church for the parish is in this village, and was erected by a loan of £1107. 13. from the late Board of First Fruits in 1829. It is a gothic structure ornamented with a tower and pinnacles: there are also a R. C. and a Wesleyan Methodist chapel. A loan fund has recently been established here.—See KILTOGHART.

DRUMSNA, a post-town, in the parish of ANNADUFF, barony and county of LEITRIM, and province of CONNAUGHT, $3\frac{1}{2}$ miles (S. E.) from Carrick-on-Shannon, and $72\frac{3}{4}$ miles (W. N. W.) from Dublin, on the river Shannon and on the mail road to Sligo; containing 427 inhabitants. It comprises about 70 slated houses, several of which are large and handsome, and is a constabulary police station. Petty sessions are held every Tuesday, and fairs on May 20th, June 22nd, Aug. 25th, Oct. 7th, and Dec. 13th. The vicinity presents some of the most beautiful scenes in the county; in one direction are seen the windings of the Shannon through a fertile district, the projection of a wooded peninsula on its course, the heights of Sheebeg and Sheemore, with the more lofty mountain of Slieve-an-erin in the distance; and in the other, the luxuriant and varied swell of Teeraroon, the adjacent part of the county of Roscommon. A pleasing walk through the woods, from which is discovered the windings of the Shannon and the lofty mountains to the north and west, conducts to a sulphureous spring issuing from the verge of a small lake. A little to the south of the town an expansion of the river forms Lough Boffin. The seats in its immediate vicinity are, Mount Campbell, the handsome residence of Vice Admiral Sir James Rowley, Bart., which is divided by the Shannon from Charlestown, that of Sir Gilbert King, Bart. In the latter is an avenue of fine limetrees through which the town is seen to great advantage. On the hill above the town is the pleasant residence of the Messrs. Walsh, commanding extensive views of the river and surrounding country; and a little below the town, on the Roscommon shore, is Clonteen, a lodge belonging to the Marquess of Westmeath.—See ANNADUFF.

DRUMSNATT, a parish, in the barony of MONAGHAN, county of MONAGHAN, and province of ULSTER, $4\frac{3}{4}$ miles (S. W.) from Monaghan, on the road from that place to Clones; containing 3411 inhabitants. According to the Ordnance survey it comprises $5019\frac{1}{4}$ statute acres, of which 4436 are applotted under the tithe act: the land is moderately fertile and chiefly under tillage. The principal seats are Thorn hill, the residence of J. Johnson, Esq.; Brookvale, of Capt. Johnston; and the Glebe-house, of the Rev. A. Mitchell. The living is a vicarage, in the diocese of Clogher, and in the patronage of the Bishop; the rectory is impropriate in Sir T. B. Lennard, Bart. The tithes amount to £189. 4. $7\frac{1}{2}$, of which £106. 3. 1. is payable to the impropriator, and £83. 1. $6\frac{1}{2}$. to the vicar. There is a glebe-house, with a glebe of 22 acres. The church, for the repairs of which the Ecclesiastical Commissioners lately granted £316, is a plain modern structure with a tower. In the R. C. divisions it is the head of a union or district, comprising the parishes of Drumsnatt and Kilmore, and containing two chapels, of which that for Drumsnatt is at Kilnaclay. About 450 children are educated in four public, and 190 in three private schools; and there is a Sunday school.

DRUMTULLAGH, a grange, in the barony of CAREY, county of ANTRIM, and province of ULSTER, on the road from Ballycastle to Coleraine; containing 1468 inhabitants. It comprises, according to the Ordnance survey, $3753\frac{1}{2}$ statute acres, and is ecclesiastically regarded as forming part of the parish of Derrykeighan.

DRUNG, a parish, in the barony of TULLAGHGARVEY, county of CAVAN, and province of ULSTER, 5 miles (E. N. E.) from Cavan, on the road from that place to Cootehill; containing 6015 inhabitants. According to the Ordnance survey it comprises 11,475 statute acres, including 78 of water. Here are several quarries of good building stone, and it is supposed that various minerals exist, but no mines have been worked. The principal seats are Rakenny, the residence of T. S. Clements, Esq., and Fort Lodge, of J. Smith, Esq. The living is a vicarage, in the diocese of Kilmore, united from time immemorial to that of Laragh, and in the patronage of the Bishop; the rectory is impropriate in the Marquess of Westmeath. The tithes amount to £475. 15. $11\frac{1}{2}$., of which £202. 4. $7\frac{1}{2}$. is payable to the impropriator, and £273. 11. $4\frac{1}{2}$. to the vicar; the entire tithes of the benefice amount to £610. 18. $6\frac{1}{2}$. There is a glebe-house, with several glebes, comprising 695 acres, and valued at £606. 16. 3. per annum. The church is a handsome building, lately repaired by a grant of £130 from the Ecclesiastical Commissioners. The R. C. parish is co-extensive with that of the Established Church, and contains two chapels, one at Dunnannah and the other at Bannow. About 350 children are educated in three public, and 320 in seven private schools, besides those who are taught in three Sunday schools. There are several raths, one of which is called Fort William, part of King William's army having occupied it after encamping near Ballyhaise on a spot since called Camp Hill.—See BALLINECARGY.

DUAGH, a parish, partly in the barony of IRAGHTICONNOR, but chiefly in that of CLANMAURICE, county of KERRY, and province of MUNSTER, on the river Feale, 3 miles (E. S. E.) from Listowel; containing 3750 inhabitants, of which number, 210 are in the village. It extends to the confines of the county of Limerick, and comprises 19,129 statute acres, as applotted under the tithe act, a large portion of which consists of coarse mountain pasture and bog. A kind of brown flagstone is found in several places. The gentlemen's seats are Duagh House, the residence of M. Fitzmaurice, Esq., pleasantly situated on the Feale, and Duagh Glebe, of the Rev. R. Hickson; part of the beautiful demesne of

Ballinruddery (a seat of the Knight of Kerry) also extends into this parish. It is in the diocese of Ardfert and Aghadoe, and is a vicarage, held by faculty with that of Kilcarragh, in the patronage of Robert Hickson, Esq.: the tithes amount to £124. 12. 5. The glebe-house was erected in 1829, when £415 was granted as a gift and £184 as a loan by the late Board of First Fruits; it stands on a glebe of 23 acres, which, with a glebe of 12½ acres in the parish of Kilcarragh, is subject to a rent of £37. 10. The church, a small plain structure, was built in 1814, by aid of a gift of £800 from the same Board. In the R. C. divisions Duagh forms a union or district of itself, with the exception of a small portion which is attached to that of Listowel; a new chapel has been lately erected. In the school superintended by the parish priest, and two other pay schools, more than 100 children are taught.

DUBLIN (County of), a maritime county of the province of Leinster, bounded on the east by the Irish Sea, on the north and west by the county of Meath, on the west and south-west by that of Kildare, and on the south by that of Wicklow. It extends from 53° 10′ to 53° 37′ (N. lat.), and from 6° 4′ to 6° 36′ (W. lon.), and comprises an area, according to the Ordnance survey, of 240,204 statute acres, of which 229,292 acres are cultivated land, and the remainder unprofitable bog and mountain. The population, in 1821, exclusively of the metropolis, was 150,011, and in 1831, 183,042.

The earliest inhabitants of this tract of whom we have any authentic notice were a native people designated by Ptolemy *Blanii* or *Eblani*, who occupied also the territory forming the present county of Meath, and whose capital city was *Eblana*, presumed on good authority to have been on the site of the present city of Dublin. By some writers it is stated that in subsequent remote ages the part of the county lying south and east of the river Liffey formed part of the principality of *Croigh Cuolan*; while that to the north was included in the principality of *Midhe*, or *Meath*. The *Eblani*, whatever may have been their origin, probably enjoyed peaceable possession of the soil until the commencement of the Danish ravages, and the seizure and occupation of Dublin by these fierce invaders. At this era, the tract now described experienced its full share of calamities, until the celebrated battle of Clontarf, which terminated in the overthrow of the military power of the Ostmen in Ireland. But that this people had made extensive settlements within its limits, which they were subsequently allowed to retain as peaceable subjects of the native Irish rulers, is proved by the fact that, at the period of the English invasion, a considerable part of the county to the north of the Liffey was wholly in their possession, and from this circumstance was designated by the Irish *Fingall*, a name signifying either the "white foreigners" or "a progeny of foreigners;" the word "*fine*" importing, in one sense, a tribe or family. The country to the south of Dublin is stated, but only on traditional authority, to have been called, at the same period, *Dubhgall*, denoting the territory of the "black foreigners," from its occupation by another body of Danes. Though all Fingall was granted by Hen. II. to Hugh de Lacy, Lord of Meath, yet the number of other proprietors, together with the circumstance of its being the centre of the English power in Ireland, prevented the county, which was one of those erected by King John in 1210, from being placed under palatine or other peculiar jurisdiction. It originally comprised the territories of the O'Birnes and O'Tooles in the south, which were separated from it and formed into the present county of Wicklow, so lately as the year 1603. At an early period, the jurisdiction of the sheriff of Dublin appears even to have extended in other directions far beyond its present limits; for, by an ordinance of parliament, about the close of the 13th century, preserved in the Black Book of Christ-Church, Dublin, it was restricted from extending, as previously, into the counties of Meath and Kildare, and into some parts even of the province of Ulster.

It is in the diocese and province of Dublin, and, for purposes of civil jurisdiction, is divided into the baronies of Balrothery, Castleknock, Coolock, Nethercross, Newcastle, Half Rathdown, and Upper Cross, exclusively of those of St. Sepulchre and Donore, which form parts of the liberties of the county of the city. The irregularities of form in the baronies are very great: that of Newcastle is composed of two portions, that of Nethercross of six, and that of Uppercross of five, of which three constituting the parishes of Ballymore-Eustace, Ballybought, and Tipperkevin, on the confines of Wicklow and Kildare, are wholly detached from the rest of the county: the irregularities of the two latter baronies are owing to their constituent parts having been formerly dispersed church lands, enjoying separate jurisdictions and privileges, but ultimately formed into baronies for the convenience of the civil authority. The county contains the ancient disfranchised boroughs and corporate towns of Swords and Newcastle; the sea-port, fishing, and post-towns of Howth, Kingstown, Balbriggan, and Malahide; the fishing-towns of Rush, Skerries, and Baldoyle; the inland post-towns of Cabin teely, Lucan, Rathcool, and Tallaght; the market-town of Ballymore-Eustace, and the town of Rathfarnham, each of which has a penny post to Dublin; besides numerous large villages, in some degree suburban to the metropolis, of which, exclusively of those of Sandymount, Booterstown, Blackrock, Donnybrook (each of which has a penny post), Dolphinsbarn, Irishtown, Rathmines, and Ringsend, which are in the county of the city, the principal are those of Finglas, Golden-Ball, Dalkey, Drumcondra, Stillorgan, Raheny, Dundrum, Roundtown, Ranelagh, Artaine, Clontarf, Castleknock, Chapelizod, Glasnevin (each of which has a twopenny post to Dublin), Donabate, Portrane, Garristown, Belgriffin, St. Doulough's, Old Connaught, Killiney, Bullock, Lusk, Newcastle, Saggard, Balrothery, Little Bray, Clondalkin, Coolock, Crumlin, Golden-Bridge, Island-Bridge, Kilmainham, Milltown, Merrion, Phibsborough, Sandford, and Williamstown. Two knights of the shire are returned to the Imperial parliament, who are elected at the county court-house at Kilmainham: the number of electors registered under the 2d of Wm. IV., c. 88, up to Feb. 1st, 1837, is 2728, of which 788 were £50, 407 £20, and 622 £10, freeholders; 18 £50, 427 £20, and 423 £10, leaseholders; and 12 £50, 30 £20, and 1 £10, rent-chargers: the number that voted at the last general election was 1480. Prior to the Union, the boroughs of Swords and Newcastle sent each two members to the Irish House of Commons. A court of assize and general gaol delivery is held every six weeks, at the court-house in Green-street, Dublin; and at

Kilmainham, where the county gaol and court-house are situated, are held the quarter sessions, at which a chairman, who exercises the same powers as the assistant barrister in other counties, presides with the magistrates. The local government is vested in a lieutenant, 17 deputy-lieutenants, and 88 magistrates, with the usual county officers. The number of constabulary police stations is 30, and the force consists of 6 chief and 29 subordinate constables and 113 men, with 6 horses, the expense of maintaining which is defrayed equally by Grand Jury presentments and by Government. The Meath Hospital, which is also the County of Dublin Infirmary, is situated on the south side of the city, and is supported by Grand Jury presentments, subscriptions, and donations, and by an annual parliamentary grant; there are 25 dispensaries. The amount of Grand Jury presentments for the county, in 1835, was £23,458. 2. 7., of which £2188. 9. 10. was expended on the public roads of the county at large; £6904. 14. 0. on the public roads, being the baronial charge; £8365. 7. 0. for public establishments, officers' salaries, &c.; £3106. 8. 8. for police; and £2895 towards repayment of advances made by Government. In military arrangements, this county is the head of all the districts throughout Ireland, the department of the commander-in-chief and his staff being at Kilmainham; it contains six military stations, besides those within the jurisdiction of the metropolis, viz., the Richmond infantry barrack, near Golden-Bridge on the Grand Canal, Island-bridge artillery station, the Portobello cavalry barrack, the Phœnix-park magazine and infantry barrack, and the recruiting depôt on the Grand Canal, all of which are described in the account of the city, affording in the whole accommodation for 161 officers, 3282 men, and 772 horses; there are, besides, 26 martello towers and nine batteries on the coast, capable of containing 684 men; and at Kilmainham stands the Royal Military Hospital, for disabled and superannuated soldiers, similar to that of Chelsea, near London. There are eight coast-guard stations, one of which (Dalkey) is in the district of Kingstown, and the rest in that of Swords, with a force consisting of 8 officers and 64 men.

The county stretches in length from north to south, and presents a sea-coast of about thirty miles, while its breadth in some places does not exceed seven. Except in the picturesque irregularities of its coast, and the grand and beautiful boundary which the mountains on its southern confines form to the rich vale below, it possesses less natural diversity of scenery than many other parts of the island; but it is superior to all in artificial decoration; and the banks of the Liffey to Leixlip present scenery of the most rich and interesting character. The grandeur of the features of the surrounding country, indeed, give the environs of the metropolis a character as striking as those, perhaps, of any city in the west of Europe. The mountains which occupy the southern border of the county are the northern extremities of the great group forming the entire adjacent county of Wicklow: the principal summits within its confines are the Three Rock Mountain and Garrycastle, at the eastern extremity of the chain, of which the former has an elevation of 1586 feet, and the latter of 1869; Montpelier hill; the group formed by Kippure, Seefinane, Seechon, and Seefin mountains, of which the first is 2527 feet high, and Seechon 2150; and the Tallaght and Rathcoole hills, which succeed each other north-westward from Seechon, and beyond the latter of which, in the same direction, is a lower range, composed of the Windmill, Athgoe, Lyons, and Rusty hills. From Rathcoole hill a long range diverges south-westward, and enters the eastern confines of Kildare county, near Blessington. In the mountains adjoining Montpelier and Kilmashogue are bogs, covering three or four square miles; but the grandest features of these elevations are the great natural ravines that open into them southward, of which the most extraordinary is the Scalp, through which the road from Dublin to the romantic scenes of Powerscourt enters the county of Wicklow. From their summits are also obtained very magnificent views of the city and bay, and the fertile and highly improved plains of which nearly all the rest of the county is composed, and which form part of the great level tract that includes also the counties of Kildare and Meath. The coast from the boldly projecting promontory of Bray head, with its serrated summit, to the Killiney hills is indented into the beautiful bay of Killiney. Dalkey Island, separated from the above-named hills by a narrow channel, is the southern limit of Dublin bay, the most northern point of which is the Bailey of Howth, on which is a lighthouse. The coast of the bay, with the exception of these two extreme points, is low and shelving, but is backed by a beautiful and highly cultivated country terminating eastward with the city. Much of the interior of the bay consists of banks of sand uncovered at low water. About a mile to the north of Howth is Ireland's Eye, and still farther north, off the peninsula of Portrane, rises Lambay Island, both described under their own heads. Between Howth and Portrane the coast is flat, and partly marshy; but hence northward it presents a varied succession of rock and strand; off Holmpatrick lie the scattered rocky islets of St. Patrick, Count, Shenex, and Rockabill.

The soil is generally shallow, being chiefly indebted to the manures from the metropolis for its high state of improvement. It is commonly argillaceous, though almost every where containing an admixture of gravel, which may generally be found in abundance within a small depth of the surface, and by tillage is frequently turned up, to the great improvement of the land. The substratum is usually a cold retentive clay, which keeps the surface in an unprofitable state, unless draining and other methods of improvement have been adopted. Rather more than one-half of the improvable surface is under tillage, chiefly in the northern and western parts, most remote from the metropolis: in the districts to the south of the Liffey, and within a few miles from its northern bank, the land is chiefly occupied by villas, gardens, nurseries, dairy farms, and for the pasturage of horses. Considerable improvement has taken place in the system of agriculture by the more extensive introduction of green crops and improved drainage, and by the extension of tillage up the mountains. The pasture lands, in consequence of drainage and manure, produce a great variety of good natural grasses, and commonly afford from four to five tons of hay per acre, and sometimes six. The salt marshes which occur along the coast from Howth northward are good, and the pastures near the sea side are of a tolerably fattening quality; but more inland they become poorer.

The only dairies are those for the supply of Dublin with milk and butter, which, however, are of great extent and number. The principal manures are lime and limestone gravel, of which the latter is a species of limestone and marl mixed, of a very fertilising quality, and found in inexhaustible quantities. Strong blue and brown marl are found in different parts, and there are likewise beds of white marl; the blue kind is preferred as producing a more durable effect: manures from Dublin, coal ashes, and shelly sand found on the coast, are also used. The implements of husbandry are of the common kind, except on the farms of noblemen and gentlemen of fortune. The breed of cattle has been much improved by the introduction of the most valuable English breeds, which have nearly superseded the native stock. The county is not well wooded with the exception of plantations in the Phœnix Park and the private grounds of the gentry: there are various nurseries for the supply of plants. The waste lands occupy 10,912 statute acres: the largest tract is that of the mountains on the southern confines, extending about fifteen miles in length and several in breadth. The scarcity of fuel, which would otherwise press severely on the industrious classes, from the want of turf nearer home, which can be had only from the mountains in the south and the distant commons of Balrothery and Garristown on the north, is greatly diminished by the ample supplies brought by both canals and by the importation of English coal.

The county presents several interesting features in its geological relations. Its southern part from Blackrock, Kingstown, and Dalkey forms the northern extremity of the great granitic range which extends through Wicklow and part of Carlow. The granite tract is bordered by a range of incumbent mica slate, which extends eastwards from Shankill and the Scalp to the hills of Killiney, and on the western side commences near Rathfarnham, passes to the south of Montpelier hill, and occupies the upper part of the hollow which separates Seefinane mountain, on the east, from Seechon on the west: in this hollow are displayed some curious intermixtures of the strata of mica slate, granite, and quartz. In the descent from Seechon mountain, both south-westward and north-westward, towards Rathcool, the mica slate passes into clay slate, containing frequent beds of greenstone, greenstone slate, and greenstone porphyry, and occasionally likewise of quartz. The Tallaght hills consist of clay slate, greenstone, and greenstone porphyry, interstratified; the latter rocks more particularly abounding in the eastern quarter. Rathcoole hills, and the range extending from them southwestward, are composed of clay slate, clay slate conglomerate, and grauwacke slate, alternating with each other. The low group west of Rathcoole is composed of clay slate, grauwacke, grauwacke slate, and granite, of which the last is found remarkably disposed in subordinate beds in the prevailing grauwacke slate of Windmill hill, whence some of them may be traced westward to near Rusty hill. This county contains the only strata of transition rocks known to exist in the eastern part of Ireland. They appear in detached portions along the coast from Portrane Head, by Loughshinny, Skerries, and Balbriggan to the Delvan stream, the northern limit of the county. The rest of the county, comprising nearly the whole of its plain surface, is based on flœtz limestone, commonly of a blueish grey colour, often tinged with black, which colour in some places entirely prevails, especially where the limestone is interstratified with slate clay, calp, or swinestone, or where it abounds in lydian stone. The black limestone in the latter case is a hard compact rock, often of a silicious nature, requiring much fuel for its conversion into lime. Calp, or "black quarry stone," which is generally of a blackish grey colour and dull fracture, and may be considered as an intimate mixture of limestone and slate clay, forms the common building stone of Dublin; it is quarried to a great extent at Crumlin and Rathgar. Besides carbonate of lime, it includes considerable quantities of silex and alumen, traces of the oxydes of iron and manganese, and a small proportion of carbon, which gives to it its dark colour: by exposure to the air it undergoes a gradual decomposition. The elevated peninsula of Howth consists of irregular alternations of clay slate and quartz rock, both pure and intermixed, on its southern coast the strata present some extraordinary contortions. The only metallic ore at present found in considerable quantity is lead, once abundantly raised near the commons of Kilmainham, and at Killiney; a much more productive vein on Shankill is now being worked by the Mining Company of Ireland. White lead is found in small quantities; the ore is smelted and refined at Ballycorus, in the immediate vicinity of the mine: on Shankill is a tower for the manufacture of shot. At Loughshinny is a copper mine, and at Clontarf a lead mine, both now abandoned. On the south-western side of Howth, grey ore of manganese and brown iron-stone have been obtained in considerable quantities; and a variety of earthy black cobalt ore has been found there. Coal is supposed to exist near the northern side of the county, and unsuccessful trials have been made for it near Lucan. Among the smaller minerals may be enumerated schorl or tourmaline and garnet, frequently found in the granite; beryl, a variety of emerald, which occurs in several places; and spodumene, which is in great request from its containing eight per cent. of a newly discovered alkali, called lithia, is procured at Killiney, as is also a mineral closely resembling spodumene, designated killinite by Dr. Taylor, its discoverer, from its locality. The limestone strata usually abound with petrifactions, specimens of which, remarkable for their perfection and variety, may be obtained at St. Doulough's, and at Feltrim, about seven miles north-east of Dublin. The shores of the county, particularly from Loughlinstown to Bray, abound with pebbles of all colours, often beautifully variegated, which bear a polish, and are applied to a variety of ornamental uses.

The manufactures are various, but of inferior importance. The most extensive is that of woollen cloth, carried on chiefly in the liberties and vicinity of Dublin. The manufacture of paper is carried on in different parts, more particularly at Rockbrook and Templeoge. There are also cotton-works, bleach and dye-works, and iron-works, besides minor establishments, all noticed in their respective localities. The banks of the numerous small streams by which the county is watered present divers advantageous sites for the erection of manufactories of every kind within a convenient distance of the metropolis. The great extent of sea-coast affords facilities for obtaining an abundant supply of fish. Nearly 90 wherries, of which the greater number belong to Skerries and Rush, and the others to Howth, Baldoyle, Malahide,

Balbriggan, and Ringsend, are employed in this occupation: there are also about twenty smacks and five seine nets occupied in the salmon fishery between Dublin and Kingstown; the former, in the season, are likewise engaged in the herring fishery; and at Kingstown and Bullock are also a number of yawls, employed in catching whiting, pollock, and herring. On the river Liffey, from Island-Bridge to the light-house at Poolbeg, there is a considerable salmon fishery. The harbours are mere fishing ports, except that of Dublin, and its dependencies Howth and Kingstown, upon the improvement of both of which vast sums have been expended, with but partial success.

The chief river is the Anna Liffey ("the water of Liffey"), which has its principal source at Sally gap, in the Wicklow mountains, and taking a circuit westward through Kildare county, enters that of Dublin near Leixlip, where it is joined by the Rye water from Kildare, and pursues a winding eastern course nearly across the middle of it, descending through a deep and rich glen by Lucan and Chapelizod: below the latter it flows through some pleasing scenes on the borders of Phœnix Park: at Island-Bridge it meets the tide, and a little below it enters the city, to the east of which it discharges its waters into the bay of Dublin. The river is navigable for vessels of 300 tons up to Carlisle bridge, the nearest to the sea; for small craft that can pass the arches, up to Island-Bridge, and for small boats beyond Chapelizod: so circuitous is its course, that although the distance from its source to its mouth, in a direct line, is only ten miles, yet, following its banks, it is no less than forty. Numerous streams, which supply water to many mills, descend into the Liffey: the principal are the Dodder, the Brittas or Cammock, and the Tolka; a stream called the Delvan forms the northern boundary of the county at Naul. The two great lines of inland navigation commence in Dublin city, but as they run in parallel directions within a few miles of each other during some parts of their course, the benefits anticipated from them have not been realised to the utmost extent. The Grand Canal was originally commenced in the year 1755, by the corporation for promoting inland navigation in Ireland: in 1772, a subscription was opened, and the subscribers were incorporated by the name of the Company of Undertakers of the Grand Canal, who, by the completion of this work, have connected the capital both with the Shannon and the Barrow. Its entire cost was £844,216, besides £122,148 expended on docks: one-third was defrayed by parliament. The Royal Canal, incorporated by a charter of Geo. III., in 1789, and afterwards aided by a grant of additional powers from the legislature, is navigable from Dublin to Longford and Tarmonbarry, near the head of the navigable course of the Shannon, an extent of 92 miles: its construction cost £776,213, which was wholly defrayed at the public expense. The roads and bridges are for the most part in excellent order, being frequently repaired at great expense. The Circular Road is a turnpike, nearly encompassing the metropolis, beyond which the Grand and Royal canals for a considerable distance run nearly parallel: from these limits of the city the great mail-coach roads branch in every direction, and all, excepting the south-east road through Wicklow to Wexford, are turnpikes.

Of the ancient round towers which form so remarkable a feature in the antiquities of Ireland, this county contains three, situated respectively at Lusk, Swords, and Clondalkin. There is a very fine cromlech at Glen Druid, near Cabinteely, and others at Killiney, Howth, Mount Venus (in the parish of Cruagh), Glen Southwell or the Little Dargle, and Larch hill, which last is within a circle of stones; and there are numerous raths or moats in various parts. The number of religious houses existing at various periods prior to the Reformation was 24, of which there are at present remains only of those of Larkfield and Monkstown; but there are several remains of ancient churches. Although always forming the centre of the English power in Ireland, the unsettled state of society caused the surface of the county, at an early period, to be studded with castles, of which the remains are still numerous; these, with the ancient castles yet inhabited, and the principal gentlemen's seats, are noticed in their respective parishes. Among the minor natural curiosities are some chalybeate springs, of which the best known are, one at Golden-Bridge, one in the Phœnix Park, and one at Lucan. Southwell's Glen, about four miles south of the metropolis, is worthy of notice as a remarkably deep dale, lined with lofty trees, and adorned by a waterfall. From the district of Fingal, which is the ancient name of a large tract of indefinite extent to the north of Dublin, the distinguished family of Plunkett derives the titles of Earl and Baron.

DUBLIN, the metropolis of Ireland, and a city and county of itself, in the province of LEINSTER, situated in 53° 21′ (N. Lat.) and 6° 17′ (W. Lon.), 339 miles (N. W.) from London; containing, in 1831, 265,316 inhabitants, of which number, 204,155 are within the boundary of the civic jurisdiction, and the remainder in the county of Dublin.

Arms.

The existence of this city, under the name of the city *Eblana*, was first noticed by Ptolemy, the Roman geographer, who lived about the year 140. Shortly after it is mentioned by the native historians, as being fixed on as the eastern boundary of a line of demarcation drawn westwards across the island to Galway, for the purpose of putting an end to a war between two rival monarchs, Con-Cead-Cathach, King of Ireland, and Mogha Nuagad, King of Munster; the portion of the island to the north of the boundary line being assigned to the former, the southern portion to the latter, of the contending parties. The city originally occupied the summit of the elevated ridge that now forms its central portion, extending from the Castle westwards towards Kilmainham, and was at first called by the native Irish *Drom-Col-Coille*, or the "Hill of Hazel wood," from the number of trees of that species which grew on it. The correctness of this conjecture as to the origin of the name is confirmed by the fact that, on clearing away the foundations of the old chapel royal in the castle, some years since, to prepare for the erection of the beautiful structure that now supplies its place, they were ascertained to have been laid on piles of hazelwood. Another ancient name, still retained by the natives, is *Bally-Ath-Cliath-Duibhlinne*, the "Town of the Ford of Hurdles on the Blackwater," given to it in consequence of the people having access to the river by means of hurdles laid over its marshy borders, before it was embanked. By the Danish settlers in the district of Fingal, to the north of the city, it was called *Divelin*, and by the Welsh it is still called *Dinas Dulin*.

The only circumstance on record connected with the city, during a long interval, is that the inhabitants of Leinster were defeated in a great battle fought at Dublin, by Fiacha Sraotine, monarch of Ireland, in 291. After which its annals present a total blank until the year 448, when, according to Josceline, Alphin Mac Eochaid, King of Bally-Ath-Cliath, was converted to Christianity by the preaching of St. Patrick, and baptised by him at a spring on the southern side of the city, near the tower of the cathedral afterwards dedicated to that saint, and still known by the name of St. Patrick's well. The Black Book of Christ-Church, a manuscript of high antiquity and repute, states that St. Patrick celebrated mass in one of the arches or vaults built by the Danish or Ostman merchants as a depository for their goods, long before the fleets of that nation appeared on the coast with the intention of taking military occupation of the country. It was not till the beginning of the ninth century that these marauders, who afterwards harassed all the northern coasts of Europe by their predatory invasions, divested themselves of the character of merchants, in which they had hitherto maintained an intercourse with the people of Ireland, to assume that of conquerors. In 836, the Ostmen or Easterlings, by which name the Danes were then known, entered the Liffey in a fleet of sixty ships in aid of their countrymen, who had ravaged the land and even fixed themselves in some districts several years before. Dublin now submitted to them for the first time; and they secured themselves in the possession of it by the erection of a strong rath, which enabled them not only to overawe the city but to extend their power through Fingal, to the north, and to Bray and the Wicklow mountains to the south. The district from that time was the principal Danish settlement in Leinster; Fin-Gal, to the north of the river, having acquired its name, as being the territory of the "White Strangers," or Norwegians; and the tract to the south being distinguished by the appellation of Dubh-Gal, or the territory of the "Black Strangers," from the Danes.

But the invaders did not enjoy their newly gained acquisition in tranquillity. On the death of their king Tor-magnus or Turgesius, who, after having reigned despotically over a great part of the island for more than 40 years, was defeated and put to death, in 845, by Malachy, King of Ireland, the Danes were driven out of Dublin, and the city plundered by the Irish of Meath and Leinster. In the year following, however, they regained possession of it and secured themselves by adding new fortifications to those already constructed, and were still further strengthened by the arrival of Amlave, or Aulaffe, who, having landed in 853 with a powerful reinforcement of Danes and Norwegians, assumed the supreme authority over all the Danish settlers; and in the hope of enjoying quiet possession of his newly acquired dignity, he concluded a truce with the neighbouring Irish chieftains, but it continued only for three years. The annals of the remainder of this century are occupied with recitals of reciprocal attacks of the Irish and the foreigners, in which the one party failed to expel the invaders, and the other was equally unsuccessful in enlarging the bounds of their authority, or even of fixing it on a permanent basis in the capital of the district that acknowledged their sway: in one of those conflicts, Clondalkin, the favourite residence of Aulaffe, was burnt and upwards of one hundred of his principal followers were slain; in another he retaliated on the enemy, by plundering and burning the city of Armagh. So firmly did the Danish king feel himself fixed in his restored dominion, that he proceeded with his son Ivar, in a fleet of 200 vessels to aid his countrymen Hinguar and Hubba, then contending against the Saxons in the West of England, and returned next year laden with booty. On the death of Aulaffe, which took place the year following, his son Ivar succeeded him in the government of Dublin, where the opinion of his power was such that the Irish annals give him the title of King of the Normans of all Ireland. A few years after, the men of Dublin fitted out an expedition under the command of Ostin Mac Aulaffe against the Picts of North Britain, in which they were successful. Encouraged by these instances of good fortune, they again invaded South Wales, but were driven out with great loss; to wipe off which disgrace they made an incursion into Anglesey, a few years after, and ravaged it with fire and sword. During all this period hostilities were carried on between them and the Irish with little intermission. The annals of the tenth century state that Dublin was four times taken by the Irish, and the Danes expelled from it, but they invariably returned in strength sufficient to re-establish themselves, and often to retaliate severely on their enemies. This century is remarkable for other events connected with Dublin. Aulaffe Mac Godfrid, the king, was defeated in Northumberland by Athelstan, King of England; and about the middle of the century, the Ostmen of Dublin embraced Christianity. The first public proof of their conversion was the foundation of the monastery of the Blessed Virgin, near Ostmanstown, on the northern bank of the Liffey. About the same time, Edgar, King of England, is said to have subdued Wales, the Isle of Man, and part of Ireland, particularly the city of Dublin, of which mention is made in his charter dated at Gloucester, in 964.

Towards the close of the century, the power of the Danes in this part of Ireland began to decline. In 980, they were defeated in a memorable battle at Taragh by Melaghlin, King of Ireland, who, following up his success, ravaged Fingal with fire and sword, and compelled the inhabitants of Dublin to pay a tribute of an ounce of gold for every capital messuage and garden in the city. Reginald, the Danish king, was so much affected by his losses that he undertook a pilgrimage to the Isle of Iona, where he died. The last year of the century was rendered still more memorable by the capture of Dublin by the celebrated Brian Boroimhe, King of Munster, who, after exacting hostages to secure his conquest, permitted the Danes to retain possession of it, a concession of which they immediately took advantage by strengthening it with several additional fortifications. Still, however, their power, though diminished, was not destroyed; for, in the commencement of the ensuing century, Brian Boriomhe, in order effectually to crush them, found it necessary to form a confederacy of most of the subordinate kings of Ireland. The result was the celebrated battle of Clontarf, fought in 1014, in which the Danes were totally defeated, and the shattered remains of their army forced to shut themselves up in Dublin. But the triumph of the conquerors was diminished by the death of their leader, who received a mortal wound at the moment of victory: his son, a number of his nobles, and 11,000 of his soldiers shared his fate. The Danes still kept possession of the city. In 1038, Christ-Church was founded by Sitric the king, and by Donat, the first Danish bishop of Dublin; Aulaffe, Sitric's son, who succeeded him, fitted out a large fleet in order to reinstate Conan, the prince of North Wales, who had fled to Ireland to escape from the cruelties of Grufydd ab Llewelyn, an usurper, and had afterwards married Sitric's daughter. The expedition, though at first so successful as to have gained possession of Grufydd's person by stratagem, ultimately failed; for the Welsh, on hearing of his capture, assembled in great numbers, rescued Grufydd, and drove Conan and his Danish auxiliaries to their ships with great slaughter. A second expedition fitted out the ensuing year was equally unfortunate: the greater part of Conan's fleet was destroyed by a tempest and himself driven back on the Irish shore. He made no further attempt to regain his throne, but spent the remainder of his life with his father-in-law in Dublin.

The city was soon after exposed to the assaults of a new enemy. In 1066, Godred Crovan, King of Man, obtained possession of it and overran a large portion of Leinster, over which he assumed the title of king, which he retained till his death, together with that of Man and of the Hebrides. On his demise the sovereign power again devolved on the Danes, who elected Godfrey Meranagh to succeed him. The Danes, though constantly exposed to the hostilities of the natives, against whom they had great difficulty in maintaining their position in the country, increased their difficulties by their internal dissensions. In 1088, those of Dublin besieged the city of Waterford, which was also inhabited by a colony of the same nation, entered it by storm and burnt it to the ground; and in the following year, the united Danish forces of Dublin, Wicklow, and Waterford proceeded to Cork with a similar intention, but were routed on their march thither and forced to return with considerable loss. For some time after the district appears to have been subject to the kings of Ireland, as no mention is made of any Danish ruler there. At the same time it appears that the kings of England endeavoured to obtain some influence in the affairs of Ireland, for it is stated that Rodolphus, Archbishop of Canterbury, by the orders of Hen. I., consecrated one Gregory Archbishop of Dublin, in 1121, and that this act was done with the concurrence of Turlogh O'Brien, then King of Ireland. Afterwards, however, Dermod Mac Murchad, or Mac Murrough, King of Leinster, exercised paramount authority in the city. He founded the nunnery of St. Mary de Hogges, and the priory of Allhallows, both in its immediate vicinity, and, after overrunning all the surrounding country, forced the Danish residents there to acknowledge his supremacy, which he retained until the commencement of the reign of Roderic O'Conor, King of Ireland, who, on his attainment of the supreme monarchy, was recognised as King of Dublin by the inhabitants, and they in return received from him a present of four thousand oxen.

After the reduction of Wexford by the English forces, who landed at Bannow bay, in 1169, under the command of Robert Fitz-Stephen, to assist Dermod Mac Murrough in the recovery of Leinster, the combined force marched upon Dublin. The garrison, intimidated by the reports of the numbers and ferocity of the assailants, sued for peace, which was granted on the payment of tribute secured by hostages. Asculph Mac Torcall, the Danish king, was suffered to retain the government, and Dermod retired with his English auxiliaries to the southern part of Leinster, where he was joined by Strongbow, Earl of Pembroke, who had landed with a reinforcement of fifteen or sixteen hundred men, and taken Waterford by storm from the Danes. The combined army thus enforced resolved upon another attack on Dublin, either in consequence of a second revolt, or, as the Irish writers assert, to gratify the vindictive feelings of Dermod, who hoped thus to revenge the injury and insult of his former expulsion. Roderic, King of Ireland, hearing of the intended movement, levied an army of 30,000 men, which he posted at Clondalkin to oppose the invaders; but on their nearer approach he disbanded his troops, and retired across the Shannon. The citizens perceiving themselves thus abandoned, again had recourse to treaty; but while they were preparing to select the hostages required of them, Milo de Cogan, one of the English leaders, forced his way into the place. Asculph and most of the Danes took shelter on board their fleet, and the city was, after much slaughter, taken possession of by the English.

Roderic now made a second attempt to expel the strangers, for which purpose he invested Dublin with an army of double the number he had formerly collected, and reduced the place to such straits, that Strongbow deputed Laurence O'Toole, the archbishop, to treat with him for a surrender. The terms offered by the Irish king were not only the surrender of all the towns held by the English, but their total evacuation of the country. When these humiliating conditions were reported, Milo de Cogan protested against thus relinquishing the earnings of so many hard-fought battles, and proposed a general sally upon the enemy. His advice was adopted. The English forces, leaving behind them in the city their Irish auxiliaries, on whose fidelity they had less reliance, and led on by Milo, proceeded to Roderic's head-quarters at Finglass, which they assaulted so suddenly that he was obliged to escape half dressed from a bath, and his whole army was dispersed.

Strongbow being soon after called to England, Asculph Mac Torcall, during his absence, arrived in the harbour of Dublin with a fleet of 60 ships and an army of 10,000 men levied in the isle of Man, the Orkneys, and Norway, and proceeded at once to storm the city. His main body was led on by John de Dene, a Norwegian of great military repute, who was repulsed by Milo de Cogan, with the loss of 500 men; and the Danes being unexpectedly attacked in the rear by another body of the garrison, which had made a sally from a different quarter, they were utterly routed, and their king Asculph made prisoner and put to death. The relics of the Danish army which escaped the sword were cut in pieces by the peasantry through the country, in revenge for their former cruelties, so that scarcely 2000 gained their ships, most of whom were destroyed by a tempest during their voyage home. This defeat put an end to the Danish power in these parts. An attempt made, soon after, to seize on the city by Tiernan O'Rourke, the chieftain of Breffny, who thought that the garrison, exhausted by its late struggle, though successful, would be incapable of making a vigorous resistance to the large force he was bringing against it, also failed.

The arrival of Hen. II., who landed at Waterford with a large fleet and a numerous train in 1172 caused a great change in the state of the city. He had compelled Strongbow to surrender to him all his conquests in Ireland: the lands were restored, to be held by feudal tenure, but the fortified places were retained in the king's hands. Henry, after having received the homage of most of the petty chieftains of the south, arrived in Dublin, in the beginning of winter, and celebrated the feast of Christmas there in great splendour; on which occasion a pavilion of hurdles, after the Irish fashion, was erected in the eastern suburb, where the court was held, and where several of the native princes did homage to him. Hugh de Lacy and William Fitz Aldelm were commissioned to receive the homage of Roderic, King of Ireland, who declined crossing the Shannon. Being unexpectedly hurried away to oppose a revolt of his own sons in Normandy, Henry quitted the city for Wexford, whence he embarked for England on Easter-Monday, leaving Hugh de Lacy in charge of the place as governor, with twenty men at arms, and Robert Fitz-Stephen and Maurice Fitz-Gerald with the same number, as wardens and constables. Milo de Cogan, to whose intrepidity the English had been indebted for their conquest, accompanied Henry on his departure. Previously to his leaving the city, the king granted it a charter, entitling it to the same privileges as Bristol then enjoyed: the original is still preserved in the archives of the corporation. By a subsequent charter of the same king, the citizens are freed from payment of toll, passage, and pontage, throughout England, Normandy, Wales, and Ireland. Three years after Henry's departure, Strongbow made an incursion into Munster, in which he was accompanied by the Ostmen of Dublin, but was surprised on his march by Donald, Prince of Ossory, and defeated, with the loss of 400 of the citizens. Elated with this success, Roderic O'Conor ravaged the country even to the walls of Dublin. Shortly after, Strongbow died of a mortification in his foot, and was buried in Christ Church, where his monument is still preserved. Previously to his death he had founded the extensive and wealthy preceptory of Knights Templars, on the site on which the Royal Hospital now stands. In the same year, Vivian, the pope's legate, held a synod in the city, at which he caused the title of Hen. II. to the lordship of Ireland to be proclaimed; and denounced an excommunication against all who should refuse allegiance to him. In 1185, John, Earl of Morton, the favourite son of Hen. II., having been invested by his father with the lordship of Ireland, arrived in Dublin, attended by a train of young noblemen; but a series of insurrections taking place, he was recalled.

From the period of the arrival of the English and their conquest of Dublin, the city was considered to be the most appropriate position to secure their possessions and to facilitate their intercourse with their native country. To promote this object, instructions were given by John, shortly after the commencement of his reign, to Meyler Fitz-Henry, to erect a castle on the eastern brow of the hill on which the city stood, for which purpose 300 marks were assigned; an order was also issued to compel the inhabitants to repair and strengthen the fortifications. The necessity of a precautionary measure of this nature was confirmed by a calamity which befel the city in 1209, in which year the citizens, while amusing themselves according to custom on Easter-Monday in Cullen's wood, near the southern suburbs, were attacked unawares by the Irish of the neighbouring mountains and driven into the town, after the slaughter of more than 500 of their number. The day was for a long time after distinguished by the name of Black Monday, and commemorated by a parade of the citizens on the field of the conflict, were they appeared in arms and challenged their enemies to renew the encounter. The castle, however, was not completed till 1220, during the government of Henry de Loundres, Archbishop of Dublin and Lord-Justice. King John on his visit to Ireland in 1210, established courts of judicature on the model of those in England, deposited an abstract of the English laws and customs in the Exchequer, and issued a coinage of pence and farthings of the same standard as the English. Hen. III. granted several charters, which were confirmed and extended by Edw. I., who also fixed a standard for coin in England, according to which that of Ireland was to be regulated: during his reign there were four mints in Dublin, besides others at Waterford and Drogheda. About the close of the 13th and beginning of the 14th century a great part of the city was destroyed by fires, one of which consumed many of the public records, which had been lodged in St. Mary's abbey. An attempt to found an university, made in 1311 by Archbishop Leck, who procured a papal bull for this purpose, failed in consequence of the unsettled state of the country, but was revived with more success in 1320 by Alexander de Bicknor, the next archbishop. In 1312, the mountain septs of the O'Byrnes and O'Tooles made an incursion into Rathcool and Saggard, when the chief force of the city had been despatched into Louth, or Orgial, to quell an insurrection of the Verdons, but on its return the southern invaders were forced to retire into their fastnesses. Three years after, when David O'Toole and some others of his sept made a similar attempt, by placing an ambush in Cullen's wood, the citizens issued out against them with their black banner displayed, and did execution on them for several miles.

The year 1315 is remarkable for the invasion of Edward Bruce, brother of Robert Bruce, King of Scotland, who landed at Carrickfergus at the head of 6000 men, to establish his claim to the crown of Ireland by force of arms. The citizens, on hearing that he was advancing southwards and had taken Greencastle, in Carlingford bay, one of the border fortresses of the English pale, sent out a strong party by sea, recovered the place, and brought the governor to Dublin, where he was starved to death in prison. This success, however, did not put a stop to the advance of Bruce, who marched upon Dublin with the intention of besieging it.

The citizens, on his approach, set fire to the suburb of Thomas-street, in consequence of which St. John's Church without Newgate, and the Magdalene chapel were burnt. The church of the Dominicans was also pulled down, in order to use the stones for repairing and extending the city walls on the north side towards the river. The gallant determination of the citizens had its effect. Bruce, after destroying St. Mary's abbey and plundering the cathedral of St. Patrick, drew off his army and marched westward into Kildare. In consideration of the sufferings and losses of the citizens, Edw. II. remitted half of their fee-farm rent. At the close of the century the city was twice visited by Rich. II.; at first, in 1394, when he marched hither from Waterford, about Michaelmas, at the head of an army of 30,000 foot and 4000 horse, and remained till the beginning of the ensuing summer. His second visit, which took place in 1399, was cut short by the unwelcome news of the insurrection of the Duke of Lancaster, afterwards Hen. IV., which hurried him back to England.

During the reign of Hen. IV. the citizens adhered firmly to him throughout the civil war excited by the Earl of Northumberland and Owain Glyndwr, and caused a diversion in his favour by fitting out a fleet with which they invaded Scotland, and, after several landings on the coast, proceeded in like manner along that of Wales, whence they carried away the shrine of St. Cubie and on their return placed it in the cathedral of Christ-Church. In consequence of these services they obtained from the king a confirmation of all their former charters, and the present of a gilded sword to be borne before the mayor in public, in the same manner as before the lord mayor of London. The border war between the citizens and the Irish of the neighbouring mountains was carried on with great fury during this and the succeeding reigns. In 1402, John Drake, the provost, led out a strong party against the O'Byrnes, whom he defeated with a slaughter, as some writers say, of 4000 men, but according to others of 400, and compelled them to surrender the castle of Newcastle-Mac-Kynegan. In 1410, the lord-deputy made another incursion into the territory of the O'Byrnes, but was forced to retreat in consequence of the desertion of a large body of his kernes; and in 1413 the O'Byrnes gave the citizens a signal defeat and carried off many prisoners. In 1431, Mac Murrough, King of Leinster, made an incursion into the vicinity of Dublin, defeated the troops sent out to oppose him, and carried off much booty; but the citizens having collected a fresh body of troops, pursued the enemy the same evening, attacked them unawares, and routed them with great loss. The city was much disturbed, about this time, by the contentions between the Kildare and Ormonde families. To decide one of their disputes, in which Thomas Fitzgerald, prior of Kilmainham, had accused the Earl of Ormonde of treason, a trial by combat was appointed at Smithfield, in Oxmantown; but the quarrel being taken up by the king was terminated without bloodshed. The mayor and citizens, having taken part with the Fitzgeralds in these broils, and grossly insulted the Earl of Ormonde, and violated the sanctity of St. Mary's abbey, were compelled to do penance, in 1434, by going barefoot to that monastery and to Christ-Church and St. Patrick's cathedrals, and craving pardon at the doors. In 1479, the fraternity of arms of St. George, consisting of thirteen of the most honourable and loyal inhabitants in the counties of Dublin, Meath, Kildare, and Louth, was formed by act of parliament, for the defence of the English pale: the mayor of Dublin was appointed one of the commanders of the force raised in the city; the fraternity was discontinued in 1492. A bull for the foundation of an university in the city was published by Pope Sextus in 1475, but was never carried into effect.

When Lambert Simnel claimed the crown of England, in the beginning of the reign of Hen. VII., his title was recognised in Dublin, where he was crowned in Christ-Church, in the presence of the lord-deputy, the lords of the council, the mayor, and all the citizens; after the ceremony was concluded, he was carried in state to the castle, according to the Irish custom, on the shoulders of Darcy of Platten, a man of extraordinary stature. On Simnel's defeat at Stoke, the mayor and citizens made a humble apology to the king for the part they had taken in the affair, pleading the authority and influence of the lord-deputy, the archbishop, and most of the clergy. Their pardon was granted through Sir Richard Edgecumbe, who was specially deputed by Henry to administer the oaths of fealty and allegiance to the Irish after the insurrection: this officer entered Dublin on the 5th of July, 1488, for the fulfilment of his mission, and embarked for England at Dalkey, on the 30th of the same month, after having successfully accomplished the objects for which he had been deputed. In 1504, the mayor and citizens contributed their share to the victory gained by the Earl of Kildare, lord-deputy, over the Irish and degenerate English of Connaught, at Knocktow, near Galway. A few years after, the revival of the controversy between the Earls of Kildare and Ormonde again subjected the citizens to ecclesiastical censures. The two Earls had a meeting in St. Patrick's cathedral, for the ostensible purpose of compromising their feud; the citizens attended the former as his guard, and on some cause of complaint between them and the Earl of Ormonde's soldiers, they let fly a volley of arrows, some of which struck the images in the rood-loft. In atonement for this sacrilegious violation of the building, the mayor was sentenced to walk barefoot before the host on Corpus Christi day yearly, a ceremony which was kept up till the Reformation.

During the early period of the reign of Hen. VIII., the people of Dublin gave several instances of loyalty and courage. In 1513 they attended the lord-deputy in a hosting against O'Carrol, which terminated without any remarkable action, in consequence of the death of their leader. In 1516 they routed the O'Tooles of the mountains, slew their chief, and sent his head a present to the mayor: a second expedition, however, was less successful; the O'Tooles drove them back with loss. Afterwards, in 1521, they performed good service under the Earl of Surrey against O'More, in Leix, and O'Conor in Meath. But the most remarkable event connected with the city, during the reign of Hen. VIII., arose out of the rebellion of Lord Thomas Fitzgerald, commonly called the Silken Knight, from the fantastical fringes with which the helmets of his followers were decorated. This young nobleman had been appointed lord-deputy in the absence of his father, the Earl of Kildare, who was summoned to appear before Henry, to answer some charges brought against him, as chief governor of Ireland; and on a false report that his father had been imprisoned and put to death in London, he proceeded, without making further inquiry into the truth of the allegation, at the head of his armed followers, to St. Mary's abbey, where the council was sitting, threw down the sword of state, and notwithstanding the paternal remonstrances of the primate, Archbishop Cromer, bade defiance to the king and declared himself his open enemy. After ravaging Fingal, where he seized and put to death Alan, then archbishop of Dublin, the enemy of his family, he laid siege to the castle, but after several ineffectual attempts to carry it by storm he surrendered to Lord Leonard Grey, and was ultimately sent to England, where he was executed with five of his uncles, who not only had taken no part in the insurrection, but had been active in dissuading him from engaging in it. In recompense for the citizens' gallant defence, the king granted them the dissolved monastery of All Hallows, without Dames Gate, confirmed a grant of £49. 6. 8. made by Rich. II., and released them from an annual rent of £20.

In 1547, the Byrnes and O'Tooles, presuming on the weakness of the government during the minority of Edw. VI., made frequent inroads into the neighbourhood of Dublin, to the great annoyance of the inhabitants. The close vicinity of the mountains and the difficulties of the passes through which they were accessible, rendered the defence of the suburbs difficult, and retaliation hazardous; but at length Sir Anthony St. Leger, lord-deputy, with a body of the standing army, and a considerable number of the city militia, made a successful inroad into their fastnesses, defeated them in a great battle, killed their chief, and brought sixteen of the Fitzgeralds prisoners to Dublin, where they were all executed as traitors. In 1552, the mayor, at the head of the armed citizens, being joined with the townsmen of Drogheda, marched against the O'Reillys of Cavan, whom they put down: but, on their return, the victory was likely to be sullied by a dispute between the two commanders, as to the honour of leading the vanguard; which was at last terminated in favour of the mayor of Dublin, by an order confirming his right of leading the van when going out, and the rear when returning home.

In the first year of Queen Mary's reign, the citizens marched out against the Cavanaghs, who with a large army were devastating the southern part of the county of Dublin, and whom they routed, killing many and compelling the remainder to shut themselves up in Powerscourt castle, whence, having been at length forced to surrender at discretion, after an obstinate resistance, they were taken to Dublin, and 74 of them executed: the rest were pardoned.

Queen Elizabeth, in the beginning of her reign, caused the castle to be fitted up as a residence for the lord-lieutenant, who, previously to this arrangement, had resided at Thomas Court. In 1579, the public records were arranged in Birmingham tower, Dublin Castle; and three years afterwards the courts of law were transferred from the castle to St. Mary's abbey, which occupied nearly the site of the buildings in which they are now held on the north side of the river. In 1586, the king's exchequer, then held without the eastern gate on the ground now called Exchequer-street, was plundered by a party of Irish from the mountains. The year 1591 is memorable for the foundation of Trinity College. In 1599, the Earl of Essex arrived in Dublin at the head of a large army, and after his removal Sir Charles Blount, afterwards Lord Mountjoy, who had been appointed to succeed him in the command of the army raised against the Earl of Tyrone, landed there with 6000 men: but his operations gave rise to no circumstances peculiarly affecting the city.

In 1607, the Government was thrown into the greatest alarm by a letter found on the floor of the council-chamber in the castle, containing intimations of a conspiracy entered into by the Earls of Tyrone and Tyrconnell, and other northern chieftains, to seize the city and excite a general insurrection against the English government. Instant measures were employed to arrest the imputed leaders, several of whom were taken and executed, but the two Earls had sufficient notice of the designs against them to save themselves by flight; their immense estates were confiscated. In 1613, a parliament was held in Dublin, after a lapse of 27 years: it was the first in which representatives were sent from all the counties, and is still more remarkable for a dispute respecting the election of a speaker between the Protestant and Roman Catholic parties, which terminated in the triumph of the former, and the secession of the latter from the House of Commons. In 1614, a convocation was held here, which established the thirty-nine articles of religion; and a subsequent convocation, in 1634, adopted a body of canons for the regulation of the Established Church.

After a period of 40 years of uninterrupted tranquillity, both to the city and the nation, the prospect of its further continuance was destroyed by the discovery of a plot to seize the castle, on the 23rd of October, 1641, as the first movement of a general insurrection against the English Government. The plan was disclosed by an accomplice, on the evening before the day it was to have been put into execution, and thus frustrated as far as the city was concerned. So little had the occurrence of such an event been apprehended that, in the year before, a large portion of the city walls was allowed to fall to ruin. To aid in their repairs, and to meet the other urgent necessities of the state, the citizens were called upon by proclamation to send in their plate, on promise of repayment, an expedient which produced only £1200 towards the relief of the public exigencies. Next year the mayor was invited to the council, to confer on a project for raising £10,000, half in money and the remainder in provisions, to enable the king's army to take the field; but such was the poverty of the place, that the project was relinquished as impracticable. On an alarm of an intended attack on Dublin, by the Irish forces of Owen Roe O'Nial and General Preston, in 1646, the Marquess of Ormonde, then lord-lieutenant, determined to strengthen the city by a line of outworks thrown up on its eastern side, between the castle and the college. On this occasion the women set a remarkable example of public spirit, the Marchioness of Ormonde and other ladies placing themselves at their head, and the whole assisting in carrying baskets of earth to the lines. Famine, however, proved the city's best safeguard. The Marquess had caused the country to be laid waste, and the mills and bridges to be destroyed for several miles round, so that the besieging army, amounting to 10,000 foot and 1000 horse, was forced to retire without any attempt of importance. So confident was Ormonde now of his own strength, that he refused admission to commissioners sent by the English parliament with 1400 men, but the very next year he was compelled, by extreme necessity, to surrender the place to them, rather than suffer it to fall into the hands of the Irish; after which, Owen Roe O'Nial, being baffled in another attempt upon the city, revenged himself by ravaging the surrounding country with such fury that from one of the town steeples 200 fires were seen blazing at once. The Marquess of Ormonde returned in 1649, with a determination to regain possession of the city. He first fixed his head-quarters at Finglas, but afterwards removed to Rathmines, on the south side. An unexpected sally of the garrison, to destroy some works he was throwing up at Bagotsrath, led to a general engagement, in which his troops, struck with an unaccountable panic, gave way with such precipitation, that he had scarcely time to make his escape. The city remained in the hands of the parliament during the remainder of the war. At the close of the same year, Oliver Cromwell landed here with a well-appointed army of 13,000 men: after remaining a short time to refresh his troops, and to arrange his affairs, he left it for Drogheda, which he took, and treated those by whom he was opposed with a degree of cruelty seldom paralleled in the annals of modern warfare. In 1652, the war having been declared at an end, a high court of justice was erected in Dublin, for the trial of persons charged with murder and other atrocities not tolerated by the rules of war, by which, among many others of less note, Sir Phelim O'Nial, the first and principal leader of the insurrection in Ulster, was condemned and executed. In 1659, a party of general officers, well inclined to the Restoration, surprised the castle, and having secured the parliamentary commissioners of Government, who resided there, declared for a free parliament; they then, upon the petition of the mayor and aldermen, summoned a convention, and though the castle was again surprised by Sir Hardress Waller, for the parliament, he was forced to surrender it, after a siege of five days, and Chas. II. was formally proclaimed. Charles, immediately after his restoration, rewarded the services of the citizens by the donation of a cap of maintenance, a golden collar of office, and a foot company to the mayor, and some years after, a pension of £500 was allowed him in lieu of the company. In 1663, several discontented officers, among whom was the notorious Col. Blood, formed a plan to seize the castle, which was discovered by one of the accomplices.

About this period the city began to increase rapidly in extent, and in the number and elegance of its public buildings. The ground to the north of the river, formerly considered as a separate jurisdiction, under the name of Oxmantown, was connected with the city by four new bridges, and has since formed an integral part of it: it had hitherto been but a single parish, but was, some years after, in consequence of the increase of houses and inhabitants, subdivided into three. Numerous improvements were successively carried into effect, and the increase of population kept pace with them. In 1688, King James visited Dublin, where he held a parliament, which passed acts to repeal the act of settlement, to attaint a number of Protestants, and to establish an enlarged system of national education. He also established a mint, in which a quantity of base metal was coined. The year 1690 is marked by the decisive battle of the Boyne, after which James passed one night in Dublin Castle, during his precipitate retreat from the kingdom; in 1701, an equestrian statue of Wm. III. was erected on College Green, to commemorate that victory. On King William's arrival, his first act was to repair in state to St. Patrick's cathedral, to return public thanks for the success which had crowned his arms. Previously to the battle of the Boyne, Sir Cloudesly Shovel, who commanded at sea for the latter monarch, took a frigate out of Dublin harbour, in which much of the plate and valuables of the Roman Catholic nobility and gentry had been embarked, under an apprehension of the event which so soon after decided the fate of their cause in Ireland.

During the period between the revolution and the legislative union, the city increased in an unprecedented manner in extent, wealth, and splendour. The effects are attributable partly to the long period of peace from the former of these eras to the commencement of the American war, but more so to the parliamentary grants which were expended on objects of utility. Afterwards, the regulation which made the lord-lieutenant a fixed resident in Dublin, instead of being a periodical visiter for a few months every second year, when he came over from England to hold a parliament; the shortening of the duration of these assemblies, the removal of the restrictions by which the national industry and the spirit of commercial speculation had been shackled, combined with the general extension of literature and science throughout the western kingdoms of Europe, tended to promote this effect. In 1798, the Leinster provisional committee of the United Irishmen were seized, with all their papers, and Lord Edward Fitzgerald, the chief leader of the insurgents, was arrested, after a desperate conflict with his captors, and lodged in prison, where he shortly after died of his wounds. The following statement will show the increase of population from about the middle of the 17th century till the legislative union: in 1682 the number of inhabitants was 64,483; in 1728, 146,075; in 1753, 128,570; in 1777, 138,208; and in 1798, 182,370.

The local events of the period which has elapsed since the Union are too numerous to particularise in a condensed narrative. The principal occurrences are the public meetings and associations for the attainment of political objects, organised insurrections, tumults resulting from those causes and embittered by the acrimony of party spirit, and visitations of famine, during which the working classes suffered great distress. Two events, however, deserve more particular notice. In 1803, a sudden and alarming insurrection broke out in the city: it was planned and carried into effect by Robert Emmet, a young gentleman of respectable family, who, at his own sole expense and with the aid of a few associates of desperate fortune, secretly formed a depôt of arms and ammunition in a retired lane off Thomas-street, whence he issued early in the night of the 23rd of July, at the head of a band chiefly brought in from the neighbouring counties of Kildare and Wicklow, and was proceeding to the castle, when the progress of his followers was checked by the coming up of Lord Kilwarden, chief justice of the king's bench, who, on hearing a rumour of insurrection at his country seat, had hurried to town in his carriage with his daughter and nephew. Both the males were killed; the lady, being allowed to pass in safety, gave the alarm at the castle, and detachments being immediately sent out, the undisciplined multitude was at once dispersed with some loss of life, and the leaders, who had escaped to the mountains, were soon after taken and executed. On the accession of Geo. IV., in 1820, his majesty received a deputation from Dublin, consisting of the lord mayor and city officers, on his throne: this was the first address from the city thus honoured. The next year, on the 12th of August, the king's birth-day, he landed in Ireland, and after remaining till Sept. 3rd, partly at the Phœnix Lodge, and partly at Slane Castle in Meath, during which time he visited most of the public institutions of Dublin, and held a chapter of the order of St. Patrick, at which nine knights were installed, he sailed from Dunleary (since called Kingstown) amidst the enthusiastic acclamations of an unprecedented multitude.

EXTENT AND GENERAL DESCRIPTION OF THE CITY.

The city, which was originally confined to the summit of the hill, on the eastern brow of which the castle now stands, and whose circuit within the walls was little more than a mile round, and its suburbs confined to the few adjacent streets, now occupies a space covering 1264 acres, and is about nine miles in circumference. It is situated at the western extremity of Dublin bay, and at the mouth of the Liffey, which passes nearly through the middle of it. The hill, which now forms the central part of the city, stands in the lowest part of the basin of the Liffey, which rises gradually on the southern side into the beautiful line of the Wicklow mountains, that skirt the boundary of the county, and still more gradually on the north and west till it loses itself in the extended plains of Fingal and Kildare. It is somewhat more than three miles long in a direct line from east to west, and of nearly equal breadth from north to south, and contains upwards of 800 streets and 22,000 houses: the foot-paths are well flagged, and the carriage ways partly paved and partly Macadamised. The paving, lighting, and cleansing of the public avenues is regulated by an act passed in the 47th, and amended by one of the 54th, of Geo. III., authorising the lord-lieutenant to appoint three commissioners, who are a corporation under the title of the "Commissioners for Paving, Cleansing, and Lighting the City of Dublin:" the total annual expenditure averages about £30,000. Several local acts have been passed for the supply of gas-light, and there are four companies,—the Dublin Gas Company, the Hibernian Gas-light Company, the Oil Gas Company, and the Alliance Company. An ample supply of water is obtained by pipes laid down from reservoirs on both sides of the river to the houses and the public fountains, under a committee appointed in pursuance of acts passed in the 42nd and 49th of Geo. III., the expense of which is defrayed by a rate called the pipe-water tax, producing about £14,000 annually. Three basins have been formed; one at the extremity of Basin-lane, in James-street, half a mile in circumference and surrounded by a broad gravel walk, formerly a favourite promenade; another at the upper end of Blessington-street, encompassed by a terrace, for the supply of the northern side of the city; and the third on the bank of the canal, near Portobello harbour, for the supply of the south-eastern part. Considerable improvements have been made by the Commissioners "for opening wide and convenient streets," appointed under an act of the 31st of Geo. II., whose powers were subsequently extended by various successive acts till the 51st of Geo. III. Their funds, till recently, were derived from a tonnage upon coal and a local rate, called "the wide street tax," the former of which ceased in 1832, and the funds arising from the latter amount to about £5500 per ann. Among the chief improvements are the opening of a passage from the Castle to Essex bridge, an enlargement of the avenue from the same place to the Parliament House (now the Bank of Ireland), the opening of Westmoreland-street and Sackville-street, the clearing away the buildings that interfered with the free thoroughfare along the quays on both sides of the river, the entrance into the city by Great Brunswick-street, besides various improvements in the vicinity of the cathedrals of Christ-Church and St. Patrick. In short, the city may be said to have been new-moulded since the year 1760, through the instrumentality of this Board, as there is no portion of it which does not exhibit in a greater or smaller degree the results of its labours in improvements tending to augment its beauty or to add to its salubrity. A circular road nearly nine miles in circuit, carried round the city, affords great facilities of communication throughout all the outlets, and also walks and drives of much beauty. Some portions of this road, however, particularly on the southern side, are already absorbed into the city by the continued extension of the streets; and most of the other parts, particularly on the eastern side, are likely, from the same cause, shortly to lose their distinguishing characteristic of an encircling avenue. On the north side of this road is the Royal Canal, and on the south, the Grand Canal; both terminating in docks near the mouth of the Liffey: and beyond these are, on the north, a small river called the Tolka, formerly called Tulkan and Tolekan, which empties itself into the sea at Ballybough bridge; and on the south, the river Dodder, which, curving northward, terminates with the Liffey at the harbour, forming two striking natural boundaries towards which the city is gradually extending itself. The city is now closely connected with the harbour of Kingstown by a railway formed under an act of parliament of the 1st and 2nd of Wm. IV., which was opened in Dec. 1834. The number of passengers conveyed upon it during the months of May, June, July, and August, 1836, was 523,080: the greatest number conveyed in one day was 13,000.

In addition to the splendid line of communication afforded by the quays on both sides of the river, there are several noble avenues of fine streets, among which, that from the northern road is peculiarly striking, especially on entering Sackville-street, which is conspicuous for its great width, the magnificence and beauty of the public buildings which embellish it, and the lofty monument to Admiral Viscount Nelson, which stands in its centre. It consists of a fluted Doric column on a massive pedestal, inscribed on each side with the name and date of his lordship's principal victories, and over that which terminated his career is a sarcophagus: the whole is surmounted with a colossal statue of the Admiral, surrounded by a balustrade, to which there is an ascent by a spiral staircase in the interior. The structure was completed at an expense of nearly £7000. On the southern side of the city, the avenue from Kingstown is equally imposing. Both meet in College-green, a spacious area surrounded with noble buildings, and having in its centre an equestrian statue of Wm. III., of cast metal, upon a pedestal of marble. Of the public squares, *St. Stephen's-green*, situated in the south-eastern quarter, is the most spacious, being nearly a mile in circuit: in the centre is an equestrian statue of Geo. II., finely executed in brass by Van Nost; *Merrion-square*, to the east of the former, is about three-quarters of a mile in circuit; on the west the lawn of the Royal Dublin Society. *Fitzwilliam-square* has been recently built and is much smaller than either of the others; the houses are built with much uniformity in a neat but unornamented style; some of them have basements of granite and the upper stories of brick. *Mountjoy-square*, in an elevated and healthy situation in the north-eastern part of the city, is more than half a mile in circuit; the houses are uniformly built and present an appearance very similar to those in Fitzwilliam-square. *Rutland-square* is on the north side of the river, at the upper end of Sackville-street: three sides of it are formed by Granby-row, Palace-row, and Cavendish-row, the fourth by the Lying-in Hospital and the Rotundo. The areas of the several squares are neatly laid out in gravel walks and planted with flowering shrubs and evergreens. A line drawn from the King's Inns, in the north of Dublin, through Capel-street, the Castle and Aungier-street, thus intersecting the Liffey at right angles, would, together with the line of that river, divide the city into four districts, strongly opposed to each other in character and appearance. The south-eastern district, including St. Stephen's-green, Merrion-square, and Fitzwilliam-square, is chiefly inhabited by the nobility, the gentry, and the members of the liberal professions. The north-eastern district, including Mountjoy and Rutland-squares, is principally inhabited by the mercantile and official classes. The south-western district, including the liberties of St. Sepulchre and Thomas-court, and formerly the seat of the woollen and silk manufactures, is in a state of lamentable dilapidation, bordering on ruin: and the north-western district, in which are the Royal barracks and Smithfield (the great market for hay and cattle), presents striking indications of poverty.

BRIDGES.

The Liffey is embanked on both sides by a range of masonry of granite, forming a continuation of spacious quays through the whole of the city, and its opposite sides are connected with nine bridges, eight of which are of elegant design and highly ornamental. *Carlisle bridge*, the nearest to the sea, and connecting Westmoreland-street on the south with Sackville-street on the north, is a very elegant structure of three arches: it is 210 feet in length and 48 feet in breadth, and was completed in 1794. *Wellington bridge*, at the end of Liffey-street, 140 feet long, consists of a single elliptic arch of cast iron, and was erected in 1816, for the accommodation of foot passengers only, at an expense of £3000, which is defrayed by a halfpenny toll. *Essex bridge*, connecting Capel-street with Parliament-street, and fronting the Royal Exchange, was built in 1755, on the site of a former structure of the same name, at an expense of £20,661; it is a handsome stone structure of five arches, 250 feet in length and 51 in width, after the model of Westminster bridge, London. *Richmond bridge*, built on the site of Ormond bridge, which had been swept away by a flood, was commenced in 1813; it connects Winetavern-street with Montrath-street, and was completed at an expense of £25,800, raised by presentments on the city and county, and opened to the public on St. Patrick's day, 1816; it is built of Portland stone, with a balustrade of cast iron, and is 220 feet long and 52 feet wide, consisting of three fine arches, the keystones of which are ornamented with colossal heads, on the one side representing Peace, Hibernia, and Commerce; and on the other, Plenty, the river Liffey, and Industry. *Whitworth bridge* supplies the place of the old bridge built by the Dominican friars, which had been for a long time the only communication between the city and its northern suburbs: the first stone was laid in 1816, by the Earl of Whitworth, then lord-lieutenant; it is an elegant structure of three arches, connecting Bridge-street with Church-street. *Queen's bridge*, a smaller structure of three arches of hewn stone, connecting Bridgefoot-street with Queen-street, is only 140 feet in length: it was built in 1768, on the site of Arran bridge, which was destroyed by a flood in 1763. *Barrack bridge*, formerly Bloody bridge, connecting Watling-street with the quay leading to the royal barracks, was originally constructed of wood, in 1671, and subsequently rebuilt of stone. *King's bridge*, of which the first stone was laid by the Marquess Wellesley in 1827, connects the military road with the south-eastern entrance to the Phœnix Park, affording to the lord-lieutenant a retired and pleasant avenue from the Castle to his country residence; it consists of a single arch of cast iron, 100 feet in span, resting on abutments of granite richly ornamented, and was completed at an expense of £13,000, raised for the purpose of erecting a national testimonial in commemoration of the visit of Geo. IV. to Ireland, in 1821. *Sarah bridge*, formerly Island bridge, but when rebuilt in its present form named after the Countess of Westmoreland, who laid the foundation stone in 1791, is a noble structure of a single arch, 104 feet in span, the keystone of which is 30 feet above low water mark: this bridge connects the suburban village of Island-Bridge with the north-western road and with one of the entrances to the Phœnix Park; from the peculiar elegance of its proportions, it has been distinguished by the name of the "Irish Rialto."

MANUFACTURE, TRADE, AND COMMERCE.

The woollen manufacture was carried on in Ireland at a very early period, and attained considerable celebrity both in the English and continental markets; but its first establishment in connection with Dublin did not take place till after the Revolution, when a number of English manufacturers, attracted by the excellent quality of the Irish wool, the cheapness of provisions, and the low price of labour, established regular and extensive factories in the liberties of the city. Soon afterwards the Coombe, Pimlico, Spitalfields, Weavers'-square, and the neighbouring streets, chiefly in the Liberties of the city, were built; and this portion of the metropolis was then inhabited by persons of opulence and respectability: but the English legislature, considering the rapid growth of the woollen manufacture of Ireland prejudicial to that of England, prevailed on King William to discourage it, in consequence of which the Liberties, by the removal of the more opulent manufacturers, soon fell into decay. The trade, however, continued to linger in that neighbourhood and even to revive in some degree by being taken, in 1773, under the protection of the Dublin Society; insomuch that, in 1792, there were 60 master clothiers, 400 broad cloth looms, and 100 narrow looms in the Liberties, giving employment to upwards of 5000 persons; but the effect was transitory: ever since, the trade has progressively declined, being at present confined to the manufacture of a few articles for home consumption. The working weavers suffered still further from the loss of time and suspension of their labours, caused by the necessity of tentering their cloths in the open air, which could only be performed during fine weather. To remedy this inconvenience, Mr. Pleasants, a philanthropic gentleman of large fortune, erected at his own cost a tenter-house near the Weavers'-square, in which that process might be performed in all states of the weather: the expense of its erection was nearly £13,000; a charge of 2*s.* 6*d.* is made on every piece of cloth, and 5*d.* on every chain of warp, brought in. The linen manufacture was carried on at a very early period for domestic consumption, long before it became the great staple of the country; in the latter point of view it owes its extension chiefly to the Earl of Strafford, who during his lieutenancy embarked £30,000 of his private property in its establishment. After the depression of the woollen trade, great encouragement was given by parliament to the linen manufacture as a substitute; and in the 8th of Queen Anne an act was passed appointing trustees, selected from among the most influential noblemen and gentlemen of large landed property in each of the four provinces, for the management and disposal of the duties granted by that statute for its promotion; and in 1728 a spacious linen hall was erected by a grant of public money under the direction of the Government, from whom the offices and warehouses are rented by the occupants: the sales commence every morning at 9 o'clock and close at 4 in the afternoon, but though the linen manufacture is still extensively carried on in some parts of Ireland, very little is made in the immediate vicinity of the city, and the sales at the hall are consequently much diminished. The cotton manufacture was first introduced about the year 1760, and was greatly promoted by Mr. R. Brook, who in 1779 embarked a large capital in the enterprise; it was further encouraged by grants from parliament and carried on with varying success in the neighbourhood of the city. Since the withdrawing of the protecting duties the trade has progressively declined in Dublin, and may now be considered as nearly extinct there.

The silk manufacture was introduced by the French refugees who settled here after the revocation of the Edict of Nantz; and an act of parliament was soon after passed by which the infant manufacture was placed under the direction of the Dublin Society. This body established an Irish silk-warehouse in Parliament-street, the management of which was vested in a board of 12 noblemen (who were directors), and a committee of 12 persons annually chosen by the guild of Weavers, to examine the quality of the goods sent in by the manufacturers, and to whom the Dublin Society allowed a premium of 5 per cent. on all goods sold in the warehouse. While the trade was thus managed, the sales on an average amounted to £70,000 per annum, and the manufacture attained a high degree of perfection; but by a subsequent act of parliament, passed in the 26th of Geo. III., the society was prohibited from disposing of any portion of its funds for the support of an establishment in which Irish silks were sold, and from that period the silk-warehouse department was discontinued and the manufacture rapidly declined. However, the tabinets and poplins, for which Dublin had been so peculiarly celebrated, are still in request, not only in Great Britain, but in the American and other foreign markets; but the demand is limited, and the number engaged in the manufacture proportionably small. The tanning and currying of leather is carried on to a considerable extent; the number of master manufacturers in both branches exceeding 100. There are 16 iron foundries, in some of which are manufactured steam-engines and agricultural implements on an extensive scale: the number of brass foundries is 25. Cabinet-making is also carried on to a considerable extent. The same may be said of the coach-making trade; the demand for jaunting cars, a vehicle peculiar to the country, is very great. There are not less than 20 porter and ale breweries, several of which are on a very large scale, particularly the former, upwards of 120,000 barrels being brewed annually, a considerable portion of which is exported. There are 14 distilleries and rectifying establishments; some of these are likewise very extensive. There are also numerous establishments in the city and its vicinity for the manufacture and production of a variety of articles both for home consumption and exportation, amongst which may be noticed, flint glass, sail-cloth, canvas, turpentine, vitriol, vinegar, soap, starch, size, glue, paper, parchment, vellum, hats, also silk and calico-printing, and in Dublin is made the celebrated Lundyfoot snuff by Messrs. Lundy Foot & Co.

Several acts of parliament have at different periods been passed for improving the port of Dublin, the last of which, 26th of Geo. III., constituted the present corporation for "preserving and improving the port of Dublin," commonly known by the name of the Ballast Board, in which was vested the care, management, and superintendence of the whole of the river and the walls bounding it. Its jurisdiction was subsequently extended by several successive acts; and the management of the port and harbour of Kingstown was also vested in this corporation; but in 1836, an act was passed by which the port was placed under the control of the Board of Works. The receipts on account of the port average about £30,000 per annum. The Ballast Board has the charge of all the lighthouses in Ireland, of which there are six connected with the port of Dublin.

The commerce of the port consists of various branches, of which the most important is the cross-channel trade, which has increased considerably, owing to the facilities afforded by steam navigation; the agricultural produce of the midland counties being brought hither for exportation, in return for which, groceries, and other commodities for domestic consumption are sent back. The first steam-boat that crossed the channel to this port was from Holyhead in 1816, but it was not till 1824 that steam-boats were employed in the transmission of merchandise: the passage by steam to Liverpool is performed on the average in 14, to London in 80, to Bristol in 24, to Cork in 20, to Belfast in 14, and to Glasgow in 24 hours. The City of Dublin Steam-packet Company, in 1824, was the first that introduced a line of packets between this port and Liverpool, also in 1825 between this port and Belfast, for the conveyance of passengers and merchandise: the capital of this company amounts to £450,000, subscribed in £50 and £100 shares, of which £350,000 is held by Dublin shareholders. It employs 18 vessels between this port and Liverpool and Belfast; nine on the river Shannon, and in the summer a vessel to Bordeaux; also 52 trade boats on the Grand and Royal Canals. Besides the above company, there are the Dublin and London Steam Marine Company, which has six vessels plying between this port and Falmouth, Plymouth, London, and Belfast; the St. George's Company, which has a vessel each to Cork, Bristol, and Greenock; also in the summer one to Whitehaven, calling at Douglas (Isle of Man); the British and Irish Steam-packet Company, which has two vessels plying between this port and Plymouth, London, and Belfast; and the Dublin and Glasgow Steam-packet Company, which has two vessels plying between this port and Glasgow and Cork: thus making 33 steam-packets trading from and to this port, from 250 to 800 tons' burden, and from 100 to 280-horse power each. The number of vessels that entered inwards at the port in the year ending Jan. 5th, 1792, was 2807, of the aggregate burden of 288,592 tons; in 1800, 2779, of 280,539 tons; in 1815, 3046, of 304,813 tons; and in 1823, 3412, of 363,685 tons. In the year ending Jan. 5th, 1836, the number of vessels that entered inwards was 34 foreign and 209 British, and that cleared outwards, 25 foreign and 107 British, exclusively of those that cleared out in ballast: during the same period, 3978 coasting vessels entered inwards and 1937 cleared outwards, exclusively of those which go out in ballast, chiefly to and from various parts of Great Britain; and 2087 colliers entered inwards, nearly the whole of which leave in ballast. The number of vessels belonging to the port in 1836 was 327. After the year 1824, no correct statement can be furnished of the imports and exports of Ireland, as the trade between that country and Great Britain was then placed on the footing of a coasting trade, and no entry was made at any custom-house except of goods on which duty was to be paid. Any statement of the quantities of corn, cattle, &c., now exported is, therefore, merely one of probable quantities. The principal articles of Irish produce and manufacture exported from Dublin for Great Britain, for the year ending Jan. 5th, 1831, were bacon, 7461 bales; barley, 10,093 barrels; wheat, 40,000 barrels; beef, 18,084 tierces; bere, 10,651 barrels; butter, 41,105 firkins; candles, 1701 boxes; eggs, 3300 crates; feathers, 1570 packs; flour, 10,356 sacks; hams, 88 casks; herrings, 259 casks; hides, 6781 bundles; lard, 365 casks; leather, 693 bales; linen, 3648 boxes; malt 103 barrels; oats, 153,191 barrels; oatmeal, 16,482 bags; porter, 29,800 hogsheads; printed cottons, 2100 packages; whiskey, 800 puncheons; wool, 3500 packs; oxen, 69,500; pigs, 58,000; and sheep, 80,000. For some years previous to 1830, the quantity of tobacco imported had been diminished by the increased cultivation of that plant in Ireland, but the legislature prohibited the cultivation in 1833, and the importation of foreign tobacco has since greatly increased. The large quantity of soap imported in 1835 is attributable to a drawback allowed on exportation from Great Britain, which was found to exceed the excise duty previously paid. The duty has since been altered, and the importation of soap has been thereby diminished. In 1830, the quantity imported into all Ireland was 6,559,461 lb. of hard and 120,992 lb. of soft soap, the drawback allowed being £82,875. 9. 11. The quantities of the principal articles imported in the year ending Jan. 5th, 1836, were—coal, 340,000 tons, chiefly from Whitehaven and Scotland; soap, 3,350,000 lb.; coffee, 2200 packages; sugar, 15,000 hogsheads; tea, 52,500 chests; pepper, 2000 packages; spirits, 700 casks,—spirits (in bottle), 1200 cases; wine, 7100 casks,—wine (in bottle), 1500 cases; tobacco, 1150 hogsheads; deals, 2000 great hundreds; staves, 3500 great hundreds; and timber, 11,600 logs. There is no sugar-refinery in Dublin, although at one period the number was very considerable; all the refined sugar now used is imported from Great Britain. It will be perceived by the above statement that the direct foreign import trade is not so great as might be expected from the consumption of a large population; but the articles required can, by steam-vessels, be expeditiously brought from Liverpool, into which port they are imported, in many instances, on much lower terms than they could be imported into Dublin direct.

There is very little foreign export from Dublin. The trade with the Baltic in timber, staves, &c., is greatly diminished by the high rate of duty imposed and the low rate at which Canada timber is admitted. From St. Petersburgh, Riga, Archangel, &c., there is a considerable import of tallow, hemp, and tar, with some linseed, bristles, &c.; from Spain and Portugal the chief import is wine, with some corkwood, raisins, barilla, and bark; from France the imports are wine in wood and bottle, claret, champagne, &c., also corkwood, prunes, dried fruits, and some brandy; from the Netherlands the imports are bark and flax; from Holland, tobacco pipes, bark, cloves, and flax-seed, and small quantities of gin, Burgundy pitch, Rhenish wines, madder, &c. With the West Indies the trade is chiefly in sugar from Jamaica, Demerara, and Trinidad, estates in the last-named island being owned in Dublin. Coffee is imported in small quantities and also rum, but very little foreign spirits are consumed in Ireland, in consequence of the low price and encouragement given to the use of whiskey. Beef and pork in casks, and soap and candles in boxes, were formerly exported to the West Indies in large quantities, but the trade is now nearly lost in consequence of permission being given to the colonists to import these articles from Hamburgh, Bremen, &c., where they can be purchased at lower prices than in Ireland. To the United States of America formerly there was a very large export of linen, principally to New York, and flax-seed, staves, turpentine, clover-seed, &c., were brought back; but the bounty on the export of linen having been withdrawn, the trade between the United States and Dublin has greatly diminished. The export of linen and import of flax-seed is now chiefly confined to Belfast and other northern ports. The American tobacco which is either sold or consumed in Dublin is brought from Liverpool. With British America the trade is very great in timber, as a return cargo of vessels sailing thither from Dublin with emigrants. With Newfoundland there is no direct trade; the cod and seal oil consumed are imported from Liverpool or brought by canal from Waterford, which has a direct trade with Newfoundland; dried codfish and ling being much used in the southern counties, but not in the northern or midland. With China there are three vessels owned in Dublin, besides others engaged in the tea trade; the number of chests directly imported is, therefore, considerable. With South America there is no direct trade, the Dublin tanners being abundantly supplied with native hides, and any foreign hides required being brought from Liverpool, whence also is imported the cotton wool consumed in the Dublin factories. With Turkey the trade is confined to the importation from Smyrna of valonia, figs, raisins, and small quantities of other articles; madder-roots and emery-stone being always transhipped for Liverpool. With Leghorn there is a considerable trade for cork-tree bark, and small quantities of hemp in bales, oil, marble, &c., are also imported, but very little communication is kept up with Trieste or other Italian ports. With Sicily the trade is in shumac and brimstone; the latter article in considerable quantities for the consumption of vitriol and other chymical works.

The markets are under the superintendence of a jury; the sheriffs being required, under the 73rd sec. of the 13th and 14th of Geo. III., cap. 22, to summon 48 of the most respectable citizens, of whom 24 are sworn in at the general quarter sessions, and any three are empowered to visit and examine the commodities, and report to the lord mayor, who is authorised to condemn the provisions, and impose a fine to the extent of £10. The principal wholesale market is in Smithfield, a narrow oblong area in the north-eastern part of the city, the site of which is the property of the corporation, as part of their manor of Oxmantown: the market days for the sale of black cattle and sheep are Monday and Thursday, and for hay and straw, Tuesday and Saturday. There is also a considerable market for hay, straw, potatoes, butter, fowls, and eggs, in Kevin-street, over which, though it is within the liberty of St. Sepulchre, and is alleged to be exempt from the corporate jurisdiction, the officers being appointed by the archbishop, the lord mayor claims a right of superintendence, and the weights and measures used there are sanctioned by his authority. The great market for the sale of potatoes is on the north side of the river, in Petticoat-lane; a small portion of the present site is corporate property, and was the ancient potatoe market of the city; it is now rented from the corporation by two persons, who are joint weighmasters and clerks of the market, under the lord mayor; the market is commodious, and the avenues to it convenient. The wholesale fish market is held in an enclosed yard in Boot-lane: there is also a wholesale fruit market in the Little Green, and one for eggs and fowls contiguous thereto in Halton-street. There are ten retail markets for butchers' meat, poultry, vegetables, and fish; namely, Northumberland market on Eden Quay, which is kept with peculiar neatness; Meath market, in the Earl of Meath's liberty; Ormond market, on Ormond quay; Castle market, between South Great-George's-street and William-street; Patrick's market, in Patrick-street; City market, in Blackhall-row; Clarendon market, in William-street; Fleet-market, in Townsend-street; Rotundo, or Norfolk-market, in Great-Britain-street; and Leinster-market, in D'Olier-street. The want of well regulated slaughter-houses, in situations which would prevent offensive exposure, is severely felt.

Fairs.—A fair is annually held at Donnybrook, about two miles from the city, but within the limits of the jurisdiction of the corporation, under several charters: the first, granted in the 16th of John, authorises its continuance for sixteen days, though of late years it has been limited to a week or eight days: it commences on Aug. 26th. The number of cattle sold is inconsiderable, as it is frequented more for purposes of amusement and conviviality than of business. The corporation have little interest in it, excepting the preservation of order; it yields the proprietor of the ground about £400 per annum. A fair is held in James'-street on St. James's day (July 25th), chiefly for pedlery. The fairs of Rathfarnham and Palmerstown, though beyond the limits of the corporate jurisdiction, are within that of the city police.

PUBLIC BUILDINGS CONNECTED WITH COMMERCE.

The Royal Exchange is situated on the ascent of Cork hill, near the principal entrance to the Castle, and also nearly opposite to Parliament-street. The building was completed in 1779, at the expense of £40,000, raised partly by parliamentary grants, partly by subscriptions, and partly by lotteries. It forms a square of 100 feet, presenting three fronts, the fourth side being concealed by the adjoining buildings of the castle. The ground plan of the interior represents a circle within a square. The circle is formed by twelve fluted columns of the composite order, forming a rotundo in the centre of the building; above their entablature is an attic, ten feet high, having a circular window corresponding with each of the subjacent intercolumniations, and above the attic rises a hemispherical dome of very chaste proportions, crowned by a large circular light, which, together with the zone of windows immediately underneath, throws an ample volume of light into the body of the building. At the eastern and western ends of the north front are geometrical staircases leading to the coffee-room and other apartments now employed as courts for the Bankrupt Commission, meeting-rooms for the trustees, and accommodations for inferior officers. In the lower hall is a fine marble statue of the late Henry Grattan, and on the staircase leading to the coffee-room another of Dr. Lucas, who preceded Grattan in the career of patriotism. The increase of commercial business since the erection of this building having required additional accommodation in a situation more convenient for mercantile transactions, the Exchange has been gradually deserted and the meetings held there transferred to the Commercial Buildings in College-green. *The Commercial Buildings* form a plain but substantial square of three stories, constituting the sides of a small quadrangle and wholly unornamented except in the principal front to College-green, which is of hewn stone and has a central entrance supported by Ionic columns. On the left of the grand entrance-hall and staircase is a news-room, 60 feet long and 28 feet wide, occupied by the members of the Chamber of Commerce (established in 1820 to protect and improve the commerce of the city); and on the right is a handsome coffee-room, connected with that part of the building which is used as an hotel. The north side of the quadrangle is occupied by the Stock Exchange and merchants' offices, and on the east and west are offices for the brokers. It was built by a proprietary of 400 £50 shareholders, and was completed in 1799, under the superintendence of Mr. Parkes. *The Corn Exchange* was built by merchants who were incorporated in 1815, under the designation of the "Corn Exchange Buildings' Company," with leave to augment their capital to £15,000; the business is managed by a committee of 15 directors. The building, which is two stories high, has a neat front of mountain granite towards Burgh Quay; the interior contains a hall, 130 feet long, separated longitudinally from walks on each side by a range of cast iron pillars supporting a cornice, which is continued round the inner hall and surmounted by an attic perforated with circular windows; the hall is furnished with tables for displaying samples of grain, and in the front of the building is a large room on the upper story for public dinners or meetings of societies, by the rent of which and of the tables the interest of the capital, estimated at £25,000, is paid. The Ouzel Galley Society was established in 1705 for the arbitration of differences respecting trade and commerce. The arbitrators must be members of the society, who are among the principal merchants in the city: the surplus of expenses incurred in this court are appropriated to the benefit of decayed merchants.

The *Bank of Ireland* was established in 1783, under an act of parliament, with a capital of £600,000, which, on a renewal of the charter in 1791, was increased to £1,000,000, and by subsequent renewals, the last in 1821, the bank was authorised to enlarge its capital to £3,000,000. The proprietors are incorporated by the name of "The Governor and Company of the Bank of Ireland," and the establishment is under the management of a governor, who must be a proprietor of £4000 stock, a deputy-governor, holding £3000, and 15 directors holding £2000 each; all these are elected by the court of proprietors, and five directors must vacate annually, but not in rotation. Agencies have been established in most of the principal cities and towns in Ireland, and connections have been formed with the Bank of England and the Royal Bank of Scotland, for facilitating the transmission of money. The building is nearly of a semicircular form, and stands on an acre and a half of ground, and previously to the Union was occupied as the Parliament House. The principal front consists of a colonnade of the Ionic order extending round three sides of a quadrangular recess, and supporting an entablature and cornice surmounted by an attic, which is broken only in the central range by a projecting portico of four columns of the same order, sustaining a triangular pediment, in the tympanum of which are the royal arms, and on the apex a statue of Hibernia, with one of Fidelity on the right, and of Commerce on the left extremity of the attic. The east front, in College-street, has a noble portico of six Corinthian columns projecting far into the surrounding area, and supporting an enriched cornice surmounted by a triangular pediment, on the apex of which is a statue of Fortitude, with Justice at one end and a figure of Liberty at the other: this portico, which differs from the style of architecture of the rest of the structure, was formerly the entrance to the House of Lords. The west front, which faces Foster-place, has in the centre an Ionic portico of four columns, supporting an entablature and cornice crowned with a triangular pediment, corresponding in style with the principal front. Within the central portico are two entrances leading to the Cash office, communicating at each end with corridors leading to the various offices in the establishment. This part of the building stands on the site of the former House of Commons. The former House of Lords, which remains unaltered, is now appropriated to the use of the court of proprietors; it is of rectangular form, with a semicircular recess at one extremity, in which the throne was placed, and in which has since been set up a statue of white marble of Geo. III. In the rear of the interior is a department for printing the bank notes, the machinery of which is wholly worked by steam, and arranged with such ingenuity as in a great measure to baffle any attempt at forgery, and at the same time to add greatly to the expedition with which the process of printing is carried on, while it likewise affords a check upon the workmen employed, by means of a self-acting register, which indicates the quantity of work done and the actual state of that in progress at any moment required. The *Hibernian Joint Stock Banking Company* is managed by a governor, deputy-governor, and 7 directors; it transacts business at a house in Castle-street, built for the late private banking establishment of Lord Newcomen. The *Provincial Bank of Ireland* is managed by a court of directors in London, and has an office in William-street and agencies throughout the country parts. The *National Bank of Ireland* was formed under the provisions of the same act, with a capital of two millions subscribed in London and Ireland, to be applied to the support of banking establishments connected with it in Ireland, by contributing to each a sum equal to that locally subscribed; it has also branches in the principal towns. The private banking establishments are those of La Touche and Co., Castle-street; Ball and Co, Henry-street; Boyle and Co., College-green; and the Royal Bank, Foster-place. There are two Savings' Banks, both formed in 1818, one in Meath-street, the other in Cuffe-street, in St. Peter's parish. The former has two branches in Marlborough-street and at the Linen-hall, by which the benefits of the system have been extended to the northern division of the city. The Money Order office, held in the general post-office, furnishes means for the secure transmission of small sums.

The *Custom-house* is a stately structure of the Doric order, situated on the north bank of the Liffey, below Carlisle bridge. It was erected under the superintendence of Mr. Gandon, in 1794, at an expense of £397,232. 4. 11., which the requisite furniture and subsequent enlargements have increased to upwards of half a million sterling. The building is 375 feet in length and 205 feet in depth, and has four fronts, of which the south is entirely of Portland stone, and the others of mountain granite. On the east of the custom-house is a wet dock capable of receiving 40 vessels, and along the quay is a range of spacious warehouses. Beyond these an extensive area, enclosed with lofty walls, contains a second wet dock, consisting of two basins, the outer 300 feet by 250 and the inner 650 by 300; still further eastward, and on the same line with the principal building, are the tobacco and general warehouses, the latter of which were burnt down in 1833, but have been rebuilt. The business of the customs and excise for all Ireland was transacted in the custom-house, until the consolidation of the boards of Customs and Excise into one general board in London, since which period it has been confined to that of the Dublin district, and a great part of the building is applied to the accommodation of the following departments:—the Stamp Office; the Commissariat; the Board of Works; the Record Office for documents connected with the Vice-Treasurer's Office; the Quit-Rent Office; and the Stationery Office. The amount of duties paid in 1836, for goods imported and exported, was £898,630. 5. 1.; and the excise duties of the Dublin district during the same period amounted to £419,935. 14. 4½.

The General Post-Office, situated in Sackville-street, is a very fine building of granite, 223 feet in length, 150 feet in depth, and three stories high. In the centre of the front is a boldly projecting portico of six fluted Ionic columns supporting an entablature and cornice, which are continued round the building and surmounted by a triangular pediment, in the tympanum of which are the Royal arms, and on the apex a figure of Hibernia, with one of Mercury on the right, and of Fidelity on the left; the whole of the building is crowned with a fine balustrade rising above the cornice. This structure was raised under the direction of Mr. Francis Johnston, architect, at an expense of £50,000. Over the mantel-piece in the Board-room is a marble bust of Earl Whitworth, by whom the first stone was laid in 1815. The establishment, which had been under the direction of two postmasters-general, was, in 1831, consolidated with the English post-office, and placed under the control of the postmaster-general of the united kingdom. Letters are delivered throughout the city three times a day by the penny post department, and once a day to 17 stations within 12 miles of it on payment of two pence.

LITERATURE AND SCIENCE.

The Royal Dublin Society originated, in 1731, in the private meetings of a few scientific gentlemen, among whom were Dr. Price and Dr. Madden, and was supported entirely by their own contributions until the year 1749, when they were incorporated by royal charter, under the name of "the Dublin Society for promoting husbandry and other useful arts in Ireland," and received an annual grant of £500, which was gradually augmented to £10,000, until lately, when it has been reduced to £5000. It is under the patronage of the king and the lord-lieutenant (the latter being president), and there are seven vice-presidents, two honorary secretaries, and an assistant secretary. The literary and scientific department consists of a professor of botany and agriculture, a professor of chymistry, a professor of mineralogy and geology, a librarian, teachers of landscape, figure, and ornamental drawing and of sculpture, and a curator of the botanic garden. The society, which in 1821 was honoured with the designation of "Royal," held its meetings in Shaws-court till 1767, when the members removed to a building which they had erected in Grafton-street, whence, in 1796, they removed to Hawkins-street, where they erected an edifice for their repository, laboratory, library, and galleries; and in 1815 they purchased, for £20,000, the spacious and splendid mansion of the Duke of Leinster, in Kildare-street. This building is 140 feet in length and 70 in depth, and is approached from the street by a massive gateway of rusticated masonry: the principal front is of the Corinthian order, richly embellished; before it is a spacious court, and in the rear an extensive lawn fronting Merrion-square. The entrance-hall is enriched with casts taken from figures by the first masters, and there are also several busts executed by artists who had been pupils of the society. The library, in the east wing, is 64 feet long and 24 feet wide, and is surrounded by a light gallery; it contains 12,000 volumes, and is rich in botanical works. The museum occupies six rooms, containing miscellaneous curiosities, specimens of animals, mineralogy, geology, &c.; the specimens of the mineralogical department are classified on the Wernerian system. The lecture-room is capable of accommodating 400 auditors. The apartments for the use of members are all on the ground-floor. The drawing schools occupy a range of detached buildings; they are appropriately fitted up, and are attended by 200 pupils. The botanical studies are under the direction of a professor, who delivers lectures both at the Society house and in the botanic gardens at Glasnevin. These are about a mile from the city, occupying a space of more than 27 acres, watered by the Tolka, and containing every requisite variety of soil for botanical purposes. The garden is formed into subdivisions for agricultural and horticultural specimens: it has the house of the professor and the lecture-rooms near the entrance, and is open to the public on Tuesdays and Fridays; the admission is free, as also to the lectures, schools, and museum. *The Royal Irish Academy* was instituted, in 1782, by a number of gentlemen, members of the University, chiefly to promote the study of polite literature, science, and antiquities, and was incorporated in 1786: it is assisted in its objects by a parliamentary grant of £300 per annum, and honoured with the patronage of the King; and is under the superintendence of a visiter (who is the lord-lieutenant for the time being), a president, four vice-presidents and a council of 21, a treasurer, librarian, and two secretaries. Its literary management is entrusted to three committees, respectively superintending the departments of science, polite literature, and antiquities. At the annual meetings premiums, accruing from the interest of £1500 bequeathed by Col. Burton Conyngham, are awarded for the best essays on given subjects, for which persons not members of the academy may become competitors; the successful essays are sometimes published in the transactions of the academy, of which 17 volumes in quarto have already appeared. The library contains some very valuable manuscripts relating to Ireland: the large room for meetings of the academy is embellished with portraits of their presidents.

LIBRARIES.

The Library of Trinity College, by much the largest not only in Dublin but in Ireland, is described under the head of the institution of which it forms a portion: the King's Inns library is also noticed in like manner. *St. Patrick's or Marsh's library* was founded by Dr. Narcissus Marsh, archbishop of Dublin, in the vicinity of St. Patrick's cathedral; it contains the celebrated Dr. Stillingfleet's collection and some manuscripts. The apartment for the books consists of two galleries meeting at a right angle, in which is the librarian's room. The library is open on liberal terms, a certificate or letter of introduction from some respectable and well-known character being all that is required: it is under the government of trustees appointed by act of parliament. *The Dublin Library Society* originated in the meeting of a few individuals at a bookseller's in Dame-street to read newspapers and periodicals. Having formed a regular society, a library was opened, in 1791, in Eustace-street, which was removed in 1809 to Burgh-quay, and finally, in 1820, to a building in D'Olier-street, erected for the special purpose, by shares. The building is plain but elegant, and contains a spacious apartment for the library, another for newspapers and periodicals, and a few smaller rooms for committees and house officers. The public rooms are ornamented with busts of John Philpot Curran, Daniel O'Connell, Henry Grattan, Archibald Hamilton Rowan, and Dean Kirwan, and with portraits of the first Earl of Charlemont and of Curran. The medical libraries of the College of Surgeons and Sir Patrick Dun's hospital are well selected and rapidly increasing. Steevens's Hospital, the Royal Hospital, Christ-Church, and Strand-street Meeting-house have each a collection of books, none of any great extent. The private library of the Earl of Charlemont is highly worthy of notice. It is contained in a building attached to the town residence in Palace-row: the entrance to it is by a long gallery, ornamented with antique busts, vases, and altars, which opens into a large vestibule lighted by a lantern, which contains the works on antiquities and numismatics, and has in a recess the statue of Venus and eight busts of ancient and modern characters of celebrity. The principal library contains a fine and well-selected collection of ancient and modern writers on most departments of literature and some of science, very judiciously and happily arranged; also some manuscripts, and an unique collection of Hogarth's engravings, mostly proofs. Over the chimney-piece is a fine bust of Homer. Attached to the library is a small museum, a medal room, and a smaller library of very elegant proportions, containing busts of the Earl of Rockingham and General Wolfe.

SURGICAL AND MEDICAL INSTITUTIONS.

The Royal College of Surgeons was incorporated in 1784, for the purpose of establishing a "liberal and extensive system of surgical education:" a parliamentary grant was afterwards conferred on it for providing the necessary accommodations. Sums amounting in the whole to £35,000 were granted for erecting and furnishing the requisite buildings; besides which, £6000, the accumulated excess of the receipts over the disbursements of the college, were expended in 1825 in the addition of a museum. The front of the building, which is situated on the west side of St. Stephen's-green, has a rusticated basement story, from which rises a range of Doric columns supporting a tier of seven large windows, the four central columns being surmounted by a triangular pediment, on which are statues of Minerva, Esculapius and Hygeia. The interior contains a large board-room, a library, an apartment for general meetings, an examination hall, with several committee-rooms and offices, four theatres for lectures, a spacious dissecting-room with several smaller apartments, and three museums, the largest of which, 84 feet by 30, with a gallery, contains a fine collection of preparations of human and comparative anatomy; the second, with two galleries, contains preparations illustrative of pathology and a collection of models in wax, presented by the Duke of Northumberland when lord-lieutenant; and the third, attached to the anatomical theatre, contains a collection for the illustration of the daily courses of lectures. The College consists of a president, vice-president, six censors, twelve assistants, secretaries, members, and licentiates. Candidates for a diploma must produce certificates of attendance on some school of medicine and surgery for five years, and of attendance at a surgical hospital for three years, and must pass four half-yearly examinations, and a final examination for letters testimonial in the presence of the members and licentiates on two days: rejected candidates have a right of appeal to a court constituted for the purpose, which is frequently resorted to. Attached to the school are two professors of anatomy and physiology, two of surgery, a professor of chymistry, one of the practice of medicine, one of materia medica, one of midwifery, and one of medical jurisprudence, with four anatomical demonstrators; the lectures commence on the last Monday in October, and close on the last day of April.

The College of Physicians was first incorporated in the reign of Chas II., but the charter being found insufficient, was surrendered in 1692, and a more ample charter was granted by William and Mary, under the designation of the King and Queen's College of Physicians in Ireland. This charter, which conferred considerable privileges, was partly confirmed by successive acts of parliament, which gave the society authority to summon all medical practitioners for examination, to inspect the shops and warehouses of apothecaries, druggists, and chymists, and to destroy all articles for medical use which are of bad quality: it has also a principal share in the superintendence of the School of Physic. No person can be a member of the College who has not graduated in one of the universities of Oxford, Cambridge, or Dublin. The officers of the college consist of a president, vice-president, four censors, a registrar, and a treasurer; the members hold their meetings at Sir Patrick Dun's hospital, of whose bequests for the promotion of medical science they are trustees. *The School of Physic* is partly under the control of the Board of the University, and partly under that of the College of Physicians; the professorships of anatomy, chymistry, and botany being in the appointment of the University, who elect the professors, thence called University professors; those of the practice of medicine, the institutes of medicine, and of the materia medica, called King's professors, derive their appointment and their salaries from the College of Physicians, being chosen by ballot from among the members of that body. The University professors deliver their lectures in Trinity College, and the King's professors in Sir Patrick Dun's hospital. No candidate is qualified for a degree in medicine until he has attended the six courses, and six months at Sir Patrick Dun's clinical hospital.

The School of Pharmacy. Previously to the company of the Apothecaries' Hall having been incorporated, the shops were supplied by the druggists, without any check on the quality of the medical articles supplied. To remedy this defect an act was passed, in 1791, incorporating a body under the title of the "Governor and Company of the Apothecaries' Hall," by whom a building was erected in Mary-street (a respectable edifice of brick, with a basement of hewn stone) for the preparation and sale of drugs, unadulterated and of the best quality, and for the delivery of courses of lectures on chymistry, the materia medica, pharmacy, botany, and the practice of physic, and for the examination of candidates for a diploma to practise as apothecaries. The establishment consists of a governor, deputy-governor, treasurer, secretary, and thirteen directors. Candidates for apprenticeship must undergo an examination in Greek and Latin, and those for the rank of master apothecary must produce certificates of attendance on a course of each of the following departments of medicine; chymistry, materia medica and pharmacy, medical botany, anatomy, and physiology, and the theory and practice of medicine. The diploma of the society of Apothecaries of London also, by the rules of the Dublin company, qualifies the holder to practise in Ireland. *The School of Anatomy, Medicine, and Surgery,* in Park-street, Merrion-square, established in 1824 by a society of surgeons and physicians, contains a museum, a chymical laboratory, an office and reading-room, a lecture-room capable of accommodating 200 persons, a dissecting-room, and rooms for preparations. Private medical schools are numerous, and, combined with the public institutions, and with the extensive practice afforded by the city hospitals, have rendered Dublin a celebrated school of medicine, resorted to by students from every part of the British empire. *The Phrenological Society,* under the direction of a president, vice-president, and two committees, was established in 1829. Its meetings are held in Upper Sackville-street, where the society has a large collection of casts illustrative of the theory of the science, and a library of phrenological treatises, which are lent out to the members: the annual subscription is one guinea. *The Association of Members of the College of Physicians* was instituted in 1816; they hold their meetings at their rooms in College-green, for receiving communications on medical subjects and on scientific matters; their object is the promotion of medical science, and among their corresponding members are some of the most eminent medical men in England and on the Continent: the society has published several volumes of transactions.

INSTITUTIONS FOR THE PROMOTION OF THE FINE ARTS, AND OTHER USEFUL AND SCIENTIFIC PURPOSES.

The Royal Hibernian Academy of painting, sculpture, and architecture, founded by royal charter in 1823, consists of fourteen academicians and ten associates, all of whom must be professional painters, sculptors, or architects: the king is patron, the lord-lieutenant vice-patron, and its affairs are under the superintendence of a council. The academy has for the last few years been encouraged by a grant from parliament of £300 per ann.; its first president, the late Francis Johnston, Esq., architect, erected an elegant and appropriate building in Abbey-street, at an expense of £10,000, which he presented to the academy for ever, at a nominal rent of 5*s.* per ann., and to which his widow subsequently added a gallery for statuary. The building, which is three stories high and of elegant design, has, on the basement story, a recess ornamented with fluted columns of the Doric order: over the entrance is a head of Palladio, emblematical of architecture; over the window on the right, a head of Michael Angelo, illustrative of sculpture; and over the window on the left, a head of Raphael, allusive to painting. The academy has a good collection of casts from the antique, some paintings by the old masters, and a library of works chiefly connected with the fine arts, and of which the greater number were presented by the late Edward Houghton, Esq. *The Royal Irish Institution for promoting the fine arts* was founded, under royal patronage, in 1815: its vice-patron is the Marquess of Anglesey, its guardian, the lord-lieutenant, and its president, the Duke of Leinster: its affairs are superintended by eight vice-presidents (all noblemen), and a committee of directors. The Artists have also formed a society, called the *Artists' and Amateurs' Conversazione,* for cultivating and maintaining a social intercourse with admirers of the fine arts, and thereby promoting their mutual interests. *The Horticultural Society,* patronised by the Lord-Lieutenant and the Duchess of Leinster, and under the direction of the Earl of Leitrim as president, several noblemen as vice-presidents, and a council, was instituted in 1813, and has rapidly increased in prosperity. Prizes are awarded at its annual exhibitions, which are numerously and most fashionably attended. *The Geological Society* was instituted in 1835, and is under the direction of a president, vice-presidents, and a council. Its attention is peculiarly directed to Ireland: it consists of honorary and ordinary members; £10 on admission, or £5 if not resident within 20 miles of Dublin for more than one month in the year, constitutes a member for life; and £1 on admission, and £1 per ann., constitutes an ordinary member. The rooms of the society are in Upper Sackville-street; two parts of a volume of its transactions have been already published. *The Zoological Society,* instituted in 1831, is under the direction of a president, vice-president, and council: £10 paid on admission constitutes a member for life, and £1 on admission and a subscription of £1 per ann., an annual member. The gardens are situated in the Phœnix Park, and occupy a piece of ground near the vice-regal lodge, given for that purpose by the Duke of Northumberland, when lord-lieutenant: they have been laid out with much taste, and are in excellent order, affording a most interesting place of resort; the council have already purchased many fine specimens of the higher classes of animals. They are open to the public daily, on payment of sixpence admission. *The Agricultural Society* was instituted in 1833, and is under the direction of a president (the Marquess of Downshire), several vice-presidents, a committee and sub-committee: it consists of 330 members, who pay an annual subscription of £1, and among whom are most of the principal landed proprietors; its object is the establishment of a central institution for concentrating the efforts made by other societies and by individuals for improving the condition of the people and the cultivation of the soil of Ireland: two annual meetings are held, one in Dublin during the April show of cattle, and the other at Ballinasloe in October. *The Civil Engineers' Society* was established in 1835, for the cultivation of science in general, and more especially of those branches of it which are connected with the engineering department; it is under the direction of a president, vice-presidents, and a committee, and consists of members who must be either civil or military engineers, or architects, who pay one guinea on admission by ballot and an annual subscription of equal amount.

THEATRES, CLUBS, AND MUSICAL SOCIETIES.

The places of public amusement are few. The Drama is little encouraged by the fashionable and wealthy; the theatre is thinly attended, except on the appearance of some first-rate performer from London, or at the special desire of the lord-lieutenant, the social character of the inhabitants inducing an almost exclusive preference to convivial intercourse within the domestic circle. The first public theatre was built in Werburgh-street, by Lord Strafford, in 1635, and was closed in 1641. After the Restoration, a theatre under the same patent was opened in Orange-street, now Smock-alley; and in 1733, a second was opened in Rainsford-street, in the liberty of Thomas-court, and a third in George's-lane. Sheridan had a theatre in Aungier-street, in 1745, which was destroyed in 1754 by a tumult of the audience; and in 1758 another was built in Crow-street, which, with that in Smock-alley, continued open for 25 years, when, after much rivalry, the latter was closed, and a patent granted to the former for the exclusive enjoyment of the privilege of performing the legitimate drama. On the expiration of this patent, Mr. Harris, of London, procured a renewal of it from Government and erected the "*New Theatre Royal*" in Hawkins-street, a pile of unsightly exterior but internally of elegant proportions, being constructed in the form of a lyre, handsomely decorated and admirably adapted to the free transmission of the actor's voice to every part of the house: attached to it is a spacious saloon, supported by pillars of the Ionic order. A smaller *theatre* has been lately opened in *Abbey-street* for dramatic performances: it is a plain building, neatly fitted up. Another small *theatre in Fishamble-street*, originally a music-hall, is occasionally opened for dramatic and other entertainments; and a third, in Great Brunswick-street, called *the Adelphi*, originally intended for a diorama, is used for amateur theatricals. In Abbey-street is a *circus*, in which equestrian performances occasionally take place. During the summer season, *the Rotundo gardens* are open on stated evenings every week, and being illuminated in a fanciful manner and enlivened by the attendance of a military band, and by occasional exhibitions of rope-dancing and fireworks, they afford an agreeable promenade in the open air, and are well attended. In *the Royal Arcade*, in College-green, are some handsome rooms for public amusements. Clubs and societies for convivial purposes are numerous: several club-houses have been opened on the principle of those in London. *The Kildare-street Club*, consisting of about 650 members, was instituted upwards of fifty years since, and takes its name from the street in which its house stands: the accommodations contain a large and elegant card-room, coffee, reading, and billiard-rooms; the terms of admission, which is by ballot, are £26. 10., and the annual subscription, £5: it is managed by a committee of 15 members chosen annually. *The Sackville-street Club*, instituted in 1795, consists of 400 members chosen by ballot, who previously pay 20 guineas, and an annual subscription of 5 guineas; the house, which contains a suite of apartments similar in character to those of the Kildare-street Club, has been recently fitted up in a very splendid style. *The Friendly Brothers' Club*, also in Upper Sackville-street, consists of many members who are in connection with similar societies in various countries; the house affords excellent accommodation. *The Hibernian United Service Club*, instituted in 1832, is limited to 500 permanent and 200 temporary members, consisting of officers of the army and navy of every rank, and of field officers and captains of militia of the United Kingdom; the terms of admission by ballot are £10. 10., and the annual subscription £4 for permanent members; honorary members are admitted on payment of the annual subscription only; the club-house is in Foster-street, near the Bank. The *Freemasons* for some years had a hall in Dawson-street: they now hold their meetings in temporary apartments in the Commercial Buildings. The leading *musical societies* are the Beefsteak Club, the Hibernian Catch Club, the Anacreontic, for the performance of instrumental music; the Dublin Philharmonic Society, for the practice of vocal and instrumental music; and the Festival Choral Society, for the cultivation of choral music. Other societies, of a more miscellaneous character, whose names indicate their objects, are the Chess, Philidorean, Shakspeare, Royal Yacht, and Rowing clubs.

MUNICIPAL GOVERNMENT.

Obverse. *Reverse.*

Seal of the Corporation.

The charters granted at various times to the city are carefully preserved from the earliest period in the archives of the corporation. The first was granted in the reign of Hen. II., from which period to the reign of Geo. III. a numerous series of them has been successively issued, either confirming previous grants, or conferring additional privileges. The present constitution of the corporate government is founded partly on the provisions of several of the earlier charters, partly on usage and ancient customs, partly on the new rules laid down in the 25th of Chas. II. and partly on the statutes of the 33rd of Geo. II., and the 11th and 12th of Geo. III. The corporation consists of a lord mayor, 24 aldermen, and a common council. The lord mayor is annually elected from among the aldermen, by a majority of that body, with the approbation of the common council; the alderman next in rotation is generally chosen. Within ten days after his election, he must be presented to the lord-lieutenant and privy council for their approbation, and is sworn into office before the lord-lieutenant on Sept. 30th; he is a justice of the peace for the county of the city, admiral of the port of Dublin, and chief Judge of the Lord Mayor's and Sheriffs' courts; he has the regulation of the assize of bread, and is clerk of the market, and, *ex officio*, a member of certain local boards and trusts. The aldermen, who are also justices of the peace for the city, are elected for life, as vacancies occur, from among such common-councilmen as have served the office of sheriff, and are therefore called sheriffs' peers; each on his election pays £400 late currency, of which £105 is for the Blue-coat hospital, and the remainder for the repair and embellishment of the Mansion-house. The sheriffs are annually elected at Easter by the lord mayor and aldermen out of eight freemen nominated by the common council, and each of them must be in possession of real or personal property to the clear amount of £2000; they must be approved by the lord-lieutenant and privy council; but on payment of a fine of £500, of which £105 is given to the Blue-coat hospital, a freeman so nominated may become a sheriffs' peer without serving the office of sheriff. The common council consists of the sheriffs' peers, and of the representatives of the guilds triennially elected, who are 96 in number, and who, in default of election by the guilds, may be chosen by the lord mayor and aldermen from each of the guilds so neglecting. The officers of the corporation are a recorder, who must be a barrister of six years' standing, but is not required to be a freeman; he is elected by the lord mayor and aldermen, with the approbation of the common council, subject to the approval of the lord-lieutenant and privy council, holds his office during good behaviour, and is permitted by the act of the 21st and 22nd of Geo. III., in case of sickness or absence, to appoint a deputy, who also, by the 39th of Geo. III., must be a barrister of six years' standing: two coroners, elected from the aldermen by the lord mayor and a majority of that body alone: a president of the court of conscience, who is the ex-lord mayor during the year after his office expires, and may appoint any alderman to officiate for him: two town-clerks, who are also clerks of the peace, either freemen or not, and elected for life in the same manner as the recorder, and subject to the approval of the privy council: a marshal, who must be a freeman, and is similarly elected, nominally for one year, but generally re-elected on its expiration: water bailiffs, elected in the same manner as the marshal, and who give security by two sureties for £1000: serjeants-at-mace, similarly elected, and who give two sureties for £250 each; and several inferior officers. The freedom of the city is obtained either by gift of the aldermen and common-councilmen in general assembly, or by admission to the freedom of one of the guilds, and afterwards to that of the city, by favour of the corporation. Freemen of the guilds, either by birth, servitude, or marriage, can only be admitted as freemen at large by the common council, who have power to reject them after passing through the guilds; hence the freedom of the guilds entitles them only to the privilege of carrying on their respective trades, but not to that of voting at elections for the city representatives in parliament. There are 25 guilds, the first of which is the Trinity guild or guild of Merchants, which returns 31 representatives out of the 96; the others, called minor guilds, are those of the Tailors, Smiths, Barber-Surgeons, Bakers, Butchers, Carpenters, Shoemakers, Saddlers, Cooks, Tanners, Tallow-chandlers, Glovers and Skinners, Weavers, Shearmen and Dyers, Goldsmiths, Coopers, Feltmakers, Cutlers, Bricklayers, Hosiers, Curriers, Brewers, Joiners, and Apothecaries. Only six of the guilds have halls; the others meet either in one of these or in a private building. The Merchants' Hall, on Aston's Quay, opposite Wellington bridge, is a new building of granite, two stories high, with little architectural ornament. The Tailors' Hall, in Back-lane, built in 1710, is ornamented with portraits of Chas. II., Dean Swift, and St. Homobon, a tailor of Cremona, canonized in 1316 for his piety and charity. The Weavers' Hall, on the Coombe, is a venerable brick building, two stories high, with a pedestrian statue of Geo. II. over the entrance, and in the Hall a portrait of the same king woven in tapestry, and one of a member of the family of La Touche, who had greatly encouraged the manufacture. The Carpenters' Hall is in Audoen's Arch, the Goldsmiths' in Golden-lane, and the Cutlers' in Capel-street.

The city returns two members to the Imperial parliament; the right of election, formerly vested in the corporation, freemen, and 40*s.* freeholders, has been extended to the £10 householders, and £20 and £10 leaseholders for the respective terms of 14 and 20 years, by the act of the 2nd of Wm. IV., cap. 88. The number of voters registered at the first general election under that act was 7041, of which number, 5126 voted. The limits of the city, for electoral purposes, include an area of 3538 statute acres, the boundaries of which are minutely detailed in the Appendix; the number of freemen is about 3500, of whom 2500 are resident and 1000 non-resident, and the number of £10 houses is 16,000: the sheriffs are the returning officers. The corporation holds general courts of quarter assembly at Christmas, Easter, Midsummer, and Michaelmas, which are occasionally adjourned, and post assemblies sometimes for particular purposes. As a justice of the peace, the lord mayor presides at the city quarter sessions, and always attends on the first day to open the court, accompanied by some of the aldermen, it being necessary that two at least of that body should be present with the lord mayor or recorder to form a quorum. The lord mayor's and sheriffs' courts are held on the Thursday after the first day of the sessions; each has cognizance of personal actions to any amount above £2; the process is by attachment of the defendant's goods. The lord mayor's court, in which he is the sole judge, is held every Thursday either at the city sessions-house, where it is an open court, or in the Mansion-house, where it may be private; it has summary jurisdiction, and takes cognizance of complaints, nuisances, informations, &c. The court of conscience, for determining causes and recovering debts not exceeding £2 late currency, is held daily before the president in the city assembly-house in William-street. The police establishment, as regulated by the Duke of

Wellington, when chief secretary for Ireland, was under the control of a chief magistrate, aided by eleven others, three of whom sat daily at one of the offices of the four divisions, according to which the city was arranged: to each office a chief constable and petty constables were attached. The police force, consisting of a horse-patrol of 29 men, a foot patrol of 169, 26 watch constables, and 539 watchmen, was maintained at an expense of about £40,000 per ann. By an act passed in 1836 the police of the metropolis is placed under two magistrates appointed by the lord-lieutenant, and the boundaries of their jurisdiction have been determined to be the rivers Dodder and Tolka to the south and north, and Knockmaroon hill to the west, which boundary may be extended according to the discretion of the lord-lieutenant and privy council to any place within five miles of Dublin castle; by whom the number of divisional offices may be reduced and also that of the magistrates, provided there be two to each office. The city is to be assessed for the payment of the establishment by a rate not exceeding 8*d.* in the pound, according to the valuation made under the act of the 5th of Geo. IV.

The *Mansion-house*, the residence of the lord mayor during his year of office, is externally a plain edifice of brick, on a detached and receding site on the south side of Dawson-street; the interior contains some large apartments fitted up in an antiquated style. On the left hand of the entrance-hall is the "Gilt Room," a small apartment in which is a portrait of Wm. III., by Gubbins; this room opens into the drawing-room, which is 50 feet long: the walls are hung with portraits of Earl Whitworth, the Earls of Hardwicke and Westmoreland, John Foster, the last speaker of the Irish House of Commons, and Alderman Alexander. Beyond this is the ball-room, used also for civic dinners, 55 feet long and wainscoted with Irish oak; in this room are placed the two city swords, the mace, the cap of maintenance and the gold collar of S S, presented by Wm. III., to replace that presented by Chas. II.; it also contains portraits of Chas. II., Geo. II., the Duke of Cumberland, and the late Duke of Richmond. A door from the ball-room opens into a noble rotundo, 90 feet in diameter, round which is continued a corridor 5 feet wide; the walls are painted in imitation of tapestry, and the room is covered with a dome; in the centre is a lantern, by which the apartment is lighted; it was built in 1821 expressly for the reception of George IV., who honoured the corporation with his presence at dinner. On the right of the entrance-hall are the Exchequer-room, wainscoted with Irish oak, and hung with portraits of the Duke of Bolton, the Earl of Buckingham, the Marquess of Buckingham, and the Earl of Harcourt; and the sheriffs' room, 40 feet long, in which are portraits of the Duke of Northumberland, Lord Townsend, John Duke of Bedford, and Aldermen Sankey, Manders, and Thorpe, the last of whom is distinguished by the title of "the good lord mayor." An equestrian statue of Geo. I., which was formerly on Essex bridge, is placed in the lawn at the side of the mansion-house; and at the extremity of the court in which the rotundo is built are colossal statues of Chas. II. and Wm. III. The *City Assembly-house*, purchased by the corporation from the artists of Dublin, by whom it was built for an exhibition-room, is a plain but commodious structure in William-street, and contains several good rooms; in the circular room the common council holds its meetings; the board of aldermen meets in another apartment; and under the common council room is a circular apartment in which the court of conscience is held.

The *Sessions-house*, in Green-street, opened for business in 1797, is ornamented in front with a central pediment and cornice supported by six engaged columns rising from a broad platform, to which is an ascent by a flight of steps extending along the whole front of the building, and on each side of the centre are the doors of entrance to the court-rooms; in another front, corresponding with this, in Halston-street, are the entrances to the apartments occupied by the agents during contested elections. The interior is spacious, lofty, and well arranged; the ceiling is supported by Ionic columns. In this building are held the court of quarter sessions, the court of oyer and terminer, the lord mayor's and sheriffs' court, and the recorder's court. The principal prison for malefactors of all classes is *Newgate*, situated near the sessions-house, in Green-street. It is a square building, flanked at each angle by a round tower with loop-hole windows. The interior is divided into two nearly equal portions by a broad passage with high walls on each side, having iron gates at intervals, through the gratings of which visiters may converse with the prisoners; the cells are neither sufficiently numerous nor large, nor is the prison well adapted for due classification. A chapel attached to it is attended by three chaplains; one of the Established Church, one of the R. C. and one of the Presbyterian religion. The *Sheriffs' Prison*, in Green-street, was built in 1794, and occupies three sides of a quadrangle with an area in the centre, which is used as a ball-court; it is visited by the chaplains of Newgate and a medical inspector. The *City Marshalsea*, a brick building attached to the preceding, is designed for prisoners committed from the lord mayor's court for debts under £10, and from the court of conscience. The *Smithfield Penitentiary* is appropriated to the confinement of juvenile convicts not exceeding 19 years of age; it is visited by three chaplains, and inspected by the divisional magistrates; an efficient classification is observed, and all the prisoners are regularly employed. The *Richmond Bridewell*, on the Circular road, erected by the city at an expense of £40,000, is a spacious structure enclosed by walls flanked with towers at the angles, and is entered by a massive gateway; between the outer wall and the main building is a wide space, intended for a rope-walk; the interior consists of two spacious quadrangles, the sides of which are all occupied by buildings; the cells, which are on the first floor, open into corridors with entrances at each end; the rooms in the second floor are used as work-rooms; the male and female prisoners occupy distinct portions of the prison; the prisoners not sentenced to the tread-mill are employed in profitable labour, and a portion of their earnings is paid to them on their discharge; they are visited by a Protestant and a R. C. chaplain, a physician, surgeon, and apothecary. A great improvement in the city prisons is now in progress. Attached to the city are the manor or liberty of St. Sepulchre, belonging to the Archbishop of Dublin; the manor of Grangegorman or Glasnevin, belonging to the dean of Christ-Church; the manor of Thomas-Court and Donore, belonging to the Earl of Meath; and the liberty of the deanery of St.

Patrick. The *Liberty of St. Sepulchre* extends over a part of the city, including the parishes of St. Patrick, St. Nicholas Without, and St. Kevin; also over a large tract of the county of Dublin to the south-east of the city, as far as the Wicklow boundary, including a small portion of the latter county and of Kildare, bordering on that of Dublin. The court is held at Longlane, in the county of Dublin, before the archbishop's seneschal, and has a very extensive criminal as well as civil jurisdiction, but exercises only the latter: the court-house and prison for the whole archbishoprick are situated there. It has a civil bill jurisdiction to any amount, extended to the Dublin manor courts in 1826. At the record side the proceedings are either by action against the body, for sums under £20 by service and above it by arrest; or, for sums above £10, by attachment against the goods. The court at the record side sits every Tuesday and Friday; the civil bill court, generally on alternate Wednesdays, except in the law terms, when it stands adjourned. At this court, in which a jury is always impannelled and sworn, sums to any amount may be recovered at a trifling expense. The jurisdiction of the *Manor Court of Glasnevin* is of great extent, comprising the baronies of Coolock, Castleknock, and Half-Rathdown, in the county of Dublin, and the lordship of St. Mary's abbey, which includes portions of the city and county. The seneschal sits in Dublin every Friday, and at Kingstown on alternate Fridays for the convenience of that town and the surrounding parishes within his jurisdiction. Causes are tried before a jury, and debts to any amount are recoverable at a small expense; from 900 to 1000 causes are heard annually. *Thomas-Court and Donore Manor Court* has a jurisdiction extending over the barony of Donore, and that part of the liberty of Thomas-Court which is within the city: the civil bill court, in which debts to any amount are recoverable, is held every Wednesday in the court-house in Thomas-Court, a plain building erected in 1160; a record court is also held there every Wednesday and Saturday.

VICE-REGAL GOVERNMENT.

Dublin is the seat of the Vice-regal government, consisting of a lord-lieutenant and privy council, assisted by a chief secretary, under-secretary, and a large establishment of inferior officers and under-clerks both for state and the despatch of business. The official residence of the lord-lieutenant is *Dublin Castle*, first appropriated to that purpose in the reign of Elizabeth; but his usual residence is the Vice-regal Lodge, in the Phœnix Park. The buildings of the Castle form two quadrangles, called the Upper and Lower Yards. The Upper, 280 feet by 130, contains the lord-lieutenant's apartments, which occupy the whole of the south and part of the east sides; the council-chamber and offices connected with it; the apartments and offices of the chief secretary, and of several of the officers of the household; and the apartments of the master of the ceremonies, and of the aides de camp of the viceroy. The entrance into this court is on the north side by a massive gateway towards the east end, ornamented by a figure of Justice above the arch; and towards the west end is a corresponding gateway, which is not used, ornamented by a figure of Fortitude; both by Van Nost. The approach to the vice-regal apartments is under a colonnade on the south side, leading into a large hall, and thence by a fine staircase to the state apartments, containing the presence chamber and the ball-room; in the former is the throne of gilt carved work, under a canopy of crimson velvet richly ornamented with gold lace; the latter, which, since the institution of the order of St. Patrick, has been called St. Patrick's Hall, has its walls decorated with paintings, and the ceiling, which is panelled in three compartments, has in the centre a full-length portrait of George III., supported by Liberty and Justice, with various allegorical devices. Between the gateways, on the north side of the court, are the apartments of the dean of the chapel royal and the chamberlain, a range of building ornamented with Ionic columns rising from a rusticated basement and supporting a cornice and pediment, above which is the Bedford Tower, embellished with Corinthian pillars and surmounted by a lofty dome, from the summit of which the royal standard is displayed on days of state. In the eastern side of the Upper Yard, is the council-chamber, a large but plain apartment, in which the lord-lieutenants are publicly sworn into office, and where the privy council holds its sittings. The privy council consists of the lord-primate, the lord-chancellor, the chief justices, and a number of prelates, noblemen, public functionaries, and others nominated by the King. This body exercises a judicial authority, especially in ecclesiastical matters, as a court of final resort, the duties of which are discharged by a committee selected from among the legal functionaries who are members of it. The Lower Yard is an irregular area, 250 feet long and 220 feet wide; in it are the treasury buildings, of antiquated style and rapidly decaying; the ordnance department, a modern brick building; and the office of the quarter-master-general, besides which are the stables, riding-house, and the official residence of the master of the horse. To the east of the Record Tower is the Castle chapel, rebuilt at an expense of £42,000, principally after a design by Johnston, and opened in 1814; it is an elegant structure, in the later style of English architecture. The interior is lighted on each side by six windows of elegant design, enriched with tracery and embellished with stained glass: the east window, which is of large dimensions and of beautiful design, is of stained glass, representing our Saviour before Pilate, and the four Evangelists in compartments, with an exquisite group of Faith, Hope, and Charity; it was purchased on the continent and presented to the chapel by Lord Whitworth, during his vice-royalty.

The Phœnix Park, situated westward of the city, and north of the Liffey, is 7 miles in circumference, comprising an area of 1759 acres enclosed by a stone wall. Its name is derived from the Irish term *Finniske*, "a spring of clear water," now corrupted into Phœnix. A lofty fluted Corinthian pillar resting on a massive pedestal, and having on the abacus a phœnix rising from the flames, was erected near the lord-lieutenant's lodge by the Earl of Chesterfield, when chief governor. *The Vice-regal Lodge* was purchased from Mr. Clements, by whom it was built, and was originally a plain mansion of brick. Lord Hardwicke, in 1802, added the wings, in one of which is the great dining-hall; the Duke of Richmond, in 1808, built the north portico of the Doric order, and the entrance lodges from the Dublin road;

and Lord Whitworth added the south front, which has a pediment supported by four Ionic columns of Portland stone, from a design by Johnston, and the whole of the façade was afterwards altered to correspond with it: the demesne attached to the lodge comprises 162 acres. The Wellington memorial occupies an elevated position: it consists of a massive truncated obelisk, 205 feet high from the ground, resting on a square pedestal 24 feet high, based on a platform 480 feet in circuit, and rising by steps to the height of 20 feet. On each side of the pedestal are sunken panels intended to receive sculptures in alto relievo, representing the principal victories of the duke; and on each side of the obelisk are enumerated all his battles, from his first career in India to the victory at Waterloo. In front of the eastern side of the pedestal rises another of small proportions, for an equestrian statue of the duke after his decease. It has been so far completed at an expense of £20,000. The park contains residences for the ranger, the principal secretary of state, the under secretary at war, and the under secretary of the civil department. The Powder magazine, erected in 1738, is a square fort, with half bastions at the angles, surrounded by a dry ditch, and entered by a drawbridge; in the interior are the magazines, which are bomb-proof and well secured against accidental fire. It is defended by ten 24-pounders. Near the Vice-regal Lodge a level space of about 50 acres, cleared of trees, is used as a place of exercise and reviews for the troops of the garrison. The park also contains the buildings of the Hibernian school for soldiers' children, the buildings erected by the Ordnance for the trigonometrical survey of Ireland, the Military Infirmary, and the garden of the Zoological society. Near one of the entrances to the Vice-regal Lodge, in a wooded glen, is a chalybeate spa surrounded with pleasure grounds, and furnished with seats for invalids, fitted up at the expense of the Duchess Dowager of Richmond for the accommodation of the public.

The military department is under the control of the commander of the forces, under whom are the departments of the adjutant-general, quarter-master-general, royal artillery, engineers, commissariat and medical staff. The garrison is under the more immediate command of the general officer commanding the eastern district of Ireland, the head-quarters of which is in the city. The commander of the forces resides in the Royal Hospital, Kilmainham, of which he is master by virtue of his office. This hospital was founded for superannuated and maimed soldiers, in 1679, by royal charter, on the site of the dissolved priory of St. John of Jerusalem, at an expense of £23,559. The building consists of a quadrangle, 306 feet by 208 on the outside, enclosing an area of 210 feet square. On the north side is the dining-hall, 100 feet by 50, the walls of which are appropriately ornamented with guns, pikes, and swords, and with standards taken from the Spaniards. The chapel is a plain but venerable structure: the east window, ornamented with stained glass, is very large, and beneath it is the communion table, of highly wrought Irish oak. The remainder of the quadrangle, round which is a covered walk, is appropriated to the use of the inmates. The present establishment is for 5 captains, an adjutant, and 200 soldiers selected from the out-pensioners, whose number is about 20,000. The building is surrounded by a space of ground laid out in lawns and avenues well planted: its principal approach is from the military road. The garrison of the city is quartered in several barracks. The largest and oldest are the Royal Barracks, situated on an eminence overlooking the Liffey, between the city and the principal gate of the Phœnix Park: the chief entrances are by two gates from Barrack-street. They are adapted for 10 field officers, 83 officers, 2003 non-commissioned officers and privates, and 460 horses, with an hospital for 240 patients. The buildings are divided into five squares, under the designation of royal, palatine, cavalry, stable, and clock squares. The barracks in South Great George's-street are adapted for 17 officers of infantry and 324 privates. The Richmond barracks, near Golden Bridge, on the bank of the Grand Canal, have accommodation for 76 officers of infantry and 1602 non-commissioned officers and privates, and an hospital for 100 patients. The Porto Bello cavalry barracks, on the Grand Canal, are adapted for 27 officers and 520 men, with stabling for 540 horses, and an hospital for 40 patients. The barracks in the Phœnix Park, for infantry, have accommodation for 10 officers and 250 non-commissioned officers and men. Connected with the powder magazine are accommodations for one officer of artillery and 18 men. The Island bridge barracks, for artillery, are adapted for 23 officers and 547 men, with stabling for 185 horses, and an hospital for 48 patients. The Recruiting Depôt at Beggar's Bush, beyond Sir Patrick Dun's Hospital, consists of a fort enclosed with a wall, and four bastions with defences for musketry, and affords accommodation for 22 officers and 360 privates, with an hospital for 39 patients. The Pigeon-house fort is situated on the south wall, midway between Ringsend and the Lighthouse, and comprises a magazine, arsenal, and custom-house, the whole enclosed with strong fortifications, and garrisoned by 16 officers of foot and artillery and 201 men, with stabling for 13 horses, and an hospital for 17 men. Adjoining the fort is a basin, 900 feet by 450, intended for a packet station; but since the formation of Howth and Kingstown harbours, it has not been used. The Military Infirmary, designed for sick and wounded soldiers who cannot be properly treated in the regimental hospital, is in the Phœnix Park, near its principal entrance.

COURTS OF JUSTICE.

The supreme courts of judicature consist of the Chancery, in which the lord-chancellor presides, assisted by the Master of the Rolls, who holds a subordinate court; the King's Bench, which is under the superintendence of a chief justice and three puisne judges; the Common Pleas, under a similar superintendence of four judges; and the Exchequer, which contains two departments, one for the management of the revenue, the other a court both of equity and law, in which a chief baron and three puisne barons preside. The courts are held in a magnificent structure, commonly called the Four Courts, situated on the north side of the river, having Richmond and Whitworth bridges at its eastern and western extremities; it consists of a central pile, 140 feet square, containing the courts, and two wings, in which are most of the offices connected with the despatch of legal business: these, with the centre, form two quadrangles. The front of the building consists of a boldly projecting central portico of six Corinthian columns on a platform, to which is an ascent by five steps, and supporting a highly enriched cornice surmounted by a triangular pediment, having on the apex a statue of Moses, and at the ends those of Justice and of Mercy. Through this portico is the principal entrance into the great circular hall, opposite to which is a passage to apartments connected with the courts, and on each side are others leading to the two quadrangles. In the intervals between these four passages are the entrances to the four chief courts; the Chancery on the north-west, the King's Bench on the north-east, the Common Pleas on the south-east, and the Exchequer on the south-west. The Rolls' Court is held in an apartment in the northern part of the central building, between the Courts of Chancery and King's Bench, where also are other apartments used as a law library and a coffee-room. The eastern wing, which forms the northern and eastern sides of one quadrangle, is appropriated to the offices belonging to the Common Pleas and some of those of the Chancery, the remainder of which, with the King's Bench and Exchequer offices, are in the northern and western sides of the other wing. A new building, for a Rolls' Court and a Nisi Prius Court, has been erected between the northern side of the main building and Pill-lane, on a piece of ground purchased for the purpose of isolating the courts, in order to diminish the risk of fire, and to provide additional accommodation for the augmentation of legal proceedings. This stately and sumptuous structure was begun by Mr. Thomas Cooley, architect, and completed by Mr. Gandon, at an expense of about £200,000, and the whole of the sculpture was executed by Mr. Edward Smith, a native artist.

INNS OF COURT.

The King's Inns are situated on a piece of elevated ground of about three acres, formerly called the Primate's Garden, at the northern end of Henrietta-street, the tenure of which having been deemed doubtful, as being held under the Dean and Chapter of Christ-Church, was secured to the society by act of parliament. The structure consists of a centre and two wings, each with a back return; the principal front has a northern aspect, looking towards the rear of the houses on Constitution Hill, but the more usual approach for purposes of business is at the rear through Henrietta-street. The centre, which is crowned with an elegant octagonal cupola and dome, forms a lofty arched gateway, with a door on each side, leading into a confined area between the wings, the northern of which contains the dining-hall, and the southern, the Prerogative and Consistorial Courts, and the repository for the registration of deeds; The Prerogative Court is established for the trial of all testamentary cases where the testator has bequeathed property in more than one diocese. Its jurisdiction is vested in the Lord-Primate, under the acts of the 28th of Hen. VIII. and 2nd of Eliz., which gives him power to appoint the judge or commissary, who ranks next after the judges of the supreme courts. In the Consistorial Court are decided all cases of ecclesiastical jurisdiction of the province of Dublin. The library of the King's Inns is kept in a separate building, erected in Henrietta-street in 1827, at an expense of £20,000, after designs by Mr. Darley: the upper story is a spacious apartment, with recesses for the books and a gallery continued all round; it contains a very extensive collection, which was partly the property of Christopher Robinson, Esq., senior puisne judge of the Court of King's Bench; the law books were chiefly selected by Earl Camden, Lord-Chancellor. The library was entitled to one of the eleven copies of new publications appropriated to the public institutions under the late copyright act, which right has been lately commuted for an equivalent in money. The lower part of the building contains accommodations for the librarian. Bankrupt cases were tried before commissioners, appointed by the lord-chancellor, of whom there were 25, arranged in five sets who presided alternately; the court was held in an upper apartment of the Royal Exchange. By a late act the duties have been transferred to a single judge, under the title of Commissioner of Bankruptcies. The court for the relief of insolvent debtors was placed by an act of the 2nd of Geo. IV. under the jurisdiction of two commissioners, to be appointed by the lord-lieutenant, who hold their court in North Strand-street, with which is connected a suite of offices on Lower Ormond Quay. Prisoners under processes from the courts of justice and insolvent debtors are confined in the Four Courts Marshalsea, a large building in Marshalsea-lane, off Thomas-street: the prison has two court-yards, two chapels, several common halls and a ball-court. The Law Club was instituted in 1791 by a number of the most respectable solicitors and attorneys: the club-house is a plain building in Dame-street. The Law Society was formed in 1830; it proposes to form a law library, and to erect a common hall for the purposes of the society: the meetings are at present held in chambers on the King's Inns' Quay. The Law Students' Society, instituted in 1830, consists exclusively of law students and barristers.

ECCLESIASTICAL STATE.

Arms.

ARCHIEPISCOPAL SEE of DUBLIN and GLENDALOUGH.—The See of Dublin comprehended both the dioceses of Dublin and Glendalough until the arrival of the Danes, who having settled themselves in the plain country on each side of the Liffey, on their conversion to Christianity established a separate bishop, who derived his spiritual authority from the Archbishop of Canterbury and acknowledged him as his superior. Donat, the first bishop of Dublin chosen by the Danes, built the conventual and cathedral church of the Holy Trinity, usually called Christ-Church, about the year 1038. His successor, Patrick, on his election by the people of Dublin, was sent to England to be consecrated by Lanfranc, Archbishop of Canterbury. Gregory, the third in succession after Patrick, on proceeding to England on a similar mission, carried with him a letter from his flock, in which notice is taken of the animosity of the Irish bishops in consequence of their acknowledgment of the jurisdiction of an English prelate. In 1152 the see was raised to an archbishoprick by Cardinal Paparo, the Pope's legate, who invested Gregory with one of the four archiepiscopal palls brought from Rome. Laurence O'Toole was the first archbishop who did not go to England for consecration; the ceremony in his case was performed in Christ-Church by Gelasius, Archbishop of Armagh; and the custom of having recourse to Canterbury was never afterwards resumed. Archbishop Laurence proceeded to Rome in 1179, where he assisted at the second council of Lateran, and obtained a bull confirming that which had decreed the dioceses of Glendalough, Kildare, Ferns, Leighlin, and Ossory, to be suffragan to the metropolitan see of Dublin. On the death of Laurence, Hen. II. bestowed the archbishoprick on John Comyn, an Englishman, and granted him the temporalities with power to hold manor courts. The archbishops henceforward were lords of parliament in right of the barony of Coillach. On Comyn's consecration, Pope Lucius III. invested the see with sole supreme ecclesiastical authority within the province, whence originated the long-continued controversy between the archbishops of Armagh and Dublin, which is fully detailed in the account of the former see. In the archiepiscopal investiture granted by Cardinal Paparo, the dioceses of Dublin and Glendalough are considered to be, strictly speaking, a single see; but in compliance with the wishes of the inhabitants of the mountain districts, which contained the latter, it was allowed to retain its name and a separate subordinate existence. But King John, in 1185, granted to Comyn the reversion of this bishoprick on its next avoidance, and the charter to this effect was confirmed by Matthew O'Heney, archbishop of Cashel, the Pope's legate, at a synod held in Dublin in 1192. But though this union was legally effected about the year 1214, the mountain clans, who were still unamenable to English law, long continued to appoint their own bishops of Glendalough. Henry de Loundres, the next archbishop, appears to have exercised the privileges of a peer of parliament in England, perhaps in right of the manor of Penkridge in Staffordshire, granted to the see by Hugh Hussey, founder of the Galtrim family in Ireland, and which long formed a peculiar of the diocese. The same prelate raised the collegiate church of St. Patrick, which had been erected by his predecessor, to the dignity of a cathedral, in consequence of which the diocese continues to have two cathedral churches. This circumstance afterwards gave rise to a violent contest between the two chapters as to the right of electing an archbishop. The dispute was terminated by an agreement that the archbishop should be consecrated and enthroned in Christ-Church, which, as being the more ancient, should have the precedency; and that the crosier, mitre, and ring of every archbishop, in whatever place he died, should be deposited in it, but that both churches should be cathedral and metropolitan. There have been always two archdeaconries in the united diocese of Dublin and Glendalough, whose jurisdictions may have been formerly coterminous with their respective sees; but the long and intimate union of these, and the little use made of the archidiaconal functions, render it nearly impossible to define their respective limits with any degree of accuracy.

The records of Christ-Church inform us that it owes its foundation to Sitric, the son of Anlaffe, king of Dublin, who, about the year 1038, gave to Donat, bishop of that see, a place where arches or vaults were built, on which to erect a church to the honour of the Blessed Trinity, to whom the building was accordingly dedicated. It was originally the conventual church of a monastery of secular canons unattached to any of the cenobitical orders, who were changed by Laurence O'Toole, in 1163, to canons regular of the order of Arras, a branch of the Augustinians. Sitric originally endowed this establishment with some small tracts on the sea coast of the present county of Dublin; and these possessions were greatly extended after the arrival of the English, when the successive augmentations of its revenue raised it to the rank of one of the most important priories in the island. Its privileges were confirmed by Henry II. and his successors; its priors were spiritual peers of parliament. This convent had anciently an endowed cell in the diocese of Armagh.

In 1541, Henry VIII. changed the monastic establishment into a dean and chapter, confirming its ancient estates and immunities, and making Payneswick, the last prior, its first dean on the new foundation, which consisted of a dean, chanter, chancellor, treasurer, and six vicars choral. Archbishop Brown, in 1544, erected in this church the three prebends of St. Michael's, St. Michan's, and St. John's; and from the time of these alterations it has generally borne the name of Christ-Church, instead of that of the Holy Trinity. King Edward VI. added six priests and two choristers or singing-boys, to whom he assigned a pension of £45. 6. 8. per annum, payable out of the exchequer during pleasure. Queen Mary confirmed this pension, and granted it in perpetuity. James I. made some further alterations, and ordained that the archdeacon of Dublin should have a stall in the choir, and a voice and seat in the chapter in all capitular acts relating to the church. Welbore Ellis, the eleventh dean, installed in 1705, was subsequently made Bishop of Kildare, from which period the deanery has continued to be held in commendam with that bishoprick. The gross annual revenue of the deanery, on an average of three years ending Dec. 31st, 1831, was £5314. 5. 11½. The cathedral establishment consists at present, therefore, of the dean (who is also Bishop of Kildare, and is guardian of the temporalities of the see during its vacancy on the death or avoidance of the archbishop), chanter, chancellor, treasurer, archdeacon, and the three above-named prebendaries, under whom are six vicars choral, six stipendiaries or choirmen, and six singing boys and a registrar. The advowsons of the Dean and Chapter are (besides the three prebends already mentioned) the rectories of St. Mary, St. Paul, and St. Thomas, and the vicarage of Balscaddan, all in Dublin diocese; the alternate presentation to the rectory of St. George, Dublin, and the fourth turn to the union of Baronstown, in the county of Louth. For the repairs of the building and the payment of the inferior officers there is an economy fund, amounting on an average of three years ending 31st of Dec., 1831, to £2386. 8. 6. per ann., arising mostly from rents, tithes, and the dividends on about £10,000 funded property, including also the above-named pension.

The *Ecclesiastical province of Dublin*, over which the Archbishop presides, comprehends the dioceses of Dublin and Glendalough, Kildare, Ossory, Ferns, and Leighlin. It is entirely included in the civil province of Leinster, and is estimated to comprise an area of 1,827,250 acres. Under the Church Temporalities' Act (3rd and 4th of Wm. IV., c. 37), on the next vacancy in the bishoprick of Kildare, that see is to be permanently united with Dublin and Glendalough; and in like manner the bishoprick of Ossory is to be permanently united with

Ferns and Leighlin. The act also provides that, on the next avoidance of the see of Cashel, that archbishoprick is to be reduced to the rank of a bishoprick, and, together, with all its dependent sees, is to be suffragan to the Archbishop of Dublin, whose jurisdiction will then extend over the whole of Munster, the greater part of Leinster, and part of Galway in Connaught.

The *Diocese of Dublin and Glendalough* extends over all the county of Dublin, together with parts of Queen's county, Wicklow, Kildare, and Wexford; and contains an estimated area of 477,950 acres, of which 142,050 are in Dublin, 600 in Queen's county, 257,400 in Wicklow, 75,000 in Kildare, and 2900 in Wexford. The lands belonging to the united sees amount to 34,040 statute acres, of which 23,926 are profitable land; and the gross income, on an average of three years ending Dec. 31st, 1831, was £9230. 12. 9. It comprises 95 benefices, exclusively of chapelries; of these, 39 are unions of two or more parishes, and 56 are single parishes or parts of parishes; 11 of them are in the gift of the Crown, 39 in lay and corporation patronage, 5 in joint or alternate presentation, and the remainder in the patronage of the Archbishop, or incumbents. The parishes or districts are 180: there are 124 churches, and 9 other buildings in which divine worship is performed, and 50 glebe-houses. The diocesan school is endowed with 10 acres of land and £100 late currency for the master.

In the R. C. divisions the Archbishop of Dublin is primate of Ireland, and his three suffragan bishops are those of Kildare and Leighlin, Ossory, and Ferns: he is styled only Archbishop of Dublin, and not of Dublin and Glendalough, as in the Established Church. The R. C. diocese of Dublin comprises 48 parochial districts, of which 9 are in the city; and contains 121 chapels, served by 153 clergymen, 48 of whom are parish priests and 105 coadjutors or curates. The Archbishop's parish is St. Mary's, in which is the R. C. cathedral, called the Metropolitan Church, or Church of the Conception. The chapter consists of the same number and denomination of officers as the chapter of St. Patrick's Cathedral, but the dean and precentor are styled vicars general.

The *Cathedral of Christ-Church* is a long cruciform building, composed of a nave with a north aisle, transepts, and choir, with a central tower. The southern transept, measuring ninety feet by twenty-five, is entered by a Norman doorway in good preservation: the tower is a low massive pile, terminating in a pointed roof. The whole of the building has recently been repaired and several improvements made, at an expense of upwards of £8000 from the economy fund. The choir is separated from the nave by an elegant skreen, above which is the organ gallery, and decorated with a noble eastern window of stained glass, representing the armorial bearings of the members of the chapter, and having its lower part ornamented with an enriched border of open work above the altar. The ceiling is intersected with quadrangular mouldings, with heavy bosses at the points of intersection serving to conceal a deviation from the straight line of direction between the entrance and the altar window, which is an irremediable defect in the original construction: a handsome border of tracery work goes round the walls. There are several remarkable monuments, the greater number of which are placed against the blank south wall of the nave. Among them are one of Strongbow, and of his wife Eva, or of his son, mutilated by the fall of the roof, and placed in its present situation by the Lord-Deputy Sidney, in 1570; a very beautiful monument of Thomas Prior, an early and zealous promoter of the Dublin Society; one of Lord Chancellor Bowes; another of Lord Chancellor Lifford; and a fourth of Robert, Earl of Kildare, who died in 1743; besides those of several successive bishops of Kildare. A very fine monument has been lately erected to the memory of Nathaniel Sneyd, Esq., who was shot by a lunatic while walking in Westmoreland-street. Various eminent prelates of the see of Dublin have been interred within the walls of this church.

St. Patrick's.

John Comyn, archbishop of Dublin, having erected a collegiate church for 13 prebendaries, in the southern suburbs of the city, on the site of an ancient parochial church, said to have been founded by St. Patrick in 448, dedicated it to God, the Blessed Virgin, and St. Patrick, and endowed it amply. Henry de Loundres, his successor, raised it to the dignity of a cathedral, consisting of a dean, precentor, chancellor, and treasurer, with thirteen prebendaries, increased its temporalities, and authorised the members to hear all pleas of their parishioners in their prebendal and economy churches. From a taxation in 1227 the number of prebendaries appears to have been increased to 22, three of whom were added by Bishop Ferings. The controversy which arose between this cathedral and that of Christ-Church, as to the right of electing the archbishop, has been noticed in the account of the latter cathedral. Among other privileges granted to the canons of this church by Henry VIII., was a dispensation from parochial residence on any other benefice, on condition of maintaining hospitality in the cathedral, but the establishment was soon after dissolved by the same monarch in 1546, together with the monastic institutions. Edward VI. disposed of the church and its appendages for a parish church, a seat for the courts of justice, a grammar school or literary college, and an hospital; the deanery was assigned for the archbishop's residence, and the lord-deputy took possession of the archiepiscopal palace; but this arrangement was revoked by Queen Mary, who at the beginning of her reign restored the cathedral to all its former privileges and possessions, by a charter commonly called the Charter of Restitution.

At present the chapter consists of a dean, precentor, chancellor, treasurer, the archdeacons of Dublin and Glendalough, and the prebendaries of Cullen, Swords, Kilmactalway, Yago, St. Audeon's, Clonmethan, Wicklow, Timothan, Mallahidart, Castleknock, Tipper, Tassagard, Dunlavan, Maynooth, Howth, Rathmichael, Monmohenock, Stagonil, Tipperkevin, and Donoughmore in Omaile. The dignity of dean has always been elective in the chapter, on the congé d'elire of the archbishop, except in cases of the promotion of the former dean to a bishoprick, the vacancy of the archiepiscopal see, or the neglect of the chapter, in which cases the appointment belongs of right to the Crown. The powers of the chapter in this regard were twice infringed upon, but they have been restored by their perseverance. By the original charter and the statute of the 14th of Edw. IV., the dean was constituted the immediate ordinary and prelate of the church of St. Patrick, and exercises episcopal jurisdiction throughout the liberties and economy thereof: he has a spiritual court in which his official or commissary, and a temporal court in which his seneschal general presides; and grants marriage licences, probate of wills, &c. The gross yearly revenue of the deanery, on an average of three years ending Dec. 31st, 1831, amounted to £1997. 8. 1. By the Church Temporalities Act the dean of St. Patrick's is to be dean of Christ-Church also; on the next avoidance of that deanery, he will be dean of Christ-Church without installation or induction. The dean and chapter have the right of presentation to the parishes of St. Bridget, St. Nicholas Within, and St. Nicholas Without. The dean, in right of his dignity, presents to the vicarage of Kilberry, and to the curacies of Malahide and Crumlin; the precentor and treasurer have the alternate presentation of the vicarage of Lusk, and the archdeacon of Dublin that of the perpetual cure of Booterstown, and three turns out of four of the united cures of Kilternan and Kilgobbin. The gross amount of the Economy fund, on an average of three years ending the 29th of Sept., 1831, was £2076. 2. 11. The archdeacon of Dublin had a stall in the chapter of the cathedral of Christ-Church, and a voice in the election of the archbishop, previously to his possessing the same in that of St. Patrick; but the archdeacon of Glendalough had neither of these rights until about the year 1267, when a new prebend was erected and annexed to the office. An additional corporation of six minor canons (since reduced to four) and six choristers was established in 1431 by Archbishop Talbot, on account of the devastations of the lands of the prebends having rendered them insufficient for the service of the church: the first in rank he styled sub-dean, and the second succentor: he endowed the entire body with the tithes of Swords, except such portions as were especially allotted to the prebendary and perpetual vicar; and vested the appointment and dismissal of the minor canons in the dean and chapter, and of the choristers in the precentor. This arrangement was sanctioned by Henry VI. and Pope Eugenius IV., who fixed the rank of the minor canons between that of prebendaries and vicars choral. In 1520 the minor canons and choristers were made a body corporate by charter. Archbishop Henry de Loundres, at the time he established the four dignitaries, instituted also the college of vicars choral, for whose common support he granted the church of Keneth (now Kinneagh), to which various endowments were subsequently added. The head of this college, styled sub-dean, or dean's vicar, enjoyed very considerable authority, possessing even a seat in the chapter, as also did the next vicar, called the sub-chanter, or chanter's vicar. They were incorporated by Richard II., and received their last charter from Charles I., who fixed their number at twelve, of whom five at least were to be priests, and the dean's vicar was to have a superior salary, and extensive power over the rest: the salary of the twelve vicars is directed by this charter to be apportioned by the dean and chapter, of whom the former enjoys the nomination to all vacancies; but out of the body thus appointed, the chanter, chancellor, and treasurer choose their respective vicars, as also does the Archdeacon of Dublin. The charter likewise secures to the Archbishop his ancient visitorial power; forms the college into a body corporate; confirms their ancient possessions; and binds them to pay a master of the choristers, and two singing boys in addition to the four choristers.

The Cathedral of St. Patrick is a venerable cruciform pile, 300 feet in length, of which the nave occupies 130 feet, the choir 90, and St. Mary's chapel 55: the transept extends 157 feet in length. The nave, the entrance to which is by a beautifully arched and deeply receding doorway, is 30 feet in width, with two aisles, each 14 feet wide, separated from it by octagonal pillars supporting plain Gothic arches of dissimilar arrangement but imposing appearance: it is lofty, and is lighted by a magnificent window at the western end, over the main entrance. In the south end of the transept is the chapter-house; the entire northern end is occupied by the parish church of St. Nicholas. The monuments in this cathedral are numerous: among the most remarkable in the nave are those of Archbishops Smith and Marsh, and that of the Earl of Cavan, who died in 1778; and on two pillars on the south side are tablets to the memory of Dean Swift and of Mrs. Johnson, the celebrated Stella. The oldest monument is a mutilated gravestone to the memory of Archbishop Tregury, who died in 1471. In the choir are many monuments: that of the first Earl of Cork, and several members of his family, which is placed on the right side of the altar, is an unsightly pile of black stone of antiquated sculpture, with ornaments of wood, painted and gilt, exhibiting sixteen unconnected figures, representing as many individuals of the family. Similar in style are the smaller monuments, on the opposite side, of Thomas Jones, Archbishop of Dublin, and Roger Jones, Viscount Ranelagh, near which is a plain slab to the memory of Duke Schomberg, with a very caustic inscription from the pen of Swift.

TRINITY COLLEGE.

Seal and Arms of the University.

The foundation of a university in Dublin was at first attempted by John Leck, archbishop of the see, who in 1311 obtained a bull from Pope Clement V. for its foundation, but it was not accomplished till 1320, when his successor, Alexander de Bicknor, having procured a confirmation of the former bull from Pope John XXII., established a school of learning in St. Patrick's cathedral, for which he framed statutes, and over which he appointed William Rodiart, then dean of St. Patrick's, chancellor. Edw. III., in 1358, granted to the scholars his letters of protection; and in 1364 confirmed a grant of land from Lionel, Duke of Clarence, to found a divinity lecture in the university; but, for want of sufficient funds, the establishment gradually declined, though it appears to have lingered till the dissolution of the cathedral establishment, in the reign of Henry VIII. In 1568, a motion was made in the Irish parliament for its re-establishment, towards which Sir Henry Sidney, then lord-deputy, offered to settle on it lands of the yearly value of £20 and £100 in money. In 1584, Sir John Perrott, lord-deputy, had it in contemplation to re-establish the university by appropriating to its support the revenues of the cathedral of St. Patrick; but in this attempt he was strenuously opposed by Dr. Adam Loftus, Archbishop of Dublin, who made application to Queen Elizabeth and to the lord-treasurer of England for the protection of his cathedral; and also prevailed upon the mayor and citizens of Dublin to give the dissolved monastery of All Saints or All Hallows, on Hoggin (now College) Green, which had been granted to them by Henry VIII., as a site for the intended building. In 1591, letters patent were issued for the erection of the present establishment, to be styled "Collegium Sanctæ et Individuæ Trinitatis juxta Dublin, a Serenissima Reginâ Elizabethâ fundatum;" to be a corporate body; under the title of the Provost, Fellows, and Scholars of the College of the Holy and Indivisible Trinity, with power to possess lands to the yearly value of £400, to have a common seal, and to be for ever exempt from local taxes. The provost and fellows were authorised by it to make laws, statutes, and ordinances for the government of the college, with liberty to select from those of Oxford or Cambridge, at their option; and to grant the degrees of bachelor, master, and doctor in all arts and faculties, provided that all fellows should vacate their fellowships after seven years' occupancy from the time of their taking the degree of master of arts. The first students were admitted in 1593. The funds of the college were so much diminished by the breaking out of the Tyrone rebellion, that the establishment must have been dissolved, had not the queen, in 1601, made the college a further grant of £200 per annum, till it should regain its possessions; and James I. granted it a revenue of £388. 15. English currency, and endowed it with many valuable lands and advowsons in Ulster; he also granted it the privilege of returning two representatives to parliament. The prosperity of the college was much retarded by internal dissensions, to which the election of the provosts frequently gave rise, and from the want of a more definite constitution to remedy this evil. In 1627 a new code of statutes was framed by Dr. Bedell, afterwards bishop of Kilmore; and in 1633 Archbishop Laud, then chancellor of the university, drew up a more complete code, founded on that of Bedell, which, together with a new charter, was enforced by royal authority, though not without considerable opposition. By this charter the power of electing the provost, and of enacting and repealing statutes, was vested in the Crown; the fellowships were distinguished into senior and junior, and made tenable for life; the extension of the number of fellows from three to sixteen, and of scholars from three to seventy, which had been previously made, was rendered permanent; and the government of the college was vested solely in the provost and the seven senior fellows, with power to enact by-laws, to be confirmed by the visiters. No subsequent alterations have taken place in the constitution of the college, except an increase in the number of junior fellows. By the Act of Settlement, the chief governor of Ireland, with the consent of the privy council, was empowered to erect another college to be of the university of Dublin, and to be called the King's College, and to raise out of the lands vested in the king by that act a sum not exceeding £2000 per ann. for its endowment. This clause has never been acted upon; and Trinity College differs in its constitution from those of Oxford and Cambridge, by combining in its own government the full privileges and powers of a university, the provost and senior fellows constituting the only senate or university convocation, and possessing the same power of electing officers and conferring degrees. A new fellowship was founded, in 1698, out of lands bequeathed to the college by Dr. John Richardson, bishop of Ardagh, who had been a fellow. Three others were added in 1724, on the foundation of Erasmus Smith; and five additional fellowships were founded, to be endowed out of the increased revenues of the university, two of them in 1762, and three in 1808. The *Senate*, or *Congregation of the University*, by which degrees are publicly conferred, consists of all masters of arts and resident doctors in the three faculties, having their names on the college books, and who are liable to a fine for non-attendance. The *Caput Senatus Academici* consists of the vice-chancellor, the provost, or vice-provost, and by election of these, with the consent of the congregation, of the senior master non-regent, resident in the college: they have each a negative voice to prevent any grace for the conferring of a degree from being proposed to the senate. Every grace must first be granted privately by the provost and senior fellows, before it can be proposed to the caput or the senate. There are now two regular days for conferring degrees; namely, Shrove-Tuesday and the Tuesday nearest to the 8th of July, whether before or after. The Board, formed by the provost and senior fellows, meets generally every Saturday to transact all business relating to the internal management of the college.

The following are the principal university and college officers: the chancellor, at present his royal highness the Duke of Cumberland; the vice-chancellor, nominated by the chancellor, at present the Rt. Hon. and Most Rev. Lord J. G. De La Poer Beresford, Archbishop of Armagh, who may appoint a pro-vice-chancellor; the provost, who, except by dispensation from the Crown, must be a doctor or bachelor in divinity, and thirty years of age, at present Bartholomew Lloyd, D. D.; the vice-provost, elected annually by the provost and senior fellows, but who is generally the senior of the senior fellows, and re-elected for many successive years; two proctors, chosen annually, one from the senior and one from the junior fellows, the former being moderator in philosophy for the masters, and the latter for the bachelors, of arts; a dean and a junior dean, chosen annually, the former from the senior and the latter from the junior fellows, and whose duty it is to superintend the morals of the students, and enforce their attendance on college duties; a senior lecturer, chosen annually from the senior fellows, to superintend the attendance of the students at lectures and examinations, and to keep a record of their merits; a censor, created in 1728, whose office is to impose literary exercises in lieu of pecuniary fines upon such students as may have incurred academic censure; a librarian and junior librarian; a librarian of the lending library; a registrar; a registrar of chambers; a bursar and junior bursar; a registrar of the university electors, appointed in 1832 for keeping the register of persons qualified to vote for the university members of parliament; an auditor; six university preachers; and four morning lecturers.

The professorships are seventeen in number. The *Regius Professorship of Divinity*, originally founded in St. Patrick's cathedral, and held in 1607 by Dr. James Ussher, afterwards Archbishop of Armagh, was more amply endowed in 1674, by Charles II., out of lands given to the college by the Act of Settlement; in 1761 it was made a regius professorship by statute of George III.; and by another, in 1814, its endowment was augmented, and the office made tenable for life. The professor is elected by the provost and senior fellows from the fellows who are doctors of divinity, and vacates his fellowship on his appointment; he acts as moderator in disputations for degrees in divinity, has to preach four times in the year in defence of the Christian religion before the university, to read publicly during the year four prelections in divinity, besides lectures twice every week during term, and to hold an annual examination of the divinity students; he has four assistants. A lectureship in divinity was founded by Archbishop King in 1718, and was formerly elected to annually from the senior fellows; but this office has been recently separated from a fellowship, and is now held with one of the college livings: its duties also have been considerably increased, and more intimately connected with the education of such students as are preparing for holy orders. Archbishop King's lecturer has now five assistants. Students in divinity must attend with diligence the lectures and examinations of this lecturer and his assistants during the first year of their course, and during the second, the lectures of the Regius Professor and his assistants; without this two years' course of study, no student can obtain the certificates necessary for admission to holy orders. The *Regius Professorship of Greek*, previously held by a lecturer under the statute of Charles I., was founded in 1761 by statute of George III.; the professor is annually elected, and has two assistants. Two *Professorships of Modern Languages*, one for the French and German, and one for the Italian and Spanish, were formed in 1777 by a royal grant of £200 each per ann. The *Professorships of Hebrew, Oratory, History, Mathematics, and Natural Philosophy* were founded by act of parliament, and endowed by Erasmus Smith; the professors are chosen from among the fellows by the provost and senior fellows, with the approbation of the governors of Erasmus Smith's schools; a lectureship in Mathematics was founded in the middle of the 17th century by Arthur, Earl of Donegal, who endowed it with £10 per annum. The *Regius Professorship of Civil and Canon Law* was founded in 1668, by letters patent of Charles II., and endowed out of revenues granted to the university by the Act of Settlement; the professor acts also as moderator in all disputations for degrees in law. The *Regius Professorship of Feudal and English Law* was founded in 1761, by statute of George III.; the professor is elected by the provost and senior fellows, either for life or for a term of years; he must be a barrister of at least two years' standing, and, if a fellow of the college, may hold the appointment for life, resigning his fellowship. The *Regius Professorship of Physic* originated in a statute appointing one of the fellows of the university to devote himself to the study of physic; but since the Restoration, the regius professor of physic and the medical fellow have been regarded as distinct, and, except in two instances, have never been united in the same person. The *Professorships of Anatomy, Chymistry and Botany*, originally lectureships established about the year 1710, were founded by an act of the 25th of George III. for the establishment of a complete school of physic in Ireland, in conjunction with three other professorships on the foundation of Sir Patrick Dun's hospital; the professors are elected for seven years, at the end of which time they may be re-elected; they deliver periodical lectures in the theatre of the college. The *Lectureship in Natural History* was founded by the provost and senior fellows in 1816: the lecturer, who is also curator of the museum, delivers lectures on such parts of natural history, including geology and mineralogy, as the provost and senior fellows may appoint. The *Professorship of Astronomy* was founded in 1774, by Dr. Francis Andrews, provost of the college, who bequeathed £3000 for the erection of an observatory, and £250 per annum for the salary of such professor and assistants as the provost and senior fellows should appoint; a statute was obtained, in 1791, for regulating the duties of the professor, who is thereby constituted astronomer-royal for Ireland, and has an assistant, appointed by himself; he resides constantly in the observatory, from which he can never be absent more than 62 days in the year, without leave of the provost or vice-provost. The *Professorship of Political Economy* was founded in 1832, by Dr. Whately, Archbishop of Dublin, upon the principle of the Drummond professorship at Oxford; the professor, who must be at least a master of arts or bachelor in civil law, and a graduate of Dublin, Oxford, or Cambridge, is elected for five years: his duty is to deliver lectures in that science to such graduates and undergraduates as may be recommended to him by their tutors, and to print one lecture annually. A *Professorship of Moral Philosophy* has been recently founded, and annexed to one of the college livings.

The *members of the university on the foundation* at present consist of the provost, seven senior fellows, eighteen junior fellows, and seventy scholars: the junior fellows are elected as vacancies occur, on Trinity Monday; candidates must have taken at least the degree of bachelor of arts; they are examined on the four last days of the week preceding the election. Only three of the fellows are allowed to be members of lay professions, one of medicine, and two of law, without a dispensation from the Crown; all the rest must devote themselves to the church, and are bound by oath, on their marriage, to vacate their fellowships. The *benefices in the gift of the college* are 21 in number, and are situated in the dioceses of Armagh, Clogher, Down, Derry, Raphoe, and Kilmore; 17 of them became forfeited to the Crown by the rebellion of O'Nial, and were bestowed on the college by James I.; many of them are of considerable value, and on the death of an incumbent are offered to the clerical fellows in rotation. These benefices, by letters patent of James I., are Arboe, Ardtrea, Clogherney, Clonfeacle, Clonoe, and Desertcreight, in the diocese of Armagh; Aghalurcher, Cleenish, Derryvullen, and Enniskillen, in the diocese of Clogher; Killileagh, in the diocese of Down; Ardstraw, Cappagh, and Drumragh, in the diocese of Derry; Clondehorky, Clondevadock, Conwall, Kilmacrenan, Ramochy, and Tullyaghnish, in the diocese of Raphoe; and Killesandra, in the diocese of Kilmore. The *terms of the university* were formerly four in the year, and as altered by Archbishop Laud corresponded nearly to those of Oxford; but by a statute obtained in 1833 they were reduced to three only; Michaelmas, Hilary, and Trinity; but if Easter fall within the limits of Hilary or Trinity term, the term for that year is continued for an additional week. These terms may be kept by answering at examinations held for the purpose, at the beginning of each; but residence, either in the college or in the city, is indispensable for students in divinity, law, and medicine, as terms in these faculties can only be kept by regular attendance on the lectures of the university professors. Members of the university are not required to subscribe to the articles, or to attend the duties, of the church of England, if they profess to have conscientious objections, except on their obtaining a fellowship or scholarship, or on admission to a degree in divinity. By charter of James I. *the university returned two members to the Irish parliament* till the Union; after which time it returned only one member to the Imperial parliament, till the recent Reform act, since which it has returned two. The right of election, which was originally vested solely in the provost, fellows, and scholars, has, by the same act, been extended to all members of the age of 21 years, who had obtained, or should hereafter obtain, a fellowship, scholarship, or the degree of Master of Arts, and whose names should be on the college books: members thus qualified, who had removed their names from the books, were allowed six months to restore them, on paying a fee of £2, and such as continued their names, merely to qualify them to vote, pay annually to the college the sum of £1, or a composition of £5 in lieu of annual payment. The number of names restored under this provision was 3005, and at present the constituency amounts to 3135. The provost is the returning officer.

The *buildings of the university*, which, from their extent and magnificence, form one of the principal ornaments of the city, consist of three spacious quadrangles, erected chiefly after designs by Sir William Chambers. The principal front, which occupies the whole of the eastern side of College-green, is 380 feet long, built of Portland stone, and consists of a projecting centre, ornamented with four three-quarter Corinthian columns supporting an enriched cornice and pediment, under which is the principal entrance; and at each extremity of the façade is a projecting pile of square building, decorated with duplicated pilasters of the same order, between which is a noble Venetian window, enriched with festoons of flowers and fruit in high relief; and above the cornice, which extends along the whole of the front, rises an attic surmounted by a balustrade. The entrance is by an octangular vestibule, the ceiling of which is formed of groined arches: it leads into the first quadrangle, called Parliament-square, from its having been rebuilt chiefly by the munificence of Parliament, which granted at different times £40,000 for the purpose. This quadrangle, which is 316 feet in length and 212 in breadth, contains, besides apartments for the fellows and students, the chapel, the theatre for examinations, and the refectory. The *chapel*, which is on the north side, is ornamented in front by a handsome portico of four Corinthian columns, supporting a rich cornice surmounted by a pediment; the interior is 80 feet in length, exclusively of a semicircular recess of 20 feet radius, 40 feet broad, and 44 feet in height; the front of the organ gallery is richly ornamented with carved oak. The *theatre*, on the south side, has a front corresponding exactly with that of the chapel, and is of the same dimensions; the walls are decorated with pilasters of the Composite order, rising from a rustic basement; between the pilasters are whole-length portraits of Queen Elizabeth, the foundress, and of the following eminent persons educated in the college; Primate Ussher, Archbishop King, Bishop Berkeley, William Molyneux, Dean Swift, Dr. Baldwin, and John Foster, Speaker of the Irish House of Commons: there is also a fine monument of black and white marble and porphyry, executed at Rome by Hewetson, a native of Ireland, at an expense of £2000, erected to the memory of Dr. Baldwin, formerly provost, who died in 1758, and bequeathed £80,000 to the university. The *refectory* is a neat building, ornamented with four Ionic pilasters supporting a cornice and pediment over the entrance; a spacious ante-hall opens into the dining-hall, in which are portraits of Henry Flood, Lord Chief Justice Downes, Lord Avonmore, Hussey Burgh, Lord Kilwarden, Henry Grattan, the Prince of Wales (father of Geo. III.), Cox, Archbishop of Cashel, and Provost Baldwin. Over the ante-hall an elegant apartment has been recently fitted up for the *Philosophy school*, and furnished with a valuable collection of philosophical and astronomical instruments; and in it are delivered the public lectures of the professors of natural philosophy and astronomy. The second quadrangle, called the *Library-square*, is 265 feet in length and 214 feet in breadth. Three sides of it are occupied by uniform ranges of brick building, containing apartments for the students; these are now the oldest buildings in the college and are fast verging to decay. The fourth side is formed by the *library*, a very fine building of granite, the basement story of which forms a piazza extending the whole length of the square, above which are two stories surmounted by an enriched entablature and crowned with a balustrade. It consists of a centre and two pavilions at the extremities: in the western pavilion are the grand staircase, the Law school, and the librarian's apartment; from the landing-place large folding doors open into the library, a magnificent gallery, 210 feet in length, 41 feet in breadth, and 40 feet high; between the windows on both sides are partitions of oak projecting at right angles from the side walls, and forming recesses in which the books are arranged; the partitions terminate in fluted Corinthian columns of carved oak, supporting a broad cornice, surmounted by a balustrade of oak richly carved, and forming a handsome front to a gallery which is continued round the whole of the room. From the gallery rises a series of Corinthian pilasters between a range of upper windows, supporting a broad entablature and cornice; at the bases of the lower range of pilasters are pedestals supporting busts, finely executed in white marble, of the most eminent of the ancient and modern philosophers, poets, orators, and men of learning, including several distinguished members of the university. At the extremity of this room is an apartment, in a transverse direction, 52 feet in length, fitted up in similar style, and containing the Fagel library, over which, and communicating with the gallery, is the apartment for MSS., containing records illustrative of Irish and English history of great value, works in the Greek, Arabic, and Persian languages, and some richly illuminated bibles and missals: the magnificent collection comprises upwards of 100,000 volumes. To the north of the Library-square is the third quadrangle, of modern structure, but with few pretensions to architectural elegance. It is wholly appropriated to chambers for the students, which occupy two of its sides, the other two being formed by the rear of the northern range of the Library-square and by one side of the dining-hall. A temporary building near its centre contains the great bell, formerly suspended in a steeple which made part of the ancient chapel of the college; it was intended by the original design of the first or principal quadrangle to be erected in a dome over the gateway. The old chapel and belfrey occupied the vacant space between the first and second quadrangles. An additional square, to contain suites of apartments for students, is laid out and the buildings of one side of it commenced, eastward of the Library-square, part of which is to be taken down when the new range of buildings is finished. The *University Museum,* a handsome apartment 60 feet long and 40 feet wide, is immediately over the vestibule of the entrance from College Green; it comprises, under the superintendence of a curator, several collections of minerals, of which there are more than 9000 specimens. The *Printing-office,* founded by Dr. Stearne, Bishop of Clogher, is a handsome structure with an elegant portico of the Doric order, and is situated on the east of the Library-square. To the south of the library is a fine garden for the fellows; and to the east of the College buildings is the Park, comprising about 20 acres, planted and tastefully laid out for the use of the students. Beyond the park are the *Chymical Laboratory* and the *School of Anatomy:* this range of building, which is 115 feet in length and 50 feet in breadth, contains a chymical laboratory and lecture-room, with apartments for the professor, a dissecting-room extending the whole length of the building, and an anatomical lecture-room, 30 feet square; an anatomical museum, 30 feet long and 28 feet wide, in which was a valuable collection of preparations of human, comparative, and morbid anatomy, the largest and by much the most valuable part of which, being the private collection of Dr. Macartney, the present professor, has been sold by him to the university of Cambridge. The *Provost's house,* a spacious and handsome edifice, is to the south of the west front of the university, and is skreened from Grafton-street by a high wall with a massive gateway in the centre. The *College Botanic Gardens* are situated in the south-eastern extremity of the city, near Ball's bridge, and comprised originally about four acres, to which two more have been lately added; they are enclosed towards the public road into the city by a dwarf wall of granite surmounted by a very high iron palisade, were first laid out in 1807, and contain an extensive collection of plants well arranged and kept in excellent order. The *College Observatory* is situated on Dunsink-hill, in Castleknock parish, about 4 miles to the north-west of the city. The building fronts to the east, and consists of a centre and two receding wings, the former surmounted by a dome which covers the equatorial room, and is moveable, having an aperture two feet six inches wide, which can be directed to any part of the horizon; around the dome is a platform, which commands an extensive and varied prospect. The first professor was Dr. Ussher, senior fellow of Dublin college, under whose direction the building was erected, and who was succeeded, on his death in 1792, by the late learned and ingenious Dr. Brinkley, afterwards Bishop of Cloyne; after whose death, in 1835, the present astronomer-royal of Ireland, Sir William Rowan Hamilton, was appointed.

PARISHES.

The Metropolitan parishes are all in the diocese of Dublin.

St. Andrew's was formerly united to St. Werburgh's, but the union having been dissolved in 1660, it was by act of parliament erected into a separate parish, and in 1707 the present parish of St. Mark was by another act formed out of it. It contains 7870 inhabitants: the number of houses valued at £5 and upwards is 731, the total annual value being £46,022. The rectory, the annual income of which is £346. 8. 3½., forms the corps of the precentorship of St. Patrick's cathedral: the vicarage is in the gift of the Lord-Chancellor, the Archbishop of Dublin, the three Chief Judges, and the Master of the Rolls; the amount of minister's money is £529. 15. 1. The church, situated in St. Andrew's-street, opposite Church-lane, was commenced in 1793, and completed in 1807, at an expense of £22,000. It is of elliptical form, 80 feet by 60, whence it has acquired the popular name of the Round Church: over the principal entrance, which is at the extremity of the lesser axis of the ellipsis, is a statue of St. Andrew bearing his cross; and at the opposite end is the communion table, reading desk, pulpit, and organ loft, with galleries for children on each side of it. The parochial school for boys and girls is supported by an annual sermon and the rent of the lands of Phrompstown. An almshouse for 28 widows, founded in 1726 by Dr. Travers, is supported by the weekly collections in the church.

St. Anne's parish was formed out of the united parishes of St. Stephen, St. Peter, and St. Bride, and made a separate parish in 1707. It contains 8363 inhabitants; the number of houses valued at £5 and upwards is 785, the total annual value being £56,812. 10. The living is a vicarage, in the patronage of the Archbishop of Dublin; the amount of minister's money is £588. 18. 5. The church, situated in Dawson-street, opposite Anne-street, was designed from a church in Rome, but remains unfinished; the front consists of a portal with Doric half columns and smaller side entrances surmounted by ornamented windows, above which the gable of the building is seen. The interior is spacious and handsome; the galleries, which surround it on three sides, are supported by Ionic pillars of carved oak: it was thoroughly repaired in 1835, towards which the Ecclesiastical Commissioners granted £736. 5. 6. There is a parochial school for boys, who are clothed, fed, educated, and apprenticed; also one for girls, an infants' school, and the model school of the Kildare-place Society. An almshouse for widows is supported by the Sunday collections. The remains of the celebrated authoress, Mrs. Hemans, were deposited in the vault beneath the church in 1835. Judge Downes was also buried in this church.

St. Audeon's, or *Owen's,* was originally a chapel dedicated to the Blessed Virgin and enlarged by the family of Fitz-Eustace of Portlester; afterwards it was given as a parish church to the priory of Grace Dieu by John Comyn; but in 1467 it was made a prebend with cure of souls in the cathedral of St. Patrick, by Archbishop Tregury. The parish contains 4599 inhabitants, and 426 houses valued at £5 and upwards, the total annual value being £19,399. The rectory or prebend is of the annual value of £243. 1. 4., and the minister's money amounts to £220. 12. 11. The present church consists only of the western end of the ancient edifice, which comprised a nave and collateral aisle, at the end of which is a modern steeple with a ring of bells; the rest of it is now in ruins. The eastern extremity still presents a fine specimen of the pointed style, and there are many curious old monuments, among which is one of Lord Portlester and his lady, erected in 1455: it is the burial-place of several ancient families. The Ecclesiastical Commissioners have granted £162. 0. 11. for the repairs of this church. There is a parochial school for boys, who are clothed, partly dieted, and apprenticed; also a school for girls, who are partly clothed; an infants' school, a Sunday school, and a female orphan school.

St. Bridget's or *St. Bride's* parish was formed out of those of St. Bride, St. Stephen, and St. Michael de la Pole, and after having belonged to Christ-Church was annexed to St. Patrick's in 1186. It contains 12,543 inhabitants; the number of houses valued at £5 and upwards is 732, and the total annual value is £23,377. 10. The living is a perpetual curacy, in the patronage of the Dean and Chapter of St. Patrick's; the minister's money amounts to £286. 4. 1., and the gross income is £405. 13. 10. The church, a very plain building, situated in the street to which it gives name, was erected in 1684: it was repaired in 1827 at an expense of between £300 and £400, by parish assessment; and the Ecclesiastical Commissioners have since granted £158. 5. 9. for its further repair. Among the monuments are those of Mr. and Mrs. Pleasants, distinguished for their munificent charitable donations and bequests. The Episcopal chapel of the Molyneux Asylum, in Peter-street, is in this parish. There is a parochial boarding school for boys, a parochial day school, a boarding school for orphans, a day and an infants' school, and a Sunday school. The school in Stephen-street is supported by the interest of a legacy of £3900 from Ralph Macklin, Esq. Two almshouses for 20 widows and 12 old men are maintained by a bequest of Mr. Pleasants; and several large legacies have been bequeathed to the parish. There is a chalybeate spa near the church.

St. Catherine's anciently formed part of the parish of St. James, but was separated from it by an act of parliament in 1710. It contains 23,237 inhabitants, and 1264 houses of the value of £5 and upwards, the total annual value being £31,921. The living is a vicarage, in the patronage of the Earl of Meath; the minister's money amounts to £395. 3. 10. The church, which had been a chapel to St. Thomas the Martyr, was rebuilt in its present form in 1769: it is situated on the south side of Thomas-street, and is built of mountain granite, in the Doric style: four semi-columns, with their entablature, enriched by triglyphs, support a noble pediment in the centre, and on each side the entablature is continued the entire length, and supported at each extremity by coupled pilasters: above the entablature, at each side of the pediment, is a stone balustrade. Between the centre columns is a handsome Ionic arched door, and the other intermediate spaces are occupied by a double range of windows. The interior is elegantly simple: eight Ionic columns support the galleries, above which the same number of Corinthian pilasters rise to the roof. At the west end of the building is an unfinished belfry. The Ecclesiastical Commissioners have granted £126 for its repair. In the interior is a tablet to the memory of Dr. Whitelaw, the historian of Dublin, who was 25 years vicar of this parish, and died in 1813; and another to that of William Mylne, engineer, who constructed the waterworks of Dublin: underneath is the family vault of the Earl of Meath. A free Episcopal church has been opened in Swift's-alley, in a building purchased from the Baptist society in 1835, and consecrated by the archbishop: it is under the management of eight trustees, one-half of whom must be clergymen of the Established Church. Another is in progress at Harold Cross, in this parish. There are a parochial boarding school for girls, a parochial day school for boys and girls, a school on Erasmus Smith's foundation, three national schools, an evening school, an infants' school, and two Sunday schools. There are two almshouses for widows, one supported by the parish and the other by a member of the La Touche family.

St. George's parish originally formed part of that of St. Mary, and though not strictly within the liberties of the city, it has been included in the new electorial boundary under the Reform act. It contains 14,692 inhabitants, and 1261 houses valued at £5 and upwards, the total annual value being £63,900. The living is a rectory, in the alternate patronage of the Dean and Chapter of Christ-Church and the representatives of the late Lord Blessington; the minister's money amounts to £628. 5. 9., and the gross income is £800. The church, erected in 1802 in Hardwicke-place, after a design by F. Johnston, and at an expense of £90,000, presents a front consisting of a central projecting portico of four fluted Doric columns resting on an elevated platform supporting a bold entablature (the frieze and cornice of which are carried entirely round the building) surmounted by a triangular pediment over which rises the steeple of four ornamented stories, terminating in a light and graceful spire tapering to a height of 200 feet from the ground. The interior is fitted up in a chaste and elegant style, and a projecting building at the east end contains the vestry-room and parish school. The Ecclesiastical Commissioners have granted £1512. 12. 5. for its repair. There are three other Episcopal places of worship: St. George's chapel, commonly called Little St. George's, in Lower Temple-street, was founded by an endowment, by Archbishop King, of £49 per ann., out of two houses in Great Britain-street, the property of Sir John Eccles, to support a lecturer; it consists of a plain building with a square tower, surrounded by a cemetery, and is a donative, in the gift of A. Eccles, Esq. The free church in Great Charles-street was originally a Methodist place of worship, and was purchased, about 1826, for its present purpose, and consecrated by the Archbishop of Dublin, in whom the appointment of the minister is vested; it is a plain neat structure. The Episcopal chapel of the female penitentiary, on the north circular road, is the third. There are three parochial schools, a boarding school for girls, a day school for both sexes, and an infants' school, also a day school for both sexes endowed with a bequest by Miss Kellett.

Grangegorman parish, situated partly within the new electoral boundary, north of the city, and partly in the county of Dublin, was formed out of those parts of the parishes of St. Michan, St. Paul, and St. George, which were in the manor of Grangegorman. It contains 7382 inhabitants, and 472 houses valued at £5 and upwards, the total annual value being £6102. The living is a perpetual curacy, in the patronage of the Prebendaries and Vicars choral of the cathedral of Christ-Church. The church was erected by a grant from the Board of First Fruits, in 1830. Within the parish are the House of Industry, the Richmond Penitentiary, the Lunatic Asylum for the district of Dublin, and the female orphan school, to the last-named of which an Episcopal chapel is attached. There are two day schools for both sexes, one of which is attached to the House of Industry, a female orphan school, and a day and infants' school, connected with the R. C. chapel. The total number of pupils in the day schools is 493.

St. James's parish contains 13,197 inhabitants, and 625 houses valued at £5 and upwards, the total annual value being £13,176. The living is a vicarage, in the patronage of the Earl of Meath; the minister's money amounts to £109. 1. 4. The church is a low and very plain building; owing to the small accommodation it affords to the numerous parishioners, it is the intention of the Ecclesiastical Commissioners to erect a new one. The cemetery is very large and situated on the north side of a hill sloping down towards the river. The episcopal chapels of the Royal and Foundling Hospitals are in this parish; and there is a chapel of ease at Golden-Bridge, chiefly for the use of Richmond barracks. There are parochial schools for boys and girls, three national schools, and an infants' school.

St. John's parish contains 4351 inhabitants, and 291 houses valued at £5 and upwards, the total annual value being £9846. 10. It was erected into a prebend with cure of souls in the cathedral of Christ-Church, in 1554, and is in the gift of the Dean and Chapter; the minister's money amounts to £118. 9. 3., and the gross income of the prebendary is £398. 2. 8. The church, situated at the corner of John's-lane, was rebuilt in 1773: it presents to Fishamble-street a neat front adorned with four Doric columns supporting a pediment, and approached by a broad flight of steps: in this front is the chief entrance to the body of the church and one to each of the galleries. In 1836 it underwent a thorough repair, for which a grant of £879. 9. 7. was made by the Ecclesiastical Commissioners. There are parochial schools for boys and girls, two national schools for boys and girls, a Sunday school, and an evening school for adult males.

St. Luke's parish contains 6605 inhabitants, and 337 houses valued at £5 and upwards, the total annual value being £7654. The living is a vicarage, in the diocese of Dublin, and in the patronage of the Dean and Chapter of Christ-Church; the minister's money is £92. 7. 8., and the gross income £171. 17. 4. The church, erected in 1708, when the parish, which had been a part of that of St. Nicholas, was formed, is approached by an avenue of trees from the Coombe, and is a plain structure entered by a large doorway between rusticated columns: it was re-roofed in 1835 by a grant of £1029. 13. 6. from the Ecclesiastical Commissioners. There are parochial schools for boys and girls, in which some of the children are clothed and some dieted; also an infants' school and a national school, all supported by charity sermons and some small bequests.

St. Mark's parish was severed from that of St. Andrew by act of parliament in 1707: it contains 14,811 inhabitants, and 1076 houses valued at £5 and upwards, the total annual value being £38,592. The living is a vicarage, in the joint patronage of the Lord-Chancellor, the Archbishop of Dublin, the three Chief Judges, and the Master of the Rolls; the minister's money is £330. 3. 3. The church is situated in Mark-street, adjacent to Brunswick-street: it was built in 1729, and is a large building perfectly plain; the interior is very neat and commodious. The Ecclesiastical Commissioners have granted £165. 13. 5. for repairing it. The Mariners' church, built in Forbes-street in 1832, and the Episcopal chapel belonging to the marine school, are in this parish; as locally is Trinity College, which is extra-parochial. There are parochial, day, and female schools, one on the foundation of Erasmus Smith, the marine school for sailors' orphans, a female orphan school, and an infants' school.

St. Mary's, originally part of St. Michan's parish, and separated from it in 1697, contains 25,305 inhabitants, and 2018 houses valued at £5 and upwards, the total annual value being £91,895. The living is a rectory, in the gift of the Dean and Chapter of Christ-Church: the minister's money amounts to £974. 16. 6., and the gross income is £1127. The church is a large building, in Stafford-street, possessing little architectural beauty. Its chief entrance is a large gate with Ionic columns on each side, surmounted by a square belfry. In the interior are many monumental tablets, among the more remarkable of which is one to the memory of Edw. Tennison, Bishop of Ossory; one to that of Dr. Robt. Law; one to that of Mr. Wm. Watson, founder of the Society for Discountenancing Vice; and one lately erected to the Hon. T. B. Vandeleur, third justice of the King's Bench, Ireland. In the crowded cemetery are the tombs of Dr. Marlay, Bishop of Waterford, and uncle to the late Henry Grattan; Mrs. Mercer, the foundress of Mercer's Hospital; and Mr. Simpson, the founder of Simpson's Hospital. The Board of First Fruits, in 1831, granted a loan of £1615 for the repair of the church, and in 1836 the Ecclesiastical Commissioners granted £205. 3. 11. for the same purpose. St. Mary's chapel of ease, built on a plot of ground in Mountjoy-street, presented to the parish by the Earl of Mountjoy, is a very elegant specimen of the modern Gothic, from a design of Mr. Semple; it has a light tapering spire surrounded by minarets of similar shape. It was opened in 1830 as a free church, and has lately received a grant of £445. 13. 0. for its repair from the Ecclesiastical Commissioners. The Episcopal chapel of the Lying-in Hospital and the Bethesda Episcopal chapel are in this parish; the latter was erected in 1786, at the sole expense of Wm. Smyth, Esq., nephew of the Archbishop of that name: he appointed two clergymen to officiate, and, in 1787, annexed to it an asylum for female orphans, in which about

24 children are entirely supported. A penitentiary adjoins it, which was opened in 1794 for the reception of females discharged from the Lock Hospital. Here are parochial schools for boys and girls, who are totally provided for; a free school for both sexes, an infants' school, and schools for boys and girls in connection with the Scots' Church. A female almshouse in Denmark-street was founded by Tristram Fostrick, Esq., in 1789. Mrs. Mary Damer, in 1753, bequeathed £1765, and Richard Cave, Esq., in 1830, £1600 to the parish for charitable uses.

St. Michael's parish was created a prebend with cure of souls in Christ Church cathedral, in 1554, by Archbishop Browne: it contains 2288 inhabitants, and 112 houses valued at £5 and upwards, the total annual value being £3670. The rectory or prebend is in the gift of the Dean and Chapter of Christ-Church; the minister's money amounts to £50. 5. 11., and the gross income is £250. 8. The church stands at the corner of Michael's-hill and High-street, and is a small building in the pointed style of architecture. The tower, which is without a spire, is ancient and of large dimensions, very disproportionate to the small structure of which it now forms the vestibule. There is a parochial school; 20 of the children are clothed.

St. Michan's parish was also erected into a prebend of Christ-Church, with cure of souls, by Archbishop Browne, in 1554, and comprehended the whole of Dublin north of the Liffey until 1697, when the parishes of St. Mary and St. Paul were severed from it. It contains 23,918 inhabitants, and 1464 houses valued at £5 and upwards, the total annual value being £43,568. 10. The prebend is in the patronage of the Dean and Chapter of Christ-Church; the minister's money is £488. 15. 7., and the gross income, £719. 7. 6. The church, situated in Church-street, is one of the oldest in the city, being supposed to have been founded by the Ostmen previously to the erection of Christ-Church, and to have been originally the cathedral church of the diocese. It is a very spacious cruciform structure, with a square tower, erected at a comparatively modern period, although the whole has an appearance of great antiquity. It was re-roofed and thoroughly repaired in 1828, at a cost of about £1500, defrayed by parish cess, since which time the Ecclesiastical Commissioners have granted £230. 19. 1. for its further repair. On one side of the communion table is an ancient figure of a bishop or an abbot; there is also a monumental tablet to the memory of the celebrated Dr. Lucas. There are a parochial school for girls, a day school for girls, and an infants' school, four day schools for boys, and two for girls, and a Sunday school.

St. Nicholas Within included also the parishes of St. Nicholas Without and St. Luke until 1707, when they were formed into separate parishes. It contains 1845 inhabitants, and 103 houses valued at £5 and upwards, the total annual value being £3929. 10. The living is a perpetual curacy, in the patronage of the Dean and Chapter of St. Patrick's; the minister's money is £3. 0. 7., and the gross income £125. The church, an unsightly edifice, situated in Nicholas-street, has been taken down and is to be rebuilt under the directions of the Ecclesiastical Commissioners, till which time divine service is performed in the school-room. There is a lectureship attached to it, which is maintained by the rent of lands in the county of Louth. There is a parochial school for 12 boys, who are clothed, educated, and apprenticed: it is supported by the rent of two houses, amounting to £36 per annum, and an annual charity sermon.

St. Nicholas Without, formed into a parish in 1707, contains 12,391 inhabitants, and 871 houses valued at £5 and upwards, the total annual value being £226.8,10.1 The living is a perpetual curacy, in the patronage of the Dean and Chapter of St. Patrick's; the minister's money is £207. 12. 6., and the gross income £264. 10. The church, which was dedicated to St. Myra, and occupied the north transept of St. Patrick's cathedral, having fallen into decay, has been restored, and still forms part of that building. The Ecclesiastical Commissioners have granted £432. 7. 7. for its repair. There are parochial schools for boys, girls, and infants, and two Sunday schools.

St. Paul's, which, previously to the year 1697, formed part of St. Michan's parish, contains 10,570 inhabitants, and 786 houses valued at £5 and upwards, the total annual value being £21,632. The living is a rectory, in the patronage of the Dean and Chapter of Christ-Church; the minister's money is £255. 4. 1., and the gross income £386. 9. 4. The church, situated in North King-street, was rebuilt in 1824, and is now a neat edifice in the Gothic style, with a small but elegant spire. The cemetery is the usual place of interment for the garrison of Dublin: it contains a monument to the memory of Lieut.-Col. Lyde Brown, of the 21st Fusileers; a mural tablet to that of three privates of the same regiment, who were killed in the insurrection of 1803; and a mausoleum for the family of Col. Ormsby. The chapel of the King's or Blue-coat Hospital is in this parish. There are parochial schools for boys and girls, an infants' school, and a Sunday school. The late Lord Netterville bequeathed £9000 to this and the adjoining parish of St. Michan for a dispensary and hospital, which is also supported by subscription.

St. Peter's parish, erected by order of council in 1680, is the largest in the city, comprising the ancient parishes of St. Peter and St. Kevin, and a portion of that of St. Stephen: it contains 27,176 inhabitants, and 2260 houses valued at £5 and upwards, the total annual value being £124,865. 10. It is a vicarage, united to the rectories of Tawney, Rathfarnham, Donnybrook, and district of Booterstown, together forming the corps of the archdeaconry of Dublin, in the patronage of the Archbishop; the minister's money is £1086. 15. 4., and the gross annual income is £2768, out of which there are 12 curates to be paid. The church, situated in Aungier-street, is a very large unornamented building, in the form of the letter T: the Ecclesiastical Commissioners have granted £735. 0. 6. for its repair. In the attached cemetery are interred the remains of many persons of rank; those of the celebrated John Fitzgibbon, Earl of Clare, lie here under a plain tombstone; Maturin, the poet, who was curate of the parish, is also buried here. There are within its limits three chapels of ease, one in Kevin-street, one in Upper Mount-street, Merrion-square, and a third at Rathmines; and within the parish are Sandford Episcopal chapel at Cullenswood, and an Episcopal chapel in Upper Baggot-street. The church or chapel of *St. Kevin* is a plain edifice, in the form of the letter T, situated to the south of

Kevin-street; it appears to have been erected on the site of an ancient chapel dedicated to St. Kevin.• The chapel in Upper Mount-street, dedicated to *St. Stephen*, is an elegant structure. The portico is of the Ionic order; over the pediment rises the belfry tower, of octangular form, covered with a cupola, the apex of which is 100 feet high. The Episcopal church in Upper Baggot-street, with a female penitentiary attached, was erected in 1835 by subscription, at a cost of upwards of £6000: the exterior is plain, but the interior is exceedingly handsome; it will accommodate 1200, and has from 300 to 400 free seats: the appointment of the chaplain is in nine trustees. The Episcopal chapel of the Magdalen Asylum, in Leeson-street, is also in this parish. There are parochial schools for boys, girls, and infants; schools at Sandford chapel for boys, girls, and infants; a Methodist female orphan school; St. Stephen's male and female day school in Mount-street; Bride-street parochial female school; day schools at Hatch-street and Cuff-lane; two in Whitefriar-street; two at Rathmines and Miltown; two other infants' schools and five Sunday schools. There is also a parochial dispensary, and a loan fund established in 1813.

St. Thomas's parish was separated from St. Mary's, in 1749, by act of parliament: it contains 20,881 inhabitants, and 1373 houses valued at £5 and upwards, the total annual value being £65,537. 10. The living is a rectory, in the patronage of the Dean and Chapter of Christ-Church; the minister's money is £684. 12. 1., and the gross income £922. 1. 10. The church, erected in 1758, presents a front to Marlborough-street, opposite to Gloucester-street, composed of two pilasters and two three-quarter columns of the Composite order, supporting an entablature and enclosing ornamented niches, and, in the centre, a Corinthian doorway, with an angular pediment: on each side of this façade is a half-pediment, supported by a Corinthian pilaster at the extremity, and a half-pilaster in the return: an intended pediment over the centre has not been erected. The Ecclesiastical Commissioners have granted £915. 17. 9. for the improvement of the building. The Episcopal chapel of the Feinaglian institution at Luxemburgh, for the use of the pupils, but open also to their friends, is in this parish. A parochial school for girls is supported by a bequest of £75. 1. 3. per ann. and voluntary contributions; there are also a day school for boys and girls, a national school, and a Sunday school. The buildings of the Board of National Education and a savings' bank are in this parish.

St. Werburgh's parish contains 3384 inhabitants, and 214 houses valued at £5 and upwards, the total annual value being £11,602. 10. It is a rectory, united to the rectory of Finglass and the chapelries of St. Margaret and Ward, together forming the corps of the chancellorship of the cathedral of St. Patrick, in the gift of the Archbishop; the minister's money is £200. 2., and the gross income £680. The church was erected in 1759. The front is composed of a basement story ornamented with six Ionic pilasters with an entablature, and a grand entrance of the same order. The second story, which is diminished, is adorned with four Corinthian pilasters, coupled, enclosing a large window, and supporting a pediment, above which rises a square tower of Composite architecture, terminating with urns placed at the angles. An elegant spire which formerly surmounted the whole was taken down in 1810, on account of its dangerous state; and, for the same reason, the entire tower was taken down in 1835. The Ecclesiastical Commissioners have granted £1140. 16. 11. for the restoration of the tower and the general repairs of the building. The Lord-Lieutenant of Ireland, attends here to qualify on his coming into office, the castle of Dublin being situated in the parish. The east window of stained glass is considered the handsomest in Dublin and cost about £600: the subject is the Presentation. In the interior are several neat monuments, and on the exterior, in the wall of the church, are some very ancient sculptured figures, evidently belonging to an older building. In the vaults are deposited the remains of Sir James Ware, the antiquary, Lord Edward Fitzgerald, and Edwin, the actor. The vice-regal chapel, Dublin Castle, is within the precincts of this parish. There is a parochial boarding school for girls, and parochial day schools for boys and girls, a day school for girls, and a Sunday school. James Southwell, Esq., in 1729, bequeathed £1250, the interest to be applied for various purposes: he also bequeathed £380 for a ring of bells, and a fund to place boys in the Blue-coat school.

ROMAN CATHOLIC PAROCHIAL DISTRICTS, PLACES OF WORSHIP, CONVENTS, AND CHARITIES CONNECTED THEREWITH.

The city is divided into nine R. C. parishes or ecclesiastical districts: St Mary's, St. Michan's, St. Paul's, St. Andrew's, St. Audeon's, St. Catherine's, St. James's, St. Michael's and John's, and St. Nicholas's: the first three are on the north side of the Liffey. The ecclesiastical duties are executed by nine parochial priests and 52 other officiating clergymen.

The parish of *St. Mary* is the mensal of the Archbishop, and comprises the Protestant parish of St. Thomas, and the principal parts of those of St. Mary and St. George: the parochial duties are performed by the Archbishop, seven officiating clergymen, and one assistant. The chapel, a spacious and magnificent building, commenced in 1815 and not yet completed, is dedicated to the Blessed Virgin Mary, and is usually styled the Church of the Conception. The front to Marlborough-street will, when finished, consist of a portico of six fluted Doric columns, supporting an entablature ornamented with triglyphs, and surmounted by a pediment. The interior is divided into a nave and side aisles by two splendid colonnades; the west end forms a circular termination, under which is the principal altar of white marble, detached from the walls and enclosed by a circular railing; in the centre of each aisle is a quadrangular recess. The total expense of completing the structure is estimated at £50,000. Besides the above, there are the chapel of St. Francis Xavier, Upper Gardiner-street; a chapel belonging to the Dominican friary, Denmark-street; and a chapel belonging to the convent of Carmelite nuns, North William-street. The chapel of St. Francis Xavier is attended by the priest of the order of "Jesuits," established here in 1817: the inmates consist of a superior and five priests, who have a classical school in Hardwicke-street. The building is cruciform and of the ancient Ionic order, with a lofty portico in the centre; and at each side are receding wings forming vestibules, crowned with domes supported by columns of the Ionic order; the interior is highly decorated, and the organ, which is considered to be one of the finest in Ireland, was built for the great musical festival at Westminster. The chapel in Denmark-street, dedicated to St. Dominic, belongs to the order of Dominicans, consisting of a prior and five friars; in connection with this is St. Patrick's Juvenile Society. The chapel in North William-street belongs to the convent of the order of Carmelites: the inmates consist of a superioress and a sisterhood of 15. The chapel is a neat building, in the later style of English architecture; a school, in which 20 girls are educated, clothed, and wholly provided for, is attached to the institution. The Sisters of Charity have an establishment in Upper Gardiner-street, consisting of a superioress and a sisterhood of 14, who superintend the education of 200 girls. The principal establishment of the Christian Doctrine Confraternity, consisting of a director and two assistants, is in North Richmond-street, where they support a model school for the novices for the other houses of the society; they also instruct 550 children in the parochial chapel and 130 in Denmark-street, every Sunday. The confraternity instruct children in all the other parochial and in most of the friary chapels: the total number of children under their tuition amounts to 5987 males and 3942 females. There are two national schools, one in Gloucester-place, and the other in King's Inns-street; an almshouse in North William-street for twenty-three widows, which is supported by subscription; and the Metropolitan Orphan Society, in which 99 children are supported, chiefly by penny weekly subscriptions of the working classes. The Asylum for Female Penitents, founded in 1833, affords shelter to 30 inmates; another in Mecklenburgh-street, founded in the same year, supports 35; a third in Dominick-street supports 34, and there is another in Marlborough-street; in all of them the penitents are employed in needlework, washing, and similar useful occupations.

St. Michan's parish comprises parts of the Protestant parishes of St. Mary, St. George, St. Michan, St. Paul, and Glasnevin. The duty is performed by a parish priest and six officiating clergymen. The chapel in North Anne-street is a splendid edifice, built entirely of granite; it is in the later English style, with three finely arched entrances in the front, which terminate above in a sharply pointed gable, embattled and surmounted with a cross; the interior is richly ornamented with sculpture, and the ceiling is elaborately groined, the intersecting arches springing from heads of saints finely sculptured; the altar is embellished with paintings of the Virgin and Child, and of St. Francis, copied from Guido. There is another chapel on George's-hill, belonging to the convent of the Presentation order, the inmates of which, consisting of a superioress and ten sisters, superintend a school, at which about 300 female children are instructed, 50 of whom are clothed, and from 16 to 20 are also boarded. The institution is chiefly supported by the profits of the work done by the children. The chapel, which is exceedingly neat, is open every morning. There is a day boys' school of about 300 pupils; also an establishment for 12 orphans who are totally provided for and when of a proper age apprenticed; the institution is supported by subscriptions. The Orphan Society of St. Vincent a Paulo was founded in 1826, in which 40 orphan children are wholly provided for, and 45 by the Society for Destitute Orphans under the tutelage of the Blessed Virgin Mary of Mount-Carmel. The Society of St. John the Evangelist, for promoting the exercise of spiritual and corporal works of mercy, is in North King-street, and has a good library in connection with it. In Paradise-row is the Josephian Orphan Society, in which 36 orphans are totally provided for; and in the same street is the House of Reception for aged females, containing 18 inmates.

St. Paul's parish comprises the Protestant parish of Grangegorman, the principal part of St. Paul's, and parts of St. Michan's and Glasnevin. The duty is performed by a parish priest and six officiating clergymen. The chapel on Arran-quay having been found to be too small, another, near the entrance of the old building, is now completed with the exception of the portico and steeple: the interior is richly ornamented; behind the altar is a painting in fresco, on which the light is thrown after the manner of the "*lumière mystérieuse*" in some of the churches of Paris. The whole cost of the erection of the building will be about £10,000, which will be wholly defrayed by voluntary subscription. There is a chapel of ease at Phibsborough, a neat Gothic structure, but too small for the increasing congregation: beneath are male and female free school-rooms, and apartments for an orphan society, and over the sacristy a residence for the clergyman and a lending library belonging to a branch society of St. John the Evangelist. The chapel of St. Francis, in Church-street, belongs to the friary of the Capuchins, the community of which consists of a guardian and six friars. The chapel is a large plain building; the altars are adorned with paintings of the Crucifixion, the Virgin and Child, and St. Francis: a free school for boys is connected with it. There is a school in Queen-street, in which about 250 boys and 150 girls are instructed; also a national boys' and girls' school connected with the chapel at Phibsborough. The convent of the Sisters of Charity, in Stanhope-street, consists of a local superioress and a sisterhood of twenty, who support a house of refuge, in which 50 industrious young women of good character are sheltered; the institution derives much of its support from the work executed by the inmates. St. Stephen's Cholera Orphan Society was first established in 1828, as a general orphan institution, but in 1830, owing to the ravages of the cholera, it assumed its present name and character.

St. Andrew's parish comprises nearly the whole of the Protestant parishes of St. Andrew, St. Mark, and St. Anne, and part of that of St. Peter. The duty is performed by a parish priest and seven officiating clergymen. The chapel, in Westland-row, was commenced in 1832, and finished in 1837: its form is that of a Roman cross; the length being 160 feet, the transept 150, the breadth and height 50 each. The walls of the interior are in compartments formed by Grecian Doric pilasters. The great altar consists of four pillars of scagliola, supporting a pediment copied from the Lantern of Demosthenes at Athens. The tabernacle is in imitation of the triumphal arch of Titus in Rome, and is surmounted by a group in white Italian marble, by Hogan, representing the Ascension; on each side of the great altar are smaller altars of Egyptian marble; several good paintings have lately been brought from Rome, and hung up over and at the sides of the altar. The portico in front consists of two pillars and four pilasters in the Grecian Doric style, prolonged at each end by a parochial house, thus presenting a façade of 160 feet in length. The cost of erection, which is defrayed by subscription, amounted to £18,000. In Clarendon-street is the chapel of St. Teresa, belonging to the order of the Discalced Carmelites, the inmates of which consist of a provincial, a prior, and six friars. It is a spacious building of plain exterior: in front of the altar is a fine statue of a Dead Christ in Italian marble, by Hogan. Attached to the convent is an almshouse for widows, and the Society of St. Joseph, for promoting the exercise of spiritual and corporal works of mercy. There is a parochial school attended by upwards of 3100 female children: it is in connection with the National Board of Education. Within the parish there are the following religious institutions; the House of Mercy, Baggot-street, the inmates of which consist of a superioress and a sisterhood of 15, who maintain a day school of about 300 children, visit the sick poor, and receive under their protection distressed women of good character; their house is a plain large building of three stories. In Stephen's-green East is St. Vincent's Hospital, containing 60 beds, and a dispensary, founded by the sisters of charity: a superioress and sisterhood of six preside over it. The Asylum for Female Penitents, in Townsend-street, is superintended by a superioress and a sisterhood of three, and affords shelter and the means of reformation to 41 penitents. The Andrean Orphans' Friend Society was revived in 1832, and supports 28 children by weekly penny subscriptions; the Orphan Society of St. John of the Cross is supported in like manner.

St. Audeon's, the smallest R. C. parish in the city, comprises the whole of the Protestant parish of the same name. The chapel, situated off Bridge-street, is in bad repair and too small for the congregation; a considerable sum has been already subscribed towards its re-erection. There is a male and female school in which 20 of each sex are clothed; also the Malachian Orphan Society for destitute children. John Power, Esq., in 1835, erected in Cook-street a building for 24 aged and destitute widows, at an expense of about £700; it is supported by subscriptions and an annual charity sermon.

St. Catherine's comprises nearly the whole of the Protestant parish of the same name. The duty is performed by a parish priest and seven officiating clergymen. The chapel was erected in Meath-street, in 1780: it is a very spacious octagon building of brick, with a gallery along five of its sides, the altar being in the centre of the other three. Near it is a school, erected in 1823 by subscription, and attended by upwards of 400 children of each sex: there are also Sunday schools. A chapel in John's-lane belongs to the Augustinian friary of St. John; the inmates consist of a prior and four friars. The chapel, a spacious structure, occupies part of the site of the priory of St. John the Baptist, which was founded in the year 1188 by A. Du Palmer; and in connection with it is a female orphan school, also an asylum for old and destitute men, in Rainsford-street. To this convent belonged the Rev. Wm. Gahan, author of many pious works.

St. James's parish comprises nearly the whole of the Protestant parish of the same name. The duty is performed by a parish priest, who is also chaplain to the county gaol of Kilmainham, and by four officiating clergymen. The chapel, which is situated at James-gate, is about to be taken down and a new building erected. There is a chapel at Dolphin's Barn for the accommodation of that populous district; and also a nunnery of the Carmelite order, consisting of a superioress and a sisterhood of 16, established in 1834, in the same neighbourhood, attached to which is a free school for girls. There is a National school for boys and girls; also St. James' and St. Joseph's Orphan Society, which maintains 50 children. The Catholic cemetery, Golden-Bridge, described under that head, is in this parish.

St. Michael's and *St. John's* parish comprises the Protestant parishes of St. Michael, St. John, St. Nicholas Within, and St. Werburgh, and parts of those of St. Peter, St. Andrew, and St. Bride. The duty is performed by a parish priest and five officiating clergymen. The chapel, situated in Exchange-street and erected in 1815, has two fronts of hewn stone in the later English style: the exterior is of elegant design, and in the interior, which is richly embellished, are three altars; over each respectively are paintings of the Crucifixion, of St. John the Evangelist by Del Frate, and of St. Michael trampling on Satan, a copy from Guido; its fine organ, made by Lawless, cost £800. It contains a handsome monument to Dr. Betagh, a celebrated preacher, who died in 1811, and another to the Rev. Dr. Anglen; at one end are six confessionals of elegant design and beautiful workmanship. The chapel was erected between 1813 and 1816, at a cost of nearly £10,000, which was defrayed by subscription. Attached to it is a house for the residence of the clergymen, containing 20 spacious apartments with a corridor to each story; the cost of its erection was about £2000, and it was completed in the short space of two months and eight days. A chapel in Whitefriar-street belongs to the order of Calced Carmelites; the inmates are a provincial, a prior, and six friars, whose residence is in an adjoining house in Aungier-street. The chapel has its front to Whitefriar-street: the interior presents a beautiful architectural view; the right side has a range of large windows, and the left is ornamented with corresponding niches, filled with statues of eminent saints; the ceiling is coved and divided into rectangular compartments; its erection cost £4000. It stands on the site of a Carmelite church founded in 1274, upon land granted by Sir Robert Bagot. The remains of St. Valentinus, martyr, have been translated from Rome by order of Pope Gregory XVI., and are deposited in this chapel in a suitable vase. Another, which is a cruciform structure, situated on Merchants'-quay, belongs to the order of Franciscans; the inmates are a prior and six friars. It is dedicated to St. Francis of Assisium, but is more generally known by the name of Adam and Eve, from an ancient chapel of that name on the site of which the present building was erected. When finished it will exhibit the ceiling divided into enriched panels; the interior ornamented with pilasters, supporting an enriched cornice of granite, over which the windows are placed; there are three elegant and commodious galleries, capable of holding 1500 persons; the altar will be constructed in the most florid style of Corinthian architecture: an Ionic portico is to front the river. In Smock-alley are parochial schools for both sexes, in connection with the National Board of Education, at which 600 children attend; also an evening and Sunday school, and two orphan schools, one for boys and the other for girls, 20 of each, who are wholly provided for and apprenticed; all these are supported by subscription, a grant from the National Board, an annual sermon, and the profits of an annual bazaar. A society was founded in Smock-alley in 1817, called "The Society of St. John the Evangelist," for administering to the spiritual and temporal wants of the sick, and for the suppressing abuses at wakes; a library is in connection with it. Near Tullow is the establishment of the Orphan Society of St. Francis of Assisium, founded in 1817, in which 24 children are supported. St. Peter's, St. Patrick's, St. Bonaventure's, and the county and city Cholera Orphan Societies are all in this parish; they are chiefly supported by subscriptions and sermons; as is also the Catholic Society for Ireland, for the gratuitous distribution of religious books, established in 1836.

The parish of *St. Nicholas* comprises the Protestant parishes of St. Nicholas Without, the city part of St. Nicholas Within, St. Luke, St. Kevin, the entire of the Liberties of Christ-Church and St. Patrick, and parts of the parishes of St. Peter and St. Bride. The duty is performed by a parish priest and six officiating clergymen. The chapel is built on the site of a Franciscan friary, erected in 1235 on a piece of ground granted by Ralph le Porter. It has a square tower, ornamented on each face with coupled Corinthian pilasters and terminating with a figure of Faith. The interior is exquisitely finished: the great altar, which is of Italian marble, was executed at Rome; over it is a group representing a "Dead Christ on the lap of Mary," by Hogan, and two relievos, "The Last Supper" and "The Marriage of Joseph and Mary," from Raphael. A monastery of the order of the Religious Brothers of the Christian Schools, in Mills-street, consists of a superior and two monks, who superintend a free school for boys. There is also a national school for boys, in which 450 are educated and 50 of them clothed; and an Orphan Institution. A convent of the order of the Institute of the Blessed Virgin Mary, in Harcourt-street, commonly called the Loretto convent, consists of a local superioress and a sisterhood of three, who educate about 40 girls.

PROTESTANT DISSENTERS.

There are four Presbyterian meeting-houses, situated respectively in Capel-street, Ushers-quay, Eustace-street, and Great Strand-street, all of the first class; the two former maintain the doctrines of the church of Scotland, and the two latter are Unitarian. Each congregation supports a school and maintains the poor of their own persuasion. That in Capel-street is possessed of a legacy called "Campbell's fund," being the interest of £500, which is distributed among four blind men; and another of the same amount, called Fenner's funds, for the relief of six widows. Those of Strand-street and Eustace-street have each a respectable collection of books for the use of the ministers and congregation, to which others can have access on very liberal terms. Dr. John Leland, author of several theological works, was one of the ministers of the Eustace-street congregation for 50 years. There are three congregations of Independents, whose places of worship are in D'Olier-street, York-street, and King's Inns-street, the last-named of which has a theological institution, or college, the object of which is to afford the means of theological instruction, according to the tenets of the Westminster and Savoy articles of faith and the doctrinal articles of the Church of England, to such young men as appear to have a call to the sacred ministry; and connected with York-street chapel are a day and Sunday school, a Dorcas and Benevolent institution, and a congregational, missionary, and a city mission, association. The Methodist congregations, the first of which was formed in 1746 by Mr. Wesley himself, have their places of worship in Whitefriar-street, Abbey-street, Cork-street, Hendrick-street, South Great George's-street, and Langrishe-place; a congregation also meets in the Weavers' hall on the Coombe. There are two Baptist congregations, one of which has a meeting-house in Lower Abbey-street, which presents a Grecian front of considerable architectural elegance; the other meets in an apartment called the Apollo Saloon, in Grafton-street. A Moravian congregation, formed in 1750, has a meeting-house in Bishop-street; and in the same street is a residentiary-house of the same sect, in which a number of the female members live in community. There is a church for German Lutherans in Poolbeg-street, the only one in Ireland. The Society of Friends, or Quakers, have a meeting-house in Eustace-street, fitted up with great neatness, and another in Meath-street, also a cemetery in Cork-street. The Jews have a synagogue in Stafford-street, and a cemetery near Ballybough bridge.

FREE SCHOOLS.

The King's Hospital, or *Free School* of Chas. II., commonly called *the Blue-coat Hospital*, was founded in 1670 by the corporation, and established by royal charter, for the reception of reduced citizens and the education of their children, to which latter object, for want of more extensive funds, it has necessarily been limited. It maintains, clothes, educates, and apprentices 100 boys, who receive a solid English and mercantile education, and such of them as are intended for the sea service are instructed in navigation. The building, erected at an expense of £21,000, consists of a centre and two wings; the centre has an Ionic portico supporting a pediment, with an unfinished cupola, and contains apartments for the principal officers: the annual income is about £4000. A Society for instructing the children of the poor in the English language and in the Protestant religion was incorporated by royal charter in 1730, under the title of the Incorporated Society for promoting English Protestant schools in Ireland, but is more generally known by that of *the Charter School Society.* It was originally maintained by donations, subscriptions, and bequests of money and lands, and subsequently by large grants of public money; but these were discontinued some years since and the society left to its own resources. At the time of this change there were forty schools under its direction, two of which were in Dublin; the number is now reduced to eight. Two schools, supported by the funds of Erasmus Smith's bequest, have been established in Dublin, one on the Coombe, the other in St. Mark's parish. *The Hibernian Soldiers' School,* situated in the Phœnix Park, was established in 1769 for the maintenance, clothing, and instruction of the children of soldiers. In addition to the usual branches of an English education, the boys are taught the trades of tailors and shoemakers, and the girls are instructed in needlework; both, when of proper age, are apprenticed to handicraft trades, and, by a new charter in 1808, the governors are empowered to place such children in the regular army, as private soldiers, as are desirous of entering into that service. The buildings consist of a centre and two wings, 300 feet in length and three stories high; there are extensive work-rooms for the children, and a farm of 13 acres is attached to the school, which is partly cultivated by the boys, whose time is divided between employment and recreation, in which athletic sports are encouraged: the school is supported by parliamentary grants and private donations: the average annual expenditure is about £4500: the number of children is about 200, of which one-third are girls. *The Hibernian Marine School* was established by charter about the year 1777, for the maintenance of children of decayed seamen in the navy and merchants' service; the number of boys in this school is 180, who, when of proper age, are placed in the navy, or apprenticed to masters of merchantmen: the building, situated on Sir John Rogerson's Quay, consists of a centre and two wings; it is supported by parliamentary grants and private benefactions. The Society for the Education of the Poor of Ireland, usually called the *Kildare-place Society*, was founded in 1811. Its object was the diffusion of a well-ordered and economical system of primary instruction throughout the country, without any interference with the religious opinions of the pupils, and the publication of cheap elementary books. It was almost wholly supported by large grants of public money, and built an extensive model school for males and females, with other accommodations for offices and stores in Kildare-place. The grants of public money have been withdrawn, and the society now proceeds on a more confined scale by voluntary contributions only. *The Association for Discountenancing Vice*, formed in 1792, and incorporated by statute in 1800, also founded and assisted schools, in which education should be conducted upon Protestant principles, and likewise received large parliamentary grants, which were withdrawn at the same time as those to the Kildare-place Society. To supply the place of these institutions, a *Board of National Education* has been formed for the education of children of all religious persuasions. The commissioners, who were appointed by the lord-lieutenant, are the Duke of Leinster; the Protestant and Roman Catholic Archbishops of Dublin; the Rev. Dr. Sadleir, senior fellow of T. C. D.; Rev. James Carlile, minister of the Scotch Church; the Rt. Hon. Anthony R. Blake, Chief Remembrancer of the Court of Exchequer; and Robert Holmes, Esq., Barrister. They transact their business in a large establishment in Marlborough-street, formerly the town residence of the Marquess of Waterford, at the rear of which three model schools have been built, and a building is now being erected for a lecture-room, museum, &c., with apartments for the secretary and inspector: it is chiefly supported by parliamentary grants. *The Dublin Free School* was opened in School-street in 1808, for the instruction of poor children of both sexes, on the system of Joseph Lancaster: it is supported wholly by private subscriptions and a small weekly stipend from the pupils, and is used both as a day and Sunday school. *The Sunday School Society* was established in 1809, and up to January, 1835, had in connection with it 2813 schools, attended by 20,596 gratuitous teachers and 214,462 pupils. There are several highly respectable schools on a new system, "The Feinaiglean," which takes its name from Professor Von Feinagle, a native of Germany, who introduced it. The principal is the Luxemburgh, formerly Aldborough House, which was purchased from Lord Aldborough, who had expended upwards of £40,000 on its erection, and £15,000 raised in shares was laid out on it to adapt it for the purpose.

INFIRMARIES FOR MEDICAL AND SURGICAL CASES.

Sir Patrick Dun's Hospital, in Canal-street, was founded for the relief of the sick, maimed, or wounded, and as an appendage to the School of Physic for extending the sphere of medical practice, by a fund arising from the produce of estates bequeathed by the founder to the College of Physicians. The institution is under the direction of a board of governors. The medical department consists of two physicians in ordinary, one extraordinary, a surgeon, and an apothecary; and the house department, of a treasurer, registrar, providore, and matron. Lectures are delivered twice every week, during the medical season, by the professors of the school of physic in rotation in the theatre, and clinical lectures are also given at the bedside of the patient. The building, which is capable of receiving 100 patients, was commenced in 1803, and completed at an expense of £40,000, of which sum, £9000 was granted by parliament, and the remainder was defrayed from the proceeds of the estates, and by subscription. The building consists of a centre and two projecting wings: the ground floor of the centre contains apartments for the matron and apothecary, the pupils' waiting-room, and the theatre; and in the upper story are the board-room of the College of Physicians, the library, and the museum; the wings contain the wards for the patients. Patients who are not objects of charity are admitted on paying £1. 10. per month during their continuance in the hospital; the average annual income is upwards of £3000.

Steevens' Hospital, near Kilmainham, was founded by a bequest of Dr. Steevens, who, in 1710, bequeathed his estate, amounting to £600 per annum for that purpose; the hospital was opened in 1733. The building forms a quadrangle, having a piazza round the interior of the lower story, and a covered gallery round that above it; attached to it is a small chapel: the board-room contains a medical library. The resident officers are a surgeon, apothecary, Protestant chaplain, steward, and matron. The funds, aided by grants of public money, support 220 beds; this is the largest infirmary in Dublin. *Meath Hospital*, originally in Meath-street, was removed to the Coombe, and ultimately to its present site in Long-lane, Kevin-street; it is now the infirmary for the county. It contains a detached ward for fever cases, a fine theatre for operations, and a spacious lecture-room. *Mercer's Hospital*, founded in 1734 by Mrs. Mary Mercer, is a large stone building, situated between Mercer-street and Stephen-street, containing 55 beds. A theatre for operations was added to it in 1831. *The Charitable Infirmary*,

Jervis-street, was the first institution of the kind in the city: the building, a plain brick structure, erected in 1800, can accommodate 60 patients. *Whitworth Hospital* was erected in 1818, on the bank of the Royal Canal, near Drumcondra; it has a ward appropriated for a class of patients who can contribute towards their own maintenance in it. *The City of Dublin Hospital*, in Upper Baggot-street, has accommodations for 52 patients: it is also the principal institution for diseases of the eye. *The United Hospital of St. Mark's and St. Anne's* was opened in Mark-street in 1808, and contains 10 beds; an establishment for vaccination is attached to it. *The Maison de Santé*, George's-place, Dorset-street, is intended for those who, though unable to defray the expense of medical advice at home, are in circumstances to prevent them from seeking admission into a public hospital; the subscription paid by a patient is a guinea per week. The Netterville and the Royal Military Hospitals are noticed under preceding heads.

LUNATICS.

The Richmond District Lunatic Asylum, which was erected in 1830 into a district asylum for the county and city of Dublin, the counties of Meath, Wicklow, and Louth, and the town of Drogheda, occupies a rectangular area of 420 feet by 372, on the western side of the House of Industry. The building forms a hollow square of three stories: the inmates are arranged in four classes of each sex, each under the charge of a keeper, whose apartment commands a view of the gallery in which the patients are confined: there are separate airing-grounds for every class. The total number of patients on the 1st of Jan., 1836, was 277, of whom 130 were males and 147 females; the expenditure for the same year was £4180. 16. In *the House of Industry* there is a department for incurable lunatics, idiots, and epileptic patients, in which those capable of any exertion are employed suitably to their unhappy circumstances. *St. Patrick's* or *Swift's Hospital*, for the reception of lunatics and idiots, was founded by the celebrated Dean Swift, who bequeathed his property, amounting to £10,000, for this purpose. The building, situated near Steevens's Hospital, was opened in 1757, and has also apartments, rated at different prices, for those whose friends can contribute either wholly or partially to their maintenance. A large garden is attached to it, in which some of the patients are employed with considerable advantage to their intellectual improvement. The Society of Friends maintain a small asylum near Donnybrook, for lunatics of their own body.

THE LYING-IN HOSPITAL AND OTHER BENEVOLENT INSTITUTIONS.

The Lying-in Hospital, in Great Britain-street, was originally a small private infirmary, opened in 1745 by Dr. Bartholomew Mosse; but the benefit resulting from it having attracted other contributors, the first stone of the present building was laid in 1750: the doctor, after expending the whole of his property in forwarding the institution, obtained from parliament two successive grants of £6000 each. In 1756 the governors were incorporated by charter, the preamble of which states the threefold object of the institution to be the providing for "destitute females in their confinement, the providing a supply of well-qualified male and female practitioners throughout the country, and the prevention of child murder;" and in the following year the hospital was opened for the admission of patients. The institution is under the direction of a board of 60 governors. The details of management are superintended by a master, always a resident and a medical practitioner, elected for seven years, and deriving his emolument from the number of his pupils, among whom eight females educated for the practice of midwifery are paid for by Government; he delivers four courses of lectures annually, and at the end of six months the students are examined before the assistants, who are appointed for three years, and if duly qualified receive a certificate. The income for the year ending March 31st, 1836, was £4770, arising mainly from the exertions of its managers. The number of cases annually admitted is about 2500. The building consists of a centre and two projecting pavilions connected with it by curved colonnades; the whole of the façade extends 125 feet in length; the principal entrance leads into a spacious hall, and a broad flight of steps leads from the hall to the chapel. The western pavilion forms an entrance to the porter's lodge, and the eastern to the rotundo; in the rear is a spacious lawn enclosed by an iron palisade, forming the interior of Rutland-square. The rotundo comprises a suite of spacious and elegant rooms appropriated to purposes of amusement; the entrance from Sackville-street leads into a waiting-room for servants, and communicates with a vestibule adjoining the great room, which is a circle of 80 feet diameter; the orchestra is of elegant design. On the east and west are respectively a spacious tea-room and card-room; and on the north is a vestibule leading to the ball-room, which is 86 feet long and 40 feet wide. Above this room is another of equal dimensions, though less ornamented; and on the same floor are two smaller apartments, which are let for exhibitions. The new rooms, built in 1786 and facing Cavendish-row, are fronted with a rusticated basement, from which rise four three-quarter columns of the Doric order, supporting a triangular pediment, in the tympanum of which are the arms of Ireland, the crest of the Duke of Rutland, and the star of the Order of St. Patrick; these rooms are elegantly fitted up and well adapted to the same uses: all the profits arising from them are appropriated to the support of the hospital.

The other institutions of a similar description are in Townsend-street; in Bishop-street, called the Anglesey Hospital; on the Coombe, in the building which was the Meath Hospital; in South Cumberland-street; and on Ellis's-quay, called the Western Lying-in Hospital. An institution is attached to Mercer's hospital, for the relief of lying-in women at their own dwellings.

The infirmaries for special complaints not already noticed are the *Fever Hospital and House of Recovery*, Cork-street, which was opened in 1804. It consists of two parallel brick buildings, 80 feet by 30, three stories high, connected by a colonnade of 116 feet. The eastern range is used for fever, the western for convalescent patients; an additional building, much larger than any of the former, was added in 1814, by which the hospital was rendered capable of containing 240 beds. The expenditure is chiefly defrayed by a parliamentary grant; the subscriptions and funded property amount to about

£1000 per annum. From the opening of the establishment to the end of March, 1835, the number of patients amounted to 104,759. *The Hardwicke Fever Hospital*, attached to the House of Industry, contains 144 beds. *The Westmorland Lock Hospital* was opened in 1792, for the reception of venereal patients of both sexes, and was originally designed for the reception of 300 inmates; but afterwards the number of beds was reduced to 150, to which females only are admissible. The building, situated in Townsend-street, consists of a centre, in which are the officers' apartments, and two wings, with additional buildings for the reception of patients; the centre and wings project a little, and the former has a plain pediment. *A Vaccine Institution* was opened in 1804, in Sackville-street, for the gratuitous vaccination of the poor, and for supplying all parts of the country with genuine matter of infection. There is an *infirmary for ophthalmic affections* in North Cumberland-street, and another in Cuffe-street, one for cutaneous diseases in Moore-street, one for the diseases of children in Pitt-street, and another in North Frederic-street. *Dispensaries* are numerous, and generally attached to hospitals and infirmaries. Among those unattached are that in Cole's-lane, for St. Mary's parish, where the poor are also in special cases attended at their own lodgings; the Dublin General Dispensary, Fleet-street; St. Thomas's Dispensary, Marlborough-green; St. Peter's Parochial Dispensary, Montague-street; South Eastern General Dispensary, Grand Canal-street, near Sir P. Dun's Hospital, to which is attached a Nourishment and Clothing society; the Sick Poor Institution, in a great measure similar, in Meath-street; St. George's Dispensary, Dorset-street; and the Charitable Institution, Kildare-street.

ORPHANS AND DESTITUTE CHILDREN.

The associations for the relief and protection of orphans and destitute children are numerous. *The Foundling Hospital*, a very extensive establishment in James-street, for the reception of infants of this description from all parts of Ireland, for many years afforded an asylum to 2000 deserted children within its walls, and to nearly 5000 who were kept at nurse in the country till of age to be admitted into the central establishment; these children were clothed, maintained, educated, and apprenticed from the funds of the hospital, which were assisted by annual parliamentary grants of from £20,000 to £30,000. The internal departments were wholly closed by order of government on the 31st of March, 1835, and all the children who are not apprenticed, amounting to 2541, are at present settled with nurses in the country. There are also about 2800 apprentices serving their time as servants and to trades, who are still under the superintendence of the governors. The buildings, which are very extensive, contain schoolrooms for both sexes, dormitories, a chapel, and accommodations for several resident officers, and attached to it is a large garden, in the cultivation of which the older inmates assist. In addition to the Blue Coat, Royal Hibernian, and Royal Marine Institutions, already noticed under the heads of their respective public establishments, the following are peculiarly worthy of notice:—*The Female Orphan House* was commenced in 1790 by Mrs. Edw. Tighe and Mrs. Este, and, owing in a great measure to the advocacy of the celebrated Dean Kirwan, who preached a succession of sermons for its support, was opened in the present buildings on the North Circular Road, which contain ample accommodations for 160 children and a large episcopal chapel. The candidates for admission must be destitute both of father and mother, and between the age of five and ten; the inmates receive an education suited to fit them for the higher class of domestic servants. Its funds are aided by a parliamentary grant equal to the sum voluntarily contributed. *The Freemasons' Orphan School*, under the patronage of the Grand Lodge of Ireland, provides for the orphan daughters of deceased members of the Society. *Pleasants' Asylum*, Camden-street, opened in 1818 by means of a bequest of the late T. Pleasants, Esq., receives 20 Protestant female orphans, who are maintained and educated till they arrive at years of maturity, when they are entitled to a respectable portion on marrying a Protestant, approved of by the trustees. The special objects of *the Protestant Orphan Society*, founded in 1828, and *the Protestant Orphan Union*, formed subsequently, appear from their names; the latter owes its origin to the ravages of the cholera, which also gave rise to three other societies for the reception of children of every religious persuasion, who had been deprived of their parents by that dreadful scourge. Most of the places of worship in Dublin have boarding-schools attached to them for boys or girls, or both, into which orphans are admitted in preference. In this department of charitable institutions may be included *the Asylum for the Deaf and Dumb* at Claremont, near Glasnevin, which, from small beginnings, is now adapted to the reception of more than 100 inmates, who are wholly maintained, clothed, and instructed; the boys, after school hours, are occupied in gardening, farming, and other mechanical works; and the girls in needlework, housewifery, laundry work, and in the management of the dairy; a printing-press has been purchased for the instruction of some of the boys in that business, and for the printing of lessons adapted to the use of the pupils. The building contains separate schoolrooms for male and female pupils: attached to it are about 19 acres of land. This institution is wholly supported by subscription and private benefactions; it has various branch establishments in different parts of the country.

AGED AND IMPOTENT.

The House of Industry was established by act of parliament in 1773, for the indiscriminate reception of paupers from every part; but it has since been limited to destitute paupers of the county and city, and to the relief of certain classes of diseases. The establishment occupies 11 acres, on which are two squares of buildings; one for the aged and infirm, the other for the insane, together with detached infirmaries for fever, chronic, medical, and surgical cases, and a dispensary. The total number of aged and impotent poor that have been admitted is 426,175, of whom 1874 are now in the institution. It is under the superintendence of a resident governor and seven visiters appointed by the lord-lieutenant, and is maintained by an annual grant of public money. *Simpson's Hospital*, in Great Britain-street, for blind and gouty men, was opened in 1781, by means of a bequest of a citizen of that name, who had himself laboured under a complication of these complaints. It is a large plain building, with a small plot of ground in the rear for the accommodation of the inmates: its interior is divided into 24 wards, containing about 70 beds, but the number supported is about 50. The annual income of the hospital averages £2700. *The Hospital for Incurables* was opened in Fleet-street, in 1744, by a musical society, the members of which applied the profits of concerts to this benevolent purpose. In 1790, by means of a bequest of £4000 by Theobald Wolfe, Esq., the institution was removed into its present building near Donnybrook, originally erected for an infirmary for small-pox patients. The governors were incorporated in 1800. The house, a substantial plain building, can accommodate 70 patients; the ground belonging to it, 14 acres, is let so advantageously, as to leave the institution rent-free. *The Old Men's Asylum,* in Russell-place, North Circular Road, was instituted in 1810 for 24 reduced old men of good character. *St. Patrick's Asylum for Old Men,* in Rainsford-street, maintains 17 inmates, the majority of whom are upwards of 80 years of age each. The literary teachers, carpenters, printers, and vintners have each an asylum or fund for the relief of decayed members of their respective bodies. *The Scottish Society of St. Andrew* is formed for the relief of distressed natives of that country while in Dublin. *The Richmond National Institution for the Industrious Blind,* in Sackville-street, affords instruction to 40 male inmates in weaving, basket-making, netting, and some other similar kinds of handicraft, and has a sale-room for the disposal of the manufactured articles. *The Molyneux Asylum* for blind females was opened in 1815, on a similar principle, in the former family mansion of Sir Capel Molyneux in Peter-street, which had been for some years employed as a circus for equestrian exhibitions. Attached to it is an Episcopal chapel. There are several asylums for destitute aged women, mostly attached to some of the places of worship. There are two places for the reception of females of virtuous character during the pressure of temporary want of employment, one in Baggot-street, under the superintendence of Protestant ladies; the other in Stanhope-street, under that of a R. C. nunnery.

FEMALE PENITENTIARIES.

The Magdalen Asylum in Leeson-street, was founded by Lady Denny in 1766; the house is adapted for the reception of 60 inmates, and the average number in the asylum is 50; after a probation of three years they are either restored to their families, or provided with the means of honest subsistence; they are employed during the time of their continuance in the asylum in profitable industry, and receive one-fourth of their earnings during their residence, and the remainder on their leaving the house: the institution has received considerable benefactions from the Latouche family. *The Lock Penitentiary* was opened in 1794 by Mr. John Walker, as a penitentiary for the special reception and employment of females discharged from the Lock Hospital; there are generally about 30 in the asylum, who are employed in needlework and other female occupations. *The Dublin Female Penitentiary,* in the North Circular Road, was opened in 1813: the house is large and commodious; there are about 35 females on the establishment. *The Asylum in Upper Baggot-street* affords shelter to 30 inmates. Each of these has a Protestant Episcopalian place of worship attached to it. The R. C. asylums of a similar character are situated respectively in Townsend-street, containing 41 penitents and superintended by the Sisters of Charity; in Mecklenburgh-street, which receives 35; in Dominick-street, late Bow-street, where 34 are sheltered; in Marlborough-street, late James's-street, which supports 45; besides St. Mary's Asylum, Drumcondra-road, in which the average number is 30. The origin of several of these institutions was attended with circumstances of peculiar interest. A house of shelter for the temporary reception of females discharged from prison is on the Circular-road, Harcourt-street. The Lock Hospital has a department in which 12 females, who had been patients, are employed in washing for the establishment, under the superintendence of a matron, and are entirely supported in the house.

GENERAL DISTRESS.

The Mendicity Association, formed in 1818, has for its object the suppression of street-begging, by supplying relief to destitute paupers, chiefly by means of employment. A large building on Ussher's Island, formerly the town residence of the Earl of Moira, and having a large space of ground attached to it, is fitted up for the purposes of the institution. The paupers are provided with food and apartments to work in, but not with lodging, and are divided into seven classes; first, those able to work at profitable employment, who receive full wages for their work; 2ndly, those whose earnings are not adequate to their entire support, who receive wages at a lower rate; 3rdly, those unable to perform full work; 4thly, the infirm; 5thly, children above six years of age, who are educated and instructed in useful employments; and lastly, children under six years of age, who are taken care of while their parents are at work: a dispensary is attached to the building and the sick are visited at their own lodgings. The institution is under the superintendence of 60 gentlemen elected annually. *The Sick and Indigent Roomkeepers' Society,* formed in 1790, gives temporary relief in money to the destitute poor at their own lodgings. At a general meeting held at the Royal Exchange, once a month, the amount of the relief to be given during the ensuing month is fixed, which is distributed by four committees for the Barrack, Workhouse, Rotundo, and Stephen's Green divisions of the city, which sit weekly. *The Strangers' Friend Society,* formed in the same year as the preceding institution, has similar objects, and is conducted on the same principle of temporary domestic relief. *The Benevolent Strangers' Friend Society,* of like character, is of later formation. *The Charitable Association,* formed in 1806, is designed for the relief of distressed persons of every description, except street beggars: relief is administered at the dwellings of the pauper. A loan fund is attached to the institution.

EMINENT MEN.

The following eminent persons were born in the city in the years attached to their names: Richard Stanyhurst, historian, 1545; Wm. Bathe, an eminent writer, 1564; Henry Fitzsimons, an eminent writer, 1569; James Ussher, the celebrated prelate, 1580; Sir James Ware, the antiquary, 1594; Arthur Annesley, Earl of Annesley, 1614; Henry Lutterel, an engraver, 1650; Nahum

Tate, a poet, 1652; Wm. Molyneux, mathematician, astronomer, and patriot, 1656; Thomas Southerne, a dramatic poet, 1659; James Butler, Duke of Ormonde, 1665; Jonathan Swift, Dean of St. Patrick's, 1667; Marmaduke Coghill, Chancellor of the Exchequer in Ireland, 1673; Dr. Robert Clayton, a celebrated prelate, 1695; Wm. Robertson, a learned divine, 1705; Thos. Frye, the first manufacturer of porcelain in England, 1710; James McArdill, engraver, 1710; Mary Barber, authoress, 1712; John Gast, an eminent divine, 1715; Springer Barry, a celebrated actor, 1719; Thos. Leland, historian, 1722; Rev. Mervyn Archdall, an antiquary, 1723; Geo. Barrett, painter, 1728; Francis Gentleman, a dramatic writer, 1728; John Cunningham, a poet, 1729; Edm. Chandler, Bishop of Durham, 1730; Nathaniel Hone, portrait painter, 1730; Isaac Bickerstaff, dramatist, 1732; Andrew Caldwell, compiler of parliamentary debates, 1732; Hugh Hamilton, painter, 1734; James Caulfeild, first Earl of Charlemont, 1738; Sir Philip Francis, author and statesman, 1740; Edward Malone, critic and antiquary, 1741; John Fitzgibbon, Earl of Clare, 1749; Henry Grattan, statesman, orator, and patriot, 1751; Wm. Mossop, medalist, 1754; John Hickey, sculptor, 1756; Joseph Cooper Walker, antiquary, 1761; Geo. McAllister, painter on glass, 1786. The birth-dates of the following natives of Dublin have not been ascertained: Edward Borlase, historian; Thomas Dogget, a celebrated actor; Robert Molesworth, Viscount Molesworth; Charles Byrne, miniature painter; Zach. Crofton, a celebrated divine; and Wm. Halliday, Irish grammarian. Dublin gave the title of Earl to His Royal Highness the late Duke of Kent.

DULEEK, a parish and village, formerly a parliamentary borough, partly in the barony of UPPER, but chiefly in that of LOWER DULEEK, county of MEATH, and province of LEINSTER, $4\frac{1}{2}$ miles (S. S. W.) from Drogheda, on the Nannywater, and on the mail coach road from Dublin to Belfast; containing 4470 inhabitants, of which number, 1217 are in the village. This place derived its name signifying, a "House of Stone," from the foundation of a church here by St. Kiernan or Ciernan, who was baptized by St. Patrick in 450 and died in 488. St. Patrick is also said to have founded an abbey at this place, over which he appointed St. Kiernan abbot; the establishment was for several ages the seat of a small surrounding diocese, which ultimately merged into that of Meath. Its situation in a maritime district exposed it to the ravages of the Danes, by whom it was frequently plundered and sometimes destroyed. It was plundered in 1171 by Milo de Cogan and his forces, who on the following day were attacked and repulsed with severe loss by the Ostmen of Dublin. A priory for Canons Regular appears to have been founded here by one of the family of O'Kelly, a long time prior to the English invasion; and in 1182, a cell of the same order was established here by Hugh de Lacy, and made subject to the priory of Llanthony; the possessions of this priory were granted at the dissolution to Sir Gerald Moore, ancestor of the Drogheda family. After the battle of the Boyne, Jas. II. retreated from Donore at the head of Sarsfield's regiment, and was followed by his whole army, which poured through the pass of Duleek pursued by a party of English dragoons. On reaching the open ground, they drew up in order of battle, and after cannonading their pursuers, effected their retreat in good order. The village comprises 240 houses. The manufacture of ticking, formerly extensive, is now very much diminished; there is an extensive corn and flour-mill in the town, and another at Beaumont, the latter recently erected and fitted up in a very complete manner with improved machinery. On the hill of Bellewstown is a course where races are held the last week in June; they are generally well attended. The market has been discontinued; but fairs are held on March 25th, May 3rd, June 24th, and Oct. 18th. A penny post to Drogheda and Ashbourne has been established; there is also a chief constabulary police station. The town was formerly governed by a portreeve and officers, annually elected under the charter of Walter de Lacy, which was confirmed by act of Edw. IV., in 1481, and by royal charter of Jas. II., in 1686. From this latter period it continued to send members to the Irish parliament till the Union, when it was disfranchised, and the corporation became extinct: the sum of £15,000, awarded as compensation for the loss of the elective privilege, was paid to the trustees of H. Bruen, Esq. Petty sessions are held every alternate week.

The parish comprises 14,343 statute acres, as applotted under the tithe act. The land is of good quality; about two-thirds are under tillage, and the eastern portion of the parish, including the hill of Bellewstown, is excellent grazing land. Annexed to the town is a considerable tract of common. Limestone is abundant, and is quarried both for building and for agricultural purposes. Platten, the seat of R. Reeves, Esq., occupies the site of an ancient castle of the D'Arcy family; it is a spacious mansion, situated in a richly planted demesne. Athcarne Castle, the seat of J. Gernon, Esq., is pleasantly situated on the Nannywater; it formerly belonged to the De Bathe family, and is a perfect specimen of the Elizabethan castellated style; it is a massive pile of building, with a still more massive keep defended by quadrangular embattled towers, and the whole was formerly surrounded by a fosse: the present proprietor has made some additions and improvements. The other seats are Annsbrook, that of H. Smith, Esq., an elegant mansion with a demesne tastefully embellished; Hiltown House, of Nicholas Boylan, Esq.; Thomastown, of Evans Kettlewell, Esq.; Beaumont, of J. McCann, Esq.; Wintergrass, of Lawrence Ball, Esq.; and Duleek House, situated in an extensive demesne, the property of the Marquess of Thomond.

The living is a vicarage, in the diocese of Meath, united, in 1816, to the vicarages of Dowth, Ardcath, Tymole, and Knockcoman, and in the patronage of the Marquess of Drogheda, in whom the rectory is impropriate. The tithes amount to £1092, the whole formerly payable to the impropriator, but on appeal to the Privy Council in 1833, £65 per ann. was made payable to the vicar; and the entire value of the benefice, tithe and glebe included, is £285. There are four glebes in the union, comprising together $48\frac{1}{2}$ acres, valued at £100. 9. per ann. The church, rebuilt in 1816 at an expense of £1500, is a handsome structure with a tower; in the porch is a marble statue of Judge Trotter, and in the churchyard a richly sculptured stone cross. In the R. C. divisions the parish is the head of a union or district, comprising also the parish of Cullinstown; the chapel is a handsome edifice in the later English style, with a school-room adjoining; and there is a chapel at Bellewstown hill, to which also a school-room is attached. The parochial school is aided by the incumbent, and there are four other public schools, one of which has a remarkably neat school-house, erected by J. Mathews, Esq.; they afford instruction to about 300 children, and about 30 children are educated in a private school. A dispensary is supported in the customary way. There are considerable remains of the ancient abbey church, with a massive square tower surmounted at the angles with embattled turrets; it was very extensive, and contains many ancient tombs, among which is one of a bishop. There are also some remains of the priory of St. Mary, on the Marquess of Thomond's demesne, and also anciently an endowed hospital, of which there are no remains. In the centre of the town and near Annsbrook are two handsome carved stone crosses bearing inscriptions, erected by the De Bathe family; and at Whitecross is another, elaborately carved. Sir William D'Arcy, treasurer of Ireland in 1523, and author of a work on the Decay of Ireland and the causes of it, was born at Platten.

DULEEN, or DULANE, a parish, in the barony of UPPER KELLS, county of MEATH, and province of LEINSTER, 2¼ miles (N.) from Kells, on the road to Moynalty; containing 1503 inhabitants. It comprises 4150 statute acres, as applotted under the tithe act: the land is generally of good quality; and the system of agriculture is improved. There is a sufficient quantity of bog for fuel, and there are quarries of limestone and freestone. The gentlemen's seats are Maprath, that of T. Taylor Rowley, Esq.; Williamston, of the Rev. G. Garnett; Willmount, of J. Radcliff, Esq.; and Oakley Park, of Capt. Graham. It is a chapelry, in the diocese of Meath, forming part of the union of Kells and corps of the archdeaconry of Meath: the tithes amount to £200; the glebe comprises 2*a.* 3*r.* 17*p.* In the R. C. divisions it is the head of a union or district called Carnaross, comprising also the parish of Loghan, in each of which is a chapel; the chapel of Duleen is a neat edifice. There is a private school, in which are about 50 children. There are some ancient crosses in Kiern churchyard, said to have been placed there by a saint of that name, which are held in great veneration by the peasantry.

DUNAGHMORE.—See DONAGHMORE, county of MEATH.

DUNAGHY, a parish, in the barony of KILCONWAY, county of ANTRIM, and province of ULSTER, 6 miles (N. W. by N.) from Broughshane; containing 3451 inhabitants. It comprises, according to the Ordnance survey, 13,743¼ statute acres, of which 12,040 are applotted under the tithe act; about one-sixth is irreclaimable mountain and bog, one-fourth rough mountain pasture, a twelfth, pasture of a better quality, and one half, arable land. Towards the east the hills attain a mountainous elevation; the highest are those of Moneyduff and Ballyboggy. A great portion of the summits of the hills towards the north is unprofitable; but nearer their base they afford good pasture to young cattle during the summer. Along the banks of the Ravel and Altakeerag are considerable tracts of low meadow land, subject to floods from the former river which pours down with great rapidity. The females are employed in spinning, and the males, in addition to their agricultural pursuits, in weaving coarse linens and calico.

The living is a rectory, in the diocese of Connor, and in the patronage of the Bishop: the tithes amount to £311. 18. 7¼. The glebe-house was built by aid of a gift of £350 and a loan of £450 from the late Board of First Fruits in 1816; the glebe comprises 25 acres. The church, a small edifice with an open belfry turret, occupies an elevated site. In the R. C. divisions the parish is the head of a union or district called Glenravel, and comprises Dunaghy and Skerry, in each of which is a chapel; the chapel for this parish, a neat edifice, is at Glenravel, near the bridge over the Ravel. There is a place of worship in the village of Clough for Presbyterians in connection with the Synod of Ulster, of the first class. There are two public schools, in which are about 260 children, and three Sunday schools. There are several Danish forts, of which the most remarkable are, one on the hill of Dungonnell, two on Dunbought, and one nearly effaced on Carnbeg, in levelling which were found an urn, a small statue, a cross, and some silver coins. There are many sepulchral monuments in the churchyard, among which those of the Crawford and Hamilton families are the most remarkable. Corby Rock is a bold precipice forming the termination of a hill; it is covered with ivy and washed at its base by the Ravel.

DUNAMANAGH, a village and post-town, in the parish of DONAGHEADY, barony of STRABANE, county of TYRONE, and province of ULSTER, on the road from Strabane to Cookstown, 6 miles (N. E. by E.) from Strabane, and 113 (N. N. W.) from Dublin: the population is returned with the parish. This village, which situated in a deed and retired glen amidst the Mounterloney mountains, was founded by Sir John Drummond in 1619. It has a station of the constabulary police, and a sub-post-office to Strabane. Fairs are held on Jan. 13th, Feb. 28th, April 14th, May 27th, July 14th, Aug. 27th, Oct. 13th, and Nov. 28th. In and around the village are extensive deposits of limestone. Here is a meeting-house for Presbyterians, in connection with the synod of Ulster, a large and handsome building: that which formerly belonged to the covenanters is in ruins. At a short distance from the village are the parochial church, and male and female schools. On the site of the bawn built by Sir John Drummond is a building which, from that circumstance, is called the Castle.—See DONAGHEADY.

DUNANY, a parish, in the barony of FERRARD, county of LOUTH, and province of LEINSTER, 5 miles (E. N. E.) from Dunleer; containing 571 inhabitants. This parish, which is situated on the eastern coast, contains, according to the Ordnance survey, 1661¾ statute acres, chiefly under tillage. Dunany House, the residence of Lady Bellingham, is surrounded by an extensive and finely-planted demesne, and commands fine views of the sea and the Carlingford mountains. Dunany Point is distinguished at sea by the church, which stands on the summit of the rising ground: at the Point is a chief station of the coast-guard. The parish is in the diocese of Armagh; the vicarage was united in the 18th century to those of Parsonstown, Marlinstown, and Salterstown, and is in the patronage of the Marquess of Drogheda; the rectory is impropriate in Lady Bellingham. The tithes amount to £154. 0. 8., of which £90. 16. 8½. is payable to the impropriator, and the remainder to the vicar; and the tithes of the entire benefice amount to £111. 18. 10½. The church, which is in excellent repair, was built in 1814, and the glebe-house about the same period, by aid of a gift of £400 and a loan of £364 from the late Board of First Fruits; the glebe comprises 20 acres, valued at £27 per annum. In the R. C. divisions the parish forms part of the union or district of Dysart. About 20 children are educated in a private school.

DUNBEG, or DOONBEG, a village, in the parish of KILLARD, barony of IBRICKANE, county of CLARE, and province of MUNSTER, 6 miles (N. W.) from Kilrush, on the bay of Dunmore; containing 213 inhabitants. The river Dunbeg flows into the harbour and is here crossed by a good bridge, near which stand the ruins of a lofty castle, formerly a defence to the harbour, and one of the ancient strong holds of the O'Briens. The harbour which is the only one, excepting Liscanor, between Loop head and the bay of Galway, an extent of nearly 40 miles, is rendered dangerous by the rocks at its entrance. The pier, built by the late Fishery Board, is small and not much frequented; sea-weed is landed here, and flags of a superior quality, raised near the village, are sent to Galway, Limerick, and Cork; it also forms a place of refuge for small craft in bad weather. Here is a station of the coast-guard. Fairs are held on May 2nd, July 26th, Oct. 8th, and Dec. 16th, for general farming stock, and for flannel and frieze of home manufacture. Near the bridge is a flour-mill. A court for the manor of Kilrush, in which small debts are recoverable, is held once in six weeks. In the village is a R. C. chapel, and about a quarter of a mile from it is the newly erected parochial church.

DUNBELL, a parish, in the barony of GOWRAN, county of KILKENNY, and province of LEINSTER, 4 miles (S. E.) from Kilkenny, on the road to Gowran; containing 567 inhabitants. This parish comprises 4299 statute acres, as applotted under the tithe act. It is a rectory and vicarage, in the diocese of Ossory, forming part of the union of Burnchurch: the tithes amount to £277. In the R. C. divisions it is part of the union or district of Gowran.

DUNBOE, or DRUMBOE, a parish, in the barony of COLERAINE, county of LONDONDERRY, and province of ULSTER, 5 miles (W. by N.) from Coleraine; containing 5018 inhabitants. This appears to have been a very important district from an early period, for, even in the 5th century, we find it mentioned under the name of *Le Bendrigi*, which seems to have comprised the northern parts of the present barony of Coleraine; and it is stated that St. Patrick founded the old church here. The parish comprises, according to the Ordnance survey, 14,811¼ statute acres, of which 14,576 are applotted under the tithe act, and valued at £5796 per ann. On the south and west it is composed of basaltic mountains, which afford good pasturage, and on the opposite sides it is washed by the ocean and the river Bann, towards which latter the surface gradually descends, and the sands at its mouth formed the most extensive rabbit warrens in the kingdom, until the decline in the price of the fur, when the warrens were mostly destroyed, and the land brought into cultivation. Numerous streams descend from the mountains, fertilizing the meadows through which they pass. Near Articlave and Downhill the land is good and under an excellent system of cultivation. Downhill, the splendid residence of Sir Jas. R. Bruce, Bart., occupies an elevated point of land between the Bann and Foyle, opening in full view on the Atlantic ocean; was erected by the late Earl of Bristol, Bishop of Derry, and is built in the Italian style, of hewn freestone; the pilasters are extremely chaste and beautiful. The interior is finished in the most costly manner, the saloons being adorned with marble statues, and the halls and galleries with statuary and paintings of the most celebrated ancient and modern masters. In the glens, the plantations are extensive, beautifully laid out, and ornamented with rustic buildings and bridges. On the lawn stands a unique and beautiful mausoleum, erected by the bishop to the memory of his brother, who was ambassador to the court of Spain, exhibiting a full-length statue of him, beneath an elevated canopy. The living is a rectory, forming the corps of the archdeaconry of Derry, and in the patronage of the Bishop: the tithes amount to £480. The glebe-house is a commodious residence, occupied by the Rev. Archdeacon Monsell; there are four glebes, containing together 550 statute acres, 382 of which are cultivated land, the remainder being hilly and affording good pasturage for cattle. The church is a large and handsome edifice, situated at Articlave, for the repair of which the Ecclesiastical Commissioners have recently granted £230; it was erected on a new site in 1691, the old church having been destroyed by King James's army, on its retreat from Derry. In the R. C. divisions the parish forms part of the union of Killowen. In the village of Articlave is a meeting-house for Presbyterians, in connection with the Synod of Ulster, and at Ballinrees is one in connection with the Seceding Synod, both of the second class. The parochial schools, situated at Articlave, are supported by the archdeacon; there are also schools at Downhill, built by Sir J. R. Bruce, and supported by him and Lady Bruce. Schools are maintained in other parts of the parish, together affording instruction to more than 500 children. There are also two private and eight Sunday schools. The parish belongs partly to Sir J. R. Bruce, and partly to the Clothworkers' Company; the latter contribute £15 per ann. to the poor on their own estate. Not far from Downhill are the ruins of the ancient abbey of Duncruthin, which became the parish church previously to 1291: and in the western part of the parish stands a great fort, called the Giant's Sconce, occupying the summit of a lofty isolated hill of basalt, strongly fortified by nature.

DUNBOLLOGE, or CARRIGNAVAR, a parish, partly in the county of the city of CORK, and partly in the barony of BARRYMORE, but chiefly in that of EAST MUSKERRY, county of CORK, and province of MUNSTER, 5 miles (N.) from Cork, on the road to Mallow; containing 4634 inhabitants. This place is said to have been the scene of a battle which took place on the confines of the parish in 1649, between the forces of Cromwell and the Irish, in which the latter were defeated. The parish comprises 15,749 statute acres, as applotted under the tithe act, and valued at £7262 per annum. The surface is hilly, and in some parts mountainous; the soil on the hills is light and stony, but of much better quality in the valleys; there is a large extent of bog, supplying the vicinity with abundance of cheap fuel; the reclaimable mountain is constantly being brought into cultivation or planted. Indications of coal have been observed in Glassaboy mountain, but no means have yet been taken to trace them; there are also quarries of limestone and some of clay-slate, which is used for building and repairing the roads. Carrignavar, the seat of Justin M[c]Carty, Esq., a descendant of the ancient royal house of the M[c]Cartys of Cork or South Desmond, is an old mansion pleasantly situated above a romantic glen, and surrounded by a very extensive demesne, richly cultivated and planted, finely embellished with stately timber, and commanding some pleasing views. The manufacture of cotton and worsted hose is carried on to a small extent, under the patronage and support of Mrs. M[c]Carty, for the employment of the poor. It is a rectory, in the diocese of Cork, and is one of the five parishes which constitute the union of St. Peter, and the corps of the archdeaconry of Cork, in the patronage of the bishop: the tithes amount to £461. 10. 9. A church has been recently built at Carrignavar by subscription, to which the incumbent and Justin M[c]Carty, Esq., were the principal contributors; the latter gave the site. It is for the use of the parishes of Dunbolloge and St. Michael. In the R. C. divisions this parish forms part of the union of Upper Glanmire: at Carrignavar is a neat chapel in the early English style, with a porch at the western entrance, and a minaret rising from the gable of the roof. The parochial school is a large and handsome edifice, built by Justin M[c]Carty, Esq., who has endowed it with two acres of land; and the female school is patronised by Mrs. M[c]Carty. About 100 children are educated in three other public schools, besides which there is a Sunday school, supported by the rector.—See CARRIGNAVAR.

DUNBOYNE, a parish and village, (formerly an incorporated town), in the barony of DUNBOYNE, county of MEATH, and province of LEINSTER, on the road from Dublin to Navan; containing, with the post-town of Clonee, 2419 inhabitants, of which number, 470 are in the village. This place, which is on the confines of the county of Dublin, appears to have been an ancient borough. In the reign of Hen. VI., a writ was issued, dated July 28th, 1423, ordering "the Provost and Commonalty of the town of Dunboyne to be at Trim with all their power for its defence." The town was burnt down in the disturbances of 1798; the present village contains 82 houses. The manufacture of straw hats is carried on here, and in the neighbourhood; and a fair, chiefly for horses and cattle, is held on July 9th, and is much frequented by the Dublin dealers. The parish is principally grazing land; there are about 50 acres of common, and a bog of about 40 acres, called the "Moor of Meath." The gentlemen's seats are Wood Park, that of the Rev. J. Auchinleck; Roosk, of — Wilson, Esq.; Ballymacall, of H. Hamilton, Esq.; Hammond, of C. Hamilton, Esq.; Court Hill, of H. Greene, Esq.; Sterling, of R. Barker, Esq; Norman's Grove, of J. Shanley, Esq.; and Priestown, of the Rev. J. Butler. The living is a vicarage, in the diocese of Meath, united in 1400 to the chapelry of Kilbride, and in the patronage of the Crown; the rectory is impropriate in Miss E. Hamilton. The tithes amount to £835. 7. 8., of which £535. 7. 8. is payable to the impropriator and £300 to the vicar; and the tithes of the union to £347. 19. The glebe-house was built by aid of a gift of £300, and a loan of £500 from the late Board of First Fruits, in 1814; the glebe comprises three acres, subject to a rent of £3 per acre. The church is an ancient edifice, for the repair of which the Ecclesiastical Commissioners have recently granted £159. The R. C. union is co-extensive with that of the Established Church, and in each parish is a chapel. About 40 children are taught in the public schools of the parish; and there are two private schools, in which are about 120 children. A dispensary is supported in the village, and adjoining it are some remains of an ancient castle, which gives the title of Baron of Dunboyne to the family of Butler.

DUNBREA, a parish, in the barony of KILKEA and MOONE, county of KILDARE, and province of LEINSTER, on the road from Athy to Carlow; containing, with the parish of Dunlost, 70 inhabitants. It is a rectory, in the diocese of Dublin, forming part of the union of St. Michael's, Athy, under which head the tithes are stated.

DUNBRODY (ST. PETER AND ST. PAUL), a parish, in the barony of SHELBURNE, county of WEXFORD, and province of LEINSTER, 2 miles (N.) from Arthurstown, on the road from New Ross to Duncannon Fort; the population is returned with the parish of St. James. Hervey de Montmorency, marshal of Hen. II., and seneschal of all the lands acquired by Strongbow, Earl of Pembroke, on his expedition to Ireland, having in consequence of some dispute resigned his commission, parcelled out the lands allotted to him among his followers, retaining only that portion which now constitutes the parishes of Dunbrody and St. James. In 1182, he founded and dedicated to St. Peter and St. Paul the Cistertian abbey of Dunbrody, which he endowed with this reserved portion of his possessions, and became himself the first abbot. The abbots sat as barons in the Irish Parliament, and the establishment flourished until the dissolution, when Alexander Devereux, the last abbot, compounded for his abbacy, and was appointed Bishop of Ferns. The parish is bounded on the west by Waterford harbour; and an inlet called Campile is navigable for small craft, bringing limestone and coal, the former of which is extensively used for manure; the land is chiefly under tillage, and an improved system of agriculture has been generally adopted. A ferry hence to Passage, on the opposite side of the harbour, affords a direct communication with the city of Waterford. Dunbrody Castle, the property of Lord Templemore, and at present in the possession of Richard Barron, Esq., is a modernised edifice, partly incorporated with the walls of the ancient castle built in the reign of Hen. II. The living is an impropriate curacy, in the diocese of Ferns, annexed to those of Rathroe and St. James, and in the patronage of Lord Templemore, in whom the rectory is impropriate. In the R. C. divisions this parish forms part of the union or district of Horeswood. The ruins of Dunbrody abbey are among the most interesting and magnificent relics of antiquity in the south of Ireland; they are situated on a verdant slope gently inclining to the shore of the harbour, and comprise the skeleton of the conventual church, the refectory, the foundations of the cloisters, and part of the domestic buildings. The church, a noble cruciform structure, 200 feet in length and 140 in breadth, is chiefly in the early style of English architecture, with a massive central tower supported on four finely pointed arches. A considerable portion of it was built by Herlewen, Bishop of Leighlin, who died in 1217, and was interred in the abbey. In 1810, a massive bronze seal, supposed to have been the ancient seal of the abbey, was discovered among the ruins.

DUNBYN, a parish, in the barony of Upper DUNDALK, county of LOUTH, and province of LEINSTER, 3¼ miles (N. W.) from Lurgan-Green, on the road from Dundalk to Carrickmacross; containing 969 inhabitants. According to the Ordnance survey it comprises 2169¼ statute acres, of which 1942 are applotted under the tithe act. It is a rectory, in the diocese of Armagh: the tithes amount to £200, and are sequestrated in the Ecclesiastical Commissioners, who pay the curate of an adjoining parish for the discharge of the occasional duties. In the R. C. divisions it forms part of the union or district of Baronstown, and has a chapel at Kilcurly. There is a public school, in which about 150 children are educated.

DUNCANELY.—See DUNKANELY.

DUNCANNON, a village, in the parish of ST. JAMES, barony of SHELBURNE, county of WEXFORD, and province of LEINSTER, 1½ mile (S.) from Arthurstown; containing 560 inhabitants. This place, which commands the entrance to the ports of Waterford and Ross, was granted by Hen. VI. to John Talbot, Earl of Shrewsbury, from whom it reverted to the Crown; and the castle, with some lands for keeping it in repair, was vested in trustees by Queen Elizabeth. On the threatened invasion of the Spaniards, in 1588, it was strongly fortified. In 1645, the fort, which was held by Laurence Esmonde for the Parliament, was surrendered to Gen. Preston for the King; and in 1649, was besieged by Ireton, whom the garrison compelled to retire. After the battle of the Boyne, Jas. II. embarked for France from this fort; and during the insurrection of 1798, it afforded an asylum to most of the loyalists in this part of the country. The fort is situated on a rock projecting from the eastern side of Waterford harbour, and has undergone frequent alterations: it is adapted for mounting 42 pieces of cannon, and, including "the bomb-proof" erected in 1815, contains barracks for 10 officers and 160 men, residences for the chaplain, fort-major, storekeeper, and other officers, and a chapel for the garrison; the whole is surrounded by a dry moat crossed by a drawbridge, and the only entrance is defended by a portcullis. On the hill overlooking the village are two martello towers, now dismantled. The village consists chiefly of one street, forming the approach to the fort, and had formerly a considerable trade, which has been mostly transferred to Arthurstown, in consequence of a steamer established by an English company to ply between Duncannon and Waterford. A new line of road is to be opened direct from Duncannon to Wexford, in consequence of which, and as the town is now in the possession of the head landlord, Lord Templemore, it promises to be soon in a flourishing state. The quay has been recently repaired, and the Harbour Commissioners are proceeding to deepen the harbour at a considerable expense. There is still a small export trade in pigs, butter, and poultry, and an import of coal. It has a daily penny post to Arthurstown, and a well-appointed mail car runs from Fethard, through Duncannon and Arthurstown, to Ross. A few boats are employed in fishing, on which and on the garrison the inhabitants depend chiefly for their support. An oyster bed just below the fort, which has been for some years only partially known, has been recently discovered to be of considerable extent, and is now much dredged. A branch from the coast-guard station at Arthurstown is quartered here. The creek is formed by the rock on which the fort is built, and the approach to the strand is rendered dangerous by shoals; but vessels of 100 tons can approach the pier at high water in fair weather. Within the fort is a lighthouse, nearly due north from that of Hook; another to the north of the Fort is nearly completed. In the village is a R. C. chapel; and two neat school-houses, one of which is for infants, have been recently built by subscription. Duncannon gives the inferior title of Viscount to the family of Ponsonby, Earls of Besborough.

DUNCORMUCK, a parish, in the barony of BARGY, county of WEXFORD, and province of LEINSTER, 3 miles (E.) from Danes-Castle; containing 1591 inhabitants, of which number, 249 are in the village. This parish is situated on a small stream that flows into the lough of Duncormuck, and comprises 5860 statute acres, which, though chiefly under tillage, contains some good grazing land. Quarries of a dark species of limestone are worked, and the produce is extensively used for manure. At Lacken a considerable trade is carried on in slates, coal, and culm from South Wales; vessels of 100 tons' burden can cross the bar at high tides and lie securely in the lough, which is still frequented by wild fowl, though not in such numbers as formerly. Petty sessions are held monthly in the village. The living is a vicarage, in the diocese of Ferns, episcopally united, in 1759, to the rectory of Ambrosetown, and in the patronage of the Bishop: the tithes amount to £306. 7. 10., of which £119. 19. 2. is payable to the impropriator, and the remainder to the vicar; and the entire tithes of the benefice amount to £324. 17. 10¾. The glebe-house, the residence of the Rev. R. B. Gordon, was erected in 1817 by a gift of £100 and a loan of £450 from the late Board of First Fruits; there are three contiguous glebes containing together 18 acres. The church is a modern edifice, erected on the site of the ancient building, and is about to be repaired by a grant of £148 from the Ecclesiastical Commissioners. In the R. C. divisions the parish is the head of the union or district of Rathangan, comprising also the parishes of Killag, Kilcowan, Kilmannon, and Ballyconnick, with the townland of Ambrosetown: there are chapels at Rathangan and Clarestown, the latter in the parish of Kilmannon. The parochial school was erected by the Rev. R. B. Gordon on a site presented by W. Richards, Esq., of Rathaspeck; it is partly supported by Mr. Gordon. A school at Rathangan is aided by the Rev. J. Barry, P. P.: the number of children educated in these schools is 110, besides which there are about 50 in a private school. In the village is a lofty tower called Duncormuck Castle, apparently of Anglo-Norman architecture.

DUNDALK, a sea-port, borough, market and post-town, and parish, in the barony of UPPER DUNDALK, county of LOUTH, and province of LEINSTER, 10¼ miles (S.) from Newry, and 40 miles (N. by W.) from Dublin, on the mail road to Belfast; containing 14,300 inhabitants, of which number, 10,078 are in the bo-

Seal.

rough and liberties. The earliest historical notice of this place occurs in 1180, when John de Courcey with 1000 men, marching against a prince of Argial who had destroyed one of his ships, was encountered by the native chiefs with a force of 7000 men, by whom he was defeated with the loss of 400 of his troops. The English power being soon afterwards firmly established, Dundalk with some other territories was granted to Bertram de Verdon, who founded here a priory for Crouched Friars of the Augustine order, which afterwards became an hospital; and in the reign of Hen. III., Lord John de Verdon founded a Franciscan friary in the town. In 1315, Edward Bruce took possession of the town and caused himself to be proclaimed King of Ireland. He maintained his assumed dignity here for nearly a whole year; but being attacked by John de Birmingham, his army was totally defeated and himself slain. Sometime after, O'Hanlon, an Irish chieftain, came with a large force to demand tribute from the inhabitants, by whom he was so vigorously repulsed that 200 of his men were left dead upon the field. In 1338, Theobald de Verdon obtained a grant of a market and fair for 15 days. Rich. II. confirmed by charter all the privileges the inhabitants had previously enjoyed, and made the town a free borough; and Hen. IV. granted the bailiffs and commonalty certain customs, to surround their town with walls, which, from its exposed situation on the north of the English pale, were necessary for its protection. In 1558, the Lord-Deputy Sidney appointed an interview with the powerful chieftain Shane O'Nial, who at last agreed to come to him here on condition of being received as his "gossip." The town was, in 1560, besieged by the O'Nials, but was so valiantly defended that they abandoned the design. A subsequent attempt was made with no better success; and in 1562, the Earl of Sussex, lord-deputy, sent some forces to the assistance of the townsmen, between whom and Shane O'Nial a mutual restitution of plunder took place. So great was the power of the native chieftains in 1596, that in a conference held at Faughart it was proposed by the English government to make this town the frontier of their dominions in Ireland; but all overtures for a pacification were rejected. On the breaking out of the war in 1641, Roger Moore and Brian Mac Mahon posted themselves near this town, of which they held possession, with a force of 2500 men, and bade defiance to the Irish government; but Sir Henry Tichborne assaulted and, after an obstinate resistance, succeeded in gaining possession of the town. Col. Monk, who had been appointed governor, was, in 1649, compelled by Lord Inchiquin to surrender it to Cromwell. In the war of the revolution, some forces of Jas. II., which had been stationed in the town, abandoned it on the approach of William's army commanded by Duke Schomberg, who encamped his forces on some low marshy ground, about a mile to the north, where they suffered much from disease. James detached a party to seize the pass at Newry, which, on the first appearance of opposition, retired to Sligo. He soon after advanced at the head of the Irish army and drew up in order of battle, but just at the moment when an engagement was expected, drew off his troops and retired to Ardee.

The town is situated on the south side of the Castletown river, which suddenly expands as it opens into the bay of Dundalk; and consists of two principal streets, each about a mile in length, intersecting each other in the market-square, and of several smaller streets. The number of houses, in 1831, was 1851, of which many are well built. The streets are paved, and the town is watched and lighted with gas, under the provisions of an act of the 9th of Geo. IV., cap. 82, by which it was assessed, in 1836, to the amount of £696. 8. 11. The southern entrance has been greatly improved by the recent erection of some handsome houses. At the northern extremity is a bridge over the Castletown river, connecting it with a small suburb on the opposite side. At the eastern extremity, near the bay, is a spacious cavalry barrack; and along the borders of the river are some lands called the town parks. A literary society has been established, and there are two subscription news-rooms, and a good assembly-room; a hunt is supported, and races are occasionally held on a course near the town. There is a very extensive distillery, employing about 100 men, consuming from 35,000 to 40,000 barrels of grain, and producing more than 300,000 gallons of whiskey annually, which is mostly for home consumption and of superior quality; there are four tanyards, two salt-works, a large malting concern, and a very extensive iron foundry and forge. The chief trade is in agricultural produce, which is shipped in great quantities to Liverpool and other British ports; its foreign trade is not inconsiderable. The exports are grain of all kinds, flour, meal, malt, butter, cattle, sheep, pigs, barrelled provisions, linen, and flax; the imports are coal, bark, soap, oil, tallow, hemp, grocery, rock-salt, and iron from British ports, and timber, tallow, wine, and bark from foreign ports. Since the introduction of steam navigation great quantities of eggs and poultry have been exported. The amount of duties paid at the Custom-house, for 1835, was £3618. 4. 10., and for 1836, £4514. 5. 10.; the excise duties paid for the district, in 1835, amounted to £112,189. 18. 7½. Two steam-packets of the first class are constantly employed between this port and Liverpool; the passage on the average is made in 16 or 17 hours. The harbour is formed by the innermost recesses of the bay, which is seven miles across at its mouth from Dunany Point to Cooley Point, and extends nearly the same distance to the town. It is very safe, and the bay affords good anchorage in from four to eight fathoms of water. There are some good bathing-places along the shore, particularly at the village of Blackrock. Two mails from the north and south of Ireland pass daily through the town. The market is on Monday; and fairs are held on the Monday next but one before Ash-Wednesday, May 17th, the first Monday in July, the last Monday in August, and the second Mondays in October and December; but the May fair is the only one of importance. At Soldiers' Point, about a mile and a half below the town, is a coast-guard station, the head of the district of Dundalk, and the residence of the inspecting commander; the district contains also the stations of Greenore, O'Meath, Cooley Point, Dunany Point, and Clogher Head.

Since the confirmation of its privileges by Rich. II., the town has received various charters from succeeding sovereigns; it is now governed by that of Chas. II., under which the corporation consists of a bailiff, 16 burgesses, and an indefinite number of freemen, assisted by a recorder, town-clerk, two town-serjeants, and other officers. The bailiff, who is also a justice of the peace, is annually elected from the burgesses by a majority of that body, and with their consent may appoint a deputy to serve the office. The burgesses, as vacancies occur are chosen from the freemen, and the freemen are elected by the corporation; the recorder and town-clerk are chosen by the corporation, and the town-serjeants by the bailiff. The borough first returned members to parliament in 1374, and continued to send two to the Irish parliament till the Union, since which period it has returned one member to the Imperial parliament. The right of election, previously limited to the corporation, was by the 2nd of Wm. IV., cap. 88, vested in the resident freemen and £10 householders; the number of registered voters at the last general election was 376; the bailiff is the returning officer. A new boundary has been drawn round the town, comprising an area of 445 statute acres, the limits of which are minutely described in the Appendix. The borough court of record, formerly held before the bailiff and recorder, has not issued any process since 1779, and may be regarded as extinct. Petty sessions are held before the bailiff daily, and by the county magistrates every Thursday. The guild-hall, which, together with nearly all the land on which the town is built, belongs to Lord Roden, is a neat edifice of brick, situated in the market-square, and containing an assembly-room, a news-room, offices for the savings' bank, an office for the sub-inspector of police, and other apartments for the transaction of municipal business and for holding public meetings. A chief constabulary police station has been established in the town, which is the residence of the sub-inspector for the county, and the head-quarters of the police force. The assizes for the county are held here, and the quarter sessions for the Dundalk division twice in the year. The court-house is a handsome modern edifice of hewn stone, with a very fine portico, after the model of that of the temple of Theseus at Athens; it is situated in the centre of the town, contains two spacious and well-arranged courts, with every requisite accommodation for the grand jury and public officers, and has a communication in the rear with the county gaol, which was erected in 1820, and is well adapted to the classification of prisoners, who are employed in breaking stones and working at their different trades; it contains a chapel, a school, and an hospital, and is kept under proper regulations; there is a treadmill, which distributes water to every part of the prison.

The parish comprises, according to the Ordnance survey, 6202 statute acres, of which 25¾ are part of Castletown river; the soil is fertile and the land in a good state of cultivation. To the west of the town is Dundalk House, the seat of the Earl of Roden, an ancient mansion situated in a well-cultivated and richly planted demesne, comprising 274 Irish acres; his lordship has it in contemplation to erect a house in a more eligible situation immediately adjoining. Fair Hill, the handsome residence of Mrs. Foster, and Lisnawilly, of Mrs. Tipping, are also in the parish. The living is a vicarage, in the diocese of Armagh, episcopally united to the rectory and vicarage of Castletown, forming the union of Dundalk, in the patronage of the Lord-Primate and the Earl of Roden, who is impropriator of the rectory. The tithes amount to £527. 9. 10., payable to the impropriator, who allows the incumbent £16, in lieu of the vicarial tithes; the tithes of the union, payable to the incumbent, amount to £216. 6. 5¼. The glebe-house was built in 1773; the glebe comprises 19½ acres. The church is a spacious and, internally, elegant cruciform structure, with a double transept; it has been frequently enlarged and improved at a very considerable expense. In the R. C. divisions the parish is the head of a union or district, comprising the parishes of Dundalk, Castletown, and Kene; a handsome chapel of hewn granite is now in progress of erection in the town, and there is also a chapel near Killen, in the parish of Kene. There is a meeting-house for Presbyterians in connection with the Synod of Ulster, of the third class; also places of worship for Wesleyan and Primitive Methodists, and Independents. Nearly 600 children are educated in the public schools of the parish: of these, the principal are the endowed classical school, to which the sons of freemen are eligible on payment of £2. 2. per ann.; the Dundalk institution, under the patronage of the Incorporated Society, in which 30 boys are received on the foundation free of all expense, 50 boarders at £12, and 20 day scholars at £1. 10. per ann.; and all are instructed in this excellent institution in every branch of useful education, except the classics; and a school on Erasmus Smith's foundation, comprehending departments for infants, for general education, and for needlework. The building cost upwards of £1700, of which £750 was given by the trustees of E. Smith's charities, who also pay the master and mistress £30 per annum each; the other expenses are defrayed by charity sermons and subscriptions. There are two others, of which one for girls is supported by Mrs. Tipping. There are also 15 private schools, affording instruction to about 500 children. The Louth Infirmary, or County hospital, with which is connected a dispensary, was built by subscription in 1835, on ground given by the Earl of Roden at a nominal rent; it is a handsome structure, in the later English style, erected at an expense of £3000, and comprising three wards for male, and three for female patients, with hot and cold baths, convalescent galleries for patients (of whom it is capable of containing forty), and every accommodation for the officers and attendants; about 4000 patients receive advice and medicine annually. The Fever Hospital, a large building, formerly the charter school, is now a pin-factory, in which 300 children, selected from the two great schools for the poor, are beneficially employed; an hour each day is allotted for their instruction at the respective schools. A Ladies' Benevolent Society, for selling clothing to the poor at reduced prices, is supported by subscription; as are also the Mendicity Association, the Destitute Sick Society, a Savings' Bank, an Association for Discountenancing Vice, and several other charitable institutions. There are some remains of the Franciscan friary on the east side of the town, consisting of the tower, a lofty square pile surmounted by a slender turret commanding an extensive prospect. After the dissolution it was granted by Hen. VIII. to James Brandon, at a rent of sixpence per annum, and a renewal fine of £9. 10. Of the religious establishment founded by Bertram de Verdon, there are no remains; its revenues were granted by Elizabeth to

Henry Draycot, who had previously obtained a lease for 21 years. Near the town is a spring, arched over with ancient massive masonry, called the Lady Well, and much resorted to on the patron day, Sept. 29th. On the plains of Ballynahatna are the remains of a Druidical temple partly enclosed by a curving rampart, on the outside of which is part of a circle of upright stones; and on a rising ground near this place is a circular fort surrounded by a double fosse and rampart, supposed to have been thrown up by the earliest inhabitants of the country. Dundalk formerly gave the title of Baron to the family of Georges.

DUNDERMOT, a grange, in the barony of KILCONWAY, county of ANTRIM, and province of ULSTER, on the Ravel water; containing 1069 inhabitants. It comprises, according to the Ordnance survey, 3003¾ statute acres: the tithes, which are impropriate, amount to £65. There is a meeting-house for Presbyterians of the Seceding Synod in connection with that at Ahoghill. Near the Ballymena road is a Danish fort or mound of an oval form, 60 feet by 30, the summit of which is level, and the base surrounded by a deep fosse and counterscarp: towards the bridge over the Ravel two parallel branches from the fosse enclose another area of a quadrangular form, now called "the parade."

DUNDERROW, a parish, partly in the county of the city of CORK, partly in the barony of KINSALE, partly in that of KINNALEA, but chiefly in the barony of EAST MUSKERRY, county of CORK, and province of MUNSTER, 4 miles (W. by N.) from Kinsale, on the road to Bandon; containing 2498 inhabitants. This parish comprises 6371¼ statute acres, as applotted under the tithe act, and valued at £4167 per annum; about 800 acres are bog and mountain, and 971¼ waste; the remainder is good land, the greater portion being arable. It consists of several detached portions, and has consequently a great variety of surface and soil; Dunderrow proper is generally composed of a light soil, which is very well cultivated, and produces abundant crops. A new line of road is in progress through the parish, leading from Kinsale to Bandon. In the Bandon river, which bounds it on the south, are several salmon weirs. The principal residences are Leoffney House, that of E. Gillman, Esq.; Killaney, of T. Markham, Esq.; Ballyvrin, of W. Dorman, Esq.; Dunderrow Cottage, of the Rev. R. Halburd; Ballinphilleck, of W. Barter, Esq.; Corron, of J. Horneybrooke, Esq.; Gortnaclough, of W. Beasley, Esq.; Hop Island, of G. Edwards, Esq.; and the glebe-house, of the Rev. M. O'Donovan: besides several good houses belonging to respectable farmers. The living is a rectory, in the diocese of Cork, and in the patronage of T. C. Kearney, Esq., of Garretstown: the tithes amount to £525, of which £150 is payable to the dean and chapter of St. Finbarr's, Cork, and the remainder to the rector. The glebe-house was built by aid of a gift of £250 and a loan of £550, from the late Board of First Fruits, in 1821: the glebe comprises 24*a.* 3*r.* 27*p.* The church, a small handsome edifice, with a lofty square tower, was erected by aid of a loan of £500, in 1812, from the same Board. In the churchyard is a handsome pyramidal monument of marble, erected over the remains of an English lady, who died at Kinsale while on a tour through Ireland. In the R. C. divisions the parish forms the union or district of Kinsale, but the detached portions belong to the several parishes by which they are surrounded: the chapel is at Ballynamona. The parochial school, situated at Leoffney, is jointly supported by Capt. Herrick and the rector; and there is a daily pay school at Ballynamona. About 100 boys and 40 girls are educated in a private school; and a Sunday school is chiefly maintained by the Rev. Robert Halburd. The doon, from which the parish derives its name, has been partly removed: the queen's forces secured themselves upon it in 1601, prior to the siege of Kinsale, when the Spanish forces were in possession.

DUNDONALD, a parish, in the barony of LOWER CASTLEREAGH, county of DOWN, and province of ULSTER, 4 miles (E.) from Belfast, on the mail coach road to Newtown-Ardes; containing 1669 inhabitants. This parish, which is called also Kirkdonald, comprises, according to the Ordnance survey, 4635 statute acres of fertile land, principally under tillage and in a high state of cultivation. Every improvement in the mode of tillage and the construction of farming implements has been eagerly adopted; there is neither bog nor waste land in the parish. The principal seats are Storemont, that of S. Cleveland, Esq.; Summerfield, of R. Gordon, Esq.; Rose Park, of Major Digby; Bessmount, of T. S. Corry, Esq.; and Donleady, of A. McDonnel, Esq. Near the village is an extensive bleach-green, where 5000 pieces of linen are annually finished. The living is a rectory, in the diocese of Down, and in the patronage of S. Cleveland, Esq.; the tithes amount to £205. The glebe-house, a handsome residence, was built in 1820 by a gift of £300 and a loan of £500 from the late Board of First Fruits; the glebe comprises 15½ acres. The church, a small edifice, was rebuilt on the site of a former church in 1771, and a tower was added to it in 1774. In the R. C. divisions the parish forms part of the union of Newtown-Ardes. There is a place of worship for Presbyterians in connection with the Synod of Ulster, of the second class, to the poor of which congregation Mr. John Crane, of London, bequeathed the interest of a sum of money. About 50 children are taught in the parochial school, which is aided by the rector; and there is a private school, in which are about 45 children. A large and handsome school-house has been built and endowed at Church Quarter, by David Gordon, Esq., the principal proprietor of the parish. In the demesne of Summerfield is a chalybeate spring; and close to the church is a large circular fort surrounded by a moat, from which the parish is supposed to derive its name. A little below, in the same ground, is a cave continued to the fort and passing under its base. Near the bleach-green is a conical hill, or rath, contiguous to which, at the mouth of a small rivulet, is a stone pillar 10 feet high. Gilbert Kennedy, a distinguished Presbyterian divine, was interred in the church in 1687.

DUNDONNELL, a parish, in the barony of LOWER CONNELLO, county of LIMERICK, and province of MUNSTER, 1 mile (W.) from Rathkeale, on the river Deel; containing 476 inhabitants. It comprises 1239 statute acres, chiefly in tillage. The land is in general good, being based on a substratum of limestone: the system of agriculture has of late been much improved. Riddlestown, the ancient mansion of Gerald Blennerhasset, Esq., is seated on the banks of the Deel; and in its vicinity is Clonarla, the residence of J. Fitzgerald Massey, Esq. It is a rectory, in the diocese of Limerick, and since 1712, has formed part of the union of Rathkeale, and the corps of the chancellorship of the cathedral of St. Mary, in the gift of the Bishop. The tithes amount to £92. 6. $1\frac{1}{2}$.; and there are 4 acres of glebe. In the R. C. divisions it forms part of the union or district of Coolcappa. There are some remains of the old church; but of the castle of Clonarla, which was taken down some years since, on clearing the site for Mr. Massey's present mansion, a few fragments only remain.

DUNDRUM, a maritime village, in that part of the parish of KILMEGAN which is in the barony of LECALE, county of DOWN, and province of ULSTER, $1\frac{1}{2}$ mile (S.) from Clough, on the road from Newry to Downpatrick: the population is returned with the parish. This place is situated on an inner bay, about $1\frac{1}{2}$ mile long by $\frac{1}{4}$ of a mile broad, at the head of the larger one to which it gives name; and was distinguished for its ancient castle, of which though twice besieged and taken by the lord-deputy, and finally demolished by Cromwell, there are still considerable and very interesting remains. It is said to have been built by Sir John de Courcy for Knights Templars, who kept possession of it till the suppression of their order in 1313, when it was transferred to the Prior of Down. On the dissolution of the monasteries, the castle, with several townlands, was given to Gerald, Earl of Kildare, and subsequently to the Maginnis family, on whose attainder it was forfeited to the Crown and granted to the Earl of Ardglass; it afterwards became the property of Viscount Blundell, from whom it descended to the Marquess of Downshire, its present proprietor. The village, which previously consisted of one narrow street, containing only a few houses very indifferently built, has been recently much improved by the Marquess of Downshire, who has widened the old street and opened several new lines of road, and has promoted the erection of many neat and comfortable dwelling-houses. He has also built a spacious and commodious hotel, hot and cold baths, and adjoining the latter a lodging-house for himself, which is occasionally let to strangers during the summer. The principal trade is the export of grain, for which a small but convenient quay has been constructed by his lordship, who has also built warehouses and stores for grain. Fairs are held on Jan. 3rd, Feb. 5th, May 12th, Aug. 6th, and Oct. 10th. The larger bay, which affords great facilities for bathing, extends from the foot of the mountain of Slieve Donard to St. John's Point, a distance of nine miles, and nearly four miles inland. The ground is mostly clean and the depth moderate; but the bay is exposed to severe gusts of wind from the Mourne mountains; the south and south-east winds send in a heavy sea, and vessels should never remain here unless when the wind is from the north or north-east. The ground immediately outside the larger bay is said to be one of the best fishing grounds in the British seas, affording always in their respective seasons large supplies of excellent haddock, cod, whiting, plaice, sole, and turbot. The western shore is a continued range of sand hills, through which is an inlet deep enough to admit vessels of 50 tons laden with coal, lime, and slate to the quay at the village. In the inlet, during the summer months, there are large shoals of sand eels, to take which several hundreds of the neighbouring peasantry assemble every tide, and provide themselves with an abundant supply for some months. The remains of the castle consist chiefly of a lofty circular tower of more than 30 feet internal diameter, built on the summit of a rock overlooking the bay; the walls and the winding staircase leading to the battlements are nearly perfect, but the roofs and the floors of the several stories have fallen in; and the vault or dungeon, deeply excavated in the rock, is exposed. The tower is surrounded by a deep fosse hewn in the solid rock, and on the east are the remains of two lofty bastions: the walls of the ancient gatehouse are still standing. Dr. Thomas Smith, consecrated Bishop of Limerick in 1695, was a native of this place. —See KILMEGAN.

DUNDRUM, a village, in the parish of TANEY, half-barony of RATHDOWN, county of DUBLIN, and province of LEINSTER, $3\frac{1}{2}$ miles (S.) from Dublin, on the road to Enniskerry; containing 680 inhabitants. This village, in which are a number of very pretty cottages, is pleasantly situated on a sheltered declivity near the base of the fine mountain range that extends along the south side of the county. It is a favourite place of resort for invalids from Dublin, for whom the mildness of its climate and the purity of the air are peculiarly favourable; and is noted for numerous herds of goats, which, browsing among the mountain pastures, afford milk of very excellent quality. An office for the twopenny post from Dublin has been established in the village, in which are a chapel belonging to the R. C. union of Booterstown, a school, and a dispensary. The environs abound with pleasing and strikingly diversified scenery, and are embellished with numerous gentlemen's seats and elegant villas, most of which are situated in tastefully ornamented grounds and command fine views of the bay of Dublin and the country adjacent. Of those in the more immediate neighbourhood the principal are Wickham, the seat of W. Farran, Esq., a handsome residence containing a richly stored museum of natural curiosities; Sweetmount, of W. Nolan, Esq.; Dundrum House, of J. Walshe, Esq.; Churchtown, of W. Corbet, Esq.; Churchtown House, of D. Lynch, Esq.; Sweetmount Villa, of J. Burke, Esq.; and Sweetmount House, of M. Ryan, Esq. The ruins of Dundrum castle consist of one tower covered with ivy.

DUNDRUM, or NEWTOWN-DUNDRUM.—See BALLINTEMPLE, county of TIPPERARY.

DUNEANE, a parish, in the barony of UPPER TOOME, county of ANTRIM, and province of ULSTER, 6 miles (W. N. W.) from Randalstown, on the road from Belfast to Londonderry; containing 6812 inhabitants. This parish is bounded on the west by Lough Beg and the river Bann, and on the south by Lough Neagh, in which, at the distance of half a mile from the shore, is a group called the Three Islands, which are within its limits. It comprises, according to the Ordnance survey, 13,128 statute acres, of which $1628\frac{1}{4}$ are in Lough Neagh, $415\frac{3}{4}$ in Lough Beg, and $29\frac{1}{2}$ in the river Bann. About two-thirds of the land are in a state of good cultivation, one-tenth is bog, and the remainder waste: the soil is fertile and the system of agriculture greatly improved. Basaltic stone is quarried in large quantities for building and for repairing the roads. The principal seats are Reymond Lodge, that of

Earl O'Neill; Moneyglass, of J. Hill, Esq.; St. Helena, of — Reford, Esq.; and Brecart, of Capt. O'Neill. The weaving of calico and union cloths, and also of fine linen, is carried on extensively. The living is a vicarage, in the diocese of Connor, united from time immemorial to the rectory of Cranfield, and in the patronage of the Marquess of Donegal; the rectory is impropriate in W. Cranston, Esq., of Belfast. The vicarial tithes, as returned by the Ecclesiastical Commissioners in 1831, amounted to £240, and of the whole union to £270; there is neither glebe nor glebe-house. The church is a small plain edifice, nearly in the centre of the union. The R. C. parish is co-extensive with that of the Established Church; there are chapels at Moneyglass and Cargin, the former built in 1826. There is also a place of worship for Presbyterians in connection with the Synod of Ulster, of the third class. About 840 children are taught in nine public schools, of which the parochial school is aided by donations from the vicar; and there are eight Sunday schools. There are some remains of a circular camp, called Ballydonnelly fort, similar to the Giant's Ring in the county of Down.

DUNFANAGHY, a sea-port and post-town, in the parish of Clondehorky, barony of Kilmacrenan, county of Donegal, and province of Ulster, 32 miles (N. W.) from Lifford, and 137¼ (N. N. W.) from Dublin; containing 464 inhabitants. It is situated on the bay of Sheephaven, and consists of one street, containing 85 houses; the inlet from Sheephaven forms a commodious bay, which takes its name from this place, and affords good anchorage to vessels of the largest burden, which find better shelter here than in Sheephaven, from the latter being too much exposed to the north and north-east winds. This place is the head of a coast-guard district, comprising also the stations of Rutland, Guidore, Innisboffin, Sheephaven, Mulroy, Rathmullen, and Knockadoon; and including a force of 7 officers and 53 men, under a resident inspecting commander. Fairs are held on the Thursday after Whit-Sunday, Aug. 5th, Oct. 2nd, and Nov. 17th. A constabulary police force is stationed in the town, and petty sessions are held every Friday. Nearly adjoining it, on the west, is a very extensive rabbit warren; and the neighbourhood is rich in mineral productions. The surrounding district, called Cloghanealy, consists chiefly of mountainous elevations covered with very indifferent herbage; and among its geological features are hills of sand and rocks of granite and crystal, rising to a great height. A commodious school-house has been built in the town, and there is also a dispensary.

DUNFEENY, or DOONFENEY, a parish, in the barony of Tyrawley, county of Mayo, and province of Connaught, 9 miles (N. W.) from Killala; containing 4110 inhabitants. This parish is situated upon the new line of road from Killala to Belmullet, now in progress through the mountains, and upon Bantraher bay. It comprises a large tract of bog; and limestone, freestone, slate, and copper are found here. The seats are Mount Glynne, the residence of J. Faussett, Esq.; Gross Lodge, of R. Faussett, Esq.; and Glynne Castle, of Mrs. Watts. It is a vicarage, in the diocese of Killala, forming part of the union of Kilbride; the rectory is appropriate to the deanery and precentorship of Killala. The tithes amount to £300, half of which is paid to the dean and precentor, and the rest to the vicar. There is a good glebe-house, and a glebe of 19½ acres. The church is a large building in good repair, erected by aid of a loan of £830, in 1810, from the late Board of First Fruits. The R. C. union is co-extensive with that of the Established Church; there is a chapel at Ballycastle, and another at Belderig. There are four public schools, one of which is aided by an annual donation from Mr. Knox, and in which about 450 children are educated; and four private schools, in which are about 70 children.

DUNFERT.—See DANESFORT.

DUNFORT, or DUNFORTH, a parish, in the barony of Carbery, county of Kildare, and province of Leinster, 5 miles (W.) from Kilcock, on the road from Enfield to Naas; containing 900 inhabitants. The land is of superior quality for grazing cattle, to which purpose it is almost exclusively devoted. A portion of the bog of Allen extends into the parish. The seats are Dunforth House, the residence of Sir F. Macdonald; Mulgeeth, of E. Ruthven, Esq., M. P.; and Metcalfe Park, of F. Metcalfe, Esq. It is a rectory, in the diocese of Kildare, entirely impropriate in the Marquess of Downshire: the tithes amount to £101. 1. 10. The clerical duties are performed by the incumbent of Carbery. In the R. C. divisions this parish forms part of the union or district of Carbery: the chapel is a plain building. At Kilshanroe is a school of about 60 children, supported by subscription. There are some remains of the old church.

Seal.

DUNGANNON, a borough, market and post-town, in the parish of Drumglass, barony of Dungannon, county of Tyrone, and province of Ulster, 10 miles (N. by W.) from Armagh, and 76 (N. N.W.) from Dublin, on the road from Armagh to Coleraine; containing 3515 inhabitants. This place appears to have been the chief seat of the O'Nials from the earliest period of Irish history; but the first direct notice of it, under its present name, is in a spirited letter addressed in 1329 to Pope John, from Dungannon, by Donald O'Nial, in which he styles himself "King of Ulster and true heir of the whole dominion of Ireland." He declares that, previously to the coming of St. Patrick, 130 of his royal ancestors had been kings of Ireland; and that from that period till the landing of Hen. II., in 1172, "sixty monarchs of the same princely family had swayed the Hibernian sceptre." In 1364, O'Nial, in his letters to Edw. III., styles himself "Prince of the Irishry in Ulster," and dated from this place, whence, in 1394, he went to make his submission to Rich. II. at Drogheda. Henry O'Nial gave a splendid entertainment here to the Primate Bole, and assigned to the church of Armagh all his lands in Moydoyn; and in 1489 Con O'Nial founded a Franciscan monastery, which he amply endowed. This establishment continued to flourish till the Reformation, when it was granted by Queen Elizabeth to the Earl of Westmeath, and it was subsequently assigned to Sir Arthur Chichester in the reign of Jas. I. In 1492, Con O'Nial, the founder, being murdered by his brother Henry, was buried in this monastery with great pomp;

and Neal McArt O'Nial rising in arms to avenge his death, the Earl of Kildare marched into Ulster to oppose him, took the fortress of Dungannon by storm, and soon reduced O'Nial to obedience. In 1501, the Albanian Scots attacked the fortress on St. Patrick's day, but were driven back with great slaughter by O'Nial, who then held it for the English government. In 1517, O'Nial was found again in rebellion against the English, but the Earl of Kildare having reduced Dundrum and taken Maginnis prisoner, marched against Dungannon, stormed the fort and burnt the town, both of which were restored by O'Nial after his submission. Con O'Nial, in 1538, took up arms against Henry VIII., in favour of the see of Rome, marched from this place with a powerful army into the English pale, and laid waste the country as far as Meath, where he was met by the Lord-Deputy Grey, who defeated him at Bellahoe, and compelled him again to retreat to his strong hold of Dungannon; he soon after submitted to the English authority, and in 1542 took the oaths of allegiance. After this battle Henry assumed the title of King, instead of Lord of Ireland; and O'Nial covenanted to renounce the name of O'Nial, to adopt the English habit and language, and to build houses and farm the lands after the English mode. For this submission he was created Earl of Tyrone, and his illegitimate son Matthew was made Baron of Dungannon, and received the estate of the O'Nials by patent. In 1552, Shane O'Nial, son of the Earl of Tyrone, appeared in arms against his father, and destroyed the fortress of Dungannon, and committed other depredations; but in 1556, Fitzwalter, then lord-deputy, marched against him, expelled him from the territory, and replaced the Earl in his possessions. Shane again revolted in 1559, and in the following year burst into the English pale, but was reduced to submission by the Lord-Deputy Sussex. From Dungannon he proceeded to England, accompanied by his body-guard, consisting of 600 soldiers, who marched through the streets of London, armed with their battle-axes, and dressed in the costume of their country. He was graciously received by Elizabeth, pardoned, and loaded with favours; but shortly after his return to Dungannon, he again appeared in arms, destroyed the city of Armagh with its venerable cathedral and monasteries, and left only a few mud cabins remaining: he also destroyed the city of Derry and laid waste the whole county; but in 1567 he was treacherously murdered in the Scottish camp. Hugh O'Nial, who by the favour of Elizabeth had been raised to the earldom of Tyrone, commenced building a magnificent castle at Dungannon, and imported large quantities of lead for its roof; in 1587 he obtained from Elizabeth the grant of a weekly market and fairs, and in 1591 the lordship of Tyrone was formed into a county, subdivided into eight baronies, and this place made the county town and a gaol built in it accordingly. In 1595, the Earl of Tyrone rebelled against the English government, and, placing himself at the head of 14,000 men, took and destroyed several forts, burnt Portmore bridge, laid siege to Monaghan, and having melted into bullets the lead which he had imported under pretence of roofing his castle, ultimately made himself master of the whole of that county. Having defeated the English in many engagements, particularly at Benburb, he was universally hailed as the champion of Ireland, and received in his fortress here the envoy of the Pope, who brought him valuable presents. The Lord-Deputy Mountjoy marched against this powerful chieftain and defeated him in several battles; and in June 1602, having secured Armagh and Charlemont, advanced towards Dungannon. Tyrone, aware of his approach, set fire to the place and retreated northward; but being thus driven from the venerable seat of his ancestors, he never regained his lost power. In the following year he made his submission at Mellifont and was pardoned; he was restored to his earldom, and obtained a grant of his lands by letters patent; but meditating new designs against the state, he was discovered, and dreading the power of Jas. I., fled to the Continent in 1607, leaving the whole of his extensive possessions to the king, who, in 1610, granted the castle and manor of Dungannon, with all their dependencies, to Sir Arthur Chichester. In 1612, Sir Arthur obtained from the king a charter of incorporation for the town which he was about to build, a grant of 1140 acres of land, and of 500 acres more for the site of the intended town; upon the former he built a bawn of limestone, 120 feet square, with bulwarks and a deep fosse; and upon the latter, previously to 1619, six large stone houses, six strong houses of frame-work timber, and a spacious church, which, with the exception of the roof, was completed at that time, whence may be dated the origin of the present town. On the breaking out of the war in 1641, Sir Phelim O'Nial, having taken the fort of Charlemont by stratagem, and made the governor prisoner, seized the castle, town, and fort of Dungannon on the same night; and having put many of the inhabitants to death, kept possession of it till after the battle of Benburb, in 1646, after which the town and church were burnt, and soon after the castle was dismantled by order of the parliament. The castle was rebuilt soon after the Restoration, and in 1688 the Rev. George Walker, rector of Donaghmore, raised a regiment in his parish and marched with it to Dungannon, to secure that garrison for the Protestants; it was entrusted to the care of Col. Lundy, who deserted his post on the 13th of March, and the inhabitants fled to Strabane. It was garrisoned in 1689 by the troops of Jas. II., who, on the 13th of April, in that year, visited this town and inspected the garrison, whence he marched to Omagh and Strabane; but his forces occupied the town and neighbourhood during the whole of that important struggle. From this period the only event of historical importance connected with the place is the meeting of delegates from 269 corps of Ulster volunteers, who, in 1782, assembled at Dungannon, and passed 20 resolutions, declaratory of the independence of the parliament of Ireland.

The town, situated about three miles from the south shore of Lough Neagh, is spacious, handsome, and well built; and consists of a square, and four principal and several smaller streets. Improvements upon a very extensive scale have been recently made, and are still in progress; handsome houses have been built within and around the town, several lines of road have been constructed, and gas-works are now being erected for lighting it. The surrounding country is richly diversified, and the situation of the town on a lofty hill of limestone, commanding interesting and extensive prospects on every side, renders it both a healthy and a pleasant place of residence. It is second only to Omagh in extent, and is rapidly increasing in opulence and importance. News-rooms are supported by subscription, and assemblies are held occasionally. At a short distance to the east is Northland Lodge, the seat of the Earl of Ranfurley, and in the immediate neighbourhood are many gentlemen's seats, which are noticed in the account of the parish. The principal trade of the town and neighbourhood is the manufacture and bleaching of linen, for which it has long been celebrated; there are several bleach-greens on a large scale, all in full operation; the manufacture of earthenware and fire-bricks, for which there are large potteries within three miles of the town, is extensive: there is a large distillery, which annually consumes 29,000 barrels of grain, and not far from it are some extensive flour-mills. A flourishing trade is also carried on in wheat, flax, oats, and barley. The Drumglass collieries, one mile distant, are the most extensive, in the North of Ireland; they were formerly worked without much success, but are now conducted by the Hibernian Mining Company and have been rendered productive of great benefit to the town and neighbourhood; the coal is of good quality and is procured in great abundance; the demand is ample, and the prices moderate from the competition of English and Scottish coal, which are brought hither by the Lagan and Newry navigations and by Lough Neagh. There are also iron-works, and some extensive lime-works near the town. The markets, originally granted in 1587, by Queen Elizabeth, to Hugh O'Nial, Earl of Tyrone, and in 1612 by Jas. I., to Sir Arthur Chichester, are held on Tuesday and Thursday; the former for grain, and the latter for brown linen, yarn, cattle, pigs, and provisions of all kinds, with all of which it is very extensively supplied. Fairs, granted in 1611 by Jas. I. to Sir Arthur Chichester, and in 1705 to T. Knox, Esq., are held on the first Thursday in every month. The market-house, shambles, grain stores, and provision sheds are commodious and well adapted to their use. A chief constabulary police station has been established in the town, which is the head-quarters of the constabulary police force of Ulster, for whose accommodation a police barrack has been built. The inhabitants under the title of the "Provost, Free Burgesses, and Commons of the borough of Dungannon," received a charter of incorporation from Jas. I., in 1612, by which the site of the town, with three parcels of land called Crosse, Brough, and Ferneskeile, (with the exception of the castle, and a space of 500 feet around it, in every direction, from its walls), was created a free borough, and the corporation made to consist of a portreeve, twelve free burgesses, and commonalty. The portreeve is chosen annually, and has power to hold a court every Friday for the recovery of debts not exceeding five marks, but this court has not been established. The charter also conferred the right of returning two members to the Irish parliament, which was exercised till the Union, since which period it has returned one member to the Imperial parliament. The right of election, formerly in the portreeve and burgesses, has, by the 2nd of Wm. IV., cap. 88, been vested in the resident freemen and £10 householders. The liberties of the borough comprised the whole of the townlands of Drumcoo and Ranaghan, a considerable portion of the townland of Gortmenon, and three small pieces in three other townlands, comprising together about 836 statute acres; but not being connected with the elective franchise, a narrower boundary has been drawn round the town, containing 224 statute acres, of which the limits are minutely described in the Appendix. In 1836 the number of registered voters was 197, consisting of 11 free burgesses and 186 £10 householders: the portreeve is the returning officer. A court for the manor of Dungannon, granted in 1621 by Jas. I. to Arthur, Lord Chichester, and now the property of the Earl of Ranfurley, is held once in three weeks, and has jurisdiction to the amount of £20 extending over 40 townlands. General sessions of the peace for the division of Dungannon, which comprises the baronies of Dungannon and Clogher, are held here and at Clogher, alternately, twice in the year; and petty sessions are also held once a fortnight before the county magistrates. The court-house is a spacious and handsome building, erected in 1830; under it is the bridewell, containing a day-room and four large cells for male prisoners, with a yard, day-room, and cells for female prisoners; the same accommodation for debtors, and apartments for the keeper.

The church of the parish of Drumglass having been destroyed in the wars during the reign of Elizabeth, a new church was erected by Sir Arthur Chichester in the town of Dungannon, in 1619. This building, which was nearly destroyed in the war of 1641, was restored in 1672, and was rebuilt in 1699, since which time it has been considerably enlarged, and is now a handsome edifice with a lofty octagonal spire. There is a R. C. chapel in the town, also places of worship for Presbyterians in connection with the Synod of Ulster and the Seceding Synod, and for Wesleyan Methodists. The free grammar school, or Royal College, was founded by letters patent of Chas. I., in 1628, which gave in trust to the Primate of Armagh and his successors six townlands in the parish of Clonoe, for the support of a school at Mountjoy, in that parish; but this place being only a garrison, the school was, after many years, removed to Dungannon, and the first account we find of it is in 1726, nearly a century after its foundation, when it was held in a lane near High-street, where it continued till 1786, when the present college was erected by order of Primate Robinson, who a few years before had erected the college of Armagh. The building comprises a centre and two deeply receding wings, erected at an expense of £4626. 8. 2., of which £2000 was given from the Primate's private purse. It is situated on a gentle eminence on the east side of the town, on grounds comprising 9 acres purchased by Primate Robinson and given to the school. The establishment is conducted by a principal and three classical assistants, two English masters, and drawing, French, and music masters, and is adapted for 100 pupils; the masters take private boarders and day scholars; at present there are no scholars on the foundation. The lands with which it is endowed comprise 3900 acres, producing a rental of £1430, and are under the management of the Commissioners of Education, who, in their report for 1834, state that "considerable improvement has been effected in the condition of the tenantry and appearance of their farms;" and there is every prospect that the rental will be nearly doubled in a few years. The principal, who is appointed by the Lord-Primate, has a salary of £500 per annum and £100 for assistants; £400 per ann. was appropriated, in 1834, to the founding of ten exhibitions in Trinity

College, Dublin, 5 of £50 and 5 of £30 per annum, tenable for 5 years by boys from this school, under the appellation of King's scholars. A school for boys and girls has also been established here by the trustees of Erasmus Smith's charity; it is situated near the court-house, and is capacious and handsome. There are also two other schools, and an infants' school, supported by subscription. There is a dispensary; and a Mendicity Society is supported by subscription. Of the castle and fortress of the Earl of Tyrone not a vestige is remaining; nor are there any traces of the castle and bawn erected by Sir Arthur Chichester. The monastery, founded by Con O'Nial, was situated near the site of the present distillery; some fragments were remaining a few years since, but every vestige has now disappeared. Dungannon gives the title of Viscount to the family of Trevor, of Brynkinalt, near Chirk, in the county of Denbigh.

DUNGANSTOWN, a parish, in the barony of Arklow, county of Wicklow, and province of Leinster, 4 miles (S. by W.) from Wicklow, on the road to Arklow; containing 3135 inhabitants. This parish, which is called also Ennisboheen, is bounded on the east by the Irish sea, and comprises 10,322 statute acres, as applotted under the tithe act, of which about three-fourths are meadow and pasture, furnishing some of the finest butter for the Dublin market, and the remainder under tillage. The soil is fertile, and the system of agriculture in the highest state of improvement; there is an adequate proportion of bog, and a quarry of good slate, which, though bordering on the sea, is not worked for want of a convenient landing-place. The surrounding scenery is pleasingly diversified, embracing extensive mountain and sea views, and the neighbourhood is enlivened with several gentlemen's seats and villas, of which the principal are West Aston, the residence of Lieut.-Col. Acton; Oatlands, of W. Shepard, Esq.; Sheep hill, of J. Shepard, Esq.; Sea Park, of J. Revell, Esq.; Ballymoney, of W. Revell, Esq.; Ballinclare, of Capt. T. Keoghoe; and Springfield, of J. Wright, Esq. Of Dunganstown Castle, the property of the coheiresses of the late F. Hoey, Esq., and now in the occupation of M. Wright, Esq., the only remains are one square tower and an extensive range of domestic buildings, partially covered with ivy. There is an extensive nursery, belonging to Messrs. Hodgens, in which are many choice plants. A ladies' association for employing the female poor in spinning, knitting, and making nets has been established. At Jack's Hole is a coast-guard station, one of the seven constituting the district of Gorey. Seven townlands have been separated from this parish to form the new parish of Redcross. The living is a rectory, in the diocese of Dublin and Glendalough, and in the patronage of the Archbishop of Dublin: the tithes amount to £700; the glebe-house is a handsome residence, and the glebe comprises 20 acres of arable land. The church, a neat plain structure, was enlarged in 1821 by a loan of £400 from the late Board of First Fruits, and the Ecclesiastical Commissioners have lately granted £200 for its repair. In the R. C. divisions this parish is the head of a union, called Kilbride, comprising also part of the parishes of Templemichael and Castlemacadam; there are chapels at Ballymurn, and Barryderry. About 190 children are taught in four public schools, one of which is supported by Lieut.-Col. Acton; and another, for which a building was erected by subscription amounting to £182, aided by £100 from the parliamentary fund, is supported by subscription. There are three private schools, in which are about 100 children; and a dispensary. A loan fund has been established, and a house is rented for the poor, who receive also the interest of two legacies of £100 each, bequeathed by Miss De Stournelles and Mrs. Frost, together producing £6. 13. 6. annually. There are several raths, and the remains of an extensive fortification, on the hill above which a shaft was sunk for copper, which was discovered, but not in sufficient quantity to work profitably. At Castletimon and Ennisboheen are remains of old churches, with burial-places; the Society of Friends have a burying-ground at Ballymurton; and on the farm of Ballincarrig several stone graves with skeletons were found a few years since.

DUNGARVAN, a parish, in the barony of Gowran, county of Kilkenny, and province of Leinster, 3 miles (S.) from Gowran, on the road from Dublin to Waterford; containing 1784 inhabitants, of which number, 75 are in the hamlet. The parish comprises 9134 statute acres, as applotted under the tithe act, and is a constabulary police station. The living is a vicarage, in the diocese of Ossory, and in the patronage of the Crown; the rectory is impropriate in J. Hamilton Bunbury, Esq. The tithes amount to £480, of which £320 is paid to the impropriator and £160 to the vicar. The glebe-house was erected in 1813, by aid of a gift of £400 and a loan of £400 from the late Board of First Fruits: there is a glebe of 15 acres. The church is a small plain building, erected by aid of a gift of £800, in 1812, from the same Board, and lately repaired by the Ecclesiastical Commissioners, at an expense of £283. In the R. C. divisions this parish forms part of the union or district of Gowran, and contains a chapel. The parish school is supported by the incumbent, and there are three pay schools, in which about 300 children are instructed. Here is a very large moat, also the ruins of a square castle at Neiglam.

DUNGARVAN, a sea-port, borough, market and post-town, and a parish, in the barony of Decies-without-Drum, county of Waterford, and province of Munster, 22 miles (S. W. by W.) from Waterford, and 97¾ miles (S. W. by S.) from Dublin, on the road from Waterford to Cork; containing 12,450 inhabitants, of which number, 8386 are in the town and borough. This place, formerly called *Achad-Garvan*, of the same import as its present appellation *Dun-Garvan*, derived that name from St. Garvan, who in the 7th century founded an abbey here for canons regular of the order of St. Augustine, of which there are no vestiges. Raymond le Gros, one of the earliest English adventurers, in 1174, brought hither the plunder he had taken in Offaly and Lismore, which he put on board some vessels he found lying at anchor; but, being detained by contrary winds, was attacked by the men of Cork, whom he repulsed with the loss of eight of their vessels, with which he sailed away in triumph. Soon afterwards the town, which then formed the frontier barrier of the dependencies of Waterford, was, together with other territories, totally surrendered to Hen. II. by Roderic, Sovereign of all Ireland; and a castle was erected for its defence by King John, who is also supposed to have surrounded the town with a wall strengthened with towers. The same monarch granted the custody of the castle, and of the territories of Waterford and Desmond, to Thomas Fitz-Anthony, at a yearly rent of 250 marks, but retained the fee in the Crown; during the minority of Edw. I., it was granted to John Fitz-Thomas at a yearly rent of 500 marks, but was subsequently recovered by Edward in a judgment against Thomas Fitz-Maurice, his cousin and heir, and in 1292 given to Thomas Fitz-Anthony. In 1447, the castle, honour, lands, and barony of Dungarvan, together with other extensive territories, were granted to John Talbot, Earl of Shrewsbury; but the unsettled state of affairs during that period prevented the improvement of the town either in extent or importance. In 1463, an act was passed at Wexford, setting forth that, "whereas the lordship of Dungarvan was of old the greatest ancient honour belonging to the King in Ireland, and that by war and trouble, and want of English governance, it is for the most part totally destroyed; for the relief and succour whereof it is ordained that the portreeve and commonalty, their heirs and successors, may have and enjoy all manner of free grants, liberties, privileges, and customs as the tenants and inhabitants of the honourable honour of Clare in England enjoyed, with a further power to take customs of all kinds of merchandise bought and sold within the franchises, as the mayor and commons of Bristol did, to be yearly expended on the walls and other defences of the town, under the inspection of the Hon. Sir Thomas, Earl of Desmond, and his heirs." By another statute of the same parliament, the entire fee farm of the town was granted to the said Earl during his life. In the 4th of Hen. VIII., an act was passed confirming the castle and all its dependencies to the Crown; but in the 26th of this reign the manor was granted to Sir Pierce Butler, who was likewise created Earl of Ossory, and appointed seneschal, constable, and governor of the castle and manor of Dungarvan, into which the Earl of Desmond had forcibly intruded. In the reign of Edw. VI., Robert St. Leger, brother to the Lord-Deputy St. Leger, was confirmed in the government of the castle, to which he had been appointed in the preceding reign, on condition of keeping a proper ward in it; and other constables for the crown were subsequently appointed with extensive powers and emoluments, to one of whom, Henry Stafford, a commission of martial law, extending over the whole county of Waterford, was directed, in the first year of the reign of Elizabeth. In 1575, the Lord-Deputy, Sir Henry Sidney, came from Waterford to this place, where he was met by the Earl of Desmond, who, with great professions of loyalty, offered his services in reducing the country to obedience; but towards the close of the year 1579, when Sir William Pelham, then Lord-Justice, was at Waterford, the Earl led a large insurgent force to this place, with which the 400 foot and 100 horse, which had been sent against him, were unable to contend. In the 2nd of James I. the manor was granted to Sir George Thornton, but subsequently was with the castle, by act of parliament, vested in the Earl of Cork, from whom it descended to its present proprietor, the Duke of Devonshire. In the 7th of his reign, James, in reward of the loyalty of the inhabitants during the reign of Elizabeth, granted them a new charter of incorporation; but early in the rebellion of 1641, they broke their allegiance, and took part with the King's enemies; in March 1642 the town was, however, taken by the Lord President of Munster, who placed in it a royal garrison, but it was soon after retaken by surprise, and the English inhabitants were plundered. The insurgents, while in occupation of this place, exported merchandise to France, and in return received warlike stores for fortifying the town and castle, of which they kept possession till 1647, when they were taken by Lord Inchiquin with a force of 1500 foot and the same number of horse. The town remained in the possession of the Royalist party till December 1649, when Cromwell, having abandoned the siege of Waterford, advanced to besiege it; after a regular investment and a few days' siege, in the course of which several neighbouring fortresses were taken by detachments from his army, the town surrendered at discretion. It is said that Cromwell ordered all the inhabitants to be put to the sword, but recalled his mandate in consequence of a female drinking to his health as he entered the town, which, with the exception of the castle and the church, he saved from being plundered by his troops. The charter of the inhabitants was renewed by Richard Cromwell in 1659, and in 1689 a new charter was granted by James II., which, on the accession of William, was annulled.

The town, which contains 1570 houses, is situated at the head of a spacious bay to which it gives name, on a peninsula formed by two arms of the bay; and under the auspices of His Grace the Duke of Devonshire has been much improved. It consists of one principal street, called Mulgrave-street, extending from west to east, and dividing in the latter direction into two short branches leading to the mouth of the port; from these several others branch off in various directions towards the line of quays, which extends along the shore. On the south and west are extensive ranges of inferior houses, and on the north is Devonshire-square, from which a handsome street leads to the bridge across the inlet, a massive structure of one arch 75 feet in span, erected at an expense of £50,000 by the Duke of Devonshire, in 1815, and communicating, by a causeway 350 yards in length, with the suburb of Abbeyside, on the main shore. The inhabitants were formerly supplied with water from the small river Phynisk, brought by an aqueduct constructed about the middle of the last century, by aid of a parliamentary grant; this source of supply having been cut off, wells have been sunk in various parts of the town, but the supply of pure water is rather scanty, that of the wells being fit only for culinary purposes. Immediately adjoining the town are fine springs of pure water, which might be conveyed into it at little expense. The barracks for infantry are adapted for four officers and sixty non-commissioned officers and privates. From its favourable and very healthy situation on the coast, this town has become a place of resort for sea-bathing, and hot and cold baths are at present in progress of erection. The fishery on the Nymph bank has always afforded employment to a considerable number of the inhabitants, and the grant of the tonnage bounty tended greatly to its increase. In 1823, 163 boats and about 1100 men were employed in the fishery, and more than 1000 tons of excellent fish were procured for the supply of the surrounding country; the sum granted in bounties (since withdrawn) was £2647; and as the wives and children of the fishermen were engaged in cleaning and salting the fish, the total number of persons that derived employment was not less than 3000. There are at present 80 hookers, of an aggregate burden of 1600 tons, exclusively employed in this trade, which, although it has greatly declined of late years, is now increasing. There are also 93 four-oared row boats engaged in fishing and cutting sea weed; besides 34 coasting vessels belonging to the port, of an aggregate burden of 2800 tons. The aggregate burden of all these is 4720 tons, and the number of men employed in them, 1229, besides whom more than 3000 persons on shore are employed in various capacities in connection with them. At Ballinacourty, on the eastern side of the parish, the property of T. Wyse, Esq., M. P., a pier for the protection of fishing boats was erected in 1832, partly by subscription, and partly by a grant from the late Fishery Board. The trade of the port consists chiefly in the exportation of corn, live stock, butter, and other provisions to the ports of the English channel; and the importation of timber, coal, culm, and the usual foreign supplies. The harbour affords good shelter for vessels drawing from 14 to 15 feet of water at any time of the tide; vessels drawing 18 feet of water may enter at spring tides, but larger ships can enter only at or near high water of spring tides. There are 3 feet at low water in the shallowest part of the channel, and at the quays there is a depth of 14 feet at high water of spring tides, and 10 feet at neap tides. The south-western recesses of the bay are separated from the rest by a bank called Cunnigar Point, between which and the town it is proposed to throw up an embankment for the purpose of reclaiming the inner recesses of the bay. According to a survey made for this purpose by Mr. Kearney, it is proposed to exclude the tides from the back strand, by making a causeway 122 perches in length, with stone walls on each side, from the garden on the east side of the churchyard to Cunnigar bank, with a roadway 22 feet wide, and sufficient openings with sluices at the bottom to discharge the surface and spring water when the tides are out. It is also proposed to cut a canal from the river Brickey, near Two-mile bridge, through the low grounds of Killongford, and along the southern verge of the back strand, for the purpose of discharging into the outer bay the waters of the Brickey, and the streams that flow into it from the hills on the south, and, by constructing a lock at the eastern end of the canal, of continuing the navigation for sand and other boats to Ballyharraghan, Killongford, and Two-mile bridge, as at present; the low parts of the Cunnigar bank, over which the waves are drifted in high tides by strong easterly and south-easterly winds, will be secured by an embankment of dry stone. The estimated expense of carrying these works into effect is £14,621. 9. 9.; and the quantity of land that would be thus reclaimed, 1234 acres, of which, by an additional expenditure of £1500 for draining and enclosing it, 1007 acres would be fit for cultivation. The causeway, among other advantages, would afford a short and easy passage to the fine bathing strand of the Cunnigar, and thus render the town, from the superior accommodation it would afford for sea-bathing, the beautiful scenery in its vicinity, and the excellence of the roads in every direction, the best-frequented watering-place on this part of the coast. Its situation is peculiarly healthy, from the constant current of air blowing or passing near it, caused by the parallelism of two chains of mountains running nearly east and west, and leaving between them a valley in which the town lies considerably protected from the north winds; in consequence, the cases of sickness are very few compared with the population. The market days are Wednesday and Saturday, chiefly for corn and provisions; and fairs are held on Feb. 7th, June 22nd, Aug. 27th, and Nov. 8th. The market-places for the sale of meat and fish were erected at the expense of the Duke of Devonshire. A chief constabulary police station has been established here.

By charter of Jas. I. the parish of St. Mary, and that of Nugent within the ancient liberties, were erected into the Borough of Dungarvan: the corporation consisted of a sovereign and twelve brethren or free burgesses, with a recorder, town-clerk, and three serjeants-at-mace, of whom one was also water-bailiff; and the borough was invested with powers and privileges nearly equal to those of any city or borough in the kingdom, which were exercised for a considerable time, till the corporation at length fell into decay. The bounds of the manor, though irregular and even uncertain, comprise an area of about 10,000 statute acres and a population of 11,858, including nearly the whole of the parish of Dungarvan East and West, together with Kilrush, and the townland of Ballyharraghan in the parish of Ringagonagh; the townlands of Knockampoor, Canty, and Ballymullalla, though entirely detached from the rest of the manor, form also part of it, while several lands much nearer the town and some wholly surrounded by the manor do not belong to it. A seneschal is appointed by the Duke of Devonshire, with power to hold a court every three weeks, for the recovery of small debts. Previously to the Union, the borough returned two members to the Irish parliament, and since that period has sent one member to the Imperial parliament. The elective franchise, vested by the charter of Jas. I. in the sovereign and burgesses, has, since the corporation fell into disuse, been exercised by the inhabitants of the town occupying houses of the yearly rent of £5, and by the freeholders of the manor, the seneschal being the returning officer. The commissioners appointed to settle the boundaries of boroughs proposed a boundary closely encircling the town, and also to raise the household qualification to £10: but a select committee subsequently determined that, as all £5 householders throughout the manor were then entitled to vote, the limits of the franchise should be so far restricted only as to exclude some of its widely detached portions, and to include some small portions of land locally within its limits, though not previously forming any part of it. The total number of electors registered up to 1835 was 620, of whom 30 were freeholders above £10, 300 forty-shilling freeholders, and 200 £10 and 90 £5 householders; about 120 are supposed to have since died. The quarter sessions of the peace for the western division of the county are held here in January, April, and October; and petty sessions are held every Thursday. It is now under the consideration of the privy council to make Dungarvan the assize town, as being in the centre of the county. The county sessions-house is a neat and well arranged building, at the entrance into the town from the bridge; and attached to it is a bridewell, containing ten cells, two day-rooms, and two airing-yards.

The parish is divided by the inlet on which the town is situated into East and West Dungarvan, of which the former comprises the more ancient parishes of Abbeyside and Ballinrode or Nugent's. On the south-east side of the channel the sea has made great encroachments. Limestone and large masses of conglomerate, or pudding-stone, are found in abundance; of the former, considerable quantities are sent in boats from Ballinacourty to Bonmahon, Stradbally, and other places along the coast. The finest view is obtained from the summit of Cushcam, on the north-east, from which are seen the castle of Clonea, the ruins of a church, and a widely extended strand, beyond which are the improvements of Clonkoskoran, and in the distance the town of Dungarvan, with its various towers as if rising from the sea. In the neighbourhood are Ballinacourty, the residence of R. Longan, Esq., commanding a fine view of the harbour and of the bay; Bay View, of R. B. H. Low, Esq.; Duckspool, of J. M. Galwey, Esq.; Tournore, of B. Boate, Esq.; Moonrudh, of the Rev. S. Dickson, vicar of the parish, a modern edifice; and the Hermitage, of W. H. Barron, Esq.; all situated on the south-eastern side of the harbour, and commanding fine marine views. On the opposite side of the bay is the marine villa of the Rt. Hon. H. Villiers Stuart, lieutenant of the county. Clonkoskoran, the seat of Lady Nugent Humble, is beautifully situated among thriving plantations, near the mail coach road from Dungarvan to Waterford, about two miles from the town; Springmount, to the west of the town, is the pleasant residence of T. E. Keily, Esq.; and in the same direction is Coolnagower, the residence of W. Giles, Esq. The living is a vicarage, in the diocese of Lismore, and in the patronage of the Duke of Devonshire, in whom the rectory is impropriate: the tithes amount to £1337. 12. 3., of which £891. 14. 10. is payable to the impropriator, and £445. 17. 5. to the vicar. The glebe comprises about 13 acres and a few houses and gardens in the town. The church is a handsome structure of hewn stone, with a tower, erected in 1831 by a loan of £800 from the late Board of First Fruits, and occupies a site commanding a fine view over the harbour and the bay. In the Roman Catholic divisions the parish is divided into West and East Dungarvan. In the former is the new R. C. chapel, dedicated to the Assumption of the Blessed Virgin: it occupies a commanding site on the south side of the town, given by the Duke of Devonshire, who has also at various times contributed nearly £1500 towards its erection; the remainder of the expense was defrayed by a collection made in London by the Rev. P. Fogarty, and divers other contributions. It is in the later English style of architecture: the roof is finely groined and supported on ranges of lofty and well-proportioned columns; the building is lighted by 14 windows of ample dimensions, and it is intended to open a large east window of stained glass; at the west end will be erected a lofty tower, under which will be the principal entrance, and over it a place has been reserved for an organ; the altar is elaborately grand: this large and handsome chapel has been erected from the designs and under the superintendence of Geo. Payne, Esq., architect, of Cork. In the East division there are two chapels, one at Abbeyside, the other at Ballinroad. Here is a convent of the order of the Presentation, in which are 16 nuns, who employ themselves in the gratuitous instruction of poor female children; and there is a chapel belonging to friars of the order of St. Augustine, the duties of which are performed by two friars, who derive their support from voluntary donations and collections at the chapel gate. A school for boys and another for girls are partly supported by the interest of a bequest of £2000 from the late Pierse Barron, Esq., out of which also the school-house was built. The girls' school is under the superintendence of the ladies of the convent, and the boys' school under that of the "Brethren of the Christian Schools," who have a residence at Shandon, adjoining the town: a branch of the boys' school is held at Shandon school-house. A new school-house has been erected at an expense of £1200, of which £100 was contributed by the Duke of Devonshire, and the remainder was defrayed by its founder, the Very Rev. Dr. Foran, P. P.; it stands on an eminence commanding an extensive and beautiful view, and is a very spacious edifice, capable of conveniently accommodating 800 boys. There is also a school for which a school-house was given by John Odell, Esq., who allows the master a salary of £12. 12. per annum. About 1050 children are educated in the public schools, and 550 in eleven private schools. Here are a fever hospital and a dispensary, towards which the Duke of Devonshire and the Marquess of Waterford contribute largely.

There are some interesting remains of the ancient castle, and of the walls and defences of the town; the former are those of a massive keep in a quadrilateral area, surmounted with a wall defended by a circular tower at each angle, and formerly mounted with cannon; the entrance is by a narrow passage under a tower gateway, flanked by circular bastions, and within the enclosure are the modern barracks. Some of the towers of the town walls are still remaining in connection with modern buildings; and to the west of the town is Cromwell's mount, supposed to have been thrown up by his forces while besieging the town. In the Abbeyside division are the ruins of a lofty square castle, of which nothing more is known than that it was anciently the property of the McGraths. There are no traces of the abbey founded by St. Garvan, but nearly adjacent to the last-named castle are the ruins of a religious house founded in the 13th century for Augustinian friars, probably by the McGraths, who, with the O'Briens of Cummeragh, were its chief benefactors. The remains form an interesting pile; the walls, windows, and arches are still entire: the old conventual church consists of a narrow nave and chancel connected by an arch of elegant design supporting a light and enriched tower, 60 feet high and still in good preservation; the entrance, at the west end, is by a small pointed doorway, and a large east window admits a fine view of the sea; below the window is a tombstone of Donald McGrath, dated 1400; on the foundation of some of the ancient cells the R. C. chapel of Abbeyside has been erected, the bell of which hangs in the old tower, and the walls and entrances of the ancient abbey are preserved in good order. An hospital for lepers, dedicated to St. Bridget, was also founded here, but nothing further has been recorded of it. At Two-mile bridge is a powerful chalybeate spa, which has its origin in the summit of a neighbouring mountain, from a basin containing a considerable portion of iron ore; thence it percolates the earth and, after a course of about four miles, issues out at the foot of the mountain; it has been found to contain, on analysis, as much carbonate of iron as the strongest chalybeate spas of Cheltenham and Leamington. At Shandon are two caves in the limestone rock, one on the sea shore, about 40 feet square, with a long passage leading to inner apartments; the other is in the middle of a plain field, near the river Colligan; in both are stalactites. To the west of the town is a large barrow, surrounded by a fosse. Dungarvan gives the inferior title of Viscount to the Earl of Cork and Orrery.

DUNGIVEN, a market and post-town, and a parish, in the barony of KENAUGHT, county of DERRY, and province of ULSTER, 16 miles (E. S. E.) from Londonderry, and 138¼ (N. N. W.) from Dublin; containing 3565 inhabitants, of which number, 1162 are in the town. This place was a seat of the O'Cahans, and was called *Dun-y-even*, or *Doon-yeven;* and here, on the summit of a rock, on the eastern bank of the Roe, Domnach O'Cahan, or O'Cathan, founded, in 1100, an abbey for Augustinian canons, which, being shortly afterwards polluted by a cruel massacre, lay for a long time in ruins, but was restored with much solemnity by the Archbishop of Armagh, and flourished till the dissolution, after which the lands were granted to the Irish Society, and are now in the possession of the Skinners' Company. It is situated on the road between Londonderry and Dublin, and on the banks of the river Roe; and comprises, according to the Ordnance survey, 30,367½ statute acres, one-third of which is mountain, everywhere affording excellent pasturage. The land around the town is fertile and well cultivated; even the mountain Benbradagh, 1,530 feet above the level of the sea, is chiefly under tillage; and Carntogher, Moneyneiney, Carn, and other mountains, all very high, afford turbary and sufficient pasturage for vast herds of cattle: grouse and other game abound in the higher parts. The town is in a vale, near the junction of the Owen-reagh and the Owen-beg, which descend in nearly parallel lines from Glenfin and Cairnaban, with the Roe, here crossed by a handsome bridge of freestone: it consists of one long street, intersected by two shorter; some of the houses are well built, but the greater number are low and only thatched. Formerly there were four extensive bleach-greens; they are now unemployed, and the manufacture is limited to a small quantity woven by the inhabitants in their own houses. A large market is held every Tuesday; the market-house is extensive, and there are stores for grain, &c.; considerable fairs are held on the second Tuesday in each month, except May and October, when they take place on the 25th. A court for the manor of Pellipar is held in the court-house at Dungiven, every third Thursday, for the recovery of debts under 40*s.*; its jurisdiction extends into the parishes of Dungiven, Banagher, Ballynascreen, and Upper and Lower Cumber. Petty sessions are likewise held monthly in the court-house. Here is a constabulary police station; adjoining the market-house is the barrack store. The gentlemen's residences are Pellipar House, that of R. Ogilby, Esq.; the Cottage, of R. Leslie Ogilby, Esq.; and Roe Lodge, of M. King, Esq.

The living is a vicarage, in the diocese of Derry, and in the patronage of the impropriator, Robert Ogilby, Esq., lessee of the manor of Pellipar under the Skinners' Company, to whom the entire tithes, amounting to £480. 14. 8., are payable; it is usually held in connection with Banagher. The glebe townland of Tirmeal comprises 654*a.* 2*r.* 17*p.*, of which 89 are mountain and bog. The church is a commodious cruciform edifice of hewn freestone, built in 1817 (on the site of a former one erected in 1711), at a cost of £1460, of which £1200 was a loan from the late Board of First Fruits. In the R. C. divisions this parish is the head of a union or district, comprising Dungiven and parts of Banagher and Bovevagh; the chapel is a large building in the town. At Scriggan is a Presbyterian meeting-house, in connection with the Synod of Ulster; and one is in course of erection at Dungiven, in connection with the Seceding Synod. The male and female parochial schools are situated on the glebe of Tirmeal, and are aided by the vicar, who also contributes principally to the support of a school at Gortnacross; a school at Ballymacallion is endowed with an acre of land by the Marquess of Waterford; and in the town are a school built and supported by R. Ogilby, Esq., and a female work school supported by the vicar and his lady. In these schools about 190 boys and 90 girls are taught; and there are five private schools, in which are about 200 boys and 80 girls, and four Sunday schools. An excellent dispensary is supported in the usual manner. The interesting remains of the abbey church occupy a remarkably picturesque situation, on a rock 200 feet in perpendicular height above the river Roe; they consist of the side walls of the nave and chancel, which are nearly entire, with the gable of the latter, in which, within a circular arch resting on corbels and cylindrical pillars, are two narrow lancet-shaped windows, with a niche on each side and a square-headed window above. The nave is separated from the chancel by a lofty circular arch, and has on the north side a low doorway of corresponding style; it was lighted by a window ornamented with tracery, in good preservation. Under a beautifully ornamented arch in the chancel is an altar-tomb, bearing a recumbent effigy of an armed warrior, said to be one of the O'Cahans; the stones in front are ornamented with figures of armed knights, sculptured in relief, in niches. The remains of the abbey have from time to time been removed, and the capitals, pillars, mullions, &c., may be seen in the churchyard, forming boundaries round the graves or head-stones. Adjoining the town are extensive ruins of a castle and bawn, built in 1618, by the Skinners' Company. A lofty stone stands near the old church, set up as the record of an ecclesiastical assembly held here in 590, at which St. Columbkill was present. Near the river Roe is Tubber-Phadrig, or St. Patrick's fountain; and a single stone, in the bed of the river, exists, around which the people assemble on certain days. There are many raths or forts in different parts of the parish: celts of stone and bronze, spear-heads, and Roman coins and other antiquities have been discovered, and are in the possession of R. L. Ogilby and M. Ross, Esqrs.

DUNGLOE, or CLOGHANLEA, a post-town, in the parish of TEMPLECROAN, barony of BOYLAGH, county of DONEGAL, and province of ULSTER, 19½ miles (N.) from Ardara, and 154 (N. W.) from Dublin, on the north-west coast: the population is returned with the parish. Here are a market-house, constabulary police station, and dispensary; also the parochial church, and R. C, chapel. The post-office is subject to that at Ardara. Petty sessions are held on the first Tuesday in each month.

DUNGOURNEY, a parish, partly in the barony of IMOKILLY, but chiefly in that of BARRYMORE, county of CORK, and province of MUNSTER, 4½ miles (N.) from Castlemartyr, on the road from Cork to Youghal; containing 2640 inhabitants. This parish comprises 8991 statute acres, of which 5925 are applotted under the tithe act, and valued at £4529 per annum; about 70 acres are woodland, nearly one-fourth of the land is waste, and the remainder is arable and pasture. The soil is generally good, but the system of agriculture is in an unimproved state; there are some quarries of common red stone, which is worked for various purposes, and there is a moderate supply of turf for fuel. The Dungourney river rises in the neighbouring hills of Clonmult, and flows through a deep glen in the parish, assuming near the church a very romantic appearance, and towards the southern boundary adding much beauty to the highly cultivated and richly wooded demesne of Brookdale, the seat of A. Ormsby, Esq. The other seats are Ballynona, that of R. Wigmore, Esq.; Ballynona Cottage, of H. Wigmore, Esq.; and Young Grove, of C. Foulke, Esq. An agricultural school, in connection with the Protestant Agricultural Society of Cork, has been established at Brookdale, under the patronage of Mr. Ormsby, for the instruction of 30 boys in the practical knowledge of agriculture, combined with a useful and religious education, and including board and clothing; the institution is maintained by a payment of £5 per annum from each of the scholars, and the produce of the farm, aided by donations and subscriptions; when qualified to become useful, the scholars are provided with situations by the Committee, and receive a gratuity of £5. There is also a female school on the same principle, in which 35 girls are boarded, clothed, and educated, under the personal superintendence of Mrs. Ormsby; on leaving the institution they are provided with situations. The buildings for both these establishments have cost more than £1000. The living is a rectory, in the diocese of Cloyne, and in the patronage of Major Fitzgerald: the tithes amount to £664. 12. 3½. The glebe-house is a good residence, and the glebe comprises 12 acres. The church, a plain building with a shingled spire, was erected by a gift of £500 from the late Board of First Fruits, in 1800, and the Ecclesiastical Commissioners have recently granted £119 for its repair. Attached to Brookdale House is a private chapel, in which a clergyman of the Established Church officiates. In the R. C. divisions the parish forms part of the union of Imogealy, or Castlemartyr. There is a private school, in which are about 170 children.

DUNHILL, or DON ISLE, anciently called DONDRONE, a parish, in the barony of MIDDLETHIRD, county of WATERFORD, and province of MUNSTER, 8 miles (S.E.) from Kilmacthomas; containing 2128 inhabitants. It is situated on St. George's channel, and comprises 6115 statute acres, as applotted under the tithe act. The high lands are principally composed of pudding-stone and clay-slate, with large masses of jasper, some of which is very beautiful. The village of Annestown has a few lodging-houses for the accommodation of visiters in the bathing season. The living is a vicarage, in the diocese of Lismore, united to the vicarages of Guilcagh and Newcastle, and in the gift of the Corporation of Waterford, in which the rectory is impropriate. The tithes amount to £210, of which £110 is payable to the impropriators, and £100 to the vicar; and the vicarial tithes of the union are £194. The glebe comprises above 6 acres. The church at Annestown was rebuilt in 1822, by aid of a gift of £900 from the late Board of First Fruits; and there is a chapel of ease at Guilcagh. In the R. C. divisions the parish is the head of a union or district, and has a commodious chapel. The most remarkable ruin is Don Isle or Donhill castle, which was a principal seat of a branch of the La Poers, and was taken by Cromwell's army, after an obstinate defence made by a female proprietor, who was called Countess of Don Isle. Near it are the ruins of the church, against one of the walls of which stood a statue with a coronet, which has lately been placed in front of the R. C. chapel. In its vicinity is a cromlech of silicious slate.

DUNISKY, a parish, in the barony of WEST MUSKERRY, county of CORK, and province of MUNSTER, 4 miles (S. S. E.) from Macroom; containing 479 inhabitants. This is a very small parish, comprising only one ploughland, situated on the south bank of the river Lee, near Warrens-court. The land is good, and the substratum consists entirely of clay-slate. It is a rectory, in the diocese of Cork, being part of the union of St. Peter's, Cork, and of the corps of the archdeaconry: the tithes amount to £107. There being no church, the parishioners attend divine service at Canaway. The ruins of the old church are a mile and a half north of Warrens-court, on rising ground, and show it to have been a small building. In the R. C. divisions the parish is part of the union or district of Kilmichael.

DUNKANELY, a village, in the parish of KILLAGHTEE, barony of BANNAGH, county of DONEGAL, and province of ULSTER, 9 miles (W.) from Donegal, near Inver bay, and on the road from Killybegs to Donegal: the population is returned with the parish. In 1618 this place was a settlement of ten British families, having a territory of 1500 acres, a bawn of lime and stone, and a castle, and able to muster 50 men at arms. It consists of one street, has a penny post to Donegal, a dispensary, a place of worship for Methodists, and a public school. Twelve fairs are held in the course of the year for farming stock, and a manor court monthly for the recovery of debts under £3. In the village are the ruins of the old parish church, and in the immediate vicinity is the present church. Half a mile to the west are the ruins of Castle Mac-Swine, occupying a point of land little broader than its foundation, which projects some yards into the sea at the head of Mac-Swine's bay.—See KILLAGHTEE.

DUNKERRIN, a parish, in the barony of CLONLISK, KING's county, and province of LEINSTER, 4½ miles (S. W. by W.) from Roscrea, on the main road from Dublin to Limerick; containing 2177 inhabitants; of which number, 127 are in the village. This parish is situated on the confines of the county of Tipperary, by which it is bounded on the east, and comprises 6515 statute acres; of which a considerable portion is bog and waste mountain land. Fairs are held on May 9th, Nov.

3rd, and Dec. 21st; and petty sessions at Shinrone every Tuesday. The village is on the estate of the Rolleston family, whose seat, Franckfort Castle, is contiguous; it is an ancient structure, defended by a regular fortification and fosse. Busherstown is the seat of G. Minchin, Esq.; Newgrove, of Westropp Smith, Esq.; Lisduff, of W. Smith, Esq.; Clyduffe, of T. Spunner, Esq.; Annegrove, of the Rev. W. Minchin; and the Glebe-house, of the Rev. Dr. Hawkins, Dean of Clonfert. It is a rectory and vicarage, in the diocese of Killaloe, forming the head of the union of Dunkerrin, Castletown-Ely, Rathnaveoge, and Finglass, and in the patronage of the Bishop. The tithes amount to £496. 15. 4¾., and of the entire benefice to £923. 1. 6. There is a glebe-house, with three glebes in the union, comprising altogether 86*a.* 2*r.* 30*p.* The church is a handsome modern structure, erected in 1818, by aid of a loan of £1200 from the late Board of First Fruits. In the R. C. divisions the parish is the head of a union or district, comprising Dunkerrin, Cullenwayne, and Castletown-Ely, in which are chapels at Dunkerrin and Barna. About 80 children are educated in three private schools. Near Dunkerrin is the old castle of Rathnaveoge, and Ballynakill castle, formerly the residence of the Minchin family.

DUNKITT, a parish, in the barony of IDA, county of KILKENNY, and province of LEINSTER, 4 miles (N. by W.) from Waterford, on the road to Thomastown; containing 2637 inhabitants. This parish is situated near the river Suir, with which it communicates by the Dunkitt pill, and comprises 6267 statute acres, as applotted under the tithe act. The land is generally good, and is based on a stratum of limestone, of which great quantities are quarried chiefly for exportation to the county of Wexford by the river Suir, from which the pill is navigable to the quarries. The principal seats are Mullinabro', that of J. Hawtrey Jones, Esq.; Greenville, of A. Fleming, Esq.; and Bishop's Hall, of Simon Blackmore, Esq. The living is a vicarage, in the diocese of Ossory, united by act of council, at a period unknown, to the vicarages of Kilcollum and Gaulskill, and in the patronage of the Crown; the rectory is impropriate in the family of Boyd. The tithes amount to £553. 16. 11½. of which £369. 4. 7½. is payable to the impropriators, and £184. 12. 4. to the vicar; and the vicarial tithes of the union amount to £519. 12. 3¾. The glebe-house was built by a gift of £200, and a loan of £600 from the late Board of First Fruits, in 1817, and the glebe comprises 23¾ acres. The church of the union is at Gaulskill. In the R. C. divisions the parish forms part of the union of Kilmacow; the chapel is at Bigwood. About 100 children are taught in a public school, and there are two private schools, in which are about the same number.

DUNLAVAN, a market and post-town, and a parish, partly in the barony of UPPERCROSS, county of DUBLIN, but chiefly in the lower half-barony of TALBOTSTOWN, county of WICKLOW, and province of LEINSTER, 7½ miles (N.) from Baltinglass, and 21 (S. W.) from Dublin, on the old road from Blessington to Timolin; containing 2528 inhabitants, of which number, 1068 are in the town. This place is situated on the confines of the counties of Wicklow, Dublin, and Kildare. The town, which is the property of the Tynte family, is built on an eminence surrounded by higher grounds, and consists of two streets, one of which branches off at right angles from the centre of the other. It contains about 180 houses, of which several are well built, is amply supplied with water from springs, and is considered a healthy place of residence. The market, chiefly for corn and potatoes, is on Wednesday; and fairs for cattle are held on March 1st, May 19th, the second Friday in July, Aug. 21st, the third Tuesday in October, and Dec. 1st. The market-house, in the centre of the principal street, and said to have been erected at an expense of £1200, by the Rt. Hon. R. Tynte, was, in 1835, thoroughly repaired, and one end of it fitted up as a court-house, by Lady Tynte; it is a handsome building of hewn stone, with four projecting porticoes, and crowned in the centre by a dome. During the disturbances of 1798, it was fortified and garrisoned for the protection of many families that fled to this town from the insurgents, who were in the neighbourhood. A chief constabulary police force has been stationed in the town, and petty sessions are held on alternate Wednesdays.

The parish comprises 6565 statute acres, as applotted under the tithe act; the lands are chiefly under tillage; the soil is fertile, and the system of agriculture is improving. There is very little waste land, and scarcely any bog. Some quarries of stone and slate are worked chiefly for building, but both are of inferior quality. A splendid mansion and out-offices have been lately built at a very great expense by Lady Tynte, on part of the estate called Loughmogue, now Tynte Park; and her grandson and heir, Mr. Tynte, who resides with her, has considerably improved the grounds by planting and fencing. The living is a rectory and vicarage, in the diocese of Dublin and Glendalough, united episcopally and by act of council to the rectory and vicarage of Uske and the vicarages of Rathsallagh and Friendstown, and, in 1833, by act of council, to the curacy of Tubber, together constituting the union and the corps of the prebend of Dunlavan in the cathedral church of St. Patrick, in the patronage of the Archbishop. It appears, from a terrier in the registry, that anciently the vicarage was endowed with one-third of the tithes, but since 1732 the vicarage and prebend have been held together. The tithes amount to £340. 9. 10½., and of the whole benefice to £472. 0. 9½. The glebe-house was built by a gift of £100, and a loan of £900 from the late Board of First Fruits, in 1812; the glebe comprises 18 acres. The church, a neat edifice in the later English style, was erected in 1816, by a loan of £1300 from the same Board, and enlarged in 1835, by a grant of £460 from the Ecclesiastical Commissioners. In the R. C. divisions the parish is the head of a union, comprising also the parishes of Donard and Donaghmore; the chapel is a neat cruciform edifice, erected on a site presented by Lady Tynte Caldwell, and her daughter Elizabeth, as appears from a tablet over the entrance; there are chapels also at Donard and Donaghmore. About 130 children are taught in two public schools, of which one is supported by Mrs. Pennefather; and there are six private schools, in which are about 230 children, a Sunday school, and a dispensary. Mr. Powell, of Tubber, about 40 years since, bequeathed £200, directing the interest to be appropriated to the apprenticing of one Protestant child of this parish, and one of the parish of Tubber; but payment has of late been withheld. On the townland of Tomant are two

Danish raths, commanding extensive views, and an ancient churchyard, near which is a well, supposed to be efficacious in various disorders, but probably owes its celebrity to its being only a fine cold spring; there is also a rath at Milltown. Dean Swift was for some time incumbent of this parish.

DUNLEARY, county of DUBLIN.—See KINGSTOWN.

DUNLECKNEY, a parish, in the barony of IDRONE EAST, county of CARLOW, and province of LEINSTER, on the road from Carlow to Burris; containing, with the post-town of Bagenalstown, 4217 inhabitants. This place, which is situated on the river Barrow, was anciently the seat of the Kavanaghs, Kings of Leinster; and in 1300 a preceptory of Knights Templars was founded here, which continued only till 1308, when it was suppressed. It was also the residence of the Bagenal family from the 16th to the 18th century, and is at present the property of Walter Newton, Esq. In 1545, a battle took place at Ballynakill, near Garry hill, in this parish, between the Kavanaghs of the latter place and those of Polmonty, in which, after 100 on each side were slain, the former were victorious and secured possession of the territory which was the object of their contention. The parish comprises 7751 statute acres, as applotted under the tithe act; the land is good and the system of agriculture in an improved state. Limestone abounds and is quarried for agricultural purposes, and there are quarries of fine granite, which is used for building: the Barrow is navigable to Waterford. The principal seats are Dunleckney, that of W. Newton, Esq.; Bagenalstown House, of Miss Newton; Garry Hill House, of Viscount Duncannon; the Lodge, of Mrs. Weld; Rathwade House, of B. B. Norton, Esq.; Lodge Mills, of S. Crosthwaite, Esq.; and Clonburrin, of W. B. Cooke, Esq. The manufacture of starch is carried on, and there is an extensive malting concern in the parish belonging to Mr. Crosthwaite; fairs and petty sessions are held at Bagenalstown. The living is a vicarage, in the diocese of Leighlin, united in 1795 to that of Agha, and in the patronage of A. Weldon, Esq., who is impropriator of the rectory. The tithes amount to £830. 15. 4½., of which £553. 16. 11. is payable to the impropriator, and £276. 18. 5½. to the vicar; and the vicarial tithes of the union, to £415. 7. 8¼. The glebe-house is a neat residence; the glebe comprises 10 acres. The church is a small edifice, and has been recently repaired. In the R. C. divisions the parish is the head of a union or district called Bagenalstown, comprising also part of the parishes of Agha, Fenagh, and Slyguff. The chapel, a handsome edifice lately erected at an expense of £2000, is situated at Bagenalstown; and there are chapels also at Newtown and Ballinkillen, and places of worship for Wesleyan Methodists and Walkerites. The parochial school-house, a neat building in the Grecian style, is in Bagenalstown, where also is a handsome court-house in the same style, lately erected at the expense of Philip Bagenal, Esq., in which quarter sessions are held at the usual periods. Besides the parochial school, there are two private schools in the town. The side walls and gables of the old parish church are still remaining in the churchyard; the interior was lighted by narrow lancet-shaped windows. At Ballymoon are the ruins of the castle of the preceptory of the Knights Templars; the walls, which are 8 feet in thickness and 30 in height, enclose a square of 130 feet, flanked by four square towers, and having a gateway entrance on the west side.—See BAGNALSTOWN.

DUNLEER, a post-town and parish (formerly a parliamentary borough), in the barony of FERRARD, county of LOUTH, and province of LEINSTER, 10 miles (S. E.) from Dundalk, and 30 (N.) from Dublin, on the great north road to Belfast; containing 1603 inhabitants, of which number, 710 are in the town. This place appears to have been first brought into notice by its proprietor, Geo. Legge, Esq., ancestor of the Dartmouth family, to whom Chas. II., in 1671, granted a market and fairs; and on whose petition, for the greater encouragement of settlers, the same monarch, in 1678, incorporated the inhabitants by charter, vesting the government in a sovereign, 12 burgesses, and an indefinite number of freemen. The sovereign, who with his deputy was a justice of the peace and coroner for the borough, was annually elected, subject to the approval of the lord of the manor, from the burgesses, who also filled up vacancies in their own body, and by a majority of whom the freemen were admitted by favour, and a recorder and town-clerk and all other corporate officers were appointed. The corporation returned two members to the Irish parliament till the Union, when the borough was disfranchised, and the £15,000 awarded as compensation was paid in equal moieties to the Right Hon. John Foster, speaker of the Irish House of Commons, and to Henry Coddington, Esq. From the Union till the year 1811 a sovereign was regularly elected, but since that period no election has taken place, and the corporation is now virtually extinct. The town contains 130 houses indifferently built, and is the property of Rodolph de Salis, Esq. The market has been long discontinued, but fairs are held under the charter on July 5th, Dec. 11th, May 14th, and Sept. 19th, and other fairs toll-free on Jan. 6th, Feb. 1st, March 9th, April 1st, June 9th, Aug. 11th, and Nov. 1st. A chief constabulary police force is stationed in the town. The parish, according to the Ordnance survey, comprises 2378¾ statute acres. The living is a rectory, in the diocese of Armagh, united by act of council, in 1682, to the rectories of Dysart, Cappog, Monasterboyce, and Moylary, and to the vicarage of Drumcar, and in the patronage of the Crown. The tithes amount to £153. 12. 3., and of the whole benefice to £741. 11. 7. The glebe-house was built by a gift of £100 and a loan of £1125 from the late Board of First Fruits; the glebe comprises 20¼ acres, of which 19¼ are subject to a rent of £3 per acre. The church has been recently enlarged and repaired, at an expense of £300 granted by the same Board. In the R. C. divisions the parish is the head of a union or district, comprising also the parishes of Cappog, Mosstown, Dromin, and Richardstown, and part of the parish of Kildemock; the chapel is a neat edifice, and there are chapels also at Dromin and Mosstown. About 50 children are taught in the parochial school, which is supported by the rector and curate; an infants' school is supported by subscription; and a handsome school-house has been built in connection with the New Board of Education. There is also a private school, in which are about 80 children; and a dispensary. The horn of a large moose deer was found some years since near the town.

DUNLOE GAP.—See KNOCKANE, county of KERRY.

DUNLOST, a chapelry, in the barony of KILKEA and MOONE, county of KILDARE, and province of LEINSTER, 3 miles (S. S. E.) from Athy, near the river Barrow; the population is returned with Dunbrea. It forms part of the union of Athy, in the diocese of Dublin.

DUNLOY.—See FINVOY.

DUNLUCE, or DOONLISS, a parish, in the barony of LOWER DUNLUCE, county of ANTRIM, and province of ULSTER, 6 miles (N. N. E.) from Coleraine, on the road to the Giants' Causeway; containing 3605 inhabitants. This parish, which gives name to the barony, was anciently called *Portramon*, and distinguished as the residence of the celebrated chieftain Mac Quillan, who was lord of a castle of which the original foundation is not precisely known. Mac Quillan, who was brave, hospitable, and improvident, unwarily suffered the Scots around him to increase in strength, till at length they expelled him from all his possessions; and Sorley Boy, brother of James Mac Donnell, having obtained possession of the district called the Glynnes, made himself master also of this place. But Sir John Perrot, the English lord-deputy, assaulted the intruder, and, after a vigorous resistance, drove him from the castle, in which he placed Sir Peter Carey, whom he thought to be a man of the English pale, as governor, with a garrison of fourteen soldiers. Sir Peter, who was in reality one of the Carews of the north, brought around him some of his own country and kindred, and unknown to the deputy discharged the English soldiers; two of his garrison, however, confederating with the party of Mac Donnell, drew up fifty of them by night into the castle, and these having taken possession of the fortress by surprise, attacked and slew the governor and a few of his companions. On this event, which took place in 1585, the lord-deputy despatched to the assault of the castle an officer named Merriman, who slew the two sons of James Mac Donnell, and Alexander, the son of Sorley Boy, and so harassed the latter by driving away the vast herds of cattle which were his only wealth, that he surrendered Dunluce, and repaired to Dublin to make his submission, which was accepted; and on condition of his fidelity to the English crown, and payment of a tribute of cattle and hawks, he received a regrant of all his possessions, with the government of Dunluce castle. This family was afterwards ennobled by the title of Earl of Antrim; and in 1642, Gen. Monroe, commander of the Scottish army in Ulster, with a party of his forces, paid a friendly visit to the Earl, by whom he was hospitably received; but at the conclusion of the entertainment, Monroe gave the signal to his armed followers, who instantly made the Earl prisoner and seized the castle, and this act was followed soon afterwards by the seizure of all his possessions.

The parish, which is within a mile and a half of the Giants' Causeway, extends for a considerable distance along the coast, and, according to the Ordnance survey, comprises 9381 statute acres. The land is fertile and generally in the highest state of cultivation; the system of agriculture is in a very improved state; there is very little waste land, some excellent pasturage, and a bog of about 500 acres. Limestone abounds, and to the westward of Dunluce castle are the White Rocks lime-works, the most extensive in the North of Ireland. There are numerous quarries of basalt, and great quantities of flint are exported. Coal exists on the estate of John Montgomery, Esq., but no mines have yet been worked. The principal gentlemen's seats are Benvarden, that of J. Montgomery, Esq.; Seaport, of J. Leslie, Esq.; Bardyville, of Sir F. W. Macnaghten, Bart.; and the Cottage, of F. D. Ward, Esq.: there are also some elegant seabathing lodges at Ballintra. The manufacture of paper affords employment to 190 persons, who, with the aid of the most improved machinery, are engaged in making the finer kinds of paper for the English, Scotch, and home markets. A facility of conveyance for the produce of the quarries and limeworks, and for the various sorts of merchandise, is afforded by the small but commodious port of Ballintra. A fair is held annually on Nov. 12th, and petty sessions for the district every fortnight at Bushmills.

The living is a consolidated rectory and vicarage, in the diocese of Connor, and in the patronage of the Bishop: the tithes amount to £369. 4. 7. The glebehouse was built by a gift of £400 and a loan of £300 from the late Board of First Fruits, in 1812; the glebe comprises 20 acres. The church, a handsome edifice, situated at the extremity of the parish, near Bushmills, was erected by aid of a gift of £900 and a loan of £300 from the same Board, in 1821, on the site of an ancient church, which was a ruin in 1625. In the R. C. divisions the parish forms part of the union or parochial benefice of Ballymoney; the chapel near Bushmills is a very small edifice. There is a place of worship for Presbyterians in connection with the Synod of Ulster, of the second class. About 80 children are taught in the public schools, of which the parochial school is chiefly supported by the rector, and a female school was built and endowed by Mrs. Montgomery. There are also three private schools, in which are about 160 children and four Sunday schools. A dispensary was established at Bushmills in 1830, for the parishes of Dunluce, Billy, and Dunseverick. A loan fund was established in 1828, for which purpose the late Hugh Montgomery, Esq., gave £100. The ruins of Dunluce castle are remarkable for their extent and picturesque appearance, especially when viewed from the shore immediately below; the fortified parts occupy the summit of a rock projecting into the sea, and separated from the adjacent cliffs by a deep chasm, over which is an arch forming the only entrance, defended on one side by a wall only 13 inches in thickness; there appears to have been a corresponding wall in a parallel direction with the former, which together were probably the parapets of the bridge. The domestic apartments and offices, of which the remains are extensive, were situated on the main land, and though at a distance appearing only as a massive rugged pile, upon a nearer approach display characteristics of architectural beauty. Underneath the castle is a natural cavern forming a noble apartment, the walls and roof of which are of rude basalt. Near the castle is a very large Danish camp. Splendid specimens of opal, jasper, and cornelian are found upon the shore. Dunluce gives the inferior title of Viscount to the Earls of Antrim.

DUNMACLOUGHY.—See ATHENRY.

DUNMANWAY, a market and post-town, in the parish of FANLOBBUS, Western Division of the barony of EAST CARBERY, county of CORK, and province of

MUNSTER, 29 miles (S. W. by W.) from Cork, and 155½ (S. W.) from Dublin, on the road from Cork to Bantry; containing 2738 inhabitants. This place, according to most authorities, derived its name, signifying "the castle of the yellow river," or "the castle on the little plain," from an ancient castle belonging to the McCarthys. The town is indebted for its origin to Sir Richard Cox, Lord Chancellor of Ireland in the reign of Wm. III., who obtained from that monarch the grant of a market and fairs, and erected a stately mansion for his own residence. Sir Richard also built the long bridge over the river Bandon, consisting of six arches, exclusively of four under the causeway, and introduced the linen manufacture, for which, under his auspices, this place became one of the principal marts, and the town, in which a colony from England had settled, one of the most flourishing in the south of Ireland. It occupies a level tract entirely surrounded on the north, west, and south by lofty hills, rocks, and mountains; and is open to the east, in which direction the river, after entering the vale to which it gives name, pursues its course between two lofty ridges diversified with tillage lands, woods, and lawns, intersected by several picturesque glens, and embellished with numerous elegant seats. It consists of one long street extending about half a mile to the west of the bridge, and in 1831 contained 419 houses, which, though indifferently built, are distinguished by an appearance of cleanliness and comfort: the post-office is subordinate to that of Bandon. Several new roads leading to the town have recently been opened, among which is a very fine and level line from Cork to Bantry. A reading-room was established in 1832, but not being generally supported it has declined. The manufacture of linen continued to flourish for some years, but at present there are very few looms at work. A porter and ale brewery, established in 1831, produces 2600 barrels annually; there are also two tanyards and two boulting-mills, the latter capable of grinding annually 15,000 bags of flour, and there are two or three smaller mills in the vicinity. Since 1810 a considerable trade in corn has been carried on. The market is on Tuesday; and fairs, chiefly for cattle, are held on May 4th, the first Tuesday in July (O. S.), Sept. 17th, and Nov. 26th. At the intersection of the principal street is a large building used as a market-house. Here is a constabulary police station; a manorial court for the recovery of debts not exceeding £2 is held every third Saturday, and petty sessions every second Monday. There is a small bridewell in the town for the temporary confinement of misdemeanants.

The church of Fanlobbus is a handsome edifice, erected in 1821, at an expense of £1100, by aid of a loan from the late Board of First Fruits; and a square tower has recently been added to it. There is a R. C. chapel in progress of erection, at an estimated expense of £2500; also a place of worship for Wesleyan Methodists. Near the R. C. chapel is a school, aided by the priest; and it is intended to establish a savings' bank and a branch of the Labourers' Friend Society: here is a dispensary. Of the stately mansion of Lord Chancellor Cox nothing remains but a part of the kitchen, now a weaver's cabin, with a fragment of the garden wall. Near the R. C. chapel is a chalybeate spring which is efficacious in cutaneous diseases; and not far distant is a small but very beautiful lake, in which Sir Richard Cox was drowned. There are several picturesque waterfalls in the midst of some very romantic scenery, and in the mountains are the ruins of Toher castle.

DUNMOE, a parish, in the barony of MORGALLION, county of MEATH, and province of LEINSTER, 2 miles (N. N. E.) from Navan, on the road to Slane; containing 112 inhabitants. The castle was built by Hugh de Lacy, and in 1641 was surrendered by Capt. Power to the insurgents, in obedience to a forged order from the Lords-Justices. It was partly rebuilt in the 17th century, and is an oblong massive pile, flanked with towers at the angles, now belonging to the D'Arcy family. The parish is in the diocese of Meath; it is a rectory, forming part of the union of Stackallen, and the tithes amount to £81. 10. In the R. C. divisions it is part of the union or district of Slane.

DUNMORE, a market and post-town, and a parish, partly in the barony of HALF-BALLYMOE, but chiefly in that of DUNMORE, county of GALWAY, and province of CONNAUGHT, 7¼ miles (N. by E.) from Tuam, and 106 (W.) from Dublin; containing 10,705 inhabitants, of which number, 847 are in the town. St. Patrick built the monastery of *Domnagh Padraig*, or "the stone house of Patrick," here, and made St. Fulartach its superintendent; and a friary for Augustine Eremites was founded on the site of this abbey, in 1425, by Lord Athenry. The parish comprises 35,571 statute acres, as applotted under the tithe act, and contains Quarrymount, the seat of J. J. Bodkin, Esq.; and Carantrila, of W. H. Handcock, Esq. The market is on Thursday; and fairs are held on May 29th, July 10th, Oct. 10th, and Dec. 11th. It has a sub-post-office to Tuam, and is a constabulary police station. The living is a rectory and vicarage, in the diocese of Tuam, and in the patronage of the Crown: the tithes amount to £646. 3. 1. The glebe-house was built in 1815, by aid of a gift of £100 and a loan of £900, and has a glebe of five acres. The church is part of the ancient friary. The R. C. parish is co-extensive with that of the Established Church, and has a small slated chapel. About 400 children are educated in two public, and 260 in eight private schools; there is also a Sunday school. Here are the ruins of a castle of the Birminghams. The Right Hon. Sir Gore Ouseley, Bart., formerly ambassador in Persia, and Sir William Ouseley, an eminent Oriental scholar, are natives of this place.

DUNMORE, a parish, in the county of the city of KILKENNY, and province of LEINSTER, 3½ miles (N.) from Kilkenny, on the road to Durrow; containing 875 inhabitants. It comprises 2264 statute acres, and has a constabulary police station. The living is a vicarage, in the diocese of Ossory, united with the vicarages of Muckalee and Kilmodum, and in the patronage of the Crown; the rectory is impropriate in the Marquess of Ormonde. The tithes amount to £175. 3., of which £85. 3. is payable to the impropriator, and £90 to the vicar; the tithes of the union are £210. The glebe-house was erected in 1816, by aid of a gift of £350 and a loan of £450 from the late Board of First Fruits: the glebe comprises 22 acres. The church is a plain building, recently repaired by the Ecclesiastical Commissioners, at an expense of £114. In the R. C. divisions the parish forms part of the union or district of Muckalee.

DUNMORE, or DUNMORE EAST, a sea-port and post-town, in the parish of KILLEA, barony of GAULTIER, county of WATERFORD, and province of MUNSTER, 9 miles (S. E.) from Waterford, and 84¾ (S. by E.) from Dublin; containing 631 inhabitants. This place, which is situated on the western shore of Waterford haven, was originally a poor fishing village, consisting only of a few cabins built of clay, and thatched with straw; but since the improvement of its harbour by government, as a station for the post-office packets from Milford, it has grown into importance and become a fashionable bathing-place. The town is situated in a valley sloping gently towards the sea, and consists chiefly of thatched cottages, which are let to visiters during the season, and of which many are about to be rebuilt by the Marquess of Waterford, the principal proprietor, by whom various important improvements are contemplated, which will render it in every respect a desirable place of resort for sea-bathing. As seen from the sea it has a very pleasing appearance, presenting several neat white houses widely interspersed among richly cultivated fields, with the church on the road to the pier, and the ruins of an ancient church crowning the hill in the back ground. The plan for improving the harbour was projected in 1814, and the expense of carrying it into effect was estimated by the late Mr. Nimmo, under whose superintendence it was conducted, at £19,385; but from the necessary additions and subsequent improvements, that sum had, in 1821, amounted to £42,500, and in 1832 to £93,286; and it was then found that £15,000 more would be requisite to complete this important work, making a total expenditure of £108,286. The pier, which extends in a north-eastern direction for more than 700 feet, is defended by a breakwater, stretching from Dunmore Head more than 800 feet into the water, varying from four to six fathoms in depth, and presenting towards the sea an inclined plane paved with massive blocks of stone, which breaks the force of the waves before they reach the parapet of the pier, which has an elevation of 70 feet. The pier and quay are built of a silicious stone quarried in the neighbouring hills, and faced with a fine granite, which, after the exhaustion of these quarries, was brought from the county of Carlow. The basin comprises an area of six acres, and is sheltered by the Mole and Dunmore hill from the west and south-west winds, on the north-east by the promontory of Creden Head, and on the east by the peninsula of Hook; the depth at the entrance is 15 feet, and at the innermost part 8 feet at the lowest ebb. At the pier head is a lighthouse, displaying a red light towards the sea, and a bright light up the harbour, which is easily accessible, but it is gradually filling with sand, whence it is in contemplation to remove the mail packet station to the quay of Waterford, thus enabling the post-office to place a superior class of steamers on the line. This is now the station of the mail packets between England and the South of Ireland, and one of the four ports for British correspondence. There are four steamers, each of 80-horse power, on this station; the packet with the mail for Milford leaves Dunmore daily at ½ past 6 o'clock in the morning, and on the arrival of the packet from Milford, a coach conveys the mail and passengers to Waterford: the distance between the two ports is 80 miles. The fishery is still carried on here, in which three hookers of from 14 to 18 tons' burden are employed in the cod and ling fishery in the deep sea, and 30 yawls in the herring and in-shore fishery. Dunmore is also the pilot station for vessels making for Waterford harbour. The limits of the harbour by the 58th of Geo. III., cap. 72, extend from Shanoon Point to Ardnamult Point; the duties of the Commissioners of this harbour have been annexed to the Board of Public Works. In the rocks in the bay of Dunmore is a fissure of no great extent, called the Cathedral, and to the west of it, near the promontory of Red Head, is another, called the Bishop's cave, 100 feet in length and 24 feet wide.

DUNMOYLAN, a parish, in the Shanid Division of the barony of LOWER CONNELLO, county of LIMERICK, and province of MUNSTER, 1½ mile (S.) from Shanagolden, on the road to Newcastle; containing 1704 inhabitants. It comprises 1774 statute acres, as applotted under the tithe act. The land is in general good, but for want of drainage is much damaged by surface water; the system of agriculture is in a backward state. It is a vicarage, in the diocese of Limerick, forming part of the union of Castlerobert, or Robertstown; the rectory is impropriate in the Earl of Cork. The tithes amount to £235, of which two-thirds are payable to the impropriator, and the remainder to the vicar. In the R. C. divisions it is part of the union or district of Kilcoleman. There are three private schools, in which about 50 children are educated. Near the ruins of the old church is the doon, or fort, whence it derives its name.

DUNMURGHILL, a parish, in the barony of IKEATHY and OUGHTERANY, county of KILDARE, and province of LEINSTER, 6½ miles (S. W.) from Maynooth; containing 234 inhabitants. It is a rectory and vicarage, in the diocese of Kildare, entirely appropriate to the dean and chapter of the cathedral of St. Bridget: the tithes amount to £18. 15. In the R. C. divisions it forms part of the union or district of Maynooth.

DUNMURRY, a village, in that part of the parish of DRUMBEG which is in the barony of UPPER BELFAST, county of ANTRIM, and province of ULSTER, 3½ miles (N. E.) from Lisburn, on the river Glenwater and the road from Belfast to Lisburn; containing 479 inhabitants. This place, which takes its name from two Danish forts, or raths, in its immediate vicinity, was formerly the parish of Ballygosh, which soon after the Reformation was annexed to that of Drumbeg. Its ancient name has been superseded by that of the village which has been recently erected, and which is beautifully situated in a sequestered and fertile vale, and remarkably neat. Over the Glenwater are two bridges, one at the village, an ancient structure, and the other, over which the Dublin road passes, a noble pile of two arches of freestone, quarried on the spot. The surrounding hills being richly planted add greatly to the beauty of the scenery, which is also embellished with several handsome seats, of which the principal are Seymour Hill, that of W. Charley, Esq.; Woodbourne, of M. Charley, Esq.; Dunmurry House, of W. Hunter, Esq.; Suffolk, of J. McCance, Esq.; Glenville, of W. McCance, Esq.; and Collin House, of W. Roberts, Esq.; besides others which are noticed in the account of the parish of Drumbeg, *which see*. In the village are some extensive flour-mills, worked partly by water and partly by steam, and attached to them are large stores for grain and malt-kilns. Near these is a large bleach-green, in which 14,000 pieces of fine linen are annually bleached; and at Glenburn, a little lower down upon the same stream, is another, in which 12,000 are annually finished. Quarries of freestone for building are wrought here; there are also quarries of basalt, which in the grounds of Glenburn consists of rude columnar masses with concave and convex joints, similar to those of the Giants' Causeway. Beneath the freestone are some thin strata of coal, which have never been worked. The church of Ballygosh has long since disappeared, and the rectorial tithes of the two townlands which constituted the parish were granted by Jas. I. to Sir Arthur Chichester, and the vicarial tithes to the incumbent of Drumbeg, in the proportions of two-thirds and one-third respectively. There is a place of worship for Presbyterians, formerly in connection with the General, but now with the Remonstrant, Synod of Ulster. Closely adjoining the bridge was discovered, while quarrying the stone for its erection, a natural basaltic wall in a direction from north to south, composed of stones of different sizes and forms, and having in a striking degree the appearance of art. On Collin mountain, to the north-west of the village, is a very conspicuous cairn of considerable extent; it consists of small stones piled together in a conical form, and is now almost covered with green sward.

DUNMURRY, a parish, in the barony of East Ophaly, county of Kildare, and province of Leinster, 2 miles (N.) from Kildare, on the road to Rathangan; containing 155 inhabitants. This parish comprises 1054 statute acres, as applotted under the tithe act, which, excepting a few acres of common, are entirely arable. It is a rectory, in the diocese of Kildare, forming part of the union of Thomastown: the tithes amount to £75. In the R. C. divisions it is part of the union or district of Kildare. Dunmurry House is the residence of E. J. Medlecott, Esq.

DUNQUIN.—See DONQUIN.

DUNSANY, a parish, in the barony of Skryne, county of Meath, and province of Leinster, 2¾ miles (N. W.) from Dunshaughlin, on the road from that place to Bective-bridge; containing 291 inhabitants. It comprises 899 statute acres, and contains a constabulary police station. The castle, which was erected in the 12th century, has been in the possession of the noble family of Plunkett at least since Sir Christopher Plunkett was created Lord Dunsany in 1461. It is incorporated with the modern castle, which is a very handsome Gothic building, containing some fine paintings and sculptures, and surrounded by a well planted demesne of more than 400 statute acres, within which is an ancient church where many members of the family have been interred. The parish is in the diocese of Meath, and is a rectory, forming part of the union of Taragh: the tithes amount to £60. In the R. C. divisions it is united with Killeen, Kilmessan, Assey, Treebly, Balsoon, and Scurloghstown, in which union or district are chapels at Dunsany and Kilmessan. About 200 children are educated in a school, for which Lord Dunsany allows a house and garden rent-free.

DUNSEVERICK, or DOONSERE, a parish, partly in the barony of Carey, and partly in that of Lower Dunluce, county of Antrim, and province of Ulster, 3½ miles (N. E.) from Bushmills; containing 1813 inhabitants. This parish is situated on the northern coast, which is here characterised by features of grandeur and sublimity. It contains the noble promontories of Pleaskin and Bengore; the latter, situated in 55° 14′ 50″ (N. Lat.) and 6° 28′ (W. Lon.), forms the commencement of that beautiful and majestic range of columnar basalt which is called the Giants' Causeway. The shore is indented with several interesting bays, of which that near Milltown is much frequented during the season; and the small creek of Portanna flows up to the village. According to the Ordnance survey it comprises 4277½ statute acres: the land is fertile and the system of agriculture rapidly improving. There are several quarries of limestone and stone for building; fossil or wood coal, found beneath the basalt and between the strata, is worked to a considerable extent, but it is of very indifferent quality; and near Pleaskin is a very fine quarry of columnar basalt. A profitable salmon fishery is carried on at Port Moon bay, where the fish are taken in great abundance. At Port Ballintrae is a coast-guard station, forming one of the eight which constitute the district of Ballycastle. The living is a perpetual curacy, in the diocese of Connor, and in the alternate patronage of the Rectors of Billy and Ballintoy, out of which parishes it was formed under the act of the 7th and 8th of Geo. IV., 1830. It is endowed with the tithes of the townlands of Lisnaguniog, Feigh, and Carncolp, in the parish of Billy, amounting to £37. 9. 3., and with those of the townlands of Artimacormick, Drimnagee, and Drimnagesson, in the parish of Ballintoy, amounting to £29. 8. 3¾., making the total endowment £66. 17. 6¾. The church, a neat edifice with a square tower, was erected in 1832, at the expense of the late Board of First Fruits. There is a place of worship for Presbyterians. Lochaber school, in which about 100 children are gratuitously instructed, was built in 1827 and is supported by subscription; and there is a pay school, in which are about 30 boys and 20 girls, and a Sunday school. In 1831, many thousand Roman coins of silver were found under a stone near Bengore Head, and fossils and minerals of every variety are found here in profusion. The venerable remains of Dunseverick castle are noticed in the account of Ballintoy, in which parish they are situated.

DUNSFORD, or DUNSPORT, a parish, in the barony of Lecale, county of Down, and province of Ulster, 3½ miles (E. S. E.) from Downpatrick; containing 1680 inhabitants. This parish, which is situated near the southern entrance to Strangford Lough, comprises, with Guns island, according to the Ordnance survey, 4239 statute acres, all under cultivation, except 40 acres of bog, and very fertile, much grain being exported from the stores at Ballyhornan, where small vessels land coal. Guns island lies off the coast, which is bold and rocky, and includes Killard Point. The parish is in the diocese of Down, and is a rectory, forming the corps of the prebend of Dunsford in the cathedral of the Holy Trinity, and in the patronage of the Bishop: the tithes amount to £382, of which £263 is payable to the incumbent and £139 to the impropriators. The church is a small plain edifice with a bell tower. In the R. C. divisions it is the head of a union or district comprising this parish and Ardglass, and containing two chapels, of which the one for Dunsford is at

Ballydock. About 350 children are educated in four public schools.

DUNSHAUGHLIN, a post-town and parish (formerly an incorporated town), in the barony of RATOATH, county of MEATH, and province of LEINSTER, 9¼ miles (S. S. E.) from Navan, and 13¾ (N. W.) from Dublin, on the road to Enniskillen; containing 1548 inhabitants, of which number, 913 are in the town. This place derives its name, signifying "Seachlan's Hill," and its origin, from St. Seachlan, nephew of St. Patrick, who founded a church or abbey here in the middle of the fifth century, which, after being sacked in 1026, and burnt in 1043, appears to have been destroyed by the sept of Hy Bruin in 1152. The provost and commonalty of the town of Dunshaghelyn were, in 1423, ordered to be at Trim with all their power for its defence. The parish comprises 7379 statute acres, of which about 200 are waste and bog, and the remainder arable and pasture land in nearly equal proportions. The town contains about 160 houses: it has fairs on June 11th and Dec. 10th, a dispensary, and is a constabulary police station. Petty sessions are held every fortnight and quarter sessions half-yearly in a neat court-house. The living is a rectory and vicarage, in the diocese of Meath, united to Rathregan, and in the patronage of the Crown. the tithes amount to £296, of which £26 is payable to the representatives of Col. Reynell, as lay impropriators of the townlands of Derks and Ballinlough: the gross value of the benefice is £436. The glebe-house, in Rathregan, was built by aid of a loan of £562, in 1822, from the late Board of First Fruits; the glebe comprises 23 acres. The church, which is in the town, was built in 1813, by aid of a loan of £700 from the same Board. In the R. C. divisions the parish is united with Colmolyn, in each of which is a chapel. There are two public schools in which are about 100 children, and a private school of about 25.

DUNTRILEAGUE.—See GALBALLY.

DUNURLIN, a parish, in the barony of CORKAGUINEY, county of KERRY, and province of MUNSTER, 6 miles (N. W.) from Dingle, on the west side of Smerwick harbour; containing 1997 inhabitants. In 1579, Saunders, the Pope's nuncio, with a party of 80 Spaniards and a few English and Irish catholics, landed here, and built a fort at Smerwick for their safety, expecting to be joined by the discontented Irish; but their ships were seized by Capt. Courtenay. In the following year a reinforcement of 700 Spaniards and Italians landed with arms for 5000 men, besides cannon, ammunition and money, and added some works to the fort, named by them "Fort del Or." The Earl of Ormonde marched directly against them, on which they retired to the fastness of Glanigalt; but finding the English not so powerful as they expected, 300 of them with their commander returned by night into the fort. The Lord-Deputy, with Captains Zouch and Raleigh, soon arriving with 800 men, and Sir William Winter at the same time returning to the coast with his fleet, the Spaniards were attacked both by sea and land, and after an arduous siege submitted at discretion. On being disarmed, all the Spaniards, except their commander and staff, were put to the sword; and the Irish who had joined them were hanged. The parish contains 5732 statute acres, as applotted under the tithe act, a large portion of which consists of coarse mountain pasture and bog. The portion under tillage is manured with seaweed, abundance of which is procured on the coast; and the state of agriculture is slowly improving. Some of the inhabitants are employed in fishing. Near the coast are three remarkable hills, called by sailors "the Three Sisters;" and between the harbour of Smerwick and Ferriter's creek is the low promontory called Dunurlin Head, forming the western point of Smerwick bay: it is situated 2¼ miles (E. N. E. ½E.) from Sybil Head, and the latter is 5½ miles (N. E. by N.) from Dunmore Head. The living is a rectory and vicarage, in the diocese of Ardfert and Aghadoe, and in the gift of the Bishop: the tithes amount to £150; there is neither church, glebe-house, nor glebe. In the R. C. divisions the parish forms part of the union or district of Keel, which also comprises the parishes of Donquin, Kilquane, Kilmelchedor, and Marhyn, and contains the chapels of Boulteen and Carrig. About 40 children are taught in a public and about 25 in a private school Overlooking the little cove, called Ferriter's creek, are the remains of Castle Sybil, or Sybilla's castle, formerly belonging to the Ferriters, and said to have been built by a widow of that family; and on the north-west side of Smerwick harbour are the remains of the Spanish fortification of Fort del Or, which consisted of a curtain 60 feet in length, a ditch, and two bastions.

DURAS, a parish, in the barony of KILTARTAN, county of GALWAY, and province of CONNAUGHT, 16 miles (E. S. E.) from Galway: the population is returned with Kinvarra. This parish, which is situated on the bay of Galway, takes its name from a small fertile island close to the shore, which was granted by Cromwell to Major John Walcot, whose grandson sold it to Mr. French, from whom it descended in the female line to the Baron de Basterot, its present proprietor. A great portion is rocky and incapable of cultivation; but some of the land is very rich and produces excellent wheat. Limestone is abundant, and much is quarried for agricultural and other purposes. The late Mr. French raised embankments in several places to prevent the encroachment of the sea, and built a long bridge to connect the island with the main land; great improvements have also been made by his successor. The principal seats are Duras Park, that of P. M. Lynch, Esq.; and Duras House, of the Baron de Basterot. Great numbers of oysters and other fish are taken off the coast, and about a mile and a half to the west of Duras Point a pier has been constructed, which, though dry at low water, is accessible to vessels of 60 or 80 tons' burden at the return of the tide; the expense of its erection was partly defrayed by a grant from Government. From the west end of the pier a ledge of foul ground extends to Deer Island. Here is a large flour-mill, worked by the tide. The parish is in the diocese of Kilmacduagh; the rectory is partly appropriate to the see, and partly to the benefice of Ardrahan; the vicarage forms part of the union of Kilcolgan; the tithes are included in the composition for Kinvarra, *which see*. In the R. C. divisions it is part of the union or district of Kinvarra; the chapel was erected by the late P. M. Lynch, Esq., and was enlarged and a spire added to it by his son, the present proprietor of Duras Park, by whom it has been also endowed with £10 per annum. On the island of Duras are the remains of an ancient friary, with a burial-ground; and there are the remains of a druidical altar, near which some ancient silver coins have been found.

DURROW, or CASTLE-DURROW, a market and post-town, and a parish, partly in the barony of UPPER OSSORY, QUEEN'S county, but chiefly in that of GALMOY, county of KILKENNY, and province of LEINSTER, 12 miles (S. by E.) from Maryborough, and 54 (S. W.) from Dublin, on the road from Athy to Cashel; containing 2911 inhabitants, of which number, 1298 are in the town. This parish comprises 6843 statute acres, as applotted under the tithe act; three-fourths of the land are arable and pasture, about 1000 acres woodland, and 300 bog. The town, which is on the bank of the river Erkin, contains 236 houses forming a square, many of which are well-built and slated. It is included in the county of Kilkenny for civil purposes, but is completely surrounded by Queen's county, of which it formed a part until the Earl of Ormonde, by act of parliament, procured its annexation to Kilkenny. Malt is made here, and there is a large boulting-mill. The market is held on Friday in the market-house; and fairs are held on the second Thursday (O. S.) in May, Aug., and Nov., and Feb. 2nd, March 4th, April 16th, July 3rd, and Oct. 8th. It is a constabulary police station, and has a dispensary. Petty sessions are held on alternate Fridays. Adjoining the town is Castle-Durrow, a large ancient mansion belonging to Viscount Ashbrook, from which he takes the title of Baron. Here are also Donmore, the residence of the Staples family; Moyne, of R. Hamilton Stubber, Esq.; and Castlewood, of R. Lawrenson, Esq. The living is a vicarage, in the diocese of Ossory, and in the gift of the Dean and Chapter of St. Canice's, Kilkenny; the rectory is appropriate to the economy estate of the cathedral. The tithes amount to £360, of which £240 is payable to the lessee under the economy estate, and £120 to the vicar. There is a glebe-house, with a glebe of more than 18 acres. A cattle show was established here, in 1801, by the Midland Farming Society. The church is a large building, with a tower and spire, and has recently been repaired by the Ecclesiastical Commissioners, at an expense of £738. In the R. C. divisions part of the parish is in the union or district of Ballyragget, and the remainder with Aghamacart forms the district of Durrow, in which is a chapel. The Wesleyan Methodists have a meeting-house in the town. The parochial school is aided by Lord Ashbrook and the incumbent, and an infants' school is supported by an annual donation of £52 from Mrs. Walker. About 70 children are educated in these schools, about 180 in four private schools, and there is also a Sunday school. At Callohill, on the estate of Lord Carbery, are the ruins of a castle. A monastery once existed at Durrow, but its history is unknown; and at Ballynasleigh was a large altar, or cromlech, which was destroyed in a search for money, also another cromlech and some enclosures and pits.

DURROW, a parish, partly in the barony of MOYCASHEL, county of WESTMEATH, but chiefly in that of BALLYCOWAN, KING'S county, and province of LEINSTER, 2¾ miles (N.) from Tullamore, on the road to Kilbeggan; containing 5192 inhabitants. This parish, which is also called Dervagh, was distinguished at a very early period for its sumptuous monastery, founded by St. Columb, in 546, and also for an abbey of Augustine Canons, which was subsequently founded and dedicated to the Blessed Virgin and St. Columb. The latter establishment, which had been endowed with the town of Durrow, by Aed McBrenaynn, King of Teaffia, who died in 585, was plundered in 832, by Fethlemid, son of Crimthan, who slew the monks and burned the town; and after having been repeatedly destroyed by fire, was, in 1175, plundered by the English, who laid waste the adjacent country. In 1186, Hugh de Lacy, while superintending the erection of a castle on the ruins of the monastery founded by St. Columb, was killed by one of the labourers, who, indignant at the profanation of the sacred spot, struck off his head with an axe while he was stooping down to give directions. In 1227, Simon Clifford built here the castle of Rahan O'Swaney, and also granted an annuity of 40*s.* to the abbey, which continued to flourish till the dissolution, when it was granted by Queen Elizabeth to Nicholas Herbert, who made it his residence, and from whose family (which took the name of Stepney) it passed to that of the Earl of Norbury, its present proprietor. The parish comprises 688 statute acres, as applotted under the tithe act. The soil is fertile, and the system of agriculture improving; there is only a small portion of bog, and the only waste land consists of sand hills. Limestone abounds and is quarried extensively for agricultural and other uses. The principal seats are Durrow Abbey, that of the Earl of Norbury, situated in an ample and highly improved demesne, in which his lordship is erecting a spacious mansion in the ancient style; Kilclare, of John Armstrong, Esq.; Coolrain, of R. B. Slater, Esq.; Ballynamona, of R. Belton, Esq., and Rostella, of Dr. Naghten. The linen manufacture was carried on here; and there was an extensive bleach-green, the property of Mr. Armstrong, in which about 50 persons were employed. The river Brosna, which bounds the parish on the north and east, and the Silver river, which bounds it on the south and west, afford facilities for trade; on the latter a flourishing distillery has been lately established. The living is a perpetual curacy, in the diocese of Meath, and in the patronage of the Earl of Norbury, in whom, and in H. Kemmis and J. Armstrong, Esqrs., the rectory is impropriate. The tithes amount to £223. 14. 1½., of which £146. 0. 7½. is payable to Lord Norbury, £60. 8. 10. to Mr. Kemmis, and £17. 4. 8. to Mr. Armstrong; the stipend of the perpetual curate is £80, payable by Lord Norbury. The glebe-house is a neat residence, and the glebe comprises 25 acres, subject to a rent of £17. 10. The church, a venerable and ancient structure, was repaired in 1802, by a gift of £450, and a loan of £50 from the late Board of First Fruits, and contains monuments to the Stepney and Armstrong families. In the churchyard is an ancient cross curiously sculptured with scriptural devices, which is supposed to have been brought from Scotland by St. Columb; it is of a different kind of stone to any in the neighbourhood. In the R. C. divisions the parish is in the union of Tullamore; the chapel is a very handsome edifice, in the later English style. There are three private schools, in which are about 200 children. Near the church is a holy well, dedicated to St. Columb. There are the remains of several towers, and also a large rath in the parish.

DURRUS-KILCROHANE, a parish, partly in the barony of BANTRY, but chiefly in the Western Division of the barony of WEST CARBERY, county of CORK, and province of MUNSTER, 5 miles (S. S. W.) from Bantry, on the road to Dunmanus bay; containing 5290 inhabitants. This parish is situated on the south side of the bay of Bantry, and comprises 9793 statute acres, as applotted under the tithe act, and valued at £3716 per annum; 2562 acres are arable, 622 pasture, and 50 bog, the remainder being coarse land. The surface is very uneven, and in some parts rises into mountains of considerable elevation, but, although parts are rocky and bare, cultivation extends, and much of the waste land is reclaimable. The principal manure used is sea-sand, which is brought up the bay and landed at many little creeks on both sides of it. The bay is a remarkable inlet, extending from Sheeps-head to Four-mile-water, a distance of 16 miles, and deep enough for the largest ships, which are occasionally driven in by adverse winds. A manor court for the recovery of debts under 40*s*. is held once a month; and petty sessions every fortnight. At Carrigboy there is a constabulary police station. The gentlemen's seats are Four-mile-water Court, that of the Rev. Alleyn Evanson; Ardoguina, of R. T. Evanson, Esq.; O'Donovan's Cove, of T. O'Donovan, Esq.; Blair's Cove, of R. L. Blair, Esq.; Fort Lodge, of R. O'Donovan, Esq.; and the glebe-house, of the Rev. E. J. Alcock. The living is a vicarage, in the diocese of Cork, united in 1792, by act of council, with that of Kilcrohane, and in the patronage of the Bishop; the rectory is impropriate in the Earl of Donoughmore: the tithes amount to £350, of which £170 is payable to the impropriator, and the remainder to the vicar; and the entire tithes of the benefice amount to £415. There are two glebes, one in Durrus of 51*a*. 2*r*. 7*p*., the other in Kilcrohane of 5*a*. 1*r*. 35*p*. The church, near Four-mile-water, is a neat building, erected in 1792 by aid of a gift of £500 from the late Board of First Fruits; the tower was considerably raised and embattled in 1830. The R. C. union or district is co-extensive with that of the Established Church; there are three chapels, one of which is near Four-mile-water, another at Aghakisky, and the third in Kilcrohane. There is also a place of worship for Wesleyan Methodists. Here are five public schools, in which about 520 children are taught. The only remains of antiquity are the ruins of Rossmore castle. Near Friendly Cove is a strong chalybeate spring efficacious in liver complaints.

DURSEY, an island, in the parish of KILNAMANNAGH, barony of BERE, county of CORK, and province of MUNSTER, 8 miles (S. W.) from Castletown; containing 198 inhabitants. On this island part of the French army landed in 1796, and on the following day were taken prisoners in Castletown. After this the government erected a signal tower on the highest point of the island, which formed the first of a line of signal stations that extended to Cork. Dursey is situated off the south-west coast, at the extremity of a peninsula whose shores border the entrances to Bantry bay and Bearhaven on one side, and to the river Kenmare on the other. It is in lat. 51° 34′ 40″, and lon. 10° 15′, extending 1¼ mile in length by ½ a mile in breadth, and comprises 754 acres, the greater part of which is a rough mountainous tract, interspersed with rocky pasture and coarse arable land. It is the property of the Earl of Bantry. Between the island and the mainland is a narrow sound, through which vessels may sail with a favourable wind and tide; and near it is Ballydonaghan bay, which is deep water, having from 20 to 30 fathoms close to the shore. Contiguous to the island are several rocks. Near the ferry crossing the sound are the remains of a very old church, called Our Lady's abbey, consisting of part of the walls only.

DYNISH, county of CLARE.—See INNISMACNAUGHTEN.

DYSART, or DISERT, a parish, partly in the barony of IRAGHTICONNOR, but chiefly in that of CLANMAURICE, county of KERRY, and province of MUNSTER, 6 miles (S. S. W.) from Listowel, on the river Brick; containing 631 inhabitants. It comprises 3608 statute acres, as applotted under the tithe act, including some excellent land. There is a considerable portion of bog, affording fuel of good quality: the state of agriculture is gradually improving. Ballinagar is the seat of the representatives of the late John Barnard, Esq. The parish is in the diocese of Ardfert and Aghadoe; the vicarage forms part of the union of Aghavallin, and the rectory is impropriate in Anthony Stoughton, Esq. The tithes amount to £133. 16. 10., payable in moieties to the impropriator and the vicar; and at Ballinagar is a glebe of 13 acres. In the R. C. divisions it is partly in the union or district of Listowel, but chiefly in that of Lixnaw, or Iveamore. About 70 children are educated in a private school. The ruins of the ancient church still remain in the burial-ground. Ennismore, the residence of J. F. Hewson, Esq., gives the titles of Baron and Viscount to the family of Hare, Earls of Listowel.

DYSART, a parish, in the barony of FASSADINING, county of KILKENNY, and province of LEINSTER, 2¼ miles (S.) from Castlecomer, on the road to Kilkenny; containing 2501 inhabitants. This parish is situated on the river Dinin; and comprises 2606 statute acres. It is a vicarage, in the diocese of Ossory, appropriate to the vicars choral of the cathedral of St. Canice, Kilkenny; the rectory is impropriate in the representatives of Sir James Tynte, Bart. The tithes amount to £300, of which £200 is paid to the impropriator, and £100 to the vicars choral. There is no church; the parishioners attend divine worship at Mothell. In the R. C. divisions it forms part of the union or district of Muckalee. About 90 children are educated in a public school.

DYSART, a parish, in the barony of FERRARD, county of LOUTH, and province of LEINSTER, 2 miles (E. by S.) from Dunleer, on the coast road from Drogheda to Dundalk; containing 699 inhabitants. The land is of superior quality and well cultivated: about two-thirds are in tillage, and there are about 50 acres of bog. The village of Grange Bellew, consisting of about 25 houses, occupied by the labourers of Sir Patrick Bellew, Bart., has a neat appearance. There is a mill for grinding oatmeal, and another for dressing flax. Barmeath, the residence of Sir Patrick Bellew, stands in a richly wooded demesne, commanding extensive views. The old castle of John Bellew (one of the lords of the English pale) is incorporated in the present mansion; and in the demesne is Windmill Hill, on which is a circular tower forming a conspicuous land mark. The parish is in the diocese of Armagh, and is a rectory, forming part of the union of Dunleer: the tithes amount to £129. 19. 7½. In the R. C. divisions it is the head of a union or district, which also comprises the parishes of Clonmore, Port, Dunany, Salterstown, and Drumcar; and contains three chapels. That of Dysart is a handsome building, the site for which was presented by Sir Patrick Bellew, who also contributed towards its erection. A school of about 160 children is aided by Sir Patrick, who also contributed largely towards the erection of the school-house. Some vestiges of the ancient church still remain in the burial-ground.

DYSART, county of ROSCOMMON.—See DISERT.

DYSART, or DESERT, a parish, in the barony of UPPERTHIRD, county of WATERFORD, and province of MUNSTER, 4 miles (E. by S.) from Clonmel; containing 1444 inhabitants. This parish is bounded by the river Suir, which separates it from the county of Tipperary, and contains 3,318 statute acres, as applotted under the tithe act. Near Churchtown is the pleasant residence of John Power, Esq. It is in the diocese of Lismore: the rectory, with that of Kilmoleran, constitutes the corps of the prebend of Dysart in the cathedral of Lismore; the vicarage was episcopally united, in 1787, to that of Kilmoleran, and in 1804 to the rectories of Fenoagh and Templemichael, forming the union of Dysart; both are in the gift of the Bishop. The tithes amount to £304. 12. 3., of which two-thirds are payable to the prebendary and the remainder to the vicar; the entire revenue of the prebend is £429, and the tithes of the benefice amount to £425. 2. 3.: the glebe-house stands on a glebe of 4½ acres. A recent grant of £188 has been made by the Ecclesiastical Board for repairing the church, which is at Churchtown. Adjacent to it are the ruins of the ancient church, within the walls of which are two large old tombs of members of the Butler and Everard families, the latter of which had a castle here in the middle of the 17th century. In the R. C. divisions the parish forms part of the union or district of Carrickbeg, and contains a chapel. The parochial school, in which about 50 children are educated, was established by Sir Moore Disney, who built the school-house.

DYSART, a parish, partly in the barony of RATHCONRATH, but chiefly in that of MOYCASHEL and MAGHERADERNAN, county of WESTMEATH, and province of LEINSTER, 5 miles (S. W.) from Mullingar, on Lough Ennel, and on the road from Mullingar to Kilbeggan; containing 1020 inhabitants. St. Colman is said to have founded an abbey here, which was eventually a house of Conventual Franciscans. One of the islands belonging to Dysart was fortified by the Irish at the close of the civil war of 1641, and made one of their chief depositories. It was taken, under capitulation, by the English, but was re-taken and the English made prisoners; it finally surrendered to a superior force. The parish comprises 4244 statute acres, as applotted under the tithe act: the land is exceedingly fertile. There is a considerable tract of bog, and an abundance of limestone. Dysart House, now in ruins, and Lilliput, also uninhabited, both the property of Andrew Savage Nugent, Esq., are in the parish. There is a constabulary police station in the village. The parish is in the diocese of Meath, and is a rectory, forming part of the union of Churchtown: the tithes amount to £120, and the glebe contains 12 acres. In the R. C. divisions it is part of the union or district of Churchtown; the chapel is near the village. There are some remains of an old church with a cemetery.

DYSARTENOS, a parish, partly in the barony of MARYBOROUGH EAST, but chiefly in that of STRADBALLY, QUEEN'S county, and province of LEINSTER, 3½ miles (W. by S.) from Stradbally, on the road to Maryborough; containing 1354 inhabitants. This place, at a very remote period, was the residence of the O'Mores, princes of Leix; and also of Dermod McMurrough, king of Leinster. A monastery was founded here by Ængus, on his retirement from Clonenagh abbey, of which he was abbot; but, though it flourished for some time, not even the site is known. The parish is the property of Sir Henry Parnell, Bart., who has fitted up a place of summer residence within the walls of the ancient fortress. Fairs are held here on Whit-Monday, and Oct. 12th. The living is a vicarage, in the diocese of Leighlin, united from time immemorial to the vicarage of Kilteel, and in the patronage of Lord Carew, in whom the rectory is impropriate. The tithes amount to £416. 10. 10½., of which £277. 13. 11¼. is payable to the impropriator, and the remainder to the vicar. The glebe-house was built in 1813, by a gift of £400, and a loan of £360 from the late Board of First Fruits; the glebe comprises seven acres. The church, towards the repair of which the Ecclesiastical Commissioners have lately granted £333, is a small edifice with a square tower, forming a very picturesque object, on the summit of one of the Dysart hills. In the R. C. divisions the parish forms part of the union or district of Maryborough; the chapel is a neat building. About 140 children are taught in a national school, and there is also a Sunday school. The fortress of Dunamase occupies the summit of a precipitous rock, rising from the midst of an extensive plain and from a very remote age was the residence of the O'Mores, and with the territory of Leinster became the property of Strongbow, Earl of Pembroke, by marriage with the daughter of Dermod McMurrough, King of Leinster, and afterwards passed again by marriage to William de Braos, the reputed founder of the castle and manor of Dunamase. In 1264 it was held by Maurice Fitzgerald, and soon after by Lord Mortimer, during whose absence in England it was, with seven other of his castles, seized by his vassal O'More, to whom he had entrusted it. Lord Mortimer, on his subsequent recovery of the fortress, increased its strength by additional fortifications; and it was for a long period an object of continued contests between the English and the native chieftains. It was further strengthened in the reign of Jas. I., but was taken in 1641 by the insurgents, who were soon after driven out by Sir Chas. Coote; it afterwards surrendered to Gen. Preston, but was retaken by the parliamentarians, who in 1646 were expelled by Owen Roe O'Neill, who carried it by assault. In 1649 it was taken by Lord Castlehaven, but the year following the garrison surrendered to the parliamentarian forces under Cols. Hewson and Reynolds, by whom it was dismantled and nearly demolished. The remains occupy the summit of a hill 200 feet high, and consist of a barbican and watch-tower defending the entrance on the south-west side, on which alone it was accessible; from the barbican a draw-bridge afforded access to the first gateway, which is defended by two towers. The interior consists of an outer and inner court; and the whole is defended by walls of great thickness surrounding the summit of the hill, which is more than 1000 feet in circuit, fortified at intervals with towers. The ruins of the keep, in which was apparently a chapel, occupy the highest ground; and adjoining it are the remains of the state apartments. Small silver coins of the early Irish kings have been found on the site of the ruins.

DYSARTGALLEN, a parish, in the barony of CULLINAGH, QUEEN'S county, and province of LEINSTER, on the road from Durrow to Abbeyleix; containing, with the post-town of Ballinakill (which is described under its own head), 4018 inhabitants. This parish comprises 10,557 statute acres, as applotted under the tithe act; the soil is generally good, and the land in a profitable state of cultivation; there is a small quantity of bog, and grit-stone is quarried for building. The only seat of importance is Monaclare, the residence of S. M. Stubber, Esq. Fairs are held monthly at Ballinakill. The living is a rectory and vicarage, in the diocese of Leighlin, and in the patronage of Earl Stanhope: the tithes amount to £406. 3. 1. The glebe-house was built by a gift of £100, and a loan of £550 from the late Board of First Fruits, in 1810; the glebe comprises 30 acres. The church, towards the repair of which the Ecclesiastical Commissioners have recently granted £292, is a handsome building with a spire, situated in Ballinakill; it has a window of stained glass, and was erected in 1821, by a loan of £1100. The R. C. parish is co-extensive with that of the Established Church; there is a chapel at Ballinakill, and another at Knockardgurt. About 680 children are taught in two public schools, of which the parochial school is supported by the rector, who also built the school-house; and there are also five private schools, in which are about 160 children. Mr. Dillon bequeathed £500 to the R. C. poor of the parish. There are some remains of the castles of Moate and Ballinakill; and at Heywood is a chalybeate spring.

DYSERT, or DYSART, a parish, in the barony of INCHIQUIN, county of CLARE, and province of MUNSTER, 4½ miles (N. W.) from Ennis, on the road to Corofin; containing 7279 inhabitants. This parish was formerly called Dysert O'Dea, from its having been the territory of the sept of that name. It comprehends the subdivisions of Inagh and Ruan, and contains 23,417 statute acres, as rated for the county cess, of which a large portion consists of coarse mountain pasture. There are about 300 plantation acres of common, 100 acres of wood, and 100 acres of bog. The waste land consists chiefly of crag and underwood, and several hundred acres are covered with water, there being a number of lakes that in winter overflow the adjoining land to a considerable extent. Limestone abounds, and is burnt for manure; and the state of agriculture is gradually improving. The river Fergus runs through the greater part of the parish, through Tedane and other lakes, to Clare Town. Fairs are held at Ruan on June 17th and Sept. 26th, the latter being one of the principal sheep fairs in the county. At Dysert and Ruan are stations of the constabulary police. A court for the manor of Inchiquin is occasionally held by the seneschal, for the recovery of small debts. The gentlemen's seats are Toonagh, the residence of C. O'Brien, Esq.; Tierna, of Hewitt Bridgeman, Esq.; Port, of H. O'Loghlen, Esq., Carhue, of E. Synge, Esq.; Fountain, of E. Powell, Esq.; Rockview, of R. O'Loghlen, Esq.; Cogia, of T. Lingard, Esq.; and Drumore, the property of R. Crowe, Esq. The parish is in the diocese of Killaloe: the rectory forms part of the union and corps of the prebend of Rath, and the vicarage, part of the union of Kilneboy. The tithes amount to £250. 13. 9., of which £165. 1. 2¾. is payable to the rector, £83. 17. 11. to the vicar, and £1. 14. 7¼. to the prebendary of Tomgraney. There is a glebe of one plantation acre. In the R. C. divisions its northern and middle portions form the union or district of Dysert; and the south-western portion (Inagh) gives name to a district, which also includes the parish of Kilnemona. In the former district are the chapels of Dysert and Ruan, and in the latter, those of Inch and Kilnemona. The chapel at Ruan was rebuilt by subscription in 1834. About 660 children are educated in two public schools at Dysert and Ruan, and about 70 in a private school; to that at Dysert, E. Synge, Esq., contributes £24 per annum. Of the ruins of the churches of Dysert, Ruan, and Kiltala, the first is distinguished by its antiquity, and by the richly sculptured Saxon arch forming the doorway. Near these ruins are the remains of an ancient round tower, of which 30 feet are still standing; about 20 feet from the ground is a doorway, and 10 feet higher are the remains of another; at each stage the dimensions of the tower diminish, and outside the second story is a projecting belting-course. An ancient cross lies on the ground, bearing the effigy of a bishop, supposed to represent St. Monalagh, and other figures. A short distance from the ruins of Dysert church are those of the castle of that name, formerly the residence of the O'Deas; and at Mahre, Ballygriffy, and Port, are the ruins of similar castles: those of Port, standing on the verge of a lake, have a picturesque appearance. In a house in this parish, the ruins of which can scarcely be traced, the old song to the air of "Carolan's receipt for drinking whiskey" is said to have been composed by three poets, of whom a ridiculous story is related concerning the manner of writing it. For an account of the ancient sepulchral monument on Mount Callan, which extends into this parish, see KILFARBOY.

DYSERT, or DISART, a parish, in the barony of TRUGHENACKMY, county of KERRY, and province of MUNSTER, 1½ mile (S.) from Castle-Island, on the road to Killarney; containing 1431 inhabitants. It comprises 8105 statute acres, as applotted under the tithe act, about one-half of which consists of coarse mountain pasture and bog: limestone abounds, and is generally burnt for manure. It is a rectory, in the diocese of Ardfert and Aghadoe, forming part of the union of Killentierna: the tithes amount to £173. 12. 9., and there is a glebe of about 5½ acres. In the R. C. divisions it forms part of the union or district of Currens, or Killentierna. The ruins of the church still remain in the burial-ground; and at Kilsarcon are the vestiges of another church or chapel, with a burial-ground attached.

DYSERTALE, a parish, in the barony of DELVIN, county of WESTMEATH, and province of LEINSTER, 2 miles (S. W.) from Castletown-Delvin; containing 2 inhabitants. It comprises 80 plantation acres only, and is a rectory, in the diocese of Meath, forming part of the union of Kilcumney, or Drumcree: the tithes amount to £3. 6. 8.

DYSERTLYN.—See DESERTLYN.

DYSERTMORE, or DESERTMOON, a parish, in the barony of IDA, county of KILKENNY, and province of LEINSTER, 4 miles (S.) from Innistioge, on the river Nore; containing 1764 inhabitants. It comprises 5773 statute acres, as applotted under the tithe act, and is a vicarage, in the diocese of Ossory, forming part of the union of Rossbercon; the rectory is impropriate in the Corporation of Waterford. The tithes, which amount to £270, are equally divided between the corporation and the vicar. In the R. C. divisions also this parish is part of the union or district of Rossbercon. About 100 children are educated in two private schools; there is also a Sunday school.

E

EAGLE ISLAND.—See KILMORE-ERRIS.

EARLSTOWN, a parish, in the barony of SHILLELOGHER, county of KILKENNY, and province of LEINSTER, 2¾ miles (E.) from Callan, on the road from Desart to Thomastown; containing 679 inhabitants. This parish is situated on the King's river, here crossed by a stone bridge, and comprises 2916 statute acres. Kilcoran is the residence of J. Baker, Esq.; and Newtown House, of the Rev. B. Morris. It is a vicarage, in the diocese of Ossory, forming part of the union of Kells: the tithes amount to £197. 9. 9¼. In the R. C. divisions it is part of the union of Callan, and contains a chapel. Here is a private school of about 100 children. At Castle-Eve are the remains of an old castle, with a moat and fortifications; in the Newtown demesne is a square tower castle, in a good state of preservation; and there are some small remains of the old church, with a burial-ground.

EASKEY, a parish, in the barony of TYRERAGH, county of SLIGO, and province of CONNAUGHT, 11½ miles (N. N. E.) from Ballina, on the old road to Sligo; containing 6124 inhabitants, of which number, 289 are in the village. This parish is situated on the north-west coast, between the entrances to the bays of Sligo and Killala; it includes the Point of Kinesharrow, called also Rathlee Point, and comprises 12,977 statute acres, principally under an improving system of tillage; there is a large quantity of bog. Limestone, which abounds with fossils, is found on the sea shore: much sea-weed is collected for manure. The village consists of one long street of 76 houses, and has petty sessions once a fortnight, a market on Wednesday for provisions, fairs on June 3rd and Nov. 18th, and is a chief constabulary police station; fairs are also held at Rosslee in July, and on Oct. 28th. Fortland, pleasantly situated on the banks of the river Easkey, is the residence of R. Jones, Esq., proprietor of the salmon fishery here; Castletown, of T. Fenton, Esq.; and Rathlee, of T. Jones, Esq. The living is a vicarage, in the diocese of Killala, and in the patronage of the Bishop: the rectory is appropriate to the see. The tithes amount to £586. 14. 5., equally divided between the bishop and the vicar. The glebe-house, on a glebe of nine acres, was built by a gift of £300, and a loan of £500 from the late Board of First Fruits, in 1815. The church is a neat building with a square tower, erected by aid of a loan of £1342, from the same Board; the Ecclesiastical Commissioners have recently granted £130 for its repair. The R. C. parish is co-extensive with that of the Established Church, and contains a chapel. Here is also a place of worship for Baptists. About 600 children are educated in five public schools; and at Killenduff is a school supported by Col. Irwin, who built the school-house, and endowed it with three acres of land. In the village are the ruins of the old parish church; and there are considerable remains of the old castle of Rosslee, formerly belonging to the O'Dowds, and, on the opposite side of the river, the remains of another, on the lands of Castletown. There are several Danish forts, and on the lands of Townamodagh is a cromlech, seven feet high, and supported by four square pillars. The shores of the parish are bold and rocky, and abound with curiosities. At Alternan is a station, holy well, and saint's bed, named after St. Ernanus, and much frequented by pilgrims; the patron is held on the last Sunday in July. Near Fortland is a chalybeate spring.

EASTERSNOW, a parish, in the barony of BOYLE, county of ROSCOMMON, and province of CONNAUGHT, 3½ miles (S. S. E.) from Boyle, on the new line of road from Tulsk, through Shankill; containing 1951 inhabitants. It comprises 3199 statute acres, of which the greater part is under tillage, and there are several large grazing farms; about one-tenth is bog, and there are some quarries of good limestone. To the west of the church are the Cavetown loughs, bounded by hills and plantations. At the head of the largest is Croghan House, the seat of the late R. Mahon, Esq., now the property of Guy Lloyd, Esq., and on a hill beyond it is an obelisk, forming a conspicuous landmark. On the opposite shore is Clogher, the seat of J. Dick, Esq. The other seats are Camlin, that of J. Irwin, Esq., and Granny, of T. Irwin, Esq.; and on the road to Elphin are several neat residences, on the property of Viscount Lorton. The living is a vicarage, in the diocese of Elphin, episcopally united, in 1813, to the vicarage of Kilcola, and in the patronage of the Bishop; the rectory is impropriate in Lord Crofton. The tithes amount to £60. 16., one-half payable to the impropriator, and the other to the vicar; and the tithes of the benefice amount to £62. 14. 2., to which is added £39 per ann. from the Augmentation fund. The glebe-house was erected by aid of a gift of £337, and a loan of £70. from the late Board of First Fruits, in 1821. The church, a very plain edifice, is situated in a deep hollow near the southern extremity of the "Plains of Boyle," of which this parish is considered to be the limit. In the R. C. divisions the parish forms part of the union or district of Croghan and Ballinameen. The parochial school, and a school under the patronage of Mrs. Irwin, of Camlin, afford instruction to about 80 children; and there is also a private school, in which are about 30 children. In Cavetown are some caves partially filled up; they are said to extend to a very great length. There are also some scarcely perceptible vestiges of an old castle, called Moylerg, which is said to have belonged to the Mac Dermotts.

EDDY ISLAND, in Galway bay, parish of DROMACOO, barony of DUNKELLIN, county of GALWAY, and province of CONNAUGHT, 5 miles (S. by E.) from Galway: the population is returned with the parish. It comprises 95 acres of land, and is a prebend in the diocese of Kilmacduagh, and in the patronage of the Bishop, endowed with a portion of the tithes of Dromacoo, amounting to £6. 6. With other lands it was granted by Chas. II., in 1667, to Dr. Robert Georges, at a rent of £1. 2. 10¾. Here are the ruins of an old castle.

EDENDERRY, a market and post-town, in the parish of Castropetre, barony of Coolestown, King's county, and province of Leinster, 9 miles (E.) from Philipstown, and 32½ (W.) from Dublin, on the mail coach road from Conard, and close to the bog of Allen; containing 1427 inhabitants. This place, in the 16th century, obtained for a time the name of Coolestown from the family of Cooley, or Cowley, who had a castle here, which in 1599 was defended by Sir George Cooley against the insurgents in the Earl of Tyrone's rebellion, and in 1691 was sacked by a part of the army of Jas. II., under Lieut.-Col. O'Connor. It is near the right bank of the Grand Canal, from which a branch has been carried for nearly half a mile close up to the town; the late Marquess of Downshire gave the ground, and contributed £1000 towards the expense. The town consists of one wide street, from which diverge several smaller streets, and contains 214 houses, well built of stone and slated; it is well paved and supplied with water, and is rapidly improving. Adjoining, and now forming a part of it, under the name of Downshire Row, on the road to Monasteroris, are several tenements, formerly the small village of Glann, which the Marquess of Downshire has greatly improved and let to occupiers with about one rood of garden to each, at a nominal rent of one shilling per ann. A coarse kind of worsted stuff is made here, affording employment to 30 families, and there are a tanyard and a brewery. The market, in which considerable business is transacted, particularly in the corn trade, is on Saturday; fairs are held on Shrove-Tuesday, the Thursday after Whitsuntide, and Nov. 4th. A constabulary police force has been stationed here, and petty sessions are held on alternate Saturdays. The town-hall, a handsome building of stone, recently erected at an expense of £5000 by the Marquess of Downshire, proprietor of two-thirds of the town, affords in the lower part accommodation for the corn-market; and the upper part contains a large handsome room for assemblies and public meetings, with several offices, and in which the sessions and other courts are held. In the town is the parochial church, also a place of worship for the Society of Friends; and about ¾ of a mile distant is a R. C. chapel. There are some remains of the old castle, and about half a mile from the town are the ruins of the old abbey of Monasteroris, formerly a place of great strength; it held out for a considerable time against the Earl of Surrey, in 1521.—See Castropetre.

EDERMINE, a parish, in the barony of Ballaghkeen, county of Wexford, and province of Leinster, 2½ miles (S. by E.) from Enniscorthy, on the mail coach road from Wexford to Dublin; containing 213 inhabitants. This parish comprises 4015 statute acres, chiefly under tillage: the soil, which is productive, contains a great quantity of blue and red marl, and the state of agriculture is improving. The gentlemen's seats are Edermine, the residence of Laurence Toole, Esq.; and Rochfort, of J. Jervis Emerson, Esq. Fairs are held at the village of Oylgate on March 1st, May 21st, and Aug. 15th, chiefly for cattle. The projected canal from Pool Darragh to Enniscorthy will pass through the parish. It is a rectory, in the diocese of Ferns, united in 1806 to the vicarage of Ballynaslaney, together constituting the union and corps of the prebend of Edermine in the cathedral of Ferns, and in the gift of the Bishop: the tithes amount to £276. 18. 5½., and the entire tithes of the union to £332. 6. 1¾. The church, a neat edifice in the later English style, with a square tower surmounted with pinnacles, was built in 1811 by a gift of £200, and a loan of £600, from the late Board of First Fruits. It is beautifully situated on an eminence near the Slaney, and being surrounded by a thriving plantation, forms a picturesque object. A grant of £134 has been lately made by the Ecclesiastical Board for its complete repair. In the R. C. divisions the parish forms part of the union or district of Oylgate, which also comprises the parishes of Ballynaslaney and Ballyhuskard; and contains the chapels of Oylgate and Glanbryan. The former has been recently rebuilt, and adjoining it a residence for the parish priest, and a public school, have been erected. In this school, and in a school supported by the Protestant clergyman, and two private schools, about 80 children are educated. A holy well, dedicated to St. Coorawn, is chiefly resorted to by the peasantry for the cure of diseases of infants.

EDERNEY, a village, in the parish of Magheraculmony, barony of Lurg, county of Fermanagh, and province of Ulster, 2 miles (N.) from Kish, on the road from Enniskillen to Derry; containing 32 houses and 132 inhabitants. It is the property of the Rev. Mr. West, who is about to erect a market-house and some good dwelling-houses. Fairs are held on March 1st, May 16th, July 18th, Oct. 6th, Nov. 28th, and the 17th of every other month.

EDGEWORTH'STOWN, or MOSTRIM, a market and post-town, and a parish, in the barony of Ardagh, county of Longford, and province of Leinster, 6¾ miles (E. by S.) from Longford, on the road to Mullingar, and 52 (W. N. W.) from Dublin; containing 4744 inhabitants, of which number, 1001 are in the town, which takes its name from its proprietors, the family of Edgeworth, distinguished for their literary talents. In 1798 it was entered by a party of the insurgents, after the landing of the French in Kilcummin bay, when the mansion, from which the family had hastily retired, was left untouched. It contains 167 houses, and has a neat and improving appearance, the greater part having been rebuilt. It has a constabulary police station, and a dispensary. The market is on Wednesday; and fairs are held on the day before Shrove-Tuesday, May 5th, July 2nd, Sept. 12th, Nov. 5th, and the third Wednesday in December. The parish comprises 8126 statute acres, as applotted under the tithe act. Edgeworth'stown House, the seat of Lovell Edgeworth, Esq., is a handsome mansion in tastefully disposed grounds, laid out in lawns and plantations; it is also the residence of Maria Edgeworth. The living is a rectory and vicarage, in the diocese of Ardagh; the rectory is partly impropriate in Messrs. Greville and Kearney, and Sir J. B. Piers, Bart., and partly united with the vicarage, which is in the patronage of the Bishop. The tithes amount to £329. 10. 9., of which £117. 4. 7. is payable to the impropriators, and £212. 6. 2. to the incumbent. The church is a handsome edifice, with a spire of iron frame-work covered with Welsh slate; it was erected by aid of a gift of £150, and a loan of £500, from the late Board of First Fruits, in 1811, and contains a mural tablet to the memory of the late R. Lovell Edgeworth, Esq., who died in 1817. In the R. C. divisions the parish is united to part of Killoe; the chapel is a large handsome building. There are two schools supported by subscription, and one by Miss Edgeworth; in these about 25 boys and 60 girls are instructed, and there are six private schools, in which are about 270 boys and 110 girls.

EFFIN, a parish, partly in the barony of COSTLEA, but chiefly in that of COSHMA, county of LIMERICK, and province of MUNSTER, 1¾ mile (S. S. W.) from Kilmallock, on the road to Charleville; containing 2090 inhabitants, and comprising 8281 statute acres, of which 5138 are applotted under the tithe act. The land is excellent and much under tillage, and the mountain pasture good; the meadows attached to dairy farms are very productive. Newpark is the residence of J. Balie, Esq.; and Maiden Hall, of R. Low Holmes, Esq. It is a rectory and vicarage, in the diocese of Limerick, constituting the corps of the prebend of Effin in the cathedral of Limerick, and in the patronage of the Earl of Dunraven; the tithes amount to £320, and there is a glebe of seven acres. The church is in ruins, and the inhabitants attend that of Kilmallock. In the R. C. divisions it is united with those of Kilbreedy-minor and Kilquane; there are two small chapels, one at Effin, the other at Kilbreedy. About 90 children are taught in two hedge schools.

EFFISHBREDA, an extra parochial district, in the barony of ENNISHOWEN, county of DONEGAL, and province of ULSTER, 2 miles (N. W.) from Buncrana, on the road to Clonmany; containing 32 inhabitants. It comprises a wild mountain district lying between Desertegney and Lower Fahan, chiefly occupied by small farmers, and is nominally in the parish of Desertegney.

EGLISH, a parish, partly in the barony of ARMAGH, but chiefly in that of TURANEY, county of ARMAGH, and province of ULSTER, 4½ miles (N. W.) from Armagh, on the road from Caledon to Charlemont; containing 5419 inhabitants, and comprising, according to the Ordnance survey, 10,574¾ statute acres, of which 7146 are in the barony of Turaney; 9840 acres are applotted under the tithe act, of which about one-fifth is pasture; 526 are tithe free; and there is a small portion of waste land. Agriculture flourishes, the land is excellent, and the country much ornamented by the plantations of Elm Park, Knappagh, and Glenaule. There are quarries of limestone, which is much used for building and burning for manure. The Ulster canal passes through this parish: the inhabitants combine with husbandry the weaving of linen cloth. The seats are Elm Park, that of the Earl of Charlemont; Knappagh, of James Johnston, Esq.; Glenaule, of Joseph Johnston, Esq.; the glebe-house, of the Rev. W. Barlow; and the modern residences of B. Eyre and R. Cross, Esqrs., bordering on the county of Tyrone. It is a rectory and perpetual cure, in the diocese of Armagh; the rectory forms part of the union of Armagh, and the perpetual cure was instituted under the act of the 7th of Geo. III., cap. 17, and is in the patronage of the Rector. The tithes amount to £469. 0. 10.: the income of the perpetual curate is £200 per ann. arising from £100 paid by the rector, and £100 derived from the glebe lands. The glebe-house is commodious, and is situated on a glebe of 64 statute acres, given for that use by the late Joseph Johnston, Esq., of Knappagh, to Primate Robinson, who built the house. The same benefactor also gave the ground on which the old church and parish school-house were built, and six acres for the use of the schoolmaster. The church is a large handsome edifice, having a square tower with pinnacles; it was erected in 1821, 1½ mile south-east from the site of the old one, at a cost of £2000, partly by subscription, and partly from a loan of £1000 from the late Board of First Fruits. In the R. C. divisions the parish forms part of the union or district of Armagh, and contains a chapel. There is a parochial school on the glebe, aided by private subscriptions; two are supported by Lord and Lady Charlemont; one by endowment of seven acres of land and a house for the master, by Primate Robinson; one by the perpetual curate; Ballymartrum school, built and supported by Mr. Johnston, who has endowed it with an acre of land; and one, the school-house of which was built by Mr. Jackson. In these schools about 330 children are instructed. There is also a private school, the master of which has a house rent-free. The strongholds and palaces of the Hy Nials, Kings of Ulster, stood in this parish, mention of which is made in the 6th century by St. Fiech, and some traces exist on the townland of Crieve-Roe; they are called "the king's stables" by the country people. The extensive and nearly perfect fort of Navan, with its deep fosses and earthworks, occupies the entire summit of a hill. Not far from Navan is Lisdown, or "the city of forts," which gives name to the townland on which it stands. The ruins of the old church form a picturesque object on the summit of a hill near the western confines of the parish.

EGLISH, a parish, partly in the barony of LOWER ORMOND, county of TIPPERARY, and province of MUNSTER, but chiefly in that of EGLISH, or FIRCAL, KING'S county, and province of LEINSTER, 3 miles (N. E.) from Parsonstown, on the road to Tullamore; containing 3290 inhabitants. This parish is six miles in length by four in breadth, and comprises 7722 statute acres: there is a great deal of bog, and some limestone for building and burning. Eglish Castle is the residence of Capt. English; Tullinisky, of Handy Dynelly, Esq.; Whigsborough, of R. Drought, Esq.; and here is the residence of the Rev. W. Parsons. The living is a vicarage, in the diocese of Meath, forming part of the union of Fircall; the rectory is impropriate in the Marquess of Downshire. The tithes amount to £148. 12. 3., of which £96. 18. 5. is payable to the impropriator, and the remainder to the vicar: the glebe comprises 116*a.* 2*r.* 38*p.*, the annual value of which is £99. 8. The church is a very old building. In the R. C. divisions the parish is the head of a union or district, comprising also Drumcullin parish, in each of which is a chapel. There are six private schools, in which about 240 children are instructed.

EGLISH, county of TIPPERARY.—See AGLISH-CLOGHANE.

EGMONT.—See CHURCHTOWN.

EIRKE, a parish, partly in the barony of UPPER OSSORY, QUEEN'S county, but chiefly in that of GAL-

MOY, county of KILKENNY, and province of LEINSTER, 8¼ miles (S. W.) from Durrow, on the road from Rathdowney to Johnstown; containing 5565 inhabitants, and comprising 15,750 statute acres, as applotted under the tithe act, valued at £10,370. 6. per annum. About 2000 acres are bog. Two fairs are held at Bawn for cattle and horses; and here is a constabulary police station. Livally is the seat of — Fitzgerald, Esq. The living is a rectory and vicarage, in the diocese of Ossory, and in the patronage of the Crown; the tithes amount to £692. 6. 1¾. The glebe-house was built by aid of a gift of £100 and a loan of £800 from the late Board of First Fruits; the glebe comprises 15*a.* 25*p.* The church is a plain building, erected in 1823, towards which the late Board lent £650. In the R. C. divisions the parish is the head of a union or district, comprising also those of Fartagh and Glashane, and containing three chapels, two in Eirke and one in Fartagh; to the chapel at Moninamuck, in this parish, Lord Courtown gave an acre of land and £50 towards the expense of its erection; it is in contemplation to rebuild the other. The parochial school is aided by the rector, and has a house and an acre of land rent-free: about 50 boys and 50 girls are taught in it. There are also nine private schools, in which are about 500 children.

ELPHIN, a market and post-town, the seat of a bishoprick, and a parish, in the barony and county of ROSCOMMON, and province of CONNAUGHT, 8½ miles (S. by E.) from Boyle, and 80½ (W. N. W.) from Dublin, on the road from Roscommon to Boyle; containing 6643 inhabitants, of which number, 1507 are in the town. This city appears to have arisen as a dependency on the religious establishment that was founded by St. Patrick in the fifth century: it was burned in 1177 and destroyed by the English in 1187. Its name appears to be derived from *Ail Fin*, "the white stone or rock," though connected by vulgar tradition with the giant Fin Mac Coul. About the year 1450, Bishop Cornelius converted the conventual church of St. Patrick into a Franciscan monastery, to which the canons and inhabitants of Elphin were likewise benefactors. Bishop King who presided over the see from 1611 to 1638, erected a castle for himself and his successors, and attached to it lands which he had purchased. This castle, in 1645, was delivered into the hands of the Lord-President of Connaught by Bishop Tilson, who retired to England: his son was then governor of Elphin and had just declared for the parliament. The town, which consists of about 260 houses, is on a ridge, and presents a pleasing appearance on entering it from the south. The main street is wide, and in the centre is a covered fountain which supplies pure water. A market has been established by the bishop on Wednesdays, for which a market-house will be erected; and fairs are held on May 3rd, June 27th, Sept. 26th, and Dec. 10th. Petty sessions are held every Wednesday, and it is a chief constabulary police station. The parish comprises 8962 statute acres, as applotted under the tithe act. It is partly under tillage, but principally in pasture, and large quantities of butter are exported by the river Shannon. Here are quarries of limestone and a considerable tract of bog. The principal seats are Smith Hill, that of the Rev. J. Lloyd; Cloonyquin, of W. French, Esq.; Foxborough, of P. Taaffe, Esq., and Raheen, of Major Fawcett.

Arms of the Bishoprick.

The DIOCESE of ELPHIN is said to have been founded by St. Patrick, who placed over it St. Asicus, an austere monk, who soon filled the cathedral with members of his own order. Several small surrounding sees appear to have been annexed to it at an early period, and a short time before the arrival of the English in Ireland it was enriched with many large estates by the annexation of the see of Roscommon. On an inquisition made in the 28th of Elizabeth, the see was valued at £1103. 18. per annum: it was greatly impoverished by Bishop John Lynch between 1584 and 1611, but was restored to its previous value by his successor, Bishop King. On the death of Bishop Hudson, in 1685, Jas. II. kept the see vacant for several years and distributed the revenue among the Catholic clergy. Elphin is one of the six dioceses which form the ecclesiastical province of Tuam, but under the Church Temporalities act of the 3rd and 4th of Wm. IV. c. 37, its temporalities are, on the next avoidance, to be transferred to the Ecclesiastical Commissioners, and the see is to be united to the bishoprick of Kilmore. It comprises parts of the counties of Galway and Sligo, and the greater part of Roscommon, and is computed to contain 420,150 acres, of which 48,800 are in Galway, 87,700 in Sligo, and the remainder in Roscommon. The gross revenue of the bishoprick, on an average of three years ending Dec. 31st, 1831, is £7034. 8. 9.; and the see lands comprise 42,843 acres, of which 29,235 are profitable. The Episcopal palace is a good building in an extensive demesne near the town, and was erected by an accumulated fund of £500 bequeathed by Bishop Hudson in 1685. The chapter consists of a dean, precentor, archdeacon, and the eight prebendaries of Kilgoghlin, Tirebrine, Kilmacallane, Kilcooley, Tibohine, Ballintubber, Oran, and Tarmon. The dean and chapter have no patronage, and there are neither minor canons nor vicars choral connected with the cathedral. The economy fund arises from a moiety of Bishop Hudson's bequest, and consists of rents arising from lands in the county of Cavan, at present amounting to £50 per ann. late currency. The consistorial court, which is held at Elphin, consists of a vicar-general, registrar, and apparitor. The diocesan school, which is also at Elphin, is endowed with £25 per annum from Bishop Hudson's fund, and has a house with 15 acres of land; the master's salary is £100 late currency. There is a diocesan society for the promotion of scriptural schools, to which the bishop subscribes £100 and Viscount Lorton £50 per annum. The diocese contains 32 benefices, of which 19 are unions and 13 are single parishes. Of these one is in the gift of the Crown, one in lay patronage, two in joint or alternate patronage, and the Bishop has the right of presentation to the remainder. The number of parishes or districts is 74, of which 71 are rectories or vicarages, and three are perpetual curacies. It contains 39 churches and three other places where divine worship is performed, also 22 glebe-houses. The R. C. diocese corresponds in extent with that of the Established Church, and is one of the six suffragan to the

Archbishoprick of Tuam. Within its limits there are 43 parochial districts, containing 80 chapels, served by 85 clergymen, of which 43 are parish priests and 42 coadjutors or curates. Sligo is the R. C. bishop's parish, in which he resides.

The rectory of Elphin is united time immemorially with the rectory of Ogulla, forming the corps of the deanery of Elphin, which is in the patronage of the Crown. The tithes of Elphin amount to £221. 10. 9., those of Ogulla to £93. 16. 5¾., and the annual value of the deanery, including 238 acres of glebe land, is £532. 12. 9. The glebe-house, or deanery, is a good residence on the western side of the town, built by aid of a gift of £100 from the late Board of First Fruits, in 1816. The cathedral, which has for more than a century been used as the parish church, is dedicated to St. Mary: the late Board of First Fruits gave £300, in 1759, and the Ecclesiastical Commissioners recently gave £121 for repairing it. It is a plain modernised building, about 80 feet long by 28 feet broad, with an ancient square tower: the interior is very neat, and at the eastern end are the bishop's throne and the dignitaries' stalls; several tombstones of bishops interred here are built in the wall of the vestry, and in the body of the church a handsome monument has been recently erected to the memory of the late Rev. Wm. Smith, V. G., and master to the diocesan school, by his pupils. In the R. C. divisions this parish is the head of a union or district, comprising Elphin, Shankill, and Kilmacumsey, and containing chapels at Elphin, Ballyroddy, and Flask. Besides the diocesan school, in which the celebrated Oliver Goldsmith was educated, there are two public schools, to which the bishop contributes £20 and the dean £7 annually: about 230 children are educated in these schools, and about 570 in nine private schools. The children who attend the public schools are clothed annually by the bishop, who also contributes largely to the support of a dispensary. Here is a loan fund, with a capital of £700. A cromlech which stood here has been thrown down, and a patron that was held at Tubbermurry is almost discontinued. Here are Rath Croghan and Rilickna Riagh, places remarkable for their caves and ancient burial-grounds, as well as for some rude remains connected by tradition with the history of the kings of Connaught, who are said to have been crowned at the former and buried at the latter place.

EMATRIS, a parish, in the barony of Dartry, county of Monaghan, and province of Ulster, 3 miles (N. E. by E.) from Cootehill, on the roads to Clones and Monaghan; containing 7541 inhabitants; and comprising, according to the Ordnance survey, 12,297¾ statute acres, of which 590½ are under water, and 10,793 are applotted under the tithe act, and valued at £8985 per annum. The soil is a rich shallow loam, on deep stiff clay, very difficult of cultivation: there is some bog, and about 400 acres of underwood. The weaving of linen to a small extent is combined with agriculture. Petty sessions are held on alternate Wednesdays at Rock Corry. Dawson Grove, the noble mansion of Lord Cremorne, stands in a demesne of more than 1000 acres, embellished with lakes adorned with islands, on which grows the finest timber; some of these islands embrace remarkable views, particularly that of Bellamont forest: in one of the woods is a temple containing a beautiful group of marble statuary to the memory of Lady Ann Dawson: on a rising ground in the demesne, and close to the public road, is a handsome column, erected by public subscription, to the memory of Richard Dawson, Esq., who represented the county of Monaghan in five successive parliaments. The other seats are Freame Mount, the residence of R. Mayne, Esq.; Glenburnie Park, of C. Stewart Corry, Esq.; Tanagh, of Capt. C. Dawson; Dromore Lodge, of Lieut. Dawson, R. N.; New Park, of Dacre Hamilton, Esq.; and Cremorne Cottage, of the Rev. N. Devereux. The living is a rectory and vicarage, in the diocese of Clogher, and in the patronage of the Bishop: the tithes amount to £365. The church, picturesquely situated in the demesne of Dawson Grove, is a handsome building with a tower, and was recently repaired by a grant of £100 from the Ecclesiastical Commissioners. The R. C. parish is co-extensive with that of the Established Church; there is a chapel at Edergole, and another at Coravockan, a neat slated building. There are a place of worship for Presbyterians in connection with the Seceding Synod, of the second class, and three for Wesleyan Methodists. The parish school is aided by an annual donation from the rector, and £10 from Lady Cremorne, with grass for a cow and a house rent-free; in this school about 60 children are instructed. There are seven other public schools, one of which is an infants' school with a sewing school attached, under the patronage of Mrs. Devereux. There are also three hedge schools, in which are about 120 boys and 50 girls; and four Sunday schools. A Clothing Society, for supplying the poor with blankets, &c., is aided by Lady Cremorne, T. C. S. Corry, Esq., and the rector; and a lending library is supported by general subscription. Near Freame Mount is a very large rath, occupying an acre of land, and commanding a number of Toghers, or bog passes, flanked by two smaller ones.

EMERICK.—See IMPHRICK.

EMLAGH, or IMLAGH, a parish, in the barony of Lower Kells, county of Meath, and province of Leinster, 4 miles (N. E. by E.) from Kells, on the road from Moynalty to Navan; containing 349 inhabitants; and comprising 2964 statute acres, as applotted under the tithe act. The river Borora runs through the parish, and joins the Blackwater at Bloomsbury. Here is a large bog, which supplies the surrounding country with fuel. It is a rectory, in the diocese of Meath, forming part of the union of Newtown: the tithes amount to £90. In the R. C. divisions it is part of the union or district of Stahalmock.

EMLY, a parish, and the seat of a diocese, in the barony of Clanwilliam, county of Tipperary, and province of Munster, 7 miles (S. W.) from Tipperary, and 15 (W.) from Cashel, on the confines of the county of Limerick; containing 3838 inhabitants, of which number, 701 are in the village. This place, noticed under the name of "Imlagh" by Ptolemy, as one of the three principal towns of Ireland, is of very remote antiquity, and was formerly an important city and the seat of a diocese. A monastery of canons regular was founded here by St. Ailbe, or Alibeus, who became its first abbot, and dying in 527, was interred in the abbey. His successors obtained many privileges for the inhabitants. The abbey and town were frequently pillaged and burnt. King John, in the 17th of his reign, granted the privilege of holding markets and fairs in the town, which, since the union of the see of Emly with that of Cashel in 1568, has gradually declined, and is now comparatively an insignificant village, containing only 115 houses. It has a constabulary police station, and fairs are held on May 21st and Sept. 22nd.

Among the successors of St. Ailbe in the SEE of EMLY, previously to the landing of the English, and who were styled indifferently abbots or bishops, were several who exercised sovereign power at Cashel, as Kings of Munster. Olchobhair Mac Cionoatha, who in 847 succeeded to the prelacy, and to the throne of Munster, aided by Lorcan, son of the King of Leinster, killed 1200 of the Danes who had plundered the monastery during the preceding year; and 1700 were slain in a subsequent battle, in which Olchobhair was killed. In 1123, during the prelacy of Moelmorda, the abbey was plundered and the mitre of St. Ailbe, which had been preserved for many ages, was burnt. Bishop Christian, who succeeded to the prelacy in 1236, was a great benefactor to the cathedral church, in which Bishop Henley, who died in 1542, erected a college of secular priests. The last bishop of this see, prior to its union with that of Cashel, to which the archbishoprick had been previously transferred, was Reymund de Burgh, after whose death, in 1562, it remained vacant till 1568, when it was united by act of parliament to the archbishoprick of Cashel, during the prelacy of Archbishop Mac Caghwell. The diocese is one of the eleven that constitute the archdiocese, or ecclesiastical province, of Cashel: it comprises an estimated superficies of 138,050 statute acres, of which 86,150 are in the county of Limerick, and 51,900 in that of Tipperary. The chapter consists of a dean, precentor, chancellor, archdeacon, treasurer, and the four prebendaries of Dollardstown Killenellick, Doon, and Lattin. It comprehends 17 benefices, of which nine are unions of two or more parishes, and eight are single parishes; of these, four are in the patronage of the Crown, and 13 in that of the Archbishop of Cashel. The total number of parishes is 44, of which 39 are rectories and vicarages, three perpetual curacies, and two without provision for the cure of souls; there are eleven churches and four other places in which divine service is performed, and nine glebe-houses. In the R. C. divisions the diocese is united with the archdiocese of Cashel, and contains 31 chapels.—See CASHEL.

The living is a vicarage, in the diocese of Emly, and in the patronage of the Archbishop of Cashel; the rectory is appropriate to the economy fund of the cathedral of Emly. The tithes amount to £450, of which £300 is payable as rectorial tithes, and the remainder to the vicar. The glebe-house is a neat building, and the glebe comprises 10 acres. The cathedral, which serves also as the parish church, is a handsome structure of hewn stone, in the later English style, with a lofty spire, erected in 1827, at an expense of £2521. 11. 9., defrayed from a surplus of the economy fund, which had been for several years accumulating for that purpose. The R. C. parish is co-extensive with that of the Established Church, and contains a chapel. There are two private schools, in which are about 80 children. In the churchyard is a large cross of rough stone, also a well, called St. Ailbe's well, which are held in veneration by the peasantry, who assemble here on the 12th of September, the anniversary of that saint's death. A very ancient canoe, resembling those of the South Sea islanders, was dug up some time since near the village; and very rich armlets of gold and brass swords have also been found in the adjacent bogs.

EMLYFADD, a parish, in the barony of CORRAN, county of SLIGO, and province of CONNAUGHT, on the road from Boyle to Coolaney; containing, with the post-town of Ballymote (which is described under its own head), 4645 inhabitants; and comprising 9915 statute acres, chiefly pasture, with some bog. Agriculture is improving: there are quarries of good limestone in the parish. The gentlemen's seats are Carrowkeel, that of F. Mac Donagh, Esq.; Drimrane, of J. Taaffe, Esq.; Temple House, of Col. A. Percival; the glebe-house, of the Rev. J. Garrett; and Earlsfield, the property of Sir R. Gore Booth, Bart. The living is a vicarage, in the diocese of Achonry, united by act of council, in 1807, to Kilmorgan, Kiltora, Tumore, and Drumratt, together forming the union of Emlyfadd, in the patronage of the Bishop; the rectory is impropriate partly in Sir H. C. Montgomery, Bart., and partly in the Earl of Kingston. The tithes amount to £407. 7. 7½., of which £168. 1. 6. is payable to Sir H. Montgomery, and £239. 6. 1½. to the vicar, from which latter sum the Earl of Kingston claims £40; and the gross amount of the tithes of the benefice is £710. The glebe-house was built by aid of a gift of £100 and a loan of £600, in 1810, from the late Board of First Fruits; the glebe comprises 20 acres. The church, at Ballymote, is a good building in the early English style, remarkable for the beauty of its tower and spire; it was erected by aid of loans of £550, in 1818, and £1000, in 1831, from the late Board, and donations of £300 from the Earl of Orkney, and £100 each from the Bishop of Killala and E. S. Cooper, Esq. The Ecclesiastical Commissioners have recently granted £190 for its repair. In the R. C. divisions this is the head of a union or district, also called Ballymote, comprising this parish and that of Kilmorgan, in each of which is a chapel; that in Ballymote is a large building. There is also a place of worship for Wesleyan Methodists. In the parish are four public schools, of which the parochial school is aided by Sir R. G. Booth, Viscount Lorton, and local subscriptions, and in which about 420 children are instructed. There are also two private schools, in which are about 100 children. The ruins of the old church, with its steeple, form a conspicuous object, from their elevated situation. An abbey is said to have been founded here by St. Columb, over which his disciple, St. Enna, presided. On the edge of Temple House lake are the ruins of an old house, once inhabited by the Knights Templars; and near Ballymote is a fort of considerable elevation.

EMLY-GRENAN, or ST. MALO, a parish, in the barony of COSTLEA, county of LIMERICK, and province of MUNSTER, 4 miles (E.) from Kilmallock, on the old road to Galbally. It comprises 2372 statute acres, as applotted under the tithe act. The land is in general good, resting for the greater part on a substratum of limestone; about two-thirds are under tillage, and the remainder meadow and pasture, of which latter about 180 acres are rough mountain. The living is a rectory, in the diocese of Limerick, and part of the corps of the treasurership of the cathedral of Limerick: the tithes amount to £150. The glebe, consisting of lands formerly belonging to the college, which was dissolved at the Reformation, comprises 39 acres. The church, formerly collegiate, was destroyed in 1641, and has not been rebuilt; the members of the Establishment attend the church of Kilmallock. In the R. C. divisions the parish forms part of the union or district of Ballinvana; there is a large modern chapel at the Red-bog.

EMO, a post-town, in the parish of COOLBANAGHER, barony of PORTNEHINCH, QUEEN'S county, and province of LEINSTER, 5 miles (E.) from Maryborough, and 34¾ (W. S. W.) from Dublin, near the high road to Maryborough; containing 14 houses and 102 inhabitants. Here are the R. C. chapel (a neat building), a public school, and a constabulary police station. Adjoining the town is Emo park, formerly Dawson's Court, the splendid mansion of the Earl of Portarlington.—See COOLBANAGHER.

EMYVALE, a post-town, in the parish of DONAGH, barony of TROUGH, county of MONAGHAN, and province of ULSTER, 5¾ miles (N. by W.) from Monaghan, and 71½ (N. W. by N.) from Dublin, on the road from Monaghan to Aughnacloy; containing 123 houses and 571 inhabitants. This town, which is nearly on the confines of the counties of Armagh and Tyrone, consists principally of one street, and is skirted by a stream tributary to the river Blackwater, which, descending from the mountains on the west, frequently, becomes a rapid and dangerous torrent after heavy rains. On its banks is a large flour-mill, and in its bed above the town is a quarry of greenstone. There is a constabulary police station, and petty sessions are held every fortnight in the town, in which is also a branch of the Glasslough dispensary. In the vicinity are several gentlemen's seats, which are noticed in the account of Donagh, *which see.*

ENERILEY.—See ENORELY.

ENFIELD, a post-town, in the parish of RATHCORE, barony of LOWER MOYFENRAGH, county of MEATH, and province of LEINSTER, 5½ miles (W.) from Kilcock, and 20 (W.) from Dublin, on the mail road to Kinnegad: the population is returned with the parish. The Royal Canal passes close by the town, which comprises about 50 houses, the property of J. H. Rorke, Esq. of Johnstown, in the immediate vicinity. Here is a station of the constabulary police.

ENNIS, a borough, and market-town, in the parish of DROMCLIFFE, barony of ISLANDS, county of CLARE, (of which it is the chief town), and province of MUNSTER, 18 miles (N. W.) from Limerick, on the mail road to Galway, and 111¾ (S. W.) from Dublin; containing 7711, and within the new electoral boundary, 9747 inhabitants. This place derives its name, formerly spelt Innis or Inish, signifying an island, from the insulation of a considerable plot of ground by the river Fergus. According to the Ulster Annals, it was anciently called *Inniscluan-ruadha,* and one of its suburbs is still called Clonroad. Mac Curtin states that it was eminent as a seat of learning, upwards of 600 scholars and 350 monks having been here supported by O'Brien, prince of Thomond, after the arrival of the English. About the year 1240, Donogh Carbrac O'Brien erected a noble monastery at Ennis for Franciscan friars, which in 1305, according to the Annals of Innisfallen, was rebuilt or repaired and much adorned by another branch of that family. It was for a long period the place of sepulture of the princes of Thomond, and occasionally of the chiefs of the sept of Mac Namara; and its prosperity appears to have been in these times dependent on this circumstance. In 1306, Dermot, grandson of Brien-Roe, at the head of a body of native and English forces, entirely destroyed the town. In 1311, Donogh, King of Thomond, bestowed the whole revenue of his principality for the enlargement and support of this monastery, and some time after the refectory and sacristy were built by Mathew Mac Namara. It is recorded in the Ulster Annals that Terence O'Brien, bishop of Killaloe, was here barbarously slain, in 1460, by Brien O'Brien. The friary was reformed by Franciscans of the Strict Observance: it remained in the Crown for some time subsequent to the Reformation, and was granted, in 1621, to Wm. Dongan, Esq. In 1609, Donogh, or Donat, Earl of Thomond, obtained a grant of a market and fairs to be held here; and in 1612 "the town of Inish," was created a borough. In 1661, the goods of some of the townspeople were seized in payment of salary due to Isaac Granier, one of their representatives in parliament, but were released on their stating, that he had agreed to serve gratuitously as their representative.

It is situated nearly in the centre of the county, on the principal or south-western branch of the river Fergus, which surrounds a portion of the town and its north-eastern suburbs; two of the principal streets form a continuous line following the winding of the river, and a third branches off from the court-house towards Limerick. The most populous of these is very narrow and irregularly built, and the entrance from Limerick is rendered equally inconvenient by a projecting angle of the court-house, which, from its dilapidated state, requires to be rebuilt. In 1831 the town comprised 1104 houses, and within the new electoral boundary, 1390; the suburbs, which are very extensive, consist chiefly of cabins. A new street of superior houses has been lately built between the county infirmary and the river; and a handsome bridge of a single arch, with parapets of hewn stone, has been recently completed, at an expense of £800, on the site of a former one nearly opposite the abbey. The town is not lighted, and the police perform the duty of a nightly patrol. A county club-house has been established; there are also two subscription news-rooms; and races are held annually in the autumn, which generally continue five days. The numerous seats in the vicinity are noticed under the head of Dromcliffe and the adjacent parishes, in which they are situated. The woollen manufacture, which formerly flourished here, has greatly declined; but the trade in corn, butter, and other produce has much increased. About 60,000 barrels of wheat, 100,000 of oats, and 30,000 of barley, are annually sold in the market, and chiefly shipped at Clare, about two miles distant, to which place the Fergus is navigable for lighters, and thence to the sea for vessels of considerable burden. A plan for improving the navigation between Ennis and Clare, is noticed in the account of the latter town, which is considered the port of Ennis. A weighing-house for butter, of which a large quantity is annually exported, was built in 1825, and there are several large corn stores. Ennis Mills, which have been recently enlarged, are capable of producing 30,000 barrels of flour annually: the produce is much esteemed in the Limerick market. At Clonroad is the extensive brewery of Messrs. Harley and Co., who are also about to re-establish a distillery formerly carried on at that place; and there is a smaller brewery in the town; the Ennis ale is in great repute. Branches of the Provincial and Agricultural Banks, and a savings' bank, have been established. A market for the sale of country produce is held daily, but the principal markets are on Tuesday and Saturday, and are abundantly supplied with provisions of every description. Fairs are held in the town on April 9th, and Sept. 3rd, and at Clonroad on May 9th, Aug. 1st, Oct. 14th, and Dec. 3rd; of the latter, the first three are large fairs for cattle and horses, and the last is chiefly for pigs.

By the charter of the 10th of Jas. I. (1612), the corporation, under the style of "The Provost, Free Burgesses, and Commonalty of the Town of Ennis," consists of a provost, twelve free burgesses, and a town-clerk, with power to admit an unlimited number of freemen to constitute a "commonalty;" but no freemen have been appointed for many years. The provost is elected by the burgesses from their own body, on the 24th of June, and sworn into office on the 29th of Sept.: until lately he appointed a deputy, called the vice-provost. The burgesses are elected for life by the provost and burgesses, who also appoint the town-clerk. The provost is empowered by the charter to hold a court of record, with cognizance of debts not exceeding £3. 6. 8. late currency, arising within the limits of the borough: this court was held until within the last 12 years, by the vice-provost, who also acted as weigh-master. By the charter the provost is a magistrate within the old borough, and the vice-provost formerly acted as such; but latterly no exclusive jurisdiction, either civil or criminal, has been exercised. The borough sent two members to the Irish parliament prior to the Union, since which period it has returned one to the Imperial parliament: the right of election, formerly limited to the provost and free burgesses, was, by the act of the 2nd of Wm. IV., cap. 88, extended to the £10 householders; and a new boundary was formed for electoral purposes, comprising an area of 469 statute acres, and comprehending the entire town and suburbs, which is minutely described in the Appendix. The number of voters registered, in March 1836, was 254, of which 7 were free burgesses, and the remainder £10 householders; and the number polled at the last election was 194: the provost is the returning officer. The spring and summer assizes, and the January, April, and October quarter sessions for the eastern division of the county, are held in the court-house. Petty sessions are held every Friday; and a court for the manor of Clonroad, which was granted by Jas. I. to the Earl of Thomond, and now belongs to the Earl of Egremont, is occasionally held by the seneschal, for the recovery of debts not exceeding £10 late currency. The county gaol, situated on the south side of the town, is an extensive modern building on the radiating principle, with detached prisons for females and debtors, lately erected in front: it contains 10 day-rooms and airing-yards, 73 sleeping cells, and 12 other bed-rooms, and has a treadmill. The total expense of the establishment, for 1835, was £2522. 7. 10. The constabulary police force, including an extra force called the peace preservation police, is under the control of a resident stipendiary chief magistrate and a sub-inspector; the barrack is a commodious building, formed out of the old county gaol. A party of the revenue police is also stationed in the town.

The parish church, which forms part of the ancient abbey, was much injured by lightning in 1817; the abbey tower was also damaged and the bell destroyed. The late Board of First Fruits granted £2000 for its renovation, and the tower was subsequently heightened by the addition of battlements and pinnacles: a grant of £146 has been recently made by the Ecclesiastical Commissioners for the further improvement of the church. The organ was presented, in 1825, by the Earl of Egremont. The R. C. district of Ennis comprises the eastern part of the parish of Dromcliffe, including the whole of the town and suburbs: the R. C. chapel is an old building, situated in an obscure part of the town. A chaste and elegant cruciform structure, from a design by Mr. Madden, was commenced in 1831, on a more eligible site, under the superintendence of the Very Rev. Dean O'Shaughnessy, P. P., which is intended for the cathedral of the R. C. diocese of Killaloe: the tower will be surmounted by a spire rising to the height of 140 feet. The estimated expense is £5000, towards which Sir Edward O'Brien, Bart., of Dromoland, contributed £100: the site was presented by Francis Gore, Esq. A small society of Franciscans has a chapel which is open to the public; and to the east of the town is an Ursuline convent, established about seven years since. There are meeting-houses for Primitive Methodists and Independents; and a congregation of Separatists meet in the court-house: the Methodist meeting-house is a modern building, erected chiefly at the expense of Mr. Leach. Ennis college is one of the four classical schools founded by the munificent bequest of Erasmus Smith. The school-house, which is situated at a short distance north of the town, was built about 70 years since by the trustees, who have recently added wings and out-offices, and made other extensive improvements, at an expense of nearly £1200: it is now capable of accommodating more than 100 boarders, and a large number of day scholars. The building, which presents an imposing front, is approached from the extremity of the promenade called the "College walk" by a handsome gateway of four octangular pillars, and, together with the extensive play-ground, is surrounded by a high wall. The head master receives a salary of £100 from the trustees, and is allowed the full benefit of the establishment as a boarding and day school; the second master also receives £100; and the third, £80. The course of instruction comprises the ancient and modern languages, mathematics, and English composition, and there are usually ten free day scholars on the foundation. The parochial school, in Jail-street, is supported by subscription; a school is held in Cook's-lane meeting-house, and a Sunday school in the church. Near the town is a large and substantial school-house, built in 1830, at an expense of £800, of which £200 was contributed by the National Board, by whom the school, in which are about 400 boys, is partly supported, and partly by collections at the R. C. chapel. About 200 girls are instructed by the nuns of the convent, by whom they are also taught every description of useful and ornamental needlework. Connected with the nunnery-school is a preparatory establishment for very young girls, under the patronage of Dean O'Shaughnessy, who contributes £6 per ann. towards its support. The County

Infirmary, situated on the north side of the town, is a substantial building, containing four wards for male and two for female patients, with a dispensary, and accommodations for a resident surgeon and apothecary. The Fever Hospital is situated in a confined part of the town, but one for the county is now being erected in a more appropriate situation and on a larger scale, to which a cholera hospital will be attached. The House of Industry immediately adjoins the infirmary, and contains three male and four female wards; it was built by subscription about the year 1775, and is governed by a corporation under an act of the Irish parliament. A loan fund, for the benefit of the poorer classes of tradesmen and farmers, has been for some time in operation, and a mendicity society was established in 1832. The remains of the Franciscan abbey, founded by the Kings of Thomond, of whom several were interred in it, still present many traces of its ancient grandeur. Of these, the principal is the grand eastern window, upwards of 30 feet high, consisting of five lancet-shaped compartments, separated by stone mullions, and universally admired for its exceedingly light proportions and beautiful workmanship. In the chancel is the "Abbot's chair," which, with the altar, is richly sculptured with figures in high relief; and some of the ancient monuments, also profusely sculptured, still exist.—See DROMCLIFFE.

ENNISBOFFIN.—See INNISBOFFIN.

ENNISCOFFEY, a parish, in the barony of FARTULLAGH, county of WESTMEATH, and province of LEINSTER, 5 miles (S. S. E.) from Mullingar, near the road to Kinnegad; containing 939 inhabitants. A battle was fought at Gaybrook, in this parish, between the forces of Wm. III. and the Irish adherents of Jas. II., in which the latter were defeated and pursued to Killucan. The parish comprises 4167 statute acres, principally grazing land, and a large proportion of bog. The chief seats are Gaybrook, the residence of Mrs. A. Smith, a handsome mansion in a fine demesne, richly planted and diversified with artificial lakes; Enniscoffey House, of M. A. Levinge, Esq.; and Birmingham, of G. Rochfort, Esq. The living is a vicarage, in the diocese of Meath, united by act of council, in 1818, to the rectory of Kilbride-Pilate, and in the patronage of the Bishop; the rectory is impropriate in the Misses Blundell. The tithes amount to £112. 12. 3½., the whole payable to the impropriators; the annual value of the benefice, including glebe, is £106. 8. The glebe-house, situated in the parish of Kilbride-Pilate, was built by aid of a gift of £450 and a loan of £200, in 1821, from the late Board of First Fruits; the glebe comprises 16 acres, valued at £6. 8. 0. per ann. The church is a neat edifice, built by aid of a gift of £900, in 1818, from the same Board. In the R. C. divisions the parish forms part of the union or district of Fartullagh. About 45 children are taught in the parochial school, which is aided by the incumbent and Mrs. Smith, and an infants' school of 50 children is entirely supported by the latter.

ENNISCORTHY, a corporate, market, and post-town, and a parish (called St. Mary's, Enniscorthy), in the barony of SCARAWALSH, county of WEXFORD, and province of LEINSTER, 11¾ miles (N.) from Wexford, and 62¾ (S. by W.) from Dublin, on the river Slaney, and on the road from Wexford to Dublin; containing, within the parish, 4938, and in the entire parish and town, which latter extends into the parish of Templeshannon and barony of Ballaghkeen, 5955 inhabitants. This place probably derives its name from a beautiful island in the bed of the Slaney, which here divides that river into two channels. It is said by Seward to have been originally the capital of the *Coriondi*, and by other writers to have been called "Corthae," and subsequently given as a portion to Basilea, sister of Strongbow, on her marriage with Raymond Le Gros, to whom is attributed the erection of its ancient castle. In 1227, the town was surrendered by Philip de Prendergast to the Bishop of Ferns, who asserted a superior claim; and in 1231 it was confirmed to that prelate by Gerald de Prendergast, the son of Philip, to whom the bishop restored it in exchange for other lands, on condition of his holding it under the see. The castle and manor afterwards came into the possession of the McMurroughs, or Kavanaghs, and were granted by Donald, surnamed Fuscus, to the Franciscan monastery which he had founded, after the dissolution of which they were given by Queen Elizabeth to John Travers, who conveyed them for a term of years to the poet Spenser, by whom they were assigned to Sir Henry Wallop, Knt., ancestor of the Earl of Portsmouth. In 1649, the town and castle were taken by Cromwell, and soon after became the property of an ancestor of the Carew family, but were subsequently restored to the Wallop family, in exchange for other lands, by Robt. Carew, Esq. In 1798, this place was the scene of much hostility: the town, which was garrisoned by 300 of the King's troops, and by several corps of yeomanry, both horse and foot, was attacked on the 28th of May by nearly 7000 of the insurgent forces, who, after a sanguinary conflict, compelled the garrison to retreat to the market-place, where, making a resolute stand, they ultimately repulsed the assailants. But the town being on fire in several places, and surrounded by an overwhelming number of the insurgents, the king's forces retreated to Wexford, and the enemy plundered the town, damaged the interior of the church, and converted the castle into a prison. On the 29th the insurgents took their station on Vinegar Hill, an adjoining eminence, where, being joined by the disaffected from the surrounding country, the numbers increased to upwards of 10,000 men. Many of the loyal inhabitants of the town, who had not been able to escape with the garrison to Wexford, were brought prisoners to the insurgents' camp, tried by a court martial, and put to death. Gen. Johnson, with a party of the royal forces, succeeded in making himself master of the town; and on the 21st of June, Gen. Lake, commander-in-chief of the royal army, attacked the insurgents in their camp, and routed them. The enemy fled with precipitation towards Wexford, leaving behind them great numbers of slain and thirteen pieces of ordnance.

The town is built on the acclivities of the hills on both sides of the Slaney, and in 1831 contained 1047 houses: the streets are in general narrow and in some parts inconveniently steep for carriages. The principal portion is on the south-west side of the river, which is connected by a substantial stone bridge of six arches with the other portion, which lies at the base of Vinegar Hill, and comprises the suburbs of Templeshannon and Drumgoold. The bridge is now being widened and its roadway lowered, partly at the expense of Lord Portsmouth's trustees and partly by a Grand Jury presentment; and a plentiful supply of spring water, from Sheill's well at Templeshannon, will be conveyed, by pipes inserted in the new work of the bridge, into several parts of the town, which is at present but badly supplied, and only partially paved. A small woollen manufacture is carried on near the town; and at Carley's bridge, on the river Urrin, which runs into the Slaney, is a manufactory for coarse pottery. In the town are a distillery, three breweries, two flour-mills, three tanyards, and a rope-factory. Flour-mills are also being erected by Mr. Pounder on the site of an extensive iron-foundry long since discontinued; and at Fairfield, about a mile and a half distant, on the road to Killan, is an extensive distillery, belonging to Mr. A. Jameson, the working of which has been suspended for the last few years. The river Slaney abounds with excellent salmon and trout, with which the markets are well supplied during the season. The trade principally consists in the exportation of agricultural produce, and the importation of coal, timber, slates, iron, salt, and various other commodities, for which its central situation and river navigation to the port of Wexford are very favourable. Large quantities of corn and butter are sent hence by lighters to Wexford, and also by land carriage, by way of New Ross, to Waterford. Two spacious quays have been lately constructed, at an expense of £9000, defrayed partly by the trustees of the Earl of Portsmouth's estate, and partly by subscription: the quay on the Templeshannon side is 450 feet, and that on the opposite side, which it is in contemplation to extend, is 500 feet in length. The tide flows up to the town, which is accessible to barges of large tonnage, and it is intended to apply for an act of parliament to construct a ship canal for vessels of 200 tons' burden from Pooldarrag, on the eastern bank of the Slaney, to the bridge of Enniscorthy, a distance of nearly seven British miles. It is also in contemplation to establish a communication by steam between this place and Wexford, and a subscription is in progress for building an iron steam-boat of 12-horse power, for the conveyance of goods and passengers. The facility of land carriage has been greatly increased by a new line of road to Wexford, avoiding the hills and shortening the distance by nearly a mile; a new road from the bridge along the western bank of the river has also been completed, communicating at Blackstoops with the Dublin road, and greatly improving that approach to the town. A branch of the National Bank of Ireland has been lately opened here; and a savings' bank has also been established. The market days are Thursday and Saturday; on the former day, which is the principal, there is an abundant supply of provisions, but corn and butter are brought to market daily. An ancient market on Tuesday, granted to Sir Henry Wallop, has been discontinued. Fairs for cattle, hogs, and various articles of merchandise are held on Jan. 20th, Feb. 21st, March 21st, April 25th, May 10th, June 7th, July 5th, Aug. 26th, Sept. 19th, Oct. 10th, Nov. 15th, and Dec. 21st. A corn market and shambles have been recently erected near the site of the ancient Franciscan monastery, and the open area, called the abbey ground, is intended to be laid out for the erection of new streets; but from some misunderstanding between the market people and the proprietors, they are not at present used, the general markets being still held in an irregular area in the centre of the town.

By the charter of incorporation granted by Jas. I., in the 11th of his reign, the government is vested in a portreeve, 12 free burgesses, and a commonalty, assisted by a recorder, town-clerk, two serjeants-at-mace, and other officers. The portreeve, who may appoint a deputy, is chosen from the free burgesses by a majority of that body on the 24th of June, and sworn into office on the 29th of September; he is a justice of the peace within the borough and liberties, in which the county magistrates have concurrent jurisdiction. The burgesses fill up vacancies in their body by a majority, either from the freemen or the inhabitants at large, and appoint all the officers of the corporation; the freemen are admitted only by favour of the corporation. The borough returned two members to the Irish parliament till the Union, when it was disfranchised, and the £15,000 awarded in compensation was paid to Cornelius, Lord Lismore, and Robert Cornwall, Esq.; to the former, £12,300, and to the latter £2700. A court of record, for debts and pleas to the amount of £3. 6. 8. late currency, is held every Tuesday before the portreeve. The Easter and Michaelmas quarter sessions for the division are held here, and petty sessions every Thursday. There is a chief constabulary police station in the town. The court-house, a neat building, erected at the expense of the county, contains also one of the two newsrooms. The market-house, built and kept in repair by the Portsmouth family, contains a large room occasionally used for concerts and public meetings.

The parish of St. Mary, Enniscorthy, comprises about 2916 statute acres, with very little wood, and no waste land. The living is a vicarage, in the diocese of Ferns, united by act of council in 1778 to the vicarage of Clonmore, and to the rectories of Templeshannon, Ballyhuskard, and St. John, and in the patronage of the Bishop: the rectory is impropriate in Cæsar Colclough, Esq. The tithes amount to £247. 10. 8., of which £71. 1. 11. is payable to the impropriator, and the remainder to the vicar; the aggregate tithes of the benefice amount to £1559. 13. 11½. There is a handsome glebe-house at Templeshannon, rebuilt by the present incumbent, with a glebe of 23 acres, and there is also a glebe of 20 acres at Ballyhuskard. The church is a plain edifice without tower or spire; in repairing it, after the disturbances of 1798, a six-pound shot fell from one of the rafters; the chancel was rebuilt a few years since. There are also churches in the parishes of Clonmore and Ballyhuskard, which have been erected into perpetual cures. In the R. C. divisions this parish is the head of a union or district, comprising also the greater part of the parish of Templeshannon, part of St. John's, and a small portion of that of Templeshambo: the chapel, a spacious and handsome edifice, erected by subscription in 1808, is the cathedral church of the R. C. diocese of Ferns: a house has been lately erected by Dr. Keating, R. C. Bishop, as a permanent residence for his curates. There is also a convent for nuns of the order of the Presentation, established in 1826 as a branch from the convent at Wexford. There are places of worship for the Society of Friends and Primitive Methodists; and another class of Methodists assemble in the market-house. About 550 children are taught in the public schools of the parish, of which the male and female parochial schools, forming a handsome range of building, erected in 1831 on the glebe, are aided by a grant of £52 from the funds of Erasmus Smith's charity, and £20 from Lord Portsmouth's trustees; a school for girls is gratuitously superintended by the ladies of the Presentation convent, by whom the children are taught reading, writing, Catechism, and every description of useful and ornamental needlework, and is supported, together with a large Lancasterian school for boys, by subscription; and an infants' school, established in 1831, is also supported by subscription. There are 11 private schools, in which are about 420 children, and one Sunday school. Bishop Vigors, in 1721, bequeathed £900 for the endowment of some almshouses, which were rebuilt in 1830 by the trustees, in a neat cottage style, at Summer Hill, near the town; they contain apartments for seven Protestant widows, who now receive £3 per annum each. Miss Toplady, late of Dublin, left £80 per annum for poor widows whose husbands were killed, or otherwise sufferers in the disturbances of 1798, ten of whom now receive £8 per annum each; and Miss Grenville left the impropriate tithes of the parish of Ballyvalloo, now amounting to about £60 per annum, for the endowment of an almshouse for the poor of this parish, which bequest is at present the subject of litigation. A fever hospital, affording accommodation for 40 patients, was erected in 1829, on an acre of ground given for its site by Lord Portsmouth's trustees, and attached to it is a dispensary, with a surgeon's ward. The ancient castle, now the property of the Earl of Portsmouth, is a venerable quadrilateral building with a round tower at each angle, and is surrounded with a high wall of more modern date. Of the Franciscan monastery the only remains are a lofty square tower on four pointed arches, a great portion of the conventual buildings having been removed in order to furnish a site for the new market; a curious brooch of gold, enriched with emeralds and garnets, was found in clearing away the ruins. About three quarters of a mile below the town, on the west bank of the Slaney, and in the parish of St. John, was a monastery for canons regular of the order of St. Victor, founded by Gerald de Prendergast in 1230, and subsequently made a cell to the abbey of St. Thomas-juxta-Dublin, by John St. John, bishop of Ferns, on which occasion it adopted the order of St. Augustine.

ENNISCRONE. — See KILGLASS, county of Sligo.

ENNISKEEN, a parish, partly in the baronies of Lower Kells and Lower Slane, county of Meath, and province of Leinster, but chiefly in the barony of Clonkee, county of Cavan, and province of Ulster, on the road from Carrickmacross to Bailieborough; containing, with the post-town of Kingscourt (which is described under its own head), 10,368 inhabitants. This place, anciently the principal seat of the Danes, was called Dunaree, and still retains that name; it is surrounded by Danish forts, and on the summits of the neighbouring hills great quantities of money and of ancient military weapons have been dug up at various times. The parish comprises 23,814 statute acres, of which about 500 are woodland, from 200 to 300 bog, and the remainder under tillage; the system of agriculture is greatly improved, and great quantities of bog and waste land have been reclaimed. Limestone abounds; there are excellent quarries of every kind of building stone, and near the rock at Carrickleck is very superior freestone, which is extensively worked for flagstones and pillars of large dimensions. On the estate of Lord Gormanstown, in the Meath district, are coal, lead and iron ore, but none is raised at present; a coal mine and an alabaster quarry were formerly worked, but have been discontinued. The principal seats are Cabra castle, the handsome residence and richly planted demesne of Col. Pratt; Corinsica, of J. Pratt, Esq.; Northlands, of the Very Rev. Dean Adams; Newcastle, of J. Smith, Esq.; Woodford, of J. Armstrong, Esq.; Lisnaboe, of — Jackson, Esq.; Plantation, of — Irwin, Esq.; Larchfield, of W. Pratt, Esq.; and Cornakill, of — Moore, Esq. An annual fair is held at Muff on the 21st of August, and there are several at Kingscourt, noticed in the account of that town, where petty sessions are also held. The living is a perpetual curacy, in the diocese of Meath, and in the patronage of the Bishop, to whom the rectory is appropriate: the tithes amount to £900. The glebe-house is a neat residence, erected by a gift of £450 and a loan of £50 from the late Board of First Fruits, in 1831; the glebe comprises 28½ acres. The church, at Kingscourt, is a neat plain edifice, to the repair of which the Ecclesiastical Commissioners have recently granted £173. The R. C. parish is co-extensive with that of the Established Church, and is called Kingscourt; the chapel in that town is a spacious and handsome edifice, in the later English style, and there is also a chapel at Muff. There is a place of worship for Presbyterians in connection with the Synod of Ulster, of the third class, and one for Wesleyan Methodists. About 130 children are taught in the public schools, and there are 16 private schools, in which are about 960 children. Between Bailieborough and Kingscourt, about two miles from the former, is a pool called *Lough-on-Leighaghs*, or the "healing lake," which is much resorted to by patients afflicted with scorbutic complaints; it is situated on the summit of a mountain, rising, according to the Ordnance survey, 1116 feet above the level of the sea. On a lofty eminence, about a mile from the lake, is a remarkable cairn; and about two miles from Kingscourt, on the Dublin road, is the singularly beautiful and romantic glen of Cabra. There are ruins of Muff and Cabra castles, and some remains of an old bridge.

ENNISKERRY, or MUTTON ISLAND, in the parish of Kilmurry, barony of Ibrickane, county of Clare, and province of Munster, ½ a mile from the shore, on the western coast: the population is returned with the parish. It lies off that part of the coast which, from its rocky and dangerous character, is called the Malbay; and contains about 210 statute acres of excellent land for feeding oxen and sheep, particularly the latter; hence the name "Mutton island," from the fine flavour of the mutton. On its shores are some curious natural caves, formerly used by smugglers for storing contraband goods. Here are an old signal tower and the ruins of an ancient structure, said to have been an abbey, founded at a very early period by St. Senan of Inniscattery: the ancient name of the island was Inniscaorach.

ENNISKERRY, a post-town, in the parish of Powerscourt, barony of Rathdown, county of Wick-

LOW, and province of LEINSTER, 3 miles (W. S. W.) from Bray, and 10 (S. by E.) from Dublin, on the road from Dublin, by Dundrum, to Roundwood; containing 497 inhabitants. This place, which is of modern origin, and has risen chiefly under the auspices of the noble family of Wingfield, Viscounts Powerscourt, occupies a beautiful situation on the acclivity of a hill rising from the bank of a mountain river called the Kerry. It contains about 70 houses, most of which are tastefully built in the cottage style and inhabited by families of respectability; and from its vicinity to the beautiful scenery of the Dargle, the Powerscourt demesne, the waterfall, the Scalp, and other objects of general attraction, is a favourite resort for strangers and visiters from Dublin, for whose accommodation two very comfortable hotels and lodging-houses have been fitted up. The air is extremely pure and mild, and the equability of its temperature is highly favourable to persons affected with pulmonary diseases; a mail and a stage coach and jaunting cars ply daily between it and Dublin. The environs are very pleasing, and, exclusively of the seats and villas noticed under the head of Powerscourt, there are several handsome villas in the immediate vicinity of the village, of which the principal are Summer Hill, that of P. Flood, Esq.; Sea View, occupied by the Rev. A. Wynne; Enniskerry Lodge, of Capt. T. Mason, R.N.; and Wingfield Terrace, of J. Gason, Esq., M.D. A constabulary police force is stationed here, and petty sessions are held on alternate Fridays. Near the bridge is a neat school-house, with apartments for a master and mistress, erected by the late Lord Powerscourt; it has lately merged into an infants' school, supported by the present lord, and part of the building is appropriated to the use of a lending library. A girls' school, a very neat building on the Scalp side of the Kerry, was erected by the late Lady Powerscourt, in 1828, and is also supported by his lordship. Here is a dispensary, and in 1828 a fever hospital was erected by subscription, towards which Lord Powerscourt contributed £200. Almshouses for six aged and infirm women were built partly by the late Lord Powerscourt and the Rev. R. Daly, the rector of the parish. A district society has been established for selling clothing to the poor at reduced prices.—See POWERSCOURT.

Seal.

ENNISKILLEN, a borough and market-town, and a parish, partly in the barony of MAGHERABOY, but chiefly in that of TYRKENNEDY, county of FERMANAGH, (of which it is the chief town), and province of ULSTER, 21½ miles (S. E.) from Ballyshannon, and 80½ (N. N. W.) from Dublin; containing 14,563 inhabitants, of which number, 13,777 are in the parish of Enniskillen, and the remainder in that part of the town which extends into the parish of Rossory; the borough and town contain 6796 inhabitants. This place, which takes its name from the island in Lough Erne, in which it is situated, and was formerly called Inniskillen, was, previously to the time of Jas. I., merely a stronghold of Maguire, chieftain of Fermanagh, who had a castle here, which was taken by the English forces under Sir Richard Bingham, in 1594; but no sooner had that general retired, leaving in it a royal garrison, than it was besieged by the forces of O'Donnel and his confederates. A detachment sent to its assistance by the lord-deputy was totally defeated, and the garrison, after holding out to the last extremity, being compelled to surrender, were inhumanly slaughtered by the assailants, who pleaded the like cruelty on the part of Bingham, when he took the town, as a justification of their revenge. The town, though it holds a conspicuous place in Irish history and is now the capital of the county, is of no great antiquity. The island being considered an important spot for the establishment of a military force, a royal fort was erected there about the commencement of the 17th century; and the advantage of its situation for a town induced Jas. I., in 1612, to make a grant of one-third of it to William Cole, Esq., ancestor of the Earl of Enniskillen, on condition of his building a town upon it, settling in it twenty British families to be incorporated as burgesses, some of whose descendants still hold burgage tenements; and assigning convenient places for a church and churchyard, a market-house, public school, 30 acres for a common, and a site for a prison to be built for the custody of prisoners and malefactors within the limits of the county of Fermanagh. This last condition seems to imply that it was intended to make this the assize town and capital of the county from the very date of its foundation.

On the breaking out of the war in 1641, the town was defended by its founder and governor, then Sir William Cole, who despatched the first intelligence of that event to the English government; and so active were the inhabitants in opposing the enemy, that they not only repulsed the insurgents with great loss, but also made themselves masters of the castle of Maguire. While the Earl of Ormonde acted in concert with the royalists, this town opposed the parliamentarian interest and firmly resisted every attack made upon it by the forces of that party; but it was finally compelled to surrender to Sir Charles Coote. During the war of the revolution the inhabitants firmly adhered to the cause of Wm. III., whom they proclaimed king; they chose Gustavus Hamilton as their governor, and bravely defended the town, which became a refuge for the Protestants of the north-west, from all assaults of the adverse party; and from the embarrassment they caused to James's forces during the siege of Londonderry, the Protestants assembled in the town soon became celebrated as the "Enniskillen men." Lord Galmoy was sent with a detachment of James's army to reduce them, and for this purpose invested Crom castle, their frontier garrison, situated on Lough Erne; after an unsuccessful stratagem to produce intimidation, by ordering two painted tin cannons to be drawn by eight horses towards the fort, the garrison, being reinforced from Enniskillen, made a vigorous sally upon the besiegers, drove them from the trenches, and returned in triumph with considerable booty and the mock cannon which had with so much apparent difficulty been drawn up and planted against them. So successful and formidable were the frequent excursions of this band, that the ruling party in Dublin actually expected them speedily at their gates; and at length a plan was formed for attacking the town at once by three different armies. For this purpose, Macarthy, an experienced officer, who had been recently created a peer, encamped at Belturbet with 7000 men; Sarsfield, another general equally distinguished, led an army from Connaught; while Fitz-James, Duke of Berwick, prepared to attack it from the north. The Enniskilleners, aware of the movements of the Connaught army only, marched out of the town with great rapidity, surprised the camp and routed the forces with much slaughter. On the approach of the Duke of Berwick, some companies sent from the town to seize a post which they might have defended against his numbers, ventured beyond the prescribed bounds and were cut to pieces; but on the approach of Hamilton, the governor of the town, the Duke of Berwick retired with his forces. Macarthy, at the head of an army which had already defeated Lord Inchiquin in Munster, marched towards Enniskillen and invested Crom castle; a detachment under an officer named Berry was sent to the relief of the castle, but finding it necessary to retreat before a very superior force, which had been detached by the enemy to intercept him, he was pursued and a skirmish followed, in which the townsmen were victorious. The arrival of the main bodies respectively under the command of Macarthy and Wolsley, the latter, one of Col. Kirk's officers, brought on a general engagement near Newtown-Butler and Lisnaskea, from both which places the battle has taken its name. The inferiority of the Enniskilleners in numbers was counterbalanced by superior resolution and energy; they defeated and pursued the assailants, granting quarter to none but officers; about 2000 were killed in the engagement, and of 500, who plunged into the lake, only one escaped drowning; about the same number of officers were taken prisoners, among whom was their general Macarthy.

The town is situated on an island in the narrowest part of Lough Erne, or rather in a strait several miles in length, which connects the great northern and southern expanses of the lake, and in which are numerous inlets. It is remarkable for its respectable and thriving appearance, and for the advantages it possesses in the navigation of the lake and the facility afforded for excursions among the rich and beautiful scenery for which it is distinguished; it has increased considerably of late, and is still improving. The principal street takes an irregular course across the island, from the bridge which connects it with the main land, on the east, to that which crosses the opposite channel on the west, which two bridges form the only outlets. Several smaller streets diverge from the main street; and contiguous to the eastern bridge, in the townland of Toneystick, and parish of Enniskillen, is a suburb in which is an old redoubt, called the East Fort; and beyond the western bridge is another suburb, in the parish of Rossory, in which is the West Fort. The total number of houses is 1036, of which 375 are slated and the remainder thatched. Here are barracks for artillery and infantry, and a constabulary police station. Among the buildings that have recently been erected, is a range of respectable houses, called Brook-place, built by Mr. Richard Kirkpatrick, on the mail coach road to Ballyshannon; a very neat house, called Brook View Lodge, pleasantly situated on the side of a hill commanding an extensive view of Lough Erne and the surrounding country; and a number of respectable houses, called Willoughby-place, which, when completed, will add much to the beauty of the town. The chief trade is in timber, coal, and slates, imported from Ballyshannon to Belleek, at the lower extremity of the lough, 18 miles distant, and brought by water to the town. The manufacture of leather is carried on upon a limited scale, and there are two distilleries and a brewery. A considerable trade is also carried on in corn, of which great quantities are sold, partly for the supply of the town and of the distilleries here and at Belturbet, and partly for exportation to Sligo and Strabane; this is also the chief retail market for a very large surrounding district. The patent granted to William Cole, in 1612, authorised the holding of a market on Thursdays, and a fair on Lammas-day, with tolls; and in 1813 a patent was granted to the Earl of Enniskillen for holding fairs on the 10th of each month, except March, May, and August. Besides the general market on Thursdays, a butter market is held on Tuesdays. A butter and grain market have been built on land belonging to the Earl, at an expense of upwards of £900; there is another market-house under the town-hall, also a pig market; and convenient shambles have been erected at an expense of £750, which was advanced by the Earl to the corporation. A linen-hall was built a few years since at an expense exceeding £400, but has never been used as a hall, and is lent gratuitously to the conductor of a private school.

By the charter of Jas. I., granted in 1613, the corporation consists of a provost, 14 burgesses, and all the inhabitants of the island as a commonalty. The provost is elected by the free burgesses on Midsummer-day, and is sworn into office on the 29th of Sept.; he is a justice of the peace for the borough, and also usually for the county. The government is vested in the provost and free burgesses, who elect members of their own body, admit freemen, appoint officers, and manage the property of the corporation. The borough court, held every Thursday, has jurisdiction to the amount of £3. 6. 8. late currency, and proceeds by attachment. The same charter conferred upon the entire corporation the privilege of sending two members to the Irish parliament, which they continued to do till the Union, since which time they have returned one to the Imperial parliament. By the act of the 2nd of Wm. IV., cap. 88, the right of election is vested in the resident burgesses and £10 householders, amounting, in 1836, to a constituency of 220, of whom 211 were £10 householders, and nine resident burgesses; the provost is the returning officer. The electoral boundaries comprehend an area of 156 statute acres, and are described in the Appendix. The assizes for the county and quarter sessions of the peace are held in the county court-house, which is a plain building near the eastern bridge. The county gaol, built about 20 years since, is near the town, on the Dublin road: it is on the radiating plan, with the governor's house in the centre, and will contain 120 prisoners; the number of cells is 36, of which four are for females; and there are five day-rooms, seven airing-yards, a treadmill, hospital, and school. The prisoners are regularly employed in breaking stones for repairing the roads: the expense of maintenance, &c., for 1835, was £1334. 8. 1.

The parish comprises, according to the Ordnance survey (including islands), 26,440½ statute acres, of which 26,387 are in the barony of Tyrkennedy, and 681¾ are water. The residences of the nobility and gentry are numerous, among which are Ely Lodge, that of the Marquess of Ely; Florence Court, of the Earl of Enniskillen; Castle Cool, of the Earl of Belmore; Rosfad, of J. Richardson, Esq.; Rockfield, of J. Irvine, Esq., D.L.; Castle Archdall, of Gen. Mervyn Archdall; Riverstown, of C. Archdall, Esq.; Prospect, of J. Nixon, Esq., Gran, of A. Nixon, Esq.; Levaghy, of Jason Hassard, Esq.; Dunbar, of T. Nixon, Esq.; Crocknacrieve, of Col. T. Stewart; Cork Hill, of the Rev. A. H. Irvine; and Bellview, of G. Knox, Esq. On the border of Lough Erne stands Bellisle, the beautiful and romantic seat of the late Earl of Rosse, now in the possession of the Rev. J. Grey Porter; it is in a dilapidated state, but is about to be rebuilt, together with the bridge leading to its extensive demesne. The living is a rectory and vicarage, in the diocese of Clogher, forming the corps of the precentorship of the cathedral, in the patronage of the Provost and Fellows of Trinity College, Dublin: the tithes amount to £550; and the glebe, consisting of 315 acres, with the glebe-house, is valued at £293. 4. 6. per annum, making the income of the precentor £843. 4. 6. The church is a plain building, erected in 1637; and there is a chapel of ease at Tempo. Divine service is also performed in the school at Derryhean. In the R. C. divisions the parish is the head of a union or district, including the town of Enniskillen, the parish of Rossory, and parts of Derryvullen, Cleenish, and Derrybrusk; there is a very large chapel in the town, in which are also a meeting-house for Presbyterians in connection with the Synod of Ulster, of the third class, and places of worship for Wesleyan and Primitive Methodists. About 670 children are educated in nine public schools, and about 900 in 25 private schools, exclusive of those taught in eight Sunday schools. The royal school of Enniskillen was founded by Chas. I., in 1626, and endowed with lands near the town, which, according to a survey made in 1795, comprise 3360 statute acres. The school-house in the town being too small, about 1777, the Rev. Mark Noble, who was then head-master, and had the absolute disposal of the school funds, built a spacious house for it at Portora, in the vicinity, capable of accommodating 70 boarders. The school contains about 65 children; the head-master has a salary of £500 per annum, late currency, besides the payments from the pupils and the house and grounds, which include 33 acres; the first classical assistant has £250, and the second £100 per annum. Four scholarships of £20 per annum each are conferred by the Commissioners of Education on those scholars who are most distinguished for proficiency in study and propriety of conduct, and are held during their stay at the school; and the Rev. — Burke bequeathed three sums of £110, late currency, for the use of three of the pupils on their entering Trinity College, Dublin. The Commissioners of Education appropriate £400 per annum of the funds of this school to the endowment of five king's scholarships of £50 each, and five of £30 each in Trinity College, Dublin, to be held for five years by scholars elected by the board of Trinity College, out of those who have been three years at least in either of the royal schools of Enniskillen, Armagh, or Dungannon. The charitable institutions are a mendicity society, a dispensary, and a county infirmary, which is a large building on an eminence outside the town, on the Dublin road. Enniskillen is the birthplace of Lord Plunket, and gives the titles of Earl and Viscount to the family of Cole, by which it was founded.

ENNISMACSAINT.—See INNISMACSAINT.

ENNISMAGRATH.—See INNISMAGRATH.

ENNISMAIN.—See ARRAN ISLANDS.

ENNISNAG, a parish, in the barony of SHILLELOGHER, county of KILKENNY, and province of LEINSTER, 5½ miles (S.) from Kilkenny, on the King's river, and on the road from Kilkenny to Waterford; containing 550 inhabitants. It comprises 1200 statute acres, of which 10 are woodland, 950 arable, 200 pasture, and about 40 waste. There are two flour-mills. The living is a rectory and vicarage, in the diocese of Ossory, and the corps of the treasurership of the cathedral of St. Canice, Kilkenny, in the patronage of the Bishop: the tithes amount to £169. The glebe-house was built by aid of a gift of £400 and a loan of £400 from the late Board of First Fruits, in 1821; the glebe comprises 18 acres. The church, a neat modern structure, was erected by aid of a gift of £900 from the same Board, in 1815, and the Ecclesiastical Commissioners have recently granted £124 for its repair. In the R. C. divisions the parish forms part of the union or district of Danesfort.

ENNISTRAHULL, an island, in the parish of CLONCHA, barony of ENNISHOWEN, county of DONEGAL, and province of ULSTER, 8 miles (E.) from Malin Head, on the northern coast; the population is returned with the parish. It is situated in lat. 55° 26′ 20″, and lon. 7° 14′ 10″. Here is a lighthouse, built by the corporation for improving the port of Dublin, exhibiting a bright revolving light, which attains its greatest brilliancy every two minutes; the lantern is elevated 167 feet above the level of the sea at high water, and may be seen from all points 18 nautical miles in clear weather. About a quarter of a mile to the north is a rocky shoal, and further northward lie the Tarmore rocks, around which are always from 11 to 18 fathoms of water. In the channel between this island and the small isles called the Garvilans the stream of tide does not flow eastward until nearly five hours after high water, nor westward until five hours after low water, when its velocity is nearly four miles an hour.

ENNISTUBRET. — See KILDYSART, county of CLARE.

ENNISTURK, or INNISTURC, an island, in the parish of OMEY, barony of BALLYNAHINCH, county of GALWAY, and province of CONNAUGHT, 4 miles (N. W.) from Clifden, on the western coast: the population is returned with the parish. It contains 85 statute acres. The sound between it and the mainland is deep and forms a harbour, within which is Kingstown, a good harbour for small vessels, but difficult of access on account of the rocks at its mouth.

ENNISTYMON, a market and post-town, in the parish of KILMANAHEEN, barony of CORCOMROE, county of CLARE, and province of MUNSTER, 16½ miles (W. by N.) from Ennis, and 128 (W. by S.) from Dublin, on the river Inagh, and on the mail road from Ennis to Miltown-Malbay; containing 241 houses and 1430 inhabitants. The town, though irregularly built, has a picturesque appearance. A little below the bridge the river, which has its source in the mountains to the south-east, rushes over an extensive ridge of rocks and forms a beautiful cascade, at a short distance from which it joins the river Derry: the latter forms a junction with the river Inagh, and the united streams fall into the Atlantic at Liscanor bay, about $2\frac{1}{2}$ miles west of the town. Races are occasionally held at Lahinch, on the bay of Liscanor, for the amusement of visiters during the bathing season. This place had formerly a considerable market for strong knit woollen stockings, which were purchased in large quantities by dealers for supplying Dublin and the north of Ireland; but since the improvement in the stocking machinery this trade has gradually declined, and is now chiefly confined to the immediate neighbourhood. The market, which is held on Saturday, is well supplied with provisions, and is also a good mart for the sale of corn and pigs; and fairs are held on March 25th, May 15th, July 2nd, Aug. 22nd, Sept. 29th, Nov. 19th, and Dec. 17th, for general farming stock. Sea-sand for manure is brought up the river, and in the vicinity are raised thin flags, used for roofing and other purposes: a body of manganese appears on the edge of a bog near the river. Coal was found in the neighbourhood several years since, and some of it sent to Galway and Limerick, but from its inferior quality the works were discontinued. Quarter sessions are held here four times in the year; also petty sessions weekly on Monday. The sessions-house and district bridewell form a neat and commodious building, considered one of the best in the county. A seneschals' court for the manor of Ennistymon is held about once in each month, for the recovery of small debts. Here is a chief constabulary police station. The church, erected in 1830, is a handsome cruciform structure, in the later English style, with an octagonal tower on its south side resting on a square base: it is advantageously situated at the northern entrance of the town; and on an eminence to the east are the ruins of the old church. The R. C. chapel is a large and substantial building, erected about 12 years since; the old chapel has been converted into a school. The male and female free schools are supported by subscriptions, and by the proceeds of an annual charity sermon at the chapel; a school is also supported partly by Archdeacon Whitty, and partly by the pupils' fees; and there is a public dispensary. Immediately adjoining the town is Ennistymon Castle, formerly a seat of the O'Brien family, descendants of the Earls of Thomond, and now the residence of Andrew Finucane, Esq.; it is boldly situated on the north bank of the river, is surrounded by a richly wooded park, and contains some fine old family pictures. At a short distance is the glebe-house, the residence of the Ven. Archdeacon Whitty, a handsome and substantial mansion of recent erection, situated in a pleasing demesne, which is ornamented by young and thriving plantations. An abbey is said to have formerly existed here, over which St. Luchtighern presided.—See Kilmanaheen.

ENORELY, or ENERILEY, a parish, in the barony of Arklow, county of Wicklow, and province of Leinster, on the road from Arklow to Wicklow, and on the eastern coast, opposite the Arklow sand-bank, 4 miles (N. by E.) from Arklow; containing 874 inhabitants, and comprising 4574 statute acres, as applotted under the tithe act, with a considerable tract of sandy coast. The gentlemen's seats are Buckroney House, the residence of M. McDonald, Esq.; Kilpatrick, of J. Byrne, Esq.; and Ballyrogan, of E. Byrne, Esq. It is a rectory, in the diocese of Dublin and Glendalough, separated from Arklow, by act of council in 1833, and now forming part of the union of Kilbride: the tithes amount to £110. A small part of the parish is included within the perpetual curacy of Redcross. In the R. C. divisions it is part of the union or district of Newbridge and Baronisky. On the grounds of Kilpatrick are two raths or moats. The church is in ruins.

ERRIGAL, or ARRIGLE, a parish, in the barony of Coleraine, county of Londonderry, and province of Ulster; containing, with the post-town of Garvagh (which is described under its own head), 5401 inhabitants. A monastery was founded here by St. Columb in 589, which flourished until the ninth century, when it was plundered and destroyed by the Danes. The parish is bounded on the south by the Agivey water, and comprises, according to the Ordnance survey, $19,625\frac{1}{4}$ statute acres, of which 18,113 are applotted under the tithe act and valued at £5163 per ann.; about 7500 acres are arable, 5500 pasture, 100 woodland, and the remainder bog and mountain; the latter affording good pasturage to large herds of cattle. The vale of Glenullen, and all the lands around Garvagh and on the banks of the Agivey water, are fertile, and even many of the more elevated lands produce excellent crops, though agriculture has been but little improved. The mountain range consists principally of the eastern slopes of Ballyness and Donald's hill, extending to the boundary of the barony, and are exclusively basalt, but everywhere produce sweet herbage. The inhabitants unite with agriculture the weaving of linen cloth. There are several handsome houses in the parish, the principal of which are Garvagh, the seat of Lord Garvagh, adjoining which is the picturesque vale of Glenullen; Ballintemple, of Mrs. Arthur Heyland; Woodbank, of Capt. Orr; Garvagh Cottage, of Capt. Crossley; and Meetigan glebe-house, of the Rev. W. Smith. The living is a rectory, in the diocese of Derry, and in the patronage of the Bishop: the tithes amount to £353, of which £300 are payable to the rector, the per centage to the landlord being about £53. The glebe-house, a small old building, is delightfully situated near the top of Glenullen; the glebe comprises about 254 acres. The church is a low plain building, adjoining the town of Garvagh, to the repairs of which the Ecclesiastical Commissioners have recently made a grant of £201. In the R. C. divisions this parish is the head of a union or district, comprising also parts of Desertog hill and Balteagh, and containing two chapels, one at Ballerin, and the other in Glenullen. There are places of worship in Garvagh for Presbyterians in connection with the Synod of Ulster and the Seceding Synod, and for Separatists from the Seceding Synod, also one for Wesleyan Methodists. There are parochial and five other public schools, some of which are aided by donations from Lord Garvagh, R. McCausland, Esq., Mrs. Heyland, the rector, and the Ironmongers' Company; they afford instruction to about 400 children. A school founded by Dr. Adam Clarke is supported by the Wesleyan Methodists; and about 120 children are educated in four private schools. Here are numerous forts, particularly in Glenullen, evidently constructed to protect the pass into the mountains. The old church at Ballintemple is a very interesting ruin. The Rev. G. V. Sampson, author of the Map and Memoir of Londonderry, and the Statistical Survey of the same county, was rector of this parish, and died at the glebe-house; he was buried at Aghanloo.

ERRIGAL-KEROGUE, a parish, in the barony of CLOGHER, county of TYRONE, and province of ULSTER, on the river Blackwater and on the road from Aughnacloy to Omagh; containing, with the greater part of the district parish and post-town of Ballygawley, 9782 inhabitants. This parish, which is also called Errigal-Kieran, from the supposed dedication of its ancient church to St. Kieran, comprises, according to the Ordnance survey, 21,139¾ statute acres, including 18 townlands, which now form part of the district parish of Ballygawley. The greater portion is rich arable, meadow, and pasture land, with a large extent of profitable mountain, and a considerable tract of waste. The hills towards the south are low and fertile, but towards the north they rise into mountains, the flat summits of which are bog and heath; the mountain of Shantavny rises, according to the Ordnance survey, 1035 feet above the level of the sea. The valleys are watered by streams which, in their descent from the mountains, form numerous picturesque cascades; and in one of them are found fossils and shells, washed down from the beds of limestone. There are extensive quarries of limestone and freestone, from the latter of which was taken the stone for building several of the churches and gentlemen's seats in the neighbourhood; and thin veins of coal have been found near Lismore, but though lying very near the surface, they have not been worked. The scenery is strikingly diversified; the glen called "Todd's Leap" abounds with romantic features, and at the southern extremity of the parish is a very handsome bridge of one arch over the Blackwater, which river is also crossed by two other bridges. The principal gentlemen's seats are Ballygawley House, the residence of Sir H. Stewart, Bart., situated on a rising ground, sheltered in the rear by the conspicuous precipice called the "Craigs;" Cleanally, of G. Spier, Esq.; Bloom Hill, of T. Simpson, Esq.; and Ballygawley Castle, of R. Armstrong, Esq. There are several large corn-mills and a tuck-mill for finishing the woollen cloths made in the various farm-houses. The manors of Donoughmore, Favour Royal, Cecil, and Ballygawley, are in this parish; in the first a court is held monthly, in which debts to any amount may be recovered; and in the three others are held similar courts every three weeks, with jurisdiction limited to £2.

The living is a rectory, in the diocese of Armagh, and in the patronage of J. C. Moutray, Esq.: the tithes amount to £380. The glebe-house is at Richmount, near Ballygawley, on a glebe of 266 acres, and there is another glebe of 297 acres, constituting the townland of Gort. The church, a handsome edifice in the later English style, with an embattled tower, was erected in 1831, near the site of the ancient structure at Ballinasaggard, at an expense of £1300, of which £1100 was a loan from the late Board of First Fruits. The R. C. parish is co-extensive with that of the Established Church; the chapel is a small plain edifice, and there are two stations or altars, where service is occasionally performed. There are places of worship for Presbyterians in connection with the Synod of Ulster of the third class, Independents, and two for Wesleyan Methodists. About 700 children are taught in the public schools, of which the parochial school is chiefly supported by the incumbent, one by Miss Montgomery, and another by Mr. Leslie; and there are three private schools, in which are about 180 children. There are some remains of the old church, in which are several of the carved stones of an ancient friary, founded by Con O'Nial; in the churchyard is a large stone cross, and near it a holy well. The friary was of the third order of Franciscans, and near it was an ancient round tower. There are many conical raths in the parish, of which the most remarkable is that on the steep height called the Craigs; it is supposed that the native chiefs of Eirgal, or Uriel, had their seat in this parish, near which a monastery was founded by St. Macartin. In the townland of Sess-Kilgreen is a carved stone, part of a kistvaen, and in that of Lismore are the ruins of a square bawn, with round towers at the angles.

ERRIGAL-TROUGH, a parish, partly in the barony of CLOGHER, county of TYRONE, but chiefly in that of TROUGH, county of MONAGHAN, and province of ULSTER, 3 miles (S.S.W.) from Aughnacloy, on the road to Emyvale, and on the river Blackwater; containing 9321 inhabitants. It comprises 24,792¼ statute acres, according to the Ordnance survey, of which 21,174¼ are in Monaghan, and 102¼ are under water; 21,834 acres are applotted under the tithe act. About four-fifths of the land are arable and pasture, and there is a great deal of mountain land used for grazing, and some bog on the western boundary: agriculture is improving. There is abundance of limestone and sandstone; and coal is supposed to exist in the Sleabea mountains, though it has not been worked. On the north-western confines of the parish is Lough More. A small factory for weaving linen has been recently erected here. The gentlemen's seats are Fort Singleton, that of T. Singleton, Esq., situated in a well wooded demesne of 200 acres; Favour Royal, the handsome residence of J. Corry Moutray, Esq., erected near the site of the ancient house, which was destroyed by fire in 1823, and surrounded by a richly wooded demesne of 740 acres; and Laurel Hill, of W. H. Mayne, Esq. The living is a vicarage, in the diocese of Clogher, and in the patronage of the Bishop; the rectory is appropriate to the see of Clogher: the tithes amount to £400, of which £215. 7. 8¼. is payable to the bishop, and the remainder to the incumbent. The glebe-house stands on a glebe of 40 acres. The church is a very neat modern structure. A handsome cruciform church, in the later English style, with a square tower at the north-east angle, was erected in the demesne of Favour Royal, in 1835, at an expense of £1000, by J. C. Moutray, Esq., who has endowed it with £50 per annum, augmented with £30 per annum by the Ecclesiastical Commissioners; it is open to the public, there being no other church within three miles of Favour Royal, and is called St. Mary's, Portclare; the living is a donative, in the patronage of the founder. There is also a chapel in the eastern part of the parish. The R. C. parish is co-extensive with that of the Established Church, and contains three chapels, one at Knockconnan, built in 1820, at an expense of £700; another on the townland of Drimbriston, built in 1823, at an expense of £500; the third, built in 1787, is in the townland of Mullyoden: the two first were erected, and the last repaired, through the exertions of the Rev. C. McDermot, the parish priest. There is a national school at Moy; and there are three other public schools, of which one at Fort Singleton is supported by T. Singleton,

Esq., who built the school-house, in which the curate of the parish performs divine service twice every Sunday. There are also four hedge, three Scriptural, and four Sunday schools. In that portion of the parish which is in the county of Tyrone is a remarkable place called Altadawin, where it is said that St. Patrick assembled the first of his followers: it is a valley, 150 feet deep, through the centre of which a tongue of land of considerable altitude extends, and on the summit stands a large rock in the form of an altar, adjoining which is another rock, in the form of a chair. The valley is covered with trees, and a beautiful stream runs nearly through its centre. A royal residence of an independent prince of the O'Nial family is reported to have stood here formerly.

ERRY, a parish, in the barony of MIDDLETHIRD, county of TIPPERARY, and province of MUNSTER, 3½ miles (N. by E.) from Cashel, on the mail coach road from Dublin to Cork; containing 772 inhabitants. It comprises 1605 statute acres, and is a rectory, in the diocese of Cashel; the tithes, amounting to £77. 1. 1., are sequestrated in the Ecclesiastical Commissioners, who pay a stipend to the curate of an adjoining parish for performing the occasional duties. In the R. C. divisions it is part of the union or district of Boherlahan. There is a private school, in which are about 50 children.

ESKER, a parish, in the barony of NEWCASTLE, county of DUBLIN, and province of LEINSTER, ¾ of a mile (E.) from Lucan; containing 1075 inhabitants. This place constitutes one of the four manors in the county which formerly belonged to the Crown. By an inquisition taken in the 15th of Henry VII. (1499), John Brownunsinge was found seized in fee of eight messuages, eight gardens, and 35 acres of land in Esker and Ballyowen, held of the Crown at an annual rent, which he bequeathed to the church of Esker, "in pure and perpetual alms." There are quarries of good building stone in the parish. The gentlemen's seats are Esker Lodge, the residence of Major Wills; Esker, of J. Cash, Esq.; St. Helen, of W. Gorman, Esq.; Esker Cottage, of J. Spring, Esq.; Esker House, of G. Clarke, Esq.; Ballyowen Lodge, of J. Cathrew, Esq.; Finstown Lodge, of S. Bell, Esq.; and the Glebe-house, of the Rev. W. Stewart. The parish is in the diocese of Dublin: the rectory forms part of the union and corps of the deanery of St. Patrick's, and the vicarage part of the union of Leixlip, under which head the tithes are stated. In the R. C. divisions it is part of the union or district of Palmerstown, Clondalkin, and Lucan. About ten boys are educated in a private classical school. The ruined church forms a conspicuous and picturesque object, appearing, from its extensive remains, to have been originally a large structure. In the vicinity are the ruins of the ancient castellated mansion of Ballyowen.

ETTAGH, a parish, partly in the barony of CLONLISK, and partly in that of BALLYBRITT, KING'S county, and province of LEINSTER, 4 miles (S. E.) from Parsonstown, on the road to Roscrea; containing 1770 inhabitants. This parish comprises 6531 statute acres, as applotted under the tithe act, and valued at £3440 per annum; the soil is generally a rich loam, and the land principally under tillage, with a small proportion of bog. The gentlemen's seats are Gloster, the residence of Hardress Lloyd, Esq., an ancient mansion situated in a fine and rather extensive demesne; and Golden Grove, of W. P. Vaughan, Esq., the demesne of which, comprising 400 Irish acres, is richly wooded, and is intersected by a small river, which separates this parish from that of Roscrea, in the adjoining county of Tipperary; it contains the hill of Knocknamace, from which are some fine views. The living is a rectory and vicarage, in the diocese of Killaloe, united to the vicarage of Kilcoleman, and in the patronage of the Bishop: the tithes amount to £148. 12. 3¾., and the tithes of the union to £217. 16. 11. There is no glebe-house; the glebe comprises 24 acres. The church is a plain small edifice, erected by aid of a loan of £600 from the late Board of First Fruits, in 1831, and the Ecclesiastical Commissioners have recently granted £100 for its repair. There is a R. C. chapel at Coolderry; and there are schools at Kilcoleman, noticed in the account of that parish.

EVELEARY.—See INCHEGEELAGH.

EYRECOURT, a market and post-town, in the parish of DONONAUGHTA, barony of LONGFORD, county of GALWAY, and province of CONNAUGHT, 11¼ miles (N. W.) from Parsonstown, on the road by Banagher to Loughrea; containing 1789 inhabitants. This town, which takes its name from the Eyre family, lords of the manor, contains 342 houses, which are neat and well built. There are some seats, which are noticed in the article on Dononaughta, *which see.* The market is on Saturday, and fairs are held on the Monday after Easter-Monday, June 29th, July 9th, Sept. 8th, Dec. 20th, and one in October. Here are a court-house (in which quarter and petty sessions are held), gaol, and a constabulary police station; also the parish church, which is in bad repair, and a R. C. chapel, built chiefly at the expense of C. B. Martin, Esq. A dispensary is supported in the usual way, and a decayed school-house is about to be restored by the Rev. Mr. Eyre, the incumbent of the parish.

EYRKE.—See EIRKE.

F

FAHAN (LOWER), a parish, in the barony of ENNISHOWEN, county of DONEGAL, and province of ULSTER; containing, with the post-town of Buncrana (which is described under its own head), 5614 inhabitants. This parish originally formed the Lower, or Northern portion of the extensive parish of Fahan, from which it was separated in 1795; it is bounded on the west by Lough Swilly, and comprises, according to the Ordnance survey, 24,782¾ statute acres. A great portion is mountain, affording good pasturage, of which Slieve Snaght, on the north-eastern boundary, rises, according to the above survey, 2019 feet above the level of the sea. The valleys are well watered and productive, and agriculture is improving. Freestone is abundant, and limestone is found in almost every part: there are also indications of lead, copper, and iron ore. There is a coast-guard station at Ballinary; and at Neids' point is a battery, erected in 1812, now under the care of a master-gunner and five artillerymen. Lough Swilly is very spacious and deep, affording anchorage for large ships; vast numbers of oysters, cod, and haddock are taken in it. Here are many gentlemen's seats, the principal of which are Buncrana Castle, the residence of Mrs. Todd, which was once the seat of the powerful sept of The O'Doherty, who governed the entire country for several centuries; the Lodge, unoccupied; Rockfort, of the Rev. W. H. Stuart; Townsend Lodge, of Col. Downing; River-View, of W. Camac, Esq.; and the Cottage, belonging to Dr. Evans. The living is a perpetual curacy, in the diocese of Derry, and in the patronage of the Rector of Upper Fahan: the tithes amount to £420. The church, in the town of Buncrana, was built in 1804, by aid of a gift of £500, and considerably enlarged by a loan of £390 in 1816, from the late Board of First Fruits; the Ecclesiastical Commissioners have recently granted £370 for its further enlargement and repair. In the R. C. divisions the parish forms part of the union or district of Upper and Lower Fahan and Desertegney; there is a large chapel at Cock Hill. At Buncrana is a meeting-house for Presbyterians in connection with the Synod of Ulster; and the Primitive and Wesleyan Methodists have each a place of worship. The parochial school, at Buncrana, is aided by the trustees of Erasmus Smith's charity: there are also male and female schools at Luddon, and a national school at Cock Hill. In these schools about 280 children are instructed; and there are eight private schools, in which are about 320 children, and a Sunday school. Not far from Ballinary is a very curious fort, or cairn, called Dooninary, chiefly composed of loose stones, having smaller ones as outposts.

FAHAN, or FOCHAN (UPPER), a parish, in the barony of Ennishowen, county of Donegal, and province of Ulster, 7 miles (N. W.) from Londonderry, on the road to Buncrana; containing 3309 inhabitants. St. Columb founded here the Abbey of Fathenmura, also called Fochan Mor, or Fothenmor, which subsequently became richly endowed and for many centuries was held in great veneration: it contained many relics of antiquity, among which was the Book of the Acts of St. Columb, written by the Abbot St. Murus, or Muran, (to whom the great church was dedicated,) in Irish verse, some fragments of which still remain; also a very large and ancient chronicle, held in high repute. The parish is bounded on the west by Lough Swilly, and comprises, according to the Ordnance survey, 10,040¼ statute acres; some of the land is very rich and well cultivated. The mountains afford good pasturage; the Scalp rises, according to the above survey, 1589 feet above the level of the sea. Near Fahan Point are slate rocks, lying close upon the shores of the Lough, which have not yet been much worked: there is also an abundance of mill-stone grit, which is quarried for making and repairing the roads, and excellent freestone. The principal seats are Glengollan, the residence of Charles Norman, Esq., proprietor of the greater part of the parish; Birdstown, of the Rev. P. B. Maxwell; Roseville, of Miss Schoales; Fahan House, of T. Kough, Esq.; and the Glebe-house, of the Rev. W. Hawkshaw. The living is a rectory, in the diocese of Derry, and in the patronage of the Bishop: the tithes amount to £360. The glebe-house was erected by aid of a gift of £100, in 1822, from the late Board of First Fruits: the glebe comprises 52 acres. The church is a large handsome edifice, built by aid of a loan of £1000, in 1820, from the same Board; it has a square tower with pinnacles. In the R. C. divisions the parish is united to Desertegney and Lower Fahan, and has a large chapel, built in 1833. At Cashel is a meeting-house for Presbyterians in connection with the Seceding Synod. The parochial school, in which are about 50 children, is aided by subscriptions; the school-house, a large and handsome building, was erected in 1828, by the Kildare-place Society. There are also two other public schools, one of which is aided by the Rev. P. B. Maxwell; and a national school is held at the R. C. chapel. About 220 children are taught in five private schools, and there are four Sunday schools. There are no remains of the abbey, but several valuable relics have been found, some of which are in the possession of the rector: the east window of the old church is nearly entire, affording an elegant specimen of the architecture of the 15th century. St. Murus's bed, or grave, and a holy well, are much resorted to by the peasantry.

FAHEERAN, a hamlet, in the parish of Kilcumreagh, barony of Kilcoursey, King's county, and province of Leinster; containing 14 houses and 70 inhabitants.

FAHEY, a parish, in the barony of Longford, county of Galway, and province of Connaught, 3¼ miles (S. W.) from Clonfert, on the road from Eyrecourt to Loughrea; containing 1233 inhabitants, and comprising 2572 statute acres, as applotted under the tithe act. It is a vicarage, in the diocese of Clonfert, forming part of the union of Dononaughta; the rectory is appropriate partly to the see of Clonfert, and partly to the prebend of Kilmeen in the cathedral of Tuam. The tithes amount to £74. 10., of which £35 is payable to the Ecclesiastical Commissioners, £12. 10. to the prebendary, and the remainder to the vicar. In the R. C. divisions it is part of the union or district of Kilquane, or Queenborough, and contains a chapel.

FAITHLEGG, a parish, in the barony of Gaultier, county of Waterford, and province of Munster, 5 miles (E.) from Waterford, at the confluence of the rivers Suir and Barrow; containing 724 inhabitants. This parish forms the termination of a promontory commanding a magnificent and highly interesting view, comprehending, towards Waterford, the course of the Suir winding between cultivated hills and encircling Little Island, with the confluence of the rivers forming an expanse of nearly three miles, terminated in the back ground by Mount Leinster, and on the right by Tory Hill, Slievekielta, and the Wexford mountains. At the extremity of the promontory is the small village of Cheekpoint, formerly the Waterford post-office packet station, and the seat of a cotton and a rope manufactory, which since the removal of the packets to Dunmore have been discontinued. The parish comprises 1291 statute acres, as applotted under the tithe act; the system of agriculture, with few exceptions, is unimproved, and there is very little bog. Limestone for burning, and other manures, are brought hither by means of the Suir; stone of good quality for building is found in abundance; and slate and lead ore, with a large proportion of cobalt, were procured till lately. Faithlegg House, the seat of N. Power, Esq., is spacious and situated in a well-planted and highly improved demesne, commanding a fine view up the river; Woodlands is the pleasant residence of M. Dobbyn, Esq.; and Ballycanvan, of R. Morris, Esq. A patent exists for fairs, but none have been held for many years. It is a rectory, in the diocese of Waterford, and forms part of the union of Kill-St. Nicholas: the tithes amount £110. In the R. C. divisions, it is part of the union or district of Passage; the chapel was built at the expense of N. Power, Esq. About 40 children are taught in a national school in the R. C. chapel, and there are two private schools, in which are about 60 children. Dr. W. Downes, who was interred in the old church (now in ruins), bequeathed £50 per annum, to be paid to the person employing the greatest number of poor persons in some useful manufacture; and large sums to the Dublin University, to be distributed as premiums among such students as had made the greatest proficiency in theology, and in reading the liturgy of the Established Church with the most impressive solemnity. There are some remains of an old castle and a rath, near which several cannon balls have been found in turning up the ground; the former was defended against the forces of Cromwell in 1649, when besieging Waterford, by its proprietor, Aylward, but surrendered to Capt. Bolton, who afterwards obtained possession of the estate, now the property of N. Power, Esq.

FALLS UPPER, a district of the parish of BELFAST, in the barony of UPPER BELFAST, county of ANTRIM, and province of ULSTER: the population is returned with Belfast. It is a perpetual cure, or chapelry, in the diocese of Connor, endowed with the small tithes, amounting to £50, and in the gift of the vicar of Belfast: the rectorial tithes, amounting to £100, are impropriate in the Marquess of Donegal.

FAMAGH CHURCH, a parish, in the barony of GOWRAN, county of KILKENNY, and province of LEINSTER, 1 mile (S. S. E.) from Thomastown, on the road to Innistiogue; containing 128 inhabitants, and comprising 623 statute acres. It is a vicarage, in the diocese of Ossory, forming part of the union of Thomastown; the rectory is impropriate in the Marquess of Ormonde, to whom the tithes, amounting to £26, are wholly payable. In the R. C. divisions also it is part of the union or district of Thomastown. Brownsbarn is the residence of John Nixon, Esq.

FANLOBBUS, a parish, in the Western Division of the barony of EAST CARBERY, county of CORK, and province of MUNSTER, on the river Bandon, and on the road from Cork to Bantry; containing, with the post-town of Dunmanway (which is described under its own head), 11,405 inhabitants. It comprises 32,743 statute acres, as applotted under the tithe act, and valued at £12,494 per annum; about 370 acres are woodland, 16,100 good arable and pasture, and the remainder mountain and bog, of which a great part is reclaimable. Much of the land was brought into cultivation for flax during the prosperity of the linen manufacture, for which the town of Dunmanway was one of the principal marts in this part of the country; but at present wheat is the principal produce and is raised in large quantities for the supply of the boulting-mills in the neighbourhood. The system of agriculture is still capable of improvement; the old heavy wooden plough is in general use. There is a large proportion of bog, and at Dareens are some remains of an extensive forest of oak. At Mohany are some small slate quarries, and at Corrigscullighy is found calcareous schist. The principal seats are the Manor House, a handsome building, erected by the late H. Cox, Esq., and now the residence of his family; Manch House, the seat of D. Conner, Esq., an elegant villa four miles from the town, situated on a terrace, and surrounded with a highly cultivated demesne; Woodbrook, of H. Gillman, Esq.; Kilronan, of N. B. Jagoe, Esq.; and Laurel Mount, of R. Townsend, Esq. There are fairs at Dunmanway, and a fair is annually held at Ballybuie on the 5th of August. The living is a vicarage, in the diocese of Cork, and in the patronage of the Bishop; the rectory is partly appropriate to the vicars choral and partly constitutes the corps of the prebend of Dromdaleague in the cathedral of St. Finbarr, Cork. The tithes amount to £923. 1. 4½., which is equally divided between the appropriators and the vicar. There is no glebe-house; the glebe comprises 23 acres. The church, situated in the town of Dunmanway, was rebuilt in 1821, by aid of a loan of £1200 from the late Board of First Fruits, and has recently been repaired by a grant of £210 from the Ecclesiastical Commissioners. In the old burial-ground, about a mile and a half from the town, are some remains of the former church, consisting only of a circular-headed window. In the R. C. divisions the parish is united to part of Ballymoney, forming the union of Dunmanway, in which are three chapels, two being in this parish, one at Dunmanway, and the other at Togher. There is a place of worship at Dunmanway for Wesleyan Methodists. About 500 children are taught in eight public schools, of which one is aided by the vicar, one supported by D. Connor, Esq., one by W. L. Shuldham, Esq., and two under the National Board; and there are 13 private schools, in which are about 480 children, and two Sunday schools. About three miles to the north of the town is Togher Castle, a lofty tower, said to have been built by Randal McCarty, who also built the castle of Ballinacorrigy, at the same distance to the south-east, in the adjoining parish of Ballymoney. In Owen Mountain, in this parish, the rivers Bandon, Ilen, and Moyalla, have their sources.

FARBANE, a post-town, partly in the parish of GALEN, and partly in that of WHERRY, barony of GARRYCASTLE, KING'S county, and province of LEINSTER, 8 miles (N. E.) from Banagher, and 57 (S. W.) from Dublin, on the river Brosna, and on the road from Clara to Banagher; containing 501 inhabitants. This town, which is within a few miles of the junction of the Brosna with the Shannon, is pleasantly situated on the banks of the former river, over which is a bridge commanding a beautiful view of the verdant plains and rich plantations through which it winds its course. It contains 106 houses, has a customary market on Thursday, fairs on Aug. 2nd and Oct. 20th, and a constabulary police station. The parochial church of Wherry is situated here, and a large R. C. chapel has been recently erected. There is also a dispensary. In the vicinity are several gentlemen's seats, which are noticed in the articles on the parishes of Galen and Wherry.

FARCET, FARSIDE, or ROSTELLAN, a village, in the parish of AGHADA, barony of IMOKILLY, county of CORK, and province of MUNSTER, 3 miles (S. W.) from Cloyne, on the road to Whitegate, and on the harbour of Cork; containing 123 inhabitants. It is situated at the head of a small creek, and consists of a range of neat houses extending along the shore and chiefly occupied by the domestics and workmen of the Marquess of

Thomond, whose seat, Rostellan Castle, immediately adjoins the village. Fairs are held on Feb. 2nd and March 25th for general farming stock. Near the village are a convenient quay and stores, where coal, sea-sand, and other articles are landed. Here is the parochial school, founded by the late Bishop Brinkley, who endowed it with two acres of land; it is almost entirely supported by the Marchioness of Thomond.—See ROSTELLAN and AGHADA.

FARIHY, a parish, in the barony of FERMOY, county of CORK, and province of MUNSTER, 6 miles (W.) from Mitchelstown, on the road to Doneraile; containing 2085 inhabitants. It comprises 4770 statute acres, as applotted under the tithe act, and valued at £3475 per annum. The land is of medium quality and chiefly under tillage; and the state of agriculture is gradually improving. There is a considerable portion of mountain pasture in the north of the parish, where it borders on the county of Limerick, from which it is separated by part of the range called the Galtees. Two small oatmeal-mills are worked by streams from these mountains, at the foot of which is situated Bowenscourt, the seat of H. C. Bowen, Esq. It is a rectory, in the diocese of Cloyne, forming the corps of the deanery of Cloyne, in the patronage of the Crown: the tithes amount to £410. The glebe-house was erected by aid of a gift of £100 and a loan of £900, in 1819, from the late Board of First Fruits, and has a glebe attached of about 25 statute acres. The church, a plain building with a tower surmounted by a small wooden spire, is now undergoing a thorough repair, for which purpose the Ecclesiastical Commissioners have recently made a grant of £317. In the R. C. divisions it forms part of the union or district of Kildorrery. About 12 children are instructed in a Sunday school, under the superintendence of the Protestant clergyman.

FARTAGH, or FERTAGH, a parish, partly in the barony of CRANAGH, but chiefly in that of GALMOY, county of KILKENNY, and province of LEINSTER, 8 miles (S. W.) from Durrow, on the mail coach road from Athy to Cashel; containing, with the post-town of Johnstown (which is described under its own head), 3205 inhabitants. A priory for Canons Regular of the order of St. Augustine was founded here in the 13th century by the Blanchfield family, which, after its dissolution, was granted by Queen Elizabeth to a member of the family of Butler. The ancient chapel is still remaining, and contains a large table monument with the recumbent figure of a warrior, and formerly of a female by his side, supposed to be members of the Fitzpatrick family; and another tomb with a female figure, having a singular head dress. A few yards to the west of this building are the roofless remains of an ancient round tower, still 96 feet high and cracked from the doorway to the summit. The parish comprises 6353 statute acres, as applotted under the tithe act, and valued at £4067 per annum, which, with the exception of a very small portion of wood and a little waste, is good arable and pasture land. Near Ballyspellan is a quarry of fine limestone used for tombstones. The principal seats are Violet Hill, the residence of Gorges Hely, Esq.; Melross, of C. Hely, Esq.; and Ellenville, of Mrs. Hely. Fowks Court, formerly the residence of Chief Justice Hely, and now the property of his descendant, G. Hely, Esq., was a very handsome seat, but is now in ruins. A fair, chiefly for pigs, is held on the 5th of March. The living is a rectory and vicarage, in the diocese of Ossory, and in the patronage of the Bishop; the tithes amount to £360. 19. The glebe-house was erected by a gift of £323 and a loan of £415 from the late Board of First Fruits, in 1828; and there is a glebe. The church is a very neat edifice, and the Ecclesiastical Commissioners have recently granted £174 for its repair. In the R. C. divisions the parish is part of the union or district of Eirke; there is a chapel at Johnstown, and another at Galmoy. About 120 girls are taught in the parochial school, and there are four private schools, in which are about 380 children. Here are the ruins of the castle of Killesheelan. The Ballyspellan spa, in this parish, is a powerful chalybeate, and is in great repute for its medicinal properties.

FAUGHANSTOWN.—See FAUGHLEY.

FAUGHANVALE, a parish, in the barony of TIRKERAN, county of LONDONDERRY, and province of ULSTER, 8 miles (S. E.) from Londonderry, on the mail coach road to Coleraine; containing 6218 inhabitants. This parish, which is bounded on the north by Lough Foyle, comprises, according to the Ordnance survey, 18,582¼ statute acres, the greater portion of which was granted in 1609, by Jas. I., to the Grocers' Company of London, who in 1619 erected a strong and handsome castle, surrounded by a bawn, in which they placed a powerful garrison. In the war of 1641 this castle sustained a siege for several months, and resolutely held out against the parliamentarians till the garrison was relieved; it was again besieged and finally taken and dismantled by the parliament; the ruins were standing till 1823, when they were removed, and the present glebe-house erected on the site. Of the remainder of the parish, part is held in perpetuity equally by Lesley Alexander, Esq., and the heirs of the late Sir Wm. Ponsonby, who pay a chief rent of £200 per ann. to the Goldsmiths' Company; part belongs to Major Scott, part to the see of Derry, and a few of the native townlands in the Grocers' proportion to the Marquess of Londonderry. The land is generally fertile, especially round the villages of Faughanvale and Muff, and the system of agriculture has been greatly improved under the auspices of the North West Agricultural Society, and the gentry resident in the district. Many thousand acres of bog and waste land have been reclaimed and brought into profitable cultivation; the lands are well drained and fenced, and there are extensive and flourishing plantations, exclusively of the ancient oak woods of Walworth, which are principally in this parish. At Creggan and Tullynee are quarries of excellent slate, but they are only partially worked, and principally for flags and tombstones. The principal seats are Willsborough, that of Major Scott; Foyle Park, of Lesley Alexander, Esq.; Campsey, of J. Quin, Esq.; Creggan, of T. Major, Esq.; Coolafeeney, of T. Lecky, Esq.; Muff House, of the Rev. J. Christie; and Tullybrisland, of T. Major, Esq. A manorial court, in which debts not exceeding 40*s*. are recoverable, is held at Muff for that part of the parish which belongs to the Grocers' Company. The living is a rectory and perpetual curacy, in the diocese of Derry; the rectory forming part of the union of Templemore and of the corps of the deanery of Derry, and the curacy in the patronage of the Dean. The tithes amount to £700, payable to the dean, and the glebe comprises 1035 statute acres. The curacy was instituted in 1823; the stipend is £92. 6. 2., of which £69. 4. 7½. is paid by the dean, and £23. 1. 6½. from Primate Boulter's fund. The glebe-house, with a glebe of 10 acres, was given to the curate by the Grocers' Company. The church, a spacious and handsome edifice, with a square tower crowned with pinnacles, was built in 1821, by a loan of £1000 from the late Board of First Fruits, near the ruins of a former church built by the Grocers' Company in 1626, in the village of Muff, and about three miles distant from the ruins of the ancient parish church. The R. C. parish is co-extensive with that of the Established church; the chapel is at Creggan. At Tullinee there is a place of worship for Presbyterians in connection with the Synod of Ulster, of the second class. About 370 children are taught in six public schools, of which the parochial school at Muff is supported by a grant of £30 per ann. from the trustees of Erasmus Smith's charity, and annual donations from the Grocers' Company and the rector; the school-house, adjoining the church, a large and handsome edifice, was erected in 1814. A school at Graceteel is under the Fishmongers' Company, who pay the whole charges for children of cottiers and one-half for those of farmers on their estate; two are aided by the Marquess of Londonderry and Major Scott; and an agricultural school is supported by shareholders and subscribers, and by the labour of the scholars on the farm. There are also three private schools, in which are about 150 children, and three Sunday schools. A valuable donation of sacramental plate and furniture for the altar and pulpit was bequeathed to the church, in 1665, by Bishop Wild, who also left £5 for the poor.

FAUGHART, or FAUGHER, a parish, in the barony of Upper Dundalk, county of Louth, and province of Leinster, 1½ mile (N. N. E.) from Dundalk, on the road, through Forkhill, to Armagh; containing 1640 inhabitants. This place, which is also called Foghard, probably takes its name from a very ancient fort of singular construction, which occupies an elevated situation in the neighbourhood. In 638 St. Monenna founded a nunnery here for 150 sisters, over whom she presided for some years, but subsequently resigned her charge to Orbila and Servila, and erected a convent for herself at Kilslieve, in the county of Armagh. A monastery for Canons Regular was also founded at an early period and dedicated to St. Bridget; but there are no remains of either of the buildings, and the only vestiges are two small pillars or crosses, called respectively the stone and pillar of St. Bridget, one having the figure of a horse-shoe sculptured in high relief, and the other a square pillar raised on two circular steps. The ancient fort of Faughart consists of an artificial mount 60 feet high, surrounded by a deep trench with a counterscarp; the whole area of the summit is circumscribed by the foundations of an octagonal building, but whether a tower or only a parapet is uncertain. It is situated near the ancient frontier of the English pale, and in 1596, the Archbishop of Cashel and the Earl of Ormonde, on the part of the English government, held a conference here with the Irish chieftains O'Nial and McDonnel, to negotiate a treaty of peace, which was rejected by the latter. During the insurrection of the Earl of Tyrone, Lord Mountjoy frequently encamped at this place and in the neighbourhood, and in 1600 remained here from the 15th of October till the 9th of November, while the Earl held the pass of Moira, about a mile distant. The parish comprises, according to the Ordnance survey, 2480½ statute acres, three-fourths of which are arable and the remainder pasture; there is neither waste land nor bog; the soil is fertile and the system of agriculture improved. Limestone of good quality abounds, and there are several limekilns. The principal gentlemen's seats are Faughart House, the residence of Neale McNeale, Esq., pleasantly situated in a well-planted demesne; Fort Hill, of the Rev. G. Tinley, beautifully situated on an eminence commanding a fine view of the town and bay of Dundalk, and having in the demesne a Danish fort, from which it takes its name; and Mount Bayly, the residence of D. Courtenay, Esq. A constabulary police force has been established here. The living is a rectory, in the diocese of Armagh, and in the patronage of the Lord-Primate: the tithes amount to £250: there is neither glebe-house nor glebe. The church, a very neat modern edifice, was erected by aid of a gift of £800 and a loan of £800 from the late Board of First Fruits, in 1815; it is situated on the townland of Kilcurry, which is a detached portion of the parish of Ballymascanlon. In the R. C. divisions this is the head of the union or district of Faughart and Jonesborough, comprising those parishes and part of Ballymascanlon, and containing two chapels, one in this parish and one in Jonesborough; the former is on the townland of Kilcurry. About 80 children are taught in the parochial school which is aided by the rector; and a school is held in the R. C. chapel. There are some remains of the ancient church of Urney, and also of the old castle of Dungooley, on the townland of that name; the latter is said to have been one of the seats of the Earl of Tyrone. St. Bridget is said to have been born in this parish.

FAUGHLEY, or FAUGHANSTOWN, a parish, in the barony of Demifore, county of Westmeath, and province of Leinster, 2 miles (S.) from Castlepollard, on the road to Mullingar; containing 1551 inhabitants, and comprising 4059 statute acres. It extends along the entire north side of Lough Derveragh, and includes within its limits the hill of Knock Ion. The land is prinpally under an improving system of tillage; limestone abounds; there is very little bog. Near the upper end of the lake stands Gartlandstown, the seat of J. Murray, Esq. It is a vicarage, in the diocese of Meath, forming part of the union of Rathoraff, or Castlepollard; the rectory is impropriate in the Marquess of Westmeath. The tithes amount to £320, of which £142. 4. 5½. is payable to the impropriators, and £177. 15. 6½. to the incumbent. In the R. C. divisions it forms part of the union or district of Mayne and Faughanstown, also called Tarbotstown, and has a chapel at Milltown. A school at Dernagaragh, in which are 46 boys and 24 girls, is aided by a bequest of the late Col. Monk; and there are three private schools, in which 76 boys and 48 girls are instructed. On contiguous eminences, overlooking Lough Derveragh, are two very large raths, and near Gartlandstown are two others. At Dernagaragh are the ruins of an old castle; and on the shore of the lake are the remains of the parochial church, near which are those of a chapel.

FAVORAN, or FOYRAN, a parish, in the barony of Demifore, county of Westmeath, and province of Leinster, 5 miles (N.) from Castle-Pollard; containing 1897 inhabitants. This parish, which is bounded on the north by Lough Sheelin, and on the west by the river Inny, which separates it from the county of Longford, contains 4187 statute acres, as rated for the county cess. The surface is mountainous towards the south; in other parts the soil is fertile, and principally under tillage, except in the lower situations towards the north, where there are large quantities of bog. Limestone abounds, but the state of agriculture is rather backward. The gentlemen's seats are Clare Island, the handsome residence of Capt. A. Walker, beautifully situated on the shore of Lough Sheelin; and Williamstown, of J. Lahy, Esq. Fairs are held at the village of Finae. It is a curacy, in the diocese of Meath, forming part of the union of Rathgraff, or Castle-Pollard; the rectory is appropriate to the vicars choral of Christ-Church cathedral, Dublin: the tithes amount to £156. 1. 11., the whole payable to the vicars choral, who allow the curate a small stipend for discharging the clerical duties. Application has been made to the Ecclesiastical Commissioners for aid in the erection of a church, and Lord Longford has guaranteed to advance the whole amount required by the Commissioners to be subscribed. In the R. C. divisions it is part of the union or district of Castle-Pollard, and has a chapel at Tullystown. About 180 children are educated in two private schools. There are the remains of an ancient church; at Togher are those of a castle; and near Finae is a breastwork, the vicinity of which was anciently the scene of several battles.—See Finae.

FEACLE, a parish, in the barony of Tulla, county of Clare, and province of Munster, 4½ miles (W.N.W.) from Scariff, on the new road to Gort; containing 8844 inhabitants. This parish, which is the largest in the county, comprises about 30,000 statute acres, of which two-fifths consist of arable and pasture land, and the remainder, with the exception of 300 acres of woodland, is coarse mountain pasture, waste, and bog, a large portion of which is improvable. It presents, throughout, a succession of mountain and valley, extending to the confines of the county of Limerick, and includes the extensive and picturesque lake called Lough Graney, or "the lake of the sun," situated nearly in its centre. Prior to the year 1828 there was scarcely a road on which a wheel carriage could be used; but through the spirited exertions of Jas. Moloney, Esq., of Kiltannan, excellent roads have been constructed, partly by the Board of Public Works and partly by the county; and this district has now a direct communication with Limerick, Gort, Ennis, Killaloe, and Loughrea. These roads encompass three sides of Lough Graney, the banks of which are in several places finely planted: the soil in the vicinity of the lake is well adapted for the growth of oak and larch; and it is expected that planting will be extensively carried on, and a considerable portion of the waste land brought into cultivation. A beautiful river flows from this lake, which is 18 feet above the level of the Shannon, through Lough O'Grady, at the south-eastern extremity and partly within the limits of the parish, and falls into the Shannon at Scariff bay, with which a navigable communication could be formed at a moderate expense, by a canal about five miles in length. A court for the manor of Doonas is occasionally held by the seneschal, in which small debts are recoverable; and it is in contemplation to establish a court of petty sessions and a dispensary in the parish. There are several tuck-mills and a large bleach-green; and there were formerly extensive iron-works at a place still called Furnace-town. The gentlemen's seats are Caher, the occasional residence of Barry O'Hara, Esq., situated in a finely planted demesne on the banks of Lough Graney; Ayle, the ancient seat of J. McNamara, Esq.; Lakeview, of T. Bridgeman, Esq.; and Kilbarron, of E. McGrath, Esq., rebuilt on the site of the old mansion. It is a rectory, vicarage, and perpetual cure, in the diocese of Killaloe; the rectory is part of the union of Omullod, the vicarage, part of the economy estate of the cathedral of Killaloe, and the perpetual cure is in the patronage of the Dean and Chapter, who, as trustees of the economy fund, allot a stipend of £69. 5. to the curate. The church, a small neat edifice, was built about the year 1823, by aid of a gift of £300 from the late Board of First Fruits. The R. C. parish is co-extensive with that of the Established Church, and contains four chapels: the principal chapel, at Feacle, is a spacious cruciform structure, built in 1827, under the superintendence of the Rev. T. McInerny, at an expense of £1300; it is provided with galleries, and has a very handsome altar embellished with well-executed paintings and a very large bell: the site was granted gratuitously by Henry Butler, of Castle Crinn, Esq., who has also contributed £50 towards its erection. A school-house on an extensive scale is now being built near the chapel by subscription. The chapel at Killenana is intended to be rebuilt, and those at Kilcleran and Cahirmurphy to be taken down, and a large chapel erected at Knockbeagh, on a site presented by J. Molony, Esq., who will also contribute liberally towards its erection. In a school, superintended and partly supported by the R. C. clergyman, and four private schools, about 360 children are educated. Lead ore has been discovered at Glendree, and on the shores of Lough Graney is found a fine sand, chiefly composed of crystals, and much used for scythe boards.

FEDAMORE, a parish, partly in the barony of Clanwilliam, but chiefly in that of Small County, county of Limerick, and province of Munster, 6 miles (S.) from Limerick, on the road to Bruff; containing 3420 inhabitants, of which number, 277 are in the village. This parish comprises 5958 statute acres, as applotted under the tithe act, and valued at £7964 per annum. The soil is remarkably fertile; about one-fourth of the land is under tillage, and the remainder, with the exception of about 800 acres of valuable bog, is good pasture and meadow land. The meadows are subject to inundation from the river Commogue, and sometimes the crops of hay are entirely swept away. The neighbourhood is highly interesting, and embellished with several gentlemen's seats, of which the principal are Ballyneguard, that of J. Croker, Esq., a handsome mansion in a well-wooded and richly varied demesne of 700 plantation acres; Sandville, of J. Barry, Esq.; Grange, of H. O'Grady, Esq.; Friarstown, the ancient residence of the Hunt family; and the Glebe-house, of the Rev. J. Bennett. The village contains 26 houses. Fairs are held here on May 5th and Oct. 9th, chiefly for cattle and pigs, and occasionally for horses; and there is a constabulary police station. The living is a vicarage, in the diocese of Limerick, united at an unknown period to the vicarage of Glenogra, and in the patronage of the Bishop; the rectory is appropriate to the vicars choral of the cathedral of Christ-Church, Dublin. The tithes amount to £553. 16. 11., of which £369. 4. 7½. is payable to the lessees of the appropriators, and the remainder to the vicar: the tithes of the benefice amount to £379. 11. 3½. The glebe-house was built by aid of a gift of £300 and a loan of £500 from the late Board of First Fruits, in 1816; there are six acres of glebe attached to it, and there are also two other small glebes in the parish. The church is a small ancient edifice. In the R. C. divisions the parish is the head of a union or district, comprising also the parishes of Ballycahane, Manister-Nenagh, and Kilpeacon, in which are two chapels; the chapel at this place is a large and handsome edifice, which cost £700. About 200 children are taught in two public schools, of which the parochial school is endowed with half an acre of land from the glebe, on which it is situated. A residence for the master was built at the expense of the Rev. Godfrey Massey, then curate of the parish. The other school, at Grange, is liberally supported by H. O'Grady, Esq., who built the school-house. At Fanningstown, near the northern boundary of the parish, are the remains of Temple Roe, a church erected by the Knights Templars in 1288. Adjoining the demesne of Ballyneguard is Rockstown Castle; and in it is Williamstown Castle, erected by the Bourke family, a plain square building in its exterior, but curiously fitted up internally in the Gothic style; it has been renovated and restored to its ancient appearance by the Messrs. Pain, architects. At Englishtown is another castle, built by Sir J. Fitzgerald.

FEIGHAN of FORE, or FOWRE (ST.), a parish, in the barony of DEMIFORE, county of WESTMEATH, and province of LEINSTER, 2½ miles (E.) from Castle-Pollard, on the road to Kells; containing, with the market-town of Collinstown (which is separately described), 2447 inhabitants, of which number, 119 are in the village. This place, which is situated on Lough Lene and is of great antiquity, was formerly a borough, comprising the parishes of St. Feighan and St. Mary, and appears to have originated in the foundation of a priory for Canons Regular by St. Fechan, about the year 630, in which, while presiding over 3000 monks, he died in 665. From this time till 1169 the priory and the town, which had risen up around it, were repeatedly destroyed by fire; but in 1209, Walter de Lacy re-founded the priory under the invocation of St. Taurin and St. Fechin, for Benedictine monks, and made it a cell to the monastery of that order at Evereux, in Normandy. The town appears to have acquired all the privileges exercised by other corporate boroughs in Meath. In 1436, Hen. VI. granted certain customs upon all merchandise coming to its market, or to any other within three miles of it, for the purpose of enclosing it with a stone wall, as a barrier against the incursions of the Irish, who had thrice destroyed it by fire; and in 1448 he made his farmer of the priory lands, though a layman, prior of the monastery, in reward for the trouble he had taken, and the expense he had incurred, in erecting a strong castle for the defence of the town. After the dissolution, the priory was granted by Queen Elizabeth, in 1588, to Christopher, Baron Delvin, whose successor, Richard, Lord Delvin, obtained for the town the grant of a fair. It appears to have been a borough by prescription, and to have sent two members to the Irish parliament till the Union, when it was disfranchised and the £15,000 awarded as compensation was paid to Arthur, Marquess of Downshire. There are still some remains of the ancient abbey and of an anchorite's cell, the latter a small massive building of very ancient character; and the ruins of several square towers, evidently built for defence, round which may be traced the walls of a very considerable town, of which two of the gates are still remaining. The present village, which is situated at the base of the Ben of Fore, in a fertile valley sheltered by some high hills, separating it from Lough Lene, contains only 20 small houses, and possesses but a few indistinct remains of its ancient importance. The parish extends along the borders of the county of Meath, having on one side the small lake called Lough Glore, and on the other the White Lake, between which is a range of heights terminating in a lofty mountain, called the Ben of Fore. It comprises 6506 statute acres, of which a small portion is mountain land, and the remainder principally under tillage; the soil is light and gravelly. Limestone abounds, but of inferior quality, and there are some quarries of good building stone. Lough Lene, about half a mile south of the village, is a fine sheet of water, studded with small islands and surrounded by rising grounds; on the south-east a stream issues from it, and passing under the hills emerges close to the village, where it turns a mill, and thence continuing its course, under the name of the Glore, falls into the river Inny; another stream, issuing from the east of the lake, takes an opposite course and falls into Lough Dele. The principal gentlemen's seats are Benison Lodge, that of the Rev. T. Smyth; Lough Park, of N. Evans, Esq.; Barbavilla, of W. B. Smyth, Esq.; Hilltown, of W. Webb, Esq.; and Sallymount, of G. S. Rotheram, Esq. A market, fairs, and petty sessions are held at Collinstown.

It is a curacy, in the diocese of Meath, forming part of the union of Rathgraff, or Castle-Pollard; the rectory is wholly appropriate to the vicars choral of the cathedral of Christ-Church, Dublin. The tithes amount to £390. In the R. C. divisions it is the head of a union or district comprising also the parishes of St. Mary and Kilcumney, and containing two chapels, situated respectively at Fore and Collinstown. A school is supported by Mr. Smyth, of Barbavilla, and there are three private schools, in which are about 100 children. On a high hill to the south-west of Lough Lene is a fort, said to have been constructed by Turgesius, the Danish king of Ireland. The family of Nugent, Marquesses of Westmeath, have a burial-place at Fore; and there are some remains of a monastery on one of the islands in Lough Lene, the property of Mr. Smyth. The surrounding country abounds with raths.

FEIGHCULLEN, a parish, partly in the barony of EAST OPHALY, but chiefly in that of CONNELL, county of KILDARE, and province of LEINSTER, 4¾ miles (N.) from Kildare, on the Grand Canal; containing 890 inhabitants. It comprises 3835 statute acres, as applotted under the tithe act, exclusively of a large tract of bog, and about 20 acres of common: the state of agriculture is gradually improving. At Grange Hill is a vein of lead ore. The gentlemen's seats are Newington, the residence of S. Neale, Esq.; Christian's Town, of J. Forbes, Esq.; Whilan, of — Cooper, Esq.; and Washington, of R. Mothersill, Esq. The living is a rectory and vicarage, in the diocese of Kildare, and in the gift of the Crown: the tithes amount to £180. There is a glebe-house, with a glebe of 10 acres. The church is a small but handsome structure, erected by a gift of £830 and a loan of £277 from the late Board of First Fruits, in 1829, and for its repair a grant of £248 has been recently made by the Ecclesiastical Commissioners. In the R. C. divisions the parish forms part of the union or district of Kilmaogue, also called Allen and Milltown: the chapel is a large building at Milltown. A public school has been established there, for which a house was built by the late Rev. J. Lawler, P. P. About 60 children are educated in two private schools.

FENAGH, a parish, partly in the barony of Mohill, but chiefly in that of Leitrim, county of Leitrim, and province of Connaught, 2½ miles (S. W.) from Ballinamore, on the road to Carrick-on-Shannon; containing 4172 inhabitants. In the time of St. Columb a monastery was founded here, over which St. Callin, or Kilian, presided, and which became celebrated as a school of divinity, being resorted to by students from all parts of Europe. The conventual church is still remaining, and has an east window of curious design; across the gable is a band carved in high relief, and on the north side is sculptured the figure of a griffin, with a cord in his mouth. The western portion, which is groined, was fitted up for the Protestant parishioners, and divine service was performed in it till the erection of the present church, about the close of the last century. The parish comprises 7279 statute acres, as applotted under the tithe act, of which about 6220 are arable and pasture land, 670 bog, and 380 waste. The surface is greatly diversified with hill and dale, and studded with several small lakes; the soil is generally poor, and the system of agriculture unimproved. Limestone of good quality is raised for burning, and there are some quarries of grit-stone at Curnagan, from which mill-stones are procured. Mough is the residence of W. Lawder, Esq. The village of Castlefore, in this parish, on the road from Ballinamore to Cashcarrigan, is of small extent, and takes its name from a castle built by Col. Coote, about the middle of the 17th century, which was plundered and burnt through the treachery of a female servant; from the present remains it appears to have consisted of three irregular sides, defended by three bastions, half of one of which is still in existence. There was anciently a furnace for smelting iron-ore found in the neighbourhood, and the iron made here was considered equal in quality to that of Sweden. The living is a rectory and vicarage, in the diocese of Ardagh, and in the patronage of the Bishop: the tithes amount to £191. The glebe-house was built by aid of a gift of £92 and a loan of £830 from the late Board of First Fruits, in 1829, and £400 from the incumbent; the glebe comprises 708 acres. The church is a plain edifice, without either tower or spire. The R. C. parish is co-extensive with that of the Established Church; the chapel is about to be rebuilt. There are two public schools, in which about 130 children are taught. About half a mile north-east of the village are the remains of a cromlech, called by the peasantry *Leaba Dearmid i Graine*, "Darby and Graine's bed." At Coolkilla, two miles north of Fenagh, was an abbey, said to have been founded by St. Columb; it is on the shore of a small lake, of which about 16 acres are in this parish, and near it is a stone with the figure of a fish carved on it; the lake abounds with fish of excellent flavour. A bell, said to have been given by St. Patrick on his landing in this country, and an Irish MS., called the "Annals of Fenagh," are preserved here with much care. In the parish is a sulphureous spring. Judge Fox and P. Dignum, both Judges in the Prerogative Court, and Edmund Bourke or de Burgo, author of the "Hibernia Dominicana," were educated in this parish.

FENIT, formerly called FENOR, an island and parish, in the barony of Clanmaurice, county of Kerry, and province of Munster, 7 miles (W. by N.) from Tralee, on the north side of Tralee bay: the population is returned with the parish of Ardfert. Between this island and the main land, with which it is connected by a long narrow isthmus, is a small creek, called Barra harbour, fit only for small craft. It is entered from the north by a narrow passage between rocky cliffs, nearly 100 feet high; and it is the opinion of scientific men that a sea wall might be constructed, and the whole of the creek drained; and as it is not much used as a harbour, a large tract of valuable land would be thus brought into cultivation. The island, which is the property of Wm. Lock, Esq., has been latterly much improved by draining, and is remarkable for producing good crops of barley. Sea-weed and sand are procured in great abundance on its shores, and used for manure: the state of agriculture is improving. The manufacture of kelp was formerly carried on here to a considerable extent, but it has been long on the decline. Opposite Samphire island are procured limestone flags of superior quality and unusual size, which have been used in the construction of the Tralee ship canal. Between Samphire island and the south shore of Fenit is good anchorage, where vessels may take shelter from the prevalent north-easterly winds. It is a rectory, in the diocese of Ardfert and Aghadoe, and forms part of the union and corps of the chancellorship of the cathedral of Ardfert: the tithes amount to £100. In the R. C. divisions it is part of the union or district of Ardfert. There are some remains of an old church; and on the north-eastern shore of the island, near the entrance of the harbour, are those of Fenit castle.

FENNAGH, or FENAGH, a parish, partly in the barony of Shillelagh, county of Wicklow, but chiefly in that of Idrone East, county of Carlow, and province of Leinster, 5 miles (S. E.) from Leighlin-Bridge, on the rivers Slaney and Burrin, and on the road from Bagnalstown to Newtown-Barry; containing 4324 inhabitants. This parish comprises 11,942 statute acres, as applotted under the tithe act, and valued at £1230 per ann.; about 600 acres are mountain, nearly 120 bog, and the remainder good arable and pasture land in a good state of cultivation; there are some quarries of fine granite. The village of Fennagh is beautifully situated, commanding picturesque and grand views of Mount Leinster; the surrounding country is thickly planted, and the gentlemen's seats afford some good specimens of ancient architecture. Here was a well-fortified castle, the seat of one of the kings of Leinster. The principal seats are Castlemore House, the residence of J. Eustace, Esq.; Hardy Mount, of J. Hardy Eustace, Esq.; Janeville, of W. Garrett, Esq.;

Lumclone, of T. H. Watson, Esq.; Kilconner, of — Watson, Esq.; Ballydarton, of J. Watson, Esq.; Upton, of I. Grey, Esq.; Clonferta, of T. Dillon, Esq.; and Garryhill House, a residence of Viscount Duncannon. A penny post to Leighlin-Bridge has been established, and here is a constabulary police station. The living is a rectory and vicarage, in the diocese of Leighlin; the rectory is in the patronage of the Crown; and the vicarage is endowed with the townlands of Castlemore, Ballybenard, Tullowbeg, Drumphey, and Ardowen (which in the vicar's title are called chapelries), and is in the patronage of the Bishop. The tithes amount to £646. 3. 1., of which £415. 7. 8¼. is payable to the rector, and £230. 15. 4¾. to the vicar. The glebe-house is a neat building, and the glebe comprises 16 acres. The church, a neat plain edifice, was erected in 1790; and the Ecclesiastical Commissioners have recently granted £206 for its repair. In the R. C. divisions the parish forms part of the union or district of Myshall; the chapel is at Drumphey. There is a place of worship for the Society of Friends. The parochial school for boys is aided by donations from the rector and vicar, and about 50 girls are taught in a school supported by subscription; there are also five private schools, in which are about 270 children, and a dispensary. At Ranegeragh are some remains of a castle, which anciently belonged to the Kavanaghs; at Drumphey are the ruins of an ancient monastery; and at Castlemore is a remarkable moat.

FENNOR, a parish, in the barony of Lower Duleek, county of Meath, and province of Leinster, ½ a mile (S.) from Slane, on the river Boyne, and on the mail road from Dublin to Londonderry; containing 225 inhabitants, and comprising 954 statute acres, as applotted under the tithe act. The Boyne, which bounds the parish on the north, is here crossed by a good stone bridge. It is a rectory, in the diocese of Meath, entirely impropriate in Blaney T. Balfour, Esq., to whom the tithes, amounting to £104, are payable. In the R. C. divisions it forms part of the union or district of Slane. There are some remains of the old church, near which are those of an ancient mansion.

FENNOR, a parish, in the barony of Slievardagh, county of Tipperary, and province of Munster, 2½ miles (S.) from Johnstown, on the mail coach road from Dublin by Cashel to Cork; containing 2073 inhabitants. This parish, which is bounded on the north and west by the bog of Allen and a small stream separating it from the barony of Eliogarty, comprises 5674 statute acres, which, with the exception of a considerable tract of bog, is chiefly under tillage. In the bog of Allen, and in this parish, is one of those verdant spots called islands, containing about 60 acres of excellent pasturage for sheep: the substratum of the island is limestone, but of almost every other part of the parish, freestone. The small river, at a very trifling expense, might be greatly improved by deepening the shallow parts, and would thus afford a facility for draining the bog, and supply abundance of water for turning the several mills upon its banks. Some limestone of a blue colour is worked for agricultural uses, but the general manure is a compost of lime and clay. Poyntstown, the property of Phanuel Cooke, Esq., is in ruins. Here is a constabulary police station. The living is a rectory, in the diocese of Cashel, forming the corps of the prebend of Fennor, in the cathedral of Cashel, in the patronage of the Archbishop: the tithes amount to £489. 4. 7½. The glebe-house was erected by aid of a grant from the late Board of First Fruits; the glebe comprises 25 acres. The church is a neat modern structure, rebuilt by aid of a gift of £800 from the same Board, in 1815. In the R. C. divisions the parish is part of the union or district of Gurtnahoe, or Buolick. About 250 children are taught in three public schools, of which the parochial school is aided by a donation of £10 per ann. from the incumbent. The ruins of the old castles of Fennor and Graigue Padeen are in the parish, in which are also the remains of the old church, and several Danish raths.

FENOAGH, or FINNOOGH, a parish, in the barony of Upperthird, county of Waterford, and province of Munster, 3 miles (S. E.) from Carrick-on-Suir; containing 881 inhabitants. This parish, which is separated by the Suir from the county of Kilkenny, comprises 2143 statute acres, as applotted under the tithe act. It is a rectory, in the diocese of Lismore, and part of the union of Dysart; the tithes amount to £193. 17.

FERBANE.—See FARBANE.

FERMANAGH, an inland county, of the province of Ulster, bounded on the east by Monaghan and Tyrone, on the north by Tyrone and Donegal, on the west by Donegal and Leitrim, and on the south by Cavan. It extends from 54° 7′ to 54° 40′ (N. Lat.), and from 7° 1′ to 8° 5′ (W. Lon.); and comprises an area, according to the Ordnance survey, of 456,538½ acres, of which 320,599 are cultivated land, 46,755 are under water, and the remainder are unprofitable bog and mountain. The population, in 1821, amounted to 130,997; and in 1831, to 149,555.

The *Erdini*, according to some authorities, were the inhabitants of this district in the time of Ptolemy; but Whitaker considers it to have been part of the territory of the *Nagnatæ*. By the ancient Irish it was called *Feor Magh Eanagh*, or "the Country of the Lakes," and *Magh Uire*, or "the Country of the Waters:" it was also called *Ernai* or *Ernagh*, and the inhabitants who lived round Lough Erne, *Ernains* and *Erenochs*, a name supposed to be derived from the Erdini. It was divided into two great portions, one called Targoll, the ancient seat of the *Facmonii*, and of the *Macmanii*, or the Mac Manuses; the other named Rosgoll, occupied by the *Guarii* or *Guirii*, from whom the Mac Guires, or Maguires, derive their origin. This family was so powerful that the greater part of the county was for several centuries known by the name of Mac Guire's country. It was made shire ground in the 11th of Elizabeth, by the name which it still retains. The unsettled state of the district at this period may be inferred from the anecdote told of its chieftain, when the lord-deputy sent to inform him that he was about to send a sheriff into his territory; Maguire's answer was, "that her majesty's officer would be received, but at the same time he desired to know his *eric*, the fine to be imposed on his murderer, in order that, if he happened to be slain by any of his followers, the amount might be levied on the offender's chattels." It was one of the six counties which escheated to the Crown by the flight of the Earls of Tyrone and Tyrconnel, on an imputed conspiracy, and which were included in the celebrated scheme of James I. for the improvement of the north of Ireland, under the name of the Plantation of Ulster. According to the arrangements therein made, the county is supposed to have consisted of 1070 tates of 30 acres each, besides 46 islands, great and small: of these, 212 tates, containing about 6360 acres, were assigned to the church, and the remainder disposed of among the English and Scotch settlers, who, from their undertaking to fulfil the conditions of the plantation, were called Undertakers. A portion, consisting of 390 tates, was assigned to the head of the Mac Guire family; and the rest of the native inhabitants were here, as in the other five counties, removed to waste lands in Munster or Connaught. The principal settlers were Sir James Belford, Sir Stephen Butler, Sir Wm. Cole, Sir John Hume, Malcolm Hamilton, John Archdall, George Hume, and John Dunbar, who were Scotchmen; John Sedborrow, Thomas Flowerdew, Edward Hatton, Sir Hugh Wirrall, George Ridgwaie, Sir Gerrard Lowther, Edw. Sibthorp, Henry Flower, Sir Edw. Blenerhasset, and Thomas Blenerhasset, Englishmen; besides whom, Sir John Davis, Capt. Harrison, Sir Henry Folliott, and Captains Gore and Atkinson, acquired large tracts in the allotments set apart for such natives as were suffered to reside. Of these, Con Mac Shane O'Neal, and Brian Mac Guire were the only persons of sufficient consequence to be noted in the report to the English government on the state of the plantation in 1619. In the war of 1688, this county became famous by the gallant stand made by its inhabitants, under the name of the Enniskillen men, in favour of King William, during which period they not only maintained themselves in the town of Enniskillen, thus preserving this important pass between Ulster and Connaught, in spite of all the attempts made to obtain possession of it, but made incursions into the neighbouring counties, from which they carried off many prisoners and much booty, and paralysed the operations of a large portion of the Irish army before Derry, from an apprehension of an attack from this quarter. After the relief of this city, they joined the army of William in Ulster, and from their gallant demeanour and knowledge of the country rendered him good service, and made the name of the Enniskilleners respected among their English friends and dreaded by the Irish enemy. The military spirit thus drawn forth has been maintained ever since, so that not only do the sons of the native farmers frequently prefer a soldier's life abroad to that of an agriculturist at home, but young men from other counties anxious to enlist travel thither to the recruiting parties which are always ready to receive them.

According to the Ecclesiastical arrangements the county is partly in the diocese of Kilmore, but chiefly in that of Clogher. For the purposes of civil jurisdiction it is divided into the baronies of Clonkelly, Coole, Glenawly, Knockninny, Lurg, Magheraboy, Magherastephana, and Tyrkennedy; it contains the borough, market and county town of Enniskillen, the market and post-towns of Irvinestown (formerly Lowtherstown), Lisnaskea, and Brookborough; the market-town of Maguires-bridge (which has a penny post); and the post-towns of Florence-Court, Kesh, Tempo, Church Hill, Newtown-Butler, Belleek, and Lisbellaw, together with the villages of Ballinamallard, Ederney, and Holywell. Prior to the Union it sent four members to the Irish parliament, *viz.*, two knights of the shire, and two burgesses for the borough of Enniskillen; and since that period it has returned three representatives to the Imperial parliament, the number for the borough having been then reduced to one, and so continued under the Reform act. The elections take place in the county town. The county constituency, as registered at the close of the January sessions, 1836, consists of 220 freeholders of £50, 246 of £20, and 1120 of £10; one leaseholder of £50, 24 of £20, and 36 of £10; two rent-chargers of £50, and 11 of £20; making a total of 1660 registered electors. The county is included in the North-west circuit. The assizes and general quarter sessions of the peace are held at Enniskillen, where the county gaol and court-house are situated: quarter sessions are also holden at Newtown-Butler, where there are a sessions-house and bridewell. The number of persons charged with criminal offences, and committed for trial in 1836, was 409. The local government is vested in a lord-lieutenant, 14 deputy-lieutenants, and 64 other magistrates, together with the usual county officers, including a coroner. The constabulary police consists of an inspector, paymaster, stipendiary magistrate, 4 officers, 21 constables, 90 sub-constables, and 5 horses, quartered in 20 stations; the expense of their maintenance is defrayed in equal proportions by Grand Jury presentments and by Government. The district lunatic asylum is at Armagh, the county infirmary is at Enniskillen, and there are dispensaries at Church Hill, Rosslea, Kesh, Brookborough, Maguires-bridge, Lisnaskea, Irvinestown, Newtown-Butler, Holywell, Ballinamallard, Belleek, and Lisbellaw. The amount of Grand Jury presentments for 1835 was £16,346. 8. $1\frac{3}{4}$., of which £3098. 19. $9\frac{1}{2}$. was for the roads, bridges, &c., of the county at large; £4380. 11. $1\frac{1}{4}$. for the roads, bridges, &c., being the baronial charge; £6566. 11. $6\frac{1}{2}$. for public buildings, charities, officers' salaries, and incidents; and £2300. 5. $8\frac{1}{2}$. for the police. In the military arrangements the county is included in the northern district, and contains barracks for artillery and infantry at Enniskillen, affording accommodation for 14 officers and 547 non-commissioned officers and men, with 98 horses.

The surface is very uneven, and presents great varieties both of soil and aspect. On the eastern verge of the county the land is elevated and sterile, and on the western still more so: indeed, with the exception of small portions in the north and south, the county may be said to consist of hills environed by mountains, and having its centre depressed into a great natural basin or reservoir, serving as a receptacle for the numerous rivers and streams from the higher grounds, whose accumulated waters form one of the noblest lakes in Ireland. Of these mountains the most elevated is Cuilcagh, which, though generally considered as belonging to Leitrim and Cavan, has its lofty eastern extremity, 2188 feet high, altogether in Fermanagh. The Slievebaught or Slabby mountain, which forms the boundary towards Monaghan and Tyrone, extends far westward into this county, and, in like manner, that of Barnesmore in Donegal penetrates southward into it. The most conspicuous of the mountains which are wholly within the county is Belmore, 1312 feet high, between the Shannon and the Erne. Tosset, or Topped mountain, of inferior elevation, commands a range of prospects, which for grandeur, variety, and extent is not surpassed by any other in the north of Ireland. Turaw mountain, rising boldly from the waters of Lough Erne, forms a beautiful and striking feature of its scenery. The other mountains of remarkable elevation are Glenkeel near Derrygonnelly, 1223 feet; North Shean, 1135; Tappahan on the borders of Tyrone, 1110; and Carnmore near Rosslea, 1034 feet. But the grand distinguishing characteristic of the county is Lough Erne, which extends forty miles from north-west to south-east, forming in reality two lakes, embayed by mountains and connected by a deep and winding strait, on an island in the centre of which stands the county town of Enniskillen. Of the two lakes, the northern or lower, between Belleek and Enniskillen, is the larger, being upwards of 20 miles in length, and 7½ in its greatest breadth; the southern or upper, between the latter town and Belturbet, is 12 miles long by 4½ broad. Both are studded with numerous islands, which in some parts of the upper lake are clustered so closely together as to present the appearance rather of a flooded country than of a spacious lake. It is a popular opinion that the number of these islands equals that of the days in the year; but accurate investigation has ascertained that there are 109 in the lower lake, and 90 in the upper. The largest is Bo or Cow island, near the northern extremity of the upper lake; it takes its name from being mostly under pasture. Ennismacsaint, also in the upper lake, is noted for a burying-ground, which is held in great veneration; Devenish island, in the same lake, near Enniskillen, is particularly remarkable for its ancient round tower and other relics of antiquity, all of which are described in the article on the parish of that name. The other more remarkable islands in this division are Eagle, Innisnakill, and Gully, all richly wooded; Cor and Ferney, mostly under pasture, and Herring island, said to derive its name from the quantities of fresh-water herring found near its shores. Innismore, the largest island in the upper lake, forms part of the two nearest parishes on the main land. Belleisle has long been celebrated for its natural beauties, which were much heightened by the judicious improvements they received when it was the residence of the Earl of Rosse: it is connected with the main land by an elegant bridge. Near it is Lady Rosse's island, so called from the improvements bestowed on it by that lady. Knockninny was used as a deer-park by the nobleman just named. In descending the lake from Belturbet, the first two miles present the appearance of a large river winding through the county without any striking features to arrest attention; but as the lake widens, a succession of rich and picturesque views opens upon the eye. The banks on each side, as well as the islands that present themselves in rapid succession, are clothed with stately timber, which rises boldly from the water's edge, occasionally interrupted by sweeps of low marsh overgrown with rushes and enlivened by herons and other aquatic fowl. After narrowing in to the strait of Enniskillen, and expanding again into a still wider sheet of water in the lower lake, it is finally contracted into a river which quits the county at the village of Belleek in a magnificent fall. The lakes called Lough Melvin, Lough Macnean, and Lough Kane, which form part of the boundary between Fermanagh and Leitrim, may be considered as partly belonging to the former county.

The soil in some parts is a rich loam upon a substratum of limestone, or calcareous gravel; in others, a light friable soil on slaty gravel; and again in others, a heavy soil mixed with stones, beneath which is blue and yellow clay on a substratum of basalt, here called whinstone; but throughout almost every part, the soil is wet and cold, obstinately retaining the surface water unless counteracted by constant draining. The size of farms varies from 3 acres to 500; those of large size are mostly near the mountains, and occupied in grazing young cattle. Considerable tracts of land are let in bulk, and the holders of them are generally middlemen, who sublet in small portions: proprietors of this description are called Terney begs, or "Little Lords." The manure, which is seldom used for any crop except potatoes, is generally a compost of stable dung, lime, and bog mould; the scourings of ditches are sometimes used as a substitute for lime. Marl is in high repute; it is of a dusky white colour, mostly found at the bottom of bogs; near Florence-Court and in some other places it shews itself in large ridges resting upon gravel, whence issue numerous springs impregnated with vitriolic acid: in the vicinity of these springs the marl is found in various curious shapes, cylindrical, spherical, oblong, and curved, highly indurated, and of a dirty red colour, but when exposed to the action of a winter's atmosphere, and used either in top-dressing or as a compost, it retains its efficacy for two or three successive seasons. The staple crops are oats and potatoes, with some wheat; flax, barley, turnips, clover, and vetches are occasionally planted; the culture of barley is every year extending, but that of all the others is chiefly confined to the gentry and wealthy farmers. In the mountain districts, much of the land is cultivated with the spade or the old heavy wooden plough; in other parts, the use of the improved iron plough and light angular harrow is universal, as well as that of all other new and improved implements. The old car with solid wooden wheels has given way to the light cart with spoke-wheels, and the slide-car is rarely used, except in the most mountainous districts to bring turf down the precipitous roads. These mountain farms are chiefly appropriated to the rearing of young cattle, great numbers of which are annually purchased in Leitrim, Sligo, and Donegal, at a year old, and kept by the mountain farmer for one or two years, when they are sold to the graziers of the adjoining counties; great numbers of milch cows are kept, and large quantities of butter made, which is mostly salted in firkins, and bought up in the neighbouring markets, chiefly for the merchants of Belfast and Newry. Perhaps less attention is paid to the breed of cattle in this than in any other county in Ireland; almost every sort of stock known in the kingdom is to be found here in a day's journey, but so crossed as to defy the possibility of distinguishing the original breeds; that best adapted to the soil and climate is the long-horned Roscommon. Sheep are numerous in some districts; they are generally a small mountain breed, and mostly kept for the purpose of furnishing wool for domestic clothing, but many of the gentry have very excellent stocks, being for the most part a cross between the Leicester and Sligo breed. Pigs, though found in all parts, are by no means so numerous as in the adjoining county of Monaghan; indeed in many instances the food which should be given to the pig is carefully saved for the cow. Goats are so numerous as to be highly detrimental to the hedges, which are everywhere stunted by the browsing of this animal.

The horses are bad, being neither of the hack nor waggon kind; larger than the poney and smaller than the galloway: but great numbers of a very superior description are brought into the county by dealers for the use of the gentry. The fences for the most part are dry stone walls, or sods, except in the lower and level districts, where white thorn and other quicksets have been planted; these, wherever properly protected, thrive remarkably well. Draining is sometimes practised, mostly by open trenches; irrigation rarely or never. Every part of the county appears to produce forest timber spontaneously, particularly ash and beech; to such an extent does the former grow, as to be called the weed of the country; and towards the northern part and in some other districts, excellent ash and beech are to be seen growing to a large size as hedgerow timber. At Crum and Castle Caldwell there are excellent and extensive woods of oak, beech, and ash, and much full-grown ornamental timber and young plantations around Florence-Court and Castle Coole; indeed, plantations are more or less connected with the residence of almost every gentleman, and they are yearly increasing. The fuel universally used is turf, cut from the numerous bogs scattered over every part of the county, from the lowest levels to the sides, and even to the summits of the mountains. Coal is sometimes brought to Enniskillen, but the expense of conveyance limits its use to the more wealthy part of the community.

In a geological point of view this county is highly interesting: the great central limestone district of Ireland terminates in it, and the western coal and iron formation commences; here the granite of Donegal forms a junction with the basaltic range, which, with little intermission, extends to the coast of Antrim; here also the Escars (that extraordinary chain of low hills, which extends from Lough Neagh to the remotest part of Galway and Mayo,) seem to form a nucleus, whence they radiate in every direction; so that within a very limited space are found almost every kind of rounded nodule, from the jasper and agate down to the softest clay slate. Generally speaking, the rock of the county is either secondary limestone, abounding with organic remains (particularly encrinites), or quartose sandstone, in some districts equal in closeness of grain, uniformity of structure, and durability to any in the British islands. Limestone of several kinds is found in the islands of Lough Erne, and in other places on the main land; the quarries of the latter are extensively worked. Near Florence-Court is brown marble beautifully veined; it receives a fine polish, and when worked into ornaments presents a surface which, for mellowness of tint and variety of veins, is not excelled even by the celebrated marble of Iona. In the parish of Killasher are large beds of marble, having a perpendicular face of 53 feet in height, projecting boldly from the neighbouring cliffs; it is of a grey colour, often beautifully clouded, but it has never been worked for ornamental purposes. Near the foot of Cuilcagh are vast deposits of ironstone, veins of which can also be traced in the bed of the neighbouring streams: numerous mines were opened, and the ore extensively wrought as long as the forest afforded fuel; but when this source failed, the works were abandoned, and the furnaces and mills have gone to decay. In this mountain and in the Tosset are thin seams of coal, which appear to form the verge of the great Leitrim and Roscommon field, the indications and strata of the base of Cuilcagh, exactly corresponding with those of the Iron mountain in the county of Leitrim; some slight excavations have been made by the peasantry, but no effort on an extended scale has been attempted to search for this valuable fossil. In the hills of Glengarron are also indications of coal; but the great quantity of turbary in every part affords so many facilities for procuring turf at a cheap rate, as to prevent any effort towards the working of the collieries. When the canal between Loughs Neagh and Erne is finished, and the navigation opened to Ballyshannon, there is every reason to hope that the mineral treasures of Fermanagh will prove a new source of national wealth and prosperity.

Fermanagh may be said to be almost exclusively an agricultural county: the only staple manufacture is that of linen, which in some districts is briskly carried on; the cloth for the most part is $\frac{7}{8}$ths; a stronger kind, principally for domestic use, is made from the refuse and tow. Flax-spinning is general throughout the county; scarcely a house is without a wheel and reel. The yarn is carried to the market-towns, and bought up in large quantities for the manufactures of the more northern counties. Wool-spinning prevails in the mountain districts, and excellent flannels and blankets are made: druggets, with linen warps of a very superior quality, are also manufactured; likewise a very useful stuff, principally for domestic wear.

The fish most common in Lough Erne are salmon, perch, pike, bream, trout, and eels. It is said that perch first appeared in this lake about the year 1760, and that they were seen in all the other lakes in Ireland and in the Shannon at the same period. There are some large eel-weirs at Enniskillen, where great quantities of that fish are caught: they come from the sea when young, and are intercepted in their return; those which are not sold fresh, or sent to Dublin, are cured in barrels containing about eight dozen each, and sold at Belturbet. There is also an eel-weir near the falls of Belleek; but this town is more remarkable for its salmon fishery, considered, in conjunction with that at Ballyshannon, a little lower down the river, to be one of the most productive in Ireland. Large flights of wild geese and swans occasionally visit Lough Erne towards the close of the year, the appearance of which is considered to prognosticate a severe winter.

The only river of any consequence is the Erne, which, entering the county a short distance from Belturbet, flows into Lough Erne at its southern extremity, and, after passing Belleek at its northern extremity, discharges itself into Donegal bay at Ballyshannon; all the other rivers empty themselves into Lough Erne. The Finn is navigable for boats as far as Cumber bridge on the confines of Monaghan; the Pettigo and the Omna rise near Lough Derg, in Donegal, and after uniting their streams fall into the lake a mile south of the town of Pettigo: the Scillies rises near Church hill, and takes a southern direction to the lake. There are upwards of fifty smaller streams, all contributing to augment the waters of the great central reservoir. The Ulster canal, intended to unite Lough Neagh and Lough Erne, will enter this county from Monaghan, not far from Clones; thence proceeding towards Belturbet, it is to fall into Lough Erne. The roads are numerous, but for the most part badly laid out; many of them are flooded during winter, exceedingly inconvenient, and kept in indifferent repair.

The number of Danish raths in all parts is very great, but none of them are peculiarly singular in their construction. Tumuli also occur, surrounded with circles of upright stones; when opened, urns and stone coffins have been found in them. At Wattle bridge, three miles from Newtown-Butler, on the banks of the Finn, are the remains of a Druidical temple. There are but few remains of monastic institutions: those of Devenish and Gola are the only structures in which traces of the original buildings can be discovered: the abbeys of Ennismacsaint, Cleenish, Kilskerry, and Rossory have been converted into parish churches: those of Ariodmuilt, Derough, Domnachmore, Inniscasin, Inniseo, Innisrocha, and Loughuva are now known only by name. About a mile from Pettigo stand the ruins of Castle Mac Grath, the residence of the first Protestant bishop of Clogher, from whom the building took its name. Lisgool, a castle on the bank of the Rale opposite to Enniskillen, also suffered during the civil war of 1641, being burnt by the Irish. The ruins of Callahill castle are near Florence-Court. Castle Hume, which was the seat of Lord Loftus, is now a pile of ruins. Enniskillen, which was little more than a fort in Elizabeth's time, has since completely changed its character; the castle is in ruins, and its defences and outworks have been gradually converted by the progress of civilization into peaceful and substantial dwelling-houses. The modern residences of the nobility and gentry are noticed in the articles on the parishes in which they are respectively situated.

The peasantry are a fine race, much superior in appearance to those of any of the other northern districts: they are tall, well formed, and robust: their countenances display the bloom of health, and they possess that uninterrupted flow of spirits which is the constant attendant on regular living and active, yet not overstrained, industry. Whether from habit or a natural propensity, the people do not rise until a late hour in the morning, and the cows are not milked until noon. The cottiers who dwell in the more retired and mountainous parts are poor, and their cabins are wretched huts, with a wattled door and a straw mat on the inside; many of the herdsmen, who are able to give their daughters a marriage portion of £20 and a feather bed, live in these cabins. The lower classes have no confidence in physicians: when one is called in, the patient despairs of life; hence a dislike is entertained for the whole medical profession. Yet, notwithstanding the reluctance to spend money upon medicine, considerable sums are lavished on the wake which precedes interment. The English language is universally spoken, and most of the children are educated in the parochial and national schools. Mineral springs are very numerous: Rutty gives a list of twenty, partly chalybeate, partly sulphureous. Of the former are those of Aghalun, Coolauran, Drumcroe, Killinshanvally, Largy, and Tullyveel; of the latter, Aghnahinch, Ashwood, Derryinch, Derrylester, Killasher, Lisbleak (two springs), Meham (two springs), Owen Brewn, and Pettigo: the water of the last-named is more strongly impregnated with the mineral than even the celebrated spring at Swanlinbar. A spring at Maguires-bridge, and two at Drumgoon, are sulphureous, with a prevailing admixture of an alkali. Four miles north-west of Enniskillen, near Ballycassidy, are some natural caves called the Daughton: the entrance is by a large arch, 25 feet high, the roof being composed of various pieces of rock in regular order; the passage leads to a second vault of the same form, but not so high, and thence it is continued by narrow windings to a brook, which, passing through unknown recesses, discharges itself at the first entrance. At Belcou, a small distance west of Enniskillen, is a celebrated well, called Davagh Phadric, reputed the best cold bath in Ireland, and in great esteem for nervous and paralytic disorders: it discharges a large stream which turns two mills at the short distance of 150 yards from its mouth. This county gave the title of Viscount to the Verney family, now extinct.

FERMOY, a market and post-town, and a parish, in the barony of CONDONS and CLONGIBBONS, county of CORK, and province of MUNSTER, 17¼ miles (N. by E.) from Cork, and 108½ (S. W.) from Dublin, on the river Blackwater, and on the mail coach road from Cork to Dublin; containing 8690 inhabitants, of which number, 6976 are in the town. This place, which is now a grand military depôt, is said to have originated in the foundation of a Cistertian abbey by the family of the Roches, in 1170, which was known as the abbey of Our Lady de Castro Dei, and after its dissolution was granted by Queen Elizabeth to Sir Rich. Grenville, Knt. The town, which commanded an important pass of the river, over which a bridge had been erected the preceding year, was, in 1690, attacked by 1500 of the Irish in the service of Jas. II., commanded by Gen. Carrol. The garrison, consisting only of a small party of Danes under Col. Donep, had recourse to the stratagem of two trumpets sounding a march as of reinforcements advancing to their aid, and the assailants retreated with precipitation. Though the inhabitants had obtained letters patent for a market and fairs, this place, at the close of the last century, consisted of a common carrier's inn and a few mud cabins only; but, in 1791, the late John Anderson, Esq., having purchased four-sixths of the manor, erected a commodious hotel and some good houses, and laid the foundation of its present prosperity. In 1797, Government wishing to form a military station in a central part of the south of Ireland, made overtures to the proprietor, who, foreseeing the advantages to be derived from such an establishment, made a free grant of a site for that purpose, and erected temporary barracks on the south side of the river. A handsome and substantial range of buildings, now called the East Barracks, was erected on the north-east side of the bridge in 1806, and in 1809 a second range, called the West Barracks. The former occupy three sides of a quadrangle, 800 feet long and 700 feet wide, with barracks in the rear for cavalry, the whole occupying an area of 16½ statute acres, and affording accommodation to 112 officers and 1478 non-commissioned officers and privates of infantry, and to 24 officers and 120 non-commissioned officers and privates of cavalry, with stabling for 112 horses, and other requisite appendages. The West Barracks are nearly similar in arrangement, but less extensive. The whole establishment is adapted for 14 field officers, 169 officers, and 2816 non-commissioned officers and privates, with stabling for 152 horses. Attached to the West Barracks is an hospital for 42 patients, and at a short distance from the East Barracks is the general military hospital for about 130 patients.

The town is finely situated on the opposite banks of the river Blackwater, over which is a handsome stone bridge of 13 arches, widened about 40 years since by the late Mr. Anderson, and consists of a spacious square of handsome houses, the south side of which was the guard-house of the temporary barracks, and of several principal streets connected with others in a parallel direction by shorter streets intersecting them at right angles; also of Barrack-street, and a range of neat houses extending from the north end of the bridge. The streets are partially paved and watched, under the provisions of an act of parliament obtained in 1808, and the inhabitants are amply supplied with water. There is a circulating library, and a news-room is supported by subscription at the principal hotel, where also is a billiard-room, and where assemblies and concerts are held. The theatre, some few years after it was built, was converted into a coach-manufactory; but a spacious warehouse on the north side of the river is occasionally fitted up for dramatic performances by the Cork company. Races are held annually about the end of September, and continue for a week, and it is in contemplation to apply for a king's plate; the race-course, a fine area of 120 acres to the north of the town, is also used as a ground for military exercises. The environs abound with pleasing scenery, and the east side of the bridge, which is the only remaining portion of any building connected with the ancient village, is richly covered with ivy, presenting a picturesque object, heightened by the water of a mill-dam, which, crossing the river diagonally under its numerous arches, has the appearance of a natural waterfall. Adjoining the bridge is the entrance to Fermoy House, the residence of the late J. Anderson, Esq., to whom not only the town owes its prosperity, but the entire country is indebted for the important advantages resulting from the introduction of the mail coach system and the formation of many new and useful lines of road: it is now occupied by the lady of the late Major Hennis, and is a handsome mansion, beautifully situated on a gently sloping lawn bounded by the river. The number of military stationed here is on an average nearly 2000, the supply of whom, in addition to its own population, affords employment to tradesmen and artisans of every kind; and hence the necessaries and luxuries of life are found here in as great profusion as in any of the larger towns in Ireland. There are some extensive flour-mills, paper-mills, and a public brewery, with a large malting establishment attached to it, formerly celebrated for its ale, but now principally brewing porter. The staple trade of the town is in corn and butter, of which considerable quantities are sent off; but a great impediment to its commercial prosperity results from the want of water conveyance, the Blackwater not being navigable within many miles of this place. Coal and culm are brought by lighters to Tallow, and thence by land carriage to Fermoy, a distance of 10 miles; and in the same tedious manner is the produce of the town and neighbourhood conveyed to the shipping-place for exportation, although it is calculated that a rail road or canal might be made at a moderate expense from this town to Tallow, the line between those places being nearly level throughout. A branch of the National Bank of Ireland, has been opened, and a savings' bank has been also established. The market is on Saturday, and is abundantly supplied with live stock, provisions of every kind, and various articles of merchandise; and fairs for general farming stock are held on June 21st, Aug. 20th, and Nov. 7th. The market-place, near the river, though well adapted to the purpose, is used only for the corn market. Two mails from Cork to Dublin, and Bianconi's cars, pass daily through the town. The quarter sessions for the East Riding are held here in January; a manorial court, formerly held every three weeks, with jurisdiction extending to debts not exceeding 40*s*., late currency, is about to be revived; petty sessions are held every Monday, and a constabulary police force is stationed in the town. The court-house, a neat and appropriate building at the east end of the town, was erected in 1808.

The parish comprises 3319 statute acres, as applotted under the tithe act, and valued at £5281 per annum. The land is generally of good quality, and the system of agriculture has within the last few years been greatly improved, under the auspices of an agricultural society established by the late Mr. Anderson, which holds its annual meetings in October for the distribution of premiums, on which occasion there is a ploughing match. The substratum on the north side of the river is limestone, and on the south a kind of brown stone; there is no bog, and but very little waste land. About a mile from the town are the extensive nursery grounds of Mr. P. Baylor, on which about 50 persons are generally employed; the produce is sent to Cork, Limerick, and other principal towns. The principal seats are Mill Bank, the residence of D. Reid, Esq.; Fermoy House, already noticed; Fermoy Lodge, of G. Shaw, Esq.; Ashfield, of J. W. Anderson, Esq.; Uplands, of S. Perrot, Esq.; Corren, of Major Coast; Grange Hill, of W. F. Austin, Esq.; Richmond, of H. Smyth, Esq.; Richmond Lodge, of Mrs. Collis; and Fairfield, of Capt. Roberts. The living is a perpetual curacy, in the diocese of Cloyne, and in the patronage of Sir Robt. Abercromby, Bart., the present lord of the manor, in whom also the rectory is impropriate, by purchase from the Anderson family. The tithes amount to £591. 9. 10., which is wholly payable to the impropriator. The curacy is endowed with £20 per annum by the late Mr. Anderson, and with £80 per annum by the late Board of First Fruits; the curate receives also a stipend for the performance of a separate service for the military every Sunday in the church. There is no glebe-house; the glebe, at the northern extremity of the parish, comprises about 4 acres. The church, a remarkably elegant structure with a square tower formerly surmounted with a spire, which has been taken down, was erected at the joint expense of the late Mr. Anderson, who presented the site, and at different times contributed nearly £3000; the late Mr. Hyde, who gave £1500; and the late Board of First Fruits, which gave £500 and granted a loan of £2000. The internal arrangement corresponds with its external appearance: the Ecclesiastical Commissioners have recently granted £172 for its repair.

In the R. C. divisions the parish is united to that of Clondullane, the greater part of Litter, and a part of the parish of Kilcrumper. The chapel, a spacious and handsome edifice on an eminence, was erected by subscription, towards which the late Mr. Anderson contributed the site rent-free and £500; the altar-piece, of light tracery, is embellished with a good painting of the Crucifixion. A convent for nuns of the order of the Presentation has been built in a very handsome style on the brow of a hill to the south of the town, to which it is a great ornament; it consists of a centre connected by corridors with two wings, of which one is a chapel and the other a school-house for girls; and was built at an expense of £2000, of which £1500 was obtained from funds appropriated by Miss Goold to the establishment of convents in this county, and the remainder raised by subscription. Adjoining the convent is a handsome dwelling-house, erected by the Rev. T. Murphy, sen., R.C.C., (and now occupied by Capt. Royce, chief officer of police), the rent of which is intended by him to be permanently applied to clothe the children educated at the convent school. There is a place of worship for Wesleyan Methodists. About 400 children are taught in three public schools, of which one was founded and endowed with £1000 by the Rev. Dr. Adair, and is kept in a house given by the late Mr. Anderson, and there are 12 private schools, in which are about 350 children, and a Sunday school. The Fermoy college school, conducted by Dr. Fahie, for the preparation of young gentlemen for the university, was originally built by the late Mr. Anderson for a military college; the buildings occupy two sides of a square, comprising, besides the usual accommodations, a gymnasium, reading-room, and a ball court, and are surrounded by 11 acres of playground. The national school is a large and substantial building, lately erected at an expense of £600, and affording accommodation for 400 children. Nothing remains of the old monastery of Our Lady de Castro Dei, which was taken down to afford materials for building several houses in the town, and the only memorial of it is preserved in the name of a street built upon the site, and thence called Abbey-street. At Corrin, under the mountain of that name, about 1½ mile south of the town, is a chalybeate spa; and at Grange, close to Castle Hyde, is a sulphureous and chalybeate spring, both strongly impregnated. Fermoy formerly gave the title of Baron to the ancient family of Roche.

FERMOYLE, or LETTERCANNON, a village, in the parish of KILLONOGHAN, barony of BURREN, county of CLARE, and province of MUNSTER; containing 42 houses and 220 inhabitants.

FERNS, a post-town and parish, and till lately the seat of a diocese, partly in the barony of GOREY, but chiefly in that of SCARAWALSH, county of WEXFORD, and province of LEINSTER, 17¾ miles (N.) from Wexford, and 56¾ (S. by W.) from Dublin, on the road from Gorey to Enniscorthy; containing 4038 inhabitants, of which number, 571 are in the town. This place, according to Colgan, derives its name from Ferna, son of Caril, King of Decies, who was slain here in battle by Gallus, son of Morna; but according to other writers from "Fearn," signifying either an alder tree, or the well-known weed so common in uncultivated districts. It is said to have been granted, in 598, by Brandubh, King of Leinster, to St. Edan, who built a monastery here, in the church of which his benefactor and himself were subsequently interred. Early in the 9th century, the growing importance of the town, which had gradually risen around the monastery, was checked by successive incursions of the Danes, in 834, 836, and 838; afterwards in 917 and 928, and in 930 they plundered the abbey and burnt the town. In 1041 the city was destroyed by Dunchad, son of Brian, and in 1165 it suffered from an accidental fire. In the following year it is said to have been burnt by Dermod Mac Murrough, the last King of Leinster, to prevent its falling into the hands of Roderic, King of Ireland; but according to more numerous authorities, it was destroyed by the confederate army under Roderic, who, advancing to Ferns during Dermod's absence in England, took the castle and restored Dervorghal, whom Dermod had forcibly carried off, to her husband O'Rourke, King of Breffny. On his return from England, towards the close of 1168, Dermod secretly took refuge in the Augustine monastery which he had founded here; and after the capture of Wexford by his English auxiliaries, concentrated his forces at this place, where he remained for three weeks refreshing his men, and concerting plans of future operations. After a successful attack on the King of Ossory, Dermod again retired to Ferns, whither Roderic, alarmed at his continued successes, advanced to give him battle. Dermod, sensible of his inferiority in numbers, stationed his troops in the bogs and woods which surrounded the castle, and awaited the contest; and Roderic, fearing to attack him in that position, concluded, at the solicitations of the clergy, a treaty of peace, in which he acknowledged Dermod's right to the crown of Leinster. Dermod died the year following, and was interred either in the cathedral of Ferns or at Baltinglass. After his death, Strongbow visited this city, where he subsequently solemnized the marriage of his daughter, by a former wife, with his standard-bearer, Robert de Quiney, whom he created Lord Daffren and appointed constable of Leinster.

The city appears never to have recovered from its previous devastations; for when it was given by Hen. II. to Robert Fitz-Aldelm, it was described as an inconsiderable place, and exposed to the hostile assaults of the native chieftains. Fitz-Aldelm, having seized the castle of Wicklow, gave this lordship in exchange to the sons of Maurice Fitzgerald, who began to build a strong castle here, which was treacherously rased to the ground before it was completed. The castle, which subsequently became the occasional residence of the bishops of the diocese, and of which there are some remains, was most probably built in the reign of John, by William Marshal, Earl of Pembroke. It was attacked, in 1312 and 1313, by the O'Tooles, who also set fire to the city; and Bishop Esmond, whose prelacy was disputed, maintained himself in it by force of arms against William Charnells, who was appointed to succeed him. The latter, after the sheriff had declared his inability to displace the former, put himself at the head of his own servants and forcibly obtained possession of the castle, in the occupation of which he was greatly annoyed by the Irish septs. In the reign of Hen. VIII., Mac Murrough, chieftain of Leinster, was made governor of the castle for the king; and during the reign of Edw. VI. and Mary, the custody of it was given to Richard Butler, Viscount Mountgarret. In 1641, Sir Chas. Coote, the parliamentary general, dismantled the fortress and greatly oppressed the inhabitants. The town is romantically situated on the river Bann, in an open and healthy district, and is sheltered on the north and west by a range of mountains. It consists chiefly of one irregular street, and contains 106 houses indifferently built, retaining no trace of its ancient importance. The market has been long discontinued; but fairs are held on Feb. 11th, March 25th, May 12th, June 29th, Sept. 4th, Oct. 29th, and Dec. 27th. Here and at Ballycarney are constabulary police stations.

The DIOCESE of FERNS appears to have been founded by St. Edan, commonly called St. Maidoc or Mogue, a descendant of Colla Vais, King of Ireland, who, having left his country, resided for some years with St. David, bishop of Menevia, in Wales, by whom he was carefully instructed in the principles of the Christian religion. After his return to Ireland, St. Maidoc founded a church at Ferns, which soon after became the seat of a diocese. In a great synod held afterwards at Leinster, Brandubh decreed that the archbishoprick of Leinster should for ever remain in the chair and see of St. Maidoc; who, after presiding over it for nearly 50 years, died in 632 and was succeeded by St. Molin. The see was governed by a regular succession of bishops till 814, from which date there is a chasm of more than a hundred years, arising probably from the ravages of the Danes of Ulster. It was afterwards governed by Laidgnene, under the title of Comorban, who died in 937: of his successors little worthy of notice is recorded till after the arrival of the English in Ireland. On the refusal of Giraldus Cambrensis to accept the see, which, with that of Leighlin, had been offered to him by John, Earl of Morton, Albin O'Mulloy succeeded in 1186; and during his prelacy it was forcibly deprived of two manors by William Marshal, Earl of Pembroke. Adam de Northampton, who succeeded in 1312, was attainted of treason for his adherence to Edward Bruce, and for furnishing Robert Bruce with provisions, arms, and men during his invasion of Ireland. The revenues of the see were greatly diminished during the prelacy of Alexander Devereux, who succeeded to it in 1539, and remained in undisturbed possession of it, notwithstanding the changes then taking place in religion; and the manor of Fethard was alienated by Hugh Allen, who succeeded in 1582, but it was subsequently recovered by Bishop Ram. During the prelacy of Bishop Graves, who was consecrated in 1600, the see of Leighlin, which had been for some time vacant, was united with Ferns; and his successors continued to be bishops of Leighlin and Ferns from that period till 1836, when, on the death of the last bishop, Dr. Elrington, both dioceses were annexed to the see of Ossory, and the temporalities of the latter became vested in the Ecclesiastical Commissioners. The diocese is one of the five which constitute the ecclesiastical province of Dublin: it comprises a small part of the county of Wicklow and of Queen's county, and nearly the whole of that of Wexford, extending 46 miles in length and 18 in breadth, and comprehending a superficies of 570,564 statute acres, of which 550,800 are in the county of Wexford, and 19,764 in that of Wicklow. The lands belonging to the see comprise 13,370 statute acres of profitable land; and the gross revenue of the bishoprick amounts to £5882. 15. 3¼. The chapter consists of a dean, precentor, chancellor, treasurer, archdeacon, and the ten prebendaries of Kilrane, Coolstuffe, Fethard, Edermine, Taghmon, Kilrush, Tomb, Clone, Crosspatrick, and Whitechurch. The consistory court, held at Enniscorthy, consists of a vicar-general, two surrogates, and a registrar, who is also keeper of the records, of which the earliest are of the date of 1618. The total number of parishes is 142, which, with the exception of two without cure of souls, are comprised within 58 benefices, of which 34 are unions of two or more parishes, and 24 single parishes; of the benefices, one (the deanery) is in the patronage of the Crown, 10 in lay patronage, and the remainder are in the patronage of the Bishop or the incumbents. The number of parish churches is 61, and there are also two other places in which divine service is performed; there are 31 glebe-houses. The diocesan school, the master of which is paid a salary by the bishop and beneficed clergy of the diocese, is at Wexford. In the R. C. divisions this diocese, as originally constituted, forms a distinct bishoprick, and is one of the three suffragan to the archiepiscopal see of Dublin: it comprises 36 parochial unions or districts, and, exclusively of the friary chapel at New Ross, contains 90 chapels, served by 36 parish priests and 54 coadjutors or curates; the episcopal parishes or districts are Enniscorthy and Camolin: the Bishop resides at the former place.

Arms of the Bishoprick.

The parish comprises 15,085 statute acres, as applotted under the tithe act: the greater portion of the land is under tillage, and there is a considerable tract of hilly pasture. The gentlemen's seats are Ballymore, the residence of R. Donovan, Esq., proprietor of the town and the largest estate in the parish; and Clobemon Hall, of T. Derinzey, Esq., beautifully situated on the eastern bank of the Slaney, which here abounds with rich and varied scenery: the latter is a handsome modern mansion of the Grecian Doric order, erected from a design by Mr. Cobden, and is surrounded by an extensive and finely wooded demesne, in which are the ruins of a castle formerly belonging to the ancestors of Lord Baltimore. The living is a vicarage, united by act of council, in 1776, to the rectory of Kilbride, and in the patronage of the Bishop, to whom the rectory is appropriate. The tithes amount to £830. 15. 4½., of which £553. 16. 11. is payable to the bishop, and £276. 18. 5½. to the vicar; the tithes of the vicarial union amount to £480. The glebe-house, the residence of the Rev. H. Newland, D. D., is pleasantly situated on a rising ground near the church; it was erected by aid of a gift of £800 from the late Board of First Fruits, in 1805. The glebe comprises more than 29 acres of cultivated land, held under the see at a yearly rent of £15, by deed executed in 1778. The present cathedral, which is also the parish church, was erected in 1816, by aid of a loan of £500 from the late Board of First Fruits; it is a small structure, in the later English style, with a square embattled tower crowned with pinnacles; and adjoining it is a small building used as a chapter-house. In removing the ruins of the old building, the date 632 (the year of St. Edan's death) was found inscribed on several pieces of timber, and also on a huge beam of oak; an ancient monument to the memory of that saint is still preserved in the present church. In the wall of the churchyard have been inserted the fragments of one of those ancient crosses which are usually referred to the 10th or 11th century. The Episcopal palace is equally conspicuous for the simple elegance of its design and the beauty of the grounds: it was commenced during the prelacy of Bishop Cope, who, in 1785, obtained an act enabling him to carry into effect two bequests, one made in 1715 and the other in 1772, for the erection of an episcopal residence at this place. The church of the ecclesiastical district of Ballycarney (*which see*), recently erected out of the parishes of Ferns, Templeshanbo, and Monart, is situated in this parish. In the R. C. divisions the parish is the head of a union or district, comprising also the parishes of Kilbride and Kilcomb: the chapel, erected in 1826, is a neat modern building, with a low tower of granite surmounted by a cupola supported on eight pillars of grit-stone; adjoining it is a good house for the priest. About 150 children are taught in two public schools, of which one is aided with £30 per ann. by the trustees of Erasmus Smith's charity, and the other is chiefly supported by Dr. Newland; there are also three private schools, in which are about 100 children, and a dispensary.

Of the Augustine monastery founded by Dermod Mac Murrough, the chief remains are the walls of a narrow building with lancet-shaped windows, and a tower of two stages, of which the lower is quadrangular and the upper polygonal and covered with moss and ivy, which give it a circular form; within is a geometrical staircase leading to the top of the square tower. There are extensive remains of the ancient castle on an eminence in the town: it appears to have been of great strength, of quadrangular form, and defended at the angles with round towers, of which one is still entire and contains a beautiful small chapel with a groined roof, the interior of which has been recently fitted up; it commands from its summit a pleasing and extensive prospect, and is the property of R. Donovan, of Ballymore, Esq., who is using every precaution to preserve it: part of one of the other towers is also remaining. Near the church-yard is St. Mogue's well, said to have been sunk by Molin, successor to St. Edan, and held in veneration for the miraculous efficacy attributed to its waters.

FERRITERS ISLANDS.—See BLASQUETS.

FERRYBANK, a village, in the parish of KILCULLIHEEN, within the liberties of the county of the city of WATERFORD, and in the province of MUNSTER, on the river Suir: the population is returned with the parish. The river is here crossed by a long and handsome wooden bridge, connecting the village with the city of Waterford, of which it may be considered a suburb. It contains a large distillery, an establishment for building and repairing vessels, and several store-houses and respectable dwelling-houses. Here are also three schools, one of which is under the patronage of Mrs. Nevins. —See KILCULLIHEEN.

FERRYCARRIGG.—See CARRIGG.

FERTAGH.—See FARTAGH.

FERTIANA, a parish, in the barony of ELIOGARTY, county of TIPPERARY, and province of MUNSTER, 2 miles (S.) from Thurles; containing 1168 inhabitants. This parish comprises 3397 statute acres, as applotted under the tithe act, and valued at £2700 per ann. It is a rectory, in the diocese of Cashel, and forms part of the mensal of the Archbishop; the tithes amount to £184. 12. $3\frac{3}{4}$.

FETHARD, an incorporated market and post-town, (formerly a parliamentary borough), and a parish, in the barony of MIDDLETHIRD, county of TIPPERARY, and province of MUNSTER, 7 miles (N.) from Clonmel, and 78 (S. W.) from Dublin by Urlingford; containing 3962 inhabitants, of which number, 3400 are in the town and liberties.

Seal.

This place, which appears to have derived its name from the Irish *Faith-Ard*, the "summit or hill of the plain," is of considerable antiquity. In 1306, the friars Eremites of the order of St. Augustine obtained from Edw. I. a full and free pardon for having acquired, contrary to the statute of mortmain, some land for rebuilding their monastery, which had been founded here at a very early period. In 1376, Edw. III. granted to the provost and commonalty certain customs, to enable them to surround their town with walls, and a similar grant was made to them by Hen. IV. The monastery, to which was attached a certain portion of the town, was granted, on its dissolution, by Hen. VIII. to Sir Edmund Butler, Knt., at an annual rent of 5*s.* 4*d.* Irish; and in 1553, Edw. VI. granted the burgesses a new charter, with liberties and immunities similar to those of Kilkenny, which was confirmed and extended by a charter of Jas. I., under which the town is now governed. In 1650, the town was besieged by Cromwell, to whom, after a short resistance, it capitulated on honourable terms; the original articles are still extant, and in the possession of W. Barton, Esq., of Grove. It is irregularly built, and contains 626 houses; the inhabitants are supplied with good water from a public pump; and there are some extensive barracks, at present occupied by infantry. The old walls, in which were five gates defended by towers, are much dilapidated. The river Clashanly, or Clashaluin (more correctly Glaisealuin, "the lovely stream," from *Glaise*, "a stream," and *Aluin*, "lovely"), which rises in the bog of Allen, passes through the town and gives motion to two flour-mills, which, except in dry seasons, are constantly at work, and furnish the principal trade of the town. The market is on Saturday, but, from its vicinity to that of Clonmel, is of very inferior importance. Fairs are held on April 20th, Friday before Trinity-Sunday, Sept. 7th, and Nov. 21st, and are well supplied with cattle; the Nov. fair is the largest in the county for fat stock. The town has latterly become a great depôt for the sale of culm from the Slievardagh collieries, eight miles distant: it is calculated that 30,000 barrels, or about 5000 tons, have been sold here in a year.

The corporation, by the charter of Jas. I., consists of a sovereign, twelve chief burgesses, a portreeve, and an indefinite number of freemen, assisted by a recorder, town-clerk, serjeant-at-mace, and other officers. The sovereign, who is also coroner and clerk of the market, is chosen annually from the burgesses by a majority of that body, and may with their consent appoint a vice-sovereign, who also is a justice of the peace within the borough. The burgesses, as vacancies occur, are chosen from the freemen by the sovereign and burgesses; the portreeve is annually elected from the freemen by the chief burgesses, and the freemen are admitted only by favour of the corporation. The recorder is chosen by the sovereign and chief burgesses, and holds his office during pleasure; the town-clerk is appointed either by the sovereign or the chief burgesses, and the serjeant-at-mace by the sovereign. The corporation, under their charter, continued to return two members to the Irish parliament till the Union, when the borough was disfranchised, and the sum of £15,000 awarded in compensation was paid in moieties to Cornelius, Lord Lismore, and T. Barton, Esq. A Tholsel court, in which the sovereign presides, assisted by two burgesses, is held every three weeks, for the recovery of debts within the borough to any amount; and petty sessions are held generally on alternate Mondays before the county magistrates. A constabulary police force is stationed here.

The parish comprises 1524 statute acres, as applotted under the tithe act, which, with the exception of a small portion of woodland and about 130 acres of common, are chiefly good arable land. Near the town are some very fine limestone quarries, whence very large blocks are procured; the stone takes a fine polish and is used for tombstones and other purposes. Grove, the handsome seat of W. Barton, Esq., is pleasantly situated in an extensive demesne intersected by the river Clashanly, and richly planted; the house commands a fine view of Kiltinan Castle and the Waterford mountains; the park is well stocked with deer, and in the grounds are the ruins of an old church. There are several other gentlemen's seats in the union, which are described in their respective parishes. The living is a rectory and vicarage, in the diocese of Cashel, united by act of council, in 1682, to the rectories and vicarages of Pepperstown, Kilbragh, Cloneen, and Rathcoole, and to the entire rectories of Kilconnel and Railstown, together forming the union of Fethard, in the patronage of the Archbishop. The tithes of the parish amount to £140, and of the whole union to £1361. 7. 5¼. The glebe-house is a neat building, and there are four glebes, comprising together 22 acres. The church is the remaining aisle of an ancient structure of which the chancel is in ruins; it is in the decorated English style with a venerable tower (in which are four fine-toned bells), and an east and west window of very elegant design, and is 100 feet in length and 50 in breadth; the Ecclesiastical Commissioners have lately granted £440 for its repair. In the R. C. divisions, the parish is the head of a union or district, comprising also the parish of Killusty; and containing a chapel in each; the chapel of this parish, a large plain modern building, was erected on ground given by W. Barton, Esq. There is also a chapel attached to the Augustinian friary in the town, an ancient edifice with a very handsome east window, the beauty of which is concealed by a modern roof, which intercepts the crown of the arch. There is a place of worship for Presbyterians, erected in 1739, in connection with the Synod of Munster, the minister of which receives a grant of £53. 10. 8. per ann. royal bounty; also a temporary place of worship for Primitive Wesleyan Methodists. The parochial school is aided by donations from the rector, W. Barton, Esq., and the parishioners: the school-house, a good slated building, was erected at an expense of £325, of which £100 was a grant from the Association for Discountenancing Vice, and Mr. Barton gave £50; the site was part of the glebe given by the rector, the Rev. H. Woodward. A national school is chiefly supported by the Very Rev. M. Laffan, and a school has been established by Mrs. Barton for females, who are also taught spinning and needlework. There are nine private schools, a charitable loan fund, and a dispensary. There are remains of the ancient walls, with four of the gateway towers; in removing some stones near one of them a gold ring was recently found, bearing the inscription, "No Frende to Fayth." At Market Hill is a mineral spring; at Kiltinan is a subterraneous stream; and in the neighbourhood are the remains of many ancient castles, one of which, at Knockelly, occupies about an acre of ground, and is surrounded by a high wall with towers at each angle, and in good preservation.

FETHARD, a small sea-port, post-town, and parish, in the barony of SHELBURNE, county of WEXFORD, and province of LEINSTER, 15¾ miles (S.) from New Ross, and 81 (S. W.) from Dublin, on the bay of Fethard; containing 2153 inhabitants, of which number, 320 are in the town. This place is supposed to have derived its ancient name, "Fiodh Ard," from the abundance of wood in the neighbourhood, though at present no part of the country is more destitute of timber. Robert Fitz-Stephen, on his first invasion of the country, landed his forces in a bay about a mile to the south of the town, since called Bagenbon bay, from the names of the ships Bag and Bon, both of which, immediately after his landing, he burnt in the presence of his men, telling them that they must either succeed in their enterprise or perish in the attempt. After the settlement of the English in Ireland, this place was given by Strongbow to Raymond le Gros, who had married his sister Basilia, and who is said to have erected a strong fortress here for the protection of his newly acquired territory. Basilia, with the concurrence of Fitz-Stephen, granted the church lands and tithes of the whole lordship to the abbey of St. Thomas near Dublin: and some of its earlier lords obtained for the inhabitants a charter of incorporation. The castle afterwards became the episcopal residence of the Bishops of Ferns, and here Alexander Devereux, the last abbot of Dunbrody, and the first Bishop of Ferns after the Reformation, died in 1556, and was buried in the church, in the aisle of which his tombstone still remains. In 1648, the manor of Ferns was exchanged by Bishop Andrews for value belonging to the Loftus family.

The town, which is neat and well built, consists principally of one wide street on the line of road from Ross to Bagenbon Head, and contains 50 houses, partly occupied by persons in the coast-guard department, of which a branch is constantly stationed here. Some trade is carried on in coal, timber, iron, and slates, and cattle and pigs are occasionally shipped from the port, for which its situation affords every facility. About 15 boats are employed in conveying limestone from the south-west side of the parish, near Loftus Hall, to this place, whence it is sent up the Scar river into the interior of the country. A considerable fishery of herrings, lobsters, and other fish of superior quality, especially plaice, is carried on off this coast. The harbour, which was constructed by Government in 1798, and is capable of receiving about four small sloops, is situated on the north side of Inguard Point. Between the pier heads are from 11 to 12 feet of water at high spring tides, and from 8 to 9 at ordinary neap tides. There is also a harbour for small craft at Slade, in the parish of Hook, between which and this place is Bagenbon bay, one of the best shipping stations on the coast, for vessels of any burden, both for its depth of water, and from its sheltered situation, from the west and north-west winds. Fairs for cattle are held on Jan. 31st, April 30th, July 28th, and Oct. 20th. The town was incorporated in 1613, by charter of Jas. I., by which the corporation was made to consist of a portreeve and 12 free burgesses, in whom was vested the right of nominating freemen to form a commonalty, and of returning two members to the Irish parliament. They had also the power of holding a court of record weekly, for the recovery of debts not exceeding five marks, with the privilege of a market and fair; but this corporation has long been extinct. The borough continued to send two members to the Irish parliament till the Union, when it was disfranchised, and the £15,000 awarded in compensation was paid to Charles, Marquess of Ely, and C. Tottenham, Esq.

The parish, which is the property of the Marquess of Ely, is on the western side of Fethard bay, and with the parishes of Hook and Templetown forms a peninsula which separates Waterford harbour from Ballyteigue bay. It comprises 3775 statute acres, of which the greater portion is under tillage, and the remainder good meadow and pasture land: the soil is fertile and the system of agriculture improved; the chief manure is sea-sand and lime. On the shore is a species of hard red granite, which is used for millstones and other purposes; several unsuccessful attempts to procure coal and slate have been made. Fethard Castle, the property of the Marquess of Ely, and in the occupation of the Rev. A. Alcock, is pleasantly situated on the left of the road to New Ross; and Innyard, the seat of the Lynn family, is situated in tastefully disposed grounds. The Turret, a bathing lodge, formerly the property of Mrs. Savage, has been recently taken down. There are numerous comfortable farmhouses and bathing lodges in the parish, which is much frequented, for the benefit of sea-bathing. The sands are firm and smooth; the surrounding country is pleasant, and the air salubrious; and the neighbourhood abounds with objects of interest, among which are the remains of the abbeys of Dunbrody, Tintern, and Clonmines. The living is a rectory, in the diocese of Ferns, and the corps of the prebend of Fethard in the cathedral of Ferns, in the patronage of the Bishop: the tithes amount to £330. The glebe-house, a handsome building, was erected in 1830 by the Rev. C. W. Doyne, the present incumbent, at an expense of £1060, towards which the late Board of First Fruits contributed a gift of £277, and a loan of £461. The glebe comprised originally 1¾ Irish acres, to which 5 acres were added by purchase in 1834. The church, an ancient structure in a very dilapidated state, is about to be rebuilt. In the R. C. divisions the parish is part of the union or district of Hook; the chapel, on the lands of Dungulph, is a neat cruciform edifice, recently built by subscription. About 70 children are taught in the public schools, which are supported by the Marquess and Marchioness of Ely; aided by an annual donation of £10 from the rector; there are also two private schools, in which are about 90 children, and a Sunday school supported by the rector. On the narrow promontory of Bagenbon Head are the remains of an encampment, said to have been formed by Fitz-Stephen on his landing; and at Fethard are the ruins of a castle, at one angle of which is a round tower in good preservation. Bagenbon Head projects considerably from the line of the coast; the land is high, and the shore bold; the water is deep, with a stiff clay bottom, covered with sand, extending nearly to the base of the cliffs. This bay has afforded refuge to many vessels in heavy gales, and the Milford packets have frequently put in and landed the mails, when it has been impracticable for them to reach Waterford; there is a martello tower on the Head.

FEWS, a parish, in the barony of Decies-without-Drum, county of Waterford, and province of Munster, 1½ mile (W. N. W.) from Kilmacthomas, on the river Mahon; containing 1247 inhabitants, and comprising 5986 statute acres, as applotted under the tithe act. Its surface is chiefly mountainous, and in several places commands fine views towards the ocean. It is a vicarage, in the diocese of Lismore, forming part of the union of Mothill; the rectory is impropriate in the Duke of Devonshire. The tithes amount to £221. 10. 9. of which £147. 13. 10., is payable to the impropriator, and the remainder to the vicar. In the R. C. divisions it is part of the union or district of Kilrosanty and Fews, and has a neat chapel.

FIDDOWN, a parish and village, in the barony of Iverk, county of Kilkenny, and province of Leinster, on the high road from Kilkenny to Carrick; containing, with the post-town of Pilltown (which is separately described), 4296 inhabitants, of which number, 193 are in the village. This parish, the name of which is said to be derived from *Fiodh*, "a wood," and *Doon*, a "rath" or "fort," is bounded on the west by the river Lingawn, which is crossed by a good stone bridge, and on the south by the river Suir; it comprises 10,485 statute acres, as applotted under the tithe act, and valued at £8145 per annum. The soil in some parts is of astonishing fertility, and there is no waste land; the system of agriculture has much improved within the last seven years, through the exertions of the Irish Farming Society. There are numerous limestone and sandstone quarries; and near Pilltown is a quarry of variegated grey marble, susceptible of a high polish. The village of Fiddown consists of 36 houses, and has fairs on April 25th, June 10th, Sept. 29th, and Nov. 30th. It is situated on the bank of the river Suir, which is navigable throughout the extent of the parish for vessels of large burden, and abounds with excellent salmon and trout. Besborough, the fine old mansion of the Earl of Besborough, and from which his lordship takes his title, is situated in a well-wooded park of more than 500 acres. The house, which is built of hewn blue limestone, is 100 feet in front by 80 in depth; the great hall is supported by four Ionic columns of Kilkenny marble, each of a single stone 10½ feet high; it was erected in 1744 from a design of David Bindon, Esq., and contains a fine collection of pictures. The other seats are Belline, the elegant residence of W. W. Currey, Esq., surrounded by a beautiful demesne; Fanningstown, of J. Walsh, Esq.; Tyburoughny Castle, of M. Rivers, Esq.; Willmount, of G. Briscoe, Esq.; Cookestown, of J. Burnett, Esq.; Garrynarca, of N. Higinbotham, Esq.; and the glebe-house, of the Rev. W. Gregory. The living is a rectory and vicarage, in the diocese of Ossory, united by act of council, in 1689, to the rectories of Owning or Bewley, and Tubrid, and the rectories and vicarages of Castlane and Tipperaghney, and in the patronage of the Bishop: the tithes of the parish amount to £687, and of the benefice to £1228. The glebe-house was built by aid of a gift of £100 and a loan of £1500 from the late Board of First Fruits, in 1817; the glebe comprises 48 acres. The church is situated in the village, on the site of an abbey, of which St. Maidoc or Momoedoc is said to have been abbot in 590: it is an ancient structure, handsomely fitted up by the late Earl of Besborough, and contains several monuments to the Ponsonby family, among which is one to Brabazon, first Earl of Besborough, who died in 1758, consisting of half-length figures of the earl and his countess, on a sarcophagus of Egyptian marble, under a pediment supported by four Corinthian columns and four pilasters of Sienna marble. In the R. C. divisions the parish forms part of the union or district of Templeorum; the chapel, a neat building, is at Pilltown. In the schools at Pilltown, an infants' school, and a national school at Tubbernabrona about 300 children are instructed: there are also a private school, in which are about 40 children, and two Sunday schools. Throughout the parish are ruins of several ancient churches, Danish forts, and druidical altars or cromlechs. Several vestiges of antiquity have been found at Belline, and many are still to be seen in its immediate neighbourhood. The horns, with a great part of the skeleton, of a moose deer were found in a bed of soft marl, and are preserved at Besborough House.—See PILLTOWN.

FIERIES.—See MOLAHIFFE.

FINAE, a village, in the parish of FAVORAN, barony of DEMIFORE, county of WESTMEATH, and province of LEINSTER, 6 miles (N. W.) from Castle-Pollard, on the road from Oldcastle to Granard, and on the confines of the county of Cavan; containing 241 inhabitants. In 1331, Sir Anthony Lucy, Lord-Justice, defeated the Irish forces near this place, after an obstinately contested battle; and in 1644, Gen. Monroe routed a detachment of Lord Castlehaven's army here, where also, in 1651, the parliamentarian forces under Cols. Hewson and Jones obtained a victory over the royalists, commanded by Pheagh Mac Hugh O'Byrne, and took the village by storm. The counties of Westmeath and Cavan are separated at this place by a stream connecting Lough Sheelin with Lough Kinale, and over which is a stone bridge of nine arches. The village consists of 45 houses, badly built, and in a state of dilapidation. Fairs are held on March 17th, the Saturday before Whitsuntide, Sept. 18th, and Nov. 15th.

FINDONAGH.—See DONAGHCAVEY.

FINGLAS, a parish, partly in the barony of NETHERCROSS, and partly in that of COOLOCK, county of DUBLIN, and province of LEINSTER, 3 miles (N.) from Dublin Castle, on the mail coach road to Ashbourne, and on a small stream which falls into the Tolka at Finglas bridge; containing 2110 inhabitants, of which number, 840 are in the village. In the reign of Hen. II., Strongbow, aided by Milo de Cogan and Raymond le Gros, with 500 men, routed the Irish army consisting of several thousands, and nearly took King O'Conor prisoner. On June 18th, 1649, the Marquess of Ormonde, with the royal army, encamped here, previous to the fatal action of Rathmines; and on July 5th, 1690, King William, after the victory of the Boyne, here took up a position and mustered his army, amounting to more than thirty thousand effective men; and hence a detachment, under the Duke of Ormonde, marched to take possession of Dublin. The manor was long vested in the Archbishop of Dublin: Fulk de Saundford, one of the prelates of this see, died here in 1271, and Archbishop Fitz-Simon, also, in 1511. The parish comprises 4663 statute acres, chiefly pasture: there are good quarries of limestone and stone for building. The Royal Canal passes through the townlands of Ballybogan and Cabra. An extensive cotton-mill was here burnt down in 1828, the ruins of which remain. A large tannery has existed at Finglas Wood for nearly two centuries, and is still carried on by J. Savage, Esq., one of the same family as the original proprietor: the residence is very ancient, and it is reported that Jas. II. slept one night there. By the 4th of Geo. I. a grant was made to the Archbishop of Dublin of markets on Tuesdays and Saturdays, fairs on April 25th and Sept. 29th, and a court of pie-poudre during the markets, by paying 6*s.* 8*d.* per ann. to the Crown. A noted pleasure fair is held here on the 1st of May. This is a station for the city of Dublin police; and in the vicinity are three private lunatic asylums. The seats are Jamestown, the residence of Mrs. Shew; Tolka Lodge, of J. W. Bayley, Esq.; Kilrisk, of J. Green, Esq.; Newtown, of Barnett Shew, Esq.; Belle Vue, of W. Gregory, Esq.; Farnham House, of J. Duncan, Esq.; St. Helena, of W. Harty, Esq., M. D.; Drogheda Lodge, of M. Farrell, Esq.; Ashfield, of Capt. Bluett, R. N.; Springmount, of C. White, Esq.; Elms, of John T. Logan, Esq., M. D.; St. Margaret's, of Mrs. Stock; Cabra House, of J. Plunkett, Esq.; Riversdale, of C. Stewart, Esq.; Rose Hill, of N. Doyle, Esq.; Tolka Park, of J. Newman, Esq.; Tolka View, of the Rev. Dr. Ledlie; Rosemount, of Capt. Walsh; Little Jamestown, of Edw. Mangan, Esq.; Rosemount, of M. Rooney, Esq.; and Cardiffe Bridge, of J. Newman, Esq. The living is a vicarage, in the diocese of Dublin, united to the curacy of Ballycoolane, and in the patronage of the Archbishop: the rectory, with the curacy of St. Werburgh's, Dublin, and the chapelries of St. Margaret's, Artaine, and the Ward, constitutes the corps of the chancellorship of St. Patrick's cathedral, Dublin. The tithes amount to £740. 5. 10., of which £462. 2. 5. is payable to the chancellor, and the remainder to the vicar. The glebe-house was erected, in 1826, by aid of a gift of £550, and a loan of £450, from the late Board of First Fruits; there is a glebe of 16 acres of profitable land, divided into three portions, two of which are at a great distance from the parsonage. The church, a plain substantial building, stands on the site of an abbey said to have been founded by St. Canice, or, as some think by St. Patrick, the former having been the first abbot: several of the early saints were interred here, and there are monuments to members of the families of Flower and Bridges, and one to Dr. Chaloner Cobbe, an eminent divine. This place gives name to a rural deanery, extending over Finglas and its chapelries, Castleknock, Clonsillagh, Chapelizod, Glasnevin, Coolock, Raheny, Clontarf, and Clonturk, or Drumcondra. In the R. C. divisions the parish is the head of a union or district, comprising Finglas, St. Margaret's, the Ward, Killeek, and Chapel-Midway, in which are two chapels, in Finglas and at St. Margaret's,

The parochial schools are aided by the chancellor of St. Patrick's and the vicar; an infants' school was established in 1835; and there are two national schools, and a dispensary. Lands producing about £41 per ann., of which £32 are expended on the schools, have been left in trust to the vicar and churchwardens for the benefit of the poor and for other pious purposes. Here are two strong ramparts, one of which, at the rear of the glebe-house, is called King William's rampart. In the grounds of J. Savage, Esq., coins of the reigns of Jas. II. and Wm. and Mary have been found. Here is a well, dedicated to St. Patrick, slightly chalybeate, and once much celebrated: and there is an ancient cross in the churchyard. The vicarage was held for the few later years of his life by Dr. T. Parnell, the intimate associate of Swift, Addison, Pope, and other distinguished literary characters.

FINGLAS, a parish, in the barony of Clonlisk, King's county, and province of Leinster, 2¼ miles (E.S.E.) from Moneygall, on the confines of the county of Tipperary; containing 271 inhabitants. It comprises only 664 statute acres, as applotted under the tithe act, and is a rectory, in the diocese of Killaloe, forming part of the union of Dunkerrin: the tithes amount to £50. 0. 6½. In the R. C. divisions it is part of the union or district of Moneygall.

FINISH, or FEENISH, an island, in the parish of Moyrus, barony of Ballynahinch, county of Galway, and province of Connaught, 17 miles (S. E.) from Clifden, near the entrance to Kilkerrin bay on the western coast; containing 103 acres of land, held in common by the inhabitants: the population is returned with the parish.

FINNOE, a parish, in the barony of Lower Ormond, county of Tipperary, and province of Munster, 1½ mile (W. S. W.) from Burris-o-Kane, on one of the roads from Nenagh to Portumna; containing 1399 inhabitants, and comprising 4003 statute acres, of which about 800 are bog; the remainder being mostly pasture land. A lake, covering about 60 acres was drained about 10 years since; the land is reclaimed, and very productive, and the state of agriculture generally is much improved. Large quantities of shell marl are found at Springfield; and there is plenty of limestone for the purposes of agriculture, and for building. A small river, called Ballyfinboy, separates this parish from Burris-o-Kane, and empties itself into the Shannon at Castle-Biggs. The principal seats are Finnoe House, the residence of T. Waller, Esq.; Ormond Cottage, of S. Waller, Esq.; Rodeen, of J. Falkiner, Esq.; Bell Park, of T. Robinson, Esq.; the glebe-house, of the Rev. Pierce Goold; and Bellgrove, the property of — Lennard, Esq. The living is a rectory and vicarage, in the diocese of Killaloe, episcopally united in 1790 to the rectory and vicarage of Cloghprior, and in the patronage of the Bishop: the tithes amount to £217. The glebe-house, situated on a glebe of 4*a.* 3*r.* 26*p.*, half a mile from the church, was built by aid of a gift of £400, and a loan of £400, in 1819, from the late Board of First Fruits; there is also a glebe of 28 acres, for which the incumbent pays £17 per annum. The church is a neat edifice, repaired and improved by aid of a loan of £323, in 1822, from the same Board. In the R. C. divisions the parish forms part of the union or district of Kilbarron; there is a chapel on the townland of Firgrove, which is on the boundary of Finnoe and Kilbarron. About 70 children are taught in a private school. Ballyfinboy castle is a square tower in good preservation. Many large elk horns have been found at Springfield bog; and on that townland there is a strong chalybeate spa, only partially used.

FINOGH, or PHINAGH, a parish, in the barony of Bunratty, county of Clare, and province of Munster, 1½ mile (N. W.) from Six-mile-bridge, on the road to Ennis; containing 1021 inhabitants, and comprising 2632 statute acres, as applotted under the tithe act. The land is in general of good quality, and chiefly under tillage, and the state of agriculture is gradually improving. Fairs are held at Rossmanaher on Jan. 6th, May 10th, June 15th, Sept. 12th, and Oct. 16th, mostly for sheep and pigs. Immediately adjoining is Rossmanagher, the seat of Lieut.-Col. Wm. O'Brien. The other seats are Deer Park, that of E. Mansell, Esq.; Springfield, of F. Morice, Esq.; and Streamstown, of E. Wilson, Esq. The parish is in the diocese of Killaloe; the rectory forms part of the union of Tomfinlough, and the vicarage, part of the union of Kilfinaghty. The tithes amount to £150, of which two-thirds are payable to the rector, and the remainder to the vicar. In the R. C. divisions it is part of the union or district of Six-mile-bridge. About 30 children are educated in a school under the superintendence of the parish priest. The ruins of the old church still remain in the burial-ground, and at Rossmanagher are those of an ancient castle.

FINTONA, a post-town, in the parish of Donaghcavey, barony of Clogher, county of Tyrone, and province of Ulster, 7 miles (S.) from Omagh, and 97¾ (N. by W.) from Dublin, on the road from Omagh to Enniskillen; containing 1714 inhabitants. At the plantation of Ulster, by Jas. I., this district was placed in the lesser proportion of Fentonagh, and was granted, in 1611, to Sir Francis Willoughby, who neglecting to comply with the terms of the grant, the lands reverted to the Crown. In 1614, 2000 acres were granted to John Leigh, Esq., who, prior to 1619, had built a bawn and house, in which he resided, and then commenced building the town. It now consists of one main and several smaller streets, very irregularly formed, comprising 354 houses, some of which are well built; and is situated in a fertile vale, on both sides of the Fintona water, occupying an advantageous position for trade, in a fine and improving country. The only manufactures are the weaving of linen and the making of spades. The market is on Friday, and is well supplied with all kinds of provisions; and large quantities of brown linens are sold every alternate Friday to the bleachers, who attend from a great distance. A fair is held on the 22nd of every month, which is large and well attended. Petty sessions are held on the second Tuesday in each month; and a court leet and baron for the manor of Castlemaine once a month, for the recovery of debts under 40*s.*, by a seneschal appointed by C. Eccles, Esq., the lord of the manor. Here is a constabulary police station, for which most convenient barracks have been recently built, and another at Barr. The gentlemen's seats in the neighbourhood are Ecclesville, that of C. Eccles, Esq.; Derrabard House, of S. Vesey, Esq.; Cavan House, of W. Dickson, Esq.; Cavan Lodge, of C. R. Lucas, Esq.; and Dundiven glebe-house, of the Rev.

Jos. McCormick. The parochial church, and a Presbyterian, and a Wesleyan Methodist meeting-house are in the town, within a short distance of which is the R. C. chapel.

FINTOWN.—See INNISKEEL.

FINUGE, a parish, in the barony of CLANMAURICE, county of KERRY, and province of MUNSTER, 2 miles (S. S. W.) from Listowel, on the river Feale, and on the road from Listowel to Tralee; containing 1431 inhabitants, of which number, 491 are in the village. The parish comprises 3583 statute acres, as applotted under the tithe act, the greater part of which consists of arable land: of the remainder, about 850 acres are coarse pasture land, 480 bog, and 100 woodland. Some of the arable land is of superior quality: the state of agriculture is gradually improving. Ballinruddery, the occasional residence of the Rt. Hon. Maurice Fitzgerald, Knt. of Kerry, is beautifully situated in a richly wooded demesne on the banks of the Feale. The house is an irregular building, partly thatched and partly slated, and the cottage front is covered with a profusion of climbing plants. A fine carriage road extends for upwards of a mile through the demesne, nearly parallel with the windings of the river. Adjoining the dwelling-house, and on the verge of the river, are the picturesque ruins of the ancient castle of Ballinruddery. The other seats are Ballyhorgan, the residence of W. Hilliard, Esq.; Finuge House, of W. Harnett, Esq.; Killocrin House, of Capt. O'Halloran; Finuge Cottage, of Miss Hewson; Bellarne, of H. Hilliard, Esq.; Tanavalla, of A. Elliott, Esq.; and Ballygrinnan, of S. Sewell, Esq. The parish is in the diocese of Ardfert and Aghadoe: the rectory is impropriate in A. Stoughton, Esq.; and the vicarage forms part of the union of Aghavallin. The tithes amount to £129. 4. 6., payable in moieties to the impropriator and the vicar. There are no remains of the church, but the ancient burial-ground is still used.

FINVARRA, a village, in the parish of OUGHTMANNA, barony of BURREN, county of CLARE, and province of MUNSTER, 2½ miles (W.) from Burren, on the bay of Galway; containing 410 inhabitants. This village, which is situated in a detached portion of the parish, is chiefly remarkable for a Point of that name which stretches into the bay from the peninsula formed by the parish of Abbey, and on which a martello tower has been erected. There is also a similar tower on Aughnish Point, to the north-east, which also forms a detached portion of the same parish. Finvarra Point is situated on the north-east side of the bay of Ballyvaughan, and to the south-west of the entrance of the harbour of New Quay.

FINVOY, a parish, in the barony of KILCONWAY, county of ANTRIM, and province of ULSTER, 5 miles (S. W.) from Ballymoney, on the road from Ballymoney to Kilrea; containing 6093 inhabitants. This parish, which is bounded on the west by the river Bann, and on the east by the Mainwater, comprises, according to the Ordnance survey, 16,474¼ statute acres, of which about one-third is bog and barren heath, and the remainder, with the exception of about 90 acres in the river Bann and a small lough of about 5 acres, is good land; about 3187 acres are applotted under the tithe act, and valued at £2281 per ann. The surface is varied: the parish is divided into three portions by two bogs which intersect it, and parallel with which are two mountainous ridges, one called the Craigs, and the other Killymorris. The system of agriculture has, within the last few years, been greatly improved; there are some quarries of basalt, which is raised for building and for mending the roads; and coal and iron stone are supposed to exist in several parts, but neither has yet been worked. Bricks are manufactured, for which there is plenty of clay along the banks of the Bann. The principal gentlemen's seats are Moore Lodge, that of G. Moore, Esq.; and Cullytrummin, of Sampson Moore, Esq. In the small village of Dunloy there is a good inn. Fairs are held there on the 15th of Feb., May, Aug., and Nov.; and it is a constabulary police station. In its immediate vicinity is the hill of Dunloy, which, according to the Ordnance survey, has an elevation of 707 feet above the level of the sea at low water. The river Bann is not navigable up to this parish, the approach being obstructed by the falls of Portna. The living is a rectory and perpetual curacy, in the diocese of Connor; the rectory forms part of the union and corps of the prebend of Rasharkin, in the cathedral of Connor; the perpetual curacy, which was instituted in 1808, is in the patronage of the Prebendary. The tithes amount to £450, of which £300 is payable to the rector, and £150 to the perpetual curate. There is neither glebe-house nor glebe. The present church was erected on the site of the original structure, by aid of a gift of £200 and a loan of £400 from the late Board of First Fruits, in 1810; and the Ecclesiastical Commissioners have lately granted £129 for its repair. In the R. C. divisions the parish is united to that of Rasharkin; the chapel is situated at Killymorris. There is a place of worship for Presbyterians in connection with the Synod of Ulster, of the second class. About 380 children are taught in four public schools, of which the parochial school was founded in 1822; and there are four private schools, in which are about 200 children, and eight Sunday schools. There are several forts, artificial caverns, and druidical remains in various parts of the parish; among the latter is a cromlech of hard black stone, between the upright pillars of which is an entrance to a chamber underneath, which communicates with two other chambers, the whole within a circle of 45 feet in diameter. This interesting relic is situated beyond the summit of the Craig; and at the distance of a furlong from it is a square fort, enclosing an area of 9000 square feet, surrounded with a deep trench. Within 300 yards of the fort are three erect tapering pillars, supposed to be monumental memorials of certain chiefs slain and buried on the spot. The view from the Craig rocks embraces that side of Lough Neagh which is towards the river Bann, and the mountains of Derry in the distance. At Lischeahan is a mineral spring, the water of which has the taste and smell of gunpowder.

FIRCALL.—See EGLISH.

FITHMONE.—See KILFITHMONE.

FIVE-MILE-TOWN, or BLESSINGBOURN, a post-town, in the parish and barony of CLOGHER, county of ANTRIM, and province of ULSTER, 6 miles (W. by S.) from Clogher, and 79¾ (N. W.) from Dublin, on the road from Lisnaskea to Clogher, and on the confines of the county of Fermanagh; containing 758 inhabitants. This place has been sometimes called Mount-Stewart, from the name of its founder, Sir Wm. Stewart, to whom Jas. I. granted 2000 acres of land, called Ballynacoole. Prior to 1619, Sir William had built the castle of Aghentine, and commenced the village, which was occupied by British tenants. He afterwards obtained a charter for markets and fairs; the latter are now held on the third Monday in every month. The town is gradually improving: it consists of one principal and two smaller streets, and comprises about 140 houses, several of which are modern and well built. A constabulary police force is stationed here, and petty sessions are held on alternate Thursdays. A neat chapel of ease, with a spire, was built in 1750, at the expense of Mr. Armor. A public school is supported by Col. Montgomery, who built the school-house; and there are two other public schools. Near the town is Blessingbourn Cottage, the neat residence of Col. Montgomery. The ruins of Aghantine castle, in the neighbourhood, are boldly situated on elevated ground: it was destroyed by Sir Phelim O'Nial, in 1641.

FLORENCE-COURT.—See KILLESHER.

FLURRY-BRIDGE.—See BALLYMASCANLAN.

FOATY, or FOTA, ISLAND, partly in the parish of CARRIGTOHILL, and partly in that of CLONMELL, barony of BARRYMORE, county of CORK, and province of MUNSTER, 6 miles (N.) from Cove, in the harbour of Cork; containing 188 inhabitants. This island, which comprises 750 statute acres, solely the demesne of the Barry family, has been connected on the north side with Carrigtohill by a handsome bridge and causeway, whence a fine line of road from Cork to Cove passes along its south-eastern side to Belvelly, where by another lofty bridge it enters the Great Island, close under the ruins of the old castle and martello tower. Near the termination of the northern bridge is an elegant entrance lodge to Foaty, the seat of the late J. Smith Barry, Esq., and near Belvelly is another lodge of similar design. The mansion is spacious and beautifully situated in the midst of thriving plantations; and the demesne extends on every side close to the shores of the harbour, of which it commands a fine view and also of the richly varied scenery of the river Lee. Not far from the house, on the shore of a picturesque bay, is a small castle of elegant design; and on the opposite shore is the castle of Blackrock, with the interesting and beautiful scenery around. Near the south-east termination of the demesne are some very neat cottages, occupied by the numerous workmen employed on the estate; and a male and female school, with residences for the master and mistress, built and wholly supported by Mr. and Mrs. Smith Barry.

FOGHARD.—See FAUGHART.

FOHENAH, or FOHANA, a parish, in the barony of KILCONNELL, county of GALWAY, and province of CONNAUGHT, 1½ mile (S. by E.) from Ahascragh, on the road from Kilconnel to Ahascragh; containing 1968 inhabitants. This parish comprises 5834 statute acres, as applotted under the tithe act. There are good limestone quarries, and an oatmeal-mill. The bog has been reclaimed by Lord Clonbrock at a large outlay of capital, according to the suggestions of Thos. Bermingham, of Caramana, Esq. The seats are Clonbrock, the residence of Lord Clonbrock, situated on an extensive demesne, finely planted and tastefully kept; and Lowville, of W. McDonagh, Esq. The living is a rectory and vicarage, in the diocese of Clonfert; the rectory is partly appropriate to the see and partly to the vicarage, which forms part of the union of Kilconnell. The tithes amount to £166. 3. 0¾., of which £32. 6. 1¾. is payable to the Ecclesiastical Commissioners and £133. 16. 11. to the incumbent. The church is in ruins and the ground used as a cemetery. In the R. C. divisions the parish is united to the half parish of Kilgerril, or Kilgirdle; the chapel is a thatched building. About 50 children are educated in a private school. The peasantry are comfortable, and agriculture is much improved. At Ballinabanaba are the remains of a castle. The skeleton of a very large elk was dug out of a bog in 1835. The title of Clonbrock, conferred on the Dillon family, is taken from the demesne.

FOLLISTOWN, or FONLISTOWN, a parish, in the barony of SKREEN, county of MEATH, and province of LEINSTER, 2½ miles (S. E.) from Navan, near the road to Duleek; containing, with the parish of Staffordstown, 137 inhabitants. It is a rectory, in the diocese of Meath, entirely impropriate in F. Murphy, Esq., of Kilcarn, to whom the tithes, amounting to £36 are payable. The clerical duties are performed gratuitously by the incumbent of Skreen.

FONSTOWN.—See BALLINTUBBER.

FONTSTOWN, formerly FULESTOWN, a parish, partly in the barony of UPPER PHILIPSTOWN, KING'S county, and partly in the barony of WEST OPHALY, but chiefly in that of NARRAGH and RHEBAN EAST, county of KILDARE, and province of LEINSTER, 5 miles (E.) from Athy, on the mail coach road from Dublin to Cork, by way of Cashel; containing 1043 inhabitants, and comprising 4579 statute acres, of which 810 are bog, the remainder being nearly equally divided into pasture and arable land: within its limits is a small part of the bog of Monavologh. There are quarries of good building stone of a flinty nature, which is worked for home consumption. The living is a rectory and vicarage, in the diocese of Dublin, and in the patronage of the Marquess of Drogheda: the tithes amount to £267. 13. 10¼. The glebe-house was built by aid of a gift of £100, and a loan of £400, in 1810, from the late Board of First Fruits, additions to which have been made at a cost of £600: the glebe comprises 16*a.* 2*r.* 16*p.* The church is a very neat structure, with a tower and spire, in imitation of the later English style of architecture, built in 1823, at an expense of £1400, of which £1200 was a gift from the late Board. In the R. C. divisions the parish forms part of the union or district of Narraghmore, or Crookstown. A handsome school-house has been erected at an expense of £376, of which £160 was a grant from the Court of Chancery, out of the estate of the Marquess of Drogheda; it is to be supported partly by a yearly allowance of £30 from the same source, and a small grant of land, and £20 annually from the rector. There is a private school, in which about 10 boys and 20 girls are instructed. In digging for marl, some time since, the skull and horns of a large elk were found, which are in the possession of Col. Bruen, of Oak Park; and about two years since a coin of the reign of Ethelred was picked up in a field here.

FOOK'S MILLS, a village, partly in the parish of CLONGEEN, and partly in that of HORETOWN, barony of SHELMALIER, county of WEXFORD, and province of

LEINSTER, 3½ miles (S. W.) from Taghmon, on the old mail road to New Ross: the population is returned with the respective parishes. It contains about 30 houses, including a good country inn, where the meetings of the South Wexford Agricultural Association are occasionally held. In the immediate vicinity are Rosegarland, the seat of F. Leigh, Esq., and Horetown Glebe, the residence of the Rev. E. Bayley.

FORAN.—See TEMPLEORAN.

FORDSTOWN, a village, in the parish of GIRLEY, barony of UPPER KELLS, county of MEATH, and province of LEINSTER, 2½ miles (N.) from Athboy, on the road to Kells; containing 14 houses and 157 inhabitants. Here is a constabulary police station; also the R. C. chapel for the union or district of Girley, a handsome modern structure.

FORE.—See FEIGHAN of FORE (ST.).

FORGNEY, or CLONCALL, a parish, in the barony of ABBEYSHRUEL, county of LONGFORD, and province of LEINSTER, 2 miles (S. E.) from Ballymahon, on the road to Mullingar; containing 2241 inhabitants, and comprising 5832 statute acres, of which 4446 are applotted under the tithe act; 32 acres are woodland, 1945 arable, 1782 pasture, and 2073 bog and waste, being almost exclusively the property of the Countess Dowager of Rosse. A canal passes within a quarter of a mile of the parish. The seats are Newcastle, that of the Countess Dowager of Rosse, situated in a demesne of more than 480 acres; Cloncallow, of W. T. Murray, Esq.; Creevagh, of R. Sandys, Esq.; Prospect, of T. Bradin, Esq.; Clinan, of Bevan C. Slator, Esq., and Forgney, of W. Atkinson, Esq. The living is a perpetual cure, in the diocese of Meath, comprehending the parishes of Forgney and Nogheval, and in the patronage of the Bishop, to whom the rectory is appropriate. The tithes amount to £200. The church is a plain building, enlarged, in 1810, by a donation from the Countess Dowager of Rosse, and to the repairs of which the Ecclesiastical Commissioners have recently granted £316. In the R. C. divisions the parish forms part of the union or district of Moyvore, and contains a chapel. A free school is supported by Lady Rosse and the Bishop of Meath; and there is a school under the National Board, in which are 80 boys and 55 girls. There are the remains of an old church, adjoining which is a burial-place. Oliver Goldsmith was born at Pallice, in 1728; the house is now in ruins.

FORKHILL, a post-town and parish, partly in the barony of LOWER ORIOR, but chiefly in that of UPPER ORIOR, county of ARMAGH, and province of ULSTER, 4½ miles (N. N. W.) from Dundalk, and 44½ (N. by W.) from Dublin, on the road from Dundalk to Armagh; containing 7063 inhabitants, of which number, 152 are in the town. This was constituted a parish by act of council in 1771, by separating 12 townlands from the parish of Loughgilly, and 11 from Killevy. It comprises, according to the Ordnance survey, 12,590 statute acres, of which 11,910 are applotted under the tithe act, and valued at £5184 per annum; 8380 acres are arable, and 3519 bog and mountain; the state of agriculture has much improved. Among the many mountains is Slieve Gullion, on the eastern boundary, rising 1895 feet above the level of the sea; they all afford pasture, and some have been lately planted. There are quarries of excellent stone, used for building. The town consists of 36 houses and is a constabulary police station. Fairs are held on May 1st, Aug. 1st, Sept. 29th, and Dec. 8th. The linen and cotton manufacture are carried on to a limited extent, and within the parish are four corn-mills, from which a considerable quantity of meal is exported through the port of Dundalk to Liverpool. The principal seats are Forkhill House, the residence of J. Foxall, Esq.; Forkhill Lodge, of Mrs. Dawson; Longfield, of Major Bernard; Bellmont, of the Rev. Mr. Smith, and of S. E. Walker, Esq.; and the Glebe-house, of the Rev. J. Campbell, L. L. D. The living is a rectory, in the diocese of Armagh, and in the patronage of the Lord-Primate: the tithes amount to £650; the glebe comprises 164 statute acres. The church is a plain structure, erected in 1767. In the R. C. divisions the parish is the head of a union or district, comprising also a portion of that of Killevy, or Meigh, in which union are two chapels; the chapel at Mullaban, in this parish, is a plain commodious building. There is a Wesleyan Methodist meeting-house in the town. Seven schools were founded and are supported by the trustees of the late Richard Jackson, Esq., of Forkhill Lodge; another is aided by an annual donation from the same source, and one by the rector. In these schools about 600 children are instructed; and there are two private schools, in which are about 90 boys and 60 girls. A dispensary in the parish is also maintained by the trustees of Mr. Jackson, who by will dated July 20th, 1776, left a great portion of his extensive property to pious and charitable uses: in consequence of some litigation as to its division, it was determined by act of parliament that a portion of the rents of the estate of Forkhill, immediately from the decease of the testator, should be applied to the use of the poor children of his tenants, as directed in the will; the lands then assigned for this purpose yielding £375 per annum. After deducting £200 per annum for agency, &c., one-half of the residue of the net revenue was appropriated to the propagation of the Christian religion in the east, and the other half to his sister and her heirs: he made also many minor charitable bequests. Mrs. Barton, by deed in 1803, gave £40 per annum, to be equally divided among 20 poor women of this parish; and Mrs. Jackson bequeathed £10 per ann., payable out of the Killesandra estate, in Cavan, to the rector, for the benefit of the poor. On the top of the mountain of Slieve Gullion there is a large heap of stones near a cave, supposed to have been the burial-place of some Druid, or ancient chieftain; near which is a deep lake. Near this was formerly Rosskugh, or the fort of Carrick-Brand, a considerable military station, with extensive outworks.

FORTH MOUNTAIN, an extra-parochial district, partly in the barony of FORTH (from which it derives its name), partly in that of BARGY, and partly in that of SHELMALIER, county of WEXFORD, and province of LEINSTER, 2 miles (S. W.) from Wexford; containing 1102 inhabitants. During the disturbances of 1798, this place was selected as a military station by the insurgents, who encamped their forces, amounting to several thousands, on the north-eastern extremity of the mountain called the Three Rocks, previously to their attack on Wexford. To reinforce the garrison of that town, a detachment of the Meath militia, with a party of artillery and two howitzers, was sent from Duncannon Fort, under the command of Capt. Adams, which on passing near the foot of the mountain was intercepted by a large party of the insurgents, the whole detachment cut to pieces, and the howitzers and ammunition captured. Immediately afterwards, Lieut.-Col. Maxwell marched out from Wexford with 200 of the Donegal regiment and about 150 of the yeoman cavalry, to support the 13th regiment commanded by Major-Gen. Fawcet, which was expected from Duncannon Fort; but the Major having heard of the disaster at the Three Rocks, fell back with his regiment, after having advanced as far as Taghmon. Col. Maxwell, who had been also apprised of the destruction of the detachment, collected his forces and advanced towards the insurgents, to co-operate with Major Watson, of whose retreat he was ignorant. On his arrival near the Three Rocks, he was attacked by a numerous body of the insurgents, who rushed down from the mountain with a view of cutting off his retreat; but they were repulsed by a steady fire from the Donegal regiment, and Col. Maxwell seeing no appearance of Major-Gen. Fawcet, and finding his forces exposed to great risk without any prospect of advantage, retreated to Wexford. This place now became the chief rendezvous of the insurgents, whose numbers were so formidable, that it was considered necessary by the garrison and inhabitants of Wexford to abandon the town, of which the former immediately took possession.

The mountain rises two miles south-west of Wexford, to an elevation of about 500 feet above the level of the sea, and extends upwards of three miles in the same direction, having a mean breadth of nearly two miles; it is chiefly composed of quartz, with a slight covering of alluvial soil, partly under cultivation and partly producing only furze and heath, which serve for fuel. Many of the peasantry have located themselves on its sides, and by immense labour have cleared away the stones from a considerable tract and converted it into good arable land, of which they remain in undisturbed possession. Its summit rises into a variety of fantastic forms, and commands a grand and very extensive prospect. In the R. C. divisions the sides of this mountain are included in the respective districts or parishes immediately adjoining. On that part which borders on Kilmannon is a public school, in which about 160 children are educated.

FOSSEY, or TIMAHOE, a parish, partly in the barony of MARYBOROUGH, but chiefly in that of CULLINAGH, QUEEN'S county, and province of LEINSTER, 2 miles (S. W.) from Stradbally, on the road from Stradbally to Ballinakill; containing 1810 inhabitants, and comprising 10,600 statute acres, as applotted under the tithe act. Fairs are held on April 5th, July 2nd, and Oct. 18th. The living is a vicarage, in the diocese of Leighlin, and in the patronage of the Bishop; the rectory is impropriate in J. Hone, Esq. The tithes amount to £387. 13. 9., of which £258. 9. 2½. is payable to the impropriator, and the remainder to the vicar. In the R. C. divisions this parish forms part of the union or district of Stradbally, and contains a handsome chapel. The parochial school is aided by Mrs. Cosby; and there are five private schools, in which about 170 children are educated.

FOUR-MILE-BURN, a hamlet, in the parish of DONEGORE, barony of UPPER ANTRIM, county of ANTRIM, and province of ULSTER; containing 15 houses and 73 inhabitants.

FOUR-MILE-WATER, a village, in the parish of KILRONAN, barony of GLANAHEIRY, county of WATERFORD, and province of MUNSTER, 5 miles (S. S. W.) from Clonmel, on the river Suir, over which is a good stone bridge: the population is returned with the parish. It has a constabulary police station, a neat and commodious R. C. chapel, and some remains of a castle.

FOWRE.—See FEIGHAN of FORE.

FOXFORD, a market and post-town, in the parish of TOOMORE, barony of GALLEN, county of MAYO, and province of CONNAUGHT, 8 miles (S.) from Ballina, and 132 (N. W. by W.) from Dublin, on the river Moy, and on the road from Ballina to Swinford; containing 1068 inhabitants, and consisting of 209 houses indifferently built. The Irish, or Celtic, term for Foxford is *Belass*, signifying the "mouth of a cataract." During the disturbances of 1798, when the French, under Gen. Humbert, had taken possession of the town of Ballina, the garrison, under Col. Sir T. Chapman and Major Keir, retreated to this place; and Gen. Humbert, on abandoning Castlebar, passed with his army through the town, on his route to Sligo. It is a place of very great antiquity, and was formerly the key of Tyrawley; from it the district, which extends a considerable distance, even into the adjoining county of Galway, takes its name: it is mostly surrounded by a chain of high mountains. The beautiful river Moy, which in its course receives the principal waters of the county of Mayo, until it discharges itself into the sea at Ballina, runs through the town, where it is crossed by a very ancient bridge of several arches, now in a state of decay. By the dissolution of the Linen Board, 140 looms in this town and neighbourhood were thrown out of employment: the only trade carried on is in corn. The market is on Thursday; and fairs are held, chiefly for cattle, on May 15th, June 25th, Oct. 3rd, and Dec. 10th. There is a market and court-house, where petty sessions are held on alternate Fridays; a constabulary police station, and an infantry barrack. This place is remarkable for the longevity of the inhabitants, being considered one of the healthiest spots in this or any of the adjoining counties. In the town stand the parish church and a R. C. chapel; and there are two public schools. About three miles distant, on the Castlebar road, are the ruins of an extensive monastery, still inhabited by a solitary individual of the order, and according as one dies his place is supplied by another. At a ford a little below the town is a huge rock, called Cromwell's rock, where it is stated the Protector's army crossed the Moy, during the civil war. A few years since, whilst the streets were undergoing some repairs, a deep pit was sunk at the corner of the main street, to raise gravel, on which occasion a great number of human skulls and skeletons was dug up, evidently indicating the scene of some battle.

FOYNE'S ISLAND, in the parish of ROBERTSTOWN, Shanid Division of the barony of LOWER CONNELLO, county of LIMERICK, and province of MUNSTER, 4 miles (N.) from Shanagolden, near Lehy's Point, on the southern shore of the river Shannon: the population is returned with the parish. This place has been recommended by Capt. Mudge, the Government engineer, as affording extensive and secure anchorage for shipping, and consequently as a proper situation for the construction of docks and quays; at present it is seldom resorted to by mariners, but the steamers plying between Limerick and Kilrush call off the island to take up passengers. There was formerly a battery of 24 guns on the island, erected for the protection of the shipping trade of the river. On the south side is a handsome marine villa, the summer residence of the Earl of Dunraven; and there are several neat cottage residences in different parts of the island.

FRACTIONS, EAST and WEST, detached portions of the barony of MAGONIHY, county of KERRY, and province of MUNSTER; the former being locally situated in the parishes of Drishane, Kilmeen, and Nohoval-Daly, in the barony of Duhallow, county of Cork, and the latter in the parishes of Glenbegh and Killorglin, barony of Magonihy, county of Kerry, containing in the whole 5296 inhabitants, of which number, 285 were in Drishane, 1045 in Kilmeen, 1304 in Nohoval-Daly, containing together 2634; and 616 in Glenbegh, and 2046 in Killorglin, together amounting to 2662 inhabitants. In the ecclesiastical divisions they are considered as forming parts of the parishes above enumerated.

FRANCIS ABBEY (ST.), an extra-parochial district, in the centre of the city of Limerick; containing 1483 inhabitants. This district comprises the site, garden, and precincts of the ancient Franciscan monastery, founded in the reign of Hen. III. by Fion de Burgo, and in which he was interred in 1287. The abbey continued to flourish till the dissolution, when it was granted to Alderman Sexton, and now forms part of the estate of the Earl of Limerick. It is situated in the Island, or Englishtown, and wholly surrounded by the parish of St. Mary, to which it nominally belongs, and in the R. C. divisions forms part of that parish. There are no vestiges of the ancient buildings, nor can their exact site be ascertained.

FRANKFORD, or KILCORMUCK, a market and post-town, in the parish and barony of BALLYBOY, KING'S county, and province of LEINSTER, 9½ miles (S. W.) from Tullamore, and 59 (S. W.) from Dublin, on the Silver river, and on the road from Tullamore to Parsonstown; containing 204 houses and 1112 inhabitants. A considerable corn market is held every Saturday; and fairs on May 28th and Nov. 8th. It is a constabulary police station, and has petty sessions on Saturdays. It gives name to the R. C. union or district, of which Ballyboy is the head, and contains the chapel. Here is a meeting-house under the Home Mission Society, and a dispensary. A monastery for Carmelites, or White Friars, was founded at this place by Odo, son of Nellan O'Molloy, dynast of the circumjacent territory of Fircal, or Fearcall; the founder died in 1454, and was buried before the high altar. On the suppression of monasteries, this house and its dependencies were granted to Robert Leycester, Esq., from whose family it passed by marriage to the Magawleys, whose seat, Temora, is in the vicinity. The present name of the town seems to be derived from the family of Frank, of whom James Frank, Esq., founded here a charter school, opened in 1753, for upwards of forty children. Near the town is Broghill castle, formerly the chief seat of the O'Molloys, and once held by the sept of O'Connor: it was taken, in 1538, by Lord Leonard Gray. The estate now belongs to the Fitzsimon family.—See BALLYBOY.

FREEMOUNT, a village, in the parish of KNOCKTEMPLE, barony of DUHALLOW, county of CORK, and province of MUNSTER, 5 miles (N. by E.) from Kanturk, on the road from Liscarrol to Newcastle: the population is returned with the parish. It is a constabulary police station, and contains the chapel which gives name to the R. C. district, a plain cruciform building, to which is attached a public school.—See KNOCKTEMPLE.

FREEPORT.—See RAHOON.

FREIGH, or FREGH ILAN, an island, in the parish of MOYRUS, barony of BALLYNAHINCH, county of GALWAY, and province of CONNAUGHT, 13 miles (S. E.) from Clifden, at the entrance of Birterbuy bay, on the western coast; containing 54 acres of land, the property of T. Martin, Esq.: the population is returned with the parish.

FRENCH-PARK, a market and post-town, in the parish of TAUGHBOYNE, barony of BOYLE, county of ROSCOMMON, and province of CONNAUGHT, 7 miles (S. S. W.) from Boyle, and 91 (N. W.) from Dublin, at the junction of the roads from Elphin, Boyle, Castlerea, and Ballaghadereen; containing 76 houses and 447 inhabitants. Much advantage is likely to result to this place from the mail coach road now constructed so as to pass through it. Silicious sandstone for building is found within a quarter of a mile, and limestone abounds. The agricultural improvements have led to preparations for the erection of a market-house, a market being held on Thursdays, which is much frequented by the Sligo merchants, who purchase butter in firkins for exportation; considerable quantities of yarn are also sold, and it is an extensive pig market. Six fairs are held during the year, on Jan. 1st, March 17th, May 21st, July 12th, Sept. 21st, and Nov. 10th. It is a constabulary police station, and has a dispensary. The noble seat and demesne of French Park, which gives name to the town, is contiguous; the mansion is a massive structure of brick, with two projecting wings, and is the property of Arthur French, Esq.; the demesne comprises about 1458 statute acres, finely wooded. Here is a R. C. chapel, towards the erection of which the French family contributed largely. Near it is the rent-office of Arthur French, Esq., where petty sessions are held. In the deer park of the demesne is a remarkable cave, consisting of five rooms, supposed to be druidical. On the verge of a bog, within half a mile of the town, are the ruins of Clonshanvill Abbey, which, from the open and level character of the surrounding country, form an imposing object: it is said to have been founded by St. Patrick, and re-erected by Mac Dermot Roe, in 1385; it was dedicated to the Holy Cross, and belonged to the Dominican friars. The remains consist of the walls of the church, the tower of which rests on pointed arches of a square building, which appears to have formed the habitable part of the monastery, and of some detached chapels within the cemetery. The chancel is now railed off for tombs, the cemetery being still much used. One of the most remarkable relics is a cross of sandstone flag, rising 11 feet from the ground, said by tradition to mark the spot beyond which a corpse might not be carried by the relatives and friends, but there be delivered up to the monks.

FRESHFORD, or AGHOURA, a post-town and parish, in the barony of CRANAGH, county of KIL-

KENNY, and province of LEINSTER, 6½ miles (W. N. W.) from Kilkenny, and 63 (S. W.) from Dublin, on the road from Kilkenny to Johnstown; containing 2277 inhabitants. This place, anciently called *Aghoure* or *Achadhur*, signifying the "green ford," was the site of an abbey founded about the commencement of the seventh century, by St. Lactan, who was its first abbot. The parish comprises 2108 statute acres, as applotted under the tithe act, and valued at £2477 per annum: there is no bog or waste land. The state of agriculture is fast improving, and the land is almost equally divided between tillage and pasturage. There are limestone quarries, in which manganese is said to exist; and a coal mine is about to be opened. The principal seats are Upperwood, the elegant mansion of W. De Montmorency, Esq., which is in a handsome and well-planted demesne; Balleen Castle, an ancient fortress, the property of the Earl of Kilkenny; Kilrush, a seat of the St. George family; and near the town is the seat of Pierse Butler, Esq. The town, which comprises 374 houses, is neat and well built, and is part of the estate of William De Montmorency, Esq. It is a station of the revenue and of the constabulary police, and has fairs on Aug. 5th and Dec. 17th, and pig fairs on Oct. 31st and Dec. 5th. Here is a dispensary, a fever hospital, and a society for relieving the bedridden poor. A flour-mill, called the manor mill, is remarkably well supplied with water from the Freshford river. A manor court is held every third week, for the recovery of debts under 40*s.*; and petty sessions are held every fortnight. The living is a rectory, in the diocese of Ossory, episcopally united to the parishes of Clomanto, Kilrush, Clashacrow, Rathbeagh, Tubridbritain, Sheffin, Clontubrid, and Coolcashin, which together form the union of Freshford and the corps of the prebend of Aghoure (anciently called the "Golden Prebend") in the cathedral of Kilkenny. The first six parishes are in the patronage of the Bishop, and the remaining three in that of the Dean and Chapter. The tithes amount to £184. 12. 5., and the gross revenue of the prebend is £860. 18. 10. The glebe-house is in Clashacrow. The church was built in 1730, and has a fine Norman porch with the date 1133, and an inscription in ancient Irish, purporting that "the priest Mac Roen and chief gave an acre of land to the church," which formerly belonged to the abbey. In the R. C. divisions the parish is the head of a union or district, comprising Freshford, Tullaroan, Ballynamara, Clashacrow, Ballylarkin, and parts of Odogh, Burnchurch, and Clomanto, in which district is a chapel at Freshford, one at Odogh, and one at Tullaroan. The parochial school is aided by an annual donation of £10 from the rector, and a bequest of £5 per annum from the late Col. Brown; the school-house, a slated building, was erected at a cost of £120, of which £60 was a grant from the lord-lieutenant's fund. There is also a national school adjoining the R. C. chapel. About 300 children are educated in these schools, and about 60 in two private schools, exclusive of those taught in a Sunday school. Near Kilrush are the ruins of Ballylarkin castle, once the seat of the Shortall family. Here are also the remains of an ancient manor-house, which belonged to Sir Toby Caulfield, and was a place of importance during the parliamentary war.

FRIENDSTOWN, a parish, in the barony of UPPER TALBOTSTOWN, county of WICKLOW, and province of LEINSTER, 2½ miles (S. E.) from Dunlavan, on the road to Stratford-upon-Slany; containing 324 inhabitants, and comprising 1572 statute acres, as applotted under the tithe act. The land is in tillage and pasture, and agriculture is improving. It is a vicarage, in the diocese of Dublin and Glendalough, forming part of the union of Dunlavan; the rectory is appropriate to the Dean and Chapter of St. Patrick's cathedral, Dublin. The tithes amount to £69, of which £43. 3. 1. is payable to the lessee of the dean and chapter, and £25. 16. 11. to the vicar. In the R. C. divisions it is part of the union or district of Dunlavan. Here are the ruins of an old church.

FUERTY, a parish, in the barony of ATHLONE, county of ROSCOMMON, and province of CONNAUGHT, 3½ miles (W. by S.) from Roscommon; containing 5611 inhabitants. It is intersected from north to south by the river Suck, which is crossed by a long causeway bridge at Castlestrange and another at Castlecoote, and comprises 8989 statute acres, of which 8782 are applotted under the tithe act, and valued at £6705 per annum; about 800 acres are bog, and 130 woodland; the remainder is arable and pasture. There are quarries of limestone, which is abundant; and an excellent quarry of grit-stone of peculiar solidity and hardness. At Castlecoote are extensive flour-mills, producing 10,000 bags annually, and employing more than 40 men; and there is a nursery of forest and fruit trees. Fairs are held on Aug. 4th and Nov. 21st, for the sale of live stock, linen, frieze, &c. The principal seats are Castlestrange, the residence of E. Mitchell, Esq.; Rockley Park, of D. Merry, Esq.; Coolmeen, of J. Mitchell, Esq.; Emla, of Edward Harrison, Esq.; Cloverhill, of J. Hurst, Esq.; and Castlecoote and Mount Prospect, both the property of Sir C. H. Coote, Bart., and the former in the occupation of Bernard Dowall, Esq. It is a vicarage, in the diocese of Elphin, forming part of the union of Athleague; the rectory is impropriate in the Earl of Essex. The tithes amount to £240, of which £156. 18. 5½ is payable to the impropriator, and the remainder to the vicar. The glebe-house was built, in 1827, by a gift of £400, and a loan of £50, from the late Board of First Fruits: there is a glebe of 18 acres, 6 of which are good arable, the remainder being very inferior land. The church is a neat building with a square tower in an unfinished state, in good repair; it contains some handsome monuments to the Mitchell family. The R. C. parish is co-extensive with that of the Established Church, and contains a chapel on the townland of Creevemully, a neat building in good repair. Here are five public schools under the Elphin Diocesan society and the London and Ladies' Hibernian societies, aided also by annual donations from Lady Coote, the Rev. Mr. Clever, and others, in which are about 370 children: there are also five private schools in which about 260 children are instructed. About a mile north-west of Athleague, on the side of the vale of the Suck, are the ruins of a large old mansion, with tall chimneys and gables, having a round tower at one of the angles. There are several Danish raths, one of which, called *Lisadaghearlagh*, or the "Fort of the two Earls," is traditionally said to have been contended for by two Earls, who at length consented to divide it between them by a trench, which still appears diametrically drawn across it.

FULESTOWN.—See FONTSTOWN.

FURNAUGHTS, or FORENAUGHTS, a parish, in the barony of South Salt, county of Kildare, and province of Leinster, 2 miles (E. by N.) from Naas, on the road to Blessington: the population is returned with the parish of Naas. This small parish comprises only 765 statute acres. The seats are Forenaughts, the residence of the Rev. R. Wolfe; and Furness, that of W. Beauman, Esq. It is a perpetual curacy, in the diocese of Kildare, united with that of Hainstown, and in the patronage of the Bishop: the tithes amount to £19. 14. 0., and those of the benefice to £26. 11. 6. In the R. C. divisions the parish forms part of the union or district of Kill. Some remains of the old church still exist, and at Furness is a rath.

FURNISH, or FURINISH, an island, in the parish of Kilcummin, barony of Moycullen, county of Galway, and province of Connaught, 22½ miles (W. by N.) from Galway, on the south side of Casheen bay, on the western coast, containing about 80 statute acres of arable and pasture land: the population is returned with the parish. The inhabitants are chiefly employed in the fisheries. There is good anchorage on the east side of the island, which is well sheltered and has a sufficient depth of water for any vessel.

FYNISH.—See INNIS-MAC-NAUGHTEN.

G

GAILE.—See GEALE.

GALBALLY, a town and parish, in the barony of Costlea, county of Limerick, and province of Munster, 8 miles (S. S. W.) from Tipperary, on the road to Mitchelstown; containing 5563 inhabitants, of which number, 560 are in the town. This place, in which are the ruins of several religious establishments, appears to have been formerly of considerable importance; an abbey for Franciscan friars was founded near the town in 1204, by Donagh Cairbre O'Brien, which flourished till the dissolution, when it was granted to John of Desmond. In 1601, the Lord-President Carew summoned the chiefs of every county in this province to meet him at this place, where he appointed Lord Barry general of the whole force of Munster. The abbey being included in the forfeiture of Sir John Fitzgerald's estates, the rectory, parsonage, and vicarage of Galbally, the parsonage and prebend of Killenellig with all the glebe and tithes, except those belonging to the vicar, and other lands belonging to the abbey were, in 1611, granted to Thomas Cantwell, Esq. The ancient town was situated at the head of the glen of Aherlow, which being the only pass into Tipperary from the northern and eastern parts of Cork, and the western parts of Limerick, was frequently contested by the rival chieftains, but remained for more than 300 years in the possession of the O'Briens and Fitzgeralds. The present town is situated near the foot of the Galtee mountains, and contains 110 houses, of which some are well built of stone and roofed with slate, but the greater number are mean thatched cabins. Fairs for black cattle and pigs are held on May 12th and October 15th, and petty sessions every alternate Wednesday. A penny post and a constabulary police force have been established in the town. The parish is mountainous, and there are large portions of waste land, which is gradually being brought into profitable cultivation; the mountains to their very summit afford good pasturage for numerous herds of cattle, and there is a considerable quantity of bog. Limestone abounds, and there are quarries of good building stone and slate, and a thin stratum of coal. The scenery is boldly diversified, and there are several handsome seats, of which the principal are Massy Lodge, the elegant residence of Lord Massy; Riversdale, of Hugh Massy, Esq.; Castlereagh, of G. Bennett, Esq.; Janeville, of the Rev. R. Lloyd; the Cottage, of W. Lewis, Esq.: Annagurra, of T. T. Adams, Esq.; and Stagdale, of W. Massy, Esq., with a fine avenue of stately beech trees. The living is a rectory and vicarage, in the diocese of Emly, forming part of the union of Duntrileague, and of the corps of the prebend of Killenellig in the cathedral church of Emly. The tithes amount to £600; the glebe-house is a large handsome residence, and the glebe comprises 14 acres. There are some remains of the parish church, consisting of the side walls, 121 feet in length, of rude masonry and perforated with narrow and circular-headed windows. In the R. C. divisions the parish is the head of a union, comprising also the parish of Clonbeg: the chapel, in the village of Galbally, is a spacious building, erected in 1834, at an expense of £900; and there is also a chapel at Clonbeg. A large and handsome parochial school-room, capable of holding 600 children, was erected at an expense of £300, and is chiefly supported by the Massy family; and there are three private schools, in which are about 200 children, and a dispensary. There are some remains of the ancient Franciscan friary.

GALEY, a parish, in the barony of Iraghticonnor, county of Kerry, and province of Munster, 8½ miles (S. W. by S.) from Tarbert, on the river Gale; containing 2920 inhabitants. It comprises 12,381 statute acres, as applotted under the tithe act, a large portion of which is in pasture: along the river the land is of excellent quality. There are large tracts of bog in the parish, amounting to nearly two-fifths of its entire surface: about one-fifth only is under tillage. The state of agriculture is improving; a considerable portion of the bog is now being drained, and other improvements are in progress by P. Mahony, Esq., who has recently purchased the Gunsborough estate (See Gunsborough). The parish is in the diocese of Ardfert and Aghadoe: the rectory is impropriate in A. Stoughton, Esq., and the vicarage forms part of the union of Aghavallin. The tithes, amounting to £203. 1. 6½. are payable in equal portions to the impropriator and the vicar. In the R. C. divisions it is partly in the district of Listowel, but chiefly in that of Lisseltin. About 220 children are educated in two private schools.

GALGORM, a village, in the parish of Ahoghill, barony of Lower Toome, county of Antrim, and province of Ulster, 1 mile (W.) from Ballymena, on the river Maine; containing 37 houses and 226 inhabitants. The castle of Galgorm, built by the celebrated Dr. Colville, is a handsome square embattled structure, now the seat of the Earl of Mountcashel: the whole of the rooms are wainscoted with Irish oak.

GALLEN or GILLEN, a parish, in the barony of Garrycastle, King's county, and province of Leinster, 6 miles (N. E.) from Banagher, on the road to

Firbane; containing, with part of that town and the post-town of Cloghan (which are separately described), 5021 inhabitants. This parish formed part of the ancient possessions of the family of the McCoghlans, proprietors of the surrounding territory, who built a strong castle here, which was surrendered to Ireton in the parliamentary war; the last male representative of this family, Thomas Coghlan, Esq., M. P. for the borough of Banagher, died in 1790. A monastery was founded here in 490 by St. Canoc, or Mocanoc, which continued to flourish till 820, when it was burnt by Felim McCroimhain; and after its restoration was occupied by some monks from Wales, who founded in it a celebrated school, from which circumstance it is supposed to have derived its name. Though repeatedly plundered and destroyed by fire, it subsisted till the dissolution, when the site and lands were granted to Sir Gerald Moore. An abbey was also founded near Firbane by St. Diarmid, who died in 563, and was succeeded by St. Coemgan; it was plundered in 1041, and destroyed by fire in 1077, soon after which it appears to have been abandoned, as no notice of it occurs since 1082. The parish comprises 16,313 statute acres, of which about one-third is bog and waste; the remainder, with the exception of a small portion of woodland, is equally divided between pasture and tillage; the system of agriculture is improving, and limestone is found in abundance. The principal seats are Gallen, the residence of A. Armstrong, Esq., beautifully situated in a richly wooded demesne bordered by the river Brosna, and containing the picturesque remains of the ancient monastery; Strawberry Hill, of Major Molloy; Castle Iver, of W. B. Armstrong, Esq.; and Clonana Castle, of — Molony, Esq. At Castle Iver are some mills for oatmeal, worked by steam. Fairs are held on May 15th, Aug. 15th, Oct. 29th, and Nov. 17th: the May and October fairs are the principal for horses, cattle, and pigs.

It is a vicarage, in the diocese of Meath, forming part of the union of Reynagh; the rectory is impropriate. The tithes amount to £415. 7. 8., and are equally divided between the impropriator and the vicar; the glebe comprises 222 statute acres, valued at £154 per annum. The church, a small neat edifice, situated at Cloghan, was built by a gift of £600 from the late Board of First Fruits, in 1813. In the R. C. divisions it is part of the union of Banagher, or Reynagh, in the diocese of Ardagh; the chapel at Cloghan is a spacious plain building. About 130 children are taught in three public schools, of which the national school is endowed with a house and garden by the Hon. Frederick Ponsonby, and one at Shillestown with a house and half an acre of land by Mr. Judge. There are also seven private schools, in which are about 280 children. There are some remains of the ancient castle of Clonana.

GALLOON, a parish, partly in the baronies of Knockninny and Clonkelly, but chiefly in that of Coole, county of Fermanagh, and province of Ulster, 5½ miles (S. S. E.) from Lisnaskea, on Lough Erne, and on the road from Cavan to Enniskillen; containing 10,506 inhabitants. The parish, according to the Ordnance survey, comprises (including islands) 25,287 statute acres, of which 432½ are in the barony of Knockninny, 9341¼ in that of Clonkelly, and 15,513¼ in that of Coole; about two-thirds are good arable and pasture land, 1455½ are in Upper Lough Erne, 1072 in small lakes, and of the remainder a very large portion is bog, which is easily reclaimable. The system of agriculture is in a very unimproved stae; limestone is abundant, and freestone of good quality is procured for building and other purposes. The only seat of importance is Crom Castle, the residence of the Earl of Erne, about three miles from Newtown-Butler, a handsome mansion recently erected, in which is still preserved the armour worn by McCarthy Moore at the battle of Kilgarret. The lake affords considerable facility of water conveyance, and it is in contemplation to open the port of Ballyshannon by the river Erne; there is a large flour-mill at Roosky, in this parish. The living is a rectory, in the diocese of Clogher, and the corps of the chancellorship of the cathedral of Clogher, in the patronage of the Bishop: the tithes amount to £410, and the gross annual value of the benefice, including glebe, is £540. There is no glebe-house; the glebe comprises 128 Irish acres. The old church was burnt by an accidental fire in 1819, and the present spacious cruciform edifice was erected in 1821, by aid of a grant of £2000 from the late Board of First Fruits. In the R. C. divisions the parish is the head of a union or district comprising also four townlands of the parish of Drummully; there are two chapels, situated at Newtown-Butler and Donagh; the former erected in 1830, at an expense of £400, and latter in 1826, at an expense of £500. There are also places of worship for Wesleyan and Primitive Wesleyan Methodists; the latter is a fine new building, one-half of the expense of which was contributed by J. Butler Danvers, Esq. About 670 children are taught in five national and four other public schools; and there are six private schools, in which are about 540 children, and ten Sunday schools. There are several raths in the parish; and at Mulnagone is a chalybeate spa, strongly impregnated with sulphur, which has been found efficacious in chronic diseases. There are some ruins of old churches on the island of Galloon and also at Donagh. —See Newtown-Butler.

GALLOW, a parish, in the barony of Upper Deece, county of Meath, and province of Leinster, 3 miles (N. N. W.) from Kilcock, on the road to Trim; containing 640 inhabitants. About one-third of it is in tillage, and the remainder is good pasture. The principal seats are Gallow, the residence of W. Maher, Esq.; Clarkstown, of T. Potterton, Esq.; and Ferrans, of I. North, Esq. It is a rectory, in the diocese of Meath, forming part of the union of Raddonstown: the tithes amount to £129. 4. 7. In the R. C. divisions it is part of the union or district of Laracor, or Summerhill. About 25 children are educated in a private school.

GALTRIM, or GAULTRIM, a parish, in the barony of Lower Deece, county of Meath, and province of Leinster, 3 miles (S.) from Summerhill, on the road to Navan; containing 716 inhabitants. This parish comprises 3953 statute acres, of which about two-thirds are under tillage. At Cloneymeath is a quarry of good building stone. Here is a constabulary police station. Galtrim House, a handsome residence in a well planted demesne, is the seat of J. Fox, Esq., who is descended from Magnus Nial, Monarch of Ireland, and is the representative of the Lords of Kilcourcy, to whom Queen Elizabeth granted large possessions. This district was anciently a palatinate: the parish was granted by the Irish parliament, in 1543, to the priory of St. Peter's near Trim. The living is a vicarage, in the diocese of Meath, and in the patronage of Thomas Hussey, Esq.; the rectory is impropriate in Joseph Ashe and George Fisher, Esqrs. The tithes amount to £176. 12. 3., of which £21. 12. 3. is payable to the impropriators and the remainder to the vicar: the great tithes of the townlands of Walterstown and Branganstown, amounting to £35, are payable to the incumbent of Kentstown. The glebe-house, which has a glebe of nine acres, was built by aid of a loan of £300 and a gift of £400, in 1815, from the late Board of First Fruits. The church, which is a neat edifice with a tower, was erected in 1800. In the R. C. divisions it is part of the union or district of Kilmore, or Monalvey, and has a neat plain chapel at Boycetown-bridge. About 70 children are educated in the parochial school, which is partly supported by the vicar and W. Disney, Esq.; and there is a small private school.

GALVOLY.—See BOLY.

GALWAY (County of), a maritime county of the province of Connaught, bounded on the east by the counties of Roscommon, King's county, and Tipperary, from the former of which it is separated by the Suck, and from the two latter by the Shannon; on the north, by those of Roscommon and Mayo; on the west, by the Atlantic Ocean; and on the south, by Galway bay and the county of Clare. It extends from 52° 57′ to 53° 42′ (N. Lat.), and from 7° 53′ to 10° 15′ (W. Lon.); and comprises an area, according to the Ordnance survey, of 1,510,592 acres, of which 955,713 are cultivated land, 476,957 are unprofitable bog and mountain, and 77,922 are under water. The population, in 1821, exclusively of the town and liberties of Galway, which forms a county of itself, was 309,599; and in 1831, 381,564.

In the time of Ptolemy, this region was inhabited by the *Auteri*, who spread themselves also into the adjoining counties of Mayo and Roscommon. At a later, though still a very remote, date it was thus parcelled out among tribes or families; Clanconow, or Clonmacnoon, among the Burkes; Clanfirgail, among the O'Hallorans; Hymaine, among the O'Dalys and O'Kellys; Maghullen, now Moycullen, among the O'Flahertys; Silnamchia, now Longford; and Hy-Fiacria-Aidne, afterwards Clanricarde, possessed by the Burkes, Burghs, or De Bourgos. The Burkes or De Bourgos alone were of Anglo Norman descent, and settled here in consequence of a grant made by Henry III. to Richard de Bourgo, of the whole kingdom of Connaught. A border warfare consequently ensued, and De Bourgo succeeded in securing some of the southern parts of the present county of Galway, making Meelick Castle one of his principal strong-holds. Under this family the towns of Athenry and Galway considerably increased; and in 1333, William de Bourgo, Earl of Ulster, being assassinated, this part of his possessions was seized by a younger male branch of the family, who assumed the Irish title of Mac William Eighter, which was also adopted by his successors, until their acquisition of that of Earl of Clanricarde. Sir William, or Ulick, was the first Mac William Eighter, and from his son Richard was the name of *Clanricarde* first given to his territory and people. The limits of his dominion were extended or curtailed according to the strength of arms possessed by the Anglo-Norman chieftain, but they commonly comprehended the six present baronies of Athenry, Clare, Dunkellin, Kiltartan, Leitrim, and Loughrea. The chief subinfeudators of the De Bourgos were the Birminghams. Another English colony was in the mean time planted in the north-western extremity of the county, now forming the barony of Ross, in the reign of Edward I., by Thomas Joyes or Joyce, who married the daughter of an Irish chieftain: they became tributary to the O'Flaherties, adopting the Irish language and customs; and that part of Connaught is known to the present day by the name of the Joyces' country. The last chieftain of Clanricarde, who bore the title of Mac William Eighter, was Sir William de Burgh, created Earl of Clanricarde by patent of the first of Edward VI. Until the reign of Elizabeth, the county of Galway was regarded as part of the county of Connaught, which comprised all the province of the same name except the county of Roscommon. The present county, therefore, called after the name of its chief town, has no earlier antiquity as a distinct shire than the re-division of Connaught into shire ground by the Lord-Deputy, Sir Henry Sidney, in 1585. At this time, and until the middle of the 17th century, the septs and families possessing the western parts of the county were the O'Flaherties, O'Malleys, and Joyces; the north-eastern districts were held by the Mac David Burkes, and the Birminghams; in the eastern quarter were the O'Naghtens, O'Fallons, O'Kellys, O'Mullallys, O'Dalys, and a branch of the Birminghams; Clanricarde contained, besides the territories immediately held by the Earl, the lands of the O'Heynes, O'Maddens, and O'Shaughnessys; bordering on Lough Corrib were the O'Hallorans; and in the immediate neighbourhood of the town of Galway were the possessions of the Kirwans, Martins, Blakes, Skerrets, Lynches, Frenches, Brownes and Darcys, all mercantile families of that town. In the rebellion of 1641, this county took part with the confederate Catholics, notwithstanding the exertions of the Marquis of Clanricarde. At the termination of the war a great proportion of the landed property passed into the hands of new families, to whom it was confirmed after the Restoration; and the war of the Revolution served but to confirm the change. The whole western portion of the county, between Lough Corrib and the Atlantic Ocean, is frequently called *Connemara*, signifying, "the Bays of the Ocean;" the name, however, is strictly applicable to only one of the three subdivisions of this district; those of the other two are *Iar-Connaught* and *Joyces' country*. These, respectively, are almost conterminous with the three existing baronies of Ballynahinch, Moycullen, and Ross.

The county is partly in the diocese of Killaloe, and partly in those of Elphin, Kilmacduagh, and Clonfert, but chiefly in the archdiocese of Tuam, and contains the episcopal cities of each of the three last-named dioceses within its limits. For purposes of civil jurisdiction it is divided into the baronies of Arran, Athenry, Half Ballymoe, Ballynahinch, Clare, Clonmacnoon, Dunkellin, Dunmore, Kilconnell, Killian, Kiltartan, Leitrim, Longford, Loughrea, Moycullen, Ross, and Tyaquin. It contains, independently of the provincial capital, which forms a separate county, the corporate and market-towns of Tuam and Athenry; the market and post-towns of Loughrea, Eyrecourt, Gort, and Headford; the greater part of the market-town of Ballinasloe; the sea-port and post town of Clifden; and the post-towns of Ahascragh, Aughrim, Castleblakeney, Dunmore, Portumna, Oranmore, Craughwell, Oughterard, Kilconnell, Monivae, and Dangan. The largest among its numerous villages are Mount Bellew, Woodford, Kinvarra, and Mount-Shannon. Prior to the Union, it sent six representatives to the Irish parliament, two for the county at large, and two for each of the boroughs of Tuam and Athenry; since that period, its sole representatives, exclusive of those of the town of Galway, have been the two sent by the county to the Imperial Parliament; the members are elected at Galway. The constituency, in January 1836, was, freeholders, 364 of £50, 224 of £20, and 3053 of £10; clergymen, registering out of their respective incumbencies, 24 of £50, 5 of £20, and 3 of £10; rent-chargers, 5 of £50, and 9 of £20; making a total of 3687 registered electors. The county is included in the Connaught circuit: the assizes are held at Galway, and general sessions of the peace are held twice in the year at each of the towns of Loughrea, Tuam, Eyrecourt, and Gort. The county court-house and gaol are in Galway; and there are bridewells at Clifden, Eyrecourt, Loughrea, Tuam, Woodford, Ballinasloe, and Gort. The number of persons charged with criminal offences and committed, in 1835, was 651. The local government is vested in a lord-lieutenant, 21 deputy-lieutenants, and 157 magistrates, besides whom there are the usual county officers, including four coroners. There are 99 constabulary police stations, in which are a force consisting of 12 chief constables, 122 constables, 540 sub-constables, and 15 horses: the expense of its maintenance is defrayed partly by the county and partly by the government. There is also a peace preservation police of one magistrate, one chief constable, 13 constables, 42 sub-constables, and 4 horses. The county infirmary and fever hospital is at Galway, and there is a fever hospital at Ballinasloe, where also is the district lunatic asylum for Connaught; and there are dispensaries at Claran Bridge, Dunmore, Ballymoe, Portumna, Tuam, Loughrea, Ballinasloe, Kiltulla, Headford, Ahascragh, Clifden, Ballygar, Miltown, Killane, Monivea, Glanmodda, Oughterard, Gort, Killyan, and Eyrecourt, maintained by private subscriptions and Grand Jury presentments. The total amount of the Grand Jury presentments, for the year 1835, was £43,938. 8. 7¼., of which £1443. 0. 6½. was for the public roads and bridges of the county at large; £11,197. 3. 1¼. for the public roads, being the baronial charge; £12,905. 7. 9. for public establishments, officers' salaries, buildings, &c., and £14,022. 7. 5½. for the police. In the military arrangements the county is included in the western district, except Mount-Shannon, which is in the south-western; and contains six barrack stations, three for cavalry at Loughrea, Gort, and Dunmore, two for infantry at Ballinasloe and Oughterard, and one for artillery at Mount-Shannon, affording in the whole accommodation for 21 officers and 415 men.

Lough Corrib divides the county into two unequal portions, which differ very considerably from each other in several important points; the eastern is, for the most part, fertile, and comparatively level; the western is rugged, mountainous, and barren. The former of these, with the exception of the Slievebaughta mountains, which separate it from Clare, is generally flat and uninteresting. A very fine vein of land, supposed by some to be a continuation of the Golden Vale of the south, proceeds from Gort by Loughrea to Aughrim and Ballinasloe; and in the northern part, about Dunmore, the country is exceedingly picturesque, being highly diversified with hill and dale, and mostly rich pasture or tillage. The land between Oranmore and Monivae exhibits a sterile surface, covered with short heath and fern, yet with a substratum of limestone gravel. Amongst the mountains of the western portion, those of Benabola, commonly called the Twelve Pins, are the most elevated: they lie midway between Lough Corrib and Aghris point, in a western direction, and between Birtirbuy and Killery bays, in a northern, covering a space of about six miles square, and consist of two ranges or groups connected by the elevated pass of Maam Ina. Knockenhiggeen, the highest, is 2400 feet high. The cliff on the south side of Glen Ina is particularly grand, being a naked perpendicular precipice of about 1200 feet, over which a considerable sheet of water falls. On the east of the same vale, a chain of hills proceeds along the boundary of the barony of Ross: the passes through which are known by the name of Maam, a term also used in the highlands of Scotland; they are called Maam-Turk in the north of Derbyshire. But the western district, although mountainous, is not an upland country like Wicklow. At least three-fourths of Connemara proper are less than 100 feet above the level of the sea. Great part of Iar-Connaught rises from the shore of Galway bay, by a gentle elevation to about 300 feet, at the upper edge of which there are some hills of about 700 feet, and beyond them a low limestone country, to the edge of Lough Corrib, which is but little elevated above the level of that lake. Joyces' country, on the other hand, is an elevated tract, with flat-topped mountains from 900 to 2000 feet high, and intersected by deep and narrow valleys. The entire western part of the county is justly regarded as one of the most uncultivated parts of Ireland, presenting in a general view a continuous tract of bog and mountain; the quantity of arable land not amounting to one-fiftieth of the whole; yet the greater portion of it is capable of being reclaimed, being every where covered with a surface of peat, with a declivity sufficient for drainage, and intersected by numerous layers of limestone rock, thus affording an inexhaustible supply of material for the best manure, and of that of fuel for its preparation.

Of the lakes, of which there are upwards of 150 of every size, the largest and most interesting is Lough Corrib, covering a surface of upwards of 30,000 acres. It derives its origin from several streams in Joyces' country, and assuming the form and magnitude of a lake near Castlekirk island, spreads to a considerable breadth near Cong where it has a subterranean communication with Lough Mask, in the county of Mayo, from which it is about two miles distant: it narrows at the ferry of Knock, and again suddenly expands, until, about two miles from Galway, it assumes the character of a river, which it retains to the sea. It receives several large rivers, and at its outlet seems to be fully equal to the Shannon, at Athlone, but more rapid. The islands in it comprehend together about 1000 acres: they are Inchiquin, Inishrater, Inishnavoe, Island Shendela, Inishgall, and Inishdarus, inhabited; and Castlekirk, Ennisdavey, Ennisrobin, and St. Francis's, uninhabited. Its level is about fourteen feet above high water mark, and it rises about three feet in floods. This lake is navigable from its head down to Galway, and a plan for a water communication by means of lockage, between it and the sea, has been estimated at a cost of £13,000. Between the mountains of Maam and Galway bay, a line of lakes, 27 in number, extends in a westerly direction from Oughterard to Ballynahinch, a distance of 23 miles; the principal are Loughs Fuogh, Baffin, Derryclare, Uriel, Poulnagopple, and Ballynahinch, which latter empties itself into the bay of Birtirbuy. Loughrea, situated near the road from Dublin to Galway, and giving name to a barony and a large town, is remarkable as well for its extent as for its picturesque scenery. Lough Ross is in Joyces' country; it receives the waters of several rivers and numerous mountain streams, yet has no visible outlet; there are numerous small but very interesting lakes near Roundstone, scattered over various parts. Lough Mask is bounded on the whole of its western shores by the county of Galway; a high ridge of land, about three miles in breadth, separates it from Lough Corrib. A subterraneous communication between these lakes serves as a vent for the waters of the former, the whole of which, after passing through a series of extensive caverns, rises again in numerous magnificent springs near Cong; and, after turning several mills, hastens by a rapid course to mingle with the waters of Lough Corrib. Some tracts, called Turloughs, which are dry in summer, assume the appearance of lakes in winter, owing to their outlets being insufficient to discharge their accumulated water. The largest is that of Turloughmore, which covers a large tract near Tuam; the next in extent is near Rahasane; and there are several smaller. They maintain seven or eight sheep to the acre, for about four months in summer, but in wet seasons are scarcely of any value.

The coast from Killery bay to the county of Clare presents a bold line of cliffs indented by numerous fine bays and inlets, many of which are adequate to receive vessels of every description. After passing Renville point, at the north of Killery, the harbour of Ballynakill presents itself, capable of accommodating large ships, and protected by Truchelaun or Heath island. The bay of Claggan, about two miles in length, is more open than the preceding, though protected in some degree by the island of Innisbofin. From Claggan to Aghris cape, the most western point of the county, the shore is low, and near it are Crua, High, and Friar islands, exhibiting only a few monastic ruins. Streamstown is a long inlet, narrow and dangerous, and, therefore, frequented only by smugglers: at some distance from it is Omey island, and within it are the cultivated islands of Tarbert and Innisturk. Ardbear harbour branches into two inlets, the northern of which terminates at the rising town of Clifden; the southern enjoys the benefit of a salmon fishery. Mannin bay, though extensive, is but little frequented by large vessels; but a good kelp shore and a valuable herring fishery bring many boats to it occasionally. Between it and Roundstone bay is the peninsula of Bunowen, terminating at Slyne Head. From Slyne Head, where two lighthouses have been erected, the coast turns eastward to Roundstone bay, the entrance to which is sheltered by the islands of Innisnee and Innislacken. Near its mouth is the new village of Roundstone: this harbour could shelter the whole navy of England. The boggy peninsula of Rosrua intervenes between Roundstone and Birtirbuy bays, which latter, though deep and with good anchorage, is little frequented: in the offing is the island of Cruanakely, used as a deer-park. The islands of Masa, Mynish, and Finish, south of this peninsula, are inhabited by a population actively engaged in the kelp trade and the fisheries. In Elanmacdara are some curious monastic remains. Kilkerran bay has a most productive kelp shore, of nearly one hundred miles in extent, including those of its islands, although the direct distance across its mouth to the western point of Costello bay is but eight miles. A series of fords, passable on foot at low water, but navigable for boats during the height of the tide, connects the islands of Garomna, Littermore, Littermullen, Knappagh, and Furrinish, which lie on its eastern coast: between Garomna and the peninsula of Killeen is Greatman's bay, a safe harbour for vessels of moderate draught. Caslah or Costello bay, to the east of Killeen, is the most eastern of the harbours of Connemara. This district, therefore, exhibits some very extraordinary features: it contains upwards of twenty safe and capacious harbours, fit for vessels of any burden, about 25 navigable lakes in the interior, each a mile or more in length, besides more than 100 smaller, and commands a coast line, including that of its islands, of not less than 400 miles. South of the county is Galway bay, having its entrance protected by the islands of Arran, described under their own head, and including the minor harbours of Oranmore, Renville or New harbour, one of the finest stations along the coast, having a natural pier with 14 feet of water at ebb tide, improved and deepened by an artificial structure. Further south are Kilcolgan Point, whence the first Marquess of Clanrickard took his final departure from Ireland during the troubles of 1641; Kinvara harbour, protected by Edey island; and the peninsula of Duras, with which is connected that of Aghnish, a detached portion of Clare, which county forms the southern boundary of this magnificent bay.

The climate, though subject to storms and rain, is peculiarly healthful; the prevalence of disease being more attributable to the habits of the humbler classes than to the influence of the atmosphere. Frost or snow seldom lies long on the western coast, and cattle of every kind remain out during the winter; but the summers are commonly wet. The soil of the eastern portion is in general suited to every kind of crop, and produces wheat of the best description, particularly to the south of Galway. Much of the land, however, being light and rocky, is better adapted for sheep-feeding. The northern parts near Tuam improve in quality, and still further north they are all rich pasture or excellent tillage ground. On the south shore of Lough Corrib, where cultivation has made the greatest progress, the arable land is interspersed with extensive tracts of naked limestone rock, of a most desolate aspect; and it appears to be only by incessant exertions that a few patches of soil have been won from the general waste. These spots are, nevertheless, of the greatest fertility, and the pasturage among the rocks is peculiarly fine. The other parts of Connemara are for the most part barren moors, consisting of bog of various depths, upon a bottom of primitive rock of difficult decomposition, and affording little soil; but several beds of limestone run through the country, and are distinguishable by the verdure in their vicinity. For improving the lands of this district there are convenient banks of shell and coral sand on all the coast, especially in the bays of Kilkerran, Birtirbuy, Bunown, and Mannin: that of Kilkerran, Birtirbuy, and Mannin is pure coralline.

Wheat is the crop at which the farmer mostly aims, and it is always sown after potatoes, except in moory soils, when oats form the succession. The want of manure for potatoes is supplied by hiring land and paring and burning the surface: the ground is skinned, or scrawed by a spade, sharp and broad at the end, with a considerable bend in the blade to prevent the necessity of stooping. Where sea weed is used, the potatoes are planted on it after it has dried; as, when used fresh, it injures the potatoe sets. A dry spring always ensures a plentiful crop of potatoes; a wet one, on the contrary, is the usual forerunner of scarcity. On the sea coast corallines are also used for manure, the succession being potatoes, wheat, oats, and, in sandy soils, barley, and then potatoes with a fresh manuring. In many places on the sea coast, very fine early potatoes are raised in several feet of pure sea sand, manured by sea weed, and after that fine barley, which is mostly consumed by the innumerable private stills of Connemara. The small farmers or cottiers till almost exclusively with the spade. Crops of every kind on the lands of cottiers are generally carefully weeded. The chief markets for grain are Galway, Loughrea, Tuam, Ballinasloe, Gort, Eyrecourt, Mount Bellew, and Clifden; they are well supplied. The numerous flour-mills lately established have tended much to increase and improve the cultivation of wheat. Among the green crops, the use of which is daily extending, that of fiorin is peculiarly encouraged, as being found among the most productive and congenial to the soil. Pasturage is carried on to a great extent. Heathy sheep-walks occupy a tract of dreary country ten miles square, between Monivae and Galway. A considerable quantity of pasture is obtained from the turloughs, particularly the Turloughmore: there is also an extensive range of many miles between Athenry and Ardrahan, stretching down to the sea at Kinvarra, chiefly occupied by sheep: the baronies of Ballynahinch, Ross, and Moycullen, are all under pasture, with the exception of patches of tillage in the valleys. To many farms large tracts of moory bottom are attached, which, if judiciously drained, a process as yet but ill understood and little practised, would amply repay the outlay.

Agriculture as a system is in a backward state, except in the neighbourhood of Ballinasloe, Tuam, Hollymount, and Gort, where the rotation and green crop systems have been introduced. The barony of Kiltartan has also made rapid strides in this respect since 1833, at which time the first clover and vetches were sown; they are generally cut and carried away as green fodder. The deepest and best soils in the county are around Ballymoe and Tyaquin. In most of the eastern portion of the county the iron plough and light angular harrow are generally used; but the land is never ploughed sufficiently deep, the antiquated system of merely turning up the old soil being adhered to: in most parts grain of every kind is sown too late, hence it sustains great injury in wet seasons. Hay is rarely cut till the month of September, and even then very injudiciously managed; the greater quantity of hay is produced on low meadows, here called Callows, where it is put up in large cocks in the field and suffered to remain until November; hence it is always much injured with rain and liable to be washed away by the autumnal floods. Although the iron plough is very general, the old wooden plough is retained in many places. Threshing and winnowing machines are sometimes seen, but only with the gentry. One-horse carts with spoke wheels are so general that the old solid wooden-wheeled car is now seldom seen, and the slide car never. Waggons of a very superior construction, drawn by two horses abreast, are frequent in the neighbourhood of Galway. In Connemara, Iar-Connaught, and Joyces' Country, wheeled vehicles are almost unknown; everything, even to the manure and grain, being carried upon the backs of men or horses. Dairy farms are by no means general, but a good deal of butter is made, particularly at Barna, in the neighbourhood of Galway. Farms are of every size; those of large extent are mostly in the mountains, and used for pasturing young and store cattle; they are always held in bulk. Those in the valleys and on the sea coast are mostly small, but in the plain, or eastern portions of the county, the size of the farms varies from 20 to 200 acres. The principal manure is the surface of the turbary, called black bog or moreen, carried home in baskets, spread over the yard, and mixed with dung, clay, or gravel. Another manure is ashes, produced by burning the surface sod, as already noticed. Coralline, commonly called oyster bank sand, is used in Connemara, with the best effect: wet moory land has been converted by it into rich meadow, mostly of fiorin grass, which has continued to throw up a fine sward for forty years. Lime and limestone gravel, found in the escars is much used, particularly to the south of Galway. Sea-weed of every kind is applied to the soil as manure, particularly for potatoes and vegetables: its effect is powerful but transient. Irrigation is little practised. The fences are walls, formerly of dry stones rudely piled up, but latterly more carefully built, from 3 to 6 feet high, and topped with sods; the clearing of the ground generally supplies the materials. Ditches are not common. The breed of black cattle has been greatly improved within the last few years. The favourite stock is a cross between the Durham and the old long-horned native cow: the cross between the old Leicester bull and the native thrives well in hilly and exposed situations. The old Irish cow is still seen. Sheep are also a very favourite stock: the new Leicester, first introduced by Mr. Taaffe, is peculiarly prized both for carcass and fleece. The cross between the new Leicester and the native sheep, though not so large as the preceding, is celebrated for the flavour of its mutton; its wool, though short, is good. The South-down sheep have degenerated, the fleece becoming short and coarse. The fairs of Ballinasloe, which are particularly noticed in the article on that place, regulate the prices of sheep and black cattle throughout Ireland. The character of the Galway horses, both as roadsters and hunters, has been long celebrated. Connemara was famed for its breed of small hardy horses, but they have latterly lost character in consequence of an injudicious cross with large stallions; the genuine breed is now extremely scarce. Pigs are numerous, and of every variety of breed. Goats are frequently met with, but not in flocks. The old red deer is sometimes seen in the mountains of Connemara and Joyces' Country, but the race is almost extinct.

The quantity of large full-grown timber found in the bogs proves that the county, though now nearly bare, was once well wooded: the hilly districts abound more in bog timber than the plain country. The trees most usually found are oak and fir, the latter of which is manufactured into ropes, which resist damp better than those of hemp. Yew of considerable size and finely grained is frequently found. Another proof that the soil is well adapted for the growth of timber may be drawn from the fact, that in almost every dry knoll or cliff the oak, beech, and hazel may be found shooting up in abundance, when not checked by the destructive browsing of goats. The plantations at present are mostly confined to skreens round gentlemen's demesnes. Although the county now exhibits such tracts of neglected waste, several attempts on a large scale to improve its natural advantages have been made. A farming society was formerly held at Loughrea; the Farming Society of Ireland held its great annual meeting at Ballinasloe till its dissolution; and the newly formed Agricultural Society of Ireland holds one of its periodical meetings in the same town. The general fuel of the county is turf, of which the stores contained in the bogs of the western districts are deemed inexhaustible, and great quantities are taken by boats to the county of Clare, as well as to the isles of Arran, and the inner shores of Galway bay. The only parts where any scarcity of this fuel is experienced are in the districts bordering on the shores of Galway bay, and in the line from the town of Galway to Athenry and Monivae: the use of sea coal is almost confined to the town of Galway.

In a geological point of view the county may be considered as divided into two great regions, the limestone and the granite: the high road from Galway to Oughterard nearly marks the division, which is also discernible to the eye of an intelligent observer by the decline of the verdant hue that enlivens the former. The country north and east of this boundary line is limestone; that to the south and west, with a few minor exceptions, is granite. The Slievebaughta mountains are silicious; the great group of Benabola chiefly quartz: Poulacopple mountain is hornblende. Between Ballynakill bay and Ardbear is a tract of mica slate and quartz interspersed with veins of primitive limestone. The same formation runs through the hills to Oughterard; it contains very beautiful serpentine and verd antique. The largest deposit of it is in the centre of the Benabola group, where it is nearly unattainable in consequence of the difficulty of conveyance; but the most valuable quarries are at Bawnanoran and Lissouter, near the head of Birtirbuy, whence the splendid chimney-piece presented to Geo. IV., and now in the Carlton Club House, was taken. A quarry at Letterlough contains a marble of a deep green porphyritic substance, unique in character and appearance. Lead ore has been found in many places, nodules of which of very pure quality are frequently met with in the mountain streams, and along the sea shore. Iron ore was extensively worked, while timber was plentiful for smelting it. At a quarry at Dunmore, millstones are made, said to be superior to those of France. A crystalline sand, of very superior quality for scythe boards, occurs at Lough Coutra, for which mowers come from twenty miles' distance. Manganese has been found in Slieve-an-oir, near the border of Clare. The limestone, except that of Connemara, contains fossil remains in various quantities, from that of Oughterard, disfigured by sections of large shells, to the beautiful marbles of Angliham, Menlo, Renville, and Merlin Park, near Galway, which are of a fine black, nearly pure, and highly prized in England and in Dublin. At Ballyleigh, near Gort, a fine black marble has long been used; some of superior quality is found near Athenry; and a very beautiful grey marble has been discovered at Woodbrook. Near Ardfry, and in Mr. D'Arcy's demesne, in Connemara, large beds of oyster shells may be seen many feet above high water mark.

Coarse linen was formerly manufactured to some extent: it was generally of the kind called bandle linen, but the fabric was not good. The principal markets for it were Loughrea and Tuam, where also a considerable quantity of linen yarn was sold. A diaper manufacture flourished for some time, but is also extinct. In Connemara some fine linen was manufactured, and a large quantity of coarse, the latter chiefly for domestic use. Canvas for bags is in good demand; a very coarse kind is bought at Tuam, for packing wool: large quantities also are sent to Cork, Waterford, and Limerick, for packing bacon for exportation. The woollen manufacture consists chiefly of flannels and friezes for home sale. A considerable quantity of white friezes and caddow blankets is manufactured and sold at Galway and Loughrea, and in the neighbourhood of the former of these towns flannels are woven to a large extent. Knit woollen stockings are made and sold in Connemara, to the amount of nearly £10,000 per annum: the wool is peculiarly fine, and they possess a much greater degree of softness and elasticity than any woven stocking, but from being made only of a single thread, they afford but little wear. The manufacture of kelp, commenced about the year 1700, was very general, and tolerably productive: when first exported it sold from 14*s.* to 16*s.* per ton, and gradually rose in price to £13 per ton: about 10,000 tons of it were annually made in Connemara, but the removal of the duty on salt has nearly destroyed the trade, and the weed is now sold as manure. Paper is manufactured in the town of Galway, and a good deal of it sent to the Dublin market. There is also in that town a considerable manufacture of black marble chimney-pieces, much prized as being wholly free from white marks. Tobacco pipes and coarse pottery are also made there, and at Creggs and Dunsandle. Coarse felt hats and straw bonnets are made at Loughrea, and some other places. The trade in grain employs 23 flour-mills, six oatmeal-mills, and two malt-mills in Galway town alone; and there are twelve other large flour-mills in different places. After supplying the home demand, the rest of the produce is sent to Dublin, to the amount of about 12,000 tons annually, from the Galway mills.

A valuable source of employment to this county is its fisheries, which, however, notwithstanding the abundance of fish on its coasts, have heretofore scarcely sufficed to supply the home demand, owing to the want of skill and systematic industry among the fishermen. The fishery for the basking shark, commonly called the sun-fish, commences in April, and continues for about six weeks: a single fish produces from four to twelve barrels, each of 30 gallons, of oil; but the boats engaged are few, and too small to venture into deep water, yet even under this defective system the fishery produces oil of the value of several thousand pounds annually. The cod and ling fishery commences in February, when these fish approach the shore from the great bank that lies seven or eight leagues from the land; the quantity of ling exceeds that of cod, in the proportion of five to one. The herring fishery commences at a later period than formerly, and is said to be less productive: the season now begins in February or March, and during its continuance all other fishing is nearly abandoned. When it commences at Galway, almost the entire of the male population of the neighbouring villages flock to the shore to assist, and have a certain share of the profits. Five thousand herrings are reckoned a middling night's capture for one boat: all that are taken are sold to supply the home demand, which is so far from being satisfied that many cargoes are brought from the north-west coast. Sometimes several men join in a boat and nets for this fishery, many of whom are tradesmen in different branches, who at this period abandon their usual occupations. The bay of Galway abounds with every kind of fish, including shell-fish, and the white fishery might consequently be made of considerable value. There are about 500 fishing-boats belonging to the bay, besides 200 or 250 belonging to the Claddagh village, near the town. Lobsters are generally in great abundance; on some parts of the coast they are put into holes in the rocks that are covered at half ebb, and fed to a large size with fish and other food. At the falls of Ballinahinch, between the lake of that name and the bay of Roundstone, is a very valuable salmon fishery, being the most profitable in Ireland, except those of Ballina and Coleraine: there is another at Galway, between Lough Corrib and the sea, and a third at the head of the Killery; and there is in Lough Corrib abundance of trout, especially the much-esteemed gillaroo trout. Oysters of superior quality abound on the coast of Connemara, and all round the bay of Galway, and are in season nearly the whole year. Pearls of great beauty, but not very large, have been taken from the pearl muscles in several rivers, particularly near Oughterard.

The Suck is the principal river: it receives the Shiven at Muckenagh, and near Ballinasloe the Ahascragh from the west, and joins the Shannon at Shannon bridge: its course is in general very sluggish, and it does much damage every year by overflowing its banks. The canal from Ballinasloe to the Shannon, an extension of the Grand Canal from Dublin, is chiefly fed from this river. The Shannon borders only a small portion of the eastern side of the county, between the confluence of the Suck and Mount Shannon, separating it from the King's county and Tipperary. The Black river, or Shruel, empties itself into Lough Corrib, as does also the Moyne: both these rivers are subject to inundations; and the former sinks into the ground through an aperture called a swallow, at a short distance from the town of Shruel, but soon emerges through several large springs. The Carnamart passes through the southern part of the county, and empties itself into the eastern extremity of the bay of Galway. The Ballynahinch river has a short but rapid course from the Twelve Pins mountains to Birtirbuy bay. The roads are numerous, and generally in excellent repair; the materials for making them being everywhere abundant and good. The principal lines are the mail-coach roads from Dublin to Galway, and to Tuam, Castlebar, and Westport, which intersect the county from east to west. Several new lines have been lately made through the western part. One line, commencing at Oughterard, proceeds by the lakes to Ballinahinch and Clifden, with numerous lines branching from it into the centre of the mountains. Another line passes from Clifden by Streamstown, Ballynakil, Kilmore, and Killery, into the county of Mayo, with several branch lines leading chiefly to the coast. These lines, with their several branches, extend through a distance of 127 miles, and although they are carried through the midst of the mountainous district, they seldom deviate from the level.

There are seven ancient round towers in the county; at Kilmacduagh, Ballygaddy, Kilbannon, Meelick, Roscam Murrough, and Ardrahan. Raths are numerous: a very fine ruin of this kind is to be seen in Arranmore. Cromlechs are also found in several places; one in good preservation in the demesne of Marble hill, another near Dunsandle, and another of very curious construction at Monument hill, near Loughrea. The remains of ancient monastic buildings are very numerous, and are noticed in the accounts of the places where they are respectively situated: the most celebrated is that of the Cistercian monastery at Knockmoy, about six miles from Tuam. Ancient castles are also numerous; some of them are in ruins, and others still kept in repair, as places of residence. Between Gort and Kilmacduagh are the remains of a round castle, a style of architecture uncommon in such buildings.

The seats of the opulent gentry are very numerous and well built, and are noticed in the articles on their respective parishes. Those of the farmers are of very defective construction; the floors are generally below the level of the soil; the windows small and often stopped up, so that the light enters only through the door; the offices badly constructed and arranged. The dwellings of the peasantry are still worse, often of dry stones or of sods, and thatched: this description applies more forcibly to the western part of the county, though even there and in other parts there are many laudable exceptions. In Connemara proper and Joyces' Country the population is thinly scattered along the coast, and by the sides of the old rugged roads; in Iar-Connaught it is dense, and the holders of land in better circumstances than those of the preceding districts, who combine fishing with farming; yet throughout the whole of the three districts there is scarcely a comfortable house, and the habits and appearance of the families, who have means sufficient to improve their condition, are little better than that of those of the indigent. The food is invariably the potato, with fish in Connemara, where also cows are a frequent appendage to the small farmer's homestead, as is a cabbage garden to his cottage. The clothing is of home-made frieze for the men: flannel jackets and petticoats, generally of blue and dark red, were the prevailing dress of the women, but they are giving way to cottons. The men in winter generally wear shoes and stockings, also home made; the women frequently go barefooted. Beer is now much more in demand than formerly. Unlicensed whiskey is still made in great quantities in the mountainous districts. The lower classes exhibit the strongest proofs of industry, when working for themselves, as is shewn by their care in clearing the ground of stones, and in the reclamation of bog, when they are secured in a profitable tenure. The use of the English language is daily increasing in all parts. The Irish language, however, is said to be still spoken better here than in any other part of the island, both with respect to idiom and pronunciation. The crying at funerals, the attendance at wakes, and other old customs are still preserved. The county almost everywhere abounds with springs of the purest water; those of Eyrecourt and Kilconnel abbey are peculiarly celebrated. A spring near the rocky summit of Knocknae is never dry. The most remarkable of the mineral springs, which are numerous and mostly chalybeate, are at Oughterard, Kiltulla, and Kingston; the last is pronounced by Kirwan to be one of the best in Europe: another near Dunsandle is much frequented. At the village of Quose is a well which instantly kills poultry that drink of its water. A spa between Clonfert and Laurencetown has been used with great effect in liver complaints; that at Oughterard attracts many invalids thither. Those at Athenry, Rathglass, near Kilconnel, Woodbrook, Killimor, Abbert, and Hampstead, are all of high repute in their respective neighbourhoods. The county gives the title of Viscount to a branch of the Arundel family, resident in England. The title of Marquess of Clanricarde expired with the first Marquess, who died without male issue, but the earldom descended to another branch of the family of De Burgh, which enjoys it to the present day, and to which the Marquesate was restored by patent, in 1825.

Seal

GALWAY, a sea-port, borough, and market-town, and a county of itself, locally between the baronies of Clare, Dunkellin, and Moycullin, county of Galway, and province of Connaught, 51¼ miles (N.N.W.) from Limerick, and 101¼ (W. by S.) from Dublin, on the bay of Galway; containing 33,120 inhabitants. Though few particulars of its early history are recorded, this place appears to have been regarded from a very remote period as a position of great importance. In the first division of Ireland, ascribed to Partholan, it was one of the chief points of partition; and in the subsequent division of the island between Heber and Heremon, adopted by Conn of the Hundred Battles and Eogan, King of Munster, it was fixed upon as the western termination of that line of demarcation, of which Dublin was the eastern extremity. There is every reason for supposing it to be identical with the *Nagnata*, or *Naguata*, of Ptolemy, described as the principal city on the western coast. Baxter adopts this opinion, from its original name, "*Cuan-na-guactie*," signifying in the Irish language "the port of the small islands," descriptive of its situation both with respect to the isles of Arran at the mouth of the bay, and to the smaller islets in the more immediate vicinity of the town. The power of the Danes having been destroyed by the decisive battle of Clontarf, the people of the surrounding district, aware of the importance of its situation, erected a strong castle for its defence; which so powerfully excited the jealousy of the people of Munster, that Conor, king of that province, in 1132, despatched a body of troops and levelled it with the ground. In 1149, the town and castle, the latter of which had been restored, were taken and destroyed by Turlough O'Brien, King of Munster; but they appear to have soon revived, for, in 1154, the ships of "Galway Dune" were sent to the northern part of the island; and it is recorded that, in 1161, strange ships were seen in the harbour, and that the town took fire; the Annals of Innisfallen notice also another conflagration, in 1170. At the time of the English invasion, the town contained only a few families and some fishermen under the protection of the O'Flahertys, who then held the castle and the surrounding territory. The first notice of it that occurs after that event is the return of Feidlim O'Conor, King of Connaught, from the English court, whither he had gone to lay before the English monarch his complaints against Richard de Burgo. Hugh O'Flaherty, embracing the cause of Feidlim, fortified the castle of Galway, and in 1230 baffled every attempt of De Burgo to dispossess him; but on the defeat of Feidlim, about two years after, the town and castle fell into the hands of De Burgo, who, though he lost them again for a short time, ultimately recovered them, and made this place his principal residence and the capital of the province; he secured it with additional fortifications, and established a municipal government under a magistrate of his own appointment. In 1270, the erection of walls for the defence of the town was commenced, and continued at intervals, by grants for that purpose, till the end of that century, when they were completed. The increased security of the place encouraged the influx of strangers, among whom was a number of new settlers, consisting of 13, or according to some, 14 families, known under the appellation of the "tribes of Galway," who enriched themselves by commerce and the purchase of lands.

The town, which rapidly increased in commerce, so as to surpass the rival city of Limerick, was, in 1312, strengthened by the erection of the great gate, and additional works under the superintendence of Nicholas Lynch, surnamed the "Black Marshall." On the death of William de Burgo, the third earl, who was assassinated by his own servants, a great change took place. That nobleman leaving only a daughter, the heads of the two younger branches of the family, fearing the alienation of the estates by marriage, threw off their allegiance, and, adopting the Irish customs, assumed the native titles of Mac William Eighter and Mac William Oughter; the former took possession of the town, with the territory towards the Shannon, and led the inhabitants into revolt; but on his returning to his allegiance, tranquillity was restored. In 1375, by grant of a charter of the staple, the merchants of Galway and Connaught were permitted for three years to pay the customs due to the Crown at Galway, which was thus placed on an equality with the cities of Cork, Dublin, and Waterford. In 1396, the town, which had hitherto exercised its corporate privileges only by prescription, obtained from Rich. II. a perpetual grant of the customs for the repair of the walls, and also a charter of incorporation, confering many privileges, which charter was confirmed in 1402, by Hen. IV. A licence for coining, which had been hitherto confined to Dublin and Trim, was, about this time, granted to Galway by statute, specifying the value and character of the coins to be struck. During the reigns of Hen. VI. and Edw. IV., the commerce of the port extended to many parts of Europe, particularly to France and Spain, whence large quantities of wine were imported. In 1484, a new charter was granted to the town, vesting its government in a mayor and bailiffs, and expressly ordaining that neither the Lord Mac William of Clanricarde, nor any of his family, should exercise any authority within its limits. In 1493 occurred the melancholy execution by the mayor, James Lynch Fitzstephen, of his own son, for murder, whom, to prevent an intended rescue, he caused to be hanged from a window of his house, under which are carved a skull and cross bones in memory of the tragical event.

During the reign of Hen. VIII., frequent disputes between the inhabitants and the men of Limerick arose from a feeling of rivalry, which were eventually terminated by treaty, and to their instigation did the former attribute the revival of a claim made on them by the Earl of Ormonde for prisage of wine, from which they had been previously exempt. The question, however, was decided in favour of Galway by the court of star chamber; the decision was of the highest importance to its merchants, who at that time supplied nearly the whole kingdom with wine, for which purpose they had vaults at Athboy, of which the remains are still to be seen. A royal ordinance was issued at the same time, by which the merchants of Galway were prohibited from forestalling the markets of Limerick; and in 1545 a new charter was granted, defining the limits of the port, which were made to extend from the isles of Arran to the town, and permitting the exportation of all goods and merchandise, except woollens and linens, with exemption from prisage and a confirmation of all former privileges. Edw. VI. granted a confirmatory charter, and the town continued to increase in prosperity; but the tyranny of Sir Edw. Fitton, the first President of Connaught, having excited an insurrection, it was harassed by the incursions of the neighbouring septs, and many of the principal inhabitants were induced to seek protection from Mac William Eighter. In 1579, the inhabitants received a charter from Elizabeth, with reversionary leases of the dissolved monasteries, the fisheries, the cocket, and lands of the value of 100 marks; but a few years after the Earl of Ormonde re-asserted his claim to the prisage of wine, which was allowed by the court of chancery. About the year 1594, Hugh Roe O'Donell having destroyed Enniskillen and burnt Athenry, appeared before the town, and being refused a supply of provisions, set fire to the suburbs, but retreated without doing further injury. In 1600, Lord Mountjoy erected a strong fort on the hill where the Augustinian monastery stood, which completely commanded the town and the harbour; and soon after the accession of Jas. I., the town and lands within a distance of two miles round it were by charter constituted a distinct county, of which the Earl of Clanricarde was appointed governor, with powers equal to those he exercised as President of Connaught.

Soon after the commencement of the war in 1641, the inhabitants joined the parliamentarians, and the Earl of Clanricarde invested the town and speedily reduced it to submission; but his exertions to retain it for the king were frustrated by the violence of Capt. Willoughby, commander of the fort, which induced the people to open their gates to the enemy. In the course of the war, Rinuncini, the pope's nuncio, took refuge here and embarked for Rome. From the great numbers that fled to the town for shelter during this period of intestine war, the plague broke out in July, 1649, and raged with violence till the April following, during which time 3700 of the inhabitants fell victims to its ravages. The Marquess of Clanricarde, wishing to borrow £20,000 for the king's service, offered the revenues of Galway and Limerick to the Duke of Lorraine as security, but the negociation failed. On this occasion a large and very accurate map of the town was drawn and engraved, two copies of which are still extant. In 1652, the town was invested by the parliamentary forces under Sir C. Coote, when Preston, the Irish commander of the garrison, having quitted it and embarked for France, the inhabitants surrendered on condition of retaining their privileges, the liberation of all native prisoners without ransom, and the restoration of all captured property. On the proclamation of Richard Cromwell, as protector, in 1658, so great a tumult was excited that the corporation was threatened with the loss of its charter. In 1690, the town was put into a state of defence, and garrisoned for Jas. II. by three companies of foot and a troop of horse, and in the following year three companies more were added, and the Protestant inhabitants removed into the western suburbs. After the battle of Aughrim, Gen. De Ginkell, with 14,000 of William's army, laid siege to it; after holding out for some time it surrendered on the 20th of July, 1691, on condition of a safe conduct for the garrison to Limerick, and a free pardon for the inhabitants, with preservation of their property and privileges. The works raised by both armies were levelled, the fort near the town was repaired, and a new one erected on Mutton Island, in the bay, for the protection of the harbour. Previously to the disturbances of 1798, 400 of the inhabitants formed themselves into eight companies of volunteers, for the preservation of the peace of the town; and on the landing of the French at Kilcummin bay, the merchants supplied Gen. Hutchinson with money, which enabled him to join Gen. Lake with the garrison and yeomanry of the town, who consequently shared in the defeat at Castlebar.

The town is most advantageously situated at the head of the spacious bay to which it gives name, and at the mouth of a river issuing from Lough Corrib, which, after a winding course from that lake through the town, falls into the bay. It consists of several streets, in general narrow, and it is in contemplation to appropriate, under parliamentary sanction, a portion of the municipal revenue for its improvement. A gas company has lately been formed to light the town, and the works are in progress. Early in the present century the greater portion of the town walls was levelled and built upon, and streets were continued into the suburbs to such an extent as to give to that part the name of the New Town. The total number of houses, in 1831, was 2683. The more ancient part is built on the plan of a Spanish town; many of the older houses are quadrangular, with an open court and an arched gateway towards the street. Two bridges connect the town with the western district of Iar-Connaught; one built in 1342, which is still in good repair; and the other higher up the stream, a handsome structure built in 1831, and connecting the county court-house and prison. From the latter is a highly interesting view, embracing up the river the fine Elizabethan structure of Menlough castle, on its right bank, and downwards the shipping in the harbour, with the suburbs and the lofty mountains of Clare. The Castle or Upper Citadel barracks, near William's gate, are a handsome range of building for 6 officers and 136 non-commissioned officers and privates, with an hospital for 60 patients; the Shambles barracks, near the river, which are also well built, are for 15 officers and 326 non-commissioned officers and privates, with stabling for six horses. There are two subscription news-rooms, belonging respectively to the Amicable and Commercial societies; and two newspapers are published in the town. Races for some years past have been held on a course about three miles distant. Several flour-mills have been erected on the banks of the river, which has a very rapid fall, and great quantities of flour are made here from the wheat grown in the neighbourhood, which is of very fine quality. The manufacture of paper is extensively carried on; the works are impelled by water, and a steam-engine has been lately erected for greater efficiency. A portion of the fine black marble found in the vicinity is made into mantel-pieces, and a turning and polishing machine and a patent saw wheel are now being constructed, which will be set in motion by the treadmill in the county gaol: a large brewery and three distilleries are in full operation, and near the town is a bleach-mill. The linen manufacture was introduced, but never flourished here; and the linen-hall erected in the western suburbs has long since fallen into decay.

The commerce, for which the port was formerly so much distinguished, has very much declined; wine is no longer imported in large quantities, and the trade in provisions is much diminished. The principal exports are corn, flour, kelp, marble, wool, and provisions; and the imports, timber, wine, salt, coal, hemp, tallow, and Swedish and British iron. In the year ending Jan. 5th, 1835, 15 British ships of the aggregate burden of 2273 tons, and 3 foreign ships of 421 tons aggregate burden, entered inwards; and 6 British ships of 1044 tons and 2 foreign ships of 301 tons cleared outwards, in the foreign trade. From British ports, 119 ships, of an aggregate burden of 12,215 tons, entered inwards; and 126 of 14,492 tons cleared outwards; and from the Irish ports, 16 ships of 700 tons entered inwards; and 19 of 1039 tons cleared outwards. The number of vessels registered as belonging to the port is 7, of the aggregate burden of 272 tons. The gross amount of customs' duties for 1835 was £31,133. 2. 5., and for 1836, £31,769. 2. 5.; and of excise duties of the district, for the former year, £50,145 12. 5. The custom-house, a small plain building, was erected in 1807. The entrances to Galway bay are, through the north sound, between the most western of the Arran isles, which are situated in the centre of its mouth, and Gulin head to the north, on which is a watch tower; and through the south sound between Dunmacfelin and Innishere island. About a mile south of Galway is Mutton island, connected with the mainland by a ridge of sand, dry at low water; a light has been erected on it, and between it and the town is the ordinary roadstead, affording good anchorage ground, though exposed to a heavy swell during winds from the south and south-south-west. There are two feet of water on the bar: the best shelter for ships of war is along the southern shore; and at the head of the bay, to the east and south of the town, are several creeks and inlets, affording good shelter to small vessels from every wind. A navigable canal from Lough Corrib to the sea at this place was recommended by the late Mr. Nimmo: some new docks planned by him are in progress, towards the completion of which the Commissioners of Public Works have granted a loan of £17,000. The docks will comprise about 9 acres, and be of sufficient depth for vessels of 500 tons' burden, and the canal will cross the town in a direction nearly parallel with the river; the level of the lake being only 14 feet above that of the sea, two locks only will be requisite in the whole distance, which is about 30 miles. The quays will be entirely of hewn limestone and 75 feet in width; the lake also will be deepened and rendered navigable for boats. The whole work, when completed, will add much to the improvement of the trade, which is now under the direction of several of the principal merchants, who have formed themselves into a chamber of commerce: A branch of the Bank of Ireland has been opened here, in a house in Eyre-square. The salmon fishery, for which there is a weir on the river, between the two bridges, has been a source of great profit from an early period, and since 1800, has frequently produced more than £500 per annum. The fishery in the bay, which is more lucrative, is wholly under the direction of the fishermen of Claddagh, *which see*. This is the head station of the Galway district coast-guard, and the residence of the inspecting commander; it comprises the subordinate stations of Ballyvaughan, Kilcolgan, Barna, Casleh Bay, Isles of Arran, Fairhill, and Kilkerran, comprehending a force of 6 officers and 51 men. The markets are on Wednesday and Saturday, the former principally for corn, and the latter also for corn, provisions of every kind, and for pigs. Fairs are held May 31st, and Sept. 21st. The corn market is held at the Little Green; that for butchers' meat and provisions in a well-arranged market-place, near William's-gate, erected in 1802.

By charter of the 29th of Chas. II., the corporation consists of a mayor, two sheriffs, an indefinite number of free burgesses, a recorder, town-clerk, mayor and two constables of the staple, sword-bearer, chamberlain, water-bailiff, and other officers. The mayor is elected annually from the free burgesses, and may appoint a deputy; the mayor, sheriffs (who are similarly elected), and free burgesses form the common council, by whom all the other officers of the corporation are elected and freemen admitted, the latter by favour only. The mayor and recorder are justices of the peace for the county of the town and also for the county at large, and there are three charter magistrates, to whom five have been recently added by an order of council. The borough appears to have first sent members to a parliament held at Tristledermot, now Castledermot, in 1377, and notices of the provost and bailiffs being summoned to subsequent parliaments till 1559 are on record. The right is recognised in the charters of Jas. I. and Chas. II., and the corporation continued to send two members to the Irish parliament till the Union, from which period they returned one member to the Imperial parliament, till, by the act of the 2nd of Wm. IV., cap. 88, the original number was restored. By that act the right of election, previously vested in freeholders of 40*s*. and upwards within the county of the town, and in all freemen, was extended to £10 householders, and to £20 leaseholders for 14 years, and £10 leaseholders for £20 years; the non-resident freemen, except within seven miles, were disfranchised, and the 40*s*. freeholders allowed to retain the franchise only for life. The number of electors registered to vote at the last general election was 2062, and the number that actually voted, 1795: the sheriffs are the returning officers. The mayor and recorder hold a court of record every Tuesday and Friday, for the recovery of debts to any amount, arising within the limits of the county of the town; the mesne process is by arrest of the person or attachment of the goods of the defendant, on an affidavit of the debt. They are also empowered to hold a criminal court, which they transfer to the general quarter sessions for the county. The assizes for the county are held here, and the quarter sessions in April and October; those for the county of the town are held in January, April, July, and October. The court-houses for the county and the borough are both handsome buildings; the former was erected in 1815, in the northern suburb, and contains two spacious court-rooms, and other requisite apartments; the front is embellished with a handsome portico of four fluted Doric columns supporting a pediment, in the tympanum of which are the royal arms. The county gaol is built in the form of a crescent, vaulted throughout, and without any timber; it contains six wards for male, and two for female criminals, with two for debtors, separated by walls converging towards the centre, in which is the governor's house; there is a tread wheel, and the prisoners are also employed in breaking stones; it will contain 300 prisoners, placing two in each cell; the whole is surrounded by a boundary wall, between which and the building is a wide gravel walk. In an open situation near it is the borough gaol, erected in 1810, but not adapted either for classification or for the maintenance of discipline; another on the improved system is in course of erection.

The county of the town comprehends an extensive rural district, comprising 23,000 statute acres. The surface is studded with lakes, and the scenery strikingly diversified; the soil is fertile and in several parts peculiarly favourable to the growth of wheat, of which large quantities are raised. The system of agriculture is improved, and there is abundance of limestone, which is quarried for building and for agricultural purposes. Black marble of a very fine quality is found at Menlough, and also at Merlin Park; both veins have been worked, but the former more extensively, from the greater facility of water carriage at that place. At Menlough is also an apparently inexhaustible vein of fine grey marble. There are strong indications of iron ore, but no attempt has yet been made to explore it; granite is also found, and in some parts, contrary to the usual order, beneath the limestone formation. After sinking a depth of six feet through the limestone stratum, a white sand of granitic quality, without a pebble, and fine enough for plaistering, has lately been discovered; its depth has not been ascertained, but in some places it is coloured as if by water running from the iron ore. The name of the lake, called by the ancient inhabitants Mine-lough, and which has both a subterranean source and outlet, tends to confirm the opinion that the townland abounds with various minerals. About 40 persons are employed in the marble quarries, and about 1300 in preparing peat for fuel. The principal seats are Menlough Castle, the residence of Sir V. Blake, Bart., a venerable castellated mansion in the Elizabethan style, beautifully situated; Villa House, the residence of the Warden of Galway; Leneboy, of J. O' Hara, Esq., recorder; Nile Lodge, of J. O'Hara, Esq.; Sea View, of Mrs. Browne; Vicar's Croft, of the Rev. J. D'Arcy; St. Helen's, of Mrs. Hynes; Renmore Lodge, of P. M. Lynch, Esq.; Merlin Park, of C. Blake, Esq.; Merview, of W. Joyce, Esq.; Rahoon, of R. O'Connor, Esq.; and Barna, of N. Lynch, Esq. The Grand Jury presentments for the county of the town, in 1835, amounted to £5701. 8. 3., of which £1035. 14. 6. was for the repairs of roads, bridges, &c.; £3568. 10. 10. for public buildings and charities, officers' salaries, and miscellaneous expenses; £453. 19. 11. for police; and £643. 3. in repayment of a loan by Government.

This district originally formed part of the diocese of *Enachdune*, an ancient bishoprick, annexed in 1324 to the archiepiscopal see of Tuam. It consists of the parish of St. Nicholas, the greater part of that of Rahoon, and part of Oranmore. The parish of St. Nicholas comprises 3046 statute acres in cultivation, as applotted under the tithe act. The living is a rectory, united to the rectories of Rahoon, Oranmore, Clare-Galway, Moycullin, Kilcommin, Ballinacourty, and Shruel, together constituting the Wardenship of Galway, instituted by the Archbishop in 1484, when the church was made collegiate, and exercising an ecclesiastical jurisdiction distinct from that of the diocese, and exempt from that of the Archbishop, with the exception only of triennial visitation. The warden is annually elected (the same person has of late been successively re-elected), and three vicars appointed for life, by the corporation under their charter. The tithes amount to £130, wholly payable to the warden, who also receives three-fourths of the tithes of the other parishes of the union, amounting, with the rent of houses and two glebes, to £1268. 15. 10½. The vicars receive each an annual stipend of £75, payable by the warden. The church, which, by letters patent granted by Edw. VI., was constituted the "Royal College of Galway," and in the reign of Elizabeth endowed with the dissolved monasteries of Annaghdown and Ballintubber, in the county of Mayo, is a spacious cruciform structure, in the decorated English style, with a tower rising from the centre. It was built in 1320, and is nearly in the centre of the town; the Ecclesiastical Commissioners have recently granted £1385 towards its repair. In the R. C. divisions Galway is the head of a see, comprising 12 parochial unions or districts, and containing 14 chapels, served by 24 clergymen, of whom 12 are parish priests and 12 coadjutors or curates. It is one of the six sees suffragan to Tuam, and the parish of St. Nicholas is the benefice and residence of the R. C. bishop; the chapel is a spacious edifice. There are friaries and nunneries of the orders of St. Francis, St. Augustine, and St. Dominick, to each of which is attached a chapel; there is also a convent for nuns of the order of the Presentation, and a place of worship for Presbyterians. In the east suburbs stands one of the four classical schools founded in Ireland by the munificent bequest of Erasmus Smith; it is a handsome building, erected at an expense of £8000 by the trustees, who allow the master a salary of £100 per ann., with the privilege of taking boarders. The parochial schools are also aided by the trustees, who allow the master a salary of £40 and the mistress £27. 13. 10. per annum; a new school-room has been built on ground given by the trustees, towards defraying the expense of which the inhabitants subscribed £300 and £250 was granted by Government. A school is conducted by the ladies of the Presentation Convent, in which 80 of the girls are maintained and clothed; and there is a large national school on the site of the barrack in Lombard-street for which two good school-rooms have been built at an expense of £600, raised by subscriptions. There are also 16 private schools, in which are about 660 children. The house of industry and the dispensary, to the latter of which the English Relief Committee of 1832 gave £700, vested in the Archbishop of Tuam as trustee, and government £500, vested in four trustees chosen by the subscribers, are supported in the customary manner. A widows' and orphans' asylum was founded by the Rev. Mr. Fynn, P.P. of St. Nicholas, and is supported under his patronage by subscription. A Protestant poor-house, in which are 20 inmates, is supported by the parochial clergy and the interest of £500, bequeathed to the Warden in trust for the Protestant poor, by the late Mr. Kirwan, of London, a native of Galway. A Magdalen asylum is supported by two R. C. ladies, who devote their time and their fortune to its management. No vestiges can be traced of the Franciscan friary without the north gate, founded in 1296 by Sir W. De Burgo; of a Dominican friary near the west gate, previously a cell to the Premonstratensian abbey of Tuam; an Augustinian friary, founded in 1508 by Stephen Lynch and Margaret his wife; a Carmelite friary, a nunnery on an island in Lough Corrib, or an hospital of Knight Templars. There are numerous ruins of ancient castles in the neighbourhood. Among the more distinguished natives of Galway may be noticed Patrick D'Arcy, author of the celebrated "Argument on the Independence of Ireland," in 1641; John Lynch, author of "Cambrensis Eversus," "Alithinologia," and other tracts; Roderick O'Flaherty, author of the "Ogygia"; Sir G. L. Staunton, secretary to Lord Macartney, and writer of the account of that nobleman's embassy to Pekin; Walter Blake Kirwan, celebrated as a popular preacher in Dublin; and Richard Kirwan, an eminent chymist and mineralogist. James Hardiman, Esq., author of the History of Galway, has a villa near the town. Galway gives the title of Viscount to the family of Monckton.

GARE.—See BALLINGARRY, county of TIPPERARY.

GARFINAGH, or GARFINEY, a parish, in the barony of CORKAGUINEY, county of KERRY, and province of MUNSTER, 2 miles (N.E.) from Dingle, on the road to Tralee; containing 938 inhabitants. It comprises 4652½ statute acres, as applotted under the tithe act, a large portion of which consists of mountain pasture; the arable portion is well manured with sea-weed and sand, brought from the strand at Bunbawn, and the state of agriculture is gradually improving. At Flemingstown is a small boulting-mill. Balintagart, the newly erected mansion of S. Murray Hickson, Esq., is finely situated on an eminence commanding an extensive view of Dingle bay and the surrounding mountains. The living is a vicarage, in the diocese of Ardfert and Aghadoe, and in the patronage of the Bishop: the rectory is impropriate in Lord Ventry. The tithes, amounting to £138. 9. 2½., are payable in the proportion of two-thirds to the impropriator and one-third to the vicar: the glebe belongs to Lord Ventry. In the R. C. divisions the parish is included in the district of Dingle. At Balintagart is an ancient burial-ground, now used for children only: it is surrounded by a circular fosse or ditch, and contains several gravestones with Ogham inscriptions. On clearing some ground in the vicinity, several small circular cells were discovered, constructed of stone work and communicating with each other: they are supposed to have formed an ancient reservoir, to which there was a descent of several steps. Near the ruins of the church is a very narrow bridge over the small river Garfinagh, on the old road from Dingle to Tralee; from its high arched form it has been termed the Rainbow bridge, and is evidently of great antiquity.

GAROMNA, an island, in the parish of KILLANIN, barony of MOYCULLEN, county of GALWAY, and province of CONNAUGHT, 20 miles (W.) from Galway, on the North side of Galway bay: the population is returned with the parish. This island forms the western side of Greatman's bay, and between it and the island of Arranmore is the North Sound, or entrance to the bay of Galway. It contains 1427 statute acres, of which about one-third consists of arable land and the remainder of mountain pasture and bog. The inhabitants depend for support chiefly on the fishery, which is here extremely precarious; and in 1831, when the famine desolated this part of the coast, they were driven to the utmost state of destitution until relieved by the London Committee. On the north-east side of the island is a small pier, originally erected by the late Fishery Board, but having been destroyed, it was subsequently rebuilt with funds from the charitable societies, and is now of great utility. The sounds between this island and the adjoining ones are dry or fordable at low water: about half a mile from the south side is Englishman's Rock, which is dry at ¾ ebb. In the R. C. divisions it forms a parish or district of itself, and has two chapels, one of which is a small thatched building. In its immediate vicinity is Innisbaraher, an island containing 32 acres of arable land and 30 of bog and mountain pasture.

GARRANAMANA, a parish, in the barony of GOWRAN, county of KILKENNY, and province of LEINSTER; containing, with the merged parish of Mocktown or Rathbin, 158 inhabitants and 834 statute acres. It is a rectory and vicarage, in the diocese of Ossory, forming part of the union of Burnchurch: the tithes amount to £38. 19. 11. In the R. C. divisions it is part of the union or district of Freshford.

GARRANEKENEFICK, a parish, in the barony of IMOKILLY, county of CORK, and province of MUNSTER; 2½ miles (W. by S.) from Cloyne, on the harbour of Cork; containing 1033 inhabitants. It is a rectory, in the diocese of Cloyne, appropriated from time immemorial to the bishop's mensal: the tithes amount to £79. 3. 4. In the R. C. divisions it is part of the union or district of Aghada, or Saleen. About 80 children are educated in two private schools. Rathcourcey, built on an inlet of the harbour, is occasionally visited for sea-bathing. The village of Saleen contains about 30 neat white-washed cottages and a R. C. chapel.

GARRANGIBBON, a parish, in the barony of SLIEVARDAGH, county of TIPPERARY, and province of MUNSTER; containing 1468 inhabitants. It is a rectory, in the diocese of Lismore, entirely impropriate in Cæsar Sutton, Esq., and the Marquess of Ormonde: the tithes amount to £180. About 130 children are educated in two private schools.

GARRISON, a village, partly in the parish of INNISMACSAINT, and partly in that of DEVENISH, barony of MAGHERABOY, county of FERMANAGH, and province of ULSTER, 7 miles (W.) from Churchhill, on the road from Ballyshannon to Manorhamilton; containing 69 inhabitants. Here are a chapel of ease to the parish church of Devenish, a R. C. chapel, and a school. It is a constabulary police station, and fairs are held on May 21st, July 19th, Oct. 21st. and Dec. 21st, besides which fairs have lately been established every alternate month.

GARRISTOWN, a parish, in the barony of BALROTHERY, county of DUBLIN, and province of LEINSTER, 4 miles (N. W.) from Ashbourne; containing 2081 inhabitants, of which number, 741 are in the village of Garristown, and 218 in that of Baldwinstown. It is a constabulary police station, and has a dispensary. There is a windmill on a hill near the village, from which is an extensive prospect, commanding a view over fourteen counties. Good building stone and turf are obtained in the parish; and fairs are held on May 5th, Aug. 15th, and Nov. 1st. The living is a vicarage, in the diocese of Dublin, and in the gift of Lord Trimleston, in whom the rectory is impropriate: the vicarial tithes were valued at £50, and there is a glebe of 25 acres. The church is a plain building: the glebe-house, which was built in 1791, is in ruins. In the R. C. divisions the parish is united to Ballymadun; there is a chapel in each parish; that of Garristown was erected in 1828, and galleries were added to the chapel of Ballymadun in 1833. There is a national school, in which about 100 boys are instructed, and there are also two private schools.

GARRYCLOYNE, a parish, partly in the barony of BARRETTS, but chiefly in that of EAST MUSKERRY, county of CORK, and province of MUNSTER, 5 miles (N. W.) from Cork, on the road to Kanturk; containing, with the village of Blarney (which is described under its own head), 2027 inhabitants. It comprises 3530 statute acres, as applotted under the tithe act, and valued at £1870 per annum. There are several extensive dairy farms, and the butter is held in high repute: the cattle are well stalled and fed with clover, turnips, and tares. Agriculture has much improved within the last few years, and the farms, particularly those belonging to the gentry, are well cultivated: the principal manure is lime. A large quantity of limestone is procured on the demesne of Blarney, the only place abounding with it from Cork to Mallow: good manure is also obtained from the cattle stalls. The establishment of a farming society, excellent roads, and other advantages have combined to improve the system of farming, but in some instances the old method is still pursued. There is neither mountain nor bog in the parish. The line of the intended canal from Cork to Limerick passes through it; and there are boulting-mills capable of producing 6000 barrels of flour annually. In the parish are several gentlemen's seats: Blarney Castle is described in the account of that village, to the north of which is Putland's Glen, the residence of George Jeffreys, Esq., by whom it was planted, and who holds a lease of it from Mr. Putland, whose ancestor was a member of the Hollow Sword Blade Company, and a large portion of this parish was allotted to him; it originally formed part of the Clancarthy estate, which being confiscated in 1692, was purchased from the Government by the company. To the north of the parish is the manor-house and castle of Garrycloyne, the property of John Travers, Esq., whose ancestor obtained a grant of it in 1604: the castle is a lofty square tower, built in 1535 by the Clancarthys; the house is spacious and well built on rising ground looking over a fine lawn of more than 100 acres, surrounded by fine plantations. Abbeyville is the seat of the Rev. W. Stopford. The living is a rectory and vicarage, in the diocese of Cloyne, united at a very early period to the rectory and vicarage of Grenaugh, and in the patronage of the Bishop: the tithes amount to £512, and of the whole benefice to £1562; there is a glebe of 21 acres. The glebe-house was erected in 1807, by aid of a gift of £100 and a loan of £800 from the late Board of First Fruits. The church is a handsome building of the Doric order, situated on rising ground commanding a view of the village and plains. In the R. C. divisions the parish is united with Whitechurch: the chapel, a neat Gothic structure, towards the erection of which Mr. Putland contributed £200, is situated at the northern extremity of Putland's Glen. The male and female parochial schools are in the village of Blarney, and are supported entirely by the rector, who provides a house rent-free for the master and mistress; he also supports a Sunday school. Adjoining the R. C. chapel is a national school, a large building recently erected.

GARRYNOE, or GARRYVOE, a parish, in the Eastern Division of the barony of EAST CARBERY, county of CORK, and province of MUNSTER, 5¾ miles (S. W. by W.) from Bandon; the population is returned with the parish of Desertserges, into which Garrynoe is considered to have merged. It is situated on the river Bandon, and comprises 8027 statute acres, as applotted under the tithe act, and valued at £3365 per annum. The living is a rectory, in the diocese of Cork, and in the patronage of Lord Kinsale: the tithes amount to £315.

GARRYVOE, or GARRYBOVE, a parish, in the barony of IMOKILLY, county of CORK, and province of MUNSTER, 4 miles (S. E. by S.) from Castlemartyr; containing 813 inhabitants. It comprises 1657 statute acres, as applotted under the tithe act, about three-fourths of which are under tillage, the remainder being pasture and furze brakes. The soil is generally poor, but is well manured with sea-weed and sand; the substratum is clay-slate. Being situated on the shore of the Atlantic, many of the inhabitants are engaged in fishing. The principal seat is Garryvoe Lodge, the residence of J. O'Neil, Esq. It is a vicarage, in the diocese of Cloyne, and forms part of the union of Kilcredan; the rectory is impropriate in A. Mann, Esq., M.D. The tithes amount to £232. 10. 10., of which £155. 0. 6½. is payable to the impropriator, and £77. 10. 3½. to the vicar. In the R. C. divisions it is part of the union or district of Ladiesbridge, or Ballymacoda. The parochial schools are supported by Capt. Hoare, Mrs. Fitzgerald, and the vicar; and there is a private school. The old church is in ruins, and near it is a small square tower, called Garryvoe Castle.

GARTAN, a parish, in the barony of KILMACRENAN, county of DONEGAL, and province of ULSTER, 6 miles (N. W.) from Letterkenny, on the road to Dunfanaghy; containing 2109 inhabitants. St. Columb founded a monastery here in 521, of which the ruins still remain. The parish comprises, according to the Ordnance survey, 44,124 statute acres, including 1590 under water; there is a considerable extent of heathy mountain and bog. A silver and lead mine was worked here in 1835, in the townland of Warrenstown, but has been discontinued. Gartan is the residence of Capt. Chambers. The living is a rectory and vicarage, in the diocese of Raphoe, and in the patronage of the Bishop: the tithes amount to £150. The glebe-house was erected in 1828 by a gift of £400 and a loan of £380 from the late Board of First Fruits: the glebe comprises 25 acres. The church, which is a small plain building, was erected in 1819. In the R. C. divisions the parish is the head of a union or district, comprising also part of Kilmacrenan, in each of which is a chapel. The parochial school, in which about 50 children are educated, is aided by an endowment from Col. Robertson's fund, and subscriptions from the rector; there is also a Sunday school.

GARVAGH, a market and post-town, in the parish of ERRIGAL, barony of COLERAINE, county of LONDONDERRY, and province of ULSTER, 8 miles (S.) from Coleraine, and 110½ (N. by W.) from Dublin, on the road from Armagh to Coleraine: the population is returned with the parish. It appears to have been a place of some importance soon after the plantation of Ulster. In 1641, Col. Rowley raised a regiment of foot and marched into the town for its protection. After keeping possession of it for some time, he was attacked by a party of forces commanded by Sir Phelim O'Nial, who, making themselves masters of the place, put the Colonel and many of the inhabitants to death, burnt the town, and plundered the country to the very gates of Coleraine. The town consists of one long spacious street intersected at right angles by two smaller streets; many of the houses are large and handsomely built, and the whole has an appearance of great respectability. Adjoining it is Garvagh House, the seat of Lord Garvagh, a spacious mansion with a well-planted demesne and an extensive park; and there are several other gentlemen's seats, which are noticed in the article on the parish. The trade of the place is considerable, and with the town owes its prosperity to the Canning family. The market is on Friday and is well supplied; and on the third Friday in every month a fair is held for the sale of brown linen, horses, cattle, sheep, and pigs, each of which is numerously attended. Petty sessions are held in a court-house on the last Monday of every month. Adjoining the town is the parish church, a small neat edifice; and there is a meeting-house for Presbyterians in connection with the Synod of Ulster, of the second class, built in 1746, rebuilt in 1790, and enlarged in 1830; another in connection with the Seceding Synod, and a third for Separatists from that synod.

GARVAGHY, a parish, partly in the barony of LOWER, but chiefly in that of UPPER, IVEAGH, county of DOWN, and province of ULSTER, 4 miles (S. E.) from Dromore, on the western branch of the river Lagan, and on the road from Banbridge to Downpatrick; containing 5036 inhabitants. This parish comprises, according to the Ordnance survey, 10,256¾ statute acres, which with the exception of about 50 acres of bog and 26 of water, are wholly under tillage; the system of agriculture is greatly improved, and the lands are well fenced and generally in a high state of cultivation. There are some quarries of stone of good quality, which is extensively worked for building, repairing the roads, and other purposes. The principal seats are Carniew, the residence of R. D. Macredy, Esq.; the Cottage, of W. Cosby, Esq.; Ballyely, of R. Maginnis, Esq.; Lion Hill, of H. Waugh, Esq.; the glebe-house, of the Rev. H. S. Hamilton, Esq.; and Waringsford, the property of J. Heron, Esq. The living is a vicarage, in the diocese of Dromore, and in the patronage of the Bishop; the rectory is partly appropriate to the see, and partly constitutes the corps of the prebend of Dromeragh in the cathedral of Dromore. The tithes amount to £514, of which £185 is payable to the bishop, £129 to the prebendary, and £200 to the vicar. The Ecclesiastical Commissioners have recommended the re-annexation of the rectorial tithes to the vicarage on the next avoidance of the prebend. The glebe-house, a handsome residence, was built by aid of a gift of £400, and a loan of £400, from the late Board of First Fruits, in 1820; the glebe comprises 74 acres. The church, a small edifice in the Grecian style, built in 1699, was thoroughly repaired in 1780, when the chancel was taken down. In the R. C. divisions the parish forms part of the union or district of Dromore; the chapel at Ballineybeg is a small edifice, erected in 1822. There are places of worship for Presbyterians in connection with the Seceding Synod (of the first class), and Antiburghers. The parochial school is on the glebe, near the church; at Carniew is a school, with a residence for the master attached, to which the Rev. C. Hamilton, in 1814, gave an acre of land; there are also a national and five other public schools. About 250 children are taught in four private schools, and there are six Sunday schools. At Ballineybeg, and also at Knockgorman, are some remains of cromlechs.

GAULSKILL, a parish, in the barony of IDA, county of KILKENNY, and province of LEINSTER, 4 miles (N. by W.) from Waterford, on the road to Thomastown; containing 322 inhabitants. It is also called Kiltokegan and Kilskegan, and comprises 1325 acres, including a lake of 100 acres. The ancient castle appears, from a a monument in the church, to have formerly belonged to the De Burgo family. It is a rectory and vicarage, in the diocese of Ossory, forming part of the union of Dunkitt: the tithes amount to £75; near the church is a small glebe. The church was built in 1792, by aid of a gift of £500 from the late Board of First Fruits, and the Ecclesiastical Commissioners have recently granted £176 for its repair. In the R. C. divisions it is part of the union or district of Kilmacow.

GEALE, or GAILE, a parish, in the barony of MIDDLETHIRD, county of TIPPERARY, and province of MUNSTER, 4 miles (S. by W.) from Thurles, on the road to Cashel; containing 707 inhabitants. It comprises 2494 statute acres, valued at £1757 per annum, which is all arable and pasture with the exception of about 30 acres of rock on Killough Hill, which, being surrounded by a flat country, is a very conspicuous object. Near it is Killough Castle, the occasional residence of the Hon. Mrs. Plunkett; and the south-west side of the hill, which is planted, forms part of the demesne of Gaile, the residence of S. Phillips, Esq. The living is a rectory, in the diocese of Cashel, and in the patronage of the Archbishop: the tithes amount to £185. There is no church, glebe-house, or glebe; the Protestant parishioners attend divine service at the church of Holy Cross, about three miles distant. On the demesne of Gaile are some remains of the old church.

GEASHILL, a post-town and parish, partly in the barony of UPPER PHILIPSTOWN, but chiefly in that of GEASHILL, KING'S county, and province of LEINSTER, 4 miles (S.) from Philipstown, and 51 (S. by W.) from Dublin, on the road from Portarlington to Tullamore; containing 13,253 inhabitants, of which number, 467 are in the town. The castle, of which there are some remains, anciently belonging to the O'Dempseys, from whom, with the surrounding territory, it passed to the Fitzgeralds, and in 1620, by marriage, to Sir Robert Digby, whose lady surviving him was besieged in it for several months, but was relieved in 1642. The town contains 87 houses arranged in a triangular form, most of which are thatched. It is a constabulary police station, has a dispensary, a patent for a market which is not held, and fairs on May 1st, Oct. 6th, and Dec. 26th, which last is one of the largest pig fairs in the kingdom; fairs are also held at Killeigh. The parish comprises 34,630 statute acres, and is the property of the Earl Digby; the soil is a deep clay, with a substratum of limestone gravel: there is a large extent of bog and some building stone, and the Earl Digby has large nurseries of forest trees; agriculture is but little improved. Sir W. Cusack Smith, Bart., has a seat at Newtown. It is a rectory and vicarage, in the diocese of Kildare, forming the corps of the prebend of Geashill in the cathedral of Kildare, and in the patronage of Earl Digby: the tithes amount to £1292. 6. 1¾. The glebe-house is a quarter of a mile from the church, and there are two glebes, comprising 82 acres. The parochial church is a plain neat edifice, rebuilt in 1814 by aid of a loan of £1500 from the late Board of First Fruits, and for the repairs of which the Ecclesiastical Commissioners have lately granted £182. At Killeigh and Cloneyhork are chapels of ease; the former, to which the Ecclesiastical Commissioners have recently granted £196 for repairs, is built on the site of the old monastery, part of which is incorporated with the present building. In the R. C. divisions the parish is partly in the union or district of Ballykeane, and partly in that of Portarlington, and has chapels at Killeigh and Ballinagar, belonging to the former union, and at Kilmalogue for the latter. There are two places of worship for Wesleyan Methodists. The parochial school is aided by an annual donation of £15 from Earl Digby; the school-house was built at the expense of the late R. E. Digby, Esq.; and there are a national and six other public schools; altogether affording instruction to about 670 children; and 15 private schools, in which are about 660 children: there are also 11 Sunday schools. Vestiges of the castle yet exist, and near Ballinagar are the ruins of a church. Geashill gives the inferior title of Baron to Earl Digby.—See BALLINAGAR and KILLEIGH.

GEEVAGH.—See KILMACTRANY.

GENEVA, NEW.—See CROOK.

GERNONSTOWN, a parish, in the barony of ARDEE, county of LOUTH, and province of LEINSTER, on the river Glyde and on the road from Drogheda to Dundalk; the population, including that of the post-town of Castle-Bellingham, is returned with the parish of Kilsaran. This parish, which for all civil purposes is considered a part of Kilsaran, comprises, according to the Ordnance survey, 1302 statute acres, of which 17 are in the river Glyde; the soil is principally clay, with some loam and gravel; the system of agriculture is greatly improved, and the land generally in a good state of cultivation. It is a rectory, in the diocese of Armagh, and part of the union of Kilsaran; the tithes amount to £146. 15. 4. The church of the union is in this parish, and is situated close to the town of Castle-Bellingham. In the R. C. divisions it is part of the union or district of Kilsaran.

GERNONSTOWN, a parish, in the barony of UPPER SLANE, county of MEATH, and province of LEINSTER, 2¼ miles (W.) from Slane, on the road from Slane to Kingscourt; containing 925 inhabitants. This parish comprises 2394 statute acres, as applotted under the tithe act; the land is of good quality and is nearly equally divided between tillage and pasture. The principal seats are Tankardstown, the residence of Mrs. Hopkins, situated in an extensive demesne surrounded by thriving plantations; and Rochestown, of J. Blakeney, Esq. The mail coach road from Dublin to Londonderry skirts the parish on the east. It is a rectory, in the diocese of Meath, and part of the union of Stackallen: the tithes amount to £230. 15. 4., and the glebe comprises 20 acres of profitable land. In the R. C. divisions it forms part of the union or district of Slane; the chapel at Rushwee is a small plain building. A R. C. school is about to be placed under the New Board of Education, and about 50 children are taught in a private school.

GIANTS' CAUSEWAY.—See BILLY.

GILBERTSTOWN, or BENDENSTOWN, a parish, in the barony of FORTH, county of CARLOW, and province of LEINSTER, 3 miles (S. W.) from Tullow, on the road to Leighlin; containing 567 inhabitants. Building stone is found, and there is some bog. Prior to 1830 the parish formed part of the union of Aghade. The living is a rectory, in the diocese of Leighlin, and in the patronage of the Bishop: the tithes amount to £250. 0. 8. In the R. C. divisions it is the head of a union or district, also called Ballon and Ratoe, comprising the parishes of Gilbertstown, Ballon, Kellistown, Templepetre, Aghade, and parts of Fennagh and Urglin, in which union are two chapels, situated at Ballon and Ratoe. About 180 children are educated in a national school.

GILFORD, a post-town, in the parish of TULLYLISH, barony of LOWER IVEAGH, county of DOWN, and province of ULSTER, 11 miles (N.) from Newry, and 65½ (N.) from Dublin, on the river Bann, and the road from Loughbrickland to Tanderagee and Portadown; containing 529 inhabitants. In 1772, a body of insurgents, calling themselves "Hearts of Oak," committed frequent outrages in this neighbourhood, and on the 6th of March attacked Gilford Castle, the residence of Sir R. Johnston, Bart., and in the assault the Rev. S. Morell, Presbyterian minister, was shot while attempting to reason with the assailants from a window of the castle; it is now the residence of Sir W. Johnston, Bart. The town is situated on both sides of the river, over which is a handsome stone bridge of two arches, and in the vicinity are a large spinning establishment, some extensive bleach-greens, flour-mills, and chemical works. The canal from Lough Neagh to Newry passes within a mile of the town, and on its banks at that place is a wharf with some good warehouses. Fairs are held on the 21st of June and November; they are toll free and well attended. There is a constabulary police station, and petty sessions are held on alternate Wednesdays. There is a chalybeate spring, the water of which has the same properties as those of Pyrmont. Several gentlemen's seats in the neighbourhood are noticed in the account of Tullylish, *which see.*

GILTOWN, a parish, in the barony of SOUTH NAAS, county of KILDARE, and province of LEINSTER, 2 miles (S. E. by S.) from Kilcullen; containing 981 inhabitants. This parish is situated on a small mountain stream, and comprises 4335 statute acres, of which about 120 are woodland, 70 roads, and the remainder good arable and pasture land, the former noted for the growth of wheat; the system of agriculture is improved. Fuel is very scarce, turf being drawn from a distance of 7 or 8 miles. Giltown House is the residence of the Rev. J. Borrowes. It is a curacy, in the diocese of Dublin, forming part of the perpetual curacy of Kilcullen; the rectory is impropriate in Cramer Roberts, Esq. The tithes amount to £69. 4. 7½., there is neither church, glebe-house, nor glebe. About 18 children are taught in a private school. There are some ruins of the old church, and in the demesne of Giltown is a Danish rath.

GIRLEY, a parish, in the barony of UPPER KELLS, county of MEATH, and province of LEINSTER, 2½ miles (N.) from Athboy, on the road from Mullingar to Navan; containing 1480 inhabitants. This parish comprises 4637 statute acres, as applotted under the tithe act: about two-thirds are grass land of excellent quality, and the remainder under good cultivation, with the exception of a considerable tract of bog extending into the neighbouring parish of Burry; there are some thriving plantations. The principal seats are Drewstown, the residence of F. McVeigh, Esq., a handsome house in a highly improved demesne; Johnsbrook, of J. Tandy, Esq., pleasantly situated in grounds tastefully embellished; and Triermore, of T. Rotheram, Esq. It is a vicarage, in the diocese of Meath, forming part of the union of Athboy; the rectory is impropriate in Dominick O'Reilly, Esq. The tithes amount to £207. 1. 7., one-half payable to the impropriator and the other to the vicar; there is no glebe-house; the glebe comprises 1½ acre. In the R. C. divisions it is part of the union or district of Kells; the chapel at Fordstown is a handsome modern building, erected in 1800. About 60 children are taught in a private school, of which the school-house is occupied rent-free. There are some remains of the ancient parish church.

GLANBANE, a parish, in the barony of CLANWILLIAM, county of TIPPERARY, and province of MUNSTER, 7 miles (W. N. W.) from Tipperary. It consists of only a single farm, and is a rectory, in the diocese of Emly, forming part of the union of Ballyscadane and of the corps of the deanery of Emly: the tithes amount to £47. 11. 6.

GLANBARAHANE.—See CASTLEHAVEN.

GLANBEHY.—See GLENBEGH.

GLANDELAGH.—See GLENDALOUGH.

GLANDORE, a small but rising village, in the parish of KILFAUGHNABEG, Western Division of the barony of EAST CARBERY, county of CORK, and province of MUNSTER, 3 miles (S. W.) from Rosscarbery; containing about 200 inhabitants. This seems to have been a place of some importance at an early period, as appears from the erection of the castles of Glandore and Kilfinnan; for many years it continued in a very impoverished state, but it has again become a place of considerable note through the spirited exertions of its present proprietor, J. Redmond Barry, Esq., who has within the last few years expended upwards of £10,000 in various improvements. It is situated on the eastern side of Glandore harbour, which affords secure anchorage to vessels of large size; and is navigable to Leap, a village on the Cork and Skibbereen mail road. The scenery at the entrance of the harbour is extremely picturesque, and is remarkable as having formed the subject of a Latin poem, called "Carberiæ Rupes," written by Dean Swift, who spent some time in the neighbourhood. A pier has been recently constructed near the village, which affords protection to about 20 fishing yawls of three tons each; fish of every kind is abundant in the bay. Many elegant houses and a comfortable hotel have been erected, and from the beauty of its situation and the salubrity of the climate, the village has become a favourite place of residence, and much frequented during the bathing season; baths have been erected and every accommodation afforded for the convenience of visiters. The principal residences are Glandore Castle, the seat of P. Morris, Esq.; Glandore House, of J. Redmond Barry, Esq.; Glandore Cottage, of H. Townsend, Esq.; Glandore Lodge, of R. Adams, Esq.; Stone Hall, of Major T. Allen; Westview House, of Major Edw. Allen; Chateau Maria, of F. Allen, Esq.; Kilfrieman Castle, of T. Raneland, Esq.; Prospect House, of John Morris, Esq.; Glenville, of Capt. E. Hart; Union Cottage, of Mrs. Donovan; and Cliff Cottage, of the Rev. Mr. Walker. A temporary church and the R. C. chapel for the parish of Kilfaughnabeg are in the village. A school-house capable of containing 600 children, has been lately erected by Mr. Barry, with the aid of the National Board of Education; the boys receive instruction in agriculture and trades from competent teachers, and a model farm and carpenters' workshop are connected with it. The management of the girls' school reflects the highest credit on Miss Adams, the acting patroness, who most benevolently devotes her time to its superintendence: an infants' school has also been established.

GLANEALY, a parish, partly in the barony of ARKLOW, but chiefly in that of NEWCASTLE, county of WICKLOW, and province of LEINSTER, 4 miles (W. S. W.) from Wicklow, on the road from Ashford to Rathdrum; containing 1531 inhabitants, of which number, 193 are in the village. It comprises 4855 statute acres, including some waste land and bog. The scenery is pleasingly diversified and enriched with timber of luxuriant growth, and there are several handsome villas; the principal are Hollywood, the residence of A. S. Broomfield, Esq., Ballyfrea, of J. Dickson, Esq.; Glencarrig, of H. J Segrave, Esq.; Favorita, of the Rev. Leek McDonnell;

and the glebe-house, of the Rev. C. Armstrong. It is a rectory, in the diocese of Dublin, forming part of the union of Wicklow; the tithes amount to £283. 10. 5., and there is a glebe of 3 acres and a glebe-house. The church, which is in the later English style, was erected in 1783, by aid of a grant from the late Board of First Fruits, and the Ecclesiastical Commissioners have recently granted £111 for its repairs. In the R. C. divisions also it is in the union of Wicklow; there is a small chapel in the village. Besides the parochial school, about 60 children are instructed in a national school, and there are two private schools.

GLANINAGH, a parish, in the barony of BURREN, county of CLARE, and province of MUNSTER, 7½ miles (W.) from Burren, on the southern shore of Galway bay; containing 545 inhabitants, of which number, 220 are in the village. It comprises about 4200 statute acres, which chiefly consist of rocky mountain pasture; the portion in tillage is manured with sea-weed, an abundance of which is procured in the bay. It comprehends the lofty headland called Blackhead, in lat. 53° 9′ 20″ and lon. 9° 13′, along the north-eastern shore of which is deep water and shelter for large vessels. Several boats belonging to this parish are engaged in the fishery of Galway bay. A new line of road, about four miles in length, is now in progress along the coast round Blackhead, which will nearly complete the line of communication round the coast of the county. It is a rectory and vicarage, in the diocese of Kilfenora, forming part of the union and corps of the treasurership of the cathedral of Kilfenora: the tithes amount to £32. 10. In the R. C. divisions it is part of the union or district of Glyn, or Glenarraha. The ruins of the church still exist in the burial-ground.

GLANKEEN, a parish, in the barony of KILNEMANAGH, county of TIPPERARY, and province of MUNSTER, on the road from Thurles to Nenagh; containing, with the post-town of Burris-o'-leagh 6585 inhabitants. It comprises 14,215 statute acres, of which 230 are reclaimable mountain. Limestone is quarried for manure, and coal is supposed to exist in the mountains. Summer Hill, the residence of J. H. Harden, Esq., and Callohill Castle are in the parish. The living is a vicarage, in the diocese of Cashel, and in the patronage of the Archbishop; the rectory forms the corps of the prebend of Glankeen in the cathedral of Cashel, and in the gift of the Crown. The tithes amount to £600, of which £400 is paid to the archbishop, as prebendary of Glankeen, and £200 to the vicar. There is a glebe-house, with a glebe of 11 acres. The church is a plain building, erected about 1776, and the Ecclesiastical Commissioners have lately granted £147 for its repairs. The R. C. parish is co-extensive with that of the Established Church, and is called Burris-o'-leagh; the chapel is at that place, and there is another at Ileigh. The parochial school, to which the late Lady Caroline Damer gave 1½ acre of land, is aided by the rector; and there are three national schools; they afford instruction to about 350 children. About 280 children are taught in seven private schools. Large horns of an elk have been dug up here. There are the ruins of an ancient church, partly covered with ivy, and containing a monument to the family of Burke; and at Kilcuilawn, situated in the mountains, the celebrated relic called *Barnaan-Cuilawn* was found in a hollow tree many years since. It is composed of iron and brass inlaid with gold and silver, having some resemblance in shape to a mitre, and is supposed to have been the top of a censer belonging to St. Cuilen, who founded a church here in the 10th century; it is now in the possession of Mr. Cooke, of Parsonstown, and forms the subject of an article in the Transactions of the Royal Irish Academy. In 1821 the remains of an ancient mill were discovered near the church.—See BURRIS-O'-LEAGH.

GLANMIRE, a village, in the parish of RATHCOONEY, North Liberties of the county and city of CORK, and province of MUNSTER, 4 miles (E.) from Cork, on the road to Dublin; containing, in 1821, 558 inhabitants; at the last census the population was returned with the parish. The village is situated on both sides of the river Glanmire, which, after meandering through a beautiful glen, empties itself under a drawbridge of cast iron into the river Lee. The vicinity is enlivened with many plantations, hanging woods, and the number of gentlemen's seats and villas with which it is adorned. The principal residences are Lota House, that of W. H. Greene, Esq.; Lotabeg, of D. Callaghan, Esq.; Lotamore, of the Hon. C. L. Bernard; Dunkittle, of A. Morris, Esq.; Sun Lodge, of W. Oliver, Esq.; Lota Lodge, of J. S. Barry, Esq.; Fort William, of Mrs. Baker; Glentown, of Mrs. McCall; Glanville, of E. Newsome, Esq.; Woodville, of N. M. Cummins, Esq.; Lota Park, lately purchased by J. J. Murphy, Esq.; Jane Mount, of W. Hickie, jun., Esq.; Lake Lodge, of John Martin, Esq.; Castle Jane House, of R. Martin, Esq.; Castle Jane, of H. Lawton, Esq.; Mina Villa, of J. Hanly, Esq.; Glanmire House, of Ed. Morrogh, Esq.: North Esk, of J. Carnegie, Esq.; Park Farm, of H. Morrogh, Esq,; Spring Hill, of G. Waters, Esq.; Glen View, of R. Young, Esq.; and Sallybrook, of J. Hodnett, Esq. In the village are extensive flour-mills, belonging to Mr. Shaw, and in the vicinity are those of Messrs. Thorley and Son, for finishing calico and linen, upwards of 1000 pieces being the weekly average; these gentlemen have also an establishment for bleaching and dyeing, and employ upwards of 200 persons; about the same number are engaged in the Glanmire woollen factory, higher up the river, by Messrs. Lyons and Hanly. The river is navigable for lighters up to the village at high water. which bring up coal, culm, sea-sand for manure, and other articles for the supply of the neighbourhood. The parochial church, a plain neat building with a tower and spire, is in the village, and was erected in 1784, on a site given by R. Rogers, Esq.; and at a short distance is the R. C. chapel for the union of Glanmire. Here are also male and female schools, supported by the rector; and a female school was built and is supported by Mr. Hickie. A dispensary is open for the relief of the poor, and a clothing society has been established.

GLANMIRE, NEW.—See CAHERLOG.

GLANWORTH, a parish, partly in the barony of CONDONS, and CLOKGIBBONS, but chiefly in that of FERMOY, county of CORK, and province of MUNSTER, 5½ miles (S. by W.) from Mitchelstown, on the new road to Cork; containing 4455 inhabitants, of which number, 1098 are in the village. This place, which is situated on the river Funcheon, and also on the road from Fermoy to Limerick, was anciently called Glanore, or "the golden glen," from its great fertility. During the parliamentary war it was the scene of several conflicts, and was among the last garrisons in the south of Ireland that held out for the king; till the castle being besieged by Ireton ultimately surrendered. The village is said to have been formerly a corporate and market-town, but no existing records afford any evidence of the fact, though probably its inhabitants may have obtained extensive privileges from the founder of the castle, and continued to enjoy them under several of the succeeding lords. In 1831 it contained 215 houses, mostly thatched; it is pleasantly situated on the south-western bank of the river, over which is an ancient narrow stone bridge of twelve arches; and as seen in the approach from the Fermoy road, with the thriving plantations around the glebe-house half concealing the spire of the church, presents a beautifully picturesque scene, of which the most interesting features are thrown into bold relief by the chain of mountains in its rear, on the confines of the county of Limerick. Near the bridge are two large flour-mills, the property of Messrs. Murphy and Killeher, producing on an average 10,000 barrels of fine flour annually. The Funcheon is remarkable for the abundance and excellence of its trout; it also affords some salmon. A constabulary police force is stationed in the village, and fairs are held on Jan. 15th, March 16th, May 13th, Aug. 10th, Sept. 24th, and Nov. 30th, for live stock, but chiefly for pigs. The parish comprises 11,232 statute acres, as applotted under the tithe act, and valued at £9878. 11. 7. per annum; the land is in general good, and chiefly under tillage; the system of agriculture is gradually improving, and there is abundance of limestone, which is quarried principally for agricultural purposes. The seats are Ballyclough, the residence of Gen. Barry, a handsome mansion, in the Elizabethan style, situated in a fine and well-planted demesne; and Glanworth Glebe, of the Rev. John Brinkley, Prebendary, a large and handsome mansion adjoining the village, and commanding a picturesque view of the bridge and ruined castle. The living is a rectory, in the diocese of Cloyne, united by act of council, at a period unknown, to the vicarages of Ballydeloughy and Derryvillane, the rectory and vicarage of Kilgullane, together with the particle of Legane (which has long since merged into the parish), constituting the union and the corps of the prebend of Glanore in the cathedral of Cloyne, and in the patronage of the Bishop. The tithes amount to £729. 16. 11¼., and of the whole benefice, to £1107. 13. 11½. The glebe-house was built by the late incumbent, at an expense of about £2000, aided by a gift of £100 and a loan of £1000 from the late Board of First Fruits, in 1809: the glebe comprised nearly seven acres, but it is all lost except one acre, which has been given to the master of the parochial school by the incumbent. The church is a plain edifice with a low tower and spire. In the R. C. divisions the parish is the head of a union or district, comprising also the parishes of Derryvillane, Kilgullane, Downmahon, and Killenemor: the chapel in the village was built on a site given by Carden Terry, Esq., of Prospect, near Cork; and there is also a chapel at Ballydangan, in the parish of Ballydeloughy. About 30 children are taught in the parochial school, which is wholly supported by the rector; and there are seven private schools, in which are about 350 children, and a Sunday school. The late Rev. J. Killeher, P. P., bequeathed £100, one-half towards the erection of a school-house and the other for repairing the chapel. On a rocky eminence on the western side of the Funcheon are the extensive and interesting ruins of Glanworth castle, an ancient seat of the Roche family, and occupied in 1601 by Lord Fermoy, by whose descendant it was forfeited in 1641. They consist of an ancient square tower of considerable strength, supposed to be the keep, and the remains of another building of more recent date and superior construction, apparently containing the state apartments; they are within a quadrilateral area, enclosed by strong walls, nearly six feet in thickness, and defended at each angle by a round tower. To the north-west are the ruins of an abbey, said to have been founded by the Roches, in 1227, for Dominican friars, and dedicated to the Holy Cross; they consist of the nave and chancel of the church, between which rises a low square tower supported on four finely pointed arches; the windows are square-headed on the outside, but finely arched in the interior. Beneath the castle, and near the margin of the river, is a well dedicated to St. Dominick, which is held in great veneration by the peasantry. On a conspicuous mountain in the Kilworth range, and on the border of the adjoining parish of Kilgullane, is a solitary tower, the sole remains of Caherdriny castle, said to have been built by the Roche family; it commands a great extent of country, and is surrounded at a short distance by a wall of loose stones. Between Glanworth and Fermoy is Labacally, or "the Witches' Bed," an ancient druidical altar, one of the covering stones of which is 17 feet long, 8 feet wide, and 3 feet thick, supported on each side by double rows of large flags fixed in the ground; the whole appears to have been nearly 30 feet long and proportionably wide, and was enclosed by a circle of flagstones of 14 feet radius; its position is nearly due east and west. About half a mile north-west of the village is a stone pillar, about 12 feet high, supposed to have been an ancient boundary, and at a short distance to the east is a similar pillar of smaller dimensions, forming part of a series between the Awbeg and Funcheon. Several brass coins bearing the date 1565, with the inscription "Paul Maylor, mayor of the city of Cork,' have been found in this parish.

GLASCARRICK, or GLASCARRIG, an ecclesiastical district, recently formed out of the parishes of Donaghmore and Kiltrisk, the former in the barony of Ballaghkeen, and the latter in that of Gorey, county of Wexford, and province of Munster. The living is a perpetual curacy, in the diocese of Ferns, and in the patronage of the Impropriator of Donaghmore and the Incumbent of Kiltrisk, which forms part of the union of Leskinfere. The stipend of £66. 3. per annum is payable in the proportion of £20 from the incumbent, £23. 1. 6. from the impropriator, and a similar sum from the Ecclesiastical Commissioners. The tithes of seven townlands in Donaghmore, called the "*Ballymonies*," amounting to £40, payable to the Crown, have been petitioned for in augmentation of the perpetual curacy, and application has been made to the Ecclesiastical Commissioners to aid a subscription already entered into for building a church on the border of Donaghmore parish, adjoining that of Kiltrisk; also to grant funds for the erection of a glebe-house.—See Donaghmore and Kiltrisk.

GLASDRUMMOND.—See KILCLUNEY.

GLASH, or GLASS, an island, in the parish of KILBELFAD, barony of TYRAWLEY, county of MAYO, and province of CONNAUGHT, 6 miles (S. W.) from Ballina: the population is returned with the parish. This small island, which is situated in Lough Conn, about a mile from the mainland, comprises some good arable land. with a portion of rocky pasture. It is remarkable chiefly as the asylum of Bishop Balefadda, who took refuge here during the times of early persecution; there are still the remains of a church, and the burial-place in which he was interred.

GLASHARE, a parish, in the barony of GALMOY, county of KILKENNY, and province of LEINSTER, 4¼ miles (S. by E.) from Rathdowney; containing 619 inhabitants. This parish comprises 2703 statute acres, as applotted under the tithe act, and valued at £1824. It is a rectory, in the diocese of Ossory, and forms part of the union of Rathdowney. The tithes amount to £100. In the R. C. divisions it is part of the union or district of Eirke. About 50 children are educated in a private school.

GLASNEVIN, a parish and village, in the barony of COOLOCK, county of DUBLIN, and province of LEINSTER, 1½ mile (N.) from Dublin, on the road to Naul; containing 1001 inhabitants, of which number, 559 are in the village. This place, which is pleasantly situated on the northern bank of the river Tolka, was, early in the last century, the residence of many families of distinction, and of several of the most eminent literary characters of that age; and from its proximity to the metropolis it is still the residence of many highly respectable families. Among the more distinguished of its earlier inhabitants were the poet Tickell, Addison, Swift, Delany, Steele, Sheridan, and Parnell. The demesne of the first-named is now the site of the botanical gardens of the Royal Dublin Society, and a large apartment of the house is appropriated as the lecture-room of that institution. Delville, formerly the seat of the Rev. Dr. Delany, Dean of Down, and now the residence of S. Gordon, Esq., was the frequent resort of Dean Swift and other distinguished literary men of that day. It is pleasantly situated on the banks of the Tolka; on an eminence in the grounds is a temple decorated with paintings by Mrs. Delany, and a medallion bust of Mrs. Johnson, the "Stella" of Swift; beneath this building were found by a former proprietor the remains of a printing press, used by Swift in printing his satires on the Irish Parliament; the house and domestic chapel still retain their original character. On the opposite side of the Tolka is the celebrated seat and demesne of Mitchel, now the residence of the Bishop of Kildare; a little beyond it is Hampstead, formerly the residence of Sir Richard Steele, subsequently that of the late Judge Parsons, and now the seat of B. O'Gorman, Esq.; and in the contiguous parish of Finglas, was the residence of Parnell, formerly vicar of that parish. In the village are many handsome houses, of which the principal are those of Capt. J. A. Crawford, the Rev. W. C. Roberts, the Rev. R. Walsh (one of the editors of the History of Dublin), Capt. R. Smyth, W. Marrable, Esq., T. Howard, Esq., G. Alker, Esq., and Fairfield, the residence of the Rev. J. Hutton. The botanical gardens occupy more than 27 statute acres, laid out with great skill and a due regard to the illustration of that interesting study. The botanical department contains an extensive range of hothouses, occupying the summit of the higher ground in the centre of the garden, and including extensive collections of beautiful and rare plants, of which the various species of each large genus are appropriated as much as possible to separate houses. In front of the hothouses is the arboretum, in which herbaceous plants trees and shrubs are arranged according to the Linnæan system, and to the north arrangements are being made for a classification of similar plants according to their natural orders, on the system of Jussieu, with a division for medical plants, and for such as are peculiar to Ireland. The horticultural department occupies the western side of the garden, and contains divisions for exhibiting the rotatory system of cropping in the cultivation of culinary vegetables; collections of the most useful grasses, clovers, grain, &c., &c.; a selection of hardy fruits, and a collection of choice fruits, to illustrate the methods of pruning and training them. The ornamental department, including the aquarium and the banks of the Tolka, is being laid out as an American garden, with a view to exhibit the various features of landscape gardening, and also contains a division for the culture of specimens of all the agricultural roots. The gardens are under the superintendence of a professor, a curator, and a foreman; and the establishment consists of eight pupils, three apprentices, three labourers, and a porter. The professor's house and lecture-room are near the entrance of the gardens, and during the season from June to September, lectures are given three times every week, and are in general numerously attended; the gardens are also open to the public two days in the week from 12 o'clock till 4. A public cemetery was opened here in 1832, comprising 6 Irish acres, neatly laid out; in the centre is a chapel for the funeral service, and the area is enclosed with walls, having at each angle a castellated watch tower: the profit of this cemetery will be appropriated to the education of poor children.

The parish, which comprises 983 statute acres, as applotted under the tithe act, and valued at £4499 per annum, is the head of an extensive manor belonging to the cathedral establishment of Christ-Church, Dublin, and frequently called Grangegorman, from its courts having been held formerly in a village of that name: courts leet and baron are regularly held, the former at Easter and Michaelmas, and the latter, in which debts to the amount of £2 are recoverable, every Friday. There is also a constabulary police station. The living is a rectory and curacy, in the diocese of Dublin, the rectory partly forming the corps of the precentorship, and partly that of the chancellorship of the cathedral of Christ-Church, and the curacy in the alternate patronage of the precentor and chancellor. The tithes amount to £184, half of which is payable to the curate. The church is a small structure, rebuilt in 1707, with the exception of the tower, which is overspread with ivy; the Ecclesiastical Commissioners have recently granted £207 for its repair: in the churchyard is a mural tablet to the memory of Dr. Delany. In the R. C. divisions the parish forms part of the union or district of Clontarf: a branch from the Carmelite convent of Clondalkin was established here in 1829, attached to which is a school. About 80 children are taught in two public schools, of which one, under the patronage of the Bishop of Kildare, was founded by Dr. Delany, who built the school-house; and there is an infants' school, founded in 1834. Claremont, an extensive institution for deaf and dumb children, was founded in 1816, under the patronage of her present Majesty and the late Duke of Gloucester; the buildings are extensive, and the grounds comprise 18½ acres, subject to a rent of £220. 10. 9. The establishment contains school-rooms and dormitories for 100 children, as poor boarders and pupils, who must be not less than 8 nor more than 12 years old at their admission; it is under the management of a committee of subscribers, and is supported by donations and annual subscriptions, entitling the contributors to the nomination of children in proportion to their subscriptions; the master has accommodations also for children of the richer class, who pay £50 per annum. The Very Rev. Dr. Barret, Vice-Provost of Trinity College, bequeathed £70,000, and Sir Gilbert King, Bart., £7000, to trustees for charitable uses; from the former this institution received £2166. 6. 10. three and a half per cent. stock, and from the latter £332. 6. 1. There is also a private lunatic asylum, under the superintendence of Dr. Eustace, well arranged for the reception of patients. An almshouse for four poor Protestants was founded and endowed by Lord Forbes, in 1723; and there is a dispensary. A field, called the "Bloody Acre," is supposed to have been part of the site of the memorable battle of Clontarf.

GLASSLOUGH, a post-town, in the parish of Donagh, barony of Trough, county of Monaghan, and province of Ulster, 5 miles (N. E.) from Monaghan, and 70¾ (N. W.) from Dublin; containing 812 inhabitants. It is situated on the road from Monaghan to Caledon, on the margin of a beautiful lake, whence the town derives its name, signifying "the green lake." It has a striking and attractive appearance, and contains excellent slated houses. It is favourably situated with regard to commerce and agriculture, but until a very late period had little or no trade. In consequence of the judicious modes which have been adopted by the present owner, Mrs. Leslie, its capabilities have been developed and it has shown decided symptoms of rapid improvement. It has now a weekly market for wheat and flax, and a fair on the third Friday in every month for cattle, sheep, pigs, and other agricultural produce. An extensive flour-mill has been lately built in the neighbourhood, for which an ample supply of wheat is obtained from Glasslough market; and mills are now being built for scutching and spinning flax, also a factory on a large scale for weaving linens by hand and power looms; the whole, when completed, will afford permanent employment to between eight and nine hundred individuals. The beautiful and extensive park and castle of Mrs. Leslie, which adjoins the town and contains upwards of 1000 acres of fine land well planted, adds much to the natural beauty of the situation. The mansion was originally of considerable grandeur, but in consequence of repeated alterations has lost all its antique features. The ancient castle was situated opposite to the town gate of the present house, and was a building of considerable strength, flanked with circular towers and defended by a moat and drawbridge, possessing also those indispensable requisites of feudal power, a keep and donjon. The site had been a place of strength long before its erection, and was granted to O'Bear McKenna by O'Nial of Ulster, on the conditions that he and his descendants should pay "Bonaghty," or tribute, and furnish white meat and oats to the Gallowglasses of O'Nial on certain days when they visited the holy well of Tubber Phadrick, near Glennan, and never to wage war with the O'Nials. This tribute was paid at stated periods in a house built of wood and osiers, at Anaghroe, or the "Red River," now the seat of William Murdoch, Esq. Near the town is the hill and rath of Drumbanagher, where, on the 13th of March, 1688, a battle was fought between a detachment of the Irish army, on its way to join the besiegers of Londonderry, and the native Protestant forces of the district, in which the latter gained a complete victory, but with the loss of their gallant colonel, Matthew Anketell, to whose memory a monument was erected in the parish church, which is still preserved. In the town is the parish church, with a tower 130 feet high: it has nothing in architectural beauty to attract notice; the interior arrangements are plain, neat, and commodious. During the erection of the tower a workman fell from the top, but escaped without suffering any material injury.

GLASSON, a village, partly in the parish of Benowen, but chiefly in that of Kilkenny West, barony of Kilkenny West, county of Westmeath, and province of Leinster, 4 miles (N. E.) from Athlone, on the road to Ballymahon; containing 33 houses and 154 inhabitants. Here are two corn-mills, one of which is also used for thickening frieze. It is a constabulary police station, and petty sessions for the barony are held on alternate Wednesdays. A patent for a market and fair exists, but they are not held. There is a dispensary, and a penny post to Athlone and Ballymahon has been established.—See Benowen.

GLAUNTANE.—See CAHERLOG.

GLENARM, a post-town, in the parish of Tickmacrevan, barony of Upper Glenarm, county of Antrim, and province of Ulster, 17½ miles (N. W.) from Carrickfergus, and 105¾ (N. by E.) from Dublin; containing 880 inhabitants. This town, which has a sub-post-office to Larne and Cushendall, is situated in a deep glen, which opens to the sea, and on the Glenarm river, which here empties itself into the bay of that name, and over which are two bridges. It contains 145 houses, and is said to have been incorporated by a charter of King John, in the 4th year of his reign; but since the conquest of Ulster it has not exercised any municipal privileges. Glenarm castle was for many years the residence of the MacDonnels, Earls of Antrim, of whom Randal MacDonnel, Marquess of Antrim, was attainted during the protectorate. It was originally built in 1639, and is now the seat of Edmund McDonnel, Esq., by whom, since his marriage with the Countess of Antrim, the present castle was erected on the site of the former structure, of which very little remains. It is a noble quadrangular pile, flanked at the angles with four large towers embellished with minarets terminating in vanes, and surmounted with stately domes; the entrance is under a large massive gateway; the hall is of large dimensions and noble appearance, and the state apartments are spacious, lofty, and magnificent. The demesne is richly planted and beautifully embellished with myrtles and other delicate shrubs; at a small distance to the south is the great deer-park, formerly enriched with stately timber, and watered by a mountain torrent, which afterwards flows through the lawn; and on the left of the road to Larne is the little park, bounded by a succession of precipitous rocks rising from the shore, and forming a bold headland, round which has been carried the Antrim coast road from Larne to Ballycastle, cut through the solid rock, and 10 feet above high water mark at spring tides, of which a detailed account is given in the article on the county. The town is much resorted to for sea-bathing; the harbour is small and chiefly frequented by vessels from the opposite coast of Scotland, which bring coal and take back grain, limestone, and other produce. Vessels may ride in safety in the bay within a quarter of a mile from the shore, in five or six fathoms of water. Fairs are held on the 26th of May and October, a chief constabulary police force has been stationed here, and there is also a coast-guard station belonging to the district of Carrickfergus. A court leet and baron for the manor of Glenarm, which is co-extensive with the barony, is held every third week, for the recovery of debts to the amount of £10, in which the proceedings are by attachment and civil bill process. Here is a handsome R. C. chapel, and a good school-house was built in 1829 from the lord-lieutenant's fund. Near the castle are some remains of an ancient Franciscan monastery, founded in 1465 by Sir Robert Bisset, and of which the site and revenues were, after the dissolution, granted to Alexander Mac Donnel, ancestor of the Earls of Antrim. Between Larne and Glenarm are the ruins of Cairn castle, situated on a rock in the sea; and near them are the remains of a castle, built by the family of Shaw in 1625.

GLENAVY, or LYNAVY, a post-town and parish, in the barony of UPPER MASSAREENE, county of ANTRIM, and province of ULSTER, 7½ miles (S.) from Lurgan, on the road to Antrim; containing 3390 inhabitants, of which number, 399 are in the town. According to the Ordnance survey it comprises 16,786 statute acres, 9219½ of which are in Lough Neagh and 342½ in Lough Portmore. The soil is well cultivated, and there is very little waste land or bog; there is some basalt. The town contains 68 houses, and is divided into two equal parts by the river Glenavy. It has four quarterly fairs, principally for horned cattle and pigs. Here is a large cotton-mill, and much flax is spun and woven in the cottages. At Glenconway is an extensive bleach-green. From its situation on Lough Neagh, this parish has a communication by water with Belfast and Newry. The principal seats are Goremount, the residence of Mrs. Gore; Ballyminimore, of W. Oakman, Esq.; and Glenconway, of Mrs. Dickson. The living is a vicarage, in the diocese of Connor, united to the vicarages of Camlin and Tullyrusk, and in the patronage of the Marquess of Hertford, who is impropriator of the rectory and proprietor of the parish: the tithes amount to £221. 19. 4., of which £172. 17. 4. is payable to the vicar, and £49. 2. 2. to the impropriator; and the gross value of the benefice is £380 per annum. The glebe-house, in the parish of Camlin, was built in 1819, on a site given by the Marquess of Hertford, at an expense of £1072, of which £500 was a loan and £300 a gift from the late Board of First Fruits. The church was rebuilt in 1814; it is a handsome edifice with a square tower, for the erection of which the Marquess of Hertford subscribed £100 and the late Board gave £200 and lent £250. In the R. C. divisions the parish is the head of a union or district, comprising also Camlin, and Killead, and containing two chapels, one of which is a large building near Glenavy. There is also a place of worship for Primitive Methodists. There are schools at Ballynacoy, Crew, Fourscore Ballyvanen, and Old Park. On Ram's island, in Lough Neagh, are the remains of a round tower; and in the parish are several raths and tumuli. From Crew hill a fine view is obtained of Lough Neagh and of parts of six counties, with several towns and seats.

GLENBEGH, or GLENBEHY, a parish, partly in the barony of IVERAGH, but chiefly in that of DUNKERRON, county of KERRY, and province of MUNSTER, 13 miles (S. W.) from Milltown; containing 2449 inhabitants. This parish, which is situated on the south-eastern shore of the bay of Dingle, derives its name from its deep seclusion and from the small river Birchen, or Begh, which rises in the mountain lakes and intersects it in its rapid course into the sea. It comprises 25,686 statute acres, as applotted under the tithe act, of which nearly two-thirds are mountain pasture, bog, and rock; and forms an extremely wild and romantic glen surrounded by steep and rugged mountains on all sides except towards the sea, where it is enclosed by a range of low but steep hills, forming a sheltered vale, through which the river Begh pursues the whole of its impetuous course. The highest of the mountains are the Drung and Cahir-Canaway, over which the old road passed into the remoter parts of the baronies of Iveragh and Dunkerron, along a range of precipitous cliffs overhanging the bay. The situation is picturesque and romantic, but its aspect is wild and savage in the extreme; and previously to the commencement of the present improvements, the glen was the inaccessible and secure retreat of lawless violence and the abode of misery and destitution. With the exception of a small detached portion, called the West Fraction, nearly the whole of the parish is the property of Lord Headley, who, in 1807, began a series of improvements, which, though gradual in their progress, have completely changed the appearance of the district and the moral and social habits of its population. The first step was the employment of the people, at his lordship's expense, in providing a facility of communication between the several farms on the estate; and many miles of good road were made, affording easy access to every part of this extensive district; a new line of mail coach road has been constructed, avoiding the steep and dangerous pass over the mountains, and preserving an easy level throughout the whole of this previously impenetrable and isolated part of the country. Since the formation of these roads, the old heavy hurdles or drags have been discontinued, and carts and wheel carriages have been brought into general use, by which great facilities have been afforded for procuring sea-sand as manure, which has greatly increased the fertility of the soil. The wretched huts, which scarcely afforded shelter to the labourers, have given place to neat and comfortable cottages, generally built of stone, most of them containing two rooms and a dairy, and several having two chambers with a dwelling-room and offices, and gardens enclosed and well planted; the old hovels have been converted into sheds for cows and pigs, and every requisite for domestic cleanliness and comfort has been provided. These houses have been erected on an economical plan, at the joint expense of his lordship and the tenants, who being regularly employed in profitable labour, derive from their industry not only the means of present support but a provision for old age. The enclosure, draining, and cultivation of waste land on the mountains and bogs have been greatly promoted, by granting to the tenants stipulated allowances for those purposes. Plantations also have been made by his lordship with very great success, and more than 350 acres have been covered with thriving trees. A spacious chapel has been erected, at the joint expense of his lordship and the tenantry; and a school, in which some hundreds of children have been taught, is partly supported by his lordship. All these improvements were effected within little more than seven years, and the tenantry were in a prosperous and thriving condition, and paid their rents with punctuality till the great depression in the prices of produce in 1815 and 1816. In 1820 his lordship undertook the embankment of 650 acres of land from the sea, which was effected by the labour of the tenantry in liquidation of their arrears: this tract has been permanently secured by a sea wall of great strength, which effectually excludes the tide, and now produces excellent crops of potatoes, oats, and hay. In 1826 a survey of the whole estate was made and further improvements undertaken and carried into effect; 80 farms were laid out varying in extent from land sufficient for 10 to what is sufficient for 40 cows; the various houses were surveyed, and proportionate allowances granted for additions or new buildings; all the best lines of road completed, and the whole regulated upon a plan of mutual benefit to landlord and tenant, and operating powerfully to their reciprocal advantage. The air of this coast is highly salubrious, and several pretty sea-bathing lodges and cottages have been built at Rossbegh, and furnished under the auspices of Lady Headley for the reception of visiters, for whose accommodation a comfortable inn has also been established; the plantations have now attained considerable maturity, and afford an abundant supply of timber; and a steep bank of about 160 acres, previously considered impracticable for planting, is universally admired for the richness and beauty of its foliage. Glencare, the seat of R. Newton, Esq., is situated on Lough Cara, on the borders of the parish. The scenery of this secluded lake is extremely beautiful and romantic, and has been rendered still more picturesque from the recent plantations on its shores. The parish is in the diocese of Ardfert and Aghadoe, and is a rectory and vicarage, forming part of the union of Cahir: the tithes amount to £130. In the R. C. divisions it is the head of a union or district, comprising also part of the parish of Killorglin, and containing a chapel here and another at Glencare, on the border of Killorglin parish. A school held in the R. C. chapel of Glenbegh is principally supported by Lord Headley; and there is a private school, in which about 100 children are educated.

GLENBROHANE, a village, in the parish of Ballingary, barony of Costlea, county of Limerick, and province of Munster, 3 miles (E.) from Kilfinane, on the road to Galbally; containing 44 houses and 233 inhabitants. Here is the R. C. chapel for the district, which was built in 1819, at an expense of £600; also a constabulary police station.

GLENCAR.—See GLENLOUGH.

GLENCOLLUMBKILLE, a parish, in the barony of Bannagh, county of Donegal, and province of Ulster, 11½ miles (N. W. by W.) from Killybegs; containing 3752 inhabitants. This parish, which is on the north-west coast, includes within its limits Tellen head and Malin bay, and, according to the Ordnance survey, comprises 32,243¾ statute acres, of which 329 are water, and 61¾ are in Rathlin O'Birne islands, belonging to Kilbarron parish. Agriculture is backward; the waste land consists of large tracts of sand, bog, and mountain, among the last of which are Malin Beg, rising 1415, Glenlough 1513, and Slieve league 1964, feet above the level of the sea. Four fairs are held at Carrick annually. The living is a consolidated rectory and vicarage, in the diocese of Raphoe, and in the patronage of the Bishop: the tithes amount to £115. The glebe-house was erected by a gift of £369. 4., and a loan of the same amount from the late Board of First Fruits, in 1828. The glebe comprises 40 acres, of which 15 are cultivated land, and the remainder bog, rock, and pasture. The church is a plain building, erected by aid of a gift of £553. 16. from the late Board, in 1828. The R. C. parish is co-extensive with that of the Established Church, and contains two chapels. About 220 children are educated in three public schools, of which the parochial school is aided by an endowment from Col. Robertson's fund. On the summit of Slieve league are the remains of a religious house: here are also some ruins of a castle. On the site of the present church formerly stood a monastery, of which scarcely a vestige is left, except a subterraneous passage, which was discovered a few years since on digging a grave. A ruin is pointed out as having been the residence of St. Columb, and a cavity in an adjoining rock is called his bed. There is a well, dedicated to St. Columb, at which a patron is held, with twelve ancient stone crosses, placed a quarter of a mile apart, as preparatory stations to visiting the well. There is a remarkable echo in the mountains.

GLENDALIGAN, a village, in the parish of Kilrosanty, barony of Decies-without-Drum, county of Waterford, and province of Munster, 6 miles (S. W.) from Kilmacthomas; containing 178 inhabitants.

GLENDALOUGH, a manor, in the parish of Derralossory, barony of Ballynacor, county of Wicklow, and province of Leinster, 6 miles (N. W.) from Rathdrum; containing 1819 inhabitants. This place, originally called Gleande, or "the town of the glen," and also Glandelagh and the Seven Churches, derives its present appellation, Glendalough, or "the glen of the two lakes," from the name of the valley in which it is situated. This valley, which abounds with the most picturesque and romantic scenery, was part of the district of Imayle which, extending widely towards the south and west, formed the ancient territory of the powerful sept of the Otothils or O'Tooles, who maintained possession of it with uncontrolled authority till the 17th century. From the numerous remains of its ancient religious foundations, from which probably it derived the name of the Seven Churches, and from the existence of one of those ancient round towers so frequently found in similar situations, it appears to have been a place of religious retreat prior to the introduction of Christianity; and from its early importance and secluded situation, it has long been regarded with feelings of veneration, as one of the most celebrated seats of ancient ecclesiastical institutions. The first Christian church established here was founded by St. Kevin, who was born of a noble family about the year 498, but choosing a monastic life retired to these solitudes, and founded an abbey in the lower part of the vale. So great was the reputation of St. Kevin, that St. Mochuorog, a Briton, also fixed his residence here; and a school was soon established, which concentrated a great portion of the learning of the times and produced some of the most eminent men of that period. A city soon arose around this monastery, which became the seat of a diocese, including the present see of Dublin, and of which St. Kevin, who also held the abbacy of Glendalough, was the first bishop. Having presided over the see till 612, he resigned the care of the bishoprick, attending solely to the duties of the abbacy, and died on the 3rd of June, 618, in the 120th year of his age. The see of Glendalough, after the resignation of St. Kevin, continued under a regular succession of bishops to flourish for 600 years, when, on the death of William Piro, in 1214, it was united to the see of Dublin, at the suggestion of Cardinal Paparo, who had delivered one of the palls to the metropolitan bishop, and this union was confirmed by Pope Honorius in 1216. The sept of the O'Tooles, however, could never be induced to acknowledge the authority of the English Archbishops of Dublin, but was still governed by Irish bishops of Glendalough for many years, till 1497, when Friar Dennis White, the last bishop, formally surrendered possession of the see of Glendalough, and the authority of the Archbishops of Dublin was fully acknowledged. It appears from the records of the see, that Glendalough, which was the depository of the wealth of the neighbouring septs, was frequently plundered by the Danes, and also by the English, after whose invasion the city was never able to preserve the importance it had previously maintained. In 1309, Piers Gavestone defeated the sept of the O'Byrnes at this place, and having rebuilt the castle of Kevin and opened the pass between it and Glendalough, presented an offering at the shrine of St. Kevin. In 1398, the English forces burnt the city, which never afterwards recovered its prosperity. In 1580, one of the Fitzgeralds, uniting with Lord Baltinglass and a chieftain of the O'Byrnes, occupied this valley in open hostility to the government, and the Lord-Deputy Grey, who had just arrived from England and was totally unacquainted with the country, gave orders for their immediate dislodgement. The officers, who had assembled to congratulate him on his arrival, accordingly led their troops to the valley; but as they began to explore its recesses, perplexed with bogs and overhung by rocks, a volley was poured in among them from an unseen enemy, and repeated with dreadful execution. Audley, Moore, Crosby, and Sir Peter Carew, all distinguished officers, fell in this rash adventure; and Lord Grey, who had awaited the result on an eminence in the vicinity, returned with the remainder of his troops to Dublin. On the suppression of the disturbances of 1798, Dwyer and his followers took refuge among the fastnesses of Glendalough, and remained in perfect security in the mountains till they procured an amnesty from the government.

The ancient city is now only a heap of scattered ruins, imparting a venerable and solitary grandeur to that part of the valley in which they are situated. The vale is about two miles in length, and about three-quarters of a mile in breadth, enclosed on the north by the mountains of Brockagh and Comaderry, and on the south by those of Derrybawn and Lugduff; it is entirely inaccessible from the west, but opens towards the east, where its waters are discharged by a powerful stream into the river Avonmore. About halfway up the valley, and at the farthest extremity to which cultivation has been extended, are the principal remains of the city, occupying a gentle eminence projecting from the base of the mountain of Comaderry, beyond which the two lakes, overshadowed by the vast precipices of the mountains of Derrybawn and Lugduff, present a scene of sombre magnificence, rendered still more impressive by the opposite heights of Comaderry, whose summit is 1567 feet above their surface. In the mountain of Derrybawn, which is composed of mica slate, is a break in the strata, where one part has sunk many feet below the other, and which is called the "Giants' Cut;" and a little farther between it and Lugduff the Glaneola brook, falling into the upper lake over some richly wooded rocks, forms several picturesque cascades. On the same side of the glen, under the gloomy brow of Lugduff, and in a precipice rising perpendicularly to the height of 30 feet from the surface of the lake, is the remarkable excavation called St. Kevin's bed, said to have been the retreat of that saint; it is large enough only for one person in a recumbent position, and is surrounded by a zone of rocky mountains encircling the lake, of which the waters, though perfectly limpid, have an appearance of sombre darkness. In storms the lake is violently agitated and sometimes overflows the meadows which separate it from the lower lake; and in calm weather an echo of surprising distinctness is formed between the rocks near the Giants' Cut and the opposite side of the valley. Amidst these scenes, to which the genius of Moore has given a high degree of celebrity, are to be found numerous vestiges of antiquity, and many objects which are intimately associated with the most pleasing and interesting periods of Irish history. These venerable remains form a group of diversified appearance, and above them rises in isolated grandeur one of those ancient round towers, the origin of which has so much excited the researches of the antiquary. The approach to these interesting relics is across the mountain torrent of Glendhasane, which descends from the back of Comaderry, on the near side of which are the traces of a paved road, leading out by Wicklow Gap, in the direction of Hollywood, and called St. Kevin's Road; also of a small paved area, said to have been the market-place of the ancient city. On the other side of the road is a gateway, the arches of which are still entire. The most conspicuous of these ruins is the ancient cathedral, of which the nave and choir were connected by a circular arch, which has fallen down; three narrow windows in the south wall of the nave, and the east window of the chancel, enriched with mouldings and allegorical sculpture on the inside, are still remaining; as is also the western doorway, which is formed of blocks of granite. Nearly adjacent are vestiges of a small building, probably the sacristy, around which are numerous crosses, mostly mutilated; one is formed of a single block of granite,

11 feet high and very neatly worked, which it is said stood on a base of masonry now visible in the market-place. There are foundations of various extensive buildings, the arrangement and design of which it is now impossible to ascertain; and beyond these is a church, with a stone roof, of very remote antiquity, called St. Kevin's Kitchen, and by far the most perfect of all the churches of which there are any remains. The interior is 22 feet 9 inches long and 15 feet wide; the vaulting of the ceiling is circular, and the roof rises to a very high pitch in horizontal courses of mica slate; in the ceiling is an opening to a circular turret at the west end, with a conical roof, built in exact resemblance of the ancient round towers; the church is lighted by one narrow window only, and at the west end is a small chapel of more recent date, similarly lighted and having a roof of lower pitch; this building was used as a R. C. chapel within the last ten years. To the west of these remains, and on the same side of the vale, are the ruins now called the Church of our Lady, the architecture of which was evidently of more ornamental character; it is very small and thickly mantled with ivy, from which it is sometimes called the Ivy Church. On the south side of the valley, near the influx of the Glaneola brook into the upper lake, are the interesting remains of Rhefeart church, or "the sepulchre of kings," so called from its being the mausoleum of the O'Tooles; and on the south side of it is a monumental stone to one of those ancient kings, who was interred here in 1010; these remains are covered with ivy and deeply embosomed in groves of hazel and other trees, and within the cemetery are some fragments of ancient crosses. On a spot of ground projecting from the base of Lugduff into the upper lake, are the ruins of the church of Teampulnaskellig, "the temple of the desert or the rock," also called the priory of the rock and St. Kevin's cell. Lower in the valley are two other churches, both enclosed in grounds that have been greatly improved; the one on the north side is called Trinity Church, and that on the south side, the Abbey or Monastery Church, but by Archdall and Ledwich, the priory of St. Saviour. Trinity Church consists of a nave and chancel, separated by a fine arch, similar in design to that which forms the entrance to the city, and has some remains of a round tower. The abbey originally consisted of two parallel ranges of building, of a style far exceeding in elegance of design and in architectural embellishment any of the other buildings of this interesting valley; there are still some portions of a very fine arch, and numerous stones richly sculptured with allegorical devices, that have formed part of the eastern window, and other ornamental portions of the building. On the summit of the gentle eminence on which the cathedral stood, and within the limits of its cemetery, is an ancient round tower, 110 feet high, with a band round its summit, from which rose a roof of conical form; it is built of the mica slate with which this place abounds, and also of granite. The cemetery of the cathedral continued for many ages to be a favourite place of interment, and monumental stones are consequently very numerous; the tomb of St. Kevin is said to have been found in a small crypt, or oratory, near the Abbey or Monastery Church, some few years since; and various relics of antiquity are scattered throughout the valley. A range of stone crosses appears to have extended along a road across the valley, and there are numerous blocks of granite with circular basins formed in them, concerning which are various traditionary legends.

The inhabitants of the valley live chiefly in cottages dispersed along the southern side; and near Derrybawn bridge the streams from the lakes of Glendalough meet the Annamoe river, which thence takes the name of Avonmore. At the base of the mountain of that name is Derrybawn, the seat of W. Bookey, Esq., pleasantly situated in the midst of natural woods and thriving plantations. From this point the road to Rathdrum runs parallel with the Avonmore, through the richly wooded and picturesque vale of Clara; the military road from Dublin crosses the mountains into Glenmalur. Near its junction with the road to Roundwood, and at the foot of Laragh hill, are the Laragh barracks, at present occupied only by a party of police, though constituting an important and formidable military station in case of need. A new road has been made leading up Glendhasane to Hollywood; and near it, at the back of Comaderry mountain, are the lead mines of Glendhasane, held under the Archbishop of Dublin by the Mining Company of Ireland. The vein of ore completely intersects the mountain, from the summit of which the view towards the east is peculiarly fine; the ore, when dressed, is conveyed to the smelting-houses of Ballycorus, in the county of Dublin, and the works employ on an average about 100 men. Lead ore is also supposed to exist in other parts, and in 1835 a search was made for it at the head of the lake in Glendalough. In the vicinity is a quarry of fine talc slate of excellent quality for making mantel-pieces. Between Comaderry and the mountain of Tonelagee, towards the north-east, and at the base of an impending precipice, is Lough Nahanaghan, about half a mile long and a quarter of a mile broad, abounding with excellent trout. In the vale of Glenmacanass, through which the military road passes, is an enormous basin formed by a curvature in the mountain's slope, down the perpendicular side of which descends a considerable stream, forming a cascade. The contiguous rocks present various interesting mineralogical specimens: and about half a mile farther is a small circular lake, called Lough Outer, overshadowed by the towering precipices of the mountain of Tonelagee, which rises to the height of 2696 feet above the level of the sea, and near which is a Danish rath. Near the village is a small rivulet, called St. Kevin's Keeve, the water of which is supposed to have peculiar efficacy in promoting the health of weakly children, who are immersed in the stream for that purpose; and on the lands of Derrybawn, on the opposite side of the river, and near St. Kevin's Kitchen, is St. Kevin's Well, which is much resorted to by the peasantry of the surrounding neighbourhood. St. Kevin's national school was built in 1832, at an expense of £140.

GLENDERMOT, or CLONDERMOT, a parish, in the barony of TIRKEERAN, county of LONDONDERRY, and province of ULSTER; containing, with the town of Waterside, which is one of the suburbs of Londonderry, 10,338 inhabitants. This parish, which is separated from the city of Londonderry by the river Foyle, over which is a fine wooden bridge, 1068 feet long, comprises 22,495 acres, of which 987 are water. A religious house is said to have been founded here by St. Patrick, which was probably the church of Kil Ard, of which the foundations are still traceable. St. Columbkill founded a monastery here in 588, at the place which still bears his name; and Ailid O'Dermit founded a nunnery at Rossnagalliagh, in 879, of which some traces remain. The founder of the extensive building, of which the ruins are on Lough Enagh, is unknown; it probably belonged to the Knights Hospitallers, and was afterwards a chapel of ease to Clondermot, and as such was confirmed to the Dean of Derry in 1609, under the name of Annagh. In the Earl of Tyrone's rebellion the church of St. Columb and the parish church were destroyed; the former was not rebuilt, but some of its ruins are visible. The soil in the northern portion of the parish is rich and well cultivated, but there is a considerable quantity of moorland in the southern part. Quarries of slate and blue limestone exist. At Ardmore is a bleach-green, the first established in this part of the country, where 25,000 pieces of linen are finished annually; there is also one at the Oaks, and a large distillery at Waterside. The water for the supply of the city of Londonderry is obtained from an elevated spot near Prehen, and conveyed in cast-iron pipes over the bridge across the Foyle into the city. Besides that bridge, there is a handsome one over the Faughan, near Enagh; another on the Coleraine road, a little lower down, and a third at Drumahoe. The Bishop's, the Goldsmiths', and the Grocers' manors extend over parts of this parish, but no manorial courts are held. The principal seats are Prehen, the residence of Col. Knox; Beech Hill, of Conolly Skipton, Esq.; Ashbrook, of W. H. Ashe, Esq.; Ardmore, of J. A. Smith, Esq.; Larchmount, of C. McClelland, Esq.; Lisdillon, of W. J. Smith, Esq.; Berryburn, of Capt. Reynolds; Ardkill, of R. Stephenson, Esq.; Bellevue, of the Rev. J. D. Maughan; Bonds Hill, of J. Murray, Esq.; St. Columbs, of G. Hill, Esq.; Glendermot glebe, of the Rev. A. G. Cary; Caw, of A. Harvey, Esq.; Lower Caw, of J. Alexander, Esq.; and Coolkeragh, of R. Young, Esq. The living is a perpetual curacy, in the diocese of Derry, and in the gift of the Dean of Derry; the rectory was united by patent in 1609, to Templemore and Faughanvale, the three forming the union of Templemore and the corps of the deanery of Derry, which is in the patronage of the Crown; the Ecclesiastical Commissioners recommend the dissolution of the union. The tithes amount to £920. 11. 8., and the perpetual curate is paid by the dean. The church is a large handsome building, in the Grecian style, erected in 1753, and for the repairs of which the Ecclesiastical Commissioners have recently granted £509. The glebe-house is situated on a glebe of 12 acres, purchased by the late Board of First Fruits in 1824, and is occupied by the perpetual curate. The rector's glebe comprises 407 acres, and the deanery lands in Clondermot consist of 1284 acres. In the R. C. divisions the parish is united to part of Lower Cumber; there is a small neat chapel at Curryneirin. At Altnagelirn are two meeting-houses for Presbyterians in connection with the Synod of Ulster, one of the first, the other of the third, class; and at Drumahoe is one connected with the Seceding Synod. There are parochial schools at Clondermot, on the glebe, and at the new church, aided by the dean; there are also schools at Salem, Ardmore, Lisdillon, and Drumahoe; the Grocers' Company have built and maintain a school at Gortnessey; a school at Prehen is supported by Col. Knox and the perpetual curate; there is a national school at Curryneirin, and female work schools at Ardmore and Bellevue; also four Sunday schools. Col. Mitchelburne, who was a native of this place, and many of the other defenders of Londonderry, are interred in the burial-ground of Clondermot, in which are considerable remains of the old church.

GLENFIN.—See KILTEEVOCK.

GLENFLESK.—See KILLAHA.

GLENGARIFF.—See KILMOCOMOGUE.

GLENLOUGH, or GLENCAR, an ecclesiastical district, in the barony of ROSSCLOGHER, county of LEITRIM, and province of CONNAUGHT; containing 1524 inhabitants. It was constituted in 1810, by separating 28 townlands from the parish of Killasnet, and comprises 3612 statute acres, chiefly under pasture. The living is a perpetual curacy, in the diocese of Kilmore, and in the patronage of the Incumbent of Killasnet: the income of the perpetual curate is £69. 5., of which £46. 3. is paid by the vicar of Killasnet, and £23. 2. from the augmentation funds at the disposal of the Ecclesiastical Commissioners. The church is a plain neat building, erected in 1821, at an expense of £553. 16. 11., being a gift from the late Board of First Fruits. In the R. C. divisions it is part of the district of Killasnet, and contains a chapel.

GLENOGRA, a parish, in the barony of SMALL COUNTY, county of LIMERICK, and province of MUNSTER, 5 miles (N. W.) from Bruff, on the road to Croom; containing 1278 inhabitants. The parish comprises 4237 statute acres, as applotted under the tithe act, about a fourth of which, though very productive, is under an unimproved system of tillage; the remainder consists principally of dairy farms. There is a patent for fairs to be held on May 11th, and Oct. 28th. The seats of Cahir Guillamore and Rockbarton form the most interesting features in the parish; the former, standing in the midst of an extensive, fertile, and well planted demesne, is the residence of the Hon. Lieut.-Col. O'Grady; and the latter is the splendid residence of his father, Viscount Guillamore, who, having for several years presided as Chief Baron of the Exchequer, was raised to the peerage in 1831, by the titles of Baron O'Grady, of Rockbarton, and Viscount Guillamore, of Cahir Guillamore. It is a vicarage, in the diocese of Limerick, forming part of the union of Fedamore; the rectory is appropriate to the vicars choral of Christ-Church cathedral, Dublin. The tithes amount to £285, of which the vicar has one-third, and two-thirds are paid to the lessee of the vicars choral. Five small glebes belong to this parish, comprising together 29½ acres: they were originally the endowments of chantries connected with the abbey church founded here by the De Lacys, which at the Reformation contained nine amply endowed chantries, and was governed by a prior. Four of the chantries can still be traced in the ruins of the church, which was a large cruciform building, and contained tombs of the De Lacys, Roches, Bourkes, O'Gradys, and Fitzgeralds. In the R. C. divisions the parish is included partly in the district of Drenin, but chiefly in that of Bruff, and has a small chapel at Meanus. On the banks of the Commogue, and near the site of the abbey, are the ruins of the castle of Glenogra. It is supposed to have been built in the 13th century by the Fitzharrises, or the De Lacys, and subsequently belonged to the

Earl of Desmond, who was unsuccessfully besieged in it by Lord Thurles, in 1536; the latter, however, captured the castle of Lough Gur, commanded by the Earl's brother, which he repaired and garrisoned. Glenogra castle was a large pile of building, and some of its walls, cellars, and underground stairs are still moderately perfect. In the demesne of Cahir are traces of some buildings which are supposed to be the ruins of an ancient city, and in their vicinity are remains of druidical structures.

GLENROE.—See DARAGH.

GLENVILLE, a village, in the parish of ARDNAGEEHY, barony of BARRYMORE, county of CORK, and province of MUNSTER; the population is returned with the parish. This village, which is situated on a hill, and is remarkable for the neatness of the houses, contains the parish church, R. C. chapel, the parochial schools, a constabulary police station, and a dispensary.

GLENWHIRRY, an extra-parochial district, in the barony of LOWER ANTRIM, county of ANTRIM, and province of ULSTER, 6 miles (W. by S.) from Larne, on the road to Broughshane; containing 1358 inhabitants. According to the Ordnance survey it comprises 11,368¼ statute acres. There is a meeting-house for Presbyterians in connection with the Synod of Ulster, of the third class. About 80 children are educated in two private schools, and there is a Sunday school.

GLIN, a market and post-town, and a parish, in the Shanid Division of the barony of LOWER CONNELLO, county of LIMERICK, and province of MUNSTER, 12 miles (W.) from Askeaton, and 117 (S. W. by W.) from Dublin, on the mail coach road from Askeaton to Tarbert; containing 4790 inhabitants, of which number, 1030 are in the town. This place, with the adjacent territory, was granted by Hen. II. to John Fitz-Thomas Fitz-Gerald, lord of Decies and Desmond, whose descendants, the Earls of Desmond, were by succeeding kings of England created princes palatine in Ireland, with the power of making tenures in capite and creating barons (by which authority they created the Knight of Glin and others) and were entitled to royal services and escheats. The manor, with all its honours and privileges, though forfeited for a short time in the 18th of Hen. VIII., and also in the 11th of Elizabeth, was restored in 1603, and has since descended through an uninterrupted succession in the male line, for more than 600 years, to John Fraunceis Fitzgerald, the 19th Knight of Glin, its present proprietor. During the rebellion of the Earl of Desmond in the reign of Elizabeth, the castle was besieged by Sir George Carew, Lord-President of Munster, assisted by the Earl of Thomond, and after two days' resolute defence by the Knight of Glin, was taken by the English. The besiegers having obtained possession of the lower part, ascended to the battlements, where the remnant of the garrison, about 80 in number, made their last desperate stand. A sanguinary conflict took place on the staircase, every step of which was fiercely contested; but the English were successful, and the Knight and his gallant band were either put to the sword, or leaped into the river and were drowned. The town, which owes much of its improvement to its present proprietor, is beautifully situated on the southern bank of the river Shannon, which is here nearly three miles in breadth; and contains about 280 houses, several of which are well built and of handsome appearance. Among the more recent improvements is a handsome terrace, built by John Hamilton, Esq., and commanding some fine views over the Shannon, which abounds with beautiful and interesting scenery; a new line of road from Askeaton to Tarbert, completed at a very great expense; and a road through the mountains to Abbeyfeale, a distance of 12 miles, which was opened in 1836. In summer the town is much resorted to for the benefit of pure air and the advantages of sea-bathing, and is admirably situated for carrying on a very extensive trade, the river affording great facilities of intercourse, and secure anchorage for vessels of any burden. The surrounding scenery is richly diversified, embracing a fine view of the opposite coast of Clare, the island of Scattery, and the fertile promontory of Tarbert, with its lofty and handsome lighthouse. This place is the great depôt of the salmon fishery of the Shannon and its tributary rivers, of which large quantities are annually shipped for England; oysters of very superior flavour and other fish are also taken in abundance. The manufacture of linen and cotton checks is carried on to some extent, and there is a considerable trade in corn and butter, which are shipped to Cork and Limerick. The market is on Saturday; and fairs are held on June 8th, the first Wednesday in Sept. (O. S.), and Dec. 3rd, for cattle and pigs. A constabulary police force is stationed here; a manorial court is held every third week, for the recovery of debts to any amount, with extensive jurisdiction; and petty sessions are held every alternate Saturday. There is a substantial bridewell, containing six cells, two day-rooms, and two spacious airing-yards.

The parish, also called *Kilfergus*, comprises 14,637 statute acres, as applotted under the tithe act, of which about one-third is under tillage, one-third mountain and bog, and the remainder pasture and demesne land. The land around the town is very fertile, and in several parts of the mountains, which everywhere afford good pasturage for young cattle, very good crops of wheat are raised. There are several large dairy farms; a large butter market is held in the town, and great quantities of butter are made here and sent to Limerick and Cork for exportation. The system of agriculture is rapidly improving; an abundance of shell manure of excellent quality is either raised in the Shannon or brought from the opposite coast; and limestone is sometimes brought from Foynes island and burnt for manure. There are some quarries of hard compact clay-slate, used for building; and flag-stones of superior quality and of very large size are found in several parts of the parish. The mountains are of silicious grit and indurated black clay, in which are several strata of coal: of these, only the upper stratum has been worked, and in a very inefficient manner; the only workings now in progress are at Cloghgough. Ironstone of very good quality is also plentiful, but has hitherto been applied solely to the making of roads. The principal seats are Glin Castle, the spacious and elegant mansion of the Knight of Glin, finely situated in a richly planted and highly embellished demesne; Westwood, of Lieut. Hyde, R. N.; Shannon View, of the Rev. R. Fitzgerald; Shannon Lawn, of D. Harnett, Esq.; Fort Shannon, of J. Evans, Esq.; Ballydonohoe, of T. Fitzgerald, Esq.; Eastwood of the Rev. E. Ashe; Cahara Lodge, of Mrs. Johnston; Villa, of

J. Hamilton, Esq.; Glin Lodge, of Mrs. Standish; Clare View, of the Rev. R. Fitzgerald; Gardenville, of Miss Sargent; and Cahara House, of R. Q. Sleeman, Esq. The living is a vicarage, in the diocese of Limerick, and in the patronage of the Vicars Choral of the cathedral of Limerick, to whom the rectory is appropriate; the tithes amount to £337. 10., of which £225 is payable to the appropriators, and the remainder to the vicar. There is neither glebe-house nor glebe. The church, a very neat edifice in the early English style, with a square tower, was erected on an eminence close to the town, in 1815, by a gift of £600 from the late Board of First Fruits. In the R. C. divisions the parish is the head of a union or district, comprising also the parish of Loughill; the chapel, near the church, is a large plain building, and there is a chapel at Loughill. About 70 children are taught in a school to which the R. C. clergyman annually contributes; and there are six private schools, in which are about 250 children; a Sunday school, and a dispensary. About half a mile to the east of the town are the ruins of the ancient church of Kilfergus, or Glin, situated within the parish of Loughill, to which that and the adjoining townland continue to pay tithes; within the ruined walls is the family vault of the Knights of Glin. The old castle, with the exception of the roof, is still nearly entire; it consists of a massive square tower on a rock, in the bed of a small river, close to its junction with the Shannon. Near it is an ancient bridge, where was the only pass over the river, which the castle was most probably built to protect. There are numerous ancient forts in various parts of the parish, five of which are within the demesne of Castle Glin; and at Flean, in the mountains, are the remains of a very ancient church, of which the history is unknown.

GLYNN, a parish, in the barony of Lower Belfast, county of Antrim, and province of Ulster, 1½ mile (S.) from Larne; containing 1668 inhabitants, of which number, 379 are in the village. This parish, anciently called Glinus, and also Gleno or Glenco, is beautifully situated in a pleasant glen, through which a mountain stream takes its course into Lough Larne, which forms the entire eastern boundary of the parish; and also on the royal military coast road. The harbour of Larne is very capacious, and may be entered at all times of the tide. In 1597, Sorley Mac Donnel, having assaulted the garrison of Carrickfergus and taken the governor, Sir John Chichester, prisoner, brought him to this place, and beheaded him on a stone that had formed the plinth of an ancient cross, and which then pointed out the boundary of North Clandeboy. The parish comprises 4484½ statute acres, which are generally in a state of high cultivation; the system of agriculture is greatly improved, and there is neither bog nor waste land. Here are some very extensive lime-works, called the Maghramorne Lime Works, the property of John Irving, Esq., from which large quantities of lime are exported to Scotland and the northern parts of England. These are the largest lime-works in the united kingdom: in 1836, there were 459 vessels, of the aggregate burden of 18,040 tons, exclusively employed in the trade; the average export is 16,228 tons, and the demand is annually increasing; the sum paid weekly for labour amounts to £1804. On a chymical analysis by Dr. Thomson, of Glasgow, the stone is found to contain 99 per cent. of pure lime, and it has been ascertained by experience that, whether employed as a manure or a cement for building, it will go twice as far as lime of the ordinary quality. Rail and tram roads have been laid down, which greatly facilitate the operations; there are also convenient wharfs, so that any quantity of the article can be furnished without delay or detention of the shipping. The principal seats are Maghramorne House, a modern mansion, beautifully situated on the bay of Larne, the residence of Mr. Irving, who is also the chief proprietor of the lands in the barony; Glynn House, that of Randall W. Johnston, Esq.; and the Cottage, of Miss McClaverty. The village is pleasantly situated and contains 75 houses neatly built. One of the first bleach-greens established in Ireland was at this place; it was subsequently the site of a cotton-mill, and in 1830 the machinery was applied to the spinning of fine linen yarn, in which about 120 persons are at present employed. The living is a vicarage, in the diocese of Connor, and in the patronage of the Marquess of Donegal, in whom the rectory is impropriate: the vicarial tithes amount to £52. There is no glebe-house or glebe, and the church is a picturesque ruin; the Protestant parishioners attend the different places of worship in Larne. About 35 children are taught in the parochial school, for which a house was built by R. W. Johnston, Esq.; and there are two private schools, in which are about 100 children. A nunnery was founded here at a very remote period, of which St. Darerca, sister of St. Patrick, was abbess; it was called Linn, and is supposed to have been situated at Glynn, near Larne, where some traces of a chapel still exist; the site, with all its possessions, was granted by Jas. I. to Sir Arthur Chichester, by the designation of the "Chapel of Glynn." Here is a powerful vitriolic spring, in which the star stone is found in great perfection.

GLYNN, county of Wexford.—See KILLURIN.

GOLDEN, a village and post-town, in the parish of Relickmurry, barony of Clanwilliam, county of Tipperary, and province of Munster, 3½ miles (W.) from Cashel (to which it has a sub-post-office), and 82 (S.) from Dublin, on the road from Cashel to Tipperary; containing 114 houses and 648 inhabitants. It is a neat and improving village, situated in what is called "the Golden Vale," and is divided into two parts by the river Suir, over which is a stone bridge, on which King William signed the charter of Cashel; and near it is an old circular stone tower. Here are flour and oatmeal-mills, and a constabulary police station; fairs are held on May 18th, Aug. 26th, Oct. 26th, and Dec. 15th, and petty sessions once a fortnight. The parochial church was erected here in 1808, and a tower was added by aid of a loan of £700 from the late Board of First Fruits, in 1812. There is also a large R. C. chapel.—See Relickmurry.

GOLDENBRIDGE, a village, in the parish of St. James, barony of Newcastle, county of Dublin, and province of Leinster, 2 miles (W.) from Dublin, on the road to Naas: the population is included in the return for the parish. The Grand Canal passes close to the village, in which are paper, flour, and pearl barley mills. Near it, in an elevated and healthy situation, are the Richmond Infantry Barracks, consisting of two fronts with extensive courts open to the north and south; these are connected by a row of light and elegant houses,

300 yards in length. On the east and west fronts are two spacious areas, and in the centre a communication through a large portal surmounted by a cupola and spire. They occupy 14 Irish acres, and afford accommodation for 76 officers and 1600 privates; there is also stabling for 25 horses, and an hospital for 100 patients. A school-house was erected here in 1827 by subscription, aided by a grant of £250 from Government, which is used on Sundays as a chapel for the troops and the inhabitants of the neighbourhood. Near it is a Wesleyan Methodist meeting-house, and an infants' school was erected by subscription in 1835. Here is a cemetery, principally for Roman Catholics, which was purchased and enclosed by the late Catholic Association, at a cost of £1000; the first stone was laid in 1829. It contains about two Irish acres tastefully laid out, with an Ionic temple in the centre, in which the burial service may be performed for persons of every denomination. In two years from the time of its being opened it was nearly filled, about 12,000 persons having been interred within that period, and several handsome monuments erected. Waterloo Spa is in this village: the waters consist principally of sulphuretted hydrogen gas united with carbonic acid and magnesia, and are said to be beneficial in bilious and liver complaints, scrofula, and several other diseases.

GOOGANE-BARRA.—See INCHEGEELA.

GORESBRIDGE, a post-town, in the parish of GRANGE-SILVAE, barony of GOWRAN, county of KILKENNY, and province of LEINSTER, 2¾ miles (E.) from Gowran, and 52 (S. W.) from Dublin, on the road from Kilkenny to Enniscorthy; containing 634 inhabitants. This town takes its name from the family of its former chief proprietor, Col. Gore, and from the bridge over the Barrow, which here connects the counties of Kilkenny and Carlow. A patent for a market is extant, but none is held. It is a constabulary and a revenue police station, and has petty sessions every fortnight, and fairs on the 18th of January and December. The cattle fairs for Barrowmount are also held here on April 13th, June 15th, Aug. 1st, and Oct. 15th. A handsome church was erected in 1811, and here is a large R. C. chapel.—See GRANGE-SILVAE.

Arms.

GOREY, or NEWBOROUGH, an incorporated market-town (formerly a parliamentary borough), and a parish, in the barony of GOREY, county of WEXFORD, and province of LEINSTER, 26¼ miles (N.) from Wexford, and 48 (S.) from Dublin; containing 4387 inhabitants, of which number, 3044 are in the town. This place derives its modern appellation, Newborough, which has never grown into general use, from a charter of incorporation obtained for the inhabitants in the 17th of Jas. I., by Dr. Thomas Ram, Bishop of Ferns. The Episcopal palace in this town, in which the bishops of that see resided, was, in 1641, attacked by the parliamentarians, who burned the library; the house was subsequently converted into an inn, afterwards into a barrack, and was taken down only within the last few years. In the disturbances of 1798, the town, after the defeat of Col. Walpole at Tubbernearing, fell into the hands of the insurgents, who destroyed the mansions of Ramsfort and Clonatin, the handsome seats of the family of Ram, and several houses belonging to their opponents. After the battle of Vinegar Hill, many of the inhabitants of the town and neighbourhood, who had taken refuge in Wicklow, thinking that order had been restored, ventured to return to their respective homes, but were met by a large party of retreating insurgents and many of them were put to death. It is situated within two miles of St. George's channel, on the mail coach road from Dublin to Wexford, and consists principally of one long street neatly and uniformly built, containing 548 houses; it is partially paved, and is amply supplied with water from the park by means of a fountain. The neighbourhood is pleasingly diversified with hill and dale, wood and water; and within the circuit of a few miles are several elegant seats and villas standing in grounds tastefully laid out and enriched with thriving plantations. The North Wexford Agricultural Association for the baronies of Gorey, Scarawalsh, and Ballaghkeen, established in 1826, holds its meetings in the town, on the second Tuesday in September, for the distribution of premiums for improvements in agriculture, and for the encouragement of neatness and comfort in cottages; towards which latter the Irish Peasantry Society contributes an annual grant of £20, and its beneficial effects are already exhibited in the superior neatness of the cottages in the neighbourhood. The great show of stock takes place on the same day, and in October is a sale for improved breeds of cattle, when also there is a show of stock; a ploughing match and a show of stock also takes place every spring. The sums distributed in premiums, on an average, amount to nearly £250 per annum; the president, the Earl of Courtown, gives two medals annually for fat cattle and breeding stock, which are adjudged at the spring show. There is an extensive brewery; flour-mills have been recently erected, and it is in contemplation to erect some cotton-mills and a distillery. A savings' bank has been established in the town. The market is on Saturday, and is abundantly supplied with provisions of all kinds and poultry, especially chickens, for which the place is noted; and on the completion of Courtown harbour the supply of fish will be equally abundant. Fairs are held on the Saturdays before Shrove-Tuesday, and St. Patrick's day; on the Saturdays nearest to April 18th, May 2nd, June 1st, Sept. 29th, and Nov. 28th, and also on the 1st of Jan., 10th of July, 31st of August, and 27th of October, for horses, cattle, and pigs. The market-house is a plain but commodious building, situated in the centre of the town; the upper part, formerly used as a court-house, is now appropriated to the use of the parochial school.

The inhabitants were incorporated by Jas. I., in the 17th of his reign, under the designation of the "Sovereign, burgesses, and free commons of the borough and town of Newborough;" they also received a new charter from Jas. II., which never came into operation. The corporation, under the former, consists of a sovereign, 12 burgesses, and an unlimited number of free commoners, assisted by a recorder, a town-clerk, and other officers. The sovereign, who is also coroner and clerk of the market, is elected by the burgesses; he is, with his predecessor, justice of the peace, and may appoint a deputy. The burgesses, as vacancies occur, are chosen by the sovereign and burgesses from the free commoners, and these are admitted by the sovereign and burgesses; the recorder, who is also town-clerk, is appointed by the corporation. The borough returned members to the Irish parliament till the Union, when it was disfranchised, and the sum of £15,000 awarded as compensation was paid to Stephen Ram, Esq. The corporation was empowered to levy tolls, and to hold courts for the recovery of debts to the amount of £20 late currency; but neither of these privileges is now exercised. Epiphany and Midsummer quarter sessions for the county are held here, and petty sessions on alternate Fridays, which latter are said to have been the first of that kind regularly held in Ireland. The court-house, a neat and appropriate building, was erected in 1819, at the expense of the county, on a site given by the late Stephen Ram, Esq. A chief constabulary police force is stationed in the town.

The parish, called also Christ-Church-Newborough, or Kilmichaelogue, comprises 5052 statute acres, as applotted under the tithe act; the soil is good, and the system of agriculture improving; much benefit has been derived from the introduction of a better system of draining, and other improvements, under the auspices of the Agricultural Association. Great quantities of poultry are reared in the parish and neighbourhood, and bought by dealers for the Dublin market; the butter also is in very high repute, and forms a material article in the exports from Enniscorthy The living is a rectory, in the diocese of Ferns, united from time immemorial to the rectories of Kilnehue, Kilkevan, and Maglass, together constituting the corps of the deanery of Ferns, in the patronage of the Crown. The tithes amount to £234. 3., and of the whole benefice to £1254. 12. 1½. The glebe-house is a neat building, and the glebe comprises 16 acres; there is also a glebe of 24½ acres in Kilkevan, and another of 6 acres in Kilnehue, which last has been allotted to the perpetual curate. The church, a spacious structure, in which the Norman and English styles are blended, was erected in 1819, on a site in the principal street given by the late Stephen Ram, Esq., and at an expense of £2200, of which £200 was a gift from Mr. Ram, and £2000 a loan from the late Board of First Fruits. In the R. C. divisions the parish is the head of a union or district, comprising also the parishes of Kilkevan and Killinor, and part of Kilnehue; the chapel is a spacious edifice at the eastern extremity of the town; there are chapels also at Killanearin in Kilkevan, and at Ballyfad in Killinor. A meeting-house for Wesleyan Methodists, a neat building, has been lately erected in the town. About 90 children are taught in two public schools, of which the parochial school is partly supported by Stephen Ram, Esq., and another by the Rev. A. J. Ram; and there are five private schools, in which are about 250 children, and a Sunday school. A fever hospital and dispensary were established in 1828; the building, which is just without the town, is of an octagonal form, and comprises four wards, capable of containing 16 beds. A charitable loan fund was formed in 1833, for lending to poor tradesmen sums not exceeding £5, to be repaid by weekly instalments of one shilling in the pound: the issues of the loans average upwards of £130 weekly. The late Hon. and Rt. Rev. Thos. Stopford, D. D., successively Dean of Ferns and Bishop of Cork, bequeathed £200; and the late Joseph Allen, Esq., also left £200, the interest to be annually divided among poor Protestants attending the Established Church. At Clonatin are the ruins of a small ecclesiastical structure, in the Norman style of architecture, supposed to have been a cell to the abbey of Ferns, founded by St. Edan; and it is supposed that the name of the place may be a modification of Cluain-Edan, signifying "the retreat or cell of Edan." Dr. Thomas Ram, Bishop of Ferns and Leighlin, was interred in the cemetery of the old church of Gorey, where is an altar-tomb to his memory, with a very curious inscription written by himself.

GORT, a market and post-town, partly in the parishes of Kiltartan and Beagh, but chiefly in that of Kilmacduagh, barony of Kiltartan, county of Galway, and province of Connaught, 17 miles (S. S. E.) from Galway, and 98½ (W. by S.) from Dublin, on the road from Galway to Ennis; containing 3627 inhabitants. This town consists of 563 houses, most of which are neat stone buildings, three or four stories high, held under perpetual leases from Viscount Gort. It is built on an eminence on the main road from Connaught to Munster, with a large square in the centre, and is in a very healthy situation on the bank of a river, which works a very large flour-mill built in 1806, and enlarged in 1836, the property of J. Mangan, Esq., in which 7000 barrels of flour may be annually made. There is a market on Saturday, for agricultural produce, at which much business is transacted; and fairs for cattle and sheep are held on May 10th, Aug. 11th, and Nov. 7th; there is also a very large pig fair on March 17th and on the Saturday preceding Easter-Sunday. The roads in the vicinity are kept in excellent order. Two mail coaches come into the town; one from Dublin, which arrives at 10 A. M. and returns at 4 P. M.; the other passes through daily from Galway to Limerick, and from Limerick to Galway. Here are an hotel, a revenue police and a chief constabulary police station, which has dependent stations at Ardrahan, Ballytiven, Granagh, Maryville, Noggira, Normongrove, Tubber, Tiernevan, and Killafin. Petty sessions are held every Saturday, and the October quarter sessions for the county are held in the court-house, which was erected in the square in 1815, and comprises a court-hall, grand and petty jury rooms, and keepers' rooms. Here is also a bridewell, built in 1814, and containing two cells, a magistrates' room, and keepers' apartments; but being now too small, is about to be rebuilt. Barracks have existed at Gort for a very long period, and £7000 have been lately expended in building houses for officers and store-rooms; they will now accommodate 8 officers, 88 men, and 116 horses. The church, which is the parish church of Kilmacduagh, was erected in 1810, by a loan of £1400 from the late Board of First Fruits, on land given by the first Lord Gort. It is an elegant cruciform building with a conical spire, and was repaired by a loan of £600 from the same Board, in 1828: the interior is handsomely fitted up with galleries and pews. A new street will be opened from Bridge-street to the church, from which a fine view of it will be obtained. The R. C. chapel was built in 1825, on a site given by Lord Gort, and at an expense of £1300, defrayed by subscription: it is a substantial cruciform building, and contains a fine paintng of the Holy Trinity, presented by Lord Gort. The infirmary, which has been recently built, contains two wards, a keeper's room, and a surgery.

The scenery in the vicinity of the town is very beautiful, comprising on the west the Burren mountains in the county of Clare, and on the east the Derrybrien, Castle Daly, and Roxborough mountains. The chief seat is Loughcooter Castle, the residence of Viscount Gort, proprietor of the town, from which he takes his title. It is a noble castellated building, erected at an immense expense, in a well-planted demesne abounding with game, by the present peer, from designs by Mr. Nash, and commanding very fine woodland, lake, and mountain views. In front of the castle is Lough Cooter, a beautiful lake three miles long, containing seven well-wooded islands, and abundance of pike, trout, perch, and eels. Besides this magnificent residence, there are many other seats near the town, which are enumerated in the articles on the surrounding parishes. In its vicinity is a river that has a subterraneous course for a considerable distance: it rises in Lough Cooter, passes through a deep ravine till it reaches "the Ladle," a precipitous hollow clothed to the water's edge with large trees, where it sinks under a perpendicular rock. About 100 yards from this spot it re-appears in "the Punch-bowl," a circular basin about thirty yards in diameter and at least fifty deep: a pathway leads down the sides of this pit, which are very steep and clothed with trees. After flowing about 300 yards from the Punch-bowl it emerges, takes the name of the Black-water, and after running rapidly for a short distance again disappears. At the "Beggarman's Hole," a smaller circular basin than the Punch-bowl, it is again visible, and soon afterwards enters the "Churn," which is like an extremely deep well, ten feet in diameter. A quarter of a mile from the Churn it re-appears from under a beautiful arch formed by nature in the rock, passes through the town, and about a mile from it sinks again, and after alternately appearing and disappearing, once more flows by a subterraneous channel into the bay of Kinvarra.

GORTIN, a village, in the parish of Lower Badony, barony of Strabane, county of Tyrone, and province of Ulster, 5 miles (E.) from Newtown-Stewart, on the road to Cookstown; containing 441 inhabitants. This place is situated in a deep valley watered by the river Nagle, and in the district of the Mounterloney mountains, of which it may be considered the chief town. It consists of one irregular street, containing 82 houses indifferently built; the surrounding scenery, though boldly picturesque, is destitute of embellishment from the want of wood, which is found only in the demesne of Beltrim, the handsome residence of A. W. C. Hamilton, Esq., which is surrounded by young and thriving plantations. There is a small distillery in the village; and fairs are held on the first Wednesday in every month, for cattle, sheep, and pigs, and a pleasure fair on Easter-Monday. It has a penny post to Omagh, and is a constabulary police station; a court baron for the manor of Eliston, in which debts to the amount of 40*s.* are recoverable, is held here on the first Tuesday in every month; and petty sessions every second Friday. The parish church, a neat small edifice, is situated here, also the parochial school, and a dispensary.

GORTROE, a parish, in the barony of Barrymore, county of Cork, and province of Munster, 2¼ miles (S. by E.) from Rathcormac, on the road to Midleton; containing, with the parish of Desert, 2856 inhabitants; and comprising 8885 statute acres, as applotted under the tithe act, and valued at £6046 per annum: about 1500 acres are bog and mountain waste, the remainder arable and pasture; the soil is in general poor. The principal seats are Ballinterry, the residence of the Rev. Archdeacon Ryder; and Holly Hill, of S. Croker, Esq. It is a rectory and vicarage, in the diocese of Cloyne, united from an early period to the rectory and vicarage of Desert, forming the corps of the archdeaconry of Cloyne, in the gift of the bishop: the tithes of the united parishes amount to £415. 7. 8. There is neither glebe-house nor glebe. The church was built in 1826. In the R. C. divisions it is part of the union or district of Rathcormac, and contains a chapel. There is a parochial school of about 20 children, to which the rector contributes £5 annually, and a private school of about 60 children.

GOWRAN, an incorporated post-town (formerly a parliamentary borough) and a parish, in the barony of Gowran, county of Kilkenny, and province of Leinster, 6 miles (E.) from Kilkenny, and 52 (S. W. by S.) from Dublin, on the road to Waterford; containing 2783 inhabitants. This place, though now comparatively insignificant, was formerly of considerable importance. In the 14th century a strong castle was built here by James, third Earl of Ormonde, who made it his principal residence till 1391, when he purchased the castle of Kilkenny. In 1399, Teigue O'Carrol, dynast of Ely, when in arms against the royal forces under the Lord-Deputy Scrope, was taken prisoner and confined in the castle of this place, from which in the following year he made his escape. Hen. V., in the second year of his reign, by charter alleging that "the town of Ballygaueran was situated far from the aid of the English, and surrounded by Irish enemies who had lately burnt it," granted the inhabitants certain customs for murage and pavage for 40 years, to enable them to build walls for its protection. The castle was subsequently repaired by Margaret, the celebrated Countess of Ormonde; and Edw. VI. granted the portreeve, burgesses, and commons an exemption from county cess, which was confirmed by Elizabeth in 1566. Jas. I., in the sixth year of his reign, made the town a parliamentary borough, and incorporated the inhabitants under the designation of the "Portreeve, Chief Burgesses, and Freemen of the Town and Borough of Gowran," by charter setting forth that the inhabitants had always been loyal, but were then greatly reduced by the war and the late plague. In 1650, the castle was besieged by the forces of Cromwell under Sankey and Hewson, to whom, after an obstinate defence by Col. Hammond, it ultimately surrendered, when the commander and the garrison were inhumanly massacred and the castle destroyed by fire. The united forces of Cromwell and Ireton soon after assembled here, where they were joined by those of Hewson, on their march to besiege Kilkenny. The town, which is the joint property of Viscount Clifden and W. Bayly, Esq., contains 193 houses, many of which have been recently rebuilt, and other improvements have also taken place. There is a flour-mill; a constabulary police force has been established here; and fairs are held on March 8th, May 9th, Aug. 10th, Oct. 6th, and Dec. 8th, but the market has been discontinued. By the charter of Jas. I. the corporation consists of a portreeve, 12 chief burgesses, and an indefinite number of freemen, assisted by a recorder, town-clerk, a serjeant-at-mace, and other officers. The portreeve, who is also coroner, clerk of the market, and master of the assay, is chosen annually from the chief burgesses, and may appoint a deputy, who with himself is justice of the peace and of the quorum. The chief burgesses, as vacancies occur, are chosen from the freemen by the portreeve and a majority of their own body, by whom also all the officers of the corporation are chosen during pleasure, and the freemen admitted. The borough continued to send two members to the Irish parliament till the Union, when it was disfranchised, and the £15,000 awarded as compensation was paid to Henry Welbore, Viscount Clifden. The corporation has power to hold a court of record, with jurisdiction extending to debts of £6. 13. 4., but no court has been held for many years; and since the Union, although a portreeve is still elected and other officers appointed, the corporation has been little more than nominal. Petty sessions are held every alternate week, and the chartered fairs are held, but the market is discontinued.

The parish comprises 7682 statute acres, as applotted under the tithe act, and valued at £7417 per ann.; the land is chiefly under tillage, and the system of agriculture improving. Limestone is plentiful and is quarried for building and for agricultural uses. Adjoining the town is Gowran House, the seat of Viscount Clifden, finely situated in a richly wooded demesne, with a deer-park attached. The living is a rectory and vicarage, in the diocese of Ossory, and in the patronage of Viscount Clifden: the tithes amount to £507. 13. 10¼. The glebe-house, a new and handsome residence, was built by the present incumbent under the provisions of Primate Robinson's act; the glebe comprises 10 acres. The church, for the repairs of which the Ecclesiastical Commissioners have recently granted £130, is part of a very ancient cruciform structure, which was restored and fitted up for divine service in 1826; the remainder, which is still a ruin, has some very interesting details in the early English style, among which are a finely pointed arch of black marble leading into the chancel; a series of similar arches supported by circular and octagonal columns; some windows of elegant design, delicately ornamented in quatrefoil, and several interior chapels; the doorways and the baptismal font are of black marble curiously sculptured; there are several ancient monuments, three of which are traditionally ascribed to the Earl of Gowran and his two sons: the founder of the castle was interred here, as were also Edmund Butler, Earl of Carrick, and his eldest son, James, first Earl of Ormonde; there is also a monument with a bust of James Agar, Viscount Clifden, who died in 1789. In the R. C. divisions the parish is the head of a union or district, comprising also the parishes of Dungarvan, Blanchfieldskill, Dunbell, Blackrath, Templemartin, Clara, and Tascoffin: the chapel is a neat modern edifice, to which a school-room for 300 children is now being added; and there are three other chapels situated respectively at Pitts, Dungarvan, and Freneystown. About 30 children are taught in the parochial school, supported by the rector; a female school is supported by Lady Dover; there is an infants' school, and also six private schools, in which are about 320 children. An almshouse was founded by Miss Diana Agar, for four poor women, who have each £5 per annum; and there is a dispensary. Gowran formerly gave the title of Baron to the family of Fitzpatrick, Earls of Upper Ossory.

GRACEHILL.—See BALLYKENNEDY.

GRAIG, or GRAIGNAMANAGH, a market and post-town, and a parish, in the barony of GOWRAN, county of KILKENNY, and province of LEINSTER, 6 miles (S.) from Goresbridge (to which it has a sub-post-office), and 58 (S. S. W.) from Dublin, on the road from Carlow to New Ross; containing 4745 inhabitants, of which number, 2130 are in the town. William Marshal, the elder, Earl of Pembroke, founded an abbey here for Cistertian monks in 1212, the abbot of which was a lord of parliament until the Reformation, when it was granted to Sir E. Butler, and is now the property of Viscount Clifden: there are considerable remains of the building. The town contains 417 houses, and is improving in appearance; it has a handsome bridge over the Barrow, on which river it has between 40 and 50 boats of about 40 tons' burden each. Markets are held on Monday and Thursday in a market-house built by Lord Clifden; and fairs on Jan. 27th, March 4th, April 7th, May 11th, June 11th, Oct. 28th, and Nov. 26th. In or near the town are a brewery and malthouse, and a flour and three grist-mills. Petty sessions and a manorial court are held occasionally, and it is a constabulary police station, and has a dispensary. The parish comprises 11,879 statute acres: there is a considerable quantity of mountain land, including Brandon Hill, and Lord Clifden has planted 300 or 400 acres. Brandon dale, the residence of D. Burtchaell, Esq., commands fine views of the river Barrow and the Blackstairs mountains. The living is a rectory, in the diocese of Leighlin, and in the patronage of the Bishop: the tithes amount to £440. The church is a plain edifice. In the R. C. divisions it is the head of a union or district, comprising this parish, Ullard, and Powerstown, and has two chapels, of which that at Graig is a very commodious building. There are two national schools, in which about 500 children are educated. Towards the erection of one of these Lord Clifden gave £50 and subscribes £10. 10. annually for its support, and it is further aided by an annual donation from D. Burtchaell, Esq. There are some remains of a castle near the river.

GRAIGUE, a suburb of the town of CARLOW, in the parish of KILLESHIN, QUEEN'S county, and province of LEINSTER; containing 1976 inhabitants. It is situated on the right bank of the river Barrow, over which there is a bridge into the town of Carlow, but is entirely exempt from the jurisdiction of the sovereign of that borough, although included within its limits for electoral purposes by the act of the 2nd and 3rd of William IV., cap. 89. It comprises 114 acres, and includes 234 houses, a large flour-mill, two tanyards, and a distillery which manufactures more than 36,000 gallons of whiskey annually. It is a constabulary police station, and has fairs on Jan. 6th, Feb. 18th, April 1st, and Oct. 6th. The parochial church (a handsome new building with a curious arched roof of stone), the R. C. chapel, and the parochial and national schools, are in the village; near which about 600 of the men who were killed in the attack upon Carlow, in 1798, were buried.—See KILLESHIN.

GRALLAGH, a parish, in the barony of BALROTHERY, county of DUBLIN, and province of LEINSTER, 12 miles (N.) from Dublin; containing 236 inhabitants. The only seat is Tralee Lodge, the residence of R. Hyland, Esq. It is a vicarage, in the diocese of Dublin, forming part of the union of Hollywood: the rectory is impropriate in W. Dutton Pollard, Esq.; the tithes are included in the composition for Hollywood. In the R. C. divisions it is part of the union or district of Naul or Damestown. There are some remains of the church and in the churchyard is a holy well.

GRANAGH.—See GRENAUGH.

GRANARD, a market and post-town (formerly a parliamentary borough), and a parish, partly in the barony of ARDAGH, but chiefly in that of GRANARD, county of LONGFORD, and province of LEINSTER, 12 miles (N. E. by E.) from Longford, and 59 (W. N. W.) from Dublin, on the road from Edgeworthstown to Virginia; containing 10,315 inhabitants. This place, of which the name is a compound of the Irish words *Grian*, the "sun," and *Ard*, an "eminence," is supposed to have been at a remote period one of the stations appropriated to the celebration of idolatrous worship. In 1315 it was burned by the Scots under Edward Bruce, and appears to have first risen to importance as a town in the reign of Jas. I., who, in 1612, granted to Sir Francis Shaen some annual fairs, to which were added a grant of a market to Sir Francis Aungier, and also of a second market in 1619. A charter of Chas. II. to the Earl of Longford in 1678, erecting the lands of Ballynelack and Longford into manors, granted that, for the better plantation, the freeholders of the market-town of Granard, which was also the property of his lordship, should have the privilege of returning two members to the Irish parliament, which they continued to do until the Union, when the £15,000 awarded as compensation was paid to G. Fulk Littleton and W. Fulk Greville, Esqrs. The town consists chiefly of one regular street, about half a mile in length, and contains 458 houses, of which several are well built and of handsome appearance. It was formerly celebrated for an institution established in 1784, by Mr. Dungan, a native of the place, for awarding annual prizes to the best performers on the Irish harp. Near one extremity of the principal street is an artificial mount, called the Moat of Granard, commanding from its summit a view into several counties; the surrounding scenery is finely diversified. The market, in which corn, provisions, and coarse linens are sold, is on Monday; and fairs are held on May 3rd, and Oct. 1st. Petty sessions are held every Thursday, and a chief constabulary police force is stationed in the town. The market-house, over which is a court-room, is a large building in the centre of the town.

The parish comprises 15,756 statute acres, as applotted under the tithe act; the land is chiefly under tillage, the system of agriculture improving, there are some small tracts of bog, and limestone of the best description is quarried for agricultural uses. In the neighbourhood are several lakes, of which the principal are Lough Gawnagh, Lough Sheelin, and Lough Kenale, all embellished with pleasing and picturesque features. Lough Gawnagh is more than 10 miles in length and from 2 to 3 miles broad; its shores, which are abruptly steep, are richly wooded. On an island called Inchmory are the remains of an abbey, founded by St. Columb, to which a cemetery is attached; there is also another island, which, from specimens of jasper having been found in it, has obtained the name of Jasper Island. This lake is also called Erne Head Lake, being regarded as the source of Lough Erne, into which it discharges its superfluous waters. Finely situated on its shores are Erne Head, the handsome seat of J. Dopping, Esq.; Woodville, of R. Lambert, Esq., a pleasing residence commanding rich and extensive views; Frankfort, of E. McEvoy, Esq.; and Kilrea, of H. Dopping, Esq. There are also in the parish, Clonfin, the handsome residence of J. Thompson, Esq., pleasantly situated in a well-cultivated demesne; Mossvale, of J. Barton, Esq.; Cartron Card, of J. W. Bond, Esq.; Moorhill, of R. Blackall, Esq.; Bessville, of C. Helden, Esq.; Castle Nugent, of W. Webb, Esq.; Furry Park, of R. R. McCally, Esq.; Creevy House, of A. Bell, Esq.; and Higginstown, of F. Tuite, Esq. The living is a vicarage, in the diocese of Ardagh, episcopally united to the vicarages of Drumloman, Cullumkill, Ballymacue, and Scrabby, and in the patronage of the Impropriator. The rectory is impropriate in W. Fulk Greville, Esq.: the tithes amount to £890, of which £400 is payable to the impropriator and £490 to the vicar; and those of the whole benefice, including glebe, to £1647. 10. 9. The glebe-house was built in 1825, by a gift of £100 and a loan of £900 from the late Board of First Fruits. Attached to it is a glebe of four acres, and there are also, in this parish, a glebe of 25 acres, valued together at £56 per annum; in the parish of Ballymacue, a glebe of 11 acres, valued at £20. 13. per annum; and in the parish of Drumloman, a glebe of 150 acres valued at £234. 0. 8. per annum. The Ecclesiastical Commissioners recommend that the union be dissolved on the next avoidance, and that each parish become a separate benefice. The church is a plain ancient structure. The R. C. parish is co-extensive with that of the Established Church; there are two chapels, one in the town and one at Granard kill. About 130 children are taught in four public schools, of which the parochial school is supported by the trustees of Erasmus Smith's charity and a donation from the vicar; and there are 15 private schools, in which are about 930 children, and a dispensary. At Granard kill are the remains of the ancient town.

GRANEY, a parish, in the barony of KILKEA and MOONE, county of KILDARE, and province of LEINSTER, 1½ mile (E. by S.) from Castledermot, on the road from Baltinglass to Carlow; containing 1135 inhabitants. A nunnery was founded here in the year 1200 by Walter de Riddlesford, which with the manor was granted by Hen. VIII. to Sir A. St. Leger, the principal seat of whose descendants was for a long period at Grangemellon, now the property of the Rev. Sir Erasmus Burrowes, Bart., near which are the gateway and some other remains of the nunnery. It comprises 4974 statute acres, as applotted under the tithe act, and valued at £3019 per annum, and is a vicarage, in the diocese of Dublin, forming part of the union of Castledermot and of the corps of the prebend of Monmohennock; the rectory is impropriate in — Bunbury, Esq. The tithes amount to £212. 6. 2. In the R. C. divisions it is part of the union or district of Baltinglass.

GRANEY, a village, in the parish of KILMACOW, barony of IVERK, county of KILKENNY, and province of LEINSTER, 2 miles (N. W.) from Waterford, on the road to Clonmel; containing 12 houses and 77 inhabitants. Fairs are held here on Jan. 6th, April 12th, May 14th, Sept. 4th, and Dec. 11th.

GRANGE, a parish, partly in the barony of O'NEILLAND WEST, but chiefly in that of ARMAGH, county of ARMAGH, and province of ULSTER, 2 miles (N.) from Armagh, on the road to Belfast; containing 4132 inhabitants. This parish, which was formed out of the parish of Armagh in 1777, comprises, according to the Ordnance survey, 6795¼ statute acres, of which 2411½ are in O'Neilland West, and 4383¾ in Armagh. The land is generally good, and well cultivated; there is a considerable quantity of bog. There are quarries of excellent limestone and freestone, from which latter the stone is raised for the restoration of Armagh cathedral. A considerable quantity of linen cloth is woven here, and there is an extensive bleach-green at Alistragh. The principal seat is Castle-Dillon, the splendid residence of Sir Thomas Molyneux, Bart., near whose extensive and richly wooded demesne is an obelisk, 60 feet high, erected by the Right Hon. Sir. Capel Molyneux, Bart., in 1782, to commemorate the passing of some acts securing the independence of the Irish parliament. Here are also Drumsill, the residence of the Misses M[c] Geough; Alistragh, of R. M[c]Bride, Esq.; the Grange, of M. Pringle, Esq.; and the glebe-house, of the Rev. C. W. Lyne. The living is a perpetual cure, in the diocese of Armagh, and in the patronage of the Dean of Armagh. The curate has a stipend of £100, paid by the dean, with the glebe-house, a large and commodious building surrounded by a fine plantation, and a glebe comprising 37¾ acres, the two latter valued at £100 per annum. The church is a handsome edifice, built in 1779, of compact limestone, with a square tower and octagonal spire. In the R. C. divisions the parish forms part of the union or district of Armagh, and has a small plain chapel. The parochial school is situated near the church, and is aided by an annual donation from the incumbent; two schools for females are aided by the dean, the incumbent, and Miss M[c]Geough; and a national school is aided by an annual donation of £20 from Lord Charlemont, who also built the school-house: they afford instruction to about 270 children. The late Rt. Hon. Sir Capel Molyneux, Bart. bequeathed a rent-charge of £30, on the Castle Dillon estate, to the poor Protestant housekeepers of this parish, which is distributed by the incumbent.

GRANGE, a tithe-free district, in the barony of SHILLELOGHER, county of KILKENNY, and province of LEINSTER, 3 miles (S. W.) from Kilkenny, on the road to Callan; the population is returned with the parish of Inchiolaghan. Grange House is the property of Major Shearman. There is a national school at Coppenna, in which are about 150 children.

GRANGE, or GRANSHAW, a parish, in the Glenquin Division of the barony of UPPER CONNELLO, county of LIMERICK, and province of MUNSTER, 2 miles (N. E.) from Newcastle, on the road to Ballingarry; containing 721 inhabitants. This parish comprises 2828 statute acres, as applotted under the tithe act. The land is very good, and much of it is under an excellent system of tillage; the remainder is rich meadow and pasture, principally in large dairy farms. The river Deel, over which there is a curious old bridge, passes through the parish, the entire of which was formerly the property of the Courtenay family, but the greater part was sold during the life of the late Earl of Devon. The seats are Knockaderry, the residence of J. D. Evans, Esq.; Chesterfield, of Major Sullivan; and Dromin House, of Nicholas Meade, Esq. It is a rectory, in the gift of the Earl of Devon: the tithes amount to £180, and there is a glebe of five acres. In the R. C. divisions it forms part of the union or district of Knockaderry. The ruins of the old church are beautifully situated on the river Deel.

GRANGE, or MANISTER GRANGE, a parish, or district, in the barony of SMALL COUNTY, county of LIMERICK, and province of MUNSTER, 3 miles (N.) from Bruff, on the road to Limerick: the population is included in the return for Manister. It comprises 1224 statute acres, as applotted under the tithe act, and consists of very good land, which is generally based on limestone, and chiefly in large dairy farms. From an inquisition taken in the reign of Elizabeth, this district appears to have belonged to the parish of Manister, of which it still forms a part for civil purposes. The village of Six-mile-bridge is within its limits. It is a rectory, in the diocese of Limerick, entirely impropriate in Lord Southwell: the tithes amount to £83. 6. 2. In the R. C. divisions it forms part of the union or district of Bruff. Here are three druidical circles, the largest of which is 44½ yards in diameter, and consists of 65 upright stones; they are principally of limestone, sandstone, and clay-slate, but the largest, which is thirteen feet high, seven broad, and four thick, is formed of breccia. The second circle is 49 yards in diameter and consists of 72 smaller stones; and the third, which consists of 15 large shapeless blocks, is 17 yards in diameter. On the summit of Knockfinnell, which overhangs Lough Gur, are two extensive earthen forts.

GRANGE, or GRANGEMONK, also called MONKSGRANGE, a parish, in the barony of BALLYADAMS, QUEEN'S county, and province of LEINSTER, 4 miles (N.) from Carlow, on the river Barrow; containing 240 inhabitants. This parish comprises 841 statute acres, as applotted under the tithe act, and valued at £490 per annum. It is a vicarage, in the diocese of Leighlin, and in the gift of G. Hartpole, Esq., in whom the rectory is impropriate. The tithes amount to £55. 7. 8¼., of which £36. 18. 5½. is payable to the impropriator, and the remainder to the vicar. There is neither church, glebe-house, nor glebe. In the R. C. divisions it forms part of the union or district of Mayo, or Arles and Ballylinan. There is an old churchyard, which is the burial-place of the Hartpole family, also the ruins of a castle.

GRANGE, a village, in the parish of AHAMPLISH, barony of LOWER CARBERY, county of SLIGO, and province of CONNAUGHT, 8 miles (N.) from Sligo, on the road to Ballyshannon; containing 221 inhabitants. It comprises 40 houses, and has two bridges over the river Banduff, which were erected at the close of the last century. It is a revenue and a constabulary police station, and has fairs, on June 2nd and 28th, July 25th, Aug. 25th, Sept. 29th, Oct. 28th, and Dec. 10th.

GRANGE (ST. JOHN BAPTIST), a parish, in the barony of MIDDLETHIRD, county of TIPPERARY, and province of MUNSTER, 2 miles (S. E.) from Fethard, on the road to Clonmel; containing 771 inhabitants. It comprises about 2754 statute acres and is well cultivated. The principal seats are Clonacody, that of E. Kellett, Esq.; and Lakefield, of W. Pennefather, Esq.; both handsome residences. It is a vicarage, in the diocese of Lismore, forming part of the union of Cahir; the rectory is impropriate in the representatives of W. Netterville, Esq. The tithes amount to £160, of which £100 is payable to the impropriators and £60 to the vicar.

GRANGE, a village, in the parish of DESERT-CREIGHT, barony of DUNGANNON, county of TYRONE, and province of ULSTER, 2½ miles (E) from Cookstown, on the road from Stewartstown to Moneymore; containing 147 inhabitants. It comprises 32 houses, generally well built, and has a fair on Nov. 12th. Here is a meeting-house for Covenanters of the third class, and a school; and near the village is Killymoon, the elegant residence of Col. Stewart.

GRANGE, county of WATERFORD.—See LISGENNAN.

GRANGE CLARE, an extra-parochial district, in the barony of EAST OPHALY, county of KILDARE, and province of LEINSTER; containing 39 inhabitants.

GRANGECLOVAN, or GRANGELORAN, a parish, in the barony of FASSADINING, county of KILKENNY, and province of LEINSTER, 1 mile (S. W.) from Ballyragget, on the river Nore; containing 949 inhabitants, and comprising 5611½ statute acres. It is a rectory and vicarage, in the diocese of Ossory, forming part of the union of Burnchurch: the tithes amount to £247. 14. 11. In the R. C. divisions it is the head of a union or district, called Conahy, which includes this parish and Maine, and part of the parishes of Kilmocar, Coolcraheen, Three Castles, and Burnchurch; and has a chapel at Conahy.

GRANGEFORTH, a parish, in the barony and county of CARLOW, and province of LEINSTER, 2 miles (S. W. by S.) from Tullow, on the road to Carlow; containing 926 inhabitants. By inquisition taken in 1601 it appears that it belonged to Fferdoroghe O'Gormogane, but it was granted to Sir John Ponsonby in 1669. It is a rectory, in the diocese of Leighlin, forming part of the union of Urglin: the tithes amount to £264. In the R. C. divisions it is part of the union or district of Tullow, and contains a chapel. There is a public school, in which about 150 children are educated.

GRANGEGEETH, a parish, in the barony of UPPER SLANE, county of MEATH. and province of LEINSTER, 2½ miles (N.) from Slane; containing 1304 inhabitants. It is a rectory, in the diocese of Meath, entirely impropriate in the Marquess of Drogheda, but it is tithe-free, from having formed part of the possessions of the abbey of Mellifont. In the R. C. divisions it is the head of a union or district, comprising this parish and Monknewtown, in each of which is a chapel. There is a national school, in which about 110 children are educated, and for which the school-house and an acre and a half of land were given by Sir J. Witchett; also a private school of about 120 children.

GRANGEGORMAN.—See City of DUBLIN.

GRANGE-KILREE, a parish, in the barony of SHILLELOGHER, county of KILKENNY, and province of LEINSTER, 5 miles (S.) from Kilkenny, on the road to West Jerpoint; containing 145 inhabitants and 1052 statute acres. It is a rectory and vicarage, in the diocese of Ossory, forming part of the union of Burnchurch: the tithes amount to £114. In the R. C. divisions it is part of the union or district of Donemagan.

GRANGE-MOCKLER, or NINE-MILE-HOUSE, a parish, in the barony of SLIEVARDAGH, county of TIPPERARY, and province of MUNSTER, 7 miles (S. by W.) from Callan, on the road to Clonmel; containing 666 inhabitants. Fairs are held here on March 25th, May 20th, Aug. 10th, Sept. 19th, Oct. 8th, Nov. 1st, and Dec. 12th. It is a rectory, in the diocese of Lismore, entirely impropriate in Cæsar Sutton, Esq.: the tithes amount to £80, and the impropriator allows £4 per ann. to the rector of Kilvemnon for the performance of the occasional duties. In the R. C. divisions it forms part of the union or district of Kilmurry, and has a chapel. There are three private schools, in which about 160 children are educated.

GRANGE O'NEILL, an extra-parochial district, locally in the parish of KILMORE, barony of LOWER ORIOR, county of ARMAGH, and province of ULSTER; containing 903 inhabitants, and more than 800 acres of excellent land. In ecclesiastical concerns it belongs to the lordship of Newry, and is under the jurisdiction of Lord Kilmorey, as abbot of Newry.

GRANGEROSNOLVIN, a parish, in the barony of KILKEA and MOONE, county of KILDARE, and province of LEINSTER, 3 miles (S. W.) from Ballytore, on the road from Kilcullen to Castledermot; containing 114 inhabitants. It comprises 1377 statute acres, as applotted under the tithe act, and valued at £615 per annum. A nunnery is traditionally stated to have existed here, but there are no traces of it. It is a rectory and vicarage, in the diocese of Dublin, forming part of the union of Castledermot: the tithes amount to £75. In the R. C. divisions also it is part of the union or district of Castledermot.

GRANGE SILVAE, a parish, in the barony of GOWRAN, county of KILKENNY, and province of LEINSTER; containing, with the post-town of Goresbridge, 2313 inhabitants. This parish, which is situated on the road from Carlow to Ross, and on the confines of the county of Carlow, is bounded on the east by the river Barrow, and comprises 7661 statute acres, as applotted under the tithe act, and valued at £4566 per annum. The land is generally of good quality and principally under tillage, and the system of agriculture is improved. Limestone is found almost in every part of the parish, and worked for agricultural purposes, except towards the southern extremity, where the strata alternate with granite. The surface, except on the demesnes, is destitute of wood, with which, from its name, it would appear to have formerly abounded. The principal gentlemen's seats are Barrowmount, formerly the residence of the late Col. Gore; Doninga, of T. T. Bookey, Esq.; and Barraghcore, of J. Handy, Esq., all handsome residences, with well-planted and improved demesnes. There are two large flour-mills, the property of Mr. Handy, worked by water and capable of producing 40,000 barrels of flour annually. The Barrow navigation, which commences at St. Mullins, about three miles below this parish, bounds it on the east and joins the Grand canal at Athy. Fairs are held at Goresbridge for cattle and pigs, and are numerously attended. The living is a rectory, in the diocese of Leighlin, and in the patronage of the Bishop; the tithes amount to £500. The glebe-house was purchased for £184. 12., a gift from the late Board of First Fruits; the glebe comprises eight acres. The church at Goresbridge, for the repair of which the Ecclesiastical Commissioners have recently granted £168, is a neat edifice with a tower, and contains a handsome marble monument to Col. Gore, who fell at Bergen-op-Zoom while leading his men to the attack of that place on the 8th of March, 1814; it was erected by the officers of the 33rd regiment of foot, as a tribute to his memory. The R. C. the chapel, a neat edifice, is at Goresbridge. About 300 children are taught in the parochial and two national schools, of which the first is aided by Mrs. Bookey with £14 per annum; there is also a private school, in which are about 50 boys.

GRANGOOLY.—See KILLALOE.

GRAYSTOWN, a parish, in the barony of SLIEVARDAGH, county of TIPPERARY, and province of MUNSTER, 1¼ mile (S. W.) from Killenaule; containing 2190 inhabitants. It comprises 5957 statute acres, as applotted under the tithe act, and valued at £3229 per annum. Here is Noan, the seat of the Taylor family. Fairs are held in July and Nov. The Killenaule coal field, which is described in the article on the county, is in this parish. It is a rectory and vicarage, in the diocese of Cashel, forming part of the union of Templeneiry and corps of the precentorship of Cashel cathedral: the tithes amount to £260. There is a public school of 130 children, also two private schools, in which 180 children are educated.

GREANE, a parish, partly in the barony of CLANWILLIAM, but chiefly in that of COONAGH, county of LIMERICK, and province of MUNSTER, on the new line of road from Limerick to Tipperary; containing, with the post-town of Pallasgreane, 4923 inhabitants. At Sulchoi pass, near Pallas, an important battle was fought in 960 between the Irish and the Danes, in which the latter were defeated and pursued to Limerick. It was formerly an incorporated town, and had a collegiate church. The parish comprises 4207 statute acres, about one-fifth of which is under tillage, three-fifths are meadow, and the remainder principally pasturage on Knock-nagreine, or the "hill of the sun." Basalt is found in Knock-na-greine, where it rises to the height of 864 feet, and appears to have been forced up by a violent convulsion, as the limestone on which it is based is very much shattered and dislocated. Near this hill is Lynfield, the fine mansion of D. O'Grady, Esq., through a wood in the neighbourhood of which is seen a magnificent façade of basaltic rock, consisting of numerous lofty columns closely joined, and forming a miniature resemblance of Fair Head, in Antrim. Dork, the handsome residence of Heffernan Considine, Esq., commands a charming view of a rich and undulating country as far as the celebrated rock of Cashel. Near the house passes the old road by which Wm. III. marched from Golden-Bridge to the siege of Limerick. The other principal mansions are Mount Catherine, the seat of H. Smithwick, Esq.; Pallas, of T. Abjohn, Esq.; Sunville, of T. Kearney, Esq.; and the glebe-house, of the Rev. W. Scott. Petty sessions are held on alternate Mondays at New Pallas. There is a constabulary police station in the village of Nicker. It is a rectory and vicarage, in the diocese of Emly, and in the patronage of the Archbishop of Cashel: the tithes amount to £450. There is a glebe-house, with a glebe of seven acres and another of 32 acres, which is subject to a rent of £30. The church, which was built in 1808, is in a dilapidated state. In the R. C. divisions it is the head of a union or district, called Pallasgreane, including the parishes of Greane and Ballyclough, and part of Drumkeen, and containing a large plain chapel at Nicker. The parochial school, for which there is a large and handsome house at New Pallas, are on the foundation of Erasmus Smith, and endowed with £30 per ann. and two acres of land. There is also a private school of 100 children. Eastward of the church is a moat, and about a mile from it is the ancient castle of Kilduff. Near Lynfield are the remains of Kilcolman church, which was founded in the 7th century.

GREAT ISLAND, or BARRYMORE ISLAND, in the harbour of CORK, barony of BARRYMORE, county of CORK, and province of MUNSTER; containing, with the post-town of Cove, (which is described under its own head), 11,089 inhabitants. It was anciently called *Ard-Neimheidh*, and is one of the first places mentioned in Irish history whose locality can be fixed with precision. A battle was fought here in 125 between Ængus, king of Ireland, and Niadh Nuaget, a tributary prince, in which the latter recovered the crown of Munster; and in the 12th century the island maintained its independence against the English for some time after they had acquired possession of Cork and the adjacent country. In 1329 it was the property of Lord Philip Hodnet, who resided at Clonmel, where he was besieged by the Barrys and Roches, and all his adherents put to death. The Barrys having obtained possession, it was called Barrymore Island. During the war of 1641, a party of Lord Castlehaven's troops coming here to plunder, were attacked by Major Power with 30 horse and two companies of foot, and about 500 of them were slain. In 1666 it was described by the Earl of Orrery as very fertile, and a place of such consequence as, were he an enemy about to invade Ireland, to be the first he would endeavour to secure. Most of the islands and headlands in its neighbourhood have since been strongly fortified.

It extends five miles from east to west, and two from north to south, comprising 221 gneeves, or 13,149 statute acres, as applotted under the tithe act, and valued at £9758 per ann., and is most advantageously situated. To the south is the magnificent harbour of Cove; on the west is the deep channel, half a mile wide, which separates it from the mainland at Passage; on the north it is bounded by the noble estuary of the Lee, and on the east by a shallow channel which separates it from Foaty Island, over which is a lofty bridge, from the extremity of which branch two roads, one leading by way of Passage to Cove, the other crossing the island to the same port. The shores are generally bold, and the interior has a pleasing variety of hill and dale, watered by several small streams that flow into the Eastern Channel. It is composed of clay-slate covered with a light productive soil, but intermingled with fragments of the substratum: two-thirds are under tillage, and the remainder in pasture or included in demesnes. Two ferries afford communication between the island and the mainland, the western ferry to Passage, the eastern to Midleton. There is also a communication by land from Belvelly, where a stone bridge and causeway connect it with Foaty island, whence is another causeway communicating with the mainland; a direct communication is thus opened by land with Cork. The beauty of its situation and salubrity of the climate have induced many genteel families to settle here. Among the principal seats are Marino, the residence of T. G. French, Esq.; Ballymore House, of J. H. Bennett, Esq.; Cuskinny, of Savage T. W. French, Esq.; Eastgrove, of J. Bagwell, Esq.; Ballymore, of R. B. Shaw, Esq.; Ashgrove, of R. Frankland, Esq.; Ballymore Cottage, of W. J. Coppinger, Esq.; Belgrove, of the Rev. G. Gumbleton; Whitepoint House, of H. H. O'Brien, Esq.; Spy Hill, of the Rev. T. L. Coghlan; the Retreat, of Mrs. O'Grady; Merton, of R. Morrison, Esq.; East Hill, of Capt. Stubbs; Bellevue, of Dr. Crotty, R. C. Bishop of Cloyne; and Ballynoe House, of A. Hargreave, Esq. Besides these are many lodges and cottages ornée for the accommodation of visiters during the bathing season.

The island is divided into the Eastern and Western parishes, which together form the union of Clonmel, or Cove, in the diocese of Cloyne, and in the patronage of the Bishop. The Eastern parish, called also Templerobin, includes, in addition to the eastern part of Great Island, part of Foaty, and the whole of Hawlbowling, Spike, and Rocky islands (each of which is described under its own head); it is a rectory and vicarage, and the tithes amount to £323. The Western parish, called Clonmel, besides the western part of the island, includes the remaining portion of Foaty island; it is a vicarage, and was anciently called Templelyra, from having belonged to the Knights Templars; the entire tithes amount to £276. 18. 5½, of which two-thirds are payable to the lessee of the economy estate of the cathedral of Cloyne, and one-third to the vicar: the tithes of the benefice amount to £415. 7. 8. A third parish was erected in 1762, by the Rev. Downes Conron, the incumbent, on a dispute between him and the Dean and Chapter of Cloyne relative to tithes; but a compromise was effected and the incumbent has to pay £100 annually to the economy estate. There is no tradition of Kilgarvan as a parish, and it is mentioned only in one of the county records; but 20 acres of arable land in Kilgarvan, with their tithes, &c., were granted by patent to Sir Richard Boyle, Knt., in 1605. The glebe-house is about to be rebuilt; there is a glebe of 18 acres belonging to the incumbent, and one of 30 acres belonging to the economy estate. The church, which is in Cove, is a large and handsome edifice. In the R. C. divisions the island forms the district of Cove, and has a chapel in that town, and one at Funnah. There is also a place of worship for Wesleyan Methodists. There are four public schools, in which about 380, and eleven private schools in which about 370, children are educated; also a Sunday school, supported by the curates: most of them are in or near Cove. The most interesting relics of antiquity are the remains of Belvelly castle, built by one of the Hodnets, formerly a potent family, and of Templerobin and Clonmel churches; within the walls of the latter are interred Tobin, the author of the "Honeymoon" and other dramatic productions; and the Rev. C. Wolfe, who wrote the ballad "Not a drum was heard," on the death of Gen. Sir John Moore.

GREAT ISLAND, in the parish of Ardcolme, barony of Shelmalier, county of Wexford, and province of Leinster, 1½ mile (N. E.) from Wexford, on the north side of Wexford harbour; containing, in 1835, five families. It comprises 80 statute acres, and to the east is a smaller island, called Breast Island.

GREENAN, or GREENANNE, a small village, in the constablewick of Ballinacor, a sub-denomination of the parish of Rathdrum, barony of Ballinacor, county of Wicklow, and province of Leinster, 2 miles (W. by S.) from Rathdrum; containing 61 inhabitants. This place is situated on the river Avonbeg, over which is a bridge leading to Glenmalur, and to the "Meeting of the Waters:" it contains the chapel of the R. C. district of Rathdrum, and a school under the patronage of W. Kemmis, Esq., by whom it is supported.

GREENISH, an island, in the parish of Dromdeeley, barony of Lower Connello East, county of Limerick, and province of Munster, 4½ miles (N.) from Askeaton; the population is returned with the parish. The ancient name of this island was *Inis Grein*, in the Irish language, signifying "the Island of the Sun," and derived from a very large heathen temple erected on its highest point, probably appropriated to the worship of that pagan divinity, and of which there are still some slight vestiges. It is situated off the southern bank of the Shannon, near the mouth of the river Deel, and comprises about 45 acres of land, being the principal of a group of islands in the bay of Tramorel.

GREENMOUNT, or DROMKEATH, a village, in the parish of Kilsaran, county of Louth, and province of Leinster, 1 mile (S.) from Castle-Bellingham, on the road from Drogheda to Dundalk; containing 44 houses and 243 inhabitants. Here is an extensive camp, consisting of a high mound with a hollow area at the top, and partly encompassed by a single trench. At one extremity is a tumulus, on the side of which is an embanked area with a circular end, in which local tradition states that the first parliament ever assembled in Ireland was held.

GREENOGUE, a parish, in the barony of Ratoath, county of Meath, and province of Leinster, 9½ miles (N. E. by N.) from Dublin, on the mail coach road to Londonderry and Belfast; containing 291 inhabitants, of which number, 195 are in the village, which in the reign of Hen. VI. was one of the borough towns of Meath. By a clause in an enrolment, dated July 28th, 1423, "The Provost and Commonalty of the town of Grenoke are ordered to be at Trim, with all their power for its defence;" it consists of 36 houses. The parish, which is on the confines of the county of Dublin, comprises 1443 acres. It is a rectory and vicarage, in the diocese of Meath, forming part of the union of Ratoath: the tithes amount to £90. 5. In the R. C. divisions it is part of the union or district of Creekstown. There are considerable remains of the old church.

GRENAUGH, or GRANAGH, a parish, in the barony of Barretts (except the ploughland of Ballymartin, which is in the barony of East Muskerry), county of Cork, and province of Munster, 7½ miles (N. N. W.) from Cork, on the new lines of road to Kanturk and Mallow; containing 5043 inhabitants. It comprises 13,250 statute acres, as applotted under the tithe act and valued at £5466 per annum. The surface is very uneven, and the substratum is entirely clay-slate. Agriculture is gradually improving under the spirited example of St. John Jefferyes, Esq., but the old heavy wooden plough is still in use in many parts, particularly towards the mountains. Here are more than 400 acres of bog, and 600 of barren mountain. Here is a woollen factory, which was built in 1806, and is worked by a mountain stream. Grenagh is the residence of H. Low, Esq. It is a rectory and vicarage, in the diocese of Cloyne, forming part of the union of Garrycloyne: the tithes amount to £1050; there is a glebe of 15 acres. In the R. C. divisions it is part of the union or district of Mourne, or Ballinamona, and has a large plain chapel at South Grenagh. The parochial schools are supported by the rector, and there are three private schools, at which about 240 children attend during the summer. At Dawestown is an extraordinary flowering lime tree, with 16 very large and wide-spreading branches. The gables and side walls of the church are nearly entire; and there are remains of druidical altars at Lyradan, Knockantoha, and Glauncoum, and several forts and raths.

GREY-ABBEY, a post-town and parish, in the barony of ARDES, county of DOWN, and province of ULSTER, 6 miles (S. E.) from Newtownards (to which it has a sub-post-office), and 95 (N. N. E.) from Dublin, on the road from Newtownards to Portaferry; containing 3700 inhabitants. This place derives its name from a monastery founded here in 1192, by Afric, wife of John de Courcy, and daughter of Godred, King of Man, in honour of the Blessed Virgin, for monks of the Cistertian order, who were brought hither from the Abbey of Holme-Cultram, in Cumberland. The establishment continued to flourish till the dissolution, and had ample possessions in Great and Little Ardes. Towards the close of the reign of Elizabeth it was nearly destroyed, in the rebellion raised by Tyrone; and in the 3rd of Jas. I. the site and precincts, together with all its possessions, were granted to Sir James Hamilton. The village is pleasantly situated on Lough Strangford, and on the road from Portaferry to Belfast; and the neighbourhood is embellished with some elegant seats and beautiful scenery. Mount Stewart, the splendid residence of the Marquess of Londonderry, is a spacious mansion, situated in an extensive demesne richly wooded and pleasingly diversified with water. On the summit of an eminence in the grounds is an elegant building, a model of the Temple of the Winds at Athens, erected under the personal superintendence of J. Stewart, Esq., whose skill and taste in Grecian architecture have procured for him the appellation of the Athenian Stewart; it is built of stone from the quarries of Scrabo, and the floors, which are of bog fir found in the peat moss on the estate, are, for beauty of material and elegance of design, unequalled by any thing of the kind in the country; nearly adjoining the village is Rosemount, the residence of Mrs. Montgomery. According to the Ordnance survey the parish, with some small islands in Strangford Lough, comprises 7689 statute acres, nearly equally divided between tillage and pasture, the land on the shore being good, but in the interior boggy and rocky; very little improvement has been made in agriculture. Excellent slate is found in the townland of Tullycaven, but the quarry is not judiciously worked. There is a very extensive bog, which supplies the inhabitants with abundance of fuel, and beneath the surface are found large oak and fir trees lying horizontally at a depth of 15 and 20 feet; the fir is in a fine state of preservation, exceedingly hard, and susceptible of a very high polish. A great quantity of calico and muslin is woven here by the peasantry at their own dwellings, and many of the females are employed in tambour-work. It is a perpetual curacy, in the diocese of Down, and in the patronage of W. Montgomery, Esq., in whom the rectory is impropriate: the tithes are included in the rent, and the perpetual curate's stipend amounts to £96. 19. 10½., of which £13. 16. 11. is paid by the impropriator, £9. 4. 7½. by the Marquess of Londonderry, £4. 12. 4. by A. Auchinleck, Esq., and £69. 6. by the Ecclesiastical Commissioners out of Primate Boulter's fund. The church is a small neat building, erected in 1778, and contains some handsome monuments of the Montgomery family. Here is a place of worship for Presbyterians in connection with the Synod of Ulster, of the third class. There is a school on Erasmus Smith's foundation, for which the school-house was built by the late Marchioness of Londonderry, and 60 of the children are supported and clothed by the present Marchioness; and a male, female, and an infants' school, to which Mrs. Montgomery annually contributes £6, £12, and £6 respectively. In these and six other schools about 460 children are educated. The remains of the abbey are beautiful and picturesque; the eastern gable is nearly entire; and contains five lancet-shaped windows, of which the stone work is quite perfect; there are also a window of the same character on the north and south sides of the choir; the nave, which till 1778 was used as the parish church, is tolerably entire, and is now the mausoleum of the family. There are the remains of several ancient monuments, and within the choir are two recumbent effigies, said to be those of John de Courcy and his wife, finely carved in freestone. There are also several other walls remaining, serving to give an idea of the former extent of the buildings, which appear to have been in the purest style of early English architecture. A very large tumulus was opened in 1825, by Dr. Stephenson, and found to contain 17 stone coffins, formed by placing together several flag-stones on edge, and covering them with one large stone; one of these in the centre was larger than the rest, and in each of them was found an urn of baked clay, containing granular earth of a dark colour.

GREY STONES.—See DELGANY.

GROGAN, a village, in the parish of LEMANAGHAN, barony of GARRYCASTLE, KING'S county, and province of LEINSTER, 4½ miles (N. W.) from Clara, on the road to Farbane; containing 52 houses and 298 inhabitants.

GROOMSPORT, a village, in the parish of BANGOR, barony of ARDES, county of DOWN, and province of ULSTER, 1½ mile (N. E. by E.) from the sea-port town of Bangor, on the coast road to Donaghadee; containing 408 inhabitants. It is situated on the south side of Belfast Lough, and has a harbour for small craft chiefly engaged in fishing. Here is a station of the coast-guard, forming part of the district of Donaghadee. On the 13th of August, 1689, the advanced army of Wm. III., consisting of about 10,000 troops under the command of Duke Schomberg, disembarked at this place from 70 transports, and encamped for the night: on the following day the Duke proceeded to invest Carrickfergus.

GUILCAGH, or GILCO, a parish, in the barony of UPPERTHIRD, county of WATERFORD, and province of MUNSTER; containing, with the post-town of Portlaw, 921 inhabitants. It comprises 2059 statute acres, as applotted under the tithe act, and is a vicarage, in the diocese of Lismore, forming part of the union of Dunhill; the rectory is impropriate in the corporation of Waterford and the Duke of Devonshire. The tithes amount to £148. 7. 1. of which £88 is payable to the corporation, £16. 7. 1. to the Duke of Devonshire, and £44 to the vicar. The church is used as a chapel of ease to Dunhill. There are two private schools, in which about 150 children are educated. Near Coolfin are the ruins of Kilbunny church.

GUNSBOROUGH, a village, in the parish of GALEY, barony of IRAGHTICONNOR, county of KERRY, and province of MUNSTER, 2¾ miles (N. N. W.) from Listowel, on the old road to Ballybunnian; containing 38 houses and 181 inhabitants. It derives its name from its former proprietor, Mr. Gun, of whose representatives it has been lately purchased by P. Mahony, Esq., of Dublin, who has commenced improvements on an extensive scale, calculated to afford constant employment to nearly 200 persons for upwards of two years. Among these are the draining of an extensive boggy district, through the centre of which a new road has been made; the rebuilding and remodelling of the village; and the formation of a large plantation, where a new mansion is about to be erected.

GURTEEN.—See KILFREE.

GURTHROE.—See GORTROE.

GURTLOWNEN, a village, in the parish of KILLERY, barony of TIRAGHRILL, county of SLIGO, and province of CONNAUGHT, 2 miles (S. W.) from Dromahaire, on the road to Collooney; containing 24 houses and 112 inhabitants.

END OF VOL. I.